Wild, Shaw, and Chiappetta: *Fundamental Accounting Principles,* offers a seamless content and technology solution to improve student engagement and comprehension, automation of assignments and grading, and easy reporting to ensure that learning objectives are being met.

Connect Plus® Accounting provides a wide array of tools and content to improve instructor productivity and student performance. In fact, the aggregated results of 34 Connect adoptions showed an 11% improvement in pass rates, a 16% improvement in retention, two times as many students receiving an A, and a 77% reduction in instructor grading time.

Connect Performance Metrics

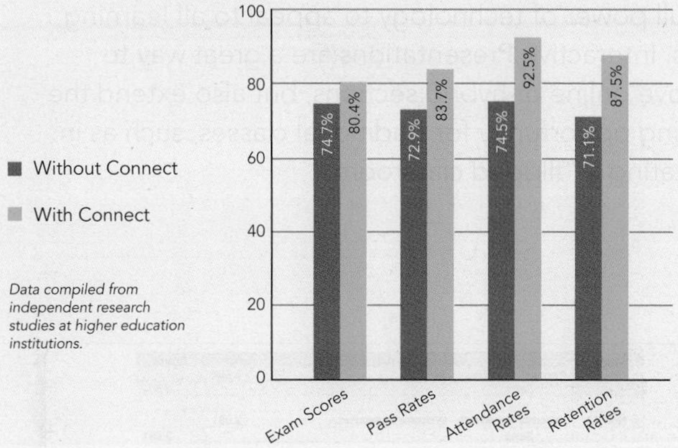

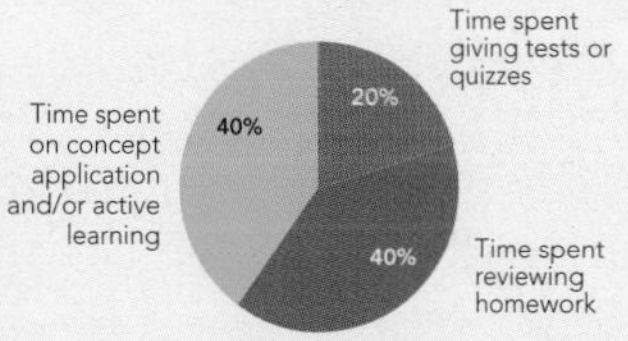

- Without Connect
- With Connect

Data compiled from independent research studies at higher education institutions.

Exam Scores: 74.7% / 80.4%
Pass Rates: 72.9% / 83.7%
Attendance Rates: 74.5% / 92.5%
Retention Rates: 71.1% / 87.5%

Average Grade Distribution

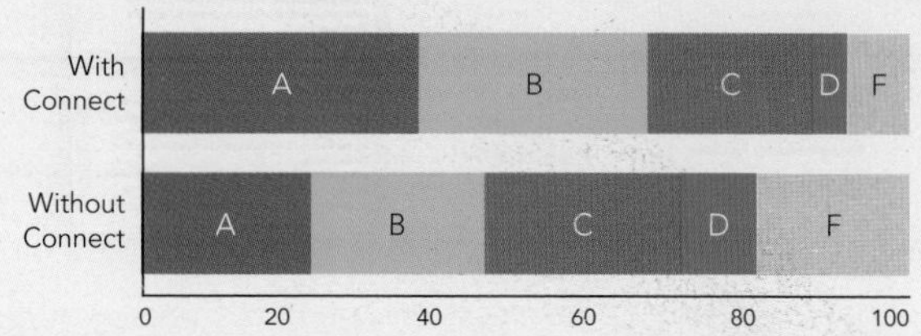

With Connect: A B C D F
Without Connect: A B C D F

Base: Seven control/test groups from six institutions.
Data compiled from independent research studies at higher education institutions.

Connect reduces time spent on administrative tasks...

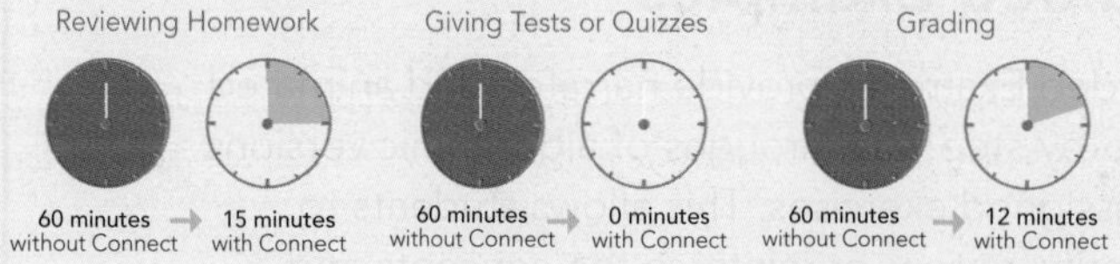

Reviewing Homework: 60 minutes without Connect → 15 minutes with Connect

Giving Tests or Quizzes: 60 minutes without Connect → 0 minutes with Connect

Grading: 60 minutes without Connect → 12 minutes with Connect

...allowing for more time to focus on concept application and other learning.

Without Connect
Time spent giving tests or quizzes: 20%
Time spent reviewing homework: 40%
Time spent on concept application and/or active learning: 40%

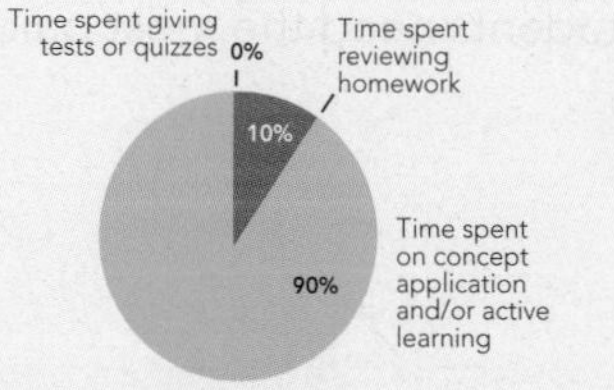

With Connect
Time spent giving tests or quizzes: 0%
Time spent reviewing homework: 10%
Time spent on concept application and/or active learning: 90%

Grade Distribution

Without LearnSmart: A 19.3%, B 38.6%, C 28.0%
With LearnSmart: A 30.5%, B 33.5%, C 22.6%

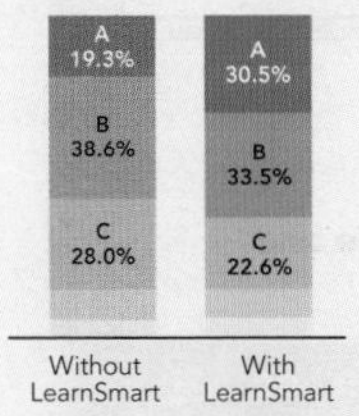

58% more A's with LearnSmart

Student Retention Rate

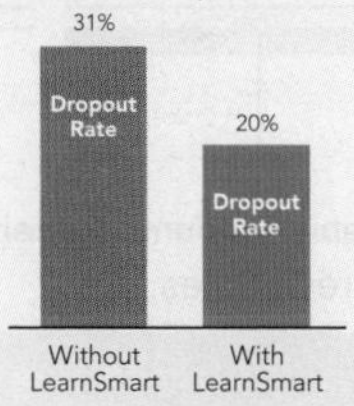

Without LearnSmart: Dropout Rate 31%
With LearnSmart: Dropout Rate 20%

35% fewer dropouts with LearnSmart

Student Pass Rate

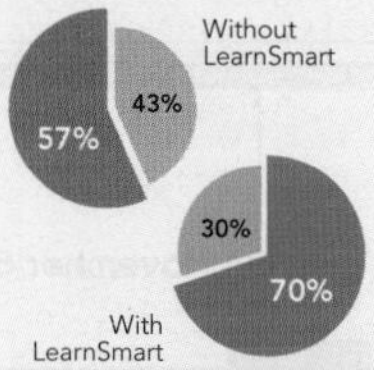

Without LearnSmart: 57% / 43%
With LearnSmart: 70% / 30%

25% more students passed with LearnSmart

LEARNSMART ADVANTAGE

LearnSmart®

LearnSmart, the most widely used adaptive learning resource, is proven to improve grades. By focusing each student on the most important information they need to learn, LearnSmart personalizes the learning experience so they study as efficiently as possible.

Smartbook™

SmartBook is an extension of LearnSmart—an adaptive eBook that helps students focus their study time more effectively. As students read, SmartBook assesses comprehension and dynamically highlights where they need to study more.

CONNECT FEATURES

Interactive Presentations

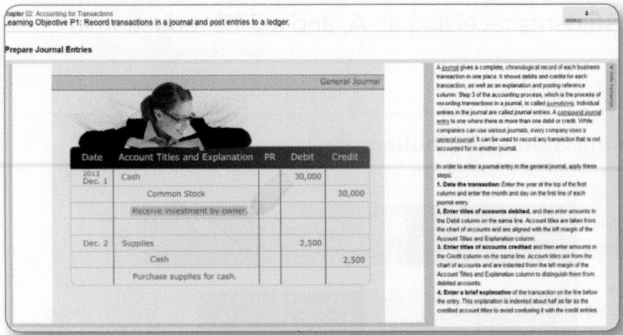

Interactive Presentations cover each chapter's core learning objectives with narrated, animated presentations that pause frequently to check for comprehension. Interactive Presentations harness the full power of technology to appeal to all learning styles. Interactive Presentations are a great way to improve online or hybrid sections, but also extend the learning opportunity for traditional classes, such as in facilitating a "flipped classroom."

Guided Examples

Guided Examples provide narrated and animated step-by-step walkthroughs of algorithmic versions of assigned exercises. This allows students to identify, review, or reinforce the concepts and activities covered in class. Guided Examples provide immediate feedback and focus on the areas where students need the most guidance.

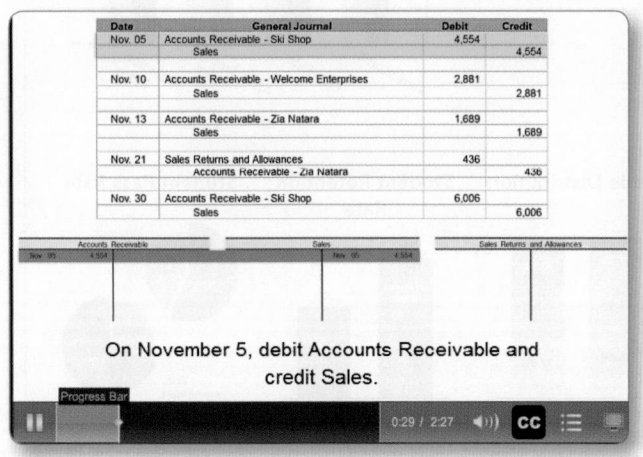

End-of-Chapter Material

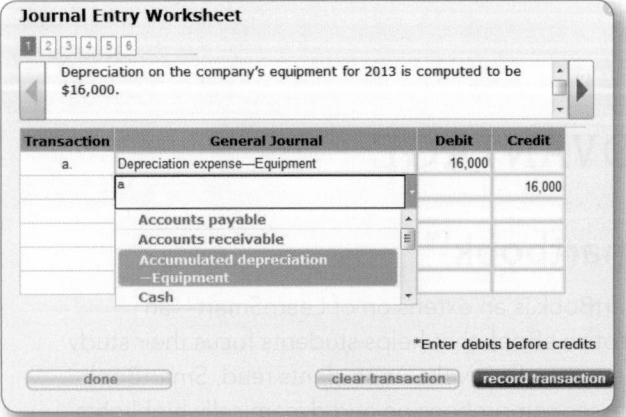

McGraw-Hill Education redesigned the student interface for our end-of-chapter assessment content. The new interface provides improved answer acceptance to reduce students' frustration with formatting issues (such as rounding) and, for select questions, provides an expanded table that guides students through the process of solving the problem. Many questions have been redesigned to more fully test students' mastery of the content.

General Ledger

New to *FAP* are General Ledger problems that offer students the ability to see how transactions post from the general journal all the way through the financial statements. General Ledger (GL) questions provide auto-grading in the same intelligent design as our end-of-chapter content. Critical thinking and analysis components are added to each GL problem to ensure understanding of the entire process.

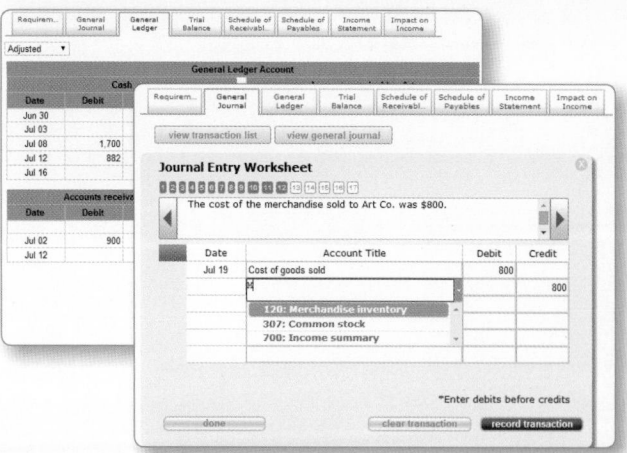

Excel Simulations

Assignable within Connect Plus Accounting, Excel Simulations allow students to practice their Excel skills—such as basic formulas and formatting—within the context of accounting. These questions feature animated, narrated Help and Show Me tutorials (when enabled). These simulations are auto-graded and provide instant feedback to the student.

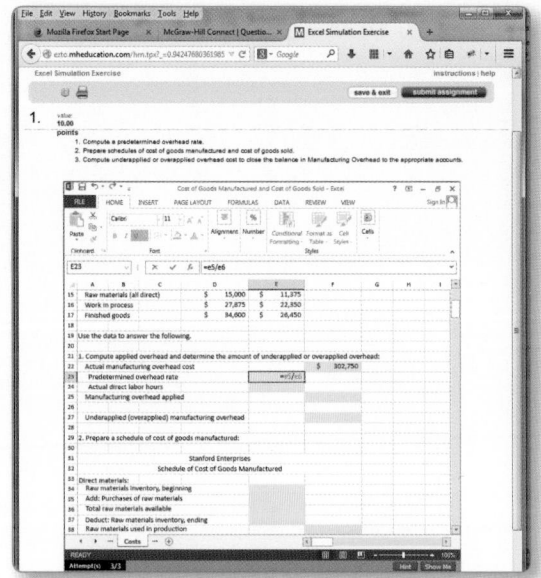

POWERFUL PERFORMANCE REPORTING

Connect generates comprehensive reports that provide instructors with an instant view of the performance of individual students, a specific section, or multiple sections. Since all content is mapped to learning objectives, Connect reporting is ideal for accreditation or other administrative documentation.

General Ledger

New to FAP are General Ledger problems that offer students the ability to see how transactions post from the general journal all the way through the financial statements. General Ledger (GL) questions provide auto-grading in the same intelligent design as our end-of-chapter content. Critical thinking and analysis components are added to each GL problem to ensure understanding of the entire process.

Excel Simulations

Assignable within Connect Plus Accounting, Excel Simulations allow students to practice their Excel skills, such as basic formulas and formatting — within the context of accounting. These questions feature animated Guided Help and Show Me tutorials (when enabled). These simulations are auto-graded and provide instant feedback to the student.

POWERFUL PERFORMANCE REPORTING

Connect generates comprehensive reports that provide instructors with an instant view of the performance of an individual student, a specific section, or multiple sections. Since all content is mapped to learning objectives, Connect reporting is ideal for accreditation or other administrative documentation.

Assignment Results & Statistics Reports

Student Performance Reports

Item Analysis Reports

Category Analysis Reports

At-Risk Student Reports

Fundamental Accounting Principles

Asia Global Edition, 2e

John J. Wild
University of Wisconsin at Madison

Winston Kwok
National University of Singapore

Sundar Venkatesh
Asian Institute of Technology

Ken W. Shaw
University of Missouri at Columbia

Barbara Chiappetta
Nassau Community College

Mc
Graw
Hill
Education

FUNDAMENTAL ACCOUNTING PRINCIPLES Second Edition
Asia Global Edition

Fundamental Accounting Principles, 21st Edition
Published by McGraw-Hill Education, 2 Penn Plaza, New York, NY, 10121. Copyright © 2013 by McGraw-Hill Education. Previous editions © 2011, 2009, 2007, 2005, 2002, 1999, 1996, 1990, 1987, 1984, 1981, 1978, 1975, 1972, 1969, 1966, 1963, 1959, 1955 by McGraw-Hill Education.

Cover image © Rook76/Istock.com

10 9 8 7 6 5 4 3 2 1
20 17 16 15

When ordering this title, use **ISBN 978-9-814-59500-1** or **MHID 9-814-59500-4**

Printed in Singapore

To my students and family, especially Kimberly, Jonathan, Stephanie, and Trevor
J.W.

To my late mother, my father, and my dearest Phuong
S.V.

To my wife Linda and children, Erin, Emily, and Jacob
K.S.

To my mother, husband Bob, and sons Michael and David
B.C.

About the Authors

JOHN J. WILD is a distinguished professor of accounting at the University of Wisconsin at Madison. He previously held appointments at Michigan State University and the University of Manchester in England. He received his BBA, MS, and PhD from the University of Wisconsin.

Professor Wild teaches accounting courses at both the undergraduate and graduate levels. He has received numerous teaching honors, including the Mabel W. Chipman Excellence-in-Teaching Award, the departmental Excellence-in-Teaching Award, and the Teaching Excellence Award from the 2003 and 2005 business graduates at the University of Wisconsin. He also received the Beta Alpha Psi and Roland F. Salmonson Excellence-in-Teaching Award from Michigan State University. Professor Wild has received several research honors and is a past KPMG Peat Marwick National Fellow and is a recipient of fellowships from the American Accounting Association and the Ernst and Young Foundation.

Professor Wild is an active member of the American Accounting Association and its sections. He has served on several committees of these organizations, including the Outstanding Accounting Educator Award, Wildman Award, National Program Advisory, Publications, and Research Committees. Professor Wild is author of *Financial Accounting, Managerial Accounting,* and *College Accounting,* each published by McGraw-Hill Education. His research articles on accounting and analysis appear in *The Accounting Review; Journal of Accounting Research; Journal of Accounting and Economics; Contemporary Accounting Research; Journal of Accounting, Auditing and Finance; Journal of Accounting and Public Policy;* and other journals. He is past associate editor of *Contemporary Accounting Research* and has served on several editorial boards including *The Accounting Review.*

In his leisure time, Professor Wild enjoys hiking, sports, travel, people, and spending time with family and friends.

WINSTON KWOK CHEE CHIU is an Associate Professor in the Department of Accounting at the National University of Singapore Business School.

He received his MBA and PhD from Richard Ivey School of Business, University of Western Ontario, Canada. Professor Kwok teaches accounting courses at both the undergraduate and graduate levels, as well as executive programs conducted in Chinese. He received Outstanding Educator Awards from the Business School in 2005, 2008, 2010, 2012, 2013 and 2014. He also received the University's Teaching Excellence Awards in 2011, 2013 and 2014. For winning the University Awards three times, Professor Kwok has been placed on the Honor Roll.

Professor Kwok's research papers appeared in Journal of Accounting Literature, Asia Pacific Journal of Management, Asian Case Research Journal and Accounting, Auditing, and Accountability Journal. Professor Kwok was an Associate Editor for the Asian Case Research Journal and has published many original teaching cases. He co-authored several accounting textbooks since 2007 and more than twenty thousand copies of the books have been sold to institutions in Hong Kong and Mainland China, Indonesia, Malaysia, Singapore, South Korea, Taiwan, and Thailand.

Being a Chartered Accountant in Singapore, Professor Kwok also served on committees such as the Singapore Corporate Awards. He regularly supervises and accompanies students to international business case competitions and study trips.

SUNDAR VENKATESH is an Adjunct Faculty in the School of Management, Asian Institute of Technology (AIT), Thailand. He serves as an advisor to the Director of AIT Extension, which runs AIT's executive and professional development programmes. He is a visiting faculty at Vietnam National University and the Maastricht School of Management's executive MBA programme in Vietnam.

He has served on the faculty of the Indian Institute of Management Bangalore, where he has been recipient of several awards for teaching excellence. He has also lectured in Bangladesh, Cambodia, China, France, Laos, Nepal, and Sri Lanka.

Dr. Venkatesh is a founder CEO of ConnectED Learning and Development, a boutique training and development company that offers blended learning, combining on-line and in class.

Dr. Venkatesh is a Chartered Accountant. He obtained his Phd from the Indian Institute of Management Ahmedabad. He also holds degrees in physics and law. He has written and published extensively. His articles have appeared in *Asia Pacific Management Journal, Asian Case Research Journal* and the *ASEAN Economic Bulletin,* among others. Several of his case studies are featured in the Ivey Case Clearing house.

KEN W. SHAW is an associate professor of accounting and the Deloitte Professor of Accounting at the University of Missouri. He previously was on the faculty at the University of Maryland at College Park. He has also taught in international programs at the University of Bergamo (Italy) and the University of Alicante (Spain). He received an accounting degree from Bradley University and an MBA and PhD from the University of Wisconsin. He is a Certified Public Accountant with work experience in public accounting.

Professor Shaw teaches accounting at the undergraduate and graduate levels. He has received numerous School of Accountancy, College of Business and university-level teaching awards. He was voted the "Most Influential Professor" by three School of Accountancy graduating classes, and is a two-time recipient of the O'Brien Excellence in Teaching Award. He is the advisor to his school's chapter of the Association of Certified Fraud Examiners.

Professor Shaw is an active member of the American Accounting Association and its sections. He has served on many committees of these organizations and presented his research papers at national and regional meetings. Professor Shaw's research appears in the *Journal of Accounting Research; The Accounting Review; Contemporary Accounting Research; Journal of Financial and Quantitative Analysis; Journal of the American Taxation Association; Strategic Management Journal; Journal of Accounting, Auditing, and Finance; Journal of Financial Research;* and other journals. He has served on the editorial boards of *Issues in Accounting Education; Journal of Business Research;* and *Research in Accounting Regulation.* Professor Shaw is co-author of *Financial and Managerial Accounting, Managerial Accounting,* and *College Accounting,* all published by McGraw-Hill Education.

In his leisure time, Professor Shaw enjoys tennis, cycling, music, and coaching his children's sports teams.

BARBARA CHIAPPETTA received her BBA in Accountancy and MS in Education from Hofstra University and is a tenured full professor at Nassau Community College. For the past two decades, she has been an active executive board member of the Teachers of Accounting at Two-Year Colleges (TACTYC), serving 10 years as vice president and as president from 1993 through 1999. As an active member of the American Accounting Association, she has served on the Northeast Regional Steering Committee, chaired the Curriculum Revision Committee of the Two-Year Section, and participated in numerous national committees. Professor Chiappetta has been inducted into the American Accounting Association Hall of Fame for the Northeast Region. She had also received the Nassau Community College dean of instruction's Faculty Distinguished Achievement Award. Professor Chiappetta was honored with the State University of New York Chancellor's Award for Teaching Excellence in 1997. As a confirmed believer in the benefits of the active learning pedagogy, Professor Chiappetta has authored *Student Learning Tools,* an active learning workbook for a first-year accounting course, published by McGraw-Hill Education.

In her leisure time, Professor Chiappetta enjoys tennis and participates on a U.S.T.A. team. She also enjoys the challenge of bridge. Her husband, Robert, is an entrepreneur in the leisure sport industry. She has two sons—Michael, a lawyer, specializing in intellectual property law in New York, and David, a composer, pursuing a career in music for film in Los Angeles.

Adapting to the Needs of Today's Students

Fundamental Accounting Principles, 2e AGE

Enhancements in technology have changed how we live and learn. Working with learning resources across devices, whether smartphones, tablets, or laptop computers, empowers students to drive their own learning by putting increasingly intelligent technology into their hands.

Whether the goal is to become an accountant, a businessperson, or simply an informed consumer of accounting information, *Fundamental Accounting Principles (FAP)* has helped generations of students succeed. Its leading-edge accounting content, paired with state-of-the-art technology, supports student learning and elevates understanding of key accounting principles.

FAP excels at **engaging students** with content that will help them see the relevance of accounting. Its chapter-opening vignettes showcase dynamic, successful entrepreneurial individuals and companies and **highlight the usefulness of accounting to business owners.** This edition's featured companies—**Nestle, Adidas,** and **Samsung**—capture student interest with their products, and their annual reports serve as a pathway for learning financial statements.

FAP also delivers innovative technology to help student performance. ***Connect Plus Accounting*** provides students with a media-rich eBook version of the textbook and offers instant grading and feedback for assignments that are completed online. Our system for completing exercise and problem material takes accounting content to the next level,
delivering assessment material in a **more intuitive, less restrictive** format that adapts to the needs of today's students.

This technology features:

- **a general journal interface** that looks and feels more like that found in practice.
- **an auto-calculation** feature that allows students to focus on concepts rather than rote tasks.
- **a smart (auto-fill) drop-down design**.

The end result is content that better prepares students for the real world.

Connect Plus Accounting also includes digitally based, interactive, adaptive learning tools that provide an opportunity to engage students more effectively by offering varied instructional methods and more personalized learning paths that build on different learning styles, interests, and abilities.

Interactive Presentations teach each chapter's core learning objectives in a rich, multimedia format, bringing the content to life. Your students will come to class prepared when you assign Interactive Presentations. Students can also review the Interactive Presentations as they study. Further, **Guided Examples** provide students with narrated, animated, step-by-step walkthroughs of algorithmic versions of assigned exercises. Students appreciate the Guided Examples, which help them learn accounting and complete assignments outside of class.

> "I believe that *FAP* is the best intro accounting text on the market—clear, concise, complete. . . . Additionally, it is clear that the authors stay in touch with the 'times'."
>
> —**JAMES L. LOCK, Northern Virginia Community College**

 **ACCOUNTING**

Easy to Use. Proven Effective.

McGraw-Hill *CONNECT PLUS ACCOUNTING*

McGraw-Hill *Connect Plus Accounting* is a digital teaching and learning environment that gives students the means to better connect with their coursework, with their instructors, and with the important concepts they will need to know for success now and in the future. With *Connect Plus Accounting,* instructors can easily deliver assignments, quizzes, and tests online. Students can review course material and practice important skills.

McGraw-Hill *Connect Plus Accounting* provides all of the following learning and teaching resources:

- Auto-graded online homework
- General ledger problems
- Auto-graded Excel simulations
- Interactive Presentations
- Guided Examples

In short, *Connect Plus Accounting* offers students powerful tools and features that optimize their time and energy, enabling them to focus on learning.

Online Assignments

Connect Plus Accounting helps students learn more efficiently by providing feedback and practice material when they need it, where they need it. *Connect Plus* grades homework automatically and gives immediate feedback on any questions students may have missed. Our assignable, gradable end-of-chapter content includes a general journal application that looks and feels more like what you would find in a general ledger software package. Also, select questions have been redesigned to test students' knowledge more fully. They now include tables for students to work through rather than requiring that all calculations be done off-line. McGraw-Hill's redesigned student interface provides a real-world feel to interactive assignments and end-of-chapter assessment content. This robust accounting software allows for flexibility in learning styles and provides opportunities for courses to be delivered in traditional, online, and blended settings.

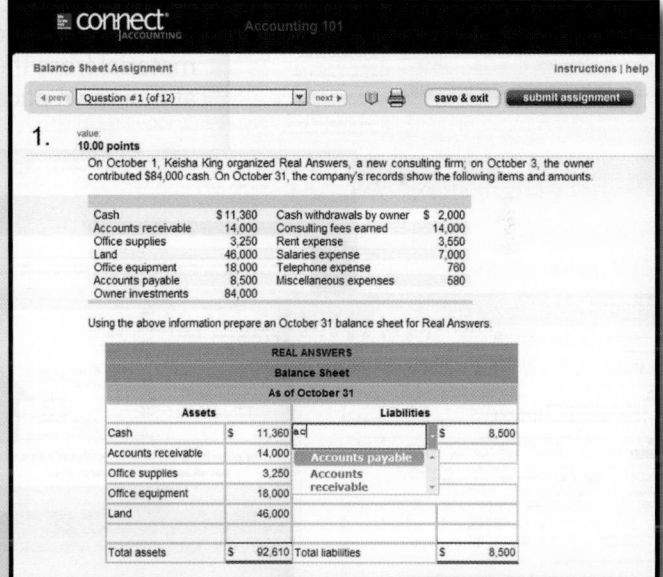

Tailored to You.

General Ledger Problems

New General Ledger problems for select questions enable students to see how transactions post from the general journal all the way through the financial statements. It provides a much-improved experience for students working with accounting cycle questions. Students' work in the general journal is automatically posted to the ledger, navigation is much simpler, scrolling is no longer an issue, and students can easily link back to their original entries simply by clicking the ledger if edits are needed. Many questions now have critical thinking components added, to maximize students' foundational knowledge of accounting concepts and principles.

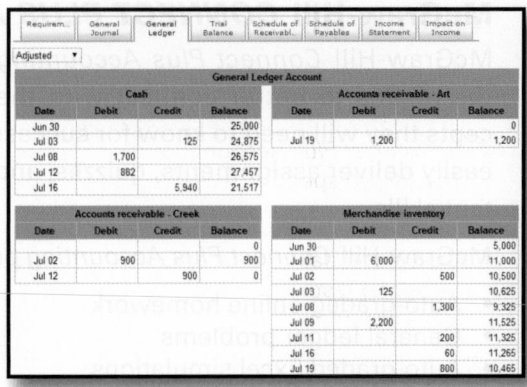

Interactive Presentations

Interactive Presentations provide engaging narratives of all chapter learning objectives in an assignable interactive online format. They follow the structure of the text and are organized to match the specific learning objectives within each chapter. While the Interactive Presentations are not meant to replace the textbook, they provide additional explanation and enhancement of material from the text chapter, allowing students to learn, study, and practice at their own pace, with instant feedback.

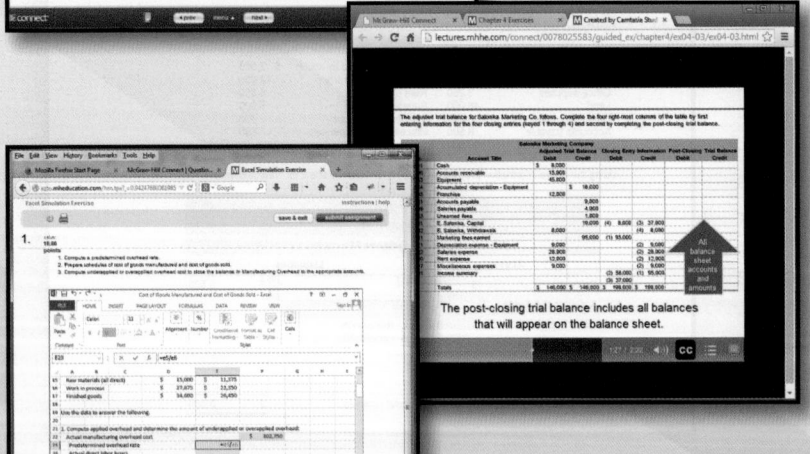

Guided Examples

The Guided Examples in *Connect Plus Accounting* provide a narrated, animated, step-by-step walk-through of select exercises similar to those assigned. These short presentations, which can be turned on or off by instructors, provide reinforcement when students need it most.

Excel Simulations

Simulated Excel questions, assignable within *Connect Plus Accounting,* allow students to practice their Excel skills—such as basic formulas and formatting—within the context of accounting. These questions feature animated, narrated Help and Show Me tutorials (when enabled), as well as automatic feedback and grading for both students and professors.

 **Easy to Use. Proven Effective.**

McGraw-Hill *CONNECT PLUS ACCOUNTING* Features

Simple Assignment Management and Smart Grading

With *Connect Plus Accounting*, creating assignments is easier than ever, enabling instructors to spend more time teaching and less time managing. Simple assignment management and smart grading allow you to:

- Create and deliver assignments easily with selectable end-of-chapter questions and Test Bank items.
- Have assignments scored automatically, giving students immediate feedback on their work and side-by-side comparisons with correct answers.
- Access and review each response, manually change grades, or leave comments for students to review.
- Reinforce classroom concepts with practice assignments and instant quizzes and exams.

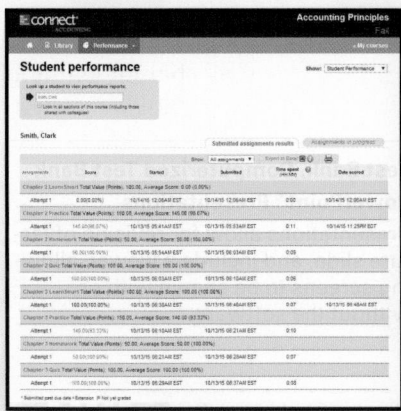

Powerful Instructor and Student Reports

Connect Plus Accounting keeps instructors informed about how each student, section, and class is performing, allowing for more productive use of lecture and office hours. The progress-tracking function enables you to:

- View scored work immediately and track individual or group performance with assignment and grade reports.
- Access an instant view of student or class performance relative to learning objectives.
- Collect data and generate reports required by many accreditation organizations, such as AACSB and AICPA.

Instructor Library

The *Connect Plus Accounting* Instructor Library is a repository for additional resources to improve student engagement in and out of class. You can select and use any asset that enhances your lecture. The *Connect Plus Accounting* Instructor Library includes:

- Presentation slides.
- Solutions Manual.
- Test Bank.
- Instructor's Resource Manual.

The *Connect Plus Accounting* Instructor Library also allows you to upload your own files.

Other Technology Offered by McGraw-Hill

Tegrity Campus: Lectures 24/7

 Tegrity Campus is a service that makes class time available 24/7 by automatically capturing every lecture. With a simple one-click start-and-stop process, you capture all computer screens and corresponding audio in a format that is easily searchable, frame by frame. Students can replay any part of any recorded class with easy-to-use browser-based viewing on a PC, Mac, or mobile device.

Help turn your students' study time into learning moments immediately supported by your lecture. With Tegrity Campus, you also increase intent listening and class participation by easing students' concerns about note-taking.

To learn more about Tegrity, watch a two-minute Flash demo at **http://tegritycampus.mhhe.com**.

For more information about *Connect Plus Accounting,* go to **www.connect.mheducation.com**, or contact your local McGraw-Hill Higher Education representative.

Tailored to You.

McGraw-Hill Campus™

Campus McGraw-Hill Campus™ is a new one-stop teaching and learning experience available to users of any learning management system. This institutional service allows faculty and students to enjoy single sign-on (SSO) access to all McGraw-Hill Higher Education materials, including the award-winning McGraw-Hill Connect Plus platform, from directly within the institution's website. To learn more about McGraw-Hill Campus, visit http://mhcampus.mhhe.com.

Custom Publishing through Create™

McGraw-Hill Create™ is a self-service website that allows instructors to create custom course materials by drawing upon McGraw-Hill's comprehensive, cross-disciplinary content. Instructors can add their own content quickly and easily and tap into other rights-secured, third-party sources as well, then arrange the content in a way that makes the most sense for their course. Through Create, you can:

- Combine material from different sources and even upload your own content.
- Personalize your product with the course name and information.
- Choose the best format for your students—color print, black-and-white print, or eBook.
- Edit and update your course materials as often as you'd like.

Begin creating now at **www.mcgrawhillcreate.com.**

Instructor Resources

Connect is your all-in-one location for a variety of instructor resources. You can create custom presentations from your own materials and access all of the following. Here's what you'll find there:

- **Instructor's Resource Manual**

This manual contains (for each chapter) a Lecture Outline, a chart linking all assignment materials to learning objectives, and additional visuals with transparency masters.

- **Solutions Manual**

- **Test Bank, Computerized Test Bank**
- **PowerPoint® Presentations**
  Presentations allow for revision of lecture slide, and include a viewer, allowing screens to be shown with or without the software.

Online Learning Center (OLC)

We offer an Online Learning Center (OLC) that follows *Fundamental Accounting Principles* chapter by chapter. It doesn't require any building or maintenance on your part. It's ready to go the moment you and your students type in the URL: *www.mheducation.asia/olc/wildkwokFAP*

As students study and learn from *Fundamental Accounting Principles*, they can visit the Student Edition of the OLC Website to work with a multitude of helpful tools:

- Chapter Learning Objectives
- PowerPoint® Presentations
- Excel Template Assignments
- Interactive Chapter Quizzes
- Video Library
- General Ledger Problems

A secured Instructor Edition stores essential course materials to save you prep time before class. Everything you need to run a lively classroom and an efficient course is included. All resources available to students, plus . . .

- Instructor's Resource Manual
- Solutions to Excel Template Assignments
- Solutions Manual
- Test Bank

The OLC Website also serves as a doorway to other technology solutions, like course management systems.

Student Supplements

Principles of Financial Accounting Chapters 1-17

ISBN: 978-9-814-59501-8
MHID: 9-814-59501-2

Written by John J. Wild.

Connect Plus Accounting Two-Semester Access Code Card
ISBN: 978-9-814-66070-9
MHID: 9-814-66070-1

Innovative Textbook Features . . .

Using Accounting for Decisions

Whether we prepare, analyze, or apply accounting information, one skill remains essential: decision making. To help develop good decision-making habits and to illustrate the relevance of accounting, we use a pedagogical framework we call the Decision Center. This framework encompasses a variety of approaches and subject areas, giving students insight into every aspect of business decision making; see the four nearby examples for the different types of decision boxes, including those that relate to fraud. Answers to Decision Maker and Ethics boxes are at the end of each chapter.

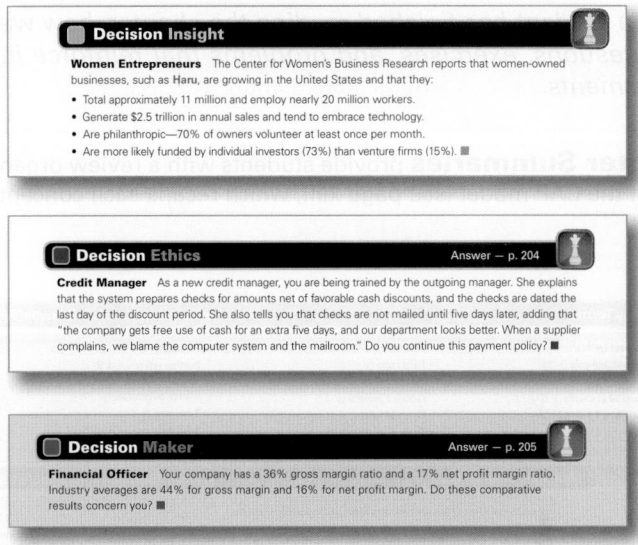

Decision Insight

Women Entrepreneurs The Center for Women's Business Research reports that women-owned businesses, such as **Haru**, are growing in the United States and that they:

- Total approximately 11 million and employ nearly 20 million workers.
- Generate $2.5 trillion in annual sales and tend to embrace technology.
- Are philanthropic—70% of owners volunteer at least once per month.
- Are more likely funded by individual investors (73%) than venture firms (15%). ■

Decision Ethics   Answer – p. 204

Credit Manager As a new credit manager, you are being trained by the outgoing manager. She explains that the system prepares checks for amounts net of favorable cash discounts, and the checks are dated the last day of the discount period. She also tells you that checks are not mailed until five days later, adding that "the company gets free use of cash for an extra five days, and our department looks better. When a supplier complains, we blame the computer system and the mailroom." Do you continue this payment policy? ■

Decision Maker   Answer – p. 205

Financial Officer Your company has a 36% gross margin ratio and a 17% net profit margin ratio. Industry averages are 44% for gross margin and 16% for net profit margin. Do these comparative results concern you? ■

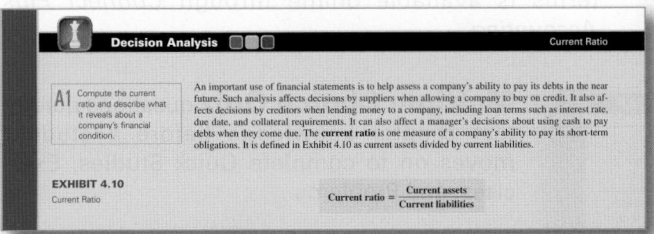

Decision Analysis   Current Ratio

A1 Compute the current ratio and describe what it reveals about a company's financial condition.

An important use of financial statements is to help assess a company's ability to pay its debts in the near future. Such analysis affects decisions by suppliers when allowing a company to buy on credit. It also affects decisions by creditors when lending money to a company, including loan terms such as interest rate, due date, and collateral requirements. It can also affect a manager's decisions about using cash to pay debts when they come due. The **current ratio** is one measure of a company's ability to pay its short-term obligations. It is defined in Exhibit 4.10 as current assets divided by current liabilities.

EXHIBIT 4.10
Current Ratio

$$\text{Current ratio} = \frac{\text{Current assets}}{\text{Current liabilities}}$$

> "Authors do a good job of relating material to real-life situations and putting students in the decision-maker role."
>
> **—Morgan Rockett, Moberly Area Community College**

Chapter Preview

Each chapter opens with a visual chapter preview. Students can begin their reading with a clear understanding of what they will learn and when, allowing them to stay more focused and organized along the way. Learning objective numbers highlight the location of related content.

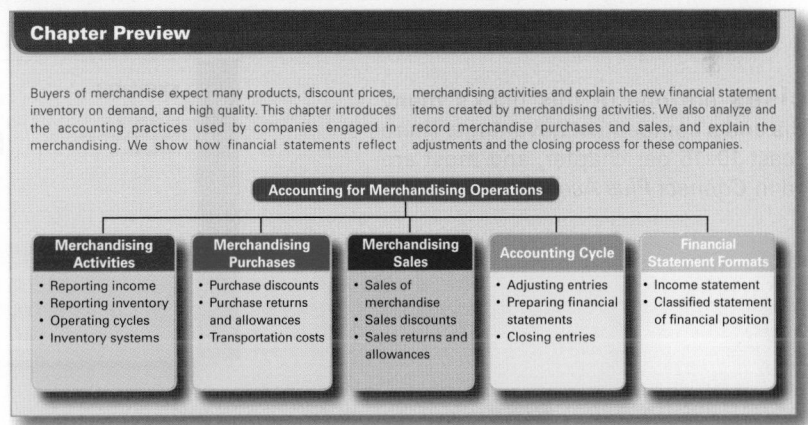

Chapter Preview

Buyers of merchandise expect many products, discount prices, inventory on demand, and high quality. This chapter introduces the accounting practices used by companies engaged in merchandising. We show how financial statements reflect merchandising activities and explain the new financial statement items created by merchandising activities. We also analyze and record merchandise purchases and sales, and explain the adjustments and the closing process for these companies.

Accounting for Merchandising Operations

Merchandising Activities	Merchandising Purchases	Merchandising Sales	Accounting Cycle	Financial Statement Formats
• Reporting income • Reporting inventory • Operating cycles • Inventory systems	• Purchase discounts • Purchase returns and allowances • Transportation costs	• Sales of merchandise • Sales discounts • Sales returns and allowances	• Adjusting entries • Preparing financial statements • Closing entries	• Income statement • Classified statement of financial position

CAP Model

The Conceptual/Analytical/Procedural (CAP) Model allows courses to be specially designed to meet the teaching needs of a diverse faculty. This model identifies learning objectives, textual materials, assignments, and test items by C, A, or P, allowing different instructors to teach from the same materials, yet easily customize their courses toward a conceptual, analytical, or procedural approach (or a combination thereof) based on personal preferences.

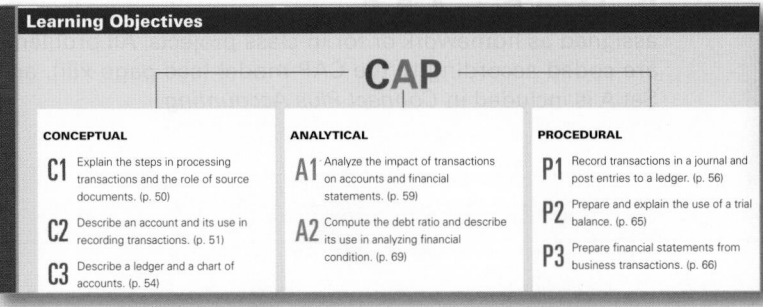

Learning Objectives

CAP

CONCEPTUAL

C1 Explain the steps in processing transactions and the role of source documents. (p. 50)

C2 Describe an account and its use in recording transactions. (p. 51)

C3 Describe a ledger and a chart of accounts. (p. 54)

ANALYTICAL

A1 Analyze the impact of transactions on accounts and financial statements. (p. 59)

A2 Compute the debt ratio and describe its use in analyzing financial condition. (p. 69)

PROCEDURAL

P1 Record transactions in a journal and post entries to a ledger. (p. 56)

P2 Prepare and explain the use of a trial balance. (p. 65)

P3 Prepare financial statements from business transactions. (p. 66)

Outstanding Assignment Material...

Once a student has finished reading the chapter, how well he or she retains the material can depend greatly on the questions, exercises, and problems that reinforce it. This book leads the way in comprehensive, accurate assignments.

Chapter Summaries provide students with a review organized by learning objectives. Chapter Summaries are a component of the CAP model (see page xiii), which recaps each conceptual, analytical, and procedural objective.

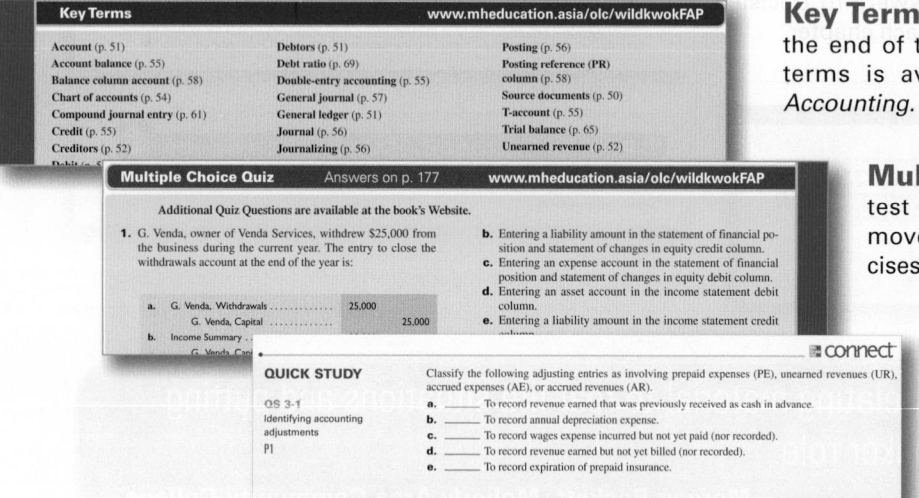

Key Terms are bolded in the text and repeated at the end of the chapter. A complete glossary of key terms is available online through *Connect Plus Accounting*.

Multiple Choice Quiz questions quickly test chapter knowledge before a student moves on to complete Quick Studies, Exercises, and Problems.

Quick Study assignments are short exercises that often focus on one learning objective. Most are included in *Connect Plus Accounting*. There are at least 10–15 Quick Study assignments per chapter.

Exercises are one of this book's many strengths and a competitive advantage. There are at least 10–15 per chapter, and most are included in *Connect Plus Accounting*.

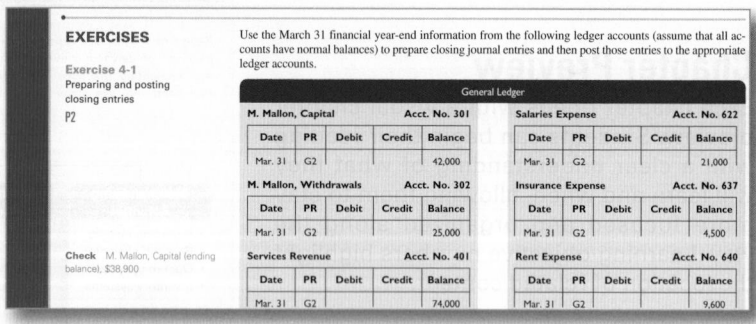

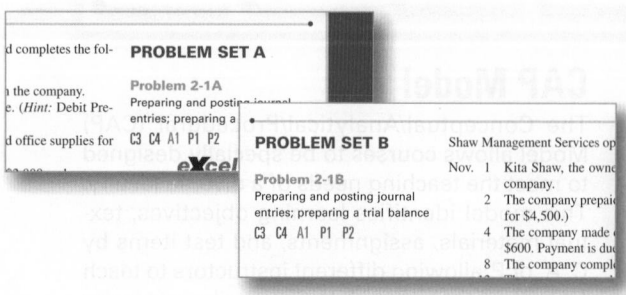

Problem Sets A & B are proven problems that can be assigned as homework or for in-class projects. All problems are coded according to the CAP model (see page xiii), and Set A is included in *Connect Plus Accounting*.

Helps Students Master Key Concepts

Beyond the Numbers exercises ask students to use accounting figures and understand their meaning. Students also learn how accounting applies to a variety of business situations. These creative and fun exercises are all new or updated and are divided into sections:

- Reporting in Action
- Comparative Analysis
- Ethics Challenge
- Communicating in Practice
- Taking It to the Net
- Teamwork in Action
- Hitting the Road
- Entrepreneurial Decision
- Global Decision

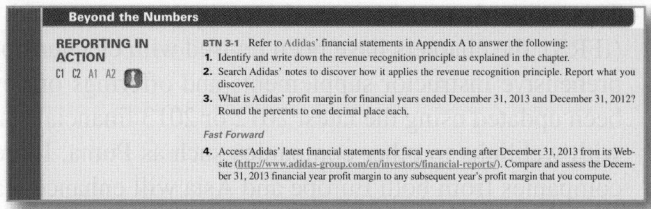

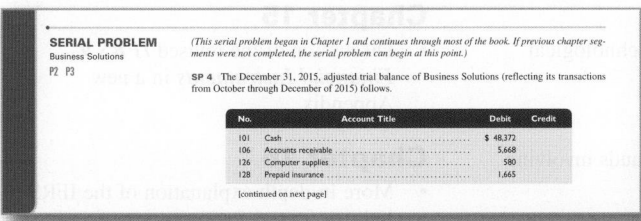

Serial Problems use a continuous running case study to illustrate chapter concepts in a familiar context. The Serial Problem can be followed continuously from the first chapter or picked up at any later point in the book; enough information is provided to ensure students can get right to work.

> "I have used many editions of this text and have been very happy with the text and all of the supplementary materials. The textbook is kept current, and is straightforward, and very usable by students. The online resources get better with each edition."
>
> **—Susan Cordes, Johnson County Community College**

General Ledger Problems New General Ledger problems enable students to see how transactions post. Students can track an amount in any financial statement all the way back to the original journal entry. Critical thinking components then challenge students to analyze the business activities in the problem.

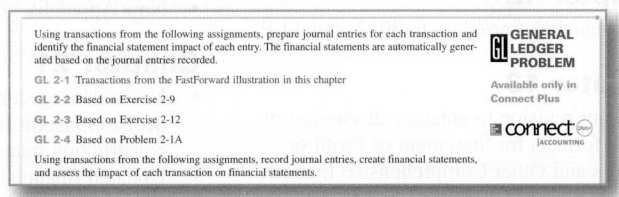

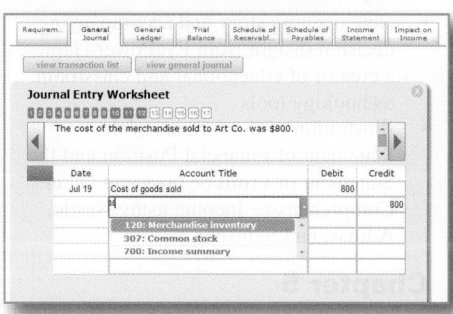

The End of the Chapter Is Only the Beginning Our valuable and proven assignments aren't just confined to the book. From problems that require technological solutions to materials found exclusively online, this book's end-of-chapter material is fully integrated with its technology package.

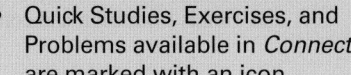

- Quick Studies, Exercises, and Problems available in *Connect* are marked with an icon.
- Assignments that focus on global accounting practices and companies are often identified with an icon.
- Assignments that involve decision analysis are identified with an icon.

New Content with a Focus on IFRS

This edition's revisions are driven by instructors and students. Based on International Financial Reporting Standards (IFRS), the chapters have been revised with chapter-opening vignettes featuring Asian entrepreneurs, and updated comprehensive instructor supplements and offerings of new questions and assignments. Learning text and questions have been updated using the latest 2012 or 2013 financial statements of Adidas, Nestle, and Samsung included as appendices, with weblinks to other companies such as Puma, L'oreal, 361 Degrees, and Li Ning. This diversity of IFRS reporting companies from both Europe and Asia will enhance learning for users.

The following gives a chapter-by-chapter synopsis, and includes revisions to the earlier edition as well as new IFRS-related material:

Chapter 1
- Expanded explanation of IASB's conceptual framework for financial reporting as part of discussion of Generally Accepted Accounting Principles
- Inclusion of updated titles and formats of IFRS financial statements including the Statement of Profit or Loss and Other Comprehensive Income

Chapter 2
- Expanded discussion and illustration on the report versus the account formats of the Statement of Financial Position

Chapter 3
- New Decision Update on the new revenue standard *IFRS 15 Revenue from Contracts with Customers*

Chapter 4
- New opening story and accompanying decision insight from EyePower Games, a creator of educational and classroom technology tools
- Illustration of the formats of the Statement of Financial Position and the Statement of Profit or Loss and Other Comprehensive Income using Nestle, Adidas, and Samsung

Chapter 5
- Detailed discussion of Statement of Profit or Loss and Other Comprehensive Income and Statement of Financial Position for a merchandising company

Chapter 6
- Enhanced discussion and illustration of IFRS inventory methods specific identification, FIFO, and weighted average cost in main text; LIFO (not allowed under IFRS) moved to Appendix for reference
- Greater clarification on lower of cost and net realizable value

Chapter 7
- Updated materials on technological advancements

Chapter 8
- Updated materials on frauds involving technology

Chapter 9
- Enhanced discussion on the allowance method used under IFRS

Chapter 10
- Revised definition of residual value as clarified in *IAS 16 Property, plant and equipment*
- Enhanced discussion and examples on the revaluation model allowed under IFRS
- Enhanced discussion of impairment

Chapter 11
- Enhanced discussion on contingent liabilities with examples using Apple, Samsung, and Nokia

Chapter 12
- Updated Net problem to 2012 actual LP

Chapter 13
- Major revision to enhance discussion of the formats for Statement of Profit or Loss and Other Comprehensive Income, Statement of Changes in Equity, and Statement of Financial Position; these formats are also explained using Nestle's financial statements
- Revised questions and problems based on the formats of the financial statements

Chapter 14
- Revised terms in line with IFRS terminology
- Secret Recipe—new opener with new entrepreneurial assignment

Chapter 15
- Discussion of the revised *IFRS 9 Financial Instruments* in a new Appendix

Chapter 16
- More in-depth explanation of the IFRS indirect format for statement of cash flows, in particular the adjustment of items from profit to cash
- Revised explanation of free cash flows

Chapter 17
- Updated 2013 financials of Adidas and Puma for all ratios and examples

Chapter 18
- Updated Financial Information (Toyota)

Chapter 19
- New opening story and accompanying decision insight from BFSI Consulting, a software services industry
- Updated financial information (Hyundai)

Chapter 20
- New Appendix on Service costing

Chapter 21
- New opening story and accompanying decision insight from Hunter Douglas, a construction materials MNC
- Updated financial information (Major Cineplex)

Chapter 23
- New opening story and accompanying decision insight from Cabela's, a sportswear industry

Chapter 24
- Updated survey of Management Tools and Trends from Bain and company

Meeting Accreditation Needs

Assurance of Learning Ready

Many educational institutions today are focused on the notion of assurance of learning, an important element of some accreditation standards. *Fundamental Accounting Principles* is designed specifically to support your assurance of learning initiatives with a simple, yet powerful solution. Each test bank question for *Fundamental Accounting Principles* maps to a specific chapter learning objective listed in the text. You can use our test bank software, EZ Test Online, or *Connect Plus Accounting* to easily query for learning objectives that directly relate to the learning objectives for your course. You can then use the EZ Test reporting features to aggregate student results in similar fashion, making the collection and presentation of assurance of learning data simple and easy.

> "*FAP...* is an old friend, dependable and true over time, with enough pizzazz and modernity to keep the relationship interesting and ongoing. The authors and publisher are dedicated to producing quality instructional materials in a variety of formats to meet the educational requirements and learning styles of a diverse audience. Hooray for them!"
>
> **—Beverly R. Beatty, Anne Arundel Community College**

AACSB Statement

The McGraw-Hill Companies is a proud corporate member of AACSB International. Understanding the importance and value of AACSB accreditation, *Fundamental Accounting Principles* recognizes the curricula guidelines detailed in the AACSB standards for business accreditation by connecting selected questions in the test bank to the six general knowledge and skill guidelines in the AACSB standards. The statements contained in *Fundamental Accounting Principles* are provided only as a guide for the users of this textbook. The AACSB leaves content coverage and assessment within the purview of individual schools, the mission of the school, and the faculty. While *Fundamental Accounting Principles* and the teaching package make no claim of any specific AACSB qualification or evaluation, we have within *Fundamental Accounting Principles* labeled select questions according to the six general knowledge and skills areas.

Preface and Acknowledgments for IFRS Edition

This is an introductory text for topics in financial accounting (Chapters 1 to 17) and managerial accounting (Chapters 18 to 25).

The major revamp is in the rewriting of the financial accounting chapters based on IFRS (including IAS). The foremost goal is to get the students interested with real-world examples and to facilitate students' application of IFRS in the shortest time possible. To generate students' interest, the real-world examples range from small entrepreneurial businesses to large multinational corporations. To facilitate quick application, questions and problems are strategically placed at checkpoints in the chapters and thoughtfully designed in graduated difficulty levels. The topics are systematically placed in sections so that instructors can assign the right amount of materials; for example, optional topics such as the periodic inventory system are placed in end-of-chapter appendices. The terminology is mainly based on IFRS, but alternative terms common to other accounting principles such as U.S. GAAP are also mentioned. For many examples and questions, the text uses the actual 2012 or 2013 financial statements of IFRS-reporting corporations of Nestlé, Adidas and Samsung, which appear in Appendix A, with website references to other IFRS corporations. As IFRS are evolving, possible future changes are strategically mentioned or placed in Decision Update boxes in the text.

All the chapter-opening stories highlight experiences of dynamic young Asian companies. Asian companies have been setting the trend in select managerial accounting practices, so the tradition of the text's previous strong points of clear exposition and enlightening questions is continued with some new Asian examples in the managerial accounting chapters. These examples present relevant findings of survey research and case studies.

Therefore, whether the reader's goal is to become an accountant, or simply an informed consumer of accounting information, this text will be an enjoyable and useful learning experience.

Winston Kwok, Sundar Venkatesh, and McGraw-Hill Education (Asia) would like to thank the following entrepreneurs for generously sharing their stories:

David Yim of U.d.d.e.r.s.

Elizabeth Seah of Haru

Violet Lim of Lunch Actually

Benson Loo of EyePower Games

George Wong of TeddyThotz 'n' OneKind

Paola Savillo, Albert Go, Bernadee Uy, and Janine Chiong of HABI Footwear

Josephine Ng of Alteration Initiative

Sam Leong of samleong@forest cooking school

Mabel Wang of Settlers Café

Janice Wong of 2am Dessert Bar

Adam Khoo and Patrick Cheo of Adam Khoo Learning Technologies Group

Michelle Tok of Home Central LLP

Douglas Young of G.O.D.

Kenny Yap of Qian Hu

Lyn Lee of Awfully Chocolate

James Tan of Scrawl Studios

Nelson Lam of Nelson and Company

Alice Zhang of Mischmasch

Prakash N. of BFSI Consulting

Desmond Yang of Abyzz

PK Sundarmoorthy of Hunter Douglas, India

Choo Yilin of Choo Yilin Artisan Jewellery

Esther Yeung of Cabela's

Derrick Lye of Mosaic Dance

Nguyen Trung Thang of Masso Group

Acknowledgments

John J. Wild, Ken W. Shaw, Barbara Chiappetta, and McGraw-Hill Education recognize the following instructors for their valuable feedback and involvement in the development of *Fundamental Accounting Principles* 2e. We are thankful for their suggestions, counsel, and encouragement.

Khaled Abdou, Penn State University - Berks

Anne Marie Anderson, Raritan Valley Community College

Elaine Anes, Heald College -Fresno

Jerome Apple, University of Akron

Jack Aschkenazi, American Intercontinental University

Sidney Askew, Borough of Manhattan Community College

Lawrence Awopetu, University of Arkansas -Pine Bluff

Jon Backman, Spartanburg Community College

Charles Baird, University of Wisconsin-Stout

Richard Barnhart, Grand Rapids Community College

Beverly R. Beatty, Anne Arundel Community College

Judy Benish, Fox Valley Tech College

Patricia Bentley, Keiser University

Teri Bernstein, Santa Monica College

Jaswinder Bhangal, Chabot College

Susan Blizzard, San Antonio College

Marvin Blye, Wor-Wic Community College

Patrick Borja, Citrus College

Anna Boulware, St. Charles Community College

Gary Bower, Community College of Rhode Island-Flanagan

Leslee Brock, Southwest Mississippi Community College

Gregory Brookins, Santa Monica College

Regina Brown, Eastfield College

Tracy L. Bundy, University of Louisiana at Lafayette

Roy Carson, Anne Arundel Community College

Deborah Carter, Coahoma Community College

Roberto Castaneda, DeVry University Online

Amy Chataginer, Mississippi Gulf Coast Community College

Gerald Childs, Waukesha County Technical College

Colleen Chung, Miami Dade College- Kendall

Shifei Chung, Rowan University

Robert Churchman, Harding University

Marilyn Ciolino, Delgado Community College

Thomas Clement, University of North Dakota

Oyinka Coakley, Broward College

Susan Cockrell, Birmingham-Southern College

Lisa Cole, Johnson County Community College

Robbie R. Coleman, Northeast Mississippi Community College

Christie Comunale, Long Island University – C.W. Post Campus

Jackie Conrecode, Florida Gulf Coast University

Debora Constable, Georgia Perimeter College

Susan Cordes, Johnson County Community College

Anne Cordozo, Broward College

Cheryl Corke, Genesse Community College

James Cosby, John Tyler Community College

Ken Couvillion, Delta College

Loretta Darche, Southwest Florida College

Judy Daulton, Piedmont Technical College

Dorothy Davis, University of Louisiana-Monroe

Walter DeAguero, Saddleback College

Mike Deschamps, MiraCosta College

Pamela Donahue, Northern Essex Community College

Steve Doster, Shawnee State University

Larry Dragosavac, Edison Community College

Samuel Duah, Bowie State University

Robert Dunlevy, Montgomery County Community College

Jerrilyn Eisenhauer, Tulsa Community College-Southeast

Ronald Elders, Virginia College

Terry Elliott, Morehead State University

Patricia Feller, Nashville State Community College

Annette Fisher, Glendale Community College

Ron Fitzgerald, Santa Monica College

David Flannery, Bryant and Stratton College

Hollie Floberg, Tennessee Wesleyan College

Linda Flowers, Houston Community College

Jeannie Folk, College of DuPage

Rebecca Foote, Middle Tennessee State University

Paul Franklin, Kaplan University

Tim Garvey, Westwood College

Barbara Gershman, Northern Virginia Community College-Woodbridge

Barbara Gershowitz, Nashville State Technical Community College

Mike Glasscock, Amarillo College

Diane Glowacki, Tarrant County College

Ernesto Gonzalez, Florida National College

Gloria Grayless, Sam Houston State University

Ann Gregory, South Plains College

Rameshwar Gupta, Jackson State University

Amy Haas, Kingsborough Community College

Pat Halliday, Santa Monica College

Keith Hallmark, Calhoun Community College

Rebecca Hancock, El Paso Community College-Valley Verde

Mechelle Harris, Bossier Parish Community College

Tracey Hawkins, University of Cincinnati-Clermont College

Thomas Hayes, University of Arkansas-Ft. Smith

Laurie Hays, Western Michigan University

Roger Hehman, University of Cincinnati-Clermont College

Cheri Hernandez, Des Moines Area Community College

Margaret Hicks, Howard University

Melanie Hicks, Liberty University

James Higgins, Holy Family University

Patricia Holmes, Des Moines Area Community College

Barbara Hopkins, Northern Virginia Community College-Manassas

Wade Hopkins, Heald College

Aileen Huang, Santa Monica College

Les Hubbard, Solano College

Deborah Hudson, Gaston College

James Hurst, National College

Constance Hylton, George Mason University
Christine Irujo, Westfield State University
Fred Jex, Macomb Community College
Gina M. Jones, Aims Community College
Jeff Jones, College of Southern Nevada
Rita Jones, Columbus State University
Dmitriy Kalyagin, Chabot College
Thomas Kam, Hawaii Pacific University
Naomi Karolinski, Monroe Community College
Shirly A. Kleiner, Johnson County Community College
Kenneth A. Koerber, Bucks County Community College
Tamara Kowalczyk, Appalachian State University
Anita Kroll, University of Wisconsin-Madison
David Krug, Johnson County Community College
Christopher Kwak, DeAnza College
Jeanette Landin, Empire College
Beth Lasky, Delgado Community College
Neal Leviton, Santa Monica College
Danny Litt, University of California Los Angeles
James L. Lock, Northern Virginia Community College
Steve Ludwig, Northwest Missouri State University
Debra Luna, El Paso Community College
Amado Mabul, Heald College
Lori Major, Luzerne County Community College
Jennifer Malfitano, Delaware County Community College
Maria Mari, Miami Dade College-Kendall
Thomas S. Marsh, Northern Virginia Community College-Annandale
Karen Martinson, University of Wisconsin-Stout
Brenda Mattison, Tri-County Technical College
Stacie Mayes, Rose State College
Jeanine Metzler, Northampton Community College
Theresa Michalow, Moraine Valley Community College
Kathleen Michele, WECA–Madison
Julie Miller, Chippewa Valley Tech College
Tim Miller, El Camino College
John Minchin, California Southern University
Edna C. Mitchell, Polk State College
Jill Mitchell, Northern Virginia Community College
Lynn Moore, Aiken Technical College
Angela Mott, Northeast Mississippi Community College
Timothy Murphy, Diablo Valley College
Kenneth F. O'Brien, Farmingdale State College
Kathleen O'Donnell, Onondaga Community College
Ahmed Omar, Burlington County College
Robert A. Pacheco, Massasoit Community College
Margaret Parilo, Cosumnes River College
Paige Paulsen, Salt Lake Community College
Yvonne Phang, Borough of Manhattan Community College
Gary Pieroni, Diablo Valley College
David Ravetch, University of California Los Angeles
Ruthie Reynolds, Howard University
Cecile Roberti, Community College of Rhode Island
Morgan Rockett, Moberly Area Community College
Patrick Rogan, Cosumnes River College

Paul Rogers, Community College of Beaver County
Helen Roybark, Radford University
Alphonse Ruggiero, Suffolk County Community College
Arjan Sadhwani, South University
Gary K. Sanborn, Northwestern Michigan College
Kin Kin Sandhu, Heald College
Marcia Sandvold, Des Moines Area Community College
Gary Schader, Kean University
Darlene Schnuck, Waukesha County Technical College
Elizabeth Serapin, Columbia Southern University
Geeta Shankhar, University of Dayton
Regina Shea, Community College of Baltimore County—Essex
James Shelton, Liberty University
Jay Siegel, Union County College
Gerald Singh, New York City College of Technology
Lois Slutsky, Broward College-South
Gerald Smith, University of Northern Iowa
Kathleen Sobieralski, University of Maryland University College
Charles Spector, State University of New York at Oswego
Diane Stark, Phoenix College
Thomas Starks, Heald College
Carolyn L. Strauch, Crowder College
Latazia Stuart, Fortis University Online
Gene Sullivan, Liberty University
David Sulzen, Ferrum College
Dominique Svarc, William Rainey Harper College
Linda Sweeney, Sam Houston State University
Margaret Tanner, University of Arkansas—Ft. Smith
Ulysses Taylor, Fayetteville State University
Anthony Teng, Saddleback College
Paula Thomas, Middle Tennessee State University
Teresa Thompson, Chaffey Community College
Leslie Thysell, John Tyler Community College
Melanie Torborg, Globe University
Shafi Ullah, Broward College
Bob Urell, Irvine Valley College
Adam Vitalis, University of Wisconsin-Madison
Patricia Walczak, Lansing Community College
Terri Walsh, Seminole State College-Oviedo
Shunda Ware, Atlanta Technical College
Dave Welch, Franklin University
Jean Wells-Jessup, Howard University
Christopher Widmer, Tidewater Community College
Andrew Williams, Edmonds Community College
Kenneth L. Wild, University of London
John Woodward, Polk State College
Gail E. Wright, Stevenson University
Wanda Wong, Chabot College
Patricia Worsham, Norco College, Riverside Community College
Lynnette Yerbury, Salt Lake Community College
Judy Zander, Grossmont College
Mary Zenner, College of Lake County
Jane Zlojutro, Northwestern Michigan College

Brief Contents

Contents

5 Merchandising Operations 178

6 Inventories and Cost of Sales 224

7 Accounting Information Systems 270

14 Long-Term Liabilities 536

15 Investments and International Operations 570

16 Statement of Cash Flows 608

Fundamental Accounting Principles

1

Accounting in Business

A Look at This Chapter

Accounting is crucial in our information age. In this chapter, we discuss the importance of accounting to different types of organizations and describe its many users and uses. We explain that ethics are essential to accounting. We also explain business transactions and how they are reflected in financial statements.

A Look Ahead

Chapter 2 describes and analyzes business transactions. We explain the analysis and recording of transactions, the ledger and trial balance, and the double-entry system. More generally, Chapters 2 through 4 show (via the accounting cycle) how financial statements reflect business activities.

Learning Objectives

Learning Objectives are classified as conceptual, analytical, or procedural.

CAP

CONCEPTUAL

C1 Explain the purpose and importance of accounting. (p. 4)

C2 Identify users and uses of, and opportunities in, accounting. (p. 5)

C3 Explain why ethics are crucial to accounting. (p. 7)

C4 Explain generally accepting accounting principles and the IASB Conceptual Framework. (p. 8)

C5 *Appendix 1B*—Identify and describe the three major activities of organizations. (p. 26)

ANALYTICAL

A1 Define and interpret the accounting equation and each of its components. (p. 13)

A2 Compute and interpret return on assets. (p. 22)

A3 *Appendix 1A*—Explain the relation between return and risk. (p. 26)

PROCEDURAL

P1 Analyze business transactions using the accounting equation. (p. 14)

P2 Identify and prepare basic financial statements and explain how they interrelate. (p. 19)

"We want to be known for our funky original flavors, and be part of people's happy memories."—**DAVID YIM**

Decision Insight

*A **Decision Feature** launches each chapter showing the relevance of accounting for a real entrepreneur. An **Entrepreneurial Decision** problem at the end of the assignments returns to this feature with a mini-case.*

Udderly Delicious

Bring together an ex-science teacher and a general manager of a café chain, and what do you get? U.d.d.e.r.s (**www. udders.com.sg**), a unique ice cream café churning out potent liqueur flavors, ice cream with a real kick! David Yim and Lillian Chan, the owners of U.d.d.e.r.s, believe passionately in great ice cream, great fun, and great creativity. When they first started, "we experimented with making ice cream day and night," says David. "My background as a science teacher helped—I treated it as one giant experiment." The name they chose for the café usually elicits chuckles, and the fun doesn't stop there—customers can put up their suggested flavors on a chalkboard in the café, and the flavors with the highest votes will be chosen for research as the next flavor creation. Says David, "Not only do customers have fun reading the suggestions and voting for them, it helps us to know what's on our customers' minds and fulfill their wish list."

When David and Lillian started out with one outlet, they did the accounts themselves. Although not formally accounting trained, they understood how important it was to have a good

grasp of the numbers of the business. "Accounting certainly ceases to be academic—it is absolutely essential when your money is on the line!" says David. "When there are so many pressing issues every day, so many things to do, it is easy to get caught up in the operational or marketing aspects of the business and assume that accounting will take care of itself." Now that business has expanded to three outlets and one central kitchen, David and Lillian have engaged professional help to set up a proper accounting system, prepare financial reports, and apply financial analysis. David stresses that "accounting is important for informed decision making, to provide an objective reference point to business decisions, which all too often could be guided by subjective 'feel' considerations, especially when everyone is offering an opinion on what should be done."

Well, one thing is certain: with great flavors like Lychee Martini, Rum Rum Raisin, and Tira-miss-u, the giant experiment has turned out to be one resounding success.

*A **Preview** opens each chapter with a summary of topics covered.*

Today's world is one of information—its preparation, communication, analysis, and use. Accounting is at the core of this information age. Knowledge of accounting gives us career opportunities and the insight to take advantage of them. This book introduces concepts, procedures, and analyses that help us make better decisions, including career choices. In this chapter we describe accounting, the users and uses of accounting information, the forms and activities of organizations, and several accounting principles. We also introduce transaction analysis and financial statements.

Accounting in Business

Importance of Accounting	Fundamentals of Accounting	Transaction Analysis	Financial Statements
• Accounting information users • Opportunities in accounting	• Ethics—key concept • Generally accepted accounting principles • International standards	• Accounting equation • Transaction analysis—illustrated	• Statement of profit or loss and other comprehensive income (including income statement) • Statement of changes in equity • Statement of financial position • Statement of cash flows

IMPORTANCE OF ACCOUNTING

C1 Explain the purpose and importance of accounting.

Why is accounting so popular on campuses? Why are there so many accounting jobs for graduates? Why is accounting so important to companies? Why do politicians and business leaders focus on accounting regulations? The answer is that we live in an information age, where that information, and its reliability, impacts the financial well-being of us all.

Accounting is an information and measurement system that identifies, records, and communicates relevant, reliable, and comparable information about an organization's business activities. *Identifying* business activities requires selecting transactions and events relevant to an organization. **Nestlé's** sale of coffee and **Adidas'** sale of sports shoes are examples. *Recording* business activities requires keeping a chronological log of transactions and events measured in dollars and classified and summarized in a useful format. *Communicating* business activities requires preparing accounting reports such as financial statements. It also requires analyzing and interpreting such reports. (The financial statements of **Nestlé** are shown in Appendix A of this book. This appendix also shows the financial statements of **Adidas**, and **Samsung**.) Exhibit 1.1 summarizes accounting activities.

Real company names are printed in bold magenta.

We must guard against a narrow view of accounting. Our most common contact with accounting is through credit approvals, checking accounts, tax forms, and payroll. These experiences are limited and tend to focus on the recordkeeping parts of accounting. **Recordkeeping,** or

EXHIBIT 1.1

Accounting Activities

Identifying	Recording	Communicating
Select transactions and events	Input, measure, and classify	Prepare, analyze, and interpret

bookkeeping, is the recording of transactions and events, either manually or electronically. This is just one part of accounting. Accounting also identifies and communicates information on transactions and events, and it includes the crucial processes of analysis and interpretation.

Technology is a key part of modern business and plays a major role in accounting. Technology reduces the time, effort, and cost of recordkeeping while improving clerical accuracy. Some small organizations continue to perform various accounting tasks manually, but even they are impacted by technology. As technology has changed the way we store, process, and summarize masses of data, accounting has been freed to expand. Consulting, planning, and other financial services are now closely linked to accounting. These services require sorting through data, interpreting their meaning, identifying key factors, and analyzing their implications.

Point: Technology is only as useful as the accounting data available, and users' decisions are only as good as their understanding of accounting. The best software and recordkeeping cannot make up for lack of accounting knowledge.

Margin notes further enhance the textual material.

Users of Accounting Information

Accounting is often called the *language of business* because all organizations set up an accounting information system to communicate data to help people make better decisions. Exhibit 1.2 shows that the accounting information system serves many kinds of users (this is a partial listing) who can be divided into two groups: external users and internal users.

EXHIBIT 1.2

Users of Accounting Information

Infographics reinforce key concepts through visual learning.

• Lenders	• Consumer groups	• Officers	• Sales staff
• Shareholders	• External auditors	• Managers	• Budget officers
• Governments	• Customers	• Internal auditors	• Controllers

External Information Users   **External users** of accounting information are *not* directly involved in running the organization. They include shareholders (investors), lenders, customers, suppliers, regulators, lawyers, brokers, and the press. External users have limited access to an organization's information. Yet their business decisions depend on information that is reliable, relevant, and comparable.

C2 Identify users and uses of, and opportunities in, accounting.

Financial accounting is the area of accounting aimed at serving external users by providing them with *general-purpose financial statements*. The term *general-purpose* refers to the broad range of purposes for which external users rely on these statements.

Each external user has special information needs depending on the types of decisions to be made. *Lenders* (creditors) loan money or other resources to an organization. Banks, savings and loans, co-ops, and mortgage and finance companies are lenders. Lenders look for information to help them assess whether an organization is likely to repay its loans with interest. *Shareholders* (investors) are the owners of a corporation. They use accounting reports in deciding whether to buy, hold, or sell shares. Shareholders typically elect a *board of directors* to oversee their interests in an organization. There be external directors not involved with the operations of the business so they can be considered as external users. *External* (independent) *auditors* examine financial statements to verify that they are prepared according to generally accepted accounting principles. *Nonexecutive employees* and *labor unions* use financial statements to judge the fairness of wages, assess job prospects, and bargain for better wages. *Regulators* often have legal authority over certain activities of organizations. For example, the Internal Revenue Service (IRS) and other tax authorities require organizations to file accounting reports in computing taxes. Other regulators include utility boards that use accounting information to set utility rates and securities regulators that require reports for companies that sell their shares to the public.

Accounting serves the needs of many other external users. *Voters, legislators,* and *government officials* use accounting information to monitor and evaluate government receipts and expenses. *Contributors* to nonprofit organizations use accounting information to evaluate the use and impact of their donations. *Suppliers* use accounting information to judge the soundness of a customer before making sales on credit, and *customers* use financial reports to assess the staying power of potential suppliers.

Internal Information Users   **Internal users** of accounting information are those directly involved in managing and operating an organization. They use the information to help improve the efficiency and effectiveness of an organization. **Managerial accounting** is the area of accounting that serves the decision-making needs of internal users. Internal reports are not subject to the same rules as external reports and instead are designed with the special needs of internal users in mind.

There are several types of internal users, and many are directors and managers of key operating activities. *Research and development managers* need information about projected costs and revenues of any proposed changes in products and services. *Purchasing managers* need to know what, when, and how much to purchase. *Human resource managers* need information about employees' payroll, benefits, performance, and compensation. *Production managers* depend on information to monitor costs and ensure quality. *Distribution managers* need reports for timely, accurate, and efficient delivery of products and services. *Marketing managers* use reports about sales and costs to target consumers, set prices, and monitor consumer needs, tastes, and price concerns. *Service managers* require information on the costs and benefits of looking after products and services. Decisions of these and other internal users depend on accounting reports.

Both internal and external users rely on internal controls to monitor and control company activities. *Internal controls* are procedures set up to protect company property and equipment, ensure reliable accounting reports, promote efficiency, and encourage adherence to company policies. Examples are good records, physical controls (locks, passwords, guards), and independent reviews.

Decision Insight boxes highlight relevant items from practice.

◼ Decision Insight

Virtuous Returns   Virtue is not always its own reward. Compare the S&P 500 with the Domini Social Index (DSI), which covers 400 companies that have especially good records of social responsibility. We see that returns for companies with socially responsible behavior are at least as high as those of the S&P 500. ◼

Copyright © 2009 by KLD Research & Analytics, Inc. The "Domini 400 Social Index" is a service mark of KLD Research & Analytics.

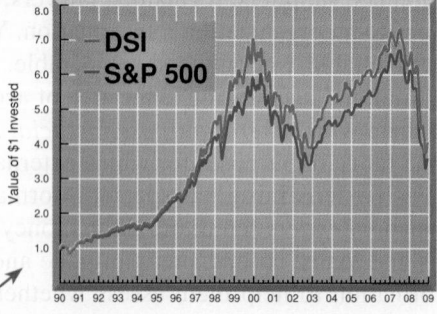

Graphical displays are often used to illustrate key points.

Opportunities in Accounting

Accounting information affects many aspects of our lives. When we earn money, pay taxes, invest savings, budget earnings, and plan for the future, we are influenced by accounting. Accounting has four broad areas of opportunities: financial, managerial, taxation, and accounting-related. Exhibit 1.3 lists selected opportunities in each area.

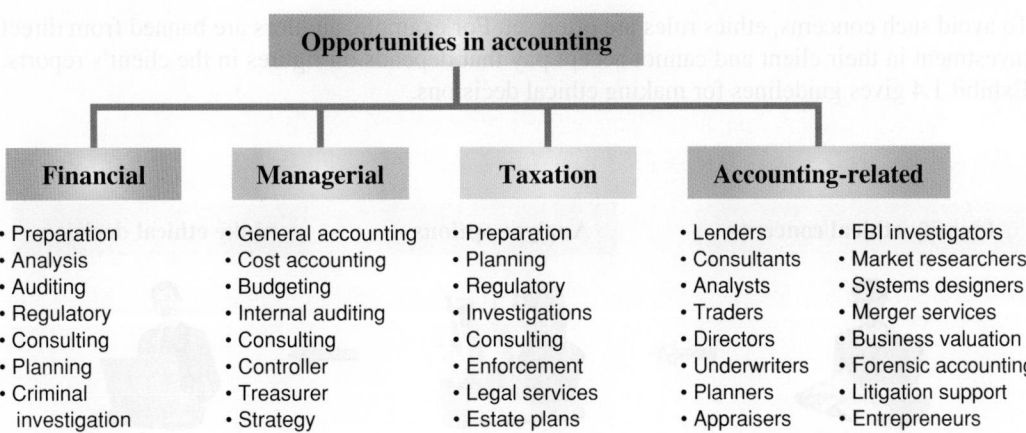

EXHIBIT 1.3

Accounting Opportunities

Accountants are highly regarded. Their professional standing often is denoted by an affiliation or certification by a professional accounting body. They must meet education and experience requirements, pass tests, and exhibit ethical character before they can use the professional designation such as Chartered Accountant (CA) used in many countries like Australia and Singapore. The approximate equivalent in the U.S. is the Certified Public Accountant (CPA). Some accountants who specialize in certain fields may hold other or additional designations such as Certified Management Accountant (CMA) or Certified Fraud Examiner (CFE).

Individuals with accounting knowledge are always in demand as they can help with financial analysis, strategic planning, e-commerce, product feasibility analysis, information technology, and financial management. Benefit packages can include flexible work schedules, telecommuting options, career path alternatives, casual work environments, extended vacation time, and child and elder care.

Point: The largest accounting firms in the world are Deloitte, Ernst & Young, KPMG, and PricewaterhouseCoopers, commonly known as the "Big Four."

Quick Check
Answers — p. 28

Quick Check *is a chance to stop and reflect on key points.*

1. What is the purpose of accounting?
2. What is the relation between accounting and recordkeeping?
3. Identify some advantages of technology for accounting.
4. Who are the internal and external users of accounting information?
5. Identify at least five types of managers who are internal users of accounting information.
6. What are internal controls and why are they important?

FUNDAMENTALS OF ACCOUNTING

Accounting is guided by principles, standards, concepts, and assumptions. This section describes several of these key fundamentals of accounting.

Ethics—A Key Concept

The goal of accounting is to provide useful information for decisions. For information to be useful, it must be trusted. This demands ethics in accounting. **Ethics** are beliefs that distinguish right from wrong. They are accepted standards of good and bad behavior.

Identifying the ethical path is sometimes difficult. The preferred path is a course of action that avoids casting doubt on one's decisions. For example, accounting users are less likely to trust an auditor's report if the auditor's pay depends on the success of the client's business.

C3 Explain why ethics are crucial to accounting.

Point: The International Ethics Standards Board for Accountants (IESBA) develops ethical standards and guidance for use by professional accountants worldwide, and is available at www.ifac.org/Ethics/.

EXHIBIT 1.4

Guidelines for Ethical Decision Making

To avoid such concerns, ethics rules are often set. For example, auditors are banned from direct investment in their client and cannot accept pay that depends on figures in the client's reports. Exhibit 1.4 gives guidelines for making ethical decisions.

Identify ethical concerns		Analyze options		Make ethical decision
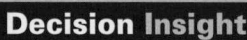	→		→	
Use personal ethics to recognize an ethical concern.		Consider all good and bad consequences.		Choose best option after weighing all consequences.

Providers of accounting information often face ethical choices as they prepare financial reports. These choices can affect the price a buyer pays and the wages paid to workers. They can even affect the success of products and services. Misleading information can lead to a wrongful closing of a division that harms workers, customers, and suppliers. There is an old saying: *Good ethics are good business.*

Some people extend ethics to *social responsibility,* which refers to a concern for the impact of actions on society. An organization's social responsibility can include donations to hospitals, colleges, community programs, and law enforcement. It also can include programs to reduce pollution, increase product safety, improve worker conditions, and support continuing education. These programs are not limited to large companies. For example, many small businesses offer discounts to students and senior citizens. Still others help sponsor events such as the Special Olympics and summer reading programs.

■ Decision Insight

They Fought the Law   Our economic and social welfare depends on reliable accounting. Some individuals forgot that and are now paying their dues. They include Bernard Madoff (in photo) of **Madoff Investment Securities**, convicted of falsifying securities records; Bernard Ebbers of **WorldCom**, convicted of an $11 billion accounting scandal; Andrew Fastow of **Enron**, guilty of hiding debt and inflating income; and Ramalinga Raju of **Satyam Computers**, accused of overstating assets by $1.5 billion. ■

Generally Accepted Accounting Principles

 C4 Explain generally accepted accounting principles and the IASB Conceptual Framework.

Financial accounting practice is governed by concepts and rules known as **generally accepted accounting principles (GAAP)**. To use and interpret financial statements effectively, we need to understand these principles, which can change over time in response to the demands of users. GAAP aims to make information in financial statements *relevant*, *reliable*, and *comparable*. Relevant information affects the decisions of its users. Reliable information is trusted by users. Comparable information is helpful in contrasting entities such as corporations.

Principles of Accounting   Accounting principles (and assumptions) are of two types. General principles are the basic concepts and guidelines for preparing financial statements. Specific principles are detailed rules used in reporting business transactions and events. *General principles* stem from long-used accounting practices. Specific principles arise more often from the pronouncements of authoritative groups and are embodied in accounting standards such as those issued by the FASB and the IASB described below.

In the United States, the **Securities and Exchange Commission (SEC)**, a government agency, has the legal authority to set GAAP. The SEC has largely delegated the task of setting U.S. GAAP to the **Financial Accounting Standards Board (FASB)**, which is a private-sector group that sets both broad and specific principles.

In today's global economy, there is increased demand by external users for comparability in accounting reports. This demand often arises when companies wish to raise money from lenders and investors in different countries. To that end, the **International Accounting Standards Board (IASB)**, an independent group (consisting of individuals from many countries), issues **International Financial Reporting Standards (IFRS)** that identify preferred accounting practices. Some old **IFRS** were issued as **International Accounting Standards (IAS)**, which are still in use. Therefore, the terms **IFRS** and **IAS** can be used interchangeably. As accounting has a rich history of accounting principles and assumptions, these will be discussed first. The description will then dwell on the IASB's Conceptual Framework which expounds some of these principles and assumptions.

We need to understand both general and specific principles to effectively use accounting information. Several general principles are described in this section that are relied on in later chapters. General principles (in purple font with white shading) and assumptions (in red font with yellow shading) are portrayed as building blocks of GAAP in Exhibit 1.5. The specific principles are described as we encounter them in the book.

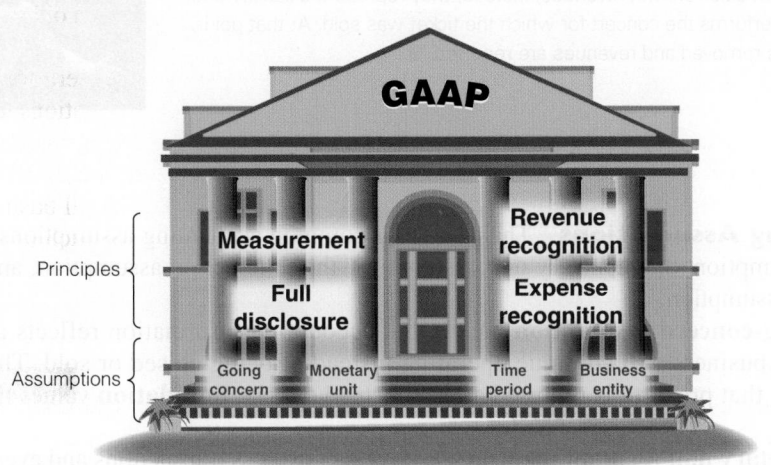

EXHIBIT 1.5

Building Blocks for GAAP

The four common general principles are measurement, revenue recognition, expense recognition, and full disclosure.

The **measurement principle,** also called the **cost principle** or **historical cost principle,** usually means that accounting information is based on actual cost (with a potential for subsequent adjustments to market). Cost is measured on a cash or equal-to-cash basis. This means if cash is given for a service, its cost is measured as the amount of cash paid. If something besides cash is exchanged (such as a car traded for a truck), cost is measured as the cash value of what is given up or received. The cost principle emphasizes reliability and verifiability, and information based on cost is considered objective. *Objectivity* means that information is supported by independent, unbiased evidence; it demands more than a person's opinion. To illustrate, suppose a company pays $5,000 for equipment. The cost principle requires that this purchase be recorded at a cost of $5,000. It makes no difference if the owner thinks this equipment is worth $7,000. Later in the book we introduce *fair value* measures.

Revenue (sales) is the amount received from selling products and services. The **revenue recognition principle** provides guidance on when a company must recognize revenue. To *recognize* means to record it. If revenue is recognized too early, a company would look more profitable than it is. If revenue is recognized too late, a company would look less profitable than it is.

Example: When a bookstore sells a textbook on credit, is its earnings process complete? *Answer:* A bookstore can record sales of the book minus an amount expected for returns.

Three criteria are important to revenue recognition. (1) *Revenue is recognized when earned.* The earnings process is normally complete when services are performed or a seller transfers ownership of products to the buyer. (2) *Proceeds from selling products and services need not be in cash.* A common noncash proceed received by a seller is a customer's promise to pay at a future date, called *credit sales.* (3) *Revenue is measured by the cash received plus the cash value of any other items received.*

The **expense recognition principle,** also called the **matching principle,** prescribes that a company record the expenses it incurred to generate the revenue reported. The principles of matching and revenue recognition are central to modern accounting.

The **full disclosure principle** prescribes that a company report the details behind financial statements that would impact users' decisions. Those disclosures are often in notes to the statements.

Decision Insight

Entertainer Lady Gaga performed in Asia during 2012
The concert tickets were sold months in advance of the performance dates. Advance ticket sales are not revenues; instead, they represent a liability until Lady Gaga performs the concert for which the ticket was sold. At that point, the liability is removed and revenues are reported. ■

Accounting Assumptions   There are four common accounting assumptions: the going concern assumption, the monetary unit assumption, the time period assumption, and the business entity assumption.

The **going-concern assumption** means that accounting information reflects a presumption that the business will continue operating instead of being closed or sold. This implies, for example, that property is reported at cost instead of, say, **liquidation** values that assume closure.

The **monetary unit assumption** means that we can express transactions and events in monetary, or money, units. Money is the common denominator in business. Examples of monetary units are the dollar in the United States, Canada, Australia, and Singapore; and the peso in Mexico, the Philippines, and Chile. The monetary unit a company uses in its accounting reports usually depends on the country where it operates, but many companies today are expressing reports in more than one monetary unit.

The **time period assumption** presumes that the life of a company can be divided into time periods, such as months and years, and that useful reports can be prepared for those periods.

The **business entity assumption** means that a business is accounted for separately from other business entities, including its owner. The reason for this assumption is that separate information about each business is necessary for good decisions. A business entity can take one of three legal forms: *proprietorship, partnership,* or *corporation.* A **sole proprietorship,** or simply **proprietorship,** is a business owned by one person. A **partnership** is a business owned by two or more people, called *partners.* A **corporation** is a business legally separate from its owners, meaning it is responsible for its own acts and its own debts. Separate legal status means that a corporation can conduct business with the rights, duties, and responsibilities of a person. A corporation acts through its managers, who are its legal agents. Separate legal status also means that its owners, who are called **shareholders,** are not personally liable for corporate acts and debts. This limited liability is its main advantage. Ownership of all corporations is divided into units called **shares,** and the owners are called **shareholders.** The type of shares issued by a corporation is usually **ordinary shares.**

Point: In the U.S., corporations issue common stock and the owners are called stockholders.

IASB Conceptual Framework   On September 28, 2010, the IASB and the FASB completed the first phase of their joint process to develop an improved conceptual framework for **IFRS** and U.S. GAAP. The objective of the conceptual framework project is to create a sound foundation for future accounting standards that are principles-based, internally consistent, and internationally converged. The new framework builds on existing IASB and FASB frameworks. The **Conceptual Framework for Financial Reporting** deals with (a) the objective of financial reporting; (b) the qualitative characteristics of useful information; (c) the definition, recognition, and measurement of the elements from which financial statements are constructed; and (d) concepts of capital and capital maintenance. The Conceptual Framework is not an **IFRS** and hence does not define standards for any particular measurement or disclosure issue. Nothing in the Conceptual Framework overrides any specific **IFRS**. The following discusses the objective of financial reporting and the qualitative characteristics. The elements directly related to the measurement of financial position are assets, liabilities and equity; the elements directly related to the measurement of performance are income and expenses. These elements will be discussed in other sections. The other parts of the Framework are discussed in more advanced accounting courses.

Objective of Financial Reporting   The objective of general purpose financial reporting is to provide financial information about the reporting entity that is useful to existing and potential investors, lenders, and other creditors in making decisions about providing resources to the entity. Those decisions involve buying, selling, or holding equity and debt instruments, and providing or settling loans and other forms of credit.

Qualitative Characteristics   The qualitative characteristics of useful financial information identify the types of information that are likely to be most useful to the existing and potential investors, lenders, and other creditors for making decisions about the reporting entity on the basis of information in its financial report (financial information). The framework identifies two fundamental qualitative characteristics and four enhancing qualitative characteristics as depicted in Exhibit 1.6.

EXHIBIT 1.6

Conceptual Framework—
Qualitative Characteristics

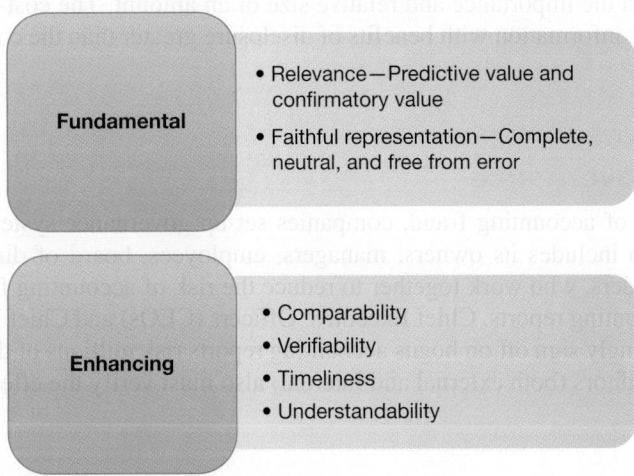

Fundamental
- Relevance—Predictive value and confirmatory value
- Faithful representation—Complete, neutral, and free from error

Enhancing
- Comparability
- Verifiability
- Timeliness
- Understandability

The two main features of **fundamental qualitative characteristics** are described in greater detail below.

1. Financial information must have **relevance**, i.e., capable of making a difference in the decisions made by users. Financial information is capable of making a difference in decisions if it has predictive value, confirmatory value, or both. **Predictive value** means that it can be used as an input to processes employed by users to predict future outcomes. **Confirmatory value** means that it provides feedback about (confirms or changes) previous evaluations. **Materiality** is also part of relevance—information is material if omitting it or misstating it could influence decisions that users make on the basis of financial information.

2. Financial information must be a **faithful representation** of the phenomena that it purports to represent. To be a faithful representation, a depiction would be complete, neutral, and free from error.

The four **enhancing qualitative characteristics** are qualitative characteristics that enhance the usefulness of information that is relevant and faithfully represented. They may also help determine which of two ways should be used to depict a phenomenon if both are considered equally relevant and faithfully represented.

1. **Comparability** enables users to identify and understand similarities in, and differences among, items. Closely related is consistency, which refers to the use of the same methods for the same items, either from period to period within a reporting entity or in a single period across entities. Comparability is the goal; consistency helps to achieve that goal.
2. **Verifiability** enables different knowledgeable and independent observers to reach consensus, although not necessarily complete agreement, that a particular depiction is a faithful representation.
3. **Timeliness** means having information available to decision makers in time to be capable of influencing their decisions. Generally, the older the information is, the less useful it is.
4. **Understandability** means classifying, characterizing, and presenting information clearly and concisely. Financial reports are prepared for users who have a reasonable knowledge of business and economic activities and who review and analyse the information diligently.

The Framework states that cost is a pervasive **constraint** on the reporting entity's ability to provide useful financial information. Reporting financial information imposes costs, and it is important that those costs are justified by the benefits of reporting that information. This constraint looks at both the importance and relative size of an amount. The cost-benefit constraint prescribes that only information with benefits of disclosure greater than the costs of providing it need be disclosed.

Corporate Governance

To reduce the risk of accounting fraud, companies set up governance systems. A company's governance system includes its owners, managers, employees, board of directors, and other important stakeholders, who work together to reduce the risk of accounting fraud and increase confidence in accounting reports. Chief Executive Officers (CEOs) and Chief Financial Officers (CFOs) who knowingly sign off on bogus accounting reports risk millions of dollars in fines and years in prison. Auditors (both external and internal) also must verify the effectiveness of internal controls.

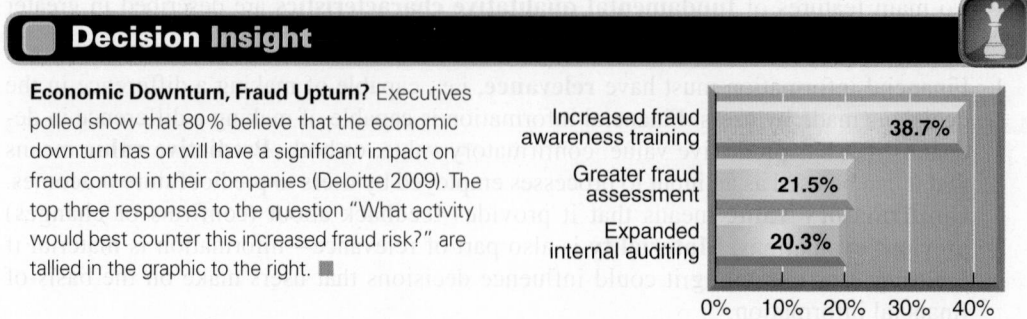

Decision Insight

Economic Downturn, Fraud Upturn? Executives polled show that 80% believe that the economic downturn has or will have a significant impact on fraud control in their companies (Deloitte 2009). The top three responses to the question "What activity would best counter this increased fraud risk?" are tallied in the graphic to the right. ■

Increased fraud awareness training	38.7%
Greater fraud assessment	21.5%
Expanded internal auditing	20.3%

0%   10%   20%   30%   40%

Quick Check

Answers — p. 28

7. What three-step guidelines can help people make ethical decisions?
8. Why are ethics and social responsibility valuable to organizations?
9. Why are ethics crucial in accounting?
10. Who sets **IFRS**?
11. State the fundamental qualitative characteristics.
12. State the enhancing qualitative characteristics.
13. Why is the business entity assumption important?
14. Why is the revenue recognition principle important?
15. What are the three basic forms of business organization?
16. Identify the owners of corporations and the terminology for ownership units.

TRANSACTION ANALYSIS AND THE ACCOUNTING EQUATION

To understand accounting information, we need to know how an accounting system captures relevant data about transactions, and then classifies, records, and reports data.

Accounting Equation

The accounting system reflects two basic aspects of a company: what it owns and what it owes. *Assets* are resources a company owns or controls. Examples are cash, supplies, equipment, and land, where each carries expected benefits. The claims on a company's assets—what it owes—are separated into owner and nonowner claims. *Liabilities* are what a company owes its nonowners (creditors) in future payments, products, or services. *Equity* (also called owner's equity or capital) refers to the claims of its owner(s). Together, liabilities and equity are the source of funds to acquire assets. The relation of assets, liabilities, and equity is reflected in the following **accounting equation:**

A1 Define and interpret the accounting equation and each of its components.

$$\text{Assets} = \text{Liabilities} + \text{Equity}$$

Liabilities are usually shown before equity in this equation because creditors' claims must be paid before the claims of owners. (The terms in this equation can be rearranged; for example, Assets − Liabilities = Equity.) The accounting equation applies to all transactions and events, to all companies and forms of organization, and to all points in time. For example, as at December 31, 2013, Nestlé's assets equal CHF 120,442, its liabilities equal CHF 56,303, and its equity equals CHF 64,139 (all in CHF millions).

Assets   Assets are resources a company owns or controls. These resources are expected to yield future benefits. Examples are Web servers for an online services company, musical instruments for a rock band, and land for a vegetable grower. The term *receivable* is used to refer to an asset that promises a future inflow of resources. A company that provides a service or product on credit is said to have an account receivable from that customer.

Point: The phrases "on credit" and "on account" imply that cash payment will occur at a future date.

Liabilities   Liabilities are creditors' claims on assets. These claims reflect company obligations to provide assets, products, or services to others. The term *payable* refers to a liability that promises a future outflow of resources. Examples are wages payable to workers, accounts payable to suppliers, notes payable to banks, and taxes payable to the government.

Equity   Equity is the owner's claim on assets. Equity is equal to assets minus liabilities. This is the reason equity is also called *net assets, net worth* or *residual equity.*

Equity for a noncorporate entity—commonly called owner's equity—increases and decreases as follows: owner investments and revenues *increase* equity, whereas owner withdrawals and expenses *decrease* equity. **Owner investments** are assets an owner puts into the company and are included under the generic account **Owner, Capital. Revenues** are sales of products or services to customers. Revenues increase equity (via net profit) and result from a company's earnings activities. Examples are consulting services provided, sales of products, facilities rented to others, and commissions from services. **Owner withdrawals** are assets an owner takes from the company for personal use. **Expenses** are the costs necessary to earn revenues. Expenses decrease equity. Examples are costs of employee time, use of supplies, and advertising, utilities, and insurance services from others. In sum, equity is the accumulated revenues and owner investments less the accumulated expenses and withdrawals since the company began. This breakdown of equity yields the following **expanded accounting equation.**

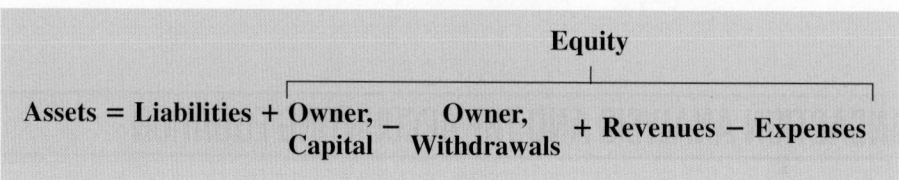

Net profit (also called **net profit**) occurs when revenues exceed expenses. Net profit increases equity. A **net loss** occurs when expenses exceed revenues, which decreases equity.

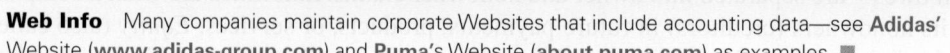

Web Info   Many companies maintain corporate Websites that include accounting data—see **Adidas'** Website (**www.adidas-group.com**) and **Puma**'s Website (**about.puma.com**) as examples. ∎

Transaction Analysis

P1 Analyze business transactions using the accounting equation.

Business activities can be described in terms of transactions and events. **External transactions** are exchanges of value between two entities, which yield changes in the accounting equation. An example is the sale of ad space by **Facebook**. **Internal transactions** are exchanges within an entity, which may or may not affect the accounting equation. An example is Facebook's use of its supplies, which are reported as expenses when used. **Events** refer to happenings that affect the accounting equation *and* are reliably measured. They include business events such as changes in the market value of certain assets and liabilities and natural events such as floods and fires that destroy assets and create losses. They do not include, for example, the signing of service or product contracts, which by themselves do not impact the accounting equation.

This section uses the accounting equation to analyze 11 selected transactions and events of FastForward, a start-up consulting (service) business, in its first month of operations. Remember that each transaction and event leaves the equation in balance and that assets *always* equal the sum of liabilities and equity.

Transaction 1: Investment by Owner   On December 1, Chas Taylor forms a consulting business, named FastForward and set up as a proprietorship, that focuses on assessing the performance of footwear and accessories. Taylor owns and manages the business. The marketing plan for the business is to focus primarily on publishing online reviews and consulting with clubs, athletes, and others who place orders for footwear and accessories with manufacturers. Taylor personally invests $30,000 cash in the new company and deposits the cash in a bank account opened under the name of FastForward. After this transaction, the cash (an asset) and the owner's equity each equal $30,000. The source of increase in equity is the owner's investment, which is included in the column titled

C. Taylor, Capital. (Owner investments are always included under the title *"Owner name," Capital.*) The effect of this transaction on FastForward is reflected in the accounting equation as follows:

	Assets	=	Liabilities	+	Equity
	Cash	=			**C. Taylor, Capital**
(1)	+$30,000	=			+$30,000

Transaction 2: Purchase Supplies for Cash FastForward uses $2,500 of its cash to buy supplies of brand name footwear for performance testing over the next few months. This transaction is an exchange of cash, an asset, for another kind of asset, supplies. It merely changes the form of assets from cash to supplies. The decrease in cash is exactly equal to the increase in supplies. The supplies of footwear are assets because of the expected future benefits from the test results of their performance. This transaction is reflected in the accounting equation as follows:

	Assets			=	Liabilities	+	Equity
	Cash	+	**Supplies**	=			**C. Taylor, Capital**
Old Bal.	$30,000			=			$30,000
(2)	−2,500	+	$2,500				
New Bal.	$27,500	+	$ 2,500	=			$30,000
		$30,000				$30,000	

Transaction 3: Purchase Equipment for Cash FastForward spends $26,000 to acquire equipment for testing footwear. Like transaction 2, transaction 3 is an exchange of one asset, cash, for another asset, equipment. The equipment is an asset because of its expected future benefits from testing footwear. This purchase changes the makeup of assets but does not change the asset total. The accounting equation remains in balance.

	Assets					=	Liabilities	+	Equity
	Cash	+	**Supplies**	+	**Equipment**	=			**C. Taylor, Capital**
Old Bal.	$27,500	+	$2,500			=			$30,000
(3)	−26,000			+	$26,000				
New Bal.	$ 1,500	+	$2,500	+	$ 26,000	=			$30,000
			$30,000					$30,000	

Transaction 4: Purchase Supplies on Credit Taylor decides more supplies of footwear and accessories are needed. These additional supplies total $7,100, but as we see from the accounting equation in transaction 3, FastForward has only $1,500 in cash. Taylor arranges to purchase them on credit from CalTech Supply Company. Thus, FastForward acquires supplies in exchange for a promise to pay for them later. This purchase increases assets by $7,100 in supplies, and liabilities (called *accounts payable* to CalTech Supply) increase by the same amount. The effects of this purchase follow:

Example: If FastForward pays $500 cash in transaction 4, how does this partial payment affect the liability to CalTech? What would be FastForward's cash balance? *Answers:* The liability to CalTech would be reduced to $6,600 and the cash balance would be reduced to $1,000.

	Assets					=	Liabilities	+	Equity
	Cash	+	**Supplies**	+	**Equipment**	=	**Accounts Payable**	+	**C. Taylor, Capital**
Old Bal.	$1,500	+	$2,500	+	$26,000	=			$30,000
(4)		+	7,100				+$7,100		
New Bal.	$1,500	+	$9,600	+	$26,000	=	$ 7,100	+	$30,000
			$37,100					$37,100	

Transaction 5: Provide Services for Cash   FastForward earns revenues by selling online ad space to manufacturers and by consulting with clients about test results on footwear and accessories. It earns net profit only if its revenues are greater than its expenses incurred in earning them. In one of its first jobs, FastForward provides consulting services to a power-walking club and immediately collects $4,200 cash. The accounting equation reflects this increase in cash of $4,200 and in equity of $4,200. This increase in equity is identified in the far right column under Revenues because the cash received is earned by providing consulting services.

	Assets					=	Liabilities	+	Equity		
	Cash	+	Supplies	+	Equipment	=	Accounts Payable	+	C. Taylor, Capital	+	Revenues
Old Bal.	$1,500	+	$9,600	+	$26,000	=	$7,100	+	$30,000		
(5)	+4,200									+	$4,200
New Bal.	$5,700	+	$9,600	+	$26,000	=	$7,100	+	$30,000	+	$ 4,200
	$41,300								$41,300		

Transactions 6 and 7: Payment of Expenses in Cash   FastForward pays $1,000 rent to the landlord of the building where its facilities are located. Paying this amount allows FastForward to occupy the space for the month of December. The rental payment is reflected in the following accounting equation as transaction 6. FastForward also pays the biweekly $700 salary of the company's only employee. This is reflected in the accounting equation as transaction 7. Both transactions 6 and 7 are December expenses for FastForward. The costs of both rent and salary are expenses, as opposed to assets, because their benefits are used in December (they have no future benefits after December). These transactions also use up an asset (cash) in carrying out FastForward's operations. The accounting equation shows that both transactions reduce cash and equity. The far right column identifies these decreases as Expenses.

By definition, increases in expenses yield decreases in equity.

	Assets					=	Liabilities	+	Equity				
	Cash	+	Supplies	+	Equipment	=	Accounts Payable	+	C. Taylor, Capital	+	Revenues	−	Expenses
Old Bal.	$5,700	+	$9,600	+	$26,000	=	$7,100	+	$30,000	+	$4,200		
(6)	−1,000											−	$1,000
Bal.	4,700	+	9,600	+	26,000	=	7,100	+	30,000	+	4,200	−	1,000
(7)	− 700											−	700
New Bal.	$4,000	+	$9,600	+	$26,000	=	$7,100	+	$30,000	+	$4,200	−	$ 1,700
	$39,600								$39,600				

Transaction 8: Provide Services and Facilities for Credit   FastForward provides consulting services of $1,600 and rents its test facilities for $300 to a podiatric services center. The rental involves allowing members to try recommended footwear and accessories at FastForward's testing area. The center is billed for the $1,900 total. This transaction results in a new asset, called *accounts receivable,* from this client. It also yields an increase in equity from the two revenue components reflected in the Revenues column of the accounting equation:

	Assets				=	Liabilities	+			Equity		
	Cash	+	Accounts Receivable	+ Supplies	+ Equipment	=	Accounts Payable	+	C. Taylor, Capital	+	Revenues	– Expenses
Old Bal.	$4,000	+		+ $9,600	+ $26,000	=	$7,100	+	$30,000	+	$4,200	– $1,700
(8)		+	$1,900							+	1,600	
										+	300	
New Bal.	$4,000	+	$1,900	+ $9,600	+ $26,000	=	$7,100	+	$30,000	+	$6,100	– $1,700
			$41,500								$41,500	

Transaction 9: Receipt of Cash from Accounts Receivable

The client in transaction 8 (the podiatric center) pays $1,900 to FastForward 10 days after it is billed for consulting services. This transaction 9 does not change the total amount of assets and does not affect liabilities or equity. It converts the receivable (an asset) to cash (another asset). It does not create new revenue. Revenue was recognized when FastForward rendered the services in transaction 8, not when the cash is now collected. This emphasis on the earnings process instead of cash flows is a goal of the revenue recognition principle and yields useful information to users. The new balances follow:

Point: Receipt of cash is not always a revenue.

	Assets				=	Liabilities	+			Equity		
	Cash	+	Accounts Receivable	+ Supplies	+ Equipment	=	Accounts Payable	+	C. Taylor, Capital	+	Revenues	– Expenses
Old Bal.	$4,000	+	$1,900	+ $9,600	+ $26,000	=	$7,100	+	$30,000	+	$6,100	– $1,700
(9)	+1,900	–	1,900									
New Bal.	$5,900	+	$ 0	+ $9,600	+ $26,000	=	$7,100	+	$30,000	+	$6,100	– $1,700
			$41,500								$41,500	

Transaction 10: Payment of Accounts Payable

FastForward pays CalTech Supply $900 cash as partial payment for its earlier $7,100 purchase of supplies (transaction 4), leaving $6,200 unpaid. The accounting equation shows that this transaction decreases FastForward's cash by $900 and decreases its liability to CalTech Supply by $900. Equity does not change. This event does not create an expense even though cash flows out of FastForward (instead the expense is recorded when FastForward derives the benefits from these supplies).

	Assets				=	Liabilities	+			Equity		
	Cash	+	Accounts Receivable	+ Supplies	+ Equipment	=	Accounts Payable	+	C. Taylor, Capital	+	Revenues	– Expenses
Old Bal.	$5,900	+	$ 0	+ $9,600	+ $26,000	=	$7,100	+	$30,000	+	$6,100	– $1,700
(10)	– 900						– 900					
New Bal.	$5,000	+	$ 0	+ $9,600	+ $26,000	=	$6,200	+	$30,000	+	$6,100	– $1,700
			$40,600								$40,600	

Transaction 11: Withdrawal of Cash by Owner

The owner of FastForward withdraws $200 cash for personal use. Withdrawals (decreases in equity) are not reported as expenses because they are not part of the company's earnings process. Since withdrawals are not company expenses, they are not used in computing net profit.

By definition, increases in withdrawals yield decreases in equity.

	Assets				=	Liabilities	+			Equity		
	Cash	+ Accounts Receivable	+ Supplies	+ Equipment	=	Accounts Payable	+	C. Taylor, Capital	− C. Taylor, Withdrawals	+ Revenues	− Expenses
Old Bal.	$5,000	+ $ 0	+ $9,600	+ $26,000	=	$6,200	+	$30,000		+ $6,100	− $1,700
(11)	− 200								− $200		
New Bal.	$4,800	+ $ 0	+ $9,600	+ $26,000	=	$6,200	+	$30,000	− $200	+ $6,100	− $1,700
	$40,400								$40,400		

Point: Knowing how financial statements are prepared improves our analysis of them. We develop the skills for analysis of financial statements throughout the book. Chapter 17 focuses on financial statement analysis.

Summary of Transactions

We summarize in Exhibit 1.7 the effects of these 11 transactions of FastForward using the accounting equation. First, we see that the accounting equation remains in balance after each transaction. Second, transactions can be analyzed by their effects on components of the accounting equation. For example, in transactions 2, 3, and 9, one asset increased while another asset decreased by equal amounts.

EXHIBIT 1.7

Summary of Transactions Using the Accounting Equation

	Assets				=	Liabilities	+			Equity		
	Cash	+ Accounts Receivable	+ Supplies	+ Equipment	=	Accounts Payable	+	C. Taylor, Capital	− C. Taylor, Withdrawals	+ Revenues	− Expenses
(1)	$30,000				=			$30,000			
(2)	− 2,500		+ $2,500								
Bal.	27,500		+ 2,500		=			30,000			
(3)	−26,000			+ $26,000							
Bal.	1,500		+ 2,500	+ 26,000	=			30,000			
(4)			+ 7,100			+$7,100					
Bal.	1,500		+ 9,600	+ 26,000	=	7,100	+	30,000			
(5)	+ 4,200									+ $4,200	
Bal.	5,700		+ 9,600	+ 26,000	=	7,100	+	30,000		+ 4,200	
(6)	− 1,000										− $1,000
Bal.	4,700		+ 9,600	+ 26,000	=	7,100	+	30,000		+ 4,200	− 1,000
(7)	− 700										− 700
Bal.	4,000		+ 9,600	+ 26,000	=	7,100	+	30,000		+ 4,200	− 1,700
(8)		+ $1,900								+ 1,600	
										+ 300	
Bal.	4,000	+ 1,900	+ 9,600	+ 26,000	=	7,100	+	30,000		+ 6,100	− 1,700
(9)	+ 1,900	− 1,900									
Bal.	5,900	+ 0	+ 9,600	+ 26,000	=	7,100	+	30,000		+ 6,100	− 1,700
(10)	− 900					− 900					
Bal.	5,000	+ 0	+ 9,600	+ 26,000	=	6,200	+	30,000		+ 6,100	− 1,700
(11)	− 200								− $200		
Bal.	$ 4,800	+ $ 0	+ $9,600	+ $26,000	=	$ 6,200	+	$ 30,000	− $200	+ $6,100	− $1,700

17. When is the accounting equation in balance, and what does that mean?

18. How can a transaction not affect any liability and equity accounts?

19. Describe a transaction increasing equity and one decreasing it.

20. Identify a transaction that decreases both assets and liabilities.

FINANCIAL STATEMENTS

This section introduces us to how financial statements are prepared from the analysis of business transactions. **IAS 1 Presentation of Financial Statements** states that a complete set of financial statements comprises:

> **P2** Identify and prepare basic financial statements and explain how they interrelate.

1. A **statement of profit or loss and other comprehensive income** for the period;
2. A **statement of changes in equity** for the period;
3. A **statement of financial position** as at the end of the period;
4. A **statement of cash flows** for the period, and
5. **Notes**, comprising a summary of significant accounting policies and other explanatory information.

When preparing these statements, there are choices or variations available, notably:

1. An entity may use titles for the statements other than those noted previously. For example, an entity may use the title "statement of comprehensive income" instead of "statement of profit or loss and other comprehensive income." As another example, the title **balance sheet** is traditionally used instead of "statement of financial position."
2. The statement of profit or loss and other comprehensive income can be shown as a single statement, with profit or loss and other comprehensive income presented in two sections. An entity may also present the profit or loss section in a separate statement of profit or loss. If so, the separate statement of profit or loss shall immediately precede the statement presenting comprehensive income, which shall begin with profit or loss. When presenting as two statements, some entities may call the first statement "income statement" or "statement of profit or loss."

We prepare these financial statements, in this order, using the 11 selected transactions of FastForward for December. (These statements are technically called unadjusted—we explain this in Chapters 2 and 3.) The most common reporting period is for a year, known as a *financial year* or a *fiscal year*. The financial year may correspond to the calendar year from January to December, but can be any 12 consecutive months mainly due to industry practice. Shorter reporting periods such as half-yearly (six months) or quarterly (three months) are possible. The following example uses one month.

Income Statement

In the chapter on Accounting for Corporations, the concept of comprehensive income—and hence the statement of profit or loss and other comprehensive income—will be explained. From now on, we will focus on the **income statement** which describes a company's revenues and expenses along with the resulting net profit or loss over a period of time due to earnings activities. FastForward's income statement for December is shown at the top of Exhibit 1.8. Information about revenues and expenses is conveniently taken from the Equity columns of Exhibit 1.7. Revenues are reported first on the income statement. They include consulting revenues of $5,800 from transactions 5 and 8 and rental revenue of $300 from transaction 8. Expenses are reported after revenues. (For convenience in this chapter, we list larger amounts first, but we can sort expenses in different ways.) Rent and salary expenses are from transactions 6 and 7. Expenses reflect the costs to generate the revenues reported. Net profit (or loss) is reported at the bottom of the statement and is the amount earned in December. Owners' investments and withdrawals are *not* part of profit.

EXHIBIT 1.8

Financial Statements and
Their Links

FASTFORWARD
Income Statement
For Month Ended December 31, 2015

Revenues		
Consulting revenue ($4,200 + $1,600)...............	$ 5,800	
Rental revenue	300	
Total revenues		$ 6,100
Expenses		
Rent expense	(1,000)	
Salaries expense	(700)	
Total expenses		(1,700)
Net profit		$ 4,400

FASTFORWARD
Statement of Changes in Equity
For Month Ended December 31, 2015

C. Taylor, Capital, December 1, 2015....................		$ 0
Investments by owner	$30,000	
Net profit	4,400	34,400
		34,400
Withdrawals by owner		(200)
C. Taylor, Capital, December 31, 2015		$34,200

FASTFORWARD
Statement of Financial Position
December 31, 2015

Assets	
Cash	$ 4,800
Supplies	9,600
Equipment..	26,000
Total assets	$40,400
Liabilities	
Accounts payable..	$ 6,200
Equity	
C. Taylor, Capital	34,200
Total liabilities and equity	$40,400

FASTFORWARD
Statement of Cash Flows
For Month Ended December 31, 2015

Cash flows from operating activities		
Cash received from clients ($4,200 + $1,900)..........	$ 6,100	
Cash paid for supplies ($2,500 + $900)...............	(3,400)	
Cash paid for rent	(1,000)	
Cash paid to employee	(700)	
Net cash from operating activities		$ 1,000
Cash flows from investing activities		
Purchase of equipment	(26,000)	
Net cash used in investing activities		(26,000)
Cash flows from financing activities		
Investments by owner	30,000	
Withdrawals by owner.............................	(200)	
Net cash from financing activities		29,800
Net increase in cash		$ 4,800
Cash balance, December 1, 2015		0
Cash balance, December 31, 2015		$ 4,800

Statement of Changes in Equity

The statement of changes in equity reports information about how equity changes over the reporting period. This statement shows beginning capital, events that increase it (owner investments and net profit), and events that decrease it (withdrawals and net loss). Ending capital is computed in this statement and is carried over and reported on the statement of financial position. FastForward's statement of changes in equity is the second report in Exhibit 1.8. The beginning capital balance is measured as at the start of business on December 1. It is zero because FastForward did not exist before then. An existing business reports a beginning balance equal to that as at the end of the prior reporting period (such as from November 30). FastForward's statement of changes in equity shows that Taylor's initial investment created $30,000 of equity. It also shows the $4,400 of net profit earned during the period. This links the income statement to the statement of changes in equity (see line ①). The statement also reports Taylor's $200 cash withdrawal and FastForward's end-of-period capital balance.

Point: Cumulative net profit (and loss) not withdrawn by owners is known as retained earnings.

Statement of Financial Position

FastForward's statement of financial position is the third report in Exhibit 1.8. This statement refers to FastForward's financial condition at the close of business on December 31. The top part of the statement of financial position lists FastForward's assets: cash, supplies, and equipment. The next part of the statement of financial position shows that FastForward owes $6,200 to creditors. Any other liabilities (such as a bank loan) would be listed here. The final part of the statement of financial position shows that the equity (capital) balance is $34,200. Line ②shows the link between the ending balance of the statement of changes in equity and the equity balance on the statement of financial position.

■ Decision Insight

Alternative Formats   There is flexibility in presenting the financial statements. For example, the format for the statement of financial position shown in Exhibit 1.8 is called the *report* or *narrative format* with assets, liabilities, and equity presented vertically (often seen in companies' published financial statements). It can also be shown in the *account* format with assets on the left and liabilities and equity on the right as follows: ■

FASTFORWARD
Statement of Financial Position
December 31, 2015

Assets		Liabilities	
Cash............	$ 4,800	Accounts payable............	$ 6,200
Supplies.........	9,600		
Equipment........	26,000		
		Equity	
		C. Taylor, Capital............	34,200
Total assets	$ 40,400	Total liabilities and equity	$ 40,400

Decision Maker boxes are role-playing exercises that stress the relevance of accounting.

■ Decision Maker    Answer — p. 28

Retailer   You open a wholesale business selling entertainment equipment to retail outlets. You find that most of your customers demand to buy on credit. How can you use the statements of financial position of these customers to help you decide which ones to extend credit to? ■

Statement of Cash Flows

FastForward's statement of cash flows is the final report in Exhibit 1.8. The first section reports cash flows from *operating activities*. It shows the $6,100 cash received from clients and the $5,100 cash paid for supplies, rent, and employee salaries. Outflows are in parentheses to denote subtraction. Net cash provided by operating activities for December is $1,000. If cash paid exceeded the $5,100 cash received, we would call it "cash used by operating activities." The second section reports *investing activities,* which involve buying and selling assets such as land and equipment that are held for *long-term use* (typically more than one year). The only investing activity is the $26,000 purchase of equipment. The third section shows cash flows from *financing activities,* which include the *long-term* borrowing and repaying of cash from lenders and the cash investments from, and withdrawals by, the owner. FastForward reports $30,000 from the owner's initial investment and the $200 cash withdrawal. The net cash effect of all financing transactions is a $29,800 cash inflow. The final part of the statement shows FastForward increased its cash balance by $4,800 in December. Since it started with no cash, the ending balance is also $4,800—see line ③. We see that cash flow numbers are different from income statement (*accrual*) numbers, which is common.

Quick Check

Answers — pp. 28

21. Explain the link between the income statement and the statement of changes in equity.
22. Describe the link between the statement of financial position and the statement of changes in equity.
23. Discuss the three major sections of the statement of cash flows.

Decision Analysis (a section at the end of each chapter) introduces and explains ratios helpful in decision making using real company data. Instructors can skip this section and cover all ratios in Chapter 17.

Decision Analysis 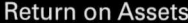   Return on Assets

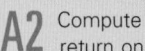 **A2** Compute and interpret return on assets.

A *Decision Analysis* section at the end of each chapter is devoted to financial statement analysis. We organize financial statement analysis into four areas: (1) liquidity and efficiency, (2) solvency, (3) profitability, and (4) market prospects—Chapter 13 has a ratio listing with definitions and groupings by area. When analyzing ratios, we need benchmarks to identify good, bad, or average levels. Common benchmarks include the company's prior levels and those of its competitors.

This chapter presents a profitability measure: return on assets. Return on assets is useful in evaluating management, analyzing and forecasting profits, and planning activities. **Return on assets (ROA),** also called *return on investment (ROI),* is defined in Exhibit 1.9.

EXHIBIT 1.9

Return on Assets

$$\text{Return on assets} = \frac{\text{Net profit}}{\text{Average total assets}}$$

To illustrate, **Adidas** reports net profit to shareholders of EUR 787 million for 2013. At the beginning of year 2013 (which is the end of year 2012), its total assets are EUR 11,651 million and at the end of year 2013, they total EUR 11,599 million. Adidas' return on assets for 2013 is therefore:

$$\text{Return on assets} = 787/(11,599 + 11,651)/2 = 6.8\%$$

Is a 6.8% return on assets good or bad for Adidas? To help answer this question, we can compare (benchmark) Adidas' return with its prior performance, the returns of competitors (such as **Puma**), and the returns from alternative investments. Adidas' return for two years is in the second column of Exhibit 1.10, which increased from 4.60% to 6.77%.

	Return on Assets	
Year	**Adidas**	**Puma**
2012	4.6%	2.7%
2013	6.8%	0.2%

EXHIBIT 1.10

Adidas and Puma Return

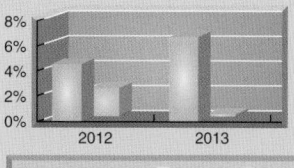

These returns show an increase in its productive use of assets over the previous year. We also compute Puma's returns in the third column of Exhibit 1.10. In both years, Adidas outperformed Puma as its return on assets is higher.

Decision Maker   Answer — p. 28

Business Owner   You own a small winter ski resort that earns a 21% return on its assets. An opportunity to purchase a winter ski equipment manufacturer is offered to you. This manufacturer earns a 19% return on its assets. The industry return for this manufacturer is 14%. Do you purchase this manufacturer? ■

*Each **Decision Analysis** section ends with a role-playing scenario to show the usefulness of ratios.*

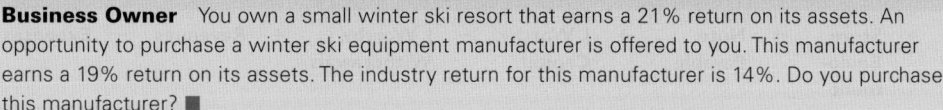

*The **Demonstration Problem** is a review of key chapter content. The Planning the Solution offers strategies in solving the problem.*

DEMONSTRATION PROBLEM

After several months of planning, Jasmine Worthy started a haircutting business called Expressions. The following events occurred during its first month of business.

a. On August 1, Worthy invested $3,000 cash and $15,000 of equipment in Expressions.

b. On August 2, Expressions paid $600 cash for furniture for the shop.

c. On August 3, Expressions paid $500 cash to rent space in a strip mall for August.

d. On August 4, it purchased $1,200 of equipment on credit for the shop (using a long-term note payable).

e. On August 5, Expressions opened for business. Cash received from haircutting services in the first week and a half of business (ended August 15) was $825.

f. On August 15, it provided $100 of haircutting services on account.

g. On August 17, it received a $100 check for services previously rendered on account.

h. On August 17, it paid $125 cash to an assistant for hours worked during the grand opening.

i. Cash received from services provided during the second half of August was $930.

j. On August 31, it paid a $400 installment toward principal on the note payable entered into on August 4.

k. On August 31, Worthy made a $900 cash withdrawal from the company for personal use.

Required

1. Arrange the following asset, liability, and equity titles in a table similar to the one in Exhibit 1.7: Cash; Accounts Receivable; Furniture; Store Equipment; Note Payable; J. Worthy, Capital; J. Worthy, Withdrawals; Revenues; and Expenses. Show the effects of each transaction using the accounting equation.

2. Prepare an income statement for August.

3. Prepare a statement of changes in equity for August.

4. Prepare a statement of financial position as at August 31.

5. Prepare a statement of cash flows for August.

6. Determine the return on assets ratio for August.

PLANNING THE SOLUTION

● Set up a table like Exhibit 1.7 with the appropriate columns for accounts.

● Analyze each transaction and show its effects as increases or decreases in the appropriate columns. Be sure the accounting equation remains in balance after each transaction.

● Prepare the income statement, and identify revenues and expenses. List those items on the statement, compute the difference, and label the result as *net profit* or *net loss*.
● Use information in the Equity columns to prepare the statement of changes in equity.
● Use information in the last row of the transactions table to prepare the statement of financial position.
● Prepare the statement of cash flows; include all events listed in the Cash column of the transactions table. Classify each cash flow as operating, investing, or financing.
● Calculate return on assets by dividing net profit by average assets.

SOLUTION TO DEMONSTRATION PROBLEM

1.

	Cash	+	Accounts Receivable	+	Furniture	+	Store Equipment	=	Note Payable	+	J. Worthy, Capital	−	J. Worthy, Withdrawals	+	Revenues	−	Expenses
a.	$3,000						$15,000				$18,000						
b.	− 600			+	$600												
Bal.	2,400	+		+	600	+	15,000	=			18,000						
c.	− 500															−	$500
Bal.	1,900	+		+	600	+	15,000	=			18,000					−	500
d.						+	1,200		+$1,200								
Bal.	1,900	+		+	600	+	16,200	=	1,200	+	18,000					−	500
e.	+ 825													+	$ 825		
Bal.	2,725	+		+	600	+	16,200	=	1,200	+	18,000			+	825	−	500
f.		+	$100											+	100		
Bal.	2,725	+	100	+	600	+	16,200	=	1,200	+	18,000			+	925	−	500
g.	+ 100	−	100														
Bal.	2,825	+	0	+	600	+	16,200	=	1,200	+	18,000			+	925	−	500
h.	− 125															−	125
Bal.	2,700	+	0	+	600	+	16,200	=	1,200	+	18,000			+	925	−	625
i.	+ 930													+	930		
Bal.	3,630	+	0	+	600	+	16,200	=	1,200	+	18,000			+	1,855	−	625
j.	− 400								− 400								
Bal.	3,230	+	0	+	600	+	16,200	=	800	+	18,000			+	1,855	−	625
k.	− 900											−	$900				
Bal.	$ 2,330	+	0	+	$600	+	$ 16,200	=	$ 800	+	$ 18,000	−	$900	+	$1,855	−	$625

2.

EXPRESSIONS		
Income Statement		
For Month Ended August 31		
Revenues		
Haircutting services revenue		$1,855
Expenses		
Rent expense	($500)	
Wages expense	(125)	
Total expenses		(625)
Net profit		$1,230

3.

EXPRESSIONS Statement of Changes in Equity For Month Ended August 31		
J. Worthy, Capital, August 1*..........		$ 0
Investments by owner	$18,000	
Net profit....................	1,230	19,230
		19,230
Withdrawals by owner..........		(900)
J. Worthy, Capital, August 31..........		$18,330

* If Expressions had been an existing business from a prior period, the beginning capital balance would equal the Capital account balance from the end of the prior period. The Capital account balance would consist of all owners' investment in the business (beginning capital plus new capital) and retained earnings (cumulative net profit or loss not withdrawn by owners).

4.

EXPRESSIONS Statement of Financial Position August 31		
Assets		
Cash		$ 2,330
Furniture		600
Store equipment		16,200
Total assets.................................		$19,130
Liabilities		
Note payable		$ 800
Equity		
J. Worthy, Capital		18,330
Total liabilities and equity......................		$19,130

5.

EXPRESSIONS Statement of Cash Flows For Month Ended August 31		
Cash flows from operating activities		
Cash received from customers	$1,855	
Cash paid for rent	(500)	
Cash paid for wages	(125)	
Net cash from operating activities		$1,230
Cash flows from investing activities		
Cash paid for furniture..........................		(600)
Cash flows from financing activities		
Cash investments by owner.......................	3,000	
Cash withdrawals by owner.......................	(900)	
Partial repayment of (long-term) note payable	(400)	
Net cash from financing activities		1,700
Net increase in cash.............................		$2,330
Cash balance, August 1		0
Cash balance, August 31		$2,330

6. Return on assets $= \dfrac{\text{Net profit}}{\text{Average assets}} = \dfrac{\$1,230}{(\$18,000^* + \$19,130)/2} = \dfrac{\$1,230}{\$18,565} = \underline{\underline{\textbf{6.63\%}}}$

* Uses the initial \$18,000 investment as the beginning balance for the *start-up period only*.

1A   Return and Risk Analysis

A3 Explain the relation between return and risk.

This appendix explains return and risk analysis and its role in business and accounting.

Net profit is often linked to **return**. Return on assets (ROA) is stated in ratio form as income divided by assets invested. For example, banks report return from a savings account in the form of an interest return which in some economic environments can be less than 1%. If we invest in debt instruments such as government bonds, we can expect a higher return. We could also invest in a company's shares, or even start our own business. How do we decide among these investment options? The answer depends on our trade-off between return and risk.

Risk is the uncertainty about the return we will earn. All business investments involve risk, but some investments involve more risk than others. The lower the risk of an investment, the lower is our expected return. The reason that savings accounts pay such a low return is the low risk of not being repaid with interest (the government guarantees most savings accounts from default). If we buy a share of Nestlé or any other company, we might obtain a large return. However, we have no guarantee of any return; there is even the risk of loss.

EXHIBIT 1A.1

Return/Risk Trade-off

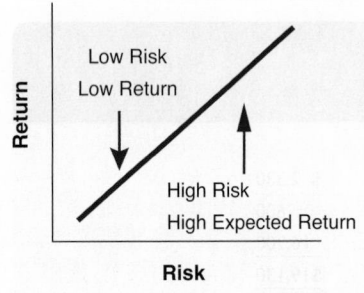

The diagram in Exhibit 1A.1 shows the tradeoff between expected return and risk. The trade-off between return and risk is a normal part of business. Higher risk implies higher, but riskier, expected returns. To help us make better decisions, we use accounting information to assess both return and risk.

1B   Business Activities and the Accounting Equation

C5 Identify and describe the three major activities of organizations.

This appendix explains how the accounting equation is derived from business activities.

There are three major types of business activities: financing, investing, and operating. Each of these requires planning. *Planning* involves defining an organization's ideas, goals, and actions. Most public corporations use the *Management Discussion and Analysis* section in their annual reports to communicate plans. However, planning is not cast in stone. This adds *risk* to both setting plans and analyzing them.

Point: Management must understand accounting data to set financial goals, make financing and investing decisions, and evaluate operating performance.

Financing   *Financing activities* provide the means organizations use to pay for resources such as land, buildings, and equipment to carry out plans. Organizations are careful in acquiring and managing financing activities because they can determine success or failure. The two sources of financing are owner and nonowner. *Owner financing* refers to resources contributed by the owner along with any income the owner leaves in the organization. *Nonowner* (or *creditor*) *financing* refers to resources contributed by creditors (lenders). *Financial management* is the task of planning how to obtain these resources and to set the right mix between owner and creditor financing.

Point: Investing (assets) and financing (liabilities plus equity) totals are *always* equal.

Investing   *Investing activities* are the acquiring and disposing of resources (assets) that an organization uses to acquire and sell its products or services. Assets are funded by an organization's financing. Organizations differ on the amount and makeup of assets. Some require land and factories to operate. Others need only an office. Determining the amount and type of assets for operations is called *asset management*. Invested amounts are referred to as *assets*. Financing is made up of creditor and owner financing, which hold claims on assets. Creditors' claims are called *liabilities*, and the owner's claim is called *equity*. This basic equality is called the *accounting equation* and can be written as:

$$\text{Assets} = \text{Liabilities} + \text{Equity.}$$

Operating   *Operating activities* involve using resources to research, develop, purchase, produce, distribute, and market products and services. Sales and revenues are the inflow of assets from selling products and services. Costs and expenses are the outflow of assets to support operating activities. *Strategic management* is the process of determining the right mix of operating activities for the type of organization, its plans, and its market.

Exhibit 1B.1 summarizes business activities. Planning is part of each activity and gives them meaning and focus. Investing (assets) and financing (liabilities and equity) are set opposite each other to stress their balance. Operating activities are below investing and financing activities to show that operating activities are the result of investing and financing.

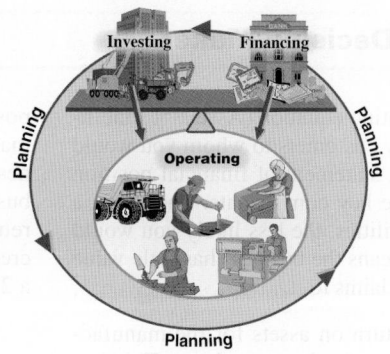

EXHIBIT 1B.1

Activities of Organizations

Summary

*A **Summary** organized by learning objectives concludes each chapter.*

C1   Explain the purpose and importance of accounting.
Accounting is an information and measurement system that aims to identify, record, and communicate relevant, reliable, and comparable information about business activities. It helps assess opportunities, products, investments, and social and community responsibilities.

C2   Identify users and uses of, and opportunities in, accounting.
Users of accounting are both internal and external. Some users and uses of accounting include (a) managers in controlling, monitoring, and planning; (b) lenders for measuring the risk and return of loans; (c) shareholders for assessing the return and risk of stock; (d) directors for overseeing management; and (e) employees for judging employment opportunities. Opportunities in accounting include financial, managerial, and tax accounting. They also include accounting-related fields such as lending, consulting, managing, and planning.

C3   Explain why ethics are crucial to accounting. The goal of accounting is to provide useful information for decision making. For information to be useful, it must be trusted. This demands ethical behavior in accounting.

C4   Explain generally accepted accounting principles and define and apply several accounting principles. Generally accepted accounting principles are a common set of standards applied by accountants. Accounting principles aid in producing relevant, reliable, and comparable information. Four principles underlying financial statements were introduced: cost, revenue recognition, matching, and full disclosure. Financial statements also reflect four assumptions: going-concern, monetary unit, time period, and business entity.

C5ᴮ   Identify and describe the three major activities of organizations. Organizations carry out three major activities: financing, investing, and operating. Financing is the means used to

pay for resources such as land, buildings, and machines. Investing refers to the buying and selling of resources used in acquiring and selling products and services. Operating activities are those necessary for carrying out the organization's plans.

A1   Define and interpret the accounting equation and each of its components. The accounting equation is: Assets = Liabilities + Equity. Assets are resources owned by a company. Liabilities are creditors' claims on assets. Equity is the owner's claim on assets (*the residual*). The expanded accounting equation is: Assets = Liabilities + [Owner Capital − Owner Withdrawals + Revenues − Expenses].

A2   Compute and interpret return on assets. Return on assets is computed as net profit divided by average assets. For example, if we have an average balance of $100 in a savings account and it earns $5 interest for the year, the return on assets is $5/$100, or 5%.

A3ᴬ   Explain the relation between return and risk. *Return* refers to income, and *risk* is the uncertainty about the return we hope to make. All investments involve risk. The lower the risk of an investment, the lower is its expected return. Higher risk implies higher, but riskier, expected return.

P1   Analyze business transactions using the accounting equation. A *transaction* is an exchange of economic consideration between two parties. Examples include exchanges of products, services, money, and rights to collect money. Transactions always have at least two effects on one or more components of the accounting equation. This equation is always in balance.

P2   Identify and prepare basic financial statements and explain how they interrelate. Four financial statements report on an organization's activities: statement of financial position, income statement, statement of changes in equity, and statement of cash flows.

Guidance Answers to Decision Maker

Retailer   You can use the accounting equation (Assets = Liabilities + Equity) to help identify risky customers to whom you would likely not want to extend credit. A statement of financial position provides amounts for each of these key components. The lower a customer's equity is relative to liabilities, the less likely you would be to extend credit. A low equity means the business has little value that does not already have creditor claims to it.

Business Owner   The 19% return on assets for the manufacturer exceeds the 14% industry return (and many others). This is a

positive factor for a potential purchase. Also, the purchase of this manufacturer is an opportunity to spread your risk over two businesses as opposed to one. Still, you should hesitate to purchase a business whose return of 19% is lower than your current resort's return of 21%. You are probably better off directing efforts to increase investment in your resort, assuming you can continue to earn a 21% return.

Guidance Answers to Quick Checks

1. Accounting is an information and measurement system that identifies, records, and communicates relevant information to help people make better decisions.

2. Recordkeeping, also called *bookkeeping,* is the recording of financial transactions and events, either manually or electronically. Recordkeeping is essential to data reliability; but accounting is this and much more. Accounting includes identifying, measuring, recording, reporting, and analyzing business events and transactions.

3. Technology offers increased accuracy, speed, efficiency, and convenience in accounting.

4. External users of accounting include lenders, shareholders, directors, customers, suppliers, regulators, lawyers, brokers, and the press. Internal users of accounting include managers, officers, and other internal decision makers involved with strategic and operating decisions.

5. Internal users (managers) include those from research and development, purchasing, human resources, production, distribution, marketing, and servicing.

6. Internal controls are procedures set up to protect assets, ensure reliable accounting reports, promote efficiency, and encourage adherence to company policies. Internal controls are crucial for relevant and reliable information.

7. Ethical guidelines are threefold: (1) identify ethical concerns using personal ethics, (2) analyze options considering all good and bad consequences, and (3) make ethical decisions after weighing all consequences.

8. Ethics and social responsibility yield good behavior, and they often result in higher income and a better working environment.

9. For accounting to provide useful information for decisions, it must be trusted. Trust requires ethics in accounting.

10. The IASB sets **IFRS**. (*Note:* Accounting rules reflect society's needs, not those of accountants or any other single constituency.)

11. The fundamental qualitative characteristics are relevance and faithful representation.

12. The enhancing qualitative characteristics are comparability, verifiability, timeliness, and understandability.

13. Users desire information about the performance of a specific entity. If information is mixed between two or more entities, its usefulness decreases.

14. The revenue recognition principle gives preparers guidelines on when to recognize (record) revenue. This is important; for example, if revenue is recognized too early, the statements report revenue sooner than it should and the business looks more profitable than it is. The reverse is also true.

15. The three basic forms of business organization are sole proprietorships, partnerships, and corporations.

16. Owners of corporations are called *shareholders.* Corporate ownership is divided into units called *shares.* The most basic of corporate shares is ordinary share.

17. The accounting equation is: Assets = Liabilities + Equity. This equation is always in balance, both before and after each transaction.

18. A transaction that changes the makeup of assets would not affect liability and equity accounts. FastForward's transactions 2 and 3 are examples. Each exchanges one asset for another.

19. Earning revenue by performing services, as in FastForward's transaction 5, increases equity (and assets). Incurring expenses while servicing clients, such as in transactions 6 and 7, decreases equity (and assets). Other examples include owner investments that increase equity and withdrawals that decrease equity.

20. Paying a liability with an asset reduces both asset and liability totals. One example is FastForward's transaction 10 that reduces a payable by paying cash.

21. An income statement reports a company's revenues and expenses along with the resulting net profit or loss. A statement of changes in equity shows changes in equity, including that from net profit or loss. Both statements report transactions occurring over a period of time.

22. The statement of financial position describes a company's financial position (assets, liabilities, and equity) at a point in time. The equity amount in the statement of financial position is obtained from the statement of changes in equity.

23. Cash flows from operating activities report cash receipts and payments from the primary business the company engages in. Cash flows from investing activities involve cash transactions from buying and selling long-term assets. Cash flows from financing activities include long-term cash borrowings and repayments to lenders and the cash investments from and withdrawals by the owner.

A list of key terms with page references concludes each chapter (a complete glossary is at the end of the book and also on the book's Website).

Key Terms   www.mheducation.asia/olc/wildkwokFAP

Accounting (p. 4)

Accounting equation (p. 13)

Assets (p. 13)

Audit (p. 12)

Bookkeeping (p. 5)

Business entity assumption (p. 10)

Common stock (p. 10)

Conceptual Framework for Financial Reporting (p. 11)

Corporation (p. 10)

Cost-benefit constraint (p. 12)

Cost principle (p. 9)

Equity (p. 13)

Ethics (p. 7)

Events (p. 14)

Expanded accounting equation (p. 14)

Expense recognition principle (p. 10)

Expenses (p. 14)

External transactions (p. 14)

External users (p. 5)

Financial accounting (p. 5)

Financial Accounting Standards Board (FASB) (p. 9)

Full disclosure principle (p. 10)

Generally accepted accounting principles (GAAP) (p. 8)

Going-concern assumption (p. 10)

Income statement (p. 19)

Internal transactions (p. 14)

Internal users (p. 6)

International Accounting Standards Board (IASB) (p. 9)

International Financial Reporting Standards (IFRS) (p. 9)

Liabilities (p. 13)

Managerial accounting (p. 6)

Matching principle (p. 10)

Materiality constraint (p. 9)

Measurement principle (p. 9)

Monetary unit assumption (p. 10)

Net profit (p. 14)

Net loss (p. 14)

Ordinary shares (p. 10)

Owner, Capital (p. 14)

Owner investment (p. 14)

Owner withdrawals (p. 14)

Partnership (p. 10)

Proprietorship (p. 10)

Recordkeeping (p. 4)

Return (p. 26)

Return on assets (p. 22)

Revenue recognition principle (p. 9)

Revenue (p. 9)

Risk (p. 26)

Securities and Exchange Commission (SEC) (p. 9)

Shareholders (p. 10)

Shares (p. 10)

Sole proprietorship (p. 10)

Statement of cash flows (p. 19)

Statement of changes in equity (p. 19)

Statement of financial position (p. 19)

Stock (p. 10)

Stockholders (p. 10)

Time period assumption (p. 10)

Withdrawals (p. 14)

Multiple Choice Quiz   Answers on p. 47   www.mheducation.asia/olc/wildkwokFAP

Additional Quiz Questions are available at the book's Website.

1. A building is offered for sale at $500,000 but is currently assessed at $400,000. The purchaser of the building believes the building is worth $475,000, but ultimately purchases the building for $450,000. The purchaser records the building at:
   a. $50,000
   b. $400,000
   c. $450,000
   d. $475,000
   e. $500,000

2. On December 30, 2015, KPMG signs a $150,000 contract to provide accounting services to one of its clients in 2016. KPMG has a December 31 year-end. Which accounting principle or assumption requires KPMG to record the accounting services revenue from this client in 2016 and not 2015?
   a. Business entity assumption
   b. Revenue recognition principle
   c. Monetary unit assumption
   d. Cost principle
   e. Going-concern assumption

3. If the assets of a company increase by $100,000 during the year and its liabilities increase by $35,000 during the same

year, then the change in equity of the company during the year must have been:
   a. An increase of $135,000.
   b. A decrease of $135,000.
   c. A decrease of $65,000.
   d. An increase of $65,000.
   e. An increase of $100,000.

4. Brunswick borrows $50,000 cash from Third National Bank. How does this transaction affect the accounting equation for Brunswick?
   a. Assets increase by $50,000; liabilities increase by $50,000; no effect on equity.
   b. Assets increase by $50,000; no effect on liabilities; equity increases by $50,000.
   c. Assets increase by $50,000; liabilities decrease by $50,000; no effect on equity.
   d. No effect on assets; liabilities increase by $50,000; equity increases by $50,000.
   e. No effect on assets; liabilities increase by $50,000; equity decreases by $50,000.

5. **Geek Squad** performs services for a customer and bills the customer for $500. How would Geek Squad record this transaction?

    a. Accounts receivable increase by $500; revenues increase by $500.

    b. Cash increases by $500; revenues increase by $500.

    c. Accounts receivable increase by $500; revenues decrease by $500.

    d. Accounts receivable increase by $500; accounts payable increase by $500.

    e. Accounts payable increase by $500; revenues increase by $500.

A(B)(C) *Superscript letter A (B) (C) denotes assignments based on Appendix 1A (1B) (1C).*

🔅 Icon denotes assignments that involve decision making.

Discussion Questions

1. What is the purpose of accounting in society?

2. Technology is increasingly used to process accounting data. Why then must we study and understand accounting?

3. 🔅 Identify four kinds of external users and describe how they use accounting information.

4. 🔅 What are at least three questions business owners and managers might be able to answer by looking at accounting information?

5. Identify three actual businesses that offer services and three actual businesses that offer products.

6. 🔅 Describe the internal role of accounting for organizations.

7. Identify three types of services typically offered by accounting professionals.

8. 🔅 What type of accounting information might be useful to the marketing managers of a business?

9. Why is accounting described as a service activity?

10. What are some accounting-related professions?

11. How do ethics rules affect auditors' choice of clients?

12. List the IASB's fundamental and enhancing qualitative characteristics of financial information.

13. What does the cost constraint imply for reporting financial information?

14. A business reports its own office stationery on the statement of financial position at its $400 cost, although it cannot be sold for more than $10 as scrap paper. Which accounting principle and/or assumption justifies this treatment?

15. Why is the revenue recognition principle needed? What does it demand?

16. Describe the three basic forms of business organization and their key attributes.

17. Define (*a*) *assets,* (*b*) *liabilities,* (*c*) *equity,* and (*d*) *net assets.*

18. What events or transactions change equity?

19. Identify the two main categories of accounting principles.

20. What do accountants mean by the term *revenue?*

21. Define *net profit* and explain its computation.

22. Identify the four basic financial statements of a business.

23. 🔅 What information is reported in an income statement?

24. Give two examples of expenses a business might incur.

25. What is the purpose of the statement of changes in equity?

26. 🔅 What information is reported in a statement of financial position?

27. The statement of cash flows reports on what major activities?

28. 🔅 Define and explain return on assets.

29.A 🔅 Define return and risk. Discuss the trade-off between them.

30.B Describe the three major business activities in organizations.

31.B Explain why investing (assets) and financing (liabilities and equity) totals are always equal.

32. Refer to the 2013 consolidated financial statements of **Adidas** in Appendix A near the end of the book. To what level of significance are the currency amounts rounded? What time period does its consolidated income statement cover?

33. Refer to **Puma**'s 2013 consolidated financial statements from its Website (http://about.puma.com/category/investors/financial-report/). Identify the currency amounts of **Puma**'s assets, liabilities, and equity shown on its statements.

34. Refer to **Samsung**'s 2012 consolidated financial statements in Appendix A. Identify its auditor. What responsibility and opinion does its auditor state regarding **Samsung**'s financial statements?

Quick Study exercises give readers a brief test of key elements.

Connect reproduces assignments online, in static or algorithmic mode, which allows instructors to monitor, promote, and assess student learning. It can be used for practice, homework, or exams.

▦ connect™

QUICK STUDY

QS 1-1

Identifying accounting terms   C1

Reading and interpreting accounting reports requires some knowledge of accounting terminology. (*a*) Identify the meaning of these accounting-related acronyms: GAAP, SEC, FASB, IASB, and **IFRS**. (*b*) Briefly explain the importance of the knowledge base or organization that is referred to for each of the accounting-related acronyms.

An important responsibility of many accounting professionals is to design and implement internal control procedures for organizations. Explain the purpose of internal control procedures. Provide two examples of internal controls applied by companies.

QS 1-2
Explaining internal control
C1

Identify the following users as either external users (E) or internal users (I).

a. Lenders   **d.** Sales staff   **g.** Brokers   **j.** Managers
b. Controllers   **e.** Tax authorities   **h.** Suppliers   **k.** Business press
c. Shareholders   **f.** Consumer group   **i.** Customers   **l.** Court judges

QS 1-3
Identifying accounting users
C2

There are many job opportunities for those with accounting knowledge. Identify at least three main areas of opportunities for accounting professionals. For each area, identify at least three job possibilities linked to accounting.

QS 1-4
Accounting opportunities C2

Accounting professionals must sometimes choose between two or more acceptable methods of accounting for business transactions and events. Explain why these situations can involve difficult matters of ethical concern.

QS 1-5
Identifying ethical concerns C3

This icon highlights assignments that enhance decision-making skills.

Identify which qualitative characteristic, accounting principle, or assumption best describes each of the following practices:

a. A corporation must present timely information to help its financial statement users to evaluate the company's past performance and predict its potential.

b. If $51,000 cash is paid to buy land, the land is reported on the buyer's statement of financial position at $51,000.

c. Kim Soo-yun owns both Sailing Passions and Dockside Supplies. In preparing financial statements for Dockside Supplies, Kim makes sure that the expense transactions of Sailing Passions are kept separate from Dockside's transactions and financial statements.

d. In December 2015, Ace Landscaping received a customer's order and cash prepayment to install a sprinkler system at a new house that would not be ready for installation until March 2016. Ace should record the revenue from the customer order in March 2016, not in December 2015.

QS 1-6
Identifying accounting principles
C4

---

a. Total assets of Caldwell Company equal $40,000 and its equity is $10,000. What is the amount of its liabilities?

b. Total assets of Waterworld equal $55,000 and its liabilities and equity amounts are equal to each other. What is the amount of its liabilities? What is the amount of its equity?

QS 1-7
Applying the accounting equation
A1

Use the accounting equation to compute the missing financial statement amounts (*a*), (*b*), and (*c*).

QS 1-8
Applying the accounting equation
A1

Company	Assets	=	Liabilities	+	Equity
1	$ 30,000		$ *(a)*		$ 20,000
2	*(b)*		50,000		30,000
3	90,000		10,000		*(c)*

[Screenshot: Microsoft Excel - Book1 with menu bar File Edit View Insert Format Tools Data Accounting Window Help and toolbar showing Arial, 10, B I U $ %. Sheet tabs: Sheet1 Sheet2 Sheet3]

Accounting provides information about an organization's business transactions and events that both affect the accounting equation and can be reliably measured. Identify at least two examples of both (*a*) business transactions and (*b*) business events that meet these requirements.

QS 1-9
Identifying transactions and events P1

QS 1-10 Identifying and computing assets, liabilities, and equity P1	Use **Adidas'** December 31, 2013, financial statements in Appendix A near the end of the book to answer the following: **a.** Identify the currency amounts of Adidas' 2013 (1) assets, (2) liabilities, and (3) equity. **b.** Using Adidas' amounts from part *a*, verify that Assets = Liabilities + Equity.

QS 1-11
Computing and interpreting
return on assets

A2

In a recent year's financial statements, **Home Depot** reported the following results. Compute and interpret Home Depot's return on assets (assume competitors average a 5% return on assets).

Sales	$71,288 million
Net profit	2,260 million
Average total assets	42,744 million

QS 1-12
Identifying items with financial
statements

P2

Indicate in which financial statement each item would most likely appear: income statement (IS), statement of financial position (SFP), statement of changes in equity (SCE), or statement of cash flows (SCF).

a. Assets   **d.** Equipment   **g.** Total liabilities and equity

b. Revenues   **e.** Withdrawals   **h.** Cash from operating activities

c. Liabilities   **f.** Expenses   **i.** Net decrease (or increase) in cash

---

connect

EXERCISES

Exercise 1-1
Classifying activities reflected in
the accounting system

C1

Accounting is an information and measurement system that identifies, records, and communicates relevant, reliable, and comparable information about an organization's business activities. Classify the following activities as part of the identifying (I), recording (R), or communicating (C) aspects of accounting.

_____ **1.** Determining employee tasks behind a service.

_____ **2.** Establishing revenues generated from a product.

_____ **3.** Maintaining a log of service costs.

_____ **4.** Measuring the costs of a product.

_____ **5.** Preparing financial statements.

_____ **6.** Analyzing and interpreting reports.

_____ **7.** Presenting financial information.

Exercise 1-2
Identifying accounting
users and uses

C2

Part A. Identify the following users of accounting information as either an internal (I) or an external (E) user.

_____ **1.** Shareholders

_____ **2.** Creditors

_____ **3.** Nonexecutive employee

_____ **4.** Research and development director

_____ **5.** Purchasing manager

_____ **6.** Human resources director

_____ **7.** Production supervisors

_____ **8.** Distribution managers

Part B. Identify the following questions as most likely to be asked by an internal (I) or an external (E) user of accounting information.

_____ **1.** What are the costs of our service to customers?

_____ **2.** Should we make a five-year loan to that business?

_____ **3.** Should we spend further research on our product?

_____ **4.** Do income levels justify the current share price?

_____ **5.** What are reasonable payroll benefits and wages?

_____ **6.** Which firm reports the highest sales and income?

_____ **7.** What are the costs of our product's ingredients?

Exercise 1-3
Describing accounting
responsibilities

C2

Many accounting professionals work in one of the following three areas:

A. Managerial accounting   **B.** Financial accounting   **C.** Tax accounting

Identify the area of accounting that is most involved in each of the following responsibilities:

_____ **1.** Reviewing reports for stock market regulators.

_____ **2.** Planning transactions to minimize taxes.

_____ **3.** Investigating violations of tax laws.

_____ **4.** Preparing external financial statements.

_____ **5.** Budgeting.

_____ **6.** Cost accounting.

_____ **7.** External auditing.

_____ **8.** Internal auditing.

Assume the following role and describe a situation in which ethical considerations play an important part in guiding your decisions and actions:

a. You are a student in an introductory accounting course.

b. You are an accounting professional with audit clients that are competitors in business.

c. You are an accounting professional preparing tax returns for clients.

d. You are a manager with responsibility for several employees.

Exercise 1-4
Identifying ethical concerns
C3

Match each of the numbered descriptions with the term or phrase it best reflects. Indicate your answer by writing the letter for the term or phrase in the blank provided.

A. Audit   **C.** Ethics   **E.** SEC   **G.** Net profit
B. GAAP   **D.** Tax accounting   **F.** Public accountants   **H.** IASB

_____ **1.** Amount a business earns after paying all expenses and costs associated with its sales and revenues.

_____ **2.** An examination of an organization's accounting system and records that adds credibility to financial statements.

_____ **3.** Principles that determine whether an action is right or wrong.

_____ **4.** Accounting professionals who provide services to many clients.

_____ **5.** An accounting area that includes planning future transactions to minimize taxes paid.

Exercise 1-5
Learning the language of business
C1–C3

Match each of the numbered descriptions with the principle or assumption it best reflects. Enter the letter for the appropriate principle or assumption in the blank space next to each description.

A. Cost principle   **E.** General accounting principle
B. Matching principle   **F.** Business entity assumption
C. Specific accounting principle   **G.** Revenue recognition principle
D. Full disclosure principle   **H.** Going-concern assumption

_____ **1.** Revenue is recorded only when the earnings process is complete.

_____ **2.** Information is based on actual costs incurred in transactions.

_____ **3.** Usually created by a pronouncement from an authoritative body.

_____ **4.** Financial statements reflect the assumption that the business continues operating.

_____ **5.** A company reports details behind financial statements that would impact users' decisions.

_____ **6.** A company records the expenses incurred to generate the revenues reported.

_____ **7.** Derived from long-used and generally accepted accounting practices.

_____ **8.** Every business is accounted for separately from its owner or owners.

Exercise 1-6
Identifying accounting principles and assumptions
C4

The IASB's Conceptual Framework for Financial Reporting stipulates the qualitative characteristics of financial statements.

a. It was reported that top investment guru Warren Buffett spends about five to six hours each day reading annual reports on the companies he wishes to invest in. Explain the characteristic(s) implicit in this statement.

b. A company changed its revenue recognition policies. Which characteristic is jeopardized by this change? Explain its importance.

c. Investors rely on financial statement to make decisions such as whether to buy or sell the shares of public companies. Which characteristic facilitates such decisions?

d. When there is agreement between a measure or description and the phenomenon it purports to represent, information possesses which characteristic? Explain its importance.

e. Yang is evaluating two companies for future investment potential. Yang's task is made easier because both companies use the same accounting methods. Which characteristic does the information Yang will be using possess? Explain its importance.

Exercise 1-7
Applying the conceptual framework
C4

Answer the following questions. (*Hint:* Use the accounting equation.)

a. Office Mart has assets equal to $123,000 and liabilities equal to $53,000 at year-end. What is the total equity for Office Mart at year-end?

b. At the beginning of the year, Logan Company's assets are $200,000 and its equity is $150,000. During the year, assets increase $70,000 and liabilities increase $30,000. What is the equity at the end of the year?

c. At the beginning of the year, Keller Company's liabilities equal $60,000. During the year, assets increase by $80,000, and at year-end assets equal $180,000. Liabilities decrease $10,000 during the year. What are the beginning and ending amounts of equity?

Exercise 1-8
Using the accounting equation
A1 P1

Check (c) Beg. equity, $40,000

Exercise 1-9

Using the accounting equation

A1

Determine the missing amount from each of the separate situations *a*, *b*, and *c* below.

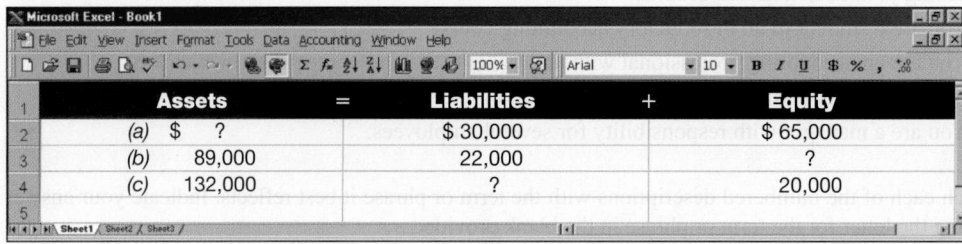

	Assets	=	Liabilities	+	Equity
(a)	$?		$ 30,000		$ 65,000
(b)	89,000		22,000		?
(c)	132,000		?		20,000

Exercise 1-10

Identifying effects of transactions on the accounting equation

P1

Provide an example of a transaction that creates the described effects for the separate cases *a* through *g*.

a. Increases an asset and decreases an asset.

b. Decreases an asset and decreases a liability.

c. Decreases a liability and increases a liability.

d. Increases an asset and increases a liability.

e. Decreases an asset and decreases equity.

f. Increases a liability and decreases equity.

g. Increases an asset and increases equity.

Exercise 1-11

Identifying effects of transactions using the accounting equation

P1

Lena Gold began a professional practice on June 1 and plans to prepare financial statements at the end of each month. During June, Gold (the owner) completed these transactions:

a. Owner invested $50,000 cash in the company along with equipment that had a $10,000 market value.

b. The company paid $1,600 cash for rent of office space for the month.

c. The company purchased $12,000 of additional equipment on credit (payment due within 30 days).

d. The company completed work for a client and immediately collected the $2,000 cash earned.

e. The company completed work for a client and sent a bill for $7,000 to be received within 30 days.

f. The company purchased additional equipment for $8,000 cash.

g. The company paid an assistant $2,400 cash as wages for the month.

h. The company collected $5,000 cash as a partial payment for the amount owed by the client in transaction *e*.

i. The company paid $12,000 cash to settle the liability created in transaction *c*.

j. Owner withdrew $500 cash from the company for personal use.

Required

Check   Net profit, $5,000

Create a table like the one in Exhibit 1.7, using the following headings for columns: Cash; Accounts Receivable; Equipment; Accounts Payable; L. Gold, Capital; L. Gold, Withdrawals; Revenues; and Expenses. Then use additions and subtractions to show the effects of the transactions on individual items of the accounting equation. Show new balances after each transaction.

Exercise 1-12

Analysis using the accounting equation

P1

Zelda began a new consulting firm on January 5. The accounting equation showed the following balances after each of the company's first five transactions. Analyze the accounting equation for each transaction and describe each of the five transactions with their amounts.

			Assets						=	Liabilities	+		Equity		
Trans-action	Cash	+	Accounts Receiv-able	+	Office Sup-plies	+	Office Furni-ture	=		Accounts Payable	+	Zelda, Capital	+	Revenues	
a.	$20,000	+	$ 0	+	$ 0	+	$ 0	=		$ 0	+	$20,000	+	$ 0	
b.	19,000	+	0	+	1,500	+	0	=		500	+	20,000	+	0	
c.	11,000	+	0	+	1,500	+	8,000	=		500	+	20,000	+	0	
d.	11,000	+	3,000	+	1,500	+	8,000	=		500	+	20,000	+	3,000	
e.	11,500	+	3,000	+	1,500	+	8,000	=		500	+	20,000	+	3,500	

The following table shows the effects of five transactions (*a* through *e*) on the assets, liabilities, and equity of Vera's Boutique. Write short descriptions of the probable nature of each transaction.

Exercise 1-13
Identifying effects of transactions on accounting equation

P1

	Assets				=	Liabilities	+	Equity		
	Cash	+ Accounts Receivable	+ Office Supplies	+ Land	=	Accounts Payable	+ Vera, Capital	+ Revenues		
	$ 10,500	+ $ 0	+ $1,500	+ $ 9,500	=	$ 0	+ $21,500	+ $ 0		
a.	− 2,000			+ 2,000						
b.			+ 500			+500				
c.		+ 950						+ 950		
d.	− 500					−500				
e.	+ 950	− 950								
	$ 8,950	+ $ 0	+ $2,000	+ $11,500	=	$ 0	+ $21,500	+ $950		

On October 1, Natalie King organized Real Solutions, a new consulting firm. On October 31, the company's records show the following items and amounts. Use this information to prepare an October income statement for the business.

Exercise 1-14
Preparing an income statement

P2

Cash	$ 2,000	Cash withdrawals by owner	$ 3,360
Accounts receivable	13,000	Consulting fees earned	15,000
Office supplies	4,250	Rent expense	2,550
Land	36,000	Salaries expense	6,000
Office equipment	28,000	Telephone expense	660
Accounts payable	7,500	Miscellaneous expenses	680
Owner investments	74,000		

Check Net profit, $5,110

Use the information in Exercise 1-14 to prepare an October statement of changes in equity for Real Solutions.

Exercise 1-15
Preparing a statement of changes in equity   P2

Use the information in Exercise 1-14 (if completed, you can also use your solution to Exercise 1-15) to prepare an October 31 statement of financial position for Real Solutions.

Exercise 1-16
Preparing a statement of financial position   P2

Use the information in Exercise 1-14 to prepare an October 31 statement of cash flows for Real Solutions. Also assume the following:

a. The owner's initial investment consists of $38,000 cash and $36,000 in land.

b. The company's $28,000 equipment purchase is paid in cash.

c. The accounts payable balance of $7,500 consists of the $4,250 office supplies purchase and $3,250 in employee salaries yet to be paid.

d. The company's rent, telephone, and miscellaneous expenses are paid in cash.

e. $2,000 has been collected on the $15,000 consulting fees earned.

Exercise 1-17
Preparing a statement of cash flows

P2

Check Net increase in cash, $2,000

Geneva Group reports net profit of $20,000 for the current year. At the beginning of the year, Geneva Group had $100,000 in assets. By the end of the year, assets had grown to $150,000. What is Geneva Group's return on assets for the current year? How would you assess its performance if competitors average a 10% return on assets?

Exercise 1-18
Analysis of return on assets

A2

Indicate the section where each of the following would appear on the statement of cash flows.

A. Cash flows from operating activity

B. Cash flows from investing activity

C. Cash flows from financing activity

Exercise 1-19
Identifying sections of the statement of cash flows

P2

_____ **1.** Cash paid for wages   _____ **5.** Cash paid on an account payable

_____ **2.** Cash withdrawal by owner   _____ **6.** Cash investment by owner

_____ **3.** Cash purchase of equipment   _____ **7.** Cash received from clients

_____ **4.** Cash paid for advertising   _____ **8.** Cash paid for rent

Exercise 1-20ᴮ
Identifying business activities

C5

Match each transaction or event to one of the following activities of an organization: financing activities (F), investing activities (I), or operating activities (O).

1. _____ An owner contributes resources to the business.

2. _____ An organization purchases equipment.

3. _____ An organization advertises a new product.

4. _____ The organization borrows money from a bank.

5. _____ An organization sells some of its land.

Problem Set B located at the end of Problem Set A is provided for each problem to reinforce the learning process.

connect

PROBLEM SET A

Problem 1-1A
Identifying effects of transactions on financial statements

A1 P1

Identify how each of the following separate transactions affects financial statements. For the statement of financial position, identify how each transaction affects total assets, total liabilities, and total equity. For the income statement, identify how each transaction affects net profit. For the statement of cash flows, identify how each transaction affects cash flows from operating activities, cash flows from financing activities, and cash flows from investing activities. For increases, place a "+" in the column or columns. For decreases, place a "−" in the column or columns. If both an increase and a decrease occur, place a "+/−" in the column or columns. The first transaction is completed as an example.

	Transaction	Statement of Financial Position			Income Statement	Statement of Cash Flows		
		Total Assets	Total Liab.	Total Equity	Net Income	Operating Activities	Financing Activities	Investing Activities
1	Owner invests cash in business	+		+			+	
2	Incurs legal costs on credit							
3	Pays cash for employee wages							
4	Borrows cash by signing long-term note payable							
5	Receives cash for services provided							
6	Buys land by signing note payable							
7	Buys office equipment for cash							
8	Provides services on credit							
9	Collects cash on receivable from (8)							
10	Owner withdraws cash							

Problem 1-2A
Computing missing information using accounting knowledge

A1 P1

The following financial statement information is from five separate companies:

	Company A	Company B	Company C	Company D	Company E
December 31, year one					
Assets.	$45,000	$35,000	$29,000	$80,000	$123,000
Liabilities	23,500	22,500	14,000	38,000	?
December 31, year two					
Assets.	48,000	41,000	?	125,000	112,500
Liabilities	?	27,500	19,000	64,000	75,000
During year two					
Owner investments.	5,000	1,500	7,750	?	4,500
Net profit (loss).	7,500	?	9,000	12,000	18,000
Owner cash withdrawals	2,500	3,000	3,875	0	9,000

Required

1. Answer the following questions about Company A:
  a. What is the amount of equity on December 31, year one?
  b. What is the amount of equity on December 31, year two?
  c. What is the amount of liabilities on December 31, year two?

2. Answer the following questions about Company B:
  a. What is the amount of equity on December 31, year one?
  b. What is the amount of equity on December 31, year two?
  c. What is net profit for year year two?

3. Calculate the amount of assets for Company C on December 31, year two.

4. Calculate the amount of owner investments for Company D during year two.

5. Calculate the amount of liabilities for Company E on December 31, year one.

Check   (1*b*) $31,500

(2*c*) $2,500

(3) $46,875

The following is selected financial information for Affiliated Company as at December 31 of the current year: liabilities, $34,000; equity, $56,000; assets, $90,000.

Required

Prepare the statement of financial position for Affiliated Company as at December 31 of the current year.

Problem 1-3A
Preparing a statement of financial position
P2

The following is selected financial information for Sun Energy Company for the current year ended December 31: revenues, $65,000; expenses, $50,000; net profit, $15,000.

Required

Prepare the current year income statement for Sun Energy Company.

Problem 1-4A
Preparing an income statement
P2

Following is selected financial information for Boardwalk for the current year ended December 31.

B. Walk, Capital, Dec. 31	$15,000	B. Walk, Withdrawals	$2,000
Net profit.	9,000	B. Walk, Capital, Jan. 1	8,000

Required

Prepare the current year statement of changes in equity for Boardwalk.

Problem 1-5A
Preparing a statement of changes in equity
P2

Following is selected financial information of Trimark for the current year ended December 31.

Cash used in investing activities.	$(3,000)
Net increase in cash	200
Cash used in financing activities	(3,800)
Cash from operating activities	7,000
Cash, December 31, beginning of year	3,300

Required

Prepare the current year statement of cash flows for Trimark Company.

Problem 1-6A
Preparing a statement of cash flows
P2

Check   Cash balance, Dec. 31, end of year, $3,500

Miranda Right started Right Consulting, a new business, and completed the following transactions during its first year of operations.

  a. M. Right invests $60,000 cash and office equipment valued at $30,000 in the company.
  b. The company purchased a $300,000 building to use as an office. Right paid $50,000 in cash and signed a note payable promising to pay the $250,000 balance over the next ten years.
  c. The company purchased office equipment for $6,000 cash.
  d. The company purchased $4,000 of office supplies and $1,000 of office equipment on credit.

Problem 1-7A
Analyzing effects of transactions
C4 P1 P2 A1

e. The company paid a local newspaper $1,000 cash for printing an announcement of the office's opening.

f. The company completed a financial plan for a client and billed that client $4,000 for the service.

g. The company designed a financial plan for another client and immediately collected an $8,000 cash fee.

h. M. Right withdrew $1,800 cash from the company for personal use.

i. The company received $3,000 cash as partial payment from the client described in transaction *f*.

j. The company made a partial payment of $500 cash on the equipment purchased in transaction *d*.

k. The company paid $2,500 cash for the office secretary's wages for this period.

Required

1. Create a table like the one in Exhibit 1.7, using the following headings for the columns: Cash; Accounts Receivable; Office Supplies; Office Equipment; Building; Accounts Payable; Notes Payable; M. Right, Capital; M. Right, Withdrawals; Revenues; and Expenses.

2. Use additions and subtractions within the table created in part *1* to show the dollar effects of each transaction on individual items of the accounting equation. Show new balances after each transaction.

3. Once you have completed the table, determine the company's net profit.

Check (2) Ending balances: Cash, $9,200; Expenses, $3,500; Notes Payable, $250,000

(3) Net profit, $8,500

Problem 1-8A
Analyzing transactions and preparing financial statements

C4 P1 P2

www.mheducation.asia/olc/wildkwokFAP

J. D. Simpson started The Simpson Co., a new business that began operations on May 1. The Simpson Co. completed the following transactions during its first month of operations.

May 1 J. D. Simpson invested $60,000 cash in the company.
1 The company rented a furnished office and paid $3,200 cash for May's rent.
3 The company purchased $1,680 of office equipment on credit.
5 The company paid $800 cash for this month's cleaning services.
8 The company provided consulting services for a client and immediately collected $4,600 cash.
12 The company provided $3,000 of consulting services for a client on credit.
15 The company paid $850 cash for an assistant's salary for the first half of this month.
20 The company received $3,000 cash payment for the services provided on May 12.
22 The company provided $2,800 of consulting services on credit.
25 The company received $2,800 cash payment for the services provided on May 22.
26 The company paid $1,680 cash for the office equipment purchased on May 3.
27 The company purchased $60 of advertising in this month's (May) local paper on credit; cash payment is due June 1.
28 The company paid $850 cash for an assistant's salary for the second half of this month.
30 The company paid $200 cash for this month's telephone bill.
30 The company paid $480 cash for this month's utilities.
31 J. D. Simpson withdrew $1,200 cash from the company for personal use.

Required

1. Arrange the following asset, liability, and equity titles in a table like Exhibit 1.7: Cash; Accounts Receivable; Office Equipment; Accounts Payable; J. D. Simpson, Capital; J. D. Simpson, Withdrawals; Revenues; and Expenses.

Check (2) Ending balances: Cash, $61,140; Expenses, $6,440

2. Show effects of the transactions on the accounts of the accounting equation by recording increases and decreases in the appropriate columns. Do not determine new account balances after each transaction. Determine the final total for each account and verify that the equation is in balance.

(3) Net profit, $3,960; Total assets, $62,820

3. Prepare an income statement for May, a statement of changes in equity for May, a May 31 statement of financial position, and a statement of cash flows for May.

Problem 1-9A
Analyzing transactions and preparing financial statements

C4 P1 P2

www.mheducation.asia/olc/wildkwokFAP

Curtis Hamilton started a new business and completed these transactions during December.

Dec. 1 Curtis Hamilton transferred $56,000 cash from a personal savings account to a checking account in the name of Hamilton Electric.
2 The company rented office space and paid $800 cash for the December rent.
3 The company purchased $14,000 of electrical equipment by paying $3,200 cash and agreeing to pay the $10,800 balance in 30 days.
5 The company purchased office supplies by paying $900 cash.
6 The company completed electrical work and immediately collected $1,000 cash for these services.
8 The company purchased $3,800 of office equipment on credit.
15 The company completed electrical work on credit in the amount of $4,000.

18 The company purchased $500 of office supplies on credit.
20 The company paid $3,800 cash for the office equipment purchased on December 8.
24 The company billed a client $600 for electrical work completed; the balance is due in 30 days.
28 The company received $4,000 cash for the work completed on December 15.
29 The company paid the assistant's salary of $1,200 cash for this month.
30 The company paid $440 cash for this month's utility bill.
31 C. Hamilton withdrew $700 cash from the company for personal use.

Required

1. Arrange the following asset, liability, and equity titles in a table like Exhibit 1.7: Cash; Accounts Receivable; Office Supplies; Office Equipment; Electrical Equipment; Accounts Payable; C. Hamilton, Capital; C. Hamilton, Withdrawals; Revenues; and Expenses.

2. Use additions and subtractions to show the effects of each transaction on the accounts in the accounting equation. Show new balances after each transaction.

3. Use the increases and decreases in the columns of the table from part 2 to prepare an income statement, a statement of changes in equity, and a statement of cash flows—each of these for the current month. Also prepare a statement of financial position as at the end of the month.

Check (2) Ending balances: Cash, $49,960, Accounts Payable, $11,300

(3) Net profit, $3,160; Total assets, $69,760

Analysis Component

4. Assume that the owner investment transaction on December 1 was $40,000 cash instead of $56,000 and that Hamilton Electric obtained another $16,000 in cash by borrowing it from a bank. Explain the effect of this change on total assets, total liabilities, and total equity.

Nolan manufactures, markets, and sells cellular telephones. The average total assets for Nolan is $250,000. In its most recent year, Nolan reported net profit of $55,000 on revenues of $455,000.

Problem 1-10A
Determining expenses, liabilities, equity, and return on assets
A1 A2

Required

1. What is Nolan's return on assets?
2. Does return on assets seem satisfactory for Nolan given that its competitors average a 12% return on assets?
3. What are total expenses for Nolan in its most recent year?
4. What is the average total amount of liabilities plus equity for Nolan?

Check (3) $400,000
(4) $250,000

Coca-Cola and PepsiCo both produce and market beverages that are direct competitors. Key financial figures for these businesses over the past year follow.

Problem 1-11A
Computing and interpreting return on assets
A2

Key Figures (US$ millions)	Coca-Cola	PepsiCo
Sales	$30,990	$43,232
Net profit.	6,906	5,979
Average assets	44,595	37,921

Required

1. Compute return on assets for (*a*) Coca-Cola and (*b*) PepsiCo.
2. Which company is more successful in its total amount of sales to consumers?
3. Which company is more successful in returning net profit from its assets invested?

Check (1*a*) 15.5%; (1*b*) 15.8%

Analysis Component

4. Write a one-paragraph memorandum explaining which company you would invest your money in and why. (Limit your explanation to the information provided.)

All business decisions involve aspects of risk and return.

Problem 1-12A[A]
Identifying risk and return
A3

Required

Identify both the risk and the return in each of the following activities:

1. Investing $1,000 in a 4% savings account.
2. Placing a $1,000 bet on your favorite sports team.
3. Investing $10,000 in shares of GOME Ltd.
4. Borrowing $10,000 student loan to study for an accounting degree.

Problem 1-13A^B
Describing organizational
activities **C5**

An organization undertakes various activities in pursuit of business success. Identify an organization's three major business activities, and describe each activity.

Problem 1-14A^B
Describing organizational
activities

C5

A start-up company often engages in the following transactions in its first year of operations. Classify those transactions in one of the three major categories of an organization's business activities.

F. Financing   **I.** Investing   **O.** Operating

_____ **1.** Owner investing land in business.
_____ **2.** Purchasing a building.
_____ **3.** Purchasing land.
_____ **4.** Borrowing cash from a bank.

_____ **5.** Purchasing equipment.
_____ **6.** Selling and distributing products.
_____ **7.** Paying for advertising.
_____ **8.** Paying employee wages.

PROBLEM SET B

Problem 1-1B
Identifying effects of
transactions on financial
statements **A1 P1**

Identify how each of the following separate transactions affects financial statements. For the statement of financial position, identify how each transaction affects total assets, total liabilities, and total equity. For the income statement, identify how each transaction affects net profit. For the statement of cash flows, identify how each transaction affects cash flows from operating activities, cash flows from financing activities, and cash flows from investing activities. For increases, place a "+" in the column or columns. For decreases, place a "−" in the column or columns. If both an increase and a decrease occur, place "+/−" in the column or columns. The first transaction is completed as an example.

	Transaction	Total Assets	Total Liab.	Total Equity	Net Profit	Operating Activities	Financing Activities	Investing Activities
		Statement of Financial Position			**Income Statement**	**Statement of Cash Flows**		
I	Owner invests cash in business	+		+			+	
2	Buys building by signing note payable							
3	Pays cash for salaries incurred							
4	Provides services for cash							
5	Pays cash for rent incurred							
6	Incurs utilities costs on credit							
7	Buys store equipment for cash							
8	Owner withdraws cash							
9	Provides services on credit							
10	Collects cash on receivable from (9)							

Problem 1-2B
Computing missing information
using accounting knowledge

A1 P1

The following financial statement information is from five separate companies.

	Company V	Company W	Company X	Company Y	Company Z
December 31, 2010					
Assets..........................	$45,000	$70,000	$121,500	$82,500	$124,000
Liabilities	30,000	50,000	58,500	61,500	?
December 31, 2011					
Assets..........................	49,000	90,000	136,500	?	160,000
Liabilities	26,000	?	55,500	72,000	52,000
During year 2011					
Owner investments.............	6,000	10,000	?	38,100	40,000
Net profit or (loss)	?	30,000	16,500	24,000	32,000
Owner cash withdrawals.........	4,500	2,000	0	18,000	6,000

Required

1. Answer the following questions about Company V:
   a. What is the amount of equity on December 31, 2010?
   b. What is the amount of equity on December 31, 2011?
   c. What is the net profit or loss for the year 2011?
2. Answer the following questions about Company W:
   a. What is the amount of equity on December 31, 2010?
   b. What is the amount of equity on December 31, 2011?
   c. What is the amount of liabilities on December 31, 2011?
3. Calculate the amount of owner investments for Company X during 2011.
4. Calculate the amount of assets for Company Y on December 31, 2011.
5. Calculate the amount of liabilities for Company Z on December 31, 2010.

Check   (1*b*) $23,000

(2*c*) $32,000

(4) $137,100

The following is selected financial information for RWB Company as at December 31 of the current year:

| Liabilities . . . . | $74,000 | Equity . . . . | $40,000 | Assets . . . . | $114,000 |

Required

Prepare the statement of financial position for RWB Company as at December 31 of the current year.

Problem 1-3B
Preparing a statement of financial position
P2

The following is selected financial information for Online Co. for the current year ended December 31: revenues,

| Revenues . . . . | $58,000 | Expenses . . . . | $30,000 | Net profit . . . . | $28,000 |

Required

Prepare the current year income statement for Online Co.

Problem 1-4B
Preparing an income statement
P2

Following is selected financial information for ComEx for the current year ended December 31.

| C. Tex, Capital, Dec. 31 . . . . | $47,000 | C. Tex, Withdrawals . . . . | $ 8,000 |
| Net profit . . . . | 6,000 | C. Tex, Capital, Jan. 1 . . . . | 49,000 |

Required

Prepare the current year statement of changes in equity for ComEx.

Problem 1-5B
Preparing a statement of changes in equity
P2

Following is selected financial information of BuyRight Company for the current year ended December 31.

Cash from investing activities	$2,600
Net increase in cash	1,400
Cash from financing activities	2,800
Cash used in operating activities	(4,000)
Cash, beginning of year	1,300

Required

Prepare the current year statement of cash flows for BuyRight Company.

Problem 1-6B
Preparing a statement of cash flows
P2

Tiana Moore started a new business, Tiana's Solutions, and completed the following transactions during its first year of operations.
   a. T. Moore invests $95,000 cash and office equipment valued at $20,000 in the company.
   b. The company purchased a $120,000 building to use as an office. It paid $20,000 in cash and signed a note payable promising to pay the $100,000 balance over the next ten years.

Problem 1-7B
Analyzing effects of transactions
C4 P1 P2 A1

c. The company purchased office equipment for $20,000 cash.

d. The company purchased $1,400 of office supplies and $3,000 of office equipment on credit.

e. The company paid a local newspaper $400 cash for printing an announcement of the office's opening.

f. The company completed a financial plan for a client and billed that client $1,800 for the service.

g. The company designed a financial plan for another client and immediately collected a $2,000 cash fee.

h. T. Moore withdrew $5,000 cash from the company for personal use.

i. The company received $1,800 cash from the client described in transaction *f*.

j. The company made a payment of $2,000 cash on the equipment purchased in transaction *d*.

k. The company paid $2,000 cash for the office secretary's wages.

Required

1. Create a table like the one in Exhibit 1.7, using the following headings for the columns: Cash; Accounts Receivable; Office Supplies; Office Equipment; Building; Accounts Payable; Notes Payable; T. Moore, Capital; T. Moore, Withdrawals; Revenues; and Expenses.

2. Use additions and subtractions within the table created in part *1* to show the dollar effects of each transaction on individual items of the accounting equation. Show new balances after each transaction.

3. Once you have completed the table, determine the company's net profit.

Check (2) Ending balances: Cash, $49,400; Expenses, $2,400; Notes Payable, $100,000

(3) Net profit, $1,400

Problem 1-8B
Analyzing transactions and preparing financial statements
C4 P1 P2

Ken Stone launched a new business, Ken's Maintenance Co., that began operations on June 1. The following transactions were completed by the company during that first month.

June	1	K. Stone invested $120,000 cash in the company.
	2	The company rented a furnished office and paid $4,500 cash for June's rent.
	4	The company purchased $2,400 of equipment on credit.
	6	The company paid $1,125 cash for this month's advertising of the opening of the business.
	8	The company completed maintenance services for a customer and immediately collected $750 cash.
	14	The company completed $6,300 of maintenance services for City Center on credit.
	16	The company paid $900 cash for an assistant's salary for the first half of the month.
	20	The company received $6,300 cash payment for services completed for City Center on June 14.
	21	The company completed $3,500 of maintenance services for Skyway Co. on credit.
	24	The company completed $825 of maintenance services for Comfort Motel on credit.
	25	The company received $3,500 cash payment from Skyway Co. for the work completed on June 21.
	26	The company made payment of $2,400 cash for equipment purchased on June 4.
	28	The company paid $900 cash for an assistant's salary for the second half of this month.
	29	K. Stone withdrew $2,000 cash from the company for personal use.
	30	The company paid $120 cash for this month's telephone bill.
	30	The company paid $525 cash for this month's utilities.

Required

1. Arrange the following asset, liability, and equity titles in a table like Exhibit 1.7: Cash; Accounts Receivable; Equipment; Accounts Payable; K. Stone, Capital; K. Stone, Withdrawals; Revenues; and Expenses.

2. Show the effects of the transactions on the accounts of the accounting equation by recording increases and decreases in the appropriate columns. Do not determine new account balances after each transaction. Determine the final total for each account and verify that the equation is in balance.

3. Prepare a June income statement, a June statement of changes in equity, a June 30 statement of financial position, and a June statement of cash flows.

Check (2) Ending balances: Cash, $118,080; Expenses, $8,070

(3) Net profit, $3,305; Total assets, $121,305

Problem 1-9B
Analyzing transactions and preparing financial statements
C4 P1 P2

Swender Excavating Co., owned by Patrick Swender, began operations in July and completed these transactions during that first month of operations.

July	1	P. Swender invested $60,000 cash in the company.
	2	The company rented office space and paid $500 cash for the July rent.
	3	The company purchased excavating equipment for $4,000 by paying $800 cash and agreeing to pay the $3,200 balance in 30 days.
	6	The company purchased office supplies for $500 cash.
	8	The company completed work for a customer and immediately collected $2,200 cash for the work.

10	The company purchased $3,800 of office equipment on credit.
15	The company completed work for a customer on credit in the amount of $2,400.
17	The company purchased $1,920 of office supplies on credit.
23	The company paid $3,800 cash for the office equipment purchased on July 10.
25	The company billed a customer $5,000 for work completed; the balance is due in 30 days.
28	The company received $2,400 cash for the work completed on July 15.
30	The company paid an assistant's salary of $1,260 cash for this month.
31	The company paid $260 cash for this month's utility bill.
31	P. Swender withdrew $1,200 cash from the company for personal use.

Required

1. Arrange the following asset, liability, and equity titles in a table like Exhibit 1.7: Cash; Accounts Receivable; Office Supplies; Office Equipment; Excavating Equipment; Accounts Payable; P. Swender, Capital; P. Swender, Withdrawals; Revenues; and Expenses.

2. Use additions and subtractions to show the effects of each transaction on the accounts in the accounting equation. Show new balances after each transaction.

3. Use the increases and decreases in the columns of the table from part 2 to prepare an income statement, a statement of changes in equity, and a statement of cash flows—each of these for the current month. Also prepare a statement of financial position as at the end of the month.

Check   (2) Ending balances: Cash, $56,280; Accounts Payable, $5,120

(3) Net profit, $7,580; Total assets, $71,500

Analysis Component

4. Assume that the $4,000 purchase of excavating equipment on July 3 was financed from an owner investment of another $4,000 cash in the business (instead of the purchase conditions described in the transaction). Explain the effect of this change on total assets, total liabilities, and total equity.

Aspen Company manufactures, markets, and sells ATV and snowmobile equipment and accessories. The average total assets for Aspen is $2,000,000. In its most recent year, Aspen reported net profit of $100,000 on revenues of $1,200,000.

Required

1. What is Aspen Company's return on assets?

2. Does return on assets seem satisfactory for Aspen given that its competitors average a 9.5% return on assets?

3. What are the total expenses for Aspen Company in its most recent year?

4. What is the average total amount of liabilities plus equity for Aspen Company?

Problem 1-10B
Determining expenses, liabilities, equity, and return on assets

A1 A2

Check   (3) $1,100,000

(4) $2,000,000

AT&T and Verizon produce and market telecommunications products and are competitors. Key financial figures for these businesses over the past year follow.

Problem 1-11B
Computing and interpreting return on assets

A2

Key Figures (US$ millions)	AT&T	Verizon
Sales	$123,018	$107,808
Net profit	12,535	10,358
Average assets	266,999	214,937

Required

1. Compute return on assets for (a) AT&T and (b) Verizon.

2. Which company is more successful in the total amount of sales to consumers?

3. Which company is more successful in returning net profit from its assets invested?

Check   (1a) 4.7%; (1b) 4.8%

Analysis Component

4. Write a one-paragraph memorandum explaining which company you would invest your money in and why. (Limit your explanation to the information provided.)

Problem 1-12B[A]
Identifying risk and return
A3

All business decisions involve aspects of risk and return.

Required

Identify both the risk and the return in each of the following activities:

1. Stashing $1,000 cash under your mattress.
2. Placing a $50 bet on roulette in Singapore's Marina Bay Sands casino.
3. Investing $10,000 in shares of Alibaba.com Ltd.
4. Investing $10,000 in Singapore government bonds.

Problem 1-13B[B]
Describing organizational
activities C5

Identify in outline format the three major business activities of an organization. For each of these activities, identify at least two specific transactions or events normally undertaken by the business's owners or its managers.

Problem 1-14B[B]
Describing organizational
activities
C5

A start-up company often engages in the following activities during its first year of operations. Classify each of the following activities into one of the three major activities of an organization.

A. Financing   **B.** Investing   **C.** Operating

_____ **1.** Providing client services.   _____ **5.** Supervising workers.
_____ **2.** Obtaining a bank loan.   _____ **6.** Owner investing money in business.
_____ **3.** Purchasing machinery.   _____ **7.** Renting office space.
_____ **4.** Research for its products.   _____ **8.** Paying utilities expenses.

This serial problem starts in this chapter and continues throughout most chapters of the book.

SERIAL PROBLEM
Business Solutions
C4 P1

On October 1, 2015, S. Rey launched a computer services company, **Business Solutions,** that is organized as a corporation or company and provides consulting services, computer system installations, and custom program development. Rey adopts the calendar year for reporting purposes and expects to prepare the company's first set of financial statements on December 31, 2015.

Required

Create a table like the one in Exhibit 1.7 using the following headings for columns: Cash; Accounts Receivable; Computer Supplies; Computer System; Office Equipment; Accounts Payable; Share Capital; Dividends; Revenues; and Expenses. Then use additions and subtractions within the table created to show the dollar effects for each of the following October transactions for Business Solutions on the individual items of the accounting equation. Show new balances after each transaction.

Oct. 1 S. Rey received shares for investing $45,000 cash, a $20,000 computer system, and $8,000 of office equipment in the company.
      3 The company purchased $1,420 of computer supplies on credit from Harris Office Products.
      6 The company billed Easy Leasing $4,800 for services performed in installing a new Web server.
      8 The company paid $1,420 cash for the computer supplies purchased from Harris Office Products on October 3.
     10 The company hired Lyn Addie as a part-time assistant for $125 per day, as needed.
     12 The company billed Easy Leasing another $1,400 for services performed.
     15 The company received $4,800 cash from Easy Leasing as partial payment toward its account.
     17 The company paid $805 cash to repair computer equipment damaged when moving it.
     20 The company paid $1,728 cash for advertisements published in the local newspaper.
     22 The company received $1,400 cash from Easy Leasing toward its account.
     28 The company billed IFM Company $5,208 for services performed.
     31 The company paid $875 cash for Lyn Addie's wages for seven days of work this month.
     31 The company paid dividend of $3,600.

Check Ending balances: Cash, $42,772; Revenues, $11,408; Expenses, $3,408

Beyond the Numbers (BTN) is a special problem section aimed at refining communication, conceptual, analysis, and research skills. It includes many activities helpful in developing an active learning environment.

Beyond the Numbers

BTN 1-1 Key financial figures for Adidas' financial year 2013 are as follows:

Key Figure	EUR millions
Liabilities and Equity	11,599
Net profit	787
Sales	14,492

REPORTING IN ACTION

A1 A2 A3

Required

1. What is the total amount of assets for Adidas?
2. What is Adidas' return on assets (net profit divided by average total assets)? Its assets as at December 31, 2012 equal EUR 11,651 million.
3. How much are total expenses for Adidas in financial year 2013?
4. Does Adidas' return on assets seem satisfactory if competitors average a 5.0% return?

Check (2) 6.77%

Fast Forward

5. Access Adidas' latest financial statements for financial years ending after December 31, 2013 from its Website (www.adidas-group.com) and compute its return on assets for those financial years. Compare the December 31, 2013's financial year-end return on assets to any subsequent years' returns you are able to compute, and interpret the results.

BTN 1-2 Key comparative figures for both Adidas and Puma are as follows:

Key Figure	Adidas (EUR millions)	Puma (EUR millions)
Liabilities and Equity	11,599	2,308
Net profit	787	5
Sales	14,492	2,985

COMPARATIVE ANALYSIS

A1 A2 A3

Required

1. What is the total amount of assets for (*a*) Adidas and (*b*) Puma?
2. What is the return on assets for (*a*) Adidas and (*b*) Puma? Adidas' beginning assets equal EUR 11,651 million and Puma's beginning assets equal EUR 2,530 million.
3. How much are expenses for (*a*) Adidas and (*b*) Puma?
4. Is return on assets satisfactory for (*a*) Adidas and (*b*) Puma? (Assume competitors average a 5% return.)
5. What can you conclude about Adidas and Puma from these computations?

Check (2b) 0.21%

BTN 1-3 Madison Thorne works in a public accounting firm and hopes to eventually be a partner. The management of Allnet Company invites Thorne to prepare a bid to audit Allnet's financial statements. In discussing the audit fee, Allnet's management suggests a fee range in which the amount depends on the reported profit of Allnet. The higher its profit, the higher will be the audit fee paid to Thorne's firm.

ETHICS CHALLENGE

C3 C4

Required

1. Identify the parties potentially affected by this audit and the fee plan proposed.
2. What are the ethical factors in this situation? Explain.
3. Would you recommend that Thorne accept this audit fee arrangement? Why or why not?
4. Describe some ethical considerations guiding your recommendation.

COMMUNICATING IN PRACTICE

A1 C2

BTN 1-4   Refer to this chapter's opening feature about **U.d.d.e.r.s.** Assume that David and Lillian desire to expand their manufacturing facilities to meet customer demand. They decide to meet with their banker to discuss a loan to allow them to expand.

Required

1. Prepare a half-page report outlining the information you would request from David and Lillian if you were the loan officer.
2. Indicate whether the information you request and your loan decision are affected by the form of business organization for U.d.d.e.r.s.

TAKING IT TO THE NET

A2

BTN 1-5   **L'Oreal, Cadbury Schweppes,** and **Heineken** are well-known companies in the personal care, food, and beverages industries respectively. They are publicly listed companies and their financial statements can be found on the Internet.

Required

Locate the financial statements of these three companies and state which of them applies **IFRS**.

TEAMWORK IN ACTION

C1

BTN 1-6   Teamwork is important in today's business world. Successful teams schedule convenient meetings, maintain regular communications, and cooperate with and support their members. This assignment aims to establish support/learning teams, initiate discussions, and set meeting times.

Required

1. Form teams and open a team discussion to determine a regular time and place for your team to meet between each scheduled class meeting. Notify your instructor via a memorandum or e-mail message as to when and where your team will hold regularly scheduled meetings.
2. Develop a list of telephone numbers and/or e-mail addresses of your teammates.

ENTREPRENEURIAL DECISION

A1 P1

BTN 1-7   Refer to this chapter's opening feature about **U.d.d.e.r.s.** Assume that David and Lillian decide to open a new manufacturing facility to produce sunscreen. This new company will be called SweetHealth Company.

Required

1. SweetHealth obtains a $500,000 loan and David and Lillian contribute $250,000 of their own assets in exchange for ordinary shares in the new company.
   a. What is the new company's total amount of liabilities plus equity?
   b. What is the new company's total amount of assets?

Check (2) 10.7%

2. If the new company earns $80,000 in net profit in the first year of operation, compute its return on asset (assume average assets equal $750,000). Assess its performance if competitors average a 10% return.

HITTING THE ROAD

C2

BTN 1-8   You are to interview a local business owner. (This can be a friend or relative.) Opening lines of communication with members of the business community can provide personal benefits of business networking. If you do not know the owner, you should call ahead to introduce yourself and explain your position as a student and your assignment requirements. You should request a thirty minute appointment for a face-to-face or phone interview to discuss the form of organization and operations of the business. Be prepared to make a good impression.

Required

1. Identify and describe the main operating activities and the form of organization for this business.
2. Determine and explain why the owner(s) chose this particular form of organization.
3. Identify any special advantages and/or disadvantages the owner(s) experiences in operating with this form of business organization.

BTN 1-9   Adidas and Li-Ning are both in the sporting goods industry. However, they are listed in different countries: Adidas in Germany and Li-Ning in Hong Kong, China. The following table shows the details and key financial figures in millions for a comparable financial year. (The amounts for average assets, net profit, and revenue are in Euro and Renminbi for Adidas and Li-Ning, respectively.)

GLOBAL DECISION

A1 A2 A3

	Adidas	Li-Ning
Listing	Germany	Hong Kong
Accounting standards	**IFRS**	**IFRS**
Average assets	10,999	6,945
Net profit	671	386
Sales/Revenue..................	13,344	8,929
Return on assets	6.1%	5.6%

Required

1. Identify any concerns you have in comparing Adidas' income and revenue figures to those of Li-Ning for purposes of making business decisions.
2. Identify any concerns you have in comparing Adidas' return on assets to that of Li-Ning for purposes of making business decisions.

ANSWERS TO MULTIPLE CHOICE QUIZ

1. c; $450,000 is the actual cost incurred.
2. b; revenue is recorded when earned.
3. d;

Assets	=	Liabilities	+	Equity
+$100,000	=	+35,000	+	?

Change in equity = $100,000 − $35,000 = $65,000

4. a
5. a

2

Analyzing and Recording Transactions

A Look Back

Chapter 1 defined accounting and introduced financial statements. We described forms of organizations and identified users and uses of accounting. We defined the accounting equation and applied it to transaction analysis.

A Look at This Chapter

This chapter focuses on the accounting process. We describe transactions and source documents, and we explain the analysis and recording of transactions. The accounting equation, T-account, general ledger, trial balance, and debits and credits are key tools in the accounting process.

A Look Ahead

Chapter 3 extends our focus on processing information. We explain the importance of adjusting accounts and the procedures in preparing financial statements.

Learning Objectives

CAP

CONCEPTUAL

C1 Explain the steps in processing transactions and the role of source documents. (p. 50)

C2 Describe an account and its use in recording transactions. (p. 51)

C3 Describe a ledger and a chart of accounts. (p. 54)

C4 Define *debits* and *credits* and explain double-entry accounting. (p. 55)

ANALYTICAL

A1 Analyze the impact of transactions on accounts and financial statements. (p. 59)

A2 Compute the debt ratio and describe its use in analyzing financial condition. (p. 69)

PROCEDURAL

P1 Record transactions in a journal and post entries to a ledger. (p. 56)

P2 Prepare and explain the use of a trial balance. (p. 65)

P3 Prepare financial statements from business transactions. (p. 66)

"As someone who likes to be different, I strongly feel that everyone should have the opportunity to discover their own unique style."—**ELIZABETH SEAH** (center front row)

Dare to Be Different

What do you do when you can't find exciting, one-of-a-kind clothes in your country? Lament about it? Not if you are Elizabeth Seah. This avid shopper and traveler decided to set up her own store, **Haru (www.facebook.com/HaruHouse)**, selling unique apparel and accessories mainly imported from Japan. "I chose the name *Haru* because it means 'Spring' in Japanese," explains Elizabeth. "Spring symbolizes a new beginning, a fresh start for people who have discovered their very own individual style. To meet the objective of uniqueness, I make it a point to bring in limited pieces of each item." The store carries apparel, accessories, and anime goods from Tokyo's well-known Harajuku Street and Akihabara Street. Haru also carries items for cosplay (costume play, where participants don costumes representing characters from manga and anime sources). To make sure prices are kept affordable for students, Elizabeth also brings in items from Taiwan.

Starting her own business presented Elizabeth with many challenges. She learned the importance of keeping proper financial records—including recording sales transactions, expenses incurred, and cash outflows—to help her better understand the financial status of her company and to better assess whether it was performing up to the target set for each period. Sales transactions are recorded in a control account on a daily basis. The total sales amount is consolidated and recorded in a general account on a monthly basis, together with a stock-taking exercise to ensure that the sales amount tallies with the stocks remaining. The sales revenue for the next period can then be roughly estimated and budgets prepared.

Elizabeth also relishes the challenges of the day-to-day running of the business. "We face different kinds of customers with different needs and budgets," says Elizabeth. "The main challenge is to be flexible and quick enough to meet their demands." The store receives a fair number of tourists: "So we need to have basic knowledge about different cultures to provide our international customers with a better customer service experience."

"I want to encourage people to be more daring in their fashion choices," adds Elizabeth. Something that seems not at all difficult to do, once you step into this eclectic shop!

Chapter Preview

Financial statements report on the financial performance and condition of an organization. Knowledge of their preparation, organization, and analysis is important. A main goal of this chapter is to illustrate how transactions are recorded, how they are reflected in financial statements, and how they impact analysis of financial statements. Debits and credits are introduced and identified as a tool in helping analyze and process transactions.

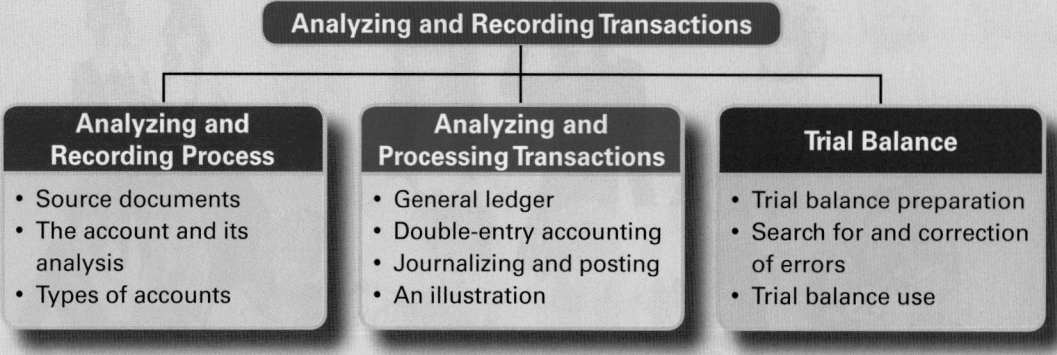

Analyzing and Recording Transactions

Analyzing and Recording Process	Analyzing and Processing Transactions	Trial Balance
• Source documents • The account and its analysis • Types of accounts	• General ledger • Double-entry accounting • Journalizing and posting • An illustration	• Trial balance preparation • Search for and correction of errors • Trial balance use

ANALYZING AND RECORDING PROCESS

EXHIBIT 2.1

The Analyzing and Recording Process

The accounting process identifies business transactions and events, analyzes and records their effects, and summarizes and presents information in reports and financial statements. These reports and statements are used for making investing, lending, and other business decisions. The steps in the accounting process that focus on *analyzing and recording* transactions and events are shown in Exhibit 2.1.

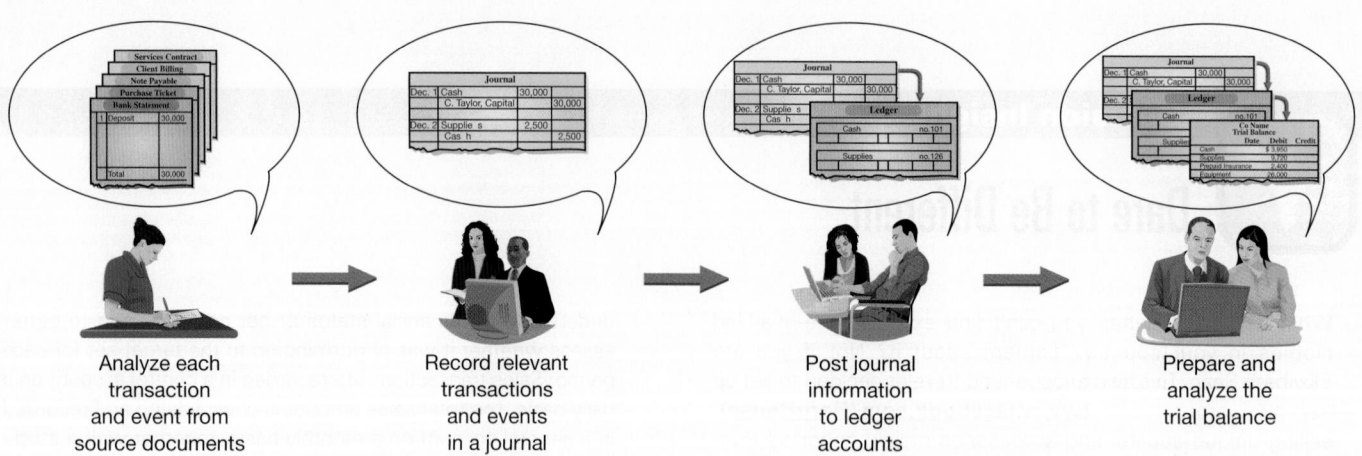

Analyze each transaction and event from source documents

Record relevant transactions and events in a journal

Post journal information to ledger accounts

Prepare and analyze the trial balance

C1 Explain the steps in processing transactions and the role of source documents.

Business transactions and events are the starting points. Relying on source documents, the transactions and events are analyzed using the accounting equation to understand how they affect company performance and financial position. These effects are recorded in accounting records, informally referred to as the *accounting books,* or simply the *books.* Additional steps such as posting and then preparing a trial balance help summarize and classify the effects of transactions and events. Ultimately, the accounting process provides information in useful reports or financial statements to decision makers.

Source Documents

Source documents identify and describe transactions and events entering the accounting process. They are the sources of accounting information and can be in either hard copy or electronic form. Examples are sales tickets, checks, purchase orders, bills from suppliers, employee earnings records, and bank statements. To illustrate, when an item is purchased on credit, the seller usually prepares at least two copies of a sales invoice. One copy is given to the buyer. Another copy, often sent electronically, results in an entry in the seller's information system to record the sale. Sellers use invoices for recording sales and for control; buyers use them for recording purchases and for monitoring purchasing activity. Many cash registers record information for each sale on a tape or electronic file locked inside the register. This record can be used as a source document for recording sales in the accounting records. Source documents, especially if obtained from outside the organization, provide objective and reliable evidence about transactions and events and their amounts.

Point: To ensure that all sales are rung up on the register, most sellers require customers to have their receipts to exchange or return purchased items.

Decision Ethics

Answer — p. 73

Cashier Your manager requires that you, as cashier, immediately enter each sale. Recently, lunch hour traffic has increased and the assistant manager asks you to avoid delays by taking customers' cash and making change without entering sales. The assistant manager says she will add up cash and enter sales after lunch. She says that, in this way, the register will always match the cash amount when the manager arrives at three o'clock. What do you do? ■

The Account and Its Analysis

An **account** is a record of increases and decreases in a specific asset, liability, equity, revenue, or expense item. Information from an account is analyzed, summarized, and presented in reports and financial statements. The **general ledger,** or simply **ledger,** is a record containing all accounts used by a company. The ledger is often in electronic form. While most companies' ledgers contain similar accounts, a company often uses one or more unique accounts because of its type of operations. As shown in Exhibit 2.2, accounts are classified into three general categories based on the accounting equation: asset, liability, or equity.

C2 Describe an account and its use in recording transactions.

EXHIBIT 2.2

Accounts Organized by the Accounting Equation

Asset Accounts Assets are resources owned or controlled by a company and that have expected future benefits. Most accounting systems include (at a minimum) separate accounts for the assets described here.

A *Cash* account reflects a company's cash balance. All increases and decreases in cash are recorded in the Cash account. It includes money and any medium of exchange that a bank accepts for deposit (coins, checks, money orders, and checking account balances).

Accounts receivable are held by a seller and refer to promises of payment from customers to sellers. These transactions are often called *credit sales* or *sales on account* (or *on credit*). Accounts receivable are increased by credit sales and are decreased by customer payments. A company needs a separate record for each customer, but for now, we use the simpler practice of recording all increases and decreases in receivables in a single account called Accounts Receivable.

A *note receivable,* or promissory note, is a written promise of another entity to pay a definite sum of money on a specified future date to the holder of the note. A company holding a promissory note signed by another entity has an asset that is recorded in a Note (or Notes) Receivable account.

Prepaid accounts (also called *prepaid expenses*) are assets that represent prepayments of future expenses (*not* current expenses). When the expenses are later incurred, the amounts in prepaid accounts are transferred to expense accounts. Common examples of prepaid accounts include prepaid insurance, prepaid rent, and prepaid services (such as club memberships). Prepaid accounts expire with the passage of time (such as with rent) or through use (such as with prepaid meal tickets). When financial statements are prepared, prepaid accounts are adjusted so that (1) all expired and used prepaid accounts are recorded as regular expenses and (2) all unexpired and unused prepaid accounts are recorded as assets (reflecting future use in

Point: Customers and others who owe a company are called its **debtors.**

Point: A college parking fee is a prepaid account from the student's standpoint. At the beginning of the term, it represents an asset that entitles a student to park on or near campus. The benefits of the parking fee expire as the term progresses. At term-end, prepaid parking (asset) equals zero as it has been entirely recorded as parking expense.

Point: Prepaid accounts that apply to current and future periods are assets. These assets are adjusted at the end of each period to reflect only those amounts that have not yet expired, and to record as expenses those amounts that have expired.

future periods). To illustrate, when an insurance fee, called a *premium,* is paid in advance, the cost is typically recorded in the asset account Prepaid Insurance. Over time, the expiring portion of the insurance cost is removed from this asset account and reported in expenses on the income statement. Any unexpired portion remains in Prepaid Insurance and is reported on the statement of financial position as an asset. (An exception exists for prepaid accounts that will expire or be used before the end of the current accounting period when financial statements are prepared. In this case, the prepayments *can* be recorded immediately as expenses.)

Supplies are assets until they are used. When they are used up, their costs are reported as expenses. The costs of unused supplies are recorded in a Supplies asset account. Supplies are often grouped by purpose—for example, office supplies and store supplies. *Office supplies* include stationery, paper, toner, and pens. *Store supplies* include packaging materials, plastic and paper bags, gift boxes and cartons, and cleaning materials. The costs of these unused supplies can be recorded in an Office Supplies or a Store Supplies asset account. When supplies are used, their costs are transferred from the asset accounts to expense accounts.

Equipment is an asset. When equipment is used and gets worn down, its cost is gradually reported as an expense (called depreciation). Equipment is often grouped by its purpose—for example, office equipment and store equipment. *Office equipment* includes computers, printers, desks, chairs, and shelves. Costs incurred for these items are recorded in an Office Equipment asset account. The Store Equipment account includes the costs of assets used in a store, such as counters, showcases, ladders, hoists, and cash registers.

Point: Some assets are described as *intangible* because they do not have physical existence or their benefits are highly uncertain.

Buildings such as stores, offices, warehouses, and factories are assets because they provide expected future benefits to those who control or own them. Their costs are recorded in a Buildings asset account. When several buildings are owned, separate accounts are sometimes kept for each of them.

The cost of *land* owned by a business is recorded in a Land account. The cost of buildings located on the land is separately recorded in one or more building accounts.

Decision Insight

Women Entrepreneurs   The Center for Women's Business Research reports that women-owned businesses, such as **Haru,** are growing in the United States and that they:

- Total approximately 11 million and employ nearly 20 million workers.
- Generate $2.5 trillion in annual sales and tend to embrace technology.
- Are philanthropic—70% of owners volunteer at least once per month.
- Are more likely funded by individual investors (73%) than venture firms (15%). ∎

Liability Accounts   Liabilities are claims (by creditors) against assets, which means they are obligations to transfer assets or provide products or services to others. **Creditors** are individuals and organizations that have rights to receive payments from a company. If a company fails to pay its obligations, the law gives creditors a right to force the sale of that company's assets to obtain the money to meet creditors' claims. When assets are sold under these conditions, creditors are paid first, but only up to the amount of their claims. Any remaining money, the residual, goes to the owners of the company. Creditors often use a statement of financial position to help decide whether to loan money to a company. A loan is less risky if the borrower's liabilities are small in comparison to assets because this means there are more resources than claims on resources. Common liability accounts are described here.

Point: Accounts payable are also called *trade payables.*

Accounts payable refer to oral or implied promises to pay later, which usually arise from purchases of merchandise. Payables can also arise from purchases of supplies, equipment, and services. Accounting systems keep separate records about each creditor. We describe these individual records in Chapter 5.

A *note payable* refers to a formal promise, usually denoted by the signing of a promissory note, to pay a future amount. It is recorded in either a short-term Note Payable account or a long-term Note Payable account, depending on when it must be repaid. We explain details of short- and long-term classification in Chapter 3.

Unearned revenue refers to a liability that is settled in the future when a company delivers its products or services. When customers pay in advance for products or services (before revenue is earned), the revenue recognition principle requires that the seller consider this payment as unearned revenue. Examples of unearned revenue include magazine subscriptions collected in advance by a publisher, sales of gift certificates by stores, and season ticket sales by sports teams. The seller would record these in liability accounts such as Unearned Subscriptions, Unearned Store Sales, and Unearned Ticket Revenue. When products and services are later delivered, the earned portion of the unearned revenue is transferred to revenue accounts such as Subscription Fees, Store Sales, and Ticket Sales.[1]

Point: If a subscription is canceled, the publisher is expected to refund the unused portion to the subscriber.

Accrued liabilities are amounts owed that are not yet paid. Examples are wages payable, taxes payable, and interest payable. These are often recorded in separate liability accounts by the same title. If they are not large in amount, one or more ledger accounts can be added and reported as a single amount on the statement of financial position. (Financial statements often have amounts reported that are a summation of several ledger accounts.)

Decision Insight

Revenue Spread   The **New Orleans Saints** have *Unearned Revenues* of about $60 million in advance ticket sales. When the team plays its home games, it settles this liability to its ticket holders and then transfers the amount earned to *Ticket Revenues.* ■

Equity Accounts   The owner's claim on a company's assets is called *equity* or *owner's equity.* Equity is the owner's *residual interest* in the assets of a business after deducting liabilities. Equity is impacted by four types of accounts: owner's capital, owner's withdrawals, revenues, and expenses. We show this visually in Exhibit 2.3 by expanding the accounting equation.

Point: Equity is also called *net assets.*

Asset Accounts	=	Liability Accounts	+	Equity Accounts			
				+ Owner's Capital	− Owner's Withdrawals	+ Revenues	− Expenses

EXHIBIT 2.3

Expanded Accounting Equation

When an owner invests in a company, the invested amount is recorded in an account titled Owner, Capital (where the owner's name is inserted in place of "owner"). The account titled *C. Taylor, Capital* is used for FastForward. Any further owner investments are recorded in this account. When an owner withdraws assets for personal use it decreases both company assets and total equity. Withdrawals are not expenses of the business; they are simply the opposite of owner investments. The Owner, Withdrawals account is used to record asset distributions to the owner. The account titled *C. Taylor, Withdrawals* is used for FastForward. (Owners of proprietorships cannot receive company salaries because they are not legally separate from their companies; and they cannot enter into company contracts with themselves.)

Point: The Owner's Withdrawals account is a *contra equity* account because it reduces the normal balance of equity.

Point: The withdrawal of assets by the owners of a corporation is called a *dividend.*

Revenues and expenses also impact equity. Examples of revenue accounts are Sales, Commissions Earned, Professional Fees Earned, Rent Revenue, and Interest Revenue. *Revenues increase equity* and result from products and services provided to customers. Examples of expense accounts are Advertising Expense, Store Supplies Expense, Office Salaries Expense, Office Supplies Expense, Rent Expense, Utilities Expense, and Insurance Expense. *Expenses decrease*

---

[1] In practice, account titles vary. As one example, Subscription Fees is sometimes called Subscription Fees Revenue, Subscription Fees Earned, or Earned Subscription Fees. As another example, Rent Earned is sometimes called Rent Revenue, Rental Revenue, or Earned Rent Revenue. We must use good judgment when reading financial statements because titles can differ even within the same industry. For example, product sales are simply called *sales* at Nestlé, but *revenue* at GOME. Generally, the term *revenues* or *fees* is more commonly used with service businesses, and *net sales* or *sales* with product businesses.

equity and result from assets and services used in a company's operations. (Different companies sometimes use different account titles. For example, some might use Interest Revenue instead of Interest Earned, or Rental Expense instead of Rent Expense. It is important only that an account title describe the item it represents.)

Decision Insight

Sporting Accounts The **Los Angeles Lakers** and the other NBA teams have the following major revenue and expense accounts:

Revenues	Expenses
Basketball ticket sales	Team salaries
TV & radio broadcast fees	Game costs
Advertising revenues	NBA franchise costs
Basketball playoff receipts	Promotional costs ■

ANALYZING AND PROCESSING TRANSACTIONS

This section explains several tools and processes that comprise an accounting system. These include a ledger, T-account, debits and credits, double-entry accounting, journalizing, and posting.

Ledger and Chart of Accounts

C3 Describe a ledger and a chart of accounts.

The collection of all accounts and their balances for an information system is called a *ledger* (or *general ledger*). If accounts are in files on a hard drive, the sum of those files is the ledger. If the accounts are pages in a file, that file is the ledger. A company's size and diversity of operations affect the number of accounts needed. A small company can get by with as few as 20 or 30 accounts; a large company can require several thousand. The **chart of accounts** is a list of all ledger accounts and includes an identification number assigned to each account. A small business might use the following numbering system for its accounts:

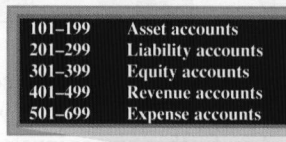

101–199	Asset accounts
201–299	Liability accounts
301–399	Equity accounts
401–499	Revenue accounts
501–699	Expense accounts

These numbers provide a three-digit code that is useful in recordkeeping. In this case, the first digit assigned to asset accounts is a 1, the first digit assigned to liability accounts is a 2, and so on. The second and third digits relate to the accounts' subcategories. Exhibit 2.4 shows a partial chart of accounts for FastForward, the focus company of Chapter 1.

EXHIBIT 2.4

Partial Chart of Accounts for FastForward

Acct. No.	Account Name	Acct. No.	Account Name	Acct. No.	Account Name
101	Cash	236	Unearned consulting revenue	622	Salaries expense
106	Accounts receivable			637	Insurance expense
126	Supplies	301	C. Taylor, Capital	640	Rent expense
128	Prepaid insurance	302	C. Taylor, Withdrawals	652	Supplies expense
167	Equipment	403	Consulting revenue	690	Utilities expense
201	Accounts payable	406	Rental revenue		

Debits and Credits

A **T-account** represents a ledger account and is a tool used to understand the effects of one or more transactions. Its name comes from its shape like the letter **T**. The layout of a T-account, shown in Exhibit 2.5, is (1) the account title on top, (2) a left, or debit side, and (3) a right, or credit, side.

C4 Define *debits* and *credits* and explain double-entry accounting.

The left side of an account is called the **debit** side, often abbreviated *Dr.* The right side is called the **credit** side, abbreviated *Cr.*[2]

Account Title	
(Left side)	(Right side)
Debit	*Credit*

EXHIBIT 2.5

The T-Account

To enter amounts on the left side of an account is to *debit* the account. To enter amounts on the right side is to *credit* the account. Do not make the error of thinking that the terms *debit* and *credit* mean increase or decrease. Whether a debit or a credit is an increase or decrease depends on the account. For an account where a debit is an increase, the credit is a decrease; for an account where a debit is a decrease, the credit is an increase. The difference between total debits and total credits for an account, including any beginning balance, is the **account balance.** When the sum of debits exceeds the sum of credits, the account has a *debit balance*. It has a *credit balance* when the sum of credits exceeds the sum of debits. When the sum of debits equals the sum of credits, the account has a *zero balance*.

Point: Think of *debit* and *credit* as accounting directions for left and right.

Double-Entry Accounting

Double-entry accounting requires that for each transaction:

- At least two accounts are involved, with at least one debit and one credit.
- The total amount debited must equal the total amount credited.
- The accounting equation must not be violated.

This means the sum of the debits for all entries must equal the sum of the credits for all entries, and the sum of debit account balances in the ledger must equal the sum of credit account balances.

The system for recording debits and credits follows from the usual accounting equation—see Exhibit 2.6. Two points are important here. First, like any simple mathematical relation, net increases or decreases on one side have equal net effects on the other side. For example, a net increase in assets must be accompanied by an identical net increase on the

"Total debits equal total credits for each entry."

Assets	=	Liabilities	+	Equity
Debit for increases / **Credit for decreases**		**Debit for decreases** / **Credit for increases**		**Debit for decreases** / **Credit for increases**
+ / **−**		**−** / **+**		**−** / **+**
Normal		**Normal**		**Normal**

EXHIBIT 2.6

Debits and Credits in the Accounting Equation

liabilities and equity side. Recall that some transactions affect only one side of the equation, meaning that two or more accounts on one side are affected, but their net effect on this one side is zero. Second, the left side is the *normal balance* side for assets, and the right side is the *normal balance* side for liabilities and equity. This matches their layout in the accounting equation where assets are on the left side of this equation, and liabilities and equity are on the right.

Recall that equity increases from revenues and owner investments and it decreases from expenses and owner withdrawals. These important equity relations are conveyed by expanding the accounting equation to include debits and credits in double-entry form as shown in Exhibit 2.7.

Increases (credits) to owner's capital and revenues *increase* equity; increases (debits) to withdrawals and expenses *decrease* equity. The normal balance of each account (asset, liability, capital, withdrawals, revenue, or expense) refers to the left or right (debit or credit) side where

Point: Debits and credits do not mean favorable or unfavorable. A debit to an asset increases it, as does a debit to an expense. A credit to a liability increases it, as does a credit to a revenue.

---

[2] These abbreviations are remnants of 18th-century English recordkeeping practices where the terms *debitor* and *creditor* were used instead of *debit* and *credit*. The abbreviations use the first and last letters of these terms, just as we still do for Saint (St.) and Doctor (Dr.).

EXHIBIT 2.7

Debit and Credit Effects for Component Accounts

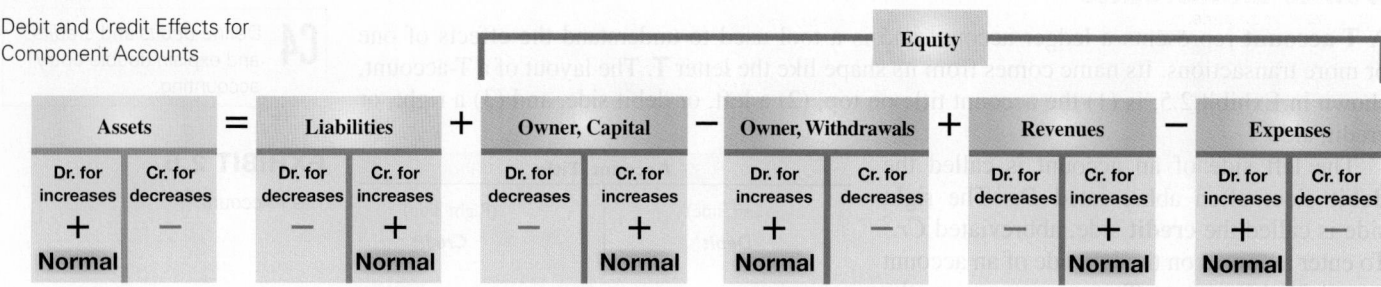

increases are recorded. Understanding these diagrams and rules is required to prepare, analyze, and interpret financial statements.

The T-account for FastForward's Cash account, reflecting its first 11 transactions (from Exhibit 1.9), is shown in Exhibit 2.8. The total increases in its Cash account are $36,100, the total decreases are $31,300, and the account's debit balance is $4,800. (We illustrate use of T-accounts later in this chapter.)

EXHIBIT 2.8

Computing the Balance for a T-Account

Point: The ending balance is on the side with the larger dollar amount. Also, a plus (+) and minus (−) are not used in a T-account.

Cash			
Receive investment by owner	30,000	Purchase of supplies	2,500
Consulting services revenue earned	4,200	Purchase of equipment	26,000
Collection of account receivable	1,900	Payment of rent	1,000
		Payment of salary	700
		Payment of account payable	900
		Withdrawal by owner	200
Balance	4,800		

Quick Check

Answers — p. 74

1. Identify examples of accounting source documents.
2. Explain the importance of source documents.
3. Identify each of the following as either an asset, a liability, or equity: (*a*) Prepaid Rent, (*b*) Unearned Fees, (*c*) Building, (*d*) Wages Payable, and (*e*) Office Supplies.
4. What is an account? What is a ledger?
5. What determines the number and types of accounts a company uses?
6. Does *debit* always mean increase and *credit* always mean decrease?
7. Describe a chart of accounts.

Journalizing and Posting Transactions

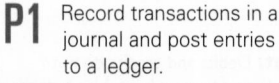

P1 Record transactions in a journal and post entries to a ledger.

Processing transactions is a crucial part of accounting. The four usual steps of this process are depicted in Exhibit 2.9. Steps 1 and 2—involving transaction analysis and the accounting equation—were introduced in prior sections. This section extends that discussion and focuses on steps 3 and 4 of the accounting process. Step 3 is to record each transaction chronologically in a journal. A **journal** gives a complete record of each transaction in one place. It also shows debits and credits for each transaction. The process of recording transactions in a journal is called **journalizing.** Step 4 is to transfer (or *post*) entries from the journal to the ledger. The process of transferring journal entry information to the ledger is called **posting.**

Journalizing Transactions The process of journalizing transactions requires an understanding of a journal. While companies can use various journals, every company uses a

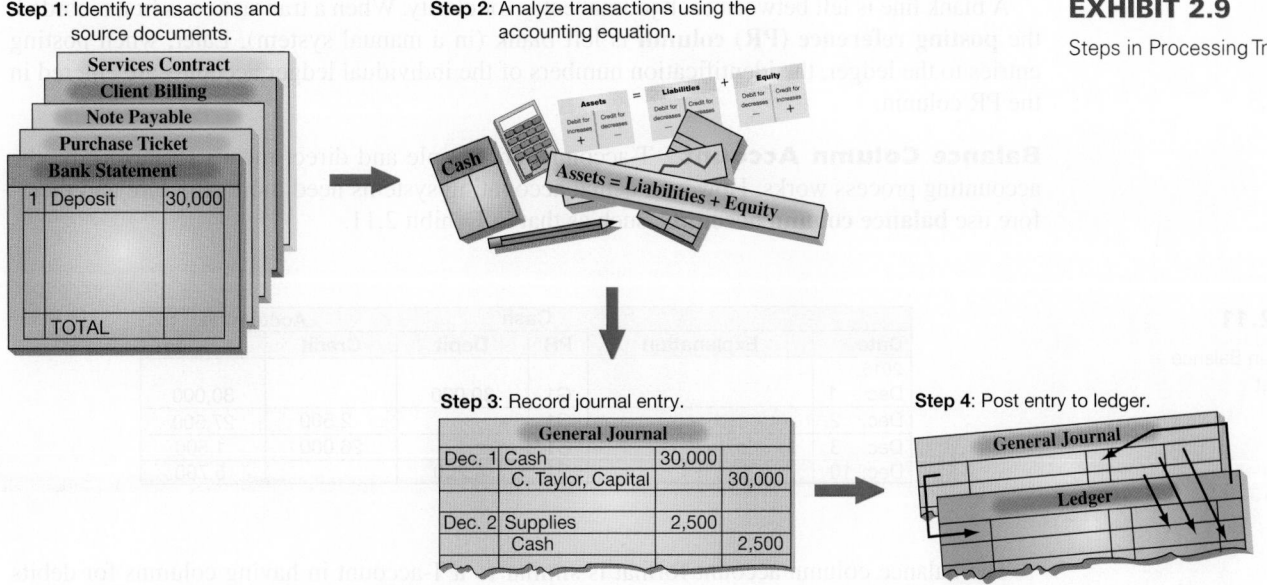

Step 1: Identify transactions and source documents.

Step 2: Analyze transactions using the accounting equation.

Assets = Liabilities + Equity

Step 3: Record journal entry.

General Journal			
Dec. 1	Cash	30,000	
	C. Taylor, Capital		30,000
Dec. 2	Supplies	2,500	
	Cash		2,500

Step 4: Post entry to ledger.

General Journal

Ledger

EXHIBIT 2.9

Steps in Processing Transactions

general journal. It can be used to record any transaction and includes the following information about each transaction: ⓐ date of transaction, ⓑ titles of affected accounts, ⓒ dollar amount of each debit and credit, and ⓓ explanation of the transaction. Exhibit 2.10 shows how the first two transactions of FastForward are recorded in a general journal. This process is similar for manual and computerized systems. Computerized journals are often designed to look like a manual journal page, and also include error-checking routines that ensure debits equal credits for each entry. Shortcuts allow recordkeepers to select account names and numbers from pull-down menus.

EXHIBIT 2.10

Partial General Journal for FastForward

```
┌─────────────────────────────────────────────────────────────────────┐
│ 🖥 General Journal Entry                                      _ □ ✕   │
│ File  Edit  Go To  Window  Help                                       │
│  ⊗     ⬜    ⊡ ▾  ⬜ ▾  ⊠     ⬜     ⬜ ▾    ⬜     ⬜                    │
│ Close  New   List   Save  Print  Delete  Recur  Row    Reports  Help  │
│                                                                        │
│                                        Journal Entry ◁▷                │
│                                                                        │
│     Date: Dec 1, 2015 ▾  Reference: _____   ☐ Reverse Transaction    │
│ ┌──────┬────────────────────────────┬─────┬─────────┬──────────┐     │
│ │ Date │ Account Titles and Explanation │ PR │  Debit  │  Credit  │     │
│ ├──────┼────────────────────────────┼─────┼─────────┼──────────┤     │
│ │2015ⓐ │                            │     │         │          │     │
│ │Dec. 1│ ⓑ Cash                     │     │ 30,000 ⓒ│          │     │
│ │      │      C. Taylor, Capital    │     │         │  30,000  │     │
│ │      │  To record investment of cash by owner. ⓓ │  │        │     │
│ │      │                            │     │         │          │     │
│ │Dec. 2│    Supplies                │     │  2,500  │          │     │
│ │      │      Cash                  │     │         │   2,500  │     │
│ │      │  To record purchase of supplies with cash. │ │        │     │
│ └──────┴────────────────────────────┴─────┴─────────┴──────────┘     │
└─────────────────────────────────────────────────────────────────────┘
```

To record entries in a general journal, apply these steps; refer to the entries in Exhibit 2.10 when reviewing these steps. (1) Date the transaction: Enter the year at the top of the first column and the month and day on the first line of each journal entry. (2) Enter titles of accounts debited and then enter amounts in the Debit column on the same line. Account titles are taken from the chart of accounts and are aligned with the left margin of the Account Titles and Explanation column. (3) Enter titles of accounts credited and then enter amounts in the Credit column on the same line. Account titles are from the chart of accounts and are indented from the left margin of the Account Titles and Explanation column to distinguish them from debited accounts. (4) Enter a brief explanation of the transaction on the line below the entry (it often references a source document). This explanation is indented about half as far as the credited account titles to avoid confusing it with accounts, and it is italicized.

Point: There are no exact rules for writing journal entry explanations. An explanation should be short yet describe why an entry is made.

A blank line is left between each journal entry for clarity. When a transaction is first recorded, the **posting reference (PR) column** is left blank (in a manual system). Later, when posting entries to the ledger, the identification numbers of the individual ledger accounts are entered in the PR column.

Balance Column Account   T-accounts are simple and direct means to show how the accounting process works. However, actual accounting systems need more structure and therefore use **balance column accounts,** such as that in Exhibit 2.11.

EXHIBIT 2.11

Cash Account in Balance
Column Format

Cash					Account No. 101
Date	Explanation	PR	Debit	Credit	Balance
2015 Dec. 1		G1	30,000		30,000
Dec. 2		G1		2,500	27,500
Dec. 3		G1		26,000	1,500
Dec. 10		G1	4,200		5,700

The balance column account format is similar to a T-account in having columns for debits and credits. It is different in including transaction date and explanation columns. It also has a column with the balance of the account after each entry is recorded. To illustrate, FastForward's Cash account in Exhibit 2.11 is debited on December 1 for the $30,000 owner investment, yielding a $30,000 debit balance. The account is credited on December 2 for $2,500, yielding a $27,500 debit balance. On December 3, it is credited again, this time for $26,000, and its debit balance is reduced to $1,500. The Cash account is debited for $4,200 on December 10, and its debit balance increases to $5,700; and so on.

Point: Explanations are typically included in ledger accounts only for unusual transactions or events.

The heading of the Balance column does not show whether it is a debit or credit balance. Instead, an account is assumed to have a *normal balance*. Unusual events can sometimes

EXHIBIT 2.12

Posting an Entry to the Ledger

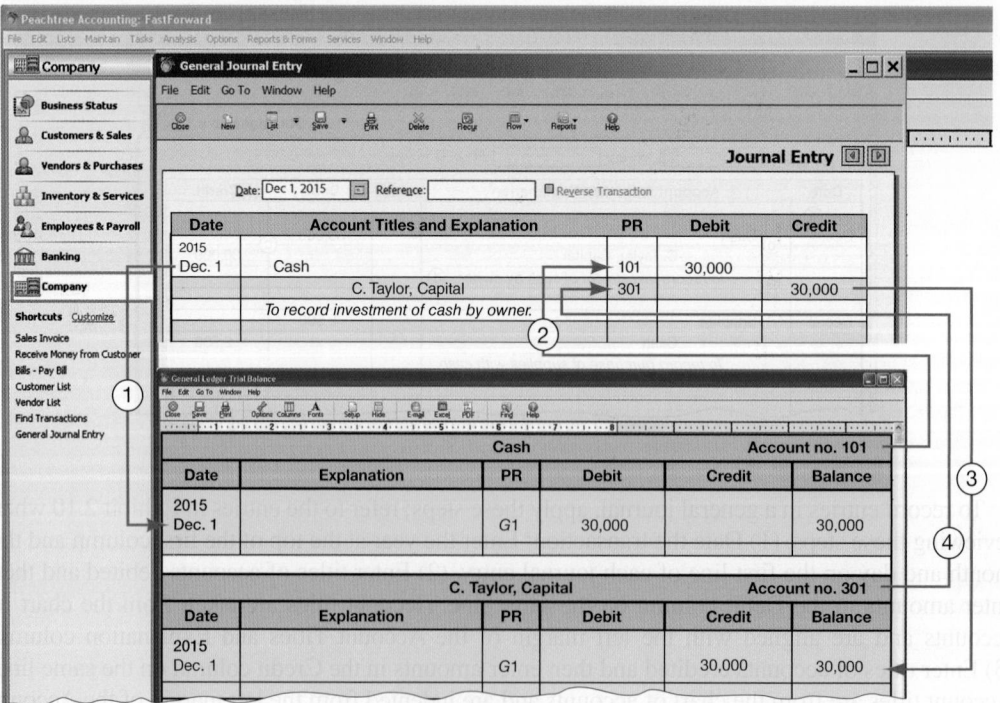

Point: The fundamental concepts of a manual (pencil-and-paper) system are identical to those of a computerized information system.

Key: ① Identify debit account in Ledger: enter date, journal page, amount, and balance.
      ② Enter the debit account number from the Ledger in the PR column of the journal.
      ③ Identify credit account in Ledger: enter date, journal page, amount, and balance.
      ④ Enter the credit account number from the Ledger in the PR column of the journal.

temporarily give an account an abnormal balance. An *abnormal balance* refers to a balance on the side where decreases are recorded. For example, a customer might mistakenly overpay a bill. This gives that customer's account receivable an abnormal (credit) balance. An abnormal balance is often identified by circling it or by entering it in red or some other unusual color. A zero balance for an account is usually shown by writing zeros or a dash in the Balance column to avoid confusion between a zero balance and one omitted in error.

Posting Journal Entries   Step 4 of processing transactions is to post journal entries to ledger accounts (see Exhibit 2.9). To ensure that the ledger is up-to-date, entries are posted as soon as possible. This might be daily, weekly, or when time permits. All entries must be posted to the ledger before financial statements are prepared to ensure that account balances are up-to-date. When entries are posted to the ledger, the debits in journal entries are transferred into ledger accounts as debits, and credits are transferred into ledger accounts as credits. Exhibit 2.12 shows the *four steps to post a journal entry*. First, identify the ledger account that is debited in the entry; then, in the ledger, enter the entry date, the journal and page in its PR column, the debit amount, and the new balance of the ledger account. (The letter *G* shows it came from the General Journal.) Second, enter the ledger account number in the PR column of the journal. Steps 3 and 4 repeat the first two steps for credit entries and amounts. The posting process creates a link between the ledger and the journal entry. This link is a useful cross-reference for tracing an amount from one record to another.

Point: Computerized systems often provide a code beside a balance such as *dr.* or *cr.* to identify its balance. Posting is automatic and immediate with accounting software.

Point: A journal is often referred to as the *book of original entry*. The ledger is referred to as the *book of final entry* because financial statements are prepared from it.

Analyzing Transactions — An Illustration

We return to the activities of FastForward to show how double-entry accounting is useful in analyzing and processing transactions. Analysis of each transaction follows the four steps of Exhibit 2.9.

A1	Analyze the impact of transactions on accounts and financial statements.

Step 1   Identify the transaction and any source documents.

Step 2   Analyze the transaction using the accounting equation.

Step 3   Record the transaction in journal entry form applying double-entry accounting.

Step 4   Post the entry (for simplicity, we use T-accounts to represent ledger accounts).

Study each transaction thoroughly before proceeding to the next. The first 11 transactions are from Chapter 1, and we analyze five additional December transactions of FastForward (numbered 12 through 16) that were omitted earlier.

1. Receive investment by Owner

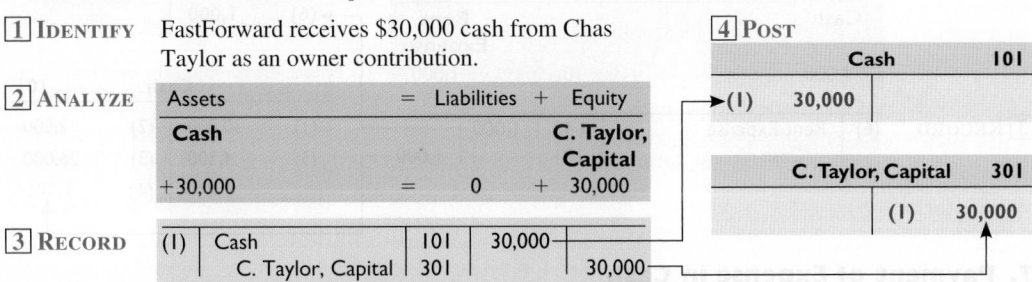

1 IDENTIFY   FastForward receives $30,000 cash from Chas Taylor as an owner contribution.

FASTForward

2. Purchase Supplies for Cash

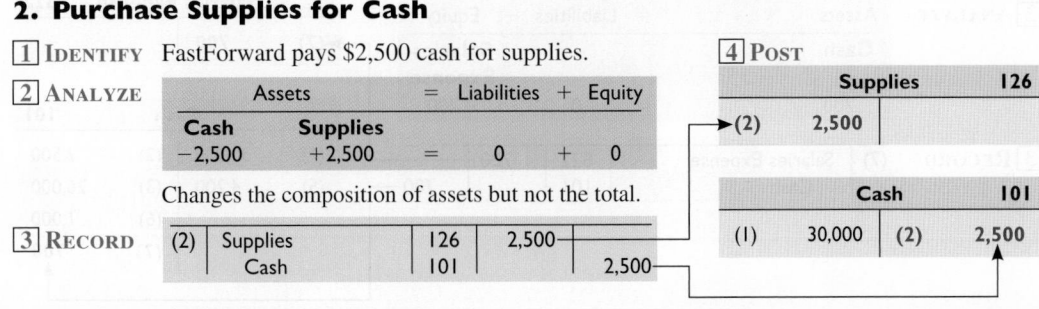

1 IDENTIFY   FastForward pays $2,500 cash for supplies.

3. Purchase Equipment for Cash

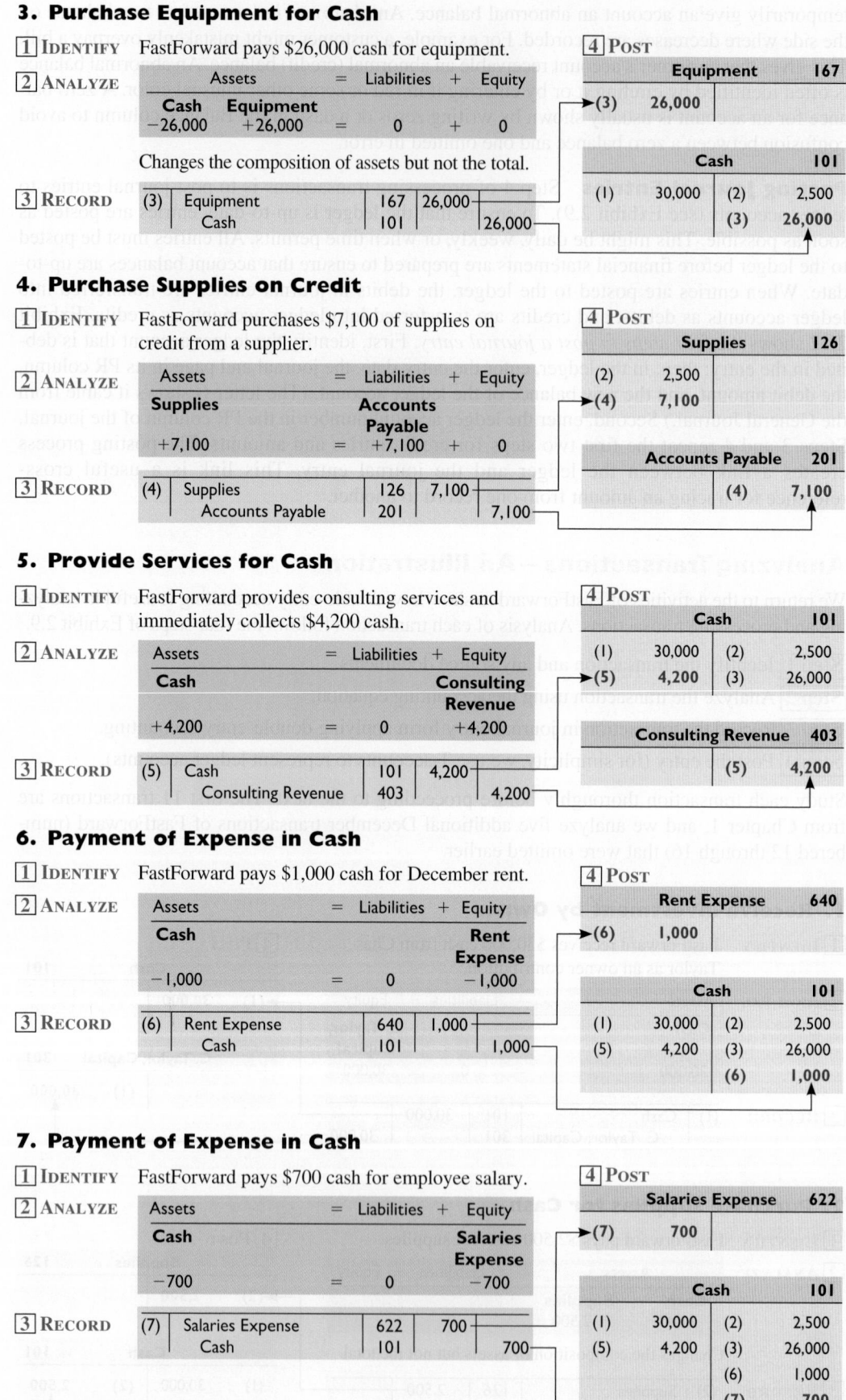

1 IDENTIFY   FastForward pays $26,000 cash for equipment.

2 ANALYZE

Assets		=	Liabilities	+	Equity
Cash	**Equipment**				
−26,000	+26,000	=	0	+	0

Changes the composition of assets but not the total.

3 RECORD

(3)	Equipment	167	26,000	
	Cash	101		26,000

4 POST

Equipment		167
(3)	26,000	

Cash		101
(1)	30,000	(2)	2,500
		(3)	26,000

4. Purchase Supplies on Credit

1 IDENTIFY   FastForward purchases $7,100 of supplies on credit from a supplier.

2 ANALYZE

Assets	=	Liabilities	+	Equity
Supplies		**Accounts Payable**		
+7,100	=	+7,100	+	0

3 RECORD

(4)	Supplies	126	7,100	
	Accounts Payable	201		7,100

4 POST

Supplies		126
(2)	2,500	
(4)	7,100	

Accounts Payable		201
		(4)	7,100

5. Provide Services for Cash

1 IDENTIFY   FastForward provides consulting services and immediately collects $4,200 cash.

2 ANALYZE

Assets	=	Liabilities	+	Equity
Cash				**Consulting Revenue**
+4,200	=	0		+4,200

3 RECORD

(5)	Cash	101	4,200	
	Consulting Revenue	403		4,200

4 POST

Cash		101
(1)	30,000	(2)	2,500
(5)	4,200	(3)	26,000

Consulting Revenue		403
		(5)	4,200

6. Payment of Expense in Cash

1 IDENTIFY   FastForward pays $1,000 cash for December rent.

2 ANALYZE

Assets	=	Liabilities	+	Equity
Cash				**Rent Expense**
−1,000	=	0		−1,000

3 RECORD

(6)	Rent Expense	640	1,000	
	Cash	101		1,000

4 POST

Rent Expense		640
(6)	1,000	

Cash		101
(1)	30,000	(2)	2,500
(5)	4,200	(3)	26,000
		(6)	1,000

7. Payment of Expense in Cash

1 IDENTIFY   FastForward pays $700 cash for employee salary.

2 ANALYZE

Assets	=	Liabilities	+	Equity
Cash				**Salaries Expense**
−700	=	0		−700

3 RECORD

(7)	Salaries Expense	622	700	
	Cash	101		700

4 POST

Salaries Expense		622
(7)	700	

Cash		101
(1)	30,000	(2)	2,500
(5)	4,200	(3)	26,000
		(6)	1,000
		(7)	700

Point: *Salary* usually refers to compensation for an employee who receives a fixed amount for a given time period, whereas *wages* usually refers to compensation based on time worked.

8. Provide Consulting and Rental Services on Credit

1 IDENTIFY   FastForward provides consulting services of $1,600 and rents its test facilities for $300. The customer is billed $1,900 for these services.

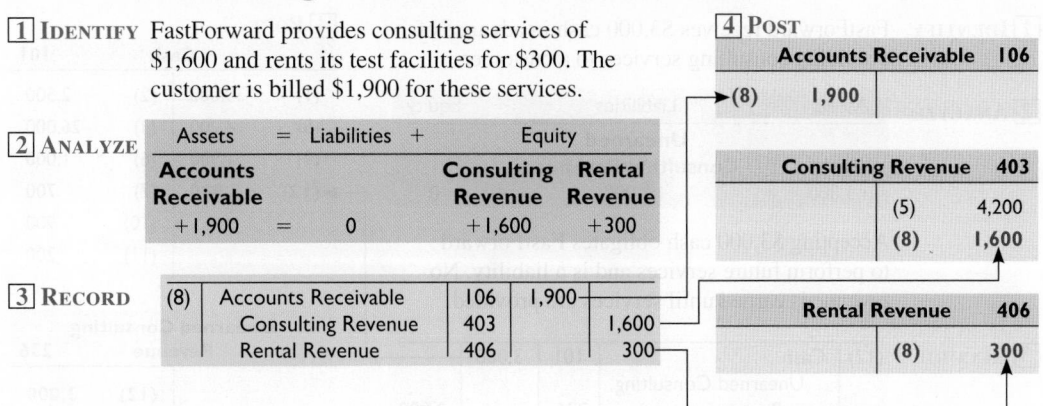

Point: Transaction 8 is a **compound journal entry,** which affects three or more accounts.

9. Receipt of Cash on Account

1 IDENTIFY   FastForward receives $1,900 cash from the client billed in transaction 8.

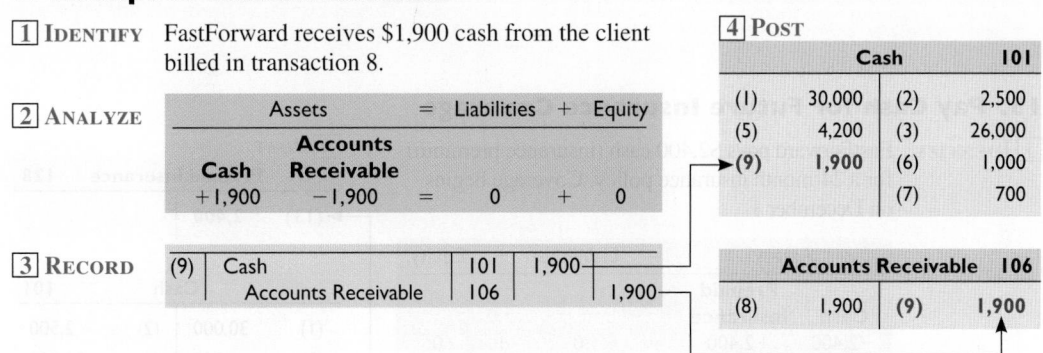

Point: The *revenue recognition principle* requires revenue to be recognized when earned, which is when the company provides products and services to a customer. This is not necessarily the same time that the customer pays. A customer can pay before or after products or services are provided.

10. Partial Payment of Accounts Payable

1 IDENTIFY   FastForward pays CalTech Supply $900 cash toward the payable of transaction 4.

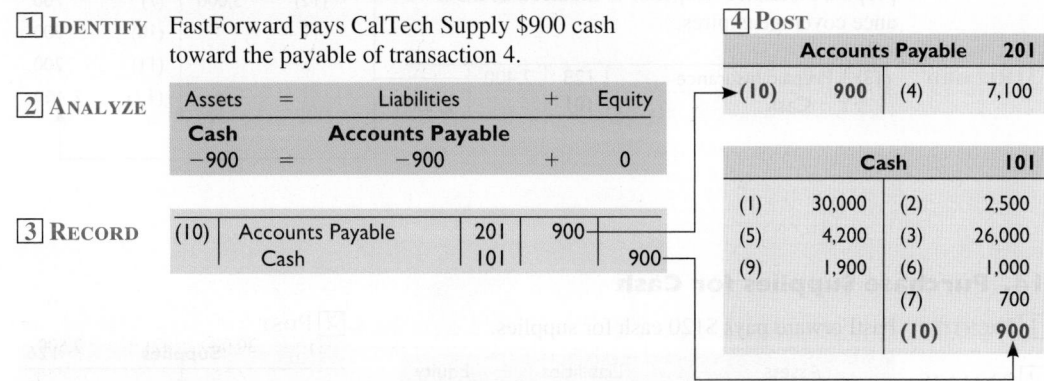

11. Withdrawal of Cash by Owner

1 IDENTIFY   Chas Taylor withdraws $200 cash from FastForward for personal use.

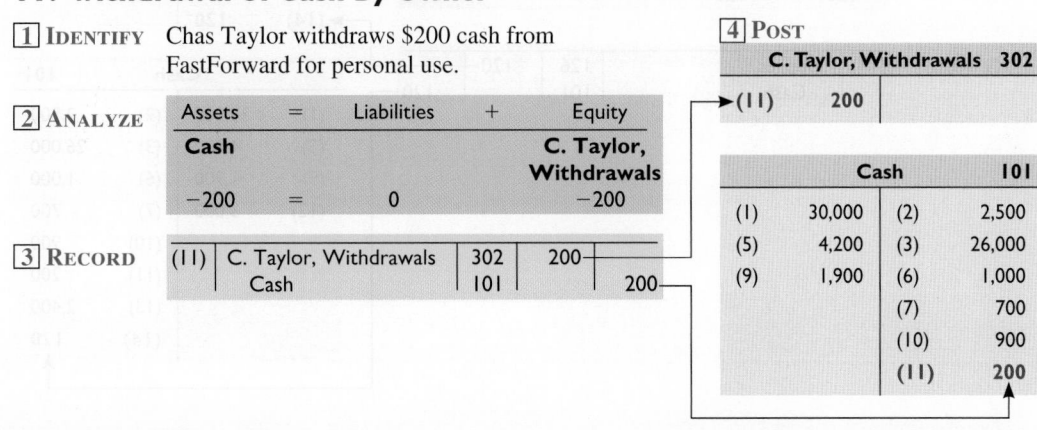

12. Receipt of Cash for Future Services

1	IDENTIFY	FastForward receives $3,000 cash in advance of providing consulting services to a customer.

2	ANALYZE

Assets	=	Liabilities	+	Equity
		Unearned		
Cash		**Consulting Revenue**		
+3,000	=	+3,000	+	0

Accepting $3,000 cash obligates FastForward to perform future services and is a liability. No revenue is earned until services are provided.

3	RECORD

(12)	Cash	101	3,000	
	Unearned Consulting Revenue	236		3,000

4	POST

Cash			101
(1)	30,000	(2)	2,500
(5)	4,200	(3)	26,000
(9)	1,900	(6)	1,000
(12)	3,000	(7)	700
		(10)	900
		(11)	200

Unearned Consulting Revenue			236
		(12)	3,000

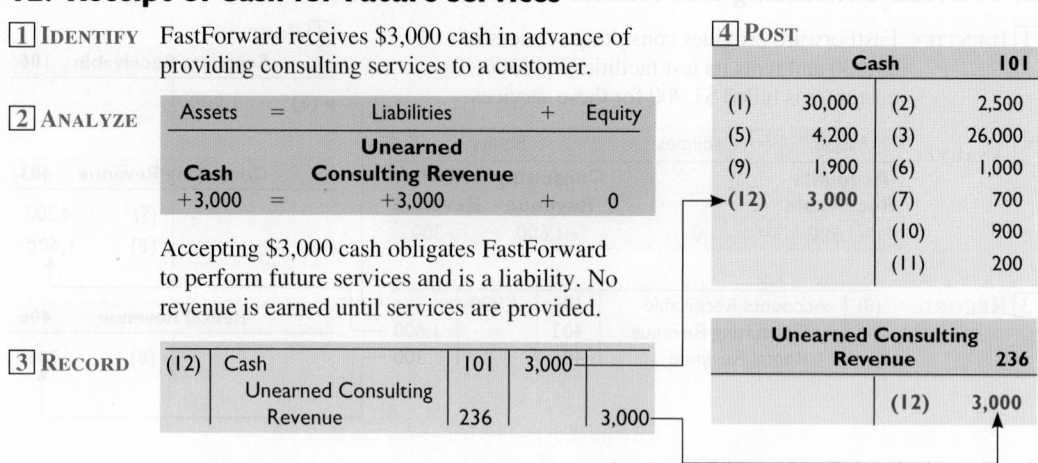

13. Pay Cash for Future Insurance Coverage

1	IDENTIFY	FastForward pays $2,400 cash (insurance premium) for a 24-month insurance policy. Coverage begins on December 1.

2	ANALYZE

Assets		=	Liabilities	+	Equity
	Prepaid				
Cash	**Insurance**				
−2,400	+2,400	=	0	+	0

Changes the composition of assets from cash to prepaid insurance. Expense is incurred as insurance coverage expires.

3	RECORD

(13)	Prepaid Insurance	128	2,400	
	Cash	101		2,400

4	POST

Prepaid Insurance		128
(13)	2,400	

Cash			101
(1)	30,000	(2)	2,500
(5)	4,200	(3)	26,000
(9)	1,900	(6)	1,000
(12)	3,000	(7)	700
		(10)	900
		(11)	200
		(13)	2,400

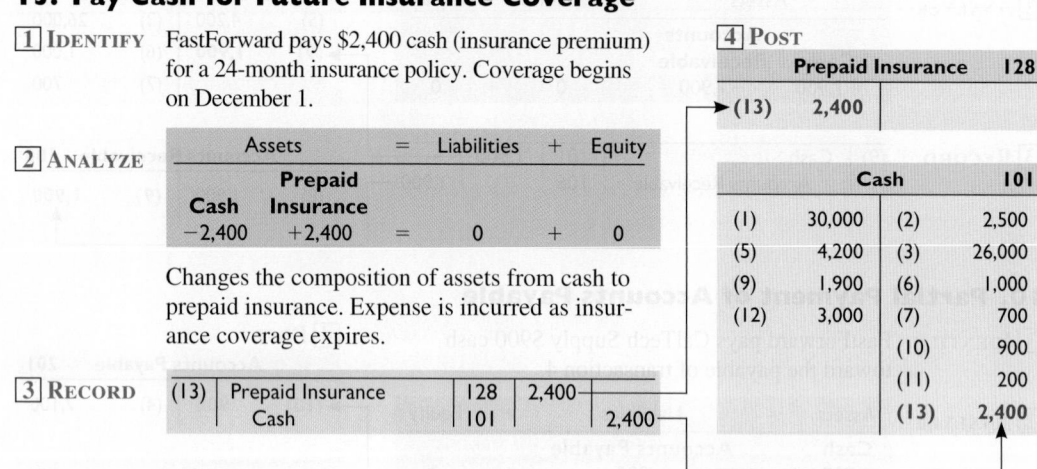

14. Purchase Supplies for Cash

1	IDENTIFY	FastForward pays $120 cash for supplies.

2	ANALYZE

Assets		=	Liabilities	+	Equity
Cash	**Supplies**				
−120	+120	=	0	+	0

3	RECORD

(14)	Supplies	126	120	
	Cash	101		120

4	POST

Supplies		126
(2)	2,500	
(4)	7,100	
(14)	120	

Cash			101
(1)	30,000	(2)	2,500
(5)	4,200	(3)	26,000
(9)	1,900	(6)	1,000
(12)	3,000	(7)	700
		(10)	900
		(11)	200
		(13)	2,400
		(14)	120

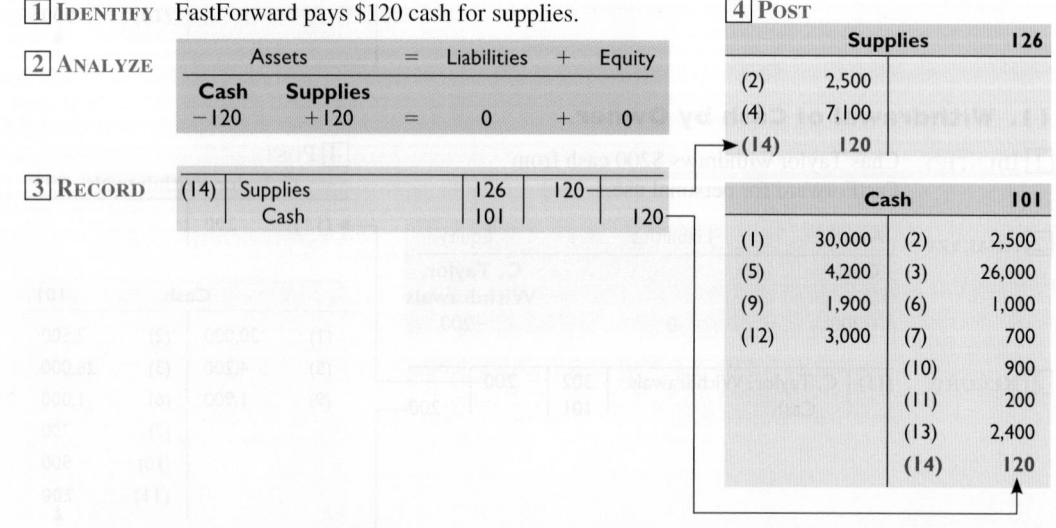

15. Payment of Expense in Cash

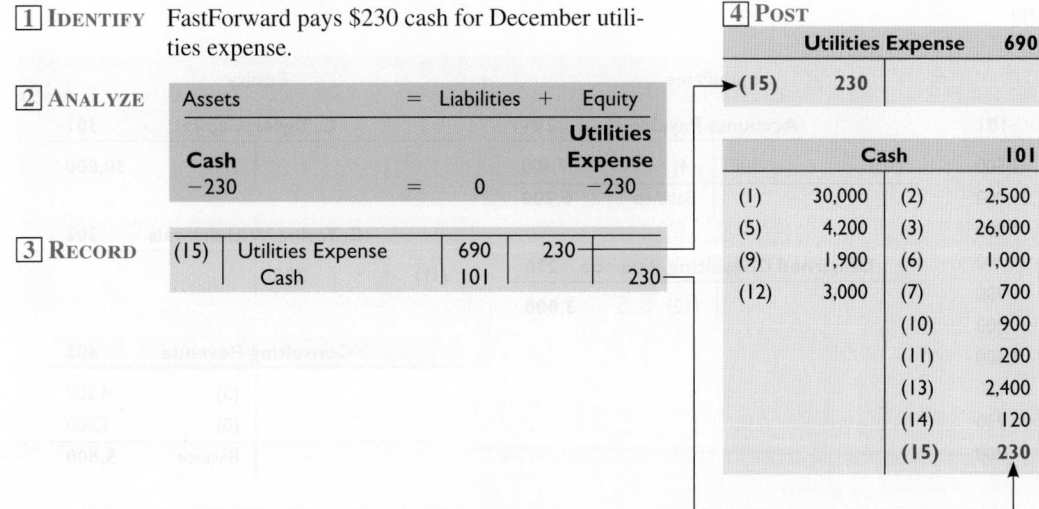

1 IDENTIFY FastForward pays $230 cash for December utilities expense.

2 ANALYZE

Assets	=	Liabilities	+	Equity
Cash				**Utilities Expense**
−230	=	0		−230

3 RECORD

(15)	Utilities Expense	690	230	
	Cash	101		230

4 POST

Utilities Expense		690
(15)	230	

Cash			101
(1)	30,000	(2)	2,500
(5)	4,200	(3)	26,000
(9)	1,900	(6)	1,000
(12)	3,000	(7)	700
		(10)	900
		(11)	200
		(13)	2,400
		(14)	120
		(15)	230

16. Payment of Expense in Cash

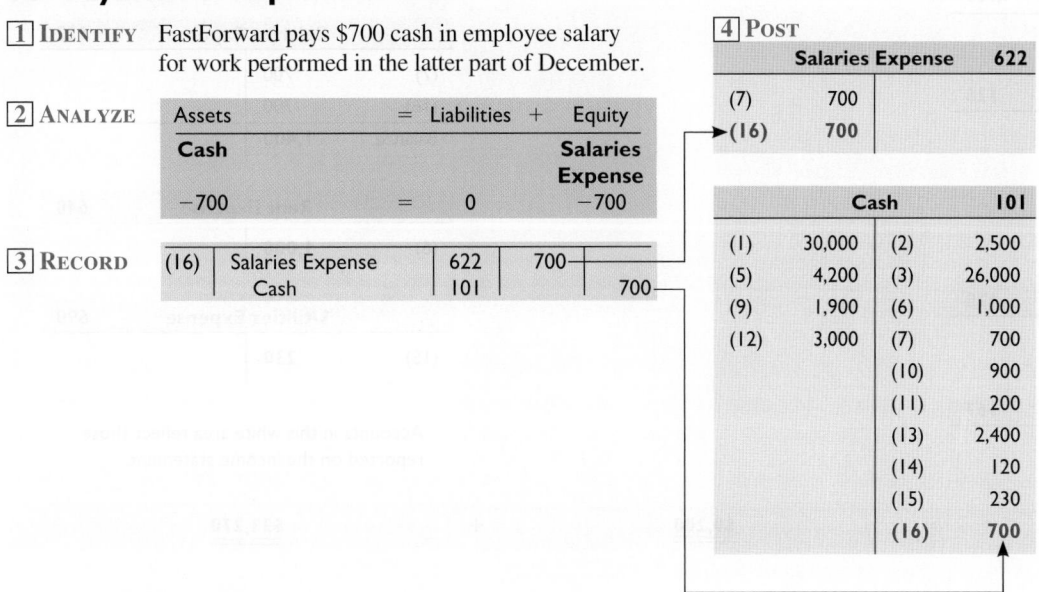

1 IDENTIFY FastForward pays $700 cash in employee salary for work performed in the latter part of December.

2 ANALYZE

Assets	=	Liabilities	+	Equity
Cash				**Salaries Expense**
−700	=	0		−700

3 RECORD

(16)	Salaries Expense	622	700	
	Cash	101		700

4 POST

Salaries Expense		622
(7)	700	
(16)	700	

Cash			101
(1)	30,000	(2)	2,500
(5)	4,200	(3)	26,000
(9)	1,900	(6)	1,000
(12)	3,000	(7)	700
		(10)	900
		(11)	200
		(13)	2,400
		(14)	120
		(15)	230
		(16)	700

Point: We could merge transactions 15 and 16 into one *compound entry.*

Accounting Equation Analysis

Exhibit 2.13 shows the ledger accounts (in T-account form) of FastForward after all 16 transactions are recorded and posted and the balances computed. The accounts are grouped into three major columns corresponding to the accounting equation: assets, liabilities, and equity. Note several important points. First, as with each transaction, the totals for the three columns must obey the accounting equation. Specifically, assets equal $42,470 ($4,350 + $0 + $9,720 + $2,400 + $26,000); liabilities equal $9,200 ($6,200 + $3,000); and equity equals $33,270 ($30,000 − $200 + $5,800 + $300 − $1,400 − $1,000 − $230). These numbers prove the accounting equation: Assets of $42,470 = Liabilities of $9,200 + Equity of $33,270. Second, the capital, withdrawals, revenue, and expense accounts reflect the transactions that change equity. These account categories underlie the statement of changes in equity. Third, the revenue and expense account balances will be summarized and reported in the income statement. Fourth, increases and decreases in the cash account make up the elements reported in the statement of cash flows.

Debit and Credit Rules

Accounts	Increase (normal bal.)	Decrease
Asset	Debit	Credit
Liability	Credit	Debit
Capital	Credit	Debit
Withdrawals	Debit	Credit
Revenue	Credit	Debit
Expense	Debit	Credit

Point: Technology does not provide the judgment required to analyze most business transactions. Analysis requires the expertise of skilled and ethical professionals.

EXHIBIT 2.13

Ledger for FastForward (in T-Account Form)

Assets		=	Liabilities		+	Equity	

Assets

Cash   **101**

(1)	30,000	(2)	2,500
(5)	4,200	(3)	26,000
(9)	1,900	(6)	1,000
(12)	3,000	(7)	700
		(10)	900
		(11)	200
		(13)	2,400
		(14)	120
		(15)	230
		(16)	700
Balance	4,350		

Accounts Receivable   **106**

(8)	1,900	(9)	1,900
Balance	0		

Supplies   **126**

(2)	2,500	
(4)	7,100	
(14)	120	
Balance	9,720	

Prepaid Insurance   **128**

(13)	2,400	

Equipment   **167**

(3)	26,000	

Liabilities

Accounts Payable   **201**

(10)	900	(4)	7,100
		Balance	6,200

Unearned Consulting Revenue   **236**

		(12)	3,000

Equity

C. Taylor, Capital   **301**

		(1)	30,000

C. Taylor, Withdrawals   **302**

(11)	200	

Consulting Revenue   **403**

		(5)	4,200
		(8)	1,600
		Balance	5,800

Rental Revenue   **406**

		(8)	300

Salaries Expense   **622**

(7)	700	
(16)	700	
Balance	1,400	

Rent Expense   **640**

(6)	1,000	

Utilities Expense   **690**

(15)	230	

Accounts in this white area reflect those reported on the income statement.

$42,470	**=**	**$9,200**	**+**	**$33,270**

Quick Check

Answers — p. 74

8. What types of transactions increase equity? What types decrease equity?

9. Why are accounting systems called *double-entry?*

10. For each transaction, double-entry accounting requires which of the following? (*a*) Debits to asset accounts must create credits to liability or equity accounts, (*b*) a debit to a liability account must create a credit to an asset account, or (*c*) total debits must equal total credits.

11. An owner invests $15,000 cash along with equipment having a market value of $23,000 in a company. Prepare the necessary journal entry.

12. Explain what a compound journal entry is.

13. Why are posting reference numbers entered in the journal when entries are posted to ledger accounts?

TRIAL BALANCE

Double-entry accounting requires the sum of debit account balances to equal the sum of credit account balances. A trial balance is used to confirm this. A **trial balance** is a list of accounts and their balances at a point in time. Account balances are reported in their appropriate debit or credit columns of a trial balance. A trial balance can be used to confirm this and to follow up on any abnormal or unusual balances. Exhibit 2.14 shows the trial balance for FastForward after its 16 entries have been posted to the ledger. (This is an *unadjusted* trial balance—Chapter 3 explains the necessary adjustments.)

EXHIBIT 2.14

Trial Balance (Unadjusted)

Peachtree Accounting: FastForward

File Edit Lists Maintain Tasks Analysis Options Reports & Forms Services Window Help

Company

- Business Status
- Customers & Sales
- Vendors & Purchases
- Inventory & Services
- Employees & Payroll
- Banking
- Company

Shortcuts Customize
Sales Invoice
Receive Money from Customer
Bills - Pay Bill
Customer List
Vendor List
Find Transactions
General Journal Entry

FASTFORWARD
Trial Balance
December 31, 2015

	Debit	Credit
Cash	$ 4,350	
Accounts receivable	0	
Supplies	9,720	
Prepaid insurance	2,400	
Equipment	26,000	
Accounts payable		$ 6,200
Unearned consulting revenue		3,000
C. Taylor, Capital		30,000
C. Taylor, Withdrawals	200	
Consulting revenue		5,800
Rental revenue		300
Salaries expense	1,400	
Rent expense	1,000	
Utilities expense	230	
Totals	$ 45,300	$ 45,300

Point: The ordering of accounts in a trial balance typically follows their identification number from the chart of accounts.

Preparing a Trial Balance

Preparing a trial balance involves three steps:

P2 Prepare and explain the use of a trial balance.

1. List each account title and its amount (from ledger) in the trial balance. If an account has a zero balance, list it with a zero in its normal balance column (or omit it entirely).
2. Compute the total of debit balances and the total of credit balances.
3. Verify (*prove*) total debit balances equal total credit balances.

The total of debit balances equals the total of credit balances for the trial balance in Exhibit 2.14. Equality of these two totals does not guarantee that no errors were made. For example, the column totals still will be equal when a debit or credit of a correct amount is made to a wrong account. Another error that does not cause unequal column totals occurs when equal debits and credits of an incorrect amount are entered.

Searching for and Correcting Errors   If the trial balance does not balance (when its columns are not equal), the error (or errors) must be found and corrected. An efficient

Point: A trial balance is *not* a financial statement but a mechanism for checking equality of debits and credits in the ledger. Financial statements do not have debit and credit columns.

way to search for an error is to check the journalizing, posting, and trial balance preparation in *reverse order.* Step 1 is to verify that the trial balance columns are correctly added. If step 1 fails to find the error, step 2 is to verify that account balances are accurately entered from the ledger. Step 3 is to see whether a debit (or credit) balance is mistakenly listed in the trial balance as a credit (or debit). A clue to this error is when the difference between total debits and total credits equals twice the amount of the incorrect account balance. If the error is still undiscovered, Step 4 is to recompute each account balance in the ledger. Step 5 is to verify that each journal entry is properly posted. Step 6 is to verify that the original journal entry has equal debits and credits. At this point, the errors should be uncovered.[3]

If an error in a journal entry is discovered before the error is posted, it can be corrected in a manual system by drawing a line through the incorrect information. The correct information is written above it to create a record of change for the auditor. Many computerized systems allow the operator to replace the incorrect information directly.

If an error in a journal entry is not discovered until after it is posted, we do not strike through both erroneous entries in the journal and ledger. Instead, we correct this error by creating a *correcting entry* that removes the amount from the wrong account and records it to the correct account. As an example, suppose a $100 purchase of supplies is journalized with an incorrect debit to Equipment, and then this incorrect entry is posted to the ledger. The Supplies ledger account balance is understated by $100, and the Equipment ledger account balance is overstated by $100. The correcting entry is: debit Supplies and credit Equipment (both for $100).

Using a Trial Balance to Prepare Financial Statements

This section shows how to prepare *financial statements* from the trial balance in Exhibit 2.14 and from information on the December transactions of FastForward. These statements differ from those in Chapter 1 because of several additional transactions. These statements are also more precisely called *unadjusted statements* because we need to make some further accounting adjustments (described in Chapter 3).

EXHIBIT 2.15

Links between Financial Statements across Time

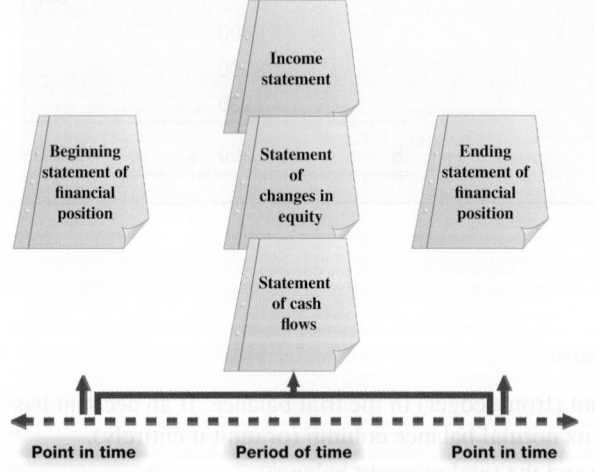

How financial statements are linked in time is illustrated in Exhibit 2.15. A statement of financial position reports on an organization's financial position at a *point in time.* The income statement, statement of changes in equity, and statement of cash flows report on financial performance over a *period of time.* The three statements in the middle column of Exhibit 2.15 link statements of financial position from the beginning to the end of a reporting period. They explain how financial position changes from one point to another.

Preparers and users (including regulatory agencies) determine the length

---

[3] *Transposition* occurs when two digits are switched, or transposed, within a number. If transposition is the only error, it yields a difference between the two trial balance totals that is evenly divisible by 9. For example, assume that a $691 debit in an entry is incorrectly posted to the ledger as $619. Total credits in the trial balance are then larger than total debits by $72 ($691 − $619). The $72 error is *evenly* divisible by 9 (72/9 = 8). The first digit of the quotient (in our example it is 8) equals the difference between the digits of the two transposed numbers (the 9 and the 1). The number of digits in the quotient also tells the location of the transposition, starting from the right. The quotient in our example had only one digit (8), so it tells us the transposition is in the first digit. Consider another example where a transposition error involves posting $961 instead of the correct $691. The difference in these numbers is $270, and its quotient is 30 (270/9). The quotient has two digits, so it tells us to check the second digit from the right for a transposition of two numbers that have a difference of 3.

of the reporting period. A one-year, or annual, reporting period is common, as are semiannual, quarterly, and monthly periods. The one-year reporting period is known as the *accounting,* or *fiscal, year.* Businesses whose accounting year begins on January 1 and ends on December 31 are known as *calendar-year* companies. Some companies choose a fiscal year ending on a date other than December 31. **Nestlé** is a calendar-year company as reflected in the headings of its December year-end financial statements in Appendix A near the end of the book.

Income Statement   An income statement reports the revenues earned less the expenses incurred by a business over a period of time. FastForward's income statement for December is shown at the top of Exhibit 2.16. Information about revenues and expenses is conveniently taken from the trial balance in Exhibit 2.14. Net profit of $3,470 is reported at the bottom of the statement. Owner investments and withdrawals are *not* part of profit.

Statement of changes in equity   The statement of changes in equity reports information about how equity changes over the reporting period. FastForward's statement of changes in equity is the second report in Exhibit 2.16. It shows the $30,000 owner investment, the $3,470

Point: A statement's heading lists the 3 W's: **W**ho—name of organization, **W**hat—name of statement, **W**hen—statement's point in time or period of time.

EXHIBIT 2.16

Financial Statements and Their Links

FASTFORWARD
Income Statement
For Month Ended December 31, 2015

Revenues		
Consulting revenue ($4,200 + $1,600)	$ 5,800	
Rental revenue	300	
Total revenues		$ 6,100
Expenses		
Rent expense	(1,000)	
Salaries expense	(1,400)	
Utilities expense	(230)	
Total expenses		(2,630)
Net profit		$ 3,470

FASTFORWARD
Statement of Changes in Equity
For Month Ended December 31, 2015

C. Taylor, Capital, December 1, 2015		$ 0
Investments by owner	$30,000	
Net profit	3,470	33,470
		33,470
Withdrawals by owner		(200)
C. Taylor, Capital, December 31, 2015		$33,270

Point: Arrow lines show how the statements are linked.

FASTFORWARD
Statement of Financial Position
December 31, 2015

Assets	
Cash	$ 4,350
Supplies	9,720
Prepaid insurance	2,400
Equipment	26,000
Total assets	$42,470
Liabilities	
Accounts payable	$ 6,200
Unearned revenue	3,000
Total liabilities	9,200
Equity	
C. Taylor, Capital	33,270
Total liabilities and equity	$ 42,470

Point: To *foot* a column of numbers is to add them.

of net profit, the $200 withdrawal, and the $33,270 end-of-period (capital) balance. (The beginning balance in the statement of changes in equity is rarely zero; an exception is for the first period of operations. The beginning capital balance in January 2016 is $33,270, which is December's ending balance.)

Point: While revenues increase equity, and expenses decrease equity, the amounts are not reported in detail in the statement of changes in equity. Instead, their effects are reflected through net profit.

Statement of Financial Position   The statement of financial position reports the financial position of a company at a point in time, usually at the end of a month, quarter, or year. FastForward's statement of financial position is the third report in Exhibit 2.16. This statement refers to financial condition at the close of business on December 31. The top portion of the statement of financial position lists its assets: cash, supplies, prepaid insurance, and equipment. The lower portion of the statement of financial position shows that it owes $6,200 to creditors and $3,000 in services to customers who paid in advance. The equity section shows an ending balance of $33,270. Note the link between the ending balance of the statement of changes in equity and the equity balance. (Recall that this presentation of the statement of financial position is called the *report* or *narrative format*: assets, liabilities, and equity presented vertically. Another presentation is the *account format*: assets on the left, liabilities and equity on the right. Either presentation is acceptable.)

Decision Maker   Answer — p. 73

Entrepreneur   You open a wholesale business selling entertainment equipment to retail outlets. You find that most of your customers demand to buy on credit. How can you use the statements of financial position of these customers to decide which ones to extend credit to? ∎

Point: Knowing how financial statements are prepared improves our analysis of them.

Presentation Issues   Currency signs are usually not used in journals and ledgers. They do often appear in financial statements and other documents such as trial balances. One practice is to put currency signs beside only the first and last numbers in a column. It is also common to place the signs beside any key amount that appears after a ruled line. Some companies just state the currency in the report headings and do not show currency signs for the column numbers. For example, the financial statements of **Nestlé** and **Adidas** in Appendix A show the reporting currency as CHF (Swiss franc) and EUR (Euro) respectively in the report headings but do not show them next to any column numbers. Companies also commonly round amounts in reports to the nearest currency unit, or even to a higher level. Nestlé is typical of many companies in that it rounds its financial statements to the nearest million. This decision is based on the perceived impact of rounding for users' business decisions.

Quick Check   Answers — p. 74

14. Where are currency signs typically entered in financial statements?
15. If a $4,000 debit to Equipment in a journal entry is incorrectly posted to the ledger as a $4,000 credit, and the ledger account has a resulting debit balance of $20,000, what is the effect of this error on the Trial Balance column totals?
16. Describe the link between the income statement and the statement of changes in equity.
17. Explain the link between the statement of financial position and the statement of changes in equity.
18. Define and describe revenues and expenses.
19. Define and describe assets, liabilities, and equity.

An important business objective is gathering information to help assess a company's risk of failing to pay its debts. Companies finance their assets with either liabilities or equity. A company that finances a relatively large portion of its assets with liabilities is said to have a high degree of *financial leverage*. Higher financial leverage involves greater risk because liabilities must be repaid and often require regular interest payments (equity financing does not). The risk that a company might not be able to meet such required payments is higher if it has more liabilities (is more highly leveraged). One way to assess the risk associated with a company's use of liabilities is to compute the **debt ratio** as in Exhibit 2.17.

> **A2** Compute the debt ratio and describe its use in analyzing financial condition.

$$\text{Debt ratio} = \frac{\text{Total liabilities}}{\text{Total assets}}$$

To see how to apply the debt ratio, let's look at Adidas' liabilities and assets. Adidas makes sports shoes and apparel. Exhibit 2.18 computes and reports its debt ratio at the end of each year from 2009 to 2013.

EXHIBIT 2.17

Debt Ratio

Point: Compare the equity amount to the liability amount to assess the extent of owner versus nonowner financing.

	2009	2010	2011	2012	2013
Total liabilities (EUR millions)	5,099	5,995	6,109	6,360	6,118
Total assets (EUR millions)	8,875	10,618	11,237	11,651	11,599
Debt ratio (%)..................	57.5	56.5	54.4	54.6	52.7

EXHIBIT 2.18

Computation and Analysis of Debt Ratio

Adidas' debt ratio ranges from 52.7% to 57.5%, and can be said to be in a downward trend for the five-year period. We can compare this ratio with that of competitors in the same industry. Does a low debt ratio mean a low risk from financial leverage, and vice-versa? To answer this question, we need to compare the company's return on the borrowed money to the rate it is paying creditors. If the return is higher, then the company is successfully borrowing money to make more money. This can quickly turn unsuccessful if the return drops below the rate it pays to creditors.

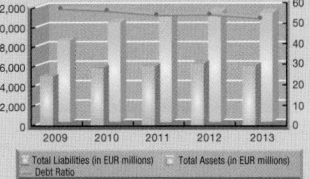

Decision Maker   Answer — p. 73

Investor You consider buying shares in Converse. As part of your analysis, you compute its debt ratio for 2009, 2010, and 2011 as: 0.35, 0.74, and 0.94, respectively. Based on the debt ratio, is Converse a low-risk investment? Has the risk of buying Converse shares changed over this period? (The industry debt ratio averages 0.40.) ■

DEMONSTRATION PROBLEM

(This problem extends the demonstration problem of Chapter 1.) After several months of planning, Jasmine Worthy started a haircutting business called Expressions. The following events occurred during its first month.

a. On August 1, Worthy invested $3,000 cash and $15,000 of equipment in Expressions.

b. On August 2, Expressions paid $600 cash for furniture for the shop.

c. On August 3, Expressions paid $500 cash to rent space in a strip mall for August.

d. On August 4, it purchased $1,200 of equipment on credit for the shop (using a long-term note payable).

e. On August 5, Expressions opened for business. Cash received from haircutting services in the first week and a half of business (ended August 15) was $825.

f. On August 15, it provided $100 of haircutting services on account.

g. On August 17, it received a $100 check for services previously rendered on account.

h. On August 17, it paid $125 to an assistant for hours worked during the grand opening.

i. Cash received from services provided during the second half of August was $930.

j. On August 31, it paid a $400 installment toward principal on the note payable entered into on August 4.

k. On August 31, Worthy withdrew $900 cash for personal use.

Required

1. Open the following ledger accounts in balance column format (account numbers are in parentheses): Cash (101); Accounts Receivable (102); Furniture (161); Store Equipment (165); Note Payable (240); J. Worthy, Capital (301); J. Worthy, Withdrawals (302); Haircutting Services Revenue (403); Wages Expense (623); and Rent Expense (640). Prepare general journal entries for the transactions.

2. Post the journal entries from (1) to the ledger accounts.

3. Prepare a trial balance as at August 31.

4. Prepare an income statement for August.

5. Prepare a statement of changes in equity for August.

6. Prepare a statement of financial position as at August 31.

7. Determine the debt ratio as at August 31.

Extended Analysis

8. In the coming months, Expressions will experience a greater variety of business transactions. Identify which accounts are debited and which are credited for the following transactions. (*Hint:* We must use some accounts not opened in part 1.)

  a. Purchase supplies with cash.

  b. Pay cash for future insurance coverage.

  c. Receive cash for services to be provided in the future.

  d. Purchase supplies on account.

PLANNING THE SOLUTION

- Analyze each transaction and use the debit and credit rules to prepare a journal entry for each.
- Post each debit and each credit from journal entries to their ledger accounts and cross-reference each amount in the posting reference (PR) columns of the journal and ledger.
- Calculate each account balance and list the accounts with their balances on a trial balance.
- Verify that total debits in the trial balance equal total credits.
- To prepare the income statement, identify revenues and expenses. List those items on the statement, compute the difference, and label the result as *net profit* or *net loss*.
- Use information in the ledger to prepare the statement of changes in equity.
- Use information in the ledger to prepare the statement of financial position.
- Calculate the debt ratio by dividing total liabilities by total assets.
- Analyze the future transactions to identify the accounts affected and apply debit and credit rules.

SOLUTION TO DEMONSTRATION PROBLEM

1. General journal entries:

General Journal Entry   _ □ ☒

Page 1

Date	Account Titles and Explanation	PR	Debit	Credit
Aug. 1	Cash	101	3,000	
	Store Equipment	165	15,000	
	J. Worthy, Capital	301		18,000
	To record investment of cash by owner.			
2	Furniture	161	600	
	Cash	101		600
	To record the purchase of furniture with cash.			
3	Rent Expense	640	500	
	Cash	101		500
	To record the payment of rent for August.			
4	Store Equipment	165	1,200	
	Note Payable	240		1,200
	To record the purchase of additional equipment on credit.			
15	Cash	101	825	
	Haircutting Services Revenue	403		825
	To record revenue received as cash from services in first half of August.			

[continued on next page]

[continued from previous page]

15	Accounts Receivable		102	100	
	Haircutting Services Revenue		403		100
	To record revenue for services provided on account.				
17	Cash		101	100	
	Accounts Receivable		102		100
	To record cash received as payment on account.				
17	Wages Expense		623	125	
	Cash		101		125
	To record the payment of wages to assistant.				
31	Cash		101	930	
	Haircutting Services Revenue		403		930
	To record revenue received as cash from services in second half of August.				
31	Note Payable		240	400	
	Cash		101		400
	To record the payment of an installment on the note payable.				
31	J. Worthy, Withdrawals		302	900	
	Cash		101		900
	To record cash withdrawal by owner.				

2. Post journal entries from part 1 to the ledger accounts:

General Ledger

Cash Account No. 101

Date	PR	Debit	Credit	Balance
Aug. 1	G1	3,000		3,000
2	G1		600	2,400
3	G1		500	1,900
15	G1	825		2,725
17	G1	100		2,825
17	G1		125	2,700
31	G1	930		3,630
31	G1		400	3,230
31	G1		900	2,330

Accounts Receivable Account No. 102

Date	PR	Debit	Credit	Balance
Aug. 15	G1	100		100
17	G1		100	0

Furniture Account No. 161

Date	PR	Debit	Credit	Balance
Aug. 2	G1	600		600

Store Equipment Account No. 165

Date	PR	Debit	Credit	Balance
Aug. 1	G1	15,000		15,000
4	G1	1,200		16,200

Note Payable Account No. 240

Date	PR	Debit	Credit	Balance
Aug. 4	G1		1,200	1,200
31	G1	400		800

J. Worthy, Capital Account No. 301

Date	PR	Debit	Credit	Balance
Aug. 1	G1		18,000	18,000

J. Worthy, Withdrawals Account No. 302

Date	PR	Debit	Credit	Balance
Aug. 31	G1	900		900

Haircutting Services Revenue Account No. 403

Date	PR	Debit	Credit	Balance
Aug. 15	G1		825	825
15	G1		100	925
31	G1		930	1,855

Wages Expense Account No. 623

Date	PR	Debit	Credit	Balance
Aug. 17	G1	125		125

Rent Expense Account No. 640

Date	PR	Debit	Credit	Balance
Aug. 3	G1	500		500

3. Prepare a trial balance from the ledger:

EXPRESSIONS
Trial Balance
August 31

	Debit	Credit
Cash	$ 2,330	
Accounts receivable	0	
Furniture	600	
Store equipment	16,200	
Note payable		$ 800
J. Worthy, Capital		18,000
J. Worthy, Withdrawals	900	
Haircutting services revenue		1,855
Wages expense	125	
Rent expense	500	
Totals	$20,655	$20,655

4.

EXPRESSIONS
Income Statement
For Month Ended August 31

Revenues		
Haircutting services revenue		$1,855
Operating expenses		
Rent expense	($500)	
Wages expense	(125)	
Total operating expenses		(625)
Net profit		$1,230

5.

EXPRESSIONS
Statement of Changes in Equity
For Month Ended August 31

J. Worthy, Capital, August 1		$ 0
Investments by owner	$18,000	
Net profit	1,230	19,230
		19,230
Withdrawals by owner		(900)
J. Worthy, Capital, August 31		$18,330

6.

EXPRESSIONS
Statement of Financial Position
August 31

Assets	
Cash	$ 2,330
Furniture	600
Store equipment	16,200
Total assets	$19,130
Liabilities	
Note payable	$ 800
Equity	
J. Worthy, Capital	18,330
Total liabilities and equity	$19,130

$$7. \text{ Debt ratio} = \frac{\text{Total liabilities}}{\text{Total assets}} = \frac{\$800}{\$19,130} = \underline{\underline{\textbf{4.18}\%}}$$

8a. Supplies *debited*
      Cash *credited*

8b. Prepaid Insurance *debited*
      Cash *credited*

8c. Cash *debited*
      Unearned Services Revenue *credited*

8d. Supplies *debited*
      Accounts Payable *credited*

Summary

C1 **Explain the steps in processing transactions and the role of source documents.** The accounting process identifies business transactions and events, analyzes and records their effects, and summarizes and prepares information useful in making decisions. Transactions and events are the starting points in the accounting process. Source documents identify and describe transactions and events. Examples are sales tickets, checks, purchase orders, bills, and bank statements. Source documents provide objective and reliable evidence, making information more useful. The effects of transactions and events are recorded in journals. Posting along with a trial balance helps summarize and classify these effects.

C2 **Describe an account and its use in recording transactions.** An account is a detailed record of increases and decreases in a specific asset, liability, equity, revenue, or expense. Information from accounts is analyzed, summarized, and presented in reports and financial statements for decision makers.

C3 **Describe a ledger and a chart of accounts.** The ledger (or general ledger) is a record containing all accounts used by a company and their balances. It is referred to as the *books*. The chart of accounts is a list of all accounts and usually includes an identification number assigned to each account.

C4 **Define *debits* and *credits* and explain double-entry accounting.** *Debit* refers to left, and *credit* refers to right. Debits increase assets, expenses, and withdrawals while credits decrease them. Credits increase liabilities, owner capital, and revenues; debits decrease them. Double-entry accounting means each transaction affects at least two accounts and has at least one debit and one credit. The system for recording debits and credits follows from the accounting equation. The left side of an account is the normal balance for assets, withdrawals, and expenses, and the right side is the normal balance for liabilities, capital, and revenues.

A1 **Analyze the impact of transactions on accounts and financial statements.** We analyze transactions using concepts of double-entry accounting. This analysis is performed by determining a transaction's effects on accounts. These effects are recorded in journals and posted to ledgers.

A2 **Compute the debt ratio and describe its use in analyzing financial condition.** A company's debt ratio is computed as total liabilities divided by total assets. It reveals how much of the assets are financed by creditor (nonowner) financing. The higher this ratio, the more risk a company faces because liabilities must be repaid at specific dates.

P1 **Record transactions in a journal and post entries to a ledger.** Transactions are recorded in a journal. Each entry in a journal is posted to the accounts in the ledger. This provides information that is used to produce financial statements. Balance column accounts are widely used and include columns for debits, credits, and the account balance.

P2 **Prepare and explain the use of a trial balance.** A trial balance is a list of accounts from the ledger showing their debit or credit balances in separate columns. The trial balance is a summary of the ledger's contents and is useful in preparing financial statements and in revealing recordkeeping errors.

P3 **Prepare financial statements from business transactions.** The statement of financial position, the statement of changes in equity, the income statement, and the statement of cash flows use data from the trial balance (and other financial statements) for their preparation.

Guidance Answers to **Decision Maker and** Decision Ethics

Cashier The advantages to the process proposed by the assistant manager include improved customer service, fewer delays, and less work for you. However, you should have serious concerns about internal control and the potential for fraud. In particular, the assistant manager could steal cash and simply enter fewer sales to match the remaining cash. You should reject her suggestion without the manager's approval. Moreover, you should have an ethical concern about the assistant manager's suggestion to ignore store policy.

Entrepreneur We can use the accounting equation (Assets = Liabilities + Equity) to help us identify risky customers to whom we

would likely not want to extend credit. A statement of financial position provides amounts for each of these key components. The lower a customer's equity is relative to liabilities, the less likely you would extend credit. A low equity means the business has little value that does not already have creditor claims to it.

Investor The debt ratio suggests the shares of Converse is of higher risk than normal and that this risk is rising. The average industry ratio of 0.40 further supports this conclusion. The 2011 debt ratio for Converse is twice the industry norm. Also, a debt ratio approaching 1.0 indicates little to no equity.

Guidance Answers to Quick Checks

1. Examples of source documents are sales tickets, checks, purchase orders, charges to customers, bills from suppliers, employee earnings records, and bank statements.

2. Source documents serve many purposes, including record-keeping and internal control. Source documents, especially if obtained from outside the organization, provide objective and reliable evidence about transactions and their amounts.

3.

Assets	Liabilities	Equity
a,c,e	b,d	—

4. An account is a record in an accounting system that records and stores the increases and decreases in a specific asset, liability, equity, revenue, or expense. The ledger is a collection of all the accounts of a company.

5. A company's size and diversity affect the number of accounts in its accounting system. The types of accounts depend on information the company needs to both effectively operate and report its activities in financial statements.

6. No. Debit and credit both can mean increase or decrease. The particular meaning in a circumstance depends on the *type of account*. For example, a debit increases the balance of asset, withdrawals, and expense accounts, but it decreases the balance of liability, capital, and revenue accounts.

7. A chart of accounts is a list of all of a company's accounts and their identification numbers.

8. Equity is increased by revenues and by owner investments. Equity is decreased by expenses and owner withdrawals.

9. The name *double-entry* is used because all transactions affect at least two accounts. There must be at least one debit in one account and at least one credit in another account.

10. The answer is (c).

11.

Cash	15,000	
Equipment	23,000	
Owner, Capital		38,000
Investment by owner of cash and equipment.		

12. A compound journal entry affects three or more accounts.

13. Posting reference numbers are entered in the journal when posting to the ledger as a cross-reference that allows the record-keeper or auditor to trace debits and credits from one record to another.

14. Currency signs are usually placed beside the first and last numbers in a column. It is also common to place currency signs beside any amount that appears after a ruled line. Some companies just state the currency in the report headings and do not show currency signs for the column numbers.

15. The Equipment account balance is incorrectly reported at $20,000—it should be $28,000. The effect of this error understates the trial balance's Debit column total by $8,000. This results in an $8,000 difference between the column totals.

16. An income statement reports a company's revenues and expenses along with the resulting net profit or loss. A statement of changes in equity reports changes in equity, including that from net profit or loss. Both statements report transactions occurring over a period of time.

17. The statement of financial position describes a company's financial position (assets, liabilities, and equity) at a point in time. The capital amount in the statement of financial position is obtained from the statement of changes in equity.

18. Revenues are inflows of assets in exchange for products or services provided to customers as part of the main operations of a business. Expenses are outflows or the using up of assets that result from providing products or services to customers.

19. Assets are the resources a business owns or controls that carry expected future benefits. Liabilities are the obligations of a business, representing the claims of others against the assets of a business. Equity reflects the owner's claims on the assets of the business after deducting liabilities.

Key Terms   www.mheducation.asia/olc/wildkwokFAP

Account (p. 51)	Debtors (p. 51)	Posting (p. 56)
Account balance (p. 55)	Debt ratio (p. 69)	Posting reference (PR)
Balance column account (p. 58)	Double-entry accounting (p. 55)	column (p. 58)
Chart of accounts (p. 54)	General journal (p. 57)	Source documents (p. 50)
Compound journal entry (p. 61)	General ledger (p. 51)	T-account (p. 55)
Credit (p. 55)	Journal (p. 56)	Trial balance (p. 65)
Creditors (p. 52)	Journalizing (p. 56)	Unearned revenue (p. 52)
Debit (p. 55)	Ledger (p. 51)	

Multiple Choice Quiz   Answers on p. 90   www.mheducation.asia/olc/wildkwokFAP

Additional Quiz Questions are available at the book's Website.

1. Amalia Company received its utility bill for the current period of $700 and immediately paid it. Its journal entry to record this transaction includes a
   a. Credit to Utility Expense for $700.
   b. Debit to Utility Expense for $700.
   c. Debit to Accounts Payable for $700.
   d. Debit to Cash for $700.
   e. Credit to capital for $700.

2. On May 1, Mattingly Lawn Service collected $2,500 cash from a customer in advance of five months of lawn service. Mattingly's journal entry to record this transaction includes a
   a. Credit to Unearned Lawn Service Fees for $2,500.
   b. Debit to Lawn Service Fees Earned for $2,500.
   c. Credit to Cash for $2,500.
   d. Debit to Unearned Lawn Service Fees for $2,500.
   e. Credit to capital for $2,500.

3. Liang Shue contributed $250,000 cash and land worth $500,000 to open his new business, Shue Consulting. Which of the following journal entries does Shue Consulting make to record this transaction?
   a. Cash Assets 750,000
         L. Shue, Capital   750,000
   b. L. Shue, Capital 750,000
         Assets   750,000
   c. Cash 250,000
      Land 500,000
         L. Shue, Capital   750,000

   d. L. Shue, Capital 750,000
         Cash   250,000
         Land   500,000

4. A trial balance prepared at year-end shows total credits exceed total debits by $765. This discrepancy could have been caused by
   a. An error in the general journal where a $765 increase in Accounts Payable was recorded as a $765 decrease in Accounts Payable.
   b. The ledger balance for Accounts Payable of $7,650 being entered in the trial balance as $765.
   c. A general journal error where a $765 increase in Accounts Receivable was recorded as a $765 increase in Cash.
   d. The ledger balance of $850 in Accounts Receivable was entered in the trial balance as $85.
   e. An error in recording a $765 increase in Cash as a credit.

5. Bonaventure Company has total assets of $1,000,000, liabilities of $400,000, and equity of $600,000. What is its debt ratio (rounded to a whole percent)?
   a. 250%
   b. 167%
   c. 67%
   d. 150%
   e. 40%

🔲 Icon denotes assignments that involve decision making.

Discussion Questions

1. Provide the names of two (a) asset accounts, (b) liability accounts, and (c) equity accounts.
2. What is the difference between a note payable and an account payable?
3. 🔲 Discuss the steps in processing business transactions.
4. What kinds of transactions can be recorded in a general journal?
5. Are debits or credits typically listed first in general journal entries? Are the debits or the credits indented?
6. If assets are valuable resources and asset accounts have debit balances, why do expense accounts also have debit balances?
7. Should a transaction be recorded first in a journal or the ledger? Why?
8. 🔲 Why does the recordkeeper prepare a trial balance?
9. If an incorrect amount is journalized and posted to the accounts, how should the error be corrected?
10. Identify the four financial statements of a business.
11. 🔲 What information is reported in an income statement?
12. 🔲 Why does the user of an income statement need to know the time period that it covers?
13. 🔲 What information is reported in a statement of financial position?
14. Define (a) assets, (b) liabilities, (c) equity, and (d) net assets.
15. Is the trial balance a financial statement? Explain.
16. Refer to Nestlé's consolidated balance sheet in Appendix A. Identify the accounts on its consolidated balance sheet that carry debit balances and the accounts on its consolidated balance sheet that carry credit balances.
17. Refer to Adidas' 2013 consolidated statement of financial position in Appendix A. Identify an asset with the word receivable(s) in its account title and a liability with the word payable(s) in its account title.
18. Refer to Samsung's 2012 consolidated financial statements in Appendix A. What currency units are reported?
19. Refer to Puma's 2013 consolidated income statement from its Website (http://about.puma.com/en/investor-relations/financial-reports). What is the title of its revenue account?
20. Refer to 361 Degrees' 2013 consolidated statement of profit and loss from its Website (http://ir.361sport.com/html/ir_report.php). State any one expense account that it has.

QUICK STUDY

QS 2-1
Identifying financial
statement items
C2 P3

Identify the financial statement(s) on which each of the following items appears. Use IS for income statement, SCE for statement of changes in equity, and SFP for statement of financial position.

a. Accounts payable
b. Cash
c. Rent expense

d. Office supplies
e. Prepaid insurance
f. Revenue

g. Office equipment
h. Cash withdrawal by owner
i. Unearned rent revenue

QS 2-2
Identifying source documents
C1

Identify the items from the following list that are likely to serve as source documents.

a. Bank statement
b. Sales ticket
c. Income statement

d. Trial balance
e. Telephone bill
f. Invoice from supplier

g. Company revenue account
h. Statement of financial position
i. Prepaid rent

QS 2-3
Analyzing debit or credit
by account
A1

Identify whether a debit or credit yields the indicated change for each of the following accounts.

a. To increase Store Equipment
b. To increase Land
c. To decrease Cash
d. To increase Utilities Expense
e. To increase Fees Earned

f. To decrease Unearned Revenue
g. To decrease Prepaid Insurance
h. To increase Notes Payable
i. To decrease Accounts Receivable
j. To increase Owner Capital

QS 2-4
Identifying normal balance
C4

Identify the normal balance (debit or credit) for each of the following accounts.

a. Equipment
b. Wages Expense
c. Repair Services Revenue

d. Office Supplies
e. Owner Withdrawals
f. Accounts Receivable

g. Prepaid Insurance
h. Wages Payable
i. Owner Capital

QS 2-5
Linking debit or credit with
normal balance
C4

Indicate whether a debit or credit *decreases* the normal balance of each of the following accounts.

a. Land
b. Service Revenue
c. Interest Payable
d. Accounts Receivable

e. Salaries Expense
f. Owner Capital
g. Prepaid Insurance
h. Buildings

i. Interest Revenue
j. Owner Withdrawals
k. Unearned Revenue
l. Accounts Payable

QS 2-6
Preparing journal entries
P1

Prepare journal entries for each of the following selected transactions.

a. On January 15, Kolby Anderson opens a remodeling company called Fancy Kitchens by investing $75,000 cash along with equipment having a $30,000 value.
b. On January 21, Fancy Kitchens purchases office supplies on credit for $650.
c. On January 25, Fancy Kitchens receives $8,700 cash for performing remodeling services.
d. On January 30, Fancy Kitchens receives $4,000 cash in advance of providing remodeling services to a customer.

QS 2-7
Identifying a posting error
P2

A trial balance has total debits of $20,000 and total credits of $24,500. Which one of the following errors would create this imbalance? Explain.

a. A $2,250 debit posting to Accounts Receivable was posted mistakenly to Cash.
b. A $4,500 debit posting to Equipment was posted mistakenly to Supplies.
c. An entry debiting Cash and crediting Accounts Payable for $4,500 was mistakenly not posted.
d. A $2,250 credit to Revenue in a journal entry is incorrectly posted to the ledger as a $2,250 debit, leaving the Revenue account with a $6,300 credit balance.

e. A $4,500 debit to Rent Expense in a journal entry is incorrectly posted to the ledger as a $4,500 credit, leaving the Rent Expense account with a $750 debit balance.

f. A $2,250 debit to Utilities Expense in a journal entry is incorrectly posted to the ledger as a $2,250 credit, leaving the Utilities Expense account with a $3,000 debit balance.

Indicate the financial statement(s) on which each of the following items appears. Use IS for income statement, SCE for statement of changes in equity, and SFP for statement of financial position.

a. Buildings
b. Interest Expense
c. Owner Withdrawals
d. Office Supplies

e. Rental Revenue
f. Insurance Expense
g. Services Revenue
h. Interest Payable

i. Accounts Receivable
j. Salaries Expense
k. Equipment
l. Prepaid Insurance

QS 2-8
Classifying accounts in financial statements
P3

---

connect _____

Order the following steps in the accounting process that focus on analyzing and recording transactions.

_____ a. Record relevant transactions in a journal.
_____ b. Prepare and analyze the trial balance.
_____ c. Analyze each transaction from source documents.
_____ d. Post journal information to ledger accounts.

EXERCISES

Exercise 2-1
Steps in analyzing and recording transactions C1

Enter the number for the item that best completes each of the descriptions below.

1. Account
2. Three
3. Asset
4. Liability
5. Equity

a. Owner, capital and owner, withdrawals are examples of _____ accounts.
b. Accounts payable, unearned revenue, and note payable are examples of _____ accounts.
c. Accounts receivable, prepaid accounts, supplies, and land are examples of _____ accounts.
d. Accounts are arranged into _____ general categories.
e. An _____ is a record of increases and decreases in a specific asset, liability, equity, revenue, or expense item.

Exercise 2-2
Identifying and classifying accounts
C2

Enter the number for the item that best completes each of the descriptions below.

1. General ledger
2. Chart

a. The _____ is a record containing all accounts used by a company.
b. A _____ of accounts is a list of all accounts a company uses.

Exercise 2-3
Identifying a ledger and chart of accounts
C3

For each of the following (1) identify the type of account as an asset, liability, equity, revenue, or expense, (2) identify the normal balance of the account, and (3) enter *debit* (*Dr.*) or *credit* (*Cr.*) to identify the kind of entry that would increase the account balance.

a. Fees Earned
b. Equipment
c. Notes Payable
d. Owner Capital

e. Cash
f. Legal Expense
g. Prepaid Insurance
h. Land

i. Accounts Receivable
j. Owner Withdrawals
k. License Fee Revenue
l. Unearned Revenue

Exercise 2-4
Identifying type and normal balances of accounts
C4

Taylor Co. bills a client $48,000 for services provided and agrees to accept the following three items in full payment: (1) $7,500 cash, (2) computer equipment worth $75,000, and (3) to assume responsibility for a $34,500 note payable related to the computer equipment. The entry Taylor makes to record this transaction includes which one or more of the following?

a. $34,500 increase in a liability account
b. $7,500 increase in the Cash account
c. $7,500 increase in a revenue account

d. $48,000 increase in an asset account
e. $48,000 increase in a revenue account
f. $34,500 increase in an equity account

Exercise 2-5
Analyzing effects of transactions on accounts
A1

Exercise 2-6

Analyzing account entries and balances

A1

Use the information in each of the following separate cases to calculate the unknown amount.

a. During October, Shandra Company had $97,500 of cash receipts and $101,250 of cash disbursements. The October 31 Cash balance was $16,800. Determine how much cash the company had at the close of business on September 30.

b. On September 30, Mordish Co. had a $97,500 balance in Accounts Receivable. During October, the company collected $88,950 from its credit customers. The October 31 balance in Accounts Receivable was $100,500. Determine the amount of sales on account that occurred in October.

c. Nasser Co. had $147,000 of accounts payable on September 30 and $136,500 on October 31. Total purchases on account during October were $270,000. Determine how much cash was paid on accounts payable during October.

Exercise 2-7

Preparing general journal entries

P1

Prepare general journal entries for the following transactions of a new company called Pose for Pics.

Aug. 1   Kasey Madison, the owner, invested $7,500 cash and $32,500 of photography equipment in the company.
       2   The company paid $3,000 cash for an insurance policy covering the next 24 months.
       5   The company purchased office supplies for $1,400 cash.
      20   The company received $2,650 cash in photography fees earned.
      31   The company paid $875 cash for August utilities.

Exercise 2-8

Preparing T-accounts (ledger) and a trial balance   P2

Use the information in Exercise 2-7 to prepare an August 31 trial balance for Pose for Pics. Begin by opening these T-accounts: Cash; Office Supplies; Prepaid Insurance; Photography Equipment; K. Madison, Capital; Photography Fees Earned; and Utilities Expense. Then, post the general journal entries to these T-accounts (which will serve as the ledger), and prepare the trial balance.

Exercise 2-9

Recording effects of transactions in T-accounts

A1

Prepare general journal entries to record the transactions below for Dexter Company by using the following accounts: Cash; Accounts Receivable; Office Supplies; Office Equipment; Accounts Payable; M. Dexter, Capital; M. Dexter, Withdrawals; Fees Earned; and Rent Expense. Use the letters beside each transaction to identify entries. After recording the transactions, post them to T-accounts, which serves as the general ledger for this assignment. Determine the ending balance of each T-account.

a. Macy Dexter, owner, invested $12,750 cash in the company.

b. The company purchased office supplies for $375 cash.

c. The company purchased $7,050 of office equipment on credit.

d. The company received $1,500 cash as fees for services provided to a customer.

e. The company paid $7,050 cash to settle the payable for the office equipment purchased in transaction c.

f. The company billed a customer $2,700 as fees for services provided.

g. The company paid $525 cash for the monthly rent.

h. The company collected $1,125 cash as partial payment for the account receivable created in transaction f.

Check   Cash ending balance, $6,425

i. Macy Dexter withdrew $1,000 cash from the company for personal use.

Exercise 2-10

Preparing a trial balance   P2

After recording the transactions of Exercise 2-9 in T-accounts and calculating the balance of each account, prepare a trial balance. Use May 31, 2011, as its report date.

Exercise 2-11

Analyzing and journalizing revenue transactions

A1 P1

Examine the following transactions and identify those that create revenues for Jade Services, a company owned by Mia Jade. Prepare general journal entries to record those revenue transactions and explain why the other transactions did not create revenues.

a. Mia Jade invests $38,250 cash in the company.

b. The company provided $1,350 of services on credit.

c. The company provided services to a client and immediately received $1,575 cash.

d. The company received $9,150 cash from a client in payment for services to be provided next year.

e. The company received $4,500 cash from a client in partial payment of an account receivable.

f. The company borrowed $150,000 cash from the bank by signing a promissory note.

Examine the following transactions and identify those that create expenses for Jade Services. Prepare general journal entries to record those expense transactions and explain why the other transactions did not create expenses.

a. The company paid $14,100 cash for payment on a 14-month old liability for office supplies.

b. The company paid $1,125 cash for the just completed two-week salary of the receptionist.

c. The company paid $45,000 cash for equipment purchased.

d. The company paid $930 cash for this month's utilities.

e. Owner (Jade) withdrew $5,000 cash from the company for personal use.

Exercise 2-12
Analyzing and journalizing
expense transactions

A1 P1

Dominick Lopez operates a consulting firm called Tech Today. On August 31, the company's records show the following accounts and amounts for the month of August. Use this information to prepare an August income statement for the business.

Exercise 2-13
Preparing an income
statement

C3 P3

Cash	$ 8,360	D. Lopez, Withdrawals	$ 3,000
Accounts receivable	17,000	Consulting fees earned	17,000
Office supplies	3,250	Rent expense	4,550
Land	46,000	Salaries expense	8,000
Office equipment	18,000	Telephone expense	560
Accounts payable	8,000	Miscellaneous expenses	280
D. Lopez, Capital, July 31	4,000	Owner investments	80,000

Check Net profit, $3,610

Use the information in Exercise 2-13 to prepare an August statement of changes in equity for Tech Today. (The owner invested $84,000 cash in the company during the first week of August.)

Exercise 2-14
Preparing a statement
of changes in equity P3

Check End. Capital, $84,610

Use the information in Exercise 2-13 (if completed, you can also use your solution to Exercise 2-14) to prepare an August 31 statement of financial position for Tech Today.

Exercise 2-15
Preparing a statement of
financial position P3

A sole proprietorship had the following assets and liabilities at the beginning and end of this year.

Exercise 2-16
Computing net profit

A1

	Assets	Liabilities
Beginning of the year	$ 70,000	$30,000
End of the year	115,000	46,000

Determine the net profit earned or net loss incurred by the business during the year for each of the following *separate* cases:

a. Owner made no investments in the business and no withdrawals were made during the year.

b. Owner made no investments in the business but withdrew $1,250 cash per month for personal use.

c. Owner made no withdrawals during the year but did invest an additional $45,000 cash.

d. Owner withdrew $1,250 cash per month for personal use and invested an additional $25,000 cash.

Compute the missing amount for each of the following separate companies *a* through *d*.

Exercise 2-17
Analyzing changes in a
company's equity

P3

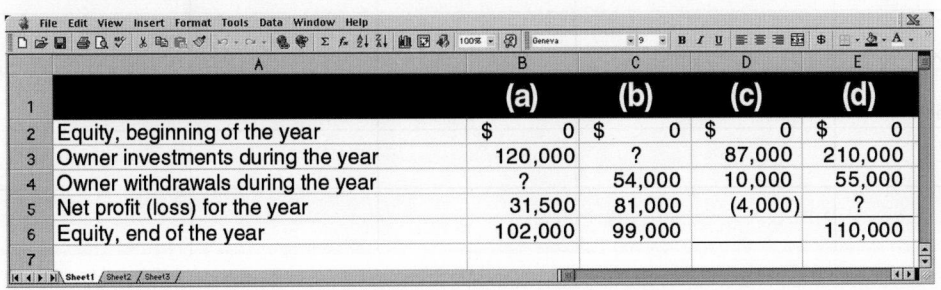

	(a)	(b)	(c)	(d)
Equity, beginning of the year	$ 0	$ 0	$ 0	$ 0
Owner investments during the year	120,000	?	87,000	210,000
Owner withdrawals during the year	?	54,000	10,000	55,000
Net profit (loss) for the year	31,500	81,000	(4,000)	?
Equity, end of the year	102,000	99,000		110,000

Exercise 2-18

Interpreting and describing transactions from T-accounts

A1

Assume the following T-accounts reflect Joy Co.'s general ledger and that seven transactions *a* through *g* are posted to them. Provide a short description of each transaction. Include the amounts in your descriptions.

Cash			
(a)	7,000	(b)	3,600
(e)	2,500	(c)	600
		(f)	2,400
		(g)	700

Office Supplies	
(c)	600
(d)	200

Prepaid Insurance	
(b)	3,600

Equipment	
(a)	5,600
(d)	9,400

Automobiles	
(a)	11,000

Accounts Payable			
(f)	2,400	(d)	9,600

D. Joy, Capital			
		(a)	23,600

Delivery Services Revenue			
		(e)	2,500

Gas and Oil Expense	
(g)	700

Exercise 2-19

Preparing general journal entries

P1

Use information from the T-accounts in Exercise 2-18 to prepare general journal entries for each of the seven transactions *a* through *g*.

Exercise 2-20

Identifying effects of posting errors on the trial balance

A1 P2

Posting errors are identified in the following table. In column (1), enter the amount of the difference between the two trial balance columns (debit and credit) due to the error. In column (2), identify the trial balance column (debit or credit) with the larger amount if they are not equal. In column (3), identify the account(s) affected by the error. In column (4), indicate the amount by which the account(s) in column (3) is under- or overstated. Item (a) is completed as an example.

	Description of Posting Error	(1) Difference between Debit and Credit Columns	(2) Column with the Larger Total	(3) Identify Account(s) Incorrectly Stated	(4) Amount that Account(s) Is Over- or Understated
a.	$2,400 debit to Rent Expense is posted as a $1,590 debit.	$810	Credit	Rent Expense	Rent Expense understated $810
b.	$4,050 credit to Cash is posted twice as two credits to Cash.				
c.	$9,900 debit to the Withdrawals account is debited to Owner's Capital.				
d.	$2,250 debit to Prepaid Insurance is posted as a debit to Insurance Expense.				
e.	$42,000 debit to Machinery is posted as a debit to Accounts Payable.				
f.	$4,950 credit to Services Revenue is posted as a $495 credit.				
g.	$1,440 debit to Store Supplies is not posted.				

You are told the column totals in a trial balance are not equal. After careful analysis, you discover only one error. Specifically, a correctly journalized credit purchase of a computer for $16,950 is posted from the journal to the ledger with a $16,950 debit to Office Equipment and another $16,950 debit to Accounts Payable. The Office Equipment account has a debit balance of $40,100 on the trial balance. Answer each of the following questions and compute the dollar amount of any misstatement.

a. Is the debit column total of the trial balance overstated, understated, or correctly stated?

b. Is the credit column total of the trial balance overstated, understated, or correctly stated?

c. Is the Office Equipment account balance overstated, understated, or correctly stated in the trial balance?

d. Is the Accounts Payable account balance overstated, understated, or correctly stated in the trial balance?

e. If the debit column total of the trial balance is $360,000 before correcting the error, what is the total of the credit column before correction?

Exercise 2-21
Analyzing a trial balance error
A1 P2

BMW reports the following statement of financial position accounts for the year ended December 31, 2009 (in EUR millions). Prepare the statement of financial position for this company as at December 31, 2009, following the usual **IFRS** formats.

Exercise 2-22
Preparing a statement of
financial position following **IFRS**
P3

Current liabilities ....EUR 8,350		Noncurrent liabilities ....EUR 10,943	
Current assets 17,663		Noncurrent assets 6,984	
Total equity 5,354			

Gary Bauer opens a computer consulting business called Technology Consultants and completes the following transactions in April.

April 1   Bauer invested $100,000 cash along with $24,000 in office equipment in the company.
2   The company prepaid $7,200 cash for twelve months' rent for an office. (*Hint:* Debit Prepaid Rent for $7,200.)
3   The company made credit purchases of office equipment for $12,000 and office supplies for $2,400. Payment is due within 10 days.
6   The company completed services for a client and immediately received $2,000 cash.
9   The company completed an $8,000 project for a client, who must pay within 30 days.
13   The company paid $14,400 cash to settle the account payable created on April 3.
19   The company paid $6,000 cash for the premium on a 12-month insurance policy. (*Hint:* Debit Prepaid Insurance for $6,000.)
22   The company received $6,400 cash as partial payment for the work completed on April 9.
25   The company completed work for another client for $2,640 on credit.
28   Bauer withdrew $6,200 cash from the company for personal use.
29   The company purchased $800 of additional office supplies on credit.
30   The company paid $700 cash for this month's utility bill.

Required

1. Prepare general journal entries to record these transactions (use the account titles listed in part 2).

2. Open the following ledger accounts—their account numbers are in parentheses (use the balance column format): Cash (101); Accounts Receivable (106); Office Supplies (124); Prepaid Insurance (128); Prepaid Rent (131); Office Equipment (163); Accounts Payable (201); G. Bauer, Capital (301); G. Bauer, Withdrawals (302); Services Revenue (403); and Utilities Expense (690). Post the journal entries from part 1 to the ledger accounts and enter the balance after each posting.

3. Prepare a trial balance as at the end of April.

PROBLEM SET A

Problem 2-1A
Preparing and posting journal
entries; preparing a trial balance
C3 C4 A1 P1 P2

e**X**cel
www.mheducation.asia/olc/wildkwokFAP

Check   (2) Ending balances: Cash,
$73,900; Accounts Receivable,
$4,240; Accounts Payable, $800
(3) Total debits, $137,440

Problem 2-2A

Preparing and posting journal
entries; preparing a trial balance

C3 C4 A1 P1 P2

Shelton Engineering completed the following transactions in the month of June.

a. Shana Shelton, the owner, invested $105,000 cash, office equipment with a value of $6,000, and $45,000 of drafting equipment to launch the company.

b. The company purchased land worth $54,000 for an office by paying $5,400 cash and signing a long-term note payable for $48,600.

c. The company purchased a portable building with $75,000 cash and moved it onto the land acquired in *b*.

d. The company paid $6,000 cash for the premium on an 18-month insurance policy.

e. The company completed and delivered a set of plans for a client and collected $5,700 cash.

f. The company purchased $22,500 of additional drafting equipment by paying $10,500 cash and signing a long-term note payable for $12,000.

g. The company completed $12,000 of engineering services for a client. This amount is to be received in 30 days.

h. The company purchased $2,250 of additional office equipment on credit.

i. The company completed engineering services for $18,000 on credit.

j. The company received a bill for rent of equipment that was used on a recently completed job. The $1,200 rent cost must be paid within 30 days.

k. The company collected $7,200 cash in partial payment from the client described in transaction *g*.

l. The company paid $1,500 cash for wages to a drafting assistant.

m. The company paid $2,250 cash to settle the account payable created in transaction *h*.

n. The company paid $675 cash for minor maintenance of its drafting equipment.

o. S. Shelton withdrew $9,360 cash from the company for personal use.

p. The company paid $1,500 cash for wages to a drafting assistant.

q. The company paid $3,000 cash for advertisements in the local newspaper during June.

Required

1. Prepare general journal entries to record these transactions (use the account titles listed in part 2).

Check   (2) Ending balances: Cash,
$2,715; Accounts Receivable,
$22,800; Accounts Payable, $1,200

2. Open the following ledger accounts—their account numbers are in parentheses (use the balance column format): Cash (101); Accounts Receivable (106); Prepaid Insurance (108); Office Equipment (163); Drafting Equipment (164); Building (170); Land (172); Accounts Payable (201); Notes Payable (250); S. Shelton, Capital (301); S. Shelton, Withdrawals (302); Engineering Fees Earned (402); Wages Expense (601); Equipment Rental Expense (602); Advertising Expense (603); and Repairs Expense (604). Post the journal entries from part 1 to the accounts and enter the balance after each posting.

(3) Trial balance totals,
$253,500

3. Prepare a trial balance as at the end of June.

Problem 2-3A

Computing net profit from
equity analysis, preparing a
statement of financial position,
and computing the debt ratio

C2 A1 A2 P3

www.mheducation.asia/olc/wildkwokFAP

The accounting records of Fabiano Distribution show the following assets and liabilities as at December 31, 2010 and 2011.

December 31	2010	2011
Cash	$ 52,500	$ 18,750
Accounts receivable	28,500	22,350
Office supplies	4,500	3,300
Office equipment	138,000	147,000
Trucks	54,000	54,000
Building	0	180,000
Land	0	45,000
Accounts payable	7,500	37,500
Note payable	0	105,000

Late in December 2011, the business purchased a small office building and land for $225,000. It paid $120,000 cash toward the purchase and a $105,000 note payable was signed for the balance. Mr. Fabiano had to invest $35,000 cash in the business to enable it to pay the $120,000 cash. Mr. Fabiano withdraws $3,000 cash per month for personal use.

Required

1. Prepare statements of financial position for the business as at December 31, 2010 and 2011. (*Hint:* Report only total equity on the statement of financial position and remember that total equity equals the difference between assets and liabilities.)

2. By comparing equity amounts from the statements of financial position and using the additional information presented in this problem, prepare a calculation to show how much net profit was earned by the business during 2011.

3. Compute the 2011 year-end debt ratio for the business.

Check (2) Net profit, $58,900

(3) Debt ratio, 30.29%

Santo Birch opens a Web consulting business called Show-Me-the-Money and completes the following transactions in its first month of operations.

March	1	Birch invests $150,000 cash along with office equipment valued at $22,000 in the company.
	2	The company prepaid $6,000 cash for twelve months' rent for office space. (*Hint:* Debit Prepaid Rent for $6,000.)
	3	The company made credit purchases for $3,000 in office equipment and $1,200 in office supplies. Payment is due within 10 days.
	6	The company completed services for a client and immediately received $4,000 cash.
	9	The company completed a $7,500 project for a client, who must pay within 30 days.
	13	The company paid $4,200 cash to settle the account payable created on March 3.
	19	The company paid $5,000 cash for the premium on a 12-month insurance policy. (*Hint:* Debit Prepaid Insurance for $5,000.)
	22	The company received $3,500 cash as partial payment for the work completed on March 9.
	25	The company completed work for another client for $3,820 on credit.
	29	Birch withdrew $5,100 cash from the company for personal use.
	30	The company purchased $600 of additional office supplies on credit.
	31	The company paid $200 cash for this month's utility bill.

Problem 2-4A

Preparing and posting journal entries; preparing a trial balance

C3 C4 A1 P1 P2

Required

1. Prepare general journal entries to record these transactions (use account titles listed in part 2).

2. Open the following ledger accounts—their account numbers are in parentheses (use the balance column format): Cash (101); Accounts Receivable (106); Office Supplies (124); Prepaid Insurance (128); Prepaid Rent (131); Office Equipment (163); Accounts Payable (201); S. Birch, Capital (301); S. Birch, Withdrawals (302); Services Revenue (403); and Utilities Expense (690). Post journal entries from part 1 to the ledger accounts and enter the balance after each posting.

3. Prepare a trial balance as at April 30.

Check (2) Ending balances:
Cash, $137,000; Accounts
Receivable, $7,820; Accounts
Payable, $600

(3) Total debits, $187,920

Business transactions completed by Eric Pense during the month of September are as follows.

a. Pense invested $23,000 cash along with office equipment valued at $12,000 in a new sole proprietorship named EP Consulting.

b. The company purchased land valued at $8,000 and a building valued at $33,000. The purchase is paid with $15,000 cash and a long-term note payable for $26,000.

c. The company purchased $600 of office supplies on credit.

d. Pense invested his personal automobile in the company. The automobile has a value of $7,000 and is to be used exclusively in the business.

e. The company purchased $1,100 of additional office equipment on credit.

f. The company paid $800 cash salary to an assistant.

g. The company provided services to a client and collected $2,700 cash.

h. The company paid $430 cash for this month's utilities.

i. The company paid $600 cash to settle the account payable created in transaction *c*.

j. The company purchased $4,000 of new office equipment by paying $4,000 cash.

k. The company completed $2,400 of services for a client, who must pay within 30 days.

l. The company paid $800 cash salary to an assistant.

m. The company received $1,000 cash in partial payment on the receivable created in transaction *k*.

n. Pense withdrew $1,050 cash from the company for personal use.

Problem 2-5A

Recording transactions; posting to ledger; preparing a trial balance

C3 A1 P1 P2

Required

1. Prepare general journal entries to record these transactions (use account titles listed in part 2).
2. Open the following ledger accounts—their account numbers are in parentheses (use the balance column format): Cash (101); Accounts Receivable (106); Office Supplies (108); Office Equipment (163); Automobiles (164); Building (170); Land (172); Accounts Payable (201); Notes Payable (250); E. Pense, Capital (301); E. Pense, Withdrawals (302); Fees Earned (402); Salaries Expense (601); and Utilities Expense (602). Post the journal entries from part 1 to the ledger accounts and enter the balance after each posting.

3. Prepare a trial balance as at the end of September.

Problem 2-6A
Analyzing account balances and reconstructing transactions

C1 C3 A1 P2

Carlos Beltran started an engineering firm called Beltran Engineering. He began operations and completed seven transactions in May, which included his initial investment of $17,000 cash. After those seven transactions, the ledger included the following accounts with normal balances.

Cash	$26,660
Office supplies	660
Prepaid insurance	3,200
Office equipment	16,500
Accounts payable	16,500
C. Beltran, Capital	17,000
C. Beltran, Withdrawals	3,740
Engineering fees earned	24,000
Rent expense	6,740

Required

1. Prepare a trial balance for this business as at the end of May.

Analysis Components

2. Analyze the accounts and their balances and prepare a list that describes each of the seven most likely transactions and their amounts.

3. Prepare a report of cash received and cash paid showing how the seven transactions in part 2 yield the $26,660 ending Cash balance.

PROBLEM SET B

Problem 2-1B
Preparing and posting journal entries; preparing a trial balance

C3 C4 A1 P1 P2

Shaw Management Services opens for business and completes these transactions in November.

Nov. 1   Kita Shaw, the owner, invested $30,000 cash along with $15,000 of office equipment in the company.
      2   The company prepaid $4,500 cash for six months' rent for an office. (*Hint:* Debit Prepaid Rent for $4,500.)
      4   The company made credit purchases of office equipment for $2,500 and of office supplies for $600. Payment is due within 10 days.
      8   The company completed work for a client and immediately received $3,400 cash.
    12   The company completed a $10,200 project for a client, who must pay within 30 days.
    13   The company paid $3,100 cash to settle the payable created on November 4.
    19   The company paid $1,800 cash for the premium on a 24-month insurance policy.
    22   The company received $5,200 cash as partial payment for the work completed on November 12.
    24   The company completed work for another client for $1,750 on credit.
    28   K. Shaw withdrew $5,300 cash from the company for personal use.
    29   The company purchased $249 of additional office supplies on credit.
    30   The company paid $531 cash for this month's utility bill.

Required

1. Prepare general journal entries to record these transactions (use account titles listed in part 2).

2. Open the following ledger accounts—their account numbers are in parentheses (use the balance column format): Cash (101); Accounts Receivable (106); Office Supplies (124); Prepaid Insurance (128); Prepaid Rent (131); Office Equipment (163); Accounts Payable (201); K. Shaw, Capital (301); K. Shaw, Withdrawals (302); Services Revenue (403); and Utilities Expense (690). Post the journal entries from part 1 to the ledger accounts and enter the balance after each posting.

3. Prepare a trial balance as at the end of November.

At the beginning of April, Brooke Gable launched a custom computer solutions company called Softways. The company had the following transactions during April.

a. Brooke Gable invested $45,000 cash, office equipment with a value of $4,500, and $28,000 of computer equipment in the company.

b. The company purchased land worth $24,000 for an office by paying $4,800 cash and signing a long-term note payable for $19,200.

c. The company purchased a portable building with $21,000 cash and moved it onto the land acquired in *b*.

d. The company paid $6,600 cash for the premium on a two-year insurance policy.

e. The company provided services to a client and immediately collected $3,200 cash.

f. The company purchased $3,500 of additional computer equipment by paying $700 cash and signing a long-term note payable for $2,800.

g. The company completed $3,750 of services for a client. This amount is to be received within 30 days.

h. The company purchased $750 of additional office equipment on credit.

i. The company completed client services for $9,200 on credit.

j. The company received a bill for rent of a computer testing device that was used on a recently completed job. The $320 rent cost must be paid within 30 days.

k. The company collected $4,600 cash in partial payment from the client described in transaction *i*.

l. The company paid $1,600 cash for wages to an assistant.

m. The company paid $750 cash to settle the payable created in transaction *h*.

n. The company paid $425 cash for minor maintenance of the company's computer equipment.

o. B. Gable withdrew $3,875 cash from the company for personal use.

p. The company paid $1,600 cash for wages to an assistant.

q. The company paid $800 cash for advertisements in the local newspaper during April.

Required

1. Prepare general journal entries to record these transactions (use account titles listed in part 2).

2. Open the following ledger accounts—their account numbers are in parentheses (use the balance column format): Cash (101); Accounts Receivable (106); Prepaid Insurance (108); Office Equipment (163); Computer Equipment (164); Building (170); Land (172); Accounts Payable (201); Notes Payable (250); B. Gable, Capital (301); B. Gable, Withdrawals (302); Fees Earned (402); Wages Expense (601); Computer Rental Expense (602); Advertising Expense (603); and Repairs Expense (604). Post the journal entries from part 1 to the accounts and enter the balance after each posting.

3. Prepare a trial balance as at the end of April.

Problem 2-2B
Preparing and posting journal entries; preparing a trial balance
C3 C4 A1 P1 P2

Check   (2) Ending balances: Cash, $10,650; Accounts Receivable, $8,350; Accounts Payable, $320

(3) Trial balance totals, $115,970

The accounting records of Schmit Co. show the following assets and liabilities as at December 31, 2010 and 2011.

December 31	2010	2011
Cash	$14,000	$ 10,000
Accounts receivable	25,000	30,000
Office supplies	10,000	12,500
Office equipment	60,000	60,000
Machinery	30,500	30,500
Building	0	260,000
Land	0	65,000
Accounts payable	5,000	15,000
Note payable	0	260,000

Late in December 2011, the business purchased a small office building and land for $325,000. It paid $65,000 cash toward the purchase and a $260,000 note payable was signed for the balance. Janet Schmit, the owner, had to invest an additional $25,000 cash to enable it to pay the $65,000 cash toward the purchase. The owner withdraws $1,000 cash per month for personal use.

Required

1. Prepare statements of financial position for the business as at December 31, 2010 and 2011. (*Hint:* Report only total equity on the statement of financial position and remember that total equity equals the difference between assets and liabilities.)

Problem 2-3B
Computing net profit from equity analysis, preparing a statement of financial position, and computing the debt ratio
C2 A1 A2 P3

2. By comparing equity amounts from the statements of financial position and using the additional information presented in the problem, prepare a calculation to show how much net profit was earned by the business during 2011.

3. Calculate the December 31, 2011, debt ratio for the business.

Problem 2-4B

Preparing and posting journal entries; preparing a trial balance

C3 C4 A1 P1 P2

Lummus Management Services opens for business and completes these transactions in September.

Sept. 1   Rhonda Lummus, the owner, invests $28,000 cash along with office equipment valued at $25,000 in the company.

2   The company prepaid $10,500 cash for 12 months' rent for office space. (*Hint:* Debit Prepaid Rent for $10,500.)

4   The company made credit purchases for $9,000 in office equipment and $1,200 in office supplies. Payment is due within 10 days.

8   The company completed work for a client and immediately received $2,600 cash.

12   The company completed a $13,400 project for a client, who must pay within 30 days.

13   The company paid $10,200 cash to settle the payable created on September 4.

19   The company paid $5,200 cash for the premium on an 18-month insurance policy. (*Hint:* Debit Prepaid Insurance for $5,200.)

22   The company received $7,800 cash as partial payment for the work completed on September 12.

24   The company completed work for another client for $1,900 on credit.

28   Lummus withdrew $5,300 cash from the company for personal use.

29   The company purchased $1,700 of additional office supplies on credit.

30   The company paid $460 cash for this month's utility bill.

Required

1. Prepare general journal entries to record these transactions (use account titles listed in part 2).

2. Open the following ledger accounts—their account numbers are in parentheses (use the balance column format): Cash (101); Accounts Receivable (106); Office Supplies (124); Prepaid Insurance (128); Prepaid Rent (131); Office Equipment (163); Accounts Payable (201); R. Lummus, Capital (301); R. Lummus, Withdrawals (302); Service Fees Earned (401); and Utilities Expense (690). Post journal entries from part 1 to the ledger accounts and enter the balance after each posting.

3. Prepare a trial balance as at the end of September.

Problem 2-5B

Recording transactions; posting to ledger; preparing a trial balance

C3 A1 P1 P2

Cooke Consulting completed the following transactions during June.

a. Chris Cooke, the owner, invested $80,000 cash along with office equipment valued at $30,000 in the new company.

b. The company purchased land valued at $30,000 and a building valued at $170,000. The purchase is paid with $40,000 cash and a long-term note payable for $160,000.

c. The company purchased $2,400 of office supplies on credit.

d. C. Cooke invested his personal automobile in the company. The automobile has a value of $18,000 and is to be used exclusively in the business.

e. The company purchased $6,000 of additional office equipment on credit.

f. The company paid $1,500 cash salary to an assistant.

g. The company provided services to a client and collected $6,000 cash.

h. The company paid $800 cash for this month's utilities.

i. The company paid $2,400 cash to settle the payable created in transaction c.

j. The company purchased $20,000 of new office equipment by paying $20,000 cash.

k. The company completed $5,200 of services for a client, who must pay within 30 days.

l. The company paid $1,500 cash salary to an assistant.

m. The company received $3,800 cash in partial payment on the receivable created in transaction k.

n. C. Cooke withdrew $6,400 cash from the company for personal use.

Required

1. Prepare general journal entries to record these transactions (use account titles listed in part 2).

2. Open the following ledger accounts—their account numbers are in parentheses (use the balance column format): Cash (101); Accounts Receivable (106); Office Supplies (108); Office Equipment (163); Automobiles (164); Building (170); Land (172); Accounts Payable (201); Notes Payable (250); C. Cooke, Capital (301); C. Cooke, Withdrawals (302); Fees Earned (402); Salaries Expense (601); and Utilities Expense (602). Post the journal entries from part 1 to the ledger accounts and enter the balance after each posting.

3. Prepare a trial balance as at the end of June.

Michael Gould started a Web consulting firm called Gould Solutions. He began operations and completed seven transactions in April that resulted in the following accounts, which all have normal balances.

Cash	$12,485
Office supplies	560
Prepaid rent	1,500
Office equipment	11,450
Accounts payable	11,450
M. Gould, Capital	10,000
M. Gould, Withdrawals	6,200
Consulting fees earned	16,400
Operating expenses	5,655

Problem 2-6B
Analyzing account balances and reconstructing transactions

C1 C3 A1 P2

Required

1. Prepare a trial balance for this business as at the end of April.

Analysis Component

2. Analyze the accounts and their balances and prepare a list that describes each of the seven most likely transactions and their amounts.

3. Prepare a report of cash received and cash paid showing how the seven transactions in part 2 yield the $12,485 ending Cash balance.

Check   (1) Trial balance total, $37,850

(3) Cash paid, $13,915

(This serial problem started in Chapter 1 and continues through most of the chapters. If the Chapter 1 segment was not completed, the problem can begin at this point.)

SERIAL PROBLEM
Business Solutions
A1 P1 P2

SP 2   On October 1, 2015, Santana Rey launched a computer services company called **Business Solutions,** which provides consulting services, computer system installations, and custom program development. Rey adopts the calendar year for reporting purposes and expects to prepare the company's first set of financial statements on December 31, 2015. The company's initial chart of accounts follows.

Account	No.	Account	No.
Cash	101	S. Rey, Capital	301
Accounts Receivable	106	S. Rey, Withdrawals	302
Computer Supplies	126	Computer Services Revenue	403
Prepaid Insurance	128	Wages Expense	623
Prepaid Rent	131	Advertising Expense	655
Office Equipment	163	Mileage Expense	676
Computer Equipment	167	Miscellaneous Expenses	677
Accounts Payable	201	Repairs Expense—Computer	684

Required

1. Prepare journal entries to record each of the following transactions for Business Solutions.

Oct. 1   S. Rey invested $45,000 cash, a $20,000 computer system, and $8,000 of office equipment in the company.
   2   The company paid $3,300 cash for four months' rent. (*Hint:* Debit Prepaid Rent for $3,300.)
   3   The company purchased $1,420 of computer supplies on credit from Harris Office Products.
   5   The company paid $2,220 cash for one year's premium on a property and liability insurance policy. (*Hint:* Debit Prepaid Insurance for $2,220.)
   6   The company billed Easy Leasing $4,800 for services performed in installing a new Web server.
   8   The company paid $1,420 cash for the computer supplies purchased from Harris Office Products on October 3.
   10   The company hired Lyn Addie as a part-time assistant for $125 per day, as needed.
   12   The company billed Easy Leasing another $1,400 for services performed.

15   The company received $4,800 cash from Easy Leasing as partial payment on its account.
17   The company paid $805 cash to repair computer equipment that was damaged when moving it.
20   The company paid $1,728 cash for advertisements published in the local newspaper.
22   The company received $1,400 cash from Easy Leasing on its account.
28   The company billed IFM Company $5,208 for services performed.
31   The company paid $875 cash for Lyn Addie's wages for seven days' work.
31   S. Rey withdrew $3,600 cash from the company for personal use.

Nov. 1   The company reimbursed S. Rey in cash for business automobile mileage allowance (Rey logged 1,000 miles at $0.32 per mile).
2   The company received $4,633 cash from Liu Corporation for computer services performed.
5   The company purchased computer supplies for $1,125 cash from Harris Office Products.
8   The company billed Gomez Co. $5,668 for services performed.
13   The company received notification from Alex's Engineering Co. that Business Solutions' bid of $3,950 for an upcoming project is accepted.
18   The company received $2,208 cash from IFM Company as partial payment of the October 28 bill.
22   The company donated $250 cash to the United Way in the company's name.
24   The company completed work for Alex's Engineering Co. and sent it a bill for $3,950.
25   The company sent another bill to IFM Company for the past-due amount of $3,000.
28   The company reimbursed S. Rey in cash for business automobile mileage (1,200 miles at $0.32 per mile).
30   The company paid $1,750 cash for Lyn Addie's wages for 14 days' work.
30   S. Rey withdrew $2,000 cash from the company for personal use.

Check (2) Cash, Nov. 30 bal., $38,264
(3) Trial bal. totals, $98,659

2. Open ledger accounts (in balance column format) and post the journal entries from part 1 to them.

3. Prepare a trial balance as at the end of November.

Beyond the Numbers

REPORTING IN ACTION

A1 A2

BTN 2-1   Refer to Adidas' financial statements in Appendix A for the following questions.

Required
Round amounts to EUR millions.

1. What amount of total liabilities does it report for each of the financial years ended December 31, 2013 and December 31, 2012?

2. What amount of total assets does it report for each of the financial years ended December 31, 2013 and December 31, 2012?

3. Compute its debt ratio for each of the financial years ended December 31, 2013 and December 31, 2012.

4. In which financial year did it employ more financial leverage (December 31, 2013 or December 31, 2012)? Explain.

Fast Forward

5. Access Adidas' latest financial statements for financial year ending after December 31, 2013 from its Website (http://www.adidas-group.com/en/investors/financial-reports/). Recompute its debt ratio for any subsequent year's data and compare it with the December 31, 2013 debt ratio.

COMPARATIVE ANALYSIS

A1 A2

BTN 2-2   Key comparative figures (in EUR millions) for both Adidas and Puma are as follows:

Key Figures	Adidas (in EUR millions)		Puma (in EUR millions)	
	Current Year	Prior Year	Current Year	Prior Year
Total liabilities	6,118	6,360	811.3	933
Total assets	11,599	11,651	2,308.6	2,530.3

Show the ratios in percents and round to one decimal place each.

1. What is the debt ratio for Adidas in the current year and for the prior year?

2. What is the debt ratio for Puma in the current year and for the prior year?

3. Which of the two companies has the higher degree of financial leverage? What does this imply?

BTN 2-3   Review the *Decision Ethics* case from the first part of this chapter involving the cashier. The guidance answer suggests that you should not comply with the assistant manager's request.

ETHICS CHALLENGE
C1

Required

Propose and evaluate two other courses of action you might consider, and explain why.

BTN 2-4   Mora Stanley is an aspiring entrepreneur and your friend. She is having difficulty understanding the purposes of financial statements and how they fit together across time.

COMMUNICATING IN PRACTICE
C1 C2 A1 P3

Required

Write a one-page memorandum to Stanley explaining the purposes of the four financial statements and how they are linked across time.

BTN 2-5   Access **L'Oréal's** 2013 annual report at **www.loreal-finance.com/eng/annual-report** and answer the following questions using its consolidated financial statements.

TAKING IT TO THE NET
A1

Required

1. What are the amounts of its net profit attributable to owners of the company for financial years 2011 to 2013?
2. Does L'Oréal's operations provide cash or use cash for each of these three years? What are the amounts?
3. If L'Oréal has a 2013 net profit attributable to owners of the company of EUR 2,958.2 million and 2013 net cash provided by operating activities of EUR 3,750.2 million, how is it possible that its cash balance at December 31, 2013, increases by only EUR 784.1 million relative to its balance at December 31, 2012?

BTN 2-6   The expanded accounting equation consists of assets, liabilities, capital, withdrawals, revenues, and expenses. It can be used to reveal insights into changes in a company's financial position.

TEAMWORK IN ACTION
C1 C2 C4 A1

Required

1. Form *learning teams* of six (or more) members. Each team member must select one of the six components and each team must have at least one expert on each component: (*a*) assets, (*b*) liabilities, (*c*) capital, (*d*) withdrawals, (*e*) revenues, and (*f*) expenses.
2. Form *expert teams* of individuals who selected the same component in part 1. Expert teams are to draft a report that each expert will present to his or her learning team addressing the following:
   a. Identify for its component the (i) increase and decrease side of the account and (ii) normal balance side of the account.
   b. Describe a transaction, with amounts, that increases its component.
   c. Using the transaction and amounts in (*b*), verify the equality of the accounting equation and then explain any effects on the income statement and statement of cash flows.
   d. Describe a transaction, with amounts, that decreases its component.
   e. Using the transaction and amounts in (*d*), verify the equality of the accounting equation and then explain any effects on the income statement and statement of cash flows.
3. Each expert should return to his/her learning team. In rotation, each member presents his/her expert team's report to the learning team. Team discussion is encouraged.

BTN 2-7   Assume Elizabeth Seah of **Haru** plans on expanding her store to accommodate more customers. She is considering financing her expansion in one of two ways: (1) contributing more of her own funds to the business or (2) borrowing the funds from a bank.

ENTREPRENEURIAL DECISION
A1 A2 P3

Required

Identify the issues that Elizabeth should consider when trying to decide on the method for financing her expansion.

**ENTREPRENEURIAL
DECISION**

A1 A2 P3

BTN 2-8   Lisa Langely is a young entrepreneur who operates Langely Music Services, offering singing lessons and instruction on musical instruments. Langely wishes to expand but needs a $15,000 loan. The bank requests Langely to prepare a statement of financial position and key financial ratios. Langely has not kept formal records but is able to provide the following accounts and their amounts as at December 31, 2011.

Cash...............	$ 1,800	Accounts Receivable....	$4,800	Prepaid Insurance	$ 750
Prepaid Rent	4,700	Store Supplies	3,300	Equipment	25,000
Accounts Payable	1,100	Unearned Lesson Fees ...	7,800	Total Equity*	31,450
Annual net profit	20,000				

* The total equity amount reflects all owner investments, withdrawals, revenues, and expenses as at December 31, 2011.

Required

1. Prepare a statement of financial position as at December 31, 2011, for Langely Music Services. (Report only the total equity amount on the statement of financial position.)

2. Compute Langely's debt ratio and its return on assets (the latter ratio is defined in Chapter 1). Assume average assets equal its ending balance.

3. Do you believe the prospects of a $15,000 bank loan are good? Why or why not?

HITTING THE ROAD

C1

BTN 2-9   Instead of obtaining an accounting degree from a college or university, a person aspiring to be an accountant can also obtain a professional accounting qualification from accredited examination bodies around the world. Visit the Websites www.accaglobal.com and www.cpaaustralia.com.au. You should at least be familiar with the qualification processes and the employment opportunities from holding these accounting qualifications.

GLOBAL DECISION

A2

BTN 2-10   361 Degrees competes with Adidas and Puma in the same product industry. Key financial ratios for these businesses for 2013 are as follows.

Financial Ratio	361 Degrees	Adidas	Puma
Return on assets........	2.9%	6.8%	0.2%
Debt ratio.............	33.4%	52.7%	35.1%

Required

1. Which company is most profitable according to its return on assets?

2. Which company is most risky according to the debt ratio?

3. Which company deserves increased investment based on a joint analysis of return of assets and the debt ratio? Explain.

ANSWERS TO MULTIPLE CHOICE QUIZ

1. b; debit Utility Expense for $700, and credit Cash for $700.

2. a; debit Cash for $2,500, and credit Unearned Lawn Service Fees for $2,500.

3. c; debit Cash for $250,000, debit Land for $500,000, and credit L. Shue, Capital for $750,000.

4. d

5. e; Debt ratio = $400,000/$1,000,000 = 40%

Adjusting Accounts and Preparing Financial Statements

A Look Back

Chapter 2 explained the analysis and recording of transactions. We showed how to apply and interpret company accounts, T-accounts, double-entry accounting, ledgers, postings, and trial balances.

A Look at This Chapter

This chapter explains the timing of reports and the need to adjust accounts. Adjusting accounts is important for recognizing revenues and expenses in the proper period. We describe the adjusted trial balance and how it is used to prepare financial statements.

A Look Ahead

Chapter 4 highlights the completion of the accounting cycle. We explain the important final steps in the accounting process. These include closing procedures, the post-closing trial balance, and reversing entries.

Learning Objectives

CAP

CONCEPTUAL

C1 Explain the importance of periodic reporting and the time period assumption. (p. 94)

C2 Explain accrual accounting and how it improves financial statements. (p. 95)

C3 Identify the types of adjustments and their purpose. (p. 96)

ANALYTICAL

A1 Explain how accounting adjustments link to financial statements. (p. 105)

A2 Compute profit margin and describe its use in analyzing company performance. (p. 108)

PROCEDURAL

P1 Prepare and explain adjusting entries. (p. 97)

P2 Explain and prepare an adjusted trial balance. (p. 106)

P3 Prepare financial statements from an adjusted trial balance. (p. 106)

P4 *Appendix 3A*—Explain the alternatives in accounting for prepaids. (p. 115)

"What I really love about managing Lunch Actually is knowing that I have made a difference in someone's life."—**VIOLET LIM**

Decision Insight

Lunch? No—Love . . . at Last

"I would be lying if I said that my childhood dream was to be a matchmaker!" exclaims Violet Lim. In fact, with a law degree and a Masters degree from the London School of Economics, Violet had her pick of jobs. Her first job was with an international bank, and it was there that she made a puzzling observation—many attractive and eligible colleagues were single, and not even dating, because they were married to the bank! So Violet set about changing this state of affairs, by starting **Lunch Actually (www.lunchactually.com)**, the company that she owns and runs with her husband, Jamie Lee. "We specialize in arranging one-to-one personalized dates for busy working professionals," says Violet. "All dates are pre-screened, pre-matched, and pre-arranged. We do all the work, and our clients just need to turn up and enjoy their dates." The concept of lunch dating, already popular in the United Kingdom, the United States, and Australia, took the local scene by storm when Violet introduced it in Singapore. Lunch Actually has offices in Singapore, Malaysia, and Hong Kong, with plans of expanding to two more Asian cities in the next few years.

For Lunch Actually to be successful, Violet has to oversee revenues and expenses. "Our membership package has two elements—one is a nonrefundable registration fee, which is recognized immediately upon the sale, and the other is the guaranteed-date segment, which we recognize as the package is being fulfilled," she explains. "Due to the upfront nature of the membership packages, the revenues of the company are lower (due to recognition) than the cash flow received from sales. There is a membership liability in the statement of financial position, which is the amount we owe to the members that has not been fulfilled yet."

Violet outsources the accounting, getting quarterly updates to see how the financial books are looking, so that she can focus on what she loves doing best—bringing people together. "When you know that some of the couples would never have met because they come from such diverse backgrounds," says Violet, "being able to get them together, seeing them eventually tie the knot, and having kids . . . it's such a great feeling!"

Financial statements reflect revenues when earned and expenses when incurred. This is known as *accrual accounting,* which was the focus of Chapter 2. We showed how companies use accounting systems to collect information about *external* transactions and events. We also explained how journals, ledgers, and other tools are useful in preparing financial statements. This chapter describes the accounting process for producing useful information involving *internal* transactions and events. An important part of this process is adjusting the account balances so that financial statements at the end of a reporting period reflect the effects of all transactions. We then explain the important steps in preparing financial statements.

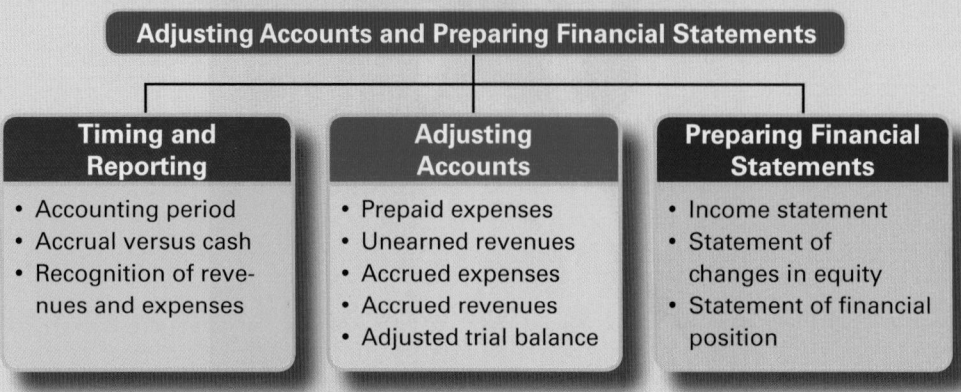

Adjusting Accounts and Preparing Financial Statements

Timing and Reporting
- Accounting period
- Accrual versus cash
- Recognition of revenues and expenses

Adjusting Accounts
- Prepaid expenses
- Unearned revenues
- Accrued expenses
- Accrued revenues
- Adjusted trial balance

Preparing Financial Statements
- Income statement
- Statement of changes in equity
- Statement of financial position

TIMING AND REPORTING

This section describes the importance of reporting accounting information at regular intervals and its impact for recording revenues and expenses.

The Accounting Period

C1 Explain the importance of periodic reporting and the time period assumption.

The value of information is often linked to its timeliness. Useful information must reach decision makers frequently and promptly. To provide timely information, accounting systems prepare reports at regular intervals. This results in an accounting process impacted by the time period (or periodicity) assumption. The **time period assumption** presumes that an organization's activities can be divided into specific time periods such as a month, a three-month quarter, a six-month interval, or a year. Exhibit 3.1 shows various **accounting,** or *reporting,* **periods.** Most organizations use a year as their primary accounting period. Reports covering a one-year period are known as **annual financial statements.** Many organizations also prepare **interim financial statements** covering one, three, or six months of activity.

"RIM announces annual income of . . ."

EXHIBIT 3.1

Accounting Periods

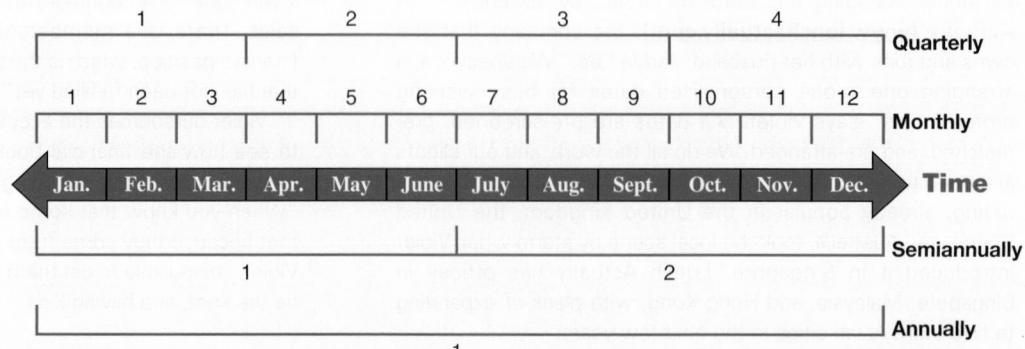

The annual reporting period is not always a calendar year ending on December 31. An organization can adopt a **financial year** consisting of any 12 consecutive months. It is also acceptable to adopt an annual reporting period of 52 weeks. For example, **Gap**'s fiscal year consistently ends the final week of January or the first week of February each year.

Companies with little seasonal variation in sales often choose the calendar year as their fiscal year. The financial statements of **The Kellogg Company** (the company that controls characters such as Tony the Tiger, Snap! Crackle! Pop!, and Keebler Elf) reflect a fiscal year that ends on the Saturday nearest December 31. Companies experiencing seasonal variations in sales often choose a **natural business year** end, which is when sales activities are at their lowest level for the year. The natural business year for retailers such as **Walmart, Target**, and **Macy**'s usually ends around January 31, after the holiday season.

Accrual Basis versus Cash Basis

After external transactions and events are recorded, several accounts still need adjustments before their balances appear in financial statements. This need arises because internal transactions and events remain unrecorded. **Accrual basis accounting** uses the adjusting process to recognize revenues when earned and expenses when incurred (matched with revenues).

C2	Explain accrual accounting and how it improves financial statements.

Cash basis accounting recognizes revenues when cash is received and records expenses when cash is paid. This means that cash basis net profit for a period is the difference between cash receipts and cash payments. Cash basis accounting is not consistent with generally accepted accounting principles.

It is commonly held that accrual accounting better reflects business performance than information about cash receipts and payments. Accrual accounting also increases the *comparability* of financial statements from one period to another. Yet cash basis accounting is useful for several business decisions—which is the reason companies must report a statement of cash flows.

To see the difference between these two accounting systems, let's consider FastForward's Prepaid Insurance account. FastForward paid $2,400 for 24 months of insurance coverage that began on December 1, 2015. Accrual accounting requires that $100 of insurance expense be reported on December 2015's income statement. Another $1,200 of expense is reported in year 2016, and the remaining $1,100 is reported as expense in the first 11 months of 2017. Exhibit 3.2 illustrates this allocation of insurance cost across these three years. Any unexpired premium is reported as a Prepaid Insurance asset on the accrual basis statement of financial position.

EXHIBIT 3.2

Accrual Accounting for Allocating Prepaid Insurance to Expense

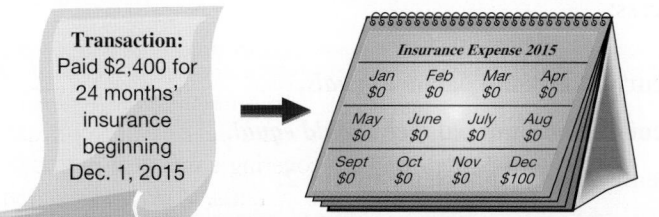

Alternatively, a cash basis income statement for December 2015 reports insurance expense of $2,400, as shown in Exhibit 3.3. The cash basis income statements for years 2016 and 2017 report no insurance expense. The cash basis statement of financial position never reports an insurance asset because it is immediately expensed. This shows that cash basis income for 2015–2017 fails to match the cost of insurance with the insurance benefits received for those years and months.

EXHIBIT 3.3

Cash Accounting for Allocating Prepaid Insurance to Expense

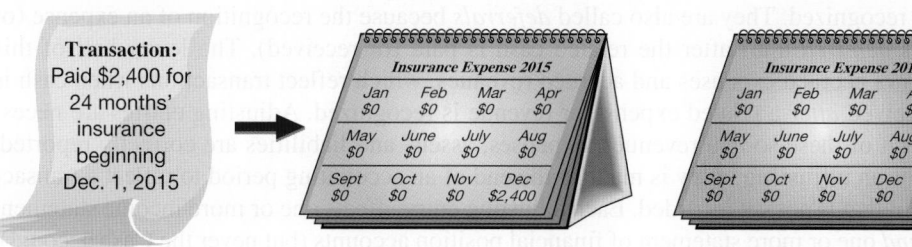

Recognizing Revenues and Expenses

We use the time period assumption to divide a company's activities into specific time periods, but not all activities are complete when financial statements are prepared. Thus, adjustments often are required to get correct account balances.

We rely on two principles in the adjusting process: revenue recognition and expense recognition (the latter is often referred to as matching). Chapter 1 explained that the *revenue recognition principle* requires that revenue be recorded when earned, not before and not after. Most companies earn revenue when they provide services and products to customers. A major goal of the adjusting process is to have revenue recognized (reported) in the time period when it is earned. The **expense recognition** (or **matching**) **principle** aims to record expenses in the same accounting period as the revenues that are earned as a result of those expenses. This matching of expenses with the revenue benefits is a major part of the adjusting process.

Matching expenses with revenues often requires us to predict certain events. When we use financial statements, we must understand that they require estimates and therefore include measures that are not precise. **Walt Disney**'s annual report explains that its production costs from movies, such as *Alice in Wonderland,* are matched to revenues based on a ratio of current revenues from the movie divided by its predicted total revenues.

Quick Check   Answers — p. 115

1. Describe a company's annual reporting period.
2. Why do companies prepare interim financial statements?
3. What two accounting principles most directly drive the adjusting process?
4. Is cash basis accounting consistent with the matching principle? Why or why not?
5. If your company pays a $4,800 premium on April 1, 2015, for two years' insurance coverage, how much insurance expense is reported in 2016 using cash basis accounting?

ADJUSTING ACCOUNTS

Adjusting accounts is a 3-step process:

> **Step 1:** Determine what the current account balance *equals*.
>
> **Step 2:** Determine what the current account balance *should equal*.
>
> **Step 3:** Record an adjusting entry to get from step *1* to step *2*.

Framework for Adjustments

Adjustments are necessary for transactions and events that extend over more than one period. It is helpful to group adjustments by the timing of cash receipt or cash payment in relation to the recognition of the related revenues or expenses. Exhibit 3.4 identifies four types of adjustments.

The upper half of this exhibit shows prepaid expenses (including depreciation) and unearned revenues, which reflect transactions when cash is paid or received *before* a related expense or revenue is recognized. They are also called *deferrals* because the recognition of an expense (or revenue) is *deferred* until after the related cash is paid (or received). The lower half of this exhibit shows accrued expenses and accrued revenues, which reflect transactions when cash is paid or received *after* a related expense or revenue is recognized. Adjusting entries are necessary for each of these so that revenues, expenses, assets, and liabilities are correctly reported. Specifically, an **adjusting entry** is made at the end of an accounting period to reflect a transaction or event that is not yet recorded. Each adjusting entry affects one or more income statement accounts *and* one or more statement of financial position accounts (but never the Cash account).

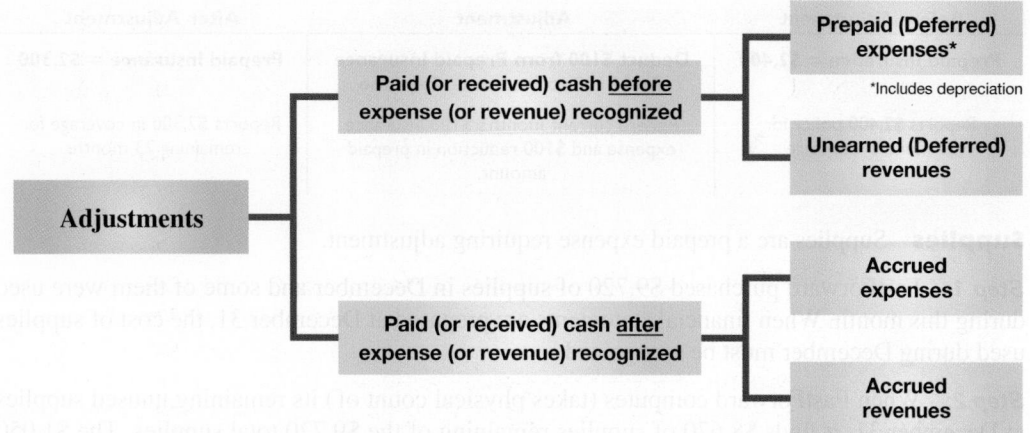

EXHIBIT 3.4

Types of Adjustments

Prepaid (Deferred) Expenses

Prepaid expenses refer to items *paid for* in advance of receiving their benefits. Prepaid expenses are assets. When these assets are used, their costs become expenses. Adjusting entries for prepaids increase expenses and decrease assets as shown in the T-accounts of Exhibit 3.5. Such adjustments reflect transactions and events that use up prepaid expenses (including passage of time). To illustrate the accounting for prepaid expenses, we look at prepaid insurance, supplies, and depreciation.

P1 Prepare and explain adjusting entries.

EXHIBIT 3.5

Adjusting for Prepaid Expenses

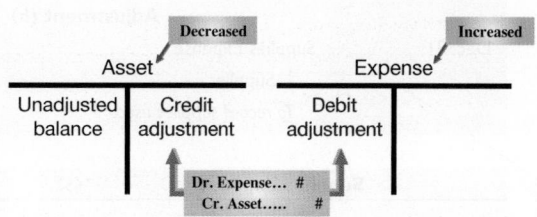

Prepaid Insurance   We use our 3-step process for this and all accounting adjustments.

Step 1:   We determine that the current balance of FastForward's prepaid insurance is equal to its $2,400 payment for 24 months of insurance benefits that began on December 1, 2015.

Step 2:   With the passage of time, the benefits of the insurance gradually expire and a portion of the Prepaid Insurance asset becomes expense. For instance, one month's insurance coverage expires by December 31, 2015. This expense is $100, or 1/24 of $2,400, which leaves $2,300.

Step 3:   The adjusting entry to record this expense and reduce the asset, along with T-account postings, follows:

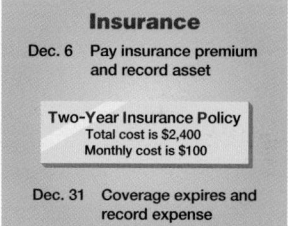

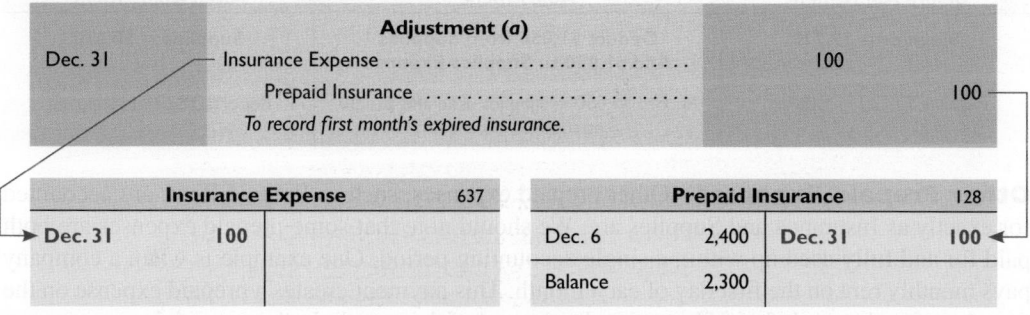

$$Assets = Liabilities + Equity$$
$$-100 \qquad\qquad\qquad -100$$

Explanation   After adjusting and posting, the $100 balance in Insurance Expense and the $2,300 balance in Prepaid Insurance are ready for reporting in financial statements. *Not* making the adjustment on or before December 31 would (1) understate expenses by $100 and overstate net profit by $100 for the December income statement and (2) overstate both prepaid insurance (assets) and equity (because of net profit) by $100 in the December 31 statement of financial position. (Exhibit 3.2 showed that 2016's adjustments must transfer a total of $1,200 from Prepaid Insurance to Insurance Expense, and 2017's adjustments must transfer the remaining $1,100 to Insurance Expense.) The following table highlights the December 31, 2015, adjustment for prepaid insurance.

Point: Many companies record adjusting entries only at the end of each year because of the time and cost necessary.

Before Adjustment	Adjustment	After Adjustment
Prepaid Insurance = $2,400	Deduct $100 from Prepaid Insurance Add $100 to Insurance Expense	Prepaid Insurance = $2,300
Reports $2,400 policy for 24-months' coverage.	Record current month's $100 insurance expense and $100 reduction in prepaid amount.	Reports $2,300 in coverage for remaining 23 months.

Supplies   Supplies are a prepaid expense requiring adjustment.

Step 1:   FastForward purchased $9,720 of supplies in December and some of them were used during this month. When financial statements are prepared at December 31, the cost of supplies used during December must be recognized.

Step 2:   When FastForward computes (takes physical count of) its remaining unused supplies at December 31, it finds $8,670 of supplies remaining of the $9,720 total supplies. The $1,050 difference between these two amounts is December's supplies expense.

Step 3:   The adjusting entry to record this expense and reduce the Supplies asset account, along with T-account postings, follows:

Supplies

Dec. 2,6,26   Purchase supplies and record asset

Dec. 31   Supplies used and record expense

Assets   =   Liabilities   +   Equity
−1,050   −1,050

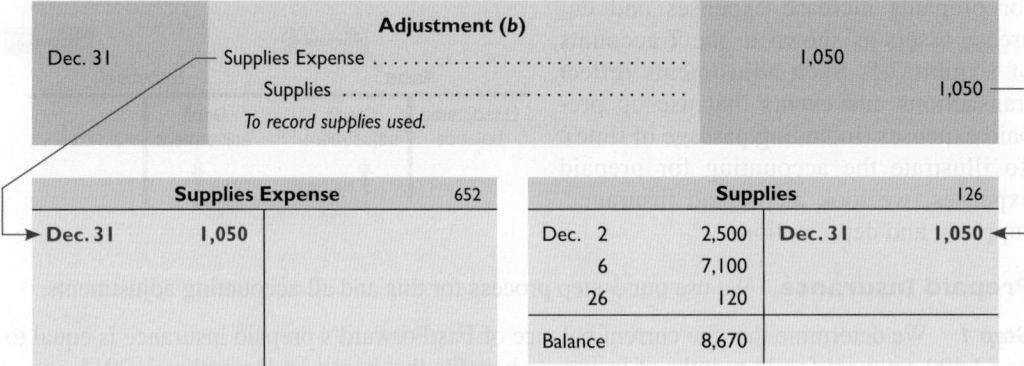

Adjustment (b)

Dec. 31	Supplies Expense	1,050	
	Supplies		1,050
	To record supplies used.		

Supplies Expense		652
Dec. 31	1,050	

Supplies			126
Dec. 2	2,500	Dec. 31	1,050
6	7,100		
26	120		
Balance	8,670		

Explanation   The balance of the Supplies account is $8,670 after posting—equaling the cost of the remaining supplies. *Not* making the adjustment on or before December 31 would (1) understate expenses by $1,050 and overstate net profit by $1,050 for the December income statement and (2) overstate both supplies and equity (because of net profit) by $1,050 in the December 31 statement of financial position. The following table highlights the adjustment for supplies.

Before Adjustment	Adjustment	After Adjustment
Supplies = $9,720	Deduct $1,050 from Supplies Add $1,050 to Supplies Expense	Supplies = $8,670
Reports $9,720 in supplies.	Record $1,050 in supplies used and $1,050 as supplies expense.	Reports $8,670 in supplies.

Other Prepaid Expenses   Other prepaid expenses, such as Prepaid Rent, are accounted for exactly as Insurance and Supplies are. We should note that some prepaid expenses are both paid for and fully used up within a single accounting period. One example is when a company pays monthly rent on the first day of each month. This payment creates a prepaid expense on the first day of each month that fully expires by the end of the month. In these special cases, we can record the cash paid with a debit to an expense account instead of an asset account. This practice is described more completely later in the chapter.

Point: We assume that prepaid and unearned items are recorded in statement of financial position accounts. An alternative is to record them in income statement accounts; Appendix 3A discusses this alternative. The adjusted financial statements are identical.

 **Decision** Maker   Answer — p. 114

Investor   A small publishing company signs a well-known athlete to write a book. The company pays the athlete $500,000 to sign plus future book royalties. A note to the company's financial statements says that "prepaid expenses include $500,000 in author signing fees to be matched against future expected sales." Is this accounting for the signing bonus acceptable? How does it affect your analysis? ■

Depreciation   A special category of prepaid expenses is **property, plant, and equipment,** which refers to long-term tangible assets used to produce and sell products and services. Property, plant, and equipment are expected to provide benefits for more than one period. Examples of property, plant, and equipment are buildings, machines, vehicles, and fixtures. All property, plant, and equipment, with a general exception for land, eventually wear out or decline in usefulness. The costs of these assets are deferred but are gradually reported as expenses in the income statement over the assets' useful lives (benefit periods). **Depreciation** is the process of allocating the costs of these assets over their expected useful lives. Depreciation expense is recorded with an adjusting entry similar to that for other prepaid expenses.

Point: Property, plant, and equipment are also called *Plant & Equipment,* or *Property, Plant & Equipment.*

Point: Depreciation does not necessarily measure decline in market value.

Point: An asset's expected value at the end of its useful life is called *residual value* or *salvage value.*

Step 1:   Recall that FastForward purchased equipment for $26,000 in early December to use in earning revenue. This equipment's cost must be depreciated.

Step 2:   The equipment is expected to have a useful life (benefit period) of four years and to be worth about $8,000 at the end of four years. This means the *net* cost of this equipment over its useful life is $18,000 ($26,000 − $8,000). We can use any of several methods to allocate this $18,000 net cost to expense. FastForward uses a method called **straight-line depreciation,** which allocates equal amounts of the asset's net cost to depreciation during its useful life. Dividing the $18,000 net cost by the 48 months in the asset's useful life gives a monthly cost of $375 ($18,000/48).

Step 3:   The adjusting entry to record monthly depreciation expense, along with T-account postings, follows:

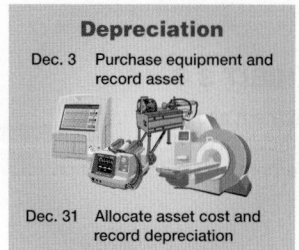

Depreciation

Dec. 3   Purchase equipment and record asset

Dec. 31   Allocate asset cost and record depreciation

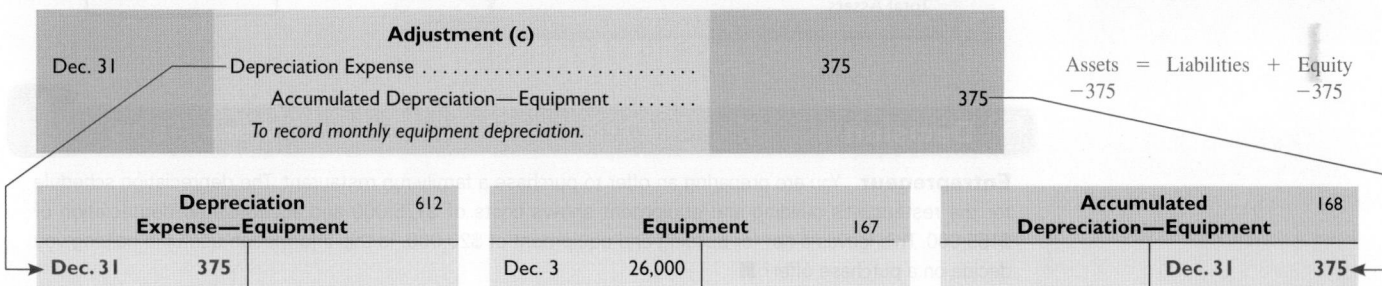

Adjustment (c)		
Dec. 31	Depreciation Expense	375	
	Accumulated Depreciation—Equipment		375
	To record monthly equipment depreciation.	

Assets = Liabilities + Equity
−375   −375

Depreciation Expense—Equipment	612		Equipment	167		Accumulated Depreciation—Equipment	168
Dec. 31	375		Dec. 3	26,000			Dec. 31	375

Explanation   After posting the adjustment, the Equipment account ($26,000) less its Accumulated Depreciation ($375) account equals the $25,625 net cost (made up of $17,625 for the 47 remaining months in the benefit period plus the $8,000 value at the end of that time). The $375 balance in the Depreciation Expense account is reported in the December income statement. *Not* making the adjustment at December 31 would (1) understate expenses by $375 and overstate net profit by $375 for the December income statement and (2) overstate both assets and equity (because of income) by $375 in the December 31 statement of financial position. The following table highlights the adjustment for depreciation.

Before Adjustment	Adjustment	After Adjustment
Equipment, net = $26,000	**Deduct $375 from Equipment, net** **Add $375 to Depreciation Expense**	**Equipment, net = $25,625**
Reports $26,000 in equipment.	Record $375 in depreciation and $375 as accumulated depreciation, which is deducted from equipment.	Reports $25,625 in equipment, net of accumulated depreciation.

Accumulated depreciation is kept in a separate contra account. A **contra account** is an account linked with another account, it has an opposite normal balance, and it is reported as a subtraction from that other account's balance. For instance, FastForward's contra account of Accumulated Depreciation—Equipment is subtracted from the Equipment account in the statement of financial position (see Exhibit 3.7). This contra account allows statement of financial position readers to know both the full costs of assets and the total depreciation.

The title of the contra account, *Accumulated Depreciation,* reveals that this account includes total depreciation expense for all prior periods for which the asset was used. To illustrate, the Equipment and the Accumulated Depreciation accounts appear as in Exhibit 3.6 on February 28, 2016, after three months of adjusting entries. The $1,125 balance in the accumulated depreciation account can be subtracted from its related $26,000 asset cost. The difference ($24,875) between these two balances is the cost of the asset that has not yet been depreciated. This difference is

Point: The cost principle requires an asset to be initially recorded at acquisition cost. Depreciation causes the asset's carrying amount (cost less accumulated depreciation) to decline over time.

EXHIBIT 3.6

Accounts after Three Months of Depreciation Adjustments

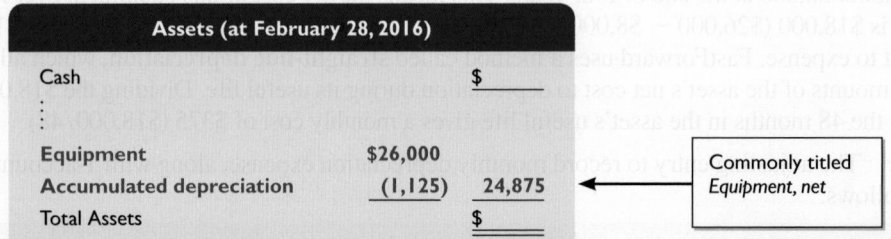

Equipment		167
Dec. 3	26,000	

	Accumulated Depreciation—Equipment	168
	Dec. 31	375
	Jan. 31	375
	Feb. 28	375
	Balance	1,125

Point: The net cost of equipment is also called the *depreciable basis.*

called the **carrying amount** (or *book value,* or *net amount*), which equals the asset's costs less its accumulated depreciation.

These account balances are reported in the assets section of the February 28 statement of financial position in Exhibit 3.7.

EXHIBIT 3.7

Equipment and Accumulated Depreciation on February 28 Statement of Financial Position

Assets (at February 28, 2016)		
Cash		$
⋮		
Equipment	$26,000	
Accumulated depreciation	(1,125)	24,875
Total Assets		$

Commonly titled *Equipment, net*

Decision Maker   Answer — p. 115

Entrepreneur You are preparing an offer to purchase a family-run restaurant. The depreciation schedule for the restaurant's building and equipment shows costs of $175,000 and accumulated depreciation of $155,000. This leaves a net for building and equipment of $20,000. Is this information useful in helping you decide on a purchase offer? ■

Unearned (Deferred) Revenues

The term **unearned revenues** refers to cash received in advance of providing products and services. Unearned revenues, also called *deferred revenues,* are liabilities. When cash is ac-

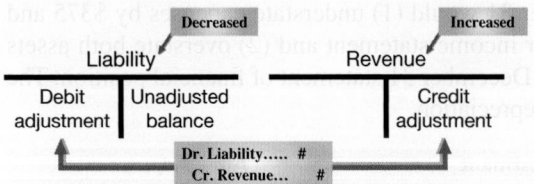

EXHIBIT 3.8

Adjusting for Unearned Revenues

cepted, an obligation to provide products or services is accepted. As products or services are provided, the unearned revenues become *earned* revenues. Adjusting entries for unearned revenues involve increasing revenues and decreasing unearned revenues, as shown in Exhibit 3.8.

Point: To *defer* is to postpone. We postpone reporting amounts received as revenues until they are earned.

An example of unearned revenues is from The New York Times Company, which reports unexpired (unearned) subscriptions of $81 million: "Proceeds from . . . subscriptions are deferred at the time of sale and are recognized in earnings on a pro rata basis over the terms of the subscriptions." Unearned revenues are nearly 10% of the current liabilities for the Times. Another example comes from the Boston Celtics. When the Celtics receive cash from advance ticket sales and broadcast fees, they record it in an unearned revenue account called *Deferred Game Revenues.* The Celtics recognize this unearned revenue with adjusting entries on a game-by-game basis. Since the NBA regular season begins in October and ends in April, revenue recognition is mainly limited to this period. For a recent season, the Celtics' quarterly revenues were $0 million for July–September; $34 million for October–December; $48 million for January–March; and $17 million for April–June.

Returning to FastForward, it also has unearned revenues. It agreed on December 26 to provide consulting services to a client for a fixed fee of $3,000 for 60 days.

Unearned Revenues

Dec. 26   Cash received in advance and record liability

Thanks for cash in advance. I'll work now through Feb. 24

Dec. 31   Provided services and record revenue

Step 1: On December 26, the client paid the 60-day fee in advance, covering the period December 27 to February 24. The entry to record the cash received in advance is

Dec. 26	Cash	3,000	
	Unearned Consulting Revenue		3,000
	To record advance payment for services over the next 60 days.		

Assets = Liabilities + Equity
+3,000   +3,000

This advance payment increases cash and creates an obligation to do consulting work over the next 60 days.

Step 2: As time passes, FastForward earns this payment through consulting. By December 31, it has provided five days' service and earned 5/60 of the $3,000 unearned revenue. This amounts to $250 ($3,000 × 5/60). The *revenue recognition principle* implies that $250 of unearned revenue must be reported as revenue on the December income statement.

Step 3: The adjusting entry to reduce the liability account and recognize earned revenue, along with T-account postings, follows:

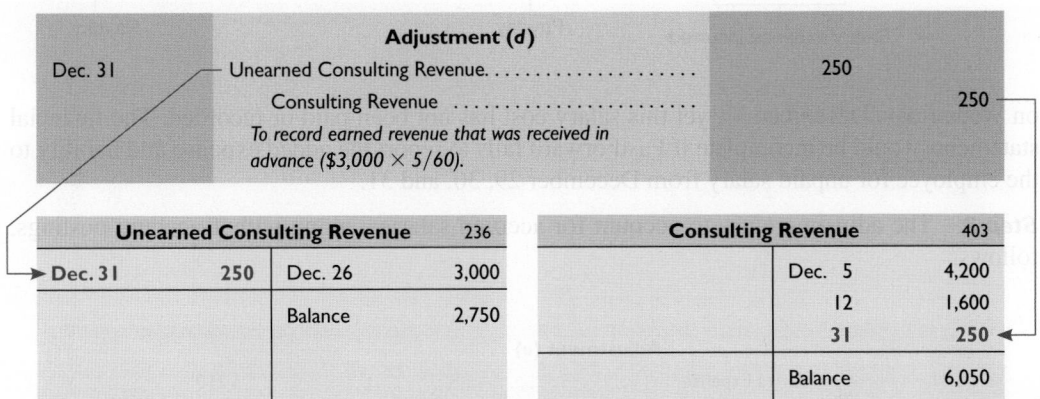

Adjustment (d)			
Dec. 31	Unearned Consulting Revenue.	250	
	Consulting Revenue		250
	To record earned revenue that was received in advance ($3,000 × 5/60).		

Assets = Liabilities + Equity
                −250   +250

Unearned Consulting Revenue			236
Dec. 31	250	Dec. 26	3,000
		Balance	2,750

Consulting Revenue			403
		Dec. 5	4,200
		12	1,600
		31	250
		Balance	6,050

Explanation The adjusting entry transfers $250 from unearned revenue (a liability account) to a revenue account. *Not* making the adjustment (1) understates revenue and net profit by $250 in the December income statement and (2) overstates unearned revenue and understates equity by $250 on the December 31 statement of financial position. The following highlights the adjustment for unearned revenue.

Before Adjustment	Adjustment	After Adjustment
Unearned Consulting Revenue = $3,000	**Deduct $250 from Unearned Consulting Revenue** **Add $250 to Consulting Revenue**	**Unearned Consulting Revenue = $2,750**
Reports $3,000 in unearned revenue for consulting services promised for 60 days.	Record 5 days of earned consulting revenue, which is 5/60 of unearned amount.	Reports $2,750 in unearned revenue for consulting services owed over next 55 days.

Accrued Expenses

Accrued expenses refer to costs that are incurred in a period but are both unpaid and unrecorded. Accrued expenses must be reported on the income statement of the period when incurred. Adjusting entries for recording accrued expenses involve increasing expenses and increasing liabilities as shown in Exhibit 3.9. This adjustment recognizes expenses incurred in a period but not yet paid. Common examples of accrued expenses are salaries, interest, rent, and taxes. We use salaries and interest to show how to adjust accounts for accrued expenses.

Point: Accrued expenses are also called accrued liabilities.

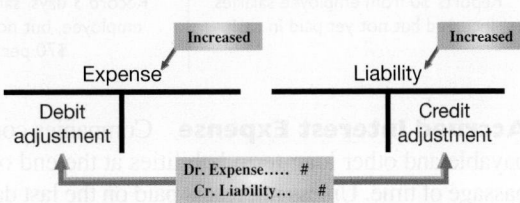

EXHIBIT 3.9

Adjusting for Accrued Expenses

Accrued Salaries Expense   FastForward's employee earns $70 per day, or $350 for a five-day workweek beginning on Monday and ending on Friday.

Step 1:   Its employee is paid every two weeks on Friday. On December 12 and 26, the wages are paid, recorded in the journal, and posted to the ledger.

Step 2:   The calendar in Exhibit 3.10 shows three working days after the December 26 payday (29, 30, and 31). This means the employee has earned three days' salary by the close of business

EXHIBIT 3.10

Salary Accrual and Paydays

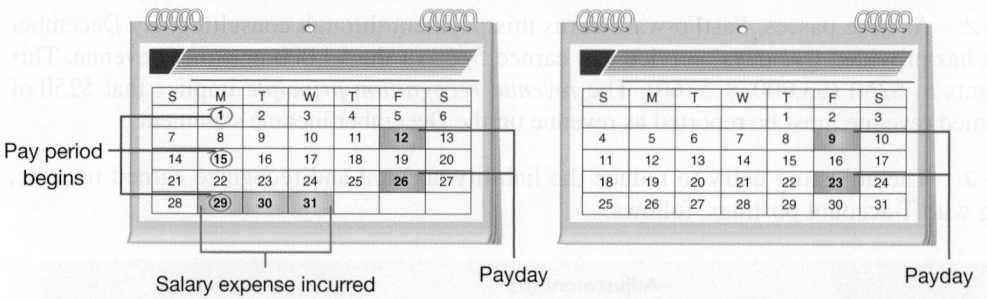

Pay period begins

Salary expense incurred   Payday   Payday

Point: An employer records salaries expense and a vacation pay liability when employees earn vacation pay.

on Wednesday, December 31, yet this salary cost has not been paid or recorded. The financial statements would be incomplete if FastForward fails to report the added expense and liability to the employee for unpaid salary from December 29, 30, and 31.

Step 3:   The adjusting entry to account for accrued salaries, along with T-account postings, follows:

Assets = Liabilities + Equity
         +210   −210

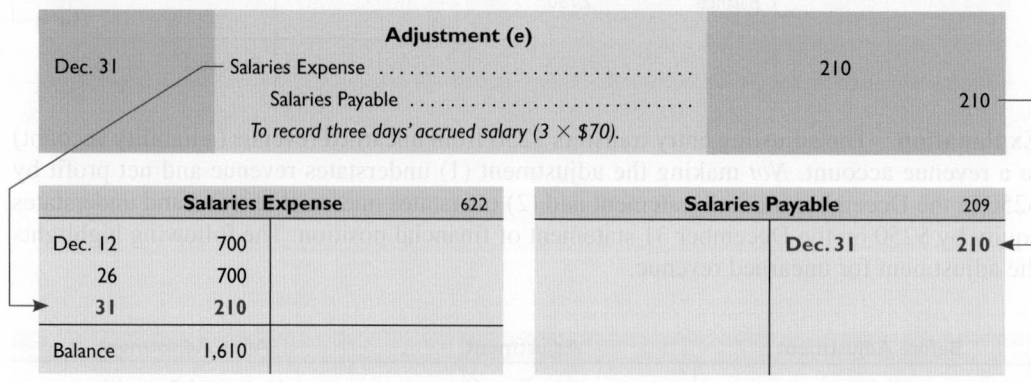

Explanation   Salaries expense of $1,610 is reported on the December income statement and $210 of salaries payable (liability) is reported in the statement of financial position. *Not* making the adjustment (1) understates salaries expense and overstates net profit by $210 in the December income statement and (2) understates salaries payable (liabilities) and overstates equity by $210 on the December 31 statement of financial position. The following highlights the adjustment for salaries incurred.

Before Adjustment	Adjustment	After Adjustment
Salaries Payable = $0	**Add $210 to Salaries Payable** **Add $210 to Salaries Expense**	**Salaries Payable = $210**
Reports $0 from employee salaries incurred but not yet paid in cash.	Record 3 days' salaries owed to employee, but not yet paid, at $70 per day.	Reports $210 salaries payable to employee but not yet paid.

Accrued Interest Expense   Companies commonly have accrued interest expense on notes payable and other long-term liabilities at the end of a period. Interest expense is incurred with the passage of time. Unless interest is paid on the last day of an accounting period, we need to adjust for interest expense incurred but not yet paid. This means we must accrue interest cost from the most recent payment date up to the end of the period. The formula for computing accrued interest is:

Principal amount owed × Annual interest rate × Fraction of year since last payment date.

To illustrate, if a company has a $6,000 loan from a bank at 6% annual interest, then 30 days' accrued interest expense is $30—computed as $6,000 × 0.06 × 30/360. The adjusting entry would be to debit Interest Expense for $30 and credit Interest Payable for $30.

Point: Interest computations assume a 360-day year; known as the *bankers' rule.*

Future Payment of Accrued Expenses Adjusting entries for accrued expenses foretell cash transactions in future periods. Specifically, accrued expenses at the end of one accounting period result in *cash payment* in a *future period*(s). To illustrate, recall that FastForward recorded accrued salaries of $210. On January 9, the first payday of the next period, the following entry settles the accrued liability (salaries payable) and records salaries expense for seven days of work in January:

Jan. 9	Salaries Payable (3 days at $70 per day)	210	
	Salaries Expense (7 days at $70 per day)	490	
	Cash		700
	To record the payment of two weeks' salary including three days accrued in December.		

Assets = Liabilities + Equity
−700   −210   −490

The $210 debit reflects the payment of the liability for the three days' salary accrued on December 31. The $490 debit records the salary for January's first seven working days (including the New Year's Day holiday) as an expense of the new accounting period. The $700 credit records the total amount of cash paid to the employee.

Accrued Revenues

The term **accrued revenues** refers to revenues earned in a period that are both unrecorded and not yet received in cash (or other assets). An example is a technician who bills customers only when the job is done. If one-third of a job is complete by the end of a period, then the technician must record one-third of the expected billing as revenue in that period—even though there is no billing or collection. The adjusting entries for accrued revenues increase assets and increase revenues as shown in Exhibit 3.11. Accrued revenues commonly arise from services, products, interest, and rent. We use service fees and interest to show how to adjust for accrued revenues.

Point: Accrued revenues are also called *accrued assets.*

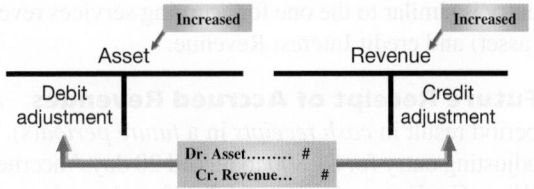

EXHIBIT 3.11

Adjusting for Accrued Revenues

Accrued Services Revenue Accrued revenues are not recorded until adjusting entries are made at the end of the accounting period. These accrued revenues are earned but unrecorded because either the buyer has not yet paid for them or the seller has not yet billed the buyer. FastForward provides an example.

Step 1: In the second week of December, it agreed to provide 30 days of consulting services to a local fitness club for a fixed fee of $2,700. The terms of the initial agreement call for Fast-Forward to provide services from December 12, 2015, through January 10, 2016, or 30 days of service. The club agrees to pay FastForward $2,700 on January 10, 2016, when the service period is complete.

Step 2: At December 31, 2015, 20 days of services have already been provided. Since the contracted services have not yet been entirely provided, FastForward has neither billed the club nor recorded the services already provided. Still, FastForward has earned two-thirds of the 30-day fee, or $1,800 ($2,700 × 20/30). The *revenue recognition principle* implies that it must report the $1,800 on the December income statement. The statement of financial position also must report that the club owes FastForward $1,800.

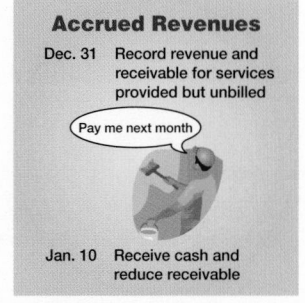

Accrued Revenues

Dec. 31 Record revenue and receivable for services provided but unbilled

Pay me next month

Jan. 10 Receive cash and reduce receivable

Step 3:   The year-end adjusting entry to account for accrued services revenue is

Assets = Liabilities + Equity
+1,800   +1,800

Adjustment (f)		
Dec. 31 Accounts Receivable	1,800	
Consulting Revenue		1,800
To record 20 days' accrued revenue.		

Accounts Receivable			106
Dec. 12	1,900	Dec. 22	1,900
31	1,800		
Balance	1,800		

Consulting Revenue		403
	Dec. 5	4,200
	12	1,600
	31	250
	31	1,800
	Balance	7,850

Example: What is the adjusting entry if the 30-day consulting period began on December 22? *Answer:* One-third of the fee is earned:

Accounts Receivable 900
    Consulting Revenue 900

Explanation   Accounts receivable are reported on the statement of financial position at $1,800, and the $7,850 total of consulting revenue is reported on the income statement. *Not* making the adjustment would understate (1) both consulting revenue and net profit by $1,800 in the December income statement and (2) both accounts receivable (assets) and equity by $1,800 on the December 31 statement of financial position. The following table highlights the adjustment for accrued revenue.

Before Adjustment	Adjustment	After Adjustment
Accounts Receivable = $0	**Add $1,800 to Accounts Receivable** **Add $1,800 to Consulting Revenue**	**Accounts Receivable = $1,800**
Reports $0 from revenue earned but not yet received in cash.	Record 20 days of earned consulting revenue, which is 20/30 of total contract amount.	Reports $1,800 in accounts receivable from consulting services provided.

Accrued Interest Revenue   In addition to the accrued interest expense we described earlier, interest can yield an accrued revenue when a debtor owes money (or other assets) to a company. If a company is holding notes or accounts receivable that produce interest revenue, we must adjust the accounts to record any earned and yet uncollected interest revenue. The adjusting entry is similar to the one for accruing services revenue. Specifically, we debit Interest Receivable (asset) and credit Interest Revenue.

Future Receipt of Accrued Revenues   Accrued revenues at the end of one accounting period result in *cash receipts* in a *future period*(s). To illustrate, recall that FastForward made an adjusting entry for $1,800 to record 20 days' accrued revenue earned from its consulting contract. When FastForward receives $2,700 cash on January 10 for the entire contract amount, it makes the following entry to remove the accrued asset (accounts receivable) and recognize the revenue earned in January. The $2,700 debit reflects the cash received. The $1,800 credit reflects the removal of the receivable, and the $900 credit records the revenue earned in January.

Assets = Liabilities + Equity
+2,700   +900
−1,800

Jan. 10	Cash	2,700	
	Accounts Receivable (20 days at $90 per day)		1,800
	Consulting Revenue (10 days at $90 per day)		900
	To record cash collected on accounts receivable and revenue earned in January.		

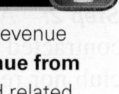

Decision Update

The IASB and the FASB announced the release of the converged standard on the recognition of revenue from contracts with customers on May 28, 2014. The guidance will be included in **IFRS 15 Revenue from Contracts with Customers** and replaces **IAS 18 Revenue, IAS 11 Construction Contracts,** and related interpretations. Companies using **IFRS** will be required to apply the revenue standard for reporting periods beginning on or after January 1, 2017, and early application is permitted.

Under the new standard, companies under contract to provide goods or services to a customer will be required to follow a five-step process to recognize revenue:

1. Identify contract(s) with a customer.
2. Identify the separate performance obligations in the contract.
3. Determine the transaction price.
4. Allocate the transaction price to the separate performance obligations.
5. Recognize revenue when the entity satisfies each performance obligation.

The rule's expanded disclosure requirements will help financial statement users understand the nature, amount, timing, and uncertainty of revenue and cash flows arising from contracts with customers. Companies that sell products and services in a bundle, or those engaged in major projects—in such industries as telecommunications, software, engineering, construction, and real estate—could see significant changes to the timing of revenue recognition. ■

Decision Maker Answer — p. 115

Loan Officer The owner of an electronics store applies for a business loan. The store's financial statements reveal large increases in current-year revenues and income. Analysis shows that these increases are due to a promotion that let consumers buy now and pay nothing until January 1 of next year. The store recorded these sales as accrued revenue. Does your analysis raise any concerns? ■

Links to Financial Statements

The process of adjusting accounts is intended to bring an asset or liability account balance to its correct amount. It also updates a related expense or revenue account. These adjustments are necessary for transactions and events that extend over more than one period. (Adjusting entries are posted like any other entry.)

Exhibit 3.12 summarizes the four types of transactions requiring adjustment. Understanding this exhibit is important to understanding the adjusting process and its importance to financial statements. Remember that each adjusting entry affects one or more income statement accounts *and* one or more statement of financial position accounts (but never cash).

A1 Explain how accounting adjustments link to financial statements.

| | BEFORE Adjusting | | |
Category	Statement of Financial Position	Income Statement	Adjusting Entry
Prepaid expenses†	Asset overstated / Equity overstated	Expense understated	Dr. Expense / Cr. Asset*
Unearned revenues†	Liability overstated / Equity understated	Revenue understated	Dr. Liability / Cr. Revenue
Accrued expenses	Liability understated / Equity overstated	Expense understated	Dr. Expense / Cr. Liability
Accrued revenues	Asset understated / Equity understated	Revenue understated	Dr. Asset / Cr. Revenue

EXHIBIT 3.12
Summary of Adjustments and Financial Statement Links

* For depreciation, the credit is to Accumulated Depreciation (contra asset).
† Exhibit assumes that prepaid expenses are initially recorded as assets and that unearned revenues are initially recorded as liabilities.

Information about some adjustments is not always available until several days or even weeks after the period-end. This means that some adjusting and closing entries are recorded later than, but dated as at, the last day of the period. One example is a company that receives a utility bill on January 10 for costs incurred for the month of December. When it receives the bill, the company records the expense and the payable as at December 31. Other examples include long-distance phone usage and costs of many Web billings. The December income statement reflects these additional expenses incurred, and the December 31 statement of financial position includes these payables, although the amounts were not actually known on December 31.

Decision Ethics Answer — p. 115

Financial Officer At year-end, the president instructs you, the financial officer, not to record accrued expenses until next year because they will not be paid until then. The president also directs you to record in current-year sales a recent purchase order from a customer that requires merchandise to be delivered two weeks after the year-end. Your company would report a net profit instead of a net loss if you carry out these instructions. What do you do? ■

6. If an adjusting entry for accrued revenues of $200 at year-end is omitted, what is this error's effect on the year-end income statement and statement of financial position?

7. What is a contra account? Explain its purpose.

8. What is an accrued expense? Give an example.

9. Describe how an unearned revenue arises. Give an example.

Adjusted Trial Balance

> **P2** Explain and prepare an adjusted trial balance.

An **unadjusted trial balance** is a list of accounts and balances prepared *before* adjustments are recorded. An **adjusted trial balance** is a list of accounts and balances prepared *after* adjusting entries have been recorded and posted to the ledger.

Exhibit 3.13 shows both the unadjusted and the adjusted trial balances for FastForward at December 31, 2015. The order of accounts in the trial balance is usually set up to match the order in the chart of accounts. Several new accounts arise from the adjusting entries.

EXHIBIT 3.13

Unadjusted and Adjusted Trial Balances

File   Edit   View   Insert   Format   Tools   Data   Window   Help

FASTFORWARD
Trial Balances
December 31, 2015

Acct. No.	Account Title	Unadjusted Trial Balance Dr.	Unadjusted Trial Balance Cr.	Adjustments Dr.	Adjustments Cr.	Adjusted Trial Balance Dr.	Adjusted Trial Balance Cr.
101	Cash	$ 4,350				$ 4,350	
106	Accounts receivable	0		(f) $1,800		1,800	
126	Supplies	9,720			(b) $1,050	8,670	
128	Prepaid insurance	2,400			(a) 100	2,300	
167	Equipment	26,000				26,000	
168	Accumulated depreciation—Equip.		$ 0		(c) 375		$ 375
201	Accounts payable		6,200				6,200
209	Salaries payable		0		(e) 210		210
236	Unearned consulting revenue		3,000	(d) 250			2,750
301	C. Taylor, Capital		30,000				30,000
302	C. Taylor, Withdrawals	200				200	
403	Consulting revenue		5,800		(d) 250		7,850
					(f) 1,800		
406	Rental revenue		300				300
612	Depreciation expense—Equip.	0		(c) 375		375	
622	Salaries expense	1,400		(e) 210		1,610	
637	Insurance expense	0		(a) 100		100	
640	Rent expense	1,000				1,000	
652	Supplies expense	0		(b) 1,050		1,050	
690	Utilities expense	230				230	
	Totals	$45,300	$45,300	$3,785	$3,785	$47,685	$47,685

Sheet1 / Sheet2 / Sheet3 /

Each adjustment (see middle columns) is identified by a letter in parentheses that links it to an adjusting entry explained earlier. Each amount in the Adjusted Trial Balance columns is computed by taking that account's amount from the Unadjusted Trial Balance columns and adding or subtracting any adjustment(s). To illustrate, Supplies has a $9,720 Dr. balance in the unadjusted columns. Subtracting the $1,050 Cr. amount shown in the adjustments columns yields an adjusted $8,670 Dr. balance for Supplies. An account can have more than one adjustment, such as for Consulting Revenue. Also, some accounts might not require adjustment for this period, such as Accounts Payable.

PREPARING FINANCIAL STATEMENTS

> **P3** Prepare financial statements from an adjusted trial balance.

We can prepare financial statements directly from information in the *adjusted* trial balance. An adjusted trial balance (see the right-most columns in Exhibit 3.13) includes all accounts and balances appearing in financial statements, and is easier to work from than the entire ledger when preparing financial statements.

Exhibit 3.14 shows how revenue and expense balances are transferred from the adjusted trial balance to the income statement (red lines). The net profit and the withdrawals amount are then used to prepare the statement of changes in equity (black lines). Asset and liability balances on the adjusted trial balance are then transferred to the statement of financial position (blue lines). The ending capital is determined on the statement of changes in equity and transferred to the statement of financial position (green lines).

EXHIBIT 3.14

Preparing Financial Statements (Adjusted Trial Balance from Exhibit 3.13)

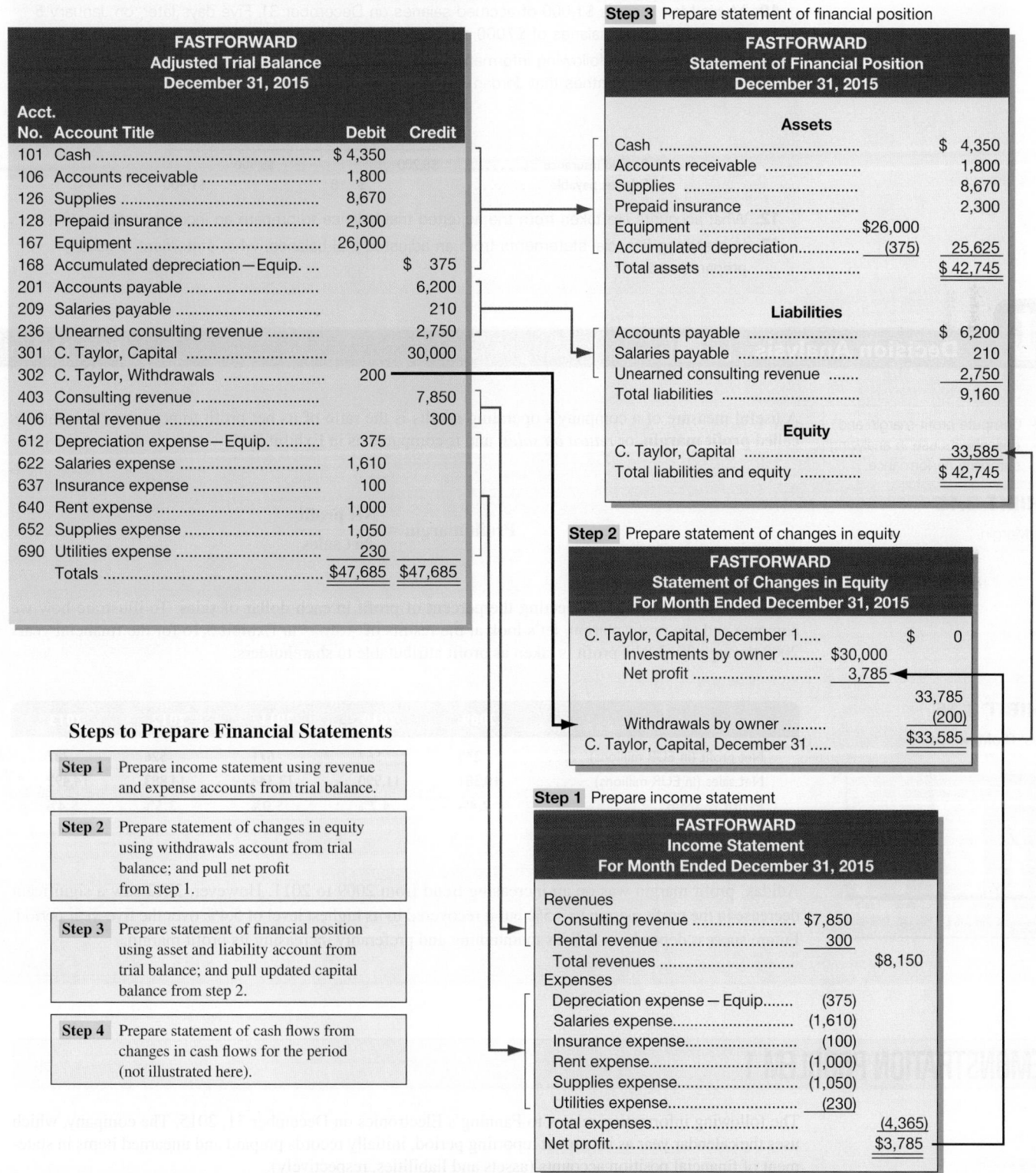

Steps to Prepare Financial Statements

Step 1 Prepare income statement using revenue and expense accounts from trial balance.

Step 2 Prepare statement of changes in equity using withdrawals account from trial balance; and pull net profit from step 1.

Step 3 Prepare statement of financial position using asset and liability account from trial balance; and pull updated capital balance from step 2.

Step 4 Prepare statement of cash flows from changes in cash flows for the period (not illustrated here).

Step 3 Prepare statement of financial position

FASTFORWARD
Statement of Financial Position
December 31, 2015

Assets

Cash	$ 4,350
Accounts receivable	1,800
Supplies	8,670
Prepaid insurance	2,300
Equipment $26,000	
Accumulated depreciation.............. (375)	25,625
Total assets	$ 42,745

Liabilities

Accounts payable	$ 6,200
Salaries payable	210
Unearned consulting revenue	2,750
Total liabilities	9,160

Equity

C. Taylor, Capital	33,585
Total liabilities and equity	$ 42,745

Step 2 Prepare statement of changes in equity

FASTFORWARD
Statement of Changes in Equity
For Month Ended December 31, 2015

C. Taylor, Capital, December 1.....		$ 0
Investments by owner	$30,000	
Net profit	3,785	
		33,785
Withdrawals by owner		(200)
C. Taylor, Capital, December 31		$33,585

Step 1 Prepare income statement

FASTFORWARD
Income Statement
For Month Ended December 31, 2015

Revenues		
Consulting revenue	$7,850	
Rental revenue	300	
Total revenues		$8,150
Expenses		
Depreciation expense — Equip.......	(375)	
Salaries expense..........................	(1,610)	
Insurance expense........................	(100)	
Rent expense................................	(1,000)	
Supplies expense..........................	(1,050)	
Utilities expense...........................	(230)	
Total expenses.............................		(4,365)
Net profit.....................................		$3,785

FASTFORWARD
Adjusted Trial Balance
December 31, 2015

Acct. No.	Account Title	Debit	Credit
101	Cash	$ 4,350	
106	Accounts receivable	1,800	
126	Supplies	8,670	
128	Prepaid insurance	2,300	
167	Equipment	26,000	
168	Accumulated depreciation—Equip. ...		$ 375
201	Accounts payable		6,200
209	Salaries payable		210
236	Unearned consulting revenue		2,750
301	C. Taylor, Capital		30,000
302	C. Taylor, Withdrawals	200	
403	Consulting revenue		7,850
406	Rental revenue		300
612	Depreciation expense—Equip.	375	
622	Salaries expense	1,610	
637	Insurance expense	100	
640	Rent expense	1,000	
652	Supplies expense	1,050	
690	Utilities expense	230	
	Totals	$47,685	$47,685

Point: Each trial balance amount is used in only *one* financial statement and, when financial statements are completed, each account will have been used once.

We prepare financial statements in the following order: income statement, statement of changes in equity, and statement of financial position. This order makes sense because the statement of financial position uses information from the statement of changes in equity, which in turn uses information from the income statement. The statement of cash flows is usually the final statement prepared.

Quick Check   Answers — p. 115

10. Music-Mart records $1,000 of accrued salaries on December 31. Five days later, on January 5 (the next payday), salaries of $7,000 are paid. What is the January 5 entry?

11. Jordan Air has the following information in its unadjusted and adjusted trial balances. What are the adjusting entries that Jordan Air likely recorded?

	Unadjusted		Adjusted	
	Debit	Credit	Debit	Credit
Prepaid insurance	$6,200		$5,900	
Salaries payable		$ 0		$1,400

12. What accounts are taken from the adjusted trial balance to prepare an income statement?

13. In preparing financial statements from an adjusted trial balance, what statement is usually prepared second?

 Decision Analysis ■■□   Profit Margin

 A2   Compute profit margin and describe its use in analyzing company performance.

A useful measure of a company's operating results is the ratio of its net profit to net sales. This ratio is called **profit margin,** or *return on sales,* and is computed as in Exhibit 3.15.

EXHIBIT 3.15

Profit Margin

$$\text{Profit margin} = \frac{\text{Net profit}}{\text{Net sales}}$$

This ratio is interpreted as reflecting the percent of profit in each dollar of sales. To illustrate how we compute and use profit margin, let's look at the results of Adidas in Exhibit 3.16 for the financial years 2009 through 2013. Net profit is taken as profit attributable to shareholders.

EXHIBIT 3.16

Adidas' Profit Margin

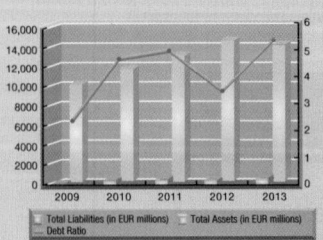

	2009	2010	2011	2012	2013
Net profit (in EUR millions)	245	567	671	526	787
Net sales (in EUR millions)	10,381	11,990	13,344	14,883	14,492
Profit margin	2.4%	4.7%	5.0%	3.5%	5.4%

Adidas' profit margin was on an increasing trend from 2009 to 2011. However, 2012 saw a significant decrease in the profit margin to 3.5% but it recovered to its highest level of 5.4% over the five-year period. Future success depends on Adidas maintaining and preferably increasing its profit margin.

DEMONSTRATION PROBLEM 1

The following information relates to Fanning's Electronics on December 31, 2015. The company, which uses the calendar year as its annual reporting period, initially records prepaid and unearned items in statement of financial position accounts (assets and liabilities, respectively).

a. The company's weekly payroll is $8,750, paid each Friday for a five-day workweek. Assume December 31, 2015, falls on a Monday, but the employees will not be paid their wages until Friday, January 4, 2016.

b. Eighteen months earlier, on July 1, 2010, the company purchased equipment that cost $20,000. Its useful life is predicted to be five years, at which time the equipment is expected to be worthless (zero residual value).

c. On October 1, 2015, the company agreed to work on a new housing development. The company is paid $120,000 on October 1 in advance of future installation of similar alarm systems in 24 new homes. That amount was credited to the Unearned Services Revenue account. Between October 1 and December 31, work on 20 homes was completed.

d. On September 1, 2015, the company purchased a 12-month insurance policy for $1,800. The transaction was recorded with an $1,800 debit to Prepaid Insurance.

e. On December 29, 2015, the company completed a $7,000 service that has not been billed and not recorded as at December 31, 2015.

Required

1. Prepare any necessary adjusting entries on December 31, 2015, in relation to transactions and events *a* through *e*.

2. Prepare T-accounts for the accounts affected by adjusting entries, and post the adjusting entries. Determine the adjusted balances for the Unearned Revenue and the Prepaid Insurance accounts.

3. Complete the following table and determine the amounts and effects of your adjusting entries on the year 2015 income statement and the December 31, 2015, statement of financial position. Use up (down) arrows to indicate an increase (decrease) in the Effect columns.

Entry	Amount in the Entry	Effect on Net profit	Effect on Total Assets	Effect on Total Liabilities	Effect on Total Equity

PLANNING THE SOLUTION

- Analyze each situation to determine which accounts need to be updated with an adjustment.
- Calculate the amount of each adjustment and prepare the necessary journal entries.
- Show the amount of each adjustment in the designated accounts, determine the adjusted balance, and identify the statement of financial position classification of the account.
- Determine each entry's effect on net profit for the year and on total assets, total liabilities, and total equity at the end of the year.

SOLUTION TO DEMONSTRATION PROBLEM 1

1. Adjusting journal entries.

(a) Dec. 31	Wages Expense	1,750	
	Wages Payable		1,750
	To accrue wages for the last day of the year ($8,750 × 1/5).		
(b) Dec. 31	Depreciation Expense—Equipment	4,000	
	Accumulated Depreciation—Equipment		4,000
	To record depreciation expense for the year ($20,000/5 years = $4,000 per year).		
(c) Dec. 31	Unearned Services Revenue	100,000	
	Services Revenue		100,000
	To recognize services revenue earned ($120,000 × 20/24).		
(d) Dec. 31	Insurance Expense	600	
	Prepaid Insurance		600
	To adjust for expired portion of insurance ($1,800 × 4/12).		
(e) Dec. 31	Accounts Receivable	7,000	
	Services Revenue		7,000
	To record services revenue earned.		

2. T-accounts for adjusting journal entries *a* through *e*.

Wages Expense		
(a)	1,750	

Wages Payable		
		(a)	1,750

Depreciation Expense—Equipment		
(b)	4,000	

Accumulated Depreciation—Equipment		
		(b)	4,000

Unearned Revenue			
		Unadj. Bal.	120,000
(c)	100,000		
		Adj. Bal.	20,000

Services Revenue			
		(c)	100,000
		(e)	7,000
		Adj. Bal.	107,000

Insurance Expense		
(d)	600	

Prepaid Insurance			
Unadj. Bal.	1,800		
		(d)	600
Adj. Bal.	1,200		

Accounts Receivable		
(e)	7,000	

3. Financial statement effects of adjusting journal entries.

Entry	Amount in the Entry	Effect on Net profit	Effect on Total Assets	Effect on Total Liabilities	Effect on Total Equity
a	$ 1,750	$ 1,750 ↓	No effect	$ 1,750 ↑	$ 1,750 ↓
b	4,000	4,000 ↓	$4,000 ↓	No effect	4,000 ↓
c	100,000	100,000 ↑	No effect	$100,000 ↓	100,000 ↑
d	600	600 ↓	$ 600 ↓	No effect	600 ↓
e	7,000	7,000 ↑	$7,000 ↑	No effect	7,000 ↑

DEMONSTRATION PROBLEM 2

Use the following adjusted trial balance to answer questions 1–3.

CHOI COMPANY Adjusted Trial Balance December 31		
	Debit	Credit
Cash	$ 3,050	
Accounts receivable	400	
Prepaid insurance	830	
Supplies	80	
Equipment	217,200	
Accumulated depreciation—Equipment		$ 29,100
Wages payable		880

[continued on next page]

[continued from previous page]

Interest payable		3,600
Unearned rent		460
Long-term notes payable		150,000
M. Choi, Capital		40,340
M. Choi, Withdrawals	21,000	
Rent earned		57,500
Wages expense	25,000	
Utilities expense	1,900	
Insurance expense	3,200	
Supplies expense	250	
Depreciation expense—Equipment	5,970	
Interest expense	3,000	
Totals	$281,880	$281,880

1. Prepare the annual income statement from the adjusted trial balance of Choi Company.

Answer:

CHOI COMPANY		
Income Statement		
For Year Ended December 31		
Revenues		
Rent earned		$57,500
Expenses		
Wages expense	($25,000)	
Utilities expense	(1,900)	
Insurance expense	(3,200)	
Supplies expense	(250)	
Depreciation expense—Equipment	(5,970)	
Interest expense	(3,000)	
Total expenses		(39,320)
Net profit		$18,180

2. Prepare a statement of changes in equity from the adjusted trial balance of Choi Company. Choi's capital account balance of $40,340 consists of a $30,340 balance from the prior year-end, plus a $10,000 owner investment during the current year.

Answer:

CHOI COMPANY		
Statement of Changes in Equity		
For Year Ended December 31		
M. Choi, Capital, December 31 prior year-end		$30,340
Owner investments	$10,000	
Net profit	18,180	28,180
		58,520
Withdrawals by owner		(21,000)
M. Choi, Capital, December 31 current year-end........		$37,520

3. Prepare a statement of financial position from the adjusted trial balance of Choi Company.

Answer:

CHOI COMPANY
Statement of Financial Position
December 31

Assets		
Cash		$ 3,050
Accounts receivable		400
Prepaid insurance		830
Supplies		80
Equipment	$217,200	
Accumulated depreciation	(29,100)	188,100
Total assets		$192,460
Liabilities		
Wages payable		$ 880
Interest payable		3,600
Unearned rent		460
Long-term notes payable		150,000
Total liabilities		$154,940
Equity		
M. Choi, Capital		37,520
Total liabilities and equity		$192,460

APPENDIX

3A Alternative Accounting for Prepayments

This appendix explains an alternative in accounting for prepaid expenses and unearned revenues.

P4 Explain the alternatives in accounting for prepaids.

Recording Prepayment of Expenses in Expense Accounts An alternative method is to record *all* prepaid expenses with debits to expense accounts. If any prepaids remain unused or unexpired at the end of an accounting period, then adjusting entries must transfer the cost of the unused portions from expense accounts to prepaid expense (asset) accounts. This alternative method is acceptable. The financial statements are identical under either method, but the adjusting entries are different. To illustrate the differences between these two methods, let's look at FastForward's cash payment of December 6 for 24 months of insurance coverage beginning on December 1. FastForward recorded that payment with a debit to an asset account, but it could have recorded a debit to an expense account. These alternatives are shown in Exhibit 3A.1.

EXHIBIT 3A.1

Alternative Initial Entries for Prepaid Expenses

		Payment Recorded as Asset		Payment Recorded as Expense	
Dec. 6	Prepaid Insurance	2,400			
	Cash		2,400		
Dec. 6	Insurance Expense			2,400	
	Cash				2,400

At the end of its accounting period on December 31, insurance protection for one month has expired. This means $100 ($2,400/24) of insurance coverage expired and is an expense for December. The adjusting entry depends on how the original payment was recorded. This is shown in Exhibit 3A.2.

		Payment Recorded as Asset	Payment Recorded as Expense
Dec. 31	Insurance Expense	100	
	Prepaid Insurance	100	
Dec. 31	Prepaid Insurance		2,300
	Insurance Expense		2,300

EXHIBIT 3A.2

Adjusting Entry for Prepaid Expenses for the Two Alternatives

When these entries are posted to the accounts in the ledger, we can see that these two methods give identical results. The December 31 adjusted account balances in Exhibit 3A.3 show Prepaid Insurance of $2,300 and Insurance Expense of $100 for both methods.

Payment Recorded as Asset		

Prepaid Insurance		128
Dec. 6	2,400	Dec. 31	100
Balance	2,300	

Insurance Expense		637
Dec. 31	100	

Payment Recorded as Expense		

Prepaid Insurance		128
Dec. 31	2,300	

Insurance Expense		637
Dec. 6	2,400	Dec. 31	2,300
Balance	100	

EXHIBIT 3A.3

Account Balances under Two Alternatives for Recording Prepaid Expenses

Recording Prepayment of Revenues in Revenue Accounts As with prepaid expenses, an alternative method is to record *all* unearned revenues with credits to revenue accounts. If any revenues are unearned at the end of an accounting period, then adjusting entries must transfer the unearned portions from revenue accounts to unearned revenue (liability) accounts. This alternative method is acceptable. The adjusting entries are different for these two alternatives, but the financial statements are identical. To illustrate the accounting differences between these two methods, let's look at FastForward's December 26 receipt of $3,000 for consulting services covering the period December 27 to February 24. FastForward recorded this transaction with a credit to a liability account. The alternative is to record it with a credit to a revenue account, as shown in Exhibit 3A.4.

		Receipt Recorded as Liability	Receipt Recorded as Revenue
Dec. 26	Cash	3,000	
	Unearned Consulting Revenue	3,000	
Dec. 26	Cash		3,000
	Consulting Revenue		3,000

EXHIBIT 3A.4

Alternative Initial Entries for Unearned Revenues

By the end of its accounting period on December 31, FastForward has earned $250 of this revenue. This means $250 of the liability has been satisfied. Depending on how the initial receipt is recorded, the adjusting entry is as shown in Exhibit 3A.5.

		Receipt Recorded as Liability	Receipt Recorded as Revenue
Dec. 31	Unearned Consulting Revenue	250	
	Consulting Revenue	250	
Dec. 31	Consulting Revenue		2,750
	Unearned Consulting Revenue		2,750

EXHIBIT 3A.5

Adjusting Entry for Unearned Revenues for the Two Alternatives

After adjusting entries are posted, the two alternatives give identical results. The December 31 adjusted account balances in Exhibit 3A.6 show unearned consulting revenue of $2,750 and consulting revenue of $250 for both methods.

EXHIBIT 3A.6

Account Balances under Two Alternatives for Recording Unearned Revenues

Receipt Recorded as Liability			
Unearned Consulting Revenue			236
Dec. 31	250	Dec. 26	3,000
		Balance	2,750

Receipt Recorded as Revenue			
Unearned Consulting Revenue			236
		Dec. 31	2,750

Consulting Revenue			403
		Dec. 31	250

Consulting Revenue			403
Dec. 31	2,750	Dec. 26	3,000
		Balance	250

Summary

C1 **Explain the importance of periodic reporting and the time period assumption.** The value of information is often linked to its timeliness. To provide timely information, accounting systems prepare periodic reports at regular intervals. The time period assumption presumes that an organization's activities can be divided into specific time periods for periodic reporting.

C2 **Explain accrual accounting and how it improves financial statements.** Accrual accounting recognizes revenue when earned and expenses when incurred—not necessarily when cash inflows and outflows occur. This information is valuable in assessing a company's financial position and performance.

C3 **Identify the types of adjustments and their purpose.** Adjustments can be grouped according to the timing of cash receipts and cash payments relative to when they are recognized as revenues or expenses as follows: prepaid expenses, unearned revenues, accrued expenses, and accrued revenues. Adjusting entries are necessary so that revenues, expenses, assets, and liabilities are correctly reported.

A1 **Explain how accounting adjustments link to financial statements.** Accounting adjustments bring an asset or liability account balance to its correct amount. They also update related expense or revenue accounts. Every adjusting entry affects one or more income statement accounts *and* one or more statement of financial position accounts. An adjusting entry never affects cash.

A2 **Compute profit margin and describe its use in analyzing company performance.** *Profit margin* is defined as the reporting period's net profit divided by its net sales. Profit margin reflects on a company's earnings activities by showing how much income is in each dollar of sales.

P1 **Prepare and explain adjusting entries.** *Prepaid expenses* refer to items paid for in advance of receiving their benefits.

Prepaid expenses are assets. Adjusting entries for prepaids involve increasing (debiting) expenses and decreasing (crediting) assets. *Unearned* (or *prepaid*) *revenues* refer to cash received in advance of providing products and services. Unearned revenues are liabilities. Adjusting entries for unearned revenues involve increasing (crediting) revenues and decreasing (debiting) unearned revenues. *Accrued expenses* refer to costs incurred in a period that are both unpaid and unrecorded. Adjusting entries for recording accrued expenses involve increasing (debiting) expenses and increasing (crediting) liabilities. *Accrued revenues* refer to revenues earned in a period that are both unrecorded and not yet received in cash. Adjusting entries for recording accrued revenues involve increasing (debiting) assets and increasing (crediting) revenues.

P2 **Explain and prepare an adjusted trial balance.** An adjusted trial balance is a list of accounts and balances prepared after recording and posting adjusting entries. Financial statements are often prepared from the adjusted trial balance.

P3 **Prepare financial statements from an adjusted trial balance.** Revenue and expense balances are reported on the income statement. Asset, liability, and equity balances are reported on the statement of financial position. We usually prepare statements in the following order: income statement, statement of changes in equity, statement of financial position, and statement of cash flows.

P4^A **Explain the alternatives in accounting for prepaids.** Charging all prepaid expenses to expense accounts when they are purchased is acceptable. When this is done, adjusting entries must transfer any unexpired amounts from expense accounts to asset accounts. Crediting all unearned revenues to revenue accounts when cash is received is also acceptable. In this case, the adjusting entries must transfer any unearned amounts from revenue accounts to unearned revenue accounts.

Guidance Answers to Decision Maker and Decision Ethics

Investor Prepaid expenses are items paid for in advance of receiving their benefits. They are assets and are expensed as they are used up. The publishing company's treatment of the signing bonus is

acceptable provided future book sales can at least match the $500,000 expense. As an investor, you are concerned about the risk of future book sales. The riskier the likelihood of future book sales is, the more likely your analysis is to treat the $500,000, or a portion of it, as an expense, not a prepaid expense (asset).

Entrepreneur Depreciation is a process of cost allocation, not asset valuation. Knowing the depreciation schedule is not especially useful in your estimation of what the building and equipment are currently worth. Your own assessment of the age, quality, and usefulness of the building and equipment is more important.

Loan Officer Your concern in lending to this store arises from analysis of current-year sales. While increased revenues and income are fine, your concern is with collectibility of these promotional sales. If the owner sold products to customers with poor records of

paying bills, then collectibility of these sales is low. Your analysis must assess this possibility and recognize any expected losses.

Financial Officer Omitting accrued expenses and recognizing revenue early can mislead financial statement users. One action is to request a second meeting with the president so you can explain that accruing expenses when incurred and recognizing revenue when earned are required practices. If the president persists, you might discuss the situation with legal counsel and any auditors involved. Your ethical action might cost you this job, but the potential pitfalls for falsification of statements, reputation and personal integrity loss, and other costs are too great.

Guidance Answers to Quick Checks

1. An annual reporting (or accounting) period covers one year and refers to the preparation of annual financial statements. The annual reporting period is not always a calendar year that ends on December 31. An organization can adopt a fiscal year consisting of any consecutive 12 months or 52 weeks.

2. Interim financial statements (covering less than one year) are prepared to provide timely information to decision makers.

3. The revenue recognition principle and the matching principle lead most directly to the adjusting process.

4. No. Cash basis accounting is not consistent with the matching principle because it reports revenue when received, not necessarily when earned, and expenses when paid, not necessarily in the period when the expenses were incurred as a result of the revenues earned.

5. No expense is reported in 2016. Under cash basis accounting, the entire $4,800 is reported as an expense in April 2015 when the premium is paid.

6. If the accrued revenues adjustment of $200 is not made, then both revenues and net profit are understated by $200 on the current year's income statement, and both assets and equity are understated by $200 on the statement of financial position.

7. A contra account is an account that is subtracted from the balance of a related account. Use of a contra account provides more information than simply reporting a net amount.

8. An accrued expense is a cost incurred in a period that is both unpaid and unrecorded prior to adjusting entries. One example is salaries earned but not yet paid at period-end.

9. An unearned revenue arises when a firm receives cash (or other assets) from a customer before providing the services or products to the customer. A magazine subscription paid in advance is one example; season ticket sales is another.

10.
Salaries Payable	1,000	
Salaries Expense	6,000	
Cash		7,000
Paid salary including accrual from December.		

11. The probable adjusting entries of Jordan Air are:
Insurance Expense	300	
Prepaid Insurance		300
To record insurance expired.		
Salaries Expense	1,400	
Salaries Payable		1,400
To record accrued salaries.		

12. Revenue accounts and expense accounts.

13. Statement of changes in equity.

Key Terms

www.mheducation.asia/olc/wildkwokFAP

Accounting period (p. 94)

Accrual basis accounting (p. 95)

Accrued expenses (p. 101)

Accrued revenues (p. 103)

Adjusted trial balance (p. 106)

Adjusting entry (p. 96)

Annual financial statements (p. 94)

Carrying amount (p. 100)

Cash basis accounting (p. 95)

Contra account (p. 99)

Depreciation (p. 99)

Expense recognition (or matching) principle (p. 96)

Financial year (p. 95)

Interim financial statements (p. 94)

Natural business year (p. 95)

Prepaid expenses (p. 97)

Profit margin (p. 108)

Property, plant, and equipment (p. 99)

Straight-line depreciation method (p. 99)

Time period assumption (p. 94)

Unadjusted trial balance (p. 106)

Unearned revenues (p. 100)

Additional Quiz Questions are available at the book's Website.

1. A company forgot to record accrued and unpaid employee wages of $350,000 at period-end. This oversight would
   a. Understate net profit by $350,000.
   b. Overstate net profit by $350,000.
   c. Have no effect on net profit.
   d. Overstate assets by $350,000.
   e. Understate assets by $350,000.

2. Prior to recording adjusting entries, the Supplies account has a $450 debit balance. A physical count of supplies shows $125 of unused supplies still available. The required adjusting entry is:
   a. Debit Supplies $125; Credit Supplies Expense $125.
   b. Debit Supplies $325; Credit Supplies Expense $325.
   c. Debit Supplies Expense $325; Credit Supplies $325.
   d. Debit Supplies Expense $325; Credit Supplies $125.
   e. Debit Supplies Expense $125; Credit Supplies $125.

3. On May 1, 2015, a two-year insurance policy was purchased for $24,000 with coverage to begin immediately. What is the amount of insurance expense that appears on the company's income statement for the year ended December 31, 2015?
   a. $4,000
   b. $8,000
   c. $12,000
   d. $20,000
   e. $24,000

4. On November 1, 2015, Stockton Co. receives $3,600 cash from Hans Co. for consulting services to be provided evenly over the period November 1, 2015, to April 30, 2016—at which time Stockton credited $3,600 to Unearned Consulting Fees. The adjusting entry on December 31, 2015 (Stockton's year-end) would include a
   a. Debit to Unearned Consulting Fees for $1,200.
   b. Debit to Unearned Consulting Fees for $2,400.
   c. Credit to Consulting Fees Earned for $2,400.
   d. Debit to Consulting Fees Earned for $1,200.
   e. Credit to Cash for $3,600.

5. If a company had $15,000 in net profit for the year, and its sales were $300,000 for the same year, what is its profit margin?
   a. 20%
   b. 2,000%
   c. $285,000
   d. $315,000
   e. 5%

A *Superscript letter A denotes assignments based on Appendix 3A.*

🎲 Icon denotes assignments that involve decision making.

Discussion Questions

1. What is the difference between the cash basis and the accrual basis of accounting?

2. 🎲 Why is the accrual basis of accounting generally preferred over the cash basis?

3. What type of business is most likely to select a fiscal year that corresponds to its natural business year instead of the calendar year?

4. What is a prepaid expense and where is it reported in the financial statements?

5. 🎲 What type of assets require adjusting entries to record depreciation?

6. 🎲 What contra account is used when recording and reporting the effects of depreciation? Why is it used?

7. Nestlé has an account called "deferred income" in its statement of financial position. Explain what you think it means.

8. What is an accrued revenue? Give an example.

9.ᴬ If a company initially records prepaid expenses with debits to expense accounts, what type of account is debited in the adjusting entries for those prepaid expenses?

10. 🎲 Refer to Adidas' consolidated statement of financial position in Appendix A. Identify one asset account that requires adjustment before annual financial statements can be prepared. What would be the effect on the consolidated income statement if this asset account were not adjusted?

11. 🎲 Refer to Samsung's 2012 consolidated statement of financial position in Appendix A. Under the section on "Current liabilities," explain the difference between "Advance received" and "Accrued expenses."

12. 🎲 Refer to Puma's 2013 consolidated statement of financial position from its Website (http://about.puma.com/en/investor-relations/financial-reports). If it made an adjustment for unpaid wages at year-end, where would the accrued wages be reported on its consolidated statement of financial position?

13. Refer to 361 Degrees' 2013 consolidated statement of financial position from its Website (http://ir.361sport.com/html/ir report.php). Identify the amount for property, plant, and equipment. What adjusting entry is necessary (no numbers required) for this account when preparing financial statements?

---

connect

QUICK STUDY

QS 3-1

Identifying accounting adjustments

P1

Classify the following adjusting entries as involving prepaid expenses (PE), unearned revenues (UR), accrued expenses (AE), or accrued revenues (AR).

a. _____ To record revenue earned that was previously received as cash in advance.

b. _____ To record annual depreciation expense.

c. _____ To record wages expense incurred but not yet paid (nor recorded).

d. _____ To record revenue earned but not yet billed (nor recorded).

e. _____ To record expiration of prepaid insurance.

a. On July 1, 2015, Baxter Company paid $1,800 for six months of insurance coverage. No adjustments have been made to the Prepaid Insurance account, and it is now December 31, 2015. Prepare the journal entry to reflect expiration of the insurance as at December 31, 2015.

b. Tyrell Company has a Supplies account balance of $1,000 on January 1, 2015. During 2015, it purchased $3,000 of supplies. As at December 31, 2015, a supplies inventory shows $1,300 of supplies available. Prepare the adjusting journal entry to correctly report the balance of the Supplies account and the Supplies Expense account as at December 31, 2015.

QS 3-2
Adjusting prepaid expenses
P1

---

a. Carlos Company purchases $30,000 of equipment on January 1, 2015. The equipment is expected to last five years and be worth $5,000 at the end of that time. Prepare the entry to record one year's depreciation expense of $5,000 for the equipment as at December 31, 2015.

b. Chaves Company purchases $40,000 of land on January 1, 2015. The land is expected to last indefinitely. What depreciation adjustment, if any, should be made with respect to the Land account as at December 31, 2015?

QS 3-3
Adjusting for depreciation
P1

---

a. Eager Co. receives $20,000 cash in advance for 4 months of legal services on October 1, 2015, and records it by debiting Cash and crediting Unearned Revenue both for $20,000. It is now December 31, 2015, and Eager has provided legal services as planned. What adjusting entry should Eager make to account for the work performed from October 1 through December 31, 2015?

b. Rutherford Co. started a new publication called *Contest News*. Its subscribers pay $48 to receive 12 issues. With every new subscriber, Rutherford debits Cash and credits Unearned Subscription Revenue for the amounts received. The company has 100 new subscribers as at July 1, 2015. It sends *Contest News* to each of these subscribers every month from July through December. Assuming no changes in subscribers, prepare the journal entry that Rutherford must make as at December 31, 2015, to adjust the Subscription Revenue account and the Unearned Subscription Revenue account.

QS 3-4
Adjusting for unearned revenues
A1 P1

Marsha Moder employs one college student every summer in her coffee shop. The student works the five weekdays and is paid on the following Monday. (For example, a student who works Monday through Friday, June 1 through June 5, is paid for that work on Monday, June 8.) Moder adjusts her books monthly, if needed, to show salaries earned but unpaid at month-end. The student works the last week of July—Friday is August 1. If the student earns $100 per day, what adjusting entry must Moder make on July 31 to correctly record accrued salaries expense for July?

QS 3-5
Accruing salaries
A1 P1

Adjusting entries affect at least one statement of financial position account and at least one income statement account. For the following entries, identify the account to be debited and the account to be credited. Indicate which of the accounts is the income statement account and which is the statement of financial position account.

a. Entry to record revenue earned that was previously received as cash in advance.

b. Entry to record annual depreciation expense.

c. Entry to record wage expenses incurred but not yet paid (nor recorded).

d. Entry to record revenue earned but not yet billed (nor recorded).

e. Entry to record expiration of prepaid insurance.

QS 3-6
Recording and analyzing adjusting entries
A1

In its first year of operations, Harden Co. earned $39,000 in revenues and received $33,000 cash from these customers. The company incurred expenses of $22,500 but had not paid $2,250 of them at year-end. The company also prepaid $3,750 cash for expenses that would be incurred the next year. Calculate the first year's net profit under both the cash basis and the accrual basis of accounting.

QS 3-7
Computing accrual and cash income
P1 C2

QS 3-8
Interpreting adjusting entries
C2 P2

The following information is taken from Cruz Company's unadjusted and adjusted trial balances.

	Unadjusted		Adjusted	
	Debit	Credit	Debit	Credit
Prepaid insurance.........	$4,100		$3,700	
Interest payable		$ 0		$800

Given this information, which of the following is likely included among its adjusting entries?

a. A $400 credit to Prepaid Insurance and an $800 debit to Interest Payable.

b. A $400 debit to Insurance Expense and an $800 debit to Interest Payable.

c. A $400 debit to Insurance Expense and an $800 debit to Interest Expense.

QS 3-9
Determining effects of
adjusting entries
C3 A1

In making adjusting entries at the end of its accounting period, Gomez Consulting failed to record $1,600 of insurance coverage that had expired. This $1,600 cost had been initially debited to the Prepaid Insurance account. The company also failed to record accrued salaries expense of $1,000. As a result of these two oversights, the financial statements for the reporting period will [choose one] (1) understate assets by $1,600; (2) understate expenses by $2,600; (3) understate net profit by $1,000; or (4) overstate liabilities by $1,000.

QS 3-10
Preparing adjusting entries
C3 P1

During the year, Lyle Co. recorded prepayments of expenses in asset accounts, and cash receipts of unearned revenues in liability accounts. At the end of its annual accounting period, the company must make three adjusting entries: (1) accrue salaries expense, (2) adjust the Unearned Services Revenue account to recognize earned revenue, and (3) record services revenue earned for which cash will be received the following period. For each of these adjusting entries (1), (2), and (3), indicate the account from *a* through *i* to be debited and the account to be credited.

a. Prepaid Salaries   **d.** Salaries Payable   **g.** Unearned Services Revenue

b. Salaries Expense   **e.** Equipment   **h.** Accounts Receivable

c. Services Revenue   **f.** Cash   **i.** Accounts Payable

QS 3-11
Analyzing profit margin
A2

Yang Company reported net profit of $37,925 and net sales of $390,000 for the current year. Calculate the company's profit margin and interpret the result. Assume that its competitors earn an average profit margin of 15%.

QS 3-12^A
Preparing adjusting entries
C3 P4

Diego Consulting initially records prepaid and unearned items in income statement accounts. Given this company's accounting practices, which of the following applies to the preparation of adjusting entries at the end of its first accounting period?

a. Earned but unbilled (and unrecorded) consulting fees are recorded with a debit to Unearned Consulting Fees and a credit to Consulting Fees Earned.

b. Unpaid salaries are recorded with a debit to Prepaid Salaries and a credit to Salaries Expense.

c. The cost of unused office supplies is recorded with a debit to Supplies Expense and a credit to Office Supplies.

d. Unearned fees (on which cash was received in advance earlier in the period) are recorded with a debit to Consulting Fees Earned and a credit to Unearned Consulting Fees.

connect

In the blank space beside each adjusting entry, enter the letter of the explanation *A* through *F* that most closely describes the entry.

A. To record this period's depreciation expense.
B. To record accrued salaries expense.
C. To record this period's use of a prepaid expense.
D. To record accrued interest revenue.
E. To record accrued interest expense.
F. To record the earning of previously unearned income.

_____ 1.	Salaries Expense	13,280	
	Salaries Payable		13,280
_____ 2.	Interest Expense	2,208	
	Interest Payable		2,208
_____ 3.	Insurance Expense	3,180	
	Prepaid Insurance		3,180
_____ 4.	Unearned Professional Fees	19,250	
	Professional Fees Earned		19,250
_____ 5.	Interest Receivable	3,300	
	Interest Revenue		3,300
_____ 6.	Depreciation Expense	38,217	
	Accumulated Depreciation		38,217

For each of the following separate cases, prepare adjusting entries required of financial statements for the year ended (date of) December 31, 2015. (Assume that prepaid expenses are initially recorded in asset accounts and that fees collected in advance of work are initially recorded as liabilities.)

a. One-third of the work related to $30,000 cash received in advance is performed this period.
b. Wages of $9,000 are earned by workers but not paid as at December 31, 2015.
c. Depreciation on the company's equipment for 2015 is $19,127.
d. The Office Supplies account had a $480 debit balance on December 31, 2014. During 2015, $5,349 of office supplies are purchased. A physical count of supplies at December 31, 2015, shows $587 of supplies available.
e. The Prepaid Insurance account had a $5,000 balance on December 31, 2014. An analysis of insurance policies shows that $2,200 of unexpired insurance benefits remain at December 31, 2015.
f. The company has earned (but not recorded) $750 of interest from investments in CDs for the year ended December 31, 2015. The interest revenue will be received on January 10, 2016.
g. The company has a bank loan and has incurred (but not recorded) interest expense of $3,500 for the year ended December 31, 2015. The company must pay the interest on January 2, 2016.

Prepare adjusting journal entries for the year ended (date of) December 31, 2015, for each of these separate situations. Assume that prepaid expenses are initially recorded in asset accounts. Also assume that fees collected in advance of work are initially recorded as liabilities.

a. Depreciation on the company's equipment for 2015 is computed to be $16,000.
b. The Prepaid Insurance account had a $7,000 debit balance at December 31, 2015, before adjusting for the costs of any expired coverage. An analysis of the company's insurance policies showed that $1,040 of unexpired insurance coverage remains.
c. The Office Supplies account had a $300 debit balance on December 31, 2014; and $2,680 of office supplies were purchased during the year. The December 31, 2015, physical count showed $354 of supplies available.
d. One-half of the work related to $10,000 of cash received in advance was performed this period.
e. The Prepaid Insurance account had a $5,600 debit balance at December 31, 2015, before adjusting for the costs of any expired coverage. An analysis of insurance policies showed that $4,600 of coverage had expired.
f. Wage expenses of $4,000 have been incurred but are not paid as at December 31, 2015.

Exercise 3-4

Adjusting and paying accrued expenses

A1 P1

The following three separate situations require adjusting journal entries to prepare financial statements as at April 30. For each situation, present both the April 30 adjusting entry and the subsequent entry during May to record the payment of the accrued expenses.

a. On April 1, the company retained an attorney for a flat monthly fee of $2,500. This amount is paid to the attorney on the 12th day of the following month in which it was earned.

b. A $780,000 note payable requires 9.6% annual interest, or $6,240 to be paid at the 20th day of each month. The interest was last paid on April 20 and the next payment is due on May 20. As at April 30, $2,080 of interest expense has accrued.

c. Total weekly salaries expense for all employees is $9,000. This amount is paid at the end of the day on Friday of each five-day workweek. April 30 falls on Tuesday of this year, which means that the employees had worked two days since the last payday. The next payday is May 3.

Exercise 3-5

Determining cost flows through accounts

C1 A1 P1

Determine the missing amounts in each of these four separate situations a through d.

	a	b	c	d
Supplies available—prior year-end	$ 300	$1,600	$1,360	?
Supplies purchased during the current year	2,100	5,400	?	$6,000
Supplies available—current year-end	750	?	1,840	800
Supplies expense for the current year..............	?	1,300	9,600	6,575

Exercise 3-6

Adjusting and paying accrued wages

C1 P1

Pablo Management has five part-time employees, each of whom earns $100 per day. They are normally paid on Fridays for work completed Monday through Friday of the same week. They were paid in full on Friday, December 28, 2015. The next week, the five employees worked only four days because New Year's Day was an unpaid holiday. Show (a) the adjusting entry that would be recorded on Monday, December 31, 2015, and (b) the journal entry that would be made to record payment of the employees' wages on Friday, January 4, 2016.

Exercise 3-7

Analyzing and preparing adjusting entries

A1 P1 P3

Following are two income statements for Kendall Co. for the year ended December 31. The left column is prepared before any adjusting entries are recorded, and the right column includes the effects of adjusting entries. The company records cash receipts and payments related to unearned and prepaid items in statement of financial position accounts. Analyze the statements and prepare the eight adjusting entries that likely were recorded. (*Note:* 30% of the $6,000 adjustment for Fees Earned has been earned but not billed, and the other 70% has been earned by performing services that were paid for in advance.)

KENDALL CO. Income Statements For Year Ended December 31		
	Unadjusted	Adjusted
Revenues		
Fees earned	$24,000	$30,000
Commissions earned	42,500	42,500
Total revenues	66,500	72,500
Expenses		
Depreciation expense—Computers	0	(1,500)
Depreciation expense—Office furniture	0	(1,750)
Salaries expense	(12,500)	(14,950)
Insurance expense	0	(1,300)
Rent expense	(4,500)	(4,500)
Office supplies expense	0	(480)
Advertising expense	(3,000)	(3,000)
Utilities expense	(1,250)	(1,320)
Total expenses	(21,250)	(28,800)
Net profit	$45,250	$43,700

On March 1, 2013, a company paid a $16,200 premium on a 36-month insurance policy for coverage beginning on that date. Refer to that policy and fill in the blanks in the following table.

Statement of Financial Position Prepaid Insurance Asset Using				Insurance Expense Using		
	Accrual Basis	Cash Basis			Accrual Basis	Cash Basis
Dec. 31, 2013	$_____	$_____	2013		$_____	$_____
Dec. 31, 2014	_____	_____	2014		_____	_____
Dec. 31, 2015	_____	_____	2015		_____	_____
Dec. 31, 2016	_____	_____	2016		_____	_____
			Total		$_____	$_____

Use the following information to compute profit margin for each separate company *a* through *e*.

	Net profit	**Net Sales**		**Net profit**	**Net Sales**
a.	$ 5,390	$ 44,830	d.	$55,234	$1,458,999
b.	87,644	398,954	e.	70,158	435,925
c.	93,385	257,082			

Which of the five companies is the most profitable according to the profit margin ratio? Interpret that company's profit margin ratio.

Corbel Company experienced the following events and transactions during July.

July   1   Received $2,000 cash in advance of performing work for Beth Oker.
     6   Received $8,400 cash in advance of performing work for Lisa Poe.
   12   Completed the job for Oker.
   18   Received $7,500 cash in advance of performing work for Henry Coe.
   27   Completed the job for Poe.
   31   None of the work for Coe has been performed.

a. Prepare journal entries (including any adjusting entries as at the end of the month) to record these events using the procedure of initially crediting the Unearned Fees account when payment is received from a customer in advance of performing services.

b. Prepare journal entries (including any adjusting entries as at the end of the month) to record these events using the procedure of initially crediting the Fees Earned account when payment is received from a customer in advance of performing services.

c. Under each method, determine the amount of earned fees reported on the income statement for July and the amount of unearned fees reported on the statement of financial position as at July 31.

On-The-Mark Construction began operations on December 1. In setting up its accounting procedures, the company decided to debit expense accounts when it prepays its expenses and to credit revenue accounts when customers pay for services in advance. Prepare journal entries for items *a* through *d* and the adjusting entries as at its December 31 period-end for items *e* through *g*.

a. Supplies are purchased on December 1 for $3,000 cash.

b. The company prepaid its insurance premiums for $1,440 cash on December 2.

c. On December 15, the company receives an advance payment of $12,000 cash from a customer for remodeling work.

d. On December 28, the company receives $3,600 cash from another customer for remodeling work to be performed in January.

e. A physical count on December 31 indicates that On-The-Mark has $1,920 of supplies available.

f. An analysis of the insurance policies in effect on December 31 shows that $240 of insurance coverage had expired.

g. As at December 31, only one remodeling project has been worked on and completed. The $6,300 fee for this project had been received in advance.

━━━━━━━━━━━━━━━━━━━━━━━━━━━━ connect

PROBLEM SET A

Problem 3-1A
Preparing adjusting and subsequent journal entries

C1 A1 P1

Meyer Co. follows the practice of recording prepaid expenses and unearned revenues in statement of financial position accounts. The company's annual accounting period ends on December 31, 2015. The following information concerns the adjusting entries to be recorded as at that date.

a. The Office Supplies account started the year with a $3,000 balance. During 2015, the company purchased supplies for $12,400, which was added to the Office Supplies account. The inventory of supplies available at December 31, 2015, totaled $2,640.

b. An analysis of the company's insurance policies provided the following facts.

Policy	Date of Purchase	Months of Coverage	Cost
A	April 1, 2014	24	$15,840
B	April 1, 2015	36	13,068
C	August 1, 2015	12	2,700

The total premium for each policy was paid in full (for all months) at the purchase date, and the Prepaid Insurance account was debited for the full cost. (Year-end adjusting entries for Prepaid Insurance were properly recorded in all prior years.)

c. The company has 15 employees, who earn a total of $2,100 in salaries each working day. They are paid each Monday for their work in the five-day workweek ending on the previous Friday. Assume that December 31, 2015, is a Tuesday, and all 15 employees worked the first two days of that week. Because New Year's Day is a paid holiday, they will be paid salaries for five full days on Monday, January 6, 2016.

d. The company purchased a building on January 1, 2015. It cost $855,000 and is expected to have a $45,000 residual value at the end of its predicted 30-year life. Annual depreciation is $27,000.

e. Since the company is not large enough to occupy the entire building it owns, it rented space to a tenant at $2,400 per month, starting on November 1, 2015. The rent was paid on time on November 1, and the amount received was credited to the Rent Earned account. However, the tenant has not paid the December rent. The company has worked out an agreement with the tenant, who has promised to pay both December and January rent in full on January 15. The tenant has agreed not to fall behind again.

f. On November 1, the company rented space to another tenant for $2,175 per month. The tenant paid five months' rent in advance on that date. The payment was recorded with a credit to the Unearned Rent account.

Required

1. Use the information to prepare adjusting entries as at December 31, 2015.

2. Prepare journal entries to record the first subsequent cash transaction in 2016 for parts c and e.

For each of the following entries, enter the letter of the explanation that most closely describes it in the space beside each entry. (You can use letters more than once.)

A. To record receipt of unearned revenue.
B. To record this period's earning of prior unearned revenue.
C. To record payment of an accrued expense.
D. To record receipt of an accrued revenue.
E. To record an accrued expense.
F. To record an accrued revenue.
G. To record this period's use of a prepaid expense.
H. To record payment of a prepaid expense.
I. To record this period's depreciation expense.

Problem 3-2A
Identifying adjusting entries with explanations

C3 P1

_____	1.	Rent Expense	2,000	
		Prepaid Rent		2,000
_____	2.	Interest Expense	1,000	
		Interest Payable		1,000
_____	3.	Depreciation Expense	4,000	
		Accumulated Depreciation		4,000
_____	4.	Unearned Professional Fees	3,000	
		Professional Fees Earned		3,000
_____	5.	Insurance Expense	4,200	
		Prepaid Insurance		4,200
_____	6.	Salaries Payable	1,400	
		Cash		1,400
_____	7.	Prepaid Rent	4,500	
		Cash		4,500
_____	8.	Salaries Expense	6,000	
		Salaries Payable		6,000
_____	9.	Interest Receivable	5,000	
		Interest Revenue		5,000
_____	10.	Cash	9,000	
		Accounts Receivable (from consulting)		9,000
_____	11.	Cash	7,500	
		Unearned Professional Fees		7,500
_____	12.	Cash	2,000	
		Interest Receivable		2,000

Watson Technical Institute (WTI), a school owned by Tom Watson, provides training to individuals who pay tuition directly to the school. WTI also offers training to groups in off-site locations. Its unadjusted trial balance as at December 31, 2015, follows. WTI initially records prepaid expenses and unearned revenues in statement of financial position accounts. Descriptions of items *a* through *h* that require adjusting entries on December 31, 2015, follow.

Problem 3-3A
Preparing adjusting entries, adjusted trial balance, and financial statements

A1 P1 P2 P3

www.mheducation.asia/olc/wildkwokFAP

Additional Information Items

a. An analysis of WTI's insurance policies shows that $3,000 of coverage has expired.

b. An inventory count shows that teaching supplies costing $2,600 are available at year-end 2015.

c. Annual depreciation on the equipment is $12,000.

d. Annual depreciation on the professional library is $6,000.

e. On November 1, WTI agreed to do a special six-month course (starting immediately) for a client. The contract calls for a monthly fee of $2,200, and the client paid the first five months' fees in advance. When the cash was received, the Unearned Training Fees account was credited. The fee for the sixth month will be recorded when it is collected in 2016.

f. On October 15, WTI agreed to teach a four-month class (beginning immediately) for an individual for $3,000 tuition per month payable at the end of the class. The class started on October 15, but no payment has yet been received. (WTI's accruals are applied to the nearest half-month; for example, October recognizes one-half month accrual.)

g. WTI's two employees are paid weekly. As at the end of the year, two days' salaries have accrued at the rate of $100 per day for each employee.

h. The balance in the Prepaid Rent account represents rent for December.

	Debit	Credit
WATSON TECHNICAL INSTITUTE Unadjusted Trial Balance December 31, 2015		
Cash	$ 26,000	
Accounts receivable	0	
Teaching supplies	10,000	
Prepaid insurance	15,000	
Prepaid rent	2,000	
Professional library	30,000	
Accumulated depreciation — Professional library		$ 9,000
Equipment	70,000	
Accumulated depreciation — Equipment		16,000
Accounts payable		36,000
Salaries payable		0
Unearned training fees		11,000
T. Watson, Capital		63,600
T. Watson, Withdrawals	40,000	
Tuition fees earned		102,000
Training fees earned		38,000
Depreciation expense — Professional library	0	
Depreciation expense — Equipment	0	
Salaries expense	48,000	
Insurance expense	0	
Rent expense	22,000	
Teaching supplies expense	0	
Advertising expense	7,000	
Utilities expense	5,600	
Totals	$ 275,600	$ 275,600

Required

1. Prepare T-accounts (representing the ledger) with balances from the unadjusted trial balance.

2. Prepare the necessary adjusting journal entries for items *a* through *h* and post them to the T-accounts. Assume that adjusting entries are made only at year-end.

3. Update balances in the T-accounts for the adjusting entries and prepare an adjusted trial balance.

4. Prepare Watson Technical Institute's income statement and statement of changes in equity for the year 2015 and prepare its statement of financial position as at December 31, 2015.

Check (2*e*) Cr. Training Fees Earned, $4,400; (2*f*) Cr. Tuition Fees Earned, $7,500; (3) Adj. Trial balance totals, $301,500; (4) Net profit, $38,500; Ending T. Watson, Capital $62,100

Problem 3-4A
Interpreting unadjusted and adjusted trial balances, and preparing financial statements

C3 A1 P1 P2 P3

www.mheducation.asia/olc/wildkwokFAP

A six-column table for JJW Company follows. The first two columns contain the unadjusted trial balance for the company as at July 31, 2015. The last two columns contain the adjusted trial balance as at the same date.

Required

Analysis Component

1. Analyze the differences between the unadjusted and adjusted trial balances to determine the eight adjustments that likely were made. Show the results of your analysis by inserting these adjustment amounts in the table's two middle columns. Label each adjustment with a letter *a* through *h* and provide a short description of it at the bottom of the table.

Preparation Component

2. Use the information in the adjusted trial balance to prepare the company's (*a*) income statement and its statement of changes in equity for the year ended July 31, 2015 (*note:* J. Winner, Capital at July 31, 2014, was $28,420, and the current-year withdrawals were $10,000), and (*b*) the statement of financial position as at July 31, 2015.

Check (2) Net profit, $37,020; J. Winner, Capital (7/31/2015), $55,440; Total assets, $131,340

	Unadjusted Trial Balance		Adjustments		Adjusted Trial Balance	
Cash	$ 27,000				$ 27,000	
Accounts receivable	12,000				22,460	
Office supplies	18,000				3,000	
Prepaid insurance	7,320				4,880	
Office equipment	92,000				92,000	
Accum. depreciation—Office equip.		$ 12,000				$ 18,000
Accounts payable		9,300				10,200
Interest payable		0				800
Salaries payable		0				6,600
Unearned consulting fees		16,000				14,300
Long-term notes payable		44,000				44,000
J. Winner, Capital		28,420				28,420
J. Winner, Withdrawals	10,000				10,000	
Consulting fees earned		156,000				168,160
Depreciation expense—Office equip.	0				6,000	
Salaries expense	71,000				77,600	
Interest expense	1,400				2,200	
Insurance expense	0				2,440	
Rent expense	13,200				13,200	
Office supplies expense	0				15,000	
Advertising expense	13,800				14,700	
Totals	$265,720	$265,720			$290,480	$290,480

The adjusted trial balance for Callahay Company as at December 31, 2015, follows.

Problem 3-5A
Preparing financial statements from the adjusted trial balance and calculating profit margin
P3 A1 A2

	Debit	Credit
Cash	$ 22,000	
Accounts receivable	44,000	
Interest receivable	10,000	
Notes receivable (due in 90 days)	160,000	
Office supplies	8,000	
Automobiles	160,000	
Accumulated depreciation—Automobiles		$ 42,000
Equipment	130,000	
Accumulated depreciation—Equipment		10,000
Land	70,000	
Accounts payable		88,000
Interest payable		12,000
Salaries payable		11,000
Unearned fees		22,000
Long-term notes payable		130,000
J. Callahay, Capital		247,800
J. Callahay, Withdrawals	38,000	

[continued on next page]

[continued from previous page]

Fees earned		420,000
Interest earned		16,000
Depreciation expense—Automobiles	18,000	
Depreciation expense—Equipment	10,000	
Salaries expense	180,000	
Wages expense	32,000	
Interest expense	24,000	
Office supplies expense	26,000	
Advertising expense	50,000	
Repairs expense—Automobiles	16,800	
Totals	$998,800	$998,800

Required

Check   (1) Total assets, $552,000

1. Use the information in the adjusted trial balance to prepare (*a*) the income statement for the year ended December 31, 2015; (*b*) the statement of changes in equity for the year ended December 31, 2015; and (*c*) the statement of financial position as at December 31, 2015.

2. Calculate the profit margin for year 2015.

Problem 3-6A[A]

Recording prepaid expenses and unearned revenues

P1 P4

Quisp Co. had the following transactions in the last two months of its year ended December 31.

Nov. 1   Paid $1,500 cash for future newspaper advertising.
       1   Paid $2,160 cash for 12 months of insurance through October 31 of the next year.
      30   Received $3,300 cash for future services to be provided to a customer.
Dec. 1   Paid $2,700 cash for a consultant's services to be received over the next three months.
      15   Received $7,650 cash for future services to be provided to a customer.
      31   Of the advertising paid for on November 1, $900 worth is not yet used.
      31   A portion of the insurance paid for on November 1 has expired. No adjustment was made in November to Prepaid Insurance.
      31   Services worth $1,200 are not yet provided to the customer who paid on November 30.
      31   One-third of the consulting services paid for on December 1 have been received.
      31   The company has performed $3,000 of services that the customer paid for on December 15.

Required

1. Prepare entries for these transactions under the method that records prepaid expenses as assets and records unearned revenues as liabilities. Also prepare adjusting entries at the end of the year.

2. Prepare entries for these transactions under the method that records prepaid expenses as expenses and records unearned revenues as revenues. Also prepare adjusting entries at the end of the year.

Analysis Component

3. Explain why the alternative sets of entries in requirements 1 and 2 do not result in different financial statement amounts.

PROBLEM SET B

Problem 3-1B

Preparing adjusting and subsequent journal entries

C1 A1 P1

Nomo Co. follows the practice of recording prepaid expenses and unearned revenues in statement of financial position accounts. The company's annual accounting period ends on October 31, 2015. The following information concerns the adjusting entries that need to be recorded as at that date.

a. The Office Supplies account started the financial year with a $500 balance. During the fiscal year, the company purchased supplies for $3,650, which was added to the Office Supplies account. The supplies available at October 31, 2015, totaled $700.

b. An analysis of the company's insurance policies provided the following facts.

Policy	Date of Purchase	Months of Coverage	Cost
A	April 1, 2014	24	$3,000
B	April 1, 2015	36	3,600
C	August 1, 2015	12	660

The total premium for each policy was paid in full (for all months) at the purchase date, and the Prepaid Insurance account was debited for the full cost. (Year-end adjusting entries for Prepaid Insurance were properly recorded in all prior fiscal years.)

c. The company has four employees, who earn a total of $800 for each workday. They are paid each Monday for their work in the five-day workweek ending on the previous Friday. Assume that October 31, 2015, is a Monday, and all four employees worked the first day of that week. They will be paid salaries for five full days on Monday, November 7, 2015.

d. The company purchased a building on November 1, 2014, that cost $155,000 and is expected to have a $20,000 residual value at the end of its predicted 25-year life. Annual depreciation is $5,400.

e. Since the company does not occupy the entire building it owns, it rented space to a tenant at $600 per month, starting on September 1, 2015. The rent was paid on time on September 1, and the amount received was credited to the Rent Earned account. However, the October rent has not been paid. The company has worked out an agreement with the tenant, who has promised to pay both October and November rent in full on November 15. The tenant has agreed not to fall behind again.

f. On September 1, the company rented space to another tenant for $525 per month. The tenant paid five months' rent in advance on that date. The payment was recorded with a credit to the Unearned Rent account.

Required

1. Use the information to prepare adjusting entries as at October 31, 2015.

2. Prepare journal entries to record the first subsequent cash transaction in November 2015 for parts *c* and *e*.

Check   (1*b*) Dr. Insurance Expense, $2,675; (1*d*) Dr. Depreciation Expense, $5,400.

For each of the following entries, enter the letter of the explanation that most closely describes it in the space beside each entry. (You can use letters more than once.)

Problem 3-2B
Identifying adjusting entries with explanations
C3 P1

A. To record payment of a prepaid expense.
B. To record this period's use of a prepaid expense.
C. To record this period's depreciation expense.
D. To record receipt of unearned revenue.
E. To record this period's earning of prior unearned revenue.
F. To record an accrued expense.
G. To record payment of an accrued expense.
H. To record an accrued revenue.
I. To record receipt of accrued revenue.

___	1.	Unearned Professional Fees	6,000
		Professional Fees Earned	6,000
___	2.	Interest Receivable	3,500
		Interest Revenue	3,500
___	3.	Salaries Payable	9,000
		Cash	9,000
___	4.	Depreciation Expense	8,000
		Accumulated Depreciation	8,000
___	5.	Cash	9,000
		Unearned Professional Fees	9,000
___	6.	Insurance Expense	4,000
		Prepaid Insurance	4,000
___	7.	Interest Expense	5,000
		Interest Payable	5,000
___	8.	Cash	1,500
		Accounts Receivable (from services)	1,500
___	9.	Salaries Expense	7,000
		Salaries Payable	7,000
___	10.	Cash	1,000
		Interest Receivable	1,000
___	11.	Prepaid Rent	3,000
		Cash	3,000
___	12.	Rent Expense	7,500
		Prepaid Rent	7,500

Problem 3-3B
Preparing adjusting entries,
adjusted trial balance, and
financial statements

A1 P1 P2 P3

Following is the unadjusted trial balance for Alcorn Institute as at December 31, 2015, which initially records prepaid expenses and unearned revenues in statement of financial position accounts. The Institute provides one-on-one training to individuals who pay tuition directly to the business and offers extension training to groups in off-site locations. Shown after the trial balance are items *a* through *h* that require adjusting entries as at December 31, 2015.

ALCORN INSTITUTE
Unadjusted Trial Balance
December 31, 2015

	Debit	Credit
Cash	$ 50,000	
Accounts receivable	0	
Teaching supplies	60,000	
Prepaid insurance	18,000	
Prepaid rent	2,600	
Professional library	10,000	
Accumulated depreciation—Professional library		$ 1,500
Equipment	30,000	
Accumulated depreciation—Equipment		16,000
Accounts payable		12,200
Salaries payable		0
Unearned training fees		27,600
M. Alcorn, Capital		68,500
M. Alcorn, Withdrawals	20,000	
Tuition fees earned		105,000
Training fees earned		62,000
Depreciation expense—Professional library	0	
Depreciation expense—Equipment	0	
Salaries expense	43,200	
Insurance expense	0	
Rent expense	28,600	
Teaching supplies expense	0	
Advertising expense	18,000	
Utilities expense	12,400	
Totals	$ 292,800	$292,800

Additional Information Items

a. An analysis of the Institute's insurance policies shows that $6,400 of coverage has expired.

b. An inventory count shows that teaching supplies costing $2,500 are available at year-end 2015.

c. Annual depreciation on the equipment is $4,000.

d. Annual depreciation on the professional library is $2,000.

e. On November 1, the Institute agreed to do a special four-month course (starting immediately) for a client. The contract calls for a $4,600 monthly fee, and the client paid the first two months' fees in advance. When the cash was received, the Unearned Training Fees account was credited. The last two month's fees will be recorded when collected in 2016.

f. On October 15, the Institute agreed to teach a four-month class (beginning immediately) to an individual for $2,200 tuition per month payable at the end of the class. The class started on October 15, but no payment has yet been received. (Alcorn's accruals are applied to the nearest half-month; for example, October recognizes one-half month accrual.)

g. The Institute's only employee is paid weekly. As at the end of the year, three days' salaries have accrued at the rate of $180 per day.

h. The balance in the Prepaid Rent account represents rent for December.

Required

1. Prepare T-accounts (representing the ledger) with balances from the unadjusted trial balance.

2. Prepare the necessary adjusting journal entries for items *a* through *h*, and post them to the T-accounts. Assume that adjusting entries are made only at year-end.

3. Update balances in the T-accounts for the adjusting entries and prepare an adjusted trial balance.

4. Prepare the company's income statement and statement of changes in equity for the year 2015, and prepare its statement of financial position as at December 31, 2015.

Check (2*e*) Cr. Training Fees Earned, $9,200; (2*f*) Cr. Tuition Fees Earned, $5,500; (3) Adj. trial balance totals, $304,840; (4) Net profit, $6,460; Ending M. Alcorn, Capital, $54,960

A six-column table for Daxu Consulting Company follows. The first two columns contain the unadjusted trial balance for the company as at December 31, 2015, and the last two columns contain the adjusted trial balance as at the same date.

Problem 3-4B
Interpreting unadjusted and adjusted trial balances, and preparing financial statements

C3 A1 P1 P2 P3

	Unadjusted Trial Balance		Adjustments		Adjusted Trial Balance	
Cash	$ 48,000				$ 48,000	
Accounts receivable	70,000				76,660	
Office supplies	30,000				7,000	
Prepaid insurance	13,200				8,600	
Office equipment	150,000				150,000	
Accumulated depreciation— Office equip.		$ 30,000				$ 40,000
Accounts payable		36,000				42,000
Interest payable		0				1,600
Salaries payable		0				11,200
Unearned consulting fees		30,000				17,800
Long-term notes payable		80,000				80,000
D. Chen, Capital		70,200				70,200
D. Chen, Withdrawals	10,000				10,000	
Consulting fees earned		264,000				282,860
Depreciation expense— Office equip.	0				10,000	
Salaries expense	115,600				126,800	
Interest expense	6,400				8,000	
Insurance expense	0				4,600	
Rent expense	24,000				24,000	
Office supplies expense	0				23,000	
Advertising expense	43,000				49,000	
Totals	$510,200	$510,200			$545,660	$545,660

Required

Analysis Component

1. Analyze the differences between the unadjusted and adjusted trial balances to determine the eight adjustments that likely were made. Show the results of your analysis by inserting these adjustment amounts in the table's two middle columns. Label each adjustment with a letter *a* through *h* and provide a short description of it at the bottom of the table.

Preparation Component

2. Use the information in the adjusted trial balance to prepare this company's (*a*) income statement and its statement of changes in equity for the year ended December 31, 2015 (*note:* D. Chen, Capital at December 31, 2014, was $70,200, and the current-year withdrawals were $10,000), and (*b*) the statement of financial position as at December 31, 2015.

Check (2) Net profit, $37,460; D. Chen, Capital (12/31/11), $97,660; Total assets, $250,260

Problem 3-5B

Preparing financial statements from the adjusted trial balance and calculating profit margin

P3 A1 A2

The adjusted trial balance for Lightning Courier as at December 31, 2015, follows.

	Debit	Credit
Cash	$ 48,000	
Accounts receivable	110,000	
Interest receivable	6,000	
Notes receivable (due in 90 days)	200,000	
Office supplies	12,000	
Trucks	124,000	
Accumulated depreciation—Trucks		$ 48,000
Equipment	260,000	
Accumulated depreciation—Equipment		190,000
Land	90,000	
Accounts payable		124,000
Interest payable		22,000
Salaries payable		30,000
Unearned delivery fees		110,000
Long-term notes payable		190,000
J. Hallam, Capital		115,000
J. Hallam, Withdrawals	40,000	
Delivery fees earned		580,000
Interest earned		24,000
Depreciation expense—Trucks	24,000	
Depreciation expense—Equipment	46,000	
Salaries expense	64,000	
Wages expense	290,000	
Interest expense	25,000	
Office supplies expense	33,000	
Advertising expense	26,400	
Repairs expense—Trucks	34,600	
Totals	$1,433,000	$1,433,000

Required

Check (1) Total assets, $612,000

1. Use the information in the adjusted trial balance to prepare (*a*) the income statement for the year ended December 31, 2015, (*b*) the statement of changes in equity for the year ended December 31, 2015, and (*c*) the statement of financial position as at December 31, 2015.

2. Calculate the profit margin for year 2015.

Problem 3-6B[A]

Recording prepaid expenses and unearned revenues

P1 P4

Quake Co. had the following transactions in the last two months of its fiscal year ended May 31.

Apr. 1 Paid $3,450 cash to an accounting firm for future consulting services.
      1 Paid $2,700 cash for 12 months of insurance through March 31 of the next year.
     30 Received $7,500 cash for future services to be provided to a customer.
May 1 Paid $3,450 cash for future newspaper advertising.
     23 Received $9,450 cash for future services to be provided to a customer.
     31 Of the consulting services paid for on April 1, $1,500 worth has been received.
     31 A portion of the insurance paid for on April 1 has expired. No adjustment was made in April to Prepaid Insurance.
     31 Services worth $3,600 are not yet provided to the customer who paid on April 30.
     31 Of the advertising paid for on May 1, $1,050 worth is not yet used.
     31 The company has performed $4,500 of services that the customer paid for on May 23.

Required

1. Prepare entries for these transactions under the method that records prepaid expenses and unearned revenues in statement of financial position accounts. Also prepare adjusting entries at the end of the year.

2. Prepare entries for these transactions under the method that records prepaid expenses and unearned revenues in income statement accounts. Also prepare adjusting entries at the end of the year.

Analysis Component

3. Explain why the alternative sets of entries in parts 1 and 2 do not result in different financial statement amounts.

(This serial problem began in Chapter 1 and continues through most of the book. If previous chapter segments were not completed, the serial problem can still begin at this point.)

SP 3 After the success of the company's first two months, Santana Rey continues to operate Business Solutions. (Transactions for the first two months are described in the serial problem of Chapter 2.) The November 30, 2015, unadjusted trial balance of Business Solutions (reflecting its transactions for October and November of 2015) follows.

SERIAL PROBLEM
Business Solutions
P1 P2 P3

No.	Account Title	Debit	Credit
101	Cash	$38,264	
106	Accounts receivable	12,618	
126	Computer supplies	2,545	
128	Prepaid insurance	2,220	
131	Prepaid rent	3,300	
163	Office equipment	8,000	
164	Accumulated depreciation—Office equipment		$ 0
167	Computer equipment	20,000	
168	Accumulated depreciation—Computer equipment		0
201	Accounts payable		0
210	Wages payable		0
236	Unearned computer services revenue		0
301	S. Rey, Capital		73,000
302	S. Rey, Withdrawals	5,600	
403	Computer services revenue		25,659
612	Depreciation expense—Office equipment	0	
613	Depreciation expense—Computer equipment	0	
623	Wages expense	2,625	
637	Insurance expense	0	
640	Rent expense	0	
652	Computer supplies expense	0	
655	Advertising expense	1,728	
676	Mileage expense	704	
677	Miscellaneous expenses	250	
684	Repairs expense—Computer	805	
	Totals	$98,659	$98,659

Business Solutions had the following transactions and events in December 2015.

Dec. 2 Paid $1,025 cash to Hillside Mall for Business Solutions' share of mall advertising costs.
    3 Paid $500 cash for minor repairs to the company's computer.
    4 Received $3,950 cash from Alex's Engineering Co. for the receivable from November.
   10 Paid cash to Lyn Addie for six days of work at the rate of $125 per day.
   14 Notified by Alex's Engineering Co. that Business Solutions' bid of $7,000 on a proposed project has been accepted. Alex's paid a $1,500 cash advance to Business Solutions.
   15 Purchased $1,100 of computer supplies on credit from Harris Office Products.
   16 Sent a reminder to Gomez Co. to pay the fee for services recorded on November 8.
   20 Completed a project for Liu Corporation and received $5,625 cash.
22–26 Took the week off for the holidays.
   28 Received $3,000 cash from Gomez Co. on its receivable.

29   Reimbursed S. Rey for business automobile mileage (600 miles at $0.32 per mile).

31   S. Rey withdrew $1,500 cash from the company for personal use.

The following additional facts are collected for use in making adjusting entries prior to preparing financial statements for the company's first three months:

a. The December 31 inventory count of computer supplies shows $580 still available.

b. Three months have expired since the 12-month insurance premium was paid in advance.

c. As at December 31, Lyn Addie has not been paid for four days of work at $125 per day.

d. The company's computer is expected to have a four-year life with no residual value.

e. The office equipment is expected to have a five-year life with no residual value.

f. Three of the four months' prepaid rent has expired.

Required

1. Prepare journal entries to record each of the December transactions and events for Business Solutions. Post those entries to the accounts in the ledger.

2. Prepare adjusting entries to reflect *a* through *f*. Post those entries to the accounts in the ledger.

Check   (3) Adjusted trial balance totals, $109,034

3. Prepare an adjusted trial balance as at December 31, 2011.

4. Prepare an income statement for the three months ended December 31, 2011.

5. Prepare a statement of changes in equity for the three months ended December 31, 2011.

(6) Total assets, $83,460

6. Prepare a statement of financial position as at December 31, 2011.

Beyond the Numbers

REPORTING IN ACTION

C1   C2   A1   A2

BTN 3-1   Refer to Adidas' financial statements in Appendix A to answer the following:

1. Identify and write down the revenue recognition principle as explained in the chapter.

2. Search Adidas' notes to discover how it applies the revenue recognition principle. Report what you discover.

3. What is Adidas' profit margin for financial years ended December 31, 2013 and December 31, 2012? Round the percents to one decimal place each.

Fast Forward

4. Access Adidas' latest financial statements for fiscal years ending after December 31, 2013 from its Website (http://www.adidas-group.com/en/investors/financial-reports/). Compare and assess the December 31, 2013 financial year profit margin to any subsequent year's profit margin that you compute.

COMPARATIVE ANALYSIS

A2

BTN 3-2   Key figures for the recent two years of both Adidas and Puma are as follows:

	Adidas (in EUR millions)		Puma (in EUR millions)	
Key Figure	**Current Year**	**Prior Year**	**Current Year**	**Prior Year**
Net profit	787	526	5.3	70.2
Net sales	14,492	14,883	2,985.3	3,270.7

Required

1. Compute profit margins for (*a*) Adidas and (*b*) Puma for the two years of data shown. Round the percents to one decimal place each.

2. Which company is more successful on the basis of profit margin? Explain.

ETHICS CHALLENGE

C1   C2   A1

BTN 3-3   Jackie Bergez works for Sea Biscuit Co. She and Bob Welch, her manager, are preparing adjusting entries for annual financial statements. Bergez computes depreciation and records it as

Depreciation Expense—Equipment	123,000	
Accumulated Depreciation—Equipment		123,000

Welch agrees with her computation but says the credit entry should be directly to the Equipment account. Welch argues that while accumulated depreciation is technically correct, "it is less hassle not to use a contra account and just credit the Equipment account directly. And besides, the statement of financial position shows the same amount for total assets under either method."

Required

1. How should depreciation be recorded? Do you support Bergez or Welch?
2. Evaluate the strengths and weaknesses of Welch's reasons for preferring his method.
3. Indicate whether the situation Bergez faces is an ethical problem. Explain.

BTN 3-4   The class should be divided into teams. Teams are to select an industry (such as automobile manufacturing, airlines, defense contractors), and each team member is to select a different company in that industry. Each team member is to acquire the annual report of the company selected. Annual reports can be downloaded from company Websites or from the SEC's EDGAR database at (www.sec.gov).

COMMUNICATING IN PRACTICE

C1 A2

Required

1. Use the annual report to compute the return on assets, debt ratio, and profit margin.
2. Communicate with team members via a meeting, e-mail, or telephone to discuss the meaning of the ratios, how different companies compare to each other, and the industry norm. The team must prepare a single memo reporting the ratios for each company and identifying the conclusions or consensus of opinion reached during the team's discussion. The memo is to be copied and distributed to the instructor and all classmates.

BTN 3-5   Access L'Oréal's Website (www.loreal-finance.com/eng) to answer the following requirements.

TAKING IT TO THE NET

C1 A2

Required

1. What are L'Oréal's main products?
2. Access L'Oréal's annual report at the company's Website. What is L'Oréal's financial year-end?
3. What is L'Oréal's net sales for the period ended December 31, 2013?
4. What is L'Oréal's net profit (use net profit attributable to owners of the company) for the period ended December 31, 2013?
5. Compute L'Oréal's profit margin (use net profit attributable to owners of the company) for the year ended December 31, 2013. Round the percent to one decimal place.
6. Do you believe L'Oréal's decision to use a year-end of December relates to its natural business year? Explain.

BTN 3-6   Four types of adjustments are described in the chapter: (1) prepaid expenses, (2) unearned revenues, (3) accrued expenses, and (4) accrued revenues.

TEAMWORK IN ACTION

C3 A1 P1

Required

1. Form *learning teams* of four (or more) members. Each team member must select one of the four adjustments as an area of expertise (each team must have at least one expert in each area).
2. Form *expert teams* from the individuals who have selected the same area of expertise. Expert teams are to discuss and write a report that each expert will present to his or her learning team addressing the following:
   a. Description of the adjustment and why it's necessary.
   b. Example of a transaction or event, with dates and amounts, that requires adjustment.
   c. Adjusting entry(ies) for the example in requirement *b*.
   d. Status of the affected account(s) before and after the adjustment in requirement *c*.
   e. Effects on financial statements of not making the adjustment.
3. Each expert should return to his or her learning team. In rotation, each member should present his or her expert team's report to the learning team. Team discussion is encouraged.

ENTREPRENEURIAL DECISION

A2

BTN 3-7   Review the opening feature of this chapter dealing with **Lunch Actually**.

Required

1. Assume that Lunch Actually collects $300 cash at the beginning of the month in advance for a package of guaranteed-three-date segment to be fulfilled in the next three months. Prepare the journal entries for the (*a*) collection of the cash and (*b*) revenue from the subsequent dates fulfilled.
2. Your classmate cannot understand why he or she cannot record the entire $300 as revenue upon receipt of the cash. Explain to him or her, citing the relevant accounting principle(s), and support with your answers from part 1.

HITTING THE ROAD

C1

BTN 3-8   Select a company that you can visit in person or interview on the telephone. Call ahead to the company to arrange a time when you can interview an employee (preferably an accountant) who helps prepare the annual financial statements. Inquire about the following aspects of its accounting cycle.

Required

1. Does the company prepare interim financial statements? What reporting period(s) is used?
2. Does the company use the cash or accrual basis of accounting?
3. Does the company use a work sheet in preparing financial statements? Why or why not?
4. Does the company use a spreadsheet program? If so, which software program is used?
5. How long does it take after the end of its reporting period to complete annual statements?

ANSWERS TO MULTIPLE CHOICE QUIZ

1. b; the forgotten adjusting entry is: *dr.* Wages Expense, *cr.* Wages Payable.
2. c; Supplies used = $450 − $125 = $325
3. b; Insurance expense = $24,000 × (8/24) = $8,000; adjusting entry is: *dr.* Insurance Expense for $8,000, *cr.* Prepaid Insurance for $8,000.

4. a; Consulting fees earned = $3,600 × (2/6) = $1,200; adjusting entry is: *dr.* Unearned Consulting Fee for $1,200, *cr.* Consulting Fees Earned for $1,200.
5. e; Profit margin = $15,000/$300,000 = 5%

4

Completing the Accounting Cycle

A Look Back

Chapter 3 explained the timing of reports. We described why adjusting accounts is key for recognizing revenues and expenses in the proper period. We prepared an adjusted trial balance and used it to prepare financial statements.

A Look at This Chapter

This chapter emphasizes the final steps in the accounting process and reviews the entire accounting cycle. We explain the closing process, including accounting procedures and the use of a post-closing trial balance. We show how a work sheet aids in preparing financial statements.

A Look Ahead

Chapter 5 looks at accounting for merchandising activities. We describe the sale and purchase of merchandise and their implications for preparing and analyzing financial statements.

Learning Objectives

CAP

CONCEPTUAL

C1 Explain why temporary accounts are closed each period. (p. 142)

C2 Identify steps in the accounting cycle. (p. 146)

C3 Explain and prepare a classified statement of financial position. (p. 147)

ANALYTICAL

A1 Compute the current ratio and describe what it reveals about a company's financial condition. (p. 150)

PROCEDURAL

P1 Prepare a work sheet and explain its usefulness. (p. 138)

P2 Describe and prepare closing entries. (p. 143)

P3 Explain and prepare a post-closing trial balance. (p. 144)

P4 *Appendix 4A*—Prepare reversing entries and explain their purpose. (p. 154)

"I love to be involved in the creative process of my company. It gives me a lot of satisfaction."—**BENSON LOO**

Decision Insight

EyePower Game's Balancing Act

Augmented reality (AR) technology was in its infancy when Benson and three others started EyePower Games in 2004. However, they believed that its application had a lot of potential, and they were excited to create games using AR because it allowed them to deliver a completely new experience for gamers. Today the ed-tech company's primary focus is on making learning fun and engaging for children using innovative technologies, but "games" remains part of the company's name to serve as a reminder of its beginning.

EyePower Games' flagship products, NewsMaker and Moo-O—targeted strategically for use in the teaching of language arts and language across the curriculum—have won awards in the United States for being outstanding educational software.

"I love to be involved in the creative process of my company," says Benson. "To actively participate in the designing of a product, to testing and gathering feedback for the product, and then to finally see its adoption by users, gives me a lot of satisfaction."

Preparing the financial statements for EyePower Games may be laborious, but they are crucial, especially when the company needs to raise capital, either from investors or through government funding. "Even bidding for projects of a certain size requires the financial statements to be in good order as they need to be part of the documents for submission during the bidding process," explains Benson.

There is often a conflict between controlling costs and monitoring revenues and customer needs because cost controls put a lid on what and how much a company can do to address revenue and customer issues. For example, the amount of time it takes to develop a project with the necessary or desired features is directly associated with costs. "Many times, during the development process, my colleagues and I have to go back to the designing table to decide whether or not we need to make changes to the original designs (or sometimes even modified designs) in order to stay within the budgeted cost of development," says Benson.

For another example, Benson explains that "in order to meet the revenue expected of a product, a certain amount of marketing is necessary, and again, that is directly associated with cost issues." When the projected marketing cost exceeds what was budgeted, EyePower Games must seek alternatives for marketing its product while still reaching the desired revenue, "and that is always a very challenging task."

Many of the important steps leading to financial statements were explained in earlier chapters. We described how transactions and events are analyzed, journalized, and posted. This chapter explains the closing process that readies revenue, expense, and withdrawal accounts for the next reporting period and updates the capital account. A work sheet is shown to be a useful tool for these final steps and in preparing financial statements. It also explains how accounts are classified on a statement of financial position to increase their usefulness to decision makers.

Completing the Accounting Cycle

Work Sheet	Closing Process	Accounting Cycle	Classified Statement of Financial Position
• Benefits of a work sheet • Use of a work sheet	• Temporary and permanent accounts • Closing entries • Post-closing trial balance	• Definition of accounting cycle • Review of accounting cycle	• Classification structure • Classification categories

WORK SHEET AS A TOOL

Information preparers use various analyses and internal documents when organizing information for internal and external decision makers. Internal documents are often called **working papers.** One widely used working paper is the **work sheet,** which is a useful tool for preparers in working with accounting information. It is usually not available to external decision makers.

Benefits of a Work Sheet (Spreadsheet)

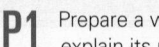

P1 Prepare a work sheet and explain its usefulness.

A work sheet is *not* a required report, yet using a manual or electronic work sheet has several potential benefits. Specifically, a work sheet

- Aids the preparation of financial statements.
- Reduces the possibility of errors when working with many accounts and adjustments.
- Links accounts and adjustments to their impacts in financial statements.
- Assists in planning and organizing an audit of financial statements—as it can be used to reflect any adjustments necessary.
- Helps in preparing interim (monthly and quarterly) financial statements when the journalizing and posting of adjusting entries are postponed until year-end.
- Shows the effects of proposed or "what-if" transactions.

Decision Insight

High-Tech Work Sheet An electronic work sheet using spreadsheet software such as Excel allows us to easily change numbers, assess the impact of alternative strategies, and quickly prepare financial statements at less cost. It can also increase the available time for analysis and interpretation. ∎

Use of a Work Sheet

Point: Since a work sheet is *not* a required report or an accounting record, its format is flexible and can be modified by its user to fit his/her preferences.

When a work sheet is used to prepare financial statements, it is constructed at the end of a period before the adjusting process. The complete work sheet includes a list of the accounts, their balances and adjustments, and their sorting into financial statement columns. It provides two columns each for the unadjusted trial balance, the adjustments, the adjusted trial balance, the income statement, and the statement of financial position (including the statement of changes in equity). To describe and interpret the work sheet, we use the information from FastForward. Preparing the work sheet has five important steps. Each step, 1 through 5, is color-coded and explained with reference to Exhibits 4.1 and 4.2.

① Step 1. Enter Unadjusted Trial Balance

Refer to Exhibit 4.1. The first step in preparing a work sheet is to list the title of every account and its account number that is expected to appear on its financial statements. This includes all accounts in the ledger plus any new ones from adjusting entries. Most adjusting entries—including expenses from salaries, supplies, depreciation, and insurance—are predictable and recurring. The unadjusted balance for each account is then entered in the appropriate Debit or Credit column of the unadjusted trial balance columns. The totals of these two columns must be equal. Exhibit 4.1 shows FastForward's work sheet after completing this first step. Sometimes blank lines are left on the work sheet based on past experience to indicate where lines will be needed for adjustments to certain accounts. Exhibit 4.1 shows Consulting Revenue as one example. An alternative is to squeeze adjustments on one line or to combine the effects of two or more adjustments in one amount. In the unusual case when an account is not predicted, we can add a new line for such an account following the *Totals* line.

② Step 2. Enter Adjustments

The second step in preparing a work sheet is to enter adjustments in the Adjustments columns. The adjustments shown are the same ones shown in Exhibit 3.13. An identifying letter links the debit and credit of each adjusting entry. This is called *keying* the adjustments. After preparing a work sheet, adjusting entries must still be entered in the journal and posted to the ledger. The Adjustments columns provide the information for those entries.

③ Step 3. Prepare Adjusted Trial Balance

The adjusted trial balance is prepared by combining the adjustments with the unadjusted balances for each account. As an example, the Prepaid Insurance account has a $2,400 debit balance in the Unadjusted Trial Balance columns. This $2,400 debit is combined with the $100 credit in the Adjustments columns to give Prepaid Insurance a $2,300 debit in the Adjusted Trial Balance columns. The totals of the Adjusted Trial Balance columns confirm the equality of debits and credits.

④ Step 4. Sort Adjusted Trial Balance Amounts to Financial Statements

This step involves sorting account balances from the adjusted trial balance to their proper financial statement columns. Expenses go to the Income Statement Debit column and revenues to the Income Statement Credit column. Assets and withdrawals go to the Statement of Financial Position & Statement of Changes in Equity Debit column. Liabilities and owner's capital go to the Statement of Financial Position & Statement of Changes in Equity Credit column.

⑤ Step 5. Total Statement Columns, Compute Income or Loss, and Balance Columns

Each financial statement column (from Step 4) is totaled. The difference between the totals of the Income Statement columns is net profit or net loss. This occurs because revenues are entered in the Credit column and expenses in the Debit column. If the Credit total exceeds the Debit total, there is net profit. If the Debit total exceeds the Credit total, there is a net loss. For FastForward, the Credit total exceeds the Debit total, giving a $3,785 net profit.

The net profit from the Income Statement columns is then entered in the Statement of Financial Position & Statement of Changes in Equity Credit column. Adding net profit to the last Credit column implies that it is to be added to owner's capital. If a loss occurs, it is added to the Debit column. This implies that it is to be subtracted from owner's capital. The ending balance of owner's capital does not appear in the last two columns as a single amount, but it is computed in the statement of changes in equity using these account balances. When net profit or net loss is added

EXHIBIT 4.1

A worksheet collects and summarizes information used to prepare adjusting entries, financial statements, and closing entries.

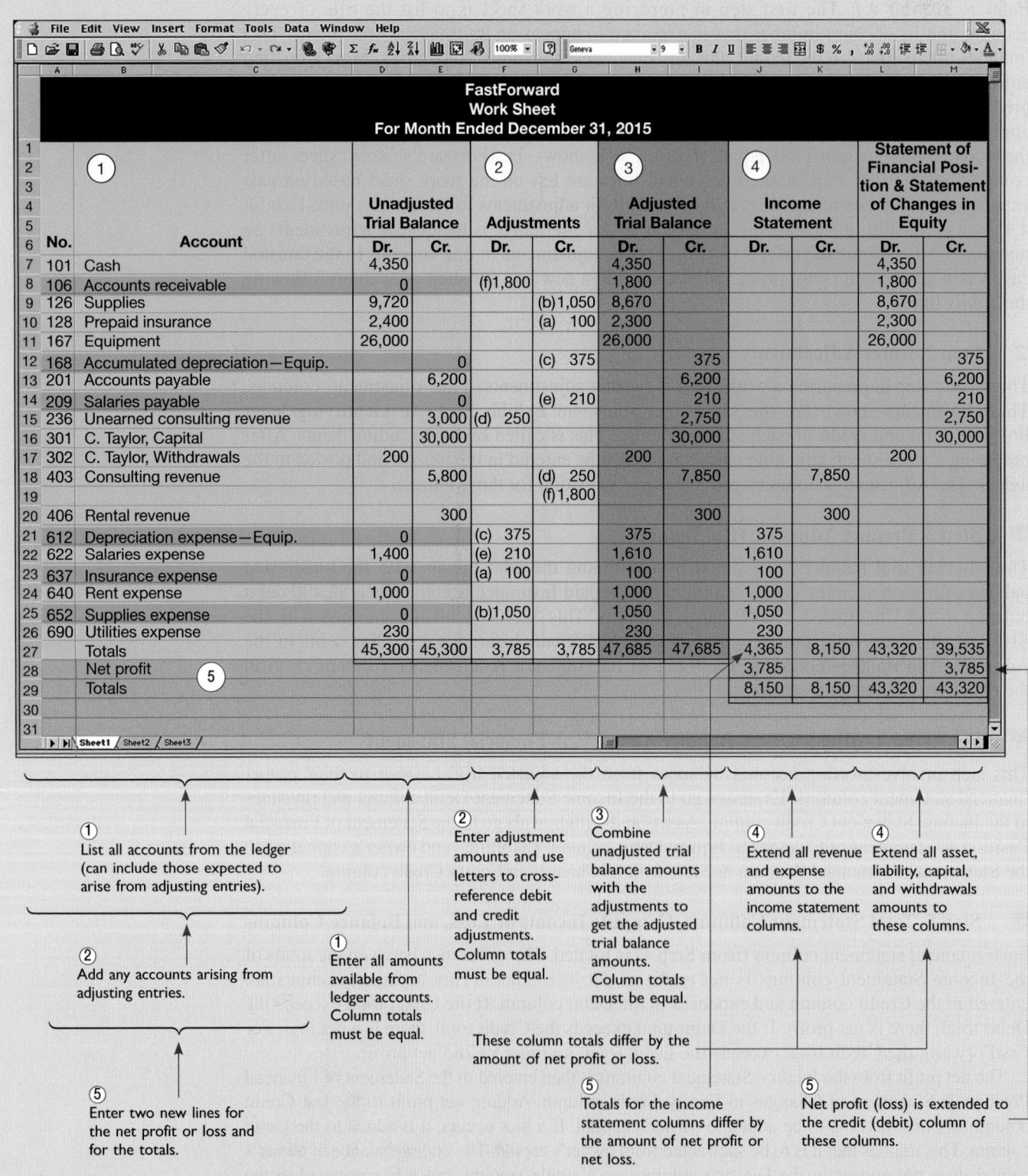

File Edit View Insert Format Tools Data Window Help												

FastForward
Work Sheet
For Month Ended December 31, 2015

		Unadjusted Trial Balance		Adjustments		Adjusted Trial Balance		Income Statement		Statement of Financial Position & Statement of Changes in Equity	
No.	Account	Dr.	Cr.	Dr.	Cr.	Dr.	Cr.	Dr.	Cr.	Dr.	Cr.
101	Cash	4,350				4,350				4,350	
106	Accounts receivable	0		(f)1,800		1,800				1,800	
126	Supplies	9,720			(b)1,050	8,670				8,670	
128	Prepaid insurance	2,400			(a) 100	2,300				2,300	
167	Equipment	26,000				26,000				26,000	
168	Accumulated depreciation—Equip.		0		(c) 375		375				375
201	Accounts payable		6,200				6,200				6,200
209	Salaries payable		0		(e) 210		210				210
236	Unearned consulting revenue		3,000	(d) 250			2,750				2,750
301	C. Taylor, Capital		30,000				30,000				30,000
302	C. Taylor, Withdrawals	200				200				200	
403	Consulting revenue		5,800		(d) 250		7,850		7,850		
					(f)1,800						
406	Rental revenue		300				300		300		
612	Depreciation expense—Equip.	0		(c) 375		375		375			
622	Salaries expense	1,400		(e) 210		1,610		1,610			
637	Insurance expense	0		(a) 100		100		100			
640	Rent expense	1,000				1,000		1,000			
652	Supplies expense	0		(b)1,050		1,050		1,050			
690	Utilities expense	230				230		230			
	Totals	45,300	45,300	3,785	3,785	47,685	47,685	4,365	8,150	43,320	39,535
	Net profit							3,785			3,785
	Totals							8,150	8,150	43,320	43,320

Sheet1 / Sheet2 / Sheet3

① List all accounts from the ledger (can include those expected to arise from adjusting entries).

② Add any accounts arising from adjusting entries.

① Enter all amounts available from ledger accounts. Column totals must be equal.

② Enter adjustment amounts and use letters to cross-reference debit and credit adjustments. Column totals must be equal.

③ Combine unadjusted trial balance amounts with the adjustments to get the adjusted trial balance amounts. Column totals must be equal.

These column totals differ by the amount of net profit or loss.

④ Extend all revenue and expense amounts to the income statement columns.

④ Extend all asset, liability, capital, and withdrawals amounts to these columns.

⑤ Enter two new lines for the net profit or loss and for the totals.

⑤ Totals for the income statement columns differ by the amount of net profit or net loss.

⑤ Net profit (loss) is extended to the credit (debit) column of these columns.

EXHIBIT 4.2

Financial Statements Prepared
from the Work Sheet

FASTFORWARD
Income Statement
For Month Ended December 31, 2015

Revenues
Consulting revenue	$ 7,850	
Rental revenue	300	
Total revenues		$ 8,150

Expenses
Depreciation expense—Equipment	(375)	
Salaries expense	(1,610)	
Insurance expense	(100)	
Rent expense	(1,000)	
Supplies expense	(1,050)	
Utilities expense	(230)	
Total expenses		(4,365)
Net profit		$ 3,785

FASTFORWARD
Statement of Changes in Equity
For Month Ended December 31, 2015

C. Taylor, Capital, December 1		$ 0
Investment by owner	$30,000	
Net profit	3,785	33,785
		33,785
Withdrawals by owner		(200)
C. Taylor, Capital, December 31		$33,585

FASTFORWARD
Statement of Financial Position
December 31, 2015

Assets
Cash		$ 4,350
Accounts receivable		1,800
Supplies		8,670
Prepaid insurance		2,300
Equipment	$26,000	
Accumulated depreciation—Equipment	(375)	25,625
Total assets		$42,745

Liabilities
Accounts payable		$ 6,200
Salaries payable		210
Unearned consulting revenue		2,750
Total liabilities		9,160

Equity
C. Taylor, Capital		33,585
Total liabilities and equity		$42,745

to the proper Statement of Financial Position & Statement of Changes in Equity column, the totals of the last two columns must balance. If they do not, one or more errors have been made. The error can either be mathematical or involve sorting one or more amounts to incorrect columns.

Decision Maker   Answer — p. 156

Entrepreneur   You make a printout of the electronic work sheet used to prepare financial statements. There is no depreciation adjustment, yet you own a large amount of equipment. Does the absence of depreciation adjustment concern you? ■

Work Sheet Applications and Analysis

A work sheet does not substitute for financial statements. It is a tool we can use at the end of an accounting period to help organize data and prepare financial statements. FastForward's financial statements are shown in Exhibit 4.2. Its income statement amounts are taken from the Income Statement columns of the work sheet. Similarly, amounts for its statement of financial position and its statement of changes in equity are taken from the Statement of Financial Position & Statement of Changes in Equity columns of the work sheet.

Information from the Adjustments columns of a work sheet can be used to journalize adjusting entries. It is important to remember that a work sheet is not a journal. This means that even when a work sheet is prepared, it is necessary to both journalize adjustments and post them to the ledger.

Work sheets are also useful in analyzing the effects of proposed, or what-if, transactions. This is done by entering financial statement amounts in the Unadjusted (what-if) columns. Proposed transactions are then entered in the Adjustments columns. We then compute "adjusted" amounts from these proposed transactions. The extended amounts in the financial statement columns show the effects of these proposed transactions. These financial statement columns yield **pro forma financial statements** because they show the statements *as if* the proposed transactions occurred.

Quick Check   Answers — p. 156

1. Where do we get the amounts to enter in the Unadjusted Trial Balance columns of a work sheet?
2. What are the advantages of using a work sheet to help prepare adjusting entries?
3. What are the overall benefits of a work sheet?

CLOSING PROCESS

C1 Explain why temporary accounts are closed each period.

The **closing process** is an important step at the end of an accounting period *after* financial statements have been completed. It prepares accounts for recording the transactions and the events of the *next* period. In the closing process we must (1) identify accounts for closing, (2) record and post the closing entries, and (3) prepare a post-closing trial balance. The purpose of the closing process is twofold. First, it resets revenue, expense, and withdrawals account balances to zero at the end of each period. This is done so that these accounts can properly measure income and withdrawals for the next period. Second, it helps in summarizing a period's revenues and expenses. This section explains the closing process.

Temporary Accounts
(closed at period-end)
Revenues
Expenses
Owner Withdrawals
Income Summary

Permanent Accounts
(not closed at period-end)
Assets
Liabilities
Owner Capital

Temporary and Permanent Accounts

Temporary (or *nominal*) **accounts** accumulate data related to one accounting period. They include all income statement accounts, the withdrawals account, and the Income Summary account. They are temporary because the accounts are opened at the beginning of a period, used to record transactions and events for that period, and then closed at the end of the period. *The closing process applies only to temporary accounts.* **Permanent** (or *real*) **accounts** report on activities related to one or more future accounting periods. They carry their ending balances into the next period and generally consist of all statement of financial position accounts. These asset, liability, and equity accounts are not closed.

Recording Closing Entries

To record and post **closing entries** is to transfer the end-of-period balances in revenue, expense, and withdrawals accounts to the permanent capital account. Closing entries are necessary at the end of each period after financial statements are prepared because

- Revenue, expense, and withdrawals accounts must begin each period with zero balances.
- Owner's capital must reflect prior periods' revenues, expenses, and withdrawals.

An income statement aims to report revenues and expenses for a *specific accounting period*. The statement of changes in equity reports similar information, including withdrawals. Since revenue, expense, and withdrawals accounts must accumulate information separately for each period, they must start each period with zero balances. To close these accounts, we transfer their balances first to an account called *Income Summary*. **Income Summary** is a temporary account (only used for the closing process) that contains a credit for the sum of all revenues (and gains) and a debit for the sum of all expenses (and losses). Its balance equals net profit or net loss and it is transferred to the capital account. Next the withdrawals account balance is transferred to the capital account. After these closing entries are posted, the revenue, expense, withdrawals, and Income Summary accounts have zero balances. These accounts are then said to be *closed* or *cleared*.

Exhibit 4.3 uses the adjusted account balances of FastForward (from the Adjusted Trial Balance columns of Exhibit 4.1 or from the left side of Exhibit 4.4) to show the four steps necessary to close its temporary accounts. We explain each step.

Point: To understand the closing process, focus on its *outcomes*—updating the capital account balance to its proper ending balance, and getting *temporary accounts* to show *zero balances* for purposes of accumulating data for the next period.

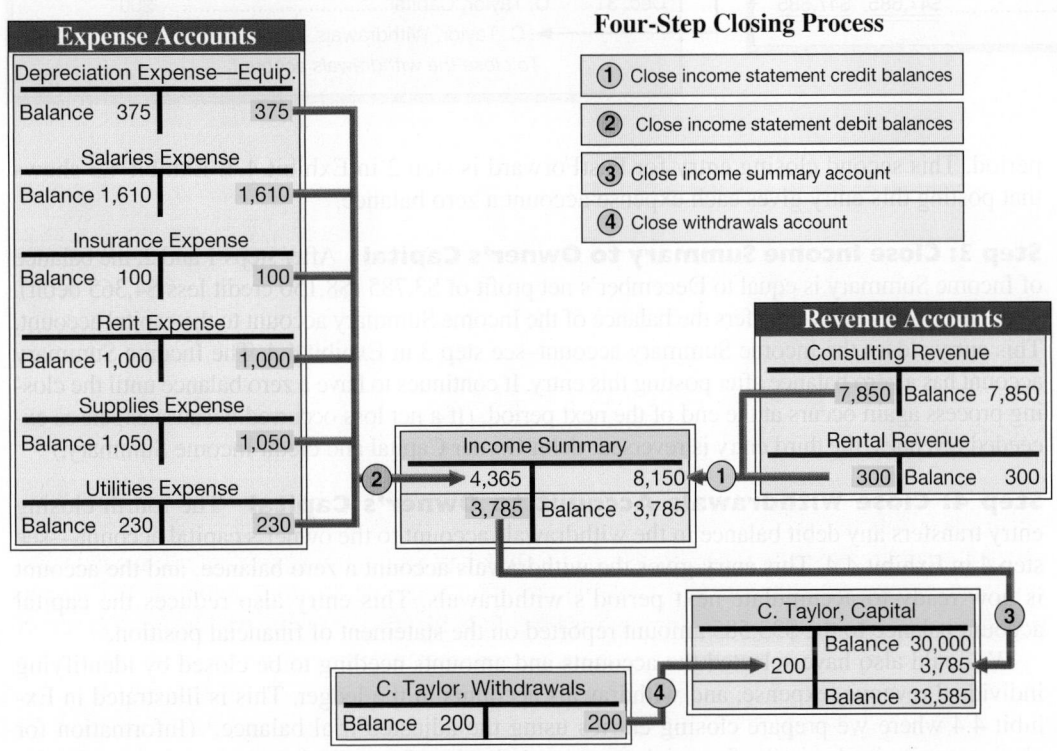

EXHIBIT 4.3

Four-Step Closing Process

Point: C. Taylor, Capital is the only *permanent account* in Exhibit 4.3.

Step 1: Close Credit Balances in Revenue Accounts to Income Summary The first closing entry transfers credit balances in revenue (and gain) accounts to the Income Summary account. We bring accounts with credit balances to zero by debiting them. For FastForward, this journal entry is step 1 in Exhibit 4.4. This entry closes revenue accounts and leaves them with zero balances. The accounts are now ready to record revenues when they occur in the next period. The $8,150 credit entry to Income Summary equals total revenues for the period.

Step 2: Close Debit Balances in Expense Accounts to Income Summary The second closing entry transfers debit balances in expense (and loss) accounts to the Income Summary account. We bring expense accounts' debit balances to zero by crediting them. With a balance of zero, these accounts are ready to accumulate a record of expenses for the next

P2 Describe and prepare closing entries.

Point: It is possible to close revenue and expense accounts directly to owner's capital. Computerized accounting systems do this.

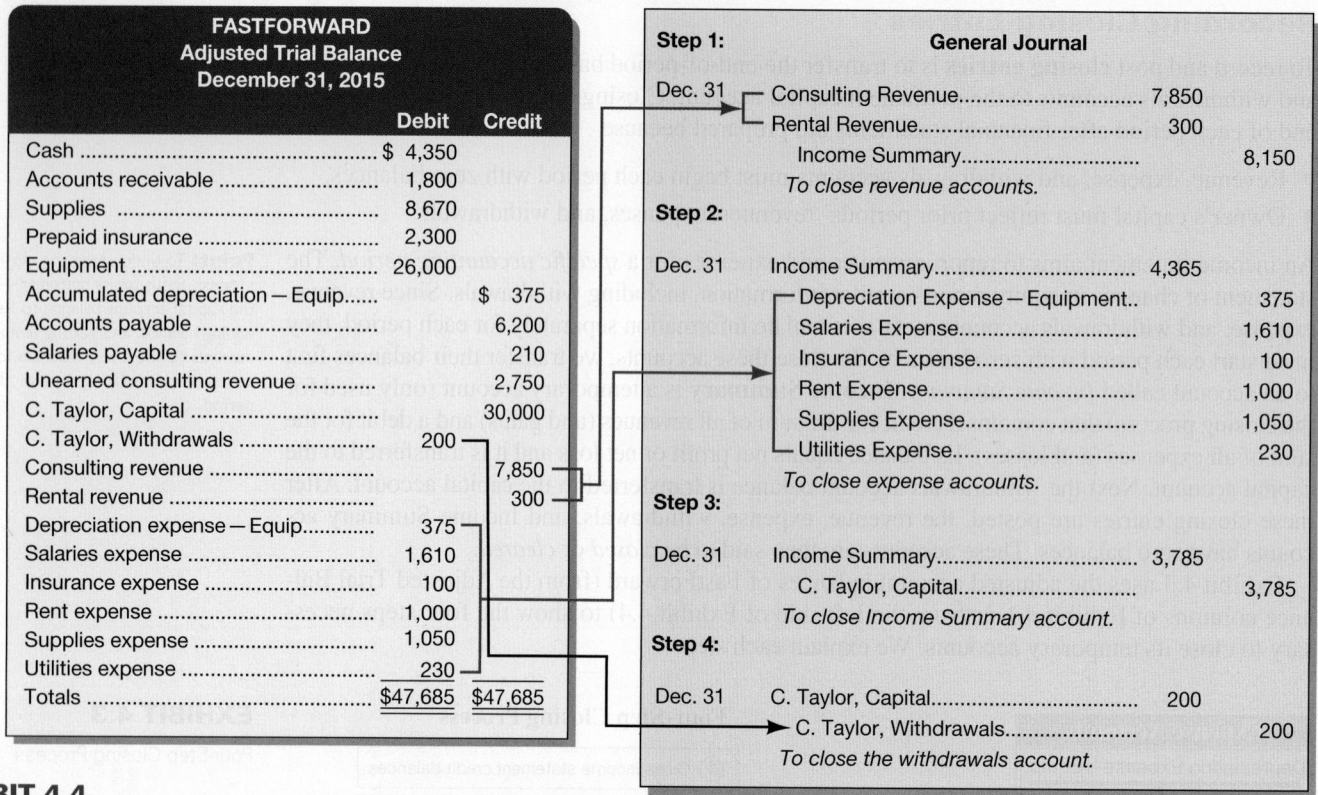

EXHIBIT 4.4

Preparing Closing Entries

period. This second closing entry for FastForward is step 2 in Exhibit 4.4. Exhibit 4.3 shows that posting this entry gives each expense account a zero balance.

Step 3: Close Income Summary to Owner's Capital   After steps 1 and 2, the balance of Income Summary is equal to December's net profit of $3,785 ($8,150 credit less $4,365 debit). The third closing entry transfers the balance of the Income Summary account to the capital account. This entry closes the Income Summary account–see step 3 in Exhibit 4.4. The Income Summary account has a zero balance after posting this entry. It continues to have a zero balance until the closing process again occurs at the end of the next period. (If a net loss occurred because expenses exceeded revenues, the third entry is reversed: debit Owner Capital and credit Income Summary.)

Step 4: Close Withdrawals Account to Owner's Capital   The fourth closing entry transfers any debit balance in the withdrawals account to the owner's capital account—see step 4 in Exhibit 4.4. This entry gives the withdrawals account a zero balance, and the account is now ready to accumulate next period's withdrawals. This entry also reduces the capital account balance to the $33,585 amount reported on the statement of financial position.

    We could also have selected the accounts and amounts needing to be closed by identifying individual revenue, expense, and withdrawals accounts in the ledger. This is illustrated in Exhibit 4.4 where we prepare closing entries using the adjusted trial balance.[1] (Information for closing entries is also in the financial statement columns of a work sheet.)

Post-Closing Trial Balance

P3	Explain and prepare a post-closing trial balance.

Exhibit 4.5 shows the entire ledger of FastForward as at December 31 after adjusting and closing entries are posted. (The transaction and adjusting entries are in Chapters 2 and 3.) The temporary accounts (revenues, expenses, and withdrawals) have ending balances equal to zero.

---

[1] The closing process has focused on proprietorships. It is identical for partnerships with the exception that each owner has separate capital and withdrawals accounts (for steps 3 and 4). The closing process for a corporation is similar with the exception that it uses a Retained Earnings account instead of a Capital account, and a Dividend account instead of a Withdrawals account.

EXHIBIT 4.5

General Ledger after the Closing Process for FastForward

Asset Accounts

Cash Acct. No. 101

Date	Explan.	PR	Debit	Credit	Balance
2015					
Dec. 1	(1)	G1	30,000		30,000
2	(2)	G1		2,500	27,500
3	(3)	G1		26,000	1,500
5	(5)	G1	4,200		5,700
6	(13)	G1		2,400	3,300
12	(6)	G1		1,000	2,300
12	(7)	G1		700	1,600
22	(9)	G1	1,900		3,500
24	(10)	G1		900	2,600
24	(11)	G1		200	2,400
26	(12)	G1	3,000		5,400
26	(14)	G1		120	5,280
26	(15)	G1		230	5,050
26	(16)	G1		700	4,350

Accounts Receivable Acct. No. 106

Date	Explan.	PR	Debit	Credit	Balance
2015					
Dec. 12	(8)	G1	1,900		1,900
22	(9)	G1		1,900	0
31	Adj.(f)	G1	1,800		1,800

Supplies Acct. No. 126

Date	Explan.	PR	Debit	Credit	Balance
2015					
Dec. 2	(2)	G1	2,500		2,500
6	(4)	G1	7,100		9,600
26	(14)	G1	120		9,720
31	Adj.(b)	G1		1,050	8,670

Prepaid Insurance Acct. No. 128

Date	Explan.	PR	Debit	Credit	Balance
2015					
Dec. 6	(13)	G1	2,400		2,400
31	Adj.(a)	G1		100	2,300

Equipment Acct. No. 167

Date	Explan.	PR	Debit	Credit	Balance
2015					
Dec. 3	(3)	G1	26,000		26,000

Accumulated Depreciation— Equipment Acct. No. 168

Date	Explan.	PR	Debit	Credit	Balance
2015					
Dec. 31	Adj.(c)	G1		375	375

Liability and Equity Accounts

Accounts Payable Acct. No. 201

Date	Explan.	PR	Debit	Credit	Balance
2015					
Dec. 6	(4)	G1		7,100	7,100
24	(10)	G1	900		6,200

Salaries Payable Acct. No. 209

Date	Explan.	PR	Debit	Credit	Balance
2015					
Dec. 31	Adj.(e)	G1		210	210

Unearned Consulting Revenue Acct. No. 236

Date	Explan.	PR	Debit	Credit	Balance
2015					
Dec. 26	(12)	G1		3,000	3,000
31	Adj.(d)	G1	250		2,750

C. Taylor, Capital Acct. No. 301

Date	Explan.	PR	Debit	Credit	Balance
2015					
Dec. 1	(1)	G1		30,000	30,000
31	Clos.(3)	G1		3,785	33,785
31	Clos.(4)	G1	200		33,585

C. Taylor, Withdrawals Acct. No. 302

Date	Explan.	PR	Debit	Credit	Balance
2015					
Dec. 24	(11)	G1	200		200
31	Clos.(4)	G1		200	0

Revenue and Expense Accounts (Including Income Summary)

Consulting Revenue Acct. No. 403

Date	Explan.	PR	Debit	Credit	Balance
2015					
Dec. 5	(5)	G1		4,200	4,200
12	(8)	G1		1,600	5,800
31	Adj.(d)	G1		250	6,050
31	Adj.(f)	G1		1,800	7,850
31	Clos.(1)	G1	7,850		0

Rental Revenue Acct. No. 406

Date	Explan.	PR	Debit	Credit	Balance
2015					
Dec. 12	(8)	G1		300	300
31	Clos.(1)	G1	300		0

Depreciation Expense— Equipment Acct. No. 612

Date	Explan.	PR	Debit	Credit	Balance
2015					
Dec. 31	Adj.(c)	G1	375		375
31	Clos.(2)	G1		375	0

Salaries Expense Acct. No. 622

Date	Explan.	PR	Debit	Credit	Balance
2015					
Dec. 12	(7)	G1	700		700
26	(16)	G1	700		1,400
31	Adj.(e)	G1	210		1,610
31	Clos.(2)	G1		1,610	0

Insurance Expense Acct. No. 637

Date	Explan.	PR	Debit	Credit	Balance
2015					
Dec. 31	Adj.(a)	G1	100		100
31	Clos.(2)	G1		100	0

Rent Expense Acct. No. 640

Date	Explan.	PR	Debit	Credit	Balance
2015					
Dec. 12	(6)	G1	1,000		1,000
31	Clos.(2)	G1		1,000	0

Supplies Expense Acct. No. 652

Date	Explan.	PR	Debit	Credit	Balance
2015					
Dec. 31	Adj.(b)	G1	1,050		1,050
31	Clos.(2)	G1		1,050	0

Utilities Expense Acct. No. 690

Date	Explan.	PR	Debit	Credit	Balance
2015					
Dec. 26	(15)	G1	230		230
31	Clos.(2)	G1		230	0

Income Summary Acct. No. 901

Date	Explan.	PR	Debit	Credit	Balance
2015					
Dec. 31	Clos.(1)	G1		8,150	8,150
31	Clos.(2)	G1	4,365		3,785
31	Clos.(3)	G1	3,785		0

A **post-closing trial balance** is a list of permanent accounts and their balances from the ledger after all closing entries have been journalized and posted. It lists the balances for all accounts not closed. These accounts comprise a company's assets, liabilities, and equity, which are identical to those in the statement of financial position. The aim of a post-closing trial balance is to verify that (1) total debits equal total credits for permanent accounts and (2) all temporary accounts have zero balances. FastForward's post-closing trial balance is shown in Exhibit 4.6. The post-closing trial balance usually is the last step in the accounting process.

EXHIBIT 4.6

Post-Closing Trial Balance

FASTFORWARD		
Post-Closing Trial Balance		
December 31, 2015		
	Debit	Credit
Cash	$ 4,350	
Accounts receivable	1,800	
Supplies	8,670	
Prepaid insurance	2,300	
Equipment	26,000	
Accumulated depreciation—Equipment		$ 375
Accounts payable		6,200
Salaries payable		210
Unearned consulting revenue		2,750
C. Taylor, Capital		33,585
Totals	$43,120	$43,120

ACCOUNTING CYCLE

 C2 Identify steps in the accounting cycle.

The term **accounting cycle** refers to the steps in preparing financial statements. It is called a *cycle* because the steps are repeated each reporting period. Exhibit 4.7 shows the 10 steps in the cycle, beginning with analyzing transactions and ending with a post-closing trial balance or

EXHIBIT 4.7

Steps in the Accounting Cycle*

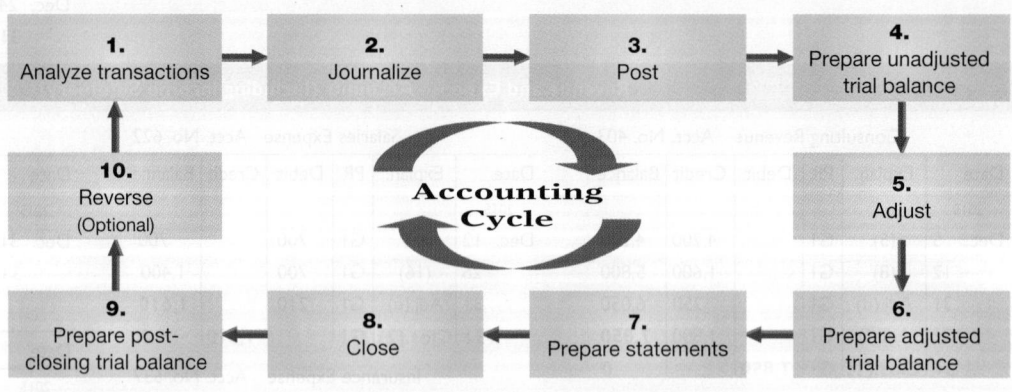

Explanations

1. Analyze transactions	Analyze transactions to prepare for journalizing.
2. Journalize	Record accounts, including debits and credits, in a journal.
3. Post	Transfer debits and credits from the journal to the ledger.
4. Prepare unadjusted trial balance	Summarize unadjusted ledger accounts and amounts.
5. Adjust	Record adjustments to bring account balances up to date; journalize and post adjustments.
6. Prepare adjusted trial balance	Summarize adjusted ledger accounts and amounts.
7. Prepare statements	Use adjusted trial balance to prepare financial statements.
8. Close	Journalize and post entries to close temporary accounts.
9. Prepare post-closing trial balance	Test clerical accuracy of the closing procedures.
10. Reverse (optional)	Reverse certain adjustments in the next period—optional step; see Appendix 4A.

* Steps 4, 6, and 9 can be done on a work sheet. A work sheet is useful in planning adjustments, but adjustments (step 5) must always be journalized and posted. Steps 3, 4, 6, and 9 are automatic with a computerized system.

reversing entries. Steps 1 through 3 usually occur regularly as a company enters into transactions. Steps 4 through 9 are done at the end of a period. *Reversing entries* in step 10 are optional and are explained in Appendix 4A.

Quick Check   Answers — p. 156

4. What are the major steps in preparing closing entries?

5. Why are revenue and expense accounts called *temporary?* Identify and list the types of temporary accounts.

6. What accounts are listed on the post-closing trial balance?

CLASSIFIED STATEMENT OF FINANCIAL POSITION

Our discussion to this point has been limited to unclassified financial statements. This section describes a classified statement of financial position. The next chapter describes a classified income statement. An **unclassified statement of financial position** is one whose items are broadly grouped into assets, liabilities, and equity. One example is FastForward's statement of financial position in Exhibit 4.2. A **classified statement of financial position** organizes assets and liabilities into important subgroups that provide more information to decision makers.

C3 Explain and prepare a classified statement of financial position.

Classification Structure

A classified statement of financial position has no required layout, but it usually contains the categories in Exhibit 4.8. One of the more important classifications is the separation between current and noncurrent items for both assets and liabilities. Current items are those expected to come due (either collected or owed) within one year or the company's operating cycle, whichever is longer. The **operating cycle** is the time span from when *cash is used* to acquire goods and services until *cash is received* from the sale of goods and services. "Operating" refers to company operations and "cycle" refers to the circular flow of cash used for company inputs and then cash received from its outputs. The length of a company's operating cycle depends on its activities. For a service company, the operating cycle is the time span between (1) paying employees who perform the services and (2) receiving cash from customers. For a merchandiser selling products, the operating cycle is the time span between (1) paying suppliers for merchandise and (2) receiving cash from customers.

Assets	Liabilities and Equity
Current assets	Current liabilities
Noncurrent assets	Noncurrent liabilities
Long-term investments	Equity
Property, plant and equipment	
Intangible assets	

EXHIBIT 4.8

Typical Categories in a Classified Statement of Financial Position

Most operating cycles are less than one year. This means most companies use a one-year period in deciding which assets and liabilities are current. A few companies have an operating cycle longer than one year. For instance, producers of certain beverages (wine) and products (ginseng) that require aging for several years have operating cycles longer than one year. A statement of financial position lists current assets before noncurrent assets and current liabilities before noncurrent liabilities. This consistency in presentation allows users to quickly identify current assets that are most easily converted to cash and current liabilities that are shortly coming due. Items in current assets and current liabilities are listed in the order of how quickly they will be converted to, or paid in, cash.

Classification Categories

This section describes the most common categories in a classified statement of financial position. The statement of financial position for Snowboarding Components in Exhibit 4.9 shows the typical categories. Its assets are classified as either current or noncurrent. Its liabilities are classified as either current or noncurrent. Not all companies use the same categories of assets and liabilities for their statement of financial positions. **K2 Inc.,** a manufacturer of snowboards, reported a statement of financial position with only three asset classes: current assets; property, plant and equipment; and other assets.

Current Assets   Current assets (also called short-term assets) are cash and other resources that are expected to be sold, collected, or used within one year or the company's

EXHIBIT 4.9

Example of a Classified
Statement of Financial Position

SNOWBOARDING COMPONENTS Statement of Financial Position January 31, 2015		
Assets		
Current assets		
Cash	$ 6,500	
Short-term investments	2,100	
Accounts receivable, net	4,400	
Merchandise inventory	27,500	
Prepaid expenses	2,400	
Total current assets		$ 42,900
Long-term financial assets	67,500	
Property, plant and equipment, net	223,400	
Intangible assets	10,000	
Total noncurrent assets		300,900
Total assets		$343,800
Liabilities		
Current liabilities		
Accounts payable	$ 15,300	
Wages payable	3,200	
Notes payable	3,000	
Current portion of long-term liabilities	7,500	
Total current liabilities		$ 29,000
Noncurrent liabilities (net of current portion)		150,000
Total liabilities		179,000
Equity		
T. Hawk, Capital		164,800
Total liabilities and equity		$343,800

operating cycle, whichever is longer. Examples are cash, short-term financial assets or investments, accounts receivable, short-term notes receivable, goods for sale (called merchandise or inventory), and prepaid expenses. The individual prepaid expenses of a company are usually small in amount compared to many other assets and are often combined and shown as a single item. The prepaid expenses in Exhibit 4.9 likely include items such as prepaid insurance, prepaid rent, office supplies, and store supplies. Prepaid expenses are usually listed last because they will not be converted to cash (instead, they are used).

Noncurrent assets Noncurrent assets (also called long-term assets) are assets not used up within one year or the operating cycle, whichever is longer. They generally include long-term financial assets which are likely to be investments in other entities' shares or bonds. Property, plant and equipment (PPE) are tangible assets that are both long-term and used to produce or sell products and services. Examples are equipment, machinery, buildings, and land that are used to produce or sell products and services. Intangible assets are long-term resources that benefit business operations, usually lack physical form, and have uncertain benefits. Examples are patents, trademarks, copyrights, franchises, and goodwill. Their value comes from the privileges or rights granted to or held by the owner.

> **Point:** Current is also called *short-term*, and noncurrent is also called *long-term*.

Current Liabilities Current liabilities (also called short-term liabilities) are obligations due to be paid or settled within one year or the operating cycle, whichever is longer. They are usually settled by paying out current assets such as cash. Current liabilities often include accounts payable, notes payable, wages payable, taxes payable, interest payable, and unearned revenues. Also, any portion of a long-term liability due to be paid within one year or the operating cycle, whichever is longer, is a current liability. Unearned revenues are current liabilities when they will be settled by delivering products or services within one year or the operating cycle, whichever is longer.

> **Point:** Property, plant and equipment are also called *fixed assets*; or *long-lived assets*.

Noncurrent Liabilities Noncurrent liabilities (also called long-term liabilities) are obligations not due within one year or the operating cycle, whichever is longer. Notes payable, mortgages payable, bonds payable, and lease obligations are common long-term liabilities. If a company has both short- and long-term items in each of these categories, they are commonly separated into two accounts in the ledger.

> **Point:** Many financial ratios are distorted if accounts are not classified correctly.

Equity Equity is the owner's claim on assets. For a proprietorship, this claim is reported in the equity section with an owner's capital account. (For a partnership, the equity section reports a capital account for each partner. For a corporation, the equity section is divided into two main subsections, share capital and retained earnings.)

> **Point:** Only assets and liabilities are classified as current or noncurrent.

Quick Check

Answers — p. 156

7. Classify the following assets as (1) current assets, (2) property, plant and equipment, or (3) intangible assets:
   (a) land used in operations, (b) office supplies, (c) receivables from customers due in 10 months, (d) insurance protection for the next 9 months, (e) trucks used to provide services to customers, (f) trademarks.
8. Cite at least two examples of assets classified as financial assets or investments on the statement of financial position.
9. Explain the operating cycle for a service company.

Decision Insight

Format of Statement of Financial Position   Guidance on implementing **IAS 1 Presentation of Financial Statements** illustrates a statement of financial position presenting noncurrent items first (and equity before liabilities). It also states, "The illustrative statement of financial position shows one way in which an entity may present a statement of financial position distinguishing between current and noncurrent items. Other formats may be equally appropriate, provided the distinction is clear." Alternative formats can be seen in Appendix A for Nestlé, Adidas, and Samsung. These three companies, which prepare their financial statements based on **IFRS**, show current assets before noncurrent assets. Current assets are listed from most liquid (usually cash and cash equivalents) to least liquid (such as inventories), where liquid refers to the ease of converting a current asset to cash (some other companies may reverse the order). These three companies also show current liabilities before noncurrent liabilities. The equity section is shown at the end. ■

Decision Analysis   Current Ratio

A1 Compute the current ratio and describe what it reveals about a company's financial condition.

An important use of financial statements is to help assess a company's ability to pay its debts in the near future. Such analysis affects decisions by suppliers when allowing a company to buy on credit. It also affects decisions by creditors when lending money to a company, including loan terms such as interest rate, due date, and collateral requirements. It can also affect a manager's decisions about using cash to pay debts when they come due. The **current ratio** is one measure of a company's ability to pay its short-term obligations. It is defined in Exhibit 4.10 as current assets divided by current liabilities.

EXHIBIT 4.10

Current Ratio

$$\text{Current ratio} = \frac{\text{Current assets}}{\text{Current liabilities}}$$

Using financial information from Nestlé, we compute its current ratio for the recent five-year period. The results are in Exhibit 4.11.

EXHIBIT 4.11

Nestlé Current Ratio

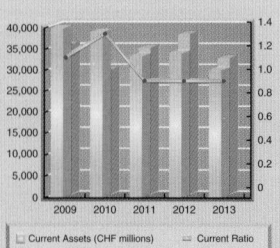

Nestle	2009	2010	2011	2012	2013
Current assets (CHF millions)	39,870	38,997	33,324	34,020	30,066
Current liabilities (CHF millions)	36,083	30,146	35,232	38,528	32,917
Current ratio	1.1	1.3	0.9	0.9	0.9

Based on its current ratio, Nestlé's liquidity position has slightly deteriorated in the recent three years. However, this does not necessarily indicate any problem in meeting its short-term obligations. Further analysis can be done by comparing its ratios with competitors and the industry average.

Decision Maker Answer — p. 156

Analyst You are analyzing the financial condition of a company to assess its ability to meet upcoming loan payments. You compute its current ratio as 1.2. You also find that a major portion of accounts receivable is due from one client who has not made any payments in the past 12 months. Removing this receivable from current assets lowers the current ratio to 0.7. What do you conclude? ∎

DEMONSTRATION PROBLEM

The partial work sheet of Midtown Repair Company at December 31, 2015, follows.

	Adjusted Trial Balance		Income Statement		Statement of Financial Position and Statement of Changes in Equity	
	Debit	Credit	Debit	Credit	Debit	Credit
Cash	95,600					
Notes receivable (current)	50,000					
Prepaid insurance	16,000					
Prepaid rent	4,000					
Equipment	170,000					
Accumulated depreciation—Equipment		57,000				
Accounts payable		52,000				
Long-term notes payable		63,000				
C. Trout, Capital		178,500				
C. Trout, Withdrawals	30,000					
Repair services revenue		180,800				
Interest revenue		7,500				
Depreciation expense—Equipment	28,500					
Wages expense	85,000					
Rent expense	48,000					
Insurance expense	6,000					
Interest expense	5,700					
Totals	538,800	538,800				

Required

1. Complete the work sheet by extending the adjusted trial balance totals to the appropriate financial statement columns.
2. Prepare closing entries for Midtown Repair Company.
3. Set up the Income Summary and the C. Trout, Capital account in the general ledger (in balance column format) and post the closing entries to these accounts.
4. Determine the balance of the C. Trout, Capital account to be reported on the December 31, 2015, statement of financial position.
5. Prepare an income statement, statement of changes in equity, and classified statement of financial position (in report form) as at December 31, 2015.

PLANNING THE SOLUTION

- Extend the adjusted trial balance account balances to the appropriate financial statement columns.
- Prepare entries to close the revenue accounts to Income Summary, to close the expense accounts to Income Summary, to close Income Summary to the capital account, and to close the withdrawals account to the capital account.

- Post the first and second closing entries to the Income Summary account. Examine the balance of income summary and verify that it agrees with the net profit shown on the work sheet.
- Post the third and fourth closing entries to the capital account.
- Use the work sheet's two right-most columns and your answer in part 4 to prepare the classified statement of financial position.

SOLUTION TO DEMONSTRATION PROBLEM

1. Completing the work sheet.

	Adjusted Trial Balance		Income Statement		Statement of Financial Position and Statement of Changes in Equity	
	Debit	Credit	Debit	Credit	Debit	Credit
Cash	95,600				95,600	
Notes receivable (current)	50,000				50,000	
Prepaid insurance	16,000				16,000	
Prepaid rent	4,000				4,000	
Equipment	170,000				170,000	
Accumulated depreciation—Equipment ...		57,000				57,000
Accounts payable		52,000				52,000
Long-term notes payable		63,000				63,000
C. Trout, Capital		178,500				178,500
C. Trout, Withdrawals	30,000				30,000	
Repair services revenue		180,800		180,800		
Interest revenue		7,500		7,500		
Depreciation expense—Equipment	28,500		28,500			
Wages expense	85,000		85,000			
Rent expense	48,000		48,000			
Insurance expense	6,000		6,000			
Interest expense	5,700		5,700			
Totals	538,800	538,800	173,200	188,300	365,600	350,500
Net profit			15,100			15,100
Totals			188,300	188,300	365,600	365,600

2. Closing entries.

Dec. 31	Repair Services Revenue	180,800	
	Interest Revenue	7,500	
	Income Summary		188,300
	To close revenue accounts.		
Dec. 31	Income Summary	173,200	
	Depreciation Expense—Equipment		28,500
	Wages Expense		85,000
	Rent Expense		48,000
	Insurance Expense		6,000
	Interest Expense		5,700
	To close expense accounts.		
Dec. 31	Income Summary	15,100	
	C. Trout, Capital		15,100
	To close the Income Summary account.		
Dec. 31	C. Trout, Capital	30,000	
	C. Trout, Withdrawals		30,000
	To close the withdrawals account.		

3. Set up the Income Summary and the capital ledger accounts and post the closing entries.

Income Summary					Account No. 901
Date	**Explanation**	**PR**	**Debit**	**Credit**	**Balance**
2015					
Jan. 1	Beginning balance				0
Dec. 31	Close revenue accounts			188,300	188,300
31	Close expense accounts		173,200		15,100
31	Close income summary		15,100		0

C. Trout, Capital					Account No. 301
Date	**Explanation**	**PR**	**Debit**	**Credit**	**Balance**
2015					
Jan. 1	Beginning balance				178,500
Dec. 31	Close Income Summary			15,100	193,600
31	Close C. Trout, Withdrawals		30,000		163,600

4. The final capital balance of $163,600 (from part 3) will be reported on the December 31, 2015, statement of financial position. The final capital balance reflects the increase due to the net profit earned during the year and the decrease for the owner's withdrawals during the year.

5.

MIDTOWN REPAIR COMPANY
Income Statement
For Year Ended December 31, 2015

Revenues		
Repair services revenue	$180,800	
Interest revenue	7,500	
Total revenues		$ 188,300
Expenses		
Depreciation expense—Equipment	(28,500)	
Wages expense	(85,000)	
Rent expense	(48,000)	
Insurance expense	(6,000)	
Interest expense	(5,700)	
Total expenses		(173,200)
Net profit		$ 15,100

MIDTOWN REPAIR COMPANY
Statement of Changes in Equity
For Year Ended December 31, 2015

C. Trout, Capital, December 31, 2014		$178,500
Investment by owner	$ 0	
Net profit	15,100	15,100
		193,600
Withdrawals by owner		(30,000)
C. Trout, Capital, December 31, 2015		$163,600

MIDTOWN REPAIR COMPANY
Statement of Financial Position
December 31, 2015

Assets

Current assets

Cash		$ 95,600
Notes receivable		50,000
Prepaid insurance		16,000
Prepaid rent		4,000
Total current assets		165,600

Property, plant and equipment

Equipment	$170,000	
Accumulated depreciation—Equipment	(57,000)	
Total property, plant and equipment		113,000
Total assets		$278,600

Liabilities

Current liabilities

Accounts payable		$ 52,000

Long-term liabilities

Long-term notes payable		63,000
Total liabilities		115,000

Equity

C. Trout, Capital		163,600
Total liabilities and equity		$278,600

APPENDIX

4A

Reversing Entries

Reversing entries are optional. They are recorded in response to accrued assets and accrued liabilities that were created by adjusting entries at the end of a reporting period. The purpose of reversing entries is to simplify a company's recordkeeping. Exhibit 4A.1 shows an example of FastForward's reversing entries. The top of the exhibit shows the adjusting entry FastForward recorded on December 31 for its employee's earned but unpaid salary. The entry recorded three days' salary of $210, which increased December's total salary expense to $1,610. The entry also recognized a liability of $210. The expense is reported on December's income statement. The expense account is then closed. The ledger on January 1, 2016, shows a $210 liability and a zero balance in the Salaries Expense account. At this point, the choice is made between using or not using reversing entries.

Point: As a general rule, adjusting entries that create new asset or liability accounts are likely candidates for reversing.

Accounting *without* Reversing Entries   The path down the left side of Exhibit 4A.1 is described in the chapter. To summarize here, when the next payday occurs on January 9, we record payment with a compound entry that debits both the expense and liability accounts and credits Cash. Posting that entry creates a $490 balance in the expense account and reduces the liability account balance to zero because the debt has been settled. The disadvantage of this approach is the slightly more complex entry required on January 9. Paying the accrued liability means that this entry differs from the routine entries made on all other paydays. To construct the proper entry on January 9, we must recall the effect of the December 31 adjusting entry. Reversing entries overcome this disadvantage.

Accounting *with* Reversing Entries   The right side of Exhibit 4A.1 shows how a reversing entry on January 1 overcomes the disadvantage of the January 9 entry when not using reversing entries. A reversing entry is the exact opposite of an adjusting entry. For FastForward, the Salaries Payable liability account is debited for $210, meaning that this account now has a zero balance after the entry is posted. The Salaries Payable account temporarily understates the liability, but this is not a problem since

P4 | Prepare reversing entries and explain their purpose.

EXHIBIT 4A.1

Reversing Entries for an Accrued Expense

Accrue salaries expense on December 31, 2015

Salaries Expense 210
    Salaries Payable 210

Salaries Expense

Date	Expl.	Debit	Credit	Balance
2015				
Dec. 12	(7)	700		700
26	(16)	700		1,400
31	(e)	210		1,610

Salaries Payable

Date	Expl.	Debit	Credit	Balance
2015				
Dec. 31	(e)		210	210

WITHOUT Reversing Entries

No reversing entry recorded on January 1, 2016

— OR —

WITH Reversing Entries

Reversing entry recorded on January 1, 2016

NO ENTRY

Salaries Expense

Date	Expl.	Debit	Credit	Balance
2016				

Salaries Payable

Date	Expl.	Debit	Credit	Balance
2015				
Dec. 31	(e)		210	210
2016				

Salaries Payable 210
    Salaries Expense 210

Salaries Expense*

Date	Expl.	Debit	Credit	Balance
2016				
Jan. 1			210	(210)

Salaries Payable

Date	Expl.	Debit	Credit	Balance
2015				
Dec. 31	(e)		210	210
2016				
Jan. 1		210		0

Pay the accrued and current salaries on January 9, the first payday in 2016

Salaries Expense 490
Salaries Payable 210
    Cash 700

Salaries Expense

Date	Expl.	Debit	Credit	Balance
2016				
Jan. 9		490		490

Salaries Payable

Date	Expl.	Debit	Credit	Balance
2015				
Dec. 31	(e)		210	210
2016				
Jan. 9		210		0

Salaries Expense 700
    Cash 700

Salaries Expense*

Date	Expl.	Debit	Credit	Balance
2016				
Jan. 1			210	(210)
Jan. 9		700		490

Salaries Payable

Date	Expl.	Debit	Credit	Balance
2015				
Dec. 31	(e)		210	210
2016				
Jan. 1		210		0

Under both approaches, the expense and liability accounts have identical balances after the cash payment on January 9.

Salaries Expense $490
Salaries Payable .... $ 0

*Circled numbers in the *Balance* column indicate abnormal balances.

financial statements are not prepared before the liability is settled on January 9. The credit to the Salaries Expense account is unusual because it gives the account an *abnormal credit balance*. We highlight an abnormal balance by circling it. Because of the reversing entry, the January 9 entry to record payment is straightforward. This entry debits the Salaries Expense account and credits Cash for the full $700 paid. It is the same as all other entries made to record 10 days' salary for the employee. Notice that after the payment entry is posted, the Salaries Expense account has a $490 balance that reflects seven days' salary of $70 per day (see the lower right side of Exhibit 4A.1). The zero balance in the Salaries Payable account is now correct. The lower section of Exhibit 4A.1 shows that the expense and liability accounts have exactly the same balances whether reversing entries are used or not. This means that both approaches yield identical results.

Summary

C1 Explain why temporary accounts are closed each period.
Temporary accounts are closed at the end of each accounting period for two main reasons. First, the closing process updates the capital account to include the effects of all transactions and events recorded for the period. Second, it prepares revenue, expense, and withdrawals accounts for the next reporting period by giving them zero balances.

C2 Identify steps in the accounting cycle. The accounting cycle consists of 10 steps: (1) analyze transactions, (2) journalize, (3) post, (4) prepare an unadjusted trial balance, (5) adjust accounts, (6) prepare an adjusted trial balance, (7) prepare statements, (8) close, (9) prepare a post-closing trial balance, and (10) prepare (optional) reversing entries.

C3 Explain and prepare a classified statement of financial position. Classified statement of financial positions report assets and liabilities in two categories: current and noncurrent. Noncurrent assets often include long-term financial assets or investments, property, plant and equipment, and intangible assets. Owner' equity for proprietorships (and partnerships) reports the capital account balance. A corporation separates equity into share capital and retained earnings.

A1 Compute the current ratio and describe what it reveals about a company's financial condition. A company's current ratio is defined as current assets divided by current liabilities. We use it to evaluate a company's ability to pay its current liabilities out of current assets.

P1 Prepare a work sheet and explain its usefulness. A work sheet can be a useful tool in preparing and analyzing financial statements. It is helpful at the end of a period in preparing adjusting entries, an adjusted trial balance, and financial statements. A work sheet usually contains five pairs of columns: Unadjusted Trial Balance, Adjustments, Adjusted Trial Balance, Income Statement, and Statement of Financial Position & Statement of changes in equity.

P2 Describe and prepare closing entries. Closing entries involve four steps: (1) close credit balances in revenue (and gain) accounts to Income Summary, (2) close debit balances in expense (and loss) accounts to Income Summary, (3) close Income Summary to the capital account, and (4) close withdrawals account to owner's capital.

P3 Explain and prepare a post-closing trial balance. A post-closing trial balance is a list of permanent accounts and their balances after all closing entries have been journalized and posted. Its purpose is to verify that (1) total debits equal total credits for permanent accounts and (2) all temporary accounts have zero balances.

P4ᴬ Prepare reversing entries and explain their purpose. Reversing entries are an optional step. They are applied to accrued expenses and revenues. The purpose of reversing entries is to simplify subsequent journal entries. Financial statements are unaffected by the choice to use or not use reversing entries.

Guidance Answers to Decision Maker and Decision Ethics

Entrepreneur Yes, you are concerned about the absence of a depreciation adjustment. Equipment does depreciate, and financial statements must recognize this occurrence. Its absence suggests an error or a misrepresentation (there is also the possibility that equipment is fully depreciated).

Analyst A current ratio of 1.2 suggests that current assets are sufficient to cover current liabilities, but it implies a minimal buffer in case of errors in measuring current assets or current liabilities. Removing the past due receivable reduces the current ratio to 0.7. Your assessment is that the company will have some difficulty meeting its loan payments.

Guidance Answers to Quick Checks

1. Amounts in the Unadjusted Trial Balance columns are taken from current account balances in the ledger. The balances for new accounts expected to arise from adjusted entries can be left blank or set at zero.

2. A work sheet offers the advantage of listing on one page all necessary information to make adjusting entries.

3. A work sheet can help in (a) accounting efficiency and avoiding errors, (b) linking transactions and events to their effects in financial statements, (c) showing adjustments for audit purposes, (d) preparing interim financial statements, and (e) showing effects from proposed, or what-if, transactions.

4. The major steps in preparing closing entries are to close (1) credit balances in revenue accounts to Income Summary, (2) debit balances in expense accounts to Income Summary, (3) Income Summary to owner's capital, and (4) any withdrawals account to owner's capital.

5. Revenue (and gain) and expense (and loss) accounts are called *temporary* because they are opened and closed each period. The Income Summary and owner's withdrawals accounts are also temporary.

6. Permanent accounts make up the post-closing trial balance, which consist of asset, liability, and equity accounts.

7. Current assets: (b), (c), (d). Property, plant and equipment: (a), (e). Item (f) is an intangible asset.

8. Investment in other entities' shares or bonds.

9. For a service company, the operating cycle is the usual time between (1) paying employees who do the services and (2) receiving cash from customers for services provided.

Key Terms   www.mheducation.asia/olc/wildkwokFAP

Accounting cycle (p. 146)

Classified statement of financial position (p. 147)

Closing entries (p. 143)

Closing process (p. 142)

Current assets (p. 148)

Current liabilities (p. 149)

Current ratio (p. 150)

Income summary (p. 143)

Noncurrent assets (p. 149)

Noncurrent liabilities (p. 149)

Operating cycle (p. 147)

Permanent accounts (p. 142)

Post-closing trial balance (p. 146)

Pro forma financial statements (p. 142)

Reversing entries (p. 154)

Temporary accounts (p. 142)

Unclassified statement of financial position (p. 147)

Working papers (p. 138)

Work sheet (p. 138)

Multiple Choice Quiz   Answers on p. 177   www.mheducation.asia/olc/wildkwokFAP

Additional Quiz Questions are available at the book's Website.

1. G. Venda, owner of Venda Services, withdrew $25,000 from the business during the current year. The entry to close the withdrawals account at the end of the year is:

a.	G. Venda, Withdrawals	25,000	
	G. Venda, Capital		25,000
b.	Income Summary	25,000	
	G. Venda, Capital		25,000
c.	G. Venda, Withdrawals	25,000	
	Cash		25,000
d.	G. Venda, Capital	25,000	
	Salary Expense		25,000
e.	G. Venda, Capital	25,000	
	G. Venda, Withdrawals		25,000

2. The following information is available for the R. Kandamil Company before closing the accounts. After all of the closing entries are made, what will be the balance in the R. Kandamil, Capital account?

Total revenues	$300,000
Total expenses	195,000
R. Kandamil, Capital	100,000
R. Kandamil, Withdrawals	45,000

a. $360,000   **d.** $150,000
b. $250,000   **e.** $60,000
c. $160,000

3. Which of the following errors would cause the statement of financial position and statement of changes in equity columns of a work sheet to be out of balance?
   a. Entering a revenue amount in the statement of financial position and statement of changes in equity debit column.

b. Entering a liability amount in the statement of financial position and statement of changes in equity credit column.

c. Entering an expense account in the statement of financial position and statement of changes in equity debit column.

d. Entering an asset account in the income statement debit column.

e. Entering a liability amount in the income statement credit column.

4. The temporary account used only in the closing process to hold the amounts of revenues and expenses before the net difference is added or subtracted from the owner's capital account is called the
   a. Closing account.
   b. Nominal account.
   c. Income Summary account.
   d. Balance Column account.
   e. Contra account.

5. Based on the following information from Repicor Company's statement of financial position, what is Repicor Company's current ratio?

Current assets	$ 75,000
Investments	30,000
Property, plant and equipment	300,000
Current liabilities	50,000
Long-term liabilities	60,000
D. Repicor, Capital	295,000

a. 2.10   **d.** 0.95
b. 1.50   **e.** 0.67
c. 1.00

^A *Superscript letter A denotes assignments based on Appendix 4A.*

Icon denotes assignments that involve decision making.

Discussion Questions

1. What accounts are affected by closing entries? What accounts are not affected?

2. What two purposes are accomplished by recording closing entries?

3. What are the steps in recording closing entries?

4. What is the purpose of the Income Summary account?

5. Explain whether an error has occurred if a post-closing trial balance includes a Depreciation Expense account.

6. What tasks are aided by a work sheet?

7. Why are the debit and credit entries in the Adjustments columns of the work sheet identified with letters?

8. What is a company's operating cycle?

9. What classes of assets and liabilities are shown on a typical classified statement of financial position?

10. How is unearned revenue classified on the statement of financial position?

11. What are the characteristics of property, plant and equipment?

12.^AHow do reversing entries simplify recordkeeping?

13.^AIf a company recorded accrued salaries expense of $500 at the end of its financial year, what reversing entry could be made? When would it be made?

14. Refer to the balance sheet for **Nestlé** in Appendix A. What noncurrent liabilities are listed on its consolidated balance sheet?

15. Refer to **Adidas'** statement of financial position in Appendix A. Identify and list its current assets.

16. Refer to **Puma's** statement of financial position from its Website (**http://about.puma.com/en/investor-relations/financial-reports**). Identify its current liabilities.

17. Refer to **Samsung's** consolidated statement of income in Appendix A. If it uses an Income Summary T-account to calculate "Profit for the year," list the items (without amounts) that should appear on the debit side.

18. Refer to **361 Degrees'** 2013 consolidated statement of financial position from its Website (**http://ir.361sport.com/html/ir_report.php**). What noncurrent assets are listed on its consolidated statement of financial position?

---

connect

QUICK STUDY

QS 4-1

Identifying the accounting cycle

C2

List the following steps of the accounting cycle in their proper order.

a. Preparing the post-closing trial balance.

b. Posting the journal entries.

c. Journalizing and posting adjusting entries.

d. Preparing the adjusted trial balance.

e. Journalizing and posting closing entries.

f. Analyzing transactions and events.

g. Preparing the financial statements.

h. Preparing the unadjusted trial balance.

i. Journalizing transactions and events.

QS 4-2

Explaining temporary and permanent accounts

C1

Complete the following descriptions related to temporary and permanent accounts.

1. Temporary accounts accumulate data related to _____ accounting period.

2. Permanent accounts report on activities related to _____ future accounting periods, and they carry their ending balances into the next period.

3. _____ accounts include all income statement accounts, the withdrawals account, and the Income Summary account.

4. _____ accounts generally consist of all statement of financial position accounts, and these accounts are not closed.

QS 4-3

Identifying current accounts and computing the current ratio

A1

Compute Jamar Company's current ratio using the following information.

Accounts receivable	$15,000	Long-term notes payable	$20,000
Accounts payable	10,000	Office supplies	1,800
Buildings	42,000	Prepaid insurance	2,500
Cash	6,000	Unearned services revenue	4,000

QS 4-4

Classifying statement of financial position items

C3

The following are common categories on a classified statement of financial position.

A. Current assets

B. Noncurrent assets

C. Current liabilities

D. Noncurrent liabilities

For each of the following items, select the letter that identifies the statement of financial position category where the item typically would appear.

_____ **1.** Trademarks   _____ **5.** Cash
_____ **2.** Accounts receivable   _____ **6.** Wages payable
_____ **3.** Land not currently used in operations   _____ **7.** Store equipment
_____ **4.** Notes payable (due in three years)   _____ **8.** Accounts payable

---

In preparing a work sheet, indicate the financial statement Debit column to which a normal balance in the following accounts should be extended. Use IS for the Income Statement Debit column and SFP/SCE for the Statement of Financial Position and Statement of Changes in Equity Debit column.

_____ **a.** Insurance expense   _____ **d.** Depreciation expense—Equipment
_____ **b.** Equipment   _____ **e.** Prepaid rent
_____ **c.** Owner, Withdrawals   _____ **f.** Accounts receivable

QS 4-5
Applying a work sheet
P1

List the following steps in preparing a work sheet in their proper order by writing numbers 1–5 in the blank spaces provided.

a. _____ Prepare an adjusted trial balance on the work sheet.
b. _____ Prepare an unadjusted trial balance on the work sheet.
c. _____ Enter adjustments data on the work sheet.
d. _____ Extend adjusted balances to appropriate financial statement columns.
e. _____ Total the statement columns, compute net profit (loss), and complete work sheet.

QS 4-6
Ordering work sheet steps
P1

The following selected information is taken from the work sheet for Wayman Company as at December 31, 2015. Using this information, determine the amount for K. Wayman, Capital, that should be reported on its December 31, 2015, statement of financial position.

QS 4-7
Interpreting a work sheet
P1

	Income Statement		Statement of Financial Position and Statement of Changes in Equity	
	Dr.	Cr.	Dr.	Cr.
K. Wayman, Capital				65,000
K. Wayman, Withdrawals			32,000	
Totals	115,000	174,000		

The ledger of Terrel Company includes the following unadjusted normal balances: Prepaid Rent $800, Services Revenue $11,600, and Wages Expense $5,000. Adjusting entries are required for **(a)** accrued rent expense $240; **(b)** accrued services revenue $180; and **(c)** accrued wages expense $160. Enter these unadjusted balances and the necessary adjustments on a work sheet and complete the work sheet for these accounts. *Note:* Also include the following accounts: Accounts Receivable, Wages Payable, and Rent Expense.

QS 4-8
Preparing a partial work sheet
P1

The ledger of Avril Company includes the following accounts with normal balances: L. Avril, Capital $6,000; L. Avril, Withdrawals $400; Services Revenue $10,000; Wages Expense $5,200; and Rent Expense $800. Prepare the necessary closing entries from the available information at December 31.

QS 4-9
Prepare closing entries from the ledger   P2

Identify the accounts listed in QS 4-9 that would be included in a post-closing trial balance.

QS 4-10
Identify post-closing accounts   P3

On December 31, 2014, Lester Co. prepared an adjusting entry for $6,700 of earned but unrecorded management fees. On January 16, 2015, Lester received $15,500 cash in management fees, which included the accrued fees earned in 2014. Assuming the company uses reversing entries, prepare the January 1, 2015, reversing entry and the January 16, 2015, cash receipt entry.

QS 4-11ᴬ
Reversing entries
P4

EXERCISES

Exercise 4-1
Preparing and posting
closing entries

P2

Check M. Mallon, Capital (ending
balance), $38,900

Use the March 31 financial year-end information from the following ledger accounts (assume that all accounts have normal balances) to prepare closing journal entries and then post those entries to the appropriate ledger accounts.

General Ledger

M. Mallon, Capital   Acct. No. 301

Date	PR	Debit	Credit	Balance
Mar. 31	G2			42,000

M. Mallon, Withdrawals   Acct. No. 302

Date	PR	Debit	Credit	Balance
Mar. 31	G2			25,000

Services Revenue   Acct. No. 401

Date	PR	Debit	Credit	Balance
Mar. 31	G2			74,000

Depreciation Expense   Acct. No. 603

Date	PR	Debit	Credit	Balance
Mar. 31	G2			17,000

Salaries Expense   Acct. No. 622

Date	PR	Debit	Credit	Balance
Mar. 31	G2			21,000

Insurance Expense   Acct. No. 637

Date	PR	Debit	Credit	Balance
Mar. 31	G2			4,500

Rent Expense   Acct. No. 640

Date	PR	Debit	Credit	Balance
Mar. 31	G2			9,600

Income Summary   Acct. No. 901

Date	PR	Debit	Credit	Balance

Exercise 4-2
Preparing closing entries and a
post-closing trial balance

P2   P3

The adjusted trial balance for Sundance Marketing Co. follows. Complete the four right-most columns of the table by first entering information for the four closing entries (keyed *1* through *4*) and second by completing the post-closing trial balance.

No.	Account Title	Adjusted Trial Balance Dr.	Adjusted Trial Balance Cr.	Closing Entry Information Dr.	Closing Entry Information Cr.	Post-Closing Trial Balance Dr.	Post-Closing Trial Balance Cr.
101	Cash	$ 8,200					
106	Accounts receivable	24,000					
153	Equipment	41,000					
154	Accumulated depreciation—Equipment		$ 16,500				
193	Franchise................................	30,000					
201	Accounts payable		14,000				
209	Salaries payable		3,200				
233	Unearned fees		2,600				
301	H. Sundance, Capital		64,500				
302	H. Sundance, Withdrawals	14,400					
401	Marketing fees earned		79,000				
611	Depreciation expense—Equipment	11,000					
622	Salaries expense	31,500					
640	Rent expense	12,000					
677	Miscellaneous expenses	7,700					
901	Income summary						
	Totals	$179,800	$179,800				

The following adjusted trial balance contains the accounts and balances of Showers Company as at December 31, 2015, the end of its financial year. (1) Prepare the December 31, 2015, closing entries for Showers Company. (2) Prepare the December 31, 2015, post-closing trial balance for Showers Company.

Exercise 4-3

Preparing closing entries and a post-closing trial balance

P2   P3

No.	Account Title	Debit	Credit
101	Cash	$18,000	
126	Supplies	12,000	
128	Prepaid insurance	2,000	
167	Equipment	23,000	
168	Accumulated depreciation—Equipment		$ 6,500
301	R. Showers, Capital		46,600
302	R. Showers, Withdrawals	6,000	
404	Services revenue		36,000
612	Depreciation expense—Equipment	2,000	
622	Salaries expense	21,000	
637	Insurance expense	1,500	
640	Rent expense	2,400	
652	Supplies expense	1,200	
	Totals	$89,100	$89,100

Check   (2) R. Showers, Capital (ending), $48,500; Total debits, $55,000

Use the following adjusted trial balance of Webb Trucking Company to prepare the (1) income statement and (2) statement of changes in equity, for the year ended December 31, 2015. The K. Webb, Capital, account balance is $161,000 at December 31, 2014.

Exercise 4-4

Preparing the financial statements

C2

Account Title	Debit	Credit
Cash	$ 7,000	
Accounts receivable	16,500	
Office supplies	2,000	
Trucks	170,000	
Accumulated depreciation—Trucks		$ 35,000
Land	75,000	
Accounts payable		11,000
Interest payable		3,000
Long-term notes payable		52,000
K. Webb, Capital		161,000
K. Webb, Withdrawals	19,000	
Trucking fees earned		128,000
Depreciation expense—Trucks	22,500	
Salaries expense	60,000	
Office supplies expense	7,000	
Repairs expense—Trucks	11,000	
Totals	$390,000	$390,000

Use the information in the adjusted trial balance reported in Exercise 4-4 to prepare Webb Trucking Company's classified statement of financial position as at December 31, 2015.

Exercise 4-5

Preparing a classified statement of financial position   **C3**

Check   Total assets, $235,500; K. Webb, Capital, $169,500

Exercise 4-6
Computing the current ratio

A1

Use the information in the adjusted trial balance reported in Exercise 4-4 to compute the current ratio as at the statement of financial position date (round the ratio to two decimals). Interpret the current ratio for the Webb Trucking Company. (Assume that the industry average for the current ratio is 1.5.)

Exercise 4-7
Computing and analyzing the current ratio

A1

Calculate the current ratio in each of the following separate cases (round the ratio to two decimals). Identify the company case with the strongest liquidity position. (These cases represent competing companies in the same industry.)

	Current Assets	Current Liabilities
Case 1	$ 78,000	$31,000
Case 2	104,000	75,000
Case 3	44,000	48,000
Case 4	84,500	80,600
Case 5	60,000	99,000

Exercise 4-8
Extending adjusted account balances on a work sheet

P1

These 16 accounts are from the Adjusted Trial Balance columns of a company's 10-column work sheet. In the blank space beside each account, write the letter of the appropriate financial statement column (A, B, C, or D) to which a normal account balance is extended.

A. Debit column for the Income Statement columns.
B. Credit column for the Income Statement columns.
C. Debit column for the Statement of Financial Position and Statement of Changes in Equity columns.
D. Credit column for the Statement of Financial Position and Statement of Changes in Equity columns.

_____ **1.** Office Supplies	_____ **9.** Service Fees Revenue
_____ **2.** Accounts Payable	_____ **10.** Insurance Expense
_____ **3.** Owner, Capital	_____ **11.** Accumulated Depreciation
_____ **4.** Wages Payable	_____ **12.** Interest Revenue
_____ **5.** Machinery	_____ **13.** Accounts Receivable
_____ **6.** Interest Receivable	_____ **14.** Rent Expense
_____ **7.** Interest Expense	_____ **15.** Depreciation Expense
_____ **8.** Owner, Withdrawals	_____ **16.** Cash

Exercise 4-9
Preparing adjusting entries from a work sheet   **P1**

Use the following information from the Adjustments columns of a 10-column work sheet to prepare the necessary adjusting journal entries (*a*) through (*e*).

	A	B	C	D	E	F	G	H	I	J	K	L
1											Statement of Financial	
2			Unadjusted				Adjusted		Income		Position and Statement	
3			Trial Balance		Adjustments		Trial Balance		Statement		of Changes in Equity	
4	No.	Account Title	Dr.	Cr.	Dr.	Cr.	Dr.	Cr.	Dr.	Cr.	Dr.	Cr.
5	109	Interest receivable					(d) $ 580					
6	124	Office supplies						(b) $1,650				
7	128	Prepaid insurance						(a) 900				
8	164	Accumulated depreciation—Office equipment						(c) 3,300				
9	209	Salaries payable						(e) 660				
10	409	Interest revenue						(d) 580				
11	612	Depreciation expense—Office equipment					(c) 3,300					
12	620	Office salaries expense					(e) 660					
13	636	Insurance expense—Office equipment					(a) 432					
14	637	Insurance expense—Store equipment					(a) 468					
15	650	Office supplies expense					(b) 1,650					
16		Totals					$7,090	$7,090				
17												

The Adjusted Trial Balance columns of a 10-column work sheet for Propel Company follow. Complete the work sheet by extending the account balances into the appropriate financial statement columns and by entering the amount of net profit for the reporting period.

Exercise 4-10
Extending accounts in a work sheet   P1

	A	B	C	D	E	F	G	H	I	J	K	L
1											Statement of Financial Position and Statement of Changes in Equity	
2-3			Unadjusted Trial Balance		Adjustments		Adjusted Trial Balance		Income Statement			
4	No.	Account Title	Dr.	Cr.	Dr.	Cr.	Dr.	Cr.	Dr.	Cr.	Dr.	Cr.
5	101	Cash					$ 6,000					
6	106	Accounts receivable					26,200					
7	153	Trucks					41,000					
8	154	Accumulated depreciation—Trucks						$ 16,500				
9	183	Land					30,000					
10	201	Accounts payable						14,000				
11	209	Salaries payable						3,200				
12	233	Unearned fees						2,600				
13	301	J. Propel, Capital						64,500				
14	302	J. Propel, Withdrawals					14,400					
15	401	Plumbing fees earned						79,000				
16	611	Depreciation expense—Trucks					5,500					
17	622	Salaries expense					37,000					
18	640	Rent expense					12,000					
19	677	Miscellaneous expenses					7,700					
20		Totals					$179,800	$179,800				

Check Net profit, $16,800

These partially completed Income Statement columns from a 10-column work sheet are for Welch's Red Sail Rental Company. (1) Use the information to determine the amount that should be entered on the net profit line of the work sheet. (2) Prepare the company's closing entries. The owner, L. Welch, did not make any withdrawals this period.

Exercise 4-11
Completing the income statement columns and preparing closing entries

P1 P2

Account Title	Debit	Credit
Rent earned		102,000
Salaries expense	45,300	
Insurance expense	6,400	
Dock rental expense	15,000	
Boat supplies expense	3,200	
Depreciation expense—Boats	19,500	
Totals		
Net profit		
Totals		

Check Net profit, $12,600

The following unadjusted trial balance contains the accounts and balances of Dalton Delivery Company as at December 31, 2015, its first year of operations.

(1) Use the following information about the company's adjustments to complete a 10-column work sheet.

a. Unrecorded depreciation on the trucks at the end of the year is $35,000.

b. The total amount of accrued interest expense at year-end is $8,000.

c. The cost of unused office supplies still available at the year-end is $1,000.

(2) Prepare the year-end closing entries for this company, and determine the capital amount to be reported on its year-end statement of financial position.

Exercise 4-12
Preparing a work sheet and recording closing entries

P1 P2

	A	B	C
1		Unadjusted Trial Balance	
2	**Account Title**	**Debit**	**Credit**
3	Cash	$ 14,000	
4	Accounts receivable	33,000	
5	Office supplies	4,000	
6	Trucks	340,000	
7	Accumulated depreciation—Trucks		$70,000
8	Land	150,000	
9	Accounts payable		22,000
10	Interest payable		6,000
11	Long-term notes payable		104,000
12	V. Dalton, Capital		322,000
13	V. Dalton, Withdrawals	38,000	
14	Delivery fees earned		256,000
15	Depreciation expense—Truck	45,000	
16	Salaries expense	120,000	
17	Office supplies expense	14,000	
18	Interest expense	6,000	
19	Repairs expense—Trucks	16,000	
20	Totals	$780,000	$780,000
21			

Check Adj. trial balance totals, $817,000; Net profit, $15,000

Exercise 4-13ᴬ
Preparing reversing entries
P4

The following two events occurred for Tanger Co. on October 31, 2015, the end of its financial year.

a. Tanger rents a building from its owner for $3,200 per month. By a prearrangement, the company delayed paying October's rent until November 5. On this date, the company paid the rent for both October and November.

b. Tanger rents space in a building it owns to a tenant for $750 per month. By prearrangement, the tenant delayed paying the October rent until November 8. On this date, the tenant paid the rent for both October and November.

Required

1. Prepare adjusting entries that the company must record for these events as at October 31.
2. Assuming Tanger does *not* use reversing entries, prepare journal entries to record Tanger's payment of rent on November 5 and the collection of rent on November 8 from Tanger's tenant.
3. Assuming that the company uses reversing entries, prepare reversing entries on November 1 and the journal entries to record Tanger's payment of rent on November 5 and the collection of rent on November 8 from Tanger's tenant.

Exercise 4-14ᴬ
Preparing reversing entries
P4

Hinson Company records prepaid assets and unearned revenues in statement of financial position accounts. The following information was used to prepare adjusting entries for the company as at August 31, the end of the company's financial year.

a. The company has earned $5,000 in service fees that were not yet recorded at period-end.
b. The expired portion of prepaid insurance is $2,700.
c. The company has earned $1,900 of its Unearned Service Fees account balance.
d. Depreciation expense for office equipment is $2,300.
e. Employees have earned but have not been paid salaries of $2,400.

Prepare any necessary reversing entries for the accounting adjustments *a* through *e* assuming that the company uses reversing entries in its accounting system.

Exercise 4-15
Determining effects of closing entries
C1

Argosy Company began the current period with a $14,000 credit balance in the D. Argosy, Capital account. At the end of the period, the company's adjusted account balances include the following temporary accounts with normal balances.

Service fees earned	$35,000	Interest revenue	$3,500
Salaries expense	19,000	D. Argosy, Withdrawals	6,000
Depreciation expense	4,000	Utilities expense	2,300

After closing the revenue and expense accounts, what will be the balance of the Income Summary account? After all closing entries are journalized and posted, what will be the balance of the D. Argosy, Capital account?

Following are **Nintendo**'s revenue and expense accounts for a recent calendar year (yen in millions). Prepare the company's closing entries for its revenues and its expenses.

Net sales	¥1,838,622
Cost of sales	1,044,981
Advertising expense	117,308
Other expense, net	397,244

Exercise 4-16
Preparing closing entries

P2

The following data are taken from the unadjusted trial balance of the Madison Company at December 31, 2015. Each account carries a normal balance and the accounts are shown here in alphabetical order.

Accounts Payable.	$ 2	Prepaid Insurance . .	$ 6	T. Madison, Withdrawals . .	$2
Accounts Receivable	4	Revenue	25	Unearned Revenue	4
Accumulated Depreciation—Equip. . .	5	Salaries Expense	6	Utilities Expense	4
Cash	7	Supplies	8		
Equipment	13	T. Madison, Capital . .	14		

Exercise 4-17
Completing a worksheet

P1

1. Use the data above to prepare a worksheet. Enter the accounts in proper order and enter their balances in the correct debit or credit column.
2. Use the following adjustment information to complete the worksheet.

   a. Depreciation on equipment, $1   **d.** Supplies available at December 31, 2015, $5

   b. Accrued salaries, $2   **e.** Expired insurance, $5

   c. The $4 of unearned revenue has been earned

connect

In the blank space beside each numbered statement of financial position item, enter the letter of its statement of financial position classification. If the item should not appear on the statement of financial position, enter a Z in the blank.

A. Current assets   **C.** Current liabilities   **E.** Equity

B. Noncurrent assets   **D.** Noncurrent liabilities

PROBLEM SET A

Problem 4-1A
Determining statement of financial position classifications

C3

_____ **1.** Office equipment	_____ **11.** Depreciation expense—Building
_____ **2.** Office supplies	_____ **12.** Prepaid rent
_____ **3.** Buildings	_____ **13.** Interest receivable
_____ **4.** Store supplies	_____ **14.** Taxes payable
_____ **5.** Accumulated depreciation—Trucks	_____ **15.** Automobiles
_____ **6.** Land (used in operations)	_____ **16.** Notes payable (due in 3 years)
_____ **7.** Repairs expense	_____ **17.** Accounts payable
_____ **8.** Cash	_____ **18.** Prepaid insurance
_____ **9.** Current portion of long-term note payable	_____ **19.** Owner, Capital
_____ **10.** Long-term investment in shares	_____ **20.** Unearned services revenue

On April 1, 2015, Jennifer Stafford created a new travel agency, See-It-Now Travel. The following transactions occurred during the company's first month.

April 1	Stafford invested $20,000 cash and computer equipment worth $40,000 in the company.
2	The company rented furnished office space by paying $1,700 cash for the first month's (April) rent.
3	The company purchased $1,100 of office supplies for cash.
10	The company paid $3,600 cash for the premium on a 12-month insurance policy. Coverage begins on April 11.
14	The company paid $1,800 cash for two weeks' salaries earned by employees.
24	The company collected $7,900 cash on commissions from airlines on tickets obtained for customers.
28	The company paid $1,800 cash for two weeks' salaries earned by employees.
29	The company paid $250 cash for minor repairs to the company's computer.
30	The company paid $650 cash for this month's telephone bill.
30	Stafford withdrew $1,500 cash from the company for personal use.

Problem 4-2A
Applying the accounting cycle

C1 C2 P2 P3

eXcel

www.mheducation.asia/olc/wildkwokFAP

The company's chart of accounts follows:

No.	Account	No.	Account
101	Cash	405	Commissions Earned
106	Accounts Receivable	612	Depreciation Expense—Computer Equip.
124	Office Supplies	622	Salaries Expense
128	Prepaid Insurance	637	Insurance Expense
167	Computer Equipment	640	Rent Expense
168	Accumulated Depreciation—Computer Equip.	650	Office Supplies Expense
209	Salaries Payable	684	Repairs Expense
301	J. Stafford, Capital	688	Telephone Expense
302	J. Stafford, Withdrawals	901	Income Summary

Required

1. Use the balance column format to set up each ledger account listed in its chart of accounts.

2. Prepare journal entries to record the transactions for April and post them to the ledger accounts. The company records prepaid and unearned items in statement of financial position accounts.

3. Prepare an unadjusted trial balance as at April 30.

4. Use the following information to journalize and post adjusting entries for the month:

   a. Two-thirds of one month's insurance coverage has expired.

   b. At the end of the month, $700 of office supplies are still available.

   c. This month's depreciation on the computer equipment is $600.

   d. Employees earned $320 of unpaid and unrecorded salaries as at month-end.

   e. The company earned $1,650 of commissions that are not yet billed at month-end.

5. Prepare the income statement and the statement of changes in equity for the month of April and the statement of financial position at April 30, 2015.

6. Prepare journal entries to close the temporary accounts and post these entries to the ledger.

7. Prepare a post-closing trial balance.

Check (3) Unadj. trial balance totals, $67,900

(4a) Dr. Insurance Expense, $200

(5) Net profit, $1,830; J. Stafford, Capital (4/30/2015), $60,330; Total assets, $60,650

(7) P-C trial balance totals, $61,250

Problem 4-3A

Preparing trial balances, closing entries, and financial statements

C3 P2 P3

www.mheducation.asia/olc/wildkwokFAP

The adjusted trial balance of Kobe Repairs on December 31, 2015, follows.

KOBE REPAIRS
Adjusted Trial Balance
December 31, 2015

No.	Account Title	Debit	Credit
101	Cash	$ 13,000	
124	Office supplies	1,200	
128	Prepaid insurance	1,950	
167	Equipment	48,000	
168	Accumulated depreciation—Equipment		$ 4,000
201	Accounts payable		12,000
210	Wages payable		500
301	S. Kobe, Capital		40,000
302	S. Kobe, Withdrawals	15,000	
401	Repair fees earned		77,750
612	Depreciation expense—Equipment	4,000	
623	Wages expense	36,500	
637	Insurance expense	700	
640	Rent expense	9,600	
650	Office supplies expense	2,600	
690	Utilities expense	1,700	
	Totals	$134,250	$134,250

Required

1. Prepare an income statement and a statement of changes in equity for the year 2015, and a classified statement of financial position at December 31, 2015. There are no owner investments in 2015.

Check (1) Ending capital balance, $47,650; net profit, $22,650

2. Enter the adjusted trial balance in the first two columns of a six-column table. Use columns three and four for closing entry information and the last two columns for a post-closing trial balance. Insert an Income Summary account as the last item in the trial balance.

(2) P-C trial balance totals, $64,150

3. Enter closing entry information in the six-column table and prepare journal entries for it.

Analysis Component

4. Assume for this part only that
   a. None of the $700 insurance expense had expired during the year. Instead, assume it is a prepayment of the next period's insurance protection.
   b. There are no earned and unpaid wages at the end of the year. (*Hint:* Reverse the $500 wages payable accrual.)

   Describe the financial statement changes that would result from these two assumptions.

The adjusted trial balance for Sharp Construction as at December 31, 2015, follows.

Problem 4-4A
Preparing closing entries, financial statements, and ratios

C3 A1 P2

SHARP CONSTRUCTION
Adjusted Trial Balance
December 31, 2015

No.	Account Title	Debit	Credit
101	Cash	$ 4,000	
104	Short-term investments	22,000	
126	Supplies	7,100	
128	Prepaid insurance	6,000	
167	Equipment	39,000	
168	Accumulated depreciation—Equipment		$ 20,000
173	Building	130,000	
174	Accumulated depreciation—Building		55,000
183	Land	45,000	
201	Accounts payable		15,500
203	Interest payable		1,500
208	Rent payable		2,500
210	Wages payable		1,500
213	Property taxes payable		800
233	Unearned professional fees		6,500
251	Long-term notes payable		66,000
301	J. Sharp, Capital		82,700
302	J. Sharp, Withdrawals	12,000	
401	Professional fees earned		96,000
406	Rent earned		13,000
407	Dividends earned		1,900
409	Interest earned		1,000
606	Depreciation expense—Building	10,000	
612	Depreciation expense—Equipment	5,000	
623	Wages expense	31,000	
633	Interest expense	4,100	
637	Insurance expense	9,000	
640	Rent expense	12,400	
652	Supplies expense	6,400	
682	Postage expense	3,200	
683	Property taxes expense	4,000	
684	Repairs expense	7,900	
688	Telephone expense	2,200	
690	Utilities expense	3,600	
	Totals	$363,900	$363,900

J. Sharp invested $50,000 cash in the business during year 2015 (the December 31, 2014, credit balance of the J. Sharp, Capital account was $32,700). Sharp Construction is required to make a $6,600 payment on its long-term notes payable during 2016.

Required

Check (1) Total assets (12/31/2015), $178,100; Net profit, $13,100

1. Prepare the income statement and the statement of changes in equity for the calendar year 2015 and the classified statement of financial position at December 31, 2015.

2. Prepare the necessary closing entries at December 31, 2015.

3. Use the information in the financial statements to compute these ratios: (*a*) return on assets (total assets at December 31, 2014, was $200,000), (*b*) debt ratio, (*c*) profit margin ratio (use total revenues as the denominator), and (*d*) current ratio.

Problem 4-5A

Preparing a work sheet, adjusting and closing entries, and financial statements

C3 P1 P2

The following unadjusted trial balance is for Adams Construction Co. as at the end of its 2015 financial year. The June 30, 2014, credit balance of the owner's capital account was $52,660, and the owner invested $25,000 cash in the company during the 2015 financial year.

	A	B	C	D
1		**ADAMS CONSTRUCTION CO.**		
2		**Unadjusted Trial Balance**		
3		**June 30, 2015**		
4	**No.**	**Account Title**	**Debit**	**Credit**
5	101	Cash	$ 17,500	
6	126	Supplies	8,900	
7	128	Prepaid insurance	6,200	
8	167	Equipment	131,000	
9	168	Accumulated depreciation—Equipment		$ 25,250
10	201	Accounts payable		5,800
11	203	Interest payable		0
12	208	Rent payable		0
13	210	Wages payable		0
14	213	Property taxes payable		0
15	251	Long-term notes payable		24,000
16	301	S. Adams, Capital		77,660
17	302	S. Adams, Withdrawals	30,000	
18	401	Construction fees earned		134,000
19	612	Depreciation expense—Equipment	0	
20	623	Wages expense	45,860	
21	633	Interest expense	2,640	
22	637	Insurance expense	0	
23	640	Rent expense	13,200	
24	652	Supplies expense	0	
25	683	Property taxes expense	4,600	
26	684	Repairs expense	2,810	
27	690	Utilities expense	4,000	
28		Totals	$266,710	$266,710
29				

Required

1. Prepare a 10-column work sheet for financial year 2015, starting with the unadjusted trial balance and including adjustments based on these additional facts.

   a. The supplies available at the end of financial year 2015 had a cost of $3,200.

   b. The cost of expired insurance for the financial year is $3,900.

   c. Annual depreciation on equipment is $8,500.

   d. The June utilities expense of $550 is not included in the unadjusted trial balance because the bill arrived after the trial balance was prepared. The $550 amount owed needs to be recorded.

   e. The company's employees have earned $1,600 of accrued wages at financial year-end.

   f. The rent expense incurred and not yet paid or recorded at financial year-end is $200.

   g. Additional property taxes of $900 have been assessed for this financial year but have not been paid or recorded in the accounts.

h. The long-term note payable bears interest at 12% per year. The unadjusted Interest Expense account equals the amount paid for the first 11 months of the 2015 financial year. The $240 accrued interest for June has not yet been paid or recorded. (The company is required to make a $5,000 payment toward the note payable during the 2016 financial year.)

2. Enter adjusting and closing information in the work sheet; then journalize the adjusting and closing entries.

3. Prepare the income statement and the statement of changes in equity for the year ended June 30 and the classified statement of financial position at June 30, 2015.

Check   (3) Total assets, $120,250; Current liabilities, $14,290; Net profit, $39,300

Analysis Component

4. Analyze the following separate errors and describe how each would affect the 10-column work sheet. Explain whether the error is likely to be discovered in completing the work sheet and, if not, the effect of the error on the financial statements.

a. Assume that the adjustment for supplies used consisted of a credit to Supplies and a debit to Supplies Expense for $3,200, when the correct amount was $5,700.

b. When the adjusted trial balance in the work sheet is completed, assume that the $17,500 Cash balance is incorrectly entered in the Credit column.

The following six-column table for Bullseye Ranges includes the unadjusted trial balance as at December 31, 2015.

Problem 4-6A[A]
Preparing adjusting, reversing, and next period entries

P4

	A	B	C	D	E	F	G
1		BULLSEYE RANGES					
2		December 31, 2015					
3		Unadjusted				Adjusted	
4		Trial Balance		Adjustments		Trial Balance	
5	Account Title	Dr.	Cr.	Dr.	Cr.	Dr.	Cr.
6	Cash	$ 13,000					
7	Accounts receivable	0					
8	Supplies	5,500					
9	Equipment	130,000					
10	Accumulated depreciation—Equipment		$ 25,000				
11	Interest payable		0				
12	Salaries payable		0				
13	Unearned member fees		14,000				
14	Notes payable		50,000				
15	T. Allen, Capital		58,250				
16	T. Allen, Withdrawals	20,000					
17	Member fees earned		53,000				
18	Depreciation expense—Equipment	0					
19	Salaries expense	28,000					
20	Interest expense	3,750					
21	Supplies expense	0					
22	Totals	$200,250	$200,250				
23							

Required

1. Complete the six-column table by entering adjustments that reflect the following information.

a. As at December 31, 2015, employees had earned $900 of unpaid and unrecorded salaries. The next payday is January 4, at which time $1,600 of salaries will be paid.

b. The cost of supplies still available at December 31, 2015, is $2,700.

c. The notes payable requires an interest payment to be made every three months. The amount of unrecorded accrued interest at December 31, 2015, is $1,250. The next interest payment, at an amount of $1,500, is due on January 15, 2016.

d. Analysis of the unearned member fees account shows $5,600 remaining unearned at December 31, 2015.

e. In addition to the member fees included in the revenue account balance, the company has earned another $9,100 in unrecorded fees that will be collected on January 31, 2016. The company is also expected to collect $8,000 on that same day for new fees earned in January 2016.

f. Depreciation expense for the year is $12,500.

Check   (1) Adjusted trial balance totals, $224,000

2. Prepare journal entries for the adjustments entered in the six-column table for part 1.

3. Prepare journal entries to reverse the effects of the adjusting entries that involve accruals.

4. Prepare journal entries to record the cash payments and cash collections described for January.

PROBLEM SET B

Problem 4-1B
Determining statement of financial position classifications
C3

In the blank space beside each numbered statement of financial position item, enter the letter of its statement of financial position classification. If the item should not appear on the statement of financial position, enter a *Z* in the blank.

A. Current assets
B. Noncurrent assets
C. Current liabilities
D. Noncurrent liabilities
E. Equity

_____ **1.** Machinery
_____ **2.** Prepaid insurance
_____ **3.** Current portion of long-term note payable
_____ **4.** Interest receivable
_____ **5.** Rent receivable
_____ **6.** Land (used in operations)
_____ **7.** Copyrights
_____ **8.** Rent revenue
_____ **9.** Depreciation expense—Trucks
_____ **10.** Long-term investment in shares

_____ **11.** Office supplies
_____ **12.** Interest payable
_____ **13.** Owner, Capital
_____ **14.** Notes receivable (due in 120 days)
_____ **15.** Accumulated depreciation—Trucks
_____ **16.** Salaries payable
_____ **17.** Commissions earned
_____ **18.** Income taxes payable
_____ **19.** Office equipment
_____ **20.** Notes payable (due in 15 years)

Problem 4-2B
Applying the accounting cycle
C1 C2 P2 P3

On July 1, 2015, Lucinda Fogle created a new self-storage business, KeepSafe Co. The following transactions occurred during the company's first month.

July 1 Fogle invested $20,000 cash and buildings worth $120,000 in the company.
2 The company rented equipment by paying $1,800 cash for the first month's (July) rent.
5 The company purchased $2,300 of office supplies for cash.
10 The company paid $5,400 cash for the premium on a 12-month insurance policy. Coverage begins on July 11.
14 The company paid an employee $900 cash for two weeks' salary earned.
24 The company collected $8,800 cash for storage fees from customers.
28 The company paid $900 cash for two weeks' salary earned by an employee.
29 The company paid $850 cash for minor repairs to a leaking roof.
30 The company paid $300 cash for this month's telephone bill.
31 Fogle withdrew $1,600 cash from the company for personal use.

The company's chart of accounts follows:

101	Cash	401	Storage Fees Earned
106	Accounts Receivable	606	Depreciation Expense—Buildings
124	Office Supplies	622	Salaries Expense
128	Prepaid Insurance	637	Insurance Expense
173	Buildings	640	Rent Expense
174	Accumulated Depreciation—Buildings	650	Office Supplies Expense
209	Salaries Payable	684	Repairs Expense
301	L. Fogle, Capital	688	Telephone Expense
302	L. Fogle, Withdrawals	901	Income Summary

Required

1. Use the balance column format to set up each ledger account listed in its chart of accounts.

2. Prepare journal entries to record the transactions for July and post them to the ledger accounts. Record prepaid and unearned items in statement of financial position accounts.

Check (3) Unadj. trial balance totals, $148,800

3. Prepare an unadjusted trial balance as at July 31.

4. Use the following information to journalize and post adjusting entries for the month:

a. Two-thirds of one month's insurance coverage has expired.

b. At the end of the month, $1,550 of office supplies are still available.

c. This month's depreciation on the buildings is $1,200.

d. An employee earned $180 of unpaid and unrecorded salary as at month-end.

e. The company earned $950 of storage fees that are not yet billed at month-end.

5. Prepare the income statement and the statement of changes in equity for the month of July and the statement of financial position at July 31, 2015.

6. Prepare journal entries to close the temporary accounts and post these entries to the ledger.

7. Prepare a post-closing trial balance.

(4a) Dr. Insurance Expense, $300

(5) Net profit, $2,570; L. Fogle, Capital (7/31/2015), $140,970; Total assets, $141,150

(7) P-C trial balance totals, $142,350

Heel-To-Toe Shoes' adjusted trial balance on December 31, 2015, follows.

Problem 4-3B
Preparing trial balances, closing entries, and financial statements

C3 P2 P3

No.	Account Title	Debit	Credit
	HEEL-TO-TOE SHOES		
	Adjusted Trial Balance		
	December 31, 2015		
101	Cash	$ 13,450	
125	Store supplies	4,140	
128	Prepaid insurance	2,200	
167	Equipment	33,000	
168	Accumulated depreciation—Equipment		$ 9,000
201	Accounts payable		1,000
210	Wages payable		3,200
301	P. Holt, Capital		31,650
302	P. Holt, Withdrawals	16,000	
401	Repair fees earned		62,000
612	Depreciation expense—Equipment	3,000	
623	Wages expense	28,400	
637	Insurance expense	1,100	
640	Rent expense	2,400	
651	Store supplies expense	1,300	
690	Utilities expense	1,860	
	Totals	$106,850	$106,850

Required

1. Prepare an income statement and a statement of changes in equity for the year 2015, and a classified statement of financial position at December 31, 2015. There are no owner investments in 2015.

2. Enter the adjusted trial balance in the first two columns of a six-column table. Use the middle two columns for closing entry information and the last two columns for a post-closing trial balance. Insert an Income Summary account (No. 901) as the last item in the trial balance.

3. Enter closing entry information in the six-column table and prepare journal entries for it.

Check (1) Ending capital balance, $39,590

(2) P-C trial balance totals, $52,790

Analysis Component

4. Assume for this part only that

a. None of the $1,100 insurance expense had expired during the year. Instead, assume it is a prepayment of the next period's insurance protection.

b. There are no earned and unpaid wages at the end of the year. (*Hint:* Reverse the $3,200 wages payable accrual.)

Describe the financial statement changes that would result from these two assumptions.

Problem 4-4B
Preparing closing entries,
financial statements, and ratios

C3 A1 P2

The adjusted trial balance for Giovanni Co. as at December 31, 2015, follows.

No.	Account Title	Debit	Credit
	GIOVANNI COMPANY		
	Adjusted Trial Balance		
	December 31, 2015		
101	Cash	$ 6,400	
104	Short-term investments	10,200	
126	Supplies	3,600	
128	Prepaid insurance	800	
167	Equipment	18,000	
168	Accumulated depreciation—Equipment		$ 3,000
173	Building	90,000	
174	Accumulated depreciation—Building		9,000
183	Land	28,500	
201	Accounts payable		2,500
203	Interest payable		1,400
208	Rent payable		200
210	Wages payable		1,180
213	Property taxes payable		2,330
233	Unearned professional fees		650
251	Long-term notes payable		32,000
301	J. Giovanni, Capital		91,800
302	J. Giovanni, Withdrawals	6,000	
401	Professional fees earned		47,000
406	Rent earned		3,600
407	Dividends earned		500
409	Interest earned		1,120
606	Depreciation expense—Building	2,000	
612	Depreciation expense—Equipment	1,000	
623	Wages expense	17,500	
633	Interest expense	1,200	
637	Insurance expense	1,425	
640	Rent expense	1,800	
652	Supplies expense	900	
682	Postage expense	310	
683	Property taxes expense	3,825	
684	Repairs expense	579	
688	Telephone expense	421	
690	Utilities expense	1,820	
	Totals	$196,280	$196,280

J. Giovanni invested $30,000 cash in the business during year 2015 (the December 31, 2014, credit balance of the J. Giovanni, Capital account was $61,800). Giovanni Company is required to make a $6,400 payment on its long-term notes payable during 2016.

Required

1. Prepare the income statement and the statement of changes in equity for the calendar year 2015 and the classified statement of financial position at December 31, 2015.

2. Prepare the necessary closing entries at December 31, 2015.

3. Use the information in the financial statements to calculate these ratios: (a) return on assets (total assets at December 31, 2014, were $150,000), (b) debt ratio, (c) profit margin ratio (use total revenues as the denominator), and (d) current ratio.

The following unadjusted trial balance is for Crush Demolition Company as at the end of its April 30, 2015, financial year. The April 30, 2014, credit balance of the owner's capital account was $36,900, and the owner invested $30,000 cash in the company during the 2015 financial year.

Problem 4-5B
Preparing a work sheet,
adjusting and closing entries,
and financial statements

C3 P1 P2

	A	B		C
1		**CRUSH DEMOLITION COMPANY**		
2		**Unadjusted Trial Balance**		
3		**April 30, 2015**		
4	**No.**	**Account Title**	**Debit**	**Credit**
5	101	Cash	$ 9,000	
6	126	Supplies	18,000	
7	128	Prepaid insurance	14,600	
8	167	Equipment	140,000	
9	168	Accumulated depreciation — Equipment		$ 10,000
10	201	Accounts payable		16,000
11	203	Interest payable		0
12	208	Rent payable		0
13	210	Wages payable		0
14	213	Property taxes payable		0
15	251	Long-term notes payable		20,000
16	301	J. Bonair, Capital		66,900
17	302	J. Bonair, Withdrawals	24,000	
18	401	Demolition fees earned		177,000
19	612	Depreciation expense — Equipment	0	
20	623	Wages expense	51,400	
21	633	Interest expense	2,200	
22	637	Insurance expense	0	
23	640	Rent expense	8,800	
24	652	Supplies expense	0	
25	683	Property taxes expense	8,400	
26	684	Repairs expense	6,700	
27	690	Utilities expense	6,800	
28		Totals	$289,900	$289,900
29				

Required

1. Prepare a 10-column work sheet for financial year 2015, starting with the unadjusted trial balance and including adjustments based on these additional facts.

   a. The supplies available at the end of financial year 2015 had a cost of $8,100.

   b. The cost of expired insurance for the financial year is $11,500.

   c. Annual depreciation on equipment is $18,000.

   d. The April utilities expense of $700 is not included in the unadjusted trial balance because the bill arrived after the trial balance was prepared. The $700 amount owed needs to be recorded.

   e. The company's employees have earned $2,200 of accrued wages at financial year-end.

   f. The rent expense incurred and not yet paid or recorded at financial year-end is $5,360.

   g. Additional property taxes of $450 have been assessed for this financial year but have not been paid or recorded in the accounts.

   h. The long-term note payable bears interest at 12% per year. The unadjusted Interest Expense account equals the amount paid for the first 11 months of the 2015 financial year. The $200 accrued interest for April has not yet been paid or recorded. (Note that the company is required to make a $4,000 payment toward the note payable during the 2016 financial year.)

2. Enter adjusting and closing information in the work sheet; then journalize the adjusting and closing entries.

3. Prepare the income statement and the statement of changes in equity for the year ended April 30 and the classified statement of financial position at April 30, 2015.

Check   (3) Total assets, $132,200;
current liabilities, $28,910; Net profit,
$44,390

Analysis Component

4. Analyze the following separate errors and describe how each would affect the 10-column work sheet. Explain whether the error is likely to be discovered in completing the work sheet and, if not, the effect of the error on the financial statements.

   a. Assume the adjustment for expiration of the insurance coverage consisted of a credit to Prepaid Insurance and a debit to Insurance Expense for $3,100, when the correct amount was $11,500.

   b. When the adjusted trial balance in the work sheet is completed, assume that the $6,700 Repairs Expense account balance is extended to the Debit column of the statement of financial position columns.

Problem 4-6B[A]
Preparing adjusting, reversing, and next period entries

P4

The following six-column table for Solutions Co. includes the unadjusted trial balance as at December 31, 2015.

	A	B	C	D	E	F	G
1		**SOLUTIONS COMPANY**					
2		**December 31, 2015**					
3		**Unadjusted**				**Adjusted**	
4		**Trial Balance**		**Adjustments**		**Trial Balance**	
5	**Account Title**	**Dr.**	**Cr.**	**Dr.**	**Cr.**	**Dr.**	**Cr.**
6	Cash	$ 9,000					
7	Accounts receivable	0					
8	Supplies	6,600					
9	Machinery	40,100					
10	Accumulated depreciation — Machinery		$15,800				
11	Interest payable		0				
12	Salaries payable		0				
13	Unearned rental fees		5,200				
14	Notes payable		20,000				
15	G. Clay, Capital		13,200				
16	G. Clay, Withdrawals	10,500					
17	Rental fees earned		37,000				
18	Depreciation expense — Machinery	0					
19	Salaries expense	23,500					
20	Interest expense	1,500					
21	Supplies expense	0					
22	Totals	$91,200	$91,200				
23							

Required

1. Complete the six-column table by entering adjustments that reflect the following information:

    a. As at December 31, 2015, employees had earned $420 of unpaid and unrecorded wages. The next payday is January 4, at which time $1,250 in wages will be paid.

    b. The cost of supplies still available at December 31, 2015, is $2,450.

    c. The notes payable requires an interest payment to be made every three months. The amount of unrecorded accrued interest at December 31, 2015, is $500. The next interest payment, at an amount of $600, is due on January 15, 2016.

    d. Analysis of the unearned rental fees shows that $3,100 remains unearned at December 31, 2015.

    e. In addition to the machinery rental fees included in the revenue account balance, the company has earned another $2,350 in unrecorded fees that will be collected on January 31, 2016. The company is also expected to collect $4,400 on that same day for new fees earned in January 2016.

Check   (1) Adjusted trial balance totals, $98,270

    f. Depreciation expense for the year is $3,800.

2. Prepare journal entries for the adjustments entered in the six-column table for part 1.

3. Prepare journal entries to reverse the effects of the adjusting entries that involve accruals.

4. Prepare journal entries to record the cash payments and cash collections described for January.

SERIAL PROBLEM
Business Solutions

P2 P3

(This serial problem began in Chapter 1 and continues through most of the book. If previous chapter segments were not completed, the serial problem can begin at this point.)

SP 4   The December 31, 2015, adjusted trial balance of Business Solutions (reflecting its transactions from October through December of 2015) follows.

No.	Account Title	Debit	Credit
101	Cash	$ 48,372	
106	Accounts receivable	5,668	
126	Computer supplies	580	
128	Prepaid insurance	1,665	

[continued on next page]

[continued from previous page]

131	Prepaid rent	825	
163	Office equipment	8,000	
164	Accumulated depreciation—Office equipment		$ 400
167	Computer equipment	20,000	
168	Accumulated depreciation—Computer equipment		1,250
201	Accounts payable		1,100
210	Wages payable		500
236	Unearned computer services revenue		1,500
301	S. Rey, Capital		73,000
302	S. Rey, Withdrawals	7,100	
403	Computer services revenue		31,284
612	Depreciation expense—Office equipment	400	
613	Depreciation expense—Computer equipment	1,250	
623	Wages expense	3,875	
637	Insurance expense	555	
640	Rent expense	2,475	
652	Computer supplies expense	3,065	
655	Advertising expense	2,753	
676	Mileage expense	896	
677	Miscellaneous expenses	250	
684	Repairs expense—Computer	1,305	
901	Income summary		0
	Totals	$109,034	$109,034

Required

1. Record and post the necessary closing entries for Business Solutions.
2. Prepare a post-closing trial balance as at December 31, 2015.

Check   Post-closing trial balance totals, $85,110

Beyond the Numbers

BTN 4-1   Refer to Nestlé's consolidated income statement in Appendix A to answer the following.

REPORTING IN ACTION

C1 P2

Required

1. For the financial year ended December 31, 2013, what amount is credited to Income Summary to summarize its revenues (including other types of income) earned?
2. For the financial year ended December 31, 2013, what amount is debited to Income Summary to summarize its expenses incurred? (Hint: Amounts for expenses are shown with negative signs in brackets.)
3. For the financial year ended December 31, 2013, what is the balance of its Income Summary account before it is closed?

Fast Forward

4. Access Nestlé's annual report for financial years ending after December 31, 2013, at its Website (http://www.nestle.com/investors). How has the amount of net profit closed to Income Summary changed in the financial years ending after December 31, 2013?

BTN 4-2   Key figures for the recent two years of both Adidas and Puma are as follows:

COMPARATIVE ANALYSIS

A1

Key Figures	Adidas (in EUR millions)		Puma (in EUR millions)	
	Current Year	Prior Year	Current Year	Prior Year
Current assets	6,875	6,877	1,514.1	1,642.6
Current liabilities	4,732	4,374	690.9	803.5

Required

1. Compute the current ratio for both years for the two companies. Round to one decimal place.
2. Which company has the better ability to pay short-term obligations according to the current ratio?
3. Analyze and comment on each company's current ratios for the two years.

ETHICS CHALLENGE
C2

BTN 4-3 On January 20, 2011, Tamira Nelson, the accountant for Picton Enterprises, is feeling pressure to complete the annual financial statements. The company president has said he needs up-to-date financial statements to share with the bank on January 21 at a dinner meeting that has been called to discuss Picton's obtaining loan financing for a special building project. Tamira knows that she will not be able to gather all the needed information in the next 24 hours to prepare the entire set of adjusting entries. Those entries must be posted before the financial statements accurately portray the company's performance and financial position for the financial period ended December 31, 2010. Tamira ultimately decides to estimate several expense accruals at the last minute. When deciding on estimates for the expenses, she uses low estimates because she does not want to make the financial statements look worse than they are. Tamira finishes the financial statements before the deadline and gives them to the president without mentioning that several account balances are estimates that she provided.

Required

1. Identify several courses of action that Tamira could have taken instead of the one she took.
2. If you were in Tamira's situation, what would you have done? Briefly justify your response.

COMMUNICATING IN PRACTICE
C1 P2

BTN 4-4 Assume that one of your classmates states that a company's books should be ongoing and therefore not closed until that business is terminated. Write a half-page memo to this classmate explaining the concept of the closing process by drawing analogies between (1) a scoreboard for an athletic event and the revenue and expense accounts of a business or (2) a sports team's record book and the capital account. (*Hint:* Think about what would happen if the scoreboard is not cleared before the start of a new game.)

TAKING IT TO THE NET
A1

BTN 4-5 Access Li-Ning's 2013 annual report from its Website (http://www.lining.com/eng/ir/finhigh.php). In the section "Five-Year Financial Highlights," it lists five years' amounts for current assets and current liabilities.

Required

1. Why do you think Li-Ning highlights these two items? What financial ratio can you calculate using these two items?
2. Calculate the ratio you identified in part 1 for each of the five years. Is the ratio improving or deteriorating over time? Explain.
3. What are the implications for a company that has a current ratio that is too high?

TEAMWORK IN ACTION
P1 P2 P3

BTN 4-6 The unadjusted trial balance and information for the accounting adjustments of Noseworthy Investigators follow. Each team member involved in this project is to assume one of the four responsibilities listed. After completing each of these responsibilities, the team should work together to prove the accounting equation utilizing information from teammates (1 and 4). If your equation does not balance, you are to work as a team to resolve the error. The team's goal is to complete the task as quickly and accurately as possible.

Unadjusted Trial Balance		
Account Title	Debit	Credit
Cash	$15,000	
Supplies	11,000	
Prepaid insurance	2,000	
Equipment	24,000	
Accumulated depreciation—Equipment		$ 6,000
Accounts payable		2,000
D. Noseworthy, Capital		31,000
D. Noseworthy, Withdrawals	5,000	
Investigation fees earned		32,000
Rent expense	14,000	
Totals	$71,000	$71,000

Additional Year-End Information

a. Insurance that expired in the current period amounts to $1,200.

b. Equipment depreciation for the period is $3,000.

c. Unused supplies total $4,000 at period-end.

d. Services in the amount of $500 have been provided but have not been billed or collected.

Responsibilities for Individual Team Members

1. Determine the accounts and adjusted balances to be extended to the statement of financial position columns of the work sheet for Noseworthy. Also determine total assets and total liabilities.

2. Determine the adjusted revenue account balance and prepare the entry to close this account.

3. Determine the adjusted account balances for expenses and prepare the entry to close these accounts.

4. Prepare T-accounts for both D. Noseworthy, Capital (reflecting the unadjusted trial balance amount) and Income Summary. Prepare the third and fourth closing entries. Ask teammates assigned to parts 2 and 3 for the postings for Income Summary. Obtain amounts to complete the third closing entry and post both the third and fourth closing entries. Provide the team with the ending capital account balance.

5. The entire team should prove the accounting equation using post-closing balances.

BTN 4-7   Review this chapter's opening feature on Benson and EyePower.

1. Explain how a classified statement of financial position can help Benson know what bills are due when, and whether he has the resources to pay those bills.

2. What objectives are met when Benson applies closing procedures each financial year-end?

ENTREPRENEURIAL DECISION

A1 C3 P2

BTN 4-8   Select a company that you can visit in person or interview on the telephone. Call ahead to the company to arrange a time when you can interview an employee (preferably an accountant) who helps prepare the annual financial statements. Inquire about the following aspects of its *accounting cycle:*

1. Does the company prepare interim financial statements? What time period(s) is used for interim statements?

2. Does the company use the cash or accrual basis of accounting?

3. Does the company use a work sheet in preparing financial statements? Why or why not?

4. Does the company use a spreadsheet program? If so, which software program is used?

5. How long does it take after the end of its reporting period to complete annual statements?

HITTING THE ROAD

C2

ANSWERS TO MULTIPLE CHOICE QUIZ

1. e   **4.** c

2. c   **5.** b

3. a

5

Merchandising Operations

A Look Back

Chapters 3 and 4 focused on the final steps of the accounting process. We explained the importance of proper revenue and expense recognition and described the adjusting and closing processes. We also prepared financial statements.

A Look at This Chapter

This chapter emphasizes merchandising activities. We explain how reporting merchandising activities differs from reporting service activities. We also analyze and record merchandise purchases and sales transactions, and explain the adjustments and closing process for merchandisers.

A Look Ahead

Chapter 6 extends our analysis of merchandising activities and focuses on the valuation of inventory. Topics include the items in inventory, costs assigned, costing methods used, and inventory estimation techniques.

Learning Objectives

CAP

CONCEPTUAL

C1 Describe merchandising activities and identify income components for a merchandising company. (p. 180)

C2 Identify and explain the inventory asset and cost flows of a merchandising company. (p. 181)

ANALYTICAL

A1 Compute the acid-test ratio and explain its use to assess liquidity. (p. 194)

A2 Compute the gross margin ratio and explain its use to assess profitability. (p. 194)

PROCEDURAL

P1 Analyze and record transactions for merchandise purchases using a perpetual system. (p. 182)

P2 Analyze and record transactions for merchandise sales using a perpetual system. (p. 187)

P3 Prepare adjustments and close accounts for a merchandising company. (p. 190)

P4 Define and prepare financial statements for a merchandising company. (p. 192)

P5 *Appendix 5A*—Record and compare merchandising transactions using both periodic and perpetual inventory systems. (p. 199)

"Being a social enterprise does not automatically bring you customers."—**JON GOH** (on right, with bear-maker Max)

Decision Insight

Building a Dream World in the Real World

"We both came from disadvantaged backgrounds," says Jon Goh candidly of his childhood and that of his friend, George Wong. Another thing the two have in common is their training in social work, plus an interest in handicraft. What's more, they share an altruistic resolve to make the world a better place. The friendship between these two similar souls led them to start **TeddyThotz 'n' OneKind (teddythotz.blogspot.com)**, which they see as a "dream world in the real world" where people can get a creatively made product and contribute to a good cause at the same time.

Our mission, says Jon of the handicraft social enterprise, is "to harness the talents and skills of the elderly, the poor, and the disadvantaged and to generate income for them." Their tagline—"where creativity and social enterprise merge"—is aptly framed around their quirky and scintillating collection of TeddyThotz handcrafted products: hand-crocheted hoody bears and animal pals; textile teddies and doggies made from lovely fabrics; bears and bunnies made from recycled jeans. The makers of these cute critters include working mothers, housewives, farmers, rural folks, and crafters. The "OneKind" range alludes to everyday things but given a creative twist—notebooks with leather cover made from leather scraps; hand-painted bags; bracelets shaped from aluminum wire; and their evergreen favorites—traditional patchwork blankets, beans sprout husks pillows, batik pouches and many more made by the elderly.

TeddyThotz sells its products mainly through a few key retail outlets. Twice a month it displays selected handicraft at a social enterprise market. "These items never fail to attract customers," says Jon. "They stop to touch and admire the patchwork blankets, and tell us about their childhoods."

Noble intentions aside, the duo understand the importance of maintaining a healthy bottom line to sustain an income for their beneficiaries. As the products are distinctively crafted and not mass-produced, there is difficulty achieving economies of scale, so "we try to keep our costs low," says Jon, adding that for each product the relevant cost has to be pinned down and a reasonably profitable price determined. All this is monitored via Microsoft Excel.

Another nagging concern of a merchandise-centered operation is inventory control. "Fortunately, we are able to keep our inventory at just the right level most of the time to avoid tying down precious cash in excess stock and renting storage space," says Jon. This involves tracking production capacity, lead time, and demand and stock levels in the retail outlets.

"Being a social enterprise does not automatically bring you customers," points out Jon. "The product must, first of all, be worth buying." Thankfully, customers are drawn to their creations and "are likely to choose the social enterprise product over the commercial product because of the social benefit behind it." Besides, who can say no to a cute smiling beanie bear?

Buyers of merchandise expect many products, discount prices, inventory on demand, and high quality. This chapter introduces the accounting practices used by companies engaged in merchandising. We show how financial statements reflect merchandising activities and explain the new financial statement items created by merchandising activities. We also analyze and record merchandise purchases and sales, and explain the adjustments and the closing process for these companies.

Accounting for Merchandising Operations

Merchandising Activities	Merchandising Purchases	Merchandising Sales	Accounting Cycle	Financial Statement Formats
• Reporting income • Reporting inventory • Operating cycles • Inventory systems	• Purchase discounts • Purchase returns and allowances • Transportation costs	• Sales of merchandise • Sales discounts • Sales returns and allowances	• Adjusting entries • Preparing financial statements • Closing entries	• Income statement • Classified statement of financial position

MERCHANDISING ACTIVITIES

C1 Describe merchandising activities and identify income components for a merchandising company.

Previous chapters emphasized the accounting and reporting activities of service companies. A merchandising company's activities differ from those of a service company. **Merchandise** consists of products, also called *goods,* that a company acquires to resell to customers. A **merchandiser** earns net profit by buying and selling merchandise. Merchandisers are often identified as either wholesalers or retailers. A **wholesaler** is an *intermediary* that buys products from manufacturers or other wholesalers and sells them to retailers or other wholesalers. A **retailer** is an intermediary that buys products from manufacturers or wholesalers and sells them to consumers. Many retailers sell both products and services.

Reporting Income for a Merchandiser

Net profit for a merchandiser equals revenues from selling merchandise minus both the cost of merchandise sold to customers and the cost of other expenses for the period, see Exhibit 5.1. The

EXHIBIT 5.1

Computing Income for a Merchandising Company versus a Service Company

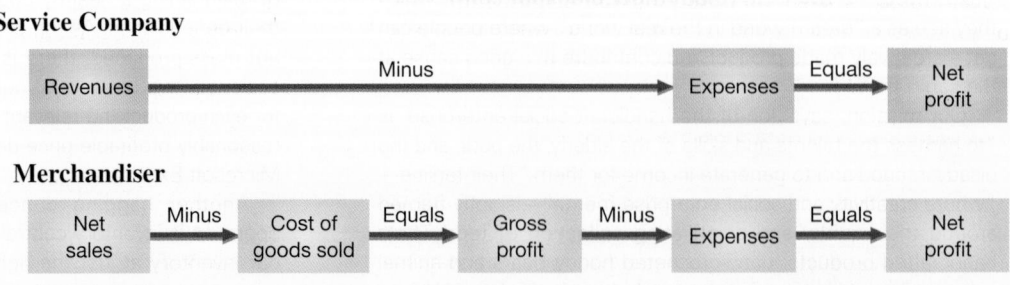

usual accounting term for revenues from selling merchandise is *sales,* and the term used for the expense of buying and preparing the merchandise is **cost of goods sold.** (Some service companies use the term *sales* instead of revenues; and cost of goods sold is also called *cost of sales.*)

The income statement for Z-Mart in Exhibit 5.2 illustrates these key components of a merchandiser's net profit. The first two lines show that products are acquired at a cost of $230,400 and sold for $314,700. The third line shows an $84,300 **gross profit,** also called

Point: Fleming, SuperValu, and SYSCO are wholesalers. Gap, Oakley, Target, and Walmart are retailers.

Z-MART **Income Statement** **For Year Ended December 31, 2015**	
Net sales	$314,700
Cost of goods sold	230,400
Gross profit	84,300
Expenses	71,400
Net Profit	$ 12,900

EXHIBIT 5.2

Merchandiser's Income Statement

gross margin, which equals net sales less cost of goods sold. Additional expenses of $71,400 are reported, which leaves $12,900 in net profit.

Point: Analysis of gross profit is important to effective business decisions, and is described later in the chapter.

Reporting Inventory for a Merchandiser

A merchandiser's statement of financial position includes a current asset called *merchandise inventory,* an item not on a service company's statement of financial position. **Merchandise inventory,** or simply *inventory,* refers to products that a company owns and intends to sell. The cost of this asset includes the cost incurred to buy the goods, ship them to the store, and make them ready for sale.

C2 Identify and explain the inventory asset and cost flows of a merchandising company.

Operating Cycle for a Merchandiser

A merchandising company's operating cycle begins by purchasing merchandise and ends by collecting cash from selling the merchandise. The length of an operating cycle differs across the types of businesses. Department stores often have operating cycles of two to five months. Operating cycles for grocery merchants usually range from two to eight weeks.

Exhibit 5.3 illustrates an operating cycle for a merchandiser with credit sales. The cycle moves from (*a*) cash purchases of merchandise to (*b*) inventory for sale to (*c*) credit sales to (*d*) accounts receivable to (*e*) cash. Companies try to keep their operating cycles short because assets tied up in inventory and receivables are not productive. Cash sales shorten operating cycles.

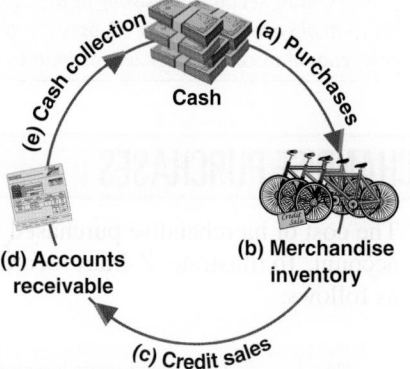

EXHIBIT 5.3

Merchandiser's Operating Cycle

Inventory Systems

Cost of goods sold is the cost of merchandise sold to customers during a period. It is often the largest single expense on a merchandiser's income statement. **Inventory** refers to products a company owns and expects to sell in its normal operations. Exhibit 5.4 shows that a company's merchandise available for sale consists of what it begins with (beginning inventory) and what it

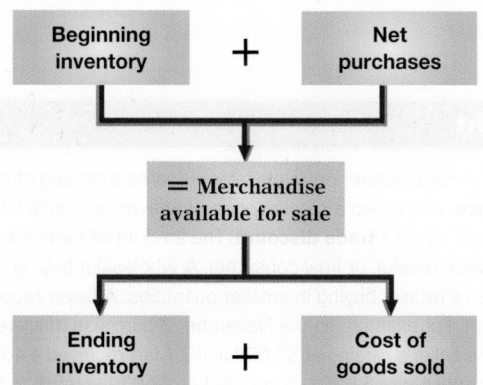

EXHIBIT 5.4

Merchandiser's Cost Flow for a Single Time Period

Point: Mathematically, Exhibit 5.4 says

$$BI + NP = MAS,$$

where BI is beginning inventory, NP is net purchases, and MAS is merchandise available for sale. Exhibit 5.4 also says

$$MAS = EI + COGS,$$

which can be rewritten as MAS − EI = COGS or MAS − COGS = EI, where EI is ending inventory and COGS is cost of goods sold.

purchases (net purchases). The merchandise available is either sold (cost of goods sold) or kept for future sales (ending inventory).

Two alternative inventory accounting systems can be used to collect information about cost of goods sold and cost of inventory: *perpetual system* or *periodic system*. The **perpetual inventory system** continually updates accounting records for merchandising transactions—specifically, for those records of inventory available for sale and inventory sold. The **periodic inventory system** updates the accounting records for merchandise transactions only at the *end of a period*. Technological advances and competitive pressures have dramatically increased the use of the perpetual system. It gives managers immediate access to detailed information on sales and inventory levels, where they can strategically react to sales trends, cost changes, consumer tastes, and so forth, to increase gross profit. (Some companies use a *hybrid* system where the perpetual system is used for tracking units available and the periodic system is used to compute cost of sales.)

Quick Check   Answers — p. 205

1. Describe a merchandiser's cost of goods sold.
2. What is gross profit for a merchandising company?
3. Explain why use of the perpetual inventory system has dramatically increased.

The following sections, consisting of the next 10 pages on purchasing, selling, and adjusting merchandise, use the perpetual system. Appendix 5A uses the periodic system (with the perpetual results on the side). An instructor can choose to cover either one or both inventory systems.

Point: Growth of superstores such as **Costco** and **Sam's** is fueled by efficient use of perpetual inventory.

ACCOUNTING FOR MERCHANDISE PURCHASES

P1 Analyze and record transactions for merchandise purchases using a perpetual system.

Assets = Liabilities + Equity
+1,200
−1,200

The cost of merchandise purchased for resale is recorded in the Merchandise Inventory asset account. To illustrate, Z-Mart records a $1,200 cash purchase of merchandise on November 2 as follows:

Nov. 2	Merchandise Inventory	1,200	
	Cash		1,200
	Purchased merchandise for cash.		

The invoice for this merchandise is shown in Exhibit 5.5. The buyer usually receives the original invoice, and the seller keeps a copy. This *source document* serves as the purchase invoice of Z-Mart (buyer) and the sales invoice for Trex (seller). The amount recorded for merchandise inventory includes its purchase cost, shipping fees, taxes, and any other costs necessary to make it ready for sale. This section explains how we compute the recorded cost of merchandise purchases.

Point: The Merchandise Inventory account reflects the cost of goods available for resale.

Decision Insight

Trade Discounts When a manufacturer or wholesaler prepares a catalog of items it has for sale, it usually gives each item a **list price,** also called a *catalog price.* However, an item's intended *selling price* equals list price minus a given percent called a **trade discount.** The amount of trade discount usually depends on whether a buyer is a wholesaler, retailer, or final consumer. A wholesaler buying in large quantities is often granted a larger discount than a retailer buying in smaller quantities. A buyer records the net amount of list price minus trade discount. For example, in the November 2 purchase of merchandise by Z-Mart, the merchandise was listed in the seller's catalog at $2,000 and Z-Mart received a 40% trade discount. This meant that Z-Mart's purchase price was $1,200, computed as $2,000 − (40% × $2,000). ∎

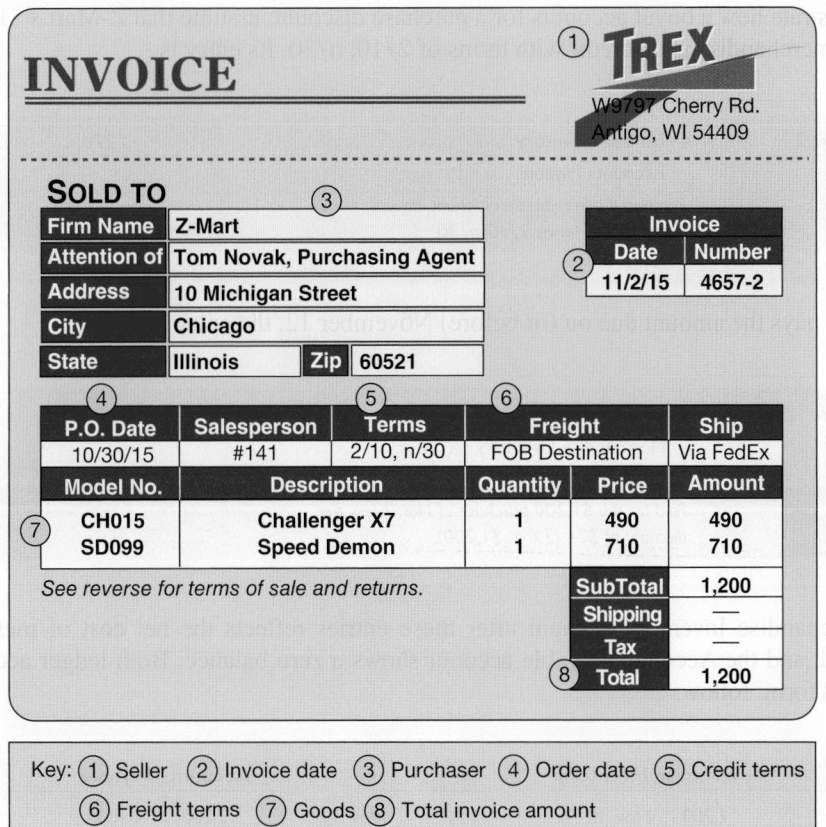

EXHIBIT 5.5

Invoice

Purchase Discounts

The purchase of goods on credit requires a clear statement of expected future payments and dates to avoid misunderstandings. **Credit terms** for a purchase include the amounts and timing of payments from a buyer to a seller. Credit terms usually reflect an industry's practices. To illustrate, when sellers require payment within 10 days after the end of the month of the invoice date, the invoice will show credit terms as "n/10 EOM," which stands for net 10 days after end of month (**EOM**). When sellers require payment within 30 days after the invoice date, the invoice shows credit terms of "n/30," which stands for *net 30 days.*

Exhibit 5.6 portrays credit terms. The amount of time allowed before full payment is due is called the **credit period.** Sellers can grant a **cash discount** to encourage buyers to pay earlier. A buyer views a cash discount as a **purchase discount.** A seller views a cash discount as a **sales discount.** Any cash discounts are described in the credit terms on the invoice. For example, credit terms of "2/10, n/60" mean that full payment is due within a 60-day credit period, but the buyer can deduct 2% of the invoice amount if payment is made within 10 days of the invoice date. This reduced payment applies only for the **discount period.**

Point: Since both the buyer and seller know the invoice date, this date is used in setting the discount and credit periods.

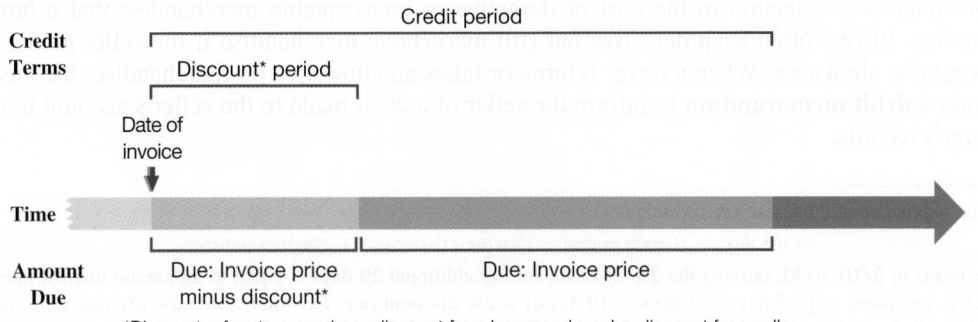

EXHIBIT 5.6

Credit Terms

Point: Appendix 5A repeats journal entries *a* through *f* using a periodic inventory system.

Assets = Liabilities + Equity
+1,200   +1,200

To illustrate how a buyer accounts for a purchase discount, assume that Z-Mart's $1,200 purchase of merchandise is on credit with terms of 2/10, n/30. Its entry is

(a) Nov. 2	Merchandise Inventory	1,200	
	Accounts Payable		1,200
	Purchased merchandise on credit, invoice dated Nov. 2, terms 2/10, n/30.		

If Z-Mart pays the amount due on (or before) November 12, the entry is

Assets = Liabilities + Equity
−24   −1,200
−1,176

(b) Nov. 12	Accounts Payable	1,200	
	Merchandise Inventory		24
	Cash		1,176
	Paid for the $1,200 purchase of Nov. 2 less the discount of $24 (2% × $1,200).		

Point: These entries illustrate what is called the *gross method* of accounting for purchases with discount terms.

The Merchandise Inventory account after these entries reflects the net cost of merchandise purchased, and the Accounts Payable account shows a zero balance. Both ledger accounts, in T-account form, follow:

Merchandise Inventory					Accounts Payable				
Nov. 2	1,200	Nov. 12	24		Nov. 12	1,200	Nov. 2	1,200	
Balance	1,176						Balance	0	

A buyer's failure to pay within a discount period can be expensive. To illustrate, if Z-Mart does not pay within the 10-day 2% discount period, it can delay payment by 20 more days. This delay costs Z-Mart $24, computed as 2% × $1,200. Most buyers take advantage of a purchase discount because of the usually high interest rate implied from not taking it.[1] Also, good cash management means that no invoice is paid until the last day of the discount or credit period.

Decision Maker   Answer — p. 204

Entrepreneur   You purchase a batch of products on terms of 3/10, n/90, but your company has limited cash and you must borrow funds at an 11% annual rate if you are to pay within the discount period. Do you take advantage of the purchase discount? ■

Purchase Returns and Allowances

Point: The sender (maker) of a *debit memorandum* will debit the account of the memo's receiver. The memo's receiver will credit the sender's account.

Purchase returns refer to merchandise a buyer acquires but then returns to the seller. A *purchase allowance* is a reduction in the cost of defective or unacceptable merchandise that a buyer acquires. Buyers often keep defective but still marketable merchandise if the seller grants an acceptable allowance. When a buyer returns or takes an allowance on merchandise, the buyer issues a **debit memorandum** to inform the seller of a debit made to the seller's account in the buyer's records.

---

[1] The *implied annual interest rate* formula is:

$$(365 \text{ days} \div [\text{Credit period} - \text{Discount period}]) \times \text{Cash discount rate.}$$

For terms of 2/10, n/30, missing the 2% discount for an additional 20 days is equal to an annual interest rate of 36.5%, computed as [365 days/(30 days − 10 days)] × 2% discount rate. *Favorable purchase discounts* are those with implied annual interest rates that exceed the purchaser's annual rate for borrowing money.

Purchase Allowances   To illustrate purchase allowances, assume that on November 15, Z-Mart (buyer) issues a $300 debit memorandum for an allowance from Trex for defective merchandise. Z-Mart's November 15 entry to update its Merchandise Inventory account to reflect the purchase allowance is

(c) Nov. 15	Accounts Payable	300	
	Merchandise Inventory		300
	Allowance for defective merchandise.		

Assets = Liabilities + Equity
−300   −300

The buyer's allowance for defective merchandise is usually offset against the buyer's current account payable balance to the seller. When cash is refunded, the Cash account is debited instead of Accounts Payable.

Purchase Returns   Returns are recorded at the net costs charged to buyers. To illustrate the accounting for returns, suppose Z-Mart purchases $1,000 of merchandise on June 1 with terms 2/10, n/60. Two days later, Z-Mart returns $100 of goods before paying the invoice. When Z-Mart later pays on June 11, it takes the 2% discount only on the $900 remaining balance. When goods are returned, a buyer can take a purchase discount on only the remaining balance of the invoice. The resulting discount is $18 (2% × $900) and the cash payment is $882 ($900 − $18). The following entries reflect this illustration.

June 1	Merchandise Inventory	1,000	
	Accounts Payable		1,000
	Purchased merchandise, invoice dated June 1,		
	terms 2/10, n/60.		
June 3	Accounts Payable	100	
	Merchandise Inventory		100
	Returned merchandise to seller.		
June 11	Accounts Payable	900	
	Merchandise Inventory		18
	Cash		882
	Paid for $900 merchandise ($1,000 − $100)		
	less $18 discount (2% × $900).		

Example: Assume Z-Mart pays $980 cash for $1,000 of merchandise purchased within its 2% discount period. Later, it returns $100 of the original $1,000 merchandise. The return entry is
Cash 98
  Merchandise Inventory 98

 Decision Ethics   Answer — p. 204

Credit Manager   As a new credit manager, you are being trained by the outgoing manager. She explains that the system prepares checks for amounts net of favorable cash discounts, and the checks are dated the last day of the discount period. She also tells you that checks are not mailed until five days later, adding that "the company gets free use of cash for an extra five days, and our department looks better. When a supplier complains, we blame the computer system and the mailroom." Do you continue this payment policy? ∎

Transportation Costs and Ownership Transfer

The buyer and seller must agree on who is responsible for paying any freight costs and who bears the risk of loss during transit for merchandising transactions. This is essentially the same as asking at what point ownership transfers from the seller to the buyer. The point of transfer is called the **FOB** (*free on board*) point, which determines who pays transportation costs (and often other incidental costs of transit such as insurance).

Exhibit 5.7 identifies two alternative points of transfer. (1) *FOB shipping point,* also called *FOB factory,* means the buyer accepts ownership when the goods depart the seller's place of business. The buyer is then responsible for paying shipping costs and bearing the risk of damage or loss when goods are in transit. The goods are part of the buyer's inventory when they are in transit since ownership has transferred to the buyer. **1-800-FLOWERS.COM**, a floral and gift

EXHIBIT 5.7

Ownership Transfer and
Transportation Costs

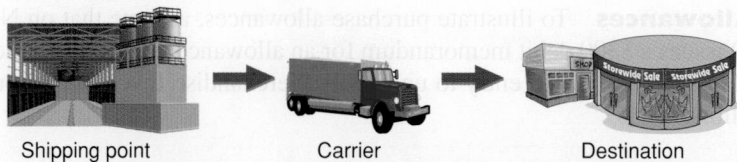

| Shipping point | Carrier | Destination |

	Ownership Transfers When Goods Passed to	Transportation Costs Paid by
FOB shipping point	Carrier	Buyer
FOB destination	Buyer	Seller

Point: The party not responsible for shipping costs sometimes pays the carrier. In these cases, the party paying these costs either bills the party responsible or, more commonly, adjusts its account payable or account receivable with the other party. For example, a buyer paying a carrier when terms are FOB destination can decrease its account payable to the seller by the amount of shipping cost.

merchandiser, and **Bare Escentuals**, a cosmetic manufacturer, both use FOB shipping point. (2) *FOB destination* means ownership of goods transfers to the buyer when the goods arrive at the buyer's place of business. The seller is responsible for paying shipping charges and bears the risk of damage or loss in transit. The seller does not record revenue from this sale until the goods arrive at the destination because this transaction is not complete before that point. **Kyocera**, a manufacturer, uses FOB destination.

Z-Mart's $1,200 purchase on November 2 is on terms of FOB destination. This means Z-Mart is not responsible for paying transportation costs. When a buyer is responsible for paying transportation costs, the payment is made to a carrier or directly to the seller depending on the agreement. The cost principle requires that any necessary transportation costs of a buyer (often called *transportation-in* or *freight-in*) be included as part of the cost of purchased merchandise. To illustrate, Z-Mart's entry to record a $75 freight charge from an independent carrier for merchandise purchased FOB shipping point is

Assets = Liabilities + Equity
+75
−75

(d) Nov. 24	Merchandise Inventory	75	
	Cash		75
	Paid freight costs on purchased merchandise.		

A seller records the costs of shipping goods to customers in a Delivery Expense account when the seller is responsible for these costs. Delivery Expense, also called *transportation-out* or *freight-out,* is reported as a selling expense in the seller's income statement.

In summary, purchases are recorded as debits to Merchandise Inventory. Any later purchase discounts, returns, and allowances are credited (decreases) to Merchandise Inventory. Transportation-in is debited (added) to Merchandise Inventory. Z-Mart's itemized costs of merchandise purchases for year 2015 are in Exhibit 5.8.

EXHIBIT 5.8

Itemized Costs of
Merchandise Purchases

Z-MART Itemized Costs of Merchandise Purchases For Year Ended December 31, 2015	
Invoice cost of merchandise purchases	$235,800
Less: Purchase discounts received	(4,200)
Purchase returns and allowances.	(1,500)
Add: Costs of transportation-in	2,300
Total cost of merchandise purchases	**$232,400**

Point: Some companies have separate accounts for purchase discounts, returns and allowances, and transportation-in. These accounts are then transferred to Merchandise Inventory at period-end. This is a *hybrid system* of perpetual and periodic. That is, Merchandise Inventory is updated on a perpetual basis but only for purchases and cost of goods sold.

The accounting system described here does not provide separate records (accounts) for total purchases, total purchase discounts, total purchase returns and allowances, and total transportation-in. Yet nearly all companies collect this information in supplementary records because managers need this information to evaluate and control each of these cost elements. **Supplementary records,** also called *supplemental records,* refer to information outside the usual general ledger accounts.

Quick Check   Answers — p. 205

4. How long are the credit and discount periods when credit terms are 2/10, n/60?

5. Identify which items are subtracted from the *list* amount and not recorded when computing purchase price: (*a*) freight-in; (*b*) trade discount; (*c*) purchase discount; (*d*) purchase return.

6. What does *FOB* mean? What does *FOB destination* mean?

ACCOUNTING FOR MERCHANDISE SALES

Merchandising companies also must account for sales, sales discounts, sales returns and allowances, and cost of goods sold. A merchandising company such as Z-Mart reflects these items in its gross profit computation, as shown in Exhibit 5.9. This section explains how this information is derived from transactions.

P2 Analyze and record transactions for merchandise sales using a perpetual system.

EXHIBIT 5.9

Gross Profit Computation

Z-MART Computation of Gross Profit For Year Ended December 31, 2015		
Sales..		$321,000
Less: Sales discounts.....................	$4,300	
Sales returns and allowances..........	2,000	6,300
Net sales		314,700
Cost of goods sold		230,400
Gross profit...............................		$ 84,300

Sales of Merchandise

Each sales transaction for a seller of merchandise involves two parts.

> 1. **Revenue received in the form of an asset from the customer.**
> 2. **Recognition of the cost of merchandise sold to the customer.**

Accounting for a sales transaction under the perpetual system requires recording information about both parts. This means that each sales transaction for merchandisers, whether for cash or on credit, requires *two entries:* one for revenue and one for cost. To illustrate, Z-Mart sold $2,400 of merchandise on credit on November 3. The revenue part of this transaction is recorded as

(e) Nov. 3	Accounts Receivable	2,400	
	Sales		2,400
	Sold merchandise on credit.		

Assets = Liabilities + Equity
+2,400   +2,400

This entry reflects an increase in Z-Mart's assets in the form of accounts receivable. It also shows the increase in revenue (Sales). If the sale is for cash, the debit is to Cash instead of Accounts Receivable.

The cost part of each sales transaction ensures that the Merchandise Inventory account under a perpetual inventory system reflects the updated cost of the merchandise available for sale. For example, the cost of the merchandise Z-Mart sold on November 3 is $1,600, and the entry to record the cost part of this sales transaction is

(e) Nov. 3	Cost of Goods Sold............................	1,600	
	Merchandise Inventory		1,600
	To record the cost of Nov. 3 sale.		

Assets = Liabilities + Equity
−1,600   −1,600

Sales Discounts

Sales discounts on credit sales can benefit a seller by decreasing the delay in receiving cash and reducing future collection efforts. At the time of a credit sale, a seller does not know whether a customer will pay within the discount period and take advantage of a discount. This means the seller usually does not record a sales discount until a customer actually pays within the discount period. To illustrate, Z-Mart completes a credit sale for $1,000 on November 12 with terms of 2/10, n/60. The entry to record the revenue part of this sale is

Assets = Liabilities + Equity
+1,000   +1,000

Nov. 12	Accounts Receivable	1,000	
	Sales		1,000
	Sold merchandise under terms of 2/10, n/60.		

This entry records the receivable and the revenue as if the customer will pay the full amount. The customer has two options, however. One option is to wait 60 days until January 11 and pay the full $1,000. In this case, Z-Mart records that payment as

Assets = Liabilities + Equity
+1,000
−1,000

Jan. 11	Cash	1,000	
	Accounts Receivable		1,000
	Received payment for Nov. 12 sale.		

The customer's second option is to pay $980 within a 10-day period ending November 22. If the customer pays on (or before) November 22, Z-Mart records the payment as

Assets = Liabilities + Equity
+980   −20
−1,000

Nov. 22	Cash	980	
	Sales Discounts	20	
	Accounts Receivable		1,000
	Received payment for Nov. 12 sale less discount.		

Sales Discounts is a contra revenue account, meaning the Sales Discounts account is deducted from the Sales account when computing a company's net sales (see Exhibit 5.9). Management monitors Sales Discounts to assess the effectiveness and cost of its discount policy.

Sales Returns and Allowances

Point: Published income statements rarely disclose sales discounts, returns and allowances.

Sales returns refer to merchandise that customers return to the seller after a sale. Many companies allow customers to return merchandise for a full refund. *Sales allowances* refer to reductions in the selling price of merchandise sold to customers. This can occur with damaged or defective merchandise that a customer is willing to purchase with a decrease in selling price. Sales returns and allowances usually involve dissatisfied customers and the possibility of lost future sales, and managers monitor information about returns and allowances.

Sales Returns   To illustrate, recall Z-Mart's sale of merchandise on November 3 for $2,400 that had cost $1,600. Assume that the customer returns part of the merchandise on

November 6, and the returned items sell for $800 and cost $600. The revenue part of this transaction must reflect the decrease in sales from the customer's return of merchandise as follows:

(f) Nov. 6	Sales Returns and Allowances	800	
	Accounts Receivable		800
	Customer returns merchandise of Nov. 3 sale.		

Assets = Liabilities + Equity
−800   −800

If the merchandise returned to Z-Mart is not defective and can be resold to another customer, Z-Mart returns these goods to its inventory. The entry to restore the cost of such goods to the Merchandise Inventory account is

Nov. 6	Merchandise Inventory	600	
	Cost of Goods Sold		600
	Returned goods added to inventory.		

Assets = Liabilities + Equity
+600   +600

This entry changes if the goods returned are defective. In this case the returned inventory is recorded at its estimated value, not its cost. To illustrate, if the goods (costing $600) returned to Z-Mart are defective and estimated to be worth $150, the following entry is made: Dr. Merchandise Inventory for $150, Dr. Loss from Defective Merchandise for $450, and Cr. Cost of Goods Sold for $600.

Decision Insight

Return to Sender   Book merchandisers such as **Barnes & Noble, Borders Books, Books-A-Million,** and **Waldenbooks** can return unsold books to publishers at purchase price. Publishers say returns of new hardcover books run between 35% and 50%. ∎

Sales Allowances   To illustrate sales allowances, assume that $800 of the merchandise Z-Mart sold on November 3 is defective but the buyer decides to keep it because Z-Mart offers a $100 price reduction. Z-Mart records this allowance as follows:

Nov. 6	Sales Returns and Allowances	100	
	Accounts Receivable		100
	To record sales allowance on Nov. 3 sale.		

Assets = Liabilities + Equity
−100   −100

The seller usually prepares a credit memorandum to confirm a buyer's return or allowance. A seller's **credit memorandum** informs a buyer of the seller's credit to the buyer's Account Receivable (on the seller's books).

Point: The sender (maker) of a credit memorandum will *credit* the account of the receiver. The receiver of a credit memorandum will *debit* the sender's account.

Quick Check   Answers — p. 205

7. Why are sales discounts and sales returns and allowances recorded in contra revenue accounts instead of directly in the Sales account?
8. Under what conditions are two entries necessary to record a sales return?
9. When merchandise is sold on credit and the seller notifies the buyer of a price allowance, does the seller create and send a credit memorandum or a debit memorandum?

COMPLETING THE ACCOUNTING CYCLE

Exhibit 5.10 shows the flow of merchandising costs during a period and where these costs are reported at period-end. Specifically, beginning inventory plus the net cost of purchases is the merchandise available for sale. As inventory is sold, its cost is recorded in cost of goods sold on the income statement; what remains is ending inventory on the statement of financial position. A period's ending inventory is the next period's beginning inventory.

EXHIBIT 5.10

Merchandising Cost Flow in the Accounting Cycle

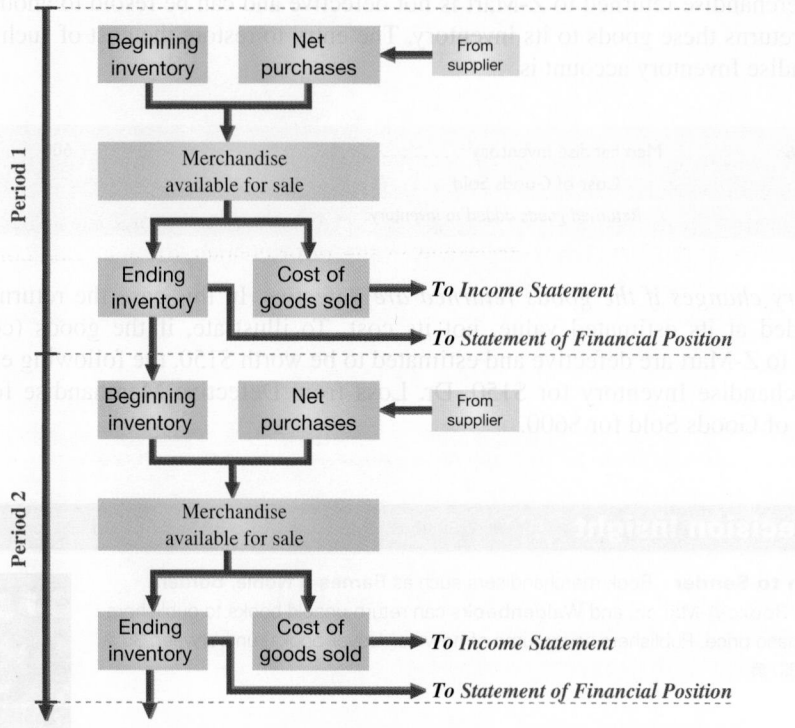

Adjusting Entries for Merchandisers

> **P3** Prepare adjustments and close accounts for a merchandising company.

Each of the steps in the accounting cycle described in the prior chapter for a service company applies to a merchandiser. This section and the next two further explain three steps of the accounting cycle for a merchandiser—adjustments, statement preparation, and closing.

Adjusting entries are generally the same for merchandising companies and service companies, including those for prepaid expenses (including depreciation), accrued expenses, unearned revenues, and accrued revenues. However, a merchandiser using a perpetual inventory system is usually required to make another adjustment to update the Merchandise Inventory account to reflect any loss of merchandise, including theft and deterioration. **Shrinkage** is the term used to refer to the loss of inventory and it is computed by comparing a physical count of inventory with recorded amounts. A physical count is usually performed at least once annually.

To illustrate, Z-Mart's Merchandise Inventory account at the end of year 2015 has a balance of $21,250, but a physical count reveals that only $21,000 of inventory exists. The adjusting entry to record this $250 shrinkage is

Point: About two-thirds of shoplifting losses are thefts by employees.

Assets = Liabilities + Equity
−250   −250

Dec. 31	Cost of Goods Sold	250	
	Merchandise Inventory		250
	To adjust for $250 shrinkage revealed by a physical count of inventory.		

Preparing Financial Statements

The financial statements of a merchandiser, and their preparation, are similar to those for a service company described in Chapters 2 through 4. The income statement mainly differs by the inclusion of *cost of goods sold* and *gross profit*. Also, net sales is affected by discounts, returns, and allowances, and some additional expenses are possible such as delivery expense and loss from defective merchandise. The statement of financial position mainly differs by the inclusion of *merchandise inventory* as part of current assets. The statement of changes in equity is unchanged. A work sheet can be used to help prepare these statements, and one is illustrated in Appendix 5B for Z-Mart.

Point: Staples's costs of shipping merchandise to its stores is included in its costs of inventories as required by the cost principle.

Closing Entries for Merchandisers

Closing entries are similar for service companies and merchandising companies using a perpetual system. The difference is that we must close some new temporary accounts that arise from merchandising activities. Z-Mart has several temporary accounts unique to merchandisers: Sales (of goods), Sales Discounts, Sales Returns and Allowances, and Cost of Goods Sold. Their existence in the ledger means that the first two closing entries for a merchandiser are slightly different from the ones described in the prior chapter for a service company. These differences are set in **red boldface** in the closing entries of Exhibit 5.11.

Point: The Inventory account is not affected by the closing process under a perpetual system.

EXHIBIT 5.11

Closing Entries for a Merchandiser

Step 1: Close Credit Balances in Temporary Accounts to Income Summary.

Dec. 31	Sales	321,000	
	Income Summary		321,000
	To close credit balances in temporary accounts.		

Step 2: Close Debit Balances in Temporary Accounts to Income Summary.

Dec. 31	Income Summary	308,100	
	Sales Discounts		4,300
	Sales Returns and Allowances		2,000
	Cost of Goods Sold		230,400
	Depreciation Expense		3,700
	Salaries Expense		43,800
	Insurance Expense		600
	Rent Expense		9,000
	Supplies Expense		3,000
	Advertising Expense		11,300
	To close debit balances in temporary accounts.		

Step 3: Close Income Summary to Owner's Capital.

The third closing entry is identical for a merchandising company and a service company. The $12,900 amount is net profit reported on the income statement.

Dec. 31	Income Summary	12,900	
	K. Marty, Capital		12,900
	To close the Income Summary account.		

Step 4: Close Withdrawals Account to Owner's Capital.

The fourth closing entry is identical for a merchandising company and a service company. It closes the Withdrawals account and adjusts the Owner's Capital account to the amount shown on the statement of financial position.

Dec. 31	K. Marty, Capital	4,000	
	K. Marty, Withdrawals		4,000
	To close the Withdrawals account.		

Summary of Merchandising Entries

Exhibit 5.12 summarizes the key adjusting and closing entries of a merchandiser (using a perpetual inventory system) that are different from those of a service company described in prior chapters (the Demonstration Problem 2 illustrates these merchandising entries).

EXHIBIT 5.12

Summary of Merchandising Entries

	Merchandising Transactions	Merchandising Entries	Dr.	Cr.
Purchases	Purchasing merchandise for resale.	Merchandise Inventory .... Cash or Accounts Payable..........	#	#
	Paying freight costs on purchases; FOB shipping point.	Merchandise Inventory .... Cash	#	#
	Paying within discount period.	Accounts Payable .... Merchandise Inventory .... Cash	#	# #
	Recording purchase returns or allowances.	Cash or Accounts Payable.............. Merchandise Inventory	#	#
Sales	Selling merchandise.	Cash or Accounts Receivable .... Sales	#	#
		Cost of Goods Sold .... Merchandise Inventory	#	#
	Receiving payment within discount period.	Cash .... Sales Discounts .... Accounts Receivable	# #	#
	Granting sales returns or allowances.	Sales Returns and Allowances .... Cash or Accounts Receivable	#	#
		Merchandise Inventory .... Cost of Goods Sold	#	#
	Paying freight costs on sales; FOB destination.	Delivery Expense .... Cash	#	#

	Merchandising Events	Adjusting and Closing Entries		
Adjusting	Adjusting due to shrinkage (occurs when recorded amount larger than physical inventory).	Cost of Goods Sold .... Merchandise Inventory	#	#
Closing	Closing temporary accounts with credit balances.	Sales .... Income Summary	#	#
	Closing temporary accounts with debit balances.	Income Summary .... Sales Returns and Allowances .... Sales Discounts .... Cost of Goods Sold .... Delivery Expense .... "Other Expenses"	#	# # # # #

Quick Check

Answers — p. 205

10. When a merchandiser uses a perpetual inventory system, why is it sometimes necessary to adjust the Merchandise Inventory balance with an adjusting entry?

11. What temporary accounts do you expect to find in a merchandising business but not in a service business?

12. Describe the closing entries normally made by a merchandising company.

FINANCIAL STATEMENT FORMATS

P4 Define and prepare financial statements for a merchandising company.

This section discusses two of the four financial statements required by **IAS 1 Presentation of Financial Statements.** One financial statement is the statement of profit or loss and other comprehensive income. This statement can be shown as a single statement, with profit or loss and other comprehensive income presented in two sections. Alternatively, the profit or loss section can be presented in a separate statement of profit or loss. If so, the separate statement of profit or loss shall immediately precede the statement presenting comprehensive income, which shall begin with profit or loss. An entity may use titles for the statements other than those used in **IAS 1**. For example, an entity may use the title "statement of comprehensive income" instead of "statement of profit or loss and other comprehensive income." When presenting as two statements, some entities may call the first statement "income statement" or "statement of profit or loss." As we will deal with comprehensive income in the chapter on corporations, we will discuss the first statement below and call it "income statement." Exhibit 5.13 shows an illustrative income statement format for Z-Mart.

EXHIBIT 5.13

Illustrative Income Statement

Z-MART Income Statement For Year Ended December 31, 2015			
Sales			$321,000
Sales discounts		($ 4,300)	
Sales returns and allowances		(2,000)	(6,300)
Net sales.			314,700
Cost of goods sold.			(230,400)
Gross profit			84,300
Expenses			
Depreciation expense		(3,700)	
Salaries expense		(43,800)	
Insurance expense		(600)	
Rent expense		(9,000)	
Supplies expense		(3,000)	
Advertising expense.		(11,300)	(71,400)
Profit before tax.			$ 12,900

Point: Amounts in brackets or parentheses indicate negative numbers in the context of the financial statement but they are optional.

Net sales is sales or revenues less any sales discounts, returns, and allowances. Cost of goods sold is also known as cost of sales. Gross profit is also known as gross margin. Depreciation, salaries, insurance, rent, supplies, and advertising are all operating expenses, so the profit amount above can be called operating profit. If there are financial items such as interest income and interest expense, they should be shown in separate categories.

Point: The example shows expenses being presented by their function. **IFRS** also permits expenses to be presented by their nature.

Classified Statement of Financial Position

The merchandiser's classified statement of financial position reports merchandise inventory as a current asset. The current asset items are normally presented in order of *liquidity,* which measures the availability of resources to meet short-term cash requirements. The partial illustrative statement of financial position in Exhibit 5.14 shows Z-Mart's current assets (other sections are as shown in Chapter 4) in decreasing order of liquidity. Inventory is usually less liquid than accounts receivable because inventory must first be sold before cash can be received; but it is more liquid than supplies and prepaid expenses.

EXHIBIT 5.14

Illustrative Classified Statement of Financial Position (Partial) of a Merchandiser

Z-MART Statements of Financial Position (Partial) December 31, 2015	
Current assets	
Cash	$ 8,200
Accounts receivable	11,200
Merchandise inventory	21,000
Office supplies	550
Store supplies	250
Prepaid expenses.	300
Total current assets	$ 41,500

Decision Insight

Merchandising Shenanigans   Accurate invoices are important to both sellers and buyers. Merchandisers rely on invoices to make certain they receive all monies for products provided—no more, no less. To achieve this, controls are set up. Still, failures arise. A survey reports that 9% of employees in sales and marketing witnessed false or misleading invoices sent to customers. Another 14% observed employees violating contract terms with customers (KPMG 2009). ∎

Decision Analysis Acid-Test and Gross Margin Ratios

Acid-Test Ratio

A1 Compute the acid-test ratio and explain its use to assess liquidity.

For many merchandisers, inventory makes up a large portion of current assets. Inventory must be sold and any resulting accounts receivable must be collected before cash is available. Chapter 4 explained that the current ratio, defined as current assets divided by current liabilities, is useful in assessing a company's ability to pay current liabilities. Because it is sometimes unreasonable to assume that inventories are a source of payment for current liabilities, we look to other measures.

One measure of a merchandiser's ability to pay its current liabilities (referred to as its *liquidity*) is the acid-test ratio. It differs from the current ratio by excluding less liquid current assets such as inventory and prepaid expenses that take longer to be converted to cash. The **acid-test ratio,** also called *quick ratio,* is defined as *quick assets* (cash, short-term investments, and current receivables) divided by current liabilities—see Exhibit 5.15.

EXHIBIT 5.15

Acid-Test (Quick) Ratio

$$\text{Acid-test ratio} = \frac{\text{Cash and cash equivalents} + \text{Short-term investments} + \text{Current receivables}}{\text{Current liabilities}}$$

Exhibit 5.16 shows both the acid-test and current ratios of Nestlé for financial years 2009 through 2013—also see graph. The worst year for Nestlé's acid-test ratio was 2009, which was probably due to the recessionary environment. However, for 2010 it increased significantly to its highest level for the five-year period, but dropped again in 2011 and remained at about 0.6. Similarly, its current ratio hit its highest level in 2010, but dropped again in 2011 and remained at about 0.9.

EXHIBIT 5.16

Nestlé Acid-Test and Current Ratios

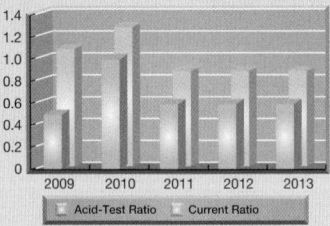

	2009	2010	2011	2012	2013
Quick assets	18,673	29,285	22,422	22,344	19,259
Current assets (CHF millions)	39,870	38,997	33,324	34,020	30,066
Current liabilities (CHF millions)	36,083	30,146	35,232	38,528	32,917
Current ratio	1.1	1.3	0.9	0.9	0.9
Acid-test ratio	0.5	1.0	0.6	0.6	0.6

Point: Successful use of a just-in-time inventory system can narrow the gap between the acid-test ratio and the current ratio.

An acid-test ratio less than 1.0 means that current liabilities exceed quick assets. A rule of thumb is that the acid-test ratio should have a value near, or higher than, 1.0 to conclude that a company is unlikely to face near-term liquidity problems. A value much less than 1.0 raises liquidity concerns unless a company can generate enough cash from inventory sales or if much of its liabilities are not due until late in the next period. Similarly, a value slightly larger than 1.0 can hide a liquidity problem if payables are due shortly and receivables are not collected until late in the next period.

Decision Maker Answer — p. 204

Supplier A retailer requests to purchase supplies on credit from your company. You have no prior experience with this retailer. The retailer's current ratio is 2.1, its acid-test ratio is 0.5, and inventory makes up most of its current assets. Do you extend credit? ■

Gross Margin Ratio

A2 Compute the gross margin ratio and explain its use to assess profitability.

The cost of goods sold makes up much of a merchandiser's expenses. Without sufficient gross profit, a merchandiser will likely fail. Users often compute the gross margin ratio to help understand this relation. It differs from the profit margin ratio in that it excludes all costs except cost of goods sold. The **gross margin ratio** (also called *gross profit ratio*) is defined as *gross margin* (net sales minus cost of goods sold) divided by net sales—see Exhibit 5.17.

EXHIBIT 5.17

Gross Margin Ratio

$$\text{Gross margin ratio} = \frac{\text{Net sales} - \text{Cost of goods sold}}{\text{Net sales}}$$

Exhibit 5.18 shows the gross margin ratio of Nestlé for financial years 2009–2013. For Nestlé, the gross margin ratio declined from 58% to 50.7% in 2010. Since 2011, it has stayed at about 47%. Any decrease in the gross margin ratio is a negative development for Nestlé, as the smaller gross margin ratio means it has less to cover all other expenses and still produce a net profit. Success for merchandisers such as Nestlé depends on adequate gross margin.

Point: The power of a ratio is often its ability to identify areas for more detailed analysis.

	2009	2010	2011	2012	2013
Gross margin (CHF millions)	62,410	47,166	39,515	42,221	44,047
Sales (CHF millions)	107,618	93,015	83,642	89,721	92,158
Gross margin ratio	58.0%	50.7%	47.2%	47.1%	47.8%

EXHIBIT 5.18

Nestlé's Gross Margin Ratio

🔲 **Decision Maker**   Answer — p. 205

Financial Officer   Your company has a 36% gross margin ratio and a 17% net profit margin ratio. Industry averages are 44% for gross margin and 16% for net profit margin. Do these comparative results concern you? ■

DEMONSTRATION PROBLEM 1

Use the following adjusted trial balance and additional information to complete the requirements.

KC ANTIQUES Adjusted Trial Balance December 31, 2015	Debit	Credit
Cash	$ 7,000	
Accounts receivable	13,000	
Merchandise inventory	60,000	
Store supplies	1,500	
Equipment	45,600	
Accumulated depreciation—Equipment		$ 16,600
Accounts payable		9,000
Salaries payable		2,000
K. Carter, Capital		79,000
K. Carter, Withdrawals	10,000	
Sales		343,250
Sales discounts	5,000	
Sales returns and allowances	6,000	
Cost of goods sold	159,900	
Depreciation expense—Store equipment	4,100	
Depreciation expense—Office equipment	1,600	
Sales salaries expense	30,000	
Office salaries expense	34,000	
Insurance expense	11,000	
Rent expense (70% is store, 30% is office)	24,000	
Store supplies expense	5,750	
Advertising expense	31,400	
Totals	$449,850	$449,850

KC Antiques' *supplementary records* for 2015 reveal the following itemized costs for merchandising activities:

Invoice cost of merchandise purchases	$150,000
Purchase discounts received	2,500
Purchase returns and allowances	2,700
Cost of transportation-in	5,000

Required

1. Use the supplementary records to compute the total cost of merchandise purchases for 2015.

2. Prepare a 2015 income statement. (Inventory at December 31, 2014, is $70,100.)

3. Prepare closing entries for KC Antiques at December 31, 2015.

4. Compute the acid-test ratio and the gross margin ratio. Explain the meaning of each ratio and interpret them for KC Antiques.

PLANNING THE SOLUTION

● Compute the total cost of merchandise purchases for 2015.

● To prepare the income statement, first compute net sales. Then, to compute cost of goods sold, add the net cost of merchandise purchases for the year to beginning inventory and subtract the cost of ending inventory. Subtract cost of goods sold from net sales to get gross profit. Then classify expenses as selling expenses or general and administrative expenses.

● The first closing entry debits all temporary accounts with credit balances and opens the Income Summary account. The second closing entry credits all temporary accounts with debit balances. The third entry closes the Income Summary account to the capital account, and the fourth entry closes the withdrawals account to the capital account.

● Identify the quick assets on the adjusted trial balance. Compute the acid-test ratio by dividing quick assets by current liabilities. Compute the gross margin ratio by dividing gross profit by net sales.

SOLUTION TO DEMONSTRATION PROBLEM 1

1.

Invoice cost of merchandise purchases	$150,000
Less: Purchases discounts received	2,500
Purchase returns and allowances	2,700
Add: Cost of transportation-in	5,000
Total cost of merchandise purchases	$149,800

2. Income statement

KC ANTIQUES
Income Statement
For Year Ended December 31, 2015

Sales		$343,250
Sales discounts.............................	($ 5,000)	
Sales returns and allowances	(6,000)	(11,000)
Net sales.....................................		332,250
Cost of goods sold*...........................		(159,900)
Gross profit		172,350
Expenses		
Selling expenses		
Depreciation expense—Store equipment	(4,100)	
Sales salaries expense	(30,000)	
Rent expense—Selling space	(16,800)	
Store supplies expense	(5,750)	
Advertising expense	(31,400)	
Total selling expenses........................	(88,050)	

[continued on next page]

[continued from previous page]

General and administrative expenses		
Depreciation expense—Office equipment	(1,600)	
Office salaries expense.........................	(34,000)	
Insurance expense	(11,000)	
Rent expense—Office space	(7,200)	
Total general and administrative expenses..........	(53,800)	
Total operating expenses		(141,850)
Net profit		$ 30,500

* Cost of goods sold can also be directly computed (applying concepts from Exhibit 5.4):

Merchandise inventory, December 31, 2014	$ 70,100
Total cost of merchandise purchases (from part 1)	149,800
Goods available for sale	219,900
Merchandise inventory, December 31, 2015	60,000
Cost of goods sold	$159,900

3.

Dec. 31	Sales	343,250	
	Income Summary		343,250
	To close credit balances in temporary accounts.		
Dec. 31	Income Summary	312,750	
	Sales Discounts		5,000
	Sales Returns and Allowances		6,000
	Cost of Goods Sold		159,900
	Depreciation Expense—Store Equipment		4,100
	Depreciation Expense—Office Equipment		1,600
	Sales Salaries Expense		30,000
	Office Salaries Expense		34,000
	Insurance Expense		11,000
	Rent Expense		24,000
	Store Supplies Expense		5,750
	Advertising Expense		31,400
	To close debit balances in temporary accounts.		
Dec. 31	Income Summary	30,500	
	K. Carter, Capital...........................		30,500
	To close the Income Summary account.		
Dec. 31	K. Carter, Capital	10,000	
	K. Carter, Withdrawals		10,000
	To close the Withdrawals account.		

4. Acid-test ratio = (Cash and equivalents + Short-term investments + Current receivables)/
  Current liabilities
  = (Cash + Accounts receivable)/(Accounts payable + Salaries payable)
  = ($7,000 + $13,000)/($9,000 + $2,000) = $20,000/$11,000 = $\underline{1.82}$

Gross margin ratio = Gross profit/Net sales = $172,350/$332,250 = $\underline{0.52}$ (or 52%)

KC Antiques has a healthy acid-test ratio of 1.82. This means it has more than $1.80 in liquid assets to satisfy each $1.00 in current liabilities. The gross margin of 0.52 shows that KC Antiques spends 48¢ ($1.00 − $0.52) of every dollar of net sales on the costs of acquiring the merchandise it sells. This leaves 52¢ of every dollar of net sales to cover other expenses incurred in the business and to provide a net profit.

DEMONSTRATION PROBLEM 2

Prepare journal entries to record the following merchandising transactions for both the seller (BMX) and buyer (Sanuk).

May 4   BMX sold $1,500 of merchandise on account to Sanuk, terms FOB shipping point, n/45, invoice dated May 4. The cost of the merchandise was $900.

May 6   Sanuk paid transportation charges of $30 on the May 4 purchase from BMX.

May 8   BMX sold $1,000 of merchandise on account to Sanuk, terms FOB destination, n/30, invoice dated May 8. The cost of the merchandise was $700.

May 10   BMX paid transportation costs of $50 for delivery of merchandise sold to Sanuk on May 8.

May 16   BMX issued Sanuk a $200 credit memorandum for merchandise returned. The merchandise was purchased by Sanuk on account on May 8. The cost of the merchandise returned was $140.

May 18   BMX received payment from Sanuk for purchase of May 8.

May 21   BMX sold $2,400 of merchandise on account to Sanuk, terms FOB shipping point, 2/10, n/EOM. BMX prepaid transportation costs of $100, which were added to the invoice. The cost of the merchandise was $1,440.

May 31   BMX received payment from Sanuk for purchase of May 21, less discount (2% × $2,400).

SOLUTION TO DEMONSTRATION PROBLEM 2

	BMX (Seller)			Sanuk (Buyer)		
May 4	Accounts Receivable—Sanuk	1,500		Merchandise Inventory	1,500	
	Sales		1,500	Accounts Payable—BMX		1,500
	Cost of Goods Sold	900				
	Merchandise Inventory		900			
6	No entry.			Merchandise Inventory	30	
				Cash		30
8	Accounts Receivable—Sanuk	1,000		Merchandise Inventory	1,000	
	Sales		1,000	Accounts Payable—BMX		1,000
	Cost of Goods Sold	700				
	Merchandise Inventory		700			
10	Delivery Expense	50		No entry.		
	Cash		50			
16	Sales Returns & Allowances	200		Accounts Payable—BMX	200	
	Accounts Receivable—Sanuk		200	Merchandise Inventory		200
	Merchandise Inventory	140				
	Cost of Goods Sold		140			
18	Cash	800		Accounts Payable—BMX	800	
	Accounts Receivable—Sanuk		800	Cash		800
21	Accounts Receivable—Sanuk	2,400		Merchandise Inventory	2,500	
	Sales		2,400	Accounts Payable—BMX		2,500
	Accounts Receivable—Sanuk	100				
	Cash		100			
	Cost of Goods Sold	1,440				
	Merchandise Inventory		1,440			
31	Cash	2,452		Accounts Payable—BMX	2,500	
	Sales Discounts	48		Merchandise Inventory		48
	Accounts Receivable—Sanuk		2,500	Cash		2,452

Periodic Inventory System

5A

A periodic inventory system requires updating the inventory account only at the *end of a period* to reflect the quantity and cost of both the goods available and the goods sold. Thus, during the period, the Merchandise Inventory balance remains unchanged. It reflects the beginning inventory balance until it is updated at the end of the period. During the period the cost of merchandise is recorded in a temporary *Purchases* account. When a company sells merchandise, it records revenue **but not the cost of the goods sold.** At the end of the period when a company prepares financial statements, it takes a *physical count of inventory* by counting the quantities and costs of merchandise available. The cost of goods sold is then computed by subtracting the ending inventory amount from the cost of merchandise available for sale.

Recording Merchandise Transactions   Under a periodic system, purchases, purchase returns and allowances, purchase discounts, and transportation-in transactions are recorded in separate temporary accounts. At period-end, each of these temporary accounts is closed and the Merchandise Inventory account is updated. To illustrate, journal entries under the periodic inventory system are shown for the most common transactions (codes *a* through *f* link these transactions to those in the chapter, and we drop explanations for simplicity). For comparison, perpetual system journal entries are shown to the right of each periodic entry, where differences are in green font.

P5 Record and compare merchandising transactions using both periodic and perpetual inventory systems.

Purchases   The periodic system uses a temporary *Purchases* account that accumulates the cost of all purchase transactions during each period. Z-Mart's November 2 entry to record the purchase of merchandise for $1,200 on credit with terms of 2/10, n/30 is

(a)

Periodic				Perpetual		
Purchases	1,200			Merchandise Inventory	1,200	
Accounts Payable		1,200		Accounts Payable		1,200

Purchase Discounts   The periodic system uses a temporary *Purchase Discounts* account that accumulates discounts taken on purchase transactions during the period. If payment in (*a*) is delayed until after the discount period expires, the entry is to debit Accounts Payable and credit Cash for $1,200 each. However, if Z-Mart pays the supplier for the previous purchase in (*a*) within the discount period, the required payment is $1,176 ($1,200 × 98%) and is recorded as

(b)

Periodic				Perpetual		
Accounts Payable	1,200			Accounts Payable	1,200	
Purchase Discounts		24		Merchandise Inventory		24
Cash		1,176		Cash		1,176

Purchase Returns and Allowances   Z-Mart returned merchandise purchased on November 2 because of defects. In the periodic system, the temporary *Purchase Returns and Allowances* account accumulates the cost of all returns and allowances during a period. The recorded cost (including discounts) of the defective merchandise is $300, and Z-Mart records the November 15 return with this entry:

(c)

Periodic				Perpetual		
Accounts Payable	300			Accounts Payable	300	
Purchase Returns and Allowances		300		Merchandise Inventory		300

Transportation-In   Z-Mart paid a $75 freight charge to transport merchandise to its store. In the periodic system, this cost is charged to a temporary *Transportation-In* account.

(d)

Periodic			Perpetual		
Transportation-In	75		Merchandise Inventory	75	
Cash		75	Cash		75

Sales   Under the periodic system, the cost of goods sold is *not* recorded at the time of each sale. (We later show how to compute total cost of goods sold at the end of a period.) Z-Mart's November 3 entry to record sales of $2,400 in merchandise on credit (when its cost is $1,600) is:

(e)

Periodic			Perpetual		
Accounts Receivable	2,400		Accounts Receivable	2,400	
Sales		2,400	Sales		2,400
			Cost of Goods Sold	1,600	
			Merchandise Inventory		1,600

Sales Returns   A customer returned part of the merchandise from the transaction in (*e*), where the returned items sell for $800 and cost $600. (*Recall:* The periodic system records only the revenue effect, not the cost effect, for sales transactions.) Z-Mart restores the merchandise to inventory and records the November 6 return as

(f)

Periodic			Perpetual		
Sales Returns and			Sales Returns and		
Allowances	800		Allowances	800	
Accounts Receivable...		800	Accounts Receivable		800
			Merchandise Inventory	600	
			Cost of Goods Sold		600

Sales Discounts   To illustrate sales discounts, assume that the remaining $1,600 of receivables (computed as $2,400 from *e* less $800 for *f*) has credit terms of 3/10, n/90 and that customers all pay within the discount period. Z-Mart records this payment as

Periodic			Perpetual		
Cash	1,552		Cash	1,552	
Sales Discounts ($1,600 × .03)	48		Sales Discounts ($1,600 × .03) ...	48	
Accounts Receivable ...		1,600	Accounts Receivable		1,600

Adjusting and Closing Entries   The periodic and perpetual inventory systems have slight differences in adjusting and closing entries. The period-end Merchandise Inventory balance (unadjusted) is $19,000 under the periodic system and $21,250 under the perpetual system. Since the periodic system does not update the Merchandise Inventory balance during the period, the $19,000 amount is the beginning inventory. However, the $21,250 balance under the perpetual system is the recorded ending inventory before adjusting for any inventory shrinkage.

A physical count of inventory taken at the end of the period reveals $21,000 of merchandise available. The adjusting and closing entries for the two systems are shown in Exhibit 5A.1. The periodic system records the ending inventory of $21,000 in the Merchandise Inventory account (which includes

EXHIBIT 5A.1

Comparison of Adjusting and Closing Entries—Periodic and Perpetual

PERIODIC			PERPETUAL		
Adjusting Entry—Shrinkage			**Adjusting Entry—Shrinkage**		
None			Cost of Goods Sold	250	
			Merchandise Inventory		250

[continued on next page]

[continued from previous page]

PERIODIC			PERPETUAL		
Closing Entries			**Closing Entries**		
(1) Sales	321,000		(1) Sales	321,000	
Merchandise Inventory	21,000				
Purchase Discounts	4,200				
Purchase Returns and Allowances	1,500				
Income Summary		347,700	Income Summary		321,000
(2) Income Summary	334,800		(2) Income Summary	308,100	
Sales Discounts		4,300	Sales Discounts		4,300
Sales Returns and Allowances		2,000	Sales Returns and Allowances		2,000
Merchandise Inventory		19,000			
Purchases		235,800	Cost of Goods Sold		230,400
Transportation-In		2,300			
Depreciation Expense		3,700	Depreciation Expense		3,700
Salaries Expense		43,800	Salaries Expense		43,800
Insurance Expense		600	Insurance Expense		600
Rent Expense		9,000	Rent Expense		9,000
Supplies Expense		3,000	Supplies Expense		3,000
Advertising Expense		11,300	Advertising Expense		11,300
(3) Income Summary	12,900		(3) Income Summary	12,900	
K. Marty, Capital		12,900	K. Marty, Capital		12,900
(4) K. Marty, Capital	4,000		(4) K. Marty, Capital	4,000	
K. Marty, Withdrawals		4,000	K. Marty, Withdrawals		4,000

shrinkage) in the first closing entry and removes the $19,000 beginning inventory balance from the account in the second closing entry.[2]

By updating Merchandise Inventory and closing Purchases, Purchase Discounts, Purchase Returns and Allowances, and Transportation-In, the periodic system transfers the cost of goods sold amount to Income Summary. Review the periodic side of Exhibit 5A.1 and notice that the **boldface** items affect Income Summary as follows.

Credit to Income Summary in the first closing entry includes amounts from:	
Merchandise inventory (ending)	$ 21,000
Purchase discounts	4,200
Purchase returns and allowances	1,500
Debit to Income Summary in the second closing entry includes amounts from:	
Merchandise inventory (beginning)	(19,000)
Purchases	(235,800)
Transportation-in	(2,300)
Net effect on Income Summary	$(230,400)

This $230,400 effect on Income Summary is the cost of goods sold amount. The periodic system transfers cost of goods sold to the Income Summary account but without using a Cost of Goods Sold account. Also, the periodic system does not separately measure shrinkage. Instead, it computes cost of goods available

---

[2] This approach is called the *closing entry method.* An alternative approach, referred to as the *adjusting entry method,* would not make any entries to Merchandise Inventory in the closing entries of Exhibit 5A.1, but instead would make two adjusting entries. Using Z-Mart data, the two adjusting entries would be: (1) Dr. Income Summary and Cr. Merchandise Inventory for $19,000 each, and (2) Dr. Merchandise Inventory and Cr. Income Summary for $21,000 each. The first entry removes the beginning balance of Merchandise Inventory, and the second entry records the actual ending balance.

for sale, subtracts the cost of ending inventory, and defines the difference as cost of goods sold, which includes shrinkage.

Preparing Financial Statements   The financial statements of a merchandiser using the periodic system are similar to those for a service company described in prior chapters. The income statement mainly differs by the inclusion of *cost of goods sold* and *gross profit*—of course, net sales is affected by discounts, returns, and allowances. The cost of goods sold section under the periodic system follows

Calculation of Cost of Goods Sold	
For Year Ended December 31, 2015	
Beginning inventory	$ 19,000
Cost of goods purchased	232,400
Cost of goods available for sale	251,400
Less ending inventory	21,000
Cost of goods sold	$230,400

The statement of financial position mainly differs by the inclusion of *merchandise inventory* in current assets—see Exhibit 5.15. The statement of changes in equity is unchanged. A work sheet can be used to help prepare these statements. The only differences under the periodic system from the work sheet illustrated in Appendix 5B using the perpetual system are highlighted as follows in blue boldface font.

File Edit View Insert Format Tools Data Accounting Window Help

	No.	Account	Unadjusted Trial Balance Dr.	Cr.	Adjustments Dr.	Cr.	Adjusted Trial Balance Dr.	Cr.	Income Statement Dr.	Cr.	Statement of Financial Position Dr.	Cr.
3	101	Cash	8,200				8,200				8,200	
4	106	Accounts receivable	11,200				11,200				11,200	
5	119	**Merchandise Inventory**	19,000				19,000		19,000	21,000	21,000	
6	126	Supplies	3,800			(b) 3,000	800				800	
7	128	Prepaid insurance	900			(a) 600	300				300	
8	167	Equipment	34,200				34,200				34,200	
9	168	Accumulated depr.—Equip.		3,700		(c) 3,700		7,400				7,400
10	201	Accounts payable		16,000				16,000				16,000
11	209	Salaries payable				(d) 800		800				800
12	301	K. Marty, Capital		42,600				42,600				42,600
13	302	K. Marty, Withdrawals	4,000				4,000				4,000	
14	413	Sales		321,000				321,000		321,000		
15	414	Sales returns and allowances	2,000				2,000		2,000			
16a	415	Sales discounts	4,300				4,300		4,300			
16b	505	**Purchases**	235,800				235,800		235,800			
16c	506	**Purchases returns & allowance**		1,500				1,500		1,500		
16d	507	**Purchases discounts**		4,200				4,200		4,200		
17	508	**Transportation-in**	2,300				2,300		2,300			
18	612	Depreciation expense—Equip.			(c) 3,700		3,700		3,700			
19	622	Salaries expense	43,000		(d) 800		43,800		43,800			
20	637	Insurance expense			(a) 600		600		600			
21	640	Rent expense	9,000				9,000		9,000			
22	652	Supplies expense			(b) 3,000		3,000		3,000			
23	655	Advertising expense	11,300				11,300		11,300			
24		Totals	389,000	389,000	8,100	8,100	393,500	393,500	334,800	347,700	79,700	66,800
25		Net profit							12,900			12,900
26		Totals							347,700	347,700	79,700	79,700

13. What account is used in a perpetual inventory system but not in a periodic system?

14. Which of the following accounts are temporary accounts under a periodic system?
(a) Merchandise Inventory; (b) Purchases; (c) Transportation-In.

15. How is cost of goods sold computed under a periodic inventory system?

16. Do reported amounts of ending inventory and net profit differ if the adjusting entry method of recording the change in inventory is used instead of the closing entry method?

APPENDIX

Work Sheet—Perpetual System

5B

Exhibit 5B.1 shows the work sheet for preparing financial statements of a merchandiser. It differs slightly from the work sheet layout in Chapter 4—the differences are in **red boldface**. Also, the adjustments in the work sheet reflect the following: (a) Expiration of $600 of prepaid insurance. (b) Use of $3,000 of supplies. (c) Depreciation of $3,700 for equipment. (d) Accrual of $800 of unpaid salaries. (e) Inventory shrinkage of $250. Once the adjusted amounts are extended into the financial statement columns, the information is used to develop financial statements.

EXHIBIT 5B.1

Work Sheet for Merchandiser (using a perpetual system)

No.	Account	Unadjusted Trial Balance Dr.	Cr.	Adjustments Dr.	Cr.	Adjusted Trial Balance Dr.	Cr.	Income Statement Dr.	Cr.	Statement of Financial Position Dr.	Cr.
101	Cash	8,200				8,200				8,200	
106	Accounts receivable	11,200				11,200				11,200	
119	Merchandise Inventory	21,250			(e) 250	21,000				21,000	
126	Supplies	3,800			(b) 3,000	800				800	
128	Prepaid insurance	900			(a) 600	300				300	
167	Equipment	34,200				34,200				34,200	
168	Accumulated depr.—Equip.		3,700		(c) 3,700		7,400				7,400
201	Accounts payable		16,000				16,000				16,000
209	Salaries payable				(d) 800		800				800
301	K. Marty, Capital		42,600				42,600				42,600
302	K. Marty, Withdrawals	4,000				4,000				4,000	
413	Sales		321,000				321,000		321,000		
414	Sales returns and allowances	2,000				2,000		2,000			
415	Sales discounts	4,300				4,300		4,300			
502	Cost of goods sold	230,150		(e) 250		230,400		230,400			
612	Depreciation expense—Equip.			(c) 3,700		3,700		3,700			
622	Salaries expense	43,000		(d) 800		43,800		43,800			
637	Insurance expense			(a) 600		600		600			
640	Rent expense	9,000				9,000		9,000			
652	Supplies expense			(b) 3,000		3,000		3,000			
655	Advertising expense	11,300				11,300		11,300			
	Totals	383,300	383,300	8,350	8,350	387,800	387,800	308,100	321,000	79,700	66,800
	Net profit							12,900			12,900
	Totals							321,000	321,000	79,700	79,700

Summary

C1 **Describe merchandising activities and identify income components for a merchandising company.** Merchandisers buy products and resell them. Examples of merchandisers include Walmart, Home Depot, The Limited, and Barnes & Noble. A merchandiser's costs on the income statement include an amount for cost of goods sold. Gross profit, or gross margin, equals sales minus cost of goods sold.

C2 **Identify and explain the inventory asset and cost flows of a merchandising company.** The current asset section of a merchandising company's statement of financial position includes *merchandise inventory,* which refers to the products a merchandiser sells and are available for sale at the statement of financial position date. Cost of merchandise purchases flows into Merchandise Inventory and from there to Cost of Goods Sold on the income statement. Any remaining inventory is reported as a current asset on the statement of financial position.

A1 **Compute the acid-test ratio and explain its use to assess liquidity.** The acid-test ratio is computed as quick assets (cash, short-term investments, and current receivables) divided by current liabilities. It indicates a company's ability to pay its current liabilities with its existing quick assets. An acid-test ratio equal to or greater than 1.0 is often adequate.

A2 **Compute the gross margin ratio and explain its use to assess profitability.** The gross margin ratio is computed as gross margin (net sales minus cost of goods sold) divided by net sales. It indicates a company's profitability before considering other expenses.

P1 **Analyze and record transactions for merchandise purchases using a perpetual system.** For a perpetual inventory system, purchases of inventory (net of trade discounts) are added to the Merchandise Inventory account. Purchase discounts and purchase returns and allowances are subtracted from Merchandise Inventory, and transportation-in costs are added to Merchandise Inventory.

P2 **Analyze and record transactions for merchandise sales using a perpetual system.** A merchandiser records sales at list price less any trade discounts. The cost of items sold is transferred from Merchandise Inventory to Cost of Goods Sold. Refunds or credits given to customers for unsatisfactory merchandise are recorded in Sales Returns and Allowances, a contra account to Sales. If merchandise is returned and restored to inventory, the cost of this merchandise is removed from Cost of Goods Sold and transferred back to Merchandise Inventory. When cash discounts from the sales price are offered and customers pay within the discount period, the seller records Sales Discounts, a contra account to Sales.

P3 **Prepare adjustments and close accounts for a merchandising company.** With a perpetual system, it is often necessary to make an adjustment for inventory shrinkage. This is computed by comparing a physical count of inventory with the Merchandise Inventory balance. Shrinkage is normally charged to Cost of Goods Sold. Temporary accounts closed to Income Summary for a merchandiser include Sales, Sales Discounts, Sales Returns and Allowances, and Cost of Goods Sold.

P4 **Define and prepare financial statements for a merchandising company.** Income statements should show the details of net sales and report expenses in categories reflecting different activities. Classified statements of financial position should show inventories as current assets.

P5ᴬ **Record and compare merchandising transactions using both periodic and perpetual inventory systems.** A perpetual inventory system continuously tracks the cost of goods available for sale and the cost of goods sold. A periodic system accumulates the cost of goods purchased during the period and does not compute the amount of inventory or the cost of goods sold until the end of a period. Transactions involving the sale and purchase of merchandise are recorded and analyzed under both the periodic and perpetual inventory systems. Adjusting and closing entries for both inventory systems are illustrated and explained.

Guidance Answers to Decision Maker and Decision Ethics

Entrepreneur For terms of 3/10, n/90, missing the 3% discount for an additional 80 days equals an implied annual interest rate of 13.69%, computed as (365 days ÷ 80 days) × 3%. Since you can borrow funds at 11% (assuming no other processing costs), it is better to borrow and pay within the discount period. You save 2.69% (13.69% − 11%) in interest costs by paying early.

Credit Manager Your decision is whether to comply with prior policy or to create a new policy and not abuse discounts offered by suppliers. Your first step should be to meet with your superior to find out if the late payment policy is the actual policy and, if so, its rationale. If it is the policy to pay late, you must apply your own sense of ethics. One point of view is that the late payment policy is unethical. A deliberate plan to make late payments means the company lies when it pretends to make payment within the discount period. Another view is that the late payment policy is acceptable. In some markets, attempts to take discounts through late payments are

accepted as a continued phase of "price negotiation." Also, your company's suppliers can respond by billing your company for the discounts not accepted because of late payments. However, this is a dubious viewpoint, especially since the prior manager proposes that you dishonestly explain late payments as computer or mail problems and since some suppliers have complained.

Supplier A current ratio of 2.1 suggests sufficient current assets to cover current liabilities. An acid-test ratio of 0.5 suggests, however, that quick assets can cover only about one-half of current liabilities. This implies that the retailer depends on money from sales of inventory to pay current liabilities. If sales of inventory decline or profit margins decrease, the likelihood that this retailer will default on its payments increases. Your decision is probably not to extend credit. If you do extend credit, you are likely to closely monitor the retailer's financial condition. (It is better to hold unsold inventory than uncollectible receivables.)

Financial Officer   Your company's net profit margin is about equal to the industry average and suggests typical industry performance. However, gross margin reveals that your company is paying far more in cost of goods sold or receiving far less in sales price than competitors. Your attention must be directed to finding the problem with cost of goods sold, sales, or both. One positive note is that your company's expenses make up 19% of sales (36% − 17%). This favorably compares with competitors' expenses that make up 28% of sales (44% − 16%).

Guidance Answers to Quick Checks

1. Cost of goods sold is the cost of merchandise purchased from a supplier that is sold to customers during a specific period.

2. Gross profit (or gross margin) is the difference between net sales and cost of goods sold.

3. Widespread use of computing and related technology has dramatically increased the use of the perpetual inventory system.

4. Under credit terms of 2/10, n/60, the credit period is 60 days and the discount period is 10 days.

5. (*b*) trade discount.

6. *FOB* means "free on board." It is used in identifying the point when ownership transfers from seller to buyer. *FOB destination* means that the seller transfers ownership of goods to the buyer when they arrive at the buyer's place of business. It also means that the seller is responsible for paying shipping charges and bears the risk of damage or loss during shipment.

7. Recording sales discounts and sales returns and allowances separately from sales gives useful information to managers for internal monitoring and decision making.

8. When a customer returns merchandise *and* the seller restores the merchandise to inventory, two entries are necessary. One entry records the decrease in revenue and credits the customer's account. The second entry debits inventory and reduces cost of goods sold.

9. Credit memorandum—seller credits accounts receivable from buyer.

10. Merchandise Inventory may need adjusting to reflect shrinkage.

11. Sales (of goods), Sales Discounts, Sales Returns and Allowances, and Cost of Goods Sold (and maybe Delivery Expense).

12. Four closing entries: (1) close credit balances in temporary accounts to Income Summary, (2) close debit balances in temporary accounts to Income Summary, (3) close Income Summary to owner's capital, and (4) close withdrawals account to owner's capital.

13. Cost of Goods Sold.

14. (*b*) Purchases and (*c*) Transportation-In.

15. Under a periodic inventory system, the cost of goods sold is determined at the end of an accounting period by adding the net cost of goods purchased to the beginning inventory and subtracting the ending inventory.

16. Both methods report the same ending inventory and income.

Key Terms   www.mheducation.asia/olc/wildkwokFAP

Acid-test ratio (p. 194)
Cash discount (p. 183)
Cost of goods sold (p. 180)
Credit memorandum (p. 189)
Credit period (p. 183)
Credit terms (p. 183)
Debit memorandum (p. 184)
Discount period (p. 183)
EOM (p. 183)

FOB (p. 185)
Gross margin (p. 181)
Gross margin ratio (p. 194)
Gross profit (p. 180)
Inventory (p. 181)
List price (p. 182)
Merchandise (p. 180)
Merchandise inventory (p. 181)
Merchandiser (p. 180)

Periodic inventory system (p. 182)
Perpetual inventory system (p. 182)
Purchase discount (p. 183)
Retailer (p. 180)
Sales discount (p. 183)
Shrinkage (p. 190)
Supplementary records (p. 186)
Trade discount (p. 182)
Wholesaler (p. 180)

Multiple Choice Quiz   Answers on p. 223   www.mheducation.asia/olc/wildkwokFAP

Additional Quiz Questions are available at the book's Website.

1. A company has $550,000 in net sales and $193,000 in gross profit. This means its cost of goods sold equals
   a. $743,000
   b. $550,000
   c. $357,000
   d. $193,000
   e. $(193,000)

2. A company purchased $4,500 of merchandise on May 1 with terms of 2/10, n/30. On May 6, it returned $250 of that merchandise. On May 8, it paid the balance owed for merchandise, taking any discount it is entitled to. The cash paid on May 8 is
   a. $4,500
   b. $4,250
   c. $4,160
   d. $4,165
   e. $4,410

3. A company has cash sales of $75,000, credit sales of $320,000, sales returns and allowances of $13,700, and sales discounts of $6,000. Its net sales equal
   a. $395,000
   b. $375,300
   c. $300,300
   d. $339,700
   e. $414,700

4. A company's quick assets are $37,500, its current assets are $80,000, and its current liabilities are $50,000. Its acid-test ratio equals
   a. 1.600
   b. 0.750
   c. 0.625
   d. 1.333
   e. 0.469

5. A company's net sales are $675,000, its costs of goods sold are $459,000, and its net profit is $74,250. Its gross margin ratio equals
   a. 32%
   b. 68%
   c. 47%
   d. 11%
   e. 34%

A(B)   *Superscript letter A (B) denotes assignments based on Appendix 5A (5B).*

🛈 Icon denotes assignments that involve decision making.

Discussion Questions

1. In comparing the accounts of a merchandising company with those of a service company, what additional accounts would the merchandising company likely use, assuming it employs a perpetual inventory system?

2. What items appear in financial statements of merchandising companies but not in the statements of service companies?

3. 🛈 Explain how a business can earn a positive gross profit on its sales and still have a net loss.

4. 🛈 Why do companies offer a cash discount?

5. How does a company that uses a perpetual inventory system determine the amount of inventory shrinkage?

6. Distinguish between cash discounts and trade discounts. Is the amount of a trade discount on purchased merchandise recorded in the accounts?

7. What is the difference between a sales discount and a purchase discount?

8. 🛈 Why would a company's manager be concerned about the quantity of its purchase returns if its suppliers allow unlimited returns?

9. Does the sender (maker) of a debit memorandum record a debit or a credit in the recipient's account? What entry (debit or credit) does the recipient record?

10. Where does merchandise inventory appear in a classified statement of financial position?

11. 🛈 Refer to Nestlé's consolidated balance sheet and consolidated income statement in Appendix A. What does the company title its inventory account? What is the amount of its cost of goods sold for financial year 2013?

12. Refer to Adidas' 2013 consolidated income statement in Appendix A. What does Adidas title its cost of goods sold account?

13. Refer to Samsung's 2012 consolidated statement of income in Appendix A. Does it report a gross profit figure? If yes, is the amount higher than the previous year's?

14. Refer to 361 Degrees' 2013 consolidated statement of profit and loss from its Website (http://ir.361sport.com/html/ir_report.php). Does it report a gross profit figure? If yes, what is the amount for financial year 2013?

15. 🛈 Buyers negotiate purchase contracts with suppliers. What type of shipping terms should a buyer attempt to negotiate to minimize freight-in costs?

🅜🅒 **connect**™

QUICK STUDY

QS 5-1

Applying merchandising terms

C1

Enter the letter for each term in the blank space beside the definition that it most closely matches.

  A. Cash discount
  B. Credit period
  C. Discount period
  D. FOB destination

  E. FOB shipping point
  F. Gross profit
  G. Merchandise inventory

  H. Purchase discount
  I. Sales discount
  J. Trade discount

_____ **1.** Ownership of goods is transferred when delivered to the buyer's place of business.

_____ **2.** Time period in which a cash discount is available.

_____ **3.** Difference between net sales and the cost of goods sold.

_____ **4.** Reduction in a receivable or payable if it is paid within the discount period.

_____ **5.** Purchaser's description of a cash discount received from a supplier of goods.

_____ **6.** Ownership of goods is transferred when the seller delivers goods to the carrier.

_____ **7.** Reduction below list or catalog price that is negotiated in setting the price of goods.

_____ **8.** Seller's description of a cash discount granted to buyers in return for early payment.

_____ **9.** Time period that can pass before a customer's payment is due.

_____ **10.** Goods a company owns and expects to sell to its customers.

The cost of merchandise inventory includes which of the following:

a. Costs incurred to buy the goods.

b. Costs incurred to ship the goods to the store(s).

c. Costs incurred to make the goods ready for sale.

d. Both a and b.

e. a, b, and c.

QS 5-2
Identifying inventory costs
C2

Prepare journal entries to record each of the following purchases transactions of a merchandising company. Show supporting calculations and assume a perpetual inventory system.

Mar. 5   Purchased 500 units of product at a cost of $5 per unit. Terms of the sale are 2/10, n/60; the invoice is dated March 5.

Mar. 7   Returned 50 defective units from the March 5 purchase and received full credit.

Mar. 15 Paid the amount due from the March 5 purchase, less the return on March 7.

QS 5-3
Recording purchases—
perpetual system
P1

Prepare journal entries to record each of the following sales transactions of a merchandising company. Show supporting calculations and assume a perpetual inventory system.

Apr. 1   Sold merchandise for $2,000, granting the customer terms of 2/10, EOM; invoice dated April 1. The cost of the merchandise is $1,400.

Apr. 4   The customer in the April 1 sale returned merchandise and received credit for $500. The merchandise, which had cost $350, is returned to inventory.

Apr. 11 Received payment for the amount due from the April 1 sale less the return on April 4.

QS 5-4
Recording sales—
perpetual system
P2

Compute net sales, gross profit, and the gross margin ratio for each separate case *a* through *d*. Interpret the gross margin ratio for case *a*.

QS 5-5
Computing and analyzing
gross margin
A2

	a	b	c	d
Sales	$130,000	$512,000	$35,700	$245,700
Sales discounts	4,200	16,500	400	3,500
Sales returns and allowances	17,000	5,000	5,000	700
Cost of goods sold	76,600	326,700	21,300	125,900

Nix'It Company's ledger on July 31, its financial year-end, includes the following selected accounts that have normal balances (Nix'It uses the perpetual inventory system).

QS 5-6
Accounting for shrinkage—
perpetual system
P3

Merchandise inventory	$ 34,800	Sales returns and allowances	$ 3,500
T. Nix, Capital	115,300	Cost of goods sold	102,000
T. Nix, Withdrawals	7,000	Depreciation expense	7,300
Sales	157,200	Salaries expense	29,500
Sales discounts	1,700	Miscellaneous expenses	2,000

A physical count of its July 31 year-end inventory discloses that the cost of the merchandise inventory still available is $32,900. Prepare the entry to record any inventory shrinkage.

QS 5-7
Closing entries   **P3**

Refer to QS 5-6 and prepare journal entries to close the balances in temporary revenue and expense accounts. Remember to consider the entry for shrinkage that is made to solve QS 5-6.

QS 5-8
Computing and interpreting acid-test ratio

A1

Use the following information on current assets and current liabilities to compute and interpret the acid-test ratio. Explain what the acid-test ratio of a company measures.

Cash	$1,200	Prepaid expenses	$ 600
Accounts receivable	2,700	Accounts payable	4,750
Inventory	5,000	Other current liabilities	950

QS 5-9
Contrasting liquidity ratios   **A1**

Identify similarities and differences between the acid-test ratio and the current ratio. Compare and describe how the two ratios reflect a company's ability to meet its current obligations.

QS 5-10
Income statement

P4

The income statement for a merchandiser normally includes which of the following:
a. Calculation of gross profit or gross margin.
b. Detailed computations of expenses, including subtotals for various expense categories.
c. Profit after tax or net profit.
d. Both a and c.
e. a, b, and c.

QS 5-11ᴬ
Contrasting periodic and perpetual systems

P5

Identify whether each description best applies to a periodic or a perpetual inventory system.
a. Provides more timely information to managers.
b. Requires an adjusting entry to record inventory shrinkage.
c. Markedly increased in frequency and popularity in business within the past decade.
d. Records cost of goods sold each time a sales transaction occurs.
e. Updates the inventory account only at period-end.

QS 5-12ᴬ
Recording purchases—
periodic system   **P5**

Refer to QS 5-3 and prepare journal entries to record each of the merchandising transactions assuming that the periodic inventory system is used.

QS 5-13ᴬ
Recording purchases—
periodic system   **P5**

Refer to QS 5-4 and prepare journal entries to record each of the merchandising transactions assuming that the periodic inventory system is used.

QS 5-14
IFRS income statement presentation

P4

Income statement information for **Adidas Group**, a German footwear, apparel, and accessories manufacturer, for the year ended December 31, 2009, follows. The company applies **IFRS**, as adopted by the European Union, and reports its results in millions of Euros. Prepare its calendar year 2009 income statement.

Net profit	EUR	245
Financial income		19
Financial expenses		169
Operating profit		508
Cost of sales		5,669
Income taxes		113
Profit before tax		358
Gross profit		4,712
Royalty and commission income		86
Other operating income		100
Other operating expenses		4,390
Net sales		10,381

■ connect

Prepare journal entries to record the following transactions for a retail store. Assume a perpetual inventory system.

Apr. 2 Purchased merchandise from Blue Company under the following terms: $3,600 price, invoice dated April 2, credit terms of 2/15, n/60, and FOB shipping point.
     3 Paid $200 for shipping charges on the April 2 purchase.
     4 Returned to Blue Company unacceptable merchandise that had an invoice price of $600.
    17 Sent a check to Blue Company for the April 2 purchase, net of the discount and the returned merchandise.
    18 Purchased merchandise from Fox Corp. under the following terms: $7,500 price, invoice dated April 18, credit terms of 2/10, n/30, and FOB destination.
    21 After negotiations, received from Fox a $2,100 allowance on the April 18 purchase.
    28 Sent check to Fox paying for the April 18 purchase, net of the discount and allowance.

EXERCISES

Exercise 5-1
Recording entries for merchandise purchases
P1

Check April 28, Cr. Cash $5,292

Taos Company purchased merchandise for resale from Tuscon Company with an invoice price of $22,000 and credit terms of 3/10, n/60. The merchandise had cost Tuscon $15,000. Taos paid within the discount period. Assume that both buyer and seller use a perpetual inventory system.

1. Prepare entries that the buyer should record for (*a*) the purchase and (*b*) the cash payment.
2. Prepare entries that the seller should record for (*a*) the sale and (*b*) the cash collection.
3. Assume that the buyer borrowed enough cash to pay the balance on the last day of the discount period at an annual interest rate of 11% and paid it back on the last day of the credit period. Compute how much the buyer saved by following this strategy. (Assume a 365-day year and round dollar amounts to the nearest cent, including computation of interest per day.)

Exercise 5-2
Analyzing and recording merchandise transactions — both buyer and seller

P1 P2

Check (3) $338.50 savings (rounded)

The operating cycle of a merchandiser with credit sales includes the following five activities. Starting with merchandise acquisition, identify the chronological order of these five activities.

a. _____ purchases of merchandise.
b. _____ credit sales to customers.
c. _____ inventory made available for sale.
d. _____ cash collections from customers.
e. _____ accounts receivable accounted for.

Exercise 5-3
Operating cycle for merchandiser
C2

Spare Parts was organized on May 1, 2011, and made its first purchase of merchandise on May 3. The purchase was for 1,000 units at a price of $10 per unit. On May 5, Spare Parts sold 600 of the units for $14 per unit to DeSoto Co. Terms of the sale were 2/10, n/60. Prepare entries for Spare Parts to record the May 5 sale and each of the following separate transactions *a* through *c* using a perpetual inventory system.

a. On May 7, DeSoto returns 200 units because they did not fit the customer's needs. Spare Parts restores the units to its inventory.
b. On May 8, DeSoto discovers that 50 units are damaged but are still of some use and, therefore, keeps the units. Spare Parts sends DeSoto a credit memorandum for $300 to compensate for the damage.
c. On May 15, DeSoto discovers that 72 units are the wrong color. DeSoto keeps 43 of these units because Spare Parts sends a $92 credit memorandum to compensate. DeSoto returns the remaining 29 units to Spare Parts. Spare Parts restores the 29 returned units to its inventory.

Exercise 5-4
Recording sales returns and allowances P2

Check (c) Dr. Merchandise Inventory $290

Refer to Exercise 5-4 and prepare the appropriate journal entries for DeSoto Co. to record the May 5 purchase and each of the three separate transactions *a* through *c*. DeSoto is a retailer that uses a perpetual inventory system and purchases these units for resale.

Exercise 5-5
Recording purchase returns and allowances P1

Exercise 5-6

Analyzing and recording merchandise transactions—both buyer and seller

P1 P2

Check (1) May 20, Cr. Cash $27,936

On May 11, Smythe Co. accepts delivery of $30,000 of merchandise it purchases for resale from Hope Corporation. With the merchandise is an invoice dated May 11, with terms of 3/10, n/90, FOB shipping point. The goods cost Hope $20,000. When the goods are delivered, Smythe pays $335 to Express Shipping for delivery charges on the merchandise. On May 12, Smythe returns $1,200 of goods to Hope, who receives them one day later and restores them to inventory. The returned goods had cost Hope $800. On May 20, Smythe mails a check to Hope Corporation for the amount owed. Hope receives it the following day. (Both Smythe and Hope use a perpetual inventory system.)

1. Prepare journal entries that Smythe Co. records for these transactions.
2. Prepare journal entries that Hope Corporation records for these transactions.

Exercise 5-7

Sales returns and allowances

C1

Business decision makers desire information on sales returns and allowances. (1) Explain why a company's manager wants the accounting system to record customers' returns of unsatisfactory goods in the Sales Returns and Allowances account instead of the Sales account. (2) Explain whether this information would be useful for external decision makers.

Exercise 5-8

Recording effects of merchandising activities

P1 P2

Check Year-End Merchandise Inventory Dec. 31, $29,200

The following supplementary records summarize Titus Company's merchandising activities for year 2015. Set up T-accounts for Merchandise Inventory and Cost of Goods Sold. Then record the summarized activities in those T-accounts and compute account balances.

Cost of merchandise sold to customers in sales transactions	$186,000
Merchandise inventory, December 31, 2014	27,000
Invoice cost of merchandise purchases	190,500
Shrinkage determined on December 31, 2015	700
Cost of transportation-in	1,900
Cost of merchandise returned by customers and restored to inventory	2,200
Purchase discounts received	1,600
Purchase returns and allowances	4,100

Exercise 5-9

Computing revenues, expenses, and income

C1 C2

Using your accounting knowledge, fill in the blanks in the following separate income statements *a* through *e*. Identify any negative amount by putting it in parentheses.

	a	b	c	d	e
Sales	$60,000	$42,500	$36,000	$?	$23,600
Cost of goods sold					
Merchandise inventory (beginning)	6,000	17,050	7,500	7,000	2,560
Total cost of merchandise purchases	36,000	?	?	32,000	5,600
Merchandise inventory (ending)	?	(2,700)	(9,000)	(6,600)	?
Cost of goods sold	34,050	15,900	?	?	5,600
Gross profit	?	?	3,750	45,600	?
Expenses	9,000	10,650	12,150	2,600	6,000
Net profit (loss)	$?	$15,950	$ (8,400)	$43,000	$?

Exercise 5-10

Preparing adjusting and closing entries for a merchandiser

P3

The following list includes selected permanent accounts and all of the temporary accounts from the December 31, 2015, unadjusted trial balance of Deacon Co., a business owned by Julie Deacon. Use these account balances along with the additional information to journalize (*a*) adjusting entries and (*b*) closing entries. Deacon Co. uses a perpetual inventory system.

	Debit	Credit
Merchandise inventory	$ 28,000	
Prepaid selling expenses	5,000	
J. Deacon, Withdrawals	2,200	
Sales		$429,000
Sales returns and allowances	16,500	
Sales discounts	4,000	
Cost of goods sold	211,000	
Sales salaries expense	47,000	
Utilities expense	14,000	
Selling expenses	35,000	
Administrative expenses	95,000	

Additional Information

Accrued sales salaries amount to $1,600. Prepaid selling expenses of $2,000 have expired. A physical count of year-end merchandise inventory shows $27,450 of goods still available.

A retail company recently completed a physical count of ending merchandise inventory to use in preparing adjusting entries. In determining the cost of the counted inventory, company employees failed to consider that $2,000 of incoming goods had been shipped by a supplier on December 31 under an FOB shipping point agreement. These goods had been recorded in Merchandise Inventory as a purchase, but they were not included in the physical count because they were in transit. Explain how this overlooked fact affects the company's financial statements and the following ratios: return on assets, debt ratio, current ratio, and acid-test ratio.

Exercise 5-11
Interpreting a physical count error as inventory shrinkage

A1

Refer to the information in Exercise 5-11 and explain how the error in the physical count affects the company's gross margin ratio and its profit margin ratio.

Exercise 5-12
Physical count error and profits

A2

Compute the current ratio and acid-test ratio for each of the following separate cases. (Round ratios to two decimals.) Which company case is in the best position to meet short-term obligations? Explain.

Exercise 5-13
Computing and analyzing acid-test and current ratios

A1

	Case A	Case B	Case C
Cash	$ 800	$ 510	$3,200
Short-term investments	0	0	1,100
Current receivables	0	790	800
Inventory	2,000	1,600	1,900
Prepaid expenses	1,200	600	300
Total current assets	$4,000	$3,500	$7,300
Current liabilities	$2,200	$1,100	$3,650

Journalize the following merchandising transactions for CSI Systems assuming it uses a perpetual inventory system.

1. On November 1, CSI Systems purchases merchandise for $1,400 on credit with terms of 2/5, n/30, FOB shipping point; invoice dated November 1.
2. On November 5, CSI Systems pays cash for the November 1 purchase.
3. On November 7, CSI Systems discovers and returns $100 of defective merchandise purchased on November 1 for a cash refund.
4. On November 10, CSI Systems pays $80 cash for transportation costs with the November 1 purchase.
5. On November 13, CSI Systems sells merchandise for $1,500 on credit. The cost of the merchandise is $750.
6. On November 16, the customer returns merchandise from the November 13 transaction. The returned items sell for $200 and cost $100.

Exercise 5-14
Preparing journal entries— perpetual system

P1   P2

A company reports the following sales related information: Sales (gross) of $100,000; Sales discounts of $2,000; Sales returns and allowances of $8,000; Sales salaries expense of $5,000. Calculate the net sales of this company's income statement.

Exercise 5-15
Income statement

P4

Refer to Exercise 5-1 and prepare journal entries to record each of the merchandising transactions assuming that the periodic inventory system is used.

Exercise 5-16^A
Recording purchases— periodic system   P5

Refer to Exercise 5-2 and prepare journal entries to record each of the merchandising transactions assuming that the periodic inventory system is used by both the buyer and the seller. (Skip the part 3 requirement.)

Exercise 5-17^A
Recording purchases and sales— periodic system   P5

Exercise 5-18ᴬ
Buyer and seller transactions—periodic system **P5**

Refer to Exercise 5-6 and prepare journal entries to record each of the merchandising transactions assuming that the periodic inventory system is used by both the buyer and the seller.

Exercise 5-19ᴬ
Recording purchases—periodic system **P5**

Refer to Exercise 5-14 and prepare journal entries to record each of the merchandising transactions assuming that the periodic inventory system is used.

Exercise 5-20
Preparing an income statement following **IFRS**

P4

L'Oréal reports the following income statement accounts for the year ended December 31, 2013 (in EUR millions). Prepare the income statement for this company for the year ended December 31, 2013, following usual **IFRS** practices.

Net profit.	EUR 2,961.4	Income tax expense	EUR 1,063.0
Finance costs	29.1	Profit before tax	4,024.4
Net sales	22,976.6	Research and development expense.	857.0
Gross profit	16,374.8	Selling, general and administrative expense	4,756.8
Other income	178.7	Advertising and promotion expense	6,886.2
Cost of sales	6,601.8		

▓ connect

PROBLEM SET A

Problem 5-1A
Preparing journal entries for merchandising activities—perpetual system

P1 P2

Prepare journal entries to record the following merchandising transactions of Stone Company, which applies the perpetual inventory system. (*Hint:* It will help to identify each receivable and payable; for example, record the purchase on August 1 in Accounts Payable—Abilene.)

Aug. 1 Purchased merchandise from Abilene Company for $6,000 under credit terms of 1/10, n/30, FOB destination, invoice dated August 1.

4 At Abilene's request, Stone paid $100 cash for freight charges on the August 1 purchase, reducing the amount owed to Abilene.

5 Sold merchandise to Lux Corp. for $4,200 under credit terms of 2/10, n/60, FOB destination, invoice dated August 5. The merchandise had cost $3,000.

8 Purchased merchandise from Welch Corporation for $5,300 under credit terms of 1/10, n/45, FOB shipping point, invoice dated August 8. The invoice showed that at Stone's request, Welch paid the $240 shipping charges and added that amount to the bill. (*Hint:* Discounts are not applied to freight and shipping charges.)

Check Aug. 9, Dr. Delivery Expense, $120

9 Paid $120 cash for shipping charges related to the August 5 sale to Lux Corp.

10 Lux returned merchandise from the August 5 sale that had cost Stone $500 and been sold for $700. The merchandise was restored to inventory.

12 After negotiations with Welch Corporation concerning problems with the merchandise purchased on August 8, Stone received a credit memorandum from Welch granting a price reduction of $800.

15 Received balance due from Lux Corp. for the August 5 sale less the return on August 10.

Aug. 18, Cr. Cash $4,695

18 Paid the amount due Welch Corporation for the August 8 purchase less the price reduction granted.

19 Sold merchandise to Trax Co. for $3,600 under credit terms of 1/10, n/30, FOB shipping point, invoice dated August 19. The merchandise had cost $2,500.

22 Trax requested a price reduction on the August 19 sale because the merchandise did not meet specifications. Stone sent Trax a $600 credit memorandum to resolve the issue.

Aug. 29, Dr. Cash $2,970

29 Received Trax's cash payment for the amount due from the August 19 sale.

30 Paid Abilene Company the amount due from the August 1 purchase.

Problem 5-2A
Preparing journal entries for merchandising activities—perpetual system

P1 P2

Prepare journal entries to record the following merchandising transactions of Bask Company, which applies the perpetual inventory system. (*Hint:* It will help to identify each receivable and payable; for example, record the purchase on July 1 in Accounts Payable—Black.)

July 1 Purchased merchandise from Black Company for $6,000 under credit terms of 1/15, n/30, FOB shipping point, invoice dated July 1.

2 Sold merchandise to Coke Co. for $800 under credit terms of 2/10, n/60, FOB shipping point, invoice dated July 2. The merchandise had cost $500.

3   Paid $100 cash for freight charges on the purchase of July 1.

8   Sold merchandise that had cost $1,200 for $1,600 cash.

9   Purchased merchandise from Lane Co. for $2,300 under credit terms of 2/15, n/60, FOB destination, invoice dated July 9.

11   Received a $200 credit memorandum from Lane Co. for the return of part of the merchandise purchased on July 9.

12   Received the balance due from Coke Co. for the invoice dated July 2, net of the discount.

16   Paid the balance due to Black Company within the discount period.

19   Sold merchandise that cost $900 to AKP Co. for $1,250 under credit terms of 2/15, n/60, FOB shipping point, invoice dated July 19.

21   Issued a $150 credit memorandum to AKP Co. for an allowance on goods sold on July 19.

24   Paid Lane Co. the balance due after deducting the discount.

30   Received the balance due from AKP Co. for the invoice dated July 19, net of discount.

31   Sold merchandise that cost $3,200 to Coke Co. for $5,000 under credit terms of 2/10, n/60, FOB shipping point, invoice dated July 31.

Check   July 12, Dr. Cash $784
July 16, Cr. Cash $5,940

July 24, Cr. Cash $2,058
July 30, Dr. Cash $1,078

The following unadjusted trial balance is prepared at financial year-end for Rex Company.

Problem 5-3A

Preparing adjusting entries and income statements; and computing gross margin, acid-test, and current ratios

A1 A2 P3 P4

www.mheducation.asia/olc/wildkwokFAP

File Edit View Insert Format Tools Data Accounting Window Help

100% Arial 10 B I U $ %

REX COMPANY
Unadjusted Trial Balance
January 31, 2015

		Debit	Credit
2	Cash	$ 2,200	
3	Merchandise inventory	11,500	
4	Store supplies	4,800	
5	Prepaid insurance	2,300	
6	Store equipment	41,900	
7	Accumulated depreciation—Store equipment		$ 15,000
8	Accounts payable		9,000
9	T. Rex, Capital		32,000
10	T. Rex, Withdrawals	2,000	
11	Sales		104,000
12	Sales discounts	1,000	
13	Sales returns and allowances	2,000	
14	Cost of goods sold	37,400	
15	Depreciation expense—Store equipment	0	
16	Salaries expense	31,000	
17	Insurance expense	0	
18	Rent expense	14,000	
19	Store supplies expense	0	
20	Advertising expense	9,900	
21	Totals	$160,000	$160,000

Sheet1 Sheet2 Sheet3

Rent expense and salaries expense are equally divided between selling activities and the general and administrative activities. Rex Company uses a perpetual inventory system.

Required

1. Prepare adjusting journal entries to reflect each of the following:

   a. Store supplies still available at financial year-end amount to $1,650.

   b. Expired insurance, an administrative expense, for the financial year is $1,500.

   c. Depreciation expense on store equipment, a selling expense, is $1,400 for the financial year.

   d. To estimate shrinkage, a physical count of ending merchandise inventory is taken. It shows $11,100 of inventory is still available at financial year-end.

Check (2) Gross profit, $63,200;
Net profit, $2,250

2. Prepare an income statement for financial year 2015.

3. Compute the current ratio, acid-test ratio, and gross margin ratio as at January 31, 2015.

Problem 5-4A
Computing merchandising
amounts and formatting
income statements

C2 P4

BizKid Company's adjusted trial balance on August 31, 2015, its financial year-end, follows.

	Debit	Credit
Merchandise inventory	$ 31,000	
Other (noninventory) assets	120,400	
Total liabilities		$ 35,000
N. Kidman, Capital		101,650
N. Kidman, Withdrawals	8,000	
Sales		212,000
Sales discounts	3,250	
Sales returns and allowances	14,000	
Cost of goods sold	82,600	
Sales salaries expense	29,000	
Rent expense—Selling space	10,000	
Store supplies expense	2,500	
Advertising expense	18,000	
Office salaries expense	26,500	
Rent expense—Office space	2,600	
Office supplies expense	800	
Totals	$348,650	$348,650

On August 31, 2014, merchandise inventory was $25,000. Supplementary records of merchandising activities for the year ended August 31, 2015, reveal the following itemized costs.

Invoice cost of merchandise purchases	$91,000
Purchase discounts received	1,900
Purchase returns and allowances..............	4,400
Costs of transportation-in	3,900

Required

1. Compute the company's net sales for the year.

Check (2) $88,600;

(3) Gross profit, $112,150;
     Net profit, $22,750;

2. Compute the company's total cost of merchandise purchased for the year.

3. Prepare an income statement that includes separate categories for selling expenses and for general and administrative expenses.

Problem 5-5A
Preparing closing entries and
interpreting information about
discounts and returns

C2 P3

Use the data for BizKid Company in Problem 5-4A to complete the following requirements.

Required

1. Prepare closing entries as at August 31, 2015 (the perpetual inventory system is used).

Analysis Component

2. The company makes all purchases on credit, and its suppliers uniformly offer a 3% sales discount. Does it appear that the company's cash management system is accomplishing the goal of taking all available discounts? Explain.

Check (1) $22,750 Dr. to close
            Income Summary
         (3) Current-year rate, 6.6%

3. In prior years, the company experienced a 5% returns and allowance rate on its sales, which means approximately 5% of its gross sales were eventually returned outright or caused the company to grant allowances to customers. How do this year's results compare to prior years' results?

Refer to the data and information in Problem 5-3A.

Required

Prepare and complete the entire 10-column work sheet for Rex Company. Follow the structure of Exhibit 5B.1 in Appendix 5B.

Problem 5-6A^B
Preparing a work sheet for a merchandiser
P3

Prepare journal entries to record the following merchandising transactions of Wave Company, which applies the perpetual inventory system. (*Hint:* It will help to identify each receivable and payable; for example, record the purchase on July 3 in Accounts Payable—CAP.)

July 3 Purchased merchandise from CAP Corp. for $15,000 under credit terms of 1/10, n/30, FOB destination, invoice dated July 3.
    4 At CAP's request, Wave paid $250 cash for freight charges on the July 3 purchase, reducing the amount owed to CAP.
    7 Sold merchandise to Morris Co. for $10,500 under credit terms of 2/10, n/60, FOB destination, invoice dated July 7. The merchandise had cost $7,500.
   10 Purchased merchandise from Murdock Corporation for $14,200 under credit terms of 1/10, n/45, FOB shipping point, invoice dated July 10. The invoice showed that at Wave's request, Murdock paid the $600 shipping charges and added that amount to the bill. (*Hint:* Discounts are not applied to freight and shipping charges.)
   11 Paid $300 cash for shipping charges related to the July 7 sale to Morris Co.
   12 Morris returned merchandise from the July 7 sale that had cost Wave $1,250 and been sold for $1,750. The merchandise was restored to inventory.
   14 After negotiations with Murdock Corporation concerning problems with the merchandise purchased on July 10, Wave received a credit memorandum from Murdock granting a price reduction of $2,000.
   17 Received balance due from Morris Co. for the July 7 sale less the return on July 12.
   20 Paid the amount due Murdock Corporation for the July 10 purchase less the price reduction granted.
   21 Sold merchandise to Ulsh for $9,000 under credit terms of 1/10, n/30, FOB shipping point, invoice dated July 21. The merchandise had cost $6,250.
   24 Ulsh requested a price reduction on the July 21 sale because the merchandise did not meet specifications. Wave sent Ulsh a credit memorandum for $1,500 to resolve the issue.
   30 Received Ulsh's cash payment for the amount due from the July 21 sale.
   31 Paid CAP Corp. the amount due from the July 3 purchase.

Problem 5-1B
Preparing journal entries for merchandising activities—perpetual system
P1 P2

Check July 17, Dr. Cash $8,575
July 20, Cr. Cash $12,678

July 30, Dr. Cash $7,425

Prepare journal entries to record the following merchandising transactions of Yang Company, which applies the perpetual inventory system. (*Hint:* It will help to identify each receivable and payable; for example, record the purchase on May 2 in Accounts Payable—Bots.)

May 2 Purchased merchandise from Bots Co. for $9,000 under credit terms of 1/15, n/30, FOB shipping point, invoice dated May 2.
    4 Sold merchandise to Chase Co. for $1,200 under credit terms of 2/10, n/60, FOB shipping point, invoice dated May 4. The merchandise had cost $750.
    5 Paid $150 cash for freight charges on the purchase of May 2.
    9 Sold merchandise that had cost $1,800 for $2,400 cash.
   10 Purchased merchandise from Snyder Co. for $3,450 under credit terms of 2/15, n/60, FOB destination, invoice dated May 10.
   12 Received a $300 credit memorandum from Snyder Co. for the return of part of the merchandise purchased on May 10.
   14 Received the balance due from Chase Co. for the invoice dated May 4, net of the discount.
   17 Paid the balance due to Bots Co. within the discount period.
   20 Sold merchandise that cost $1,450 to Tex Co. for $2,800 under credit terms of 2/15, n/60, FOB shipping point, invoice dated May 20.
   22 Issued a $400 credit memorandum to Tex Co. for an allowance on goods sold from May 20.
   25 Paid Snyder Co. the balance due after deducting the discount.
   30 Received the balance due from Tex Co. for the invoice dated May 20, net of discount and allowance.
   31 Sold merchandise that cost $4,800 to Chase Co. for $7,500 under credit terms of 2/10, n/60, FOB shipping point, invoice dated May 31.

Problem 5-2B
Preparing journal entries for merchandising activities—perpetual system
P1 P2

Check May 14, Dr. Cash $1,176
May 17, Cr. Cash $8,910

May 30, Dr. Cash $2,352

Problem 5-3B
Preparing adjusting entries
and income statements; and
computing gross margin,
acid-test, and current ratios

A1 A2 P3 P4

The following unadjusted trial balance is prepared at financial year-end for FAB Products Company.

File Edit View Insert Format Tools Data Accounting Window Help

FAB PRODUCTS COMPANY Unadjusted Trial Balance October 31, 2015		
	Debit	**Credit**
Cash	$ 4,400	
Merchandise inventory	23,000	
Store supplies	9,600	
Prepaid insurance	4,600	
Store equipment	83,800	
Accumulated depreciation—Store equipment		$ 30,000
Accounts payable		16,000
A. Fab, Capital		64,000
A. Fab, Withdrawals	2,000	
Sales		208,000
Sales discounts	2,000	
Sales returns and allowances	4,000	
Cost of goods sold	74,800	
Depreciation expense—Store equipment	0	
Salaries expense	62,000	
Insurance expense	0	
Rent expense	28,000	
Store supplies expense	0	
Advertising expense	19,800	
Totals	$318,000	$318,000

Sheet1 / Sheet2 / Sheet3 /

Rent expense and salaries expense are equally divided between selling activities and the general and administrative activities. FAB Products Company uses a perpetual inventory system.

Required

1. Prepare adjusting journal entries to reflect each of the following.
   a. Store supplies still available at financial year-end amount to $3,300.
   b. Expired insurance, an administrative expense, for the financial year is $3,000.
   c. Depreciation expense on store equipment, a selling expense, is $2,800 for the financial year.
   d. To estimate shrinkage, a physical count of ending merchandise inventory is taken. It shows $22,200 of inventory is still available at financial year-end.

Check (2) Gross profit, $126,400;

2. Prepare an income statement for financial year 2015.
3. Compute the current ratio, acid-test ratio, and gross margin ratio as at October 31, 2015.

Problem 5-4B
Computing merchandising
amounts and formatting
income statements

C1 C2 P4

Albin Company's adjusted trial balance on March 31, 2015, its fiscal year-end, follows.

	Debit	Credit
Merchandise inventory	$ 46,500	
Other (noninventory) assets	190,600	
Total liabilities		$ 52,500
R. Albin, Capital		152,475
R. Albin, Withdrawals	2,000	

[continued on next page]

[continued from previous page]

Sales		318,000
Sales discounts	4,875	
Sales returns and allowances	21,000	
Cost of goods sold	123,900	
Sales salaries expense	43,500	
Rent expense—Selling space	15,000	
Store supplies expense	3,750	
Advertising expense	27,000	
Office salaries expense	39,750	
Rent expense—Office space	3,900	
Office supplies expense	1,200	
Totals	$522,975	$522,975

On March 31, 2014, merchandise inventory was $37,500. Supplementary records of merchandising activities for the year ended March 31, 2015, reveal the following itemized costs.

Invoice cost of merchandise purchases	$136,500
Purchase discounts received	2,850
Purchase returns and allowances	6,600
Costs of transportation-in	5,850

Required

1. Calculate the company's net sales for the year.
2. Calculate the company's total cost of merchandise purchased for the year.
3. Prepare an income statement that includes separate categories for selling expenses and for general and administrative expenses.

Check   (2) $132,900;

(3) Gross profit, $168,225;
Net profit, $34,125

Use the data for Albin Company in Problem 5-4B to complete the following requirements.

Required

1. Prepare closing entries as at March 31, 2015 (the perpetual inventory system is used).

Analysis Component

2. The company makes all purchases on credit, and its suppliers uniformly offer a 3% sales discount. Does it appear that the company's cash management system is accomplishing the goal of taking all available discounts? Explain.
3. In prior years, the company experienced a 5% returns and allowance rate on its sales, which means approximately 5% of its gross sales were eventually returned outright or caused the company to grant allowances to customers. How do this year's results compare to prior years' results?

Problem 5-5B
Preparing closing entries and interpreting information about discounts and returns

C2 P3

Check   (1) $34,125 Dr. to close
Income Summary

(3) Current-year rate, 6.6%

Refer to the data and information in Problem 5-3B.

Required

Prepare and complete the entire 10-column work sheet for FAB Products Company. Follow the structure of Exhibit 5B.1 in Appendix 5B.

Problem 5-6B[B]
Preparing a work sheet for a merchandiser

P3

SERIAL PROBLEM

Business Solutions

P1 P2 P3 P4

(This serial problem began in Chapter 1 and continues through most of the book. If previous chapter segments were not completed, the serial problem can begin at this point.)

SP 5   Santana Rey created Business Solutions on October 1, 2015. The company has been successful, and its list of customers has grown. To accommodate the growth, the accounting system is modified to set up separate accounts for each customer. The following chart of accounts includes the account number used for each account and any balance as at December 31, 2015. Santana Rey decided to add a fourth digit with a decimal point to the 106 account number that had been used for the single Accounts Receivable account. This change allows the company to continue using the existing chart of accounts.

No.	Account Title	Dr.	Cr.
101	Cash	$48,372	
106.1	Alex's Engineering Co.	0	
106.2	Wildcat Services	0	
106.3	Easy Leasing	0	
106.4	IFM Co.	3,000	
106.5	Liu Corp.	0	
106.6	Gomez Co.	2,668	
106.7	Delta Co.	0	
106.8	KC, Inc.	0	
106.9	Dream, Inc.	0	
119	Merchandise inventory	0	
126	Computer supplies	580	
128	Prepaid insurance	1,665	
131	Prepaid rent	825	
163	Office equipment	8,000	
164	Accumulated depreciation—Office equipment		$ 400
167	Computer equipment	20,000	
168	Accumulated depreciation—Computer equipment		1,250
201	Accounts payable		1,100

No.	Account Title	Dr.	Cr.
210	Wages payable		$ 500
236	Unearned computer services revenue		1,500
301	S. Rey, Capital		80,360
302	S. Rey, Withdrawals	$0	
403	Computer services revenue		0
413	Sales		0
414	Sales returns and allowances	0	
415	Sales discounts	0	
502	Cost of goods sold	0	
612	Depreciation expense—Office equipment	0	
613	Depreciation expense—Computer equipment	0	
623	Wages expense	0	
637	Insurance expense	0	
640	Rent expense	0	
652	Computer supplies expense	0	
655	Advertising expense	0	
676	Mileage expense	0	
677	Miscellaneous expenses	0	
684	Repairs expense—Computer	0	

In response to requests from customers, S. Rey will begin selling computer software. The company will extend credit terms of 1/10, n/30, FOB shipping point, to all customers who purchase this merchandise. However, no cash discount is available on consulting fees. Additional accounts (Nos. 119, 413, 414, 415, and 502) are added to its general ledger to accommodate the company's new merchandising activities. Also, Business Solutions does not use reversing entries and, therefore, all revenue and expense accounts have zero beginning balances as at January 1, 2016. Its transactions for January through March follow:

Jan.   4   The company paid cash to Lyn Addie for five days' work at the rate of $125 per day. Four of the five days relate to wages payable that were accrued in the prior year.

      5   Santana Rey invested an additional $25,000 cash in the company.

      7   The company purchased $5,800 of merchandise from Kansas Corp. with terms of 1/10, n/30, FOB shipping point, invoice dated January 7.

      9   The company received $2,668 cash from Gomez Co. as full payment on its account.

    11   The company completed a five-day project for Alex's Engineering Co. and billed it $5,500, which is the total price of $7,000 less the advance payment of $1,500.

Check   Jan. 11, Dr. Unearned Computer Services Revenue $1,500

13 The company sold merchandise with a retail value of $5,200 and a cost of $3,560 to Liu Corp., invoice dated January 13.

15 The company paid $600 cash for freight charges on the merchandise purchased on January 7.

16 The company received $4,000 cash from Delta Co. for computer services provided.

17 The company paid Kansas Corp. for the invoice dated January 7, net of the discount.

20 Liu Corp. returned $500 of defective merchandise from its invoice dated January 13. The returned merchandise, which had a $320 cost, is discarded. (The policy of Business Solutions is to leave the cost of defective products in cost of goods sold.)

Check Jan. 20, No entry to Cost of Goods Sold

22 The company received the balance due from Liu Corp., net of both the discount and the credit for the returned merchandise.

24 The company returned defective merchandise to Kansas Corp. and accepted a credit against future purchases. The defective merchandise invoice cost, net of the discount, was $496.

26 The company purchased $9,000 of merchandise from Kansas Corp. with terms of 1/10, n/30, FOB destination, invoice dated January 26.

26 The company sold merchandise with a $4,640 cost for $5,800 on credit to KC, Inc., invoice dated January 26.

29 The company received a $496 credit memorandum from Kansas Corp. concerning the merchandise returned on January 24.

31 The company paid cash to Lyn Addie for 10 days' work at $125 per day.

Feb. 1 The company paid $2,475 cash to Hillside Mall for another three months' rent in advance.

3 The company paid Kansas Corp. for the balance due, net of the cash discount, less the $496 amount in the credit memorandum.

5 The company paid $600 cash to the local newspaper for an advertising insert in today's paper.

11 The company received the balance due from Alex's Engineering Co. for fees billed on January 11.

15 Santana Rey withdrew $4,800 cash from the company for personal use.

23 The company sold merchandise with a $2,660 cost for $3,220 on credit to Delta Co., invoice dated February 23.

26 The company paid cash to Lyn Addie for eight days' work at $125 per day.

27 The company reimbursed Santana Rey for business automobile mileage (600 miles at $0.32 per mile).

Mar. 8 The company purchased $2,730 of computer supplies from Harris Office Products on credit, invoice dated March 8.

9 The company received the balance due from Delta Co. for merchandise sold on February 23.

11 The company paid $960 cash for minor repairs to the company's computer.

16 The company received $5,260 cash from Dream, Inc., for computing services provided.

19 The company paid the full amount due to Harris Office Products, consisting of amounts created on December 15 (of $1,100) and March 8.

24 The company billed Easy Leasing for $9,047 of computing services provided.

25 The company sold merchandise with a $2,002 cost for $2,800 on credit to Wildcat Services, invoice dated March 25.

30 The company sold merchandise with a $1,048 cost for $2,220 on credit to IFM Company, invoice dated March 30.

31 The company reimbursed Santana Rey for business automobile mileage (400 miles at $0.32 per mile).

The following additional facts are available for preparing adjustments on March 31 prior to financial statement preparation:

a. The March 31 amount of computer supplies still available totals $2,005.

b. Three more months have expired since the company purchased its annual insurance policy at a $2,220 cost for 12 months of coverage.

c. Lyn Addie has not been paid for seven days of work at the rate of $125 per day.

d. Three months have passed since any prepaid rent has been transferred to expense. The monthly rent expense is $825.

e. Depreciation on the computer equipment for January 1 through March 31 is $1,250.

f. Depreciation on the office equipment for January 1 through March 31 is $400.

g. The March 31 amount of merchandise inventory still available totals $704.

Required

1. Prepare journal entries to record each of the January through March transactions.

2. Post the journal entries in part 1 to the accounts in the company's general ledger. (*Note:* Begin with the ledger's post-closing adjusted balances as at December 31, 2015.)

3. Prepare a partial work sheet consisting of the first six columns (similar to the one shown in Exhibit 5B.1) that includes the unadjusted trial balance, the March 31 adjustments (*a*) through (*g*), and the adjusted trial balance. Do not prepare closing entries and do not journalize the adjustments or post them to the ledger.

4. Prepare an income statement (from the adjusted trial balance in part 3) for the three months ended March 31, 2016. List all expenses without differentiating between selling expenses and general and administrative expenses.

5. Prepare a statement of changes in equity (from the adjusted trial balance in part 3) for the three months ended March 31, 2016.

6. Prepare a classified statement of financial position (from the adjusted trial balance) as at March 31, 2016.

Beyond the Numbers

REPORTING IN ACTION

A1

BTN 5-1   Refer to Nestlé's financial statements in Appendix A to answer the following.

Required

1. Assume that the amounts reported for inventories and cost of sales reflect items purchased in a form ready for resale. Compute the net cost of goods purchased for the financial year ended December 31, 2013.

2. Compute the current ratio and acid-test ratio as at December 31, 2013 and December 31, 2012 (Take quick assets as Cash and cash equivalents + Short-term investments + Trade and other receivables and round the ratios to one decimal place each). Interpret and comment on the ratio results. How does Nestlé compare to the industry average of 0.9 for the current ratio and 0.5 for the acid-test ratio?

Fast Forward

3. Access Nestlé's financial statements for financial years ending after December 31, 2013 from its Website (http://www.nestle.com/investors). Recompute and interpret the current ratio and acid-test ratio for these current financial years.

COMPARATIVE ANALYSIS

A2

BTN 5-2   Key comparative figures for both Adidas and Puma follow.

	Adidas (in EUR millions)		Puma (in EUR millions)	
	Current Year	**Prior Year**	**Current Year**	**Prior Year**
Net sales	14,492	14,883	2,985.3	3,270.7
Cost of goods sold	7,352	7,780	1,597.8	1,691.7

Required

1. Compute the gross margin amounts and the gross margin ratios for the two years shown for both companies.

2. Which company earns more in gross margin for each EUR of net sales?

3. Did the gross margin ratio improve or decline for these companies?

BTN 5-3 Ashton Martin is a student who plans to attend approximately four professional events a year at her college. Each event necessitates a financial outlay of $100 to $200 for a new suit and accessories. After incurring a major hit to her savings for the first event, Ashton developed a different approach. She buys the suit on credit the week before the event, wears it to the event, and returns it the next week to the store for a full refund on her charge card.

Required

1. Comment on the ethics exhibited by Ashton and possible consequences of her actions.

2. How does the merchandising company account for the suits that Ashton returns?

BTN 5-4 You are the financial officer for Music Plus, a retailer that sells goods for home entertainment needs. The business owner, Jamie Madsen, recently reviewed the annual financial statements you prepared and sent you an e-mail stating that he thinks you overstated net profit. He explains that although he has invested a great deal in security, he is sure shoplifting and other forms of inventory shrinkage have occurred, but he does not see any deduction for shrinkage on the income statement. The store uses a perpetual inventory system.

Required

Prepare a brief memorandum that responds to the owner's concerns.

BTN 5-5 Access L'Oréal's Website (www.loreal-finance.com/eng) to answer the following requirements:

Required

Prepare a table that reports the gross margin ratios for L'Oréal using the revenues and cost of goods sold data from L'Oréal's income statement for each of its most recent three years. Analyze and comment on the trend in its gross margin ratio.

BTN 5-6 Best Brands' general ledger and supplementary records at the end of its current period reveal the following.

Sales	$430,000	Merchandise inventory (beginning of period)	$ 49,000
Sales returns	18,000	Invoice cost of merchandise purchases	180,000
Sales discounts	6,600	Purchase discounts received	4,500
Cost of transportation-in	11,000	Purchase returns and allowances	5,500
Operating expenses	20,000	Merchandise inventory (end of period)	42,000

Required

1. *Each* member of the team is to assume responsibility for computing *one* of the following items. You are not to duplicate your teammates' work. Get any necessary amounts to compute your item from the appropriate teammate. Each member is to explain his or her computation to the team in preparation for reporting to the class.

   a. Net sales   **d.** Gross profit

   b. Total cost of merchandise purchases   **e.** Net profit

   c. Cost of goods sold

2. Check your net profit with the instructor. If correct, proceed to step 3.

3. Assume that a physical inventory count finds that actual ending inventory is $38,000. Discuss how this affects previously computed amounts in step 1.

Point: In teams of four, assign the same student *a* and *e*. Rotate teams for reporting on a different computation and the analysis in step 3.

ENTREPRENEURIAL DECISION

C1 C2 P4

BTN 5-7 Refer to the opening feature about TeddyThotz 'n' OneKind. Assume that Jon Goh and George Wong report current annual sales at approximately $500,000 and disclose the following income statement.

TeddyThotz 'n' OneKind Income Statement For Year Ended January 31, 2011	
Net sales	$500,000
Cost of sales	305,000
Expenses (other than cost of sales)	100,000
Net profit	$ 95,000

Jon and George sell to various individuals and retailers, ranging from small shops to large chains. Assume that they currently offer credit terms of 1/15, n/60, and ship FOB destination. To improve their cash flow, they are considering changing credit terms to 3/10, n/30. In addition, they propose to change shipping terms to FOB shipping point. They expect that the increase in discount rate will increase net sales by 9%, but the gross margin ratio (and ratio of cost of sales divided by net sales) is expected to remain unchanged. They also expect that delivery expenses will be zero under this proposal; thus, expenses other than cost of sales are expected to increase only 6%.

Required

1. Prepare a forecasted income statement for the year ended January 31, 2011, based on the proposal.
2. Based on the forecasted income statement alone (from your part 1 solution), do you recommend that Jon and George implement the new sales policies? Explain.
3. What else should Jon and George consider before deciding whether or not to implement the new policies? Explain.

HITTING THE ROAD

C1

Point: This activity complements the Ethics Challenge assignment.

BTN 5-8 Arrange an interview (in person or by phone) with the manager of a retail shop in a mall or in the downtown area of your community. Explain to the manager that you are a student studying merchandising activities and the accounting for sales returns and sales allowances. Ask the manager what the store policy is regarding returns. Also find out if sales allowances are ever negotiated with customers. Inquire whether management perceives that customers are abusing return policies and what actions management takes to counter potential abuses. Be prepared to discuss your findings in class.

GLOBAL DECISION

A2 P4

BTN 5-9 Apple, Nokia, and Samsung are competitors in the global marketplace. Key comparative figures for each company follow.

	Net Sales	Cost of Sales
Apple (in US$ millions)	156,508	87,846
Nokia (in EUR millions).......	13,372	9,917
Samsung (in KRW millions)	201,103,613	126,651,931

Required

Rank the three companies (highest to lowest) based on the gross margin ratio.

ANSWERS TO MULTIPLE CHOICE QUIZ

1. c; Gross profit = $550,000 − $193,000 = $357,000

2. d; ($4,500 − $250) × (100% − 2%) = $4,165

3. b; Net sales = $75,000 + $320,000 − $13,700 − $6,000 = $375,300

4. b; Acid-test ratio = $37,500/$50,000 = 0.750

5. a; Gross margin ratio = ($675,000 − $459,000)/$675,000 = 32%

6

Inventories and Cost of Sales

A Look Back

Chapter 5 focused on merchandising activities and how they are reported. We analyzed and recorded purchases and sales and explained accounting adjustments and closing for merchandisers.

A Look at This Chapter

This chapter emphasizes accounting for inventory. We describe methods for assigning costs to inventory and we explain the items and costs making up merchandise inventory. We also discuss methods of estimating and measuring inventory.

A Look Ahead

Chapter 7 emphasizes accounting information systems. We describe system principles, the system components, use of special journals and subsidiary ledgers, and technology-based systems.

Learning Objectives

CAP

CONCEPTUAL

C1 Identify the items making up merchandise inventory. (p. 226)

C2 Identify the costs of merchandise inventory. (p. 227)

ANALYTICAL

A1 Analyze the effects of inventory methods for both financial and tax reporting. (p. 233)

A2 Analyze the effects of inventory errors on current and future financial statements. (p. 236)

A3 Assess inventory management using both inventory turnover and days' sales in inventory. (p. 238)

PROCEDURAL

P1 Compute inventory in a perpetual system using the methods of specific identification, FIFO, and weighted average cost. (p. 228)

P2 Compute the lower of cost and net realizable value of inventory. (p. 234)

P3 *Appendix 6A*—Compute inventory in a periodic system using the methods of specific identification, FIFO, and weighted average cost. (p. 243)

P4 *Appendix 6B*—Apply both the retail inventory and gross profit methods to estimate inventory. (p. 247)

P5 *Appendix 6C*—Compute inventory in a perpetual system and a periodic system using LIFO. (p. 249)

"HABI Footwear seeks for efficient inventory management by regulating its production based on anticipated demand and consumer trends."—**BERNADEE UY, ALBERT GO, JANINE CHIONG, AND PAOLA SAVILLO** (front row, left to right)

Decision Insight

Weave to Walk Happy!

Habi means *weave* in Tagalog. **HABI Footwear** (**www.habifootwear.com**) is about a step towards a new lifestyle.

HABI Footwear is a social enterprise founded in the Philippines that makes fashionable and comfortable shoes from scrap textile and recycled rubber. Scrap textile is used for the upper parts of the shoes while the soles are made from recycled tyres. A partner community weaves the cloth used for the shoes while truck tyres are provided by a supplier. HABI Footwear aims to develop the partner community by providing them with a source of livelihood and, therefore, giving them an opportunity to escape poverty.

Paola Savillo, Albert Go, Bernadee Uy, and Janine Chiong—all thesis mates at Ateneo de Manila University—started the company as a school project in 2011. HABI Footwear bagged the top prize in the Fifth Business Development (BiD) Challenge Philippines, a business plan competition for small and medium enterprises.

The growing business poses a challenge to inventory stocking. Inventory decisions are made based on sales and the number of bazaars for the month. Insufficient stock of a particular size, bestsellers, number of bazaars in the month—all these are taken into account in inventory stocking.

HABI Footwear tries to avoid excess and insufficient inventory by regulating the procurement of raw materials and manufacturing of shoes based on anticipated demand. Excess inventory are sold at below cost at clearance sales and bazaars. Problems with insufficient inventory are usually in the form of lack of a particular design or particular size. This problem is addressed with willing customers waiting one to two weeks for the shoes to be delivered directly to their homes.

One of the pressing issues faced by HABI Footwear is keeping track of inventory. This is due to the absence of a physical office—where inventory can be stored—and a system for financial recording and tracking. Sometimes, this results in excess raw materials (rags) and insufficient capital to turn these into finished products (shoes). This problem is addressed by forecasting monthly sales and ordering an appropriate amount from the community.

Physical counts of the finished product (shoes) are conducted monthly. This enables the company to check any missing items, ensure stocks are in good condition, and that stocks are moved on a first-in, first-out basis.

Merchandisers' activities include the purchasing and reselling of merchandise. We explained accounting for merchandisers in Chapter 5, including that for purchases and sales. In this chapter, we extend the study and analysis of inventory by explaining the methods used to assign costs to merchandise inventory *and* to cost of goods sold. Retailers, wholesalers, and other merchandising companies that purchase products for resale use the principles and methods described here. Understanding inventory accounting helps in the analysis and interpretation of financial statements and helps people run their businesses.

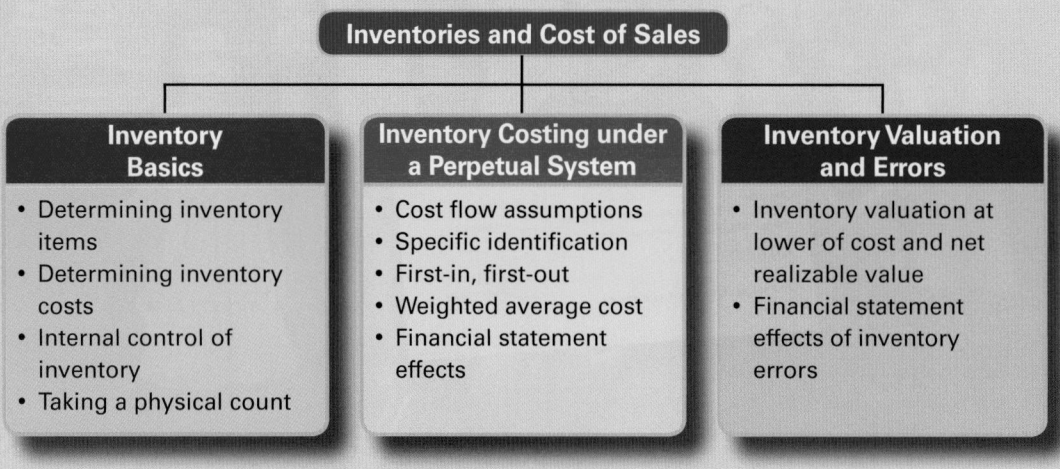

Inventories and Cost of Sales

Inventory Basics	Inventory Costing under a Perpetual System	Inventory Valuation and Errors
• Determining inventory items • Determining inventory costs • Internal control of inventory • Taking a physical count	• Cost flow assumptions • Specific identification • First-in, first-out • Weighted average cost • Financial statement effects	• Inventory valuation at lower of cost and net realizable value • Financial statement effects of inventory errors

IMPORTANCE OF ACCOUNTING

This section identifies the items and costs making up merchandise inventory. It also describes the importance of internal controls in taking a physical count of inventory.

Determining Inventory Items

 C1 Identify the items making up merchandise inventory.

Merchandise inventory includes all goods that a company owns and holds for sale. This rule holds regardless of where the goods are located when inventory is counted. Certain inventory items require special attention, including goods in transit, goods on consignment, and goods that are damaged or obsolete.

Goods in Transit Does a purchaser's inventory include goods in transit from a supplier? The answer is that if ownership has passed to the purchaser, the goods are included in the purchaser's inventory. We determine this by reviewing the shipping terms: *FOB destination* or *FOB shipping point*. If the purchaser is responsible for paying freight, ownership passes when goods are loaded on the transport vehicle. If the seller is responsible for paying freight, ownership passes when goods arrive at their destination.

Goods on Consignment Goods on consignment are goods shipped by the owner, called the **consignor**, to another party, the **consignee.** A consignee sells goods for the owner. The consignor continues to own the consigned goods and reports them in its inventory. **Upper Deck**, for instance, pays sports celebrities such as Tony Romo of the Dallas Cowboys to sign memorabilia, which are offered to shopping networks on consignment. Upper Deck, the consignor, must report these items in its inventory until sold.

Goods Damaged or Obsolete Damaged and obsolete (and deteriorated) goods are not counted in inventory if they cannot be sold. If these goods can be sold at a reduced price, they are included in inventory at an estimate of their **net realizable value.** Net realizable value is the estimated selling price in the ordinary course of business less the estimated costs of completion and the estimated costs necessary to make the sale. The period when damage or obsolescence (or deterioration) occurs is the period when the loss in value is reported.

Decision Insight

A wireless portable device with a two-way radio allows clerks to quickly record inventory by scanning bar codes and to instantly send and receive inventory data. It gives managers access to up-to-date information on inventory and its location. ∎

Determining Inventory Costs

Merchandise inventory includes costs of expenditures necessary, directly or indirectly, to bring an item to a salable condition and location. This means that the cost of an inventory item includes its invoice cost minus any discount, and plus any incidental costs necessary to put it in a place and condition for sale. Incidental costs can include import duties, freight, storage, insurance, and costs incurred in an aging process (for example, aging wine or cheese).

Accounting principles prescribe that incidental costs be added to inventory. However, some companies cite materiality (a feature of relevance which is a fundamental qualitative characteristic in the Conceptual Framework) to avoid assigning some incidental costs of acquiring merchandise to inventory. Instead, they expense them when incurred. These companies argue that those incidental costs are immaterial.

C2 Identify the costs of merchandise inventory.

Internal Controls and Taking a Physical Count

The Inventory account under a perpetual system is updated for each purchase and sale, but events can cause the Inventory account balance to differ from the actual inventory available. Such events include theft, loss, damage, and errors. Thus, nearly all companies take a *physical count of inventory* at least once each year—informally called *taking an inventory*. This often occurs at the end of a financial year or when inventory amounts are low. This physical count is used to adjust the Inventory account balance to the actual inventory available.

A company applies internal controls when taking a physical count of inventory that usually include the following:

- *Prenumbered inventory tickets* are prepared and distributed to the *counters*—each ticket must be accounted for.
- Counters of inventory are assigned and do not include those responsible for inventory.
- Counters confirm the validity of inventory, including its existence, amount, and quality.
- A second count is taken by a different counter.
- A manager confirms that all inventories are ticketed once, and only once.

Point: The Inventory account is a controlling account for the inventory subsidiary ledger. This *subsidiary ledger* contains a separate record (units and costs) for each separate product, and it can be in electronic or paper form. Subsidiary records assist managers in planning and monitoring inventory.

Quick Check
Answers — p. 252

1. Why are incidental costs such as import duties, freight, storage, and insurance added to the cost of inventory?
2. If **Skechers** sells goods to **Target** with terms FOB shipping point, which company reports these goods in its inventory while they are in transit?
3. An art gallery purchases a painting for $11,400 on terms FOB shipping point. Additional costs in obtaining and offering the artwork for sale include $130 for transportation-in, $150 for import duties, $100 for insurance during shipment, $180 for advertising, $400 for framing, and $800 for office salaries. For computing inventory, what cost is assigned to the painting?

INVENTORY COSTING UNDER A PERPETUAL SYSTEM

Accounting for inventory affects both the statement of financial position and the income statement. Management decisions in accounting for inventory involve the following:

- Items included in inventory and their costs.
- Costing method (specific identification, FIFO, or weighted average cost).

- Inventory system (perpetual or periodic).
- Use of costs or net realizable values.

The first point was explained on the prior two pages. The second and third points will be addressed now. The fourth point is the focus at the end of this chapter. Decisions on these points affect the reported amounts for inventory, cost of goods sold, gross profit, net profit, current assets, and other accounts.

One of the most important issues in accounting for inventory is determining the per unit costs assigned to inventory items. When all units are purchased at the same unit cost, this process is simple. When identical items are purchased at different costs, however, a question arises as to which amounts to record in cost of goods sold and which amounts remain in inventory.

Three methods are commonly used to assign costs to inventory and to cost of goods sold: (1) specific identification; (2) first-in, first-out; and (3) weighted average cost. Each method assumes a particular pattern for how costs flow through inventory. Each of these three methods is acceptable whether or not the actual physical flow of goods follows the cost flow assumption. Physical flow of goods depends on the type of product and the way it is stored. (Perishable goods such as fresh fruit demand that a business attempt to sell them in a first-in, first-out physical flow. Other products such as crude oil and minerals such as coal, gold, and decorative stone can be sold in a last-in, first-out physical flow.) **Physical flow and cost flow need not be the same.**

Decision Insight

For inventory accounting, U.S. GAAP allows the use of last-in, first-out (LIFO), but **IFRS** does not (currently) allow use of LIFO. As the U.S. GAAP and **IFRS** convergence project progresses, this prohibition may or may not persist. LIFO is discussed in Appendix 6C. ■

Inventory Cost Flow Assumptions

P1 Compute inventory in a perpetual system using the methods of specific identification, FIFO, and weighted average cost.

This section introduces inventory cost flow assumptions. For this purpose, assume that three identical units are purchased separately at the following three dates and costs: May 1 at $45, May 3 at $65, and May 6 at $70. One unit is then sold on May 7 for $100. Exhibit 6.1 gives a visual layout of the flow of costs to either the gross profit section of the income statement or the inventory reported on the statement of financial position for FIFO and weighted average cost.

Point: It is helpful to recall the cost flow of inventory from Exhibit 5.4.

(1) *FIFO assumes costs flow in the order incurred.* The unit purchased on May 1 for $45 is the earliest cost incurred—it is sent to cost of goods sold on the income statement first. The remaining two units ($65 and $70) are reported in inventory on the statement of financial position.

(2) *Weighted average cost assumes costs flow at an average of the costs available.* The units available at the May 7 sale average $60 in cost, computed as ($45 + $65 + $70)/3. One unit's $60 average cost is sent to cost of goods sold on the income statement. The remaining two units' average costs are reported in inventory at $120 on the statement of financial position.

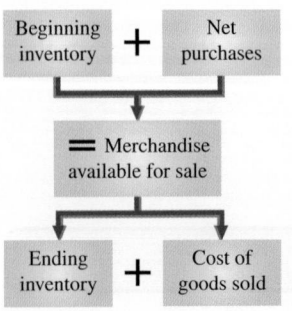

Cost flow assumptions can markedly impact gross profit and inventory numbers. Exhibit 6.1 shows that gross profit as a percent of net sales can change from 55% to 40% due to nothing else but the cost flow assumption.

The following sections on inventory costing use the perpetual system. Appendix 6A uses the periodic system. An instructor can choose to cover either one or both systems. If the perpetual system is skipped, then read Appendix 6A and return to the section titled "Valuing Inventory at Lower of Cost and NRV and The Effects of Inventory Errors" on page 241.

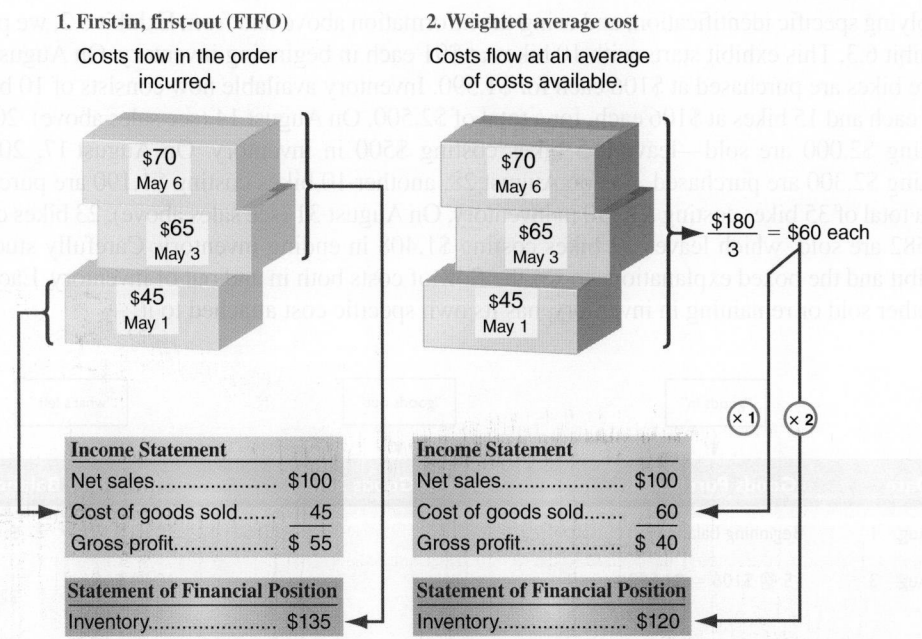

EXHIBIT 6.1

Cost Flow Assumptions

Inventory Costing Illustration

This section provides a comprehensive illustration of inventory costing methods. We use information from Trekking, a sporting goods store. Among its many products, Trekking carries one type of mountain bike whose sales are directed at resorts that provide inexpensive mountain bikes for complimentary guest use. Its customers usually purchase in amounts of 10 or more bikes. We use Trekking's data from August. Its mountain bike (unit) inventory at the beginning of August and its purchases and sales during August are shown in Exhibit 6.2. It ends August with 12 bikes remaining in inventory.

EXHIBIT 6.2

Purchases and Sales of Goods

Date	Activity	Units Acquired at Cost	Units Sold at Retail	Unit Inventory
Aug. 1	Beginning inventory	10 units @ $ 91 = $ 910		10 units
Aug. 3	Purchases	15 units @ $106 = $ 1,590		25 units
Aug. 14	Sales		20 units @ $130	5 units
Aug. 17	Purchases	20 units @ $115 = $ 2,300		25 units
Aug. 28	Purchases	10 units @ $119 = $ 1,190		35 units
Aug. 31	Sales		23 units @ $150	12 units
	Total	55 units $5,990	43 units	

Trekking uses the perpetual inventory system, which means that its merchandise inventory account is continually updated to reflect purchases and sales. (**Appendix 6A describes the assignment of costs to inventory using a periodic system.**) Regardless of what inventory method or system is used, cost of goods available for sale must be allocated between cost of goods sold and ending inventory.

Specific Identification

When each item in inventory can be identified with a specific purchase and invoice, we can use **specific identification** to assign costs. We also need sales records that identify exactly which items were sold and when. Trekking's internal documents reveal the following specific unit sales:

August 14   Sold 8 bikes costing $91 each and 12 bikes costing $106 each
August 31   Sold 2 bikes costing $91 each, 3 bikes costing $106 each, 15 bikes costing $115 each, and 3 bikes costing $119 each

Point: Given the proliferation of computer technology which facilitates perpetual recording, the perpetual inventory system is now the most dominant system for businesses.

Point: Cost of goods sold plus ending inventory equals cost of goods available for sale.

Applying specific identification, and using the information above and from Exhibit 6.2, we prepare Exhibit 6.3. This exhibit starts with 10 bikes at $91 each in beginning inventory. On August 3, 15 more bikes are purchased at $106 each for $1,590. Inventory available now consists of 10 bikes at $91 each and 15 bikes at $106 each, for a total of $2,500. On August 14 (see sales above), 20 bikes costing $2,000 are sold—leaving 5 bikes costing $500 in inventory. On August 17, 20 bikes costing $2,300 are purchased, and on August 28, another 10 bikes costing $1,190 are purchased, for a total of 35 bikes costing $3,990 in inventory. On August 31 (see sales above), 23 bikes costing $2,582 are sold, which leaves 12 bikes costing $1,408 in ending inventory. Carefully study this exhibit and the boxed explanations to see the flow of costs both in and out of inventory. Each unit, whether sold or remaining in inventory, has its own specific cost attached to it.

EXHIBIT 6.3

Specific Identification
Computations

For the 20 units sold on August 14, the company specifically identified that 8 of those had cost $91 and 12 had cost $106.

For the 23 units sold on August 31, the company specifically identified each bike sold and its acquisition cost from prior purchases.

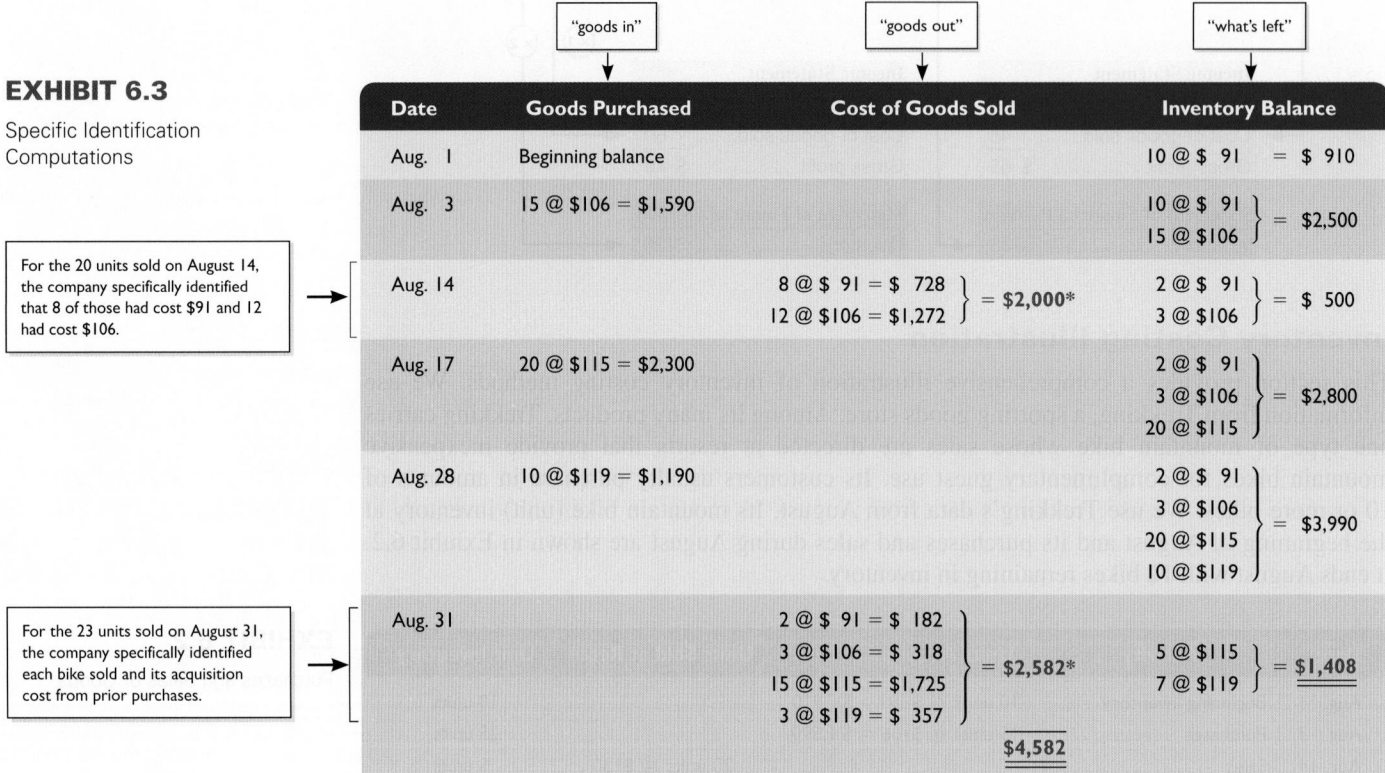

Date	Goods Purchased	Cost of Goods Sold	Inventory Balance
Aug. 1	Beginning balance		10 @ $ 91 = $ 910
Aug. 3	15 @ $106 = $1,590		10 @ $ 91 ⎫ = $2,500 15 @ $106 ⎭
Aug. 14		8 @ $ 91 = $ 728 ⎫ = $2,000* 12 @ $106 = $1,272 ⎭	2 @ $ 91 ⎫ = $ 500 3 @ $106 ⎭
Aug. 17	20 @ $115 = $2,300		2 @ $ 91 ⎫ 3 @ $106 ⎬ = $2,800 20 @ $115 ⎭
Aug. 28	10 @ $119 = $1,190		2 @ $ 91 ⎫ 3 @ $106 ⎪ 20 @ $115 ⎬ = $3,990 10 @ $119 ⎭
Aug. 31		2 @ $ 91 = $ 182 ⎫ 3 @ $106 = $ 318 ⎪ = $2,582* 15 @ $115 = $1,725 ⎬ 3 @ $119 = $ 357 ⎭ $4,582	5 @ $115 ⎫ = $1,408 7 @ $119 ⎭

* Identification of items sold (and their costs) is obtained from internal documents that track each unit from its purchase to its sale.

When using specific identification, Trekking's cost of goods sold reported on the income statement totals **$4,582**, the sum of $2,000 and $2,582 from the third column of Exhibit 6.3. Trekking's ending inventory reported on the statement of financial position is **$1,408**, which is the final inventory balance from the fourth column of Exhibit 6.3.

All purchases and sales are made on credit. The journal entries for Exhibit 6.3 follow (the colored boldface numbers are those impacted by the cost flow assumption).

Purchases

Aug. 3	Merchandise Inventory	1,590	
	Accounts Payable		1,590
17	Merchandise Inventory	2,300	
	Accounts Payable		2,300
28	Merchandise Inventory	1,190	
	Accounts Payable		1,190

Sales

Aug. 14	Accounts Receivable	2,600	
	Sales		2,600
14	Cost of Goods Sold	2,000	
	Merchandise Inventory		2,000
31	Accounts Receivable	3,450	
	Sales		3,450
31	Cost of Goods Sold	2,582	
	Merchandise Inventory		2,582

First-In, First-Out

The **first-in, first-out (FIFO)** method of assigning costs to both inventory and cost of goods sold assumes that inventory items are sold in the order acquired. When sales occur, the costs of the earliest units acquired are charged to cost of goods sold. This leaves the costs from the most recent purchases in ending inventory. Use of FIFO for computing the cost of inventory and cost of goods sold is shown in Exhibit 6.4.

This exhibit starts with beginning inventory of 10 bikes at $91 each. On August 3, 15 more bikes costing $106 each are bought for $1,590. Inventory now consists of 10 bikes at $91 each and 15 bikes at $106 each, for a total of $2,500. On August 14, 20 bikes are sold—applying FIFO, the first 10 sold cost $91 each and the next 10 sold cost $106 each, for a total cost of $1,970. This leaves 5 bikes costing $106 each, or $530, in inventory. On August 17, 20 bikes costing $2,300 are purchased, and on August 28, another 10 bikes costing $1,190 are purchased, for a total of 35 bikes costing $4,020 in inventory. On August 31, 23 bikes are sold—applying FIFO, the first 5 bikes sold cost $530 and the next 18 sold cost $2,070, which leaves 12 bikes costing $1,420 in ending inventory.

Point: The "Goods Purchased" column is identical for all methods. Data are taken from Exhibit 6.2.

Date	Goods Purchased	Cost of Goods Sold	Inventory Balance
Aug. 1	Beginning balance		10 @ $ 91 = $ 910
Aug. 3	15 @ $106 = $1,590		10 @ $ 91 ⎫ = $2,500 15 @ $106 ⎭
Aug. 14		10 @ $ 91 = $ 910 ⎫ = $1,970 10 @ $106 = $1,060 ⎭	5 @ $106 = $ 530
Aug. 17	20 @ $115 = $2,300		5 @ $106 ⎫ = $2,830 20 @ $115 ⎭
Aug. 28	10 @ $119 = $1,190		5 @ $106 ⎫ 20 @ $115 ⎬ = $4,020 10 @ $119 ⎭
Aug. 31		5 @ $106 = $ 530 ⎫ = $2,600 18 @ $115 = $2,070 ⎭ $4,570	2 @ $115 ⎫ = $1,420 10 @ $119 ⎭

EXHIBIT 6.4

FIFO Computations—Perpetual System

For the 20 units sold on August 14, the first 10 sold are assigned the earliest cost of $91 (from beginning balance). The next 10 sold are assigned the next earliest cost of $106.

For the 23 units sold on August 31, the first 5 sold are assigned the earliest available cost of $106 (from August 3 purchase). The next 18 sold are assigned the next earliest cost of $115 (from August 17 purchase).

Trekking's FIFO cost of goods sold reported on its income statement (reflecting the 43 units sold) is **$4,570** ($1,970 + $2,600), and its ending inventory reported on the statement of financial position (reflecting the 12 units unsold) is **$1,420**.

All purchases and sales are made on credit. The journal entries for Exhibit 6.4 follow (the colored boldface numbers are those impacted by the cost flow assumption).

Point: Under FIFO, a unit sold is assigned the earliest (oldest) cost from inventory. This leaves the most recent costs in ending inventory.

Purchases

Aug. 3	Merchandise Inventory	1,590	
	Accounts Payable		1,590
17	Merchandise Inventory	2,300	
	Accounts Payable		2,300
28	Merchandise Inventory	1,190	
	Accounts Payable		1,190

Sales

Aug. 14	Accounts Receivable	2,600	
	Sales		2,600
14	Cost of Goods Sold	1,970	
	Merchandise Inventory		1,970
31	Accounts Receivable	3,450	
	Sales		3,450
31	Cost of Goods Sold	2,600	
	Merchandise Inventory		2,600

Weighted Average Cost

The **weighted average cost** (also called **average cost**) method of assigning cost requires that we use the weighted average cost per unit of inventory at the time of each sale. Weighted average cost per unit at the time of each sale equals the cost of goods available for sale divided by the units available. The results using weighted average cost (WAC) for Trekking are shown in Exhibit 6.5.

EXHIBIT 6.5

Weighted Average
Computations—Perpetual System

Date	Goods Purchased	Cost of Goods Sold	Inventory Balance	
Aug. 1	Beginning balance		10 @ $ 91	= $ 910
Aug. 3	15 @ $106 = $1,590		10 @ $ 91 ⎫ 15 @ $106 ⎭	= $2,500 (or $100 per unit)ᵃ
Aug. 14		20 @ $100 = $2,000	5 @ $100	= $ 500 (or $100 per unit)ᵇ
Aug. 17	20 @ $115 = $2,300		5 @ $100 ⎫ 20 @ $115 ⎭	= $2,800 (or $112 per unit)ᶜ
Aug. 28	10 @ $119 = $1,190		5 @ $100 ⎫ 20 @ $115 ⎬ 10 @ $119 ⎭	= $3,990 (or $114 per unit)ᵈ
Aug. 31		23 @ $114 = $2,622	12 @ $114	= $1,368 (or $114 per unit)ᵉ
		$4,622		

> For the 20 units sold on August 14, the cost assigned is the $100 *average cost* per unit from the inventory balance column at the time of sale.

> For the 23 units sold on August 31, the cost assigned is the $114 *average cost* per unit from the inventory balance column at the time of sale.

ᵃ $100 per unit = ($2,500 inventory balance ÷ 25 units in inventory).
ᵇ $100 per unit = ($500 inventory balance ÷ 5 units in inventory).
ᶜ $112 per unit = ($2,800 inventory balance ÷ 25 units in inventory).
ᵈ $114 per unit = ($3,990 inventory balance ÷ 35 units in inventory).
ᵉ $114 per unit = ($1,368 inventory balance ÷ 12 units in inventory).

This exhibit starts with beginning inventory of 10 bikes at $91 each. On August 3, 15 more bikes costing $106 each are bought for $1,590. Inventory now consists of 10 bikes at $91 each and 15 bikes at $106 each, for a total of $2,500. The average cost per bike for that inventory is $100, computed as $2,500/(10 bikes + 15 bikes). On August 14, 20 bikes are sold—applying WAC, the 20 sold are assigned the $100 average cost, for a total cost of $2,000. This leaves 5 bikes with an average cost of $100 each, or $500, in inventory. On August 17, 20 bikes costing $2,300 are purchased, and on August 28, another 10 bikes costing $1,190 are purchased, for a total of 35 bikes costing $3,990 in inventory at August 28. The average cost per bike for the August 28 inventory is $114, computed as $3,990/(5 bikes + 20 bikes +10 bikes). On August 31, 23 bikes are sold—applying WAC, the 23 sold are assigned the $114 average cost, for a total cost of $2,622. This leaves 12 bikes costing $1,368 in ending inventory.

Trekking's cost of goods sold reported on the income statement (reflecting the 43 units sold) is **$4,622** ($2,000 + $2,622), and its ending inventory reported on the statement of financial position (reflecting the 12 units unsold) is **$1,368**.

All purchases and sales are made on credit. The journal entries for Exhibit 6.5 follow (the colored boldface numbers are those impacted by the cost flow assumption).

> **Point:** Under weighted average cost, a unit sold is assigned the average cost of all items currently available for sale at the date of each sale.

Purchases			
Aug. 3	Merchandise Inventory	1,590	
	Accounts Payable		1,590
17	Merchandise Inventory	2,300	
	Accounts Payable		2,300
28	Merchandise Inventory	1,190	
	Accounts Payable		1,190

Sales			
Aug. 14	Accounts Receivable	2,600	
	Sales		2,600
14	Cost of Goods Sold	**2,000**	
	Merchandise Inventory		**2,000**
31	Accounts Receivable	3,450	
	Sales		3,450
31	Cost of Goods Sold	**2,622**	
	Merchandise Inventory		**2,622**

This completes computations under the three most common perpetual inventory costing methods. Advances in technology have greatly reduced the cost of a perpetual inventory system. Many companies now ask whether they can afford *not* to have a perpetual inventory system because timely access to inventory information is a competitive advantage and it can help reduce the amount of inventory, which reduces costs.

Financial Statement Effects of Costing Methods

When purchase prices do not change, each inventory costing method assigns the same cost amounts to inventory and to cost of goods sold. When purchase prices are different, however, the methods nearly always assign different cost amounts. We show these differences in Exhibit 6.6 using Trekking's data.

A1 Analyze the effects of inventory methods for both financial and tax reporting.

EXHIBIT 6.6

Financial Statement Effects of Inventory Costing Methods

TREKKING COMPANY For Month Ended August 31			
	Specific Identification	FIFO	Weighted Average Cost
Income Statement			
Sales	$ 6,050	$ 6,050	$ 6,050
Cost of goods sold	4,582	4,570	4,622
Gross profit	1,468	1,480	1,428
Expenses	450	450	450
Profit before tax	1,018	1,030	978
Income tax expense (30%)	305	309	293
Net profit	$ 713	$ 721	$ 685
Statement of financial position			
Inventory	$1,408	$1,420	$1,368

This exhibit reveals two important results. First, when purchase costs *regularly rise*, as in Trekking's case, the following occurs:

- FIFO assigns the lower amount to cost of goods sold—yielding the higher gross profit and net profit.
- Weighted average cost yields the higher cost of goods sold and lower profit as it averages the recent higher costs with the earlier lower costs.
- Specific identification always yields results that depend on which units are sold.

Second, when costs *regularly decline*, the reverse occurs, namely, FIFO gives the higher cost of goods sold—yielding the lower gross profit and income. However, weighted average cost then gives the lower cost of goods sold—yielding the higher gross profit and net profit.

All three inventory costing methods are acceptable. However, a company must disclose the inventory method it uses in its financial statements or notes. Each method offers certain advantages as follows:

- FIFO assigns an amount to inventory on the statement of financial position that approximates its current cost; it also mimics the actual flow of goods for most businesses.
- Weighted average cost tends to smooth out erratic changes in costs.
- Specific identification exactly matches the costs of items with the revenues they generate.

Point: Managers prefer FIFO when costs are rising *and* incentives exist to report higher net profit for reasons such as bonus plans, job security, and reputation.

Decision Maker   Answer — p. 252

Financial Planner   One of your clients asks if the inventory account of a company using FIFO needs any "adjustments" for analysis purposes in light of recent inflation. What is your advice? Does your advice depend on changes in the costs of these inventories? ■

Tax Effects of Costing Methods   Trekking's income statement in Exhibit 6.6 includes income tax expense (at a rate of 30%) because it was formed as a corporation. Since inventory costs affect net profit, they have potential tax effects. Trekking gains a temporary tax advantage by using weighted average cost.

Consistency in Using Costing Methods

The IASB's Conceptual Framework states that comparability is an enhancing qualitative characteristic of financial information. Comparability enables users to identify and understand similarities in—and differences among—items. Related to comparability is consistency which refers to the use of the same methods for the same items, either from period to period within a reporting entity or in a single period across entities. Comparability is the goal; consistency helps to achieve that goal. When a change from one method to another will improve its financial reporting, the entity can do so but the notes to the financial statements must report the type of change, its justification, and its effect on profit.

Consistency does *not* require a company to use one method exclusively. For example, it can use different methods to value different categories of inventory.

Decision Ethics   Answer — p. 252

Inventory Manager   Your compensation as inventory manager includes a bonus plan based on gross profit. Your superior asks your opinion on changing the inventory costing method from FIFO to weighted average cost. Since costs are expected to continue to rise, your superior predicts that weighted average cost would match higher current costs against sales, thereby lowering taxable profit (and gross profit). What do you recommend? ■

Quick Check   Answers — p. 252

4. Describe one advantage for each of the inventory costing methods: specific identification, FIFO, and weighted average cost.

5. When costs are rising, which method reports higher net profit—weighted average cost or FIFO?

6. When costs are rising, what effect does weighted average cost have on a statement of financial position compared to FIFO?

VALUING INVENTORY AT LOWER OF COST AND NRV AND THE EFFECTS OF INVENTORY ERRORS

Lower of Cost and Net Realizable Value

P2 Compute the lower of cost and net realizable value of inventory.

We explained how to assign costs to ending inventory and cost of goods sold using one of three costing methods (FIFO, weighted average cost, or specific identification). However, **IAS 2** requires that inventory be reported at the net realizable value of inventory when the net realizable value is lower than cost. Merchandise inventory is then said to be reported on the statement of financial position at the **lower of cost and net realizable value (NRV).** This prevents the cost of inventories or assets from being overstated on the statement of financial position. Overstated assets will paint an overly optimistic picture to users of financial statements, which can result in inappropriate economic decisions.

Computing the Lower of Cost and Net Realizable Value   Net realizable value (NRV) is the estimated selling price in the ordinary course of business less the estimated costs of completion and the estimated costs necessary to make the sale. The practice of writing inventories down below cost to NRV is consistent with the view that assets should not be carried in excess of amounts expected to be realized from their sale or use.

A decline in NRV reflects a loss of value in inventory. When the recorded cost of inventory is higher than the NRV, a loss is recognized. When the recorded cost is lower, no adjustment is made.

IAS 2 requires that inventories be written down to net realizable value item by item but allows some circumstances where it may be appropriate to group similar or related items. With the increasing application of technology and inventory tracking, companies increasingly apply lower of cost and NRV to each individual item separately. Accordingly, we show this method only. To illustrate, we apply it to the ending inventory of a motorsports retailer in Exhibit 6.7.

Point: Advances in technology encourage the individual-item approach for Lower of cost and NRV.

EXHIBIT 6.7

Lower of Cost and Net Realizable Value Computations

Inventory Items	Units	Per Unit Cost	Per Unit NRV	Total Cost	Total NRV	Lower of Cost and NRV Applied to Items
Cycles						
Roadster	20	$8,000	$7,000	$160,000	$140,000	$ 140,000
Sprint	10	5,000	6,000	50,000	60,000	50,000
Off-Road						
Trax-4	8	5,000	6,500	40,000	52,000	40,000
Blazer	5	9,000	7,000	45,000	35,000	35,000
Totals				$295,000		$265,000

$140,000 is the lower of $160,000 or $140,000

Lower of Cost and NRV Applied to Individual Items When lower of cost and NRV is applied to individual items of inventory, the number of comparisons equals the number of items. For Roadster, $140,000 is the lower of the $160,000 cost and the $140,000 NRV. For Sprint, $50,000 is the lower of the $50,000 cost and the $60,000 NRV. For Trax-4, $40,000 is the lower of the $40,000 cost and the $52,000 NRV. For Blazer, $35,000 is the lower of the $45,000 cost and the $35,000 NRV. This yields a $265,000 reported inventory, computed from $140,000 for Roadster plus $50,000 for Sprint plus $40,000 for Trax-4 plus $35,000 for Blazer. Therefore, the final total of $265,000 is a combination of cost and NRV figures, thus the "and" in lower of cost and NRV.

Point: Net realizable value for inventories may not equal fair value less costs to sell. Fair value is the price that would be received to sell an asset or paid to transfer a liability in an orderly transaction between market participants at the measurement date.

Recording the Lower of Cost and NRV Inventory must be adjusted downward when NRV is less than cost. To illustrate, if lower of cost and NRV is applied to the individual items of inventory in Exhibit 6.7, the Merchandise Inventory account must be adjusted from the $295,000 recorded cost down to the $265,000 NRV amount as follows.

Cost of Goods Sold	30,000	
Merchandise Inventory		30,000
To adjust inventory cost to NRV.		

IAS 2 allows reversals of those write-downs up to the original acquisition cost but not beyond. This occurs, for example, when an item of inventory that is carried at net realizable value—because its selling price has declined—is still on hand in a subsequent period and its selling price has increased. The amount of any reversal of any write-down shall be recognized as a reduction in the amount of inventories recognized as an expense in the period in which the reversal occurs. However, the reversal is limited to the amount of the original write-down.

Financial Statement Effects of Inventory Errors

A2 Analyze the effects of inventory errors on current and future financial statements.

Companies must take care in both taking a physical count of inventory and in assigning a cost to it. An inventory error causes misstatements in cost of goods sold, gross profit, net profit, current assets, and equity. It also causes misstatements in the next period's statements because ending inventory of one period is the beginning inventory of the next. As we consider the financial statement effects in this section, it is helpful if we recall the following *inventory relation*.

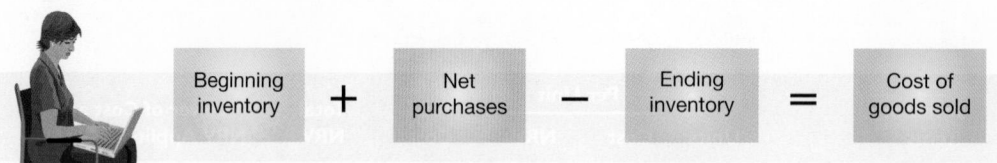

Income Statement Effects Exhibit 6.8 shows the effects of inventory errors on key amounts in the current and next periods' income statements. Let's look at row 1 and year 1. We see that understating ending inventory overstates cost of goods sold. This can be seen from the above inventory relation where we subtract a smaller ending inventory amount in computing cost of goods sold. Then a higher cost of goods sold yields a lower profit.

To understand year 2 of row 1, remember that an understated ending inventory for year 1 becomes an understated beginning inventory for year 2. Using the above inventory relation, we see that if beginning inventory is understated, then cost of goods sold is understated (because we are starting with a smaller amount). A lower cost of goods sold yields a higher profit.

Turning to overstatements, let's look at row 2 and year 1. If ending inventory is overstated, we use the inventory relation to see that cost of goods sold is understated. A lower cost of goods sold yields a higher profit.

For year 2 of row 2, we again recall that an overstated ending inventory for year 1 becomes an overstated beginning inventory for year 2. If beginning inventory is overstated, we use the inventory relation to see that cost of goods sold is overstated. A higher cost of goods sold yields a lower profit.

EXHIBIT 6.8

Effects of Inventory Errors on the Income Statement

| | Year 1 | | Year 2 | |
Ending Inventory	Cost of Goods Sold	Net Profit	Cost of Goods Sold	Net Profit
Understated ↓	Overstated ↑	Understated ↓	Understated ↓	Overstated ↑
Overstated* ↑	Understated ↓	Overstated ↑	Overstated ↑	Understated ↓

* This error is less likely under a perpetual system because it implies more inventory than is recorded (or less shrinkage than expected). Factors that contribute to inventory shrinkage are breakage, loss, deterioration, decay, and theft. Management will normally follow up and discover and correct this error before it impacts any accounts.

To illustrate, consider an inventory error for a company with $100,000 in sales for each of the years 2010, 2011, and 2012. If this company maintains a steady $20,000 inventory level during this period and makes $60,000 in purchases in each of these years, its cost of goods sold is $60,000 and its gross profit is $40,000 each year.

Ending Inventory Understated—Year 1 Assume that this company errs in computing its 2010 ending inventory and reports $16,000 instead of the correct amount of $20,000. The effects of this error are shown in Exhibit 6.9. The $4,000 understatement of 2010 ending inventory causes a $4,000 overstatement in 2010 cost of goods sold and a $4,000 understatement in both gross profit and net profit for 2010. We see that these effects match the effects predicted in Exhibit 6.8.

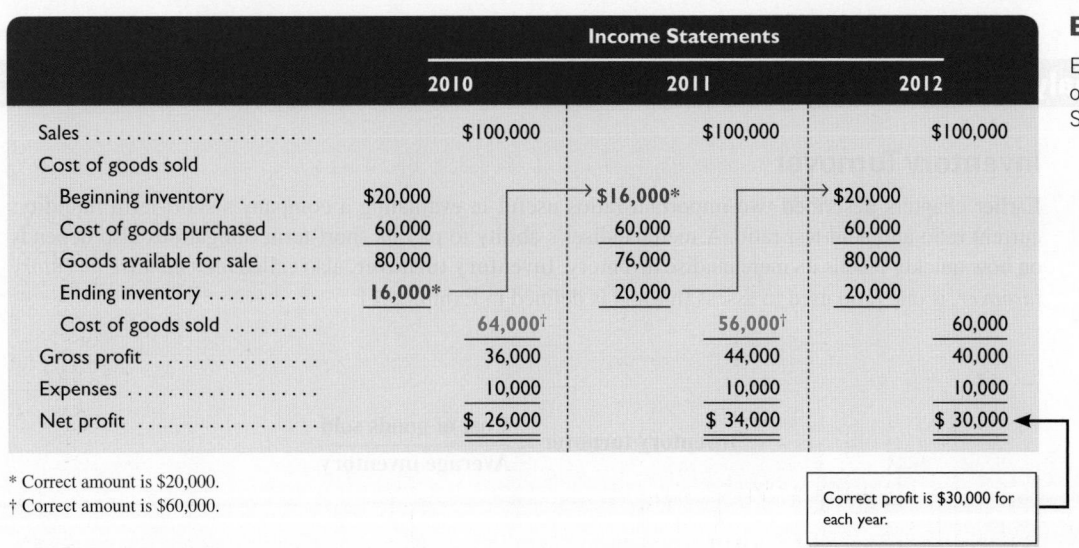

EXHIBIT 6.9

Effects of Inventory Errors on Three Periods' Income Statements

* Correct amount is $20,000.
† Correct amount is $60,000.

Ending Inventory Understated—Year 2   The 2010 understated ending inventory becomes the 2011 understated *beginning* inventory. We see in Exhibit 6.9 that this error causes an understatement in 2011 cost of goods sold and a $4,000 overstatement in both gross profit and net profit for 2011.

Ending Inventory Understated—Year 3   Exhibit 6.9 shows that the 2010 ending inventory error affects only that period and the next. It does not affect 2012 results or any period thereafter. An inventory error is said to be *self-correcting* because it always yields an offsetting error in the next period. This does not reduce the severity of inventory errors. Managers, lenders, owners, and others make important decisions from analysis of profit and costs.

We can also do an analysis of beginning inventory errors. The income statement effects are the opposite of those for ending inventory.

Statement of Financial Position Effects   Statement of financial position effects of an inventory error can be seen by considering the accounting equation: Assets = Liabilities + Equity. For example, understating ending inventory understates both current and total assets. An understatement in ending inventory also yields an understatement in equity because of the understatement in net profit. Exhibit 6.10 shows the effects of inventory errors on the current period's statement of financial position amounts.

Example: If 2010 ending inventory in Exhibit 6.9 is overstated by $3,000 (not understated by $4,000), what is the effect on cost of goods sold, gross profit, assets, and equity? *Answer:* Cost of goods sold is understated by $3,000 in 2010 and overstated by $3,000 in 2011. Gross profit and net profit are overstated in 2010 and understated in 2011. Assets and equity are overstated in 2010.

Point: A former internal auditor at **Coca-Cola** alleges that just before midnight at a prior calendar year-end, fully loaded Coke trucks were ordered to drive about 2 feet away from the loading dock so that Coke could record millions of dollars in extra sales.

Ending Inventory	Assets	Equity
Understated ↓	Understated ↓	Understated ↓
Overstated ↑	Overstated ↑	Overstated ↑

EXHIBIT 6.10

Effects of Inventory Errors on Current Period's Statement of Financial Position

Quick Check   Answers — p. 252

7. A company takes a physical count of inventory at the end of 2010 and finds that ending inventory is understated by $10,000. Would this error cause cost of goods sold to be overstated or understated in 2010? In year 2011? If so, by how much?

8. Use lower of cost and NRV applied separately to the following individual items to compute ending inventory.

Product	Units	Unit Recorded Cost	Unit NRV
A	20	$ 6	$ 5
B	40	9	8
C	10	12	15

Decision Analysis ▣ ▣ ▣   Inventory Turnover and Days' Sales in Inventory

Inventory Turnover

A3 Assess inventory management using both inventory turnover and days' sales in inventory.

Earlier chapters described two important ratios useful in evaluating a company's short-term liquidity: current ratio and acid-test ratio. A merchandiser's ability to pay its short-term obligations also depends on how quickly it sells its merchandise inventory. **Inventory turnover**, also called *merchandise inventory turnover*, is one ratio used to assess this and is defined in Exhibit 6.11.

EXHIBIT 6.11

Inventory Turnover

$$\text{Inventory turnover} = \frac{\text{Cost of goods sold}}{\text{Average inventory}}$$

Point: We must take care when comparing turnover ratios across companies that use different costing methods (such as FIFO and weighted average cost).

This ratio reveals how many *times* a company turns over (sells) its inventory during a period. If a company's inventory greatly varies within a year, average inventory amounts can be computed from interim periods such as quarters or months.

Users apply inventory turnover to help analyze short-term liquidity and to assess whether management is doing a good job controlling the amount of inventory available. A low ratio compared to that of competitors suggests inefficient use of assets. The company may be holding more inventory than it needs to support its sales volume. Similarly, a very high ratio compared to that of competitors suggests inventory might be too low. This can cause lost sales if customers must back-order merchandise. Inventory turnover has no simple rule except to say *a high ratio is preferable provided inventory is adequate to meet demand.*

Days' Sales in Inventory

Point: Inventory turnover is higher and days' sales in inventory is lower for industries such as foods and other perishable products. The reverse holds for nonperishable product industries.

To better interpret inventory turnover, many users measure the adequacy of inventory to meet sales demand. **Days' sales in inventory** is a ratio that reveals how much inventory is available in terms of the number of days' sales. It can be interpreted as the number of days one can sell from inventory if no new items are purchased. This ratio is often viewed as a measure of the buffer against out-of-stock inventory and is useful in evaluating liquidity of inventory. It is defined in Exhibit 6.12.

EXHIBIT 6.12

Days' Sales in Inventory

$$\text{Days' sales in inventory} = \frac{\text{Ending inventory}}{\text{Cost of goods sold}} \times 365$$

Days' sales in inventory focuses on ending inventory and it estimates how many days it will take to convert inventory at the end of a period into accounts receivable or cash. Days' sales in inventory focuses on *ending* inventory whereas inventory turnover focuses on *average* inventory.

Analysis of Inventory Management

Inventory management is a major emphasis for manufacturers and merchandisers. They must both plan and control inventory purchases and sales. Adidas is one of those businesses. Its inventory in financial year 2013 was EUR 2,634 million. This inventory constituted 38.4% of its current assets and 22.7% of its total assets. We apply the analysis tools in this section to Adidas, as shown in Exhibit 6.13—also see bar graph.

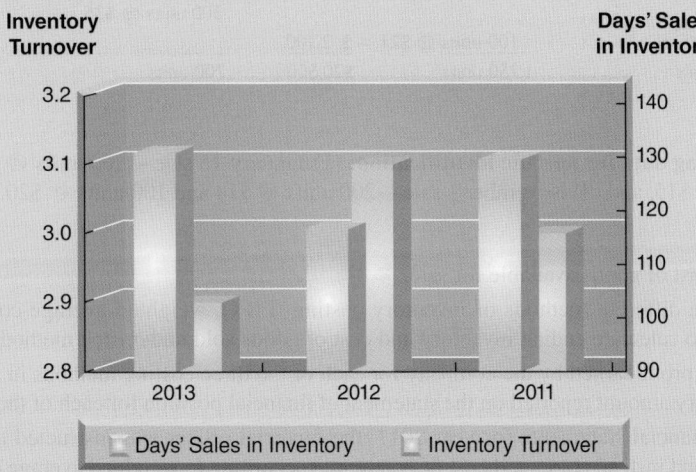

	2013	2012	2011
Cost of sales (in EUR millions)	7,352	7,780	7,000
Ending inventory (in EUR millions)	2,634	2,486	2,484
Inventory turnover	2.9 times	3.1 times	3.0 times
Days' sales in inventory	130.8 days	116.6 days	129.5 days

EXHIBIT 6.13

Inventory Turnover and Days' Sales in Inventory for Adidas

Its 2013 inventory turnover of 2.9 times means that Adidas turns over its inventory 2.9 times per year. We prefer inventory turnover to be high provided inventory is not out of stock and the company is not losing customers. The second metric, the 2013 days' sales in inventory of 130.8 days, reveals that it is carrying 130.8 days of sales in inventory. This inventory buffer seems more than adequate. Adidas would benefit from further management efforts to increase inventory turnover and reduce inventory levels.

Decision Maker   Answer — p. 252

Entrepreneur   Analysis of your retail store yields an inventory turnover of 5.0 and a days' sales in inventory of 73 days. The industry norm for inventory turnover is 4.4 and for days' sales in inventory is 74 days. What is your assessment of inventory management? ■

DEMONSTRATION PROBLEM

Craig Company uses a perpetual inventory system for its one product. Its beginning inventory, purchases, and sales during calendar year 2011 follow.

Date		Activity	Units Acquired at Cost	Units Sold at Retail	Unit Inventory
Jan.	1	Beg. Inventory	400 units @ $14 = $ 5,600		400 units
Jan.	15	Sale		200 units @ $30	200 units
Mar.	10	Purchase	200 units @ $15 = $ 3,000		400 units
April	1	Sale		200 units @ $30	200 units
May	9	Purchase	300 units @ $16 = $ 4,800		500 units
Sept.	22	Purchase	250 units @ $20 = $ 5,000		750 units
Nov.	1	Sale		300 units @ $35	450 units
Nov.	28	Purchase	100 units @ $21 = $ 2,100		550 units
		Totals	1,250 units $20,500	700 units	

Additional tracking data for specific identification: (1) January 15 sale—200 units @ $14, (2) April 1 sale—200 units @ $15, and (3) November 1 sale—200 units @ $14 and 100 units @ $20.

Required

1. Calculate the cost of goods available for sale.

2. Apply the three different methods of inventory costing (FIFO, weighted average cost, and specific identification) to calculate ending inventory and cost of goods sold under each method.

3. Compute gross profit earned by the company for each of the three costing methods in part 2. Also, report the inventory amount reported on the statement of financial position for each of the three methods.

4. In preparing financial statements for year 2011, the financial officer was instructed to use FIFO but failed to do so and instead computed cost of goods sold according to weighted average cost. Determine the impact on year 2011's profit from the error. Also determine the effect of this error on year 2012's profit. Assume no income taxes.

5. Management wants a report that shows how changing from FIFO to another method would change net profit. Prepare a table showing (1) the cost of goods sold amount under each of the three methods, (2) the amount by which each cost of goods sold total is different from the FIFO cost of goods sold, and (3) the effect on net profit if another method is used instead of FIFO.

PLANNING THE SOLUTION

- Compute cost of goods available for sale by multiplying the units of beginning inventory and each purchase by their unit costs to determine the total cost of goods available for sale.

- Prepare a perpetual FIFO table starting with beginning inventory and showing how inventory changes after each purchase and after each sale (see Exhibit 6.4).

- Make a table of purchases and sales recalculating the average cost of inventory prior to each sale to arrive at the weighted average cost of ending inventory. Total the average costs associated with each sale to determine cost of goods sold (see Exhibit 6.5).

- Prepare a table showing the computation of cost of goods sold and ending inventory using the specific identification method (see Exhibit 6.3).

- Compare the year-end 2011 inventory amounts under FIFO and weighted average cost to determine the misstatement of year 2011 profit that results from using weighted average cost. The errors for year 2011 and 2012 are equal in amount but opposite in effect.

- Create a table showing cost of goods sold under each method and how net profit would differ from FIFO net profit if an alternate method is adopted.

SOLUTION TO DEMONSTRATION PROBLEM

1. Cost of goods available for sale (this amount is the same for all methods).

Date			Units	Unit Cost	Cost
Jan.	1	Beg. Inventory	400	$14	$ 5,600
Mar.	10	Purchase	200	15	3,000
May	9	Purchase	300	16	4,800
Sept.	22	Purchase	250	20	5,000
Nov.	28	Purchase	100	21	2,100
		Total goods available for sale	1,250		$20,500

2a. FIFO perpetual method.

Date	Goods Purchased	Cost of Goods Sold	Inventory Balance
Jan. 1	Beginning balance		400 @ $14 = $ 5,600
Jan. 15		200 @ $14 = $2,800	200 @ $14 = $ 2,800
Mar. 10	200 @ $15 = $3,000		200 @ $14 200 @ $15 } = $ 5,800
April 1		200 @ $14 = $2,800	200 @ $15 = $ 3,000
May 9	300 @ $16 = $4,800		200 @ $15 300 @ $16 } = $ 7,800
Sept. 22	250 @ $20 = $5,000		200 @ $15 300 @ $16 250 @ $20 } = $12,800
Nov. 1		200 @ $15 = $3,000 100 @ $16 = $1,600	200 @ $16 250 @ $20 } = $ 8,200
Nov. 28	100 @ $21 = $2,100		200 @ $16 250 @ $20 100 @ $21 } = $10,300
Total cost of goods sold		**$10,200**	

Note to students: **In a classroom situation**, once we compute cost of goods available for sale, we can compute the amount for either cost of goods sold or ending inventory—it is a matter of preference. **In practice**, the costs of items sold are identified as sales are made and immediately transferred from the inventory account to the cost of goods sold account. The previous solution showing the line-by-line approach illustrates actual application in practice. The following alternate solutions illustrate that, once the concepts are understood, other solution approaches are available. Although this is only shown for FIFO, it could be shown for all methods.

Alternate Methods to Compute FIFO Perpetual Numbers

[FIFO Alternate No. 1: Computing cost of goods sold first]

Cost of goods available for sale (from part 1)			$ 20,500
Cost of goods sold			
Jan. 15	Sold (200 @ $14)	$2,800	
April 1	Sold (200 @ $14)	2,800	
Nov. 1	Sold (200 @ $15 and 100 @ $16)	4,600	10,200
Ending inventory			**$10,300**

[FIFO Alternate No. 2: Computing ending inventory first]

Cost of goods available for sale (from part 1)			$ 20,500
Ending inventory*			
Nov. 28	Purchase (100 @ $21).	$2,100	
Sept. 22	Purchase (250 @ $20).	5,000	
May 9	Purchase (200 @ $16).	3,200	
Ending inventory			10,300
Cost of goods sold			**$10,200**

* Since FIFO assumes that the earlier costs are the first to flow out, we determine ending inventory by assigning the most recent costs to the remaining items.

2b. Weighted average cost perpetual method.

Date	Goods Purchased	Cost of Goods Sold	Inventory Balance	
------	-----------------	--------------------	--------------------	
Jan. 1	Beginning balance		400 @ $14	= $ 5,600
Jan. 15		200 @ $14 = $2,800	200 @ $14	= $ 2,800
Mar. 10	200 @ $15 = $3,000		200 @ $14 ⎱ 200 @ $15 ⎰ (avg. cost is $14.5)	= $ 5,800
Apr. 1		200 @ $14.5 = $2,900	200 @ $14.5	= $ 2,900
May 9	300 @ $16 = $4,800		200 @ $14.5 ⎱ 300 @ $16 ⎰ (avg. cost is $15.4)	= $ 7,700
Sept. 22	250 @ $20 = $5,000		200 @ $14.5 ⎱ 300 @ $16 ⎰ 250 @ $20 (avg. cost is $16.93)	= $ 12,700
Nov. 1		300 @ $16.93 = $5,079	450 @ $16.93	= $ 7,618.5
Nov. 28	100 @ $21 = $2,100		450 @ $16.93 ⎱ 100 @ $21 ⎰	= $9,718.5
Total cost of goods sold*		**$10,779**		

* The cost of goods sold ($10,779) plus ending inventory ($9,718.5) is $2.5 less than the cost of goods available for sale ($20,500) due to rounding.

2c. Specific identification method.

Date	Goods Purchased	Cost of Goods Sold	Inventory Balance	
------	-----------------	--------------------	--------------------	
Jan. 1	Beginning balance		400 @ $14	= $ 5,600
Jan. 15		200 @ $14 = $2,800	200 @ $14	= $ 2,800
Mar. 10	200 @ $15 = $3,000		200 @ $14 ⎱ 200 @ $15 ⎰	= $ 5,800
Apr. 1		200 @ $15 = $3,000	200 @ $14	= $ 2,800
May 9	300 @ $16 = $4,800		200 @ $14 ⎱ 300 @ $16 ⎰	= $ 7,600
Sept. 22	250 @ $20 = $5,000		200 @ $14 ⎱ 300 @ $16 ⎰ 250 @ $20	= $ 12,600
Nov. 1		200 @ $14 = $2,800 100 @ $20 = $2,000	300 @ $16 ⎱ 150 @ $20 ⎰	= $ 7,800
Nov. 28	100 @ $21 = $2,100		300 @ $16 ⎱ 150 @ $20 100 @ $21 ⎰	= $ 9,900
Total cost of goods sold		**$10,600**		

3.

	FIFO	Weighted Average Cost	Specific Identification
Income Statement			
Sales*	$22,500	$ 22,500	$22,500
Cost of goods sold..................	10,200	10,779	10,600
Gross profit	$12,300	$ 11,721	$11,900
Statement of Financial Position			
Inventory	$10,300	$9,718.5	$ 9,900

* Sales = (200 units × $30) + (200 units × $30) + (300 units × $35) = $22,500

4. Mistakenly using weighted average cost when FIFO should have been used overstates cost of goods sold in year 2011 by $579. It understates profit in 2011 by $579. In year 2012, profit is overstated because of the understatement in beginning inventory. The inventory difference of $2.5 in the inventory numbers ($10,300 − $9,718.5 = $581.5) is due to rounding.

5. Analysis of the effects of alternative inventory methods.

	Cost of Goods Sold	Difference from FIFO Cost of Goods Sold	Effect on Net Profit If Adopted Instead of FIFO
FIFO	$10,200	—	—
Weighted average cost	10,779	+ $579	$579 lower
Specific identification	10,600	+ 400	400 lower

APPENDIX

Inventory Costing under a Periodic System

6A

The basic aim of the periodic system and the perpetual system is the same: to assign costs to inventory and cost of goods sold. The same three methods are used to assign costs under both systems: specific identification; first-in, first-out; and weighted average cost. We use information from Trekking to show how to assign costs using these three methods with a periodic system. Data for sales and purchases are shown in Exhibit 6A.1. Also, recall that we explained the accounting entries under a periodic system in Appendix 5A.

P3 Compute inventory in a periodic system using the methods of specific identification, FIFO, and weighted average cost.

EXHIBIT 6A.1

Purchases and Sales of Goods

Date	Activity	Units Acquired at Cost	Units Sold at Retail	Unit Inventory
Aug. 1	Beginning inventory	10 units @ $ 91 = $ 910		10 units
Aug. 3	Purchases	15 units @ $106 = $ 1,590		25 units
Aug. 14	Sales		20 units @ $130	5 units
Aug. 17	Purchases	20 units @ $115 = $ 2,300		25 units
Aug. 28	Purchases............	10 units @ $119 = $ 1,190		35 units
Aug. 31	Sales...............		23 units @ $150	12 units
	Totals...............	55 units $5,990	43 units	

Specific Identification We use the above sales and purchases information and the specific identification method to assign costs to ending inventory and units sold. Trekking's internal data reveal the following specific unit sales:

August 14 Sold 8 bikes costing $91 each and 12 bikes costing $106 each

August 31 Sold 2 bikes costing $91 each, 3 bikes costing $106 each, 15 bikes costing $115 each, and 3 bikes costing $119 each

Applying specific identification and using the information above, we prepare Exhibit 6A.2. This exhibit starts with 10 bikes at $91 each in beginning inventory. On August 3, 15 more bikes are purchased at $106 each for $1,590. Inventory available now consists of 10 bikes at $91 each and 15 bikes at $106 each, for a total of $2,500. On August 14 (see specific sales data above), 20 bikes costing $2,000 are sold—leaving 5 bikes costing $500 in inventory. On August 17, 20 bikes costing $2,300 are purchased, and on August 28, another 10 bikes costing $1,190 are purchased, for a total of 35 bikes costing $3,990 in inventory. On August 31 (see specific sales above), 23 bikes costing $2,582 are sold, which leaves 12 bikes costing $1,408 in ending inventory. Carefully study Exhibit 6A.2 to see the flow of costs both in and out of inventory. Each unit, whether sold or remaining in inventory, has its own specific cost attached to it.

EXHIBIT 6A.2

Specific Identification
Computations

For the 20 units sold on August 14, the company specifically identified that 8 of those had cost $91 and 12 had cost $106.

For the 23 units sold on August 31, the company specifically identified each bike sold and its acquisition cost from prior purchases.

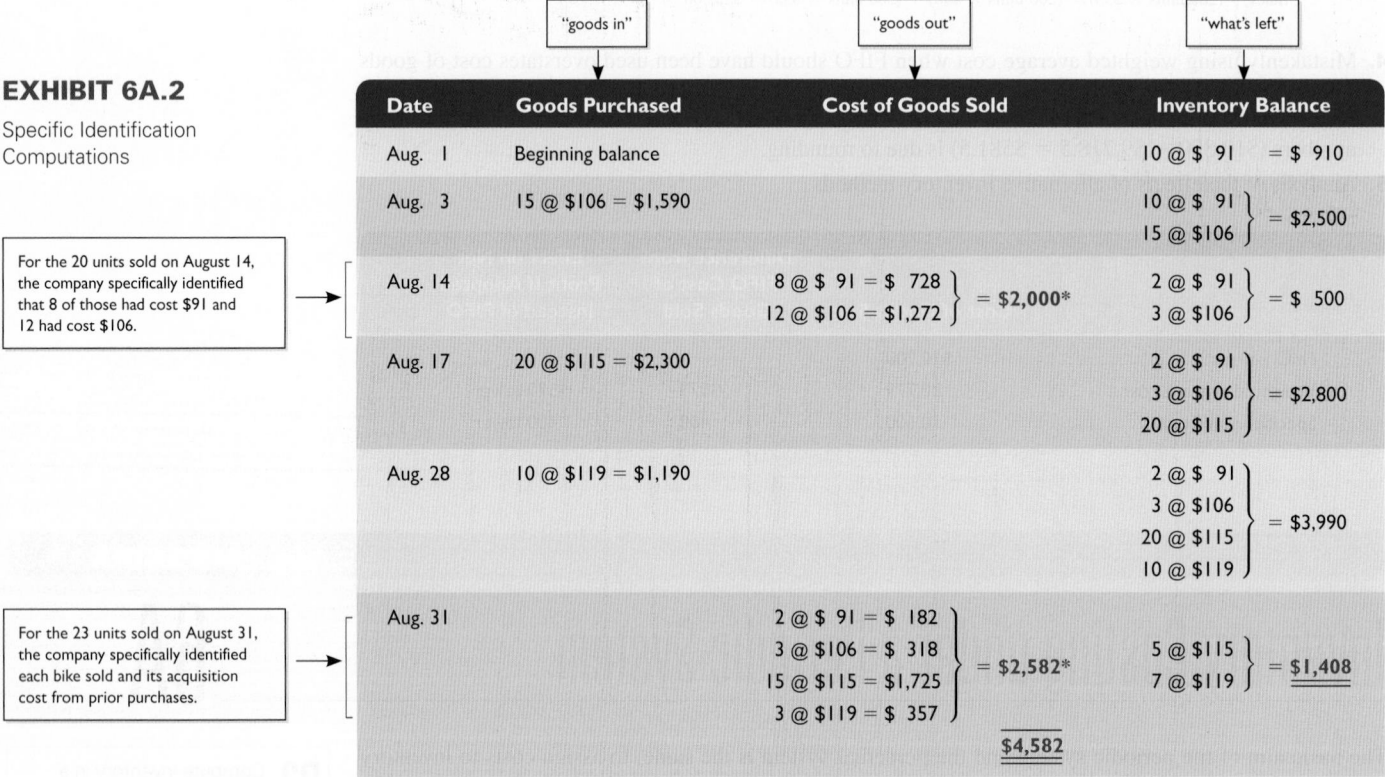

Date	Goods Purchased	Cost of Goods Sold	Inventory Balance
Aug. 1	Beginning balance		10 @ $ 91 = $ 910
Aug. 3	15 @ $106 = $1,590		10 @ $ 91 ⎫ = $2,500 15 @ $106 ⎭
Aug. 14		8 @ $ 91 = $ 728 ⎫ = $2,000* 12 @ $106 = $1,272 ⎭	2 @ $ 91 ⎫ = $ 500 3 @ $106 ⎭
Aug. 17	20 @ $115 = $2,300		2 @ $ 91 ⎫ 3 @ $106 ⎬ = $2,800 20 @ $115 ⎭
Aug. 28	10 @ $119 = $1,190		2 @ $ 91 ⎫ 3 @ $106 ⎪ 20 @ $115 ⎬ = $3,990 10 @ $119 ⎭
Aug. 31		2 @ $ 91 = $ 182 ⎫ 3 @ $106 = $ 318 ⎪ = $2,582* 15 @ $115 = $1,725 ⎬ 3 @ $119 = $ 357 ⎭	5 @ $115 ⎫ = $1,408 7 @ $119 ⎭
		$4,582	

* Identification of items sold (and their costs) is obtained from internal documents that track each unit from its purchase to its sale.

Point: The assignment of costs to the goods sold and to inventory using specific identification is the same for both the perpetual and periodic systems.

When using specific identification, Trekking's cost of goods sold reported on the income statement totals **$4,582**, the sum of $2,000 and $2,582 from the third column of Exhibit 6A.2. Trekking's ending inventory reported on the statement of financial position is **$1,408**, which is the final inventory balance from the fourth column. All purchases and sales are made on credit. The journal entries for Exhibit 6A.2 follow (the colored boldface numbers are those impacted by the cost flow assumption).

	Purchases		
Aug. 3	Purchases	1,590	
	Accounts Payable		1,590
17	Purchases	2,300	
	Accounts Payable		2,300
28	Purchases	1,190	
	Accounts Payable		1,190

	Sales		
Aug. 14	Accounts Receivable	2,600	
	Sales....................		2,600
31	Accounts Receivable	3,450	
	Sales....................		3,450
	Adjusting Entry		
31	Merchandise Inventory	1,408	
	Income Summary.........		498
	Merchandise Inventory		910

First-In, First-Out   The first-in, first-out (FIFO) method of assigning costs to inventory assumes that inventory items are sold in the order acquired. When sales occur, the costs of the earliest units acquired are charged to cost of goods sold. This leaves the costs from the most recent purchases in ending inventory. Use of FIFO for computing the cost of inventory and cost of goods sold is shown in Exhibit 6A.3.

This exhibit starts with computing $5,990 in total units available for sale—this is given to us at the start of this appendix. Applying FIFO, we know that the 12 units in ending inventory will be reported at the cost of the most recent 12 purchases. Reviewing purchases in reverse order, we assign costs to the 12 bikes in ending inventory as follows: $119 cost to 10 bikes and $115 cost to 2 bikes. This yields 12 bikes costing $1,420 in ending inventory. We then subtract this $1,420 in ending inventory from $5,990 in cost of goods available to get $4,570 in cost of goods sold.

Total cost of 55 units available for sale (from Exhibit 6A.1)		$5,990
Less ending inventory priced using FIFO		
10 units from August 28 purchase at $119 each	$1,190	
2 units from August 17 purchase at $115 each	230	
Ending inventory		1,420
Cost of goods sold		$4,570

EXHIBIT 6A.3

FIFO Computations— Periodic System

Exhibit 6A.1 shows that the 12 units in ending inventory consist of 10 units from the latest purchase on August 28 and 2 units from the next latest purchase on August 17.

Trekking's ending inventory reported on the statement of financial position is **$1,420**, and its cost of goods sold reported on the income statement is **$4,570**. These amounts are the same as those computed using the perpetual system. This always occurs because the most recent purchases are in ending inventory under both systems. All purchases and sales are made on credit. The journal entries for Exhibit 6A.3 follow (the colored boldface numbers are those impacted by the cost flow assumption).

Point: The assignment of costs to the goods sold and to inventory using FIFO is the same for both the perpetual and periodic systems.

Purchases				**Sales**		
Aug. 3	Purchases....................	1,590		Aug. 14	Accounts Receivable	2,600
	Accounts Payable..........		1,590		Sales	2,600
17	Purchases....................	2,300		31	Accounts Receivable	3,450
	Accounts Payable..........		2,300		Sales	3,450
28	Purchases....................	1,190			**Adjusting Entry**	
	Accounts Payable..........		1,190	31	Merchandise Inventory 1,420	
					Income Summary	510
					Merchandise Inventory	910

Weighted Average Cost   The weighted average cost method of assigning cost requires that we use the average cost per unit of inventory at the end of the period. Weighted average cost per unit equals the cost of goods available for sale divided by the units available. The weighted average cost method of assigning cost involves three important steps. The first two steps are shown in Exhibit 6A.4. First, multiply the per unit cost for beginning inventory and each particular purchase by the corresponding number of units (from Exhibit 6A.1). Second, add these amounts and divide by the total number of units available for sale to find the weighted average cost per unit.

Step 1:	10 units @ $ 91 =	$ 910
	15 units @ $106 =	1,590
	20 units @ $115 =	2,300
	10 units @ $119 =	1,190
	55	$5,990
Step 2:	$5,990/55 units = **$108.91** weighted average cost per unit	

EXHIBIT 6A.4

Weighted Average Cost per Unit

Example: In Exhibit 6A.4, if 5 more units had been purchased at $120 each, what would be the weighted average cost per unit?
Answer: $109.83 ($6,590/60)

The third step is to use the weighted average cost per unit to assign costs to inventory and to the units sold as shown in Exhibit 6A.5.

Step 3:	Total cost of 55 units available for sale (from Exhibit 6A.1).........	$ 5,990
	Less **ending inventory** priced on a weighted average cost basis: 12 units at $108.91 each (from Exhibit 6A.4)...........	1,307
	Cost of goods sold	$4,683

EXHIBIT 6A.5

Weighted Average Computations—Periodic

Trekking's ending inventory reported on the statement of financial position is $1,307, and its cost of goods sold reported on the income statement is $4,683 when using the weighted average cost (periodic) method. All purchases and sales are made on credit. The journal entries for Exhibit 6A.5 follow (the colored boldface numbers are those impacted by the cost flow assumption).

Purchases				Sales		
Aug. 3	Purchases	1,590		Aug. 14	Accounts Receivable	2,600
	Accounts Payable		1,590		Sales		2,600
17	Purchases	2,300		31	Accounts Receivable	3,450
	Accounts Payable		2,300		Sales		3,450
28	Purchases	1,190			**Adjusting Entry**		
	Accounts Payable		1,190				
				31	Merchandise Inventory	1,307	
					Income Summary		397
					Merchandise Inventory		910

Financial Statement Effects   When purchase prices do not change, each inventory costing method assigns the same cost amounts to inventory and to cost of goods sold. When purchase prices are different, however, the methods nearly always assign different cost amounts. We show these differences in Exhibit 6A.6 using Trekking's data.

EXHIBIT 6A.6

Financial Statement Effects of Inventory Costing Methods

	TREKKING COMPANY		
	For Month Ended August 31		
	Specific Identification	FIFO	Weighted Average Cost
Income Statement			
Sales	$ 6,050	$ 6,050	$ 6,050
Cost of goods sold	4,582	4,570	4,683
Gross profit	1,468	1,480	1,367
Expenses	450	450	450
Profit before tax	1,018	1,030	917
Income tax expense (30%)	305	309	275
Net profit	$ 713	$ 721	$ 642
Statement of financial position			
Inventory	$1,408	$1,420	$1,307

This exhibit reveals two important results. First, when purchase costs *regularly rise*, as in Trekking's case, observe the following:

- FIFO assigns the lower amount to cost of goods sold—yielding the higher gross profit and net profit.
- Weighted average cost yields the higher cost of goods sold and lower profit as it averages the recent higher costs with the earlier lower costs.
- Specific identification always yields results that depend on which units are sold.

Second, when costs *regularly decline*, the reverse occurs for FIFO and weighted average cost. FIFO gives the higher cost of goods sold—yielding the lower gross profit and net profit. And weighted average cost gives the lower cost of goods sold—yielding the higher gross profit and net profit.

     All three inventory costing methods are acceptable in **IAS 2**. A company must disclose the inventory method it uses. Each method offers certain advantages as follows:

- FIFO assigns an amount to inventory on the statement of financial position that approximates its current cost; it also mimics the actual flow of goods for most businesses.
- Weighted average cost tends to smooth out erratic changes in costs.
- Specific identification exactly matches the costs of items with the revenues they generate.

Quick Check

Answers — p. 252

9. A company reports the following beginning inventory and purchases, and it ends the period with 30 units in inventory.

Beginning inventory	100 units at $10 cost per unit
Purchase 1	40 units at $12 cost per unit
Purchase 2	20 units at $14 cost per unit

Compute ending inventory using the FIFO periodic system.

APPENDIX

Inventory Estimation Methods

6B

Inventory sometimes requires estimation for two reasons. First, companies often require **interim financial statements** (financial statements prepared for periods of less than one year), but they only annually take a physical count of inventory. Second, companies may require an inventory estimate if some casualty such as fire or flood makes taking a physical count impossible. Estimates are usually only required for companies that use the periodic system. Companies using a perpetual system would presumably have updated inventory data.

This appendix describes two methods to estimate inventory.

P4 Apply both the retail inventory and gross profit methods to estimate inventory.

Retail Inventory Method   To avoid the time-consuming and expensive process of taking a physical inventory each month or quarter, some companies use the **retail inventory method** to estimate cost of goods sold and ending inventory. Some companies even use the retail inventory method to prepare the annual statements. A company may also estimate inventory for audit purposes or when inventory is damaged or destroyed.

The retail inventory method uses a three-step process to estimate ending inventory. We need to know the amount of inventory a company had at the beginning of the period in both *cost* and *retail* amounts. We already explained how to compute the cost of inventory. The *retail amount of inventory* refers to its dollar amount measured using selling prices of inventory items. We also need to know the net amount of goods purchased (minus returns, allowances, and discounts) in the period, both at cost and at retail. The amount of net sales at retail is also needed. The process is shown in Exhibit 6B.1.

The reasoning behind the retail inventory method is that if we can get a good estimate of the cost-to-retail ratio, we can multiply ending inventory at retail by this ratio to estimate ending inventory at cost. We show in Exhibit 6B.2 how these steps are applied to estimate ending inventory for a typical company. First, we find that $100,000 of goods (at retail selling prices) were available for sale. We see that $70,000 of these goods were sold, leaving $30,000 (retail value) of merchandise in ending inventory. Second, the cost of these goods is 60% of the $100,000 retail value. Third, since cost for these goods is 60% of retail, the estimated cost of ending inventory is $18,000.

Point: When a retailer takes a physical inventory, it can restate the retail value of inventory to a cost basis by applying the cost-to-retail ratio. It can also estimate the amount of shrinkage by comparing the inventory computed with the amount from a physical inventory.

Step 1   Goods available for sale at retail **−** Net sales at retail **=** Ending inventory at retail

Step 2   Goods available for sale at cost **÷** Goods available for sale at retail **=** Cost-to-retail ratio

Step 3   Ending inventory at retail **×** Cost-to-retail ratio **=** Estimated ending inventory at cost

EXHIBIT 6B.1

Retail Inventory Method of Inventory Estimation

Example: What is the cost of ending inventory in Exhibit 6B.2 if the cost of beginning inventory is $22,500 and its retail value is $34,500? *Answer:* $30,000 × 62% = $18,600

EXHIBIT 6B.2

Estimated Inventory Using the
Retail Inventory Method

	At Cost	At Retail
Goods available for sale		
Beginning inventory	$ 20,500	$ 34,500
Cost of goods purchased.	39,500	65,500
Goods available for sale	60,000	100,000
Step 1: **Deduct net sales at retail**		70,000
Ending inventory at retail		$ 30,000
Step 2: **Cost-to-retail ratio: ($60,000 ÷ $100,000) = 60%**		
Step 3: **Estimated ending inventory at cost ($30,000 × 60%)**	$18,000	

Gross Profit Method

The **gross profit method** estimates the cost of ending inventory by applying the gross profit ratio to net sales (at retail). This type of estimate often is needed when inventory is destroyed, lost, or stolen. These cases require an inventory estimate so that a company can file a claim with its insurer. Users also apply this method to see whether inventory amounts from a physical count are reasonable. This method uses the historical relation between cost of goods sold and net sales to estimate the proportion of cost of goods sold making up current sales. This cost of goods sold estimate is then subtracted from cost of goods available for sale to estimate the ending inventory at cost. These two steps are shown in Exhibit 6B.3.

EXHIBIT 6B.3

Gross Profit Method of
Inventory Estimation

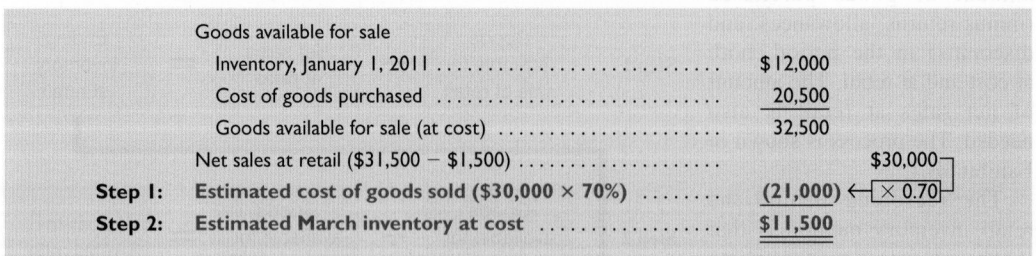

Point: A fire or other catastrophe can result in an insurance claim for lost inventory or profit. Backup and off-site storage of data help ensure coverage for such losses.

Point: Reliability of the gross profit method depends on a good estimate of the gross profit ratio.

To illustrate, assume that a company's inventory is destroyed by fire in March 2011. When the fire occurs, the company's accounts show the following balances for January through March: sales, $31,500; sales returns, $1,500; inventory (January 1, 2011), $12,000; and cost of goods purchased, $20,500. If this company's gross profit ratio is 30%, then 30% of each net sales dollar is gross profit and 70% is cost of goods sold. We show in Exhibit 6B.4 how this 70% is used to estimate lost inventory of $11,500. To understand this exhibit, think of subtracting the cost of goods sold from the goods available for sale to get the ending inventory.

EXHIBIT 6B.4

Estimated Inventory Using the
Gross Profit Method

Goods available for sale		
Inventory, January 1, 2011	$12,000	
Cost of goods purchased	20,500	
Goods available for sale (at cost)	32,500	
Net sales at retail ($31,500 − $1,500)		$30,000
Step 1: **Estimated cost of goods sold ($30,000 × 70%)**	(21,000) ← × 0.70	
Step 2: **Estimated March inventory at cost**	$11,500	

Quick Check

Answers – p. 252

10. Using the retail method and the following data, estimate the cost of ending inventory.

	Cost	Retail
Beginning inventory	$324,000	$530,000
Cost of goods purchased	195,000	335,000
Net sales		320,000

LIFO Inventory Systems

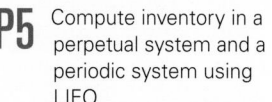

LIFO is not allowed under **IAS 2** but allowed under U.S. GAAP. As shown in Exhibit 6C.1, LIFO assumes that the costs flow in the reverse order incurred. Therefore, an appeal of LIFO is that by assigning costs from the most recent purchases to cost of goods sold, LIFO comes closest to matching current costs of goods sold with revenues (compared to FIFO or weighted average).

P5	Compute inventory in a perpetual system and a periodic system using LIFO.

Costs flow in the *reverse* order incurred.

$70
May 6

$65
May 3

$45
May 1

Income Statement

Net sales......................	$100
Cost of goods sold.......	70
Gross profit..................	$ 30

Statement of Financial Position

| Inventory...................... | $110 |

EXHIBIT 6C.1

LIFO Cost Flow Assumption

For detailed calculations, we start by illustrating a perpetual system using LIFO, followed by a periodic system using LIFO.

Perpetual System We use the same information in the chapter from Trekking, a sporting goods store. Among its many products, Trekking carries one type of mountain bike whose sales are directed at resorts that provide inexpensive mountain bikes for complimentary guest use. Its customers usually purchase in amounts of 10 or more bikes. We use Trekking's data from August. Its mountain bike (unit) inventory at the beginning of August and its purchases and sales during August are shown in Exhibit 6C.2. It ends August with 12 bikes remaining in inventory.

Date	Activity	Units Acquired at Cost	Units Sold at Retail	Unit Inventory
Aug. 1	Beginning inventory	10 units @ $ 91 = $ 910		10 units
Aug. 3	Purchases	15 units @ $106 = $ 1,590		25 units
Aug. 14	Sales		20 units @ $130	5 units
Aug. 17	Purchases	20 units @ $115 = $ 2,300		25 units
Aug. 28	Purchases.............	10 units @ $119 = $ 1,190		35 units
Aug. 31	Sales.................		23 units @ $150	12 units
	Totals...............	55 units $5,990	43 units	

EXHIBIT 6C.2

Purchases and Sales of Goods

Trekking uses the perpetual inventory system, which means that its merchandise inventory account is continually updated to reflect purchases and sales. Regardless of what inventory method or system is used, cost of goods available for sale must be allocated between cost of goods sold and ending inventory.

Exhibit 6C.3 shows the LIFO computations. It starts with beginning inventory of 10 bikes at $91 each. On August 3, 15 more bikes costing $106 each are bought for $1,590. Inventory now consists of 10 bikes at $91 each and 15 bikes at $106 each, for a total of $2,500. On August 14, 20 bikes are sold—applying LIFO, the first 15 sold are from the most recent purchase costing $106 each, and the next 5 sold are from the next most recent purchase costing $91 each, for a total cost of $2,045. This leaves 5 bikes costing $91 each, or $455, in inventory. On August 17, 20 bikes costing $2,300 are purchased, and on August 28, another 10 bikes costing $1,190 are purchased, for a total of 35 bikes costing $3,945 in inventory. On August 31, 23 bikes are sold—applying LIFO, the first 10 bikes sold are from the most recent purchase costing $1,190, and the next 13 sold are from the next most recent purchase costing $1,495, which leaves 12 bikes costing $1,260 in ending inventory.

EXHIBIT 6C.3

LIFO Computations—
Perpetual System

For the 20 units sold on August 14, the first 15 sold are assigned the most recent cost of $106. The next 5 sold are assigned the next most recent cost of $91.

For the 23 units sold on August 31, the first 10 sold are assigned the most recent cost of $119. The next 13 sold are assigned the next most recent cost of $115.

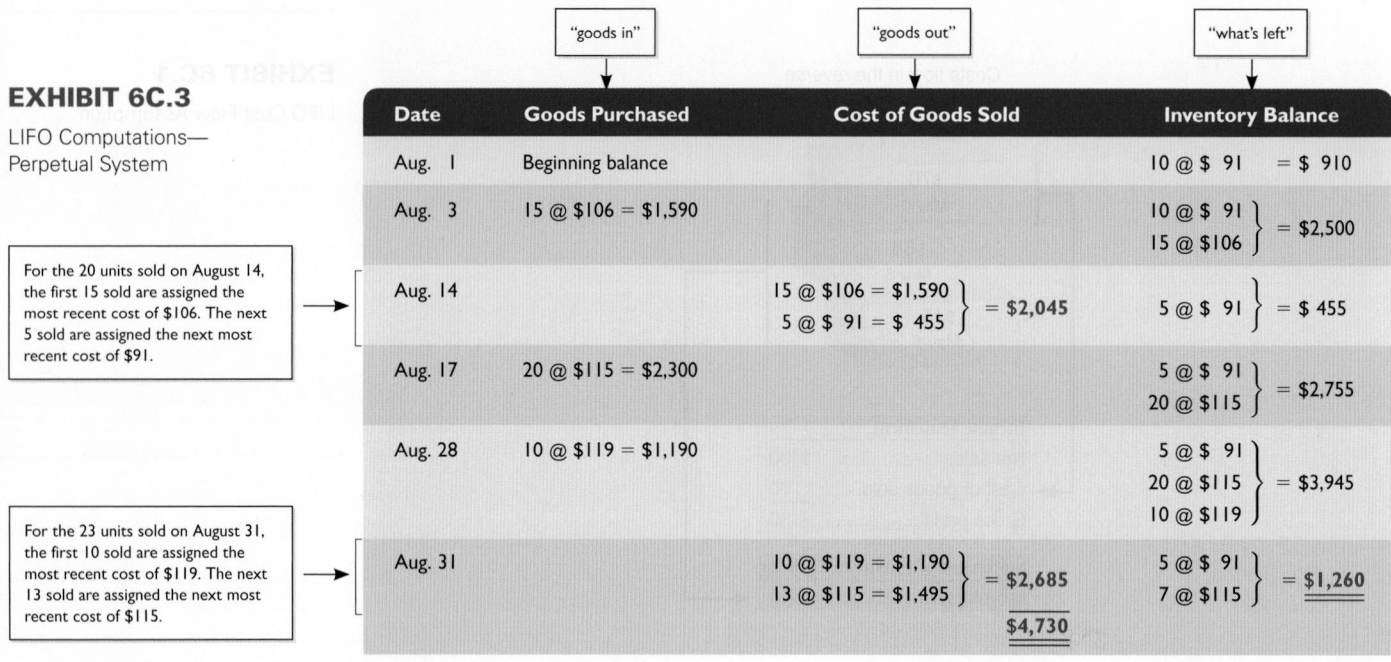

Date	Goods Purchased	Cost of Goods Sold	Inventory Balance
Aug. 1	Beginning balance		10 @ $ 91 = $ 910
Aug. 3	15 @ $106 = $1,590		10 @ $ 91 } = $2,500 15 @ $106 }
Aug. 14		15 @ $106 = $1,590 } = $2,045 5 @ $ 91 = $ 455 }	5 @ $ 91 } = $ 455
Aug. 17	20 @ $115 = $2,300		5 @ $ 91 } = $2,755 20 @ $115 }
Aug. 28	10 @ $119 = $1,190		5 @ $ 91 } 20 @ $115 } = $3,945 10 @ $119 }
Aug. 31		10 @ $119 = $1,190 } = $2,685 13 @ $115 = $1,495 } $4,730	5 @ $ 91 } = $1,260 7 @ $115 }

Trekking's LIFO cost of goods sold reported on the income statement is **$4,730** ($2,045 + $2,685), and its ending inventory reported on the statement of financial position is **$1,260**. All purchases and sales are made on credit. The journal entries for Exhibit 6C.3 follow (the colored boldface numbers are those impacted by the cost flow assumption).

Purchases

Aug. 3	Merchandise Inventory	1,590	
	Accounts Payable.		1,590
17	Merchandise Inventory	2,300	
	Accounts Payable.		2,300
28	Merchandise Inventory	1,190	
	Accounts Payable.		1,190

Sales

Aug. 14	Accounts Receivable	2,600	
	Sales		2,600
14	Cost of Goods Sold.	2,045	
	Merchandise Inventory		2,045
31	Accounts Receivable	3,450	
	Sales		3,450
31	Cost of Goods Sold.	2,685	
	Merchandise Inventory		2,685

Periodic System   Using the same data from Trekking, Exhibit 6C.4 starts with computing $5,990 in total units available for sale—this is given to us at the start of this appendix. Applying LIFO, we know that the 12 units in ending inventory will be reported at the cost of the earliest 12 purchases. Reviewing the earliest purchases in order, we assign costs to the 12 bikes in ending inventory as follows: $91 cost to 10 bikes and $106 cost to 2 bikes. This yields 12 bikes costing $1,122 in ending inventory. We then subtract this $1,122 in ending inventory from $5,990 in cost of goods available to get $4,868 in cost of goods sold.

Total cost of 55 units available for sale (from Exhibit 6A.1)		$5,990
Less ending inventory priced using LIFO		
10 units in beginning inventory at $91 each	$910	
2 units from August 3 purchase at $106 each	212	
Ending inventory		1,122
Cost of goods sold		$4,868

EXHIBIT 6C.4

LIFO Computations—
Periodic System

Exhibit 6C.4 shows that the 12 units in ending inventory consist of 10 units from the earliest purchase (beginning inventory) and 2 units from the next earliest purchase on August 3.

Trekking's ending inventory reported on the statement of financial position is **$1,122**, and its cost of goods sold reported on the income statement is **$4,868**. When LIFO is used with the periodic system, cost of goods sold is assigned costs from the most recent purchases for the period. With a perpetual system, cost of goods sold is assigned costs from the most recent purchases at the point of *each sale*. All purchases and sales are made on credit. The journal entries for Exhibit 6C.4 follow (the colored boldface numbers are those impacted by the cost flow assumption).

Purchases

Aug. 3	Purchases	1,590	
	Accounts Payable		1,590
17	Purchases	2,300	
	Accounts Payable		2,300
28	Purchases	1,190	
	Accounts Payable		1,190

Sales

Aug. 14	Accounts Receivable	2,600	
	Sales		2,600
31	Accounts Receivable	3,450	
	Sales		3,450

Adjusting Entry

31	Merchandise Inventory	1,122	
	Income Summary		212
	Merchandise Inventory		910

Summary

C1 Identify the items making up merchandise inventory. Merchandise inventory refers to goods owned by a company and held for resale. Three special cases merit our attention. Goods in transit are reported in inventory of the company that holds ownership rights. Goods on consignment are reported in the consignor's inventory. Goods damaged or obsolete are reported in inventory at their net realizable value.

C2 Identify the costs of merchandise inventory. Costs of merchandise inventory include expenditures necessary to bring an item to a salable condition and location. This includes its invoice cost minus any discount plus any added or incidental costs necessary to put it in a place and condition for sale.

A1 Analyze the effects of inventory methods for both financial and tax reporting. When purchase costs are rising or falling, the inventory costing methods are likely to assign different costs to inventory. Specific identification exactly matches costs and revenues. Weighted average cost smooths out cost changes. FIFO assigns an amount to inventory closely approximating current cost.

A2 Analyze the effects of inventory errors on current and future financial statements. An error in the amount of ending inventory affects assets (inventory), net profit (cost of goods sold), and equity for that period. Since ending inventory is next period's beginning inventory, an error in ending inventory affects next period's cost of goods sold and net profit. Inventory errors in one period are offset in the next period.

A3 Assess inventory management using both inventory turnover and days' sales in inventory. We prefer a high

inventory turnover, provided that goods are not out of stock and customers are not turned away. We use days' sales in inventory to assess the likelihood of goods being out of stock. We prefer a small number of days' sales in inventory if we can serve customer needs and provide a buffer for uncertainties.

P1 Compute inventory in a perpetual system using the methods of specific identification, FIFO, and weighted average cost. Costs are assigned to the cost of goods sold account *each time* a sale occurs in a perpetual system. Specific identification assigns a cost to each item sold by referring to its actual cost (for example, its net invoice cost). Weighted average cost assigns a cost to items sold by dividing the current balance in the inventory account by the total items available for sale to determine cost per unit. We then multiply the number of units sold by this cost per unit to get the cost of each sale. FIFO assigns cost to items sold assuming that the earliest units purchased are the first units sold.

P2 Compute the lower of cost and net realizable value (NRV) of inventory. Inventory is reported at NRV when NRV is lower than recorded cost, called the lower of cost and NRV. NRV is the estimated selling price in the ordinary course of business less the estimated costs of completion and the estimated costs necessary to make the sale. Lower of cost and NRV can be applied separately to each item or to major categories of items.

P3A Compute inventory in a periodic system using the methods of specific identification, FIFO, and weighted average cost. Periodic inventory systems allocate the cost of goods available for sale between cost of goods sold and ending inventory *at the end of a period.* Specific identification and FIFO give identical results whether the periodic or perpetual system is used. The weighted average cost per unit is computed by dividing the total cost of beginning inventory and net purchases for the period by the total number of units available. Then, it multiplies cost per unit by the number of units sold to give cost of goods sold.

P4ᴮ Apply both the retail inventory and gross profit methods to estimate inventory. The retail inventory method involves three steps (1) goods available at retail minus net sales at retail equals ending inventory at retail, (2) goods available at cost divided by goods available at retail equals the cost-to-retail ratio, and (3) ending inventory at retail multiplied by the cost-to-retail ratio equals

estimated ending inventory at cost. The gross profit method involves two steps: (1) net sales at retail multiplied by 1 minus the gross profit ratio equals estimated cost of goods sold, and (2) goods available at cost minus estimated cost of goods sold equals estimated ending inventory at cost.

P5ᶜ Compute inventory in a perpetual system and a periodic system using LIFO. LIFO assigns cost to items sold assuming that the most recent units purchased are the first units sold. For a perpetual system, costs are assigned to the cost of goods sold account *each time* a sale occurs in a perpetual system. In contrast, a periodic inventory system allocates the cost of goods available for sale between cost of goods sold and ending inventory *at the end of a period.*

Guidance Answers to Decision Maker and Decision Ethics

Financial Planner   The FIFO method implies that the oldest costs are the first ones assigned to cost of goods sold. This leaves the most recent costs in ending inventory. You report this to your client and note that in most cases, the ending inventory of a company using FIFO is reported at or near its recent cost. This means that your client need not in most cases adjust the reported value of inventory. (*Note:* Decreases in costs of purchases are recognized under the lower of cost and net realizable value adjustment.)

Inventory Manager   It seems your company can save (or at least postpone) taxes by switching to weighted average cost, but the switch is likely to reduce bonus money that you think you have earned and deserve. You also should discuss your bonus plan and how this is

likely to hurt you unfairly. You might propose to compute inventory under the weighted average cost method for reporting purposes but use the FIFO method for your bonus calculations. Another solution is to revise the bonus plan to reflect the company's use of the weighted average cost method.

Entrepreneur   Your inventory turnover is markedly higher than the norm, whereas days' sales in inventory approximates the norm. Since your turnover is already 14% better than average, you are probably best served by directing attention to days' sales in inventory. You should see whether you can reduce the level of inventory while maintaining service to customers. Given your higher turnover, you should be able to hold less inventory.

Guidance Answers to Quick Checks

1. Incidental costs are added because they are necessary to bring the inventory item to a salable condition and location.

2. Target reports these goods in its inventory.

3. Total cost assigned to the painting is $12,180, computed as $11,400 + $130 + $150 + $100 + $400.

4. Specific identification exactly matches costs and revenues. FIFO assigns an amount to inventory that closely approximates current cost. Weighted average cost tends to smooth out cost changes.

5. FIFO—it gives a lower cost of goods sold, a higher gross profit, and a higher net profit when costs are rising.

6. When costs are rising, weighted average cost gives a lower inventory figure on the statement of financial position as compared to FIFO.

7. Cost of goods sold would be overstated by $10,000 in 2010 and understated by $10,000 in year 2011.

8. The reported lower of cost and NRV inventory amount (using items) is $540, computed as $[(20 \times \$5) + (40 \times \$8) + (10 \times \$12)]$.

9.ᴬ FIFO periodic inventory $= (20 \times \$14) + (10 \times \$12)$
$$= \$400$$

10.ᴮ Estimated ending inventory (at cost) is $327,000. It is computed as follows:

Step 1: $(\$530,000 + \$335,000) - \$320,000 = \$545,000$

Step 2: $\dfrac{\$324,000 + \$195,000}{\$530,000 + \$335,000} = 60\%$

Step 3: $\$545,000 \times 60\% = \underline{\$327,000}$

Key Terms   www.mheducation.asia/olc/wildkwokFAP

Multiple Choice Quiz   Answers on p. 268   **www.mheducation.asia/olc/wildkwokFAP**

Use the following information from Marvel Company for the month of July to answer questions 1 through 3.

July 1	Beginning inventory	75 units @ $25 each
July 3	Purchase	348 units @ $27 each
July 8	Sale	300 units
July 15	Purchase	257 units @ $28 each
July 23	Sale	275 units

1. Assume that Marvel uses a perpetual FIFO inventory system. What is the dollar value of its ending inventory?
   a. $2,940   c. $2,625   e. $2,705
   b. $2,685   d. $2,852

2. Assume that Marvel uses a perpetual specific identification inventory system. Its ending inventory consists of 20 units from beginning inventory, 40 units from the July 3 purchase, and 45 units from the July 15 purchase. What is the dollar value of its ending inventory?
   a. $2,940   c. $2,625   e. $2,840
   b. $2,685   d. $2,852

3.^A Assume that Marvel uses *periodic* FIFO inventory system. What is the dollar value of its ending inventory?
   a. $2,940   c. $2,625   e. $2,705
   b. $2,685   d. $2,852

4. A company has cost of goods sold of $85,000 and ending inventory of $18,000. Its days' sales in inventory equals:
   a. 49.32 days   c. 4.72 days   e. 1,723.61 days
   b. 0.21 days   d. 77.29 days

^A(A)(B) *Superscript letters (A) and (B) denotes assignments based on Appendices 6A and 6B*
[icon] Icon denotes assignments that involve decision making.

Discussion Questions

1. Describe how costs flow from inventory to cost of goods sold for FIFO method.

2. Where is the amount of merchandise inventory disclosed in the financial statements?

3. Why are incidental costs sometimes ignored in inventory costing? Under what accounting constraint is this permitted?

4. [icon] If costs are declining, will the weighted average or FIFO method of inventory valuation yield the lower cost of goods sold? Why?

5. Do "comparability" and "consistency" mean the same thing? Explain.

6. Can a company change its inventory method each accounting period? Explain.

7. [icon] Does the accounting concept of consistency preclude any changes from one accounting method to another?

8. [icon] If inventory errors are said to correct themselves, why are accounting users concerned when such errors are made?

9. Explain the following statement: "Inventory errors correct themselves."

10. What is the meaning of *net realizable value* as it is used in determining the lower of cost and net realizable value (NRV) for inventory?

11. [icon] How does an error in ending inventory affect equity?

12. What factors contribute to (or cause) inventory shrinkage?

13.^A What accounts are used in a periodic inventory system but not in a perpetual inventory system?

14. Refer to **Nestlé**'s consolidated balance sheet as at December 31, 2013 in Appendix A. What percent of current assets are represented by inventories?

15. [icon] Refer to **Adidas**' consolidated financial statements in Appendix A. Compute its cost of goods available for sale for the year ended December 31, 2013.

16. [icon] Refer to the consolidated statements of financial position of **Samsung** in Appendix A. What percent of Samsung's current assets are inventories as at December 31, 2012, and as at December 31, 2011?

17. [icon] Refer to **Puma**'s consolidated financial statements from its Website (http://about.puma.com/en/investor-relations/financial-reports). Compute its cost of goods available for sale for the year ended December 31, 2013.

18.^B When preparing interim financial statements, what two methods can companies utilize to estimate cost of goods sold and ending inventory?

[McGraw Hill] **connect**

A company reports the following beginning inventory and purchases for the month of January. On January 26, the company sells 360 units. What is the cost of the 155 units that remain in ending inventory at January 31, assuming costs are assigned based on a perpetual inventory system and use of FIFO? (Round per unit costs to three decimals, but inventory balances to the dollar.)

QUICK STUDY

QS 6-1

Inventory costing with FIFO perpetual

P1

	Units	Unit Cost
Beginning inventory on January 1	320	$6.00
Purchase on January 9	85	6.40
Purchase on January 25	110	6.60

QS 6-2^c

Inventory costing with LIFO perpetual

P5

Refer to the information in QS 6-1 and assume the perpetual inventory system is used. Determine the costs assigned to ending inventory when costs are assigned based on LIFO. (Round per unit costs to three decimals, but inventory balances to the dollar.)

QS 6-3

Inventory costing with weighted average cost perpetual

P1

Check $960

Refer to the information in QS 6-1 and assume the perpetual inventory system is used. Determine the costs assigned to ending inventory when costs are assigned based on weighted average cost. (Round per unit costs to three decimals, but inventory balances to the dollar.)

QS 6-4

Computing goods available for sale

P1

Segoe Company reports beginning inventory of 10 units at $50 each. Every week for four weeks it purchases an additional 10 units at respective costs of $51, $52, $55, and $60 per unit for weeks 1 through 4. Calculate the cost of goods available for sale and the units available for sale for this four-week period. Assume that no sales occur during those four weeks.

QS 6-5

Assigning costs with FIFO perpetual

P1

Mercedes Brown starts a merchandising business on December 1 and enters into three inventory purchases:

December 7	10 units @ $ 9 cost
December 14	20 units @ $10 cost
December 21	15 units @ $12 cost

Brown sells 18 units for $35 each on December 15. Seven of the sold units are from the December 7 purchase and 11 are from the December 14 purchase. Brown uses a perpetual inventory system. Determine the costs assigned to the December 31 ending inventory based on FIFO. (Round per unit costs to three decimals, but inventory balances to the dollar.)

QS 6-6^c

Inventory costing with LIFO perpetual

P5

Refer to the information in QS 6-5 and assume the perpetual inventory system is used. Determine the costs assigned to ending inventory when costs are assigned based on LIFO. (Round per unit costs to three decimals, but inventory balances to the dollar.)

QS 6-7

Inventory costing with weighted average perpetual

P1

Check End. Inv. = $296

Refer to the information in QS 6-5 and assume the perpetual inventory system is used. Determine the costs assigned to ending inventory when costs are assigned based on weighted average cost. (Round per unit costs to three decimals, but inventory balances to the dollar.)

QS 6-8

Inventory costing with specific identification perpetual

P1

Refer to the information in QS 6-5 and assume the perpetual inventory system is used. Determine the costs assigned to ending inventory when costs are assigned based on specific identification. (Round per unit costs to three decimals, but inventory balances to the dollar.)

QS 6-9

Contrasting inventory costing methods

A1

Identify the inventory costing method best described by each of the following separate statements. Assume a period of increasing costs.

1. The preferred method when each unit of product has unique features that markedly affect cost.
2. Tends to smooth out erratic changes in costs.
3. Assigns an amount to inventory on the statements of financial position that approximates its current cost.

Crafts Galore, a distributor of handmade gifts, operates out of owner Jenny Finn's house. At the end of the current period, Jenny reports she has 1,500 units (products) in her basement, 30 of which were damaged by water and cannot be sold. She also has another 250 units in her van, ready to deliver per a customer order, terms FOB destination, and another 70 units out on consignment to a friend who owns a retail store. How many units should Jenny include in her company's period-end inventory?

QS 6-10
Inventory ownership
C1

A car dealer acquires a used car for $3,000, terms FOB shipping point. Additional costs in obtaining and offering the car for sale include $150 for transportation-in, $200 for import duties, $50 for insurance during shipment, $25 for advertising, and $250 for sales staff salaries. For computing inventory, what cost is assigned to the used car?

QS 6-11
Inventory costs
C2

Tailspin Trading Co. has the following products in its ending inventory. Compute lower of cost and net realizable value for inventory applied separately to each product.

Product	Quantity	Cost per Unit	NRV per Unit
Mountain bikes	9	$360	$330
Skateboards	12	210	270
Gliders	25	480	420

QS 6-12
Applying lower of cost and NRV to inventories
P2

In taking a physical inventory at the end of year 2011, Nadir Company forgot to count certain units. Explain how this error affects the following: (*a*) 2011 cost of goods sold, (*b*) 2011 gross profit, (*c*) 2011 net profit, (*d*) 2012 net profit, (*e*) the combined two-year profit, and (*f*) profit for years after 2012.

QS 6-13
Inventory errors
A2

Market Company begins the year with $200,000 of goods in inventory. At year-end, the amount in inventory has increased to $230,000. Cost of goods sold for the year is $1,600,000. Compute Market's inventory turnover and days' sales in inventory. Assume that there are 365 days in the year.

QS 6-14
Analyzing inventory
A3

Refer to the information in QS 6-1 and assume the periodic inventory system is used. Determine the costs assigned to the ending inventory when costs are assigned based on FIFO. (Round per unit costs to three decimals, but inventory balances to the dollar.)

QS 6-15^A
Assigning costs with FIFO periodic
P3

Refer to the information in QS 6-1 and assume the periodic inventory system is used. Determine the costs assigned to ending inventory when costs are assigned based on LIFO. (Round per unit costs to three decimals, but inventory balances to the dollar.)

QS 6-16^C
Inventory costing with LIFO periodic
P5

Refer to the information in QS 6-1 and assume the periodic inventory system is used. Determine the costs assigned to ending inventory when costs are assigned based on weighted average cost. (Round per unit costs to three decimals, but inventory balances to the dollar.)

QS 6-17^A
Inventory costing with weighted average cost periodic
P3

Refer to the information in QS 6-5 and assume the periodic inventory system is used. Determine the costs assigned to the December 31 ending inventory when costs are assigned based on FIFO. (Round per unit costs to three decimals, but inventory balances to the dollar.)

QS 6-18^A
Inventory costing with FIFO periodic
P3

Refer to the information in QS 6-5 and assume the periodic inventory system is used. Determine the costs assigned to ending inventory when costs are assigned based on LIFO. (Round per unit costs to three decimals, but inventory balances to the dollar.)

QS 6-19^C
Inventory costing with LIFO periodic
P5

QS 6-20ᴬ

Inventory costing with weighted average cost periodic

P3

Refer to the information in QS 6-5 and assume the periodic inventory system is used. Determine the costs assigned to ending inventory when costs are assigned based on weighted average cost. (Round per unit costs to three decimals, but inventory balances to the dollar.)

QS 6-21ᴬ

Inventory costing with specific identification periodic

P3

Refer to the information in QS 6-5 and assume the periodic inventory system is used. Determine the costs assigned to ending inventory when costs are assigned based on specific identification. (Round per unit costs to three decimals, but inventory balances to the dollar.)

QS 6-22ᴮ

Estimating inventories—gross profit method

P4

Dooling Store's inventory is destroyed by a fire on September 5, 2011. The following data for year 2011 are available from the accounting records. Estimate the cost of the inventory destroyed.

Jan. I inventory	$180,000
Jan. I through Sept. 5 purchases (net)	$342,000
Jan. I through Sept. 5 sales (net)	$675,000
Year 2011 estimated gross profit rate	42%

⬛ connect™

EXERCISES

Exercise 6-1

Inventory ownership

C1

1. Jolie Company has shipped $500 of goods to China Co., and China Co. has arranged to sell the goods for Jolie. Identify the consignor and the consignee. Which company should include any unsold goods as part of its inventory?

2. At year-end, Jolie Co. had shipped $850 of merchandise FOB destination to China Co. Which company should include the $850 of merchandise in transit as part of its year-end inventory?

Exercise 6-2

Inventory costs

C2

Duke Associates, antique dealers, purchased the contents of an estate for $37,500. Terms of the purchase were FOB shipping point, and the cost of transporting the goods to Duke Associates' warehouse was $1,200. Duke Associates insured the shipment at a cost of $150. Prior to putting the goods up for sale, they cleaned and refurbished them at a cost of $490. Determine the cost of the inventory acquired from the estate.

Exercise 6-3

Inventory costing methods—perpetual

P1

Park Company reported the following March purchases and sales data for its only product.

Date	Activities	Units Acquired at Cost	Units Sold at Retail
Mar. 1	Beginning inventory	150 units @ $7.00 = $1,050	
Mar. 10	Sales		90 units @ $15
Mar. 20	Purchase	220 units @ $6.00 = 1,320	
Mar. 25	Sales		145 units @ $15
Mar. 30	Purchase	90 units @ $5.00 = 450	
	Totals	460 units $2,820	235 units

Check Ending inventory: WAC, $1,289

Park uses a perpetual inventory system. Determine the cost assigned to ending inventory and to cost of goods sold using (*a*) specific identification, (*b*) weighted average cost, and (*c*) FIFO. (Round per unit costs to three decimals, but inventory balances to the dollar.) For specific identification, ending inventory consists of 225 units, where 90 are from the March 30 purchase, 80 are from the March 20 purchase, and 55 are from beginning inventory.

Exercise 6-4

Profit effects of inventory methods

A1 ⬛

Use the data in Exercise 6-3 to prepare comparative income statements for the month of January for Park Company similar to those shown in Exhibit 6.6 for the four inventory methods. Assume expenses are $1,600, and that the applicable income tax rate is 30%.

1. Which method yields the highest net profit?

2. If costs were rising instead of falling, which method would yield the highest net profit?

Harold Co. reported the following current-year purchases and sales data for its only product.

Date	Activities	Units Acquired at Cost	Units Sold at Retail
Jan. 1	Beginning inventory	100 units @ $10 = $ 1,000	
Jan. 10	Sales		90 units @ $40
Mar. 14	Purchase	250 units @ $15 = 3,750	
Mar. 15	Sales		140 units @ $40
July 30	Purchase	400 units @ $20 = 8,000	
Oct. 5	Sales		300 units @ $40
Oct. 26	Purchase	600 units @ $25 = 15,000	
	Totals	1,350 units $27,750	530 units

Harold uses a perpetual inventory system. Determine the costs assigned to ending inventory and to cost of goods sold using (*a*) FIFO and (*b*) LIFO. Compute the gross margin for each method.

Exercise 6-5[C]
Inventory costing methods (perpetual)—FIFO and LIFO
P1 P5

Check Ending inventory: LIFO, $18,750

Refer to the data in Exercise 6-5. Assume that ending inventory is made up of 100 units from the March 14 purchase, 120 units from the July 30 purchase, and all 600 units from the October 26 purchase. Using the specific identification method, calculate (*a*) the cost of goods sold and (*b*) the gross profit.

Exercise 6-6
Specific identification
P1

Ripken Company's ending inventory includes the following items. Compute the lower of cost and net realizable value for ending inventory applied separately to each product.

Product	Units	Per Unit Cost	Per Unit NRV
Helmets	22	$50	$54
Bats	15	78	72
Shoes	36	95	91
Uniforms	40	36	36

Exercise 6-7
Lower of cost and net realizable value
P2

Check Lower of cost and NRV = $6,896

Ringo Company had $900,000 of sales in each of three consecutive years 2010–2012, and it purchased merchandise costing $500,000 in each of those years. It also maintained a $200,000 physical inventory from the beginning to the end of that three-year period. In accounting for inventory, it made an error at the end of year 2010 that caused its year-end 2010 inventory to appear on its statements as $180,000 rather than the correct $200,000.

1. Determine the correct amount of the company's gross profit in each of the years 2010–2012.

2. Prepare comparative income statements as in Exhibit 6.9 to show the effect of this error on the company's cost of goods sold and gross profit for each of the years 2010–2012.

Exercise 6-8
Analysis of inventory errors
A2

Check 2010 reported gross profit, $380,000

Use the following information for Ryder Co. to compute inventory turnover for 2011 and 2010, and its days' sales in inventory at December 31, 2011 and 2010. (Round answers to one decimal.) Comment on Ryder's efficiency in using its assets to increase sales from 2010 to 2011.

	2011	2010	2009
Cost of goods sold	$643,825	$426,650	$391,300
Ending inventory	96,400	86,750	91,500

Exercise 6-9
Inventory turnover and days' sales in inventory
A3

Refer to Exercise 6-3 and assume the periodic inventory system is used. Determine the costs assigned to ending inventory and to cost of goods sold using (*a*) specific identification, (*b*) weighted average cost, (*c*) FIFO, and (*d*) LIFO. (Round per unit costs to three decimals, but inventory balances to the dollar.)

Exercise 6-10[A,C]
Inventory costing— periodic system
P3 P5

Exercise 6-11[A,C]
Inventory costing—periodic system
P3 **P5**

Refer to Exercise 6-5 and assume the periodic inventory system is used. Determine the costs assigned to ending inventory and to cost of goods sold using (a) FIFO and (b) LIFO. Then (c) compute the gross margin for each method.

Exercise 6-12[A,C]
Alternative cost flow assumptions—periodic
P3 **P5**

Lopez Co. reported the following current-year data for its only product. The company uses a periodic inventory system, and its ending inventory consists of 300 units—100 from each of the last three purchases. Determine the cost assigned to ending inventory and to cost of goods sold using (a) specific identification, (b) weighted average cost, (c) FIFO, and (d) LIFO. (Round per unit costs to three decimals, but inventory balances to the dollar.) Which method yields the highest net profit?

Jan.	1	Beginning inventory	200 units @ $2.00 = $	400
Mar.	7	Purchase	440 units @ $2.25 =	990
Jul.	28	Purchase	1,080 units @ $2.50 =	2,700
Oct.	3	Purchase	960 units @ $2.80 =	2,688
Dec.	19	Purchase	320 units @ $2.90 =	928
		Totals	3,000 units	$7,706

Check   Inventory; LIFO, $625; FIFO, $870

Exercise 6-13[A,C]
Alternative cost flow assumptions—periodic
P3 **P5**

Candis Gifts reported the following current-year data for its only product. The company uses a periodic inventory system, and its ending inventory consists of 300 units—100 from each of the last three purchases. Determine the cost assigned to ending inventory and to cost of goods sold using (a) specific identification, (b) weighted average cost, (c) FIFO, and (d) LIFO. (Round per unit costs to three decimals, but inventory balances to the dollar.) Which method yields the lowest net profit?

Jan.	1	Beginning inventory	280 units @ $3.00 = $	840
Mar.	7	Purchase	600 units @ $2.80 =	1,680
Jul.	28	Purchase	800 units @ $2.50 =	2,000
Oct.	3	Purchase	1,100 units @ $2.30 =	2,530
Dec.	19	Purchase	250 units @ $2.00 =	500
		Totals	3,030 units	$7,550

Check   Inventory: LIFO, $896; FIFO, $615

Exercise 6-14[B]
Estimating ending inventory—retail method
P4

In 2011, Wichita Company had net sales (at retail) of $130,000. The following additional information is available from its records at the end of 2011. Use the retail inventory method to estimate Wichita's 2011 ending inventory at cost.

	At Cost	At Retail
Beginning inventory	$ 31,900	$64,200
Cost of goods purchased	57,810	98,400

Check   End. Inventory, $17,930

Exercise 6-15[B]
Estimating ending inventory—gross profit method
P4

On March 1, KB Shop had $450,000 of inventory at cost. In the first quarter of the year, it purchased $1,590,000 of merchandise, returned $23,100, and paid freight charges of $37,600 on purchased merchandise, terms FOB shipping point. The company's gross profit averages 30%, and the store had $2,000,000 of net sales (at retail) in the first quarter of the year. Use the gross profit method to estimate its cost of inventory at the end of the first quarter.

Exercise 6-16
Accounting for inventory value changes
P2

Li Ning Company Limited reports the following regarding its accounting for inventories for financial year 2011.

> Inventories are stated at the lower of cost and net realizable value. Cost is determined using the weighted average method. The cost of finished goods and work in progress comprises costs of merchandise, raw materials, direct labour, other direct costs, and related production overheads. The Group realized a loss of approximately RMB72,427,000 for the year ended 31 December 2011 (2010: RMB42,556,000) in respect of the write-down of inventories to their net realizable value. These amounts have been included in administrative expenses in the consolidated income statement.

1. What cost flow assumption(s) does Li Ning apply in assigning costs to its inventories?
2. What has Li Ning recorded for 2011 as a write-down on valuation of its inventories?
3. If at year-end 2011 there was an increase in the value of its inventories such that there was a reversal for the 2011 write-down, how would Li Ning account for this? Explain.

connect

Anthony Company uses a perpetual inventory system. It entered into the following purchases and sales transactions for March.

PROBLEM SET A

Problem 6-1A
Alternative cost flows—perpetual
P1

Date	Activities	Units Acquired at Cost	Units Sold at Retail
Mar. 1	Beginning inventory	50 units @ $50/unit	
Mar. 5	Purchase...................	200 units @ $55/unit	
Mar. 9	Sales		210 units @ $85/unit
Mar. 18	Purchase...................	60 units @ $60/unit	
Mar. 25	Purchase...................	100 units @ $62/unit	
Mar. 29	Sales		80 units @ $95/unit
	Totals	410 units	290 units

Required

1. Compute cost of goods available for sale and the number of units available for sale.
2. Compute the number of units in ending inventory.
3. Compute the cost assigned to ending inventory using (a) FIFO, (b) weighted average cost, and (c) specific identification. (Round per unit costs to three decimals, but inventory balances to the dollar.) For specific identification, the March 9 sale consisted of 40 units from beginning inventory and 170 units from the March 5 purchase; the March 29 sale consisted of 20 units from the March 18 purchase and 60 units from the March 25 purchase.
4. Compute gross profit earned by the company for each of the four costing methods in part 3.

Check (3) Ending Inventory: FIFO, $7,400; WAC, $7,176

Marlow Company uses a perpetual inventory system. It entered into the following calendar-year 2011 purchases and sales transactions.

Problem 6-2A
Alternative cost flows—perpetual
P1

Date	Activities	Units Acquired at Cost	Units Sold at Retail
Jan. 1	Beginning inventory	600 units @ $44/unit	
Feb. 10	Purchase...................	200 units @ $40/unit	
Mar. 13	Purchase...................	100 units @ $20/unit	
Mar. 15	Sales		400 units @ $75/unit
Aug. 21	Purchase...................	160 units @ $60/unit	
Sept. 5	Purchase...................	280 units @ $48/unit	
Sept. 10	Sales		200 units @ $75/unit
	Totals	1,340 units	600 units

Required

1. Compute cost of goods available for sale and the number of units available for sale.
2. Compute the number of units in ending inventory.
3. Compute the cost assigned to ending inventory using (a) FIFO, (b) specific identification—units sold consist of 500 units from beginning inventory and 100 units from the March 13 purchase, and (c) weighted average cost. (Round per unit costs to three decimals, but inventory balances to the dollar.)
4. Compute gross profit earned by the company for each of the three costing methods in part 3.

Check (3) Ending inventory: FIFO, $33,040; WAC, $34,055;

Analysis Component

5. If the company's manager earns a bonus based on a percent of gross profit, which method of inventory costing will the manager likely prefer?

Problem 6-3A
Lower of cost and net realizable value

P2

A physical inventory of Helmke Company taken at December 31 reveals the following.

		Per Unit	
Item	**Units**	**Cost**	**NRV**
Audio equipment			
Receivers	335	$ 90	$ 98
CD players	250	111	100
MP3 players	316	86	95
Speakers	194	52	41
Video equipment			
Handheld LCDs	470	150	125
VCRs	281	93	84
Camcorders	202	310	322
Car audio equipment			
Satellite radios	175	70	84
CD/MP3 radios	160	97	105

Required

Check $263,024

1. Calculate the lower of cost and net realizable value for the inventory applied separately to each item.
2. If the NRV amount is less than the recorded cost of the inventory, then record the lower of cost and NRV adjustment to the Merchandise Inventory account.

Problem 6-4A
Analysis of inventory errors

A2

www.mheducation.asia/olc/wildkwokFAP

Doubletree Company's financial statements show the following. The company recently discovered that in making physical counts of inventory, it had made the following errors: Inventory on December 31, 2010, is understated by $50,000, and inventory on December 31, 2011, is overstated by $20,000.

For Year Ended December 31	2010	2011	2012
(a) Cost of goods sold	$ 725,000	$ 955,000	$ 790,000
(b) Net profit	268,000	275,000	250,000
(c) Total current assets	1,247,000	1,360,000	1,230,000
(d) Total equity.	1,387,000	1,580,000	1,245,000

Required

1. For each key financial statement figure—(a), (b), (c), and (d) above—prepare a table similar to the following to show the adjustments necessary to correct the reported amounts.

Figure: _____	2010	2011	2012
Reported amount	____	____	____
Adjustments for: 12/31/2010 error	____	____	____
12/31/2011 error	____	____	____
Corrected amount	____	____	____

Check (1) Corrected net profit:
2010, $318,000; 2011, $205,000;
2012, $270,000

Analysis Component

2. What is the error in total net profit for the combined three-year period resulting from the inventory errors? Explain.
3. Explain why the understatement of inventory by $50,000 at the end of 2010 results in an understatement of equity by the same amount in that year.

Viper Company began year 2011 with 20,000 units of product in its January 1 inventory costing $15 each. It made successive purchases of its product in year 2011 as follows. The company uses a periodic inventory system. On December 31, 2011, a physical count reveals that 35,000 units of its product remain in inventory.

Mar. 7	28,000 units @ $18 each
May 25	30,000 units @ $22 each
Aug. 1	20,000 units @ $24 each
Nov. 10	33,000 units @ $27 each

Problem 6-5A[A]

Alternative cost flows—periodic

P3

www.mheducation.asia/olc/wildkwokFAP

Required

1. Compute the number and total cost of the units available for sale in year 2011.
2. Compute the amounts assigned to the 2011 ending inventory and the cost of goods sold using (*a*) FIFO and (*b*) weighted average cost. (Round per unit costs to three decimals, but inventory balances to the dollar.)

Check   (2) Cost of goods sold: FIFO, $1,896,000; WAC, $2,077,557

Botch Corp. sold 5,500 units of its product at $45 per unit in year 2011 and incurred operating expenses of $6 per unit in selling the units. It began the year with 600 units in inventory and made successive purchases of its product as follows.

Jan. 1	Beginning inventory	600 units @ $18 per unit
Feb. 20	Purchase	1,500 units @ $19 per unit
May 16	Purchase	700 units @ $20 per unit
Oct. 3	Purchase	400 units @ $21 per unit
Dec. 11	Purchase	3,300 units @ $22 per unit
	Total	6,500 units

Problem 6-6A[A]

Profit comparisons and cost flows—periodic

A1 P3

Required

1. Prepare comparative income statements similar to Exhibit 6.6 for the three inventory costing methods of FIFO, and weighted average cost. (Round per unit costs to three decimals, but inventory balances to the dollar.) Include a detailed cost of goods sold section as part of each statement. The company uses a periodic inventory system, and its income tax rate is 30%.
2. How would the financial results from using the two alternative inventory costing methods change if Botch had been experiencing declining costs in its purchases of inventory?
3. What advantages and disadvantages are offered by using (*a*) weighted average cost and (*b*) FIFO? Assume the continuing trend of increasing costs.

Check   (1) Net profit: FIFO, $71,540; WAC, $70,603

The records of Nilson Company provide the following information for the year ended December 31.

	At Cost	At Retail
January 1 beginning inventory	$ 471,350	$ 927,150
Cost of goods purchased	3,276,030	6,279,350
Sales		5,495,700
Sales returns		44,600

Problem 6-7A[B]

Retail inventory method

P4

Required

1. Use the retail inventory method to estimate the company's year-end inventory at cost.
2. A year-end physical inventory at retail prices yields a total inventory of $1,675,800. Prepare a calculation showing the company's loss from shrinkage at cost and at retail.

Check   (1) Inventory, $912,808 cost; (2) Inventory shortage at cost, $41,392

Wayman Company wants to prepare interim financial statements for the first quarter. The company wishes to avoid making a physical count of inventory. Wayman's gross profit rate averages 35%. The following information for the first quarter is available from its records.

Problem 6-8A[B]

Gross profit method

P4

January 1 beginning inventory	$ 300,260
Cost of goods purchased	939,050
Sales.............................	1,191,150
Sales returns	9,450

Required

Use the gross profit method to estimate the company's first quarter ending inventory.

PROBLEM SET B

Problem 6-1B
Alternative cost flows—perpetual

P1

CCO Company uses a perpetual inventory system. It entered into the following purchases and sales transactions for April.

Date	Activities	Units Acquired at Cost	Units Sold at Retail
Apr. 1	Beginning inventory	15 units @ $3,000/unit	
Apr. 6	Purchase	35 units @ $3,500/unit	
Apr. 9	Sales		18 units @ $12,000/unit
Apr. 17	Purchase	8 units @ $4,500/unit	
Apr. 25	Purchase	10 units @ $4,580/unit	
Apr. 30	Sales		30 units @ $14,000/unit
	Total	68 units	48 units

Required

1. Compute cost of goods available for sale and the number of units available for sale.
2. Compute the number of units in ending inventory.

3. Compute the cost assigned to ending inventory using (a) FIFO, (b) weighted average cost, and (c) specific identification. (Round per unit costs to three decimals, but inventory balances to the dollar.) For specific identification, the April 9 sale consisted of 8 units from beginning inventory and 10 units from the April 6 purchase; the April 30 sale consisted of 20 units from the April 6 purchase and 10 units from the April 25 purchase.
4. Compute gross profit earned by the company for each of the three costing methods in part 3.

Problem 6-2B
Alternative cost flows—perpetual

P1

Venus Company uses a perpetual inventory system. It entered into the following calendar-year 2011 purchases and sales transactions.

Date	Activities	Units Acquired at Cost	Units Sold at Retail
Jan. 1	Beginning inventory	600 units @ $55/unit	
Jan. 10	Purchase	450 units @ $56/unit	
Feb. 13	Purchase	200 units @ $57/unit	
Feb. 15	Sales		430 units @ $90/unit
July 21	Purchase	230 units @ $58/unit	
Aug. 5	Purchase	345 units @ $59/unit	
Aug. 10	Sales		335 units @ $90/unit
	Total	1,825 units	765 units

Required

1. Compute cost of goods available for sale and the number of units available for sale.
2. Compute the number of units in ending inventory.

3. Compute the cost assigned to ending inventory using (a) FIFO, (b) specific identification—units sold consist of 600 units from beginning inventory and 165 units from the February 13 purchase, and (c) weighted average cost. (Round per unit costs to three decimals, but inventory balances to the dollar.)
4. Compute gross profit earned by the company for each of the three costing methods in part 3.

Analysis Component

5. If the company's manager earns a bonus based on a percent of gross profit, which method of inventory costing will the manager likely prefer?

A physical inventory of Office Deals taken at December 31 reveals the following.

Problem 6-3B
Lower of cost and net realizable value
P2

File Edit View Insert Format Tools Data Accounting Window Help

100%

Item	Units	Per Unit	
		Cost	NRV
Office furniture			
Desks	436	$261	$305
Credenzas	295	227	256
Chairs	587	49	43
Bookshelves	321	93	82
Filing cabinets			
Two-drawer	214	81	70
Four-drawer	398	135	122
Lateral	175	104	118
Office equipment			
Fax machines	430	168	200
Copiers	545	317	288
Telephones	352	125	117

Sheet1 Sheet2 Sheet3

Required

1. Compute the lower of cost and net realizable value for the inventory applied separately to each item.

2. If the NRV amount is less than the recorded cost of the inventory, then record the lower of cost and NRV adjustment to the Merchandise Inventory account.

Check $584,444

Watson Company's financial statements show the following. The company recently discovered that in making physical counts of inventory, it had made the following errors: Inventory on December 31, 2010, is overstated by $70,000, and inventory on December 31, 2011, is understated by $55,000.

Problem 6-4B
Analysis of inventory errors
A2

For Year Ended December 31	2010	2011	2012
(a) Cost of goods sold	$ 655,000	$ 957,000	$ 799,000
(b) Net profit	225,000	277,000	244,000
(c) Total current assets	1,251,000	1,360,000	1,200,000
(d) Total equity	1,387,000	1,520,000	1,250,000

Required

1. For each key financial statement figure—(*a*), (*b*), (*c*), and (*d*) above—prepare a table similar to the following to show the adjustments necessary to correct the reported amounts.

Check (1) Corrected net profit: 2010, $155,000; 2011, $402,000; 2012, $189,000

Figure: _____	2010	2011	2012
Reported amount	_____	_____	_____
Adjustments for: 12/31/2010 error	_____	_____	_____
12/31/2011 error	_____	_____	_____
Corrected amount	_____	_____	_____

Analysis Component

2. What is the error in total net profit for the combined three-year period resulting from the inventory errors? Explain.

3. Explain why the overstatement of inventory by $70,000 at the end of 2010 results in an overstatement of equity by the same amount in that year.

Problem 6-5B^A

Alternative cost flows—periodic

P3

Check (2) Cost of goods sold:
FIFO, $1,302,000; WAC, $1,234,681

Solaris Co. began year 2011 with 6,300 units of product in its January 1 inventory costing $35 each. It made successive purchases of its product in year 2011 as follows. The company uses a periodic inventory system. On December 31, 2011, a physical count reveals that 16,500 units of its product remain in inventory.

Jan. 4	....	10,500 units @ $33 each
May 18	....	13,000 units @ $32 each
Jul. 9	....	12,000 units @ $29 each
Nov. 21	....	15,500 units @ $26 each

Required

1. Compute the number and total cost of the units available for sale in year 2011.
2. Compute the amounts assigned to the 2011 ending inventory and the cost of goods sold using (a) FIFO and (b) weighted average cost. (Round per unit costs to three decimals, but inventory balances to the dollar.)

Problem 6-6B^A

Profit comparisons and cost flows—periodic

A1 P3

Check (1) Net profit: FIFO,
$44,805; WAC, $42,519

Rikkers Company sold 2,500 units of its product at $98 per unit in year 2011 and incurred operating expenses of $14 per unit in selling the units. It began the year with 740 units in inventory and made successive purchases of its product as follows.

Jan. 1	Beginning inventory	....	740 units @ $58 per unit
Apr. 2	Purchase	....	700 units @ $59 per unit
Jun. 14	Purchase	....	600 units @ $61 per unit
Aug. 29	Purchase	....	500 units @ $64 per unit
Nov. 18	Purchase	....	800 units @ $65 per unit
	Total	....	3,340 units

Required

1. Prepare comparative income statements similar to Exhibit 6.6 for the two inventory costing methods of FIFO and weighted average cost. (Round per unit costs to three decimals, but inventory balances to the dollar.) Include a detailed cost of goods sold section as part of each statement. The company uses a periodic inventory system, and its income tax rate is 25%.
2. How would the financial results from using the three alternative inventory costing methods change if the company had been experiencing decreasing prices in its purchases of inventory?
3. What advantages and disadvantages are offered by using (a) weighted average cost and (b) FIFO? Assume the continuing trend of increasing costs.

Problem 6-7B^B

Retail inventory method

P4

Check (1) Inventory, $55,902 cost;

  (2) Inventory shortage at
  cost, $4,059

The records of Saturn Co. provide the following information for the year ended December 31.

	At Cost	At Retail
January 1 beginning inventory	$ 81,670	$114,610
Cost of goods purchased	492,250	751,730
Sales		786,120
Sales returns		4,480

Required

1. Use the retail inventory method to estimate the company's year-end inventory.
2. A year-end physical inventory at retail prices yields a total inventory of $78,550. Prepare a calculation showing the company's loss from shrinkage at cost and at retail.

Problem 6-8B^B

Gross profit method

P4

Ernst Equipment Co. wants to prepare interim financial statements for the first quarter. The company wishes to avoid making a physical count of inventory. Ernst's gross profit rate averages 30%. The following information for the first quarter is available from its records.

January 1 beginning inventory	$ 752,880
Cost of goods purchased	2,159,630
Sales	3,710,250
Sales returns	74,200

Required

Use the gross profit method to estimate the company's first quarter ending inventory.

Check Estim. ending inventory, $367,275

*This **serial problem** began in Chapter 1 and continues through most of the book. If previous chapter segments were not completed, the serial problem can begin at this point.*

SERIAL PROBLEM
Business Solutions
P2 A3

Part A

SP 6 S. Rey of Business Solutions is evaluating her inventory to determine whether it must be adjusted based on the lower of cost and net realizable value rule. Business Solutions has three different types of software in its inventory and the following information is available for each.

Inventory Items	Units	Per Unit Cost	Per Unit NRV
Office productivity	3	$ 76	$ 74
Desktop publishing	2	103	100
Accounting	3	90	96

Required

Compute the lower of cost and net realizable value for ending inventory assuming Rey applies it to each product in inventory. Under this assumption, must Rey adjust the reported inventory value? Explain.

Part B

Selected accounts and balances for the three months ended March 31, 2012, for Business Solutions follow.

January 1 beginning inventory	$ 0
Cost of goods sold	14,052
March 31 ending inventory	704

Required

1. Compute inventory turnover and days' sales in inventory for the three months ended March 31, 2012.
2. Assess the company's performance if competitors average 15 times for inventory turnover and 25 days for days' sales in inventory.

Beyond the Numbers

BTN 6-1 Refer to Nestlé's statement of financial position in Appendix A.

REPORTING IN ACTION
C2 A3

Required

1. What amount of inventories did Nestlé hold as current asset as at December 31, 2013? As at December 31, 2012?
2. Inventories represent what percent of current assets as at December 31, 2013? As at December 31, 2012?
3. What accounting method(s) did Nestlé use to compute inventory amounts on its statement of financial position?
4. Compute inventory turnover for financial year ended December 31, 2013 and days' sales in inventory as at December 31, 2012. Round to one decimal place each.

Fast Forward

5. Access Nestlé's financial statements for financial years ended after December 31, 2013 from its Website (http://www.nestle.com/investors). Answer questions 1 through 4 using the current Nestlé information and compare results to those prior years.

COMPARATIVE ANALYSIS

A3

BTN 6-2   Key comparative figures for both Adidas and Puma follow.

	Adidas (in EUR millions)			Puma (in EUR millions)		
	Current Year	One Year Prior	Two Years Prior	Current Year	One Year Prior	Two Years Prior
Inventories	2,634	2,486	2,482	521.3	552.5	536.8
Cost of sales	7,352	7,780	7,000	1,597.8	1,691.7	1,515.6

Required

1. Compute inventory turnover for both companies for the most recent two years shown.
2. Compute days' sales in inventory for both companies for the three years shown.
3. Comment on and interpret your findings from parts 1 and 2.

ETHICS CHALLENGE

A1 P5

BTN 6-3   Golf Mart is a retail sports store carrying golf apparel and equipment. The store is at the end of its second year of operation and is struggling. A major problem is that its cost of inventory has continually increased in the past two years. In the first year of operations, the store assigned inventory costs using weighted average cost. A loan agreement the store has with its bank, its prime source of financing, requires the store to maintain a certain profit margin and current ratio. The store's owner is currently looking over Golf Mart's preliminary financial statements for its second year. The numbers are not favorable. The only way the store can meet the required financial ratios agreed on with the bank is to change from weighted average cost to FIFO. The owner recalculates ending inventory using FIFO and submits those numbers and statements to the loan officer at the bank for the required bank review. The owner thankfully reflects on the available latitude in choosing the inventory costing method.

Required

1. How does Golf Mart's use of FIFO improve its net profit margin and current ratio?
2. Is the action by Golf Mart's owner ethical? Explain.

TAKING IT TO THE NET

A3

BTN 6-4   Access L'Oréal's Website (www.loreal-finance.com/eng) to answer the following.

Required

1. What inventory method does L'Oréal use? (Hint: See the notes to its financial statements.)
2. Compute L'Oréal's gross margin and gross margin ratio for the financial year 2013. Comment on your computations—assume an industry average of 60% for the gross margin ratio.
3. Compute L'Oréal's inventory turnover and days' sales in inventory for the year ended December 31, 2013. Comment on your computations—assume an industry average of 3.0 for inventory turnover and 120 days for days' sale in inventory.

TEAMWORK IN ACTION

A1 P1 P5

BTN 6-5   Each team member has the responsibility to become an expert on an inventory method. This expertise will be used to facilitate teammates' understanding of the concepts relevant to that method.

1. Each learning team member should select an area for expertise by choosing one of the following inventory methods: specific identification, LIFO, FIFO, or weighted average cost.
2. Form expert teams made up of students who have selected the same area of expertise. The instructor will identify where each expert team will meet.
3. Using the following data, each expert team must collaborate to develop a presentation that illustrates the relevant concepts and procedures for its inventory method. Each team member must write the presentation in a format that can be shown to the learning team.

Point: Step 1 allows four choices or areas for expertise. Larger teams will have some duplication of choice, but the specific identification method should not be duplicated.

Data

The company uses a perpetual inventory system. It had the following beginning inventory and current year purchases of its product.

Jan. 1	Beginning inventory.........	50 units @ $10 =	$ 500
Jan. 14	Purchase	150 units @ $12 =	1,800
Apr. 30	Purchase	200 units @ $15 =	3,000
Sept. 26	Purchase	300 units @ $20 =	6,000

The company transacted sales on the following dates at a $35 per unit sales price.

Jan. 10	30 units	(specific cost: 30 @ $10)
Feb. 15	100 units	(specific cost: 100 @ $12)
Oct. 5	350 units	(specific cost: 100 @ $15 and 250 @ $20)

Concepts and Procedures to Illustrate in Expert Presentation

a. Identify and compute the costs to assign to the units sold. (Round per unit costs to three decimals.)

b. Identify and compute the costs to assign to the units in ending inventory. (Round inventory balances to the dollar.)

c. How likely is it that this inventory costing method will reflect the actual physical flow of goods? How relevant is that factor in determining whether this is an acceptable method to use?

d. What is the impact of this method versus others in determining net profit and income taxes?

4. Re-form learning teams. In rotation, each expert is to present to the team the presentation developed in part 3. Experts are to encourage and respond to questions.

BTN 6-6 Review the chapter's opening feature highlighting **HABI Footwear**. Assume that HABI Footwear consistently maintains an inventory level of $30,000, meaning that its average and ending inventory levels are the same. Also assume its annual cost of sales is $120,000. To cut costs, HABI Footwear proposes to slash inventory to a constant level of $15,000 with no impact on cost of sales. HABI Footwear plans to work with suppliers to get quicker deliveries and to order smaller quantities more often.

ENTREPRENEURIAL DECISION

A3

Required

1. Compute the company's inventory turnover and its days' sales in inventory under (*a*) current conditions and (*b*) proposed conditions.

2. Evaluate and comment on the merits of HABI Footwear's proposal given your analysis in part 1. Identify any concerns you might have about the proposal.

BTN 6-7 Visit four retail stores with another classmate. In each store, identify whether the store uses a bar-coding system to help manage its inventory. Try to find at least one store that does not use bar-coding. If a store does not use bar-coding, ask the store's manager or clerk whether he or she knows which type of inventory method the store employs. Create a table that shows columns for the name of store visited, type of merchandise sold, use or nonuse of bar-coding, and the inventory method used if bar-coding is not employed. You might also inquire as to what the store's inventory turnover is and how often physical inventory is taken.

HITTING THE ROAD

C1 C2

BTN 6-8 **Adidas**, **Puma**, and **Nike** are all competitors in the global marketplace. Key comparative figures for each company follow.

GLOBAL DECISION

A3

	Adidas (in EUR millions)			Puma (in EUR millions)			Nike (in US$ millions)		
	Current Year	One Year Prior	Two Years Prior	Current Year	One Year Prior	Two Years Prior	Current Year	One Year Prior	Two Years Prior
Inventories.........	2,482	2,119	1,471	536.8	439.7	344.4	2,175	2,041	2,357
Cost of Sales	7,000	6,260	—	1,515.6	1,361.6	—	11,354	10,214	—

Required

1. Use these data to compute (*a*) inventory turnover and (*b*) days' sales in inventory for the most recent two years shown for **Adidas**, **Puma**, and **Nike**.

2. Comment on and interpret your findings from part 1.

ANSWERS TO MULTIPLE CHOICE QUIZ

1. a; FIFO perpetual

Date	Goods Purchased	Cost of Goods Sold	Inventory Balance
Jul. 1			75 units @ $25 = $ 1,875
Jul. 3	348 units @ $27 = $9,396		75 units @ $25 ⎱ = $ 11,271 348 units @ $27 ⎰
Jul. 8		75 units @ $25 ⎱ = $ 7,950 225 units @ $27 ⎰	123 units @ $27 = $ 3,321
Jul. 15	257 units @ $28 = $7,196		123 units @ $27 ⎱ = $ 10,517 257 units @ $28 ⎰
Jul. 23		123 units @ $27 ⎱ = $ 7,577 152 units @ $28 ⎰	105 units @ $28 = $ 2,940
		$15,527	

2. e; Specific identification perpetual—Ending inventory computation.

20 units @ $25	$ 500
40 units @ $27	1,080
45 units @ $28	1,260
105 units	$2,840

3. a; FIFO periodic—Ending inventory computation.
105 units @ $28 each = $2,940; The FIFO periodic inventory computation is identical to the FIFO perpetual inventory computation (see question 1).

4. d; Days' sales in inventory = (Ending inventory/Cost of goods sold × 365)
= ($18,000/$85,000) × 365 = 77.29 days

7

Accounting Information Systems

A Look Back

Chapters 5 and 6 focused on merchandising activities and accounting for inventory. We explained inventory systems, accounting for inventory transactions, and assigning costs to inventory.

A Look at This Chapter

This chapter emphasizes accounting information systems. We describe fundamental system principles, the system's components, use of special journals and subsidiary ledgers, and technology-based systems.

A Look Ahead

Chapter 8 focuses on internal controls and accounting for cash and cash equivalents. We explain good internal control procedures and their importance.

Learning Objectives

CAP

CONCEPTUAL

C1 Identify the principles and components of accounting information systems. (p. 272)

C2 Explain the goals and uses of special journals. (p. 275)

C3 Describe the use of controlling accounts and subsidiary ledgers. (p. 276)

ANALYTICAL

A1 Compute segment return on assets and use it to evaluate segment performance. (p. 288)

PROCEDURAL

P1 Journalize and post transactions using special journals. (p. 278)

P2 Prepare and prove the accuracy of subsidiary ledgers. (p. 279)

P3 *Appendix 7A*—Journalize and post transactions using special journals in a periodic inventory system. (p. 292)

"Managing this social enterprise gives me great joy." —**JOSEPHINE NG**

Sew Something Good

Making people look good is her business. But the real deal is the good she does. Meet Josephine Ng, owner of **Alteration Initiative (www.alteration.com.sg)**, an enterprise she co-founded with her husband of 15 years. Being her own boss is nothing new to Josephine. "I was a co-founder of an integrated marketing agency until 2001, when it was acquired by an international marketing group," says Josephine. She took a six-year break, and instead of rejoining the rat race, started thinking of setting up a social enterprise "to give back to society." What could be more timely than a social entrepreneurship and philanthropy event at the National University of Singapore in 2009 during which she learned from a friend the challenges faced by single mothers? She knew instantly who her beneficiaries would be.

The next step was to find the right fit of jobs for them. "Many people I know, including myself, face much frustration at the lack of professional alteration centers in Singapore," she says. The outcome was Alteration Initiative, a high-quality apparel alteration service, which she launched with three outlets in Singapore in 2010. It works closely with government agencies, community councils, and voluntary welfare organizations to recruit beneficiaries who include both single mothers and women in need.

Managing a social enterprise is no different from overseeing a business concern, as Josephine will tell you, though it means you need to work harder to meet both business and social objectives in terms of training and employing disadvantaged women. She faces the same challenges as all business owners, and understands the importance of grasping the fundamentals of accounting principles for effective decision making. Josephine's accounting and point-of-sale systems were developed in-house. The accounting system was designed using Microsoft Excel, with automated macros and formula, to manipulate financial data. FileMaker Pro, with automated summary of closing cash, nets, and credit card transactions, keeps track of customers, items, and sales.

"Managing this social enterprise gives me great joy as it allows me to fulfill both my social and entrepreneurial aspirations," says Josephine, community proprietor with a heart of gold, whose initiative to "do good together" will surely light a path for others to follow.

With increases in the number and complexity of business activities, the demands placed on accounting information systems increase. Accounting information systems must meet this challenge in an efficient and effective manner. In this chapter, we learn about fundamental principles guiding information systems, and we study components making up these systems. We also explain procedures that use special journals and subsidiary ledgers to make accounting information systems more efficient. An understanding of the details of accounting reports makes us better decision makers when using financial information, and it improves our ability to analyze and interpret financial statements.

Accounting Information Systems

System Principles	System Components	Special Journals	System Technology
• Control • Relevance • Compatibility • Flexibility • Cost-Benefit	• Source documents • Input devices • Processors • Storage • Output devices	• Subsidiary ledgers • Sales journal • Cash receipts journal • Purchases journal • Cash disbursements journal	• Computers • Data processing • Networks • Enterprise resource planning (ERP)

FUNDAMENTAL SYSTEM PRINCIPLES

C1 Identify the principles and components of accounting information systems.

Accounting information systems collect and process data from transactions and events, organize them in useful reports, and communicate results to decision makers. With the increasing complexity of business and the growing need for information, accounting information systems are more important than ever. All decision makers need to have a basic knowledge of how accounting information systems work. This knowledge gives decision makers a competitive edge as they gain a better understanding of information constraints, measurement limitations, and potential applications. It allows them to make more informed decisions and to better balance the risks and returns of different strategies. This section explains five basic principles of accounting information systems, shown in Exhibit 7.1.

EXHIBIT 7.1

System Principles

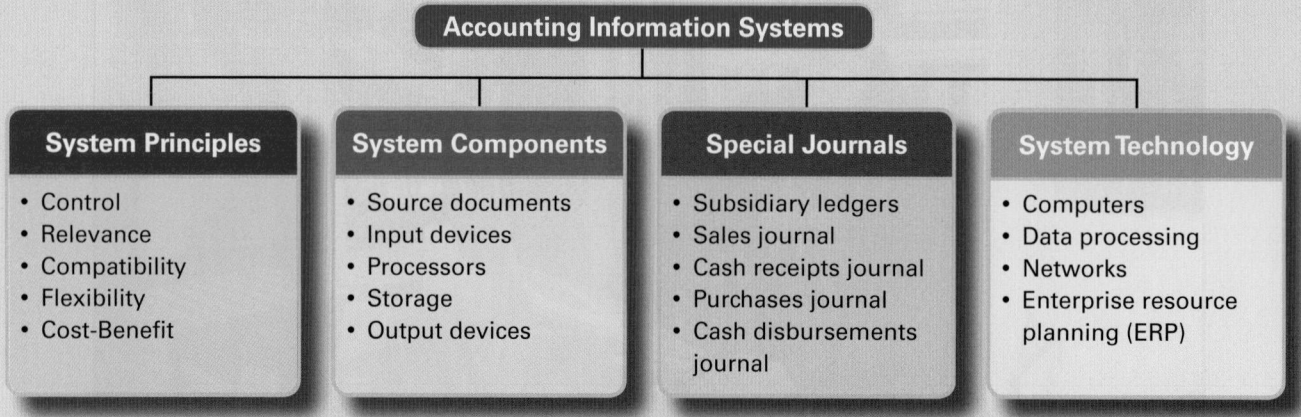

Control Principle

Managers need to control and monitor business activities. The **control principle** prescribes that an accounting information system have internal controls. **Internal controls** are methods and procedures allowing managers to control and monitor business activities. They include policies to direct operations toward common goals, procedures to ensure reliable financial reports, safeguards to protect company assets, and methods to achieve compliance with laws and regulations.

Relevance Principle

Decision makers need relevant information to make informed decisions. The **relevance principle** prescribes that an accounting information system report useful, understandable, timely, and pertinent information for effective decision making. The system must be designed to capture data that make a difference in decisions. To ensure this, we must consider all decision makers when identifying relevant information for disclosure.

Point: Albert Gonzalez is an American computer hacker who is accused of masterminding the combined credit card theft and subsequent reselling of more than 170 million card and ATM numbers from 2005 through 2007—the biggest such fraud in history as at year 2013. Gonzalez and his accomplices used SQL injection to deploy backdoors on several corporate systems in order to launch packet sniffing (specifically, ARP Spoofing) attacks, which allowed him to steal computer data from internal corporate networks.

Compatibility Principle

Accounting information systems must be consistent with the aims of a company. The **compatibility principle** prescribes that an accounting information system conform with a company's activities, personnel, and structure. It also must adapt to a company's unique characteristics. The system must not be intrusive but must work in harmony with and be driven by company goals. Most start-up entrepreneurs require only a simple information system. **Harley-Davidson**, on the other hand, demands both a merchandising and a manufacturing information system able to assemble data from its global operations.

Flexibility Principle

Accounting information systems must be able to adjust to changes. The **flexibility principle** prescribes that an accounting information system be able to adapt to changes in the company, business environment, and needs of decisions makers. Technological advances, competitive pressures, consumer tastes, regulations, and company activities constantly evolve. A system must be designed to adapt to these changes.

Cost-Benefit Principle

The **cost-benefit principle** prescribes that the benefits from an activity in an accounting information system outweigh the costs of that activity. The costs and benefits of an activity such as producing a specific report will impact the decisions of both external and internal users. Decisions regarding other systems principles (control, relevance, compatibility, and flexibility) are also affected by the cost-benefit principle.

Point: Law requires that *all* employers destroy credit-check and other employee records *before* tossing them. A cross-cut shredder is the tool of choice.

Decision Insight

Digital Is Forever E-communications have helped bring down many employees, including the former CEO of **Boeing**. To comply with Sarbanes-Oxley, more and more companies now archive and monitor e-mails, instant messages, blog postings, and Net-based phone calls. Using natural-language software, companies sift through digital communications in milliseconds, checking for trade secrets, bad language, porn, and pirated files. ■

COMPONENTS OF ACCOUNTING SYSTEMS

Accounting information systems consist of people, records, methods, and equipment. The systems are designed to capture information about a company's transactions and to provide output including financial, managerial, and tax reports. All accounting information systems have these same goals, and thus share some basic components. These components apply whether or not a system is heavily computerized, yet the components of computerized systems usually provide more accuracy, speed, efficiency, and convenience than those of manual systems.

The five basic **components of accounting systems** are source documents, input devices, information processors, information storage, and output devices. Exhibit 7.2 shows these components as a series of steps, yet we know that much two-way communication occurs between many of these components. We briefly describe each of these key components in this section.

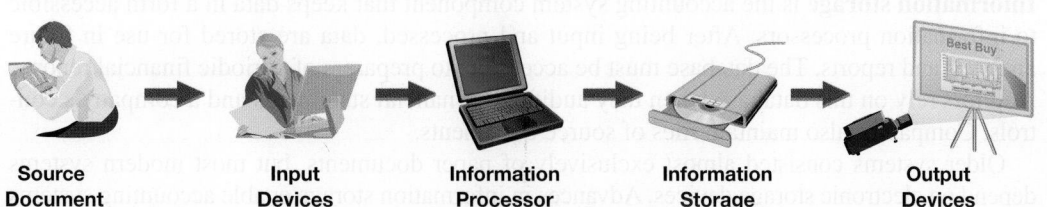

| Source Document | Input Devices | Information Processor | Information Storage | Output Devices |

EXHIBIT 7.2

Accounting System Components

Source Documents

We introduced source documents in Chapters 1 and 2 and explained their importance for both business transactions and information collection. Source documents provide the basic information processed by an accounting system. Examples of source documents include bank statements and checks, invoices from suppliers, billings to customers, cash register files, and employee earnings records. Source documents can be paper, although they increasingly are taking the form of electronic files and Web communications. A growing number of companies are sending documents directly from their systems to their customers' and suppliers' systems. The Web is playing a major role in this transformation from paper-based to *paperless* systems.

Accurate source documents are crucial to accounting information systems. Input of faulty or incomplete information seriously impairs the reliability and relevance of the information system. We commonly refer to this as "garbage in, garbage out." Information systems are set up with attention on control procedures to limit the possibility of entering faulty data in the system.

Input Devices

Point: Understanding a manual accounting system is useful in understanding an electronic system.

Input devices capture information from source documents and enable its transfer to the system's information processing component. These devices often involve converting data on source documents from written or electronic form to a form usable for the system. Journal entries, both electronic and paper based, are a type of input device. Keyboards, scanners, and modems are some of the most common input devices in practice today. For example, bar code readers capture code numbers and transfer them to the organization's computer for processing. Moreover, a scanner can capture writing samples and other input directly from source documents.

Controls are used to ensure that only authorized individuals input data to the system. Controls increase the system's reliability and allow information to be traced back to its source.

Decision Insight

Geek Chic   Cyberfashion pioneers are creating geek chic, a kind of wearable computer. Cyberfashion draws on digital cellular phones, lithium batteries, and miniature monitors. Special thread is woven into clothing to carry low-voltage signals from one part of the system to another, and fabric keyboards are sewn into clothes. These creations give new meaning to the term *software*. ■

Information Processors

Information processors are systems that interpret, transform, and summarize information for use in analysis and reporting. An important part of an information processor in accounting systems is professional judgment. Accounting principles are never so structured that they limit the need for professional judgment. Other parts of an information processor include journals, ledgers, working papers, and posting procedures. Each assists in transforming raw data to useful information.

Point: Roughly three-quarters of the world's email traffic was spam during December 2013, according to Russian security firm Kaspersky Lab.

Increasingly, computer technology (both computing hardware and software) is assisting manual information processors. This assistance is freeing accounting professionals to take on increased analysis, interpretive, and managerial roles. Web-based application service providers (ASPs) offer another type of information processor.

Information Storage

Point: A financial accounting database can be designed to support a wide range of internal reports for management.

Information storage is the accounting system component that keeps data in a form accessible to information processors. After being input and processed, data are stored for use in future analyses and reports. The database must be accessible to preparers of periodic financial reports. Auditors rely on this database when they audit both financial statements and a company's controls. Companies also maintain files of source documents.

Older systems consisted almost exclusively of paper documents, but most modern systems depend on electronic storage devices. Advances in information storage enable accounting systems to increasingly store more detailed data. This means managers have more data to access and work with in planning and controlling business activities. Information storage can be online, meaning that data can be accessed whenever, and from wherever, it is needed. Off-line storage means access often requires assistance and authorization. Information storage is increasingly augmented by Web sources such as SEC databases, benchmarking services, and financial and product markets.

Decision Insight

Direct Output A screenless computer display, called *virtual retinal display* (VRD), scans rows of pixels directly onto the user's retina by means of a laser. VRDs can simulate three-dimensional virtual worlds, including 3D financial graphics. ■

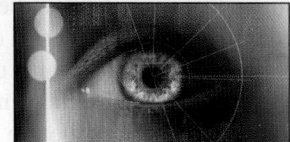

Output Devices

Output devices are the means to take information out of an accounting system and make it available to users. Common output devices are printers, monitors, projectors, and Web communications. Output devices provide users a variety of items including graphics, analysis reports, bills to customers, checks to suppliers, employee paychecks, financial statements, and internal reports. When requests for output occur, an information processor takes the needed data from a database and prepares the necessary report, which is then sent to an output device. A special type of output is an electronic funds transfer (EFT). One example is the transfer of payroll from the company's bank account to its employees' bank accounts. This requires an interface to allow a company's accounting system to send payroll data directly to the bank's accounting system. This interface can involve a company recording its payroll data in an encrypted zip file and forwarding it to the bank. The bank then uses this output to transfer wages earned to employees' accounts.

Decision Ethics   Answer — p. 297

Accountant Your client requests advice in purchasing software for its accounting system. You have been offered a 10% commission by a software company for each purchase of its system by one of your clients. Does this commission arrangement affect your evaluation of software? Do you tell your client about the commission arrangement? ■

Quick Check   Answers — p. 297

1. Identify the five primary components of an accounting information system.
2. What is the aim of information processors in an accounting system?
3. How are data in the information storage component of an accounting system used?

SPECIAL JOURNALS IN ACCOUNTING

This section describes the underlying records of accounting information systems. Designed correctly, these records support efficiency in processing transactions and events. They are part of all systems in various forms and are increasingly electronic. Even in technologically advanced systems, a basic understanding of the records we describe in this section aids in using, interpreting, and applying accounting information. It also improves our knowledge of computer-based systems. Remember that all accounting systems have common purposes and internal workings whether or not they depend on technology.

This section focuses on special journals and subsidiary ledgers that are an important part of accounting systems. We describe how special journals are used to capture transactions, and we explain how subsidiary ledgers are set up to capture details of accounts. This section uses a *perpetual*

 C2 Explain the goals and uses of special journals.

inventory system, and the special journals are set up using this system. Appendix 7A describes the change in special journals required for a *periodic* system. We also include a note at the bottom of each of the special journals explaining the change required if a company uses a periodic system.

Basics of Special Journals

A **general journal** is an all-purpose journal in which we can record any transaction. Use of a general journal for all transactions is usually more costly for a business *and* is a less effective control procedure. Moreover, for less technologically advanced systems, use of a general journal requires that each debit and each credit entered be individually posted to its respective ledger account. To enhance internal control and reduce costs, transactions are organized into common groups. A **special journal** is used to record and post transactions of similar type. Most transactions of a merchandiser, for instance, can be categorized into the journals shown in Exhibit 7.3. This section assumes the use of these four special journals along with the general journal. The general journal continues to be used for transactions not covered by special journals and for adjusting, closing, and correcting entries. We show in the following discussion that special journals are *efficient tools in helping journalize and post transactions.* This is done, for instance, by accumulating debits and credits of similar transactions, which allows posting of amounts as column *totals* rather than as individual amounts. The advantage of this system increases as the number of transactions increases. Special journals allow an *efficient division of labor,* which is also an effective control procedure.

EXHIBIT 7.3

Using Special Journals with a General Journal

Sales Journal	Cash Receipts Journal	Purchases Journal	Cash Disbursements Journal	General Journal
For recording credit sales	For recording cash receipts	For recording credit purchases	For recording cash payments	For transactions not in special journals

It is important to note that special journals and subsidiary ledgers *are designed in a manner that is best suited for each business.* The most likely candidates for special journal status are recurring transactions—for many businesses those are sales, cash receipts, purchases, and cash disbursements. However, good systems design for a business could involve collapsing sales and cash receipts in one journal, or purchases and cash disbursements in another. It could also involve adding more special journals or additional subsidiary ledgers for other recurring transactions. This design decision extends to journal and ledger format. That is, the selection on number of columns, column headings, and so forth is based on what is best suited for each business. Thus, read the following sections as one example of a common systems design, but not the only design.

Subsidiary Ledgers

 C3 Describe the use of controlling accounts and subsidiary ledgers.

To understand special journals, it is necessary to understand the workings of a **subsidiary ledger,** which is a list of individual accounts with a common characteristic. A subsidiary ledger contains detailed information on specific accounts in the general ledger. Information systems often include several subsidiary ledgers. Two of the most important are:

- *Accounts receivable ledger*—stores transaction data of individual customers.
- *Accounts payable ledger*—stores transaction data of individual suppliers.

Individual accounts in subsidiary ledgers are often arranged alphabetically, which is the approach taken here. We describe accounts receivable and accounts payable ledgers in this section. Our discussion of special journals uses these ledgers.

Accounts Receivable Ledger   When we recorded credit sales in prior chapters, we debited (increased) Accounts Receivable. When a company has more than one credit customer, the accounts receivable records must show how much *each* customer purchased, paid, and has yet to pay. This information is collected by keeping a separate account receivable for each credit customer. A separate account for each customer *could* be kept in the general ledger with the other financial statement accounts, but this is uncommon. Instead, the general ledger usually has a single Accounts Receivable account, and a *subsidiary ledger* is set up to keep a separate account for each customer. This subsidiary ledger is called the **accounts receivable ledger** (also called *accounts receivable subsidiary ledger* or *customers ledger*), and it can exist in electronic or paper form.

Exhibit 7.4 shows the relation between the Accounts Receivable account and its individual accounts in the subsidiary ledger. After all items are posted, the balance in the Accounts Receivable account must equal the sum of all balances of its customers' accounts. The Accounts Receivable account is said to control the accounts receivable ledger and is called a **controlling account.** Since the accounts receivable ledger is a supplementary record controlled by an account in the general ledger, it is called a *subsidiary* ledger.

Point: When a general ledger account has a subsidiary ledger, any transaction that impacts one of them also impacts the other—some refer to this as *general and subsidiary ledgers kept in tandem.*

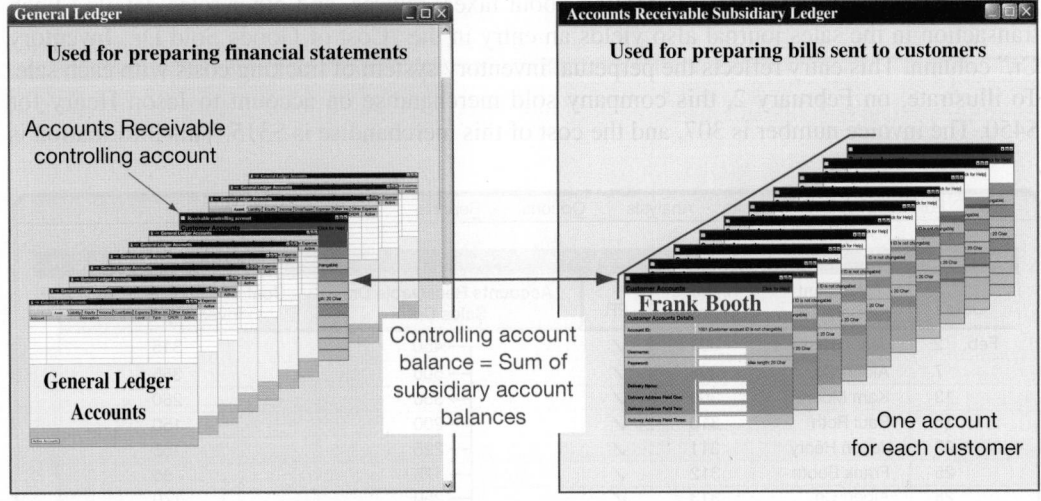

EXHIBIT 7.4

Accounts Receivable Controlling Account and Its Subsidiary Ledger

Point: A control account refers to any general ledger account that summarizes subsidiary ledger data.

Accounts Payable Ledger   There are other controlling accounts and subsidiary ledgers. We know, for example, that many companies buy on credit from several suppliers. This means that companies must keep a separate account for each supplier by keeping an Accounts Payable controlling account in the general ledger and a separate account for each supplier (creditor) in an **accounts payable ledger** (also called *accounts payable subsidiary ledger* or *creditors ledger*).

Other Subsidiary Ledgers   Subsidiary ledgers are common for several other accounts. A company with many classes of equipment, for example, might keep only one Equipment account in its general ledger, but its Equipment account would control a subsidiary ledger in which each class of equipment is recorded in a separate account. Similar treatment is common for investments, inventory, and any accounts needing separate detailed records. **Genmar Holdings,** which manufactures boats by Champion, Glastron, Four Winns, and Larson, reports sales information by product line in its report. Yet its accounting system keeps much more detailed sales records. Genmar Holdings, for instance, sells hundreds of different products and must be able to analyze the sales performance of each. This detail can be captured by many different general ledger sales accounts but is instead captured by using supplementary records that function like subsidiary ledgers. Overall, subsidiary ledgers are applied in many different ways to ensure that the accounting system captures sufficient details to support analyses that decision makers need. At least four benefits derive from subsidiary ledgers:

1. Removal of excessive details, and detailed accounts, from the general ledger.
2. Up-to-date information readily available on specific customers and suppliers.
3. Aid in error identification for specific accounts.
4. Potential efficiencies in recordkeeping through division of labor in posting.

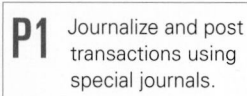

P1 Journalize and post transactions using special journals.

Point: Each transaction in the sales journal includes a debit to accounts receivable and a credit to sales.

Sales Journal

A typical **sales journal** is used to record sales of inventory *on credit*. Sales of inventory for cash are not recorded in a sales journal but in a cash receipts journal. Sales of noninventory assets on credit are recorded in the general journal.

Journalizing   Credit sale transactions are recorded with information about each sale entered separately in a sales journal. This information is often taken from a copy of the sales ticket or invoice prepared at the time of sale. The top portion of Exhibit 7.5 shows a typical sales journal from a merchandiser. It has columns for recording the date, customer's name, invoice number, posting reference, and the retail and cost amounts of each credit sale. The sales journal in this exhibit is called a **columnar journal,** which is any journal with more than one column.

Each transaction recorded in the sales journal yields an entry in the "Accounts Receivable Dr., Sales Cr." column. We usually need only one column for these two accounts. (An exception is when managers need more information about taxes, returns, and other sales details.) Each transaction in the sales journal also yields an entry in the "Cost of Goods Sold Dr., Inventory Cr." column. This entry reflects the perpetual inventory system of tracking costs with each sale. To illustrate, on February 2, this company sold merchandise on account to Jason Henry for $450. The invoice number is 307, and the cost of this merchandise is $315. This information is

EXHIBIT 7.5

Sales Journal with Posting*

Totals are posted at the end of the period to General Ledger accounts.

Individual line item amounts in the Accounts Receivable Dr. and Sales Cr. column are posted immediately to the subsidiary ledger.

Customer accounts are in a subsidiary ledger and the financial statement accounts are in the General Ledger.

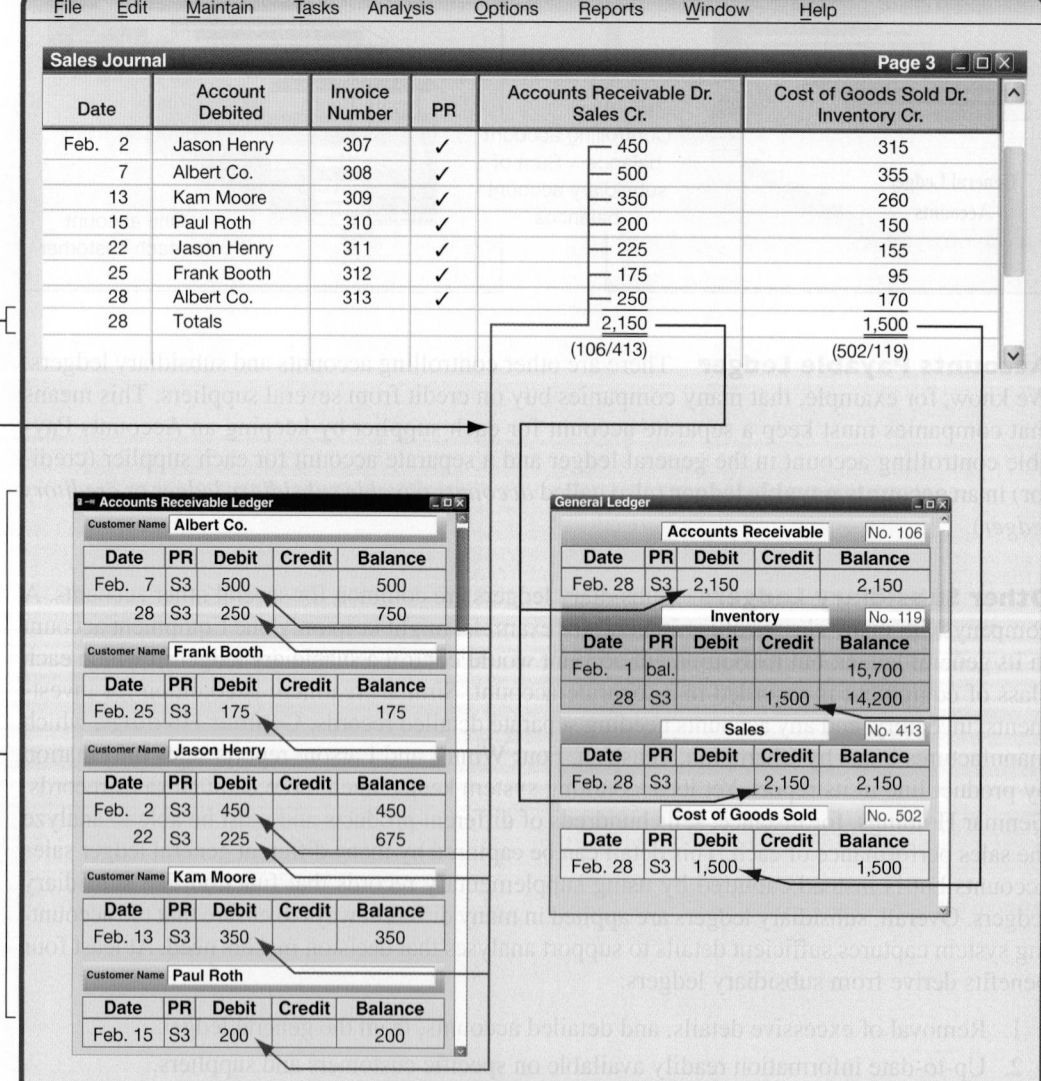

*The Sales Journal in a *periodic* system would exclude the column on the far right titled "Cost of Goods Sold Dr., Inventory Cr." (see Exhibit 7A.1).

captured on one line in the sales journal. No further explanations or entries are necessary, saving time and effort. Moreover, this sales journal is consistent with most inventory systems that use bar codes to record both sales and costs with each sale transaction. Note that the Posting Reference (PR) column is not used when entering transactions but instead is used when posting.

Posting A sales journal is posted as reflected in the arrow lines of Exhibit 7.5. Two types of posting can be identified: (1) posting to the subsidiary ledger(s) and (2) posting to the general ledger.

Posting to subsidiary ledger. Individual transactions in the sales journal are posted regularly (typically concurrently) to customer accounts in the accounts receivable ledger. These postings keep customer accounts up-to-date, which is important for the person granting credit to customers. When sales recorded in the sales journal are individually posted to customer accounts in the accounts receivable ledger, check marks are entered in the sales journal's PR column. Check marks are used rather than account numbers because customer accounts usually are arranged alphabetically in the accounts receivable ledger. Note that posting debits to Accounts Receivable twice—once to Accounts Receivable and once to the customer's subsidiary account—does not violate the accounting equation of debits equal credits. The equality of debits and credits is always maintained in the general ledger.

Posting to general ledger. The sales journal's account columns are totaled at the end of each period (the month of February in this case). For the "sales" column, the $2,150 total is debited to Accounts Receivable and credited to Sales in the general ledger (see Exhibit 7.5). For the "cost" column, the $1,500 total is debited to Cost of Goods Sold and credited to Inventory in the general ledger. When totals are posted to accounts in the general ledger, the account numbers are entered below the column total in the sales journal for tracking. For example, we enter (106/413) below the total in the sales column after this amount is posted to account number 106 (Accounts Receivable) and account number 413 (Sales).

A company identifies in the PR column of its subsidiary ledgers the journal and page number from which an amount is taken. We identify a journal by using an initial. Items posted from the sales journal carry the initial **S** before their journal page numbers in a PR column. Likewise, items from the cash receipts journal carry the initial **R**; items from the cash disbursements journal carry the initial **D**; items from the purchases journal carry the initial **P**; and items from the general journal carry the initial **G**.

Proving the Ledgers Account balances in the general ledger and subsidiary ledgers are periodically proved (or reviewed) for accuracy after posting. To do this we first prepare a trial balance of the general ledger to confirm that debits equal credits. Second, we test a subsidiary ledger by preparing a *schedule* of individual accounts and amounts. A **schedule of accounts receivable** lists each customer and the balance owed. If this total equals the balance of the Accounts Receivable controlling account, the accounts in the accounts receivable ledger are assumed correct. Exhibit 7.6 shows a schedule of accounts receivable drawn from the accounts receivable ledger of Exhibit 7.5.

P2 Prepare and prove the accuracy of subsidiary ledgers.

Schedule of Accounts Receivable February 28	
Albert Co.	$ 750
Frank Booth	175
Jason Henry	675
Kam Moore	350
Paul Roth	200
Total accounts receivable	$2,150

Additional Issues We consider three additional issues with the sales journal: (1) recording sales taxes, (2) recording sales returns and allowances, and (3) using actual sales invoices as a journal.

Sales taxes.   Governmental agencies such as cities and states often require sellers to collect sales taxes from customers and to periodically send these taxes to the appropriate agency. When using a columnar sales journal, we can keep a record of taxes collected by adding a Sales Taxes Payable column as follows.

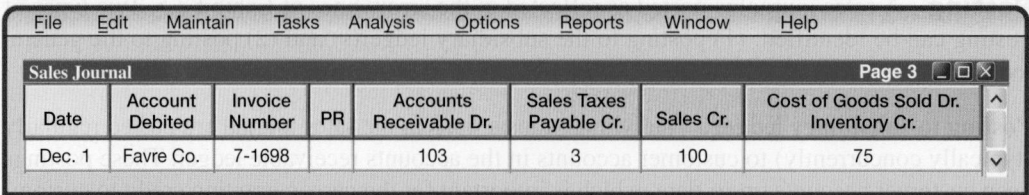

File	Edit	Maintain	Tasks	Analysis	Options	Reports	Window	Help

Sales Journal   Page 3

Date	Account Debited	Invoice Number	PR	Accounts Receivable Dr.	Sales Taxes Payable Cr.	Sales Cr.	Cost of Goods Sold Dr. Inventory Cr.
Dec. 1	Favre Co.	7-1698		103	3	100	75

Individual amounts in the Accounts Receivable column would continue to be posted immediately to customer accounts in the accounts receivable ledger. Individual amounts in the Sales Taxes Payable and Sales columns are not posted. Column totals would continue to be posted as usual. (A company that collects sales taxes on its cash sales can also use a Sales Taxes Payable column in its cash receipts journal.)

Sales returns and allowances.   A company with only a few sales returns and allowances can record them in a general journal with an entry such as the following:

Assets = Liabilities + Equity
−175   −175

May 17	Sales Returns and Allowances	414	175	
	Accounts Receivable—Ray Ball	106/✓		175
	Customer returned merchandise.			

The debit in this entry is posted to the Sales Returns and Allowances account (no. 414). The credit is posted to both the Accounts Receivable controlling account (no. 106) and to the customer's account. When we enter the account number and the check mark, 106/✓, in the PR column on the credit line, this means both the Accounts Receivable controlling account in the general ledger and the Ray Ball account in the accounts receivable ledger are credited for $175. [*Note:* If the returned goods can be resold to another customer, the company would debit (increase) the Inventory account and credit (decrease) the Cost of Goods Sold account. If the returned goods are defective (worthless), the company could simply leave their costs in the Cost of Goods Sold account (see Chapter 5).] A company with a large number of sales returns and allowances can save time by recording them in a separate sales returns and allowances journal.

Sales invoices as a sales journal.   To save costs, some small companies avoid using a sales journal for credit sales and instead post each sales invoice amount directly to the customer's account in the accounts receivable ledger. They then put copies of invoices in a file. At the end of the period, they total all invoices for that period and make a general journal entry to debit Accounts Receivable and credit Sales for the total amount. The file of invoice copies acts as a sales journal. This is called *direct posting of sales invoices*.

Quick Check   Answers — p. 297

4. When special journals are used, where are cash payments by check recorded?
5. How does a columnar journal save posting time and effort?
6. How do debits and credits remain equal when credit sales are posted twice (once to Accounts Receivable and once to the customer's subsidiary account)?
7. How do we identify the journal from which an amount in a ledger account was posted?
8. How are sales taxes recorded in the context of special journals?
9. What is direct posting of sales invoices?

Cash Receipts Journal

A **cash receipts journal** is typically used to record all receipts of cash. Exhibit 7.7 shows one common form of the cash receipts journal.

Journalizing and Posting Cash receipts can be separated into one of three types: (1) cash from credit customers in payment of their accounts, (2) cash from cash sales, and (3) cash from other sources. The cash receipts journal in Exhibit 7.7 has a separate credit

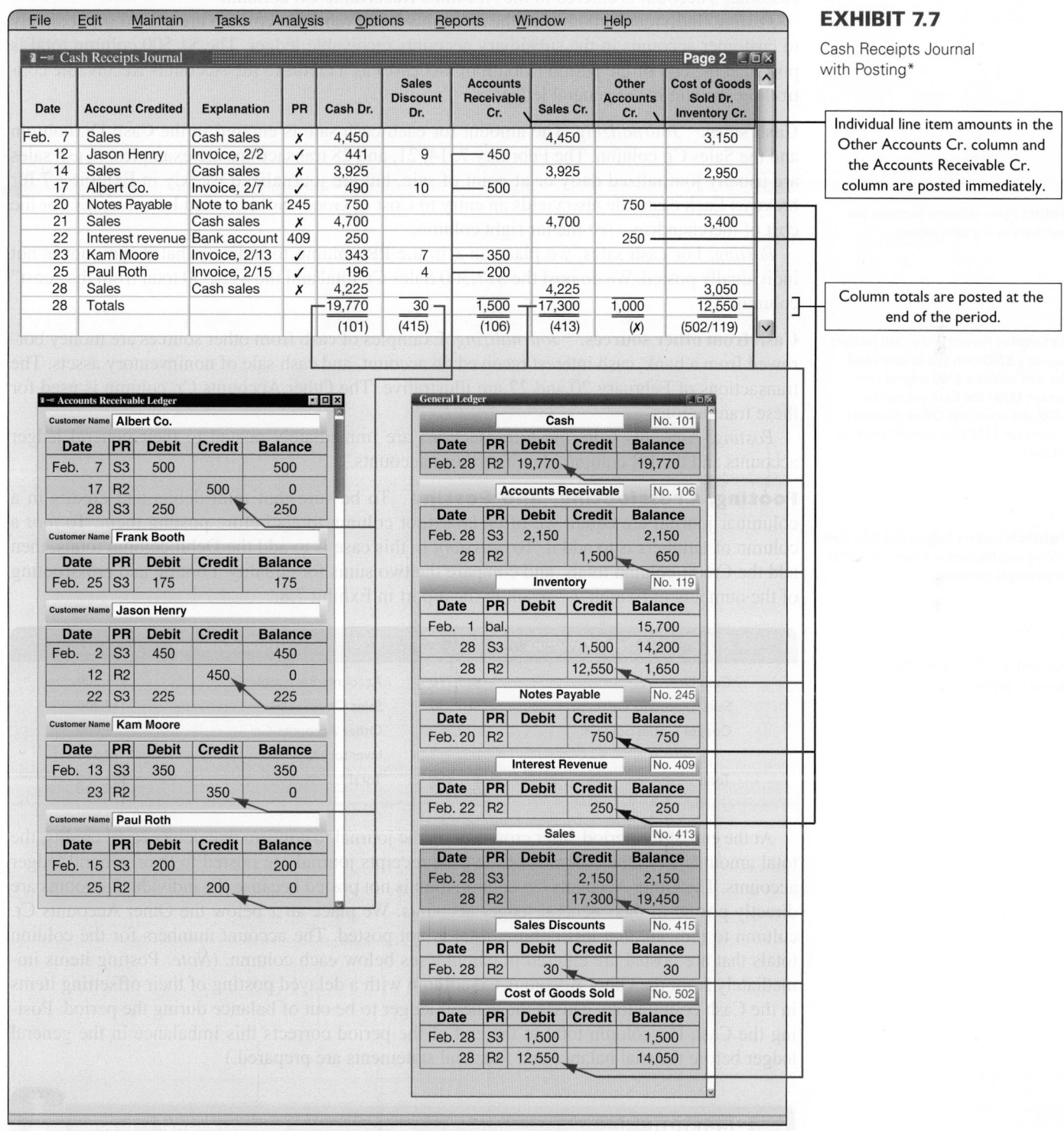

EXHIBIT 7.7

Cash Receipts Journal with Posting*

Individual line item amounts in the Other Accounts Cr. column and the Accounts Receivable Cr. column are posted immediately.

Column totals are posted at the end of the period.

*The Cash Receipts Journal in a *periodic* system would exclude the column on the far right titled "Cost of Goods Sold Dr., Inventory Cr." (see Exhibit 7A.2).

column for each of these three sources. We describe how to journalize transactions from each of these three sources. (An Explanation column is included in the cash receipts journal to identify the source.)

Point: Each transaction in the cash receipts journal involves a debit to Cash. Credit accounts will vary.

Cash from credit customers.   *Journalizing.* To record cash received in payment of a customer's account, the customer's name is first entered in the Account Credited column—see transactions dated February 12, 17, 23, and 25. Then the amounts debited to both Cash and the Sales Discount (if any) are entered in their respective columns, and the amount credited to the customer's account is entered in the Accounts Receivable Cr. column.

Posting. Individual amounts in the Accounts Receivable Cr. column are posted immediately to customer accounts in the subsidiary accounts receivable ledger. The $1,500 column total is posted at the end of the period (month in this case) as a credit to the Accounts Receivable controlling account in the general ledger.

Cash sales.   *Journalizing.* The amount for each cash sale is entered in the Cash Dr. column and the Sales Cr. column. The February 7, 14, 21, and 28 transactions are examples. (Cash sales are usually journalized daily or at point of sale, but are journalized weekly in Exhibit 7.7 for brevity.) Each cash sale also yields an entry to Cost of Goods Sold Dr. and Inventory Cr. for the cost of merchandise—see the far right column.

Point: Some software packages put cash sales in the sales journal.

Posting. For cash sales, we place an *x* in the PR column to indicate that its amount is not individually posted. We do post the $17,300 Sales Cr. total and the $12,550 total from the "cost" column.

Cash from other sources.   *Journalizing.* Examples of cash from other sources are money borrowed from a bank, cash interest received on account, and cash sale of noninventory assets. The transactions of February 20 and 22 are illustrative. The Other Accounts Cr. column is used for these transactions.

Example: Record in the cash receipts journal a $700 cash sale of land when the land carries a $700 original cost. *Answer:* Debit the Cash column for $700, and credit the Other Accounts column for $700 (the account credited is Land).

Posting. Amounts from these transactions are immediately posted to their general ledger accounts and the PR column identifies those accounts.

Footing, Crossfooting, and Posting   To be sure that total debits and credits in a columnar journal are equal, we often crossfoot column totals before posting them. To *foot* a column of numbers is to add it. To *crossfoot* in this case is to add the Debit column totals, then add the Credit column totals, and compare the two sums for equality. Footing and crossfooting of the numbers in Exhibit 7.7 result in the report in Exhibit 7.8.

Point: Subsidiary ledgers and their controlling accounts are *in balance* only after all posting is complete.

EXHIBIT 7.8

Footing and Crossfooting Journal Totals

Debit Columns		Credit Columns	
Cash Dr.	$19,770	Accounts Receivable Cr.	$ 1,500
Sales Discounts Dr.	30	Sales Cr.	17,300
Cost of Goods Sold Dr.	12,550	Other Accounts Cr.	1,000
		Inventory Cr.	12,550
Total	$32,350	Total	$32,350

At the end of the period, after crossfooting the journal to confirm that debits equal credits, the total amounts from the columns of the cash receipts journal are posted to their general ledger accounts. The Other Accounts Cr. column total is not posted because the individual amounts are directly posted to their general ledger accounts. We place an *x* below the Other Accounts Cr. column to indicate that this column total is not posted. The account numbers for the column totals that are posted are entered in parentheses below each column. (*Note:* Posting items immediately from the Other Accounts Cr. column with a delayed posting of their offsetting items in the Cash column total causes the general ledger to be out of balance during the period. Posting the Cash Dr. column total at the end of the period corrects this imbalance in the general ledger before the trial balance and financial statements are prepared.)

 **Decision** Maker   Answer — p. 297

Entrepreneur   You want to know how promptly customers are paying their bills. This information can help you decide whether to extend credit and to plan your cash payments. Where do you find this information? ∎

Purchases Journal

A **purchases journal** is typically used to record all credit purchases, including those for inventory. Purchases for cash are recorded in the Cash Disbursements Journal.

Journalizing Entries in the purchases journal in Exhibit 7.9 reflect purchase invoices or other source documents. We use the invoice date and terms to compute the date when payment for each purchase is due. The Accounts Payable Cr. column is used to record the amounts owed to each creditor. Inventory purchases are recorded in the Inventory Dr. column.

To illustrate, inventory costing $200 is purchased from Ace Manufacturing on February 5. The creditor's name (Ace) is entered in the Account column, the invoice date is entered in the Date of Invoice column, the purchase terms are entered in the Terms column, and the $200 amount is entered in the Accounts Payable Cr. and the Inventory Dr. columns. When a purchase involves an amount recorded in the Other Accounts Dr. column, we use the Account column to identify the general ledger account debited. For example, the February 28 transaction involves purchases of inventory, office supplies, and store supplies from ITT. The journal has no column for store supplies, so the Other Accounts Dr. column is used. In this case, Store Supplies is entered in the Account column along with the creditor's name (ITT). This purchases journal also includes a separate column for credit purchases of office supplies. A separate column such as this is useful when several transactions involve debits to the same account. Each company uses its own judgment in deciding on the number of separate columns necessary.

Posting The amounts in the Accounts Payable Cr. column are immediately posted to individual creditor accounts in the accounts payable subsidiary ledger. Individual amounts in the Other Accounts Dr. column are immediately posted to their general ledger accounts. At the end

Point: The number of special journals and the design of each are based on a company's specific needs.

Point: Each transaction in the purchases journal has a credit to Accounts Payable. Debit accounts will vary.

Point: The Other Accounts Dr. column allows the purchases journal to be used for any purchase on credit.

EXHIBIT 7.9

Purchases Journal with Posting*

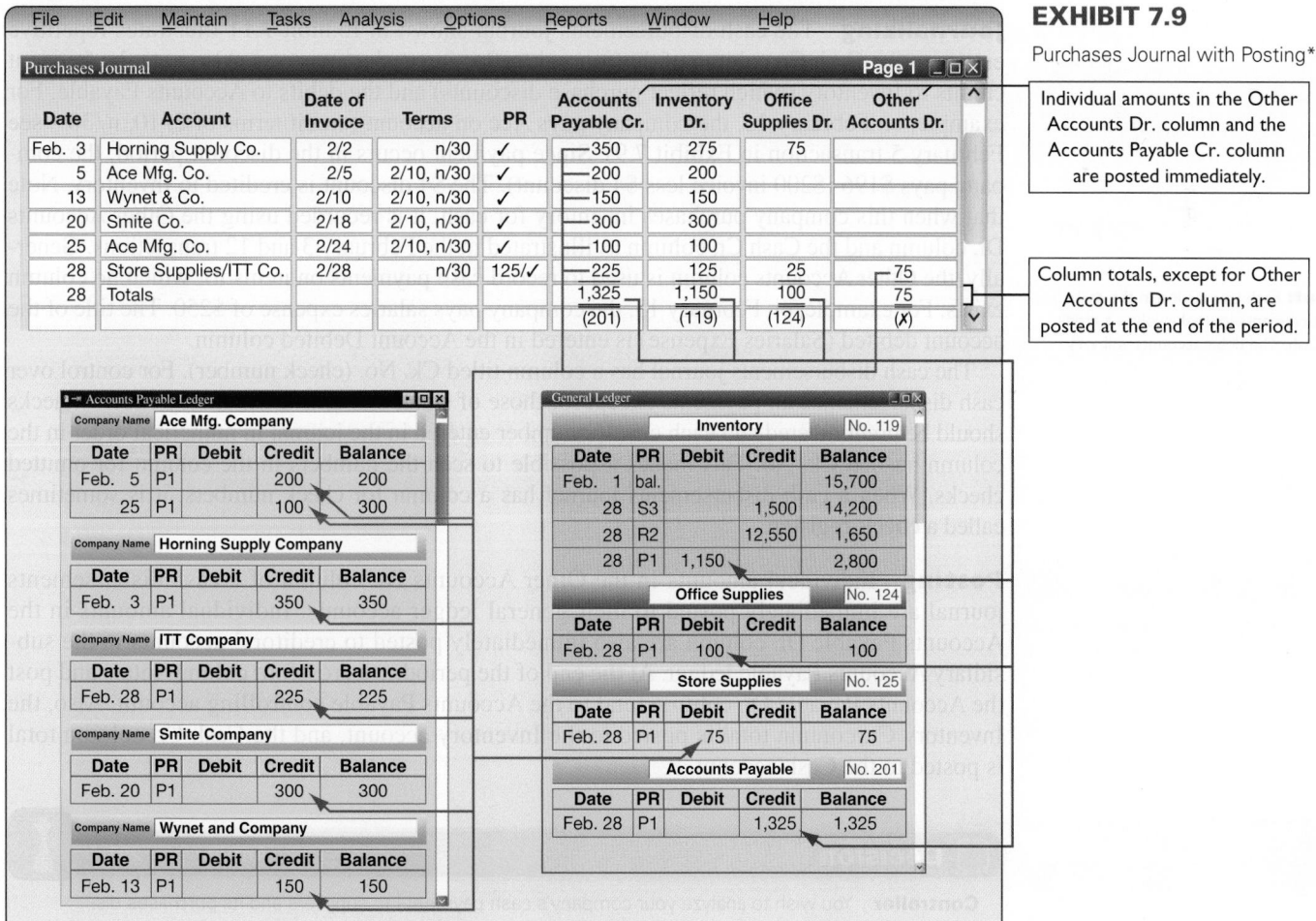

Individual amounts in the Other Accounts Dr. column and the Accounts Payable Cr. column are posted immediately.

Column totals, except for Other Accounts Dr. column, are posted at the end of the period.

*The Purchases Journal in a *periodic* system replaces "Inventory Dr." with "Purchases Dr." (see Exhibit 7A.3).

of the period, all column totals except the Other Accounts Dr. column are posted to their general ledger accounts.

Point: The balance in the Accounts Payable controlling account must equal the sum of the individual account balances in the accounts payable subsidiary ledger after posting.

Proving the Ledger   Accounts payable balances in the subsidiary ledger can be periodically proved after posting. We prove the subsidiary ledger by preparing a **schedule of accounts payable,** which is a list of accounts from the accounts payable ledger with their balances and the total. If this total of the individual balances equals the balance of the Accounts Payable controlling account, the accounts in the accounts payable ledger are assumed correct. Exhibit 7.10 shows a schedule of accounts payable drawn from the accounts payable ledger of Exhibit 7.9. (This schedule can be done after any posting; for example, we could prepare another schedule of accounts payable after the postings in Exhibit 7.11.)

EXHIBIT 7.10

Schedule of Accounts Payable

Schedule of Accounts Payable February 28	
Ace Mfg. Company	$ 300
Horning Supply Company	350
ITT Company	225
Smite Company	300
Wynet & Company	150
Total accounts payable	$1,325

Cash Disbursements Journal

A **cash disbursements journal,** also called a *cash payments journal,* is typically used to record all cash payments.

Journalizing   The cash disbursements journal shown in Exhibit 7.11 illustrates repetitive entries to the Cash Cr. column of this journal (reflecting cash payments). Also note the frequent credits to Inventory (which reflect purchase discounts) and the debits to Accounts Payable. For example, on February 15, the company pays Ace on account (credit terms of 2/10, n/30—see February 5 transaction in Exhibit 7.9). Since payment occurs in the discount period, the company pays $196 ($200 invoice less $4 discount). The $4 discount is credited to Inventory. Note that when this company purchases inventory for cash, it is recorded using the Other Accounts Dr. column and the Cash Cr. column as illustrated in the February 3 and 12 transactions. Generally, the Other Accounts column is used to record cash payments on items for which no column exists. For example, on February 15, the company pays salaries expense of $250. The title of the account debited (Salaries Expense) is entered in the Account Debited column.

Point: Each transaction in the cash disbursements journal involves a credit to Cash. The debit accounts will vary.

The cash disbursements journal has a column titled Ck. No. (check number). For control over cash disbursements, all payments except for those of small amounts are made by check. Checks should be prenumbered and each check's number entered in the journal in numerical order in the column headed Ck. No. This makes it possible to scan the numbers in the column for omitted checks. When a cash disbursements journal has a column for check numbers, it is sometimes called a **check register.**

Posting   Individual amounts in the Other Accounts Dr. column of a cash disbursements journal are immediately posted to their general ledger accounts. Individual amounts in the Accounts Payable Dr. column are also immediately posted to creditors' accounts in the subsidiary Accounts Payable ledger. At the end of the period, we crossfoot column totals and post the Accounts Payable Dr. column total to the Accounts Payable controlling account. Also, the Inventory Cr. column total is posted to the Inventory account, and the Cash Cr. column total is posted to the Cash account.

Decision Maker   Answer — p. 297

Controller   You wish to analyze your company's cash payments to suppliers and its purchases discounts. Where do you find this information? ■

EXHIBIT 7.11

Cash Disbursements Journal with Posting*

Cash Disbursements Journal — Page 2

	Date	Ck. No.	Payee	Account Debited	PR	Cash Cr.	Inventory Cr.	Other Accounts Dr.	Accounts Payable Dr.
	Feb. 3	105	L. & N. Railroad	Inventory	119	15		15	
	12	106	East Sales Co.	Inventory	119	25		25	
	15	107	Ace Mfg. Co.	Ace Mfg. Co.	✓	196	4		200
	15	108	Jerry Hale	Salaries Expense	622	250		250	
	20	109	Wynet & Co.	Wynet & Co.	✓	147	3		150
	28	110	Smite Co.	Smite Co.	✓	294	6		300
	28		Totals			927	13	290	650
						(101)	(119)	(X)	(201)

File   Edit   Maintain   Tasks   Analysis   Options   Reports   Window   Help

Individual amounts in the Other Accounts Dr. column and the Accounts Payable Dr. column are posted immediately.

Column totals, except for Other Accounts column, are posted at the end of the period.

General Ledger

Cash — No. 101

Date	PR	Debit	Credit	Balance
Feb. 28	R2	19,770		19,770
28	D2		927	18,843

Inventory — No. 119

Date	PR	Debit	Credit	Balance
Feb. 1	bal.			15,700
3	D2	15		15,715
12	D2	25		15,740
28	S3		1,500	14,240
28	R2		12,550	1,690
28	P1	1,150		2,840
28	D2		13	2,827

Accounts Payable — No. 201

Date	PR	Debit	Credit	Balance
Feb. 28	P1		1,325	1,325
28	D2	650		675

Salaries Expense — No. 622

Date	PR	Debit	Credit	Balance
Feb. 15	D2	250		250

Accounts Payable Ledger

Company Name **Ace Mfg. Company**

Date	PR	Debit	Credit	Balance
Feb. 5	P1		200	200
15	D2	200		0
25	P1		100	100

Company Name **Horning Supply Company**

Date	PR	Debit	Credit	Balance
Feb. 3	P1		350	350

Company Name **ITT Company**

Date	PR	Debit	Credit	Balance
Feb. 28	P1		225	225

Company Name **Smite Company**

Date	PR	Debit	Credit	Balance
Feb. 20	P1		300	300
28	D2	300		0

Company Name **Wynet & Company**

Date	PR	Debit	Credit	Balance
Feb. 13	P1		150	150
20	D2	150		0

*The Cash Disbursements Journal in a *periodic* system replaces "Inventory Cr." with "Purchases Discounts Cr." (see Exhibit 7A.4).

General Journal Transactions

When special journals are used, we still need a general journal for adjusting, closing, and any other transactions for which no special journal has been set up. Examples of these other transactions might include purchases returns and allowances, purchases of plant assets by issuing a note payable, sales returns if a sales returns and allowances journal is not used, and receipt of a note receivable from a customer. We described the recording of transactions in a general journal in Chapters 2 and 3.

Quick Check   Answers — p. 297

10. What are the normal recording and posting procedures when using special journals and controlling accounts with subsidiary ledgers?

11. What is the process for posting to a subsidiary ledger and its controlling account?

12. How do we prove the accuracy of account balances in the general ledger and subsidiary ledgers after posting?

13. Why does a company need a general journal when using special journals for sales, purchases, cash receipts, and cash disbursements?

TECHNOLOGY-BASED ACCOUNTING SYSTEMS

Accounting information systems are supported with technology, which can range from simple calculators to advanced computerized systems. Since technology is increasingly important in accounting information systems, we discuss the impact of computer technology, how data processing works with accounting data, and the role of computer networks.

Computer Technology in Accounting

Computer technology provides accuracy, speed, efficiency, and convenience in performing accounting tasks. A program can be written, for instance, to process customers' merchandise orders. Multipurpose off-the-shelf software applications exist for a variety of business operations. These include familiar accounting programs such as Peachtree® and QuickBooks®. Off-the-shelf programs are designed to be user friendly and menu driven, and many operate more efficiently as *integrated* systems. In an integrated system, actions taken in one part of the system automatically affect related parts. When a credit sale is recorded in an integrated system, for instance, several parts of the system are automatically updated, such as posting.

Computer technology can dramatically reduce the time and effort devoted to recordkeeping. Less effort spent on recordkeeping means more time for accounting professionals to concentrate on analysis and managerial decision making. These advances have created a greater demand for accounting professionals who understand financial reports and can draw insights and information from mountains of processed data. Accounting professionals have expertise in determining relevant and reliable information for decision making. They also can assess the effects of transactions and events on a company and its financial statements.

Point: Companies that have reported missing or stolen employee data such as Social Security numbers include Time Warner, Polo Ralph Lauren, Lexis/Nexis, ChoicePoint, and DSW Shoes.

Decision Insight

Middleware is software allowing different computer programs in a company or across companies to work together. It allows transfer of purchase orders, invoices, and other electronic documents between accounting systems. For example, suppliers can monitor inventory levels of their buyers for production and shipping purposes. ∎

Data Processing in Accounting

Accounting systems differ with regard to how input is entered and processed. **Online processing** enters and processes data as soon as source documents are available. This means that databases are immediately updated. **Batch processing** accumulates source documents for a period of time and then processes them all at once such as daily, weekly, or monthly. The advantage of online processing is timeliness. This often requires additional costs related to both software and hardware requirements. Companies such as **Intuit** (**Intuit.com**) are making online processing of accounting data a reality for many businesses. The advantage of batch processing is that it requires only periodic updating of databases. Records used to send bills to customers, for instance, might require updating only once a month. The disadvantage of batch processing is the lack of updated databases for management to use when making business decisions.

Computer Networks in Accounting

Networking, or linking computers with each other, can create information advantages (and cost efficiencies). **Computer networks** are links among computers giving different users and different computers access to common databases, programs, and hardware. Many college computer labs, for instance, are networked. A small computer network is called a *local area* *network (LAN);* it links machines with *hard-wire* hookups. Large computer networks extending over long distances often rely on *modem* or *wireless* communication.

Demand for information sometimes requires advanced networks such as the systems **Federal Express** and **UPS** use to track packages and bill customers and the system **Walmart** uses to monitor inventory levels in its stores. These networks include many computers and satellite communications to gather information and to provide ready access to its databases from all locations.

Enterprise Resource Planning Software

Enterprise resource planning (ERP) software includes the programs that manage a company's vital operations. They extend from order taking to manufacturing to accounting. When working properly, these integrated programs can speed decision making, identify costs for reduction, and give managers control over operations with the click of a mouse. For many managers, this software can help a company slash production planning, trim inventories, and has huge savings. ERP has several suppliers. **SAP** leads the market, with **Oracle**, a distant second (Forbes). SAP software is used by more than half of the world's 500 largest companies. It links ordering, inventory, production, purchasing, planning, tracking, and human resources. A transaction or event triggers an immediate chain reaction of events throughout the enterprise. It is making companies more efficient and profitable.

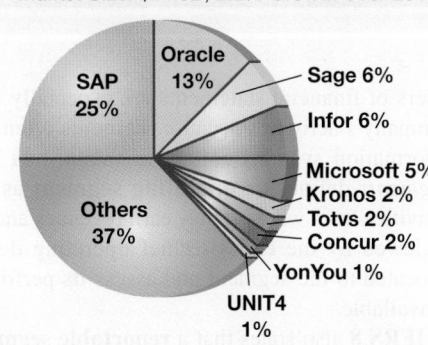

Worldwide ERP Software Market Share, 2012
Market Size: $24.5B; 2.2% Growth Over 2011

- SAP 25%
- Oracle 13%
- Sage 6%
- Infor 6%
- Microsoft 5%
- Kronos 2%
- Totvs 2%
- Concur 2%
- YonYou 1%
- UNIT4 1%
- Others 37%

ERP is pushing into cyberspace and customer relationship management (CRM). Now companies can share data with customers and suppliers. Applesauce maker **Mott's** is using SAP so that distributors can check the status of orders and place them over the Net, and the **Coca-Cola Company** uses it to ship soda on time. ERP is also increasingly used by small business. For example, **NetSuite**'s accounting services to small and medium businesses are powered by Oracle's system.

Companies can choose between on-premise ERP and cloud ERP: On-premise ERP solutions are installed locally on a company's hardware and servers and then managed by its IT staff while cloud ERP—also called SaaS, or Software-as-a-Service—is provided as a service. With this type of deployment, a company's ERP software and its associated data are managed centrally (in the Internet "cloud") by the ERP vendor and are accessed by customers using a Web browser.

Decision Insight

A new generation of accounting support is available. With the touch of a key, users can create real-time inventory reports showing all payments, charges, and credit limits at any point in the accounting cycle. Many services also include "alert signals" notifying the company when, for example, a large order exceeds a customer's credit limit or when purchases need to be made or when a bank balance is running low. These alerts occur via e-mail, fax, PDA, or phone. ∎

Quick Check Answers — p. 297

14. Identify an advantage of an integrated computer-based accounting system.
15. What advantages do computer systems offer over manual systems?
16. Identify an advantage of computer networks.
17. Describe ERP software and its potential advantages to businesses.

Decision Maker Answer — p. 297

Banker A bicycle merchandiser requests a loan from you to expand operations. Its net profit is $220,000, reflecting a 10% increase over the prior year. You ask about segment results. The owner reports that $160,000 of net profit is from Cuban operations, reflecting a 60% increase over the prior year. The remaining $60,000 of net profit is from U.S. operations, reflecting a 40% decrease. Does this segment information impact your loan decision? ■

Decision Analysis  | Segment Return on Assets

A1 Compute segment return on assets and use it to evaluate segment performance.

Users of financial statements are especially interested in segment information to better understand a company's activities because segments often vary on profitability, risk, and growth. Good accounting information systems collect financial data for a company's various segments. **IFRS 8** *Operating Segments* defines an **operating segment** as a component of an entity (a) that engages in business activities from which it may earn revenues and incur expenses, (b) whose operating results are regularly reviewed by the entity's chief operating decision maker to make decisions about resources to be allocated to the segment and assess its performance, and (c) for which discrete financial information is available.

IFRS 8 also states that a **reportable segment** is an operating segment or aggregations of operating segments that meet specified criteria and quantitative thresholds. Companies report segment information, including their revenues, operating profit, assets, liabilities, additions to noncurrent assets, depreciation, and amortization.

While segment financial ratios are not required to be presented in the annual report, we can calculate them to analyze segments' performance, such as the **segment return on assets ratio** defined as follows.

$$\text{Segment return on assets} = \frac{\text{Segment operating profit or income}}{\text{Segment average assets}}$$

EXHIBIT 7.12

Nestlé's Segment Return on Assets

Nestlé Segment (CHF millions)	Zone Europe	Zone America	Zone Asia, Oceania, and Africa
Profit*	2,331	5,151	3,558
2013 assets	11,779	21,252	14,169
2012 assets	11,804	22,485	14,329
Average assets	11,791.5	21,868.5	14,249.0
Segment return on assets	19.8%	23.6%	25.0%

* Trading operating profit

Nestlé's best performing segment in terms of return on assets is Zone Asia, Oceania, and Africa. This is especially impressive considering this segment ranks second in terms of the amount of assets.

DEMONSTRATION PROBLEM—PERPETUAL SYSTEM

Pepper Company completed the following selected transactions and events during March of this year. (Terms of all credit sales for the company are 2/10, n/30.)

Mar. 4 Sold merchandise on credit to Jennifer Nelson, Invoice No. 954, for $16,800 (cost is $12,200).

6 Purchased $1,220 of office supplies on credit from Mack Company. Invoice dated March 3, terms n/30.

6 Sold merchandise on credit to Dennie Hoskins, Invoice No. 955, for $10,200 (cost is $8,100).

11 Purchased $52,600 of merchandise, invoice dated March 6, terms 2/10, n/30, from Defore Industries.

12 Borrowed $26,000 cash by giving Commerce Bank a long-term promissory note payable.

14 Received cash payment from Jennifer Nelson for the March 4 sale less the discount (Invoice No. 954).

16 Received a $200 credit memorandum from Defore Industries for unsatisfactory merchandise Pepper purchased on March 11 and later returned.

16 Received cash payment from Dennie Hoskins for the March 6 sale less the discount (Invoice No. 955).

18 Purchased $22,850 of store equipment on credit from Schmidt Supply, invoice dated March 15, terms n/30.

20 Sold merchandise on credit to Marjorie Allen, Invoice No. 956, for $5,600 (cost is $3,800).

21 Sent Defore Industries Check No. 516 in payment of its March 6 dated invoice less the return and the discount.

22 Purchased $41,625 of merchandise, invoice dated March 18, terms 2/10, n/30, from Welch Company.

26 Issued a $600 credit memorandum to Marjorie Allen for defective merchandise Pepper sold on March 20 and Allen later returned.

31 Issued Check No. 517, payable to Payroll, in payment of $15,900 sales salaries for the month. Cashed the check and paid the employees.

31 Cash sales for the month are $134,680 (cost is $67,340). (Cash sales are recorded daily but are recorded only once here to reduce repetitive entries.)

Required

1. Open the following selected general ledger accounts: Cash (101), Accounts Receivable (106) Inventory (119), Office Supplies (124), Store Equipment (165), Accounts Payable (201), Long-Term Notes Payable (251), Sales (413), Sales Returns and Allowances (414), Sales Discounts (415), Cost of Goods Sold (502), and Sales Salaries Expense (621). Open the following accounts receivable ledger accounts: Marjorie Allen, Dennie Hoskins, and Jennifer Nelson. Open the following accounts payable ledger accounts: Defore Industries, Mack Company, Schmidt Supply, and Welch Company.

2. Enter the transactions using a sales journal, a purchases journal, a cash receipts journal, a cash disbursements journal, and a general journal similar to the ones illustrated in the chapter. Regularly post to the individual customer and creditor accounts. Also, post any amounts that should be posted as individual amounts to general ledger accounts. Foot and crossfoot the journals and make the month-end postings. *Pepper Co. uses the perpetual inventory system.*

3. Prepare a trial balance for the selected general ledger accounts in part 1 and prove the accuracy of subsidiary ledgers by preparing schedules of accounts receivable and accounts payable.

PLANNING THE SOLUTION

- Set up the required general ledger, the subsidiary ledger accounts, and the five required journals as illustrated in the chapter.
- Read and analyze each transaction and decide in which special journal (or general journal) the transaction is recorded.

- Record each transaction in the proper journal (and post the appropriate individual amounts).
- Once you have recorded all transactions, total the journal columns. Post from each journal to the appropriate ledger accounts.
- Prepare a trial balance to prove the equality of the debit and credit balances in your general ledger.
- Prepare schedules of accounts receivable and accounts payable. Compare the totals of these schedules to the Accounts Receivable and Accounts Payable controlling account balances, making sure that they agree.

SOLUTION TO DEMONSTRATION PROBLEM—PERPETUAL SYSTEM

Sales Journal   Page 2

Date	Account Debited	Invoice Number	PR	Accounts Receivable Dr. Sales Cr.	Cost of Goods Sold Dr. Inventory Cr.
Mar. 4	Jennifer Nelson	954	✓	16,800	12,200
6	Dennie Hoskins	955	✓	10,200	8,100
20	Marjorie Allen	956	✓	5,600	3,800
31	Totals			32,600	24,100
				(106/413)	(502/119)

Cash Receipts Journal   Page 3

Date	Account Credited	Explanation	PR	Cash Dr.	Sales Discount Dr.	Accounts Receivable Cr.	Sales Cr.	Other Accounts Cr.	Cost of Goods Sold Dr. Inventory Cr.
Mar. 12	L.T. Notes Payable	Note to bank	251	26,000				26,000	
14	Jennifer Nelson	Invoice 954, 3/4	✓	16,464	336	16,800			
16	Dennie Hoskins	Invoice 955, 3/6	✓	9,996	204	10,200			
31	Sales	Cash sales	x	134,680			134,680		67,340
31	Totals			187,140	540	27,000	134,680	26,000	67,340
				(101)	(415)	(106)	(413)	(x)	(502/119)

Purchases Journal   Page 3

Date	Account	Date of Invoice	Terms	PR	Accounts Payable Cr.	Inventory Dr.	Office Supplies Dr.	Other Accounts Dr.
Mar. 6	Office Supplies/Mack Co	3/3	n/30	✓	1,220		1,220	
11	Defore Industries	3/6	2/10, n/30	✓	52,600	52,600		
18	Store Equipment/Schmidt Supp	3/15	n/30	165/✓	22,850			22,850
22	Welch Company	3/18	2/10, n/30	✓	41,625	41,625		
31	Totals				118,295	94,225	1,220	22,850
					(201)	(119)	(124)	(x)

Cash Disbursements Journal   Page 3

Date	Ck. No.	Payee	Account Debited	PR	Cash Cr.	Inventory Cr.	Other Accounts Dr.	Accounts Payable Dr.
Mar. 21	516	Defore Industries	Defore Industries	✓	51,352	1,048		52,400
31	517	Payroll	Sales Salaries Expense	621	15,900		15,900	
31		Totals			67,252	1,048	15,900	52,400
					(101)	(119)	(x)	(201)

General Journal				Page 2
Mar. 16	Accounts Payable—Defore Industries	201/✓	200	
	Inventory	119		200
	To record credit memorandum received.			
26	Sales Returns and Allowances	414	600	
	Accounts Receivable—Marjorie Allen	106/✓		600
	To record credit memorandum issued.			

Accounts Receivable Ledger

Marjorie Allen

Date	PR	Debit	Credit	Balance
Mar. 20	S2	5,600		5,600
26	G2		600	5,000

Dennie Hoskins

Date	PR	Debit	Credit	Balance
Mar. 6	S2	10,200		10,200
16	R3		10,200	0

Jennifer Nelson

Date	PR	Debit	Credit	Balance
Mar. 4	S2	16,800		16,800
14	R3		16,800	0

Accounts Payable Ledger

Defore Industries

Date	PR	Debit	Credit	Balance
Mar. 11	P3		52,600	52,600
16	G2	200		52,400
21	D3	52,400		0

Mack Company

Date	PR	Debit	Credit	Balance
Mar. 6	P3		1,220	1,220

Schmidt Supply

Date	PR	Debit	Credit	Balance
Mar. 18	P3		22,850	22,850

Welch Company

Date	PR	Debit	Credit	Balance
Mar. 22	P3		41,625	41,625

General Ledger (Partial Listing)

Cash   Acct. No. 101

Date	PR	Debit	Credit	Balance
Mar. 31	R3	187,140		187,140
31	D3		67,252	119,888

Accounts Receivable   Acct. No. 106

Date	PR	Debit	Credit	Balance
Mar. 26	G2		600	(600)
31	S2	32,600		32,000
31	R3		27,000	5,000

Inventory   Acct. No. 119

Date	PR	Debit	Credit	Balance
Mar. 16	G2		200	(200)
21	D3		1,048	(1,248)
31	P3	94,225		92,977
31	S2		24,100	68,877
31	R3		67,340	1,537

Office Supplies   Acct. No. 124

Date	PR	Debit	Credit	Balance
Mar. 31	P3	1,220		1,220

Store Equipment   Acct. No. 165

Date	PR	Debit	Credit	Balance
Mar. 18	P3	22,850		22,850

Accounts Payable   Acct. No. 201

Date	PR	Debit	Credit	Balance
Mar. 16	G2	200		(200)
31	P3		118,295	118,095
31	D3	52,400		65,695

Long-Term Notes Payable   Acct. No. 251

Date	PR	Debit	Credit	Balance
Mar. 12	R3		26,000	26,000

Sales   Acct. No. 413

Date	PR	Debit	Credit	Balance
Mar. 31	S2		32,600	32,600
31	R3		134,680	167,280

Sales Returns and Allowances   Acct. No. 414

Date	PR	Debit	Credit	Balance
Mar. 26	G2	600		600

Sales Discounts   Acct. No. 415

Date	PR	Debit	Credit	Balance
Mar. 31	R3	540		540

Cost of Goods Sold   Acct. No. 502

Date	PR	Debit	Credit	Balance
Mar. 31	R3	67,340		67,340
31	S2	24,100		91,440

Sales Salaries Expense   Acct. No. 621

Date	PR	Debit	Credit	Balance
Mar. 31	D3	15,900		15,900

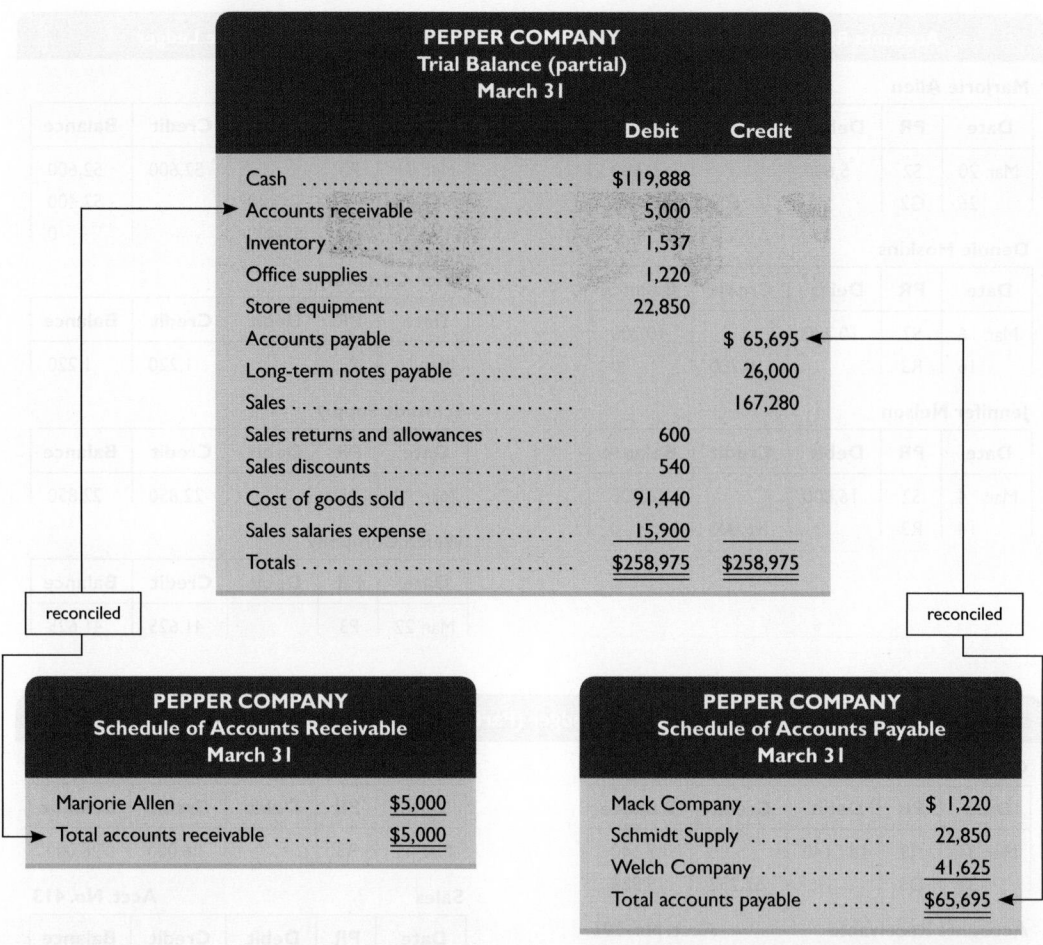

7A Special Journals under a Periodic System

> **P3** Journalize and post transactions using special journals in a periodic inventory system.

This appendix describes special journals under a periodic inventory system. Each journal is slightly impacted. The sales journal and the cash receipts journal both require one less column (namely that of Cost of Goods Sold Dr., Inventory Cr.). The Purchases Journal replaces the Inventory Dr. column with a Purchases Dr. column in a periodic system. The cash disbursements journal replaces the Inventory Cr. column with a Purchases Discounts Cr. column in a periodic system. These changes are illustrated.

Sales Journal The sales journal using the periodic inventory system is shown in Exhibit 7A.1. The difference in the sales journal between the perpetual and periodic system is the exclusion of the column to record cost of goods sold and inventory amounts for each sale. The periodic system does *not* record the increase in cost of goods sold and the decrease in inventory at the time of each sale.

EXHIBIT 7A.1

Sales Journal—Periodic System

Sales Journal				Page 3 ⬛▢✕
Date	**Account Debited**	**Invoice Number**	**PR**	**Accounts Receivable Dr. Sales Cr.**
Feb. 2	Jason Henry	307	✓	450
7	Albert Co.	308	✓	500
13	Kam Moore	309	✓	350
15	Paul Roth	310	✓	200
22	Jason Henry	311	✓	225
25	Frank Booth	312	✓	175
28	Albert Co.	313	✓	250
28	Total			2,150
				(106/413)

Cash Receipts Journal The cash receipts journal using the periodic system is shown in Exhibit 7A.2. Note the absence of the column on the far right side to record debits to Cost of Goods Sold and credits to Inventory for the cost of merchandise sold (seen under the perpetual system). Consistent with the cash receipts journal shown in Exhibit 7.7, we show only the weekly (summary) cash sale entries.

EXHIBIT 7A.2

Cash Receipts Journal—
Periodic System

Cash Receipts Journal   Page 2

Date	Account Credited	Explanation	PR	Cash Dr.	Sales Discount Dr.	Accounts Receivable Cr.	Sales Cr.	Other Accounts Cr.
Feb. 7	Sales	Cash sales	x	4,450			4,450	
12	Jason Henry	Invoice 307, 2/2	✓	441	9	450		
14	Sales	Cash sales	x	3,925			3,925	
17	Albert Co.	Invoice 308, 2/7	✓	490	10	500		
20	Notes Payable	Note to bank	245	750				750
21	Sales	Cash sales	x	4,700			4,700	
22	Interest revenue	Bank account	409	250				250
23	Kam Moore	Invoice 309, 2/13	✓	343	7	350		
25	Paul Roth	Invoice 310, 2/15	✓	196	4	200		
28	Sales	Cash sales	x	4,225			4,225	
28	Totals			19,770	30	1,500	17,300	1,000
				(101)	(415)	(106)	(413)	(x)

Purchases Journal The purchases journal using the periodic system is shown in Exhibit 7A.3. This journal under a perpetual system included an Inventory column where the periodic system now has a Purchases column.

EXHIBIT 7A.3

Purchases Journal—Periodic System

Purchases Journal   Page 1

Date	Account	Date of Invoice	Terms	PR	Accounts Payable Cr.	Purchases Dr.	Office Supplies Dr.	Other Accounts Dr.
Feb. 3	Horning Supply Co.	2/2	n/30	✓	350	275	75	
5	Ace Mfg. Co.	2/5	2/10, n/30	✓	200	200		
13	Wynet and Co.	2/10	2/10, n/30	✓	150	150		
20	Smite Co.	2/18	2/10, n/30	✓	300	300		
25	Ace Mfg. Co.	2/24	2/10, n/30	✓	100	100		
28	Store Supplies/ITT Co.	2/28	n/30	125/✓	225	125	25	75
28	Totals				1,325	1,150	100	75
					(201)	(505)	(124)	(x)

Cash Disbursements Journal The cash disbursements journal using a periodic system is shown in Exhibit 7A.4. This journal under the perpetual system included an Inventory column where the periodic system now has the Purchases Discounts column.

EXHIBIT 7A.4

Cash Disbursements Journal—Periodic System

Cash Disbursements Journal   Page 2

Date	Ck. No.	Payee	Account Debited	PR	Cash Cr.	Purchases Discounts Cr.	Other Accounts Dr.	Accounts Payable Dr.
Feb. 3	105	L. and N. Railroad	Purchases	505	15		15	
12	106	East Sales Co.	Purchases	505	25		25	
15	107	Ace Mfg. Co.	Ace Mfg. Co.	✓	196	4		200
15	108	Jerry Hale	Salaries Expense	622	250		250	
20	109	Wynet and Co.	Wynet and Co.	✓	147	3		150
28	110	Smite Co.	Smite Co.	✓	294	6		300
28		Totals			927	13	290	650
					(101)	(507)	(x)	(201)

DEMONSTRATION PROBLEM—PERIODIC SYSTEM

Refer to Pepper Company's selected transactions described under the Demonstration Problem—Perpetual System to fulfill the following requirements.

Required

1. Open the following selected general ledger accounts: Cash (101), Accounts Receivable (106), Office Supplies (124), Store Equipment (165), Accounts Payable (201), Long-Term Notes Payable (251), Sales (413), Sales Returns and Allowances (414), Sales Discounts (415), Purchases (505), Purchases

Returns and Allowances (506), Purchases Discounts (507), and Sales Salaries Expense (621). Open the following accounts receivable ledger accounts: Marjorie Allen, Dennie Hoskins, and Jennifer Nelson. Open the following accounts payable ledger accounts: Defore Industries, Mack Company, Schmidt Supply, and Welch Company.

2. Enter the transactions using a sales journal, a purchases journal, a cash receipts journal, a cash disbursements journal, and a general journal similar to the ones illustrated in Appendix 7A. Regularly post to the individual customer and creditor accounts. Also, post any amounts that should be posted as individual amounts to general ledger accounts. Foot and crossfoot the journals and make the month-end postings. *Pepper Co. uses the periodic inventory system in this problem.*

3. Prepare a trial balance for the selected general ledger accounts in part 1 and prove the accuracy of subsidiary ledgers by preparing schedules of accounts receivable and accounts payable.

SOLUTION TO DEMONSTRATION PROBLEM—PERIODIC SYSTEM

Sales Journal — Page 2

Date	Account Debited	Invoice Number	PR	Accounts Receivable Dr. Sales Cr.
Mar. 4	Jennifer Nelson	954	✓	16,800
6	Dennie Hoskins	955	✓	10,200
20	Marjorie Allen	956	✓	5,600
31	Totals			32,600
				(106/413)

Cash Receipts Journal — Page 3

Date	Account Credited	Explanation	PR	Cash Dr.	Sales Discount Dr.	Accounts Receivable Cr.	Sales Cr.	Other Accounts Cr.
Mar. 12	L.T. Notes Payable	Note to bank	251	26,000				26,000
14	Jennifer Nelson	Invoice 954, 3/4	✓	16,464	336	16,800		
16	Dennie Hoskins	Invoice 955, 3/6	✓	9,996	204	10,200		
31	Sales	Cash sales	x	134,680			134,680	
31	Totals			187,140	540	27,000	134,680	26,000
				(101)	(415)	(106)	(413)	(x)

Purchases Journal — Page 3

Date	Account	Date of Invoice	Terms	PR	Accounts Payable Cr.	Purchases Dr.	Office Supplies Dr.	Other Accounts Dr.
Mar. 6	Office Supplies/Mack Co	3/3	n/30	✓	1,220		1,220	
11	Defore Industries	3/6	2/10, n/30	✓	52,600	52,600		
18	Store Equipment/Schmidt Supp	3/15	n/30	165/✓	22,850			22,850
22	Welch Company	3/18	2/10, n/30	✓	41,625	41,625		
31	Totals				118,295	94,225	1,220	22,850
					(201)	(505)	(124)	(x)

Cash Disbursements Journal — Page 3

Date	Ck. No.	Payee	Account Debited	PR	Cash Cr.	Purchases Discount Cr.	Other Accounts Dr.	Accounts Payable Dr.
Mar. 21	516	Defore Industries	Defore Industries	✓	51,352	1,048		52,400
31	517	Payroll	Sales Salaries Expense	621	15,900		15,900	
31		Totals			67,252	1,048	15,900	52,400
					(101)	(507)	(x)	(201)

General Journal — Page 2

Mar. 16	Accounts Payable—Defore Industries	201/✓	200	
	Purchases Returns and Allowances	506		200
	To record credit memorandum received.			
26	Sales Returns and Allowances	414	600	
	Accounts Receivable—Marjorie Allen..........	106/✓		600
	To record credit memorandum issued.			

Accounts Receivable Ledger

Marjorie Allen

Date	PR	Debit	Credit	Balance
Mar. 20	S2	5,600		5,600
26	G2		600	5,000

Dennie Hoskins

Date	PR	Debit	Credit	Balance
Mar. 6	S2	10,200		10,200
16	R3		10,200	0

Jennifer Nelson

Date	PR	Debit	Credit	Balance
Mar. 4	S2	16,800		16,800
14	R3		16,800	0

Accounts Payable Ledger

Defore Industries

Date	PR	Debit	Credit	Balance
Mar. 11	P3		52,600	52,600
16	G2	200		52,400
21	D3	52,400		0

Mack Company

Date	PR	Debit	Credit	Balance
Mar. 6	P3		1,220	1,220

Schmidt Supply

Date	PR	Debit	Credit	Balance
Mar. 18	P3		22,850	22,850

Welch Company

Date	PR	Debit	Credit	Balance
Mar. 22	P3		41,625	41,625

General Ledger (Partial Listing)

Cash   Acct. No. 101

Date	PR	Debit	Credit	Balance
Mar. 31	R3	187,140		187,140
31	D3		67,252	119,888

Accounts Receivable   Acct. No. 106

Date	PR	Debit	Credit	Balance
Mar. 26	G2		600	(600)
31	S2	32,600		32,000
31	R3		27,000	5,000

Office Supplies   Acct. No. 124

Date	PR	Debit	Credit	Balance
Mar. 31	P3	1,220		1,220

Store Equipment   Acct. No. 165

Date	PR	Debit	Credit	Balance
Mar. 18	P3	22,850		22,850

Accounts Payable   Acct. No. 201

Date	PR	Debit	Credit	Balance
Mar. 16	G2	200		(200)
31	P3		118,295	118,095
31	D3	52,400		65,695

Long-Term Notes Payable   Acct. No. 251

Date	PR	Debit	Credit	Balance
Mar. 12	R3		26,000	26,000

Sales   Acct. No. 413

Date	PR	Debit	Credit	Balance
Mar. 31	S2		32,600	32,600
31	R3		134,680	167,280

Sales Returns and Allowances   Acct. No. 414

Date	PR	Debit	Credit	Balance
Mar. 26	G2	600		600

Sales Discounts   Acct. No. 415

Date	PR	Debit	Credit	Balance
Mar. 31	R3	540		540

Purchases   Acct. No. 505

Date	PR	Debit	Credit	Balance
Mar. 31	P3	94,225		94,225

Purchases Returns and Allowances   Acct. No. 506

Date	PR	Debit	Credit	Balance
Mar. 16	G2		200	200

Purchases Discounts   Acct. No. 507

Date	PR	Debit	Credit	Balance
Mar. 31	D3		1,048	1,048

Sales Salaries Expense   Acct. No. 621

Date	PR	Debit	Credit	Balance
Mar. 31	D3	15,900		15,900

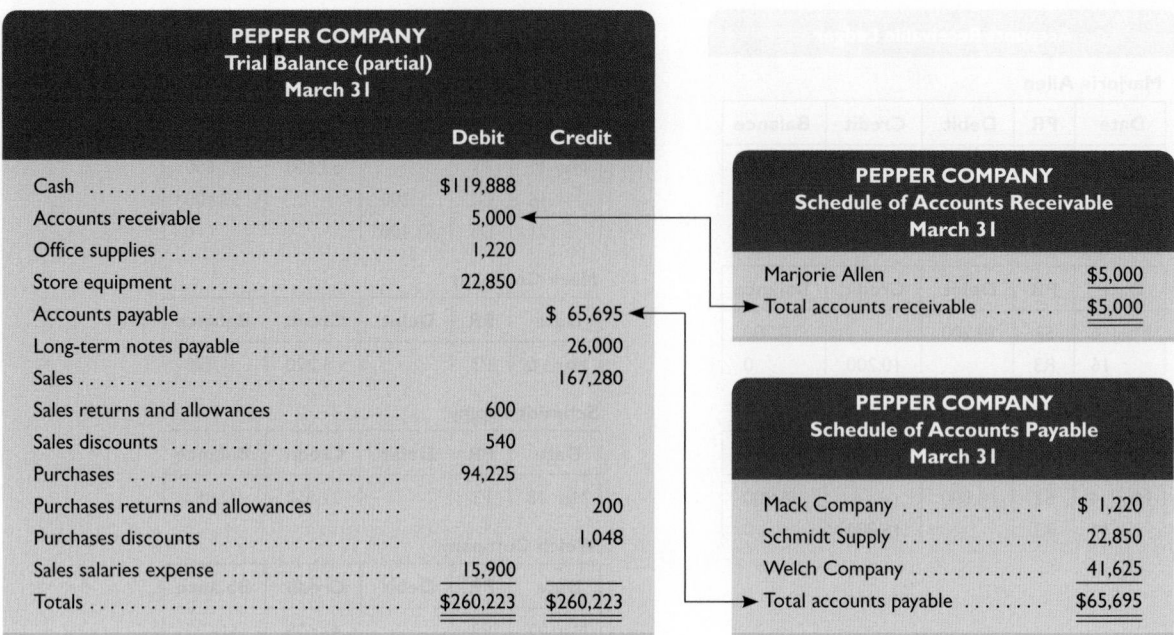

PEPPER COMPANY
Trial Balance (partial)
March 31

	Debit	Credit
Cash	$119,888	
Accounts receivable	5,000	
Office supplies	1,220	
Store equipment	22,850	
Accounts payable		$ 65,695
Long-term notes payable		26,000
Sales		167,280
Sales returns and allowances	600	
Sales discounts	540	
Purchases	94,225	
Purchases returns and allowances		200
Purchases discounts		1,048
Sales salaries expense	15,900	
Totals	$260,223	$260,223

PEPPER COMPANY
Schedule of Accounts Receivable
March 31

Marjorie Allen	$5,000
Total accounts receivable	$5,000

PEPPER COMPANY
Schedule of Accounts Payable
March 31

Mack Company	$ 1,220
Schmidt Supply	22,850
Welch Company	41,625
Total accounts payable	$65,695

Summary

C1 Identify the principles and components of accounting information systems. Accounting information systems are governed by five fundamental principles: control, relevance, compatibility, flexibility, and cost-benefit. The five basic components of an accounting information system are source documents, input devices, information processors, information storage, and output devices.

C2 Explain the goals and uses of special journals. Special journals are used for recording transactions of similar type, each meant to cover one kind of transaction. Four of the most common special journals are the sales journal, cash receipts journal, purchases journal, and cash disbursements journal. Special journals are efficient and cost-effective tools in the journalizing and posting processes.

C3 Describe the use of controlling accounts and subsidiary ledgers. A general ledger keeps controlling accounts such as Accounts Receivable and Accounts Payable, but details on individual accounts making up the controlling account are kept in subsidiary ledgers (such as an accounts receivable ledger). The balance in a controlling account must equal the sum of its subsidiary account balances after posting is complete.

A1 Compute segment return on assets and use it to evaluate segment performance. IFRS 8 *Operating Segments* defines an operating segment as a component of an entity (*a*) that engages in business activities from which it may earn revenues and incur expenses, (*b*) whose operating results are regularly reviewed by the entity's chief operating decision maker to make decisions about resources to be allocated to the segment and assess its performance, and (*c*) for which discrete financial information is available. **IFRS 8** also states that a *reportable segment* is an operating segment or aggregations of operating segments that meet specified

criteria and quantitative threshold. Analysis of a company's segments is aided by the segment return on assets (segment profit or income divided by segment average assets).

P1 Journalize and post transactions using special journals. Each special journal is devoted to similar kinds of transactions. Transactions are journalized on one line of a special journal, with columns devoted to specific accounts, dates, names, posting references, explanations, and other necessary information. Posting is threefold: (1) individual amounts in the Other Accounts column are posted to their general ledger accounts on a regular (daily) basis, (2) individual amounts in a column whose total is *not* posted to a controlling account at the end of a period (month) are posted regularly (daily) to their general ledger accounts, and (3) total amounts for all columns except the Other Accounts column are posted at the end of a period (month) to their column's account title in the general ledger.

P2 Prepare and prove the accuracy of subsidiary ledgers. Account balances in the general ledger and its subsidiary ledgers are tested for accuracy after posting is complete. This procedure is twofold: (1) prepare a trial balance of the general ledger to confirm that debits equal credits and (2) prepare a schedule to confirm that the controlling account's balance equals the subsidiary ledger's balance.

P3A Journalize and post transactions using special journals in a periodic inventory system. Transactions are journalized and posted using special journals in a periodic system. The methods are similar to those in a perpetual system; the primary difference is that both cost of goods sold and inventory are not adjusted at the time of each sale. This usually results in the deletion (or renaming) of one or more columns devoted to these accounts in each special journal.

Guidance Answers to Decision Maker and Decision Ethics

Accountant   The main issue is whether commissions have an actual or perceived impact on the integrity and objectivity of your advice. You probably should not accept a commission arrangement. In any event, you should tell the client of your commission arrangement. Also, you need to seriously examine the merits of agreeing to a commission arrangement when you are in a position to exploit it.

Entrepreneur   The accounts receivable ledger has much of the information you need. It lists detailed information for each customer's account, including the amounts, dates for transactions, and dates of payments. It can be reorganized into an "aging schedule" to show how long customers wait before paying their bills.

Controller   Much of the information you need is in the accounts payable ledger. It contains information for each supplier, the amounts due, and when payments are made. This subsidiary ledger along with information on credit terms should enable you to conduct your analyses.

Banker   This merchandiser's segment information is likely to greatly impact your loan decision. The risks associated with the company's two sources of net profit are quite different. While net profit is up by 10%, U.S. operations are performing poorly and Cuban operations are subject to many uncertainties. These uncertainties depend on political events, legal issues, business relationships, Cuban economic conditions, and a host of other risks. Overall, net profit results suggested a low-risk loan opportunity, but the segment information reveals a high-risk situation.

Guidance Answers to Quick Checks

1. The five components are source documents, input devices, information processors, information storage, and output devices.
2. Information processors interpret, transform, and summarize the recorded accounting information so that it can be used in analysis, interpretation, and decision making.
3. Data saved in information storage are used to prepare periodic financial reports and special-purpose internal reports as well as source documentation for auditors.
4. All cash payments by check are recorded in the cash disbursements journal.
5. Columnar journals allow us to accumulate repetitive debits and credits and post them as column totals rather than as individual amounts from each entry.
6. The equality of debits and credits is kept within the general ledger. The subsidiary ledger keeps the customer's individual account and is used only for supplementary information.
7. An initial and the page number of the journal from which the amount was posted are entered in the PR column next to the amount.
8. A separate column for Sales Taxes Payable can be included in both the cash receipts journal and the sales journal.
9. This refers to a procedure of using copies of sales invoices as a sales journal. Each invoice amount is posted directly to the customer's account. All invoices are totaled at period-end for posting to the general ledger accounts.
10. The normal recording and posting procedures are threefold. First, transactions are entered in a special journal if applicable. Second, individual amounts are posted to any subsidiary ledger accounts. Third, column totals are posted to general ledger accounts if not already individually posted.
11. Controlling accounts are debited periodically for an amount or amounts equal to the sum of their respective debits in the subsidiary ledgers (equals journal column totals), and they are credited periodically for an amount or amounts equal to the sum of their respective credits in the subsidiary ledgers (from journal column totals).
12. Tests for accuracy of account balances in the general ledger and subsidiary ledgers are twofold. First, we prepare a trial balance of the general ledger to confirm that debits equal credits. Second, we prove the subsidiary ledgers by preparing schedules of accounts receivable and accounts payable.
13. The general journal is still needed for adjusting, closing, and correcting entries and for special transactions such as sales returns, purchases returns, and certain asset purchases.
14. Integrated systems can save time and minimize errors. This is so because actions taken in one part of the system automatically affect and update related parts.
15. Computer systems offer increased accuracy, speed, efficiency, and convenience.
16. Computer networks can create advantages by linking computers, and giving different users and different computers access to common databases, programs, and hardware.
17. ERP software involves integrated programs, from order taking to manufacturing to accounting. It can speed decision making, help identify costs for reduction, and aid managers in controlling operations.

Key Terms   www.mheducation.asia/olc/wildkwokFAP

Accounting information systems (p. 272)
Accounts payable ledger (p. 277)
Accounts receivable ledger (p. 277)
Batch processing (p. 286)
Cash disbursements journal (p. 284)
Cash receipts journal (p. 281)
Check register (p. 284)
Columnar journal (p. 278)
Compatibility principle (p. 273)

Components of accounting systems (p. 273)

Computer network (p. 286)

Control principle (p. 272)

Controlling account (p. 277)

Cost-benefit principle (p. 273)

Enterprise resource planning (ERP) software (p. 287)

Flexibility principle (p. 273)

General journal (p. 276)

Information processor (p. 274)

Information storage (p. 274)

Input device (p. 274)

Internal controls (p. 272)

Online processing (p. 286)

Operating segment (p. 288)

Output devices (p. 275)

Purchases journal (p. 283)

Relevance principle (p. 272)

Reportable segment (p. 288)

Sales journal (p. 278)

Schedule of accounts payable (p. 284)

Schedule of accounts receivable (p. 279)

Segment return on assets ratio (p. 288)

Special journal (p. 276)

Subsidiary ledger (p. 276)

Multiple Choice Quiz   Answers on p. 313   www.mheducation.asia/olc/wildkwokFAP

Additional Quiz Questions are available at the book's Website.

1. The sales journal is used to record
 a. Credit sales
 b. Cash sales
 c. Cash receipts
 d. Cash purchases
 e. Credit purchases

2. The purchases journal is used to record
 a. Credit sales
 b. Cash sales
 c. Cash receipts
 d. Cash purchases
 e. Credit purchases

3. The ledger that contains the financial statement accounts of a company is the
 a. General journal
 b. Column balance journal

 c. Special ledger
 d. General ledger
 e. Special journal

4. A subsidiary ledger that contains a separate account for each supplier (creditor) to the company is the
 a. Controlling account
 b. Accounts payable ledger
 c. Accounts receivable ledger
 d. General ledger
 e. Special journal

5. Enterprise resource planning software
 a. Refers to programs that help manage company operations.
 b. Is another name for spreadsheet programs.
 c. Uses batch processing of business information.
 d. Is substantially declining in use.
 e. Is another name for database programs.

A   *Superscript letter A denotes assignments based on Appendix 7A.*

🔘 Icon denotes assignments that involve decision making.

Discussion Questions

1. What are the five fundamental principles of accounting information systems?

2. What are five basic components of an accounting system?

3. What are source documents? Give two examples.

4. What is the purpose of an input device? Give examples of input devices for computer systems.

5. What is the difference between data that are stored off-line and data that are stored online?

6. What purpose is served by the output devices of an accounting system?

7. When special journals are used, they are usually used to record each of four different types of transactions. What are these four types of transactions?

8. What notations are entered into the Posting Reference column of a ledger account?

9. 🔘 When a general journal entry is used to record sales returns, the credit of the entry must be posted twice. Does this cause the trial balance to be out of balance? Explain.

10. Describe the procedures involving the use of copies of a company's sales invoices as a sales journal.

11. Credits to customer accounts and credits to Other Accounts are individually posted from a cash receipts journal such as the one in Exhibit 7.7. Why not put both types of credits in the same column and save journal space?

12. 🔘 Why should sales to and receipts of cash from credit customers be recorded and posted immediately?

13. 🔘 Locate the note that discusses Nestlé's operations by segments in Appendix A. How many reportable segments does it have?

14. 🔘 Does the income statement of Adidas in Appendix A indicate the profit earned by its segments? If so, list them.

15. Locate the note that discusses Puma's segments in its 2013 annual report on its Website www.about.puma.com/?page_id=8. What segments does Puma have?

16. 🔘 Refer to 361 Degrees' 2013 consolidated statement of financial position from its Website http://ir.361sport.com/html/ir_report.php. Does its statement of financial position indicate the identifiable assets owned by segments? If so, list them.

McGraw Hill connect™

Identify the most likely role in an accounting system played by each of the numbered items 1 through 12 by assigning a letter from the list A through E on the left.

A. Source documents	_____	**1.** Bar code reader
B. Input devices	_____	**2.** Filing cabinet
C. Information processors	_____	**3.** Bank statement
D. Information storage	_____	**4.** Computer scanner
E. Output devices	_____	**5.** Computer keyboard
	_____	**6.** Zip drive
	_____	**7.** Computer monitor
	_____	**8.** Invoice from a supplier
	_____	**9.** Computer software
	_____	**10.** Computer printer
	_____	**11.** Digital camera
	_____	**12.** MP3 player

Enter the letter of each system principle in the blank next to its best description.

A. Control principle   **D.** Flexibility principle
B. Relevance principle   **E.** Cost-benefit principle
C. Compatibility principle

1. _____ The principle prescribes the accounting information system to change in response to techno-logical advances and competitive pressures.

2. _____ The principle prescribes the accounting information system to help monitor activities.

3. _____ The principle prescribes the accounting information system to provide timely information for effective decision making.

4. _____ The principle prescribes the accounting information system to adapt to the unique character-istics of the company.

5. _____ The principle that affects all other accounting information system principles.

Fill in the blanks to complete the following descriptions.

1. _____ _____ _____ software comprises programs that help manage a company's vital operations, from manufacturing to accounting.

2. A computer _____ allows different computer users to share access to data and programs.

3. A _____ is an input device that captures writing and other input directly from source documents.

4. With _____ processing, source documents are accumulated for a period and then processed all at the same time, such as once a day, week, or month.

General Electronics uses a sales journal, a purchases journal, a cash receipts journal, a cash disbursements journal, and a general journal as illustrated in this chapter. General recently completed the following transactions *a* through *h*. Identify the journal in which each transaction should be recorded.

a. Paid cash to a creditor.
b. Sold merchandise on credit.
c. Purchased shop supplies on credit.
d. Paid an employee's salary in cash.
e. Borrowed cash from the bank.
f. Sold merchandise for cash.
g. Purchased merchandise on credit.
h. Purchased inventory for cash.

Lue Gifts uses a sales journal, a purchases journal, a cash receipts journal, a cash disbursements journal, and a general journal as illustrated in this chapter. Journalize its March transactions that should be recorded in the general journal. For those not recorded in the general journal, identify the special journal where each should be recorded.

Mar. 2 The company purchased $2,900 of merchandise on credit from the Elko Co., terms 2/10, n/30.
   12 The owner, T. Lue, contributed an automobile worth $15,000 to the company.
   16 The company sold $1,100 of merchandise (cost is $700) on credit to K. Gould, terms n/30.
   19 K. Gould returned $150 of (worthless) merchandise to the company originally purchased on March 16 (assume the cost of this merchandise is left in cost of goods sold).

QS 7-6
Controlling accounts and
subsidiary ledgers
C3

Following is information from Thompson Company for its initial month of business. (1) Identify the balances listed in the accounts receivable subsidiary ledger. (2) Identify the accounts receivable balance listed in the general ledger at month's end.

Credit Sales			Cash Collections		
Jan. 10	Boerman Company	$3,000	Jan. 20	Boerman Company	$2,000
19	Lehman Brothers	1,600	28	Lehman Brothers	1,600
23	Finger Company	2,200	31	Finger Company	1,300

QS 7-7
Purchases journal—perpetual
P1

Redmon Company uses a sales journal, a purchases journal, a cash receipts journal, a cash disbursements journal, and a general journal. The following transactions occur in the month of June.

June 1 Purchased $8,100 of merchandise on credit from Krause, Inc., terms n/30.
      8 Sold merchandise costing $900 on credit to G. Seles for $1,500 subject to a $30 sales discount if paid by the end of the month.
     14 Purchased $240 of store supplies from Chang Company on credit, terms n/30.
     17 Purchased $260 of office supplies on credit from Monder Company, terms n/30.
     24 Sold merchandise costing $400 to D. Lee for $630 cash.
     28 Purchased store supplies from Porter's for $90 cash.
     29 Paid Krause, Inc., $8,100 cash for the merchandise purchased on June 1.

Prepare headings for a purchases journal like the one in Exhibit 7.9. Journalize the June transactions that should be recorded in the purchases journal.

QS 7-8
Identifying journal of entry   C2

Refer to QS 7-7 and for each of the June transactions identify the journal in which it would be recorded. Assume the company uses a sales journal, purchases journal, cash receipts journal, cash disbursements journal, and general journal as illustrated in this chapter.

QS 7-9ᴬ
Purchases journal—periodic   P3

Prepare headings for a purchases journal like the one in Exhibit 7A.3. Journalize the June transactions from QS 7-7 that should be recorded in the purchases journal assuming the periodic inventory system is used.

QS 7-10
Accounts receivable ledger;
posting from sales journal
P2

Winslow Company posts its sales invoices directly and then binds them into a Sales Journal. Winslow had the following credit sales to these customers during June.

June	2	Joe Mack	$ 3,600
	8	Eric Horner	6,100
	10	Tess Wilson	13,400
	14	Hong Jiang	20,500
	20	Tess Wilson	11,200
	29	Joe Mack	7,300
		Total credit sales	$62,100

Required
1. Open an accounts receivable subsidiary ledger having a T-account for each customer. Post the invoices to the subsidiary ledger.
2. Open an Accounts Receivable controlling T-account and a Sales T-account to reflect general ledger accounts. Post the end-of-month total from the sales journal to these accounts.
3. Prepare a schedule of accounts receivable and prove that its total equals the Accounts Receivable controlling account balance.

QS 7-11
Analyzing segment reports
A1

Nestlé reports the following profit (and average assets in parentheses) for each of its reportable segments in 2013 in CHF (Swiss franc) millions: Zone Europe, 2,331 (11,792); Zone Americas, 5,151 (21,869); Zone Asia, Oceania, and Africa, 3,558 (14,249); Nestlé Waters, 680 (6,201); Nestlé Nutrition, 1,961 (23,398); Other, 2,175 (9,323). Compute Nestlé's return on assets for each of its segments, and assess the relative performance of these segments. Round the percents to one decimal place each.

Nestlé uses a sales journal, a purchases journal, a cash receipts journal, a cash disbursements journal, and a general journal in a manner similar to that explained in this chapter. Journalize the following summary transactions of Nestlé transactions that should be recorded in the general journal. For those not recorded in the general journal, identify only the special journal where each should be recorded. (All amounts in CHF millions.)

1. Nestlé purchased CHF 8,000 of merchandise on credit from the suppliers.

2. Nestlé sold CHF 100,000 of merchandise (cost is CHF 44,000) on credit to customers.

3. A key customer returned CHF 900 of (worthless) merchandise to Nestlé (assume the cost of this merchandise is left in cost of goods sold).

QS 7-12
International accounting and special journals
C2

connect

Hutton Company uses a sales journal, a purchases journal, a cash receipts journal, a cash disbursements journal, and a general journal. The following transactions occur in the month of March.

Mar. 2 Sold merchandise costing $300 to B. Fager for $450 cash, invoice no. 5703.
5 Purchased $2,300 of merchandise on credit from Marsh Corp.
7 Sold merchandise costing $800 to J. Dryer for $1,150, terms 2/10, n/30, invoice no. 5704.
8 Borrowed $8,000 cash by signing a note payable to the bank.
12 Sold merchandise costing $200 to R. Land for $320, terms n/30, invoice no. 5705.
16 Received $1,127 cash from J. Dryer to pay for the purchase of March 7.
19 Sold used store equipment for $900 cash to Malone, Inc.
25 Sold merchandise costing $350 to T. Burton for $550, terms n/30, invoice no. 5706.

Prepare headings for a sales journal like the one in Exhibit 7.5. Journalize the March transactions that should be recorded in this sales journal.

EXERCISES

Exercise 7-1
Sales journal—perpetual
P1

Refer to Exercise 7-1 and for each of the March transactions identify the journal in which it would be recorded. Assume the company uses a sales journal, purchases journal, cash receipts journal, cash disbursements journal, and general journal as illustrated in this chapter.

Exercise 7-2
Identifying journal of entry C2

Prepare headings for a sales journal like the one in Exhibit 7A.1. Journalize the March transactions shown in Exercise 7-1 that should be recorded in the sales journal assuming that the periodic inventory system is used.

Exercise 7-3ᴬ
Sales journal—periodic P3

Moeder Co. uses a sales journal, a purchases journal, a cash receipts journal, a cash disbursements journal, and a general journal. The following transactions occur in the month of November.

Nov. 3 The company purchased $3,100 of merchandise on credit from Hargrave Co., terms n/20.
7 The company sold merchandise costing $840 on credit to J. York for $900, subject to an $18 sales discount if paid by the end of the month.
9 The company borrowed $2,750 cash by signing a note payable to the bank.
13 J. Emling, the owner, contributed $4,000 cash to the company.
18 The company sold merchandise costing $130 to B. Box for $230 cash.
22 The company paid Hargrave Co. $3,100 cash for the merchandise purchased on November 3.
27 The company received $882 cash from J. York in payment of the November 7 purchase.
30 The company paid salaries of $1,600 in cash.

Prepare headings for a cash receipts journal like the one in Exhibit 7.7. Journalize the November transactions that should be recorded in the cash receipts journal.

Exercise 7-4
Cash receipts journal—perpetual
P1

Refer to Exercise 7-4 and for each of the November transactions identify the journal in which it would be recorded. Assume the company uses a sales journal, purchases journal, cash receipts journal, cash disbursements journal, and general journal as illustrated in this chapter.

Exercise 7-5
Identifying journal of entry C2

Prepare headings for a cash receipts journal like the one in Exhibit 7A.2. Journalize the November transactions shown in Exercise 7-4 that should be recorded in the cash receipts journal assuming that the periodic inventory system is used.

Exercise 7-6ᴬ
Cash receipts journal—periodic
P3

Exercise 7-7
Controlling accounts and
subsidiary ledgers
C3

Following is information from Ryan Company for its initial month of business. (1) Identify the balances listed in the accounts payable subsidiary ledger. (2) Identify the accounts payable balance listed in the general ledger at month's end.

Credit Purchases			Cash Paid		
Jan. 9	Boeder Company	$7,000	Jan. 19	Boeder Company	$5,100
18	Johnson Brothers	6,600	27	Johnson Brothers	6,600
22	Padley Company	4,200	31	Padley Company	3,400

Exercise 7-8
Cash disbursements
journal—perpetual
P1

Pebblebrook Supply uses a sales journal, a purchases journal, a cash receipts journal, a cash disbursements journal, and a general journal. The following transactions occur in the month of April.

Apr. 3 Purchased merchandise for $2,750 on credit from Scott, Inc., terms 2/10, n/30.
9 Issued check no. 210 to Kidman Corp. to buy store supplies for $450.
12 Sold merchandise costing $400 on credit to C. Meyers for $670, terms n/30.
17 Issued check no. 211 for $1,500 to pay off a note payable to City Bank.
20 Purchased merchandise for $3,500 on credit from LeBron, terms 2/10, n/30.
28 Issued check no. 212 to LeBron to pay the amount due for the purchase of April 20, less the discount.
29 Paid salary of $1,700 to B. Decker by issuing check no. 213.
30 Issued check no. 214 to Scott, Inc., to pay the amount due for the purchase of April 3.

Prepare headings for a cash disbursements journal like the one in Exhibit 7.11. Journalize the April transactions that should be recorded in the cash disbursements journal.

Exercise 7-9
Identifying journal of entry   **C2**

Refer to Exercise 7-8 and for each of the April transactions identify the journal in which it would be recorded. Assume the company uses a sales journal, purchases journal, cash receipts journal, cash disbursements journal, and general journal as illustrated in this chapter.

Exercise 7-10^A
Cash disbursements
journal—periodic   **P3**

Prepare headings for a cash disbursements journal like the one in Exhibit 7A.4. Journalize the April transactions from Exercise 7-8 that should be recorded in the cash disbursements journal assuming that the periodic inventory system is used.

Exercise 7-11
Special journal transactions and
error discovery
P1

Porter Pharmacy uses the following journals: sales journal, purchases journal, cash receipts journal, cash disbursements journal, and general journal. On June 5, Porter purchased merchandise priced at $12,000, subject to credit terms of 2/10, n/30. On June 14, the pharmacy paid the net amount due for the merchandise. In journalizing the payment, the pharmacy debited Accounts Payable for $12,000 but failed to record the cash discount on the purchases. Cash was properly credited for the actual $11,760 paid. (a) In what journals would the June 5 and the June 14 transactions be recorded? (b) What procedure is likely to discover the error in journalizing the June 14 transaction?

Exercise 7-12
Posting to subsidiary ledger
accounts; preparing a schedule
of accounts receivable
P2

At the end of May, the sales journal of Clear View appears as follows.

Sales Journal					Page 2 ☐☐☒
Date	Account Debited	Invoice Number	PR	Accounts Receivable Dr. Sales Cr.	Cost of Goods Sold Dr. Inventory Cr.
May 6	Aaron Reckers	190		2,880	2,200
10	Sara Reed	191		1,940	1,600
17	Anna Page	192		850	500
25	Sara Reed	193		340	200
31	Totals			6,010	4,500

Clear View also recorded the return of defective merchandise with the following entry.

May 20	Sales Returns and Allowances	250	
	Accounts Receivable—Anna Page		250
	Customer returned (worthless) merchandise.		

Required

1. Open an accounts receivable subsidiary ledger that has a T-account for each customer listed in the sales journal. Post to the customer accounts the entries in the sales journal and any portion of the general journal entry that affects a customer's account.

2. Open a general ledger that has T-accounts for Accounts Receivable, Inventory, Sales, Sales Returns and Allowances, and Cost of Goods Sold. Post the sales journal and any portion of the general journal entry that affects these accounts.

3. Prepare a schedule of accounts receivable and prove that its total equals the balance in the Accounts Receivable controlling account.

Check (3) Ending Accounts Receivable, $5,760

A company that records credit purchases in a purchases journal and records purchases returns in a general journal made the following errors. Indicate when each error should be discovered.

1. Posted a purchases return to the Accounts Payable account and to the creditor's subsidiary account but did not post the purchases return to the Inventory account.

2. Posted a purchases return to the Inventory account and to the Accounts Payable account but did not post to the creditor's subsidiary account.

3. Correctly recorded a $4,000 purchase in the purchases journal but posted it to the creditor's subsidiary account as a $400 purchase.

4. Made an addition error in determining the balance of a creditor's subsidiary account.

5. Made an addition error in totaling the Office Supplies column of the purchases journal.

Exercise 7-13
Purchases journal and error identification

P1

Refer to the table below and complete the segment return on assets. Analyze your findings and identify the segment with the highest, and that with the lowest, segment return on assets.

Exercise 7-14
Computing and analyzing segment return on assets

A1

Segment	Segment Operating Profit (in $ mil.)		Segment Assets (in $ mil.)		Segment Return on Assets
	2015	2014	2015	2014	2015
Specialty					
Skiing Group	$ 62	$ 58	$ 581	$440	
Skating Group	9	6	53	42	
Specialty Footwear	22	19	155	136	
Other Specialty	11	4	37	24	
Subtotal	104	87	826	642	
General Merchandise					
South America	32	36	305	274	
United States	7	8	52	35	
Europe	5	3	14	12	
Subtotal	44	47	371	321	
Total	$148	$134	$1197	$963	

Check Europe segment return, 38.5%

---

connect

Wise Company completes these transactions during April of the current year (the terms of all its credit sales are 2/10, n/30).

Apr. 2 Purchased $13,300 of merchandise on credit from Negi Company, invoice dated April 2, terms 2/10, n/60.
   3 Sold merchandise on credit to Brooke Sledd, Invoice No. 760, for $3,000 (cost is $2,000).
   3 Purchased $1,380 of office supplies on credit from Madison, Inc. Invoice dated April 2, terms n/10 EOM.
   4 Issued Check No. 587 to *U.S. View* for advertising expense, $999.
   5 Sold merchandise on credit to Paul Kohr, Invoice No. 761, for $8,000 (cost is $6,500).
   6 Received an $85 credit memorandum from Madison, Inc., for the return of some of the office supplies received on April 3.
   9 Purchased $11,125 of store equipment on credit from Ned's Supply, invoice dated April 9, terms n/10 EOM.

PROBLEM SET A

Problem 7-1A
Special journals, subsidiary ledgers, and schedule of accounts receivable—perpetual

C3 P1 P2

11   Sold merchandise on credit to Amy Nilson, Invoice No 762, for $9,500 (cost is $7,000).

12   Issued Check No. 588 to Negi Company in payment of its April 2 invoice, less the discount.

13   Received payment from Brooke Sledd for the April 3 sale, less the discount.

13   Sold $4,100 of merchandise on credit to Brooke Sledd (cost is $2,600), Invoice No. 763.

14   Received payment from Paul Kohr for the April 5 sale, less the discount.

16   Issued Check No. 589, payable to Payroll, in payment of sales salaries expense for the first half of the month, $9,750. Cashed the check and paid employees.

16   Cash sales for the first half of the month are $50,840 (cost is $33,880). (Cash sales are recorded daily from cash register data but are recorded only twice in this problem to reduce repetitive entries.)

17   Purchased $12,750 of merchandise on credit from Price Company, invoice dated April 17, terms 2/10, n/30.

18   Borrowed $50,000 cash from First State Bank by signing a long-term note payable.

20   Received payment from Amy Nilson for the April 11 sale, less the discount.

20   Purchased $730 of store supplies on credit from Ned's Supply, invoice dated April 19, terms n/10 EOM.

23   Received a $400 credit memorandum from Price Company for the return of defective merchandise received on April 17.

23   Received payment from Brooke Sledd for the April 13 sale, less the discount.

25   Purchased $10,375 of merchandise on credit from Negi Company, invoice dated April 24, terms 2/10, n/60.

26   Issued Check No. 590 to Price Company in payment of its April 17 invoice, less the return and the discount.

27   Sold $3,070 of merchandise on credit to Paul Kohr, Invoice No. 764 (cost is $2,420).

27   Sold $5,700 of merchandise on credit to Amy Nilson, Invoice No. 765 (cost is $3,305).

30   Issued Check No. 591, payable to Payroll, in payment of the sales salaries expense for the last half of the month, $9,750.

30   Cash sales for the last half of the month are $70,975 (cost is $55,900).

Required

1. Prepare a sales journal like that in Exhibit 7.5 and a cash receipts journal like that in Exhibit 7.7. Number both journal pages as page 3. Then review the transactions of Wise Company and enter those that should be journalized in the sales journal and those that should be journalized in the cash receipts journal. Ignore any transactions that should be journalized in a purchases journal, a cash disbursements journal, or a general journal.

2. Open the following general ledger accounts: Cash, Accounts Receivable, Inventory, Long-Term Notes Payable, B. Wise, Capital, Sales, Sales Discounts, and Cost of Goods Sold. Enter the March 31 balances for Cash ($85,000), Inventory ($125,000), Long-Term Notes Payable ($110,000), and B. Wise, Capital ($100,000). Also open accounts receivable subsidiary ledger accounts for Paul Kohr, Brooke Sledd, and Amy Nilson.

3. Verify that amounts that should be posted as individual amounts from the journals have been posted. (Such items are immediately posted.) Foot and crossfoot the journals and make the month-end postings.

Check   Trial balance totals, $415,185

4. Prepare a trial balance of the general ledger and prove the accuracy of the subsidiary ledger by preparing a schedule of accounts receivable.

Analysis Component

5. Assume that the total for the schedule of Accounts Receivable does not equal the balance of the controlling account in the general ledger. Describe steps you would take to discover the error(s).

Problem 7-2A^A

Special journals, subsidiary ledgers, and schedule of accounts receivable—periodic

C3 P2 P3

Assume that Wise Co. in Problem 7-1A uses the periodic inventory system.

Required

1. Prepare headings for a sales journal like the one in Exhibit 7A.1. Prepare headings for a cash receipts journal like the one in Exhibit 7A.2. Journalize the April transactions shown in Problem 7-1A that should be recorded in the sales journal and the cash receipts journal assuming the *periodic* inventory system is used.

2. Open the general ledger accounts with balances as shown in Problem 7-1A (do not open a Cost of Goods Sold ledger account). Also open accounts receivable subsidiary ledger accounts for

Brooke Sledd, Paul Kohr, and Amy Nilson. Under the periodic system, an Inventory account exists but is inactive until its balance is updated to the correct inventory balance at year-end. In this problem, the Inventory account remains inactive but must be included to correctly complete the trial balance.

3. Complete parts 3, 4, and 5 of Problem 7-1A using the results of parts 1 and 2 of this problem.

Check   Trial balance totals, $415,185

The April transactions of Wise Company are described in Problem 7-1A.

Problem 7-3A
Special journals, subsidiary ledgers, and schedule of accounts payable—perpetual

C3 P1 P2

Required

1. Prepare a general journal, a purchases journal like that in Exhibit 7.9, and a cash disbursements journal like that in Exhibit 7.11. Number all journal pages as page 3. Review the April transactions of Wise Company and enter those transactions that should be journalized in the general journal, the purchases journal, or the cash disbursements journal. Ignore any transactions that should be journalized in a sales journal or cash receipts journal.

2. Open the following general ledger accounts: Cash, Inventory, Office Supplies, Store Supplies, Store Equipment, Accounts Payable, Long-Term Notes Payable, B. Wise, Capital, Sales Salaries Expense, and Advertising Expense. Enter the March 31 balances of Cash ($85,000), Inventory ($125,000), Long-Term Notes Payable ($110,000), and B. Wise, Capital ($100,000). Also open accounts payable subsidiary ledger accounts for Ned's Supply, Negi Company, Price Company, and Madison, Inc.

3. Verify that amounts that should be posted as individual amounts from the journals have been posted. (Such items are immediately posted.) Foot and crossfoot the journals and make the month-end postings.

4. Prepare a trial balance of the general ledger and a schedule of accounts payable.

Check   Trial balance totals, $233,525

Refer to Problem 7-1A and assume that Wise Co. uses the periodic inventory system.

Problem 7-4A[A]
Special journals, subsidiary ledgers, and schedule of accounts payable—periodic

C3 P2 P3

Required

1. Prepare a general journal, a purchases journal like that in Exhibit 7A.3, and a cash disbursements journal like that in Exhibit 7A.4. Number all journal pages as page 3. Review the April transactions of Wise Company (Problem 7-1A) and enter those transactions that should be journalized in the general journal, the purchases journal, or the cash disbursements journal. Ignore any transaction that should be journalized in a sales journal or cash receipts journal.

2. Open the following general ledger accounts: Cash, Inventory, Office Supplies, Store Supplies, Store Equipment, Accounts Payable, Long-Term Notes Payable, B. Wise, Capital, Purchases, Purchases Returns and Allowances, Purchases Discounts, Sales Salaries Expense, and Advertising Expense. Enter the March 31 balances of Cash ($85,000), Inventory ($125,000), Long-Term Notes Payable ($110,000), and B. Wise, Capital ($100,000). Also open accounts payable subsidiary ledger accounts for Ned's Supply, Negi Company, Price Company, and Madison, Inc.

3. Complete parts 3 and 4 of Problem 7-3A using the results of parts 1 and 2 of this problem.

Check   Trial balance totals, $234,438

Bishop Company completes these transactions and events during March of the current year (terms for all its credit sales are 2/10, n/30).

Problem 7-5A
Special journals, subsidiary ledgers, trial balance—perpetual

C3 P1 P2

www.mheducation.asia/olc/wildkwokFAP

Mar.	1	Purchased $42,600 of merchandise from Soy Industries, invoice dated March 1, terms 2/15, n/30.
	2	Sold merchandise on credit to Min Cho, Invoice No. 854, for $15,800 (cost is $7,900).
	3	Purchased $1,120 of office supplies on credit from Stacy Company, invoice dated March 3, terms n/10 EOM.
	3	Sold merchandise on credit to Lance Snow, Invoice No. 855, for $9,200 (cost is $4,600).
	6	Borrowed $72,000 cash from Federal Bank by signing a long-term note payable.
	9	Purchased $20,850 of office equipment on credit from Tells Supply, invoice dated March 9, terms n/10 EOM.
	10	Sold merchandise on credit to Taylor Few, Invoice No. 856, for $4,600 (cost is $2,300).
	12	Received payment from Min Cho for the March 2 sale less the discount.
	13	Sent Soy Industries Check No. 416 in payment of the March 1 invoice less the discount.
	13	Received payment from Lance Snow for the March 3 sale less the discount.
	14	Purchased $31,625 of merchandise from the JW Company, invoice dated March 13, terms 2/10, n/30.
	15	Issued Check No. 417, payable to Payroll, in payment of sales salaries expense for the first half of the month, $15,900. Cashed the check and paid the employees.

15   Cash sales for the first half of the month are $164,680 (cost is $138,000). (Cash sales are recorded daily, but are recorded only twice here to reduce repetitive entries.)

16   Purchased $1,670 of store supplies on credit from Stacy Company, invoice dated March 16, terms n/10 EOM.

17   Received a $2,425 credit memorandum from JW Company for the return of unsatisfactory merchandise purchased on March 14.

19   Received a $630 credit memorandum from Tells Supply for office equipment received on March 9 and returned for credit.

20   Received payment from Taylor Few for the sale of March 10 less the discount.

23   Issued Check No. 418 to JW Company in payment of the invoice of March 13 less the March 17 return and the discount.

27   Sold merchandise on credit to Taylor Few, Invoice No. 857, for $13,910 (cost is $6,220).

28   Sold merchandise on credit to Lance Snow, Invoice No. 858, for $5,315 (cost is $2,280).

31   Issued Check No. 419, payable to Payroll, in payment of sales salaries expense for the last half of the month, $15,900. Cashed the check and paid the employees.

31   Cash sales for the last half of the month are $174,590 (cost is $143,000).

31   Verify that amounts impacting customer and creditor accounts were posted and that any amounts that should have been posted as individual amounts to the general ledger accounts were posted. Foot and crossfoot the journals and make the month-end postings.

Required

1. Open the following general ledger accounts: Cash; Accounts Receivable; Inventory (March 1 beg. bal. is $300,000); Office Supplies; Store Supplies; Office Equipment; Accounts Payable; Long-Term Notes Payable; M. Bishop, Capital (March 1 beg. bal. is $300,000); Sales; Sales Discounts; Cost of Goods Sold; and Sales Salaries Expense. Open the following accounts receivable subsidiary ledger accounts: Taylor Few, Min Cho, and Lance Snow. Open the following accounts payable subsidiary ledger accounts: Stacy Company, Soy Industries, Tells Supply, and JW Company.

2. Enter these transactions in a sales journal like Exhibit 7.5, a purchases journal like Exhibit 7.9, a cash receipts journal like Exhibit 7.7, a cash disbursements journal like Exhibit 7.11, or a general journal. Number all journal pages as page 2.

Check   Trial balance totals, $783,105

3. Prepare a trial balance of the general ledger and prove the accuracy of the subsidiary ledgers by preparing schedules of both accounts receivable and accounts payable.

Problem 7-6A[A]
Special journals, subsidiary ledgers, trial balance—periodic

C3 P2 P3

www.mheducation.asia/olc/wildkwokFAP

Assume that Bishop Company in Problem 7-5A uses the periodic inventory system.

Required

1. Open the following general ledger accounts: Cash; Accounts Receivable; Inventory (March 1 beg. bal. is $300,000); Office Supplies; Store Supplies; Office Equipment; Accounts Payable; Long-Term Notes Payable; M. Bishop, Capital (March 1 beg. bal. is $300,000); Sales; Sales Discounts; Purchases; Purchases Returns and Allowances; Purchases Discounts; and Sales Salaries Expense. Open the following accounts receivable subsidiary ledger accounts: Taylor Few, Min Cho, and Lance Snow. Open the following accounts payable subsidiary ledger accounts: Stacy Company, Soy Industries, Tells Supply, and JW Company.

2. Enter the transactions from Problem 7-5A in a sales journal like that in Exhibit 7A.1, a purchases journal like that in Exhibit 7A.3, a cash receipts journal like that in Exhibit 7A.2, a cash disbursements journal like that in Exhibit 7A.4, or a general journal. Number journal pages as page 2.

Check   Trial balance totals, $786,966

3. Prepare a trial balance of the general ledger and prove the accuracy of the subsidiary ledgers by preparing schedules of both accounts receivable and accounts payable.

PROBLEM SET B

Problem 7-1B
Special journals, subsidiary ledgers, schedule of accounts receivable—perpetual

C3 P1 P2

Alcorn Industries completes these transactions during July of the current year (the terms of all its credit sales are 2/10, n/30).

July 1   Purchased $6,300 of merchandise on credit from Tahoe Company, invoice dated June 30, terms 2/10, n/30.

3   Issued Check No. 300 to *The Weekly* for advertising expense, $575.

5   Sold merchandise on credit to Kim Newsom, Invoice No. 918, for $18,400 (cost is $9,700).

6   Sold merchandise on credit to Ruth Baker, Invoice No. 919, for $7,500 (cost is $4,300).

7   Purchased $1,050 of store supplies on credit from Pryor, Inc., invoice dated July 7, terms n/10 EOM.

8   Received a $150 credit memorandum from Pryor, Inc., for the return of store supplies received on July 7.

9   Purchased $37,710 of store equipment on credit from Caro's Supply, invoice dated July 8, terms n/10 EOM.

10   Issued Check No. 301 to Tahoe Company in payment of its June 30 invoice, less the discount.

13   Sold merchandise on credit to Stephanie Meyer, Invoice No. 920, for $8,350 (cost is $5,030).

14   Sold merchandise on credit to Kim Newsom, Invoice No. 921, for $4,100 (cost is $2,800).

15   Received payment from Kim Newsom for the July 5 sale, less the discount.

15   Issued Check No. 302, payable to Payroll, in payment of sales salaries expense for the first half of the month, $30,620. Cashed the check and paid employees.

15   Cash sales for the first half of the month are $121,370 (cost is $66,330). (Cash sales are recorded daily using data from the cash registers but are recorded only twice in this problem to reduce repetitive entries.)

16   Received payment from Ruth Baker for the July 6 sale, less the discount.

17   Purchased $8,200 of merchandise on credit from Dixon Company, invoice dated July 17, terms 2/10, n/30.

20   Purchased $750 of office supplies on credit from Caro's Supply, invoice dated July 19, terms n/10 EOM.

21   Borrowed $20,000 cash from College Bank by signing a long-term note payable.

23   Received payment from Stephanie Meyer for the July 13 sale, less the discount.

24   Received payment from Kim Newsom for the July 14 sale, less the discount.

24   Received a $2,400 credit memorandum from Dixon Company for the return of defective merchandise received on July 17.

26   Purchased $9,770 of merchandise on credit from Tahoe Company, invoice dated July 26, terms 2/10, n/30.

27   Issued Check No. 303 to Dixon Company in payment of its July 17 invoice, less the return and the discount.

29   Sold merchandise on credit to Ruth Baker, Invoice No. 922, for $28,090 (cost is $22,850).

30   Sold merchandise on credit to Stephanie Meyer, Invoice No. 923, for $15,750 (cost is $9,840).

31   Issued Check No. 304, payable to Payroll, in payment of the sales salaries expense for the last half of the month, $30,620.

31   Cash sales for the last half of the month are $79,020 (cost is $51,855).

Required

1. Prepare a sales journal like that in Exhibit 7.5 and a cash receipts journal like that in Exhibit 7.7. Number both journals as page 3. Then review the transactions of Alcorn Industries and enter those transactions that should be journalized in the sales journal and those that should be journalized in the cash receipts journal. Ignore any transactions that should be journalized in a purchases journal, a cash disbursements journal, or a general journal.

2. Open the following general ledger accounts: Cash, Accounts Receivable, Inventory, Long-Term Notes Payable, R. Alcorn, Capital, Sales, Sales Discounts, and Cost of Goods Sold. Enter the June 30 balances for Cash ($100,000), Inventory ($200,000), Long-Term Notes Payable ($200,000), and R. Alcorn, Capital ($100,000). Also open accounts receivable subsidiary ledger accounts for Kim Newsom, Stephanie Meyer, and Ruth Baker.

3. Verify that amounts that should be posted as individual amounts from the journals have been posted. (Such items are immediately posted.) Foot and crossfoot the journals and make the month-end postings.

4. Prepare a trial balance of the general ledger and prove the accuracy of the subsidiary ledger by preparing a schedule of accounts receivable.

Check   Trial balance totals, $602,580

Analysis Component

5. Assume that the total for the schedule of Accounts Receivable does not equal the balance of the controlling account in the general ledger. Describe steps you would take to discover the error(s).

Problem 7-2B^A

Special journals, subsidiary ledgers, and schedule of accounts receivable—periodic

C3 P2 P3

Assume that Alcorn Industries in Problem 7-1B uses the periodic inventory system.

Required

1. Prepare headings for a sales journal like the one in Exhibit 7A.1. Prepare headings for a cash receipts journal like the one in Exhibit 7A.2. Journalize the July transactions shown in Problem 7-1B that should be recorded in the sales journal and the cash receipts journal assuming the periodic inventory system is used.

2. Open the general ledger accounts with balances as shown in Problem 7-1B (do not open a Cost of Goods Sold ledger account). Also open accounts receivable subsidiary ledger accounts for Ruth Baker, Stephanie Meyer, and Kim Newsom. Under the periodic system, an Inventory account exists but is inactive until its balance is updated to the correct inventory balance at year-end. In this problem, the Inventory account remains inactive but must be included to correctly complete the trial balance.

Check Trial balance totals, $602,580

3. Complete parts 3, 4, and 5 of Problem 7-1B using the results of parts 1 and 2 of this problem.

Problem 7-3B

Special journals, subsidiary ledgers, and schedule of accounts payable—perpetual

C3 P1 P2

The July transactions of Alcorn Industries are described in Problem 7-1B.

Required

1. Prepare a general journal, a purchases journal like that in Exhibit 7.9, and a cash disbursements journal like that in Exhibit 7.11. Number all journal pages as page 3. Review the July transactions of Alcorn Industries and enter those transactions that should be journalized in the general journal, the purchases journal, or the cash disbursements journal. Ignore any transactions that should be journalized in a sales journal or cash receipts journal.

2. Open the following general ledger accounts: Cash, Inventory, Office Supplies, Store Supplies, Store Equipment, Accounts Payable, Long-Term Notes Payable, R. Alcorn, Capital, Sales Salaries Expense, and Advertising Expense. Enter the June 30 balances of Cash ($100,000), Inventory ($200,000), Long-Term Notes Payable ($200,000), and R. Alcorn, Capital ($100,000). Also open accounts payable subsidiary ledger accounts for Caro's Supply, Tahoe Company, Dixon Company, and Pryor, Inc.

3. Verify that amounts that should be posted as individual amounts from the journals have been posted. (Such items are immediately posted.) Foot and crossfoot the journals and make the month-end postings.

Check Trial balance totals, $349,130

4. Prepare a trial balance of the general ledger and a schedule of accounts payable.

Problem 7-4B^A

Special journals, subsidiary ledgers, and schedule of accounts payable—periodic

C3 P2 P3

Refer to Problem 7-1B and assume that Alcorn uses the periodic inventory system.

Required

1. Prepare a general journal, a purchases journal like that in Exhibit 7A.3, and a cash disbursements journal like that in Exhibit 7A.4. Number all journal pages as page 3. Review the July transactions of Alcorn Company (Problem 7-1B) and enter those transactions that should be journalized in the general journal, the purchases journal, or the cash disbursements journal. Ignore any transaction that should be journalized in a sales journal or cash receipts journal.

2. Open the following general ledger accounts: Cash, Inventory, Office Supplies, Store Supplies, Store Equipment, Accounts Payable, Long-Term Notes Payable, R. Alcorn, Capital, Purchases, Purchases Returns and Allowances, Purchases Discounts, Sales Salaries Expense, and Advertising Expense. Enter the June 30 balances of Cash ($100,000), Inventory ($200,000), Long-Term Notes Payable ($200,000), and R. Alcorn, Capital ($100,000). Also open accounts payable subsidiary ledger accounts for Tahoe Company, Pryor, Inc., Caro's Supply, and Dixon Company.

Check Trial balance totals, $351,772

3. Complete parts 3 and 4 of Problem 7-3B using the results of parts 1 and 2 of this problem.

Problem 7-5B

Special journals, subsidiary ledgers, trial balance—perpetual

C3 P2 P3

Suppan Company completes these transactions during November of the current year (terms for all its credit sales are 2/10, n/30).

Nov. 1 Purchased $5,062 of office equipment on credit from Blix Supply, invoice dated November 1, terms n/10 EOM.

2 Borrowed $86,250 cash from Kansas Bank by signing a long-term note payable.

4 Purchased $11,400 of merchandise from ATM Industries, invoice dated November 3, terms 2/10, n/30.

5 Purchased $1,020 of store supplies on credit from Globe Company, invoice dated November 5, terms n/10 EOM.

8   Sold merchandise on credit to Sid Ragan, Invoice No. 439, for $6,350 (cost is $3,710).

10   Sold merchandise on credit to Carlos Mane, Invoice No. 440, for $12,500 (cost is $7,500).

11   Purchased $2,887 of merchandise from Xu Company, invoice dated November 10, terms 2/10, n/30.

12   Sent ATM Industries Check No. 633 in payment of its November 3 invoice less the discount.

15   Issued Check No. 634, payable to Payroll, in payment of sales salaries expense for the first half of the month, $8,435. Cashed the check and paid the employees.

15   Cash sales for the first half of the month are $27,170 (cost is $17,000). (Cash sales are recorded daily but are recorded only twice in this problem to reduce repetitive entries.)

15   Sold merchandise on credit to Tony Timmons, Invoice No. 441, for $4,250 (cost is $1,450).

16   Purchased $559 of office supplies on credit from Globe Company, invoice dated November 16, terms n/10 EOM.

17   Received a $487 credit memorandum from Xu Company for the return of unsatisfactory merchandise purchased on November 11.

18   Received payment from Sid Ragan for the November 8 sale less the discount.

19   Received payment from Carlos Mane for the November 10 sale less the discount.

19   Issued Check No. 635 to Xu Company in payment of its invoice of November 10 less the return and the discount.

22   Sold merchandise on credit to Carlos Mane, Invoice No. 442, for $2,595 (cost is $1,060).

24   Sold merchandise on credit to Tony Timmons, Invoice No. 443, for $3,240 (cost is $1,090).

25   Received payment from Tony Timmons for the sale of November 15 less the discount.

26   Received a $922 credit memorandum from Blix Supply for the return of office equipment purchased on November 1.

30   Issued Check No. 636, payable to Payroll, in payment of sales salaries expense for the last half of the month, $8,435. Cashed the check and paid the employees.

30   Cash sales for the last half of the month are $35,703 (cost is $20,400).

30   Verify that amounts impacting customer and creditor accounts were posted and that any amounts that should have been posted as individual amounts to the general ledger accounts were posted. Foot and crossfoot the journals and make the month-end postings.

Required

1. Open the following general ledger accounts: Cash; Accounts Receivable; Inventory (November 1 beg. bal. is $40,000); Office Supplies; Store Supplies; Office Equipment; Accounts Payable; Long-Term Notes Payable; J. Suppan, Capital (Nov. 1 beg. bal. is $40,000); Sales; Sales Discounts; Cost of Goods Sold; and Sales Salaries Expense. Open the following accounts receivable subsidiary ledger accounts: Carlos Mane, Tony Timmons, and Sid Ragan. Open the following accounts payable subsidiary ledger accounts: Globe Company, ATM Industries, Blix Supply, and Xu Company.

2. Enter these transactions in a sales journal like that in Exhibit 7.5, a purchases journal like that in Exhibit 7.9, a cash receipts journal like that in Exhibit 7.7, a cash disbursements journal like that in Exhibit 7.11, or a general journal. Number all journal pages as page 2.

3. Prepare a trial balance of the general ledger and prove the accuracy of the subsidiary ledgers by preparing schedules of both accounts receivable and accounts payable.

Check   Trial balance totals, $223,777

Assume that Suppan Company in Problem 7-5B uses the periodic inventory system.

Required

1. Open the following general ledger accounts: Cash; Accounts Receivable; Inventory (November 1 beg. bal. is $40,000); Office Supplies; Store Supplies; Office Equipment; Accounts Payable; Long-Term Notes Payable; J. Suppan, Capital (Nov. 1 beg. bal. is $40,000); Sales; Sales Discounts; Purchases; Purchases Returns and Allowances; Purchases Discounts; and Sales Salaries Expense. Open the following accounts receivable subsidiary ledger accounts: Carlos Mane, Tony Timmons, and Sid Ragan. Open the following accounts payable subsidiary ledger accounts: Globe Company, ATM Industries, Blix Supply, and Xu Company.

2. Enter the transactions from Problem 7-5B in a sales journal like that in Exhibit 7A.1, a purchases journal like that in Exhibit 7A.3, a cash receipts journal like that in Exhibit 7A.2, a cash disbursements journal like that in Exhibit 7A.4, or a general journal. Number journal pages as page 2.

3. Prepare a trial balance of the general ledger and prove the accuracy of the subsidiary ledgers by preparing schedules of both accounts receivable and accounts payable.

Problem 7-6B[A]
Special journals, subsidiary ledgers, trial balance—periodic

C3 P2 P3

Check   Trial balance totals, $224,540

SERIAL PROBLEM
Business Solutions   P1

(This serial problem began in Chapter 1 and continues through most of the book. If previous chapter segments were not completed, the serial problem can begin at this point.)

SP 7   Assume that Santana Rey expands Business Solutions' accounting system to include special journals.

Required

1. Locate the transactions related to January through March 2016 for Business Solutions in Chapter 5.
2. Enter the Business Solutions transactions for January through March in a sales journal like that in Exhibit 7.5 (insert "n/a" in the Invoice column), a cash receipts journal like that in Exhibit 7.7, a purchases journal like that in Exhibit 7.9 (use Computer Supplies heading instead of Office Supplies), and a cash disbursements journal like that in Exhibit 7.11 (insert "n/a" in the Check Number column), or a general journal. Number journal pages as page 2. If the transaction does not specify the name of the payee, state "not specified" in the Payee column of the cash disbursements journal.
3. The transactions on the following dates should be journalized in the general journal: January 5, 11, 20, 24, and 29 (no entry required) and March 24. Do not record and post the adjusting entries for the end of March.

COMPREHENSIVE PROBLEM
Colo Company

www.mheducation.asia/olc/wildkwokFAP

(If the Working Papers that accompany this book are not available, omit this comprehensive problem.)
Assume it is Monday, May 1, the first business day of the month, and you have just been hired as the accountant for Colo Company, which operates with monthly accounting periods. All of the company's accounting work is completed through the end of April and its ledgers show April 30 balances. During your first month on the job, the company experiences the following transactions and events (terms for all its credit sales are 2/10, n/30 unless stated differently):

May 1   Issued Check No. 3410 to S&P Management Co. in payment of the May rent, $3,710. (Use two lines to record the transaction. Charge 80% of the rent to Rent Expense—Selling Space and the balance to Rent Expense—Office Space.)

2   Sold merchandise on credit to Hensel Company, Invoice No. 8785, for $6,100 (cost is $4,100).

2   Issued a $175 credit memorandum to Knox Co., for defective (worthless) merchandise sold on April 28 and returned for credit. The total selling price (gross) was $4,725.

3   Received a $798 credit memorandum from Peyton Products for the return of merchandise purchased on April 29.

4   Purchased the following on credit from Gear Supply Co.: merchandise, $37,072; store supplies, $574; and office supplies, $83. Invoice dated May 4, terms n/10 EOM.

5   Received payment from Knox Co., for the balance from the April 28 sale less the May 2 return and the discount.

8   Issued Check No. 3411 to Peyton Products to pay for the $7,098 of merchandise purchased on April 29 less the May 3 return and a 2% discount.

9   Sold store supplies to the merchant next door at their cost of $350 cash.

10   Purchased $4,074 of office equipment on credit from Gear Supply Co., invoice dated May 10, terms n/10 EOM.

11   Received payment from Hensel Company for the May 2 sale less the discount.

11   Purchased $8,800 of merchandise from Garcia, Inc., invoice dated May 10, terms 2/10, n/30.

12   Received an $854 credit memorandum from Gear Supply Co. for the return of defective office equipment received on May 10.

15   Issued Check No. 3412, payable to Payroll, in payment of sales salaries, $5,320, and office salaries, $3,150. Cashed the check and paid the employees.

15   Cash sales for the first half of the month are $59,220 (cost is $38,200). (Cash sales are recorded daily but are recorded only twice here to reduce repetitive entries.)

15   Post to the customer and creditor accounts. Also post individual items that are not included in column totals at the end of the month to the general ledger accounts. (Such items are posted daily but are posted only twice each month because they are few in number.)

16   Sold merchandise on credit to Hensel Company, Invoice No. 8786, for $3,990 (cost is $1,890).

17   Purchased $13,650 of merchandise from Fink Corp., invoice dated May 14, terms 2/10, n/60.

19   Issued Check No. 3413 to Garcia, Inc., in payment of its May 10 invoice less the discount.

22   Sold merchandise to Lee Services, Invoice No. 8787, for $6,850 (cost is $4,990), terms 2/10, n/60.

23   Issued Check No. 3414 to Fink Corp. in payment of its May 14 invoice less the discount.

24   Purchased the following on credit from Gear Supply Co.: merchandise, $8,120; store supplies, $630; and office supplies, $280. Invoice dated May 24, terms n/10 EOM.

25   Purchased $3,080 of merchandise from Peyton Products, invoice dated May 23, terms 2/10, n/30.

26   Sold merchandise on credit to Crane Corp., Invoice No. 8788, for $14,210 (cost is $8,230).

26   Issued Check No. 3415 to Perennial Power in payment of the May electric bill, $1,283.

29   The owner of Colo Company, Jenny Colo, used Check No. 3416 to withdraw $7,000 cash from the business for personal use.

30   Received payment from Lee Services for the May 22 sale less the discount.

30   Issued Check No. 3417, payable to Payroll, in payment of sales salaries, $5,320, and office salaries, $3,150. Cashed the check and paid the employees.

31   Cash sales for the last half of the month are $66,052 (cost is $42,500).

31   Post to the customer and creditor accounts. Also post individual items that are not included in column totals at the end of the month to the general ledger accounts. Foot and crossfoot the journals and make the month-end postings.

Required

1. Enter these transactions in a sales journal, a purchases journal, a cash receipts journal, a cash disbursements journal, or a general journal as illustrated in this chapter (number all journal pages as page 2). Post when instructed to do so. Assume a perpetual inventory system.

2. Prepare a trial balance in the Trial Balance columns of the work sheet form provided with the working papers. Complete the work sheet using the following information for accounting adjustments.

  a. Expired insurance, $553.

  b. Ending store supplies inventory, $2,632.

  c. Ending office supplies inventory, $504.

  d. Depreciation of store equipment, $567.

  e. Depreciation of office equipment, $329.

  Prepare and post adjusting and closing entries.

3. Prepare a May 2015 income statement, a May 2015 statement of changes in equity, and a May 31, 2015, classified statement of financial position.

4. Prepare a post-closing trial balance. Also prove the accuracy of subsidiary ledgers by preparing schedules of both accounts receivable and accounts payable.

Check (2) Unadjusted trial balance totals, $545,020; Adjustments column totals, $2,407

(3) Net profit, $31,647; Total assets, $385,791

Beyond the Numbers

BTN 7-1   Refer to Nestlé's financial statements in Appendix A to answer the following.

1. Identify the note that reports on Nestlé's segments.

2. Describe the focus and activities of each of Nestlé's segments.

Fast Forward

3. Access Nestlé's annual report for financial years ending after December 31, 2013 from its Website (http://www.nestle.com/investors/publications). Has Nestlé changed its reporting policy regarding segment information? Explain.

REPORTING IN ACTION

A1

BTN 7-2   Samsung and Nokia Siemens are competitors in some products. In its 2012 annual report, Samsung reports the following three segments:

COMPARATIVE ANALYSIS

A1

(KRW millions)	Consumer Electronics		Information Technology and Mobile Communication		Semi-conductor	
	2012	2011	2012	2011	2012	2011
Segment operating profit	2,301,431	1,256,788	19,440,840	8,122,626	4,173,730	6,383,875
Segment net sales	48,443,749	47,296,625	108,506,036	67,447,953	34,886,606	36,989,551

In its 2012 annual report, Nokia Siemens reports the following two segments:

(EUR millions)	Mobile Broadband		Global Services	
	2012	2011	2012	2011
Segment operating profit	488	214	332	229
Segment net sales	6,043	6,335	6,929	6,737

Required

1. Compute the ratio of segment operating profit divided by segment net sales for both companies for years 2012 and 2011.

2. Why do Samsung and Nokia Siemens define their segments differently? Given the differences, is it still worthwhile to analyze segment information?

ETHICS
CHALLENGE

C1

BTN 7-3   Erica Gray, CPA, is a sole practitioner. She has been practicing as an auditor for 10 years. Recently a long-standing audit client asked Gray to design and implement an integrated computer-based accounting information system. The fees associated with this additional engagement with the client are very attractive. However, Gray wonders if she can remain objective on subsequent audits in her evaluation of the client's accounting system and its records if she was responsible for its design and implementation. Gray knows that professional auditing standards require her to remain independent in fact and appearance from her auditing clients.

Required

1. What do you believe auditing standards are mainly concerned with when they require independence in fact? In appearance?

2. Why is it important that auditors remain independent of their clients?

3. Do you think Gray can accept this engagement and remain independent? Justify your response.

COMMUNICATING
IN PRACTICE

C2 C3

BTN 7-4   Your friend, Wendy Geiger, owns a small retail store that sells candies and nuts. Geiger acquires her goods from a few select vendors. She generally makes purchase orders by phone and on credit. Sales are primarily for cash. Geiger keeps her own manual accounting system using a general journal and a general ledger. At the end of each business day, she records one summary entry for cash sales. Geiger recently began offering items in creative gift packages. This has increased sales substantially, and she is now receiving orders from corporate and other clients who order large quantities and prefer to buy on credit. As a result of increased credit transactions in both purchases and sales, keeping the accounting records has become extremely time consuming. Geiger wants to continue to maintain her own manual system and calls you for advice. Write a memo to her advising how she might modify her current manual accounting system to accommodate the expanded business activities. Geiger is accustomed to checking her ledger by using a trial balance. Your memo should explain the advantages of what you propose and of any other verification techniques you recommend.

TAKING IT TO
THE NET

A1

BTN 7-5   Access the 2013 annual report of L'Oréal at www.loreal-finance.com/eng/annualreport#. Read its Note 3.1 that details L'Oréal's business activities and answer the following.

1. L'Oréal's cosmetics branch is divided among which four divisions?

2. Which segment had the largest dollar amount of operating profit? Which had the largest percentage of operating profit as a percent of sales?

TEAMWORK IN
ACTION

C3 P1 P2

BTN 7-6   Each member of the team is to assume responsibility for one of the following tasks:

a. Journalizing in the purchases journal.

b. Journalizing in the cash disbursements journal.

c. Maintaining and verifying the Accounts Payable ledger.

d. Journalizing in the sales journal and the general journal.

e. Journalizing in the cash receipts journal.

f. Maintaining and verifying the Accounts Receivable ledger.

The team should abide by the following procedures in carrying out responsibilities.

Required

1. After tasks *a–f* are assigned, each team member is to quickly read the list of transactions in Problem 7-5A, identifying with initials the journal in which each transaction is to be recorded. Upon

completion, the team leader is to read transaction dates, and the appropriate team member is to vocalize responsibility. Any disagreement between teammates must be resolved.

2. Journalize and continually update subsidiary ledgers. Journal recorders should alert teammates assigned to subsidiary ledgers when an entry must be posted to their subsidiary.

3. Team members responsible for tasks *a*, *b*, *d*, and *e* are to summarize and prove journals; members responsible for tasks *c* and *f* are to prepare both payables and receivables schedules.

4. The team leader is to take charge of the general ledger, rotating team members to obtain amounts to be posted. The person responsible for a journal must complete posting references in that journal. Other team members should verify the accuracy of account balance computations. To avoid any abnormal account balances, post in the following order: P, S, G, R, D. (*Note:* Posting any necessary individual general ledger amounts is also done at this time.)

5. The team leader is to read out general ledger account balances while another team member fills in the trial balance form. Concurrently, one member should keep a running balance of debit account balance totals and another credit account balance totals. Verify the final total of the trial balance and the schedules. If necessary, the team must resolve any errors. Turn in the trial balance and schedules to the instructor.

BTN 7-7 Refer to the chapter's opening feature about Josephine Ng and her company, Alteration Initiative. Her service business deals with numerous suppliers and customers.

ENTREPRENEURIAL DECISION

P1

Required

1. Identify the special journals that Alteration Initiative would be likely to use in its operations. Also identify any subsidiary ledgers that it would likely use.

2. Alteration Initiative hopes to double yearly sales within five years hence from its current $500,000 amount. Assume that its sales growth projections are as follows.

Year	One Year Hence	Two Years Hence	Three Years Hence	Four Years Hence	Five Years Hence
Projected growth in sales (from the preceding year)	0%	20%	15%	25%	20%

Estimate Alteration Initiative's projected sales for each year (round to the nearest dollar). If this pattern of sales growth holds, will Alteration Initiative achieve its goal of doubling sales in five years?

ANSWERS TO MULTIPLE CHOICE QUIZ

1. a
2. e
3. d

4. b
5. a

8

Cash and Internal Controls

A Look Back

Chapter 7 focused on accounting information systems. We explained the principles and components of information systems, the use of special journals and subsidiary ledgers, and technology-based systems.

A Look at This Chapter

This chapter extends our study of accounting to internal control and the analysis of cash. We describe procedures that are good for internal control. We also explain the control of and the accounting for cash, including control features of banking activities.

A Look Ahead

Chapter 9 focuses on receivables. We explain how to account and report on receivables and their related accounts. This includes estimating uncollectible receivables and computing interest earned.

Learning Objectives

CAP

CONCEPTUAL

C1 Define internal control and identify its purpose and principles. (p. 316)

C2 Define cash and cash equivalents and explain how to report them. (p. 321)

ANALYTICAL

A1 Compute the days' sales uncollected ratio and use it to assess liquidity. (p. 335)

PROCEDURAL

P1 Apply internal control to cash receipts and disbursements. (p. 322)

P2 Explain and record petty cash fund transactions. (p. 326)

P3 Prepare a bank reconciliation. (p. 331)

P4 *Appendix 8A*—Describe the use of documentation and verification to control cash disbursements. (p. 338)

P5 *Appendix 8B*—Apply the net method to control purchase discounts. (p. 341)

"I wanted to go back to the basics of food production and cooking."—**SAM LEONG**

Decision Insight

What's Cooking, Sam?

At **sam.leong@forest cooking school (www.samatforest. com),** you can ask any question about cooking without fearing a verbal tirade or a pot being rattled. For this culinary school is no hell's kitchen—its founders, husband-and-wife team Sam and Forest Leong, believe in more than teaching their students to make the perfect soft-boiled egg or hold a kitchen knife. What this dynamic couple ultimately want cooking in their kitchen is their students "getting the best out of their time here".

On a personal level, "I wanted to go back to the basics of food production and cooking," says Sam, Singapore's award-winning celebrity chef, who brings to the table a gastronomic wealth of culinary skills honed through years of working in some of Singapore's most reputable restaurants. "I also wanted to give my service and time back to the community," he stresses, adding that his entrepreneurial inspiration was in part sparked by a desire "to work closely with my wife." Forest is Thai and spent her childhood in the kitchen helping her father, a traditional Thai cuisine chef. Their partnership has given the culinary school a piquant flavor with its Asian fusion of Thai and Chinese cuisine.

The couple conduct different classes based on their forte, though sometimes, "we conduct cooking classes together, especially when we are abroad," says Sam.

With a regular travel schedule, Sam and Forest keep the business operation simple to avoid fretting over management issues. Unlike most companies that delegate responsibilities and rely on formal procedures to control business activities, the couple maintain close personal supervision by doing most of the tasks themselves ("I do the grocery shopping," says Sam). Financial records—receipts of cash and cash equivalents—are vigilantly monitored and meticulously recorded by Forest, even though "we do not incur a lot of petty cash transactions and set aside only a small amount as daily petty cash."

Sam, who has represented Singapore at some of the world's most prestigious culinary events, has no grandiose plans to expand his operations yet, preferring to keep it personalized and manageable. "One thing I love about teaching a class and managing a culinary school is that I can interact personally with the participants," he says. This is one chef instructor a novice cook wouldn't mind being in the kitchen with!

We all are aware of theft and fraud. They affect us in several ways: We lock doors, chain bikes, review sales receipts, and acquire alarm systems. A company also takes actions to safeguard, control, and manage what it owns. Experience tells us that small companies are most vulnerable, usually due to weak internal controls. It is management's responsibility to set up policies and procedures to safeguard a company's assets, especially cash. To do so, management *and* employees must understand and apply principles of internal control. This chapter describes these principles and how to apply them. It focuses special attention on cash because it is easily transferable and is often at high risk of loss.

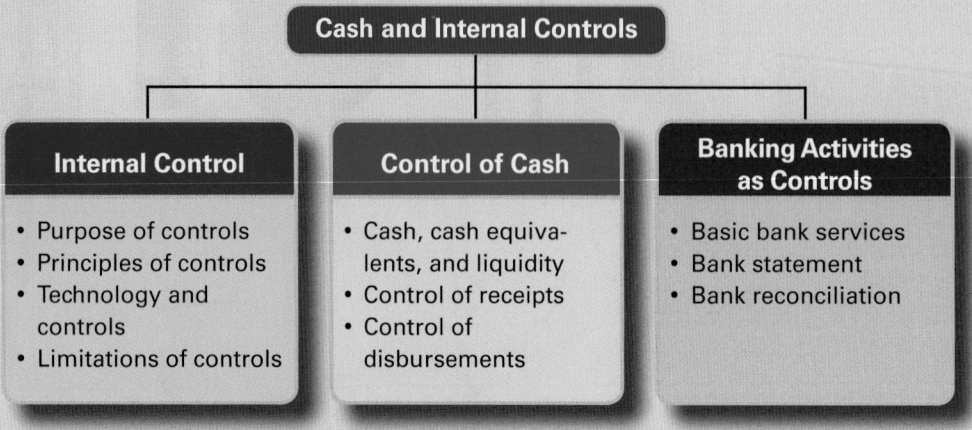

INTERNAL CONTROL

This section describes internal control and its fundamental principles. We also discuss the impact of technology on internal control and the limitations of control procedures.

Purpose of Internal Control

C1 Define internal control and identify its purpose and principles.

Managers (or owners) of small businesses often control the entire operation. These managers usually purchase all assets, hire and manage employees, negotiate all contracts, and sign all checks. They know from personal contact and observation whether the business is actually receiving the assets and services paid for. Most companies, however, cannot maintain this close personal supervision. They must delegate responsibilities and rely on formal procedures rather than personal contact in controlling business activities.

Internal Control System Managers use an internal control system to monitor and control business activities. An **internal control system** consists of the policies and procedures managers use to

- Protect assets.
- Ensure reliable accounting.
- Promote efficient operations.
- Urge adherence to company policies.

A properly designed internal control system is a key part of systems design, analysis, and performance. Managers place a high priority on internal control systems because they can prevent avoidable losses, help managers plan operations, and monitor company and employee performance. Internal controls do not provide guarantees, but they lower the company's risk of loss.

Principles of Internal Control

Internal control policies and procedures vary from company to company according to such factors as the nature of the business and its size. Certain fundamental internal control principles apply to all companies. The **principles of internal control** are to

1. Establish responsibilities.
2. Maintain adequate records.
3. Insure assets and bond key employees.
4. Separate recordkeeping from custody of assets.
5. Divide responsibility for related transactions.
6. Apply technological controls.
7. Perform regular and independent reviews.

This section explains these seven principles and describes how internal control procedures minimize the risk of fraud and theft. These procedures also increase the reliability and accuracy of accounting records. A framework for how these seven principles improve the quality of financial reporting is provided by the **Committee of Sponsoring Organizations (COSO)** (www.COSO.org). Specifically, these principles link to five aspects of internal control: control activities, control environment, risk assessment, monitoring, and communication.

Establish Responsibilities   Proper internal control means that responsibility for a task is clearly established and assigned to one person. When a problem occurs in a company where responsibility is not identified, determining who is at fault is difficult. For instance, if two salesclerks share the same cash register and there is a cash shortage, neither clerk can be held accountable. To prevent this problem, one clerk might be given responsibility for handling all cash sales. Alternately, a company can use a register with separate cash drawers for each clerk. Most of us have waited at a retail counter during a shift change while employees swap cash drawers.

Maintain Adequate Records   Good recordkeeping is part of an internal control system. It helps protect assets and ensures that employees use prescribed procedures. Reliable records are also a source of information that managers use to monitor company activities. When detailed records of equipment are kept, for instance, items are unlikely to be lost or stolen without detection. Similarly, transactions are less likely to be entered in wrong accounts if a chart of accounts is set up and carefully used. Many preprinted forms and internal documents are also designed for use in a good internal control system. When sales slips are properly designed, for instance, sales personnel can record needed information efficiently with less chance of errors or delays to customers. When sales slips are prenumbered and controlled, each one issued is the responsibility of one salesperson, preventing the salesperson from pocketing cash by making a sale and destroying the sales slip. Computerized point-of-sale systems achieve the same control results.

Point: Many companies have a mandatory vacation policy for employees who handle cash. When another employee must cover for the one on vacation, it is more difficult to hide cash frauds.

Insure Assets and Bond Key Employees   Good internal control means that assets are adequately insured against casualty and that employees handling large amounts of cash and easily transferable assets are bonded. An employee is *bonded* when a company purchases an insurance policy, or a bond, against losses from theft by that employee. Bonding reduces the risk of loss. It also discourages theft because bonded employees know an independent bonding company will be involved when theft is uncovered and is unlikely to be sympathetic with an employee involved in theft.

Point: The Association of Certified Fraud Examiners (cfenet.com) estimates that employee fraud costs small companies more than $100,000 per incident.

Separate Recordkeeping from Custody of Assets   A person who controls or has access to an asset must not keep that asset's accounting records. This principle reduces

Decision Insight

Tag Control A novel technique exists for marking physical assets. It involves embedding a less than one-inch-square tag of fibers that creates a unique optical signature recordable by scanners. Manufacturers hope to embed tags in everything from compact discs and credit cards to designer clothes for purposes of internal control and efficiency. ■

the risk of theft or waste of an asset because the person with control over it knows that another person keeps its records. Also, a recordkeeper who does not have access to the asset has no reason to falsify records. This means that to steal an asset and hide the theft from the records, two or more people must *collude*—or agree in secret to commit the fraud.

Divide Responsibility for Related Transactions Good internal control divides responsibility for a transaction or a series of related transactions between two or more individuals or departments. This is to ensure that the work of one individual acts as a check on the other. This principle, often called *separation of duties,* is not a call for duplication of work. Each employee or department should perform unduplicated effort. Examples of transactions with divided responsibility are placing purchase orders, receiving merchandise, and paying vendors. These tasks should not be given to one individual or department. Assigning responsibility for two or more of these tasks to one party increases mistakes and perhaps fraud. Having an independent person, for example, check incoming goods for quality and quantity encourages more care and attention to detail than having the person who placed the order do the checking. Added protection can result from identifying a third person to approve payment of the invoice. A company can even designate a fourth person with authority to write checks as another protective measure.

Point: There's a new security device—a person's ECG (electrocardiogram) reading—that is as unique as a fingerprint and a lot harder to lose or steal than a PIN. ECGs can be read through fingertip touches. An ECG also shows that a living person is actually there, whereas fingerprint and facial recognition software can be fooled.

Apply Technological Controls Cash registers, check protectors, time clocks, and personal identification scanners are examples of devices that can improve internal control. Technology often improves the effectiveness of controls. A cash register with a locked-in tape or electronic file makes a record of each cash sale. A check protector perforates the amount of a check into its face and makes it difficult to alter the amount. A time clock registers the exact time an employee both arrives at and departs from the job. Mechanical change and currency counters quickly and accurately count amounts, and personal scanners limit access to only authorized individuals. Each of these and other technological controls are an effective part of many internal control systems.

Decision Insight

About Face Face-recognition software snaps a digital picture of the face and converts key facial features—say, the distance between the eyes—into a series of numerical values. These can be stored on an ID or ATM card as a simple bar code to prohibit unauthorized access. ■

Perform Regular and Independent Reviews Changes in personnel, stress of time pressures, and technological advances present opportunities for shortcuts and lapses. To counter these factors, regular reviews of internal control systems are needed to ensure that procedures are followed. These reviews are preferably done by internal auditors not directly involved in the activities. Their impartial perspective encourages an evaluation of the efficiency as well as the effectiveness of the internal control system. Many companies also pay for audits by independent, external auditors. These external auditors test the company's financial records to give an opinion as to whether its financial statements are presented fairly. Before external auditors decide on how much testing is needed, they evaluate the effectiveness of the internal control system. This evaluation is often helpful to a client.

Decision Maker   Answer — p. 343

Entrepreneur   As owner of a start-up information services company, you hire a systems analyst. One of her first recommendations is to require all employees to take at least one week of vacation per year. Why would she recommend a "forced vacation" policy? ■

Technology and Internal Control

The fundamental principles of internal control are relevant no matter what the technological state of the accounting system, from purely manual to fully automated systems. Technology impacts an internal control system in several important ways. Perhaps the most obvious is that technology allows us quicker access to databases and information. Used effectively, technology greatly improves managers' abilities to monitor and control business activities. This section describes some technological impacts we must be alert to.

Reduced Processing Errors   Technologically advanced systems reduce the number of errors in processing information. Provided the software and data entry are correct, the risk of mechanical and mathematical errors is nearly eliminated. However, we must remember that erroneous software or data entry does exist. Also, less human involvement in data processing can cause data entry errors to go undiscovered. Moreover, errors in software can produce consistent but erroneous processing of transactions. Continually checking and monitoring all types of systems are important.

More Extensive Testing of Records   A company's review and audit of electronic records can include more extensive testing when information is easily and rapidly accessed. When accounting records are kept manually, auditors and others likely select only small samples of data to test. When data are accessible with computer technology, however, auditors can quickly analyze large samples or even the entire database.

Limited Evidence of Processing   Many data processing steps are increasingly done by computer. Accordingly, fewer hard-copy items of documentary evidence are available for review. Yet technologically advanced systems can provide new evidence. They can, for instance, record who made the entries, the date and time, the source of the entry, and so on. Technology can also be designed to require the use of passwords or other identification before access to the system is granted. This means that internal control depends more on the design and operation of the information system and less on the analysis of its resulting documents.

Crucial Separation of Duties   Technological advances in accounting information systems often yield some job eliminations or consolidations. While those who remain have the special skills necessary to operate advanced programs and equipment, a company with a reduced workforce risks losing its crucial separation of duties. The company must establish ways to control and monitor employees to minimize risk of error and fraud. For instance, the person who designs and programs the information system must not be the one who operates it. The company must also separate control over programs and files from the activities related to cash receipts and disbursements. For instance, a computer operator should not control check-writing activities. Achieving acceptable separation of duties can be especially difficult and costly in small companies with few employees.

Increased E-Commerce   Technology has encouraged the growth of e-commerce. Amazon.com and eBay are examples of companies that have successfully exploited e-commerce. Most companies have some e-commerce transactions. All such transactions involve at least three risks. (1) *Credit card number theft* is a risk of using, transmitting, and storing such data online. This increases the cost of e-commerce. (2) *Computer viruses* are malicious programs that attach themselves to innocent files for purposes of infecting and harming other files and programs. (3) *Impersonation* online can result in charges of sales to bogus accounts, purchases of inappropriate materials, and the unknowing giving up of confidential information to hackers. Companies use both firewalls and encryption

Point: Information on Internet fraud can be found at these Websites: **sec.gov/investor/pubs/cyberfraud.htm** **ftc.gov/bcp/consumer.shtm** **www.fraud.org**

Point: Evidence of any internal control failure for a company reduces user confidence in its financial statements.

Point: We look to several sources when assessing a company's internal controls. Sources include the auditor's report, management report on controls (if available), management discussion and analysis, and financial press.

Point: COSO organizes control components into five types:
- Control environment
- Control activities
- Risk assessment
- Monitoring
- Information and communication

"Worst case of identity theft I've ever seen!"

Copyright 2004 by Randy Glasbergen. www.glasbergen.com

to combat some of these risks—firewalls are points of entry to a system that require passwords to continue, and encryption is a mathematical process to rearrange contents that cannot be read without the process code. Nearly 5% of Americans already report being victims of identity theft, and roughly 10 million say their privacy has been compromised.

Decision Insight

Cheery Fraud Victim   Certified Fraud Examiners Website reports the following: Andrew Cameron stole Jacqueline Boanson's credit card. Cameron headed to the racetrack and promptly charged two bets for $150 on the credit card—winning $400. Unfortunately for Cameron the racetrack refused to pay him cash as its internal control policy is to credit winnings from bets made on a credit card to that same card. Cameron was later nabbed; and the racetrack let Ms. Boanson keep the winnings. ■

Limitations of Internal Control

All internal control policies and procedures have limitations that usually arise from either (1) the human element or (2) the cost–benefit principle.

Internal control policies and procedures are applied by people. This human element creates several potential limitations that we can categorize as either (1) human error or (2) human fraud. *Human error* can occur from negligence, fatigue, misjudgment, or confusion. *Human fraud* involves intent by people to defeat internal controls, such as *management override,* for personal gain. Fraud also includes collusion to thwart the separation of duties. The human element highlights the importance of establishing an *internal control environment* to convey management's commitment to internal control policies and procedures. Human fraud is driven by the *triple-threat* of fraud:

- **Opportunity**—refers to internal control deficiencies in the workplace.
- **Pressure**—refers to financial, family, society, and other stresses to succeed.
- **Rationalization**—refers to employees justifying fraudulent behavior.

The second major limitation on internal control is the *cost–benefit principle,* which dictates that the costs of internal controls must not exceed their benefits. Analysis of costs and benefits must consider all factors, including the impact on morale. Most companies, for instance, have a legal right to read employees' e-mails, yet companies seldom exercise that right unless they are confronted with evidence of potential harm to the company. The same holds for drug testing, phone tapping, and hidden cameras. The bottom line is that managers must establish internal control policies and procedures with a net benefit to the company. ■

Point: **Cybercrime.gov** pursues computer and intellectual property crimes, including that of e-commerce.

Address   www.hacker'sguidetocyberspace.com   GO

Hacker's Guide to Cyberspace

Pharming   Viruses attached to e-mails and Websites load software onto your PC that monitors keystrokes; when you sign on to financial Websites, it steals your passwords.

Phishing   Hackers send e-mails to you posing as banks; you are asked for information using fake Websites where they reel in your passwords and personal data.

WI-Phishing   Cybercrooks set up wireless networks hoping you use them to connect to the Web; your passwords and data are stolen as you use their network.

Bot-Networking   Hackers send remote-control programs to your PC that take control to send out spam and viruses; they even rent your bot to other cybercrooks.

Typo-Squatting   Hackers set up Websites with addresses similar to legit outfits; when you make a typo and hit their sites, they infect your PC with viruses or take them over as bots.

Quick Check   Answers — p. 343

1. Principles of internal control suggest that (choose one): (*a*) Responsibility for a series of related transactions (such as placing orders, receiving and paying for merchandise) should be assigned to one employee; (*b*) Responsibility for individual tasks should be shared by more than one employee so that one serves as a check on the other; or (*c*) Employees who handle considerable cash and easily transferable assets should be bonded.

2. What are some impacts of computing technology on internal control?

CONTROL OF CASH

Cash is a necessary asset of every company. Most companies also own *cash equivalents* (defined below), which are assets similar to cash. Cash and cash equivalents are the most liquid of all assets and are easily hidden and moved. An effective system of internal controls protects these assets and it should meet three basic guidelines:

1. Handling cash is separate from recordkeeping of cash.
2. Cash receipts are promptly deposited in a bank.
3. Cash disbursements are made by check.

The first guideline applies separation of duties to minimize errors and fraud. When duties are separated, two or more people must collude to steal cash and conceal this action in the accounting records. The second guideline uses immediate (say, daily) deposits of all cash receipts to produce a timely independent record of the cash received. It also reduces the likelihood of cash theft (or loss) and the risk that an employee could personally use the money before depositing it. The third guideline uses payments by check to develop an independent bank record of cash disbursements. This guideline also reduces the risk of cash theft (or loss).

This section begins with definitions of cash and cash equivalents. Discussion then focuses on controls and accounting for both cash receipts and disbursements. The exact procedures used to achieve control over cash vary across companies. They depend on factors such as company size, number of employees, volume of cash transactions, and sources of cash.

Cash, Cash Equivalents, and Liquidity

Good accounting systems help in managing the amount of cash and controlling who has access to it. Cash is the usual means of payment when paying for assets, services, or liabilities. **Liquidity** refers to a company's ability to pay for its near-term obligations. Cash and similar assets are called **liquid assets** because they can be readily used to settle such obligations. A company needs liquid assets to effectively operate.

Cash includes currency and coins along with the amounts on deposit in bank accounts, checking accounts (called *demand deposits*), and many savings accounts (called *time deposits*). Cash also includes items that are acceptable for deposit in these accounts such as customer checks, cashier's checks, certified checks, and money orders. **Cash equivalents** are short-term, highly liquid investment assets meeting two criteria: (1) readily convertible to a known cash amount and (2) sufficiently close to their due date so that their market value is not sensitive to interest rate changes. Only investments purchased within three months of their due date usually satisfy these criteria. Examples of cash equivalents are short-term investments in assets such as U.S. Treasury bills and money market funds. To increase their return, many companies invest idle cash in cash equivalents. Most companies combine cash equivalents with cash as a single item on the statement of financial position.

C2 Define cash and cash equivalents and explain how to report them.

Point: The most liquid assets are usually reported first on a statement of financial position; the least liquid assets are reported last.

Point: Google reports cash and cash equivalents of $10,198 million in its statement of financial position. This amount makes up nearly 25% of its total assets.

Cash Management

When companies fail, one of the most common causes is their inability to manage cash. Companies must plan both cash receipts and cash payments. The goals of cash management are twofold:

1. Plan cash receipts to meet cash payments when due.
2. Keep a minimum level of cash necessary to operate.

The *treasurer* of the company is responsible for cash management. Effective cash management involves applying the following cash management principles.

- **Encourage collection of receivables.** The more quickly customers and others pay the company, the more quickly that company can use the money. Some companies have cash-only sales policies. Others might offer discounts for payments received early.
- **Delay payment of liabilities.** The more delayed a company is in paying others, the more time it has to use the money. Some companies regularly wait to pay their bills until the last possible day allowed—although, a company must take care not to hurt its credit standing.
- **Keep only necessary levels of assets.** The less money tied up in idle assets, the more money to invest in productive assets. Some companies maintain *just-in-time* inventory; meaning they plan inventory to be available at the same time orders are filled. Others might lease out excess warehouse space or rent equipment instead of buying it.
- **Plan expenditures.** Money should be spent only when it is available. Companies must look at seasonal and business cycles to plan expenditures.
- **Invest excess cash.** Excess cash earns no return and should be invested. Excess cash from seasonal cycles can be placed in a bank account or other short-term investment for income. Excess cash beyond what's needed for regular business should be invested in productive assets like factories and inventories.

◼ Decision Insight

Days' Cash Expense Coverage   The ratio of *cash (and cash equivalents) to average daily cash expenses* indicates the number of days a company can operate without additional cash inflows. It reflects on company liquidity and on the potential of excess cash. ◼

Control of Cash Receipts

P1 Apply internal control to cash receipts and disbursements.

Internal control of cash receipts ensures that cash received is properly recorded and deposited. Cash receipts can arise from transactions such as cash sales, collections of customer accounts, receipts of interest earned, bank loans, sales of assets, and owner investments. This section explains internal control over two important types of cash receipts: over-the-counter and by mail.

Over-the-Counter Cash Receipts   For purposes of internal control, over-the-counter cash receipts from sales should be recorded on a cash register at the time of each sale. To help ensure that correct amounts are entered, each register should be located so customers can read the amounts entered. Clerks also should be required to enter each sale before wrapping merchandise and to give the customer a receipt for each sale. The design of each cash register should provide a permanent, locked-in record of each transaction. In many systems, the register is directly linked with computing and accounting services. Less advanced registers simply print a record of each transaction on a paper tape or electronic file locked inside the register.

Proper internal control prescribes that custody over cash should be separate from its record-keeping. For over-the-counter cash receipts, this separation begins with the cash sale. The clerk who has access to cash in the register should not have access to its locked-in record. At the end of the clerk's work period, the clerk should count the cash in the register, record the amount, and turn over the cash and a record of its amount to the company cashier. The cashier, like the clerk, has access to the cash but should not have access to accounting records (or the register tape or file). A third employee, often a supervisor, compares the record of total register transactions (or the register tape or file) with the cash receipts reported by the cashier. This record is the basis for a journal entry recording over-the-counter cash receipts. The third employee has access to the records for cash but not to the actual cash. The clerk and the cashier have access to cash but not to the accounting records. None of them can make a mistake or divert cash without the difference being revealed—see the following diagram.

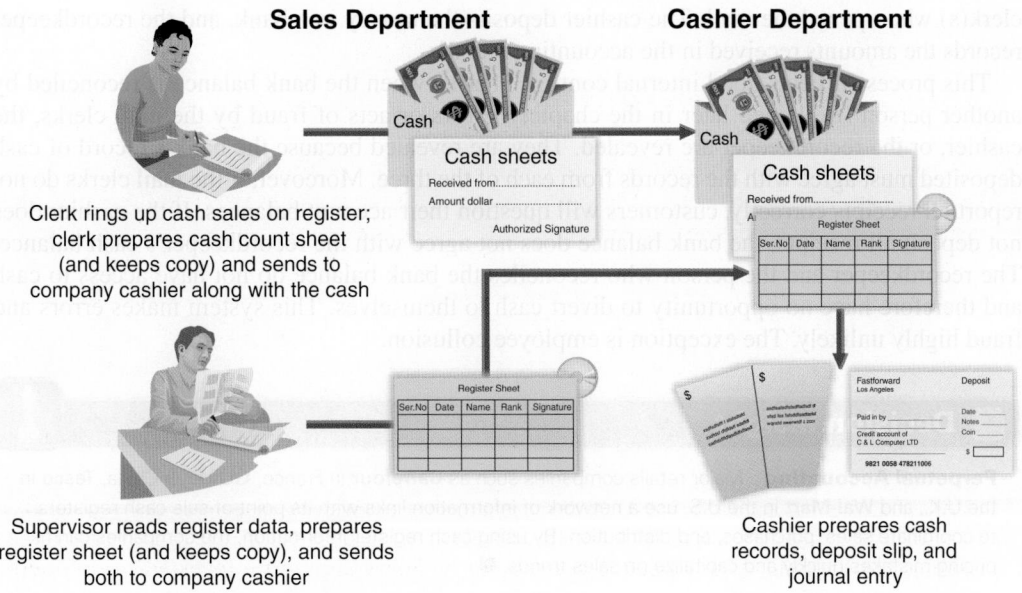

Sales Department

Clerk rings up cash sales on register; clerk prepares cash count sheet (and keeps copy) and sends to company cashier along with the cash

Supervisor reads register data, prepares register sheet (and keeps copy), and sends both to company cashier

Cashier Department

Cashier prepares cash records, deposit slip, and journal entry

Cash over and short. Sometimes errors in making change are discovered from differences between the cash in a cash register and the record of the amount of cash receipts. Although a clerk is careful, one or more customers can be given too much or too little change. This means that at the end of a work period, the cash in a cash register might not equal the record of cash receipts. This difference is reported in the **Cash Over and Short** account, also called *Cash Short and Over,* which is an income statement account recording the income effects of cash overages and cash shortages. To illustrate, if a cash register's record shows $550 but the count of cash in the register is $555, the entry to record cash sales and its overage is

Point: Retailers often require cashiers to restrictively endorse checks immediately on receipt by stamping them "For deposit only."

Cash	555	
Cash Over and Short		5
Sales		550
To record cash sales and a cash overage.		

Assets = Liabilities + Equity
+555   +   5
                         +550

On the other hand, if a cash register's record shows $625 but the count of cash in the register is $621, the entry to record cash sales and its shortage is

Cash	621	
Cash Over and Short	4	
Sales		625
To record cash sales and a cash shortage.		

Assets = Liabilities + Equity
+621   −   4
                         +625

Since customers are more likely to dispute being shortchanged than being given too much change, the Cash Over and Short account usually has a debit balance at the end of an accounting period. A debit balance reflects an expense. It is reported on the income statement as part of general and administrative expenses. (Since the amount is usually small, it is often combined with other small expenses and reported as part of *miscellaneous expenses*—or as part of *miscellaneous revenues* if it has a credit balance.)

Point: Merchants begin a business day with a *change fund* in their cash register. The accounting for a change fund is similar to that for petty cash, including that for cash shortages or overages.

Cash Receipts by Mail Control of cash receipts that arrive through the mail starts with the person who opens the mail. Preferably, two people are assigned the task of, and are present for, opening the mail. In this case, theft of cash receipts by mail requires collusion between these two employees. Specifically, the person(s) opening the mail enters a list (in triplicate) of money received. This list should contain a record of each sender's name, the amount, and an explanation of why the money is sent. The first copy is sent with the money to the cashier. A second copy is sent to the recordkeeper in the accounting area. A third copy is kept by the

Point: Collusion implies that two or more individuals are knowledgeable or involved with the activities of the other(s).

clerk(s) who opened the mail. The cashier deposits the money in a bank, and the recordkeeper records the amounts received in the accounting records.

This process reflects good internal control. That is, when the bank balance is reconciled by another person (explained later in the chapter), errors or acts of fraud by the mail clerks, the cashier, or the recordkeeper are revealed. They are revealed because the bank's record of cash deposited must agree with the records from each of the three. Moreover, if the mail clerks do not report all receipts correctly, customers will question their account balances. If the cashier does not deposit all receipts, the bank balance does not agree with the recordkeeper's cash balance. The recordkeeper and the person who reconciles the bank balance do not have access to cash and therefore have no opportunity to divert cash to themselves. This system makes errors and fraud highly unlikely. The exception is employee collusion.

Decision Insight

Perpetual Accounting   Major retails companies such as **Carrefour** in France, **GOME** in China, **Tesco** in the U.K., and **Wal-Mart** in the U.S. use a network of information links with its point-of-sale cash registers to coordinate sales, purchases, and distribution. By using cash register information, the companies can fix pricing mistakes quickly and capitalize on sales trends. ■

Control of Cash Disbursements

Control of cash disbursements is especially important as most large thefts occur from payment of fictitious invoices. One key to controlling cash disbursements is to require all expenditures to be made by check. The only exception is small payments made from petty cash. Another key is to deny access to the accounting records to anyone other than the owner who has the authority to sign checks. A small business owner often signs checks and knows from personal contact that the items being paid for are actually received. This arrangement is impossible in large businesses. Instead, internal control procedures must be substituted for personal contact. Such procedures are designed to assure the check signer that the obligations recorded are properly incurred and should be paid. This section describes these and other internal control procedures, including the voucher system and petty cash system. A method for management of cash disbursements for purchases is described in Appendix 8B.

Decision Insight

Cash Budget   Projected cash receipts and cash disbursements are often summarized in a *cash budget*. Provided that sufficient cash exists for effective operations, companies wish to minimize the cash they hold because of its risk of theft and its low return versus other investment opportunities. ■

Voucher System of Control   A **voucher system** is a set of procedures and approvals designed to control cash disbursements and the acceptance of obligations. The voucher system of control establishes procedures for

- Verifying, approving, and recording obligations for eventual cash disbursement.
- Issuing checks for payment of verified, approved, and recorded obligations.

A reliable voucher system follows standard procedures for every transaction. This applies even when multiple purchases are made from the same supplier.

A voucher system's control over cash disbursements begins when a company incurs an obligation that will result in payment of cash. A key factor in this system is that only approved departments and individuals are authorized to incur such obligations. The system often limits the type of obligations that a department or individual can incur. In a large retail store, for instance, only a purchasing department should be authorized to incur obligations for merchandise inventory. Another key factor is that procedures for purchasing, receiving, and paying for merchandise are divided among several departments (or individuals). These departments include the one requesting the purchase, the purchasing department, the receiving department, and the accounting department. To coordinate and control responsibilities of these departments, a company uses

EXHIBIT 8.1

Document Flow in a
Voucher System

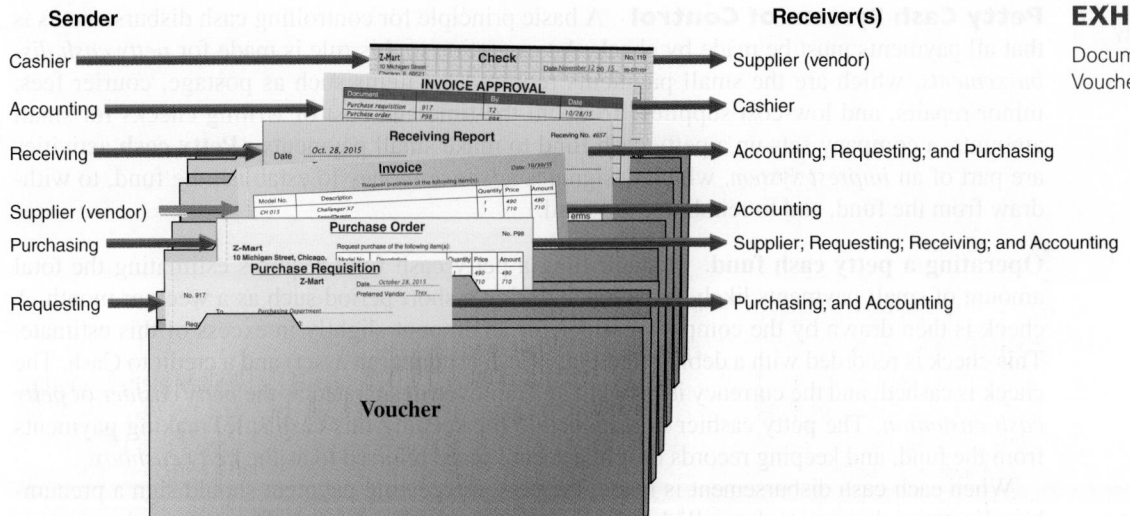

Sender	Receiver(s)
Cashier	Supplier (vendor)
Accounting	Cashier
Receiving	Accounting; Requesting; and Purchasing
Supplier (vendor)	Accounting
Purchasing	Supplier; Requesting; Receiving; and Accounting
Requesting	Purchasing; and Accounting

several different business documents. Exhibit 8.1 shows how documents are accumulated in a **voucher,** which is an internal document (or file) used to accumulate information to control cash disbursements and to ensure that a transaction is properly recorded. This specific example begins with a *purchase requisition* and concludes with a *check* drawn against cash. Appendix 8A describes the documentation and verification necessary for a voucher system of control. It also describes the internal control objective served by each document.

A voucher system should be applied not only to purchases of inventory but to all expenditures. To illustrate, when a company receives a monthly telephone bill, it should review and verify the charges, prepare a voucher (file), and insert the bill. This transaction is then recorded with a journal entry. If the amount is currently due, a check is issued. If not, the voucher is filed for payment on its due date. If no voucher is prepared, verifying the invoice and its amount after several days or weeks can be difficult. Also, without records, a dishonest employee could collude with a dishonest supplier to get more than one payment for an obligation, payment for excessive amounts, or payment for goods and services not received. An effective voucher system helps prevent such frauds.

Point: A *voucher* is an internal document (or file).

Point: The basic purposes of paper and electronic documents are similar. However, the internal control system must change to reflect different risks, including confidential and competitive-sensitive information that is at greater risk in electronic systems.

Decision Insight

Cyber Setup The FTC is on the cutting edge of cyber-sleuthing. Opportunists in search of easy money are lured to **WeMarket4U.net/SundaeStation** and **WeMarket4U.net/FatFoe.** Take the bait and you get warned. The top 5 fraud complaints as compiled by the Bureau of Consumer Protection are shown to the right. ■

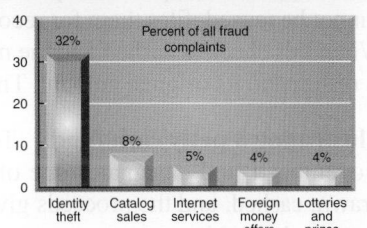

Quick Check

Answers — p. 343

3. Why must a company hold liquid assets?
4. Why does a company hold cash equivalent assets in addition to cash?
5. Identify at least two assets that are classified as cash equivalents.
6. Good internal control procedures for cash include which of the following? (a) All cash disbursements, other than those for very small amounts, are made by check; (b) One employee counts cash received from sales and promptly deposits cash receipts; or (c) Cash receipts by mail are opened by one employee who is then responsible for recording and depositing them.
7. Should all companies require a voucher system? At what point in a company's growth would you recommend a voucher system?

Petty Cash System of Control   A basic principle for controlling cash disbursements is that all payments must be made by check. An exception to this rule is made for *petty cash disbursements,* which are the small payments required for items such as postage, courier fees, minor repairs, and low-cost supplies. To avoid the time and cost of writing checks for small amounts, a company sets up a petty cash fund to make small payments. (**Petty cash** activities are part of an *imprest system,* which designates advance money to establish the fund, to withdraw from the fund, and to reimburse the fund.)

Operating a petty cash fund.   Establishing a petty cash fund requires estimating the total amount of small payments likely to be made during a short period such as a week or month. A check is then drawn by the company cashier for an amount slightly in excess of this estimate. This check is recorded with a debit to the Petty Cash account (an asset) and a credit to Cash. The check is cashed, and the currency is given to an employee designated as the *petty cashier* or *petty cash custodian.* The petty cashier is responsible for keeping this cash safe, making payments from the fund, and keeping records of it in a secure place referred to as the *petty cashbox.*

When each cash disbursement is made, the person receiving payment should sign a prenumbered *petty cash receipt,* also called *petty cash ticket*—see Exhibit 8.2. The petty cash receipt is then placed in the petty cashbox with the remaining money. Under this system, the sum of all receipts plus the remaining cash equals the total fund amount. A $100 petty cash fund, for instance, contains any combination of cash and petty cash receipts that totals $100 (examples are $80 cash plus $20 in receipts, or $10 cash plus $90 in receipts). Each disbursement reduces cash and increases the amount of receipts in the petty cashbox.

Point: A petty cash fund is used only for business expenses.

EXHIBIT 8.2

Petty Cash Receipt

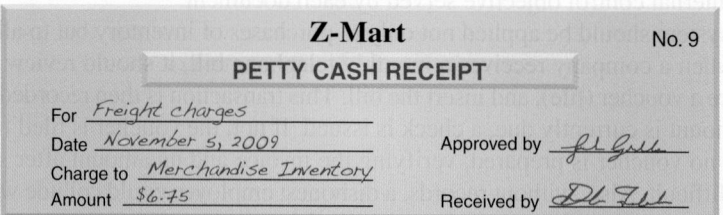

Z-Mart   No. 9

PETTY CASH RECEIPT

For *Freight charges*
Date *November 5, 2009*   Approved by *f.l.Gull*
Charge to *Merchandise Inventory*
Amount *$6.75*   Received by *DL Fll*

Point: Petty cash receipts with either no signature or a forged signature usually indicate misuse of petty cash. Companies respond with surprise petty cash counts for verification.

The petty cash fund should be reimbursed when it is nearing zero and at the end of an accounting period when financial statements are prepared. For this purpose, the petty cashier sorts the paid receipts by the type of expense or account and then totals the receipts. The petty cashier presents all paid receipts to the company cashier, who stamps all receipts *paid* so they cannot be reused, files them for recordkeeping, and gives the petty cashier a check for their sum. When this check is cashed and the money placed in the cashbox, the total money in the cashbox is restored to its original amount. The fund is now ready for a new cycle of petty cash payments.

Illustrating a petty cash fund.   To illustrate, assume Z-Mart establishes a petty cash fund on November 1 and designates one of its office employees as the petty cashier. A $75 check is drawn, cashed, and the proceeds given to the petty cashier. The entry to record the setup of this petty cash fund is

Assets = Liabilities + Equity
+75
−75

Nov. 1	Petty Cash	75	
	Cash		75
	To establish a petty cash fund.		

Point: Reducing or eliminating a petty cash fund requires a credit to Petty Cash.

Point: Although *individual* petty cash disbursements are not evidenced by a check, the initial petty cash fund is evidenced by a check, and later petty cash expenditures are evidenced by a check to replenish them *in total.*

After the petty cash fund is established, the Petty Cash account is not debited or credited again unless the amount of the fund is changed. (A fund should be increased if it requires reimbursement too frequently. On the other hand, if the fund is too large, some of its money should be redeposited in the Cash account.)

Next, assume that Z-Mart's petty cashier makes several November payments from petty cash. Each person who received payment is required to sign a receipt. On November 27, after making a $26.50 cash payment for tile cleaning, only $3.70 cash remains in the fund. The petty cashier then summarizes and totals the petty cash receipts as shown in Exhibit 8.3.

EXHIBIT 8.3

Petty Cash Payments Report

Z-MART		
Petty Cash Payments Report		
Miscellaneous Expenses		
Nov. 2 Cleaning of LCD panels	$20.00	
Nov. 27 Tile cleaning	26.50	$ 46.50
Merchandise Inventory (transportation-in)		
Nov. 5 Transport of merchandise purchased	6.75	
Nov. 20 Transport of merchandise purchased	8.30	15.05
Delivery Expense		
Nov. 18 Customer's package delivered		5.00
Office Supplies Expense		
Nov. 15 Purchase of office supplies immediately used		4.75
Total		**$71.30**

The petty cash payments report and all receipts are given to the company cashier in exchange for a $71.30 check to reimburse the fund. The petty cashier cashes the check and puts the $71.30 cash in the petty cashbox. The company records this reimbursement as follows.

Nov. 27	Miscellaneous Expenses	46.50	
	Merchandise Inventory	15.05	
	Delivery Expense	5.00	
	Office Supplies Expense	4.75	
	Cash		71.30
	To reimburse petty cash.		

Assets = Liabilities + Equity
−71.30   −46.50
                              −15.05
                              − 5.00
                              − 4.75

Point: This report can also include receipt number and names of those who approved and received cash payment (see Demo Problem 2).

A petty cash fund is usually reimbursed at the end of an accounting period so that expenses are recorded in the proper period, even if the fund is not low on money. If the fund is not reimbursed at the end of a period, the financial statements would show both an overstated cash asset and understated expenses (or assets) that were paid out of petty cash. Some companies do not reimburse the petty cash fund at the end of each period under the notion that this amount is immaterial to users of financial statements.

Point: To avoid errors in recording petty cash reimbursement, follow these steps: (1) prepare payments report, (2) compute cash needed by subtracting cash remaining from total fund amount, (3) record entry, and (4) check "Dr. = Cr." in entry. Any difference is Cash Over and Short.

Increasing or decreasing a petty cash fund.   A decision to increase or decrease a petty cash fund is often made when reimbursing it. To illustrate, assume Z-Mart decides to *increase* its petty cash fund from $75 to $100 on November 27 when it reimburses the fund. The entries required are to (1) reimburse the fund as usual (see the preceding November 27 entry) and (2) increase the fund amount as follows.

Nov. 27	Petty Cash	25	
	Cash		25
	To increase the petty cash fund amount.		

Alternatively, if Z-Mart *decreases* the petty cash fund from $75 to $55 on November 27, the entry is to (1) credit Petty Cash for $20 (decreasing the fund from $75 to $55) and (2) debit Cash for $20 (reflecting the $20 transfer from Petty Cash to Cash).

Cash over and short.   Sometimes a petty cashier fails to get a receipt for payment or overpays for the amount due. When this occurs and the fund is later reimbursed, the petty cash payments report plus the cash remaining will not total to the fund balance. This mistake causes the fund to be *short*. This shortage is recorded as an expense in the reimbursing entry with a debit to the Cash Over and Short account. (An overage in the petty cash fund is recorded with a credit to Cash Over and Short in the reimbursing entry.) To illustrate, prepare the June 1 entry

Summary of Petty Cash Accounting			
Event	**Petty Cash**	**Cash**	**Expenses**
Set up fund	Dr.	Cr.	—
Reimburse fund ..	—	Cr.	Dr.
Increase fund	Dr.	Cr.	—
Decrease fund ...	Cr.	Dr.	—

$200 Petty Cash Fund

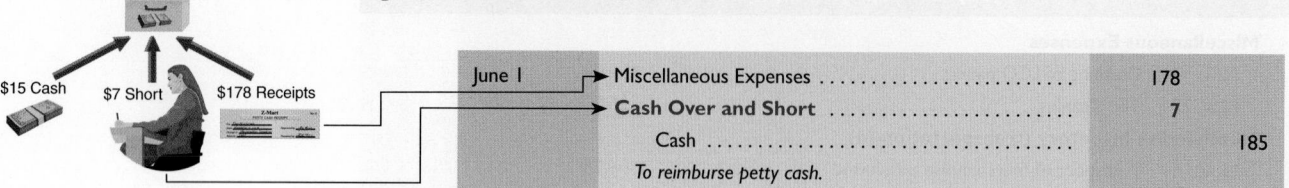

to reimburse a $200 petty cash fund when its payments report shows $178 in miscellaneous expenses and $15 cash remains.

June 1	Miscellaneous Expenses	178	
	Cash Over and Short	7	
	Cash		185
	To reimburse petty cash.		

Decision Insight

Warning Signs   There are clues to internal control violations. Warning signs from accounting include (1) an increase in customer refunds—could be fake, (2) missing documents—could be used for fraud, (3) differences between bank deposits and cash receipts—could be cash embezzled, and (4) delayed recording—could reflect fraudulent records. Warning signs from employees include (1) lifestyle change—could be embezzlement, (2) too close with suppliers—could signal fraudulent transactions, and (3) failure to leave job, even for vacations—could conceal fraudulent activities. ■

Quick Check   Answers — p. 343

8. Why are some cash payments made from a petty cash fund and not by check?
9. Why should a petty cash fund be reimbursed at the end of an accounting period?
10. Identify at least two results of reimbursing a petty cash fund.

BANKING ACTIVITIES AS CONTROLS

Banks (and other financial institutions) provide many services, including helping companies control cash. Banks safeguard cash, provide detailed and independent records of cash transactions, and are a source of cash financing. This section describes these services and the documents provided by banking activities that increase managers' control over cash.

Basic Bank Services

This section explains basic bank services—such as the bank account, the bank deposit, and checking—that contribute to the control of cash.

Bank Account, Deposit, and Check   A *bank account* is a record set up by a bank for a customer. It permits a customer to deposit money for safekeeping and helps control withdrawals. To limit access to a bank account, all persons authorized to write checks on the account must sign a **signature card,** which bank employees use to verify signatures on checks. Many companies have more than one bank account to serve different needs and to handle special transactions such as payroll.

Each bank deposit is supported by a **deposit ticket,** which lists items such as currency, coins, and checks deposited along with their corresponding dollar amounts. The bank gives the customer a copy of the deposit ticket or a deposit receipt as proof of the deposit. Exhibit 8.4 shows one type of deposit ticket.

To withdraw money from an account, the depositor can use a **check,** which is a document signed by the depositor instructing the bank to pay a specified amount of money to a designated recipient. A check involves three parties: a *maker* who signs the check, a *payee* who is the recipient, and a *bank* (or *payer*) on which the check is drawn. The bank provides a depositor the checks that are serially numbered and imprinted with the name and address of both the depositor and bank. Both checks and deposit tickets are imprinted with identification codes in magnetic ink

Point: Online banking services include the ability to stop payment on a check, move money between accounts, get up-to-date balances, and identify cleared checks and deposits.

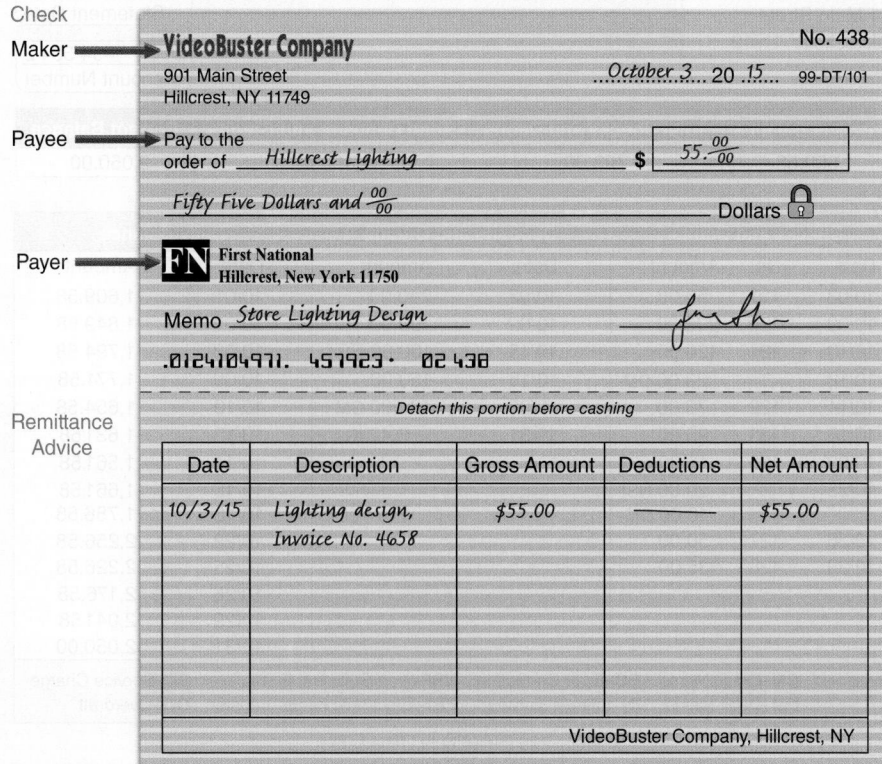

EXHIBIT 8.4

Deposit Ticket

DEPOSIT TICKET

Date *October 2* 20 *15*

VideoBuster Company
901 Main Street
Hillcrest, NY 11749

Front

CASH	CURRENCY	36	50
	COIN		
LIST CHECKS SINGLY			
TOTAL FROM OTHER SIDE		203	50
TOTAL		240	00
NET DEPOSIT		240	00

Deposit checks
(Memo)

FN First National
Hillcrest, New York 11750

⑈0124104971⑈ 457923 · 02 75

USE OTHER SIDE FOR ADDITIONAL
LISTINGS. BE SURE EACH ITEM IS
PROPERLY ENDORSED

Checks and other items are received for deposit subject to the provisions of the uniform commercial code or any applicable collection agreement

99-DT/101

Back

CHECKS LIST SINGLY	DOLLARS	CENTS
1 14-287/939	90	50
2 82-759/339	82	80
3 76-907/919	30	20
4		
5		
6		
7		
8		
9		
10		
11		
12		
13		
14		
15		
16		
17		
18		
19		
20		
21		
22		
TOTAL	203	50

ENTER TOTAL ON THE FRONT OF THIS TICKET

for computer processing. Exhibit 8.5 shows one type of check. It is accompanied with an optional *remittance advice* explaining the payment. When a remittance advice is unavailable, the *memo* line is often used for a brief explanation.

Electronic Funds Transfer **Electronic funds transfer (EFT)** is the electronic transfer of cash from one party to another. No paper documents are necessary. Banks simply transfer cash from one account to another with a journal entry. Companies are increasingly using EFT

EXHIBIT 8.5

Check with Remittance Advice

Check

Maker → **VideoBuster Company**   No. 438
901 Main Street   *October 3* 20 *15*   99-DT/101
Hillcrest, NY 11749

Payee → Pay to the
order of   *Hillcrest Lighting* $ 55.00/00

Fifty Five Dollars and 00/00   Dollars 🔒

Payer → **FN** First National
Hillcrest, New York 11750

Memo *Store Lighting Design*   *[signature]*

.0124104971. 457923 · 02 438

- -
Detach this portion before cashing

Remittance
Advice

Date	Description	Gross Amount	Deductions	Net Amount
10/3/15	Lighting design, Invoice No. 4658	$55.00	——————	$55.00

VideoBuster Company, Hillcrest, NY

because of its convenience and low cost. For instance, it can cost up to 50 cents to process a check through the banking system, whereas EFT cost is near zero. We now commonly see items such as payroll, rent, utilities, insurance, and interest payments being handled by EFT. The bank statement lists cash withdrawals by EFT with the checks and other deductions. Cash receipts by EFT are listed with deposits and other additions. A bank statement is sometimes a depositor's only notice of an EFT. *Automated teller machines (ATMs)* are one form of EFT, which allows bank customers to deposit, withdraw, and transfer cash.

Bank Statement

Point: Good internal control is to deposit all cash receipts daily and make all payments for goods and services by check. This controls access to cash and creates an independent record of all cash activities.

Usually once a month, the bank sends each depositor a **bank statement** showing the activity in the account. Although a monthly statement is common, companies often regularly access information on their banking transactions. (Companies can choose to record any accounting adjustments required from the bank statement immediately or later, say, at the end of each day, week, month, or when reconciling a bank statement.) Different banks use different formats for their bank statements, but all of them include the following items of information:

1. Beginning-of-period balance of the depositor's account.
2. Checks and other debits decreasing the account during the period.
3. Deposits and other credits increasing the account during the period.
4. End-of-period balance of the depositor's account.

This information reflects the bank's records. Exhibit 8.6 shows one type of bank statement. Identify each of these four items in that statement. Part Ⓐ of Exhibit 8.6 summarizes changes in the account. Part Ⓑ lists paid checks along with other debits. Part Ⓒ lists deposits and credits to the account, and part Ⓓ shows the daily account balances.

EXHIBIT 8.6

Bank Statement

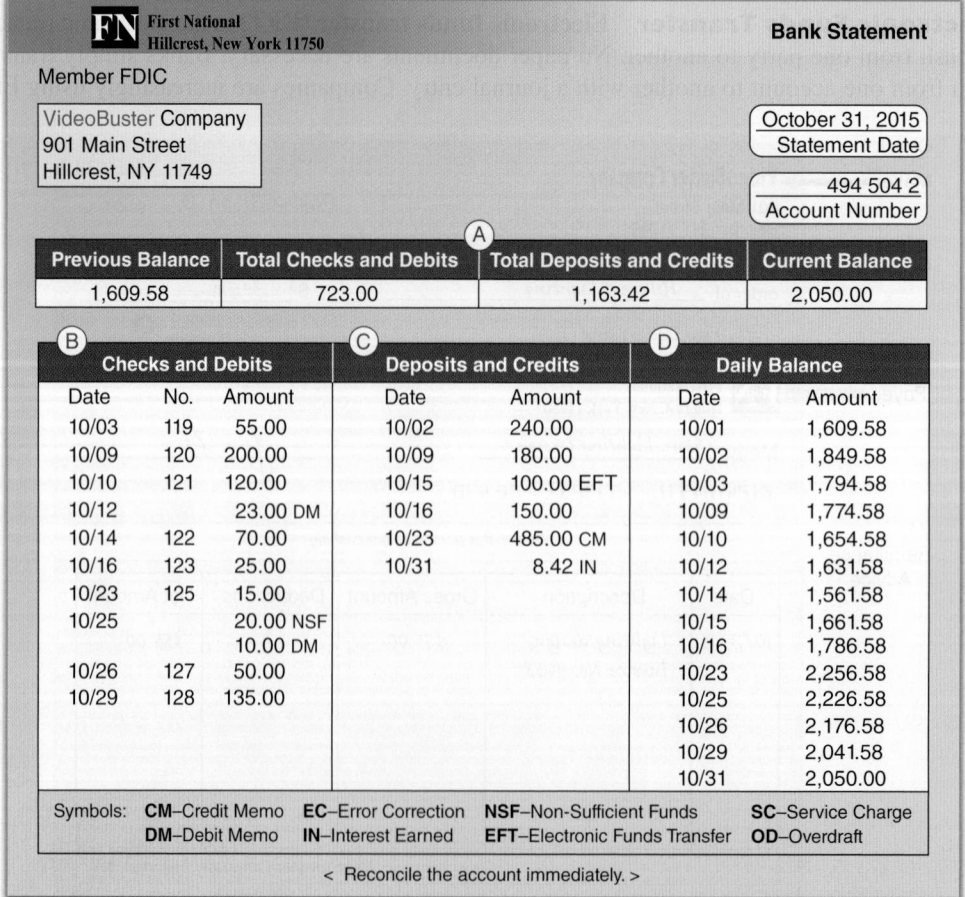

Point: Many banks separately report other debits and credits apart from checks and deposits.

In reading a bank statement note that a depositor's account is a liability on the bank's records. This is so because the money belongs to the depositor, not the bank. When a depositor increases the account balance, the bank records it with a *credit* to that liability account. This means that debit memos from the bank produce *credits* on the depositor's books, and credit memos from the bank produce *debits* on the depositor's books.

Enclosed with a bank statement is a list of the depositor's canceled checks (or the actual canceled checks) along with any debit or credit memoranda affecting the account. Increasingly, banks are showing canceled checks electronically via online access to accounts. **Canceled checks** are checks the bank has paid and deducted from the customer's account during the period. Other deductions that can appear on a bank statement include (1) service charges and fees assessed by the bank, (2) checks deposited that are uncollectible, (3) corrections of previous errors, (4) withdrawals through automated teller machines (ATMs), and (5) periodic payments arranged in advance by a depositor. (Most company checking accounts do not allow ATM withdrawals because of the company's desire to make all disbursements by check.) Except for service charges, the bank notifies the depositor of each deduction with a debit memorandum when the bank reduces the balance. A copy of each debit memorandum is usually sent with the statement (again, this information is often available earlier via online access and notifications).

Transactions that increase the depositor's account include amounts the bank collects on behalf of the depositor and the corrections of previous errors. Credit memoranda notify the depositor of all increases when they are recorded. A copy of each credit memorandum is often sent with the bank statement. Banks that pay interest on checking accounts often compute the amount of interest earned on the average cash balance and credit it to the depositor's account each period. In Exhibit 8.6, the bank credits $8.42 of interest to the account.

Bank Reconciliation

P3 Prepare a bank reconciliation.

When a company deposits all cash receipts and makes all cash payments (except petty cash) by check, it can use the bank statement for proving the accuracy of its cash records. This is done using a **bank reconciliation,** which is a report explaining any differences between the checking account balance according to the depositor's records and the balance reported on the bank statement. The figure below reflects this process, which we describe in the following sections.

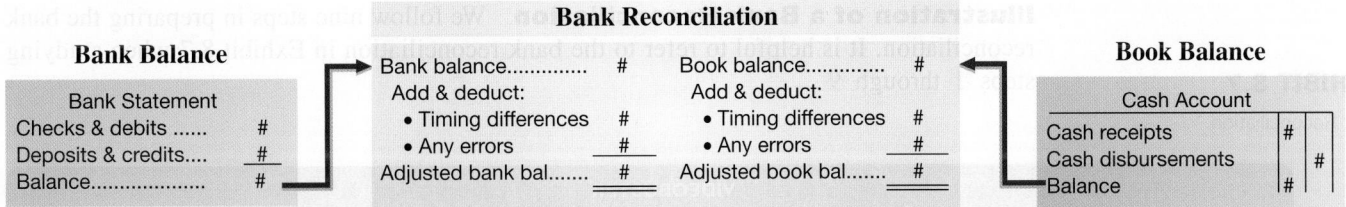

Purpose of Bank Reconciliation   The balance of a checking account reported on the bank statement rarely equals the balance in the depositor's accounting records. This is usually due to information that one party has that the other does not. We must therefore prove the accuracy of both the depositor's records and those of the bank. This means we must *reconcile* the two balances and explain or account for any differences in them. Among the factors causing the bank statement balance to differ from the depositor's book balance are these:

- **Outstanding checks. Outstanding checks** are checks written (or drawn) by the depositor, deducted on the depositor's records, and sent to the payees but not yet received by the bank for payment at the bank statement date.

- **Deposits in transit** (also called **outstanding deposits**). **Deposits in transit** are deposits made and recorded by the depositor but not yet recorded on the bank statement. For example,

Forms of Check Fraud (CkFraud.org)

- Forged signatures—legitimate blank checks with fake payer signature
- Forged endorsements—stolen check that is endorsed and cashed by someone other than the payee
- Counterfeit checks—fraudulent checks with fake payer signature
- Altered checks—legitimate check altered (such as changed payee or amount) to benefit perpetrator
- Check kiting—deposit check from one bank account (without sufficient funds) into a second bank account

companies can make deposits (in the night depository) at the end of a business day after the bank is closed. If such a deposit occurred on a bank statement date, it would not appear on this period's statement. The bank would record such a deposit on the next business day, and it would appear on the next period's bank statement. Deposits mailed to the bank near the end of a period also can be in transit and unrecorded when the statement is prepared.

- **Deductions for uncollectible items and for services.** A company sometimes deposits another party's check that is uncollectible (usually meaning the balance in that party's account is not large enough to cover the check). This check is called a *non-sufficient funds (NSF)* check. The bank would have initially credited the depositor's account for the amount of the check. When the bank learns the check is uncollectible, it debits (reduces) the depositor's account for the amount of that check. The bank may also charge the depositor a fee for processing an uncollectible check and notify the depositor of the deduction by sending a debit memorandum. The depositor should record each deduction when a debit memorandum is received, but an entry is sometimes not made until the bank reconciliation is prepared. Other possible bank charges to a depositor's account that are first reported on a bank statement include printing new checks and service fees.

- **Additions for collections and for interest.** Banks sometimes act as collection agents for their depositors by collecting notes and other items. Banks can also receive electronic funds transfers to the depositor's account. When a bank collects an item, it is added to the depositor's account, less any service fee. The bank also sends a credit memorandum to notify the depositor of the transaction. When the memorandum is received, the depositor should record it; yet it sometimes remains unrecorded until the bank reconciliation is prepared. The bank statement also includes a credit for any interest earned.

- **Errors.** Both banks and depositors can make errors. Bank errors might not be discovered until the depositor prepares the bank reconciliation. Also, depositor errors are sometimes discovered when the bank balance is reconciled. Error testing includes: (a) comparing deposits on the bank statement with deposits in the accounting records and (b) comparing canceled checks on the bank statement with checks recorded in the accounting records.

Illustration of a Bank Reconciliation   We follow nine steps in preparing the bank reconciliation. It is helpful to refer to the bank reconciliation in Exhibit 8.7 when studying steps ① through ⑨.

Point: Small businesses with few employees often allow recordkeepers to both write checks and keep the general ledger. If this is done, it is essential that the owner do the bank reconciliation.

Point: The person preparing the bank reconciliation should not be responsible for processing cash receipts, managing checks, or maintaining cash records.

EXHIBIT 8.7

Bank Reconciliation

	VIDEOBUSTER Bank Reconciliation October 31, 2015						
①	Bank statement balance		$ 2,050.00	⑤	Book balance		$ 1,404.58
②	Add			⑥	Add		
	Deposit of Oct. 31 in transit		145.00		Collect $500 note less $15 fee	$485.00	
			2,195.00		Interest earned	8.42	493.42
③	Deduct						1,898.00
	Outstanding checks			⑦	Deduct		
	No. 124	$150.00			Check printing charge	23.00	
	No. 126	200.00	350.00		NSF check plus service fee	30.00	53.00
④	**Adjusted bank balance**		**$1,845.00**	⑧	**Adjusted book balance**		**$1,845.00**
				⑨ Balances are equal (reconciled)			

1. Identify the bank statement balance of the cash account (*balance per bank*). VideoBuster's bank balance is $2,050.

2. Identify and list any unrecorded deposits and any bank errors understating the bank balance. Add them to the bank balance. VideoBuster's $145 deposit placed in the bank's night depository on October 31 is not recorded on its bank statement.

3. Identify and list any outstanding checks and any bank errors overstating the bank balance. Deduct them from the bank balance. VideoBuster's comparison of canceled checks with its books shows two checks outstanding: No. 124 for $150 and No. 126 for $200.

4. Compute the *adjusted bank balance,* also called the *corrected* or *reconciled balance.*

5. Identify the company's book balance of the cash account (*balance per book*). VideoBuster's book balance is $1,404.58.

6. Identify and list any unrecorded credit memoranda from the bank, any interest earned, and errors understating the book balance. Add them to the book balance. VideoBuster's bank statement includes a credit memorandum showing the bank collected a note receivable for the company on October 23. The note's proceeds of $500 (minus a $15 collection fee) are credited to the company's account. VideoBuster's bank statement also shows a credit of $8.42 for interest earned on the average cash balance. There was no prior notification of this item, and it is not yet recorded.

7. Identify and list any unrecorded debit memoranda from the bank, any service charges, and errors overstating the book balance. Deduct them from the book balance. Debits on Video-Buster's bank statement that are not yet recorded include (a) a $23 charge for check printing and (b) an NSF check for $20 plus a related $10 processing fee. (The NSF check is dated October 16 and was included in the book balance.)

8. Compute the *adjusted book balance,* also called *corrected* or *reconciled balance.*

9. Verify that the two adjusted balances from steps 4 and 8 are equal. If so, they are reconciled. If not, check for accuracy and missing data to achieve reconciliation.

Point: Outstanding checks are identified by comparing canceled checks on the bank statement with checks recorded. This includes identifying any outstanding checks listed on the *previous* period's bank reconciliation that are not included in the canceled checks on this period's bank statement.

Adjusting Entries from a Bank Reconciliation

A bank reconciliation often identifies unrecorded items that need recording by the company. In VideoBuster's reconciliation, the adjusted balance of $1,845 is the correct balance as at October 31. But the company's accounting records show a $1,404.58 balance. We must prepare journal entries to adjust the book balance to the correct balance. It is important to remember that only the items reconciling the *book balance* require adjustment. A review of Exhibit 8.7 indicates that four entries are required for VideoBuster.

Point: Adjusting entries can be combined into one compound entry.

Collection of note.   The first entry is to record the proceeds of its note receivable collected by the bank less the expense of having the bank perform that service.

Oct. 31	Cash	485	
	Collection Expense	15	
	Notes Receivable		500
	To record the collection fee and proceeds for a note collected by the bank.		

Assets = Liabilities + Equity
+485   −15
−500

Interest earned.   The second entry records interest credited to its account by the bank.

Oct. 31	Cash	8.42	
	Interest Revenue		8.42
	To record interest earned on the cash balance in the checking account.		

Assets = Liabilities + Equity
+8.42   +8.42

Check printing.   The third entry records expenses for the check printing charge.

Assets = Liabilities + Equity
−23   −23

Oct. 31	Miscellaneous Expenses	23	
	Cash		23
	Check printing charge.		

NSF check.   The fourth entry records the NSF check that is returned as uncollectible. The $20 check was originally received from T. Woods in payment of his account and then deposited. The bank charged $10 for handling the NSF check and deducted $30 total from VideoBuster's account. This means the entry must reverse the effects of the original entry made when the check was received and must record (add) the $10 bank fee.

Assets = Liabilities + Equity
+30
−30

Oct. 31	Accounts Receivable—T. Woods.	30	
	Cash		30
	To charge Woods' account for $20 NSF check		
	and $10 bank fee.		

Point: The company will try to collect the entire NSF amount of $30 from customer.

Point: The Demo Problem I shows an adjusting entry for an error correction.

Cash			
Unadj. bal.	1,404.58		
⑥	485.00	⑦	23.00
⑥	8.42	⑦	30.00
Adj. bal.	1,845.00		

After these four entries are recorded, the book balance of cash is adjusted to the correct amount of $1,845 (computed as $1,404.58 + $485 + $8.42 − $23 − $30). The Cash T-account to the side shows the same computation, where entries are keyed to the numerical codes in Exhibit 8.7.

Decision Insight

Fraud often the result of inadequate internal controls   Almost a third (29%) of respondents in the KPMG-SMU Singapore Fraud Survey 2014 report said that at least one fraud incident had occurred in their company in the past two years, up from 22% when the survey was last published in 2011. Notably, the survey found that the bulk of fraud was still being perpetrated by insiders—with the proportion of fraud carried out by employees rising to 58%, from 47% in 2011. There was no change in the percentage of fraud incidents carried out by management, such as board members and senior management (17%). Overall, internal fraud constituted 75% of fraud in 2014, up from 64% in 2011. The report noted that fraud committed by internal parties was identified as a top concern in the 2011 edition. Fraud perpetrated by external parties dropped to 25% from 36%. ■

Quick Check   Answers — pp. 343–344

11. What is a bank statement?

12. What is the meaning of the phrase *to reconcile a bank balance?*

13. Why do we reconcile the bank statement balance of cash and the depositor's book balance of cash?

14. List at least two items affecting the *bank balance* side of a bank reconciliation and indicate whether the items are added or subtracted.

15. List at least three items affecting the *book balance* side of a bank reconciliation and indicate whether the items are added or subtracted.

Days' Sales Uncollected  **Decision Analysis**

An important part of cash management is monitoring the receipt of cash from receivables. If customers and others who owe money to a company are delayed in payment, then that company can find it difficult to pay its obligations when they are due. A company's customers are crucial partners in its cash management. Many companies attract customers by selling to them on credit. This means that cash receipts from customers are delayed until accounts receivable are collected.

> **A1** Compute the days' sales uncollected ratio and use it to assess liquidity.

One measure of how quickly a company can convert its accounts receivable into cash is the **days' sales uncollected,** also called *days' sales in receivables.* This measure is computed by dividing the current balance of receivables by net credit sales over the year just completed and then multiplying by 365 (number of days in a year). Since net credit sales usually are not reported to external users, the net sales (or revenues) figure is commonly used in the computation as in Exhibit 8.8.

$$\text{Days' sales uncollected} = \frac{\text{Accounts receivable}}{\text{Net sales}} \times 365$$

EXHIBIT 8.8

Days' Sales Uncollected

We use days' sales uncollected to estimate how much time is likely to pass before the current amount of accounts receivable is received in cash. For evaluation purposes, we need to compare this estimate to that for other companies in the same industry. We also make comparisons between current and prior periods.

To illustrate, we select data from the annual reports of two companies in the same industry, Adidas and Puma. Their days' sales uncollected figures are shown in Exhibit 8.9.

EXHIBIT 8.9

Analysis Using Days' Sales Uncollected

		2009	2010	2011	2012	2013
Adidas	Accounts receivable	1,429	1,667	1,595	1,688	1,809
	Net Sales	10,381	11,990	13,344	14,883	14,492
	Days' sales uncollected	**50.2**	**50.7**	**43.6**	**41.4**	**45.6**
Puma	Accounts receivable	347.4	447.0	533.1	507.0	423.4
	Net Sales	2,447.3	2,706.4	3,009.0	3,270.7	2,985.3
	Days' sales uncollected	**51.8**	**60.3**	**64.7**	**56.6**	**51.8**

Days' sales uncollected for Adidas in 2013 is computed as (1,809/14,492) × 365 days = 45.6 days. This means that it will take about 45.6 days to collect cash from ending accounts receivable. This number reflects one or more of the following factors: a company's ability to collect receivables, customer financial health, customer payment strategies, and discount terms. To further assess days' sales uncollected for Adidas, we compare it to four prior years and to those of Puma. We see that Adidas' days' sales uncollected has generally improved from the beginning of the period. It is better (shorter) than those of Puma for the period.

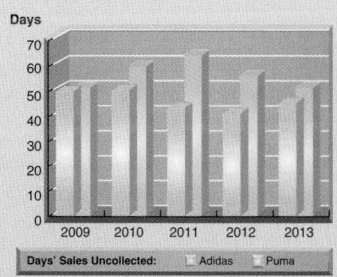

 Decision Maker Answer — p. 343

Sales Representative   The sales staff is told to take action to help reduce days' sales uncollected for cash management purposes. What can you, a salesperson, do to reduce days' sales uncollected? ∎

DEMONSTRATION PROBLEM 1

Prepare a bank reconciliation for Jamboree Enterprises for the month ended November 30, 2015. The following information is available to reconcile Jamboree Enterprises' book balance of cash with its bank statement balance as at November 30, 2015:

a. After all posting is complete on November 30, the company's book balance of Cash has a $16,380 debit balance, but its bank statement shows a $38,520 balance.

b. Checks No. 2024 for $4,810 and No. 2026 for $5,000 are outstanding.

c. In comparing the canceled checks on the bank statement with the entries in the accounting records, it is found that Check No. 2025 in payment of rent is correctly drawn for $1,000 but is erroneously entered in the accounting records as $880.

d. The November 30 deposit of $17,150 was placed in the night depository after banking hours on that date, and this amount does not appear on the bank statement.

e. In reviewing the bank statement, a check written by Jumbo Enterprises in the amount of $160 was erroneously drawn against Jamboree's account.

f. A credit memorandum enclosed with the bank statement indicates that the bank collected a $30,000 note and $900 of related interest on Jamboree's behalf. This transaction was not recorded by Jamboree prior to receiving the statement.

g. A debit memorandum for $1,100 lists a $1,100 NSF check received from a customer, Marilyn Welch. Jamboree had not recorded the return of this check before receiving the statement.

h. Bank service charges for November total $40. These charges were not recorded by Jamboree before receiving the statement.

PLANNING THE SOLUTION

- Set up a bank reconciliation with a bank side and a book side (as in Exhibit 8.7). Leave room to both add and deduct items. Each column will result in a reconciled, equal balance.
- Examine each item *a* through *h* to determine whether it affects the book or the bank balance and whether it should be added or deducted from the bank or book balance.
- After all items are analyzed, complete the reconciliation and arrive at a reconciled balance between the bank side and the book side.
- For each reconciling item on the book side, prepare an adjusting entry. Additions to the book side require an adjusting entry that debits Cash. Deductions on the book side require an adjusting entry that credits Cash.

SOLUTION TO DEMONSTRATION PROBLEM 1

JAMBOREE ENTERPRISES
Bank Reconciliation
November 30, 2015

Bank statement balance		$ 38,520	Book balance		$ 16,380
Add			Add		
Deposit of Nov. 30	$17,150		Collection of note	$30,000	
Bank error (Jumbo)	160	17,310	Interest earned	900	30,900
		55,830			47,280
Deduct			Deduct		
Outstanding checks			NSF check (M. Welch)	1,100	
No. 2024	4,810		Recording error (# 2025)	120	
No. 2026	5,000	9,810	Service charge	40	1,260
Adjusted bank balance		**$46,020**	**Adjusted book balance**		**$46,020**

Required Adjusting Entries for Jamboree

Nov. 30	Cash	30,900	
	Notes Receivable		30,000
	Interest Earned		900
	To record collection of note with interest.		
Nov. 30	Accounts Receivable—M. Welch.	1,100	
	Cash		1,100
	To reinstate account due from an NSF check.		
Nov. 30	Rent Expense	120	
	Cash		120
	To correct recording error on check no. 2025.		
Nov. 30	Bank Service Charges	40	
	Cash		40
	To record bank service charges.		

Point: Error correction can alternatively involve (1) reversing the error entry, and (2) recording the correct entry.

DEMONSTRATION PROBLEM 2

Bacardi Company established a $150 petty cash fund with Dean Martin as the petty cashier. When the fund balance reached $19 cash, Martin prepared a petty cash payment report, which follows.

Petty Cash Payments Report				
Receipt No.	**Account Charged**		**Approved by**	**Received by**
12	Delivery Expense	$ 29	Martin	A. Smirnoff
13	Merchandise Inventory	18	Martin	J. Daniels
15	(Omitted)	32	Martin	C. Carlsberg
16	Miscellaneous Expense	41	(Omitted)	J. Walker
	Total	$120		

Required

1. Identify four internal control weaknesses from the payment report.
2. Prepare general journal entries to record:
   a. Establishment of the petty cash fund.
   b. Reimbursement of the fund. (Assume for this part only that petty cash receipt no. 15 was issued for miscellaneous expenses.)
3. What is the Petty Cash account balance immediately before reimbursement? Immediately after reimbursement?

SOLUTION TO DEMONSTRATION PROBLEM 2

1. Four internal control weaknesses are
   a. Petty cash ticket no. 14 is missing. Its omission raises questions about the petty cashier's management of the fund.
   b. The $19 cash balance means that $131 has been withdrawn ($150 − $19 = $131). However, the total amount of the petty cash receipts is only $120 ($29 + $18 + $32 + $41). The fund is $11 short of cash ($131 − $120 = $11). Was petty cash receipt no. 14 issued for $11? Management should investigate.
   c. The petty cashier (Martin) did not sign petty cash receipt no. 16. This omission could have been an oversight on his part or he might not have authorized the payment. Management should investigate.
   d. Petty cash receipt no. 15 does not indicate which account to charge. This omission could have been an oversight on the petty cashier's part. Management could check with C. Carlsberg and the petty cashier (Martin) about the transaction. Without further information, debit Miscellaneous Expense.

2. Petty cash general journal entries.

    a. Entry to establish the petty cash fund.   **b.** Entry to reimburse the fund.

Petty Cash	150	
Cash		150

Delivery Expense	29	
Merchandise Inventory	18	
Miscellaneous Expense ($41 + $32)	73	
Cash Over and Short	11	
Cash		131

3. The Petty Cash account balance *always* equals its fund balance, in this case $150. This account balance does not change unless the fund is increased or decreased.

APPENDIX

8A   Documentation and Verification

This appendix describes the important business documents of a voucher system of control.

P4   Describe the use of documentation and verification to control cash disbursements.

Purchase Requisition   Department managers are usually not allowed to place orders directly with suppliers for control purposes. Instead, a department manager must inform the purchasing department of its needs by preparing and signing a **purchase requisition,** which lists the merchandise needed and requests that it be purchased—see Exhibit 8A.1. Two copies of the purchase requisition are sent to the purchasing department, which then sends one copy to the accounting department. When the accounting department receives a purchase requisition, it creates and maintains a voucher for this transaction. The requesting department keeps the third copy.

EXHIBIT 8A.1

Purchase Requisition

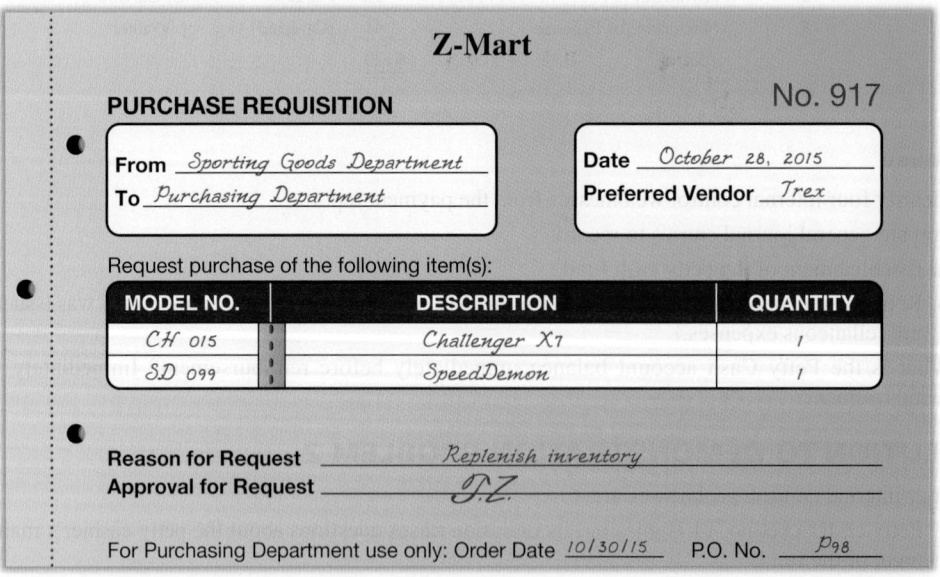

Point: A voucher system is designed to uniquely meet the needs of a specific business. Thus, we should read this appendix as one example of a common voucher system design, but *not* the only design.

Purchase Order   A **purchase order** is a document the purchasing department uses to place an order with a **vendor** (seller or supplier). A purchase order authorizes a vendor to ship ordered merchandise at the stated price and terms—see Exhibit 8A.2. When the purchasing department receives a purchase requisition, it prepares at least five copies of a purchase order. The copies are distributed as follows: *copy 1* to the vendor as a purchase request and as authority to ship merchandise; *copy 2,* along with a copy of the purchase requisition, to the accounting department, where it is entered in the voucher and used in approving payment of the invoice; *copy 3* to the requesting department to inform its manager that action is being taken; *copy 4* to the receiving department without order quantity so it can compare with goods received and provide independent count of goods received; and *copy 5* retained on file by the purchasing department.

Z-Mart
10 Michigan Street
Chicago, Illinois 60521

PURCHASE ORDER

No. P98

Date	10/30/11
FOB	Destination
Ship by	As soon as possible
Terms	2/15, n/30

To: Trex
W9797 Cherry Road
Antigo, Wisconsin 54409

Request shipment of the following item(s):

Model No.	Description	Quantity	Price	Amount
CH 015	Challenger X7	1	490	490
SD 099	SpeedDemon	1	710	710

All shipments and invoices must include purchase order number

J. W.

ORDERED BY

Invoice   An **invoice** is an itemized statement of goods prepared by the vendor listing the customer's name, items sold, sales prices, and terms of sale. An invoice is also a bill sent to the buyer from the supplier. From the vendor's point of view, it is a *sales invoice*. The buyer, or **vendee,** treats it as a *purchase invoice*. When receiving a purchase order, the vendor ships the ordered merchandise to the buyer and includes or mails a copy of the invoice covering the shipment to the buyer. The invoice is sent to the buyer's accounting department where it is placed in the voucher. (Refer back to Exhibit 8.5, which shows Z-Mart's purchase invoice.)

Receiving Report   Many companies maintain a separate department to receive all merchandise and purchased assets. When each shipment arrives, this receiving department counts the goods and checks them for damage and agreement with the purchase order. It then prepares four or more copies of a **receiving report,** which is used within the company to notify the appropriate persons that ordered goods have been received and to describe the quantities and condition of the goods. One copy is sent to accounting and placed in the voucher. Copies are also sent to the requesting department and the purchasing department to notify them that the goods have arrived. The receiving department retains a copy in its files.

Invoice Approval   When a receiving report arrives, the accounting department should have copies of the following documents in the voucher: purchase requisition, purchase order, and invoice. With the information in these documents, the accounting department can record the purchase and approve its payment. In approving an invoice for payment, it checks and compares information across all documents. To facilitate this checking and to ensure that no step is omitted, it often uses an **invoice approval,** also called *check authorization*—see Exhibit 8A.3. An invoice approval is a checklist of steps necessary for approving an invoice for recording and payment. It is a separate document either filed in the voucher or preprinted (or stamped) on the voucher.

INVOICE APPROVAL

DOCUMENT		BY	DATE
Purchase requisition	917	TZ	10/28/15
Purchase order	P98	JW	10/30/15
Receiving report	R85	SK	11/03/15
Invoice:	4657		11/12/15
Price		JK	11/12/15
Calculations		JK	11/12/15
Terms		JK	11/12/15
Approved for payment		BC	

Point: Recording a purchase is initiated by an invoice approval, not an invoice. An invoice approval verifies that the amount is consistent with that requested, ordered, and received. This controls and verifies purchases and related liabilities.

As each step in the checklist is approved, the person initials the invoice approval and records the current date. Final approval implies the following steps have occurred:

1. **Requisition check:** Items on invoice are requested per purchase requisition.
2. **Purchase order check:** Items on invoice are ordered per purchase order.
3. **Receiving report check:** Items on invoice are received per receiving report.
4. **Invoice check: Price:** Invoice prices are as agreed with the vendor.
   Calculations: Invoice has no mathematical errors.
   Terms: Terms are as agreed with the vendor.

Voucher   Once an invoice has been checked and approved, the voucher is complete. A complete voucher is a record summarizing a transaction. Once the voucher certifies a transaction, it authorizes recording an obligation. A voucher also contains approval for paying the obligation on an appropriate date. The physical form of a voucher varies across companies. Many are designed so that the invoice and other related source documents are placed inside the voucher, which can be a folder.

Completion of a voucher usually requires a person to enter certain information on both the inside and outside of the voucher. Typical information required on the inside of a voucher is shown in Exhibit 8A.4, and that for the outside is shown in Exhibit 8A.5. This information is taken from the invoice and the supporting documents filed in the voucher. A complete voucher is sent to an authorized individual (often called an *auditor*). This person performs a final review, approves the accounts and amounts for debiting (called the *accounting distribution*), and authorizes recording of the voucher.

EXHIBIT 8A.4

Inside of a Voucher

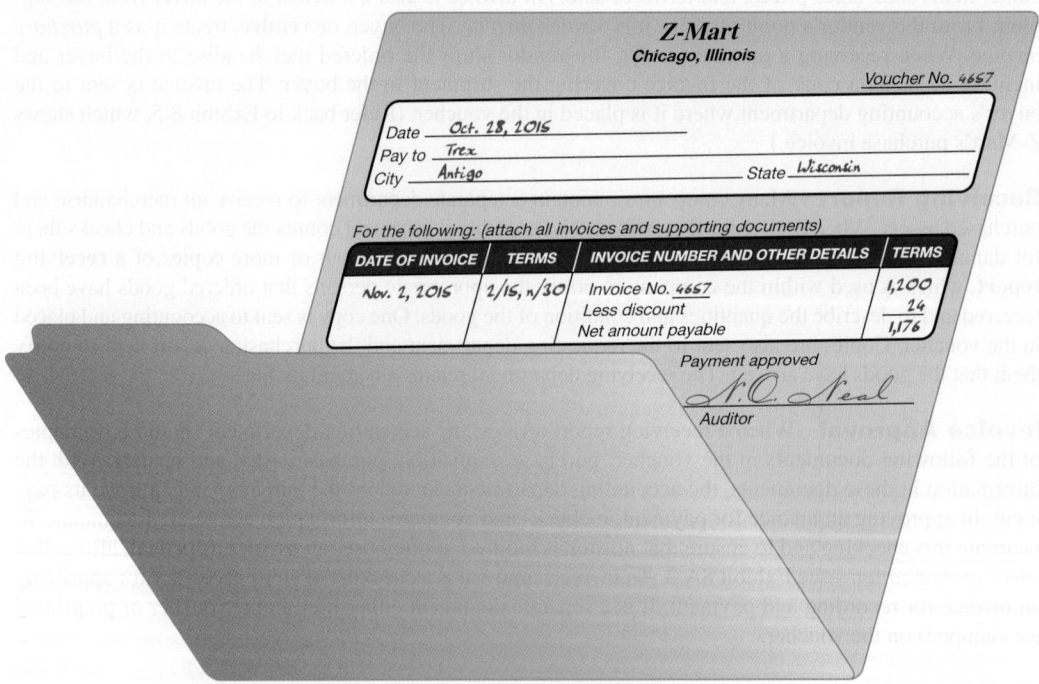

After a voucher is approved and recorded (in a journal called a **voucher register**), it is filed by its due date. A check is then sent on the payment date from the cashier, the voucher is marked "paid," and the voucher is sent to the accounting department and recorded (in a journal called the **check register**). The person issuing checks relies on the approved voucher and its signed supporting documents as proof that an obligation has been incurred and must be paid. The purchase requisition and purchase order confirm the purchase was authorized. The receiving report shows that items have been received, and the invoice approval form verifies that the invoice has been checked for errors. There is little chance for error and even less chance for fraud without collusion unless all the documents and signatures are forged.

EXHIBIT 8A.5

Outside of a Voucher

Voucher No. 4657

Accounting Distribution	
ACCOUNT DEBITED	**AMOUNT**
Merch. Inventory	1,200
Store Supplies	
Office Supplies	
Sales Salaries	
Other	
Total Vouch. Pay. Cr.	1,200

Due Date November 12, 2015
Pay to Trex
City Antigo
State Wisconsin

Summary of charges:
Total charges _____ 1,200
Discount _____ 24
Net payment _____ 1,176

Record of payment:
Paid _____
Check No. _____

APPENDIX

Control of Purchase Discounts

8B

This appendix explains how a company can better control its cash *disbursements* to take advantage of favorable purchases discounts. Chapter 5 described the entries to record the receipt and payment of an invoice for a merchandise purchase with and without discount terms. Those entries were prepared under what is called the **gross method** of recording purchases, which initially records the invoice at its *gross* amount ignoring any cash discount.

The **net method** is another means of recording purchases, which initially records the invoice at its *net* amount of any cash discount. The net method gives management an advantage in controlling and monitoring cash payments involving purchase discounts.

To explain, when invoices are recorded at *gross* amounts, the amount of any discounts taken is deducted from the balance of the Merchandise Inventory account when cash payment is made. This means that the amount of any discounts lost is not reported in any account or on the income statement. Lost discounts recorded in this way are unlikely to come to the attention of management. When purchases are recorded at *net* amounts, a **Discounts Lost** expense account is recorded and brought to management's attention. Management can then seek to identify the reason for discounts lost such as oversight, carelessness, or unfavorable terms. (Chapter 5 explains how managers assess whether a discount is favorable or not.)

Perpetual Inventory System   To illustrate, assume that a company purchases merchandise on November 2 at a $1,200 invoice price with terms of 2/10, n/30. Its November 2 entries under the gross and net methods are

Gross Method—Perpetual			**Net Method—Perpetual**		
Merchandise Inventory	1,200		Merchandise Inventory	1,176	
Accounts Payable		1,200	Accounts Payable		1,176

If the invoice is paid on November 12 within the discount period, it records the following:

Gross Method—Perpetual			**Net Method—Perpetual**		
Accounts Payable	1,200		Accounts Payable	1,176	
Merchandise Inventory		24	Cash		1,176
Cash		1,176			

P5 Apply the net method to control purchase discounts.

If the invoice is *not* paid within the discount period, it records the following November 12 entry (which is the date corresponding to the end of the discount period):

Gross Method—Perpetual		Net Method—Perpetual	
No entry		Discounts Lost	24
		Accounts Payable	24

Then, when the invoice is later paid on December 2, outside the discount period, it records the following:

Gross Method—Perpetual		Net Method—Perpetual	
Accounts Payable	1,200	Accounts Payable	1,200
Cash	1,200	Cash	1,200

(The discount lost can be recorded when the cash payment is made with a single entry. However, in this case, when financial statements are prepared after a discount is lost and before the cash payment is made, an adjusting entry is required to recognize any unrecorded discount lost in the period when incurred.)

Periodic Inventory System   The preceding entries assume a perpetual inventory system. If a company is using a periodic system, its November 2 entries under the gross and net methods are

Gross Method—Periodic		Net Method—Periodic	
Purchases	1,200	Purchases	1,176
Accounts Payable.............	1,200	Accounts Payable	1,176

If the invoice is paid on November 12 within the discount period, it records the following:

Gross Method—Periodic		Net Method—Periodic	
Accounts Payable	1,200	Accounts Payable	1,176
Purchases Discounts	24	Cash	1,176
Cash	1,176		

If the invoice is *not* paid within the discount period, it records the following November 12 entry:

Gross Method—Periodic		Net Method—Periodic	
No entry		Discounts Lost	24
		Accounts Payable	24

Then, when the invoice is later paid on December 2, outside the discount period, it records the following:

Gross Method—Periodic		Net Method—Periodic	
Accounts Payable	1,200	Accounts Payable	1,200
Cash	1,200	Cash	1,200

Summary

C1   Define internal control and identify its purpose and principles. An internal control system consists of the policies and procedures managers use to protect assets, ensure reliable accounting, promote efficient operations, and urge adherence to company policies. It can prevent avoidable losses and help managers both plan operations and monitor company and human performance. Principles of good internal control include establishing responsibilities, maintaining adequate records, insuring assets and bonding employees, separating recordkeeping from custody of assets, dividing responsibilities for related transactions, applying technological controls, and performing regular independent reviews.

C2   Define cash and cash equivalents and explain how to report them. Cash includes currency, coins, and amounts on (or acceptable for) deposit in checking and savings accounts. Cash equivalents are short-term, highly liquid investment assets readily convertible to a known cash amount and sufficiently close to their maturity date so that market value is not sensitive to interest rate changes. Cash and cash equivalents are liquid assets because they are readily converted into other assets or can be used to pay for goods, services, or liabilities.

A1 **Compute the days' sales uncollected ratio and use it to assess liquidity.** Many companies attract customers by selling to them on credit. This means that cash receipts from customers are delayed until accounts receivable are collected. Users want to know how quickly a company can convert its accounts receivable into cash. The days' sales uncollected ratio, one measure reflecting company liquidity, is computed by dividing the ending balance of receivables by annual net sales, and then multiplying by 365.

P1 **Apply internal control to cash receipts and disbursements.** Internal control of cash receipts ensures that all cash received is properly recorded and deposited. Attention focuses on two important types of cash receipts: over-the-counter and by mail. Good internal control for over-the-counter cash receipts includes use of a cash register, customer review, use of receipts, a permanent transaction record, and separation of the custody of cash from its record-keeping. Good internal control for cash receipts by mail includes at least two people assigned to open mail and a listing of each sender's name, amount, and explanation. (Banks offer several services that promote the control and safeguarding of cash.)

P2 **Explain and record petty cash fund transactions.** Petty cash disbursements are payments of small amounts for items such as postage, courier fees, minor repairs, and supplies. A company usually sets up one or more petty cash funds. A petty cash fund cashier is responsible for safekeeping the cash, making payments from this fund, and keeping receipts and records. A Petty Cash account

is debited only when the fund is established or increased in amount. When the fund is replenished, petty cash disbursements are recorded with debits to expense (or asset) accounts and a credit to cash.

P3 **Prepare a bank reconciliation.** A bank reconciliation proves the accuracy of the depositor's and the bank's records. The bank statement balance is adjusted for items such as outstanding checks and unrecorded deposits made on or before the bank statement date but not reflected on the statement. The book balance is adjusted for items such as service charges, bank collections for the depositor, and interest earned on the account.

P4A **Describe the use of documentation and verification to control cash disbursements.** A voucher system is a set of procedures and approvals designed to control cash disbursements and acceptance of obligations. The voucher system of control relies on several important documents, including the voucher and its supporting files. A key factor in this system is that only approved departments and individuals are authorized to incur certain obligations.

P5B **Apply the net method to control purchase discounts.** The net method aids management in monitoring and controlling purchase discounts. When invoices are recorded at gross amounts, the amount of discounts taken is deducted from the balance of the Inventory account. This means that the amount of any discounts lost is not reported in any account and is unlikely to come to the attention of management. When purchases are recorded at net amounts, a Discounts Lost account is brought to management's attention as an operating expense. Management can then seek to identify the reason for discounts lost, such as oversight, carelessness, or unfavorable terms.

Guidance Answers to Decision Maker and Decision Ethics

Entrepreneur A forced vacation policy is part of a good system of internal controls. When employees are forced to take vacations, their ability to hide any fraudulent behavior decreases because others must perform the vacationers' duties. A replacement employee potentially can uncover fraudulent behavior or falsified records. A forced vacation policy is especially important for employees in sensitive positions of handling money or in control of easily transferable assets.

Sales Representative A salesperson can take several steps to reduce days' sales uncollected. These include (1) decreasing the ratio of sales on account to total sales by encouraging more cash sales, (2) identifying customers most delayed in their payments and encouraging earlier payments or cash sales, and (3) applying stricter credit policies to eliminate credit sales to customers that never pay.

Guidance Answers to Quick Checks

1. (c)
2. Technology reduces processing errors. It also allows more extensive testing of records, limits the amount of hard evidence, and highlights the importance of separation of duties.
3. A company holds liquid assets so that it can purchase other assets, buy services, and pay obligations.
4. It owns cash equivalents because they yield a return greater than what cash earns (and are readily exchanged for cash).
5. Examples of cash equivalents are 90-day (or less) U.S. Treasury bills, money market funds, and commercial paper (notes).
6. (a)
7. A voucher system is used when an owner/manager can no longer control purchasing procedures through personal supervision and direct participation.

8. If all cash payments are made by check, numerous checks for small amounts must be written. Since this practice is expensive and time-consuming, a petty cash fund is often established for making small (immaterial) cash payments.
9. If the petty cash fund is not reimbursed at the end of an accounting period, the transactions involving petty cash are not yet recorded and the petty cash asset is overstated.
10. First, petty cash transactions are recorded when the petty cash fund is reimbursed. Second, reimbursement provides cash to allow the fund to continue being used. Third, reimbursement identifies any cash shortage or overage in the fund.
11. A bank statement is a report prepared by the bank describing the activities in a depositor's account.

12. To reconcile a bank balance means to explain the difference between the cash balance in the depositor's accounting records and the cash balance on the bank statement.

13. The purpose of the bank reconciliation is to determine whether the bank or the depositor has made any errors and whether the bank has entered any transactions affecting the account that the depositor has not recorded.

14. Unrecorded deposits—added
Outstanding checks—subtracted

15. Interest earned—added   Debit memos—subtracted
Credit memos—added   NSF checks—subtracted
                             Bank service charges—subtracted

Key Terms   www.mheducation.asia/olc/wildkwokFAP

Bank reconciliation (p. 331)
Bank statement (p. 330)
Canceled checks (p. 331)
Cash (p. 321)
Cash equivalents (p. 321)
Cash Over and Short (p. 323)
Check (p. 328)
Check register (p. 340)
Committee of Sponsoring Organizations (COSO) (p. 317)
Days' sales uncollected (p. 335)
Deposit ticket (p. 328)

Deposits in transit (p. 331)
Discounts lost (p. 341)
Electronic funds transfer (EFT) (p. 329)
Gross method (p. 341)
Internal control system (p. 316)
Invoice (p. 339)
Invoice approval (p. 339)
Liquid assets (p. 321)
Liquidity (p. 321)
Net method (p. 341)
Outstanding checks (p. 331)

Petty cash (p. 326)
Principles of internal control (p. 317)
Purchase order (p. 338)
Purchase requisition (p. 338)
Receiving report (p. 339)
Signature card (p. 328)
Vendee (p. 339)
Vendor (p. 338)
Voucher (p. 325)
Voucher register (p. 340)
Voucher system (p. 324)

Multiple Choice Quiz   Answers on p. 357   www.mheducation.asia/olc/wildkwokFAP

Additional Quiz Questions are available at the book's Website.

1. A company needs to replenish its $500 petty cash fund. Its petty cash box has $75 cash and petty cash receipts of $420. The journal entry to replenish the fund includes
   a. A debit to Cash for $75.
   b. A credit to Cash for $75.
   c. A credit to Petty Cash for $420.
   d. A credit to Cash Over and Short for $5.
   e. A debit to Cash Over and Short for $5.

2. The following information is available for Hapley Company:
   • The November 30 bank statement shows a $1,895 balance.
   • The general ledger shows a $1,742 balance at November 30.
   • A $795 deposit placed in the bank's night depository on November 30 does not appear on the November 30 bank statement.
   • Outstanding checks amount to $638 at November 30.
   • A customer's $335 note was collected by the bank in November. A collection fee of $15 was deducted by the bank and the difference deposited in Hapley's account.
   • A bank service charge of $10 is deducted by the bank and appears on the November 30 bank statement.

How will the customer's note appear on Hapley's November 30 bank reconciliation?
   a. $320 appears as an addition to the book balance of cash.
   b. $320 appears as a deduction from the book balance of cash.
   c. $320 appears as an addition to the bank balance of cash.

   d. $320 appears as a deduction from the bank balance of cash.
   e. $335 appears as an addition to the bank balance of cash.

3. Using the information from question 2, what is the reconciled balance on Hapley's November 30 bank reconciliation?
   a. $2,052
   b. $1,895
   c. $1,742
   d. $2,201
   e. $1,184

4. A company had net sales of $84,000 and accounts receivable of $6,720. Its days' sales uncollected is
   a. 3.2 days
   b. 18.4 days
   c. 230.0 days
   d. 29.2 days
   e. 12.5 days

5.[B] A company records its purchases using the net method. On August 1, it purchases merchandise on account for $6,000 with terms of 2/10, n/30. The August 1 journal entry to record this transaction includes a
   a. Debit to Merchandise Inventory for $6,000.
   b. Debit to Merchandise Inventory for $5,880.
   c. Debit to Merchandise Inventory for $120.
   d. Debit to Accounts Payable for $5,880.
   e. Credit to Accounts Payable for $6,000.

A(B) *Superscript letter A(B) denotes assignments based on Appendix 8A (8B).*

🔒 Icon denotes assignments that involve decision making.

Discussion Questions

1. List the seven broad principles of internal control.

2. 🔒 Internal control procedures are important in every business, but at what stage in the development of a business do they become especially critical?

3. 🔒 Why should responsibility for related transactions be divided among different departments or individuals?

4. 🔒 Why should the person who keeps the records of an asset not be the person responsible for its custody?

5. 🔒 When a store purchases merchandise, why are individual departments not allowed to directly deal with suppliers?

6. What are the limitations of internal controls?

7. Which of the following assets is most liquid? Which is least liquid? Inventory, building, accounts receivable, or cash.

8. What is a petty cash receipt? Who should sign it?

9. Why should cash receipts be deposited on the day of receipt?

10. Examine Nestlé's consolidated cash flow statement for financial year 2013 in Appendix A. What amount is from (used in) investing activities? What amount is from (used in) financing activities?

11. Refer to Adidas' consolidated statement of financial position in Appendix A. How does its cash and cash equivalents compare with its other current assets (both in amount and percent) as at December 31, 2013? Compare and assess the cash and cash equivalents amount as at December 31, 2013 with its amount at December 31, 2012.

12. 🔒 Examine Samsung's consolidated statement of cash flow statement for financial year 2012 in Appendix A. What amount is from (used in) operating activities? What amount is from (used in) investing activities?

13. Refer to Puma's consolidated statement of financial position from its Website (http://about.puma.com/en/investor-relations/financial-reports), which shows that cash and cash equivalents decreased during the financial year ended December 31, 2013. Identify at least three major causes of this change in cash and equivalents.

▦ connect

An internal control system consists of all policies and procedures used to protect assets, ensure reliable accounting, promote efficient operations, and urge adherence to company policies.

1. What is the main objective of internal control procedures? How is that objective achieved?

2. Why should recordkeeping for assets be separated from custody over those assets?

3. Why should the responsibility for a transaction be divided between two or more individuals or departments?

QUICK STUDY

QS 8-1
Internal control objectives
C1 🔒

A good system of internal control for cash provides adequate procedures for protecting both cash receipts and cash disbursements.

1. What are three basic guidelines that help achieve this protection?

2. Identify two control systems or procedures for cash disbursements.

QS 8-2
Internal control for cash
P1

Good accounting systems help in managing cash and controlling who has access to it.

1. What items are included in the category of cash?

2. What items are included in the category of cash equivalents?

3. What does the term *liquidity* refer to?

QS 8-3
Cash and equivalents
C2

---

1. The petty cash fund of the Rio Agency is established at $75. At the end of the current period, the fund contained $14 and had the following receipts: film rentals, $19, refreshments for meetings, $23 (both expenditures to be classified as Entertainment Expense); postage, $6; and printing, $13. Prepare journal entries to record (*a*) establishment of the fund and (*b*) reimbursement of the fund at the end of the current period.

2. Identify the two events that cause a Petty Cash account to be credited in a journal entry.

QS 8-4
Petty cash accounting
P2

---

1. For each of the following items, indicate whether its amount (i) affects the bank or book side of a bank reconciliation and (ii) represents an addition or a subtraction in a bank reconciliation.

   a. Outstanding checks   **d.** Unrecorded deposits   **g.** Bank service charges
   b. Debit memos   **e.** Interest on cash balance
   c. NSF checks   **f.** Credit memos

2. Which of the items in part 1 require an adjusting journal entry?

QS 8-5
Bank reconciliation
P3

QS 8-6
Bank reconciliation
P3

Cruz Company deposits all cash receipts on the day when they are received and it makes all cash payments by check. At the close of business on June 30, 2015, its Cash account shows an $11,352 debit balance. Cruz's June 30 bank statement shows $10,332 on deposit in the bank. Prepare a bank reconciliation for Cruz Company using the following information.

a. Outstanding checks as at June 30 total $1,713.

b. The June 30 bank statement included a $23 debit memorandum for bank services; Cruz has not yet recorded the cost of these services.

c. In reviewing the bank statement, a $90 check written by Cruz Company was mistakenly recorded in Cruz Company's books at $99.

d. June 30 cash receipts of $2,724 were placed in the bank's night depository after banking hours and were not recorded on the June 30 bank statement.

e. The bank statement included a $5 credit for interest earned on the cash in the bank.

QS 8-7
Days' sales uncollected
A1

The following annual account balances are taken from ProTeam Sports at December 31.

	2015	2014
Accounts receivable	$ 75,692	$ 70,484
Net sales	2,591,933	2,296,673

What is the change in the number of days' sales uncollected between years 2014 and 2015? According to this analysis, is the company's collection of receivables improving? Explain.

QS 8-8ᴬ
Documents in a voucher system
P4

Management uses a voucher system to help control and monitor cash disbursements. Identify and describe at least four key documents that are part of a voucher system of control.

QS 8-9ᴮ
Purchase discounts   **P5**

An important part of cash management is knowing when, and if, to take purchase discounts.

a. Which accounting method uses a Discounts Lost account?

b. What is the advantage of this method for management?

QS 8-10
Internal controls and cash
C1 P1

Answer the following related to internal controls and cash.

a. Explain the purposes and principles of internal controls.

b. What are the special internal control challenges when accounting for cash?

QS 8-11
Reviewing bank statements
P3

An entrepreneur commented that a bank reconciliation may not be necessary as she regularly reviews her online bank statement for any unusual items and errors.

a. Describe how a bank reconciliation and an online review (or reading) of the bank statement are not equivalent.

b. Identify and explain at least two frauds or errors that would be uncovered through a bank reconciliation and that would *not* be uncovered through an online review of the bank statement.

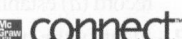

EXERCISES

Exercise 8-1
Internal control recommendations
C1

What internal control procedures would you recommend in each of the following situations?

1. A concession company has one employee who sells towels, coolers, and sunglasses at the beach. Each day, the employee is given enough towels, coolers, and sunglasses to last through the day and enough cash to make change. The money is kept in a box at the stand.

2. An antique store has one employee who is given cash and sent to garage sales each weekend. The employee pays cash for any merchandise acquired that the antique store resells.

Cantu Company is a rapidly growing start-up business. Its recordkeeper, who was hired nine months ago, left town after the company's manager discovered that a large sum of money had disappeared over the past three months. An audit disclosed that the recordkeeper had written and signed several checks made payable to her fiancé and then recorded the checks as salaries expense. The fiancé, who cashed the checks but never worked for the company, left town with the recordkeeper. As a result, the company incurred an uninsured loss of $84,000. Evaluate Cantu's internal control system and indicate which principles of internal control appear to have been ignored.

Exercise 8-2

Analyzing internal control

C1

Some of Chester Company's cash receipts from customers are received by the company with the regular mail. Chester's recordkeeper opens these letters and deposits the cash received each day. (*a*) Identify any internal control problem(s) in this arrangement. (*b*) What changes to its internal control system do you recommend?

Exercise 8-3

Control of cash receipts by mail

P1

Good accounting systems help with the management and control of cash and cash equivalents.

1. Define and contrast the terms *liquid asset* and *cash equivalent*.
2. Why would companies invest their idle cash in cash equivalents?
3. Identify five principles of effective cash management.

Exercise 8-4

Cash, liquidity, and return

C2

Hawk Company establishes a $400 petty cash fund on September 9. On September 30, the fund shows $166 in cash along with receipts for the following expenditures: transportation-in, $32; postage expenses, $113; and miscellaneous expenses, $87. The petty cashier could not account for a $2 shortage in the fund. Hawk uses the perpetual system in accounting for merchandise inventory. Prepare (1) the September 9 entry to establish the fund, (2) the September 30 entry to reimburse the fund, and (3) an October 1 entry to decrease the fund to $300.

Exercise 8-5

Petty cash fund with a shortage

P2

Check   (2) Cr. Cash $234 and (3) Dr. Cash $100

NetPerks Co. establishes a $200 petty cash fund on January 1. On January 8, the fund shows $28 in cash along with receipts for the following expenditures: postage, $64; transportation-in, $19; delivery expenses, $36; and miscellaneous expenses, $53. NetPerks uses the perpetual system in accounting for merchandise inventory. Prepare journal entries to (1) establish the fund on January 1, (2) reimburse it on January 8, and (3) both reimburse the fund and increase it to $500 on January 8, assuming no entry in part 2. (*Hint*: Make two separate entries for part 3.)

Exercise 8-6

Petty cash fund accounting

P2

Check   (3) Cr. Cash $472 (total)

Prepare a table with the following headings for a monthly bank reconciliation dated September 30.

Exercise 8-7

Bank reconciliation and adjusting entries

P3

Bank Balance		Book Balance			Not Shown on the Reconciliation
Add	Deduct	Add	Deduct	Adjust	

For each item 1 through 12, place an *x* in the appropriate column to indicate whether the item should be added to or deducted from the book or bank balance, or whether it should not appear on the reconciliation. If the book balance is to be adjusted, place a *Dr.* or *Cr.* in the Adjust column to indicate whether the Cash balance should be debited or credited. At the left side of your table, number the items to correspond to the following list.

1. Bank service charge for September.
2. Checks written and mailed to payees on October 2.
3. Checks written by another depositor but charged against this company's account.
4. Principal and interest on a note receivable to this company is collected by the bank but not yet recorded by the company.
5. Special bank charge for collection of note in part 4 on this company's behalf.
6. Check written against the company's account and cleared by the bank; erroneously not recorded by the company's recordkeeper.
7. Interest earned on the September cash balance in the bank.
8. Night deposit made on September 30 after the bank closed.
9. Checks outstanding on August 31 that cleared the bank in September.
10. NSF check from customer is returned on September 25 but not yet recorded by this company.
11. Checks written by the company and mailed to payees on September 30.
12. Deposit made on September 5 and processed by the bank on September 6.

Exercise 8-8 Voucher system P1	The voucher system of control is designed to control cash disbursements and the acceptance of obligations. **1.** The voucher system of control establishes procedures for what two processes? **2.** What types of expenditures should be overseen by a voucher system of control? **3.** When is the voucher initially prepared? Explain.

Exercise 8-9 Bank reconciliation P3 **Check** Reconciled bal., $15,025	Frederick Clinic deposits all cash receipts on the day when they are received and it makes all cash payments by check. At the close of business on June 30, 2015, its Cash account shows a $15,141 debit balance. Frederick Clinic's June 30 bank statement shows $14,275 on deposit in the bank. Prepare a bank reconciliation for Frederick Clinic using the following information: **a.** Outstanding checks as at June 30 total $2,500. **b.** The June 30 bank statement included a $125 debit memorandum for bank services. **c.** Check No. 919, listed with the canceled checks, was correctly drawn for $645 in payment of a utility bill on June 15. Frederick Clinic mistakenly recorded it with a debit to Utilities Expense and a credit to Cash in the amount of $654. **d.** The June 30 cash receipts of $3,250 were placed in the bank's night depository after banking hours and were not recorded on the June 30 bank statement.

Exercise 8-10 Adjusting entries from bank reconciliation P3	Prepare the adjusting journal entries that Frederick Clinic must record as a result of preparing the bank reconciliation in Exercise 8-9.

Exercise 8-11 Bank reconciliation P3 **Check** Reconciled bal., $14,800	Chung Company deposits all cash receipts on the day when they are received and it makes all cash payments by check. At the close of business on May 31, 2015, its Cash account shows a $15,500 debit balance. Chung's May 31 bank statement shows $13,800 on deposit in the bank. Prepare a bank reconciliation for Chung Company using the following information. **a.** May 31 cash receipts of $2,200 were placed in the bank's night depository after banking hours and were not recorded on the May 31 bank statement. **b.** Outstanding checks as at May 31 total $1,600. **c.** The May 31 bank statement included a $100 debit memorandum for bank services; Chung has not yet recorded the cost of these services. **d.** In reviewing the bank statement, a $400 check written by Wald Company was mistakenly drawn against Chung's account. **e.** A debit memorandum for $600 refers to a $600 NSF check from a customer; Chung has not yet recorded this NSF check.

Exercise 8-12 Liquid assets and accounts receivable A1	Deacon Co. reported annual net sales for 2014 and 2015 of $565,000 and $647,000, respectively. Its year-end balances of accounts receivable follow: December 31, 2014, $51,000; and December 31, 2015, $83,000. (*a*) Calculate its days' sales uncollected at the end of each year. (*b*) Evaluate and comment on any changes in the amount of liquid assets tied up in receivables.

Exercise 8-13ᴬ Documents in a voucher system P4	Match each document in a voucher system in column one with its description in column two. **Document** **1.** Voucher **2.** Invoice approval **3.** Receiving report **4.** Invoice **5.** Purchase order **6.** Purchase requisition **Description** **A.** A document used to notify the appropriate persons that ordered goods have arrived, including a description of the quantities and condition of goods. **B.** An internal file used to store documents and information to control cash disbursements and to ensure that a transaction is properly authorized and recorded. **C.** A document used to place an order with a vendor that authorizes the vendor to ship ordered merchandise at the stated price and terms. **D.** A checklist of steps necessary for the approval of an invoice for recording and payment; also known as a check authorization. **E.** A document used by department managers to inform the purchasing department to place an order with a vendor. **F.** An itemized statement of goods prepared by the vendor listing the customer's name, items sold, sales prices, and terms of sale.

USA Imports uses the perpetual system in accounting for merchandise inventory and had the following transactions during the month of October. Prepare entries to record these transactions assuming that USA Imports records invoices (*a*) at gross amounts and (*b*) at net amounts.

Oct. 2   Purchased merchandise at a $4,000 price, invoice dated October 2, terms 2/10, n/30.
      10   Received a $400 credit memorandum (at full invoice price) for the return of merchandise that it purchased on October 2.
      17   Purchased merchandise at a $4,400 price, invoice dated October 16, terms 2/10, n/30.
      26   Paid for the merchandise purchased on October 17, less the discount.
      31   Paid for the merchandise purchased on October 2. Payment was delayed because the invoice was mistakenly filed for payment today. This error caused the discount to be lost.

■**connect**

For each of these five separate cases, identify the principle(s) of internal control that is violated. Recommend what the business should do to ensure adherence to principles of internal control.

1. Heather Flat records all incoming customer cash receipts for her employer and posts the customer payments to their respective accounts.
2. At Netco Company, Jeff and Jose alternate lunch hours. Jeff is the petty cash custodian, but if someone needs petty cash when he is at lunch, Jose fills in as custodian.
3. Nadine Cox posts all patient charges and payments at the Dole Medical Clinic. Each night Nadine backs up the computerized accounting system to a tape and stores the tape in a locked file at her desk.
4. Barto Sayles prides himself on hiring quality workers who require little supervision. As office manager, Barto gives his employees full discretion over their tasks and for years has seen no reason to perform independent reviews of their work.
5. Desi West's manager has told her to reduce costs. Desi decides to raise the deductible on the plant's property insurance from $5,000 to $10,000. This cuts the property insurance premium in half. In a related move, she decides that bonding the plant's employees is a waste of money since the company has not experienced any losses due to employee theft. Desi saves the entire amount of the bonding insurance premium by dropping the bonding insurance.

Shawnee Co. set up a petty cash fund for payments of small amounts. The following transactions involving the petty cash fund occurred in May (the last month of the company's financial year).

May 1   Prepared a company check for $250 to establish the petty cash fund.
     15   Prepared a company check to replenish the fund for the following expenditures made since May 1.
           a. Paid $78 for janitorial services.
           b. Paid $63.68 for miscellaneous expenses.
           c. Paid postage expenses of $43.50.
           d. Paid $57.15 to *The County Gazette* (the local newspaper) for an advertisement.
           e. Counted $11.15 remaining in the petty cash box.
     16   Prepared a company check for $200 to increase the fund to $450.
     31   The petty cashier reports that $293.39 cash remains in the fund. A company check is drawn to replenish the fund for the following expenditures made since May 15.
           f. Paid postage expenses of $48.36.
           g. Reimbursed the office manager for business mileage, $38.50.
           h. Paid $39.75 to deliver merchandise to a customer, terms FOB destination.
     31   The company decides that the May 16 increase in the fund was too large. It reduces the fund by $50, leaving a total of $400.

Required

1. Prepare journal entries to establish the fund on May 1, to replenish it on May 15 and on May 31, and to reflect any increase or decrease in the fund balance on May 16 and May 31.

Analysis Component

2. Explain how the company's financial statements are affected if the petty cash fund is not replenished and no entry is made on May 31.

Problem 8-3A
Establish, reimburse, and
increase petty cash

P2

Shelton Gallery had the following petty cash transactions in February of the current year.

Feb. 2 Wrote a $300 check, cashed it, and gave the proceeds and the petty cashbox to Bo Brown, the
        petty cashier.
     5 Purchased bond paper for the copier for $10.13 that is immediately used.
     9 Paid $22.50 COD shipping charges on merchandise purchased for resale, terms FOB shipping
        point. Shelton uses the perpetual system to account for merchandise inventory.
    12 Paid $9.95 postage to express mail a contract to a client.
    14 Reimbursed Alli Buck, the manager, $58 for business mileage on her car.
    20 Purchased stationery for $77.76 that is immediately used.
    23 Paid a courier $18 to deliver merchandise sold to a customer, terms FOB destination.
    25 Paid $15.10 COD shipping charges on merchandise purchased for resale, terms FOB shipping
        point.
    27 Paid $64 for postage expenses.
    28 The fund had $21.23 remaining in the petty cash box. Sorted the petty cash receipts by accounts
        affected and exchanged them for a check to reimburse the fund for expenditures.
    28 The petty cash fund amount is increased by $100 to a total of $400.

Required

1. Prepare the journal entry to establish the petty cash fund.
2. Prepare a petty cash payments report for February with these categories: delivery expense, mileage expense, postage expense, merchandise inventory (for transportation-in), and office supplies expense. Sort the payments into the appropriate categories and total the expenditures in each category.
3. Prepare the journal entries for part 2 to both (a) reimburse and (b) increase the fund amount.

Check (3a & 3b) Total Cr. to Cash
$378.77

Problem 8-4A
Prepare a bank reconciliation
and record adjustments

P3

www.mheducation.asia/olc/wildkwokFAP

The following information is available to reconcile Clark Company's book balance of cash with its bank
statement cash balance as at July 31, 2015.

a. On July 31, the company's Cash account has a $26,193 debit balance, but its July bank statement
   shows a $28,020 cash balance.
b. Check No. 3031 for $1,380 and Check No. 3040 for $552 were outstanding on the June 30 bank reconciliation. Check No. 3040 is listed with the July canceled checks, but Check No. 3031 is not. Also,
   Check No. 3065 for $336 and Check No. 3069 for $2,148, both written in July, are not among the
   canceled checks on the July 31 statement.
c. In comparing the canceled checks on the bank statement with the entries in the accounting records, it
   is found that Check No. 3056 for July rent was correctly written and drawn for $1,250 but was erroneously entered in the accounting records as $1,230.
d. A credit memorandum enclosed with the July bank statement indicates the bank collected $9,000 cash
   on a non-interest-bearing note for Clark, deducted a $45 collection fee, and credited the remainder to
   its account. Clark had not recorded this event before receiving the statement.
e. A debit memorandum for $805 lists a $795 NSF check plus a $10 NSF charge. The check had been
   received from a customer, Jim Shaw. Clark has not yet recorded this check as NSF.
f. Enclosed with the July statement is a $15 debit memorandum for bank services. It has not yet been
   recorded because no previous notification had been received.
g. Clark's July 31 daily cash receipts of $10,152 were placed in the bank's night depository on that date,
   but do not appear on the July 31 bank statement.

Required

1. Prepare the bank reconciliation for this company as at July 31, 2015.
2. Prepare the journal entries necessary to bring the company's book balance of cash into conformity
   with the reconciled cash balance as at July 31, 2015.

Check (1) Reconciled balance,
$34,308; (2) Cr. Note Receivable
$9,000

Analysis Component

3. Assume that the July 31, 2015, bank reconciliation for this company is prepared and some items are
   treated incorrectly. For each of the following errors, explain the effect of the error on (i) the adjusted
   bank statement cash balance and (ii) the adjusted cash account book balance.
   a. The company's unadjusted cash account balance of $26,193 is listed on the reconciliation as $26,139.
   b. The bank's collection of the $9,000 note less the $45 collection fee is added to the bank statement
      cash balance on the reconciliation.

Els Company most recently reconciled its bank statement and book balances of cash on August 31 and it reported two checks outstanding, No. 5888 for $1,038.05 and No. 5893 for $484.25. The following information is available for its September 30, 2015, reconciliation.

Problem 8-5A
Prepare a bank reconciliation and record adjustments
P3

www.mheducation.asia/olc/wildkwokFAP

From the September 30 Bank Statement

PREVIOUS BALANCE	TOTAL CHECKS AND DEBITS	TOTAL DEPOSITS AND CREDITS	CURRENT BALANCE
16,800.45	9,620.05	11,182.85	18,363.25

CHECKS AND DEBITS			DEPOSITS AND CREDITS		DAILY BALANCE	
Date	No.	Amount	Date	Amount	Date	Amount
09/03	5888	1,038.05	09/05	1,103.75	08/31	16,800.45
09/04	5902	731.90	09/12	2,226.90	09/03	15,762.40
09/07	5901	1,824.25	09/21	4,093.00	09/04	15,030.50
09/17		588.25 NSF	09/25	2,351.70	09/05	16,134.25
09/20	5905	937.00	09/30	22.50 IN	09/07	14,310.00
09/22	5903	399.10	09/30	1,385.00 CM	09/12	16,536.90
09/22	5904	2,080.00			09/17	15,948.65
09/28	5907	213.85			09/20	15,011.65
09/29	5909	1,807.65			09/21	19,104.65
					09/22	16,625.55
					09/25	18,977.25
					09/28	18,763.40
					09/29	16,955.75
					09/30	18,363.25

From Els Company's Accounting Records

Cash Receipts Deposited				Cash Disbursements		
Date		Cash Debit		Check No.		Cash Credit
Sept.	5	1,103.75		5901		1,824.25
	12	2,226.90		5902		731.90
	21	4,093.00		5903		399.10
	25	2,351.70		5904		2,050.00
	30	1,582.75		5905		937.00
		11,358.10		5906		859.30
				5907		213.85
				5908		276.00
				5909		1,807.65
						9,099.05

Cash						Acct. No. 101
Date		Explanation	PR	Debit	Credit	Balance
Aug.	31	Balance				15,278.15
Sept.	30	Total receipts	R12	11,358.10		26,636.25
	30	Total disbursements	D23		9,099.05	17,537.20

Additional Information

Check No. 5904 is correctly drawn for $2,080 to pay for computer equipment; however, the recordkeeper misread the amount and entered it in the accounting records with a debit to Computer Equipment and a credit to Cash of $2,050. The NSF check shown in the statement was originally received from a customer, S. Nilson, in payment of her account. Its return has not yet been recorded by the company. The credit memorandum is from the collection of a $1,400 note for Els Company by the bank. The bank deducted a $15 collection fee. The collection and fee are not yet recorded.

Required

1. Prepare the September 30, 2015, bank reconciliation for this company.
2. Prepare the journal entries to adjust the book balance of cash to the reconciled balance.

Analysis Component

3. The bank statement reveals that some of the prenumbered checks in the sequence are missing. Describe three situations that could explain this.

PROBLEM SET B

Problem 8-1B

Analyzing internal control

C1

For each of these five separate cases, identify the principle(s) of internal control that is violated. Recommend what the business should do to ensure adherence to principles of internal control.

1. Latoya Tally is the company's computer specialist and oversees its computerized payroll system. Her boss recently asked her to put password protection on all office computers. Latoya has put a password in place that allows only the boss access to the file where pay rates are changed and personnel are added or deleted from the payroll.
2. Lake Theater has a computerized order-taking system for its tickets. The system is active all week and backed up every Friday night.
3. X2U Company has two employees handling acquisitions of inventory. One employee places purchase orders and pays vendors. The second employee receives the merchandise.
4. The owner of Super-Aid Pharmacy uses a check protector to perforate checks, making it difficult for anyone to alter the amount of the check. The check protector is on the owner's desk in an office that contains company checks and is normally unlocked.
5. LeAnn Company is a small business that has separated the duties of cash receipts and cash disbursements. The employee responsible for cash disbursements reconciles the bank account monthly.

Problem 8-2B

Establishing, reimbursing, and adjusting petty cash

P2

Pepco Co. establishes a petty cash fund for payments of small amounts. The following transactions involving the petty cash fund occurred in January (the last month of the company's financial year).

Jan. 3   A company check for $150 is written and made payable to the petty cashier to establish the petty cash fund.

     14   A company check is written to replenish the fund for the following expenditures made since January 3.
        a.   Purchased office supplies for $16.29 that are immediately used up.
        b.   Paid $17.60 COD shipping charges on merchandise purchased for resale, terms FOB shipping point. Pepco uses the perpetual system to account for inventory.
        c.   Paid $36.57 to All-Tech for minor repairs to a computer.
        d.   Paid $14.82 for items classified as miscellaneous expenses.
        e.   Counted $62.28 remaining in the petty cash box.

     15   Prepared a company check for $25 to increase the fund to $175.
     31   The petty cashier reports that $17.35 remains in the fund. A company check is written to replenish the fund for the following expenditures made since January 14.
        f.   Paid $40 to *The Smart Shopper* for an advertisement in January's newsletter.
        g.   Paid $38.19 for postage expenses.
        h.   Paid $58 to Take-You-There for delivery of merchandise, terms FOB destination.

     31   The company decides that the January 15 increase in the fund was too little. It increases the fund by another $75, leaving a total of $250.

Required

1. Prepare journal entries to establish the fund on January 3, to replenish it on January 14 and January 31, and to reflect any increase or decrease in the fund balance on January 15 and 31.

Analysis Component

2. Explain how the company's financial statements are affected if the petty cash fund is not replenished and no entry is made on January 31.

RPM Music Center had the following petty cash transactions in March of the current year.

Problem 8-3B
Establish, reimburse, and
increase petty cash

P2

March 5 Wrote a $200 check, cashed it, and gave the proceeds and the petty cashbox to Liz Buck, the
petty cashier.
6 Paid $14.50 COD shipping charges on merchandise purchased for resale, terms FOB shipping
point. RPM uses the perpetual system to account for merchandise inventory.
11 Paid $8.75 delivery charges on merchandise sold to a customer, terms FOB destination.
12 Purchased file folders for $12.13 that are immediately used.
14 Reimbursed Will Nelson, the manager, $9.65 for office supplies purchased and used.
18 Purchased printer paper for $22.54 that is immediately used.
27 Paid $47.10 COD shipping charges on merchandise purchased for resale, terms FOB shipping
point.
28 Paid postage expenses of $16.
30 Reimbursed Nelson $58.80 for business car mileage.
31 Cash of $11.53 remained in the fund. Sorted the petty cash receipts by accounts affected and
exchanged them for a check to reimburse the fund for expenditures.
31 The petty cash fund amount is increased by $50 to a total of $250.

Required

1. Prepare the journal entry to establish the petty cash fund.

2. Prepare a petty cash payments report for March with these categories: delivery expense, mileage expense, postage expense, merchandise inventory (for transportation-in), and office supplies expense. Sort the payments into the appropriate categories and total the expenses in each category.

3. Prepare the journal entries for part 2 to both (*a*) reimburse and (*b*) increase the fund amount.

Check   (2) Total expenses $189.47

(3a & 3b) Total Cr. to Cash
$238.47

The following information is available to reconcile Style Co.'s book balance of cash with its bank statement cash balance as at December 31, 2015.

Problem 8-4B
Prepare a bank reconciliation
and record adjustments

P3

a. The December 31 cash balance according to the accounting records is $31,743.70, and the bank statement cash balance for that date is $45,091.80.

b. Check No. 1273 for $1,084.20 and Check No. 1282 for $390, both written and entered in the accounting records in December, are not among the canceled checks. Two checks, No. 1231 for $2,289 and No. 1242 for $370.50, were outstanding on the most recent November 30 reconciliation. Check No. 1231 is listed with the December canceled checks, but Check No. 1242 is not.

c. When the December checks are compared with entries in the accounting records, it is found that Check No. 1267 had been correctly drawn for $2,435 to pay for office supplies but was erroneously entered in the accounting records as $2,453.

d. Two debit memoranda are enclosed with the statement and are unrecorded at the time of the reconciliation. One debit memorandum is for $749.50 and dealt with an NSF check for $732 received from a customer, Titus Industries, in payment of its account. The bank assessed a $17.50 fee for processing it. The second debit memorandum is a $79 charge for check printing. Style did not record these transactions before receiving the statement.

e. A credit memorandum indicates that the bank collected $20,000 cash on a note receivable for the company, deducted a $20 collection fee, and credited the balance to the company's Cash account. Style did not record this transaction before receiving the statement.

f. Style's December 31 daily cash receipts of $7,666.10 were placed in the bank's night depository on that date, but do not appear on the December 31 bank statement.

Required

1. Prepare the bank reconciliation for this company as at December 31, 2015.

2. Prepare the journal entries necessary to bring the company's book balance of cash into conformity with the reconciled cash balance as at December 31, 2015.

Check   (1) Reconciled balance,
$50,913.20; (2) Cr. Note Receivable
$20,000

Analysis Component

3. Explain the nature of the communications conveyed by a bank when the bank sends the depositor (*a*) a debit memorandum and (*b*) a credit memorandum.

Problem 8-5B
Prepare a bank reconciliation
and record adjustments

P3

Safe Systems most recently reconciled its bank balance on April 30 and reported two checks outstanding at that time, No. 1771 for $781 and No. 1780 for $1,325.90. The following information is available for its May 31, 2015, reconciliation.

From the May 31 Bank Statement

PREVIOUS BALANCE	TOTAL CHECKS AND DEBITS	TOTAL DEPOSITS AND CREDITS	CURRENT BALANCE
18,290.70	12,898.90	16,416.80	21,808.60

CHECKS AND DEBITS			DEPOSITS AND CREDITS		DAILY BALANCE	
Date	No.	Amount	Date	Amount	Date	Amount
05/01	1771	781.00	05/04	2,438.00	04/30	18,290.70
05/02	1783	195.30	05/14	2,898.00	05/01	17,509.70
05/04	1782	1,285.50	05/22	1,801.80	05/02	17,314.40
05/11	1784	1,449.60	05/25	7,200.00 CM	05/04	18,466.90
05/18		431.80 NSF	05/26	2,079.00	05/11	17,017.30
05/25	1787	8,032.50			05/14	19,915.30
05/26	1785	157.20			05/18	19,483.50
05/29	1788	554.00			05/22	21,285.30
05/31		12.00 SC			05/25	20,452.80
					05/26	22,374.60
					05/29	21,820.60
					05/31	21,808.60

From Safe Systems' Accounting Records

Cash Receipts Deposited				Cash Disbursements		
Date		Cash Debit		Check No.		Cash Credit
May	4	2,438.00		1782		1,285.50
	14	2,898.00		1783		195.30
	22	1,801.80		1784		1,449.60
	26	2,079.00		1785		157.20
	31	2,526.30		1786		353.10
		11,743.10		1787		8,032.50
				1788		544.00
				1789		639.50
						12,656.70

Cash						Acct. No. 101
Date		Explanation	PR	Debit	Credit	Balance
Apr.	30	Balance				16,183.80
May	31	Total receipts	R7	11,743.10		27,926.90
	31	Total disbursements	D8		12,656.70	15,270.20

Additional Information

Check No. 1788 is correctly drawn for $554 to pay for May utilities; however, the recordkeeper misread the amount and entered it in the accounting records with a debit to Utilities Expense and a credit to Cash for $544. The bank paid and deducted the correct amount. The NSF check shown in the statement was originally received from a customer, S. Bax, in payment of her account. The company has not yet recorded its return. The credit memorandum is from a $7,300 note that the bank collected for the company. The bank deducted a $100 collection fee and deposited the remainder in the company's account. The collection and fee have not yet been recorded.

Required

1. Prepare the May 31, 2015, bank reconciliation for Safe Systems.
2. Prepare the journal entries to adjust the book balance of cash to the reconciled balance.

Check   (1) Reconciled balance, $22,016.40; (2) Cr. Note Receivable $7,300

Analysis Component

3. The bank statement reveals that some of the prenumbered checks in the sequence are missing. Describe three possible situations to explain this.

(This serial problem began in Chapter 1 and continues through most of the book. If previous chapter segments were not completed, the serial problem can begin at this point.)

SERIAL PROBLEM
Business Solutions

P3

SP 8   Santana Rey receives the March bank statement for Business Solutions on April 11, 2016. The March 31 bank statement shows an ending cash balance of $67,566. A comparison of the bank statement with the general ledger Cash account, No. 101, reveals the following.

a. S. Rey notices that the bank erroneously cleared a $500 check against her account in March that she did not issue. The check documentation included with the bank statement shows that this check was actually issued by a company named Business Systems.

b. On March 25, the bank issued a $50 debit memorandum for the safety deposit box that Business Solutions agreed to rent from the bank beginning March 25.

c. On March 26, the bank issued a $102 debit memorandum for printed checks that Business Solutions ordered from the bank.

d. On March 31, the bank issued a credit memorandum for $33 interest earned on Business Solutions' checking account for the month of March.

e. S. Rey notices that the check she issued for $128 on March 31, 2016, has not yet cleared the bank.

f. S. Rey verifies that all deposits made in March do appear on the March bank statement.

g. The general ledger Cash account, No. 101, shows an ending cash balance per books of $68,057 as at March 31 (prior to any reconciliation).

Required

1. Prepare a bank reconciliation for Business Solutions for the month ended March 31, 2016.
2. Prepare any necessary adjusting entries. Use Miscellaneous Expenses, No. 677, for any bank charges. Use Interest Revenue, No. 404, for any interest earned on the checking account for the month of March.

Check   (1) Adj. bank bal. $67,938

Beyond the Numbers

BTN 8-1   Refer to Nestlé's financial statements in Appendix A to answer the following.

1. For both financial year-ends December 31, 2013, and December 31, 2012, identify the total amount of cash and cash equivalents. Determine the percent this amount represents of total current assets, total current liabilities, total equity, and total assets for both years. Comment on any trends.
2. For financial years ended December 31, 2013, and December 31, 2012, use the information in the consolidated cash flow statement to determine the percent change between the beginning and ending year amounts of cash and cash equivalents.
3. Compute the days' sales uncollected as at December 31, 2013, and December 31, 2012. Has the collection of receivables improved? Are accounts receivable an important asset for Nestlé? Explain.

REPORTING IN ACTION

C2 A1

Fast Forward

4. Access Nestlé's financial statements for financial years ending after December 31, 2013, from its Website (http://www.nestle.com/investors/publications). Recompute its days' sales uncollected for financial years ending after December 31, 2013. Compare this to the days' sales uncollected for 2013 and 2012.

COMPARATIVE ANALYSIS

A1

BTN 8-2 Key comparative figures for both **Samsung** and **Apple** follow.

	Samsung (KRW millions)		Apple (US$ millions)	
	Current Year	Prior Year	Current Year	Prior Year
Accounts receivable	26,674,596	24,153,028	10,930	5,369
Net sales	201,103,613	165,001,771	156,508	108,249

Required

Compute days' sales uncollected for both companies for each of the two years shown. Comment on any trends for the companies. Which company has the largest percent change in days' sales uncollected?

ETHICS CHALLENGE

C1

BTN 8-3 Carol Benton, Sue Knox, and Marcia Diamond work for a family physician, Dr. Gwen Conrad, who is in private practice. Dr. Conrad is knowledgeable about office management practices and has segregated the cash receipt duties as follows. Benton opens the mail and prepares a triplicate list of money received. She sends one copy of the list to Knox, the cashier, who deposits the receipts daily in the bank. Diamond, the recordkeeper, receives a copy of the list and posts payments to patients' accounts. About once a month the office clerks have an expensive lunch they pay for as follows. First, Knox endorses a patient's check in Dr. Conrad's name and cashes it at the bank. Benton then destroys the remittance advice accompanying the check. Finally, Diamond posts payment to the customer's account as a miscellaneous credit. The three justify their actions by their relatively low pay and knowledge that Dr. Conrad will likely never miss the money.

Required

1. Who is the best person in Dr. Conrad's office to reconcile the bank statement?
2. Would a bank reconciliation uncover this office fraud?
3. What are some procedures to detect this type of fraud?
4. Suggest additional internal controls that Dr. Conrad could implement.

COMMUNICATING IN PRACTICE

P5

BTN 8-4[B] Assume you are a business consultant. The owner of a company sends you an e-mail expressing concern that the company is not taking advantage of its discounts offered by vendors. The company currently uses the gross method of recording purchases. The owner is considering a review of all invoices and payments from the previous period. Due to the volume of purchases, however, the owner recognizes that this is time-consuming and costly. The owner seeks your advice about monitoring purchase discounts in the future. Provide a response in memorandum form.

TAKING IT TO THE NET

C1 P1

BTN 8-5 Visit the Association of Certified Fraud Examiners Website at www.acfe.com. Research the fraud facts (see *Fraud Resources* tab) presented at this site and report to your instructor about how the information can help you prepare for your future career.

TEAMWORK IN ACTION

C1

BTN 8-6 Organize the class into teams. Each team must prepare a list of 10 internal controls a consumer could observe in a typical retail department store. When called upon, the team's spokesperson must be prepared to share controls identified by the team that have not been shared by another team's spokesperson.

ENTREPRENEURIAL DECISION

C1 P1

BTN 8-7 Review the opening feature of this chapter that highlights Sam and Forest Leong and their business sam.leong@forest cooking school.

Required

Do you believe that Sam and Forest Leong will need to add controls as their business expands? Explain and suggest some internal controls for them.

BTN 8-8   Visit an area of your college that serves the student community with either products or services. Some examples are food services, libraries, and bookstores. Identify and describe between four and eight internal controls being implemented.

HITTING THE ROAD

C1

BTN 8-9   The following information is from **361 Degrees** (http://ir.361sport.com/html/ir_report.php), which is a Chinese corporation engaged in the manufacturing and trading of sporting goods, including footwear, apparel, and accessories.

GLOBAL DECISION

C2 A1

RMB (in RMB thousands)	Current Year	Prior Year
Inventories	409,358	460,715
Accounts receivable.	1,831,184	1,928,040
Cash and cash equivalents	2,494,280	2,107,018
Current assets	5,816,082	5,932,987
Total assets	7,119,265	7,212,210
Current liabilities.	1,605,653	1,726,168
Total equity	4,740,681	4,730,463
Net sales	3,583,477	4,950,578

Required

1. For each year, compute the percentage that cash and cash equivalents represents of current assets, total assets, current liabilities, and total equity. Comment on any trends in these percentages.
2. Determine the percent change between the current and prior year cash and cash equivalents balances.
3. Compute the days' sales uncollected at the end of both the current year and the prior year. Has the collection of receivables improved? Explain.

ANSWERS TO MULTIPLE CHOICE QUIZ

1. e; The entry follows.

Debits to expenses (or assets)	420	
Cash Over and Short	5	
Cash		425

2. a; recognizes cash collection of note by bank.
3. a; the bank reconciliation follows.

4. d; ($6,720/$84,000) × 365 = 29.2 days
5. b; The entry follows.

Merchandise Inventory*	5,880	
Accounts Payable		5,880

*$6,000 × 98%

Bank Reconciliation November 30			
Balance per bank statement	$1,895	Balance per books	$1,742
Add: Deposit in transit	795	Add: Note collected less fee	320
Deduct: Outstanding checks	(638)	Deduct: Service charge	(10)
Reconciled balance	$2,052	Reconciled balance	$2,052

9

Receivables

A Look Back

Chapter 8 focused on internal control and reporting for cash. We described internal control procedures and the accounting for and management of cash.

A Look at This Chapter

This chapter emphasizes receivables. We explain that they are liquid assets and describe how companies account for and report them. We also discuss the importance of estimating uncollectibles.

A Look Ahead

Chapter 10 focuses on property, plant and equipment, natural resources, and intangible assets. We explain how to account for, report, and analyze these long-term assets.

Learning Objectives

CAP

CONCEPTUAL

C1 Describe accounts receivable and how they occur and are recorded. (p. 360)

C2 Describe a note receivable, the computation of its maturity date, and the recording of its existence. (p. 370)

C3 Explain how receivables can be converted to cash before maturity. (p. 373)

ANALYTICAL

A1 Compute accounts receivable turnover and use it to help assess financial condition. (p. 374)

PROCEDURAL

P1 Apply the direct write-off method to account for accounts receivable. (p. 364)

P2 Apply the allowance method and estimate uncollectibles based on accounts receivable. (p. 367)

P3 Record the honoring and dishonoring of a note and adjustments for interest. (p. 372)

"Boardgames can bring people together."—**COLIN LIM**

Decision Insight

All On Board for Boardgames

It all started, innocuously enough, with an enjoyable pastime. Colin Lim and his five friends used to take turns visiting each other's homes to play boardgames bought with their own money. "While we enjoyed playing, we certainly didn't enjoy cleaning up after each session," recalls Colin with a laugh. The group of friends realized that they had a winning formula for a viable business model—provide a place where gamers could settle down and play without the hassle of cleaning up or buying food and drink. At **Settlers Café** (**www.settlerscafe.com**) clients can take their pick from a huge selection of over 600 different boardgame titles, including Lost Cities, Taboo, Fullhouse, Masterpiece, Guillotine, Management Material, and Cashflow—a very popular game that trains your entrepreneurial mind and financial IQ. Don't know how to play? Not to worry— the friendly, well-trained staff at Settlers is always on hand to help. And last but not least, the café's mouthwatering specials ensure that gamers will never go hungry!

"We want to give our customers the chance to dine and play at the same time, and enjoy our excellent service, all at a reasonable price," says Colin. Colin seldom has to worry about bad debts, as Settlers usually receives payment from customers immediately via cash, NETS (Network for Electronic Transfers), or credit card. For hosting of events or purchase of games, Settlers collects a down payment, and then receives full payment immediately after delivery.

Perhaps as an indication of its sound financial practices, Settlers Café has found itself hosting many financial talks and workshops, as well as seminars, corporate retreats, and career-building exercises. But at the heart of it all is the simple, pure enjoyment that comes from gaming with friends and loved ones. "Knowing that we are promoting a healthy and somewhat 'rare' form of entertainment brings us much satisfaction," says Colin. "We love to see the smiles on our customers' faces when they leave after a gaming session!"

This chapter focuses on accounts receivable and short-term notes receivable. We describe each of these assets, their uses, and how they are accounted for and reported in financial statements. This knowledge helps us use accounting information to make better business decisions. It can also help in predicting future company performance and financial condition as well as in managing one's own business.

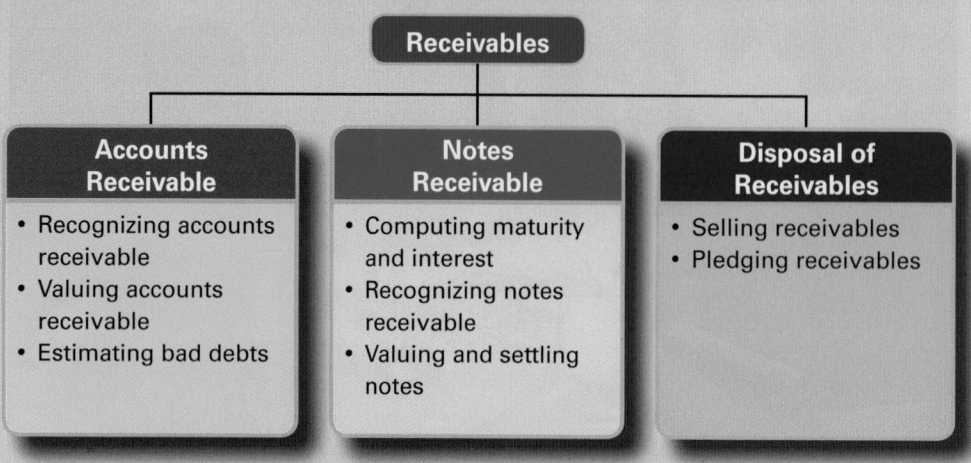

Receivables

Accounts Receivable	Notes Receivable	Disposal of Receivables
• Recognizing accounts receivable • Valuing accounts receivable • Estimating bad debts	• Computing maturity and interest • Recognizing notes receivable • Valuing and settling notes	• Selling receivables • Pledging receivables

ACCOUNTS RECEIVABLE

A *receivable* is an amount due from another party. The two most common receivables are accounts receivable and notes receivable. Other receivables include interest receivable, rent receivable, tax refund receivable, and receivables from employees. **Accounts receivable** are amounts due from customers for credit sales. This section begins by describing how accounts receivable occur. It includes receivables that occur when customers use credit cards issued by third parties and when a company gives credit directly to customers. When a company does extend credit directly to customers, it (1) maintains a separate account receivable for each customer and (2) accounts for bad debts from credit sales.

Recognizing Accounts Receivable

C1	Describe accounts receivable and how they occur and are recorded.

Accounts receivable occur from credit sales to customers. The amount of credit sales has increased in recent years, reflecting several factors including an efficient financial system. Retailers such as **Carrefour** (France), **TESCO** (U.K.), **Walmart** (U.S.), and **GOME** (China) hold certain amounts in accounts or trade receivables. Exhibit 9.1 shows their recent currency amounts of accounts receivables as percents of their total assets.

EXHIBIT 9.1

Accounts Receivable for Selected Companies

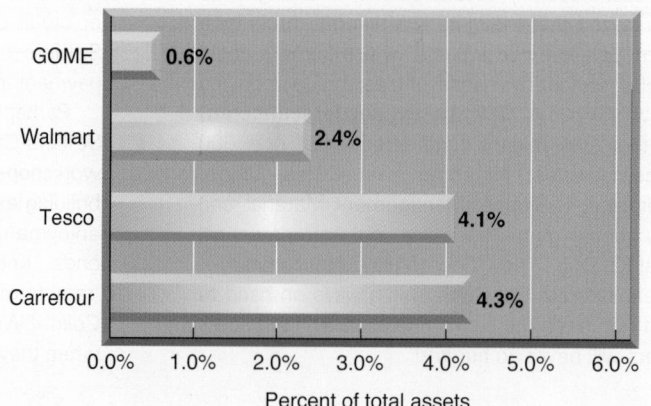

Percent of total assets

Sales on Credit   Credit sales are recorded by increasing (debiting) Accounts Receivable. A company must also maintain a separate account for each customer that tracks how much that customer purchases, has already paid, and still owes. This information provides the basis for sending bills to customers and for other business analyses. To maintain this information, companies that extend credit directly to their customers keep a separate account receivable for each one of them. The general ledger continues to have a single Accounts Receivable account along with the other financial statement accounts, but a supplementary record is created to maintain a separate account for each customer. This supplementary record is called the *accounts receivable ledger*.

Exhibit 9.2 shows the relation between the Accounts Receivable account in the general ledger and its individual customer accounts in the accounts receivable ledger for TechCom, a small electronics wholesaler. This exhibit reports a $3,000 ending balance of TechCom's accounts receivable for June 30. TechCom's transactions are mainly in cash, but it has two major credit customers: CompStore and RDA Electronics. Its *schedule of accounts receivable* shows that the $3,000 balance of the Accounts Receivable account in the general ledger equals the total of its two customers' balances in the accounts receivable ledger.

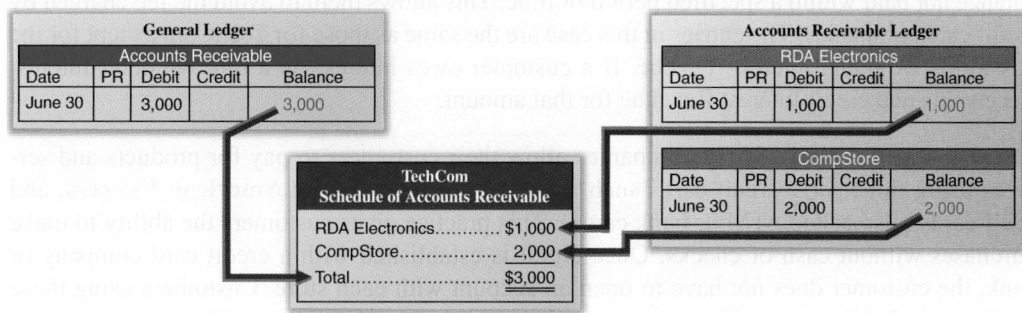

EXHIBIT 9.2

General Ledger and the Accounts Receivable Ledger (before July 1 transactions)

To see how accounts receivable from credit sales are recognized in the accounting records, we look at two transactions on July 1 between TechCom and its credit customers—see Exhibit 9.3. The first is a credit sale of $950 to CompStore. A credit sale is posted with both a debit to the Accounts Receivable account in the general ledger and a debit to the customer account in the accounts receivable ledger. The second transaction is a collection of $720 from RDA Electronics from a prior credit sale. Cash receipts from a credit customer are posted with a credit to the Accounts Receivable account in the general ledger and flow through to credit the customer account in the accounts receivable ledger. (Posting debits or credits to Accounts Receivable in two separate ledgers does not violate the requirement that debits equal credits. The equality of debits and credits is maintained in the general ledger. The accounts receivable ledger is a *supplementary* record providing information on each customer.)

EXHIBIT 9.3

Accounts Receivable Transactions

July 1	Accounts Receivable—CompStore	950	
	Sales		950
	*To record credit sales**		
July 1	Cash	720	
	Accounts Receivable—RDA Electronics		720
	To record collection of credit sales.		

Assets = Liabilities + Equity
+ 950   +950

Assets = Liabilities + Equity
+720
−720

* We omit the entry to Dr. Cost of Sales and Cr. Merchandise Inventory to focus on sales and receivables.

Exhibit 9.4 shows the general ledger and the accounts receivable ledger after recording the two July 1 transactions. The general ledger shows the effects of the sale, the collection, and the resulting balance of $3,230. These events are also reflected in the individual customer accounts: RDA Electronics has an ending balance of $280, and CompStore's ending balance is $2,950.

The $3,230 sum of the individual accounts equals the debit balance of the Accounts Receivable account in the general ledger.

EXHIBIT 9.4

General Ledger and
the Accounts Receivable Ledger
(after July 1 transactions)

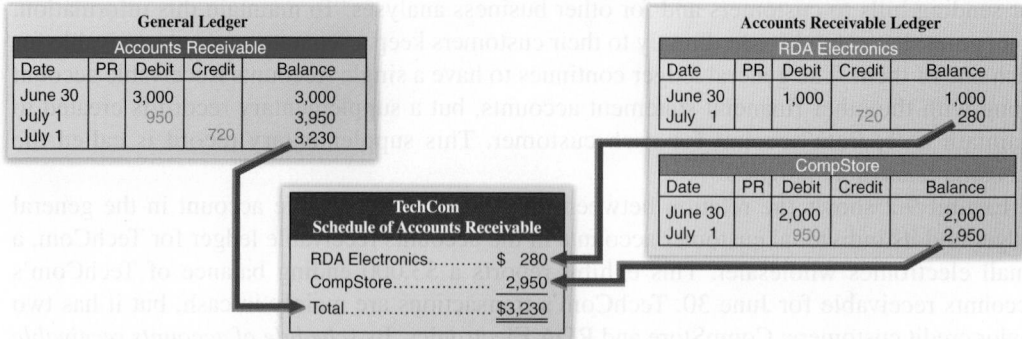

General Ledger				
Accounts Receivable				
Date	PR	Debit	Credit	Balance
June 30		3,000		3,000
July 1		950		3,950
July 1			720	3,230

Accounts Receivable Ledger				
RDA Electronics				
Date	PR	Debit	Credit	Balance
June 30		1,000		1,000
July 1			720	280
CompStore				
Date	PR	Debit	Credit	Balance
June 30		2,000		2,000
July 1		950		2,950

TechCom
Schedule of Accounts Receivable

RDA Electronics............	$ 280
CompStore..................	2,950
Total..........................	$3,230

Like TechCom, many large retailers such as **Tesco** and **Walmart** sell on credit. Many also maintain their own credit cards to grant credit to approved customers and to earn interest on any balance not paid within a specified period of time. This allows them to avoid the fee charged by credit card companies. The entries in this case are the same as those for TechCom except for the possibility of added interest revenue. If a customer owes interest on a bill, we debit Interest Receivable and credit Interest Revenue for that amount.

Point: Visa USA now transacts more than $1 trillion from its credit, debit, and prepaid cards.

Credit Card Sales   Many companies allow their customers to pay for products and services using third-party credit cards such as **Visa**, **MasterCard**, or **American Express**, and debit cards (also called ATM or bank cards). This practice gives customers the ability to make purchases without cash or checks. Once credit is established with a credit card company or bank, the customer does not have to open an account with each store. Customers using these cards can make single monthly payments instead of several payments to different creditors and can defer their payments.

Many sellers allow customers to use third-party credit cards and debit cards instead of granting credit directly for several reasons. First, the seller does not have to evaluate each customer's credit standing or make decisions about who gets credit and how much. Second, the seller avoids the risk of extending credit to customers who cannot or do not pay. This risk is transferred to the card company. Third, the seller typically receives cash from the card company sooner than had it granted credit directly to customers. Fourth, a variety of credit options for customers offers a potential increase in sales volume. In addition to their own credit cards, most retail companies permit customers to charge purchases to third-party credit card companies such as Visa, MasterCard, and American Express in a desire to increase sales.

There are guidelines in how companies account for credit card and debit card sales. Some credit cards, but nearly all debit cards, credit a seller's Cash account immediately upon deposit. In this case the seller deposits a copy of each card sales receipt in its bank account just as it deposits a customer's check. The majority of credit cards, however, require the seller to remit a copy (often electronically) of each receipt to the card company. Until payment is received, the seller has an account receivable from the card company. In both cases, the seller pays a fee for services provided by the card company, often ranging from 1% to 5% of card sales. This charge is deducted from the credit to the seller's account or the cash payment to the seller.

Decision Insight

Debit Card vs. Credit Card   A buyer's debit card purchase reduces the buyer's cash account balance at the card company, which is often a bank. Since the buyer's cash account balance is a liability (with a credit balance) for the card company to the buyer, the card company would debit that account for a buyer's purchase—hence, the term *debit card*. A credit card reflects authorization by the card company of a line of credit for the buyer with preset interest rates and payment terms—hence, the term *credit card*. Most card companies waive interest charges if the buyer pays its balance each month. ■

The procedures used in accounting for credit card sales depend on whether cash is received immediately on deposit or cash receipt is delayed until the credit card company makes the payment.

Cash Received Immediately on Deposit   To illustrate, if TechCom has $100 of credit card sales with a 4% fee, and its $96 cash is received immediately on deposit, the entry is

July 15	Cash	96	
	Credit Card Expense	4	
	Sales		100
	*To record credit card sales less a 4% credit card expense.**		

Assets = Liabilities + Equity
+96   +100
                          −4

* We omit the entry to Dr. Cost of Sales and Cr. Merchandise Inventory to focus on credit card expense.

Cash Received Some Time after Deposit   However, if instead TechCom must remit electronically the credit card sales receipts to the credit card company and wait for the $96 cash payment, the entry on the date of sale is

July 15	**Accounts Receivable—Credit Card Co.**	96	
	Credit Card Expense	4	
	Sales		100
	*To record credit card sales less 4% credit card expense.**		

Assets = Liabilities + Equity
+96   +100
                          −4

* We omit the entry to Dr. Cost of Sales and Cr. Merchandise Inventory to focus on credit card expense.

When cash is later received from the credit card company, usually through electronic funds transfer, the entry is

July 20	Cash	96	
	Accounts Receivable—Credit Card Co.		96
	To record cash receipt.		

Assets = Liabilities + Equity
+96
−96

Some firms report credit card expense in the income statement as a type of discount deducted from sales to get net sales. Other companies classify it as a selling expense or even as an administrative expense. Arguments can be made for each approach.

Point: Third-party credit card costs can be large. JCPenney reported third-party credit card costs exceeding $10 million.

Installment Sales and Receivables   Many companies allow their credit customers to make periodic payments over several months. For example, **Ford Motor Company** reports more than $75 billion in installment receivables. The seller refers to such assets as *installment accounts* (or *finance*) *receivable,* which are amounts owed by customers from credit sales for which payment is required in periodic amounts over an extended time period. Source documents for installment accounts receivable include sales slips or invoices describing the sales transactions. The customer is usually charged interest. Although installment accounts receivable can have credit periods of more than one year, they are classified as current assets if the seller regularly offers customers such terms.

Decision Maker   Answer — p. 377

Entrepreneur   As a small retailer, you are considering allowing customers to buy merchandise using credit cards. Until now, your store accepted only cash and checks. What analysis do you use to make this decision? ∎

Quick Check   Answers — p. 378

1. In recording credit card sales, when do you debit Accounts Receivable and when do you debit Cash?

2. A company accumulates sales receipts and remits them to the credit card company for payment. When are the credit card expenses recorded? When are these expenses incurred?

Valuing Accounts Receivable—Direct Write-Off Method

When a company directly grants credit to its customers, it expects that some customers will not pay what they promised. The accounts of these customers are *uncollectible accounts,* commonly called **bad debts.** The total amount of uncollectible accounts is an expense of selling on credit. Why do companies sell on credit if they expect some accounts to be uncollectible? The answer is that companies believe that granting credit will increase total sales and net profit enough to offset bad debts. Companies use two methods to account for uncollectible accounts: (1) direct write-off method and (2) allowance method. We describe both.

Point: Managers realize that some portion of credit sales will be uncollectible, but which credit sales are uncollectible is unknown.

Recording and Writing Off Bad Debts The **direct write-off method** of accounting for bad debts records the loss from an uncollectible account receivable when it is determined to be uncollectible. No attempt is made to predict bad debts expense. To illustrate, if Tech-Com determines on January 23 that it cannot collect $520 owed to it by its customer J. Kent, it recognizes the loss using the direct write-off method as follows:

Assets = Liabilities + Equity
−520   −520

Jan. 23	Bad Debts Expense	520	
	Accounts Receivable—J. Kent.		520
	To write off an uncollectible account.		

The debit in this entry charges the uncollectible amount directly to the current period's Bad Debts Expense account. The credit removes its balance from the Accounts Receivable account in the general ledger (and its subsidiary ledger).

Point: If a customer fails to pay within the credit period, most companies send out repeated billings and make other efforts to collect.

Recovering a Bad Debt Although uncommon, sometimes an account written off is later collected. This can be due to factors such as continual collection efforts or a customer's good fortune. If the account of J. Kent that was written off directly to Bad Debts Expense is later collected in full, the following two entries record this recovery.

Assets = Liabilities + Equity
+520   +520

Assets = Liabilities + Equity
+520
−520

Mar. 11	Accounts Receivable—J. Kent.	520	
	Bad Debts Expense		520
	To reinstate account previously written off.		
Mar. 11	Cash	520	
	Accounts Receivable—J. Kent		520
	To record full payment of account.		

Assessing the Direct Write-Off Method Strictly speaking, the direct write-off method may not be in line with **IFRS** for reasons explained in the next section on the allowance method. It is discussed here because (1) it is useful in illustrating the superiority of the allowance method, and (2) in practice, some companies use it under circumstances that do not lend themselves to the allowance method.

Valuing Accounts Receivable—Allowance Method

The IASB's Conceptual Framework states that the concept of probability is used in the recognition criteria to refer to the degree of uncertainty that the future economic benefits associated with the item will flow to or from the entity. For example, when it is probable that a receivable owed to an entity will be paid, it is then justifiable to recognize the receivable as an asset. For a large population of receivables, however, some degree of nonpayment is normally considered probable; hence an expense representing the expected reduction in economic benefits is recognized.

The **allowance method** achieves the measurement of such assets.[1] Such a method of accounting for bad debts has two advantages over the direct write-off method: (1) it records estimated bad debts expense in the period when the related sales are recorded, and (2) it reports accounts receivable on the statement of financial position at the estimated amount of cash to be collected.

Recording Bad Debts Expense   The allowance method estimates bad debts expense at the end of each accounting period and records it with an adjusting entry. TechCom, for instance, had credit sales of $300,000 during its first year of operations. At the end of the first year, $20,000 of credit sales remained uncollected. Based on the experience of similar businesses, TechCom estimated that $1,500 of its accounts receivable would be uncollectible. This estimated expense is recorded with the following adjusting entry.

Dec. 31	Bad Debts Expense	1,500	
	Allowance for Doubtful Accounts..............		1,500
	To record estimated bad debts.		

Assets = Liabilities + Equity
−1,500   −1,500

The estimated Bad Debts Expense of $1,500 is reported on the income statement (as either a selling expense or an administrative expense) and offsets the $300,000 credit sales it helped produce. The **Allowance for Doubtful Accounts** is a contra asset account. A contra account is used instead of reducing accounts receivable directly because at the time of the adjusting entry, the company does not know which customers will not pay. After the bad debts adjusting entry is posted, TechCom's account balances (in T-account form) for Accounts Receivable and its Allowance for Doubtful Accounts are as shown in Exhibit 9.5.

Point: Credit approval is usually not assigned to the selling dept. because its goal is to increase sales, and it may approve customers at the cost of increased bad debts. Instead, approval is assigned to a separate credit-granting or administrative dept.

Accounts Receivable			**Allowance for Doubtful Accounts**		
Dec. 31	20,000			Dec. 31	1,500

EXHIBIT 9.5

General Ledger Entries after Bad Debts Adjusting Entry

The Allowance for Doubtful Accounts credit balance of $1,500 has the effect of reducing accounts receivable to its expected cash collections. Although credit customers owe $20,000 to TechCom, only $18,500 is expected to be collected as cash. The original $20,000 can be referred to as the **gross accounts receivable,** and the $18,500 can be referred to as the **net accounts receivable,** the **realizable value,** or the **carrying amount**. In the statement of financial position, the Allowance for Doubtful Accounts is subtracted from Accounts Receivable and is often reported as shown in Exhibit 9.6.

Point: Bad Debts Expense is also called *Uncollectible Accounts Expense.* The Allowance for Doubtful Accounts is also called *Allowance for Uncollectible Accounts.*

Current assets		
Accounts receivable.............................	$20,000	
Less allowance for doubtful accounts	1,500	$18,500

EXHIBIT 9.6

Statement of Financial Position Presentation of the Allowance for Doubtful Accounts

---

[1] *IAS 39* states that financial assets are recognized initially at fair values and are subsequently measured at amortized cost using the effective interest method less provision for impaired receivables. If there is objective evidence that an impairment loss on financial assets measured at amortized cost has been incurred, the amount of the loss is measured as the difference between the asset's carrying amount and the present value of estimated future cash flows discounted at the financial asset's original effective interest rate. The carrying amount of the asset shall be reduced either directly or through use of an allowance account. The amount of the loss shall be recognized in profit or loss. Cash flows relating to short-term receivables are not discounted if the effect of discounting is immaterial.

Sometimes the Allowance for Doubtful Accounts is not reported separately. This alternative presentation is shown in Exhibit 9.7.

Current assets	
Accounts receivable (net of $1,500 doubtful accounts)	$18,500

Writing Off a Bad Debt   When specific accounts are identified as uncollectible, they are written off against the Allowance for Doubtful Accounts. To illustrate, TechCom decides that J. Kent's $520 account is uncollectible and makes the following entry to write it off.

Assets = Liabilities + Equity
+520
−520

Jan. 23	Allowance for Doubtful Accounts	520	
	Accounts Receivable—J. Kent.		520
	To write off an uncollectible account.		

Point: The Bad Debts Expense account is not debited in the write-off entry because it was recorded in the period when sales occurred.

Posting this write-off entry to the Accounts Receivable account removes the amount of the bad debt from the general ledger (it is also posted to the accounts receivable subsidiary ledger). The general ledger accounts now appear as in Exhibit 9.8 (assuming no other transactions affecting these accounts).

EXHIBIT 9.8

General Ledger Entries after Write-Off

Accounts Receivable					Allowance for Doubtful Accounts			
Dec. 31	20,000						Dec. 31	1,500
		Jan. 23	520		Jan. 23	520		

Point: In posting a write-off, the ledger's Explanation column indicates the reason for this credit so it is not misinterpreted as payment in full.

The write-off does *not* affect the realizable value of accounts receivable as shown in Exhibit 9.9. Neither total assets nor net profit is affected by the write-off of a specific account. Instead, both assets and net profit are affected in the period when bad debts expense is predicted and recorded with an adjusting entry.

EXHIBIT 9.9

Realizable Value before and after Write-Off of a Bad Debt

	Before Write-Off	After Write-Off
Accounts receivable	$ 20,000	$ 19,480
Less allowance for doubtful accounts	1,500	980
Estimated realizable accounts receivable	**$18,500**	**$18,500**

Recovering a Bad Debt   When a customer fails to pay and the account is written off as uncollectible, his or her credit standing is jeopardized. To help restore credit standing, a customer sometimes volunteers to pay all or part of the amount owed. A company makes two entries when collecting an account previously written off by the allowance method. The first is to reverse the write-off and reinstate the customer's account. The second entry records the collection of the reinstated account. To illustrate, if on March 11 Kent pays in full his account previously written off, the entries are

Assets = Liabilities + Equity
+520
−520

Assets = Liabilities + Equity
+520
−520

Mar. 11	Accounts Receivable—J. Kent.	520	
	Allowance for Doubtful Accounts.		520
	To reinstate account previously written off.		
Mar. 11	Cash	520	
	Accounts Receivable—J. Kent.		520
	To record full payment of account.		

Example: If TechCom used a collection agency and paid a 35% commission on $520 collected from Kent, how is this recorded? *Answer:*
Cash 338
Collection Expense 182
   Accts. Recble.—J. Kent 520

In this illustration, Kent paid the entire amount previously written off, but sometimes a customer pays only a portion of the amount owed. A question then arises as to whether the entire balance of the account or just the amount paid is returned to accounts receivable. This is a matter of judgment. If we believe this customer will later pay in full, we return the entire amount owed to accounts receivable, but if we expect no further collection, we return only the amount paid.

Decision Update

Accounting for Receivables   Receivables are included as financial assets in **IAS 39** *Financial Instruments*, which states that financial assets are impaired and impairment losses are incurred if, and only if, there is objective evidence of impairment as a result of one or more loss events that occurred after the initial recognition of the asset having an impact on the estimated future cash flows of the financial assets that can be reliably estimated. Examples of loss events are:

- significant financial difficulty of the debtor, including probable bankruptcy
- adverse changes in national or local economic conditions that affect the debtors.

The current practice may be changed by **IFRS 9** *Financial Instruments*, which should replace **IAS 39**. The current effective date for implementation of **IFRS 9** is January 1, 2015. The impairment requirements for short-term trade receivables are still in the process of being re-deliberated by the IASB. However, it has been decided that short-term receivables should be considered together with the measurement of revenue (which is also the initial measurement of an accounts receivable) as part of the IASB's project on revenue recognition. ∎

Estimating Bad Debts—Percent of Receivables Method

The *accounts receivable methods,* also referred to as *statement of financial position methods,* use statement of financial position relations to estimate bad debts—mainly the relation between accounts receivable and the allowance amount. The goal of the bad debts adjusting entry for these methods is to make the Allowance for Doubtful Accounts balance equal to the portion of accounts receivable that is estimated to be uncollectible. The estimated balance for the allowance account is obtained in one of two ways: (1) computing the percent uncollectible from the total accounts receivable or (2) aging accounts receivable.

The *percent of accounts receivable method* assumes that a given percent of a company's receivables is uncollectible. This percent is based on past experience and is impacted by current conditions such as economic trends and customer difficulties. The total dollar amount of all receivables is multiplied by this percent to get the estimated dollar amount of uncollectible accounts—reported in the statement of financial position as the Allowance for Doubtful Accounts.

To illustrate, assume that Musicland has $50,000 of accounts receivable on December 31, 2015. Experience suggests 5% of its receivables is uncollectible. This means that *after* the adjusting entry is posted, we want the Allowance for Doubtful Accounts to show a $2,500 credit balance (5% of $50,000). We are also told that its beginning balance is $2,200, which is 5% of the $44,000 accounts receivable on December 31, 2014—see Exhibit 9.10.

P2 Apply the allowance method and estimate uncollectibles based on accounts receivable.

Point: When using an accounts receivable method for estimating uncollectibles, the allowance account balance is adjusted to equal the estimate of uncollectibles.

EXHIBIT 9.10

Allowance for Doubtful Accounts after Bad Debts Adjusting Entry

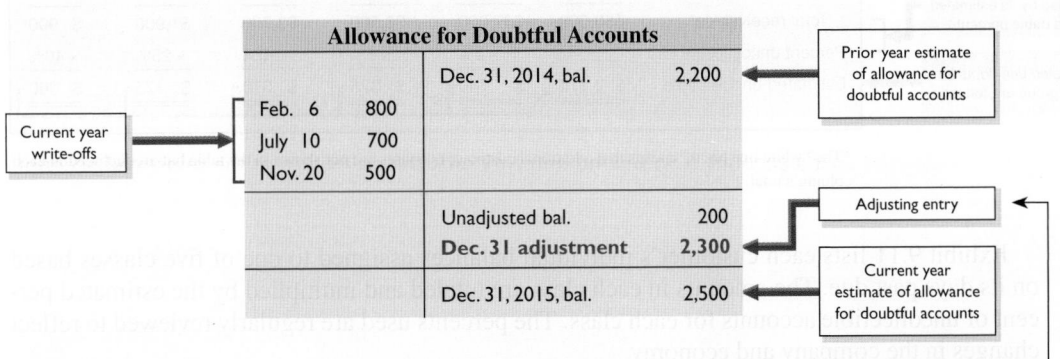

During 2015, accounts of customers are written off on February 6, July 10, and November 20. Thus, the account has a $200 credit balance *before* the December 31, 2015, adjustment. The adjusting entry to give the allowance account the estimated $2,500 balance is

Dec. 31	Bad Debts Expense	2,300	
	Allowance for Doubtful Accounts		2,300
	To record estimated bad debts.		

Assets = Liabilities + Equity
−2,300   −2,300

Aging Pains Experience shows that the longer a receivable is past due, the lower is the likelihood of its collection. An *aging schedule* uses this knowledge to estimate bad debts. The chart here is from a survey that reported estimates of bad debts for receivables grouped by how long they were past their due dates. Each company sets its own estimates based on its customers and its experiences with those customers' payment patterns. ■

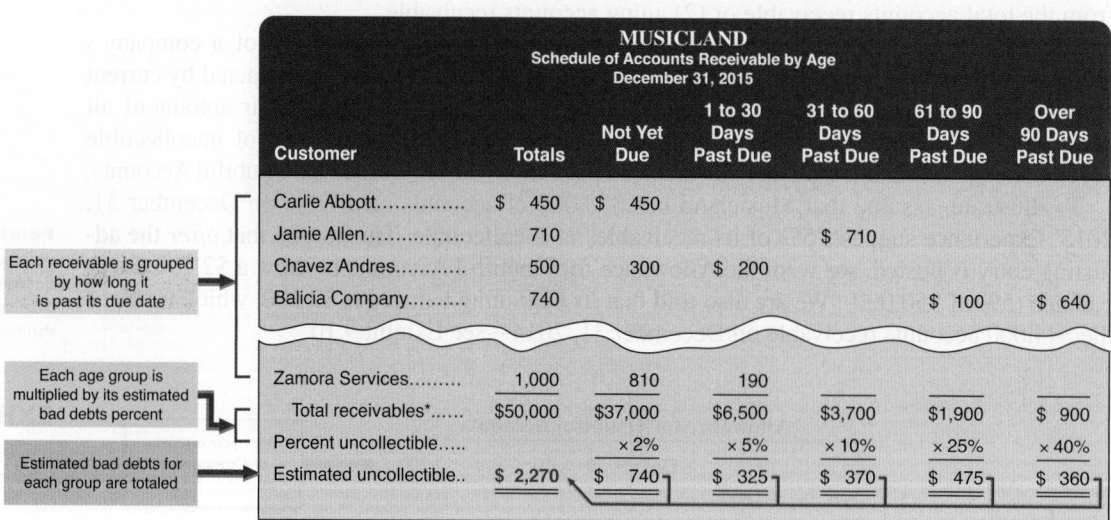

Estimating Bad Debts—Aging of Receivables Method

The **aging of accounts receivable** method uses both past and current receivables information to estimate the allowance amount. Specifically, each receivable is classified by how long it is past its due date. Then estimates of uncollectible amounts are made assuming that the longer an amount is past due, the more likely it is to be uncollectible. Classifications are often based on 30-day periods. After the amounts are classified (or aged), experience is used to estimate the percent of each uncollectible class. These percents are applied to the amounts in each class and then totaled to get the estimated balance of the Allowance for Doubtful Accounts. This computation is performed by setting up a schedule such as Exhibit 9.11.

EXHIBIT 9.11

Aging of Accounts Receivable

MUSICLAND
Schedule of Accounts Receivable by Age
December 31, 2015

Customer	Totals	Not Yet Due	1 to 30 Days Past Due	31 to 60 Days Past Due	61 to 90 Days Past Due	Over 90 Days Past Due
Carlie Abbott...............	$ 450	$ 450				
Jamie Allen.................	710			$ 710		
Chavez Andres............	500	300	$ 200			
Balicia Company..........	740				$ 100	$ 640
Zamora Services.........	1,000	810	190			
Total receivables*......	$50,000	$37,000	$6,500	$3,700	$1,900	$ 900
Percent uncollectible.....		× 2%	× 5%	× 10%	× 25%	× 40%
Estimated uncollectible..	$ 2,270	$ 740	$ 325	$ 370	$ 475	$ 360

Each receivable is grouped by how long it is past its due date

Each age group is multiplied by its estimated bad debts percent

Estimated bad debts for each group are totaled

*The "white line break" means that additional customer accounts are not shown in the table but are included in each column's total.

Exhibit 9.11 lists each customer's individual balances assigned to one of five classes based on its days past due. The amounts in each class are totaled and multiplied by the estimated percent of uncollectible accounts for each class. The percents used are regularly reviewed to reflect changes in the company and economy.

To explain, Musicland has $3,700 in accounts receivable that are 31 to 60 days past due. Its management estimates 10% of the amounts in this age class are uncollectible, or a total of $370 (computed as $3,700 × 10%). Similar analysis is done for each of the other four classes. The final

EXHIBIT 9.12

Computation of the Required Adjustment for the Accounts Receivable Method

Unadjusted balance	$ 200 credit
Estimated balance	2,270 credit
Required adjustment	**$2,070 credit**

total of $2,270 ($740 + $325 + 370 + $475 + $360) shown in the first column is the estimated balance for the Allowance for Doubtful Accounts. Exhibit 9.12 shows that since the allowance account has an unadjusted credit balance of $200, the required adjustment to the Allowance for Doubtful Accounts is $2,070. (We could also use a T-account for this analysis as shown in the margin.) This yields the following end-of-period adjusting entry.

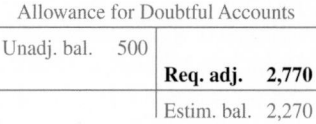

Allowance for Doubtful Accounts	
	Unadj. bal. 200
	Req. adj. 2,070
	Estim. bal. 2,270

Dec. 31	Bad Debts Expense	2,070	
	Allowance for Doubtful Accounts		2,070
	To record estimated bad debts.		

Assets = Liabilities + Equity
−2,070   −2,070

Alternatively, if the allowance account had an unadjusted *debit* balance of $500 (instead of the $200 credit balance), its required adjustment would be computed as follows. (Again, a T-account can be used for this analysis as shown in the margin.)

Point: A debit balance implies that write-offs for that period exceed the total allowance.

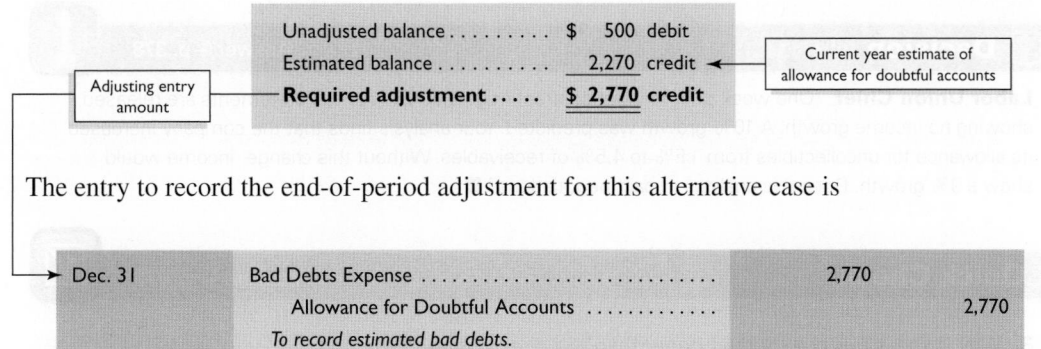

Unadjusted balance.........	$ 500 debit
Estimated balance..........	2,270 credit ← Current year estimate of allowance for doubtful accounts
Required adjustment	**$ 2,770 credit**

Adjusting entry amount

Allowance for Doubtful Accounts	
Unadj. bal. 500	
	Req. adj. 2,770
	Estim. bal. 2,270

The entry to record the end-of-period adjustment for this alternative case is

Dec. 31	Bad Debts Expense	2,770	
	Allowance for Doubtful Accounts		2,770
	To record estimated bad debts.		

Assets = Liabilities + Equity
−2,770   −2,770

The aging of accounts receivable method is an examination of specific accounts and is usually the most reliable of the estimation methods.

Allowance for Doubtful Accounts	
Debit balance when the total amount of accounts receivable written off is greater than the estimated allowance. Must adjust to become a credit balance before preparing the financial statements.	**Credit balance** when the total amount of accounts receivable written off is less than the estimated allowance. This is the normal balance for this account.

EXHIBIT 9.13

Total Accounts Receivable Written Off During a Period Will Rarely Equal the Estimated Allowance

Individual and Group Estimation of Bad Debts

Assessment of impairment losses for financial assets can be categorized into three types:

(a) Assessment at the "individual" asset level for all individually significant items.

(b) For individually non-significant items, the entity has a choice either to assess it individually or collectively for a group of assets with similar credit risk features.

(c) Collective assessment of impairment for items where no individual impairment exists but forms part of a group of assets with similar credit characteristics.

We illustrate these ideas to receivables using the example below.

At the beginning of the period, GlobeCom has a credit balance of $1,700 in its allowance for doubtful accounts. At the end of the period, GlobeCom has gross accounts receivable of $71,200. There was objective evidence that 10% of a $6,000 debt owed by a debtor, Island-Com, would most probably be uncollectible. The rest of the accounts receivables were reviewed collectively, and the results indicated that an estimated 2% of these accounts would not be collectible.

The required ending balance in the allowance for doubtful accounts is calculated as 10% × $6,000 + 2% × ($71,200 − $6,000) = $1,904. Since we already have a beginning balance of $1,700, we need to credit another $204.

The estimated expense is recorded with the following adjusting entry.

Dec. 31	Bad Debts Expense	204	
	Allowance for Doubtful Accounts		204
	To record estimated bad debts.		

Reversal of Bad Debts

If, in a subsequent period, an objective event occurs (such as an improvement in the debtor's credit rating) which results in a decrease in the allowance, the previously recognized amount can be reversed by adjusting the allowance account. However, the reversal amount cannot exceed the amount recorded previously. The reduction in the allowance is accompanied by a reversal of the expense to profit.

 **Decision Maker**   Answer —p. 378

Labor Union Chief   One week prior to labor contract negotiations, financial statements are released showing no income growth. A 10% growth was predicted. Your analysis finds that the company increased its allowance for uncollectibles from 1.5% to 4.5% of receivables. Without this change, income would show a 9% growth. Does this analysis impact negotiations? ■

Quick Check   Answers — p. 378

3. Why is the allowance method better than the direct write-off method?

4. What is the difference between gross accounts receivable and net accounts receivable?

5. Why is estimated bad debts expense credited to a contra account (Allowance for Doubtful Accounts) rather than to the Accounts Receivable account?

6. SnoBoard Company's year-end balance in its Allowance for Doubtful Accounts is a credit of $440. By aging accounts receivable, it estimates that $6,142 is uncollectible. Prepare SnoBoard's year-end adjusting entry for bad debts.

7. Record entries for these transactions assuming the allowance method is used:

   Jan. 10   The $300 account of customer Cool Jam is determined uncollectible.

   April 12   Cool Jam unexpectedly pays in full the account deemed uncollectible on Jan. 10.

NOTES RECEIVABLE

C2 Describe a note receivable, the computation of its maturity date, and the recording of its existence.

A **promissory note** is a written promise to pay a specified amount of money, usually with interest, either on demand or at a definite future date. Promissory notes are used in many transactions, including paying for products and services, and lending and borrowing money. Sellers sometimes ask for a note to replace an account receivable when a customer requests additional time to pay a past-due account. For legal reasons, sellers generally prefer to receive notes when the credit period is long and when the receivable is for a large amount. If a lawsuit is needed to collect from a customer, a note is the buyer's written acknowledgment of the debt, its amount, and its terms.

Exhibit 9.14 shows a simple promissory note dated July 10, 2015. For this note, Julia Browne promises to pay TechCom or to its order (according to TechCom's instructions) a specified amount of money ($1,000), called the **principal of a note,** at a definite future date (October 8, 2015). As the one who signed the note and promised to pay it at maturity, Browne is the **maker of the note.** As the person to whom the note is payable, TechCom is the **payee of the note.** To Browne, the note is a liability called a *note payable*. To TechCom, the same note is an asset called a *note receivable*. This note bears interest at 12%, as written on the note. **Interest** is the charge for using the money until its due date. To a borrower, interest is an expense. To a lender, it is revenue.

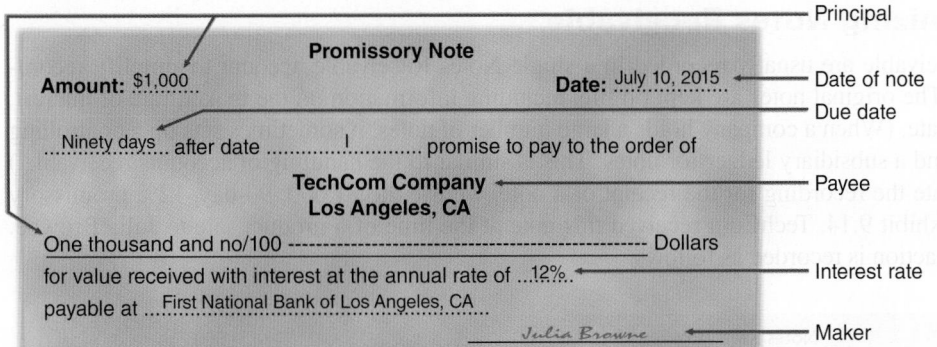

EXHIBIT 9.14
Promissory Note

Computing Maturity and Interest

This section describes key computations for notes including the determination of maturity date, period covered, and interest computation.

Maturity Date and Period   The **maturity date of a note** is the day the note (principal and interest) must be repaid. The *period* of a note is the time from the note's (contract) date to its maturity date. Many notes mature in less than a full year, and the period they cover is often expressed in days. When the time of a note is expressed in days, its maturity date is the specified number of days after the note's date. As an example, a five-day note dated June 15 matures and is due on June 20. A 90-day note dated July 10 matures on October 8. This October 8 due date is computed as shown in Exhibit 9.15. The period of a note is sometimes expressed in months or years. When months are used, the note matures and is payable in the month of its maturity on the *same day of the month* as its original date. A nine-month note dated July 10, for instance, is payable on April 10. The same analysis applies when years are used.

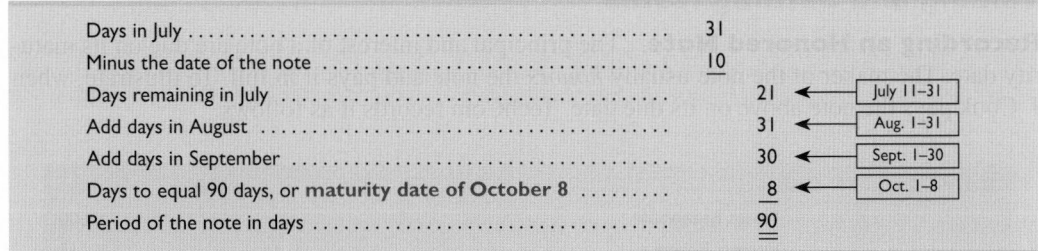

EXHIBIT 9.15

Maturity Date Computation

Days in July	31	
Minus the date of the note	10	
Days remaining in July	21 ←	July 11–31
Add days in August	31 ←	Aug. 1–31
Add days in September	30 ←	Sept. 1–30
Days to equal 90 days, or **maturity date of October 8**	8 ←	Oct. 1–8
Period of the note in days	90	

Interest Computation   *Interest* is the cost of borrowing money for the borrower or, alternatively, the profit from lending money for the lender. Unless otherwise stated, the rate of interest on a note is the rate charged for the use of the principal for one year. The formula for computing interest on a note is shown in Exhibit 9.16.

$$\boxed{\begin{array}{ccccccc} \textbf{Principal} & & \textbf{Annual} & & \textbf{Time expressed} & & \\ \textbf{of the note} & \times & \textbf{interest rate} & \times & \textbf{in fraction of year} & = & \textbf{Interest} \end{array}}$$

EXHIBIT 9.16

Computation of Interest Formula

To simplify interest computations, a year is commonly treated as having 360 days (called the *banker's rule* in the business world and widely used in commercial transactions). **We treat a year as having 360 days for interest computations in the examples and assignments.** Using the promissory note in Exhibit 9.14 where we have a 90-day, 12%, $1,000 note, the total interest is computed as follows.

$$\$1,000 \times 12\% \times \frac{90}{360} = \$1,000 \times 0.12 \times 0.25 = \$30$$

Recognizing Notes Receivable

Notes receivable are usually recorded in a single Notes Receivable account to simplify record-keeping. The original notes are kept on file, including information on the maker, rate of interest, and due date. (When a company holds a large number of notes, it sometimes sets up a controlling account and a subsidiary ledger for notes. This is similar to the handling of accounts receivable.) To illustrate the recording for the receipt of a note, we use the $1,000, 90-day, 12% promissory note in Exhibit 9.14. TechCom received this note at the time of a product sale to Julia Browne. This transaction is recorded as follows.

Assets = Liabilities + Equity
+1,000   +1,000

July 10*	Notes Receivable	1,000	
	Sales		1,000
	Sold goods in exchange for a 90-day, 12% note.		

* We omit the entry to Dr. Cost of Sales and Cr. Merchandise Inventory to focus on sales and receivables.

When a seller accepts a note from an overdue customer as a way to grant a time extension on a past-due account receivable, it will often collect part of the past-due balance in cash. This partial payment forces a concession from the customer, reduces the customer's debt (and the seller's risk), and produces a note for a smaller amount. To illustrate, assume that TechCom agreed to accept $232 in cash along with a $600, 60-day, 15% note from Jo Cook to settle her $832 past-due account. TechCom made the following entry to record receipt of this cash and note.

Point: Notes receivable often are a major part of a company's assets. Likewise, notes payable often are a large part of a company's liabilities.

Assets = Liabilities + Equity
+232
+600
−832

Oct. 5	Cash	232	
	Notes Receivable	600	
	Accounts Receivable—J. Cook		832
	Received cash and note to settle account.		

Valuing and Settling Notes

P3 Record the honoring and dishonoring of a note and adjustments for interest.

Recording an Honored Note   The principal and interest of a note are due on its maturity date. The maker of the note usually *honors* the note and pays it in full. To illustrate, when J. Cook pays the note above on its due date, TechCom records it as follows.

Assets = Liabilities + Equity
+615   +15
−600

Dec. 4	Cash	615	
	Notes Receivable		600
	Interest Revenue		15
	Collect note with interest of $600 × 15% × 60/360.		

Interest Revenue, also called *Interest Earned,* is reported on the income statement.

Recording a Dishonored Note   When a note's maker is unable or refuses to pay at maturity, the note is *dishonored.* The act of dishonoring a note does not relieve the maker of the obligation to pay. The payee should use every legitimate means to collect. How do companies report this event? The balance of the Notes Receivable account should include only those notes that have not matured. Thus, when a note is dishonored, we remove the amount of this note from the Notes Receivable account and charge it back to an account receivable from its maker. To illustrate, TechCom holds an $800, 12%, 60-day note of Greg Hart. At maturity, Hart dishonors the note. TechCom records this dishonoring of the note as follows.

Point: When posting a dishonored note to a customer's account, an explanation is included so as not to misinterpret the debit as a sale on account.

Assets = Liabilities + Equity
+816   +16
−800

Oct. 14	Accounts Receivable—G. Hart	816	
	Interest Revenue		16
	Notes Receivable		800
	To charge account of G. Hart for a dishonored note and interest of $800 × 12% × 60/360.		

Charging a dishonored note back to the account of its maker serves two purposes. First, it removes the amount of the note from the Notes Receivable account and records the dishonored note in the maker's account. Second, and more important, if the maker of the dishonored note applies for credit in the future, his or her account will reveal all past dealings, including the dishonored note. Restoring the account also reminds the company to continue collection efforts from Hart for both principal and interest. The entry records the full amount, including interest, to ensure that it is included in collection efforts.

Point: Reporting the details of notes is consistent with the **full disclosure principle,** which requires financial statements (including footnotes) to report all relevant information.

Recording End-of-Period Interest Adjustment   When notes receivable are outstanding at the end of a period, any accrued interest earned is computed and recorded. To illustrate, on December 16, TechCom accepts a $3,000, 60-day, 12% note from a customer in granting an extension on a past-due account. When TechCom's accounting period ends on December 31, $15 of interest has accrued on this note ($3,000 × 12% × 15/360). The following adjusting entry records this revenue.

Dec. 31	Interest Receivable	15	
	Interest Revenue		15
	To record accrued interest earned.		

Assets = Liabilities + Equity
+15   +15

Interest Revenue appears on the income statement, and Interest Receivable appears on the statement of financial position as a current asset. When the December 16 note is collected on February 14, TechCom's entry to record the cash receipt is

Feb. 14	Cash	3,060	
	Interest Revenue		45
	Interest Receivable		15
	Notes Receivable		3,000
	Received payment of note and its interest.		

Assets = Liabilities + Equity
+3,060   +45
−15
−3,000

Total interest earned on the 60-day note is $60. The $15 credit to Interest Receivable on February 14 reflects the collection of the interest accrued from the December 31 adjusting entry. The $45 interest earned reflects TechCom's revenue from holding the note from January 1 to February 14 of the current period.

Quick Check

Answers — p. 378

8. Irwin purchases $7,000 of merchandise from Stamford on December 16, 2015. Stamford accepts Irwin's $7,000, 90-day, 12% note as payment. Stamford's accounting period ends on December 31, and it does not make reversing entries. Prepare entries for Stamford on December 16, 2015, and December 31, 2015.

9. Using the information in Quick Check 8, prepare Stamford's March 16, 2016, entry if Irwin dishonors the note.

DISPOSAL OF RECEIVABLES

Companies can convert receivables to cash before they are due. Reasons for this include the need for cash or the desire not to be involved in collection activities. Converting receivables is usually done either by (1) selling them or (2) using them as security for a loan. A recent survey shows that about 20% of companies obtain cash from either selling receivables or pledging them as security. In some industries such as textiles, apparel and furniture, this is common practice.

C3 Explain how receivables can be converted to cash before maturity.

Selling Receivables

A company can sell all or a portion of its receivables to a finance company or bank. The buyer, called a *factor,* charges the seller a *factoring fee* and then the buyer takes ownership of the receivables and receives cash when they come due. By incurring a factoring fee, the seller receives cash earlier and can pass the risk of bad debts to the factor. The seller can also choose to avoid costs of billing and accounting for the receivables. To illustrate, if TechCom sells $20,000 of its accounts receivable and is charged a 4% factoring fee, it records this sale as follows.

Global: Firms in export sales increasingly sell their receivables to factors.

Assets = Liabilities + Equity
+19,200   −800
−20,000

Aug. 15	Cash	19,200	
	Factoring Fee Expense	800	
	Accounts Receivable		20,000
	Sold accounts receivable for cash, less 4% fee.		

The accounting for sales of notes receivable is similar to that for accounts receivable. The detailed entries are covered in advanced courses.

Pledging Receivables

A company can raise cash by borrowing money and *pledging* its receivables as security for the loan. Pledging receivables does not transfer the risk of bad debts to the lender because the borrower retains ownership of the receivables. If the borrower defaults on the loan, the lender has a right to be paid from the cash receipts of the receivable when collected. To illustrate, when TechCom borrows $35,000 and pledges its receivables as security, it records this transaction as follows.

Assets = Liabilities + Equity
+35,000   +35,000

Aug. 20	Cash	35,000	
	Notes Payable		35,000
	Borrowed money with a note secured by pledging receivables.		

Since pledged receivables are committed as security for a specific loan, the borrower's financial statements disclose the pledging of them. TechCom, for instance, includes the following note with its statements: Accounts receivable of $40,000 are pledged as security for a $35,000 note payable.

Decision Insight

What's the Proper Allowance? How can we assess whether a company has properly estimated its allowance for uncollectibles? One way is to compute the ratio of the allowance account to the gross accounts receivable. When this ratio is analyzed over several consecutive periods, trends often emerge that reflect on the adequacy of the allowance amount. ■

Decision Analysis   Accounts Receivable Turnover

A1 Compute accounts receivable turnover and use it to help assess financial condition.

For a company selling on credit, we want to assess both the quality and liquidity of its accounts receivable. *Quality* of receivables refers to the likelihood of collection without loss. Experience shows that the longer receivables are outstanding beyond their due date, the lower the likelihood of collection. *Liquidity* of receivables refers to the speed of collection. **Accounts receivable turnover** is a measure of both the quality and liquidity of accounts receivable. It indicates how often, on average, receivables are received and collected during the period. The formula for this ratio is shown in Exhibit 9.17.

EXHIBIT 9.17

Accounts Receivable Turnover

$$\text{Accounts receivable turnover} = \frac{\text{Net sales}}{\text{Average accounts receivable, net}}$$

We prefer to use net *credit* sales in the numerator because cash sales do not create receivables. However, since financial statements rarely report net credit sales, our analysis uses net sales. The denominator is the *average* accounts receivable balance, computed as (Beginning balance + Ending balance) ÷ 2. TechCom has an accounts receivable turnover of 5.1. This indicates its average accounts receivable balance is converted into cash 5.1 times during the period. Exhibit 9.18 shows graphically this turnover activity for TechCom.

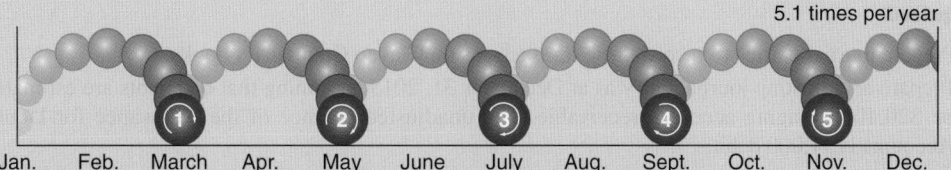

5.1 times per year

| Jan. | Feb. | March | Apr. | May | June | July | Aug. | Sept. | Oct. | Nov. | Dec. |

EXHIBIT 9.18

Rate of Accounts Receivable Turnover for TechCom

Accounts receivable turnover also reflects how well management is doing in granting credit to customers in a desire to increase sales. A high turnover in comparison with competitors suggests that management should consider using more liberal credit terms to increase sales. A low turnover suggests management should consider stricter credit terms and more aggressive collection efforts to avoid having its resources tied up in accounts receivable.

To illustrate, we take data from two major retailers: **Carrefour** (France) and **Tesco** (United Kingdom) Exhibit 9.19 shows accounts receivable turnover for both companies.

Point: Credit risk ratio is computed by dividing the Allowance for Doubtful Accounts by Accounts Receivable. The higher this ratio, the higher is credit risk.

Company	Figure (currency millions)	2007	2008	2009	2010	2011
Carrefour	Net sales	82,149	86,967	85,963	80,511	81,271
	Average accounts receivable	3,522	3,172	2,697	2,397	2,669
	Accounts receivable turnover	23.3	27.4	31.9	33.6	30.4
Tesco	Net sales	42,641	47,298	54,327	56,910	60,931
	Average accounts receivable	986	1,195	1,555	1,843	2,101
	Accounts receivable turnover	43.2	39.6	34.9	30.9	29.0

EXHIBIT 9.19

Analysis Using Accounts Receivable Turnover

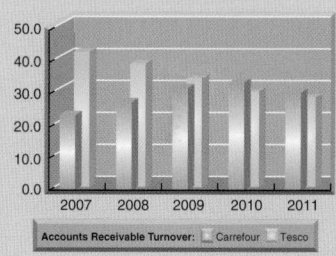

Even though the reporting currency of each company is different (Carrefour in Euro and Tesco in British Pound), by converting the amounts in ratios, the performance can be compared. Carrefour's 2011 turnover is computed as $81,271/2,669 = 30.4$. This means that Carrefour's average accounts receivable balance was converted into cash 30.4 times in 2011. Its turnover deteriorated in 2011 (versus its previous two years) and has overtaken Tesco's, which has been continually decreasing over the five-year period.

 **Decision** Maker   Answer — p. 378

Family Physician   Your medical practice is barely profitable, so you hire a health care analyst. The analyst highlights several points including the following: *"Accounts receivable turnover is too low. Tighter credit policies are recommended along with discontinuing service to those most delayed in payments."* How do you interpret these recommendations? What actions do you take? ∎

DEMONSTRATION PROBLEM

Clayco Company completes the following selected transactions during year 2015.

July 14   Writes off a $750 account receivable arising from a sale to Briggs Company that dates to 10 months ago. (Clayco Company uses the allowance method.)

　　 30   Clayco Company receives a $1,000, 90-day, 10% note in exchange for merchandise sold to Sumrell Company (the merchandise cost $600).

Aug. 15   Receives $2,000 cash plus a $10,000 note from JT Co. in exchange for merchandise that sells for $12,000 (its cost is $8,000). The note is dated August 15, bears 12% interest, and matures in 120 days.

Nov. 1   Completed a $200 credit card sale with a 4% fee (the cost of sales is $150). The cash is received immediately from the credit card company.

　　 3   Sumrell Company refuses to pay the note that was due to Clayco Company on October 28. Prepare the journal entry to charge the dishonored note plus accrued interest to Sumrell Company's accounts receivable.

　　 5   Completed a $500 credit card sale with a 5% fee (the cost of sales is $300). The payment from the credit card company is received on Nov. 9.

　　 15   Received the full amount of $750 from Briggs Company that was previously written off on July 14. Record the bad debts recovery.

Dec. 13   Received payment of principal plus interest from JT for the August 15 note.

Required

1. Prepare journal entries to record these transactions on Clayco Company's books.
2. Prepare an adjusting journal entry as at December 31, 2015, assuming that bad debts are estimated to be $20,400 by aging accounts receivable. The unadjusted balance of the Allowance for Doubtful Accounts is $1,000 debit.

PLANNING THE SOLUTION

- Examine each transaction to determine the accounts affected, and then record the entries.
- For the year-end adjustment, record the bad debts expense for the two approaches.

SOLUTION TO DEMONSTRATION PROBLEM

1.

July 14	Allowance for Doubtful Accounts	750	
	Accounts Receivable—Briggs Co.		750
	Wrote off an uncollectible account.		
July 30	Notes Receivable—Sumrell Co.	1,000	
	Sales		1,000
	Sold merchandise for a 90-day, 10% note.		
July 30	Cost of Goods Sold	600	
	Merchandise Inventory		600
	To record the cost of July 30 sale.		
Aug. 15	Cash	2,000	
	Notes Receivable—JT Co.	10,000	
	Sales		12,000
	Sold merchandise to customer for $2,000 cash and $10,000 note.		
Aug. 15	Cost of Goods Sold	8,000	
	Merchandise Inventory		8,000
	To record the cost of Aug. 15 sale.		
Nov. 1	Cash	192	
	Credit Card Expense	8	
	Sales		200
	To record credit card sale less a 4% credit card expense.		
Nov. 1	Cost of Goods Sold	150	
	Merchandise Inventory		150
	To record the cost of Nov. 1 sale.		
Nov. 3	Accounts Receivable—Sumrell Co.	1,025	
	Interest Revenue		25
	Notes Receivable—Sumrell Co.		1,000
	To charge account of Sumrell Company for a $1,000 dishonored note and interest of $1,000 × 10% × 90/360.		
Nov. 5	Accounts Receivable—Credit Card Co.	475	
	Credit Card Expense	25	
	Sales		500
	To record credit card sale less a 5% credit card expense.		
Nov. 5	Cost of Goods Sold	300	
	Merchandise Inventory		300
	To record the cost of Nov. 5 sale.		
Nov. 9	Cash	475	
	Accounts Receivable—Credit Card Co.		475
	To record cash receipt from Nov. 5 sale.		
Nov. 15	Accounts Receivable—Briggs Co.	750	
	Allowance for Doubtful Accounts		750
	To reinstate the account of Briggs Company previously written off.		

Nov. 15	Cash	750	
	Accounts Receivable—Briggs Co.		750
	Cash received in full payment of account.		
Dec. 13	Cash	10,400	
	Interest Revenue		400
	Note Receivable—JT Co.		10,000
	Collect note with interest of		
	$10,000 × 12% × 120/360.		

2. Aging of accounts receivable method.

Dec. 31	Bad Debts Expense	21,400	
	Allowance for Doubtful Accounts..............		21,400
	To adjust allowance account from a $1,000		
	debit balance to a $20,400 credit balance.		

Summary

C1 **Describe accounts receivable and how they occur and are recorded.** Accounts receivable are amounts due from customers for credit sales. A subsidiary ledger lists amounts owed by each customer. Credit sales arise from at least two sources: (1) sales on credit and (2) credit card sales. *Sales on credit* refers to a company's granting credit directly to customers. Credit card sales involve customers' use of third-party credit cards.

C2 **Describe a note receivable, the computation of its maturity date, and the recording of its existence.** A note receivable is a written promise to pay a specified amount of money at a definite future date. The maturity date is the day the note (principal and interest) must be repaid. Interest rates are normally stated in annual terms. The amount of interest on the note is computed by expressing time as a fraction of one year and multiplying the note's principal by this fraction and the annual interest rate. A note received is recorded at its principal amount by debiting the Notes Receivable account. The credit amount is to the asset, product, or service provided in return for the note.

C3 **Explain how receivables can be converted to cash before maturity.** Receivables can be converted to cash before maturity in three ways. First, a company can sell accounts receivable to a factor, who charges a factoring fee. Second, a company can borrow money by signing a note payable that is secured by pledging the accounts receivable. Third, notes receivable can be discounted at (sold to) a financial institution.

A1 **Compute accounts receivable turnover and use it to help assess financial condition.** Accounts receivable turnover is a measure of both the quality and liquidity of accounts receivable.

The accounts receivable turnover measure indicates how often, on average, receivables are received and collected during the period. Accounts receivable turnover is computed as net sales divided by average accounts receivable.

P1 **Apply the direct write-off method to account for accounts receivable.** The direct write-off method charges Bad Debts Expense when accounts are written off as uncollectible. This method is acceptable only when the amount of bad debts expense is immaterial.

P2 **Apply the allowance method and estimate uncollectibles based on accounts receivable.** Under the allowance method, bad debts expense is recorded with an adjustment at the end of each accounting period that debits the Bad Debts Expense account and credits the Allowance for Doubtful Accounts. The uncollectible accounts are later written off with a debit to the Allowance for Doubtful Accounts. Uncollectibles are estimated by focusing on the statement of financial position relation between accounts receivable and the allowance for doubtful accounts. This should be done at individual and group receivables levels.

P3 **Record the honoring and dishonoring of a note and adjustments for interest.** When a note is honored, the payee debits the money received and credits both Notes Receivable and Interest Revenue. Dishonored notes are credited to Notes Receivable and debited to Accounts Receivable (to the account of the maker in an attempt to collect), and Interest Revenue is recorded for interest earned for the time the note is held.

Guidance Answers to Decision Maker and Decision Ethics

Entrepreneur   Analysis of credit card sales should weigh the benefits against the costs. The primary benefit is the potential to increase sales by attracting customers who prefer the convenience

of credit cards. The primary cost is the fee charged by the credit card company for providing this service. Analysis should therefore estimate the expected increase in dollar sales from allowing credit card sales and then subtract (1) the normal costs and expenses and (2) the credit card fees associated with this expected increase in dollar sales. If your analysis shows an increase in profit from allowing credit card sales, your store should probably accept them.

Labor Union Chief   Yes, this information is likely to impact your negotiations. The obvious question is why the company markedly increased this allowance. The large increase in this allowance means a substantial increase in bad debts expense *and* a decrease in earnings. This change (coming immediately prior to labor contract discussions) also raises concerns since it reduces the union's bargaining power for increased compensation. You want to ask management for supporting documentation justifying this increase. You also want data for two or three prior years and similar data from

competitors. These data should give you some sense of whether the change in the allowance for uncollectibles is justified.

Family Physician   The recommendations are twofold. First, the analyst suggests more stringent screening of patients' credit standing. Second, the analyst suggests dropping patients who are most overdue in payments. You are likely bothered by both suggestions. They are probably financially wise recommendations, but you are troubled by eliminating services to those less able to pay. One alternative is to follow the recommendations while implementing a care program directed at patients less able to pay for services. This allows you to continue services to patients less able to pay and lets you discontinue services to patients able but unwilling to pay.

Guidance Answers to Quick Checks

1. If cash is immediately received when credit card sales receipts are deposited, the company debits Cash at the time of sale. If the company does not receive payment until after it submits receipts to the credit card company, it debits Accounts Receivable at the time of sale. (Cash is later debited when payment is received from the credit card company.)

2. Credit card expenses are usually *recorded* and *incurred* at the time of their related sales, not when cash is received from the credit card company.

3. The allowance method is better than the direct write-off method because: (1) it records estimated bad debts expense in the period when the related sales are recorded, and (2) it reports accounts receivable on the statement of financial position at the estimated amount of cash to be collected.

4. The sales amount can be referred to as the **gross accounts receivable**, and that amount after deducting the allowance for doubtful accounts can be referred to as the **net accounts receivable**, the **realizable value**, or the **carrying amount**.

5. The estimated amount of bad debts expense cannot be credited to the Accounts Receivable account because the specific customer accounts that will prove uncollectible cannot yet be identified and removed from the accounts receivable subsidiary ledger. Moreover, if only the Accounts Receivable account is credited, its balance would not equal the sum of its subsidiary account balances.

6.

Dec. 31	Bad Debts Expense	5,702	
	Allowance for Doubtful Accounts		5,702

7.

Jan. 10	Allowance for Doubtful Accounts	300	
	Accounts Receivable—Cool Jam		300
Apr. 12	Accounts Receivable—Cool Jam	300	
	Allowance for Doubtful Accounts		300
Apr. 12	Cash	300	
	Accounts Receivable—Cool Jam		300

8.

Dec. 16	Note Receivable—Irwin	7,000	
	Sales		7,000
Dec. 31	Interest Receivable	35	
	Interest Revenue		35
	($7,000 × 12% × 15/360)		

9.

Mar. 16	Accounts Receivable—Irwin	7,210	
	Interest Revenue		175
	Interest Receivable		35
	Notes Receivable—Irwin		7,000

Key Terms   www.mheducation.asia/olc/wildkwokFAP

Accounts receivable (p. 360)

Accounts receivable turnover (p. 374)

Aging of accounts receivable (p. 368)

Allowance for Doubtful Accounts (p. 365)

Allowance method (p. 365)

Bad debts (p. 364)

Direct write-off method (p. 364)

Interest (p. 370)

Maker of the note (p. 370)

Maturity date of a note (p. 371)

Payee of the note (p. 370)

Principal of a note (p. 370)

Promissory note (or note) (p. 370)

Realizable value (p. 365)

Multiple Choice Quiz   Answers on p. 390   www.mheducation.asia/olc/wildkwokFAP

Additional Quiz Questions are available at the book's Website.

1. A company's Accounts Receivable balance at its December 31 year-end is $125,650, and its Allowance for Doubtful Accounts has a credit balance of $328 before year-end adjustment. Its net sales are $572,300. It estimates that 4% of outstanding accounts receivable are uncollectible. What amount of Bad Debts Expense is recorded at December 31?
   a. $5,354
   b. $328
   c. $5,026
   d. $4,698
   e. $34,338

2. A company's Accounts Receivable balance at its December 31 year-end is $489,300, and its Allowance for Doubtful Accounts has a debit balance of $554 before year-end adjustment. Its net sales are $1,300,000. It estimates that 6% of outstanding accounts receivable are uncollectible. What amount of Bad Debts Expense is recorded at December 31?
   a. $29,912
   b. $28,804
   c. $78,000
   d. $29,358
   e. $554

3. Total interest to be earned on a $7,500, 5%, 90-day note is
   a. $93.75
   b. $375.00
   c. $1,125.00
   d. $31.25
   e. $125.00

4. A company receives a $9,000, 8%, 60-day note. The maturity value of the note is
   a. $120
   b. $9,000
   c. $9,120
   d. $720
   e. $9,720

5. A company has net sales of $489,600 and average accounts receivable of $40,800. What is its accounts receivable turnover?
   a. 0.08
   b. 30.41
   c. 1,341.00
   d. 12.00
   e. 111.78

🔲 Icon denotes assignments that involve decision making.

Discussion Questions

1. 🔲 How do sellers benefit from allowing their customers to use credit cards?
2. Explain the difference between a debit card and a credit card.
3. 🔲 Why do companies sell on credit if they expect some accounts to be uncollectible?
4. Explain why writing off a bad debt against the Allowance for Doubtful Accounts does not reduce the estimated realizable value of a company's accounts receivable.
5. 🔲 Why does the Bad Debts Expense account usually not have the same adjusted balance as the Allowance for Doubtful Accounts?
6. Why might a business prefer a note receivable to an account receivable?
7. 🔲 Refer to Nestlé's consolidated balance sheet in Appendix A. In its presentation of "trade and other receivables," Nestlé does not mention uncollectible accounts, nor does it list its receivables as "net." Where would you find the information to ascertain that Nestlé does account for uncollectibles?

8. 🔲 Refer to Adidas' consolidated statement of financial position in Appendix A. Given that the amount reported on the statement of financial position for accounts receivable are net amounts and the allowance for 2013 is EUR 120 million, what is Adidas' gross accounts receivable as at December 31, 2013? What percentage of its accounts receivable does Adidas believe to be uncollectible as at December 31, 2013?
9. Refer to Samsung's consolidated statement of financial position in Appendix A. Given that the amount reported on the statement of financial position for accounts receivable are net amounts and the allowance for 2012 is KRW 276,787 million, what is Samsung's gross accounts receivable as at December 31, 2012? What percentage of its accounts receivable does Samsung believe to be uncollectible as at December 31, 2012?
10. Refer to 361 Degrees' statement of financial position from its Website http://ir.361sport.com/html/ir_report.php. What does it title its accounts receivable?

connect

QUICK STUDY

Prepare journal entries for the following credit card sales transactions (the company uses the perpetual inventory system).

QS 9-1
Credit card sales
C1

1. Sold $10,000 of merchandise, that cost $7,500, on MasterCard credit cards. The net cash receipts from sales are immediately deposited in the seller's bank account. MasterCard charges a 5% fee.

2. Sold $3,000 of merchandise, that cost $1,500, on an assortment of credit cards. Net cash receipts are received 7 days later, and a 4% fee is charged.

QS 9-2
Allowance method for bad debts
P2

Milner Corp. uses the allowance method to account for uncollectibles. On October 31, it wrote off a $1,000 account of a customer, C. Schaub. On December 9, it receives a $200 payment from Schaub.

1. Prepare the journal entry or entries for October 31.

2. Prepare the journal entry or entries for December 9; assume no additional money is expected from Schaub.

QS 9-3
Percent of accounts receivable method
P2

Wecker Company's year-end unadjusted trial balance shows accounts receivable of $89,000, allowance for doubtful accounts of $500 (credit), and sales of $270,000. Uncollectibles are estimated to be 1.5% of accounts receivable.

1. Prepare the December 31 year-end adjusting entry for uncollectibles.

2. What amount would have been used in the year-end adjusting entry if the allowance account had a year-end unadjusted debit balance of $200?

QS 9-4
Note receivable   C2

On August 2, 2015, JLK Co. receives a $5,500, 90-day, 12% note from customer Tom Menke as payment on his $9,000 account. (1) Compute the maturity date for this note. (2) Prepare JLK's journal entry for August 2.

QS 9-5
Note receivable   P3

Refer to the information in QS 9-4 and prepare the journal entry assuming the note is honored by the customer on October 31, 2015.

QS 9-6
Note receivable   P3

Dekon Company's December 31 year-end unadjusted trial balance shows a $8,000 balance in Notes Receivable. This balance is from one 6% note dated December 1, with a period of 45 days. Prepare any necessary journal entries for December 31 and for the note's maturity date assuming it is honored.

QS 9-7
Disposing receivables   C3

Record the sale by Kroll Company of $1,000 in accounts receivable on May 1. Kroll is charged a 3% factoring fee.

QS 9-8
Direct write-off method   P1

Krugg Company determines on May 1 that it cannot collect $1,000 of its accounts receivable from its customer P. Carroll. Apply the direct write-off method to record this loss as at May 1.

QS 9-9
Recovering a bad debt   P1

Refer to the information in QS 9-8. On May 30, P. Carroll unexpectedly paid his account in full to Krugg Company. Record Krugg's entry(ies) to reflect this recovery of this bad debt.

QS 9-10
Accounts receivable turnover
A1

The following data are taken from the comparative statement of financial positions of Fulton Company. Compute and interpret its accounts receivable turnover for year 2015 (competitors average a turnover of 7.5).

	2015	2014
Accounts receivable, net	$152,900	$133,700
Net sales	754,200	810,600

connect

Petri Company uses the perpetual inventory system and allows customers to use two credit cards in charging purchases. With the Omni Bank Card, Petri receives an immediate credit to its account when it deposits sales receipts. Omni assesses a 4% service charge for credit card sales. The second credit card that Petri accepts is the Continental Card. Petri sends its accumulated receipts to Continental on a weekly basis and is paid by Continental about a week later. Continental assesses a 2.5% charge on sales for using its card. Prepare journal entries to record the following selected credit card transactions of Petri Company.

Apr. 8   Sold merchandise for $9,200 (that had cost $6,800) and accepted the customer's Omni Bank Card. The Omni receipts are immediately deposited in Petri's bank account.
   12   Sold merchandise for $5,400 (that had cost $3,500) and accepted the customer's Continental Card. Transferred $5,400 of credit card receipts to Continental, requesting payment.
   20   Received Continental's check for the April 12 billing, less the service charge.

Exercise 9-1
Accounting for credit card sales
C1

Sami Company recorded the following selected transactions during November 2015.

Nov. 5	Accounts Receivable—Surf Shop	4,417	
	Sales		4,417
10	Accounts Receivable—Yum Enterprises	1,250	
	Sales		1,250
13	Accounts Receivable—Matt Albin	733	
	Sales		733
21	Sales Returns and Allowances	189	
	Accounts Receivable—Matt Albin		189
30	Accounts Receivable—Surf Shop	2,606	
	Sales		2,606

1. Open a general ledger having T-accounts for Accounts Receivable, Sales, and Sales Returns and Allowances. Also open an accounts receivable subsidiary ledger having a T-account for each customer. Post these entries to both the general ledger and the accounts receivable ledger.
2. Prepare a schedule of accounts receivable (see Exhibit 9.4) and compare its total with the balance of the Accounts Receivable controlling account as at November 30.

Exercise 9-2
Accounts receivable subsidiary ledger; schedule of accounts receivable
C1

Check   Accounts Receivable ending balance, $8,817

Diablo Company applies the direct write-off method in accounting for uncollectible accounts. Prepare journal entries to record the following selected transactions of Diablo.

June 11   Diablo determines that it cannot collect $9,000 of its accounts receivable from its customer Chaffey Company.
   29   Chaffey Company unexpectedly pays its account in full to Diablo Company. Diablo records its recovery of this bad debt.

Exercise 9-3
Direct write-off method
P1

At each calendar year-end, Cabool Supply Co. uses the percent of accounts receivable method to estimate bad debts. On December 31, 2015, it has outstanding accounts receivable of $53,000, and it estimates that 4% will be uncollectible. Prepare the adjusting entry to record bad debts expense for year 2015 under the assumption that the Allowance for Doubtful Accounts has (a) a $915 credit balance before the adjustment and (b) a $1,332 debit balance before the adjustment.

Exercise 9-4
Percent of accounts receivable method
P2

Hecter Company estimates uncollectible accounts using the allowance method at December 31. It prepared the following aging of receivables analysis.

Exercise 9-5
Aging of receivables method
P2

			Days Past Due			
	Total	0	1 to 30	31 to 60	61 to 90	Over 90
Accounts receivable	$190,000	$132,000	$30,000	$12,000	$6,000	$10,000
Percent uncollectible		1%	2%	4%	7%	12%

a. Estimate the balance of the Allowance for Doubtful Accounts using the aging of accounts receivable method.

b. Prepare the adjusting entry to record Bad Debts Expense using the estimate from part *a*. Assume the unadjusted balance in the Allowance for Doubtful Accounts is a $600 credit.

c. Prepare the adjusting entry to record Bad Debts Expense using the estimate from part *a*. Assume the unadjusted balance in the Allowance for Doubtful Accounts is a $400 debit.

Exercise 9-6
Percent of receivables method
P2

Refer to the information in Exercise 9-5 to complete the following requirements.

a. Estimate the balance of the Allowance for Doubtful Accounts assuming the company uses 3.5% of total accounts receivable to estimate uncollectibles, instead of the aging of receivables method.

b. Prepare the adjusting entry to record Bad Debts Expense using the estimate from part *a*. Assume the unadjusted balance in the Allowance for Doubtful Accounts is a $300 credit.

c. Prepare the adjusting entry to record Bad Debts Expense using the estimate from part *a*. Assume the unadjusted balance in the Allowance for Doubtful Accounts is a $200 debit.

Exercise 9-7
Writing off receivables
P2

Refer to the information in Exercise 9-5 to complete the following requirements.

a. On February 1 of the next period, the company determined that $1,900 in customer accounts is uncollectible; specifically, $400 for Oxford Co. and $1,500 for Brookes Co. Prepare the journal entry to write off those accounts.

b. On June 5 of that next period, the company unexpectedly received a $400 payment on a customer account, Oxford Company, that had previously been written off in part *a*. Prepare the entries necessary to reinstate the account and to record the cash received.

Exercise 9-8
Estimating bad debts
P2

At December 31, GreenTea Company reports the following results for its calendar year.

Cash sales	$1,200,000
Credit sales	900,000

Its year-end unadjusted trial balance includes the following items.

Accounts receivable	$195,000 debit
Allowance for doubtful accounts	3,000 debit

Check Dr. Bad Debts Expense: $15,100

There was objective evidence that 10% of a $10,000 debt owed by a debtor, Black Coffee Company, would most probably be uncollectible. The rest of the accounts receivables were reviewed collectively and the results indicated that an estimated 6% of these accounts would not be collectible. Prepare the adjusting entry to record Bad Debts Expense.

Exercise 9-9
Selling and pledging accounts receivable
C3

On June 30, Roman Co. has $125,900 of accounts receivable. Prepare journal entries to record the following selected July transactions. Also prepare any footnotes to the July 31 financial statements that result from these transactions. (The company uses the perpetual inventory system.)

July 4 Sold $6,295 of merchandise (that had cost $4,000) to customers on credit.
     9 Sold $18,000 of accounts receivable to Center Bank. Center charges a 4% factoring fee.
   17 Received $3,436 cash from customers in payment on their accounts.
   27 Borrowed $10,000 cash from Center Bank, pledging $13,000 of accounts receivable as security for the loan.

Exercise 9-10
Honoring a note
P3

Prepare journal entries to record these selected transactions for Eduardo Company.

Nov. 1 Accepted a $5,000, 180-day, 6% note dated November 1 from Melosa Allen in granting a time extension on her past-due account receivable.
Dec. 31 Adjusted the year-end accounts for the accrued interest earned on the Allen note.
Apr. 30 Allen honors her note when presented for payment; February has 28 days for the current year.

Prepare journal entries to record the following selected transactions of Paloma Company for 2015.

Mar. 21 Accepted a $3,100, 180-day, 10% note dated March 21 from Salma Hernandez in granting a time extension on her past-due account receivable.
Sept. 17 Hernandez dishonors her note when it is presented for payment.
Dec. 31 After exhausting all legal means of collection, Paloma Company writes off Hernandez's account against the Allowance for Doubtful Accounts.

Exercise 9-11
Dishonoring a note
P3

Prepare journal entries for the following selected transactions of Deshawn Company for 2014.

2014

Dec. 13 Accepted a $10,000, 45-day, 8% note dated December 13 in granting Latisha Clark a time extension on her past-due account receivable.
31 Prepared an adjusting entry to record the accrued interest on the Clark note.

Exercise 9-12
Notes receivable transactions
C2

Check Dec. 31, Cr. Interest Revenue $40

Refer to the information in Exercise 9-12 and prepare the journal entries for the following selected transactions of Deshawn Company for 2015.

2015

Jan. 27 Received Clark's payment for principal and interest on the note dated December 13.
Mar. 3 Accepted a $4,000, 10%, 90-day note dated March 3 in granting a time extension on the past-due account receivable of Shandi Company.
17 Accepted a $2,000, 30-day, 9% note dated March 17 in granting Juan Torres a time extension on his past-due account receivable.
Apr. 16 Torres dishonors his note when presented for payment.
May 1 Wrote off the Torres account against the Allowance for Doubtful Accounts.
June 1 Received the Shandi payment for principal and interest on the note dated March 3.

Exercise 9-13
Notes receivable transactions
P3

Check Jan. 27, Dr. Cash $10,100

June 1, Dr. Cash $4,100

The following information is from the annual financial statements of Waseem Company. Compute its accounts receivable turnover for 2014 and 2015. Compare the two years results and give a possible explanation for any change (competitors average a turnover of 11).

Exercise 9-14
Accounts receivable turnover
A1

	2015	2014	2013
Net sales	$305,000	$236,000	$288,000
Accounts receivable, net (year-end)	22,900	20,700	17,400

connect

Atlas Co. allows select customers to make purchases on credit. Its other customers can use either of two credit cards: Zisa or Access. Zisa deducts a 3% service charge for sales on its credit card and credits the bank account of Atlas immediately when credit card receipts are deposited. Atlas deposits the Zisa credit card receipts each business day. When customers use Access credit cards, Atlas accumulates the receipts for several days before submitting them to Access for payment. Access deducts a 2% service charge and usually pays within one week of being billed. Atlas completes the following transactions in June. (The terms of all credit sales are 2/15, n/30, and all sales are recorded at the gross price.)

PROBLEM SET A

Problem 9-1A
Sales on account and credit card sales
C1

June 4 Sold $750 of merchandise (that had cost $500) on credit to Anne Cianci.
5 Sold $5,900 of merchandise (that had cost $3,200) to customers who used their Zisa cards.
6 Sold $4,800 of merchandise (that had cost $2,800) to customers who used their Access cards.
8 Sold $3,200 of merchandise (that had cost $1,900) to customers who used their Access cards.

10 Submitted Access card receipts accumulated since June 6 to the credit card company for payment.

13 Wrote off the account of Nakia Wells against the Allowance for Doubtful Accounts. The $329 balance in Wells's account stemmed from a credit sale in October of last year.

17 Received the amount due from Access.

18 Received Cianci's check in full payment for the purchase of June 4.

Check   June 17, Dr. Cash $7,840

Required

Prepare journal entries to record the preceding transactions and events. (The company uses the perpetual inventory system. Round amounts to the nearest dollar.)

Problem 9-2A
Accounts receivable transactions and bad debts adjustments
C1 P2

Lopez Company began operations on January 1, 2014. During its first two years, the company completed a number of transactions involving sales on credit, accounts receivable collections, and bad debts. These transactions are summarized as follows.

2014

a. Sold $1,803,750 of merchandise (that had cost $1,475,000) on credit, terms n/30.

b. Wrote off $20,300 of uncollectible accounts receivable.

c. Received $789,200 cash in payment of accounts receivable.

Check   (d) Dr. Bad Debts Expense
$35,214

d. In adjusting the accounts on December 31, the company estimated that 1.5% of accounts receivable will be uncollectible.

2015

e. Sold $1,825,700 of merchandise (that had cost $1,450,000) on credit, terms n/30.

f. Wrote off $28,800 of uncollectible accounts receivable.

g. Received $1,304,800 cash in payment of accounts receivable.

(h) Dr. Bad Debts Expense
$36,181

h. In adjusting the accounts on December 31, the company estimated that 1.5% of accounts receivable will be uncollectible.

Required

Prepare journal entries to record Lopez's 2014 and 2015 summarized transactions and its year-end adjustments to record bad debts expense. (The company uses the perpetual inventory system. Round amounts to the nearest dollar.)

Problem 9-3A
Estimating and reporting bad debts
P2

At December 31, 2015, Ethan Company reports the following results for its calendar year.

Cash sales	$1,803,750
Credit sales	3,534,000

In addition, its unadjusted trial balance includes the following items.

Accounts receivable	$1,070,100 debit
Allowance for doubtful accounts	15,750 debit

There was objective evidence that 10% of a $150,000 debt owed by a debtor, Nathan Company, would most probably be uncollectible. An aging analysis of the rest of the accounts receivables indicated that an estimated 5% of these accounts would not be collectible.

Required

Check   Bad Debts Expense:
$76,755

1. Prepare the adjusting entry for this company to recognize bad debts.

2. Show how Accounts Receivable and the Allowance for Doubtful Accounts appear on its December 31, 2015 statement of financial position.

Carmack Company has credit sales of $2.6 million for year 2015. On December 31, 2015, the company's Allowance for Doubtful Accounts has an unadjusted credit balance of $13,400. Carmack prepares a schedule of its December 31, 2015, accounts receivable by age. On the basis of past experience, it estimates the percent of receivables in each age category that will become uncollectible. This information is summarized here.

File Edit View Insert Format Tools Data Accounting Window Help		
December 31, 2015 Accounts Receivable	**Age of Accounts Receivable**	**Expected Percent Uncollectible**
$730,000	Not yet due	1.25%
354,000	1 to 30 days past due	2.00
76,000	31 to 60 days past due	6.50
48,000	61 to 90 days past due	32.75
12,000	Over 90 days past due	68.00

Required

1. Estimate the required balance of the Allowance for Doubtful Accounts at December 31, 2015, using the aging of accounts receivable method.

2. Prepare the adjusting entry to record bad debts expense at December 31, 2015.

Analysis Component

3. On June 30, 2016, Carmack Company concludes that a customer's $3,750 receivable (created in 2015) is uncollectible and that the account should be written off. What effect will this action have on Carmack's 2016 net profit? Explain.

The following selected transactions are from Ohlde Company.

2014

Dec. 16   Accepted a $9,600, 60-day, 9% note dated this day in granting Todd Duke a time extension on his past-due account receivable.

    31   Made an adjusting entry to record the accrued interest on the Duke note.

2015

Feb. 14   Received Duke's payment of principal and interest on the note dated December 16.

Mar. 2   Accepted an $4,120, 8%, 90-day note dated this day in granting a time extension on the past-due account receivable from Mare Co.

    17   Accepted a $2,400, 30-day, 7% note dated this day in granting Jolene Halaam a time extension on her past-due account receivable.

Apr. 16   Halaam dishonored her note when presented for payment.

June 2   Mare Co. refuses to pay the note that was due to Ohlde Co. on May 31. Prepare the journal entry to charge the dishonored note plus accrued interest to Mare Co.'s accounts receivable.

July 17   Received payment from Mare Co. for the maturity value of its dishonored note plus interest for 46 days beyond maturity at 8%.

Aug. 7   Accepted an $5,440, 90-day, 10% note dated this day in granting a time extension on the past-due account receivable of Birch and Byer Co.

Sept. 3   Accepted a $2,080, 60-day, 10% note dated this day in granting Kevin York a time extension on his past-due account receivable.

Nov. 2   Received payment of principal plus interest from York for the September 3 note.

Nov. 5   Received payment of principal plus interest from Birch and Byer for the August 7 note.

Dec. 1   Wrote off the Jolene Halaam account against Allowance for Doubtful Accounts.

Required

1. Prepare journal entries to record these transactions and events. (Round amounts to the nearest dollar.)

Analysis Component

2. What reporting is necessary when a business pledges receivables as security for a loan and the loan is still outstanding at the end of the period? Explain the reason for this requirement and the accounting principle being satisfied.

PROBLEM SET B

Problem 9-1B
Sales on account and credit
card sales

C1

Able Co. allows select customers to make purchases on credit. Its other customers can use either of two credit cards: Commerce Bank or Aztec. Commerce Bank deducts a 3% service charge for sales on its credit card and immediately credits the bank account of Able when credit card receipts are deposited. Able deposits the Commerce Bank credit card receipts each business day. When customers use the Aztec card, Able accumulates the receipts for several days and then submits them to Aztec for payment. Aztec deducts a 2% service charge and usually pays within one week of being billed. Able completed the following transactions in August (terms of all credit sales are 2/10, n/30; and all sales are recorded at the gross price).

Aug. 4 Sold $2,780 of merchandise (that had cost $1,750) on credit to Stacy Dalton.
      10 Sold $3,248 of merchandise (that had cost $2,456) to customers who used their Commerce Bank credit cards.
      11 Sold $1,575 of merchandise (that had cost $1,150) to customers who used their Aztec cards.
      14 Received Dalton's check in full payment for the purchase of August 4.
      15 Sold $2,960 of merchandise (that had cost $1,758) to customers who used their Aztec cards.
      18 Submitted Aztec card receipts accumulated since August 11 to the credit card company for payment.
      22 Wrote off the account of Ness City against the Allowance for Doubtful Accounts. The $398 balance in Ness City's account stemmed from a credit sale in November of last year.

Check Aug. 25, Dr. Cash $4,444

      25 Received the amount due from Aztec.

Required

Prepare journal entries to record the preceding transactions and events. (The company uses the perpetual inventory system. Round amounts to the nearest dollar.)

Problem 9-2B
Accounts receivable transactions
and bad debts adjustments

C1 P2

Crist Co. began operations on January 1, 2014, and completed several transactions during 2014 and 2015 that involved sales on credit, accounts receivable collections, and bad debts. These transactions are summarized as follows.

2014

a. Sold $673,490 of merchandise (that had cost $500,000) on credit, terms n/30.
b. Received $437,250 cash in payment of accounts receivable.
c. Wrote off $8,330 of uncollectible accounts receivable.

Check (d) Dr. Bad Debts Expense
$10,609

d. In adjusting the accounts on December 31, the company estimated that 1% of accounts receivable will be uncollectible.

2015

e. Sold $930,100 of merchandise (that had cost $650,000) on credit, terms n/30.
f. Received $890,220 cash in payment of accounts receivable.
g. Wrote off $10,090 of uncollectible accounts receivable.

(h) Dr. Bad Debts Expense
$10,388

h. In adjusting the accounts on December 31, the company estimated that 1% of accounts receivable will be uncollectible.

Required

Prepare journal entries to record Crist's 2014 and 2015 summarized transactions and its year-end adjusting entry to record bad debts expense. (The company uses the perpetual inventory system. Round amounts to the nearest dollar.)

Problem 9-3B
Estimating and reporting
bad debts

P2

At December 31, 2015, Klimek Company reports the following results for the year.

Cash sales	$1,015,000
Credit sales	1,241,000

In addition, its unadjusted trial balance includes the following items.

Accounts receivable	$475,000 debit
Allowance for doubtful accounts	5,200 credit

There was objective evidence that 9% of a $50,000 debt owed by a debtor, Kem Company, would most probably be uncollectible. An aging analysis of the rest of the accounts receivables indicated that an estimated 4% of these accounts would not be collectible.

Required

1. Prepare the adjusting entry for Klimek Co. to recognize bad debts.
2. Show how Accounts Receivable and the Allowance for Doubtful Accounts appear on its December 31, 2015, statement of financial position.

Check Bad debts expense: $16,300

Quisp Company has credit sales of $3.5 million for year 2015. At December 31, 2015, the company's Allowance for Doubtful Accounts has an unadjusted debit balance of $4,100. Quisp prepares a schedule of its December 31, 2015, accounts receivable by age. On the basis of past experience, it estimates the percent of receivables in each age category that will become uncollectible. This information is summarized here.

Problem 9-4B

Aging accounts receivable and accounting for bad debts

P2

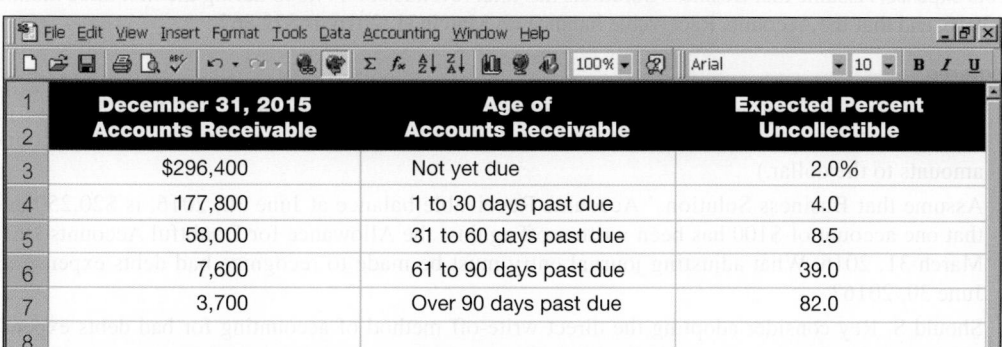

December 31, 2015 Accounts Receivable	Age of Accounts Receivable	Expected Percent Uncollectible
$296,400	Not yet due	2.0%
177,800	1 to 30 days past due	4.0
58,000	31 to 60 days past due	8.5
7,600	61 to 90 days past due	39.0
3,700	Over 90 days past due	82.0

Required

1. Compute the required balance of the Allowance for Doubtful Accounts at December 31, 2015, using the aging of accounts receivable method.
2. Prepare the adjusting entry to record bad debts expense at December 31, 2015.

Analysis Component

3. On July 31, 2016, Quisp concludes that a customer's $2,345 receivable (created in 2015) is uncollectible and that the account should be written off. What effect will this action have on Quisp's 2016 net profit? Explain.

Check (2) Dr. Bad Debts Expense $28,068

The following selected transactions are from Seeker Company.

2014

Nov.   1   Accepted a $4,800, 90-day, 8% note dated this day in granting Julie Stephens a time extension on her past-due account receivable.
Dec. 31   Made an adjusting entry to record the accrued interest on the Stephens note.

2015

Jan. 30   Received Stephens's payment for principal and interest on the note dated November 1.
Feb. 28   Accepted a $12,600, 6%, 30-day note dated this day in granting a time extension on the past-due account receivable from Kramer Co.
Mar.   1   Accepted a $6,200, 60-day, 8% note dated this day in granting Shelly Myers a time extension on her past-due account receivable.
      30   The Kramer Co. dishonored its note when presented for payment.
April 30   Received payment of principal plus interest from Myers for the March 1 note.
June 15   Accepted a $2,000, 60-day, 10% note dated this day in granting a time extension on the past-due account receivable of Rhonda Rye.
      21   Accepted a $9,500, 90-day, 12% note dated this day in granting J. Striker a time extension on his past-due account receivable.
Aug. 14   Received payment of principal plus interest from R. Rye for the note of June 15.
Sep. 19   Received payment of principal plus interest from J. Striker for the June 21 note.
Nov. 30   Wrote off Kramer's account against Allowance for Doubtful Accounts.

Problem 9-5B

Analyzing and journalizing notes receivable transactions

C2 C3 P3

Check Jan. 30, Cr. Interest Revenue $32

April 30, Cr. Interest Revenue $83

Sep. 19, Cr. Interest Revenue $285

Required

1. Prepare journal entries to record these transactions and events. (Round amounts to the nearest dollar.)

Analysis Component

2. What reporting is necessary when a business pledges receivables as security for a loan and the loan is still outstanding at the end of the period? Explain the reason for this requirement and the accounting principle being satisfied.

SERIAL PROBLEM
Business Solutions

P1 P2

(This serial problem began in Chapter 1 and continues through most of the book. If previous chapter segments were not completed, the serial problem can begin at this point.)

SP 9   Santana Rey, owner of Business Solutions, realizes that she needs to begin accounting for bad debts expense. Assume that Business Solutions has total revenues of $44,000 during the first three months of 2016, and that the Accounts Receivable balance on March 31, 2016, is $22,867.

Required

1. Prepare the adjusting entry needed for Business Solutions to recognize bad debts expense on March 31, 2016, given that bad debts are estimated to be 2% of accounts receivable. (Round amounts to the dollar.)

2. Assume that Business Solutions' Accounts Receivable balance at June 30, 2016, is $20,250 and that one account of $100 has been written off against the Allowance for Doubtful Accounts since March 31, 2016. What adjusting journal entry must be made to recognize bad debts expense on June 30, 2016?

Check   Bad Debts Expense, $48

3. Should S. Rey consider adopting the direct write-off method of accounting for bad debts expense rather than the allowance method? Explain.

Beyond the Numbers

REPORTING IN ACTION
A1

BTN 9-1   Refer to Nestlé's consolidated financial statements in Appendix A.
1. What is the amount of Nestlé's accounts receivable as at December 31, 2013?
2. Compute Nestlé's accounts receivable turnover as at December 31, 2013.
3. How long does it take, *on average*, for Nestlé to collect receivables?
4. Nestlé's most liquid assets include (*a*) cash and cash equivalents, (*b*) short-term investments, (*c*) inventories, and (*d*) trade and other receivables. Compute the percentage that these liquid assets make up of current liabilities as at December 31, 2013. Do the same computations for December 31, 2012. Comment on the company's ability to satisfy its current liabilities at the 2013 financial year-end compared to the 2012 financial year.

Fast Forward

5. Access Nestlé's financial statements for financial years after December 31, 2013, at its Website (www.nestle.com). Recompute parts 2 and 4 and comment on any changes since December 31, 2013.

COMPARATIVE ANALYSIS
A1 P2

BTN 9-2   Comparative figures for both Adidas and Puma follow.

	Adidas (EUR millions)			Puma (EUR millions)		
	2013	2012	2011	2013	2012	2011
Accounts receivable, net	1,809	1,688	1,595	423.4	507.0	533.1
Net sales	14,492	14,883	13,322	2,985.3	3,270.7	3,009.0

Required

1. Compute the accounts receivable turnover for both Adidas and Puma for each of the two most recent years using the data shown (Round to one decimal place).
2. Using results from part 1, compute how many days it takes each company, on average, to collect receivables. (Round to one decimal place.)
3. Which company is more efficient in collecting its accounts receivable? Explain.

Hint: Average collection period equals 365 divided by the accounts receivable turnover.

BTN 9-3   Kelly Steinman is the manager of a medium-size company. A few years ago, Steinman persuaded the owner to base a part of her compensation on the net profit the company earns each year. Each December she estimates year-end financial figures in anticipation of the bonus she will receive. If the bonus is not as high as she would like, she offers several recommendations to the accountant for year-end adjustments. One of her favorite recommendations is for the controller to reduce the estimate of doubtful accounts.

ETHICS CHALLENGE
P2

Required

1. What effect does lowering the estimate for doubtful accounts have on the income statement and statement of financial position?
2. Do you believe Steinman's recommendation to adjust the allowance for doubtful accounts is within her right as manager, or do you believe this action is an ethics violation? Justify your response.
3. What type of internal control(s) might be useful for this company in overseeing the manager's recommendations for accounting changes?

BTN 9-4   As the accountant for Pure-Air Distributing, you attend a sales managers' meeting devoted to a discussion of credit policies. At the meeting, you report that bad debts expense is estimated to be $59,000 and accounts receivable at year-end amount to $1,750,000 less a $43,000 allowance for doubtful accounts. Sid Omar, a sales manager, expresses confusion over why bad debts expense and the allowance for doubtful accounts are different amounts. Write a one-page memorandum to him explaining why a difference in bad debts expense and the allowance for doubtful accounts is not unusual. The company estimates bad debts expense based on aging of its accounts receivable.

COMMUNICATING IN PRACTICE
P2

BTN 9-5   Access L'Oréal's Website (www.loreal-finance.com/eng) to answer the following.

TAKING IT TO THE NET
C1

Required

1. What is the amount of L'Oréal's net accounts receivable as at December 31, 2013, and as at December 31, 2012?
2. Refer to Note 17 to its financial statements which lists L'Oréal's gross accounts receivable, allowance for doubtful accounts, and net accounts receivable. For the two years ended December 31, 2013 and 2012, compute its allowance for doubtful accounts as a percent of gross accounts receivable.
3. Do you believe that these percentages are reasonable based on what you know about L'Oréal? Explain.

BTN 9-6   Each member of a team is to participate in estimating uncollectibles using the aging schedule and percents shown in Problem 9-4A. The division of labor is up to the team. Your goal is to accurately complete this task as soon as possible. After estimating uncollectibles, check your estimate with the instructor. If the estimate is correct, the team then should prepare the adjusting entry and the presentation of accounts receivable (net) for the December 31, 2015, statement of financial position.

TEAMWORK IN ACTION
P2

BTN 9-7   Colin Lim of Settlers Café is introduced in the chapter's opening feature. In order to diversify his business, Colin is considering two proposals (all $ are annual amounts).

ENTREPRENEURIAL DECISION
C1

Plan A. Colin would begin selling boardgames online directly to customers through his Website. Online customers would use their credit cards. Settlers Café currently has the capability of selling through its Website with no additional investment in hardware or software. Credit sales are expected to be $25,000.

Costs associated with this plan are as follows: cost of these sales will be $13,550, credit card fees will be 5% of sales, and additional recordkeeping and shipping costs will be 6% of sales.

Plan B. Colin would expand his market by opening more cafés. He would make additional sales of $50,000 in these cafés. Costs associated with those sales are as follows: cost of sales will be $34,000, additional recordkeeping expenses will be 6% of sales, and new fixed annual expenses will be $5,000.

Required

Check   (1b) Net profit, $74,000

1. Compute the additional annual net profit or loss expected under (a) Plan A and (b) Plan B.
2. Should Colin pursue either plan? Discuss both the financial and nonfinancial factors relevant to this decision.

HITTING THE ROAD

C1

BTN 9-8 Many commercials include comments similar to the following: "We accept **VISA**" or "We do not accept **American Express**." Conduct your own research by contacting at least five companies via interviews, phone calls, or the Internet to determine the reason(s) companies discriminate in their use of credit cards. Collect information on the fees charged by the different cards for the companies contacted. (The instructor can assign this as a team activity.)

ANSWERS TO MULTIPLE CHOICE QUIZ

1. d; Desired balance in Allowance for Doubtful Accounts = $ 5,026 cr.
   ($125,650 × 0.04)
   Current balance in Allowance for Doubtful Accounts = ___(328)__ cr.
   Bad Debts Expense to be recorded   = $ 4,698

2. a; Desired balance in Allowance for Doubtful Accounts   = $29,358 cr.
   ($489,300 × 0.06)
   Current balance in Allowance for Doubtful Accounts = ___554__ dr.
   Bad Debts Expense to be recorded   = $29,912

3. a; $7,500 × 0.05 × 90/360 = $93.75

4. c; Principal amount $9,000
   Interest accrued . . . .   ___120__ ($9,000 × 0.08 × 60/360)
   Maturity value $9,120

5. d; $489,600/$40,800 = 12

10

Long-Term Assets

A Look Back

Chapters 8 and 9 focused on short-term assets: cash, cash equivalents, and receivables. We explained why they are known as liquid assets and described how companies account and report for them.

A Look at This Chapter

This chapter introduces us to long-term or noncurrent assets. We explain how to account for a long-term asset's cost, the allocation of an asset's cost to periods benefiting from it, the recording of additional costs after an asset is purchased, and the disposal of an asset.

A Look Ahead

Chapter 11 focuses on current liabilities. We explain how they are computed, recorded, and reported in financial statements. We also explain the accounting for company payroll and contingencies.

Learning Objectives

CAP

CONCEPTUAL

C1 Explain the cost principle for computing the cost of property, plant and equipment. (p. 395)

C2 Explain depreciation for partial years and changes in estimates. (p. 402)

C3 Distinguish between revenue and capital expenditures, and account for them. (p. 404)

C4 Explain the revaluation model to account for property, plant and equipment. (p. 405)

ANALYTICAL

A1 Compute total asset turnover and apply it to analyze a company's use of assets. (p. 412)

PROCEDURAL

P1 Compute and record depreciation using the straight-line, units-of-production, and declining-balance methods. (p. 398)

P2 Account for asset disposal through discarding or selling an asset. (p. 407)

P3 Account for natural resource assets and their depletion. (p. 409)

P4 Account for intangible assets. (p. 410)

P5 *Appendix 10A*—Account for asset exchanges. (p. 415)

"I love the freedom of creating and experimenting with new techniques and ingredients."—JANICE WONG

Decision Insight

A Delectable Dessert Bar

Her midnight craving for hot chocolate and chocolate desserts was what inspired Chef Janice Wong to open **2am Dessert Bar** (**www.2amdessertbar.com**), a veritable haven for chocoholics and dessert lovers everywhere. Just imagine a restaurant where the entire menu of main courses comprises delectable desserts, sophisticated creations that customers can enjoy with carefully selected wines. "2am Dessert Bar is an open-concept restaurant where we prepare everything in front of the guests," says Janice, who received her education from the world's most prestigious culinary school, Le Cordon Bleu. Janice focuses on quality and bringing the best out of the ingredients that she uses, and the result is a host of dessert creations that are to die for.

People management is a crucial factor in her business. "In our industry the turnover is high and you have to find a way to keep your staff happy and growing," says Janice. "I believe strongly in growth and I always have a long-term plan for the people working with me. It's important for them to grow

together with the bar and continue to learn and experiment with new techniques." Equally important is making wise investments in property, plant and equipment—heavy-duty machinery such as ovens, refrigerators, and chocolate-tempering machines—all of which are susceptible to depreciation. Adds Janice, "It is a high-risk business with heavy startup costs." Such heavy costs can materially change the depreciation expenses of the business. Adding to the costs is the constant investment in new equipment, technology, and ingredients, which Janice firmly believes in: "Most of our profits are put back into research and development. This helps us not only to grow with the rest of the world but to be ahead in our industry."

"I aim to elevate the status of desserts to that of their savory counterparts in top restaurants in Singapore and the rest of the world," enthuses Janice. And as you bite into one of her heavenly confections, you absolutely believe that she will succeed.

This chapter focuses on long-term assets, which can be grouped into property, plant and equipment, natural resource assets, and intangible assets. Property, plant and equipment make up a large part of assets on most statements of financial position, and they yield depreciation, often one of the largest expenses on income statements. The acquisition or building of an item of property, plant and equipment is often referred to as a *capital expenditure*. Capital expenditures are important events because they impact both the short- and long-term success of a company. Natural resource assets and intangible assets have similar impacts. This chapter describes the purchase and use of these assets. We also explain what distinguishes these assets from other types of assets, how to determine their cost, how to allocate their costs to periods benefiting from their use, and how to dispose of them.

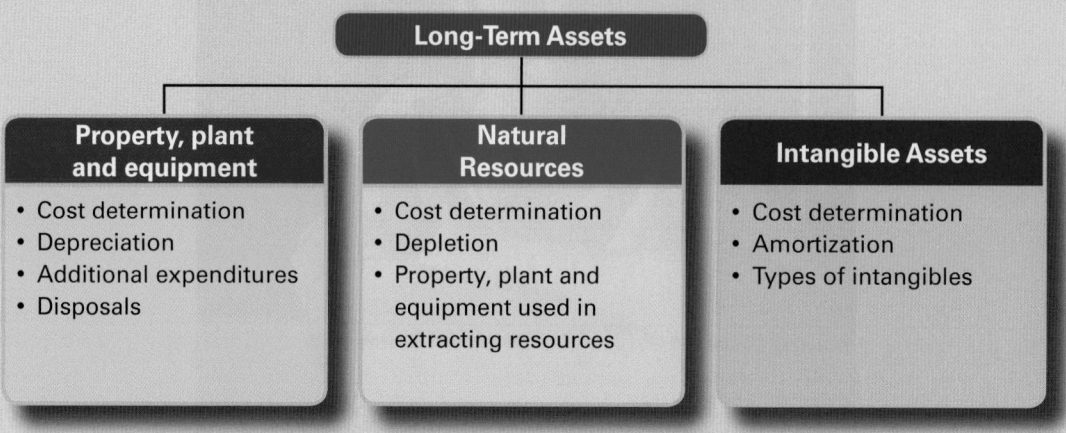

Section 1—Property, Plant and Equipment

Property, plant and equipment are tangible assets used in a company's operations that have a useful life of more than one accounting period. They are also called *plant assets* or *fixed assets*. For many companies, property, plant and equipment amounts are large. **Adidas**' 2013 property, plant and equipment, for instance, are reported at about EUR 1,238 million, and **Puma**'s 2013 property, plant and equipment are about EUR 213 million. In addition, property, plant and equipment can be a significant proportion of a company's total assets. **Nestlé**'s 2013 property, plant and equipment of CHF 26,895 million make up about 30% of its noncurrent assets and 22% of its total assets.

Property, plant and equipment are set apart from other assets by two important features. First, *property, plant and equipment are used in operations*. This makes them different from, for instance, inventory that is held for sale and not used in operations. The distinctive feature here is use, not type of asset. A company that purchases a computer to resell it reports it on the statement of financial position as inventory. If the same company purchases this computer to use in operations, however, it is an item of property, plant and equipment. Another example is land held for future expansion, which is reported as a long-term investment. However, if this land holds a factory used in operations, the land is part of property, plant and equipment. Another example is equipment held for use in the event of a breakdown or for peak periods of production, which is reported in property, plant and equipment. If this same equipment is removed from use and held for sale, however, it is not reported in property, plant and equipment.

The second important feature is that *property, plant and equipment have useful lives extending over more than one accounting period*. This makes property, plant and equipment different from current assets such as supplies that are normally consumed in a short time period after they are placed in use.

The accounting for property, plant and equipment reflects these two features. Since property, plant and equipment are used in operations, we try to match their costs against the revenues they generate. Also, since their useful lives extend over more than one period, our matching of costs and revenues must extend over several periods. Specifically, we value property, plant and equipment (statement of financial position effect) and then, for many of them, we allocate their costs to periods benefiting from their use (income statement effect). An important exception is land; land cost is not allocated to expense when we expect it to have an indefinite life.

Exhibit 10.1 shows four main issues in accounting for property, plant and equipment: (1) computing the costs of property, plant and equipment, (2) allocating the costs of most property, plant and equipment (less any residual values) against revenues for the periods they benefit, (3) accounting for expenditures such as repairs and improvements to property, plant and equipment, and (4) recording the disposal of property, plant and equipment. The following sections discuss these issues.

Point: It can help to view property, plant and equipment as prepaid expenses that benefit several future accounting periods.

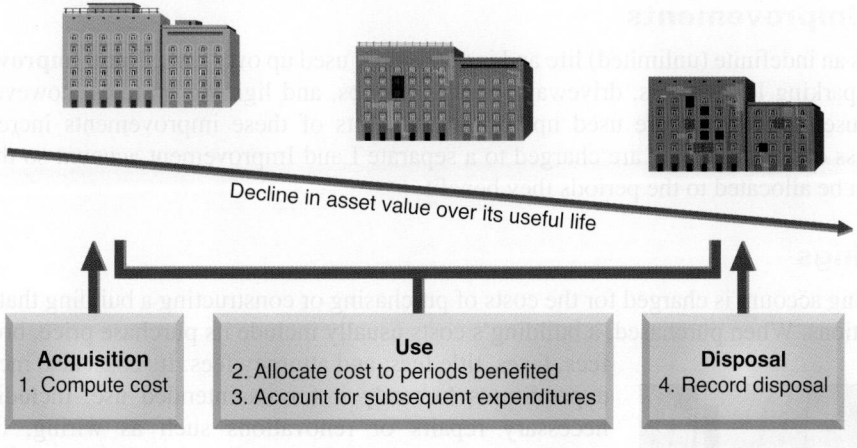

EXHIBIT 10.1

Issues in Accounting for Property, Plant and Equipment

COST DETERMINATION

Property, plant and equipment are recorded at cost when acquired. This is consistent with the *cost principle.* **Cost** includes all normal and reasonable expenditures necessary to get the asset in place and ready for its intended use. The cost of a factory machine, for instance, includes its invoice cost less any cash discount for early payment, plus any necessary freight, unpacking, assembling, installing, and testing costs. Examples are the costs of building a base or foundation for a machine, providing electrical hookups, and testing the asset before using it in operations.

To be recorded as part of the cost of an item of property, plant and equipment, an expenditure must be normal, reasonable, and necessary in preparing it for its intended use. If an asset is damaged during unpacking, the repairs are not added to its cost. Instead, they are charged to an expense account. Nor is a paid traffic fine for moving heavy machinery on city streets without a proper permit part of the machinery's cost; but payment for a proper permit is included in the cost of machinery. Charges are sometimes incurred to modify or customize a new item of property, plant and equipment. These charges are added to the asset's cost. We explain in this section how to determine the cost of property, plant and equipment for each of its four major classes.

C1 Explain the cost principle for computing the cost of property, plant and equipment.

Land

When land is purchased for a building site, its cost includes the total amount paid for the land, including any real estate commissions, title insurance fees, legal fees, and any accrued property taxes paid by the purchaser. Payments for surveying, clearing, grading, and draining also are included in the cost of land. Other costs include government assessments, whether incurred at the time of purchase or later, for items such as public roadways, sewers, and sidewalks. These assessments are included because they permanently add to the land's value. Land purchased as a building site sometimes includes structures that must be removed. In such cases, the total purchase price is charged to the Land account as is the cost of removing the structures, less any amounts recovered through sale of salvaged materials. To illustrate, assume that **Starbucks** paid $167,000 cash to acquire land for a retail store. This land had an old service garage that was removed at a net

EXHIBIT 10.2

Computing Cost of Land

Cash price of land	$ 167,000
Net cost of garage removal	13,000
Closing costs	10,000
Cost of land	**$190,000**

cost of $13,000 ($15,000 in costs less $2,000 proceeds from salvaged materials). Additional closing costs total $10,000, consisting of brokerage fees ($8,000), legal fees ($1,500), and title costs ($500). The cost of this land to Starbucks is $190,000 and is computed as shown in Exhibit 10.2.

Land Improvements

Land has an indefinite (unlimited) life and is not usually used up over time. **Land improvements** such as parking lot surfaces, driveways, fences, shrubs, and lighting systems, however, have limited useful lives and are used up. While the costs of these improvements increase the usefulness of the land, they are charged to a separate Land Improvement account so that their costs can be allocated to the periods they benefit.

Buildings

A Building account is charged for the costs of purchasing or constructing a building that is used in operations. When purchased, a building's costs usually include its purchase price, brokerage

fees, taxes, title fees, and attorney fees. Its costs also include all expenditures to ready it for its intended use, including any necessary repairs or renovations such as wiring, lighting, flooring, and wall coverings. When a company constructs a building or any item of property, plant and equipment for its own use, its costs include materials and labor plus a reasonable amount of indirect overhead cost. Overhead includes the costs of items such as heat, lighting, power, and depreciation on machinery used to construct the asset. Costs of construction also include design fees, building permits, and insurance during construction. However, costs such as insurance to cover the asset *after* it is placed in use are operating expenses.

Machinery and Equipment

The costs of machinery and equipment consist of all costs normal and necessary to purchase them and prepare them for their intended use. These include the purchase price, taxes, transportation charges, insurance while in transit, and the installing, assembling, and testing of the machinery and equipment.

Lump-Sum Purchase

Example: If appraised values in Exhibit 10.3 are land, $24,000; land improvements, $12,000; and building, $84,000, what cost is assigned to the building? *Answer:*
(1) $24,000 + $12,000 + $84,000 = $120,000 (total appraisal)
(2) $84,000/$120,000 = 70% (building's percent of total)
(3) 70% × $90,000 = $63,000 (building's apportioned cost)

Property, plant and equipment sometimes are purchased as a group in a single transaction for a lump-sum price. This transaction is called a *lump-sum purchase,* or *group, bulk,* or *basket purchase.* When this occurs, we allocate the cost of the purchase among the different types of assets acquired based on their *relative market values,* which can be estimated by appraisal or by using the tax-assessed valuations of the assets. To illustrate, assume **CarMax** paid $90,000 cash to acquire a group of items consisting of land appraised at $30,000, land improvements appraised at $10,000, and a building appraised at $60,000. The $90,000 cost is allocated on the basis of these appraised values as shown in Exhibit 10.3.

EXHIBIT 10.3

Computing Costs in a Lump-Sum Purchase

	Appraised Value	Percent of Total	Apportioned Cost
Land	$ 30,000	30% ($30,000/$100,000)	$27,000 ($90,000 × 30%)
Land improvements	10,000	10 ($10,000/$100,000)	9,000 ($90,000 × 10%)
Building	60,000	60 ($60,000/$100,000)	54,000 ($90,000 × 60%)
Totals	$100,000	100%	$ 90,000

Quick Check

Answers — p. 417–418

1. Identify the asset class for each of the following: (*a*) supplies, (*b*) office equipment, (*c*) inventory, (*d*) land for future expansion, and (*e*) trucks used in operations.

2. Identify the account charged for each of the following: (*a*) the purchase price of a vacant lot to be used in operations and (*b*) the cost of paving that same vacant lot.

3. Compute the amount recorded as the cost of a new machine given the following payments related to its purchase: gross purchase price, $700,000; sales tax, $49,000; purchase discount taken, $21,000; freight cost—terms FOB shipping point, $3,500; normal assembly costs, $3,000; cost of necessary machine platform, $2,500; cost of parts used in maintaining machine, $4,200.

DEPRECIATION

Depreciation is the process of allocating the cost of an item of property, plant and equipment to expense in the accounting periods benefiting from its use. Depreciation does not measure the decline in the asset's market value each period, nor does it measure the asset's physical deterioration. Since depreciation reflects the cost of using property, plant and equipment, depreciation charges are only recorded when the asset is actually in service. This section describes the factors we must consider in computing depreciation, the depreciation methods used, revisions in depreciation, and depreciation for partial periods.

Factors in Computing Depreciation

Factors that determine depreciation are (1) cost, (2) residual value, and (3) useful life.

Cost   The **cost** of an item of property, plant and equipment consists of all necessary and reasonable expenditures to acquire it and to prepare it for its intended use.

Residual Value   The **residual value** is estimated amount that an entity would currently obtain from disposal of the asset, after deducting the estimated costs of disposal, if the asset were already of the age and in the condition expected at the end of its useful life. The total amount of depreciation to be charged off over an asset's benefit period equals the asset's cost minus its residual value.

Useful Life   The **useful life** of an item of property, plant and equipment is the length of time it is productively used in a company's operations. Useful life, also called *service life,* might not be as long as the asset's total productive life. For example, the productive life of a computer can be eight years or more. Some companies, however, trade in old computers for new ones every two years. In this case, these computers have a two-year useful life, meaning the cost of these computers (less their expected trade-in values) is charged to depreciation expense over a two-year period.

Several variables often make the useful life of an item of property, plant and equipment difficult to predict. A major variable is the wear and tear from use in operations. Two other variables, inadequacy and obsolescence, also require consideration. **Inadequacy** refers to the insufficient capacity of a company's property, plant and equipment to meet its growing productive demands. **Obsolescence** refers to the condition of a property, plant and equipment that is no longer useful in producing goods or services with a competitive advantage because of new inventions and improvements. Both inadequacy and obsolescence are difficult to predict because of demand changes, new inventions, and improvements. A company usually disposes of an inadequate or obsolete asset before it wears out.

A company is often able to better predict a new asset's useful life when it has past experience with a similar asset. When it has no such experience, a company relies on the experience of

Point: Useful life and residual value are estimates which require judgment based on all available information. **IAS 16** requires that useful life and residual value be reviewed at least at each financial year-end and, if expectations differ from previous estimates, the change(s) shall be accounted for as a change in an accounting estimate in accordance with **IAS 8** *Accounting Policies, Changes in Accounting Estimates and Errors.*

others or on engineering studies and judgment. In note 1 of its annual report, **Nestlé** reports the following useful lives:

Buildings	20–40 years
Machinery and Equipment	10–25 years

Decision Insight

Component Depreciation   IAS 16 *Property, Plant and Equipment* does not prescribe the unit of measure for an item of property, plant and equipment and states that each part of an item of property, plant and equipment with a cost that is significant in relation to the total cost of the item shall be depreciated separately. Some accountants express concern that this may require an entity to subdivide its property, plant and equipment into dozens of component parts. As with everything in **IFRS**, there are key words which state that "judgement is required." Practically, there is little point in allocating the cost of an asset to components if the effect of doing so is immaterial. Still, some assets have components with useful lives that are significantly different from one another, and some jurisdictions already separate assets into components. For example, a building's elevators, and heating/air conditioning equipment may have lives that are shorter than that of the building shell. **IFRS** requires allocation among those component parts for purposes of computing depreciation. ∎

Depreciation Methods

P1 Compute and record depreciation using the straight-line, units-of-production, and declining-balance methods.

Depreciation methods are used to allocate the cost of an item of property, plant and equipment over the accounting periods in its useful life. The most frequently used method of depreciation is the straight-line method. Another common depreciation method is the units-of-production method. We explain both of these methods in this section. This section also describes accelerated depreciation methods, with a focus on the declining-balance method.

The computations in this section use information about a machine that inspects athletic shoes before packaging. Manufacturers such as **Adidas** and **Puma** use this machine. Data for this machine are in Exhibit 10.4.

EXHIBIT 10.4

Data for Athletic Shoe-Inspecting Machine

Cost	$10,000
Residual value	1,000
Depreciable amount	$ 9,000
Useful life	
Accounting periods	5 years
Units inspected	36,000 shoes

Straight-Line Method   **Straight-line depreciation** charges the same amount of expense to each period of the asset's useful life. A two-step process is used. We first compute the *depreciable amount* of the asset, also called the *depreciable cost* or *amount to be depreciated*. It is computed by subtracting the asset's residual value from its total cost (or other amount substituted for cost). Second, depreciable amount is divided by the number of accounting periods in the asset's useful life. The formula for straight-line depreciation, along with its computation for the inspection machine just described, is shown in Exhibit 10.5.

EXHIBIT 10.5

Straight-Line Depreciation Formula and Example

$$\frac{\text{Cost} - \text{Residual value}}{\text{Useful life in periods}} = \frac{\$10,000 - \$1,000}{5 \text{ years}} = \$1,800 \text{ per year}$$

If this machine is purchased on December 31, 2010, and used throughout its predicted useful life of five years, the straight-line method allocates an equal amount of depreciation to each of the years 2011 through 2015. We make the following adjusting entry at the end of each of the five years to record straight-line depreciation of this machine.

Dec. 31	Depreciation Expense	1,800	
	Accumulated Depreciation—Machinery		1,800
	To record annual depreciation.		

Assets = Liabilities + Equity
−1,800   −1,800

The $1,800 Depreciation Expense is reported on the income statement among operating expenses. The $1,800 Accumulated Depreciation is a contra asset account to the Machinery account in the statement of financial position. The graph on the left in Exhibit 10.6 shows the $1,800 per year expenses reported in each of the five years. The graph on the right shows the amounts reported on each of the six December 31 statements of financial position.

Example: If the residual value of the machine is $2,500, what is the annual depreciation? *Answer:*
($10,000 − $2,500)/5 years = $1,500

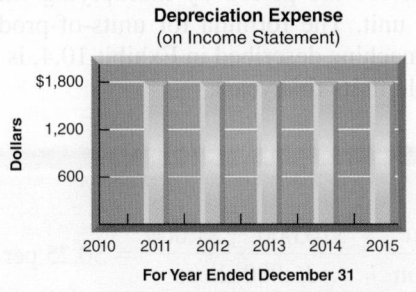

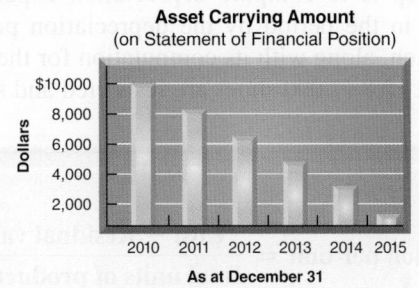

EXHIBIT 10.6

Financial Statement Effects of Straight-Line Depreciation

The net statement of financial position amount is the **asset carrying amount**, also called *book value*, and is computed as the asset's total cost less its accumulated depreciation (or accumulated amortization and accumulated impairment losses explained later). For example, at the end of year 2 (December 31, 2012), its carrying amount is $6,400 and is reported in the statement of financial position as follows:

Machinery	$10,000	
Less accumulated depreciation	3,600	$6,400

The carrying amount of this machine declines by $1,800 each year due to depreciation. From the graphs in Exhibit 10.6 we can see why this method is called straight-line.

We also can compute the *straight-line depreciation rate,* defined as 100% divided by the number of periods in the asset's useful life. For the inspection machine, this rate is 20% (100% ÷ 5 years, or 1/5 per period). We use this rate, along with other information, to compute the machine's *straight-line depreciation schedule* shown in Exhibit 10.7. Note three points in this exhibit. First, depreciation expense is the same each period. Second, accumulated depreciation is the sum of current and prior periods' depreciation expense. Third, carrying amount declines each period until it equals residual value at the end of the machine's useful life.

Point: Depreciation requires estimates for residual value and useful life. Ethics are relevant when managers might be tempted to choose estimates to achieve desired results on financial statements.

EXHIBIT 10.7

Straight-Line Depreciation Schedule

	Depreciation for the Period			End of Period	
Annual Period	Depreciable Cost*	Depreciation Rate	Depreciation Expense	Accumulated Depreciation	Carrying Amount†
2010	—	—	—	—	$10,000
2011	$9,000	20%	$1,800	$1,800	8,200
2012	9,000	20	1,800	3,600	6,400
2013	9,000	20	1,800	5,400	4,600
2014	9,000	20	1,800	7,200	2,800
2015	9,000	20	1,800	9,000	1,000

* $10,000 − $1,000.   † Carrying amount is total cost minus accumulated depreciation.

Units-of-Production Method   The straight-line method charges an equal share of an asset's cost to each period. If property, plant and equipment are used up in about equal amounts each accounting period, this method produces a reasonable matching of expenses with revenues. However, the use of some items of property, plant and equipment varies greatly from one period to the next. A builder, for instance, might use a piece of construction equipment for a month and then not use it again for several months. When equipment use varies from period to period, the units-of-production depreciation method can better match expenses with revenues. **Units-of-production depreciation** charges a varying amount to expense for each period of an asset's useful life depending on its usage.

A two-step process is used to compute units-of-production depreciation. We first compute *depreciation per unit* by subtracting the asset's residual value from its total cost and then dividing by the total number of units expected to be produced during its useful life. Units of production can be expressed in product or other units such as hours used or miles driven. The second step is to compute depreciation expense for the period by multiplying the units produced in the period by the depreciation per unit. The formula for units-of-production depreciation, along with its computation for the machine described in Exhibit 10.4, is shown in Exhibit 10.8 (7,000 shoes are inspected and sold in its first year).

EXHIBIT 10.8

Units-of-Production Depreciation Formula and Example

Step 1

$$\text{Depreciation per unit} = \frac{\text{Cost} - \text{Residual value}}{\text{Total units of production}} = \frac{\$10,000 - \$1,000}{36,000 \text{ shoes}} = \$0.25 \text{ per shoe}$$

Step 2

$$\text{Depreciation expense} = \text{Depreciation per unit} \times \text{Units produced in period}$$
$$\$0.25 \text{ per shoe} \times 7,000 \text{ shoes} = \$1,750$$

Using data on the number of shoes inspected by the machine, we can compute the *units-of-production depreciation schedule* shown in Exhibit 10.9. For example, depreciation for the first year is $1,750 (7,000 shoes at $0.25 per shoe). Depreciation for the second year is $2,000 (8,000 shoes at $0.25 per shoe). Other years are similarly computed. Exhibit 10.9 shows that (1) depreciation expense depends on unit output, (2) accumulated depreciation is the sum of current and prior periods' depreciation expense, and (3) carrying amount declines each period until it equals residual value at the end of the asset's useful life. **Deltic Timber** is one of many companies using the units-of-production depreciation method. It reports that depreciation "is calculated over the estimated useful lives of the assets by using the units of production method for machinery and equipment."

Example: Refer to Exhibit 10.9. If the number of shoes inspected in 2015 is 5,500, what is depreciation for 2015? *Answer:* $1,250 (never depreciate below residual value)

EXHIBIT 10.9

Units-of-Production Depreciation Schedule

| Annual Period | Depreciation for the Period | | | End of Period | |
	Number of Units	Depreciation per Unit	Depreciation Expense	Accumulated Depreciation	Carrying Amount
2010	—	—	—	—	$10,000
2011	7,000	$0.25	$1,750	$1,750	8,250
2012	8,000	0.25	2,000	3,750	6,250
2013	9,000	0.25	2,250	6,000	4,000
2014	7,000	0.25	1,750	7,750	2,250
2015	5,000	0.25	1,250	9,000	1,000

Declining-Balance Method   An **accelerated depreciation method** yields larger depreciation expenses in the early years of an asset's life and less depreciation in later years. The most common accelerated method is the **declining-balance method** of depreciation, which uses a depreciation rate that is a multiple of the straight-line rate and applies it to the asset's beginning-of-period carrying amount. The amount of depreciation declines each period because carrying amount declines each period.

A common depreciation rate for the declining-balance method is double the straight-line rate. This is called the *double-declining-balance* (*DDB*) method. This method is applied in three steps: (1) compute the asset's straight-line depreciation rate, (2) double the straight-line rate, and (3) compute depreciation expense by multiplying this rate by the asset's beginning-of-period carrying amount. To illustrate, let's return to the machine in Exhibit 10.4 and apply the double-declining-balance method to compute depreciation expense. Exhibit 10.10 shows the first-year depreciation computation for the machine. The three-step process is to (1) divide 100% by five years to determine the straight-line rate of 20%, or 1/5, per year, (2) double this 20% rate to get the declining-balance rate of 40%, or 2/5, per year, and (3) compute depreciation expense as 40%, or 2/5, multiplied by the beginning-of-period carrying amount.

Point: In the DDB method, *double* refers to the rate and *declining balance* refers to carrying amount. The rate is applied to beginning carrying amount each period.

EXHIBIT 10.10

Double-Declining-Balance Depreciation Formula*

Step 1

Straight-line rate = 100% ÷ Useful life = 100% ÷ 5 years = 20%

Step 2

Double-declining-balance rate = 2 × Straight-line rate = 2 × 20% = 40%

Step 3

Depreciation expense = Double-declining-balance rate × Beginning-period carrying amount

40% × \$10,000 = \$4,000 (for 2011)

* To simplify: DDB depreciation = (2 × Beginning-period carrying amount)/Useful life.

The *double-declining-balance depreciation schedule* is shown in Exhibit 10.11. The schedule follows the formula except for year 2015, when depreciation expense is \$296. This \$296 is not equal to 40% × \$1,296, or \$518.40. If we had used the \$518.40 for depreciation expense in 2015, the ending carrying amount would equal \$777.60, which is less than the \$1,000 residual value. Instead, the \$296 is computed by subtracting the \$1,000 residual value from the \$1,296 carrying amount at the beginning of the fifth year (the year when DDB depreciation cuts into residual value).

Example: What is the DDB depreciation expense in year 2014 if the residual value is \$2,000? *Answer:* \$2,160 − \$2,000 = \$160

EXHIBIT 10.11

Double-Declining-Balance Depreciation Schedule

	Depreciation for the Period			End of Period	
Annual Period	Beginning of Period Carrying Amount	Depreciation Rate	Depreciation Expense	Accumulated Depreciation	Carrying Amount
2010	—	—	—	—	\$10,000
2011	\$10,000	40%	\$4,000	\$4,000	6,000
2012	6,000	40	2,400	6,400	3,600
2013	3,600	40	1,440	7,840	2,160
2014	2,160	40	864	8,704	1,296
2015	1,296	40	296*	9,000	1,000

* Year 2015 depreciation is \$1,296 − \$1,000 = \$296 (never depreciate carrying amount below residual value).

Comparing Depreciation Methods   Exhibit 10.12 shows depreciation expense for each year of the machine's useful life under each of the three depreciation methods. While depreciation expense per period differs for different methods, total depreciation expense of \$9,000 is the same over the machine's useful life.

EXHIBIT 10.12

Depreciation Expense for the Different Methods

Period	Straight-Line	Units-of-Production	Double-Declining-Balance
2011	\$1,800	\$1,750	\$4,000
2012	1,800	2,000	2,400
2013	1,800	2,250	1,440
2014	1,800	1,750	864
2015	1,800	1,250	296
Totals	\$9,000	\$9,000	\$9,000

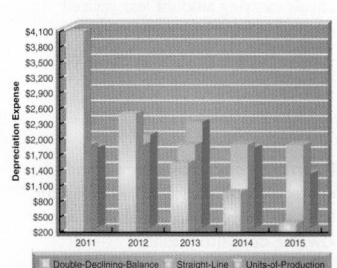

Each method starts with a total cost of $10,000 and ends with a residual value of $1,000. The difference is the pattern in depreciation expense over the useful life. The carrying amount of the asset when using straight-line is always greater than the carrying amount from using double-declining-balance, except at the beginning and end of the asset's useful life, when it is the same. Also, the straight-line method yields a steady pattern of depreciation expense while the units-of-production depreciation depends on the number of units produced. Each of these methods is acceptable because it allocates cost in a systematic and rational manner.

Depreciation for Tax Reporting Depending on the country, the records a company keeps for financial accounting purposes can be separate from the records it keeps for tax accounting purposes. This is so because financial accounting aims to report useful information on financial performance and position, whereas tax accounting reflects government objectives in raising revenues. Differences between these two accounting systems are normal and expected. Depreciation is a common example of how the records differ. For example, many companies use accelerated depreciation in computing taxable income. Reporting higher depreciation expense in the early years of an asset's life reduces the company's taxable income in those years and increases it in later years, when the depreciation expense is lower. The company's goal here is to *postpone* its tax payments.

Partial-Year Depreciation

Property, plant and equipment are purchased and disposed of at various times. When an asset is purchased (or disposed of) at a time other than the beginning or end of an accounting period, depreciation is recorded for part of a year. This is done so that the year of purchase or the year of disposal is charged with its share of the asset's depreciation.

To illustrate, assume that the machine in Exhibit 10.4 is purchased and placed in service on October 8, 2010, and the annual accounting period ends on December 31. Since this machine is purchased and used for nearly three months in 2010, the calendar-year income statement should report depreciation expense on the machine for that part of the year. Normally, depreciation assumes that the asset is purchased on the first day of the month nearest the actual date of purchase. In this case, since the purchase occurred on October 8, we assume an October 1 purchase date. This means that three months' depreciation is recorded in 2010. Using straight-line depreciation, we compute three months' depreciation of $450 as follows.

$$\frac{\$10,000 - \$1,000}{5 \text{ years}} \times \frac{3}{12} = \$450$$

A similar computation is necessary when an asset disposal occurs during a period. To illustrate, assume that the machine is sold on June 24, 2015. Depreciation is recorded for the period January 1 through June 24 when it is disposed of. This partial year's depreciation, computed to the nearest whole month, is

$$\frac{\$10,000 - \$1,000}{5 \text{ years}} \times \frac{6}{12} = \$900$$

Change in Estimates for Depreciation

Depreciation is based on estimates of residual value and useful life. During the useful life of an asset, new information may indicate that these estimates are inaccurate. If our estimate of an asset's useful life and/or residual value changes, what should we do? The answer is to use the new estimate to compute depreciation for current and future periods. This means that we revise the depreciation expense computation by spreading the cost yet to be depreciated over the remaining useful life. This approach is used for all depreciation methods.

Let's return to the machine described in Exhibit 10.7 using straight-line depreciation. At the beginning of this asset's third year, its carrying amount is $6,400, computed as $10,000 minus $3,600. Assume that at the beginning of its third year, the estimated number of years remaining in its useful life changes from three to four years *and* its estimate of residual value changes from $1,000 to $400. Straight-line depreciation for each of the four remaining years is computed as shown in Exhibit 10.13.

$$\frac{\text{Carrying amount} - \text{Revised residual value}}{\text{Revised remaining useful life}} = \frac{\$6,400 - \$400}{4 \text{ years}} = \$1,500 \text{ per year}$$

EXHIBIT 10.13

Computing Revised Straight-Line Depreciation

Thus, $1,500 of depreciation expense is recorded for the machine at the end of the third through sixth years—each year of its remaining useful life. Since this asset was depreciated at $1,800 per year for the first two years, it is tempting to conclude that depreciation expense was overstated in the first two years. However, these expenses reflected the best information available at that time. We do not go back and restate prior years' financial statements for this type of new information. Instead, we adjust the current and future periods' statements to reflect this new information. Revising an estimate of the useful life or residual value of an item of property, plant and equipment is referred to as a **change in an accounting estimate** and is reflected in current and future financial statements, not in prior statements.

Example: If at the beginning of its second year the machine's remaining useful life changes from four to three years and residual value from $1,000 to $400, how much straight-line depreciation is recorded in remaining years?
Answer: Revised depreciation = ($8,200 − $400)/3 = $2,600.

Reporting Depreciation

Both the cost and accumulated depreciation of property, plant and equipment are reported on the statement of financial position or in its notes. **Nestlé** for instance, reports the following carrying amounts or net amounts in Note 7 of its 2013 annual report (in CHF millions).

Land and building	15,988
Less accumulated depreciation and impairment	5,300
Carrying amount	10,688
Machinery and equipment	28,433
Less accumulated depreciation and impairment	15,098
Carrying amount	13,335
Tools, furniture and other equipment	7,817
Less accumulated depreciation and impairment	5,323
Carrying amount	2,494
Vehicles	880
Less accumulated depreciation and impairment	502
Carrying amount	378

Note: Impairment to be discussed in section on Measurement Subsequent to Initial Reporting

Point: A company usually keeps records for each asset showing its cost and depreciation to date. The combined records for individual assets are a type of *property, plant and equipment subsidiary ledger.*

Many companies also show property, plant and equipment on one line with the net amount of cost less accumulated depreciation. When this is done, the amount of accumulated depreciation is disclosed in a note. **Nestlé** reports only the net amount of its property, plant and equipment in its statement of financial position. To satisfy the full-disclosure principle, Nestlé describes its depreciation methods and the amounts comprising property, plant and equipment in its notes to its financial statements.

Reporting both the cost and accumulated depreciation of property, plant and equipment helps users compare the assets of different companies. For example, a company holding assets costing $50,000 and accumulated depreciation of $40,000 is likely in a situation different from a company with new assets costing $10,000. While the net undepreciated cost of $10,000 is the same in both cases, the first company may have more productive capacity available but likely is facing the need to replace older assets. These insights are not provided if the two statements of financial position report only the $10,000 carrying amounts.

Decision Ethics   Answer — p. 417

Controller   You are the controller for a struggling company. Its operations require regular investments in equipment, and depreciation is its largest expense. Its competitors frequently replace equipment—often depreciated over three years. The company president instructs you to revise useful lives of equipment from three to six years and to use a six-year life on all new equipment. What actions do you take? ■

Quick Check   Answers — p. 418

4. On January 1, 2015, a company pays $77,000 to purchase office furniture with a zero residual value. The furniture's useful life is somewhere between 7 and 10 years. What is the year 2015 straight-line depreciation on the furniture using (a) a 7-year useful life and (b) a 10-year useful life?

5. What does the term *depreciation* mean in accounting?

6. A company purchases a machine for $96,000 on January 1, 2015. Its useful life is five years or 100,000 units of product, and its residual value is $8,000. During 2015, 10,000 units of product are produced. Compute the carrying amount of this machine on December 31, 2015, assuming (a) straight-line depreciation and (b) units-of-production depreciation.

7. In early January 2015, a company acquires equipment for $3,800. The company estimates this equipment to have a useful life of three years and a residual value of $200. Early in 2017, the company changes its estimates to a total four-year useful life and zero residual value. Using the straight-line method, what is depreciation for the year ended 2017?

ADDITIONAL EXPENDITURES

C3 Distinguish between revenue and capital expenditures, and account for them.

After a company acquires an item of property, plant and equipment and puts it into service, it often makes additional expenditures for that asset's operation, maintenance, repair, and improvement. In recording these expenditures, it must decide whether to capitalize or expense them (to capitalize an expenditure is to debit the asset account). The issue is whether these expenditures are reported as current period expenses or added to the cost of property, plant and equipment and depreciated over its remaining useful life.

Revenue expenditures, also called *income statement expenditures*, are additional costs of property, plant and equipment that do not materially increase the asset's life or productive capabilities. They are recorded as expenses and deducted from revenues in the current period's income statement. The purpose of these expenditures is often described as for the "repairs and maintenance" of the item of property, plant and equipment. Examples of revenue expenditures are cleaning, repainting, adjustments, and lubricants.

Capital expenditures, also called *statement of financial position expenditures*, are additional costs of property, plant and equipment that provide benefits extending beyond the current period. They are debited to asset accounts and reported on the statement of financial position. Capital expenditures increase or improve the type or amount of service an asset provides. Examples are roofing replacement, plant expansion, and major overhauls of machinery and equipment.

The decision to record an expenditure as revenue or capital in nature requires judgment. Financial statements are affected for several years by the accounting choice of recording costs as either revenue expenditures or capital expenditures. As an example of the journal entry for revenue expenditures, **Brunswick** reports that "maintenance and repair costs are expensed as incurred." If Brunswick's current year repair costs are $9,500, it makes the following entry.

	Financial Statement Effect	
	Accounting	Expense Timing
Revenue expenditure	Income stmt. account debited	Expensed currently
Capital expenditure	Statement of financial position account debited	Expensed in future

Point: Many companies apply materiality to treat *low-cost property, plant and equipment* (say, less than $500) as revenue expenditures. This practice is referred to as a "capitalization policy."

Assets = Liabilities + Equity
−9,500   −9,500

Dec. 31	Repairs Expense	9,500	
	Cash		9,500
	To record ordinary repairs of equipment.		

For examples of capital expenditures, suppose a company pays $8,000 for a machine with an eight-year useful life and no residual value. After three years and $3,000 of depreciation, it adds an automated control system to the machine at a cost of $1,800. This results in reduced labor costs in future periods. The journal entry is as follows:

Jan. 2	Machinery	1,800	
	Cash		1,800
	To record installation of automated system.		

Assets = Liabilities + Equity
+1,800
−1,800

Adidas reports that renewals and improvements are capitalized and depreciated separately, if the recognition criteria are met.

Example: Assume a firm owns a Web server. Identify each cost as a revenue or capital expenditure: (1) purchase price, (2) necessary wiring, (3) platform for operation, (4) circuits to increase capacity, (5) cleaning after each month of use, (6) repair of a faulty switch, and (7) replaced a worn fan. *Answer:* Capital expenditures: 1, 2, 3, 4; revenue expenditures: 5, 6, 7.

■ **Decision Maker**   Answer — p. 417

Entrepreneur Your start-up Internet services company needs cash, and you are preparing financial statements to apply for a short-term loan. A friend suggests that you treat as many expenses as possible as capital expenditures. What are the impacts on financial statements of this suggestion? What do you think is the aim of this suggestion? ■

MEASUREMENT SUBSEQUENT TO INITIAL RECORDING

Measurement Models

C4 Explain the revaluation model to account for property, plant and equipment.

IAS 16 allows a reporting entity to choose either the cost model or the revaluation model and apply that policy to an entire class of property, plant and equipment.

The Cost Model states that after recognition as an asset, an item of property, plant and equipment shall be carried at its cost less any accumulated depreciation and any accumulated impairment losses (impairment discussed below).

The Revaluation Model states that after recognition as an asset, an item of property, plant and equipment whose fair value can be measured reliably shall be carried at a revalued amount, being its fair value at the date of the revaluation less any subsequent accumulated depreciation and subsequent accumulated impairment losses. The fair value of property, plant and equipment is usually determined from market-based evidence by professional appraisal or valuation. For example, if land which was bought for $1 million in 2013 is revalued to $1.5 million on June 30, 2015 (no depreciation for land), the journal entry for the revaluation on that date is:

June 30	Land	500,000	
	Revaluation Surplus-Land		500,000
	To revalue land.		

Revaluation surplus is part of other comprehensive income discussed in the chapter on accounting for corporations. For depreciable assets, we have to account for accumulated depreciation using the following example.

KC Corp has equipment bought on July 1, 2013 with a cost of $200,000, no residual value, and estimated useful life of five years. After two years on June 30, 2015, KC obtains market information for revaluation suggesting that the fair value of the equipment is $300,000. **IAS 16** allows two methods to account for the accumulated depreciation of $80,000. At the date of the revaluation, the accumulated depreciation is either:

a. restated proportionately with the change in the gross carrying amount of the asset so that the carrying amount of the asset after revaluation equals its revalued amount; or

b. eliminated against the gross carrying amount of the asset and the net amount restated to the revalued amount of the asset.

For KC Corp, to apply method **a**:

The fair value (gross carrying amount) must be $5/3 \times \$300,000 = \$500,000$. In order to have the carrying amount equal to the fair value after two years, the balance in accumulated depreciation needs to be $200,000. Therefore, the cost of the equipment must increase by $300,000 ($500,000 − $200,000), and accumulated depreciation must increase by $120,000 ($200,000 − $80,000). In other words, we must restate the equipment and the accumulated depreciation so that the ratio of net carrying amount to gross carrying amount is 60% ($120,000/$200,000) and the net carrying amount is thus $300,000. New gross carrying amount is calculated as $300,000/60% = $500,000.

	Original		Revaluation		Total	Percent
Gross Amount............	$200,000	+	$300,000	=	$500,000	100
Accumulated Amortization ...	80,000	+	120,000	=	200,000	40
Carrying Amount	$120,000	+	$180,000	=	$300,000	60

The journal entry for revaluation on June 30, 2015 is:

June 30	Equipment	30,000	
	Accumulated Depreciation—Equipment		120,000
	Revaluation Surplus—Equipment..............		180,000
	To revalue equipment with accumulated depreciation.		

For KC Corp, to apply method **b**:

Eliminate accumulated depreciation of $80,000 and then increase the equipment by $180,000 so the carrying amount is $300,000 (= $200,000 − $80,000 + $180,000).

The journal entries for revaluation on June 30, 2015 are:

June 30	Accumulated Depreciation—Equipment	8,000	
	Equipment		80,000
	To eliminate accumulated depreciation for revaluation.		

June 30	Equipment	18,000	
	Revaluation Surplus—Equipment..............		180,000
	To revalue equipment.		

Impairment

A reporting entity has to calculate its assets' carrying amounts, which are after deducting any accumulated depreciation (amortization) and accumulated impairment losses. An **impairment** is the amount by which the carrying amount of an asset exceeds its recoverable amount. **IAS 36 Impairment of Assets** provides detailed guidance on this matter. For example, if a company has specialized machines that can manufacture only DVDs, then these machines would be useless once the market switches completely to Blu-ray disks. These machines have to be tested for impairment losses (details on impairment test are in advanced courses).

For example, equipment bought before 2015 has a carrying amount of $8,000 ($9,000 cost less $1,000 accumulated depreciation) and a recoverable amount of $7,500. The journal entry to record this impairment on December 31, 2015 is:

December 31	Impairment Loss on Equipment	500	
	Accumulated Impairment Losses—Equipment ...		500
	To record impairment loss on equipment.		

Some companies record depreciation and impairment in the same accumulated accounting as shown above.

DISPOSALS OF PROPERTY, PLANT AND EQUIPMENT

Property, plant and equipment are disposed of for several reasons. Some are discarded because they wear out or become obsolete. Others are sold because of changing business plans. Regardless of the reason, disposals of property, plant and equipment occur in one of three basic ways: discarding, sale, or exchange. The general steps in accounting for a disposal of property, plant and equipment are described in Exhibit 10.14.

1. Record depreciation up to the date of disposal—this also updates Accumulated Depreciation.
2. Record the removal of the disposed asset's account balances—including its Accumulated Depreciation.
3. Record any cash (and/or other assets) received or paid in the disposal.
4. Record any gain or loss—computed by comparing the disposed asset's carrying amount with the market value of any assets received.

EXHIBIT 10.14

Accounting for Disposals of Property, Plant and Equipment

Discarding Property, Plant and Equipment

An item of property, plant and equipment is *discarded* when it is no longer useful to the company and it has no market value. To illustrate, assume that a machine costing $9,000 with accumulated depreciation of $9,000 is discarded. When accumulated depreciation equals the asset's cost, it is said to be *fully depreciated* (zero carrying amount). The entry to record the discarding of this asset is

P2 Account for asset disposal through discarding or selling an asset.

June 5	Accumulated Depreciation—Machinery	9,000	
	Machinery		9,000
	To discard fully depreciated machinery.		

Assets = Liabilities + Equity
+9,000
−9,000

This entry reflects all four steps of Exhibit 10.14. Step 1 is unnecessary since the machine is fully depreciated. Step 2 is reflected in the debit to Accumulated Depreciation and credit to Machinery. Since no other asset is involved, step 3 is irrelevant. Finally, since carrying amount is zero and no other asset is involved, no gain or loss is recorded in step 4.

How do we account for discarding an asset that is not fully depreciated or one whose depreciation is not up-to-date? To answer this, consider equipment costing $8,000 with accumulated depreciation of $6,000 on December 31 of the prior financial year-end. This equipment is being depreciated using the straight-line method over eight years with zero residual value. On July 1 of the current year it is discarded. Step 1 is to bring depreciation up-to-date.

Point: Recording depreciation expense up-to-date gives an up-to-date carrying amount for determining gain or loss.

July 1	Depreciation Expense	500	
	Accumulated Depreciation—Equipment		500
	To record 6 months' depreciation ($1,000 × 6/12).		

Assets = Liabilities + Equity
−500   −500

Steps 2 through 4 of Exhibit 10.14 are reflected in the second (and final) entry.

July 1	Accumulated Depreciation—Equipment	6,500	
	Loss on Disposal of Equipment	1,500	
	Equipment		8,000
	To discard equipment with a $1,500 carrying amount.		

Assets = Liabilities + Equity
+6,500   −1,500
−8,000

This loss is computed by comparing the equipment's $1,500 carrying amount ($8,000 − $6,000 − $500) with the zero net cash proceeds. The loss is reported in the Other Expenses and Losses section of the income statement. Discarding an asset can sometimes require a cash payment that would increase the loss.

Point: Gain or loss is determined by comparing "value given" (carrying amount) to "value received."

Selling Property, Plant and Equipment

Companies often sell property, plant and equipment when they restructure or downsize operations. To illustrate the accounting for selling property, plant and equipment, we consider BTO's March 31 sale of equipment that cost $16,000 and has accumulated depreciation of

$12,000 at December 31 of the prior calendar year-end. Annual depreciation on this equipment is $4,000 computed using straight-line depreciation. Step 1 of this sale is to record depreciation expense and update accumulated depreciation to March 31 of the current year.

Assets = Liabilities + Equity
−1,000   −1,000

March 31	Depreciation Expense	1,000	
	Accumulated Depreciation—Equipment		1,000
	To record 3 months' depreciation ($4,000 × 3/12).		

Steps 2 through 4 of Exhibit 10.14 can be reflected in one final entry that depends on the amount received from the asset's sale. We consider three different possibilities.

Sale price = Carrying amount →
No gain or loss

Sale at Carrying Amount If BTO receives $3,000 cash, an amount equal to the equipment's carrying amount as at March 31 (carrying amount = $16,000 − $12,000 − $1,000), no gain or loss occurs on disposal. The entry is

Assets = Liabilities + Equity
+3,000
+13,000
−16,000

March 31	Cash	3,000	
	Accumulated Depreciation—Equipment	13,000	
	Equipment		16,000
	To record sale of equipment for no gain or loss.		

Sale price > Carrying amount → Gain

Sale above Carrying Amount If BTO receives $7,000, an amount that is $4,000 above the equipment's $3,000 carrying amount as at March 31, a gain on disposal occurs. The entry is

Assets = Liabilities + Equity
+7,000   +4,000
+13,000
−16,000

March 31	Cash	7,000	
	Accumulated Depreciation—Equipment	13,000	
	Gain on Disposal of Equipment		4,000
	Equipment		16,000
	To record sale of equipment for a $4,000 gain.		

Sale price < Carrying amount → Loss

Sale below Carrying Amount If BTO receives $2,500, an amount that is $500 below the equipment's $3,000 carrying amount as at March 31, a loss on disposal occurs. The entry is

Assets = Liabilities + Equity
+2,500   −500
+13,000
−16,000

March 31	Cash	2,500	
	Loss on Disposal of Equipment	500	
	Accumulated Depreciation—Equipment	13,000	
	Equipment		16,000
	To record sale of equipment for a $500 loss.		

IAS 16 clarifies that an entity cannot classify as revenue a gain it realizes on the disposal of an item of property, plant and equipment. Therefore, gains or losses on disposal of property, plant and equipment should be shown separately on the income statement before calculation of profit.

Quick Check

Answers — p. 418

8. Early in the fifth year of a machine's six-year useful life, it is overhauled, and its useful life is extended to nine years. This machine originally cost $108,000 and the overhaul cost is $12,000. Prepare the entry to record the overhaul cost.

9. Explain the difference between revenue expenditures and capital expenditures and how both are recorded.

10. If a piece of equipment is sold at its carrying amount, how is net profit affected?

11. A company acquires equipment on January 10, 2015, at a cost of $42,000. Straight-line depreciation is used with a five-year life and $7,000 residual value. On June 27, 2016, the company sells this equipment for $32,000. Prepare the entry(ies) for June 27, 2016.

Section 2—Natural Resources

Natural resources are assets that are physically consumed when used. Examples are standing timber, mineral deposits, and oil and gas fields. Since they are consumed when used, they are often called *wasting assets*. These assets represent soon-to-be inventories of raw materials that will be converted into one or more products by cutting, mining, or pumping. Until that conversion takes place, they are noncurrent assets and are shown in a statement of financial position using titles such as timberlands, mineral deposits, or oil reserves. Natural resources are reported under either property, plant and equipment or their own separate category. **Alcoa**, for instance, reports its natural resources under the statement of financial position title *Properties, plants and equipment.* In a note to its financial statements, Alcoa reports a separate amount for *Land and land rights, including mines.* **Weyerhaeuser**, on the other hand, reports its timber holdings in a separate statement of financial position category titled *Timber and timberlands.*

> **P3** Account for natural resource assets and their depletion.

Cost Determination and Depletion

Natural resources are recorded at cost, which includes all expenditures necessary to acquire the resource and prepare it for its intended use. **Depletion** is the process of allocating the cost of a natural resource to the period when it is consumed. Natural resources are reported on the statement of financial position at cost less *accumulated depletion.* The depletion expense per period is usually based on units extracted from cutting, mining, or pumping. This is similar to units-of-production depreciation. **Exxon Mobil** uses this approach to amortize the costs of discovering and operating its oil wells.

To illustrate depletion of natural resources, let's consider a mineral deposit with an estimated 250,000 tons of available ore. It is purchased for $500,000, and we expect zero residualvalue. The depletion charge per ton of ore mined is $2, computed as $500,000 ÷ 250,000 tons. If 85,000 tons are mined and sold in the first year, the depletion charge for that year is $170,000. These computations are detailed in Exhibit 10.15.

Step 1

$$\text{Depletion per unit} = \frac{\text{Cost} - \text{Residual value}}{\text{Total units of capacity}} = \frac{\$500,000 - \$0}{250,000 \text{ tons}} = \$2 \text{ per ton}$$

Step 2

$$\text{Depletion expense} = \text{Depletion per unit} \times \text{Units extracted and sold in period}$$
$$= \$2 \times 85,000 = \$170,000$$

EXHIBIT 10.15

Depletion Formula and Example

Depletion expense for the first year is recorded as follows.

Dec. 31	Depletion Expense—Mineral Deposit	170,000	
	Accumulated Depletion—Mineral Deposit		170,000
	To record depletion of the mineral deposit.		

Assets	= Liabilities +	Equity
−170,000		−170,000

The period-end statement of financial position reports the mineral deposit as shown in Exhibit 10.16

| Mineral deposit . . . . | $500,000 | |
| **Less accumulated depletion** . . . . | **170,000** | $330,000 |

EXHIBIT 10.16

Statement of Financial Position Presentation of Natural Resources

Since all 85,000 tons of the mined ore are sold during the year, the entire $170,000 of depletion is reported on the income statement. If some of the ore remains unsold at year-end, however, the depletion related to the unsold ore is carried forward on the statement of financial position and reported as Ore Inventory, a current asset. To illustrate, and continuing with our example, assume that 40,000 tons are mined in the second year, but only 34,000 tons are sold. We record depletion of $68,000 (34,000 tons × $2 depletion per unit) and the remaining Ore Inventory of $12,000 (6,000 tons × $2 depletion per unit) as follows.

Assets = Liabilities + Equity
−80,000   −68,000
+12,000

Dec. 31	Depletion Expense—Mineral Deposit	68,000	
	Ore Inventory	12,000	
	Accumulated Depletion—Mineral Deposit		80,000
	To record depletion and inventory of mineral deposit.		

Property, Plant and Equipment Used in Extracting

The conversion of natural resources by mining, cutting, or pumping usually requires machinery, equipment, and buildings. When the usefulness of these items of property, plant and equipment is directly related to the depletion of a natural resource, their costs are depreciated using the units-of-production method in proportion to the depletion of the natural resource. For example, if a machine is permanently installed in a mine and 10% of the ore is mined and sold in the period, then 10% of the machine's cost (less any residual value) is allocated to depreciation expense. The same procedure is used when a machine is abandoned once resources have been extracted. If, however, a machine will be moved to and used at another site when extraction is complete, the machine is depreciated over its own useful life.

Decision Insight

Asset Control   Long-term assets must be safeguarded against theft, misuse, and other damages. Controls take many forms depending on the asset, including use of security tags, the legal monitoring of rights infringements, and approvals of all asset disposals. A study reports that 44% of employees in operations and service areas witnessed the wasting, mismanaging, or abusing of assets in the past year (KPMG 2009). Another 21% in general management and administration observed stealing or misappropriation of assets. ∎

Section 3—Intangible Assets

P4 Account for intangible assets.

Intangible assets are nonphysical assets (used in operations) that confer on their owners long-term rights, privileges, or competitive advantages. Examples are patents, copyrights, licenses, franchises, goodwill, and trademarks. Lack of physical substance does not necessarily imply an intangible asset. Notes and accounts receivable, for instance, lack physical substance, but they are not intangibles. This section identifies the more common types of intangible assets and explains the accounting for them.

Cost Determination and Amortization

An intangible asset is recorded at cost when purchased. Intangibles are then separated into those with limited lives or indefinite lives. If an intangible has a **limited life**, its cost is systematically allocated to expense over its estimated useful life through the process of **amortization**. If an intangible asset has an **indefinite life**—meaning that no legal, regulatory, contractual, competitive, economic, or other factors limit its useful life—it should not be amortized. (If an intangible with an indefinite life is later judged to have a limited life, it is amortized over that limited life.) Amortization of intangible assets is similar to depreciation of property, plant and equipment and the depletion of natural resources in that it is a process of cost allocation. However, only the straight-line method is used for amortizing intangibles *unless* the company can show that another method is preferred. The effects of amortization are recorded in a contra account (Accumulated Amortization). The gross acquisition cost of intangible assets is disclosed in the statement of financial position along with their accumulated amortization (these disclosures are new).

The eventual disposal of an intangible asset involves removing its carrying amount, recording any other asset(s) received or given up, and recognizing any gain or loss for the difference.

Many intangibles have limited lives due to laws, contracts, or other asset characteristics. Examples are patents and copyrights. Other intangibles such as goodwill, trademarks, and trade names have lives that cannot be easily determined. The cost of intangible assets is amortized over the periods expected to benefit by their use, but in no case can this period be longer than the asset's legal existence. The values of some intangible assets such as goodwill continue indefinitely into the future and are not amortized. (An intangible asset that is not amortized is tested annually for impairment—if necessary, an impairment loss is recorded. Details for this test are in advanced courses.)

Intangible assets are often shown in a separate section of the statement of financial position immediately after property, plant and equipment. **Heineken**, for instance, follows this approach in reporting almost EUR 16 billion of intangible assets in its 2013 statement of financial position. Companies usually disclose their amortization periods for intangibles. The remainder of our discussion focuses on accounting for specific types of intangible assets.

Types of Intangibles

Patents Patents are granted by the relevant authorities in different countries to encourage the invention of new technology, mechanical devices, and production processes. A **patent** is an exclusive right to its owner to manufacture and sell a patented item or to use a process for 20 years. For example, the European Patent Office (EPO) provides a uniform application procedure for individual inventors and companies seeking patent protection in up to 38 European countries.

A patent's cost is amortized over its estimated useful life. If we purchase a patent costing $25,000 with a useful life of 10 years, we make the following adjusting entry at the end of each of the 10 years to amortize one-tenth of its cost.

Dec. 31	Amortization Expense—Patents	2,500	
	Accumulated Amortization—Patents		2,500
	To amortize patent costs over its useful life.		

The $2,500 debit to Amortization Expense appears on the income statement as a cost of the product or service provided under protection of the patent. The Accumulated Amortization—Patents account is a contra asset account to Patents.

Assets = Liabilities + Equity
−2,500   −2,500

Decision Insight

Mention "drug war" and most people think of illegal drug trade. But another drug war is under way: Brand-name drugmakers are fighting to stop generic copies of their products from hitting the market once patents expire. Delaying a generic rival can yield millions in extra sales. ■

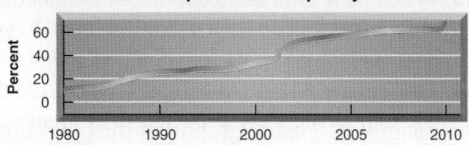

Percent of Prescriptions That Specify Generics

Copyrights A **copyright** gives its owner the exclusive right to publish and sell a musical, literary, or artistic work during the life of the creator plus 70 years, although the useful life of most copyrights is much shorter. The costs of a copyright are amortized over its useful life. The only identifiable cost of many copyrights is the fee paid to the Copyright Office of the federal government or international agency granting the copyright. If this fee is immaterial, it is charged directly to an expense account; but if the identifiable costs of a copyright are material, they are capitalized (recorded in an asset account) and periodically amortized by debiting an account called Amortization Expense—Copyrights.

Franchises and Licenses **Franchises** and **licenses** are rights that a company or government grants an entity to deliver a product or service under specified conditions. Many organizations grant franchise and license rights—**McDonald's**, **Pizza Hut**, and **Major League Baseball** are just a few examples. The costs of franchises and licenses are debited to a Franchises and Licenses asset account and are amortized over the lives of the agreements. If an agreement is for an indefinite or perpetual period, those costs are not amortized.

Trademarks and Trade Names   Companies often adopt unique symbols or select unique names and brands in marketing their products. A **trademark** or **trade (brand) name** is a symbol, name, phrase, or jingle identified with a company, product, or service. Examples are **Adidas'** 3-stripes, **L'Oréal's** slogan "Because you're worth it" and **McDonald's** Big Mac. Ownership and exclusive right to use a trademark or trade name is often established by showing that one company used it before another. Ownership is best established by registering a trademark or trade name with the government's Patent Office. The cost of developing a trademark or trade name (such as advertising) is charged to expense when incurred. If a trademark or trade name is purchased, however, its cost is debited to an asset account and then amortized over its expected life. If the company plans to renew indefinitely its right to the trademark or trade name, the cost is not amortized.

Goodwill   **Goodwill** has a specific meaning in accounting. Goodwill is the amount by which a company's value exceeds the value of its individual assets and liabilities. This usually implies that the company as a whole has certain valuable attributes not measured among its individual assets and liabilities. These can include superior management, skilled workforce, good supplier or customer relations, quality products or services, good location, or other competitive advantages.

To keep accounting information from being too subjective, goodwill is not recorded unless an entire company or business segment is purchased. Purchased goodwill is measured by taking the purchase price of the company and subtracting the fair market value of its individual net assets (excluding goodwill). For instance, **Yahoo!** paid nearly $3.0 billion to acquire **GeoCities**; about $2.8 of the $3.0 billion was for goodwill and other intangibles.

Goodwill is measured as the excess of the cost of an acquired entity over the value of the acquired net assets. Goodwill is recorded as an asset, and it is *not* amortized. Instead, goodwill is tested annually for impairment. If the carrying amount of goodwill does not exceed its recoverable amount, goodwill is not impaired. However, if the carrying amount of goodwill does exceed its recoverable amount, an impairment loss is recorded equal to that excess. (Details of the impairment test are in advanced courses.)

Other Intangibles   There are other types of intangible assets such as *software, noncompete covenants, customer lists,* and so forth. Our accounting for them is the same. First, we record the intangible asset's costs. Second, we determine whether the asset has a limited or indefinite life. If limited, we allocate its costs over that period. If indefinite, its costs are not amortized.

Quick Check   Answers — p. 418

12. Give an example of a natural resource and of an intangible asset.
13. A company pays $650,000 for an ore deposit. The deposit is estimated to have 325,000 tons of ore that will be mined over the next 10 years. During the first year, it mined, processed, and sold 91,000 tons. What is that year's depletion expense?
14. On January 6, 2015, a company pays $120,000 for a patent with a remaining 17-year legal life to produce a toy expected to be marketable for three years. Prepare entries to record its acquisition and the December 31, 2015, amortization entry.

Decision Analysis   Total Asset Turnover

A1 Compute total asset turnover and apply it to analyze a company's use of assets.

A company's assets are important in determining its ability to generate sales and earn income. Managers devote much attention to deciding what assets a company acquires, how much it invests in assets, and how to use assets most efficiently and effectively. One important measure of a company's ability to use its assets is **total asset turnover,** defined in Exhibit 10.17.

EXHIBIT 10.17

Total Asset Turnover

$$\text{Total asset turnover} = \frac{\text{Net sales}}{\text{Average total assets}}$$

The numerator reflects the net amounts earned from the sale of products and services. The denominator reflects the average total resources devoted to operating the company and generating sales.

To illustrate, let's look at total asset turnover in Exhibit 10.18 for two competing companies: Adidas and Puma.

		2011	2012	2013
Adidas	Net sales	13,344	14,883	14,492
(EUR millions)	Average Assets	10,999	11,515.5	11,625
	Total asset turnover	1.2	1.3	1.2
Puma	Net sales	3,009	3270.7	2530.3
(EUR millions)	Average Assets	2,474.2	2,556.05	2,419.4
	Total asset turnover	1.2	1.3	1.0

EXHIBIT 10.18

Analysis Using Total Asset Turnover

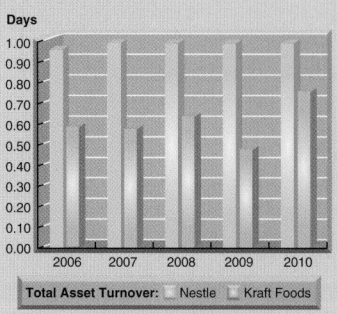

To show how we use total asset turnover, let's look at Adidas. We express Adidas' use of assets in generating net sales by saying "it turned its assets over 1.2 times during 2013." This means that each Euro of assets produced 1.2 Euro of net sales. Is a total asset turnover of 1.2 good or bad? It is safe to say that all companies desire a high total asset turnover. Like many ratio analyses, however, a company's total asset turnover must be interpreted in comparison with that of prior years and of its competitors. Interpreting the total asset turnover also requires an understanding of the company's operations. Some operations are capital intensive, meaning that a relatively large amount is invested in assets to generate sales. This suggests a relatively lower total asset turnover. Other companies' operations are labor intensive, meaning that they generate sales more by the efforts of people than the use of assets. In that case, we expect a higher total asset turnover. Companies with low total asset turnover require higher profit margins (examples are hotels and real estate); companies with high total asset turnover can succeed with lower profit margins (examples are food stores and toy merchandisers). Adidas' turnover has been the same with Puma's over the last two years, but has been higher than that for Puma in 2013.

Point: An estimate of **property, plant and equipment useful life** equals the property, plant and equipment cost divided by depreciation expense.

Point: The **property, plant and equipment age** is estimated by dividing accumulated depreciation by depreciation expense. Older property, plant and equipment can signal needed asset replacements; they may also signal less efficient assets.

Decision Maker Answer — p. 417

Environmentalist A paper manufacturer claims it cannot afford more environmental controls. It points to its low total asset turnover of 1.9 and argues that it cannot compete with companies whose total asset turnover is much higher. Examples cited are food stores (5.5) and auto dealers (3.8). How do you respond? ∎

DEMONSTRATION PROBLEM

On July 14, 2015, Tulsa Company pays $600,000 to acquire a fully equipped factory. The purchase involves the following assets and information.

Asset	Appraised Value	Residual Value	Useful Life	Depreciation Method
Land	$160,000			Not depreciated
Land improvements	80,000	$ 0	10 years	Straight-line
Building	320,000	100,000	10 years	Double-declining-balance
Machinery	240,000	20,000	10,000 units	Units-of-production*
Total	$800,000			

* The machinery is used to produce 700 units in 2015 and 1,800 units in 2016.

Required

1. Allocate the total $600,000 purchase cost among the separate assets.

2. Compute the 2015 (six months) and 2016 depreciation expense for each asset, and compute the company's total depreciation expense for both years.

3. On the last day of calendar year 2017, Tulsa discarded machinery that had been on its books for five years. The machinery's original cost was $12,000 (estimated life of five years) and its residual value was $2,000. No depreciation had been recorded for the fifth year when the disposal occurred. Journalize the fifth year of depreciation (straight-line method) and the asset's disposal.

4. At the beginning of year 2017, Tulsa purchased a patent for $100,000 cash. The company estimated the patent's useful life to be 10 years. Journalize the patent acquisition and its amortization for the year 2017.

5. Late in the year 2017, Tulsa acquired an ore deposit for $600,000 cash. It added roads and built mine shafts for an additional cost of $80,000. Residual value of the mine is estimated to be $20,000. The company estimated 330,000 tons of available ore. In year 2017, Tulsa mined and sold 10,000 tons of ore. Journalize the mine's acquisition and its first year's depletion.

PLANNING THE SOLUTION

- Complete a three-column table showing the following amounts for each asset: appraised value, percent of total value, and apportioned cost.
- Using allocated costs, compute depreciation for 2015 (only one-half year) and 2016 (full year) for each asset. Summarize those computations in a table showing total depreciation for each year.
- Remember that depreciation must be recorded up-to-date before discarding an asset. Calculate and record depreciation expense for the fifth year using the straight-line method. Since residual value is not received at the end of a discarded asset's life, the amount of any residual value becomes a loss on disposal. Record the loss on the disposal as well as the removal of the discarded asset and its related accumulated depreciation.
- Record the patent (an intangible asset) at its purchase price. Use straight-line amortization over its useful life to calculate amortization expense.
- Record the ore deposit (a natural resource asset) at its cost, including any added costs to ready the mine for use. Calculate depletion per ton using the depletion formula. Multiply the depletion per ton by the amount of tons mined and sold to calculate depletion expense for the year.

SOLUTION TO DEMONSTRATION PROBLEM

1. Allocation of the total cost of $600,000 among the separate assets.

Asset	Appraised Value	Percent of Total Value	Apportioned Cost
Land	$160,000	20%	$120,000 ($600,000 × 20%)
Land improvements	80,000	10	60,000 ($600,000 × 10%)
Building	320,000	40	240,000 ($600,000 × 40%)
Machinery	240,000	30	180,000 ($600,000 × 30%)
Total	$800,000	100%	$ 600,000

2. Depreciation for each asset. (Land is not depreciated.)

Land Improvements

Cost	$ 60,000
Residual value	0
Depreciable amount.	$ 60,000
Useful life	10 years
Annual depreciation expense ($60,000/10 years)	$ 6,000
2015 depreciation ($6,000 × 6/12)	$ 3,000
2016 depreciation	$ 6,000

Building

Straight-line rate = 100%/10 years = 10%
Double-declining-balance rate = 10% × 2 = 20%

2015 depreciation ($240,000 × 20% × 6/12)	$ 24,000
2016 depreciation [($240,000 − $24,000) × 20%].	$ 43,200

Machinery

Cost	$180,000
Residual value	20,000
Depreciable amount.	$160,000
Total expected units of production.	10,000 units
Depreciation per unit ($160,000/10,000 units)	$ 16
2015 depreciation ($16 × 700 units).	$ 11,200
2016 depreciation ($16 × 1,800 units)	$ 28,800

Total depreciation expense for each year:

	2015	2016
Land improvements	$ 3,000	$ 6,000
Building	24,000	43,200
Machinery	11,200	28,800
Total	$38,200	$78,000

3. Record the depreciation up-to-date on the discarded asset.

Depreciation Expense—Machinery	2,000	
Accumulated Depreciation—Machinery		2,000
To record depreciation on date of disposal: ($12,000 − $2,000)/5		

Record the removal of the discarded asset and its loss on disposal.

Accumulated Depreciation—Machinery	10,000	
Loss on Disposal of Machinery	2,000	
Machinery		12,000
To record the discarding of machinery with a $2,000 carrying amount.		

4.

Patent	100,000	
Cash		100,000
To record patent acquisition.		

Amortization Expense—Patent	10,000	
Accumulated Amortization—Patent.		10,000
To record amortization expense: $100,000/10 years = $10,000.		

5.

Ore Deposit	680,000	
Cash		680,000
To record ore deposit acquisition and its related costs.		

Depletion Expense—Ore Deposit	20,000	
Accumulated Depletion—Ore Deposit		20,000
To record depletion expense: ($680,000 − $20,000)/330,000 tons =		
$2 per ton. 10,000 tons mined and sold × $2 = $20,000 depletion.		

APPENDIX

Exchanging Property, Plant and Equipment

10A

P5A Account for asset exchanges.

Many items of property, plant and equipment such as machinery, automobiles, and office equipment are disposed of by exchanging them for newer assets. The cost of such an item of property, plant and equipment is measured at fair value unless (*a*) the exchange transaction lacks commercial substance or (*b*) the fair value of neither the asset received nor the asset given up is reliably measurable. The acquired item is measured in this way even if an entity cannot immediately derecognize the asset given up. An entity determines whether an exchange transaction has commercial substance by considering the extent to which its future cash flows are expected to change as a result of the transaction. If the acquired item is not measured at fair value, its cost is measured at the carrying amount of the asset given up. The following will consider only exchanges with commercial substance (other instances are covered in more advanced courses).

Exchange with Commercial Substance: A Loss   A company acquires $42,000 in new equipment. In exchange, the company pays $33,000 cash and trades in old equipment. The old equipment originally cost $36,000 and has accumulated depreciation of $20,000, which implies a $16,000 carrying amount at the time of exchange. This exchange yields a loss as computed in the middle (Loss) columns of Exhibit 10A.1; the loss is computed as Asset received – Assets given = $42,000 – $49,000 = $(7,000).

EXHIBIT 10A.1

Computing Gain or Loss on Asset Exchange with Commercial Substance

Asset Exchange Has Commercial Substance	Loss		Gain	
Market value of asset received		$ 42,000		$ 52,000
Carrying amount of assets given:				
Equipment ($36,000 − $20,000)	$16,000		$16,000	
Cash	33,000	49,000	33,000	49,000
Gain (loss) on exchange		$(7,000)		$ 3,000

The entry to record this asset exchange is

Assets = Liabilities + Equity
+42,000   −7,000
+20,000
−36,000
−33,000

Jan. 3	Equipment (**new**).	42,000	
	Loss on Exchange of Assets	7,000	
	Accumulated Depreciation—Equipment (**old**)	20,000	
	Equipment (**old**)		36,000
	Cash		33,000
	To record exchange (with commercial substance) of old equipment and cash for new equipment.		

Point: Parenthetical notes to "new" and "old" equipment are for illustration only. Both the debit and credit are to the same Equipment account.

Exchange with Commercial Substance: A Gain   Let's assume the same facts as in the preceding asset exchange *except* that the new equipment received has a fair value of $52,000 instead of $42,000. This exchange yields a gain as computed in the right-most (Gain) columns of Exhibit 10A.1; the gain is computed as Asset received – Assets given = $52,000 – $49,000 = $3,000. The entry to record this asset exchange is

Assets = Liabilities + Equity
+52,000   +3,000
+20,000
−36,000
−33,000

Jan. 3	Equipment (**new**)	52,000	
	Accumulated Depreciation—Equipment (**old**)	20,000	
	Equipment (**old**)		36,000
	Cash		33,000
	Gain on Exchange of Assets		3,000
	To record exchange (with commercial substance) of old equipment and cash for new equipment.		

Quick Check   Answer — p. 418 ✓

15. A company trades an old Web server for a new one. The cost of the old server is $30,000, and its accumulated depreciation at the time of the trade is $23,400. The new server has a cash price (fair value) of $45,000 but the company pays cash of $42,000. Prepare entries to record the trade assuming that the exchange has commercial substance.

Summary

C1 Explain the cost principle for computing the cost of property, plant and equipment. Property, plant and equipment are set apart from other tangible assets by two important features: use in operations and useful lives longer than one period. Property, plant and equipment are recorded at cost when purchased. Cost includes all normal and reasonable expenditures necessary to get the asset in place and ready for its intended use. The cost of a lump-sum purchase is allocated among its individual assets.

C2 Explain depreciation for partial years and changes in estimates. Partial-year depreciation is often required because assets are bought and sold throughout the year. Depreciation is revised when changes in estimates such as residual value and useful life occur. If the useful life of an item of property, plant and equipment changes, for instance, the remaining cost to be depreciated is spread over the remaining (revised) useful life of the asset.

C3 **Distinguish between revenue and capital expenditures, and account for them.** Revenue expenditures expire in the current period and are debited to expense accounts and matched with current revenues. Ordinary repairs are an example of revenue expenditures. Capital expenditures benefit future periods and are debited to asset accounts.

C4 **Explain the revaluation model to account for property, plant and equipment.** After initially recording an item of property, plant and equipment at cost, the company can subsequently choose to keep it at cost or revalue it. The revalued amount is its fair value at the date of the revaluation less any subsequent accumulated depreciation and subsequent accumulated impairment losses. The increase in value is credited to a revaluation surplus account which is under other comprehensive income.

A1 **Compute total asset turnover and apply it to analyze a company's use of assets.** Total asset turnover measures a company's ability to use its assets to generate sales. It is defined as net sales divided by average total assets. While all companies desire a high total asset turnover, it must be interpreted in comparison with those for prior years and its competitors.

P1 **Compute and record depreciation using the straight-line, units-of-production, and declining-balance methods.** *Depreciation* is the process of allocating to expense the cost of an item of property, plant and equipment over the accounting periods that benefit from its use. Depreciation does not measure the decline in the market value of an item of property, plant and equipment or its physical deterioration. Three factors determine depreciation: cost, residual value, and useful life. Residual value is the estimated amount that an entity would currently obtain from disposal of the asset, after deducting the estimated costs of disposal, if the asset were already of the age and in the condition expected at the end of

its useful life. Useful (service) life is the length of time an asset is productively used. The straight-line method divides cost less residual value by the asset's useful life to determine depreciation expense per period. The units-of-production method divides cost less residual value by the estimated number of units the asset will produce over its life to determine depreciation per unit. The declining-balance method multiplies the asset's beginning-of-period carrying amount by a factor that is often double the straight-line rate.

P2 **Account for asset disposal through discarding or selling an asset.** When an item of property, plant and equipment is discarded or sold, its cost and accumulated depreciation are removed from the accounts. Any cash proceeds from discarding or selling an asset are recorded and compared to the asset's carrying amount to determine gain or loss.

P3 **Account for natural resource assets and their depletion.** The cost of a natural resource is recorded in a noncurrent asset account. Depletion of a natural resource is recorded by allocating its cost to depletion expense using the units-of-production method. Depletion is credited to an Accumulated Depletion account.

P4 **Account for intangible assets.** An intangible asset is recorded at the cost incurred to purchase it. The cost of an intangible asset with a definite useful life is allocated to expense using the straight-line method, and is called *amortization*. Goodwill and intangible assets with an indefinite useful life are not amortized—they are annually tested for impairment. Intangible assets include patents, copyrights, goodwill, and trademarks.

P5ᴬ **Account for asset exchanges.** For an asset exchange with commercial substance, a gain or loss is recorded based on the difference between the carrying amount of the asset given up and the market value of the asset received.

Guidance Answers to Decision Maker and Decision Ethics

Controller The president's instructions may reflect an honest and reasonable prediction of the future. Since the company is struggling financially, the president may have concluded that the normal pattern of replacing assets every three years cannot continue. Perhaps the strategy is to avoid costs of frequent replacements and stretch use of equipment a few years longer until financial conditions improve. However, if you believe the president's decision is unprincipled, you might confront the president with your opinion that it is unethical to change the estimate to increase income. Another possibility is to wait and see whether the auditor will prohibit this change in estimate. In either case, you should insist that the statements be based on reasonable estimates.

Entrepreneur Treating an expense as a capital expenditure means that reported expenses will be lower and income higher in the short run. This is so because a capital expenditure is not expensed

immediately but is spread over the asset's useful life. Treating an expense as a capital expenditure also means that asset and equity totals are reported at larger amounts in the short run. This continues until the asset is fully depreciated. Your friend is probably trying to help, but the suggestion is misguided. Only an expenditure benefiting future periods is a capital expenditure.

Environmentalist The paper manufacturer's comparison of its total asset turnover with food stores and auto dealers is misdirected. These other industries' turnovers are higher because their profit margins are lower (about 2%). Profit margins for the paper industry are usually 3% to 3.5%. You need to collect data from competitors in the paper industry to show that a 1.9 total asset turnover is about the norm for this industry. You might also want to collect data on this company's revenues and expenses, along with compensation data for its high-ranking officers and employees.

Guidance Answers to Quick Checks

1. a. Supplies—current assets
  b. Office equipment—property, plant and equipment
  c. Inventory—current assets
  d. Land for future expansion—long-term investments
  e. Trucks used in operations—property, plant and equipment

2. a. Land   **b.** Land Improvements

3. $700,000 + $49,000 − $21,000 + $3,500 + $3,000 + $2,500 = $737,000

4. a. Straight-line with 7-year life: ($77,000/7) = $11,000

   b. Straight-line with 10-year life: ($77,000/10) = $7,700

5. Depreciation is a process of allocating the cost of property, plant and equipment to the accounting periods that benefit from the assets' use.

6. a. Carrying amount using straight-line depreciation:
$96,000 − [($96,000 − $8,000)/5] = $78,400

   b. Carrying amount using units of production:
$96,000 − [($96,000 − $8,000) × (10,000/100,000)] = $87,200

7. ($3,800 − $200)/3 = $1,200 (original depreciation per year)
$1,200 × 2 = $2,400 (accumulated depreciation)
($3,800 − $2,400)/2 = $700 (revised depreciation)

8.

Machinery	12,000	
Cash		12,000

9. A revenue expenditure benefits only the current period and should be charged to expense in the current period. A capital expenditure yields benefits that extend beyond the end of the current period and should be charged to an asset.

10. No gain or loss occurs so net profit is not affected.

11.

Depreciation Expense	3,500	
Accumulated Depreciation		3,500
Cash	32,000	
Accumulated Depreciation	10,500	
Gain on Sale of Equipment		500
Equipment		42,000

12. Examples of natural resources are timberlands, mineral deposits, and oil reserves. Examples of intangible assets are patents, copyrights, goodwill, trademarks, and licenses.

13. ($650,000/325,000 tons) × 91,000 tons = $182,000

14.

Jan. 6	Patents	120,000	
	Cash		120,000
Dec. 31	Amortization Expense	40,000*	
	Accumulated Amortization—Patents		40,000

* $120,000/3 years = $40,000.

15.

Equipment (new)	45,000	
Loss on Exchange of Assets	3,600	
Accumulated Depreciation—Equipment (old)	23,400	
Equipment (old)		30,000
Cash ($45,000 − $3,000)		42,000

Key Terms   www.mheducation.asia/olc/wildkwokFAP

Accelerated depreciation method (p. 400)
Amortization (p. 410)
Asset carrying amount (p. 399)
Capital expenditures (p. 404)
Change in an accounting estimate (p. 403)
Copyright (p. 411)
Cost (p. 395)
Declining-balance method (p. 400)
Depletion (p. 409)
Depreciation (p. 397)
Franchises (p. 411)

Goodwill (p. 412)
Impairment (p. 406)
Inadequacy (p. 397)
Indefinite life (p. 410)
Intangible assets (p. 410)
Land improvements (p. 396)
Licenses (p. 411)
Limited life (p. 410)
Natural resources (p. 409)
Obsolescence (p. 397)

Patent (p. 411)
Property, plant and equipment (p. 394)
Property, plant and equipment age (p. 413)
Residual value (p. 397)
Revenue expenditures (p. 404)
Straight-line depreciation (p. 397)
Total asset turnover (p. 412)
Trademark or trade (brand) name (p. 412)
Units-of-production depreciation (p. 400)
Useful life (p. 397)

Multiple Choice Quiz   Answers on p. 432   www.mheducation.asia/olc/wildkwokFAP

Additional Quiz Questions are available at the book's Website.

1. A company paid $326,000 for property that included land, land improvements, and a building. The land was appraised at $175,000, the land improvements were appraised at $70,000, and the building was appraised at $105,000. What is the allocation of property costs to the three assets purchased?

a. Land, $150,000; Land Improvements, $60,000; Building, $90,000

b. Land, $163,000; Land Improvements, $65,200; Building, $97,800

c. Land, $150,000; Land Improvements, $61,600; Building, $92,400

d. Land, $159,000; Land Improvements, $65,200; Building, $95,400

e. Land, $175,000; Land Improvements, $70,000; Building, $105,000

2. A company purchased a truck for $35,000 on January 1, 2015. The truck is estimated to have a useful life of four years and an estimated residual value of $1,000. Assuming that the company uses straight-line depreciation, what is the depreciation expense on the truck for the year ended December 31, 2016?
  a. $8,750
  b. $17,500
  c. $8,500
  d. $17,000
  e. $25,500

3. A company purchased machinery for $10,800,000 on January 1, 2015. The machinery has a useful life of 10 years and an estimated residual value of $800,000. What is the depreciation expense on the machinery for the year ended December 31, 2016, assuming that the double-declining-balance method is used?
  a. $2,160,000
  b. $3,888,000
  c. $1,728,000

  d. $2,000,000
  e. $1,600,000

4. A company sold a machine that originally cost $250,000 for $120,000 when accumulated depreciation on the machine was $100,000. The gain or loss recorded on the sale of this machine is
  a. $0 gain or loss.
  b. $120,000 gain.
  c. $30,000 loss.
  d. $30,000 gain.
  e. $150,000 loss.

5. A company had average total assets of $500,000, gross sales of $575,000, and net sales of $550,000. The company's total asset turnover is
  a. 1.15
  b. 1.10
  c. 0.91
  d. 0.87
  e. 1.05

^A *Superscript letter A denotes assignments based on Appendix 10A.*
🔲 Icon denotes assignments that involve decision making.

Discussion Questions

1. 🔲 What characteristics of an item of property, plant and equipment make it different from other assets?

2. What is the general rule for cost inclusion for property, plant and equipment?

3. What is different between land and land improvements?

4. Why is the cost of a lump-sum purchase allocated to the individual assets acquired?

5. 🔲 Does the balance in the Accumulated Depreciation—Machinery account represent funds to replace the machinery when it wears out? If not, what does it represent?

6. Must the depreciation method used for financial accounting purposes be the same as that used for tax accounting purposes?

7. 🔲 What accounting concept justifies charging low-cost property, plant and equipment purchases immediately to an expense account?

8. What is the difference between costs on ordinary repairs and those that increase or improve the type or amount of service an asset provides? How should each be recorded?

9. 🔲 Identify events that might lead to disposal of an item of property, plant and equipment.

10. What is the process of allocating the cost of natural resources to expense as they are used?

11. Is the declining-balance method an acceptable way to compute depletion of natural resources? Explain.

12. What are the characteristics of an intangible asset?

13. What general procedures are applied in accounting for the acquisition and potential cost allocation of intangible assets?

14. 🔲 When do we know that a company has goodwill? When can goodwill appear in a company's statement of financial position?

15. 🔲 Assume that a company buys another business and pays for its goodwill. If the company plans to incur costs each year to maintain the value of the goodwill, must it also amortize this goodwill?

16. 🔲 How is total asset turnover computed? Why would a financial statement user be interested in total asset turnover?

17. Refer to **Nestlé**'s 2013 consolidated balance sheet in Appendix A. What are the three largest long-term assets by amounts?

18. Refer to **Adidas**' 2013 consolidated statement of financial position in Appendix A. What is the carrying amount of its property, plant and equipment as at December 31, 2013?

19. Refer to **Samsung**'s 2012 consolidated statement of financial position in Appendix A. What is the carrying amount of its property, plant and equipment as at December 31, 2012?

QUICK STUDY

QS 10-1

Cost of property, plant and equipment C1

Strike Bowling installs automatic scorekeeping equipment with an invoice cost of $180,000. The electrical work required for the installation costs $8,000. Additional costs are $3,000 for delivery and $12,600 for sales tax. During the installation, a component of the equipment is carelessly left on a lane and hit by the automatic lane-cleaning machine. The cost of repairing the component is $2,250. What is the total recorded cost of the automatic scorekeeping equipment?

QS 10-2

Defining assets C1

Identify the main difference between (1) property, plant and equipment and inventory, (2) property, plant and equipment and current assets, and (3) property, plant and equipment and long-term investments.

QS 10-3

Straight-line depreciation

P1

On January 2, 2015, the Crossover Band acquires sound equipment for concert performances at a cost of $55,900. The band estimates it will use this equipment for four years, during which time it anticipates performing about 120 concerts. It estimates that after four years it can sell the equipment for $1,900. During year 2015, the band performs 40 concerts. Compute the year 2015 depreciation using the straight-line method.

QS 10-4

Units-of-production depreciation

P1

Refer to the information in QS 10-3. Compute the year 2015 depreciation using the units-of-production method.

QS 10-5

Computing revised depreciation

C2

Refer to the facts in QS 10-3. Assume that the Crossover Band uses straight-line depreciation but realizes at the start of the second year that due to concert bookings beyond expectations, this equipment will last only a total of three years. The residual value remains unchanged. Compute the revised depreciation for both the second and third years.

QS 10-6

Double-declining-balance method P1

A fleet of refrigerated delivery trucks is acquired on January 5, 2015, at a cost of $930,000 with an estimated useful life of eight years and an estimated residual value of $150,000. Compute the depreciation expense for the first three years using the double-declining-balance method.

QS 10-7

Recording property, plant and equipment impairment C2

Assume a company's equipment carrying amount is $4,000 ($4,500 cost less $500 accumulated depreciation) and a recoverable amount of $3,750, and that the $250 decline meets the impairment test. Prepare the entry to record this $250 impairment.

QS 10-8

Revenue and capital expenditures

C3

1. Classify the following as either revenue or capital expenditures.
   a. Completed an addition to an office building for $250,000 cash.
   b. Paid $160 for the monthly cost of replacement filters on an air-conditioning system.
   c. Paid $300 cash per truck for the cost of their annual tune-ups.
   d. Paid $50,000 cash to replace a compressor on a refrigeration system that extends its useful life by four years.
2. Prepare the journal entries to record transactions *a* and *d* of part 1.

QS 10-9

Disposal of assets P2

Horizon Co. owns equipment that cost $138,750, with accumulated depreciation of $81,000. Horizon sells the equipment for cash. Record the sale of the equipment assuming Horizon sells the equipment for (1) $63,000 cash, (2) $57,750 cash, and (3) $46,500 cash.

QS 10-10

Natural resources and depletion

P3

Diamond Company acquires an ore mine at a cost of $1,300,000. It incurs additional costs of $200,000 to access the mine, which is estimated to hold 500,000 tons of ore. The estimated value of the land after the ore is removed is $150,000.

1. Prepare the entry(ies) to record the cost of the ore mine.
2. Prepare the year-end adjusting entry if 90,000 tons of ore are mined and sold the first year.

Which of the following assets are reported on the statement of financial position as intangible assets? Which are reported as natural resources? (*a*) oil well, (*b*) trademark, (*c*) gold mine, (*d*) building, (*e*) copyright, (*f*) franchise, (*g*) timberland.

QS 10-11
Classify assets
P3 P4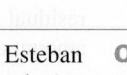

At the beginning of financial year 2014, Asti purchased a patent for $150,000 cash. The company estimated the patent's useful life to be 10 years. Journalize the patent acquisition and its amortization for the financial year 2014.

QS 10-12
Intangible assets and amortization **P4**

Eastman Company reports the following ($ 000s): net sales of $13,557 for 2015 and $12,670 for 2014; end-of-year total assets of $14,968 for 2015 and $18,810 for 2014. Compute its total asset turnover for 2015, and assess its level if competitors average a total asset turnover of 2.0 times.

QS 10-13
Computing total asset turnover
A1

Esteban Co. owns a machine that costs $38,400 with accumulated depreciation of $20,400. Esteban exchanges the machine for a newer model that has a market value of $48,000. (1) Record the exchange assuming Esteban paid $32,000 cash and the exchange has commercial substance. (2) Record the exchange assuming Esteban pays $24,000 cash and the exchange lacks commercial substance.

QS 10-14[A]
Asset exchange
P5

■■ connect™ ——————————————————————————————————————

Farha Co. purchases a machine for $11,500, terms 2/10, n/60, FOB shipping point. The seller prepaid the $260 freight charges, adding the amount to the invoice and bringing its total to $11,760. The machine requires special steel mounting and power connections costing $795. Another $375 is paid to assemble the machine and get it into operation. In moving the machine to its steel mounting, $190 in damages occurred. Materials costing $30 are used in adjusting the machine to produce a satisfactory product. The adjustments are normal for this machine and are not the result of the damages. Compute the cost recorded for this machine. (Farha pays for this machine within the cash discount period.)

EXERCISES

Exercise 10-1
Cost of property, plant and equipment
C1

Cerner Manufacturing purchases a large lot on which an old building is located as part of its plans to build a new plant. The negotiated purchase price is $225,000 for the lot plus $120,000 for the old building. The company pays $34,500 to tear down the old building and $51,000 to fill and level the lot. It also pays a total of $1,440,000 in construction costs—this amount consists of $1,354,500 for the new building and $85,500 for lighting and paving a parking area next to the building. Prepare a single journal entry to record these costs incurred by Cerner, all of which are paid in cash.

Exercise 10-2
Recording costs of assets
C1

Ming Yue Company pays $368,250 for real estate plus $19,600 in closing costs. The real estate consists of land appraised at $166,320; land improvements appraised at $55,440; and a building appraised at $174,240. Allocate the total cost among the three purchased assets and prepare the journal entry to record the purchase.

Exercise 10-3
Lump-sum purchase of property, plant and equipment
C1

In early January 2015, LabTech purchases computer equipment for $147,000 to use in operating activities for the next four years. It estimates the equipment's residual value at $30,000. Prepare a table showing depreciation and carrying amount for each of the four years assuming straight-line depreciation.

Exercise 10-4
Straight-line depreciation **P1**

Refer to the information in Exercise 10-4. Prepare a table showing depreciation and carrying amount for each of the four years assuming double-declining-balance depreciation.

Exercise 10-5
Double-declining-balance depreciation **P1**

Feng Company installs a computerized manufacturing machine in its factory at the beginning of the year at a cost of $42,300. The machine's useful life is estimated at 10 years, or 363,000 units of product, with a $6,000 residual value. During its second year, the machine produces 35,000 units of product. Determine the machine's second-year depreciation under the straight-line method.

Exercise 10-6
Straight-line depreciation
P1

Refer to the information in Exercise 10-6. Determine the machine's second-year depreciation using the units-of-production method.

Exercise 10-7
Units-of-production depreciation
P1

Refer to the information in Exercise 10-6. Determine the machine's second-year depreciation using the double-declining-balance method.

Exercise 10-8
Double-declining-balance depreciation **P1**

Exercise 10-9 Straight-line, partial-year depreciation C2	On April 1, 2014, Stone's Backhoe Co. purchases a trencher for $250,000. The machine is expected to last five years and have a residual value of $25,000. Compute depreciation expense for both 2014 and 2015 assuming the company uses the straight-line method.
Exercise 10-10 Double-declining-balance, partial-year depreciation C2	Refer to the information in Exercise 10-9. Compute depreciation expense for both 2014 and 2015 assuming the company uses the double-declining-balance method.
Exercise 10-11 Revising depreciation C2 **Check**　(2) $3,400	Supreme Fitness Club uses straight-line depreciation for a machine costing $21,750, with an estimated four-year life and a $2,250 residual value. At the beginning of the third year, Supreme determines that the machine has three more years of remaining useful life, after which it will have an estimated $1,800 residual value. Compute (1) the machine's carrying amount at the end of its second year and (2) the amount of depreciation for each of the final three years given the revised estimates.
Exercise 10-12 Straight-line depreciation and income effects P1	Mulan Enterprises pays $235,200 for equipment that will last five years and have a $52,500 residual value. By using the equipment in its operations for five years, the company expects to earn $85,500 annually, after deducting all expenses except depreciation. Prepare a table showing income before depreciation, depreciation expense, and net (pretax) income for each year and for the total five-year period, assuming straight-line depreciation.
Exercise 10-13 Double-declining-balance depreciation P1 **Check**　Year 3 NI, $53,328	Refer to the information in Exercise 10-12. Prepare a table showing income before depreciation, depreciation expense, and net (pretax) income for each year and for the total five-year period, assuming double-declining-balance depreciation is used.
Exercise 10-14 Cost of repairs C3 **Check**　(3) $207,450	Passat Company owns a building that appears on its prior year-end statement of financial position at its original $561,000 cost less $420,750 accumulated depreciation. The building is depreciated on a straight-line basis assuming a 20-year life and no residual value. During the first week in January of the current calendar year, major structural repairs are completed on the building at a $67,200 cost. The repairs extend its useful life for 7 years beyond the 20 years originally estimated. **1.** Determine the building's age (property, plant and equipment age) as at the prior year-end statement of financial position date. **2.** Prepare the entry to record the cost of the structural repairs that are paid in cash. **3.** Determine the carrying amount of the building immediately after the repairs are recorded. **4.** Prepare the entry to record the current calendar year's depreciation.
Exercise 10-15 Cost of repairs C3	Patterson Company pays $262,500 for equipment expected to last four years and have a $30,000 residual value. Prepare journal entries to record the following costs related to the equipment. **1.** During the second year of the equipment's life, $21,000 cash is paid for a new component expected to increase the equipment's productivity by 10% a year. **2.** During the third year, $5,250 cash is paid for normal repairs necessary to keep the equipment in good working order. **3.** During the fourth year, $13,950 is paid for repairs expected to increase the useful life of the equipment from four to five years.
Exercise 10-16 Disposal of assets P2	Millworks Company owns a milling machine that cost $125,000 and has accumulated depreciation of $91,000. Prepare the entry to record the disposal of the milling machine on January 5 under each of the following independent situations. **1.** The machine needed extensive repairs, and it was not worth repairing. Millworks disposed of the machine, receiving nothing in return. **2.** Millworks sold the machine for $17,500 cash. **3.** Millworks sold the machine for $34,000 cash. **4.** Millworks sold the machine for $40,000 cash.

Finesse Co. purchases and installs a machine on January 1, 2015, at a total cost of $92,750. Straight-line depreciation is taken each year for four years assuming a seven-year life and no residual value. The machine is disposed of on July 1, 2019, during its fifth year of service. Prepare entries to record the partial year's depreciation on July 1, 2019, and to record the disposal under the following separate assumptions: (1) the machine is sold for $35,000 cash and (2) Finesse receives an insurance settlement of $30,000 resulting from the total destruction of the machine in a fire.

Exercise 10-17
Partial-year depreciation; disposal of property, plant and equipment
P2

On April 2, 2015, Idaho Mining Co. pays $3,633,750 for an ore deposit containing 1,425,000 tons. The company installs machinery in the mine costing $171,000, with an estimated seven-year life and no residual value. The machinery will be abandoned when the ore is completely mined. Idaho begins mining on May 1, 2015, and mines and sells 156,200 tons of ore during the remaining eight months of 2015. Prepare the December 31, 2015, entries to record both the ore deposit depletion and the mining machinery depreciation. Mining machinery depreciation should be in proportion to the mine's depletion.

Exercise 10-18
Depletion of natural resources
P1 P3

Busch Gallery purchases the copyright on an oil painting for $236,700 on January 1, 2015. The copyright legally protects its owner for 12 more years. The company plans to market and sell prints of the original for 15 years. Prepare entries to record the purchase of the copyright on January 1, 2015, and its annual amortization on December 31, 2015.

Exercise 10-19
Amortization of intangible assets
P4

On January 1, 2015, Timothy Company purchased Macys Company at a price of $3,750,000. The fair market value of the net assets purchased equals $2,700,000.

1. What is the amount of goodwill that Timothy records at the purchase date?

2. Explain how Timothy would determine the amount of goodwill amortization for the year ended December 31, 2015.

3. Timothy Company believes that its employees provide superior customer service, and through their efforts, Timothy Company believes it has created $1,350,000 of goodwill. How would Timothy Company record this goodwill?

Exercise 10-20
Goodwill
P4

Ajay Company bought land on January 1, 2014 for $2 million. It constructed a building during the year for a total of $500,000. The amount included a crane which was damaged during the construction due to an accident and the repair cost was $20,000. The building was completed on December 31, 2014 (the financial year-end of Ajay) with an estimated useful life of 20 years and no residual value. Ajay uses straight-line depreciation. On June 30, 2015, Ajay revalued the land to $2.3 million.

1. What amounts should appear on Ajay's statement of financial position as at December 31, 2014 relating to the carrying amounts of land and building?

2. What amounts should appear on Ajay's statement of financial position as at December 31, 2015 relating to the carrying amounts of land and building?

Exercise 10-21
Costs related to property, plant and equipment
C1 C4

Joy Co. reports net sales of $4,862,000 for 2010 and $7,542,000 for 2015. End-of-year balances for total assets are 2013, $1,586,000; 2014, $1,700,000; and 2015, $1,882,000. (a) Compute Joy's total asset turnover for 2014 and 2015. (b) Comment on Joy's efficiency in using its assets if its competitors average a total asset turnover of 3.0.

Exercise 10-22
Evaluating efficient use of assets
A1

Ramond Construction trades in an old tractor for a new tractor with a fair market value of $125,125 and paying $93,275 in cash. The old tractor had cost $107,900, and straight-line accumulated depreciation of $58,500 had been recorded to date under the assumption that it would last eight years and have a $14,300 residual value. Answer the following questions assuming the exchange has commercial substance.

1. What is the carrying amount of the old tractor at the time of exchange?

2. What is the loss on this asset exchange?

3. What amount should be recorded (debited) in the asset account for the new tractor?

Exercise 10-23^A
Exchanging assets
P5

Check (2) $17,550

At year-end, land (no accumulated depreciation) with a cost of $1.5 million is revalued to its fair value of $2 million.

Required

Record the journal entry for the revaluation of the land.

Exercise 10-24
Applying the revaluation model to property, plant and equipment
C4

Exercise 10-25

Applying the revaluation model to property, plant and equipment

C4

At year-end, equipment with a cost of $100,000 and accumulated depreciation of $40,000 (adjusted to end of year) has been revalued to its fair value of $90,000.

Required

Record the journal entry for the revaluation of the equipment, by restating the accumulated depreciation proportionately with the change in the gross carrying amount of the asset so that the carrying amount of the asset after revaluation equals its revalued amount.

Exercise 10-26

Applying the revaluation model to property, plant and equipment

C4

At year-end, equipment with a cost of $100,000 and accumulated depreciation of $40,000 (adjusted to end of year) has been revalued to its fair value of $90,000.

Required

Record the journal entry for the revaluation of the equipment, by eliminating the accumulated depreciation against the gross carrying amount of the asset and the net amount restated to the revalued amount of the asset.

Exercise 10-27

Accounting for property, plant and equipment under **IFRS**

C2 P1 P2

Volkswagen Group reports the following information for property, plant and equipment as at December 31, 2008, along with additions, disposals, depreciation, and impairments for the year ended December 31, 2008 (in EUR millions):

Property, plant and equipment, net	23,121
Additions to property, plant and equipment	6,651
Disposals of property, plant and equipment	2,322
Depreciation on property, plant and equipment	4,625
Impairments to property, plant and equipment	184

Required

1. Prepare Volkswagen's journal entry to record its depreciation for 2008.
2. Prepare Volkswagen's journal entry to record its additions for 2008 assuming they are paid in cash and are treated as "improvements" to the assets.
3. Prepare Volkswagen's journal entry to record its EUR 2,322 in disposals for 2008 assuming it receives EUR 700 cash in return and the accumulated depreciation on the disposed assets totals EUR 1,322.
4. Volkswagen reports EUR 184 of impairments. Do these impairments increase or decrease the property, plant and equipment account? And, by what amount?

PROBLEM SET A

Problem 10-1A

Property, plant and equipment costs; depreciation methods

C1 P1

www.mheducation.asia/olc/wildkwokFAP

Check (2) $23,490

(3) $15,750

Xavier Construction negotiates a lump-sum purchase of several assets from a company that is going out of business. The purchase is completed on January 1, 2015, at a total cash price of $787,500 for a building, land, land improvements, and four vehicles. The estimated market values of the assets are building, $408,000; land, $289,000; land improvements, $42,500; and four vehicles, $110,500. The company's financial year ends on December 31.

Required

1. Prepare a table to allocate the lump-sum purchase price to the separate assets purchased (round percents to the nearest 1%). Prepare the journal entry to record the purchase.
2. Compute the depreciation expense for year 2015 on the building using the straight-line method, assuming a 15-year life and a $25,650 residual value.
3. Compute the depreciation expense for year 2015 on the land improvements assuming a five-year life and double-declining-balance depreciation.

Analysis Component

4. Defend or refute this statement: Accelerated depreciation results in payment of less taxes over the asset's life.

In January 2015, Keona Co. pays $2,800,000 for a tract of land with two buildings on it. It plans to demolish Building 1 and build a new store in its place. Building 2 will be a company office; it is appraised at $641,300, with a useful life of 20 years and an $80,000 residual value. A lighted parking lot near Building 1 has improvements (Land Improvements 1) valued at $408,100 that are expected to last another 14 years with no residual value. Without the buildings and improvements, the tract of land is valued at $1,865,600. The company also incurs the following additional costs:

Cost to demolish Building 1	$ 422,600
Cost of additional land grading	167,200
Cost to construct new building (Building 3), having a useful life of 25 years and a $390,100 residual value	2,019,000
Cost of new land improvements (Land Improvements 2) near Building 2 having a 20-year useful life and no residual value	158,000

Required

1. Prepare a table with the following column headings: Land, Building 2, Building 3, Land Improvements 1, and Land Improvements 2. Allocate the costs incurred by Keona to the appropriate columns and total each column (round percents to the nearest 1%).

2. Prepare a single journal entry to record all the incurred costs assuming they are paid in cash on January 1, 2015.

3. Using the straight-line method, prepare the December 31 adjusting entries to record depreciation for the 12 months of 2015 when these assets were in use.

Clarion Contractors completed the following transactions and events involving the purchase and operation of equipment in its business.

2014

Jan.   1   Paid $255,440 cash plus $15,200 in sales tax and $2,500 in transportation (FOB shipping point) for a new loader. The loader is estimated to have a four-year life and a $34,740 residual value. Loader costs are recorded in the Equipment account.

Jan.   3   Paid $3,660 to enclose the cab and install air conditioning in the loader to enable operations under harsher conditions. This increased the estimated residual value of the loader by another $1,110.

Dec. 31   Recorded annual straight-line depreciation on the loader.

2015

Jan.   1   Paid $4,500 to overhaul the loader's engine, which increased the loader's estimated useful life by two years.

Feb. 17   Paid $920 to repair the loader after the operator backed it into a tree.

Dec. 31   Recorded annual straight-line depreciation on the loader.

Required

Prepare journal entries to record these transactions and events.

Chen Company completed the following transactions and events involving its delivery trucks.

2014

Jan.   1   Paid $19,415 cash plus $1,165 in sales tax for a new delivery truck estimated to have a five-year life and a $3,000 residual value. Delivery truck costs are recorded in the Trucks account.

Dec. 31   Recorded annual straight-line depreciation on the truck.

2015

Dec. 31   Due to new information obtained earlier in the year, the truck's estimated useful life was changed from five to four years, and the estimated residual value was increased to $3,500. Recorded annual straight-line depreciation on the truck.

Problem 10-2A
Asset cost allocation; straight-line depreciation
C1 P1

www.mheducation.asia/olc/wildkwokFAP

Check (1) Land costs, $2,381,800; Building 2 costs, $616,000

(3) Depr.—Land Improv. 1 and 2, $28,000 and $7,900

Problem 10-3A
Computing and revising depreciation; revenue and capital expenditures
C1 C2 C3

Check Dec. 31, 2014, Dr. Depr. Expense—Equip., $60,238

Check Dec. 31, 2015, Dr. Depr. Expense—Equip., $37,042

Problem 10-4A
Computing and revising depreciation; selling property, plant and equipment
C2 P1 P2

Check Dec. 31, 2015, Dr. Depr. Expense—Trucks, $4,521

2016

Dec. 31   Recorded annual straight-line depreciation on the truck.
Dec. 31   Sold the truck for $6,200 cash.

Required

Prepare journal entries to record these transactions and events.

Problem 10-5A

Depreciation methods

P1

A machine costing $210,000 with a four-year life and an estimated $20,000 residual value is installed in Calhoon Company's factory on January 1. The factory manager estimates the machine will produce 475,000 units of product during its life. It actually produces the following units: year 1, 121,400; year 2, 122,400; year 3, 119,600; and year 4, 118,200. The total number of units produced by the end of year 4 exceeds the original estimate—this difference was not predicted. (The machine must not be depreciated below its estimated residual value.)

Required

Prepare a table with the following column headings and compute depreciation for each year (and total depreciation of all years combined) for the machine under each depreciation method.

Check Year 4: units-of-production depreciation, $44,640; DDB depreciation, $6,250

Year	Straight-Line	Units-of-Production	Double-Declining-Balance

---

Problem 10-6A

Disposal of property, plant and equipment

C1 P1 P2

Saturn Co. purchases a used machine for $167,000 cash on January 2 and readies it for use the next day at an $3,420 cost. On January 3, it is installed on a required operating platform costing $1,080, and it is further readied for operations. The company predicts the machine will be used for six years and have a $14,600 residual value. Depreciation is to be charged on a straight-line basis. On December 31, at the end of its fifth year in operations, it is disposed of.

Required

Check (2b) Depr. Exp., $26,150

(3c) Dr. Loss from Fire, $16,750

1. Prepare journal entries to record the machine's purchase and the costs to ready and install it. Cash is paid for all costs incurred.

2. Prepare journal entries to record depreciation of the machine at December 31 of (a) its first year in operations and (b) the year of its disposal.

3. Prepare journal entries to record the machine's disposal under each of the following separate assumptions: (a) it is sold for $13,500 cash; (b) it is sold for $45,000 cash; and (c) it is destroyed in a fire and the insurance company pays $24,000 cash to settle the loss claim.

Problem 10-7A

Natural resources

P3

On July 23 of the current year, Dakota Mining Co. pays $4,836,000 for land estimated to contain 7,800,000 tons of recoverable ore. It installs machinery costing $390,000 that has a 10-year life and no residual value and is capable of mining the ore deposit in eight years. The machinery is paid for on July 25, seven days before mining operations begin. The company removes and sells 400,000 tons of ore during its first five months of operations ending on December 31. Depreciation of the machinery is in proportion to the mine's depletion as the machinery will be abandoned after the ore is mined.

Required

Check (c) Depletion, $248,000
(d) Depreciation, $20,000

Prepare entries to record (a) the purchase of the land, (b) the cost and installation of machinery, (c) the first five months' depletion assuming the land has a net residual value of zero after the ore is mined, and (d) the first five months' depreciation on the machinery.

Analysis Component

Describe both the similarities and differences in amortization, depletion, and depreciation.

Racerback Company negotiates a lump-sum purchase of several assets from a contractor who is relocating. The purchase is completed on January 1, 2015, at a total cash price of $1,610,000 for a building, land, land improvements, and six trucks. The estimated market values of the assets are building, $784,800; land, $540,640; land improvements, $226,720; and six trucks, $191,840. The company's financial year ends on December 31.

Required

1. Prepare a table to allocate the lump-sum purchase price to the separate assets purchased (round percents to the nearest 1%). Prepare the journal entry to record the purchase.

2. Compute the depreciation expense for year 2015 on the building using the straight-line method, assuming a 12-year life and a $100,500 residual value.

3. Compute the depreciation expense for year 2015 on the land improvements assuming a 10-year life and double-declining-balance depreciation.

Analysis Component

4. Defend or refute this statement: Accelerated depreciation results in payment of more taxes over the asset's life.

In January 2015, InTech Co. pays $1,350,000 for a tract of land with two buildings. It plans to demolish Building A and build a new shop in its place. Building B will be a company office; it is appraised at $472,770, with a useful life of 15 years and a $90,000 residual value. A lighted parking lot near Building B has improvements (Land Improvements B) valued at $125,145 that are expected to last another six years with no residual value. Without the buildings and improvements, the tract of land is valued at $792,585. The company also incurs the following additional costs.

Cost to demolish Building A	$ 117,000
Cost of additional land grading	172,500
Cost to construct new building (Building C), having a useful life of 20 years and a $295,500 residual value	1,356,000
Cost of new land improvements (Land Improvements C) near Building C, having a 10-year useful life and no residual value	101,250

Required

1. Prepare a table with the following column headings: Land, Building B, Building C, Land Improvements B, and Land Improvements C. Allocate the costs incurred by InTech to the appropriate columns and total each column (round percents to the nearest 1%).

2. Prepare a single journal entry to record all incurred costs assuming they are paid in cash on January 1, 2015.

3. Using the straight-line method, prepare the December 31 adjusting entries to record depreciation for the 12 months of 2015 when these assets were in use.

Xpress Delivery Service completed the following transactions and events involving the purchase and operation of equipment for its business.

2014

Jan. 1 Paid $24,950 cash plus $1,950 in sales tax for a new delivery van that was estimated to have a five-year life and a $3,400 residual value. Van costs are recorded in the Equipment account.

Jan. 3 Paid $1,550 to install sorting racks in the van for more accurate and quicker delivery of packages. This increases the estimated residual value of the van by another $200.

Dec. 31 Recorded annual straight-line depreciation on the van.

2015

Jan. 1 Paid $1,970 to overhaul the van's engine, which increased the van's estimated useful life by two years.

PROBLEM SET B

Problem 10-1B
Property, plant and equipment costs; depreciation methods

C1 P1

Check (2) $52,000

(3) $41,860

Problem 10-2B
Asset cost allocation; straight-line depreciation

C1 P1

Check (1) Land costs, $1,059,000;
Building B costs, $459,000

(3) Depr.—Land Improv.
B and C, $20,250 and $10,125

Problem 10-3B
Computing and revising depreciation; revenue and capital expenditures

C1 C2 C3

Check Dec. 31, 2014, Dr. Depr.
Expense—Equip., $4,970

May 10   Paid $600 to repair the van after the driver backed it into a loading dock.
Dec. 31   Record annual straight-line depreciation on the van. (Round to the nearest dollar.)

Required

Prepare journal entries to record these transactions and events.

Problem 10-4B
Computing and revising depreciation; selling property, plant and equipment

C2 P1 P2

Field Instruments completed the following transactions and events involving its machinery.

2014

Jan.   1   Paid $106,600 cash plus $6,400 in sales tax for a new machine. The machine is estimated to have a six-year life and a $9,800 residual value.
Dec. 31   Recorded annual straight-line depreciation on the machinery.

2015

Dec. 31   Due to new information obtained earlier in the year, the machine's estimated useful life was changed from six to four years, and the estimated residual value was increased to $13,050. Recorded annual straight-line depreciation on the machinery.

2016

Dec. 31   Recorded annual straight-line depreciation on the machinery.
Dec. 31   Sold the machine for $25,240 cash.

Required

Prepare journal entries to record these transactions and events.

Problem 10-5B
Depreciation methods

P1

On January 2, Gannon Co. purchases and installs a new machine costing $312,000 with a five-year life and an estimated $28,000 residual value. Management estimates the machine will produce 1,136,000 units of product during its life. Actual production of units is as follows: year 1, 245,600; year 2, 230,400; year 3, 227,000; year 4, 232,600; and year 5, 211,200. The total number of units produced by the end of year 5 exceeds the original estimate—this difference was not predicted. (The machine must not be depreciated below its estimated residual value.)

Required

Prepare a table with the following column headings and compute depreciation for each year (and total depreciation of all years combined) for the machine under each depreciation method.

Year	Straight-Line	Units-of-Production	Double-Declining-Balance

Problem 10-6B
Disposal of property, plant and equipment

C1 P1 P2

On January 1, Jefferson purchases a used machine for $130,000 and readies it for use the next day at a cost of $3,390. On January 4, it is mounted on a required operating platform costing $4,800, and it is further readied for operations. Management estimates the machine will be used for seven years and have an $18,000 residual value. Depreciation is to be charged on a straight-line basis. On December 31, at the end of its sixth year of use, the machine is disposed of.

Required

1. Prepare journal entries to record the machine's purchase and the costs to ready and install it. Cash is paid for all costs incurred.

2. Prepare journal entries to record depreciation of the machine at December 31 of (a) its first year in operations and (b) the year of its disposal.

3. Prepare journal entries to record the machine's disposal under each of the following separate assumptions: (a) it is sold for $30,000 cash; (b) it is sold for $50,000 cash; and (c) it is destroyed in a fire and the insurance company pays $20,000 cash to settle the loss claim.

Problem 10-7B
Natural resources

P3

On February 19 of the current year, Rock Chalk Co. pays $4,450,000 for land estimated to contain 5 million tons of recoverable ore. It installs machinery costing $200,000 that has a 16-year life and no residual value and is capable of mining the ore deposit in 12 years. The machinery is paid for on March

21, eleven days before mining operations begin. The company removes and sells 352,000 tons of ore during its first nine months of operations ending on December 31. Depreciation of the machinery is in proportion to the mine's depletion as the machinery will be abandoned after the ore is mined.

Check   (*c*) Depletion, $313,280;
           (*d*) Depreciation, $14,080

Required

Prepare entries to record (*a*) the purchase of the land, (*b*) the cost and installation of the machinery, (*c*) the first nine months' depletion assuming the land has a net residual value of zero after the ore is mined, and (*d*) the first nine months' depreciation on the machinery.

Analysis Component

Describe both the similarities and differences in amortization, depletion, and depreciation.

(This serial problem began in Chapter 1 and continues through most of the book. If previous chapter segments were not completed, the serial problem can begin at this point.)

SERIAL PROBLEM
Business Solutions

P1

SP 10   Selected ledger account balances for Business Solutions follow.

	For Three Months Ended December 31, 2015	For Three Months Ended March 31, 2016
Office equipment	$ 8,000	$ 8,000
Accumulated depreciation— Office equipment	400	800
Computer equipment	20,000	20,000
Accumulated depreciation— Computer equipment	1,250	2,500
Total revenue	31,284	44,000
Total assets	83,460	120,268

Required

1. Assume that Business Solutions does not acquire additional office equipment or computer equipment in 2016. Compute amounts for *the year ended* December 31, 2016, for Depreciation Expense—Office Equipment and for Depreciation Expense—Computer Equipment (assume use of the straight-line method).

2. Given the assumptions in part 1, what is the carrying amount of both the office equipment and the computer equipment as at December 31, 2016?

Check   Dr. Rent Expense: (2*a*) $6,000, (2*c*) $26,400

3. Compute the three-month total asset turnover for Business Solutions as at March 31, 2016. Use total revenue for the numerator and average the December 31, 2015, total assets and the March 31, 2016, total assets for the denominator. Interpret its total asset turnover if competitors average 2.5 for annual periods. (Round turnover to two decimals.)

Beyond the Numbers

BTN 10-1   Refer to Nestlé's financial statements in Appendix A.

REPORTING IN ACTION

A1

1. As is typical of companies' statements of financial position, Nestlé reports the carrying amount (total cost less its accumulated depreciation and accumulated impairment losses) of its property, plant and equipment on its statement of financial position. Given that it reports accumulated depreciation for its property, plant and equipment as at December 31, 2013 of CHF 26,223 million, what percent of the original cost of Nestlé's property, plant and equipment remains to be depreciated as at December 31, 2013?

2. Compute its total asset turnover for the year ended December 31, 2013 and the year ended December 31, 2012. Assume total assets as at January 1, 2012 are CHF 114,091 million.

Fast Forward

3. Access Nestlé's financial statements for financial years ending after December 31, 2013 at its Website (**nestle.com/investors**). Recompute Nestlé's total asset turnover for the additional years' data you collect. Comment on any differences relative to the turnover computed in part 3.

COMPARATIVE ANALYSIS

A1

BTN 10-2   Key comparative figures for Adidas and Puma follow:

	Adidas (EUR millions)			Puma (EUR millions)		
	Current Year	One Year Prior	Two Years Prior	Current Year	One Year Prior	Two Years Prior
Net sales	14,492	14,883	13,344	2,530.3	3,270.7	3,009.0
Total assets	11,599	11,651	11,380	2,308.5	2,530.3	2,581.8

Required

1. Compute total asset turnover for the most recent two years for both Adidas and Puma using the data shown.
2. Which company is more efficient in generating net sales given the total assets it employs? Assume an industry average of 1.0.

ETHICS CHALLENGE

C1

BTN 10-3   Flo Choi owns a small business and manages its accounting. Her company just finished a year in which a large amount of borrowed funds was invested in a new building addition as well as in equipment and fixture additions. Choi's banker requires her to submit semiannual financial statements so he can monitor the financial health of her business. He has warned her that if profit margins erode, he might raise the interest rate on the borrowed funds to reflect the increased loan risk from the bank's point of view. Choi knows profit margin is likely to decline this year. As she prepares year-end adjusting entries, she decides to apply the following depreciation rule: All asset additions are considered to be in use on the first day of the following month. (The previous rule assumed assets are in use on the first day of the month nearest to the purchase date.)

Required

1. Identify decisions that managers like Choi must make in applying depreciation methods.
2. Is Choi's rule an ethical violation, or is it a legitimate decision in computing depreciation?
3. How will Choi's new depreciation rule affect the profit margin of her business?

COMMUNICATING IN PRACTICE

A1

BTN 10-4   Teams are to select an industry, and each team member is to select a different company in that industry. Each team member is to acquire the financial statements of the company selected—visit the company's Website or the stock exchange on which the company is listed. Use the financial statements to compute total asset turnover. Communicate with teammates via a meeting, e-mail, or telephone to discuss the meaning of this ratio, how different companies compare to each other, and the industry norm. The team must prepare a one-page report that describes the ratios for each company and identifies the conclusions reached during the team's discussion.

TAKING IT TO THE NET

P4

BTN 10-5   Go to www.loreal-finance.com/eng and download L'Oréal's 2013 relevant financial statements to answer the following.

Required

1. What amount of property, plant and equipment is reported on L'Oréal's consolidated statement of financial position? What percentage of noncurrent and total assets does its property, plant and equipment represent? Is property, plant and equipment a major asset for L'Oréal? Explain.
2. What amount of intangible assets is reported on L'Oréal's consolidated statement of financial position? What percentage of noncurrent and total assets does its goodwill represent? Is goodwill a major asset for L'Oréal? Explain.
3. Locate Note 14 to its financial statements. Identify the categories of property, plant and equipment.
4. Locate Note 12 to its financial statements. Identify the five categories of other intangible assets.

BTN 10-6 Each team member is to become an expert on one depreciation method to facilitate teammates' understanding of that method. Follow these procedures:

a. Each team member is to select an area for expertise from one of the following depreciation methods: straight-line, units-of-production, or double-declining-balance.

b. Expert teams are to be formed from those who have selected the same area of expertise. The instructor will identify the location where each expert team meets.

c. Using the following data, expert teams are to collaborate and develop a presentation answering the requirements. Expert team members must write the presentation in a format they can show to their learning teams.

Data and Requirements On January 8, 2009, Waverly Riders purchases a van to transport rafters back to the point of departure at the conclusion of the rafting adventures they operate. The cost of the van is $44,000. It has an estimated residual value of $2,000 and is expected to be used for four years and driven 60,000 miles. The van is driven 12,000 miles in 2009, 18,000 miles in 2010, 21,000 in 2011, and 10,000 in 2012.

  1. Compute the annual depreciation expense for each year of the van's estimated useful life.

  2. Explain when and how annual depreciation is recorded.

  3. Explain the impact on income of this depreciation method versus others over the van's life.

  4. Identify the van's carrying amount for each year of its life and illustrate the reporting of this amount for any one year.

d. Re-form original learning teams. In rotation, experts are to present to their teams the results from part *c*. Experts are to encourage and respond to questions.

TEAMWORK IN ACTION

P1

Point: This activity can follow an overview of each method. Step 1 allows for three areas of expertise. Larger teams will have some duplication of areas, but the straight-line choice should not be duplicated. Expert teams can use the book and consult with the instructor.

BTN 10-7 Review the chapter's opening feature involving **2am Dessert Bar**. The company currently has net sales of $800,000. Assume that it is planning an expansion that will increase net sales by $400,000. To accomplish this expansion, 2am Dessert Bar must increase its average total assets from $250,000 to $300,000.

ENTREPRENEURIAL DECISION

A1

Required

1. Compute the company's total asset turnover under (*a*) current conditions and (*b*) proposed conditions.

2. Evaluate and comment on the merits of the proposal given your analysis in part 1. Identify any concerns you would express about the proposal.

BTN 10-8 Team up with one or more classmates for this activity. Identify companies in your community or area that must account for at least one of the following assets: natural resource; patent; copyright; trademark; or goodwill. You might find a company having more than one type of asset. Once you identify a company with a specific asset, describe the accounting this company uses to allocate the cost of that asset to the periods benefited from its use.

HITTING THE ROAD

P3 P4

BTN 10-9 **Adidas**, **Puma**, and **Nike** are all competitors in the global marketplace. Key comparative figures for each company follow.

GLOBAL DECISION

A1

Key Figures	Nike (US$ millions)		Adidas (EUR millions)		Puma (EUR millions)	
	Current Year	Prior Year	Current Year	Prior Year	Current Year	Prior Year
Average total assets	13,834	12,846.2	9,747	9,204	2,145.6	1,880.1
Net sales	19,014	19,176	11,990	10,381	2,706.4	2,447.3
Total asset turnover	?	?	1.23	1.13	1.26	1.30

Required

1. Compute total asset turnover for the most recent two years for Nike using the data shown.

2. Which company of the three is most efficient in generating net sales given the total assets it employs?

ANSWERS TO MULTIPLE CHOICE QUIZ

1. b;

	Appraisal Value	%	Total Cost	Allocated
Land	$175,000	50%	$326,000	$163,000
Land improvements	70,000	20	326,000	65,200
Building	105,000	30	326,000	97,800
Totals	$350,000			$326,000

2. c; ($35,000 − $1,000)/4 years = $8,500 per year.

3. c; 2011: $10,800,000 × (2 × 10%) = $2,160,000

   2012: ($10,800,000 − $2,160,000) × (2 × 10%) = $1,728,000

4. c;

Cost of machine	$250,000
Accumulated depreciation	100,000
Carrying amount	150,000
Cash received	120,000
Loss on sale	$ 30,000

5. b; $550,000/$500,000 = 1.10

11

Current Liabilities

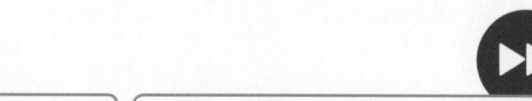

A Look Back	A Look at This Chapter	A Look Ahead
Chapter 10 focused on long-term assets including property, plant and equipment, natural resources, and intangibles. We showed how to account for and analyze those assets.	This chapter explains how to identify, compute, record, and report current liabilities in financial statements. We also analyze and interpret these liabilities, including those related to employee costs.	Chapter 12 explains the partnership form of organization. It also describes the accounting concepts and procedures for partnership transactions.

Learning Objectives

CAP

CONCEPTUAL

C1 Describe current and long-term liabilities and their characteristics. (p. 436)

C2 Identify and describe known current liabilities. (p. 438)

C3 Explain how to account for contingent liabilities. (p. 444)

ANALYTICAL

A1 Compute the times interest earned ratio and use it to analyze liabilities. (p. 446)

PROCEDURAL

P1 Prepare entries to account for short-term notes payable. (p. 439)

P2 Compute and record *employee* payroll deductions and liabilities. (p. 442)

P3 Compute and record *employer* payroll expenses and liabilities. (p. 442)

P4 Account for estimated liabilities (p. 443)

"There is always something to innovate and improvise. The drive to push for new boundaries keeps us growing year after year."—**PATRICK CHEO** (on left, Adam Khoo on right)

Decision Insight

A Promise of Success

"Empowering Lives, Designing Destinies"—this is the fervent promise that Adam Khoo, founder and Executive Chairman of **Adam Khoo Learning Technologies Group** (AKLTG) **(www.akltg.com)**, is committed to. AKLTG is a leading regional personal and professional development organization. Its aim is to help individuals, schools, and corporate organizations to realize their greatest potential and achieve their visions and dreams. "For many years, the training scene in Singapore was dominated by foreign trainers. AKLTG was inspired by our drive to start and excel in a business that is run and trained by locals for the local market," says Chief Executive Officer Patrick Cheo. Headquartered in Singapore, the company has operations in Malaysia, Indonesia, Bangkok, and Hong Kong.

"As a training company where most of our assets are our people, employee wages and benefits take up more than 60% of our total operating expenses. As such, we monitor this area

of investment closely," says Patrick. "We also work toward long-term relations with all our suppliers, treating them as partners in our business." Accounts payable are tracked on a weekly basis. Suppliers are paid according to payment terms or based on urgency of the payments required.

All the public training programs at AKLTG come with unlimited re-attendance, where customers only need to pay a one-time fee for the chosen program, and thereafter get to attend it as many times as they wish. "This is to ensure that our customers master the skill-sets and gain the life-changing experience they intended to have," says Patrick. "We also offer a 100% money-back guarantee. This policy works for those who think they have signed up for a program that does not match their needs." Which all goes to prove how dedicated the people at AKLTG are in delivering their promise to realize the highest potential in every person.

Chapter Preview

Previous chapters introduced liabilities such as accounts payable, notes payable, wages payable, and unearned revenues. This chapter further explains these liabilities and additional ones such as warranties, taxes, payroll, and bonuses. It also describes contingent liabilities and introduces long-term liabilities. The focus is on how to define, classify, measure, report, and analyze these liabilities so that this information is useful to business decision makers.

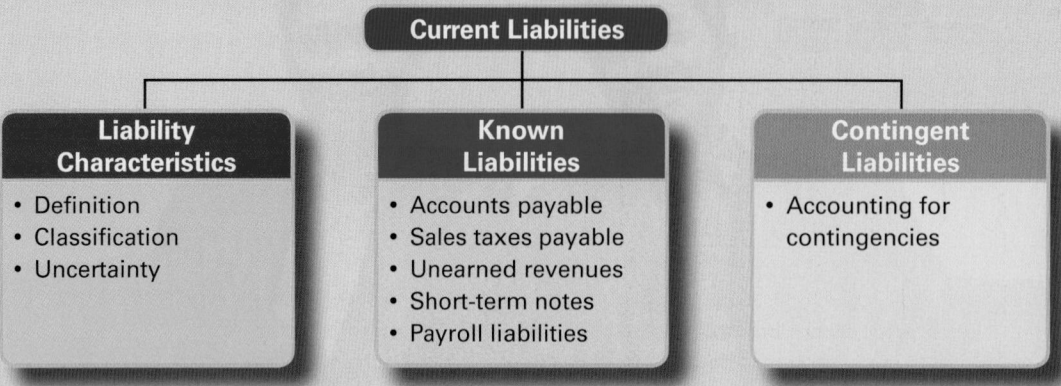

CHARACTERISTICS OF LIABILITIES

This section discusses important characteristics of liabilities and how liabilities are classified and reported.

Defining Liabilities

C1 Describe current and long-term liabilities and their characteristics.

A liability is defined in **IAS 37 Provisions, Continent Liabilities and Contingent Assets** as a present obligation of the entity arising from past events, the settlement of which is expected to result in an outflow from the entity of resources embodying economic benefits. This definition includes three crucial factors:

1. A past transaction or event.
2. A present obligation.
3. A future payment of assets or services.

These three important elements are portrayed visually in Exhibit 11.1. Liabilities reported in financial statements exhibit those characteristics. No liability is reported when one or more of those characteristics is absent. For example, most companies expect to pay wages to their employees in upcoming months and years, but these future payments are *not* liabilities because no past event such as employee work resulted in a present obligation. Instead, such liabilities arise when employees perform their work and earn the wages.

EXHIBIT 11.1

Characteristics of a Liability

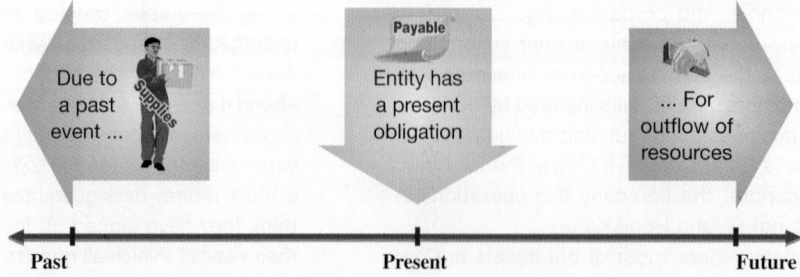

Classifying Liabilities

Information about liabilities is more useful when the statement of financial position identifies them as either current or long term. Decision makers need to know when obligations are due so they can plan for them and take appropriate action.

Current Liabilities   **Current liabilities,** also called *short-term liabilities,* are obligations due within one year or the company's operating cycle, whichever is longer. They are expected to be paid using current assets or by creating other current liabilities. Common examples of current liabilities are accounts payable, short-term notes payable, wages payable, warranty liabilities, taxes payable, and unearned revenues.

Current liabilities differ across companies because they depend on the type of company operations. **MGM Mirage**, for instance, included the following current liabilities related to its gaming, hospitality and entertainment operations ($000s):

Advance deposits and ticket sales	$104,911
Casino outstanding chip liability	83,957
Casino front money deposits	80,944

Nokia reports a much different set of current liabilities. It discloses current liabilities made up of items such as warranty and intellectual property rights liabilities.

Noncurrent Liabilities   **Noncurrent liabilities,** also called *long-term liabilities,* are obligations not expected to be paid within the longer of one year or the company's operating cycle. They can include long-term notes payable and bonds payable. They are shown separately from current liabilities. **Nestlé**, for instance, reports total noncurrent liabilities of CHF 23,386 million for financial year 2013. They are reported after current liabilities of CHF 32,917 million. Exhibit 11.2 shows amounts of current liabilities and as a percent of total liabilities for selected companies for financial year 2013.

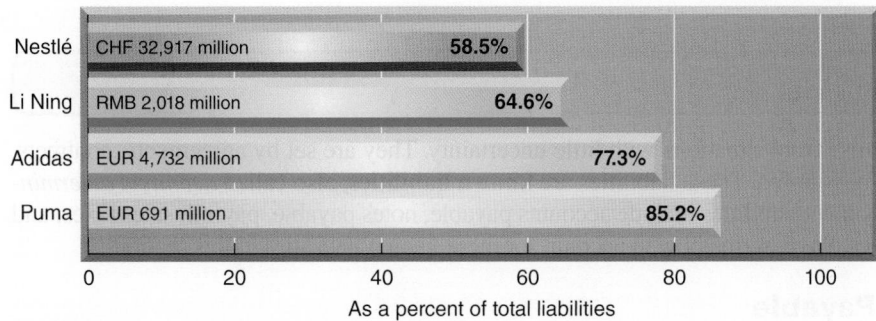

Company	Amount	As a percent of total liabilities
Nestlé	CHF 32,917 million	58.5%
Li Ning	RMB 2,018 million	64.6%
Adidas	EUR 4,732 million	77.3%
Puma	EUR 691 million	85.2%

As a percent of total liabilities

EXHIBIT 11.2

Current Liabilities of Selected Companies

Uncertainty in Liabilities

Accounting for liabilities involves addressing three important questions: Whom to pay? When to pay? How much to pay? Answers to these questions are often decided when a liability is incurred. For example, if a company has a $100 account payable to a specific individual, payable on March 15, the answers are clear. The company knows whom to pay, when to pay, and how much to pay. However, the answers to one or more of these questions are uncertain for some liabilities.

Uncertainty in Whom to Pay   Liabilities can involve uncertainty in whom to pay. For instance, a company can create a liability with a known amount when issuing a note that is payable to its holder. In this case, a specific amount is payable to the note's holder at a specified date, but the company does not know who the holder is until that date. Despite this uncertainty, the company reports this liability on its statement of financial position.

Uncertainty in When to Pay A company can have an obligation of a known amount to a known creditor but not know when it must be paid. For example, a legal services firm can accept fees in advance from a client who plans to use the firm's services in the future. This means that the firm has a liability that it settles by providing services at an unknown future date. Although this uncertainty exists, the legal firm's statement of financial position must report this liability. These types of obligations are reported as current liabilities because they are likely to be settled in the short term.

Uncertainty in How Much to Pay A company can be aware of an obligation but not know how much will be required to settle it. For example, a company using electrical power is billed only after the meter has been read. This cost is incurred and the liability created before a bill is received. A liability to the power company is reported as an estimated amount if the statement of financial position is prepared before a bill arrives.

Quick Check
Answers — p. 450

1. What is a liability? Identify its crucial characteristics.
2. Is every expected future payment a liability?
3. If a liability is payable in 15 months, is it classified as current or long term?

KNOWN LIABILITIES

C2 Identify and describe known current liabilities.

Most liabilities arise from situations with little uncertainty. They are set by agreements, contracts, or laws and are measurable. These liabilities are **known liabilities,** also called *definitely determinable liabilities.* Known liabilities include accounts payable, notes payable, payroll, sales taxes, and unearned revenues. We describe how to account for these known liabilities in this section.

Accounts Payable

Accounts payable, or trade accounts payable, are amounts owed to suppliers for products or services purchased on credit. Accounting for accounts payable is primarily explained and illustrated in our discussion of merchandising activities in Chapters 5 and 6.

Sales Taxes Payable

Many countries levy sales taxes on retail sales; some countries such as Australia and Singapore call them **goods and services tax (GST)**. **Harvey Norman**, for instance, paid almost A$50 million GST in its 2010 annual report. In its notes, it states that "Revenues, expenses and assets are recognised net of the amount of GST." The net amount of GST recoverable from, or payable to, the taxation authority is included as part of receivables or payables in the statement of financial position. To illustrate, if Harvey Norman sells goods on August 31 for $6,000 cash that are subject to a 10% GST, the revenue portion of this transaction is recorded as follows:

Assets = Liabilities + Equity
6,600   600   +6,000

Aug. 31	Cash	6,600	
	Sales		6,000
	GST Payable ($6,000 × 0.10)		600
	To record cash sales and 10% GST.		

GST (or Sales Taxes Payable) is debited and Cash credited when it remits these collections to the government. GST Payable is not an expense. It arises because laws require sellers to collect this cash from customers for the government.

Unearned Revenues

Unearned revenues (also called *deferred revenues, collections in advance,* and *prepayments*) are amounts received in advance from customers for future products or services. Advance ticket sales for sporting events or music concerts are examples. **Beyonce**, for instance, has "deferred revenues" from advance ticket sales. To illustrate, assume that Beyonce sells $5 million in tickets for eight concerts; the entry is

Point: To *defer* a revenue means to postpone recognition of a revenue collected in advance until it is earned. Sport teams must defer recognition of ticket sales until games are played.

June 30	Cash	5,000,000	
	Unearned Ticket Revenue		5,000,000
	To record sale of concert tickets.		

Assets = Liabilities + Equity
+5,000,000   +5,000,000

When a concert (out of eight) is played, Beyonce would record revenue for the portion earned.

Oct. 31	Unearned Ticket Revenue	625,000	
	Ticket Revenue		625,000
	To record concert ticket revenues earned.		

Assets = Liabilities + Equity
              −625,000   +625,000

Unearned Ticket Revenue is an unearned revenue account and is reported as a current liability. Unearned revenues also arise with airline ticket sales, magazine subscriptions, construction projects, hotel reservations, and custom orders.

Decision Insight

Frequent Flyer Programs   Many airlines operate frequent flyer or loyalty programs that provide travel awards to program members based on accumulated mileage. A portion of passenger revenue attributable to the award of frequent flyer benefits, estimated based on expected utilization of these benefits, is deferred until they are utilized. These are included under Deferred Revenue on the statement of financial position. Any remaining unutilized benefits are recognized as revenue upon expiry. ■

Short-Term Notes Payable

A **short-term note payable** is a written promise to pay a specified amount on a definite future date within one year or the company's operating cycle, whichever is longer. These promissory notes are negotiable (as are checks), meaning they can be transferred from party to party by endorsement. The written documentation provided by notes is helpful in resolving disputes and for pursuing legal actions involving these liabilities. Most notes payable bear interest to compensate for use of the money until payment is made. Short-term notes payable can arise from many transactions. A company that purchases merchandise on credit can sometimes extend the credit period by signing a note to replace an account payable. Such notes also can arise when money is borrowed from a bank. We describe both of these cases.

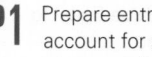 **P1** Prepare entries to account for short-term notes payable.

Point: Required characteristics for negotiability of a note: (1) unconditional promise, (2) in writing, (3) specific amount, and (4) definite due date.

Note Given to Extend Credit Period   A company can replace an account payable with a note payable. A common example is a creditor that requires the substitution of an interest-bearing note for an overdue account payable that does not bear interest. A less common situation occurs when a debtor's weak financial condition motivates the creditor to accept a note, sometimes for a lesser amount, and to close the account to ensure that this customer makes no additional credit purchases.

To illustrate, let's assume that on August 23, Brady Company asks to extend its past-due $600 account payable to McGraw. After some negotiations, McGraw agrees to accept $100 cash and a 60-day, 12%, $500 note payable to replace the account payable. Brady records the transaction with this entry:

Assets = Liabilities + Equity
−100   −600
              +500

Aug. 23	Accounts Payable—McGraw	600	
	Cash		100
	Notes Payable—McGraw		500
	Gave $100 cash and a 60-day, 12% note for payment on account.		

Point: Accounts payable are detailed in a subsidiary ledger, but notes payable are sometimes not. A file with copies of notes can serve as a subsidiary ledger.

Signing the note does not resolve Brady's debt. Instead, the form of debt is changed from an account payable to a note payable. McGraw prefers the note payable over the account payable because it earns interest and it is written documentation of the debt's existence, term, and amount. When the note comes due, Brady pays the note and interest by giving McGraw a check for $510. Brady records that payment with this entry:

Assets = Liabilities + Equity
−510   −500   −10

Oct. 22	Notes Payable—McGraw	500	
	Interest Expense	10	
	Cash		510
	Paid note with interest ($500 × 12% × 60/360).		

Point: Commercial companies commonly compute interest using a 360-day year. This is known as the *banker's rule*.

Interest expense is computed by multiplying the principal of the note ($500) by the annual interest rate (12%) for the fraction of the year the note is outstanding (60 days/360 days).

Note Given to Borrow from Bank   A bank nearly always requires a borrower to sign a promissory note when making a loan. When the note matures, the borrower repays the note with an amount larger than the amount borrowed. The difference between the amount borrowed and the amount repaid is *interest*. This section considers a type of note whose signer promises to pay *principal* (the amount borrowed) plus interest. In this case, the *face value* of the note equals principal. Face value is the value shown on the face (front) of the note. To illustrate, assume that a company needs $2,000 for a project and borrows this money from a bank at 12% annual interest. The loan is made on September 30, 2011, and is due in 60 days. Specifically, the borrowing company signs a note with a face value equal to the amount borrowed. The note includes a statement similar to this: *"I promise to pay $2,000 plus interest at 12% within 60 days after September 30."* This simple note is shown in Exhibit 11.3.

Point: When money is borrowed from a bank, the loan is reported as an asset (receivable) on the bank's statement of financial position.

EXHIBIT 11.3

Note with Face Value Equal to Amount Borrowed

Promissory Note

$2,000   Sept. 30, 2011
Face Value   **Date**

Sixty days   after date, _____ I _____ promise to pay to the order of

National Bank
Boston, MA

Two thousand and no/100 ---------------------- **Dollars**

plus interest at the annual rate of   12% .

                                   Janet Lee

The borrower records its receipt of cash and the new liability with this entry:

Sept. 30	Cash	2,000	
	Notes Payable		2,000
	Borrowed $2,000 cash with a 60-day, 12%, $2,000 note.		

Assets = Liabilities + Equity
+2,000   +2,000

When principal and interest are paid, the borrower records payment with this entry:

Nov. 29	Notes Payable	2,000	
	Interest Expense	40	
	Cash		2,040
	Paid note with interest ($2,000 × 12% × 60/360).		

Assets = Liabilities + Equity
−2,040   −2,000   −40

End-of-period interest adjustment.   When the end of an accounting period occurs between the signing of a note payable and its maturity date, the *matching principle* requires us to record the accrued but unpaid interest on the note. To illustrate, let's return to the note in Exhibit 11.3, but assume that the company borrows $2,000 cash on December 16, 2011, instead of September 30. This 60-day note matures on February 14, 2012, and the company's financial year ends on December 31. Thus, we need to record interest expense for the final 15 days in December. This means that one-fourth (15 days/60 days) of the $40 total interest is an expense of year 2011. The borrower records this expense with the following adjusting entry:

2011			
Dec. 31	Interest Expense	10	
	Interest Payable		10
	To record accrued interest on note ($2,000 × 12% × 15/360).		

Assets = Liabilities + Equity
              +10   −10

When this note matures on February 14, the borrower must recognize 45 days of interest expense for year 2012 and remove the balances of the two liability accounts:

Example: If this note is dated Dec. 1 instead of Dec. 16, how much expense is recorded on Dec. 31? *Answer:* $2,000 × 12% × 30/360 = $20

2012			
Feb. 14	Interest Expense*	30	
	Interest Payable	10	
	Notes Payable	2,000	
	Cash		2,040
	*Paid note with interest. *($2,000 × 12% × 45/360)*		

Assets = Liabilities + Equity
−2,040   −10   −30
                −2,000

> ### Decision Insight
> Many franchisors such as **Baskin-Robbins**, **Dunkin' Donuts**, and **Cold Stone Creamery**, use notes to help entrepreneurs acquire their own franchises, including using notes to pay for the franchise fee and any equipment. Payments on these notes are usually collected monthly and often are secured by the franchisees' assets. ■

Payroll Liabilities

An employer incurs several expenses and liabilities from having employees. These expenses and liabilities are often large and arise from salaries and wages earned, from employee benefits, and from payroll taxes levied on the employer. **Heineken**, for instance, reports employee benefits liabilities of EUR 1.202 billion as at end of 2013. We discuss payroll liabilities and related accounts in this section.

P2 Compute and record *employee* payroll deductions and liabilities.

Payroll, also called employee compensation, is a major expense for most companies, especially for service entities such as accounting firms, law firms, real estate agencies, and travel agencies.

Such employee compensation takes several forms. *Wages* usually refer to payments to employees at an hourly rate. *Salaries* usually refer to payments to employees at a monthly or yearly rate. *Commissions* to sales people are stated at a percentage of the sales the person has made. *Bonuses* are amounts over and above normal compensation. Companies may also pay some employer payroll taxes and expense for employee benefits.

Using Singapore as an example, under the law, both the employee and his employer will have to contribute to the Central Provident Fund (CPF), which is primarily for the employee's retirement needs. An employee will have to contribute 20%, which is to be deducted from his salary and bonus and paid into his account with the CPF Board. His employer has to contribute 16% to the employee's CPF account. Assuming that the employee earns $50,000 of salary and bonus:

Assets = Liabilities + Equity
+10,000   −58,000
+8,000
+40,000

Salary and Bonus Expense	58,000	
Employee CPF Contribution Payable.		10,000
Employer CPF Contribution Payable.		8,000
Salary Payable to Employee		40,000

P3 Compute and record *employer* payroll expenses and liabilities.

Salary expense thus represents **gross pay** (that is, pay before subtractions for CPF contributions and other deductions). Salary expense creates several payroll liabilities.

- Salary payable to the employee is the employee's **net pay** (also called *take-home pay*).
- Employee CPF contribution payable is the employee's pay that is withheld from his paycheck.
- Employer CPF contribution payable is additional pay for the employee paid directly to his CPF account.

Multi-Period Known Liabilities

Many known liabilities extend over multiple periods. These often include unearned revenues and notes payable. For example, if **Sports Illustrated** sells a four-year magazine subscription, it records amounts received for this subscription in an Unearned Subscription Revenues account. Amounts in this account are liabilities, but are they current or long term? They are *both*. The portion of the Unearned Subscription Revenues account that will be fulfilled in the next year is reported as a current liability. The remaining portion is reported as a long-term liability.

Point: Some accounting systems do make an entry to transfer the current amount due out of Long-Term Debt and into the Current Portion of Long-Term Debt as follows:

Long-Term Debt 1,500
    Current Portion of L-T Debt 1,500

The same analysis applies to notes payable. For example, a borrower reports a three-year note payable as a long-term liability in the first two years it is outstanding. In the third year, the borrower reclassifies this note as a current liability since it is due within one year or the operating cycle, whichever is longer. The **current portion of long-term debt** refers to that part of long-term debt due within one year or the operating cycle, whichever is longer. Long-term debt is reported under long-term liabilities, but the *current portion due* is reported under current liabilities. To illustrate, assume that a $7,500 debt is paid in installments of $1,500 per year for five years. The $1,500 due within the year is reported as a current liability. No journal entry is necessary for this reclassification. Instead, we simply classify the amounts for debt as either current or long term when the statement of financial position is prepared.

Some known liabilities are rarely reported in long-term liabilities. These include accounts payable, sales taxes, and wages and salaries.

Decision Insight

Liability Limits   Probably the greatest number of frauds involve payroll. Companies must safeguard payroll activities. Controls include proper approvals and processes for employee additions, deletions, and pay rate changes. A common fraud is a manager adding a fictitious employee to the payroll and then cashing the fictitious employee's check. A study reports that 28% of employees in operations and service areas witnessed violations of employee wage, overtime, or benefit rules in the past year (KPMG 2009). Another 21% observed falsifying of time and expense reports. ■

4. Why does a creditor prefer a note payable to a past-due account payable?

ESTIMATED LIABILITIES

An **estimated liability** is a known obligation that is of an uncertain amount but that can be reliably estimated. Common examples are employee benefits such as pensions and warranties offered by a seller. Topics such as pensions are discussed in more advanced accounting texts; we will discuss only warranties in this section. Other examples of estimated liabilities include property taxes and certain contracts to provide future services. **IAS 37 Provisions, Contingent Liabilities and Contingent Assets** defines a liability of uncertain timing or amount as a *provision*.

> **P4** Account for estimated liabilities.

Warranty Liabilities

A **warranty** is a seller's obligation to replace or correct a product (or service) that fails to perform as expected within a specified period. Most new cars, for instance, are sold with a warranty covering parts for a specified period of time. **Ford Motor Company** reported more than $15 billion in "dealer and customer allowances and claims" in its annual report. To comply with the *full disclosure* and *matching principles,* the seller reports the expected warranty expense in the period when revenue from the sale of the product or service is reported. The seller reports this warranty obligation as a liability, although the existence, amount, payee, and date of future sacrifices are uncertain. This is because such warranty costs are probable and the amount can be estimated using, for instance, past experience with warranties.

> **Point:** **Nokia** recently reported EUR 928 million on its statement of financial position for warranty provisions.

To illustrate, a dealer sells a used car for $16,000 on December 1, 2011, with a maximum one-year or 12,000-mile warranty covering parts. This dealer's experience shows that warranty expense averages about 4% of a car's selling price, or $640 in this case ($16,000 × 4%). The dealer records the estimated expense and liability related to this sale with this entry:

2011			
Dec. 1	Warranty Expense	640	
	Estimated Warranty Liability		640
	To record estimated warranty expense.		

Assets = Liabilities + Equity
+640   −640

This entry alternatively could be made as part of end-of-period adjustments. Either way, the estimated warranty expense is reported on the 2011 income statement and the warranty liability on the 2011 statement of financial position. To further extend this example, suppose the customer returns the car for warranty repairs on January 9, 2012. The dealer performs this work by replacing parts costing $200. The entry to record partial settlement of the estimated warranty liability is

> **Point:** Recognition of warranty liabilities is necessary to comply with the matching and full disclosure principles.

2012			
Jan. 9	Estimated Warranty Liability	200	
	Auto Parts Inventory		200
	To record costs of warranty repairs.		

Assets = Liabilities + Equity
−200   −200

This entry reduces the balance of the estimated warranty liability. Warranty expense was previously recorded in 2011, the year the car was sold with the warranty. Finally, what happens if total warranty expenses are more or less than the estimated 4%, or $640? The answer is that management should monitor actual warranty expenses to see whether the 4% rate is accurate. If experience reveals a large difference from the estimate, the rate for current and future sales should be changed. Differences are expected, but they should be small.

> **Point:** Both U.S. GAAP and **IFRS** account for restructuring costs in a manner similar to accounting for warranties.

Multi-Period Estimated Liabilities

Estimated liabilities can be both current and long term. For example, pension liabilities to employees are long term to workers who will not retire within the next period. For employees who are retired or will retire within the next period, a portion of pension liabilities is current. Other examples include employee health benefits and warranties. Specifically, many warranties are for 30 or 60 days in length. Estimated costs under these warranties are properly reported in current liabilities. Many other automobile warranties are for three years or 36,000 miles. A portion of these warranties is reported as long term.

<table>
<tr><td>Quick Check</td><td>Answers — p. 450</td><td></td></tr>
</table>

5. Estimated liabilities or provisions involve an obligation to pay which of these: (*a*) an uncertain but reliably estimated amount owed on a known obligation, or (*b*) a known amount to a specific entity on an uncertain due date?

6. A car is sold for $15,000 on June 1, 2011, with a one-year warranty on parts. Warranty expense is estimated at 1.5% of selling price at each calendar year-end. On March 1, 2012, the car is returned for warranty repairs costing $135. The amount recorded as warranty expense on March 1 is (*a*) $0; (*b*) $60; (*c*) $75; (*d*) $135; (*e*) $225.

CONTINGENT LIABILITIES

C3 Explain how to account for contingent liabilities.

A **contingent liability** is a potential obligation that depends on a future event arising from a past transaction or event. An example is a pending lawsuit. Here, a past transaction or event leads to a lawsuit whose result depends on the outcome of the suit. Future payment of a contingent liability depends on whether an uncertain future event occurs.

Accounting for Contingent Liabilities

IAS 37 defines a contingent liability as:

a. a possible obligation that arises from past events and whose existence will be confirmed only by the occurrence or nonoccurrence of one or more uncertain future events not wholly within the control of the entity; or

b. a present obligation that arises from past events but is not recognized because:

   i. it is not probable that an outflow of resources embodying economic benefits will be required to settle the obligation; or

   ii. the amount of the obligation cannot be measured with sufficient reliability.

Point: A contingency is an *if*. Namely, if a future event occurs, then financial consequences are likely for the entity.

The standard also states that where it is not probable that a present obligation exists, an entity discloses a contingent liability, unless the possibility of an outflow of resources embodying economic benefits is remote.

Point: Accounting standards generally do not give a probability threshold: **IFRS** defines *probable* as "more likely than not" while U.S. GAAP defines it as "likely to occur."

Given the above, accounting for contingent liabilities therefore depends on the likelihood that a future event will occur and the ability to estimate the future amount owed if this event occurs. Three different possibilities are identified in the following chart: record liability, disclose in notes, or no disclosure.

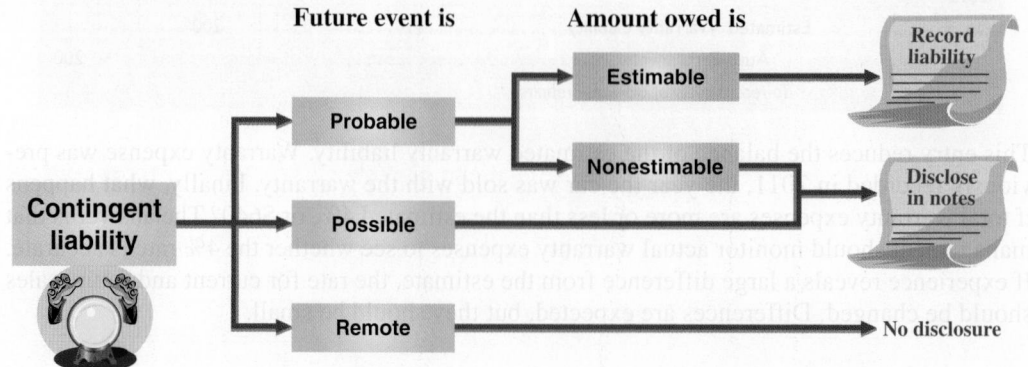

The conditions that determine each of these three possibilities follow.

1. The future event is *probable* (more likely than not) and the amount owed can be *reliably estimated*. We then record this amount as a liability.
2. The future event is *possible* (could occur). We disclose information about this type of contingent liability in notes to the financial statements.
3. The future event is *remote* (unlikely). We do not record or disclose information on remote contingent liabilities.

IAS 37 does not assign any numerical measure of probability. Accountants would generally agree that "more likely than not" implies a probability of more than 50% and "remote" would be as low as 5% or less.

Probable Contingent Liabilities

This section describes the accounting treatment for a probable contingent liability using a common example of legal claims or lawsuits. Many companies are sued or at risk of being sued. The accounting issue is whether the defendant should recognize a liability on its statement of financial position while a lawsuit is outstanding and not yet settled. The answer is that a potential claim is recorded in the accounts *only* if payment for damages is probable and the amount can be reliably estimated. For example, if company A is sued for $10 million and in the opinion of its management and legal experts it is probable that the company will lose this amount, then the journal entry recorded by company A should be

Loss from Lawsuit	10,000,000	
Lawsuit Payable.		10,000,000
To record probable loss from lawsuit.		

This journal entry will make the company's financials look less favorable to investors and creditors as it reduces profits in the income statement and increases liabilities in the statement of financial position. Such a liability is called a *provision* by **IAS 37** as there is uncertainty about the timing or amount of the future expenditure required in settlement.

Possible Contingent Liabilities

This section identifies and discusses contingent liabilities that commonly fall in the second category—when the future event is possible. Disclosing information about contingencies in this category is motivated by the *full-disclosure principle,* which requires information relevant to decision makers be reported and not ignored.

If a legal claim or lawsuit cannot be reliably estimated or is less than probable but possible, then it is disclosed. **Adidas**, for example, includes the following note in its annual report: "The Adidas Group is exposed to the risk of claims and litigation for infringement of third-party trademark, patent and other rights."

Another common example of a possible contingent liability is a company guaranteeing the payment of debt owed by a supplier, customer, or another company. The guarantor usually discloses the guarantee in its financial statement notes as a contingent liability. If it is probable that the debtor will default, then the guarantor needs to record and report the guarantee in its financial statements as a liability. The **Boston Celtics** report a unique guarantee when it comes to coaches and players: "Certain of the contracts provide for guaranteed payments which must be paid even if the employee [player] is injured or terminated."

Remote Contingent Liabilities

The accounting standard seems to allow a company to not record and not disclose any contingent liability with a remote probability. In this modern tech world where information is easily accessible on the Internet, it may be good transparency practice for a company to voluntarily disclose even remote contingent liabilities.

Point: Auditors and managers often have different views about whether a contingency is recorded, disclosed, or omitted.

Other Contingencies   Other examples of contingencies include environmental damages, possible tax assessments, insurance losses, and government investigations. **Nokia**, for example, includes the following note in its annual report: "Allegations of possible health risks from the electromagnetic fields generated by base stations and mobile devices, and the lawsuits and publicity relating to this matter, regardless of merit, could have a material adverse effect on our sales, results of operations, share price, reputation and brand value by leading consumers to reduce their use of mobile devices, by increasing difficulty in obtaining sites for base stations, or by leading regulatory bodies to set arbitrary use restrictions and exposure limits, or by causing us to allocate additional monetary and personnel resources to these issues." Many of Nokia's contingencies are only revealed in notes.

Decision Insight

Apple versus Samsung   In the spring of 2011, Apple began litigating against Samsung in patent infringement suits. By July 2012, the two companies were still embroiled in more than 50 lawsuits around the globe, with billions of dollars in damages claimed between them. If the companies decide to record these potential liabilities, then these provisions would affect profits on the income statements and liabilities on the statements of financial position. ■

Uncertainties That Are Not Contingencies

All organizations face uncertainties from future events such as natural disasters and the development of new competing products or services. These uncertainties are not contingent liabilities because they are future events *not* arising from past transactions. Accordingly, they are not disclosed.

Quick Check   Answers — p. 450

7. A future payment is reported as a liability on the statement of financial position if payment is contingent on a future event that (*a*) is reliably possible but the payment cannot be reliably estimated; (*b*) is probable and the payment can be reliably estimated; or (*c*) is not probable but the payment is known.

8. Under what circumstances is a future payment reported in the notes to the financial statements as a contingent liability?

Decision Analysis ▢▢▢   Times Interest Earned Ratio

A1 Compute the times interest earned ratio and use it to analyze liabilities.

A company incurs interest expense on many of its current and long-term liabilities. Examples extend from its short-term notes and the current portion of long-term liabilities to its long-term notes and bonds. Interest expense is often viewed as a *fixed expense* because the amount of these liabilities is likely to remain in one form or another for a substantial period of time. This means that the amount of interest is unlikely to vary due to changes in sales or other operating activities. While fixed expenses can be advantageous when a company is growing, they create risk. This risk stems from the possibility that a company might be unable to pay fixed expenses if sales decline. To illustrate, consider **IAS** Company's results for 2015 and two possible outcomes for year 2016 in Exhibit 11.5.

EXHIBIT 11.5

Actual and Projected Results

(US$ thousands)	2015	2016 Projections	
		Sales Increase	Sales Decrease
Sales	$600	$900	$300
Expenses (75% of sales)	450	675	225
Profit before interest and tax.	150	225	75
Interest expense (fixed)	60	60	60
Net profit	$ 90	$165	$ 15

Expenses excluding interest are at, and are expected to remain at, 75% of sales. Expenses such as these that change with sales volume are called *variable expenses*. However, interest expense is at, and is expected to remain at, $60,000 per year due to its fixed nature.

The middle numerical column of Exhibit 11.5 shows that **IAS** Company's profit nearly doubles to $165,000 if sales increase by 50% to $900,000. In contrast, the far right column shows that profit falls sharply if sales decline by 50%. These results reveal that the amount of fixed interest expense affects a company's risk of its ability to pay interest, which is numerically reflected in the **times interest earned** ratio in Exhibit 11.6.

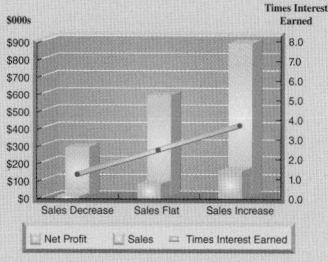

EXHIBIT 11.6

$$\text{Times interest earned} = \frac{\text{Profit before interest expense and income tax}}{\text{Interest expense}}$$

For 2015, **IAS** Company's times interest earned is computed as $150,000/$60,000, or 2.5 times. This ratio suggests that **IAS** Company faces low to moderate risk because its sales must decline sharply before it would be unable to cover its interest expenses.

Experience shows that when times interest earned falls below 1.5 to 2.0 and remains at that level or lower for several periods, the default rate on liabilities increases sharply. This reflects increased risk for companies and their creditors. We also must interpret the times interest earned ratio in light of information about the variability of a company's profit. If profit is stable from year to year or if it is growing, the company can afford to take on added risk by borrowing. If its profit greatly varies from year to year, fixed interest expense can increase the risk that it will not earn enough profit to pay interest. For the two projected sales in 2016, time interest earned is (1) 3.75 for a sales increase and (2) 1.25 for a sales decrease.

■ **Decision** Maker   Answer — p. 450

Entrepreneur   You wish to invest in a franchise for either one of two national chains. Each franchise has an expected annual net profit *after* interest and taxes of $100,000. Net profit for the first franchise includes a regular fixed interest charge of $200,000. The fixed interest charge for the second franchise is $40,000. Which franchise is riskier to you if sales forecasts are not met? Does your decision change if the first franchise has more variability in its income stream? ■

DEMONSTRATION PROBLEM

The following transactions and events took place at Kern Company during its recent calendar-year reporting period (Kern does not use reversing entries).

a. In September 2015, Kern sold $140,000 of merchandise covered by a 180-day warranty. Prior experience shows that costs of the warranty equal 5% of sales. Compute September's warranty expense and prepare the adjusting journal entry for the warranty liability as recorded at September 30. Also prepare the journal entry on October 8 to record a $300 cash expenditure to provide warranty service on an item sold in September.

b. On October 12, 2015, Kern arranged with a supplier to replace Kern's overdue $10,000 account payable by paying $2,500 cash and signing a note for the remainder. The note matures in 90 days and has a 12% interest rate. Prepare the entries recorded on October 12, December 31, and January 10, 2016, related to this transaction.

c. In late December, Kern learns it is facing a product liability suit filed by an unhappy customer. Kern's lawyer advises that although it will probably suffer a loss from the lawsuit, it is not possible to estimate the amount of damages at this time.

d. Sally Kline works for Kern. For the pay period ended November 30, her earnings are $3,000. Kline has $600 deducted for Employee CPF Contribution from each paycheck. Additionally, Kern is liable for Employer CPF Contribution Payable of $480 payable to the CPF Board. Journalize the accrual of salaries expense of Kline's wages by Kern.

e. On November 1, Kern borrows $5,000 cash from a bank in return for a 60-day, 12%, $5,000 note. Record the note's issuance on November 1 and its repayment with interest on December 31.

f. Kern has estimated and recorded its quarterly income tax payments. In reviewing its year-end tax adjustments, it identifies an additional $5,000 of income tax expense that should be recorded. Record this year-end income tax expense adjusting entry.

g. For this calendar-year, Kern's net profit is $1,000,000, its interest expense is $275,000, and its income tax expense is $225,000. Calculate Kern's times interest earned ratio.

PLANNING THE SOLUTION

- For *a*, compute the warranty expense for September and record it with an estimated liability. Record the October expenditure as a decrease in the liability.
- For *b*, eliminate the liability for the account payable and create the liability for the note payable. Compute interest expense for the 80 days that the note is outstanding in 2015 and record it as an additional liability. Record the payment of the note, being sure to include the interest for the 10 days in 2016.
- For *c*, decide whether the company's contingent liability needs to be disclosed or accrued (recorded) according to the two necessary criteria: probable loss and reliably estimable.
- For *d*, first calculate the gross amount that the employer is liable for (the salaries plus the employer CPF contribution), then set up payable accounts for all items in Kline's paycheck that require deductions. After deducting all necessary items, credit the remaining amount to Salary Payable to Employee.
- For *e*, record the issuance of the note. Calculate 60 days' interest due using the 360-day convention in the interest formula.
- For *f*, determine how much of the income tax expense is payable in the current year.
- For *g*, apply and compute times interest earned.

SOLUTION TO DEMONSTRATION PROBLEM

a. Warranty expense = 5% × $140,000 = $7,000

Sept. 30	Warranty Expense	7,000	
	Estimated Warranty Liability		7,000
	To record warranty expense for the month.		
Oct. 8	Estimated Warranty Liability	300	
	Cash		300
	To record the cost of the warranty service.		

b. Interest expense for 2011 = 12% × $7,500 × 80/360 = $200

     Interest expense for 2012 = 12% × $7,500 × 10/360 = $25

Oct. 12	Accounts Payable	10,000	
	Notes Payable		7,500
	Cash		2,500
	Paid $2,500 cash and gave a 90-day, 12% note to extend the due date on the account.		
Dec. 31	Interest Expense	200	
	Interest Payable		200
	To accrue interest on note payable.		
Jan. 10	Interest Expense	25	
	Interest Payable	200	
	Notes Payable	7,500	
	Cash		7,725
	Paid note with interest, including the accrued interest payable.		

c. Disclose the pending lawsuit in the financial statement notes. Although the loss is probable, no liability can be accrued since the loss cannot be reliably estimated.

d.

Salaries Expense	3,480	
Employee CPF Contribution Payable		600
Employer CPF Contribution Payable		480
Salaries Payable to Employee		2,400
To record Kern's payroll expense and liability.		

e.

Nov. 1	Cash	5,000	
	Notes Payable		5,000
	Borrowed cash with a 60-day, 12% note.		

When the note and interest are paid 60 days later, Kern Company records this entry:

Dec. 31	Notes Payable	5,000	
	Interest Expense	100	
	Cash		5,100
	Paid note with interest ($5,000 × 12% × 60/360).		

f.

Income Tax Expense	5,000	
Income Tax Payable		5,000
To record Kern's tax expense and liability.		

g. Times interest earned $= \dfrac{\$1,000,000 + \$275,000 + \$225,000}{\$275,000} = \underline{5.45 \text{ times}}$

Summary

C1 Describe current and long-term liabilities and their characteristics. Liabilities are probable future payments of assets or services that past transactions or events obligate an entity to make. Current liabilities are due within one year or the operating cycle, whichever is longer. All other liabilities are long term.

C2 Identify and describe known current liabilities. Known (determinable) current liabilities are set by agreements or laws and are measurable with little uncertainty. They include accounts payable, sales taxes payable, unearned revenues, notes payable, payroll liabilities, and the current portion of long-term debt.

C3 Explain how to account for contingent liabilities. If an uncertain future payment depends on a probable future event and the amount can be reliably estimated, the payment is recorded as a liability. The uncertain future payment is reported as a contingent liability (in the notes) if (a) the future event is possible but not probable or (b) the event is probable but the payment amount cannot be reliably estimated.

A1 Compute the times interest earned ratio and use it to analyze liabilities. Times interest earned is computed by dividing a company's profit before interest expense and income tax by the amount of interest expense. The times interest earned ratio reflects a company's ability to pay interest obligations.

P1 Prepare entries to account for short-term notes payable. Short-term notes payable are current liabilities; most bear interest. When a short-term note's face value equals the amount borrowed, it identifies a rate of interest to be paid at maturity.

P2 Compute and record *employee* payroll deductions and liabilities. Employee payroll deductions include compulsory and voluntary deductions such as for retirement savings. They make up the difference between gross and net pay.

P3 Compute and record *employer* payroll expenses and liabilities. An employer's payroll expenses include employees' gross earnings and any employee benefits.

P4 Account for estimated liabilities. A common estimated liability is warranties, which are recorded as expenses when incurred and matched with revenues generated.

Guidance Answers to Decision Maker

Entrepreneur   Risk is partly reflected by the times interest earned ratio. This ratio for the first franchise is 1.5 [($100,000 + $200,000)/$200,000], whereas the ratio for the second franchise is 3.5 [($100,000 + $40,000)/$40,000]. This analysis shows that the first franchise is more at risk of incurring a loss if its sales decline.

The second question asks about variability of income. If income greatly varies, this increases the risk an owner will not earn sufficient income to cover interest. Since the first franchise has the greater variability, it is a riskier investment.

Guidance Answers to Quick Checks

1. A liability involves a probable future payment of assets or services that an entity is presently obligated to make as a result of past transactions or events.

2. No, an expected future payment is not a liability unless an existing obligation was created by a past event or transaction.

3. In most cases, a liability due in 15 months is classified as long term. It is classified as a current liability if the company's operating cycle is 15 months or longer.

4. A creditor prefers a note payable instead of a past-due account payable so as to (a) charge interest and/or (b) have evidence of the debt and its terms for potential litigation or disputes.

5. (a)

6. (a) Warranty expense was previously estimated and recorded.

7. (b)

8. A future payment is reported in the notes as a contingent liability if (a) the uncertain future event is probable but the amount of payment cannot be reliably estimated or (b) the uncertain future event is not probable but has a possibility of occurring.

Key Terms   www.mheducation.asia/olc/wildkwokFAP

Contingent liability (p. 444)
Current liabilities (p. 437)
Current portion of long-term debt (p. 442)
Estimated liability (p. 443)

Goods and services tax (GST) (p. 438)
Gross pay (p. 442)
Known liabilities (p. 438)
Noncurrent liabilities (p. 437)

Net pay (p. 442)
Short-term note payable (p. 439)
Times interest earned (p. 447)
Warranty (p. 443)

Multiple Choice Quiz   Answers on p. 461   www.mheducation.asia/olc/wildkwokFAP

Additional Quiz Questions are available at the book's Website.

1. On December 1, a company signed a $6,000, 90-day, 5% note payable, with principal plus interest due on March 1 of the following year. What amount of interest expense should be accrued at December 31 on the note?
   a. $300
   b. $25
   c. $100
   d. $75
   e. $0

2. A company sells big screen televisions for $3,000 each. Each television has a two-year warranty that covers the replacement of defective parts. It is estimated that 1% of all televisions sold will be returned under warranty at an average cost of $250 each. During July, the company sold 10,000 big screen televisions, and 80 were serviced under the warranty during July at a total cost of $18,000. The credit balance in the Estimated Warranty Liability account at July 1 was $26,000. What is the company's warranty expense for the month of July?
   a. $51,000
   b. $1,000
   c. $25,000
   d. $33,000
   e. $18,000

Icon denotes assignments that involve decision making.

Discussion Questions

1. What are the three important questions concerning the uncertainty of liabilities?
2. What is the difference between a current and a long-term liability?
3. What is an estimated liability?
4. If $988 is the total of a sale that includes its sales tax of 4%, what is the selling price of the item only?
5. Why is an employee's gross pay often not the same as the net pay?
6. Why are warranty liabilities usually recognized on the statement of financial position as liabilities even when they are uncertain?
7. Suppose that a company has a facility located where disastrous weather conditions often occur. Should it report a probable loss from a future disaster as a liability on its statement of financial position? Explain.
8. Refer to the consolidated balance sheet of **Nestlé** in Appendix A. What is the amount of Nestlé's accounts payable (trade and other payables) as at December 31, 2013?
9. Refer to **Adidas**' consolidated statement of financial position in Appendix A. What is the amount of Adidas' accounts payable as at December 31, 2013?
10. Refer to **Puma**'s statement of financial position from its Website (http://about.puma.com/en/investor-relations/financial-reports). Identify its current liabilities.
11. Refer to **Samsung**'s consolidated statement of financial position in Appendix A. Which current liability is the largest amount as at December 31, 2012?
12. Refer to **361 Degrees**' consolidated statement of financial position from its Website (http://ir.361sport.com/html/ir_report.php). Which current liability is the largest amount as at December 31, 2013?

connect

QUICK STUDY

QS 11-1
Classifying liabilities C1

Which of the following items are normally classified as a current liability for a company that has a 15-month operating cycle?

1. Salaries payable.
2. Note payable due in 19 months.
3. Sales taxes payable.
4. Note payable maturing in 3 years.
5. Note payable due in 10 months.
6. Portion of long-term note due in 15 months.

QS 11-2
Accounting for sales taxes C2

Wrecker Computing sells merchandise for $5,000 cash on September 30 (cost of merchandise is $2,900). The sales tax law requires Wrecker to collect 4% sales tax on every dollar of merchandise sold. Record the entry for the $5,000 sale and its applicable sales tax. Also record the entry that shows the remittance of the 4% tax on this sale to the state government on October 15.

QS 11-3
Unearned revenue C2

Tickets, Inc., receives $5,500,000 cash in advance ticket sales for a four-date tour of Bruce Springsteen. Record the advance ticket sales on October 31. Record the revenue earned for the first concert date of November 8, assuming it represents one-fourth of the advance ticket sales.

QS 11-4
Accounting for contingent liabilities C3

The following legal claims exist for Kalamazoo Co. Identify the accounting treatment for each claim as either (*a*) a liability that is recorded or (*b*) an item described in notes to its financial statements.

1. Kalamazoo (defendant) estimates that a pending lawsuit could result in damages of $1,000,000; it is possible that the plaintiff will win the case.
2. Kalamazoo faces a probable loss on a pending lawsuit; the amount is not reliably estimable.
3. Kalamazoo estimates damages in a case at $2,500,000 with a high probability of losing the case.

QS 11-5
Interest-bearing note transactions P1

On November 7, 2015, Ortez Company borrows $150,000 cash by signing a 90-day, 8% note payable with a face value of $150,000. (1) Compute the accrued interest payable on December 31, 2015, (2) prepare the journal entry to record the accrued interest expense at December 31, 2015, and (3) prepare the journal entry to record payment of the note at maturity.

QS 11-6

Compute and record employee and employer payroll **P2 P3**

Edmund Tan works for Jane. For the pay period ended November 30, his earnings are $4,000. Edmund has $800 deducted for Employee CPF Contribution from each paycheck. Additionally, Jane is liable for Employer CPF Contribution of $640 payable to the CPF Board. Journalize the accrual of salaries expense of Edmund's wages by Jane.

QS 11-7

Recording warranty repairs

P4

On September 11, 2014, Home Store sells a mower for $400 with a one-year warranty that covers parts. Warranty expense is estimated at 5% of sales. On July 24, 2015, the mower is brought in for repairs covered under the warranty requiring $35 in materials taken from the Repair Parts Inventory. Prepare the July 24, 2015, entry to record the warranty repairs.

QS 11-8

Times interest earned **A1**

Compute the times interest earned for Weltin Company, which reports profit before interest expense and income tax of $2,044,000, and interest of $350,000. Interpret its times interest earned (assume that its competitors average a times interest earned of 4.0).

 connect

EXERCISES

Exercise 11-1

Classifying liabilities

C1

The following items appear on the statement of financial position of a company with a two-month operating cycle. Identify the proper classification of each item as follows: *C* if it is a current liability, *L* if it is a long-term liability, or *N* if it is not a liability.

_____ **1.** Sales taxes payable.

_____ **2.** Accounts payable.

_____ **3.** Accounts receivable.

_____ **4.** Wages payable.

_____ **5.** Salaries payable.

_____ **6.** Notes payable (due in 6 to 12 months).

_____ **7.** Notes payable (due in 120 days).

_____ **8.** Current portion of long-term debt.

_____ **9.** Notes payable (mature in five years).

_____ **10.** Notes payable (due in 13 to 24 months).

Exercise 11-2

Recording known current liabilities

C2

Prepare any necessary adjusting entries at December 31, 2015, for Yacht Company's year-end financial statements for each of the following separate transactions and events.

1. Yacht Company records an adjusting entry for $2,000,000 of previously unrecorded cash sales (costing $1,000,000) and its sales taxes at a rate of 5%.

2. The company earned $40,000 of $100,000 previously received in advance for services.

Exercise 11-3

Accounting for contingent liabilities

C3

Prepare any necessary adjusting entries at December 31, 2015, for Moor Company's year-end financial statements for each of the following separate transactions and events.

1. A disgruntled employee is suing Moor Company. Legal advisers believe that the company will probably need to pay damages, but the amount cannot be reliably estimated.

2. Moor Company guarantees the $5,000 debt of a supplier. The supplier will probably not default on the debt.

Exercise 11-4

Accounting for note payable

P1

Check (2b) Interest expense, $1,880

Perfect Systems borrows $94,000 cash on May 15, 2015, by signing a 60-day, 12% note.

1. On what date does this note mature?

2. Suppose the face value of the note equals $94,000, the principal of the loan. Prepare the journal entries to record (*a*) issuance of the note and (*b*) payment of the note at maturity.

Exercise 11-5

Interest-bearing notes payable with year-end adjustments

P1

Check (2) $2,250
(3) $1,125

Kwon Co. borrows $150,000 cash on November 1, 2015, by signing a 90-day, 9% note with a face value of $150,000.

1. On what date does this note mature? (Assume that February of 2015 has 28 days.)

2. How much interest expense results from this note in 2015? (Assume a 360-day year.)

3. How much interest expense results from this note in 2016? (Assume a 360-day year.)

4. Prepare journal entries to record (*a*) issuance of the note, (*b*) accrual of interest at the end of 2015, and (*c*) payment of the note at maturity.

During December, Jester Company sold 3,000 units of a product that carries a 60-day warranty. December sales for this product total $120,000. The company expects 8% of the units to need warranty repairs, and it estimates the average repair cost per unit will be $15. Prepare any necessary adjusting entries at December 31, 2015, for Jester Company's year-end financial statements for each of the following separate transactions and events.

Exercise 11-6
Accounting for estimated liabilities
P4

Chang Co. sold a copier costing $3,800 with a two-year parts warranty to a customer on August 16, 2015, for $5,500 cash. Chang uses the perpetual inventory system. On November 22, 2016, the copier requires on-site repairs that are completed the same day. The repairs cost $199 for materials taken from the Repair Parts Inventory. These are the only repairs required in 2016 for this copier. Based on experience, Chang expects to incur warranty costs equal to 4% of dollar sales. It records warranty expense with an adjusting entry at the end of each year.

Exercise 11-7
Warranty expense and liability computations and entries
P4

1. How much warranty expense does the company report in 2015 for this copier?
2. How much is the estimated warranty liability for this copier as at December 31, 2015?
3. How much warranty expense does the company report in 2016 for this copier?
4. How much is the estimated warranty liability for this copier as at December 31, 2016?
5. Prepare journal entries to record (*a*) the copier's sale; (*b*) the adjustment on December 31, 2015, to recognize the warranty expense; and (*c*) the repairs that occur in November 2016.

Check   (1) $220

(4) $21

Use the following information from separate companies *a* through *f* to compute times interest earned. Which company indicates the strongest ability to pay interest expense as it comes due?

Exercise 11-8
Computing and interpreting times interest earned

A1

	Net profit (Loss)	Interest Expense	Income tax
a.	$140,000	$48,000	$ 35,000
b.	140,000	15,000	50,000
c.	140,000	8,000	70,000
d.	265,000	12,000	130,000
e.	79,000	12,000	30,000
f.	(4,000)	12,000	0

Check   (b) 13.67

Volvo Group reports the following information for its product warranty costs as at December 31, 2008, along with provisions and utilizations of warranty liabilities for the year ended December 31, 2008 (SEK in millions).

Exercise 11-9
Accounting for current liabilities under **IFRS**
P4

Product warranty costs

Estimated costs for product warranties are charged to cost of sales when the products are sold. Estimated warranty costs include contractual warranty and goodwill warranty. Warranty provisions are estimated with consideration of historical claims statistics, the warranty period, the average time-lag between faults occurring and claims to the company, and anticipated changes in quality indexes. Differences between actual warranty claims and the estimated claims generally affect the recognized expense and provisions in future periods. At December 31, 2008, warranty cost provisions amounted to 10,354.

Product warranty liabilities, December 31, 2007	SEK 9,373
Additional provisions to product warranty liabilities	6,201
Utilizations and reductions of product warranty liabilities	(5,220)
Product warranty liabilities, December 31, 2008	10,354

1. Prepare Volvo's journal entry to record its estimated warranty liabilities (provisions) for 2008.
2. Prepare Volvo's journal entry to record its costs (utilizations) related to its warranty program for 2008. Assume those costs involve replacements taken out of Inventory, with no cash involved.
3. How much warranty expense does Volvo report for 2008?

PROBLEM SET A

Problem 11-1A
Short-term notes payable
transactions and entries

P1

www.mheducation.asia/olc/wildkwokFAP

Tytus Co. entered into the following transactions involving short-term liabilities in 2014 and 2015.

2014

Apr. 20   Purchased $38,500 of merchandise on credit from Frier, terms are 1/10, n/30. Tytus uses the perpetual inventory system.

May 19   Replaced the April 20 account payable to Frier with a 90-day, $30,000 note bearing 9% annual interest along with paying $8,500 in cash.

July 8   Borrowed $60,000 cash from Community Bank by signing a 120-day, 10% interest-bearing note with a face value of $60,000.

___?___   Paid the amount due on the note to Frier at the maturity date.

___?___   Paid the amount due on the note to Community Bank at the maturity date.

Nov. 28   Borrowed $21,000 cash from UMB Bank by signing a 60-day, 8% interest-bearing note with a face value of $21,000.

Dec. 31   Recorded an adjusting entry for accrued interest on the note to UMB Bank.

2015

___?___   Paid the amount due on the note to UMB Bank at the maturity date.

Required

Check (2) Frier, $675
(3) $154
(4) $126

1. Determine the maturity date for each of the three notes described.
2. Determine the interest due at maturity for each of the three notes. (Assume a 360-day year.)
3. Determine the interest expense to be recorded in the adjusting entry at the end of 2014.
4. Determine the interest expense to be recorded in 2015.
5. Prepare journal entries for all the preceding transactions and events for years 2014 and 2015.

Problem 11-2A
Warranty expense and
liability estimation

P4

On October 29, 2010, Lue Co. began operations by purchasing razors for resale. Lue uses the perpetual inventory method. The razors have a 90-day warranty that requires the company to replace any nonworking razor. When a razor is returned, the company discards it and mails a new one from Merchandise Inventory to the customer. The company's cost per new razor is $18 and its retail selling price is $80 in both 2010 and 2011. The manufacturer has advised the company to expect warranty costs to equal 7% of dollar sales. The following transactions and events occurred.

2010

Nov. 11   Sold 75 razors for $6,000 cash.
      30   Recognized warranty expense related to November sales with an adjusting entry.
Dec. 9   Replaced 15 razors that were returned under the warranty.
      16   Sold 210 razors for $16,800 cash.
      29   Replaced 30 razors that were returned under the warranty.
      31   Recognized warranty expense related to December sales with an adjusting entry.

2011

Jan. 5   Sold 130 razors for $10,400 cash.
      17   Replaced 50 razors that were returned under the warranty.
      31   Recognized warranty expense related to January sales with an adjusting entry.

Required

Check (3) $728
(4) $786 Cr.
(5) $614 Cr.

1. Prepare journal entries to record these transactions and adjustments for 2010 and 2011.
2. How much warranty expense is reported for November 2010 and for December 2010?
3. How much warranty expense is reported for January 2011?
4. What is the balance of the Estimated Warranty Liability account as at December 31, 2010?
5. What is the balance of the Estimated Warranty Liability account as at January 31, 2011?

Shown here are condensed income statements for two different companies (both are organized as LLCs and pay no income tax).

Problem 11-3A
Computing and analyzing times interest earned

A1

Ace Company	
Sales	$500,000
Variable expenses (80%)	400,000
Profit before interest	100,000
Interest expense (fixed)	30,000
Net profit	$ 70,000

Deuce Company	
Sales	$500,000
Variable expenses (60%)	300,000
Profit before interest	200,000
Interest expense (fixed)	130,000
Net profit	$ 70,000

Required

1. Compute times interest earned for Ace Company.
2. Compute times interest earned for Deuce Company.
3. What happens to each company's net profit if sales increase by 30%?
4. What happens to each company's net profit if sales increase by 50%?
5. What happens to each company's net profit if sales increase by 80%?
6. What happens to each company's net profit if sales decrease by 10%?
7. What happens to each company's net profit if sales decrease by 20%?
8. What happens to each company's net profit if sales decrease by 40%?

Check   (3) Ace net profit, $100,000 (43% increase)

(6) Deuce net profit, $50,000 (29% decrease)

Analysis Component

9. Comment on the results from parts 3 through 8 in relation to the fixed-cost strategies of the two companies and the ratio values you computed in parts 1 and 2.

Bargen Co. entered into the following transactions involving short-term liabilities in 2014 and 2015.

PROBLEM SET B

Problem 11-1B
Short-term notes payable transactions and entries

P1

2014

Apr. 22   Purchased $4,000 of merchandise on credit from Quinn Products, terms are 1/10, n/30. Bargen uses the perpetual inventory system.
May 23   Replaced the April 22 account payable to Quinn Products with a 60-day, $3,600 note bearing 15% annual interest along with paying $400 in cash.
July 15   Borrowed $9,000 cash from Blackhawk Bank by signing a 120-day, 10% interest-bearing note with a face value of $9,000.
___?___   Paid the amount due on the note to Quinn Products at maturity.
___?___   Paid the amount due on the note to Blackhawk Bank at maturity.
Dec. 6   Borrowed $16,000 cash from City Bank by signing a 45-day, 9% interest-bearing note with a face value of $16,000.
    31   Recorded an adjusting entry for accrued interest on the note to City Bank.

2015

___?___   Paid the amount due on the note to City Bank at maturity.

Required

1. Determine the maturity date for each of the three notes described.
2. Determine the interest due at maturity for each of the three notes. (Assume a 360-day year.)
3. Determine the interest expense to be recorded in the adjusting entry at the end of 2014.
4. Determine the interest expense to be recorded in 2015.
5. Prepare journal entries for all the preceding transactions and events for years 2014 and 2015.

Check   (2) Quinn, $90
(3) $100
(4) $80

Problem 11-2B
Warranty expense and
liability estimation

P4

On November 10, 2015, Byung Co. began operations by purchasing coffee grinders for resale. Byung uses the perpetual inventory method. The grinders have a 60-day warranty that requires the company to replace any nonworking grinder. When a grinder is returned, the company discards it and mails a new one from Merchandise Inventory to the customer. The company's cost per new grinder is $14 and its retail selling price is $35 in both 2015 and 2016. The manufacturer has advised the company to expect warranty costs to equal 10% of dollar sales. The following transactions and events occurred.

2015

Nov. 16   Sold 50 grinders for $1,750 cash.
    30   Recognized warranty expense related to November sales with an adjusting entry.
Dec. 12   Replaced six grinders that were returned under the warranty.
    18   Sold 150 grinders for $5,250 cash.
    28   Replaced 17 grinders that were returned under the warranty.
    31   Recognized warranty expense related to December sales with an adjusting entry.

2016

Jan.   7   Sold 60 grinders for $2,100 cash.
    21   Replaced 38 grinders that were returned under the warranty.
    31   Recognized warranty expense related to January sales with an adjusting entry.

Required

1. Prepare journal entries to record these transactions and adjustments for 2015 and 2016.
2. How much warranty expense is reported for November 2015 and for December 2015?
3. How much warranty expense is reported for January 2016?
4. What is the balance of the Estimated Warranty Liability account as at December 31, 2015?
5. What is the balance of the Estimated Warranty Liability account as at January 31, 2016?

Check   (3) $210
        (4) $378 Cr.
        (5) $56 Cr.

Problem 11-3B
Computing and analyzing times
interest earned

A1

Shown here are condensed income statements for two different companies (both are organized as LLCs and pay no income tax).

Virgo Company	
Sales	$120,000
Variable expenses (50%)	60,000
Profit before interest	60,000
Interest expense (fixed)	45,000
Net profit	$ 15,000

Zodiac Company	
Sales	$120,000
Variable expenses (75%)	90,000
Profit before interest	30,000
Interest expense (fixed)	15,000
Net profit	$ 15,000

Required

1. Compute times interest earned for Virgo Company.
2. Compute times interest earned for Zodiac Company.
3. What happens to each company's net profit if sales increase by 10%?
4. What happens to each company's net profit if sales increase by 40%?
5. What happens to each company's net profit if sales increase by 90%?
6. What happens to each company's net profit if sales decrease by 20%?
7. What happens to each company's net profit if sales decrease by 50%?
8. What happens to each company's net profit if sales decrease by 80%?

Check   (4) Virgo net profit, $39,000
(160% increase)

      (6) Zodiac net profit, $9,000
(40% decrease)

Analysis Component

9. Comment on the results from parts 3 through 8 in relation to the fixed-cost strategies of the two companies and the ratio values you computed in parts 1 and 2.

COMPREHENSIVE PROBLEM
Bug-Off Exterminators
(Review of Chapters 1–11)

CP 11 Bug-Off Exterminators provides pest control services and sells extermination products manufactured by other companies. The following six-column table contains the company's unadjusted trial balance as at December 31, 2015.

BUG-OFF EXTERMINATORS December 31, 2015	Unadjusted Trial Balance		Adjustments		Adjusted Trial Balance	
Cash	$ 17,000					
Accounts receivable	4,000					
Allowance for doubtful accounts		$ 828				
Merchandise inventory	11,700					
Trucks	32,000					
Accum. depreciation—Trucks		0				
Equipment	45,000					
Accum. depreciation—Equipment		12,200				
Accounts payable		5,000				
Estimated warranty liability		1,400				
Unearned services revenue		0				
Interest payable		0				
Long-term notes payable		15,000				
D. Buggs, Capital		59,700				
D. Buggs, Withdrawals	10,000					
Extermination services revenue		60,000				
Interest revenue		872				
Sales (of merchandise)		71,026				
Cost of goods sold	46,300					
Depreciation expense—Trucks	0					
Depreciation expense—Equipment	0					
Wages expense	35,000					
Interest expense	0					
Rent expense	9,000					
Bad debts expense	0					
Miscellaneous expense	1,226					
Repairs expense	8,000					
Utilities expense	6,800					
Warranty expense	0					
Totals	$226,026	$226,026				

The following information in *a* through *h* applies to the company at the end of the current year.

a. The bank reconciliation as at December 31, 2015, includes the following facts.

Cash balance per bank	$15,100
Cash balance per books	17,000
Outstanding checks	1,800
Deposit in transit	2,450
Interest earned (on bank account)	52
Bank service charges (miscellaneous expense)	15

Reported on the bank statement is a canceled check that the company failed to record. (Information from the bank reconciliation allows you to determine the amount of this check, which is a payment on an account payable.)

b. An examination of customers' accounts shows that accounts totaling $679 should be written off as uncollectible. Using an aging of receivables, the company determines that the ending balance of the Allowance for Doubtful Accounts should be $700.

c. A truck is purchased and placed in service on January 1, 2015. Its cost is being depreciated with the straight-line method using the following facts and estimates.

Original cost	$32,000
Expected residual value	8,000
Useful life (years)	4

d. Two items of equipment (a sprayer and an injector) were purchased and put into service in early January 2013. They are being depreciated with the straight-line method using these facts and estimates.

	Sprayer	Injector
Original cost	$27,000	$18,000
Expected residual value	3,000	2,500
Useful life (years)	8	5

e. On August 1, 2015, the company is paid $3,840 cash in advance to provide monthly service for an apartment complex for one year. The company began providing the services in August. When the cash was received, the full amount was credited to the Extermination Services Revenue account.

f. The company offers a warranty for the services it sells. The expected cost of providing warranty service is 2.5% of the extermination services revenue of $57,760 for 2015. No warranty expense has been recorded for 2015. All costs of servicing warranties in 2015 were properly debited to the Estimated Warranty Liability account.

g. The $15,000 long-term note is an 8%, five-year, interest-bearing note with interest payable annually on December 31. The note was signed with First National Bank on December 31, 2015.

h. The ending inventory of merchandise is counted and determined to have a cost of $11,700. Bug-Off uses a perpetual inventory system.

Required

1. Use the preceding information to determine amounts for the following items.

   a. Correct (reconciled) ending balance of Cash, and the amount of the omitted check.

   b. Adjustment needed to obtain the correct ending balance of the Allowance for Doubtful Accounts.

   c. Depreciation expense for the truck used during year 2015.

   d. Depreciation expense for the two items of equipment used during year 2015.

   e. The adjusted 2015 ending balances of the Extermination Services Revenue and Unearned Services Revenue accounts.

   f. The adjusted 2015 ending balances of the accounts for Warranty Expense and Estimated Warranty Liability.

   g. The adjusted 2015 ending balances of the accounts for Interest Expense and Interest Payable. (Round amounts to nearest whole dollar.)

2. Use the results of part 1 to complete the six-column table by first entering the appropriate adjustments for items *a* through *g* and then completing the adjusted trial balance columns. (*Hint:* Item *b* requires two adjustments.)

3. Prepare journal entries to record the adjustments entered on the six-column table. Assume Bug-Off's adjusted balance for Merchandise Inventory matches the year-end physical count.

4. Prepare Prepare an income statement, a statement of changes in equity (cash withdrawals during 2015 were $10,000), and a classified statement of financial position.

Beyond the Numbers

BTN 11-1 The following is extracted from **361 Degrees'** financial statements.

1. Complete the following table for financial years 2013 and 2012. Comment on 361 Degrees' ability to cover its interest expense for both years.

(RMB thousands)	2013	2012
Net profit	214,731	715,229
Add income tax	100,193	115,415
Profit before tax	?	?
Add interest expense	53,169	23,535
Profit before interest and taxe		
Times interest earned ratio		

Fast Forward

2. Access 361 Degrees' financial statements for financial years ending after December 31, 2013 at its Website (http://ir.361sport.com/html/ir_report.php). Compute its times interest earned for years ending after December 31, 2013 and compare your results to those in part 1.

BTN 11-2 Key comparative figures for both Adidas and Puma follow.

COMPARATIVE ANALYSIS

A1

	Adidas (in EUR millions)			Puma (in EUR millions)		
(Euro millions)	Current Year	One Year Prior	Two Years Prior	Current Year	One Year Prior	Two Years Prior
Net income	787	526	613	5.3	70.2	230.1
Income taxes	344	327	261	32.5	32.5	90.0
Interest expense	73	97	108	7.8	8.4	19.1

Required

1. Compute times interest earned for the three years' data shown for each company.

2. Comment on which company appears stronger in its ability to pay interest obligations if income should decline.

BTN 11-3 Connor Bly is a sales manager for an automobile dealership. He earns a bonus each year based on revenue from the number of autos sold in the year less related warranty expenses. Actual warranty expenses have varied over the prior 10 years from a low of 3% of an automobile's selling price to a high of 10%. In the past, Bly has tended to estimate warranty expenses on the high end to be conservative. He must work with the dealership's accountant at year-end to arrive at the warranty expense accrual for cars sold each year.

ETHICS CHALLENGE

P4

1. Does the warranty accrual decision create any ethical dilemma for Bly?

2. Since warranty expenses vary, what percent do you think Bly should choose for the current year? Justify your response.

BTN 11-4 Dustin Clemens is the accounting and finance manager for a manufacturer. At year-end, he must determine how to account for the company's contingencies. His manager, Madeline Pretti, objects to Clemens's proposal to recognize an expense and a liability for warranty service on units of a new product introduced in the fourth quarter. Pretti comments, "There's no way we can estimate this warranty cost. We don't owe anyone anything until a product fails and it is returned. Let's report an expense if and when we do any warranty work."

COMMUNICATING IN PRACTICE

C3

Required

Prepare a one-page memorandum for Clemens to send to Pretti defending his proposal.

TAKING IT TO THE NET

C1 A1

BTN 11-5 Access L'Oréal's 2013 annual report at www.loreal-finance.com/eng/annual-report

Required

1. Identify the current liabilities on L'Oréal's consolidated balance sheet as at December 31, 2013.
2. Use the consolidated income statement for the year ended December 31, 2013, to compute L'Oréal's times interest earned ratio, assuming the interest expense is EUR 29.1 million and net profit is net profit attributable to owners of the company of Euro 2,958.2 million.

TEAMWORK IN ACTION

C2 P1

BTN 11-6 Assume that your team is in business and you must borrow $6,000 cash for short-term needs. You have been shopping banks for a loan, and you have the following two options.
A. Sign a $6,000, 90-day, 10% interest-bearing note dated June 1.
B. Sign a $6,000, 120-day, 8% interest-bearing note dated June 1.

Required

1. Discuss these two options and determine the best choice. Ensure that all teammates concur with the decision and understand the rationale.
2. Each member of the team is to prepare *one* of the following journal entries.
    a. Option A—at date of issuance.
    b. Option B—at date of issuance.
    c. Option A—at maturity date.
    d. Option B—at maturity date.
3. In rotation, each member is to explain the entry he or she prepared in part 2 to the team. Ensure that all team members concur with and understand the entries.
4. Assume that the funds are borrowed on December 1 (instead of June 1) and your business operates on a calendar-year reporting period. Each member of the team is to prepare *one* of the following entries.
    a. Option A—the year-end adjustment.
    b. Option B—the year-end adjustment.
    c. Option A—at maturity date.
    d. Option B—at maturity date.
5. In rotation, each member is to explain the entry he or she prepared in part 4 to the team. Ensure that all team members concur with and understand the entries.

ENTREPRENEURIAL DECISION

A1

BTN 11-7 Review the chapter's opening feature about Adam Khoo Learning Technologies Group (AKLTG). Assume that Adam and Patrick are considering expanding their business to open a branch in India. Assume AKLTG's current income statement is as follows.

AKLTG Income Statement For Year Ended December 31, 2008	
Sales	$1,000,000
Wages and benefits (30%)	300,000
Other operating expenses (25%)	250,000
Net profit	$ 450,000

AKLTG currently has no interest-bearing debt. If AKLTG expands to open an Indian location, the business will require a $300,000 loan. AKLTG has found a bank that will loan the money on a 7% note payable. Adam and Patrick believe that, at least for the first few years, sales at the new Indian location will be $250,000, and that all expenses will follow the same patterns as the current locations.

Required

1. Prepare an income statement (separately for current locations, India, and total) for **AKLTG** assuming that the business borrows the funds and expands to India. Annual revenues at the current locations are expected to remain at $1,000,000.

2. Compute **AKLTG's** times interest earned under the expansion assumptions in part 1.

3. Assume sales at the Indian location are $400,000. Prepare an income statement (separately for current locations, India, and total) for **AKLTG** and compute times interest earned.

4. Assume sales at the Indian location are $100,000. Prepare an income statement (separately for current locations, India, and total) for **AKLTG** and compute times interest earned.

5. Comment on your results from parts 1 through 4.

BTN 11-8   Nike and Puma are competitors in the global marketplace. Key comparative figures follow.

GLOBAL DECISION

A1

Key Figures	Nike (US$ millions) Current Year	Nike (US$ millions) Prior Year	Puma (EUR millions) Current Year	Puma (EUR millions) Prior Year
Net profit	1906.7	1486.7	202.2	77.3
Income tax	610.2	469.8	99.3	61.1
Interest expense	36.4	40.3	11.5	11.8
Times interest earned	?	?	27.2	12.7

Required

1. Compute the times interest earned ratio for the most recent two years for Nike using the data shown.

2. Which company presented provides the better coverage of interest expense? Explain.

ANSWERS TO MULTIPLE CHOICE QUIZ

1. b; $6,000 × 0.05 × 30/360 = $25

2. c; 10,000 television sets × .01 × $250 = $25,000

12

Accounting for Partnerships

 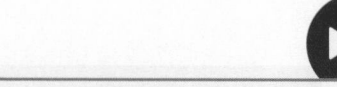

A Look Back

Chapter 11 focused on how current liabilities are identified, computed, recorded, and reported. Attention was directed at notes, payroll, sales taxes, warranties, employee benefits, and contingencies.

A Look at This Chapter

This chapter explains the partnership form of organization. Important partnership characteristics are described along with the accounting concepts and procedures for its most fundamental transactions.

A Look Ahead

Chapter 13 extends our discussion to the corporate form of organization. We describe the accounting and reporting for share issuances, dividends, and other equity transactions.

Learning Objectives

CAP

CONCEPTUAL

C1 Identify characteristics of partnerships and similar organizations. (p. 464)

ANALYTICAL

A1 Compute partner return on equity and use it to evaluate partnership performance. (p. 476)

PROCEDURAL

P1 Prepare entries for partnership formation. (p. 467)

P2 Allocate and record income and loss among partners. (p. 467)

P3 Account for the admission and withdrawal of partners. (p. 470)

P4 Prepare entries for partnership liquidation. (p. 473)

"We try to…maintain the 'personal touch' with our customers by not overly emphasizing the bottom line."—**MICHELLE TOK**

No Dirty Business

Michelle Tok and her two partners know that there's one thing that most busy working people do not enjoy—the dreaded housework. "We see a demand for such home services in Singapore," says Michelle. To tap the huge potential in a traditional manual business where cleaning ladies typically work freelance to earn some pocket money, Michelle, together with partners Patrick Cheong and Jobina Ow, set up **Home Central (www.homecentral.com.sg),** a professional housekeeping outfit that provides services ranging from dusting and mopping to ironing and cleaning. "Modern cleaning technology has greatly helped us, especially in servicing large corporate clients," says Michelle.

Not only do the trio, who have university degrees, display their business insight by learning about the technical know-how, they also exhibit their marketing ingenuity by offering exclusive Home Central gift vouchers for special occasions such as birthdays and wedding anniversaries. Showing someone your love? "What better way than to give them a good day's rest!" their Website tagline reads.

When not mapping out exciting marketing plans, the partners have to brave business challenges such as a tight labor market and the increased cost of living, which inadvertently translates into higher labor, transport, and material costs. Moreover, the nature of its set-up—a partnership—can be a limiting factor in the procurement of funds from investors or financial institutions, such financing especially required in securing tenders or bids for large corporate projects, according to Michelle. A partnership may also slow down decision making, as obviously business strategies or decisions have to be made collectively. On the upside, "A partnership is easier to manage in terms of accounting and tax reporting," says Michelle.

It's not all dirty business at Home Central. "We try to manage our growth by expanding at a comfortable rate so that we are able to maintain the 'personal touch' with our customers by not overly emphasizing the bottom line," explains Michelle. Accolades from customers for "transforming a house into a home" keep the three partners going, as do the smiles on their workers' faces when they receive their paychecks. "It makes us happy that we are in a position to provide a living for them and their families," says Michelle.

The three basic types of business organizations are proprietorships, partnerships, and corporations. Partnerships are similar to proprietorships, except they have more than one owner. This chapter explains partnerships and looks at several variations of them such as limited partnerships, limited liability partnerships, S corporations, and limited liability companies. Understanding the advantages and disadvantages of the partnership form of business organization is important for making informed business decisions.

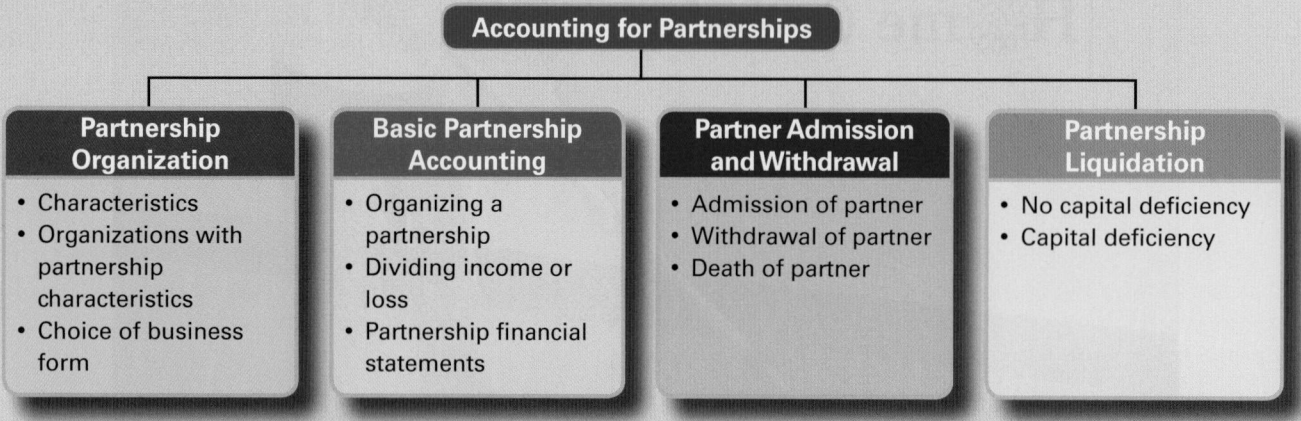

Accounting for Partnerships

Partnership Organization	Basic Partnership Accounting	Partner Admission and Withdrawal	Partnership Liquidation
• Characteristics • Organizations with partnership characteristics • Choice of business form	• Organizing a partnership • Dividing income or loss • Partnership financial statements	• Admission of partner • Withdrawal of partner • Death of partner	• No capital deficiency • Capital deficiency

PARTNERSHIP FORM OF ORGANIZATION

C1 Identify characteristics of partnerships and similar organizations.

A **partnership** is an unincorporated association of two or more people to pursue a business for profit as co-owners. Many businesses are organized as partnerships. They are especially common in small retail and service businesses. Many professional practitioners, including physicians, lawyers, investors, and accountants, also organize their practices as partnerships.

Characteristics of Partnerships

Partnerships are an important type of organization because they offer certain advantages with their unique characteristics. We describe these characteristics in this section.

Voluntary Association A partnership is a voluntary association between partners. Joining a partnership increases the risk to one's personal financial position. Some courts have ruled that partnerships are created by the actions of individuals even when there is no *express agreement* to form one.

Partnership Agreement Forming a partnership requires that two or more legally competent people (who are of age and of sound mental capacity) agree to be partners. Their agreement becomes a **partnership contract,** also called *articles of copartnership*. Although it should be in writing, the contract is binding even if it is only expressed verbally. Partnership agreements normally include details of the partners' (1) names and contributions, (2) rights and duties, (3) sharing of income and losses, (4) withdrawal arrangement, (5) dispute procedures, (6) admission and withdrawal of partners, and (7) rights and duties in the event a partner dies.

Point: When a new partner is admitted, all parties usually must agree to the admission.

Limited Life The life of a partnership is limited. Death, bankruptcy, or any event taking away the ability of a partner to enter into or fulfill a contract ends a partnership. Any one of the partners can also terminate a partnership at will.

Point: The end of a partnership is referred to as its *dissolution*.

Taxation A partnership is not subject to taxes on its income. The income or loss of a partnership is allocated to the partners according to the partnership agreement, and it is included in determining the taxable income for each partner's tax return. Partnership income or loss is allocated each year whether or not cash is distributed to partners.

Point: Partners are taxed on their share of partnership income, not on their withdrawals.

Mutual Agency Mutual agency implies that each partner is a fully authorized agent of the partnership. As its agent, a partner can commit or bind the partnership to any contract within the scope of the partnership business. For instance, a partner in a merchandising business can sign

contracts binding the partnership to buy merchandise, lease a store building, borrow money, or hire employees. These activities are all within the scope of a merchandising firm. A partner in a law firm, acting alone, however, cannot bind the other partners to a contract to buy snowboards for resale or rent an apartment for parties. These actions are outside the normal scope of a law firm's business. Partners also can agree to limit the power of any one or more of the partners to negotiate contracts for the partnership. This agreement is binding on the partners and on outsiders who know it exists. It is not binding on outsiders who do not know it exists. Outsiders unaware of the agreement have the right to assume each partner has normal agency powers for the partnership. Mutual agency exposes partners to the risk of unwise actions by any one partner.

Point: The majority of states adhere to the Uniform Partnership Act for the basic rules of partnership formation, operation, and dissolution.

Unlimited Liability   **Unlimited liability** implies that each partner can be called on to pay a partnership's debts. When a partnership cannot pay its debts, creditors usually can apply their claims to partners' *personal* assets. If a partner does not have enough assets to meet his or her share of the partnership debt, the creditors can apply their claims to the assets of the other partners. A partnership in which all partners have *mutual agency* and *unlimited liability* is called a **general partnership.** Mutual agency and unlimited liability are two main reasons that most general partnerships have only a few members.

Point: Limited life, mutual agency, and unlimited liability are disadvantages of a partnership.

Co-Ownership of Property   Partnership assets are owned jointly by all partners. Any investment by a partner becomes the joint property of all partners. Partners have a claim on partnership assets based on their capital account and the partnership contract.

Organizations with Partnership Characteristics

Organizations exist that combine certain characteristics of partnerships with other forms of organizations. We discuss several of these forms in this section.

Limited Partnerships   Some individuals who want to invest in a partnership are unwilling to accept the risk of unlimited liability. Their needs can be met with a **limited partnership.** This type of organization is identified in its name with the words "Limited Partnership" or "Ltd." or "LP." A limited partnership has two classes of partners, general and limited. At least one partner must be a **general partner,** who assumes management duties and unlimited liability for the debts of the partnership. The **limited partners** have no personal liability beyond the amounts they invest in the partnership. Limited partners have no active role except as specified in the partnership agreement. A limited partnership agreement often specifies unique procedures for allocating income and losses between general and limited partners. The accounting procedures are similar for both limited and general partnerships.

♞ Decision **Insight**

Nutty Partners   The Hawaii-based **ML Macadamia Orchards LP** is one of the world's largest growers of macadamia nuts. It reported the following partners' capital balances ($ 000s) in its balance sheet: ∎

| General Partner . . . . . . | $ 81 |
| Limited Partners . . . . . . | $43,560 |

Limited Liability Partnerships   Most states allow individuals to form a **limited liability partnership.** This is identified in its name with the words "Limited Liability Partnership" or by "LLP." This type of partnership is designed to protect innocent partners from malpractice or negligence claims resulting from the acts of another partner. When a partner provides service resulting in a malpractice claim, that partner has personal liability for the claim. The remaining partners who were not responsible for the actions resulting in the claim are not personally liable for it. However, most states hold all partners personally liable for other partnership debts. Accounting for a limited liability partnership is the same as for a general partnership.

Point: Many accounting services firms are set up as LLPs.

S Corporations   Certain corporations with 100 or fewer shareholders can elect to be treated as a partnership for income tax purposes. These corporations are called *Sub-Chapter S* or simply **S corporations.** This distinguishes them from other corporations, called *Sub-Chapter C* or simply **C corporations.** S corporations provide shareholders the same limited liability feature that C corporations do. The advantage of an S corporation is that it does not pay income taxes. If shareholders work for an S corporation, their salaries are treated as expenses of the corporation. The remaining income or loss of the corporation is allocated to shareholders for inclusion on their personal tax returns. Except for C corporations having to account for income tax expenses and liabilities, the accounting procedures are the same for both S and C corporations.

Limited Liability Companies   A relatively new form of business organization is the **limited liability company.** The names of these businesses usually include the words "Limited Liability Company" or an abbreviation such as "LLC" or "LC." This form of business has certain features similar to a corporation and others similar to a limited partnership. The owners, who are called *members,* are protected with the same limited liability feature as owners of corporations. While limited partners cannot actively participate in the management of a limited partnership, the members of a limited liability company can assume an active management role. A limited liability company usually has a limited life. For income tax purposes, a limited liability company is typically treated as a partnership. This treatment depends on factors such as whether the members' equity interests are freely transferable and whether the company has continuity of life. A limited liability company's accounting system is designed to help management comply with the dictates of the articles of organization and company regulations adopted by its members. The accounting system also must provide information to support the company's compliance with state and federal laws, including taxation.

Choosing a Business Form

Choosing the proper business form is crucial. Many factors should be considered, including taxes, liability risk, tax and financial year-end, ownership structure, estate planning, business risks, and earnings and property distributions. The following table summarizes several important characteristics of business organizations:

	Proprietorship	Partnership	LLP	LLC	S Corp.	Corporation
Business entity	Yes	Yes	Yes	Yes	Yes	Yes
Legal entity	No	No	No	Yes	Yes	Yes
Limited liability	No	No	Limited*	Yes	Yes	Yes
Business taxed	No	No	No	No	No	Yes
One owner allowed	Yes	No	No	Yes	Yes	Yes

* A partner's personal liability for LLP debts is limited. Most LLPs carry insurance to protect against malpractice.

We must remember that this table is a summary, not a detailed list. Many details underlie each of these business forms, and several details differ across states. Also, state and federal laws change, and a body of law is still developing around LLCs. Business owners should look at these details and consider unique business arrangements such as organizing various parts of their businesses in different forms.

Point: The majority of proprietorships and partnerships that are organized today are set up as LLCs.

Point: Accounting for LLCs is similar to that for partnerships (and proprietorships). One difference is that Owner (Partner), Capital is usually called *Members, Capital* for LLCs.

Point: The Small Business Administration provides suggestions and information on setting up the proper form for your organization—see **SBA.gov**.

Quick Check   Answers – p. 479

1. A partnership is terminated in the event (*a*) a partnership agreement is not in writing, (*b*) a partner dies, (*c*) a partner exercises mutual agency.
2. What does the term *unlimited liability* mean when applied to a general partnership?
3. Which of the following forms of organization do not provide limited liability to *all* of its owners? (*a*) S corporation, (*b*) limited liability company, (*c*) limited partnership.

BASIC PARTNERSHIP ACCOUNTING

Since ownership rights in a partnership are divided among partners, partnership accounting

- Uses a capital account for each partner.
- Uses a withdrawals account for each partner.
- Allocates net income or loss to partners according to the partnership agreement.

This section describes partnership accounting for organizing a partnership, distributing income and loss, and preparing financial statements.

Organizing a Partnership

When partners invest in a partnership, their capital accounts are credited for the invested amounts. Partners can invest both assets and liabilities. Each partner's investment is recorded at an agreed-on value, normally the market values of the contributed assets and liabilities at the date of contribution. To illustrate, Kayla Zayn and Hector Perez organize a partnership on January 11 called BOARDS that offers year-round facilities for skateboarding and snowboarding. Zayn's initial net investment in BOARDS is $30,000, made up of cash ($7,000), boarding facilities ($33,000), and a note payable reflecting a bank loan for the new business ($10,000). Perez's initial investment is cash of $10,000. These amounts are the values agreed on by both partners. The entries to record these investments follow.

P1 Prepare entries for partnership formation.

Zayn's Investment

Jan. 11	Cash	7,000	
	Boarding facilities	33,000	
	Note payable		10,000
	K. Zayn, Capital		30,000
	To record the investment of Zayn.		

Assets = Liabilities + Equity
+7,000   +10,000   +30,000
+33,000

Perez's Investment

Jan. 11	Cash	10,000	
	H. Perez, Capital		10,000
	To record the investment of Perez.		

Assets = Liabilities + Equity
+10,000   +10,000

In accounting for a partnership, the following additional relations hold true: (1) Partners' withdrawals are debited to their own separate withdrawals accounts. (2) Partners' capital accounts are credited (or debited) for their shares of net income (or net loss) when closing the accounts at the end of a period. (3) Each partner's withdrawals account is closed to that partner's capital account. Separate capital and withdrawals accounts are kept for each partner.

Point: Both equity and cash are reduced when a partner withdraws cash from a partnership.

Decision Insight

Broadway Partners **Big River Productions** is a partnership that owns the rights to the play *Big River*. The play is performed on tour and periodically on Broadway. For a recent year-end, its Partners' Capital was approximately $300,000, and it was distributed in its entirety to the partners. ■

Dividing Income or Loss

Partners are not employees of the partnership but are its owners. If partners devote their time and services to their partnership, they are understood to do so for profit, not for salary. This means there are no salaries to partners that are reported as expenses on the partnership income statement. However, when net income or loss of a partnership is allocated among partners, the partners can agree to allocate "salary allowances" reflecting the relative value of services

P2 Allocate and record income and loss among partners.

provided. Partners also can agree to allocate "interest allowances" based on the amount invested. For instance, since Zayn contributes three times the investment of Perez, it is only fair that this be considered when allocating income between them. Like salary allowances, these interest allowances are not expenses on the income statement.

Partners can agree to any method of dividing income or loss. In the absence of an agreement, the law says that the partners share income or loss of a partnership equally. If partners agree on how to share income but say nothing about losses, they share losses the same way they share income. Three common methods to divide income or loss use (1) a stated ratio basis, (2) the ratio of capital balances, or (3) salary and interest allowances and any remainder according to a fixed ratio. We explain each of these methods in this section.

Allocation on Stated Ratios The *stated ratio* (also called the *income-and-loss-sharing ratio,* the *profit and loss ratio,* or the *P&L ratio*) method of allocating partnership income or loss gives each partner a fraction of the total. Partners must agree on the fractional share each receives. To illustrate, assume the partnership agreement of K. Zayn and H. Perez says Zayn receives two-thirds and Perez one-third of partnership income and loss. If their partnership's net income is $60,000, it is allocated to the partners when the Income Summary account is closed as follows.

Dec. 31	Income Summary	60,000	
	K. Zayn, Capital		40,000
	H. Perez, Capital		20,000
	To allocate income and close Income Summary.		

Allocation on Capital Balances The *capital balances* method of allocating partnership income or loss assigns an amount based on the ratio of each partner's relative capital balance. If Zayn and Perez agree to share income and loss on the ratio of their beginning capital balances—Zayn's $30,000 and Perez's $10,000—Zayn receives three-fourths of any income or loss ($30,000/$40,000) and Perez receives one-fourth ($10,000/$40,000). The journal entry follows the same format as that using stated ratios (see the preceding entries).

Allocation on Services, Capital, and Stated Ratios The *services, capital, and stated ratio* method of allocating partnership income or loss recognizes that service and capital contributions of partners often are not equal. Salary allowances can make up for differences in service contributions. Interest allowances can make up for unequal capital contributions. Also, the allocation of income and loss can include *both* salary and interest allowances. To illustrate, assume that the partnership agreement of K. Zayn and H. Perez reflects differences in service and capital contributions as follows: (1) annual salary allowances of $36,000 to Zayn and $24,000 to Perez, (2) annual interest allowances of 10% of a partner's beginning-year capital balance, and (3) equal share of any remaining balance of income or loss. These salaries and interest allowances are *not* reported as expenses on the income statement. They are simply a means of dividing partnership income or loss. The remainder of this section provides two illustrations using this three-point allocation agreement.

Illustration when income exceeds allowance. If BOARDS has first-year net income of $70,000, and Zayn and Perez apply the three-point partnership agreement described in the prior paragraph, income is allocated as shown in Exhibit 12.1. Zayn gets $42,000 and Perez gets $28,000 of the $70,000 total.

Illustration when allowances exceed income. The sharing agreement between Zayn and Perez must be followed even if net income is less than the total of the allowances. For example, if BOARDS' first-year net income is $50,000 instead of $70,000, it is allocated to the partners as shown in Exhibit 12.2. Computations for salaries and interest are identical to those in Exhibit 12.1. However, when we apply the total allowances against income, the balance of income is negative. This $(14,000) negative balance is allocated equally to the partners per their sharing agreement. This means that a negative $(7,000) is allocated to each partner. In this case, Zayn ends up with $32,000 and Perez with $18,000. If BOARDS had experienced a net loss, Zayn and Perez would share it in the same manner as the $50,000 income. The only difference is that they would have begun with a negative amount because of the loss. Specifically, the partners would still have been

	Zayn	Perez	Total
Net income			**$70,000**
Salary allowances			
Zayn	$ 36,000		
Perez		$ 24,000	
Interest allowances			
Zayn (10% × $30,000)	3,000		
Perez (10% × $10,000)		1,000	
Total salaries and interest	39,000	25,000	64,000
Balance of income			6,000
Balance allocated equally			
Zayn	3,000 ←		
Perez		3,000 ←	
Total allocated			6,000
Balance of income			$ 0
Income of each partner	**$42,000**	**$28,000**	

EXHIBIT 12.1

Dividing Income When Income Exceeds Allowances

	Zayn	Perez	Total
Net income			**$50,000**
Salary allowances			
Zayn	$ 36,000		
Perez		$ 24,000	
Interest allowances			
Zayn (10% × $30,000)	3,000		
Perez (10% × $10,000)		1,000	
Total salaries and interest	39,000	25,000	64,000
Balance of income			(14,000)
Balance allocated equally			
Zayn	(7,000) ←		
Perez		(7,000) ←	
Total allocated			(14,000)
Balance of income			$ 0
Income of each partner	**$32,000**	**$18,000**	

EXHIBIT 12.2

Dividing Income When Allowances Exceed Income

allocated their salary and interest allowances, further adding to the negative balance of the loss. This *total* negative balance *after* salary and interest allowances would have been allocated equally between the partners. These allocations would have been applied against the positive numbers from any allowances to determine each partner's share of the loss.

Point: When a loss occurs, it is possible for a specific partner's capital to increase (when closing income summary) if that partner's allowance is in excess of his or her share of the negative balance. This implies that decreases to the capital balances of other partners exceed the partnership's loss amount.

Quick Check   Answer — p. 479

4. Denzel and Shantell form a partnership by contributing $70,000 and $35,000, respectively. They agree to an interest allowance equal to 10% of each partner's capital balance at the beginning of the year, with the remaining income shared equally. Allocate first-year income of $40,000 to each partner.

Partnership Financial Statements

Partnership financial statements are similar to those of other organizations. The **statement of partners' equity,** also called *statement of partners' capital,* is one exception. It shows *each* partner's beginning capital balance, additional investments, allocated income or loss, withdrawals, and ending capital balance. To illustrate, Exhibit 12.3 shows the statement of partners' equity for BOARDS prepared using the sharing agreement of Exhibit 12.1. Recall that BOARDS' income was $70,000; also, assume that Zayn withdrew $20,000 and Perez $12,000 at year-end.

EXHIBIT 12.3

Statement of Partners' Equity

BOARDS			
Statement of Partners' Equity			
For Year Ended December 31, 2015			
	Zayn	Perez	Total
Beginning capital balances	$ 0	$ 0	$ 0
Plus			
Investments by owners	30,000	10,000	40,000
Net income			
Salary allowances $36,000		$24,000	
Interest allowances 3,000		1,000	
Balance allocated 3,000		3,000	
Total net income	42,000	28,000	70,000
	72,000	38,000	110,000
Less partners' withdrawals	(20,000)	(12,000)	(32,000)
Ending capital balances	**$52,000**	**$26,000**	**$78,000**

The equity section of the balance sheet of a partnership usually shows the separate capital account balance of each partner. In the case of BOARDS, both K. Zayn, Capital, and H. Perez, Capital, are listed in the equity section along with their balances of $52,000 and $26,000, respectively.

Decision Insight

Gambling Partners   **Trump Entertainment Resorts LP** and subsidiaries operate three casino hotel properties in Atlantic City: Trump Taj Mahal Casino Resort ("Trump Taj Mahal"), Trump Plaza Hotel and Casino ("Trump Plaza"), and Trump Marina Hotel Casino ("Trump Marina"). Its recent statement of partners' equity reports $1,020,000 in partners' withdrawals, leaving $605,314,000 in partners' capital balances. ■

ADMISSION AND WITHDRAWAL OF PARTNERS

P3 Account for the admission and withdrawal of partners.

A partnership is based on a contract between individuals. When a partner is admitted or withdraws, the present partnership ends. Still, the business can continue to operate as a new partnership consisting of the remaining partners. This section considers how to account for the admission and withdrawal of partners.

Admission of a Partner

A new partner is admitted in one of two ways: by purchasing an interest from one or more current partners or by investing cash or other assets in the partnership.

Purchase of Partnership Interest   The purchase of partnership interest is a *personal transaction between one or more current partners and the new partner.* To become a partner, the current partners must accept the purchaser. Accounting for the purchase of partnership interest involves reallocating current partners' capital to reflect the transaction. To illustrate, at the end of BOARDS' first year, H. Perez sells one-half of his partnership interest to Tyrell Rasheed for $18,000. This means that Perez gives up a $13,000 recorded interest ($26,000 × 1/2) in the partnership (see the ending capital balance in Exhibit 12.3). The partnership records this January 4 transaction as follows.

Assets = Liabilities + Equity
−13,000
+13,000

Jan. 4	H. Perez, Capital	13,000	
	T. Rasheed, Capital		13,000
	To record admission of Rasheed by purchase.		

After this entry is posted, BOARDS' equity shows K. Zayn, Capital; H. Perez, Capital; and T. Rasheed, Capital, and their respective balances of $52,000, $13,000, and $13,000.

Two aspects of this transaction are important. First, the partnership does *not* record the $18,000 Rasheed paid Perez. The partnership's assets, liabilities, and *total equity* are unaffected by this transaction among partners. Second, Zayn and Perez must agree that Rasheed is to become a partner. If they agree to accept Rasheed, a new partnership is formed and a new contract with a new income-and-loss-sharing agreement is prepared. If Zayn or Perez refuses to accept Rasheed as a partner, then (under the Uniform Partnership Act) Rasheed gets Perez's sold share of partnership income and loss. If the partnership is liquidated, Rasheed gets Perez's sold share of partnership assets. Rasheed gets no voice in managing the company unless Rasheed is admitted as a partner.

Point: Partners' withdrawals are not constrained by the partnership's annual income or loss.

Investing Assets in a Partnership   Admitting a partner by accepting assets is a *transaction between the new partner and the partnership*. The invested assets become partnership property. To illustrate, if Zayn (with a $52,000 interest) and Perez (with a $26,000 interest) agree to accept Rasheed as a partner in BOARDS after an investment of $22,000 cash, this is recorded as follows.

Jan. 4	Cash...	22,000	
	T. Rasheed, Capital		22,000
	To record admission of Rasheed by investment.		

Assets = Liabilities + Equity
+22,000   +22,000

After this entry is posted, both assets (cash) and equity (T. Rasheed, Capital) increase by $22,000. Rasheed now has a 22% equity in the assets of the business, computed as $22,000 divided by the entire partnership equity ($52,000 + $26,000 + $22,000). Rasheed does not necessarily have a right to 22% of income. Dividing income and loss is a separate matter on which partners must agree.

Bonus to old partners.   When the current value of a partnership is greater than the recorded amounts of equity, the partners usually require a new partner to pay a bonus for the privilege of joining. To illustrate, assume that Zayn and Perez agree to accept Rasheed as a partner with a 25% interest in BOARDS if Rasheed invests $42,000. Recall that the partnership's accounting records show that Zayn's recorded equity in the business is $52,000 and Perez's recorded equity is $26,000 (see Exhibit 12.3). Rasheed's equity is determined as follows.

Equities of existing partners ($52,000 + $26,000)	$ 78,000
Investment of new partner	42,000
Total partnership equity	$120,000
Equity of Rasheed (25% × $120,000)	$ 30,000

Although Rasheed invests $42,000, the equity attributed to Rasheed in the new partnership is only $30,000. The $12,000 difference is called a *bonus* and is allocated to existing partners (Zayn and Perez) according to their income-and-loss-sharing agreement. A bonus is shared in this way because it is viewed as reflecting a higher value of the partnership that is not yet reflected in income. The entry to record this transaction follows.

Jan. 4	Cash...	42,000	
	T. Rasheed, Capital		30,000
	K. Zayn, Capital ($12,000 × ½)		6,000
	H. Perez, Capital ($12,000 × ½)		6,000
	To record admission of Rasheed and bonus.		

Assets = Liabilities + Equity
+42,000   +30,000
                               +6,000
                               +6,000

Bonus to new partner.   Alternatively, existing partners can grant a bonus to a new partner. This usually occurs when they need additional cash or the new partner has exceptional talents. The bonus to the new partner is in the form of a larger share of equity than the amount invested. To illustrate, assume that Zayn and Perez agree to accept Rasheed as a partner with a

25% interest in the partnership, but they require Rasheed to invest only $18,000. Rasheed's equity is determined as follows.

Equities of existing partners ($52,000 + $26,000)	$78,000
Investment of new partner	18,000
Total partnership equity	$96,000
Equity of Rasheed (25% × $96,000)	$24,000

The old partners contribute the $6,000 bonus (computed as $24,000 minus $18,000) to Rasheed according to their income-and-loss-sharing ratio. Moreover, Rasheed's 25% equity does not necessarily entitle Rasheed to 25% of future income or loss. This is a separate matter for agreement by the partners. The entry to record the admission and investment of Rasheed is

Assets = Liabilities + Equity
+18,000   −3,000
                            −3,000
                            +24,000

Jan. 4	Cash	18,000	
	K. Zayn, Capital ($6,000 × ½)	3,000	
	H. Perez, Capital ($6,000 × ½)	3,000	
	T. Rasheed, Capital		24,000
	To record Rasheed's admission and bonus.		

Withdrawal of a Partner

A partner generally withdraws from a partnership in one of two ways. (1) First, the withdrawing partner can sell his or her interest to another person who pays for it in cash or other assets. For this, we need only debit the withdrawing partner's capital account and credit the new partner's capital account. (2) The second case is when cash or other assets of the partnership are distributed to the withdrawing partner in settlement of his or her interest. To illustrate these cases, assume that Perez withdraws from the partnership of BOARDS in some future period. The partnership shows the following capital balances at the date of Perez's withdrawal: K. Zayn, $84,000; H. Perez, $38,000; and T. Rasheed, $38,000. The partners (Zayn, Perez, and Rasheed) share income and loss equally. Accounting for Perez's withdrawal depends on whether a bonus is paid. We describe three possibilities.

No Bonus   If Perez withdraws and takes cash equal to Perez's capital balance, the entry is

Assets = Liabilities + Equity
−38,000   −38,000

Oct. 31	H. Perez, Capital	38,000	
	Cash		38,000
	To record withdrawal of Perez from partnership with no bonus.		

Perez can take any combination of assets to which the partners agree to settle Perez's equity. Perez's withdrawal creates a new partnership between the remaining partners. A new partnership contract and a new income-and-loss-sharing agreement are required.

Bonus to Remaining Partners   A withdrawing partner is sometimes willing to take less than the recorded value of his or her equity to get out of the partnership or because the recorded value is overstated. Whatever the reason, when this occurs, the withdrawing partner in effect gives the remaining partners a bonus equal to the equity left behind. The remaining partners share this unwithdrawn equity according to their income-and-loss-sharing ratio. To illustrate, if Perez withdraws and agrees to take $34,000 cash in settlement of Perez's capital balance, the entry is

Assets = Liabilities + Equity
−34,000   −38,000
                             +2,000
                             +2,000

Oct. 31	H. Perez, Capital	38,000	
	Cash		34,000
	K. Zayn, Capital		2,000
	T. Rasheed, Capital		2,000
	To record withdrawal of Perez and bonus to remaining partners.		

Perez withdrew $4,000 less than Perez's recorded equity of $38,000. This $4,000 is divided between Zayn and Rasheed according to their income-and-loss-sharing ratio.

Bonus to Withdrawing Partner   A withdrawing partner may be able to receive more than his or her recorded equity for at least two reasons. First, the recorded equity may be understated. Second, the remaining partners may agree to remove this partner by giving assets of greater value than this partner's recorded equity. In either case, the withdrawing partner receives a bonus. The remaining partners reduce their equity by the amount of this bonus according to their income-and-loss-sharing ratio. To illustrate, if Perez withdraws and receives $40,000 cash in settlement of Perez's capital balance, the entry is

Oct. 31	H. Perez, Capital	38,000	
	K. Zayn, Capital	1,000	
	T. Rasheed, Capital	1,000	
	Cash		40,000
	To record Perez's withdrawal from partnership with a bonus to Perez.		

Assets = Liabilities + Equity
−40,000   −38,000
                     −1,000
                     −1,000

Falcon Cable Communications set up a partnership withdrawal agreement. Falcon owns and operates cable television systems and had two managing general partners. The partnership agreement stated that either partner "can offer to sell to the other partner the offering partner's entire partnership interest . . . for a negotiated price. If the partner receiving such an offer rejects it, the offering partner may elect to cause [the partnership] . . . to be liquidated and dissolved."

Death of a Partner

A partner's death dissolves a partnership. A deceased partner's estate is entitled to receive his or her equity. The partnership contract should contain provisions for settlement in this case. These provisions usually require (1) closing the books to determine income or loss since the end of the previous period and (2) determining and recording current market values for both assets and liabilities. The remaining partners and the deceased partner's estate then must agree to a settlement of the deceased partner's equity. This can involve selling the equity to remaining partners or to an outsider, or it can involve withdrawing assets.

Decision Ethics   Answer − p. 479

Financial Planner   You are hired by the two remaining partners of a three-member partnership after the third partner's death. The partnership agreement states that a deceased partner's estate is entitled to a "share of partnership assets equal to the partner's relative equity balance" (partners' equity balances are equal). The estate argues that it is entitled to one-third of the current value of partnership assets. The remaining partners say the distribution should use asset book values, which are 75% of current value. They also point to partnership liabilities, which equal 40% of total asset book value and 30% of current value. How would you resolve this situation? ■

LIQUIDATION OF A PARTNERSHIP

When a partnership is liquidated, its business ends and four concluding steps are required.

 P4 Prepare entries for partnership liquidation.

1. Record the sale of noncash assets for cash and any gain or loss from their liquidation.
2. Allocate any gain or loss from liquidation of the assets in step 1 to the partners *using their income-and-loss-sharing ratio.*
3. Pay or settle all partner liabilities.
4. Distribute any remaining cash to partners *based on their capital balances.*

Partnership liquidation usually falls into one of two cases, as described in this section.

No Capital Deficiency

No capital deficiency means that all partners have a zero or credit balance in their capital accounts for final distribution of cash. To illustrate, assume that Zayn, Perez, and Rasheed operate their partnership in BOARDS for several years, sharing income and loss equally. The partners then decide to liquidate. On the liquidation date, the current period's income or loss is transferred to the partners' capital accounts according to the sharing agreement. After that transfer, assume the partners' recorded account balances (immediately prior to liquidation) are:

Cash	$178,000	Accounts payable	$20,000	H. Perez, Capital	$66,000
Land	40,000	K. Zayn, Capital	70,000	T. Rasheed, Capital	62,000

We apply three steps for liquidation. ① *The partnership sells its noncash assets, and any losses or gains from liquidation are shared among partners according to their income-and-loss-sharing agreement* (equal for these partners). Assume that BOARDS sells its noncash assets consisting of $40,000 in land for $46,000 cash, yielding a net gain of $6,000. In a liquidation, gains or losses usually result from the sale of noncash assets, which are called *losses and gains from liquidation*. The entry to sell its assets for $46,000 follows.

Assets = Liabilities + Equity
−40,000   +6,000
+46,000

Jan. 15	Cash	46,000	
	Land		40,000
	Gain from Liquidation		6,000
	Sold noncash assets at a gain.		

Allocation of the gain from liquidation per the partners' income-and-loss-sharing agreement follows.

Assets = Liabilities + Equity
                        −6,000
                        +2,000
                        +2,000
                        +2,000

Jan. 15	Gain from Liquidation	6,000	
	K. Zayn, Capital		2,000
	H. Perez, Capital		2,000
	T. Rasheed, Capital		2,000
	To allocate liquidation gain to partners.		

② *The partnership pays its liabilities, and any losses or gains from liquidation of liabilities are shared among partners according to their income-and-loss-sharing agreement.* BOARDS' only liability is $20,000 in accounts payable, and no gain or loss occurred.

Assets = Liabilities + Equity
−20,000   −20,000

Jan. 15	Accounts Payable	20,000	
	Cash		20,000
	To pay claims of creditors.		

After step 2, we have the following capital balances along with the remaining cash balance.

K. Zayn			H. Perez, Capital			T. Rasheed, Capital			Cash			
	Bal.	70,000		Bal.	66,000		Bal.	62,000	Bal.	178,000	(3)	20,000
	(2)	2,000		(2)	2,000		(2)	2,000	(1)	46,000		
	Bal.	72,000		Bal.	68,000		Bal.	64,000	Bal.	204,000		

③ *Any remaining cash is divided among the partners **according to their capital account balances.*** The entry to record the final distribution of cash to partners follows.

Assets = Liabilities + Equity
−204,000   −72,000
                        −68,000
                        −64,000

Jan. 15	K. Zayn, Capital	72,000	
	H. Perez, Capital	68,000	
	T. Rasheed, Capital	64,000	
	Cash		204,000
	To distribute remaining cash to partners.		

It is important to remember that the final cash payment is distributed to partners according to their capital account balances, whereas gains and losses from liquidation are allocated according to the income-and-loss-sharing ratio. The following *statement of liquidation* summarizes the three steps in this section.

Statement of Liquidation	Cash	Noncash Assets	=	Liabilities	K. Zayn, Capital	H. Perez, Capital	T. Rasheed, Capital
Balances prior to liquidation....	$178,000	$ 40,000		$ 20,000	$ 70,000	$66,000	$62,000
① Sale of noncash assets	46,000	(40,000)			2,000	2,000	2,000
② Payment of liabilities	(20,000)			(20,000)	0	0	0
Balances for distribution	204,000				72,000	68,000	64,000
③ Distribution of cash to partners	(204,000)				(72,000)	(68,000)	(64,000)

Capital Deficiency

Capital deficiency means that at least one partner has a debit balance in his or her capital account at the point of final cash distribution (during step ③ as explained in the prior section). This can arise from liquidation losses, excessive withdrawals before liquidation, or recurring losses in prior periods. A partner with a capital deficiency must, if possible, cover the deficit by paying cash into the partnership.

To illustrate, assume that Zayn, Perez, and Rasheed operate their partnership in BOARDS for several years, sharing income and losses equally. The partners then decide to liquidate. Immediately prior to the final distribution of cash, the partners' recorded capital balances are Zayn, $19,000; Perez, $8,000; and Rasheed, $(3,000). Rasheed's capital deficiency means that Rasheed owes the partnership $3,000. Both Zayn and Perez have a legal claim against Rasheed's personal assets. The final distribution of cash in this case depends on how this capital deficiency is handled. Two possibilities exist: the partner pays the deficiency or the partner cannot pay the deficiency.

Partner Pays Deficiency   Rasheed is obligated to pay $3,000 into the partnership to cover the deficiency. If Rasheed is willing and able to pay, the entry to record receipt of payment from Rasheed follows.

Jan. 15	Cash	3,000	
	T. Rasheed, Capital		3,000
	To record payment of deficiency by Rasheed.		

Assets = Liabilities + Equity
+3,000   +3,000

After the $3,000 payment, the partners' capital balances are Zayn, $19,000; Perez, $8,000; and Rasheed, $0. The entry to record the final cash distributions to partners is

Jan. 15	K. Zayn, Capital	19,000	
	H. Perez, Capital	8,000	
	Cash		27,000
	To distribute remaining cash to partners.		

Assets = Liabilities + Equity
−27,000   −19,000
                   −8,000

Partner Cannot Pay Deficiency   The remaining partners with credit balances absorb any partner's unpaid deficiency according to their income-and-loss-sharing ratio. To illustrate, if Rasheed is unable to pay the $3,000 deficiency, Zayn and Perez absorb it. Since they share income and loss equally, Zayn and Perez each absorb $1,500 of the deficiency. This is recorded as follows.

Jan. 15	K. Zayn, Capital	1,500	
	H. Perez, Capital	1,500	
	T. Rasheed, Capital		3,000
	To transfer Rasheed deficiency to Zayn and Perez.		

Assets = Liabilities + Equity
                   −1,500
                   −1,500
                   +3,000

After Zayn and Perez absorb Rasheed's deficiency, the capital accounts of the partners are Zayn, $17,500; Perez, $6,500; and Rasheed, $0. The entry to record the final cash distribution to the partners is

Jan. 15	K. Zayn, Capital	17,500	
	H. Perez, Capital	6,500	
	Cash		24,000
	To distribute remaining cash to partners.		

Assets = Liabilities + Equity
−24,000   −17,500
                   −6,500

Rasheed's inability to cover this deficiency does not relieve Rasheed of the liability. If Rasheed becomes able to pay at a future date, Zayn and Perez can each collect $1,500 from Rasheed.

Decision Analysis ▢▢▢

Partner Return on Equity

A1 Compute partner return on equity and use it to evaluate partnership performance.

An important role of partnership financial statements is to aid current and potential partners in evaluating partnership success compared with other opportunities. One measure of this success is the **partner return on equity** ratio:

$$\text{Partner return on equity} = \frac{\text{Partner net income}}{\text{Average partner equity}}$$

This measure is separately computed for each partner. To illustrate, Exhibit 12.4 reports selected data from the Boston Celtics LP. The return on equity for the *total* partnership is computed as $216/[(\$85 + \$253)/2] = 127.8\%$. However, return on equity is quite different across the partners. For example, the Boston Celtics LP I partner return on equity is computed as $44/[(\$122 + \$166)/2] = 30.6\%$, whereas the Celtics LP partner return on equity is computed as $111/[(\$270 + \$333)/2] = 36.8\%$. Partner return on equity provides *each* partner an assessment of its return on its equity invested in the partnership. A specific partner often uses this return to decide whether additional investment or withdrawal of resources is best for that partner. Exhibit 12.4 reveals that the year shown produced good returns for all partners (the Boston Celtics LP II return is not computed because its average equity is negative due to an unusual and large distribution in the prior year).

EXHIBIT 12.4

Selected Data from Boston Celtics LP

(US$ thousands)	Total*	Boston Celtics LP I	Boston Celtics LP II	Celtics LP
Beginning-year balance	$ 85	$122	$(307)	$270
Net income (loss) for year	216	44	61	111
Cash distribution	(48)	—	—	(48)
Ending-year balance	$253	$166	$(246)	$333
Partner return on equity	127.8%	30.6%	n.a.	36.8%

* Totals may not add up due to rounding.

DEMONSTRATION PROBLEM

The following transactions and events affect the partners' capital accounts in several successive partnerships. Prepare a table with six columns, one for each of the five partners along with a total column to show the effects of the following events on the five partners' capital accounts.

Part 1

4/13/2013   Ries and Bax create R&B Company. Each invests $10,000, and they agree to share income and losses equally.

12/31/2013   R&B Co. earns $15,000 in income for its first year. Ries withdraws $4,000 from the partnership, and Bax withdraws $7,000.

1/1/2014   Royce is made a partner in RB&R Company after contributing $12,000 cash. The partners agree that a 10% interest allowance will be given on each partner's beginning-year capital balance. In addition, Bax and Royce are to receive $5,000 salary allowances. The remainder of the income or loss is to be divided evenly.

12/31/2014   The partnership's income for the year is $40,000, and withdrawals at year-end are Ries, $5,000; Bax, $12,500; and Royce, $11,000.

1/1/2015   Ries sells her interest for $20,000 to Murdock, whom Bax and Royce accept as a partner in the new BR&M Co. Income or loss is to be shared equally after Bax and Royce receive $25,000 salary allowances.

12/31/2015   The partnership's income for the year is $35,000, and year-end withdrawals are Bax, $2,500, and Royce, $2,000.

1/1/2016   Elway is admitted as a partner after investing $60,000 cash in the new Elway & Associates partnership. He is given a 50% interest in capital after the other partners transfer $3,000 to his account from each of theirs. A 20% interest allowance (on the beginning-year capital balances) will be used in sharing any income or loss, there will be no salary allowances, and Elway will receive 40% of the remaining balance—the other three partners will each get 20%.

12/31/2016   Elway & Associates earns $127,600 in income for the year, and year-end withdrawals are Bax, $25,000; Royce, $27,000; Murdock, $15,000; and Elway, $40,000.

1/1/2017   Elway buys out Bax and Royce for the balances of their capital accounts after a revaluation of the partnership assets. The revaluation gain is $50,000, which is divided in using a 1:1:1:2 ratio (Bax:Royce:Murdock:Elway). Elway pays the others from personal funds. Murdock and Elway will share income on a 1:9 ratio.

2/28/2017   The partnership earns $10,000 of income since the beginning of the year. Murdock retires and receives partnership cash equal to her capital balance. Elway takes possession of the partnership assets in his own name, and the partnership is dissolved.

Part 2

Journalize the events affecting the partnership for the year ended December 31, 2014.

PLANNING THE SOLUTION

- Evaluate each transaction's effects on the capital accounts of the partners.
- Each time a new partner is admitted or a partner withdraws, allocate any bonus based on the income-or-loss-sharing agreement.
- Each time a new partner is admitted or a partner withdraws, allocate subsequent net income or loss in accordance with the new partnership agreement.
- Prepare entries to (1) record Royce's initial investment; (2) record the allocation of interest, salaries, and remainder; (3) show the cash withdrawals from the partnership; and (4) close the withdrawal accounts on December 31, 2014.

SOLUTION TO DEMONSTRATION PROBLEM

Part 1

Event	Ries	Bax	Royce	Murdock	Elway	Total
4/13/2013						
Initial investment	$10,000	$10,000				$ 20,000
12/31/2013						
Income (equal)	7,500	7,500				15,000
Withdrawals	(4,000)	(7,000)				(11,000)
Ending balance	$13,500	$10,500				$ 24,000
1/1/2014						
New investment			$12,000			$ 12,000
12/31/2014						
10% interest	1,350	1,050	1,200			3,600
Salaries		5,000	5,000			10,000
Remainder (equal)	8,800	8,800	8,800			26,400
Withdrawals	(5,000)	(12,500)	(11,000)			(28,500)
Ending balance	$18,650	$12,850	$16,000			$ 47,500
1/1/2015						
Transfer interest	(18,650)			$18,650		$ 0

[continued on next page]

[continued from previous page]

Event	Ries	Bax	Royce	Murdock	Elway	Total
12/31/2015						
Salaries		25,000	25,000			50,000
Remainder (equal)		(5,000)	(5,000)	(5,000)		(15,000)
Withdrawals		(2,500)	(2,000)			(4,500)
Ending balance	$ 0	$30,350	$34,000	$13,650		$ 78,000
1/1/2016						
New investment					$ 60,000	60,000
Bonuses to Elway		(3,000)	(3,000)	(3,000)	9,000	0
Adjusted balance		$27,350	$31,000	$10,650	$ 69,000	$138,000
12/31/2016						
20% interest		5,470	6,200	2,130	13,800	27,600
Remainder (1:1:1:2)		20,000	20,000	20,000	40,000	100,000
Withdrawals		(25,000)	(27,000)	(15,000)	(40,000)	(107,000)
Ending balance		$27,820	$30,200	$17,780	$ 82,800	$158,600
1/1/2017						
Gain (1:1:1:2)		10,000	10,000	10,000	20,000	50,000
Adjusted balance		$37,820	$40,200	$27,780	$102,800	$208,600
Transfer interests		(37,820)	(40,200)		78,020	0
Adjusted balance		$ 0	$ 0	$27,780	$180,820	$208,600
2/28/2017						
Income (1:9)				1,000	9,000	10,000
Adjusted balance				$28,780	$189,820	$218,600
Settlements				(28,780)	(189,820)	(218,600)
Final balance				$ 0	$ 0	$ 0

Part 2

2014			
Jan. 1	Cash	12,000	
	Royce, Capital		12,000
	To record investment of Royce.		
Dec. 31	Income Summary	40,000	
	Ries, Capital		10,150
	Bax, Capital		14,850
	Royce, Capital		15,000
	To allocate interest, salaries, and remainders.		
Dec. 31	Ries, Withdrawals	5,000	
	Bax, Withdrawals	12,500	
	Royce, Withdrawals	11,000	
	Cash		28,500
	To record cash withdrawals by partners.		
Dec. 31	Ries, Capital	5,000	
	Bax, Capital	12,500	
	Royce, Capital	11,000	
	Ries, Withdrawals		5,000
	Bax, Withdrawals		12,500
	Royce, Withdrawals		11,000
	To close withdrawal accounts.		

Summary

C1 **Identify characteristics of partnerships and similar organizations.** Partnerships are voluntary associations, involve partnership agreements, have limited life, are not subject to income tax, include mutual agency, and have unlimited liability. Organizations that combine selected characteristics of partnerships and corporations include limited partnerships, limited liability partnerships, S corporations, and limited liability companies.

A1 **Compute partner return on equity and use it to evaluate partnership performance.** Partner return on equity provides each partner an assessment of his or her return on equity invested in the partnership.

P1 **Prepare entries for partnership formation.** A partner's initial investment is recorded at the market value of the assets contributed to the partnership.

P2 **Allocate and record income and loss among partners.** A partnership agreement should specify how to allocate partnership income or loss among partners. Allocation can be based on a stated ratio, capital balances, or salary and interest allowances to

compensate partners for differences in their service and capital contributions.

P3 **Account for the admission and withdrawal of partners.** When a new partner buys a partnership interest directly from one or more existing partners, the amount of cash paid from one partner to another does not affect the partnership total recorded equity. When a new partner purchases equity by investing additional assets in the partnership, the new partner's investment can yield a bonus either to existing partners or to the new partner. The entry to record a withdrawal can involve payment from either (1) the existing partners' personal assets or (2) partnership assets. The latter can yield a bonus to either the withdrawing or remaining partners.

P4 **Prepare entries for partnership liquidation.** When a partnership is liquidated, losses and gains from selling partnership assets are allocated to the partners according to their income-and-loss-sharing ratio. If a partner's capital account has a deficiency that the partner cannot pay, the other partners share the deficit according to their relative income-and-loss-sharing ratio.

Guidance Answers to Decision Ethics

Financial Planner The partnership agreement apparently fails to mention liabilities or use the term *net assets*. To give the estate one-third of total assets is not fair to the remaining partners because if the partner had lived and the partners had decided to liquidate, the liabilities would need to be paid out of assets before any liquidation. Also, a settlement based on the deceased partner's recorded equity would fail to recognize excess of current value over book value. This value increase would be realized if the partnership were liquidated. A fair settlement would seem to be a payment to the estate for the balance of the deceased partner's equity based on the *current value of net assets.*

Guidance Answers to Quick Checks

1. (*b*)
2. *Unlimited liability* means that the creditors of a partnership require each partner to be personally responsible for all partnership debts.
3. (*c*)

4.

	Denzel	Shantell	Total
Net income			$40,000
Interest allowance (10%)	$ 7,000	$ 3,500	10,500
Balance of income			**$29,500**
Balance allocated equally	14,750	14,750	29,500
Balance of income			$ 0
Income of partners	**$21,750**	**$18,250**	

Key Terms   www.mheducation.asia/olc/wildkwokFAP

C corporation (p. 466)
General partner (p. 465)
General partnership (p. 465)
Limited liability company (LLC) (p. 466)
Limited liability partnership (p. 465)

Limited partners (p. 465)
Limited partnership (p. 465)
Mutual agency (p. 464)
Partner return on equity (p. 476)
Partnership (p. 464)

Partnership contract (p. 464)
Partnership liquidation (p. 473)
S corporation (p. 466)
Statement of partners' equity (p. 469)
Unlimited liability (p. 465)

Multiple Choice Quiz   Answers on p. 489   www.mheducation.asia/olc/wildkwokFAP

Additional Quiz Questions are available at the book's Website.

1. Stokely and Leder are forming a partnership. Stokely invests a building that has a market value of $250,000; and the partnership assumes responsibility for a $50,000 note secured by a mortgage on that building. Leder invests $100,000 cash. For the partnership, the amounts recorded for the building and for Stokely's Capital account are these:
   a. Building, $250,000; Stokely, Capital, $250,000.
   b. Building, $200,000; Stokely, Capital, $200,000.
   c. Building, $200,000; Stokely, Capital, $100,000.
   d. Building, $200,000; Stokely, Capital, $250,000.
   e. Building, $250,000; Stokely, Capital, $200,000.

2. Katherine, Alliah, and Paulina form a partnership. Katherine contributes $150,000, Alliah contributes $150,000, and Paulina contributes $100,000. Their partnership agreement calls for the income or loss division to be based on the ratio of capital invested. If the partnership reports income of $90,000 for its first year of operations, what amount of income is credited to Paulina's capital account?
   a. $22,500
   b. $25,000
   c. $45,000
   d. $30,000
   e. $90,000

3. Jamison and Blue form a partnership with capital contributions of $600,000 and $800,000, respectively. Their partnership agreement calls for Jamison to receive $120,000 per year in salary. Also, each partner is to receive an interest allowance equal to 10% of the partner's beginning capital contributions, with any remaining income or loss divided equally. If net income for its initial year is $270,000, then Jamison's and Blue's respective shares are
   a. $135,000; $135,000.
   b. $154,286; $115,714.
   c. $120,000; $150,000.
   d. $185,000; $85,000.
   e. $85,000; $185,000.

4. Hansen and Fleming are partners and share equally in income or loss. Hansen's current capital balance in the partnership is $125,000 and Fleming's is $124,000. Hansen and Fleming agree to accept Black with a 20% interest. Black invests $75,000 in the partnership. The bonus granted to Hansen and Fleming equals
   a. $13,000 each.
   b. $5,100 each.
   c. $4,000 each.
   d. $5,285 to Hansen; $4,915 to Fleming.
   e. $0; Hansen and Fleming grant a bonus to Black.

5. Mee Su is a partner in Hartford Partners, LLC. Her partnership capital balance at the beginning of the current year was $110,000, and her ending balance was $124,000. Her share of the partnership income is $10,500. What is her partner return on equity?
   a. 8.97%
   b. 1060.00%
   c. 9.54%
   d. 1047.00%
   e. 8.47%

🔘 Icon denotes assignments that involve decision making.

Discussion Questions

1. 🔘 If a partnership contract does not state the period of time the partnership is to exist, when does the partnership end?

2. What does the term *mutual agency* mean when applied to a partnership?

3. 🔘 Can partners limit the right of a partner to commit their partnership to contracts? Would such an agreement be binding (*a*) on the partners and (*b*) on outsiders?

4. 🔘 Assume that Amey and Lacey are partners. Lacey dies, and her son claims the right to take his mother's place in the partnership. Does he have this right? Why or why not?

5. 🔘 Assume that the Barnes and Ardmore partnership agreement provides for a two-third/one-third sharing of income but says nothing about losses. The first year of partnership operation resulted in a loss, and Barnes argues that the loss should be shared equally because the partnership agreement said nothing about sharing losses. Is Barnes correct? Explain.

6. Allocation of partnership income among the partners appears on what financial statement?

7. What does the term *unlimited liability* mean when it is applied to partnership members?

8. How does a general partnership differ from a limited partnership?

9. 🔘 George, Burton, and Dillman have been partners for three years. The partnership is being dissolved. George is leaving the firm, but Burton and Dillman plan to carry on the business. In the final settlement, George places a $75,000 salary claim against the partnership. He contends that he has a claim for a salary of $25,000 for each year because he devoted all of his time for three years to the affairs of the partnership. Is his claim valid? Why or why not?

10. 🔘 Kay, Kat, and Kim are partners. In a liquidation, Kay's share of partnership losses exceeds her capital account balance. Moreover, she is unable to meet the deficit from her personal assets, and her partners shared the excess losses. Does this relieve Kay of liability?

11. After all partnership assets have been converted to cash and all liabilities paid, the remaining cash should equal the sum of the balances of the partners' capital accounts. Why?

12. Assume a partner withdraws from a partnership and receives assets of greater value than the book value of his equity. Should the remaining partners share the resulting reduction in their equities in the ratio of their relative capital balances or according to their income-and-loss-sharing ratio?

connect

Kent and Davis are partners in operating a store. Without consulting Kent, Davis enters into a contract to purchase merchandise for the store. Kent contends that he did not authorize the order and refuses to pay for it. The vendor sues the partners for the contract price of the merchandise. (*a*) Must the partnership pay for the merchandise? Why? (*b*) Does your answer differ if Kent and Davis are partners in a public accounting firm? Explain.

Lamb organized a limited partnership and is the only general partner. Maxi invested $20,000 in the partnership and was admitted as a limited partner with the understanding that she would receive 10% of the profits. After two unprofitable years, the partnership ceased doing business. At that point, partnership liabilities were $85,000 larger than partnership assets. How much money can the partnership's creditors obtain from Maxi's personal assets to satisfy the unpaid partnership debts?

Ann Keeley and Susie Norton are partners in a business they started two years ago. The partnership agreement states that Keeley should receive a salary allowance of $40,000 and that Norton should receive a $30,000 salary allowance. Any remaining income or loss is to be shared equally. Determine each partner's share of the current year's net income of $210,000.

Jake and Ness are partners who agree that Jake will receive a $60,000 salary allowance and that any remaining income or loss will be shared equally. If Ness's capital account is credited for $1,000 as his share of the net income in a given period, how much net income did the partnership earn in that period?

Jones and Bordan are partners, each with $30,000 in their partnership capital accounts. Holly is admitted to the partnership by investing $30,000 cash. Make the entry to show Holly's admission to the partnership.

Mintz agrees to pay Bogg and Heyer $10,000 each for a one-third (33⅓%) interest in the Bogg and Heyer partnership. Immediately prior to Mintz's admission, each partner had a $30,000 capital balance. Make the journal entry to record Mintz's purchase of the partners' interest.

The Red, White & Blue partnership was begun with investments by the partners as follows: Red, $175,000; White, $220,000; and Blue, $205,000. The operations did not go well, and the partners eventually decided to liquidate the partnership, sharing all losses equally. On August 31, after all assets were converted to cash and all creditors were paid, only $60,000 in partnership cash remained.

1. Compute the capital account balance of each partner after the liquidation of assets and the payment of creditors.
2. Assume that any partner with a deficit agrees to pay cash to the partnership to cover the deficit. Present the journal entries on August 31 to record (*a*) the cash receipt from the deficient partner(s) and (*b*) the final disbursement of cash to the partners.
3. Assume that any partner with a deficit is not able to reimburse the partnership. Present journal entries (*a*) to transfer the deficit of any deficient partners to the other partners and (*b*) to record the final disbursement of cash to the partners.

Gilson and Lott's company is organized as a partnership. At the prior year-end, partnership equity totaled $300,000 ($200,000 from Gilson and $100,000 from Lott). For the current year, partnership net income is $50,000 ($40,000 allocated to Gilson and $10,000 allocated to Lott), and year-end total partnership equity is $400,000 ($280,000 from Gilson and $120,000 from Lott). Compute the total partnership return on equity *and* the individual partner return on equity ratios.

QUICK STUDY

QS 12-1
Partnership liability

C1

QS 12-2
Liability in limited partnerships

P1

QS 12-3
Partnership income allocation

P2

QS 12-4
Partnership income allocation

P2

QS 12-5
Admission of a partner

P3

QS 12-6
Partner admission through purchase of interest

P3

QS 12-7
Liquidation of partnership

P4

Check (1) Red, $(5,000)

QS 12-8
Partner return on equity

A1

EXERCISES

Exercise 12-1
Forms of organization

C1

For each of the following separate cases, recommend a form of business organization. With each recommendation, explain how business income would be taxed if the owners adopt the form of organization recommended. Also list several advantages that the owners will enjoy from the form of business organization that you recommend.

a. Milan has been out of school for about six years and has become quite knowledgeable about the residential real estate market. He would like to organize a company that buys and sells real estate. Milan believes he has the expertise to manage the company but needs funds to invest in residential property.

b. Dr. Langholz and Dr. Clark are recent graduates from medical residency programs. Both are family practice physicians and would like to open a clinic in an underserved rural area. Although neither has any funds to bring to the new venture, an investor has expressed interest in making a loan to provide start-up funds for their practice.

c. Ross, Jenks and Keim are recent college graduates in computer science. They want to start a Website development company. They all have college debts and currently do not own any substantial computer equipment needed to get the company started.

Exercise 12-2
Characteristics of partnerships

C1

Next to the following list of eight characteristics of business organizations, enter a brief description of how each characteristic applies to general partnerships.

Characteristic	Application to General Partnerships
1. Ease of formation	
2. Transferability of ownership	
3. Ability to raise large amounts of capital	
4. Life	
5. Owners' liability	
6. Legal status	
7. Tax status of income	
8. Owners' authority	

Exercise 12-3
Journalizing partnership formation

P2

Anita Kroll and Aaron Rogers organize a partnership on January 1. Kroll's initial net investment is $60,000, consisting of cash ($14,000), equipment ($66,000), and a note payable reflecting a bank loan for the new business ($20,000). Rogers's initial investment is cash of $25,000. These amounts are the values agreed on by both partners. Prepare journal entries to record (1) Kroll's investment and (2) Rogers's investment.

Exercise 12-4
Journalizing partnership transactions

P2

On March 1, 2015, Abbey and Dames formed a partnership. Abbey contributed $88,000 cash and Dames contributed land valued at $70,000 and a building valued at $100,000. The partnership also assumed responsibility for Dames's $80,000 long-term note payable associated with the land and building. The partners agreed to share income as follows: Abbey is to receive an annual salary allowance of $30,000, both are to receive an annual interest allowance of 10% of their beginning-year capital investment, and any remaining income or loss is to be shared equally. On October 20, 2015, Abbey withdrew $32,000 cash and Dames withdrew $25,000 cash. After the adjusting and closing entries are made to the revenue and expense accounts at December 31, 2015, the Income Summary account had a credit balance of $79,000.

1. Prepare journal entries to record (a) the partners' initial capital investments, (b) their cash withdrawals, and (c) the December 31 closing of both the Withdrawals and Income Summary accounts.

Check (2) Dames, $89,600

2. Determine the balances of the partners' capital accounts as at December 31, 2015.

Exercise 12-5
Income allocation in a partnership

P2

Cosmo and Ellis began a partnership by investing $50,000 and $75,000, respectively. During its first year, the partnership earned $165,000. Prepare calculations showing how the $165,000 income should be allocated to the partners under each of the following three separate plans for sharing income and loss: (1) the partners failed to agree on a method to share income; (2) the partners agreed to share income and loss in proportion to their initial investments (round amounts to the nearest dollar); and (3) the partners agreed to share income by granting a $55,000 per year salary allowance to Cosmo, a $45,000 per year salary allowance to Ellis, 10% interest on their initial capital investments, and the remaining balance shared equally.

Check Plan 3, Cosmo, $86,250

Assume that the partners of Exercise 12-5 agreed to share net income and loss by granting annual salary allowances of $55,000 to Cosmo and $45,000 to Ellis, 10% interest allowances on their investments, and any remaining balance shared equally.

1. Determine the partners' shares of Cosmo and Ellis given a first-year net income of $94,400.

2. Determine the partners' shares of Cosmo and Ellis given a first-year net loss of $15,700.

Exercise 12-6
Income allocation in a partnership
P2

Check   (2) Cosmo, $(4,100)

The partners in the Biz Partnership have agreed that partner Mona may sell her $90,000 equity in the partnership to Seal, for which Seal will pay Mona $75,000. Present the partnership's journal entry to record the sale of Mona's interest to Seal on September 30.

Exercise 12-7
Sale of partnership interest
P3

The Treed Partnership has total partners' equity of $510,000, which is made up of Elm, Capital, $400,000, and Oak, Capital, $110,000. The partners share net income and loss in a ratio of 80% to Elm and 20% to Oak. On November 1, Ash is admitted to the partnership and given a 15% interest in equity and a 15% share in any income and loss. Prepare the journal entry to record the admission of Ash under each of the following separate assumptions: Ash invests cash of (1) $90,000; (2) $125,000; and (3) $60,000.

Exercise 12-8
Admission of new partner
P3

Holland, Flowers, and Tulip have been partners while sharing net income and loss in a 5:3:2 ratio. On January 31, the date Tulip retires from the partnership, the equities of the partners are Holland, $350,000; Flowers, $240,000; and Tulip, $180,000. Present journal entries to record Tulip's retirement under each of the following separate assumptions: Tulip is paid for her equity using partnership cash of (1) $180,000; (2) $200,000; and (3) $150,000.

Exercise 12-9
Retirement of partner
P3

Tuttle, Ritter, and Lee are partners who share income and loss in a 1:4:5 ratio. After lengthy disagreements among the partners and several unprofitable periods, the partners decide to liquidate the partnership. Immediately before liquidation, the partnership balance sheet shows total assets, $116,000; total liabilities, $88,000; Tuttle, Capital, $1,200; Ritter, Capital, $11,700; and Lee, Capital, $15,100. The cash proceeds from selling the assets were sufficient to repay all but $24,000 to the creditors. (*a*) Calculate the loss from selling the assets. (*b*) Allocate the loss to the partners. (*c*) Determine how much of the remaining liability should be paid by each partner.

Exercise 12-10
Liquidation of partnership
P4

Check   (b) Lee, Capital after allocation, $(10,900)

Assume that the Tuttle, Ritter, and Lee partnership of Exercise 12-10 is a limited partnership. Tuttle and Ritter are general partners and Lee is a limited partner. How much of the remaining $24,000 liability should be paid by each partner? (Round amounts to the nearest dollar.)

Exercise 12-11
Liquidation of limited partnership
P4

Hunt Sports Enterprises LP is organized as a limited partnership consisting of two individual partners: Soccer LP and Football LP. Both partners separately operate a minor league soccer team and a semipro football team. Compute partner return on equity for each limited partnership (and the total) for the year ended June 30, 2015, using the following selected data on partner capital balances from Hunt Sports Enterprises LP.

Exercise 12-12
Partner return on equity
A1

	Soccer LP	Football LP	Total
Balance at 6/30/2014	$378,000	$1,516,000	$1,894,000
Annual net income	44,268	891,796	936,064
Cash distribution	—	(100,000)	(100,000)
Balance at 6/30/2015	$422,268	$2,307,796	$2,730,064

PROBLEM SET A

Problem 12-1A
Allocating partnership income

P2

Check (3) Thomas, Capital, $48,900

Kim Ries, Tere Bax, and Josh Thomas invested $40,000, $56,000, and $64,000, respectively, in a partnership. During its first calendar year, the firm earned $124,500.

Required

Prepare the entry to close the firm's Income Summary account as at its December 31 year-end and to allocate the $124,500 net income to the partners under each of the following separate assumptions: The partners (1) have no agreement on the method of sharing income and loss; (2) agreed to share income and loss in the ratio of their beginning capital investments; and (3) agreed to share income and loss by providing annual salary allowances of $33,000 to Ries, $28,000 to Bax, and $40,000 to Thomas; granting 10% interest on the partners' beginning capital investments; and sharing the remainder equally.

Problem 12-2A
Allocating partnership income and loss; sequential years

P2

www.mheducation.asia/olc/wildkwokFAP

Rex Baker and Ty Farney are forming a partnership to which Baker will devote one-half time and Farney will devote full time. They have discussed the following alternative plans for sharing income and loss: (*a*) in the ratio of their initial capital investments, which they have agreed will be $21,000 for Baker and $31,500 for Farney; (*b*) in proportion to the time devoted to the business; (*c*) a salary allowance of $3,000 per month to Farney and the balance in accordance with the ratio of their initial capital investments; or (*d*) a salary allowance of $3,000 per month to Farney, 10% interest on their initial capital investments, and the balance shared equally. The partners expect the business to perform as follows: year 1, $18,000 net loss; year 2, $45,000 net income; and year 3, $75,000 net income.

Required

Prepare three tables with the following column headings.

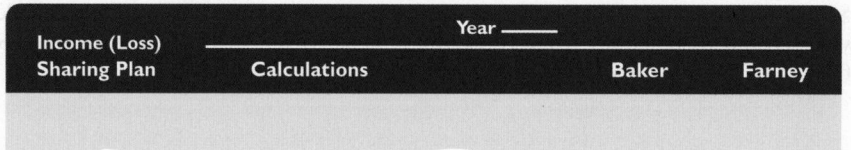

Income (Loss) Sharing Plan	Calculations	Year ———		
			Baker	Farney

Check Plan d, year 1, Farney's share, $9,525

Complete the tables, one for each of the first three years, by showing how to allocate partnership income or loss to the partners under each of the four plans being considered. (Round answers to the nearest whole dollar.)

Problem 12-3A
Partnership income allocation, statement of partners' equity, and closing entries

P2

www.mheducation.asia/olc/wildkwokFAP

Will Beck, Ron Beck, and Barb Beck formed the BBB Partnership by making capital contributions of $183,750, $131,250, and $210,000, respectively. They predict annual partnership net income of $225,000 and are considering the following alternative plans of sharing income and loss: (*a*) equally; (*b*) in the ratio of their initial capital investments; or (*c*) salary allowances of $40,000 to Will, $30,000 to Ron, and $45,000 to Barb; interest allowances of 10% on their initial capital investments; and the balance shared equally.

Required

1. Prepare a table with the following column headings.

Income (Loss) Sharing Plan	Calculations	Will	Ron	Barb	Total

Check (2) Barb, Ending Capital, $223,000

Use the table to show how to distribute net income of $225,000 for the calendar year under each of the alternative plans being considered. (Round answers to the nearest whole dollar.)

2. Prepare a statement of partners' equity showing the allocation of income to the partners assuming they agree to use plan (*c*), that income earned is $104,500, and that Will, Ron, and Barb withdraw $17,000, $24,000, and $32,000, respectively, at year-end.

3. Prepare the December 31 journal entry to close Income Summary assuming they agree to use plan (*c*) and that net income is $104,500. Also close the withdrawals accounts.

Part 1. Goering, Zarcus, and Schmit are partners and share income and loss in a 3:2:5 ratio. The partnership's capital balances are as follows: Goering, $84,000; Zarcus, $69,000; and Schmit, $147,000. Zarcus decides to withdraw from the partnership, and the partners agree to not have the assets revalued upon Zarcus's retirement. Prepare journal entries to record Zarcus's February 1 withdrawal from the partnership under each of the following separate assumptions: Zarcus (*a*) sells her interest to Getz for $80,000 after Goering and Schmit approve the entry of Getz as a partner; (*b*) gives her interest to a son-in-law, Swanson, and thereafter Goering and Schmit accept Swanson as a partner; (*c*) is paid $69,000 in partnership cash for her equity; (*d*) is paid $107,000 in partnership cash for her equity; and (*e*) is paid $15,000 in partnership cash plus equipment recorded on the partnership books at $35,000 less its accumulated depreciation of $11,600.

Part 2. Assume that Zarcus does not retire from the partnership described in Part 1. Instead, Ford is admitted to the partnership on February 1 with a 25% equity. Prepare journal entries to record Ford's entry into the partnership under each of the following separate assumptions: Ford invests (*a*) $100,000; (*b*) $74,000; and (*c*) $131,000.

Quick, Drake, and Sage share income and loss in a 3:2:1 ratio. The partners have decided to liquidate their partnership. On the day of liquidation their balance sheet appears as follows.

QUICK, DRAKE, AND SAGE
Balance Sheet
May 31

Assets		Liabilities and Equity	
Cash	$ 90,400	Accounts payable	$122,750
Inventory	268,600	Quick, Capital	46,500
		Drake, Capital	106,250
		Sage, Capital	83,500
Total assets	$359,000	Total liabilities and equity	$359,000

Required

Prepare journal entries for (*a*) the sale of inventory, (*b*) the allocation of its gain or loss, (*c*) the payment of liabilities at book value, and (*d*) the distribution of cash in each of the following separate cases: Inventory is sold for (1) $300,000; (2) $250,000; (3) $160,000 and any partners with capital deficits pay in the amount of their deficits; and (4) $125,000 and the partners have no assets other than those invested in the partnership. (Round to the nearest dollar.)

Matt Albin, Ryan Peters and Seth Ramsey invested $82,000, $49,200 and $32,800, respectively, in a partnership. During its first calendar year, the firm earned $135,000.

Required

Prepare the entry to close the firm's Income Summary account as at its December 31 year-end and to allocate the $135,000 net income to the partners under each of the following separate assumptions. (Round answers to whole dollars.) The partners (1) have no agreement on the method of sharing income and loss; (2) agreed to share income and loss in the ratio of their beginning capital investments; and (3) agreed to share income and loss by providing annual salary allowances of $48,000 to Albin, $36,000 to Peters, and $25,000 to Ramsey; granting 10% interest on the partners' beginning capital investments; and sharing the remainder equally.

Maria Karto and J.R. Black are forming a partnership to which Karto will devote one-third time and Black will devote full time. They have discussed the following alternative plans for sharing income and loss: (*a*) in the ratio of their initial capital investments, which they have agreed will be $52,000 for Karto and $78,000 for Black; (*b*) in proportion to the time devoted to the business; (*c*) a salary allowance of $2,000 per month to Black and the balance in accordance with the ratio of their initial capital investments; or

---

Problem 12-4A
Partner withdrawal and admission
P3

Check (1*e*) Cr. Schmit, Capital, $19,125

(2*c*) Cr. Zarcus, Capital, $4,650

Problem 12-5A
Liquidation of a partnership
P4

Check (4) Cash distribution: Sage, $51,134

PROBLEM SET B

Problem 12-1B
Allocating partnership income
P2

Check (3) Ramsey, Capital, $31,480

Problem 12-2B
Allocating partnership income and loss; sequential years
P2

(*d*) a salary allowance of $2,000 per month to Black, 10% interest on their initial capital investments, and the balance shared equally. The partners expect the business to perform as follows: year 1, $18,000 net loss; year 2, $38,000 net income; and year 3, $94,000 net income.

Required

Prepare three tables with the following column headings.

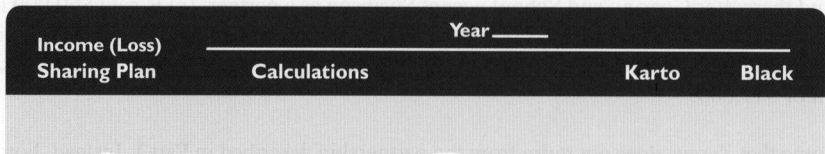

Complete the tables, one for each of the first three years, by showing how to allocate partnership income or loss to the partners under each of the four plans being considered. (Round answers to the nearest whole dollar.)

Check   Plan d, year 1, Black's share, $4,300

Problem 12-3B

Partnership income allocation, statement of partners' equity, and closing entries

P2

Staci Cook, Lin Xi, and Kevin Schwartz formed the CXS Partnership by making capital contributions of $72,000, $108,000, and $60,000, respectively. They predict annual partnership net income of $120,000 and are considering the following alternative plans of sharing income and loss: (*a*) equally; (*b*) in the ratio of their initial capital investments; or (*c*) salary allowances of $20,000 to Cook, $15,000 to Xi, and $40,000 to Schwartz; interest allowances of 12% on their initial capital investments; and the balance shared equally.

Required

1. Prepare a table with the following column headings.

Use the table to show how to distribute net income of $120,000 for the calendar year under each of the alternative plans being considered. (Round answers to the nearest whole dollar.)

Check   (2) Schwartz, Ending Capital, $75,200

2. Prepare a statement of partners' equity showing the allocation of income to the partners assuming they agree to use plan (*c*), that income earned is $43,800, and that Cook, Xi, and Schwartz withdraw $9,000, $19,000, and $12,000, respectively, at year-end.

3. Prepare the December 31 journal entry to close Income Summary assuming they agree to use plan (*c*) and that net income is $43,800. Also close the withdrawals accounts.

Problem 12-4B

Partner withdrawal and admission

P3

Part 1. Gibbs, Mier, and Hill are partners and share income and loss in a 5:1:4 ratio. The partnership's capital balances are as follows: Gibbs, $303,000; Mier, $74,000; and Hill, $223,000. Gibbs decides to withdraw from the partnership, and the partners agree not to have the assets revalued upon Gibbs's retirement. Prepare journal entries to record Gibbs's April 30 withdrawal from the partnership under each of the following separate assumptions: Gibbs (*a*) sells her interest to Brady for $250,000 after Mier and Hill approve the entry of Brady as a partner; (*b*) gives her interest to a daughter-in-law, Cannon, and thereafter Mier and Hill accept Cannon as a partner; (*c*) is paid $303,000 in partnership cash for her equity; (*d*) is paid $175,000 in partnership cash for her equity; and (*e*) is paid $100,000 in partnership cash plus manufacturing equipment recorded on the partnership books at $269,000 less its accumulated depreciation of $168,000.

Check   (1*e*) Cr. Hill, Capital, $81,600

Part 2. Assume that Gibbs does not retire from the partnership described in Part 1. Instead, Brise is admitted to the partnership on April 30 with a 20% equity. Prepare journal entries to record the entry of Brise under each of the following separate assumptions: Brise invests (*a*) $150,000; (*b*) $98,000; and (*c*) $213,000.

Check   (2*c*) Cr. Mier, Capital, $5,040

Asure, Ramirez, and Soney, who share income and loss in a 2:1:2 ratio, plan to liquidate their partnership. At liquidation, their balance sheet appears as follows.

Problem 12-5B
Liquidation of a partnership
P4

ASURE, RAMIREZ, AND SONEY
Balance Sheet
January 18

Assets		Liabilities and Equity	
Cash	$174,300	Accounts payable	$171,300
Equipment	308,600	Asure, Capital	150,200
		Ramirez, Capital	97,900
		Soney, Capital	63,500
Total assets	$482,900	Total liabilities and equity	$482,900

Required

Prepare journal entries for (*a*) the sale of equipment, (*b*) the allocation of its gain or loss, (*c*) the payment of liabilities at book value, and (*d*) the distribution of cash in each of the following separate cases: Equipment is sold for (1) $325,000; (2) $265,000; (3) $100,000 and any partners with capital deficits pay in the amount of their deficits; and (4) $75,000 and the partners have no assets other than those invested in the partnership. (Round amounts to the nearest dollar.)

Check (4) Cash distribution: Asure, $36,800

(*This serial problem began in Chapter 1 and continues through most of the book. If previous chapter segments were not completed, the serial problem can begin at this point.*)

SERIAL PROBLEM
Business Solutions
P3

SP 12   At the start of 2016, Santana Rey is considering adding a partner to her business. She envisions the new partner taking the lead in generating sales of both services and merchandise for Business Solutions. S. Rey's equity in Business Solutions as at January 1, 2016, is reflected in the following capital balance.

S. Rey, Capital.	$80,360

Required

1. S. Rey is evaluating whether the prospective partner should be an equal partner with respect to capital investment and profit sharing (1:1) or whether the agreement should be 4:1 with Rey retaining four-fifths interest with rights to four-fifths of the net income or loss. What factors should she consider in deciding which partnership agreement to offer?

2. Prepare the January 1, 2016, journal entry(ies) necessary to admit a new partner to Business Solutions through the purchase of a partnership interest for each of the following two separate cases: (*a*) 1:1 sharing agreement and (*b*) 4:1 sharing agreement.

3. Prepare the January 1, 2016, journal entry(ies) required to admit a new partner if the new partner invests cash of $20,090.

4. After posting the entry in part 3, what would be the new partner's equity percentage?

Beyond the Numbers

BTN 12-1   Take a step back in time and imagine **Adidas** in its infancy as a business.

REPORTING IN ACTION
C1

Required

1. Find out from its Website or search the Internet about who started the business.

2. Assume that Adidas was originally organized as a partnership. Adidas's income statement in Appendix A varies in several key ways from what it would look like for a partnership. Identify at least two ways in which a corporate income statement differs from a partnership income statement.

3. Compare the Adidas statement of financial position in Appendix A to what a partnership balance sheet would have shown. Identify and explain any account differences we would anticipate.

COMPARATIVE ANALYSIS

C1

BTN 12-2   Over the years Adidas and Puma have evolved into large corporations. Today it is difficult to imagine them as fledgling start-ups. Research each company's history online.

Required

1. Which company is older? How are the founder(s) of each company related?
2. In what years did each company have its first public offering of shares?

ETHICS CHALLENGE

P2

BTN 12-3   Doctors Maben, Orlando, and Clark have been in a group practice for several years. Maben and Orlando are family practice physicians, and Clark is a general surgeon. Clark receives many referrals for surgery from his family practice partners. Upon the partnership's original formation, the three doctors agreed to a two-part formula to share income. Every month each doctor receives a salary allowance of $3,000. Additional income is divided according to a percent of patient charges the doctors generate for the month. In the current month, Maben generated 10% of the billings, Orlando 30%, and Clark 60%. The group's income for this month is $50,000. Clark has expressed dissatisfaction with the income-sharing formula and asks that income be split entirely on patient charge percents.

Required

1. Compute the income allocation for the current month using the original agreement.
2. Compute the income allocation for the current month using Clark's proposed agreement.
3. Identify the ethical components of this partnership decision for the doctors.

COMMUNICATING IN PRACTICE

C1

BTN 12-4   Assume that you are studying for an upcoming accounting exam with a good friend. Your friend says that she has a solid understanding of general partnerships but is less sure that she understands organizations that combine certain characteristics of partnerships with other forms of business organization. You offer to make some study notes for your friend to help her learn about limited partnerships, limited liability partnerships, S corporations, and limited liability companies. Prepare a one-page set of well-organized, complete study notes on these four forms of business organization.

TAKING IT TO THE NET

P1 P2

BTN 12-5   Access the 2012 10-K of America First Tax Exempt Investors LP. This company deals with tax exempt mortgage revenue bonds that, among other things, finance student housing properties.

1. Locate its December 31, 2012 balance sheet and list the account titles reported in the equity section of the balance sheet.
2. Locate its statement of partners' capital and comprehensive income (loss). How many units of limited partnership (known as "beneficial unit certificate holders") are outstanding as at December 31, 2012?
3. What is the partnership's largest asset and its amount as at December 31, 2012?

TEAMWORK IN ACTION

P2

BTN 12-6   This activity requires teamwork to reinforce understanding of accounting for partnerships.

Required

1. Assume that Baker, Warner, and Rice form the BWR Partnership by making capital contributions of $200,000, $300,000, and $500,000, respectively. BWR predicts annual partnership net income of $600,000. The partners are considering various plans for sharing income and loss. Assign a different team member to compute how the projected $600,000 income would be shared under each of the following separate plans:

   a. Shared equally.
   b. In the ratio of the partners' initial capital investments.
   c. Salary allowances of $50,000 to Baker, $60,000 to Warner, and $70,000 to Rice, with the remaining balance shared equally.
   d. Interest allowances of 10% on the partners' initial capital investments, with the remaining balance shared equally.

2. In sequence, each member is to present his or her income-sharing calculations with the team.

3. As a team, identify and discuss at least one other possible way that income could be shared.

BTN 12-7 Recall the chapter's opening feature involving Michelle Tok, Patrick Cheong, and Jobina Ow, and their company, **Home Central**. Assume that Michelle, Patrick, and Jobina decide to expand their business with the help of general partners.

ENTREPRENEURIAL DECISION

C1

Required

1. What details should Michelle, Patrick, Jobina, and their future partners specify in the general partnership agreements?

2. What advantages should Michelle, Patrick, Jobina, and their future partners be aware of with respect to organizing as a general partnership?

3. What disadvantages should Michelle, Patrick, Jobina, and their future partners be aware of with respect to organizing as a general partnership?

BTN 12-8 Access Nokia's Website (www.Nokia.com) and research the company's history.

1. When was the company founded?

2. What three companies merged to create Nokia Corporation?

3. What are some of the companies that are part of Nokia?

GLOBAL DECISION

C1

ANSWERS TO MULTIPLE CHOICE QUIZ

1. e; Capital = $250,000 − $50,000

2. a; $90,000 × [$100,000/($150,000 + $150,000 + $100,000)]
= $22,500

3. d;

	Jamison	Blue	Total
Net income			$ 270,000
Salary allowance	$120,000		(120,000)
Interest allowance	60,000	$80,000	(140,000)
Balance of income			10,000
Balance divided equally	5,000	5,000	(10,000)
Totals	$185,000	$85,000	$ 0

4. b; Total partnership equity = $125,000 + $124,000 + $75,000
= $324,000
Equity of Black = $324,000 × 20% = $64,800
Bonus to old partners = $75,000 − $64,800 = $10,200, split equally

5. a; $10,500/[($110,000 + $124,000)/2] = 8.97%

13

Accounting for Corporations

A Look Back

Chapter 12 focused on the partnership form of organization. We described crucial characteristics of partnerships and the accounting and reporting of their important transactions.

A Look at This Chapter

This chapter focuses on equity transactions. The first part of the chapter describes the basics of the corporate form of organization. We then focus on the accounting concepts and procedures for equity transactions. The final section describes how to report and analyze comprehensive income, earnings per share, and changes in equity.

A Look Ahead

Chapter 14 focuses on long-term liabilities. We explain how to value, record, amortize, and report these liabilities in financial statements.

Learning Objectives

CAP

CONCEPTUAL

C1 Identify characteristics of corporations and their organization. (p. 492)

C2 Explain characteristics of, and distribute dividends between, ordinary and preference shares. (p. 501)

C3 Explain the items reported in comprehensive income and equity. (p. 507)

ANALYTICAL

A1 Compute earnings per share and describe its use. (p. 511)

A2 Compute price-earnings ratio and describe its use in analysis. (p. 511)

A3 Compute dividend yield and explain its use in analysis. (p. 512)

A4 Compute book value and explain its use in analysis. (p. 513)

PROCEDURAL

P1 Record the issuance of corporate shares. (p. 496)

P2 Record transactions involving cash dividends, share dividends, and share splits. (p. 498)

P3 Record purchases and sales of treasury shares and the retirement of shares. (p. 504)

"I get to do something I am passionate about every day."—**DOUGLAS YOUNG**

G.O.D. Designs

In an era of rising Western influences and industrial chic, some entre-preneurs see a future in the past. Douglas Young, a Hong Kong native and architect by training, is one such designer–entrepreneur. "Many of us see the need to be proud of being who we are," says Douglas. Against a backdrop of Hong Kong's impending handover to China in 1997, he recognized the people's yearning to own a nostalgic bit of history. "At the time, there was a void in the market for a Hong Kong-based brand that was truly local in inspiration," he adds. Taking inspira-tion from the East-meets-West concept to create a uniquely Hong Kong imprint, Douglas set up **G.O.D. (www.god.com.hk)** in 1996, a lifestyle brand company offering an eclectic range of furniture and household products designed to embrace the old and the new as-pects of this city-state.

The company's Chinese name means "to live better" and in the local dialect sounds like G.O.D, the acronym for "Goods of Desire." Check out its online catalog and you might ferret out a coir floor mat embroidered with a retro punk rock song title, a carpet framed by huge prints of the popular "Double Happiness" Chinese character,

and a retro-chic coffee table with an unmistakably modern twist. G.O.D. isn't all furniture chic—it also flexes its hipster muscles in a quirky clothing and fashion line. Think handbags covered with Chinese newspaper print and you get an idea of the witty resourcefulness that goes into the design of a G.O.D. product.

Like any company that has enjoyed a successful corporate structure and equity financing, G.O.D. is poised for new opportunities and challenges. With five stores under his stewardship and plans to expand in the region, Douglas understands very well the importance of being updated on corporate information and practices, equity issuance, stock types, retained earnings, and dividend policies, in order to take the business to greater heights. The key is to effectively use accounting for equity as a tool to achieve the company's objectives.

"I get to do something I am passionate about every day!" says Douglas. That "something," without question, embodies the forging of a national identity through designs that infuse the good old days into modern living.

This chapter focuses on equity transactions. The first part of the chapter describes the basics of the corporate form of organization and explains the accounting for ordinary and preference shares. We then focus on several special financing transactions, including cash and share dividends, share splits, and treasury shares. The final section considers accounting for comprehensive income and changes in equity.

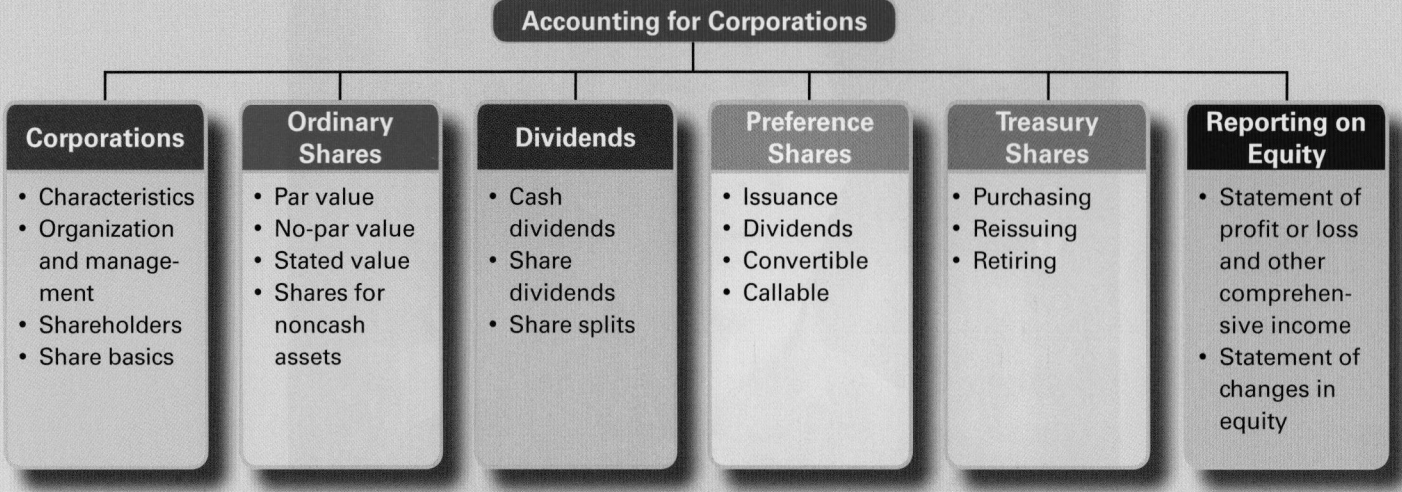

CORPORATE FORM OF ORGANIZATION

C1 Identify characteristics of corporations and their organization.

A **corporation** or a company is an entity created by law that is separate from its owners. It has most of the rights and privileges granted to individuals. Owners of corporations are called *shareholders*. Corporations can be separated into two types. A *privately held* (or *closely held*) corporation does not offer its shares for public sale and usually has few shareholders. A *publicly held* corporation offers its shares for public sale and can have thousands of shareholders. *Public sale* usually refers to issuance and trading on an organized stock market.

Characteristics of Corporations

Corporations represent an important type of organization. Their unique characteristics offer advantages and disadvantages.

Advantages of Corporate Characteristics

Point: The *business entity assumption* requires a corporation to be accounted for separately from its owners (shareholders).

Point: North American corporations issue *common stock* and *preferred stock*, so the related terms are *stockholders*, *stock dividends*, *stock splits*, *stock options*, and *treasury stock*.

- **Separate legal entity:** A corporation conducts its affairs with the same rights, duties, and responsibilities of a person. It takes actions through its agents, who are its officers and managers.
- **Limited liability of shareholders:** Shareholders are liable for neither corporate acts nor corporate debt.
- **Transferable ownership rights:** The transfer of shares from one shareholder to another usually has no effect on the corporation or its operations except when this causes a change in the directors who control or manage the corporation.
- **Continuous life:** A corporation's life continues indefinitely because it is not tied to the physical lives of its owners.
- **Lack of mutual agency for shareholders:** A corporation acts through its agents, who are its officers and managers. Shareholders, who are not its officers and managers, do not have the power to bind the corporation to contracts—referred to as *lack of mutual agency*.
- **Ease of capital accumulation:** Buying shares is attractive to investors because (1) shareholders are not liable for the corporation's acts and debts, (2) shares usually are transferred easily, (3) the life of the corporation is unlimited, and (4) shareholders are not corporate agents. These advantages enable corporations to accumulate large amounts of capital from the combined investments of many shareholders.

Disadvantages of Corporate Characteristics

- **Government regulation:** A corporation must comply with many rules and regulations. Proprietorships and partnerships avoid many of these regulations and governmental reports.
- **Corporate taxation:** Corporations are subject to the same property and payroll taxes as proprietorships and partnerships plus *additional* taxes. Moreover, corporate profit may be taxed a second time as part of shareholders' personal income when they receive cash distributed as dividends. This is called **double taxation.**

Decision Insight

Share Financing   In 1999, Ma Yun (Jack Ma) and 18 others founded **Alibaba Group** in China, an Internet-based business that includes business-to-business international trade, online retail and payment platforms, and data-centric cloud computing services. On November 6, 2007, **Alibaba.com**, its flagship company, listed on the Hong Kong Stock Exchange. The initial public offering (IPO) price was HK$13.5, raising HK$13.1 billion (US$1.7 billion) in the second-largest IPO sale of an Internet company after Google Inc. ■

Corporate Organization and Management

This section describes the incorporation, costs, and management of corporate organizations.

Incorporation   In general, the creation of a corporation begins when its organizers, called the promoters or incorporators, obtain a registration from a government body or the court. When the process is complete and fees paid, the registration is complete and the corporation is formed.

Organization Expenses   **Organization expenses** (also called *organization costs*) are the costs to organize a corporation; they include legal fees, promoters' fees, and amounts paid to obtain a registration. The corporation records (debits) these costs to an expense account called *Organization Expenses*. Organization costs are expensed as incurred because it is difficult to determine the amount and timing of their future benefits.

Management of a Corporation   The ultimate control of a corporation rests with shareholders who control a corporation by electing its *board of directors*, or simply, *directors*. Each shareholder usually has one vote for each share owned. This control relation is shown in Exhibit 13.1. Directors are responsible for and have final authority for managing corporate activities. A board can act only as a collective body and usually limits its actions to setting general policy.

A corporation usually holds a shareholder meeting at least once a year to elect directors and transact business as its bylaws require. A group of shareholders owning or controlling votes of more than a 50% share of a corporation's shares can elect the board and control the corporation. Shareholders who do not attend shareholders' meetings must have an opportunity to delegate their voting rights to an agent by signing a **proxy**, a document that gives a designated agent the right to vote the shares.

Day-to-day direction of corporate business is delegated to executive officers appointed by the board. A corporation's chief executive officer (CEO) is often its president. Several vice presidents, who report to the president, are commonly assigned specific areas of management responsibility such as finance, production, and marketing. One person often has the dual role of chairperson of the board of directors and CEO. In this case, the president is usually designated the chief operating officer (COO).

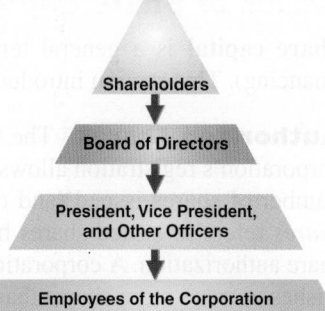

Global: Some corporate labels are:

Country	Label
United States	Inc.
France	SA
United Kingdom	
Public	PLC
Private	Ltd
Germany & Austria	
Public	AG
Private	GmbH
Sweden & Finland	AB
Italy	SpA
Netherlands	NV
Australia	AG
Mexico	SA
Bahamas	IBC

Decision Insight

Seed Money   Sources for start-up money include (1) "angel" investors such as family, friends, or anyone who believes in a company, (2) employees, investors, and even suppliers who can be paid with shares, and (3) venture capitalists (investors) who have a record of entrepreneurial success. Different countries have their own organizations, such as National Venture Capital Association (**www.nvca.org**), British Private Equity & Venture Capital Association (**www.bvca.co.uk**), and Singapore Venture Capital & Private Equity Association (**www.svca.org.sg**). ■

Shareholders of Corporations

This section explains shareholder rights, share purchases and sales, and the role of registrar and transfer agents.

Rights of Shareholders   When investors buy shares, they acquire all *specific* rights the corporation grants to shareholders. They also acquire *general* rights granted shareholders by the laws of the country in which the company is incorporated. When a corporation has only one class of shares, it is identified as **ordinary shares**. State laws vary, but ordinary shareholders usually have the general right to

1. Vote at shareholders' meetings.
2. Sell or otherwise dispose of their shares.
3. Purchase their proportional share of any ordinary shares later issued by the corporation. This **preemptive right** protects shareholders' proportionate interest in the corporation. For example, a shareholder who owns 25% of a corporation's ordinary shares has the first opportunity to buy 25% of any new ordinary shares issued.
4. Receive the same dividend, if any, on each ordinary share of the corporation.
5. Share in any assets remaining after creditors and preference shareholders are paid when, and if, the corporation is liquidated. Each ordinary share receives the same amount.

Shareholders also have the right to receive timely financial reports.

Decision Insight

Pricing Shares   A prospectus accompanies a share's initial public offering (IPO), giving financial information about the company issuing the shares. A prospectus should help answer these questions to price an IPO: (1) Is the underwriter reliable? (2) Is there growth in revenues, profits, and cash flows? (3) What is management's view of operations? (4) Are current owners selling? (5) What are the risks? ■

Basics of Share Capital

Share capital is a general term that refers to any shares issued to obtain capital (owner financing). This section introduces terminology and accounting for share capital.

Subcategories of Authorized Shares

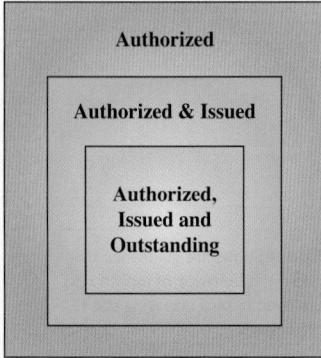

Authorized Shares   The term **authorized shares** refers to the number of shares that a corporation's registration allows it to sell. The number of authorized shares usually exceeds the number of shares issued (and outstanding), often by a large amount. (The term *outstanding shares* refers to issued shares held by shareholders.) No formal journal entry is required for share authorization. A corporation must generally apply to a government body for a change if it wishes to issue more shares than previously authorized. A corporation discloses the number of shares authorized in the equity section of its statement of financial position or notes. Nestlé's 2013 annual report Note 19 states that it has 3.2248 billion authorized ordinary shares.

   Some countries such as Australia, New Zealand, and Singapore have abolished the concept of authorized capital. The reason for the abolition is that the authorized capital is an artificial ceiling that can, in practice, be easily raised (or lowered) though a government body's approval or even as simply as a shareholder's resolution.

Selling (Issuing) Shares   A corporation can sell shares directly or indirectly. To *sell directly*, it advertises its share issuance to potential buyers. This type of issuance is most common with privately held corporations. To *sell indirectly*, a corporation pays a brokerage house (investment banker) to issue its shares. Some brokerage houses *underwrite* an indirect issuance of shares; that is, they buy the shares from the corporation and take all gains or losses from its resale.

Market Value of Shares   **Market value per share** is the price at which a share is bought and sold. Expected future earnings, dividends, growth, and other company and economic factors influence market value. Traded shares' market values are available daily in newspapers such as *The Wall Street Journal* and online. The current market value of previously issued shares (for example, the price of shares in trades between investors) does not impact the issuing corporation's shareholders' equity.

Classes of Shares   When all authorized shares have the same rights and characteristics, the share are called *ordinary shares*. A corporation is sometimes authorized to issue more than one class of shares, including preference shares and different classes of ordinary shares. **American Greetings**, for instance, has two types of ordinary shares: Class A share has 1 vote per share and Class B share has 10 votes per share.

Par Value Share   **Par value share** is a share that is assigned a **par value**, which is an amount assigned per share by the corporation. Historically, the par value was equal to the share price upon initial public offering (IPO). The issuing company promised not to issue further shares below par value, so a shareholder could be confident that no one else was receiving a more favorable issue price. Current thinking is leaning toward no-par value share, to be explained next.

Point: The term *nominal value* or *face value* is sometimes used instead of *par value*. **Nestlé** uses the term nominal value.

No-Par Value Share   **No-par value share**, or simply *no-par share*, is a share not assigned a value per share. It is better for a company to issue shares with no par value, in order to avoid a liability to shareholders should the share price plunge. For example, if a share was trading at $5 per share and the par value on the share was $10, theoretically, the company would have a $5-per-share liability. Par value has no relation to the market value (share price). A no-par value share can still trade for tens or hundreds of dollars—it all depends on what the market feels the company is worth.

Point: Par, no-par, and stated value do *not* set the share's market value.

Stated Value Share   **Stated value share** is a no-par share to which the directors assign a "stated" value per share and this value is used to calculate the amounts to be recorded upon issuance of the shares.

Shareholders' Equity   **Shareholders' equity**, or simply equity, consists basically of (1) share capital, and (2) retained earnings; see Exhibit 13.2. Share capital is the total amount of cash and other assets the corporation receives from its shareholders in exchange for its shares. Retained earnings is the cumulative net profit (and loss) not distributed as dividends to its shareholders. There could be other components of equity such as share premium or reserves discussed in the following sections.

Share Capital	
	Normal balance

Retained Earnings	
	Normal balance

EXHIBIT 13.2

Equity Composition

♛ Decision Insight

Share Price Quote
Adidas' share price quote for April 9, 2010 is interpreted as (left to right): **Hi**, highest

52 Wks				Yld		Avg				Net
Hi	Lo	Sym	Div	%	PE	Vol	Hi	Lo	Close	Chg
41.28	31.35	ADS.DE	0.35	0.87	32.90	1,266,760	41.28	40.28	41.12	0.95

price in past 52 weeks; **Lo**, lowest price in past 52 weeks; **Sym**, company exchange symbol; **Div**, dividends paid per share in past year; **Yld %**, dividend divided by closing price; **PE**, share price divided by earnings per share; **Avg Vol** of shares traded in 3 months; **Hi**, highest price for the day; **Lo**, lowest price for the day; **Close**, closing price for the day; **Net Chg**, change in closing price from prior day. ∎

1. Which of the following is *not* a characteristic of the corporate form of business? (*a*) Ease of capital accumulation, (*b*) Shareholder responsibility for corporate debts, (*c*) Ease in transferability of ownership rights, or (*d*) Double taxation.
2. Why is a corporation's profit said to be taxed twice?
3. What is a proxy?

ORDINARY SHARES

 P1 Record the issuance of corporate shares.

Accounting for the issuance of ordinary shares affects share capital accounts (including share premium); no retained earnings accounts are affected.

Issuing Par Value Shares

The following covers the common situations of issuing par value shares at par and at a premium (above par). In each case, shares can be exchanged for either cash or noncash assets.

Issuing Par Value Shares at Par When ordinary shares are issued at par value, we record amounts for both the asset(s) received and the par value shares issued. To illustrate, the entry to record Dillon Snowboards' issuance of 30,000 shares of $10 par value shares for $300,000 cash on June 5, 2015, follows.

Assets = Liabilities + Equity
+300,000   +300,000

$10 par value × 30,000 shares

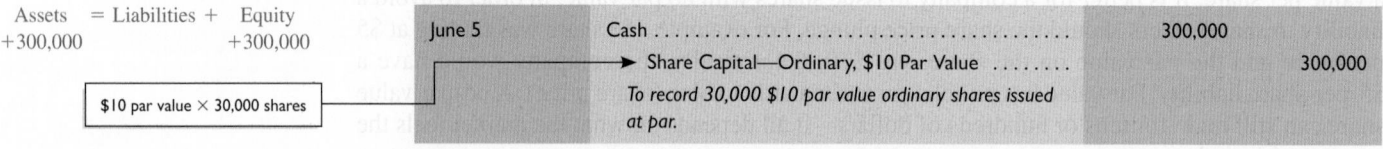

June 5	Cash	300,000	
	Share Capital—Ordinary, $10 Par Value		300,000
	To record 30,000 $10 par value ordinary shares issued at par.		

Exhibit 13.3 shows the shareholders' equity of Dillon Snowboards at year-end 2015 (its first year of operations) after profit of $65,000 and no dividend payments.

EXHIBIT 13.3

Shareholders' Equity for Shares Issued at Par

Shareholders' Equity	
Share Capital—Ordinary, $10 par value; 50,000 shares authorized;	
30,000 shares issued and outstanding	$300,000
Retained earnings	65,000
Total shareholders' equity	$365,000

Point: A *premium* is the amount by which issue price exceeds par (or stated) value. It is recorded in the "Share Premium, Ordinary" account; also called "Additional Paid-In Capital, Ordinary shares."

Issuing Par Value Shares at a Premium A **premium on shares** occurs when a corporation sells its shares for more than par (or stated) value. To illustrate, if Dillon Snowboards issues its $10 par value ordinary shares at $12 per share, its shares are sold at a $2 per share premium. The premium, known as **share premium**, is reported as part of equity; it is not revenue and is not listed on the income statement. The entry to record Dillon Snowboards' issuance of 30,000 shares of $10 par value shares for $12 per shares on June 5, 2015, follows.

Assets = Liabilities + Equity
+360,000   +300,000
                  +60,000

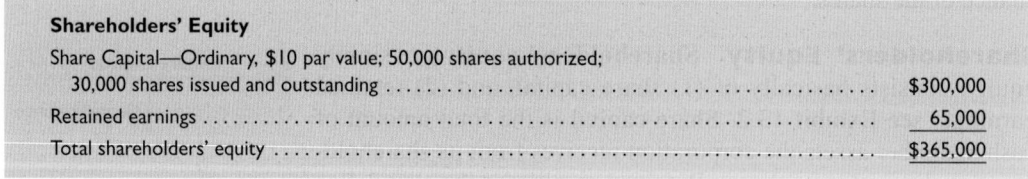

June 5	Cash	360,000	
	Share Capital—Ordinary, $10 Par Value		300,000
	Share Premium—Ordinary		60,000
	To record 30,000 $10 par value ordinary shares issued at $12 per share.		

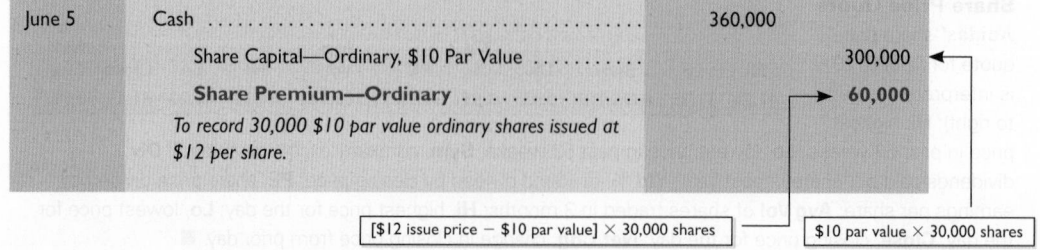

[$12 issue price − $10 par value] × 30,000 shares

$10 par value × 30,000 shares

The Share Premium account is added to the par value of the shares in the equity section of the statement of financial position as shown in Exhibit 13.4.

Shareholders' Equity	
Share Capital—Ordinary, $10 par value; 50,000 shares authorized;	
30,000 shares issued and outstanding	$300,000
Share Premium—Ordinary	60,000
Retained earnings	65,000
Total shareholders' equity	$425,000

EXHIBIT 13.4

Shareholders' Equity for Shares Issued at a Premium

Issuing No-Par Value Shares

When a no-par share is issued and not assigned a stated value, the amount the corporation receives is recorded as Share Capital—Ordinary (If the corporation has only one type of shares, then the word "ordinary" may be omitted.) This means that the entire proceeds are credited to a no-par share account. To illustrate, a corporation records its October 20 issuance of 1,000 shares of no-par share for $40 cash per share as follows.

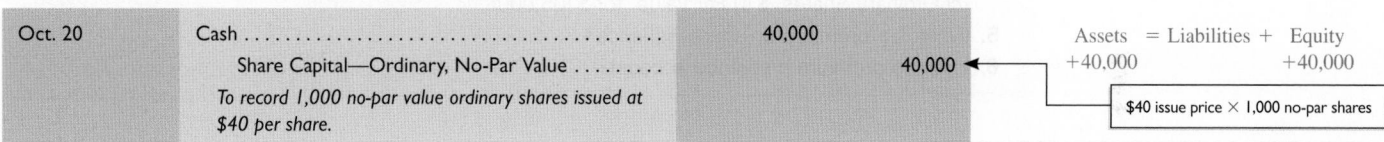

Oct. 20	Cash	40,000	
	Share Capital—Ordinary, No-Par Value		40,000
	To record 1,000 no-par value ordinary shares issued at $40 per share.		

Assets = Liabilities + Equity
+40,000   +40,000

$40 issue price × 1,000 no-par shares

Assuming that stated value shares are issued at an amount in excess of stated value (the usual case), the excess is credited to Share Premium—Ordinary, which is reported in the shareholders' equity section. To illustrate, a corporation that issues 1,000 shares of no-par ordinary shares having a stated value of $40 per share in return for $50 cash per share records this as follows.

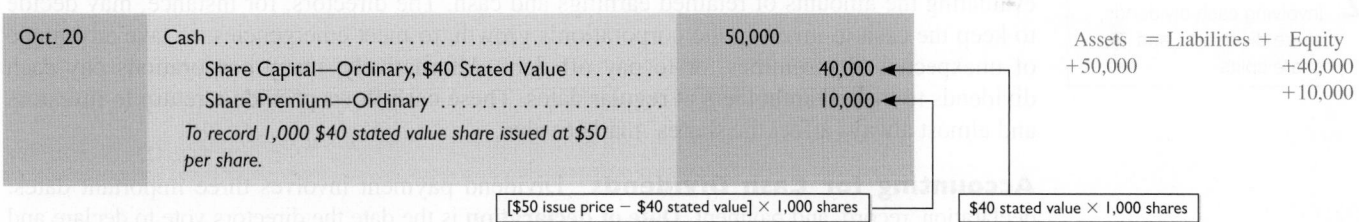

Oct. 20	Cash	50,000	
	Share Capital—Ordinary, $40 Stated Value		40,000
	Share Premium—Ordinary		10,000
	To record 1,000 $40 stated value share issued at $50 per share.		

Assets = Liabilities + Equity
+50,000   +40,000
                   +10,000

[$50 issue price − $40 stated value] × 1,000 shares

$40 stated value × 1,000 shares

Issuing Shares for Noncash Assets

A corporation can receive assets other than cash in exchange for its shares. (It can also assume liabilities on the assets received such as a mortgage on property received.) The corporation records the assets received at their market values as of the date of the transaction. The shares given in exchange is recorded at its par (or stated) value with any excess recorded in the Share Premium account. (If no-par shares are issued, the shares are recorded at the assets' market value.) To illustrate, the entry to record receipt of land valued at $105,000 in return for issuance of 4,000 shares of $20 par value ordinary shares on June 10 is

Point: Shares issued for noncash assets should be recorded at the market value of either the shares or the noncash asset, whichever is more clearly determinable.

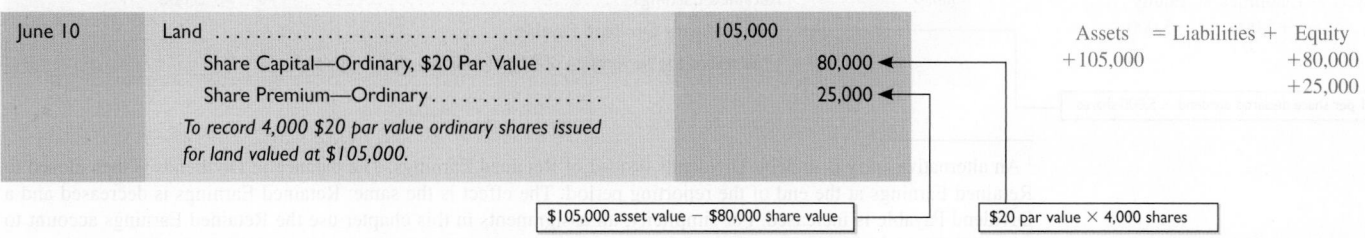

June 10	Land	105,000	
	Share Capital—Ordinary, $20 Par Value		80,000
	Share Premium—Ordinary		25,000
	To record 4,000 $20 par value ordinary shares issued for land valued at $105,000.		

Assets = Liabilities + Equity
+105,000   +80,000
                   +25,000

$105,000 asset value − $80,000 share value

$20 par value × 4,000 shares

A corporation sometimes gives shares to promoters in exchange for their services in organizing the corporation, which the corporation records as *Organization Expenses*. The entry to record receipt of services valued at $12,000 in organizing the corporation in return for 600 shares of $15 par value ordinary shares on June 5 is

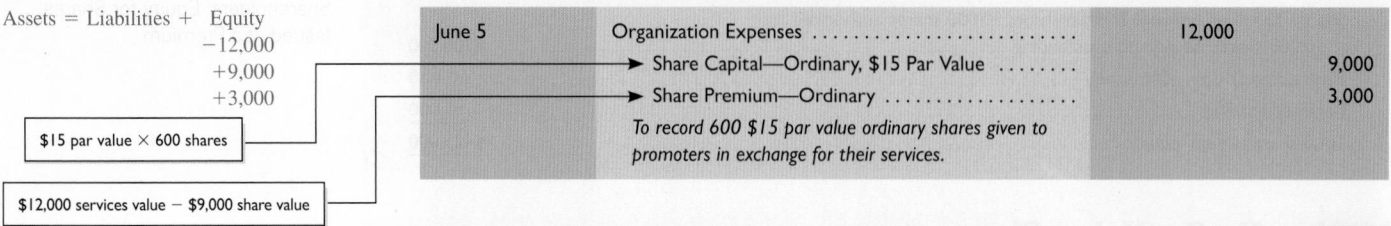

Assets = Liabilities + Equity
−12,000
+9,000
+3,000

$15 par value × 600 shares

$12,000 services value − $9,000 share value

June 5	Organization Expenses	12,000	
	Share Capital—Ordinary, $15 Par Value		9,000
	Share Premium—Ordinary		3,000
	To record 600 $15 par value ordinary shares given to promoters in exchange for their services.		

Quick Check

Answers — p. 518

4. A company issues 7,000 shares of its $10 par value ordinary shares in exchange for equipment valued at $105,000. The entry to record this transaction includes a credit to
   (*a*) Share Premium, Ordinary, for $35,000.
   (*b*) Retained Earnings for $35,000.
   (*c*) Ordinary Shares, $10 Par Value, for $105,000.
5. What is a premium on share issuance?
6. Is share premium a revenue account?

DIVIDENDS

This section describes both cash and share dividend transactions.

Cash Dividends

The decision to pay cash dividends rests with the board of directors and involves more than evaluating the amounts of retained earnings and cash. The directors, for instance, may decide to keep the cash to invest in the corporation's growth, to meet emergencies, to take advantage of unexpected opportunities, or to pay off debt. Alternatively, many corporations pay cash dividends to their shareholders at regular dates. These cash flows provide a return to investors and almost always affect the shares' market value.

Accounting for Cash Dividends Dividend payment involves three important dates: declaration, record, and payment. **Date of declaration** is the date the directors vote to declare and pay a dividend. This creates a legal liability of the corporation to its shareholders. **Date of record** is the future date specified by the directors for identifying those shareholders listed in the corporation's records to receive dividends. The date of record usually follows the date of declaration by at least two weeks. Persons who own shares on the date of record receive dividends. **Date of payment** is the date when the corporation makes payment; it follows the date of record by enough time to allow the corporation to arrange checks, money transfers, or other means to pay dividends.

To illustrate, the entry to record a January 9 declaration of a $1 per share cash dividend by the directors of Z-Tech, Inc., with 5,000 outstanding shares is

Date of Declaration

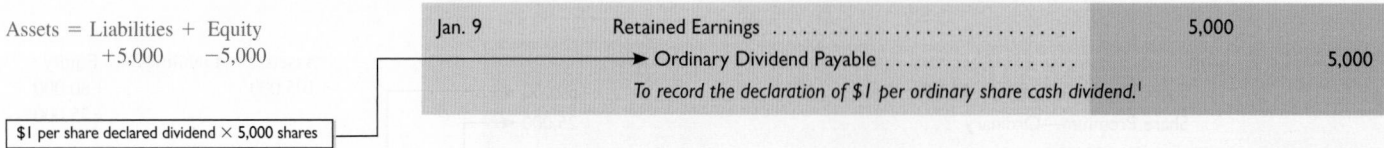

Assets = Liabilities + Equity
+5,000   −5,000

$1 per share declared dividend × 5,000 shares

Jan. 9	Retained Earnings	5,000	
	Ordinary Dividend Payable		5,000
	To record the declaration of $1 per ordinary share cash dividend.[1]		

---

[1] An alternative entry is to debit Dividends instead of Retained Earnings. The balance in Dividends is then closed to Retained Earnings at the end of the reporting period. The effect is the same: Retained Earnings is decreased and a Dividend Payable is increased. For simplicity, all assignments in this chapter use the Retained Earnings account to record dividend declarations.

Ordinary Dividend Payable is a current liability. The date of record for the Z-Tech dividend is January 22. *No formal journal entry is needed on the date of record*. The February 1 date of payment requires an entry to record both the settlement of the liability and the reduction of the cash balance, as follows:

Date of Payment

Feb. 1	Ordinary Dividend Payable	5,000	
	Cash		5,000
	To record the payment of $1 per ordinary share cash dividend.		

Assets = Liabilities + Equity
−5,000   −5,000

Quick Check
Answers — p. 518

7. What type of an account is the Ordinary Dividend Payable account?

8. What three crucial dates are involved in the process of paying a cash dividend?

9. When does a dividend become a company's legal obligation?

Ordinary shares may be issued, or the number of ordinary shares outstanding may be reduced, without a corresponding change in resources. The common ways to do this is through a bonus issue (also called a **share dividend**), or a share split.

Bonus Issue

A **bonus issue,** declared by a corporation's directors, is a distribution of additional shares of the corporation's own shares to its shareholders without the receipt of any payment in return. Therefore, the number of ordinary shares outstanding is increased without an increase in resources. The number of ordinary shares outstanding before the event is adjusted for the proportionate change in the number of ordinary shares outstanding as if the event had occurred at the beginning of the earliest period presented. For example, on a two-for-one bonus issue, the number of ordinary shares outstanding before the issue is multiplied by three to obtain the new total number of ordinary shares, or by two to obtain the number of additional ordinary shares. Bonus issue and cash dividends are different. A bonus issue does not reduce assets and equity but instead transfers a portion of equity from retained earnings to share capital.

Reasons for Bonus Issue   A bonus issue exists for at least two reasons. First, directors are said to use a bonus issue to keep the market price of the shares affordable. For example, if a corporation continues to earn profit but does not issue cash dividends, the price of its ordinary shares likely increases. The share price may become so high that it discourages some investors from buying the shares (especially in lots of 100 and 1,000 shares which are the common sizes on stock exchanges). When a corporation has a bonus issue, it increases the number of outstanding shares and lowers the share price. Another reason for a bonus issue is to provide evidence of management's confidence that the company is doing well and will continue to do well.

Accounting for Bonus Issue   IAS 33 Earnings per Share describes a bonus issue as "a capitalization." This suggests transferring a portion of equity from retained earnings to share capital. The journal entry should be to debit Retained Earnings and to credit Share Capital. The new shares are issued at a price to be decided by a director's resolution. This price is likely to be made with reference to a market price, if available.

Assume that Orient Ltd declared on December 31, 2014, a one-for-five (20%) bonus issue; the number of shares in issue before the bonus issue was 100,000 shares, no-par value. The bonus issue of 20,000 shares computed as 20% of its original 100,000 shares, is to be distributed on January 20, 2015 to the shareholders on record on January 15, 2015. Given that the share price of Orient Ltd on December 31, 2014 is $1.50 per share, this bonus issue is recorded as follows.

Dec. 31	Retained Earnings	30,000	
	Ordinary Share Dividend Distributable		30,000
	To record the declaration of a 20% bonus issue or 20,000 shares.		

No entry is made on the date of record for a bonus issue. On January 20, 2015, the date of payment, Orient Ltd distributes the new shares to shareholders and records this entry:

Jan. 20	Ordinary Share Dividend Distributable	30,000	
	Share Capital—Ordinary		30,000
	To record the issuance of bonus shares.		

The combined effect of these journal entries is to transfer (or capitalize) $30,000 of retained earnings to share capital accounts. The amount of capitalized retained earnings equals the market value of the 20,000 issued shares ($30,000). A bonus issue has no effect on the ownership percent of individual shareholders.

Share Splits

A **share split** is the distribution of additional shares to shareholders according to their percent ownership. When a share split occurs, the corporation "calls in" its outstanding shares and issues more than one new share in exchange for each old share. Splits can be done in any ratio, including 2-for-1, 3-for-1, or higher. Share splits reduce the par or stated value (if applicable) per share. The reasons for share splits are similar to those for bonus issues. To illustrate, CompTec has 100,000 outstanding shares of $20 par value ordinary shares with a current market value of $88 per share. A 2-for-1 share split cuts par value in half as it replaces 100,000 shares of $20 par value shares with 200,000 shares of $10 par value shares. Market value is reduced from $88 per share to about $44 per share. The split does not affect any equity amounts reported on the statement of financial position or any individual shareholder's percent ownership. Both the Share Capital and Retained Earnings accounts are unchanged by a split, and *no journal entry is made*. The only effect on the accounts is a change in the share account description. CompTec's 2-for-1 split on its $20 par value shares means that after the split, it changes its share account title to Share Capital—Ordinary, $10 Par Value. This share's description on the statement of financial position also changes to reflect the additional authorized, issued, and outstanding shares and the new par value. The difference between share splits and bonus issue is often blurred.

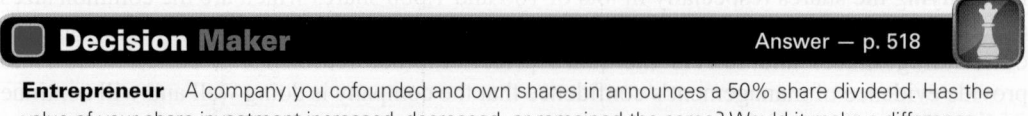

Decision Maker   Answer — p. 518

Entrepreneur   A company you cofounded and own shares in announces a 50% share dividend. Has the value of your share investment increased, decreased, or remained the same? Would it make a difference if it was a 3-for-2 share split? ■

Quick Check   Answers — p. 518

10. How does a share dividend impact assets and retained earnings?

11. What distinguishes a cash dividend from a bonus issue or share dividend?

12. Explain how a bonus issue or share dividend "capitalizes" retained earnings.

PREFERENCE SHARES

A corporation can issue two basic kinds of shares, ordinary and preference. **Preference shares** have special rights that give them priority (or senior status) over ordinary shares in one or more areas. Special rights typically include a preference for receiving dividends and for the distribution of assets if the corporation is liquidated. Preference shares carries all rights of ordinary shares unless the corporate registration nullifies them. Most preference shares, for instance, does not confer the right to vote.

C2 Explain characteristics of, and distribute dividends between, ordinary and preference shares.

Issuance of Preference Shares

Preference shares usually have a par value. Like ordinary shares, it can be sold at a price different from par. Preference shares are recorded in their own separate capital accounts. To illustrate, if Dillon Snowboards issues 50 shares of $100 par value preference shares for $6,000 cash on July 1, 2015, the entry is

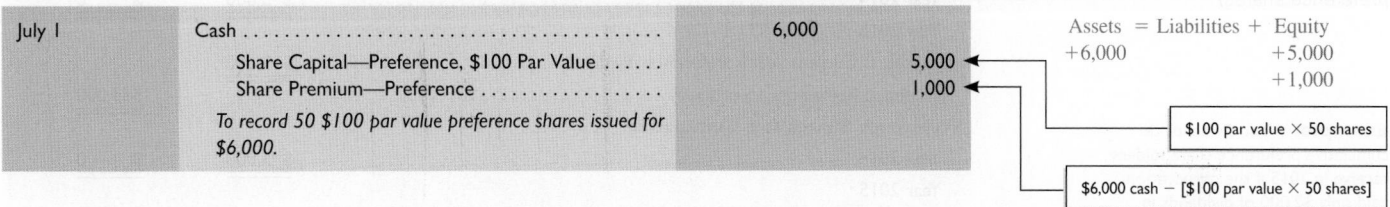

July 1	Cash	6,000	
	Share Capital—Preference, $100 Par Value		5,000
	Share Premium—Preference		1,000
	To record 50 $100 par value preference shares issued for $6,000.		

Assets = Liabilities + Equity
+6,000   +5,000
                            +1,000

$100 par value × 50 shares

$6,000 cash − [$100 par value × 50 shares]

The equity section of the year-end statement of financial position for Dillon Snowboards, including preference shares, is shown in Exhibit 13.5. (This exhibit assumes that ordinary shares was issued at par.) Issuing no-par preference shares is similar to issuing no-par ordinary shares. Also, the entries for issuing preference shares for noncash assets are similar to those for ordinary shares.

Shareholders' Equity	
Share Capital—Ordinary, $10 par value; 50,000 shares authorized;	
30,000 shares issued and outstanding	$300,000
Share Capital—Preference, $100 par value; 1,000 shares authorized;	
50 shares issued and outstanding	5,000
Share Premium—Preference	1,000
Retained earnings	65,000
Total shareholders' equity	$371,000

EXHIBIT 13.5

Shareholders' Equity with Ordinary and Preference Shares

Dividends of Preference Shares

Preference shares usually carry a preference for dividends, meaning that preference shareholders are allocated their dividends before any dividends are allocated to ordinary shareholders. The dividends allocated to preference shareholders are usually expressed as a dollar amount per share or a percent applied to par value. A preference for dividends does *not* ensure dividends. If the directors do not declare a dividend, neither the preference nor the ordinary shareholders receive one.

Cumulative or Noncumulative Dividend Most preference shares carry a cumulative dividend right. **Cumulative preference shares** have a right to be paid both the current and all prior periods' unpaid dividends before any dividend is paid to ordinary shareholders. When preference shares are cumulative and the directors either do not declare a dividend to preference shareholders or declare one that does not cover the total amount of cumulative dividend, the unpaid dividend amount is called **dividend in arrears**. Accumulation of dividends in arrears on cumulative preference shares does not guarantee they will be paid. **Noncumulative preference shares** confer no right to prior periods' unpaid dividends if they were not declared in those prior periods.

Point: "Preference" does not imply that preference shareholders receive more dividends than ordinary shareholders, nor does it guarantee a dividend.

To illustrate the difference between cumulative and noncumulative preference shares, assume that a corporation's outstanding shares include (1) 1,000 shares of $100 par, 9% preference shares—yielding $9,000 per year in potential dividends, and (2) 4,000 shares of $50 par value ordinary shares. During 2014, the first year of operations, the directors declare cash dividends of $5,000. In year 2015, they declare cash dividends of $42,000. See Exhibit 13.6 for the allocation of dividends for these two years. Allocation of year 2015 dividends depends on whether the preference shares are noncumulative or cumulative. With noncumulative preference, the preference shareholders never receive the $4,000 skipped in 2014. If the preference shares are cumulative, the $4,000 in arrears is paid in 2015 before any other dividends are paid.

EXHIBIT 13.6

Allocation of Dividends (noncumulative vs. cumulative preference shares)

Example: What dividends do cumulative preference shareholders receive in 2015 if the corporation paid only $2,000 of dividends in 2014? How does this affect dividends to ordinary shareholders in 2015? *Answers:* $16,000 ($7,000 dividends in arrears, plus $9,000 current preference dividends). Dividends to ordinary shareholders decrease to $26,000.

	Preference	Ordinary
Preference Shares Are Noncumulative		
Year 2014	$ 5,000	$ 0
Year 2015		
Step 1: Current year's preference dividend	$ 9,000	
Step 2: Remainder to ordinary		$33,000
Preference Shares Are Cumulative		
Year 2014	$ 5,000	$ 0
Year 2015		
Step 1: Dividend in arrears	$ 4,000	
Step 2: Current year's preference dividend	9,000	
Step 3: Remainder to ordinary		$29,000
Totals for year 2015	$13,000	$29,000

A liability for a dividend does not exist until the directors declare a dividend. If a preference dividend date passes and the corporation's board fails to declare the dividend on its cumulative preference shares, the dividend in arrears is not a liability. The *full-disclosure principle* requires a corporation to report (usually in a note) the amount of preference dividends in arrears as at the statement of financial position date.

Participating or Nonparticipating Dividend   **Nonparticipating preference shares** have a feature that limits dividends to a maximum amount each year. This maximum is often stated as a percent of the share's par value or as a specific dollar amount per share. Once preference shareholders receive this amount, the ordinary shareholders receive any and all additional dividends. **Participating preference shares** have a feature allowing preference shareholders to share with ordinary shareholders in any dividends paid in excess of the percent or dollar amount stated on the preference shares. This participation feature does not apply until ordinary shareholders receive dividends equal to the preference shares' dividend percent. Many corporations are authorized to issue participating preference shares but rarely do, and most managers never expect to issue it.[2]

---

[2] Participating preference shares are usually authorized as a defense against a possible corporate *takeover* by an "unfriendly" investor (or a group of investors) who intends to buy enough voting ordinary shares to gain control. Taking a term from spy novels, the financial world refers to this type of plan as a *poison pill* that a company swallows if enemy investors threaten its capture. A poison pill usually works as follows: A corporation's ordinary shareholders on a given date are granted the right to purchase a large amount of participating preference shares at a very low price. This right to purchase preference shares is *not* transferable. If an unfriendly investor buys a large block of ordinary shares (whose right to purchase participating preference shares does *not* transfer to this buyer), the board can issue preference shares at a low price to the remaining ordinary shareholders who retained the right to purchase. Future dividends are then divided between the newly issued participating preference shares and the ordinary shares. This usually transfers value from ordinary shares to preference shares, causing the unfriendly investor's ordinary shares to lose much of its value and reduces the potential benefit of a hostile takeover.

Convertible Preference Shares

Preference shares are more attractive to investors if these shares carry a right to exchange preference shares for a fixed number of ordinary shares. **Convertible preference shares** give holders the option to exchange their preference shares for ordinary shares at a specified rate. When a company prospers and its ordinary shares increase in value, convertible preference shareholders can share in this success by converting their preference shares into more valuable ordinary shares.

Callable Preference Shares

Callable preference shares give the issuing corporation the right to purchase (retire) these shares from the holders at specified future prices and dates. The amount paid to call and retire a preference share is its **call price**, or *redemption value*, and is set when the shares are issued. The call price normally includes the share's par value plus a premium giving holders additional return on their investment. When the issuing corporation calls and retires preference shares, the terms of the agreement often require it to pay the call price *and* any dividends in arrears.

Point: The issuing corporation has the right, or option, to retire its callable preference shares.

Classification of Preference Shares

IAS 32 Financial Instruments: Presentation requires that preference shares be classified as debt or equity based on analysis of the shares' contractual terms. For example, when preference shares are nonredeemable, the appropriate classification is determined by the other rights that attach to them. Classification is based on an assessment of the substance of the contractual arrangements and the definitions of a financial liability and an equity instrument. When distributions to holders of the preference shares, whether cumulative or noncumulative, are at the discretion of the issuer, the shares are equity instruments.

Reasons for Issuing Preference Shares

Corporations issue preference shares for several reasons. One is to raise capital without sacrificing control. For example, suppose a company's organizers have $100,000 cash to invest and organize a corporation that needs $200,000 of capital to start. If they sell $200,000 worth of ordinary shares (with $100,000 to the organizers), they would have only 50% control and would need to negotiate extensively with other shareholders in making policy. However, if they issue $100,000 worth of ordinary shares to themselves and sell outsiders $100,000 of 8%, cumulative preference shares with no voting rights, they retain control.

A second reason to issue preference shares is to boost the return earned by ordinary shareholders. To illustrate, suppose a corporation's organizers expect to earn an annual after-tax profit of $24,000 on an investment of $200,000. If they sell and issue $200,000 worth of ordinary shares, the $24,000 income produces a 12% return on the $200,000 of ordinary shareholders' equity. However, if they issue $100,000 of 8% preference shares to outsiders and $100,000 of ordinary shares to themselves, their own return increases to 16% per year, as shown in Exhibit 13.7.

Net (after-tax) profit	$24,000
Less preference dividends at 8%	(8,000)
Balance to ordinary shareholders	$16,000
Return to ordinary shareholders ($16,000/$100,000)	16%

EXHIBIT 13.7

Return to Ordinary Shareholders When Preference Shares Are Issued

Ordinary shareholders earn 16% instead of 12% because assets contributed by preferred shareholders are invested to earn $12,000 while the preference dividend is only $8,000. Use of preference shares to increase return to ordinary shareholders is an example of **financial leverage** (also called *trading on the equity*). As a general rule, when the dividend rate on preference

Point: Financial leverage also occurs when debt is issued and the interest rate paid on it is less than the rate earned from using the assets the creditors lend the company.

shares is less than the rate the corporation earns on its assets, the effect of issuing preference shares is to increase (or *lever*) the rate earned by ordinary shareholders.

Other reasons for issuing preference shares include its appeal to some investors who believe that the corporation's ordinary shares are too risky or that the expected return on ordinary shares is too low.

Decision Maker   Answer — p. 518

Concert Organizer   Assume that you alter your business strategy from organizing concerts targeted at under 1,000 people to those targeted at between 5,000 to 20,000 people. You also incorporate because of increased risk of lawsuits and a desire to issue shares for financing. It is important that you control the company for decisions on whom to schedule. What types of shares do you offer? ∎

Quick Check   Answers — p. 519

13. In what ways does preference shares often have priority over ordinary shares?

14. Increasing the return to ordinary shareholders by issuing preference shares is an example of (*a*) Financial leverage. (*b*) Cumulative earnings. (*c*) Dividend in arrears.

15. A corporation has issued an outstanding (i) 9,000 shares of $50 par value, 10% cumulative, nonparticipating preference shares and (ii) 27,000 shares of $10 par value ordinary shares. No dividends have been declared for the two prior years. During the current year, the corporation declares $288,000 in dividends. The amount paid to ordinary shareholders is (*a*) $243,000. (*b*) $153,000. (*c*) $135,000.

TREASURY SHARES

P3 Record purchases and sales of treasury shares and the retirement of shares.

Corporations acquire their own shares for several reasons: (1) to use their shares to acquire another corporation, (2) to purchase shares to avoid a hostile takeover of the company, (3) to reissue them to employees as compensation, and (4) to maintain a strong market for their shares or to show management confidence in the current price.

A corporation's reacquired shares are called **treasury shares**, which is similar to unissued shares in several ways: (1) neither treasury shares nor unissued shares are assets, (2) neither receive cash dividends, and (3) neither allow the exercise of voting rights. When a corporation has treasury shares, it is important to distinguish between issued shares and outstanding shares. Assume that ABC Ltd had 100,000 issued shares. It then repurchased 10,000 shares as treasury shares (par value $1) at $1.50 per share and cancelled the shares. The number of outstanding shares is 90,000 (100,000 issued shares minus 10,000 treasury shares), and this is the number used in the computation of ratios such as the book value per share, and basic earnings per share.

No gain or loss is recognized in profit or loss on the purchase, sale, issue, or cancellation of a corporation's own shares.

Purchasing Treasury Shares

Purchasing treasury shares reduces the corporation's assets and equity by equal amounts. (We describe the *cost method* of accounting for treasury shares, which is the most widely used method.) To illustrate, Exhibit 13.8 shows Cyber Corporation's account balances *before* any treasury share purchase.

Assets		Shareholders' Equity	
Cash	$ 30,000	Share capital, ordinary no-par, 10,000 shares	
Other assets	95,000	issued and outstanding	$100,000
		Retained earnings	25,000
Total assets	$125,000	Total shareholders' equity	$125,000

EXHIBIT 13.8

Account Balances *before* Purchasing Treasury Shares

Cyber then purchases 1,000 of its own shares for $11,500 on May 1, which is recorded as follows.

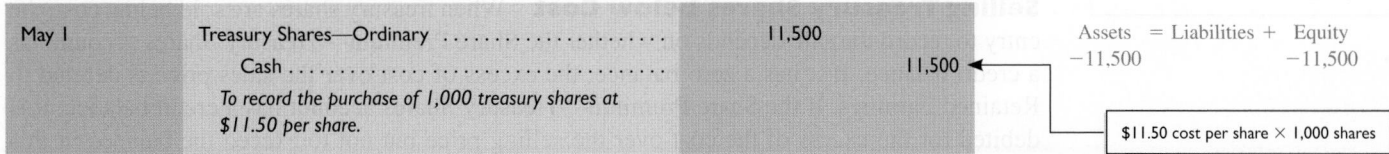

May 1	Treasury Shares—Ordinary	11,500	
	Cash		11,500
	To record the purchase of 1,000 treasury shares at *$11.50 per share.*		

Assets = Liabilities + Equity
−11,500   −11,500

$11.50 cost per share × 1,000 shares

This entry reduces equity through the debit to the Treasury Share account, which is a *contra equity account*. Exhibit 13.9 shows account balances *after* this transaction.

Assets		Shareholders' Equity	
Cash	$ 18,500	Share capital, ordinary no-par; 10,000 shares	
Other assets	95,000	issued and outstanding	$100,000
		Retained earnings	25,000
		Less cost of treasury shares	**(11,500)**
Total assets	$113,500	Total shareholders' equity	$113,500

EXHIBIT 13.9

Account Balances *after* Purchasing Treasury Shares

The treasury share purchase reduces Cyber's cash, total assets, and total equity by $11,500 but does not reduce the balance of either the Share Capital or the Retained Earnings account. The equity reduction is reported by deducting the cost of treasury shares in the equity section. While the company holds the treasury shares, there is no need to recognize changes in fair value, because treasury shares are not considered investments or financial assets.

Reissuing Treasury Shares

Treasury shares can be reissued by selling it at cost, above cost, or below cost.

Selling Treasury Shares at Cost If treasury shares are reissued at cost, the entry is the reverse of the one made to record the purchase. For instance, if on May 21 Cyber reissues 100 of the treasury shares purchased on May 1 at the same $11.50 per share cost, the entry is

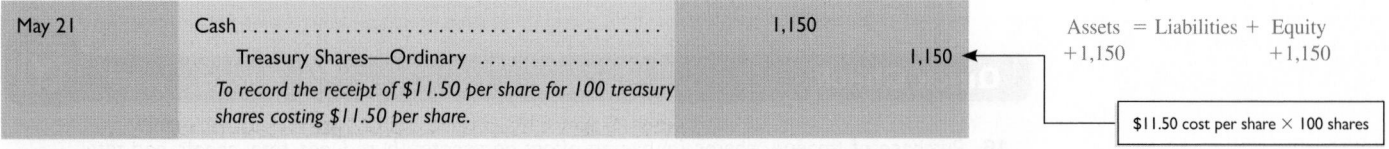

May 21	Cash	1,150	
	Treasury Shares—Ordinary		1,150
	To record the receipt of $11.50 per share for 100 treasury *shares costing $11.50 per share.*		

Assets = Liabilities + Equity
+1,150   +1,150

$11.50 cost per share × 100 shares

Selling Treasury Shares above Cost Since no gain or loss can be recognized in profit or loss on the sale of a corporation's own shares, if treasury shares are sold for more than cost, the amount received in excess of cost must be credited to another capital account: the Share Premium—Treasury Shares account. It is logical to use a separate capital account to record any gain or loss from treasury share transactions. To illustrate, if Cyber receives $12 cash per share for 400 treasury shares costing $11.50 per share on June 3, the entry is

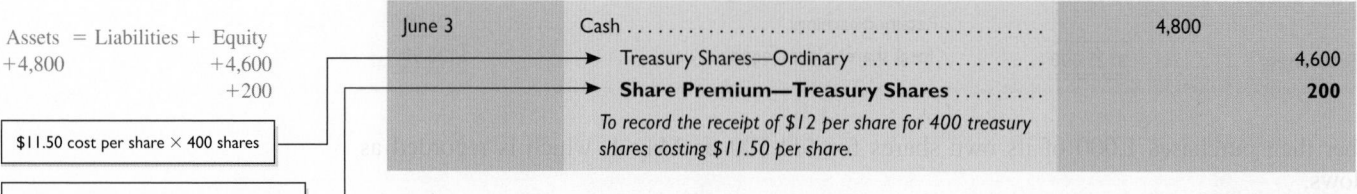

Assets = Liabilities + Equity
+4,800   +4,600
                          +200

$11.50 cost per share × 400 shares

[$12 issue price − $11.50 cost per share] × 400 shares

Selling Treasury Shares below Cost   When treasury shares are sold below cost, the entry to record the sale depends on whether the Share Premium—Treasury Shares account has a credit balance. If it has a zero balance, the excess of cost over the sales price is debited to Retained Earnings. If the Share Premium—Treasury Shares account has a credit balance, it is debited for the excess of the cost over the selling price but not to exceed the balance in this account. When the credit balance in this premium account is eliminated, any remaining difference between the cost and selling price is debited to Retained Earnings. To illustrate, if Cyber sells its remaining 500 shares of treasury shares at $10 per share on July 10, equity is reduced by $750 (500 shares × $1.50 per share excess of cost over selling price), as shown in this entry:

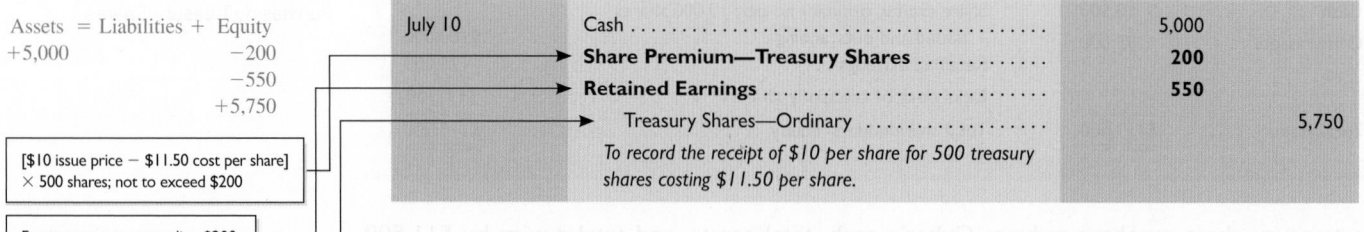

Assets = Liabilities + Equity
+5,000   −200
                          −550
                          +5,750

[$10 issue price − $11.50 cost per share] × 500 shares; not to exceed $200

For any amount exceeding $200

$11.50 cost per share × 500 shares

This entry eliminates the $200 credit balance in the Share Premium—Treasury Shares account created on June 3 and then reduces the Retained Earnings balance by the remaining $550 excess of cost over selling price. A company never reports a loss (or gain) from the sale of treasury shares. Note that in all the sale transactions, we credit the account Treasury Shares at cost.

Cancelling or Retiring Shares

Point: Amendments to **IAS 1** effective July 1, 2012 changes title for "Statement of Comprehensive Income" to "Statement of Profit and Loss and Other Comprehensive Income." However, an entity may use other titles for the statements.

A corporation can purchase its own shares and cancel or retire them. No gain or loss is recognized in profit or loss on the cancellation. Cancelling shares reduces the number of issued shares. When shares are purchased for cancellation, we remove all capital amounts related to the cancelled shares. Corporations will probably explicitly specify whether the repurchase and cancellation is made out of capital or retained earnings, or a mixture of both, and so the debit is to share capital and/or retained earnings as appropriate.

Quick Check   Answers — p. 519

16. Purchase of treasury shares (a) has no effect on assets; (b) reduces total assets and total equity by equal amounts; or (c) is recorded with a debit to Retained Earnings.
17. Southern Co. purchases shares of Northern Corp. Should either company classify these shares as treasury shares?
18. How does treasury shares affect the issued and outstanding shares?
19. When a company sells treasury shares, (a) there can be a gain or loss; (b) these shares are cancelled; or (c) outstanding shares are increased.

REPORTING OF INCOME AND EQUITY

Exhibits 13.10 shows typical layouts for a single statement of profit or loss and other comprehensive income and a statement of changes in equity and their links.

C3 Explain the items reported in comprehensive income and equity.

EXHIBIT 13.10

Statement of Profit or Loss and Other Comprehensive Income and Statement of Changes in Equity with Their Links

IFRS Corp Statement of Profit or Loss and Other Comprehensive Income For Year Ended December 31, 2015		
Revenue		$ 198,000
Cost of goods sold		(100,000)
Gross profit		98,000
Other income		10,000
Selling expenses		(30,000)
Administrative expenses		(25,000)
Other expenses		(14,500)
Interest expense		(12,500)
Profit before tax		26,000
Income tax expense		(6,000)
Net profit		20,000
Other comprehensive income		
Revaluation surplus on property, plant and equipment	$40,000	
Foreign currency translation differences	8,000	
Other comprehensive income for year, net of tax		48,000
Total comprehensive income for the year		$ 68,000

IFRS Corp Statement of Changes in Equity For Year Ended December 31, 2015				
	Share Capital	Retained Earnings	Reserves	Total Equity
Balance as at December 31, 2014	$1,000,000	$570,000	–	$1,570,000
Changes in accounting policy or correction of prior period error	–	1,000	–	1,000
Restated balance	1,000,000	571,000	–	1,571,000
Net profit	–	20,000	–	20,000
Other comprehensive income	–	–	48,000	48,000
Issuance of shares	200,000	–	–	200,000
Purchase of treasury shares	–	–	(150,000)	(150,000)
Dividends	–	(10,000)	–	(10,000)
Balance as at December 31, 2015	$1,200,000	$581,000	$(102,000)	$1,679,000

Statement of Profit or Loss and Other Comprehensive Income

The corporation must present a **statement of profit or loss and other comprehensive income**, which is intended to show all nonowner changes in equity and other comprehensive income. A corporation may use other titles such as "statement of comprehensive income." This statement can be shown as a single statement or presented as two statements: (1) an income statement (or statement of profit or loss) that presents revenues and expenses recognized in the calculation of profit or loss, and (2) a statement of profit or loss and other comprehensive income, which

Point: According to the business entity assumption, a corporation (the parent) which controls one or more other companies (*subsidiaries*) must present consolidated financial statements. Noncontrolling interest refers to the equity in a subsidiary not attributable, directly or indirectly, to a parent. The statements must allocate profit or loss and other comprehensive income for the period attributable to: (i) noncontrolling interests, and (ii) owners of the parent (shareholders).

begins with the profit or loss from the income statement and then lists other items of income and expense to show total comprehensive income. These other items of income and expense (that are not recognized in profit or loss or permitted by **IFRS**) include:

- Exchange differences on translating foreign operations.
- Gains and losses from investments in equity instruments measured at fair value through other comprehensive income.
- For particular liabilities designated as at fair value through profit or loss, the amount of the change in fair value that is attributable to changes in the liability's credit risk.
- Effective portion of gains and losses on hedging instruments in cash flow hedges.
- Changes in revaluation surplus.
- Remeasurements of defined benefit pension plans.

In **Nestlé**'s case, it chose to show the statement of profit or loss and other comprehensive income as two separate statements in its 2013 annual report (Appendix A). It titles them as income statement and statement of comprehensive income, and these statements are reproduced as Exhibit 13.11 and Exhibit 13.12 respectively.

EXHIBIT 13.11

Nestlé's Income Statement

Consolidated Income Statement for the Year Ended 31 December 2013

In millions of CHF	Notes	2013
Sales	3	**92 158**
Other revenue		215
Cost of goods sold		(48 111)
Distribution expenses		(8 156)
Marketing and administration expenses		(19 711)
Research and development costs		(1 503)
Other trading income	4	120
Other trading expenses	4	(965)
Trading operating profit	3	**14 047**
Other operating income	4	616
Other operating expenses	4	(1 595)
Operating profit		**13 068**
Financial income	5	219
Financial expense	5	(850)
Profit before taxes, associates and joint ventures		**12 437**
Taxes	15	(3 256)
Share of results of associates and joint ventures	16	1 264
Profit for the year		**10 445**
of which attributable to non-controlling interests		430
of which attributable to shareholders of the parent (Net profit)		10 015

The top line of the income statement shows sales or revenue, which must be recorded in accordance with the revenue recognition principle. Cost of goods sold would be the major operating expense for a manufacturing or merchandizing company such as **Nestlé**. After considering all other operating income and expenses, we arrive at operating profit, which would often be used by financial analysts to predict the company's future operating performance. Financial income and financial expense (or interest income and interest expense) are shown separately before we arrive at profit before tax. Profit for the year after tax of which attributable to shareholders of the parent is the bottom line or net profit for the corporation.

Nestlé's statement of comprehensive income begins with the profit or loss from the income statement and then lists other items of income and expense to show total comprehensive income. There may be reclassification adjustments, which are amounts reclassified to profit or loss in the current period that were recognized in other comprehensive income in the current or previous periods.

EXHIBIT 13.12

Nestlé's Statement of Comprehensive Income

Consolidated Statement of Comprehensive Income for the Year Ended 31 December 2013

In millions of CHF	Notes	2013
Profit for the year recognised in the income statement		10 445
Currency retranslations		
– Recognised in translation reserve		(3 160)
– Reclassified from translation reserve to income statement		214
Fair value adjustments on available-for-sale financial instruments		
– Recognised in fair value reserve		9
– Reclassified from fair value reserve to income statement		(532)
Fair value adjustments on cash flow hedges		
– Recognised in hedging reserve		161
– Reclassified from hedging reserve		85
Taxes	15	290
Share of other comprehensive income of associates and joint ventures	16	40
Items that are or may be reclassified subsequently to the income statement		(2 893)
Remeasurement of defined benefit plans	11	1 632
Taxes	15	(848)
Share of other comprehensive income of associates and joint ventures	16	47
Items that will never be reclassified to the income statement		831
Other comprehensive income for the year	19	(2 062)
Total comprehensive income for the year		8 383
of which attributable to non-controlling interests		371
of which attributable to shareholders of the parent		8 012

Statement of Changes in Equity

The corporation must present a statement of changes in equity, which is intended to show all owner changes in equity and dividends. Dividends to shareholders must not be shown in the income statement or in the statement of profit or loss and other comprehensive income; they belong in the statement of changes in equity. This statement includes the total amount of comprehensive income, but its main purpose is to show the amounts of transactions with shareholders (e.g., issuances of shares and distributions of dividends) and to provide a reconciliation of the opening and closing balances of each class of equity and each type of reserve. The statement of changes in equity also shows the effects of any changes in accounting policies and correction of prior period errors. The minimum headings are share capital, retained earnings, and reserves, although corporations can have more headings depending on their business transactions and events.

Changes in Accounting Policies and Correction of Prior Period Errors   Such adjustments are handled retrospectively by adjusting the beginning balance of retained earnings. A change in accounting policy means that the corporation changes from one accounting principle or method to another. For example, the corporation adopts a new mandatory accounting standard, or voluntarily changes its inventory costing method. An error may be caused by a transaction being recorded incorrectly or not at all, a mathematical mistake, an inaccurate physical count of inventory, or failure to record an adjusting entry.

Correction of prior period errors are different from changes in estimates. Many items reported in financial statements are based on estimates. Future events may reveal that some of these estimates were inaccurate even when based on the best data available at the time. These inaccuracies are not considered errors and are not reported as prior period adjustments. Instead, they are identified as **changes in accounting estimates** and are accounted for in current and future periods. To illustrate, we know that depreciation is based on estimated useful lives and residual values. As time passes and new information becomes available, managers may need to change these estimates and the resulting depreciation expense for current and future periods.

Retained Earnings   Retained earnings generally consist of a company's cumulative net profit less any net losses and dividends declared since its inception. Some companies labeled retained earnings as revenue reserves. Retained earnings are part of shareholders' claims on the company's net assets, but this does *not* imply that a certain amount of cash or other assets is available to pay shareholders. For example, **Nestlé** has CHF 85,260 million in retained earnings and other reserves as at December 31, 2013, but only CHF 6,415 million in cash and cash equivalents as at December 31, 2013 (consolidated balance sheet in Appendix A).

Reserves   Most **reserves** result from accounting standards to reflect certain measurement changes in equity rather than the income statement: for example, asset revaluation surplus or reserve, foreign currency translation reserve, and other statutory reserves. Some companies may show share premium (for shares issued above par or stated value) as a separate column, or include it in reserves. For example, **Puma** states in its notes that its capital reserve includes the premium from the issuing of shares; **Nestlé** also states that its retained earnings and other reserves include share premium.

Nestlé's statement of changes in equity (from Appendix A) is reproduced as Exhibit 13.13.

EXHIBIT 13.13

Nestlé's Statement of Changes in Equity

Consolidated Statement of Changes in Equity for the Year Ended 31 December 2013

In millions of CHF

	Share capital	Treasury shares	Translation reserve	Retained earnings and other reserves	Total equity attributable to shareholders of the parent	Non-controlling interests	Total equity
Equity as at 31 December 2011 as originally published	330	(6 722)	(16 927)	80 116	56 797	1 477	58 274
First application of IAS 19 revised				68	68	—	68
Equity restated as at 1 January 2012	330	(6 722)	(16 927)	80 184	56 865	1 477	58 342
Profit for the year[b]	—	—	—	10 228	10 228	449	10 677
Other comprehensive income for the year[a]	—	—	(997)	(202)	(1 199)	(56)	(1 255)
Total comprehensive income for the year[a]	—	—	(997)	10 026	9 029	393	(9 422)
Dividend paid to shareholders of the parent	—	—	—	(6 213)	(6 213)	—	(6 213)
Dividends paid to non-controlling interests	—	—	—			(204)	(204)
Movement of treasury shares[b]	—	501	—	599	1 100	—	1 100
Equity compensation plans	—	212	—	(39)	173	—	173
Changes in non-controlling interests	—	—	—	(94)	(94)	(9)	(103)
Reduction in share capital	(8)	3 931	—	(3 923)	—	—	—
Total transactions with owners	(8)	4 644	—	(9 670)	(5 034)	(213)	(5 247)
Other movements[c]	—	—	—	147	147	—	147
Equity restated as at 31 December 2012[a]	322	(2 078)	(17 924)	80 687	61 007	1 657	62 664
Profit for the year	—	—	—	10 015	(10 015)	430	10 445
Other comprehensive income for the year	—	—	(2 887)	884	(2 003)	(59)	(2 062)
Other comprehensive income for the year	—	—	(2 887)	10 899	8 012	371	8 383
Dividend paid to shareholders of the parent	—	—	—	(6 552)	(6 552)	—	(6 552)
Dividends paid to non-controlling interests	—	—	—		—	(328)	(328)
Movement of treasury shares	—	(612)	—	190	(422)	—	(422)
Equity compensation plans	—	214	—	(39)	175	—	175
Other transactions settled with treasury shares[d]	—	280	—	—	280	—	280
Changes in non-controlling interests	—	—	—	(297)	(297)	(136)	(433)
Total transactions with owners	—	(118)	—	(6 698)	(6 816)	(464)	(7 280)
Other movements[c]	—	—	—	372	372	—	372
Equity as at 31 December 2013	322	(2 196)	(20 811)	85 260	62 575	1 564	64 139

Nestlé's statement of changes in equity shows separate columns for share capital, treasury shares, translation reserve, retained earnings, and other reserves (including share premium). As required by **IAS 1**, it shows separately the total amounts attributable to shareholders of the parent and to noncontrolling interests.

Earnings per Share, Price-Earnings Ratio, Dividend Yield, and Book Value per Share    **Decision Analysis**

Earnings per Share

The income statement reports **earnings per share**, also called *EPS* or *net profit per share*, which is the amount of profit earned per each share of a company's outstanding ordinary shares. The **basic earnings per share** formula is shown in Exhibit 13.14. When a company has no preference shares, then preference dividends are zero. The weighted-average ordinary shares outstanding is measured over the income reporting period; its computation is explained in advanced courses.

$$\text{Basic earnings per share} = \frac{\text{Net profit} - \text{Preference dividends}}{\text{Weighted-average ordinary shares outstanding}}$$

A1 Compute earnings per share and describe its use.

EXHIBIT 13.14
Basic Earnings per Share

To illustrate, assume that Quantum Co. earns $40,000 net profit in 2015 and declares dividends of $7,500 on its noncumulative preference shares. (If preference shares are *non*cumulative, the profit available [numerator] is the current period net profit less any preference dividends *declared* in that same period. If preference shares are cumulative, the profit available [numerator] is the current period net profit less the preference dividends whether declared or not.) Quantum has 5,000 weighted-average ordinary shares outstanding during 2015. Its basic EPS[3] is

Point: EPS is the only ratio required by IFRS to be calculated and shown in the corporation's financial statements.

$$\text{Basic earnings per share} = \frac{\$40,000 - \$7,500}{5,000 \text{ shares}} = \$6.50$$

Earnings per share is the only financial ratio required to be calculated and shown in the company's financial statements and has an entire accounting standard **IAS 33 Earnings Per Share** devoted to it. IAS 33 also clarifies that for the purpose of calculating EPS based on the consolidated financial statements, the numerator net profit refers to profit or loss of the consolidated entity after adjusting for noncontrolling interests.

Price-Earnings Ratio

The market value of shares is determined by its *expected* future cash flows. A comparison of a company's EPS and its market value per share reveals information about market expectations. This comparison is traditionally made using a **price-earnings (or PE) ratio**, expressed also as *price earnings*, *price to earnings*, or *PE*. Some analysts interpret this ratio as what price the market is willing to pay for a

A2 Compute price-earnings ratio and describe its use in analysis.

---

[3] A corporation can be classified as having either a simple or complex capital structure. The term **simple capital structure** refers to a company with only ordinary shares and nonconvertible preference shares outstanding. The term **complex capital structure** refers to companies with dilutive securities. **Dilutive securities** include options, rights to purchase ordinary shares, and any bonds or preference shares that are convertible into ordinary shares. A company with a complex capital structure must often report two EPS figures: basic and diluted. **Diluted earnings per share** is computed by adding all dilutive securities to the denominator of the basic EPS computation. It reflects the decrease in basic EPS *assuming* that all dilutive securities are converted into ordinary shares.

company's current earnings stream. Price-earnings ratios can differ across companies that have similar earnings because of either higher or lower expectations of future earnings. The price-earnings ratio is defined in Exhibit 13.15.

EXHIBIT 13.15

Price-Earnings Ratio

$$\text{Price-earnings ratio} = \frac{\text{Market value (price) per share}}{\text{Earnings per share}}$$

This ratio is often computed using EPS from the most recent period. However, many users compute this ratio using *expected* EPS for the next period because they are investing for the future.

Some analysts view shares with high PE ratios (higher than 20 to 25) as more likely to be overpriced and shares with low PE ratios (less than 5 to 8) as more likely to be underpriced. These investors prefer to sell or avoid buying shares with high PE ratios and to buy or hold shares with low PE ratios. However, investment decision making is rarely so simple as to rely on a single ratio. For instance, shares with a high PE ratio can prove to be a good investment if their earnings continue to increase beyond current expectations. Similarly, shares with a low PE ratio can prove to be a poor investment if their earnings decline below expectations.

☐ Decision Maker   Answer — p. 518

Money Manager   You plan to invest in one of two companies identified as having identical future prospects. One has a PE of 19 and the other a PE of 25. Which do you invest in? Does it matter if your *estimate* of PE for these two companies is 29 as opposed to 22? ■

Dividend Yield

A3 Compute dividend yield and explain its use in analysis.

Investors buy a company's shares in anticipation of receiving a return from either or both cash dividends and share price increases. Shares that pay large dividends on a regular basis, called *income shares*, are attractive to investors who want recurring cash flows from their investments. In contrast, some shares pay little or no dividends but are still attractive to investors because of their expected share price increases. The shares of companies that distribute little or no cash but use their cash to finance expansion are called *growth shares*. One way to help identify whether shares are income shares or growth shares is to analyze its dividend yield. **Dividend yield**, defined in Exhibit 13.16, shows the annual amount of cash dividends distributed to ordinary shares relative to their market value.

EXHIBIT 13.16

Dividend Yield

$$\text{Dividend yield} = \frac{\text{Annual cash dividends per share}}{\text{Market value per share}}$$

Dividend yield can be computed for current and prior periods using actual dividends and share prices and for future periods using expected values. Exhibit 13.17 shows recent dividend and share price data for **Alibaba.com** (Internet business listed in Hong Kong) and **SMRT** (public transport operator listed in Singapore) to compute dividend yield.

EXHIBIT 13.17

Dividend and Share Price Information

Company	Currency	Cash Dividends per Share	Market Value per Share	Dividend Yield
Alibaba.com....................	HKD	0.00	8.19	0.0%
SMRT........................	SGD	0.0745	1.74	4.3%

Point: The *payout ratio* equals cash dividends declared on ordinary shares divided by net profit. A low payout ratio suggests that a company is retaining earnings for future growth.

Dividend yield is zero for Alibaba.com; the nature of its business makes it a growth share as opposed to an income share. An investor in Alibaba.com would look for increases in share prices (and eventual cash from the sale of shares). On the other hand, the nature of SMRT's business makes it an income share. Its dividend yield of 4.3% is an important ratio for evaluation by investors desiring a steady flow of income.

Book Value per Share

Book value per ordinary share, defined in Exhibit 13.18, reflects the amount of equity applicable to *ordinary* shares on a per share basis. To illustrate, we use Dillon Snowboards' data from Exhibit 13.3. Dillon has 30,000 outstanding ordinary shares, and the shareholders' equity applicable to ordinary shares is $365,000. Dillon's book value per ordinary share is $12.17, computed as $365,000 divided by 30,000 shares.

 A4 Compute book value and explain its use in analysis.

$$\text{Book value per ordinary share} = \frac{\text{Shareholders' equity applicable to ordinary shares}}{\text{Number of ordinary shares outstanding}}$$

EXHIBIT 13.18

Book Value per Ordinary Share

Book value per share reflects the value per share if a company is liquidated at the carrying amounts on its statement of financial position. Book value is also the starting point in many share valuation models, merger negotiations, price setting for public utilities, and loan contracts. The main limitation in using book value is the potential difference between recorded value and market value for assets and liabilities. Investors often adjust their analysis for estimates of these differences.

Point: Book value per share is also referred to as *shareholders' claim to assets on a per share basis.*

Decision Maker Answer — p. 518

Investor You are considering investing in **BMX**, whose book value per ordinary share is $4 and price per ordinary share on the stock exchange is $7. From this information, are BMX's net assets priced higher or lower than its recorded values? ■

DEMONSTRATION PROBLEM 1

Barton Corporation began operations on January 1, 2015. The following transactions relating to shareholders' equity occurred in the first two years of the company's operations.

2015

Jan. 1   Authorized the issuance of 2 million shares of $5 par value ordinary shares and 100,000 shares of $100 par value, 10% cumulative, preference shares.

Jan. 2   Issued 200,000 ordinary shares for $12 cash per share.

Jan. 3   Issued 100,000 ordinary shares in exchange for a building valued at $820,000 and merchandise inventory valued at $380,000.

Jan. 4   Paid $10,000 cash to the company's founders for organization activities.

Jan. 5   Issued 12,000 preference shares for $110 cash per share.

2016

June 4   Issued 100,000 ordinary shares for $15 cash per share.

Required

1. Prepare journal entries to record these transactions.

2. Prepare the shareholders' equity section of the statement of financial position as at December 31, 2015, and December 31, 2016, based on these transactions.

3. Prepare a table showing dividend allocations for 2015 and 2016 assuming Barton declares the following cash dividends: 2015, $50,000, and 2016, $300,000.

4. Prepare the January 2, 2015, journal entry for Barton's issuance of 200,000 ordinary shares for $12 cash per share assuming

   a. Ordinary shares are no-par shares without a stated value.

   b. Ordinary shares are no-par shares with a stated value of $10 per share.

PLANNING THE SOLUTION

- Record journal entries for the transactions for 2015 and 2016.
- Determine the balances for the 2015 and 2016 equity accounts for the statement of financial position.
- Prepare the contributed capital portion of the 2015 and 2016 statements of financial position.
- Prepare a table similar to Exhibit 13.6 showing dividend allocations for 2015 and 2016.
- Record the issuance of ordinary shares under both specifications of no-par shares.

SOLUTION TO DEMONSTRATION PROBLEM 1

1. Journal entries.

2015			
Jan. 2	Cash	2,400,000	
	Share Capital—Ordinary, $5 Par Value		1,000,000
	Share Premium—Ordinary		1,400,000
	To record 200,000 $5 par value ordinary shares issued at $12 per share.		
Jan. 3	Building	820,000	
	Merchandise Inventory	380,000	
	Share Capital—Ordinary, $5 Par Value		500,000
	Share Premium—Ordinary		700,000
	To record 100,000 $5 par value ordinary shares issued for building valued at $820,000 and merchandise inventory valued at $380,000.		
Jan. 4	Organization Expenses	10,000	
	Cash		10,000
	To record the payment to company's founders.		
Jan. 5	Cash	1,320,000	
	Share Capital—Preference, $100 Par Value		1,200,000
	Share Premium—Preference		120,000
	To record 12,000 $100 par value preference shares issued at $110 per share.		
2015			
June 4	Cash	1,500,000	
	Share Capital—Ordinary, $5 Par Value		500,000
	Share Premium—Ordinary		1,000,000
	To record 100,000 $5 par value ordinary shares issued at $15 per share.		

2. Statement of financial position presentations (at December 31 year-end).

	2016	2015
Shareholders' Equity		
Share Capital—Preference, $100 par value, 10% cumulative, 100,000 shares authorized, 12,000 shares issued and outstanding	$1,200,000	$1,200,000
Share Premium—Preference	120,000	120,000
Total share capital by preference shareholders	$1,320,000	$1,320,000
Share Capital—Ordinary, $5 par value, 2,000,000 shares authorized, 300,000 shares issued and outstanding in 2015, and 400,000 shares issued and outstanding in 2016......................	2,000,000	1,500,000
Share Premium—Ordinary...	3,100,000	2,100,000
Total share capital by ordinary shareholders	$5,100,000	$3,600,000
Total share capital	$6,420,000	$4,920,000

3. Dividend allocation table.

	Ordinary	Preference
2015 ($50,000)		
Preference—current year (12,000 shares × $10 = $120,000)	$ 0	$ 50,000
Ordinary—remainder (300,000 shares outstanding)....................	0	0
Total for the year	$ 0	$ 50,000
2016 ($300,000)		
Preference—dividend in arrears from 2015 ($120,000 − $50,000)	$ 0	$ 70,000
Preference—current year	0	120,000
Ordinary—remainder (400,000 shares outstanding)...................	110,000	0
Total for the year	$110,000	$190,000

4. Journal entries.

   a. For 2015 (no-par shares without a stated value):

Jan. 2	Cash	2,400,000	
	Share Capital—Ordinary, No-Par Value		2,400,000
	To record 200,000 no-par value share issued at $12 per share.		

   b. For 2015 (no-par shares with a stated value):

Jan. 2	Cash	2,400,000	
	Share Capital—Ordinary, $10 Stated Value.......		2,000,000
	Share Premium—Ordinary		400,000
	To record 200,000 $10 stated value shares at $12 per share.		

DEMONSTRATION PROBLEM 2

Precision Company began year 2016 with the following balances in its shareholders' equity accounts.

Share Capital—Ordinary, $10 par, 500,000 shares authorized, 200,000 shares issued and outstanding	$2,000,000
Share Premium—Ordinary	1,000,000
Retained earnings	5,000,000
Total	$8,000,000

All outstanding ordinary shares were issued for $15 per share when the company was created. Prepare journal entries to account for the following transactions during year 2016.

Jan. 10   The board declared a $0.10 cash dividend per share to shareholders of record Jan. 28.
Feb. 15   Paid the cash dividend declared on January 10.
July 1   Purchased 30,000 treasury shares at $20 per share.
Sept. 1   Sold 20,000 treasury shares at $26 cash per share.
Dec. 1   Sold the remaining 10,000 treasury shares at $7 cash per share.

PLANNING THE SOLUTION

● Calculate the total cash dividend to record by multiplying the cash dividend declared by the number of shares as at the date of record.

● Analyze each event to determine the accounts affected and the appropriate amounts to be recorded.

SOLUTION TO DEMONSTRATION PROBLEM 2

Jan. 10	Retained Earnings	20,000	
	Ordinary Dividend Payable		20,000
	To record the declaration of $0.10 per ordinary share cash dividend.		
Feb. 15	Ordinary Dividend Payable	20,000	
	Cash		20,000
	To record the payment of $0.10 per ordinary share cash dividend.		
July 1	Treasury Shares—Ordinary	600,000	
	Cash		600,000
	To record the purchase of 30,000 treasury shares at $20 per share.		
Sept. 1	Cash	520,000	
	Treasury Shares—Ordinary		400,000
	Share Premium—Treasury Shares		120,000
	To record the receipt of $26 per share for 20,000 treasury shares costing $20 per share.		
Dec. 1	Cash	70,000	
	Share Premium—Treasury Shares	120,000	
	Retained Earnings	10,000	
	Treasury Shares—Ordinary		200,000
	To record the receipt of $7 per share for 10,000 treasury shares costing $20 per share.		

DEMONSTRATION PROBLEM 3

Selected account balances from the adjusted trial balance for Olinda Corporation as at its calendar year-end December 31, 2016, follow.

a.	Interest income	$ 14,000
b.	Depreciation expense—Equipment	34,000
c.	Loss on sale of equipment	25,850
d.	Accounts payable	44,000
e.	Other operating expenses	106,400
f.	Accumulated depreciation—Equipment.................	71,600
g.	Gain from settlement of lawsuit......................	44,000
h.	Accumulated depreciation—Buildings..................	174,500
i.	Net sales	998,500
j.	Depreciation expense—Buildings......................	52,000
k.	Income tax expense.................................	12,000
l.	Cost of goods sold	482,500
m.	Revaluation surplus on property, plant and equipment	10,000

Required

Prepare its statement of profit or loss and other comprehensive income for calendar year 2016. (Omit the earnings per share section.)

PLANNING THE SOLUTION

- Identify the items that belong in a statement of profit or loss and other comprehensive income.
- Separate the items into (1) items for the first part of the statement, which consists of income statement items, and (2) items for the second part of the statement, which consists of other comprehensive income items.
- Prepare the complete statement of profit or loss and other comprehensive income.

SOLUTION TO DEMONSTRATION PROBLEM 3

● Items *d, f,* and *h* are items that belong in a statement of financial position.
● Interest income is also known as interest revenue or finance income.

OLINDA CORPORATION Statement of Profit or Loss and Other Comprehensive Income For Year Ended December 31, 2016	
Net sales	$ 998,500
Cost of goods sold	(482,500)
Gross profit	516,000
Depreciation expense—Equipment	(34,000)
Depreciation expense—Buildings	(52,000)
Other operating expenses	(106,400)
Gain from settlement of lawsuit	44,000
Loss on sale of equipment	(25,850)
Operating profit	341,750
Interest income	14,000
Profit before tax	355,750
Income tax expense	(12,000)
Net profit	343,750
Other comprehensive income	
Revaluation surplus on property, plant and equipment	10,000
Total comprehensive income for the year	$ 353,750

Summary

C1 **Identify characteristics of corporations and their organization.** Corporations are legal entities whose shareholders are not liable for its debts. Shares are easily transferred, and the life of a corporation does not end with the incapacity of a shareholder. A corporation acts through its agents, who are its officers and managers. Corporations are regulated and subject to income taxes. An authorized share is a share that a corporation has been authorized to sell. Issued share is an authorized share sold. Par value share is a value per share assigned. No-par value share is a share not assigned a value per share. Stated value share is a no-par share to which the directors assign a value per share.

C2 **Explain characteristics of, and distribute dividends between, ordinary and preference shares.** Preference shares has a priority (or senior status) relative to ordinary shares in one or more areas, usually (1) dividends and (2) assets in case of liquidation. Preference shares usually does not carry voting rights and can be convertible or callable. Convertibility permits the holder to convert preference shares to ordinary shares. Callability permits the issuer to buy back preference shares under specified conditions. Preference shareholders usually hold the right to dividend distributions before ordinary shareholders. When preference shares are cumulative and in arrears, the amount in arrears must be distributed to preference shareholders before any dividends are distributed to ordinary shareholders.

C3 **Explain the items reported in comprehensive income and equity.** The company must present a statement of profit or loss and other comprehensive income, which is intended to show all nonowner changes in equity and other comprehensive income. This statement can be shown as a single statement or as two statements: (1) an income statement that presents revenues and expenses recognized in the calculation of profit or loss, and (2) a statement of profit or loss and other comprehensive income that begins with the profit or loss from the income statement and then lists other items of income and expense (e.g., revaluation gains) to show total comprehensive income. The company must present a statement of changes in equity, which is intended to show all owner changes in equity and dividends, as well as the effects of any changes in accounting policies and correction of prior period errors.

A1 **Compute earnings per share and describe its use.** A company with a simple capital structure computes basic EPS by dividing net profit less any preference dividends by the weighted-average number of outstanding ordinary shares. A company with a complex capital structure must usually report both basic and diluted EPS.

A2 **Compute price-earnings ratio and describe its use in analysis.** The price-earnings (PE) ratio of ordinary shares is computed by dividing the share's market value (price) per share by its EPS. A share's PE is based on expectations that can prove to be better or worse than eventual performance.

A3   **Compute dividend yield and explain its use in analysis.**
Dividend yield is the ratio of the shares' annual cash dividends per share to its market value (price) per share. Dividend yield can be compared with the yield of other companies to determine whether the shares are expected to be income or growth shares.

A4   **Compute book value and explain its use in analysis.**
Book value per ordinary share is equity applicable to ordinary shares divided by the number of outstanding ordinary shares.

P1   **Record the issuance of corporate shares.** When shares are issued, their par or stated value is credited to the share account and any excess is credited to a separate contributed capital account. If the shares have neither par nor stated value, the entire proceeds are credited to the share capital account.

P2   **Record transactions involving cash dividends, share dividends, and share splits.** Cash dividends involve three events. On the date of declaration, the directors bind the company to pay the dividend. A dividend declaration reduces

retained earnings and creates a current liability. On the date of record, recipients of the dividend are identified. On the date of payment, cash is paid to shareholders and the current liability is removed. Neither a share dividend nor a share split alters the value of the company. However, the value of each share is less due to the distribution of additional shares. Share splits do not necessitate journal entries but do necessitate changes in the description of shares.

P3   **Record purchases and sales of treasury shares and the retirement of shares.** When a corporation purchases its own previously issued shares, it debits the cost of these shares to Treasury Shares. Treasury shares are subtracted from equity in the statement of financial position. If treasury shares are reissued, any proceeds in excess of cost are credited to Share Premium—Treasury Shares. If the proceeds are less than cost, they are debited to Share Premium—Treasury Shares to the extent a credit balance exists. Any remaining amount is debited to Retained Earnings. When shares are retired, all accounts related to the shares are removed.

Guidance Answers to **Decision Maker and** Decision Ethics

Entrepreneur   The 50% share dividend provides you no direct income. A share dividend often reveals management's optimistic expectations about the future and can improve a share's marketability by making it affordable to more investors. Accordingly, a share dividend usually reveals "good news" and because of this, it likely increases (slightly) the market value for your shares. The same conclusions apply to the 3-for-2 share split.

Concert Organizer   You have two basic options: (1) different classes of ordinary shares or (2) ordinary and preference shares. Your objective is to issue to yourself shares that have all or a majority of the voting power. The other class of shares would carry limited or no voting rights. In this way, you maintain control and are able to raise the necessary funds.

Money Manager   Since one company requires a payment of $19 for each $1 of earnings, and the other requires $25, you would

prefer the shares with the PE of 19; it is a better deal given identical prospects. You should make sure these companies' earnings computations are roughly the same. Also, your PE estimates for these companies do matter. If you are willing to pay $29 for each $1 of earnings for these companies, you obviously expect both to exceed current market expectations.

Investor   Book value reflects recorded values. BMX's book value is $4 per ordinary share. Share price reflects the market's expectation of net asset value (both tangible and intangible items). BMX's market value is $7 per ordinary share. Comparing these figures suggests BMX's market value of net assets is higher than its recorded values (by an amount of $7 versus $4 per share).

Guidance Answers to **Quick Checks**

1. (*b*)

2. A corporation pays taxes on its profit, and its shareholders normally pay personal income taxes (at the 15% rate or lower) on any cash dividends received from the corporation.

3. A proxy is a legal document used to transfer a shareholder's right to vote to another person.

4. (*a*)

5. A share premium is an amount in excess of par (or stated) value paid by purchasers of newly issued shares.

6. No, it is an equity account.

7. Ordinary Dividend Payable is a current liability account.

8. The date of declaration, date of record, and date of payment.

9. A dividend is a legal liability at the date of declaration, on which date it is recorded as a liability.

10. A share dividend does not transfer assets to shareholders, but it does require an amount of retained earnings to be transferred to a contributed capital account(s).

11. A cash dividend results in reduction in both assets and equity; a bonus issue or share dividend does not affect asset and equity.

12. This means transferring retained earnings to share capital resulting in no change to equity.

13. Typically, preference shares have a preference in receipt of dividends and in distribution of assets.

14. (*a*)

15. (*b*)

Total cash dividend	$288,000
To preference shareholders	135,000*
Remainder to ordinary shareholders	$153,000

* 9,000 × $50 × 10% × 3 years = $135,000.

16. (*b*)

17. No. The shares are an investment for Southern Co. and are issued and outstanding shares for Northern Corp.

18. Treasury shares do not affect the number of issued shares, but reduce the outstanding shares.

19. (*c*)

Key Terms   www.mheducation.asia/olc/wild

Authorized shares (p. 494)
Basic earnings per share (p. 511)
Bonus issue (p. 499)
Book value per ordinary share (p. 513)
Call price (p. 503)
Callable preference shares (p. 503)
Changes in accounting estimates (p. 509)
Complex capital structure (p. 511)
Contributed capital (p. 497)
Convertible preference shares (p. 503)
Corporation (p. 492)
Cumulative preference shares (p. 501)
Date of declaration (p. 498)
Date of payment (p. 498)
Date of record (p. 498)
Diluted earnings per share (p. 511)

Dilutive securities (p. 511)
Dividend in arrears (p. 501)
Dividend yield (p. 512)
Double taxation (p. 493)
Earnings per share (EPS) (p. 511)
Financial leverage (p. 503)
Market value per share (p. 495)
Noncumulative preference shares (p. 501)
Nonparticipating preference shares (p. 502)
No-par value share (p. 495)
Ordinary shares (p. 494)
Organization expenses (p. 493)
Participating preference shares (p. 502)
Par value (p. 495)
Par value share (p. 495)
Preemptive right (p. 494

Preference shares (p. 501)
Premium on shares (p. 496)
Price-earnings (PE) ratio (p. 511)
Proxy (p. 493)
Reserves (p. 510)
Retained earnings (p. 510)
Share capital (p. 494)
Share dividend (p. 499)
Share premium (p. 496)
Share split (p. 500)
Shareholders' equity (p. 495)
Simple capital structure (p. 511)
Stated value share (p. 495)
Statement of profit or loss and other comprehensive income (p. 507)
Treasury shares (p. 504)

Multiple Choice Quiz   Answers on p. 535   www.mheducation.asia/olc/wild

1. A corporation issues 6,000 shares of $5 par value ordinary shares for $8 cash per share. The entry to record this transaction includes:
  a. A debit to Share Premium—Ordinary for $18,000.
  b. A credit to Share Capital—Ordinary for $48,000.
  c. A credit to Share Premium—Ordinary for $30,000.
  d. A credit to Cash for $48,000.
  e. A credit to Share Capital—Ordinary for $30,000.

2. A company reports net profit of $75,000. Its weighted-average ordinary shares outstanding is 19,000. It has no other shares outstanding. Its earnings per share is:
  a. $4.69
  b. $3.95
  c. $3.75
  d. $2.08
  e. $4.41

3. A company has 5,000 shares of $100 par value preference shares and 50,000 shares of $10 par value ordinary shares outstanding. Its total shareholders' equity is $2,000,000. Its book value per ordinary share is:

  a. $100.00
  b. $ 10.00
  c. $ 40.00
  d. $ 30.00
  e. $ 36.36

4. A company paid cash dividends of $0.81 per share. Its earnings per share is $6.95 and its market price per share is $45.00. Its dividend yield is:
  a. 1.8%
  b. 11.7%
  c. 15.4%
  d. 55.6%
  e. 8.6%

5. A company's shares have a market value of $85 per share. Its net profit is $3,500,000, and its weighted-average ordinary shares outstanding is 700,000. Its price-earnings ratio is:
  a. 5.9
  b. 425.0
  c. 17.0
  d. 10.4
  e. 41.2

ℹ The icon denotes assignments that involve decision making.

Discussion Questions

1. What are organization expenses? Provide examples.
2. How are organization expenses reported?
3. **ℹ** Who is responsible for directing a corporation's affairs?
4. What is the preemptive right of ordinary shareholders?
5. List the general rights of ordinary shareholders.
6. What is the difference between authorized shares and outstanding shares?
7. **ℹ** Why would an investor find convertible preference shares attractive?
8. What is the difference between the market value per share and the par value per share?
9. What is the difference between the par value and the call price of a share of preference shares?
10. Identify and explain the importance of the three dates relevant to corporate dividends.
11. How does paying cash dividends affect the corporation's assets, liabilities, and total equity?
12. **ℹ** How does declaring a share dividend affect the corporation's assets, liabilities, and total equity? What are the effects of the eventual distribution of those shares?
13. **ℹ** What is the difference between a share dividend and a share split?
14. **ℹ** Do you think that shareholders receiving bonus shares or share dividends should be taxed on these dividends?

15. How does the purchase of treasury shares affect the purchaser's assets and total equity?
16. **ℹ** Are purchased treasury shares considered outstanding shares?
17. How are EPS results computed for a corporation with a simple capital structure?
18. Why should an investor look at a company's dividend yield?
19. How is book value per share computed for a corporation with no preference shares? What is the main limitation of using book value per share to value a corporation?
20. **ℹ** Refer to Nestlé's financial statements in Appendix A. Is the number of ordinary shares issued stated in the financial statements? If not, where can you find the information for the number of ordinary shares issued in 2013?
21. Refer to Adidas' 2013 consolidated statement of financial position in Appendix A. List the shareholders' equity items discussed in this chapter.
22. **ℹ** Refer to Samsung's 2012 consolidated statement of cash flows in Appendix A. What are its cash proceeds from disposal of treasury shares?
23. **ℹ** Refer to Puma's 2013 consolidated statement of financial position from its Website (http://about.puma.com/en/investor-relations/financial-reports) and list the amounts for treasury shares and retained earnings.

---

connect

QUICK STUDY

QS 13-1
Characteristics of corporations
C1

Of the following statements, which are true for the corporate form of organization?
1. Owners are not agents of the corporation.
2. It is a separate legal entity.
3. It has a limited life.
4. Capital is more easily accumulated than with most other forms of organization.
5. Corporate profit that is distributed to shareholders is usually taxed twice.
6. Owners have unlimited liability for corporate debts.
7. Ownership rights cannot be easily transferred.

QS 13-2
Issuance of ordinary shares
P1

Prepare the journal entry to record Channel One Company's issuance of 100,000 shares of $0.50 par value ordinary shares assuming the shares are issued for:
a. $0.50 cash per share.
b. $2 cash per share.

QS 13-3
Issuance of no-par ordinary shares
P1

Prepare the journal entry to record Selectist Company's issuance of 104,000 shares of no-par value ordinary shares assuming the shares:
a. Are issued for $15 cash per share.
b. Are exchanged for land valued at $1,560,000.

Prepare the journal entry to record Typist Company's issuance of 250,000 ordinary shares assuming the shares have a:

a. $1 par value and sell for $10 cash per share.

b. $1 stated value and sell for $10 cash per share.

QS 13-4
Issuance of par and stated value ordinary shares
P1

Prepare the issuer's journal entry for each separate transaction. (*a*) On March 1, Edgar Co. issues 44,500 shares of $4 par value ordinary shares for $255,000 cash. (*b*) On April 1, GT Co. issues no-par value ordinary shares for $50,000 cash. (*c*) On April 6, MTV issues 2,000 $20 par value ordinary shares for $35,000 of inventory, $135,000 of machinery, and acceptance of an $84,000 note payable.

QS 13-5
Issuance of ordinary shares
P1

---

a. Prepare the journal entry to record Stefan Company's issuance of 12,000 $50 par value 6% cumulative preference shares for $75 cash per share.

b. Assuming the facts in part 1, if Stefan declares a year-end cash dividend, what is the amount of dividend paid to preference shareholders? (Assume no dividends in arrears.)

QS 13-6
Issuance of preference shares
P1 P2

Prepare journal entries to record the following transactions for Emerson Corporation.

April 15   Declared a cash dividend payable to ordinary shareholders of $40,000.
May 15   Date of record is May 15 for the cash dividend declared on April 15.
May 31   Paid the dividend declared on April 15.

QS 13-7
Accounting for cash dividends
P2

Shareholders' equity of STIX Company consists of 75,000 shares of $5 par value, 8% cumulative preference shares and 200,000 $1 par value ordinary shares. Both classes of shares have been outstanding since the company's inception. STIX did not declare any dividends in the prior year, but it now declares and pays a $108,000 cash dividend at the current year-end. Determine the amount distributed to each class of shareholders for this two-year-old company.

QS 13-8
Dividend allocation between classes of shareholders
C2

Explain how each of the following will affect the financial statements:

1. After using an expected useful life of 20 years and no residual value to depreciate its office equipment over the preceding 15 years, the company decided early this year that the equipment will last only two more years.

2. A review of the notes payable files discovers that two years ago the company reported the entire amount of a payment (principal and interest) on an installment note payable as interest expense. This mistake had a material effect on the amount of profit in that year.

QS 13-9
Accounting for changes in estimates; error adjustments
C3

On May 3, Lassman Corporation purchased 3,000 of its own shares for $27,000 cash. On November 4, Lassman reissued 750 treasury shares for $7,080. Prepare the May 3 and November 4 journal entries to record Lassman's purchase and reissuance of treasury shares.

QS 13-10
Purchase and sale of treasury shares
P3

Barnes Company earned net profit of $450,000 this year. The weighted-average ordinary shares outstanding during the entire year was 200,000, and preference shareholders received a $10,000 cash dividend. Compute Barnes Company's basic earnings per share.

QS 13-11
Basic earnings per share
A1

Campbell Company reports net profit of $1,200,000 for the year. It has no preference shares, and its weighted-average ordinary shares outstanding is 300,000 shares. Compute its basic earnings per share.

QS 13-12
Basic earnings per share
A1

Compute Fox Company's price-earnings ratio if its ordinary shares have a market value of $30.75 per share and its EPS is $4.10. Would an analyst likely consider these shares potentially over- or underpriced? Explain.

QS 13-13
Price-earnings ratio
A2

QS 13-14

Dividend yield

A3

Fiona Company expects to pay a $2.10 per share cash dividend this year on its ordinary shares. The current market value of Fiona shares is $28.50 per share. Compute the expected dividend yield on the Fiona shares. Would you classify the Fiona shares as growth or income shares? Explain.

QS 13-15

Book value per ordinary share

A4

The shareholders' equity section of Axel Company's statement of financial position follows. Determine the book value per share of the ordinary shares.

Share Capital—Ordinary, $5 par value, 100,000 shares	
authorized, 75,000 shares issued and outstanding	375,000
Retained earnings	445,000
Total shareholders' equity	$820,000

QS 13-16

International equity disclosures

P1

Air France-KLM reports the following equity information for its financial year ended March 31, 2009 (in EUR millions). Prepare its journal entry, using its account titles, to record the issuance of share capital assuming that its entire par value shares were issued on March 31, 2009, for cash.

March 31	2009
Issued capital	EUR 2,552
Additional share capital	765

EXERCISES

Describe how each of the following characteristics of organizations applies to corporations.

Exercise 13-1

Characteristics of corporations

C1

1. Duration of life	5. Owner authority and control
2. Owner liability	6. Ease of formation
3. Legal status	7. Transferability of ownership
4. Tax status of profit	8. Ability to raise large capital amounts

---

Exercise 13-2

Accounting for par, stated, and no-par share issuances

P1

Aloha Corporation issues 6,000 of its ordinary shares for $144,000 cash on February 20. Prepare journal entries to record this event under each of the following separate situations.

1. The shares have neither par nor stated value.

2. The shares have a $20 par value.

3. The shares have an $8 stated value.

Exercise 13-3

Recording share issuances

P1

Prepare journal entries to record the following four separate issuances of shares.

1. A corporation issued 2,000 no-par ordinary shares to its promoters in exchange for their efforts, estimated to be worth $30,000. The shares have no stated value.

2. A corporation issued 2,000 no-par ordinary shares to its promoters in exchange for their efforts, estimated to be worth $30,000. The shares have a $1 per share stated value.

3. A corporation issued 4,000 $10 par value ordinary shares for $70,000 cash.

4. A corporation issued 1,000 $100 par value preference shares for $120,000 cash.

Exercise 13-4

Share issuance for noncash assets

P1

Soku Company issues 36,000 $9 par value ordinary shares in exchange for land and a building. The land is valued at $225,000 and the building at $360,000. Prepare the journal entry to record issuance of the shares in exchange for the land and building.

Match each description 1 through 6 with the characteristic of preference shares that it best describes by writing the letter of that characteristic in the blank next to each description.

A. Cumulative
B. Noncumulative
C. Convertible
D. Callable
E. Nonparticipating
F. Participating

_____ **1.** Holders of the shares lose any dividends that are not declared in the current year.
_____ **2.** The issuing corporation can retire the shares by paying a prespecified price.
_____ **3.** Holders of the shares can receive dividends exceeding the stated rate under certain conditions.
_____ **4.** Holders of the shares are not entitled to receive dividends in excess of the stated rate.
_____ **5.** Holders of the shares can exchange it for ordinary shares.
_____ **6.** Holders of the shares are entitled to receive current and all past dividends before ordinary shareholders receive any dividends.

Exercise 13-5
Identifying characteristics of preference shares

C2

Wade's outstanding shares consist of 40,000 *noncumulative* 7.5% preference shares with a $10 par value and also 100,000 ordinary shares with a $1 par value. During its first four years of operation, the corporation declared and paid the following total cash dividends.

2011	$ 10,000
2012	24,000
2013	100,000
2014	196,000

Determine the amount of dividends paid each year to each of the two classes of shareholders: preference and ordinary. Also compute the total dividends paid to each class for the four years combined.

Exercise 13-6
Dividends on ordinary and noncumulative preference shares

C2

Check 4-year total paid to preference, $94,000

Use the data in Exercise 13-6 to determine the amount of dividends paid each year to each of the two classes of shareholders assuming that the preference shares are *cumulative*. Also determine the total dividends paid to each class for the four years combined.

Exercise 13-7
Dividends on ordinary and cumulative preference shares

C2

On October 10, the shareholders' equity of Noble Systems appears as follows.

Share Capital—Ordinary, $10 par value, 36,000 shares authorized, issued, and outstanding	$360,000
Share Premium—Ordinary	108,000
Retained earnings	432,000
Total shareholders' equity	$900,000

1. Prepare journal entries to record the following transactions for Noble Systems.
    a. Purchased 4,500 of its own ordinary shares at $30 per share on October 11.
    b. Sold 1,200 treasury shares on November 1 for $36 cash per share.
    c. Sold all remaining treasury shares on November 25 for $25 cash per share.
2. Explain how the company's equity section changes after the October 11 treasury share purchase, and prepare the revised equity section of its statement of financial position at that date.

Exercise 13-8
Recording and reporting treasury share transactions

P3

Check (1c) Dr. Retained Earnings, $9,300

Exercise 13-9

Items in statement of profit or loss and other comprehensive income and statement of changes in equity

C3

Indicate the financial statement on which each of the following items appears. Use SPLOCI for statement of profit or loss and comprehensive income, and SCE for statement of changes in equity. Assume that the company prepares the statement of profit or loss and comprehensive income as one statement.

a. Increase in building revaluation surplus

b. Loss on translation of foreign currencies

c. Retained earnings

d. Share premium

e. An accounting error made in the previous period

f. Revenue

g. Dividends

h. Change in inventory method from the previous year

Exercise 13-10

Interpreting a statement of changes in equity

C3

Refer to Amatrep Holdings Limited's statement of changes in equity below.

	Share Capital $'000	Foreign Currency Translation Reserve $'000	Share Option Reserve $'000	Revenue Reserve $'000	Revaluation Reserve $'000	Total Reserves $'000	Total Equity $'000
Balance as at July 1, 2014	66,654	(6,310)	407	42,109	437	36,643	103,297
Profit for the financial year	—	—	—	6,699	—	6,699	6,699
Other comprehensive income for the financial year	—	(286)	—	—	—	(286)	(286)
Total comprehensive income for the financial year	—	(286)	—	6,699	—	6,413	6,413
Share option expense	—	—	20	—	—	20	20
Dividend paid	—	—	—	(5,811)	—	(5,811)	(5,811)
Balance as at June 30, 2015	66,654	(6,596)	427	42,997	437	37,265	103,919
Balance as at July 1, 2015	66,654	(6,596)	427	42,997	437	37,265	103,919
Profit for the financial year	—	—	—	9,036	—	9,036	9,036
Other comprehensive income for the financial year	—	1,379	—	—	—	1,379	1,379
Total comprehensive income for the financial year	—	1,379	—	9,036	—	10,415	10,415
Acquisition of noncontrolling interest	—	43	—	(1,334)	—	(1,291)	(1,291)
Dividend paid	—	—	—	(5,858)	—	(5,858)	(5,858)
Balance as at June 30, 2016	66,654	(5,174)	427	44,841	437	40,531	107,185

1. Did the company pay more dividends in the year ended June 30, 2016 than the previous financial year?

2. Which item is mainly responsible for the increase in total equity in the year ended June 30, 2016?

Exercise 13-11

Earnings per share

A1

Check   (2) $2.10

Guess Company reports $648,500 of net profit for 2015 and declares $102,500 of cash dividends on its preference shares for 2015. At the end of 2015, the company had 260,000 weighted-average ordinary shares outstanding.

1. What amount of net profit is available to ordinary shareholders for 2015?

2. What is the company's basic EPS for 2015?

Exercise 13-12

Earnings per share

A1

Franklin Company reports $698,000 of net profit for 2015 and declares $75,500 of cash dividends on its preference shares for 2015. At the end of 2015, the company had 175,000 weighted-average ordinary shares outstanding.

1. What amount of net profit is available to ordinary shareholders for 2015?

2. What is the company's basic EPS for 2015? Round your answer to the nearest whole cent.

Check   (2) $3.56

Compute the dividend yield for each of these four separate companies. Which company's shares would probably *not* be classified as income shares? Explain.

Exercise 13-13
Dividend yield computation and interpretation

A3

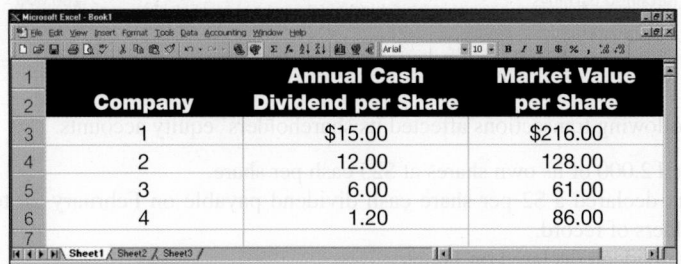

Company	Annual Cash Dividend per Share	Market Value per Share
1	$15.00	$216.00
2	12.00	128.00
3	6.00	61.00
4	1.20	86.00

Compute the price-earnings ratio for each of these four separate companies. Which shares might an analyst likely investigate as being potentially undervalued by the market? Explain.

Exercise 13-14
Price-earnings ratio computation and interpretation

A2

Company	Earnings per Share	Market Value per Share
1	$10.00	$166.00
2	9.00	90.00
3	6.50	84.50
4	40.00	240.00

The equity section of Webster Corporation's statement of financial position shows the following.

Exercise 13-15
Book value per share

A4

Share Capital—Ordinary, $10 par value, 55,000 shares issued and outstanding	$550,000
Retained earnings	267,500
Total shareholders' equity	$817,500

Determine the book value per share of the ordinary shares.

Unilever Group reports the following equity information for the years ended December 31, 2007 and 2008 (in EUR millions).

Exercise 13-16
Accounting for equity

C3 P1

December 31	2008	2007
Share capital	EUR 484	EUR 484
Share premium	121	153
Other reserves	(6,469)	(3,412)
Retained profit	15,812	15,162
Shareholders' equity	EUR 9,948	EUR 12,387

1. Prepare Unilever's journal entry, using its account titles, to record the issuance of share capital assuming that its entire par value shares were issued on December 31, 2007, for cash.

2. What were Unilever's 2008 dividends assuming that only dividends and profit impacted retained profit for 2008 and that its 2008 profit totaled EUR 2,692?

Exercise 13-17

Cash dividends, treasury shares, and statement of changes in equity

C3 P2 P3

Kroll Corporation reports the following components of shareholders' equity on December 31, 2015.

Share capital—Ordinary, $25 par value; 40,000 shares authorized; 30,000 shares issued and outstanding	$ 750,000
Share Premium—Ordinary	50,000
Retained earnings	260,000
Total shareholders' equity	$1,060,000

In year 2016, the following transactions affected its shareholders' equity accounts.

Jan. 2   Purchased 2,000 of its own shares at $25 cash per share.
Jan. 7   Directors declared a $2 per share cash dividend payable on February 28 to the February 9 shareholders of record.
Feb. 28   Paid the dividend declared on January 7.
July 9   Sold 500 of its treasury shares at $30 cash per share.
Aug. 27   Sold 1,500 of its treasury shares at $23 cash per share.
Sept. 9   Directors declared a $2 per share cash dividend payable on October 22 to the September 23 shareholders of record.
Oct. 22   Paid the dividend declared on September 9.
Dec. 31   Closed the $8,000 credit balance (from net profit) in the Income Summary account to Retained Earnings.

Required

1. Prepare journal entries to record each of these transactions for 2016.
2. Prepare a statement of changes in equity for the year ended December 31, 2016.
3. Prepare the shareholders' equity section of the company's statement of financial position as at December 31, 2016.

connect

PROBLEM SET A

Problem 13-1A

Shareholders' equity transactions and analysis

C2 P1

Oxygen Co. is incorporated at the beginning of this year and engages in a number of transactions. The following journal entries impacted its shareholders' equity during its first year of operations.

a.	Cash	150,000	
	Share Capital—Ordinary, $25 Par Value		125,000
	Share Premium—Ordinary		25,000
b.	Organization Expenses	75,000	
	Share Capital—Ordinary, $25 Par Value		62,500
	Share Premium—Ordinary		12,500
c.	Cash	21,500	
	Accounts Receivable	7,500	
	Building	30,000	
	Notes Payable		19,000
	Share Capital—Ordinary, $25 Par Value		25,000
	Share Premium—Ordinary		15,000
d.	Cash	60,000	
	Share Capital—Ordinary, $25 Par Value		37,500
	Share Premium—Ordinary		22,500

Required

1. Explain the transaction(s) underlying each journal entry (a) through (d).
2. How many ordinary shares are outstanding at year-end?
3. What is the total share capital (contributed capital) at year-end?

4. What is the book value per share of the ordinary shares at year-end if total share capital plus retained earnings equals $347,500?

Context Corporation reports the following components of shareholders' equity on December 31, 2015.

Problem 13-2A
Cash dividends, treasury shares, and statement of changes in equity

C3 P2 P3

Share Capital—Ordinary, $10 par value, 50,000 shares authorized, 20,000 shares issued and outstanding	$200,000
Share Premium—Ordinary	30,000
Retained earnings	135,000
Total shareholders' equity	$365,000

In year 2016, the following transactions affected its shareholders' equity accounts.

Jan. 1 Purchased 2,000 of its own shares at $20 cash per share.
Jan. 5 Directors declared a $2 per share cash dividend payable on February 28 to the February 5 shareholders of record.
Feb. 28 Paid the dividend declared on January 5.
July 6 Sold 750 of its treasury shares at $24 cash per share.
Aug. 22 Sold 1,250 of its treasury shares at $17 cash per share.
Sept. 5 Directors declared a $2 per share cash dividend payable on October 28 to the September 25 shareholders of record.
Oct. 28 Paid the dividend declared on September 5.
Dec. 31 Closed the $194,000 credit balance (from net profit) in the Income Summary account to Retained Earnings.

Required

1. Prepare journal entries to record each of these transactions for 2016.

2. Prepare a statement of changes in equity for the year ended December 31, 2016.

Check (2) Retained earnings, Dec. 31, 2012, $252,250.

As at September 30, the end of Excel Company's third quarter, the following shareholders' equity accounts are reported.

Problem 13-3A
Equity analysis—journal entries and account balances

P2

Share Capital—Ordinary, $12 par value	$720,000
Share premium—Ordinary	180,000
Retained earnings	640,000

In the fourth quarter, the following entries related to its equity are recorded.

Oct. 2	Retained Earnings	120,000	
	Ordinary Dividend Payable		120,000
Oct. 25	Ordinary Dividend Payable	120,000	
	Cash		120,000
Oct. 31	Cash	150,000	
	Share Capital—Ordinary, $12 Par Value		72,000
	Share Premium—Ordinary		78,000
Dec. 1	Memo—Change the title of the ordinary shares account to reflect the new par value of $4.		
Dec. 31	Income Summary	420,000	
	Retained Earnings		420,000

Required

1. Explain the transaction(s) underlying each journal entry.

2. Complete the following table showing the equity account balances at each indicated date (include the balances from September 30).

	Oct. 2	Oct. 25	Oct. 31	Dec. 1	Dec. 31
Share Capital—Ordinary	$____	$____	$____	$____	$____
Share Premium—Ordinary	____	____	____	____	____
Retained earnings	____	____	____	____	____
Total equity	$____	$____	$____	$____	$____

Check Total equity: Oct. 2,
$1,420,000; Dec. 31, $1,840,000

Problem 13-4A
Analysis of changes in
shareholders' equity accounts

C3 P2 P3

The equity sections from Salazar Group's 2015 and 2016 year-end statements of financial position follow.

Shareholders' Equity (December 31, 2015)

Share Capital—Ordinary, $4 par value, 50,000 shares authorized,	
20,000 shares issued and outstanding	$ 80,000
Share Premium—Ordinary	60,000
Retained earnings	160,000
Total shareholders' equity	$300,000

Shareholders' Equity (December 31, 2016)

Share Capital—Ordinary, $4 par value, 50,000 shares authorized,	
23,700 shares issued, 1,500 shares in treasury	$ 94,800
Share Premium—Ordinary	89,600
Retained earnings	200,000
	$384,400
Less cost of treasury shares	(15,000)
Total shareholders' equity	$369,400

The following transactions and events affected its equity during year 2016.

Jan. 5 Declared a $0.50 per share cash dividend, date of record January 10.
Mar. 20 Purchased treasury shares for cash.
Apr. 5 Declared a $0.50 per share cash dividend, date of record April 10.
July 5 Declared a $0.50 per share cash dividend, date of record July 10.
July 31 Declared a 20% share dividend when the shares' market value is $12 per share.
Aug. 14 Issued the share dividend that was declared on July 31.
Oct. 5 Declared a $0.50 per share cash dividend, date of record October 10.

Required

1. How many ordinary shares are outstanding on each cash dividend date?
2. What is the total dollar amount for each of the four cash dividends?
3. What is the amount of the capitalization of retained earnings for the share dividend?
4. What is the per share cost of the treasury shares purchased?
5. How much net profit did the company earn during year 2016?

Check (3) $44,400

(4) $10

(5) $124,000

Problem 13-5A
Computation of book values and
dividend allocations

C2 A4

Razz Corporation's ordinary shares is currently selling on a stock exchange at $170 per share, and its current statement of financial position shows the following shareholders' equity section.

Share Capital—Preference, 5% cumulative, $___ par value, 1,000 shares	
authorized, issued, and outstanding	$100,000
Share Capital—Ordinary, $___ par value, 4,000 shares authorized, issued,	
and outstanding	160,000
Retained earnings	300,000
Total shareholders' equity	$560,000

Required (Round per share amounts to cents.)

1. What is the current market value (price) of this corporation's ordinary shares?

2. What are the par values of the corporation's preference shares and its ordinary shares?

3. If two years' preference dividends are in arrears and the board of directors declares cash dividends of $20,000, what total amount will be paid to the preference and to the ordinary shareholders? What is the amount of dividends per share for the ordinary shares? (Round per share values to the nearest cent.)

Check   (2) Par value of preference, $100; par value of ordinary, $40

Analysis Component

4. What are some factors that can contribute to a difference between the book value of ordinary shares and its market value (price)?

Ideo Company manufactures tablet PCs and started the financial year 2016 with the following equity balances.

As at December 31, 2015	
Share Capital (no-par value ordinary shares)	$1,200,000
Retained earnings	213,000

Problem 13-6A
Preparation of statement of profit or loss and other comprehensive income and statement of changes in equity

C3

For the year 2016, the following information is given.

a. Additional 50,000 no-par value shares were issued in exchange for land worth $375,000.

b. Cost of goods sold was $482,500 and other operating expenses was $106,000.

c. Cash dividends of $100,000 were declared.

d. Corporate tax rate was 20%.

e. Ending retained earnings was $158,000.

f. The land acquired through the issuance of shares during the year was not depreciated and revalued to $450,000 on December 31, 2016.

g. Management chose to present the statement of profit or loss and other comprehensive income as one statement and to present revaluation surplus under "Reserves" in the statement of changes in equity.

Required

Prepare Ideo Company's statement of profit or loss and other comprehensive income and statement of changes in equity for year ended December 31, 2016.

Check   Total comprehensive income for year, $120,000

Nilson Company is incorporated at the beginning of this year and engages in a number of transactions. The following journal entries impacted its shareholders' equity during its first year of operations.

PROBLEM SET B

Problem 13-1B
Shareholders' equity transactions and analysis

C2 P1

a.	Cash	60,000	
	Share Capital—Ordinary, $1 Par Value		1,500
	Share Premium—Ordinary		58,500
b.	Organization Expenses	20,000	
	Share Capital—Ordinary, $1 Par Value		500
	Share Premium—Ordinary		19,500
c.	Cash	6,650	
	Accounts Receivable	4,000	
	Building	12,500	
	Notes Payable		3,150
	Share Capital—Ordinary, $1 Par Value		400
	Share Premium—Ordinary		19,600
d.	Cash	30,000	
	Share Capital—Ordinary, $1 Par Value		600
	Share Premium—Ordinary		29,400

Required

1. Explain the transaction(s) underlying each journal entry (*a*) through (*d*).

2. How many ordinary shares are outstanding at year-end?
3. What is the total share capital (contributed capital) at year-end?
4. What is the book value per share of the ordinary shares at year-end if total share capital plus retained earnings equals $347,500?

Problem 13-2B

Cash dividends, treasury shares, and statement of changes in equity

C3 P2 P3

Baycore Corp. reports the following components of shareholders' equity on December 31, 2015.

Share Capital—Ordinary, $1 par value, 160,000 shares authorized, 100,000 shares issued and outstanding	$ 100,000
Share Premium—Ordinary	700,000
Retained earnings	1,080,000
Total shareholders' equity	$1,880,000

It completed the following transactions related to shareholders' equity in year 2016.

Jan. 10   Purchased 20,000 of its own shares at $12 cash per share.
Mar. 2   Directors declared a $1.50 per share cash dividend payable on March 31 to the March 15 shareholders of record.
Mar. 31   Paid the dividend declared on March 2.
Nov. 11   Sold 12,000 of its treasury shares at $13 cash per share.
Nov. 25   Sold 8,000 of its treasury shares at $9.50 cash per share.
Dec. 1   Directors declared a $2.50 per share cash dividend payable on January 2 to the December 10 shareholders of record.
Dec. 31   Closed the $536,000 credit balance (from net profit) in the Income Summary account to Retained Earnings.

Required

1. Prepare journal entries to record each of these transactions for 2016.

2. Prepare a statement of changes in equity for the year ended December 31, 2016.

Problem 13-3B

Equity analysis—journal entries and account balances

P2

At December 31, the end of Intertec Communication's third quarter, the following shareholders' equity accounts are reported.

Share Capital—Ordinary, $10 par value	$480,000
Share Premium—Ordinary	192,000
Retained earnings	800,000

In the fourth quarter, the following entries related to its equity are recorded.

Jan. 17	Retained Earnings	48,000	
	Ordinary Dividend Payable		48,000
Feb. 5	Ordinary Dividend Payable	48,000	
	Cash		48,000
Feb. 28	Cash	126,000	
	Share Capital—Ordinary, $10 Par Value		60,000
	Share Premium—Ordinary		66,000
Mar. 25	Memo—Change the title of the ordinary shares account to reflect the new par value of $5.		
Mar. 31	Income Summary	360,000	
	Retained Earnings		360,000

Required

1. Explain the transaction(s) underlying each journal entry.

2. Complete the following table showing the equity account balances at each indicated date (include the balances from December 31).

	Jan. 17	Feb. 5	Feb. 28	Mar. 25	Mar. 31
Share Capital—Ordinary	$_____	$_____	$_____	$_____	$_____
Share Premium—Ordinary	_____	_____	_____	_____	_____
Retained earnings	_____	_____	_____	_____	_____
Total equity	$_____	$_____	$_____	$_____	$_____

Check Total equity: Jan. 17, $1,424,000; Mar. 31, $1,910,000

The equity sections from Jetta Corporation's 2015 and 2016 statements of financial position follow.

Problem 13-4B
Analysis of changes in shareholders' equity accounts

C3 P2 P3

Shareholders' Equity (December 31, 2015)

Share Capital—Ordinary, $20 par value, 15,000 shares authorized, 8,500 shares issued and outstanding	$170,000
Share Premium—Ordinary	30,000
Retained earnings	$135,000
Total shareholders' equity	$335,000

Shareholders' Equity (December 31, 2016)

Share Capital—Ordinary, $20 par value, 15,000 shares authorized, 9,500 shares issued, 500 shares in treasury	$190,000
Share Premium—Ordinary	52,000
Retained earnings	147,600
	$389,600
Less cost of treasury shares	(20,000)
Total shareholders' equity	$369,600

The following transactions and events affected its equity during year 2016.

Feb.	15	Declared a $0.40 per share cash dividend, date of record five days later.
Mar.	2	Purchased treasury shares for cash.
May	15	Declared a $0.40 per share cash dividend, date of record five days later.
Aug.	15	Declared a $0.40 per share cash dividend, date of record five days later.
Oct.	4	Declared a 12.5% share dividend when the shares' market value is $42 per share.
Oct.	20	Issued the share dividend that was declared on October 4.
Nov.	15	Declared a $0.40 per share cash dividend, date of record five days later.

Required

1. How many ordinary shares are outstanding on each cash dividend date?
2. What is the total dollar amount for each of the four cash dividends?
3. What is the amount of the capitalization of retained earnings for the share dividend?
4. What is the per share cost of the treasury share purchased?
5. How much net profit did the company earn during year 2016?

Check (3) $42,000
(4) $40
(5) $68,000

Scotch Company's ordinary shares are currently selling on a stock exchange at $45 per share, and its current statement of financial position shows the following shareholders' equity section.

Problem 13-5B
Computation of book values and dividend allocations

C2 A4

Share Capital—Preference, 8% cumulative, $___ par value, 1,500 shares authorized, issued, and outstanding	$ 187,500
Share Capital—Ordinary, $___ par value, 18,000 shares authorized, issued, and outstanding	450,000
Retained earnings	562,500
Total shareholders' equity	$1,200,000

Required (Round per share amounts to cents.)

1. What is the current market value (price) of this corporation's ordinary shares?
2. What are the par values of the corporation's preference shares and its ordinary shares?
3. If two years' preference dividends are in arrears and the board of directors declares cash dividends of $50,000, what total amount will be paid to the preference and to the ordinary shareholders? What is the amount of dividends per share for the ordinary shares? (Round per share values to the nearest cent.)

Analysis Component

4. Discuss why the book value of ordinary shares is not always a good estimate of its market value.

Problem 13-6B
Preparation of statement of profit or loss and other comprehensive income and statement of changes in equity

C3

Ananda Company manufactures smartphones and started the financial year 2016 with the following equity balances.

As at December 31, 2015	
Share Capital (no-par value ordinary shares)	$1,000,000
Retained earnings	571,000

For the year 2016, the following information is given.

a. Additional 20,000 no-par value shares were issued in exchange for land worth $200,000.
b. Cost of goods sold was $300,000 and other operating expenses was $98,000.
c. No dividends declared.
d. Corporate tax rate was 20%.
e. Ending retained earnings was $639,000.
f. The land acquired through the issuance of shares during the year was not depreciated and revalued to $250,000 on December 31, 2016.
g. A total of 15,000 shares were bought back at $10 per share.
h. Management chose to present the statement of profit or loss and other comprehensive income as one statement and to present revaluation surplus and purchase of treasury shares under "Reserves" in the statement of changes in equity.

Required

Prepare Ananda Company's statement of profit or loss and other comprehensive income and statement of changes in equity for year ended December 31, 2016.

This serial problem began in Chapter 1 and continues through most of the book. If previous chapter segments were not completed, the serial problem can begin at this point.

SERIAL PROBLEM
Business Solutions
P1 C1 C2

S. Rey created Business Solutions on October 1, 2015. The company has been successful, and Santana plans to expand her business. She believes that an additional $86,000 is needed and is investigating three funding sources.

a. Santana's sister Cicely is willing to invest $86,000 in the business as an ordinary shareholder. Since Santana currently has about $129,000 invested in the business, Cicely's investment will mean that Santana will maintain about 60% ownership, and Cicely will have 40% ownership of Business Solutions.
b. Santana's uncle Marcello is willing to invest $86,000 in the business as a preference shareholder. Marcello would purchase 860 shares of $100 par value, 7% preference shares.
c. Santana's banker is willing to lend her $86,000 on a 7%, 10-year note payable. She would make monthly payments of $1,000 per month for 10 years.

Required

1. Prepare the journal entry to reflect the initial $86,000 investment under each of the options (a), (b), and (c).
2. Evaluate the three proposals for expansion, providing the pros and cons of each option.
3. Which option do you recommend Santana adopt? Explain.

Beyond the Numbers

BTN 13-1   Refer to Nestlé's financial statements in Appendix A, as well as its Notes 17 and 19.

REPORTING IN ACTION

C2 A1 A4

1. How many ordinary shares are issued as at December 31, 2013? How does this number compare with the basic weighted-average ordinary shares outstanding used in the calculation of basic earnings per share as at December 31, 2013?

2. What is the carrying amount or book value of equity applicable to ordinary shares as at December 31, 2013?

3. What is the total amount of cash dividends paid to ordinary shareholders for the year ended December 31, 2013?

4. Identify and compare basic EPS amounts across financial years 2013 and 2012. Comment on any notable changes.

5. List the largest item that reduces equity for 2013 on Nestlé's consolidated statement of changes in equity. Why does this item appear on the statement of changes in equity and not the statement of profit or loss and other comprehensive income?

Fast Forward

6. Access Nestlé's financial statements for financial years ending after December 31, 2013, from its Website (www.nestle.com). Has the number of ordinary shares outstanding increased since that date? Has the company increased the total amount of cash dividends paid compared to the total amount for financial year 2013?

BTN 13-2   Key comparative figures for Nike, Adidas, and Puma follow.

COMPARATIVE ANALYSIS

A1 A2 A3 A4

Key Figures	Nike (US$)	Adidas (EUR)	Puma (EUR)
Net profit (in currency millions)	1,907	568	202.2
Cash dividends declared per ordinary share	1.06	0.80	1.80
Ordinary shares outstanding (in millions)	484.0	209.2	15.0
Weighted-average ordinary shares outstanding (in millions)	485.5	209.2	15.0
Market value (price) per share	72.38	48.89	248.0
Equity applicable to ordinary shares (in millions)	9,753.7	4,623	1,386.4

Required

1. Compute the book value per ordinary share for each company using these data.

2. Compute the basic EPS for each company using these data.

3. Compute the dividend yield for each company using these data. Does the dividend yield of any of the companies characterize it as an income or growth share? Explain.

4. Compute, compare, and interpret the price-earnings ratio for each company using these data.

BTN 13-3   Gianna Tuck is an accountant for Post Pharmaceuticals. Her duties include tracking research and development spending in the new product development division. Over the course of the past six months, Gianna notices that a great deal of funds have been spent on a particular project for a new drug. She hears "through the grapevine" that the company is about to patent the drug and expects it to be a major advance in antibiotics. Gianna believes that this new drug will greatly improve company performance and will cause the company's shares to increase in value. Gianna decides to purchase shares of Post in order to benefit from this expected increase.

ETHICS CHALLENGE

C3

Required

What are Gianna's ethical responsibilities, if any, with respect to the information she has learned through her duties as an accountant for Post Pharmaceuticals? What are the implications to her planned purchase of Post shares?

COMMUNICATING IN PRACTICE

A1 A2

Hint: Make a transparency of each team's memo for a class discussion.

BTN 13-4   Teams are to select an industry, and each team member is to select a different company in that industry. Each team member then is to acquire the selected company's financial statements (from its Website or the stock exchange where it is listed). Use these data to identify basic EPS. Use the financial press (e.g., **finance.yahoo.com**) to determine the market price of its shares, and then compute the price-earnings ratio. Communicate with teammates via a meeting, e-mail, or telephone to discuss the meaning of this ratio, how companies compare, and the industry norm. The team must prepare a single memorandum reporting the ratio for each company and identifying the team conclusions or consensus of opinion. The memorandum is to be duplicated and distributed to the instructor and teammates.

TAKING IT TO THE NET

C1 C3

BTN 13-5   Access the December 31, 2013 annual report of L'Oréal from **www.lorealfinance.com/eng/annual-review-2013**.

Required

1. Review L'Oréal's consolidated balance sheet and notes to identify the types of shares it has issued.
2. What are the par values and issued shares of the classes of shares you identified in part 1?
3. Review its consolidated statement of cash flows and identify what total amount of cash it paid or received in 2013 to purchase or dispose of treasury shares.
4. What amount did L'Oréal pay out in ordinary cash dividends for 2013?

TEAMWORK IN ACTION

P3

Hint: Instructor should be sure each team accurately completes part 1 before proceeding.

BTN 13-6   This activity requires teamwork to reinforce understanding of accounting for treasury shares.

1. Write a brief team statement (*a*) generalizing what happens to a corporation's financial position when it engages in a share "buyback" and (*b*) identifying reasons why a corporation would engage in this activity.
2. Assume that an entity acquires 100 shares of its $100 par value ordinary shares at a cost of $134 cash per share. Discuss the entry to record this acquisition. Next, assign *each* team member to prepare *one* of the following entries (assume each entry applies to all shares):
    a. Reissue treasury shares at cost.
    b. Reissue treasury shares at $150 per share.
    c. Reissue treasury shares at $120 per share; assume the share capital account from treasury shares has a $1,500 balance.
    d. Reissue treasury shares at $120 per share; assume the share capital account from treasury shares has a $1,000 balance.
    e. Reissue treasury shares at $120 per share; assume the share capital account from treasury shares has a zero balance.
3. In sequence, each member is to present his/her entry to the team and explain the *similarities* and *differences* between that entry and the previous entry.

ENTREPRENEURIAL DECISION

C2 P2

BTN 13-7   Assume that Douglas Young of **G.O.D.** decides to launch a new apparel retail chain. This chain requires $500,000 of start-up capital. Douglas contributes $375,000 of personal assets in return for 15,000 ordinary shares, but he must raise another $125,000 in cash. There are two alternative plans for raising the additional cash. Plan A is to sell 3,750 ordinary shares to one or more investors for $125,000 cash. Plan B is to sell 1,250 shares of cumulative preference shares to one or more investors for $125,000 cash (this preference share would have a $100 par value, an annual 8% dividend rate, and be issued at par).

1. If the new business is expected to earn $72,000 of after-tax net profit in the first year, what rate of return on beginning equity will Douglas earn under each alternative plan? Which plan will provide the higher expected return?
2. If the new business is expected to earn $16,800 of after-tax net profit in the first year, what rate of return on beginning equity will Douglas earn under each alternative plan? Which plan will provide the higher expected return?
3. Analyze and interpret the differences between the results for parts 1 and 2.

HITTING THE ROAD

A1 A2 A3

BTN 13-8   Review 30 to 60 minutes of financial news programming on television. Take notes on companies that are catching analysts' attention. You might hear reference to over- and undervaluation of firms and to reports about PE ratios, dividend yields, and earnings per share. Be prepared to give a brief description to the class of your observations.

BTN 13-9   Financial information for Nokia Corporation (www.nokia.com) follows.

GLOBAL DECISION

A1 C3

Net profit (in millions)	EUR	260
Cash dividends declared (in millions)	EUR	1,481
Cash dividends declared per share	EUR	0.40
Number of shares outstanding (in millions)*		3,708
Equity applicable to shares (in millions)	EUR	14,749

* Assume that for Nokia the year-end number of shares outstanding approximates the weighted-average shares outstanding.

Required

1. Compute book value per share for Nokia.

2. Compute earnings per share (EPS) for Nokia.

3. Compare Nokia's dividends per share with its EPS. Is Nokia paying out a large or small amount of its profit as dividends? Explain.

ANSWERS TO MULTIPLE CHOICE QUIZ

1. e; Entry to record this shares issuance is:

Cash (6,000 × $8)	48,000	
Share Capital—Ordinary (6,000 × $5)		30,000
Share Premium—Ordinary		18,000

2. b; $75,000/19,000 shares = $3.95 per share

3. d; Preference shares = 5,000 × $100 = $500,000
Book value per share = ($2,000,000 − $500,000)/50,000 shares = $30 per ordinary share

4. a; $0.81/$45.00 = 1.8%

5. c; Earnings per share = $3,500,000/700,000 shares = $5 per share
PE ratio = $85/$5 = 17.0

14

Long-Term Liabilities

A Look Back

Chapter 13 focused on corporate equity transactions, including share issuances and dividends. We also explained how to analyze comprehensive income and changes in equity.

A Look at This Chapter

This chapter describes the accounting for and analysis of bonds and notes. We explain their characteristics, payment patterns, interest computations, retirement, and reporting requirements.

A Look Ahead

Chapter 15 focuses on how to classify, account for, and report investments in both debt and equity securities. We also describe accounting for transactions listed in a foreign currency.

Learning Objectives

CAP

CONCEPTUAL

C1 Explain the types and payment patterns of notes. (p. 548)

C2 *Appendix 14A*—Explain and compute the present value of an amount(s) to be paid at a future date(s). (p. 554)

ANALYTICAL

A1 Compare bond financing with share financing. (p. 538)

A2 Assess debt features and their implications. (p. 551)

A3 Compute the debt-to-equity ratio and explain its use. (p. 551)

PROCEDURAL

P1 Prepare entries to record bond issuance and interest expense. (p. 540)

P2 Compute and record amortization of bond discount. (p. 542)

P3 Compute and record amortization of bond premium. (p. 544)

P4 Record the retirement of bonds. (p. 547)

P5 Prepare entries to account for notes. (p. 549)

"Our customers are the lifeblood of Qian Hu."—**KENNY YAP**

Decision Insight

A Fishy Tale Worth Telling

At **Qian Hu (www.qianhu.com)**, fishy business is nothing to be frowned upon; in fact, it's incredibly profitable. Just ask Kenny Yap, one of the executive directors and founders of Qian Hu. "Currently, Qian Hu operates in four countries—Singapore, Malaysia, Thailand, and China—and exports over 500 species and varieties of ornamental fish directly to more than 65 countries, as well as distributes to local retailers and exporters," says Kenny. "In our business, the ability to source for new varieties of fish, prompt response in processing orders, and timely delivery are of utmost importance to our customers." Kenny also strongly believes in preserving the natural environment, and explains that "throughout our farm, we recycle rain water in order to reduce the burden on our water resources. All waste or effluent water is treated before being released into the public waterways. Our staff is trained to recycle plastic bags, styrofoam and paper carton boxes, and even rubber bands."

Qian Hu was publicly listed in 2000 and has achieved increasing profits. Despite its success, Kenny is cautiously optimistic: "Qian Hu is no longer satisfied being Southeast Asia's biggest exporter of ornamental fish. We want to pursue bigger oceans of opportunities and growth, and we have specific strategies to achieve it. To fund our growth, we have to ensure we have sufficient cash flow." Since 2005, Qian Hu's debt-to-equity ratio has been increasing because of increasing liabilities in the form of bank loans to fund its expansion. The challenge is to balance funding needs and expansion gains.

Under Kenny's able helmsmanship, it looks like the future is bright for Qian Hu to chart more exciting journeys in newer oceans.

Individuals, companies, and governments issue bonds to finance their activities. In return for financing, bonds promise to repay the lender with interest. This chapter explains the basics of bonds and the accounting for their issuance and retirement. The chapter also describes long-term notes as another financing source. We explain how present value concepts impact both the accounting for and reporting of bonds and notes. The appendix to this chapter discusses present value concepts applicable to liabilities.

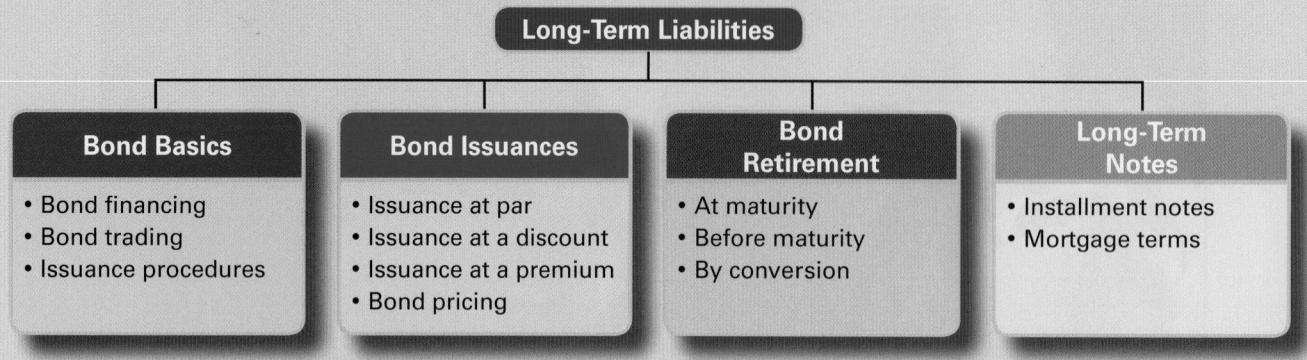

Long-Term Liabilities

Bond Basics
- Bond financing
- Bond trading
- Issuance procedures

Bond Issuances
- Issuance at par
- Issuance at a discount
- Issuance at a premium
- Bond pricing

Bond Retirement
- At maturity
- Before maturity
- By conversion

Long-Term Notes
- Installment notes
- Mortgage terms

BASICS OF BONDS

This section explains the basics of bonds and a company's motivation for issuing them.

Bond Financing

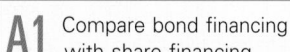

A1 Compare bond financing with share financing.

Projects that demand large amounts of money often are funded from bond issuances. (Both for-profit and nonprofit companies, as well as governmental units, such as nations, states, cities, and school districts, issue bonds.) A **bond** is its issuer's written promise to pay an amount identified as the par value of the bond with interest. The **par value of a bond,** also called the *face amount* or *face value,* is paid at a specified future date known as the bond's *maturity date.* Most bonds also require the issuer to make semiannual interest payments. The amount of interest paid each period is determined by multiplying the par value of the bond by the bond's contract rate of interest for that same period. This section explains both advantages and disadvantages of bond financing.

Advantages of Bonds   There are three main advantages of bond financing:

1. *Bonds do not affect owner control.* Equity financing reflects ownership in a company, whereas bond financing does not. A person who contributes $1,000 of a company's $10,000 equity financing typically controls one-tenth of all owner decisions. A person who owns a $1,000, 11%, 20-year bond has no ownership right. This person, or bondholder, is to receive from the bond issuer 11% interest, or $110, each year the bond is outstanding and $1,000 when it matures in 20 years.
2. *Interest on bonds is tax deductible.* Bond interest payments are tax deductible for the issuer, but equity payments (distributions) to owners are not. To illustrate, assume that a corporation with no bond financing earns $15,000 in profit *before* paying taxes at a 40% tax rate, which amounts to $6,000 ($15,000 × 40%) in taxes. If a portion of its financing is in bonds, however, the resulting bond interest is deducted in computing taxable profit. That is, if bond interest expense is $10,000, the taxes owed would be $2,000 ([$15,000 − $10,000] × 40%), which is less than the $6,000 owed with no bond financing.
3. *Bonds can increase return on equity.* A company that earns a higher return with borrowed funds than it pays in interest on those funds increases its return on equity. This process is called *financial leverage* or *trading on the equity.*

Point: Financial leverage reflects issuance of bonds, notes, or preference shares.

To illustrate the third point, consider Magnum Co., which has $1 million in equity and is planning a $500,000 expansion to meet increasing demand for its product. Magnum predicts the $500,000 expansion will yield $125,000 in additional profit before paying any interest. It currently earns $100,000 per year and has no interest expense. Magnum is considering three plans. Plan A is to not expand. Plan B is to expand and raise $500,000 from equity financing. Plan C is to expand and issue $500,000 of bonds that pay 10% annual interest ($50,000). Exhibit 14.1 shows how these three plans affect Magnum's net profit, equity, and return on equity (net profit/equity). The owner(s) will earn a higher return on equity if expansion occurs. Moreover, the preferred expansion plan is to issue bonds. Projected net profit under Plan C ($175,000) is smaller than under Plan B ($225,000), but the return on equity is larger because of less equity investment. Plan C has another advantage if profit is taxable. This illustration reflects a general rule: *Return on equity increases when the expected rate of return from the new assets is higher than the rate of interest expense on the debt financing.*

Example: Compute return on equity for all three plans if Magnum currently earns $150,000 instead of $100,000.
Answer ($ 000s):
Plan A = 15%   ($150/$1,000)
Plan B = 18.3%   ($275/$1,500)
Plan C = 22.5%   ($225/$1,000)

	Plan A: Do Not Expand	Plan B: Equity Financing	Plan C: Bond Financing
Profit before interest expense	$ 100,000	$ 225,000	$ 225,000
Interest expense	—	—	(50,000)
Net profit	**$ 100,000**	**$ 225,000**	**$ 175,000**
Equity	$1,000,000	$1,500,000	$1,000,000
Return on equity	**10.0%**	**15.0%**	**17.5%**

EXHIBIT 14.1

Financing with Bonds versus Equity

Disadvantages of Bonds   The two main disadvantages of bond financing are these:

1. *Bonds can decrease return on equity.* When a company earns a lower return with the borrowed funds than it pays in interest, it decreases its return on equity. This downside risk of financial leverage is more likely to arise when a company has periods of low profit or net losses.

2. *Bonds require payment of both periodic interest and the par value at maturity.* Bond payments can be especially burdensome when profit and cash flow are low. Equity financing, in contrast, does not require any payments because cash withdrawals (dividends) are paid at the discretion of the owner (or board).

Point: Debt financing is desirable when interest is tax deductible, when owner control is preferred, and when return on equity exceeds the debt's interest rate.

A company must weigh the risks and returns of the disadvantages and advantages of bond financing when deciding whether to issue bonds to finance operations.

Bond Trading

Bonds are securities that can be readily bought and sold. According to McKinsey & Co's publication, "Mapping Global Capital Markets 2011", global bonds take up 74% or US$ 157 trillion of the global capital (bonds and shares) of US$212 trillion. A bond *issue* consists of a number of bonds, usually in denominations of $1,000 or $5,000, and is sold to many different lenders. After bonds are issued, they often are bought and sold by investors, meaning that any particular bond probably has a number of owners before it matures. Since bonds are exchanged (bought and sold) in the market, they have a market value (price). For convenience, bond market values are expressed as a percent of their par (face) value. For example, a company's bonds might be trading at 103½, meaning they can be bought or sold for 103.5% of their par value. Bonds can also trade below par value. For instance, if a company's bonds are trading at 95, they can be bought or sold at 95% of their par value.

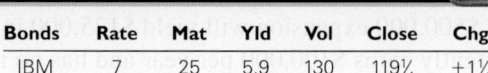

Decision Insight

Quotes The **IBM** bond quote here is interpreted (left to right) as **Bonds,** issuer name; **Rate,** contract interest rate (7%); **Mat,** matures in year 2025 when principal is paid; **Yld,** yield rate (5.9%) of bond at current price; **Vol,** daily dollar worth ($130,000) of trades (in 1,000s); **Close,** closing price (119.25) for the day as percentage of par value; **Chg,** change (+1.25) in closing price from prior day's close. ■

Bonds	Rate	Mat	Yld	Vol	Close	Chg
IBM	7	25	5.9	130	119¼	+1¼

Bond-Issuing Procedures

In the United States, state and federal laws govern bond issuances. Bond issuers also want to ensure that they do not violate any of their existing contractual agreements when issuing bonds. Authorization of bond issuances includes the number of bonds authorized, their par value, and the contract interest rate. The legal document identifying the rights and obligations of both the bondholders and the issuer is called the **bond indenture,** which is the legal contract between the issuer and the bondholders. A bondholder may also receive a bond certificate as evidence of the company's debt. A **bond certificate,** such as that shown in Exhibit 14.2, includes specifics such as the issuer's name, the par value, the contract interest rate, and the maturity date. Many companies reduce costs by not issuing paper certificates to bondholders.[1]

EXHIBIT 14.2

Bond Certificate

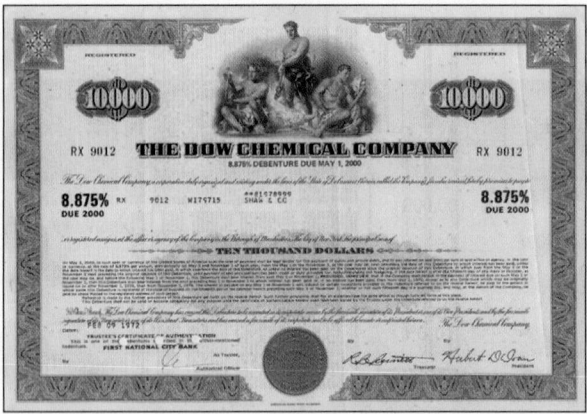

Point: *Indenture* refers to a bond's legal contract; *debenture* refers to an unsecured bond.

BOND ISSUANCES

This section explains accounting for bond issuances at par, below par (discount), and above par (premium). It also describes how to amortize a discount or premium and record bonds issued between interest payment dates.

Issuing Bonds at Par

P1 Prepare entries to record bond issuance and interest expense.

To illustrate an issuance of bonds at par value, suppose a company receives authorization to issue $800,000 of 9%, 20-year bonds dated January 1, 2011, that mature on December 31, 2030, and pay interest semiannually on each June 30 and December 31. After accepting the bond indenture on behalf of the bondholders, the trustee can sell all or a portion of the bonds to an underwriter. If all bonds are sold at par value, the issuer records the sale as follows.

Assets = Liabilities + Equity
+800,000   +800,000

2011				
Jan. 1	Cash		800,000	
	Bonds Payable			800,000
	Sold bonds at par.			

Global: In the United Kingdom, government bonds are called *gilts*—short for gilt-edged investments. *Gilt account* is also a term used by the Reserve Bank of India to refer to a constituent account maintained by a custodian bank for maintenance and servicing of dematerialized government securities owned by a retail customer.

---

[1] The issuing company normally sells its bonds to an investment firm called an *underwriter,* which resells them to the public. An issuing company can also sell bonds directly to investors. When an underwriter sells bonds to a large number of investors, a *trustee* represents and protects the bondholders' interests. The trustee monitors the issuer to ensure that it complies with the obligations in the bond indenture. Most trustees are large banks or trust companies. The trustee writes and accepts the terms of a bond indenture before it is issued. When bonds are offered to the public, called *floating an issue,* they must be registered with the Securities and Exchange Commission (SEC). SEC registration requires the issuer to file certain financial information. Most company bonds are issued in par value units of $1,000 or $5,000. *A baby bond* has a par value of less than $1,000, such as $100.

This entry reflects increases in the issuer's cash *and* long-term liabilities.

The issuer records the first semiannual interest payment as follows.

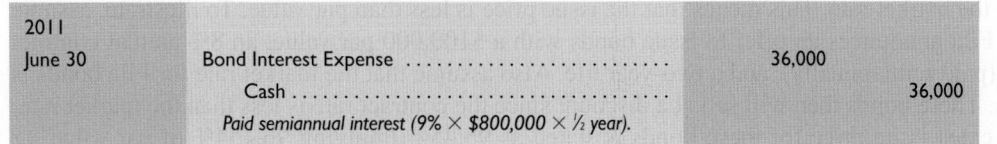

2011			
June 30	Bond Interest Expense	36,000	
	Cash		36,000
	Paid semiannual interest (9% × $800,000 × ½ year).		

Assets = Liabilities + Equity
−36,000   −36,000

The issuer pays and records its semiannual interest obligation every six months until the bonds mature. When they mature, the issuer records its payment of principal as follows.

2030			
Dec. 31	Bonds Payable	800,000	
	Cash		800,000
	Paid bond principal at maturity.		

Assets = Liabilities + Equity
−800,000   −800,000

Bond Discount or Premium

The bond issuer pays the interest rate specified in the indenture, the **contract rate,** also referred to as the *coupon rate, stated rate,* or *nominal rate.* The annual interest paid is determined by multiplying the bond par value by the contract rate. The contract rate is usually stated on an annual basis, even if interest is paid semiannually. For example, if a company issues a $1,000, 8% bond paying interest semiannually, it pays annual interest of $80 (8% × $1,000) in two semiannual payments of $40 each.

The contract rate sets the amount of interest the issuer pays in *cash,* which is not necessarily the *bond interest expense* actually incurred by the issuer. Bond interest expense depends on the bond's market value at issuance, which is determined by market expectations of the risk of lending to the issuer. The bond's **market rate** of interest is the rate that borrowers are willing to pay and lenders are willing to accept for a particular bond and its risk level. As the risk level increases, the rate increases to compensate purchasers for the bonds' increased risk. Also, the market rate is generally higher when the time period until the bond matures is longer due to the risk of adverse events occurring over a longer time period.

Many bond issuers try to set a contract rate of interest equal to the market rate they expect as at the bond issuance date. When the contract rate and market rate are equal, a bond sells at par value, but when they are not equal, a bond does not sell at par value. Instead, it is sold at a *premium* above par value or at a *discount* below par value. Exhibit 14.3 shows the relation between the contract rate, market rate, and a bond's issue price.

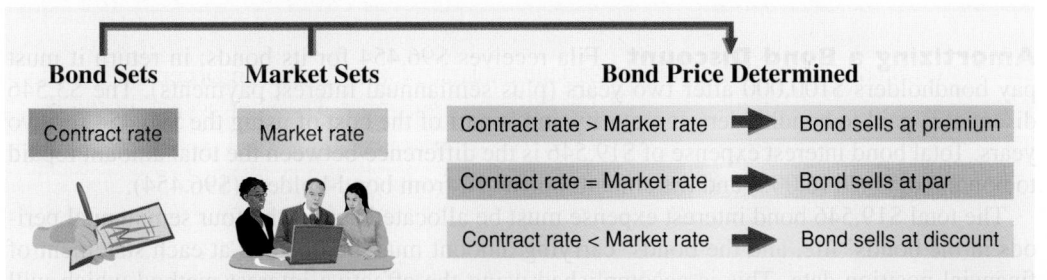

EXHIBIT 14.3

Relation between Bond Issue Price, Contract Rate, and Market Rate

Quick Check

Answers — p. 558

1. A company issues $10,000 of 9%, 5-year bonds dated January 1, 2011, that mature on December 31, 2015, and pay interest semiannually on each June 30 and December 31. Prepare the entry to record this bond issuance and the first semiannual interest payment.

2. How do you compute the amount of interest a bond issuer pays in cash each year?

3. When the contract rate is above the market rate, do bonds sell at a premium or a discount? Do purchasers pay more or less than the par value of the bonds?

Point: The difference between the
contract rate and the market rate of
interest on a new bond issue is usually
a fraction of a percent. We use a
difference of 2% to emphasize the
effects.

Issuing Bonds at a Discount

A **discount on bonds payable** occurs when a company issues bonds with a contract rate less
than the market rate. This means that the issue price is less than par value. To illustrate, assume
that Fila announces an offer to issue bonds with a $100,000 par value, an 8% annual contract
rate (paid semiannually), and a two-year life. Also assume that the market rate for Fila bonds is
10%. These bonds then will sell at a discount since the contract rate is less than the market rate.
The exact issue price for these bonds is stated as 96.454 (implying 96.454% of par value, or
$96,454); we show how to compute this issue price later in the chapter. These bonds obligate the
issuer to pay two separate types of future cash flows:

1. Par value of $100,000 cash at the end of the bonds' two-year life.
2. Cash interest payments of $4,000 (4% × $100,000) at the end of each semiannual period
   during the bonds' two-year life.

The exact pattern of cash flows for the Fila bonds is shown in Exhibit 14.4.

EXHIBIT 14.4

Cash Flows for Fila Bonds

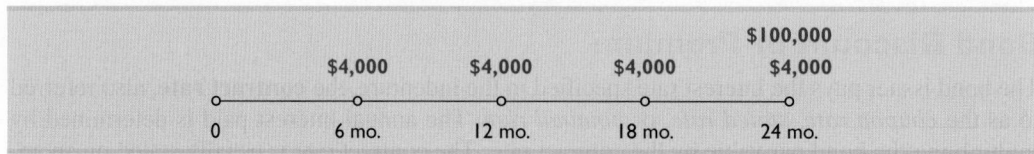

When Fila accepts $96,454 cash for its bonds on the issue date of December 31, 2011, it records
the sale as follows.

Assets = Liabilities + Equity
+96,454   +100,000
             −3,546

Dec. 31	Cash	96,454	
	Discount on Bonds Payable	3,546	
	Bonds Payable		100,000
	Sold bonds at a discount on their issue date.		

Point: Carrying amount at issuance
always equals the issuer's cash borrowed.

These bonds are reported in the long-term liability section of the issuer's December 31, 2011,
statement of financial position as shown in Exhibit 14.5. A discount is deducted from the par
value of bonds to yield the **carrying amount (book value) of bonds.** Discount on Bonds Payable is a contra liability account.

EXHIBIT 14.5

Statement of Financial Position
Presentation of Bond Discount

Long-term liabilities		
Bonds payable, 8%, due December 31, 2013	$100,000	
Less discount on bonds payable	3,546	$96,454

Point: *Zero-coupon bonds* do not pay
periodic interest (contract rate is zero).
These bonds always sell at a discount
because their 0% contract rate is always
below the market rate.

Amortizing a Bond Discount   Fila receives $96,454 for its bonds; in return it must
pay bondholders $100,000 after two years (plus semiannual interest payments). The $3,546
discount is paid to bondholders at maturity and is part of the cost of using the $96,454 for two
years. Total bond interest expense of $19,546 is the difference between the total amount repaid
to bondholders ($116,000) and the amount borrowed from bond-holders ($96,454).

The total $19,546 bond interest expense must be allocated across the four semiannual peri-
ods in the bonds' life, and the bonds' carrying amount must be updated at each statement of
financial position date. This is accomplished using the effective interest method which will
systematically reduce the bond discount to zero over the two-year life. This process is called
amortizing a bond discount.

Effective Interest Amortization

IFRS requires the use of the **effective interest method**, or simply *interest method*. This method
allocates total bond interest expense over the bonds' life in a way that yields a constant rate of
interest. This constant rate of interest is the market rate at the issue date. Thus, bond interest
expense for a period equals the carrying amount of the bond at the beginning of that period
multiplied by the market rate when issued.

Exhibit 14.6 shows an effective interest amortization table for the Fila bonds (as described in Exhibit 14.4). The effective interest method assigns a bond interest expense amount that increases over the life of a discount bond. Specifically, the amortization table shows that the balance of the discount (column D) is amortized until it reaches zero. Also, the bonds' carrying amount (column E) changes each period until it equals par value at maturity. Total bond interest expense is $19,546, consisting of $16,000 of semiannual cash payments and $3,546 of the original bond discount.

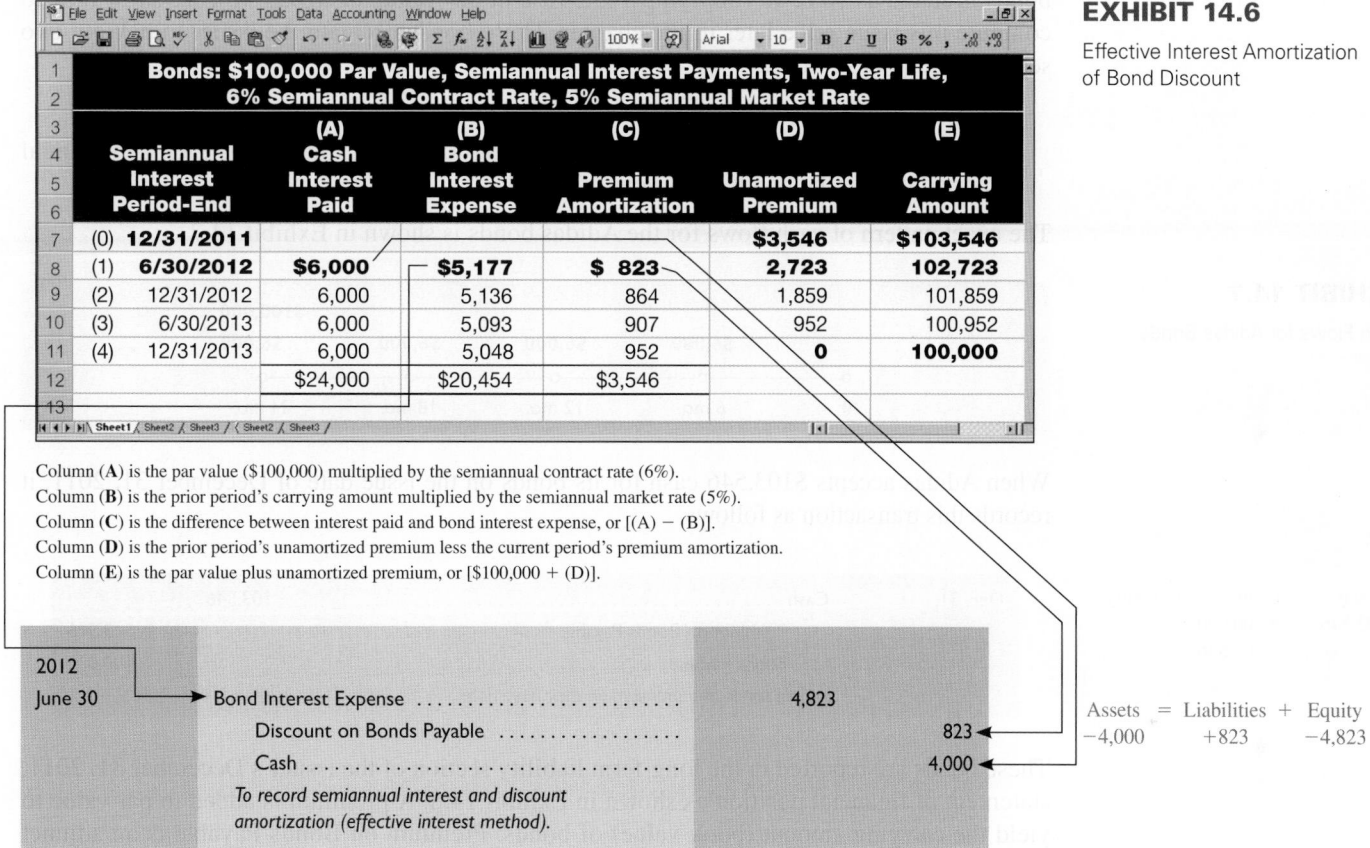

EXHIBIT 14.6

Effective Interest Amortization of Bond Discount

Bonds: $100,000 Par Value, Semiannual Interest Payments, Two-Year Life, 6% Semiannual Contract Rate, 5% Semiannual Market Rate

Semiannual Interest Period-End	(A) Cash Interest Paid	(B) Bond Interest Expense	(C) Premium Amortization	(D) Unamortized Premium	(E) Carrying Amount
(0) 12/31/2011				$3,546	$103,546
(1) 6/30/2012	$6,000	$5,177	$ 823	2,723	102,723
(2) 12/31/2012	6,000	5,136	864	1,859	101,859
(3) 6/30/2013	6,000	5,093	907	952	100,952
(4) 12/31/2013	6,000	5,048	952	0	100,000
	$24,000	$20,454	$3,546		

Column (**A**) is the par value ($100,000) multiplied by the semiannual contract rate (6%).
Column (**B**) is the prior period's carrying amount multiplied by the semiannual market rate (5%).
Column (**C**) is the difference between interest paid and bond interest expense, or [(A) − (B)].
Column (**D**) is the prior period's unamortized premium less the current period's premium amortization.
Column (**E**) is the par value plus unamortized premium, or [$100,000 + (D)].

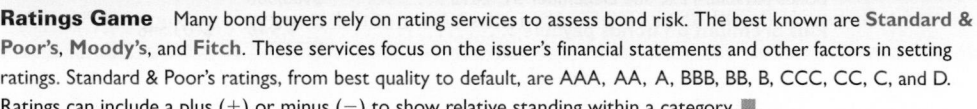

2012		
June 30	Bond Interest Expense	4,823	
	Discount on Bonds Payable		823
	Cash		4,000
	To record semiannual interest and discount amortization (effective interest method).		

Assets	=	Liabilities	+	Equity
−4,000		+823		−4,823

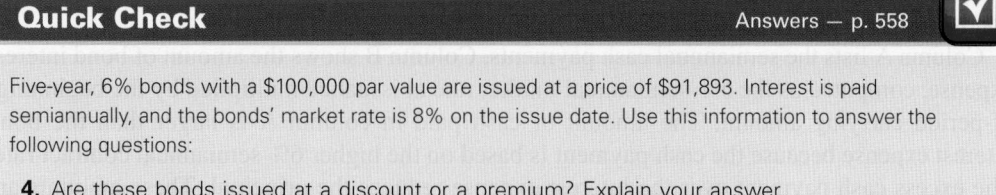

Decision Insight

Ratings Game Many bond buyers rely on rating services to assess bond risk. The best known are **Standard & Poor's**, **Moody's**, and **Fitch**. These services focus on the issuer's financial statements and other factors in setting ratings. Standard & Poor's ratings, from best quality to default, are AAA, AA, A, BBB, BB, B, CCC, CC, C, and D. Ratings can include a plus (+) or minus (−) to show relative standing within a category. ∎

Quick Check

Answers — p. 558

Five-year, 6% bonds with a $100,000 par value are issued at a price of $91,893. Interest is paid semiannually, and the bonds' market rate is 8% on the issue date. Use this information to answer the following questions:

4. Are these bonds issued at a discount or a premium? Explain your answer.

5. What is the issuer's journal entry to record the issuance of these bonds?

6. What is the amount of bond interest expense recorded at the first semiannual period using the effective interest method?

Issuing Bonds at a Premium

When the contract rate of bonds is higher than the market rate, the bonds sell at a price higher than par value. The amount by which the bond price exceeds par value is the **premium on bonds.** To illustrate, assume that **Adidas** issues bonds with a $100,000 par value, a 12% annual contract rate, semiannual interest payments, and a two-year life. Also assume that the market rate for Adidas bonds is 10% on the issue date. The Adidas bonds will sell at a premium because the contract rate is higher than the market rate. The issue price for these bonds is stated as 103.546 (implying 103.546% of par value, or $103,546); we show how to compute this issue price later in the chapter. These bonds obligate the issuer to pay out two separate future cash flows:

1. Par value of $100,000 cash at the end of the bonds' two-year life.
2. Cash interest payments of $6,000 (6% × $100,000) at the end of each semiannual period during the bonds' two-year life.

The exact pattern of cash flows for the Adidas bonds is shown in Exhibit 14.7.

EXHIBIT 14.7

Cash Flows for Adidas Bonds

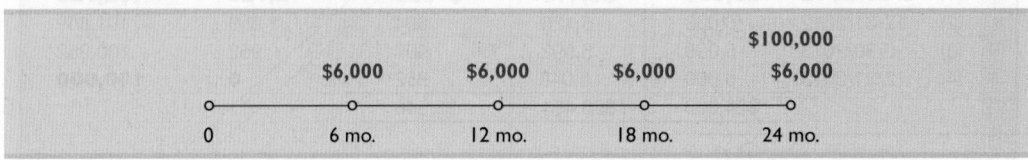

When Adidas accepts $103,546 cash for its bonds on the issue date of December 31, 2011, it records this transaction as follows.

Assets = Liabilities + Equity
+103,546   +100,000
           +3,546

Dec. 31	Cash	103,546	
	Premium on Bonds Payable		3,546
	Bonds Payable		100,000
	Sold bonds at a premium on their issue date.		

These bonds are reported in the long-term liability section of the issuer's December 31, 2011, statement of financial position as shown in Exhibit 14.8. A premium is added to par value to yield the carrying amount (book value) of bonds. Premium on Bonds Payable is an adjunct (also called *accretion*) liability account.

EXHIBIT 14.8

Statement of Financial Position Presentation of Bond Premium

Long-term liabilities		
Bonds payable, 12%, due December 31, 2013	$100,000	
Plus premium on bonds payable	3,546	$103,546

Amortizing a Bond Premium

Exhibit 14.9 shows the amortization table using the effective interest method for the Adidas bonds (as described in Exhibit 14.7).

Column A lists the semiannual cash payments. Column B shows the amount of bond interest expense, computed as the 5% semiannual market rate at issuance multiplied by the beginning-of-period carrying amount. The amount of cash paid in column A is larger than the bond interest expense because the cash payment is based on the higher 6% semiannual contract rate. The excess cash payment over the interest expense reduces the principal. These amounts are shown in column C. Column E shows the carrying amount after deducting the amortized premium in column C from the prior period's carrying amount. Column D shows the premium's reduction by periodic amortization. When the issuer makes the first semiannual interest payment, the effect of premium amortization on bond interest expense and bond liability is recorded as follows:

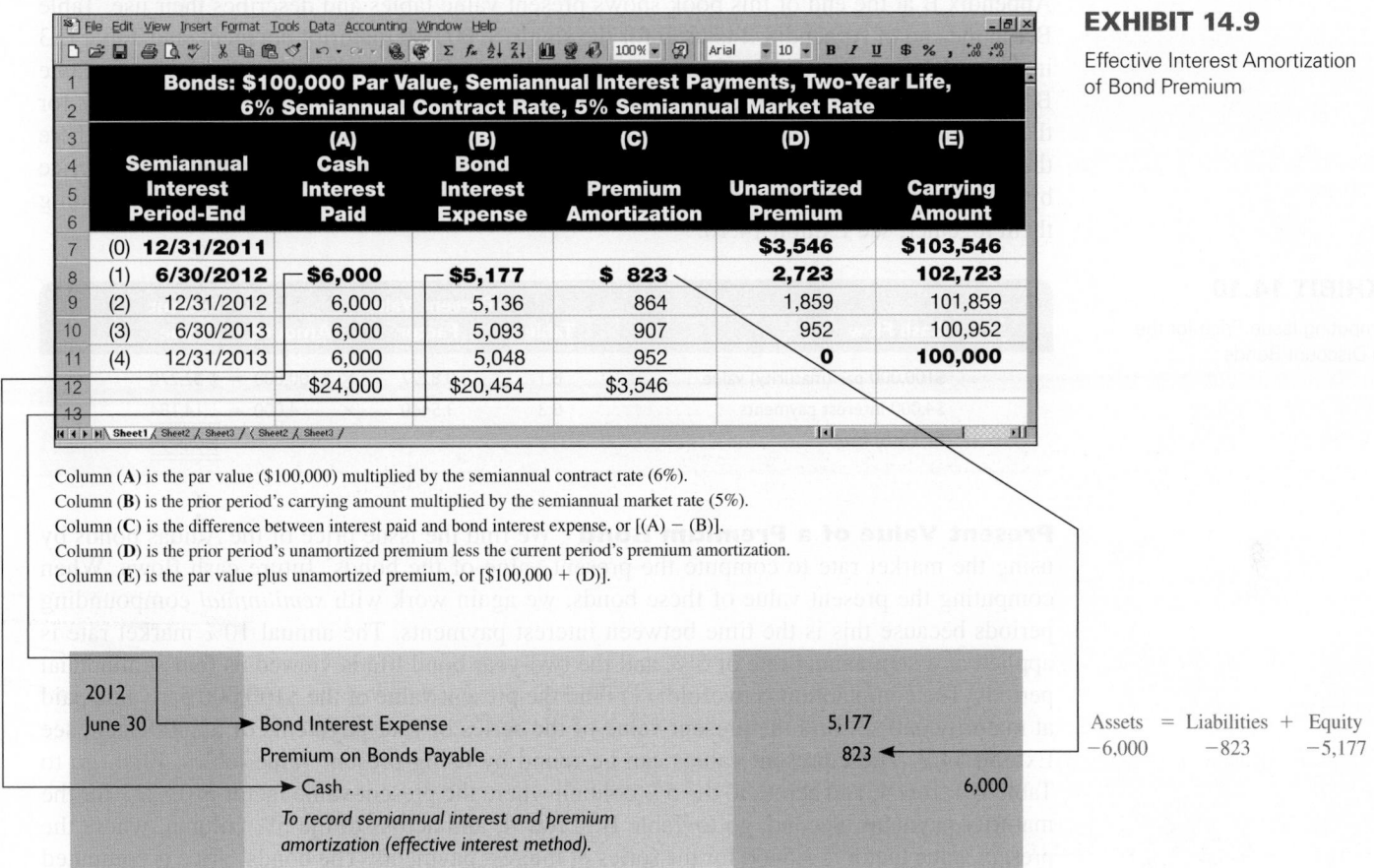

EXHIBIT 14.9

Effective Interest Amortization
of Bond Premium

Similar entries with different amounts are recorded at each payment date until the bond matures at the end of 2013. The effective interest method yields decreasing amounts of bond interest expense and increasing amounts of premium amortization over the bonds' life.

Bond Pricing

Prices for bonds traded on an organized exchange are often published in newspapers and through online services. This information normally includes the bond price (called *quote*), its contract rate, and its current market (called *yield*) rate. However, only a fraction of bonds are traded on organized exchanges. To compute the price of a bond, we apply present value concepts. This section explains how to use *present value concepts* to price the Fila discount bond and the Adidas premium bond described earlier.

Present Value of a Discount Bond The issue price of bonds is found by computing the present value of the bonds' cash payments, discounted at the bonds' market rate. When computing the present value of the Fila bonds, we work with *semiannual* compounding periods because this is the time between interest payments; the annual market rate of 10% is considered a semiannual rate of 5%. Also, the two-year bond life is viewed as four semiannual periods.

Point: InvestingInBonds.com is a
bond research and learning source.

Point: A bond's market value (price) at
issuance equals the present value of its
future cash payments, where the interest
(discount) rate used is the bond's market
rate.

Point: Many calculators have present
value functions for computing bond
prices.

The price computation is twofold: (1) Find the present value of the $100,000 par value paid at maturity and (2) find the present value of the series of four semiannual payments of $4,000 each; see Exhibit 14.4. These present values can be found by using *present value tables*. Appendix B at the end of this book shows present value tables and describes their use. Table B.1 at the end of Appendix B is used for the single $100,000 maturity payment, and Table B.3 in Appendix B is used for the $4,000 series of interest payments. Specifically, we go to Table B.1, row 4, and across to the 5% column to identify the present value factor of 0.8227 for the maturity payment. Next, we go to Table B.3, row 4, and across to the 5% column, where the present value factor is 3.5460 for the series of interest payments. We compute bond price by multiplying the cash flow payments by their corresponding present value factors and adding them together; see Exhibit 14.10.

EXHIBIT 14.10

Computing Issue Price for the Fila Discount Bonds

Cash Flow	Table	Present Value Factor	Amount	Present Value
$100,000 par (maturity) value	B.1	0.8227	× $100,000 =	$ 82,270
$4,000 interest payments	B.3	3.5460	× 4,000 =	14,184
Price of bond				$96,454

Present Value of a Premium Bond   We find the issue price of the Adidas bonds by using the market rate to compute the present value of the bonds' future cash flows. When computing the present value of these bonds, we again work with *semiannual* compounding periods because this is the time between interest payments. The annual 10% market rate is applied as a semiannual rate of 5%, and the two-year bond life is viewed as four semiannual periods. The computation is twofold: (1) Find the present value of the $100,000 par value paid at maturity and (2) find the present value of the series of four payments of $6,000 each; see Exhibit 14.7. These present values can be found by using present value tables. First, go to Table B.1, row 4, and across to the 5% column where the present value factor is 0.8227 for the maturity payment. Second, go to Table B.3, row 4, and across to the 5% column, where the present value factor is 3.5460 for the series of interest payments. The bonds' price is computed by multiplying the cash flow payments by their corresponding present value factors and adding them together; see Exhibit 14.11.

EXHIBIT 14.11

Computing Issue Price for the Adidas Premium Bonds

Cash Flow	Table	Present Value Factor	Amount	Present Value
$100,000 par (maturity) value	B.1	0.8227	× $100,000 =	$ 82,270
$6,000 interest payments	B.3	3.5460	× 6,000 =	21,276
Price of bond				$103,546

Quick Check

Answers — p. 558

On December 31, 2014, a company issues 16%, 10-year bonds with a par value of $100,000. Interest is paid on June 30 and December 31. The bonds are sold to yield a 14% annual market rate at an issue price of $110,592. Use this information to answer questions 7 through 9:

7. Are these bonds issued at a discount or a premium? Explain your answer.

8. Using the effective interest method to allocate bond interest expense, the issuer records the second interest payment (on December 31, 2015) with a debit to Premium on Bonds Payable in the amount of (*a*) $7,723, (*b*) $530, (*c*) $8,000, or (*d*) $277.

9. How are these bonds reported in the long-term liability section of the issuer's statement of financial position as at December 31, 2015?

BOND RETIREMENT

This section describes the retirement of bonds (1) at maturity, (2) before maturity, and (3) by conversion to shares.

P4 Record the retirement of bonds.

Bond Retirement at Maturity

The carrying amount of bonds at maturity always equals par value. The retirement of these bonds at maturity, assuming interest is already paid and entered, is recorded as follows:

2013			
Dec. 31	Bonds Payable	100,000	
	Cash		100,000
	To record retirement of bonds at maturity.		

Assets = Liabilities + Equity
−100,000   −100,000

Bond Retirement before Maturity

Issuers sometimes wish to retire some or all of their bonds prior to maturity. For instance, if interest rates decline greatly, an issuer may wish to replace high-interest-paying bonds with new low-interest bonds. Two common ways to retire bonds before maturity are to (1) exercise a call option or (2) purchase them on the open market. In the first instance, an issuer can reserve the right to retire bonds early by issuing callable bonds. The bond indenture can give the issuer an option to *call* the bonds before they mature by paying the par value plus a *call premium* to bondholders. In the second case, the issuer retires bonds by repurchasing them on the open market at their current price. Whether bonds are called or repurchased, the issuer is unlikely to pay a price that exactly equals their carrying amount. When a difference exists between the bonds' carrying amount and the amount paid, the issuer records a gain or loss equal to the difference.

Point: Bond retirement is also referred to as *bond redemption.*

Point: Gains and losses from retiring bonds should be reported in other comprehensive income.

   To illustrate the accounting for retiring callable bonds, assume that a company issued callable bonds with a par value of $100,000. The call option requires the issuer to pay a call premium of $3,000 to bondholders in addition to the par value. Next, assume that after the June 30, 2011, interest payment, the bonds have a carrying amount of $104,500. Then on July 1, 2011, the issuer calls these bonds and pays $103,000 to bondholders. The issuer recognizes a $1,500 gain from the difference between the bonds' carrying amount of $104,500 and the retirement price of $103,000. The issuer records this bond retirement as follows.

July 1	Bonds Payable	100,000	
	Premium on Bonds Payable	4,500	
	Gain on Bond Retirement		1,500
	Cash		103,000
	To record retirement of bonds before maturity.		

Assets = Liabilities + Equity
−103,000   −100,000   +1,500
              −4,500

An issuer usually must call all bonds when it exercises a call option. However, to retire as many or as few bonds as it desires, an issuer can purchase them on the open market. If it retires less than the entire class of bonds, it recognizes a gain or loss for the difference between the carrying amount of those bonds retired and the amount paid to acquire them.

Bond Retirement by Conversion

Holders of convertible bonds have the right to convert their bonds to shares. When conversion occurs, the bonds' carrying amount is transferred to equity accounts and no gain or loss is recorded. (We further describe convertible bonds in the Decision Analysis section of this chapter.)

   To illustrate, assume that on January 1 the $100,000 par value bonds of **Converse**, with a carrying amount of $100,000, are converted to 15,000 shares of $2 par value ordinary shares. The

Convertible Bond

entry to record this conversion follows (the market prices of the bonds and shares are *not* relevant to this entry; the material in Chapter 13 is helpful in understanding this transaction):

Assets = Liabilities + Equity
      −100,000   +30,000
                 +70,000

Jan. 1	Bonds Payable	100,000	
	Share Capital—Ordinary		30,000
	Share Premium—Ordinary		70,000
	To record retirement of bonds by conversion.		

Decision Insight

Junk Bonds   Junk bonds are company bonds with low credit ratings due to a higher than average likelihood of default. On the upside, the high risk of junk bonds can yield high returns if the issuer survives and repays its debt. ∎

Quick Check   Answer — p. 558

10. Six years ago, a company issued $500,000 of 6%, eight-year bonds at a price of 95. The current carrying amount is $493,750. The company decides to retire 50% of these bonds by buying them on the open market at a price of 102½. What is the amount of gain or loss on the retirement of these bonds?

LONG-TERM NOTES PAYABLE

C1   Explain the types and payment patterns of notes.

Like bonds, notes are issued to obtain assets such as cash. Unlike bonds, notes are typically transacted with a *single* lender such as a bank. An issuer initially records a note at its selling price—that is, the note's face value minus any discount or plus any premium. Over the note's life, the amount of interest expense allocated to each period is computed by multiplying the market rate (at issuance of the note) by the beginning-of-period note balance. The note's carrying amount at any time equals its face value minus any unamortized discount or plus any unamortized premium; carrying amount is also computed as the present value of all remaining payments, discounted using the market rate at issuance.

Installment Notes

An **installment note** is an obligation requiring a series of payments to the lender. Installment notes are common for franchises and other businesses when lenders and borrowers agree to spread payments over several periods. To illustrate, assume that Foghog borrows $60,000 from a bank to purchase equipment. It signs an 8% installment note requiring six annual payments of principal plus interest and it records the note's issuance at January 1, 2011, as follows.

Assets = Liabilities + Equity
+60,000   +60,000

Jan. 1	Cash	60,000	
	Notes Payable		60,000
	Borrowed $60,000 by signing an 8%, six-year installment note.		

Payments on an installment note normally include the accrued interest expense plus a portion of the amount borrowed (the *principal*). This section describes an installment note with equal payments.

The equal total payments pattern consists of changing amounts of both interest and principal. To illustrate, assume that Foghog borrows $60,000 by signing a $60,000 note that requires six *equal payments* of $12,979 at the end of each year. (The present value of an **annuity** of six annual payments of $12,979, discounted at 8%, equals $60,000; we show this computation in footnote 2 on the next page.) The $12,979 includes both interest and principal, the amounts of which change with each payment. Exhibit 14.12 shows the pattern of equal total payments and its two parts, interest and principal. Column A shows the note's beginning balance. Column B shows accrued interest for each year at 8% of the beginning note balance. Column C shows the impact on the note's principal, which equals the difference between the total payment in column D and the interest expense in column B. Column E shows the note's year-end balance.

Years

2011 2012 2013 2014 2015 2016

Point: Most consumer notes are installment notes that require equal total payments.

EXHIBIT 14.12

Installment Note: Equal Total Payments

			Payments		
	(A)	(B)	(C)	(D)	(E)
Period Ending Date	Beginning Balance	*Debit* Interest Expense 8% × (A) +	*Debit* Notes Payable (D) − (B) =	*Credit* Cash (computed)	Ending Balance (A) − (C)
(1) 12/31/2011	$60,000	$ 4,800	$ 8,179	$12,979	$51,821
(2) 12/31/2012	51,821	4,146	8,833	12,979	42,988
(3) 12/31/2013	42,988	3,439	9,540	12,979	33,448
(4) 12/31/2014	33,448	2,676	10,303	12,979	23,145
(5) 12/31/2015	23,145	1,852	11,127	12,979	12,018
(6) 12/31/2016	12,018	961	12,018	12,979	0
		$17,874	$60,000	$77,874	

☐ Interest ☐ Principal

Decreasing Accrued Interest

Increasing Principal Component

Equal Total Payments

End of Year		
2011	$4,800	$8,179
2012	$4,146	$8,833
2013	$3,439	$9,540
2014	$2,676	$10,303
2015	$1,852	$11,127
2016	$961	$12,018

0   $2,500 $5,000 $7,500 $10,000 $12,500 $15,000

Cash Payment Pattern

Decision Insight

Hidden Debt A study reports that 13% of employees in finance and accounting witnessed the falsifying or manipulating of accounting information in the past year (KPMG 2009). This is of special concern with long-term liabilities. For example, Enron violated GAAP to keep debt off its statement of financial position. This concern extends to hidden environment liabilities. That same study reports 27% of employees in quality, safety, and environmental areas observed violations of environmental standards, which can yield massive liabilities. ■

Although the six cash payments are equal, accrued interest decreases each year because the principal balance of the note declines. As the amount of interest decreases each year, the portion of each payment applied to principal increases. This pattern is graphed in the lower part of

P5 Prepare entries to account for notes.

Exhibit 14.12. Foghog uses the amounts in Exhibit 14.12 to record its first two payments (for years 2011 and 2012) as follows:

Assets	=	Liabilities	+	Equity
−12,979		−8,179		−4,800

2011
Dec. 31

Interest Expense	4,800	
Notes Payable	8,179	
Cash		12,979
To record first installment payment.		

Assets	=	Liabilities	+	Equity
−12,979		−8,833		−4,146

2012
Dec. 31

Interest Expense	4,146	
Notes Payable	8,833	
Cash		12,979
To record second installment payment.		

Foghog records similar entries but with different amounts for each of the remaining four payments. After six years, the Notes Payable account balance is zero.[2]

Mortgage Notes and Bonds

A **mortgage** is a legal agreement that helps protect a lender if a borrower fails to make required payments on notes or bonds. A mortgage gives the lender a right to be paid from the cash proceeds of the sale of a borrower's assets identified in the mortgage. A legal document, called a *mortgage contract,* describes the mortgage terms.

Mortgage notes carry a mortgage contract pledging title to specific assets as security for the note. Mortgage notes are especially popular in the purchase of homes and the acquisition of plant assets. Less common *mortgage bonds* are backed by the issuer's assets. Accounting for mortgage notes and bonds is similar to that for unsecured notes and bonds, except that the mortgage agreement must be disclosed. For example, **TIBCO Software** reports that its "mortgage note payable . . . is collateralized by the commercial real property acquired [corporate headquarters]."

Decision Maker   Answer — p. 557

Entrepreneur   You are an electronics retailer planning a holiday sale on a custom stereo system that requires no payments for two years. At the end of two years, buyers must pay the full amount. The system's suggested retail price is $4,100, but you are willing to sell it today for $3,000 cash. What is your holiday sale price if payment will not occur for two years and the market interest rate is 10%? ■

Quick Check   Answers — p. 558

11. Which of the following is true for an installment note requiring a series of equal total cash payments? (*a*) Payments consist of increasing interest and decreasing principal; (*b*) payments consist of changing amounts of principal but constant interest; or (*c*) payments consist of decreasing interest and increasing principal.

12. How is the interest portion of an installment note payment computed?

13. When a borrower records an interest payment on an installment note, how are the statement of financial position and income statement affected?

---

[2] Table B.3 in Appendix B is used to compute the dollar amount of the six payments that equal the initial note balance of $60,000 at 8% interest. We go to Table B.3, row 6, and across to the 8% column, where the present value factor is 4.6229. The dollar amount is then computed by solving this relation:

Table	Present Value Factor		Dollar Amount		Present Value
B.3	4.6229	×	?	=	$60,000

The dollar amount is computed by dividing $60,000 by 4.6229, yielding $12,979.

Collateral agreements can reduce the risk of loss for both bonds and notes. Unsecured bonds and notes are riskier because the issuer's obligation to pay interest and principal has the same priority as all other unsecured liabilities in the event of bankruptcy. If a company is unable to pay its debts in full, the unsecured creditors (including the holders of debentures) lose all or a portion of their balances. These types of legal agreements and other characteristics of long-term liabilities are crucial for effective business decisions. The first part of this section describes the different types of features sometimes included with bonds and notes. The second part explains and applies the debt-to-equity ratio.

Features of Bonds and Notes

This section describes common features of debt securities.

A2 Assess debt features and their implications.

Secured or Unsecured **Secured bonds** (and notes) have specific assets of the issuer pledged (or *mortgaged*) as collateral. This arrangement gives holders added protection against the issuer's default. If the issuer fails to pay interest or par value, the secured holders can demand that the collateral be sold and the proceeds used to pay the obligation. **Unsecured bonds** (and notes), also called *debentures*, are backed by the issuer's general credit standing. Unsecured debt is riskier than secured debt. *Subordinated debentures* are liabilities that are not repaid until the claims of the more senior, unsecured (and secured) liabilities are settled.

Secured Debt   Unsecured Debt

Term or Serial **Term bonds** (and notes) are scheduled for maturity on one specified date. **Serial bonds** (and notes) mature at more than one date (often in series) and thus are usually repaid over a number of periods. For instance, $100,000 of serial bonds might mature at the rate of $10,000 each year from 6 to 15 years after they are issued. Many bonds are **sinking fund bonds,** which to reduce the holder's risk require the issuer to create a *sinking fund* of assets set aside at specified amounts and dates to repay the bonds.

Registered or Bearer Bonds issued in the names and addresses of their holders are **registered bonds.** The issuer makes bond payments by sending checks (or cash transfers) to registered holders. A registered holder must notify the issuer of any ownership change. Registered bonds offer the issuer the practical advantage of not having to actually issue bond certificates. Bonds payable to whoever holds them (the *bearer*) are called **bearer bonds** or *unregistered bonds*. Sales or exchanges might not be recorded, so the holder of a bearer bond is presumed to be its rightful owner. As a result, lost bearer bonds are difficult to replace. Many bearer bonds are also **coupon bonds.** This term reflects interest coupons that are attached to the bonds. When each coupon matures, the holder presents it to a bank or broker for collection. At maturity, the holder follows the same process and presents the bond certificate for collection. Issuers of coupon bonds cannot deduct the related interest expense for taxable profit. This is to prevent abuse by taxpayers who own coupon bonds but fail to report interest profit on their tax returns.

Convertible and/or Callable **Convertible bonds** (and notes) can be exchanged for a fixed number of shares of the issuing corporation's ordinary shares. Convertible debt offers holders the potential to participate in future increases in share price. Holders still receive periodic interest while the debt is held and the par value if they hold the debt to maturity. In most cases, the holders decide whether and when to convert debt to shares. **Callable bonds** (and notes) have an option exercisable by the issuer to retire them at a stated dollar amount before maturity.

Convertible Debt   Callable Debt

Decision Insight

Munis More than a million municipal bonds, or "munis," exist, and many are tax exempt. Munis are issued by state, city, town, and county governments to pay for public projects including schools, libraries, roads, bridges, and stadiums. ■

Debt-to-Equity Ratio

Beyond assessing different characteristics of debt as just described, we want to know the level of debt, especially in relation to total equity. Such knowledge helps us assess the risk of a company's financing

A3 Compute the debt-to-equity ratio and explain its use.

structure. A company financed mainly with debt is more risky because liabilities must be repaid—usually with periodic interest—whereas equity financing does not. A measure to assess the risk of a company's financing structure is the **debt-to-equity ratio** (see Exhibit 14.13).

EXHIBIT 14.13

Debt-to-Equity Ratio

$$\text{Debt-to-equity} = \frac{\text{Total liabilities}}{\text{Total equity}}$$

The debt-to-equity ratio varies across companies and industries. To apply the debt-to-equity ratio, let's look at this measure for Adidas in Exhibit 14.14.

EXHIBIT 14.14

Adidas' Debt-to-Equity Ratio

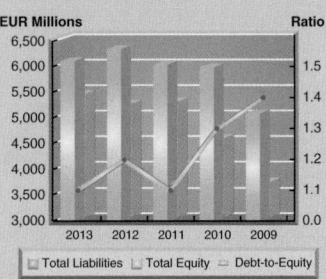

(EUR millions)	2013	2012	2011	2010	2009
Total liabilities	6,118	6,360	6,049	5,995	5,099
Total equity	5,481	5,291	5,331	4,623	3,776
Debt-to-equity.	1.1	1.2	1.1	1.3	1.4

Adidas' 2013 debt-to-equity ratio is 1.1, meaning that creditors contributed EUR 1.1 for each EUR 1 contributed by shareholders. This implies a low risk financing structure for Adidas. Analysis across the years shows that Adidas' financing structure has become less risky in recent years. Given its stable revenues and profits in recent years (see its annual report), Adidas is not at risk of financial distress.

■ **Decision Maker**   Answer — p. 557

Bond Investor   You plan to purchase debenture bonds from one of two companies in the same industry that are similar in size and performance. The first company has $350,000 in total liabilities, and $1,750,000 in equity. The second company has $1,200,000 in total liabilities, and $1,000,000 in equity. Which company's debenture bonds are less risky based on the debt-to-equity ratio? ■

DEMONSTRATION PROBLEM

Water Sports Company (WSC) patented and successfully test-marketed a new product. To expand its ability to produce and market the new product, WSC needs to raise $800,000 of financing. On January 1, 2011, the company obtained the money in two ways:

a. WSC signed a $400,000, 10% installment note to be repaid with five equal annual installments to be made on December 31 of 2011 through 2015.

b. WSC issued five-year bonds with a par value of $400,000. The bonds have a 12% annual contract rate and pay interest on June 30 and December 31. The bonds' annual market rate is 10% as at January 1, 2011.

Required

1. For the installment note, (*a*) compute the size of each annual payment, (*b*) prepare an amortization table such as Exhibit 14.12, and (*c*) prepare the journal entry for the first payment.

2. For the bonds, (*a*) compute their issue price; (*b*) prepare the January 1, 2011, journal entry to record their issuance; (*c*) prepare an amortization table using the effective interest method; (*d*) prepare the June 30, 2011, journal entry to record the first interest payment; and (*e*) prepare a journal entry to record retiring the bonds at a $416,000 call price on January 1, 2013.

PLANNING THE SOLUTION

● For the installment note, divide the borrowed amount by the annuity factor (from Table B.3) using the 10% rate and five payments to compute the amount of each payment. Prepare a table similar to Exhibit 14.12 and use the numbers in the table's first line for the journal entry.

● Compute the bonds' issue price by using the market rate to find the present value of their cash flows (use tables found in Appendix B). Then use this result to record the bonds' issuance. Next, prepare an amortization table and use it to get the numbers needed for the journal entry. Also use the table to find the carrying amount as at the date of the bonds' retirement that you need for the journal entry.

SOLUTION TO DEMONSTRATION PROBLEM

Part 1: Installment Note

a. Annual payment = Note balance/Annuity factor = $400,000/3.7908 = $105,519 (The annuity factor is for five payments and a rate of 10%.)

b. An amortization table follows.

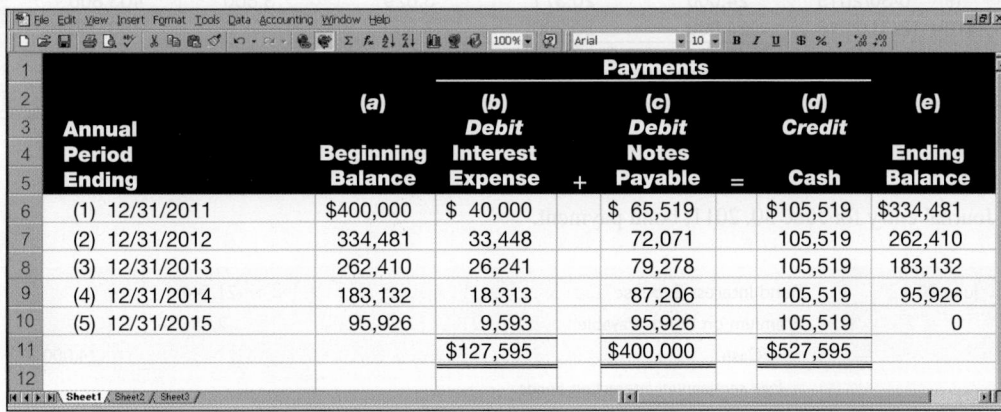

Annual Period Ending	(a) Beginning Balance	(b) Debit Interest Expense	+	(c) Debit Notes Payable	=	(d) Credit Cash	(e) Ending Balance
(1) 12/31/2011	$400,000	$ 40,000		$ 65,519		$105,519	$334,481
(2) 12/31/2012	334,481	33,448		72,071		105,519	262,410
(3) 12/31/2013	262,410	26,241		79,278		105,519	183,132
(4) 12/31/2014	183,132	18,313		87,206		105,519	95,926
(5) 12/31/2015	95,926	9,593		95,926		105,519	0
		$127,595		$400,000		$527,595	

c. Journal entry for December 31, 2011, payment.

Dec. 31	Interest Expense	40,000	
	Notes Payable	65,519	
	Cash		105,519
	To record first installment payment.		

Part 2: Bonds (Effective Interest Method)

a. Compute the bonds' issue price.

Cash Flow	Table	Present Value Factor*	Amount		Present Value
Par (maturity) value	B.1 in App. B (PV of 1)	0.6139	× 400,000	=	$245,560
Interest payments	B.3 in App. B (PV of annuity)	7.7217	× 24,000	=	185,321
Price of bond					$430,881

* Present value factors are for 10 payments using a semiannual market rate of 5%.

b. Journal entry for January 1, 2011, issuance.

Jan. 1	Cash	430,881	
	Premium on Bonds Payable		30,881
	Bonds Payable		400,000
	Sold bonds at a premium.		

c. Effective interest amortization table for premium bonds.

Semiannual Interest Period	(A) Cash Interest Paid 6% × $400,000	(B) Interest Expense 5% × Prior (E)	(C) Premium Amortization (A) − (B)	(D) Unamortized Premium Prior (D) − (C)	(E) Carrying Amount $400,000 + (D)
(0) 1/1/2011				$30,881	$430,881
(1) 6/30/2011	$ 24,000	$ 21,544	$ 2,456	28,425	428,425
(2) 12/31/2011	24,000	21,421	2,579	25,846	425,846
(3) 6/30/2012	24,000	21,292	2,708	23,138	423,138
(4) 12/31/2012	24,000	21,157	2,843	20,295	420,295
(5) 6/30/2013	24,000	21,015	2,985	17,310	417,310
(6) 12/31/2013	24,000	20,866	3,134	14,176	414,176
(7) 6/30/2014	24,000	20,709	3,291	10,885	410,885
(8) 12/31/2014	24,000	20,544	3,456	7,429	407,429
(9) 6/30/2015	24,000	20,371	3,629	3,800	403,800
(10) 12/31/2015	24,000	20,200*	3,800	0	400,000
	$240,000	$209,119	$30,881		

* Adjusted for rounding

d. Journal entry for June 30, 2011, bond payment.

June 30	Bond Interest Expense	21,544	
	Premium on Bonds Payable	2,456	
	Cash		24,000
	Paid semiannual interest on bonds.		

e. Journal entry for January 1, 2013, bond retirement.

Jan. 1	Bonds Payable	400,000	
	Premium on Bonds Payable	20,295	
	Cash		416,000
	Gain on Retirement of Bonds		4,295
	To record bond retirement (carrying amount as at December 31, 2012).		

APPENDIX

14A — Present Values of Bonds and Notes

This appendix explains how to apply present value techniques to measure a long-term liability when it is created and to assign interest expense to the periods until it is settled. Appendix B at the end of the book provides additional discussion of present value concepts.

C2 Explain and compute the present value of an amount(s) to be paid at a future date(s).

Present Value Concepts The basic present value concept is that cash paid (or received) in the future has less value now than the same amount of cash paid (or received) today. To illustrate, if we must pay $1 one year from now, its present value is less than $1. To see this, assume that we borrow $0.9259 today that must be paid back in one year with 8% interest. Our interest expense for this loan is computed as $0.9259 × 8%, or $0.0741. When the $0.0741 interest is added to the $0.9259 borrowed, we get the $1 payment necessary to repay our loan with interest. This is formally computed in Exhibit 14A.1. The

$0.9259 borrowed is the present value of the $1 future payment. More generally, an amount borrowed equals the present value of the future payment. (This same interpretation applies to an investment. If $0.9259 is invested at 8%, it yields $0.0741 in revenue after one year. This amounts to $1, made up of principal and interest.)

Amount borrowed	$0.9259
Interest for one year at 8%	0.0741
Amount owed after 1 year	$ 1.0000

EXHIBIT 14A.1

Components of a One-Year Loan

To extend this example, assume that we owe $1 two years from now instead of one year, and the 8% interest is compounded annually. *Compounded* means that interest during the second period is based on the total of the amount borrowed plus the interest accrued from the first period. The second period's interest is then computed as 8% multiplied by the sum of the amount borrowed plus interest earned in the first period. Exhibit 14A.2 shows how we compute the present value of $1 to be paid in two years. This amount is $0.8573. The first year's interest of $0.0686 is added to the principal so that the second year's interest is based on $0.9259. Total interest for this two-year period is $0.1427, computed as $0.0686 plus $0.0741.

Point: Benjamin Franklin is said to have described compounding as "the money, money makes, makes more money."

Amount borrowed	$0.8573
Interest for first year ($0.8573 × 8%)	0.0686
Amount owed after 1 year	0.9259
Interest for second year ($0.9259 × 8%)	0.0741
Amount owed after 2 years	$ 1.0000

EXHIBIT 14A.2

Components of a Two-Year Loan

Present Value Tables   The present value of $1 that we must repay at some future date can be computed by using this formula: $1/(1 + i)^n$. The symbol i is the interest rate per period and n is the number of periods until the future payment must be made. Applying this formula to our two-year loan, we get $1/(1.08)^2$, or $0.8573. This is the same value shown in Exhibit 14A.2. We can use this formula to find any present value. However, a simpler method is to use a *present value table,* which lists present values computed with this formula for various interest rates and time periods. Many people find it helpful in learning present value concepts to first work with the table and then move to using a calculator.

Exhibit 14A.3 shows a present value table for a future payment of 1 for up to 10 periods at three different interest rates. Present values in this table are rounded to four decimal places. This table is drawn from the larger and more complete Table B.1 in Appendix B at the end of the book. Notice that the first value in the 8% column is 0.9259, the value we computed earlier for the present value of a $1 loan for one year at 8% (see Exhibit 14A.1). Go to the second row in the same 8% column and find the present value of 1 discounted at 8% for two years, or 0.8573. This $0.8573 is the present value of our obligation to repay $1 after two periods at 8% interest (see Exhibit 14A.2).

	Rate		
Periods	6%	8%	10%
1	0.9434	**0.9259**	0.9091
2	0.8900	**0.8573**	0.8264
3	0.8396	0.7938	0.7513
4	0.7921	0.7350	0.6830
5	0.7473	0.6806	0.6209
6	0.7050	0.6302	0.5645
7	0.6651	0.5835	0.5132
8	0.6274	0.5403	0.4665
9	0.5919	0.5002	0.4241
10	0.5584	0.4632	0.3855

EXHIBIT 14A.3

Present Value of 1

Example: Use Exhibit 14A.3 to find the present value of $1 discounted for 2 years at 6%. *Answer:* $0.8900

Applying a Present Value Table   To illustrate how to measure a liability using a present value table, assume that a company plans to borrow cash and repay it as follows: $2,000 after one year, $3,000 after two years, and $5,000 after three years. How much does this company receive today if the interest rate on this loan is 10%? To answer, we need to compute the present value of the three future payments, discounted at 10%. This computation is shown in Exhibit 14A.4 using present values from Exhibit 14A.3. The company can borrow $8,054 today at 10% interest in exchange for its promise to make these three payments at the scheduled dates.

Periods	Payments	Present Value of 1 at 10%	Present Value of Payments
1	$2,000	0.9091	$ 1,818
2	3,000	0.8264	2,479
3	5,000	0.7513	3,757
Present value of all payments			$8,054

EXHIBIT 14A.4

Present Value of a Series of Unequal Payments

Present Value of an Annuity   The $8,054 present value for the loan in Exhibit 14A.4 equals the sum of the present values of the three payments. When payments are not equal, their combined present value is best computed by adding the individual present values as shown in Exhibit 14A.4. Sometimes payments follow an **annuity,** which is a series of *equal* payments at equal time intervals. The present value of an annuity is readily computed.

EXHIBIT 14A.5

Present Value of a Series of Equal Payments (Annuity) by Discounting Each Payment

Periods	Payments	Present Value of 1 at 6%	Present Value of Payments
1	$5,000	0.9434	$ 4,717
2	5,000	0.8900	4,450
3	5,000	0.8396	4,198
4	5,000	0.7921	3,961
Present value of all payments		**3.4651**	**$17,326**

To illustrate, assume that a company must repay a 6% loan with a $5,000 payment at each year-end for the next four years. This loan amount equals the present value of the four payments discounted at 6%. Exhibit 14A.5 shows how to compute this loan's present value of $17,326 by multiplying each payment by its matching present value factor taken from Exhibit 14A.3.

However, the series of $5,000 payments is an annuity, so we can compute its present value with either of two shortcuts. First, the third column of Exhibit 14A.5 shows that the sum of the present values of 1 at 6% for periods 1 through 4 equals 3.4651. One shortcut is to multiply this total of 3.4651 by the $5,000 annual payment to get the combined present value of $17,326. It requires one multiplication instead of four.

EXHIBIT 14A.6

Present Value of an Annuity of 1

Periods	Rate 6%	Rate 8%	Rate 10%
1	0.9434	0.9259	0.9091
2	1.8334	1.7833	1.7355
3	2.6730	2.5771	2.4869
4	3.4651	3.3121	3.1699
5	4.2124	3.9927	3.7908
6	4.9173	4.6229	4.3553
7	5.5824	5.2064	4.8684
8	6.2098	5.7466	5.3349
9	6.8017	6.2469	5.7590
10	7.3601	6.7101	6.1446

Example: Use Exhibit 14A.6 to find the present value of an annuity of eight $15,000 payments with an 8% interest rate. *Answer:* $15,000 × 5.7466 = $86,199

The second shortcut uses an *annuity table* such as the one shown in Exhibit 14A.6, which is drawn from the more complete Table B.3 in Appendix B. We go directly to the annuity table to get the present value factor for a specific number of payments and interest rate. We then multiply this factor by the amount of the payment to find the present value of the annuity. Specifically, find the row for four periods and go across to the 6% column, where the factor is 3.4651. This factor equals the present value of an annuity with four payments of 1, discounted at 6%. We then multiply 3.4651 by $5,000 to get the $17,326 present value of the annuity.

Compounding Periods Shorter Than a Year   The present value examples all involved periods of one year. In many situations, however, interest is compounded over shorter periods. For example, the interest rate on bonds is usually stated as an annual rate but interest is often paid every six months (semiannually). This means that the present value of interest payments from such bonds must be computed using interest periods of six months.

Assume that a borrower wants to know the present value of a series of 10 *semiannual payments* of $4,000 made over five years at an *annual interest rate* of 12%. The interest rate is stated as an annual rate of 12%, but it is actually a rate of 6% per semiannual interest period. To compute the present value of this series of $4,000 payments, go to row 10 of Exhibit 14A.6 and across to the 6% column to find the factor 7.3601. The present value of this annuity is $29,440 (7.3601 × $4,000).

Example: If this borrower makes five semiannual payments of $8,000, what is the present value of this annuity at a 12% rate? *Answer:* 4.2124 × $8,000 = $33,699

Appendix B further describes present value concepts and includes more complete present value tables and assignments.

Quick Check   Answers — p. 558

14. A company enters into an agreement to make four annual year-end payments of $1,000 each, starting one year from now. The annual interest rate is 8%. The present value of these four payments is (a) $2,923, (b) $2,940, or (c) $3,312.

15. Suppose a company has an option to pay either (a) $10,000 after one year or (b) $5,000 after six months and another $5,000 after one year. Which choice has the lower present value?

Summary

C1 Explain the types and payment patterns of notes. Notes repaid over a period of time are called *installment notes* and usually follow one of two payment patterns: (1) decreasing payments of interest plus equal amounts of principal or (2) equal total payments. Mortgage notes also are common.

C2A Explain and compute the present value of an amount(s) to be paid at a future date(s). The basic concept of present value is that an amount of cash to be paid or received in the future is worth less than the same amount of cash to be paid or received today. Another important present value concept is that interest is compounded, meaning interest is added to the balance and used to determine interest for succeeding periods. An annuity is a series of equal payments occurring at equal time intervals. An annuity's present value can be computed using the present value table for an annuity (or a calculator).

A1 Compare bond financing with share financing. Bond financing is used to fund business activities. Advantages of bond financing versus share financing include (1) no effect on owner control, (2) tax savings, and (3) increased earnings due to financial leverage. Disadvantages include (1) interest and principal payments and (2) amplification of poor performance.

A2 Assess debt features and their implications. Certain bonds are secured by the issuer's assets; other bonds, called *debentures,* are unsecured. Serial bonds mature at different points in time; term bonds mature at one time. Registered bonds have each bondholder's name recorded by the issuer; bearer bonds are payable to the holder. Convertible bonds are exchangeable for shares of the issuer's shares. Callable bonds can be retired by the issuer at a set price. Debt features alter the risk of loss for creditors.

A3 Compute the debt-to-equity ratio and explain its use. Both creditors and equity holders are concerned about the relation between the amount of liabilities and the amount of equity. A company's financing structure is at less risk when the debt-to-equity ratio is lower, as liabilities must be paid and usually with periodic interest.

P1 Prepare entries to record bond issuance and interest expense. When bonds are issued at par, Cash is debited and Bonds Payable is credited for the bonds' par value. At bond interest payment dates (usually semiannual), Bond Interest Expense is debited and Cash credited—the latter for an amount equal to the bond par value multiplied by the bond contract rate.

P2 Compute and record amortization of bond discount. Bonds are issued at a discount when the contract rate is less than the market rate, making the issue (selling) price less than par. When this occurs, the issuer records a credit to Bonds Payable (at par) and debits both Discount on Bonds Payable and Cash. The amount of bond interest expense assigned to each period is computed using the effective interest method.

P3 Compute and record amortization of bond premium. Bonds are issued at a premium when the contract rate is higher than the market rate, making the issue (selling) price greater than par. When this occurs, the issuer records a debit to Cash and credits both Premium on Bonds Payable and Bonds Payable (at par). The amount of bond interest expense assigned to each period is computed using the effective interest method. The Premium on Bonds Payable is allocated to reduce bond interest expense over the life of the bonds.

P4 Record the retirement of bonds. Bonds are retired at maturity with a debit to Bonds Payable and a credit to Cash at par value. The issuer can retire the bonds early by exercising a call option or purchasing them in the market. Bondholders can also retire bonds early by exercising a conversion feature on convertible bonds. The issuer recognizes a gain or loss for the difference between the amount paid and the bond carrying amount.

P5 Prepare entries to account for notes. Interest is allocated to each period in a note's life by multiplying its beginning-period carrying amount by its market rate at issuance. If a note is repaid with equal payments, the payment amount is computed by dividing the borrowed amount by the present value of an annuity factor (taken from a present value table) using the market rate and the number of payments.

Guidance Answers to **Decision Maker**

Entrepreneur This is a "present value" question. The market interest rate (10%) and present value ($3,000) are known, but the payment required two years later is unknown. This amount ($3,630) can be computed as $3,000 \times 1.10 \times 1.10$. Thus, the sale price is $3,630 when no payments are received for two years. The $3,630 received two years from today is equivalent to $3,000 cash today.

Bond Investor The debt-to-equity ratio for the first company is 0.2 ($350,000/$1,750,000) and for the second company is 1.2 ($1,200,000/$1,000,000), suggesting that the financing structure of the second company is more risky than that of the first company. Consequently, as a buyer of unsecured debenture bonds, you prefer the first company (all else equal).

Guidance Answers to Quick Checks

1.

2011			
Jan. 1	Cash	10,000	
	Bonds Payable		10,000
June 30	Bond Interest Expense	450	
	Cash		450

Semiannual Interest Period-end	Cash Interest Paid	Bond Interest Expense	Premium Amortization	Unamortized Premium	Carrying Amount
Dec 31 10				10,592	110,592
Jun 30 11	8,000	7,741	259	10,333	110,333
Dec 31 11	8,000	7,723	277	10,057	110,057

2. Multiply the bond's par value by its contract rate of interest.

3. Bonds sell at a premium when the contract rate exceeds the market rate and the purchasers pay more than their par value.

4. The bonds are issued at a discount, meaning that issue price is less than par value. A discount occurs because the bond contract rate (6%) is less than the market rate (8%).

5.

Cash	91,893	
Discount on Bonds Payable	8,107	
Bonds Payable		100,000

6. $3,676 (beginning carrying amount of $91,893 multiplied by the annual market rate of 8% for 6 months or semiannual market rate of 4%).

7. The bonds are issued at a premium, meaning issue price is higher than par value. A premium occurs because the bonds' contract rate (16%) is higher than the market rate (14%).

8. (d) See partial amortization table:

Bonds: $100,000 Par Value, Semiannual Interest Payments, Ten-Year Life, 16% Annual Contract Rate, 14% Annual Market Rate

9.

Bonds payable, 16%, due 12/31/2020	$100,000
Plus premium on bonds payable	10,057* $110,057

* Original premium balance of $10,592 less $259 and $277 amortized on 6/30/2011 and 12/31/2011, respectively (some rounding difference).

10. $9,375 loss, computed as the difference between the repurchase price of $256,250 [50% of ($500,000 × 102.5%)] and the carrying amount of $246,875 (50% of $493,750).

11. (c)

12. The interest portion of an installment payment equals the period's beginning loan balance multiplied by the market interest rate at the time of the note's issuance.

13. On the statement of financial position, the account balances of the related liability (note payable) and asset (cash) accounts are decreased. On the income statement, interest expense is recorded.

14. (c), computed as 3.3121 × $1,000 = $3,312.

15. The option of paying $10,000 after one year has a lower present value. It postpones paying the first $5,000 by six months. More generally, the present value of a further delayed payment is always lower than a less delayed payment.

Key Terms   www.mheducation.asia/olc/wildkwokFAP

Annuity (p. 549)

Bearer bonds (p. 551)

Bond (p. 538)

Bond certificate (p. 540)

Bond indenture (p. 540)

Callable bonds (p. 551)

Carrying amount (book value) of bonds (p. 542)

Contract rate (p. 541)

Convertible bonds (p. 551)

Coupon bonds (p. 551)

Debt-to-equity ratio (p. 552)

Discount on bonds payable (p. 542)

Effective interest method (p. 542)

Installment note (p. 548)

Market rate (p. 541)

Mortgage (p. 550)

Par value of a bond (p. 538)

Premium on bonds (p. 544)

Registered bonds (p. 551)

Secured bonds (p. 551)

Serial bonds (p. 551)

Sinking fund bonds (p. 551)

Term bonds (p. 551)

Unsecured bonds (p. 551)

Multiple Choice Quiz   Answers on p. 568   www.mheducation.asia/olc/wildkwokFAP

Additional Quiz Questions are available at the book's Website.

1. A bond traded at 97½ means that
   a. The bond pays 97½% interest.
   b. The bond trades at $975 per $1,000 bond.
   c. The market rate of interest is below the contract rate of interest for the bond.
   d. The bonds can be retired at $975 each.
   e. The bond's interest rate is 2½%.

2. A bondholder that owns a $1,000, 6%, 15-year bond has
  a. The right to receive $1,000 at maturity.
  b. Ownership rights in the bond issuing entity.
  c. The right to receive $60 per month until maturity.
  d. The right to receive $1,900 at maturity.
  e. The right to receive $600 per year until maturity.

3. A company issues 8%, 20-year bonds with a par value of $500,000. The current market rate for the bonds is 8%.

The amount of interest owed to the bondholders for each semi-annual interest payment is
  a. $40,000.
  b. $0.
  c. $20,000.
  d. $800,000.
  e. $400,000.

🔲 Icon denotes assignments that involve decision making.

Discussion Questions

1. What is the main difference between a bond and an ordinary share?

2. What is the main difference between notes payable and bonds payable?

3. 🔲 What is the advantage of issuing bonds instead of obtaining financing from the company's owners?

4. What are the duties of a trustee for bondholders?

5. What is a bond indenture? What provisions are usually included in it?

6. What are the *contract* rate and the *market* rate for bonds?

7. 🔲 What factors affect the market rates for bonds?

8. 🔲 If you know the par value of bonds, the contract rate, and the market rate, how do you compute the bonds' price?

9. What is the issue price of a $2,000 bond sold at 98¼? What is the issue price of a $6,000 bond sold at 101½?

10. Describe the debt-to-equity ratio and explain how creditors and owners would use this ratio to evaluate a company's risk?

11. 🔲 What obligation does an entrepreneur (owner) have to investors that purchase bonds to finance the business?

12. Refer to Nestlé's 2013 consolidated cash flow statement in Appendix A. Is there any indication that Nestlé has issued bonds?

13. Refer to Adidas' 2013 consolidated statement of financial position in Appendix A. By what amount did Adidas's long-term borrowing increase or decrease in 2013?

14. Refer to Samsung's 2012 consolidated statement of cash flows in Appendix A. For the year ended December 31, 2012, did Samsung receive cash on long-term borrowings and debentures or repay cash on long-term borrowings and debentures?

15. Refer to Puma's 2013 consolidated statement of financial position from its Website (**http://about.puma.com/en/investor-relations/financial-reports**). For the year ended December 31, 2013, what is its debt-to-equity ratio? What does this ratio tell us?

---

connect

Round dollar amounts to the nearest whole dollar.

Enter the letter of the description A through H that best fits each term or phrase 1 through 8.

A. Records and tracks the bondholders' names.

B. Is unsecured; backed only by the issuer's credit standing.

C. Has varying maturity dates for amounts owed.

D. Identifies rights and responsibilities of the issuer and the bondholders.

E. Can be exchanged for the issuer's ordinary shares.

F. Is unregistered; interest is paid to whoever possesses them.

G. Maintains a separate asset account from which bondholders are paid at maturity.

H. Pledges specific assets of the issuer as collateral.

1. _____ Debenture

2. _____ Bond indenture

3. _____ Bearer bond

4. _____ Registered bond

5. _____ Sinking fund bond

6. _____ Convertible bond

7. _____ Secured bond

8. _____ Serial bond

QUICK STUDY

QS 14-1
Bond features and terminology

A2

QS 14-2
Bond computations—
effective interest

P1 P3

Sanchez Company issues 10%, 15-year bonds with a par value of $120,000 and semiannual interest payments. On the issue date, the annual market rate for these bonds is 8%, which implies a selling price of 117¼. The effective interest method is used to allocate interest expense.

1. What are the issuer's cash proceeds from issuance of these bonds?

2. What total amount of bond interest expense will be recognized over the life of these bonds?

3. What amount of bond interest expense is recorded on the first interest payment date?

QS 14-3
Journalize bond issuance   **P1**

Prepare the journal entries for the issuance of the bonds in both QS 14-2. Assume that the bonds are issued for cash on January 1, 2011.

QS 14-4
Computing bond price   **P2 P3**

Using the bond details in QS 14-2, confirm that the bonds' selling prices given in the problem is approximately correct. Use the present value tables B.1 and B.3 in Appendix B.

QS 14-5
Bond retirement by call option

P4

On July 1, 2011, Jackson Company exercises a $5,000 call option (plus par value) on its outstanding bonds that have a carrying amount of $208,000 and par value of $200,000. The company exercises the call option after the semiannual interest is paid on June 30, 2011. Record the entry to retire the bonds.

QS 14-6
Bond retirement by share
conversion   **P4**

On January 1, 2011, the $1,000,000 par value bonds of Gruden Company with a carrying amount of $1,000,000 are converted to 500,000 shares of $0.50 par value ordinary shares. Record the entry for the conversion of the bonds.

QS 14-7
Computing payments for
an installment note   **C1**

Valdez Company borrows $170,000 cash from a bank and in return signs an installment note for five annual payments of equal amount, with the first payment due one year after the note is signed. Use Table B.3 in Appendix B to compute the amount of the annual payment for each of the following annual market rates: (*a*) 4%, (*b*) 8%, and (*c*) 12%.

QS 14-8
Debt-to-equity ratio

A2

Compute the debt-to-equity ratio for each of the following companies. Which company appears to have a riskier financing structure? Explain.

	Canal Company	Sears Company
Total liabilities	$492,000	$ 384,000
Total equity	656,000	1,200,000

QS 14-9
International liabilities
disclosures

P1 P2

Vodafone Group Plc reports the following information among its bonds payable as at March 31, 2009 (pounds in millions).

Financial Long-Term Liabilities Measured at Amortised Cost			
(£ in GBP millions)	Nominal (par) Value	Carrying Amount	Fair Value
4.625% (US$ 500 million) bond due July 2018	GBP 350	GBP 392	GBP 315

a. What is the par value of the 4.625% bond issuance? What is its carrying amount (book value)?

b. Was the 4.625% bond sold at a discount or a premium? Explain.

Refer to the information in QS 14-9 for **Vodafone Group Plc.** The following price quotes (from Yahoo! Finance Bond Center) relate to its bonds payable as at late 2009. For example, the price quote indicates that the 4.625% bonds have a market price of 98.0 (98.0% of par value), resulting in a yield to maturity of 4.899%.

QS 14-10
International liabilities disclo-sures and interpretations

P1   P2

Price	Contract Rate (coupon)	Maturity Date	Market Rate (YTM)
98.0	4.625%	15-Jul-2018	4.899%

a. Assuming that the 4.625% bonds were originally issued at par value, what does the market price reveal about interest rate changes since bond issuance? (Assume that Vodafone's credit rating has remained the same.)

b. Does the change in market rates since the issuance of these bonds affect the amount of interest expense reported on Vodafone's income statement? Explain.

c. How much cash would Vodafone need to pay to repurchase the 4.625% bonds at the quoted market price of 98.0? (Assume no interest is owed when the bonds are repurchased.)

d. Assuming that the 4.625% bonds remain outstanding until maturity, at what market price will the bonds sell on the due date in 2018?

connect

Round dollar amounts to the nearest whole dollar. Assume no reversing entries are used.

On January 1, 2011, Kidman Enterprises issues bonds that have a $1,700,000 par value, mature in 20 years, and pay 9% interest semiannually on June 30 and December 31. The bonds are sold at par.

1. How much interest will Kidman pay (in cash) to the bondholders every six months?

2. Prepare journal entries to record (*a*) the issuance of bonds on January 1, 2011; (*b*) the first interest payment on June 30, 2011; and (*c*) the second interest payment on December 31, 2011.

3. Prepare the journal entry for issuance assuming the bonds are issued at (*a*) 98 and (*b*) 102.

EXERCISES

Exercise 14-1
Recording bond issuance and interest
P1

Welch issues bonds dated January 1, 2011, with a par value of $250,000. The bonds' annual contract rate is 9%, and interest is paid semiannually on June 30 and December 31. The bonds mature in three years. The annual market rate at the date of issuance is 12%, and the bonds are sold for $231,570.

1. What is the amount of the discount on these bonds at issuance?

2. How much total bond interest expense will be recognized over the life of these bonds?

3. Prepare an amortization table like the one in Exhibit 14.9 for these bonds; use the effective interest method to amortize the discount.

Exercise 14-2
Effective interest amortization of bond discount
P2

Prairie Dunes Co. issues bonds dated January 1, 2011, with a par value of $800,000. The bonds' annual contract rate is 13%, and interest is paid semiannually on June 30 and December 31. The bonds mature in three years. The annual market rate at the date of issuance is 12%, and the bonds are sold for $819,700.

1. What is the amount of the premium on these bonds at issuance?

2. How much total bond interest expense will be recognized over the life of these bonds?

3. Prepare an amortization table like the one in Exhibit 14.9 for these bonds; use the effective interest method to amortize the premium.

Exercise 14-3
Effective interest amortization of bond premium
P3

Jester Company issues bonds with a par value of $600,000 on their stated issue date. The bonds mature in 10 years and pay 6% annual interest in semiannual payments. On the issue date, the annual market rate for the bonds is 8%.

1. What is the amount of each semiannual interest payment for these bonds?

2. How many semiannual interest payments will be made on these bonds over their life?

3. Use the interest rates given to determine whether the bonds are issued at par, at a discount, or at a premium.

4. Compute the price of the bonds as at their issue date.

5. Prepare the journal entry to record the bonds' issuance.

Exercise 14-4
Computing bond interest and price; recording bond issuance
P2

Check (4) $518,465

Exercise 14-5
Computing bond interest and price; recording bond issuance

P3

Metro Company issues bonds with a par value of $75,000 on their stated issue date. The bonds mature in five years and pay 10% annual interest in semiannual payments. On the issue date, the annual market rate for the bonds is 8%.

1. What is the amount of each semiannual interest payment for these bonds?

2. How many semiannual interest payments will be made on these bonds over their life?

3. Use the interest rates given to determine whether the bonds are issued at par, at a discount, or at a premium.

4. Compute the price of the bonds as at their issue date.

5. Prepare the journal entry to record the bonds' issuance.

Exercise 14-6
Installment note with equal total payments **C1 P5**

Check   (1) $7,381

On January 1, 2011, Randa borrows $25,000 cash by signing a four-year, 7% installment note. The note requires four equal total payments of accrued interest and principal on December 31 of each year from 2011 through 2014.

1. Compute the amount of each of the four equal total payments.

2. Prepare an amortization table for this installment note like the one in Exhibit 14.12.

Exercise 14-7
Installment note entries **P5**

Use the information in Exercise 14-6 to prepare the journal entries for Randa to record the loan on January 1, 2011, and the four payments from December 31, 2011, through December 31, 2014.

Exercise 14-8
Applying debt-to-equity ratio

A3

Ramirez Company is considering a project that will require a $500,000 loan. It presently has total liabilities of $220,000, and total assets of $620,000.

1. Compute Ramirez's (a) present debt-to-equity ratio and (b) the debt-to-equity ratio assuming it borrows $500,000 to fund the project.

2. Evaluate and discuss the level of risk involved if Ramirez borrows the funds to pursue the project.

Exercise 14-9
Accounting for long-term liabilities under **IFRS**

P1 P2 P3

Heineken N.V. reports the following information for its Loans and Borrowings as at December 31, 2008, including proceeds and repayments for the year ended December 31, 2008 (in EUR millions).

Loans and borrowings (noncurrent liabilities)	
Loans and borrowings, December 31, 2008.	EUR 9,084
Proceeds (cash) from issuances of loans and borrowings.	6,361
Repayments (in cash) of loans and borrowings	(2,532)

1. Prepare Heineken's journal entry to record its cash proceeds from issuances of its loans and borrowings for 2008. Assume that the par value of these issuances is EUR 6,000.

2. Prepare Heineken's journal entry to record its cash repayments of its loans and borrowings for 2008. Assume that the par value of these issuances is EUR 2,400, and the premium on them is EUR 32.

3. Compute the discount or premium on its loans and borrowings as at December 31, 2008, assuming that the par value of these liabilities is EUR 9,000.

4. Given the facts in part 3 and viewing the entirety of loans and borrowings as one issuance, was the contract rate on these loans and borrowings higher or lower than the market rate at the time of issuance? Explain. (Assume that Heineken's credit rating has remained the same.)

connect

Round dollar amounts to the nearest whole dollar. Assume no reversing entries are used.

Stowers Research issues bonds dated January 1, 2011, that pay interest semiannually on June 30 and December 31. The bonds have a $20,000 par value and an annual contract rate of 10%, and they mature in 10 years.

Required

For each of the following three separate situations, (*a*) determine the bonds' issue price on January 1, 2011, and (*b*) prepare the journal entry to record their issuance.
1. The market rate at the date of issuance is 8%.
2. The market rate at the date of issuance is 10%.
3. The market rate at the date of issuance is 12%.

PROBLEM SET A

Problem 14-1A
Computing bond price and recording issuance
P1 P2 P3

Check (1) Premium, $2,718

(3) Discount, $2,294

Saturn issues 6.5%, five-year bonds dated January 1, 2011, with a $500,000 par value. The bonds pay interest on June 30 and December 31 and are issued at a price of $510,666. The annual market rate is 6% on the issue date.

Required

1. Compute the total bond interest expense over the bonds' life.
2. Prepare an effective interest amortization table like the one in Exhibit 14.9 for the bonds' life.
3. Prepare the journal entries to record the first two interest payments.
4. Use the market rate at issuance to compute the present value of the remaining cash flows for these bonds as at December 31, 2013. Compare your answer with the amount shown on the amortization table as the balance for that date (from part 2) and explain your findings.

Problem 14-2A
Effective interest amortization of bond premium; computing bond price
P1 P3

Patton issues $650,000 of 5%, four-year bonds dated January 1, 2011, that pay interest semiannually on June 30 and December 31. They are issued at $584,361 and their market rate is 8% at the issue date.

Required

1. Prepare the January 1, 2011, journal entry to record the bonds' issuance.
2. Determine the total bond interest expense to be recognized over the bonds' life.
3. Prepare an effective interest amortization table like the one in Exhibit 14.6 for the bonds' first two years.
4. Prepare the journal entries to record the first two interest payments.

Problem 14-3A
Effective interest amortization of bond discount
P1 P2

McFad issues $90,000 of 11%, three-year bonds dated January 1, 2011, that pay interest semiannually on June 30 and December 31. They are issued at $92,283. Their market rate is 10% at the issue date.

Required

1. Prepare the January 1, 2011, journal entry to record the bonds' issuance.
2. Determine the total bond interest expense to be recognized over the bonds' life.
3. Prepare an effective interest amortization table like Exhibit 14.9 for the bonds' first two years.
4. Prepare the journal entries to record the first two interest payments.
5. Prepare the journal entry to record the bonds' retirement on January 1, 2013, at 98.

Analysis Component

6. Assume that the market rate on January 1, 2011, is 12% instead of 10%. Without presenting numbers, describe how this change affects the amounts reported on McFad's financial statements.

Problem 14-4A
Effective interest amortization of bond premium; retiring bonds
P1 P3 P4

Check (3) 6/30/2012 carrying amount, $91,224

(5) $2,635 gain

www.mheducation.asia/olc/wildkwokFAP

Problem 14-5A
Installment notes

C1 P5

Check (2) 10/31/2015 ending balance, $92,759

On November 1, 2011, Leetch Ltd. borrows $400,000 cash from a bank by signing a five-year installment note bearing 8% interest. The note requires equal total payments each year on October 31.

Required

1. Compute the total amount of each installment payment.
2. Complete an amortization table for this installment note similar to the one in Exhibit 14.12.
3. Prepare the journal entries in which Leetch records (*a*) accrued interest as at December 31, 2011 (the end of its annual reporting period), and (*b*) the first annual payment on the note.

Problem 14-6A
Applying the debt-to-equity ratio

A3

At the end of the current year, the following information is available for both Kumar Company and Asher Company.

	Kumar Company	Asher Company
Total assets	$2,254,500	$1,123,500
Total liabilities	904,500	598,500
Total equity	1,350,000	525,000

Required

1. Compute the debt-to-equity ratios for both companies.
2. Comment on your results and discuss the riskiness of each company's financing structure.

PROBLEM SET B

> Round dollar amounts to the nearest whole dollar. Assume no reversing entries are used.

Problem 14-1B
Computing bond price and recording issuance

P1 P2 P3

Check (1) Premium, $3,475

(3) Discount, $3,162

Sedona Systems issues bonds dated January 1, 2011, that pay interest semiannually on June 30 and December 31. The bonds have a $45,000 par value and an annual contract rate of 12%, and they mature in five years.

Required

For each of the following three separate situations, (*a*) determine the bonds' issue price on January 1, 2011, and (*b*) prepare the journal entry to record their issuance.

1. The market rate at the date of issuance is 10%.
2. The market rate at the date of issuance is 12%.
3. The market rate at the date of issuance is 14%.

Problem 14-2B
Effective interest amortization of bond premium; computing bond price

P1 P3

Zooba Company issues 9%, five-year bonds dated January 1, 2011, with a $160,000 par value. The bonds pay interest on June 30 and December 31 and are issued at a price of $166,494. Their annual market rate is 8% on the issue date.

Required

1. Compute the total bond interest expense over the bonds' life.
2. Prepare an effective interest amortization table like the one in Exhibit 14.9 for the bonds' life.
3. Prepare the journal entries to record the first two interest payments.
4. Use the market rate at issuance to compute the present value of the remaining cash flows for these bonds as at December 31, 2013. Compare your answer with the amount shown on the amortization table as the balance for that date (from part 2) and explain your findings.

Roney issues $120,000 of 6%, 15-year bonds dated January 1, 2011, that pay interest semiannually on June 30 and December 31. They are issued at $99,247, and their market rate is 8% at the issue date.

Required

1. Prepare the January 1, 2011, journal entry to record the bonds' issuance.
2. Determine the total bond interest expense to be recognized over the bonds' life.
3. Prepare an effective interest amortization table like the one in Exhibit 14.6 for the bonds' first two years.
4. Prepare the journal entries to record the first two interest payments.

Problem 14-3B
Effective interest amortization of bond discount
P1 P2

Hutton issues $900,000 of 13%, four-year bonds dated January 1, 2011, that pay interest semiannually on June 30 and December 31. They are issued at $987,217, and their market rate is 10% at the issue date.

Required

1. Prepare the January 1, 2011, journal entry to record the bonds' issuance.
2. Determine the total bond interest expense to be recognized over the bonds' life.
3. Prepare an effective interest amortization table like the one in Exhibit 14.9 for the bonds' first two years.
4. Prepare the journal entries to record the first two interest payments.
5. Prepare the journal entry to record the bonds' retirement on January 1, 2013, at 106.

Analysis Component

6. Assume that the market rate on January 1, 2011, is 14% instead of 10%. Without presenting numbers, describe how this change affects the amounts reported on Hutton's financial statements.

Problem 14-4B
Effective interest amortization of bond premium; retiring bonds
P1 P3 P4

Check (3) 6/30/2012 carrying amount, $958,406

(5) $6,174 loss

On October 1, 2011, Milan Enterprises borrows $300,000 cash from a bank by signing a three-year installment note bearing 10% interest. The note requires equal total payments each year on September 30.

Required

1. Compute the total amount of each installment payment.
2. Complete an amortization table for this installment note similar to the one in Exhibit 14.12.
3. Prepare the journal entries to record (a) accrued interest as at December 31, 2011 (the end of its annual reporting period) and (b) the first annual payment on the note.

Problem 14-5B
Installment notes
C1 P5

Check (2) 9/30/2013 ending balance, $109,673

At the end of the current year, the following information is available for both West Elm Company and East Park Company.

Problem 14-6B
Applying the debt-to-equity ratio
A3

	West Elm Company	East Park Company
Total assets	$396,396	$1,650,000
Total liabilities	178,596	1,237,500
Total equity	217,800	412,500

Required

1. Compute the debt-to-equity ratios for both companies.
2. Comment on your results and discuss what they imply about the relative riskiness of these companies.

SERIAL PROBLEM
Business Solutions

A1 A3

(This serial problem began in Chapter 1 and continues through most of the book. If previous chapter segments were not completed, the serial problem can begin at this point.)

SP 14 Santana Rey has consulted with her local banker and is considering financing an expansion of her business by obtaining a long-term bank loan. Selected account balances at March 31, 2012, for Business Solutions follow.

Total assets	$120,268	Total liabilities.......	$875	Total equity	$119,393

Check (1) $94,639

Required

1. The bank has offered a long-term secured note to Business Solutions. The bank's loan procedures require that a client's debt-to-equity ratio not exceed 0.8. As at March 31, 2012, what is the maximum amount that Business Solutions could borrow from this bank (rounded to nearest dollar)?
2. If Business Solutions borrows the maximum amount allowed from the bank, what percentage of assets would be financed (*a*) by debt and (*b*) by equity?
3. What are some factors Santana Rey should consider before borrowing the funds?

Beyond the Numbers

REPORTING IN ACTION

A1 A2

BTN 14-1   Refer to Nestlé's financial statements in Appendix A to answer the following.

1. Identify the items, if any, that make up Nestlé's long-term liabilities as reported on its consolidated balance sheet as at December 31, 2013.
2. Assume that Nestlé has CHF 9,000 millions in bonds that carry a 2.25% contract rate of interest. How much annual cash interest must be paid on those bonds?
3. How much cash did it generate from issuance of bonds for the year ended December 31, 2013? How much cash did it use for repayments of bonds for that same year?

Fast Forward

4. Access Nestlé's financial statements for the years ending after December 31, 2013, from its Website (www.nestle.com). Has it issued additional bonds since the year ended December 31, 2013? If yes, identify the amount(s).

COMPARATIVE ANALYSIS

A3

BTN 14-2   Key figures for Adidas and Puma follow.

	Adidas (EUR millions)		Puma (EUR millions)	
	Current Year	Prior Year	Current Year	Prior Year
Total assets	11,599	11,651	2,308.5	2,530.3
Total liabilities	6,118	6,360	811.2	932.9
Total equity	5,481	5,291	1,497.3	1,597.4

Required

1. Compute the debt-to-equity ratios for Adidas and Puma for both the current year and the prior year (round to one decimal place).
2. Use the ratios you computed in part 1 to determine which company's financing structure is less risky.

BTN 14-3 Your business associate mentions that she is considering investing in corporate bonds currently selling at a premium. She says that since the bonds are selling at a premium, they are highly valued and her investment will yield more than the going rate of return for the risk involved. Reply with a memorandum to confirm or correct your associate's interpretation of premium bonds.

COMMUNICATING IN PRACTICE

P3

BTN 14-4 Access the 2013 annual report of L'Oréal from its Website (www.loreal-finance.com/eng). Refer to its consolidated balance sheet, including its Note 23.

TAKING IT TO THE NET

A2

Required

1. State the amount of L'Oréal's noncurrent borrowings and debt as at December 31, 2013.
2. Review L'Oréal's Note 23. List the items and amounts for the noncurrent borrowings and debt stated in Part 1.

BTN 14-5 Break into teams and complete the following requirements related to effective interest amortization for a premium bond.

TEAMWORK IN ACTION

P2 P3

1. Each team member is to independently prepare a blank table with proper headings for amortization of a bond premium. When all have finished, compare tables and ensure that all are in agreement.

Parts 2 and 3 require use of these facts: On January 1, 2010, Caleb issues $100,000, 9%, five-year bonds at 104.1. The market rate at issuance is 8%. Caleb pays interest semiannually on June 30 and December 31.

2. In rotation, *each* team member must explain how to complete *one* line of the bond amortization table, including all computations for his or her line. (Round amounts to the nearest dollar.) All members are to fill in their tables during this process. You need not finish the table; stop after all members have explained a line.

3. In rotation, *each* team member is to identify a separate column of the table and indicate what the final number in that column will be and explain the reasoning.

4. Reach a team consensus as to what the total bond interest expense on this bond issue will be if the bond is not retired before maturity.

Hint: Rotate teams to report on parts 4 and 5. Consider requiring entries for issuance and interest payments.

5. As a team, prepare a list of similarities and differences between the amortization table just prepared and the amortization table if the bond had been issued at a discount.

BTN 14-6 Kenny Yap is the founder of Qian Hu, which is listed on the Singapore Exchange. As at end 2008, his company has about S$63 million in equity and he is considering a S$10 million expansion to meet increased demand. This S$10 million expansion would yield S$1.6 million in additional annual profit before interest expense. The business currently earns S$8,277,000 annual profit before interest expense of S$877,000, yielding a return on equity of 11.7% (S$7,400,000/S$63,000,000). To fund the expansion, he is considering borrowing long-term debt of S$10 million with annual interest payments (the principal due at the end of 10 years).

ENTREPRENEURIAL DECISION

A1

Required

1. Using return on equity as the decision criterion, show computations to support or reject the expansion if interest on the $10 million debt is (a) 10%, (b) 15%, (c) 16%, (d) 17%, and (e) 20%.
2. What general rule do the results in part 1 illustrate?

Chapter 14 Long-Term Liabilities

A3

BTN 14-7 Nike, Adidas, and Puma are competitors in the global marketplace. Selected results from these companies follow.

Key Figures	Nike (US$ millions)		Adidas (EUR millions)		Puma (EUR millions)	
	Current Year	Prior Year	Current Year	Prior Year	Current Year	Prior Year
Total assets	17,584	15,465	11,599	11,651	2,308.5	2,530.3
Total liabilities	6,428	5,084	6,118	6,360	811.2	932.9
Total equity	11,156	10,381	5,481	5,291	1,497.3	1,597.4
Debt-to-equity ratio	?	?	1.1	1.2	0.5	0.6

Required

1. Compute Nike's debt-to-equity ratios for the current year and the prior year.
2. Use the data provided and the ratios computed in part 1 to determine which company's financing structure is least risky.

ANSWERS TO MULTIPLE CHOICE QUIZ

1. b
2. a

3. c; $500,000 × 0.08 × ½ year = $20,000

15

Investments and International Operations

A Look Back

Chapter 14 focused on long-term liabilities—a main part of most companies' financing. We explained how to value, record, amortize, and report these liabilities in financial statements.

A Look at This Chapter

This chapter focuses on investments in securities. We explain how to identify, account for, and report investments in both debt and equity securities. We also explain accounting for transactions listed in a foreign currency.

A Look Ahead

Chapter 16 focuses on reporting and analyzing a company's cash flows. Special emphasis is directed at the statement of cash flows reported under the indirect method.

Learning Objectives

CAP

CONCEPTUAL

C1 Distinguish between debt and equity securities and between short-term and long-term investments. (p. 572)

C2 Describe how to report equity with control. (p. 577)

C3 *Appendix 15A*—Explain foreign exchange rates and record transactions listed in a foreign currency. (p. 584)

C4 *Appendix 15B*—Understand the new requirements under **IFRS 9**. (p. 586)

ANALYTICAL

A1 Compute and analyze the components of return on total assets. (p. 579)

PROCEDURAL

P1 Account for held-for-trading securities. (p. 573)

P2 Account for available-for-sale securities. (p. 574)

P3 Account for held-to-maturity debt. (p. 575)

P4 Account for equity with significant influence. (p. 576)

P5 *Appendix 15B*—Account for securities measured at fair value through other comprehensive income (FVTOCI). (p. 586)

"Without franchising, it would have been difficult to expand as quickly as we did."—LYN LEE

 **Decision Insight**

Franchising Success, Chocolatey Sweet

At **Awfully Chocolate (www.awfullychocolate.com)**, a slice of dark indulgence is not a sinful matter but a small miracle. "It had to be simple, really good dark chocolate, not too sweet and not creamy at all...the perfect dark chocolate cake that you could eat all the time and not get tired of," Lyn Lee says of the cake that she was conceptualizing and selling before she traded in her law books for cookbooks and set up shop in Singapore more than a decade ago. For a good year, Lyn and a small group of close friends would meet in the kitchen every weekend and experiment with ingredients and portions. The final product was an enormous sweet success. To date, Awfully Chocolate has franchises around the world, in such diverse places as Beijing, Jakarta, and Hong Kong.

"Everything else, really, followed on from that single-minded premise," says Lyn. For many years, they sold only whole cakes and later, one kind of dark chocolate ice cream. They have since introduced other chocolate confections such as the Cold Poached Chocolate and two new cakes sold in slices by weight—the Super Stacked Cake and the White Chocolate Butterscotch Block. "You could say that everything, from the design and branding to our culture, was built on that passion and energy," explains Lyn, a self-confessed chocoholic who loves managing her company because "I get to eat my chocolate cake and the now much-expanded variety of products and restaurant food" that the company has added to its staple of cakes.

"Without franchising, it would have been difficult to expand as quickly as we did. The local knowledge and administration are valuable in successfully rolling out the brand," remarks Lyn while acknowledging that franchise success doesn't come without a few financial snags. "Our franchisees pay us royalties in their own currencies, so there would usually be some shortfall due to currency fluctuations—other Asian currencies seldom strengthen against the Singapore dollar," she explains. "Moreover, we may calculate and book our franchise revenues—based on a percentage of sales—at the end of the month, but the actual payments would come in later. This needs to be accounted for as well." Managing a franchising business may not be all chocolate-coated, but thankfully, to her legions of chocoholic fans, her cakes are.

This chapter's main focus is investments in securities. Many companies have investments, and many of these are in the form of debt and equity securities issued by other companies. We describe investments in these securities and how to account for them. An increasing number of companies also invest in international operations. We explain how to account for and report international transactions listed in foreign currencies.

Investments and International Operations

Basics of Investments

- Motivation for investments
- Short-term versus long-term
- Classification and reporting
- Accounting basics

Types of Investments

- Held-for-trading equity and debt
- Available-for-sale equity and debt
- Held-to-maturity debt
- Equity with significant influence
- Equity with control

BASICS OF INVESTMENTS

C1 Distinguish between debt and equity securities and between short-term and long-term investments.

This section describes the motivation for investments, the distinction between short- and long-term investments, and the different classes of investments.

Motivation for Investments

Companies make investments for at least three reasons. First, companies transfer *excess cash* into investments to produce higher income. Second, some entities, such as mutual funds and pension funds, are set up to produce income from investments. Third, companies make investments for strategic reasons. Examples are investments in competitors, suppliers, and even customers.

Short-Term Investments Cash equivalents are investments that are both readily converted to known amounts of cash and mature within three months. Many investments, however, mature between 3 and 12 months. These investments are **short-term investments,** also called *temporary investments* and *marketable securities*. Specifically, short-term investments are securities that (1) management intends to convert to cash within one year or the operating cycle, whichever is longer, and (2) are readily convertible to cash. Short-term investments are reported under current assets and serve a purpose similar to cash equivalents.

Long-Term Investments **Long-term investments** in securities are defined as those securities that are not readily convertible to cash or are not intended to be converted into cash in the short term. Long-term investments can also include funds earmarked for a special purpose, such as bond sinking funds and investments in land or other assets not used in the company's operations. Long-term investments are reported in the noncurrent section of the statement of financial position, often in its own separate line titled *Long-Term Investments*.

Nestlé's statement of financial position (Appendix A) lists under its current assets "short-term investments" of CHF 638 million. In its notes, it explains that these short-term investments are classified as "available-for-sale assets" (more on this later). Under its noncurrent assets, Nestlé lists "Investment in associates and joint ventures" of CHF 12,315 million and "Financial assets" of CHF 4,550 million.

Classification and Reporting

Accounting for investments in securities depends on some or all of the following:

1. Purpose, e.g., trading or long-term investment, the company's intent to hold the security either short-term or long-term,

2. Its contractual characteristics, e.g., debt or equity;

3. The industry in which the reporting entity operates; and

4. The accounting policy choice of the reporting entity.

The accounting for such securities is covered in **IAS 39 Financial Instruments**, including loans and receivables. Since loans and receivables are covered in Chapter 9, this chapter will cover the other common possibilities, as laid out in Exhibit 15.1.[1]

EXHIBIT 15.1

Investments in Equity and Debt Securities

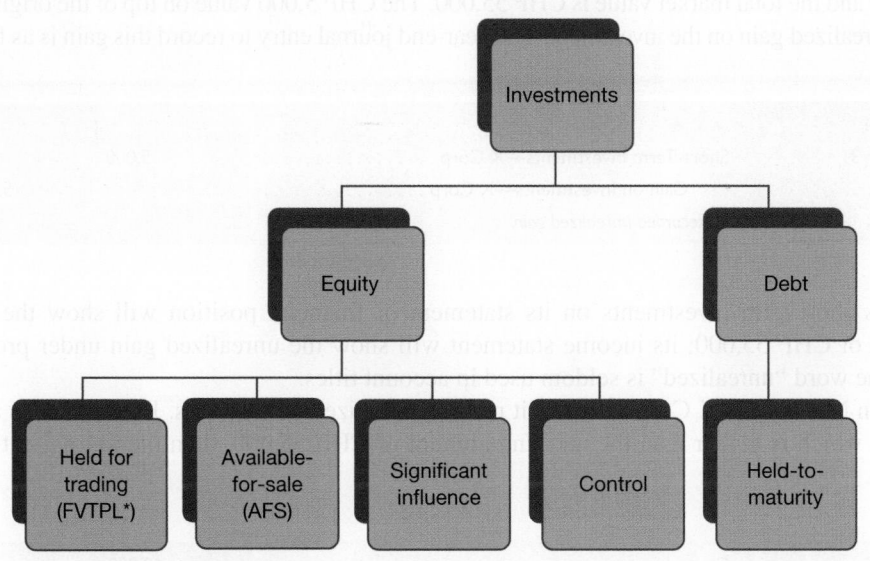

* Fair value through profit or loss (FVTPL).

HELD-FOR-TRADING AND AVAILABLE-FOR-SALE INVESTMENTS IN EQUITY

Held-for-Trading Securities

P1 Account for held-for-trading securities.

Usually a financial asset at fair value through profit or loss is a **held-for-trading**. A financial asset is classified as held for trading if it is: (i) acquired or incurred principally for the purpose of selling or repurchasing it in the near term; (ii) part of a portfolio of identified financial instruments that are managed together and for which there is evidence of a recent actual pattern of short-term profit-taking; or (iii) a derivative (except for a derivative that is a designated and effective hedging instrument).

Nestlé states in its notes that "held-for-trading assets are carried at fair value and all their gains and losses, realized and unrealised, are recognised in the income statement."

"Held-for-trading securities" are classified as securities measures at fair value through profit and loss (FVTPL). These **FVTPL securities** are acquired principally for the purpose of selling or repurchasing them in the near term, with a pattern of short-term profit-taking. Such investments are accounted for by the fair value approach, in contrast to the historical cost approach generally used for other assets like land, buildings, and equipment. The reason is that the fair values for them are readily determinable, and the periodic fluctuations have a definite economic impact

---

[1] Although debt securities can also be classified as held-for-trading or available-for-sale, the reporting is detailed in advanced accounting courses.

that should be reported. Fair value is the amount for which an asset could be exchanged between knowledgeable and willing parties, in an arm's length transaction.

Assume that Nestlé buys X Corp's shares on October 1, with the intention to sell within a few months. The journal entry at purchase is as follows

2014			
Oct. 1	Short-Term Investments—X Corp	50,000	
	Cash		50,000
	Purchased shares in X Corp.		

When Nestlé's financial year ends on December 31, 2014, the share price of X Corp has risen in value and the total market value is CHF 55,000. The CHF 5,000 value on top of the original cost is an unrealized gain on the investment. The year-end journal entry to record this gain is as follows.

2014			
Dec. 31	Short-Term Investments—X Corp	5,000	
	Gain on Investments—X Corp		5,000
	Recorded unrealized gain.		

Nestlé's short-term investments on its statement of financial position will show the higher amount of CHF 55,000; its income statement will show the unrealized gain under profit and loss. The word "unrealized" is seldom used in account titles.

When Nestlé sells X Corp's shares, it records a realized gain or loss. If Nestlé sells at CHF 60,000, which is higher than the carrying amount of CHF 55,000, then the journal entry is as follows.

2015	Cash	60,000	
Jan. 10	Short-Term Investments—X Corp		55,000
	Gain on Sale of Short-Term Investments		5,000
	Recorded shares of investment at a gain.		

The above examples show unrealized and realized gains but the same ideas apply to unrealized and realized losses. An entity can also present on a net basis the gains and losses arising from a group of similar transactions, including gains and losses arising on financial instruments held for trading. However, it must present such gains and losses separately if they are material.

Available-for-Sale Securities

Nestlé states in its notes that "available-for-sale assets are those non-derivative financial assets that are either designated as such upon initial recognition or are not classified in any of the other financial assets categories."

Available-for-sale (AFS) securities are purchased to yield dividends or increases in fair value. They are not actively managed like held-for-trading securities. If the intent is to sell available-for-sale securities within the longer of one year or operating cycle, they are classified as short-term investments. Otherwise, they are classified as long-term. As with held-for-trading securities, companies adjust the cost of available-for-sale securities to reflect changes in fair value. This is done with a fair value adjustment to its total portfolio cost. However, any unrealized gain or loss for the portfolio of available-for-sale securities is not reported as part of profit or loss but as part of other comprehensive income. To illustrate, assume that Nestlé buys Y Corp's shares at CHF 100,000. Nestlé intends to hold this investment for longer than a year and decided to treat it as an available-for-sale (AFS) investment.

P2 Account for available-for-sale securities.

2014			
Sept. 1	Long-Term Investments—AFS (Y Corp)	100,000	
	Cash		100,000
	Purchased shares in Y Corp as AFS Investment.		

Assume that at year-end, the fair market value of Y Corp's shares is CHF 120,000. The journal entry is as follows.

2014			
Dec. 31	Fair Value Adjustment—Y Corp	20,000	
	Unrealized Gain on Investment (OCI)		20,000
	Recorded adjustment to fair value of AFS investments		
	in Y Corp.		

It is also common to combine the cost of investments with the balance in the Fair Value Adjustment account and report the net as a single amount in the statement of financial position. Upon sale at CHF 110,000, the journal entry is as follows.

2015	Cash	110,000	
Nov. 1	Realized Gain on Investment (P&L)		10,000
	Long-Term Investments—AFS (Y Corp)		100,000
	Recorded sales of AFS investments in Y Corp at a gain.		

In addition, the company must make adjusting entries to the Fair Value Adjustment account and the unrealized account. More details are provided in advanced accounting courses.

INVESTMENTS IN DEBT

Held-to-Maturity Debt

Nestlé states in its notes that "loans and receivables are non-derivative financial assets with fixed or determinable payments that are not quoted in an active market. . . Loans and receivables are further classified as current and non-current depending whether these will be realized within twelve months after the statement of financial position date or beyond."

Held-to-maturity (HTM) debt are debt a company intends and is able to hold until maturity. They are reported in current assets if their maturity dates are within one year or the operating cycle, whichever is longer. Held-to-maturity debt are reported in long-term assets when the maturity dates extend beyond one year or the operating cycle, whichever is longer. All held-to-maturity debt are recorded at cost when purchased, and interest revenue is recorded when earned.

P3 Account for held-to-maturity debt.

To illustrate, assume that Music City paid $29,500 plus a $500 brokerage fee on September 1, 2014, to buy Dell's 7%, two-year bonds payable with a $30,000 par value. The bonds pay interest semi-annually on August 31 and February 28. Music City intends to hold the bonds until they mature on August 31, 2016; consequently, they are classified as held-to-maturity debt. The entry to record this purchase follows. (If the maturity of the debt was short term, and management's intent was to hold them until they mature, then they would be classified as Short-Term Investments—HTM.)

2014			
Sept. 1	Long-Term Investments—HTM (Dell)	30,000	
	Cash		30,000
	Purchased bonds to be held to maturity.		

Interest revenue for investments in debt is recorded when earned. To illustrate, on December 31, 2014, at the end of its accounting period, Music City accrues interest receivable as follows.

2014			
Dec. 31	Interest Receivable..............................	700	
	Interest Revenue		700
	Accrued interest earned ($30,000 × 7% × 412).		

The $700 reflects 4/6 of the semi-annual cash receipt of interest—the portion Music City earned as at December 31. The portfolio of held-to-maturity debt is usually reported at **(amortized) cost**, which is explained in advanced courses. There is no fair value adjustment to the portfolio of held-to-maturity debt—neither to the short-term nor long-term portfolios.

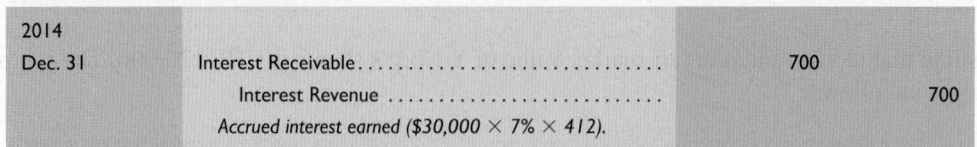

Quick Check   Answers — p. 590

1. How are held-for-trading securities reported (valued) on the statement of financial position?
2. How are available-for-sale securities reported (valued) on the statement of financial position?
3. Where are unrealized gains and losses on held-for-trading securities reported?
4. Where are unrealized gains and losses on available-for-sale securities reported?

INVESTMENTS IN EQUITY WITH SIGNIFICANT INFLUENCE

P4 Account for equity with significant influence.

Nestlé states in notes that it holds 178,381,021 shares of **L'Oréal** representing a 29.7% participation. Nestlé is said to have significant influence over L'Oréal. Companies that Nestlé has significant influence over are said to be "associates." A long-term investment classified as **equity with significant influence** implies that the investor can exert significant influence over the investee. An investor that owns 20% or more (but not more than 50%) of a company's voting shares is usually presumed to have a significant influence over the investee. In some cases, however, the 20% test of significant influence is overruled by other, more persuasive, evidence. This evidence can either lower the 20% requirement or increase it. The **equity method** of accounting and reporting is used for long-term investments in equity with significant influence, which is explained in this section.

Long-term investments in equity with significant influence are recorded at cost when acquired. To illustrate, Micron Co. records the purchase of 3,000 shares (30%) of Star Co. ordinary shares at a total cost of $70,650 on January 1, 2014, as follows.

Assets = Liabilities + Equity
+70,650
−70,650

Jan. 1	Long-Term Investments—Star	70,650	
	Cash		70,650
	To record purchase of 3,000 Star shares.		

The investee's (Star) earnings increase both its net assets and the claim of the investor (Micron) on the investee's net assets. Thus, when the investee reports its earnings, the investor records its share of those earnings in its investment account. To illustrate, assume that Star reports net profit of $20,000 for 2014. Micron then records its 30% share of those earnings as follows.

Dec. 31	Long-Term Investments—Star	6,000	
	Share of Earnings of Associates		6,000
	To record 30% equity in investee earnings.		

Assets = Liabilities + Equity
+6,000   +6,000

The debit reflects the increase in Micron's equity in Star. The credit reflects 30% of Star's net profit. Earnings from Long-Term Investment is a *temporary* account (closed to Income Summary at each period-end) and is reported on the investor's (Micron's) income statement. If the investee incurs a net loss instead of a net profit, the investor records its share of the loss and reduces (credits) its investment account. The investor closes this earnings or loss account to Income Summary.

The receipt of cash dividends is not revenue under the equity method because the investor has already recorded its share of the investee's earnings. Instead, cash dividends received by an investor from an investee are viewed as a conversion of one asset to another; that is, dividends reduce the balance of the investment account. To illustrate, Star declares and pays $10,000 in cash dividends on its ordinary shares. Micron records its 30% share of these dividends received on January 9, 2015, as:

Jan. 9	Cash	3,000	
	Long-Term Investments—Star		3,000
	To record share of dividend paid by Star.		

Assets = Liabilities + Equity
+3,000
−3,000

The book value of an investment under the equity method equals the cost of the investment plus (minus) the investor's equity in the *undistributed* (*distributed*) earnings of the investee. Once Micron records these transactions, its Long-Term Investments account appears as in Exhibit 15.2.

Long-Term Investment—Star				
1/ 1/2014 Investment acquisition	70,650			
12/31/2014 Share of earnings	6,000			
12/31/2014 Balance	76,650			
		1/ 9/2015 Share of dividend	3,000	
1/ 9/2015 Balance	73,650			

EXHIBIT 15.2

Investment in Star Ordinary Shares (Ledger Account)

Micron's account balance on January 9, 2015, for its investment in Star is $73,650. This is the investment's cost *plus* Micron's equity in Star's earnings since its purchase *less* Micron's equity in Star's cash dividends since its purchase. When an investment in equity securities is sold, the gain or loss is computed by comparing proceeds from the sale with the carrying amount of the investment on the date of sale. If Micron sells its Star shares for $80,000 on January 10, 2015, it records the sale as:

Point: Security prices are sometimes listed in fractions. For example, a debt security with a price of $22\frac{1}{4}$ is the same as $22.25.

Jan. 10	Cash	80,000	
	Long-Term Investments—Star		73,650
	Gain on Sale of Investment		6,350
	Sold 3,000 shares for $80,000.		

Assets = Liabilities + Equity
+80,000   +6,350
−73,650

INVESTMENTS IN EQUITY WITH CONTROL

A long-term investment classified as **equity with control** implies that the investor can exert a controlling influence over the investee. An investor who owns more than 50% of a company's voting shares has control over the investee. This investor can dominate all other shareholders in electing the corporation's board of directors and has control over the investee's management. In

 C2 Describe how to report equity with control.

EXHIBIT 15.3

Accounting for Equity Investments by Percent of Ownership

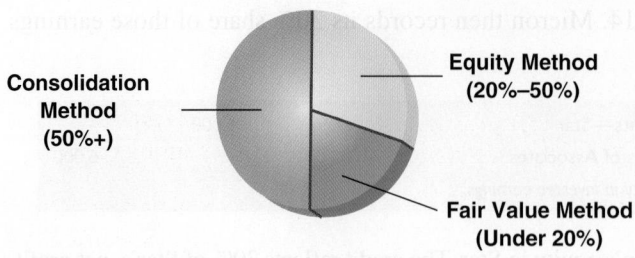

Consolidation Method (50%+)

Equity Method (20%–50%)

Fair Value Method (Under 20%)

some cases, control can extend to situations of less than 50% ownership. Exhibit 15.3 summarizes the accounting for investments in equity securities based on an investor's ownership in the shares.

The *consolidation method* is used to account for long-term investments in equity with control. The investor reports *consolidated financial statements* when owning such securities. The controlling investor is called the **parent,** and the investee is called the **subsidiary.** Many companies are parents with subsidiaries. Examples are (1) McGraw-Hill, the parent of J.D. Power and Associates, Standard & Poor's, and Platt's; (2) Gap, Inc., the parent of Gap, Old Navy, and Banana Republic; and (3) Brunswick, the parent of Mercury Marine, Sea Ray, and U.S. Marine. A company owning all the outstanding shares of a subsidiary can, if it desires, take over the subsidiary's assets, retire the subsidiary's shares, and merge the subsidiary into the parent. However, there often are financial, legal, and tax advantages if a business operates as a parent controlling one or more subsidiaries. When a company operates as a parent with subsidiaries, each entity maintains separate accounting records. From a legal viewpoint, the parent and each subsidiary are separate entities with all rights, duties, and responsibilities of individual companies.

Consolidated financial statements show the financial position, results of operations, and cash flows of all entities under the parent's control, including all subsidiaries. These statements are prepared as if the business were organized as one entity. The parent uses the equity method in its accounts, but the investment account is *not* reported on the parent's financial statements. Instead, the individual assets and liabilities of the parent and its subsidiaries are combined on one statement of financial position. Their revenues and expenses also are combined on one income statement, and their cash flows are combined on one statement of cash flows. The procedures for preparing consolidated financial statements are in advanced courses.

Accounting Summary for Investments in Securities

Exhibit 15.4 summarizes the standard accounting for investments in securities. Recall that many investment securities are classified as either short term or long term depending on management's intent and ability to convert them in the future. Understanding the accounting for these investments enables us to draw better conclusions from financial statements in making business decisions.

EXHIBIT 15.4

Accounting for Investments in Securities

Classification	Accounting
Short-Term Investment in Securities	
Held-for-trading (equity and debt)	**Fair value** (with fair value adjustment to profit or loss)
Available-for-sale (equity and debt)	**Fair value** (with fair value adjustment to other comprehensive income, transferred ("recycled") to P&L at disposal.)
Held-to-maturity (debt)	Cost
Long-Term Investment in Securities	
Available-for-sale (equity and debt)	**Fair value** (with fair value adjustment to other comprehensive income, transferred ("recycled") to P&L at disposal.)
Equity with significant influence	Equity method
Equity with control	Consolidation
Held-to-maturity (debt)	Cost

Users of financial statements often differentiate between fair value changes arising from equity investments held for purposes other than generating investment returns and equity investments held for trading. Therefore, the separate presentation in other comprehensive income of gains and losses for some investments could provide useful information to users of financial statements because it would allow them to identify easily, and value accordingly, the associated fair value changes.

In addition, all financial assets, except for those measured at fair value through profit or loss, are subject to review for impairment. Therefore, AFS and HTM Securities are subject to impairment tests if circumstances warrant them. Details are in advanced accounting courses.

Comprehensive Income   **Comprehensive income** is defined as all changes in equity during a period except those from owners' investments and dividends. Specifically, comprehensive income is computed by adding or subtracting *other comprehensive income* to net profit:

Net profit	$ #
Other comprehensive income	#
Comprehensive income	$ #

Other comprehensive income includes gains and losses from investments in equity instruments measured at fair value through other comprehensive income, and gains and losses arising from translating the financial statements.

Comprehensive income is shown in:

1. The statement of comprehensive income.
2. The statement of changes in equity.

In Appendix A, **Nestlé** shows its fair value adjustments on available-for-sale investments in the statement of comprehensive income.

Quick Check

Answers – p. 590

5. What is the difference between significant influence and control?
6. What is the purpose of consolidated financial statements?

Components of Return on Total Assets  **Decision Analysis**

A company's **return on total assets** (or simply *return on assets*) is important in assessing financial performance. The return on total assets can be separated into two components, profit margin and total asset turnover, for additional analyses. Exhibit 15.5 shows how these two components determine return on total assets.

 A1   Compute and analyze the components of return on total assets.

$$\text{Return on total assets} = \text{Profit margin} \times \text{Total asset turnover}$$

$$\frac{\text{Net profit}}{\text{Average total assets}} = \frac{\text{Net profit}}{\text{Net sales}} \times \frac{\text{Net sales}}{\text{Average total assets}}$$

EXHIBIT 15.5

Components of Return on Total Assets

Profit margin reflects the percent of net profit in each dollar of net sales. Total asset turnover reflects a company's ability to produce net sales from total assets. All companies desire a high return on total assets. By considering these two components, we can often discover strengths and weaknesses not revealed by return on total assets alone. This improves our ability to assess future performance and company strategy.

To illustrate, consider return on total assets and its components for Gap Inc. in Exhibit 15.6.

EXHIBIT 15.6

Gap's Components of Return on Total Assets

Financial Year	Return on Total Assets	=	Profit Margin	×	Total Asset Turnover
2012	11.5%	=	5.7%	×	2.01
2011	16.0*	=	8.2	×	1.95
2010	14.1*	=	7.7	×	1.83
2009	12.6	=	6.66	×	1.89
2008	10.2*	=	5.28	×	1.92

* Differences due to rounding.

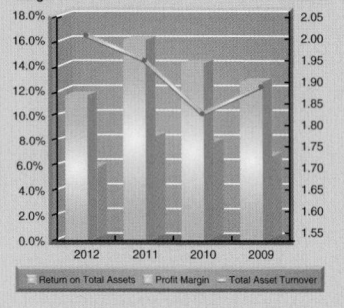

At least three findings emerge. First, Gap's return on total assets improved from 10.2% in 2008 to 11.5% in 2012. Second, total asset turnover has slightly improved over this period, from 1.92 to 2.01. Third, Gap's profit margin steadily increased over this period, from 2008's level of 5.28%. These components reveal the dual role of profit margin and total asset turnover in determining return on total assets. They also reveal that the driver of Gap's recent improvement in return on total assets is not total asset turnover but profit margin.

Generally, if a company is to maintain or improve its return on total assets, it must meet any decline in either profit margin or total asset turnover with an increase in the other. If not, return on assets will decline. Companies consider these components in planning strategies. A component analysis can also reveal where a company is weak and where changes are needed, especially in a competitor analysis. If asset turnover is lower than the industry norm, for instance, a company should focus on raising asset turnover at least to the norm. The same applies to profit margin.

Decision Maker   Answer — p. 590

Retailer   You are an entrepreneur and owner of a retail sporting goods store. The store's recent annual performance reveals (industry norms in parentheses): return on total assets = 11% (11.2%); profit margin = 4.4% (3.5%); and total asset turnover = 2.5 (3.2). What does your analysis of these figures reveal? ∎

DEMONSTRATION PROBLEM 1

Garden Company completes the following selected transactions related to its short-term investments during 2015.

May 8   Purchased 300 shares of FedEx shares as a short-term investment in available-for-sale securities at $40 per share plus $975 in broker fees.

Sept. 2   Sold 100 shares of its investment in FedEx shares at $47 per share and held the remaining 200 shares; broker's commission was $225.

Oct. 2   Purchased 400 shares of Ajay shares for $60 per share plus $1,600 in commissions. The shares are held as a short-term investment in available-for-sale securities.

Required

1. Prepare journal entries for the above transactions of Garden Company for 2015.

2. Prepare an adjusting journal entry as at December 31, 2015, if the fair values of the equity securities held by Garden Company are $48 per share for FedEx and $55 per share for Ajay. (Year 2015 is the first year Garden Company acquired short-term investments.)

SOLUTION TO DEMONSTRATION PROBLEM 1

1.

May 8	Short-Term Investments—AFS (FedEx)	12,975	
	Cash		12,975
	Purchased 300 shares of FedEx shares		
	(300 × $40) + $975.		

[continued on next page]

[continued from previous page]

Sept. 2	Cash	4,475	
	Gain on Sale of Short-Term Investment		150
	Short-Term Investments—AFS (FedEx)		4,325
	Sold 100 shares of FedEx for $47 per share less		
	a $225 commission. The original cost is		
	($12,975 × 100/300).		
Oct. 2	Short-Term Investments—AFS (Ajay)	25,600	
	Cash		25,600
	Purchased 400 shares of Ajay for $60 per share		
	plus $1,600 in commissions.		

2. Computation of unrealized gain or loss follows.

Short-Term Investments in Available-for-Sale Securities	Shares	Cost per Share	Total Cost	Fair Value per Share	Total Fair Value	Unrealized Gain (Loss)
FedEx	200	$43.25	$ 8,650	$48.00	$ 9,600	
Ajay	400	64.00	25,600	55.00	22,000	
Totals			$34,250		$31,600	$(2,650)

The adjusting entry follows.

Dec. 31	Unrealized Loss—Equity	2,650	
	Fair Value Adjustment—Available-for-Sale (ST)		2,650
	To reflect an unrealized loss in fair values		
	of available-for-sale securities.		

DEMONSTRATION PROBLEM 2

The following transactions relate to Euro Company's long-term investments during 2014 and 2015. Euro did not own any long-term investments prior to 2014. Show (1) the appropriate journal entries and (2) the relevant portions of each year's statement of financial position and statement of comprehensive income that reflect these transactions for both 2014 and 2015.

2014

Sept. 9 Purchased 1,000 shares of Heineken's ordinary shares for EUR 80,000 cash. These shares represent 30% of Heineken's outstanding shares.

Oct. 2 Purchased 2,000 shares of Adidas' ordinary shares for EUR 60,000 cash as a long-term investment. These shares represent less than a 1% ownership in Adidas.

17 Purchased as a long-term investment 1,000 shares of Puma's ordinary shares for EUR 40,000 cash. These shares are less than 1% of Puma's outstanding shares.

Nov. 1 Received EUR 5,000 cash dividend from Heineken.

30 Received EUR 3,000 cash dividend from Adidas.

Dec. 15 Received EUR 1,400 cash dividend from Puma.

31 Heineken's net profit for this year is EUR 70,000.

31 Fair values for the investments in equity securities are Heineken, EUR 84,000; Adidas, EUR 48,000; and Puma, EUR 45,000.

31 For preparing financial statements, note the following post-closing account balances: Share Capital (Ordinary Shares), EUR 500,000, and Retained Earnings, EUR 350,000.

2015

Jan. 1 Sold Heineken's shares for EUR 108,000 cash.

May 30 Received EUR 3,100 cash dividend from Adidas.

June 15 Received EUR 1,600 cash dividend from Puma.

Aug. 17   Sold the Adidas shares for EUR 52,000 cash.
19   Purchased 2,000 shares of L'Oreal ordinary shares for EUR 50,000 cash as a long-term investment. The shares represent less than a 5% ownership in L'Oreal.
Dec. 15   Received EUR 1,800 cash dividend from Puma.
31   Fair values of the investments in equity securities are Puma, EUR 39,000, and L'Oreal, EUR 48,000.
31   For preparing financial statements, note the following post-closing account balances: Share
Capital (Ordinary Shares), EUR 500,000, and Retained Earnings, EUR 410,000.

PLANNING THE SOLUTION

● Account for the investment in Heineken under the equity method.
● Account for the investments in Adidas, Puma, and L'Oreal as long-term investments in available-for-sale
securities.
● Prepare the information for the two years' statement of financial positions by including the relevant asset and equity accounts, and the two years' statements of comprehensive income by identifying the
relevant revenues, earnings, gains, and losses.

SOLUTION TO DEMONSTRATION PROBLEM 2

1. Journal entries for 2014.

Sept. 9	Long-Term Investments—Heineken	80,000	
	Cash		80,000
	Acquired 1,000 shares, representing a 30% equity in Heineken.		
Oct. 2	Long-Term Investments—AFS (Adidas)	60,000	
	Cash		60,000
	Acquired 2,000 shares as a long-term investment in available-for-sale securities.		
Oct. 17	Long-Term Investments—AFS (Puma)	40,000	
	Cash		40,000
	Acquired 1,000 shares as a long-term investment in available-for-sale securities.		
Nov. 1	Cash	5,000	
	Long-Term Investments—Heineken		5,000
	Received dividend from Heineken.		
Nov. 30	Cash	3,000	
	Dividend Revenue.		3,000
	Received dividend from Adidas.		
Dec. 15	Cash	1,400	
	Dividend Revenue.		1,400
	Received dividend from Puma.		
Dec. 31	Long-Term Investments—Heineken	21,000	
	Earnings from Investment (Heineken)		21,000
	To record 30% share of Heineken's annual earnings of EUR 70,000.		
Dec. 31	Loss on Investments.	7,000	
	Fair Value Adjustment—Available-for-Sale (LT)* . . .		7,000
	To record change in fair value of long-term available-for-sale securities.		

* Fair value adjustment computations:

EUR	Cost	Fair Value	Unrealized Gain (Loss)
Adidas	60,000	48,000	(12,000)
Puma	40,000	45,000	5,000
Total	100,000	93,000	(7,000)

Required balance of the Fair Value
Adjustment—Available-for-Sale
(LT) account (credit) . . . . (7,000)
Existing balance 0
Necessary adjustment (credit) . . . . . . (7,000)

2. The December 31, 2014, selected statement of financial position items appear as follows.

Assets	
Long-term investments	
Available-for-sale securities (at fair value; cost is EUR 100,000)	EUR 93,000
Investment in equity securities	96,000
Total long-term investments	189,000
Equity	
Share Capital	500,000
Retained earnings.	343,000

The relevant statement of comprehensive income items for the year ended December 31, 2014, follow.

Dividend revenue	EUR 4,400
Share of Earnings of Associates (Heineken)	21,000
Other Comprehensive Income	
Fair Value Adjustment—AFS Investments	(7,000)

1. Journal entries for 2015.

Jan. 1	Cash	108,000	
	Long-Term Investments—Heineken		96,000
	Gain on Sale of Long-Term Investments		12,000
	Sold 1,000 shares for cash.		
May 30	Cash	3,100	
	Dividend Revenue.		3,100
	Received dividend from Adidas.		
June 15	Cash	1,600	
	Dividend Revenue.		1,600
	Received dividend from Puma.		
Aug. 17	Cash	52,000	
	Loss on Sale of Long-Term Investments	8,000	
	Long-Term Investments—AFS (Adidas)		60,000
	Sold 2,000 shares for cash.		
Aug. 19	Long-Term Investments—AFS (L'Oreal)	50,000	
	Cash		50,000
	Acquired 2,000 shares as a long-term investment in available-for-sale securities.		
Dec. 15	Cash	1,800	
	Dividend Revenue.		1,800
	Received dividend from Puma.		
Dec. 31	Fair Value Adjustment—Available-for-Sale (LT)*	4,000	
	Unrealized Loss—Equity		4,000
	To record change in fair value of long-term available-for-sale securities.		

* Fair value adjustment computations:

	Cost	Fair Value	Unrealized Gain (Loss)		
				Required balance of the Fair Value Adjustment—Available-for-Sale (LT) account (credit)	$(3,000)
Puma	$40,000	$39,000	$(1,000)	Existing balance (credit)	(7,000)
L'Oreal	50,000	48,000	(2,000)	Necessary adjustment (debit)	$ 4,000
Total	$90,000	$87,000	$(3,000)		

2. The December 31, 2015, statement of financial position items appear as follows.

Assets	
Long-term investments	
Available-for-sale securities (at fair value; cost is EUR 90,000)	EUR 87,000
Equity	
Share capital	500,000
Retained earnings	407,000

The relevant statement of comprehensive income items for the year ended December 31, 2015, follow.

Dividend revenue	EUR 6,500
Gain on sale of long-term investments	12,000
Loss on sale of long-term investments........................	(8,000)
Other Comprehensive Income:	
Fair Value Adjustment—AFS Investments	4,000

15A   Investments in International Operations

Many entities from small entrepreneurs to large corporations conduct business internationally. Some entities' operations occur in so many different countries that the companies are called **multinationals.** Nestlé, for example, defines itself as operating in three significant geographic zones: Zone Europe, Zone Americas, and Zone Asia, Oceania and Africa. Managing and accounting for multinationals present challenges. This section describes some of these challenges and how to account for and report these activities.

    Two major accounting challenges that arise when companies have international operations relate to transactions that involve more than one currency. The first is to account for sales and purchases listed in a foreign currency. The second is to prepare consolidated financial statements with international subsidiaries. For ease in this discussion, we use companies with a U.S. base of operations and assume the need to prepare financial statements in U.S. dollars. This means the *reporting currency* of these companies is the U.S. dollar.

Point: Transactions *listed* or *stated* in a foreign currency are said to be *denominated* in that currency.

C3 Explain foreign exchange rates and record transactions listed in a foreign currency.

Exchange Rates between Currencies   Markets for the purchase and sale of foreign currencies exist all over the world. In these markets, U.S. dollars can be exchanged for Canadian dollars, British pounds, Japanese yen, Euros, or any other legal currencies. The price of one currency stated in terms of another currency is called a **foreign exchange rate**. Exhibit 15A.1 lists recent exchange rates for selected currencies. The exchange rate for British pounds and U.S. dollars is $1.8980, meaning 1 British pound could be purchased for $1.8980. On that same day, the exchange rate between Mexican pesos and U.S. dollars is $0.0925, or 1 Mexican peso can be purchased for $0.0925. Exchange rates fluctuate due to changing economic and political conditions, including the supply and demand for currencies and expectations about future events.

Point: To convert currency, see XE.com

Decision Insight

Greek Haircut   Investors in government debt securities in the Eurozone must be careful of the heightened default risk associated with securities issued by certain Eurozone member nations. For example, in 2012, buyers of certain Greek bonds were repaid only 30% of principal because of the government's inability to honor its full obligation on the bonds. ∎

EXHIBIT 15A.1

Foreign Exchange Rates for
Selected Currencies*

Source (unit)	Price in US$	Source (unit)	Price in US$
Britain (pound)	$1.8980	Canada (dollar)	$0.9793
Mexico (peso)	0.0925	Japan (yen)	0.0090
Taiwan (dollar)	0.0305	Europe (EUR)	1.2920

* Rates will vary over time based on economic, political, and other changes.

Sales and Purchases Listed in a Foreign Currency

When a U.S. company makes a credit sale to an international customer, accounting for the sale and the account receivable is straightforward if sales terms require the international customer's payment in U.S. dollars. If sale terms require (or allow) payment in a foreign currency, however, the U.S. company must account for the sale and the account receivable in a different manner.

Sales in a Foreign Currency To illustrate, consider the case of the U.S.-based manufacturer Boston Company, which makes credit sales to London Outfitters, a British retail company. A sale occurs on December 12, 2015, for a price of GBP 10,000 with payment due on February 10, 2017. Boston Company keeps its accounting records in U.S. dollars. To record the sale, Boston Company must translate the sales price from pounds to dollars. This is done using the exchange rate on the date of the sale. Assuming the exchange rate on December 12, 2016, is $1.80, Boston records this sale as follows.

Dec. 12	Accounts Receivable—London Outfitters	18,000	
	Sales*		18,000
	To record a sale at EUR 10,000, when the exchange rate equals $1.80. * (EUR 10,000 × $1.80/EUR)		

Assets = Liabilities + Equity
+18,000   +18,000

When Boston Company prepares its annual financial statements on December 31, 2016, the current exchange rate is $1.84. Thus, the current dollar value of Boston Company's receivable is $18,400 (EUR 10,000 × $1.84/EUR). This amount is $400 higher than the amount recorded on December 12. Accounting principles require a receivable to be reported in the statement of financial position at its current dollar value. Thus, Boston Company must make the following entry to record the increase in the dollar value of this receivable at year-end.

Dec. 31	Accounts Receivable—London Outfitters	400	
	Foreign Exchange Gain		400
	To record the increased value of the British pound for the receivable.		

Assets = Liabilities + Equity
+400   +400

On February 10, 2017, Boston Company receives London Outfitters' payment of EUR 10,000. It immediately exchanges the pounds for U.S. dollars. On this date, the exchange rate for pounds is $1.78. Thus, Boston Company receives only $17,800 (EUR 10,000 × $1.78/EUR). It records the cash receipt and the loss associated with the decline in the exchange rate as follows.

Point: Foreign exchange gains are credits, and foreign exchange losses are debits.

Feb. 10	Cash	17,800	
	Foreign Exchange Loss	600	
	Accounts Receivable—London Outfitters		18,400
	Received foreign currency payment of an account and converted it into dollars.		

Assets = Liabilities + Equity
+17,800   −600
−18,400

Gains and losses from foreign exchange transactions are accumulated in the Foreign Exchange Gain (or Loss) account. After year-end adjustments, the balance in the Foreign Exchange Gain (or Loss) account is reported on the income statement and closed to the Income Summary account.

Purchases in a Foreign Currency Accounting for credit purchases from an international seller is similar to the case of a credit sale to an international customer. In particular, if the U.S. company is required to make payment in a foreign currency, the account payable must be translated into dollars before the U.S. company can record it. If the exchange rate is different when preparing financial statements and when paying for the purchase, the U.S. company must recognize a foreign exchange gain or loss at those dates. To illustrate, assume NC Imports, a U.S. company, purchases products costing EUR 20,000 from Hamburg Brewing on January 15, when the exchange rate is $1.20 per EUR. NC records this transaction as follows.

Example: Assume that a U.S. company makes a credit purchase from a British company for EUR 10,000 when the exchange rate is $1.62. At the statement of financial position date, this rate is $1.72. Does this imply a gain or loss for the U.S. company? *Answer:* A loss.

Assets = Liabilities + Equity
+24,000   +24,000

Jan. 15	Inventory	24,000	
	Accounts Payable—Hamburg Brewing		24,000
	To record a EUR 20,000 purchase when exchange rate is $1.20 (EUR 20,000 × $1.20/EUR).		

NC Imports makes payment in full on February 14 when the exchange rate is $1.25 per EUR, which is recorded as follows.

Assets = Liabilities + Equity
−25,000   −24,000   −1,000

Feb. 14	Accounts Payable—Hamburg Brewing	24,000	
	Foreign Exchange Loss	1,000	
	Cash		25,000
	To record cash payment towards EUR 20,000 account when exchange rate is $1.25 (EUR 20,000 × $1.25/EUR).		

Decision Insight

Global Greenback What do changes in foreign exchange rates mean? A decline in the price of the U.S. dollar against other currencies usually yields increased international sales for U.S. companies, without hiking prices or cutting costs, and puts them on a stronger competitive footing abroad. At home, they can raise prices without fear that foreign rivals will undercut them. ■

Consolidated Statements with International Subsidiaries
A second challenge in accounting for international operations involves preparing consolidated financial statements when the parent company has one or more international subsidiaries. Consider a U.S.-based company that owns a controlling interest in a French subsidiary. The reporting currency of the U.S. parent is the dollar. The French subsidiary maintains its financial records in euros. Before preparing consolidated statements, the parent must translate financial statements of the French company into U.S. dollars. After this translation is complete (including that for accounting differences), it prepares consolidated statements the same as for domestic subsidiaries. Procedures for translating an international subsidiary's account balances depend on the nature of the subsidiary's operations. The process requires the parent company to select appropriate foreign exchange rates and to apply those rates to the foreign subsidiary's account balances. This is described in advanced courses.

Global: A weaker U.S. dollar often increases global sales for U.S. companies.

Decision Maker
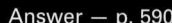
Answer — p. 590

Entrepreneur You are a U.S. home builder that purchases lumber from mills in both the U.S. and Canada. The price of the Canadian dollar in terms of the U.S. dollar jumps from US$0.70 to US$0.80. Are you now more or less likely to buy lumber from Canadian or U.S. mills? ■

APPENDIX
15B   New requirements under IFRS 9

C4 Understand the new requirements under **IFRS 9**.

The International Accounting Standards Board (IASB) first issued **IFRS 9 Financial Instruments** in November 2009. **IFRS 9** Financial Instruments sets out the requirements for recognising and measuring financial assets, financial liabilities, and some contracts to buy or sell non-financial items. It is designed to replace **IAS 39 Financial Instruments: Recognition and Measurement** with a new standard designed to simply the recognition, classification and measurement requirements for financial instruments. The project was conducted in three phases:

Phase 1: Classification and measurement

Phase 2: Impairment methodology

Phase 3: Hedge accounting

IFRS 9 was subsequently modified in 2010 and 2013. Due to various reasons the mandatory adoption date had been deferred. On July 24 2014, the International Accounting Standards Board completed the final element of its comprehensive response to the financial crisis by issuing **IFRS 9 Financial Instruments**. The new Standard will come into effect on 1 January 2018 with early application permitted.

General principles

Classification determines how financial assets are accounted for in financial statements and how they are measured on an ongoing basis. Classification is made at the time the financial asset is initially recognized. **IFRS 9** retains a mixed-measurement model, but classifies financial instruments into two categories:

1. at amortised cost; or
2. at fair value.

IFRS 9 uses two criteria to determine how financial assets should be classified and measured:

(a) the entity's business model for managing the financial assets (the "business model approach"); and
(b) the contractual cash flow characteristics of the financial assets.

For debt instruments, if the objective of the entity's business model is to collect the contractual cash flows and those contractual cash flows are solely payments of principal and interest ("SPPI"), the financial asset is measured at amortised cost. This is usually the case for a simple debt instrument. Otherwise, the financial asset is measured at fair value.

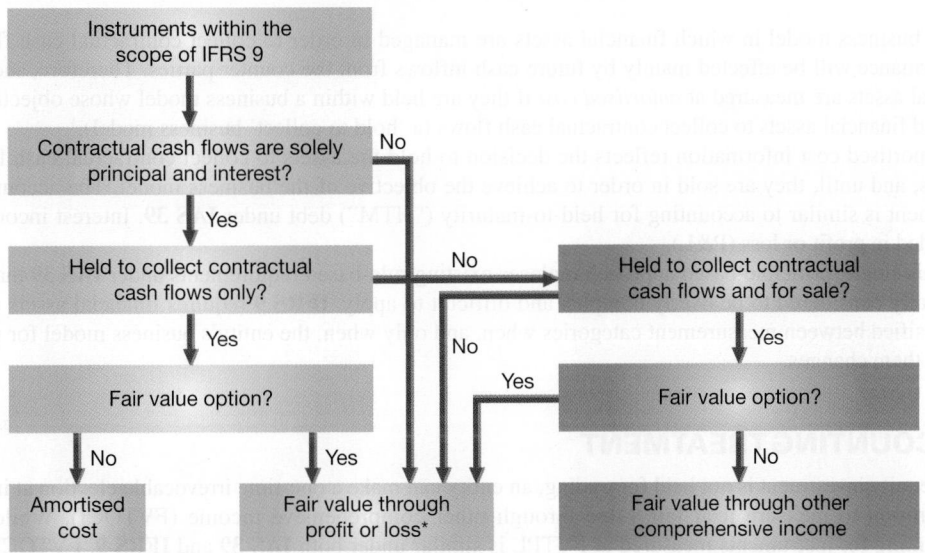

Process for determining the classification and measurement of financial assets

* Presentation option for equity investments to present fair value changes in OCI.

For equity instruments, if the financial assets are managed for sale, performance will be affected mainly by the realisation of fair values. Such financial assets are reported at fair value, either:

1. through profit or loss (FVTPL), or
2. through other comprehensive income (FVTOCI).

IASB believes that fair value information reflects the cash flows that would be realised if, and when, they were sold. Dividends are a form of income that should be presented in profit or loss whether the financial assets are measured at FVTPL or FVTOCI.

WHAT IS A BUSINESS MODEL?

The objective of **IFRS 9** to replace **IAS 39** is to make it easier for users of financial statements to assess the amounts, timing and uncertainty of cash flows arising from financial assets. **IFRS 9** achieves this objective by aligning the measurement of financial assets with the way the entity manages its financial assets (its 'business model') and with their contractual cash flow characteristics. A business model refers to how an entity manages its financial assets in order to generate cash flows—by collecting contractual cash flows, selling financial assets or both.

The business model should be determined on a level that reflects how financial assets are managed to achieve a particular business objective. However, the determination is not dependent on management's intentions for an individual instrument, and should be made on a higher level of aggregation. In order to assess the business model, an entity needs to consider the frequency and significance of past sales and the reason for those sales, as well as expectations for the future. This is done to determine whether the cash flows from financial assets will arise from the collection of contractual cash flows or from sale. Judgment needs to be used when assessing a business model and that assessment should consider all relevant available evidence.

A quick summary:

Business Model	Classification
Objective is to hold assets in order to collect contractual cash flows	Amortized cost
Objective is both collect contractual cash flows and sell financial assets	FVTOCI
Other objectives, including for example, trading	FVTPL

For a business model in which financial assets are managed in order to collect contractual cash flows, performance will be affected mainly by future cash inflows from the counter parties. Therefore, such financial assets are measured at *amortised cost* if they are held within a business model whose objective is to hold financial assets to collect contractual cash flows (a 'hold to collect' business model).[1]

Amortised cost information reflects the decision to hold the assets to collect contractual cash flows unless, and until, they are sold in order to achieve the objective of the business model. The accounting treatment is similar to accounting for held-to-maturity ("HTM") debt under **IAS 39**. Interest income is recorded in profit or loss (P&L).

This single, principle-based approach replaces existing rule-based requirements under **IAS 39** that are generally considered to be overly complex and difficult to apply. **IFRS 9** requires financial assets to be reclassified between measurement categories when, and only when, the entity's business model for managing them changes.

ACCOUNTING TREATMENT

If an equity investment is not held for trading, an entity can make a one-time irrevocable election at initial recognition to measure it at fair value through other comprehensive income (FVTOCI). While the accounting for instruments measured at FVTPL is similar under both **IAS 39** and **IFRS 9**, FVTOCI is a new category under **IFRS 9**. Unlike AFS securities, **IFRS 9** prohibit subsequent transfer ('recycling') of fair value changes to profit or loss on sale of the investments for FVTOCI. In other words, *both* realized and unrealized changes in carrying amount (gains or losses) "by pass" the P&L and are reported in the OCI. Only dividend income is recognised in profit or loss.

IASB argue that a gain or loss on those investments should be recognised once only; therefore, recognising a gain or loss in other comprehensive income and subsequently transferring it to profit or loss is inappropriate.

---

[1] This is subject to the contractual cash flow characteristics assessment, i.e. whether the financial asset has only contractual cash flows representing principal and interest on that principal. If a debt instrument does not meet such requirement, it is reported at FVTPL. **IFRS 9** also contains a "fair value option" to designate a financial liability as measured at FVTPL if doing so eliminates or significantly reduces a measurement or recognition inconsistency ("accounting mismatch"). This is often the case for financial institutions. Accounting for such instruments is beyond our scope at the introductory level.

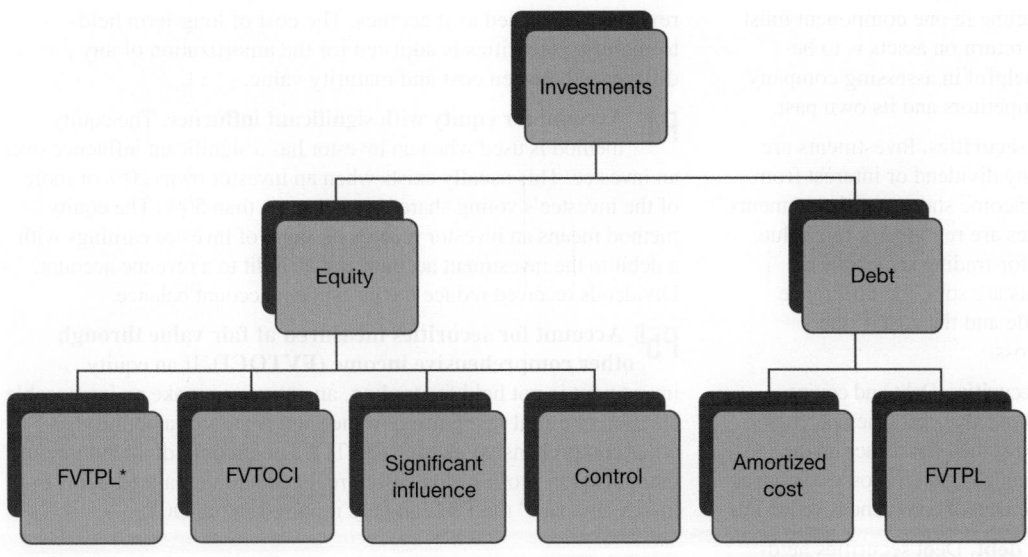

* Fair value through profit or loss (FVTPL).

RATIONALE FOR FVTOCI

IAS 39 maintains a distinction between realised and unrealised gains and losses because an entity's performance should include all *realised* gains and losses. **IFRS 9** intends to reduce the complexity of the financial reporting for financial assets. Accordingly, the Board decided to prohibit recycling of gains and losses into profit or loss when an equity instrument is derecognised.

To prevent an entity from "cherry picking" and reclassifying equity instruments into and out of the fair value through other comprehensive income category, the election to measure an instrument at FVTOCI is *irrevocable* once made at initial recognition. The fair value through other comprehensive income measurement category should result in a fair value carrying amount in the statement of financial position, but fluctuation in fair values would not affect P&L.

Summary

C1 Distinguish between debt and equity securities and between short-term and long-term investments. *Debt securities* reflect a creditor relationship and include investments in notes, bonds, and certificates of deposit. *Equity securities* reflect an owner relationship and include shares issued by other companies. Short-term investments in securities are current assets that meet two criteria: (1) They are expected to be converted into cash within one year or the current operating cycle of the business, whichever is longer and (2) they are readily convertible to cash, or *marketable*. All other investments in securities are long-term. Long-term investments also include assets not used in operations and those held for special purposes, such as land for expansion.

C2 Describe how to report equity with control. If an investor owns more than 50% of another company's voting shares and controls the investee, the investor's financial reports are prepared on a consolidated basis. These reports are prepared as if the company were organized as one entity.

C3ᴬ Explain foreign exchange rates and record transactions listed in a foreign currency. A foreign exchange rate is the price of one currency stated in terms of another. An entity with

transactions in a foreign currency when the exchange rate changes between the transaction dates and their settlement will experience exchange gains or losses. When a company makes a credit sale to a foreign customer and sales terms call for payment in a foreign currency, the company must translate the foreign currency into dollars to record the receivable. If the exchange rate changes before payment is received, exchange gains or losses are recognized in the year they occur. The same treatment is used when a company makes a credit purchase from a foreign supplier and is required to make payment in a foreign currency.

C4ᴮ Understand the new requirements under IFRS 9. IFRS 9 classifies financial instruments into two categories: measured at amortised cost and at fair value. A financial asset shall be measured at amortised cost if it is held within a business model whose objective is to hold assets in order to collect contractual cash flows and such cash flows are solely payments of principal and interest on the principal amount outstanding. A financial asset shall be measured at fair value unless it is measured at amortised cost.

A1 Compute and analyze the components of return on total assets. Return on total assets has two components: profit margin and total asset turnover. A decline in one component must be met with an increase in another if return on assets is to be maintained. Component analysis is helpful in assessing company performance compared to that of competitors and its own past.

P1 **Account for held-for-trading securities.** Investments are initially recorded at cost, and any dividend or interest from these investments is recorded in the income statement. Investments classified as held-for-trading securities are reported at fair value. Unrealized gains and losses on held-for-trading securities are reported in income. When investments are sold, the difference between the net proceeds from the sale and the cost of the securities is recognized as a gain or loss.

P2 **Account for available-for-sale securities.** Debt and equity securities available-for-sale are recorded at cost when purchased. Available-for-sale securities are reported at their fair values on the statement of financial position with unrealized gains or losses shown as other comprehensive income in the statement of comprehensive income.

P3 **Account for held-to-maturity debt.** Debt securities held-to-maturity are reported at cost when purchased. Interest

revenue is recorded as it accrues. The cost of long-term held-to-maturity securities is adjusted for the amortization of any difference between cost and maturity value.

P4 **Account for equity with significant influence.** The equity method is used when an investor has a significant influence over an investee. This usually exists when an investor owns 20% or more of the investee's voting shares but not more than 50%. The equity method means an investor records its share of investee earnings with a debit to the investment account and a credit to a revenue account. Dividends received reduce the investment account balance.

P5ᴮ **Account for securities measured at fair value through other comprehensive income (FVTOCI).** If an equity investment is not held for trading, an entity can make an irrevocable election at initial recognition to measure it at fair value through other comprehensive income (FVTOCI) with only dividend income recognised in profit or loss. Both realized and unrealized gains or losses "by pass" the P&L and are reported in the OCI.

Guidance Answers to Decision Maker

Retailer Your store's return on assets is 11%, which is similar to the industry norm of 11.2%. However, disaggregation of return on assets reveals that your store's profit margin of 4.4% is much higher than the norm of 3.5%, but your total asset turnover of 2.5 is much lower than the norm of 3.2. These results suggest that, as compared with competitors, you are less efficient in using assets. You need to focus on increasing sales or reducing assets. You might consider reducing prices to increase sales, provided such a strategy does not reduce your return on assets. For instance, you could reduce your profit margin to 4% to increase sales. If total asset turnover

increases to more than 2.75 when profit margin is lowered to 4%, your overall return on assets is improved.

Entrepreneur You are now less likely to buy Canadian lumber because it takes more U.S. money to buy a Canadian dollar (and lumber). For instance, the purchase of lumber from a Canadian mill with a C$1,000 price would have cost the U.S. builder US$700 (computed as C$1,000 × US$0.70) before the rate change, and $800 (US dollars, computed as C$1,000 × US$0.80) after the rate change.

Guidance Answers to Quick Checks

1. Held-for-trading securities are reported (valued) at fair value.
2. Available-for-sale securities are reported (valued) at fair value.
3. As part of profit and loss.
4. As part of other comprehensive income.
5. An investor that owns 20% or more (but not more than 50%) of a company's voting shares is usually presumed to have a significant

influence over the investee. An investor who owns more than 50% of a company's voting shares has control over the investee.

6. Consolidated financial statements show the financial position, results of operations, and cash flows of all entities under the parent's control, including all subsidiaries. These statements are prepared as if the business were organized as one entity.

Key Terms

www.mheducation.asia/olc/wildkwokFAP

Additional Quiz Questions are available at the book's Website.

1. A company purchased $30,000 of 5% bonds for investment purposes on May 1. The bonds pay interest on February 1 and August 1. The amount of interest revenue accrued at December 31 (the company's year-end) is:
   a. $1,500
   b. $1,375
   c. $1,000
   d. $625
   e. $300

2. Earlier this period, Amadeus Co. purchased its only available-for-sale investment in the shares of Bach Co. for $83,000. The period-end fair value of the shares is $84,500. Amadeus records a:
   a. Credit to Unrealized Gain—Equity for $1,500.
   b. Debit to Unrealized Loss—Equity for $1,500.
   c. Debit to Investment Revenue for $1,500.
   d. Credit to Fair Value Adjustment—Available-for-Sale for $3,500.
   e. Credit to Cash for $1,500.

3. Mozart Co. owns 35% of Melody Inc. Melody pays $50,000 in cash dividends to its shareholders for the period. Mozart's entry to record the Melody dividend includes a:
   a. Credit to Investment Revenue for $50,000.
   b. Credit to Long-Term Investments for $17,500.

c. Credit to Cash for $17,500.
d. Debit to Long-Term Investments for $17,500.
e. Debit to Cash for $50,000.

4. A company has net profit of $300,000, net sales of $2,500,000, and total assets of $2,000,000. Its return on total assets equals:
   a. 6.7%
   b. 12.0%
   c. 8.3%
   d. 80.0%
   e. 15.0%

5. A company had net profit of $80,000, net sales of $600,000, and total assets of $400,000. Its profit margin and total asset turnover are:

	Profit Margin	Total Asset Turnover
a.	1.5%	13.3
b.	13.3%	1.5
c.	13.3%	0.7
d.	7.0%	13.3
e.	10.0%	26.7

[A] Superscript A denotes assignments based on Appendix 15A.

[B] Superscript B denotes assignments based on Appendix 15B.

🔲 Icon denotes assignments that involve decision making.

Discussion Questions

1. Under what two conditions should investments be classified as current assets?

2. 🔲 On a statement of financial position, what valuation must be reported for short-term investments in held-for-trading securities?

3. If a short-term investment in available-for-sale securities costs $6,780 and is sold for $7,500, how should the difference between these two amounts be recorded?

4. Explain what is meant by long-term investments having "significant influence" and "control" and the appropriate accounting for each.

5. Under what conditions should investments be classified as current assets? As long-term assets?

6. If a company purchases its only long-term investments in available-for-sale debt securities this period and their fair value is below cost at the statement of financial position date, what entry is required to recognize this unrealized loss?

7. On a statement of financial position, what valuation must be reported for debt securities classified as available-for-sale?

8. Under what circumstances are long-term investments in debt securities reported at cost and adjusted for amortization of any difference between cost and maturity value?

9. For investments in available-for-sale securities, how are unrealized (holding) gains and losses reported?

10. In accounting for investments in equity securities, when should the equity method be used?

11. Under what circumstances does a company prepare consolidated financial statements?

12.[A] What are two major challenges in accounting for international operations?

13.[A] Assume a U.S. company makes a credit sale to a foreign customer that is required to make payment in its foreign currency. In the current period, the exchange rate is $1.40 on the date of the sale and is $1.30 on the date the customer pays the receivable. Will the U.S. company record an exchange gain or loss?

14.[A] 🔲 If a U.S. company makes a credit sale to a foreign customer required to make payment in U.S. dollars, can the U.S. company have an exchange gain or loss on this sale?

15.[A] 🔲 Refer to Nestlé's statement of comprehensive income in Appendix A. What is the amount of foreign currency translation adjustment for the year ended December 31, 2013? Is this adjustment a gain or a loss?

16. Refer to Nestlé's statement of comprehensive income in Appendix A. What was the amount of its financial 2013 unrealized gain or loss on available-for sale investments?

17. Refer to the statement of financial position of Adidas in Appendix A. How can you tell that Adidas uses the consolidated method of accounting?

18. Refer to the financial statements of Adidas in Appendix A. Compute its return on total assets for the year ended December 31, 2013.

19.ᴮ For equity investments at FVTOCI, how are unrealized (holding) gains and losses reported?

20.ᴮ For equity investments at FVTOCI, how are realized (actual) gains and losses reported?

connect

QUICK STUDY

QS 15-1

Describing investments in securities

C1 C2

Complete the following descriptions by filling in the blanks.

1. Accrual of interest on bonds held as long-term investments requires a credit to _____ _____.

2. The controlling investor (more than 50% ownership) is called the _____, and the investee company is called the _____.

3. Held-for-trading securities are classified as _____ assets.

4. Equity securities giving an investor significant influence are accounted for using the _____ _____.

5. Available-for-sale debt securities are reported on the statement of financial position at _____ _____.

QS 15-2

Identifying long-term investments

C1

Which of the following statements are true of long-term investments?

a. They can include investments in held-for-trading securities.

b. They are always easily sold and therefore qualify as being marketable.

c. They can include debt and equity securities available-for-sale.

d. They are held as an investment of cash available for current operations.

e. They can include debt held-to-maturity.

f. They can include bonds and shares not intended to serve as a ready source of cash.

g. They can include funds earmarked for a special purpose, such as bond sinking funds.

QS 15-3

Short-term equity investments P1

On April 18, Dice Co. made a short-term investment in 500 ordinary shares of XLT Co. The purchase price is $45 per share and the broker's fee is $150. The intent is to actively manage these shares for profit. On May 30, Dice Co. receives $1 per share from XLT in dividends. Prepare the April 18 and May 30 journal entries to record these transactions.

QS 15-4

Available-for-sale securities

P2

Fender Co. purchased short-term investments in available-for-sale securities at a cost of $100,000 on November 25, 2014. At December 31, 2014, these securities had a fair value of $94,000. This is the first and only time the company has purchased such securities.

1. Prepare the December 31, 2014, year-end adjusting entry for the securities' portfolio.

2. For each account in the entry for part 1, explain how it is reported in financial statements.

3. Prepare the April 6, 2015, entry when Fender sells one-half of these securities for $52,000.

QS 15-5

Available-for-sale securities

P2

Prepare Hoffman Company's journal entries to reflect the following transactions for the current year.

May 7   Purchases 100 shares of Lov shares as a short-term investment in available-for-sale securities at a cost of $25 per share plus $200 in broker fees.

June 6   Sells 100 shares of its investment in Lov shares at $28 per share. The broker's commission on this sale is $75.

QS 15-6

Available-for-sale securities

P2

Galaxy Company completes the following transactions during the current year.

May 9   Purchases 400 shares of X&O shares as a short-term investment in available-for-sale securities at a cost of $50 per share plus $400 in broker fees.

June 2   Sells 200 shares of its investment in X&O shares at $56 per share. The broker's commission on this sale is $180.

Dec. 31   The closing market price (fair value) of the X&O shares is $46 per share.

Prepare the May 9 and June 2 journal entries and the December 31 adjusting entry. This is the first and only time the company purchased such securities.

On May 20, 2014, Alexis Co. paid $750,000 to acquire 25,000 ordinary shares (10%) of TKR Corp. as a long-term investment. On August 5, 2015, Alexis sold one-half of these shares for $475,000. What valuation method should be used to account for this shares investment? Prepare entries to record both the acquisition and the sale of these shares.

QS 15-7
Recording equity securities
P2

Assume the same facts as in QS 15-7 except that the shares acquired represent 40% of TKR Corp.'s outstanding shares. Also assume that TKR Corp. paid a $125,000 dividend on November 1, 2014, and reported a net profit of $550,000 for 2014. Prepare the entries to record (*a*) the receipt of the dividend and (*b*) the December 31, 2014, year-end adjustment required for the investment account.

QS 15-8
Equity method transactions
P4

On February 1, 2014, Charo Mendez purchased 6% bonds issued by CR Utilities at a cost of $30,000, which is their par value. The bonds pay interest semiannually on July 31 and January 31. For 2014, prepare entries to record Mendez's July 31 receipt of interest and its December 31 year-end interest accrual.

QS 15-9
Debt securities transactions
P3

During the current year, Patton Consulting Group acquired long-term available-for-sale securities at a $35,000 cost. At its December 31 year-end, these securities had a fair value of $29,000. This is the first and only time the company purchased such securities.
1. Prepare the necessary year-end adjusting entry related to these securities.
2. Explain how each account used in part 1 is reported in the financial statements.

QS 15-10
Recording fair value adjustment for securities
P2

The return on total assets is the focus of analysts, creditors, and other users of financial statements.
1. How is the return on total assets computed?
2. What does this important ratio reflect?

QS 15-11
Return on total assets   A1

Return on total assets can be separated into two important components.
1. Write the formula to separate the return on total assets into its two basic components.
2. Explain how these components of the return on total assets are helpful to financial statement users for business decisions.

QS 15-12
Component return on total assets   A1

A U.S. company sells a product to a British company with the transaction listed in British pounds. On the date of the sale, the transaction total of $16,000 is billed as EUR 10,000, reflecting an exchange rate of 1.60 (that is, $1.60 per pound). Prepare the entry to record (1) the sale and (2) the receipt of payment in pounds when the exchange rate is 1.50.

QS 15-13[A]
Foreign currency transactions
C3

On March 1, 2014, a U.S. company made a credit sale requiring payment in 30 days from a Malaysian company, Hamac Sdn. Bhd., in 20,000 Malaysian ringgit. Assuming the exchange rate between Malaysian ringgit and U.S. dollars is $0.6811 on March 1 and $0.6985 on March 31, prepare the entries to record the sale on March 1 and the cash receipt on March 31.

QS 15-14[A]
Foreign currency transactions
C3

Complete the following descriptions by filling in the blanks.
1. A long-term investment classified as equity with control implies that the investor can exert _____ over the investee.
2. The controlling investor is called the _____, and the investee is called the _____.

QS 15-15
Equity control
C2

The **Carrefour Group** reports the following description of its held-for-trading securities (titled "financial assets reported at fair value in the income statement").

These are financial assets held by the Group in order to make a short-term profit on the sale. These assets are valued at their fair value with variations in value recognized in the income statement.

QS 15-16
International accounting for investments
P1

Note 10 to Carrefour's 2008 financial statements reports EUR 7 million in unrealized gains for 2008 and EUR 26 million in unrealized losses for 2008, both included in the fair value of those financial assets held for trading. What amount of these unrealized gains and unrealized losses, if any, are reported in its 2008 income statement? Explain.

EXERCISES

Exercise 15-1

Accounting for short-term held-to-maturity debt   P3

Prepare journal entries to record the following transactions involving the short-term securities investments of Maxwell Co., all of which occurred during year 2015.

a. On February 15, paid $100,000 cash to purchase FTR's 90-day short-term debt securities ($100,000 principal), dated February 15, that pay 8% interest (categorized as held-to-maturity debt).

b. On May 16, received a check from FTR in payment of the principal and 90 days' interest on the debt purchased in transaction *a*.

Exercise 15-2

Accounting for short-term held-for-trading securities

P1

(c) Dr. Cash $13,860

Prepare journal entries to record the following transactions involving the short-term securities investments of Smart Co., all of which occurred during year 2015.

a. On March 22, purchased 700 shares of FIX Company shares at $30 per share plus a $150 brokerage fee. These shares are categorized as held-for-trading securities.

b. On September 1, received a $1.00 per share cash dividend on the FIX Company shares purchased in transaction *a*.

c. On October 8, sold 350 shares of FIX Co. shares for $40 per share, less a $140 brokerage fee.

Exercise 15-3

Accounting for short-term available-for-sale securities

P2

Prepare journal entries to record the following transactions involving the short-term securities investments of Prairie Co., all of which occurred during year 2015.

a. On August 1, paid $60,000 cash to purchase Better Buy's 10% debt securities ($60,000 principal), dated July 30, 2015, and maturing January 30, 2016 (categorized as available-for-sale securities).

b. On October 30, received a check from Better Buy for 90 days' interest on the debt securities purchased in transaction *a*.

Exercise 15-4

Debt and equity securities and short- and long-term investments

C1

Complete the following descriptions by filling in the blanks.

1. Short-term investments are securities that (1) management intends to convert to cash within ___ ___ or the ___ ___ whichever is longer, and (2) are readily convertible to ___.

2. Long-term investments in securities are defined as those securities that are ___ ___ convertible to cash or are ___ ___ to be converted into cash in the short term.

3. Debt securities reflect a ___ relationship such as investments in notes, bonds, and certificates of deposit.

4. Equity securities reflect an ___ relationship such as shares issued by companies.

Exercise 15-5

Equity with control

C2

Complete the following descriptions by filling in the blanks.

1. ___ is used to account for long-term investments in equity with control.

2. Consolidated ___ ___ show the financial position, results of operations, and cash flows of all entities under the parent's control, including all subsidiaries.

Exercise 15-6

Accounting for held-for-trading securities

P1

Check   (3) Gain, $2,000

Forex Co. purchases various investments in held-for-trading securities at a cost of $56,000 on December 27, 2015. (This is its first and only purchase of such securities.) At December 31, 2015, these securities had a fair value of $66,000.

1. Prepare the December 31, 2015, year-end adjusting entry for the held-for-trading securities' portfolio.

2. Explain how each account in the entry of part 1 is reported in financial statements.

3. Prepare the January 3, 2016, entry when Forex sells a portion of its held-for-trading securities (that had originally cost $28,000) for $30,000.

Exercise 15-7

Adjusting available-for-sale securities to fair value

P2

On December 31, 2015, Rollo Company held the following short-term investments in its portfolio of available-for-sale securities. Rollo had no short-term investments in its prior accounting periods. Prepare the December 31, 2015, adjusting entry to report these investments at fair value.

	Cost	Fair Value
Vicks Corporation bonds payable	$79,600	$90,600
Pace Corporation notes payable	60,600	52,900
Lake Lugano Company ordinary shares	85,500	82,100

Check   Unrealized loss, $100

Prepare journal entries to record the following transactions involving both the short-term and long-term investments of Sophia Corp., all of which occurred during calendar year 2015. Use the account Short-Term Investments for any transactions that you determine are short term.

a. On February 15, paid $150,000 cash to purchase American General's 120-day short-term notes at par, which are dated February 15 and pay 10% interest (classified as held-to-maturity).

b. On March 22, bought 700 Frain Industries' ordinary shares at $25 cash per share plus a $250 brokerage fee (classified as long-term available-for-sale securities).

c. On June 15, received a check from American General in payment of the principal and 120 days' interest on the notes purchased in transaction *a*.

d. On July 30, paid $50,000 cash to purchase MP3 Electronics' 8% notes at par, dated July 30, 2015, and maturing on January 30, 2016 (classified as held-for-trading securities).

e. On September 1, received a $0.50 per share cash dividend on the Frain Industries ordinary shares purchased in transaction *b*.

f. On October 8, sold 350 Frain Industries' ordinary shares for $32 cash per share, less a $175 brokerage fee.

g. On October 30, received a check from MP3 Electronics for three months' interest on the notes purchased in transaction *d*.

Exercise 15-8
Transactions in short-term and long-term investments
P1 P2 P3

On December 31, 2015, Manhattan Co. held the following short-term available-for-sale securities.

	Cost	Fair Value
Nintendo Co. ordinary shares	$68,900	$75,300
Atlantic bonds payable	24,500	22,800
Kellogg Co. notes payable	50,000	47,200
McDonald's Corp. ordinary shares	91,400	86,600

Manhattan had no short-term investments prior to the current period. Prepare the December 31, 2015, year-end adjusting entry to record the fair value adjustment for these securities.

Exercise 15-9
Fair value adjustment to available-for-sale securities
P2

Berroa Co. began operations in 2014. The cost and fair values for its long-term investments portfolio in available-for-sale securities are shown below. Prepare Berroa's December 31, 2015, adjusting entry to reflect any necessary fair value adjustment for these investments.

	Cost	Fair Value
December 31, 2014	$79,483	$72,556
December 31, 2015	85,120	90,271

Exercise 15-10
Fair value adjustment to available-for-sale securities
P2

Ticker Services began operations in 2013 and maintains long-term investments in available-for-sale securities. The year-end cost and fair values for its portfolio of these investments follow. Prepare journal entries to record each year-end fair value adjustment for these securities.

	Cost	Fair Value
December 31, 2013	$374,000	$362,560
December 31, 2014	426,900	453,200
December 31, 2015	580,700	686,450
December 31, 2016	875,500	778,800

Exercise 15-11
Multiyear fair value adjustments to available-for-sale securities
P2

Exercise 15-12

Classifying investments in securities; recording fair values

C1 P2 P3 P4

Information regarding Central Company's individual investments in securities during its calendar-year 2015, along with the December 31, 2015, fair values, follows.

a. Investment in Beeman Company's bonds: $418,500 cost, $455,000 fair value. Central intends to hold these bonds until they mature in 2020.

b. Investment in Baybridge's ordinary shares: 29,500 shares; $332,450 cost; $361,375 fair value. Central owns 32% of Baybridge's voting shares and has a significant influence over Baybridge.

c. Investment in Carroll's ordinary shares: 12,000 shares; $169,750 cost; $183,000 fair value. This investment amounts to 3% of Carroll's outstanding shares, and Central's goal with this investment is to earn dividends over the next few years.

d. Investment in Newtech's ordinary shares: 3,500 shares; $95,300 cost; $93,625 fair value. Central's goal with this investment is to reap an increase in fair value of the shares over the next three to five years. Newtech has 30,000 ordinary shares outstanding.

e. Investment in Flock's ordinary shares: 16,300 shares; $102,860 cost; $109,210 fair value. These shares are marketable and are held as an investment of cash available for operations.

Required

1. Identify whether each investment should be classified as a short-term or long-term investment. For each long-term investment, indicate in which of the long-term investment classifications it should be placed.

2. Prepare a journal entry dated December 31, 2015, to record the fair value adjustment of the long-term investments in available-for-sale securities. Central had no long-term investments prior to year 2015.

Check (2) Unrealized gain, $11,575

Exercise 15-13

Securities transactions; equity method

P4

Prepare journal entries to record the following transactions and events of Kash Company.

2015

Jan. 2   Purchased 30,000 Bushtex Co.'s ordinary shares for $204,000 cash plus a broker's fee of $3,480 cash. Bushtex has 90,000 ordinary shares outstanding and its policies will be significantly influenced by Kash.

Sept. 1   Bushtex declared and paid a cash dividend of $3.10 per share.

Dec. 31 Bushtex announced that net profit for the year is $624,900.

2016

June 1   Bushtex declared and paid a cash dividend of $3.60 per share.

Dec. 31 Bushtex announced that net profit for the year is $699,750.

Dec. 31 Kash sold 10,000 shares of Bushtex for $162,500 cash.

Exercise 15-14

Return on total assets

A1

The following information is available from the financial statements of Wright Industries. Compute Wright's return on total assets for 2015 and 2016. (Round returns to one-tenth of a percent.) Comment on the company's efficiency in using its assets in 2015 and 2016.

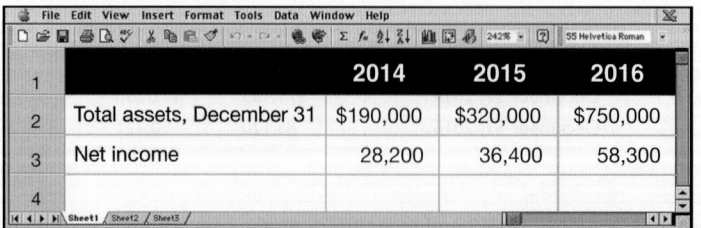

	2014	2015	2016
Total assets, December 31	$190,000	$320,000	$750,000
Net income	28,200	36,400	58,300

Exercise 15-15^A

Foreign currency transactions

C3

Desi of New York sells its products to customers in the United States and the United Kingdom. On December 16, 2015, Desi sold merchandise on credit to Bronson Ltd. of London at a price of GBP 17,000. The exchange rate on that day for EUR 1 was $1.5238. On December 31, 2015, when Desi prepared its financial statements, the rate was EUR 1 for $1.4990. Bronson paid its bill in full on January 15, 2016, at which time the exchange rate was EUR 1 for $1.5156. Desi immediately exchanged the GBP 17,000 for U.S. dollars. Prepare Desi's journal entries on December 16, December 31, and January 15 (round to the nearest dollar).

On May 8, 2015, Jett Company (a U.S. company) made a credit sale to Lopez (a Mexican company). The terms of the sale required Lopez to pay MXN 80,000 on February 10, 2016. Jett prepares quarterly financial statements on March 31, June 30, September 30, and December 31. The exchange rates for pesos during the time the receivable is outstanding follow.

Exercise 15-16A
Computing foreign exchange gains and losses on receivables
C3

May 8, 2015	$0.1984
June 30, 2015	0.2013
September 30, 2015	0.2029
December 31, 2015	0.1996
February 10, 2016	0.2047

Compute the foreign exchange gain or loss that Jett should report on each of its quarterly income statements for the last three quarters of 2015 and the first quarter of 2016. Also compute the amount reported on Jett's statement of financial positions at the end of each of its last three quarters of 2015.

connect

Ryder Company, which began operations in 2015, invests its idle cash in held-for-trading securities. The following transactions are from its short-term investments in its held-for-trading securities.

PROBLEM SET A

Problem 15-1A
Recording transactions and fair value adjustments for held-for-trading securities
P1

2015

Jan. 20 Purchased 900 ordinary shares of Ford Motor Co. at $36 per share plus a $125 commission.
Feb. 9 Purchased 4,400 ordinary shares of Lucent at $10 per share plus a $200 commission.
Oct. 12 Purchased 500 ordinary shares of Z-Seven at $8 per share plus a $100 commission.

2016

Apr. 15 Sold 900 ordinary shares of Ford Motor Co. at $39 per share less a $185 commission.
July 5 Sold 500 ordinary shares of Z-Seven at $10.25 per share less a $100 commission.
July 22 Purchased 800 ordinary shares of Hunt Corp. at $30 per share plus a $225 commission.
Aug. 19 Purchased 1,000 ordinary shares of Donna Karan at $12 per share plus a $100 commission.

2017

Feb. 27 Purchased 3,400 ordinary shares of HCA at $22 per share plus a $220 commission.
Mar. 3 Sold 800 ordinary shares of Hunt at $25 per share less a $125 commission.
June 21 Sold 4,400 ordinary shares of Lucent at $8 per share less a $180 commission.
June 30 Purchased 1,000 ordinary shares of Black & Decker at $47.50 per share plus a $195 commission.
Nov. 1 Sold 1,000 ordinary shares of Donna Karan at $22 per share less a $208 commission.

Required

1. Prepare journal entries to record these short-term investment activities for the years shown. (Ignore any year-end adjusting entries.)

2. On December 31, 2017, prepare the adjusting entry to record any necessary fair value adjustment for the portfolio of held-for-trading securities when HCA's share price is $24 and Black & Decker's share price is $43.50. (Assume the Fair Value Adjustment—Trading account had an unadjusted balance of zero.)

Check (2) Dr. Short-term Investment—Trading $2,385

Perry Company had no short-term investments prior to year 2015. It had the following transactions involving short-term investments in available-for-sale securities during 2015.

Problem 15-2A
Recording, adjusting, and reporting short-term available-for-sale securities

P3

Apr. 16 Purchased 8,000 ordinary shares of Gem Co. at $24.25 per share plus a $360 brokerage fee.
May 1 Paid $200,000 to buy 90-day U.S. Treasury bills (debt securities): $200,000 principal amount, 6% interest, securities dated May 1.
July 7 Purchased 4,000 ordinary shares of PepsiCo at $49.25 per share plus a $350 brokerage fee.
20 Purchased 2,000 ordinary shares of Xerox at $16.75 per share plus a $410 brokerage fee.

Aug.   3   Received a check for principal and accrued interest on the U.S. Treasury bills that matured on July 29.
      15   Received an $0.85 per share cash dividend on the Gem Co. shares.
      28   Sold 4,000 shares of Gem Co. shares at $30 per share less a $450 brokerage fee.
Oct.   1   Received a $1.90 per share cash dividend on the PepsiCo shares.
Dec. 15   Received a $1.05 per share cash dividend on the remaining Gem Co. shares.
      31   Received a $1.30 per share cash dividend on the PepsiCo shares.

Required

1. Prepare journal entries to record the preceding transactions and events.

Check   (2) Cost = $328,440

2. Prepare a table to compare the year-end cost and fair values of Perry's short-term investments in available-for-sale securities. The year-end fair values per share are: Gem Co., $26.50; PepsiCo, $46.50; and Xerox, $13.75.

(3) Dr. Loss on Investments $8,940

3. Prepare an adjusting entry, if necessary, to record the year-end fair value adjustment for the portfolio of short-term investments in available-for-sale securities.

Analysis Component

4. Explain the statement of financial position presentation of the fair value adjustment for Perry's short-term investments.

5. How do these short-term investments affect Perry's statement of comprehensive income?

Problem 15-3A
Recording, adjusting, and reporting long-term available-for-sale securities

P2

Shaq Security, which began operations in 2015, invests in long-term available-for-sale securities. Following is a series of transactions and events determining its long-term investment activity.

2015

Jan. 20   Purchased 900 ordinary shares of Johnson & Johnson at $18.75 per share plus a $590 commission.
Feb.   9   Purchased 2,200 ordinary shares of Sony at $46.88 per share plus a $2,578 commission.
June 12   Purchased 500 ordinary shares of Mattel at $55.50 per share plus an $832 commission.
Dec. 31   Per share fair values for shares in the portfolio are Johnson & Johnson, $20.38; Mattel, $57.25; Sony, $39.

2016

Apr. 15   Sold 900 ordinary shares of Johnson & Johnson at $21.75 per share less a $685 commission.
July   5   Sold 500 ordinary shares of Mattel at $49.13 per share less a $491 commission.
July 22   Purchased 1,600 ordinary shares of Sara Lee at $36.25 per share plus a $1,740 commission.
Aug. 19   Purchased 1,800 ordinary shares of Eastman Kodak at $28 per share plus a $1,260 commission.
Dec. 31   Per share fair values for shares in the portfolio are: Kodak, $31.75; Sara Lee, $30.00; Sony, $36.50.

2017

Feb. 27   Purchased 3,400 ordinary shares of Microsoft at $23.63 per share plus a $1,606 commission.
June 21   Sold 2,200 ordinary shares of Sony at $40.00 per share less a $2,640 commission.
June 30   Purchased 1,200 ordinary shares of Black & Decker at $47.50 per share plus a $1,995 commission.
Aug.   3   Sold 1,600 ordinary shares of Sara Lee at $31.25 per share less a $1,750 commission.
Nov.   1   Sold 1,800 ordinary shares of Eastman Kodak at $42.75 per share less a $2,309 commission.
Dec. 31   Per share fair values for shares in the portfolio are: Black & Decker, $56.50; Microsoft, $28.

Required

1. Prepare journal entries to record these transactions and events and any year-end fair value adjustments to the portfolio of long-term available-for-sale securities.

Check   (2b) Fair Value Adjustment bal.: 12/31/11, $(18,994); 12/31/12; $(31,664)

2. Prepare a table that summarizes the (*a*) total cost, (*b*) total fair value adjustment, and (*c*) total fair value of the portfolio of long-term available-for-sale securities at each year-end.

(3b) Unrealized Gain at 12/31/2013, $22,057

3. Prepare a table that summarizes (*a*) the realized gains and losses and (*b*) the unrealized gains or losses for the portfolio of long-term available-for-sale securities at each year-end.

Park Co.'s long-term available-for-sale portfolio at December 31, 2014, consists of the following.

Available-for-Sale Securities	Cost	Fair Value
80,000 ordinary shares of Company A	$1,070,600	$ 980,000
14,000 ordinary shares of Company B	318,750	308,000
35,000 ordinary shares of Company C	1,325,500	1,281,875

Park enters into the following long-term investment transactions during year 2015.

Jan. 29   Sold 7,000 ordinary shares of Company B for $158,375 less a brokerage fee of $3,100.
Apr. 17   Purchased 20,000 ordinary shares of Company W for $395,000 plus a brokerage fee of $3,500.
          The shares represent a 30% ownership in Company W.
July   6   Purchased 9,000 ordinary shares of Company X for $253,125 plus a brokerage fee of $3,500.
          The shares represent a 10% ownership in Company X.
Aug. 22   Purchased 100,000 ordinary shares of Company Y for $750,000 plus a brokerage fee of $8,200.
          The shares represent a 51% ownership in Company Y.
Nov. 13   Purchased 17,000 ordinary shares of Company Z for $533,800 plus a brokerage fee of $6,900.
          The shares represent a 5% ownership in Company Z.
Dec. 9   Sold 80,000 ordinary shares of Company A for $1,030,000 less a brokerage fee of $4,100.

The fair values of its investments at December 31, 2015, are: B, $162,750; C, $1,220,625; W, $382,500;
X, $236,250; Y, $1,062,500; and Z, $557,600.

Required

1. Determine the amount Park should report on its December 31, 2015, statement of financial position
   for its long-term investments in available-for-sale securities.
2. Prepare any necessary December 31, 2015, adjusting entry to record the fair value adjustment for the
   long-term investments in available-for-sale securities.
3. What amount of gains or losses on transactions relating to long-term investments in available-for-sale
   securities should Park report on its December 31, 2015, income statement?

Problem 15-4A
Long-term investment
transactions; unrealized and
realized gains and losses
C2 P2 P4

Check (2) Cr. Loss on Investments,
$40,000

Pillar Steel Co., which began operations on January 4, 2015, had the following subsequent transactions
and events in its long-term investments.

2015

Jan. 5   Pillar purchased 30,000 ordinary shares (20% of total) of Kildaire for $780,000.
Oct. 23   Kildaire declared and paid a cash dividend of $1.60 per share.
Dec. 31   Kildaire's net profit for 2015 is $582,000, and the fair value of its shares at December 31 is
          $27.75 per share.

2016

Oct. 15   Kildaire declared and paid a cash dividend of $1.30 per share.
Dec. 31   Kildaire's net profit for 2016 is $738,000, and the fair value of its shares at December 31 is
          $30.45 per share.

2017

Jan. 2   Pillar sold all of its investment in Kildaire for $947,000 cash.

Part 1

Assume that Pillar has a significant influence over Kildaire with its 20% share of ordinary shares.

Required

1. Prepare journal entries to record these transactions and events for Pillar.
2. Compute the carrying amount (book value) per share of Pillar's investment in Kildaire's ordinary
   shares as reflected in the investment account on January 1, 2017.
3. Compute the net increase or decrease in Pillar's equity from January 5, 2015, through January 2, 2017,
   resulting from its investment in Kildaire.

Problem 15-5A
Accounting for long-term
investments in securities; with
and without significant influence
P2 P4

Check (2) Carrying amount per
share, $31.90

Part 2

Assume that although Pillar owns 20% of Kildaire's outstanding shares, circumstances indicate that it does not have a significant influence over the investee and that it is classified as an available-for-sale security investment.

Required

(1) 1/2/2017 Dr. Gain on Investments $133,500

1. Prepare journal entries to record the preceding transactions and events for Pillar. Also prepare an entry dated January 2, 2017, to remove any balance related to the fair value adjustment.

2. Compute the cost per share of Pillar's investment in Kildaire ordinary shares as reflected in the investment account on January 1, 2017.

(3) Net increase, $254,000

3. Compute the net increase or decrease in Pillar's equity from January 5, 2015, through January 2, 2017, resulting from its investment in Kildaire.

Problem 15-6A^A

Foreign currency transactions

C3

Roundtree Company, a U.S. corporation with customers in several foreign countries, had the following selected transactions for 2015 and 2016.

2015

Apr. 8 Sold merchandise to Salinas & Sons of Mexico for MXN 7,938 cash. The exchange rate for pesos is $0.1323 on this day.

July 21 Sold merchandise on credit to Sumito Corp. in Japan. The price of JPY 1.5 million is to be paid 120 days from the date of sale. The exchange rate for yen is $0.0096 on this day.

Oct. 14 Sold merchandise for GBP 19,000 to Smithers Ltd. of Great Britain, payment in full to be received in 90 days. The exchange rate for pounds is $1.5181 on this day.

Nov. 18 Received Sumito's payment in yen for its July 21 purchase and immediately exchanged the yen for dollars. The exchange rate for yen is $0.0091 on this day.

Dec. 20 Sold merchandise for MYR 17,000 to Hamid Albar of Malaysia, payment in full to be received in 30 days. On this day, the exchange rate for ringgit is $0.6852.

Dec. 31 Recorded adjusting entries to recognize exchange gains or losses on Roundtree's annual financial statements. Rates for exchanging foreign currencies on this day follow.

Pesos (Mexico)	$0.1335
Yen (Japan)	0.0095
Pounds (Britain)	1.5235
Ringgit (Malaysia)	0.6807

2016

Jan. 12 Received full payment in pounds from Smithers for the October 14 sale and immediately exchanged the pounds for dollars. The exchange rate for pounds is $1.5314 on this day.

Jan. 19 Received Hamid Albar's full payment in ringgit for the December 20 sale and immediately exchanged the ringgit for dollars. The exchange rate for ringgit is $0.6771 on this day.

Required

1. Prepare journal entries for the Roundtree transactions and adjusting entries (round amounts to the nearest dollar).

Check (2) 2015 total foreign exchange loss, $723

2. Compute the foreign exchange gain or loss to be reported on Roundtree's 2015 income statement.

Analysis Component

3. What actions might Roundtree consider to reduce its risk of foreign exchange gains or losses?

PROBLEM SET B

Problem 15-1B

Recording transactions and fair value adjustments for held-for-trading securities P1

Deal Company, which began operations in 2015, invests its idle cash in held-for-trading securities. The following transactions relate to its short-term investments in its held-for-trading securities.

2015

Mar. 10 Purchased 1,200 ordinary shares of AOL at $59.15 per share plus a $773 commission.

May 7 Purchased 2,500 ordinary shares of MTV at $36.25 per share plus a $1,428 commission.

Sept. 1 Purchased 600 ordinary shares of UPS at $57.25 per share plus a $625 commission.

2016

Apr. 26 Sold 2,500 ordinary shares of MTV at $34.50 per share less a $1,025 commission.

Apr. 27 Sold 600 ordinary shares of UPS at $60.50 per share less an $894 commission.

June 2 Purchased 1,800 ordinary shares of SPW at $172 per share plus a $1,625 commission.
June 14 Purchased 450 ordinary shares of Walmart at $50.25 per share plus a $541.50 commission.

2017

Jan. 28 Purchased 1,000 ordinary shares of PepsiCo at $43 per share plus a $1,445 commission.
Jan. 31 Sold 1,800 ordinary shares of SPW at $168 per share less a $1,020 commission.
Aug. 22 Sold 1,200 ordinary shares of AOL at $56.75 per share less a $1,240 commission.
Sept. 3 Purchased 750 ordinary shares of Vodaphone at $40.50 per share plus an $840 commission.
Oct. 9 Sold 450 ordinary shares of Walmart at $53.75 per share less a $610.50 commission.

Required

1. Prepare journal entries to record these short-term investment activities for the years shown. (Ignore any year-end adjusting entries.)
2. On December 31, 2017, prepare the adjusting entry to record any necessary fair value adjustment for the portfolio of held-for-trading securities when PepsiCo's share price is $41 and Vodaphone's share price is $37. (Assume the Fair Value Adjustment—Trading account had an unadjusted balance of zero.)

Check (2) Cr. Short-term
Investments—Trading $6,910

Day Systems had no short-term investments prior to 2015. It had the following transactions involving short-term investments in available-for-sale securities during 2015.

Feb. 6 Purchased 1,700 ordinary shares of Nokia at $41.25 per share plus a $1,500 brokerage fee.
15 Paid $10,000 to buy six-month U.S. Treasury bills (debt securities): $10,000 principal amount, 6% interest, securities dated February 15.
Apr. 7 Purchased 600 ordinary shares of Dell Co. at $39.50 per share plus a $627 brokerage fee.
June 2 Purchased 1,250 ordinary shares of Merck at $72.50 per share plus a $1,945 brokerage fee.
30 Received a $0.19 per share cash dividend on the Nokia shares.
Aug. 11 Sold 425 ordinary shares of Nokia at $46 per share less a $525 brokerage fee.
16 Received a check for principal and accrued interest on the U.S. Treasury bills purchased February 15.
24 Received a $0.10 per share cash dividend on the Dell shares.
Nov. 9 Received a $0.20 per share cash dividend on the remaining Nokia shares.
Dec. 18 Received a $0.15 per share cash dividend on the Dell shares.

Required

1. Prepare journal entries to record the preceding transactions and events.
2. Prepare a table to compare the year-end cost and fair values of the short-term investments in available-for-sale securities. The year-end fair values per share are: Nokia, $40.25; Dell, $41; and Merck, $59.
3. Prepare an adjusting entry, if necessary, to record the year-end fair value adjustment for the portfolio of short-term investments in available-for-sale securities.

Analysis Component

4. Explain the statement of financial position presentation of the fair value adjustment to Day's short-term investments.
5. How do these short-term investments affect (*a*) its income statement for year 2015 and (*b*) the equity section of its statement of financial position at the 2015 year-end?

Problem 15-2B
Recording, adjusting, and reporting short-term available-for-sale securities

P2

Check (2) Cost = $170,616

(3) Dr. Loss on Investments, $20,947

Venice Enterprises, which began operations in 2015, invests in long-term available-for-sale securities. Following is a series of transactions and events involving its long-term investment activity.

2015

Mar. 10 Purchased 2,400 ordinary shares of Apple at $33.25 per share plus $1,995 commission.
Apr. 7 Purchased 5,000 ordinary shares of Ford at $17.50 per share plus $2,625 commission.
Sept. 1 Purchased 1,200 ordinary shares of Polaroid at $49.00 per share plus $1,176 commission.
Dec. 31 Per share fair values for shares in the portfolio are: Apple, $35.50; Ford, $17.00; Polaroid, $51.75.

2016

Apr. 26 Sold 5,000 ordinary shares of Ford at $16.38 per share less a $2,237 commission.
June 2 Purchased 3,600 ordinary shares of Duracell at $18.88 per share plus a $2,312 commission.
June 14 Purchased 900 ordinary shares of Sears at $24.50 per share plus a $541 commission.
Nov. 27 Sold 1,200 ordinary shares of Polaroid at $52 per share less a $1,672 commission.
Dec. 31 Per share fair values for shares in the portfolio are: Apple, $35.50; Duracell, $18.00; Sears, $26.00.

Problem 15-3B
Recording, adjusting, and reporting long-term available-for-sale securities

P2

2017

Jan.	28	Purchased 2,000 ordinary shares of Coca-Cola Co. at $41 per share plus a $3,280 commission.
Aug.	22	Sold 2,400 ordinary shares of Apple at $29.75 per share less a $2,339 commission.
Sept.	3	Purchased 1,500 ordinary shares of Motorola at $29 per share plus a $870 commission.
Oct.	9	Sold 900 ordinary shares of Sears at $27.50 per share less a $619 commission.
Oct.	31	Sold 3,600 ordinary shares of Duracell at $16.00 per share less a $1,496 commission.
Dec.	31	Per share fair values for shares in the portfolio are: Coca-Cola, $46.00; Motorola, $22.00.

Required

1. Prepare journal entries to record these transactions and events and any year-end fair value adjustments to the portfolio of long-term available-for-sale securities.

Check   (2b) Fair Value Adjustment bal.: 12/31/15, $404; 12/31/16, $(1,266)

(3b) Unrealized Loss at 12/31/2017, $4,650

2. Prepare a table that summarizes the (*a*) total cost, (*b*) total fair value adjustment, and (*c*) total fair value for the portfolio of long-term available-for-sale securities at each year-end.

3. Prepare a table that summarizes (*a*) the realized gains and losses and (*b*) the unrealized gains or losses for the portfolio of long-term available-for-sale securities at each year-end.

Problem 15-4B
Long-term investment transactions; unrealized and realized gains and losses

C2 P2 P4

Capollo's long-term available-for-sale portfolio at December 31, 2014, consists of the following.

Available-for-Sale Securities	Cost	Fair Value
45,000 ordinary shares of Company R	$1,118,250	$1,198,125
17,000 ordinary shares of Company S	616,760	586,500
22,000 ordinary shares of Company T	294,470	303,600

Capollo enters into the following long-term investment transactions during year 2015.

Jan.	13	Sold 4,250 ordinary shares of Company S for $144,500 less a brokerage fee of $2,390.
Mar.	24	Purchased 31,000 ordinary shares of Company U for $565,750 plus a brokerage fee of $9,900. The shares represent a 62% ownership interest in Company U.
Apr.	5	Purchased 85,000 ordinary shares of Company V for $267,750 plus a brokerage fee of $4,500. The shares represent a 10% ownership in Company V.
Sept.	2	Sold 22,000 ordinary shares of Company T for $313,500 less a brokerage fee of $5,400.
Sept.	27	Purchased 5,000 ordinary shares of Company W for $101,000 plus a brokerage fee of $2,100. The shares represent a 25% ownership interest in Company W.
Oct.	30	Purchased 10,000 ordinary shares of Company X for $97,500 plus a brokerage fee of $2,340. The shares represent a 13% ownership interest in Company X.

The fair values of its investments at December 31, 2015, are: R, $1,136,250; S, $420,750; U, $545,600; V, $269,875; W, $109,375; and X, $91,250.

Required

1. Determine the amount Capollo should report on its December 31, 2015, statement of financial position for its long-term investments in available-for-sale securities.

Check   (2) Dr. Loss on Investments, $34,785; Cr. Fair Value Adjustment— AFS (LT), $93,530

2. Prepare any necessary December 31, 2015, adjusting entry to record the fair value adjustment of the long-term investments in available-for-sale securities.

3. What amount of gains or losses on transactions relating to long-term investments in available-for-sale securities should Capollo report on its December 31, 2015, income statement?

Problem 15-5B
Accounting for long-term investments in securities; with and without significant influence

P2 P4

Bengal Company, which began operations on January 3, 2015, had the following subsequent transactions and events in its long-term investments.

2015

Jan.	5	Bengal purchased 15,000 ordinary shares (25% of total) of Bloch for $187,500.
Aug.	1	Bloch declared and paid a cash dividend of $0.95 per share.
Dec.	31	Bloch's net profit for 2015 is $92,000, and the fair value of its shares is $12.90 per share.

2016

Aug.	1	Bloch declared and paid a cash dividend of $1.25 per share.
Dec.	31	Bloch's net profit for 2016 is $76,000, and the fair value of its shares is $13.55 per share.

2017

Jan.   8   Bengal sold all of its investment in Bloch for $204,750 cash.

Part 1

Assume that Bengal has a significant influence over Bloch with its 25% share.

Required

1. Prepare journal entries to record these transactions and events for Bengal.

2. Compute the carrying amount (book value) per share of Bengal's investment in Bloch ordinary shares as reflected in the investment account on January 7, 2017.

3. Compute the net increase or decrease in Bengal's equity from January 5, 2015, through January 8, 2017, resulting from its investment in Bloch.

Part 2

Assume that although Bengal owns 25% of Bloch's outstanding shares, circumstances indicate that it does not have a significant influence over the investee and that it is classified as an available-for-sale security investment.

Required

1. Prepare journal entries to record these transactions and events for Bengal. Also prepare an entry dated January 8, 2017, to remove any balance related to the fair value adjustment.

2. Compute the cost per share of Bengal's investment in Bloch ordinary shares as reflected in the investment account on January 7, 2017.

3. Compute the net increase or decrease in Bengal's equity from January 5, 2015, through January 8, 2017, resulting from its investment in Bloch.

Check (2) Carrying amount per share, $13.10

(1) 1/8/2017 Dr. Gain on Investments, $15,750

(3) Net increase, $50,250

Datamix, a U.S. corporation with customers in several foreign countries, had the following selected transactions for 2015 and 2016.

2015

May 26   Sold merchandise for JPY 6.5 million to Fuji Company of Japan, payment in full to be received in 60 days. On this day, the exchange rate for yen is $0.0094.

June   1   Sold merchandise to Fordham Ltd. of Great Britain for $72,613 cash. The exchange rate for pounds is $1.5277 on this day.

July   25   Received Fuji's payment in yen for its May 26 purchase and immediately exchanged the yen for dollars. The exchange rate for yen is $0.0090 on this day.

Oct.   15   Sold merchandise on credit to Martinez Brothers of Mexico. The price of MXN 373,000 is to be paid 90 days from the date of sale. On this day, the exchange rate for pesos is $0.1340.

Dec.   6   Sold merchandise for CNY 242,000 to Chi-Ying Company of China, payment in full to be received in 30 days. The exchange rate for yuan is $0.1975 on this day.

Dec. 31   Recorded adjusting entries to recognize exchange gains or losses on Datamix's annual financial statements. Rates of exchanging foreign currencies on this day follow.

Yen (Japan)	$0.0094
Pounds (Britain)	1.5318
Pesos (Mexico)	0.1560
Yuan (China)	0.2000

2016

Jan.   5   Received Chi-Ying's full payment in yuan for the December 6 sale and immediately exchanged the yuan for dollars. The exchange rate for yuan is $0.2060 on this day.

Jan. 13   Received full payment in pesos from Martinez for the October 15 sale and immediately exchanged the pesos for dollars. The exchange rate for pesos is $0.1420 on this day.

Required

1. Prepare journal entries for the Datamix transactions and adjusting entries.

2. Compute the foreign exchange gain or loss to be reported on Datamix's 2015 income statement.

Analysis Component

3. What actions might Datamix consider to reduce its risk of foreign exchange gains or losses?

Problem 15-6B[A]
Foreign currency transactions

C3

Check (2) 2015 total foreign exchange gain, $6,211

SERIAL PROBLEM
Business Solutions

P1

(This serial problem began in Chapter 1 and continues through most of the book. If previous chapter segments were not completed, the serial problem can begin at this point.)

SP 15 While reviewing the March 31, 2016, statement of financial position of Business Solutions, Santana Rey notes that the business has built a large cash balance of $68,057. Its most recent bank money market statement shows that the funds are earning an annualized return of 0.75%. S. Rey decides to make several investments with the desire to earn a higher return on the idle cash balance. Accordingly, in April 2016, Business Solutions makes the following investments in held-for-trading securities:

April 16   Purchases 400 ordinary shares of Johnson & Johnson at $50 per share plus $300 commission.
April 30   Purchases 200 ordinary shares of Starbucks Corporation at $22 per share plus $250 commission.

On June 30, 2016, the per share market price (fair value) of the Johnson & Johnson shares is $55 and the Starbucks shares is $19.

Required

1. Prepare journal entries to record the April purchases of trading securities by Business Solutions.
2. On June 30, 2016, prepare the adjusting entry to record any necessary fair value adjustment to its portfolio of held-for-trading securities.

Beyond the Numbers

REPORTING IN ACTION

C3   A1

BTN 15-1   Refer to Nestlé's financial statements in Appendix A to answer the following.

Required

1. Are Nestlé's financial statements consolidated? How can you tell?
2. Does Nestlé have any short-term investments for the year ended December 31, 2013?
3. Does Nestlé have any foreign operations? How can you tell?
4. Compute Nestlé's return on total assets for the year ended December 31, 2013.

Fast Forward

5. Access Nestlé's annual report for a financial year ending after December 31, 2013 from its Website (**www.nestle.com/INVESTORS/REPORTS/Pages/Reports.aspx**). Recompute Nestlé's return on total assets for the years subsequent to December 31, 2013.

COMPARATIVE ANALYSIS

A1

BTN 15-2   Key figures for Nestlé and Kraft Foods follow.

Key Figures	Nestlé (in CHF millions)			Kraft Foods (in US$ millions)		
	Current Year	1 Year Prior	2 Years Prior	Current Year	1 Year Prior	2 Years Prior
Net profit..........	10,015	10,228	9,487	2,703	1,637	1,775
Net sales	92,158	89,721	83,642	18,218	18,271	18,576
Total assets	120,442	125,877	114,091	23,148	23,329	21,539

Required

1. Compute return on total assets for Nestlé and Kraft Foods for the two most recent years.
2. Separate the return on total assets computed in part 1 into its components for both companies and both years according to the formula in Exhibit 15.5.
3. Which company has the higher total return on assets? The higher profit margin? The higher total asset turnover? What does this comparative analysis reveal? (Assume an industry average of 10.0% for return on assets for both years.)

ETHICS CHALLENGE

P2   P3

BTN 15-3   Kendra Wecker is the controller for Wildcat Company, which has numerous long-term investments in debt securities. Wildcat's investments are mainly in 10-year bonds. Wecker is preparing its year-end financial statements. In accounting for long-term debt securities, she knows that each long-term investment must be designated as a held-to-maturity or an available-for-sale security. Interest rates rose sharply this past year causing the portfolio's fair value to substantially decline. The company does not intend to hold the bonds for the entire 10 years. Wecker also earns a bonus each year, which is computed as a percent of net profit.

Required

1. Will Wecker's bonus depend in any way on the classification of the debt securities? Explain.
2. What criteria must Wecker use to classify the securities as held-to-maturity or available-for-sale?
3. Is there likely any company oversight of Wecker's classification of the securities? Explain.

BTN 15-4   Assume that you are Jackson Company's accountant. Company owner Abel Terrio has reviewed the 2015 financial statements you prepared and questions the $6,000 loss reported on the sale of its investment in Blackhawk Co. ordinary shares. Jackson acquired 50,000 shares of Blackhawk's ordinary shares on December 31, 2013, at a cost of $500,000. This shares purchase represented a 40% interest in Blackhawk. The 2014 income statement reported that earnings from all investments were $126,000. On January 3, 2015, Jackson Company sold the Blackhawk shares for $575,000. Blackhawk did not pay any dividends during 2014 but reported a net profit of $202,500 for that year. Terrio believes that because the Blackhawk share purchase price was $500,000 and was sold for $575,000, the 2015 income statement should report a $75,000 gain on the sale.

Required

Draft a one-half page memorandum to Terrio explaining why the $6,000 loss on sale of Blackhawk's shares is correctly reported.

COMMUNICATING IN PRACTICE

P4

BTN 15-5   Access the 2013 annual report of L'Oréal from its Website (www.loreal-finance.com/eng/annual-report). Review its Note 15, "Noncurrent financial assets."

Required

1. State the noncurrent financial assets held as at December 31, 2013.
2. What is the percentage stake in Sanofi-Aventis and the original cost of this investment?

TAKING IT TO THE NET

C1

BTN 15-6ᴮ   Each team member is to become an expert on a specific classification of long-term investments. This expertise will be used to facilitate other teammates' understanding of the concepts and procedures relevent to the classification chosen.

1. Each team member must select an area for expertise by choosing one of the following classifications of long-term investments.
   a. At amortized cost
   b. At FVTPL
   c. At FVTOCI
   d. Equity with significant influence
   e. Equity with control
2. Learning teams are to disburse and expert teams are to be formed. Expert teams are made up of those who select the same area of expertise. The instructor will identify the location where each expert team will meet.
3. Expert teams will collaborate to develop a presentation based on the following requirements. Students must write the presentation in a format they can show to their learning teams in part (4).

Requirements for Expert Presentation

   a. Write a transaction for the acquisition of this type of investment security. The transaction description is to include all necessary data to reflect the chosen classification.
   b. Prepare the journal entry to record the acquisition.
   [*Note:* The expert team on equity with control will substitute requirements (*d*) and (*e*) with a discussion of the reporting of these investments.]
   c. Identify information necessary to complete the end-of-period adjustment for this investment.
   d. Assuming that this is the only investment owned, prepare any necessary year-end entries.
   e. Present the relevant statement of financial position section(s).
4. Re-form learning teams. In rotation, experts are to present to their teams the presentations they developed in part 3. Experts are to encourage and respond to questions.

TEAMWORK IN ACTION

C1 C2 P1 P2 P3 P4

ENTREPRENEURIAL DECISION

C3

BTN 15-7ᴬ   Refer to the opening feature in this chapter about Lyn Lee and her business, **Awfully Chocolate**. Assume that she is accounting for the royalties from Japanese franchises. Assume Awfully Chocolate earns royalties on January 1, 2014 of JPY 12 million per year but will receive two equal amounts on March 31 and June 30, 2014. On January 1, 2014, the yen is worth SG$0.015096.

Required

1. Prepare the journal entry to record the royalties earned on January 1, 2014.
2. Prepare the journal entries to record the receipts on March 31 and June 30, 2014. The value of the yen on those dates follows.

March 31	$0.014972
June 30	0.015776

HITTING THE ROAD

C3

BTN 15-8ᴬ   Assume that you are planning a spring break trip to Europe. Identify three locations where you can find exchange rates for the dollar relative to the Euro or other currencies.

GLOBAL DECISION

A1

BTN 15-9   **Samsung**, **Nokia**, and **Apple** are competitors in the global marketplace. Following are selected data from each company.

Key Figures	Samsung (in billions of KRW) Current Year 2013	One Year Prior 2012	Two Year Prior 2011	Nokia (in millions of EUR) Current Year 2013	One Year Prior 2012	Two Year Prior 2011	Apple (in millions of US$) Current Year 2013	One Year Prior 2012	Two Year Prior 2011
Net profit	29,821	23,185	13,359	−615	−3105	−1,163	37,037	41,733	25,922
Net sales	214,075	181,072	165,002	12,709	15,400	15,968	170,910	156,508	108,249
Total assets	214,075	181,072	155,632	25,191	29,984	36,205	207,000	176,064	116,371
Profit margin	—	—	—	−4.8%	−20.2%	—	21.7%	26.7%	—
Total asset turnover	—	—	—	0.46	0.47	—	0.89	1.07	—

Required

1. Compute Samsung return on total assets, and its components of profit margin and total asset turnover, for the most recent two years using the data provided.
2. Which of these three companies has the highest return on total assets? Highest profit margin? Highest total asset turnover? Interpret these results.

ANSWERS TO MULTIPLE CHOICE QUIZ

1. d; $30,000 × 5% × 5/12 = $625
2. a; Unrealized gain = $84,500 − $83,000 = $1,500
3. b; $50,000 × 35% = $17,500
4. e; $300,000/$2,000,000 = 15%
5. b; Profit margin = $80,000/$600,000 = 13.3%
      Total asset turnover = $600,000/$400,000 = 1.5

16

Statement of Cash Flows

A Look Back

Chapter 15 focused on how to identify, account for, and report investments in securities. We also accounted for transactions listed in a foreign currency.

A Look at This Chapter

This chapter focuses on reporting and analyzing cash inflows and cash outflows. We emphasize how to prepare and interpret the statement of cash flows.

A Look Ahead

Chapter 17 focuses on tools to help us analyze financial statements. We also describe comparative analysis and the application of ratios for financial analysis.

Learning Objectives

CAP

CONCEPTUAL

C1 Distinguish between operating, investing, and financing activities, and describe how noncash investing and financing activities are disclosed. (p. 611)

ANALYTICAL

A1 Analyze the statement of cash flows and apply the cash flow on total assets ratio. (p. 628)

PROCEDURAL

P1 Prepare a statement of cash flows. (p. 614)

P2 Compute cash flows from operating activities using the indirect method. (p. 617)

P3 Determine cash flows from both investing and financing activities. (p. 624)

P4 *Appendix 16A*—Compute cash flows from operating activities using the direct method. (p. 633)

"I enjoy being part of a team effort to bring an idea to fruition as an animated television series or feature film."
—**SENG CHOON MENG** (center)

Decision Insight

Scrawling Their Way to Success

Scrawl Studios (www.scrawlstudios.com) is the brainchild of Seng Choon Meng, Wong Chi Kong, and James Tan, three friends who are passionate about animation. Avid illustrators themselves, they manage a talented team of top creative people and have enabled Scrawl Studios to become one of the most prolific animation companies in Asia, selling original series to broadcasters like Discovery Kids and Nickelodeon. "For us, human resources are our most important asset, and managing our large and diverse pool of talents has always been a significant challenge," says Choon Meng. "We are constantly on the lookout for the right talent, which, in practically all markets, from the United States to Japan, is a scarce resource as animation requires extremely unique skills and a creative mindset."

Another challenge is managing cash flow. "Cash flow is the lifeblood of any company, and particularly for a studio like Scrawl, which operates based on projects," stresses Choon Meng. "We

develop our financing plan and cash flow plan based on the production budget before the work actually gets started. This helps us track our project receivables—such as grants, commissioning fees, and other cash inflows, as well as our payables, such as supplier and vendor payments, and direct production salaries—ensuring a healthy cash flow. The project cash flows are also integrated with our company cash flow, which also includes other payables such as management overheads and operating expenses. All this information is updated monthly to monitor our cash position and ensure we have sufficient cash flow to continue operations effectively." The company tries to constantly streamline its operating model, adopting technology tools or processes that help to reduce manpower costs, which is its single largest cost item.

With such a great combination of creative energy and astute accounting, Scrawl Studios can only grow from strength to strength.

A company cannot achieve or maintain profits without carefully managing cash. Managers and other users of information pay attention to a company's cash position and the events and transactions affecting cash. This chapter explains how we prepare, analyze, and interpret a statement of cash flows. It also discusses the importance of cash flow information for predicting future performance and making managerial decisions. More generally, effectively using the statement of cash flows is crucial for managing and analyzing the operating, investing, and financing activities of businesses.

Statement of Cash Flows

Basics of Cash Flow Reporting
- Purpose
- Importance
- Measurement
- Classification
- Noncash activities
- Format and preparation

Cash Flows from Operating
- Indirect and direct methods of reporting
- Application of indirect method of reporting
- Summary of indirect method adjustments

Cash Flows from Investing
- Three-stage process of analysis
- Analysis of noncurrent assets
- Analysis of other assets

Cash Flows from Financing
- Three-stage process of analysis
- Analysis of non-current liabilities
- Analysis of equity

BASICS OF CASH FLOW REPORTING

This section describes the basics of cash flow reporting, including its purpose, measurement, classification, format, and preparation.

Purpose of the Statement of Cash Flows

The purpose of the **statement of cash flows** is to report cash receipts (inflows) and cash payments (outflows) during a period. This includes separately identifying the cash flows related to operating, investing, and financing activities. The statement of cash flows does more than simply report changes in cash. It is the detailed disclosure of individual cash flows that makes this statement useful to users. Information in this statement helps users answer questions such as these:

- How does a company obtain its cash?
- Where does a company spend its cash?
- What explains the change in the cash balance?

The statement of cash flows addresses important questions such as these by summarizing, classifying, and reporting a company's cash inflows and cash outflows for each period.

Point: Internal users rely on the statement of cash flows to make investing and financing decisions. External users rely on this statement to assess the amount and timing of a company's cash flows.

Importance of Cash Flows

Information about cash flows can influence decision makers in important ways. For instance, we look more favorably at a company that is financing its expenditures with cash from operations than one that does it by selling its assets. Information about cash flows helps users decide whether a company has enough cash to pay its existing debts as they mature. It is also relied upon to evaluate a company's ability to meet unexpected obligations and pursue unexpected opportunities. External information users especially want to assess a company's ability to take advantage of new business opportunities. Internal users such as managers use cash flow information to plan day-to-day operating activities and make long-term investment decisions.

    Macy's striking turnaround is an example of how analysis and management of cash flows can lead to improved financial stability. Several years ago Macy's obtained temporary protection from bankruptcy, at which time it desperately needed to improve its cash flows. It did so by engaging in aggressive cost-cutting measures. As a result, Macy's annual cash flow rose to $210 million, up from a negative cash flow of $38.9 million in the prior year. Macy's eventually met its financial obligations and then successfully merged with **Federated Department Stores**.

The case of **W. T. Grant Co.** is a classic example of the importance of cash flow information in predicting a company's future performance and financial strength. Grant reported net profit of more than $40 million per year for three consecutive years. At that same time, it was experiencing an alarming decrease in cash from operations. For instance, net cash outflow was more than $90 million by the end of that three-year period. Grant soon went bankrupt. Users who relied solely on Grant's profit numbers were unpleasantly surprised. This reminds us that cash flows as well as income statement and statement of financial position information are crucial in making business decisions.

■ Decision Insight

Cash Savvy "A lender must have a complete understanding of a borrower's cash flows to assess both the borrowing needs and repayment sources. This requires information about the major types of cash inflows and outflows. I have seen many companies, whose financial statements indicate good profitability, experience severe financial problems because the owners or managers lacked a good understanding of cash flows."—Mary E. Garza, **Bank of America** ■

Measurement of Cash Flows

Cash flows are defined to include both *cash* and *cash equivalents*. The statement of cash flows explains the difference between the beginning and ending balances of cash and cash equivalents. We continue to use the phrases *cash flows* and the *statement of cash flows*, but we must remember that both phrases refer to cash and cash equivalents. Recall that a cash equivalent must satisfy two criteria: (1) be readily convertible to a known amount of cash and (2) be sufficiently close to its maturity so its market value is unaffected by interest rate changes. In most cases, a debt security must be within three months of its maturity to satisfy these criteria. Companies must disclose and follow a clear policy for determining cash and cash equivalents and apply it consistently from period to period. **Nestlé**, for example, in its annual report 2013, defines its cash and cash equivalents as cash at bank and in hand and other short-term highly liquid investments with maturities of three months or less from the initial recognition.

Classification of Cash Flows

Since cash and cash equivalents are combined, the statement of cash flows does not report transactions between cash and cash equivalents such as cash paid to purchase cash equivalents and cash received from selling cash equivalents. However, all other cash receipts and cash payments are classified and reported on the statement as operating, investing, or financing activities. Individual cash receipts and payments for each of these three categories are labeled to identify their originating transactions or events. A net cash inflow (source) occurs when the receipts in a category exceed the payments. A net cash outflow (use) occurs when the payments in a category exceed the receipts.

C1 Distinguish between operating, investing, and financing activities, and describe how noncash investing and financing activities are disclosed.

Operating Activities IAS 7 **Statement of Cash Flows** states that **operating activities** are the principal revenue-producing activities of the entity and other activities that are not investing or financing activities. These generally include those transactions and events that determine net profit or net profit. Examples are:

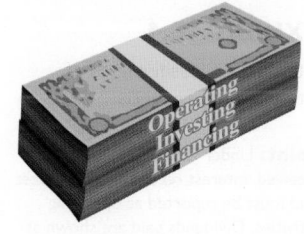

- cash receipts from the sale of goods and the rendering of services;
- cash receipts from royalties, fees, commissions, and other revenue;
- cash payments to suppliers for goods and services;
- cash payments to and on behalf of employees;
- cash payments or refunds of income taxes unless they can be specifically identified with financing and investing activities; and
- cash receipts and payments from contracts held for dealing or trading purposes.

Investing activities IAS 7 states that **investing activities** are the acquisition and disposal of long-term assets and other investments not included in cash equivalents. Examples are:

- cash payments to acquire property, plant and equipment, intangibles and other long-term assets. These payments include those relating to capitalized development costs and self-constructed property, plant and equipment;

- cash receipts from sales of property, plant and equipment, intangibles and other long-term assets;
- cash payments to acquire equity or debt instruments of other entities and interests in joint ventures (other than payments for those instruments considered to be cash equivalents or those held for dealing or trading purposes);
- cash receipts from sales of equity or debt instruments of other entities and interests in joint ventures (other than receipts for those instruments considered to be cash equivalents and those held for dealing or trading purposes);
- cash advances and loans made to other parties (other than advances and loans made by a financial institution);
- cash receipts from the repayment of advances and loans made to other parties (other than advances and loans of a financial institution).

Financing activities   IAS 7 states that **financing activities** are activities that result in changes in the size and composition of the contributed equity and borrowings of the entity. Examples are:

- cash proceeds from issuing shares or other equity instruments;
- cash payments to owners to acquire or redeem the entity's shares;
- cash proceeds from issuing debentures, loans, notes, bonds, mortgages, and other short-term or long-term borrowings;
- cash repayments of amounts borrowed.

Interest and Dividends: Alternative Classifications

IAS 7 allows alternative classifications of interest and dividends received, as well as interest and dividends paid. Interest and dividends received may be classified as operating cash flows because they enter into the determination of profit or loss. Alternatively, interest and dividends received may be classified as investing cash flows because they are returns on investments.

Interest paid may be operating or financing because it enters into the determination of profit or loss and is also a cost of obtaining financial resources. Dividends paid may be classified as a financing cash flow because they are a cost of obtaining financial resources. Alternatively, dividends paid may be classified as cash flows from operating activities in order to assist users to determine the ability of an entity to pay dividends out of operating cash flows. Exhibit 16.1 summarizes these alternatives.

EXHIBIT 16.1

Alternative Classifications of Interest and Dividends

Point: Under U.S. GAAP, dividends received, interest received, and interest paid must be reported as operating activities. Dividends paid are shown as financing activities.

	Operating	Investing	Financing
Interest received	Yes	Yes	
Dividends received	Yes	Yes	
Interest paid	Yes		Yes
Dividends paid	Yes		Yes

Decision Insight

Cash Monitoring   Cash flows can be delayed or accelerated at the end of a period to improve or reduce current period cash flows. Also, cash flows can be misclassified. Cash outflows reported under operations are interpreted as expense payments. However, cash outflows reported under investing activities are interpreted as a positive sign of growth potential. Thus, managers face incentives to misclassify cash flows. For these reasons, cash flow reporting warrants our scrutiny. ∎

Noncash Investing and Financing

When important investing and financing activities do not affect cash receipts or payments, they are still disclosed because of their importance and the *full-disclosure principle*. **IAS 7** states that investing and financing transactions that do not require the use of cash or cash equivalents shall be excluded from a statement of cash flows. Such transactions shall be disclosed elsewhere in the financial statements in a way that provides all the relevant information about these investing and financing activities. One example of such a transaction is the purchase of long-term assets using a long-term note payable (loan). This transaction involves both investing and financing activities but does not affect any cash inflow or outflow and is not reported in any of the three sections of the statement of cash flows. This disclosure rule also extends to transactions with partial cash receipts or payments.

To illustrate, assume that Goorin purchases land for $12,000 by paying $5,000 cash and trading in used equipment worth $7,000. The investing section of the statement of cash flows reports only the $5,000 cash outflow for the land purchase. The $12,000 investing transaction is only partially described in the body of the statement of cash flows, yet this information is potentially important to users because it changes the makeup of assets. Goorin should describe the transaction in the notes to the financial statements that list the $12,000 land purchase along with the cash financing of $5,000 and a $7,000 trade-in of equipment. As another example, Borg Co. acquired $900,000 of assets in exchange for $200,000 cash and a $700,000 long-term note, which should be reported as follows:

Fair value of assets acquired	$900,000
Less cash paid	200,000
Liabilities incurred or assumed	$700,000

IAS 7 lists examples of noncash transactions as:

- the acquisition of assets either by assuming directly related liabilities or by means of a finance lease;
- the acquisition of an entity by means of an equity issue; and
- the conversion of debt to equity.

Format of the Statement of Cash Flows

IFRS requires companies to include a statement of cash flows in a complete set of financial statements. This statement must report information about a company's cash receipts and cash payments during the period. Exhibit 16.2 shows the usual format. A company must report cash flows from three activities: operating, investing, and financing. The statement explains how

EXHIBIT 16.2

Format of the Statement of Cash Flows

COMPANY NAME
Statement of Cash Flows
For *period* Ended *date*

Cash flows from operating activities		
[List of individual inflows and outflows]		
Net cash from (used in) operating activities	$ #	
Cash flows from investing activities		
[List of individual inflows and outflows]		
Net cash from (used in) investing activities	#	
Cash flows from financing activities		
[List of individual inflows and outflows]		
Net cash from (used in) financing activities	#	
Net increase (decrease) in cash	$ #	
Cash (and equivalents) balance at prior period-end	#	
Cash (and equivalents) balance at current period-end	$ #	

Separate note disclosure of any "noncash investing and financing transactions" is required.

transactions and events impact the prior period-end cash (and cash equivalents) balance to produce its current period-end balance.

Decision Maker   Answer — p. 638

Entrepreneur You are considering purchasing a start-up business that recently reported a $110,000 annual net loss and a $225,000 annual net cash inflow. How are these results possible? ■

Quick Check   Answers — p. 638

1. Does a statement of cash flows report the cash payments to purchase cash equivalents? Does it report the cash receipts from selling cash equivalents?
2. Identify the three categories of cash flows reported separately on the statement of cash flows.
3. Identify the cash activity category for each transaction: (*a*) purchase equipment for cash, (*b*) cash payment of wages, (*c*) sale of ordinary shares for cash, (*d*) receipt of cash dividends from share investment, (*e*) cash collection from customers, (*f*) notes issued for cash.

Preparing the Statement of Cash Flows

P1 Prepare a statement of cash flows.

Preparing a statement of cash flows involves five steps: ☐1 compute the net increase or decrease in cash; ☐2 compute and report the net cash from or used in operating activities (using either the direct or indirect method; both are explained); ☐3 compute and report the net cash from or used in investing activities; ☐4 compute and report the net cash from or used in financing activities; and ☐5 compute the net cash flow by combining net cash from or used in operating, investing, and financing activities and then *prove it* by adding it to the beginning cash balance to show that it equals the ending cash balance.

Step☐1 Compute net increase or decrease in cash

Step☐2 Compute net cash from operating activities

Step☐3 Compute net cash from investing activities

Step☐4 Compute net cash from financing activities

Step☐5 Prove and report beginning and ending cash balances

Point: View the change in cash as a *target* number that we will fully explain and prove in the statement of cash flows.

Computing the net increase or net decrease in cash is a simple but crucial computation. It equals the current period's cash balance minus the prior period's cash balance. This is the *bottom-line* figure for the statement of cash flows and is a check on accuracy. The information we need to prepare a statement of cash flows comes from various sources including comparative statements of financial position at the beginning and end of the period, and an income statement for the period. There are two alternative approaches to preparing the statement: (1) analyzing the Cash account and (2) analyzing noncash accounts.

Analyzing the Cash Account A company's cash receipts and cash payments are recorded in the Cash account in its general ledger. The Cash account is therefore a natural place to look for information about cash flows from operating, investing, and financing activities. To illustrate, review the summarized Cash T-account of Genesis, Inc., in Exhibit 16.3. Individual cash transactions are summarized in this Cash account according to the major types of cash receipts and cash payments. For instance, only the total of cash receipts from all customers is listed. Individual cash transactions underlying these totals can number in the thousands. Accounting software is available to provide summarized cash accounts.

Preparing a statement of cash flows from Exhibit 16.3 requires determining whether an individual cash inflow or outflow is an operating, investing, or financing activity, and then listing each by activity. This yields the statement shown in Exhibit 16.4. However, preparing the statement

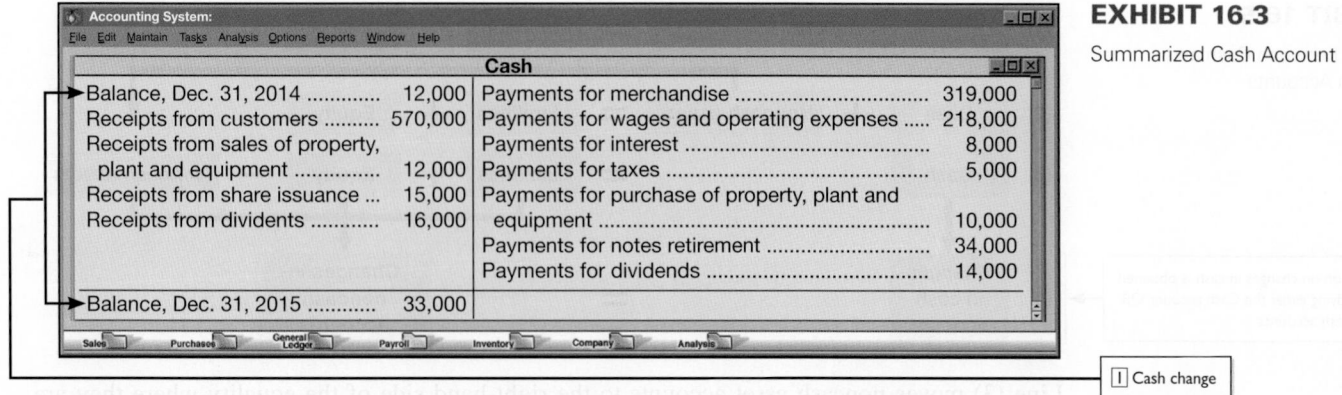

EXHIBIT 16.3

Summarized Cash Account

of cash flows from an analysis of the summarized Cash account has two limitations. First, most companies have many individual cash receipts and payments, making it difficult to review them all. Accounting software minimizes this burden, but it is still a task requiring professional judgment for many transactions. Second, the Cash account does not usually carry an adequate description of each cash transaction, making assignment of all cash transactions according to activity difficult.

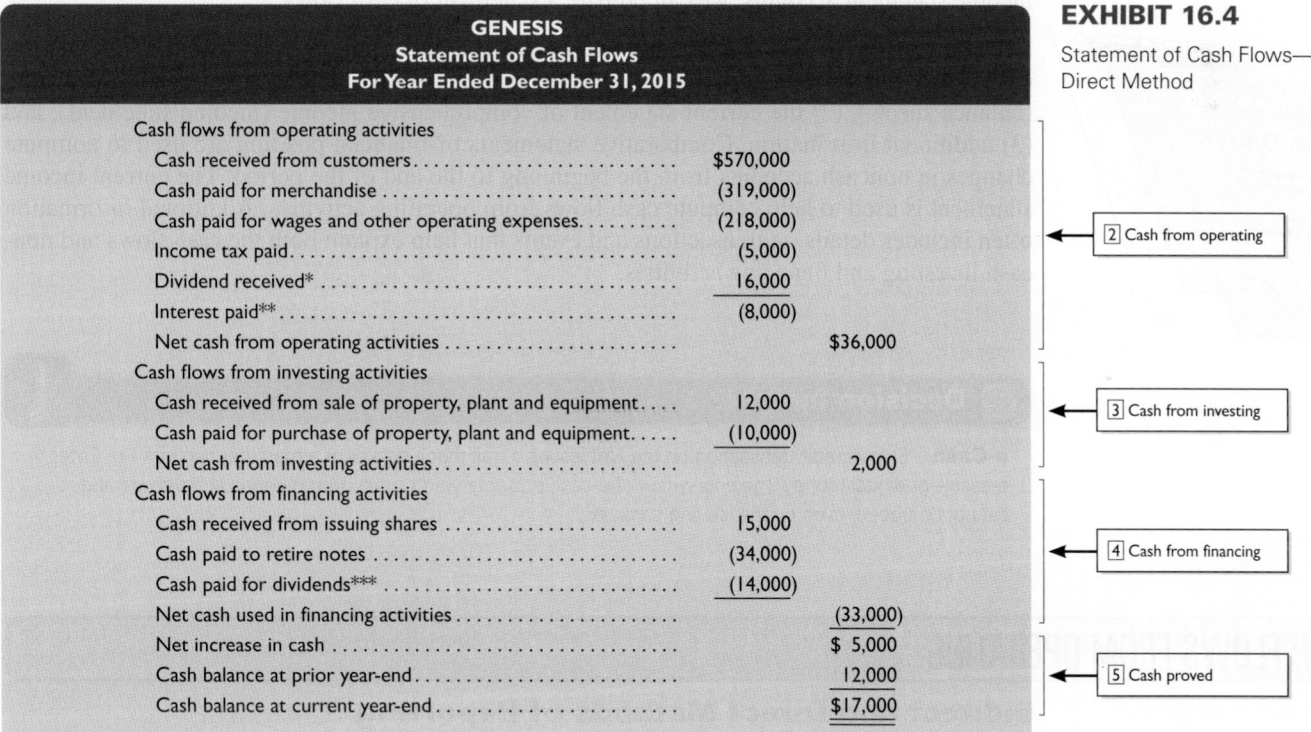

EXHIBIT 16.4

Statement of Cash Flows—
Direct Method

*Can also be classified as investing.
**Can also be classified as financing.
***Can also be classified as operating.

Analyzing Noncash Accounts   A second approach to preparing the statement of cash flows is analyzing noncash accounts. This approach uses the fact that when a company records cash inflows and outflows with debits and credits to the Cash account (see Exhibit 16.3), it also records credits and debits in noncash accounts (reflecting double-entry accounting). Many of these noncash accounts are statement of financial position accounts—for instance, from the sale of land for cash. Others are revenue and expense accounts that are closed to equity. For instance, the sale of services for cash yields a credit to Services Revenue that is closed to Retained Earnings for a corporation. In sum, *all cash transactions eventually affect noncash statement of financial position accounts.* Thus, we can determine cash inflows and outflows by analyzing changes in noncash statement of financial position accounts.

Exhibit 16.5 uses the accounting equation to show the relation between the Cash account and the noncash statement of financial position accounts. This exhibit starts with the accounting equation at the top. It is then expanded in line (2) to separate cash from noncash asset accounts.

EXHIBIT 16.5

Relation between Cash and
Noncash Accounts

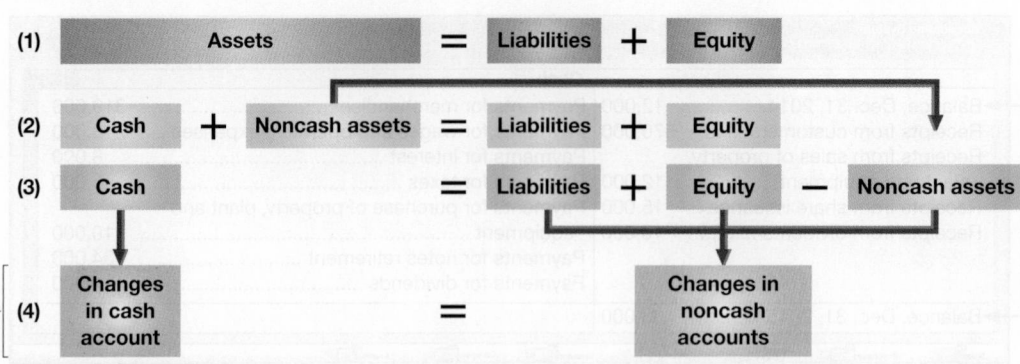

Information on changes in cash is obtained from studying *either* the Cash account OR the noncash accounts

Line (3) moves noncash asset accounts to the right-hand side of the equality where they are subtracted. This shows that cash equals the sum of the liability and equity accounts *minus* the noncash asset accounts. Line (4) points out that *changes* on one side of the accounting equation equal *changes* on the other side. It shows that we can explain changes in cash by analyzing changes in the noncash accounts consisting of liability accounts, equity accounts, and noncash asset accounts. By analyzing noncash statement of financial position accounts and any related income statement accounts, we can prepare a statement of cash flows.

Information to Prepare the Statement   Information to prepare the statement of cash flows usually comes from three sources: (1) comparative statements of financial position (balance sheets), (2) the current statement of comprehensive income (income statement), and (3) additional information. Comparative statements of financial position are used to compute changes in noncash accounts from the beginning to the end of the period. The current income statement is used to help compute cash flows from operating activities. Additional information often includes details on transactions and events that help explain both the cash flows and noncash investing and financing activities.

Decision Insight

e-Cash   Every credit transaction on the Net leaves a trail that a hacker or a marketer can pick up. Enter e-cash—or digital money. The encryption of e-cash protects your money from snoops and thieves and cannot be traced, even by the issuing bank. ■

CASH FLOWS FROM OPERATING

Indirect and Direct Methods of Reporting

Cash flows from (used in) operating activities are reported in one of two ways: the *direct method* or the *indirect method*. **These two different methods apply only to the operating activities section.**

The **direct method** separately lists each major item of operating cash receipts (such as cash received from customers) and each major item of operating cash payments (such as cash paid for merchandise). The cash payments are subtracted from cash receipts to determine the net cash from (used in) operating activities. The operating activities section of Exhibit 16.4 reflects the direct method of reporting operating cash flows.

The **indirect method** reports profit and then adjusts it for items necessary to obtain net cash from or used in operating activities. It does *not* report individual items of cash inflows and cash outflows from operating activities. Instead, the indirect method reports the necessary adjustments to reconcile profit to net cash from or used in operating activities. **The net cash amount from operating activities is *identical* under both the direct and indirect methods.**

This equality always exists. The difference in these methods is with the computation and presentation of this amount. The **IASB** recommends the direct method, but because it is not required and the indirect method is arguably easier to compute for accountants, nearly all companies report operating cash flows using the indirect method.

Application of the Indirect Method of Reporting

Profit is computed using accrual accounting, which recognizes revenues when earned and expenses when incurred. Revenues and expenses do not necessarily reflect the receipt and payment of cash. The indirect method of computing and reporting net cash flows from operating activities involves adjusting the profit figure to obtain the net cash from or used in operating activities. This includes subtracting noncash increases (credits) from profit and adding noncash charges (debits) back to profit. Noncash credits refer to revenue amounts reported on the income statement that are not collected in cash this period. Noncash charges refer to expense amounts reported on the income statement that are not paid this period.

> **P2** Compute cash flows from operating activities using the indirect method.

IAS 7 states that cash flows arising from taxes on income shall be separately disclosed and shall be classified as cash flows from operating activities unless they can be specifically identified with financing and investing activities. **IAS 7** also states that cash flows from interest and dividends received and paid shall each be disclosed separately. For example, a company with interest income and interest expense reporting under the indirect method would have to start with profit before tax, make adjustments by subtracting interest income and adding back interest expense. It would show tax paid under operating activities, and has the choice of putting interest received in operating or investing activities, as well as the choice of putting interest paid in operating or financing activities.

A company with dividend income (e.g., from investing in financial assets) would have to adjust by subtracting dividend income, and has the choice of putting dividend received in operating or investing activities. As dividend declared by the company is below the bottom line (i.e., after calculation of profit), there is no adjustment and the dividend paid can be classified in operating or financing activities.

Therefore, before presenting the statement of cash flows, we may have to solve for interest and tax amounts as follows (numbers from Exhibit 16.6):

Income tax payable (GENESIS)

	Income tax payable	
	Bal., Dec. 31, 2014	12,000
Income tax paid	Income tax expense	15,000
	Bal., Dec. 31, 2015	22,000

Numbers in black are taken from Exhibit 16.6. The red number is the computed (plug) figure.

Beginning balance + Income tax expense – Income tax paid = Ending balance
12,000 + 15,000 – Income tax paid = 22,000
Solving for Income tax paid = 5,000

Interest payable (GENESIS)

	Interest payable	
	Bal., Dec.31, 2014	4,000
Interest paid	Interest expense	7,000
	Bal., Dec. 31, 2015	3,000

Beginning balance + Interest expense – Interest paid = Ending balance
4,000 + 7,000 – Interest paid = 3,000
Solving for Interest paid = 8,000

To illustrate, we prepare the operating activities section of the statement of cash flows for Genesis. Exhibit 16.6 shows the December 31, 2014 and 2015 statements of financial position of Genesis along with its 2015 income statement. To prepare the indirect method statement of cash flows, we begin with net profit of $38,000 and add back income tax expense of $15,000 to get profit before tax of $53,000 (remember we have to add back because income tax paid must be shown separately).

EXHIBIT 16.6

Financial Statements

GENESIS Income Statement For Year Ended December 31, 2015		
Sales		$590,000
Cost of goods sold		(300,000)
Gross profit......................		290,000
Wages and other operating expenses ...	(216,000)	
Depreciation expense..............	(24,000)	
Loss on sale of property, plant and equipment	(6,000)	(246,000)
Operating profit		44,000
Dividend income on financial assets		16,000
Interest expense		(7,000)
Profit before tax		53,000
Income tax expense		(15,000)
Net profit		$ 38,000

GENESIS Statements of Financial Position December 31, 2015 and 2014	2015	2014
Assets		
Current assets		
Cash	$ 17,000	$ 12,000
Accounts receivable	60,000	40,000
Merchandise inventory	84,000	70,000
Prepaid expenses	6,000	4,000
Total current assets................	167,000	126,000
Noncurrent assets		
Property, plant and equipment	250,000	210,000
Accumulated depreciation	(60,000)	(48,000)
Total assets	$357,000	$288,000
Liabilities		
Current liabilities		
Accounts payable	$ 35,000	$ 40,000
Interest payable	3,000	4,000
Income tax payable	22,000	12,000
Total current liabilities	60,000	56,000
Long-term notes payable	90,000	64,000
Total liabilities	150,000	120,000
Equity		
Share capital—Ordinary, no-par value	95,000	80,000
Retained earnings	112,000	88,000
Total equity	207,000	168,000
Total liabilities and equity	$357,000	$288,000

Point: Other common names for profit before tax are *pretax income, income before tax,* or *earnings before tax.* Tax can also be in the plural form (i.e., *taxes* or written as *taxation.*)

We use the following additional information to prepare a statement of cash flows that explains the $5,000 increase in cash for 2015 as reflected in its statements of financial position. This $5,000 is computed as Cash of $17,000 at the end of 2015 minus Cash of $12,000 at the end of 2014.

a. The accounts payable balances result from merchandise inventory purchases.

b. Purchased $70,000 in property, plant and equipment by paying $10,000 cash and issuing $60,000 of notes payable.

c. Sold property, plant and equipment with an original cost of $30,000 and accumulated depreciation of $12,000 for $12,000 cash, yielding a $6,000 loss.

d. Received $15,000 cash from issuing 3,000 no-par ordinary shares.

e. Paid $34,000 cash to retire notes with a $34,000 carrying amount.

f. Declared and paid cash dividends of $14,000.

g. Received all its dividend income on financial assets in cash of $16,000.

Exhibit 16.7 shows the results of the indirect method of reporting operating cash flows, which in general has four types of adjustments. There are adjustments (1) to income statement items involving operating activities that do not affect cash inflows or outflows, (2) to eliminate gains and losses resulting from investing and financing activities (not part of operating activities), (3) to reflect changes in noncash current assets and current liabilities related to operating activities, and (4) to show dividend received, interest received, or interest paid separately.

EXHIBIT 16.7

Statement of Cash Flows—Indirect Method

GENESIS
Statement of Cash Flows
For Year Ended December 31, 2015

Cash flows from operating activities		
Net profit	$38,000	
Income tax expense	15,000	
Profit before tax	53,000	
Adjustments to reconcile profit to net cash from operating activities		
① { Depreciation expense	24,000	
② { Loss on sale of property, plant and equipment	6,000	
③ { Increase in accounts receivable	(20,000)	
Increase in merchandise inventory	(14,000)	
Increase in prepaid expenses	(2,000)	
Decrease in accounts payable	(5,000)	
④ { Dividend income	(16,000)	
Interest expense	7,000	
Cash generated from operating activities	33,000	
Income tax paid	(5,000)	
Dividend received*	16,000	
Interest paid**	(8,000)	
Net cash from operating activities		$36,000
Cash flows from investing activities		
Cash received from sale of property, plant and equipment	12,000	
Cash paid for purchase of property, plant and equipment	(10,000)	
Net cash from investing activities		2,000
Cash flows from financing activities		
Cash received from issuing shares	15,000	
Cash paid to retire notes	(34,000)	
Cash paid for dividends***	(14,000)	
Net cash used in financing activities		(33,000)
Net increase in cash		$ 5,000
Cash balance at prior year-end		12,000
Cash balance at current year-end		$17,000

*Can also be classified as investing.
**Can also be classified as financing.
***Can also be classified as operating. Interest expense can also be called finance cost.

① Adjustments for Operating Items Not Providing or Using Cash   The

income statement usually includes some expenses (e.g., depreciation, amortization, depletion, bad debts) or losses (e.g., impairment) that do not reflect cash outflows in the period. The indirect method for reporting operating cash flows requires that

Expense or losses with no cash outflows are added back to profit.

To see the logic of this adjustment, recall that items such as depreciation expense and impairment loss are debited to expense or loss accounts (reducing profit) and credited to noncash accounts. These entries have *no* cash effect, and we add them back to profit when computing net cash flows from operating activities. Adding them back cancels their deductions.

Similarly, when profit includes revenues or gains that do not reflect cash inflows in the period, the indirect method for reporting operating cash flows requires that

Revenues or gains with no cash inflows are subtracted from profit.

We apply these adjustments to the Genesis operating items that do not provide or use cash.

Depreciation.   Depreciation expense is the only Genesis operating item that has no effect on cash flows in the period (the account depreciation expense was debited and the account accumulated depreciation was credited). We must add back the $24,000 depreciation expense to profit when computing cash from operating activities as shown in Exhibit 16.7. (We later explain that any cash outflow to acquire an item of property, plant and equipment is reported as an investing activity.)

② **Adjustments for Nonoperating Items**   Profit often includes losses that are not part of operating activities but are part of investing activities. An example is a loss from the sale of an item of property, plant and equipment. The indirect method for reporting operating cash flows requires that

Nonoperating losses are added back to profit.

To see the logic, consider that items such as a property, plant and equipment sale are normally recorded by recognizing the cash, removing all property, plant and equipment, and recognizing any loss or gain. The cash received or paid is not part of operating activities but is part of investing activities. *No* operating cash flow effect occurs. However, because the nonoperating loss is a deduction in computing profit, we need to add it back to profit when computing cash flow from operating activities. Adding it back cancels the deduction.

Similarly, profit can include gains that are not part of operating activities, and the indirect method for reporting operating cash flows requires that

Nonoperating gains are subtracted from profit.

To illustrate these adjustments, we consider the nonoperating item of Genesis.

Loss on sale of property, plant and equipment.   Genesis reports a $6,000 loss on sale of property, plant and equipment as part of profit. This loss is a proper deduction in computing profit, but it is *not part of operating activities*. Instead, a sale of property, plant and equipment is part of investing activities. Thus, the $6,000 nonoperating loss is added back to profit (see Exhibit 16.7). Adding it back cancels the loss. We later explain how to report the cash inflow from the asset sale in investing activities.

③ **Adjustments for Changes in Noncash Current Assets and Current Liabilities**   This section describes adjustments for changes in noncash current assets and current liabilities.

Point: Operating activities are typically those that determine profit, which are often reflected in changes in current assets and current liabilities.

Adjustments for changes in noncash current assets.   Changes in noncash current assets normally result from operating activities. Examples are sales affecting accounts receivable and building usage affecting prepaid rent. Decreases in noncash current assets yield the following adjustment:

Decreases in noncash current assets are added to profit.

To see the logic for this adjustment, consider that a decrease in a noncash current asset such as accounts receivable suggests more available cash at the end of the period compared to the beginning. This is so because a decrease in accounts receivable implies higher cash receipts than reflected in sales. We add these higher cash receipts (from decreases in noncash current assets) to profit when computing cash flow from operating activities.

In contrast, an increase in noncash current assets such as accounts receivable implies less cash receipts than reflected in sales. As another example, an increase in prepaid rent indicates that more cash is paid for rent than is deducted as rent expense. Increases in noncash current assets yield the following adjustment:

Increases in noncash current assets are subtracted from profit.

To illustrate, these adjustments are applied to the noncash current assets in Exhibit 16.6.

Accounts receivable. Accounts receivable *increase* $20,000, from a beginning balance of $40,000 to an ending balance of $60,000. This increase implies that Genesis collects less cash than is reported in sales. That is, some of these sales were in the form of accounts receivable and that amount increased during the period. To see this it is helpful to use *account analysis*. This usually involves setting up a T-account and reconstructing its major entries to compute cash receipts or payments. The following reconstructed Accounts Receivable T-account reveals that cash receipts are less than sales:

Accounts Receivable			
Bal., Dec. 31, 2014	40,000		
Sales	590,000	Cash receipts =	570,000
Bal., Dec. 31, 2015	60,000		

Numbers in black are taken from Exhibit 16.6. The red number is the computed (plug) figure.

We see that sales are $20,000 greater than cash receipts. This $20,000—as reflected in the $20,000 increase in Accounts Receivable—is subtracted from profit when computing cash from operating activities (see Exhibit 16.7).

Merchandise inventory. Merchandise inventory *increases* by $14,000, from a $70,000 beginning balance to an $84,000 ending balance. This increase implies that Genesis had greater cash purchases than cost of goods sold. This larger amount of cash purchases is in the form of inventory, as reflected in the following account analysis:

Merchandise Inventory			
Bal., Dec. 31, 2014	70,000		
Purchases =	314,000	Cost of goods sold	300,000
Bal., Dec. 31, 2015	84,000		

The amount by which purchases exceed cost of goods sold—as reflected in the $14,000 increase in inventory—is subtracted from profit when computing cash from operating activities (see Exhibit 16.7).

Prepaid expenses. Prepaid Expenses *increase* $2,000, from a $4,000 beginning balance to a $6,000 ending balance, implying that Genesis's cash payments exceed its recorded prepaid expenses. These higher cash payments increase the amount of Prepaid Expenses, as reflected in its reconstructed T-account:

Prepaid Expenses			
Bal., Dec. 31, 2014	4,000		
Cash payments =	218,000	Wages and other operating exp.	216,000
Bal., Dec. 31, 2015	6,000		

The amount by which cash payments exceed the recorded operating expenses—as reflected in the $2,000 increase in Prepaid Expenses—is subtracted from profit when computing cash from operating activities (see Exhibit 16.7).

Adjustments for changes in current liabilities. Changes in current liabilities normally result from operating activities. An example is a purchase that affects accounts payable. Increases in current liabilities yield the following adjustment to profit when computing operating cash flows:

Increases in current liabilities are added to profit.

To see the logic for this adjustment, consider that an increase in the Accounts Payable account suggests that cash payments are less than the related (cost of goods sold) expense. As another example, an increase in wages payable implies that cash paid for wages is less than the recorded wages expense. Since the recorded expense is greater than the cash paid, we add the increase in wages payable to profit to compute net cash flow from operating activities.

Conversely, when current liabilities decrease, the following adjustment is required:

Decreases in current liabilities are subtracted from profit.

To illustrate, these adjustments are applied to the current liabilities in Exhibit 16.6.

Accounts payable. Accounts payable *decrease* $5,000, from a beginning balance of $40,000 to an ending balance of $35,000. This decrease implies that cash payments to suppliers exceed purchases by $5,000 for the period, which is reflected in the reconstructed Accounts Payable T-account:

		Accounts Payable	
Cash payments =	319,000	Bal., Dec. 31, 2014	40,000
		Purchases	314,000
		Bal., Dec. 31, 2015	35,000

The amount by which cash payments exceed purchases—as reflected in the $5,000 decrease in Accounts Payable—is subtracted from profit when computing cash from operating activities (see Exhibit 16.7).

Exhibit 16.8 summarizes the adjustments we make to profit for noncash current assets and current liabilities.

EXHIBIT 16.8

Summary of Adjustments for Noncash Current Assets and Current Liabilities

	Change in Account Balance During Year	
	Increase	**Decrease**
Noncash current assets	Subtract from profit	Add to profit
Current liabilities	Add to profit	Subtract from profit

④ **Adjustments for Separate Disclosure of Dividend Received, Interest Received, or Interest Paid.** Under **IFRS**, dividend received and interest received, as well as interest paid must be separately shown. Since dividend income and interest income are added to derive the profit amount, adjustments involve deducting these amounts from profit so that dividend received and interest received can be shown separately.

Dividend income and interest income are subtracted from profit.

Since interest expense is deducted to derive profit, the adjustment involves adding the amount to profit so that interest paid can be shown separately.

Interest expense is added back to profit.

If there is no receivable or payable for the item, the adjusted amount and the cash amount are the same but appear with opposite signs in the statement of cash flows. This is the case with Genesis as all the dividend income of $160,000 for the year is received as cash and no dividend receivable as at year end. The dividend income of $16,000 is first deducted as an adjustment and then the dividend received which is the same amount of $16,000 is then shown separately.

Summary of Adjustments for Indirect Method

Exhibit 16.9 summarizes the most common adjustments to profit when computing net cash from or used in operating activities under the indirect method. This is not an exhaustive list but the concepts are applicable to any item needing adjustment. See the end-of-chapter demonstration problem involving adjustment for nonoperating item using retirement of notes payable.

EXHIBIT 16.9

Summary of Selected Adjustments for Indirect Method

Profit before tax

+ Depreciation, depletion, amortization, and impairment ① Adjustments for operating items not providing or using cash

+ Losses from disposal of long-term assets

– Gains from disposal of long-term assets ② Adjustments for nonoperating items

+ Decrease in noncash current asset

– Increase in noncash current asset ③ Adjustments for changes in noncash current assets and current liabilities

+ Increase in current liability*

– Decrease in current liability*

+ Interest expense

– Interest income ④ Adjustments for separate disclosure of dividend received, interest received, or interest paid

– Dividend income

Net cash from (used in) operating activities

* Excludes current portion of long-term debt and any (non-sales-related) short-term notes payable—both are financing activities.

Decision Insight

Cash or Profit The difference between net profit and operating cash flows can be large and sometimes reflects on the quality of earnings. This bar chart shows the net profit and operating cash flows of three companies. Operating cash flows can be either higher or lower than net profit. ■

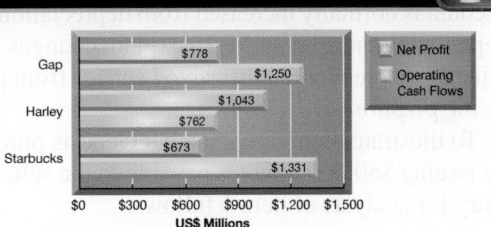

Quick Check

Answers — p. 638

4. Determine net cash flows from operating activities using the following data: profit before tax, $79,000; decrease in accounts receivable, $4,600; increase in inventory, $11,700; decrease in accounts payable, $1,000; loss on sale of equipment, $3,400; income tax paid, $4,100.

5. Why are expenses such as depreciation and amortization added to profit when cash flow from operating activities is computed by the indirect method?

6. A company reports profit of $15,000 that includes a $3,000 gain on the sale of property, plant and equipment. Why is this gain subtracted from profit in computing cash flow from operating activities using the indirect method?

CASH FLOWS FROM INVESTING

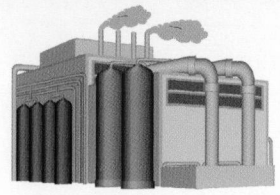

P3 Determine cash flows from both investing and financing activities.

The third major step in preparing the statement of cash flows is to compute and report cash flows from investing activities. We normally do this by identifying changes in (1) all noncurrent asset accounts and (2) the current accounts for both notes receivable and investments in securities (excluding trading securities). We then analyze changes in these accounts to determine their effect, if any, on cash and report the cash flow effects in the investing activities section of the statement of cash flows. **Reporting of investing activities is identical under the direct method and indirect method.**

Three-Stage Process of Analysis

Information to compute cash flows from investing activities is usually taken from beginning and ending statements of financial position and the income statement. We use a three-stage process to determine cash from or used in investing activities: (1) identify changes in investing-related accounts, (2) explain these changes using reconstruction analysis, and (3) report their cash flow effects.

Analysis of Noncurrent Assets

Information about the Genesis transactions provided earlier reveals that the company both purchased and sold property, plant and equipment during the period. Both transactions are investing activities and are analyzed for their cash flow effects in this section.

Point: Investing activities include (1) purchasing and selling long-term assets, (2) lending and collecting on notes receivable, and (3) purchasing and selling short-term investments other than cash equivalents and trading securities.

Property, Plant and Equipment Transactions   The first stage in analyzing the Property, Plant and Equipment account and its related Accumulated Depreciation is to identify any changes in these accounts from comparative statements of financial position in Exhibit 16.6. This analysis reveals a $40,000 increase in property, plant and equipment from $210,000 to $250,000 and a $12,000 increase in accumulated depreciation from $48,000 to $60,000.

The second stage is to explain these changes. Items *b* and *c* of the additional information for Genesis (page 611) are relevant in this case. Recall that the Property, Plant and Equipment account is affected by both asset purchases and sales, while its Accumulated Depreciation account is normally increased from depreciation and decreased from the removal of accumulated depreciation in asset sales. To explain changes in these accounts and to identify their cash flow effects, we prepare *reconstructed entries* from prior transactions; *they are not the actual entries by the preparer.*

Point: Financing and investing info is available in ledger accounts to help explain changes in comparative statements of financial position. Post references lead to relevant entries and explanations.

To illustrate, item *b* reports that Genesis purchased property, plant and equipment of $70,000 by issuing $60,000 in notes payable to the seller and paying $10,000 in cash. The reconstructed entry for analysis of item *b* follows:

Reconstruction	Property, plant and equipment	70,000	
	Notes Payable		60,000
	Cash		**10,000**

This entry reveals a $10,000 cash outflow for property, plant and equipment and a $60,000 noncash investing and financing transaction involving notes exchanged for property, plant and equipment.

Next, item *c* reports that Genesis sold property, plant and equipment costing $30,000 (with $12,000 of accumulated depreciation) for $12,000 cash, resulting in a $6,000 loss. The reconstructed entry for analysis of item *c* follows:

Reconstruction	**Cash**	**12,000**	
	Accumulated Depreciation	12,000	
	Loss on Sale of Property, Plant and Equipment	6,000	
	Property, Plant and Equipment		30,000

This entry reveals a $12,000 cash inflow from assets sold. The $6,000 loss is computed by comparing the asset carrying amount to the cash received and does not reflect any cash inflow or outflow. We also reconstruct the entry for Depreciation Expense using information from the income statement.

Reconstruction	Depreciation Expense	24,000	
	Accumulated Depreciation		24,000

This entry shows that Depreciation Expense results in no cash flow effect. These three reconstructed entries are reflected in the following property, plant and equipment and related T-accounts.

Property, Plant and Equipment					Accumulated Depreciation—Property, Plant and Equipment			
Bal., Dec. 31, 2014	210,000						Bal., Dec. 31, 2014	48,000
Purchase	70,000	Sale	30,000		Sale	12,000	Depr. expense	24,000
Bal., Dec. 31, 2015	250,000						Bal., Dec. 31, 2015	60,000

This reconstruction analysis is complete in that the change in property, plant and equipment from $210,000 to $250,000 is fully explained by the $70,000 purchase and the $30,000 sale. Also, the change in accumulated depreciation from $48,000 to $60,000 is fully explained by depreciation expense of $24,000 and the removal of $12,000 in accumulated depreciation from an asset sale. (Preparers of the statement of cash flows have the entire ledger and additional information at their disposal, but for brevity reasons only the information needed for reconstructing accounts is given.)

The third stage looks at the reconstructed entries for identification of cash flows. The two identified cash flow effects are reported in the investing section of the statement as follows (also see Exhibit 16.4 or 16.7):

Example: If an item of property, plant and equipment costing $40,000 with $37,000 of accumulated depreciation is sold at a $1,000 loss, what is the cash flow? What is the cash flow if this asset is sold at a gain of $3,000? *Answers:* +$2,000; +$6,000.

Cash flows from investing activities	
Cash received from sale of property, plant and equipment	$12,000
Cash paid for purchase of property, plant and equipment	(10,000)

The $60,000 portion of the purchase described in item *b* and financed by issuing notes is a noncash investing and financing activity. It is reported in a note or in a separate schedule to the statement as follows:

Noncash investing and financing activity	
Purchased property, plant and equipment with issuance of notes	$60,000

Analysis of Other Assets

Many other asset transactions (including those involving current notes receivable and investments in certain securities) are considered investing activities and can affect a company's cash flows. Since Genesis did not enter into other investing activities impacting assets, we do not need to extend our analysis to these other assets. If such transactions did exist, we would analyze them using the same three-stage process illustrated for property, plant and equipment.

Quick Check   Answer — p. 638

> **7.** Equipment costing $80,000 with accumulated depreciation of $30,000 is sold at a loss of $10,000. What is the cash receipt from this sale? In what section of the statement of cash flows is this transaction reported?

CASH FLOWS FROM FINANCING

The fourth major step in preparing the statement of cash flows is to compute and report cash flows from financing activities. We normally do this by identifying changes in all noncurrent liability accounts (including the current portion of any notes and bonds) and the equity accounts. These accounts include long-term debt, notes payable, bonds payable, ordinary shares, and retained earnings. Changes in these accounts are then analyzed using available information to determine their effect, if any, on cash. Results are reported in the financing activities section of the statement. **Reporting of financing activities is identical under the direct method and indirect method.**

Three-Stage Process of Analysis

We again use a three-stage process to determine cash from or used in financing activities: (1) identify changes in financing-related accounts, (2) explain these changes using reconstruction analysis, and (3) report their cash flow effects.

Analysis of Noncurrent Liabilities

Point: Financing activities generally refer to changes in the noncurrent liability and the equity accounts. Examples are (1) receiving cash from issuing debt or repaying amounts borrowed and (2) receiving cash from or distributing cash to owners.

Information about Genesis provided earlier reveals two transactions involving noncurrent liabilities. We analyzed one of those, the $60,000 issuance of notes payable to purchase property, plant and equipment. This transaction is reported as a significant noncash investing and financing activity in a footnote or a separate schedule to the statement of cash flows. The other remaining transaction involving noncurrent liabilities is the cash retirement of notes payable.

Notes Payable Transactions   The first stage in analysis of notes is to review the comparative statements of financial position from Exhibit 16.6. This analysis reveals an increase in notes payable from $64,000 to $90,000.

The second stage explains this change. Item *e* of the additional information for Genesis reports that notes with a carrying amount of $34,000 are retired for $34,000 cash.

Also, item *b* of the additional information reports that Genesis purchased property, plant and equipment costing $70,000 by issuing $60,000 in notes payable to the seller and paying $10,000 in cash. We reconstructed this entry when analyzing investing activities: It showed a $60,000 increase to notes payable that is reported as a noncash investing and financing transaction. The Notes Payable account reflects (and is fully explained by) these reconstructed entries as follows:

Notes Payable			
		Bal., Dec. 31, 2014	64,000
Retired notes	**34,000**	**Issued notes**	**60,000**
		Bal., Dec. 31, 2015	90,000

The third stage is to report the cash flow effect of the notes' retirement in the financing section of the statement as follows (also see Exhibit 16.4 or 16.7):

Cash flows from financing activities	
Cash paid to retire notes	$(34,000)

Analysis of Equity

The Genesis information reveals two transactions involving equity accounts. The first is the issuance of ordinary shares for cash. The second is the declaration and payment of cash dividends. We analyze both.

Share Capital Transactions   The first stage in analyzing share capital is to review the comparative statements of financial position from Exhibit 16.6, which reveal an increase in share capital from $80,000 to $95,000. The second stage explains this change. Item *d* of the additional information (page 618) reports that 3,000 ordinary shares are issued at $15,000. The reconstructed entry for analysis of item *d* follows:

Reconstruction	Cash.	15,000	
	Share Capital		15,000

This entry reveals a $15,000 cash inflow from share issuance and reflects (and explains) the Share Capital account as follows:

Share Capital	
Bal., Dec. 31, 2014	80,000
Issued shares	**15,000**
Bal., Dec. 31, 2015	95,000

The third stage discloses the cash flow effect from share issuance in the financing as follows (also see Exhibit 16.4 or 16.7):

Cash flows from financing activities	
Cash received from issuing shares.	$15,000

Retained Earnings Transactions   The first stage in analyzing the Retained Earnings account is to review the comparative statements of financial position from Exhibit 16.6. This reveals an increase in retained earnings from $88,000 to $112,000.

The second stage explains this change. Item *f* of the additional information (page •••) reports that cash dividends of $14,000 are paid. The reconstructed entry follows:

Reconstruction	Retained Earnings	14,000	
	Cash		14,000

This entry reveals a $14,000 cash outflow for cash dividends. Also see that the Retained Earnings account is impacted by net profit of $38,000. (Net profit was analyzed under the operating section of the statement of cash flows.) The reconstructed Retained Earnings account follows:

Retained Earnings			
		Bal., Dec. 31, 2014	88,000
Cash dividend	**14,000**	**Net profit**	**38,000**
		Bal., Dec. 31, 2015	112,000

The third stage reports the cash flow effect from the cash dividend in the financing section of the statement as follows (also see Exhibit 16.4 or 16.7). Remember that the company can also choose to classify this item in the operating section.

Cash flows from financing activities	
Cash paid for dividends.	$(14,000)

We now have identified and explained all of the Genesis cash inflows and cash outflows and one noncash investing and financing transaction. Specifically, our analysis has reconciled changes in all noncash statement of financial position accounts.

Global: There are no requirements to separate domestic and international cash flows, leading some users to ask, "Where in the world is cash flow?"

Proving Cash Balances

The fifth and final step in preparing the statement is to report the beginning and ending cash balances and prove that the *net change in cash* is explained by operating, investing, and financing cash flows. This step is shown here for Genesis.

Net cash from operating activities	$36,000
Net cash from investing activities	2,000
Net cash used in financing activities	(33,000)
Net increase in cash	**$ 5,000**
Cash balance at 2014 year-end	12,000
Cash balance at 2015 year-end	$17,000

The preceding table shows that the $5,000 net increase in cash, from $12,000 at the beginning of the period to $17,000 at the end, is reconciled by net cash flows from operating ($36,000 inflow), investing ($2,000 inflow), and financing ($33,000 outflow) activities. This is formally reported at the bottom of the statement of cash flows as shown in both Exhibits 16.4 and 16.7.

Decision Maker   Answer — p. 638

Reporter   Management is in labor contract negotiations and grants you an interview. It highlights a recent $600,000 net loss that involves a $930,000 exceptional loss (not expected to repeat in near future) and a total net cash outflow of $550,000 (which includes net cash outflows of $850,000 for investing activities and $350,000 for financing activities). What is your assessment of this company? ∎

Decision Analysis    Cash Flow Analysis

Analyzing Cash Sources and Uses

A1 Analyze the statement of cash flows and apply the cash flow on total assets ratio.

Most managers stress the importance of understanding and predicting cash flows for business decisions. Creditors evaluate a company's ability to generate cash before deciding whether to lend money. Investors also assess cash inflows and outflows before buying and selling shares. Information in the statement of cash flows helps address these and other questions such as (1) How much cash is generated from or used in operations? (2) What expenditures are made with cash from operations? (3) What is the source of cash for debt payments? (4) What is the source of cash for distributions to owners? (5) How is the increase in investing activities financed? (6) What is the source of cash for new property, plant and equipment? (7) Why is cash flow from operations different from profit? (8) How is cash from financing used?

To effectively answer these questions, it is important to separately analyze investing, financing, and operating activities. To illustrate, consider data from three different companies in Exhibit 16.10. These companies operate in the same industry and have been in business for several years.

EXHIBIT 16.10

Cash Flows of Competing Companies

(in US$ thousands)	BMX	ATV	Trex
Cash from (used in) operating activities	$90,000	$40,000	$(24,000)
Cash from (used in) investing activities			
Proceeds from sale of property, plant and equipment			26,000
Purchase of property, plant and equipment	(48,000)	(25,000)	
Cash from (used in) financing activities			
Proceeds from issuance of debt			13,000
Repayment of debt.	(27,000)		
Net increase (decrease) in cash.	$15,000	$15,000	$ 15,000

Each company generates an identical $15,000 net increase in cash, but its sources and uses of cash flows are very different. BMX's operating activities provide net cash flows of $90,000, allowing it to purchase property, plant and equipment of $48,000 and repay $27,000 of its debt. ATV's operating activities provide $40,000 of cash flows, limiting its purchase of property, plant and equipment to $25,000. Trex's $15,000 net cash increase is due to selling property, plant and equipment and incurring additional debt. Its operating activities yield a net cash outflow of $24,000. Overall, analysis of these cash flows reveals that BMX is more capable of generating future cash flows than is ATV or Trex.

Cash Flow on Total Assets

Cash flow information has limitations, but it can help measure a company's ability to meet its obligations, pay dividends, expand operations, and obtain financing. Users often compute and analyze a cash-based ratio similar to return on total assets except that its numerator is net cash flows from operating activities. The **cash flow on total assets** ratio is in Exhibit 16.11.

$$\text{Cash flow on total assets} = \frac{\text{Net cash flow from operating activities}}{\text{Average total assets}}$$

EXHIBIT 16.11

Cash Flow on Total Assets

This ratio reflects actual cash flows and is not affected by accounting profit recognition and measurement. It can help business decision makers estimate the amount and timing of cash flows when planning and analyzing operating activities.

To illustrate, the 2013 cash flow on total assets ratio for Nestlé is 12.2%—see Exhibit 16.12. Is a 12.2% ratio good or bad? To answer this question, we compare this ratio with the ratios of prior years (we could also compare its ratio with those of its competitors and the market). Nestlé's cash flow on total assets ratio for two prior years is in the second column of Exhibit 16.12. Results show that its 2013's return is lower than the previous year's but much higher than 2011's.

Year	Cash Flow on Total Assets	Return on Total Assets
2013.........	12.2%	8.1%
2012.........	13.1%	8.5%
2011.........	8.7%	8.4%

EXHIBIT 16.12

Nestlé's Cash Flow on Total Assets

As an indicator of earnings quality, some analysts compare the cash flow on total assets ratio to the return on total assets ratio. Nestlé's return on total assets is provided in the third column of Exhibit 16.12. For each of the three years, Nestlé's cash flow on total assets ratio exceeds its return on total assets, so some analysts may infer that the earnings quality has been consistently high because more profit was realized in the form of cash.

◼ Decision Insight

Free Cash Flows   Many investors use cash flows to value company shares. However, cash-based valuation models often yield different share values due to differences in measurement of cash flows. Most models require cash flows that are "free" for distribution to shareholders.

Free cash flows = Net cash flow from operating activities − Capital expenditures

Free cash flows represent the cash that a company is able to generate after setting aside the money required to maintain or expand its asset base, which is important because it allows the company to pursue opportunities that enhance shareholder value. Without sufficient cash, it is difficult to develop new products, make acquisitions, pay dividends, and reduce debt. A company's growth and financial flexibility depend on adequate free cash flows. ◼

Point: Similar to financial ratios, calculations of free cash flows vary in practice as some analysts may deduct dividends or debt repayments as well.

DEMONSTRATION PROBLEM

Umlauf's comparative statements of financial position, income statement, and additional information follow.

UMLAUF COMPANY
Statements of Financial Position
December 31, 2015 and 2014

Assets	2015	2014
Cash	$ 43,050	$ 23,925
Accounts receivable	34,125	39,825
Merchandise inventory	156,000	146,475
Prepaid expenses	3,600	1,650
Equipment	135,825	146,700
Accum. depreciation—Equipment	(61,950)	(47,550)
Total assets	$310,650	$311,025
Liabilities and Equity		
Accounts payable	$ 28,800	$ 33,750
Income tax payable	5,100	4,425
Dividends payable	0	4,500
Bonds payable	0	37,500
Share capital—Ordinary, $10 par value	168,750	168,750
Retained earnings	108,000	62,100
Total liabilities and equity	$310,650	$311,025

UMLAUF COMPANY
Income Statement
For Year Ended December 31, 2015

Sales		$446,100
Cost of goods sold	$222,300	
Other operating expenses	120,300	
Depreciation expense	25,500	(368,100)
		78,000
Other gains (losses)		
Loss on sale of equipment	3,300	
Loss on retirement of bonds	825	(4,125)
Profit before tax		73,875
Income tax expense		(13,725)
Net profit		$ 60,150

Additional Information

a. Equipment costing $21,375 with accumulated depreciation of $11,100 is sold for cash.

b. Equipment purchases are for cash.

c. Accumulated Depreciation is affected by depreciation expense and the sale of equipment.

d. The balance of Retained Earnings is affected by dividend declarations and net profit.

e. Accounts Payable balances result from merchandise inventory purchases.

f. Prepaid expenses relate to "other operating expenses."

Required

1. Prepare a statement of cash flows using the indirect method for year 2015.

2.^APrepare a statement of cash flows using the direct method for year 2015.

PLANNING THE SOLUTION

● Prepare two blank statements of cash flows with sections for operating, investing, and financing activities using the (1) indirect method format and (2) direct method format.

● Compute the cash paid for equipment and the cash received from the sale of equipment using the additional information provided along with the amount for depreciation expense and the change in the balances of equipment and accumulated depreciation. Use T-accounts to help chart the effects of the sale and purchase of equipment on the balances of the Equipment account and the Accumulated Depreciation account.

- Compute the effect of net profit on the change in the Retained Earnings account balance. Assign the difference between the change in retained earnings and the amount of net profit to dividends declared. Adjust the dividends declared amount for the change in the Dividends Payable balance.
- Compute cash received from customers, cash paid for merchandise, cash paid for other operating expenses, and cash paid for taxes as illustrated in the chapter.
- Enter the cash effects of reconstruction entries to the appropriate section(s) of the statement.
- Total each section of the statement, determine the total net change in cash, and add it to the beginning balance to get the ending balance of cash.

SOLUTION TO DEMONSTRATION PROBLEM

Supporting computations for cash receipts and cash payments.

(1) *Cost of equipment sold	$ 21,375
Accumulated depreciation of equipment sold	(11,100)
Carrying amount of equipment sold	10,275
Loss on sale of equipment	(3,300)
Cash received from sale of equipment	$ 6,975
Cost of equipment sold	$ 21,375
Less decrease in the equipment account balance	(10,875)
Cash paid for new equipment	$ 10,500
(2) Loss on retirement of bonds	$ 825
Carrying amount of bonds retired	37,500
Cash paid to retire bonds	$ 38,325
(3) Net profit	$ 60,150
Less increase in retained earnings	45,900
Dividends declared	14,250
Plus decrease in dividends payable	4,500
Cash paid for dividends	$ 18,750
(4)A Sales	$ 446,100
Add decrease in accounts receivable	5,700
Cash received from customers	$451,800
(5)A Cost of goods sold	$ 222,300
Plus increase in merchandise inventory	9,525
Purchases	231,825
Plus decrease in accounts payable	4,950
Cash paid for merchandise	$236,775
(6)A Other operating expenses	$ 120,300
Plus increase in prepaid expenses	1,950
Cash paid for other operating expenses	$122,250
(7)A Income tax expense	$ 13,725
Less increase in income tax payable	(675)
Cash paid for income tax	$ 13,050

* Supporting T-account analysis for part 1 follows:

Equipment			
Bal., Dec. 31, 2014	146,700		
Cash purchase	10,500	Sale	21,375
Bal., Dec. 31, 2015	135,825		

Accumulated Depreciation—Equipment			
		Bal., Dec. 31, 2014	47,550
Sale	11,100	Depr. expense	25,500
		Bal., Dec. 31, 2015	61,950

UMLAUF COMPANY
Statement of Cash Flows (Indirect Method)
For Year Ended December 31, 2015

Cash flows from operating activities		
Profit before tax	$73,875	
Adjustments to reconcile profit to net cash from operating activities		
Decrease in accounts receivables	5,700	
Increase in merchandise inventory	(9,525)	
Increase in prepaid expenses	(1,950)	
Decrease in accounts payable	(4,950)	
Depreciation expense	25,500	
Loss on sale of property, plant and equipment	3,300	
Loss on retirement of bonds	825	
Cash flows generated from operating activities	92,775	
Income tax paid	(13,050)	
Net cash from operating activities		$79,725
Cash flows from investing activities		
Cash received from sale of equipment	6,975	
Cash paid for equipment	(10,500)	
Net cash used in investing activities		(3,525)
Cash flows from financing activities		
Cash paid to retire bonds payable	(38,325)	
Cash paid for dividends	(18,750)	
Net cash used in financing activities		(57,075)
Net increase in cash		$19,125
Cash balance at prior year-end		23,925
Cash balance at current year-end		$43,050

UMLAUF COMPANY
Statement of Cash Flows (Direct Method)
For Year Ended December 31, 2015

Cash flows from operating activities		
Cash received from customers	$451,800	
Cash paid for merchandise	(236,775)	
Cash paid for other operating expenses	(122,250)	
Cash paid for profit tax	(13,050)	
Net cash from operating activities		$79,725
Cash flows from investing activities		
Cash received from sale of equipment	6,975	
Cash paid for equipment	(10,500)	
Net cash used in investing activities		(3,525)
Cash flows from financing activities		
Cash paid to retire bonds payable	(38,325)	
Cash paid for dividends	(18,750)	
Net cash used in financing activities		(57,075)
Net increase in cash		$19,125
Cash balance at prior year-end		23,925
Cash balance at current year-end		$43,050

Direct Method of Reporting Operating Cash Flows

16A

We compute cash flows from operating activities under the direct method by adjusting accrual-based income statement items to the cash basis. The usual approach is to adjust income statement accounts related to operating activities for changes in their related statement of financial position accounts as follows:

P4 Compute cash flows from operating activities using the direct method.

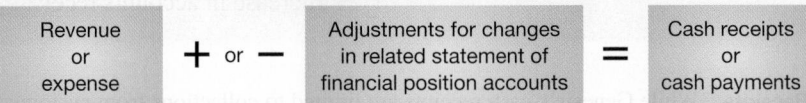

The framework for reporting cash receipts and cash payments for the operating section of the cash flow statement under the direct method is shown in Exhibit 16A.1. We consider cash receipts first and then cash payments.

EXHIBIT 16A.1

Major Classes of Operating Cash Flows

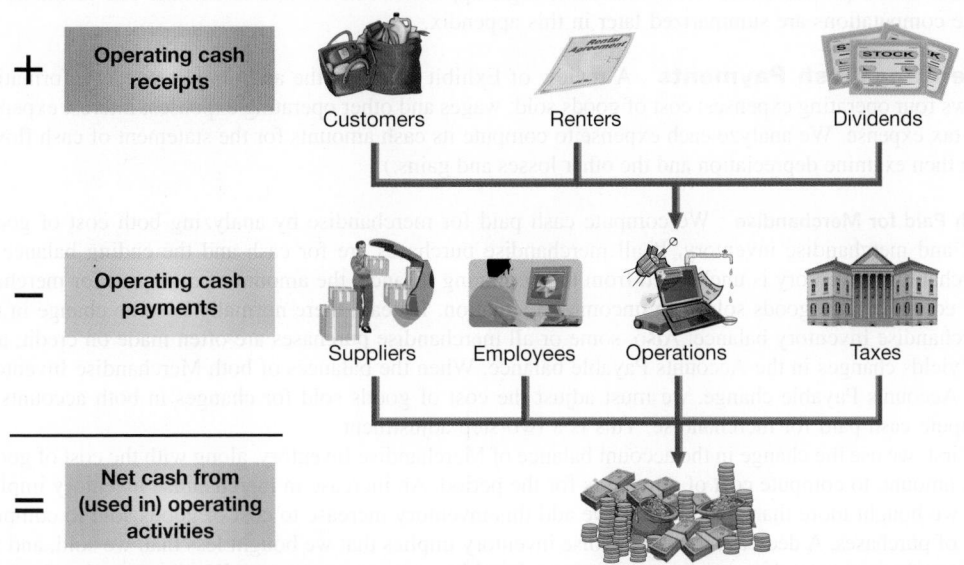

Operating Cash Receipts   A review of Exhibit 16.6 and the additional information reported by Genesis suggests only one potential cash receipt: sales to customers. This section, therefore, starts with sales to customers as reported on the income statement and then adjusts it as necessary to obtain cash received from customers to report on the statement of cash flows.

Cash Received from Customers   If all sales are for cash, the amount received from customers equals the sales reported on the income statement. When some or all sales are on account, however, we must adjust the amount of sales for the change in Accounts Receivable. It is often helpful to use *account analysis* to do this. This usually involves setting up a T-account and reconstructing its major entries, with emphasis on cash receipts and payments. To illustrate, we use a T-account that includes accounts receivable balances for Genesis on December 31, 2014 and 2015. The beginning balance is $40,000 and the ending balance is $60,000. Next, the income statement shows sales of $590,000, which we enter on the debit side of this account. We now can reconstruct the Accounts Receivable account to determine the amount of cash received from customers as follows:

Point: An accounts receivable increase implies that cash received from customers is less than sales (the converse is also true).

Accounts Receivable			
Bal., Dec. 31, 2014	40,000		
Sales	590,000	Cash receipts =	570,000
Bal., Dec. 31, 2015	60,000		

EXHIBIT 16A.2

Formula to Compute Cash Received from Customers—Direct Method

This T-account shows that the Accounts Receivable balance begins at $40,000 and increases to $630,000 from sales of $590,000, yet its ending balance is only $60,000. This implies that cash receipts from customers are $570,000, computed as $40,000 + $590,000 − [?] = $60,000. This computation can be rearranged to express cash received as equal to sales of $590,000 minus a $20,000 increase in accounts receivable. This computation is summarized as a general rule in Exhibit 16A.2. The statement of cash flows in Exhibit 16.4 reports the $570,000 cash received from customers as a cash inflow from operating activities.

$$\text{Cash received from customers} = \text{Sales} \left[\begin{array}{c} + \text{ Decrease in accounts receivable} \\ \text{or} \\ - \text{ Increase in accounts receivable} \end{array} \right.$$

Other Cash Receipts   While Genesis's cash receipts are limited to collections from customers, we often see other types of cash receipts, most commonly cash receipts involving rent, interest, and dividends. We compute cash received from these items by subtracting an increase in their respective receivable or adding a decrease. For instance, if rent receivable increases in the period, cash received from renters is less than rent revenue reported on the income statement. If rent receivable decreases, cash received is more than reported rent revenue. The same logic applies to interest and dividends. The formulas for these computations are summarized later in this appendix.

Operating Cash Payments   A review of Exhibit 16.6 and the additional Genesis information shows four operating expenses: cost of goods sold; wages and other operating expenses; interest expense; and tax expense. We analyze each expense to compute its cash amounts for the statement of cash flows. (We then examine depreciation and the other losses and gains.)

Cash Paid for Merchandise   We compute cash paid for merchandise by analyzing both cost of goods sold and merchandise inventory. If all merchandise purchases are for cash and the ending balance of Merchandise Inventory is unchanged from the beginning balance, the amount of cash paid for merchandise equals cost of goods sold—an uncommon situation. Instead, there normally is some change in the Merchandise Inventory balance. Also, some or all merchandise purchases are often made on credit, and this yields changes in the Accounts Payable balance. When the balances of both Merchandise Inventory and Accounts Payable change, we must adjust the cost of goods sold for changes in both accounts to compute cash paid for merchandise. This is a two-step adjustment.

First, we use the change in the account balance of Merchandise Inventory, along with the cost of goods sold amount, to compute cost of purchases for the period. An increase in merchandise inventory implies that we bought more than we sold, and we add this inventory increase to cost of goods sold to compute cost of purchases. A decrease in merchandise inventory implies that we bought less than we sold, and we subtract the inventory decrease from cost of goods sold to compute purchases. We illustrate the *first step* by reconstructing the Merchandise Inventory account of Genesis:

Merchandise Inventory			
Bal., Dec. 31, 2014	70,000		
Purchases =	314,000	Cost of goods sold	300,000
Bal., Dec. 31, 2015	84,000		

The beginning balance is $70,000, and the ending balance is $84,000. The income statement shows that cost of goods sold is $300,000, which we enter on the credit side of this account. With this information, we determine the amount for cost of purchases to be $314,000. This computation can be rearranged to express cost of purchases as equal to cost of goods sold of $300,000 plus the $14,000 increase in inventory.

The second step uses the change in the balance of Accounts Payable, and the amount of cost of purchases, to compute cash paid for merchandise. A decrease in accounts payable implies that we paid for more goods than we acquired this period, and we would then add the accounts payable decrease to cost of purchases to compute cash paid for merchandise. An increase in accounts payable implies that we paid for less than the amount of goods acquired, and we would subtract the accounts payable increase from purchases to compute cash paid for merchandise. The *second step* is applied to Genesis by reconstructing its Accounts Payable account:

Accounts Payable			
		Bal., Dec. 31, 2014	40,000
Cash payments =	319,000	Purchases	314,000
		Bal., Dec. 31, 2015	35,000

Its beginning balance of $40,000 plus purchases of $314,000 minus an ending balance of $35,000 yields cash paid of $319,000 (or $40,000 + $314,000 − [?] = $35,000). Alternatively, we can express cash paid for merchandise as equal to purchases of $314,000 plus the $5,000 decrease in accounts payable. The $319,000 cash paid for merchandise is reported on the statement of cash flows in Exhibit 16.4 as a cash outflow under operating activities.

We summarize this two-step adjustment to cost of goods sold to compute cash paid for merchandise inventory in Exhibit 16A.3.

Example: If the ending balances of Inventory and Accounts Payable are $60,000 and $50,000, respectively (instead of $84,000 and $35,000), what is cash paid for merchandise? *Answer:* $280,000

EXHIBIT 16A.3

Two Steps to Compute Cash Paid for Merchandise—Direct Method

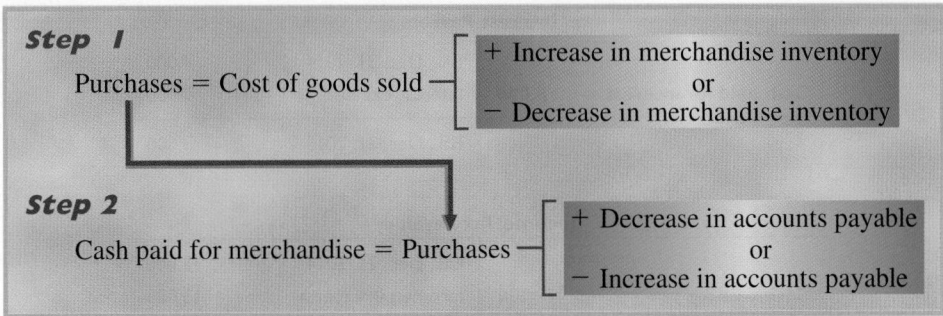

Cash Paid for Wages and Operating Expenses (Excluding Depreciation)   The income statement of Genesis shows wages and other operating expenses of $216,000 (see Exhibit 16.6). To compute cash paid for wages and other operating expenses, we adjust this amount for any changes in their related statement of financial position accounts. We begin by looking for any prepaid expenses and accrued liabilities related to wages and other operating expenses in the statements of financial position of Genesis in Exhibit 16.6. The statements of financial position show prepaid expenses but no accrued liabilities. Thus, the adjustment is limited to the change in prepaid expenses. The amount of adjustment is computed by assuming that all cash paid for wages and other operating expenses is initially debited to Prepaid Expenses. This assumption allows us to reconstruct the Prepaid Expenses account:

Prepaid Expenses			
Bal., Dec. 31, 2014	4,000		
Cash payments =	218,000	Wages and other operating exp.	216,000
Bal., Dec. 31, 2015	6,000		

Prepaid Expenses increase by $2,000 in the period, meaning that cash paid for wages and other operating expenses exceeds the reported expense by $2,000. Alternatively, we can express cash paid for wages and other operating expenses as equal to its reported expenses of $216,000 plus the $2,000 increase in prepaid expenses.[1]

Exhibit 16A.4 summarizes the adjustments to wages (including salaries) and other operating expenses. The Genesis statement of financial position did not report accrued liabilities, but we include them in the formula to explain the adjustment to cash when they do exist. A decrease in accrued liabilities implies that we paid cash for more goods or services than received this period, so we add the decrease in accrued liabilities to the expense amount to obtain cash paid for these goods or services. An increase in accrued liabilities implies that we paid cash for less than what was acquired, so we subtract this increase in accrued liabilities from the expense amount to get cash paid.

Point: A decrease in prepaid expenses implies that reported expenses include an amount(s) that did not require a cash outflow in the period.

[1] The assumption that all cash payments for wages and operating expenses are initially debited to Prepaid Expenses is not necessary for our analysis to hold. If cash payments are debited directly to the expense account, the total amount of cash paid for wages and other operating expenses still equals the $216,000 expense plus the $2,000 increase in Prepaid Expenses (which arise from end-of-period adjusting entries).

EXHIBIT 16A.4

Formula to Compute Cash Paid for Wages and Operating Expenses—Direct Method

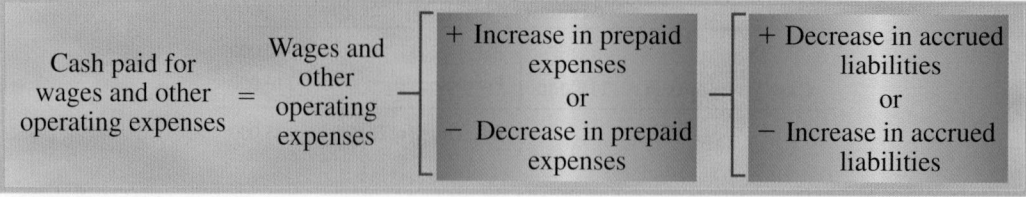

Cash paid for interest and income tax   Computing operating cash flows for interest and tax is similar to that for operating expenses. Both require adjustments to their amounts reported on the income statement for changes in their related statement of financial position accounts. We begin with the Genesis income statement showing interest expense of $7,000 and income tax expense of $15,000. To compute the cash paid, we adjust interest expense for the change in interest payable and then the income tax expense for the change in income tax payable. These computations involve reconstructing both liability accounts:

		Interest Payable	
		Bal., Dec. 31, 2014	4,000
Cash paid for interest =	8,000	Interest expense	7,000
		Bal., Dec. 31, 2015	3,000

		Income Tax Payable	
		Bal., Dec. 31, 2014	12,000
Cash paid for tax =	5,000	Income tax expense	15,000
		Bal., Dec. 31, 2015	22,000

These accounts reveal cash paid for interest of $8,000 and cash paid for income tax of $5,000. The formulas to compute these amounts are in Exhibit 16A.5. Both of these cash payments are reported as operating cash outflows on the statement of cash flows in Exhibit 16.4.

EXHIBIT 16A.5

Formulas to Compute Cash Paid for Both Interest and Tax—Direct Method

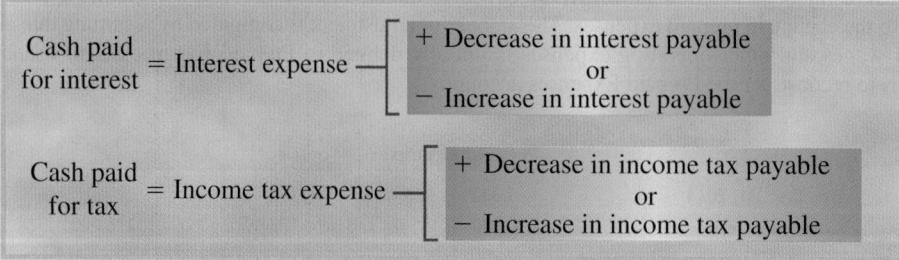

Analysis of Additional Expenses, Gains, and Losses   Genesis has three additional items reported on its income statement: depreciation, loss on sale of assets, and gain on retirement of debt. We must consider each for its potential cash effects.

Depreciation Expense   Depreciation expense is $24,000. It is often called a *noncash expense* because depreciation has no cash flows. Depreciation expense is an allocation of an asset's depreciable cost. The cash outflow with an item of property, plant and equipment is reported as part of investing activities when it is paid for. Thus, depreciation expense is *never* reported on a statement of cash flows using the direct method; nor is depletion or amortization expense.

Loss on Sale of Assets   Sales of assets frequently result in gains and losses reported as part of net profit, but the amount of recorded gain or loss does *not* reflect any cash flows in these transactions. Asset sales result in cash inflow equal to the cash amount received, regardless of whether the asset was sold at a gain or a loss. This cash inflow is reported under investing activities. Thus, the loss or gain on a sale of assets is *never* reported on a statement of cash flows using the direct method.

Point: The direct method is usually viewed as *user friendly* because less accounting knowledge is required to understand and use it.

Gain on Retirement of Debt   Retirement of debt usually yields a gain or loss reported as part of net profit, but that gain or loss does *not* reflect cash flow in this transaction. Debt retirement results in cash outflow equal to the cash paid to settle the debt, regardless of whether the debt is retired at a gain or loss. This cash outflow is reported under financing activities; the loss or gain from retirement of debt is *never* reported on a statement of cash flows using the direct method.

Summary of Adjustments for Direct Method   Exhibit 16A.6 summarizes common adjustments for net profit to yield net cash from or used in operating activities under the direct method.

EXHIBIT 16A.6

Summary of Selected Adjustments for Direct Method

Item	From Income Statement	Adjustments to Obtain Cash Flow Numbers	
Receipts			
From sales	Sales Revenue	+Decrease in Accounts Receivable −Increase in Accounts Receivable	
From rent	Rent Revenue	+Decrease in Rent Receivable −Increase in Rent Receivable	
From interest	Interest Revenue	+Decrease in Interest Receivable −Increase in Interest Receivable	
From dividends	Dividend Revenue	+Decrease in Dividends Receivable −Increase in Dividends Receivable	
Payments			
To suppliers	Cost of Goods Sold	+Increase in Inventory −Decrease in Inventory	+Decrease in Accounts Payable −Increase in Accounts Payable
For operations	Operating Expense	+Increase in Prepaids −Decrease in Prepaids	+Decrease in Accrued Liabilities −Increase in Accrued Liabilities
To employees	Wages (Salaries) Expense	+Decrease in Wages (Salaries) Payable −Increase in Wages (Salaries) Payable	
For interest	Interest Expense	+Decrease in Interest Payable −Increase in Interest Payable	
For taxes	Income Tax Expense	+Decrease in Income Tax Payable −Increase in Income Tax Payable	

Direct Method Format of Operating Activities Section   Exhibit 16.4 shows the Genesis statement of cash flows using the direct method. Major items of cash inflows and cash outflows are listed separately in the operating activities section. The format requires that operating cash outflows be subtracted from operating cash inflows to get net cash from (used in) operating activities. The **IASB** recommends that the operating activities section of the statement of cash flows be reported using the direct method, which is considered more useful to financial statement users.

Point: Some preparers argue that it is easier to prepare a statement of cash flows using the indirect method. This likely explains its greater frequency in financial statements.

Quick Check

Answers — p. 638

8. Net sales in a period are $590,000, beginning accounts receivable are $120,000, and ending accounts receivable are $90,000. What cash amount is collected from customers in the period?

9. The Merchandise Inventory account balance decreases in the period from a beginning balance of $32,000 to an ending balance of $28,000. Cost of goods sold for the period is $168,000. If the Accounts Payable balance increases $2,400 in the period, what is the cash amount paid for merchandise inventory?

10. This period's wages and other operating expenses total $112,000. Beginning-of-period prepaid expenses totaled $1,200, and its ending balance is $4,200. There were no beginning-of-period accrued liabilities, but end-of-period wages payable equal $5,600. How much cash is paid for wages and other operating expenses?

Summary

C1 **Distinguish between operating, investing, and financing activities, and describe how noncash investing and financing activities are disclosed.** The purpose of the statement of cash flows is to report major cash receipts and cash payments relating to operating, investing, or financing activities. Operating activities include transactions and events that determine net profit. Investing activities include transactions and events that mainly affect long-term assets. Financing activities include transactions and events that mainly affect long-term liabilities and equity. Noncash investing and financing activities must be disclosed in either a note or a separate schedule to the statement of cash flows. Examples are the retirement of debt by issuing equity and the exchange of a note payable for property, plant and equipment.

A1 **Analyze the statement of cash flows and apply the cash flow on total assets ratio.** To understand and predict cash flows, users stress identification of the sources and uses of cash flows by operating, investing, and financing activities. Emphasis is on operating cash flows since they derive from continuing operations. The cash flow on total assets ratio is defined as operating cash flows divided by average total assets. Analysis of current and past values for this ratio can reflect a company's ability to yield regular and positive cash flows. It is also viewed as a measure of earnings quality.

P1 **Prepare a statement of cash flows.** Preparation of a statement of cash flows involves five steps: (1) Compute the net increase or decrease in cash; (2) compute net cash from or used in operating

activities (*using either the direct or indirect method*); (3) compute net cash from or used in investing activities; (4) compute net cash from or used in financing activities; and (5) report the beginning and ending cash balance and prove that it is explained by net cash flows. Noncash investing and financing activities are also disclosed.

P2 **Compute cash flows from operating activities using the indirect method.** The indirect method for reporting net cash from or used in operating activities starts with net profit and then adjusts it for three items: (1) changes in noncash current assets and current liabilities related to operating activities, (2) revenues and expenses not providing or using cash, and (3) gains and losses from investing and financing activities.

P3 **Determine cash flows from both investing and financing activities.** Cash flows from both investing and financing activities are determined by identifying the cash flow effects of transactions and events affecting each statement of financial position account related to these activities. All cash flows from these activities are identified when we can explain changes in these accounts from the beginning to the end of the period.

P4^A **Compute cash flows from operating activities using the direct method.** The direct method for reporting net cash from or used in operating activities lists major operating cash inflows less cash outflows to yield net cash inflow or outflow from operations.

Guidance Answers to Decision Maker

Entrepreneur Several factors might explain an increase in net cash flows when a net loss is reported, including (1) early recognition of expenses relative to revenues generated (such as research and development), (2) cash advances on long-term sales contracts not yet recognized in profit, (3) issuances of debt or equity for cash to finance expansion, (4) cash sale of assets, (5) delay of cash payments, and (6) cash prepayment on sales. Analysis needs to focus on the components of both the net loss and the net cash flows and their implications for future performance.

Reporter Your initial reaction based on the company's $600,000 loss with a $550,000 decrease in net cash flows is not positive. However, closer scrutiny reveals a more positive picture of this company's performance. Cash flow from operating activities is $650,000, computed as [?] − $850,000 − $350,000 = $(550,000). You also note that net profit *before* the exceptional loss not expected to repeat in the near future is $330,000, computed as[?] − $930,000 = $(600,000).

Guidance Answers to Quick Checks

1. No to both. The statement of cash flows reports changes in the sum of cash plus cash equivalents. It does not report transfers between cash and cash equivalents.

2. The three categories of cash inflows and outflows are operating activities, investing activities, and financing activities.

3. **a.** Investing   **d.** Operating or investing
      b. Operating   **e.** Operating
      c. Financing   **f.** Financing

4. $79,000 + $4,600 − $11,700 − $1,000 + $3,400 − $4,100 = $70,200

5. Expenses such as depreciation and amortization do not require current cash outflows. Therefore, adding these expenses back to

profit eliminates these noncash items from the income number, converting it to a cash basis.

6. A gain on the sale of property, plant and equipment is subtracted from profit because a sale of property, plant and equipment is not an operating activity; it is an investing activity for the amount of cash received from its sale. Also, such a gain yields no cash effects.

7. $80,000 − $30,000 − $10,000 = $40,000 cash receipt. The $40,000 cash receipt is reported as an investing activity.

8. $590,000 + ($120,000 − $90,000) = $620,000

9. $168,000 − ($32,000 − $28,000) − $2,400 = $161,600

10. $112,000 + ($4,200 − $1,200) − $5,600 = $109,400

Multiple Choice Quiz   Answers on p. 656   www.mheducation.asia/olc/wildkwokFAP

Additional Quiz Questions are available at the book's Website.

1. A company uses the indirect method to determine its cash flows from operating activities. Use the following information to determine its net cash from or used in operating activities. The company does not pay taxes.

Net profit	$15,200
Depreciation expense	10,000
Cash payment on notes payable	8,000
Gain on sale of land	3,000
Increase in inventory	1,500
Increase in accounts payable	2,850

  a. $23,550 used in operating activities
  b. $23,550 from operating activities
  c. $15,550 from operating activities
  d. $42,400 from operating activities
  e. $20,850 from operating activities

2. A machine with a cost of $175,000 and accumulated depreciation of $94,000 is sold for $87,000 cash. The amount reported as a source of cash under cash flows from investing activities is
  a. $81,000.
  b. $6,000.
  c. $87,000.
  d. Zero; this is a financing activity.
  e. Zero; this is an operating activity.

3. A company settles a long-term note payable plus interest by paying $68,000 cash toward the principal amount and $5,440 cash for interest. The amount reported as a use of cash under cash flows from financing activities is
  a. Zero; this is an investing activity.
  b. Zero; this is an operating activity.

  c. $73,440.
  d. $68,000.
  e. *c* or *d*.

4. The following information is available regarding a company's annual salaries and wages. What amount of cash is paid for salaries and wages?

Salaries and wages expense	$255,000
Salaries and wages payable, prior year-end	8,200
Salaries and wages payable, current year-end	10,900

  a. $252,300
  b. $257,700
  c. $255,000
  d. $274,100
  e. $235,900

5. The following information is available for a company. What amount of cash is paid for merchandise for the current year?

Cost of goods sold	$545,000
Merchandise inventory, prior year-end	105,000
Merchandise inventory, current year-end	112,000
Accounts payable, prior year-end	98,500
Accounts payable, current year-end	101,300

  a. $545,000
  b. $554,800
  c. $540,800
  d. $535,200
  e. $549,200

^A *Superscript letter A denotes assignments based on Appendix 16A.*

ⓘ Icon denotes assignments that involve decision making.

Discussion Questions

1. What is the reporting purpose of the statement of cash flows? Identify at least two questions that this statement can answer.

2. Describe the direct method of reporting cash flows from operating activities.

3. When a statement of cash flows is prepared using the direct method, what are some of the operating cash flows?

4. Describe the indirect method of reporting cash flows from operating activities.

5. What are some investing activities reported on the statement of cash flows?

6. What are some financing activities reported on the statement of cash flows?

7. Where on the statement of cash flows is the payment of cash dividends reported?

8. Assume that a company purchases land for $100,000, paying $20,000 cash and borrowing the remainder with a long-term note payable. How should this transaction be reported on a statement of cash flows?

9. On June 3, a company borrows $50,000 cash by giving its bank a 160-day, interest-bearing note. On the statement of cash flows, where should this be reported?

10. If a company reports positive net profit for the year, can it also show a net cash outflow from operating activities? Explain.

11. Is depreciation a source of cash flow?

12. Refer to Nestlé's consolidated cash flow statement in Appendix A. List its net cash for each of the three types of activities: operating, investing, and financing.

13. Refer to Adidas' consolidated statement of cash flows in Appendix A. What are its cash flows from financing activities for the year ended December 31, 2013? List items and amounts.

14. Refer to Samsung's consolidated statement of cash flows in Appendix A. (*a*) Which method is used to compute its net cash from operating activities? (*b*) While its consolidated statement of financial position shows an increase in trade and other receivables from financial years 2011 to 2012, why is this increase in trade and other receivables deducted when computing cash provided by operating activities for the year ended December 31, 2012?

15. Refer to 361 Degrees' 2013 consolidated cash flow statement from its Website (http://ir.361sport.com/html/ir_report.php). What investing activities result in cash outflows for the year ended December 31, 2013? List items and amounts.

≡ connect™

QUICK STUDY

QS 16-1
Transaction classification by activity

C1

Classify the following cash flows as operating, investing, or financing activities (some items may be classified in more than one way).

1. Paid cash for property tax on building.
2. Paid cash dividends.
3. Paid cash for wages and salaries.
4. Purchased inventories for cash.
5. Received cash payments from customers.

6. Received cash from sale of land at a loss.
7. Received cash interest on a note.
8. Paid cash interest on outstanding notes.
9. Issued ordinary shares for cash.
10. Sold long-term investments for cash.

QS 16-2
Statement of cash flows

C1

The statement of cash flows is one of the four primary financial statements.

1. Describe the content and layout of a statement of cash flows, including its three sections.

2. List at least three transactions classified as significant noncash financing and investing activities in the statement of cash flows.

3. List at least three transactions classified as financing activities in a statement of cash flows.

4. List at least three transactions classified as investing activities in a statement of cash flows.

QS 16-3
Computing cash from operations (indirect)

P2

Use the following information to determine this company's cash flows from operating activities using the indirect method.

LING COMPANY Income Statement For Year Ended December 31, 2015		
Sales		$2,060,000
Cost of goods sold		1,326,400
Gross profit		733,600
Operating expenses		
Depreciation expense	$144,000	
Other expenses	486,000	630,000
Profit before tax		103,600
Income tax expense		30,800
Net profit		$ 72,800

LING COMPANY Selected Statement of Financial Position Information December 31, 2015 and 2014		
	2015	**2014**
Current assets		
Cash	$338,600	$107,200
Accounts receivable	100,000	128,000
Inventory	240,000	216,400
Current liabilities		
Accounts payable	121,600	102,800
Income tax payable	8,200	8,800

The following selected information is from Mooney Company's comparative statements of financial position.

At December 31	2015	2014
Furniture.	$155,000	$ 260,000
Accumulated depreciation—Furniture	(74,400)	(121,400)

The income statement reports depreciation expense for the year of $36,000. Also, furniture costing $105,000 was sold for its carrying amount. Compute the cash received from the sale of furniture.

QS 16-4
Computing cash from asset sales
P3

The following selected information is from the Teeter Company's comparative statements of financial position.

At December 31	2015	2014
Share capital—Ordinary, $10 par value	$ 310,000	$300,000
Share premium	1,134,000	684,000
Retained earnings	627,000	575,000

The company's net profit for the year ended December 31, 2015, was $196,000.
1. Compute the cash received from the sale of its ordinary shares during 2015.
2. Compute the cash paid for dividends during 2015.

QS 16-5
Computing financing cash flows
P3

For each of the following separate cases, compute cash flows from operations. The list includes all statement of financial position accounts related to operating activities. For each year, the tax expense is the same as the tax paid.

	Case A	Case B	Case C
Profit before tax	$ 30,000	$145,000	$120,000
Income tax paid	10,000	20,000	15,000
Depreciation expense	60,000	16,000	48,000
Accounts receivable increase (decrease)	80,000	40,000	(8,000)
Inventory increase (decrease)	(40,000)	(20,000)	21,000
Accounts payable increase (decrease)	28,000	(44,000)	16,000
Accrued liabilities increase (decrease)	(88,000)	10,000	(16,000)

QS 16-6
Computing cash flows from operations (indirect)
P2

Compute cash flows from investing activities using the following company information.

Sale of short-term investments	$16,000
Cash collections from customers	44,000
Purchase of used equipment	10,000
Depreciation expense	6,000

QS 16-7
Computing cash flows from investing
P3

Compute cash flows from financing activities using the following company information. Assume that cash dividends paid and interest paid are classified as financing.

Additional short-term borrowings	$88,000
Purchase of short-term investments	25,000
Cash dividends paid	32,000
Interest paid	17,000

QS 16-8
Computing cash flows from financing
P3

QS 16-9

Computing cash from
operations (indirect) **P2**

Use the following statements of financial position and income statement to answer QS 16-9 through
QS 16-14.

Use the indirect method to prepare the cash from or used in operating activities section only of the
statement of cash flows for this company.

ORWELL, INC. Comparative Statements of Financial Position December 31, 2015		
	2015	**2014**
Assets		
Cash	$ 95,800	$ 25,000
Accounts receivable, net	42,000	52,000
Inventory	86,800	96,800
Prepaid expenses	6,400	5,200
Furniture	110,000	120,000
Accum. depreciation—Furniture	(18,000)	(10,000)
Total assets	$323,000	$289,000
Liabilities and Equity		
Accounts payable	$ 16,000	$ 22,000
Wages payable	10,000	6,000
Income tax payable	2,400	3,600
Notes payable (long-term)	30,000	70,000
Share capital—Ordinary, 5 par value	230,000	180,000
Retained earnings	34,600	7,400
Total liabilities and equity	$323,000	$289,000

ORWELL, INC. Income Statement For Year Ended December 31, 2015		
Sales		$468,000
Cost of goods sold		312,000
Gross profit		156,000
Operating expenses		
Depreciation expense	$38,600	
Other expenses	57,000	95,600
Profit before tax		60,400
Income tax expense		24,600
Net profit		$ 35,800

QS 16-10

Computing cash from asset sales
P3

Refer to the data in QS 16-9.
Furniture costing $54,000 is sold at its carrying amount in 2015. Acquisitions of furniture total $44,000
cash, on which no depreciation is necessary because it is acquired at year-end. What is the cash inflow
related to the sale of furniture?

QS 16-11

Computing financing cash
outflows **P3**

Refer to the data in QS 16-9.

1. Assume that all ordinary shares are issued for cash. What amount of cash dividends is paid during 2015?
2. Assume that no additional notes payable are issued in 2015. What cash amount is paid to reduce the
   notes payable balance in 2015?

QS 16-12^A

Computing cash received from
customers **P4**

Refer to the data in QS 16-9.

1. How much cash is received from sales to customers for year 2015?
2. What is the net increase or decrease in cash for year 2015?

QS 16-13^A

Computing operating cash
outflows **P4**

Refer to the data in QS 16-9.

1. How much cash is paid to acquire merchandise inventory during year 2015?
2. How much cash is paid for operating expenses during year 2015?

QS 16-14^A

Computing cash from operations
(direct) **P4**

Refer to the data in QS 16-9.
Use the direct method to prepare the cash from or used in operating activities section only of the statement
of cash flows for this company.

QS 16-15

Analyses of sources and uses
of cash **A1**

Financial data from three competitors in the same industry follow.

1. Which of the three competitors is in the strongest position as shown by its statement of cash flows?
2. Analyze and compare the strength of Z-Best's cash flow on total assets ratio to that of Lopez.

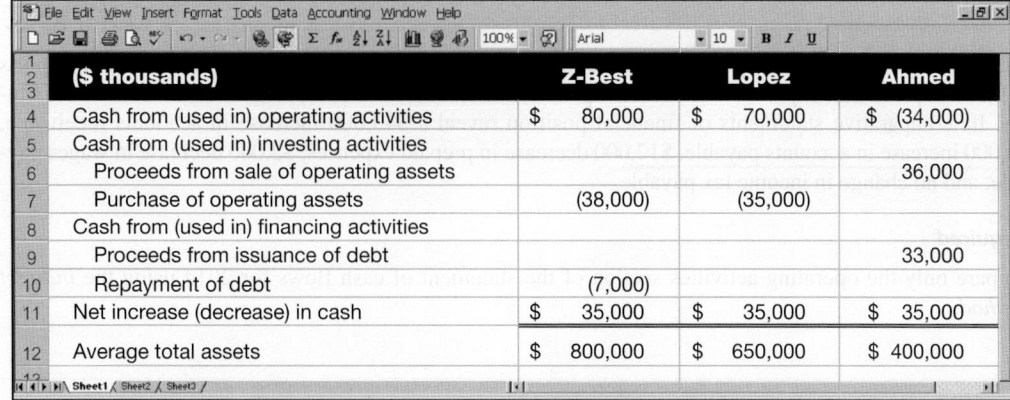

($ thousands)	Z-Best	Lopez	Ahmed
Cash from (used in) operating activities	$ 80,000	$ 70,000	$ (34,000)
Cash from (used in) investing activities			
Proceeds from sale of operating assets			36,000
Purchase of operating assets	(38,000)	(35,000)	
Cash from (used in) financing activities			
Proceeds from issuance of debt			33,000
Repayment of debt	(7,000)		
Net increase (decrease) in cash	$ 35,000	$ 35,000	$ 35,000
Average total assets	$ 800,000	$ 650,000	$ 400,000

Use the following financial statements and additional information to (1) prepare a statement of cash flows for the year ended December 31, 2016, using the *indirect method,* and (2) analyze and briefly discuss the statement prepared in part 1 with special attention to operating activities and to the company's cash level.

QS 16-16
Preparation of statement of cash flows (indirect)
P1

KRUG INC.
Income Statement
For Year Ended December 31, 2016

Sales		$47,575
Cost of goods sold		(17,950)
Gross profit		29,625
Operating expenses		
Depreciation expense	$4,200	
Other expenses	8,550	
Total operating expense		12,750
Profit before tax		16,875
Income tax expense		3,375
Net profit		$13,500

KRUG INC.
Comparative Statements of Financial Position
December 31, 2016 and 2015

	2016	2015
Assets		
Cash	$ 26,400	$ 30,550
Accounts receivable, net	14,050	12,150
Inventory	90,100	70,150
Equipment	49,900	44,500
Accum. depreciation—Equipment	(22,500)	(18,300)
Total assets	$157,950	$139,050
Liabilities and Equity		
Accounts payable	$ 23,350	$ 25,400
Salaries payable	1,050	600
Share capital—Ordinary, no par value	107,000	100,000
Retained earnings	26,550	13,050
Total liabilities and equity	$157,950	$139,050

Additional Information

a. No dividends are declared or paid in 2016.

b. Issued additional shares for $7,000 cash in 2016.

c. Purchased equipment for cash in 2016; no equipment was sold in 2016.

Answer each of the following related to international accounting standards.

1. Which method, indirect or direct, is acceptable for reporting operating cash flows under **IFRSv**?

2. For each of the following four cash flows, identify whether it is reported under the operating, investing, or financing section (or some combination) within the indirect format of the statement of cash flows reported under **IFRS** and under U.S. GAAP.

QS 16-17
International cash flow disclosures
C1

Cash Flow Source	US GAAP Reporting	IFRS Reporting
a. Interest paid		
b. Dividends paid		
c. Interest received		
d. Dividends received		

EXERCISES

Exercise 16-1

Cash flow from operations (indirect)

P2

Salud Company reports net profit of $420,000 for the year ended December 31, 2014. It also reports $80,000 depreciation expense, income tax expense of $20,000, and a $20,000 gain on the sale of machinery. Its comparative statements of financial position reveal a $40,000 increase in accounts receivable, $6,000 increase in accounts payable, $12,000 decrease in prepaid expenses, $2,000 decrease in wages payable, and no change in income tax payable.

Required

Prepare only the operating activities section of the statement of cash flows for 2014 using the *indirect method*.

Exercise 16-2

Cash flow classification (indirect)

C1

The following transactions and events occurred during the year. Assuming that this company uses the *indirect method* to report cash provided by operating activities, indicate where each item would appear on its statement of cash flows by placing an *x* in the appropriate column.

	Statement of Cash Flows			Noncash Investing and Financing Activities	Not Reported on Statement or in Notes
	Operating Activities	Investing Activities	Financing Activities		
a. Accounts receivable decreased in the year	____	____	____	____	____
b. Purchased land by issuing ordinary shares	____	____	____	____	____
c. Paid cash to purchase inventory	____	____	____	____	____
d. Sold equipment for cash, yielding a loss	____	____	____	____	____
e. Accounts payable decreased in the year	____	____	____	____	____
f. Income tax payable increased in the year	____	____	____	____	____
g. Declared and paid a cash dividend	____	____	____	____	____
h. Recorded depreciation expense	____	____	____	____	____
i. Paid cash to settle long-term note payable	____	____	____	____	____
j. Prepaid expenses increased in the year	____	____	____	____	____

Exercise 16-3^A

Cash flow classification (direct)

C1 P4

The following transactions and events occurred during the year. Assuming that this company uses the *direct method* to report cash provided by operating activities, indicate where each item would appear on the statement of cash flows by placing an *x* in the appropriate column.

	Statement of Cash Flows			Noncash Investing and Financing Activities	Not Reported on Statement or in Notes
	Operating Activities	Investing Activities	Financing Activities		
a. Accepted six-month note receivable in exchange for property, plant and equipment	____	____	____	____	____
b. Recorded depreciation expense	____	____	____	____	____
c. Paid cash to acquire treasury shares	____	____	____	____	____
d. Collected cash from sales	____	____	____	____	____
e. Borrowed cash from bank by signing a nine-month note payable	____	____	____	____	____
f. Paid cash to purchase a patent	____	____	____	____	____
g. Retired long-term notes payable by issuing ordinary shares	____	____	____	____	____
h. Paid cash toward accounts payable	____	____	____	____	____
i. Sold inventory for cash	____	____	____	____	____
j. Paid cash dividend that was declared in a prior period	____	____	____	____	____

Olhstead Company's calendar-year 2014 income statement shows the following: Net Profit, $374,000; Income Tax Expense, $31,000; Depreciation Expense, $44,000; Amortization Expense, $7,200; Gain on Sale of Property, Plant and Equipment, $6,000.

An examination of the company's current assets and current liabilities reveals the following changes (all from operating activities): Accounts Receivable decrease, $17,100; Merchandise Inventory decrease, $42,000; Prepaid Expenses increase, $4,700; Accounts Payable decrease, $8,200; Other Payables increase, $1,200; but no change in Income Tax Payable. Use the *indirect method* to compute cash flow from operating activities.

Exercise 16-4
Cash flows from operating activities (Indirect)
P2

For each of the following three separate cases, use the information provided about the calendar-year 2016 operations of Sahim Company to compute the required cash flow information.

Exercise 16-5ᴬ
Computation of cash flows (direct)
P5

Case A: Compute cash received from customers:

Sales	$510,000
Accounts receivable, December 31, 2015	25,200
Accounts receivable, December 31, 2016	34,800

Case B: Compute cash paid for rent:

Rent expense	$140,800
Rent payable, December 31, 2015	8,800
Rent payable, December 31, 2016	7,200

Case C: Compute cash paid for merchandise:

Cost of goods sold	$528,000
Merchandise inventory, December 31, 2015	159,600
Accounts payable, December 31, 2015	67,800
Merchandise inventory, December 31, 2016	131,400
Accounts payable, December 31, 2016	84,000

Use the following income statement and information about changes in noncash current assets and current liabilities to prepare only the cash flows from operating activities section of the statement of cash flows using the *indirect* method. The income tax expenses and tax paid for the year are the same.

Exercise 16-6
Cash flows from operating activities (indirect)
P2

BEKHAM COMPANY
Income Statement
For Year Ended December 31, 2015

Sales		$1,818,000
Cost of goods sold		891,000
Gross profit		927,000
Operating expenses		
Salaries expense	$248,535	
Depreciation expense	43,200	
Rent expense	48,600	
Amortization expenses—Patents	5,400	
Utilities expense	19,125	364,860
		562,140
Gain on sale of equipment		7,200
profit before tax		$ 569,340
Income tax expense		$ 10,000
Net profit		$ 559,340

Changes in current asset and current liability accounts for the year that relate to operations follow.

Accounts receivable	$40,500 increase	Accounts payable	$13,500 decrease
Merchandise inventory	27,000 increase	Salaries payable	4,500 decrease

Exercise 16-7^A
Cash flows from operating
activities (direct) **P4**

Refer to the information about Bekham Company in Exercise 16-6.
Use the *direct method* to prepare only the cash from or used in operating activities section of the statement
of cash flows for this company.

Exercise 16-8
Cash flows from investing
activities

P3

Use the following information to determine this company's cash flows from investing activities.

a. Sold land costing $315,000 for $400,000 cash, yielding a gain of $15,000.

b. Paid $106,000 cash for a new truck.

c. Equipment with a carrying amount of $80,500 and an original cost of $165,000 was sold at a loss of $34,000.

d. Long-term investments in shares were sold for $94,700 cash, yielding a gain of $15,750.

Exercise 16-9
Cash flows from financing
activities

P3

Use the following information to determine this company's cash flows from financing activities.

a. Net profit was $472,000.

b. Issued ordinary shares for $75,000 cash.

c. Paid cash dividend of $13,000. Assume this is classified as financing.

d. Paid $120,000 cash to settle a note payable at its $120,000 maturity value.

e. Paid $118,000 cash to acquire its treasury shares.

f. Purchased equipment for $92,000 cash.

Exercise 16-10
Preparation of statement of
cash flows (indirect) **P1**

Use the following financial statements and additional information to (1) prepare a statement of cash flows
for the year ended June 30, 2015, using the *indirect method,* and (2) compute the company's cash flow on
total assets ratio for its financial year 2015.

GECKO INC. Comparative Statements of Financial Position June 30, 2015 and 2014		
	2015	**2014**
Assets		
Cash	$ 85,800	$ 45,000
Accounts receivable, net	70,000	52,000
Inventory	66,800	96,800
Prepaid expenses	5,400	5,200
Equipment	130,000	120,000
Accum. depreciation—Equipment	(28,000)	(10,000)
Total assets	$330,000	$309,000
Liabilities and Equity		
Accounts payable	$ 26,000	$ 32,000
Wages payable	7,000	16,000
Income tax payable	2,400	3,600
Notes payable (long term)	40,000	70,000
Share capital—Ordinary, $5 par value	230,000	180,000
Retained earnings	24,600	7,400
Total liabilities and equity	$330,000	$309,000

GECKO INC. Income Statement For Year Ended June 30, 2015		
Sales		$668,000
Cost of goods sold		412,000
Gross profit		256,000
Operating expenses		
Depreciation expense	$58,600	
Other expenses	67,000	
Total operating expenses		125,600
		130,400
Other gains (losses)		
Gain on sale of equipment		2,000
Profit before tax		132,400
Income tax expense		45,640
Net profit		$ 86,760

Additional Information

a. A $30,000 note payable is retired at its $30,000 carrying amount in exchange for cash.

b. The only changes affecting retained earnings are net profit and cash dividends paid. Cash dividends are classified as financing.

c. New equipment is acquired for $58,600 cash.

d. Received cash for the sale of equipment that had cost $48,600, yielding a $2,000 gain.

e. Prepaid Expenses and Wages Payable relate to Other Expenses on the income statement.

f. All purchases and sales of merchandise inventory are on credit.

Check   (b) Cash dividends, $69,560

(d) Cash from equip. sale, $10,000

Refer to the data in Exercise 16-10.

Using the *direct method,* prepare the statement of cash flows for the year ended June 30, 2015.

Exercise 16-11^A

Preparation of statement of cash flows (direct)

P1

Use the following information about the cash flows of Kansas Company to prepare a complete statement of cash flows (*direct method*) for the year ended December 31, 2015. Use a note disclosure for any noncash investing and financing activities. Assume that interest received is classified as operating and cash dividends paid is classified as financing.

Exercise 16-12^A

Preparation of statement of cash flows (direct) and supporting note

P1

Cash and cash equivalents balance, December 31, 2014	$ 25,000
Cash and cash equivalents balance, December 31, 2015	70,000
Cash received as interest	2,500
Cash paid for salaries	72,500
Bonds payable retired by issuing ordinary shares (no gain or loss on retirement)	187,500
Cash paid to retire long-term notes payable.	125,000
Cash received from sale of equipment	61,250
Cash received in exchange for six-month note payable	25,000
Land purchased by issuing long-term note payable	106,250
Cash paid for store equipment	23,750
Cash dividends paid	15,000
Cash paid for other expenses	40,000
Cash received from customers	485,000
Cash paid for merchandise	252,500

The following summarized Cash T-account reflects the total debits and total credits to the Cash account of Texas Corporation for calendar year 2015.

(1) Use this information to prepare a complete statement of cash flows for year 2015. The cash from or used in operating activities should be reported using the *direct method.* The management of Texas Corporation wants to classify receipts from dividends and payments for interest as operating activities, and payments for dividends as financing activities.

(2) Refer to the statement of cash flows prepared for part 1 to answer the following questions *a* through *d*: (*a*) Which section—operating, investing, or financing—shows the largest cash (i) inflow and (ii) outflow? (*b*) What is the largest individual item among the investing cash outflows? (*c*) Are the cash proceeds larger from issuing notes or issuing shares? (*d*) Does the company have a net cash inflow or outflow from borrowing activities?

Exercise 16-13^A

Preparation of statement of cash flows (direct) from Cash T-account

P1

Accounting System: ▫◻✕

File Edit Maintain Tasks Analysis Options Reports Window Help

Cash			
Balance, Dec. 31, 2014	135,200		
Receipts from customers	6,000,000	Payments for merchandise	1,590,000
Receipts from dividends	208,400	Payments for wages	550,000
Receipts from land sale	220,000	Payments for rent	320,000
Receipts from machinery sale	710,000	Payments for interest	218,000
Receipts from issuing shares	1,540,000	Payments for tax	450,000
Receipts from borrowing	2,600,000	Payments for machinery	2,236,000
		Payments for long-term investments	2,260,000
		Payments for note payable	386,000
		Payments for dividends	500,000
		Payments for treasury shares	218,000
Balance, Dec. 31, 2015	$?		

Sales   Purchases   General Ledger   Payroll   Inventory   Company   Analysis

Exercise 16-14
Reporting cash flows from
operations (indirect)
P2

Harold Company reports the following information for its recent calendar year.

Sales	$70,000
Expenses	
Cost of goods sold	40,000
Salaries expense	12,000
Depreciation expense	6,000
Net profit........................	$12,000
Accounts receivable increase.........	$ 9,000
Inventory decrease	3,000
Salaries payable increase	800

Required

Prepare the operating activities section of the statement of cash flows for Harold Company using the indirect method. The company did not have any tax expense or paid tax for the year.

Exercise 16-15
Reporting and interpreting cash
flows from operations (indirect)
P2

Oregon Company disclosed the following information for its recent calendar year.

Revenues	$100,000
Expenses	
Salaries expense	68,000
Utilities expense	28,000
Depreciation expense	29,200
Other expenses	6,800
Net loss	$ (32,000)
Accounts receivable decrease	$ 28,000
Purchased a machine	20,000
Salaries payable increase	26,000
Other accrued liabilities decrease	16,000

Required

1. Prepare the operating activities section of the statement of cash flows using the indirect method. The company did not have any tax expense or paid tax for the year.
2. What were the major reasons that this company was able to report a net loss but positive cash flow from operations?
3. Of the potential causes of differences between cash flow from operations and net profit, which are the most important to investors?

Exercise 16-16
Analyses of cash flow on
total assets   A1

A company reported average total assets of $248,000 in 2014 and $302,000 in 2015. Its net operating cash flow in 2014 was $20,575 and $27,750 in 2015. Calculate its cash flow on total assets ratio for both years. Comment on the results and any change in performance.

connect

Kazaam Company, a merchandiser, recently completed its calendar-year 2015 operations. For the year, (1) all sales are credit sales, (2) all credits to Accounts Receivable reflect cash receipts from customers, (3) all purchases of inventory are on credit, (4) all debits to Accounts Payable reflect cash payments for inventory, and (5) Other Expenses are paid in advance and are initially debited to Prepaid Expenses. The company's statements of financial position and income statement follow.

PROBLEM SET A

Problem 16-1A
Statement of cash flows (indirect method)

A1 P1 P2 P3

KAZAAM COMPANY
Comparative Statements of Financial Position
December 31, 2015 and 2014

	2015	2014
Assets		
Cash	$ 53,875	$ 76,625
Accounts receivable	65,000	49,625
Merchandise inventory	273,750	252,500
Prepaid expenses	5,375	6,250
Equipment	159,500	110,000
Accum. depreciation—Equipment	(34,625)	(44,000)
Total assets	$522,875	$451,000
Liabilities and Equity		
Accounts payable	$ 88,125	$116,625
Short-term notes payable	10,000	6,250
Long-term notes payable	93,750	53,750
Share capital—Ordinary, $5 par value	168,750	156,250
Share premium—Ordinary	32,500	0
Retained earnings	129,750	118,125
Total liabilities and equity	$522,875	$451,000

KAZAAM COMPANY
Income Statement
For Year Ended December 31, 2015

Sales		$496,250
Cost of goods sold		250,000
Gross profit		246,250
Operating expenses		
Depreciation expense	$ 18,750	
Other expenses.................	136,500	155,250
Other gains (losses)		
Loss on sale of equipment		5,125
Profit before tax....................		85,875
Income tax expense		12,125
Net profit.........................		$ 73,750

Additional Information on Year 2015 Transactions

a. The loss on the cash sale of equipment was $5,125 (details in *b*).

b. Sold equipment costing $46,875, with accumulated depreciation of $28,125, for $13,625 cash.

c. Purchased equipment costing $96,375 by paying $25,000 cash and signing a long-term note payable for the balance.

d. Borrowed $3,750 cash by signing a short-term note payable.

e. Paid $31,375 cash to reduce the long-term notes payable.

f. Issued 2,500 ordinary shares for $18 cash per share.

g. Declared and paid cash dividends of $62,125. The company's management wants to classify payments for dividends as financing activities.

Required

1. Prepare a complete statement of cash flows; report its operating activities using the *indirect method*. Disclose any noncash investing and financing activities in a note.

Check Cash from operating activities, $33,375

Analysis Component

2. Analyze and discuss the statement of cash flows prepared in part 1, giving special attention to the wisdom of the cash dividend payment.

Refer to Kazaam Company's financial statements and related information in Problem 16-1A.

Required

Prepare a complete statement of cash flows; report its operating activities according to the *direct method*. Disclose any noncash investing and financing activities in a note.

Problem 16-2A^A
Statement of cash flows (direct method) P1 P3 P4

Check Cash used in financing activities, $(44,750)

Problem 16-3A
Statement of cash flows
(indirect method)

P1 P2 P3

www.mheducation.asia/olc/wildkwokFAP

Galley Corp., a merchandiser, recently completed its 2015 operations. For the year, (1) all sales are credit sales, (2) all credits to Accounts Receivable reflect cash receipts from customers, (3) all purchases of inventory are on credit, (4) all debits to Accounts Payable reflect cash payments for inventory, (5) Other Expenses are all cash expenses, and (6) any change in Income Tax Payable reflects the accrual and cash payment of tax. The company's statements of financial position and income statement follow.

GALLEY CORPORATION
Comparative Statements of Financial Position
December 31, 2015 and 2014

	2015	2014
Assets		
Cash	$ 174,000	$117,000
Accounts receivable	93,000	81,000
Merchandise inventory	609,000	534,000
Equipment	333,000	297,000
Accum. depreciation—Equipment	(156,000)	(102,000)
Total assets	$1,053,000	$927,000
Liabilities and Equity		
Accounts payable	$ 69,000	$ 96,000
Income tax payable	27,000	24,000
Share capital—Ordinary, $2 par value	582,000	558,000
Share premium—Ordinary	198,000	162,000
Retained earnings	177,000	87,000
Total liabilities and equity	$1,053,000	$927,000

GALLEY CORPORATION
Income Statement
For Year Ended December 31, 2015

Sales		$1,992,000
Cost of goods sold		1,194,000
Gross profit		798,000
Operating expenses		
Depreciation expense	$ 54,000	
Other expenses	501,000	555,000
Profit before tax		243,000
Income tax expense		42,000
Net profit		$ 201,000

Additional Information on Year 2015 Transactions

a. Purchased equipment for $36,000 cash.

b. Issued 12,000 ordinary shares for $5 cash per share.

c. Declared and paid $111,000 in cash dividends. The company's management wants to classify payments for dividends as financing activities.

Check Cash from operating activities, $144,000

Required

Prepare a complete statement of cash flows; report its cash inflows and cash outflows from operating activities according to the *indirect method*.

Problem 16-4A[A]
Statement of cash flows (direct method) P1 P3 P4

www.mheducation.asia/olc/wildkwokFAP

Check Cash used in financing activities, $(51,000)

Refer to Galley Corporation's financial statements and related information in Problem 16-3A.

Required

Prepare a complete statement of cash flows; report its cash flows from operating activities according to the *direct method*.

Problem 16-5A
Computing cash flows from operations (indirect)

P2

Rapture Company's 2015 income statement and selected statement of financial position data at December 31, 2014 and 2015, follow ($ thousands).

RAPTURE COMPANY Selected Statement of Financial Position Accounts		
At December 31	**2015**	**2014**
Accounts receivable	$380	$390
Inventory	99	77
Accounts payable...........	120	130
Salaries payable	44	35
Utilities payable	11	8
Prepaid insurance	13	14
Prepaid rent	11	9

RAPTURE COMPANY Income Statement For Year Ended December 31, 2015	
Sales revenue	$58,600
Expenses	
Cost of goods sold	21,000
Depreciation expense	6,000
Salaries expense	11,000
Rent expense	2,500
Insurance expense	1,900
Interest expense	1,800
Utilities expense	1,400
Net profit.....................	$13,000

Required

Prepare the cash flows from operating activities section only of the company's 2015 statement of cash flows using the indirect method. The company's income is tax-exempt due to a concession from the government to encourage its type of business.

Check Cash from operating activities, $18,989

Refer to the information in Problem 16-5A.

Problem 16-6A[A]
Computing cash flows from operations (direct)
P4

Required

Prepare the cash flows from operating activities section only of the company's 2015 statement of cash flows using the direct method. The company's profit is tax-exempt due to a concession from the government to encourage its type of business.

Kite Corporation, a merchandiser, recently completed its calendar-year 2015 operations. For the year, (1) all sales are credit sales, (2) all credits to Accounts Receivable reflect cash receipts from customers, (3) all purchases of inventory are on credit, (4) all debits to Accounts Payable reflect cash payments for inventory, and (5) Other Expenses are paid in advance and are initially debited to Prepaid Expenses. The company's statements of financial position and income statement follow.

PROBLEM SET B

Problem 16-1B
Statement of cash flows (indirect method)
A1 P1 P2 P3

KITE CORPORATION Income Statement For Year Ended December 31, 2015		
Sales		$1,083,000
Cost of goods sold		585,000
Gross profit		498,000
Operating expenses		
Depreciation expense	$ 36,600	
Other expenses	392,850	
Total operating expenses		429,450
		68,550
Other gains (losses)		
Loss on sale of equipment		2,100
Profit before tax....................		66,450
Income tax expense		9,450
Net profit.......................		$ 57,000

KITE CORPORATION Comparative Statements of Financial Position December 31, 2015 and 2014		
	2015	**2014**
Assets		
Cash	$136,500	$ 71,550
Accounts receivable	74,100	90,750
Merchandise inventory	454,500	490,200
Prepaid expenses	17,100	19,200
Equipment	278,250	216,000
Accum. depreciation—Equipment	(108,750)	(93,000)
Total assets	$851,700	$794,700
Liabilities and Equity		
Accounts payable	$117,450	$123,450
Short-term notes payable	17,250	11,250
Long-term notes payable	112,500	82,500
Share capital—Ordinary, $5 par value......	465,000	450,000
Share premium—Ordinary	18,000	0
Retained earnings	121,500	127,500
Total liabilities and equity	$851,700	$794,700

Additional Information on Year 2015 Transactions

a. The loss on the cash sale of equipment was $2,100 (details in *b*).

b. Sold equipment costing $51,000, with accumulated depreciation of $20,850, for $28,050 cash.

c. Purchased equipment costing $113,250 by paying $38,250 cash and signing a long-term note payable for the balance.

d. Borrowed $6,000 cash by signing a short-term note payable.

e. Paid $45,000 cash to reduce the long-term notes payable.

f. Issued 3,000 ordinary shares for $11 cash per share.

g. Declared and paid cash dividends of $63,000. The company's management wants to classify payments for dividends as financing activities.

Check Cash from operating activities, $144,150

Required

1. Prepare a complete statement of cash flows; report its operating activities using the *indirect method*. Disclose any noncash investing and financing activities in a note.

Analysis Component

2. Analyze and discuss the statement of cash flows prepared in part 1, giving special attention to the wisdom of the cash dividend payment.

Problem 16-2B[A]
Statement of cash flows
(direct method) **P1 P3 P4**

Check Cash used in financing activities, $(69,000)

Refer to Kite Corporation's financial statements and related information in Problem 16-1B.

Required

Prepare a complete statement of cash flows; report its operating activities according to the *direct method*. Disclose any noncash investing and financing activities in a note.

Problem 16-3B
Statement of cash flows
(indirect method)

P1 P2 P3

Taurasi Company, a merchandiser, recently completed its 2015 operations. For the year, (1) all sales are credit sales, (2) all credits to Accounts Receivable reflect cash receipts from customers, (3) all purchases of inventory are on credit, (4) all debits to Accounts Payable reflect cash payments for inventory, (5) Other Expenses are cash expenses, and (6) any change in Income Tax Payable reflects the accrual and cash payment of tax. The company's statements of financial position and income statement follow.

TAURASI COMPANY
Comparative Statements of Financial Position
December 31, 2015 and 2014

	2015	2014
Assets		
Cash	$ 53,925	$ 31,800
Accounts receivable	19,425	23,250
Merchandise inventory	175,350	139,875
Equipment	105,450	76,500
Accum. depreciation—Equipment	(48,300)	(30,600)
Total assets	$305,850	$240,825
Liabilities and Equity		
Accounts payable	$ 38,475	$ 35,625
Income tax payable	4,500	6,750
Share capital—Ordinary, $2 par value	165,000	150,000
Share premium—Ordinary	42,000	15,000
Retained earnings	55,875	33,450
Total liabilities and equity	$305,850	$240,825

TAURASI COMPANY
Income Statement
For Year Ended December 31, 2015

Sales		$609,750
Cost of goods sold		279,000
Gross profit		330,750
Operating expenses		
Depreciation expense	$ 17,700	
Other expenses	179,775	197,475
Profit before tax		133,275
Income tax expense		44,850
Net profit		$ 88,425

Additional Information on Year 2015 Transactions

a. Purchased equipment for $28,950 cash.

b. Issued 3,000 ordinary shares for $14 cash per share.

c. Declared and paid $66,000 of cash dividends. The company's management wants to classify payments for dividends as financing activities.

Required

Prepare a complete statement of cash flows; report its cash inflows and cash outflows from operating activities according to the *indirect method*.

Check Cash from operating activities, $75,075

Refer to Taurasi Company's financial statements and related information in Problem 16-3B.

Required

Prepare a complete statement of cash flows; report its cash flows from operating activities according to the *direct method*.

Problem 16-4B[A]
Statement of cash flows (direct method) P1 P3 P4

Check Cash used by financing activities, $(24,000)

Tyra Company's 2015 income statement and selected statement of financial position data at December 31, 2014 and 2015, follow ($ thousands).

Problem 16-5B
Computing cash flows from operations (indirect)
P2

TYRA COMPANY Income Statement For Year Ended December 31, 2015	
Sales revenue	$412,000
Expenses	
Cost of goods sold	244,000
Depreciation expense	64,000
Salaries expense	30,000
Rent expense	20,000
Insurance expense	5,200
Interest expense	4,800
Utilities expense	4,000
Net profit.	$ 40,000

TYRA COMPANY Selected Statement of Financial Position Accounts		
At December 31	2015	2014
Accounts receivable	$820	$700
Inventory	272	296
Accounts payable	480	520
Salaries payable	280	220
Utilities payable	40	0
Prepaid insurance	28	36
Prepaid rent	40	60

Required

Prepare the cash flows from operating activities section only of the company's 2015 statement of cash flows using the indirect method. The company's profit is tax-exempt due to a concession from the government to encourage its type of business.

Check Cash from operating activities, $103,992

Refer to the information in Problem 16-5B.

Required

Prepare the cash flows from operating activities section only of the company's 2015 statement of cash flows using the direct method.

Problem 16-6B[A]
Computing cash flows from operations (direct)
P4

(This serial problem began in Chapter 1 and continues through most of the book. If previous chapter segments were not completed, the serial problem can begin at this point.)

SERIAL PROBLEM
Business Solutions
P1 P2 P3

SP 16 Santana Rey, owner of Business Solutions, decides to prepare a statement of cash flows for her business. (Although the serial problem allowed for various ownership changes in earlier chapters, we will prepare the statement of cash flows using the following financial data.)

BUSINESS SOLUTIONS
Comparative Statements of Financial Position
December 31, 2015, and March 31, 2016

	2016	2015
Assets		
Cash	$ 68,057	$48,372
Accounts receivable	22,867	5,668
Merchandise inventory	704	0
Computer supplies	2,005	580
Prepaid insurance	1,110	1,665
Prepaid rent	825	825
Office equipment	8,000	8,000
Accumulated depreciation—Office equipment	(800)	(400)
Computer equipment	20,000	20,000
Accumulated depreciation—Computer equipment	(2,500)	(1,250)
Total assets	$120,268	$83,460
Liabilities and Equity		
Accounts payable	$ 0	$ 1,100
Wages payable	875	500
Unearned computer service revenue	0	1,500
Share capital	98,000	73,000
Retained earnings	21,393	7,360
Total liabilities and equity	$120,268	$83,460

BUSINESS SOLUTIONS
Income Statement
For Three Months Ended March 31, 2016

Computer services revenue		$25,307
Net sales		18,693
Total revenue		44,000
Cost of goods sold	$14,052	
Depreciation expense—Office equipment	400	
Depreciation expense—Computer equipment	1,250	
Wages expense	3,250	
Insurance expense	555	
Rent expense	2,475	
Computer supplies expense	1,305	
Advertising expense	600	
Mileage expense	320	
Repairs expense—Computer	960	
Total expenses		25,167
Net profit		$18,833

Required

Prepare a statement of cash flows for Business Solutions using the *indirect method* for the three months ended March 31, 2016. Recall that the owner Santana Rey contributed $25,000 to the business in exchange for additional shares in the first quarter of 2016 and has received $4,800 in cash dividends. The company's profit is tax-exempt due to a concession from the government to encourage its type of business. Classify cash paid for dividends as financing activities.

Check Cash flows used by operations: $(515)

Beyond the Numbers

REPORTING IN ACTION

A1

BTN 16-1   Refer to Nestlé's consolidated cash flow statement in Appendix A.

Required

1. Is Nestlé's consolidated statement of cash flows prepared under the direct method or the indirect method? How do you know?

2. For each financial year 2013 and 2012, is the amount of operating cash flow larger or smaller than the dividends paid?

3. Identify the largest cash flows for investing and for financing activities in 2013 and in 2012.

Fast Forward

4. Obtain Nestlé's financial statements for financial years ending after December 31, 2013 from its Website (www.nestle.com). Since December 31, 2013, what are Nestlé's largest cash outflows and cash inflows in the investing and in the financing sections of its statement of cash flows?

BTN 16-2 Key comparative figures for Adidas and Puma are as follows:

COMPARATIVE ANALYSIS

A1

	Adidas (in EUR millions)			Puma (in EUR millions)		
	Current Year	One Year Prior	Two Years Prior	Current Year	One Year Prior	Two Years Prior
Operating cash flows	634	942	807	109.3	156.7	126.8
Total assets	11,599	11,651	11,237	2,308.5	2,530.3	2,581.8

Required

1. Compute the recent two years' cash flow on total assets ratios for both Adidas and Puma.
2. What does the cash flow on total assets ratio measure?
3. Which company has the higher cash flow on total assets ratio for the periods shown?
4. Does the cash flow on total assets ratio reflect the quality of earnings? Explain.

BTN 16-3 Lisa Gish is preparing for a meeting with her banker. Her business is finishing its fourth year of operations. In the first year, it had negative cash flows from operations. In the second and third years, cash flows from operations were positive. However, inventory costs rose significantly in year 4, and cash flows from operations will probably be down 25%. Gish wants to secure a line of credit from her banker as a financing buffer. From experience, she knows the banker will scrutinize operating cash flows for years 1 through 4 and will want a projected number for year 5. Gish knows that a steady progression upward in operating cash flows for years 1 through 4 will help her case. She decides to use her discretion as owner and considers several business actions that will turn her operating cash flow in year 4 from a decrease to an increase.

ETHICS CHALLENGE

C1 A1

Required

1. Identify two business actions Gish might take to improve cash flows from operations.
2. Comment on the ethics and possible consequences of Gish's decision to pursue these actions.

BTN 16-4 Your friend, Jessica Willard, recently completed the second year of her business and just received annual financial statements from her accountant. Willard finds the income statement and statement of financial position informative but does not understand the statement of cash flows. She says the first section is especially confusing because it contains a lot of additions and subtractions that do not make sense to her. Willard adds, "The income statement tells me the business is more profitable than last year and that's most important. If I want to know how cash changes, I can look at comparative statements of financial position."

COMMUNICATING IN PRACTICE

C1

Required

Write a half-page memorandum to your friend explaining the purpose of the statement of cash flows. Speculate as to why the first section is so confusing and how it might be rectified.

BTN 16-5 Access L'Oréal's financial statements at its Website (www.loreal-finance.com/eng).

TAKING IT TO THE NET

A1

Required

1. Does L'Oréal use the direct or indirect method to construct its consolidated statement of cash flows?
2. For the financial year ended December 31, 2013, what is the largest item in reconciling the profit to net cash from operating activities?
3. For the last three years, has the company been more successful in generating cash from operating activities than in generating profit?
4. In the year ended December 31, 2013, did the company acquire long-term assets? If so, how much?
5. In the year ended December 31, 2013, did the company pay out cash dividends? If so, how much?

TEAMWORK IN ACTION

C1   A1   P2   P4

BTN 16-6   Team members are to coordinate and independently answer one question within each of the following three sections. Team members should then report to the team and confirm or correct teammates' answers.

1. Answer *one* of the following questions about the statement of cash flows.

    a. What are this statement's reporting objectives?

    b. What two methods are used to prepare it? Identify similarities and differences between them.

    c. What steps are followed to prepare the statement?

    d. What types of analyses are often made from this statement's information?

2. Identify and explain the adjustment from net profit to obtain cash flows from operating activities using the indirect method for *one* of the following items.

    a. Noncash operating revenues and expenses.

    b. Nonoperating gains and losses.

    c. Increases and decreases in noncash current assets.

    d. Increases and decreases in current liabilities.

Note: For teams of more than four, some pairing within teams is necessary. Use as an in-class activity or as an assignment. If used in class, specify a time limit on each part. Conclude with reports to the entire class, using team rotation. Each team can prepare responses on a transparency.

3.^BIdentify and explain the formula for computing cash flows from operating activities using the direct method for *one* of the following items.

    a. Cash receipts from sales to customers.

    b. Cash paid for merchandise inventory.

    c. Cash paid for wages and operating expenses.

    d. Cash paid for interest and taxes.

ENTREPRENEURIAL DECISION

C1   A1

BTN 16-7   Review the chapter's opener involving **Scrawl Studios**.

Required

1. In a business such as Scrawl Studios, monitoring cash flow is always a priority. Can a profitable business have cash flow lagging behind earnings?

2. Scrawl Studio is a private company. What are potential sources of financing for its future expansion?

C1   A1

BTN 16-8   Jenna and Matt Wilder are completing their second year operating Mountain High, a downhill ski area and resort. Mountain High reports a net loss of $(10,000) for its second year, which includes an $85,000 loss from fire. This past year also involved major purchases of property, plant and equipment for renovation and expansion, yielding a year-end total asset amount of $800,000. Mountain High's net cash outflow for its second year is $(5,000); a summarized version of its statement of cash flows follows:

Net cash flow from operating activities	$295,000
Net cash flow used in investing activities	(310,000)
Net cash flow from financing activities	10,000

Required

Write a one-page memorandum to the Wilders evaluating Mountain High's current performance and assessing its future. Give special emphasis to cash flow data and their interpretation.

ANSWERS TO MULTIPLE CHOICE QUIZ

1. b;

Net profit.	$15,200
Depreciation expense	10,000
Gain on sale of land	(3,000)
Increase in inventory	(1,500)
Increase in accounts payable	2,850
Net cash from operating activities	$23,550

2. c; cash received from sale of machine is reported as an investing activity.

3. c or d; The **IASB** allows cash interest paid to be reported under operating or financing.

4. a; Cash paid for salaries and wages = $255,000 + $8,200 − $10,900 = $252,300

5. e; Increase in inventory = $112,000 − $105,000 = $7,000

    Increase in accounts payable = $101,300 − $98,500 = $2,800

    Cash paid for merchandise = $545,000 + $7,000 − $2,800 = $549,200

17

Financial Statement Analysis

A Look Back

Chapter 16 focused on reporting and analyzing cash inflows and cash outflows. We explained how to prepare, analyze, and interpret the statement of cash flows.

A Look at This Chapter

This chapter emphasizes the analysis and interpretation of financial statement information. We learn to apply horizontal, vertical, and ratio analyses to better understand company performance and financial condition.

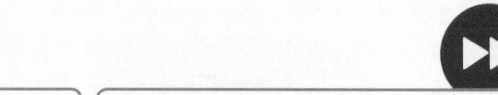

A Look Ahead

Chapter 18 introduces us to managerial accounting. We discuss its purposes, concepts, and roles in helping managers gather and organize information for decisions. We also explain basic management principles.

Learning Objectives

CAP

CONCEPTUAL

C1 Explain the purpose and identify the building blocks of analysis. (p. 660)

C2 Describe standards for comparisons in analysis. (p. 662)

ANALYTICAL

A1 Summarize and report results of analysis. (p. 681)

PROCEDURAL

P1 Explain and apply methods of horizontal analysis. (p. 662)

P2 Describe and apply methods of vertical analysis. (p. 667)

P3 Define and apply ratio analysis. (p. 670)

"It is good for the ordinary man to learn how to use financial information." —**NELSON LAM**

In Good Company

Navigating through the financial maze of a company's accounts, especially in a climate of rapidly changing **IFRS**, can be a daunting affair. Not when you are a client of **Nelson and Company (www.nelsoncpa.com.hk).** Its owner, Nelson Lam, who established the professional accountancy company in Hong Kong, will walk you through complicated figures and tables by using simple layman's language and even highlighting one or two interesting elements in the financial statements to fuel your curiosity. "Showing how financial ratios can help in critical decision making is one of the easiest ways to draw their attention and interest," says Nelson of his clients.

His imaginative approach to an apparently technical subject— "Many regard accounting as a necessary evil," quips Nelson— has no wonder attracted an extensive overseas client base from China and Africa to the United States and France, ranging from garment producers and electronic product manufacturers to property investors and retail chain owners. This, despite the self-acknowledged humble fact: "We are a small CPA company, providing mainly auditing, assurance, and tax services to small and medium companies." For large clients, including listed entities and Fortune 500 companies, instead of auditing services, Nelson and Company provides consultancy and other services in the areas of **IFRS** compliance, income tax evaluation, and corporate training on the new accounting standards.

When he is not donning a business suit, Nelson plays accounting coach to other people who want advice on using financial information through e-mail and Facebook. He even takes phone calls. "It is good for the ordinary man to learn how to use financial information," says Nelson, who is also committed to helping others by sharing his expertise. "It is applicable in every facet of life, from buying food in the supermarket to buying shares in the stock market."

Following Nelson's sage advice, this chapter, besides analyzing financial ratios, introduces horizontal and vertical analyses—tools used to measure a company's performance and to interpret vital trends and insights from financial statements. As Nelson puts it, not only does learning how to use financial information "provide a good framework for sound monetary decisions, it also improves logical and quantitative thinking." What better place to start than here?

This chapter shows how we use financial statements to evaluate a company's financial performance and condition. We explain financial statement analysis, its basic building blocks, the information available, standards for comparisons, and tools of analysis. Three major analysis tools are presented: horizontal analysis, vertical analysis, and ratio analysis. We illustrate the application of each of these tools using **Adidas'** financial statements. We also introduce comparative analysis using **Puma**'s financial statements. This chapter expands and organizes the ratio analyses introduced at the end of each chapter.

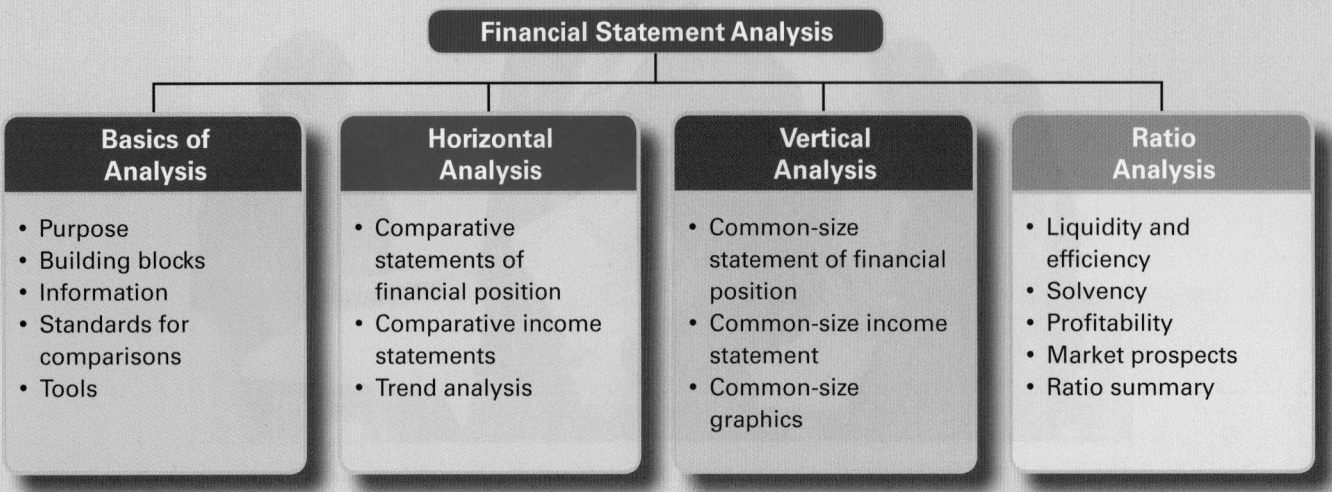

Financial Statement Analysis

Basics of Analysis	Horizontal Analysis	Vertical Analysis	Ratio Analysis
• Purpose • Building blocks • Information • Standards for comparisons • Tools	• Comparative statements of financial position • Comparative income statements • Trend analysis	• Common-size statement of financial position • Common-size income statement • Common-size graphics	• Liquidity and efficiency • Solvency • Profitability • Market prospects • Ratio summary

BASICS OF ANALYSIS

C1 Explain the purpose and identify the building blocks of analysis.

Financial statement analysis applies analytical tools to general-purpose financial statements and related data for making business decisions. It involves transforming accounting data into more useful information. Financial statement analysis reduces our reliance on hunches, guesses, and intuition as well as our uncertainty in decision making. It does not lessen the need for expert judgment; instead, it provides us an effective and systematic basis for making business decisions. This section describes the purpose of financial statement analysis, its information sources, the use of comparisons, and some issues in computations.

Purpose of Analysis

Internal users of accounting information are those involved in strategically managing and operating the company. They include managers, officers, internal auditors, consultants, budget directors, and market researchers. The purpose of financial statement analysis for these users is to provide strategic information to improve company efficiency and effectiveness in providing products and services.

Point: Financial statement analysis tools are also used for personal financial investment decisions.

External users of accounting information are *not* directly involved in running the company. They include shareholders, lenders, directors, customers, suppliers, regulators, lawyers, brokers, and the press. External users rely on financial statement analysis to make better and more informed decisions in pursuing their own goals.

We can identify other uses of financial statement analysis. Shareholders and creditors assess company prospects to make investing and lending decisions. A board of directors analyzes financial statements in monitoring management's decisions. Employees and unions use financial statements in labor negotiations. Suppliers use financial statement information in establishing credit terms. Customers analyze financial statements in deciding whether to establish supply relationships. Public utilities set customer rates by analyzing financial statements. Auditors use financial statements in assessing the "fair presentation" of their clients' financial results. Analyst services such as **Dun & Bradstreet, Moody's,** and **Standard & Poor's** use financial statements in making buy-sell recommendations and in setting credit ratings. The common

Point: Financial statement analysis is a topic on the CPA, CMA, CIA, and CFA exams.

goal of these users is to evaluate company performance and financial condition. This includes evaluating (1) past and current performance, (2) current financial position, and (3) future performance and risk.

Building Blocks of Analysis

Financial statement analysis focuses on one or more elements of a company's financial condition or performance. Our analysis emphasizes four areas of inquiry—with varying degrees of importance. These four areas are described and illustrated in this chapter and are considered the *building blocks* of financial statement analysis:

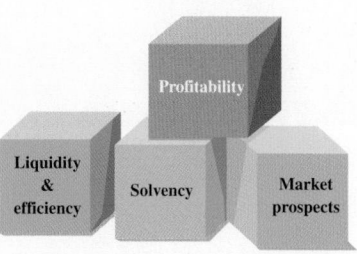

- **Liquidity** and **efficiency**—ability to meet short-term obligations and to efficiently generate revenues.
- **Solvency**—ability to generate future revenues and meet long-term obligations.
- **Profitability**—ability to provide financial rewards sufficient to attract and retain financing.
- **Market prospects**—ability to generate positive market expectations.

Applying the building blocks of financial statement analysis involves determining (1) the objectives of analysis and (2) the relative emphasis among the building blocks. We distinguish among these four building blocks to emphasize the different aspects of a company's financial condition or performance, yet we must remember that these areas of analysis are inter-related. For instance, a company's operating performance is affected by the availability of financing and short-term liquidity conditions. Similarly, a company's credit standing is not limited to satisfactory short-term liquidity but depends also on its profitability and efficiency in using assets. Early in our analysis, we need to determine the relative emphasis of each building block. Emphasis and analysis can later change as a result of evidence collected.

♟ Decision Insight

Chips and Brokers The phrase *blue chips* refers to stock of big, profitable companies. The phrase comes from poker; where the most valuable chips are blue. The term *brokers* refers to those who execute orders to buy or sell stock. The term comes from wine retailers—individuals who broach (break) wine casks. ■

Information for Analysis

Some users, such as managers and regulatory authorities, are able to receive special financial reports prepared to meet their analysis needs. However, most users must rely on the **general-purpose financial statements** that include the (1) statement of profit or loss and comprehensive income (income statement), (2) statement of financial position (balance sheet), (3) statement of changes in equity, (4) statement of cash flows, and (5) notes to these statements.

Financial reporting refers to the communication of financial information useful for making investment, credit, and other business decisions. Financial reporting includes not only general-purpose financial statements but also information from stock exchange filings, press releases, shareholders' meetings, forecasts, management letters, auditors' reports, and Webcasts.

♟ Decision Insight

Analysis Online Many Websites offer free access and screening of companies by key numbers such as earnings, sales, and book value. For instance, **Standard & Poor's** has information for more than 10,000 stocks (**www.standardandpoors.com**). ■

<table>
<tr><td>

C2 Describe standards for comparisons in analysis.
</td></tr>
</table>

Standards for Comparisons

When interpreting measures from financial statement analysis, we need to decide whether the measures indicate good, bad, or average performance. To make such judgments, we need standards (benchmarks) for comparisons that include the following:

● *Intracompany*—The company under analysis can provide standards for comparisons based on its own prior performance and relations between its financial items. **Adidas'** current net profit, for instance, can be compared with its prior years' net profit and in relation to its revenues or total assets.

● *Competitor*—One or more direct competitors of the company being analyzed can provide standards for comparisons. **Adidas'** profit margin, for instance, can be compared with **Puma's** profit margin.

● *Industry*—Industry statistics can provide standards of comparisons. Such statistics are available from services such as **Dun & Bradstreet**, **Standard & Poor's**, and **Moody's**.

● *Guidelines (rules of thumb)*—General standards of comparisons can develop from experience. Examples are the 2:1 level for the current ratio or 1:1 level for the acid-test ratio. Guidelines, or rules of thumb, must be carefully applied because context is crucial.

Point: Each chapter's *Reporting in Action* problems engage students in *intracompany* analysis, whereas *Comparative Analysis* problems require competitor analysis.

All of these comparison standards are useful when properly applied, yet measures taken from a selected competitor or group of competitors are often best. Intracompany and industry measures are also important. Guidelines or rules of thumb should be applied with care, and then only if they seem reasonable given past experience and industry norms.

Tools of Analysis

Three of the most common tools of financial statement analysis are

1. **Horizontal analysis**—Comparison of a company's financial condition and performance across time.
2. **Vertical analysis**—Comparison of a company's financial condition and performance to a base amount.
3. **Ratio analysis**—Measurement of key relations between financial statement items.

The remainder of this chapter describes these analysis tools and how to apply them.

Quick Check   Answers — p. 685

1. Who are the intended users of general-purpose financial statements?
2. General-purpose financial statements consist of what information?
3. Which of the following is *least* useful as a basis for comparison when analyzing ratios? (*a*) Company results from a different economic setting. (*b*) Standards from past experience. (*c*) Rule-of-thumb standards. (*d*) Industry averages.
4. What is the preferred basis of comparison for ratio analysis?

HORIZONTAL ANALYSIS

Analysis of any single financial number is of limited value. Instead, much of financial statement analysis involves identifying and describing relations between numbers, groups of numbers, and changes in those numbers. Horizontal analysis refers to examination of financial statement data *across time*. [The term *horizontal analysis* arises from the left-to-right (or right-to-left) movement of our eyes as we review comparative financial statements across time.]

Comparative Statements

P1 Explain and apply methods of horizontal analysis.

Comparing amounts for two or more successive periods often helps in analyzing financial statements. **Comparative financial statements** facilitate this comparison by showing financial amounts in side-by-side columns on a single statement, called a *comparative format*. Using figures from **Adidas'** financial statements, this section explains how to compute dollar changes and percent changes for comparative statements.

Computation of Dollar Changes and Percent Changes   Comparing financial statements over relatively short time periods—two to three years—is often done by analyzing changes in line items. A change analysis usually includes analyzing absolute dollar amount changes and percent changes. Both analyses are relevant because dollar changes can yield large percent changes inconsistent with their importance. For instance, a 50% change from a base figure of $100 is less important than the same percent change from a base amount of $100,000 in the same statement. Reference to dollar amounts is necessary to retain a proper perspective and to assess the importance of changes. We compute the *dollar change* for a financial statement item as follows:

$$\text{Dollar change} = \text{Analysis period amount} - \text{Base period amount}$$

Analysis period is the point or period of time for the financial statements under analysis, and *base period* is the point or period of time for the financial statements used for comparison purposes. The prior year is commonly used as a base period. We compute the *percent change* by dividing the dollar change by the base period amount and then multiplying this quantity by 100 as follows:

$$\text{Percent change} (\%) = \frac{\text{Analysis period amount} - \text{Base period amount}}{\text{Base period amount}} \times 100$$

We can always compute a dollar change, but we must be aware of a few rules in working with percent changes. To illustrate, look at four separate cases in this chart:

Case	Analysis Period	Base Period	Change Analysis Dollar	Change Analysis Percent
A	$ 1,500	$(4,500)	$ 6,000	—
B	(1,000)	2,000	(3,000)	—
C	8,000	—	8,000	—
D	0	10,000	(10,000)	(100%)

When a negative amount appears in the base period and a positive amount in the analysis period (or vice versa), we cannot compute a meaningful percent change; see cases A and B. Also, when no value is in the base period, no percent change is computable; see case C. Finally, when an item has a value in the base period and zero in the analysis period, the decrease is 100%; see case D.

It is common when using horizontal analysis to compare amounts to either average or median values from prior periods (average and median values smooth out erratic or unusual fluctuations).[1] We also commonly round percents and ratios to one or two decimal places, but practice on this matter is not uniform. Computations are as detailed as necessary, which is judged by whether rounding potentially affects users' decisions. Computations should not be excessively detailed so that important relations are lost among a mountain of decimal points and digits.

Comparative Statements of Financial Position   Comparative statements of financial position consist of statement of financial position amounts from two or more statement of financial position dates arranged side by side. Its usefulness is often improved by showing each item's dollar change and percent change to highlight large changes.

Analysis of comparative financial statements begins by focusing on items that show large dollar or percent changes. We then try to identify the reasons for these changes and, if possible, determine whether they are favorable or unfavorable. We also follow up on items with small changes when we expected the changes to be large.

Example: What is a more significant change, a 70% increase on a $1,000 expense or a 30% increase on a $400,000 expense? *Answer:* The 30% increase.

Example: When there is a value in the base period and zero in the analysis period, the decrease is 100%. Why isn't the reverse situation an increase of 100%? *Answer:* A 100% increase of zero is still zero.

Point: Spreadsheet programs can help with horizontal, vertical, and ratio analyses, including graphical depictions of financial relations.

---

[1] *Median* is the middle value in a group of numbers. For instance, if five prior years' incomes are (in 000s) $15, $19, $18, $20, and $22, the median value is $19. When there are two middle numbers, we can take their average. For instance, if four prior years' sales are (in 000s) $84, $91, $96, and $93, the median is $92 (computed as the average of $91 and $93).

Point: Business consultants use comparative statement analysis to provide management advice.

Exhibit 17.1 shows comparative statements of financial position for **Adidas**. These are based on the consolidated financial numbers which include its subsidiaries' financial numbers. A few items stand out. Most asset categories decrease slightly, which indicates that is not

EXHIBIT 17.1

Comparative Statements of Financial Position

ADIDAS Comparative Statements of Financial Position December 31, 2013 and December 31, 2012				
(in EUR millions)	2013	2012	Euro Change	Percent Change
Cash and cash equivalents	1,587	1,670	(83)	(5.0)
Short-term financial assets	41	265	(224)	(84.5)
Accounts receivable	1,809	1,688	121	7.2
Other current financial assets	183	192	(9)	(4.7)
Inventories	2,634	2,486	148	6.0
Income tax receivables	86	76	10	13.2
Other current assets	506	489	17	3.5
Assets classified as held for sale	11	11	0	0.0
Total current assets	6,857	6,877	(20)	(0.3)
Property, plant and equipment	1,238	1,095	143	13.1
Goodwill	1,204	1,281	(77)	(6.0)
Trademarks	1,419	1,484	(65)	(4.4)
Other intangible assets	164	167	(3)	(1.8)
Long-term financial assets	120	112	8	7.1
Other noncurrent financial assets	30	21	9	42.9
Deferred tax assets	486	528	(42)	(8.0)
Other noncurrent assets	81	86	(5)	(5.8)
Total noncurrent assets	4,742	4,774	(32)	(0.7)
Total assets	11,599	11,651	(52)	(0.4)
Short-term borrowings	681	280	401	143.2
Accounts payable	1,825	1,790	35	2.0
Other current financial liabilities	113	83	30	36.1
Income taxes	240	275	(35)	(12.7)
Other current provisions	450	563	(113)	(20.1)
Current accrued liabilities	1,147	1,084	63	5.8
Other current liabilities	276	299	(23)	(7.7)
Total current liabilities	4,732	4,374	358	8.2
Long-term borrowings	653	1,207	(554)	(45.9)
Other noncurrent financial liabilities	22	17	5	29.4
Pensions and similar obligations	255	251	4	1.6
Deferred tax liabilities	338	368	(30)	(8.2)
Other noncurrent provisions	25	69	(44)	(63.8)
Noncurrent accrued liabilities	64	40	24	60.0
Other noncurrent liabilities	29	34	(5)	(14.7)
Total noncurrent liabilities	1,386	1,986	(600)	(30.2)
Share capital	209	209	0	0.0
Reserves	321	641	(320)	(49.9)
Retained earnings	4,959	4,454	505	11.3
Shareholders' equity	5,489	5,304	185	3.5
Noncontrolling interests	(8)	(13)	5	38.5
Total equity	5,481	5,291	190	3.6
Total liabilities and equity	11,599	11,651	(52)	(0.4)

expanding probably in light of the uncertain global economic environment. Adidas increases its funding from short-term liabilities and decreases its funding from long-term liabilities.

Comparative Income Statements   As Adidas presents its income statement separately from its statement of profit or loss and comprehensive income (allowed under **IFRS**), we will focus on its income statement. Comparative income statements are prepared similarly to comparative statements of financial position. Amounts for two or more periods are placed side by side, with additional columns for dollar and percent changes. Exhibit 17.2 shows Adidas' comparative income statements.

EXHIBIT 17.2

Comparative Income Statements

ADIDAS Comparative Income Statements December 31, 2013 and December 31, 2012				
(in EUR millions, except per share data)	**2013**	**2012**	**Euro Change**	**Percent Change**
Net sales	14,492	14,883	(391)	(2.6)
Cost of sales	7,352	7,780	(428)	(5.5)
Gross profit	7,140	7,103	37	0.5
Royalty and commission income	104	105	(1)	(1.0)
Other operating income	143	127	16	12.6
Other operating expenses	6,133	6,150	(17)	(0.3)
Goodwill impairment losses	52	265	(213)	(80.4)
Operating profit	1,202	920	282	30.7
Financial income	26	36	10	(27.8)
Financial expenses	94	105	(11)	(10.5)
Income before taxes	1,134	851	283	33.3
Income taxes	344	327	17	5.2
Net profit	790	524	266	50.8
Net profit attributable to shareholders	787	526	261	49.6

Adidas' net sales declines slightly in 2013. However, it still manages an increase of about 50% growth in profit (net profit attributable to shareholders). This is primarily due to decreases in cost of sales and goodwill impairment losses.

Trend Analysis

Trend analysis, also called *trend percent analysis* or *index number trend analysis,* is a form of horizontal analysis that can reveal patterns in data across successive periods. It involves computing trend percents for a series of financial numbers and is a variation on the use of percent changes. The difference is that trend analysis does not subtract the base period amount in the numerator. To compute trend percents, we do the following:

1. Select a *base period* and assign each item in the base period a weight of 100%.
2. Express financial numbers as a percent of their base period number.

Specifically, a *trend percent,* also called an *index number,* is computed as follows:

$$\text{Trend percent (\%)} = \frac{\text{Analysis period amount}}{\text{Base period amount}} \times 100$$

Point: *Index* refers to the comparison of the analysis period to the base period. Percents determined for each period are called *index numbers.*

To illustrate trend analysis, we use the **Adidas** data shown in Exhibit 17.3.

EXHIBIT 17.3

Revenue and Expenses

(EUR millions)	2009	2010	2011	2012	2013
Net sales	10,381	11,990	13,344	14,883	14,492
Cost of sales	5,669	6,260	6,344	7,780	7,352

EXHIBIT 17.4

Trend Percents for Revenue and Expenses

(EUR millions)	2009	2010	2011	2012	2013
Net sales	100.0%	115.5%	128.5%	143.4%	139.6%
Cost of sales	100.0%	110.4%	111.9%	137.2%	129.7%

Point: Trend analysis expresses a percent of base, not a percent of change.

Graphical depictions often aid analysis of trend percents. Exhibit 17.5 shows the trend percents from Exhibit 17.4 in a line graph, which can help us identify trends and detect changes in direction or magnitude. It reveals that for years the trend lines are tracking each other closely.

EXHIBIT 17.5

Trend Percent Lines for Revenue and Expenses of Research In Motion

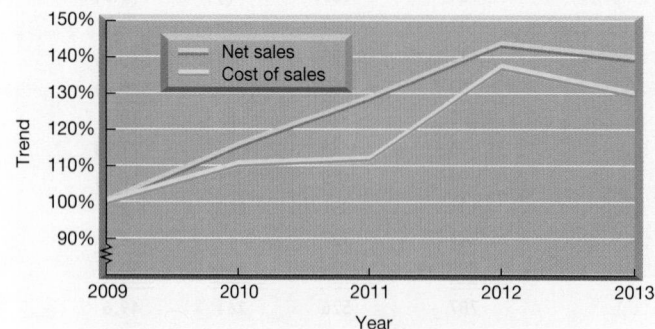

It is important for Adidas to control cost of sales as it is by far its largest cost. The line graph also reveals a consistent increase in each of these accounts which both start to decrease in the latest year.

Exhibit 17.6 compares **Adidas'** sales trend line to that of Puma for this same period.

Trend analysis of financial statement items can include comparisons of relations between items on different financial statements. For instance, Exhibit 17.7 compares Adidas' sales and total assets. The rate of increase in net sales (139.6%) is greater than the increase in total assets (130.7%) since 2009. Is this result favorable or not? It suggests that Adidas was more efficient in using its assets in 2013.

EXHIBIT 17.6

Trend Percent Lines—Adidas vs. Puma

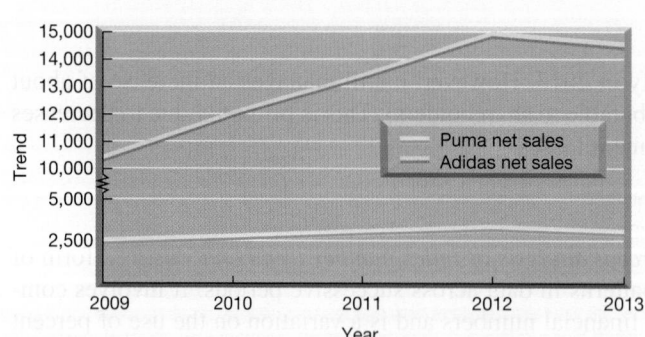

EXHIBIT 17.7

Sales and Asset Data for Adidas

(in EUR millions)	2009	2013	Trend Percent (2013 vs. 2009)
Net sales	10,381	14,492	139.6%
Total assets	8,875	11,599	130.7%

Overall we must remember that an important role of financial statement analysis is identifying questions and areas of interest, which often direct us to important factors bearing on a company's future. Accordingly, financial statement analysis should be seen as a continuous process of refining our understanding and expectations of company performance and financial condition.

Decision Maker   Answer — p. 684

Auditor   Your tests reveal a 3% increase in sales from $200,000 to $206,000 and a 4% decrease in expenses from $190,000 to $182,400. Both changes are within your "reasonableness" criterion of ±5%, and thus you don't pursue additional tests. The audit partner in charge questions your lack of follow-up and mentions the *joint relation* between sales and expenses. To what is the partner referring? ■

VERTICAL ANALYSIS

Vertical analysis is a tool to evaluate individual financial statement items or a group of items in terms of a specific base amount. We usually define a key aggregate figure as the base, which for an income statement is usually revenue and for a statement of financial position is usually total assets. This section explains vertical analysis and applies it to **Adidas**. [The term *vertical analysis* arises from the up-down (or down-up) movement of our eyes as we review common-size financial statements. Vertical analysis is also called *common-size analysis*.]

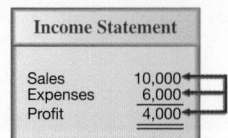

Income Statement	
Sales	10,000
Expenses	6,000
Profit	4,000

Common-Size Statements

The comparative statements in Exhibits 17.1 and 17.2 show the change in each item over time, but they do not emphasize the relative importance of each item. We use **common-size financial statements** to reveal changes in the relative importance of each financial statement item. All individual amounts in common-size statements are redefined in terms of common-size percents. A *common-size percent* is measured by dividing each individual financial statement amount under analysis by its base amount:

P2	Describe and apply methods of vertical analysis.

$$\text{Common-size percent } (\%) = \frac{\text{Analysis amount}}{\text{Base amount}} \times 100$$

Common-Size Statements of Financial Position   Common-size statements express each item as a percent of a *base amount,* which for a common-size statement of financial position is usually total assets. The base amount is assigned a value of 100%. (This implies that the total amount of liabilities plus equity equals 100% since this amount equals total assets.) We then compute a common-size percent for each asset, liability, and equity item using total assets as the base amount. When we present a company's successive statements of financial position in this way, changes in the mixture of assets, liabilities, and equity are apparent.

   Exhibit 17.8 shows common-size comparative statements of financial position for Adidas. Some relations that stand out on both a magnitude and percentage basis include (1) slight increase in inventories which is the largest asset item taking up about one-fifth of total assets; (2) the next two largest asset items are accounts receivable and cash (including cash equivalents); (3) intangible assets of goodwill and trademarks take up about one-fifth of total assets, even higher than property, plant and equipment; (4) a marked decrease in noncurrent liabilities; and (5) a slight increase in retained earnings. Most of these changes are characteristic of a mature stable company. The concern is whether Adidas can continue to generate sufficient revenues and profit in a very competitive industry.

Point: The *base* amount in common-size analysis is an *aggregate* amount from that period's financial statement.

Point: Common-size statements often are used to compare two or more companies in the same industry.

Point: Common-size statements are also useful in comparing firms that report in different currencies.

Common-Size Income Statements   Analysis also benefits from use of a common-size income statement. Revenue is usually the base amount, which is assigned a value of 100%. Each common-size income statement item appears as a percent of revenue. If we think of the 100% revenue amount as representing one sales dollar, the remaining items show how each revenue dollar is distributed among costs, expenses, and profit.

EXHIBIT 17.8

Common-Size Comparative
Statements of Financial Position

ADIDAS Comparative Statements of Financial Position December 31, 2013 and December 31, 2012			Common-Size Percents*	
(in EUR millions)	2013	2012	2013	2012
Cash and cash equivalents	1,587	1,670	13.7%	14.3%
Short-term financial assets.	41	265	0.4%	2.3%
Accounts receivable.	1,809	1,688	15.6%	14.5%
Other current financial assets	183	192	1.6%	1.6%
Inventories	2,634	2,486	22.7%	21.3%
Income tax receivables.	86	76	0.7%	0.7%
Other current assets	506	489	4.4%	4.2%
Assets classified as held for sale.	11	11	0.1%	0.1%
Total current assets.	6,857	6,877	59.1%	59.0%
Property, plant and equipment.	1,238	1,095	10.7%	9.4%
Goodwill.	1,204	1,281	10.4%	11.0%
Trademarks.	1,419	1,484	12.2%	12.7%
Other intangible assets	164	167	1.4%	1.4%
Long-term financial assets	120	112	1.0%	1.0%
Other noncurrent financial assets	30	21	0.3%	0.2%
Deferred tax assets	486	528	4.2%	4.5%
Other noncurrent assets	81	86	0.7%	0.7%
Total noncurrent assets	4,742	4,774	40.9%	41.0%
Total assets	11,599	11,651	100.0%	100.0%
Short-term borrowings	681	280	5.9%	2.4%
Accounts payable	1,825	1,790	15.7%	15.4%
Other current financial liabilities	113	83	1.0%	0.7%
Income taxes	240	275	2.1%	2.4%
Other current provisions.	450	563	3.9%	4.8%
Current accrued liabilities	1,147	1,084	9.9%	9.3%
Other current liabilities	276	299	2.4%	2.6%
Total current liabilities	4,732	4,374	40.8%	37.5%
Long-term borrowings	653	1,207	5.6%	10.4%
Other noncurrent financial liabilities	22	17	0.2%	0.1%
Pensions and similar obligations.	255	251	2.2%	2.2%
Deferred tax liabilities	338	368	2.9%	3.2%
Other noncurrent provisions.	25	69	0.2%	0.6%
Noncurrent accrued liabilities	64	40	0.6%	0.3%
Other noncurrent liabilities	29	34	0.3%	0.3%
Total noncurrent liabilities	1,386	1,986	11.9%	17.0%
Share capital	209	209	1.8%	1.8%
Reserves	321	641	2.8%	5.5%
Retained earnings	4,959	4,454	42.8%	38.2%
Shareholders' equity	5,489	5,304	47.3%	45.5%
Noncontrolling interests	(8)	(13)	−0.1%	−0.1%
Total equity	5,481	5,291	47.3%	45.4%
Total liabilities and equity	11,599	11,651	100.0%	100.0%

* Percents are rounded to tenths and thus may not exactly sum to totals and subtotals.

Exhibit 17.9 shows common-size comparative income statements for each Euro of Adidas' sales. The good news is that Adidas has been able to squeeze an extra EUR 1.9 in earnings per sales Euro—evidenced by the 3.5% to 5.4% rise in earnings as a percentage of sales. This implies that management is effectively controlling costs and/or the company is reaping growth benefits, so-called economies of scale. The other good news is that cost of sales and goodwill impairment losses have decreased as a percentage of sales. Analysis here shows that common-size percents for successive income statements can uncover potentially important changes in a company's expenses. Evidence of no changes, especially when changes are expected, is also informative.

EXHIBIT 17.9

Common-Size Comparative Income Statements

			Common-Size Percents*	
ADIDAS Comparative Income Statements December 31, 2013 and December 31, 2012				
(in EUR millions)	2013	2012	2013	2012
Net sales	14,492	14,883	100.0%	100.0%
Cost of sales	7,352	7,780	50.7%	52.3%
Gross profit	7,140	7,103	49.3%	47.7%
Royalty and commission income	104	105	0.7%	0.7%
Other operating income	143	127	1.0%	0.9%
Other operating expenses	6,133	6,150	42.3%	41.3%
Goodwill impairment losses	52	265	0.4%	1.8%
Operating profit.	1,202	920	8.3%	6.2%
Financial income.	26	36	0.2%	0.2%
Financial expenses	94	105	0.6%	0.7%
Income before taxes	1,134	851	7.8%	5.7%
Income taxes	344	327	2.4%	2.2%
Net profit.	790	524	5.5%	3.5%
Net profit attributable to shareholders	787	526	5.4%	3.5%

* Percents are rounded to tenths and thus may not exactly sum to totals and subtotals.

Common-Size Graphics

Two of the most common tools of common-size analysis are trend analysis of common-size statements and graphical analysis. The trend analysis of common-size statements is similar to that of comparative statements discussed under vertical analysis. It is not illustrated here because the only difference is the substitution of common-size percents for trend percents. Instead, this section discusses graphical analysis of common-size statements.

An income statement readily lends itself to common-size graphical analysis. This is so because revenues affect nearly every item in an income statement. Exhibit 17.10 shows

EXHIBIT 17.10

Common-Size Graphic of Income Statement

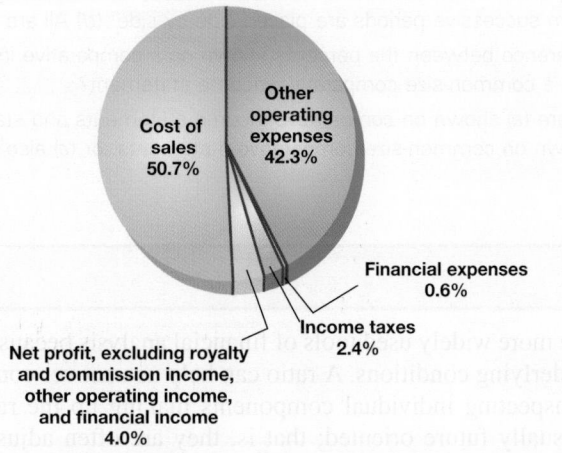

EXHIBIT 17.11

Common-Size Graphic of
Asset Components

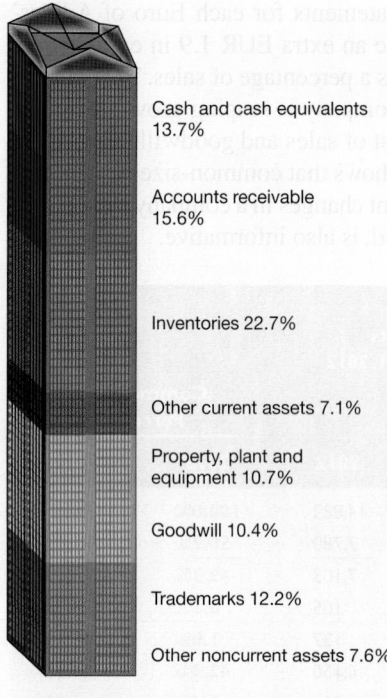

Cash and cash equivalents
13.7%

Accounts receivable
15.6%

Inventories 22.7%

Other current assets 7.1%

Property, plant and
equipment 10.7%

Goodwill 10.4%

Trademarks 12.2%

Other noncurrent assets 7.6%

Adidas' 2013 common-size income statement in graphical form. This pie chart highlights the contribution of each component of sales for operating profit (% do not add exactly to 100 due to rounding).

Graphical analysis is also useful in identifying (1) sources of financing including the distribution among current liabilities, noncurrent liabilities, and equity capital and (2) focuses of investing activities, including the distribution among current and noncurrent assets. To illustrate, Exhibit 17.11 shows a common-size graphical display of Adidas' assets (current asset items of less than 5% are combined as other current assets, similarly for noncurrent assets). Common-size statement of financial position analysis can be extended to examine the composition of these subgroups. For instance, in assessing liquidity of current assets, knowing what proportion of current assets consists of inventories is usually important, and not simply what proportion inventories are of total assets. Common-size financial statements are also useful in comparing different companies. Exhibit 17.12 shows common-size graphics of both Adidas and Puma on financing sources. This graphic highlights the much larger percent of equity financing (and less noncurrent liability financing) for Puma than for Adidas. Comparison of a company's common-size statements with competitors' or industry common-size statistics alerts us to differences in the structure or distribution of its financial statements but not to their dollar magnitude.

EXHIBIT 17.12

Common-Size Graphic of Financing
Sources—Competitor Analysis

Adidas

Equity 47.3%

Noncurrent liabilities 11.9%

Current Liabilities 40.8%

Puma

Equity 64.9%

Noncurrent liabilities 5.2%

Current Liabilities 29.9%

Quick Check
Answers — p. 685

5. Which of the following is true for common-size comparative statements? (a) Each item is expressed as a percent of a base amount. (b) Total assets often are assigned a value of 100%. (c) Amounts from successive periods are placed side by side. (d) All are true. (e) None is true.

6. What is the difference between the percents shown on a comparative income statement and those shown on a common-size comparative income statement?

7. Trend percents are (a) shown on comparative income statements and statements of financial position, (b) shown on common-size comparative statements, or (c) also called *index numbers*.

RATIO ANALYSIS

P3 Define and apply ratio analysis.

Ratios are among the more widely used tools of financial analysis because they provide clues to and symptoms of underlying conditions. A ratio can help us uncover conditions and trends difficult to detect by inspecting individual components making up the ratio. Ratios, like other analysis tools, are usually future oriented; that is, they are often adjusted for their probable future trend and magnitude, and their usefulness depends on skillful interpretation.

A ratio expresses a mathematical relation between two quantities. It can be expressed as a percent, rate, or proportion. For instance, a change in an account balance from $100 to $250 can be expressed as (1) 150% increase, (2) 2.5 times, or (3) 2.5 to 1 (or 2.5:1). Computation of a ratio is a simple arithmetic operation, but its interpretation is not. To be meaningful, a ratio must refer to an economically important relation. For example, a direct and crucial relation exists between an item's sales price and its cost. Accordingly, the ratio of cost of goods sold to sales is meaningful. In contrast, no obvious relation exists between freight costs and the balance of long-term investments.

This section describes an important set of financial ratios and its application. The selected ratios are organized into the four building blocks of financial statement analysis: (1) liquidity and efficiency, (2) solvency, (3) profitability, and (4) market prospects. All of these ratios were explained at relevant points in prior chapters. The purpose here is to organize and apply them under a summary framework. We use four common standards, in varying degrees, for comparisons: intracompany, competitor, industry, and guidelines.

Point: Some sources for industry norms are *Annual Statement Studies* by Robert Morris Associates, *Industry Norms & Key Business Ratios* by Dun & Bradstreet, *Standard & Poor's Industry Surveys*, and Reuters.com/finance.

Liquidity and Efficiency

Liquidity refers to the availability of resources to meet short-term cash requirements. It is affected by the timing of cash inflows and outflows along with prospects for future performance. Analysis of liquidity is aimed at a company's funding requirements. *Efficiency* refers to how productive a company is in using its assets. Efficiency is usually measured relative to how much revenue is generated from a certain level of assets.

Both liquidity and efficiency are important and complementary. If a company fails to meet its current obligations, its continued existence is doubtful. Viewed in this light, all other measures of analysis are of secondary importance. Although accounting measurements assume the company's continued existence, our analysis must always assess the validity of this assumption using liquidity measures. Moreover, inefficient use of assets can cause liquidity problems. A lack of liquidity often precedes lower profitability and fewer opportunities. It can foretell a loss of owner control. To a company's creditors, lack of liquidity can yield delays in collecting interest and principal payments or the loss of amounts due them. A company's customers and suppliers of goods and services also are affected by short-term liquidity problems. Implications include a company's inability to execute contracts and potential damage to important customer and supplier relationships. This section describes and illustrates key ratios relevant to assessing liquidity and efficiency.

Working Capital and Current Ratio The amount of current assets less current liabilities is called **working capital,** or *net working capital.* A company needs adequate working capital to meet current debts, to carry sufficient inventories, and to take advantage of cash discounts. A company that runs low on working capital is less likely to meet current obligations or to continue operating. When evaluating a company's working capital, we must not only look at the dollar amount of current assets less current liabilities, but also at their ratio. The *current ratio* is defined as follows (see Chapter 3 for additional explanation):

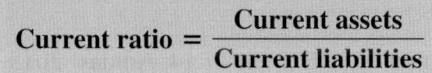

$$\text{Current ratio} = \frac{\text{Current assets}}{\text{Current liabilities}}$$

Drawing on information in Exhibit 17.1, **Adidas'** working capital and current ratio for both 2013 and 2012 are shown in Exhibit 17.13. **Puma's** current ratio of 2.2 is shown in the margin. Adidas' ratio (1.4) is lower than Puma's but does not appear in danger of defaulting on loan payments. A high current ratio suggests a strong liquidity position and an ability to meet current obligations. A company can, however, have a current ratio that is too high. An excessively high current ratio means that the company has invested too much in current assets compared to its current obligations. An excessive investment in current assets is not an efficient use of funds because current assets normally generate a low return on investment (compared with long-term assets).

EXHIBIT 17.13

Adidas' Working Capital and Current Ratio

(in EUR millions)	2013	2012
Current assets	6,857	6,877
Current liabilities	4,732	4,374
Working capital	2,125	2,503
Current ratio		
6,857/4,732	1.4 to 1	
6,877/4,374		1.6 to 1

Puma
Current ratio = 2.2

Many users apply a guideline of 2:1 (or 1.5:1) for the current ratio in helping evaluate a company's debt-paying ability. A company with a 2:1 or higher current ratio is generally thought to be a good credit risk in the short run. Such a guideline or any analysis of the current ratio must recognize at least three additional factors: (1) type of business, (2) composition of current assets, and (3) turnover rate of current asset components.

Type of business.   A service company that grants little or no credit and carries few inventories can probably operate on a current ratio of less than 1:1 if its revenues generate enough cash to pay its current liabilities. On the other hand, a company selling high-priced clothing or furniture requires a higher ratio because of difficulties in judging customer demand and cash receipts. For instance, if demand falls, inventory may not generate as much cash as expected. Accordingly, analysis of the current ratio should include a comparison with ratios from successful companies in the same industry and from prior periods. We must also recognize that a company's accounting methods, especially choice of inventory method, affect the current ratio. For instance, when costs are rising, a company using average method tends to report a smaller amount of current assets than when using FIFO method.

Composition of current assets.   The composition of a company's current assets is important to an evaluation of short-term liquidity. For instance, cash, cash equivalents, and short-term investments are more liquid than accounts and notes receivable. Also, short-term receivables normally are more liquid than inventory. Cash, of course, can be used to immediately pay current debts. Items such as accounts receivable and inventory, however, normally must be converted into cash before payment is made. An excessive amount of receivables and inventory weakens a company's ability to pay current liabilities. The acid-test ratio (see below) can help with this assessment.

Turnover rate of assets.   Asset turnover measures a company's efficiency in using its assets. One relevant measure of asset efficiency is the revenue generated. A measure of total asset turnover is revenues divided by total assets, but evaluation of turnover for individual assets is also useful. We discuss both receivables turnover and inventory turnover on the next page.

▢ Decision Maker   Answer — p. 685

Banker   A company requests a one-year, $200,000 loan for expansion. This company's current ratio is 4:1, with current assets of $160,000. Key competitors carry a current ratio of about 1.9:1. Using this information, do you approve the loan application? Does your decision change if the application is for a 10-year loan? ▪

Acid-Test Ratio   Quick assets are cash, short-term investments, and current receivables. These are the most liquid types of current assets. The *acid-test ratio,* also called *quick ratio,* and introduced in Chapter 5, reflects on a company's short-term liquidity.

$$\text{Acid-test ratio} = \frac{\text{Cash + Short-term investments + Current receivables}}{\text{Current liabilities}}$$

Adidas' acid-test ratio is computed in Exhibit 17.14. Adidas' 2013 acid-test ratio of 0.8 is less than that for Puma of 2.2, as well as less than the 1:1 common guideline for an acceptable

---

EXHIBIT 17.14

Acid-Test Ratio

Puma
Acid-test ratio = 2.2

(in EUR millions)	2013	2012
Cash and cash equivalents	1,587	1,670
Short-term financial assets	41	265
Accounts receivable	1,809	1,688
Other current financial assets	183	192
Total quick assets	3,620	3,815
Current liabilities	4,732	4,374
Acid-test ratio		
3,620/4,732	0.8 to 1	
3,815/4,374		0.9 to 1

acid-test ratio. As with analysis of the current ratio, we need to consider other factors. For instance, the frequency with which a company converts its current assets into cash affects its working capital requirements. This implies that analysis of short-term liquidity should also include an analysis of receivables and inventories, which we consider next.

Accounts Receivable Turnover   We can measure how frequently a company converts its receivables into cash by computing the *accounts receivable turnover*. This ratio is defined as follows (see Chapter 9 for additional explanation):

$$\text{Accounts receivable turnover} = \frac{\text{Net sales}}{\text{Average accounts receivable, net}}$$

Short-term receivables from customers are often included in the denominator along with accounts receivable. Also, accounts receivable turnover is more precise if credit sales are used for the numerator, but external users generally use net sales (or net revenues) because information about credit sales is typically not reported. Adidas' 2013 accounts receivable turnover is computed as follows.

$$\frac{14,492}{(1,809 + 1,688)/2} = 8.3 \text{ times}$$

Adidas' value of 8.3 times is larger than Puma's 6.4. Accounts receivable turnover is high when accounts receivable are quickly collected. A high turnover is favorable because it means the company need not commit large amounts of funds to accounts receivable. However, an accounts receivable turnover can be too high; this can occur when credit terms are so restrictive that they negatively affect sales volume.

Inventory Turnover   How long a company holds inventory before selling it will affect working capital requirements. One measure of this effect is *inventory turnover*, also called *merchandise turnover* or *merchandise inventory turnover*, which is defined as follows (see Chapter 6 for additional explanation):

$$\text{Inventory turnover} = \frac{\text{Cost of goods sold}}{\text{Average inventory}}$$

Using Adidas' cost of goods sold and inventories information, we compute its inventory turnover as follows.

$$\frac{7,352}{(2,634 + 2,486)/2} = 2.9 \text{ times}$$

Adidas' inventory turnover of 2.9 is slightly lower than Puma's 3.0. A company with a high turnover requires a smaller investment in inventory than one producing the same sales with a lower turnover. Inventory turnover can be too high, however, if the inventory a company keeps is so small that it restricts sales volume.

Accounts Payable Turnover   Inventories are often financed by accounts payable. Such payables usually represent interest-free financing and are therefore less expensive than using borrowed money to finance inventory purchases or production. We compute account payable turnover as follows:

$$\text{Accounts payable turnover} = \frac{\text{Cost of goods sold}}{\text{Average accounts payable}}$$

Point: As two points do not always accurately represent changes in inventory, average inventory can be calculated by using 13 points. We could use the end of each month over the course of one financial year, including the base month. These points are then added together and divided by 13 (the number of points) to determine the average inventory. Another method is to calculate each month's average inventory, adding these figures and dividing by the number of points.

Point: Some users prefer using gross accounts receivable (before subtracting the allowance for doubtful accounts) to avoid the influence of a manager's bad debts estimate.

Puma
Accounts receivable turnover
= 6.4

Point: Ending accounts receivable can be substituted for the average balance in computing accounts receivable turnover if the difference between ending and average receivables is small.

Puma
Inventory turnover = 3.0 times

Like inventories, payables are reported at cost, not retail prices. Thus, for consistency with the denominator, cost of goods sold (not sales) is used in the numerator. All else equal, companies prefer to use this cheap source of financing as much as possible and therefore, have a lower accounts payable turnover (meaning a higher level of payables.)

Adidas' 2013 accounts payable turnover is computed as follows.

Puma
Accounts payable turnover = 4.3 times

$$\frac{7,352}{(1,825 + 1,790)/2} = 4.1 \text{ times}$$

Days' Sales Uncollected Accounts receivable turnover provides insight into how frequently a company collects its accounts. Days' sales uncollected is one measure of this activity, which is defined as follows (Chapter 8 provides additional explanation):

$$\text{Days' sales uncollected} = \frac{\text{Accounts receivable, net}}{\text{Net sales}} \times 365$$

Any short-term notes receivable from customers are normally included in the numerator.

Adidas' 2013 days' sales uncollected follows.

Puma
Day's sales uncollected = 51.8

$$\frac{1,809}{14,492} \times 365 = 45.6 \text{ days}$$

Puma's days' sales uncollected of 51.8 days is longer than the 45.6 days for Adidas. Days' sales uncollected is more meaningful if we know company credit terms. A rough guideline states that days' sales uncollected should not exceed $1\frac{1}{3}$ times the days in its (1) credit period, *if* discounts are not offered or (2) discount period, *if* favorable discounts are offered.

Days' Sales in Inventory *Days' sales in inventory* is a useful measure in evaluating inventory liquidity. Days' sales in inventory is linked to inventory in a way that days' sales uncollected is linked to receivables. We compute days' sales in inventory as follows (Chapter 6 provides additional explanation).

$$\text{Days' sales in inventory} = \frac{\text{Ending inventory}}{\text{Cost of goods sold}} \times 365$$

Adidas' days' sales in inventory for 2013 follows.

Puma
Day's sales in inventory = 119.1

$$\frac{2,634}{7,352} \times 365 = 130.8 \text{ days}$$

If the products in Adidas' inventory are in demand by customers, this formula estimates that its inventory will be converted into receivables (or cash) in 130.8 days. If all of Adidas' sales were credit sales, the conversion of inventory to receivables in 130.8 days plus the conversion of receivables to cash in 45.6 days implies that inventory will be converted to cash in about 176.4 days (130.8 + 45.6).

Days' Purchases in Accounts Payable In addition to accounts payable turnover, we can compute another ratio, days' purchases in accounts payable.

$$\text{Days' purchases in accounts payable} = \frac{\text{Accounts payable}}{\text{Cost of goods sold}} \times 365$$

Adidas' 2013 days' purchases in accounts payable is computed as follows:

$$\frac{1,825}{7,352} \times 365 = 90.6 \text{ days}$$

Puma
Days' purchases in accounts payable = 85.2

Adidas takes slightly longer (90.6 days) than Puma (85.2 days) to pay its credit suppliers.

Cash Conversion Cycle The cash conversion cycle of a company is defined by the sum of the days' sales uncollected and the days' sales in inventory subtracting the days' purchases in accounts payable. It represents the number of days a firm's cash remains tied up within the operations of the business. It is also a powerful tool for assessing how well a company is managing its working capital. The lower the cash conversion cycle, the more healthy a company generally is.

It is possible for a company to have a negative cash conversion cycle. If this occurs it means that it is selling inventory and collecting receivables before it has to pay its payables. Companies such as Walmart and Dell Computers sell a large part of their inventory before they have to pay for it.

Adidas' cash conversion cycle for 2013 is computed as follows.

Ratio	2013
Days' sales uncollected	45.6
Days' sales in inventory	130.8
Days' purchases in accounts payable	(90.6)
Cash conversion cycle	85.8

Puma
Cash conversion cycle = 85.7

Total Asset Turnover *Total asset turnover* reflects a company's ability to use its assets to generate sales and is an important indication of operating efficiency. The definition of this ratio follows (Chapter 10 offers additional explanation).

$$\text{Total asset turnover} = \frac{\text{Net sales}}{\text{Average total assets}}$$

Adidas' total asset turnover for 2013 follows and is the same as Puma's.

$$\frac{14,492}{(11,599 + 11,651)/2} = 1.2 \text{ times}$$

Puma
Total asset turnover = 1.2

Quick Check Answers — p. 685

8. Information from Paff Co. at Dec. 31, 2014, follows: cash, $820,000; accounts receivable, $240,000; inventories, $470,000; property, plant and equipment, $910,000; accounts payable, $350,000; and income taxes payable, $180,000. Compute its (a) current ratio and (b) acid-test ratio.

9. On Dec. 31, 2015, Paff Company (see question 8) had accounts receivable of $290,000, inventories of $530,000, and accounts payable of $370,000. During 2015, net sales amounted to $2,500,000 and cost of goods sold was $750,000. Compute (a) accounts receivable turnover, (b) days' sales uncollected, (c) inventory turnover, (d) days' sales in inventory, (e) accounts payable turnover, and (f) days' purchases in accounts payable.

Solvency

Solvency refers to a company's long-run financial viability and its ability to cover long-term obligations. All of a company's business activities—financing, investing, and operating—affect its solvency. Analysis of solvency is long term and uses less precise but more encompassing measures than liquidity. One of the most important components of solvency analysis is the composition of a company's capital structure. *Capital structure* refers to a company's financing sources. It ranges from relatively permanent equity financing to riskier or more temporary short-term financing. Assets represent security for financiers, ranging from loans secured by specific assets to the assets available as general security to unsecured creditors. This section describes the tools of solvency analysis. Our analysis focuses on a company's ability to both meet its obligations and provide security to its creditors *over the long run*. Indicators of this ability include *debt* and *equity* ratios, the relation between *pledged assets and secured liabilities,* and the company's capacity to earn sufficient profit to *pay fixed interest charges*.

Point: For analysis purposes, Noncontrolling Interest is usually added to equity.

Debt and Equity Ratios   One element of solvency analysis is to assess the portion of a company's assets contributed by its owners and the portion contributed by creditors. This relation is reflected in the debt ratio (also described in Chapter 2). The *debt ratio* expresses total liabilities as a percent of total assets. The **equity ratio** provides complementary information by expressing total equity as a percent of total assets. **Adidas**' debt and equity ratios follow.

Puma

Debt ratio = 35.1%

Equity ratio = 64.9%

(in EUR millions)	2013	Ratios	
Total liabilities	6,116	52.7%	[Debt ratio]
Total equity	5,481	47.3%	[Equity ratio]
Total liabilities and equity	11,599	100.0%	

Adidas's financial statements reveal more debt than equity. A company is considered less risky if its capital structure (equity and long-term debt) contains more equity. One risk factor is the required payment for interest and principal when debt is outstanding. Another factor is the greater the stockholder financing, the more losses a company can absorb through equity before the assets become inadequate to satisfy creditors' claims. From the shareholders' point of view, if a company earns a return on borrowed capital that is higher than the cost of borrowing, the difference represents increased profit to shareholders. The inclusion of debt is described as *financial leverage* because debt can have the effect of increasing the return to shareholders. Companies are said to be highly leveraged if a large portion of their assets is financed by debt.

Debt-to-Equity Ratio   The ratio of total liabilities to equity is another measure of solvency. We compute the ratio as follows (Chapter 14 offers additional explanation).

$$\text{Debt-to-equity ratio} = \frac{\text{Total liabilities}}{\text{Total equity}}$$

Adidas' debt-to-equity ratio for 2013 is

$$6,116/5,481 = 1.1$$

Puma (Industry)

Debt-to-equity = 0.5

Adidas' 1.1 debt-to-equity ratio is higher than the 0.5 ratio for Puma. Consistent with our inferences from the debt ratio, Adidas' capital structure has more debt than equity, which increases risk. Recall that debt must be repaid with interest, while equity does not. These debt requirements can be burdensome when the industry and/or the economy experience a downturn. A larger debt-to-equity ratio also implies less opportunity to expand through use of debt financing.

Times Interest Earned   The amount of profit before deductions for interest expense and income taxes is the amount available to pay interest expense. The following *times* *interest earned* ratio reflects the creditors' risk of loan repayments with interest (see Chapter 11 for additional explanation).

Point: The times interest earned ratio and the debt and equity ratios are of special interest to bank lending officers.

$$\text{Times interest earned} = \frac{\text{Income before interest expense and income taxes}}{\text{Interest expense}}$$

The larger this ratio, the less risky is the company for creditors. One guideline says that creditors are reasonably safe if the company earns its fixed interest expense two or more times each year. Adidas' times interest earned ratio (also known as interest coverage ratio) follows; its value suggests that its creditors have little risk of nonrepayment.

Puma
Times interest earned = 7.9

$$\frac{1,134 + 73 \text{ (Interest expense from statement of cash flows)}}{73} = 16.5$$

Decision Insight

Bears and Bulls A *bear market* is a declining market. The phrase comes from bear-skin jobbers who often sold the skins before the bears were caught. The term *bear* was then used to describe investors who sold shares they did not own in anticipation of a price decline. A *bull market* is a rising market. This phrase comes from the once popular sport of bear and bull baiting. The term *bull* came to mean the opposite of *bear*. ■

Profitability

We are especially interested in a company's ability to use its assets efficiently to produce profits (and positive cash flows). *Profitability* refers to a company's ability to generate an adequate return on invested capital. Return is judged by assessing earnings relative to the level and sources of financing. Profitability is also relevant to solvency. This section describes key profitability measures and their importance to financial statement analysis.

Profit Margin A company's operating efficiency and profitability can be expressed by two components. The first is *profit margin,* which reflects a company's ability to earn net profit from sales (Chapter 3 offers additional explanation). It is measured by expressing net profit as a percent of sales (*sales* and *revenues* are similar terms). **Adidas**' profit margin follows.

Puma
Profit margin = 0.2%

$$\text{Profit margin} = \frac{\text{Net profit}}{\text{Net sales}} = \frac{787}{14,492} = 5.4\%$$

The numerator is taken from Adidas' net profit attributable to shareholders although some analysts may use the net profit of EUR 790 million, which includes noncontrolling interests.

To evaluate profit margin, we must consider the industry. For instance, an appliance company might require a profit margin between 10% and 15%; whereas a retail supermarket might require a profit margin of 1% or 2%. Both profit margin and *total asset turnover* make up the two basic components of operating efficiency. These ratios reflect on management because managers are ultimately responsible for operating efficiency. The next section explains how we use both measures to analyze return on total assets.

Return on Total Assets *Return on total assets* is defined as follows.

$$\text{Return on total assets} = \frac{\text{Net profit}}{\text{Average total assets}}$$

Adidas' 2013 return on total assets is

Puma
Return on total assets = 0.2%

$$\frac{787}{(11,599 + 11,651)/2} = 6.8\%$$

Point: Many analysts add back *Interest expense* × *(1 − Tax rate)* to net profit in computing return on total assets.

Adidas' 6.8% return on total assets is higher than Puma's return of 0.2%. We also should evaluate any trend in the rate of return.

The following equation shows the important relation between profit margin, total asset turnover, and return on total assets.

$$\text{Profit margin} \times \text{Total asset turnover} = \text{Return on total assets}$$

or

$$\frac{\text{Net profit}}{\text{Net sales}} \times \frac{\text{Net sales}}{\text{Average total assets}} = \frac{\text{Net profit}}{\text{Average total assets}}$$

Both profit margin and total asset turnover contribute to overall operating efficiency, as measured by return on total assets.

Return on Ordinary Shareholders' Equity   Perhaps the most important goal in operating a company is to earn net profit for its owner(s). *Return on ordinary shareholders' equity* measures a company's success in reaching this goal and is defined as follows.

$$\text{Return on ordinary shareholders' equity} = \frac{\text{Net profit} - \text{Preference dividends}}{\text{Average ordinary shareholders' equity}}$$

Adidas' 2013 return on ordinary shareholders' equity is computed as follows:

Puma
Return on ordinary shareholders' equity = 1.4%

$$\frac{787}{(5,481 + 5,291)/2} = 14.6\%$$

The denominator in this computation is the book value of ordinary equity (including any non-controlling interest). In the numerator, the dividends on cumulative preference shares are subtracted whether they are declared or are in arrears. If preference shares are noncumulative, their dividends are subtracted only if declared.

▶ **Decision Insight**

Wall Street   *Wall Street* is synonymous with financial markets, but its name comes from the street location of the original New York Stock Exchange. The street's name derives from stockades built by early settlers to protect New York from pirate attacks. ■

Market Prospects

Market measures are useful for analyzing corporations with publicly traded shares. These market measures use share or stock price, which reflects the market's (public's) expectations for the company. This includes expectations of both company return and risk—as the market perceives it.

Price-Earnings Ratio   Computation of the *price-earnings ratio* follows (Chapter 13 provides additional explanation).

$$\text{Price-earnings ratio} = \frac{\text{Market price per ordinary share}}{\text{Earnings per share}}$$

Point: PE ratio can be viewed as an indicator of the market's expected growth and risk for a share. High expected risk suggests a low PE ratio. High expected growth suggests a high PE ratio.

Predicted earnings per share for the next period is often used in the denominator of this computation. Reported earnings per share for the most recent period is also commonly used. In both cases, the ratio is used as an indicator of the future growth and risk of a company's earnings as perceived by the shares' buyers and sellers.

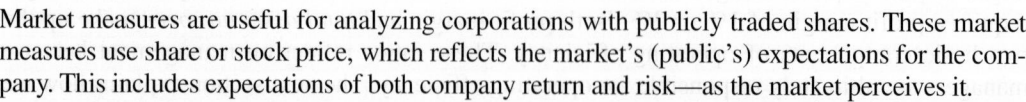

The market price of Adidas' ordinary shares at the end of financial year 2013 was EUR 92.64. Using Adidas' EUR 3.76 basic earnings per share, we compute its price-earnings ratio as follows (some analysts compute this ratio using the median of the low and high share prices):

$$\frac{92.64}{3.76} = 24.6$$

The PE ratio is sometimes referred to as the "multiple", because it shows how much investors are willing to pay per dollar of earnings. Adidas' PE ratio is 24.6; the interpretation is that an investor is willing to pay EUR 24.6 for EUR 1 of current earnings. This ratio is very sensitive to the market price and EPS so Puma's 2013 PE ratio was triple digit as its EPS was very low for that year. Some analysts may thus view Puma's shares as over-valued.

Puma
PE = 652.8

Dividend Yield   *Dividend yield* is used to compare the dividend-paying performance of different investment alternatives. We compute dividend yield for ordinary shares as follows (Chapter 13 offers additional explanation):

$$\text{Dividend yield} = \frac{\textbf{Annual cash dividends per share}}{\textbf{Market price per share}}$$

Adidas' dividend yield, based on its financial year-end market price per share of EUR 92.64 and its policy of EUR 1.50 cash dividends per share, is computed as follows:

$$\frac{1.50}{92.64} = 1.6\%$$

Puma
Dividend yield = 0.2%

Some companies do not declare and pay dividends because they wish to reinvest the cash.

Summary of Ratios

Exhibit 17.15 summarizes the major financial statement analysis ratios illustrated in this chapter and throughout the book. This summary includes each ratio's title, its formula, and the purpose for which it is commonly used.

> **Point:** Some investors avoid shares with high PE ratios under the belief they are "overpriced." Alternatively, some investors sell these shares short—hoping for price declines.

> **Point:** Corporate PE ratios and dividend yields are found in daily stock market quotations listed in *The Wall Street Journal*, *Investor's Business Daily*, or other publications and Web services.

Decision Insight

Ticker Prices   *Ticker prices* refer to a band of moving data on a monitor carrying up-to-the-minute stock prices. The phrase comes from *ticker tape,* a 1-inch-wide strip of paper spewing stock prices from a printer that ticked as it ran. Most of today's investors have never seen actual ticker tape, but the phrase survives. ■

Quick Check   Answers — p. 685

10. Which ratio best reflects a company's ability to meet immediate interest payments? (*a*) Debt ratio. (*b*) Equity ratio. (*c*) Times interest earned.

11. Which ratio best measures a company's success in earning net profit for its owner(s)? (*a*) Profit margin. (*b*) Return on ordinary shareholders' equity. (*c*) Price-earnings ratio. (*d*) Dividend yield.

12. If a company has net sales of $8,500,000, net profit of $945,000, and total asset turnover of 1.8 times, what is its return on total assets?

EXHIBIT 17.15

Financial Statement Analysis Ratios*

Ratio	Formula	Measure of
Liquidity and Efficiency		
Current ratio	$= \dfrac{\text{Current assets}}{\text{Current liabilities}}$	Short-term debt-paying ability
Acid-test ratio	$= \dfrac{\text{Cash + Short-term investments + Current receivables}}{\text{Current liabilities}}$	Immediate short-term debt-paying ability
Accounts receivable turnover	$= \dfrac{\text{Net sales}}{\text{Average accounts receivable, net}}$	Efficiency of collection
Inventory turnover	$= \dfrac{\text{Cost of goods sold}}{\text{Average inventory}}$	Efficiency of inventory management
Accounts payable turnover	$= \dfrac{\text{Cost of goods sold}}{\text{Average accounts payable}}$	Frequency of trade credit payments
Days' sales uncollected	$= \dfrac{\text{Accounts receivable, net}}{\text{Net sales}} \times 365$	Liquidity of receivables
Days' sales in inventory	$= \dfrac{\text{Ending inventory}}{\text{Cost of goods sold}} \times 365$	Liquidity of inventory
Days' purchases in accounts payable	$= \dfrac{\text{Accounts payable}}{\text{Cost of goods sold}} \times 365$	Speed of trade credit payments
Total asset turnover	$= \dfrac{\text{Net sales}}{\text{Average total assets}}$	Efficiency of assets in producing sales
Solvency		
Debt ratio	$= \dfrac{\text{Total liabilities}}{\text{Total assets}}$	Creditor financing and leverage
Equity ratio	$= \dfrac{\text{Total equity}}{\text{Total assets}}$	Owner financing
Debt-to-equity ratio	$= \dfrac{\text{Total liabilities}}{\text{Total equity}}$	Debt versus equity financing
Times interest earned	$= \dfrac{\text{Income before interest expense and income taxes}}{\text{Interest expense}}$	Protection in meeting interest payments
Profitability		
Profit margin ratio	$= \dfrac{\text{Net profit}}{\text{Net sales}}$	Net profit in each sales dollar
Gross margin ratio	$= \dfrac{\text{Net sales − Cost of goods sold}}{\text{Net sales}}$	Gross margin in each sales dollar
Return on total assets	$= \dfrac{\text{Net profit}}{\text{Average total assets}}$	Overall profitability of assets
Return on ordinary shareholders' equity	$= \dfrac{\text{Net profit − Preference dividends}}{\text{Average ordinary shareholders' equity}}$	Profitability of owner investment
Basic earnings per share	$= \dfrac{\text{Net profit − Preference dividends}}{\text{Weighted-average ordinary shares outstanding}}$	Net profit per ordinary share
Market Prospects		
Price-earnings ratio	$= \dfrac{\text{Market price per ordinary share}}{\text{Earnings per share}}$	Market value relative to earnings
Dividend yield	$= \dfrac{\text{Annual cash dividends per share}}{\text{Market price per share}}$	Cash return per ordinary share

* Additional ratios also examined in previous chapters included credit risk ratio; property, plant and equipment useful life; property, plant and equipment age; days' cash expense coverage; cash coverage of growth; cash coverage of debt; free cash flow; cash flow on total assets; and payout ratio.

 **Decision Analysis**

Understanding the purpose of financial statement analysis is crucial to the usefulness of any analysis. This understanding leads to efficiency of effort, effectiveness in application, and relevance in focus. The purpose of most financial statement analyses is to reduce uncertainty in business decisions through a rigorous and sound evaluation. A *financial statement analysis report* helps by directly addressing the building blocks of analysis and by identifying weaknesses in inference by requiring explanation: It forces us to organize our reasoning and to verify its flow and logic. A report also serves as a communication link with readers, and the writing process reinforces our judgments and vice versa. Finally, the report helps us (re)evaluate evidence and refine conclusions on key building blocks. A good analysis report usually consists of six sections:

A1 Summarize and report results of analysis.

1. **Executive summary**—brief focus on important analysis results and conclusions.
2. **Analysis overview**—background on the company, its industry, and its economic setting.
3. **Evidential matter**—financial statements and information used in the analysis, including ratios, trends, comparisons, statistics, and all analytical measures assembled; often organized under the building blocks of analysis.
4. **Assumptions**—identification of important assumptions regarding a company's industry and economic environment, and other important assumptions for estimates.
5. **Key factors**—list of important favorable and unfavorable factors, both quantitative and qualitative, for company performance; usually organized by areas of analysis.
6. **Inferences**—forecasts, estimates, interpretations, and conclusions drawing on all sections of the report.

We must remember that the user dictates relevance, meaning that the analysis report should include a brief table of contents to help readers focus on those areas most relevant to their decisions. All irrelevant matter must be eliminated. For example, decades-old details of obscure transactions and detailed miscues of the analysis are irrelevant. Ambiguities and qualifications to avoid responsibility or hedging inferences must be eliminated. Finally, writing is important. Mistakes in grammar and errors of fact compromise the report's credibility.

Decision Insight

Short Selling *Short selling* refers to selling shares before you buy it. Here's an example: You borrow 100 Nike shares, sell them at $40 each, and receive money from their sale. You then wait. You hope that Nike's share price falls to, say, $35 each and you can replace the borrowed shares for less than you sold it for, reaping a profit of $5 each less any transaction costs. ∎

DEMONSTRATION PROBLEM

Use the following financial statements of Precision Co. to complete these requirements.

1. Prepare comparative income statements showing the percent increase or decrease for year 2015 in comparison to year 2014.
2. Prepare common-size comparative statements of financial position for years 2015 and 2014.
3. Compute the following ratios as at December 31, 2015, or for the year ended December 31, 2015, and identify its building block category for financial statement analysis.

   a. Current ratio
   b. Acid-test ratio
   c. Accounts receivable turnover
   d. Days' sales uncollected
   e. Inventory turnover
   f. Debt ratio

   g. Debt-to-equity ratio
   h. Times interest earned
   i. Profit margin ratio
   j. Total asset turnover
   k. Return on total assets
   l. Return on ordinary shareholders' equity

PRECISION COMPANY Comparative Income Statements For Years Ended December 31, 2015 and 2014		
	2015	**2014**
Sales	$2,486,000	$2,075,000
Cost of goods sold	1,523,000	1,222,000
Gross profit	963,000	853,000
Operating expenses		
Advertising expense	145,000	100,000
Sales salaries expense	240,000	280,000
Office salaries expense	165,000	200,000
Insurance expense	100,000	45,000
Supplies expense	26,000	35,000
Depreciation expense	85,000	75,000
Miscellaneous expenses	17,000	15,000
Total operating expenses	778,000	750,000
Operating profit	185,000	103,000
Interest expense	44,000	46,000
Profit before tax	141,000	57,000
Income tax expense	47,000	19,000
Net profit	$ 94,000	$ 38,000
Earnings per share	$ 0.99	$ 0.40

PRECISION COMPANY Comparative Statements of Financial Position December 31, 2015 and 2014		
	2015	**2014**
Assets		
Current assets		
Cash	$ 79,000	$ 42,000
Short-term investments	65,000	96,000
Accounts receivable, net	120,000	100,000
Merchandise inventory	250,000	265,000
Total current assets	514,000	503,000
Property, plant and equipment		
Store equipment, net	400,000	350,000
Office equipment, net	45,000	50,000
Buildings, net	625,000	675,000
Land	100,000	100,000
Total property, plant and equipment	1,170,000	1,175,000
Total assets	$1,684,000	$1,678,000
Liabilities		
Current liabilities		
Accounts payable	$ 164,000	$ 190,000
Short-term notes payable	75,000	90,000
Taxes payable	26,000	12,000
Total current liabilities	265,000	292,000
Long-term liabilities		
Notes payable (secured by mortgage on buildings)	400,000	420,000
Total liabilities	665,000	712,000
Shareholders' Equity		
Share capital	475,000	475,000
Retained earnings	544,000	491,000
Total shareholders' equity	1,019,000	966,000
Total liabilities and equity	$1,684,000	$1,678,000

PLANNING THE SOLUTION

- Set up a four-column income statement; enter the 2015 and 2014 amounts in the first two columns and then enter the dollar change in the third column and the percent change from 2014 in the fourth column.
- Set up a four-column statement of financial position; enter the 2015 and 2014 year-end amounts in the first two columns and then compute and enter the amount of each item as a percent of total assets.
- Compute the required ratios using the data provided. Use the average of beginning and ending amounts when appropriate (see Exhibit 17.15 for definitions).

SOLUTION TO DEMONSTRATION PROBLEM

1.

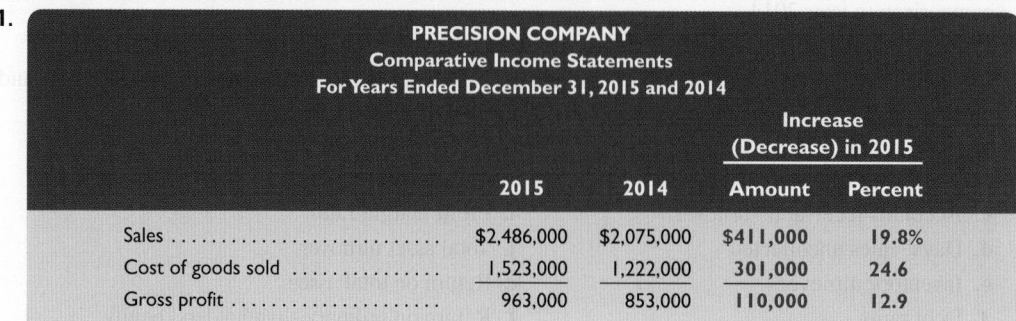

PRECISION COMPANY Comparative Income Statements For Years Ended December 31, 2015 and 2014				
			Increase (Decrease) in 2015	
	2015	**2014**	**Amount**	**Percent**
Sales	$2,486,000	$2,075,000	$411,000	19.8%
Cost of goods sold	1,523,000	1,222,000	301,000	24.6
Gross profit	963,000	853,000	110,000	12.9

[continued on next page]

[continued from previous page]

Operating expenses				
Advertising expense	145,000	100,000	45,000	45.0
Sales salaries expense	240,000	280,000	(40,000)	(14.3)
Office salaries expense	165,000	200,000	(35,000)	(17.5)
Insurance expense	100,000	45,000	55,000	122.2
Supplies expense	26,000	35,000	(9,000)	(25.7)
Depreciation expense	85,000	75,000	10,000	13.3
Miscellaneous expenses	17,000	15,000	2,000	13.3
Total operating expenses	778,000	750,000	28,000	3.7
Operating profit	185,000	103,000	82,000	79.6
Interest expense	44,000	46,000	(2,000)	(4.3)
Profit before tax	141,000	57,000	84,000	147.4
Income tax expense	47,000	19,000	28,000	147.4
Net profit	$ 94,000	$ 38,000	$ 56,000	147.4
Earnings per share	$ 0.99	$ 0.40	$ 0.59	147.5

2.

PRECISION COMPANY Common-Size Comparative Statements of Financial Position December 31, 2015 and 2014				
	December 31		**Common-Size Percents**	
	2015	**2014**	**2015***	**2014***
Assets				
Current assets				
Cash	$ 79,000	$ 42,000	4.7%	2.5%
Short-term investments	65,000	96,000	3.9	5.7
Accounts receivable, net	120,000	100,000	7.1	6.0
Merchandise inventory	250,000	265,000	14.8	15.8
Total current assets	514,000	503,000	30.5	30.0
Property, plant and equipment				
Store equipment, net	400,000	350,000	23.8	20.9
Office equipment, net	45,000	50,000	2.7	3.0
Buildings, net	625,000	675,000	37.1	40.2
Land	100,000	100,000	5.9	6.0
Total property, plant and equipment	1,170,000	1,175,000	69.5	70.0
Total assets	$1,684,000	$1,678,000	100.0	100.0
Liabilities				
Current liabilities				
Accounts payable	$ 164,000	$ 190,000	9.7%	11.3%
Short-term notes payable	75,000	90,000	4.5	5.4
Taxes payable	26,000	12,000	1.5	0.7
Total current liabilities	265,000	292,000	15.7	17.4
Long-term liabilities				
Notes payable (secured by mortgage on buildings)	400,000	420,000	23.8	25.0
Total liabilities	665,000	712,000	39.5	42.4
Shareholders' equity				
Share capital	475,000	475,000	28.2	28.3
Retained earnings	544,000	491,000	32.3	29.3
Total shareholders' equity	1,019,000	966,000	60.5	57.6
Total liabilities and equity	$1,684,000	$1,678,000	100.0	100.0

* Columns do not always exactly add to 100 due to rounding.

3. **Ratios for 2015:**

   a. Current ratio: $514,000/$265,000 = 1.9:1 (liquidity and efficiency)

   b. Acid-test ratio: ($79,000 + $65,000 + $120,000)/$265,000 = 1.0:1 (liquidity and efficiency)

   c. Average receivables: ($120,000 + $100,000)/2 = $110,000

      Accounts receivable turnover: $2,486,000/$110,000 = 22.6 times (liquidity and efficiency)

   d. Days' sales uncollected: ($120,000/$2,486,000) × 365 = 17.6 days (liquidity and efficiency)

   e. Average inventory: ($250,000 + $265,000)/2 = $257,500

      Inventory turnover: $1,523,000/$257,500 = 5.9 times (liquidity and efficiency)

   f. Debt ratio: $665,000/$1,684,000 = 39.5% (solvency)

   g. Debt-to-equity ratio: $665,000/$1,019,000 = 0.65 (solvency)

   h. Times interest earned: $185,000/$44,000 = 4.2 times (solvency)

   i. Profit margin ratio: $94,000/$2,486,000 = 3.8% (profitability)

   j. Average total assets: ($1,684,000 + $1,678,000)/2 = $1,681,000

      Total asset turnover: $2,486,000/$1,681,000 = 1.48 times (liquidity and efficiency)

   k. Return on total assets: $94,000/$1,681,000 = 5.6% or 3.8% × 1.48 = 5.6% (profitability)

   l. Average total ordinary equity: ($1,019,000 + $966,000)/2 = $992,500

      Return on ordinary shareholders' equity: $94,000/$992,500 = 9.5% (profitability)

Summary

C1   **Explain the purpose and identify the building blocks of analysis.** The purpose of financial statement analysis is to help users make better business decisions. Internal users want information to improve company efficiency and effectiveness in providing products and services. External users want information to make better and more informed decisions in pursuing their goals. The common goals of all users are to evaluate a company's (1) past and current performance, (2) current financial position, and (3) future performance and risk. Financial statement analysis focuses on four "building blocks" of analysis: (1) liquidity and efficiency—ability to meet short-term obligations and efficiently generate revenues; (2) solvency—ability to generate future revenues and meet long-term obligations; (3) profitability—ability to provide financial rewards sufficient to attract and retain financing; and (4) market prospects—ability to generate positive market expectations.

C2   **Describe standards for comparisons in analysis.** Standards for comparisons include (1) intracompany—prior performance and relations between financial items for the company under analysis; (2) competitor—one or more direct competitors of the company; (3) industry—industry statistics; and (4) guidelines (rules of thumb)—general standards developed from past experiences and personal judgments.

A1   **Summarize and report results of analysis.** A financial statement analysis report is often organized around the building blocks of analysis. A good report separates interpretations and conclusions of analysis from the information underlying them.

An analysis report often consists of six sections: (1) executive summary, (2) analysis overview, (3) evidential matter, (4) assumptions, (5) key factors, and (6) inferences.

P1   **Explain and apply methods of horizontal analysis.** Horizontal analysis is a tool to evaluate changes in data across time. Two important tools of horizontal analysis are comparative statements and trend analysis. Comparative statements show amounts for two or more successive periods, often with changes disclosed in both absolute and percent terms. Trend analysis is used to reveal important changes occurring from one period to the next.

P2   **Describe and apply methods of vertical analysis.** Vertical analysis is a tool to evaluate each financial statement item or group of items in terms of a base amount. Two tools of vertical analysis are common-size statements and graphical analyses. Each item in common-size statements is expressed as a percent of a base amount. For the statement of financial position, the base amount is usually total assets, and for the income statement, it is usually sales.

P3   **Define and apply ratio analysis.** Ratio analysis provides clues to and symptoms of underlying conditions. Ratios, properly interpreted, identify areas requiring further investigation. A ratio expresses a mathematical relation between two quantities such as a percent, rate, or proportion. Ratios can be organized into the building blocks of analysis: (1) liquidity and efficiency, (2) solvency, (3) profitability, and (4) market prospects.

Guidance Answers to Decision Maker

Auditor   The *joint relation* referred to is the combined increase in sales and the decrease in expenses yielding more than a 5% increase in profit. Both *individual* accounts (sales and expenses) yield percent changes within the ±5% acceptable range. However, a joint analysis suggests a different picture. For example, consider a joint analysis using the profit margin ratio. The client's profit margin is 11.46% ($206,000 − $182,400/$206,000) for the current year compared with 5.0% ($200,000 − $190,000/$200,000) for the prior year—yielding a 129% increase in profit margin! This is what concerns the partner, and it suggests expanding audit tests to verify or refute the client's figures.

Banker Your decision on the loan application is positive for at least two reasons. First, the current ratio suggests a strong ability to meet short-term obligations. Second, current assets of $160,000 and a current ratio of 4:1 imply current liabilities of $40,000 (one-fourth

of current assets) and a working capital excess of $120,000. This working capital excess is 60% of the loan amount. However, if the application is for a 10-year loan, our decision is less optimistic. The current ratio and working capital suggest a good safety margin, but indications of inefficiency in operations exist. In particular, a 4:1 current ratio is more than double its key competitors' ratio. This is characteristic of inefficient asset use.

Guidance Answers to Quick Checks

1. General-purpose financial statements are intended for a variety of users interested in a company's financial condition and performance—users without the power to require specialized financial reports to meet their specific needs.

2. General-purpose financial statements include the statement of comprehensive income, statement of financial position, statement of changes in equity, statement of cash flows, and notes to these statements.

3. *a*

4. Data from one or more direct competitors are usually preferred for comparative purposes.

5. *d*

6. Percents on comparative income statements show the increase or decrease in each item from one period to the next. On common-size comparative income statements, each item is shown as a percent of net sales for that period.

7. *c*

8. (*a*) ($820,000 + $240,000 + $470,000)/($350,000 + $180,000) = 2.9 to 1.
   (*b*) ($820,000 + $240,000)/($350,000 + $180,000) = 2:1.

9. (*a*) $2,500,000/[($290,000 + $240,000)/2] = 9.43 times.
   (*b*) ($290,000/$2,500,000) × 365 = 42 days.
   (*c*) $750,000/[($530,000 + $470,000)/2] = 1.5 times.
   (*d*) ($530,000/$750,000) × 365 = 258 days.
   (*e*) $750,000/[($350,000 + $370,000)/2] = 2.08 times.
   (*f*) ($370,000/$750,000) × 365 = 180 days.

10. *c*

11. *b*

12. Profit margin × $\dfrac{\text{Total asset}}{\text{turnover}}$ = $\dfrac{\text{Return on}}{\text{total assets}}$

    $\dfrac{\$945,000}{\$8,500,000}$ × 1.8 = 20%

Key Terms   www.mheducation.asia/olc/wildkwokFAP

Common-size financial statement (p. 667)

Comparative financial statements (p. 662)

Efficiency (p. 661)

Equity ratio (p. 676)

Financial reporting (p. 661)

Financial statement analysis (p. 660)

General-purpose financial statements (p. 661)

Horizontal analysis (p. 662)

Liquidity (p. 661)

Market prospects (p. 661)

Profitability (p. 661)

Ratio analysis (p. 662)

Solvency (p. 661)

Vertical analysis (p. 662)

Working capital (p. 671)

Multiple Choice Quiz   Answers on p. 699   www.mheducation.asia/olc/wildkwokFAP

Additional Quiz Questions are available at the book's Website.

1. A company's sales in 2014 were $300,000 and in 2015 were $351,000. Using 2014 as the base year, the sales trend percent for 2015 is:
   a. 17%
   b. 85%
   c. 100%
   d. 117%
   e. 48%

Use the following information for questions 2 through 5.

GALLOWAY COMPANY
Statement of Financial Position
December 31, 2015

Assets

Cash	$ 86,000
Accounts receivable	76,000
Merchandise inventory	122,000
Prepaid insurance	12,000
Long-term investments	98,000
Property, plant and equipment, net	436,000
Total assets	$830,000

Liabilities and Equity

Current liabilities	$124,000
Long-term liabilities	90,000
Share capital	300,000
Retained earnings	316,000
Total liabilities and equity	$830,000

2. What is Galloway Company's current ratio?
 a. 0.69
 b. 1.31
 c. 3.88
 d. 6.69
 e. 2.39

3. What is Galloway Company's acid-test ratio?
 a. 2.39
 b. 0.69
 c. 1.31
 d. 6.69
 e. 3.88

4. What is Galloway Company's debt ratio?
 a. 25.78%
 b. 100.00%
 c. 74.22%
 d. 137.78%
 e. 34.74%

5. What is Galloway Company's equity ratio?
 a. 25.78%
 b. 100.00%
 c. 34.74%
 d. 74.22%
 e. 137.78%

🔲 Icon denotes assignments that involve decision making.

Discussion Questions

1. What is the difference between comparative financial statements and common-size comparative statements?

2. Which items are usually assigned a 100% value on (*a*) a common-size statement of financial position and (*b*) a common-size income statement?

3. Explain the difference between financial reporting and financial statements.

4. 🔲 What three factors would influence your evaluation as to whether a company's current ratio is good or bad?

5. 🔲 Suggest several reasons why a 2:1 current ratio might not be adequate for a particular company.

6. 🔲 Why is working capital given special attention in the process of analyzing statements of financial position?

7. 🔲 What does the number of days' sales uncollected indicate?

8. 🔲 What does a relatively high accounts receivable turnover indicate about a company's short-term liquidity?

9. 🔲 Why is a company's capital structure, as measured by debt and equity ratios, important to financial statement analysts?

10. 🔲 How does inventory turnover provide information about a company's short-term liquidity?

11. 🔲 What ratios would you compute to evaluate management performance?

12. 🔲 What does a negative conversion cycle ratio mean?

13. Where on the income statement does a company report an unusual gain not expected to occur more often than once every two years or so?

14. If you intend to hold the shares over many years but desire to have some cash return over the years, which ratio would be most relevant to you and why?

15. Use Nestlé's financial statements in Appendix A to compute its return on total assets for the years ended December 31, 2012, and December 31, 2013. Total assets as at December 31, 2011, were 114,091 (in CHF millions). For the numerator, use profit attributable to shareholders of the parent.

16. Refer to Adidas' financial statements in Appendix A to compute its equity ratio as at December 31, 2012, and December 31, 2013.

17. Refer to Samsung's financial statements in Appendix A. Compute its profit margin for the financial year ended December 31, 2012. For the numerator, use profit attributable to owners of the parent.

≣ connect

Which of the following items (1) through (9) are part of financial reporting but are not included as part of general-purpose financial statements? (1) share price information and analysis, (2) statement of cash flows, (3) management discussion and analysis of financial performance, (4) statement of comprehensive income, (5) company news releases, (6) statement of financial position, (7) financial statement notes, (8) statement of changes in equity, (9) prospectus for initial public offering.

QUICK STUDY

QS 17-1
Financial reporting C1

What are four possible standards of comparison used to analyze financial statement ratios? Which of these is generally considered to be the most useful? Which one is least likely to provide a good basis for comparison?

QS 17-2
Standard of comparison C2

Use the following information for Ciolino Corporation to determine (1) the 2014 and 2015 common-size percents for cost of goods sold using net sales as the base and (2) the 2014 and 2015 trend percents for net sales using 2014 as the base year.

QS 17-3
Common-size and trend percents
P1

($ thousands)	2015	2014
Net sales	$202,800	$116,200
Cost of goods sold.	110,600	61,400

Compute the annual dollar changes and percent changes for each of the following accounts.

QS 17-4
Horizontal analysis
P1

	2015	2014
Short-term investments.	$220,000	$160,000
Accounts receivable.	38,000	44,000
Notes payable	60,000	0

Match the ratio to the building block of financial statement analysis to which it best relates.

A. Liquidity and efficiency   **C.** Profitability
B. Solvency   **D.** Market prospects

1. _____ Price-earnings ratio   **6.** _____ Gross margin ratio
2. _____ Days' sales in inventory   **7.** _____ Acid-test ratio
3. _____ Accounts receivable turnover **8.** _____ Equity ratio
4. _____ Debt-to-equity   **9.** _____ Return on total assets
5. _____ Times interest earned   **10.** _____ Dividend yield

QS 17-5
Building blocks of analysis
C1 P3

1. Which two short-term liquidity ratios measure how frequently a company collects its accounts?
2. What measure reflects the difference between current assets and current liabilities?
3. Which two ratios are key components in measuring a company's operating efficiency? Which ratio summarizes these two components?

QS 17-6
Identifying financial ratios
P3

For each ratio listed, identify whether the change in ratio value from 2014 to 2015 is usually regarded as favorable or unfavorable.

QS 17-7
Ratio interpretation
P3

Ratio	2015	2014	Ratio	2015	2014
1. Profit margin	9%	8%	5. Accounts receivable turnover	5.5	6.7
2. Debt ratio	47%	42%	6. Basic earnings per share	$1.25	$1.10
3. Gross margin	34%	46%	7. Inventory turnover	3.6	3.4
4. Acid-test ratio	1.00	1.15	8. Dividend yield	2%	1.2%

EXERCISES

Exercise 17-1

Computation and analysis of trend percents

P1

Compute trend percents for the following financial items, using 2011 as the base year. State whether the situation as revealed by the trends appears to be favorable or unfavorable for each item.

	2015	2014	2013	2012	2011
Sales	$282,880	$270,800	$252,600	$234,560	$150,000
Cost of goods sold	128,200	122,080	115,280	106,440	67,000
Accounts receivable	18,100	17,300	16,400	15,200	9,000

Exercise 17-2

Determination of income effects from common-size and trend percents

P1 P2

Common-size and trend percents for Skelton Company's sales, cost of goods sold, and expenses follow. Determine whether net profit increased, decreased, or remained unchanged in this three-year period.

	Common-Size Percents			Trend Percents		
	2014	2013	2012	2014	2013	2012
Sales	100.0%	100.0%	100.0%	105.4%	104.2%	100.0%
Cost of goods sold	63.4	61.9	59.1	103.0	101.1	100.0
Total expenses	15.3	14.8	15.1	95.0	91.0	100.0

Exercise 17-3

Common-size percent computation and interpretation

P2

Express the following comparative income statements in common-size percents and assess whether or not this company's situation has improved in the most recent year.

MACHIKO CORPORATION Comparative Income Statements For Years Ended December 31, 2015 and 2014		
	2015	2014
Sales	$740,000	$625,000
Cost of goods sold	560,300	290,800
Gross profit	179,700	334,200
Operating expenses	128,200	218,500
Net profit	$ 51,500	$115,700

Exercise 17-4

Analysis of short-term financial condition

A1 P3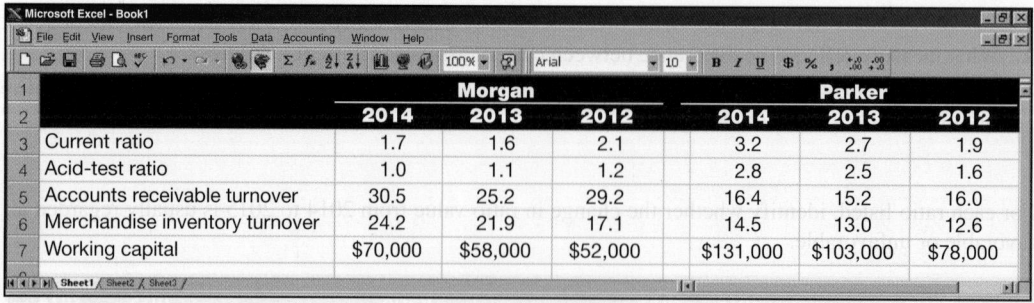

Team Project: Assume that the two companies apply for a one-year loan from the team. Identify additional information the companies must provide before the team can make a loan decision.

The following information is available for Morgan Company and Parker Company, similar firms operating in the same industry. Write a half-page report comparing Morgan and Parker using the available information. Your discussion should include their ability to meet current obligations and to use current assets efficiently.

Microsoft Excel - Book1						
	Morgan			**Parker**		
	2014	**2013**	**2012**	**2014**	**2013**	**2012**
Current ratio	1.7	1.6	2.1	3.2	2.7	1.9
Acid-test ratio	1.0	1.1	1.2	2.8	2.5	1.6
Accounts receivable turnover	30.5	25.2	29.2	16.4	15.2	16.0
Merchandise inventory turnover	24.2	21.9	17.1	14.5	13.0	12.6
Working capital	$70,000	$58,000	$52,000	$131,000	$103,000	$78,000

Exercise 17-5

Analysis of efficiency and financial leverage

A1 P3

Roak Company and Clay Company are similar firms that operate in the same industry. Clay began operations in 2013 and Roak in 2006. In 2015, both companies pay 7% interest on their debt to creditors. The following additional information is available.

	Roak Company			Clay Company		
	2015	**2014**	**2013**	**2015**	**2014**	**2013**
Total asset turnover	3.1	2.8	3.0	1.7	1.5	1.2
Return on total assets.........	9.0%	9.6%	8.8%	5.9%	5.6%	5.3%
Profit margin ratio............	2.4%	2.5%	2.3%	2.8%	3.0%	2.9%
Sales......................	$410,000	$380,000	$396,000	$210,000	$170,000	$110,000

Write a half-page report comparing Roak and Clay using the available information. Your analysis should include their ability to use assets efficiently to produce profits. Also comment on their success in employing financial leverage in 2015.

Simeon Company's year-end statements of financial position follow. Express the statements of financial position in common-size percents. Round amounts to the nearest one-tenth of a percent. Analyze and comment on the results.

Exercise 17-6
Common-size percents
P2

At December 31	2014	2013	2012
Assets			
Cash...	$ 31,800	$ 35,625	$ 37,800
Accounts receivable, net	89,500	62,500	50,200
Merchandise inventory...........................	112,500	82,500	54,000
Prepaid expenses	10,700	9,375	5,000
Property, plant and equipment, net.................	278,500	255,000	230,500
Total assets.....................................	$523,000	$445,000	$377,500
Liabilities and Equity			
Accounts payable.................................	$129,900	$ 75,250	$ 51,250
Long-term notes payable secured by mortgages on property, plant and equipment.......	98,500	101,500	83,500
Share capital....................................	163,500	163,500	163,500
Retained earnings................................	131,100	104,750	79,250
Total liabilities and equity	$523,000	$445,000	$377,500

Refer to Simeon Company's statements of financial position in Exercise 17-6. Analyze its year-end short-term liquidity position at the end of 2014, 2013, and 2012 by computing (1) the current ratio and (2) the acid-test ratio. Comment on the ratio results.

Exercise 17-7
Liquidity analysis
P3

Refer to the Simeon Company information in Exercise 17-6. The company's income statements for the years ended December 31, 2014 and 2013, follow. Assume that all sales are on credit and then compute: (1) accounts receivable turnover, (2) days' sales uncollected, (3) inventory turnover, (4) days' sales in inventory, (5) accounts payable turnover, (6) days' purchases in accounts payable, and (7) conversion cycle. Comment on the changes in the ratios from 2013 to 2014.

Exercise 17-8
Liquidity analysis and conversion cycle
P3

For Year Ended December 31	2014		2013	
Sales		$673,500		$532,000
Cost of goods sold...............	$411,225		$345,500	
Other operating expenses.........	209,550		134,980	
Interest expense.................	12,100		13,300	
Income taxes	9,525		8,845	
Total costs and expenses..........		642,400		502,625
Net profit.....................		$ 31,100		$ 29,375
Earnings per share		$ 1.90		$ 1.80

Exercise 17-9
Risk and capital structure analysis

P3

Refer to the Simeon Company information in Exercises 17-6 and 17-8. Compare the company's long-term risk and capital structure positions at the end of 2014 and 2013 by computing these ratios: (1) debt and equity ratios, (2) debt-to-equity ratio, and (3) times interest earned. Comment on these ratio results.

Exercise 17-10
Efficiency and profitability analysis

P3

Refer to Simeon Company's financial information in Exercises 17-6 and 17-8. Evaluate the company's efficiency and profitability by computing the following for 2014 and 2013: (1) profit margin ratio, (2) total asset turnover, and (3) return on total assets. Comment on these ratio results.

Exercise 17-11
Profitability analysis

P3

Refer to Simeon Company's financial information in Exercises 17-6 and 17-8. Additional information about the company follows. To help evaluate the company's profitability, compute and interpret the following ratios for 2014 and 2013: (1) return on ordinary shareholders' equity, (2) price-earnings ratio on December 31, and (3) dividend yield.

Market price per ordinary share, December 31, 2014......	$30.00
Market price per ordinary share, December 31, 2013......	28.00
Annual cash dividends per share in 2014................	0.29
Annual cash dividends per share in 2013................	0.24

■■ connect™

PROBLEM SET A

Problem 17-1A
Ratios, common-size statements, and trend percents

P1 P2 P3

eXcel

www.mheducation.asia/olc/wildkwokFAP

Selected comparative financial statements of Korbin Company follow.

KORBIN COMPANY
Comparative Income Statements
For Years Ended December 31, 2014, 2013, and 2012

	2014	2013	2012
Sales........................	$555,000	$340,000	$278,000
Cost of goods sold..............	283,500	212,500	153,900
Gross profit	271,500	127,500	124,100
Selling expenses................	102,900	46,920	50,800
Administrative expenses	50,668	29,920	22,800
Total expenses.................	153,568	76,840	73,600
Profit before tax...............	117,932	50,660	50,500
Income tax expense.............	40,800	10,370	15,670
Net profit.....................	$ 77,132	$ 40,290	$ 34,830

KORBIN COMPANY
Comparative Statements of Financial Position
December 31, 2014, 2013, and 2012

	2014	2013	2012
Assets			
Current assets......................	$ 52,390	$ 37,924	$ 51,748
Long-term investments	0	500	3,950
Property, plant and equipment, net.....	100,000	96,000	60,000
Total assets	$152,390	$134,424	$115,698
Liabilities and Equity			
Current liabilities....................	$ 22,800	$ 19,960	$ 20,300
Share capital	72,000	72,000	60,000
Share premium.....................	9,000	9,000	6,000
Retained earnings..................	48,590	33,464	29,398
Total liabilities and equity	$152,390	$134,424	$115,698

Required

1. Compute each year's current ratio.
2. Express the income statement data in common-size percents.
3. Express the statement of financial position data in trend percents with 2012 as the base year.

Analysis Component

4. Comment on any significant relations revealed by the ratios and percents computed.

Check (3) 2014, Total assets trend, 131.71%

Selected comparative financial statements of Haroun Company follow.

Problem 17-2A
Calculation and analysis of trend percents

A1 P1

HAROUN COMPANY Comparative Income Statements ($000) For Years Ended December 31, 2010–2004							
	2010	**2009**	**2008**	**2007**	**2006**	**2005**	**2004**
Sales	$1,694	$1,496	$1,370	$1,264	$1,186	$1,110	$928
Cost of goods sold.	1,246	1,032	902	802	752	710	586
Gross profit	448	464	468	462	434	400	342
Operating expenses.	330	256	234	170	146	144	118
Net profit.	$ 118	$ 208	$ 234	$ 292	$ 288	$ 256	$224

HAROUN COMPANY Comparative Statements of Financial Position ($000) December 31, 2010–2004							
	2010	**2009**	**2008**	**2007**	**2006**	**2005**	**2004**
Assets							
Cash	$ 58	$ 78	$ 82	$ 84	$ 88	$ 86	$ 89
Accounts receivable, net	490	514	466	360	318	302	216
Merchandise inventory.	1,838	1,364	1,204	1,032	936	810	615
Other current assets	36	32	14	34	28	28	9
Long-term investments	0	0	0	146	146	146	146
Property, plant and equipment, net.	2,020	2,014	1,752	944	978	860	725
Total assets.	$4,442	$4,002	$3,518	$2,600	$2,494	$2,232	$1,800
Liabilities and Equity							
Current liabilities	$1,220	$1,042	$ 718	$ 614	$ 546	$ 522	$ 282
Long-term liabilities	1,294	1,140	1,112	570	580	620	400
Share capital	1,000	1,000	1,000	850	850	650	650
Share premium.	250	250	250	170	170	150	150
Retained earnings.	678	570	438	396	348	290	318
Total liabilities and equity	$4,442	$4,002	$3,518	$2,600	$2,494	$2,232	$1,800

Required

1. Compute trend percents for all components of both statements using 2004 as the base year.

Check (1) 2014, Total assets trend, 246.8%

Analysis Component

2. Analyze and comment on the financial statements and trend percents from part 1.

Plum Corporation began the month of May with $700,000 of current assets, a current ratio of 2.50:1, and an acid-test ratio of 1.10:1. During the month, it completed the following transactions (the company uses a perpetual inventory system).

May 2 Purchased $50,000 of merchandise inventory on credit.
     8 Sold merchandise inventory that cost $55,000 for $110,000 cash.
   10 Collected $20,000 cash on an account receivable.
   15 Paid $22,000 cash to settle an account payable.

Problem 17-3A
Transactions, working capital, and liquidity ratios

P3

17   Wrote off a $5,000 bad debt against the Allowance for Doubtful Accounts account.
22   Declared a $1 per share cash dividend on the 50,000 outstanding ordinary shares.
26   Paid the dividend declared on May 22.
27   Borrowed $100,000 cash by giving the bank a 30-day, 10% note.
28   Borrowed $80,000 cash by signing a long-term secured note.
29   Used the $180,000 cash proceeds from the notes to buy new machinery.

Required

Prepare a table showing Plum's (1) current ratio, (2) acid-test ratio, and (3) working capital, after each transaction. Round ratios to hundredths.

Problem 17-4A
Calculation of financial statement ratios
P3

www.mheducation.asia/olc/wildkwokFAP

Selected year-end financial statements of Cabot Corporation follow. (All sales were on credit; selected statement of financial position amounts at December 31, 2014, were inventory, $48,900; total assets, $189,400; share capital, $90,000; and retained earnings, $22,748.)

CABOT CORPORATION
Income Statement
For Year Ended December 31, 2015

Sales	$448,600
Cost of goods sold	297,250
Gross profit	151,350
Operating expenses	98,600
Interest expense	4,100
Profit before tax	48,650
Income tax expense	19,598
Net profit	$ 29,052

CABOT CORPORATION
Statement of Financial Position
December 31, 2015

Assets		Liabilities and Equity	
Cash	$ 10,000	Accounts payable	$ 17,500
Short-term investments	8,400	Accrued wages payable	3,200
Accounts receivable, net	29,200	Income taxes payable	3,300
Notes receivable (trade)*	4,500	Long-term note payable, secured by mortgage	
Merchandise inventory	32,150	on property, plant and equipment	63,400
Prepaid expenses	2,650	Share capital	90,000
Property, plant and equipment, net	153,300	Retained earnings	62,800
Total assets	$240,200	Total liabilities and equity	$240,200

* These are short-term notes receivable arising from customer (trade) sales.

Required

Compute the following: (1) current ratio, (2) acid-test ratio, (3) days' sales uncollected, (4) inventory turnover, (5) days' sales in inventory, (6) debt-to-equity ratio, (7) times interest earned, (8) profit margin ratio, (9) total asset turnover, (10) return on total assets, and (11) return on ordinary shareholders' equity.

Problem 17-5A
Comparative ratio analysis

A1   P3

Summary information from the financial statements of two companies competing in the same industry follows.

	Barco Company	Kyan Company			Barco Company	Kyan Company
Data from the current year-end statements of financial position				**Data from the current year's income statement**		
Assets				Sales	$770,000	$880,200
Cash	$ 19,500	$ 34,000		Cost of goods sold	585,100	632,500
Accounts receivable, net	37,400	57,400		Interest expense	7,900	13,000
Current notes receivable (trade)	9,100	7,200		Income tax expense.	14,800	24,300
Merchandise inventory	84,440	132,500		Net profit	$162,200	$210,400
Prepaid expenses	5,000	6,950		Basic earnings per share.	$ 4.51	$ 5.11
Property, plant and equipment, net	290,000	304,400				
Total assets	$445,440	$542,450				
				Beginning-of-year statement of financial position data		
Liabilities and Equity				Accounts receivable, net	$ 29,800	$ 54,200
Current liabilities	$ 61,340	$ 93,300		Current notes receivable (trade).	0	0
Long-term notes payable	80,800	101,000		Merchandise inventory.	55,600	107,400
Share capital	180,000	206,000		Total assets	398,000	382,500
Retained earnings	123,300	142,150		Share capital	180,000	206,000
Total liabilities and equity	$445,440	$542,450		Retained earnings.	98,300	93,600

Required

1. For both companies compute the (*a*) current ratio, (*b*) acid-test ratio, (*c*) accounts (including notes) receivable turnover, (*d*) inventory turnover, (*e*) days' sales in inventory, and (*f*) days' sales uncollected. Identify the company you consider to be the better short-term credit risk and explain why.

2. For both companies compute the (*a*) profit margin ratio, (*b*) total asset turnover, (*c*) return on total assets, and (*d*) return on ordinary shareholders' equity. Assuming that each company paid cash dividends of $3.80 per share and each company's shares can be purchased at $75 per share, compute their (*e*) price-earnings ratios and (*f*) dividend yields. Identify which company's shares you would recommend as the better investment and explain why.

Check (1) Kyan: Accounts receivable turnover, 14.8; Inventory turnover, 3.5

(2) Barco: Profit margin, 21.1%; PE, 16.6

Selected comparative financial statement information of Bluegrass Corporation follows.

PROBLEM SET B

Problem 17-1B
Ratios, common-size statements, and trend percents

P1 P2 P3

BLUEGRASS CORPORATION Comparative Income Statements For Years Ended December 31, 2014, 2013, and 2012			
	2014	2013	2012
Sales	$198,800	$166,000	$143,800
Cost of goods sold.	108,890	86,175	66,200
Gross profit	89,910	79,825	77,600
Selling expenses	22,680	19,790	18,000
Administrative expenses	16,760	14,610	15,700
Total expenses	39,440	34,400	33,700
Profit before tax.	50,470	45,425	43,900
Income tax expense.	6,050	5,910	5,300
Net profit	$ 44,420	$ 39,515	$ 38,600

BLUEGRASS CORPORATION Comparative Statements of Financial Position December 31, 2014, 2013, and 2012			
	2014	2013	2012
Assets			
Current assets	$ 54,860	$ 32,660	$ 36,300
Long-term investments	0	1,700	10,600
Property, plant and equipment, net.	112,810	113,660	79,000
Total assets.	$167,670	$148,020	$125,900
Liabilities and Equity			
Current liabilities	$ 22,370	$ 19,180	$ 16,500
Share capital.	46,500	46,500	37,000
Share premium.	13,850	13,850	11,300
Retained earnings.	84,950	68,490	61,100
Total liabilities and equity	$167,670	$148,020	$125,900

Required

1. Compute each year's current ratio.
2. Express the income statement data in common-size percents.
3. Express the statement of financial position data in trend percents with 2012 as the base year.

Check (3) 2014, Total assets trend, 133.18%

Analysis Component

4. Comment on any significant relations revealed by the ratios and percents computed.

Problem 17-2B
Calculation and analysis of trend percents

A1 P1

Selected comparative financial statements of Tripoly Company follow.

TRIPOLY COMPANY Comparative Income Statements ($000) For Years Ended December 31, 2010–2004							
	2010	2009	2008	2007	2006	2005	2004
Sales	$560	$610	$630	$680	$740	$770	$860
Cost of goods sold.	276	290	294	314	340	350	380
Gross profit	284	320	336	366	400	420	480
Operating expenses.	84	104	112	126	140	144	150
Net profit.	$200	$216	$224	$240	$260	$276	$330

TRIPOLY COMPANY Comparative Statements of Financial Position ($000) December 31, 2010–2004							
	2010	2009	2008	2007	2006	2005	2004
Assets							
Cash	$ 44	$ 46	$ 52	$ 54	$ 60	$ 62	$ 68
Accounts receivable, net	130	136	140	144	150	154	160
Merchandise inventory.	166	172	178	180	186	190	208
Other current assets	34	34	36	38	38	40	40
Long-term investments	36	30	26	110	110	110	110
Property, plant and equipment, net.	510	514	520	412	420	428	454
Total assets.	$920	$932	$952	$938	$964	$984	$1,040
Liabilities and Equity							
Current liabilities	$148	$156	$186	$190	$210	$260	$ 280
Long-term liabilities	92	120	142	148	194	214	260
Share capital.	160	160	160	160	160	160	160
Share premium.	70	70	70	70	70	70	70
Retained earnings.	450	426	394	370	330	280	270
Total liabilities and equity	$920	$932	$952	$938	$964	$984	$1,040

Required

1. Compute trend percents for all components of both statements using 2004 as the base year.

Analysis Component

2. Analyze and comment on the financial statements and trend percents from part 1.

Check   (1) 2014, Total assets trend, 88.5%

Koto Corporation began the month of June with $300,000 of current assets, a current ratio of 2.5:1, and an acid-test ratio of 1.4:1. During the month, it completed the following transactions (the company uses a perpetual inventory system).

June 1   Sold merchandise inventory that cost $75,000 for $120,000 cash.
      3   Collected $88,000 cash on an account receivable.
      5   Purchased $150,000 of merchandise inventory on credit.
      7   Borrowed $100,000 cash by giving the bank a 60-day, 10% note.
     10   Borrowed $120,000 cash by signing a long-term secured note.
     12   Purchased machinery for $275,000 cash.
     15   Declared a $1 per share cash dividend on the 80,000 outstanding ordinary shares.
     19   Wrote off a $5,000 bad debt against the Allowance for Doubtful Accounts account.
     22   Paid $12,000 cash to settle an account payable.
     30   Paid the dividend declared on June 15.

Required

Prepare a table showing the company's (1) current ratio, (2) acid-test ratio, and (3) working capital after each transaction. Round ratios to hundredths.

Problem 17-3B

Transactions, working capital, and liquidity ratios   **P3**

Check   June 1: Current ratio, 2.88; Acid-test, 2.40

June 30: Working capital, $(10,000); Current ratio, 0.97

Selected year-end financial statements of Overton Corporation follow. (All sales were on credit; selected statement of financial position amounts at December 31, 2014, were inventory, $17,400; total assets, $94,900; share capital, $35,500; and retained earnings, $18,800.)

Problem 17-4B

Calculation of financial statement ratios

P3

OVERTON CORPORATION
Income Statement
For Year Ended December 31, 2015

Sales	$315,500
Cost of goods sold.	236,100
Gross profit	79,400
Operating expenses.	49,200
Interest expense.	2,200
Profit before tax.	28,000
Income tax expense.	4,200
Net profit.	$ 23,800

OVERTON CORPORATION
Statement of Financial Position
December 31, 2015

Assets		Liabilities and Equity	
Cash.	$ 6,100	Accounts payable	$ 11,500
Short-term investments	6,900	Accrued wages payable	3,300
Accounts receivable, net.	12,100	Income taxes payable.	2,600
Notes receivable (trade)*	3,000	Long-term note payable, secured by mortgage	
Merchandise inventory	13,500	on property, plant and equipment.	30,000
Prepaid expenses.	2,000	Share capital	35,000
Property, plant and equipment, net . . .	73,900	Retained earnings.	35,100
Total assets	$117,500	Total liabilities and equity.	$117,500

* These are short-term notes receivable arising from customer (trade) sales.

Required

Compute the following: (1) current ratio, (2) acid-test ratio, (3) days' sales uncollected, (4) inventory turnover, (5) days' sales in inventory, (6) debt-to-equity ratio, (7) times interest earned, (8) profit margin ratio, (9) total asset turnover, (10) return on total assets, and (11) return on ordinary shareholders' equity.

Problem 17-5B
Comparative ratio analysis

A1 P3

Summary information from the financial statements of two companies competing in the same industry follows.

	Fargo Company	Ball Company		Fargo Company	Ball Company
Data from the current year-end statements of financial position			**Data from the current year's income statement**		
Assets			Sales	$393,600	$667,500
Cash	$ 20,000	$ 36,500	Cost of goods sold.	290,600	480,000
Accounts receivable, net	77,100	70,500	Interest expense.	5,900	12,300
Current notes receivable (trade).	11,600	9,000	Income tax expense.	5,700	12,300
Merchandise inventory.	86,800	82,000	Net profit.	33,850	61,700
Prepaid expenses	9,700	10,100	Basic earnings per share.	1.27	2.19
Property, plant and equipment, net	176,900	252,300			
Total assets.	$382,100	$460,400			
			Beginning-of-year statement of financial position data		
			Accounts receivable, net	$ 72,200	$ 73,300
Liabilities and Equity					
Current liabilities	$ 90,500	$ 97,000	Current notes receivable (trade).	0	0
Long-term notes payable	93,000	93,300	Merchandise inventory.	105,100	80,500
Share capital	133,000	141,000	Total assets.	383,400	443,000
Retained earnings	65,600	129,100	Share capital.	133,000	141,000
Total liabilities and equity.	$382,100	$460,400	Retained earnings.	49,100	109,700

Required

1. For both companies compute the (*a*) current ratio, (*b*) acid-test ratio, (*c*) accounts (including notes) receivable turnover, (*d*) inventory turnover, (*e*) days' sales in inventory, and (*f*) days' sales uncollected. Identify the company you consider to be the better short-term credit risk and explain why.

2. For both companies compute the (*a*) profit margin ratio, (*b*) total asset turnover, (*c*) return on total assets, and (*d*) return on ordinary shareholders' equity. Assuming that each company paid cash dividends of $1.50 per share and each company's shares can be purchased at $25 per share, compute their (*e*) price-earnings ratios and (*f*) dividend yields. Identify which company's shares you would recommend as the better investment and explain why.

SERIAL PROBLEM
Business Solutions

P3

(This serial problem began in Chapter 1 and continues through most of the book. If previous chapter segments were not completed, the serial problem can begin at this point.)

SP 17 Use the following selected data from Business Solutions' income statement for the three months ended March 31, 2016, and from its March 31, 2016, statement of financial position to complete the requirements below: computer services revenue, $25,307; net sales (of goods), $18,693; total sales and revenue, $44,000; cost of goods sold, $14,052; net profit, $18,833; quick assets, $90,924; current assets, $95,568; total assets, $120,268; current liabilities, $875; total liabilities, $875; and total equity, $119,393.

Required

1. Compute the gross margin ratio (both with and without services revenue) and net profit margin ratio.
2. Compute the current ratio and acid-test ratio.
3. Compute the debt ratio and equity ratio.
4. What percent of its assets are current? What percent are long term?

Beyond the Numbers

BTN 17-1   Answer the following on Nestlé using its financial statements in Appendix A.

Required

1. Compute common-size percents for financial years 2012 and 2013 for the following categories of assets: (a) total current assets, (b) property and equipment, net, and (c) intangible assets. Round to the nearest tenth of a percent.

2. Comment on any significant changes across the years for the statement of financial position percents computed in part 1.

Fast Forward

3. Access Nestlé's financial statements for financial years ending after December 31, 2013, from Nestlé's Website (www.nestle.com). Update your work for parts 1 and 2 using the new information accessed.

REPORTING IN ACTION

A1 P1 P2

BTN 17-2   Key 2013 comparative figures for both Adidas and Puma follow.

(EUR millions)	Adidas	Puma
Cash and cash equivalents	1,587	390.1
Accounts receivable, net	1,809	423.4
Inventories	2,634	521.3
Retained earnings	4,959	1,355.40
Cost of goods sold	7,352	1,597.80
Sales	14,492	2,985.30
Total assets	11,599	2,308.50

COMPARATIVE ANALYSIS

C2 P2

Required

1. Compute common-size percents for each of the companies using the data provided. Round to the nearest tenth of a percent.

2. Which company retains a higher portion of cumulative net profit in the company?

3. Which company has a higher gross margin ratio on sales?

4. Which company holds a higher percent of its total assets as inventory?

BTN 17-3   As Beacon Company controller, you are responsible for informing the board of directors about its financial activities. At the board meeting, you present the following information.

ETHICS CHALLENGE

A1

	2015	2014	2013
Sales trend percent	147.0%	135.0%	100.0%
Selling expenses to sales	10.1%	14.0%	15.6%
Sales to property, plant and equipment ratio	3.8 to 1	3.6 to 1	3.3 to 1
Current ratio	2.9 to 1	2.7 to 1	2.4 to 1
Acid-test ratio	1.1 to 1	1.4 to 1	1.5 to 1
Inventory turnover	7.8 times	9.0 times	10.2 times
Accounts receivable turnover	7.0 times	7.7 times	8.5 times
Total asset turnover	2.9 times	2.9 times	3.3 times
Return on total assets	10.4%	11.0%	13.2%
Return on shareholders' equity	10.7%	11.5%	14.1%
Profit margin ratio	3.6%	3.8%	4.0%

After the meeting, the company's CEO holds a press conference with analysts in which she mentions the following ratios.

	2015	2014	2013
Sales trend percent	147.0%	135.0%	100.0%
Selling expenses to sales	10.1%	14.0%	15.6%
Sales to property, plant and equipment ratio	3.8 to 1	3.6 to 1	3.3 to 1
Current ratio	2.9 to 1	2.7 to 1	2.4 to 1

Required

1. Why do you think the CEO decided to report 4 ratios instead of the 11 prepared?
2. Comment on the possible consequences of the CEO's reporting of the ratios selected.

COMMUNICATING IN PRACTICE
A1 P3

BTN 17-4   Each team is to select a different industry, and each team member is to select a different company in that industry and acquire its financial statements. Use those statements to analyze the company, including at least one ratio from each of the four building blocks of analysis. When necessary, use the financial press to determine the market price of its shares. Communicate with teammates via a meeting, e-mail, or telephone to discuss how different companies compare to each other and to industry norms. The team is to prepare a single one-page memorandum reporting on its analysis and the conclusions reached.

TAKING IT TO THE NET
P3

BTN 17-5   Locate L'Oréal's 2013 annual report at **www.loreal-finance.com/eng/annual-report** and complete the following requirements.

Required

Compute or identify the following profitability ratios of L'Oréal for its years ending December 31, 2013, and December 31, 2012. Interpret its profitability using the following ratio results. Show the first four ratios in percents and round to one decimal place each; round basic EPS to two decimal places.

1. Profit margin ratio.
2. Gross profit ratio.
3. Return on total assets.
4. Return on ordinary shareholders' equity.
5. Basic earnings per share.

TEAMWORK IN ACTION
P1 P2 P3

BTN 17-6   A team approach to learning financial statement analysis is often useful.

Required

1. Each team should write a description of horizontal and vertical analysis that all team members agree with and understand. Illustrate each description with an example.
2. *Each* member of the team is to select *one* of the following categories of ratio analysis. Explain what the ratios in that category measure. Choose one ratio from the category selected, present its formula, and explain what it measures.
   a. Liquidity and efficiency
   b. Solvency
   c. Profitability
   d. Market prospects
3. Each team member is to present his or her notes from part 2 to teammates. Team members are to confirm or correct other teammates' presentation.

Hint: Pairing within teams may be necessary for part 2. Use as an in-class activity or as an assignment. Consider presentations to the entire class using team rotation with transparencies.

BTN 17-7   Assume that Nelson Lam of Nelson and Company has impressed you since you first heard of him. You learn of a staff opening at Nelson and Company and decide to apply for it. Your resume is successfully screened from the thousands received and you advance to the interview process. You learn that the interview consists of analyzing the following financial facts and answering analysis questions. (*Note:* The data are taken from a small merchandiser in outdoor recreational equipment.)

ENTREPRENEURIAL DECISION

A1 P1 P2 P3

	2010	2009	2008
Sales trend percents	137.0%	125.0%	100.0%
Selling expenses to sales	9.8%	13.7%	15.3%
Sales to property, plant and equipment ratio	3.5 to 1	3.3 to 1	3.0 to 1
Current ratio	2.6 to 1	2.4 to 1	2.1 to 1
Acid-test ratio	0.8 to 1	1.1 to 1	1.2 to 1
Merchandise inventory turnover	7.5 times	8.7 times	9.9 times
Accounts receivable turnover	6.7 times	7.4 times	8.2 times
Total asset turnover	2.6 times	2.6 times	3.0 times
Return on total assets	8.8%	9.4%	11.1%
Return on equity	9.75%	11.50%	12.25%
Profit margin ratio	3.3%	3.5%	3.7%

Required

Use these data to answer each of the following questions with explanations.

1. Is it becoming easier for the company to meet its current liabilities on time and to take advantage of any available cash discounts? Explain.
2. Is the company collecting its accounts receivable more rapidly? Explain.
3. Is the company's investment in accounts receivable decreasing? Explain.
4. Is the company's investment in property, plant and equipment increasing? Explain.
5. Is the owner's investment becoming more profitable? Explain.
6. Did the dollar amount of selling expenses decrease during the three-year period? Explain.

BTN 17-8   Nike, Adidas, and Puma are competitors in the global marketplace. Locate Nike's annual report (known as 10-K) from its Website http://invest.nike.com/phoenix.zhtml?c=100529&p=irol-reportsannual.

GLOBAL DECISION

A1

Required

Compare Nike's annual report to one of its European competitor's reports (Adidas or Puma, presented in Appendix A). Identify five ways that the U.S. report differs from the European report.

ANSWERS TO MULTIPLE CHOICE QUIZ

1. d; ($351,000/$300,000) × 100 = 117%
2. e; ($86,000 + $76,000 + $122,000 + $12,000)/$124,000 = 2.39
3. c; ($86,000 + $76,000)/$124,000 = 1.31
4. a; ($124,000 + $90,000)/$830,000 = 25.78%
5. d; ($300,000 + $316,000)/$830,000 = 74.22%

18

Managerial Accounting Concepts and Principles

A Look Back

Chapter 17 described the analysis and interpretation of financial statement information. We applied horizontal, vertical, and ratio analyses to better understand company performance and financial condition.

A Look at This Chapter

We begin our study of managerial accounting by explaining its purpose and describing its major characteristics. We also discuss cost concepts and describe how they help managers gather and organize information for making decisions. The reporting of manufacturing activities is also discussed.

A Look Ahead

The remaining chapters discuss the types of decisions managers must make and how managerial accounting helps with those decisions. The first of these chapters, Chapter 19, considers how we measure costs assigned to certain types of projects.

Learning Objectives

CAP

CONCEPTUAL

C1 Explain the purpose and nature of, and the role of ethics in, managerial accounting. (p. 702)

C2 Describe accounting concepts useful in classifying costs. (p. 706)

C3 Define product and period costs and explain how they impact financial statements. (p. 708)

C4 Explain how statements of financial position and income statements for manufacturing and merchandising companies differ. (p. 710)

C5 Explain manufacturing activities and the flow of manufacturing costs. (p. 714)

C6 Describe trends in managerial accounting. (p. 717)

ANALYTICAL

A1 Compute cycle time and cycle efficiency, and explain their importance to production management (p. 719)

PROCEDURAL

P1 Compute cost of goods sold for a manufacturer. (p. 711)

P2 Prepare a manufacturing statement and explain its purpose and links to financial statements. (p. 715)

"The world is big enough for everyone to play in."—**ALICE ZHANG**

Decision Insight

Artistic Mischmasch

Mischmasch was the name of a magazine that Lewis Carrol, author of *Alice in Wonderland*, wrote for his family's entertainment. It is also a German word meaning a mixture of things. Today it may refer to the online art gallery founded by Alice Zhang, a graduate of the Rhode Island School of Design. Why Mischmasch? "The gallery features a hodgepodge of art around the world," explains Alice, "and that's the core of our business."

Alice's wandering into a virtual museum started when she was working as a designer in London. "I saw a lot of independently organized exhibitions. They were great works but they weren't getting a lot of attention," she explains. So with some entrepreneurial instinct and artistic foresight she started **Mischmasch (www.mischmaschonline.com)**, designing it as a "well-branded" artist community connecting the artist, the gallery, and the general public. Mischmasch members can upload as many art pieces as they want, comment and vote on others' works, and participate in discussion forums. Buyers can also buy art online. It uses a five-point voting system that constantly rearranges the listing of art pieces on the homepage to rank their popularity.

Initially, Mischmasch was often mistaken as a German Website, which turned out to be a lucky stroke. Picked up by German blogs, Mischmasch attracted many European artists to join. So successful was the venture that it launched Mischmasch Gallery, a physical exhibition space in Central Hong Kong, where popular works on its online counterpart are featured.

While managing the creative process, Alice ensures that she does not lose sight of the financials. Paying close attention to the managerial aspects of accounting and using accounting information to make informed business decisions have paid off bountifully. She is ready to take her company to the next level. In the pipeline is an online auction house to Mischmasch. To woo the mobile, tech-savvy crowd, it is rolling out smartphone video games and apps based on members' artwork.

Just like Alice in the famous story, this young woman is not afraid to go down the rabbit hole to seek new adventures. "The world is big enough for everyone to play in," says Alice. "The challenge is to create a fresh, interactive environment and design an effective user interface to make online art viewing a fun and compelling experience."

Managerial accounting, like financial accounting, provides information to help users make better decisions. However, managerial accounting and financial accounting differ in important ways, which this chapter explains. This chapter also compares the accounting and reporting practices used by manufacturing and merchandising companies. A merchandising company sells products without changing their condition. A manufacturing company buys raw materials and turns them into finished products for sale to customers. A third type of company earns revenues by providing services rather than products. The skills, tools, and techniques developed for measuring a manufacturing company's activities apply to service companies as well. The chapter concludes by explaining the flow of manufacturing activities and preparing the manufacturing statement.

Managerial Accounting Concepts and Principles

Managerial Accounting Basics	**Managerial Cost Concepts**	**Reporting Manufacturing Activities**
• Purpose of managerial accounting • Nature of managerial accounting • Managerial decisions • Fraud and ethics in managerial accounting	• Types of cost classifications • Identification of cost classifications • Cost concepts for service companies	• Statement of financial position • Income statement • Flow of activities • Manufacturing statement • Trends in managerial accounting

MANAGERIAL ACCOUNTING BASICS

Managerial accounting is an activity that provides financial and nonfinancial information to an organization's managers and other internal decision makers. This section explains the purpose of managerial accounting (also called *management accounting*) and compares it with financial accounting. The main purpose of the financial accounting system is to prepare general-purpose financial statements. That information is incomplete for internal decision makers who manage organizations.

Purpose of Managerial Accounting

C1 Explain the purpose and nature of, and the role of ethics in, managerial accounting.

The purpose of both managerial accounting and financial accounting is providing useful information to decision makers. They do this by collecting, managing, and reporting information in demand by their users. Both areas of accounting also share the common practice of reporting monetary information, although managerial accounting includes the reporting of nonmonetary information. They even report some of the same information. For instance, a company's financial statements contain information useful for both its managers (insiders) and other persons interested in the company (outsiders).

The remainder of this book looks carefully at managerial accounting information, how to gather it, and how managers use it. We consider the concepts and procedures used to determine the costs of products and services as well as topics such as budgeting, break-even analysis, product costing, profit planning, and cost analysis. Information about the costs of products and services is important for many decisions that managers make. These decisions include predicting the future costs of a product or service. Predicted costs are used in product pricing, profitability analysis, and in deciding whether to make or buy a product or component. More generally, much of managerial accounting involves gathering information about costs for planning and control decisions.

Point: Nonfinancial information, also called nonmonetary information, includes customer and employee satisfaction data, the percentage of on-time deliveries, and product defect rates.

One of the purposes of managerial accounting is an accurate measurement of costs. These are costs of products, services, processes, or projects. These may be collectively referred to as *cost objects*, objects for which cost is sought to be measured. Typically, measurement involves a correct assignment of traceable costs to a cost object and an allocation of nontraceable costs following some scientific basis. The output of the measurement function provides the basis for most managerial decisions using costs as an input.

Planning is the process of setting goals and making plans to achieve them. Companies formulate long-term strategic plans that usually span a 5- to 10-year horizon and then refine them with medium-term and short-term plans. Strategic plans usually set a firm's long-term direction by developing a road map based on opportunities such as new products, new markets, and capital investments. A strategic plan's goals and objectives are broadly defined given its long-term orientation. Medium- and short-term plans are more operational in nature. They translate the strategic plan into actions. These plans are more concrete and consist of better defined objectives and goals. A short-term plan often covers a one-year period that, when translated in monetary terms, is known as a budget.

Control is the process of monitoring planning decisions and evaluating an organization's activities and employees. It includes the measurement and evaluation of actions, processes, and outcomes. Feedback provided by the control function allows managers to revise their plans. Measurement of actions and processes also allows managers to take corrective actions to avoid undesirable outcomes. For example, managers periodically compare actual results with planned results. Exhibit 18.1 portrays the important management functions of planning and control.

Point: Costs are important to managers because they impact both the financial position and profitability of a business. Managerial accounting assists in analysis, planning, and control of costs.

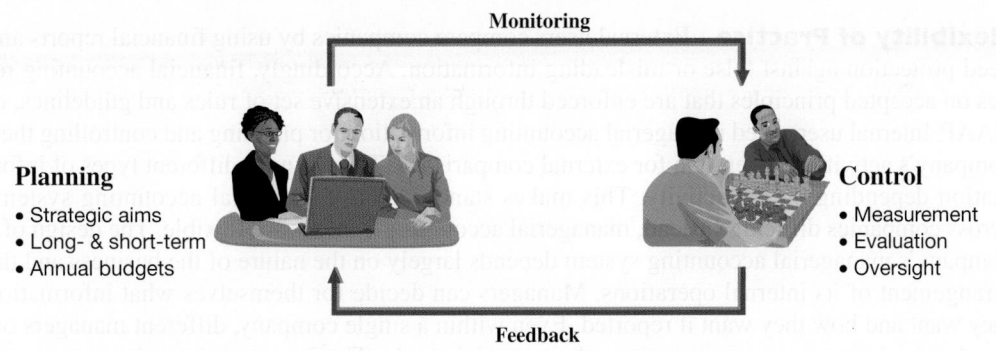

EXHIBIT 18.1

Planning and Control (including monitoring and feedback)

Managers use information to plan and control business activities. In later chapters, we explain how managers also use this information to direct and improve business operations.

Nature of Managerial Accounting

Managerial accounting has its own special characteristics. To understand these characteristics, we compare managerial accounting to financial accounting; they differ in at least seven important ways. These differences are summarized in Exhibit 18.2. This section discusses each of these characteristics.

	Financial Accounting	Managerial Accounting
1. Users and decision makers	Investors, creditors, and other users external to the organization	Managers, employees, and decision makers internal to the organization
2. Purpose of information	Assist external users in making investment, credit, and other decisions	Assist managers in making planning and control decisions
3. Flexibility of practice	Structured and often controlled by GAAP	Relatively flexible (no GAAP constraints)
4. Timeliness of information	Often available only after an audit is complete	Available quickly without the need to wait for an audit
5. Time dimension	Focus on historical information with some predictions	Many projections and estimates; historical information also presented
6. Focus of information	Emphasis on whole organization	Emphasis on an organization's products, services, projects, processes, and subdivisions
7. Nature of information	Monetary information	Mostly monetary; but also nonmonetary information

Point: It is desirable to accumulate certain information for management reports in a database separate from financial accounting records.

Users and Decision Makers   Companies accumulate, process, and report financial accounting and managerial accounting information for different groups of decision makers. Financial accounting information is provided primarily to external users including investors, creditors, analysts, and regulators. External users rarely have a major role in managing a company's daily activities. Managerial accounting information is provided primarily to internal users who are responsible for making and implementing decisions about a company's business activities.

Purpose of Information   Investors, creditors, and other external users of financial accounting information must often decide whether to invest in or lend to a company. If they have already done so, they must decide whether to continue owning the company or carrying the loan. Internal decision makers must plan a company's future. They seek to take advantage of opportunities or to overcome obstacles. They also try to control activities and ensure their effective and efficient implementation. Managerial accounting information helps these internal users make both planning and control decisions.

Point: The *Institute of Management Accountants* issues statements that govern the practice of managerial accounting. Accountants who pass a qualifying exam are awarded the CMA.

Flexibility of Practice   External users compare companies by using financial reports and need protection against false or misleading information. Accordingly, financial accounting relies on accepted principles that are enforced through an extensive of rules and guidelines, or GAAP. Internal users need managerial accounting information for planning and controlling their company's activities rather than for external comparisons. They require different types of information depending on the activity. This makes standardizing managerial accounting systems across companies difficult. Instead, managerial accounting systems are flexible. The design of a company's managerial accounting system depends largely on the nature of the business and the arrangement of its internal operations. Managers can decide for themselves what information they want and how they want it reported. Even within a single company, different managers often design their own systems to meet their special needs. The important question a manager must ask is whether the information being collected and reported is useful for planning, decision making, and control purposes.

Point: Financial statements are usually issued several weeks after the period-end. GAAP requires the reporting of important events that occur while the statements are being prepared. These events are called *subsequent events.*

Point: Independent auditors test the integrity of managerial accounting records when they are used in preparing financial statements.

Timeliness of Information   Formal financial statements reporting past transactions and events are not immediately available to outside parties. Independent certified public accountants often must *audit* a company's financial statements before it provides them to external users. Thus, because audits often take several weeks to complete, financial reports to outsiders usually are not available until well after the period-end. However, managers can quickly obtain managerial accounting information. External auditors need not review it. Estimates and projections are acceptable. To get information quickly, managers often accept less precision in reports. As an example, an early internal report to management prepared right after the year-end could report net profit for the year between $4.2 and $4.8 million. An audited income statement could later show net profit for the year at $4.6 million. The internal report is not precise, but its information can be more useful because it is available earlier.

   Internal auditing plays an important role in managerial accounting. Internal auditors evaluate the flow of information not only inside but also outside the company. Managers are responsible for preventing and detecting fraudulent activities in their companies.

Time Dimension   To protect external users from false expectations, financial reports deal primarily with results of both past activities and current conditions. While some predictions such as service lives and salvage values of property, plant and equipment are necessary, financial accounting avoids predictions whenever possible. Managerial accounting regularly includes predictions of conditions and events. As an example, one important managerial accounting report is a budget, which predicts revenues, expenses, and other items. If managerial accounting reports were restricted to the past and present, managers would be less able to plan activities and less effective in managing and evaluating current activities.

EXHIBIT 18.3

Focus of External Reports

Focus of Information   Companies often organize into divisions and departments, but investors rarely can buy shares in one division or department. Nor do creditors lend money to a company's single division or department. Instead, they own shares in or make loans to the entire company. Financial accounting focuses primarily on a company as a whole as depicted in Exhibit

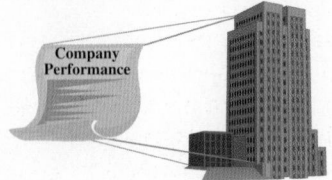

Company Performance

18.3. The focus of managerial accounting is different. While top-level managers are responsible for managing the whole company, most other managers are responsible for much smaller sets of activities. These middle-level and lower-level managers need managerial accounting reports dealing with specific activities, projects, and subdivisions for which they are responsible. For instance, division sales managers are directly responsible only for the results achieved in their divisions. Accordingly, division sales managers need information about results achieved in their own divisions to improve their performance. This information includes the level of success achieved by each individual, product, or department in each division as depicted in Exhibit 18.4.

EXHIBIT 18.4

Focus of Internal Reports

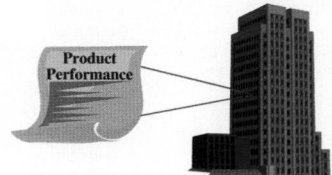

Nature of Information Both financial and managerial accounting systems report monetary information. Managerial accounting systems also report considerable nonmonetary information. Monetary information is an important part of managerial decisions, and nonmonetary information plays a crucial role, especially when monetary effects are difficult to measure. Common examples of nonmonetary information are the quality and delivery criteria of purchasing decisions.

Decision Ethics   Answer — p. 724

Production Manager You invite three friends to a restaurant. When the dinner check arrives, David, a self-employed entrepreneur, picks it up saying, "Here, let me pay. I'll deduct it as a business expense on my tax return." Denise, a salesperson, takes the check from David's hand and says, "I'll put this on my company's credit card. It won't cost us anything." Derek, a factory manager for a company, laughs and says, "Neither of you understands. I'll put this on my company's credit card and call it overhead on a cost-plus contract my company has with a client." (*A cost-plus contract means the company receives its costs plus a percent of those costs.*) Adds Derek, "That way, my company pays for dinner *and* makes a profit." Who should pay the bill? Why? ■

Managerial Decision Making

The previous section emphasized differences between financial and managerial accounting, but they are not entirely separate. Similar information is useful to both external and internal users. For instance, information about costs of manufacturing products is useful to all users in making decisions. Also, both financial and managerial accounting affect peoples' actions. For example, Atlas Cycles's design of a sales compensation plan affects the behavior of its salesforce when selling its manufactured bikes. It also must estimate the dual effects of promotion and sales compensation plans on buying patterns of customers. These estimates impact the equipment purchase decisions for manufacturing and can affect the supplier selection criteria established by purchasing. Thus, financial and managerial accounting systems do more than measure; they also affect people's decisions and actions.

Fraud and Ethics in Managerial Accounting

Fraud, and the role of ethics in reducing fraud, are important factors in running business operations. Fraud involves the use of one's job for personal gain through the deliberate misuse of the employer's assets. Examples include theft of the employer's cash or other assets, overstating reimbursable expenses, payroll schemes, and financial statement fraud. Fraud affects all business and it is costly: According to the Association of Certified Fraud Examiners, a 2010 survey of 338 fraud cases revealed that the median fraud loss for organizations in Asia is about US$300,000, significantly higher than the global median loss of US$160,000. Asset misappropriation was the most common form of occupational fraud.

The most common type of fraud, where employees steal or misuse the employer's resources, results in an average loss of $175,000 per occurrence. For example, in a billing fraud, an employee sets up a bogus supplier. The employee then prepares bills from the supplier and pays these bills from the employer's checking account. The employee cashes the checks sent to the bogus supplier and uses them for his or her own personal benefit.

More generally, although there are many types of fraud schemes, all fraud:

● Is done to provide direct or indirect benefit to the employee.
● Violates the employee's obligations to the employer.
● Costs the employer money or loss of other assets.
● Is hidden from the employer.

Implications for Managerial Accounting   Fraud increases a business's costs. Left undetected, these inflated costs can result in poor pricing decisions, an improper product mix, and faulty performance evaluations. Management can develop accounting systems to closely track costs and identify deviations from expected amounts. In addition, managers rely on an **internal control system** to monitor and control business activities. An internal control system is the policies and procedures managers use to:

● Urge adherence to company policies.
● Promote efficient operations.
● Ensure reliable accounting.
● Protect assets.

Point: The IMA also issues the Certified Management Accountant (CMA) and the Certified Financial Manager (CFM) certifications. Employees with the CMA or CFM certifications typically earn higher salaries than those without.

Point: The **Sarbanes-Oxley Act** requires each issuer of securities to disclose whether it has adopted a code of ethics for its senior officers and the content of that code.

Combating fraud and other dilemmas requires ethics in accounting. **Ethics** are beliefs that distinguish right from wrong. They are accepted standards of good and bad behavior. Identifying the ethical path can be difficult. The preferred path is a course of action that avoids casting doubt on one's decisions.

The Institute of Cost and Works Accountants of India (ICWAI) is the professional body that controls the qualifications and ethical conduct of management accountants in India. Management Accountants in India should preferably, though not necessarily, hold a qualification granted by the ICWAI. The institute's code of ethics requires its members to possess integrity, objectivity, competence, confidentiality, and professional behavior.

Quick Check   Answers — p. 725

1. Managerial accounting produces information (*a*) to meet internal users' needs, (*b*) to meet a user's specific needs, (*c*) often focusing on the future, or (*d*) all of these.
2. What is the difference between the intended users of financial and managerial accounting?
3. Do generally accepted accounting principles (GAAP) control and dictate managerial accounting?

MANAGERIAL COST CONCEPTS

C2 Describe accounting concepts useful in classifying costs.

An organization incurs many different types of costs that are classified differently, depending on management needs (different costs for different purposes). We can classify costs on the basis of their (1) behavior, (2) traceability, (3) controllability, (4) relevance, and (5) function. This section explains each concept for assigning costs to products and services.

Types of Cost Classifications

Classification by Behavior   At a basic level, a cost can be classified as fixed or variable. A **fixed cost** does not change with changes in the volume of activity (within a range of activity known as an activity's *relevant range*). For example, straight-line depreciation on equipment is a fixed cost. A **variable cost** changes in proportion to changes in the volume of activity. Sales commissions computed as a percent of sales revenue are variable costs. Additional examples of fixed and variable costs for a bike manufacturer are provided in Exhibit 18.5. When cost items are combined, total cost can be fixed, variable, or mixed. *Mixed* refers to a combination of fixed and variable costs. Equipment rental often includes a fixed cost for some minimum amount and a variable cost based on amount of usage. Classification of costs by behavior is helpful in cost-volume-profit analyses and short-term decision making. We discuss these in Chapters 22 and 25.

Fixed Cost: Rent for Mount Fuji Bikes' building is $22,000, and it doesn't change with the number of bikes produced.

Variable Cost: Cost of bicycle tires is variable with the number of bikes produced—this cost is $15 per pair.

EXHIBIT 18.5
Fixed and Variable Costs

Classification by Traceability   A cost is often traced to a **cost object,** which is a product, process, department, or customer to which costs are assigned. **Direct costs** are those traceable to a single cost object. For example, if a product is a cost object, its material and labor costs are usually directly traceable. **Indirect costs** are those that cannot be easily and cost–beneficially traced to a single cost object. An example of an indirect cost is a maintenance plan that benefits two or more departments. Exhibit 18.6 identifies examples of both direct and indirect costs for the maintenance department in a manufacturing plant. Thus, salaries of Mount Fuji Bikes' maintenance department employees are considered indirect if the cost object is bicycles and direct if the cost object is the maintenance department. Classification of costs by traceability is useful for cost allocation. This is discussed in Chapter 21.

EXHIBIT 18.6
Direct and Indirect Costs of a Maintenance Department

Direct Costs		Indirect Costs	
• Salaries of maintenance department employees	• Materials purchased by maintenance department	• Factory accounting	• Factory light and heat
• Equipment purchased by maintenance department	• Maintenance department equipment depreciation	• Factory administration	• Factory internal audit
		• Factory rent	• Factory intranet
		• Factory manager's salary	• Insurance on factory

Decision Maker   Answer — p. 724

Entrepreneur   You wish to trace as many of your assembly department's direct costs as possible. You can trace 90% of them in an economical manner. To trace the other 10%, you need sophisticated and costly accounting software. Do you purchase this software? ■

Classification by Controllability   A cost can be defined as **controllable** or **not controllable.** Whether a cost is controllable or not depends on the employee's responsibilities, as shown in Exhibit 18.7. This is referred to as *hierarchical levels* in management, or *pecking order.* For example, investments in machinery are controllable by upper-level managers but not lower-level managers. Many daily operating expenses such as overtime often are controllable by lower-level managers. Classification of costs by controllability is especially useful for assigning responsibility to and evaluating managers.

EXHIBIT 18.7
Controllability of Costs

Senior Manager
Controls costs of investments in land, buildings, and equipment.

Supervisor
Controls daily expenses such as supplies, maintenance, and overtime.

Classification by Relevance   A cost can be classified by relevance by identifying it as either a sunk cost or an out-of-pocket cost. A **sunk cost** has already been incurred and cannot be avoided or changed. It is irrelevant to future decisions. One example is the cost of a company's

Point: Opportunity costs are not recorded by the accounting system.

office equipment previously purchased. An **out-of-pocket cost** requires a future outlay of cash and is relevant for decision making. Future purchases of equipment involve out-of-pocket costs. A discussion of relevant costs must also consider opportunity costs. An **opportunity cost** is the potential benefit lost by choosing a specific action from two or more alternatives. One example is a student giving up wages from a job to attend evening classes. Consideration of opportunity cost is important when, for example, an insurance company must decide whether to outsource its payroll function or maintain it internally. This is discussed in Chapter 25.

C3	Define product and period costs and explain how they impact financial statements.

Classification by Function   Another cost classification (for manufacturers) is capitalization as inventory or to expense as incurred. Costs capitalized as inventory are called **product costs,** which refer to expenditures necessary and integral to finished products. They include direct materials, direct labor, and indirect manufacturing costs called *overhead costs.* Product costs pertain to activities carried out to manufacture the product. Costs expensed are called **period costs,** which refer to expenditures identified more with a time period than with finished products. They include selling and general administrative expenses. Period costs pertain to activities that are not part of the manufacturing process. A distinction between product and period costs is important because period costs are expensed in the income statement and product costs are assigned to inventory on the statement of financial position until that inventory is sold. An ability to understand and identify product costs and period costs is crucial to using and interpreting a *manufacturing statement* described later in this chapter.

Point: Only costs of production and purchases are classed as product costs.

Exhibit 18.8 shows the different effects of product and period costs. Period costs flow directly to the current income statement as expenses. They are not reported as assets. Product costs are first assigned to inventory. Their final treatment depends on when inventory is sold or disposed of. Product costs assigned to finished goods that are sold in year 2011 are reported on the 2011 income statement as part of cost of goods sold. Product costs assigned to unsold inventory are carried forward on the statement of financial position at the end of year 2011. If this inventory is sold in year 2012 product costs assigned to it are reported as part of cost of goods sold in that year's income statement.

Point: Product costs are either in the income statement as part of cost of goods sold or in the statement of financial position as inventory. Period costs appear only on the income statement under operating expenses. See Exhibit 18.8.

Point: For a team approach to identifying period and product costs, see *Teamwork in Action* in the *Beyond the Numbers* section.

The difference between period and product costs explains why the year 2011 income statement does not report operating expenses related to either factory workers' wages or depreciation on factory buildings and equipment. Instead, both costs are combined with the cost of raw materials to compute the product cost of finished goods. A portion of these manufacturing costs (related to the goods sold) is reported in the year 2011 income statement as part of Cost of Goods Sold. The other portion is reported on the statement of financial position at the end of that year as part of Inventory. The portion assigned to inventory could be included in any or all of raw materials, goods in process, or finished goods inventories.

EXHIBIT 18.8

Period and Product Costs in Financial Statements

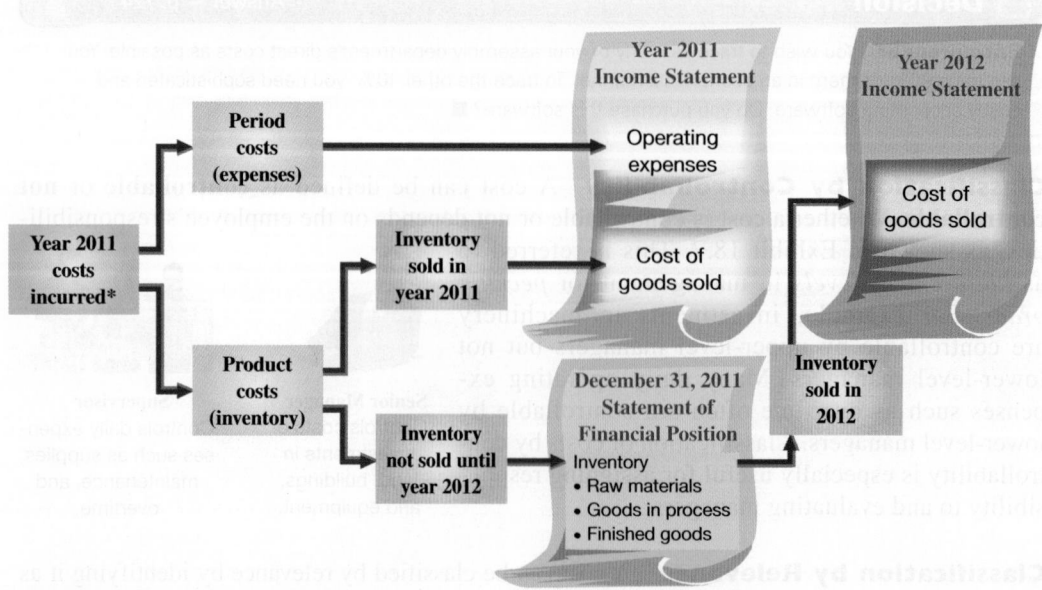

* This diagram excludes costs to acquire assets other than inventory.

Decision Maker   Answer — p. 725

Purchase Manager You are evaluating two potential suppliers of seats for the manufacturing of motor-cycles. One supplier (A) quotes a $145 price per seat and ensures 100% quality standards and on-time delivery. The second supplier (B) quotes a $115 price per seat but does not give any written assurances on quality or delivery. You decide to contract with the second supplier (B), saving $30 per seat. Does this decision have opportunity costs? ■

Identification of Cost Classifications

It is important to understand that a cost can be classified using any one (or combination) of the five different means described here. To do this we must understand costs and operations. Specifically, for the five classifications, we must be able to identify the *activity* for behavior, *cost object* for traceability, *management hierarchical level* for controllability, *opportunity cost* for relevance, and *benefit period* for function. Factory rent, for instance, can be classified as a product cost; it is fixed with respect to number of units produced, it is indirect with respect to the product, and it is not controllable by a production supervisor. Potential multiple classifications are shown in Exhibit 18.9 using different cost items incurred in manufacturing mountain bikes. The finished bike is the cost object. Proper allocation of these costs and the managerial decisions based on cost data depend on a correct cost classification.

Cost Item	By Behavior	By Traceability	By Function
Bicycle tires	Variable	Direct	Product
Wages of assembly worker*	Variable	Direct	Product
Advertising	Fixed	Indirect	Period
Production manager's salary	Fixed	Indirect	Product
Office depreciation	Fixed	Indirect	Period

EXHIBIT 18.9

Examples of Multiple Cost Classifications

* Although an assembly worker's wages are classified as variable costs, their actual behavior depends on how workers are paid and whether their wages are based on a union contract (such as piece rate or monthly wages).

Cost Concepts for Service Companies

The cost concepts described are generally applicable to service organizations. For example, consider **Singapore Airlines**. Its cost of beverages for passengers is a variable cost based on number of passengers. The cost of leasing an aircraft is fixed with respect to number of passengers. We can also trace a flight crew's salary to a specific flight whereas we likely cannot trace wages for the ground crew to a specific flight. Classification by function (such as product versus period costs) is not relevant to service companies because services are not inventoried. Instead, costs incurred by a service firm are expensed in the reporting period when incurred. Nevertheless, service companies also make a distinction between cost of service and other functional costs such as selling and administrative costs. Some service companies such as those providing software services report *cost of sales*. For example, **Infosys**, one of the leading software service companies in the world, reports "Software development and business process management expenses" as something that can be considered equivalent to the cost of goods sold in manufacturing companies.

Managers in service companies must understand and apply cost concepts. They seek and rely on accurate cost estimates for many decisions. For example, an airline manager must often decide between canceling or rerouting flights. The manager must also be able to estimate costs saved by canceling a flight versus rerouting. Knowledge of fixed costs is equally important. We explain more about the cost requirements for these and other managerial decisions in Chapter 25.

Point: All expenses of service companies are period costs because these companies do not have inventory.

Service Costs
- Beverages and snacks
- Cleaning fees
- Pilot and copilot salaries
- Attendant salaries
- Fuel and oil costs
- Travel agent fees
- Ground crew salaries

Quick Check   Answers — p. 725

4. Which type of cost behavior increases total costs when volume of activity increases?

5. How could traceability of costs improve managerial decisions?

REPORTING MANUFACTURING ACTIVITIES

Companies with manufacturing activities differ from both merchandising and service companies. The main difference between merchandising and manufacturing companies is that merchandisers buy goods ready for sale while manufacturers produce goods from materials and labor. **BigC** is an example of a merchandising company. It buys and sells goods without physically changing them. **Li Ning** is primarily a manufacturer of shoes, apparel, and accessories. It purchases materials such as leather, cloth, dye, plastic, rubber, glue, and laces and then uses employees' labor to convert these materials to products. **Singapore Airlines** is a service company that transports people and items.

Manufacturing activities differ from both selling merchandise and providing services. Also, the financial statements for manufacturing companies differ slightly. This section considers some of these differences and compares them to accounting for a merchandising company.

Manufacturer's Statement of Financial Position

C4 Explain how statements of financial position and income statements for manufacturing and merchandising companies differ.

Manufacturers carry several unique assets and usually have three inventories instead of the single inventory that merchandisers carry. Exhibit 18.10 shows three different inventories in the current asset section of the statement of financial position for Mount Fuji Bikes, a manufacturer. The three inventories are raw materials, goods in process, and finished goods.

Raw Materials Inventory   **Raw materials inventory** refers to the goods a company acquires to use in making products. It uses raw materials in two ways: directly and indirectly. Most raw materials physically become part of a product and are identified with specific units or batches of a product. Raw materials used directly in a product are called *direct materials*. Other materials used to support production processes are sometimes not as clearly identified with specific units or batches of product. These materials are called **indirect materials** because they are not clearly identified with specific product units or batches. Items used as indirect materials often appear on a statement of financial position as factory supplies or are included in raw materials. Some direct materials are classified as indirect materials when their costs are low (insignificant). Examples include screws and nuts used in assembling mountain bikes and staples and glue used in manufacturing

Point: Reducing the size of inventories saves storage costs and frees money for other uses.

EXHIBIT 18.10

Statement of financial position for a Manufacturer

MOUNT FUJI BIKES				
Statement of Financial Position				
December 31, 2011				
Assets			**Liabilities and Equity**	
Current assets			Current liabilities	
Cash	$ 11,000		Accounts payable	$ 14,000
Accounts receivable, net	30,150		Wages payable	540
Raw materials inventory	9,000		Interest payable	2,000
Goods in process inventory	7,500		income tax payable	32,600
Finished goods inventory	10,300		Total current liabilities	49,140
Factory supplies	350			
Prepaid insurance	300		Long-term liabilities	
Total current assets	68,600		Long-term notes payable	50,000
Property, plant and equipment			Total liabilities	99,140
Small tools, net	1,100			
Delivery equipment, net	5,000		Shareholders' equity	
Office equipment, net	1,300		Share capital—ordinary $1.2 par	24,000
Factory machinery, net	65,500		Paid-in capital	76,000
Factory building, net	86,700		Retained earnings	49,760
Land	9,500		Total shareholders' equity	149,760
Total property, plant and equipment, net	169,100			
Intangible assets (patents), net	11,200		Total liabilities and equity	$248,900
Total assets	$248,900			

shoes. Using the *materiality principle,* individually tracing the costs of each of these materials and classifying them separately as direct materials does not make much economic sense. For instance, keeping detailed records of the amount of glue used to manufacture one shoe is not cost beneficial.

Inventories of Mount Fuji Bikes

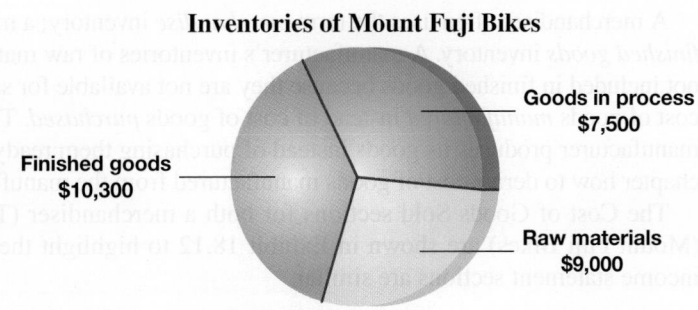

Goods in process $7,500

Finished goods $10,300

Raw materials $9,000

Goods in Process Inventory   Another inventory held by manufacturers is **goods in process inventory,** also called *work in process inventory.* It consists of products in the process of being manufactured but not yet complete. The amount of goods in process inventory depends on the type of production process. If the time required to produce a unit of product is short, the goods in process inventory is likely small; but if weeks or months are needed to produce a unit, the goods in process inventory is usually larger.

Finished Goods Inventory   A third inventory owned by a manufacturer is **finished goods inventory,** which consists of completed products ready for sale. This inventory is similar to merchandise inventory owned by a merchandising company. Manufacturers also often own unique items of property, plant and equipment such as small tools, factory buildings, factory equipment, and patents to manufacture products. The statement of financial position in Exhibit 18.10 shows that Mount Fuji Bikes owns all of these assets. Some manufacturers invest millions or even billions of dollars in production facilities and patents. As at March 31, 2014, the **Toyota Motor** company carried inventories of more than JPY 1,894 billion. As on the same date, the company's total property, plant and equipment *at cost* was over JPY 19,764 billion. Toyota is among the top three car producers in the world.

Manufacturer's Income Statement

The main difference between the income statement of a manufacturer and that of a merchandiser involves the items making up cost of goods sold. Exhibit 18.11 compares the components of cost of goods sold for a manufacturer and a merchandiser. A merchandiser adds cost of goods purchased to beginning merchandise inventory and then subtracts ending merchandise inventory to get cost of goods sold. A manufacturer adds cost of goods manufactured to beginning finished goods inventory and then subtracts ending finished goods inventory to get cost of goods sold.

P1 Compute cost of goods sold for a manufacturer.

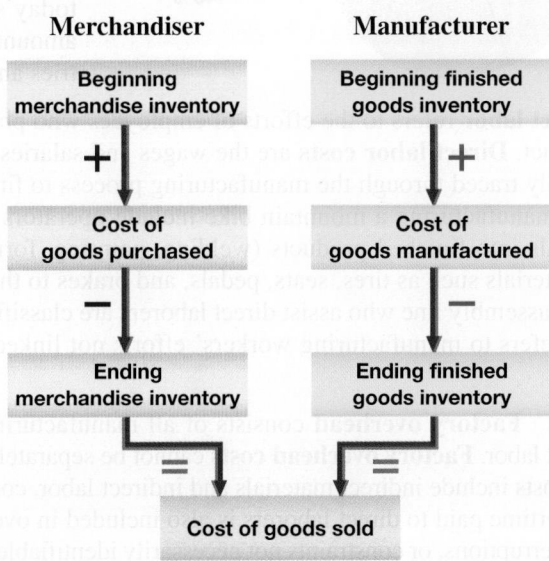

EXHIBIT 18.11

Cost of Goods Sold Computation

A merchandiser often uses the term *merchandise* inventory; a manufacturer often uses the term *finished goods* inventory. A manufacturer's inventories of raw materials and goods in process are not included in finished goods because they are not available for sale. A manufacturer also shows cost of goods *manufactured* instead of cost of goods *purchased.* This difference occurs because a manufacturer produces its goods instead of purchasing them ready for sale. We show later in this chapter how to derive cost of goods manufactured from the manufacturing statement.

EXHIBIT 18.12

Cost of Goods Sold for a
Merchandiser and Manufacturer

The Cost of Goods Sold sections for both a merchandiser (Tele-Mart) and a manufacturer (Mount Fuji Bikes) are shown in Exhibit 18.12 to highlight these differences. The remaining income statement sections are similar.

Merchandising (Tele-Mart) Company		Manufacturing (Mount Fuji Bikes) Company	
Cost of goods sold		Cost of goods sold	
Beginning *merchandise* inventory	$ 14,200	**Beginning *finished goods* inventory**	$ 11,200
Cost of merchandise *purchased*	234,150	**Cost of goods *manufactured****	170,500
Goods available for sale	248,350	Goods available for sale	181,700
Less ending *merchandise* inventory	12,100	**Less ending *finished goods* inventory**	10,300
Cost of goods sold	$236,250	Cost of goods sold	$171,400

* Cost of goods manufactured is reported in the income statement of Exhibit 18.14.

Although the cost of goods sold computations are similar, the numbers in these computations reflect different activities. A merchandiser's cost of goods purchased is the cost of buying products to be sold. A manufacturer's cost of goods manufactured is the sum of direct materials, direct labor, and factory overhead costs incurred in producing products. The remainder of this section further explains these three manufacturing costs and describes prime and conversion costs.

Direct Materials   **Direct materials** are tangible components of a finished product. **Direct material costs** are the expenditures for direct materials that are separately and readily traced through the manufacturing process to finished goods. Examples of direct materials in manufacturing a mountain bike include its tires, seat, frame, pedals, brakes, cables, gears, and handlebars. The chart in the margin shows that direct materials generally make up about 45% of manufacturing costs in today's products, but this amount varies across industries and companies.

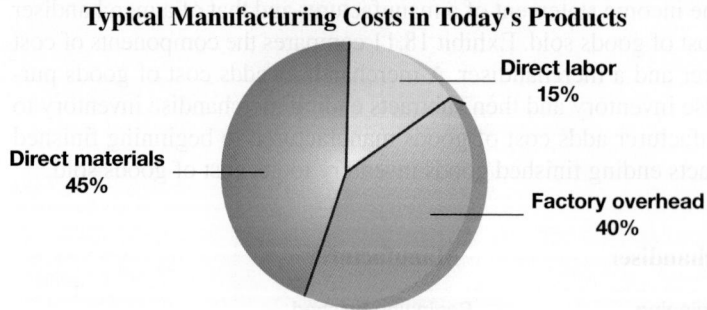

Typical Manufacturing Costs in Today's Products

Direct labor 15%
Direct materials 45%
Factory overhead 40%

Direct Labor   **Direct labor** refers to the efforts of employees who physically convert materials to finished product. **Direct labor costs** are the wages and salaries for direct labor that are separately and readily traced through the manufacturing process to finished goods. Examples of direct labor in manufacturing a mountain bike include operators directly involved in converting raw materials into finished products (welding, painting, forming) and assembly workers who attach materials such as tires, seats, pedals, and brakes to the bike frames. Costs of other workers on the assembly line who assist direct laborers are classified as **indirect labor costs.** **Indirect labor** refers to manufacturing workers' efforts not linked to specific units or batches of the product.

Point: Indirect labor costs are part of factory overhead.

Factory Overhead   **Factory overhead** consists of all manufacturing costs that are not direct materials or direct labor. **Factory overhead costs** cannot be separately or readily traced to finished goods. These costs include indirect materials and indirect labor, costs not directly traceable to the product. Overtime paid to direct laborers is also included in overhead because overtime is due to delays, interruptions, or constraints not necessarily identifiable to a specific product or batches of product. Factory overhead costs also include maintenance of the mountain bike

Point: Factory overhead is also called *manufacturing overhead.*

factory, supervision of its employees, repairing manufacturing equipment, factory utilities (water, gas, electricity), production manager's salary, factory rent, depreciation on factory buildings and equipment, factory insurance, property taxes on factory buildings and equipment, and factory accounting and legal services. Factory overhead does *not* include selling and administrative expenses because they are not incurred in manufacturing products. These expenses are called *period costs* and are recorded as expenses on the income statement when incurred.

Direct material, direct labor, and factory overhead together constitute the cost of goods sold. For **Toyota Motors**, for the year ended March 31, 2014, the cost of goods sold was JPY 19,988 billion. This was just over 82% of its revenues from the sale of its products.

Prime and Conversion Costs   Direct material costs and direct labor costs are also called **prime costs**—expenditures directly associated with the manufacture of finished goods. Direct labor costs and overhead costs are called **conversion costs**—expenditures incurred in the process of converting raw materials to finished goods. Direct labor costs are considered both prime costs and conversion costs. Exhibit 18.13 conveys the relation between prime and conversion costs and their components of direct material, direct labor, and factory overhead.

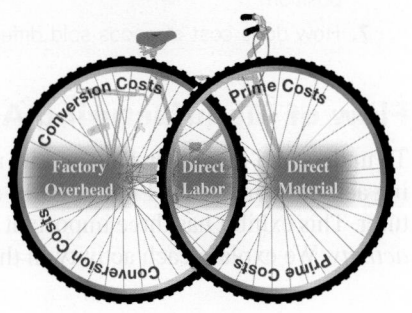

EXHIBIT 18.13

Prime and Conversion Costs and Their Makeup

Prime costs =
Direct materials + Direct labor.
Conversion costs =
Direct labor + Factory overhead.

Reporting Performance   Exhibit 18.14 shows the income statement for Mount Fuji Bikes. Its operating expenses include sales salaries, office salaries, and depreciation of delivery

EXHIBIT 18.14

Income Statement for a Manufacturer

MOUNT FUJI BIKES Income Statement For Year Ended December 31, 2011		
Sales		$310,000
Cost of goods sold		
Finished goods inventory, Dec. 31, 2010	$ 11,200	
Cost of goods manufactured	170,500	
Goods available for sale	181,700	
Less finished goods inventory, Dec. 31, 2011	(10,300)	
Cost of goods sold		171,400
Gross profit		138,600
Operating expenses		
Selling expenses		
Sales salaries expense	18,000	
Advertising expense	5,500	
Delivery wages expense	12,000	
Shipping supplies expense	250	
Insurance expense—Delivery equipment	300	
Depreciation expense—Delivery equipment	2,100	
Total selling expenses		38,150
General and administrative expenses		
Office salaries expense	15,700	
Miscellaneous expense	200	
Bad debts expense	1,550	
Office supplies expense	100	
Depreciation expense—Office equipment	200	
Interest expense	4,000	
Total general and administrative expenses		21,750
Total operating expenses		59,900
Income before income taxes		78,700
income tax payable		32,600
Net profit		$ 46,100

Point: Manufacturers treat costs such as depreciation and rent as product costs if they are related to manufacturing.

and office equipment. Operating expenses do not include manufacturing costs such as factory workers' wages and depreciation of production equipment and the factory buildings. These manufacturing costs are reported as part of cost of goods manufactured and included in cost of goods sold. We explained why and how this is done in the section "Classification by Function."

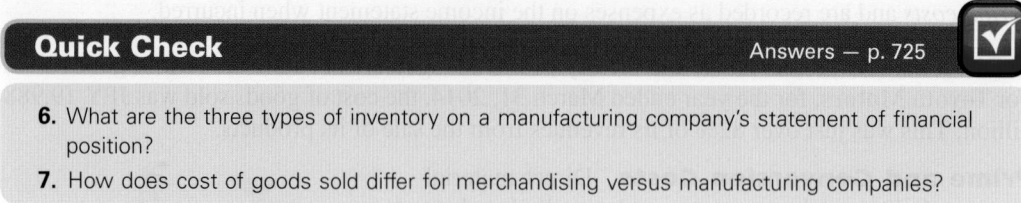

Quick Check

Answers — p. 725

6. What are the three types of inventory on a manufacturing company's statement of financial position?
7. How does cost of goods sold differ for merchandising versus manufacturing companies?

Flow of Manufacturing Activities

C5 Explain manufacturing activities and the flow of manufacturing costs.

To understand manufacturing and its reports, we must first understand the flow of manufacturing activities and costs. Exhibit 18.15 shows the flow of manufacturing activities for a manufacturer. This exhibit has three important sections: *materials activity, production activity,* and *sales activity.* We explain each activity in this section.

EXHIBIT 18.15

Activities and Cost Flows in Manufacturing

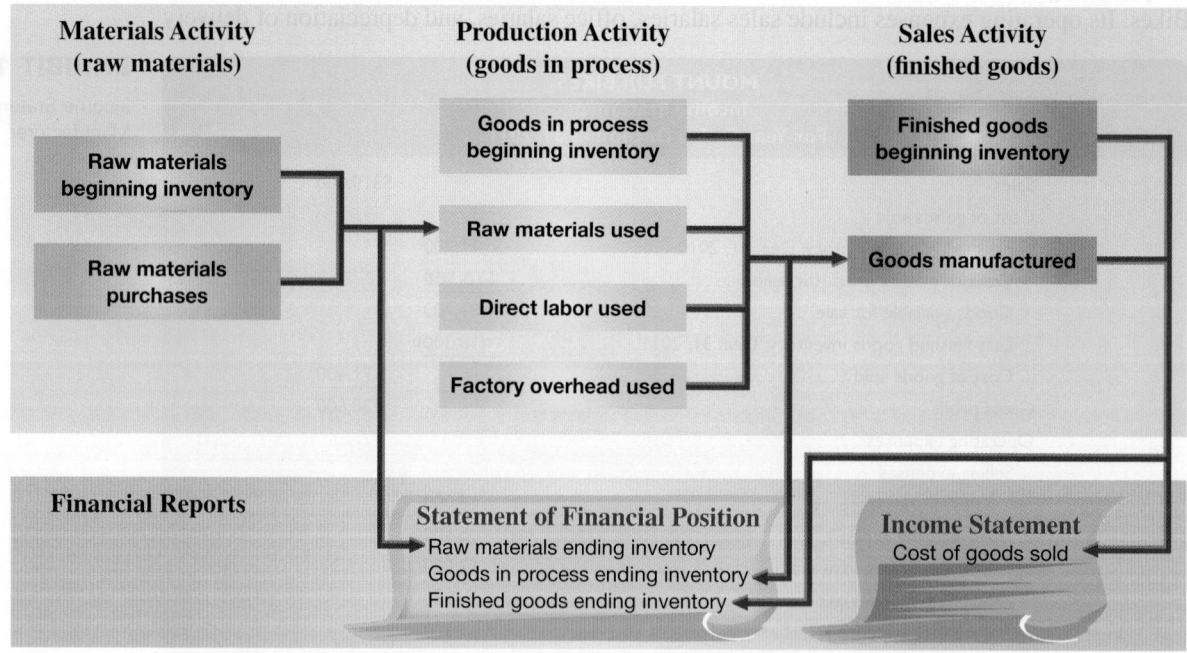

Materials Activity   The far left side of Exhibit 18.15 shows the flow of raw materials. Manufacturers usually start a period with some beginning raw materials inventory carried over from the previous period. The company then acquires additional raw materials in the current period. Adding these purchases to beginning inventory gives total raw materials available for use in production. These raw materials are then either used in production in the current period or remain in inventory at the end of the period for use in future periods.

Point: Knowledge of managerial accounting provides us a means of measuring manufacturing costs and is a sound foundation for studying advanced business topics.

Production Activity   The middle section of Exhibit 18.15 describes production activity. Four factors come together in production: beginning goods in process inventory, direct materials, direct labor, and overhead. Beginning goods in process inventory consists of partly assembled products from the previous period. Production activity results in products that are either finished or remain unfinished. The cost of finished products makes up the cost of goods manufactured for the current period. Unfinished products are identified as ending goods in process inventory. The cost of unfinished products consists of direct materials, direct labor, and factory overhead, and is reported on the current period's statement of financial position. The costs of both finished goods manufactured and goods in process are *product costs.*

Sales Activity   The company's sales activity is portrayed in the far right side of Exhibit 18.15. Newly completed units are combined with beginning finished goods inventory to make up total finished goods available for sale in the current period. The cost of finished products sold is reported on the income statement as cost of goods sold. The cost of products not sold is reported on the current period's statement of financial position as ending finished goods inventory.

Manufacturing Statement

A company's manufacturing activities are described in a **manufacturing statement,** also called the *schedule of manufacturing activities* or the *schedule of cost of goods manufactured.* The manufacturing statement summarizes the types and amounts of costs incurred in a company's manufacturing process. Exhibit 18.16 shows the manufacturing statement for Mount Fuji Bikes. The statement is divided into four parts: *direct materials, direct labor, overhead,* and *computation of cost of goods manufactured.* We describe each of these parts in this section.

① The manufacturing statement begins by computing direct materials used. We start by adding beginning raw materials inventory of $8,000 to the current period's purchases of $86,500. This yields $94,500 of total raw materials available for use. A physical count of inventory shows $9,000 of ending raw materials inventory. This implies a total cost of raw materials used during the period of $85,500 ($94,500 total raw materials available for use − $9,000 ending inventory). (*Note:* All raw materials are direct materials for Mount Fuji Bikes.)

P2 Prepare a manufacturing statement and explain its purpose and links to financial statements.

EXHIBIT 18.16

Manufacturing Statement

MOUNT FUJI BIKES Manufacturing Statement For Year Ended December 31, 2011		
Direct materials		
Raw materials inventory, Dec. 31, 2010	$ 8,000	
Raw materials purchases	86,500	
Raw materials available for use	94,500	
Less raw materials inventory, Dec. 31, 2011	9,000	
Direct materials used		$ 85,500
Direct labor		60,000
Factory overhead		
Indirect labor	9,000	
Factory supervision	6,000	
Factory utilities	2,600	
Repairs—Factory equipment	2,500	
Property taxes—Factory building	1,900	
Factory supplies used	600	
Factory insurance expired	1,100	
Depreciation expense—Small tools	200	
Depreciation expense—Factory equipment	3,500	
Depreciation expense—Factory building	1,800	
Amortization expense—Patents	800	
Total factory overhead		30,000
Total manufacturing costs		175,500
Add goods in process inventory, Dec. 31, 2010		2,500
Total cost of goods in process		178,000
Less goods in process inventory, Dec. 31, 2011		7,500
Cost of goods manufactured		$170,500

Point: Direct material and direct labor costs increase with increases in production volume and are called *variable costs*. Overhead can be both variable and fixed. When overhead costs vary with production, they are called *variable overhead*. When overhead costs don't vary with production, they are called *fixed overhead*.

Point: Manufacturers sometimes report variable and fixed overhead separately in the manufacturing statement to provide more information to managers about cost behavior.

② The second part of the manufacturing statement reports direct labor costs. Mount Fuji Bikes had total direct labor costs of $60,000 for the period. This amount includes payroll taxes and fringe benefits.

③ The third part of the manufacturing statement reports overhead costs. The statement lists each important factory overhead item and its cost. Total factory overhead cost for the period is $30,000. Some companies report only *total* factory overhead on the manufacturing statement and attach a separate schedule listing individual overhead costs.

④ The final section of the manufacturing statement computes and reports the *cost of goods manufactured*. (Total manufacturing costs for the period are $175,500 [$85,500 + $60,000 + $30,000], the sum of direct materials used and direct labor and overhead costs incurred.) This amount is first added to beginning goods in process inventory. This gives the total goods in process inventory of $178,000 ($175,500 + $2,500). We then compute the current period's cost of goods manufactured of $170,500 by taking the $178,000 total goods in process and subtracting the $7,500 cost of ending goods in process inventory that consists of direct materials, direct labor, and factory overhead. The cost of goods manufactured amount is also called *net cost of goods manufactured* or *cost of goods completed*. Exhibit 18.14 shows that this item and amount are listed in the Cost of Goods Sold section of Mount Fuji Bikes' income statement and the statement of financial position.

A managerial accounting system records costs and reports them in various reports that eventually determine financial statements. Exhibit 18.17 shows how overhead costs flow through the system: from an initial listing of specific costs, to a section of the manufacturing statement, to the reporting on the income statement and the statement of financial position.

Management uses information in the manufacturing statement to plan and control the company's manufacturing activities. To provide timely information for decision making, the statement is often prepared monthly, weekly, or even daily. In anticipation of release of its much-hyped iPad, **Apple** grew its inventory of critical components, and its finished goods inventory. The manufacturing statement contains information useful to external users but is not a general-purpose financial statement. Companies rarely publish the manufacturing statement because managers view this information as proprietary and potentially harmful to them if released to competitors.

EXHIBIT 18.17

Overhead Cost Flows across Accounting Reports

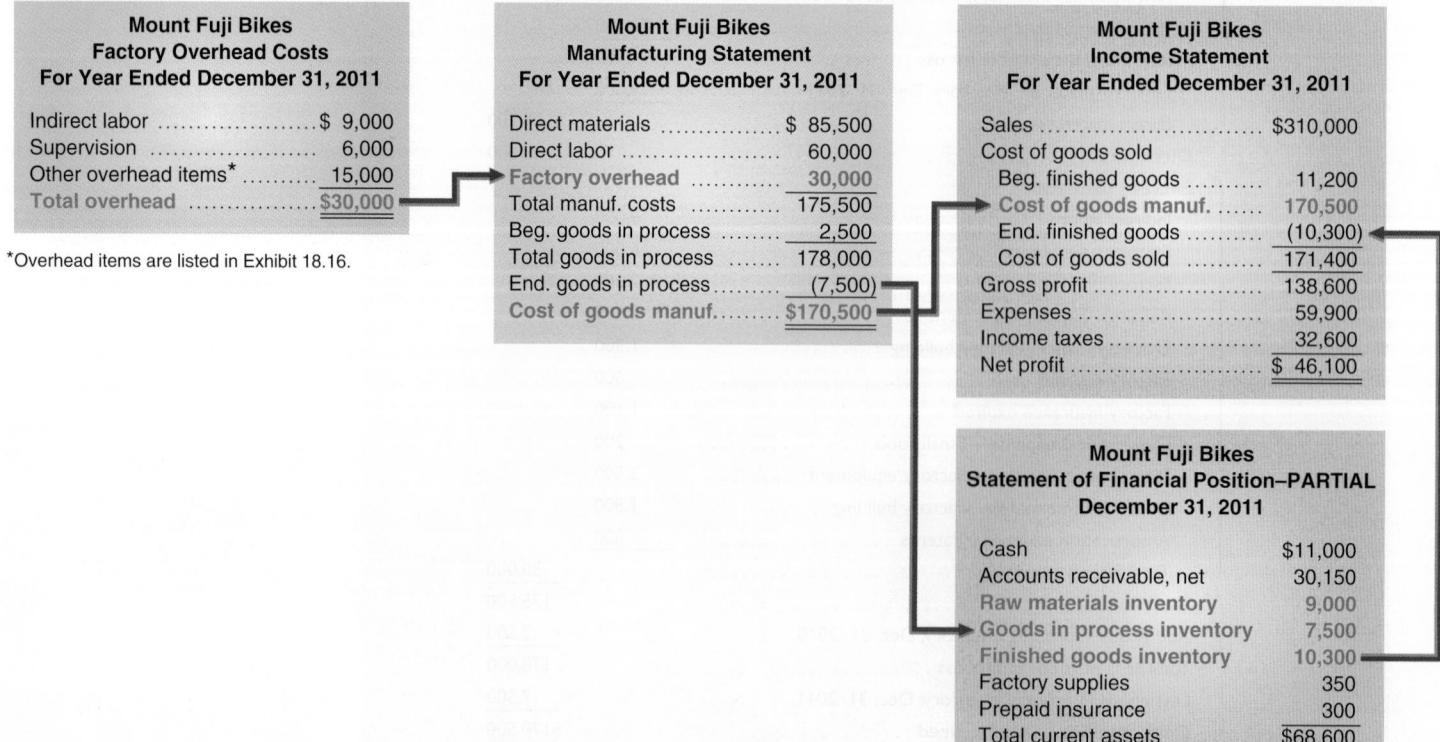

Mount Fuji Bikes — Factory Overhead Costs — For Year Ended December 31, 2011	
Indirect labor	$ 9,000
Supervision	6,000
Other overhead items*	15,000
Total overhead	$30,000

*Overhead items are listed in Exhibit 18.16.

Mount Fuji Bikes — Manufacturing Statement — For Year Ended December 31, 2011	
Direct materials	$ 85,500
Direct labor	60,000
Factory overhead	30,000
Total manuf. costs	175,500
Beg. goods in process	2,500
Total goods in process	178,000
End. goods in process	(7,500)
Cost of goods manuf.	$170,500

Mount Fuji Bikes — Income Statement — For Year Ended December 31, 2011	
Sales	$310,000
Cost of goods sold	
Beg. finished goods	11,200
Cost of goods manuf.	170,500
End. finished goods	(10,300)
Cost of goods sold	171,400
Gross profit	138,600
Expenses	59,900
Income taxes	32,600
Net profit	$ 46,100

Mount Fuji Bikes — Statement of Financial Position–PARTIAL — December 31, 2011	
Cash	$11,000
Accounts receivable, net	30,150
Raw materials inventory	9,000
Goods in process inventory	7,500
Finished goods inventory	10,300
Factory supplies	350
Prepaid insurance	300
Total current assets	$68,600

8. A manufacturing statement (*a*) computes cost of goods manufactured for the period, (*b*) computes cost of goods sold for the period, or (*c*) reports operating expenses incurred for the period.

9. Are companies required to report a manufacturing statement?

10. How are both beginning and ending goods in process inventories reported on a manufacturing statement?

Trends in Managerial Accounting

The analytical tools and techniques of managerial accounting have always been useful, and their relevance and importance continue to increase. This is so because of changes in the business environment. This section describes some of these changes and their impact on managerial accounting.

C6 Describe trends in managerial accounting.

Customer Orientation   There is an increased emphasis on *customers* as the most important constituent of a business. Customers expect to derive a certain value for the money they spend to buy products and services. Specifically, they expect that their suppliers will offer them the right service (or product) at the right time and the right price. This implies that companies accept the notion of **customer orientation,** which means that employees understand the changing needs and wants of their customers and align their management and operating practices accordingly.

Global Economy   Our *global economy* expands competitive boundaries and provides customers more choices. The global economy also produces changes in business activities. One notable case that reflects these changes in customer demand and global competition is auto manufacturing. The top three Japanese auto manufacturers (**Honda, Nissan,** and **Toyota**) once controlled more than 40% of the U.S. auto market. Customers perceived that Japanese auto manufacturers provided value not available from other manufacturers. Many European and North American auto manufacturers responded to this challenge and regained much of the lost market share.

E-Commerce   People have become increasingly interconnected via smartphones, text messaging, and other electronic applications. Consumers thus expect and demand to be able to buy items electronically, whenever and wherever they want. Many businesses have enhanced their Websites to allow for online transactions. Online sales now make up over 7% of total retail sales.

Service Economy   Businesses that provide services, such as telecommunications and health care, constitute an ever-growing part of our economy. In developed economies like the United States, service businesses typically account for over 60% to 70% of total economic activity.

Companies must be alert to these and other factors. Many companies have responded by adopting the **lean business model,** whose goal is to *eliminate waste* while "satisfying the customer" and "providing a positive return" to the company.

Lean Practices   **Continuous improvement** rejects the notions of "good enough" or "acceptable" and challenges employees and managers to continuously experiment with new and improved business practices. This has led companies to adopt practices such as total quality management (TQM) and just-in-time (JIT) manufacturing. The philosophy underlying both practices is continuous improvement; the difference is in the focus.

Total quality management focuses on quality improvement and applies this standard to all aspects of business activities. In doing so, managers and employees seek to uncover waste in business activities including accounting activities such as payroll and disbursements. The Deming Application Prize is given to companies or divisions of companies that have achieved distinctive performance improvement through the application of TQM. Recent winners include **Sanden International (Singapore) Pte Limited**, **Tata Steel Limited** from India and **Siam White Cement Company** from Thailand.

Just-in-time manufacturing is a system that acquires inventory and produces only when needed. An important aspect of JIT is that companies manufacture products only after they receive an order (a *demand-pull* system) and then deliver the customer's requirements on time. This means that processes must be aligned to eliminate any delays and inefficiencies including inferior inputs and outputs. Companies must also establish good relations and communications with their suppliers. On the downside, JIT is more susceptible to disruption than traditional systems. As one example, several **General Motors** plants were temporarily shut down due to a strike at an assembly division; the plants supplied components *just in time* to the assembly division.

Value Chain   The **value chain** refers to the series of activities that add value to a company's products or services. Exhibit 18.18 illustrates a possible value chain for a retail cookie company. Companies can use lean practices to increase efficiency and profits.

EXHIBIT 18.18

Typical Value Chain (Cookie Retailer)

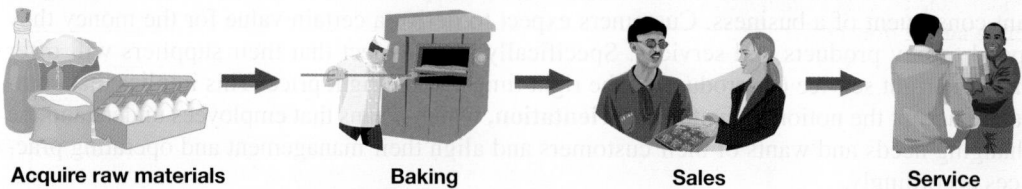

Acquire raw materials   Baking   Sales   Service

▢ Decision Insight

Global Lean   Toyota Motor Corporation pioneered lean manufacturing, and it has since spread to other manufacturers throughout the world. The goals include improvements in quality, reliability, inventory turnover, productivity, exports, and—above all—sales and income. ∎

"My boss wants us to appeal to a younger and hipper crowd. So, I'd like to get a tattoo that says-- 'Accounting rules!'"

Copyright © Jerry King. www.artizans.com

Implications for Managerial Accounting   Adopting the lean business model can be challenging because to foster its implementation, all systems and procedures that a company follows must be realigned. Managerial accounting has an important role to play by providing accurate cost and performance information. Companies must understand the nature and sources of cost and must develop systems that capture costs accurately. Developing such a system is important to measuring the "value" provided to customers. The price that customers pay for acquiring goods and services is an important determinant of value. In turn, the costs a company incurs are key determinants of price. All else being equal, the better a company is at controlling its costs, the better its performance.

▢ Decision Insight

Balanced Scorecard   The *balanced scorecard* aids continuous improvement by augmenting financial measures with information on the "drivers" (indicators) of future financial performance along four dimensions: (1) *financial*—profitability and risk, (2) *customer*—value creation and product and service differentiation, (3) *internal business processes*—business activities that create customer and owner satisfaction, and (4) *learning and growth*—organizational change, innovation, and growth. ∎

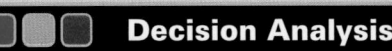

As lean manufacturing practices help companies move toward just-in-time manufacturing, it is important for these companies to reduce the time to manufacture their products and to improve manufacturing efficiency. One metric that measures that time element is **cycle time (CT).** A definition of cycle time is in Exhibit 18.19.

> **A1** Compute cycle time and cycle efficiency, and explain their importance to production management.

> **Cycle time = Process time + Inspection time + Move time + Wait time**

EXHIBIT 18.19

Cycle Time

Process time is the time spent producing the product. *Inspection time* is the time spent inspecting (1) raw materials when received, (2) goods in process while in production, and (3) finished goods prior to shipment. *Move time* is the time spent moving (1) raw materials from storage to production and (2) goods in process from one factory location to another factory location. *Wait time* is the time that an order or job sits with no production applied to it; this can be due to order delays, bottlenecks in production, and poor scheduling.

Process time is considered **value-added time** because it is the only activity in cycle time that adds value to the product from the customer's perspective. The other three time activities are considered **non-value-added time** because they add no value to the customer.

Companies strive to reduce non-value-added time to improve **cycle efficiency (CE).** Cycle efficiency is the ratio of value-added time to total cycle time—see Exhibit 18.20.

> $$\text{Cycle efficiency} = \frac{\text{Value-added time}}{\text{Cycle time}}$$

EXHIBIT 18.20

Cycle Efficiency

To illustrate, assume that Mount Fuji Bikes receives and produces an order for 500 Tracker® mountain bikes. Assume that the following times were measured during production of this order.

Process time... 1.8 days   **Inspection time... 0.5 days**   **Move time... 0.7 days**   **Wait time... 3.0 days**

In this case, cycle time is 6.0 days, computed as 1.8 days + 0.5 days + 0.7 days + 3.0 days. Also, cycle efficiency is 0.3, or 30%, computed as 1.8 days divided by 6.0 days. This means that Mount Fuji Bikes spends 30% of its time working on the product (value-added time). The other 70% is spent on non-value-added activities.

If a company has a CE of 1, it means that its time is spent entirely on value-added activities. If the CE is low, the company should evaluate its production process to see if it can identify ways to reduce non-value-added activities. The 30% CE for Mount Fuji Bikes is low and its management should look for ways to reduce non-value-added activities.

DEMONSTRATION PROBLEM 1: COST BEHAVIOR AND CLASSIFICATION

Understanding the classification and assignment of costs is important. Consider a company that manufactures computer chips. It incurs the following costs in manufacturing chips and in operating the company.

1. Plastic board used to mount the chip, $3.50 each.
2. Assembly worker pay of $15 per hour to attach chips to plastic board.
3. Salary for factory maintenance workers who maintain factory equipment.
4. Factory supervisor pay of $55,000 per year to supervise employees.

5. Real estate taxes paid on the factory, $14,500.

6. Real estate taxes paid on the company office, $6,000.

7. Depreciation costs on machinery used by workers, $30,000.

8. Salary paid to the chief financial officer, $95,000.

9. Advertising costs of $7,800 paid to promote products.

10. Salespersons' commissions of $0.50 for each assembled chip sold.

11. Management has the option to rent the manufacturing plant to six local hospitals to store medical records instead of producing and assembling chips.

Classify each cost in the following table according to the categories listed in the table header. A cost can be classified under more than one category. For example, the plastic board used to mount chips is classified as a direct material product cost and as a direct unit cost.

	Period Costs	Product Costs			Unit Cost Classification		Sunk Cost	Opportunity Cost
Cost	**Selling and Administrative**	**Direct Material (Prime Cost)**	**Direct Labor (Prime and Conversion)**	**Factory Overhead (Conversion Cost)**	**Direct**	**Indirect**		
1. Plastic board used to mount the chip, $3.50 each		✔			✔			

SOLUTION TO DEMONSTRATION PROBLEM 1

	Period Costs	Product Costs			Unit Cost Classification		Sunk Cost	Opportunity Cost
Cost*	**Selling and Administrative**	**Direct Material (Prime Cost)**	**Direct Labor (Prime and Conversion)**	**Factory Overhead (Conversion Cost)**	**Direct**	**Indirect**		
1.		✔			✔			
2.			✔		✔			
3.				✔		✔		
4.				✔		✔		
5.				✔		✔		
6.	✔							
7.				✔		✔	✔	
8.	✔							
9.	✔							
10.	✔							
11.								✔

* Costs 1 through 11 refer to the 11 cost items described at the beginning of the problem.

DEMONSTRATION PROBLEM 2: REPORTING FOR MANUFACTURERS

A manufacturing company's statement of financial position and income statement differ from those for a merchandising or service company.

Required

1. Fill in the [BLANK] descriptors on the partial statements of financial position for both the manufacturing company and the merchandising company. Explain why a different presentation is required.

Manufacturing Company

ADIDAS GROUP Partial Statement of Financial Position December 31, 2011	
Current assets	
Cash	$10,000
[BLANK]	8,000
[BLANK]	5,000
[BLANK]	7,000
Supplies	500
Prepaid insurance	500
Total current assets	$31,000

Merchandising Company

PAYLESS SHOE OUTLET Partial Statement of Financial Position December 31, 2011	
Current assets	
Cash	$ 5,000
[BLANK]	12,000
Supplies	500
Prepaid insurance	500
Total current assets	$18,000

2. Fill in the [BLANK] descriptors on the income statements for the manufacturing company and the merchandising company. Explain why a different presentation is required.

Manufacturing Company

ADIDAS GROUP Partial Income Statement For Year Ended December 31, 2011	
Sales	$200,000
Cost of goods sold	
Finished goods inventory, Dec. 31, 2010	10,000
[BLANK]	120,000
Goods available for sale	130,000
Finished goods inventory, Dec. 31, 2011	(7,000)
Cost of goods sold	123,000
Gross profit	$ 77,000

Merchandising Company

PAYLESS SHOE OUTLET Partial Income Statement For Year Ended December 31, 2011	
Sales	$190,000
Cost of goods sold	
Merchandise inventory, Dec. 31, 2010	8,000
[BLANK]	108,000
Goods available for sale	116,000
Merchandise inventory, Dec. 31, 2011	(12,000)
Cost of goods sold	104,000
Gross profit	$ 86,000

3. A manufacturer's cost of goods manufactured is the sum of (a) _____, (b) _____, and (c) _____ costs incurred in producing the product.

SOLUTION TO DEMONSTRATION PROBLEM 2

1. Inventories for a manufacturer and for a merchandiser.

Manufacturing Company

ADIDAS GROUP Partial Statement of Financial Position December 31, 2011	
Current assets	
Cash	$10,000
Raw materials inventory	8,000
Goods in process inventory	5,000
Finished goods inventory	7,000
Supplies	500
Prepaid insurance	500
Total current assets	$31,000

Merchandising Company

PAYLESS SHOE OUTLET Partial Statement of Financial Position December 31, 2011	
Current assets	
Cash	$ 5,000
Merchandise inventory	12,000
Supplies	500
Prepaid insurance	500
Total current assets	$18,000

Explanation: A manufacturing company must control and measure three types of inventories: raw materials, goods in process, and finished goods. In the sequence of making a product, the raw materials move into production—called *goods in process inventory*—and then to finished goods. All raw materials and goods in process inventory at the end of each accounting period are considered current assets. All unsold finished inventory is considered a current asset at the end of each accounting period. The merchandising company must control and measure only one type of inventory, purchased goods.

2. Cost of goods sold for a manufacturer and for a merchandiser.

Manufacturing Company

ADIDAS GROUP Partial Income Statement For Year Ended December 31, 2011	
Sales	$ 200,000
Cost of goods sold	
Finished goods inventory, Dec. 31, 2010	10,000
Cost of goods manufactured	120,000
Goods available for sale	130,000
Finished goods inventory, Dec. 31, 2011	(7,000)
Cost of goods sold	123,000
Gross profit	$ 77,000

Merchandising Company

PAYLESS SHOE OUTLET Partial Income Statement For Year Ended December 31, 2011	
Sales	$ 190,000
Cost of goods sold	
Merchandise inventory, Dec. 31, 2010	8,000
Cost of purchases	108,000
Goods available for sale	116,000
Merchandise inventory, Dec. 31, 2011	(12,000)
Cost of goods sold	104,000
Gross profit	$ 86,000

Explanation: Manufacturing and merchandising companies use different reporting terms. In particular, the terms *finished goods* and *cost of goods manufactured* are used to reflect the production of goods, yet the concepts and techniques of reporting cost of goods sold for a manufacturing company and merchandising company are similar.

3. A manufacturer's cost of goods manufactured is the sum of (a) *direct material,* (b) *direct labor,* and (c) *factory overhead* costs incurred in producing the product.

DEMONSTRATION PROBLEM 3: MANUFACTURING STATEMENT

The following account balances and other information are from SUNN Corporation's accounting records for year-end December 31, 2011. Use this information to prepare (1) a table listing factory overhead costs, (2) a manufacturing statement (show only the total factory overhead cost), and (3) an income statement.

Advertising expense	$ 85,000	Goods in process inventory, Dec. 31, 2010	$ 8,000
Amortization expense—Factory Patents	16,000	Goods in process inventory, Dec. 31, 2011	9,000
Bad debts expense	28,000	Income taxes	53,400
Depreciation expense—Office equipment	37,000	Indirect labor	26,000
Depreciation expense—Factory building	133,000	Interest expense	25,000
Depreciation expense—Factory equipment	78,000	Miscellaneous expense	55,000
Direct labor	250,000	Property taxes on factory equipment	14,000
Factory insurance expired	62,000	Raw materials inventory, Dec. 31, 2010	60,000
Factory supervision	74,000	Raw materials inventory, Dec. 31, 2011	78,000
Factory supplies used	21,000	Raw materials purchases	313,000
Factory utilities	115,000	Repairs expense—Factory equipment	31,000
Finished goods inventory, Dec. 31, 2010	15,000	Salaries expense	150,000
Finished goods inventory, Dec. 31, 2011	12,500	Sales	1,630,000

PLANNING THE SOLUTION

- Analyze the account balances and select those that are part of factory overhead costs.
- Arrange these costs in a table that lists factory overhead costs for the year.
- Analyze the remaining costs and select those related to production activity for the year; selected costs should include the materials and goods in process inventories and direct labor.

- Prepare a manufacturing statement for the year showing the calculation of the cost of materials used in production, the cost of direct labor, and the total factory overhead cost. When presenting overhead cost on this statement, report only total overhead cost from the table of overhead costs for the year. Show the costs of beginning and ending goods in process inventory to determine cost of goods manufactured.

- Organize the remaining revenue and expense items into the income statement for the year. Combine cost of goods manufactured from the manufacturing statement with the finished goods inventory amounts to compute cost of goods sold for the year.

SOLUTION TO DEMONSTRATION PROBLEM 3

SUNN CORPORATION
Factory Overhead Costs
For Year Ended December 31, 2011

Amortization expense—Factory patents	$ 16,000
Depreciation expense—Factory building	133,000
Depreciation expense—Factory equipment	78,000
Factory insurance expired	62,000
Factory supervision	74,000
Factory supplies used	21,000
Factory utilities	115,000
Indirect labor	26,000
Property taxes on factory equipment	14,000
Repairs expense—Factory equipment	31,000
Total factory overhead	$570,000

SUNN CORPORATION
Manufacturing Statement
For Year Ended December 31, 2011

Direct materials		
Raw materials inventory, Dec. 31, 2010.............	$ 60,000	
Raw materials purchase	313,000	
Raw materials available for use	373,000	
Less raw materials inventory, Dec. 31, 2011	78,000	
Direct materials used		295,000
Direct labor		250,000
Factory overhead		570,000
Total manufacturing costs		1,115,000
Goods in process inventory, Dec. 31, 2010............		8,000
Total cost of goods in process		1,123,000
Less goods in process inventory, Dec. 31, 2011		9,000
Cost of goods manufactured		$1,114,000

SUNN CORPORATION
Income Statement
For Year Ended December 31, 2011

Sales		$1,630,000
Cost of goods sold		
Finished goods inventory, Dec. 31, 2010	$ 15,000	
Cost of goods manufactured	1,114,000	
Goods available for sale	1,129,000	
Less finished goods inventory, Dec. 31, 2011.........	(12,500)	
Cost of goods sold		1,116,500
Gross profit		513,500
Operating expenses		
Advertising expense	85,000	
Bad debts expense	28,000	
Depreciation expense—Office equipment	37,000	
Interest expense	25,000	
Miscellaneous expense	55,000	
Salaries expense	150,000	
Total operating expenses........................		380,000
Income before income taxes		133,500
Income taxes		53,400
Net profit..		$ 80,100

Summary

C1 **Explain the purpose and nature of, and the role of ethics in, managerial accounting.** The purpose of managerial accounting is to provide useful information to management and other internal decision makers. It does this by collecting, managing, and reporting both monetary and nonmonetary information in a manner useful to internal users. Major characteristics of managerial accounting include (1) focus on internal decision makers, (2) emphasis on planning and control, (3) flexibility, (4) timeliness, (5) reliance on forecasts and estimates, (6) focus on segments and projects, and (7) reporting both monetary and nonmonetary information. Ethics are beliefs that distinguish right from wrong. Ethics can be important in reducing fraud in business operations.

C2 **Describe accounting concepts useful in classifying costs.** We can classify costs on the basis of their (1) behavior—fixed vs. variable, (2) traceability—direct vs. indirect, (3) controllability—controllable vs. uncontrollable, (4) relevance—sunk vs. out of pocket, and (5) function—product vs. period. A cost can be classified in more than one way, depending on the purpose for which the cost is being determined. These classifications help us understand cost patterns, analyze performance, and plan operations.

C3 **Define product and period costs and explain how they impact financial statements.** Costs that are capitalized because they are expected to have future value are called *product costs;* costs that are expensed are called *period costs.* This classification is important because it affects the amount of costs expensed in the income statement and the amount of costs assigned to inventory on the statement of financial position. Product costs are commonly made up of direct materials, direct labor, and overhead. Period costs include selling and administrative expenses.

C4 **Explain how statements of financial position and income statements for manufacturing and merchandising companies differ.** The main difference is that manufacturers usually carry three inventories on their statements of financial position—raw materials, goods in process, and finished goods—instead of one inventory that merchandisers carry. The main difference between income statements of manufacturers and merchandisers is the items making up cost of goods sold. A merchandiser adds beginning merchandise inventory to cost of goods purchased and then subtracts ending merchandise inventory to get cost of goods sold. A manufacturer adds beginning finished goods inventory to cost of goods manufactured and then subtracts ending finished goods inventory to get cost of goods sold.

C5 **Explain manufacturing activities and the flow of manufacturing costs.** Manufacturing activities consist of materials, production, and sales activities. The materials activity consists of the purchase and issuance of materials to production. The production activity consists of converting materials into finished goods. At this stage in the process, the materials, labor, and overhead costs have been incurred and the manufacturing statement is prepared. The sales activity consists of selling some or all of finished goods available for sale. At this stage, the cost of goods sold is determined.

C6 **Describe trends in managerial accounting.** Important trends in managerial accounting include an increased focus on satisfying customers, the impact of a global economy, and the growing presence of e-commerce and service-based businesses. The lean business model, designed to eliminate waste and satisfy customers, can be useful in responding to recent trends. Concepts such as total quality management, just-in-time production, and the value chain often aid in application of the lean business model.

A1 **Compute cycle time and cycle efficiency, and explain their importance to production management.** It is important for companies to reduce the time to produce their products and to improve manufacturing efficiency. One measure of that time is cycle time (CT), defined as Process time + Inspection time + Move time + Wait time. Process time is value-added time; the others are non-value-added time. Cycle efficiency (CE) is the ratio of value-added time to total cycle time. If CE is low, management should evaluate its production process to see if it can reduce non-value-added activities.

P1 **Compute cost of goods sold for a manufacturer.** A manufacturer adds beginning finished goods inventory to cost of goods manufactured and then subtracts ending finished goods inventory to get cost of goods sold.

P2 **Prepare a manufacturing statement and explain its purpose and links to financial statements.** The manufacturing statement reports computation of cost of goods manufactured for the period. It begins by showing the period's costs for direct materials, direct labor, and overhead and then adjusts these numbers for the beginning and ending inventories of the goods in process to yield cost of goods manufactured.

Guidance Answers to Decision Maker and Decision Ethics

Production Manager It appears that all three friends want to pay the bill with someone else's money. David is using money belonging to the tax authorities, Denise is taking money from her company, and Derek is defrauding the client. To prevent such practices, companies have internal audit mechanisms. Many companies also adopt ethical codes of conduct to help guide employees. We must recognize that some entertainment expenses are justifiable and even encouraged. For example, the tax law allows certain deductions for entertainment that have a business purpose. Corporate policies also sometimes allow and encourage reimbursable spending for social activities, and contracts can include entertainment as allowable costs.

Nevertheless, without further details, payment for this bill should be made from personal accounts.

Entrepreneur Tracing all costs directly to cost objects is always desirable, but you need to be able to do so in an economically feasible manner. In this case, you are able to trace 90% of the assembly department's direct costs. It may not be economical to spend more money on a new software to trace the final 10% of costs. You need to make a cost–benefit trade-off. If the software offers benefits beyond tracing the remaining 10% of the assembly department's costs, your decision should consider this.

Purchase Manager Opportunity costs relate to the potential quality and delivery benefits given up by not choosing supplier (A). Selecting supplier (B) might involve future costs of poor-quality seats (inspection, repairs, and returns). Also, potential delivery delays could interrupt work and increase manufacturing costs. Your company could also incur sales losses if the product quality of supplier (B) is low. As purchase manager, you are responsible for these costs and must consider them in making your decision.

Guidance Answers to Quick Checks

1. *d*
2. Financial accounting information is intended for users external to an organization such as investors, creditors, and government authorities. Managerial accounting focuses on providing information to managers, officers, and other decision makers within the organization.
3. No, GAAP do not control the practice of managerial accounting. Unlike external users, the internal users need managerial accounting information for planning and controlling business activities rather than for external comparison. Different types of information are required, depending on the activity. Therefore it is difficult to standardize managerial accounting.
4. Variable costs increase when volume of activity increases.
5. By being able to trace costs to cost objects (say, to products and departments), managers better understand the total costs associated with a cost object. This is useful when managers consider making changes to the cost object (such as when dropping the product or expanding the department).
6. Raw materials inventory, goods in process inventory, and finished goods inventory.
7. The cost of goods sold for merchandising companies includes all costs of acquiring the merchandise; the cost of goods sold for manufacturing companies includes the three costs of manufacturing: direct materials, direct labor, and overhead.
8. *a*
9. No; companies rarely report a manufacturing statement.
10. Beginning goods in process inventory is added to total manufacturing costs to yield total goods in process. Ending goods in process inventory is subtracted from total goods in process to yield cost of goods manufactured for the period.

Key Terms   www.mheducation.asia/olc/wildkwokFAP

Continuous improvement (p. 717)
Control (p. 702)
Controllable or not controllable cost (p. 707)
Conversion costs (p. 713)
Cost object (p. 707)
Customer orientation (p. 717)
Cycle efficiency (CE) (p. 719)
Cycle time (CT) (p. 719)
Direct costs (p. 707)
Direct labor (p. 712)
Direct labor costs (p. 712)
Direct material (p. 712)
Direct material costs (p. 712)

Ethics (p. 706)
Factory overhead (p. 712)
Factory overhead costs (p. 712)
Finished goods inventory (p. 711)
Fixed cost (p. 706)
Goods in process inventory (p. 711)
Indirect costs (p. 707)
Indirect labor (p. 712)
Indirect labor costs (p. 712)
Indirect material (p. 710)
Internal control system (p. 706)
Just-in-time (JIT) manufacturing (p. 718)
Lean business model (p. 717)
Managerial accounting (p. 702)

Manufacturing statement (p. 715)
Non-value-added time (p. 719)
Opportunity cost (p. 708)
Out-of-pocket cost (p. 708)
Period costs (p. 708)
Planning (p. 702)
Prime costs (p. 713)
Product costs (p. 708)
Raw materials inventory (p. 710)
Sunk cost (p. 707)
Total quality management (TQM) (p. 717)
Value-added time (p. 719)
Value chain (p. 718)
Variable cost (p. 706)

Multiple Choice Quiz   Answers on p. 742   www.mheducation.asia/olc/wildkwokFAP

Additional Quiz Questions are available at the book's Website.

1. Continuous improvement
   a. Is used to reduce inventory levels.
   b. Is applicable only in service businesses.
   c. Rejects the notion of "good enough."
   d. Is used to reduce ordering costs.
   e. Is applicable only in manufacturing businesses.

2. A direct cost is one that is
   a. Variable with respect to the cost object.
   b. Traceable to the cost object.
   c. Fixed with respect to the cost object.
   d. Allocated to the cost object.
   e. A period cost.

3. Costs that are incurred as part of the manufacturing process, but are not clearly traceable to the specific unit of product or batches of product, are called
   a. Period costs.
   b. Factory overhead.
   c. Sunk costs.
   d. Opportunity costs.
   e. Fixed costs.

4. The three major cost components of manufacturing a product are
   a. Direct materials, direct labor, and factory overhead.
   b. Period costs, product costs, and sunk costs.

c. Indirect labor, indirect materials, and fixed expenses.
d. Variable costs, fixed costs, and period costs.
e. Opportunity costs, sunk costs, and direct costs.

5. A company reports the following for the current year.

Finished goods inventory, beginning year	$6,000
Finished goods inventory, ending year	3,200
Cost of goods sold	7,500

Its cost of goods manufactured for the current year is
a. $1,500.
b. $1,700.
c. $7,500.
d. $2,800.
e. $4,700.

 Icon denotes assignments that involve decision making.

Discussion Questions

1. Describe the managerial accountant's role in business planning, control, and decision making.

2. Distinguish between managerial and financial accounting on
   a. Users and decision makers.   b. Purpose of information.
   c. Flexibility of practice.   d. Time dimension.
   e. Focus of information.   f. Nature of information.

3. Identify the usual changes that a company must make when it adopts a customer orientation.

4. Distinguish between direct material and indirect material.

5. Distinguish between direct labor and indirect labor.

6. Distinguish between (a) factory overhead and (b) selling and administrative overhead.

7. What product cost is listed as both a prime cost and a conversion cost?

8. Assume that you tour Apple's factory where it makes its products. List three direct costs and three indirect costs that you are likely to see.

9. Should we evaluate a manager's performance on the basis of controllable or noncontrollable costs? Why?

10. Explain why knowledge of cost behavior is useful in product performance evaluation.

11. Explain why product costs are capitalized but period costs are expensed in the current accounting period.

12. Explain how business activities and inventories for a manufacturing company, a merchandising company, and a service company differ.

13. Why does managerial accounting often involve working with numerous predictions and estimates?

14. How do an income statement and a statement of financial position for a manufacturing company and a merchandising company differ?

15. Besides inventories, what other assets often appear on manufacturers' statements of financial position but not on merchandisers' statements of financial position?

16. Why does a manufacturing company require three different inventory categories?

17. Manufacturing activities of a company are described in the _____. This statement summarizes the types and amounts of costs incurred in its manufacturing _____.

18. What are the three categories of manufacturing costs?

19. List several examples of factory overhead.

20. List the four components of a manufacturing statement and provide specific examples of each for Apple.

21. Prepare a proper title for the annual "manufacturing statement" of Palm. Does the date match the statement of financial position or income statement? Why?

22. Describe the relations among the income statement, the manufacturing statement, and a detailed listing of factory overhead costs.

23. Define and describe cycle time and identify the components of cycle time.

24. Explain the difference between value-added time and non-value-added time.

25. Define and describe cycle efficiency.

26. Can management of a company such as Research In Motion use cycle time and cycle efficiency as useful measures of performance? Explain.

27. Access Dell's annual report (10-K) for the financial year ended January 29, 2010, at the SEC's EDGAR database (SEC.gov) or its Website (Dell.com). From its financial statement notes, identify the titles and amounts of its inventory components.

connect

Identify whether each description most likely applies to managerial or financial accounting.

1. _____ Its primary focus is on the organization as a whole.
2. _____ Its principles and practices are very flexible.
3. _____ It is directed at external users in making investment, credit, and other decisions.
4. _____ Its primary users are company managers.
5. _____ Its information is often available only after an audit is complete.

QUICK STUDY

QS 18-1
Managerial accounting versus
financial accounting
C1

Managerial accounting (choose one)

1. Must follow generally accepted accounting principles.
2. Provides information to aid management in planning and controlling business activities.
3. Is directed at reporting aggregate data on the company as a whole.
4. Provides information that is widely available to all interested parties.

QS 18-2
Managerial accounting defined
C1

Which of these statements is true regarding fixed and variable costs?

1. Fixed costs increase and variable costs decrease in total as activity volume decreases.
2. Fixed costs stay the same and variable costs increase in total as activity volume increases.
3. Both fixed and variable costs increase as activity volume increases.
4. Both fixed and variable costs stay the same in total as activity volume increases.

QS 18-3
Fixed and variable costs
C2

Kasey Anthony Company produces sporting equipment, including basketballs. Identify each of the following costs as direct or indirect if the cost object is a basketball produced by Kasey Anthony.

1. Materials used to produce basketballs.
2. Electricity used in the production plant.
3. Labor used on the basketball production line.
4. Salary of manager who supervises the entire plant.
5. Depreciation on equipment used to produce basketballs.

QS 18-4
Direct and indirect costs
C2

Which of these statements is true regarding product and period costs?

1. Sales commission is a product cost and factory rent is a period cost.
2. Factory wages are a product cost and direct material is a period cost.
3. Factory maintenance is a product cost and sales commission is a period cost.
4. Sales commission is a product cost and depreciation on factory equipment is a product cost.

QS 18-5
Product and period costs
C3

Three inventory categories are reported on a manufacturing company's statement of financial position: (i) raw materials, (ii) goods in process, and (iii) finished goods. Identify the usual order in which these inventory items are reported on the statement of financial position.

1. (i)(ii)(iii)   2. (ii)(i)(iii)   3. (ii)(iii)(i)   4. (iii)(ii)(i)

QS 18-6
Inventory reporting for
manufacturers   C4

A company has year-end cost of goods manufactured of $5,000, beginning finished goods inventory of $700, and ending finished goods inventory of $850. Its cost of goods sold is

1. $4,250   2. $4,000   3. $4,850   4. $6,550

QS 18-7
Cost of goods sold   P1

Identify the usual sequence of manufacturing activities by filling in the blank (with i, ii or iii) corresponding to its order: _____ Production activities; _____ sales activities; _____ materials activities.

QS 18-8
Manufacturing flows identified
C5

QS 18-9

Lean business concepts

C6

Match each lean business concept with its best description by entering its letter in the blank.

1. _____ Customer orientation
2. _____ Total quality management
3. _____ Just-in-time manufacturing
4. _____ Continuous improvements

A. Inventory is acquired or produced only as needed.

B. Flexible product designs can be modified to accommodate customer choices.

C. Every manager and employee constantly looks for ways to improve company operations.

D. Focuses on quality throughout the production process.

QS 18-10

Cost of goods sold

P1

Compute cost of goods sold for year 2011 using the following information.

Finished goods inventory, Dec. 31, 2010	$321,500
Goods in process inventory, Dec. 31, 2010	74,550
Goods in process inventory, Dec. 31, 2011	81,200
Cost of goods manufactured, year 2011	972,345
Finished goods inventory, Dec. 31, 2011	297,200

QS 18-11

Cost of goods manufactured

P2

Prepare the 2011 manufacturing statement for Carmichael Company using the following information.

Direct materials	$192,500
Direct labor	65,150
Factory overhead costs	26,000
Goods in process, Dec. 31, 2010	159,600
Goods in process, Dec. 31, 2011	144,750

QS 18-12

Manufacturing cycle time and efficiency

A1

Compute and interpret (*a*) manufacturing cycle time and (*b*) manufacturing cycle efficiency using the following information from a manufacturing company.

Process time	15 minutes
Inspection time	2 minutes
Move time	6.4 minutes
Wait time	36.6 minutes

QS 18-13

Direct materials used

C5

Nestlé reports beginning raw materials inventory of 3,590 and ending raw materials inventory of 3,708 (both numbers in millions of Swiss francs). If Nestlé purchased 12,000 (in millions of Swiss francs) of raw materials during the year, what is the amount of raw materials it used during the year?

EXERCISES

Exercise 18-1

Sources of accounting information

C1

Both managerial accounting and financial accounting provide useful information to decision makers. Indicate in the following chart the most likely source of information for each business decision (a decision can require major input from both sources, in which case both can be marked).

	Primary Information Source	
Business Decision	**Managerial**	**Financial**
1. Plan the budget for next quarter	_____	_____
2. Measure profitability of all individual stores	_____	_____
3. Prepare financial reports according to GAAP	_____	_____
4. Determine location and size for a new plant	_____	_____
5. Determine amount of dividends to pay shareholders	_____	_____
6. Evaluate a purchasing department's performance	_____	_____
7. Report financial performance to board of directors	_____	_____
8. Estimate product cost for a new line of shoes	_____	_____

In the following chart, compare financial accounting and managerial accounting by describing how each differs for the items listed. Be specific in your responses.

	Financial Accounting	Managerial Accounting
1. Nature of information	_____	_____
2. Flexibility of practice	_____	_____
3. Focus of information	_____	_____
4. Time dimension	_____	_____
5. Users and decision makers	_____	_____
6. Timeliness of information	_____	_____
7. Purpose of information	_____	_____

Exercise 18-2
Characteristics of financial accounting and managerial accounting
C1

Complete the following statements by filling in the blanks.

1. _____ is the process of setting goals and making plans to achieve them.

2. _____ _____ usually covers a period of 5 to 10 years.

3. _____ _____ usually covers a period of one year.

4. _____ is the process of monitoring planning decisions and evaluating an organization's activities and employees.

Exercise 18-3
Planning and control descriptions
C1

Georgia Pacific, a manufacturer, incurs the following costs. (1) Classify each cost as either a product or a period cost. If a product cost, identify it as a prime and/or conversion cost. (2) Classify each product cost as either a direct cost or an indirect cost using the product as the cost object.

Exercise 18-4
Cost analysis and identification
C3

	Product Cost		Period Cost	Direct Cost	Indirect Cost
Cost	Prime	Conversion			
1. Office supplies used	___	___	___	___	___
2. Bad debts expense	___	___	___	___	___
3. Small tools used	___	___	___	___	___
4. Factory utilities	___	___	___	___	___
5. Advertising..............................	___	___	___	___	___
6. Amortization of patents on factory machine...	___	___	___	___	___
7. Payroll taxes for production supervisor	___	___	___	___	___
8. Accident insurance on factory workers	___	___	___	___	___
9. Depreciation—Factory building	___	___	___	___	___
10. State and federal income taxes	___	___	___	___	___
11. Wages to assembly workers	___	___	___	___	___
12. Direct materials used	___	___	___	___	___

(1) Identify each of the five cost classifications discussed in the chapter. (2) List two purposes of identifying these separate cost classifications.

Exercise 18-5
Cost classifications C2

Listed here are product costs for the production of soccer balls. (1) Classify each cost (a) as either fixed or variable and (b) as either direct or indirect. (2) What pattern do you see regarding the relation between costs classified by behavior and costs classified by traceability?

Exercise 18-6
Cost analysis and classification
C2

	Cost by Behavior		Cost by Traceability	
Product Cost	Variable	Fixed	Direct	Indirect
1. Taxes on factory	___	___	___	___
2. Machinery depreciation	___	___	___	___
3. Coolants for machinery	___	___	___	___
4. Wages of assembly workers	___	___	___	___
5. Lace to hold leather together	___	___	___	___
6. Leather covers for soccer balls	___	___	___	___
7. Annual flat fee paid for office security	___	___	___	___

Exercise 18-7
Statement of financial position
identification and preparation

C4

Current assets for two different companies at calendar year-end 2011 are listed here. One is a manufacturer, Roller Blades Mfg., and the other, Sunny Foods, is a grocery distribution company. (1) Identify which set of numbers relates to the manufacturer and which to the merchandiser. (2) Prepare the current asset section for each company from this information. Discuss why the current asset section for these two companies is different.

Account	Company 1	Company 2
Cash	$ 9,000	$ 7,000
Raw materials inventory	—	44,000
Merchandise inventory	47,000	—
Goods in process inventory	—	32,000
Finished goods inventory	—	52,000
Accounts receivable, net	64,000	77,000
Prepaid expenses	3,500	700

Exercise 18-8
Cost of goods sold computation

P1

Compute cost of goods sold for each of these two companies for the year ended December 31, 2011.

		Century Merchandising	New Homes Manufacturing
1			
2			
3	Beginning inventory		
4	Merchandise	$250,000	
5	Finished goods		$500,000
6	Cost of purchases	460,000	
7	Cost of goods manufactured		886,000
8	Ending inventory		
9	Merchandise	150,000	
10	Finished goods		144,000

Check Century Merchandising
COGS, $560,000

Exercise 18-9
Cost of goods manufactured and
cost of goods sold computation

P1 P2

Using the following data, compute (1) the cost of goods manufactured and (2) the cost of goods sold for both Canyon Company and Rossings Company.

	Canyon Company	Rossings Company
Beginning finished goods inventory	$14,000	$18,450
Beginning goods in process inventory	16,500	21,950
Beginning raw materials inventory	9,250	11,000
Rental cost on factory equipment	29,000	24,750
Direct labor.............................	21,000	37,000
Ending finished goods inventory	19,650	15,300
Ending goods in process inventory	24,000	18,000
Ending raw materials inventory	7,300	9,200
Factory utilities	11,000	14,000
Factory supplies used	10,200	5,200
General and administrative expenses	23,000	45,000
Indirect labor...........................	3,250	9,660
Repairs—Factory equipment	6,780	3,500
Raw materials purchases	35,000	54,000
Sales salaries	52,000	48,000

Check Canyon COGS, $105,030

For each of the following accounts for a manufacturing company, place a ✔ in the appropriate column indicating that it appears on the statement of financial position, the income statement, the manufacturing statement, and/or a detailed listing of factory overhead costs. Assume that the income statement shows the calculation of cost of goods sold and the manufacturing statement shows only the total amount of factory overhead. (An account can appear on more than one report.)

Exercise 18-10
Components of accounting reports
P2

Account	Statement of Financial Position	Income Statement	Manufacturing Statement	Overhead Report
3 Accounts receivable				
4 Computer supplies used in office				
5 Beginning finished goods inventory				
6 Beginning goods in process inventory				
7 Beginning raw materials inventory				
8 Cash				
9 Depreciation expense—Factory building				
10 Depreciation expense—Factory equipment				
11 Depreciation expense—Office building				
12 Depreciation expense—Office equipment				
13 Direct labor				
14 Ending finished goods inventory				
15 Ending goods in process inventory				
16 Ending raw materials inventory				
17 Factory maintenance wages				
18 Computer supplies used in factory				
19 Income taxes				
20 Insurance on factory building				
21 Rent cost on office building				
22 Office supplies used				
23 Property taxes on factory building				
24 Raw materials purchases				
25 Sales				

Given the following selected account balances of Randa Company, prepare its manufacturing statement for the year ended on December 31, 2011. Include a listing of the individual overhead account balances in this statement.

Exercise 18-11
Manufacturing statement preparation
P2

Sales	$1,252,000
Raw materials inventory, Dec. 31, 2010	39,000
Goods in process inventory, Dec. 31, 2010	55,900
Finished goods inventory, Dec. 31, 2010	64,750
Raw materials purchases	177,600
Direct labor	227,000
Factory computer supplies used	19,840
Indirect labor	49,000
Repairs—Factory equipment	7,250
Rent cost of factory building	59,000
Advertising expense	96,000
General and administrative expenses	131,300
Raw materials inventory, Dec. 31, 2011	44,700
Goods in process inventory, Dec. 31, 2011	43,500
Finished goods inventory, Dec. 31, 2011	69,300

Check   Cost of goods manufactured, $546,390

Use the information in Exercise 18-11 to prepare an income statement for Randa Company (a manufacturer). Assume that its cost of goods manufactured is $546,390.

Exercise 18-12
Income statement preparation
P2

Exercise 18-13

Cost flows in manufacturing

C5

The following chart shows how costs flow through a business as a product is manufactured. Some boxes in the flowchart show cost amounts. Compute the cost amounts for the boxes that contain question marks.

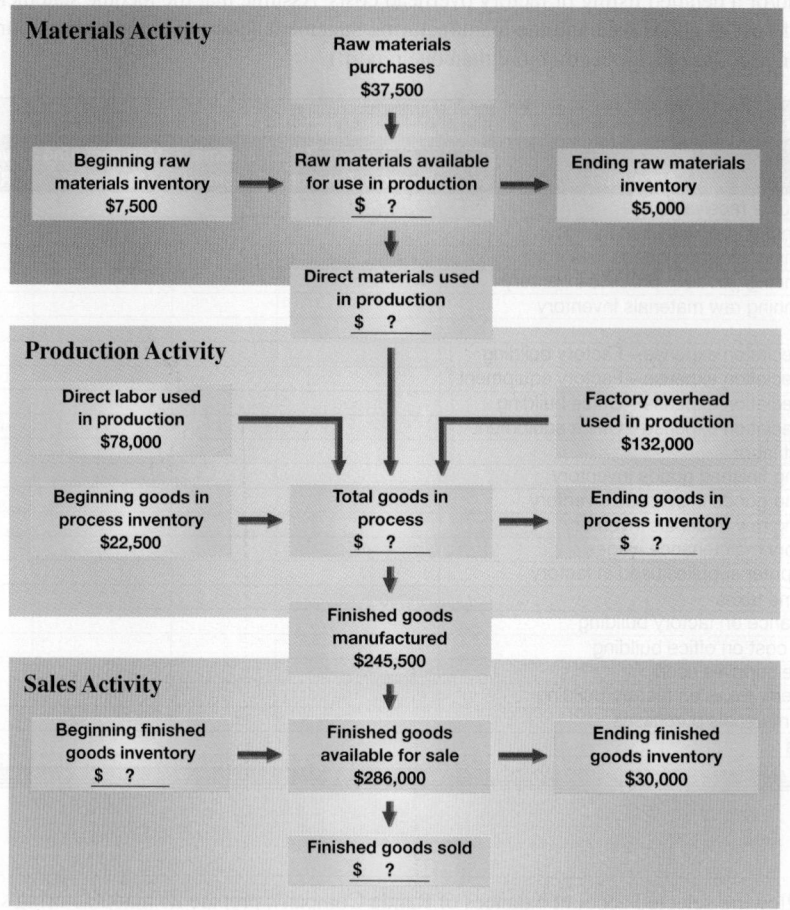

Exercise 18-14

Customer orientation in practice

C6

Customer orientation means that a company's managers and employees respond to customers' changing wants and needs. A manufacturer of metal parts has created a customer satisfaction survey that it asks each of its customers to complete. The survey asks about the following factors: (A) product performance; (B) price; (C) lead time; (D) delivery. Each factor is to be rated as unsatisfactory, marginal, average, satisfactory, or very satisfied.

a. Match the competitive forces 1 through 4 to the factors on the survey. A factor can be matched to more than one competitive force.

Survey Factor	Competitive Force
A. Product performance	_____ **1.** Cost
B. Price	_____ **2.** Time
C. Lead time	_____ **3.** Quality
D. Delivery	_____ **4.** Flexibility of service

b. How can managers of this company use the information from this customer satisfaction survey to better meet competitive forces and satisfy their customers?

Exercise 18-15

Management concepts

C6

Following are three separate events affecting the managerial accounting systems for different companies. Match the management concept(s) that the company is likely to adopt for the event identified. There is some overlap in the meaning of customer orientation and total quality management and, therefore, some responses can include more than one concept.

Event	Management Concept
_____ 1. The company starts measuring inventory turnover and discontinues elaborate inventory records. Its new focus is to pull inventory through the system.	a. Total quality management (TQM)
	b. Just-in-time (JIT) system
_____ 2. The company starts reporting measures on customer complaints and product returns from customers.	c. Continuous improvement (CI)
	d. Customer orientation (CO)
_____ 3. The company starts reporting measures such as the percent of defective products and the number of units scrapped.	

▦ connect

This chapter explained the purpose of managerial accounting in the context of the current business environment. Review the *automobile* section of your local newspaper; the Sunday paper is often best. Review advertisements of sport-utility vehicles and identify the manufacturers that offer these products and the factors on which they compete.

PROBLEM SET A

Problem 18-1A
Managerial accounting role

C1

Required

Discuss the potential contributions and responsibilities of the managerial accounting professional in helping an automobile manufacturer succeed. (*Hint:* Think about information and estimates that a managerial accountant might provide new entrants into the sport-utility market.)

Listed here are the total costs associated with the 2011 production of 1,000 drum sets manufactured by NeatBeat. The drum sets sell for $300 each.

Problem 18-2A
Cost computation, classification, and analysis

C2   C3

	Cost by Behavior		Cost by Function	
Costs	**Variable**	**Fixed**	**Product**	**Period**
1. Plastic for casing—$12,000	$12,000		$12,000	
2. Wages of assembly workers—$60,000				
3. Property taxes on factory—$6,000				
4. Accounting staff salaries—$45,000....................				
5. Drum stands (1,000 stands outsourced)—$25,000........				
6. Rent cost of equipment for sales staff—$7,000				
7. Upper management salaries—$100,000				
8. Annual flat fee for maintenance service—$9,000				
9. Sales commissions—$10 per unit				
10. Machinery depreciation—$10,000				

Required

1. Classify each cost and its amount as (*a*) either fixed or variable and (*b*) either product or period. (The first cost is completed as an example.)

Check   (1) Total variable manufacturing cost, $97,000

2. Compute the manufacturing cost per drum set.

Analysis Component

3. Assume that 1,200 drum sets are produced in the next year. What do you predict will be the total cost of plastic for the casings and the per unit cost of the plastic for the casings? Explain.

4. Assume that 1,200 drum sets are produced in the next year. What do you predict will be the total cost of property taxes and the per unit cost of the property taxes? Explain.

Assume that you must make a presentation to the marketing staff explaining the difference between product and period costs. Your supervisor tells you the marketing staff would also like clarification regarding prime and conversion costs and an explanation of how these terms fit with product and period cost. You are told that many on the staff are unable to classify costs in their merchandising activities.

Problem 18-3A
Cost classification and explanation

C2   C3

Required

Prepare a one-page memorandum to your supervisor outlining your presentation to the marketing staff.

Problem 18-4A

Opportunity cost
estimation and application

C1 C2

Refer to *Decision Maker,* **Purchase Manager,** in this chapter. Assume that you are the motorcycle manufacturer's managerial accountant. The purchasing manager asks you about preparing an estimate of the related costs for buying motorcycle seats from supplier (B). She tells you this estimate is needed because unless dollar estimates are attached to nonfinancial factors, such as lost production time, her supervisor will not give it full attention. The manager also shows you the following information.

● Production output is 3,000 motorcycles per year based on 250 production days a year.
● Production time per day is 8 hours at a cost of $2,000 per hour to run the production line.
● Lost production time due to poor quality is 1%.
● Satisfied customers purchase, on average, three motorcycles during a lifetime.
● Satisfied customers recommend the product, on average, to 10 other people.
● Marketing predicts that using seat (B) will result in 10 lost customers per year from repeat business and referrals.
● Average gross profit per motorcycle is $3,000.

Required

Estimate the costs (including opportunity costs) of buying motorcycle seats from supplier (B). This problem requires that you think creatively and make reasonable estimates; thus there could be more than one correct answer. (*Hint:* Reread the answer to *Decision Maker* and compare the cost savings for buying from supplier [B] to the sum of lost customer revenue from repeat business and referrals and the cost of lost production time.)

Check Estimated cost of lost
production time, $40,000

Problem 18-5A

Ending inventory computation
and evaluation

C4

Shepler Boot Company makes specialty boots for the rodeo circuit. On December 31, 2010, the company had (*a*) 500 pairs of boots in finished goods inventory and (*b*) 1,500 heels at a cost of $5 each in raw materials inventory. During 2011, the company purchased 50,000 additional heels at $5 each and manufactured 20,000 pairs of boots.

Required

Check (1) Ending (heel) inventory,
11,500 units; $57,500

1. Determine the unit and dollar amounts of raw materials inventory in heels at December 31, 2011.

Analysis Component

2. Write a one-half page memorandum to the production manager explaining why a just-in-time inventory system for heels should be considered. Include the amount of working capital that can be reduced at December 31, 2011, if the ending heel raw material inventory is cut by half.

Problem 18-6A

Inventory computation
and reporting

C4 P1

www.mheducation.asia/olc/wildkwokFAP

Shown here are annual financial data at December 31, 2011, taken from two different companies.

	Pinnacle Retail	Slope Board Manufacturing
Beginning inventory		
Merchandise	$150,000	
Finished goods		$300,000
Cost of purchases	250,000	
Cost of goods manufactured		586,000
Ending inventory		
Merchandise	100,000	
Finished goods		200,000

Required

Check (1) Slope Board's cost of
goods sold, $686,000

1. Compute the cost of goods sold section of the income statement at December 31, 2011, for each company. Include the proper title and format in the solution.

2. Write a half-page memorandum to your instructor (*a*) identifying the inventory accounts and (*b*) describing where each is reported on the income statement and statement of financial position for both companies.

Many fast-food restaurants compete on lean business concepts. Match each of the following activities at a fast-food restaurant with the lean business concept it strives to achieve. Some activities might relate to more than one lean business concept.

_____ **1.** Clean tables and floors	**a.** Just-in-time (JIT)
_____ **2.** Orders filled within three minutes	**b.** Continuous improvement (CI)
_____ **3.** Standardized food making processes	**c.** Total quality management (TQM)
_____ **4.** Courteous employees	
_____ **5.** Food produced to order	
_____ **6.** New product development	
_____ **7.** Customer satisfaction surveys	
_____ **8.** Continually changing menus	
_____ **9.** Drive-through windows	
_____ **10.** Standardized menus from location to location	

The following calendar year-end information is taken from the December 31, 2011, adjusted trial balance and other records of Plaza Company.

Advertising expense	$ 30,750	Direct labor	$ 677,480
Depreciation expense—Office equipment	9,250	income tax payable	235,725
Depreciation expense—Selling equipment	10,600	Indirect labor	58,875
Depreciation expense—Factory equipment	35,550	Miscellaneous production costs	10,425
Factory supervision	104,600	Office salaries expense	65,000
Factory supplies used	9,350	Raw materials purchases	927,000
Factory utilities	35,000	Rent expense—Office space	24,000
Inventories		Rent expense—Selling space	28,100
Raw materials, December 31, 2010	168,850	Rent expense—Factory building	78,800
Raw materials, December 31, 2011	184,000	Maintenance expense—Factory equipment	37,400
Goods in process, December 31, 2010	17,700	Sales	4,527,000
Goods in process, December 31, 2011	21,380	Sales discounts	64,500
Finished goods, December 31, 2010	169,350	Sales salaries expense	394,560
Finished goods, December 31, 2011	138,490		

Required

1. Prepare the company's 2011 manufacturing statement.

2. Prepare the company's 2011 income statement that reports separate categories for (*a*) selling expenses and (*b*) general and administrative expenses.

Check (1) Cost of goods manufactured, $1,955,650

Analysis Component

3. Compute the (*a*) inventory turnover, defined as cost of goods sold divided by average inventory, and (*b*) days' sales in inventory, defined as 365 times ending inventory divided by cost of goods sold, for both its raw materials inventory and its finished goods inventory. (To compute turnover and days' sales in inventory for raw materials, use raw materials used rather than cost of goods sold.) Discuss some possible reasons for differences between these ratios for the two types of inventories. Round answers to one decimal place.

White Maple Company produces maple bookcases to customer order. It received an order from a customer to produce 15,000 bookcases. The following information is available for the production of the bookcases.

Process time	16.0 days
Inspection time	0.5 days
Move time	5.5 days
Wait time	18.0 days

Required

1. Compute the company's manufacturing cycle time.

Check (2) Manufacturing cycle efficiency, 0.40

2. Compute the company's manufacturing cycle efficiency. Interpret your answer.

Analysis Component

3. Assume that White Maple wishes to increase its manufacturing cycle efficiency to 0.75. What are some ways that it can accomplish this?

PROBLEM SET B

Problem 18-1B
Managerial accounting role

C1

This chapter described the purpose of managerial accounting in the context of the current business environment. Review the *home electronics* section of your local newspaper; the Sunday paper is often best. Review advertisements of home electronics and identify the manufacturers that offer these products and the factors on which they compete.

Required

Discuss the potential contributions and responsibilities of the managerial accounting professional in helping a home electronics manufacturer succeed. (*Hint:* Think about information and estimates that a managerial accountant might provide new entrants into the home electronics market.)

Problem 18-2B
Cost computation, classification, and analysis

C2 C3

Listed here are the total costs associated with the 2011 production of 10,000 Blu-ray Discs (BDs) manufactured by Hip-Hop. The BDs sell for $15 each.

Costs	Cost by Behavior		Cost by Function	
	Variable	Fixed	Product	Period
1. Plastic for BDs—$1,000	$1,000			$1,000
2. Wages of assembly workers—$20,000				
3. Cost of factory rent—$4,500				
4. Systems staff salaries—$10,000				
5. Labeling (outsourced)—$2,500				
6. Cost of office equipment rent—$700				
7. Upper management salaries—$100,000				
8. Annual fixed fee for cleaning service—$3,000				
9. Sales commissions—$0.50 per BD				
10. Machinery depreciation—$15,000				

Required

1. Classify each cost and its amount as (*a*) either fixed or variable and (*b*) either product or period. (The first cost is completed as an example.)

Check (2) Total variable manufacturing cost, $23,500

2. Compute the manufacturing cost per BD.

Analysis Component

3. Assume that 15,000 BDs are produced in the next year. What do you predict will be the total cost of plastic for the BDs and the per unit cost of the plastic for the BDs? Explain.

4. Assume that 15,000 BDs are produced in the next year. What do you predict will be the total cost of factory rent and the per unit cost of the factory rent? Explain.

Problem 18-3B
Cost classification and explanation

C2 C3

Assume that you must make a presentation to a client explaining the difference between prime and conversion costs. The client makes and sells 50,000 cookies per week. The client tells you that her sales staff also would like a clarification regarding product and period costs. She tells you that most of the staff lack training in managerial accounting.

Required

Prepare a one-page memorandum to your client outlining your planned presentation to her sales staff.

Refer to *Decision Maker,* **Purchase Manager,** in this chapter. Assume that you are the motorcycle manufacturer's managerial accountant. The purchasing manager asks you about preparing an estimate of the related costs for buying motorcycle seats from supplier (B). She tells you this estimate is needed because unless dollar estimates are attached to nonfinancial factors such as lost production time, her supervisor will not give it full attention. The manager also shows you the following information.

Problem 18-4B
Opportunity cost estimation
and application
C1 C2

- Production output is 2,000 motorcycles per year based on 250 production days a year.
- Production time per day is 8 hours at a cost of $500 per hour to run the production line.
- Lost production time due to poor quality is 1%.
- Satisfied customers purchase, on average, three motorcycles during a lifetime.
- Satisfied customers recommend the product, on average, to 10 other people.
- Marketing predicts that using seat (B) will result in 8 lost customers per year from repeat business and referrals.
- Average gross profit per motorcycle is $4,000.

Required

Estimate the costs (including opportunity costs) of buying motorcycle seats from supplier (B). This problem requires that you think creatively and make reasonable estimates; thus there could be more than one correct answer. (*Hint:* Reread the answer to *Decision Maker,* and compare the cost savings for buying from supplier [B] to the sum of lost customer revenue from repeat business and referrals and the cost of lost production time.)

Check   Cost of lost gross profit, $32,000

The Edge Company makes specialty skates for the ice skating circuit. On December 31, 2010, the company had (*a*) 500 skates in finished goods inventory and (*b*) 2,000 blades at a cost of $15 each in raw materials inventory. During 2011, Edge Company purchased 45,000 additional blades at $15 each and manufactured 20,000 pairs of skates.

Problem 18-5B
Ending inventory computation
and evaluation
C4

Required

1. Determine the unit and dollar amounts of raw materials inventory in blades at December 31, 2011.

Check   (1) Ending (blade) inventory, 7,000 units; $105,000

Analysis Component

2. Write a one-half page memorandum to the production manager explaining why a just-in-time inventory system for blades should be considered. Include the amount of working capital that can be reduced at December 31, 2011, if the ending blade raw material inventory is cut in half.

Shown here are annual financial data at December 31, 2011, taken from two different companies.

Problem 18-6B
Inventory computation and
reporting
C4 P1

	Cardinal Drug (Retail)	Nandina (Manufacturing)
Beginning inventory		
Merchandise	$ 50,000	
Finished goods		$200,000
Cost of purchases	350,000	
Cost of goods manufactured		686,000
Ending inventory		
Merchandise	25,000	
Finished goods		300,000

Required

1. Compute the cost of goods sold section of the income statement at December 31, 2011, for each company. Include the proper title and format in the solution.

2. Write a half-page memorandum to your instructor (*a*) identifying the inventory accounts and (*b*) identifying where each is reported on the income statement and statement of financial position for both companies.

Check   (1) Cardinal Drug cost of goods sold, $375,000

Problem 18-7B
Lean business concepts

C6

Eastman-Kodak manufactures digital cameras and must compete on lean manufacturing concepts. Match each of the following activities that it engages in with the lean manufacturing concept it strives to achieve. (Some activities might relate to more than one lean manufacturing concept.)

_____ **1.** Kodak monitors the market to determine what features its competitors are offering on digital cameras.

_____ **2.** Kodak asks production workers for ideas to improve production.

_____ **3.** Lenses are received daily based on customer orders.

_____ **4.** Customers receive a satisfaction survey with each camera purchased.

_____ **5.** The manufacturing process is standardized and documented.

_____ **6.** Cameras are produced in small lots, and only to customer order.

_____ **7.** Manufacturing facilities are arranged to reduce move time and wait time.

_____ **8.** Kodak conducts focus groups to determine new features that customers want in digital cameras.

_____ **9.** Orders received are filled within two business days.

_____ **10.** Kodak works with suppliers to reduce inspection time of incoming materials.

a. Just-in-time (JIT)

b. Continuous improvement (CI)

c. Total quality management (TQM)

Problem 18-8B
Manufacturing and income statements; analysis of inventories **P2**

The following calendar year-end information is taken from the December 31, 2011, adjusted trial balance and other records of Firethorn Furniture.

Advertising expense	$ 22,250	Direct labor	$ 564,500
Depreciation expense—Office equipment	10,440	income tax payable	138,700
Depreciation expense—Selling equipment	12,125	Indirect labor	61,000
Depreciation expense—Factory equipment	37,400	Miscellaneous production costs	10,440
Factory supervision	123,500	Office salaries expense	72,875
Factory supplies used	8,060	Raw materials purchases	896,375
Factory utilities	39,500	Rent expense—Office space	25,625
Inventories		Rent expense—Selling space	29,000
Raw materials, December 31, 2010	42,375	Rent expense—Factory building	95,500
Raw materials, December 31, 2011	72,430	Maintenance expense—Factory equipment	32,375
Goods in process, December 31, 2010	14,500	Sales	5,002,000
Goods in process, December 31, 2011	16,100	Sales discounts	59,375
Finished goods, December 31, 2010	179,200	Sales salaries expense	297,300
Finished goods, December 31, 2011	143,750		

Required

Check (1) Cost of goods manufactured, $1,836,995

1. Prepare the company's 2011 manufacturing statement.

2. Prepare the company's 2011 income statement that reports separate categories for (*a*) selling expenses and (*b*) general and administrative expenses.

Analysis Component

3. Compute the (*a*) inventory turnover, defined as cost of goods sold divided by average inventory, and (*b*) days' sales in inventory, defined as 365 times ending inventory divided by cost of goods sold, for both its raw materials inventory and its finished goods inventory. (To compute turnover and days' sales in inventory for raw materials, use raw materials used rather than cost of goods sold.) Discuss some possible reasons for differences between these ratios for the two types of inventories. Round answers to one decimal place.

Quick Dry Ink produces ink-jet printers for personal computers. It received an order for 600 printers from a customer. The following information is available for this order.

Process time	16.0 hours
Inspection time	3.4 hours
Move time	9.0 hours
Wait time	21.6 hours

Required

1. Compute the company's manufacturing cycle time.

2. Compute the company's manufacturing cycle efficiency. Interpret your answer.

Analysis Component

3. Assume that Quick Dry Ink wishes to increase its manufacturing cycle efficiency to 0.80. What are some ways that it can accomplish this?

(This serial problem begins in Chapter 1 and continues through most of the book. If previous chapter segments were not completed, the serial problem can begin at this point.)

SERIAL PROBLEM

Business Solutions

C2 C4 P2

SP 18   Santana Rey, owner of Business Solutions, decides to diversify her business by also manufacturing computer workstation furniture.

Required

1. Classify the following manufacturing costs of Business Solutions by behavior and traceability.

	Cost by Behavior		Cost by Traceability	
Product Costs	**Variable**	**Fixed**	**Direct**	**Indirect**
1. Monthly flat fee to clean workshop	___	___	___	___
2. Laminate coverings for desktops	___	___	___	___
3. Taxes on assembly workshop	___	___	___	___
4. Glue to assemble workstation component parts	___	___	___	___
5. Wages of desk assembler	___	___	___	___
6. Electricity for workshop	___	___	___	___
7. Depreciation on tools	___	___	___	___

2. Prepare a manufacturing statement for Business Solutions for the month ended January 31, 2012. Assume the following manufacturing costs:

Direct materials: $2,200

Factory overhead: $490

Direct labor: $900

Beginning goods in process: none (December 31, 2011)

Ending goods in process: $540 (January 31, 2012)

Beginning finished goods inventory: none (December 31, 2011)

Ending finished goods inventory: $350 (January 31, 2012)

3. Prepare the cost of goods sold section of a partial income statement for Business Solutions for the month ended January 31, 2012.

Check   (3) COGS, $2,700

Beyond the Numbers

REPORTING IN ACTION

C1

BTN 18-1   Managerial accounting is more than recording, maintaining, and reporting financial results. Managerial accountants must provide managers with both financial and nonfinancial information including estimates, projections, and forecasts. There are many accounting estimates that management accountants must make, and **Research In Motion** must notify shareholders of these estimates.

Required

1. Access Research In Motion's 2010 annual report from its Website www.rim.com. Read the "Use of Estimates" section of the "Summary of Significant Accounting Policies" footnote to its financial statements. What are some of the accounting estimates that Research In Motion made in preparing its financial statements? What are some of the effects if the company's actual results differ from its estimates?

2. What is the management accountant's role in determining those estimates?

Fast Forward

3. Access **Research In Motion**'s annual report for a financial year ending after February 27, 2010, from either its Website or the SEC's EDGAR database [www.SEC.gov]. Answer the questions in parts (1) and (2) after reading the current "Summary of Significant Accounting Policies". Identify any major changes.

COMPARATIVE ANALYSIS

C1

BTN 18-2   Manufacturing companies must decide whether to operate their own manufacturing facilities or instead outsource the manufacturing function to a third-party (outside) company. This decision impacts both company managers and also financial statement items. Access the 2010 annual report for **Research In Motion** (RIM) and **Apple**. The RIM report is for the year ended February 27, 2010 and the Apple report is for the year ended September 26, 2009.

Required

1. Determine whether RIM operates its own manufacturing facilities or outsources the manufacturing function. (*Hint:* Search for "Manufacturing Capacity.")

2. Determine whether Apple operates its own manufacturing facilities or outsources the manufacturing function. (*Hint:* Search for "product manufacturing.")

3. For both companies, determine the amounts they report for (a) raw materials inventory, (b) work-in-process inventory, and (c) finished goods inventory. Explain how the decision on outsourcing (or not) of manufacturing operations is related to the components of inventory.

ETHICS CHALLENGE

C1 C3

BTN 18-3   Assume that you are the managerial accountant at Infostore, a manufacturer of hard drives, CDs, and DVDs. Its reporting year-end is December 31. The chief financial officer is concerned about having enough cash to pay the expected income tax bill because of poor cash flow management. On November 15, the purchasing department purchased excess inventory of CD raw materials in anticipation of rapid growth of this product beginning in January. To decrease the company's tax liability, the chief financial officer tells you to record the purchase of this inventory as part of supplies and expense it in the current year; this would decrease the company's tax liability by increasing expenses.

Required

1. In which account should the purchase of CD raw materials be recorded?

2. How should you respond to this request by the chief financial officer?

COMMUNICATING IN PRACTICE

C6

BTN 18-4   Write a one-page memorandum to a prospective college student about salary expectations for graduates in business. Compare and contrast the expected salaries for accounting (including different subfields such as public, corporate, tax, audit, and so forth), marketing, management, and finance majors. Prepare a graph showing average starting salaries (and those for experienced professionals in those fields if available). To get this information, stop by your school's career services office; libraries also have this information. The Website JobStar.org (click on *Salary Info*) also can get you started.

BTN 18-5 Managerial accounting professionals follow a code of ethics. As a member of the Institute of Management Accountants, the managerial accountant must comply with Standards of Ethical Conduct.

TAKING IT TO THE NET

C1

Required

1. Identify, print, and read the *Statement of Ethical Professional Practice* posted at www.IMAnet.org. (Search using "ethical professional practice.")

2. What four overarching ethical principles underlie the IMA's statement?

3. Describe the courses of action the IMA recommends in resolving ethical conflicts.

BTN 18-6 The following calendar-year information is taken from the December 31, 2011, adjusted trial balance and other records of Azalea Company.

TEAMWORK IN ACTION

C5 P2

Advertising expense	$ 19,125	Direct labor	$ 650,750
Depreciation expense—Office equipment	8,750	Indirect labor	60,000
Depreciation expense—Selling equipment	10,000	Miscellaneous production costs	8,500
Depreciation expense—Factory equipment	32,500	Office salaries expense	100,875
Factory supervision	122,500	Raw materials purchases	872,500
Factory supplies used	15,750	Rent expense—Office space	21,125
Factory utilities	36,250	Rent expense—Selling space	25,750
Inventories		Rent expense—Factory building	79,750
Raw materials, December 31, 2010	177,500	Maintenance expense—Factory equipment	27,875
Raw materials, December 31, 2011	168,125	Sales	3,275,000
Goods in process, December 31, 2010	15,875	Sales discounts	57,500
Goods in process, December 31, 2011	14,000	Sales salaries expense	286,250
Finished goods, December 31, 2010	164,375		
Finished goods, December 31, 2011	129,000		

Required

1. *Each* team member is to be responsible for computing **one** of the following amounts. You are not to duplicate your teammates' work. Get any necessary amounts from teammates. Each member is to explain the computation to the team in preparation for reporting to class.

   a. Materials used.

   b. Factory overhead.

   c. Total manufacturing costs.

   d. Total cost of goods in process.

   e. Cost of goods manufactured.

2. Check your cost of goods manufactured with the instructor. If it is correct, proceed to part (3).

3. *Each* team member is to be responsible for computing **one** of the following amounts. You are not to duplicate your teammates' work. Get any necessary amounts from teammates. Each member is to explain the computation to the team in preparation for reporting to class.

   a. Net sales.

   b. Cost of goods sold.

   c. Gross profit.

   d. Total operating expenses.

   e. Net profit or loss before taxes.

Point: Provide teams with transparencies and markers for presentation purposes.

ENTREPRENEURIAL DECISION

C1 C2 C6

BTN 18-7   Alice Zhang of Mischmasch must keep a close watch on her costs as would any entrepreneur. However, given the nature of her business, which is creating an online community of artists and providing a platform for the sale of art works, the costs she would have to monitor are likely to be different from those of traditional manufacturing businesses.

Required

1. What are the main categories of costs that Alice would have to monitor closely? Give examples.
2. E-commerce now accounts for 7% or more of global sales. How does e-commerce affect the practice of management accounting? Answer with reference to Alice's venture.
3. What are the likely sources of Mischmasch's sources of revenues and cost of goods sold?
4. Visit Mischmasch's Website. What are the some of the key factors likely to affect Mischmasch's growth in revenues and profits?

HITTING THE ROAD

C1 C2

BTN 18-8   Visit your favorite fast-food restaurant. Observe its business operations.

Required

1. Describe all business activities from the time a customer arrives to the time that customer departs.
2. List all costs you can identify with the separate activities described in part 1.
3. Classify each cost from part 2 as fixed or variable, and explain your classification.

GLOBAL DECISION

C1

BTN 18-9   Access Nestle's Corporate Governance Report, 2010 at http://www.nestle.com/Common/ NestleDocuments/Documents/Library/Documents/Corporate_Governance/Corp_ Governance_Report_2010_EN.pdf. Section 3.5 describes the Board's responsibilities.

Required

What is the role of a management accountant in helping the Board fulfill its responsibilities?

ANSWERS TO MULTIPLE CHOICE QUIZ

1. c
2. b
3. b
4. a

5. Beginning finished goods + Cost of goods manufactured (COGM) − Ending finished goods = Cost of goods sold
   $6,000 + COGM − $3,200 = $7,500
   COGM = $4,700

19

Job Order Cost Accounting

A Look Back

Chapter 18 introduced managerial accounting and explained basic cost concepts. We also described the lean business model and the reporting of manufacturing activities, including the manufacturing statement.

A Look at This Chapter

We begin this chapter by describing a cost accounting system. We then explain the procedures used to determine costs using a job order costing system. We conclude with a discussion of over- and underapplied overhead.

A Look Ahead

Chapter 20 focuses on measuring costs in process production companies. We explain process production, describe how to assign costs to processes, and compute and analyze cost per equivalent unit.

Learning Objectives

CAP

CONCEPTUAL

C1 Describe important features of job order production. (p. 746)

C2 Explain job cost sheets and how they are used in job order cost accounting. (p. 748)

ANALYTICAL

A1 Apply job order costing in pricing services. (p. 759)

PROCEDURAL

P1 Describe and record the flow of materials costs in job order cost accounting. (p. 750)

P2 Describe and record the flow of labor costs in job order cost accounting. (p. 752)

P3 Describe and record the flow of overhead costs in job order cost accounting. (p. 753)

P4 Determine adjustments for overapplied and underapplied factory overhead. (p. 758)

"On budget, on time, and on specification."—**PRAKASH**

BFSI Consulting's Three *O*s

"On budget, on time, and on specification," says Prakash N. That is the philosophy of **BFSI Consulting** (**www.bfsiconsulting.com**), an Oracle Gold partner that provides consulting, training, and implementation support to banks and financial institutions that have adopted Oracle's financial services products. Its clients can be found in more than 30 countries around the world.

Prakash, an experienced executive in the banking industry, is one of the company's founders and a member of its top management team. As such, he spends much of his time traveling to meet clients to ensure that BFSI's projects conform to the three *O*s.

The company, which started operating in 2007, offers consulting services that include providing custom built solutions and customized user training, conducting module-specific sessions, developing operating guidelines, conducting requirement analysis and documentation, developing interfaces and reports, and offering expertise in process improvement, project management, and testing and quality assurance.

The training support allows BFSI's clients to maximize their return on investment in technology. It includes generic end-user training to support daily operations, customized training aligned to a bank's business processes and the skill level of its staff, and technical training for support staff.

The company's own Egalite is a financial inclusion product that provides technological solutions to the logistical challenges of making banking accessible to those for whom "brick and mortar" banks are not easily accessible.

With such a vast array of services, Prakash notes there are challenges in costing jobs and bidding well. Among other things, jobs differ based on the size of the client and the scope of the work. Because each project constitutes a unique "job," bids are based on the estimated costs and a target margin. "Cost estimates and margins could go wrong for many reasons," he explains, "such as unexpected complexities in implementation." Though it would be safer for BFSI to follow a time-and-material model (i.e., bill for the time spent by each BFSI staff on the project), clients prefer a turnkey approach.

Under the turnkey approach, BFSI estimates the time each type of human resource will spend on the project. Typically, senior managers cost more than juniors, and managers with special technical skills also cost more. Prakash points out that when costing a job, "generally, labor costs account for more than 60 percent of a job. Overhead and margins account for the remaining 40 percent."

This chapter introduces a system for assigning costs to the flow of goods through a production process. We then describe the details of a *job order cost accounting system*. Job order costing is frequently used by manufacturers of custom products or providers of custom services. Manufacturers that use job order costing typically base it on a perpetual inventory system, which provides a continuous record of materials, goods in process, and finished goods inventories.

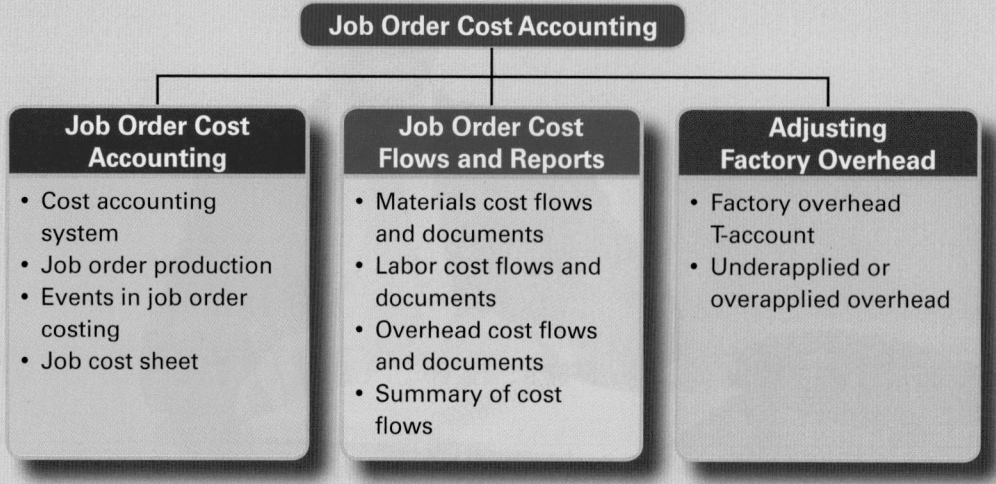

Job Order Cost Accounting

Job Order Cost Accounting	Job Order Cost Flows and Reports	Adjusting Factory Overhead
• Cost accounting system • Job order production • Events in job order costing • Job cost sheet	• Materials cost flows and documents • Labor cost flows and documents • Overhead cost flows and documents • Summary of cost flows	• Factory overhead T-account • Underapplied or overapplied overhead

JOB ORDER COST ACCOUNTING

This section describes a cost accounting system and job order production and costing.

Cost Accounting System

An ever-increasing number of companies use a cost accounting system to generate timely and accurate inventory information. A **cost accounting system** records manufacturing activities using a *perpetual* inventory system, which continuously updates records for costs of materials, goods in process, and finished goods inventories. A cost accounting system also provides timely information about inventories and manufacturing costs per unit of product. This is especially helpful for managers' efforts to control costs and determine selling prices. (A **general accounting system** records manufacturing activities using a *periodic* inventory system. Some companies still use a general accounting system, but its use is declining as competitive forces and customer demands have increased pressures on companies to better manage inventories.)

The two basic types of cost accounting systems are *job order cost accounting* and *process cost accounting*. We describe job order cost accounting in this chapter. Process cost accounting is explained in the next chapter.

Job Order Production

 C1 Describe important features of job order production.

Many companies produce products individually designed to meet the needs of a specific customer. Each customized product is manufactured separately and its production is called **job order production,** or *job order manufacturing* (also called *customized production,* which is the production of products in response to special orders). Examples of such products include synthetic football fields, special-order machines, a factory building, custom jewelry, wedding invitations, and artwork.

The production activities for a customized product represent a **job.** The principle of customization is equally applicable to both manufacturing *and* service companies. Most service companies meet customers' needs by performing a custom service for a specific customer. Examples of such services include an accountant auditing a client's financial statements, an interior designer remodeling an office, a wedding consultant planning and supervising a reception, and a lawyer defending a client. Whether the setting is manufacturing or services, job order operations involve meeting the needs of customers by producing or performing custom jobs.

Hyundai Heavy Industries, a Korean company, is the leading shipbuilder in the world. Its annual sales for the year 2013 was just over KRW 54,188 billion. Its shipbuilding business produces submarines, drill ships, LNG carriers, LPG carriers, container ships, and bulk carriers all built to specification. The company would use job costing to estimate, measure, and manage costs on its different jobs.

When a job involves producing more than one unit of a custom product, it is often called a **job lot.** Products produced as job lots could include benches for a church, imprinted T-shirts for a 10K race or company picnic, or advertising signs for a chain of stores. Although these orders involve more than one unit, the volume of production is typically low, such as 50 benches, 200 T-shirts, or 100 signs. Another feature of job order production is the diversity, often called *heterogeneity,* of the products produced. Namely, each customer order is likely to differ from another in some important respect. These variations can be minor or major.

Decision Insight

Custom Design   Managers once saw companies as the center of a solar system orbited by suppliers and customers. Now the customer has become the center of the business universe. The online store of **Tanishq,** a famous Asian jewelry brand, allows customers to compare, choose and order from among a range of metals, precious stones, sizes, prices, and type. Soon consumers may be able to personalize almost any product, from cellular phones to appliances to furniture. ■

Events in Job Order Costing

The initial event in a normal job order operation is the receipt of a customer order for a custom product. This causes the company to begin work on a job. A less common case occurs when management decides to begin work on a job before it has a signed contract. This is referred to as *jobs produced on speculation.*

Step 1: **Predict the cost to complete the job.** This cost depends on the product design prepared by either the customer or the producer.

Step 2: **Negotiate price and decide whether to pursue the job.** Other than for government or other cost-plus contracts, the selling price is determined by market factors. Producers evaluate the market price, compare it to cost, and determine whether the profit on the job is reasonable. If the profit is not reasonable, the producer would determine a desired **target cost.**

Step 3: **Schedule production of the job.** This must meet the customer's needs and fit within the company's own production constraints. Preparation of this work schedule should consider workplace facilities including equipment, personnel, and supplies. Once this schedule is complete, the producer can place orders for raw materials. Production occurs as materials and labor are applied to the job.

An overview of job order production activity is shown in Exhibit 19.1. This exhibit shows the March production activity of Road Warriors, which installs security devices into cars and trucks. The company converts any vehicle by adding alarms, reinforced exterior, bulletproof glass, and bomb detectors. The company began by catering to high-profile celebrities, but it now caters to anyone who desires added security in a vehicle.

Job order production for Road Warriors requires materials, labor, and overhead costs. Recall that direct materials are goods used in manufacturing that are clearly identified with a particular job. Similarly, direct labor is effort devoted to a particular job. Overhead costs support production of more than one job. Common overhead items are depreciation on factory buildings and equipment, factory supplies, supervision, maintenance, cleaning, and utilities.

Exhibit 19.1 shows that materials, labor, and overhead are added to Jobs B15, B16, B17, B18, and B19, which were started during March. Special tires and bulletproof glass are added to Jobs B15 and B16, while Job B17 receives a reinforced exterior and bulletproof glass. Road Warriors completed Jobs B15, B16, and B17 in March and delivered Jobs B15 and B16 to customers. At the end of March, Jobs B18 and B19 remain in goods in process inventory and Job B17 is in finished goods inventory. Both labor and materials costs are also separated into their direct and indirect components. Their indirect amounts are added to overhead. Total overhead cost is then allocated to the various jobs.

Point: Some jobs are priced on a *cost-plus basis:* The customer pays the manufacturer for costs incurred on the job plus a negotiated amount or rate of profit.

Point: Many professional examinations including the CPA and CMA exams require knowledge of job order and process cost accounting.

EXHIBIT 19.1

Job Order Production Activities

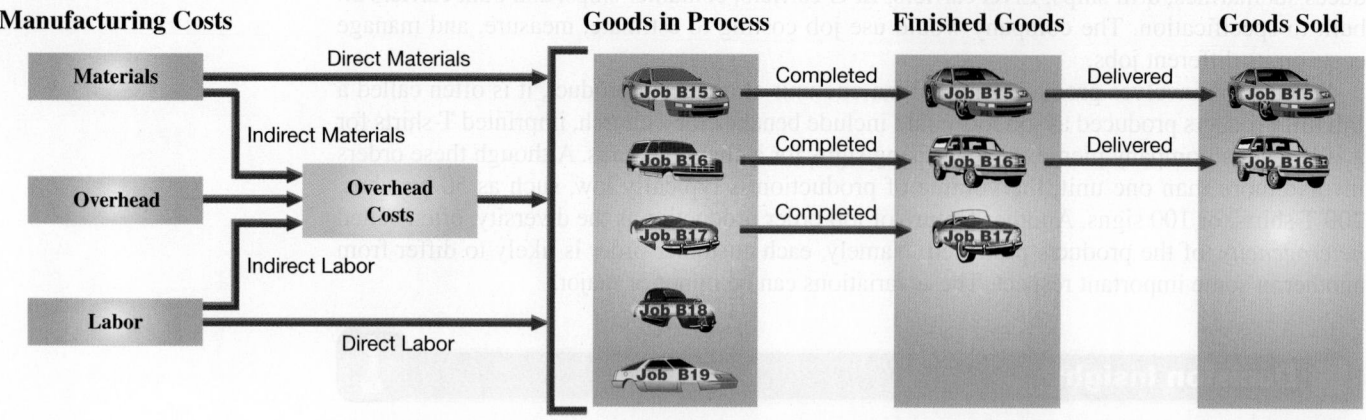

▣ Decision Insight

Target Costing   Many producers determine a target cost for their jobs. Target cost is determined as follows: Expected selling price − Desired profit = Target cost. If the projected target cost of the job as determined by job costing is too high, the producer can apply *value engineering,* which is a method of determining ways to reduce job cost until the target cost is met. Japanese companies are pioneers in the application of target costing. *Kaizen,* a philosophy of continuous improvement, led to the idea of kaizen costing which is an emphasis on gradual and ongoing cost reduction. Target costing, as pioneered by Japanese companies, is an extension of kaizen costing, in which acceptable levels of costs are determined by what is an acceptable selling price of the product in the market. Pioneering companies include **Isuzu, Toyota, Nissan, Sony,** and **Sharp.** ▣

Job Cost Sheet

 C2 Explain job cost sheets and how they are used in job order cost accounting.

General ledger accounts usually do not provide the accounting information that managers of job order cost operations need to plan and control production activities. This is so because the needed information often requires more detailed data. Such detailed data are usually stored in subsidiary records controlled by general ledger accounts. Subsidiary records store information about raw materials, overhead costs, jobs in process, finished goods, and other items. This section describes the use of these records.

A major aim of a **job order cost accounting system** is to determine the cost of producing each job or job lot. In the case of a job lot, the system also aims to compute the cost per unit. The accounting system must include separate records for each job to accomplish this, and it must capture information about costs incurred and charge these costs to each job.

A **job cost sheet** is a separate record maintained for each job. Exhibit 19.2 shows a job cost sheet for an alarm system that Road Warriors produced for a customer. This job cost sheet identifies the customer, the job number assigned, the product, and key dates. Costs incurred on the job are immediately recorded on this sheet. When each job is complete, the supervisor enters the date of completion, records any remarks, and signs the sheet. The job cost sheet in Exhibit 19.2 classifies costs as direct materials, direct labor, or overhead. It shows that a total of $600 in direct materials is added to Job B15 on four different dates. It also shows seven entries for direct labor costs that total $1,000. Road Warriors *allocates* (also termed *applies, assigns,* or *charges*) factory overhead costs of $1,600 to this job using an allocation rate of 160% of direct labor cost (160% × $1,000)—we discuss overhead allocation later in this chapter.

Point: Factory overhead consists of costs (other than direct materials and direct labor) that ensure the production activities are carried out.

Cost Flows: During Production

While a job is being produced, its accumulated costs are kept in Goods in Process Inventory. The collection of job cost sheets for all jobs in process makes up a subsidiary ledger controlled by the **Goods in Process Inventory** account in the general ledger. Managers use job cost sheets to monitor costs incurred to date and to predict and control costs for each job.

EXHIBIT 19.2

Job Cost Sheet

Accounting System: Exhibit 19-2   ⬓ ◻ ☒

File Edit Maintain Tasks Analysis Options Reports Window Help

Road Warriors, Los Angeles, California   **JOB COST SHEET**

Customer's Name	Carroll Connor	Job No.	B15
Address	1542 High Point Dr.	City & State	Malibu, California
Job Description	Level 1 Alarm System on Ford Expedition		
Date promised	March 15	Date started	March 3	Date completed	March 11

Direct Materials			Direct Labor			Overhead		
Date	Requisition	Cost	Date	Time Ticket	Cost	Date	Rate	Cost
3/3/2011	R-4698	100.00	3/3/2011	L-3393	120.00	3/11/2011	160% of	1,600.00
3/7/2011	R-4705	225.00	3/4/2011	L-3422	150.00		Direct	
3/9/2011	R-4725	180.00	3/5/2011	L-3456	180.00		Labor	
3/10/2011	R-4777	95.00	3/8/2011	L-3479	60.00		Cost	
			3/9/2011	L-3501	90.00			
			3/10/2011	L-3535	240.00			
			3/11/2011	L-3559	160.00			
	Total	600.00		Total	1,000.00		Total	1,600.00

REMARKS: Completed job on March 11, and shipped to customer on March 15. Met all specifications and requirements.

SUMMARY:

Materials	600.00
Labor	1,000.00
Overhead	1,600.00

Signed: *C. Luther, Supervisor*

| Total cost | 3,200.00 |

Cost Flows: Job Completion   When a job is finished, its job cost sheet is completed and moved from the jobs in process file to the finished jobs file. This latter file acts as a subsidiary ledger controlled by the **Finished Goods Inventory** account.

Cost Flows: Job Delivery   When a finished job is delivered to a customer, the job cost sheet is moved to a permanent file supporting the total cost of goods sold. This permanent file contains records from both current and prior periods. When the job is finished, the company also prepares a journal entry that credits Sales and debits Cash (or Accounts Receivable).

Point: Documents (electronic and paper) are crucial in a job order system, and the job cost sheet is a cornerstone. Understanding it aids in grasping concepts of capitalizing product costs and product cost flow.

◻ **Decision Maker**   Answer — p. 763

Management Consultant   One of your tasks is to control and manage costs for a consulting company. At the end of a recent month, you find that three consulting jobs were completed and two are 60% complete. Each unfinished job is estimated to cost $10,000 and to earn a revenue of $12,000. You are unsure how to recognize goods in process inventory and record costs and revenues. Do you recognize any inventory? If so, how much? How much revenue is recorded for unfinished jobs this month? ■

✓ **Quick Check**   Answers — p. 763

1. Which of these products is likely to involve job order production? (*a*) inexpensive watches, (*b*) racing bikes, (*c*) bottled soft drinks, or (*d*) athletic socks.

2. What is the difference between a job and a job lot?

3. Which of these statements is correct? (*a*) The collection of job cost sheets for unfinished jobs makes up a subsidiary ledger controlled by the Goods in Process Inventory account, (*b*) Job cost sheets are financial statements provided to investors, or (*c*) A separate job cost sheet is maintained in the general ledger for each job in process.

4. What three costs are normally accumulated on job cost sheets?

JOB ORDER COST FLOWS AND REPORTS

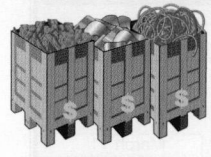

P1 Describe and record the flow of materials costs in job order cost accounting.

Materials

Materials Cost Flows and Documents

This section focuses on the flow of materials costs and the related documents in a job order cost accounting system. We begin analysis of the flow of materials costs by examining Exhibit 19.3. When materials are first received from suppliers, the employees count and inspect them and record the items' quantity and cost on a receiving report. The receiving report serves as the *source document* for recording materials received in both a materials ledger card and in the general ledger. In nearly all job order cost systems, **materials ledger cards** (or files) are perpetual records that are updated each time units are purchased and each time units are issued for use in production.

To illustrate the purchase of materials, Road Warriors acquired $450 of wiring and related materials on March 4, 2011. This purchase is recorded as follows.

Point: Some companies certify certain suppliers based on the quality of their materials. Goods received from these suppliers are not always inspected by the purchaser to save costs.

Assets = Liabilities + Equity
+450   +450

Mar. 4	Raw Materials Inventory—M-347	450	
	Accounts Payable		450
	To record purchase of materials for production.		

EXHIBIT 19.3

Materials Cost Flows through Subsidiary Records

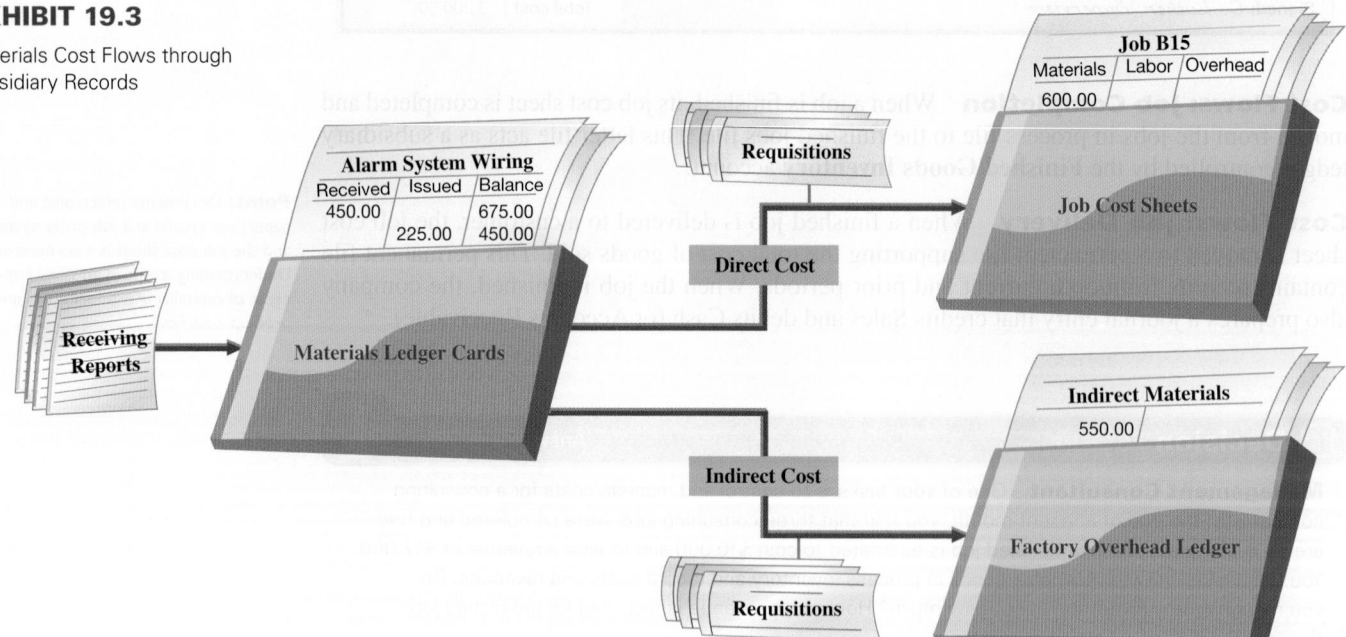

Exhibit 19.3 shows that materials can be requisitioned for use either on a specific job (direct materials) or as overhead (indirect materials). Cost of direct materials flows from the materials ledger card to the job cost sheet. The cost of indirect materials flows from the materials ledger card to the Indirect Materials account in the factory overhead ledger, which is a subsidiary ledger controlled by the Factory Overhead account in the general ledger.

Exhibit 19.4 shows a materials ledger card for material received and issued by Road Warriors. The card identifies the item as alarm system wiring and shows the item's stock number, its location in the storeroom, information about the maximum and minimum quantities that should be available, and the reorder quantity. For example, alarm system wiring is issued

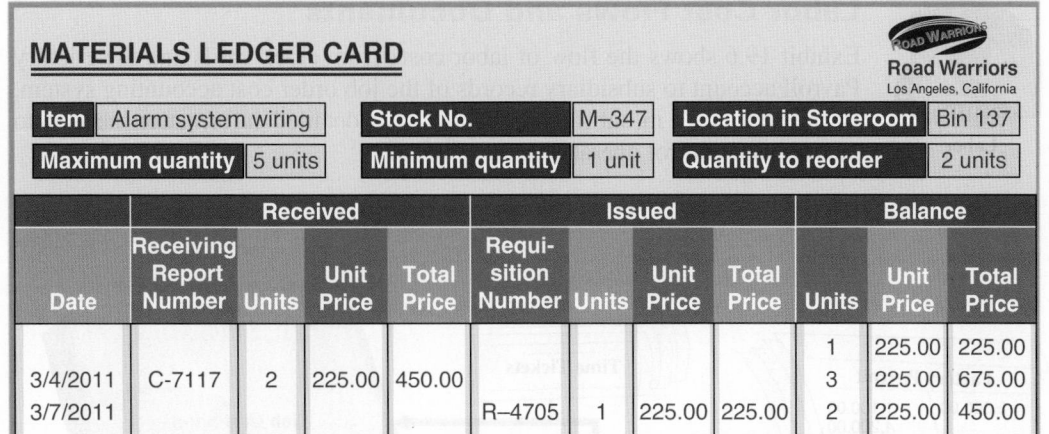

EXHIBIT 19.4

Materials Ledger Card

and recorded on March 7, 2011. The job cost sheet in Exhibit 19.2 showed that Job B15 used this wiring.

When materials are needed in production, a production manager prepares a **materials requisition** and sends it to the materials manager. The requisition shows the job number, the type of material, the quantity needed, and the signature of the manager authorized to make the requisition. Exhibit 19.5 shows the materials requisition for alarm system wiring for Job B15. To see how this requisition ties to the flow of costs, compare the information on the requisition with the March 7, 2011, data in Exhibits 19.2 and 19.4.

Point: Requisitions are often accumulated and recorded in one entry. The frequency of entries depends on the job, the industry, and management procedures.

MATERIALS REQUISITION

Road Warriors
Los Angeles, California

No. R–4705

Job No. _____ B15	Date _____ 3/7/2011
Material Stock No. _____ M–347	Material Description _____ Alarm system wiring
Quantity Requested _____ 1	Requested By _____ *C. Luther*
Quantity Provided _____ 1	Date Provided _____ 3/7/2011
Filled By _____ *M. Bateman*	Material Received By _____ *C. Luther*
Remarks _____	

EXHIBIT 19.5

Materials Requisition

The use of alarm system wiring on Job B15 yields the following entry (locate this cost item in the job cost sheet shown in Exhibit 19.2).

Mar. 7	Goods in Process Inventory—Job B15	225	
	Raw Materials Inventory—M-347		225
	To record use of material on Job B15.		

Assets = Liabilities + Equity
+225
−225

This entry is posted both to its general ledger accounts and to subsidiary records. Posting to subsidiary records includes a debit to a job cost sheet and a credit to a materials ledger card. (*Note:* An entry to record use of indirect materials is the same as that for direct materials *except* the debit is to Factory Overhead. In the subsidiary factory overhead ledger, this entry is posted to Indirect Materials.)

P2 Describe and record the flow of labor costs in job order cost accounting.

Labor

Labor Cost Flows and Documents

Exhibit 19.6 shows the flow of labor costs from clock cards and the Factory Payroll account to subsidiary records of the job order cost accounting system. Recall that costs in subsidiary records give detailed information needed to manage and control operations.

EXHIBIT 19.6

Labor Cost Flows through Subsidiary Records

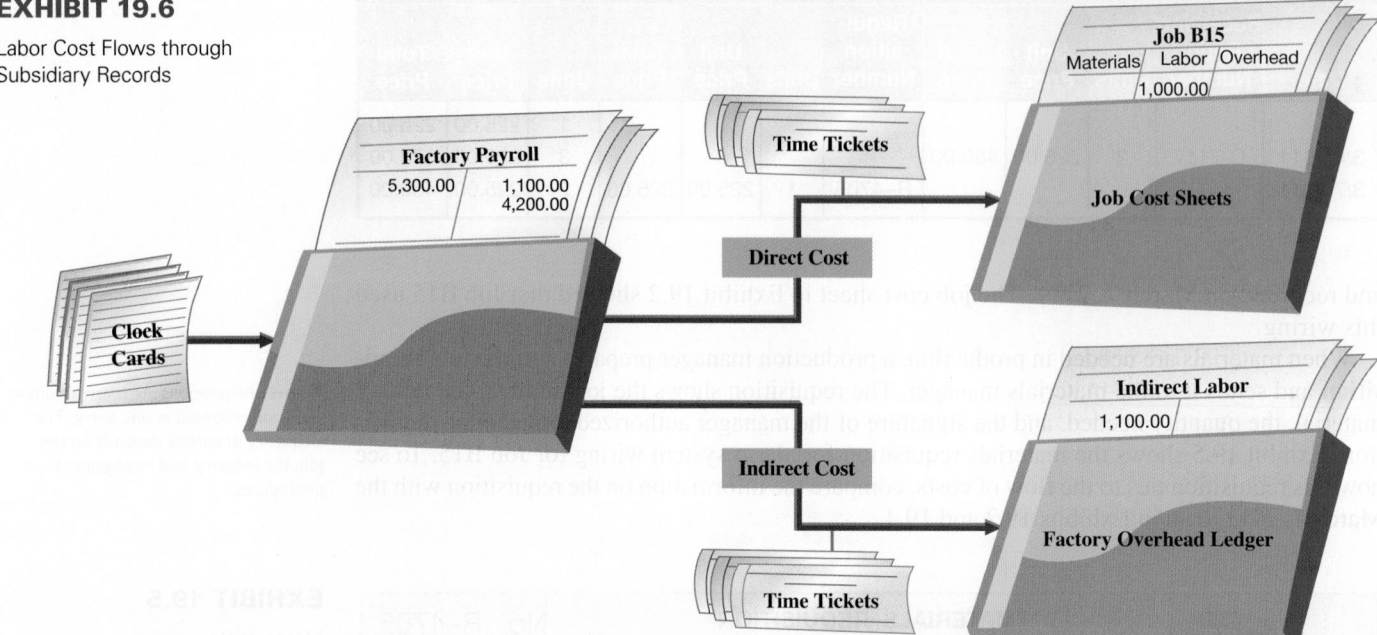

The flow of costs in Exhibit 19.6 begins with **clock cards.** Employees commonly use these cards to record the number of hours worked, and they serve as source documents for entries to record labor costs. Clock card data on the number of hours worked is used at the end of each pay period to determine total labor cost. This amount is then debited to the Factory Payroll account, a temporary account containing the total payroll cost (both direct and indirect). Payroll cost is later allocated to both specific jobs and overhead.

According to clock card data, workers earned $1,500 for the week ended March 5. Illustrating the flow of labor costs, the accrual and payment of these wages are recorded as follows.

Assets = Liabilities + Equity
−1,500   −1,500

Mar. 6	Factory Payroll	1,500	
	Cash		1,500
	To record the weekly payroll.		

"It's on Corporate Standard Time... It loses an hour of your pay every day."

To assign labor costs to specific jobs and to overhead, we must know how each employee's time is used and its costs. Source documents called **time tickets** usually capture these data. Employees regularly fill out time tickets to report how much time they spent on each job. An employee who works on several jobs during a day completes a separate time ticket for each job. Tickets are also prepared for time charged to overhead as indirect labor. A supervisor signs an employee's time ticket to confirm its accuracy.

Exhibit 19.7 shows a time ticket reporting the time a Road Warrior employee spent working on Job B15. The employee's supervisor signed the ticket to confirm its accuracy. The hourly rate and total labor cost are computed after the time ticket is turned in. To see the effect of this time ticket on the job cost sheet, look at the entry dated March 8, 2011, in Exhibit 19.2.

EXHIBIT 19.7

Time Ticket

TIME TICKET

Road Warriors
Los Angeles, California

No. L–3479

Date ...March 8... 20 ...11...

Employee Name	Employee Number	Job No.
T. Zeller	3969	B15

TIME AND RATE INFORMATION:

Remarks

	Start Time	Finish Time	Elapsed Time	Hourly Rate
	9:00	12:00	3.0	$20.00

Approved By ....C. Luther........... | **Total Cost** | $60.00

When time tickets report labor used on a specific job, this cost is recorded as direct labor. The following entry records the data from the time ticket in Exhibit 19.7.

Mar. 8	Goods in Process Inventory—Job B15	60	
	Factory Payroll		60
	To record direct labor used on Job B15.		

Assets = Liabilities + Equity
+60   +60

The debit in this entry is posted both to the general ledger account and to the appropriate job cost sheet. (*Note:* An entry to record indirect labor is the same as for direct labor *except* that it debits Factory Overhead and credits Factory Payroll. In the subsidiary factory overhead ledger, the debit in this entry is posted to the Indirect Labor account.)

Overhead Cost Flows and Documents

Factory overhead (or simply overhead) cost flows are shown in Exhibit 19.8. Factory overhead includes all production costs other than direct materials and direct labor. Two sources of overhead costs are indirect materials and indirect labor. These costs are recorded from requisitions for indirect materials and time tickets for indirect labor. Two other sources of overhead are (1) vouchers authorizing payments for items such as supplies or utilities and (2) adjusting entries for costs such as depreciation on factory assets.

Overhead

P3 Describe and record the flow of overhead costs in job order cost accounting.

Factory overhead usually includes many different costs and, thus, a separate account for each is often maintained in a subsidiary factory overhead ledger. This ledger is controlled by the Factory Overhead account in the general ledger. Factory Overhead is a temporary account that accumulates costs until they are allocated to jobs.

Recording Overhead   Recall that overhead costs are recorded with debits to the Factory Overhead account and with credits to other accounts such as Cash, Accounts Payable, and

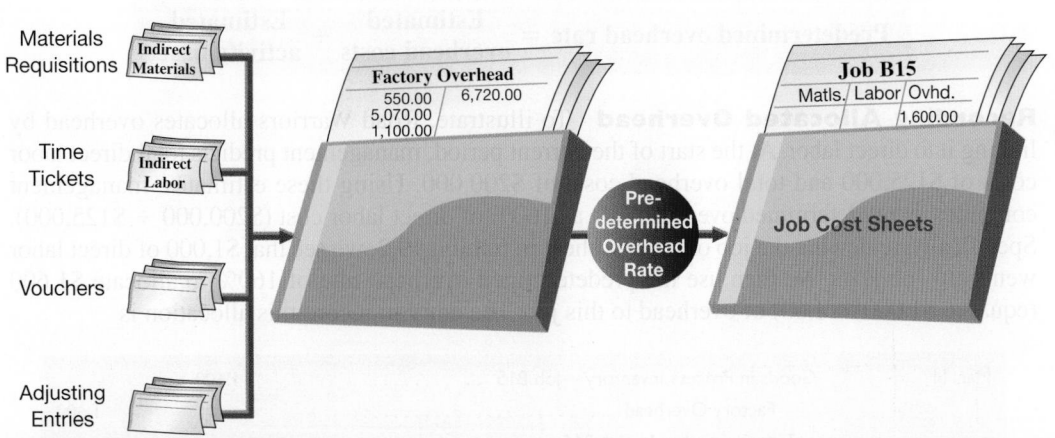

EXHIBIT 19.8

Overhead Cost Flows through Subsidiary Records

Accumulated Depreciation—Equipment. In the subsidiary factory overhead ledger, the debits are posted to their respective accounts such as Depreciation Expense—Equipment, Insurance Expense—Warehouse, or Amortization Expense—Patents.

To illustrate the recording of overhead, the following two entries reflect the depreciation of factory equipment and the accrual of utilities, respectively, for the week ended March 6.

Assets = Liabilities + Equity
−600   −600

Assets = Liabilities + Equity
              +250   −250

Mar. 6	Factory Overhead	600	
	Accumulated Depreciation—Equipment		600
	To record depreciation on factory equipment.		
Mar. 6	Factory Overhead	250	
	Utilities Payable		250
	To record the accrual of factory utilities.		

Exhibit 19.8 shows that overhead costs flow from the Factory Overhead account to job cost sheets. Because overhead is made up of costs not directly associated with specific jobs or job lots, we cannot determine the dollar amount incurred on a specific job. We know, however, that overhead costs represent a necessary part of business activities. If a job cost is to include all costs needed to complete the job, some amount of overhead must be included. Given the difficulty in determining the overhead amount for a specific job, however, we allocate overhead to individual jobs in some reasonable manner.

Overhead Allocation Bases   We generally allocate overhead by linking it to another factor used in production, such as direct labor or machine hours. The factor to which overhead costs are linked is known as the *allocation base.* A manager must think carefully about how many and which allocation bases to use. This managerial decision influences the accuracy with which overhead costs are allocated to individual jobs. In turn, the cost of individual jobs might impact a manager's decisions for pricing or performance evaluation. In Exhibit 19.2, overhead is expressed as 160% of direct labor. We then allocate overhead by multiplying 160% by the estimated amount of direct labor on the jobs.

Overhead Allocation Rates   We cannot wait until the end of a period to allocate overhead to jobs because perpetual inventory records are part of the job order costing system (demanding up-to-date costs). Instead, we must predict overhead in advance and assign it to jobs so that a job's total costs can be estimated prior to its completion. This estimated cost is useful for managers in many decisions including setting prices and identifying costs that are out of control. Being able to estimate overhead in advance requires a **predetermined overhead rate,** also called *predetermined overhead allocation* (or *application*) *rate.* This rate requires an estimate of total overhead cost and an allocation factor such as total direct labor cost before the start of the period. Exhibit 19.9 shows the usual formula for computing a predetermined overhead rate (estimates are commonly based on annual amounts). This rate is used during the period to allocate overhead to jobs. It is common for companies to use multiple activity (allocation) bases and multiple predetermined overhead rates for different types of products and services.

Point: The predetermined overhead rate is computed at the start of the period and is used throughout the period to allocate overhead to jobs.

Point: Predetermined overhead rates can be estimated using mathematical equations, statistical analysis, or professional experience.

EXHIBIT 19.9

Predetermined Overhead Allocation Rate Formula

$$\text{Predetermined overhead rate} = \frac{\text{Estimated}}{\text{overhead costs}} \div \frac{\text{Estimated}}{\text{activity base}}$$

Recording Allocated Overhead   To illustrate, Road Warriors allocates overhead by linking it to direct labor. At the start of the current period, management predicts total direct labor costs of $125,000 and total overhead costs of $200,000. Using these estimates, management computes its predetermined overhead rate as 160% of direct labor cost ($200,000 ÷ $125,000). Specifically, reviewing the job order cost sheet in Exhibit 19.2, we see that $1,000 of direct labor went into Job B15. We then use the predetermined overhead rate of 160% to allocate $1,600 (equal to $1,000 × 1.60) of overhead to this job. The entry to record this allocation is

Example: If management predicts total direct labor costs of $100,000 and total overhead costs of $200,000, what is its predetermined overhead rate? *Answer:* 200% of direct labor cost.

Assets = Liabilities + Equity
+1,600   +1,600

Mar. 11	Goods in Process Inventory—Job B15	1,600	
	Factory Overhead		1,600
	To assign overhead to Job B15.		

Since the allocation rate for overhead is estimated at the start of a period, the total amount assigned to jobs during a period rarely equals the amount actually incurred. We explain how this difference is treated later in this chapter.

Decision Ethics   Answer — p. 763

Web Consultant   You are working on seven client engagements. Two clients reimburse your firm for actual costs plus a 10% markup. The other five pay a fixed fee for services. Your firm's costs include overhead allocated at $47 per labor hour. The managing partner of your firm instructs you to record as many labor hours as possible to the two markup engagements by transferring labor hours from the other five. What do you do? ■

Summary of Cost Flows

We showed journal entries for charging Goods in Process Inventory (Job B15) with the cost of (1) direct materials requisitions, (2) direct labor time tickets, and (3) factory overhead. We made separate entries for each of these costs, but they are usually recorded in one entry. Specifically, materials requisitions are often collected for a day or a week and recorded with a single entry summarizing them. The same is done with labor time tickets. When summary entries are made, supporting schedules of the jobs charged and the types of materials used provide the basis for postings to subsidiary records.

Point: Study the flow of manufacturing costs through general ledger accounts and job cost sheets. Use Exhibit 19.11 as reinforcement.

To show all production cost flows for a period and their related entries, we again look at Road Warriors' activities. Exhibit 19.10 shows costs linked to all of Road Warriors' production activities for March. Road Warriors did not have any jobs in process at the beginning of March, but it did apply materials, labor, and overhead costs to five new jobs in March. Jobs B15 and B16 are completed and delivered to customers in March, Job B17 is completed but not delivered, and Jobs B18 and B19 are still in process. Exhibit 19.10 also shows purchases of raw materials for $2,750, labor costs incurred for $5,300, and overhead costs of $6,720.

EXHIBIT 19.10

Job Order Costs of All Production Activities

Explanation	Materials	Labor	Overhead Incurred	Overhead Allocated	Goods in Process	Finished Goods	Cost of Goods Sold
ROAD WARRIORS Job Order Manufacturing Costs For Month Ended March 31, 2011							
Job B15	$ 600	$1,000		$1,600			$3,200
Job B16	300	800		1,280			2,380
Job B17	500	1,100		1,760		$3,360	
Job B18	150	700		1,120	$1,970		
Job B19	250	600		960	1,810		
Total job costs	1,800	4,200		$6,720	$3,780	$3,360	$5,580
Indirect materials	550		$ 550				
Indirect labor		1,100	1,100				
Other overhead			5,070				
Total costs used in production............	2,350	$5,300	$6,720				
Ending materials inventory	1,400						
Materials available	3,750						
Less beginning materials inventory	(1,000)						
Materials purchased	$2,750						

The upper part of Exhibit 19.11 shows the flow of these costs through general ledger accounts and the end-of-month balances in key subsidiary records. Arrow lines are numbered to show the flows of costs for March. Each numbered cost flow reflects several entries made in March. The lower part of Exhibit 19.11 shows summarized job cost sheets and their status at the end of March. The sum of costs assigned to the jobs in process ($1,970 + $1,810) equals the $3,780

EXHIBIT 19.11

Job Order Cost Flows and Ending Job Cost Sheets

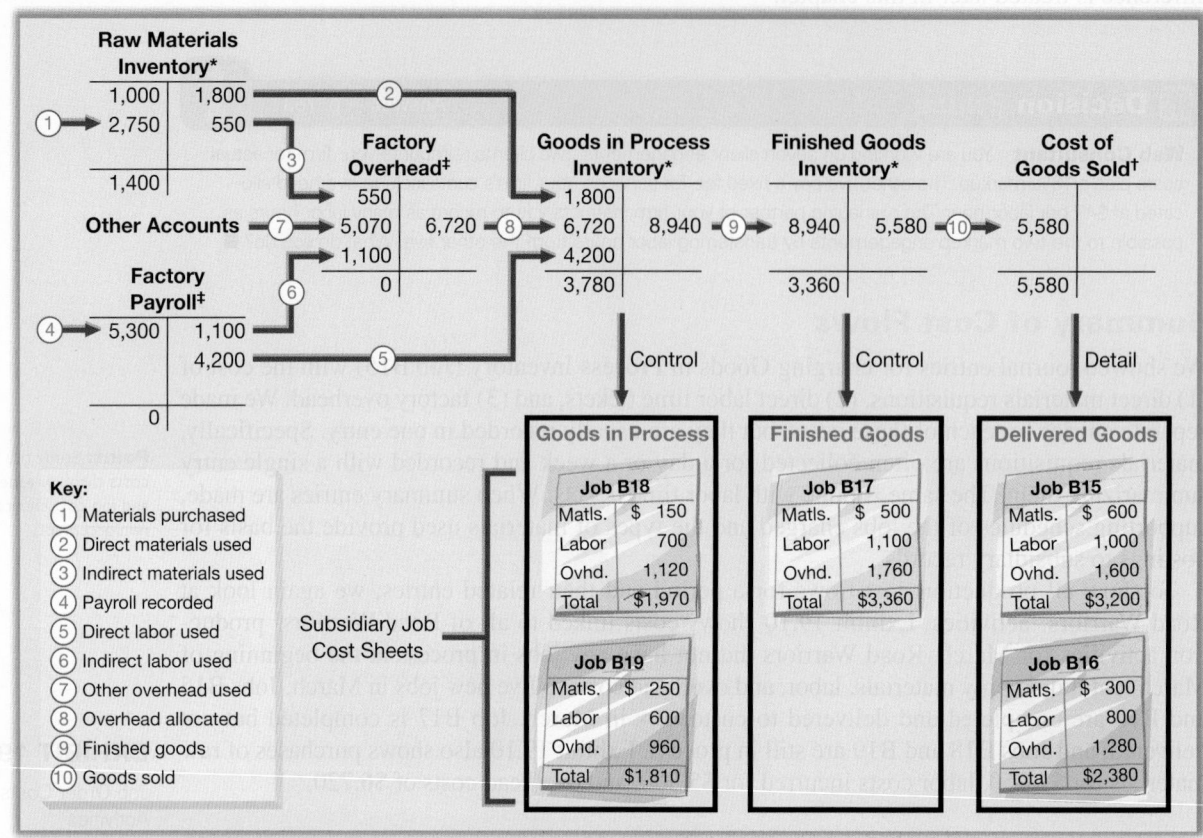

* The ending balances in the inventory accounts are carried to the statement of financial position.
† The Cost of Goods Sold balance is carried to the income statement.
‡ Factory Payroll and Factory Overhead are considered temporary accounts; when these costs are allocated to jobs, the balances in these accounts are reduced.

balance in Goods in Process Inventory shown in Exhibit 19.10. Also, costs assigned to Job B17 equal the $3,360 balance in Finished Goods Inventory. The sum of costs assigned to Jobs B15 and B16 ($3,200 + $2,380) equals the $5,580 balance in Cost of Goods Sold.

Exhibit 19.12 shows each cost flow with a single entry summarizing the actual individual entries made in March. Each entry is numbered to link with the arrow lines in Exhibit 19.11.

Decision Maker   Answer — p. 763

Entrepreneur   Competitors' prices on one of your product segments are lower than yours. Of the total product cost used in setting your prices, 53% is overhead allocated using direct labor hours. You believe that product costs are distorted and wonder whether there is a better way to allocate overhead and to set product price. What do you suggest? ■

Quick Check   Answers — p. 763

5. In job order cost accounting, which account is debited in recording a raw materials requisition? (a) Raw Materials Inventory, (b) Raw Materials Purchases, (c) Goods in Process Inventory if for a job, or (d) Goods in Process Inventory if they are indirect materials.

6. What are four sources of information for recording costs in the Factory Overhead account?

7. Why does job order cost accounting require a predetermined overhead rate?

8. What events result in a debit to Factory Payroll? What events result in a credit?

EXHIBIT 19.12

Entries for Job Order Production Costs*

①	Raw Materials Inventory	2,750	
	Accounts Payable		2,750
	Acquired materials on credit for factory use.		
②	Goods in Process Inventory	1,800	
	Raw Materials Inventory		1,800
	To assign costs of direct materials used.		
③	Factory Overhead	550	
	Raw Materials Inventory		550
	To record use of indirect materials.		
④	Factory Payroll	5,300	
	Cash (and other accounts)		5,300
	To record salaries and wages of factory workers (including various payroll liabilities).		
⑤	Goods in Process Inventory	4,200	
	Factory Payroll		4,200
	To assign costs of direct labor used.		

⑥	Factory Overhead	1,100	
	Factory Payroll		1,100
	To record indirect labor costs as overhead.		
⑦	Factory Overhead	5,070	
	Cash (and other accounts)		5,070
	To record factory overhead costs such as insurance, utilities, rent, and depreciation.		
⑧	Goods in Process Inventory	6,720	
	Factory Overhead		6,720
	To apply overhead at 160% of direct labor.		
⑨	Finished Goods Inventory	8,940	
	Goods in Process Inventory		8,940
	To record completion of Jobs B15, B16, and B17.		
⑩	Cost of Goods Sold	5,580	
	Finished Goods Inventory		5,580
	To record sale of Jobs B15 and B16.		

* Exhibit 19.12 provides summary journal entries. Remember, applied overhead is recorded *during* the period, while actual overhead is recorded at the end of the period. *Actual* overhead is debited to Factory Overhead. *Allocated* overhead is credited to Factory Overhead.

ADJUSTING FACTORY OVERHEAD

Refer to the debits in the Factory Overhead account in Exhibit 19.11 (or Exhibit 19.12). The total cost of factory overhead incurred during March is $6,720 ($550 + $5,070 + $1,100). The $6,720 exactly equals the amount assigned to goods in process inventory (see ⑧). Therefore, the overhead incurred equals the overhead applied in March. The amount of overhead incurred rarely equals the amount of overhead applied, however, because estimates rarely equal the exact amounts actually incurred. This section explains what we do when too much or too little overhead is applied to jobs.

Factory Overhead T-Account

Exhibit 19.13 shows a Factory Overhead T-account. The company applies overhead using a predetermined rate estimated at the beginning of the period. At the end of the period, the company receives bills for its actual overhead costs.

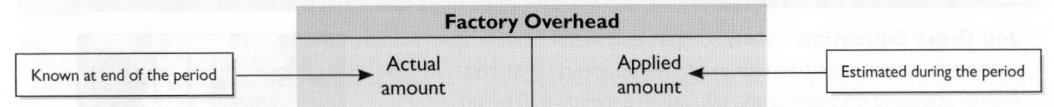

EXHIBIT 19.13

Factory Overhead T-account

Exhibit 19.14 shows what to do when actual overhead does not equal applied overhead. When less overhead is applied than is actually incurred, the remaining debit balance in the Factory Overhead account is called **underapplied overhead.** When the overhead applied in a period exceeds the overhead incurred, the resulting credit balance in the Factory Overhead account is called **overapplied overhead.** In either case, a journal entry is needed to adjust Factory Overhead and Cost of Goods Sold. Exhibit 19.14 summarizes this entry.

EXHIBIT 19.14

Adjusting Factory Overhead

Overhead Costs	Factory Overhead Balance Is	Overhead Is	Journal Entry Needed Is		
Actual > Applied	Debit	Underapplied	Cost of Goods Sold	#	
			Factory Overhead		#
Actual < Applied	Credit	Overapplied	Factory Overhead	#	
			Cost of Goods Sold		#

Underapplied or Overapplied Overhead

P4 Determine adjustments for overapplied and underapplied factory overhead.

To illustrate, assume that Road Warriors actually incurred *other overhead costs* of $5,550 instead of the $5,070 shown in Exhibit 19.11. This yields an actual total overhead cost of $7,200 in March. Since the amount of overhead applied was only $6,720, the Factory Overhead account is left with a $480 debit balance as shown in the ledger account in Exhibit 19.15.

EXHIBIT 19.15

Underapplied Overhead in the Factory Overhead Ledger Account

Factory Overhead				Acct. No. 540
Date	Explanation	Debit	Credit	Balance
Mar. 31	Indirect materials cost	550		550 Dr.
31	Indirect labor cost	1,100		1,650 Dr.
31	Other overhead cost	5,550		7,200 Dr.
31	Overhead costs applied to jobs		6,720	480 Dr.

Example: If we do not adjust for underapplied overhead, will net profit be overstated or understated? *Answer:* Overstated.

The $480 debit balance reflects manufacturing costs not assigned to jobs. This means that the balances in Goods in Process Inventory, Finished Goods Inventory, and Cost of Goods Sold do not include all production costs incurred. When the underapplied overhead amount is immaterial, it is allocated (closed) to the Cost of Goods Sold account with the following adjusting entry.

Assets = Liabilities + Equity
          −480
          +480

Mar. 31	Cost of Goods Sold..............................	480	
	Factory Overhead		480
	To adjust for underapplied overhead costs.		

The $480 debit (increase) to Cost of Goods Sold reduces income by $480. (When the underapplied (or overapplied) overhead is material, the amount is normally allocated to the Cost of Goods Sold, Finished Goods Inventory, and Goods in Process Inventory accounts. This process is covered in advanced courses.)

We treat overapplied overhead at the end of the period in the same way we treat underapplied overhead, except that we debit Factory Overhead and credit Cost of Good Sold for the amount.

Decision Insight

Job Order Education Many companies invest in their employees, and the demand for executive education is strong. Annual spending on training and education exceeds $20 billion. Annual revenues for providers of executive education continue to rise, with about 40% of revenues coming from custom programs designed for one or a select group of companies. ■

Quick Check

Answers — p. 764

9. In a job order cost accounting system, why does the Factory Overhead account usually have an overapplied or underapplied balance at period-end?

10. When the Factory Overhead account has a debit balance at period-end, does this reflect overapplied or underapplied overhead?

◻◻◻ **Decision Analysis**

The chapter described job order costing mainly using a manufacturing setting. However, these concepts and procedures are applicable to a service setting. Consider AdWorld, an advertising agency that develops Web-based ads for small firms. Each of its customers has unique requirements, so costs for each individual job must be tracked separately.

A1 Apply job order costing in pricing services.

AdWorld uses two types of labor: Web designers ($65 per hour) and computer staff ($50 per hour). It also incurs overhead costs that it assigns using two different predetermined overhead allocation rates: $125 per designer hour and $96 per staff hour. For each job, AdWorld must estimate the number of designer and staff hours needed. Then total costs pertaining to each job are determined using the procedures in the chapter. (*Note:* Most service firms have neither the category of materials cost nor inventory.)

To illustrate, a manufacturer of golf balls requested a quote from AdWorld for an advertising engagement. AdWorld estimates that the job will require 43 designer hours and 61 staff hours, with the following total estimated cost for this job.

Direct Labor		
Designers (43 hours × $65)	$ 2,795	
Staff (61 hours × $50)	3,050	
Total direct labor		$ 5,845
Overhead		
Designer related (43 hours × $125)	5,375	
Staff related (61 hours × $96)	5,856	
Total overhead		11,231
Total estimated job cost		$17,076

AdWorld can use this cost information to help determine the price quote for the job (see *Decision Maker, Sales Manager,* scenario in this chapter).

Another source of information that AdWorld must consider is the market, that is, how much competitors will quote for this job. Competitor information is often unavailable; therefore, AdWorld's managers must use estimates based on their assessment of the competitive environment.

◼ **Decision** Maker Answer — p. 763

Sales Manager As AdWorld's sales manager, assume that you estimate costs pertaining to a proposed job as $17,076. Your normal pricing policy is to apply a markup of 18% from total costs. However, you learn that three other agencies are likely to bid for the same job, and that their quotes will range from $16,500 to $22,000. What price should you quote? What factors other than cost must you consider? ◼

DEMONSTRATION PROBLEM—JOB ORDER COSTING

The following information reflects Walczak Company's job order production activities for May.

Raw materials purchases	$16,000
Factory payroll cost	15,400
Overhead costs incurred	
Indirect materials	5,000
Indirect labor	3,500
Other factory overhead	9,500

Walczak's predetermined overhead rate is 150% of direct labor cost. Costs are allocated to the three jobs worked on during May as follows.

	Job 401	Job 402	Job 403
In-process balances on April 30			
Direct materials	$3,600		
Direct labor	1,700		
Applied overhead	2,550		
Costs during May			
Direct materials	3,550	$3,500	$1,400
Direct labor	5,100	6,000	800
Applied overhead	?	?	?
Status on May 31	**Finished (sold)**	**Finished (unsold)**	**In process**

Required

1. Determine the total cost of:
   a. The April 30 inventory of jobs in process.
   b. Materials used during May.
   c. Labor used during May.
   d. Factory overhead incurred and applied during May and the amount of any over- or underapplied overhead on May 31.
   e. Each job as at May 31, the May 31 inventories of both goods in process and finished goods, and the goods sold during May.

2. Prepare summarized journal entries for the month to record:
   a. Materials purchases (on credit), the factory payroll (paid with cash), indirect materials, indirect labor, and the other factory overhead (paid with cash).
   b. Assignment of direct materials, direct labor, and overhead costs to the Goods in Process Inventory account. (Use separate debit entries for each job.)
   c. Transfer of each completed job to the Finished Goods Inventory account.
   d. Cost of goods sold.
   e. Removal of any underapplied or overapplied overhead from the Factory Overhead account. (Assume the amount is not material.)

3. Prepare a manufacturing statement for May.

PLANNING THE SOLUTION

- Determine the cost of the April 30 goods in process inventory by totaling the materials, labor, and applied overhead costs for Job 401.
- Compute the cost of materials used and labor by totaling the amounts assigned to jobs and to overhead.
- Compute the total overhead incurred by summing the amounts for the three components. Compute the amount of applied overhead by multiplying the total direct labor cost by the predetermined overhead rate. Compute the underapplied or overapplied amount as the difference between the actual cost and the applied cost.
- Determine the total cost charged to each job by adding the costs incurred in April (if any) to the cost of materials, labor, and overhead applied during May.
- Group the costs of the jobs according to their completion status.
- Record the direct materials costs assigned to the three jobs, using a separate Goods in Process Inventory account for each job; do the same for the direct labor and the applied overhead.
- Transfer costs of Jobs 401 and 402 from Goods in Process Inventory to Finished Goods.
- Record the costs of Job 401 as cost of goods sold.
- Record the transfer of underapplied overhead from the Factory Overhead account to the Cost of Goods Sold account.
- On the manufacturing statement, remember to include the beginning and ending goods in process inventories and to deduct the underapplied overhead.

SOLUTION TO DEMONSTRATION PROBLEM

1. Total cost of

a. April 30 inventory of
jobs in process (Job 401).

Direct materials	$3,600
Direct labor	1,700
Applied overhead	2,550
Total cost	$7,850

b. Materials used during May.

Direct materials	
Job 401	$ 3,550
Job 402	3,500
Job 403	1,400
Total direct materials	8,450
Indirect materials	5,000
Total materials used	$13,450

c. Labor used during May.

Direct labor	
Job 401	$ 5,100
Job 402	6,000
Job 403	800
Total direct labor	11,900
Indirect labor	3,500
Total labor used	$15,400

d. Factory overhead incurred in May.

Actual overhead	
Indirect materials	$ 5,000
Indirect labor	3,500
Other factory overhead	9,500
Total actual overhead	18,000
Overhead applied (150% × $11,900)	17,850
Underapplied overhead	$ 150

e. Total cost of each job.

	401	402	403
In-process costs from April			
Direct materials	$ 3,600		
Direct labor	1,700		
Applied overhead*	2,550		
Cost incurred in May			
Direct materials	3,550	$ 3,500	$1,400
Direct labor	5,100	6,000	800
Applied overhead*	7,650	9,000	1,200
Total costs	$24,150	$18,500	$3,400

* Equals 150% of the direct labor cost.

Total cost of the May 31 inventory of goods in process (Job 403) = $3,400

Total cost of the May 31 inventory of finished goods (Job 402) = $18,500

Total cost of goods sold during May (Job 401) = $24,150

2. Journal entries.

a.

Raw Materials Inventory.	16,000	
Accounts Payable		16,000
To record materials purchases.		
Factory Payroll	15,400	
Cash		15,400
To record factory payroll.		
Factory Overhead	5,000	
Raw Materials Inventory		5,000
To record indirect materials.		
Factory Overhead	3,500	
Factory Payroll		3,500
To record indirect labor.		
Factory Overhead	9,500	
Cash		9,500
To record other factory overhead.		

b. Assignment of costs to Goods in Process Inventory.

Goods in Process Inventory (Job 401)	3,550	
Goods in Process Inventory (Job 402)	3,500	
Goods in Process Inventory (Job 403)	1,400	
Raw Materials Inventory		8,450
To assign direct materials to jobs.		
Goods in Process Inventory (Job 401)	5,100	
Goods in Process Inventory (Job 402)	6,000	
Goods in Process Inventory (Job 403)	800	
Factory Payroll		11,900
To assign direct labor to jobs.		
Goods in Process Inventory (Job 401)	7,650	
Goods in Process Inventory (Job 402)	9,000	
Goods in Process Inventory (Job 403)	1,200	
Factory Overhead		17,850
To apply overhead to jobs.		

c. Transfer of completed jobs to Finished Goods Inventory.

Finished Goods Inventory	42,650	
Goods in Process Inventory (Job 401)		24,150
Goods in Process Inventory (Job 402)		18,500
To record completion of jobs.		

d.

Cost of Goods Sold	24,150	
Finished Goods Inventory		24,150
To record sale of Job 401.		

e.

Cost of Goods Sold	150	
Factory Overhead		150
To assign underapplied overhead.		

3.

WALCZAK COMPANY Manufacturing Statement For Month Ended May 31		
Direct materials		$ 8,450
Direct labor		11,900
Factory overhead		
Indirect materials	$5,000	
Indirect labor	3,500	
Other factory overhead	9,500	18,000
Total production costs		38,350
Add goods in process, April 30		7,850
Total cost of goods in process		46,200
Less goods in process, May 31		3,400
Less underapplied overhead		150
Cost of goods manufactured		$42,650

Note how underapplied overhead is reported. Overapplied overhead is similarly reported, but is added.

Summary

C1 **Describe important features of job order production.** Certain companies called *job order manufacturers* produce custom-made products for customers. These customized products are produced in response to a customer's orders. A job order manufacturer produces products that usually are different and, typically, produced in low volumes. The production systems of job order companies are flexible and are not highly standardized.

C2 **Explain job cost sheets and how they are used in job order cost accounting.** In a job order cost accounting system, the costs of producing each job are accumulated on a separate job cost sheet. Costs of direct materials, direct labor, and overhead are accumulated separately on the job cost sheet and then added to determine the total cost of a job. Job cost sheets for jobs in process, finished jobs, and jobs sold make up subsidiary records controlled by general ledger accounts.

A1 **Apply job order costing in pricing services.** Job order costing can usefully be applied to a service setting. The resulting job cost estimate can then be used to help determine a price for services.

P1 **Describe and record the flow of materials costs in job order cost accounting.** Costs of materials flow from receiving reports to materials ledger cards and then to either job cost sheets or the Indirect Materials account in the factory overhead ledger.

P2 **Describe and record the flow of labor costs in job order cost accounting.** Costs of labor flow from clock cards to the Factory Payroll account and then to either job cost sheets or the Indirect Labor account in the factory overhead ledger.

P3 **Describe and record the flow of overhead costs in job order cost accounting.** Overhead costs are accumulated in the Factory Overhead account that controls the subsidiary factory overhead ledger. Then, using a predetermined overhead rate, overhead costs are charged to jobs.

P4 **Determine adjustments for overapplied and underapplied factory overhead.** At the end of each period, the Factory Overhead account usually has a residual debit (underapplied overhead) or credit (overapplied overhead) balance. If the balance is not material, it is transferred to Cost of Goods Sold, but if it is material, it is allocated to Goods in Process Inventory, Finished Goods Inventory, and Cost of Goods Sold.

Guidance Answers to Decision Maker and Decision Ethics

Management Consultant Service companies (such as this consulting firm) do not recognize goods in process inventory or finished goods inventory—an important difference between service and manufacturing companies. For the two jobs that are 60% complete, you could recognize revenues and costs at 60% of the total expected amounts. This means you could recognize revenue of $7,200 (0.60 × $12,000) and costs of $6,000 (0.60 × $10,000), yielding net profit of $1,200 from each job.

Web Consultant The partner has a monetary incentive to *manage* the numbers and assign more costs to the two cost-plus engagements. This also would reduce costs on the fixed-price engagements. To act in such a manner is unethical. As a professional and an honest person, it is your responsibility to engage in ethical behavior. You must not comply with the partner's instructions. If the partner insists you act in an unethical manner, you should report the matter to a higher authority in the organization.

Entrepreneur An inadequate cost system can distort product costs. You should review overhead costs in detail. Once you know the different cost elements in overhead, you can classify them into groups such as material related, labor related, or machine related. Other groups can also be formed (we discuss this in Chapter 21). Once you have classified overhead items into groups, you can better establish overhead allocation bases and use them to compute predetermined overhead rates. These multiple rates and bases can then be used to assign overhead costs to products. This will likely improve product pricing.

Sales Manager The price based on AdWorld's normal pricing policy is $20,150 ($17,076 × 1.18), which is within the price range offered by competitors. One option is to apply normal pricing policy and quote a price of $20,150. On the other hand, assessing the competition, particularly in terms of their service quality and other benefits they might offer, would be useful. Although price is an input customers use to select suppliers, factors such as quality and timeliness (responsiveness) of suppliers are important. Accordingly, your price can reflect such factors.

Guidance Answers to Quick Checks

1. *b*
2. A job is a special order for a custom product. A job lot consists of a quantity of identical, special-order items.
3. *a*
4. Three costs normally accumulated on a job cost sheet are direct materials, direct labor, and factory overhead.
5. *c*

6. Four sources of factory overhead are materials requisitions, time tickets, vouchers, and adjusting entries.
7. Since a job order cost accounting system uses perpetual inventory records, overhead costs must be assigned to jobs before the end of a period. This requires the use of a predetermined overhead rate.
8. Debits are recorded when wages and salaries of factory employees are paid or accrued. Credits are recorded when direct labor

costs are assigned to jobs and when indirect labor costs are transferred to the Factory Overhead account.

9. Overapplied or underapplied overhead usually exists at the end of a period because application of overhead is based on

estimates of overhead and another variable such as direct labor. Estimates rarely equal actual amounts incurred.

10. A debit balance reflects underapplied factory overhead.

Key Terms   www.mheducation.asia/olc/wildkwokFAP

Clock card (p. 752)
Cost accounting system (p. 746)
Finished Goods Inventory (p. 749)
General accounting system (p. 746)
Goods in Process Inventory (p. 748)
Job (p. 746)

Job cost sheet (p. 748)
Job lot (p. 747)
Job order cost accounting system (p. 748)
Job order production (p. 746)
Materials ledger card (p. 750)

Materials requisition (p. 751)
Overapplied overhead (p. 757)
Predetermined overhead rate (p. 754)
Target cost (p. 747)
Time ticket (p. 752)
Underapplied overhead (p. 757)

Multiple Choice Quiz   Answers on p. 781   www.mheducation.asia/olc/wildkwokFAP

Additional Quiz Questions are available at the book's Website.

1. A company's predetermined overhead allocation rate is 150% of its direct labor costs. How much overhead is applied to a job that requires total direct labor costs of $30,000?
   a. $15,000
   b. $30,000
   c. $45,000
   d. $60,000
   e. $75,000

2. A company's cost accounting system uses direct labor costs to apply overhead to goods in process and finished goods inventories. Its production costs for the period are: direct materials, $45,000; direct labor, $35,000; and overhead applied, $38,500. What is its predetermined overhead allocation rate?
   a. 10%
   b. 110%
   c. 86%
   d. 91%
   e. 117%

3. A company's ending inventory of finished goods has a total cost of $10,000 and consists of 500 units. If the overhead applied to these goods is $4,000, and the predetermined overhead rate is 80% of direct labor costs, how much direct materials cost was incurred in producing these 500 units?
   a. $10,000
   b. $ 6,000
   c. $ 4,000
   d. $ 5,000
   e. $ 1,000

4. A company's Goods in Process Inventory T-account follows.

Goods in Process Inventory			
Beginning balance	9,000		
Direct materials	94,200		
Direct labor	59,200	?	Finished goods
Overhead applied	31,600		
Ending balance	17,800		

The cost of units transferred to Finished Goods inventory is
   a. $193,000
   b. $211,800
   c. $185,000
   d. $144,600
   e. $176,200

5. At the end of its current year, a company learned that its overhead was underapplied by $1,500 and that this amount is not considered material. Based on this information, the company should
   a. Close the $1,500 to Finished Goods Inventory.
   b. Close the $1,500 to Cost of Goods Sold.
   c. Carry the $1,500 to the next period.
   d. Do nothing about the $1,500 because it is not material and it is likely that overhead will be overapplied by the same amount next year.
   e. Carry the $1,500 to the Income Statement as "Other Expense."

🖊 Icon denotes assignments that involve decision making.

Discussion Questions

1. Why must a company estimate the amount of factory overhead assigned to individual jobs or job lots?

2. 🖊 The chapter used a percent of labor cost to assign factory overhead to jobs. Identify another factor (or base) a company might reasonably use to assign overhead costs.

3. What information is recorded on a job cost sheet? How do management and employees use job cost sheets?

4. In a job order cost accounting system, what records serve as a subsidiary ledger for Goods in Process Inventory? For Finished Goods Inventory?

5. What journal entry is recorded when a materials manager receives a materials requisition and then issues materials (both direct and indirect) for use in the factory?

6. How does the materials requisition help safeguard a company's assets?

7. Palm uses a "time ticket" for some employees. What is the difference between a clock card and a time ticket?

8. What events cause debits to be recorded in the Factory Overhead account? What events cause credits to be recorded in the Factory Overhead account?

9. Nokia applies overhead to product costs. What account(s) is(are) used to eliminate overapplied or underapplied overhead from the Factory Overhead account, assuming the amount is not material?

10. Assume that Apple produces a batch of 1,000 iPods. Does it account for this as 1,000 individual jobs or as a job lot? Explain (consider costs and benefits).

11. Why must a company prepare a predetermined overhead rate when using job order cost accounting?

12. How would a hospital apply job order costing? Explain.

13. Harley-Davidson manufactures 30 custom-made, luxury-model motorcycles. Does it account for these motorcycles as 30 individual jobs or as a job lot? Explain.

14. Assume Research In Motion will install and service a server to link all of a customer's employees' smartphones to a centralized company server, for an upfront flat price. How can RIM use a job order costing system?

---

connect _____

Determine which products are most likely to be manufactured as a job and which as a job lot.

1. A hand-crafted table.
2. A 90-foot motor yacht.
3. Wedding dresses for a chain of stores.

4. A custom-designed home.
5. Hats imprinted with company logo.
6. Little League trophies.

QUICK STUDY

QS 19-1
Jobs and job lots C1

List the three types of costs that are typically recorded on a job cost sheet. How can managers use job cost sheets?

QS 19-2
Job cost sheets C2

During the current month, a company that uses a job order cost accounting system purchases $70,000 in raw materials for cash. It then uses $22,000 of raw materials indirectly as factory supplies and uses $42,000 of raw materials as direct materials. Prepare entries to record these three transactions.

QS 19-3
Direct materials journal entries
P1

During the current month, a company that uses a job order cost accounting system incurred a monthly factory payroll of $120,000, paid in cash. Of this amount, $30,000 is classified as indirect labor and the remainder as direct. Prepare entries to record these transactions.

QS 19-4
Direct labor journal entries P2

A company incurred the following manufacturing costs this period: direct labor, $605,000; direct materials, $672,000; and factory overhead, $129,500. Compute its overhead cost as a percent of (1) direct labor and (2) direct materials. Express your answers as percents, rounded to one decimal place.

QS 19-5
Factory overhead rates P3

During the current month, a company that uses a job order cost accounting system incurred a monthly factory payroll of $120,000, paid in cash. Of this amount, $30,000 is classified as indirect labor and the remainder as direct for the production of Job 65A. Factory overhead is applied at 150% of direct labor. Prepare the entry to apply factory overhead to this job lot.

QS 19-6
Factory overhead journal entries
P3

A company allocates overhead at a rate of 140% of direct labor cost. Actual overhead cost for the current period is $745,000, and direct labor cost is $500,000. Prepare the entry to close over- or underapplied overhead to cost of goods sold.

QS 19-7
Entry for over- or underapplied overhead P4

A company's Factory Overhead T-account shows total debits of $325,000 and total credits of $331,000 at the end of a period. Prepare the journal entry to close the balance in the Factory Overhead account to Cost of Goods Sold.

QS 19-8
Entry for over- or underapplied overhead P4

QS 19-9
Pricing services   A1

An advertising agency is estimating costs for advertising a music festival. The job will require 50 direct labor hours at a cost of $60 per hour. Overhead costs are applied at a rate of $95 per direct labor hour. What is the total estimated cost for this job?

QS 19-10
Predetermined overhead rate
P3

At the beginning of a period a company predicts total direct materials costs of $175,000 and total overhead costs of $218,750. If the company uses direct materials costs as its activity base to allocate overhead, what is the predetermined overhead rate it should use during the period?

QS 19-11
Job cost sheets   C2

Road Warriors' job cost sheet for job A75 shows that the cost to add security features to a car was $13,500. The car was delivered to the customer, who paid $18,900 in cash for the added features. What journal entries should Road Warriors record for the completion and delivery of job A75?

EXERCISES

Exercise 19-1

Job order production

C1

Match the terms below with their definitions.

1. Job
2. Job order production
3. Job lot
4. Cost accounting system
5. Target cost
6. General accounting system

a. The expected selling price of a job minus its desired profit.
b. Production activities for a customized product.
c. A system that records manufacturing costs using a perpetual inventory system.
d. Production of products in response to customer orders.
e. Production of more than one unit of a custom product.
f. A system that records manufacturing costs using a periodic inventory system.

Exercise 19-2

Documents in job order cost accounting

P1 P2 P3

The left column lists the titles of documents and accounts used in job order cost accounting. The right column presents short descriptions of the purposes of the documents. Match each document in the left column to its numbered description in the right column.

A. Factory Payroll account
B. Materials ledger card
C. Time ticket
D. Voucher
E. Materials requisition
F. Factory Overhead account
G. Clock card

_____ 1. Communicates the need for materials to complete a job.
_____ 2. Shows only total time an employee works each day.
_____ 3. Shows amount approved for payment of an overhead or other cost.
_____ 4. Shows amount of time an employee works on a job.
_____ 5. Temporarily accumulates the cost of incurred overhead until the cost is assigned to specific jobs.
_____ 6. Temporarily accumulates incurred labor costs until they are assigned to specific jobs or to overhead.
_____ 7. Perpetual inventory record of raw materials received, used, and available for use.

Exercise 19-3

Job cost computation

C2

The following information is from the materials requisitions and time tickets for Job 9-1005 completed by Wright Boats. The requisitions are identified by code numbers starting with the letter Q and the time tickets start with W. At the start of the year, management estimated that overhead cost would equal 140% of direct labor cost for each job. Determine the total cost on the job cost sheet for Job 9-1005.

Date	Document	Amount
7/1/2011	Q-4698	$1,350
7/1/2011	W-3393	700
7/5/2011	Q-4725	1,100
7/5/2011	W-3479	550
7/10/2011	W-3559	400

As of the end of June, the job cost sheets at Racing Wheels, Inc., show the following total costs accumulated on three custom jobs.

Exercise 19-4
Analysis of cost flows
C2 P1 P2 P3

	Job 102	Job 103	Job 104
Direct materials..........	$30,000	$66,000	$54,000
Direct labor	16,000	28,400	42,000
Overhead...............	8,000	14,200	21,000

Job 102 was started in production in May and the following costs were assigned to it in May: direct materials, $12,000; direct labor, $3,600; and overhead, $1,800. Jobs 103 and 104 are started in June. Overhead cost is applied with a predetermined rate based on direct labor cost. Jobs 102 and 103 are finished in June, and Job 104 is expected to be finished in July. No raw materials are used indirectly in June. Using this information, answer the following questions. (Assume this company's predetermined overhead rate did not change across these months).

1. What is the cost of the raw materials requisitioned in June for each of the three jobs?
2. How much direct labor cost is incurred during June for each of the three jobs?
3. What predetermined overhead rate is used during June?
4. How much total cost is transferred to finished goods during June?

Check (4) $162,600

In December 2010, Kent Computer's management establishes the year 2011 predetermined overhead rate based on direct labor cost. The information used in setting this rate includes estimates that the company will incur $756,000 of overhead costs and $540,000 of direct labor cost in year 2011. During March 2011, Kent began and completed Job No. 13-56.

Exercise 19-5
Overhead rate; costs assigned to jobs
P3

1. What is the predetermined overhead rate for year 2011?
2. Use the information on the following job cost sheet to determine the total cost of the job.

Check (2) $23,280

JOB COST SHEET

Customer's Name	Keiser Co.		Job No.	13-56

Job Description   5 color monitors—21 inch

	Direct Materials		Direct Labor		Overhead Costs Applied	
Date	Requisition No.	Amount	Time-Ticket No.	Amount	Rate	Amount
Mar. 8	4-129	$5,000	T-306	$ 640		
Mar. 11	4-142	7,050	T-432	1,280		
Mar. 18	4-167	3,550	T-456	1,280		
Totals						

Lopez Company uses a job order cost accounting system that charges overhead to jobs on the basis of direct material cost. At year-end, the Goods in Process Inventory account shows the following.

Exercise 19-6
Analysis of costs assigned to goods in process
P3

Accounting System
File Edit Maintain Tasks Analysis Options Reports Window Help

Goods in Process Inventory   Acct. No. 121

Date	Explanation	Debit	Credit	Balance
2011				
Dec. 31	Direct materials cost	1,500,000		1,500,000
31	Direct labor cost	240,000		1,740,000
31	Overhead costs	450,000		2,190,000
31	To finished goods		2,100,000	90,000

Sales   Purchases   General Ledger   Payroll   Inventory   Company   Analysis

1. Determine the overhead rate used (based on direct material cost).
2. Only one job remained in the goods in process inventory at December 31, 2011. Its direct materials cost is $30,000. How much direct labor cost and overhead cost are assigned to it?

Check (2) Direct labor cost, $51,000

Exercise 19-7
Cost flows in a job order cost system

P1 P2 P3 P4

The following information is available for Lock-Down Company, which produces special-order security products and uses a job order cost accounting system.

	April 30	May 31
Inventories		
Raw materials	$40,000	$ 50,000
Goods in process	9,600	19,500
Finished goods	60,000	33,200
Activities and information for May		
Raw materials purchases (paid with cash)		189,000
Factory payroll (paid with cash)		400,000
Factory overhead		
Indirect materials		12,000
Indirect labor		75,000
Other overhead costs		100,500
Sales (received in cash)		1,200,000
Predetermined overhead rate based on direct labor cost		65%

Compute the following amounts for the month of May.

1. Cost of direct materials used.
2. Cost of direct labor used.
3. Cost of goods manufactured.
4. Cost of goods sold.*
5. Gross profit.
6. Overapplied or underapplied overhead.

Check (3) $693,350

*Do not consider any underapplied or overapplied overhead.

Exercise 19-8
Journal entries for materials

P1

Use information in Exercise 19-7 to prepare journal entries for the following events for the month of May.
1. Raw materials purchases for cash.
2. Direct materials usage.
3. Indirect materials usage.

Exercise 19-9
Journal entries for labor

P2

Use information in Exercise 19-7 to prepare journal entries for the following events for the month of May.
1. Factory payroll costs in cash.
2. Direct labor usage.
3. Indirect labor usage.

Exercise 19-10
Journal entries for overhead

P3

Use information in Exercise 19-7 to prepare journal entries for the following events for the month of May.
1. Factory overhead excluding indirect materials and indirect labor (record credit to Other Accounts).
2. Application of overhead to goods in process.

Exercise 19-11
Adjusting factory overhead   P4

Refer to information in Exercise 19-7. Prepare the journal entry to allocate (close) overapplied or underapplied overhead to Cost of Goods Sold.

Exercise 19-12
Adjusting factory overhead

P4

Record the journal entry to close over- or underapplied factory overhead to Cost of Goods Sold for each of the independent cases below.

	JK Concert Promotions	EL Home Builders
Actual indirect materials costs	$12,000	$ 6,500
Actual indirect labor costs	56,000	46,500
Other overhead costs	17,000	49,000
Overhead applied	96,200	106,800

In December 2010, Ultravision established its predetermined overhead rate for movies produced during year 2011 by using the following cost predictions: overhead costs, $1,800,000, and direct labor costs, $450,000. At year end 2011, the company's records show that actual overhead costs for the year are $1,770,000. Actual direct labor cost had been assigned to jobs as follows.

Exercise 19-13
Factory overhead computed, applied, and adjusted
P3 P4

Movies completed and released	$400,000
Movies still in production	45,000
Total actual direct labor cost	$445,000

1. Determine the predetermined overhead rate for year 2011.

2. Set up a T-account for overhead and enter the overhead costs incurred and the amounts applied to movies during the year using the predetermined overhead rate.

3. Determine whether overhead is overapplied or underapplied (and the amount) during the year.

Check   (3) $10,000 overapplied

4. Prepare the adjusting entry to allocate any over- or underapplied overhead to Cost of Goods Sold.

In December 2010, Perez Company established its predetermined overhead rate for jobs produced during year 2011 by using the following cost predictions: overhead costs, $600,000, and direct labor costs, $500,000. At year end 2011, the company's records show that actual overhead costs for the year are $680,000. Actual direct labor cost had been assigned to jobs as follows.

Exercise 19-14
Factory overhead computed, applied, and adjusted
P3 P4

Jobs completed and sold	$420,000
Jobs in finished goods inventory	84,000
Jobs in goods in process inventory	56,000
Total actual direct labor cost	$560,000

1. Determine the predetermined overhead rate for year 2011.

2. Set up a T-account for Factory Overhead and enter the overhead costs incurred and the amounts applied to jobs during the year using the predetermined overhead rate.

3. Determine whether overhead is overapplied or underapplied (and the amount) during the year.

Check   (3) $8,000 underapplied

4. Prepare the adjusting entry to allocate any over- or underapplied overhead to Cost of Goods Sold.

Red Wing Company applies factory overhead based on direct labor costs. The company incurred the following costs during 2011: direct materials costs, $637,500; direct labor costs, $2,500,000; and factory overhead costs applied, $1,000,000.

Exercise 19-15
Overhead rate calculation, allocation, and analysis
P3

1. Determine the company's predetermined overhead rate for year 2011.

2. Assuming that the company's $57,000 ending Goods in Process Inventory account for year 2011 had $18,000 of direct labor costs, determine the inventory's direct materials costs.

3. Assuming that the company's $337,485 ending Finished Goods Inventory account for year 2011 had $137,485 of direct materials costs, determine the inventory's direct labor costs and its overhead costs.

Check   (3) $57,143 overhead costs

Vegas Company's ending Goods in Process Inventory account consists of 4,500 units of partially completed product, and its Finished Goods Inventory account consists of 11,700 units of product. The factory manager determines that Goods in Process Inventory includes direct materials cost of $10 per unit and direct labor cost of $7 per unit. Finished goods are estimated to have $12 of direct materials cost per unit and $9 of direct labor cost per unit. The company established the predetermined overhead rate using the following predictions: estimated direct labor cost, $300,000, and estimated factory overhead, $360,000. The company allocates factory overhead to its goods in process and finished goods inventories based on direct labor cost. During the period, the company incurred these costs: direct materials, $460,000; direct labor, $277,000; and factory overhead applied, $332,400.

Exercise 19-16
Costs allocated to ending inventories
P1 P2 P3

1. Determine the predetermined overhead rate.

2. Compute the total cost of the two ending inventories.

3. Compute cost of goods sold for the year (assume no beginning inventories and no underapplied or overapplied overhead).

Check   (3) Cost of goods sold, $583,040

Exercise 19-17
Cost-based pricing

A1

Multiplex Corporation has requested bids from several architects to design its new corporate headquarters. Friesen Architects is one of the firms bidding on the job. Friesen estimates that the job will require the following direct labor.

Labor	Estimated Hours	Hourly Rate
Architects	200	$300
Staff	400	75
Clerical	700	20

Friesen applies overhead to jobs at 160% of direct labor cost. Friesen would like to earn at least $80,000 profit on the architectural job. Based on past experience and market research, it estimates that the competition will bid between $325,000 and $400,000 for the job.

Check (1) $270,400

1. What is Friesen's estimated cost of the architectural job?
2. What bid would you suggest that Friesen submit?

Exercise 19-18
Direct materials journal entries

P1

A recent statement of financial position for **Porsche AG** shows beginning raw materials inventory of EUR 83 million and ending raw materials inventory of EUR 85 million. Assume the company purchased raw materials (on account) for EUR 3,108 million during the year. (1) Prepare journal entries to record (a) the purchase of raw materials and (b) the use of raw materials in production. (2) What do you notice about the Euro amounts in your journal entries?

PROBLEM SET A

Problem 19-1A
Production costs computed and recorded; reports prepared

C2 P1 P2 P3 P4

Winfrey Co.'s March 31 inventory of raw materials is $150,000. Raw materials purchases in April are $400,000, and factory payroll cost in April is $220,000. Overhead costs incurred in April are: indirect materials, $30,000; indirect labor, $14,000; factory rent, $20,000; factory utilities, $12,000; and factory equipment depreciation, $30,000. The predetermined overhead rate is 50% of direct labor cost. Job 306 is sold for $380,000 cash in April. Costs of the three jobs worked on in April follow.

	Job 306	Job 307	Job 308
Balances on March 31			
Direct materials	$ 14,000	$ 18,000	
Direct labor	18,000	16,000	
Applied overhead	9,000	8,000	
Costs during April			
Direct materials	100,000	170,000	$ 80,000
Direct labor	30,000	56,000	120,000
Applied overhead	?	?	?
Status on April 30	Finished (sold)	Finished (unsold)	In process

Required

1. Determine the total of each production cost incurred for April (direct labor, direct materials, and applied overhead), and the total cost assigned to each job (including the balances from March 31).

2. Prepare journal entries for the month of April to record the following.

   a. Materials purchases (on credit), factory payroll (paid in cash), and actual overhead costs including indirect materials and indirect labor. (Factory rent and utilities are paid in cash.)

   b. Assignment of direct materials, direct labor, and applied overhead costs to the Goods in Process Inventory.

   c. Transfer of Jobs 306 and 307 to the Finished Goods Inventory.

   d. Cost of goods sold for Job 306.

   e. Revenue from the sale of Job 306.

   f. Assignment of any underapplied or overapplied overhead to the Cost of Goods Sold account. (The amount is not material.)

Check (2f) $3,000 underapplied

(3) Cost of goods
   manufactured, $482,000

3. Prepare a manufacturing statement for April (use a single line presentation for direct materials and show the details of overhead cost).

4. Compute gross profit for April. Show how to present the inventories on the April 30 statement of financial position.

Analysis Component

5. The over- or underapplied overhead is closed to Cost of Goods Sold. Discuss how this adjustment impacts business decision making regarding individual jobs or batches of jobs.

Thai Bay's computer system generated the following trial balance on December 31, 2011. The company's manager knows something is wrong with the trial balance because it does not show any balance for Goods in Process Inventory but does show balances for the Factory Payroll and Factory Overhead accounts.

Problem 19-2A
Source documents, journal entries, overhead, and financial reports

P1 P2 P3 P4

	Debit	Credit
Cash	$ 48,000	
Accounts receivable	42,000	
Raw materials inventory	26,000	
Goods in process inventory	0	
Finished goods inventory	9,000	
Prepaid rent	3,000	
Accounts payable		$ 10,500
Notes payable		13,500
Share capital—ordinary		30,000
Retained earnings		87,000
Sales		180,000
Cost of goods sold	105,000	
Factory payroll	16,000	
Factory overhead	27,000	
Operating expenses	45,000	
Totals	$321,000	$321,000

After examining various files, the manager identifies the following six source documents that need to be processed to bring the accounting records up to date.

Materials requisition 21-3010:	$4,600 direct materials to Job 402
Materials requisition 21-3011:	$7,600 direct materials to Job 404
Materials requisition 21-3012:	$2,100 indirect materials
Labor time ticket 6052:	$5,000 direct labor to Job 402
Labor time ticket 6053:	$8,000 direct labor to Job 404
Labor time ticket 6054:	$3,000 indirect labor

Jobs 402 and 404 are the only units in process at year-end. The predetermined overhead rate is 200% of direct labor cost.

Required

1. Use information on the six source documents to prepare journal entries to assign the following costs.
  a. Direct materials costs to Goods in Process Inventory.
  b. Direct labor costs to Goods in Process Inventory.
  c. Overhead costs to Goods in Process Inventory.
  d. Indirect materials costs to the Factory Overhead account.
  e. Indirect labor costs to the Factory Overhead account.
2. Determine the revised balance of the Factory Overhead account after making the entries in part 1. Determine whether there is any under- or overapplied overhead for the year. Prepare the adjusting entry to allocate any over- or underapplied overhead to Cost of Goods Sold, assuming the amount is not material.
3. Prepare a revised trial balance.
4. Prepare an income statement for year 2011 and a statement of financial position as at December 31, 2011.

Check (2) $6,100 underapplied overhead

(3) T. B. totals, $321,000
(4) Net profit, $23,900

Analysis Component

5. Assume that the $2,100 on materials requisition 21-3012 should have been direct materials charged to Job 404. Without providing specific calculations, describe the impact of this error on the income statement for 2011 and the statement of financial position at December 31, 2011.

Problem 19-3A

Source documents, journal entries, and accounts in job order cost accounting

P1   P2   P3

Westin Watercraft's predetermined overhead rate for year 2011 is 200% of direct labor. Information on the company's production activities during May 2011 follows.

a. Purchased raw materials on credit, $125,000.

b. Paid $84,000 cash for factory wages.

c. Paid $11,000 cash to a computer consultant to reprogram factory equipment.

d. Materials requisitions record use of the following materials for the month.

Job 136.	$30,000
Job 137.	20,000
Job 138.	12,000
Job 139.	14,000
Job 140.	4,000
Total direct materials.	80,000
Indirect materials	12,000
Total materials used.	$92,000

e. Time tickets record use of the following labor for the month.

Job 136	$ 8,000
Job 137	7,000
Job 138	25,000
Job 139	26,000
Job 140	2,000
Total direct labor	68,000
Indirect labor	16,000
Total	$84,000

f. Applied overhead to Jobs 136, 138, and 139.

g. Transferred Jobs 136, 138, and 139 to Finished Goods.

h. Sold Jobs 136 and 138 on credit at a total price of $340,000.

i. The company incurred the following overhead costs during the month (credit Prepaid Insurance for expired factory insurance).

Depreciation of factory building	$37,000
Depreciation of factory equipment	21,000
Expired factory insurance	7,000
Accrued property tax payable.	31,000

j. Applied overhead at month-end to the Goods in Process (Jobs 137 and 140) using the predetermined overhead rate of 200% of direct labor cost.

Required

1. Prepare a job cost sheet for each job worked on during the month. Use the following simplified form.

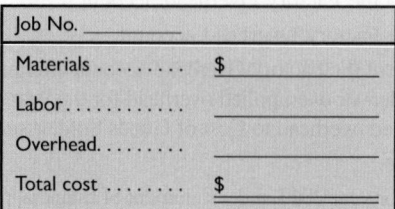

Job No. _____	
Materials	$_____
Labor.	_____
Overhead.	_____
Total cost	$_____

Check   (2f) Cr. Factory Overhead, $118,000

2. Prepare journal entries to record the events and transactions *a* through *j*.

3. Set up T-accounts for each of the following general ledger accounts, each of which started the month with a zero balance: Raw Materials Inventory; Goods in Process Inventory; Finished Goods Inventory;

Factory Payroll; Factory Overhead; Cost of Goods Sold. Then post the journal entries to these T-accounts and determine the balance of each account.

4. Prepare a report showing the total cost of each job in process and prove that the sum of their costs equals the Goods in Process Inventory account balance. Prepare similar reports for Finished Goods Inventory and Cost of Goods Sold.

Check   (4) Finished Goods
Inventory, $92,000

In December 2010, Gomez Company's manager estimated next year's total direct labor cost assuming 50 persons working an average of 2,000 hours each at an average wage rate of $15 per hour. The manager also estimated the following manufacturing overhead costs for year 2011.

Problem 19-4A
Overhead allocation and adjustment using a predetermined overhead rate

P3   P4

www.mheducation.asia/olc/wildkwokFAP

Indirect labor	$159,600
Factory supervision	120,000
Rent on factory building.	70,000
Factory utilities	44,000
Factory insurance expired	34,000
Depreciation—Factory equipment	240,000
Repairs expense—Factory equipment.	30,000
Factory supplies used	34,400
Miscellaneous production costs	18,000
Total estimated overhead costs	$750,000

At the end of 2011, records show the company incurred $725,000 of actual overhead costs. It completed and sold five jobs with the following direct labor costs: Job 201, $354,000; Job 202, $330,000; Job 203, $175,000; Job 204, $420,000; and Job 205, $184,000. In addition, Job 206 is in process at the end of 2011 and had been charged $10,000 for direct labor. No jobs were in process at the end of 2010. The company's predetermined overhead rate is based on direct labor cost.

Required

1. Determine the following.

  a. Predetermined overhead rate for year 2011.

  b. Total overhead cost applied to each of the six jobs during year 2011.

  c. Over- or underapplied overhead at year-end 2011.

Check   (1c) $11,500 overapplied

(2) Dr. Factory Overhead
$11,500

2. Assuming that any over- or underapplied overhead is not material, prepare the adjusting entry to allocate any over- or underapplied overhead to Cost of Goods Sold at the end of year 2011.

If the working papers that accompany this book are unavailable, do not attempt to solve this problem.
Sagrillo Company manufactures variations of its product, a technopress, in response to custom orders from its customers. On May 1, the company had no inventories of goods in process or finished goods but held the following raw materials.

Problem 19-5A
Production transactions, subsidiary records, and source documents

P1   P2   P3   P4

Material M	120 units @ $200 =	$24,000
Material R	80 units @ 160 =	12,800
Paint	44 units @ 72 =	3,168
Total cost		$39,968

On May 4, the company began working on two technopresses: Job 102 for Global Company and Job 103 for Rolf Company.

Required

Follow the instructions in this list of activities and complete the sheets provided in the working papers.

a. Purchased raw materials on credit and recorded the following information from receiving reports and invoices.

Receiving Report No. 426, Material M, 150 units at $200 each.
Receiving Report No. 427, Material R, 70 units at $160 each.

Instructions: Record these purchases with a single journal entry and post it to general ledger T-accounts, using the transaction letter *a* to identify the entry. Enter the receiving report information on the materials ledger cards.

b. Requisitioned the following raw materials for production.

> Requisition No. 35, for Job 102, 80 units of Material M.
> Requisition No. 36, for Job 102, 60 units of Material R.
> Requisition No. 37, for Job 103, 40 units of Material M.
> Requisition No. 38, for Job 103, 30 units of Material R.
> Requisition No. 39, for 12 units of paint.

Instructions: Enter amounts for direct materials requisitions on the materials ledger cards and the job cost sheets. Enter the indirect material amount on the materials ledger card and record a debit to the Indirect Materials account in the subsidiary factory overhead ledger. Do not record a journal entry at this time.

c. Received the following employee time tickets for work in May.

> Time tickets Nos. 1 to 10 for direct labor on Job 102, $40,000.
> Time tickets Nos. 11 to 30 for direct labor on Job 103, $32,000.
> Time tickets Nos. 31 to 36 for equipment repairs, $12,000.

Instructions: Record direct labor from the time tickets on the job cost sheets and then debit indirect labor to the Indirect Labor account in the subsidiary factory overhead ledger. Do not record a journal entry at this time.

d. Paid cash for the following items during the month: factory payroll, $84,000, and miscellaneous overhead items, $36,000.

Instructions: Record these payments with journal entries and then post them to the general ledger accounts. Also record a debit in the Miscellaneous Overhead account in the subsidiary factory overhead ledger.

e. Finished Job 102 and transferred it to the warehouse. The company assigns overhead to each job with a predetermined overhead rate equal to 70% of direct labor cost.

Instructions: Enter the allocated overhead on the cost sheet for Job 102, fill in the cost summary section of the cost sheet, and then mark the cost sheet "Finished." Prepare a journal entry to record the job's completion and its transfer to Finished Goods and then post it to the general ledger accounts.

f. Delivered Job 102 and accepted the customer's promise to pay $290,000 within 30 days.

Instructions: Prepare journal entries to record the sale of Job 102 and the cost of goods sold. Post them to the general ledger accounts.

g. Applied overhead to Job 103 based on the job's direct labor to date.

Instructions: Enter overhead on the job cost sheet but do not make a journal entry at this time.

Check (h) Dr. Goods in Process Inventory, $38,400

h. Recorded the total direct and indirect materials costs as reported on all the requisitions for the month.

Instructions: Prepare a journal entry to record these costs and post it to general ledger accounts.

i. Recorded the total direct and indirect labor costs as reported on all time tickets for the month.

Instructions: Prepare a journal entry to record these costs and post it to general ledger accounts.

Check Balance in Factory Overhead, $1,536 Cr., overapplied

j. Recorded the total overhead costs applied to jobs.

Instructions: Prepare a journal entry to record the allocation of these overhead costs and post it to general ledger accounts.

PROBLEM SET B

Problem 19-1B
Production costs computed and recorded; reports prepared

C2 P1 P2 P3 P4

Pak Co.'s August 31 inventory of raw materials is $16,000. Raw materials purchases in September are $60,000, and factory payroll cost in September is $68,000. Overhead costs incurred in September are: indirect materials, $6,000; indirect labor, $4,000; factory rent, $24,000; factory utilities, $22,000; and factory equipment depreciation, $25,000. The predetermined overhead rate is 130% of direct labor cost. Job 114 is sold for $100,000 cash in September. Costs for the three jobs worked on in September follow.

	Job 114	Job 115	Job 116
Balances on August 31			
Direct materials	$ 4,000	$ 6,000	
Direct labor	2,000	2,200	
Applied overhead	2,600	2,860	
Costs during September			
Direct materials	10,000	30,000	$16,000
Direct labor	16,000	28,000	20,000
Applied overhead	?	?	?
Status on September 30	Finished (sold)	Finished (unsold)	In process

Required

1. Determine the total of each production cost incurred for September (direct labor, direct materials, and applied overhead), and the total cost assigned to each job (including the balances from August 31).

2. Prepare journal entries for the month of September to record the following.

    a. Materials purchases (on credit), factory payroll (paid in cash), and actual overhead costs including indirect materials and indirect labor. (Factory rent and utilities are paid in cash.)

    b. Assignment of direct materials, direct labor, and applied overhead costs to Goods in Process Inventory.

    c. Transfer of Jobs 114 and 115 to the Finished Goods Inventory.

    d. Cost of Job 114 in the Cost of Goods Sold account.

    e. Revenue from the sale of Job 114.

    f. Assignment of any underapplied or overapplied overhead to the Cost of Goods Sold account. (The amount is not material.)

    Check (2f) $2,200 overapplied

3. Prepare a manufacturing statement for September (use a single line presentation for direct materials and show the details of overhead cost).

    (3) Cost of goods manufactured, $160,860

4. Compute gross profit for September. Show how to present the inventories on the September 30 statement of financial position.

Analysis Component

5. The over- or underapplied overhead adjustment is closed to Cost of Goods Sold. Discuss how this adjustment impacts business decision making regarding individual jobs or batches of jobs.

Metro's computer system generated the following trial balance on December 31, 2011. The company's manager knows that the trial balance is wrong because it does not show any balance for Goods in Process Inventory but does show balances for the Factory Payroll and Factory Overhead accounts.

Problem 19-2B
Source documents, journal entries, overhead, and financial reports

P1 P2 P3 P4

	Debit	Credit
Cash	$ 40,000	
Accounts receivable	80,000	
Raw materials inventory	24,000	
Goods in process inventory	0	
Finished goods inventory	50,000	
Prepaid rent	4,000	
Accounts payable		$ 16,000
Notes payable		30,000
Share capital—ordinary		60,000
Retained earnings		33,800
Sales		250,000
Cost of goods sold	140,000	
Factory payroll	20,000	
Factory overhead	9,800	
Operating expenses	22,000	
Totals	$389,800	$389,800

After examining various files, the manager identifies the following six source documents that need to be processed to bring the accounting records up to date.

Materials requisition 94-231:	$ 5,000 direct materials to Job 603
Materials requisition 94-232:	$ 8,000 direct materials to Job 604
Materials requisition 94-233:	$ 1,500 indirect materials
Labor time ticket 765:	$ 6,000 direct labor to Job 603
Labor time ticket 766:	$12,000 direct labor to Job 604
Labor time ticket 777:	$ 2,000 indirect labor

Jobs 603 and 604 are the only units in process at year-end. The predetermined overhead rate is 80% of direct labor cost.

Required

1. Use information on the six source documents to prepare journal entries to assign the following costs.
    a. Direct materials costs to Goods in Process Inventory.
    b. Direct labor costs to Goods in Process Inventory.
    c. Overhead costs to Goods in Process Inventory.
    d. Indirect materials costs to the Factory Overhead account.
    e. Indirect labor costs to the Factory Overhead account.

Check (2) $1,100 overapplied overhead

(3) T. B. totals, $389,800

(4) Net profit, $89,100

2. Determine the revised balance of the Factory Overhead account after making the entries in part 1. Determine whether there is under- or overapplied overhead for the year. Prepare the adjusting entry to allocate any over- or underapplied overhead to Cost of Goods Sold, assuming the amount is not material.
3. Prepare a revised trial balance.
4. Prepare an income statement for year 2011 and a statement of financial position as at December 31, 2011.

Analysis Component

5. Assume that the $1,500 indirect materials on materials requisition 94-233 should have been direct materials charged to Job 604. Without providing specific calculations, describe the impact of this error on the income statement for 2011 and the statement of financial position at December 31, 2011.

Problem 19-3B
Source documents, journal entries, and accounts in job order cost accounting

P1 P2 P3

Troupe Company's predetermined overhead rate is 90% of direct labor. Information on the company's production activities during September 2011 follows.
a. Purchased raw materials on credit, $57,000.
b. Paid $99,750 cash for factory wages.
c. Paid $11,250 cash for miscellaneous factory overhead costs.
d. Materials requisitions record use of the following materials for the month.

Job 487	$13,500
Job 488	9,000
Job 489	12,000
Job 490	10,500
Job 491	1,500
Total direct materials	46,500
Indirect materials	3,750
Total materials used	$50,250

e. Time tickets record use of the following labor for the month.

Job 487	$16,500
Job 488	19,500
Job 489	25,500
Job 490	18,000
Job 491	7,500
Total direct labor	87,000
Indirect labor	12,750
Total	$99,750

f. Allocated overhead to Jobs 487, 489, and 490.

g. Transferred Jobs 487, 489, and 490 to Finished Goods.

h. Sold Jobs 487 and 489 on credit for a total price of $225,000.

i. The company incurred the following overhead costs during the month (credit Prepaid Insurance for expired factory insurance).

Depreciation of factory building	$24,750
Depreciation of factory equipment	18,750
Expired factory insurance	2,250
Accrued property tax payable.	5,250

j. Applied overhead at month-end to the Goods in Process (Jobs 488 and 491) using the predetermined overhead rate of 90% of direct labor cost.

Required

1. Prepare a job cost sheet for each job worked on in the month. Use the following simplified form.

Job No. _____	
Materials	$ _____
Labor.	_____
Overhead.	_____
Total cost	$ _____

2. Prepare journal entries to record the events and transactions *a* through *j*.

3. Set up T-accounts for each of the following general ledger accounts, each of which started the month with a zero balance: Raw Materials Inventory, Goods in Process Inventory, Finished Goods Inventory, Factory Payroll, Factory Overhead, Cost of Goods Sold. Then post the journal entries to these T-accounts and determine the balance of each account.

4. Prepare a report showing the total cost of each job in process and prove that the sum of their costs equals the Goods in Process Inventory account balance. Prepare similar reports for Finished Goods Inventory and Cost of Goods Sold.

Check   (2f) Cr. Factory Overhead, $54,000

(3) Finished goods inventory, $44,700

In December 2010, Monk Company's manager estimated next year's total direct labor cost assuming 40 persons working an average of 1,500 hours each at an average wage rate of $50 per hour. The manager also estimated the following manufacturing overhead costs for year 2011.

Problem 19-4B
Overhead allocation and adjustment using a predetermined overhead rate

P3   P4

Indirect labor	$ 540,000
Factory supervision	450,000
Rent on factory building.	360,000
Factory utilities	200,000
Factory insurance expired	60,000
Depreciation—Factory equipment	300,000
Repairs expense—Factory equipment	180,000
Factory supplies used	110,000
Miscellaneous production costs	200,000
Total estimated overhead costs	$2,400,000

At the end of 2011, records show the company incurred $2,200,000 of actual overhead costs. It completed and sold five jobs with the following direct labor costs: Job 625, $300,000; Job 626, $225,000; Job 627, $975,000; Job 628, $240,000; and Job 629, $375,000. In addition, Job 630 is in process at the end of 2011 and had been charged $75,000 for direct labor. No jobs were in process at the end of 2010. The company's predetermined overhead rate is based on direct labor cost.

Required

1. Determine the following.

   a. Predetermined overhead rate for year 2011.

   b. Total overhead cost applied to each of the six jobs during year 2011.

   c. Over- or underapplied overhead at year-end 2011.

2. Assuming that any over- or underapplied overhead is not material, prepare the adjusting entry to allocate any over- or underapplied overhead to Cost of Goods Sold at the end of year 2011.

Check   (1c) $448,000 underapplied

(2) Cr. Factory Overhead, $448,000

Problem 19-5B
Production transactions, subsidiary records, and source documents

P1 P2 P3 P4

If the working papers that accompany this book are unavailable, do not attempt to solve this problem.
Sim Company produces variations of its product, a megatron, in response to custom orders from its customers. On June 1, the company had no inventories of goods in process or finished goods but held the following raw materials.

Material M	150 units @ $ 40 =	$ 6,000
Material R	50 units @ 160 =	8,000
Paint	20 units @ 20 =	400
Total cost		$14,400

On June 3, the company began working on two megatrons: Job 450 for Olivas Company and Job 451 for Ireland, Inc.

Required

Follow instructions in this list of activities and complete the sheets provided in the working papers.

a. Purchased raw materials on credit and recorded the following information from receiving reports and invoices.

> Receiving Report No. 20, Material M, 150 units at $40 each.
> Receiving Report No. 21, Material R, 200 units at $160 each.

Instructions: Record these purchases with a single journal entry and post it to general ledger T-accounts, using the transaction letter *a* to identify the entry. Enter the receiving report information on the materials ledger cards.

b. Requisitioned the following raw materials for production.

> Requisition No. 223, for Job 450, 60 units of Material M.
> Requisition No. 224, for Job 450, 100 units of Material R.
> Requisition No. 225, for Job 451, 30 units of Material M.
> Requisition No. 226, for Job 451, 75 units of Material R.
> Requisition No. 227, for 10 units of paint.

Instructions: Enter amounts for direct materials requisitions on the materials ledger cards and the job cost sheets. Enter the indirect material amount on the materials ledger card and record a debit to the Indirect Materials account in the subsidiary factory overhead ledger. Do not record a journal entry at this time.

c. Received the following employee time tickets for work in June.

> Time tickets Nos. 1 to 10 for direct labor on Job 450, $24,000.
> Time tickets Nos. 11 to 20 for direct labor on Job 451, $20,000.
> Time tickets Nos. 21 to 24 for equipment repairs, $4,000.

Instructions: Record direct labor from the time tickets on the job cost sheets and then debit indirect labor to the Indirect Labor account in the subsidiary factory overhead ledger. Do not record a journal entry at this time.

d. Paid cash for the following items during the month: factory payroll, $48,000, and miscellaneous overhead items, $47,000.

Instructions: Record these payments with journal entries and post them to the general ledger accounts. Also record a debit in the Miscellaneous Overhead account in the subsidiary factory overhead ledger.

e. Finished Job 450 and transferred it to the warehouse. The company assigns overhead to each job with a predetermined overhead rate equal to 120% of direct labor cost.

Instructions: Enter the allocated overhead on the cost sheet for Job 450, fill in the cost summary section of the cost sheet, and then mark the cost sheet "Finished." Prepare a journal entry to record the job's completion and its transfer to Finished Goods and then post it to the general ledger accounts.

f. Delivered Job 450 and accepted the customer's promise to pay $130,000 within 30 days.

Instructions: Prepare journal entries to record the sale of Job 450 and the cost of goods sold. Post them to the general ledger accounts.

g. Applied overhead cost to Job 451 based on the job's direct labor used to date.

Instructions: Enter overhead on the job cost sheet but do not make a journal entry at this time.

h. Recorded the total direct and indirect materials costs as reported on all the requisitions for the month.

Instructions: Prepare a journal entry to record these costs and post it to general ledger accounts.

Check   (h) Dr. Goods in Process Inventory, $31,600

i. Recorded the total direct and indirect labor costs as reported on all time tickets for the month.

Instructions: Prepare a journal entry to record these costs and post it to general ledger accounts.

j. Recorded the total overhead costs applied to jobs.

Instructions: Prepare a journal entry to record the allocation of these overhead costs and post it to general ledger accounts.

Check   Balance in Factory Overhead, $1,600 Cr., overapplied

(This serial problem began in Chapter 1 and continues through most of the book. If previous chapter segments were not completed, the serial problem can begin at this point.)

SERIAL PROBLEM
Business Solutions

P1 P2 P3

SP 19 The computer workstation furniture manufacturing that Santana Rey started in January is progressing well. As of the end of June, Business Solutions' job cost sheets show the following total costs accumulated on three furniture jobs.

Job 6.02 was started in production in May, and these costs were assigned to it in May: direct materials,

	Job 6.02	Job 6.03	Job 6.04
Direct materials.........	$1,500	$3,300	$2,700
Direct labor............	800	1,420	2,100
Overhead..............	400	710	1,050

$600; direct labor, $180; and overhead, $90. Jobs 6.03 and 6.04 were started in June. Overhead cost is applied with a predetermined rate based on direct labor costs. Jobs 6.02 and 6.03 are finished in June, and Job 6.04 is expected to be finished in July. No raw materials are used indirectly in June. (Assume this company's predetermined overhead rate did not change over these months).

Required

1. What is the cost of the raw materials used in June for each of the three jobs and in total?
2. How much total direct labor cost is incurred in June?
3. What predetermined overhead rate is used in June?
4. How much cost is transferred to finished goods inventory in June?

Check   (1) Total materials, $6,900

(3) 50%

Beyond the Numbers

BTN 19-1 Access **Research In Motion**'s 2010 annual report from its Website www.rim.com. The report provides evidence of growth potential in its sales.

REPORTING IN ACTION

C1

Required

1. Identify at least two types of costs that will predictably increase as a percent of sales with growth in sales.
2. Explain why you believe the types of costs identified for part 1 will increase, and describe how you might assess RIM's success with these costs. (*Hint:* You might consider the gross margin ratio.)

Fast Forward

3. Access RIM's annual report for a financial year ending after February 27, 2010, from its Website. Review and report its growth in sales along with its cost and income levels (including its gross margin ratio).

COMPARATIVE ANALYSIS

C1

BTN 19-2   Retailers as well as manufacturers can apply just-in-time (JIT) to their inventory management. Both **Research In Motion** and **Apple** want to know the impact of a JIT inventory system for their operating cash flows. Access the 2010 annual report of Research In Motion from www. rim. com and look at Apple's financial report in Appendix A. Review each company's statement of cash flows to answer the following. (For RIM, also review Note 16.)

Required

1. Identify the impact on operating cash flows (increase or decrease) for changes in inventory levels (increase or decrease) for both companies for each of the three most recent years.

2. What impact would a JIT inventory system have on both RIM's and Apple's operating income? Link the answer to your response for part 1.

3. Would the move to a JIT system have a one-time or recurring impact on operating cash flow?

ETHICS CHALLENGE

P3

BTN 19-3   An accounting professional requires at least two skill sets. The first is to be technically competent. Knowing how to capture, manage, and report information is a necessary skill. Second, the ability to assess manager and employee actions and biases for accounting analysis is another skill. For instance, knowing how a person is compensated helps anticipate information biases. Draw on these skills and write a one-half page memo to the financial officer on the following practice of allocating overhead.

Background: Assume that your company sells portable housing to both general contractors and the government. It sells jobs to contractors on a bid basis. A contractor asks for three bids from different manufacturers. The combination of low bid and high quality wins the job. However, jobs sold to the government are bid on a cost-plus basis. This means price is determined by adding all costs plus a profit based on cost at a specified percent, such as 10%. You observe that the amount of overhead allocated to government jobs is higher than that allocated to contract jobs. These allocations concern you and motivate your memo.

Point: Students could compare responses and discuss differences in concerns with allocating overhead.

COMMUNICATING IN PRACTICE

C1 C2

BTN 19-4   Assume that you are preparing for a second interview with a manufacturing company. The company is impressed with your credentials but has indicated that it has several qualified applicants. You anticipate that in this second interview, you must show what you offer over other candidates. You learn the company currently uses a periodic inventory system and is not satisfied with the timeliness of its information and its inventory management. The company manufactures custom-order holiday decorations and display items. To show your abilities, you plan to recommend that it use a cost accounting system.

Required

In preparation for the interview, prepare notes outlining the following:

1. Your cost accounting system recommendation and why it is suitable for this company.

2. A general description of the documents that the proposed cost accounting system requires.

3. How the documents in part 2 facilitate the operation of the cost accounting system.

Point: Have students present a mock interview, one assuming the role of the president of the company and the other the applicant.

TAKING IT TO THE NET

C1

BTN 19-5   Many contractors work on custom jobs that require a job order costing system.

Required

Access the Website AMSI.com and click on *Construction Management Software,* and then on STARBUILDER. Prepare a one-page memorandum for the CEO of a construction company providing information about the job order costing software this company offers. Would you recommend that the company purchase this software?

BTN 19-6   Consider the activities undertaken by a medical clinic in your area.

TEAMWORK IN ACTION

C1

Required

1. Do you consider a job order cost accounting system appropriate for the clinic?

2. Identify as many factors as possible to lead you to conclude that it uses a job order system.

BTN 19-7   Prakash of BFSI (refer to the Decision Insight at the beginning of the chapter) contrasts time and materials approach with a turnkey approach to costing and pricing for software jobs.

ENTREPRENEURIAL DECISION

C1

Required

List three items on which the approach to job costing for times and materials contract would be different from that of a turnkey contract.

BTN 19-8   Visit the office of the student union in your university. Interview the president and treasurer to ascertain how the union budgeted for and tracked a recent event that it organized. Can you find any scope for improvements in the system?

HITTING THE ROAD

C2 P1 P2 P3

BTN 19-9   Refer to the annual report of Adidas for 2010 at http://adidas-group.corporate-publications.com/2010/gb/files/pdf/en/ADS_GB_2010_En.pdf. Pages 134 to 136 analyze the revenues and expenses performance.

GLOBAL DECISION

C1

Required

1. What is the difference between the sales working budget and the marketing working budget as employed by Adidas?

2. What factors are likely to influence the sales working budget? What factors are likely to influence the marketing working budget?

ANSWERS TO MULTIPLE CHOICE QUIZ

1. c; $30,000 × 150% = $45,000

2. b; $38,500/$35,000 = 110%

3. e; Direct materials + Direct labor + Overhead = Total cost;
 Direct materials + ($4,000/.80) + $4,000 = $10,000
 Direct materials = $1,000

4. e; $9,000 + $94,200 + $59,200 + $31,600 − Finished goods = $17,800
 Thus, finished goods = $176,200

5. b

20

Process Cost Accounting

A Look Back

Chapter 18 introduced managerial accounting and described cost concepts and the reporting of manufacturing activities. Chapter 19 explained job order costing—an important cost accounting system for customized products and services.

A Look at This Chapter

This chapter focuses on how to measure and account for costs in process operations. We explain process production, describe how to assign costs to processes, and compute cost per equivalent unit for a process.

A Look Ahead

Chapter 21 explains how to allocate factory overhead costs to different products and introduces the activity-based costing method of overhead allocation. It also explains responsibility accounting and measures of departmental performance.

Learning Objectives

CAP

CONCEPTUAL

C1 Explain process operations and the way they differ from job order operations. (p. 784)

C2 Define and compute equivalent units and explain their use in process cost accounting. (p. 791)

C3 Define and prepare a process cost summary and describe its purposes. (p. 796)

C4 *Appendix 20A*—Explain and illustrate the accounting for production activity using FIFO. (p. 803)

ANALYTICAL

A1 Compare process cost accounting and job order cost accounting. (p. 787)

A2 Explain and illustrate a hybrid costing system. (p. 799)

PROCEDURAL

P1 Record the flow of direct materials costs in process cost accounting. (p. 788)

P2 Record the flow of direct labor costs in process cost accounting. (p. 789)

P3 Record the flow of factory overhead costs in process cost accounting. (p. 789)

P4 Record the transfer of completed goods to Finished Goods Inventory and Cost of Goods Sold. (p. 797)

"Balancing creativity and commerciality is a constant challenge."—**DESMOND YANG**

Wearing Yang

"Why Abyzz and not Desmond Yang?" is a question he gets all the time of his fashion label. Well, use your name by all means if you're famous, according to Desmond. For him, he is happy with Abyzz, derived from the word "abyss," which means "an immeasurably deep chasm," alluding to mysterious hidden treasure within. And that is how he wants his wearer to approach his clothing line—with a sense of explorative spirit toward the apparel's mystical quality and alluring details.

"Having your own label is every designer's dream," says Desmond, who fulfilled his young ambition barely four years after graduating from a design school when he launched his own label, **Abyzz (ww.abyzz.com.sg)**. The initial collection he put out was the basic day-to-day wearable range. When the line took off, he added more versatile, "transformational" garments to the mix—dresses that can be worn as tops, skirts, or cardigans. The revolutionary design was a hit. In July 2008, Desmond opened his first standalone boutique under the Abyzz label.

"Balancing creativity and commerciality is a constant challenge," remarks Desmond, who also struggles with the high cost of retail space, as well as intense competition from international and mass market brands. "There are also the fluctuations in actual and forecast sales to deal with," he adds. To keep costs low, Desmond works with a variety of fabrics, accessories, and materials, which he sources from regular overseas trips. For clothing lines that carry standard designs, he applies process cost summaries to help him monitor and control the costs of material, labor, and overhead, "which are comparatively high in Singapore." However, Desmond asserts that he will not compromise on quality, preferring to acquire premium fabric by buying in bulk to save costs.

Desmond attributes his success partly to a dedicated team who has helped shave off training and other expenses. His two full-time workshop assistants, a sample sewer, and a drafter are experienced and independent workers, as are the boutique's full-time sales assistant and a part-timer, both of whom wear many hats, tackling administrative and inventory matters between them.

"What I love about managing Abyzz is the encouraging feedback from the customers," says Desmond. With a strong client base and a committed staff, this fashion aficionado can now put to rest the initial doubts he had about his business and start enjoying every minute of his dream job!

The type of product or service a company offers determines its cost accounting system. Job order costing is used to account for custom products and services that meet the demands of a particular customer. Not all products are manufactured in this way; many carry standard designs so that one unit is no different than any other unit. Such a system often produces large numbers of units on a continuous basis, all of which pass through similar processes.

This chapter describes how to use a process cost accounting system to account for these types of products. It also explains how costs are accumulated for each process and then assigned to units passing through those processes. This information helps us understand and estimate the cost of each process as well as find ways to reduce costs and improve processes.

Process Cost Accounting

Process Operations
- Comparing job order and process operations
- Organization of process operations
- GenX Company—an illustration

Process Cost Accounting
- Direct and indirect costs
- Accounting for materials costs
- Accounting for labor costs
- Accounting for factory overhead

Equivalent Units of Production (EUP)
- Accounting for goods in process
- Differences between EUP for materials, labor, and overhead

Process Costing Illustration
- Physical flow of units
- EUP
- Cost per EUP
- Cost reconciliation
- Process cost summary
- Transfers to finished goods and to cost of goods sold

PROCESS OPERATIONS

C1 Explain process operations and the way they differ from job order operations.

Process operations, also called *process manufacturing* or *process production,* is the mass production of products in a continuous flow of steps. This means that products pass through a series of sequential processes. The steel production activities of **Bao Steel**, one of the leading steel manufacturers in the world, reflect a process operation. Bao Steel's process for manufacturing cold rolled sheet can be viewed at http://tv.baosteel.com/web/plc/p-pdf/LB0904C0101.pdf. An important characteristic of process operations is the high level of standardization necessary if the system is to produce large volumes of products. Process operations also extend to services. Examples include order processing in large mail-order firms and mail sorting in large postal organizations like **Singapore Post**. Irrespective of the brand or type of delivery service, postal services involve bulk processing. You can view this process at http://www.singpost.com.sg/singpost_01consumer_mail.htm. The common feature in these service organizations is that operations are performed in a sequential manner using a series of standardized processes. Other companies using process operations include:

Company	Product or Service	Company	Product or Service
Kellogg	Cereals	Heinz	Ketchup
Pfizer	Pharmaceuticals	Penn	Tennis balls
Proctor & Gamble	Household products	Hershey	Chocolate
Coca-Cola	Soft drinks	Jiffy Lube	Oil changes

Watersecure is an Australian company that takes polluted water and purifies it to meet or exceed drinking water standards by passing the water through seven different processes. For a virtual tour of a water purification plant visit Watersecure's site at **www.watersecure.com.au/virtualtours/bundamba/.**

Each of these examples of products and services involves operations having a series of *processes*, or steps. Each process involves a different set of activities. A production operation that processes chemicals, for instance, might include the four steps shown in Exhibit 20.1.

Understanding such processes for companies with process operations is crucial for measuring their costs. Increasingly, process operations use machines and automation to control product quality and reduce manufacturing costs.

EXHIBIT 20.1

Process Operations: Chemicals

| Preparing the chemicals | → | Mixing the chemicals | → | Bottling the chemical mix | → | Packaging the bottles |

Comparing Job Order and Process Operations

Job order and process operations can be considered as two ends of a continuum. Important features of both systems are shown in Exhibit 20.2. We often describe job order and process operations with manufacturing examples, but both also apply to service companies. In a job order costing system, the measurement focus is on the individual job or batch. In a process costing system, the measurement focus is on the process itself and the standardized units produced.

EXHIBIT 20.2

Comparing Job Order and Process Operations

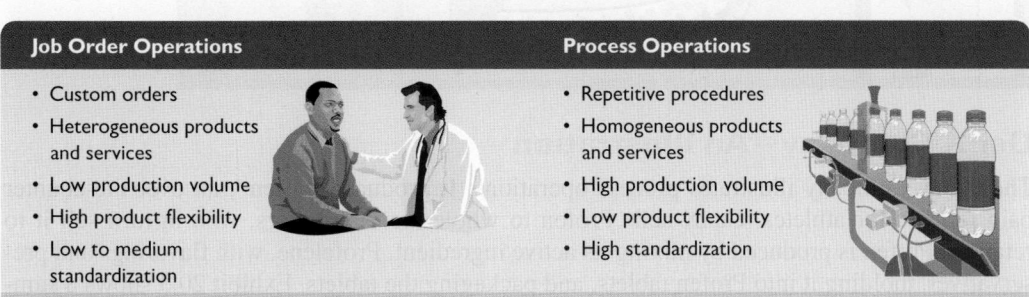

Job Order Operations
- Custom orders
- Heterogeneous products and services
- Low production volume
- High product flexibility
- Low to medium standardization

Process Operations
- Repetitive procedures
- Homogeneous products and services
- High production volume
- Low product flexibility
- High standardization

Organization of Process Operations

In a process operation, each process is identified as a separate *production department, workstation,* or *work center.* With the exception of the first process or department, each receives the output from the prior department as a partially processed product. Depending on the nature of the process, a company applies direct labor, overhead, and, perhaps, additional direct materials to move the product toward completion. Only the final process or department in the series produces finished goods ready for sale to customers.

Tracking costs for several related departments can seem complex. Yet because process costing procedures are applied to the activity of each department or process separately, we need to consider only one process at a time. This simplifies the procedures.

When the output of one department becomes an input to another department, as is the case in sequential processing, we simply transfer the costs associated with those units from the first department into the next. We repeat these steps from department to department until the final process is complete. At that point the accumulated costs are transferred with the product from Goods in Process Inventory to Finished Goods Inventory. The next section illustrates a company with a single process, but the methods illustrated apply to a multiprocess scenario as each department's costs are handled separately for each department.

Decision Insight

Accounting for Health   Many service companies use process departments to perform specific tasks for consumers. Hospitals, for instance, have radiology and physical therapy facilities with special equipment and trained employees. When patients need services, they are processed through departments to receive prescribed care. Service companies need process cost accounting information as much as manufacturers to estimate costs of services, to plan future operations, to control costs, and to determine customer charges. ■

EXHIBIT 20.3

Floor Plan of GenX's Factory

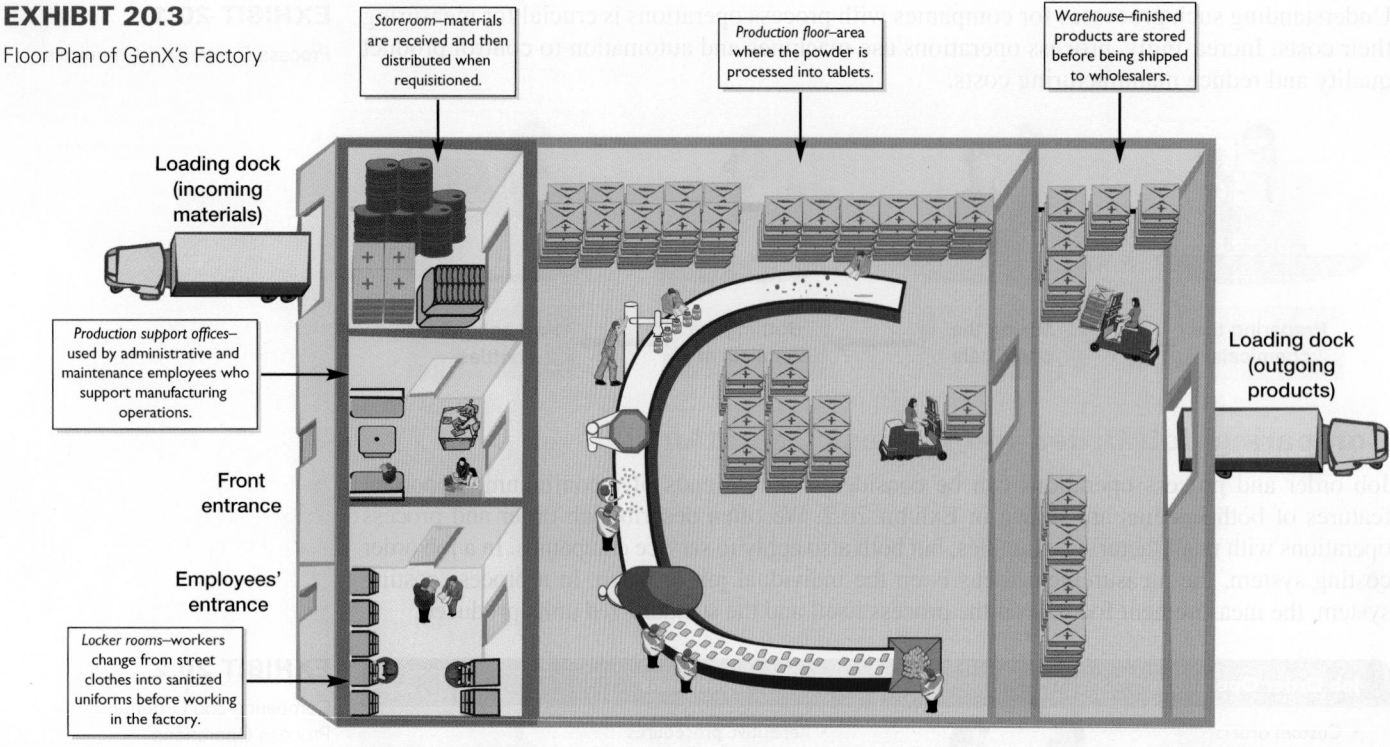

Storeroom—materials are received and then distributed when requisitioned.

Production floor—area where the powder is processed into tablets.

Warehouse—finished products are stored before being shipped to wholesalers.

Loading dock (incoming materials)

Production support offices—used by administrative and maintenance employees who support manufacturing operations.

Front entrance

Employees' entrance

Locker rooms—workers change from street clothes into sanitized uniforms before working in the factory.

Loading dock (outgoing products)

Point: Electronic monitoring of operations is common in factories.

GenX Company—An Illustration

The GenX Company illustrates process operations. It produces Profen®, an over-the-counter pain reliever for athletes. GenX sells Profen to wholesale distributors, who in turn sell it to retailers. Profen is produced by mixing its active ingredient, Profelene, with flavorings and preservatives, molding it into Profen tablets, and packaging the tablets. Exhibit 20.3 shows a summary floor plan of the GenX factory, which has five areas.

The first step in process manufacturing is to decide when to produce a product. Management determines the types and quantities of materials and labor needed and then schedules the work. Unlike a job order process, where production often begins only after receipt of a custom order, managers of companies with process operations often forecast the demand expected for their products. Based on these plans, production begins. The flowchart in Exhibit 20.4 shows the production steps for GenX. The following sections explain how GenX uses a process cost accounting system to compute these costs. Many of the explanations refer to this exhibit and its numbered cost flows ① through ⑩. (*Hint:* The amounts for the numbered cost flows in Exhibit 20.4 are summarized in Exhibit 20.21. Those amounts are explained in the following pages, but it can help to refer to Exhibit 20.21 as we proceed through the explanations.)

EXHIBIT 20.4

Process Operations and Costs: GenX

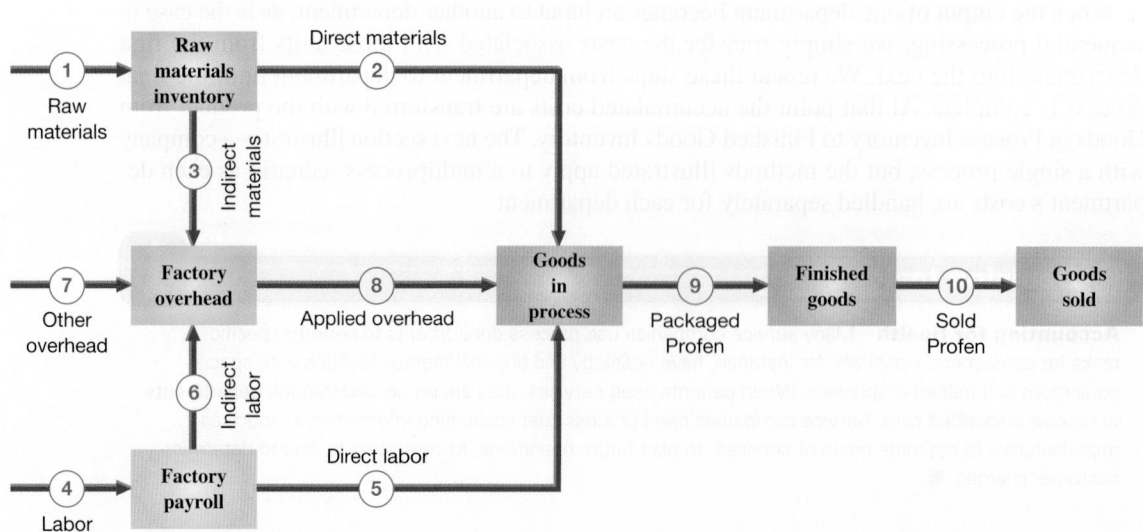

PROCESS COST ACCOUNTING

Comparing Job Order and Process Cost Accounting Systems

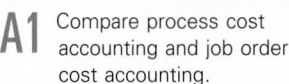

A1 Compare process cost accounting and job order cost accounting.

Process and job order operations are similar in that both combine materials, labor, and overhead in the process of producing products. They differ in how they are organized and managed. The measurement focus in a job order costing system is on the individual job or batch, whereas in a process costing system, it is on the individual process. Regardless of the measurement focus, we are ultimately interested in determining the cost per unit of product (or service) resulting from either system.

Specifically, the **job order cost accounting system** assigns direct materials, direct labor, and overhead to jobs. The total job cost is then divided by the number of units to compute a cost per unit for that job. The **process cost accounting system** assigns direct materials, direct labor, and overhead to specific processes (or departments). The total costs associated with each process are then divided by the number of units passing through that process to determine the cost per equivalent unit (defined later in the chapter) for that process. Differences in the way these two systems apply materials, labor, and overhead costs are highlighted in Exhibit 20.5.

Point: The cost object in a job order system is the specific job; the cost object in a process costing system is the process.

EXHIBIT 20.5

Comparing Job Order and Process Cost Accounting Systems

Job order systems

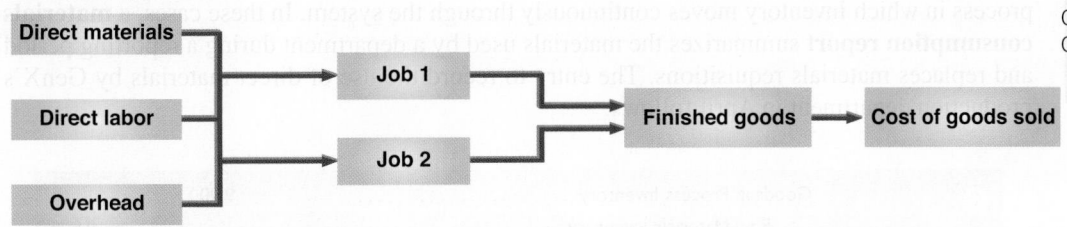

Process systems

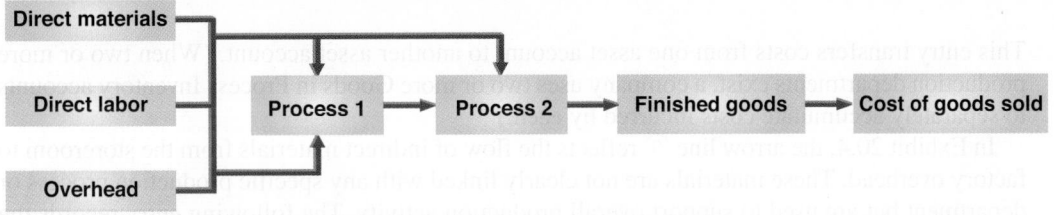

Direct and Indirect Costs

Like job order operations, process cost accounting systems use the concepts of direct and indirect costs. If a cost can be traced to the cost object, it is direct; if it cannot, it is indirect. Materials and labor that can be traced to specific processes are assigned to those processes as direct costs. Materials and labor that cannot be traced to a specific process are indirect costs and are assigned to overhead. Some costs classified as overhead in a job order system may be classified as direct costs in process cost accounting. For example, depreciation of a machine used entirely by one process is a direct cost of that process.

Decision Insight

JIT and BPR Boon to Process Operations   Companies that adopt JIT manufacturing often organize their production system as a series of sequential processes. One survey found 60% of companies that converted to JIT used process operations; this compares to only 20% before converting to JIT. Business Process Reengineering (BPR) is an idea that is related to JIT. BPR involves the redesigning of core business processes to achieve improvements in productivity, cycle time, and quality. According to a survey by **Bain & Company**, a leading global management consulting company, BPR is one of the top ten management tools used by companies globally. While the use of BPR as a management tool is popular globally, its use is more pronounced in regions such as North America where companies are more focused on cost cutting for competitiveness than in countries like China and India where the focus is more on growth. ■

Accounting for Materials Costs

In Exhibit 20.4, arrow line ① reflects the arrival of materials at GenX's factory. These materials include Profelene, flavorings, preservatives, and packaging. They also include supplies for the production support office. GenX uses a perpetual inventory system and makes all purchases on credit. The summary entry for receipts of raw materials in April follows (dates in journal entries numbered ① through ⑩ are omitted because they are summary entries, often reflecting two or more transactions or events).

Assets = Liabilities + Equity
+11,095   +11,095

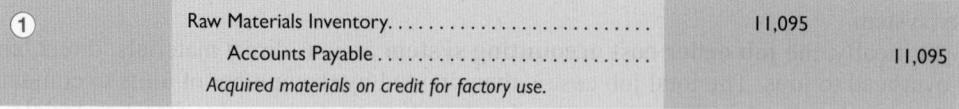

①	Raw Materials Inventory.............................	11,095	
	Accounts Payable.............................		11,095
	Acquired materials on credit for factory use.		

Arrow line ② in Exhibit 20.4 reflects the flow of direct materials to production, where they are used to produce Profen. Most direct materials are physically combined into the finished product; the remaining direct materials include those used and clearly linked with a specific process. The manager of a process usually obtains materials by submitting a *materials requisition* to the materials storeroom manager. In some situations, materials move continuously from raw materials inventory through the manufacturing process. **Pepsi Bottling**, for instance, uses a process in which inventory moves continuously through the system. In these cases, a **materials consumption report** summarizes the materials used by a department during a reporting period and replaces materials requisitions. The entry to record the use of direct materials by GenX's production department in April follows.

Assets = Liabilities + Equity
+9,900
−9,900

②	Goods in Process Inventory	9,900	
	Raw Materials Inventory		9,900
	To assign costs of direct materials used in production.		

This entry transfers costs from one asset account to another asset account. (When two or more production departments exist, a company uses two or more Goods in Process Inventory accounts to separately accumulate costs incurred by each.)

In Exhibit 20.4, the arrow line ③ reflects the flow of indirect materials from the storeroom to factory overhead. These materials are not clearly linked with any specific production process or department but are used to support overall production activity. The following entry records the cost of indirect materials used by GenX in April.

Example: What types of materials might the flow of arrow line ③ in Exhibit 20.4 reflect? *Answer:* Goggles, gloves, protective clothing, recordkeeping supplies, and cleaning supplies.

Assets = Liabilities + Equity
−1,195   −1,195

③	Factory Overhead	1,195	
	Raw Materials Inventory		1,195
	To record indirect materials used in April.		

After the entries for both direct and indirect materials are posted, the Raw Materials Inventory account appears as shown in Exhibit 20.6. The April 30 statement of financial position reports the $4,000 Raw Materials Inventory account as a current asset.

EXHIBIT 20.6

Raw Materials Inventory

Raw Materials Inventory				Acct. No. 132		
Date		Explanation	Debit	Credit	Balance
Mar.	31	Balance			4,000
Apr.	30	Materials purchases	11,095		15,095
	30	Direct materials usage		9,900	5,195
	30	Indirect materials usage		1,195	4,000

Accounting for Labor Costs

Exhibit 20.4 shows GenX factory payroll costs as reflected in arrow line ④. Total labor costs of $8,920 are paid in cash and are recorded in the Factory Payroll account.

P2 Record the flow of direct labor costs in process cost accounting.

④	Factory Payroll	8,920	
	Cash		8,920
	To record factory wages for April.		

Assets = Liabilities + Equity
−8,920   −8,920

Time reports from the production department and the production support office triggered this entry. (For simplicity, we do not separately identify withholdings and additional payroll taxes for employees.) In a process operation, the direct labor of a production department includes all labor used exclusively by that department. This is the case even if the labor is not applied to the product itself. If a production department in a process operation, for instance, has a full-time manager and a full-time maintenance worker, their salaries are direct labor costs of that process and are not factory overhead.

Arrow line ⑤ in Exhibit 20.4 shows GenX's use of direct labor in the production department. The following entry transfers April's direct labor costs from the Factory Payroll account to the Goods in Process Inventory account.

⑤	Goods in Process Inventory	5,700	
	Factory Payroll		5,700
	To assign costs of direct labor used in production.		

Assets = Liabilities + Equity
+5,700   +5,700

Arrow line ⑥ in Exhibit 20.4 reflects GenX's indirect labor costs. These employees provide clerical, maintenance, and other services that help produce Profen efficiently. For example, they order materials, deliver them to the factory floor, repair equipment, operate and program computers used in production, keep payroll and other production records, clean up, and move the finished goods to the warehouse. The following entry charges these indirect labor costs to factory overhead.

Point: A department's indirect labor cost might include an allocated portion of the salary of a manager who supervises two or more departments. Allocation of costs between departments is discussed in a later chapter.

⑥	Factory Overhead	3,220	
	Factory Payroll		3,220
	To record indirect labor as overhead.		

Assets = Liabilities + Equity
                        −3,220
                        +3,220

After these entries for both direct and indirect labor are posted, the Factory Payroll account appears as shown in Exhibit 20.7. The temporary Factory Payroll account is now closed to another temporary account, Factory Overhead, and is ready to receive entries for May. Next we show how to apply overhead to production and close the temporary Factory Overhead account.

EXHIBIT 20.7

Factory Payroll

Factory Payroll				Acct. No. 530	
Date		Explanation	Debit	Credit	Balance
Mar.	31	Balance			0
Apr.	30	Total payroll for April	8,920		8,920
	30	Direct labor costs		5,700	3,220
	30	Indirect labor costs		3,220	0

Accounting for Factory Overhead

Overhead costs other than indirect materials and indirect labor are reflected by arrow line ⑦ in Exhibit 20.4. These overhead items include the costs of insuring production assets, renting the factory building, using factory utilities, and depreciating equipment not directly related to a specific process. The following entry records overhead costs for April.

P3 Record the flow of factory overhead costs in process cost accounting.

Assets = Liabilities + Equity
−180   +645   −2,425
−750
−850

(7)	Factory Overhead	2,425	
	Prepaid Insurance		180
	Utilities Payable		645
	Cash		750
	Accumulated Depreciation—Factory Equipment ...		850
	To record overhead items incurred in April.		

After this entry is posted, the Factory Overhead account balance is $6,840, comprising indirect materials of $1,195, indirect labor of $3,220, and $2,425 of other overhead.

Arrow line ⑧ in Exhibit 20.4 reflects the application of factory overhead to production. Factory overhead is applied to processes by relating overhead cost to another variable such as direct labor hours or machine hours used. With increasing automation, companies with process operations are more likely to use machine hours to allocate overhead. In some situations, a single allocation basis such as direct labor hours (or a single rate for the entire plant) fails to provide useful allocations. As a result, management can use different rates for different production departments. Based on an analysis of its operations, GenX applies its April overhead at a rate of 120% of direct labor cost, as shown in Exhibit 20.8.

Point: The time it takes to process (cycle) products through a process is sometimes used to allocate costs.

EXHIBIT 20.8

Applying Factory Overhead
(Production Department)

Overhead applied = Direct labor cost × Predetermined rate
$$\$6,840 \quad = \quad \$5,700 \quad \times \quad 120\%$$

GenX records its applied overhead with the following entry.

Assets = Liabilities + Equity
+6,840   +6,840

(8)	Goods in Process Inventory	6,840	
	Factory Overhead		6,840
	Allocated overhead costs to production at 120% of direct labor cost.		

After posting this entry, the Factory Overhead account appears as shown in Exhibit 20.9. For GenX, the amount of overhead applied equals the actual overhead incurred during April. In most cases, using a predetermined overhead rate leaves an overapplied or underapplied balance in the Factory Overhead account. At the end of the period, this overapplied or underapplied balance should be closed to the Cost of Goods Sold account, as described in the job order costing chapter.

EXHIBIT 20.9

Factory Overhead

Example: If applied overhead results in a $6,940 credit to the factory overhead account, does it yield an over- or underapplied overhead amount?
Answer: $100 overapplied overhead

Factory Overhead					Acct. No. 540
Date		Explanation	Debit	Credit	Balance
Mar.	31	Balance			0
Apr.	30	Indirect materials usage	1,195		1,195
	30	Indirect labor costs	3,220		4,415
	30	Other overhead costs	2,425		6,840
	30	Applied to production departments		6,840	0

☐ **Decision Ethics**   Answer — p. 809

Budget Officer You are working to identify the direct and indirect costs of a new processing department that has several machines. This department's manager instructs you to classify a majority of the costs as indirect to take advantage of the direct labor-based overhead allocation method so it will be charged a lower amount of overhead (because of its small direct labor cost). This would penalize other departments with higher allocations. It also will cause the performance ratings of managers in these other departments to suffer. What action do you take? ■

Answers — p. 809

Quick Check

1. A process operation (*a*) is another name for a job order operation, (*b*) does not use the concepts of direct materials or direct labor, or (*c*) typically produces large quantities of homogeneous products or services.
2. Under what conditions is a process cost accounting system more suitable for measuring production costs than a job order cost accounting system?
3. When direct materials are assigned and used in production, the entry to record their use includes (*a*) a credit to Goods in Process Inventory, (*b*) a debit to Goods in Process Inventory, or (*c*) a debit to Raw Materials Inventory.
4. What are the three cost categories incurred by both job order and process operations?
5. How many Goods in Process Inventory accounts are needed in a process cost system?

EQUIVALENT UNITS OF PRODUCTION

We explained how materials, labor, and overhead costs for a period are accumulated in the Goods in Process Inventory account, but we have not explained the arrow lines labeled ⑨ and ⑩ in Exhibit 20.4. These lines reflect the transfer of products from the production department to finished goods inventory, and from finished goods inventory to cost of goods sold. To determine the costs recorded for these flows, we must first determine the cost per unit of product and then apply this result to the number of units transferred.

 C2 Define and compute equivalent units and explain their use in process cost accounting.

Accounting for Goods in Process

If a process has *no beginning and no ending goods in process inventory,* the unit cost of goods transferred out of a process is computed as follows.

> **Total cost assigned to the process (direct materials, direct labor, and overhead)**
> **Total number of units started and finished in the period**

If a process has a beginning or ending inventory of partially processed units (or both), then the total cost assigned to the process must be allocated to all completed and incomplete units worked on during the period. Therefore, the denominator must measure the entire production activity of the process for the period, called **equivalent units of production** (or **EUP**), a phrase that refers to the number of units that could have been started *and* completed given the cost incurred during a period. This measure is then used to compute the cost per equivalent unit and to assign costs to finished goods and goods in process inventory.

To illustrate, assume that GenX adds (or introduces) 100 units into its process during a period. Suppose at the end of that period, the production supervisor determines that those 100 units are 60% of the way through the process. Therefore, equivalent units of production for that period total 60 EUP (100 units × 60%). This means that with the resources used to put 100 units 60% of the way through the process, GenX could have started and completed 60 whole units.

Point: For GenX, "units" might refer to individual Profen tablets. For a juice maker, units might refer to gallons.

Differences in Equivalent Units for Materials, Labor, and Overhead

In many processes, the equivalent units of production for direct materials are not the same with respect to direct labor and overhead. To illustrate, consider a five-step process operation shown in Exhibit 20.10.

EXHIBIT 20.10

An Illustrative Five-Step Process
Operation

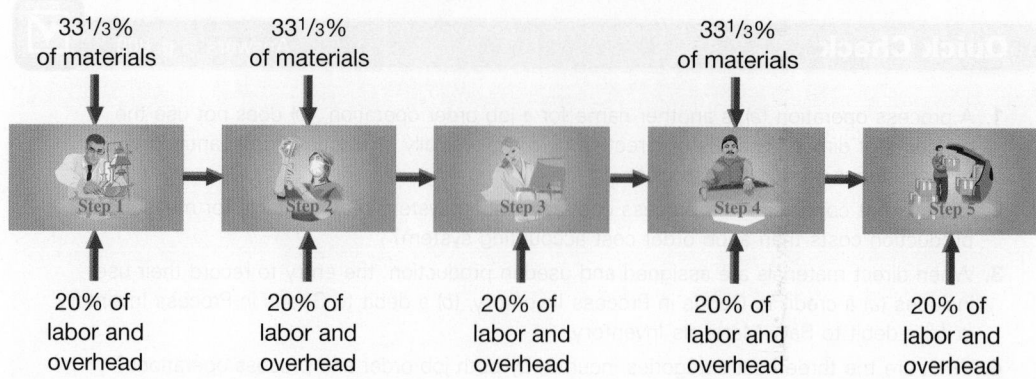

This exhibit shows that one-third of the direct material cost is added at each of three steps: 1, 2, and 4. One-fifth of the direct labor cost is added at each of the five steps. One-fifth of the overhead also is added at each step because overhead is applied as a percent of direct labor for this company.

When units finish step 1, they are one-third complete with respect to direct materials but only one-fifth complete with respect to direct labor and overhead. When they finish step 2, they are two-thirds complete with respect to direct materials but only two-fifths complete with respect to direct labor and overhead. When they finish step 3, they remain two-thirds complete with respect to materials but are now three-fifths complete with respect to labor and overhead. When they finish step 4, they are 100% complete with respect to materials (all direct materials have been added) but only four-fifths complete with respect to labor and overhead.

For example, if 300 units of product are started and processed through step 1 of Exhibit 20.10, they are said to be one-third complete *with respect to materials*. Expressed in terms of equivalent finished units, the processing of these 300 units is equal to finishing 100 EUP with respect to materials (300 units × 33⅓%). However, only one-fifth of direct labor and overhead has been applied to the 300 units at the end of step 1. This means that the equivalent units of production *with respect to labor and overhead* total 60 EUP (300 units × 20%).

▢ Decision Insight

Process Services   Customer interaction software is a hot item in customer service processes. Whether in insurance, delivery, or technology services, companies are finding that this software can turn their customer service process into an asset. How does it work? For starters, it cuts time spent on service calls because a customer describes a problem only once. It also yields a database of customer questions and complaints that gives insights into needed improvements. It recognizes incoming phone numbers and accesses previous dealings. For an example of the use of customer interaction software in an Asian company, visit the following site: www.aspect.com/Documents/CaseStudies/Aspect_AsianPaints-CS.pdf. ▪

PROCESS COSTING ILLUSTRATION

This section applies process costing concepts and procedures to GenX. **This illustration uses the weighted-average method for inventory costs. The FIFO method is illustrated in Appendix 20A.** (Assume a weighted-average cost flow for all computations and assignments in this chapter unless explicitly stated differently. When using a just-in-time inventory system, different inventory methods yield similar results because inventories are immaterial.)

Exhibit 20.11 shows selected information from the production department for the month of April. Accounting for a department's activity for a period includes four steps involving analysis of (1) physical flow, (2) equivalent units, (3) cost per equivalent unit, and (4) cost assignment and reconciliation. The next sections describe each step.

Beginning goods in process inventory (March 31)	
Units of product	30,000 units
Percentage of completion—Direct materials..................	100%
Percentage of completion—Direct labor	65%
Direct materials costs	$ 3,300
Direct labor costs	$ 600
Factory overhead costs applied (120% of direct labor)	$ 720
Activities during the current period (April)	
Units started this period	90,000 units
Units transferred out (completed)	100,000 units
Direct materials costs.....................................	$ 9,900
Direct labor costs	$ 5,700
Factory overhead costs applied (120% of direct labor)	$ 6,840
Ending goods in process inventory (April 30)	
Units of product	20,000 units
Percentage of completion—Direct materials	100%
Percentage of completion—Direct labor....................	25%

EXHIBIT 20.11

Production Data

Step 1: Determine the Physical Flow of Units

A *physical flow reconciliation* is a report that reconciles (1) the physical units started in a period with (2) the physical units completed in that period. A physical flow reconciliation for GenX is shown in Exhibit 20.12 for April.

Units to Account For		Units Accounted For	
Beginning goods in process inventory.........	30,000 units	Units completed and transferred out	100,000 units
Units started this period	90,000 units	Ending goods in process inventory.....	20,000 units
Total units to account for	**120,000 units**	Total units accounted for	**120,000 units**

reconciled

EXHIBIT 20.12

Physical Flow Reconciliation

The weighted-average method does not require us to separately track the units in beginning work in process from those units started this period. Instead, the units are treated as part of a large pool with an average cost per unit.

Step 2: Compute Equivalent Units of Production

The second step is to compute *equivalent units of production* for direct materials, direct labor, and factory overhead for April. Overhead is applied using direct labor as the allocation base for GenX. This also implies that equivalent units are the same for both labor and overhead.

GenX used its direct materials, direct labor, and overhead to make finished units of Profen and to begin processing some units that are not yet complete. We must convert the physical units measure to equivalent units based on how each input has been used. Equivalent units are computed by multiplying the number of physical units by the percentage of completion for each input—see Exhibit 20.13.

Equivalent Units of Production	Direct Materials	Direct Labor	Factory Overhead
Equivalent units completed and transferred out (100,000 × 100%)	100,000 EUP	100,000 EUP	100,000 EUP
Equivalent units for ending goods in process			
Direct materials (20,000 × 100%).................	20,000		
Direct labor (20,000 × 25%)		5,000	
Factory overhead (20,000 × 25%)			5,000
Equivalent units of production	120,000 EUP	105,000 EUP	105,000 EUP

EXHIBIT 20.13

Equivalent Units of Production— Weighted Average

The first row of Exhibit 20.13 reflects units transferred out in April. The production department entirely completed its work on the 100,000 units transferred out. These units have 100% of the materials, labor, and overhead required, or 100,000 equivalent units of each input (100,000 × 100%).

The second row references the ending goods in process, and rows three, four, and five break it down by materials, labor, and overhead. For direct materials, the units in ending goods in process inventory (20,000 physical units) include all materials required, so there are 20,000 equivalent units (20,000 × 100%) of materials in the unfinished physical units. Regarding labor, the units in ending goods in process inventory include 25% of the labor required, which implies 5,000 equivalent units of labor (20,000 × 25%). These units are only 25% complete and labor is used uniformly through the process. Overhead is applied on the basis of direct labor for GenX, so equivalent units for overhead are computed identically to labor (20,000 × 25%).

The final row reflects the whole units of product that could have been manufactured with the amount of inputs used to create some complete and some incomplete units. For GenX, the amount of inputs used to produce 100,000 complete units and to start 20,000 additional units is equivalent to the amount of direct materials in 120,000 whole units, the amount of direct labor in 105,000 whole units, and the amount of overhead in 105,000 whole units.

Step 3: Compute the Cost per Equivalent Unit

Equivalent units of production for each product (from step 2) is used to compute the average cost per equivalent unit. Under the **weighted-average method,** the computation of EUP does not separate the units in beginning inventory from those started this period; similarly, this method combines the costs of beginning goods in process inventory with the costs incurred in the current period. This process is illustrated in Exhibit 20.14.

EXHIBIT 20.14

Cost per Equivalent Unit of Production—Weighted Average

Cost per Equivalent Unit of Production	Direct Materials	Direct Labor	Factory Overhead
Costs of beginning goods in process inventory	$ 3,300	$ 600	$ 720
Costs incurred this period	9,900	5,700	6,840
Total costs	$13,200	$6,300	$7,560
÷ Equivalent units of production (from Step 2)	120,000 EUP	105,000 EUP	105,000 EUP
= Cost per equivalent unit of production	$0.11 per EUP*	$0.06 per EUP†	$0.072 per EUP‡

*$13,200 ÷ 120,000 EUP   †$6,300 ÷ 105,000 EUP   ‡$7,560 ÷ 105,000 EUP

For direct materials, the cost averages $0.11 per EUP, computed as the sum of direct materials cost from beginning goods in process inventory ($3,300) and the direct materials cost incurred in April ($9,900), and this sum ($13,200) is then divided by the 120,000 EUP for materials (from step 2). The costs per equivalent unit for labor and overhead are similarly computed. Specifically, direct labor cost averages $0.06 per EUP, computed as the sum of labor cost in beginning goods in process inventory ($600) and the labor costs incurred in April ($5,700), and this sum ($6,300) divided by 105,000 EUP for labor. Overhead costs averages $0.072 per EUP, computed as the sum of overhead cost in the beginning goods in process inventory ($720) and the overhead costs applied in April ($6,840), and this sum ($7,560) divided by 105,000 EUP for overhead.

Step 4: Assign and Reconcile Costs

The EUP from step 2 and the cost per EUP from step 3 are used in step 4 to assign costs to (a) units that production completed and transferred to finished goods and (b) units that remain in process. This is illustrated in Exhibit 20.15.

EXHIBIT 20.15

Report of Costs Accounted
For—Weighted Average

Cost of units completed and transferred out		
Direct materials (100,000 EUP × $0.11 per EUP)	$11,000	
Direct labor (100,000 EUP × $0.06 per EUP)	6,000	
Factory overhead (100,000 EUP × $0.072 per EUP)	7,200	
Cost of units completed this period		$ 24,200
Cost of ending goods in process inventory		
Direct materials (20,000 EUP × $0.11 per EUP)	2,200	
Direct labor (5,000 EUP × $0.06 per EUP)	300	
Factory overhead (5,000 EUP × $0.072 per EUP)	360	
Cost of ending goods in process inventory		2,860
Total costs accounted for		**$27,060**

Cost of Units Completed and Transferred The 100,000 units completed and transferred to finished goods inventory required 100,000 EUP of direct materials. Thus, we assign $11,000 (100,000 EUP × $0.11 per EUP) of direct materials cost to those units. Similarly, those units had received 100,000 EUP of direct labor and 100,000 EUP of factory overhead (recall Exhibit 20.13). Thus, we assign $6,000 (100,000 EUP × $0.06 per EUP) of direct labor and $7,200 (100,000 EUP × $0.072 per EUP) of overhead to those units. The total cost of the 100,000 completed and transferred units is $24,200 ($11,000 + $6,000 + $7,200) and their average cost per unit is $0.242 ($24,200 ÷ 100,000 units).

Cost of Units for Ending Goods in Process There are 20,000 incomplete units in goods in process inventory at period-end. For direct materials, those units have 20,000 EUP of material (from step 2) at a cost of $0.11 per EUP (from step 3), which yields the materials cost of goods in process inventory of $2,200 (20,000 EUP × $0.11 per EUP). For direct labor, the in-process units have 25% of the required labor, or 5,000 EUP (from step 2). Using the $0.06 labor cost per EUP (from step 3) we obtain the labor cost of goods in process inventory of $300 (5,000 EUP × $0.06 per EUP). For overhead, the in-process units reflect 5,000 EUP (from step 2). Using the $0.072 overhead cost per EUP (from step 3) we obtain overhead costs with in-process inventory of $360 (5,000 EUP × $0.072 per EUP). Total cost of goods in process inventory at period-end is $2,860 ($2,200 + $300 + $360).

As a check, management verifies that total costs assigned to those units completed and transferred plus the costs of those in process (from Exhibit 20.15) equal the costs incurred by production. Exhibit 20.16 shows the costs incurred by production this period. We then reconcile the *costs accounted for* in Exhibit 20.15 with the *costs to account for* in Exhibit 20.16.

EXHIBIT 20.16

Report of Costs to Account
For—Weighted Average

Cost of beginning goods in process inventory		
Direct materials	$3,300	
Direct labor	600	
Factory overhead	720	$ 4,620
Cost incurred this period		
Direct materials	9,900	
Direct labor	5,700	
Factory overhead	6,840	22,440
Total costs to account for		**$27,060**

At GenX, the production department manager is responsible for $27,060 in costs: $4,620 that is assigned to the goods in process at the start of the period plus $22,440 of materials, labor, and overhead incurred in the period. At period-end, that manager must show where these costs are assigned. The manager for GenX reports that $2,860 are assigned to units in process and $24,200 are assigned to units completed (per Exhibit 20.15). The sum of these amounts equals $27,060. Thus, the total *costs to account for* equal the total *costs accounted for* (minor differences can sometimes occur from rounding).

C3	Define and prepare a process cost summary and describe its purposes.

Point: Managers can examine changes in monthly costs per equivalent unit to help control the production process. When prices are set in a competitive market, managers can use process cost summary information to determine which costs should be cut to achieve a profit.

Process Cost Summary An important managerial accounting report for a process cost accounting system is the **process cost summary** (also called *production report*), which is prepared separately for each process or production department. Three reasons for the summary are to (1) help department managers control and monitor their departments, (2) help factory managers evaluate department managers' performances, and (3) provide cost information for financial statements. A process cost summary achieves these purposes by describing the costs charged to each department, reporting the equivalent units of production achieved by each department, and determining the costs assigned to each department's output. For our purposes, it is prepared using a combination of Exhibits 20.13, 20.14, 20.15, and 20.16.

The process cost summary for GenX is shown in Exhibit 20.17. The report is divided into three sections. Section ①︎ lists the total costs charged to the department, including direct materials, direct labor, and overhead costs incurred, as well as the cost of the beginning goods in process inventory. Section ②︎ describes the equivalent units of production for the department. Equivalent units for materials, labor, and overhead are in separate columns. It also reports direct

EXHIBIT 20.17

Process Cost Summary

GenX COMPANY
Process Cost Summary
For Month Ended April 30, 2011

Costs Charged to Production

Costs of beginning goods in process

Direct materials	$3,300	
Direct labor	600	
Factory overhead	720	$ 4,620

Costs incurred this period

Direct materials	9,900	
Direct labor	5,700	
Factory overhead	6,840	22,440
Total costs to account for		$27,060

Unit Cost Information

Units to account for:		Units accounted for:	
Beginning goods in process	30,000	Completed and transferred out	100,000
Units started this period	90,000	Ending goods in process	20,000
Total units to account for	120,000	Total units accounted for	120,000

Equivalent Units of Production (EUP)	**Direct Materials**	**Direct Labor**	**Factory Overhead**
Units completed and transferred out	100,000 EUP	100,000 EUP	100,000 EUP
Units of ending goods in process			
Direct materials (20,000 × 100%)	20,000		
Direct labor (20,000 × 25%)		5,000	
Factory overhead (20,000 × 25%)			5,000
Equivalent units of production	120,000 EUP	105,000 EUP	105,000 EUP

Cost per EUP	**Direct Materials**	**Direct Labor**	**Factory Overhead**
Costs of beginning goods in process	$ 3,300	$ 600	$ 720
Costs incurred this period	9,900	5,700	6,840
Total costs	$13,200	$6,300	$7,560
÷EUP	120,000 EUP	105,000 EUP	105,000 EUP
Cost per EUP	$0.11 per EUP	$0.06 per EUP	$0.072 per EUP

Cost Assignment and Reconciliation

Costs transferred out (cost of goods manufactured)

Direct materials (100,000 EUP × $0.11 per EUP)	$11,000	
Direct labor (100,000 EUP × $0.06 per EUP)	6,000	
Factory overhead (100,000 EUP × $0.072 per EUP)	7,200	$ 24,200

Costs of ending goods in process

Direct materials (20,000 EUP × $0.11 per EUP)	2,200	
Direct labor (5,000 EUP × $0.06 per EUP)	300	
Factory overhead (5,000 EUP × $0.072 per EUP)	360	2,860
Total costs accounted for		$27,060

reconciled

materials, direct labor, and overhead costs per equivalent unit. Section ◇3◇ allocates total costs among units worked on in the period. The $24,200 is the total cost of goods transferred out of the department, and the $2,860 is the cost of partially processed ending inventory units. The assigned costs are then added to show that the total $27,060 cost charged to the department in section ◇1◇ is now assigned to the units in section ◇3◇.

Quick Check

Answers — p. 809

6. Equivalent units are (*a*) a measure of a production department's productivity in using direct materials, direct labor, or overhead; (*b*) units of a product produced by a foreign competitor that are similar to units produced by a domestic company; or (*c*) generic units of a product similar to brand name units of a product.

7. Interpret the meaning of a department's equivalent units with respect to direct labor.

8. A department began the period with 8,000 units that were one-fourth complete with respect to direct labor. It completed 58,000 units, and ended with 6,000 units that were one-third complete with respect to direct labor. What were its direct labor equivalent units for the period using the weighted-average method?

9. A process cost summary for a department has three sections. What information is presented in each of them?

Transfers to Finished Goods Inventory and Cost of Goods Sold

Arrow line ⑨ in Exhibit 20.4 reflects the transfer of completed products from production to finished goods inventory. The process cost summary shows that the 100,000 units of finished Profen are assigned a cost of $24,200. The entry to record this transfer follows.

P4 Record the transfer of completed goods to Finished Goods Inventory and Cost of Goods Sold.

⑨	Finished Goods Inventory	24,200	
	Goods in Process Inventory.		24,200
	To record transfer of completed units.		

Assets = Liabilities + Equity
+24,200
−24,200

The credit to Goods in Process Inventory reduces that asset balance to reflect that 100,000 units are no longer in production. The cost of these units has been transferred to Finished Goods Inventory, which is recognized as a $24,200 increase in this asset. After this entry is posted, there remains a balance of $2,860 in the Goods in Process Inventory account, which is the amount computed in Step 4 previously. The cost of units transferred from Goods in Process Inventory to Finished Goods Inventory is called the **cost of goods manufactured.** Exhibit 20.18 reveals the activities in the Goods in Process Inventory account for this period. The ending balance of this account equals the cost assigned to the partially completed units in section ◇3◇ of Exhibit 20.17.

Goods in Process Inventory				Acct. No. 134	
Date		Explanation	Debit	Credit	Balance
Mar.	31	Balance			4,620
Apr.	30	Direct materials usage	9,900		14,520
	30	Direct labor costs incurred	5,700		20,220
	30	Factory overhead applied	6,840		27,060
	30	Transfer completed product to warehouse		24,200	2,860

EXHIBIT 20.18

Goods in Process Inventory

Arrow line ⑩ in Exhibit 20.4 reflects the sale of finished goods. Assume that GenX sold 106,000 units of Profen this period, and that its beginning inventory of finished goods consisted of 26,000 units with a cost of $6,292. Also assume that its ending finished goods inventory consists of 20,000 units at a cost of $4,840. Using this information, we can compute its cost of goods sold for April as shown in Exhibit 20.19.

Point: We omit the journal entry for sales, but it totals the number of units sold times price per unit.

EXHIBIT 20.19

Cost of Goods Sold

Beginning finished goods inventory	$ 6,292
+ Cost of goods manufactured this period	24,200
= Cost of goods available for sale	$30,492
− Ending finished goods inventory	4,840
= Cost of goods sold	$25,652

The summary entry to record cost of goods sold for this period follows.

Assets = Liabilities + Equity
−25,652   −25,652

		Debit	Credit
⑩	Cost of Goods Sold	25,652	
	Finished Goods Inventory		25,652
	To record cost of goods sold for April.		

The Finished Goods Inventory account now appears as shown in Exhibit 20.20.

EXHIBIT 20.20

Finished Goods Inventory

Finished Goods Inventory					Acct. No. 135	
Date		**Explanation**		**Debit**	**Credit**	**Balance**
Mar.	31	Balance				6,292
Apr.	30	Transfer in cost of goods manufactured		24,200		30,492
	30	Cost of goods sold			25,652	4,840

Summary of Cost Flows   Exhibit 20.21 shows GenX's manufacturing cost flows for April. Each of these cost flows and the entries to record them have been explained. The flow of costs through the accounts reflects the flow of production activities and products.

EXHIBIT 20.21*

Cost Flows through GenX

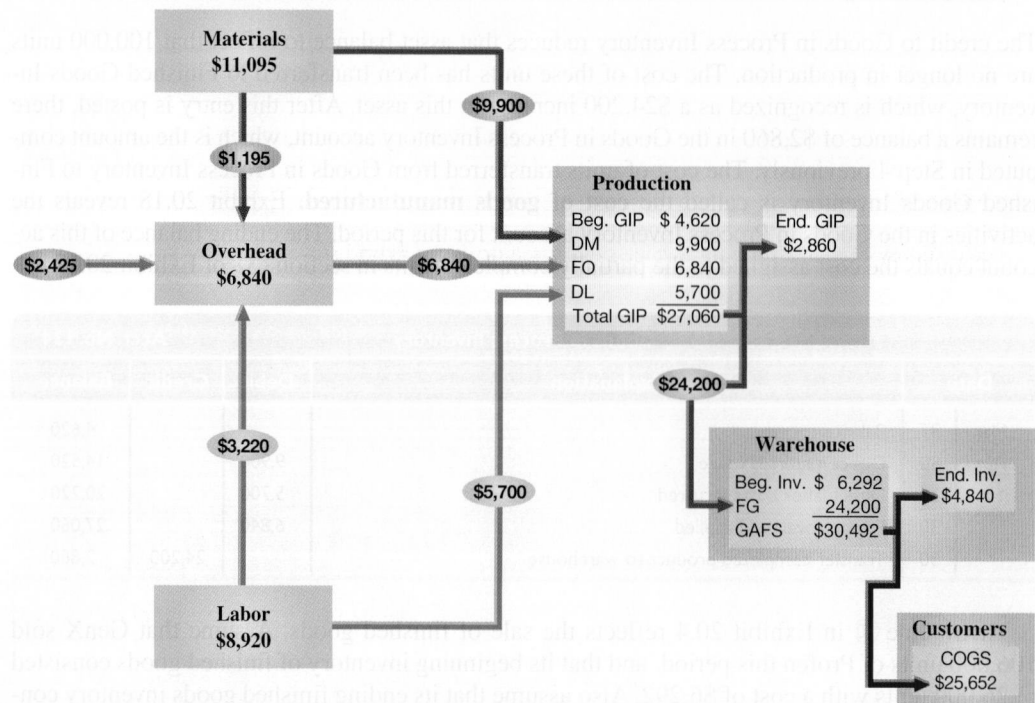

*Abbreviations: GIP (goods in process); DM (direct materials); DL (direct labor); FO (factory overhead);
FG (finished goods); GAFS (goods available for sale); COGS (cost of goods sold).

Trends in Process Operations

Some of the recent trends in process operations are discussed in the following paragraphs.

Process Design Management concerns with production efficiency can lead companies to entirely reorganize production processes. For example, instead of producing different types of computers in a series of departments, a separate work center for each computer can be established in one department. The process cost system is then changed to account for each work center's costs.

Just-in-Time Production Companies are increasingly adopting just-in-time techniques. With a just-in-time inventory system, inventory levels can be minimal. If raw materials are not ordered or received until needed, a Raw Materials Inventory account might be unnecessary. Instead, materials cost is immediately debited to the Goods in Process Inventory account. Similarly, a Finished Goods Inventory account may not be needed. Instead, cost of finished goods may be immediately debited to the Cost of Goods Sold account.

Automation Advances in technology increasingly enable companies to automate their production processes. This allows them to reduce direct labor costs. Reflecting this, some companies focus on **conversion costs per equivalent unit,** which is the combined costs of direct labor and factory overhead per equivalent unit.

Services Service-based businesses are increasingly prevalent. For routine, standardized services like oil changes and simple tax returns, computing costs based on the process is simpler and more useful than a cost per individual job.

Customer Orientation Focus on customer orientation also leads to improved processes. A manufacturer of control devices improved quality and reduced production time by forming teams to study processes and suggest improvements. An ice cream maker studied customer tastes to develop a more pleasing ice cream texture.

Hybrid Costing System		Decision Analysis

This chapter explained the process costing system and contrasted it with the job order costing system. Many organizations use a *hybrid system* that contains features of both process and job order operations. A recent survey of manufacturers revealed that a majority use hybrid systems.

 **A2** Explain and illustrate a hybrid costing system.

To illustrate, consider a car manufacturer's assembly line. On one hand, the line resembles a process operation in that the assembly steps for each car are nearly identical. On the other hand, the specifications of most cars have several important differences. At the Ford Mustang plant, each car assembled on a given day can be different from the previous car and the next car. This means that the costs of materials (subassemblies or components) for each car can differ. Accordingly, while the conversion costs (direct labor and overhead) can be accounted for using a process costing system, the component costs (direct materials) are accounted for using a job order system (separately for each car or type of car).

A hybrid system of processes requires a *hybrid costing system* to properly cost products or services. In the Ford plant, the assembly costs per car are readily determined using process costing. The costs of additional components can then be added to the assembly costs to determine each car's total cost (as in job order costing). To illustrate, consider the following information for a daily assembly process at Ford.

Assembly process costs	
Direct materials	$10,600,000
Direct labor	$5,800,000
Factory overhead	$6,200,000
Number of cars assembled	1,000
Costs of three different types of steering wheels	$240, $330, $480
Costs of three different types of seats	$620, $840, $1,360

The assembly process costs $22,600 per car. Depending on the type of steering wheel and seats the customer requests, the cost of a car can range from $23,460 to $24,440 (a $980 difference).

Today companies are increasingly trying to standardize processes while attempting to meet individual customer needs. To the extent that differences among individual customers' requests are large, understanding the costs to satisfy those requests is important. Thus, monitoring and controlling both process and job order costs are important.

■ Decision Ethics   Answer — p. 809

Entrepreneur   You operate a process production company making similar products for three different customers. One customer demands 100% quality inspection of products at your location before shipping. The added costs of that inspection are spread across all customers, not just the one demanding it. If you charge the added costs to that customer, you could lose that customer and experience a loss. Moreover, your other two customers have agreed to pay 110% of full costs. What actions (if any) do you take? ■

DEMONSTRATION PROBLEM

Pennsylvania Company produces a product that passes through a single production process. Then completed products are transferred to finished goods in its warehouse. Information related to its manufacturing activities for July follows.

Raw Materials

Beginning inventory	$100,000
Raw materials purchased on credit	211,400
Direct materials used	(190,000)
Indirect materials used	(51,400)
Ending inventory	$ 70,000

Factory Payroll

Direct labor incurred	$ 55,500
Indirect labor incurred	50,625
Total payroll (paid in cash)	$106,125

Factory Overhead

Indirect materials used	$ 51,400
Indirect labor used	50,625
Other overhead costs	71,725
Total factory overhead incurred	$173,750

Factory Overhead Applied

Overhead applied (200% of direct labor)	$111,000

Production Department

Beginning goods in process inventory (units)	5,000
Percentage completed—Materials	100%
Percentage completed—Labor and overhead	60%
Beginning goods in process inventory (costs)	
Direct materials used	$ 20,000
Direct labor incurred	9,600
Overhead applied (200% of direct labor)	19,200
Total costs of beginning goods in process	$ 48,800
Units started this period	20,000
Units completed this period	17,000
Ending goods in process inventory (units)	8,000
Percentage completed—Materials	100%
Percentage completed—Labor and overhead	20%

Finished Goods Inventory

Beginning finished goods inventory	$ 96,400
Cost transferred in from production	321,300
Cost of goods sold	(345,050)
Ending finished goods inventory	$ 72,650

Required

1. Prepare a physical flow reconciliation for July as illustrated in Exhibit 20.12.
2. Compute the equivalent units of production in July for direct materials, direct labor, and factory overhead.
3. Compute the costs per equivalent units of production in July for direct materials, direct labor, and factory overhead.
4. Prepare a report of costs accounted for and a report of costs to account for.
5. Prepare summary journal entries to record the transactions and events of July for (a) raw materials purchases, (b) direct materials usage, (c) indirect materials usage, (d) factory payroll costs, (e) direct labor usage, (f) indirect labor usage, (g) other overhead costs (credit Other Accounts), (h) application of overhead to production, (i) transfer of finished goods from production, and (j) the cost of goods sold.

PLANNING THE SOLUTION

- Track the physical flow to determine the number of units completed in July.
- Compute the equivalent unit of production for direct materials, direct labor, and factory overhead.
- Compute the costs per equivalent unit of production with respect to direct materials, direct labor, and overhead; and determine the cost per unit for each.
- Compute the total cost of the goods transferred to production by using the equivalent units and unit costs. Determine (a) the cost of the beginning in-process inventory, (b) the materials, labor, and overhead costs added to the beginning in-process inventory, and (c) the materials, labor, and overhead costs added to the units started and completed in the month.
- Determine the cost of goods sold using balances in finished goods and cost of units completed this period.
- Use the information to record the summary journal entries for July.

SOLUTION TO DEMONSTRATION PROBLEM

1. Physical flow reconciliation.

Units to Account For		Units Accounted For	
Beginning goods in process inventory..........	5,000 units	Units completed and transferred out	17,000 units
Units started this period......	20,000 units	Ending goods in process inventory......	8,000 units
Total units to account for	**25,000 units**	Total units accounted for	**25,000 units**

reconciled

2. Equivalent units of production.

Equivalent Units of Production	Direct Materials	Direct Labor	Factory Overhead
Equivalent units completed and transferred out	17,000 EUP	17,000 EUP	17,000 EUP
Equivalent units in ending goods in process			
Direct materials (8,000 × 100%)	8,000		
Direct labor (8,000 × 20%)		1,600	
Factory overhead (8,000 × 20%)			1,600
Equivalent units of production	25,000 EUP	18,600 EUP	18,600 EUP

3. Costs per equivalent unit of production.

Costs per Equivalent Unit of Production	Direct Materials	Direct Labor	Factory Overhead
Costs of beginning goods in process	$ 20,000	$ 9,600	$ 19,200
Costs incurred this period	190,000	55,500	111,000*
Total costs	$210,000	$65,100	$130,200
÷ Equivalent units of production (from part 2)..	25,000 EUP	18,600 EUP	18,600 EUP
= Costs per equivalent unit of production	$8.40 per EUP	$3.50 per EUP	$7.00 per EUP

*Factory overhead applied

4. Reports of costs accounted for and of costs to account for

Report of Costs Accounted For

Cost of units transferred out (cost of goods manufactured)

Direct materials ($8.40 per EUP × 17,000 EUP)	$142,800	
Direct labor ($3.50 per EUP × 17,000 EUP)	59,500	
Factory overhead ($7.00 per EUP × 17,000 EUP)	119,000	
Cost of units completed this period		$ 321,300

Cost of ending goods in process inventory

Direct materials ($8.40 per EUP × 8,000 EUP)	67,200	
Direct labor ($3.50 per EUP × 1,600 EUP)	5,600	
Factory overhead ($7.00 per EUP × 1,600 EUP)	11,200	
Cost of ending goods in process inventory		84,000
Total costs accounted for		**$405,300**

Report of Costs to Account For

Cost of beginning goods in process inventory

Direct materials	$ 20,000	
Direct labor	9,600	
Factory overhead	19,200	$ 48,800

Cost incurred this period

Direct materials	190,000	
Direct labor	55,500	
Factory overhead	111,000	356,500
Total costs to account for		**$405,300**

reconciled

5. Summary journal entries for the transactions and events in July.

a.	Raw Materials Inventory	211,400	
	Accounts Payable		211,400
	To record raw materials purchases.		
b.	Goods in Process Inventory	190,000	
	Raw Materials Inventory		190,000
	To record direct materials usage.		
c.	Factory Overhead	51,400	
	Raw Materials Inventory		51,400
	To record indirect materials usage.		
d.	Factory Payroll	106,125	
	Cash		106,125
	To record factory payroll costs.		
e.	Goods in Process Inventory	55,500	
	Factory Payroll		55,500
	To record direct labor usage.		
f.	Factory Overhead	50,625	
	Factory Payroll		50,625
	To record indirect labor usage.		

g.	Factory Overhead	71,725	
	Other Accounts		71,725
	To record other overhead costs.		
h.	Goods in Process Inventory	111,000	
	Factory Overhead		111,000
	To record application of overhead.		
i.	Finished Goods Inventory	321,300	
	Goods in Process Inventory		321,300
	To record transfer of finished goods from production.		
j.	Cost of Goods Sold	345,050	
	Finished Goods Inventory		345,050
	To record cost of goods sold.		

FIFO Method of Process Costing

20A

C4	Explain and illustrate the accounting for production activity using FIFO.

The **FIFO method** of process costing assigns costs to units assuming a first-in, first-out flow of product. The objectives, concepts, and journal entries (not amounts) are the same as for the weighted-average method, but computation of equivalent units of production and cost assignment are slightly different.

Exhibit 20A.1 shows selected information from GenX's production department for the month of April. Accounting for a department's activity for a period includes four steps: (1) determine physical flow, (2) compute equivalent units, (3) compute cost per equivalent unit, and (4) determine cost assignment and reconciliation. This appendix describes each of these steps using the FIFO method for process costing.

EXHIBIT 20A.1

Production Data

Beginning goods in process inventory (March 31)	
Units of product	30,000 units
Percentage of completion—Direct materials	100%
Percentage of completion—Direct labor	65%
Direct materials costs	$ 3,300
Direct labor costs	$ 600
Factory overhead costs applied (120% of direct labor)	$ 720
Activities during the current period (April)	
Units started this period	90,000 units
Units transferred out (completed)	100,000 units
Direct materials costs	$ 9,900
Direct labor costs	$ 5,700
Factory overhead costs applied (120% of direct labor)	$ 6,840
Ending goods in process inventory (April 30)	
Units of product	20,000 units
Percentage of completion—Direct materials	100%
Percentage of completion—Direct labor	25%

Step 1: Determine Physical Flow of Units A *physical flow reconciliation* is a report that reconciles (1) the physical units started in a period with (2) the physical units completed in that period. The physical flow reconciliation for GenX is shown in Exhibit 20A.2 for April.

EXHIBIT 20A.2

Physical Flow Reconciliation

Units to Account For		Units Accounted For	
Beginning goods in process inventory.	30,000 units	Units completed and transferred out	100,000 units
Units started this period	90,000 units	Ending goods in process inventory	20,000 units
Total units to account for	**120,000 units**	Total units accounted for	**120,000 units**

reconciled

FIFO assumes that the 100,000 units transferred to finished goods during April include the 30,000 units from the beginning goods in process inventory. The remaining 70,000 units transferred out are from units started in April. Of the total 90,000 units started in April, 70,000 were completed, leaving 20,000 units unfinished at period-end.

Step 2: Compute Equivalent Units of Production—FIFO GenX used its direct materials, direct labor, and overhead both to make complete units of Profen and to start some units that are not yet complete. We need to convert the physical measure of units to equivalent units based on how much of each input has been used. We do this by multiplying the number of physical units by the percentage of processing applied to those units in the current period; this is done for each input (materials, labor, and overhead). The FIFO method accounts for cost flow in a sequential manner—earliest costs are the first to flow out. (This is different from the weighted-average method, which combines prior period costs—those in beginning Goods in Process Inventory—with costs incurred in the current period.)

Three distinct groups of units must be considered in determining the equivalent units of production under the FIFO method: (a) units in beginning Goods in Process Inventory that were completed this period, (b) units started *and* completed this period, and (c) units in ending Goods in Process Inventory. We must determine how much material, labor, and overhead are used for each of these unit groups. These computations are shown in Exhibit 20A.3. The remainder of this section explains these computations.

EXHIBIT 20A.3

Equivalent Units of Production—FIFO

Equivalent Units of Production	Direct Materials	Direct Labor	Factory Overhead
(a) Equivalent units to complete beginning goods in process			
Direct materials (30,000 × 0%)	0 EUP		
Direct labor (30,000 × 35%)		10,500 EUP	
Factory overhead (30,000 × 35%)			10,500 EUP
(b) Equivalent units started and completed*	70,000	70,000	70,000
(c) Equivalent units in ending goods in process			
Direct materials (20,000 × 100%)	20,000		
Direct labor (20,000 × 25%)		5,000	
Factory overhead (20,000 × 25%)			5,000
Equivalent units of production	90,000 EUP	85,500 EUP	85,500 EUP

*Units completed this period .... 100,000 units
Less units in beginning goods in process 30,000
Units started and completed this period .... 70,000 units

(a) Beginning Goods in Process   Under FIFO, we assume that production first completes any units started in the prior period. There were 30,000 physical units in beginning goods in process inventory. Those units were 100% complete with respect to direct materials as at the end of the prior period. This means that no materials (0%) are needed in April to complete those 30,000 units. So the equivalent units of *materials* to complete beginning goods in process are zero (30,000 × 0%)—see first row under row "(a)" in Exhibit 20A.3. The units in process as at April 1 had already been through 65% of production prior to this period and need only go through the remaining 35% of production. The equivalent units of *labor* to complete the beginning goods in process are 10,500 (30,000 × 35%)—see the second row under row "(a)." This implies that the amount of labor required this period to complete the 30,000 units started in the prior period is the amount of labor needed to make 10,500 units, start-to-finish. Finally, overhead is applied based on direct labor costs, so GenX computes equivalent units for overhead as it would for direct labor.

(b) Units Started and Completed This Period   After completing any beginning goods in process, FIFO assumes that production begins on newly started units. GenX began work on 90,000 new units this period. Of those units, 20,000 remain incomplete at period-end. This means that 70,000 of the units started in April were completed in April. These complete units have received 100% of materials, labor, and overhead. Exhibit 20A.3 reflects this by including 70,000 equivalent units (70,000 × 100%) of materials, labor, and overhead in its equivalent units of production—see row "(b)."

(c) Ending Goods in Process   The 20,000 units started in April that GenX was not able to complete by period-end consumed materials, labor, and overhead. Specifically, those 20,000 units received 100% of materials and, therefore, the equivalent units of materials in ending goods in process inventory are 20,000 (20,000 × 100%)—see the first row under row "(c)." For labor and overhead, the units in ending goods in process were 25% complete in production. This means the equivalent units of labor and overhead for those units are 5,000 (20,000 × 25%) as GenX incurs labor and overhead costs uniformly throughout its production process. Finally, for each input (direct materials, direct labor, and factory overhead), the equivalent units for each of the unit groups (a), (b), and (c) are added to determine the total equivalent units of production with respect to each—see the final row in Exhibit 20A.3.

Step 3: Compute Cost per Equivalent Unit—FIFO   To compute cost per equivalent unit, we take the product costs (for each of direct materials, direct labor, and factory overhead from Exhibit 20A.1) added in April and divide by the equivalent units of production from step 2. Exhibit 20A.4 illustrates these computations.

EXHIBIT 20A.4

Cost per Equivalent Unit of Production—FIFO

Cost per Equivalent Unit of Production	Direct Materials	Direct Labor	Factory Overhead
Costs incurred this period	$9,900	$5,700	$6,840
÷ Equivalent units of production (from Step 2)	90,000 EUP	85,500 EUP	85,500 EUP
Cost per equivalent unit of production	$0.11 per EUP	$0.067 per EUP	$0.08 per EUP

It is essential to compute costs per equivalent unit for *each* input because production inputs are added at different times in the process. The FIFO method computes the cost per equivalent unit based solely on this period's EUP and costs (unlike the weighted-average method, which adds in the costs of the beginning goods in process inventory).

Step 4: Assign and Reconcile Costs   The equivalent units determined in step 2 and the cost per equivalent unit computed in step 3 are both used to assign costs (1) to units that the production department completed and transferred to finished goods and (2) to units that remain in process at period-end.

In Exhibit 20A.5, under the section for cost of units transferred out, we see that the cost of units completed in April includes the $4,620 cost carried over from March for work already applied to the 30,000 units that make up beginning Goods in Process Inventory, plus the $1,544 incurred in April to complete those units. This section also includes the $17,990 of cost assigned to the 70,000 units started and completed this period. Thus, the total cost of goods manufactured in April is $24,154 ($4,620 + $1,544 + $17,990). The average cost per unit for goods completed in April is $0.242 ($24,154 ÷ 100,000 completed units).

EXHIBIT 20A.5

Report of Costs Accounted
For—FIFO

Cost of units transferred out (cost of goods manufactured)		
Cost of beginning goods in process inventory.............................		$ 4,620
Cost to complete beginning goods in process		
Direct materials ($0.11 per EUP × 0 EUP).............................	$ 0	
Direct labor ($0.067 per EUP × 10,500 EUP)	704	
Factory overhead ($0.08 per EUP × 10,500 EUP)	840	1,544
Cost of units started and completed this period		
Direct materials ($0.11 per EUP × 70,000 EUP)	7,700	
Direct labor ($0.067 per EUP × 70,000 EUP)	4,690	
Factory overhead ($0.08 per EUP × 70,000 EUP)	5,600	17,990
Total cost of units finished this period................................		24,154
Cost of ending goods in process inventory		
Direct materials ($0.11 per EUP × 20,000 EUP)	2,200	
Direct labor ($0.067 per EUP × 5,000 EUP)	335	
Factory overhead ($0.08 per EUP × 5,000 EUP)	400	
Total cost of ending goods in process inventory		2,935
Total costs accounted for		**$27,089**

The computation for cost of ending goods in process inventory is in the lower part of Exhibit 20A.5. The cost of units in process includes materials, labor, and overhead costs corresponding to the percentage of these resources applied to those incomplete units in April. That cost of $2,935 ($2,200 + $335 + $400) also is the ending balance for the Goods in Process Inventory account.

Management verifies that the total costs assigned to units transferred out and units still in process equal the total costs incurred by production. We reconcile the costs accounted for (in Exhibit 20A.5) to the costs that production was charged for as shown in Exhibit 20A.6.

EXHIBIT 20A.6

Report of Costs to
Account For—FIFO

Cost of beginning goods in process inventory		
Direct materials	$3,300	
Direct labor	600	
Factory overhead...	720	$ 4,620
Costs incurred this period		
Direct materials	9,900	
Direct labor..	5,700	
Factory overhead...	6,840	22,440
Total costs to account for		**$27,060**

The production manager is responsible for $27,060 in costs: $4,620 that had been assigned to the department's Goods in Process Inventory as at April 1 plus $22,440 of materials, labor, and overhead costs the department incurred in April. At period-end, the manager must identify where those costs were assigned. The production manager can report that $24,154 of cost was assigned to units completed in April and $2,935 was assigned to units still in process at period-end. The sum of these amounts is $29 different from the $27,060 total costs incurred by production due to rounding in step 3—rounding errors are common and not a concern.

The final report is the process cost summary, which summarizes key information from Exhibits 20A.3, 20A.4, 20A.5, and 20A.6. Reasons for the summary are to (1) help managers control and monitor costs, (2) help upper management assess department manager performance, and (3) provide cost information for financial reporting. The process cost summary, using FIFO, for GenX is in Exhibit 20A.7. Section ◇ lists

EXHIBIT 20A.7

Process Cost Summary

GenX COMPANY
Process Cost Summary
For Month Ended April 30, 2011

Costs charged to production

Costs of beginning goods in process inventory

Direct materials	$3,300	
Direct labor	600	
Factory overhead	720	$ 4,620

Costs incurred this period

Direct materials	9,900	
Direct labor	5,700	
Factory overhead	6,840	22,440
Total costs to account for		$27,060

Unit cost information

Units to account for		Units accounted for	
Beginning goods in process	30,000	Transferred out	100,000
Units started this period	90,000	Ending goods in process	20,000
Total units to account for	120,000	Total units accounted for	120,000

Equivalent units of production	Direct Materials	Direct Labor	Factory Overhead
Equivalent units to complete beginning goods in process			
Direct materials (30,000 × 0%)	0 EUP		
Direct labor (30,000 × 35%)		10,500 EUP	
Factory overhead (30,000 × 35%)			10,500 EUP
Equivalent units started and completed	70,000	70,000	70,000
Equivalent units in ending goods in process			
Direct materials (20,000 × 100%)	20,000		
Direct labor (20,000 × 25%)		5,000	
Factory overhead (20,000 × 25%)			5000
Equivalent units of production	90,000 EUP	85,500 EUP	85,500 EUP

Cost per equivalent unit of production	Direct Materials	Direct Labor	Factory Overhead
Costs incurred this period	$9,900	$5,700	$6,840
÷ Equivalent units of production	90,000 EUP	85,500 EUP	85,500 EUP
Cost per equivalent unit of production	$0.11 per EUP	$0.067 per EUP	$0.08 per EUP

Cost assignment and reconciliation

(cost of units completed and transferred out)

Cost of beginning goods in process		$ 4,620

Cost to complete beginning goods in process

Direct materials ($0.11 per EUP × 0 EUP)	$ 0	
Direct labor ($0.067 per EUP × 10,500 EUP)	704	
Factory overhead ($0.08 per EUP × 10,500 EUP)	840	1,544

Cost of units started and completed this period

Direct materials ($0.11 per EUP × 70,000 EUP)	7,700	
Direct labor ($0.067 per EUP × 70,000 EUP)	4,690	
Factory overhead ($0.08 per EUP × 70,000 EUP)	5,600	17,990
Total cost of units finished this period		24,154

Cost of ending goods in process

Direct materials ($0.11 per EUP × 20,000 EUP)	2,200	
Direct labor ($0.067 per EUP × 5,000 EUP)	335	
Factory overhead ($0.08 per EUP × 5,000 EUP)	400	
Total cost of ending goods in process		2,935
Total costs accounted for		$27,089*

reconciled

*$29 difference due to rounding

the total costs charged to the department, including direct materials, direct labor, and overhead costs incurred, as well as the cost of the beginning goods in process inventory. Section ② describes the equivalent units of production for the department. Equivalent units for materials, labor, and overhead are in separate columns. It also reports direct materials, direct labor, and overhead costs per equivalent unit. Section ③ allocates total costs among units worked on in the period.

Decision Maker   Answer — p. 809

Cost Manager   As cost manager for an electronics manufacturer, you apply a process costing system using FIFO. Your company plans to adopt a just-in-time system and eliminate inventories. What is the impact of the use of FIFO (versus the weighted-average method) given these plans? ∎

SERVICE COSTING

What is a Service?   *Service* refers to the act of doing work for someone. In the context of a business, service can refer to the work done by an organization for a customer. An example is legal service provided by a law firm to a client. Service can also be provided by a department within an organization to another department within the same organization. Legal services could be provided by the legal department to the purchasing department, both within the same organization.

Service organizations are all around us. These include hospitals providing medical services, audit firms providing auditing services, travel agencies providing ticketing services, software companies providing programming services, and universities providing educational services.

Special features in costing for services: In costing for services, three key points need to be noted:

1. Labor is a more significant element of cost than materials. In manufacturing, materials cost is more significant than labor.
2. In general, service cost cannot be inventoried. There are some exceptions to this rule, which will be discussed later in this section.
3. Cost objects can be distinctive to the service being provided.

Programming services provided by a software company can be used to illustrate the three points made above. Software programs are written by programmers. Programming requires the labor of programmers but no significant materials as inputs. The cost of programming service will predominantly consist of labor, both direct and indirect.

While programmers may need furniture and computers to work with, the programs they write are not inventoried. Contrast a software company with a steel manufacturer. A steel manufacturer would carry inventories of raw materials such as iron ore, work-in-process inventory of steel in the making, and inventories of finished steel waiting to be shipped to customers. Programming services require no raw materials nor can they be inventoried as finished products. There can, however, be work-in-process inventory of programming services.

Continuing with the example of a software company, consider a multiyear project being executed by the company. The company would invoice a customer periodically during the course of the contract, based on achievement of milestones as laid out in the contract. At the end of an accounting period, the company may have incurred costs on services which remain not billed because no billable milestone has been achieved. The company would treat costs not billed at the end of an accounting period as work-in-process, to be carried forward to the next accounting period as an asset in the statement of financial position.

In manufacturing, final outputs are measured in weight or volume. In service organizations definitions of the final output are based on the distinctive nature of their services. An audit or a consulting firm would compile its costs per *person hour*. A passenger airline would use *passenger miles* as its cost object. The rooms division of a hotel would use *room nights*.

Methods of costing: As in manufacturing, either job, process, or a hybrid method of costing can be used to cost for services. Services such as audit or consulting for a client are costed using job costing. Each audit or consulting assignment is a distinct block of service that can be treated as a job. Services such as lodging services provided by hotels are costed using process costing. The costs of maintaining and servicing a room are accumulated over a period and divided by the number of room nights available for that period. Likewise, universities would use process costing to divide the accumulated costs of providing services by the number of students to determine the cost per student. A hotel that uses process costing to cost its room night would also use job costing to cost for and price its conferencing services. Each conference would constitute a job for a single distinctive client. Use of a hybrid comprising of both job and process costing is quite common in many service organizations such as hotels.

Direct costs are *assigned* to jobs or processes while indirect costs are *allocated*. Typically, the overheads (i.e., indirect costs in a service business) is much larger as a proportion of total costs than in a manufacturing business. Incorrect allocation can result in incorrect costing and pricing with consequent losses to the business. Overestimating the cost and price of a service can result in loss of customers; underestimating the cost and price of a service can result in financial losses.

To better estimate costs and prices, service businesses make use of Activity Based Costing (ABC). ABC can result in improved allocation of overheads and improve the quality of cost estimates.

In their article, "Activity-Based Costing in Services: Literature Bibliometric Review," Stefano* and Filho report the adoption of ABC in service organizations such as hotels, hospitals, libraries, logistic services, postal services, transportation companies, police services, and financial services.

Summary

C1 Explain process operations and the way they differ from job order operations. Process operations produce large quantities of similar products or services by passing them through a series of processes, or steps, in production. Like job order operations, they combine direct materials, direct labor, and overhead in the operations. Unlike job order operations that assign the responsibility for each job to a manager, process operations assign the responsibility for each *process* to a manager.

C2 Define and compute equivalent units and explain their use in process cost accounting. Equivalent units of production measure the activity of a process as the number of units that would be completed in a period if all effort had been applied to units that were started and finished. This measure of production activity is used to compute the cost per equivalent unit and to assign costs to finished goods and goods in process inventory. To compute equivalent units, determine the number of units that would have been finished if all materials (or labor or overhead) had been used to produce units that were started and completed during the period. The costs incurred by a process are divided by its equivalent units to yield cost per unit.

C3 Define and prepare a process cost summary and describe its purposes. A process cost summary reports on the activities of a production process or department for a period. It describes the costs charged to the department, the equivalent units of production for the department, and the costs assigned to the output. The report aims to (1) help managers control their departments, (2) help factory managers evaluate department managers' performances, and (3) provide cost information for financial statements. A process cost summary includes the physical flow of units, equivalent units of production, costs per equivalent unit, and a cost reconciliation. It reports the units and costs to account for during the period and how they were accounted for during the period. In terms of units, the summary includes the beginning goods in process inventory and the units started during the month. These units are accounted for in terms of the goods completed and transferred out, and the ending goods in process inventory. With respect to costs, the summary

includes materials, labor, and overhead costs assigned to the process during the period. It shows how these costs are assigned to goods completed and transferred out, and to ending goods in process inventory.

C4 Explain and illustrate the accounting for production activity using FIFO. The FIFO method for process costing is applied and illustrated to (1) report the physical flow of units, (2) compute the equivalent units of production, (3) compute the cost per equivalent unit of production, and (4) assign and reconcile costs.

A1 Compare process cost accounting and job order cost accounting. Process and job order manufacturing operations are similar in that both combine materials, labor, and factory overhead to produce products or services. They differ in the way they are organized and managed. In job order operations, the job order cost accounting system assigns materials, labor, and overhead to specific jobs. In process operations, the process cost accounting system assigns materials, labor, and overhead to specific processes. The total costs associated with each process are then divided by the number of units passing through that process to get cost per equivalent unit. The costs per equivalent unit for all processes are added to determine the total cost per unit of a product or service.

A2 Explain and illustrate a hybrid costing system. A hybrid costing system contains features of both job order and process costing systems. Generally, certain direct materials are accounted for by individual products as in job order costing, but direct labor and overhead costs are accounted for similar to process costing.

P1 Record the flow of direct materials costs in process cost accounting. Materials purchased are debited to a Raw Materials Inventory account. As direct materials are issued to processes, they are separately accumulated in a Goods in Process Inventory account for that process.

P2 Record the flow of direct labor costs in process cost accounting. Direct labor costs are initially debited to the Factory Payroll account. The total amount in it is then assigned to the Goods in Process Inventory account pertaining to each process.

---

* Stefano, Nara Medianeira, and Nelson Casarotto Filho. "Activity-based costing in services: literature bibliometric review." SpringerPlus 2.1 (2013): 1-11.

P3 Record the flow of factory overhead costs in process cost accounting. The different factory overhead items are first accumulated in the Factory Overhead account and are then allocated, using a predetermined overhead rate, to the different processes. The allocated amount is debited to the Goods in Process Inventory account pertaining to each process.

P4 Record the transfer of completed goods to Finished Goods Inventory and Cost of Goods Sold. As units complete the final process and are eventually sold, their accumulated cost is transferred to Finished Goods Inventory and finally to Cost of Goods Sold.

Guidance Answers to Decision Maker and Decision Ethics

Budget Officer By instructing you to classify a majority of costs as indirect, the manager is passing some of his department's costs to a common overhead pool that other departments will partially absorb. Since overhead costs are allocated on the basis of direct labor for this company and the new department has a relatively low direct labor cost, the new department will be assigned less overhead. Such action suggests unethical behavior by this manager. You must object to such reclassification. If this manager refuses to comply, you must inform someone in a more senior position.

Entrepreneur By spreading the added quality-related costs across three customers, the entrepreneur is probably trying to remain competitive with respect to the customer that demands the 100%

quality inspection. Moreover, the entrepreneur is partly covering the added costs by recovering two-thirds of them from the other two customers who are paying 110% of total costs. This act likely breaches the trust placed by the two customers in this entrepreneur's application of its costing system. The costing system should be changed, and the entrepreneur should consider renegotiating the pricing and/or quality test agreement with this one customer (at the risk of losing this currently loss-producing customer).

Cost Manager Differences between the FIFO and weighted-average methods are greatest when large work in process inventories exist and when costs fluctuate. The method used if inventories are eliminated does not matter; both produce identical costs.

Guidance Answers to Quick Checks

1. *c*
2. When a company produces large quantities of similar products/services, a process cost system is often more suitable.
3. *b*
4. The costs are direct materials, direct labor, and overhead.
5. A goods in process inventory account is needed for *each* production department.
6. *a*
7. Equivalent units with respect to direct labor are the number of units that would have been produced if all labor had been used on units that were started and finished during the period.

8.

Units completed and transferred out	58,000 EUP
Units of ending goods in process	
Direct labor (6,000 × 1/3)	2,000 EUP
Units of production	60,000 EUP

9. The first section shows the costs charged to the department. The second section describes the equivalent units produced by the department. The third section shows the assignment of total costs to units worked on during the period.

Key Terms   www.mheducation.asia/olc/wildkwokFAP

Conversion costs per equivalent unit (p. 799)	**FIFO method** (p. 803)	**Process cost accounting system** (p. 787)
Cost of goods manufactured (p. 797)	**Job order cost accounting**	**Process cost summary** (p. 796)
Equivalent units of production	**system** (p. 787)	**Process operations** (p. 784)
(EUP) (p. 791)	**Materials consumption report** (p. 788)	**Weighted-average method** (p. 794)

Multiple Choice Quiz   Answers on p. 826   www.mheducation.asia/olc/wildkwokFAP

Additional Quiz Questions are available at the book's Website.

1. Equivalent units of production are equal to
   a. Physical units that were completed this period from all effort being applied to them.
   b. The number of units introduced into the process this period.
   c. The number of finished units actually completed this period.
   d. The number of units that could have been started and completed given the cost incurred.
   e. The number of units in the process at the end of the period.

2. Recording the cost of raw materials purchased for use in a process costing system includes a
   a. Credit to Raw Materials Inventory.
   b. Debit to Goods in Process Inventory.
   c. Debit to Factory Overhead.
   d. Credit to Factory Overhead.
   e. Debit to Raw Materials Inventory.

3. The production department started the month with a beginning goods in process inventory of $20,000. During the month, it was assigned the following costs: direct materials, $152,000; direct labor, $45,000; overhead applied at the rate of 40% of direct labor cost. Inventory with a cost of $218,000 was transferred to finished goods. The ending balance of goods in process inventory is
   a. $330,000.
   b. $ 17,000.
   c. $220,000.
   d. $112,000.
   e. $118,000.

4. A company's beginning work in process inventory consists of 10,000 units that are 20% complete with respect to direct labor

costs. A total of 40,000 units are completed this period. There are 15,000 units in goods in process, one-third complete for direct labor, at period-end. The equivalent units of production (EUP) with respect to direct labor at period-end, assuming the weighted-average method, are
   a. 45,000 EUP.
   b. 40,000 EUP.
   c.   5,000 EUP.
   d. 37,000 EUP.
   e. 43,000 EUP.

5. Assume the same information as in question 4. Also assume that beginning work in process had $6,000 in direct labor cost and that $84,000 in direct labor is added during this period. What is the cost per EUP for labor?
   a. $0.50 per EUP
   b. $1.87 per EUP
   c. $2.00 per EUP
   d. $2.10 per EUP
   e. $2.25 per EUP

> Assume the weighted-average inventory method is used for all assignments unless stated differently.

A   *Superscript letter A denotes assignments based on Appendix 20A.*
   ⚊ Icon denotes assignments that involve decision making.

Discussion Questions

1. **⚊** Can services be delivered by means of process operations? Support your answer with an example.

2. **⚊** What is the main factor for a company in choosing between the job order costing and process costing accounting systems? Give two likely applications of each system.

3. Identify the control document for materials flow when a materials requisition slip is not used.

4. The focus in a job order costing system is the job or batch. Identify the main focus in process costing.

5. Are the journal entries that match cost flows to product flows in process costing primarily the same or much different than those in job order costing? Explain.

6. **⚊** Explain in simple terms the notion of equivalent units of production (EUP). Why is it necessary to use EUP in process costing?

7. **⚊** What are the two main inventory methods used in process costing? What are the differences between these methods?

8. **⚊** Why is it possible for direct labor in process operations to include the labor of employees who do not work directly on products or services?

9. Assume that a company produces a single product by processing it first through a single production department.

Direct labor costs flow through what accounts in this company's process cost system?

10. After all labor costs for a period are allocated, what balance should remain in the Factory Payroll account?

11. **⚊** Is it possible to have under- or overapplied overhead costs in a process cost accounting system? Explain.

12. Explain why equivalent units of production for both direct labor and overhead can be the same as, and why they can be different from, equivalent units for direct materials.

13. Companies such as **Palm** apply process operations. List the four steps in accounting for production activity in a reporting period (for process operations).

14. Companies such as **Nokia** commonly prepare a process cost summary. What purposes does a process cost summary serve?

15. **⚊** Are there situations where **Research In Motion** can use process costing? Identify at least one and explain it.

16. **⚊** **Apple** produces iMacs with a multiple production line. Identify and list some of its production processing steps and departments.

For each of the following products and services, indicate whether it is most likely produced in a process operation or in a job order operation.

1. Luxury cars   **3.** Apple juice

2. Vanilla ice cream   **4.** Tennis courts

QUICK STUDY

QS 20-1
Process vs. job order operations
C1

Sturdy Packaging makes cardboard shipping cartons in a single operation. This period, Sturdy purchased $125,000 in raw materials. Its production department requisitioned $90,000 of those materials for use in producing cartons. Prepare journal entries to record its (1) purchase of raw materials and (2) requisition of direct materials.

QS 20-2
Recording costs of direct materials   P1

Refer to the information in QS 20-2. Sturdy Packaging incurred $165,000 in factory payroll costs, of which $110,000 was direct labor. Prepare journal entries to record its (1) total factory payroll incurred and (2) direct labor used in production.

QS 20-3
Recording costs of direct labor
P2

Refer to the information in QS 20-2 and QS 20-3. Sturdy Packaging requisitioned $62,000 of indirect materials from its raw materials and used $55,000 of indirect labor in its production of boxes. Also, it incurred $220,000 of other factory overhead costs. It applies factory overhead at the rate of 130% of direct labor costs. Prepare journal entries to record its (1) indirect materials requisitioned, (2) indirect labor used in production, (3) other factory overhead costs incurred, and (4) application of overhead to production.

QS 20-4
Recording costs of factory overhead
P3

Refer to the information in QS 20-2, QS 20-3, and QS 20-4. Sturdy Packaging completed 175,000 boxes costing $335,000 and transferred them to finished goods. Prepare its journal entry to record the transfer of the boxes from production to finished goods inventory.

QS 20-5
Recording transfer of costs to finished goods   P4

The following refers to units processed in Heath Printing's binding department in June. Compute the total equivalent units of production with respect to labor for June using the weighted-average inventory method.

QS 20-6
Computing equivalent units of production
C2

	Units of Product	Percent of Labor Added
Beginning goods in process	150,000	85%
Goods started	310,000	100
Goods completed	340,000	100
Ending goods in process	120,000	25

The cost of beginning inventory plus the costs added during the period should equal the cost of units _____ plus the cost of _____.

QS 20-7
Computing EUP cost   C2

Explain how a car maintenance and repair garage might use a hybrid costing system.

QS 20-8
Hybrid costing   A2

Refer to QS 20-6 and compute the total equivalent units of production with respect to labor for June using the FIFO inventory method.

QS 20-9ᴬ
Computing equivalent units—FIFO   C4

Put the four steps in accounting for production activities in the order in which they would occur.

a. Assign and reconcile costs
b. Compute the cost per equivalent unit
c. Compute equivalent units of production
d. Determine physical flow of units

QS 20-10
Steps in process costing
C3

QS 20-11
Process cost summary   C3

List the headings of the three major sections of a process cost summary. Refer to Exhibit 20.17.

QS 20-12
Process cost summary   C3

Anheuser-Busch InBev is attempting to reduce its water usage. How could a company manager use a process cost summary to determine if the program to reduce water usage is successful?

QS 20-13
Process vs. job order costing
A1

Label each statement below as either true ("T") or false ("F").

1. Job order and process operations both combine materials, labor, and overhead in producing products or services.
2. Costs per job are computed in both job order and process costing systems.
3. Service companies are not able to use process costing.
4. The cost per equivalent unit is computed as the total costs of a process divided by the number of equivalent units passing through that process.

EXERCISES

Exercise 20-1
Terminology in process cost accounting

C1   A1   P1   P2   P3

Match each of the following items A through G with the best numbered description of its purpose.

A. Process cost summary
B. Equivalent units of production
C. Goods in Process Inventory account
D. Raw Materials Inventory account
E. Materials requisition
F. Finished Goods Inventory account
G. Factory Overhead account

_____ **1.** Holds costs of materials until they are used in production or as factory overhead.
_____ **2.** Holds costs of indirect materials, indirect labor, and similar costs until assigned to production.
_____ **3.** Holds costs of direct materials, direct labor, and applied overhead until products are transferred from production to finished goods (or another department).
_____ **4.** Standardizes partially completed units into equivalent completed units.
_____ **5.** Holds costs of finished products until sold to customers.
_____ **6.** Describes the activity and output of a production department for a period.
_____ **7.** Notifies the materials manager to send materials to a production department.

Exercise 20-2
Recording costs of materials
P1

Prepare journal entries to record its following production activities.

1. Purchased $80,000 of raw materials on credit.
2. Used $34,000 of direct materials in production.
3. Used $41,000 of indirect materials.

Exercise 20-3
Recording costs of labor
P2

Prepare journal entries to record the following production activities.

1. Incurred total labor cost of $77,000, which is paid in cash.
2. Used $58,000 of direct labor in production.
3. Used $19,000 of indirect labor.

Exercise 20-4
Recording overhead costs
P3

Refer to information in Exercise 20-3. Prepare journal entries to record the following production activities.

1. Paid overhead costs (other than indirect materials and indirect labor) of $22,000.
2. Applied overhead at 90% of direct labor costs.

Exercise 20-5
Recording cost of completed goods
P4

Prepare journal entries to record the following production activities.

1. Transferred completed products with a cost of $137,000 to finished goods inventory.
2. Sold $450,000 of products on credit. Their cost is $150,000.

Lowes Lumber produces bagged bark for use in landscaping. Production involves packaging bark chips in plastic bags in a bagging department. The following information describes production operations for October.

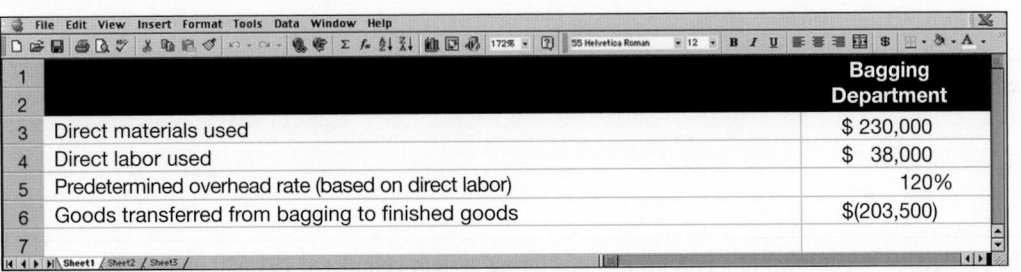

	Bagging Department
3 Direct materials used	$ 230,000
4 Direct labor used	$ 38,000
5 Predetermined overhead rate (based on direct labor)	120%
6 Goods transferred from bagging to finished goods	$(203,500)

The company's revenue for the month totaled $450,000 from credit sales, and its cost of goods sold for the month is $250,000. Prepare summary journal entries dated October 31 to record its October production activities for (1) direct material usage, (2) direct labor usage, (3) overhead allocation, (4) goods transfer from production to finished goods, and (5) sales.

Exercise 20-6
Recording cost flows in a process cost system
P1 P2 P3 P4

Check (3) Cr. Factory Overhead, $45,600

The following journal entries are recorded in Kiera Co.'s process cost accounting system. Kiera produces handbags and scarves. Overhead is applied to production based on direct labor cost for the period. Prepare a brief explanation (including any overhead rates applied) for each journal entry *a* through *j*.

Exercise 20-7
Interpretation of journal entries in process cost accounting
P1 P2 P3 P4

a.	Raw Materials Inventory	54,000		**g.**	Factory Overhead	8,000	
	Accounts Payable		54,000		Factory Payroll		8,000
b.	Goods in Process Inventory	44,000		**h.**	Goods in Process Inventory	35,000	
	Raw Materials Inventory		44,000		Factory Overhead		35,000
c.	Factory Payroll	36,000		**i.**	Finished Goods Inventory	98,000	
	Cash		36,000		Goods in Process Inventory		98,000
d.	Goods in Process Inventory	28,000		**j.**	Accounts Receivable	256,000	
	Factory Payroll		28,000		Sales		256,000
e.	Factory Overhead	10,500			Cost of Goods Sold	104,000	
	Cash		10,500		Finished Goods Inventory		104,000
f.	Factory Overhead	3,000					
	Raw Materials Inventory		3,000				

During April, the production department of a process manufacturing system completed a number of units of a product and transferred them to finished goods. Of these transferred units, 37,500 were in process in the production department at the beginning of April and 150,000 were started and completed in April. April's beginning inventory units were 60% complete with respect to materials and 40% complete with respect to labor. At the end of April, 51,250 additional units were in process in the production department and were 80% complete with respect to materials and 30% complete with respect to labor.

1. Compute the number of units transferred to finished goods.
2. Compute the number of equivalent units with respect to both materials used and labor used in the production department for April using the weighted-average method.

Exercise 20-8
Computing equivalent units of production—weighted average
C2

Check (2) EUP for materials, 228,500

The production department described in Exercise 20-8 had $531,480 of direct materials and $407,689 of direct labor cost charged to it during April. Also, its beginning inventory included $74,075 of direct materials cost and $28,493 of direct labor.

1. Compute the direct materials cost and the direct labor cost per equivalent unit for the department.
2. Using the weighted-average method, assign April's costs to the department's output—specifically, its units transferred to finished goods and its ending goods in process inventory.

Exercise 20-9
Costs assigned to output and inventories—weighted average
C2 P4

Check (1) $2.65 per EUP of direct materials

Exercise 20-10ᴬ
Computing equivalent units of production—FIFO **C4**

Refer to the information in Exercise 20-8 to compute the number of equivalent units with respect to both materials used and labor used in the production department for April using the FIFO method.

Exercise 20-11ᴬ
Costs assigned to output—FIFO
C4 P4

Refer to the information in Exercise 20-8 and complete its parts (1) and (2) using the FIFO method.

Exercise 20-12
Equivalent units computed—weighted average

C2

The production department in a process manufacturing system completed 191,500 units of product and transferred them to finished goods during a recent period. Of these units, 31,500 were in process at the beginning of the period. The other 160,000 units were started and completed during the period. At period-end, 29,500 units were in process. Compute the department's equivalent units of production with respect to direct materials under each of three separate assumptions:

1. All direct materials are added to products when processing begins.

2. Direct materials are added to products evenly throughout the process. Beginning goods in process inventory was 40% complete, and ending goods in process inventory was 75% complete.

Check   (3) EUP for materials, 206,250

3. One-half of direct materials is added to products when the process begins and the other half is added when the process is 75% complete as to direct labor. Beginning goods in process inventory is 40% complete as to direct labor, and ending goods in process inventory is 60% complete as to direct labor.

Exercise 20-13ᴬ
Equivalent units computed—FIFO **C4**

Refer to the information in Exercise 20-12 and complete it for each of the three separate assumptions using the FIFO method for process costing.

Check   (3) EUP for materials, 190,500

Exercise 20-14
Flowchart of costs for a process operation **P1 P2 P3 P4**

The following flowchart shows the August production activity of the The Spade Company. Use the amounts shown on the flowchart to compute the missing four numbers identified by blanks.

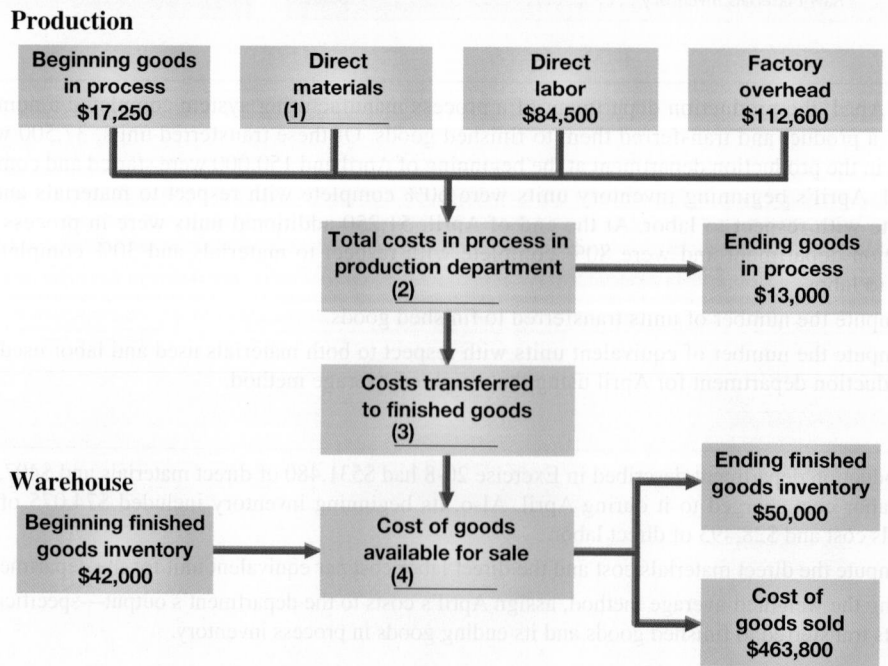

The following partially completed process cost summary describes the May production activities of Raman Company. Its production output is sent to its warehouse for shipping. Prepare its process cost summary using the weighted-average method.

Equivalent Units of Production	Direct Materials	Direct Labor	Factory Overhead
Units transferred out	128,000	128,000	128,000
Units of ending goods in process	10,000	6,000	6,000
Equivalent units of production	138,000	134,000	134,000

Costs per EUP	Direct Materials	Direct Labor	Factory Overhead
Costs of beginning goods in process	$ 37,100	$ 1,520	$ 3,040
Costs incurred this period	715,000	125,780	251,560
Total costs	$752,100	$127,300	$254,600

Units in beginning goods in process	8,000
Units started this period	130,000
Units completed and transferred out	128,000
Units in ending goods in process	10,000

Ebony Company uses the weighted-average method of process costing to assign production costs to its products. Information for April follows. Assume that all materials are added at the beginning of its production process, and that direct labor and factory overhead are added uniformly throughout the process.

Goods in process inventory, April 1 (4,000 units, 100% complete with respect to direct materials, 80% complete with respect to direct labor and overhead; includes $90,000 of direct material cost, $51,200 in direct labor cost, $61,440 overhead cost)	$202,640
Units started in April	56,000
Units completed and transferred to finished goods inventory	46,000
Goods in process inventory, April 30 (? units, 100% complete with respect to direct materials, 40% complete with respect to direct labor and overhead)	?
Costs incurred in April	
Direct materials	$750,000
Direct labor	$310,000
Overhead applied at 120% of direct labor cost	?

Required

Fill in the blanks labeled *a* through *uu* in the following process cost summary.

EBONY COMPANY Process Cost Summary For Month Ended April 30		
Costs Charged to Production		
Costs of beginning goods in process		
Direct materials	$ 90,000	
Direct labor	51,200	
Factory overhead	61,440	$202,640
Costs incurred this period		
Direct materials	$750,000	
Direct labor	310,000	
Factory overhead	(a)_____	(b)_____
Total costs to account for		(c)_____

[continued on next page]

Check   (c) $1,634,640

[continued from previous page]

Unit Cost Information

Units to account for		Units accounted for	
Beginning goods in process	4,000	Completed and transferred out	46,000
Units started this period	56,000	Ending goods in process	(d)_____
Total units to account for	(e)_____	Total units accounted for	(f)_____

Equivalent Units of Production (EUP)

				Direct Materials	Direct Labor	Factory Overhead
Units completed and transferred out				(g)_____ EUP	(h)_____ EUP	(i)_____ EUP
Units of ending goods in process						
Materials	(j)_____	×	100%	(k)_____ EUP		
Direct labor	(l)_____	×	40%		(m)_____ EUP	
Factory overhead	(n)_____	×	40%			(o)_____ EUP
Equivalent units of production (EUP)				(p)_____ EUP	(q)_____ EUP	(r)_____ EUP

Cost per EUP

	Direct Materials	Direct Labor	Factory Overhead
Costs of beginning goods in process	$ 90,000	$ 51,200	$61,440
Costs incurred this period	750,000	310,000	(s)_____
Total costs	$840,000	$361,200	(t)_____
÷ EUP	(u)_____	(v)_____	(w)_____
Cost per EUP	(x)_____	(y)_____	(z)_____

Check   (z) $8.40 per EUP

Cost Assignment and Reconciliation

Costs transferred out	Cost/EUP	×	EUP		
Direct materials	(aa)_____	×	(bb)_____	(cc)_____	
Direct labor	(dd)_____	×	(ee)_____	(ff)_____	
Factory overhead	(gg)_____	×	(hh)_____	(ii)_____	
Costs of goods completed and transferred out					(jj)_____
Costs of ending goods in process					
Direct materials	(kk)_____	×	(ll)_____	(mm)_____	
Direct labor	(nn)_____	×	(oo)_____	(pp)_____	
Factory overhead	(qq)_____	×	(rr)_____	(ss)_____	
Costs of ending goods in process					(tt)_____
Total costs accounted for					(uu)_____

Exercise 20-17

Matching of product to cost accounting system

C1

For each of the following products and services, indicate whether it is most likely produced in a process operation or in a job order operation.

1. Door hardware
2. Cut flower arrangements
3. House paints
4. Concrete swimming pools
5. Custom tailored dresses
6. Grand pianos
7. Table lamps
8. Beach towels
9. Bolts and nuts
10. Lawn chairs
11. Headphones
12. Designed patio

Exercise 20-18

Compare process and job order operations

C1

Label each item *a* through *h* below as a feature of either a job order or process operation.

a. Routine, repetitive procedures
b. Custom orders
c. Low production volume
d. Heterogeneous products and services
e. Low product flexibility
f. Low product standardization
g. Focus on individual batch
h. Focus on standardized units

Exercise 20-19

Hybrid costing system

A2

Explain a hybrid costing system. Identify a product or service operation that might well fit a hybrid costing system.

Edison Company manufactures wool blankets and accounts for product costs using process costing. The following information is available regarding its May inventories.

PROBLEM SET A

Problem 20-1A
Production cost flow and measurement; journal entries

P1 P2 P3 P4

	Beginning Inventory	Ending Inventory
Raw materials inventory	$ 28,000	$ 25,500
Goods in process inventory	220,750	252,000
Finished goods inventory	319,000	277,000

The following additional information describes the company's production activities for May.

Raw materials purchases (on credit)	$ 135,000
Factory payroll cost (paid in cash)	791,500
Other overhead cost (Other Accounts credited)	43,000
Materials used	
Direct	$ 93,500
Indirect	31,000
Labor used	
Direct	$ 352,000
Indirect	439,500
Overhead rate as a percent of direct labor..............	110%
Sales (on credit)	$1,500,000

Required

1. Compute the cost of (a) products transferred from production to finished goods, and (b) goods sold.
2. Prepare summary journal entries dated May 31 to record the following production activities during May: (a) raw materials purchases, (b) direct materials usage, (c) indirect materials usage, (d) payroll costs, (e) direct labor costs, (f) indirect labor costs, (g) other overhead costs, (h) overhead applied, (i) goods transferred from production to finished goods, and (j) sale of finished goods.

Check   (1b) Cost of goods sold $843,450

Fairfax Company uses weighted-average process costing to account for its production costs. Direct labor is added evenly throughout the process. Direct materials are added at the beginning of the process. During September, the company transferred 735,000 units of product to finished goods. At the end of September, the goods in process inventory consists of 207,000 units that are 90% complete with respect to labor. Beginning inventory had $244,920 of direct materials and $69,098 of direct labor cost. The direct labor cost added in September is $1,312,852, and the direct materials cost added is $1,639,080.

Problem 20-2A
Cost per equivalent unit; costs assigned to products

C2 C3

e**X**cel

www.mheducation.asia/olc/wildkwokFAP

Required

1. Determine the equivalent units of production with respect to (a) direct labor and (b) direct materials.
2. Compute both the direct labor cost and the direct materials cost per equivalent unit.
3. Compute both direct labor cost and direct materials cost assigned to (a) units completed and transferred out, and (b) ending goods in process inventory.

Check   (2) Direct labor cost per equivalent unit, $1.50

(3b) $693,450

Analysis Component

4. The company sells and ships all units to customers as soon as they are completed. Assume that an error is made in determining the percentage of completion for units in ending inventory. Instead of being 90% complete with respect to labor, they are actually 65% complete. Write a one-page memo to the plant manager describing how this error affects its September financial statements.

Problem 20-3A

Journalizing in process costing; equivalent units and costs

C2 P1 P2 P3

Li Company produces large quantities of a standardized product. The following information is available for its production activities for January.

Raw materials		Factory overhead incurred	
Beginning inventory	$ 26,000	Indirect materials used	$ 81,500
Raw materials purchased (on credit)	255,000	Indirect labor used	50,000
Direct materials used	(172,000)	Other overhead costs	159,308
Indirect materials used	(81,500)	Total factory overhead incurred	$290,808
Ending inventory	$ 27,500		
		Factory overhead applied	
Factory payroll		**(140% of direct labor cost)**	
Direct labor used	$207,720	Total factory overhead applied	$290,808
Indirect labor used	50,000		
Total payroll cost (paid in cash)	$257,720		

Additional information about units and costs of production activities follows.

Units		Costs		
Beginning goods in process inventory	2,200	Beginning goods in process inventory		
Started	30,000	Direct materials	$3,500	
Ending goods in process inventory	5,900	Direct labor	3,225	
		Factory overhead	4,515	$ 11,240
Status of ending goods in process inventory		Direct materials added		172,000
Materials—Percent complete	50%	Direct labor added		207,720
Labor and overhead—Percent complete	65%	Overhead applied (140% of direct labor)		290,808
		Total costs		$681,768
		Ending goods in process inventory		$ 82,128

During January, 55,000 units of finished goods are sold for $50 cash each. Cost information regarding finished goods follows.

Beginning finished goods inventory	$155,000
Cost transferred in	599,640
Cost of goods sold	(612,500)
Ending finished goods inventory	$142,140

Required

1. Prepare journal entries dated January 31 to record the following January activities: (a) purchase of raw materials, (b) direct materials usage, (c) indirect materials usage, (d) factory payroll costs, (e) direct labor costs used in production, (f) indirect labor costs, (g) other overhead costs—credit Other Accounts, (h) overhead applied, (i) goods transferred to finished goods, and (j) sale of finished goods.

Check (2) Cost per equivalent unit: materials, $6.00; labor, $7.00; overhead, $9.80

2. Prepare a process cost summary report for this company, showing costs charged to production, units cost information, equivalent units of production, cost per EUP, and its cost assignment and reconciliation.

Analysis Component

3. The company provides incentives to its department managers by paying monthly bonuses based on their success in controlling costs per equivalent unit of production. Assume that the production department underestimates the percentage of completion for units in ending inventory with the result that

its equivalent units of production in ending inventory for January are understated. What impact does this error have on the January bonuses paid to the production managers? What impact, if any, does this error have on February bonuses?

Easton Co. produces its product through a single processing department. Direct materials are added at the start of production, and direct labor and overhead are added evenly throughout the process. The company uses monthly reporting periods for its weighted-average process cost accounting system. Its Goods in Process Inventory account follows after entries for direct materials, direct labor, and overhead costs for October.

Problem 20-4A
Process cost summary; equivalent units

C2 C3 P4

www.mheducation.asia/olc/wildkwokFAP

Goods in Process Inventory				Acct. No. 133
Date	Explanation	Debit	Credit	Balance
Oct. 1	Balance			348,638
31	Direct materials	104,090		452,728
31	Direct labor	416,360		869,088
31	Applied overhead	244,920		1,114,008

Its beginning goods in process consisted of $60,830 of direct materials, $176,820 of direct labor, and $110,988 of factory overhead. During October, the company started 280,000 units and transferred 306,000 units to finished goods. At the end of the month, the goods in process inventory consisted of 41,200 units that were 80% complete with respect to direct labor and factory overhead.

Required

1. Prepare the company's process cost summary for October using the weighted-average method.
2. Prepare the journal entry dated October 31 to transfer the cost of the completed units to finished goods inventory.

Check   (1) Costs transferred to finished goods, $1,002,150

Ogden Co. manufactures a single product in one department. All direct materials are added at the beginning of the manufacturing process. Direct labor and overhead are added evenly throughout the process. The company uses monthly reporting periods for its weighted-average process cost accounting. During October, the company completed and transferred 22,200 units of product to finished goods inventory. Its 3,000 units of beginning goods in process consisted of $9,900 of direct materials, $61,650 of direct labor, and $49,320 of factory overhead. It has 2,400 units (100% complete with respect to direct materials and 80% complete with respect to direct labor and overhead) in process at month-end. After entries to record direct materials, direct labor, and overhead for October, the company's Goods in Process Inventory account follows.

Problem 20-5A
Process cost summary, equivalent units, cost estimates

C2 C3 P4

Goods in Process Inventory				Acct. No. 133
Date	Explanation	Debit	Credit	Balance
Oct. 1	Balance			120,870
31	Direct materials	248,400		369,270
31	Direct labor	601,650		970,920
31	Applied overhead	481,320		1,452,240

Required

1. Prepare the company's process cost summary for October using the weighted-average method.
2. Prepare the journal entry dated October 31 to transfer the cost of completed units to finished goods inventory.

Check   (1) EUP for labor and overhead, 24,120 EUP

(2) Cost transferred to finished goods, $1,332,000

Analysis Components

3. The cost accounting process depends on numerous estimates.

   a. Identify two major estimates that determine the cost per equivalent unit.

   b. In what direction might you anticipate a bias from management for each estimate in part 3a (assume that management compensation is based on maintaining low inventory amounts)? Explain your answer.

Problem 20-6A^A

Process cost summary; equivalent units; cost estimates—FIFO

C3 C4 P4

Refer to the data in Problem 20-5A. Assume that Ogden uses the FIFO method to account for its process costing system. The following additional information is available:

● Beginning goods in process consisted of 3,000 units that were 100% complete with respect to direct materials and 40% complete with respect to direct labor and overhead.

● Of the 22,200 units completed, 3,000 were from beginning goods in process. The remaining 19,200 were units started and completed during October.

Required

Check (1) EUP for labor and overhead, 22,920 EUP

       (2) Cost transferred to finished goods, $1,333,920

1. Prepare the company's process cost summary for October using FIFO.

2. Prepare the journal entry dated October 31 to transfer the cost of completed units to finished goods inventory.

PROBLEM SET B

Problem 20-1B

Production cost flow and measurement; journal entries

P1 P2 P3 P4

Tarick Toys Company manufactures video game consoles and accounts for product costs using process costing. The following information is available regarding its June inventories.

	Beginning Inventory	Ending Inventory
Raw materials inventory	$ 54,000	$ 82,500
Goods in process inventory	117,000	187,500
Finished goods inventory	120,000	148,500

The following additional information describes the company's production activities for June.

Raw materials purchases (on credit)	$150,000
Factory payroll cost (paid in cash)	300,000
Other overhead cost (Other Accounts credited)	127,875
Materials used	
Direct	$ 90,000
Indirect	31,500
Labor used	
Direct	$262,500
Indirect	37,500
Overhead rate as a percent of direct labor	75%
Sales (on credit)	$750,000

Required

Check (1b) Cost of goods sold, $450,375

1. Compute the cost of (a) products transferred from production to finished goods, and (b) goods sold.

2. Prepare journal entries dated June 30 to record the following production activities during June: (a) raw materials purchases, (b) direct materials usage, (c) indirect materials usage, (d) payroll costs, (e) direct labor costs, (f) indirect labor costs, (g) other overhead costs, (h) overhead applied, (i) goods transferred from production to finished goods, and (j) sale of finished goods.

Problem 20-2B

Cost per equivalent unit; costs assigned to products

C2 C3

Eden Company uses process costing to account for its production costs. Direct labor is added evenly throughout the process. Direct materials are added at the beginning of the process. During April, the production department transferred 40,000 units of product to finished goods. Beginning goods in process had $116,000 of direct materials and $172,800 of direct labor cost. At the end of April, the goods in process inventory consists of 4,000 units that are 25% complete with respect to labor. The direct materials cost added in April is $1,424,000, and direct labor cost added is $3,960,000.

Required

1. Determine the equivalent units of production with respect to (a) direct labor and (b) direct materials.

2. Compute both the direct labor cost and the direct materials cost per equivalent unit.

Check   (2) Direct labor cost per equivalent unit, $100.80

3. Compute both direct labor cost and direct materials cost assigned to (a) units completed and transferred out, and (b) ending goods in process inventory.

(3b) $240,800

Analysis Component

4. The company sells and ships all units to customers as soon as they are completed. Assume that an error is made in determining the percentage of completion for units in ending inventory. Instead of being 30% complete with respect to labor, they are actually 75% complete. Write a one-page memo to the plant manager describing how this error affects its April financial statements.

Ying Company produces large quantities of a standardized product. The following information is available for its production activities for March.

Problem 20-3B
Journalizing in process costing; equivalent units and costs

C2 P1 P2 P3 P4

Raw materials		**Factory overhead incurred**	
Beginning inventory	$ 16,000	Indirect materials used	$20,280
Raw materials purchased (on credit)	110,560	Indirect labor used	18,160
Direct materials used	(98,560)	Other overhead costs	17,216
Indirect materials used	(20,280)	Total factory overhead incurred	$55,656
Ending inventory	$ 7,720		
		Factory overhead applied	
Factory payroll		**(90% of direct labor cost)**	
Direct labor used	$61,840	Total factory overhead applied	$55,656
Indirect labor used	18,160		
Total payroll cost (paid in cash)	$80,000		

Additional information about units and costs of production activities follows.

Units		**Costs**		
Beginning goods in process inventory	8,000	Beginning goods in process inventory		
Started	24,000	Direct materials	$2,240	
Ending goods in process inventory	6,000	Direct labor	1,410	
		Factory overhead	1,269	$ 4,919
Status of ending goods in process inventory		Direct materials added		98,560
Materials—Percent complete	100%	Direct labor added		61,840
Labor and overhead—Percent complete	25%	Overhead applied (90% of direct labor)		55,656
		Total costs		$220,975
		Ending goods in process inventory		$ 25,455

During March, 45,000 units of finished goods are sold for $25 cash each. Cost information regarding finished goods follows.

Beginning finished goods inventory	$ 74,200
Cost transferred in from production	195,520
Cost of goods sold	(225,000)
Ending finished goods inventory	$ 44,720

Required

1. Prepare journal entries dated March 31 to record the following March activities: (a) purchase of raw materials, (b) direct materials usage, (c) indirect materials usage, (d) factory payroll costs, (e) direct labor costs used in production, (f) indirect labor costs, (g) other overhead costs—credit Other Accounts, (h) overhead applied, (i) goods transferred to finished goods, and (j) sale of finished goods.

2. Prepare a process cost summary report for this company, showing costs charged to production, unit cost information, equivalent units of production, cost per EUP, and its cost assignment and reconciliation.

Check   (2) Cost per equivalent unit: materials, $3.15; labor, $2.30; overhead, $2.07

Analysis Component

3. This company provides incentives to its department managers by paying monthly bonuses based on their success in controlling costs per equivalent unit of production. Assume that production over-estimates the percentage of completion for units in ending inventory with the result that its equivalent units of production in ending inventory for March are overstated. What impact does this error have on bonuses paid to the managers of the production department? What impact, if any, does this error have on these managers' April bonuses?

Problem 20-4B

Process cost summary; equivalent units

C2 C3 P4

Basilex Company produces its product through a single processing department. Direct materials are added at the beginning of the process. Direct labor and overhead are added to the product evenly throughout the process. The company uses monthly reporting periods for its weighted-average process cost accounting. Its Goods in Process Inventory account follows after entries for direct materials, direct labor, and overhead costs for November.

		Goods in Process Inventory			Acct. No. 133
Date		Explanation	Debit	Credit	Balance
Nov.	1	Balance			10,650
	30	Direct materials	58,200		68,850
	30	Direct labor	213,400		282,250
	30	Applied overhead	320,100		602,350

The 7,500 units of beginning goods in process consisted of $3,400 of direct materials, $2,900 of direct labor, and $4,350 of factory overhead. During November, the company finished and transferred 100,000 units of its product to finished goods. At the end of the month, the goods in process inventory consisted of 12,000 units that were 100% complete with respect to direct materials and 25% complete with respect to direct labor and factory overhead.

Required

Check   (1) Cost transferred to finished goods, $580,000

1. Prepare the company's process cost summary for November using the weighted-average method.

2. Prepare the journal entry dated November 30 to transfer the cost of the completed units to finished goods inventory.

Problem 20-5B

Process cost summary; equivalent units; cost estimates

C2 C3 P4

Oakley International Co. manufactures a single product in one department. Direct labor and overhead are added evenly throughout the process. Direct materials are added as needed. The company uses monthly reporting periods for its weighted-average process cost accounting. During March, Oakley completed and transferred 220,000 units of product to finished goods inventory. Its 10,000 units of beginning goods in process consisted of $16,800 of direct materials, $27,920 of direct labor, and $69,800 of factory overhead. 40,000 units (50% complete with respect to direct materials and 30% complete with respect to direct labor and overhead) are in process at month-end. After entries for direct materials, direct labor, and overhead for March, the company's Goods in Process Inventory account follows.

		Goods in Process Inventory			Acct. No. 133
Date		Explanation	Debit	Credit	Balance
Mar.	1	Balance			114,520
	31	Direct materials	223,200		337,720
	31	Direct labor	352,560		690,280
	31	Applied overhead	881,400		1,571,680

Required

Check   (1) EUP for labor and overhead, 232,000

         (2) Cost transferred to finished goods, $1,482,800

1. Prepare the company's process cost summary for March using the weighted-average method.

2. Prepare the journal entry dated March 31 to transfer the cost of completed units to finished goods inventory.

Analysis Components

3. The cost accounting process depends on several estimates.

    a. Identify two major estimates that affect the cost per equivalent unit.

    b. In what direction might you anticipate a bias from management for each estimate in part 3a (assume that management compensation is based on maintaining low inventory amounts)? Explain your answer.

Refer to the information in Problem 20-5B. Assume that Oakley International uses the FIFO method to account for its process costing system. The following additional information is available.

● Beginning goods in process consists of 10,000 units that were 75% complete with respect to direct materials and 60% complete with respect to direct labor and overhead.

● Of the 220,000 units completed, 10,000 were from beginning goods in process; the remaining 210,000 were units started and completed during March.

Required

1. Prepare the company's process cost summary for March using FIFO. Round cost per EUP to one-tenth of a cent.

2. Prepare the journal entry dated March 31 to transfer the cost of completed units to finished goods inventory.

Problem 20-6B[A]

Process cost summary; equivalent units; cost estimates—FIFO

C3   C4   P4

Check (1) Labor and overhead EUP, 226,000

      (2) Cost transferred, $1,486,960

(This serial problem began in Chapter 1 and continues through most of the book. If previous chapter segments were not completed, the serial problem can begin at this point.)

SP 20 The computer workstation furniture manufacturing that Santana Rey started is progressing well. At this point, Santana is using a job order costing system to account for the production costs of this product line. Santana has heard about process costing and is wondering whether process costing might be a better method for her to keep track of and monitor her production costs.

Required

1. What are the features that distinguish job order costing from process costing?

2. Do you believe that Santana should continue to use job order costing or switch to process costing for her workstation furniture manufacturing? Explain.

SERIAL PROBLEM

Business Solutions

C1   A1

CP 20 Major League Bat Company manufactures baseball bats. In addition to its goods in process inventories, the company maintains inventories of raw materials and finished goods. It uses raw materials as direct materials in production and as indirect materials. Its factory payroll costs include direct labor for production and indirect labor. All materials are added at the beginning of the process, and direct labor and factory overhead are applied uniformly throughout the production process.

Required

You are to maintain records and produce measures of inventories to reflect the July events of this company. Set up the following general ledger accounts and enter the June 30 balances: Raw Materials Inventory, $25,000; Goods in Process Inventory, $8,135 ($2,660 of direct materials, $3,650 of direct labor, and $1,825 of overhead); Finished Goods Inventory, $110,000; Sales, $0; Cost of Goods Sold, $0; Factory Payroll, $0; and Factory Overhead, $0.

1. Prepare journal entries to record the following July transactions and events.

    a. Purchased raw materials for $125,000 cash (the company uses a perpetual inventory system).

    b. Used raw materials as follows: direct materials, $52,440; and indirect materials, $10,000.

    c. Incurred factory payroll cost of $227,250 paid in cash (ignore taxes).

    d. Assigned factory payroll costs as follows: direct labor, $202,250; and indirect labor, $25,000.

    e. Incurred additional factory overhead costs of $80,000 paid in cash.

    f. Allocated factory overhead to production at 50% of direct labor costs.

COMPREHENSIVE PROBLEM

Major League Bat Company

(Review of Chapters 2, 5, 18, 20)

Check (1f) Cr. Factory Overhead, $101,125

2. Information about the July inventories follows. Use this information with that from part 1 to prepare a process cost summary, assuming the weighted-average method is used.

Units	
Beginning inventory	5,000 units
Started	14,000 units
Ending inventory	8,000 units
Beginning inventory	
Materials—Percent complete	100%
Labor and overhead—Percent complete	75%
Ending inventory	
Materials—Percent complete	100%
Labor and overhead—Percent complete	40%

3. Using the results from part 2 and the available information, make computations and prepare journal entries to record the following:

  a. Total costs transferred to finished goods for July (label this entry g).

  b. Sale of finished goods costing $265,700 for $625,000 in cash (label this entry h).

4. Post entries from parts 1 and 3 to the ledger accounts set up at the beginning of the problem.

5. Compute the amount of gross profit from the sales in July. (*Note:* Add any underapplied overhead to, or deduct any overapplied overhead from, the cost of goods sold. Ignore the corresponding journal entry.)

Beyond the Numbers

REPORTING IN ACTION

C2

BTN 20-1   **Research In Motion** reports in notes to its financial statements that, in addition to its merchandise sold, it includes the following costs (among others) in cost of goods sold: customer shipping and handling expenses, warranty expenses, and depreciation expense on assets used in manufacturing.

Required

1. Why do you believe Research In Motion includes these costs in its cost of goods sold?

2. What effect does this cost accounting policy for its cost of goods sold have on Research In Motion's financial statements and any analysis of these statements? Explain.

Fast Forward

3. Access Research In Motion's financial statements for the financial years after February 27, 2010, from its Website (www.rim.com). Review its footnote relating to Critical Accounting Policies and Estimates. Has Research In Motion changed its policy with respect to what costs are included in the cost of goods sold? Explain.

COMPARATIVE ANALYSIS

C1

BTN 20-2   Manufacturers such as **Research In Motion, Apple,** and **Palm** usually work to maintain a high-quality and low-cost operation. One ratio routinely computed for this assessment is the cost of goods sold divided by total expenses. A decline in this ratio can mean that the company is spending too much on selling and administrative activities. An increase in this ratio beyond a reasonable level can mean that the company is not spending enough on selling activities. (Assume for this analysis that total expenses equal the cost of goods sold plus selling, general, and administrative expenses.)

Required

1. For Research In Motion, refer to its 2010 annual report from its Website, and for Apple and Palm refer to Appendix A. Compute the ratios of cost of goods sold to total expenses for their two most recent financial years. (Record answers as percents, rounded to one decimal.)

2. Comment on the similarities or differences in the ratio results across both years among the companies.

BTN 20-3   Many accounting and accounting-related professionals are skilled in financial analysis, but most are not skilled in manufacturing. This is especially the case for process manufacturing environments (for example, a bottling plant or chemical factory). To provide professional accounting and financial services, one must understand the industry, product, and processes. We have an ethical responsibility to develop this understanding before offering services to clients in these areas.

ETHICS CHALLENGE
C1

Required

Write a one-page action plan, in memorandum format, discussing how you would obtain an understanding of key business processes of a company that hires you to provide financial services. The memorandum should specify an industry, a product, and one selected process and should draw on at least one reference, such as a professional journal or industry magazine.

BTN 20-4   You hire a new assistant production manager whose prior experience is with a company that produced goods to order. Your company engages in continuous production of homogeneous products that go through various production processes. Your new assistant e-mails you questioning some cost classifications on an internal report—specifically why the costs of some materials that do not actually become part of the finished product, including some labor costs not directly associated with producing the product, are classified as direct costs. Respond to this concern via memorandum.

COMMUNICATING IN PRACTICE
A1 C1 P1 P2

BTN 20-5   Many companies acquire software to help them monitor and control their costs and as an aid to their accounting systems. One company that supplies such software is **proDacapo** (prodacapo.com). There are many other such vendors. Access proDacapo's Website, click on "Prodacapo Process Management," and review the information displayed.

TAKING IT TO THE NET
C1

Required

How is process management software helpful to businesses? Explain with reference to costs, efficiency, and examples, if possible.

BTN 20-6   The purpose of this team activity is to ensure that each team member understands process operations and the related accounting entries. Find the activities and flows identified in Exhibit 20.4 with numbers ①–⑩. Pick a member of the team to start by describing activity number ① in this exhibit, then verbalizing the related journal entry, and describing how the amounts in the entry are computed. The other members of the team are to agree or disagree; discussion is to continue until all members express understanding. Rotate to the next numbered activity and next team member until all activities and entries have been discussed. If at any point a team member is uncertain about an answer, the team member may pass and get back in the rotation when he or she can contribute to the team's discussion.

TEAMWORK IN ACTION
C1 P1 P2 P3 P4

BTN 20-7   Desmond Yang's **Abyzz** faces the challenge of maintaining a balance between a wide variety of clothing and keeping costs down through bulk buying and production.

ENTREPRENEURIAL DECISION
C3 A2

Required

1. Can you design a costing system that will help him to accurately cost his standard and premium products?
2. Prepare a presentation for Desmond, explaining your logic in the choice of the system and the key challenges in implementing it.

HITTING THE ROAD

C2

Point: The class can compare and discuss the different processes studied and the answers provided.

BTN 20-8 In process costing, the process is analyzed first and then a unit measure is computed in the form of equivalent units for direct materials, direct labor, overhead, and all three combined. The same analysis applies to both manufacturing and service processes.

Required

Visit your local bank. Introduce yourself to the customer relations officer. Interview him/her to understand the steps involved in clearing a check issued by a customer. Make your assumptions about the cost of materials, labor, and overhead. Compute the cost of clearing a check. Explain your overhead allocation method.

GLOBAL DECISION

C1

BTN 20-9 Visit Puma's link on product development:

http://ir2.flife.de/data/puma/igb_html/index.php?bericht_id=1000004&index=&lang=ENG

Puma has three main product categories: Footwear, Apparel, and Accesories. It has several brands and categories under each of these three main categories.

Required

How might Puma's product management philosophy affect production costs across the three main categories and the various subcategories?

ANSWERS TO MULTIPLE CHOICE QUIZ

1. d
2. e
3. b; $20,000 + $152,000 + $45,000 + $18,000 − $218,000 = $17,000

4. a; 40,000 + (15,000 × 1/3) = 45,000 EUP
5. c; ($6,000 + $84,000) ÷ 45,000 EUP = $2 per EUP

21

Cost Allocation and Performance Measurement

A Look Back

Chapter 20 focused on how to measure and account for costs in process operations. It explained process production, described how to assign costs to processes, and computed cost per equivalent unit.

A Look at This Chapter

This chapter describes cost allocation and activity-based costing. It identifies managerial reports useful in directing a company's activities. It also describes responsibility accounting, measuring departmental performance, transfer pricing, and allocating common costs across departments.

A Look Ahead

Chapter 22 looks at cost behavior and explains how its identification is useful to managers in performing cost-volume-profit analyses. It also shows how to apply cost-volume-profit analysis for managerial decisions.

Learning Objectives

CAP

CONCEPTUAL

C1 Distinguish between direct and indirect expenses and identify bases for allocating indirect expenses to departments. (p. 837)

C2 Explain controllable costs and responsibility accounting. (p. 847)

C3 *Appendix 21A*—Explain transfer pricing and methods to set transfer prices. (p. 854)

C4 *Appendix 21B*—Describe allocation of joint costs across products. (p. 855)

ANALYTICAL

A1 Analyze investment centers using return on assets, residual income, and balanced scorecard. (p. 845)

A2 Analyze investment centers using profit margin and investment turnover. (p. 850)

PROCEDURAL

P1 Assign overhead costs using two-stage cost allocation. (p. 830)

P2 Assign overhead costs using activity-based costing. (p. 832)

P3 Prepare departmental income statements and contribution reports. (p. 839)

"Idle assets are detrimental to business unit performance."—**SUNDARMOORTHY**

 **Decision Insight**

No Idle Assets at Hunter Douglas

Hunter Douglas is a leading global manufacturer and distributor of window coverings and architectural products. Headquartered in Rotterdam, the Netherlands, and with 17,000 employees around the world, the company has a significant presence in Asia and has its main Asian office in Kuala Lumpur, Malaysia.

The company's strong research base helps it deliver innovative products to the market—products that serve as window coverings, acoustical and metal ceilings, and solar controls. The company works with architects, designers, and builders to manage heat, light, and acoustics. It provides customization, fabrication, installation, and technical support services to help its customers derive maximum value from its products. The company's portfolio includes a range of high profile projects covering a variety of buildings and spaces, such as homes, hotels, hospitals, IT parks, commercial buildings, and airports.

PK Sundaramoorthy (Sundar) is the managing director of Hunter Douglas's Indian business (**http://wf.hunterdouglas.asia/in/en/sb.cn**). Sundar, who has an MBA from the Indian Institute of Management, Bengaluru, uses cost accounting information in a variety of decision-making situations, including bidding on projects.

Sundar is also required to track and report on divisional performance. The Indian business, for example, reports its business performance under five product-based business units. Each unit and the Indian business as a whole is evaluated on a measure of profit computed after net asset charge. The net asset charge is computed as a percentage of net fixed assets plus net current assets. To enhance business unit performance, Sundar has to keep a tight control on net assets while improving its profits. "Idle assets are detrimental to business unit performance," he explains.

This chapter describes how to allocate costs shared by more than one product across those different products and how to allocate indirect costs of shared items such as utilities, advertising, and rent. The chapter also describes activity-based costing and how it traces the costs of individual activities. This knowledge helps managers better understand how to assign costs and assess company performance. The chapter also introduces additional managerial accounting reports useful in managing a company's activities and explains how and why management divides companies into departments.

Cost Allocation and Performance Measurement

Overhead Cost Allocation Methods	Departmental Accounting	Departmental Expense Allocation	Investment Centers	Responsibility Accounting
• Two-stage cost allocation • Activity-based cost allocation • Comparison of allocation methods	• Motivation for departmentalization • Departmental evaluation	• Direct and indirect expenses • Allocation of indirect expenses • Departmental income statements and contribution to overhead	• Financial performance measures • Nonfinancial performance measures	• Controllable versus direct costs • Responsibility accounting system • Transfer pricing

Section 1—Allocating Costs for Product Costing

Managers focus on different costs for different decisions. This requires different cost allocation methods to fit these decisions. This first of two sections in this chapter focuses on alternatives for allocation of costs to products and services. We explain and illustrate two basic methods: (1) traditional two-stage cost allocation and (2) activity-based cost allocation. The second section describes and illustrates the allocation of costs for performance evaluation.

OVERHEAD COST ALLOCATION METHODS

P1 Assign overhead costs using two-stage cost allocation.

Point: Use of a single overhead allocation rate is known as using a *plantwide rate*.

We previously explained how to assign overhead costs to jobs (and processes) by using a predetermined overhead rate per unit of an allocation base such as direct labor cost. When a single overhead rate is used on a companywide basis, all overhead is lumped together, and a predetermined overhead rate per unit of an allocation base is computed and used to assign overhead to jobs (and processes). The use of a single predetermined overhead rate suggests that this allocation process is simple. In reality, it can be complicated. This chapter explains the traditional two-stage cost allocation procedure and then introduces the activity-based cost allocation procedure.

Two-Stage Cost Allocation

An organization incurs overhead costs in many activities. These activities can be identified with various departments, which can be broadly classified as either operating or service departments. *Operating departments* perform an organization's main functions. For example, an accounting firm's main functions usually include auditing, tax, and advisory services. Similarly, the production and selling departments of a manufacturing firm perform its main functions and serve as operating departments. *Service departments* provide support to an organization's operating departments. Examples of service departments are payroll, human resource management, accounting, and executive management. Service departments do not engage in activities that generate revenues, yet their support is crucial for the operating departments' success. In this section, we apply a two-stage cost allocation procedure to assign (1) service department costs to operating departments and (2) operating department costs, including those assigned from service departments, to the organization's output.

Illustration of Two-Stage Cost Allocation   Exhibit 21.1 shows the two-stage cost allocation procedure. This exhibit uses data from **AutoGrand**, a custom automobile manufacturer. AutoGrand has five manufacturing-related departments: janitorial, maintenance, factory accounting, machining, and assembly. Expenses incurred by each of these departments are considered product costs. There are three service departments—janitorial, maintenance, and factory accounting; each incurs expenses of $10,000, $15,000 and $8,000, respectively. There are two operating departments, machining and assembly; they incur expenses of $10,000 and $18,000, respectively. As shown in Exhibit 21.1, the first stage of the two-stage procedure involves allocating the costs of the three service departments to the two operating departments (machining and assembly). The two operating departments use the resources of these service departments.

EXHIBIT 21.1

Two-Stage Cost Allocation

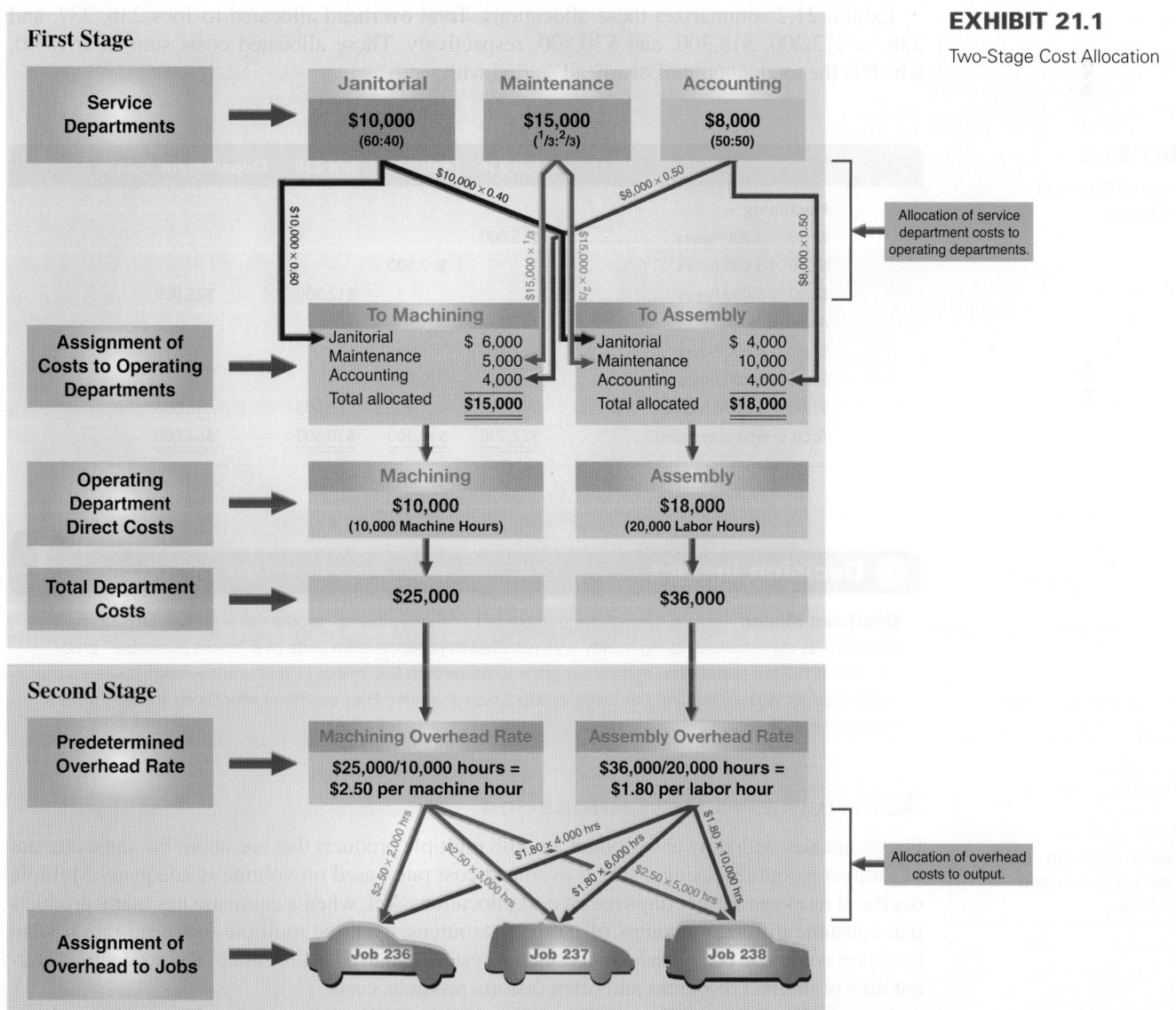

First Stage   To illustrate the first stage of cost allocation, we use the janitorial department. Its costs are allocated to machining and assembly in the ratio 60:40. This means that 60%, or $6,000, of janitorial costs are assigned to the machining department and 40%, or $4,000, to the assembly department. The expenses incurred by the maintenance and factory accounting departments are similarly assigned to machining and assembly. We then add the expenses directly incurred by each operating department to these assigned costs to determine the total expenses for each operating department. This yields total costs of $25,000 for machining and $36,000 for assembly.

Second Stage   In the second stage, predetermined overhead rates are computed for each operating department. The allocation base is machine hours for machining and labor hours for assembly. The predetermined overhead rate is $2.50 per machine hour for the machining department and $1.80 per labor hour for the assembly department. These predetermined overhead rates are then used to assign overhead to output.

To illustrate this second stage, assume that three jobs were started and finished in a recent month. These jobs consumed resources as follows: Job 236—2,000 machine hours in machining and 4,000 labor hours in assembly; Job 237—3,000 machine hours and 6,000 labor hours; Job 238—5,000 machine hours and 10,000 labor hours. The overhead assigned to these three jobs is shown with the arrow lines in the bottom row of Exhibit 21.1.

Exhibit 21.2 summarizes these allocations. Total overhead allocated to Jobs 236, 237, and 238, is $12,200, $18,300, and $30,500, respectively. These allocated costs sum to $61,000, which is the total amount of overhead started with.

EXHIBIT 21.2

Assignment of Overhead Costs to Output

	Job 236	Job 237	Job 238	Department Totals
Machining				
$2.50 × 2,000 hours	$ 5,000			
$2.50 × 3,000 hours		$ 7,500		
$2.50 × 5,000 hours			$12,500	$25,000
Assembly				
$1.80 × 4,000 hours	7,200			
$1.80 × 6,000 hours		10,800		
$1.80 × 10,000 hours			18,000	36,000
Total overhead assigned	$12,200	$18,300	$30,500	$61,000

Decision Insight

Overhead Misled   **Futura Computer** outsourced a "money-losing" product to a Korean firm for manufacturing. Its own manufacturing facility was retooled to produce extra units of a "more profitable" product. Profits did not materialize, and losses grew to more than $20 million! What went wrong? It seems the better product was a loser and the losing product was a winner. Poor overhead allocations misled Futura's management. ■

Activity-Based Cost Allocation

For companies with only one product, or with multiple products that use about the same amount of indirect resources, using a single overhead cost rate based on volume is adequate. Multiple overhead rates can further improve on cost allocations. Yet, when a company has many products that consume different amounts of indirect resources, even the multiple overhead rate system based on volume is often inadequate. Such a system usually fails to reflect the products' different uses of indirect resources and often distorts products costs.

Specifically, low-volume complex products are usually undercosted, whereas high-volume simpler products are overcosted. This can cause companies to believe that their complex products

EXHIBIT 21.3

Activity-Based Cost Allocation

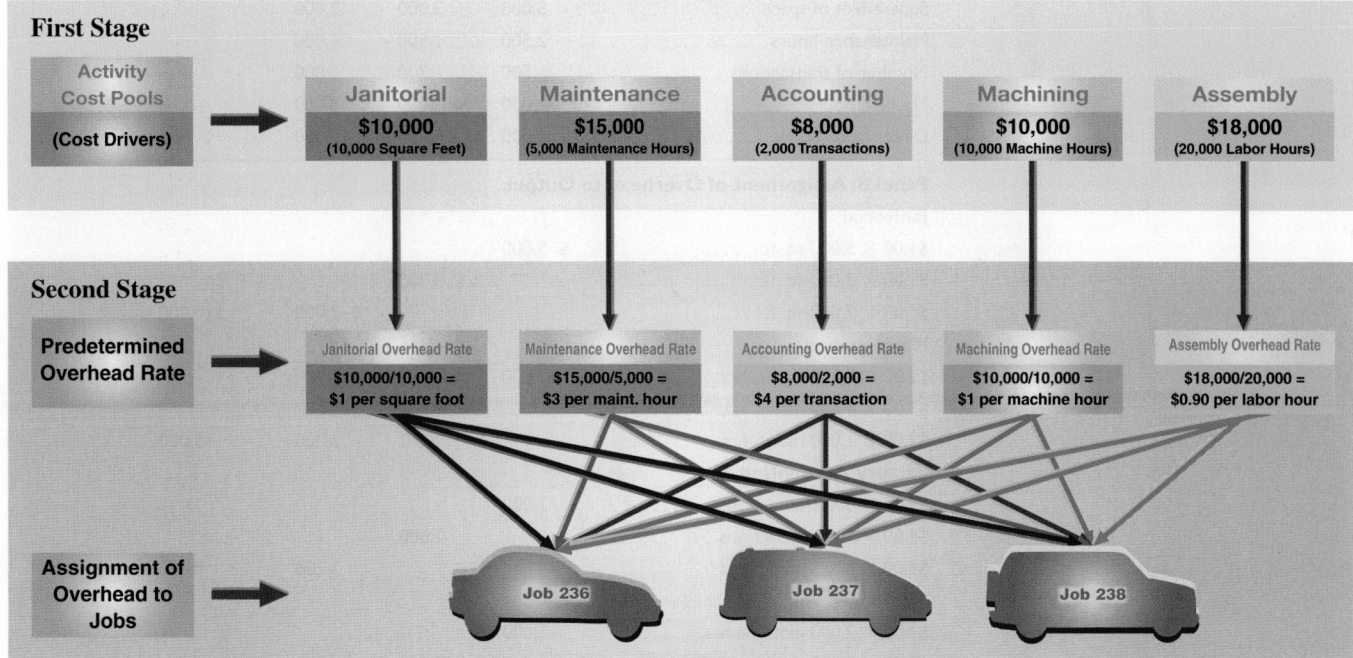

are more profitable than they really are, which can lead those companies to focus on them to the detriment of high-volume simpler products. This creates a demand for a better cost allocation system for these indirect (overhead) costs.

Activity-based costing (ABC) attempts to better allocate costs to the proper users of overhead by focusing on *activities*. Costs are traced to individual activities and then allocated to cost objects. Exhibit 21.3 shows the (two-stage) activity-based cost allocation method. The first stage identifies the activities involved in processing Jobs 236, 237, and 238 and forms activity cost *pools* by combining those activities. The second stage involves computing predetermined overhead cost rates for each cost pool and then assigning costs to jobs.

We begin our explanation at the top of Exhibit 21.3. The first stage identifies individual activities, which are pooled in a logical manner into homogenous groups, or *cost pools*. A homogeneous cost pool consists of activities that belong to the same process and/or are caused by the same cost driver. An **activity cost driver,** or simply *cost driver,* is a factor that causes the cost of an activity to go up or down. For example, preparing an invoice, checking it, and dispatching it are activities of the "invoicing" process and can therefore be grouped in a single cost pool. Moreover, the number of invoices processed likely drives the costs of these activities.

An **activity cost pool** is a temporary account accumulating the costs a company incurs to support an identified set of activities. Costs accumulated in an activity cost pool include the variable and fixed costs of the activities in the pool. Variable costs pertain to resources acquired as needed (such as materials); fixed costs pertain to resources acquired in advance (such as equipment). An activity cost pool account is handled like a factory overhead account.

In the second stage, after all activity costs are accumulated in an activity cost pool account, overhead rates are computed. Then, costs are allocated to cost objects (users) based on cost drivers (allocation bases).

Illustration of Activity-Based Costing To illustrate, let's return to AutoGrand's three jobs. Assume that resources used to complete Jobs 236, 237, and 238 are shown in panel A at the top of Exhibit 21.4.

The $61,000 of total costs are assigned to these three jobs using activity-based costing as shown in panel B at the bottom of Exhibit 21.4 (rates are taken from the second stage of Exhibit 21.3).

Point: Activity-based costing is used in many settings. A study found that activity-based costing improves health care costing accuracy, enabling improved profitability analysis and decision making. However, identifying cost drivers in a health care setting is challenging.

Point: Although the use of activity-based allocation of overheads can lead to more accurate measurement of costs, according to some surveys, the adoption of activity-based costing across countries in Asia is very low.

Point: A cost driver is different from an allocation base. An allocation base is used as a basis for assigning overhead but need not have a cause-effect relation with the costs assigned. However, a cost driver has a cause-effect relation with the cost assigned.

EXHIBIT 21.4

Activity Resource Use and Assignment of Overhead to Output

	Job 236	Job 237	Job 238	Activity Totals
Panel A: Resources Used				
Square feet of space	5,000	3,000	2,000	
Maintenance hours	2,500	1,500	1,000	
Number of transactions	500	700	800	
Machine hours	2,000	3,000	5,000	
Direct labor hours	4,000	6,000	10,000	
Panel B: Assignment of Overhead to Output				
Janitorial				
$1.00 × 5,000 sq. ft.	$ 5,000			
$1.00 × 3,000 sq. ft.		$ 3,000		
$1.00 × 2,000 sq. ft.			$ 2,000	$10,000
Maintenance				
$3.00 × 2,500 maint. hrs.	7,500			
$3.00 × 1,500 maint. hrs.		4,500		
$3.00 × 1,000 maint. hrs.			3,000	15,000
Factory Accounting				
$4.00 × 500 transactions	2,000			
$4.00 × 700 transactions		2,800		
$4.00 × 800 transactions			3,200	8,000
Machining				
$1.00 × 2,000 machine hrs.	2,000			
$1.00 × 3,000 machine hrs.		3,000		
$1.00 × 5,000 machine hrs.			5,000	10,000
Assembly				
$0.90 × 4,000 labor hrs.	3,600			
$0.90 × 6,000 labor hrs.		5,400		
$0.90 × 10,000 labor hrs.			9,000	18,000
Total overhead assigned	$20,100	$18,700	$22,200	$61,000

From Exhibit 21.5, we see that the costs assigned to the three jobs vary markedly depending on whether two-stage (departmental) cost allocation or activity-based costing is used. Costs assigned to Job 236 go from $12,200 under two-stage cost allocation to $20,100 under activity-based costing. Costs assigned to Job 238 decline from $30,500 to $22,200. These differences in assigned amounts result from more accurately tracing costs to each job using activity-based costing where the allocation bases reflect actual cost drivers.

EXHIBIT 21.5

Comparing Overhead Costs Assigned under Alternative Methods

Overhead Assigned	Job 236	Job 237	Job 238	Total
Two-stage cost allocation (Exhibit 21.2)	$12,200	$18,300	$30,500	$61,000
Activity-based costing (Exhibit 21.4)	20,100	18,700	22,200	61,000

Decision Maker   Answer — p. 858

Director of Operations Two department managers at your ad agency complain to you that overhead costs assigned to them are too high. Overhead is assigned on the basis of labor hours for designers. These managers argue that overhead depends not only on designers' hours but on many activities unrelated to these hours. What is your response? ■

Comparison of Two-Stage and Activity-Based Cost Allocation

Traditional cost systems capture overhead costs by individual department (or function) and accumulate these costs in one or more overhead accounts. Companies then assign these overhead costs using a single allocation base such as direct labor or multiple volume-based allocation bases.

Unfortunately, traditional cost systems have tended to use allocation bases that are often not closely related to the way these costs are actually incurred.

In contrast, activity-based cost systems capture costs by individual activity. These activities and their costs are then accumulated into activity cost pools. A company selects a cost driver (allocation base) for each activity pool. It uses this cost driver to assign the accumulated activity costs to cost objects (such as jobs or products) benefiting from the activity. As shown in Exhibit 21.5, the activity-based costing (ABC) system can more accurately trace costs to individual jobs. More generally, we can conclude the following:

- ABC uses more allocation bases than a traditional cost system. For example, a Chicago-based manufacturer currently uses nearly 20 different activity cost drivers to assign overhead costs to its products. Exhibit 21.6 lists common examples of overhead cost pools and their usual cost drivers.

- ABC is especially effective when the same department or departments produce many different types of products. For instance, more complex products often require more help from service departments such as engineering, maintenance, and materials handling. If the same amount of direct labor is applied to the complex and simple products, a traditional overhead allocation system assigns the same overhead cost to both. With activity-based costing, however, the complex products are assigned a larger portion of overhead. The difference in overhead assigned can affect product pricing, make-or-buy, and other managerial decisions.

- ABC encourages managers to focus on *activities* as well as the use of those activities. For instance, assume AutoGrand can reduce the number of transactions processed in Factory Accounting to 1,500 (375 transactions for Job 236, 525 transactions for Job 237, and 600 transactions for Job 238) and that through continuous improvement it can reduce costs of processing those transactions to $4,500. The resulting rate to process a transaction is $3 per transaction ($4,500/1,500 transactions—down from $4 per Exhibit 21.3). The cost of transaction processing is reduced for all jobs (Job 236, $1,125; Job 237, $1,575; Job 238, $1,800). However, if those accounting costs were grouped in a single overhead cost pool, it is more difficult to identify cost savings and understand their effects on product costs.

- ABC requires managers to look at each item and encourages them to manage each cost to increase the benefit from each dollar spent. It also encourages managers to cooperate because it shows how their efforts are interrelated. This results in *activity-based management.*

Activity Cost Pool	Cost Driver
Materials purchasing	Number of purchase orders
Materials handling	Number of materials requisitions
Personnel processing	Number of employees hired or laid off
Equipment depreciation	Number of products produced or hours of use
Quality inspection	Number of units inspected
Indirect labor in setting up equipment	Number of setups required
Engineering costs for product modifications	Number of modifications (engineering change orders)

EXHIBIT 21.6

Cost Pools and Cost Drivers in Activity-Based Costing

Decision Ethics   Answer — p. 858

Accounting Officer   Your company produces expensive garments, whose production involves many complex and specialized activities. Your general manager recently learned about activity-based costing (ABC) and asks your advice. However, your supervisor does not want to disturb the existing cost system and instructs you to prepare a report stating that "implementation of ABC is a complicated process involving too many steps and not worth the effort." You believe ABC will actually help the company identify sources of costs and control them. What action do you take? ∎

1. What is a cost driver?

2. When activity-based costing is used rather than traditional allocation methods, (*a*) managers must identify cost drivers for various items of overhead cost, (*b*) individual cost items in service departments are allocated directly to products or services, (*c*) managers can direct their attention to the activities that drive overhead cost, or (*d*) all of the above.

Section 2—Allocating Costs for Performance Evaluation

This second section of the chapter describes and illustrates allocation of costs for performance evaluation. We begin with departmental accounting and expense allocations and conclude with responsibility accounting.

DEPARTMENTAL ACCOUNTING

Companies are divided into *departments,* also called *subunits,* when they are too large to be managed effectively as a single unit. Managerial accounting for departments has two main goals. The first is to set up a **departmental accounting system** to provide information for managers to evaluate the profitability or cost effectiveness of each department's activities. The second goal is to set up a **responsibility accounting system** to control costs and expenses and evaluate managers' performances by assigning costs and expenses to the managers responsible for controlling them. Departmental and responsibility accounting systems are related and share much information.

Motivation for Departmentalization

Point: Major Cineplex, Thailand's lifestyle entertainment company, is divided into several divisions or business units: cinema, bowling and karaoke, advertising, rental and services, and film distribution. In its financial reports Major Cineplex reports revenues and operating profits for each of these units. This helps various users understand each business unit performance in addition to the overall corporate performance. Business units may be somewhat interdependent, as in the case of Major Cineplex (for example, advertising revenues also depend on success of the cinema business) or completely independent of each other.

Many companies are so large and complex that they are broken into separate divisions for efficiency and/or effectiveness purposes. Divisions then are usually organized into separate departments. When a company is departmentalized, each department is often placed under the direction of a manager. As a company grows, management often divides departments into new departments so that responsibilities for a department's activities do not overwhelm the manager's ability to oversee and control them. A company also creates departments to take advantage of the skills of individual managers. Departments are broadly classified as either operating or service departments.

Departmental Evaluation

When a company is divided into departments, managers need to know how each department is performing. The accounting system must supply information about resources used and outputs achieved by each department. This requires a system to measure and accumulate revenue and expense information for each department whenever possible. Exhibit 21.7 shows the divisional numbers for Major Cineplex from its annual report of 2013.

EXHIBIT 21.7

Divisional Numbers for Major Cineplex

(in THB million)	Cinema	Advertising	Bowling and Karaoke	Rental	Movie Content Business	Consolidated
Net revenues	5,451	788	490	481	500	7,710
Segment results	794	569	46	31	−295	1,145
Net profit						1024
Unallocated costs and income						121

Departmental information is rarely distributed publicly because of its potential usefulness to competitors. Information about departments is prepared for internal managers to help control operations, appraise performance, allocate resources, and plan strategy. If a department is highly profitable, management may decide to expand its operations, or if a department is performing poorly, information about revenues or expenses can suggest useful changes.

More companies are emphasizing customer satisfaction as a main responsibility of many departments. This has led to changes in the measures reported. Increasingly, financial measurements are being supplemented with quality and customer satisfaction indexes. At **Haier**, one of China's leading brands and a global name in household electrical and electronic appliances, divisional control is based on a combination of financial and nonfinancial measures. Nonfinancial measures include capacity utilization, productivity, management quality, new product introduction, and breakthroughs in R&D. The set of measures used changes with the strategy emphasized by the company at any point in time.

Financial information used to evaluate a department depends on whether it is evaluated as a profit center, cost center, revenue center, or investment center. A **profit center** incurs costs and generates revenues; selling departments are often evaluated as profit centers. Depending on how costs are defined for the purpose, a profit center could be responsible for gross profits, operating profits before central administrative costs, or operating profits after central administrative costs. Interest costs or taxes are rarely assigned to profit centers. A **cost center** incurs costs without directly generating revenues. Cost centers are responsible for keeping cost per unit of production at or below a standard. The manufacturing departments of a manufacturer and its service departments such as accounting, advertising, and purchasing, are all cost centers. A **revenue center** is responsible for achieving or exceeding budgeted revenues. Costs, except the relatively minor administrative costs of running the center, are not considered important in the evaluation of revenue centers. An **investment center** incurs costs and generates revenues, and is responsible for effectively using center assets. The manager of an investment center is required to maximize profits while minimizing the assets deployed as much as possible. Profit, cost, revenue, and investment centers are collectively known as *responsibility centers*, as they fix financial responsibility on the specific center and its managers.

Evaluating managers' performance depends on whether they are responsible for profit centers, cost centers, or investment centers. Profit center managers are judged on their abilities to generate revenues in excess of the department's costs. They are assumed to influence both revenue generation and cost incurrence. Cost center managers are judged on their abilities to control costs by keeping them within a satisfactory range under an assumption that only they influence costs. Investment center managers are evaluated on their use of center assets to generate income.

Point: Selling departments are often treated as *revenue centers*; their managers are responsible for maximizing sales revenues.

Quick Check

Answers — p. 858

3. What is the difference between a departmental accounting system and a responsibility accounting system?
4. Service departments (a) manufacture products, (b) make sales directly to customers, (c) produce revenues, (d) assist operating departments.
5. Explain the difference between a cost center and a profit center. Cite an example of each.

DEPARTMENTAL EXPENSE ALLOCATION

When a company computes departmental profits, it confronts some accounting challenges that involve allocating its expenses across its operating departments.

Direct and Indirect Expenses

Direct expenses are costs readily traced to a department because they are incurred for that department's sole benefit. They require no allocation across departments. For example, the salary of an employee who works in only one department is a direct expense of that one department.

Indirect expenses are costs that are incurred for the joint benefit of more than one department and cannot be readily traced to only one department. For example, if two or more departments share a single building, all enjoy the benefits of the expenses for rent, heat, and light. Indirect expenses are allocated across departments benefiting from them when we need information about departmental profits. Ideally, we allocate indirect expenses by using a cause-effect relation. When we cannot identify cause-effect relations, we allocate each indirect expense on a basis approximating the relative benefit each department receives. Measuring the benefit for each department from an indirect expense can be difficult.

C1 Distinguish between direct and indirect expenses and identify bases for allocating indirect expenses to departments.

Point: Utility expense has elements of both direct and indirect expenses.

Illustration of Indirect Expense Allocation   To illustrate how to allocate an indirect expense, we consider a retail store that purchases janitorial services from an outside company. Management allocates this cost across the store's three departments according to the floor space each occupies. Costs of janitorial services for a recent month are $300. Exhibit 21.8 shows the square feet of floor space each department occupies. The store computes the percent of total square feet allotted to each department and uses it to allocate the $300 cost.

EXHIBIT 21.8

Indirect Expense Allocation

Department	Square Feet	Percent of Total	Allocated Cost
Jewelry	2,400	60%	$180
Watch repair	600	15	45
China and silver	1,000	25	75
Totals	4,000	100%	$300

Specifically, because the jewelry department occupies 60% of the floor space, 60% of the total $300 cost is assigned to it. The same procedure is applied to the other departments. When the allocation process is complete, these and other allocated costs are deducted from the gross profit for each department to determine net profit for each. One consideration in allocating costs is to motivate managers and employees to behave as desired. As a result, a cost incurred in one department might be best allocated to other departments when one of the other departments caused the cost.

Allocation of Indirect Expenses

This section describes how to identify the bases used to allocate indirect expenses across departments. No standard rule identifies the best basis because expense allocation involves several factors, and the relative importance of these factors varies across departments and organizations. Judgment is required, and people do not always agree. Employee morale suffers when allocations are perceived as unfair. Thus, it is important to carefully design and explain the allocation of service department costs. In our discussion, note the parallels between activity-based costing and the departmental expense allocation procedures described here.

Wages and Salaries   Employee wages and salaries can be either direct or indirect expenses. If their time is spent entirely in one department, their wages are direct expenses of that department. However, if employees work for the benefit of more than one department, their wages are indirect expenses and must be allocated across the departments benefited. An employee's contribution to a department usually depends on the number of hours worked in contributing to that department. Thus, a reasonable basis for allocating employee wages and salaries is the *relative amount of time spent in each department*. In the case of a supervisor who manages more than one department, recording the time spent in each department may not always be practical. Instead, a company can allocate the supervisor's salary to departments on the basis of the number of employees in each department—a reasonable basis if a supervisor's main task is managing people. Another basis of allocation is on sales across departments, also a reasonable basis if a supervisor's job reflects on departmental sales.

Point: Some companies ask supervisors to estimate time spent supervising specific departments for purposes of expense allocation.

Rent and Related Expenses   Rent expense for a building is reasonably allocated to a department on the basis of floor space it occupies. Location can often make some floor space more valuable than other space. Thus, the allocation method can charge departments that occupy more valuable space a higher expense per square foot. Ground floor retail space, for instance, is often more valuable than basement or upper-floor space because all customers pass departments near the entrance but fewer go beyond the first floor. When no precise measures of floor space values exist, basing allocations on data such as customer traffic and real estate assessments is helpful. When a company owns its building, its expenses for depreciation, taxes, insurance, and other related building expenses are allocated like rent expense.

Advertising Expenses   Effective advertising of a department's products increases its sales and customer traffic. Moreover, advertising products for some departments usually helps other departments' sales because customers also often buy unadvertised products. Thus, many stores treat advertising as an indirect expense allocated on the basis of each department's proportion of total sales. For example, a department with 10% of a store's total sales is assigned 10% of advertising expense. Another method is to analyze each advertisement to compute the Web/newspaper space or TV/radio time devoted to the products of a department and charge that department for the proportional costs of advertisements. Management must consider whether this more detailed and costly method is justified.

Equipment and Machinery Depreciation Depreciation on equipment and machinery used only in one department is a direct expense of that department. Depreciation on equipment and machinery used by more than one department is an indirect expense to be allocated across departments. Accounting for each department's depreciation expense requires a company to keep records showing which departments use specific assets. The number of hours that a department uses equipment and machinery is a reasonable basis for allocating depreciation.

Utilities Expenses Utilities expenses such as heating and lighting are usually allocated on the basis of floor space occupied by departments. This practice assumes their use is uniform across departments. When this is not so, a more involved allocation can be necessary, although there is often a trade-off between the usefulness of more precise allocations and the effort to compute them. Manufacturers often allocate electricity cost to departments on the basis of the horsepower of equipment located in each department.

Service Department Expenses To generate revenues, operating departments require support services provided by departments such as personnel, payroll, advertising, and purchasing. Such service departments are typically evaluated as cost centers because they do not produce revenues. (Evaluating them as profit centers requires the use of a system that "charges" user departments a price that then serves as the "revenue" generated by service departments.) A departmental accounting system can accumulate and report costs incurred directly by each service department for this purpose. The system then allocates a service department's expenses to operating departments benefiting from them. This is often done, for example, using traditional two-stage cost allocation (see Exhibit 21.1). Exhibit 21.9 shows some commonly used bases for allocating service department expenses to operating departments.

Point: When a service department "charges" its user departments within a company, a *transfer pricing system* must be set up to determine the "revenue" from its services provided.

Service Department	Common Allocation Bases
Office expenses	Number of employees or sales in each department
Personnel expenses	Number of employees in each department
Payroll expenses	Number of employees in each department
Advertising expenses	Sales or amount of advertising charged directly to each department
Purchasing costs	Dollar amounts of purchases or number of purchase orders processed
Cleaning expenses	Square feet of floor space occupied
Maintenance expenses	Square feet of floor space occupied

EXHIBIT 21.9

Bases for Allocating Service Department Expenses

Departmental Income Statements

An income statement can be prepared for each operating department once expenses have been assigned to it. Its expenses include both direct expenses and its share of indirect expenses. For this purpose, compiling all expenses incurred in service departments before assigning them to operating departments is useful. We illustrate the steps to prepare departmental income statements using **A-1 Hardware** and its five departments. Two of them (office and purchasing) are service departments and the other three (hardware, housewares, and appliances) are operating (selling) departments. Allocating costs to operating departments and preparing departmental income statements involves four steps.

P3 Prepare departmental income statements and contribution reports.

1. Accumulating direct expenses by department.
2. Allocating indirect expenses across departments.
3. Allocating service department expenses to operating department.
4. Preparing departmental income statements.

Step 1 Step 1 accumulates direct expenses for each service and operating department as shown in Exhibit 21.10. Direct expenses include salaries, wages, and other expenses that each department incurs but does not share with any other department. This information is accumulated in departmental expense accounts.

EXHIBIT 21.10

Step 1: Direct Expense Accumulation

Accumulate Direct Expenses in Departmental Expense Accounts

General office · Purchasing · Hardware · Housewares · Appliances

Point: We sometimes allocate service department costs across other service departments before allocating them to operating departments. This "step-wise" process is in advanced courses.

Step 2 Step 2 allocates indirect expenses across all departments as shown in Exhibit 21.11. Indirect expenses can include items such as depreciation, rent, advertising, and any other expenses that cannot be directly assigned to a department. Indirect expenses are recorded in company expense accounts, an allocation base is identified for each expense, and costs are allocated using a *departmental expense allocation spreadsheet* described in step 3.

EXHIBIT 21.11

Step 2: Indirect Expense Allocation

Accumulate Indirect Expenses in Company Accounts and Allocate

General office · Purchasing · Hardware · Housewares · Appliances

Step 3 Step 3 allocates expenses of the service departments (office and purchasing) to the operating departments. Service department costs are not allocated to other service departments. Exhibit 21.12 reflects the allocation of service department expenses using the allocation base(s). All of the direct and indirect expenses of service departments are allocated to operating departments.[1]

EXHIBIT 21.12

Step 3: Service Department Expense Allocation to Operating Departments

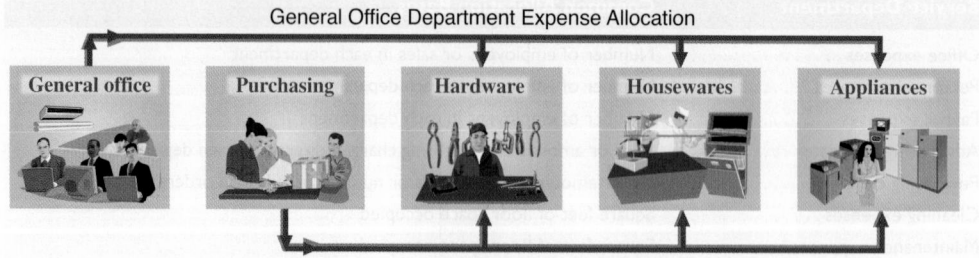

General Office Department Expense Allocation

General office · Purchasing · Hardware · Housewares · Appliances

Purchasing Department Expense Allocation

Computations for both steps 2 and 3 are commonly made using a departmental expense allocation spreadsheet as shown in Exhibit 21.13. The first two sections of this spreadsheet list direct expenses and indirect expenses by department. The third section lists the service department expenses and their allocations to operating departments. The allocation bases are identified in the second column, and total expense amounts are reported in the third column.

Illustration of Steps 1, 2, and 3 The departmental expense allocation spreadsheet is useful in implementing the first three steps. To illustrate, first (step 1) the three direct expenses of salaries, depreciation, and supplies are accumulated in each of the five departments.

---

[1] In some cases we allocate a service department's expenses to other service departments when they use its services. For example, expenses of a payroll office benefit all service and operating departments and can be assigned to all departments. Nearly all examples and assignment materials in this book allocate service expenses only to operating departments for simplicity.

EXHIBIT 21.13

Departmental Expense Allocation Spreadsheet

			File Edit View Insert Format Tools Data Window Help				

A-1 HARDWARE
Departmental Expense Allocations
For Year Ended December 31, 2011

			Allocation of Expenses to Departments				
	Allocation Base	Expense Account Balance	General Office Dept.	Purchas- ing Dept.	Hard- ware Dept.	House- wares Dept.	Appli- ances Dept.
Direct expenses							
Salaries expense.....................	Payroll records.......................	$51,900	$13,300	$8,200	$15,600	$ 7,000	$ 7,800
Depreciation—Equipment......	Depreciation records.............	1,500	500	300	400	100	200
Supplies expense....................	Requisitions...........................	900	200	100	300	200	100
Indirect expenses							
Rent expense	Amount and value of space..	12,000	600	600	4,860	3,240	2,700
Utilities expense......................	Floor space...........................	2,400	300	300	810	540	450
Advertising expense	Sales.....................................	1,000			500	300	200
Insurance expense..................	Value of insured assets	2,500	400	200	900	600	400
Total department expenses		72,200	15,300	9,700	23,370	11,980	11,850
Service department expenses							
General office department.....	Sales.....................................		(15,300)		↳7,650	↳4,590	↳3,060
Purchasing department	Purchase orders....................			(9,700)	→3,880	→2,630	→3,190
Total expenses allocated to operating departments................................		$72,200	$ 0	$ 0	$34,900	$19,200	$18,100

	Sheet1 Sheet2 Sheet3	

Second (step 2), the four indirect expenses of rent, utilities, advertising, and insurance are allocated to all departments using the allocation bases identified. For example, consider rent allocation. Exhibit 21.14 lists the five departments' square footage of space occupied.

Department	Floor Space (Square Feet)	Value of Insured Assets ($)	Sales ($)	Number of Purchase Orders
General office	1,500	$ 38,000		—
Purchasing	1,500	19,000		*
Hardware	4,050	85,500	$119,500	394
Housewares	2,700	57,000	71,700	267
Appliances	2,250	38,000	47,800	324
Total	12,000	$237,500	$239,000	985

EXHIBIT 21.14

Departments' Allocation Bases

* Purchasing department tracks purchase orders by department.

The two service departments (office and purchasing) occupy 25% of the total space (3,000 sq. feet/ 12,000 sq. feet). However, they are located near the back of the building, which is of lower value than space near the front that is occupied by operating departments. Management esti- mates that space near the back accounts for $1,200 of the total rent expense of $12,000. Exhibit 21.15 shows how we allocate the $1,200 rent expense between these two service departments in proportion to their square footage. Exhibit 21.15 shows a simple rule for cost

Department	Square Feet	Percent of Total	Allocated Cost
General office	1,500	50.0%	$ 600
Purchasing	1,500	50.0	600
Totals	3,000	100.0%	$1,200

EXHIBIT 21.15

Allocating Indirect (Rent) Expense to Service Departments

allocations: Allocated cost = Percentage of allocation base × Total cost. We then allocate the remaining $10,800 of rent expense to the three operating departments as shown in Exhibit 21.16.

EXHIBIT 21.16

Allocating Indirect (Rent)
Expense to Operating Departments

Department	Square Feet	Percent of Total	Allocated Cost
Hardware	4,050	45.0%	$ 4,860
Housewares	2,700	30.0	3,240
Appliances	2,250	25.0	2,700
Totals	9,000	100.0%	$10,800

We continue step 2 by allocating the $2,400 of utilities expense to all departments based on the square footage occupied as shown in Exhibit 21.17.

EXHIBIT 21.17

Allocating Indirect (Utilities)
Expense to All Departments

Department	Square Feet	Percent of Total	Allocated Cost
General office	1,500	12.50%	$ 300
Purchasing	1,500	12.50	300
Hardware	4,050	33.75	810
Housewares	2,700	22.50	540
Appliances	2,250	18.75	450
Totals	12,000	100.00%	$2,400

Exhibit 21.18 shows the allocation of $1,000 of advertising expense to the three operating departments on the basis of sales dollars. We exclude service departments from this allocation because they do not generate sales.

EXHIBIT 21.18

Allocating Indirect (Advertising)
Expense to Operating Departments

Department	Sales	Percent of Total	Allocated Cost
Hardware	$119,500	50.0%	$ 500
Housewares	71,700	30.0	300
Appliances	47,800	20.0	200
Totals	$239,000	100.0%	$1,000

To complete step 2 we allocate insurance expense to each service and operating department as shown in Exhibit 21.19.

EXHIBIT 21.19

Allocating Indirect (Insurance)
Expense to All Departments

Department	Value of Insured Assets	Percent of Total	Allocated Cost
General office	$ 38,000	16.0%	$ 400
Purchasing	19,000	8.0	200
Hardware	85,500	36.0	900
Housewares	57,000	24.0	600
Appliances	38,000	16.0	400
Total	$237,500	100.0%	$2,500

Third (step 3), total expenses of the two service departments are allocated to the three operating departments as shown in Exhibits 21.20 and 21.21.

EXHIBIT 21.20

Allocating Service Department
(General Office) Expenses to
Operating Departments

Department	Sales	Percent of Total	Allocated Cost
Hardware	$119,500	50.0%	$ 7,650
Housewares	71,700	30.0	4,590
Appliances	47,800	20.0	3,060
Total	$239,000	100.0%	$15,300

Department	Number of Purchase Orders	Percent of Total	Allocated Cost
Hardware	394	40.00%	$3,880
Housewares	267	27.11	2,630
Appliances	324	32.89	3,190
Total	985	100.00%	$9,700

EXHIBIT 21.21

Allocating Service Department (Purchasing) Expenses to Operating Departments

Step 4 The departmental expense allocation spreadsheet can now be used to prepare performance reports for the company's service and operating departments. The general office and purchasing departments are cost centers, and their managers will be evaluated on their control of costs. Actual amounts of service department expenses can be compared to budgeted amounts to help assess cost center manager performance.

Amounts in the operating department columns are used to prepare departmental income statements as shown in Exhibit 21.22. This exhibit uses the spreadsheet for its operating expenses; information on sales and cost of goods sold comes from departmental records.

Example: If the $15,300 general office expenses in Exhibit 21.13 are allocated equally across departments, what is net profit for the hardware department and for the combined company? *Answer:* Hardware income, $13,350; combined income, $19,000.

EXHIBIT 21.22

Departmental Income Statements

A-I HARDWARE Departmental Income Statements For Year Ended December 31, 2011	Hardware Department	Housewares Department	Appliances Department	Combined
Sales	$119,500	$71,700	$47,800	$239,000
Cost of goods sold	73,800	43,800	30,200	147,800
Gross profit	45,700	27,900	17,600	91,200
Operating expenses				
Salaries expense	(15,600)	(7,000)	(7,800)	(30,400)
Depreciation expense—Equipment	(400)	(100)	(200)	(700)
Supplies expense	(300)	(200)	(100)	(600)
Rent expense........................	(4,860)	(3,240)	(2,700)	(10,800)
Utilities expense	(810)	(540)	(450)	(1,800)
Advertising expense	(500)	(300)	(200)	(1,000)
Insurance expense....................	(900)	(600)	(400)	(1,900)
Share of general office expenses	(7,650)	(4,590)	(3,060)	(15,300)
Share of purchasing expenses	(3,880)	(2,630)	(3,190)	(9,700)
Total operating expenses	(34,900)	(19,200)	(18,100)	(72,200)
Net profit (loss)	$10,800	$8,700	$ (500)	$19,000

Departmental Contribution to Overhead

Data from departmental income statements are not always best for evaluating each profit center's performance, especially when indirect expenses are a large portion of total expenses and when weaknesses in assumptions and decisions in allocating indirect expenses can markedly affect net profit. In these and other cases, we might better evaluate profit center performance using the **departmental contribution to overhead,** which is a report of the amount of sales less *direct* expenses.[2] We can also examine cost center performance by focusing on control of direct expenses.

---

[2] A department's contribution is said to be "to overhead" because of the practice of considering all indirect expenses as overhead. Thus, the excess of a department's sales over direct expenses is a contribution toward at least a portion of its total overhead.

EXHIBIT 21.23

Departmental Contribution
to Overhead

A-I HARDWARE Income Statement Showing Departmental Contribution to Overhead For Year Ended December 31, 2011				
	Hardware Department	Housewares Department	Appliances Department	Combined
Sales	$119,500	$ 71,700	$47,800	$239,000
Cost of goods sold	73,800	43,800	30,200	147,800
Gross profit	45,700	27,900	17,600	91,200
Direct expenses				
Salaries expense	(15,600)	(7,000)	(7,800)	(30,400)
Depreciation expense—Equipment	(400)	(100)	(200)	(700)
Supplies expense	(300)	(200)	(100)	(600)
Total direct expenses.	(16,300)	(7,300)	(8,100)	(31,700)
Departmental contributions				
to overhead.	**$29,400**	**$20,600**	**$ 9,500**	**$59,500**
Indirect expenses				
Rent expense				(10,800)
Utilities expense				(1,800)
Advertising expense.				(1,000)
Insurance expense				(1,900)
General office department expense				(15,300)
Purchasing department expense				(9,700)
Total indirect expenses				(40,500)
Net profit.				$ 19,000
Contribution as percent of sales	24.6%	28.7%	19.9%	24.9%

Point: Net profit is the same in
Exhibits 21.22 and 21.23. The method of
reporting indirect expenses in Exhibit
21.23 does not change total net profit
but does identify each department's contribution to overhead and net profit.

The upper half of Exhibit 21.23 shows a departmental (profit center) contribution to overhead
as part of an expanded income statement. This format is common when reporting departmental
contributions to overhead. Using the information in Exhibits 21.22 and 21.23, we can evaluate
the profitability of the three profit centers. For instance, let's compare the performance of the
appliances department as described in these two exhibits. Exhibit 21.22 shows a $500 net loss
resulting from this department's operations, but Exhibit 21.23 shows a $9,500 positive contribu-
tion to overhead, which is 19.9% of the appliance department's sales. The contribution of the
appliances department is not as large as that of the other selling departments, but a $9,500 con-
tribution to overhead is better than a $500 loss. This tells us that the appliances department
is not a money loser. On the contrary, it is contributing $9,500 toward defraying total indirect
expenses of $40,500.

Quick Check   Answers — p. 858

6. If a company has two operating (selling) departments (shoes and hats) and two service
   departments (payroll and advertising), which of the following statements is correct? (a) Wages
   incurred in the payroll department are direct expenses of the shoe department, (b) Wages
   incurred in the payroll department are indirect expenses of the operating departments, or
   (c) Advertising department expenses are allocated to the other three departments.

7. Which of the following bases can be used to allocate supervisors' salaries across operating
   departments? (a) Hours spent in each department, (b) number of employees in each
   department, (c) sales achieved in each department, or (d) any of the above, depending on
   which information is most relevant and accessible.

8. What three steps are used to allocate expenses to operating departments?

9. An income statement showing departmental contribution to overhead, (a) subtracts indirect
   expenses from each department's revenues, (b) subtracts only direct expenses from each
   department's revenues, or (c) shows net profit for each department.

EVALUATING INVESTMENT CENTER PERFORMANCE

This section introduces both financial and nonfinancial measures of investment center performance.

Financial Performance Evaluation Measures

Investment center managers are typically evaluated using performance measures that combine income and assets. Consider the following data for ZTel, a company which operates two divisions: LCD and S-Phone. The LCD division manufactures liquid crystal display (LCD) touch-screen monitors and sells them for use in computers, cellular phones, and other products. The S-Phone division sells smartphones, mobile phones that also function as personal computers, MP3 players, cameras, and global positioning satellite (GPS) systems. Exhibit 21.24 shows current year income and assets for those divisions.

> **A1** Analyze investment centers using return on assets, residual income, and balanced scorecard.

	LCD	S-Phone
Net profit....................	$ 526,500	$ 417,600
Average invested assets.........	2,500,000	1,850,000

EXHIBIT 21.24

Investment Center Income and Assets

Investment Center Return on Total Assets   One measure to evaluate division performance is the **investment center return on total assets,** also called *return on investment* (ROI). This measure is computed as follows

$$\text{Return on investment} = \frac{\text{Investment center net profit}}{\text{Investment center average invested assets}}$$

The return on investment for the LCD division is 21% (rounded), computed as $526,500/ $2,500,000. The S-Phone division's return on investment is 23% (rounded), computed as $417,600/$1,850,000. Though the LCD division earned more dollars of net profit, it was less efficient in using its assets to generate income compared to the S-Phone division.

Investment Center Residual Income   Another way to evaluate division performance is to compute **investment center residual income,** which is computed as follows

$$\text{Residual income} = \text{Investment center actual net profit} - \text{Investment center target net profit}$$

Assume ZTel's top management sets target net profit at 8% of divisional assets. For an investment center, this **hurdle rate** is typically the cost of obtaining financing. Applying this hurdle rate using the data from Exhibit 21.24 yields the residual income for ZTel's divisions in Exhibit 21.25.

	LCD	S-Phone
Net profit............................	$526,500	$417,600
Target net profit		
$2,500,000 × 8%.....................	(200,000)	
$1,850,000 × 8%.....................		(148,000)
Investment center residual income	$326,500	$269,600

EXHIBIT 21.25

Investment Center Residual Income

Unlike return on assets, residual income is expressed in dollars. The LCD division outperformed the S-Phone division on the basis of residual income. However, this result is due in part to the LCD division having a larger asset base than the S-Phone division.

Using residual income to evaluate division performance encourages division managers to accept all opportunities that return more than the target net profit, thus increasing company value. For example, the S-Phone division might not want to accept a new customer that will provide a 15% return on investment, since that will reduce the S-Phone division's overall return on investment (23% as shown above). However, the S-Phone division should accept this opportunity because the new customer would increase residual income by providing net profit above the target net profit.

Nonfinancial Performance Evaluation Measures

Evaluating performance solely on financial measures such as return on investment or residual income has limitations. For example, some investment center managers might forgo profitable opportunities to keep their return on investment high. Also, residual income is less useful when comparing investment centers of different size. And, both return on investment and residual income can encourage managers to focus too heavily on short-term financial goals.

In response to these limitations, companies consider nonfinancial measures. For example, **Haier** uses the speed of a new product development and launch as a key nonfinancial measure to track its strategy of meeting customer needs as quickly as possible. **Rang Dong Plastics**, a company that manufactures and markets plastic products out of Vietnam, has its vision expressed in the motto "Innovation, competence and performance." To monitor its technological competence the company uses "number of products involving special solutions for customers" as an evaluation measure.

Balanced Scorecard   The **balanced scorecard** is a system of performance measures, including nonfinancial measures, used to assess company and division manager performance. The balanced scorecard requires managers to think of their company from four perspectives:

1. **Customer:** What do customers think of us?
2. **Internal processes:** Which of our operations are critical to meeting customer needs?
3. **Innovation and learning:** How can we improve?
4. **Financial:** What do our owners think of us?

The balanced scorecard collects information on several key performance indicators within each of the four perspectives. These key indicators vary across companies. Exhibit 21.26 lists common performance measures.

EXHIBIT 21.26

Balanced Scorecard Performance Indicators

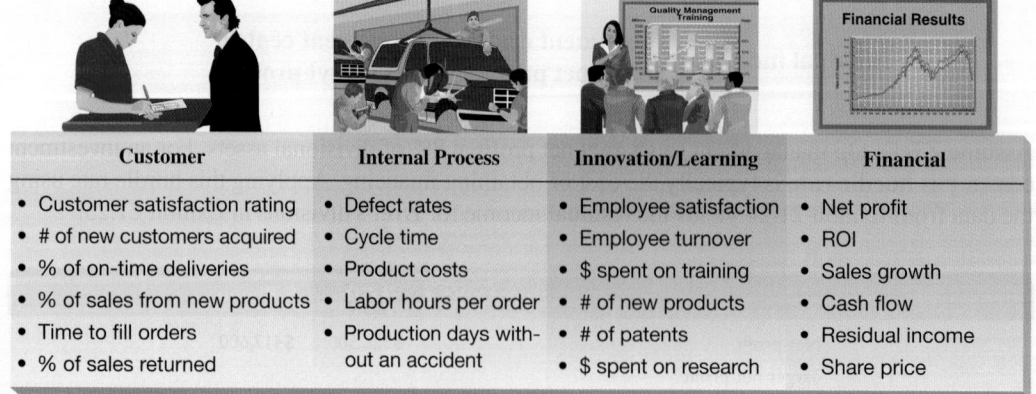

Customer	Internal Process	Innovation/Learning	Financial
• Customer satisfaction rating	• Defect rates	• Employee satisfaction	• Net profit
• # of new customers acquired	• Cycle time	• Employee turnover	• ROI
• % of on-time deliveries	• Product costs	• $ spent on training	• Sales growth
• % of sales from new products	• Labor hours per order	• # of new products	• Cash flow
• Time to fill orders	• Production days without an accident	• # of patents	• Residual income
• % of sales returned		• $ spent on research	• Share price

After selecting key performance indicators, companies collect data on each indicator and compare actual amounts to expected amounts to assess performance. For example, a company might have a goal of filling 98% of customer orders within two hours. Balanced scorecard reports are often presented in graphs or tables that can be updated frequently. Such timely information aids division managers in their decisions, and can be used by top management to evaluate division manager performance.

One important factor that affects the choice of measures under each of the four perspectives is the strategy of the business. For example, a luxury retail store might emphasize profit margins while a discount retail store might emphasize sales volumes. Another factor that can affect the choice of measures is the industry to which a company belongs.

Exhibit 21.27 is an example of balanced scorecard reporting on the customer perspective for an Internet retailer. This scorecard reports for example that the retailer is getting 62% of its potential customers successfully through the checkout process, and that 2.2% of all orders are returned. The *color* of the arrows in the right-most column reveals whether the company is exceeding its goal (green), barely meeting the goal (yellow), or not meeting the goal (red). The *direction* of the arrows reveals any trend in performance: an upward arrow indicates improvement, a downward arrow indicates declining performance, and an arrow pointing sideways indicates no change. A review of these arrows' color and direction suggests the retailer is meeting or exceeding its goals on checkout success, orders returned, and customer satisfaction. Further, checkout success and customer satisfaction are improving. The red arrow shows the company has received more customer complaints than was hoped for; however, the number of customer complaints is declining. A manager would combine this information with similar information on the internal process, innovation and learning, and financial perspectives to get an overall view of division performance.

Customer Perspective	Actual	Goal
Checkout success	62%	⬆
Orders returned	2.2%	⬌
Customer satisfaction rating	9.5	⬆
Number of customer complaints	142	⬇

EXHIBIT 21.27

Balanced Scorecard Reporting: Internet Retailer

🔲 **Decision Maker**   Answer — p. 858

Center Manager   Your center's usual return on total assets is 19%. You are considering two new investments for your center. The first requires a $250,000 average investment and is expected to yield annual net profit of $50,000. The second requires a $1 million average investment with an expected annual net profit of $175,000. Do you pursue either? ■

RESPONSIBILITY ACCOUNTING

Departmental accounting reports often provide data used to evaluate a department's performance, but are they useful in assessing how well a department *manager* performs? Neither departmental income nor its contribution to overhead may be useful because many expenses can be outside a manager's control. Instead, we often evaluate a manager's performance using responsibility accounting reports that describe a department's activities in terms of **controllable costs.**[3] A cost is controllable if a manager has the power to determine or at least significantly affect the amount incurred. **Uncontrollable costs** are not within the manager's control or influence.

  C2 Explain controllable costs and responsibility accounting.

---

[3] The terms *cost* and *expense* are often used interchangeably in managerial accounting, but they are not necessarily the same. *Cost* often refers to the monetary outlay to acquire some resource that can have present and future benefit. *Expense* usually refers to an expired cost. That is, as the benefit of a resource expires, a portion of its cost is written off as an expense.

Controllable versus Direct Costs

Controllable costs are not always the same as direct costs. Direct costs are readily traced to a department, but the department manager might or might not control their amounts. For example, department managers often have little or no control over depreciation expense because they cannot affect the amount of equipment assigned to their departments. Also, department managers rarely control their own salaries. However, they can control or influence items such as the cost of supplies used in their department. When evaluating managers' performances, we should use data reflecting their departments' outputs along with their controllable costs and expenses.

Distinguishing between controllable and uncontrollable costs depends on the particular manager and time period under analysis. For example, the cost of property insurance is usually not controllable at the department manager's level but by the executive responsible for obtaining the company's insurance coverage. Likewise, this executive might not control costs resulting from insurance policies already in force. However, when a policy expires, this executive can renegotiate a replacement policy and then controls these costs. Therefore, all costs are controllable at some management level if the time period is sufficiently long. We must use good judgment in identifying controllable costs.

Responsibility Accounting System

A *responsibility accounting system* uses the concept of controllable costs to assign managers the responsibility for costs and expenses under their control. Prior to each reporting period, a company prepares plans that identify costs and expenses under each manager's control. These plans are called **responsibility accounting budgets.** To ensure the cooperation of managers and the reasonableness of budgets, managers should be involved in preparing their budgets.

Point: Responsibility accounting does not place blame. Instead, responsibility accounting is used to identify opportunities for improving performance.

A responsibility accounting system also involves performance reports. A **responsibility accounting performance report** accumulates and reports costs and expenses that a manager is responsible for and their budgeted amounts. Management's analysis of differences between budgeted amounts and actual costs and expenses often results in corrective or strategic managerial actions. Upper-level management uses performance reports to evaluate the effectiveness of lower-level managers in controlling costs and expenses and keeping them within budgeted amounts.

A responsibility accounting system recognizes that control over costs and expenses belongs to several levels of management. We illustrate this by considering the organization chart in Exhibit 21.28. The lines in this chart connecting the managerial positions reflect channels of authority. For example, the four department managers of this consulting firm (benchmarking, cost management, outsourcing, and service) are responsible for controllable costs and expenses incurred in their departments, but these same costs are subject to the overall control of the vice president (VP) for operational consulting. Similarly, this VP's costs are subject to the control of the executive vice president (EVP) for operations, the president, and, ultimately, the board of directors.

At lower levels, managers have limited responsibility and relatively little control over costs and expenses. Performance reports for low-level management typically cover few controllable costs. Responsibility and control broaden for higher-level managers; therefore, their reports span a wider range of costs. However, reports to higher-level managers seldom contain the details reported to their subordinates but are summarized for two reasons: (1) lower-level managers are often responsible for these detailed costs and (2) detailed reports can obscure broader, more important issues facing a company.

Exhibit 21.29 shows summarized performance reports for the three management levels identified in Exhibit 21.28. Exhibit 21.29 shows that costs under the control of the benchmarking department manager are totaled and included among controllable costs of the VP for operational consulting. Also, costs under the control of the VP are totaled and included among controllable costs of the EVP for operations. In this way, a responsibility accounting system provides relevant information for each management level.

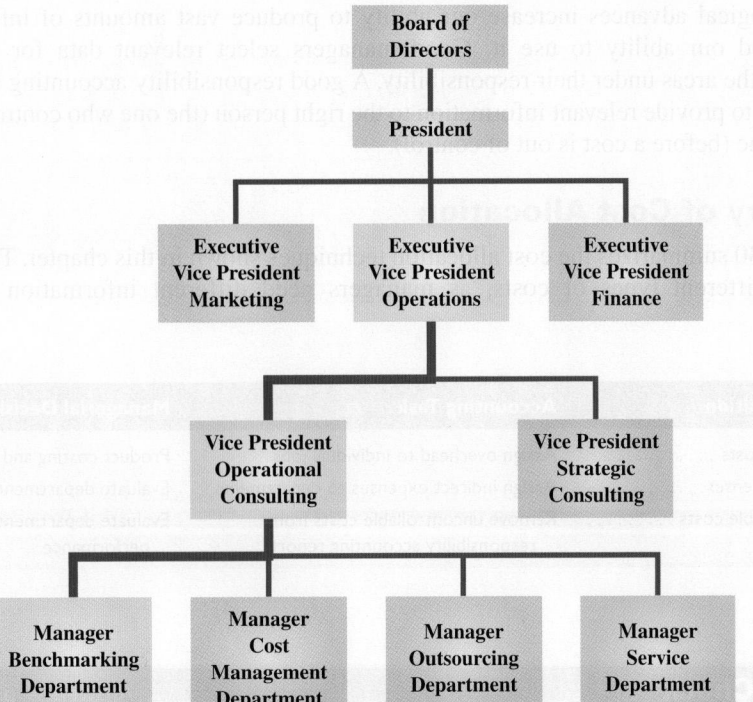

EXHIBIT 21.28

Organizational Responsibility Chart

EXHIBIT 21.29

Responsibility Accounting
Performance Reports

Executive Vice President, Operations	For July		
Controllable Costs	**Budgeted Amount**	**Actual Amount**	**Over (Under) Budget**
Salaries, VPs	$ 80,000	$ 80,000	$ 0
Quality control costs	21,000	22,400	1,400
Office costs	29,500	28,800	(700)
Operational consulting	276,700	279,500	2,800
Strategic consulting	390,000	380,600	(9,400)
Totals	$ 797,200	$ 791,300	$ (5,900)

Vice President, Operational Consulting	For July		
Controllable Costs	**Budgeted Amount**	**Actual Amount**	**Over (Under) Budget**
Salaries, department managers	$ 75,000	$ 78,000	$ 3,000
Depreciation	10,600	10,600	0
Insurance	6,800	6,300	(500)
Benchmarking department	79,600	79,900	300
Cost management department	61,500	60,200	(1,300)
Outsourcing department	24,300	24,700	400
Service department	18,900	19,800	900
Totals	$276,700	$279,500	$2,800

Manager, Benchmarking Department	For July		
Controllable Costs	**Budgeted Amount**	**Actual Amount**	**Over (Under) Budget**
Salaries	$ 51,600	$ 52,500	$ 900
Supplies	8,000	7,800	(200)
Other controllable costs	20,000	19,600	(400)
Totals	$ 79,600	$ 79,900	$ 300

Technological advances increase our ability to produce vast amounts of information that often exceed our ability to use it. Good managers select relevant data for planning and controlling the areas under their responsibility. A good responsibility accounting system makes every effort to provide relevant information to the right person (the one who controls the cost) at the right time (before a cost is out of control).

Summary of Cost Allocation

Exhibit 21.30 summarizes the cost allocation techniques shown in this chapter. These methods focus on different types of costs, as managers need different information for different decisions.

EXHIBIT 21.30

Cost Allocation Methods

Cost Definition	Accounting Task	Managerial Decision
Overhead costs	Assign overhead to individual jobs	Product costing and pricing
Indirect expenses.	Assign indirect expenses to departments	Evaluate department performance
Uncontrollable costs	Remove uncontrollable costs from responsibility accounting reports	Evaluate department manager performance

Quick Check

Answers — p. 858

10. Are the reports of departmental net profit and the departmental contribution to overhead useful in assessing a department manager's performance? Explain.

11. Performance reports to evaluate managers should (*a*) include data about controllable expenses, (*b*) compare actual results with budgeted levels, or (*c*) both (*a*) and (*b*).

 Decision Analysis  Investment Center Profit Margin and Investment Turnover

A2 Analyze investment centers using profit margin and investment turnover.

We can further examine investment center (division) performance by splitting return on investment into **profit margin** and **investment turnover** as follows

$$\text{Return on investment} \quad = \quad \text{Profit margin} \quad \times \quad \text{Investment turnover}$$

$$\frac{\text{Investment center net profit}}{\text{Investment center average assets}} = \frac{\text{Investment center net profit}}{\text{Investment center sales}} \times \frac{\text{Investment center sales}}{\text{Investment center average assets}}$$

Profit margin measures the income earned per dollar of sales. **Investment turnover** measures how efficiently an investment center generates sales from its invested assets. Higher profit margin and higher investment turnover indicate better performance. To illustrate, consider **Best Buy** which reports in Exhibit 21.31 results for two divisions (segments): Domestic and International.

EXHIBIT 21.31

Best Buy Division Sales, Income, and Assets

(US$ millions)	Domestic	International
Sales.	$37,314	$12,380
Net profit.	2,071	164
Average invested assets	9,745	7,319

Profit margin and investment turnover for its Domestic and International divisions are computed and shown in Exhibit 21.32:

($ millions)	Domestic	International
Profit Margin		
$2,071/$37,314	5.55%	
$164/$12,380		1.32%
Investment Turnover		
$37,314/9,745	3.83	
$12,380/$7,319		1.69

Best Buy's Domestic division generates 5.55 cents of profit per $1 of sales, while its International division generates only 1.32 cents of profit per dollar of sales. Its Domestic division also uses its assets more efficiently; its investment turnover of 3.83 is over twice that of its International division's 1.69. Top management can use profit margin and investment turnover to evaluate the performance of division managers. The measures can also aid management when considering further investment in its divisions.

◼ Decision Maker   Answer — p. 858

Division Manager   You manage a division in a highly competitive industry. You will receive a cash bonus if your division achieves an ROI above 12%. Your division's profit margin is 7%, equal to the industry average, and your division's investment turnover is 1.5. What actions can you take to increase your chance of receiving the bonus? ◼

DEMONSTRATION PROBLEM

Management requests departmental income statements for Hacker's Haven, a computer store that has five departments. Three are operating departments (hardware, software, and repairs) and two are service departments (general office and purchasing).

	General Office	Purchasing	Hardware	Software	Repairs
Sales	—	—	$960,000	$600,000	$840,000
Cost of goods sold	—	—	500,000	300,000	200,000
Direct expenses					
Payroll	$60,000	$45,000	80,000	25,000	325,000
Depreciation	6,000	7,200	33,000	4,200	9,600
Supplies	15,000	10,000	10,000	2,000	25,000

The departments incur several indirect expenses. To prepare departmental income statements, the indirect expenses must be allocated across the five departments. Then the expenses of the two service departments must be allocated to the three operating departments. Total cost amounts and the allocation bases for each indirect expense follow.

Indirect Expense	Total Cost	Allocation Basis
Rent	$150,000	Square footage occupied
Utilities	50,000	Square footage occupied
Advertising	125,000	Dollars of sales
Insurance	30,000	Value of assets insured
Service departments		
General office	?	Number of employees
Purchasing	?	Dollars of cost of goods sold

The following additional information is needed for indirect expense allocations.

Department	Square Feet	Sales	Insured Assets	Employees	Cost of Goods Sold
General office	500		$ 60,000		
Purchasing	500		72,000		
Hardware	4,000	$ 960,000	330,000	5	$ 500,000
Software............	3,000	600,000	42,000	5	300,000
Repairs	2,000	840,000	96,000	10	200,000
Totals	10,000	$2,400,000	$600,000	20	$1,000,000

Required

1. Prepare a departmental expense allocation spreadsheet for Hacker's Haven.
2. Prepare a departmental income statement reporting net profit for each operating department and for all operating departments combined.

PLANNING THE SOLUTION

● Set up and complete four tables to allocate the indirect expenses—one each for rent, utilities, advertising, and insurance.
● Allocate the departments' indirect expenses using a spreadsheet like the one in Exhibit 21.13. Enter the given amounts of the direct expenses for each department. Then enter the allocated amounts of the indirect expenses that you computed.
● Complete two tables for allocating the general office and purchasing department costs to the three operating departments. Enter these amounts on the spreadsheet and determine the total expenses allocated to the three operating departments.
● Prepare departmental income statements like the one in Exhibit 21.22. Show sales, cost of goods sold, gross profit, individual expenses, and net profit for each of the three operating departments and for the combined company.

SOLUTION TO DEMONSTRATION PROBLEM

Allocations of the four indirect expenses across the five departments.

Rent	Square Feet	Percent of Total	Allocated Cost
General office	500	5.0%	$ 7,500
Purchasing	500	5.0	7,500
Hardware............	4,000	40.0	60,000
Software	3,000	30.0	45,000
Repairs	2,000	20.0	30,000
Totals	10,000	100.0%	$150,000

Utilities	Square Feet	Percent of Total	Allocated Cost
General office	500	5.0%	$ 2,500
Purchasing	500	5.0	2,500
Hardware............	4,000	40.0	20,000
Software	3,000	30.0	15,000
Repairs	2,000	20.0	10,000
Totals	10,000	100.0%	$50,000

Advertising	Sales Dollars	Percent of Total	Allocated Cost
Hardware...........	$ 960,000	40.0%	$ 50,000
Software............	600,000	25.0	31,250
Repairs	840,000	35.0	43,750
Totals	$2,400,000	100.0%	$125,000

Insurance	Assets Insured	Percent of Total	Allocated Cost
General office	$ 60,000	10.0%	$ 3,000
Purchasing	72,000	12.0	3,600
Hardware	330,000	55.0	16,500
Software	42,000	7.0	2,100
Repairs	96,000	16.0	4,800
Totals	$600,000	100.0%	$30,000

1. Allocations of service department expenses to the three operating departments.

General Office Allocations to	Employees	Percent of Total	Allocated Cost
Hardware..............	5	25.0%	$23,500
Software..............	5	25.0	23,500
Repairs	10	50.0	47,000
Totals	20	100.0%	$94,000

Purchasing Allocations to	Cost of Goods Sold	Percent of Total	Allocated Cost
Hardware..............	$ 500,000	50.0%	$37,900
Software..............	300,000	30.0	22,740
Repairs	200,000	20.0	15,160
Totals	$1,000,000	100.0%	$75,800

HACKER'S HAVEN
Departmental Expense Allocations
For Year Ended December 31, 2011

	Allocation Base	Expense Account Balance	General Office Dept.	Purchasing Dept.	Hardware Dept.	Software Dept.	Repairs Dept.
Direct Expenses							
Payroll..............................		$ 535,000	$ 60,000	$ 45,000	$ 80,000	$ 25,000	$ 325,000
Depreciation		60,000	6,000	7,200	33,000	4,200	9,600
Supplies		62,000	15,000	10,000	10,000	2,000	25,000
Indirect Expenses							
Rent	Square ft.	150,000	7,500	7,500	60,000	45,000	30,000
Utilities............................	Square ft.	50,000	2,500	2,500	20,000	15,000	10,000
Advertising..........................	Sales	125,000	—	—	50,000	31,250	43,750
Insurance	Assets	30,000	3,000	3,600	16,500	2,100	4,800
Total expenses.......................		1,012,000	94,000	75,800	269,500	124,550	448,150
Service Department Expenses							
General office	Employees		(94,000)		23,500	23,500	47,000
Purchasing	Goods sold			(75,800)	37,900	22,740	15,160
Total expenses allocated to operating departments		$1,012,000	$ 0	$ 0	$330,900	$170,790	$510,310

2. Departmental income statements for Hacker's Haven.

HACKER'S HAVEN
Departmental Income Statements
For Year Ended December 31, 2011

	Hardware	Software	Repairs	Combined
Sales	$ 960,000	$ 600,000	$ 840,000	$2,400,000
Cost of goods sold	500,000	300,000	200,000	1,000,000
Gross profit	460,000	300,000	640,000	1,400,000
Expenses				
Payroll	(80,000)	(25,000)	(325,000)	(430,000)
Depreciation	(33,000)	(4,200)	(9,600)	(46,800)
Supplies	(10,000)	(2,000)	(25,000)	(37,000)
Rent	(60,000)	(45,000)	(30,000)	(135,000)
Utilities	(20,000)	(15,000)	(10,000)	(45,000)
Advertising..................	(50,000)	(31,250)	(43,750)	(125,000)
Insurance	(16,500)	(2,100)	(4,800)	(23,400)
Share of general office	(23,500)	(23,500)	(47,000)	(94,000)
Share of purchasing	(37,900)	(22,740)	(15,160)	(75,800)
Total expenses...............	(330,900)	(170,790)	(510,310)	(1,012,000)
Net profit	$129,100	$129,210	$129,690	$ 388,000

21A

Transfer Pricing

C3 Explain transfer pricing and methods to set transfer prices.

Divisions in decentralized companies sometimes do business with one another. For example, a separate division of **Harley-Davidson** manufactures its plastic and fiberglass parts used in the company's motorcycles. **Anheuser-Busch**'s metal container division makes cans and lids used in its brewing operations, and also sells cans and lids to soft-drink companies. A division of **Prince** produces strings used in tennis rackets made by Prince and other manufacturers.

Determining the price that should be used to record transfers between divisions in the same company is the focus of this appendix. Because these transactions are transfers within the same company, the price to record them is called the **transfer price.** In decentralized organizations, division managers have input on or decide those prices. Transfer prices can be used in cost, profit, and investment centers. Since these transfers are not with customers outside the company, the transfer price has no direct impact on the company's overall profits. However, transfer prices can impact performance evaluations and, if set incorrectly, lead to bad decisions.

Point: Transfer pricing can impact company profits when divisions are located in countries with different tax rates; this is covered in advanced courses.

Alternative Transfer Prices   Exhibit 21A.1 reports data on the LCD division of ZTel. LCD manufactures liquid crystal display (LCD) touch-screen monitors for use in ZTel's S-Phone division's smartphones, which sell for $400 each. The monitors can also be used in other products. So, LCD can sell its monitors to buyers other than S-Phone. Likewise, the S-Phone division can purchase monitors from suppliers other than LCD.

EXHIBIT 21A.1

LCD Division Manufacturing Information—Monitors

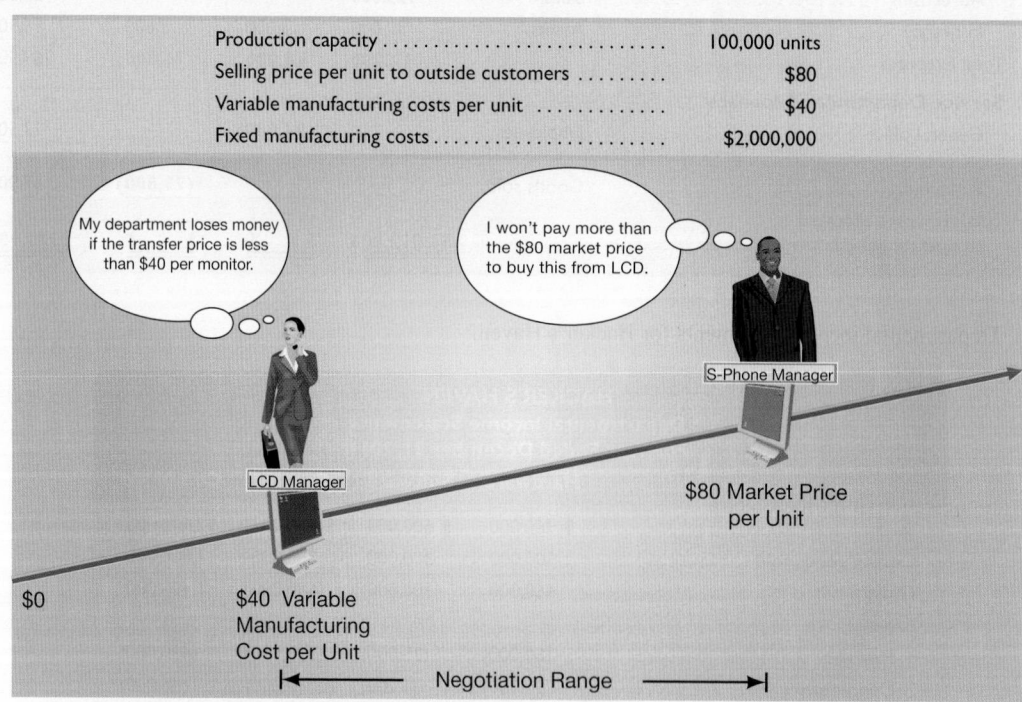

Exhibit 21A.1 reveals the range of transfer prices for transfers of monitors from LCD to S-Phone. The manager of LCD wants to report a division profit; thus, this manager will not accept a transfer price less than $40 (variable manufacturing cost per unit) because doing so would cause the division to lose money on each monitor transferred. The LCD manager will only consider transfer prices of $40 or more. On the other hand, the S-Phone division manager also wants to report a division profit. Thus, this manager will not pay more than $80 per monitor because similar monitors can be bought from outside suppliers at that price. The S-Phone manager will only consider transfer prices of $80 or less. As any transfer price between $40 and $80 per monitor is possible, how does ZTel determine the transfer price? The answer depends in part on whether the LCD division has excess capacity to manufacture monitors.

No Excess Capacity   Assume the LCD division can sell every monitor it produces, and thus is producing 100,000 units. In that case, a **market-based transfer price** of $80 per monitor is preferred. At that price, the LCD division manager is willing to either transfer monitors to S-Phone or sell to outside customers. The S-Phone manager cannot buy monitors for less than $80 from outside suppliers, so the $80 price is acceptable. Further, with a transfer price of $80 per monitor, top management of ZTel is indifferent to S-Phone buying from LCD or buying similar-quality monitors from outside suppliers.

With no excess capacity, the LCD manager will not accept a transfer price less than $80 per monitor. For example, suppose the S-Phone manager suggests a transfer price of $70 per monitor. At that price the LCD manager incurs an unnecessary *opportunity cost* of $10 per monitor (computed as $80 market price minus $70 transfer price). This would lower the LCD division's income and hurt its performance evaluation.

Excess Capacity   Assume that the LCD division has excess capacity. For example, the LCD division might currently be producing only 80,000 units. Because LCD has $2,000,000 of fixed manufacturing costs, both LCD and the top management of ZTel prefer that S-Phone purchases its monitors from LCD. For example, if S-Phone purchases its monitors from an outside supplier at the market price of $80 each, LCD manufactures no units. Then, LCD reports a division loss equal to its fixed costs, and ZTel overall reports a lower net profit as its costs are higher. Consequently, with excess capacity, LCD should accept any transfer price of $40 per unit or greater and S-Phone should purchase monitors from LCD. This will allow LCD to recover some (or all) of its fixed costs and increase ZTel's overall profits. For example, if a transfer price of $50 per monitor is used, the S-Phone manager is pleased to buy from LCD, since that price is below the market price of $80. For each monitor transferred from LCD to S-Phone at $50, the LCD division receives a *contribution margin* of $10 (computed as $50 transfer price less $40 variable cost) to contribute towards recovering its fixed costs. This form of transfer pricing is called **cost-based transfer pricing.** Under this approach the transfer price might be based on variable costs, total costs, or variable costs plus a markup. Determining the transfer price under excess capacity is complex and is covered in advanced courses.

Additional Issues in Transfer Pricing   Several additional issues arise in determining transfer prices which include the following:

- **No market price exists.** Sometimes there is no market price for the product being transferred. The product might be a key component that requires additional conversion costs at the next stage and is not easily replicated by an outside company. For example, there is no market for a console for a **Nissan** Maxima and there is no substitute console **Nissan** can use in assembling a Maxima. In this case a market-based transfer price cannot be used.
- **Cost control.** To provide incentives for cost control, transfer prices might be based on standard, rather than actual costs. For example, if a transfer price of actual variable costs plus a markup of $20 per unit is used in the case above, LCD has no incentive to control its costs.
- **Division managers' negotiation.** With excess capacity, division managers will often negotiate a transfer price that lies between the variable cost per unit and the market price per unit. In this case, the **negotiated transfer price** and resulting departmental performance reports reflect, in part, the negotiating skills of the respective division managers. This might not be best for overall company performance.
- **Nonfinancial factors.** Factors such as quality control, reduced lead times, and impact on employee morale can be important factors in determining transfer prices.

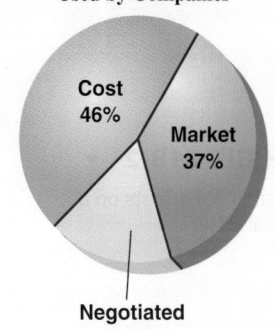

Transfer Pricing Approaches Used by Companies

Cost 46%

Market 37%

Negotiated 17%

APPENDIX

Joint Costs and Their Allocation

21B

C4   Describe allocation of joint costs across products.

Most manufacturing processes involve **joint costs,** which refer to costs incurred to produce or purchase two or more products at the same time. A joint cost is like an indirect expense in the sense that more than one cost object share it. For example, a sawmill company incurs a joint cost when it buys logs that it cuts into lumber as shown in Exhibit 21B.1. The joint cost includes the logs (raw material) and its cutting (conversion) into boards classified as Clear, Select, No. 1 Common, No. 2 Common, No. 3 Common, and other types of lumber and by-products.

When a joint cost is incurred, a question arises as to whether to allocate it to different products resulting from it. The answer is that when management wishes to estimate the costs of individual products, joint

EXHIBIT 21B.1

Joint Products from Logs

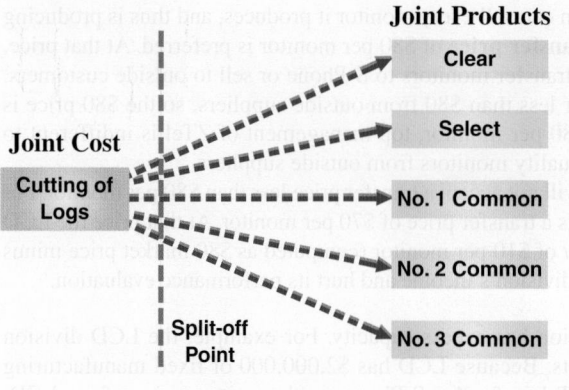

costs are included and must be allocated to these joint products. However, when management needs information to help decide whether to sell a product at a certain point in the production process or to process it further, the joint costs are ignored.

Financial statements prepared according to GAAP must assign joint costs to products. To do this, management must decide how to allocate joint costs across products benefiting from these costs. If some products are sold and others remain in inventory, allocating joint costs involves assigning costs to both cost of goods sold and ending inventory.

The two usual methods to allocate joint costs are the (1) *physical basis* and (2) the *value basis*. The physical basis typically involves allocating joint cost using physical characteristics such as the ratio of pounds, cubic feet, or gallons of each joint product to the total pounds, cubic feet, or gallons of all joint products flowing from the cost. This method is not preferred because the resulting cost allocations do not reflect the relative market values the joint cost generates. The preferred approach is the value basis, which allocates joint cost in proportion to the sales value of the output produced by the process at the "split-off point"; see Exhibit 21B.1.

Physical Basis Allocation of Joint Cost   To illustrate the physical basis of allocating a joint cost, we consider a sawmill that bought logs for $30,000. When cut, these logs produce 100,000 board feet of lumber in the grades and amounts shown in Exhibit 21B.2. The logs produce 20,000 board feet of No. 3 Common lumber, which is 20% of the total. With physical allocation, the No. 3 Common lumber is assigned 20% of the $30,000 cost of the logs, or $6,000 ($30,000 × 20%). Because this low-grade lumber sells for $4,000, this allocation gives a $2,000 loss from its production and sale. The physical basis for allocating joint costs does not reflect the extra value flowing into some products or the inferior value flowing into others. That is, the portion of a log that produces Clear and Select grade lumber is worth more than the portion used to produce the three grades of common lumber, but the physical basis fails to reflect this.

EXHIBIT 21B.2

Allocating Joint Costs on a Physical Basis

Grade of Lumber	Board Feet Produced	Percent of Total	Allocated Cost	Sales Value	Gross Profit
Clear and Select............	10,000	10.0%	$ 3,000	$12,000	$ 9,000
No. 1 Common	30,000	30.0	9,000	18,000	9,000
No. 2 Common	40,000	40.0	12,000	16,000	4,000
No. 3 Common	20,000	20.0	6,000	4,000	(2,000)
Totals	100,000	100.0%	$30,000	$50,000	$20,000

Value Basis Allocation of Joint Cost   Exhibit 21B.3 illustrates the value basis method of allocation. It determines the percents of the total costs allocated to each grade by the ratio of each grade's sales value to the total sales value of $50,000 (sales value is the unit selling price multiplied by the number of units produced). The Clear and Select lumber grades receive 24% of the total cost ($12,000/$50,000) instead of the 10% portion using a physical basis. The No. 3 Common lumber receives only 8% of the total cost, or $2,400, which is much less than the $6,000 assigned to it using the physical basis.

EXHIBIT 21B.3

Allocating Joint Costs on a Value Basis

Grade of Lumber	Sales Value	Percent of Total	Allocated Cost	Gross Profit
Clear and Select	$12,000	24.0%	$ 7,200	$ 4,800
No. 1 Common............	18,000	36.0	10,800	7,200
No. 2 Common............	16,000	32.0	9,600	6,400
No. 3 Common............	4,000	8.0	2,400	1,600
Totals..................	$50,000	100.0%	$30,000	$20,000

An outcome of value basis allocation is that *each* grade produces exactly the same 40% gross profit at the split-off point. This 40% rate equals the gross profit rate from selling all the lumber made from the $30,000 logs for a combined price of $50,000.

Example: Refer to Exhibit 21B.3. If the sales value of Clear and Select lumber is changed to $10,000, what is the revised ratio of the market value of No. 1 Common to the total? *Answer:* $18,000/$48,000 = 37.5%

Quick Check   Answers — p. 858 ✓

12. A company produces three products, B1, B2, and B3. The joint cost incurred for the current month for these products is $180,000. The following data relate to this month's production:

Product	Units Produced	Unit Sales Value
B1	96,000	$3.00
B2	64,000	6.00
B3	32,000	9.00

The amount of joint cost allocated to product B3 using the value basis allocation is (a) $30,000, (b) $54,000, or (c) $90,000.

Summary

C1 **Distinguish between direct and indirect expenses and identify bases for allocating indirect expenses to departments.** Direct expenses are traced to a specific department and are incurred for the sole benefit of that department. Indirect expenses benefit more than one department. Indirect expenses are allocated to departments when computing departmental net profit. Ideally, we allocate indirect expenses by using a cause-effect relation for the allocation base. When a cause-effect relation is not identifiable, each indirect expense is allocated on a basis reflecting the relative benefit received by each department.

C2 **Explain controllable costs and responsibility accounting.** A controllable cost is one that is influenced by a specific management level. The total expenses of operating a department often include some items a department manager does not control. Responsibility accounting systems provide information for evaluating the performance of department managers. A responsibility accounting system's performance reports for evaluating department managers should include only the expenses (and revenues) that each manager controls.

C3 **Explain transfer pricing and methods to set transfer prices.** Transfer prices are used to record transfers of items between divisions of the same company. Transfer prices can be based on costs or market prices, or can be negotiated by division managers.

C4 **Describe allocation of joint costs across products.** A joint cost refers to costs incurred to produce or purchase two or more products at the same time. When income statements are prepared, joint costs are usually allocated to the resulting joint products using either a physical or value basis.

A1 **Analyze investment centers using return on assets, residual income, and balanced scorecard.** A financial measure often used to evaluate an investment center manager is the *investment center return on total assets*, also called *return on investment*. This measure is computed as the center's net profit divided by the center's average total assets. Residual income, computed as investment center net profit minus a target net profit is an alternative financial

measure of investment center performance. A balanced scorecard uses a combination of financial and non-financial measures to evaluate performance.

A2 **Analyze investment centers using profit margin and investment turnover.** Return on investment can also be computed as profit margin times investment turnover. Profit margin (equal to net profit/sales) measures the income earned per dollar of sales and investment turnover (equal to sales/assets) measures how efficiently a division uses its assets.

P1 **Assign overhead costs using two-stage cost allocation.** In the traditional two-stage cost allocation procedure, service department costs are first assigned to operating departments. Then, in the second stage, a predetermined overhead allocation rate is computed for each operating department and is used to assign overhead to output.

P2 **Assign overhead costs using activity-based costing.** In activity-based costing, the costs of related activities are collected and then pooled in some logical manner into activity cost pools. After all activity costs have been accumulated in an activity cost pool account, users of the activity, termed *cost objects*, are assigned a portion of the total activity cost using a cost driver (allocation base).

P3 **Prepare departmental income statements and contribution reports.** Each profit center (department) is assigned its expenses to yield its own income statement. These costs include its direct expenses and its share of indirect expenses. The departmental income statement lists its revenues and costs of goods sold to determine gross profit. Its operating expenses (direct expenses and its indirect expenses allocated to the department) are deducted from gross profit to yield departmental net profit. The departmental contribution report is similar to the departmental income statement in terms of computing the gross profit for each department. Then the direct operating expenses for each department are deducted from gross profit to determine the contribution generated by each department. Indirect operating expenses are deducted *in total* from the company's combined contribution.

Guidance Answers to Decision Maker and Decision Ethics

Director of Operations You should collect details on overhead items and review them to see whether direct labor drives these costs. If it does not, overhead might be improperly assigned to departments. The situation also provides an opportunity to consider other overhead allocation bases, including use of activity-based costing.

Accounting Officer You should not author a report that you disagree with. You are responsible for ascertaining all the facts of ABC (implementation procedures, advantages and disadvantages, and costs). You should then approach your supervisor with these facts and suggest that you would like to modify the report to request, for example, a pilot test. The pilot test will allow you to further assess the suitability of ABC. Your suggestion might be rejected, at which time you may wish to speak with a more senior-level manager.

Center Manager We must first realize that the two investment opportunities are not comparable on the basis of absolute dollars of income or on assets. For instance, the second investment provides a higher income in absolute dollars but requires a higher investment.

Accordingly, we need to compute return on total assets for each alternative: (1) $50,000 ÷ $250,000 = 20%, and (2) $175,000 ÷ $1 million = 17.5%. Alternative 1 has the higher return and is preferred over alternative 2. Do you pursue one, both, or neither? Because alternative 1's return is higher than the center's usual return of 19%, it should be pursued, assuming its risks are acceptable. Also, since alternative 1 requires a small investment, top management is likely to be more agreeable to pursuing it. Alternative 2's return is lower than the usual 19% and is not likely to be acceptable.

Division Manager Your division's ROI without further action is 10.5% (equal to 7% × 1.5). In a highly competitive industry, it is difficult to increase profit margins by raising prices. Your division might be better able to control its costs to increase its profit margin. In addition, you might engage in a marketing program to increase sales without increasing your division's invested assets. Investment turnover and thus ROI will increase if the marketing campaign attracts customers.

Guidance Answers to Quick Checks

1. Cost drivers are the factors that have a cause-effect relation with costs (or activities that pertain to costs).

2. d

3. A departmental accounting system provides information used to evaluate the performance of *departments*. A responsibility accounting system provides information used to evaluate the performance of *department managers*.

4. d

5. A cost center, such as a service department, incurs costs without directly generating revenues. A profit center, such as a product division, incurs costs but also generates revenues.

6. b

7. d

8. (1) Assign the direct expenses to each department. (2) Allocate indirect expenses to all departments. (3) Allocate the service department expenses to the operating departments.

9. b

10. No, because many expenses that enter into these calculations are beyond the manager's control, and managers should not be evaluated using costs they do not control.

11. c

12. b; $180,000 × ([32,000 × $9]/[96,000 × $3 + 64,000 × $6 + 32,000 × $9]) = $54,000.

Additional Quiz Questions are available at the book's Website.

1. A retailer has three departments—housewares, appliances, and clothing—and buys advertising that benefits all departments. Advertising expense is $150,000 for the year, and departmental sales for the year follow: housewares, $356,250; appliances, $641,250; clothing, $427,500. How much advertising expense is allocated to appliances if allocation is based on departmental sales?
   a. $37,500
   b. $67,500
   c. $45,000
   d. $150,000
   e. $641,250

2. An activity-based costing system
   a. Does not require the level of detail that a traditional costing system requires.
   b. Does not enable the calculation of unit cost data.
   c. Allocates costs to products on the basis of activities performed on them.
   d. Cannot be used by a service company.
   e. Allocates costs to products based on the number of direct labor hours used.

3. A company produces two products, Grey and Red. The following information is available relating to those two products. Assume that the company's total setup cost is $162,000. Using activity-based costing, how much setup cost is allocated to each unit of Grey?

	Grey	Red
Units produced	500	40,000
Number of setups	50	100
Direct labor hours per unit	15	15

   a. $1,080
   b. $ 72
   c. $ 162
   d. $2,000
   e. $ 108

4. A company operates three retail departments as profit centers, and the following information is available for each. Which department has the largest dollar amount of departmental contribution to overhead and what is the dollar amount contributed?

Department	Sales	Cost of Goods Sold	Direct Expenses	Allocated Indirect Expenses
X	$500,000	$350,000	$50,000	$40,000
Y	200,000	75,000	20,000	50,000
Z	350,000	150,000	75,000	10,000

   a. Department Y, $ 55,000
   b. Department Z, $125,000
   c. Department X, $500,000
   d. Department Z, $200,000
   e. Department X, $ 60,000

5. Using the data in question 4, Department X's contribution to overhead as a percentage of sales is
   a. 20%
   b. 30%
   c. 12%
   d. 48%
   e. 32%

A(B) *Superscript letter A (B) denotes assignments based on Appendix 21A (21B).*

🔲 Icon denotes assignments that involve decision making.

Discussion Questions

1. Why are many companies divided into departments?
2. Complete the following for a traditional two-stage allocation system: In the first stage, service department costs are assigned to _____ departments. In the second stage, a predetermined overhead rate is computed for each operating department and used to assign overhead to _____.
3. What is the difference between operating departments and service departments?
4. What is activity-based costing? What is its goal?
5. 🔲 Identify at least four typical cost pools for activity-based costing in most organizations.
6. In activity-based costing, costs in a cost pool are allocated to _____ using predetermined overhead rates.

7. 🔲 What company circumstances especially encourage use of activity-based costing?
8. 🔲 What are two main goals in managerial accounting for reporting on and analyzing departments?
9. 🔲 Is it possible to evaluate a cost center's profitability? Explain.
10. What is the difference between direct and indirect expenses?
11. 🔲 Suggest a reasonable basis for allocating each of the following indirect expenses to departments: (a) salary of a supervisor who manages several departments, (b) rent, (c) heat, (d) electricity for lighting, (e) janitorial services, (f) advertising, (g) expired insurance on equipment, and (h) property taxes on equipment.

12. Research In Motion has many departments. How is a department's contribution to overhead measured?

13. What are controllable costs?

14. Controllable and uncontrollable costs must be identified with a particular _____ and a definite _____ period.

15. Why should managers be closely involved in preparing their responsibility accounting budgets?

16. Nokia aims to give its managers timely cost reports. In responsibility accounting, who receives timely cost reports and specific cost information? Explain.

17.^AWhat is a transfer price? Under what conditions is a market-based transfer price most likely to be used?

18.^B What is a joint cost? How are joint costs usually allocated among the products produced from them?

19.^B Give two examples of products with joint costs.

20. Each retail store of Apple has several departments. Why is it useful for its management to (a) collect accounting information about each department and (b) treat each department as a profit center?

21. Palm delivers its products to locations around the world. List three controllable and three uncontrollable costs for its delivery department.

---

connect

QUICK STUDY

QS 21-1

Allocation and measurement terms

C1

In each blank next to the following terms, place the identifying letter of its best description.

1. _____ Operating department
2. _____ Profit center
3. _____ Responsibility accounting system
4. _____ Cost center
5. _____ Investment center
6. _____ Departmental accounting system
7. _____ Service department

A. Holds manager responsible for revenues, costs, and investments.

B. Does not directly manufacture products but contributes to profitability of the entire company.

C. Incurs costs and also generates revenues.

D. Provides information used to evaluate the performance of a department.

E. Incurs costs without directly yielding revenues.

F. Provides information used to evaluate the performance of a department manager.

G. Engages directly in manufacturing or in making sales directly to customers.

QS 21-2

Basis for cost allocation

C1

For each of the following types of indirect expenses and service department expenses, identify one allocation basis that could be used to distribute it to the departments indicated.

1. Electric utility expenses of all departments.
2. General office department expenses of the operating departments.
3. Maintenance department expenses of the operating departments.
4. Computer service expenses of production scheduling for operating departments.

QS 21-3

Activity-based costing and overhead cost allocation

P2

The following is taken from Maxwell Co.'s internal records of its factory with two operating departments. The cost driver for indirect labor and supplies is direct labor costs, and the cost driver for the remaining overhead items is number of hours of machine use. Compute the total amount of overhead cost allocated to Operating Department 1 using activity-based costing.

	Direct Labor	Machine Use Hours
Operating department 1	$10,400	2,200
Operating department 2	9,600	3,000
Totals	$20,000	5,200

Factory overhead costs	
Rent and utilities	$ 7,100
Indirect labor	3,700
General office expense	2,700
Depreciation—Equipment	4,500
Supplies	300
Total factory overhead	$18,300

Check   Dept. 1 allocation, $8,130

Use the information in the following table to compute each department's contribution to overhead (both in dollars and as a percent). Which department contributes the largest dollar amount to total overhead? Which contributes the highest percent (as a percent of sales)? Round percents to one decimal.

QS 21-4
Departmental contribution to overhead
P3

	Dept. A	Dept. B	Dept. C
Sales	$53,000	$170,000	$84,000
Cost of goods sold	34,185	103,700	49,560
Gross profit	18,815	66,300	34,440
Total direct expenses	6,360	37,060	8,736
Contribution to overhead	$	$	$
Contribution percent	%	%	%

Compute return on assets for each of these **Best Buy** divisions (each is an investment center). Comment on the relative performance of each investment center. Round percents to one decimal.

QS 21-5
Investment center analysis
A1

Investment Center	Net profit	Average Assets	Return on Assets
Cameras and camcorders	$4,500,000	$20,000,000	
Phones and communications	1,500,000	12,500,000	
Computers and accessories	800,000	10,000,000	

Refer to information in QS 21-5. Assume a target income of 12% of average invested assets. Compute residual income for each of Best Buy's divisions.

QS 21-6
Computing residual income
A1

A company's shipping division (an investment center) has sales of $4,700,000, net profit of $916,000, and average invested assets of $3,000,000. Compute the division's profit margin and investment turnover.

QS 21-7
Computing performance measures A2

Fill in the blanks in the schedule below for two separate investment centers A and B.

QS 21-8
Performance measures
A1 A2

	Investment Center	
	A	B
Sales	$	$6,400,000
Net profit	$ 252,000	$
Average invested assets	$1,400,000	
Profit margin	6%	%
Investment turnover		1.6
Return on assets	%	10%

Classify each of the performance measures below into the most likely balanced scorecard perspective it relates to. Label your answers using C (customer), P (internal process), I (innovation and growth), or F (financial).

QS 21-9
Performance measures— balanced scorecard
A1

1. Number of new products introduced ____

2. Length of time raw materials are in inventory ____

3. Profit margin ____

4. Customer wait time ____

5. Change in market share ____

6. Employee training sessions attended ____

7. Number of days of employee absences ____

8. Customer satisfaction index ____

QS 21-10

Performance measures—
balanced scorecard

A1

Walt Disney reports the following information for its two Parks and Resorts divisions.

	East Coast		West Coast	
	Current year	Prior year	Current year	Prior year
Hotel occupancy rates	89%	86%	92%	93%

Assume Walt Disney uses a balanced scorecard and sets a target of 90% occupancy in its resorts. Using Exhibit 21.27 as a guide, show how the company's performance on hotel occupancy would appear on a balanced scorecard report.

QS 21-11^A

Determining transfer prices
without excess capacity

C3

The Windshield division of Cargo Co. makes windshields for use in Cargo's Assembly division. The Windshield division incurs variable costs of $350 per windshield and has capacity to make 100,000 windshields per year. The market price is $600 per windshield. The Windshield division incurs total fixed costs of $3,000,000 per year. If the Windshield division is operating at full capacity, what transfer price should be used on transfers between the Windshield and Assembly divisions? Explain.

QS 21-12^A

Determining transfer prices with
excess capacity   C3

Refer to information in QS 21-11. If the Windshield division has excess capacity, what is the range of possible transfer prices that could be used on transfers between the Windshield and Assembly divisions? Explain.

QS 21-13^B

Joint cost allocation

C4

A company purchases a 10,000 square foot commercial building for $400,000 and spends an additional $65,000 to divide the space into two separate rental units and prepare it for rent. Unit A, which has the desirable location on the corner and contains 2,500 square feet, will be rented for $2.00 per square foot. Unit B contains 7,500 square feet and will be rented for $1.50 per square foot. How much of the joint cost should be assigned to Unit B using the value basis of allocation?

QS 21-14

Rent expense allocated
to departments

P1

Auto Market pays $128,000 rent each year for its two-story building. The space in this building is occupied by five departments as specified here.

Paint department	1,200 square feet of first-floor space
Engine department	3,600 square feet of first-floor space
Window department	1,920 square feet of second-floor space
Electrical department	1,056 square feet of second-floor space
Accessory department	1,824 square feet of second-floor space

Check   Allocated to Paint Dept.,
$20,800

The company allocates 65% of total rent expense to the first floor and 35% to the second floor, and then allocates rent expense for each floor to the departments occupying that floor on the basis of space occupied. Determine the rent expense to be allocated to each department. (Round percents to the nearest one-tenth and dollar amounts to the nearest whole dollar.)

QS 21-15

Return on investment

A1

For a recent year **L'Oreal** reported operating profit of EUR 3,110 million for its Cosmetics division. Total assets were EUR 11,314 million at the beginning of the year and EUR 12,988 million at the end of the year. Compute return on investment for the year. State your answer as a percent, rounded to one decimal.

connect

EXERCISES

Exercise 21-1

Departmental expense
allocations

P1

Won Han Co. has four departments: materials, personnel, manufacturing, and packaging. In a recent month, the four departments incurred three shared indirect expenses. The amounts of these indirect expenses and the bases used to allocate them follow.

Indirect Expense	Cost	Allocation Base
Supervision	$ 75,000	Number of employees
Utilities	60,000	Square feet occupied
Insurance	16,500	Value of assets in use
Total.	$151,500	

Departmental data for the company's recent reporting period follow.

Department	Employees	Square Feet	Asset Values
Materials	18	27,000	$ 6,000
Personnel	6	4,500	1,200
Manufacturing	66	45,000	37,800
Packaging	30	13,500	15,000
Total	120	90,000	$60,000

(1) Use this information to allocate each of the three indirect expenses across the four departments.
(2) Prepare a summary table that reports the indirect expenses assigned to each of the four departments.

Check (2) Total of $30,900 assigned to Materials Dept.

Pane Company produces two types of glass shelving, rounded edge and squared edge, on the same production line. For the current period, the company reports the following data.

Exercise 21-2
Activity-based costing of overhead

P2

	Rounded Edge	Squared Edge	Total
Direct materials	$ 9,500	$21,600	$ 31,100
Direct labor	6,100	11,900	18,000
Overhead (300% of direct labor cost)	18,300	35,700	54,000
Total cost..............................	$33,900	$69,200	$103,100
Quantity produced	10,500 ft.	14,100 ft.	
Average cost per ft.	$ 3.23	$ 4.91	

Pane's controller wishes to apply activity-based costing (ABC) to allocate the $54,000 of overhead costs incurred by the two product lines to see whether cost per foot would change markedly from that reported above. She has collected the following information.

Overhead Cost Category (Activity Cost Pool)	Cost
Supervision	$ 2,160
Depreciation of machinery	28,840
Assembly line preparation............................	23,000
Total overhead	$54,000

She has also collected the following information about the cost drivers for each category (cost pool) and the amount of each driver used by the two product lines.

Overhead Cost Category (Activity Cost Pool)	Driver	Usage		
		Rounded Edge	Squared Edge	Total
Supervision	Direct labor cost($)	$6,100	$11,900	$18,000
Depreciation of machinery	Machine hours	300 hours	700 hours	1,000 hours
Assembly line preparation	Setups (number)	31 times	94 times	125 times

Use this information to (1) assign these three overhead cost pools to each of the two products using ABC, (2) determine average cost per foot for each of the two products using ABC, and (3) compare the average cost per foot under ABC with the average cost per foot under the current method for each product. For part 3, explain why a difference between the two cost allocation methods exists.

Check (2) Rounded edge, $2.92; Squared edge, $5.14

Below are departmental income statements for a guitar manufacturer. The manufacturer is considering dropping its electric guitar department since it has a net loss. The company classifies advertising, rent, and utilities expenses as indirect. (1) Prepare a departmental contribution report that shows each department's contribution to overhead. (2) Based on contribution to overhead, should the electric guitar department be eliminated?

Exercise 21-3
Departmental contribution report

P3

BEST GUITAR
Departmental Income Statements
For Year Ended December 31, 2011

	Acoustic	Electric
Sales	$101,500	$85,000
Cost of goods sold	45,675	46,750
Gross profit	55,825	38,250
Operating expenses		
Advertising expense	5,075	4,250
Depreciation expense—equipment	10,150	8,500
Salaries expense	20,300	17,000
Supplies expense	2,030	1,700
Rent expense	7,105	5,950
Utilities expense	3,045	2,550
Total operating expenses	47,705	39,950
Net profit (loss)	$ 8,120	($1,700)

Exercise 21-4
Departmental expense allocation spreadsheet

P1

Overroad Cycle Shop has two service departments (advertising and administration) and two operating departments (cycles and clothing). During 2011, the departments had the following direct expenses and occupied the following amount of floor space.

Department	Direct Expenses	Square Feet
Advertising	$ 16,000	1,088
Administrative	18,500	1,152
Cycles	101,600	6,336
Clothing	11,900	4,224

The advertising department developed and distributed 100 advertisements during the year. Of these, 76 promoted cycles and 24 promoted clothing. The store sold $300,000 of merchandise during the year. Of this amount, $225,000 is from the cycles department, and $75,000 is from the clothing department. The utilities expense of $64,000 is an indirect expense to all departments. Prepare a departmental expense allocation spreadsheet for Overroad Cycle Shop. The spreadsheet should assign (1) direct expenses to each of the four departments, (2) the $64,000 of utilities expense to the four departments on the basis of floor space occupied, (3) the advertising department's expenses to the two operating departments on the basis of the number of ads placed that promoted a department's products, and (4) the administrative department's expenses to the two operating departments based on the amount of sales. Provide supporting computations for the expense allocations.

Check Total expenses allocated to Cycles Dept., $167,769

Exercise 21-5
Service department expenses allocated to operating departments **P3**

The following is a partially completed lower section of a departmental expense allocation spreadsheet for Bookworm Bookstore. It reports the total amounts of direct and indirect expenses allocated to its five departments. Complete the spreadsheet by allocating the expenses of the two service departments (advertising and purchasing) to the three operating departments.

File Edit View Insert Format Tools Data Window Help

	Allocation Base	Expense Account Balance	Advertising Dept.	Purchasing Dept.	Books Dept.	Magazines Dept.	Newspapers Dept.
			Allocation of Expenses to Departments				
Total department expenses		$654,000	$22,000	$30,000	$425,000	$86,000	$91,000
Service department expenses							
Advertising department	Sales		?		?	?	?
Purchasing department	Purch. orders			?	?	?	?
Total expenses allocated to							
operating departments		?	$ 0	$ 0	?	?	?

Sheet1 Sheet2 Sheet3

Advertising and purchasing department expenses are allocated to operating departments on the basis of dollar sales and purchase orders, respectively. Information about the allocation bases for the three operating departments follows.

Department	Sales	Purchase Orders
Books...............	$448,000	424
Magazines............	144,000	312
Newspapers..........	208,000	264
Total...............	$800,000	1,000

Check Total expenses allocated to Books Dept., $450,040

Monica Gellar works in both the jewelry department and the hosiery department of a retail store. Gellar assists customers in both departments and arranges and stocks merchandise in both departments. The store allocates Gellar's $30,000 annual wages between the two departments based on a sample of the time worked in the two departments. The sample is obtained from a diary of hours worked that Gellar kept in a randomly chosen two-week period. The diary showed the following hours and activities spent in the two departments. Allocate Gellar's annual wages between the two departments. (Round percents to one decimal.)

Exercise 21-6
Indirect payroll expense allocated to departments
C1

Selling in jewelry department..................................	64 hours
Arranging and stocking merchandise in jewelry department.......................	6 hours
Selling in hosiery department	14 hours
Arranging and stocking merchandise in hosiery department	12 hours
Idle time spent waiting for a customer to enter one of the selling departments	4 hours

Check Assign $8,130 to Hosiery

Bob Daniels manages an auto dealership's service department. The recent month's income statement for his department follows. (1) Analyze the items on the income statement and identify those that definitely should be included on a performance report used to evaluate Daniels's performance. List them and explain why you chose them. (2) List and explain the items that should definitely be excluded. (3) List the items that are not definitely included or excluded and explain why they fall into that category.

Exercise 21-7
Managerial performance evaluation
C2

Revenues		
Sales of parts	$144,000	
Sales of services..........................	210,000	$354,000
Costs and expenses		
Cost of parts sold	(60,000)	
Building depreciation	(18,600)	
Income taxes allocated to department.........	(17,400)	
Interest on long-term debt	(15,000)	
Manager's salary..........................	(24,000)	
Payroll taxes.............................	(16,200)	
Supplies	(31,800)	
Utilities.................................	(8,800)	
Wages (hourly)...........................	(32,000)	
Total costs and expenses...................		(223,800)
Departmental net profit		$130,200

You must prepare a return on investment analysis for the regional manager of Out-and-In Burgers. This growing chain is trying to decide which outlet of two alternatives to open. The first location (A) requires a $500,000 investment and is expected to yield annual net profit of $80,000. The second location (B) requires a $200,000 investment and is expected to yield annual net profit of $38,000. Compute the return on investment for each Out-and-In Burgers alternative and then make your recommendation in a one-half page memorandum to the regional manager. (The chain currently generates an 18% return on total assets.)

Exercise 21-8
Investment center analysis
A1

Exercise 21-9

Computing performance measures

A1

Comart, a retailer of consumer goods, provides the following information on two of its departments (each considered an investment center).

Investment Center	Sales	Net Income	Average Invested Assets
Electronics	$20,000,000	$1,500,000	$ 7,500,000
Sporting goods.	16,000,000	1,600,000	10,000,000

(1) Compute return on investment for each department. Using return on investment, which department is most efficient at using assets to generate returns for the company? (2) Assume a target income level of 12% of average invested assets. Compute residual income for each department. Which department generated the most residual income for the company? (3) Assume the Electronics department is presented with a new investment opportunity that will yield a 15% return on assets. Should the new investment opportunity be accepted? Explain.

Exercise 21-10

Computing performance measures   A2

Refer to information in Exercise 21-9. Compute profit margin and investment turnover for each department. Which department generates the most net profit per dollar of sales? Which department is most efficient at generating sales from average invested assets?

Exercise 21-11

Performance measures—balanced scorecard

A1

MidCoast Airlines uses the following performance measures. Classify each of the performance measures below into the most likely balanced scorecard perspective it relates to. Label your answers using C (customer), P (internal process), I (innovation and growth), or F (financial).

  1. Flight attendant training sessions attended _____

  2. Customer complaints _____

  3. Percentage of on-time departures _____

  4. Market value _____

  5. Percentage of ground crew trained _____

  6. Return on investment _____

  7. On-time flight percentage _____

  8. Accidents or safety incidents per mile flown _____

  9. Number of reports of mishandled or lost baggage _____

10. Cash flow from operations _____

11. Time airplane is on ground between flights _____

12. Airplane miles per gallon of fuel _____

13. Revenue per seat _____

14. Cost of leasing airplanes _____

Exercise 21-12^A

Determining transfer prices

C3

The Trailer department of Soni Bicycles makes bike trailers that attach to bicycles and can carry children or cargo. The trailers have a retail price of $100 each. Each trailer incurs $40 of variable manufacturing costs. The Trailer department has capacity for 40,000 trailers per year, and incurs fixed costs of $800,000 per year.

Required

  1. Assume the Assembly division of Soni Bicycles wants to buy 10,000 trailers per year from the Trailer division. If the Trailer division can sell all of the trailers it manufactures to outside customers, what price should be used on transfers between Soni Bicycle's divisions? Explain.

  2. Assume the Trailer division currently only sells 20,000 trailers to outside customers, and the Assembly division wants to buy 10,000 trailers per year from the Trailer division. What is the range of acceptable prices that could be used on transfers between Soni Bicycle's divisions? Explain.

  3. Assume transfer prices of either $40 per trailer or $70 per trailer are being considered. Comment on the preferred transfer prices from the perspectives of the Trailer division manager, the Assembly division manager, and the top management of Soni Bicycles.

Exercise 21-13^B

Joint real estate costs assigned

C4

Tidy Home Properties is developing a subdivision that includes 300 home lots. The 225 lots in the Garden section are below a ridge and do not have views of the neighboring gardens and hills; the 75 lots in the Premier section offer unobstructed views. The expected selling price for each Garden lot is $50,000 and for each Premier lot is $100,000. The developer acquired the land for $2,500,000 and spent another $2,000,000 on street and utilities improvements. Assign the joint land and improvement costs to the lots using the value basis of allocation and determine the average cost per lot.

Check Total Garden cost, $2,700,000

Pike Seafood Company purchases lobsters and processes them into tails and flakes. It sells the lobster tails for $20 per pound and the flakes for $15 per pound. On average, 100 pounds of lobster are processed into 57 pounds of tails and 24 pounds of flakes, with 19 pounds of waste. Assume that the company purchased 3,000 pounds of lobster for $6.00 per pound and processed the lobsters with an additional labor cost of $1,800. No materials or labor costs are assigned to the waste. If 1,510 pounds of tails and 710 pounds of flakes are sold, what is (1) the allocated cost of the sold items and (2) the allocated cost of the ending inventory? The company allocates joint costs on a value basis. (Round the dollar cost per pound to the nearest thousandth.)

Exercise 21-14[B]
Joint product costs assigned
C4

Check (2) Inventory cost, $1,826

L'Oreal reports the following for a recent year for the major divisions in its Cosmetics branch.

Exercise 21-15
Profit margin and investment turnover

A2

(in EUR millions)	Sales	Income	Total Assets End of Year	Total Assets Beginning of Year
Professional products	2,472	519	2,516	2,440
Consumer products	8,355	1,578	5,496	5,361
Luxury products	4,170	766	4,059	2,695
Active cosmetics	1,289	259	817	818
Total	16,286	3,122	12,888	11,314

1. Compute profit margin for each division. State your answers as percents, rounded to two decimal places. Which L'Oreal division has the highest profit margin?

2. Compute investment turnover for each division. Round your answers to two decimal places. Which L'Oreal division has the best investment turnover?

connect _____

City Bank has several departments that occupy both floors of a two-story building. The departmental accounting system has a single account, Building Occupancy Cost, in its ledger. The types and amounts of occupancy costs recorded in this account for the current period follow.

PROBLEM SET A

Problem 21-1A
Allocation of building occupancy costs to departments

P1

www.mheducation.asia/olc/wildkwokFAP

Depreciation—Building	$18,000
Interest—Building mortgage	27,000
Taxes—Building and land	8,000
Gas (heating) expense..............	2,500
Lighting expense	3,000
Maintenance expense	5,500
Total occupancy cost	$64,000

The building has 4,000 square feet on each floor. In prior periods, the accounting manager merely divided the $64,000 occupancy cost by 8,000 square feet to find an average cost of $8 per square foot and then charged each department a building occupancy cost equal to this rate times the number of square feet that it occupied.

Laura Diaz manages a first-floor department that occupies 1,000 square feet, and Lauren Wright manages a second-floor department that occupies 1,800 square feet of floor space. In discussing the departmental reports, the second-floor manager questions whether using the same rate per square foot for all departments makes sense because the first-floor space is more valuable. This manager also references a recent real estate study of average local rental costs for similar space that shows first-floor space worth $30 per square foot and second-floor space worth $20 per square foot (excluding costs for heating, lighting, and maintenance).

Required

1. Allocate occupancy costs to the Diaz and Wright departments using the current allocation method.

2. Allocate the depreciation, interest, and taxes occupancy costs to the Diaz and Wright departments in proportion to the relative market values of the floor space. Allocate the heating, lighting, and maintenance costs to the Diaz and Wright departments in proportion to the square feet occupied (ignoring floor space market values).

Check (1) Total allocated to Diaz and Wright, $22,400 (2) Total occupancy cost to Diaz, $9,330

Analysis Component

3. Which allocation method would you prefer if you were a manager of a second-floor department? Explain.

Problem 21-2A
Activity-based costing

P2

We Care is an outpatient surgical clinic that was profitable for many years, but Medicare has cut its reimbursements by as much as 50%. As a result, the clinic wants to better understand its costs. It decides to prepare an activity-based cost analysis, including an estimate of the average cost of both general surgery and orthopedic surgery. The clinic's three cost centers and their cost drivers follow.

Cost Center	Cost	Cost Driver	Driver Quantity
Professional salaries...............	$1,500,000	Professional hours	10,000
Patient services and supplies.........	25,000	Number of patients	500
Building cost	150,000	Square feet	1,500

The two main surgical units and their related data follow.

Service	Hours	Square Feet*	Patients
General surgery............	2,500	500	400
Orthopedic surgery.........	7,500	1,000	100

* Orthopedic surgery requires more space for patients, supplies, and equipment.

Required

1. Compute the cost per cost driver for each of the three cost centers.

Check   (2) Average cost of general (orthopedic) surgery, $1,113 ($12,300) per patient

2. Use the results from part 1 to allocate costs from each of the three cost centers to both the general surgery and the orthopedic surgery units. Compute total cost and average cost per patient for both the general surgery and the orthopedic surgery units.

Analysis Component

3. Without providing computations, would the average cost of general surgery be higher or lower if all center costs were allocated based on the number of patients? Explain.

Problem 21-3A
Departmental income statements; forecasts

P3

eXcel
www.mheducation.asia/olc/wildkwokFAP

Time-To-See Company began operations in January 2011 with two operating (selling) departments and one service (office) department. Its departmental income statements follow.

TIME-TO-SEE COMPANY Departmental Income Statements For Year Ended December 31, 2011			
	Clock	**Mirror**	**Combined**
Sales.......................................	$122,500	$52,500	$175,000
Cost of goods sold	60,000	32,000	92,000
Gross profit................................	62,500	20,500	83,000
Direct expenses			
Sales salaries	20,000	7,000	27,000
Advertising	1,200	500	1,700
Store supplies used	900	400	1,300
Depreciation—Equipment	1,500	300	1,800
Total direct expenses.....................	23,600	8,200	31,800
Allocated expenses			
Rent expense............................	7,020	3,780	10,800
Utilities expense	2,600	1,400	4,000
Share of office department expenses	10,500	4,500	15,000
Total allocated expenses	20,120	9,680	29,800
Total expenses.............................	43,720	17,880	61,600
Net profit.................................	$ 18,780	$ 2,620	$ 21,400

Time-To-See plans to open a third department in January 2012 that will sell paintings. Management predicts that the new department will generate $35,000 in sales with a 55% gross profit margin and will require the following direct expenses: sales salaries, $8,000; advertising, $800; store supplies, $500; and equipment depreciation, $200. It will fit the new department into the current rented space by taking some square footage from the other two departments. When opened the new painting department will fill one-fifth of the space presently used by the clock department and one-sixth used by the mirror department. Management does not predict any increase in utilities costs, which are allocated to the departments in proportion to occupied space (or rent expense). The company allocates office department expenses to the operating departments in proportion to their sales. It expects the painting department to increase total office department expenses by $7,000. Since the painting department will bring new customers into the store, management expects sales in both the clock and mirror departments to increase by 7%. No changes for those departments' gross profit percents or their direct expenses are expected except for store supplies used, which will increase in proportion to sales.

Required

Prepare departmental income statements that show the company's predicted results of operations for calendar year 2012 for the three operating (selling) departments and their combined totals. (Round percents to the nearest one-tenth and dollar amounts to the nearest whole dollar.)

Check 2012 forecasted combined net profit (sales), $29,869 ($222,250)

Becky Hoefer, the plant manager of Travel Far's Indiana plant, is responsible for all of that plant's costs other than her own salary. The plant has two operating departments and one service department. The camper and trailer operating departments manufacture different products and have their own managers. The office department, which Hoefer also manages, provides services equally to the two operating departments. A budget is prepared for each operating department and the office department. The company's responsibility accounting system must assemble information to present budgeted and actual costs in performance reports for each operating department manager and the plant manager. Each performance report includes only those costs that a particular operating department manager can control: raw materials, wages, supplies used, and equipment depreciation. The plant manager is responsible for the department managers' salaries, utilities, building rent, office salaries other than her own, and other office costs plus all costs controlled by the two operating department managers. The annual departmental budgets and actual costs for the two operating departments follow.

Problem 21-4A
Responsibility accounting performance reports; controllable and budgeted costs
C2

	Budget			Actual		
	Campers	Trailers	Combined	Campers	Trailers	Combined
Raw materials	$160,000	$250,000	$ 410,000	$159,400	$246,500	$ 405,900
Employee wages	99,000	191,000	290,000	102,300	193,700	296,000
Dept. manager salary	40,000	44,000	84,000	41,000	47,000	88,000
Supplies used	34,000	83,000	117,000	31,900	84,600	116,500
Depreciation—Equip.	58,000	110,000	168,000	58,000	110,000	168,000
Utilities...................	2,800	4,200	7,000	2,700	3,800	6,500
Building rent	5,000	8,000	13,000	4,800	7,200	12,000
Office department costs	56,000	56,000	112,000	54,450	54,450	108,900
Totals	$454,800	$746,200	$1,201,000	$454,550	$747,250	$1,201,800

The office department's annual budget and its actual costs follow.

	Budget	Actual
Plant manager salary	$ 60,000	$ 62,000
Other office salaries	30,000	27,700
Other office costs	22,000	19,200
Totals	$112,000	$108,900

Required

1. Prepare responsibility accounting performance reports like those in Exhibit 21.29 that list costs controlled by the following:

    a. Manager of the camper department.

    b. Manager of the trailer department.

    c. Manager of the Indiana plant.

In each report, include the budgeted and actual costs and show the amount that each actual cost is over or under the budgeted amount.

Analysis Component

2. Did the plant manager or the operating department managers better manage costs? Explain.

Problem 21-5A^B

Allocation of joint costs

C4

Bloom Orchards produced a good crop of peaches this year. After preparing the following income statement, the company believes it should have given its No. 3 peaches to charity and saved its efforts.

BLOOM ORCHARDS Income Statement For Year Ended December 31, 2011				
	No. 1	**No. 2**	**No. 3**	**Combined**
Sales (by grade)				
No. 1: 300,000 lbs. @ $1.50/lb	$450,000			
No. 2: 300,000 lbs. @ $1.00/lb		$300,000		
No. 3: 750,000 lbs. @ $0.20/lb			$ 150,000	
Total sales				$900,000
Costs				
Tree pruning and care @ $0.20/lb	60,000	60,000	150,000	270,000
Picking, sorting, and grading @ $0.12/lb	36,000	36,000	90,000	162,000
Delivery costs $0.03/lb	9,000	9,000	22,500	40,500
Total costs	105,000	105,000	262,500	472,500
Net profit (loss)	$345,000	$195,000	$(112,500)	$427,500

In preparing this statement, the company allocated joint costs among the grades on a physical basis as an equal amount per pound. The company's delivery cost records show that $30,000 of the $40,500 relates to crating the No. 1 and No. 2 peaches and hauling them to the buyer. The remaining $10,500 of delivery costs is for crating the No. 3 peaches and hauling them to the cannery.

Required

1. Prepare reports showing cost allocations on a sales value basis to the three grades of peaches. Separate the delivery costs into the amounts directly identifiable with each grade. Then allocate any shared delivery costs on the basis of the relative sales value of each grade.

2. Using your answers to part 1, prepare an income statement using the joint costs allocated on a sales value basis.

Analysis Component

3. Do you think delivery costs fit the definition of a joint cost? Explain.

PROBLEM SET B

Problem 21-1B

Allocation of building occupancy costs to departments

P1

Dixon's has several departments that occupy all floors of a two-story building that includes a basement floor. Dixon rented this building under a long-term lease negotiated when rental rates were low. The departmental accounting system has a single account, Building Occupancy Cost, in its ledger. The types and amounts of occupancy costs recorded in this account for the current period follow.

Building rent	$300,000
Lighting expense	24,000
Cleaning expense	16,000
Total occupancy cost	$340,000

The building has 7,500 square feet on each of the upper two floors but only 5,000 square feet in the basement. In prior periods, the accounting manager merely divided the $340,000 occupancy cost by 20,000 square feet to find an average cost of $17 per square foot and then charged each department a building occupancy cost equal to this rate times the number of square feet that it occupies.

Alex Ferrero manages a department that occupies 2,000 square feet of basement floor space. In discussing the departmental reports with other managers, she questions whether using the same rate per square foot for all departments makes sense because different floor space has different values. Ferrero checked a recent real estate report of average local rental costs for similar space that shows first-floor space worth $40 per square foot, second-floor space worth $20 per square foot, and basement space worth $10 per square foot (excluding costs for lighting and cleaning).

Required

1. Allocate occupancy costs to Ferrero's department using the current allocation method.
2. Allocate the building rent cost to Ferrero's department in proportion to the relative market value of the floor space. Allocate to Ferrero's department the lighting and heating costs in proportion to the square feet occupied (ignoring floor space market values). Then, compute the total occupancy cost allocated to Ferrero's department.

Check Total costs allocated to Ferrero's Dept., (1) $34,000; (2) Total occupancy cost to Ferrero $16,000

Analysis Component

3. Which allocation method would you prefer if you were a manager of a basement department?

Prairie Landscaping has enjoyed profits for many years, but new competition has cut service revenue by as much as 30%. As a result, the company wants to better understand its costs. It decides to prepare an activity-based cost analysis, including an estimate of the average cost of both general landscaping services and custom design landscaping services. The company's three cost centers and their cost drivers follow.

Problem 21-2B
Activity-based costing
P2

Cost Center	Cost	Cost Driver	Driver Quantity
Professional salaries	$500,000	Professional hours	10,000
Customer supplies	125,000	Number of customers	500
Building cost	150,000	Square feet	1,500

The two main landscaping units and their related data follow.

Service	Hours	Square Feet*	Customers
General landscaping..............	2,500	500	400
Custom design landscaping	7,500	1,000	100

* Custom design landscaping requires more space for equipment, supplies, and planning.

Required

1. Compute the cost per cost driver for each of the three cost centers.
2. Use the results from part 1 to allocate costs from each of the three cost centers to both the general landscaping and the custom design landscaping units. Compute total cost and average cost per customer for both the general landscaping and the custom design landscaping units.

Check (2) Average cost of general (custom) landscaping, $687.50 ($5,000) per customer

Analysis Component

3. Without providing computations, would the average cost of general landscaping be higher or lower if all center costs were allocated based on the number of customers? Explain.

Hollywood Entertainment began operations in January 2011 with two operating (selling) departments and one service (office) department. Its departmental income statements follow.

Problem 21-3B
Departmental income
statements; forecasts   P3

HOLLYWOOD ENTERTAINMENT
Departmental Income Statements
For Year Ended December 31, 2011

	Movies	Video Games	Combined
Sales	$540,000	$180,000	$720,000
Cost of goods sold	378,000	138,600	516,600
Gross profit	162,000	41,400	203,400
Direct expenses			
Sales salaries	35,000	14,000	49,000
Advertising	10,500	5,500	16,000
Store supplies used	3,300	700	4,000
Depreciation—Equipment	4,200	2,800	7,000
Total direct expenses	53,000	23,000	76,000
Allocated expenses			
Rent expense	29,520	6,480	36,000
Utilities expense	4,100	900	5,000
Share of office department expenses	39,000	14,000	53,000
Total allocated expenses	72,620	21,380	94,000
Total expenses	125,620	44,380	170,000
Net profit (loss)	$ 36,380	$ (2,980)	$ 33,400

The company plans to open a third department in January 2012 that will sell compact discs. Management predicts that the new department will generate $250,000 in sales with a 35% gross profit margin and will require the following direct expenses: sales salaries, $18,000; advertising, $10,000; store supplies, $1,500; and equipment depreciation, $1,000. The company will fit the new department into the current rented space by taking some square footage from the other two departments. When opened, the new compact disc department will fill one-fourth of the space presently used by the movie department and one-third of the space used by the video game department. Management does not predict any increase in utilities costs, which are allocated to the departments in proportion to occupied space (or rent expense). The company allocates office department expenses to the operating departments in proportion to their sales. It expects the compact disc department to increase total office department expenses by $8,000. Since the compact disc department will bring new customers into the store, management expects sales in both the movie and video game departments to increase by 10%. No changes for those departments' gross profit percents or for their direct expenses are expected, except for store supplies used, which will increase in proportion to sales.

Required

Check   2012 forecasted movies net profit (sales), $64,885 ($594,000)

Prepare departmental income statements that show the company's predicted results of operations for calendar year 2012 for the three operating (selling) departments and their combined totals. (Round percents to the nearest one-tenth and dollar amounts to the nearest whole dollar.)

Problem 21-4B
Responsibility accounting performance reports; controllable and budgeted costs

C2

Aaron Braun, the plant manager of SOS Co.'s Chicago plant, is responsible for all of that plant's costs other than his own salary. The plant has two operating departments and one service department. The refrigerator and dishwasher operating departments manufacture different products and have their own managers. The office department, which Braun also manages, provides services equally to the two operating departments. A monthly budget is prepared for each operating department and the office department. The company's responsibility accounting system must assemble information to present budgeted and actual costs in performance reports for each operating department manager and the plant manager. Each performance report includes only those costs that a particular operating department manager can control: raw materials, wages, supplies used, and equipment depreciation. The plant manager is responsible for the department managers' salaries, utilities, building rent, office salaries other than his own, and other office costs plus all costs controlled by the two operating department managers. The April departmental budgets and actual costs for the two operating departments follow.

	Budget			Actual		
	Refrigerators	Dishwashers	Combined	Refrigerators	Dishwashers	Combined
Raw materials	$400,000	$200,000	$ 600,000	$375,000	$200,000	$ 575,000
Employee wages	172,000	80,000	252,000	174,700	76,800	251,500
Dept. manager salary	55,000	49,000	104,000	55,000	46,500	101,500
Supplies used	15,000	9,000	24,000	14,000	10,000	24,000
Depreciation—Equip.	53,000	37,000	90,000	53,000	37,000	90,000
Utilities.......................	30,000	18,000	48,000	34,500	20,700	55,200
Building rent	63,000	17,000	80,000	61,000	15,000	76,000
Office department costs	70,500	70,500	141,000	75,000	75,000	150,000
Totals	$858,500	$480,500	$1,339,000	$842,200	$481,000	$1,323,200

The office department's budget and its actual costs for April follow.

	Budget	Actual
Plant manager salary	$ 80,000	$ 85,000
Other office salaries	40,000	35,200
Other office costs	21,000	29,800
Totals	$141,000	$150,000

Required

1. Prepare responsibility accounting performance reports like those in Exhibit 21.28 that list costs controlled by the following:

    a. Manager of the refrigerator department.

    b. Manager of the dishwasher department.

    c. Manager of the Chicago plant.

In each report, include the budgeted and actual costs for the month and show the amount by which each actual cost is over or under the budgeted amount.

Check (1a) $23,300 total under budget

(1c) Chicago plant controllable costs, $20,800 total under budget

Analysis Component

2. Did the plant manager or the operating department managers better manage costs? Explain.

Sarah and Stew Salsa own and operate a tomato grove. After preparing the following income statement, Sarah believes they should have offered the No. 3 tomatoes to the public for free and saved themselves time and money.

Problem 21-5B[B]
Allocation of joint costs
C4

SARAH AND STEW SALSA Income Statement For Year Ended December 31, 2011				
	No. 1	No. 2	No. 3	Combined
Sales (by grade)				
No. 1: 400,000 lbs. @ $1.50/lb	$600,000			
No. 2: 300,000 lbs. @ $1.00/lb		$300,000		
No. 3: 100,000 lbs. @ $0.30/lb			$ 30,000	
Total sales.				$930,000
Costs				
Land preparation, seeding, and cultivating @ $0.50/lb	200,000	150,000	50,000	400,000
Harvesting, sorting, and grading @ $0.02/lb..................	8,000	6,000	2,000	16,000
Delivery costs @ $0.01/lb	4,000	3,000	1,000	8,000
Total costs	212,000	159,000	53,000	424,000
Net profit (loss)..	$388,000	$141,000	$(23,000)	$506,000

In preparing this statement, Sarah and Stew allocated joint costs among the grades on a physical basis as an equal amount per pound. Also, their delivery cost records show that $7,000 of the $8,000 relates to crating the No. 1 and No. 2 tomatoes and hauling them to the buyer. The remaining $1,000 of delivery costs is for crating the No. 3 tomatoes and hauling them to the cannery.

Required

Check (1) $512 harvesting, sorting and grading costs allocated to No. 3

1. Prepare reports showing cost allocations on a sales value basis to the three grades of tomatoes. Separate the delivery costs into the amounts directly identifiable with each grade. Then allocate any shared delivery costs on the basis of the relative sales value of each grade. (Round percents to the nearest one-tenth and dollar amounts to the nearest whole dollar.)

(2) Net profit from No. 1 & No. 2 tomatoes, $327,011 & $163,301

2. Using your answers to part 1, prepare an income statement using the joint costs allocated on a sales value basis.

Analysis Component

3. Do you think delivery costs fit the definition of a joint cost? Explain.

SERIAL PROBLEM
Business Solutions

P1 P2

(This serial problem began in Chapter 1 and continues through most of the book. If previous chapter segments were not completed, the serial problem can begin at this point.)

SP 21   After reading an article about activity-based costing in a trade journal for the furniture industry, Santana Rey wondered if it was time to critically analyze overhead costs at Business Solutions. In a recent month, Rey found that setup costs, inspection costs, and utility costs made up most of its overhead. Additional information about overhead follows.

Activity	Cost	Driver
Setting up machines............	$20,000	25 batches
Inspecting components	$ 7,500	5,000 parts
Providing utilities	$10,000	5,000 machine hours

Overhead has been applied to output at a rate of 50% of direct labor costs. The following data pertain to Job 6.15.

Direct materials..........	$2,500	Number of parts	400 parts
Direct labor.............	$3,500	Machine hours	600 machine hours
Batches.................	2 batches		

Required

1. What is the total cost of Job 6.15 if Business Solutions applies overhead at 50% of direct labor cost?
2. What is the total cost of Job 6.15 if Business Solutions uses activity-based costing?
3. Which approach to assigning overhead gives a better representation of the costs incurred to produce Job 6.15? Explain.

Beyond the Numbers

REPORTING IN ACTION

C1

BTN 21-1   Access **Research In Motion's** 2010 annual report from its Website www.rim.com. Review the income statement and identify its revenues for the years ended February 27, 2010, February 28, 2009, and March 1, 2008. For the year ended February 27, 2010, Research In Motion reports the following product revenue mix. (Assume that its product revenue mix is the same for each of the three years reported when answering the requirements.)

Devices	Service	Software	Other
81%	14%	2%	3%

Required

1. Compute the amount of revenue from each of its product lines for the years ended February 27, 2010, February 28, 2009, and March 1, 2008.

2. If Research In Motion wishes to evaluate each of its product lines, how can it allocate its operating expenses to each of them to determine each product line's profitability?

Fast Forward

3. Access Research In Motion's annual report for a financial year ending after February 27, 2010, from its Website. Compute its revenues for its product lines for the most recent year(s). Compare those results to those from part 1. How has its product mix changed?

BTN 21-2   Research In Motion, Apple, and Palm compete across the world in several markets.

Required

1. Design a three-tier responsibility accounting organizational chart assuming that you have available internal information for all three companies. Use Exhibit 21.28 as an example. The goal of this assignment is to design a reporting framework for the companies; numbers are not required. Limit your reporting framework to sales activity only.

2. Explain why it is important to have similar performance reports when comparing performance within a company (and across different companies). Be specific in your response.

COMPARATIVE ANALYSIS

P3

BTN 21-3   Senior Security Co. offers a range of security services for senior citizens. Each type of service is considered within a separate department. Mary Pincus, the overall manager, is compensated partly on the basis of departmental performance by staying within the quarterly cost budget. She often revises operations to make sure departments stay within budget. Says Pincus, "I will not go over budget even if it means slightly compromising the level and quality of service. These are minor compromises that don't significantly affect my clients, at least in the short term."

Required

1. Is there an ethical concern in this situation? If so, which parties are affected? Explain.

2. Can Mary Pincus take action to eliminate or reduce any ethical concerns? Explain.

3. What is Senior Security's ethical responsibility in offering professional services?

ETHICS CHALLENGE

P3

BTN 21-4   Home Station is a national home improvement chain with more than 100 stores throughout the country. The manager of each store receives a salary plus a bonus equal to a percent of the store's net profit for the reporting period. The following net profit calculation is on the Denver store manager's performance report for the recent monthly period.

COMMUNICATING IN PRACTICE

P3

Sales	$2,500,000
Cost of goods sold	800,000
Wages expense	500,000
Utilities expense	200,000
Home office expense	75,000
Net profit.	$ 925,000
Manager's bonus (0.5%)	$ 4,625

In previous periods, the bonus had also been 0.5%, but the performance report had not included any charges for the home office expense, which is now assigned to each store as a percent of its sales.

Required

Assume that you are the national office manager. Write a one-half page memorandum to your store managers explaining why home office expense is in the new performance report.

TAKING IT TO THE NET

P1

BTN 21-5   This chapter described and used spreadsheets to prepare various managerial reports (see Exhibit 21-13). You can download from Websites various tutorials showing how spreadsheets are used in managerial accounting and other business applications.

Required

1. Link to the Website Lacher.com. Select "Excel Examples." Identify and list three tutorials for review.
2. Describe in a one-half page memorandum to your instructor how the applications described in each tutorial are helpful in business and managerial decision making.

TEAMWORK IN ACTION

P2

BTN 21-6   Activity-based costing (ABC) is increasingly popular as a useful managerial tool to (1) measure the cost of resources consumed and (2) assign cost to products and services. This managerial tool has been available to accounting and business decision makers for more than 25 years.

Required

Break into teams and identify at least three likely reasons that activity-based costing has gained popularity in recent years. Be prepared to present your answers in a class discussion. (*Hint:* What changes have occurred in products and services over the past 25 years?)

ENTREPRENEURIAL DECISION

P3

BTN 21-7   Refer to the Decision Insight that describes measurement of divisional performance in Hunter Douglas, India. All divisions are subject to a net asset charge.

Required

What would be the impact on behavior of divisional managers if the divisional performance was computed *without* a net asset charge?

HITTING THE ROAD

C1 C2

BTN 21-8   Visit a large hotel, preferably one that is listed on a stock exchange. Observe the different kind of services it provides.

Required

1. Look up its financials and see if you can find financials reported for the different segments of services you identified.
2. Comment on the financial performance of each segment.

GLOBAL DECISION

P3

BTN 21-9   Refer to Nestle's 2010 financial statements in Appendix A.

Required

1. Examine the performance reported by Nestle for different geographical segments and different product segments from pages A-20 through A-23.
2. Choose three measures of performance. Compare the performance of the different metrics using these measures on the 2010 data.

ANSWERS TO MULTIPLE CHOICE QUIZ

1. b; [$641,250/($356,250 + $641,250 + $427,500)] × $150,000 = $67,500

2. c;

3. e; $162,000 × 50/150 setup. $54,000; $54,000/500 units = $108 per Grey unit. (Red is $2.70 per unit.)

4. b;

	Department X	Department Y	Department Z
Sales	$500,000	$200,000	$350,000
Cost of goods sold	350,000	75,000	150,000
Gross profit	150,000	125,000	200,000
Direct expenses.	50,000	20,000	75,000
Departmental contribution.	$100,000	$105,000	$125,000

5. a; $100,000/$500,000 = 20%

22

Cost-Volume-Profit Analysis

A Look Back

Chapter 21 focused on cost allocation, activity-based costing, and performance measurement. We identified ways to measure and analyze company activities, its departments, and its managers.

A Look at This Chapter

This chapter shows how information on both costs and sales behavior is useful to managers in performing cost-volume-profit analysis. This analysis is an important part of successful management and sound business decisions.

A Look Ahead

Chapter 23 introduces and describes the budgeting process and its importance to management. It also explains the master budget and its usefulness to the planning of future company activities.

Learning Objectives

CAP

CONCEPTUAL

C1 Describe different types of cost behavior in relation to production and sales volume. (p. 880)

C2 Describe several applications of cost-volume-profit analysis. (p. 891)

ANALYTICAL

A1 Compute the contribution margin and describe what it reveals about a company's cost structure. (p. 886)

A2 Analyze changes in sales using the degree of operating leverage. (p. 896)

PROCEDURAL

P1 Determine cost estimates using the scatter diagram, high-low, and regression methods of estimating costs. (p. 883)

P2 Compute the break-even point for a single product company. (p. 886)

P3 Graph costs and sales for a single product company. (p. 888)

P4 Compute the break-even point for a multiproduct company. (p. 893)

"I wanted a business that is not only profitable but socially meaningful."—**CHOO YILIN**

Decision Insight

Art Choo!

It started out as a hobby-cum-side-business when Choo Yilin was working full time as an analyst, selling her jewelry pieces to independent luxury boutiques in Singapore. Today it is **Choo Yilin Artisan Jewellery (www.chooyilin.com)**, an international award-winning luxury brand seeking to infuse sustainability into a luxurious lifestyle.

The journey to entrepreneurship, however, was anything but gemstone-smooth. With her husband's job relocation to Bangkok, Yilin followed suit, and with time on her side, she experimented with jewelry design and creations, pushing her merchandise from door to door, braving one rejection after another. "If I had known what I was going into, I might not have started!" Yilin would joke when relating the experience to her friends. She remained steadfast, thanks to a Frenchman and veteran in the jewelry industry who helped her unravel the intricacies of the gem business.

Yilin embraced the opportunity to start her own jewelry business when she encountered the Karen hilltribe artisans in northern Thailand. "I wanted a business that is not only profitable but socially meaningful," she explains. Drawn by a deep connection to the centuries-old culture of their silversmithing craft, she collaborated with these indigenous artisans, expanding her efforts to working with nonprofit groups and using their conservation campaigns as inspirations for her signature pieces. In her interaction with World Wildlife Fund, for example, the conservation message is weaved into her jewelry design with peripheral pieces—leaves, roots, vines—twisting and writhing around a distinctively luminescent centerpiece.

Yilin agrees that sustaining a business means understanding cost behavior and performing cost-volume-profit analyses to determine the break-even points. To do this, she needs to identify fixed and variable costs and to monitor variables such as the sales volume needed to achieve a target income and the change in income if selling prices decline and sales volume increases. With a diverse design line, it is even more important to understand how costs relate to volume and profits to ensure the right mix of design choices and profitability.

Once a business novice who had doors shut on her, the now director and chief designer of a jewelry label has this sage advice for aspiring entrepreneurs: "Don't be afraid to fail." She is proof that you can make it happen, that is, turn raw passionate ambition into a gem of a business!

This chapter describes different types of costs and shows how changes in a company's operating volume affect these costs. The chapter also analyzes a company's costs and sales to explain how different operating strategies affect profit or loss. Managers use this type of analysis to forecast what will happen if changes are made to costs, sales volume, selling prices, or product mix. They then use these forecasts to select the best business strategy for the company.

Cost-Volume-Profit Analysis

Identifying Cost Behavior	**Measuring Cost Behavior**	**Using Break-Even Analysis**	**Applying Cost-Volume-Profit Analysis**
• Fixed costs • Variable costs • Mixed costs • Step-wise costs • Curvilinear costs	• Scatter diagrams • High-low method • Least-squares regression • Comparison of cost estimation methods	• Computing contribution margin • Computing break-even • Preparing a cost-volume-profit chart • Making assumptions in cost-volume-profit analysis	• Computing income from sales and costs • Computing sales for target income • Computing margin of safety • Using sensitivity analysis • Computing multiproduct break-even

IDENTIFYING COST BEHAVIOR

Planning a company's future activities and events is a crucial phase in successful management. One of the first steps in planning is to predict the volume of activity, the costs to be incurred, sales to be made, and profit to be received. An important tool to help managers carry out this step is **cost-volume-profit (CVP) analysis,** which helps them predict how changes in costs and sales levels affect income. In its basic form, CVP analysis involves computing the sales level at which a company neither earns an income nor incurs a loss, called the *break-even point.* For this reason, this basic form of cost-volume-profit analysis is often called *break-even analysis.* Managers use variations of CVP analysis to answer questions such as these:

Point: *Profit* is another term for *income.*

- What sales volume is needed to earn a target income?
- What is the change in income if selling prices decline and sales volume increases?
- How much does income increase if we install a new machine to reduce labor costs?
- What is the income effect if we change the sales mix of our products or services?

Consequently, cost-volume-profit analysis is useful in a wide range of business decisions.

Conventional cost-volume-profit analysis requires management to classify all costs as either *fixed* or *variable* with respect to production or sales volume. The remainder of this section discusses the concepts of fixed and variable cost behavior as they relate to CVP analysis.

▮ Decision Insight

No Free Lunch   Hardly a week goes by without a company advertising a free product with the purchase of another. Examples are a free printer with a digital camera purchase or a free monitor with a computer purchase. Can these companies break even, let alone earn profits? We are reminded of the *no-free-lunch* adage, meaning that companies expect profits from the companion or add-on purchase to make up for the free product. ▮

Fixed Costs

C1 Describe different types of cost behavior in relation to production and sales volume.

A *fixed cost* remains unchanged in amount when the volume of activity varies from period to period within a relevant range. For example, $5,000 in monthly rent paid for a factory building remains the same whether the factory operates with a single eight-hour shift or around the clock with three shifts. This means that rent cost is the same each month at any level of output from zero to the plant's full productive capacity. Notice that while *total* fixed cost does not change as the level of production changes, the fixed cost *per unit* of output decreases as volume increases. For instance, if 20 units are produced when monthly rent is $5,000, the average rent cost per unit is $250 (computed as $5,000/20 units). When production increases to 100 units per month, the average cost per unit decreases to $50 (computed as $5,000/100 units). The average cost decreases to $10 per unit if production increases to 500 units per month. Common examples of fixed costs include depreciation, property taxes, office salaries, and many service department costs.

When production volume and costs are graphed, units of product are usually plotted on the *horizontal axis* and dollars of cost are plotted on the *vertical axis.* Fixed costs then are represented as a horizontal line because they remain constant at all levels of production. To illustrate, the graph in Exhibit 22.1 shows that fixed costs remain at $32,000 at all production levels up to the company's monthly capacity of 2,000 units of output. The *relevant range* for fixed costs in Exhibit 22.1 is 0 to 2,000 units. If the relevant range changes (that is, production capacity extends beyond this range), the amount of fixed costs will likely change.

Example: If the fixed cost line in Exhibit 22.1 is shifted upward, does the total cost line shift up, down, or remain in the same place? *Answer:* It shifts up by the same amount.

EXHIBIT 22.1

Relations of Fixed and Variable Costs to Volume

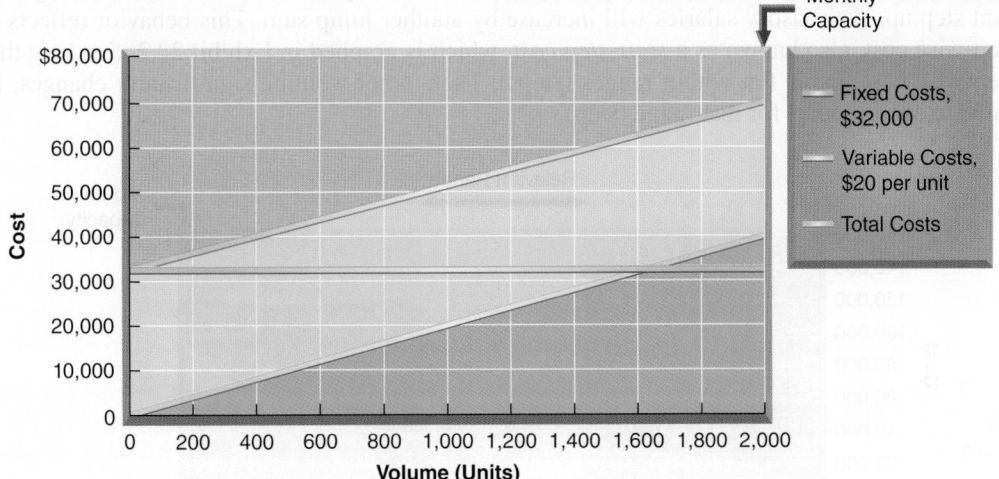

Variable Costs

A *variable cost* changes in proportion to changes in volume of activity. The direct materials cost of a product is one example of a variable cost. If one unit of product requires materials costing $20, total materials costs are $200 when 10 units of product are manufactured, $400 for 20 units, $600 for 30 units, and so on. Notice that variable cost *per unit* remains constant but the *total* amount of variable cost changes with the level of production. In addition to direct materials, common variable costs include direct labor (if employees are paid per unit), sales commissions, shipping costs, and some overhead costs.

When variable costs are plotted on a graph of cost and volume, they appear as a straight line starting at the zero cost level. This straight line is upward (positive) sloping. The line rises as volume of activity increases. A variable cost line using a $20 per unit cost is graphed in Exhibit 22.1.

Point: Fixed costs are constant in total but vary (decline) per unit as more units are produced. Variable costs vary in total but are fixed per unit.

Mixed Costs

A **mixed cost** includes both fixed and variable cost components. For example, compensation for sales representatives often includes a fixed monthly salary and a variable commission based on sales.

Total Costs

Total cost is the sum of fixed and variable costs. The total cost line in Exhibit 22.1 starts on the vertical axis at the $32,000 fixed cost point. Thus, at the zero volume level, total cost equals the fixed costs. As the activity level increases, the total cost line increases at an amount equal to the variable cost per unit. This line is highest when volume of activity is at 2,000 units (the end point of the relevant range). In CVP analysis, total cost is often separated into fixed and variable components. The fixed component is added to other fixed costs, and the variable component is added to other variable costs.

Example: If the level of fixed costs in Exhibit 22.1 changes, does the slope of the total cost line change? *Answer:* No, the slope doesn't change. The total cost line is simply shifted upward or downward.

The table below shows a comparison between fixed, variable, mixed, and total costs.

	Per Unit	Total	At Zero Volume
Fixed cost	Changes with volume	Fixed, within a range of volume	Fixed amount
Variable cost	Does not change with volume	Changes with volume	No cost
Mixed cost	Partly changes with volume	Partly changes with volume	Fixed component of the cost
Total cost	Partly changes with volume	Partly changes with volume	Fixed component of the cost

Step-Wise Costs

A **step-wise cost** reflects a step pattern in costs. Salaries of production supervisors often behave in a step-wise manner in that their salaries are fixed within a *relevant range* of the current production volume. However, if production volume expands significantly (for example, with the addition of another shift), additional supervisors must be hired. This means that the total cost for supervisory salaries goes up by a lump-sum amount. Similarly, if volume takes another significant step up, supervisory salaries will increase by another lump sum. This behavior reflects a step-wise cost, also known as a *stair-step cost,* which is graphed in Exhibit 22.2. See how the step-wise cost line is flat within ranges (steps). Then, when volume significantly changes, it shifts to another level for that range (step).

EXHIBIT 22.2

Step-Wise and Curvilinear Costs

Point: Computer spreadsheets are important and effective tools for CVP analysis and for analyzing alternative "what-if" strategies.

In a conventional CVP analysis, a step-wise cost is usually treated as either a fixed cost or a variable cost. This treatment involves manager judgment and depends on the width of the range and the expected volume. To illustrate, suppose after the production of every 25 snowboards, an operator lubricates the finishing machine. The cost of this lubricant reflects a step-wise pattern. Also, suppose that after the production of every 1,000 units, the snowboard cutting tool is replaced. Again, this is a step-wise cost. Note that the range of 25 snowboards is much narrower than the range of 1,000 snowboards. Some managers might treat the lubricant cost as a variable cost and the cutting tool cost as a fixed cost.

Curvilinear Costs

A variable cost, as explained, is a *linear* cost; that is, it increases at a constant rate as volume of activity increases. A **curvilinear cost,** also called a *nonlinear cost,* increases at a nonconstant rate as volume increases. When graphed, curvilinear costs appear as a curved line. Exhibit 22.2 shows a curvilinear cost beginning at zero when production is zero and then increasing at different rates.

Point: Cost-volume-profit analysis helped Rod Canion, Jim Harris, and Bill Murto raise start-up capital of $20 million to launch **Compaq Computer.** They showed that break-even volumes were attainable within the first year.

An example of a curvilinear cost is total direct labor cost when workers are paid by the hour. At low to medium levels of production, adding more employees allows each of them to specialize by doing certain tasks repeatedly instead of doing several different tasks. This often yields additional units of output at lower costs. A point is eventually reached at which adding more employees creates inefficiencies. For instance, a large crew demands more time and effort in communicating and coordinating their efforts. While adding employees in this case increases output, the labor cost per unit increases, and the total labor cost goes up at a steeper slope. This pattern is seen in Exhibit 22.2 where the curvilinear cost curve starts at zero, rises, flattens out, and then increases at a faster rate as output nears the maximum.

1. Which of the following statements is typically true? (a) Variable cost per unit increases as volume increases, (b) fixed cost per unit decreases as volume increases, or (c) a curvilinear cost includes both fixed and variable elements.
2. Describe the behavior of a fixed cost.
3. If cost per unit of activity remains constant (fixed), why is it called a variable cost?

MEASURING COST BEHAVIOR

Identifying and measuring cost behavior requires careful analysis and judgment. An important part of this process is to identify costs that can be classified as either fixed or variable, which often requires analysis of past cost behavior. Three methods are commonly used to analyze past costs: scatter diagrams, high-low method, and least-squares regression. Each method is discussed in this section using the unit and cost data shown in Exhibit 22.3, which are taken from a start-up company that uses units produced as the activity base in estimating cost behavior.

P1 Determine cost estimates using the scatter diagram, high-low, and regression methods of estimating costs.

EXHIBIT 22.3

Data for Estimating Cost Behavior

Month	Units Produced	Total Cost
January	17,500	$20,500
February.	27,500	21,500
March	25,000	25,000
April	35,000	21,500
May.	47,500	25,500
June	22,500	18,500
July	30,000	23,500
August	52,500	28,500
September	37,500	26,000
October	57,500	26,000
November	62,500	31,000
December	67,500	29,000

Scatter Diagrams

Scatter diagrams display past cost and unit data in graphical form. In preparing a scatter diagram, units are plotted on the horizontal axis and cost is plotted on the vertical axis. Each individual point on a scatter diagram reflects the cost and number of units for a prior period. In Exhibit 22.4, the prior 12 months' costs and numbers of units are graphed. Each point reflects total costs incurred and units produced for one of those months. For instance, the point labeled March had units produced of 25,000 and costs of $25,000.

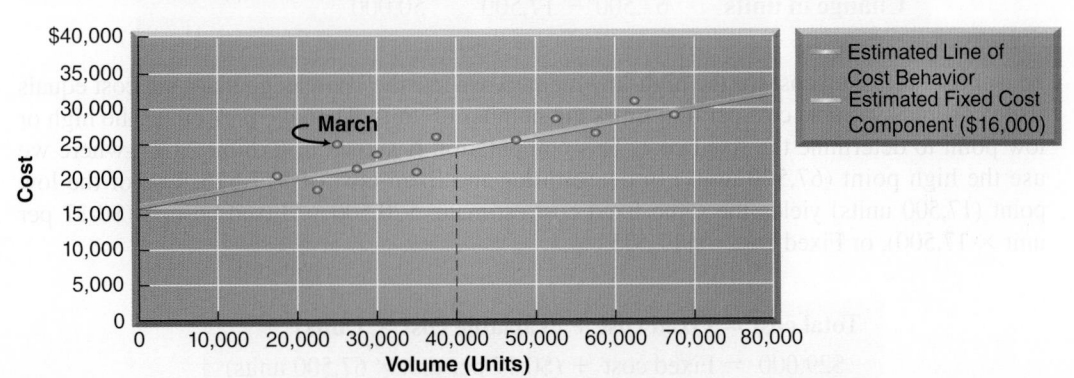

EXHIBIT 22.4

Scatter Diagram

The **estimated line of cost behavior** is drawn on a scatter diagram to reflect the relation between cost and unit volume. This line best visually "fits" the points in a scatter diagram. Fitting this line demands judgment. The line drawn in Exhibit 22.4 intersects the vertical axis at approximately $16,000, which reflects fixed cost. To compute variable cost per unit, or the slope, we perform three steps. First, we select any two points on the horizontal axis (units), say 0 and 40,000. Second, we draw a vertical line from each of these points to intersect the estimated line of cost behavior. The point on the vertical axis (cost) corresponding to the 40,000 units point that intersects the estimated line is roughly $24,000. Similarly, the cost corresponding to zero units is $16,000 (the fixed cost point). Third, we compute the slope of the line, or variable cost, as the change in cost divided by the change in units. Exhibit 22.5 shows this computation.

EXHIBIT 22.5

Variable Cost per Unit
(Scatter Diagram)

$$\frac{\textbf{Change in cost}}{\textbf{Change in units}} = \frac{\$24,000 - \$16,000}{40,000 - 0} = \frac{\$8,000}{40,000} = \$0.20 \text{ per unit}$$

Example: In Exhibits 22.4 and 22.5, if units are projected at 30,000, what is the predicted cost? *Answer:* Approximately $22,000.

Variable cost is $0.20 per unit. Thus, the cost equation that management will use to estimate costs for different unit levels is **$16,000 plus $0.20 per unit**.

High-Low Method

The **high-low method** is a way to estimate the cost equation by graphically connecting the two cost amounts at the highest and lowest unit volumes. In our case, the lowest number of units is 17,500, and the highest is 67,500. The costs corresponding to these unit volumes are $20,500 and $29,000, respectively (see the data in Exhibit 22.3). The estimated line of cost behavior for the high-low method is then drawn by connecting these two points on the scatter diagram corresponding to the lowest and highest unit volumes as follows.

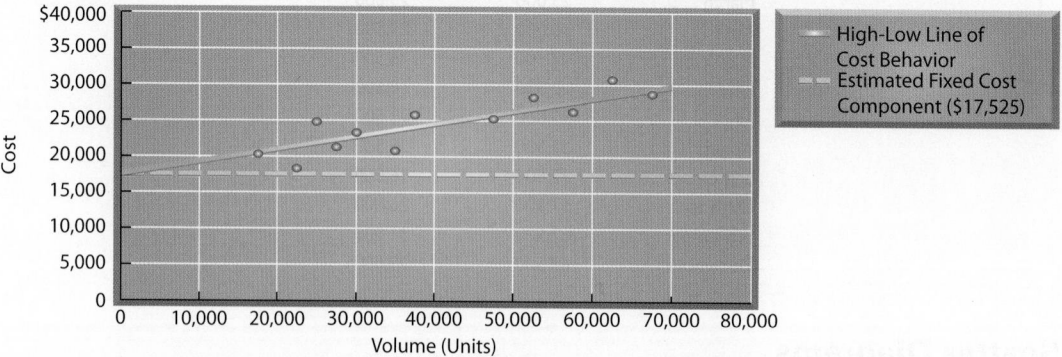

Point: Note that the high-low method identifies the high and low points of the volume (activity) base, and the costs linked with those extremes—which may not be the highest and lowest costs.

The variable cost per unit is determined as the change in cost divided by the change in units and uses the data from the high and low unit volumes. This results in a slope, or variable cost per unit, of $0.17 as computed in Exhibit 22.6.

EXHIBIT 22.6

Variable Cost per Unit
(High-Low Method)

$$\frac{\textbf{Change in cost}}{\textbf{Change in units}} = \frac{\$29,000 - \$20,500}{67,500 - 17,500} = \frac{\$8,500}{50,000} = \$0.17 \text{ per unit}$$

To estimate the fixed cost for the high-low method, we use the knowledge that total cost equals fixed cost plus variable cost per unit times the number of units. Then we pick either the high or low point to determine the fixed cost. This computation is shown in Exhibit 22.7—where we use the high point (67,500 units) in determining the fixed cost of $17,525. Use of the low point (17,500 units) yields the same fixed cost estimate: $20,500 = Fixed cost + ($0.17 per unit × 17,500), or Fixed cost = $17,525.

EXHIBIT 22.7

Fixed Cost (High-Low Method)

Total cost = Fixed cost + (Variable cost × Units)

$29,000 = Fixed cost + ($0.17 per unit × 67,500 units)

Then,　　　Fixed cost = $17,525

Thus, the cost equation used to estimate costs at different units is **$17,525 plus $0.17 per unit.** This cost equation differs slightly from that determined from the scatter diagram method. A deficiency of the high-low method is that it ignores all cost points except the highest and lowest. The result is less precision because the high-low method uses the most extreme points rather than the more usual conditions likely to recur.

Least-Squares Regression

Least-squares regression is a statistical method for identifying cost behavior. For our purposes, we use the cost equation estimated from this method but leave the computational details for more advanced courses. Such computations for least-squares regression are readily done using most spreadsheet programs or calculators. We illustrate this using Excel® in Appendix 22A.

The regression cost equation for the data presented in Exhibit 22.3 is **$16,947 plus $0.19 per unit**; that is, the fixed cost is estimated as $16,947 and the variable cost at $0.19 per unit. Both costs are reflected in the following graph.

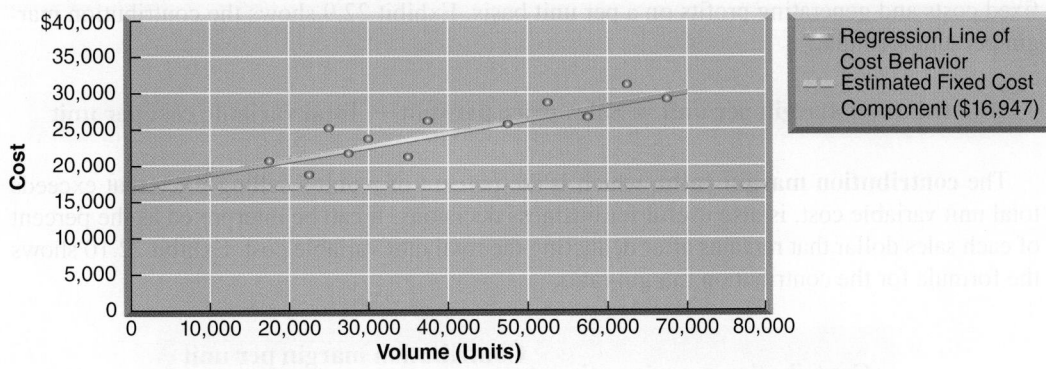

Comparison of Cost Estimation Methods

The three cost estimation methods result in slightly different estimates of fixed and variable costs as summarized in Exhibit 22.8. Estimates from the scatter diagram are based on a visual fit of the cost line and are subject to interpretation. Estimates from the high-low method use only two sets of values corresponding to the lowest and highest unit volumes. Estimates from least-squares regression use a statistical technique and all available data points.

Estimation Method	Fixed Cost	Variable Cost
Scatter diagram	$16,000	$0.20 per unit
High-low method	17,525	0.17 per unit
Least-squares regression	16,947	0.19 per unit

EXHIBIT 22.8

Comparison of Cost Estimation Methods

We must remember that all three methods use *past data.* Thus, cost estimates resulting from these methods are only as good as the data used for estimation. Managers must establish that the data are reliable in deriving cost estimates for the future.

Quick Check

Answers — p. 900

4. Which of the following methods is likely to yield the most precise estimated line of cost behavior? (*a*) High-low, (*b*) least-squares regression, or (*c*) scatter diagram.

5. What is the primary weakness of the high-low method?

6. Using conventional CVP analysis, a mixed cost should be (*a*) disregarded, (*b*) treated as a fixed cost, or (*c*) separated into fixed and variable components.

USING BREAK-EVEN ANALYSIS

Break-even analysis is a special case of cost-volume-profit analysis. This section describes break-even analysis by computing the break-even point and preparing a CVP (or break-even) chart.

Contribution Margin and Its Measures

A1 Compute the contribution margin and describe what it reveals about a company's cost structure.

We explained how managers classify costs by behavior. This often refers to classifying costs as being fixed or variable with respect to volume of activity. In manufacturing companies, volume of activity usually refers to the number of units produced. We then classify a cost as either fixed or variable, depending on whether total cost changes as the number of units produced changes. Once we separate costs by behavior, we can then compute a product's contribution margin. **Contribution margin per unit,** or *unit contribution margin,* is the amount by which a product's unit selling price exceeds its total unit variable cost. This excess amount contributes to covering fixed costs and generating profits on a per unit basis. Exhibit 22.9 shows the contribution margin per unit formula.

EXHIBIT 22.9

Contribution Margin per Unit

> **Contribution margin per unit = Sales price per unit − Total variable cost per unit**

The **contribution margin ratio,** which is the percent of a unit's selling price that exceeds total unit variable cost, is also useful for business decisions. It can be interpreted as the percent of each sales dollar that remains after deducting the total unit variable cost. Exhibit 22.10 shows the formula for the contribution margin ratio.

EXHIBIT 22.10

Contribution Margin Ratio

> $$\text{Contribution margin ratio} = \frac{\text{Contribution margin per unit}}{\text{Sales price per unit}}$$

To illustrate the use of contribution margin, let's consider Ridwan, which sells soccer balls for $100 per unit and incurs variable costs of $70 per unit sold. Its fixed costs are $24,000 per month with monthly capacity of 1,800 units (soccer balls). Ridwan's contribution margin per unit is $30, which is computed as follows.

Selling price per unit	$100
Variable cost per unit	70
Contribution margin per unit	$ 30

Its contribution margin ratio is 30%, computed as $30/$100. This reveals that for each unit sold, Ridwan has $30 that contributes to covering fixed cost and profit. If we consider sales in dollars, a contribution margin of 30% implies that for each $1 in sales, Ridwan has $0.30 that contributes to fixed cost and profit.

◻ **Decision** Maker   Answer — p. 899

Sales Manager   You are evaluating orders from two customers but can accept only one of the orders because of your company's limited capacity. The first order is for 100 units of a product with a contribution margin ratio of 60% and a selling price of $1,000. The second order is for 500 units of a product with a contribution margin ratio of 20% and a selling price of $800. The incremental fixed costs are the same for both orders. Which order do you accept? ■

Computing the Break-Even Point

P2 Compute the break-even point for a single product company.

The **break-even point** is the sales level at which a company neither earns a profit nor incurs a loss. The concept of break-even is applicable to nearly all organizations, activities, and events. One of the most important items of information when launching a project is whether it will break even—that is, whether sales will at least cover total costs. The break-even point can be expressed in either units or dollars of sales.

To illustrate the computation of break-even analysis, let's again look at Ridwan, which sells soccer balls for $100 per unit and incurs $70 of variable costs per unit sold. Its fixed costs are $24,000 per month. Ridwan breaks even for the month when it sells 800 soccer balls (sales volume of $80,000). We compute this break-even point using the formula in Exhibit 22.11. This formula uses the contribution margin per unit, which for Ridwan is $30 ($100 − $70). From this we can compute the break-even sales volume as $24,000/$30, or 800 units per month.

$$\text{Break-even point in units} = \frac{\text{Fixed costs}}{\text{Contribution margin per unit}}$$

EXHIBIT 22.11

Formula for Computing Break-Even Sales (in Units)

At a price of $100 per unit, monthly sales of 800 units yield sales dollars of $80,000 (called *break-even sales dollars*). This $80,000 break-even sales can be computed directly using the formula in Exhibit 22.12.

$$\text{Break-even point in dollars} = \frac{\text{Fixed costs}}{\text{Contribution margin ratio}}$$

EXHIBIT 22.12

Formula for Computing Break-Even Sales (in Dollars)

Ridwan's break-even point in dollars is computed as $24,000/0.30, or $80,000 of monthly sales. To verify that Ridwan's break-even point equals $80,000 (or 800 units), we prepare a simplified income statement in Exhibit 22.13. It shows that the $80,000 revenue from sales of 800 units exactly equals the sum of variable and fixed costs.

Point: Even if a company operates at a level in excess of its break-even point, management may decide to stop operating because it is not earning a reasonable return on investment.

EXHIBIT 22.13

Contribution Margin Income Statement for Break-Even Sales

RIDWAN COMPANY	
Contribution Margin Income Statement (at Break-Even)	
For Month Ended January 31, 2011	
Sales (800 units at $100 each)	$80,000
Variable costs (800 units at $70 each)	56,000
Contribution margin	24,000
Fixed costs	24,000
Net profit	$ 0

The statement in Exhibit 22.13 is called a *contribution margin income statement*. It differs in format from a conventional income statement in two ways. First, it separately classifies costs and expenses as variable or fixed. Second, it reports contribution margin (Sales − Variable costs). The contribution margin income statement format is used in this chapter's assignment materials because of its usefulness in CVP analysis.

Point: A contribution margin income statement is also referred to as a *variable costing income statement*. This differs from the traditional *absorption costing* approach where all product costs are assigned to units sold and to units in ending inventory. Recall that variable costing expenses all fixed product costs. Thus, income for the two approaches differs depending on the level of finished goods inventory; the lower inventory is, the more similar the two approaches are.

Decision Insight

Trade Offs in Managing Break-Even Point A high break-even point indicates that a business has to sell larger volumes before it reaches break even and eventually makes a profit. Sometimes this is seen as being risky. In terms of decision making, the dilemma facing a manager could be: "Should we build a large capacity (and incur high fixed costs, thus raising the break-even point) or should we build a small capacity and keep the fixed costs and break-even point low?" For example, a hotel chain could build a 500-room hotel or a 200-room hotel. If it does the former, the fixed costs and break-even point would be higher than if it does the latter. In making this decision, a manager faces uncertainty about eventual demand. If he chooses to build a 200-room hotel and the demand turns out to be very high, he may have kept the break-even point low but he could well lose out to competitors who have the capacity to absorb the large demand. In summary, a high or low break-even point is not a good or bad thing in itself. Forecasting market demand is the key. ■

Preparing a Cost-Volume-Profit Chart

<table>
<tr><td>**P3**</td><td>Graph costs and sales for a single product company.</td></tr>
</table>

Exhibit 22.14 is a graph of Ridwan's cost-volume-profit relations. This graph is called a **cost-volume-profit (CVP) chart,** or a *break-even chart* or *break-even graph.* The horizontal axis is the number of units produced and sold and the vertical axis is dollars of sales and costs. The lines in the chart depict both sales and costs at different output levels.

EXHIBIT 22.14

Cost-Volume-Profit Chart

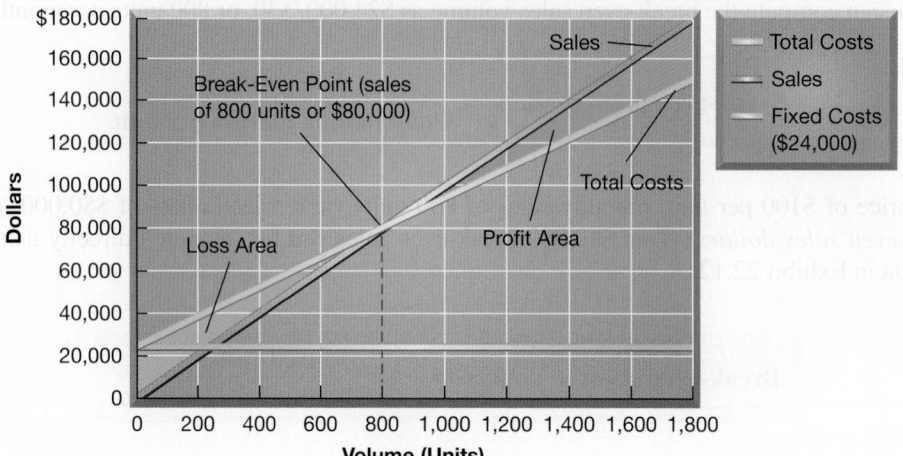

We follow three steps to prepare a CVP chart, which can also be drawn with computer programs that convert numeric data to graphs:

1. Plot fixed costs on the vertical axis ($24,000 for Ridwan). Draw a horizontal line at this level to show that fixed costs remain unchanged regardless of output volume (drawing this fixed cost line is not essential to the chart).

2. Draw the total (variable plus fixed) costs line for a relevant range of volume levels. This line starts at the fixed costs level on the vertical axis because total costs equal fixed costs at zero volume. The slope of the total cost line equals the variable cost per unit ($70). To draw the line, compute the total costs for any volume level, and connect this point with the vertical axis intercept ($24,000). Do not draw this line beyond the productive capacity for the planning period (1,800 units for Ridwan).

3. Draw the sales line. Start at the origin (zero units and zero dollars of sales) and make the slope of this line equal to the selling price per unit ($100). To sketch the line, compute dollar sales for any volume level and connect this point with the origin. Do not extend this line beyond the productive capacity. Total sales will be at the highest level at maximum capacity.

Example: In Exhibit 22.14, the sales line intersects the total cost line at 800 units. At what point would the two lines intersect if selling price is increased by 20% to $120 per unit? *Answer:* $24,000/($120 − $70) = 480 units

The total costs line and the sales line intersect at 800 units in Exhibit 22.14, which is the break-even point—the point where total dollar sales of $80,000 equals the sum of both fixed and variable costs ($80,000).

On either side of the break-even point, the vertical distance between the sales line and the total costs line at any specific volume reflects the profit or loss expected at that point. At volume levels to the left of the break-even point, this vertical distance is the amount of the expected loss because the total costs line is above the total sales line. At volume levels to the right of the break-even point, the vertical distance represents the expected profit because the total sales line is above the total costs line.

Decision Maker   Answer — p. 899

Operations Manager   As a start-up manufacturer, you wish to identify the behavior of manufacturing costs to develop a production cost budget. You know three methods can be used to identify cost behavior from past data, but past data are unavailable because this is a start-up. What do you do? ■

Making Assumptions in Cost-Volume-Profit Analysis

Cost-volume-profit analysis assumes that relations can normally be expressed as simple lines similar to those in Exhibits 22.4 and 22.14. Such assumptions allow users to answer several important questions, but the usefulness of the answers depends on the validity of three assumptions: (1) constant selling price per unit, (2) constant variable costs per unit, and (3) constant total fixed costs. These assumptions are not always realistic, but CVP analysis can be very useful for business decision making even when its assumptions are not strictly met. This section discusses these assumptions and other issues for CVP analysis.

Working with Assumptions   The behavior of individual costs and sales often is not perfectly consistent with CVP assumptions. If the expected costs and sales behavior differ from the assumptions, the results of CVP analysis can be limited. Still, we can perform useful analyses in spite of limitations with these assumptions for several reasons.

Summing costs can offset individual deviations.   Deviations from assumptions with individual costs are often minor when these costs are summed. That is, individual variable cost items may not be perfectly variable, but when we sum these variable costs, their individual deviations can offset each other. This means the assumption of variable cost behavior can be proper for total variable costs. Similarly, an assumption that total fixed costs are constant can be proper even when individual fixed cost items are not exactly constant.

CVP is applied to a relevant range of operations.   Sales, variable costs, and fixed costs often are reasonably reflected in straight lines on a graph when the assumptions are applied over a relevant range. The **relevant range of operations** is the normal operating range for a business. Except for unusually difficult or prosperous times, management typically plans for operations within a range of volume neither close to zero nor at maximum capacity. The relevant range excludes extremely high and low operating levels that are unlikely to occur. The validity of assuming that a specific cost is fixed or variable is more acceptable when operations are within the relevant range. As shown in Exhibit 22.2, a curvilinear cost can be treated as variable and linear if the relevant range covers volumes where it has a nearly constant slope. If the normal range of activity changes, some costs might need reclassification.

CVP analysis yields estimates.   CVP analysis yields approximate answers to questions about costs, volumes, and profits. These answers do not have to be precise because the analysis makes rough estimates about the future. As long as managers understand that CVP analysis gives estimates, it can be a useful tool for starting the planning process. Other qualitative factors also must be considered.

Working with Output Measures   CVP analysis usually describes the level of activity in terms of *sales volume,* which can be expressed in terms of either units sold or dollar sales. However, other measures of output exist. For instance, a manufacturer can use the number of units produced as a measure of output. Also, to simplify analysis, we sometimes assume that the production level is the same as the sales level. That is, inventory levels do not change. This often is justified by arguing that CVP analysis provides only approximations.

Example: If the selling price declines, what happens to the break-even point? *Answer:* It increases.

Quick Check

Answers — p. 900

7. Fixed cost divided by the contribution margin ratio yields the (*a*) break-even point in dollars, (*b*) contribution margin per unit, or (*c*) break-even point in units.

8. A company sells a product for $90 per unit with variable costs of $54 per unit. What is the contribution margin ratio?

9. Refer to Quick Check (8). If fixed costs for the period are $90,000, what is the break-even point in dollars?

10. What three basic assumptions are used in CVP analysis?

Working with Changes in Estimates   Because CVP analysis uses estimates, knowing how changes in those estimates impact break-even is useful. For example, a manager might form three estimates for each of the components of break-even: optimistic, most likely, and pessimistic. Then ranges of break-even points in units can be computed using the formula in Exhibit 22.11.

To illustrate, assume Ridwan's managers provide the set of estimates in Exhibit 22.15.

EXHIBIT 22.15

Alternative Estimates for Break-Even Analysis

	Selling Price per Unit	Variable Cost per Unit	Total Fixed Costs
Optimistic	$105	$68	$21,000
Most likely	100	70	24,000
Pessimistic	95	72	27,000

If, for example, Ridwan's managers believe they can raise the selling price of a soccer ball to $105, without any change in variable or fixed costs, then the revised contribution margin per soccer ball is $35, and the revised break-even in units follows in Exhibit 22.16.

EXHIBIT 22.16

Revised Break-Even in Units

$$\text{Revised break-even point in units} = \frac{\$24,000}{\$35} = 686 \text{ units}$$

EXHIBIT 22.17

Scatter Diagrams—Break-Even Points for Alternative Estimates

Repeating this calculation using each of the other eight separate estimates above, and graphing the results, yields the three scatter diagrams in Exhibit 22.17.

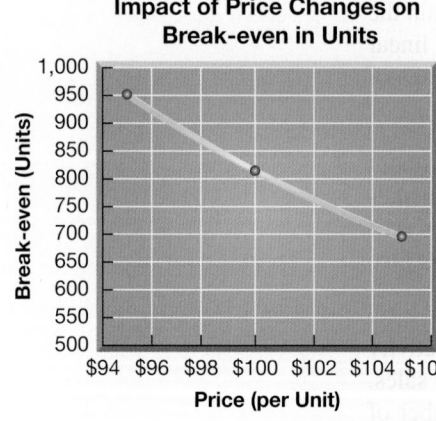

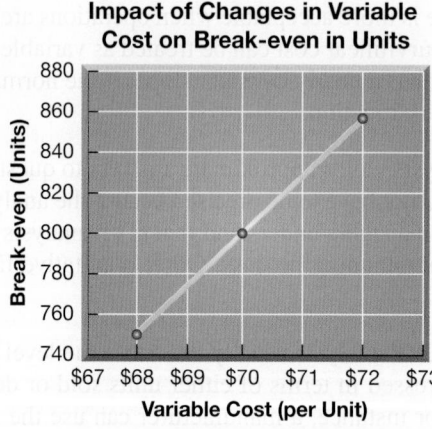

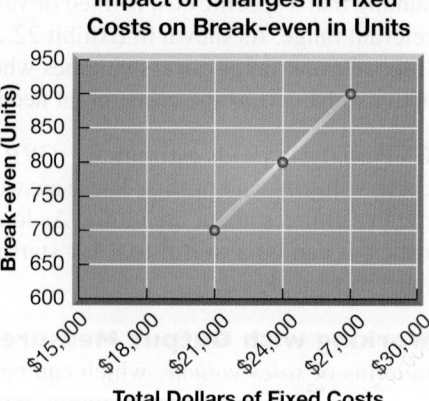

These scatter diagrams show how changes in selling prices, variable costs, and fixed costs impact break-even. When selling prices can be increased without impacting costs, break-even decreases. When competition drives selling prices down, and the company cannot reduce costs, break-even increases. Increases in either variable or fixed costs, if they cannot be passed on to customers via higher selling prices, will increase break-even. If costs can be reduced and selling prices held constant, the break-even decreases.

Point: This analysis changed only one estimate at a time; managers can examine how combinations of changes in estimates will impact break-even.

APPLYING COST-VOLUME-PROFIT ANALYSIS

Managers consider a variety of strategies in planning business operations. Cost-volume-profit analysis is useful in helping managers evaluate the likely effects of these strategies, which is the focus of this section.

Computing Income from Sales and Costs

An important question managers often need an answer to is "What is the predicted income from a predicted level of sales?" To answer this, we look at four variables in CVP analysis. These variables and their relations to income (pretax) are shown in Exhibit 22.18. We use these relations to compute expected income from predicted sales and cost levels.

 C2 Describe several applications of cost-volume-profit analysis.

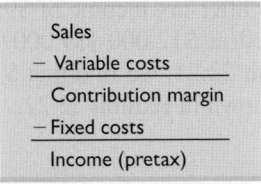

Sales
− Variable costs
Contribution margin
− Fixed costs
Income (pretax)

EXHIBIT 22.18

Income Relations in CVP Analysis

To illustrate, let's assume that Ridwan's management expects to sell 1,500 units in January 2011. What is the amount of income if this sales level is achieved? Following Exhibit 22.18, we compute Ridwan's expected income in Exhibit 22.19.

RIDWAN COMPANY	
Contribution Margin Income Statement	
For Month Ended January 31, 2011	
Sales (1,500 units at $100 each)	$150,000
Variable costs (1,500 units at $70 each)	105,000
Contribution margin	45,000
Fixed costs	24,000
Income (pretax)	$ 21,000

EXHIBIT 22.19

Computing Expected Pretax Income from Expected Sales

The $21,000 income is pretax. To find the amount of *after-tax* income from selling 1,500 units, management must apply the proper tax rate. Assume that the tax rate is 25%. Then we can prepare the after-tax income statement shown in Exhibit 22.20. We can also compute pretax income as after-tax income divided by (1 − tax rate); for Ridwan, this is $15,750/(1 − 0.25), or $21,000.

RIDWAN COMPANY	
Contribution Margin Income Statement	
For Month Ended January 31, 2011	
Sales (1,500 units at $100 each)	$150,000
Variable costs (1,500 units at $70 each)	105,000
Contribution margin	45,000
Fixed costs	24,000
Pretax income	21,000
Income taxes (25%)	5,250
Net profit (after tax)	$ 15,750

EXHIBIT 22.20

Computing Expected After-Tax Income from Expected Sales

Management then assesses whether this income is an adequate return on assets invested. Management should also consider whether sales and income can be increased by raising or lowering prices. CVP analysis is a good tool for addressing these kinds of "what-if" questions.

Computing Sales for a Target Income

Many companies' annual plans are based on certain income targets (sometimes called *budgets*). Ridwan's income target for this year is to increase income by 10% over the prior year. When prior year income is known, Ridwan easily computes its target income. CVP analysis helps to determine the sales level needed to achieve the target income. Computing this sales level is important because planning for the year is then based on this level. We use the formula shown in Exhibit 22.21 to compute sales for a target *after-tax* income.

"How many units must I sell to earn $50,000?"

EXHIBIT 22.21

Computing Sales (Dollars) for a Target After-Tax Income

$$\text{Dollar sales at target after-tax income} = \frac{\text{Fixed costs} + \text{Target pretax income}}{\text{Contribution margin ratio}}$$

To illustrate, Ridwan has monthly fixed costs of $24,000 and a 30% contribution margin ratio. Assume that it sets a target monthly after-tax income of $9,000 when the tax rate is 25%. This means the pretax income is targeted at $12,000 [$9,000/(1 − 0.25)] with a tax expense of $3,000. Using the formula in Exhibit 22.21, we find that $120,000 of sales are needed to produce a $9,000 after-tax income as shown in Exhibit 22.22.

EXHIBIT 22.22

Ridwan's Dollar Sales for a Target Income

$$\text{Dollar sales at target after-tax income} = \frac{\$24,000 + \$12,000}{30\%} = \$120,000$$

Point: Break-even is a special case of the formulas in Exhibits 22.21 and 22.23; simply set target pretax income to $0 and the formulas reduce to those in Exhibits 22.11 and 22.12.

We can alternatively compute *unit sales* instead of dollar sales. To do this, we substitute *contribution margin per unit* for the contribution margin ratio in the denominator. This gives the number of units to sell to reach the target after-tax income. Exhibit 22.23 illustrates this for Ridwan. The two computations in Exhibits 22.22 and 22.23 are equivalent because sales of 1,200 units at $100 per unit equal $120,000 of sales.

EXHIBIT 22.23

Computing Sales (Units) for a Target After-Tax Income

$$\text{Unit sales at target after-tax income} = \frac{\text{Fixed costs} + \text{Target pretax income}}{\text{Contribution margin per unit}}$$

$$= \frac{\$24,000 + \$12,000}{\$30} = 1,200 \text{ units}$$

Computing the Margin of Safety

All companies wish to sell more than the break-even number of units. The excess of expected sales over the break-even sales level is called a company's **margin of safety,** the amount that sales can drop before the company incurs a loss. It can be expressed in units, dollars, or even as a percent of the predicted level of sales. To illustrate, if Ridwan's expected sales are $100,000, the margin of safety is $20,000 above break-even sales of $80,000. As a percent, the margin of safety is 20% of expected sales as shown in Exhibit 22.24.

EXHIBIT 22.24

Computing Margin of Safety (in Percent)

$$\text{Margin of safety (in percent)} = \frac{\text{Expected sales} - \text{Break-even sales}}{\text{Expected sales}}$$

$$= \frac{\$100,000 - \$80,000}{\$100,000} = 20\%$$

Management must assess whether the margin of safety is adequate in light of factors such as sales variability, competition, consumer tastes, and economic conditions.

■ **Decision Ethics**   Answer — p. 899

Supervisor   Your team is conducting a cost-volume-profit analysis for a new product. Different sales projections have different incomes. One member suggests picking numbers yielding favorable income because any estimate is "as good as any other." Another member points to a scatter diagram of 20 months' production on a comparable product and suggests dropping unfavorable data points for cost estimation. What do you do? ■

Using Sensitivity Analysis

Earlier we showed how changing one of the estimates in a CVP analysis impacts break-even. We can also examine strategies that impact several estimates in the CVP analysis. For instance, we might want to know what happens to income if we automate a currently manual process. We can use CVP analysis to predict income if we can describe how these changes affect a company's fixed costs, variable costs, selling price, and volume.

To illustrate, assume that Ridwan Company is looking into buying a new machine that would increase monthly fixed costs from $24,000 to $30,000 but decrease variable costs from $70 per unit to $60 per unit. The machine is used to produce output whose selling price will remain unchanged at $100. This results in increases in both the unit contribution margin and the contribution margin ratio. The revised contribution margin per unit is $40 ($100 − $60), and the revised contribution margin ratio is 40% of selling price ($40/$100). Using CVP analysis, Ridwan's revised break-even point in dollars would be $75,000 as computed in Exhibit 22.25.

Example: If fixed costs decline, what happens to the break-even point? *Answer:* It decreases.

EXHIBIT 22.25

Revising Break-even When Changes Occur

$$\text{Revised break-even point in dollars} = \frac{\text{Revised fixed costs}}{\text{Revised contribution margin ratio}} = \frac{\$30,000}{40\%} = \$75,000$$

The revised fixed costs and the revised contribution margin ratio can be used to address other issues including computation of (1) expected income for a given sales level and (2) the sales level needed to earn a target income. Once again, we can use sensitivity analysis to generate different sets of revenue and cost estimates that are *optimistic, pessimistic,* and *most likely.* Different CVP analyses based on these estimates provide different scenarios that management can analyze and use in planning business strategy.

Decision Insight

Eco-CVP Auto makers are increasingly offering hybrid cars, including the **Ford** Fusion, **Toyota** Prius, and **Nissan** Altima Hybrid. Hybrids yield better gas mileage and generate fewer greenhouse gases, but they are priced higher. Are hybrid models economically feasible for buyers? A study by **Edmunds.com** shows it take several years for consumers to break even (save enough money on gas to offset the higher purchase price) on most hybrid models. When break-even point is computed in years, the expenses and revenues are adjusted for their time value. The resulting number is called a *discounted break even.* ∎

Quick Check

Answers — p. 900

11. A company has fixed costs of $50,000 and a 25% contribution margin ratio. What dollar sales are necessary to achieve an after-tax net profit of $120,000 if the tax rate is 20%? (*a*) $800,000, (*b*) $680,000, or (*c*) $600,000.

12. If a company's contribution margin ratio decreases from 50% to 25%, what can be said about the unit sales needed to achieve the same target income level?

13. What is a company's margin of safety?

Computing a Multiproduct Break-Even Point

To this point, we have looked only at cases where the company sells a single product or service. This was to keep the basic CVP analysis simple. However, many companies sell multiple products or services, and we can modify the CVP analysis for use in these cases. An important assumption in a multiproduct setting is that the sales mix of different products is known and remains constant during the planning period. **Sales mix** is the ratio (proportion) of the sales volumes for the various products. For instance, if a company normally sells 10,000 soccer balls, 5,000 softballs, and 4,000 basketballs per month, its sales mix can be expressed as 10:5:4 for soccer balls, softballs, and basketballs.

 P4 Compute the break-even point for a multiproduct company.

To apply multiproduct CVP analysis, we can estimate the break-even point by using a **composite unit,** which consists of a specific number of units of each product in proportion to their expected sales mix. Multiproduct CVP analysis treats this composite unit as a single product. To illustrate, let's look at Hair-Today, a styling salon that offers three cuts: basic, ultra, and budget in the ratio of 4 basic units to 2 ultra units to 1 budget unit (expressed as 4:2:1). Management wants to estimate its break-even point for next year. Unit selling prices for these three cuts are basic, $20; ultra, $32; and budget, $16. Using the 4:2:1 sales mix, the selling price of a composite unit of the three products is computed as follows.

4 units of basic @ $20 per unit	$ 80
2 units of ultra @ $32 per unit	64
1 unit of budget @ $16 per unit	16
Selling price of a composite unit	**$160**

Point: Selling prices and variable costs are usually expressed in per unit amounts. Fixed costs are usually expressed in total amounts.

Hair-Today's fixed costs are $192,000 per year, and its variable costs of the three products are basic, $13; ultra, $18.00; and budget, $8.00. Variable costs for a composite unit of these products follow.

4 units of basic @ $13 per unit	$52
2 units of ultra @ $18 per unit	36
1 unit of budget @ $8 per unit	8
Variable costs of a composite unit	**$96**

Hair-Today's $64 contribution margin for a composite unit is computed by subtracting the variable costs of a composite unit ($96) from its selling price ($160). We then use the contribution margin to determine Hair-Today's break-even point in composite units in Exhibit 22.26.

EXHIBIT 22.26

Break-Even Point in Composite Units

$$\text{Break-even point in composite units} = \frac{\text{Fixed costs}}{\text{Contribution margin per composite unit}}$$

$$= \frac{\$192,000}{\$64} = 3,000 \text{ composite units}$$

Point: The break-even point in dollars for Exhibit 22.26 is $192,000/($64/$160) = $480,000.

This computation implies that Hair-Today breaks even when it sells 3,000 composite units. To determine how many units of each product it must sell to break even, we multiply the number of units of each product in the composite by 3,000 as follows.

Basic:	4 × 3,000	. . . .	12,000 units
Ultra:	2 × 3,000	. . . .	6,000 units
Budget:	1 × 3,000	. . . .	3,000 units

Instead of computing contribution margin per composite unit, a company can compute a **weighted-average contribution margin.** Given the 4:2:1 product mix, basic cuts comprise 57.14% (computed as 4/7) of the company's haircuts, ultra makes up 28.57% of its business, and budget cuts comprise 14.29%. The weighted-average contribution margin follows in Exhibit 22.27.

EXHIBIT 22.27

Weighted-Average Contribution Margin

	Unit contribution margin	×	Percentage of sales mix	=	Weighted unit contribution margin
Basic.	$ 7		57.14%		$4.000
Ultra	14		28.57		4.000
Budget	8		14.29		1.143
Weighted-average contribution margin					**$9.143**

The company's break-even point in units is computed in Exhibit 22.28 as follows:

EXHIBIT 22.28

Break-Even in Units using
Weighted-Average
Contribution Margin

$$\text{Break-even point in units} = \frac{\text{Fixed costs}}{\text{Weighted-average contribution margin}}$$

$$= \frac{\$192,000}{\$9.143} = 21,000 \text{ units}$$

We see that the weighted-average contribution margin method yields 21,000 whole units as the break-even amount, the same total as the composite unit approach.

Exhibit 22.29 verifies the results for composite units by showing Hair-Today's sales and costs at this break-even point using a contribution margin income statement.

EXHIBIT 22.29

Multiproduct Break-Even
Income Statement

HAIR-TODAY
Forecasted Contribution Margin Income Statement (at Break-even)

	Basic	Ultra	Budget	Totals
Sales				
Basic (12,000 @ $20)	$240,000			
Ultra (6,000 @ $32)		$192,000		
Budget (3,000 @ $16)			$48,000	
Total sales				$480,000
Variable costs				
Basic (12,000 @ $13)	156,000			
Ultra (6,000 @ $18)		108,000		
Budget (3,000 @ $8)			24,000	
Total variable costs				288,000
Contribution margin	$ 84,000	$ 84,000	$24,000	192,000
Fixed costs				192,000
Net profit				$ 0

A CVP analysis using composite units can be used to answer a variety of planning questions. Once a product mix is set, all answers are based on the assumption that the mix remains constant at all relevant sales levels as other factors in the analysis do. We also can vary the sales mix to see what happens under alternative strategies.

Decision Maker Answer — p. 900

Entrepreneur A CVP analysis indicates that your start-up, which markets electronic products, will break even with the current sales mix and price levels. You have a target income in mind. What analysis might you perform to assess the likelihood of achieving this income? ■

Quick Check Answers — p. 900

14. The sales mix of a company's two products, X and Y, is 2:1. Unit variable costs for both products are $2, and unit sales prices are $5 for X and $4 for Y. What is the contribution margin per composite unit? (a) $5, (b) $10, or (c) $8.

15. What additional assumption about sales mix must be made in doing a conventional CVP analysis for a company that produces and sells more than one product?

> **A2** Analyze changes in sales using the degree of operating leverage.

CVP analysis is especially useful when management begins the planning process and wishes to predict outcomes of alternative strategies. These strategies can involve changes in selling prices, fixed costs, variable costs, sales volume, and product mix. Managers are interested in seeing the effects of changes in some or all of these factors.

One goal of all managers is to get maximum benefits from their fixed costs. Managers would like to use 100% of their output capacity so that fixed costs are spread over the largest number of units. This would decrease fixed cost per unit and increase income. The extent, or relative size, of fixed costs in the total cost structure is known as **operating leverage.** Companies having a higher proportion of fixed costs in their total cost structure are said to have higher operating leverage. An example of this is a company that chooses to automate its processes instead of using direct labor, increasing its fixed costs and lowering its variable costs. A useful managerial measure to help assess the effect of changes in the level of sales on income is the **degree of operating leverage (DOL)** defined in Exhibit 22.30.

EXHIBIT 22.30

Degree of Operating Leverage

$$\text{DOL} = \text{Total contribution margin (in dollars)/Pretax income}$$

To illustrate, let's return to Ridwan Company. At a sales level of 1,200 units, Ridwan's total contribution margin is $36,000 (1,200 units × $30 contribution margin per unit). Its pretax income, after subtracting fixed costs of $24,000, is $12,000 ($36,000 − $24,000). Ridwan's degree of operating leverage at this sales level is 3.0, computed as contribution margin divided by pretax income ($36,000/$12,000). We then use DOL to measure the effect of changes in the level of sales on pretax income. For instance, suppose Ridwan expects sales to increase by 10%. If this increase is within the relevant range of operations, we can expect this 10% increase in sales to result in a 30% increase in pretax income computed as DOL multiplied by the increase in sales (3.0 × 10%). Similar analyses can be done for expected decreases in sales.

DEMONSTRATION PROBLEM

Sport Caps Co. manufactures and sells caps for different sporting events. The fixed costs of operating the company are $150,000 per month, and the variable costs for caps are $5 per unit. The caps are sold for $8 per unit. The fixed costs provide a production capacity of up to 100,000 caps per month.

Required

1. Use the formulas in the chapter to compute the following:
    a. Contribution margin per cap.
    b. Break-even point in terms of the number of caps produced and sold.
    c. Amount of net profit at 30,000 caps sold per month (ignore taxes).
    d. Amount of net profit at 85,000 caps sold per month (ignore taxes).
    e. Number of caps to be produced and sold to provide $45,000 of after-tax income, assuming an income tax rate of 25%.
2. Draw a CVP chart for the company, showing cap output on the horizontal axis. Identify (a) the break-even point and (b) the amount of pretax income when the level of cap production is 70,000. (Omit the fixed cost line.)
3. Use the formulas in the chapter to compute the
    a. Contribution margin ratio.
    b. Break-even point in terms of sales dollars.

c. Amount of net profit at $250,000 of sales per month (ignore taxes).

d. Amount of net profit at $600,000 of sales per month (ignore taxes).

e. Dollars of sales needed to provide $45,000 of after-tax income, assuming an income tax rate of 25%.

PLANNING THE SOLUTION

● Identify the formulas in the chapter for the required items expressed in units and solve them using the data given in the problem.

● Draw a CVP chart that reflects the facts in the problem. The horizontal axis should plot the volume in units up to 100,000, and the vertical axis should plot the total dollars up to $800,000. Plot the total cost line as upward sloping, starting at the fixed cost level ($150,000) on the vertical axis and increasing until it reaches $650,000 at the maximum volume of 100,000 units. Verify that the break-even point (where the two lines cross) equals the amount you computed in part 1.

● Identify the formulas in the chapter for the required items expressed in dollars and solve them using the data given in the problem.

SOLUTION TO DEMONSTRATION PROBLEM

1. a. Contribution margin per cap = Selling price per unit − Variable cost per unit
= $8 − $5 = $\underline{\underline{\$3}}$

b. Break-even point in caps = $\dfrac{\text{Fixed costs}}{\text{Contribution margin per cap}} = \dfrac{\$150,000}{\$3} = \underline{\underline{50,000 \text{ caps}}}$

c. Net profit at 30,000 caps sold = (Units × Contribution margin per unit) − Fixed costs
= (30,000 × $3) − $150,000 = $\underline{\underline{\$(60,000) \text{ loss}}}$

d. Net profit at 85,000 caps sold = (Units × Contribution margin per unit) − Fixed costs
= (85,000 × $3) − $150,000 = $\underline{\underline{\$105,000 \text{ profit}}}$

e. Pretax income = $45,000/(1 − 0.25) = $60,000
Income taxes = $60,000 × 25% = $15,000

Units needed for $45,000 income = $\dfrac{\text{Fixed costs} + \text{Target pretax income}}{\text{Contribution margin per cap}}$
= $\dfrac{\$150,000 + \$60,000}{\$3} = \underline{\underline{70,000 \text{ caps}}}$

2. CVP chart.

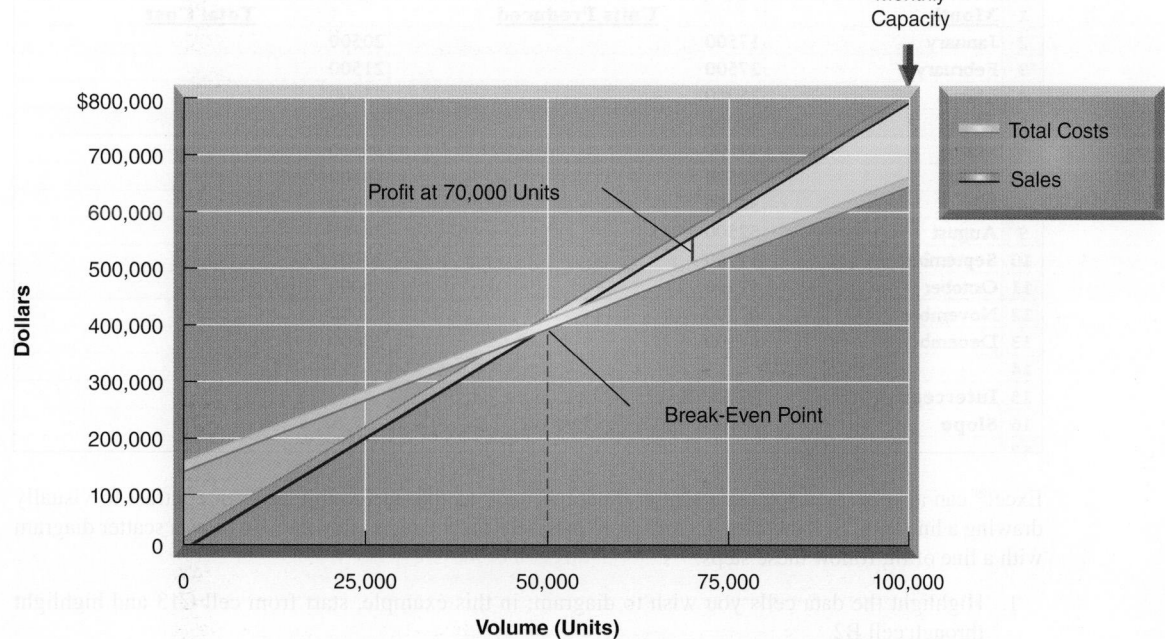

3. a. Contribution margin ratio

$$= \frac{\text{Contribution margin per unit}}{\text{Selling price per unit}} = \frac{\$3}{\$8} = 0.375, \text{ or } 37.5\%$$

b. Break-even point in dollars

$$= \frac{\text{Fixed costs}}{\text{Contribution margin ratio}} = \frac{\$150,000}{37.5\%} = \$400,000$$

c. Net profit at sales of $250,000

$$= (\text{Sales} \times \text{Contribution margin ratio}) - \text{Fixed costs}$$
$$= (\$250,000 \times 37.5\%) - \$150,000 = \$(56,250) \text{ loss}$$

d. Net profit at sales of $600,000

$$= (\text{Sales} \times \text{Contribution margin ratio}) - \text{Fixed costs}$$
$$= (\$600,000 \times 37.5\%) - \$150,000 = \$75,000 \text{ income}$$

e. Dollars of sales to yield
  $45,000 after-tax income

$$= \frac{\text{Fixed costs} + \text{Target pretax income}}{\text{Contribution margin ratio}}$$
$$= \frac{\$150,000 + \$60,000}{37.5\%} = \$560,000$$

APPENDIX

22A   Using Excel to Estimate Least-Squares Regression

Microsoft Excel® 2007 and other spreadsheet software can be used to perform least-squares regressions to identify cost behavior. In Excel®, the INTERCEPT and SLOPE functions are used. The following screen shot reports the data from Exhibit 22.3 in cells Al through C13 and shows the cell contents to find the intercept (cell B16) and slope (cell B17). Cell B16 uses Excel® to find the intercept from a least-squares regression of total cost (shown as C2:C13 in cell B16) on units produced (shown as B2:B13 in cell B16). Spreadsheet software is useful in understanding cost behavior when many data points (such as monthly total costs and units produced) are available.

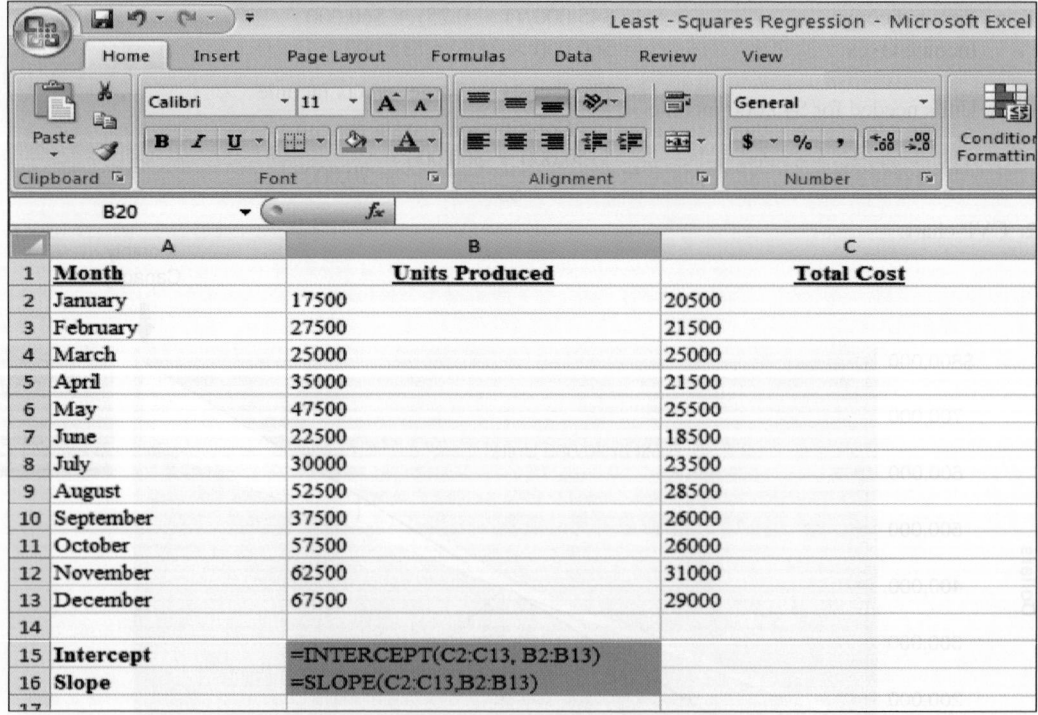

Excel® can also be used to create scatter diagrams such as that in Exhibit 22.4. In contrast to visually drawing a line that "fits" the data, Excel® more precisely fits the regression line. To draw a scatter diagram with a line of fit, follow these steps:

1. Highlight the data cells you wish to diagram; in this example, start from cell C13 and highlight through cell B2.

2. Then select "Insert" and "Scatter" from the drop-down menus. Selecting the chart type in the upper left corner of the choices under Scatter will produce a diagram that looks like that in Exhibit 22.4, without a line of fit.

3. To add a line of fit (also called trend line), select "Layout" and "Trendline" from the drop-down menus. Selecting "Linear Trendline" will produce a diagram that looks like that in Exhibit 22.4, including the line of fit.

Summary

C1 **Describe different types of cost behavior in relation to production and sales volume.** Cost behavior is described in terms of how its amount changes in relation to changes in volume of activity within a relevant range. Fixed costs remain constant to changes in volume. Total variable costs change in direct proportion to volume changes. Mixed costs display the effects of both fixed and variable components. Step-wise costs remain constant over a small volume range, then change by a lump sum and remain constant over another volume range, and so on. Curvilinear costs change in a nonlinear relation to volume changes.

C2 **Describe several applications of cost-volume-profit analysis.** Cost-volume-profit analysis can be used to predict what can happen under alternative strategies concerning sales volume, selling prices, variable costs, or fixed costs. Applications include "what-if" analysis, computing sales for a target income, and break-even analysis.

A1 **Compute the contribution margin and describe what it reveals about a company's cost structure.** Contribution margin per unit is a product's sales price less its total variable costs. Contribution margin ratio is a product's contribution margin per unit divided by its sales price. Unit contribution margin is the amount received from each sale that contributes to fixed costs and income. The contribution margin ratio reveals what portion of each sales dollar is available as contribution to fixed costs and income.

A2 **Analyze changes in sales using the degree of operating leverage.** The extent, or relative size, of fixed costs in a company's total cost structure is known as *operating leverage*. One tool useful in assessing the effect of changes in sales on income is the degree of operating leverage, or DOL. DOL is the ratio of the contribution margin divided by pretax income. This ratio can be used to determine the expected percent change in income given a percent change in sales.

P1 **Determine cost estimates using the scatter diagram, high-low, and regression methods of estimating costs.** Three different methods used to estimate costs are the scatter diagram, the high-low method, and least-squares regression. All three methods use past data to estimate costs. Cost estimates from a scatter diagram are based on a visual fit of the cost line. Estimates from the high-low method are based only on costs corresponding to the lowest and highest sales. The least-squares regression method is a statistical technique and uses all data points.

P2 **Compute the break-even point for a single product company.** A company's break-even point for a period is the sales volume at which total revenues equal total costs. To compute a break-even point in terms of sales units, we divide total fixed costs by the contribution margin per unit. To compute a break-even point in terms of sales dollars, divide total fixed costs by the contribution margin ratio.

P3 **Graph costs and sales for a single product company.** The costs and sales for a company can be graphically illustrated using a CVP chart. In this chart, the horizontal axis represents the number of units sold and the vertical axis represents dollars of sales or costs. Straight lines are used to depict both costs and sales on the CVP chart.

P4 **Compute the break-even point for a multiproduct company.** CVP analysis can be applied to a multiproduct company by expressing sales volume in terms of composite units. A composite unit consists of a specific number of units of each product in proportion to their expected sales mix. Multiproduct CVP analysis treats this composite unit as a single product.

Guidance Answers to Decision Maker and Decision Ethics

Sales Manager The contribution margin per unit for the first order is $600 (60% of $1,000); the contribution margin per unit for the second order is $160 (20% of $800). You are likely tempted to accept the first order based on its high contribution margin per unit, but you must compute the total contribution margin based on the number of units sold for each order. Total contribution margin is $60,000 ($600 per unit × 100 units) and $80,000 ($160 per unit × 500 units) for the two orders, respectively. The second order provides the largest return in absolute dollars and is the order you would accept. Another factor to consider in your selection is the potential for a long-term relationship with these customers including repeat sales and growth.

Operations Manager Without the availability of past data, none of the three methods described in the chapter can be used to measure cost behavior. Instead, the manager must investigate whether data from similar manufacturers can be accessed. This is likely difficult due to the sensitive nature of such data. In the absence of data, the manager should develop a list of the different production inputs and identify input-output relations. This provides guidance to the manager in measuring cost behavior. After several months, actual cost data will be available for analysis.

Supervisor Your dilemma is whether to go along with the suggestions to "manage" the numbers to make the project look like it will achieve sufficient profits. You should not succumb to these suggestions. Many people will likely be affected negatively if you manage the predicted numbers and the project eventually is unprofitable. Moreover, if it does fail, an investigation would likely reveal that data in the proposal were "fixed" to make it look good. Probably the only benefit from managing the numbers is the short-term payoff of pleasing those who proposed the product. One way to deal with this dilemma is to prepare several analyses showing results under different assumptions and then let senior management make the decision.

Entrepreneur   You must first compute the level of sales required to achieve the desired net profit. Then you must conduct sensitivity

analysis by varying the price, sales mix, and cost estimates. Results from the sensitivity analysis provide information you can use to assess the possibility of reaching the target sales level. For instance, you might have to pursue aggressive marketing strategies to push the high-margin products, or you might have to cut prices to increase sales and profits, or another strategy might emerge.

Guidance Answers to Quick Checks

1. *b*

2. A fixed cost remains unchanged in total amount regardless of output levels. However, fixed *cost per unit* declines with increased output.

3. Such a cost is considered variable because the *total* cost changes in proportion to volume changes.

4. *b*

5. The high-low method ignores all costs and sales (activity base) volume data points except the costs corresponding to the highest and lowest (most extreme) sales (activity base) volume.

6. *c*

7. *a*

8. ($90 − $54)/$90 = 40%

9. $90,000/40% = $225,000

10. Three basic CVP assumptions are that (1) selling price per unit is constant, (2) variable costs per unit are constant, and (3) total fixed costs are constant.

11. *a*; Two steps are required for explanation:
(1) Pretax income = $120,000/(1 − 0.20) = $150,000
(2) $\dfrac{\$50,000 + \$150,000}{25\%} = \$800,000$

12. If the contribution margin ratio decreases from 50% to 25%, unit sales would have to double.

13. A company's margin of safety is the excess of the predicted sales level over its break-even sales level.

14. *c*; Selling price of a composite unit:

2 units of X @ $5 per unit	$10
1 unit of Y @ $4 per unit	4
Selling price of a composite unit	$14

Variable costs of a composite unit:

2 units of X @ $2 per unit	$4
1 unit of Y @ $2 per unit	2
Variable costs of a composite unit	$6

Therefore, the contribution margin per composite unit is $8.

15. It must be assumed that the sales mix remains unchanged at all sales levels in the relevant range.

Key Terms   www.mheducation.asia/olc/wildkwokFAP

Absorption costing (p. 887)

Break-even point (p. 886)

Composite unit (p. 894)

Contribution margin per unit (p. 886)

Contribution margin ratio (p. 886)

Cost-volume-profit (CVP) analysis (p. 880)

Cost-volume-profit (CVP) chart (p. 888)

Curvilinear cost (p. 882)

Degree of operating leverage (DOL) (p. 896)

Estimated line of cost behavior (p. 883)

High-low method (p. 884)

Least-squares regression (p. 885)

Margin of safety (p. 892)

Mixed cost (p. 881)

Operating leverage (p. 896)

Relevant range of operations (p. 889)

Sales mix (p. 893)

Scatter diagram (p. 883)

Step-wise cost (p. 882)

Total cost (p. 881)

Variable costing income statement (p. 887)

Weighted-average contribution margin (p. 894)

Multiple Choice Quiz   Answers on p. 915   www.mheducation.asia/olc/wildkwokFAP

Additional Quiz Questions are available at the book's Website.

1. A company's only product sells for $150 per unit. Its variable costs per unit are $100, and its fixed costs total $75,000. What is its contribution margin per unit?
   a. $50
   b. $250
   c. $100
   d. $150
   e. $25

2. Using information from question 1, what is the company's contribution margin ratio?
   a. 66⅔%
   b. 100%
   c. 50%
   d. 0%
   e. 33⅓%

3. Using information from question 1, what is the company's break-even point in units?
- **a.** 500 units
- **b.** 750 units
- **c.** 1,500 units
- **d.** 3,000 units
- **e.** 1,000 units

4. A company's forecasted sales are $300,000 and its sales at break-even are $180,000. Its margin of safety in dollars is
- **a.** $180,000.
- **b.** $120,000.
- **c.** $480,000.

- **d.** $60,000.
- **e.** $300,000.

5. A product sells for $400 per unit and its variable costs per unit are $260. The company's fixed costs are $840,000. If the company desires $70,000 pretax income, what is the required dollar sales?
- **a.** $2,400,000
- **b.** $200,000
- **c.** $2,600,000
- **d.** $2,275,000
- **e.** $1,400,000

A   *Superscript letter A denotes assignments based on Appendix 22A*

Icon denotes assignments that involve decision making.

Discussion Questions

1. How is cost-volume-profit analysis useful?

2. What is a variable cost? Identify two variable costs.

3. When output volume increases, do variable costs per unit increase, decrease, or stay the same within the relevant range of activity? Explain.

4. When output volume increases, do fixed costs per unit increase, decrease, or stay the same within the relevant range of activity? Explain.

5. How do step-wise costs and curvilinear costs differ?

6. Define and describe *contribution margin* per unit.

7. Define and explain the *contribution margin ratio*.

8. Describe the contribution margin ratio in layperson's terms.

9. In performing CVP analysis for a manufacturing company, what simplifying assumption is usually made about the volume of production and the volume of sales?

10. What two arguments tend to justify classifying all costs as either fixed or variable even though individual costs might not behave exactly as classified?

11. How does assuming that operating activity occurs within a relevant range affect cost-volume-profit analysis?

12. List three methods to measure cost behavior.

13. How is a scatter diagram used to identify and measure the behavior of a company's costs?

14. In cost-volume-profit analysis, what is the estimated profit at the break-even point?

15. Assume that a straight line on a CVP chart intersects the vertical axis at the level of fixed costs and has a positive slope that rises with each additional unit of volume by the amount of the variable costs per unit. What does this line represent?

16. Palm has both fixed and variable costs. Why are fixed costs depicted as a horizontal line on a CVP chart?

17. Each of two similar companies has sales of $20,000 and total costs of $15,000 for a month. Company A's total costs include $10,000 of variable costs and $5,000 of fixed costs. If Company B's total costs include $4,000 of variable costs and $11,000 of fixed costs, which company will enjoy more profit if sales double?

18. _____ of _____ reflects expected sales in excess of the level of break-even sales.

19. Apple produces iPods for sale. Identify some of the variable and fixed product costs associated with that production. [*Hint:* Limit costs to product costs.]

20. Should Research In Motion use single product or multiproduct break-even analysis? Explain.

21. Nokia is thinking of expanding sales of its most popular cell-phone model by 65%. Do you expect its variable and fixed costs for this model to stay within the relevant range? Explain.

---

connect _____

Determine whether each of the following is best described as a fixed, variable, or mixed cost with respect to product units.

1. Maintenance of factory machinery.
2. Depreciation expense of warehouse.
3. Taxes on factory building.
4. Factory supervisor's salary.

5. Wages of an assembly-line worker paid on the basis of acceptable units produced.
6. Packaging expense.
7. Rubber used to manufacture athletic shoes.

QUICK STUDY

QS 22-1
Cost behavior identification

C1

QS 22-2

Cost behavior identification

C1

Listed here are four series of separate costs measured at various volume levels. Examine each series and identify whether it is best described as a fixed, variable, step-wise, or curvilinear cost. (It can help to graph the cost series.)

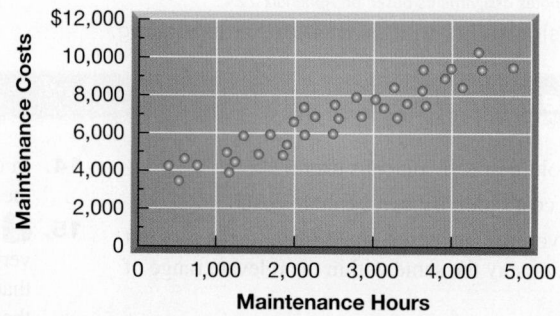

Volume (Units)	Series 1	Series 2	Series 3	Series 4
0	$ 0	$900	$ 400	$200
100	400	900	400	210
200	800	900	400	240
300	1,200	900	800	290
400	1,600	900	800	380
500	2,000	900	1,200	500
600	2,400	900	1,200	640

QS 22-3

Cost behavior estimation—
scatter diagram

P1

This scatter diagram reflects past maintenance hours and their corresponding maintenance costs.

1. Draw an estimated line of cost behavior.
2. Estimate the fixed and variable components of maintenance costs.

QS 22-4

Cost behavior estimation—
high-low method

P1

The following information is available for a company's maintenance cost over the last seven months. Using the high-low method, estimate both the fixed and variable components of its maintenance cost.

Month	Maintenance Hours	Maintenance Cost
June.	20	$6,020
July	48	8,100
August	24	5,100
September	38	7,000
October	42	6,900
November	36	6,900
December	12	3,600

QS 22-5

Contribution margin ratio

A1

Compute and interpret the contribution margin ratio using the following data: sales, $150,000; total variable cost, $90,000.

QS 22-6

Contribution margin per unit and break-even units

P2

MCU Phone Company sells its cordless phone for $300 per unit. Fixed costs total $540,000, and variable costs are $120 per unit. Determine the (1) contribution margin per unit and (2) break-even point in units.

QS 22-7

Assumptions in CVP analysis

C2

Refer to the information from QS 22-6. How will the break-even point in units change in response to each of the following independent changes in selling price per unit, variable cost per unit, or total fixed costs? Use I for increase and D for decrease. (It is not necessary to compute new break-even points.)

Change	Break-even in Units Will
1. Total fixed cost to $520,000	_____
2. Variable cost to $134 per unit......	_____
3. Selling price per unit to $290	_____
4. Variable cost to $100 per unit.......	_____
5. Total fixed cost to $544,000	_____
6. Selling price per unit to $320	_____

Refer to QS 22-6. Determine the (1) contribution margin ratio and (2) break-even point in dollars.

QS 22-8
Contribution margin ratio and break-even dollars P2

Refer to QS 22-6. Assume that MCU Phone Co. is subject to a 30% income tax rate. Compute the units of product that must be sold to earn after-tax income of $504,000.

QS 22-9
CVP analysis and target income
P2

Which one of the following is an assumption that underlies cost-volume-profit analysis?
1. All costs have approximately the same relevant range.
2. The selling price per unit must change in proportion to the number of units sold.
3. For costs classified as variable, the costs per unit of output must change constantly.
4. For costs classified as fixed, the costs per unit of output must remain constant.

QS 22-10
CVP assumptions
C2

A high proportion of Company X's total costs are variable with respect to units sold; a high proportion of Company Y's total costs are fixed with respect to units sold. Which company is likely to have a higher degree of operating leverage (DOL)? Explain.

QS 22-11
Operating leverage analysis A2

M-Mobile Company manufactures and sells two products, black phones and white phones, in the ratio of 5:3. Fixed costs are $85,000, and the contribution margin per composite unit is $170. What number of both black and white phones is sold at the break-even point?

QS 22-12
Multiproduct break-even P4

Corme Company expects sales of $34 million (400,000 units). The company's total fixed costs are $17.5 million and its variable costs are $35 per unit. Prepare a CVP chart from this information.

QS 22-13
CVP graph P3

A recent income statement for **Volkswagen** reports the following (in EUR millions). Assume 70% of the cost of sales and 70% of the selling and administrative costs are variable costs, and the remaining 30% of each is fixed. Compute the contribution margin (in EUR millions). (Round computations using percentages to the nearest whole Euro.)

QS 22-14
Contribution margin A1

Sales	105,187
Cost of sales	91,608
Selling and administrative expenses	13,276

≡ connect

A company reports the following information about its sales and its cost of sales. Each unit of its product sells for $500. Use these data to prepare a scatter diagram. Draw an estimated line of cost behavior and determine whether the cost appears to be variable, fixed, or mixed.

EXERCISES

Exercise 22-1
Measurement of cost behavior using a scatter diagram
P1

Period	Sales	Cost of Sales	Period	Sales	Cost of Sales
1	$15,000	$10,100	4	7,500	5,500
2	11,500	7,500	5	9,000	6,000
3	10,500	7,000	6	12,500	9,500

Exercise 22-2
Cost behavior in graphs

C1

Following are five graphs representing various cost behaviors. (1) Identify whether the cost behavior in each graph is mixed, step-wise, fixed, variable, or curvilinear. (2) Identify the graph (by number) that best illustrates each cost behavior: (a) Factory policy requires one supervisor for every 30 factory workers; (b) real estate taxes on factory; (c) electricity charge that includes the standard monthly charge plus a charge for each kilowatt hour; (d) commissions to salespersons; and (e) costs of hourly paid workers that provide substantial gains in efficiency when a few workers are added but gradually smaller gains in efficiency when more workers are added.

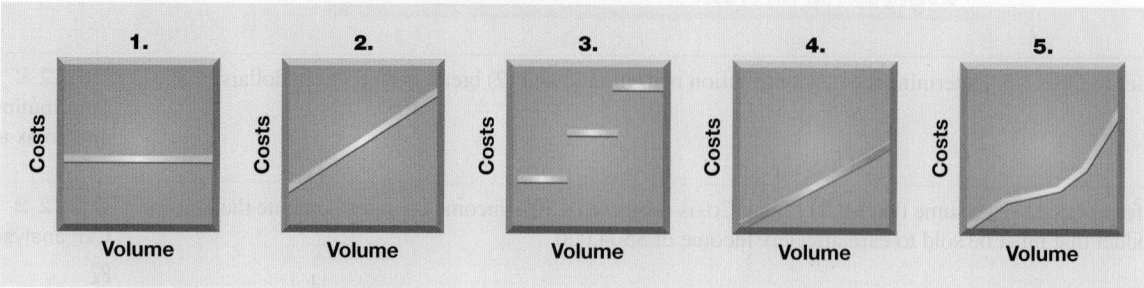

Exercise 22-3
Cost behavior defined

C1

The left column lists several cost classifications. The right column presents short definitions of those costs. In the blank space beside each of the numbers in the right column, write the letter of the cost best described by the definition.

A. Curvilinear cost

B. Step-wise cost

C. Fixed cost

D. Mixed cost

E. Variable cost

F. Total cost

_____ **1.** This cost increases in direct proportion to increases in volume; its amount is constant for each unit produced.

_____ **2.** This cost remains constant over a limited range of volume; when it reaches the end of its limited range, it changes by a lump sum and remains at that level until it exceeds another limited range.

_____ **3.** This cost has a component that remains the same over all volume levels and another component that increases in direct proportion to increases in volume.

_____ **4.** This cost increases when volume increases, but the increase is not constant for each unit produced.

_____ **5.** This cost remains constant over all volume levels within the productive capacity for the planning period.

_____ **6.** This cost is the combined amount of all the other costs.

Exercise 22-4
Cost behavior identification

C1

Following are five series of costs *A* through *E* measured at various volume levels. Examine each series and identify which is fixed, variable, mixed, step-wise, or curvilinear.

Volume (Units)	Series A	Series B	Series C	Series D	Series E
0	$ 0	$2,500	$ 0	$2,000	$4,000
200	3,600	3,100	6,000	2,000	4,000
400	7,200	3,700	6,600	4,000	4,000
600	10,800	4,300	7,200	4,000	4,000
800	14,400	4,900	8,200	6,000	4,000
1,000	18,000	5,500	9,600	6,000	4,000
1,200	21,600	6,100	13,500	8,000	4,000

Exercise 22-5
Predicting sales and variable costs using contribution margin

C2

Orlando Company management predicts that it will incur fixed costs of $250,000 and earn pretax income of $350,000 in the next period. Its expected contribution margin ratio is 60%. Use this information to compute the amounts of (1) total dollar sales and (2) total variable costs.

Use the following information about sales and costs to prepare a scatter diagram. Draw a cost line that reflects the behavior displayed by this cost. Determine whether the cost is variable, step-wise, fixed, mixed, or curvilinear.

Exercise 22-6
Scatter diagram and measurement of cost behavior

P1

Period	Sales	Costs	Period	Sales	Costs
1.............	$760	$590	9.............	$580	$390
2.............	800	560	10.............	320	240
3.............	200	230	11.............	240	230
4.............	400	400	12.............	720	550
5.............	480	390	13.............	280	260
6.............	620	550	14.............	440	410
7.............	680	590	15.............	380	260
8.............	540	430			

Felix & Co. reports the following information about its sales and cost of sales. Draw an estimated line of cost behavior using a scatter diagram, and compute fixed costs and variable costs per unit sold. Then use the high-low method to estimate the fixed and variable components of the cost of sales.

Exercise 22-7
Cost behavior estimation—scatter diagram and high-low

P1

Period	Units Sold	Cost of Sales	Period	Units Sold	Cost of Sales
1.............	0	$2,500	6.............	2,000	5,500
2.............	400	3,100	7.............	2,400	6,100
3.............	800	3,700	8.............	2,800	6,700
4.............	1,200	4,300	9.............	3,200	7,300
5.............	1,600	4,900	10.............	3,600	7,900

Refer to the information from Exercise 22-7. Use spreadsheet software to use ordinary least-squares regression to estimate the cost equation, including fixed and variable cost amounts.

Exercise 22-8[A]
Measurement of cost behavior using regression P1

A pants maker is designing a new line of pants called the Redbird. The pants will sell for $325 per pair and cost $260 per pair in variable costs to make. (1) Compute the contribution margin per pair. (2) Compute the contribution margin ratio. (3) Describe what the contribution margin ratio reveals about this new pants line.

Exercise 22-9
Contribution margin

A2

Apollo Company manufactures a single product that sells for $168 per unit and whose total variable costs are $126 per unit. The company's annual fixed costs are $630,000. (1) Use this information to compute the company's (a) contribution margin, (b) contribution margin ratio, (c) break-even point in units, and (d) break-even point in dollars of sales.

Exercise 22-10
Contribution margin, break-even, and CVP chart P2

Refer to the information in Exercise 22-10. Prepare a CVP chart for the company.

Exercise 22-11
CVP chart P3

Refer to Exercise 22-10. (1) Prepare a contribution margin income statement for Apollo Company showing sales, variable costs, and fixed costs at the break-even point. (2) If the company's fixed costs increase by $135,000, what amount of sales (in dollars) is needed to break even? Explain.

Exercise 22-12
Income reporting and break-even analysis C2

Apollo Company management (in Exercise 22-10) targets an annual after-tax income of $840,000. The company is subject to a 20% income tax rate. Assume that fixed costs remain at $630,000. Compute the (1) unit sales to earn the target after-tax net profit and (2) dollar sales to earn the target after-tax net profit.

Exercise 22-13
Computing sales to achieve target income C2

Exercise 22-14
Forecasted income statement
C2

Check Forecasted income, $1,416,000

Apollo Company's sales manager (in Exercise 22-10) predicts that annual sales of the company's product will soon reach 40,000 units and its price will increase to $200 per unit. According to the production manager, the variable costs are expected to increase to $140 per unit but fixed costs will remain at $630,000. The income tax rate is 20%. What amounts of pretax and after-tax income can the company expect to earn from these predicted changes? (*Hint:* Prepare a forecasted contribution margin income statement as in Exhibit 22.20.)

Exercise 22-15
Predicting unit and dollar sales
C2

Greenspan Company management predicts $500,000 of variable costs, $800,000 of fixed costs, and a pretax income of $100,000 in the next period. Management also predicts that the contribution margin per unit will be $60. Use this information to compute the (1) total expected dollar sales for next period and (2) number of units expected to be sold next period.

Exercise 22-16
Computation of variable and fixed costs
C2

Cinquante Company expects to sell 100,000 units of its product next year, which would generate total sales of $12 million. Management predicts that pretax net profit for next year will be $3,000,000 and that the contribution margin per unit will be $40. Use this information to compute next year's total expected (a) variable costs and (b) fixed costs.

Exercise 22-17
CVP analysis using composite units P4

Check (3) 1,000 composite units

Home Builders sells windows and doors in the ratio of 8:2 (windows:doors). The selling price of each window is $100 and of each door is $250. The variable cost of a window is $62.50 and of a door is $175. Fixed costs are $450,000. Use this information to determine the (1) selling price per composite unit, (2) variable costs per composite unit, (3) break-even point in composite units, and (4) number of units of each product that will be sold at the break-even point.

Exercise 22-18
CVP analysis using weighted-average contribution margin
P4

Refer to the information from Exercise 22-17. Use the information to determine the (1) weighted-average contribution margin, (2) break-even point in units, and (3) number of units of each product that will be sold at the break-even point.

Exercise 22-19
CVP analysis using composite units
P4

Hubert Tax Service offers tax and consulting services to individuals and small businesses. Data for fees and costs of three types of tax returns follow. Hubert provides services in the ratio of 4:4:2 (easy, moderate, business). Fixed costs total $20,000 for the tax season. Use this information to determine the (1) selling price per composite unit, (2) variable costs per composite unit, (3) break-even point in composite units, and (4) number of units of each product that will be sold at the break-even point. Round answer to part (3) to two decimals.

Type of Return	Fee Charged	Variable Cost per Return
Easy (form 1040EZ)	$ 50	$ 30
Moderate (form 1040)	125	75
Business	275	100

Exercise 22-20
CVP analysis using weighted-average contribution margin
P4

Refer to the information from Exercise 22-19. Use the information to determine the (1) weighted-average contribution margin, (2) break-even point in units, and (3) number of units of each product that will be sold at the break-even point. Round answer to part (2) to one decimal.

Exercise 22-21
Operating leverage computed and applied
A2

Company A is a manufacturer with current sales of $3,000,000 and a 60% contribution margin. Its fixed costs equal $1,300,000. Company B is a consulting firm with current service revenues of $3,000,000 and a 25% contribution margin. Its fixed costs equal $250,000. Compute the degree of operating leverage (DOL) for each company. Identify which company benefits more from a 20% increase in sales and explain why.

The following costs result from the production and sale of 4,000 drum sets manufactured by Vince Drum Company for the year ended December 31, 2011. The drum sets sell for $250 each. The company has a 25% income tax rate.

Variable production costs	
Plastic for casing	$ 68,000
Wages of assembly workers	328,000
Drum stands	104,000
Variable selling costs	
Sales commissions	60,000
Fixed manufacturing costs	
Taxes on factory	10,000
Factory maintenance	20,000
Factory machinery depreciation	80,000
Fixed selling and administrative costs	
Lease of equipment for sales staff.	20,000
Accounting staff salaries	70,000
Administrative management salaries	150,000

PROBLEM SET A

Problem 22-1A
Contribution margin income statement and contribution margin ratio

A1

Check (1) Net profit, $67,500

Required

1. Prepare a contribution margin income statement for the company.
2. Compute its contribution margin per unit and its contribution margin ratio.

Analysis Component

3. Interpret the contribution margin and contribution margin ratio from part 2.

Edge Equipment Co. manufactures and markets a number of rope products. Management is considering the future of Product XT, a special rope for hang gliding, that has not been as profitable as planned. Since Product XT is manufactured and marketed independently of the other products, its total costs can be precisely measured. Next year's plans call for a $150 selling price per 100 yards of XT rope. Its fixed costs for the year are expected to be $200,000, up to a maximum capacity of 550,000 yards of rope. Forecasted variable costs are $100 per 100 yards of XT rope.

Required

1. Estimate Product XT's break-even point in terms of (a) sales units and (b) sales dollars.
2. Prepare a CVP chart for Product XT like that in Exhibit 22.14. Use 5,500 units (550,000 yards/100 yards) as the maximum number of sales units on the horizontal axis of the graph, and $900,000 as the maximum dollar amount on the vertical axis.
3. Prepare a contribution margin income statement showing sales, variable costs, and fixed costs for Product XT at the break-even point.

Problem 22-2A
CVP analysis and charting

P2 P3

Check (1) Break-even sales, 4,000 units

Alden Co.'s monthly sales and cost data for its operating activities of the past year follow. Management wants to use these data to predict future fixed and variable costs.

Problem 22-3A
Scatter diagram and cost behavior estimation

P1

Month	Sales	Total Cost	Month	Sales	Total Cost
1	$325,000	$162,500	7	$355,000	$242,000
2	170,000	106,250	8	275,000	156,750
3	270,000	210,600	9	75,000	60,000
4	210,000	105,000	10	155,000	135,625
5	295,000	206,500	11	99,000	99,000
6	195,000	117,000	12	105,000	76,650

Required

1. Prepare a scatter diagram for these data with sales volume (in $) plotted on the horizontal axis and total cost plotted on the vertical axis.

2. Estimate both the variable costs per sales dollar and the total monthly fixed costs using the high-low method. Draw the total costs line on the scatter diagram in part 1.

3. Use the estimated line of cost behavior and results from part 2 to predict future total costs when sales volume is (a) $380,000 and (b) $420,000.

Problem 22-4A

Break-even analysis; income targeting and forecasting

C2 P2 A1

Jetson Co. sold 20,000 units of its only product and incurred a $50,000 loss (ignoring taxes) for the current year as shown here. During a planning session for year 2012's activities, the production manager notes that variable costs can be reduced 50% by installing a machine that automates several operations. To obtain these savings, the company must increase its annual fixed costs by $150,000. The maximum output capacity of the company is 40,000 units per year.

JETSON COMPANY	
Contribution Margin Income Statement	
For Year Ended December 31, 2011	
Sales	$750,000
Variable costs	600,000
Contribution margin	150,000
Fixed costs	200,000
Net loss	$ (50,000)

Required

1. Compute the break-even point in dollar sales for year 2011.

2. Compute the predicted break-even point in dollar sales for year 2012 assuming the machine is installed and there is no change in the unit sales price.

3. Prepare a forecasted contribution margin income statement for 2012 that shows the expected results with the machine installed. Assume that the unit sales price and the number of units sold will not change, and no income taxes will be due.

4. Compute the sales level required in both dollars and units to earn $140,000 of after-tax income in 2012 with the machine installed and no change in the unit sales price. Assume that the income tax rate is 30%. (*Hint:* Use the procedures in Exhibits 22.21 and 22.23.)

5. Prepare a forecasted contribution margin income statement that shows the results at the sales level computed in part 4. Assume an income tax rate of 30%.

Problem 22-5A

Break-even analysis, different cost structures, and income calculations

C2 A1 P4

Letter Co. produces and sells two products, T and O. It manufactures these products in separate factories and markets them through different channels. They have no shared costs. This year, the company sold 50,000 units of each product. Sales and costs for each product follow.

	Product T	Product O
Sales	$800,000	$800,000
Variable costs.................	560,000	100,000
Contribution margin	240,000	700,000
Fixed costs	100,000	560,000
Profit before tax	140,000	140,000
Income taxes (32% rate)	44,800	44,800
Net profit.....................	$ 95,200	$ 95,200

Required

1. Compute the break-even point in dollar sales for each product.

2. Assume that the company expects sales of each product to decline to 33,000 units next year with no change in unit sales price. Prepare forecasted financial results for next year following the format of the contribution margin income statement as just shown with columns for each of the two products (assume a 32% tax rate). Also, assume that any loss before taxes yields a 32% tax savings.

3. Assume that the company expects sales of each product to increase to 64,000 units next year with no change in unit sales price. Prepare forecasted financial results for next year following the format of the contribution margin income statement shown with columns for each of the two products (assume a 32% tax rate).

Check (2) After-tax income:
T, $39,712; O, $(66,640)

(3) After-tax income:
T, $140,896; O, $228,480

Analysis Component

4. If sales greatly decrease, which product would experience a greater loss? Explain.

5. Describe some factors that might have created the different cost structures for these two products.

This year Cairo Company sold 35,000 units of its only product for $16 per unit. Manufacturing and selling the product required $120,000 of fixed manufacturing costs and $180,000 of fixed selling and administrative costs. Its per unit variable costs follow.

Problem 22-6A

Analysis of price, cost, and volume changes for contribution margin and net profit

P2   A1

Material	$4.00
Direct labor (paid on the basis of completed units)..........	3.00
Variable overhead costs	0.40
Variable selling and administrative costs..................	0.20

Next year the company will use new material, which will reduce material costs by 60% and direct labor costs by 40% and will not affect product quality or marketability. Management is considering an increase in the unit sales price to reduce the number of units sold because the factory's output is nearing its annual output capacity of 40,000 units. Two plans are being considered. Under plan 1, the company will keep the price at the current level and sell the same volume as last year. This plan will increase income because of the reduced costs from using the new material. Under plan 2, the company will increase price by 25%. This plan will decrease unit sales volume by 10%. Under both plans 1 and 2, the total fixed costs and the variable costs per unit for overhead and for selling and administrative costs will remain the same.

Required

1. Compute the break-even point in dollar sales for both (a) plan 1 and (b) plan 2.

2. Prepare a forecasted contribution margin income statement with two columns showing the expected results of plan 1 and plan 2. The statements should report sales, total variable costs, contribution margin, total fixed costs, profit before tax, income taxes (30% rate), and net profit.

Check (1) Break-even: Plan 1, $400,000; Plan 2, $375,000

(2) Net profit: Plan 1, $84,000; Plan 2, $142,800

National Co. manufactures and sells three products: red, white, and blue. Their unit sales prices are red, $55; white, $85; and blue, $110. The per unit variable costs to manufacture and sell these products are red, $40; white, $60; and blue, $80. Their sales mix is reflected in a ratio of 5:4:2 (red:white:blue). Annual fixed costs shared by all three products are $150,000. One type of raw material has been used to manufacture all three products. The company has developed a new material of equal quality for less cost. The new material would reduce variable costs per unit as follows: red, by $10; white, by $20; and blue, by $10. However, the new material requires new equipment, which will increase annual fixed costs by $20,000. (Round answers to whole composite units.)

Problem 22-7A

Break-even analysis with composite units

P4

Required

1. If the company continues to use the old material, determine its break-even point in both sales units and sales dollars of each individual product.

2. If the company uses the new material, determine its new break-even point in both sales units and sales dollars of each individual product.

Check (1) Old plan break-even, 639 composite units (rounded)

(2) New plan break-even, 442 composite units (rounded)

Analysis Component

3. What insight does this analysis offer management for long-term planning?

PROBLEM SET B

Problem 22-1B
Contribution margin income statement and contribution margin ratio

A1

The following costs result from the production and sale of 480,000 CD sets manufactured by Trace Company for the year ended December 31, 2011. The CD sets sell for $4.50 each. The company has a 25% income tax rate.

Variable manufacturing costs	
Plastic for CD sets	$ 43,200
Wages of assembly workers	600,000
Labeling	86,400
Variable selling costs	
Sales commissions	48,000
Fixed manufacturing costs	
Rent on factory	100,000
Factory cleaning service	75,000
Factory machinery depreciation	125,000
Fixed selling and administrative costs	
Lease of office equipment	120,000
Systems staff salaries	600,000
Administrative management salaries	300,000

Required

Check (1) Net profit, $46,800

1. Prepare a contribution margin income statement for the company.

2. Compute its contribution margin per unit and its contribution margin ratio.

Analysis Component

3. Interpret the contribution margin and contribution margin ratio from part 2.

Problem 22-2B
CVP analysis and charting

P2 P3

Jammin Co. manufactures and markets several products. Management is considering the future of one product, electronic keyboards, that has not been as profitable as planned. Since this product is manufactured and marketed independently of the other products, its total costs can be precisely measured. Next year's plans call for a $225 selling price per unit. The fixed costs for the year are expected to be $30,000, up to a maximum capacity of 700 units. Forecasted variable costs are $150 per unit.

Required

Check (1) Break-even sales, 400 units

1. Estimate the keyboards' break-even point in terms of (a) sales units and (b) sales dollars.

2. Prepare a CVP chart for keyboards like that in Exhibit 22.14. Use 700 keyboards as the maximum number of sales units on the horizontal axis of the graph, and $180,000 as the maximum dollar amount on the vertical axis.

3. Prepare a contribution margin income statement showing sales, variable costs, and fixed costs for keyboards at the break-even point.

Problem 22-3B
Scatter diagram and cost behavior estimation

P1

Koto Co.'s monthly sales and costs data for its operating activities of the past year follow. Management wants to use these data to predict future fixed and variable costs.

Month	Sales	Total Cost	Month	Sales	Total Cost
1	$390	$194	7	$290	$186
2	250	174	8	370	210
3	210	146	9	270	170
4	310	178	10	170	116
5	190	162	11	350	190
6	430	220	12	230	158

Required

1. Prepare a scatter diagram for these data with sales volume (in $) plotted on the horizontal axis and total costs plotted on the vertical axis.

2. Estimate both the variable costs per sales dollar and the total monthly fixed costs using the high-low method. Draw the total costs line on the scatter diagram in part 1.

3. Use the estimated line of cost behavior and results from part 2 to predict future total costs when sales volume is (a) $150 and (b) $250.

Check   (2) Variable costs, $0.40 per sales dollar; fixed costs, $48

Caruso Co. sold 40,000 units of its only product and incurred a $100,000 loss (ignoring taxes) for the current year as shown here. During a planning session for year 2012's activities, the production manager notes that variable costs can be reduced 50% by installing a machine that automates several operations. To obtain these savings, the company must increase its annual fixed costs by $300,000. The maximum output capacity of the company is 80,000 units per year.

Problem 22-4B
Break-even analysis; income targeting and forecasting
C2   P2   A1

CARUSO COMPANY Contribution Margin Income Statement For Year Ended December 31, 2011	
Sales	$1,500,000
Variable costs.	1,200,000
Contribution margin	300,000
Fixed costs	400,000
Net loss	$ (100,000)

Required

1. Compute the break-even point in dollar sales for year 2011.

2. Compute the predicted break-even point in dollar sales for year 2012 assuming the machine is installed and no change occurs in the unit sales price. (Round the change in variable costs to a whole number.)

3. Prepare a forecasted contribution margin income statement for 2012 that shows the expected results with the machine installed. Assume that the unit sales price and the number of units sold will not change, and no income taxes will be due.

4. Compute the sales level required in both dollars and units to earn $280,000 of after-tax income in 2012 with the machine installed and no change in the unit sales price. Assume that the income tax rate is 30%. (*Hint:* Use the procedures in Exhibits 22.21 and 22.23.)

5. Prepare a forecasted contribution margin income statement that shows the results at the sales level computed in part 4. Assume an income tax rate of 30%.

Check   (3) Net profit, $200,000

(4) Required sales, $1,833,333 or 48,889 units

Dominico Co. produces and sells two products, BB and TT. It manufactures these products in separate factories and markets them through different channels. They have no shared costs. This year, the company sold 120,000 units of each product. Sales and costs for each product follow.

Problem 22-5B
Break-even analysis, different cost structures, and income calculations
C2   P4   A1

	Product BB	Product TT
Sales	$3,000,000	$3,000,000
Variable costs.	1,800,000	600,000
Contribution margin	1,200,000	2,400,000
Fixed costs	600,000	1,800,000
Profit before tax	600,000	600,000
Income taxes (35% rate)	210,000	210,000
Net profit.	$ 390,000	$ 390,000

Required

1. Compute the break-even point in dollar sales for each product.

2. Assume that the company expects sales of each product to decline to 104,000 units next year with no change in the unit sales price. Prepare forecasted financial results for next year following the format of the contribution margin income statement as shown here with columns for each of the two products (assume a 35% tax rate, and that any loss before taxes yields a 35% tax savings).

3. Assume that the company expects sales of each product to increase to 190,000 units next year with no change in the unit sales prices. Prepare forecasted financial results for next year following the format of the contribution margin income statement as shown here with columns for each of the two products (assume a 35% tax rate).

Check   (2) After-tax income: BB, $286,000; TT, $182,000

(3) After-tax income: BB, $845,000; TT, $1,300,000

Analysis Component

4. If sales greatly increase, which product would experience a greater increase in profit? Explain.

5. Describe some factors that might have created the different cost structures for these two products.

Problem 22-6B

Analysis of price, cost, and volume changes for contribution margin and net profit

A1   P2

This year Jostens Company earned a disappointing 4.2% after-tax return on sales (Net profit/Sales) from marketing 100,000 units of its only product. The company buys its product in bulk and repackages it for resale at the price of $25 per unit. Jostens incurred the following costs this year.

Total variable unit costs.	$1,000,000
Total variable packaging costs	$ 100,000
Fixed costs	$1,250,000
Income tax rate	30%

The marketing manager claims that next year's results will be the same as this year's unless some changes are made. The manager predicts the company can increase the number of units sold by 80% if it reduces the selling price by 20% and upgrades the packaging. This change would increase variable packaging costs by 25%. Increased sales would allow the company to take advantage of a 20% quantity purchase discount on the cost of the bulk product. Neither the packaging change nor the volume discount would affect fixed costs, which provide an annual output capacity of 200,000 units.

Required

Check   (1) Break-even sales for new strategy, $2,325,581

1. Compute the break-even point in dollar sales under the (a) existing business strategy and (b) new strategy that alters both unit sales price and variable costs.

(2) Net profit: Existing strategy, $105,000; new strategy, $479,500

2. Prepare a forecasted contribution margin income statement with two columns showing the expected results of (a) the existing strategy and (b) changing to the new strategy. The statements should report sales, total variable costs (unit and packaging), contribution margin, fixed costs, profit before tax, income taxes, and net profit. Also determine the after-tax return on sales for these two strategies.

Problem 22-7B

Break-even analysis with composite units

P4

Texon Co. manufactures and sells three products: product 1, product 2, and product 3. Their unit sales prices are product 1, $40; product 2, $30; and product 3, $14. The per unit variable costs to manufacture and sell these products are product 1, $30; product 2, $20; and product 3, $8. Their sales mix is reflected in a ratio of 6:3:5. Annual fixed costs shared by all three products are $200,000. One type of raw material has been used to manufacture products 1 and 2. The company has developed a new material of equal quality for less cost. The new material would reduce variable costs per unit as follows: product 1 by $10, and product 2, by $5. However, the new material requires new equipment, which will increase annual fixed costs by $50,000.

Required

Check   (1) Old plan break-even, 1,667 composite units (rounded)

1. If the company continues to use the old material, determine its break-even point in both sales units and sales dollars of each individual product.

(2) New plan break-even, 1,282 composite units (rounded)

2. If the company uses the new material, determine its new break-even point in both sales units and sales dollars of each individual product.

Analysis Component

3. What insight does this analysis offer management for long-term planning?

SERIAL PROBLEM

Business Solutions

P4

(This serial problem began in Chapter 1 and continues through most of the book. If previous chapter segments were not completed, the serial problem can begin at this point.)

SP 22   Business Solutions sells upscale modular desk units and office chairs in the ratio of 3:2 (desk unit:chair). The selling prices are $1,250 per desk unit and $500 per chair. The variable costs are $750 per desk unit and $250 per chair. Fixed costs are $120,000.

Required

1. Compute the selling price per composite unit.
2. Compute the variable costs per composite unit.
3. Compute the break-even point in composite units.
4. Compute the number of units of each product that would be sold at the break-even point.

Check   (3) 60 composite units

Beyond the Numbers

BTN 22-1   **Research In Motion** offers services to Blackberry customers that allows them subscription access for wireless connectivity via a mobile carrier. As you complete the following requirements, assume that the Blackberry services department uses many of Research In Motion's existing resources such as its software, phone systems, account databases and buildings.

REPORTING IN ACTION

C1

Required

1. Identify several of the variable, mixed, and fixed costs that the Blackberry services department is likely to incur in carrying out its services.
2. Assume that Blackberry services revenues are expected to grow by 25% in the next year. How do you expect the costs identified in part 1 to change, if at all?
3. Based on your answer to part 2, can Research In Motion use the contribution margin ratio to predict how income will change in response to increases in Blackberry services revenues?

BTN 22-2   Both **Research In Motion** and **Apple** sell numerous hand-held consumer products, and each of these companies has a different product mix.

COMPARATIVE ANALYSIS

P2   A2

Required

1. Assume the following data are available for both companies. Compute each company's break-even point in unit sales. (Each company sells many hand-held consumer products at many different selling prices, and each has its own variable costs. This assignment assumes an *average* selling price per unit and an *average* cost per item.)

	Research In Motion	Apple
Average selling price per item sold	$350	$280
Average variable cost per item sold	$140	$110
Total fixed costs.	$14,980 million	$12,580 million

2. If unit sales were to decline, which company would experience the larger decline in operating profit? Explain.

BTN 22-3   Labor costs of an auto repair mechanic are seldom based on actual hours worked. Instead, the amount paid a mechanic is based on an industry average of time estimated to complete a repair job. The repair shop bills the customer for the industry average amount of time at the repair center's billable cost per hour. This means a customer can pay, for example, $120 for two hours of work on a car when the actual time worked was only one hour. Many experienced mechanics can complete repair jobs faster than the industry average. The average data are compiled by engineering studies and surveys conducted in the auto repair business. Assume that you are asked to complete such a survey for a repair center. The survey calls for objective input, and many questions require detailed cost data and analysis. The mechanics and owners know you have the survey and encourage you to complete it in a way that increases the average billable hours for repair work.

ETHICS CHALLENGE

C1

Required

Write a one-page memorandum to the mechanics and owners that describes the direct labor analysis you will undertake in completing this survey.

COMMUNICATING IN PRACTICE

C2

BTN 22-4   Several important assumptions underlie CVP analysis. Assumptions often help simplify and focus our analysis of sales and costs. A common application of CVP analysis is as a tool to forecast sales, costs, and income.

Required

Assume that you are actively searching for a job. Prepare a one-half page report identifying (1) three assumptions relating to your expected revenue (salary) and (2) three assumptions relating to your expected costs for the first year of your new job. Be prepared to discuss your assumptions in class.

TAKING IT TO THE NET

C1

BTN 22-5   Access and review the entrepreneurial information at **Business Owner's Toolkit** [Toolkit. cch.com]. Access and review its *New Business Cash Needs Estimate* under the Business Tools/Business Finance menu bar or similar worksheets related to controls of cash and costs.

Required

Write a one-half page report that describes the information and resources available at the Business Owner's Toolkit to help the owner of a start-up business to control and monitor its costs.

TEAMWORK IN ACTION

C2

BTN 22-6   A local movie theater owner explains to you that ticket sales on weekends and evenings are strong, but attendance during the weekdays, Monday through Thursday, is poor. The owner proposes to offer a contract to the local grade school to show educational materials at the theater for a set charge per student during school hours. The owner asks your help to prepare a CVP analysis listing the cost and sales projections for the proposal. The owner must propose to the school's administration a charge per child. At a minimum, the charge per child needs to be sufficient for the theater to break even.

Required

Your team is to prepare two separate lists of questions that enable you to complete a reliable CVP analysis of this situation. One list is to be answered by the school's administration, the other by the owner of the movie theater.

ENTREPRENEURIAL DECISION

C1 A1

BTN 22-7   Visit Choo Yilin's company Website (www.chooyilin.com). Refer to her different collections.

Required

1. Can you identify whether and why the contribution margins would be different across different collections?
2. What would be the items of the company's fixed costs?
3. What would be the fixed costs, if any, of each collection?
4. How can Choo Yilin make use of BEP in launching a new collection?

HITTING THE ROAD

P4

BTN 22-8   Multiproduct break-even analysis is often viewed differently when actually applied in practice. You are to visit a local fast-food restaurant and count the number of items on the menu. To apply multiproduct break-even analysis to the restaurant, similar menu items must often be fit into groups. A reasonable approach is to classify menu items into approximately five groups. We then estimate average selling price and average variable cost to compute average contribution margin. (*Hint:* For fast-food restaurants, the highest contribution margin is with its beverages, at about 90%.)

Required

1. Prepare a one-year multiproduct break-even analysis for the restaurant you visit. Begin by establishing groups. Next, estimate each group's volume and contribution margin. These estimates are necessary to compute each group's contribution margin. Assume that annual fixed costs in total are $500,000 per year. (*Hint:* You must develop your own estimates on volume and contribution margin for each group to obtain the break-even point and sales.)

2. Prepare a one-page report on the results of your analysis. Comment on the volume of sales necessary to break even at a fast-food restaurant.

BTN 22-9   Refer to Puma's product development philosophy and strategy at the following link: http://ir2.flife.de/data/puma/igb_html/index.php?bericht_id=1000004&index=&lang=ENG.

GLOBAL DECISION

P4

Required

1. If you are a financial analyst at Puma, what data would you need to perform a BEP analysis supporting a decision to launch a new range of shoes?

2. What are the likely challenges in obtaining this data?

ANSWERS TO MULTIPLE CHOICE QUIZ

1. a; $150 − $100 = $50
2. e; ($150 − $100)/$150 = 33⅓%
3. c; $75,000/$50 CM per unit = 1,500 units

4. b; $300,000 − $180,000 = $120,000
5. c; Contribution margin ratio = ($400 − $260)/$400 = 0.35
   Targeted sales = ($840,000 + $70,000)/0.35 = $2,600,000

23

Master Budgets and Planning

A Look Back

Chapter 22 looked at cost behavior and its use by managers in performing cost-volume-profit analysis. It also illustrated the application of cost-volume-profit analysis.

A Look at This Chapter

This chapter explains the importance of budgeting and describes the master budget and its preparation. It also discusses the value of the master budget to the planning of future business activities.

A Look Ahead

Chapter 24 focuses on flexible budgets, standard costs, and variance reporting. It explains the usefulness of these procedures and reports for business decisions.

Learning Objectives

CAP

CONCEPTUAL

C1 Describe the importance and benefits of budgeting and the process of budget administration. (p. 918)

C2 Describe a master budget and the process of preparing it. (p. 922)

ANALYTICAL

A1 Analyze expense planning using activity-based budgeting. (p. 932)

PROCEDURAL

P1 Prepare each component of a master budget and link each to the budgeting process. (p. 924)

P2 Link both operating and capital expenditures budgets to budgeted financial statements. (p. 928)

P3 *Appendix 23A*—Prepare production and manufacturing budgets. (p. 938)

"Cost data is crucial in everyday decision making in the supply chain team." — **ESTHER YEUNG**

 **Decision Insight**

Managing Cabela's Social Compliance Audits

Cabela's is a leading specialty retailer and the world's largest direct marketer of hunting, fishing, camping, and related outdoor merchandise (**www.cabelas.com**). Founded in 1961, Cabela's is one of the most well known outdoor recreation brands in the world, and it is recognized as the world's foremost outfitter.

The Hong Kong office, established in 2005, includes a supply chain team that is responsible for social compliance audits. These audits are conducted to make sure that Cabela's vendors, factories, and suppliers are in compliance with requirements in social responsibility and the Customs-Trade Partnership Against Terrorism (C-TPAT), a voluntary supply chain security program led by U.S. Customs and Border Protection.

Esther Yeung, manager of the supply chain team, knows that cost data is crucial in everyday decision making in the supply chain team. Some of her challenges involve answering questions from her management such as, "How can we increase the number of audits by 20% while keeping the total budget unchanged?" and "How can we increase the proportion of unannounced audits while keeping the budget unchanged, though unannounced audits cost more?"

In order to answer these questions, Esther prepares a cost analysis every time she plans an audit trip. She has found that identifying factories located in the same region and combining them into a single audit trip increases output while keeping the budget constant. She has also been able to outsource some audits to qualified third parties.

Management seeks to turn its strategies into action plans. These action plans include financial details that are compiled in a master budget. The budgeting process serves several purposes, including motivating employees and communicating with them. The budget process also helps coordinate a company's activities toward common goals and is useful in evaluating results and management performance. This chapter explains how to prepare a master budget and use it as a formal plan of a company's future activities. The ability to prepare this type of plan is of enormous help in starting and operating a company. Such planning gives managers a glimpse into the future, and it can help translate ideas into actions.

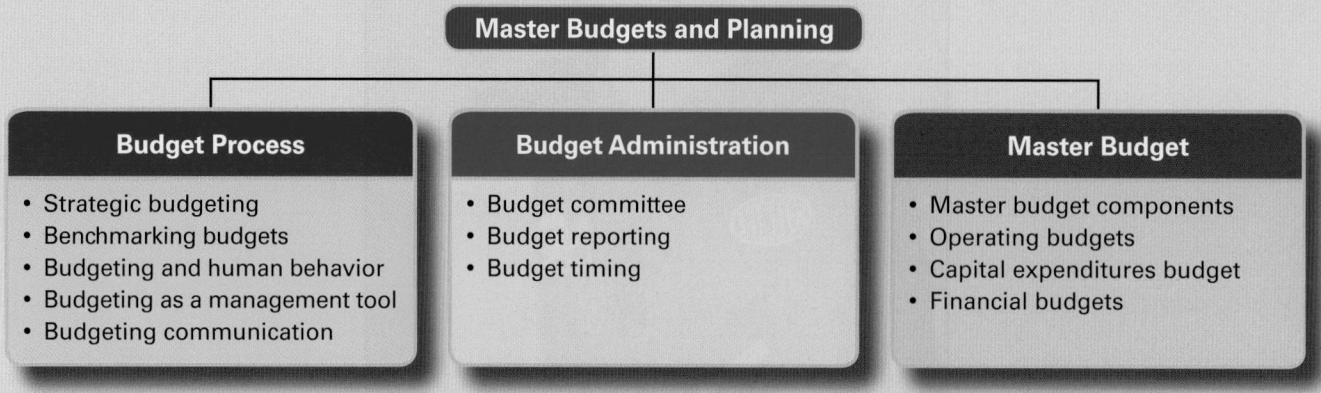

Master Budgets and Planning

Budget Process	Budget Administration	Master Budget
• Strategic budgeting • Benchmarking budgets • Budgeting and human behavior • Budgeting as a management tool • Budgeting communication	• Budget committee • Budget reporting • Budget timing	• Master budget components • Operating budgets • Capital expenditures budget • Financial budgets

BUDGET PROCESS

Strategic Budgeting

C1 Describe the importance and benefits of budgeting and the process of budget administration.

Most companies prepare long-term strategic plans spanning 5 to 10 years. They then fine-tune them in preparing medium-term and short-term plans. Strategic plans usually set a company's long-term direction. They provide a road map for the future about potential opportunities such as new products, markets, and investments. The strategic plan can be inexact, given its long-term focus. Medium- and short-term plans are more operational and translate strategic plans into actions. These action plans are fairly concrete and consist of defined objectives and goals.

Short-term financial plans are called *budgets* and typically cover a one-year period. A **budget** is a formal statement of a company's future plans. It is usually expressed in monetary terms because the economic or financial aspects of the business are the primary factors driving management's decisions. All managers should be involved in **budgeting,** the process of planning future business actions and expressing them as formal plans. Managers who plan carefully and formalize plans in a budgeting process increase the likelihood of both personal and company success. (Although most firms prepare annual budgets, it is not unusual for organizations to prepare three-year and five-year budgets that are revised at least annually.)

The relevant focus of a budgetary analysis is the future. Management must focus on future transactions and events and the opportunities available. A focus on the future is important because the pressures of daily operating problems often divert management's attention and take precedence over planning. A good budgeting system counteracts this tendency by formalizing the planning process and demanding relevant input. Budgeting makes planning an explicit management responsibility.

Companies Performing Annual Budgeting

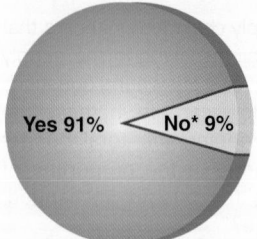

Yes 91%   No* 9%

*Most of the 9% have eliminated annual budgeting in favor of rolling or continual budgeting.

Benchmarking Budgets

The control function requires management to evaluate (benchmark) business operations against some norm. Evaluation involves comparing actual results against one of two usual alternatives: (1) past performance or (2) expected performance.

An evaluation assists management in identifying problems and taking corrective actions if necessary. Evaluation using expected, or budgeted, performance is potentially superior to using past performance to decide whether actual results trigger a need for corrective actions. This is so because past performance fails to consider several changes that can affect current and future activities. Changes in economic conditions, shifts in competitive advantages within the industry, new product developments, increased or decreased advertising, and other factors reduce the usefulness of comparisons with past results. In hi-tech industries, for instance, increasing competition, technological advances, and other innovations often reduce the usefulness of performance comparisons across years.

Budgeted performance is computed after careful analysis and research that attempts to anticipate and adjust for changes in important company, industry, and economic factors. Therefore, budgets usually provide management an effective control and monitoring system.

Budgeting and Human Behavior

Budgeting provides standards for evaluating performance and can affect the attitudes of employees evaluated by them. It can be used to create a positive effect on employees' attitudes, but it can also create negative effects if not properly applied. Budgeted levels of performance, for instance, must be realistic to avoid discouraging employees. Personnel who will be evaluated should be consulted and involved in preparing the budget to increase their commitment to meeting it. Performance evaluations must allow the affected employees to explain the reasons for apparent performance deficiencies.

The budgeting process has three important guidelines: (1) Employees affected by a budget should be consulted when it is prepared (*participatory budgeting*), (2) goals reflected in a budget should be attainable, and (3) evaluations should be made carefully with opportunities to explain any failures. Budgeting can be a positive motivating force when these guidelines are followed. Budgeted performance levels can provide goals for employees to attain or even exceed as they carry out their responsibilities. This is especially important in organizations that consider the annual budget a "sacred" document.

Managers must also be aware of potential negative outcomes of budgeting. Under participatory budgeting, some employees might understate sales budgets and overstate expense budgets to allow them a cushion, or *budgetary slack,* to aid in meeting targets. For some businesses, pressure to meet budgeted results might lead employees to engage in unethical behavior or commit fraud. Finally, some employees might always spend their budgeted amounts, even on unnecessary items, to ensure their budgets aren't reduced for the next period.

Culture affects budgeting and the use of budgets. A good example of this is the use of budgets in measuring and rewarding performance in Japanese companies. Japanese culture is usually characterized as being "collectivist." This means that a manager in a typical Japanese company is responsible for and rewarded on group performance, which could be measured against a business-unit or company-level budget. As a famous Japanese saying goes, "The nail that stands out gets banged down." In other cultures, which are characterized as being more individualistic, most performance evaluation and rewards are based on individual performance rather than group performance. Such cultural differences pose a challenge for multinationals to find the right balance in adapting to local conditions and cultures in different countries while implementing their budgeting systems.

Point: Surveys show widespread use of budgets across countries in Asia. Budgets are regarded as one of the most important management accounting tools by Asian companies. Companies and countries differ in the purposes for which they use budgets. Use of budgets as planning and controlling tools is more common than their use in performance evaluation.

Point: The practice of involving employees in the budgeting process is known as *participatory budgeting.*

Example: Assume a company's sales force receives a bonus when sales exceed the budgeted amount. How would this arrangement affect the participatory sales forecasts? *Answer:* Sales reps may understate their budgeted sales.

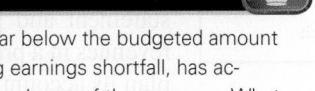

Decision Ethics   Answer — p. 940

Budget Staffer Your company's earnings for the current period will be far below the budgeted amount reported in the press. One of your superiors, who is aware of the upcoming earnings shortfall, has accepted a management position with a competitor. This superior is selling her shares of the company. What are your ethical concerns, if any? ■

Budgeting as a Management Tool

An important management objective in large companies is to ensure that activities of all departments contribute to meeting the company's overall goals. This requires coordination. Budgeting helps to achieve this coordination.

We describe later in this chapter that a company's budget, or operating plan, is based on its objectives. This operating plan starts with the sales budget, which drives all other budgets including production, materials, labor, and overhead. The budgeting process coordinates the activities of these various departments to meet the company's overall goals.

Budgeting Communication

Managers of small companies can adequately explain business plans directly to employees through conversations and other informal communications. However, conversations can create uncertainty and confusion if not supported by clear documentation of the plans. A written budget is preferred and can inform employees in all types of organizations about management's plans. The budget can also communicate management's specific action plans for the employees in the budget period.

Decision Insight

Budgets Exposed   When companies go public and their securities trade on an organized stock exchange, management usually develops specific future plans and budgets. For this purpose, companies often develop detailed six- to twelve-month budgets and less-detailed budgets spanning two to five years. ∎

BUDGET ADMINISTRATION

Budget Committee

Point: In a large company, developing a budget through a bottom-up process can involve hundreds of employees and take several weeks to finalize.

The task of preparing a budget should not be the sole responsibility of any one department. Similarly, the budget should not be simply handed down as top management's final word. Instead, budget figures and budget estimates developed through a *bottom-up* process usually are more useful. This includes, for instance, involving the sales department in preparing sales estimates. Likewise, the production department should have initial responsibility for preparing its own expense budget. Without active employee involvement in preparing budget figures, there is a risk these employees will feel that the numbers fail to reflect their special problems and needs.

Most budgets should be developed by a bottom-up process, but the budgeting system requires central guidance. This guidance is supplied by a budget committee of department heads and other executives responsible for seeing that budgeted amounts are realistic and coordinated. If a department submits initial budget figures not reflecting efficient performance, the budget committee should return them with explanatory comments on how to improve them. Then the originating department must either adjust its proposals or explain why they are acceptable. Communication between the originating department and the budget committee should continue as needed to ensure that both parties accept the budget as reasonable, attainable, and desirable.

The concept of continuous improvement applies to budgeting as well as production. At **Aedas**, a leading international consultancy firm on architecture, interiors, and master planning, CFO Vincent Liew uses the profit funnel to budget and monitor performance. As a company that manages projects, Aedas recognizes three different types of revenues: accounting revenues, billing revenues, and cash revenues. Even though accounting revenues are what finally enter the income statement and profit computations, planning and monitoring billing and cash revenues in a profit funnel are important too. This innovation helps Aedas not only plan its accounting profit but also its unbilled work-in-process and collections.

Profit Funnel

Budget Reporting

The budget period usually coincides with the accounting period. Most companies prepare at least an annual budget, which reflects the objectives for the next year. To provide specific guidance, the annual budget usually is separated into quarterly or monthly budgets. These short-term budgets allow management to periodically evaluate performance and take needed corrective action.

Managers can compare actual results to budgeted amounts in a report such as that shown in Exhibit 23.1. This report shows actual amounts, budgeted amounts, and their differences. A difference is called a *variance*. Management examines variances, particularly large ones, to identify areas for improvement and corrective action.

ECCENTRIC MUSIC Income Statement with Variances from Budget For Month Ended April 30, 2011	Actual	Budget	Variance
Net sales	$60,500	$57,150	$+3,350
Cost of goods sold	41,350	39,100	+2,250
Gross profit	19,150	18,050	+1,100
Operating expenses			
Selling expenses			
Sales salaries	(6,250)	(6,000)	+250
Advertising	(900)	(800)	+100
Store supplies	(550)	(500)	+50
Depreciation—Store equipment	(1,600)	(1,600)	
Total selling expenses	(9,300)	(8,900)	+400
General and administrative expenses			
Office salaries	(2,000)	(2,000)	
Office supplies used	(165)	(150)	+15
Rent	(1,100)	(1,100)	
Insurance	(200)	(200)	
Depreciation—Office equipment	(100)	(100)	
Total general and administrative expenses	(3,565)	(3,550)	+15
Total operating expenses	(12,865)	(12,450)	+415
Net profit	$ 6,285	$ 5,600	$ +685

EXHIBIT 23.1

Comparing Actual Performance with Budgeted Performance

Example: Assume that you must explain variances to top management. Which variances in Exhibit 23.1 would you research and why? *Answer:* Sales and cost of goods sold—due to their large variances.

Budget Timing

The time period required for the annual budgeting process can vary considerably. For example, budgeting for 2012 can begin as early as January 2011 or as late as December 2011. Large, complex organizations usually require a longer time to prepare their budgets than do smaller organizations. This is so because considerable effort is required to coordinate the different units (departments) within large organizations.

Many companies apply **continuous budgeting** by preparing **rolling budgets.** As each monthly or quarterly budget period goes by, these companies revise their entire set of budgets for the months or quarters remaining and add new monthly or quarterly budgets to replace the ones that have lapsed. At any point in time, monthly or quarterly budgets are available for the next 12 months or four quarters. Exhibit 23.2 shows rolling budgets prepared at the end of five consecutive

Companies Using Rolling Budgets

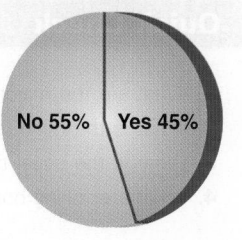

No 55%   Yes 45%

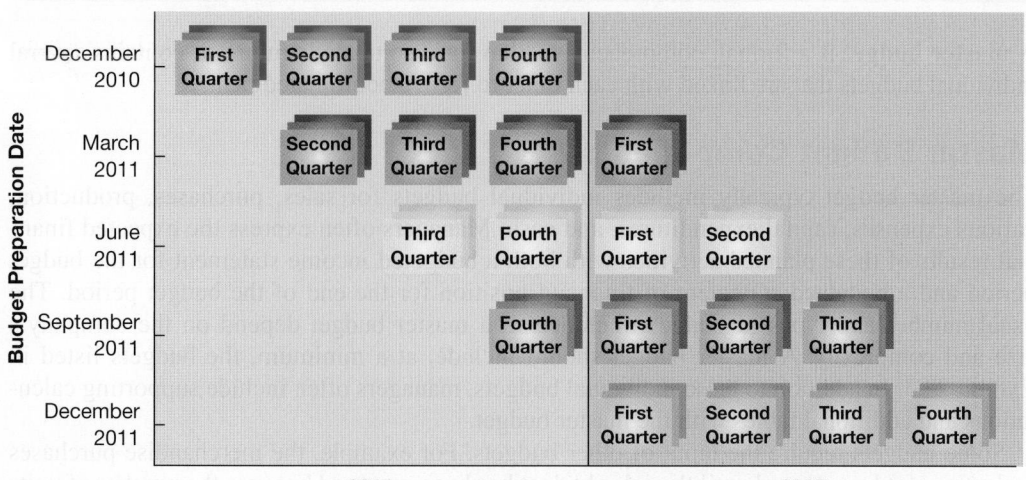

EXHIBIT 23.2

Rolling Budgets

periods. The first set (at top) is prepared in December 2010 and covers the four calendar quarters of 2011. In March 2011, the company prepares another rolling budget for the next four quarters through March 2012. This same process is repeated every three months. As a result, management is continuously planning ahead.

Exhibit 23.2 reflects an annual budget composed of four quarters prepared four times per year using the most recent information available. For example, the budget for the fourth quarter of 2011 is prepared in December 2010 and revised in March, June, and September of 2011. When continuous budgeting is not used, the fourth-quarter budget is nine months old and perhaps out of date when applied.

Decision Insight

Budget Calendar   Many companies use long-range operating budgets. For large companies, three groups usually determine or influence the budgets: creditors, directors, and management. All three are interested in the companies' future cash flows and earnings. The annual budget process often begins six months or more before the budget is due to the board of directors. A typical budget calendar, shown here, provides insight into the budget process during a typical calendar year. ■

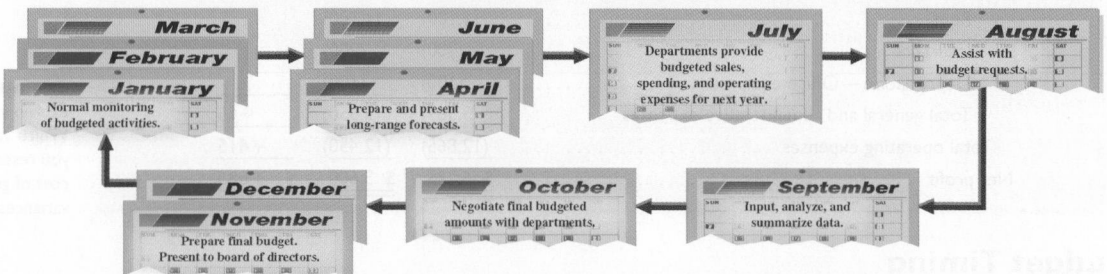

Quick Check

Answers — p. 940

1. What are the major benefits of budgeting?
2. What is the main responsibility of the budget committee?
3. What is the usual time period covered by a budget?
4. What are rolling budgets?

MASTER BUDGET

C2 Describe a master budget and the process of preparing it.

A **master budget** is a formal, comprehensive plan for a company's future. It contains several individual budgets that are linked with each other to form a coordinated plan.

Master Budget Components

The master budget typically includes individual budgets for sales, purchases, production, various expenses, capital expenditures, and cash. Managers often express the expected financial results of these planned activities with both a budgeted income statement for the budget period and a budgeted statement of financial position for the end of the budget period. The usual number and types of budgets included in a master budget depend on the company's size and complexity. A master budget should include, at a minimum, the budgets listed in Exhibit 23.3. In addition to these individual budgets, managers often include supporting calculations and additional tables with the master budget.

Some budgets require the input of other budgets. For example, the merchandise purchases budget cannot be prepared until the sales budget has been prepared because the number of units

EXHIBIT 23.3
Basic Components of a
Master Budget

Operating budgets
- *Sales budget*
- For merchandisers add: *Merchandise purchases budget* (units to be purchased)
- For manufacturers add: *Production budget* (units to be produced)
  Manufacturing budget (manufacturing costs)
- *Selling expense budget*
- *General and administrative expense budget*

Capital expenditures budget (expenditures for property, plant and equipment)

Financial budgets
- *Cash budget* (cash receipts and disbursements)
- *Budgeted income statement*
- *Budgeted statement of financial position*

to be purchased depends on how many units are expected to be sold. As a result, we often must sequentially prepare budgets within the master budget.

A typical sequence for a master budget consists of the five steps in Exhibit 23.4. Any stage in this budgeting process might reveal undesirable outcomes, so changes often must be made to prior budgets by repeating the previous steps. For instance, an early version of the cash budget could show an insufficient amount of cash unless cash outlays are reduced. This could yield a reduction in planned equipment purchases. A preliminary budgeted statement of financial position could also reveal too much debt from an ambitious capital expenditures budget. Findings such as these often result in revised plans and budgets.

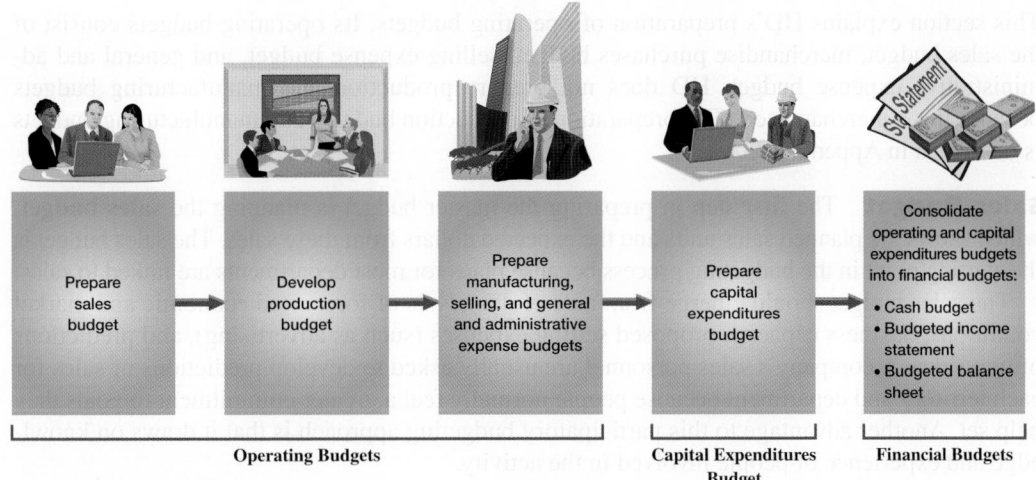

EXHIBIT 23.4
Master Budget Sequence

The remainder of this section explains how Hockey Den (HD), a retailer of youth hockey sticks, prepares its master budget. Its master budget includes operating, capital expenditures, and cash budgets for each month in each quarter. It also includes a budgeted income statement for each quarter and a budgeted statement of financial position as of the last day of each quarter. We show how HD prepares budgets for October, November, and December 2011. Exhibit 23.5 presents HD's statement of financial position at the start of this budgeting period, which we often refer to as we prepare the component budgets.

Decision Insight

Budgeting Targets Budgeting is a crucial part of any acquisition. Analysis begins by projecting annual sales volume and prices. It then estimates cost of sales, expenses, and income for the next several years. Using the present value of this projected income stream, buyers determine an offer price. ∎

EXHIBIT 23.5

Statement of financial position
Prior to the Budgeting Periods

HOCKEY DEN Statement of Financial Position September 30, 2011		
Assets		
Cash		$ 20,000
Accounts receivable		42,000
Inventory (900 units @ $60)		54,000
Equipment*	$200,000	
Less accumulated depreciation	36,000	164,000
Total assets		$280,000
Liabilities and Equity		
Liabilities		
Accounts payable	$ 58,200	
Income taxes payable (due 10/31/2011)	20,000	
Note payable to bank	10,000	$ 88,200
Shareholders' equity		
Share capital—ordinary	150,000	
Retained earnings	41,800	191,800
Total liabilities and equity		$280,000

* Equipment is depreciated on a straight-line basis over 10 years (residual value is $20,000).

Operating Budgets

P1 Prepare each component of a master budget and link each to the budgeting process.

This section explains HD's preparation of operating budgets. Its operating budgets consist of the sales budget, merchandise purchases budget, selling expense budget, and general and administrative expense budget. HD does not prepare production and manufacturing budgets because it is a merchandiser. (The preparation of production budgets and manufacturing budgets is described in Appendix 23A.)

Sales Budget The first step in preparing the master budget is planning the **sales budget,** which shows the planned sales units and the expected dollars from these sales. The sales budget is the starting point in the budgeting process because plans for most departments are linked to sales.

The sales budget should emerge from a careful analysis of forecasted economic and market conditions, business capacity, proposed selling expenses (such as advertising), and predictions of unit sales. A company's sales personnel are usually asked to develop predictions of sales for each territory and department because people normally feel a greater commitment to goals they help set. Another advantage to this participatory budgeting approach is that it draws on knowledge and experience of people involved in the activity.

To illustrate, in September 2011, HD sold 700 hockey sticks at $100 per unit. After considering sales predictions and market conditions, HD prepares its sales budget for the next quarter (three months) plus one extra month (see Exhibit 23.6). The sales budget includes

EXHIBIT 23.6

Sales Budget for Planned Unit and Dollar Sales

HOCKEY DEN Monthly Sales Budget October 2011–January 2012	Budgeted Unit Sales	Budgeted Unit Price	Budgeted Total Sales
September 2011 (actual)	700	$100	$ 70,000
October 2011	1,000	$100	$100,000
November 2011	800	100	80,000
December 2011	1,400	100	140,000
Totals for the quarter	3,200	100	$320,000
January 2012	900	100	$ 90,000

January 2012 because the purchasing department relies on estimated January sales to decide on December 2011 inventory purchases. The sales budget in Exhibit 23.6 includes forecasts of both unit sales and unit prices. Some sales budgets are expressed only in total sales dollars, but most are more detailed. Management finds it useful to know budgeted units and unit prices for many different products, regions, departments, and sales representatives.

Decision Maker   Answer — p. 940

Entrepreneur You run a start-up that manufactures designer clothes. Business is seasonal, and fashions and designs quickly change. How do you prepare reliable annual sales budgets? ■

Merchandise Purchases Budget   Companies use various methods to help managers make inventory purchasing decisions. These methods recognize that the number of units added to inventory depends on budgeted sales volume. Whether a company manufactures or purchases the product it sells, budgeted future sales volume is the primary factor in most inventory management decisions. A company must also consider its inventory system and other factors that we discuss next.

Just-in-time inventory systems.   Managers of *just-in-time* (JIT) inventory systems use sales budgets for short periods (often as few as one or two days) to order just enough merchandise or materials to satisfy the immediate sales demand. This keeps the amount of inventory to a minimum (or zero in an ideal situation). A JIT system minimizes the costs of maintaining inventory, but it is practical only if customers are content to order in advance or if managers can accurately determine short-term sales demand. Suppliers also must be able and willing to ship small quantities regularly and promptly.

> **Point:** Accurate estimates of future sales are crucial in a JIT system.

Safety stock inventory systems.   Market conditions and manufacturing processes for some products do not allow use of a just-in-time system. Companies in these cases maintain sufficient inventory to reduce the risk and cost of running short. This practice requires enough purchases to satisfy the budgeted sales amounts and to maintain a **safety stock,** a quantity of inventory that provides protection against lost sales caused by unfulfilled demands from customers or delays in shipments from suppliers.

Merchandise purchases budget preparation.   A merchandiser usually expresses a **merchandise purchases budget** in both units and dollars. Exhibit 23.7 shows the general layout for this budget in equation form. If this formula is expressed in units and only one product is involved, we can compute the number of dollars of inventory to be purchased for the budget by multiplying the units to be purchased by the cost per unit.

| Inventory to be purchased | = | Budgeted ending inventory | + | Budgeted cost of sales for the period | − | Budgeted beginning inventory |

EXHIBIT 23.7

General Formula for a Merchandise Purchases Budget

Example: Assume Hockey Den adopts a JIT system in purchasing merchandise. How will its sales budget differ from its merchandise purchases budget? *Answer:* The two budgets will be similar because future inventory should be near zero.

To illustrate, after assessing the cost of keeping inventory along with the risk and cost of inventory shortages, HD decided that the number of units in its inventory at each month-end should equal 90% of next month's predicted sales. For example, inventory at the end of October should equal 90% of budgeted November sales, and the November ending inventory should equal 90% of budgeted December sales, and so on. Also, HD's suppliers expect the September 2011 per unit cost of $60 to remain unchanged through January 2012. This information along with knowledge of 900 units in inventory at September 30 (see Exhibit 23.5) allows the company to prepare the merchandise purchases budget shown in Exhibit 23.8.

The first three lines of HD's merchandise purchases budget determine the required ending inventories (in units). Budgeted unit sales are then added to the desired ending inventory to give the required units of available merchandise. We then subtract beginning inventory to

EXHIBIT 23.8

Merchandise Purchases Budget

HOCKEY DEN Merchandise Purchases Budget October 2011–December 2011	October	November	December
Next month's budgeted sales (units)	800	1,400	900
Ratio of inventory to future sales	× 90%	× 90%	× 90%
Budgeted ending inventory (units)	720	1,260	810
Add budgeted sales (units)	1,000	800	1,400
Required units of available merchandise	1,720	2,060	2,210
Deduct beginning inventory (units)	900	720	1,260
Units to be purchased	820	1,340	950
Budgeted cost per unit	$ 60	$ 60	$ 60
Budgeted cost of merchandise purchases	$49,200	$80,400	$57,000

Example: If ending inventory in Exhibit 23.8 is required to equal 80% of next month's predicted sales, how many units must be purchased each month? *Answer:* Budgeted ending inventory: Oct. = 640 units; Nov. = 1,120 units; Dec. = 720 units. Required purchases: Oct. = 740 units; Nov. = 1,280 units; Dec. = 1,000 units.

determine the budgeted number of units to be purchased. The last line is the budgeted cost of the purchases, computed by multiplying the number of units to be purchased by the predicted cost per unit.

We already indicated that some budgeting systems describe only the total dollars of budgeted sales. Likewise, a system can express a merchandise purchases budget only in terms of the total cost of merchandise to be purchased, omitting the number of units to be purchased. This method assumes a constant relation between sales and cost of goods sold. HD, for instance, might assume the expected cost of goods sold to be 60% of sales, computed from the budgeted unit cost of $60 and the budgeted sales price of $100. However, it still must consider the effects of changes in beginning and ending inventories in determining the amounts to be purchased.

Selling Expense Budget   The **selling expense budget** is a plan listing the types and amounts of selling expenses expected during the budget period. Its initial responsibility usually rests with the vice president of marketing or an equivalent sales manager. The selling expense budget is normally created to provide sufficient selling expenses to meet sales goals reflected in the sales budget. Predicted selling expenses are based on both the sales budget and the experience of previous periods. After some or all of the master budget is prepared, management might decide that projected sales volume is inadequate. If so, subsequent adjustments in the sales budget can require corresponding adjustments in the selling expense budget.

To illustrate, HD's selling expense budget is in Exhibit 23.9. The firm's selling expenses consist of commissions paid to sales personnel and a $2,000 monthly salary paid to the sales manager. Sales commissions equal 10% of total sales and are paid in the month sales occur. Sales commissions are variable with respect to sales volume, but the sales manager's salary is fixed. No advertising expenses are budgeted for this particular quarter.

EXHIBIT 23.9

Selling Expense Budget

HOCKEY DEN Selling Expense Budget October 2011–December 2011	October	November	December	Totals
Budgeted sales	$100,000	$80,000	$140,000	$320,000
Sales commission percent	× 10%	× 10%	× 10%	× 10%
Sales commissions	10,000	8,000	14,000	32,000
Salary for sales manager	2,000	2,000	2,000	6,000
Total selling expenses	$ 12,000	$10,000	$ 16,000	$ 38,000

Example: If sales commissions in Exhibit 23.9 are increased, which budgets are affected? *Answer:* Selling expenses budget, cash budget, and budgeted income statement.

General and Administrative Expense Budget   The **general and administrative expense budget** plans the predicted operating expenses not included in the selling expenses budget. General and administrative expenses can be either variable or fixed with respect to sales volume. The office manager responsible for general administration often is responsible for preparing the initial general and administrative expense budget.

Exhibit 23.10 shows HD's general and administrative expense budget. It includes salaries of $54,000 per year, or $4,500 per month (paid each month when they are earned). Using information in Exhibit 23.5, the depreciation on equipment is computed as $18,000 per year [($200,000 − $20,000)/10 years], or $1,500 per month ($18,000/12 months).

EXHIBIT 23.10

General and Administrative Expense Budget

HOCKEY DEN General and Administrative Expense Budget October 2011–December 2011				
	October	November	December	Totals
Administrative salaries	$4,500	$4,500	$4,500	$13,500
Depreciation of equipment	1,500	1,500	1,500	4,500
Total general and administrative expenses	$6,000	$6,000	$6,000	$18,000

Interest expense and income tax expense are often classified as general and administrative expenses in published income statements but normally cannot be planned at this stage of the budgeting process. The prediction of interest expense follows the preparation of the cash budget and the decisions regarding debt. The predicted income tax expense depends on the budgeted amount of pretax income. Both interest and income taxes are usually beyond the control of the office manager. As a result, they are not used in comparison to the budget to evaluate that person's performance.

Example: In Exhibit 23.10, how would a rental agreement of $5,000 per month plus 1% of sales affect the general and administrative expense budget? (Budgeted sales are in Exhibit 23.6.) *Answer: Rent expense:* Oct. = $6,000; Nov. = $5,800; Dec. = $6,400; Total = $18,200; *Revised total general and administrative expenses:* Oct. = $12,000; Nov. = $11,800; Dec. = $12,400; Total = $36,200.

Decision Insight

No Biz Like Snow Biz   Ski resorts' costs of making snow are in the millions of dollars for equipment alone. Snowmaking involves spraying droplets of water into the air, causing them to freeze and come down as snow. Making snow can cost more than $2,000 an hour. Snowmaking accounts for 40 to 50 percent of the operating budgets for many ski resorts. ■

Quick Check

Answers — p. 940

5. What is a master budget?

6. A master budget (a) always includes a manufacturing budget specifying the units to be produced; (b) is prepared with a process starting with the operating budgets and continues with the capital expenditures budget and then financial budgets; or (c) is prepared with a process ending with the sales budget.

7. What are the three primary categories of budgets in the master budget?

8. In preparing monthly budgets for the third quarter, a company budgeted sales of 120 units for July and 140 units for August. Management wants each month's ending inventory to be 60% of next month's sales. The June 30 inventory consists of 50 units. How many units of product for July acquisition should the merchandise purchases budget specify for the third quarter? (a) 84, (b) 120, (c) 154, or (d) 204.

9. How do the operating budgets for merchandisers and manufacturers differ?

10. How does a just-in-time inventory system differ from a safety stock system?

Capital Expenditures Budget

The **capital expenditures budget** lists dollar amounts to be both received from disposals of property, plant and equipment and spent to purchase additional items of property, plant and equipment to carry out the budgeted business activities. It is usually prepared after the operating budgets. Since a company's property, plant and equipment determine its productive capacity, this budget is usually affected by long-range plans for the business. Yet the process of preparing a sales or purchases budget can reveal that the company requires more (or less) capacity, which implies more (or less) property, plant and equipment.

Capital budgeting is the process of evaluating and planning for capital (property, plant and equipment) expenditures. This is an important management task because these expenditures often involve long-run commitments of large amounts, affect predicted cash flows, and impact future debt and equity financing. This means that the capital expenditures budget is often linked with management's evaluation of the company's ability to take on more debt. We describe capital budgeting in Chapter 25.

Hockey Den does not anticipate disposal of any property, plant and equipment through December 2011, but it does plan to acquire additional equipment for $25,000 cash near the end of December 2011. This is the only budgeted capital expenditure from October 2011 through January 2012. Thus, no separate budget is shown. Hockey Den's cash budget will reflect this $25,000 planned expenditure.

Financial Budgets

After preparing its operating and capital expenditures budgets, a company uses information from these budgets to prepare at least three financial budgets: the cash budget, budgeted income statement, and budgeted statement of financial position.

P2 Link both operating and capital expenditures budgets to budgeted financial statements.

Cash Budget   After developing budgets for sales, merchandise purchases, expenses, and capital expenditures, the next step is to prepare the **cash budget,** which shows expected cash inflows and outflows during the budget period. It is especially important to maintain a cash balance necessary to meet ongoing obligations. By preparing a cash budget, management can prearrange loans to cover anticipated cash shortages before they are needed. A cash budget also helps management avoid a cash balance that is too large. Too much cash is undesirable because it earns a relatively low (if any) return. Exhibit 23.11 shows the general formula for the cash budget.

EXHIBIT 23.11

General Formula for Cash Budget

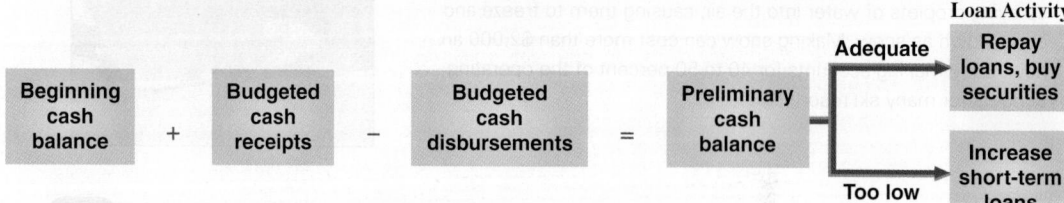

When preparing a cash budget, we add expected cash receipts to the beginning cash balance and deduct expected cash disbursements. If the expected (preliminary) ending cash balance is too low, additional cash requirements appear in the budget as planned increases from short-term loans. If the expected ending cash balance exceeds the desired balance, the excess is used to repay loans or to acquire short-term investments. Information for preparing the cash budget is mainly taken from the operating and capital expenditures budgets.

Cash Receipts from Sales   To illustrate, Exhibit 23.12 presents HD's budgeted cash receipts.

EXHIBIT 23.12

Computing Budgeted Cash Receipts

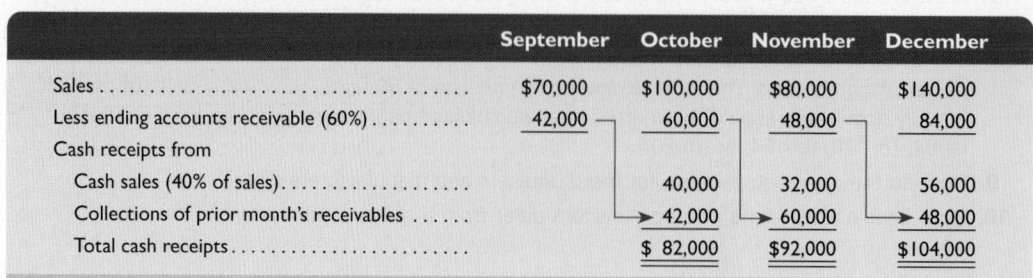

	September	October	November	December
Sales	$70,000	$100,000	$80,000	$140,000
Less ending accounts receivable (60%)	42,000	60,000	48,000	84,000
Cash receipts from				
Cash sales (40% of sales)		40,000	32,000	56,000
Collections of prior month's receivables		42,000	60,000	48,000
Total cash receipts		$ 82,000	$92,000	$104,000

We begin with reference to HD's budgeted sales (Exhibit 23.6). Analysis of past sales indicates that 40% of the firm's sales are for cash. The remaining 60% are credit sales; these customers are expected to pay in full in the month following the sales. We now can compute the budgeted cash receipts from customers as shown in Exhibit 23.12. October's budgeted cash receipts consist of $40,000 from expected cash sales ($100,000 × 40%) plus the anticipated collection of $42,000 of accounts receivable from the end of September.

Cash Disbursements for Merchandise Next, we see that HD's merchandise purchases are entirely on account. It makes full payment during the month following its purchases. Therefore, cash disbursements for purchases can be computed from the September 30, 2011, statement of financial position (Exhibit 23.5), for October disbursements, and the merchandise purchases budget (Exhibit 23.8), for November and December disbursements. This is shown in Exhibit 23.13.

EXHIBIT 23.13

Computing Cash Disbursements for Purchases

	October	November	December
Purchases (from Exhibit 23.8)	$49,200	$80,400	$57,000
Cash disbursements for			
Current month purchases (0%)	0	0	0
Prior month purchases (100%)	58,200*	49,200	80,400
Total cash disbursements for purchases	$58,200	$49,200	$80,400

*From September 30 statement of financial position (Exhibit 23.5)

The schedule above can be modified for alternative payment timing. For example, if Hockey Den paid for 20% of its purchases in the month of purchase, and paid the remaining 80% of a month's purchases in the following month, its cash disbursements in December would equal $75,720, computed as (20% × $57,000) plus (80% × $80,400).

Exhibit 23.14 shows the full cash budget for Hockey Den, beginning with information on budgeted cash receipts from Exhibit 23.13 and budgeted cash purchases for merchandise from Exhibit 23.13. Next we discuss HD's other cash disbursements and loan activity on its cash budget.

EXHIBIT 23.14

Cash Budget

HOCKEY DEN Cash Budget October 2011–December 2011			
	October	November	December
Beginning cash balance	$ 20,000	$ 20,000	$ 22,272
Cash receipts from customers (Exhibit 23.12)	82,000	92,000	104,000
Total cash available	102,000	112,000	126,272
Cash disbursements			
Payments for merchandise (Exhibit 23.13)	58,200	49,200	80,400
Sales commissions (Exhibit 23.9)	10,000	8,000	14,000
Salaries			
Sales (Exhibit 23.9)	2,000	2,000	2,000
Administrative (Exhibit 23.10)	4,500	4,500	4,500
Income taxes payable (Exhibit 23.5)	20,000		
Dividends ($150,000 × 2%)			3,000
Interest on bank loan			
October ($10,000 × 1%)*	100		
November ($22,800 × 1%)		228	
Purchase of equipment			25,000
Total cash disbursements	94,800	66,928	125,900
Preliminary cash balance	$ 7,200	$ 45,072	$ 372
Loan activity			
Additional loan from bank	12,800		19,628
Repayment of loan to bank		22,800	
Ending cash balance	$ 20,000	$ 22,272	$ 20,000
Loan balance, end of month	$ 22,800	$ 0	$ 19,628

* Beginning loan balance from Exhibit 23.5

Example: If the minimum ending cash balance in Exhibit 23.14 is changed to $25,000 for each month, what is the projected loan balance at Dec. 31, 2011?
Answer:
Loan balance, Oct. 31	$27,800
November interest.........	278
November payment........	25,022
Loan balance, Nov. 30	2,778
December interest	28
Additional loan in Dec.	21,928
Loan balance, Dec. 31	$24,706

The monthly budgeted cash disbursements for sales commissions and salaries are taken from the selling expense budget (Exhibit 23.9) and the general and administrative expense budget (Exhibit 23.10). The cash budget is unaffected by depreciation as reported in the general and administrative expenses budget.

Cash Disbursements for Other Items   Income taxes are due and payable in October as shown in the September 30, 2011, statement of financial position (Exhibit 23.5). The cash budget in Exhibit 23.14 shows this $20,000 expected payment in October. Predicted income tax expense for the quarter ending December 31 is 40% of net profit and is due in January 2012. It is therefore not reported in the October–December 2011 cash budget but in the budgeted income statement as income tax expense and on the budgeted statement of financial position as income tax liability.

Hockey Den also pays a cash dividend equal to 2% of the par value of ordinary shares in the second month of each quarter. The cash budget in Exhibit 23.14 shows a November payment of $3,000 for this purpose (2% of $150,000; see Exhibit 23.5).

Loan Activity   Analyzing Hockey Den's loan activity is necessary in computing its budgeted cash disbursements for interest. Hockey Den has an agreement with its bank that promises additional loans at each month-end, if necessary, to keep a minimum cash balance of $20,000. If the cash balance exceeds $20,000 at a month-end, HD uses the excess to repay loans. Interest is paid at each month-end at the rate of 1% of the beginning balance of these loans. For October, this payment is 1% of the $10,000 amount reported in the statement of financial position of Exhibit 23.5. For November, HD expects to pay interest of $228, computed as 1% of the $22,800 expected loan balance at October 31. No interest is budgeted for December because the company expects to repay the loans in full at the end of November. Exhibit 23.14 shows that the October 31 cash balance declines to $7,200 (before any loan-related activity). This amount is less than the $20,000 minimum. Hockey Den will bring this balance up to the minimum by borrowing $12,800 with a short-term note. At the end of November, the budget shows an expected cash balance of $45,072 before any loan activity. This means that HD expects to repay $22,800 of debt. The equipment purchase budgeted for December reduces the expected cash balance to $372, far below the $20,000 minimum. The company expects to borrow $19,628 in that month to reach the minimum desired ending balance.

Decision Insight

Cash Cushion   Why do some companies maintain a minimum cash balance when the budget shows extra cash is not needed? For example, iPhone sales have pushed Apple's cash and investments balance to over $40 billion. Per CEO Steve Jobs the cushion provides "flexibility and security," important in navigating uncertain economic times. ∎

Budgeted Income Statement   One of the final steps in preparing the master budget is to summarize the income effects. The **budgeted income statement** is a managerial accounting report showing predicted amounts of sales and expenses for the budget period. Information needed for preparing a budgeted income statement is primarily taken from already prepared budgets. The volume of information summarized in the budgeted income statement is so large for some companies that they often use spreadsheets to accumulate the budgeted transactions and classify them by their effects on income. We condense HD's budgeted income statement and show it in Exhibit 23.15. All information in this exhibit is taken from earlier budgets. Also, we now can predict the amount of income tax expense for the quarter, computed as 40% of the budgeted pretax income. This amount is included in the cash budget and/or the budgeted statement of financial position as necessary.

Budgeted Statement of Financial Position   The final step in preparing the master budget is summarizing the company's financial position. The **budgeted statement of financial position** shows predicted amounts for the company's assets, liabilities, and equity as at the end

Point: Lenders often require potential borrowers to provide cash budgets, budgeted income statements, and budgeted statement of financial positions, as well as data on past performance.

EXHIBIT 23.15

Budgeted Income Statement

HOCKEY DEN
Budgeted Income Statement
For Three Months Ended December 31, 2011

Sales (Exhibit 23.6, 3,200 units @ $100)		$320,000
Cost of goods sold (3,200 units @ $60)		192,000
Gross profit		128,000
Operating expenses		
Sales commissions (Exhibit 23.9)	$32,000	
Sales salaries (Exhibit 23.9)	6,000	
Administrative salaries (Exhibit 23.10)	13,500	
Depreciation on equipment (Exhibit 23.10)	4,500	
Interest expense (Exhibit 23.14)	328	56,328
Profit before tax		71,672
Income tax expense ($71,672 × 40%)		28,669
Net profit		$ 43,003

of the budget period. HD's budgeted statement of financial position in Exhibit 23.16 is prepared using information from the other budgets. The sources of amounts are reported in the notes to the budgeted statement of financial position.[1]

EXHIBIT 23.16

Budgeted Statement of Financial Position

HOCKEY DEN
Budgeted Statement of Financial Position
December 31, 2011

Assets

Cash[a]		$ 20,000
Accounts receivable[b]		84,000
Inventory[c]		48,600
Equipment[d]	$225,000	
Less accumulated depreciation[e]	40,500	184,500
Total assets		$337,100

Liabilities and Equity

Liabilities		
Accounts payable[f]	$ 57,000	
Income taxes payable[g]	28,669	
Bank loan payable[h]	19,628	$105,297
Shareholders' equity		
Share capital—ordinary[i]	150,000	
Retained earnings[j]	81,803	231,803
Total liabilities and equity		$337,100

[a] Ending balance for December from the cash budget in Exhibit 23.14.

[b] 60% of $140,000 sales budgeted for December from the sales budget in Exhibit 23.6.

[c] 810 units in budgeted December ending inventory at the budgeted cost of $60 per unit (from the purchases budget in Exhibit 23.8).

[d] September 30 balance of $200,000 from the beginning statement of financial position in Exhibit 23.5 plus $25,000 cost of new equipment from the cash budget in Exhibit 23.14.

[e] September 30 balance of $36,000 from the beginning statement of financial position in Exhibit 23.5 plus $4,500 expense from the general and administrative expense budget in Exhibit 23.10.

[f] Budgeted cost of purchases for December from the purchases budget in Exhibit 23.8.

[g] Income tax expense from the budgeted income statement for the fourth quarter in Exhibit 23.15.

[h] Budgeted December 31 balance from the cash budget in Exhibit 23.14.

[i] Unchanged from the beginning statement of financial position in Exhibit 23.5.

[j] September 30 balance of $41,800 from the beginning statement of financial position in Exhibit 23.5 plus budgeted net profit of $43,003 from the budgeted income statement in Exhibit 23.15 minus budgeted cash dividends of $3,000 from the cash budget in Exhibit 23.14.

---

[1] An eight-column spreadsheet, or work sheet, can be used to prepare a budgeted statement of financial position (and income statement). The first two columns show the ending statement of financial position amounts from the period prior to the budget period. The budgeted transactions and adjustments are entered in the third and fourth columns in the same manner as adjustments are entered on an ordinary work sheet. After all budgeted transactions and adjustments have been entered, the amounts in the first two columns are combined with the budget amounts in the third and fourth columns and sorted to the proper Income Statement (fifth and sixth columns) and Statement of Financial Position columns (seventh and eighth columns). Amounts in these columns are used to prepare the budgeted income statement and statement of financial position.

Plan Ahead   Most companies allocate dollars based on budgets submitted by department managers. These managers verify the numbers and monitor the budget. Managers must remember, however, that a budget is judged by its success in helping achieve the company's mission. One analogy is that a hiker must know the route to properly plan a hike and monitor hiking progress. ▦

Quick Check   Answers — p. 940

11. In preparing a budgeted statement of financial position, (*a*) property, plant and equipment are determined by analyzing the capital expenditures budget and the statement of financial position from the beginning of the budget period, (*b*) liabilities are determined by analyzing the general and administrative expense budget, or (*c*) retained earnings are determined from information contained in the cash budget and the statement of financial position from the beginning of the budget period.

12. What sequence is followed in preparing the budgets that constitute the master budget?

Decision Analysis ▢▢▢   Activity-Based Budgeting

A1 Analyze expense planning using activity-based budgeting.

Activity-based budgeting (ABB) is a budget system based on expected activities. Knowledge of expected activities and their levels for the budget period enables management to plan for resources required to perform the activities. To illustrate, we consider the budget of a company's accounting department. Traditional budgeting systems list items such as salaries, supplies, equipment, and utilities. Such an itemized budget informs management of the use of the funds budgeted (for example, salaries), but management cannot assess the basis for increases or decreases in budgeted amounts as compared to prior periods. Accordingly, management often makes across-the-board cuts or increases. In contrast, ABB requires management to list activities performed by, say, the accounting department such as auditing, tax reporting, financial reporting, and cost accounting. Exhibit 23.17 contrasts a traditional budget with an activity-based budget for a company's accounting department. An understanding of the resources required to perform the activities, the costs associated with these resources, and the way resource use changes with changes in activity levels allows management to better assess how expenses will change to accommodate changes in activity levels. Moreover, by knowing the relation between activities and costs, management can attempt to reduce costs by eliminating nonvalue-added activities.

EXHIBIT 23.17

Activity-Based Budgeting versus Traditional Budgeting (for an accounting department)

Activity-Based Budget		Traditional Budget	
Auditing	$ 58,000	Salaries	$152,000
Tax reporting	71,000	Supplies	22,000
Financial reporting	63,000	Depreciation	36,000
Cost accounting	32,000	Utilities	14,000
Total	$224,000	Total	$224,000

☐ **Decision Maker**

Answer — p. 940

Environmental Manager You hold the new position of environmental control manager for a chemical company. You are asked to develop a budget for your job and identify job responsibilities. How do you proceed? ■

DEMONSTRATION PROBLEM

Wild Wood Company's management asks you to prepare its master budget using the following information. The budget is to cover the months of April, May, and June of 2011.

WILD WOOD COMPANY Statement of Financial Position March 31, 2011				
Assets			**Liabilities and Equity**	
Cash	$ 50,000		Accounts payable	$156,000
Accounts receivable	175,000		Short-term notes payable	12,000
Inventory	126,000		Total current liabilities	168,000
Total current assets	351,000		Long-term note payable	200,000
Equipment, gross	480,000		Total liabilities	368,000
Accumulated depreciation	(90,000)		Share capital—ordinary	235,000
Equipment, net	390,000		Retained earnings	138,000
			Total shareholders' equity	373,000
Total assets	$741,000		Total liabilities and equity	$741,000

Additional Information

a. Sales for March total 10,000 units. Each month's sales are expected to exceed the prior month's results by 5%. The product's selling price is $25 per unit.

b. Company policy calls for a given month's ending inventory to equal 80% of the next month's expected unit sales. The March 31 inventory is 8,400 units, which complies with the policy. The purchase price is $15 per unit.

c. Sales representatives' commissions are 12.5% of sales and are paid in the month of the sales. The sales manager's monthly salary will be $3,500 in April and $4,000 per month thereafter.

d. Monthly general and administrative expenses include $8,000 administrative salaries, $5,000 depreciation, and 0.9% monthly interest on the long-term note payable.

e. The company expects 30% of sales to be for cash and the remaining 70% on credit. Receivables are collected in full in the month following the sale (none is collected in the month of the sale).

f. All merchandise purchases are on credit, and no payables arise from any other transactions. One month's purchases are fully paid in the next month.

g. The minimum ending cash balance for all months is $50,000. If necessary, the company borrows enough cash using a short-term note to reach the minimum. Short-term notes require an interest payment of 1% at each month-end (before any repayment). If the ending cash balance exceeds the minimum, the excess will be applied to repaying the short-term notes payable balance.

h. Dividends of $100,000 are to be declared and paid in May.

i. No cash payments for income taxes are to be made during the second calendar quarter. Income taxes will be assessed at 35% in the quarter.

j. Equipment purchases of $55,000 are scheduled for June.

Required

Prepare the following budgets and other financial information as required:
 1. Sales budget, including budgeted sales for July.
 2. Purchases budget, the budgeted cost of goods sold for each month and quarter, and the cost of the June 30 budgeted inventory.
 3. Selling expense budget.
 4. General and administrative expense budget.
 5. Expected cash receipts from customers and the expected June 30 balance of accounts receivable.
 6. Expected cash payments for purchases and the expected June 30 balance of accounts payable.
 7. Cash budget.
 8. Budgeted income statement.
 9. Budgeted statement of retained earnings.
10. Budgeted statement of financial position.

PLANNING THE SOLUTION

- The sales budget shows expected sales for each month in the quarter. Start by multiplying March sales by 105% and then do the same for the remaining months. July's sales are needed for the purchases budget. To complete the budget, multiply the expected unit sales by the selling price of $25 per unit.

- Use these results and the 80% inventory policy to budget the size of ending inventory for April, May, and June. Add the budgeted sales to these numbers and subtract the actual or expected beginning inventory for each month. The result is the number of units to be purchased each month. Multiply these numbers by the per unit cost of $15. Find the budgeted cost of goods sold by multiplying the unit sales in each month by the $15 cost per unit. Compute the cost of the June 30 ending inventory by multiplying the expected units available at that date by the $15 cost per unit.

- The selling expense budget has only two items. Find the amount of the sales representatives' commissions by multiplying the expected dollar sales in each month by the 12.5% commission rate. Then include the sales manager's salary of $3,500 in April and $4,000 in May and June.

- The general and administrative expense budget should show three items. Administrative salaries are fixed at $8,000 per month, and depreciation is $5,000 per month. Budget the monthly interest expense on the long-term note by multiplying its $200,000 balance by the 0.9% monthly interest rate.

- Determine the amounts of cash sales in each month by multiplying the budgeted sales by 30%. Add to this amount the credit sales of the prior month (computed as 70% of prior month's sales). April's cash receipts from collecting receivables equals the March 31 balance of $175,000. The expected June 30 accounts receivable balance equals 70% of June's total budgeted sales.

- Determine expected cash payments on accounts payable for each month by making them equal to the merchandise purchases in the prior month. The payments for April equal the March 31 balance of accounts payable shown on the beginning statement of financial position. The June 30 balance of accounts payable equals merchandise purchases for June.

- Prepare the cash budget by combining the given information and the amounts of cash receipts and cash payments on account that you computed. Complete the cash budget for each month by either borrowing enough to raise the preliminary balance to the minimum or paying off short-term debt as much as the balance allows without falling below the minimum. Show the ending balance of the short-term note in the budget.

- Prepare the budgeted income statement by combining the budgeted items for all three months. Determine the income before income taxes and multiply it by the 35% rate to find the quarter's income tax expense.

- The budgeted statement of retained earnings should show the March 31 balance plus the quarter's net profit minus the quarter's dividends.

- The budgeted statement of financial position includes updated balances for all items that appear in the beginning statement of financial position and an additional liability for unpaid income taxes. Amounts for all asset, liability, and equity accounts can be found either in the budgets, other calculations, or by adding amounts found there to the beginning balances.

SOLUTION TO DEMONSTRATION PROBLEM

1. Sales budget

	April	May	June	July
Prior period's unit sales	10,000	10,500	11,025	11,576
Plus 5% growth	500	525	551	579
Projected unit sales	10,500	11,025	11,576	12,155

	April	May	June	Quarter
Projected unit sales	10,500	11,025	11,576	
Selling price per unit	× $25	× $25	× $25	
Projected sales	$262,500	$275,625	$289,400	$827,525

2. Purchases budget

	April	May	June	Quarter
Next period's unit sales (part 1)	11,025	11,576	12,155	
Ending inventory percent	× 80%	× 80%	× 80%	
Desired ending inventory	8,820	9,261	9,724	
Current period's unit sales (part 1)	10,500	11,025	11,576	
Units to be available	19,320	20,286	21,300	
Less beginning inventory	8,400	8,820	9,261	
Units to be purchased	10,920	11,466	12,039	
Budgeted cost per unit	× $15	× $15	× $15	
Projected purchases	$163,800	$171,990	$180,585	$516,375

Budgeted cost of goods sold

	April	May	June	Quarter
This period's unit sales (part 1)	10,500	11,025	11,576	
Budgeted cost per unit	× $15	× $15	× $15	
Projected cost of goods sold	$157,500	$165,375	$173,640	$496,515

Budgeted inventory for June 30

Units (part 2).........	9,724
Cost per unit	× $15
Total...............	$145,860

3. Selling expense budget

	April	May	June	Quarter
Budgeted sales (part 1)	$262,500	$275,625	$289,400	$827,525
Commission percent	× 12.5%	× 12.5%	× 12.5%	× 12.5%
Sales commissions	32,813	34,453	36,175	103,441
Manager's salary	3,500	4,000	4,000	11,500
Projected selling expenses	$ 36,313	$ 38,453	$ 40,175	$114,941

4. General and administrative expense budget

	April	May	June	Quarter
Administrative salaries	$ 8,000	$ 8,000	$ 8,000	$24,000
Depreciation	5,000	5,000	5,000	15,000
Interest on long-term note payable (0.9% × $200,000)	1,800	1,800	1,800	5,400
Projected expenses	$14,800	$14,800	$14,800	$44,400

5. Expected cash receipts from customers

	April	May	June	Quarter
Budgeted sales (part 1)	$262,500	$275,625	$289,400	
Ending accounts receivable (70%)	$183,750	$192,938	$202,580	
Cash receipts				
Cash sales (30% of budgeted sales)	$ 78,750	$ 82,687	$ 86,820	$248,257
Collections of prior month's receivables	175,000	183,750	192,938	551,688
Total cash to be collected	$253,750	$266,437	$279,758	$799,945

6. Expected cash payments to suppliers

	April	May	June	Quarter
Cash payments (equal to prior month's purchases)	$156,000	$163,800	$171,990	$491,790
Expected June 30 balance of accounts payable (June purchases)			$180,585	

7. Cash budget

	April	May	June
Beginning cash balance	$ 50,000	$ 89,517	$ 50,000
Cash receipts (part 5)	253,750	266,437	279,758
Total cash available	303,750	355,954	329,758
Cash payments			
Payments for merchandise (part 6)	156,000	163,800	171,990
Sales commissions (part 3)	32,813	34,453	36,175
Salaries			
Sales (part 3)	3,500	4,000	4,000
Administrative (part 4)	8,000	8,000	8,000
Interest on long-term note (part 4)	1,800	1,800	1,800
Dividends		100,000	
Equipment purchase			55,000
Interest on short-term notes			
April ($12,000 × 1.0%)	120		
June ($6,099 × 1.0%)			61
Total cash payments	202,233	312,053	277,026
Preliminary balance	101,517	43,901	52,732
Loan activity			
Additional loan		6,099	
Loan repayment	(12,000)		(2,732)
Ending cash balance	$ 89,517	$ 50,000	$ 50,000
Ending short-term notes	$ 0	$ 6,099	$ 3,367

8.

WILD WOOD COMPANY
Budgeted Income Statement
For Quarter Ended June 30, 2011

Sales (part 1)		$827,525
Cost of goods sold (part 2)		496,515
Gross profit		331,010
Operating expenses		
Sales commissions (part 3)	($103,441)	
Sales salaries (part 3)	(11,500)	
Administrative salaries (part 4)	(24,000)	
Depreciation (part 4)	(15,000)	
Interest on long-term note (part 4)	(5,400)	
Interest on short-term notes (part 7)	(181)	
Total operating expenses		(159,522)
Profit before tax		171,488
Income taxes (35%)		60,021
Net profit		$111,467

9.

WILD WOOD COMPANY
Budgeted Statement of Retained Earnings
For Quarter Ended June 30, 2011

Beginning retained earnings (given)	$138,000
Net profit (part 8)	111,467
	249,467
Less cash dividends (given)	100,000
Ending retained earnings	$149,467

10.

WILD WOOD COMPANY
Budgeted Statement of Financial Position
June 30, 2011

Assets		
Cash (part 7)		$ 50,000
Accounts receivable (part 5)		202,580
Inventory (part 2)		145,860
Total current assets		398,440
Equipment (given plus purchase)	$535,000	
Less accumulated depreciation (given plus expense)	105,000	430,000
Total assets		$828,440
Liabilities and Equity		
Accounts payable (part 6)		$180,585
Short-term notes payable (part 7)		3,367
Income taxes payable (part 8)		60,021
Total current liabilities		243,973
Long-term note payable (given)		200,000
Total liabilities		443,973
Share capital—ordinary (given)		235,000
Retained earnings (part 9)		149,467
Total shareholders' equity		384,467
Total liabilities and equity		$828,440

23A Production and Manufacturing Budgets

P3 Prepare production and manufacturing budgets.

Unlike a merchandising company, a manufacturer must prepare a **production budget** instead of a merchandise purchases budget. A production budget, which shows the number of units to be produced each month, is similar to merchandise purchases budgets except that the number of units to be purchased each month (as shown in Exhibit 23.8) is replaced by the number of units to be manufactured each month. A production budget does not show costs; it is *always expressed in units of product*. Exhibit 23A.1 shows the production budget for Toronto Sticks Company (TSC), a manufacturer of hockey sticks. TSC is an exclusive supplier of hockey sticks to Hockey Den, meaning that TSC uses HD's budgeted sales figures (Exhibit 23.6) to determine its production and manufacturing budgets.

EXHIBIT 23A.1

Production Budget

TSC Production Budget October 2011–December 2011	October	November	December
Next period's budgeted sales (units)	800	1,400	900
Ratio of inventory to future sales	× 90%	× 90%	× 90%
Budgeted ending inventory (units)	720	1,260	810
Add budgeted sales for the period (units)	1,000	800	1,400
Required units of available production	1,720	2,060	2,210
Deduct beginning inventory (units)	(900)	(720)	(1,260)
Units to be produced	820	1,340	950

A **manufacturing budget** shows the budgeted costs for direct materials, direct labor, and overhead. It is based on the budgeted production volume from the production budget. The manufacturing budget for most companies consists of three individual budgets: direct materials budget, direct labor budget, and overhead budget. Exhibits 23A.2–23A.4 show these three manufacturing budgets for TSC. These budgets yield the total expected cost of goods to be manufactured in the budget period.

The *direct materials budget* is driven by the budgeted materials needed to satisfy each month's production requirement. To this we must add the desired ending inventory requirements. The desired ending inventory of direct materials as shown in Exhibit 23A.2 is 50% of next month's budgeted materials requirements of wood. For instance, in October 2011, an ending inventory of 335 units of material is desired (50% of November's 670 units). The desired ending inventory for December 2011 is 225 units, computed from the direct material requirement of 450 units for a production level of 900 units in January 2012. The total materials requirements are computed by adding the desired ending inventory figures to that month's budgeted production material requirements. For October 2011, the total materials requirement is 745 units (335 + 410). From the total materials requirement, we then subtract the units of

EXHIBIT 23A.2

Direct Materials Budget

TSC Direct Materials Budget October 2011–December 2011	October	November	December
Budget production (units)	820	1,340	950
Materials requirements per unit	× 0.5	× 0.5	× 0.5
Materials needed for production (units)	410	670	475
Add budgeted ending inventory (units)	335	237.5	225
Total materials requirements (units)	745	907.5	700
Deduct beginning inventory (units)	(205)	(335)	(237.5)
Materials to be purchased (units)	540	572.5	462.5
Material price per unit	$ 20	$ 20	$ 20
Total cost of direct materials purchases	$10,800	$11,450	$9,250

materials available in beginning inventory. For October 2011, the materials available from September 2011 are computed as 50% of October's materials requirements to satisfy production, or 205 units (50% of 410). Therefore, direct materials purchases in October 2011 are budgeted at 540 units (745 − 205). See Exhibit 23A.2.

TSC's *direct labor budget* is shown in Exhibit 23A.3. About 15 minutes of labor time is required to produce one unit. Labor is paid at the rate of $12 per hour. Budgeted labor hours are computed by multiplying the budgeted production level for each month by one-quarter (0.25) of an hour. Direct labor cost is then computed by multiplying budgeted labor hours by the labor rate of $12 per hour.

TSC Direct Labor Budget October 2011–December 2011			
	October	November	December
Budgeted production (units)	820	1,340	950
Labor requirements per unit (hours)	× 0.25	× 0.25	× 0.25
Total labor hours needed	205	335	237.5
Labor rate (per hour)	$ 12	$ 12	$ 12
Labor dollars	$2,460	$4,020	$2,850

EXHIBIT 23A.3

Direct Labor Budget

TSC's *factory overhead budget* is shown in Exhibit 23A.4. The variable portion of overhead is assigned at the rate of $2.50 per unit of production. The fixed portion stays constant at $1,500 per month. The budget in Exhibit 23A.4 is in condensed form; most overhead budgets are more detailed, listing each overhead cost item.

TSC Factory Overhead Budget October 2011–December 2011			
	October	November	December
Budgeted production (units)	820	1,340	950
Variable factory overhead rate	× $2.50	× $2.50	× $2.50
Budgeted variable overhead	2,050	3,350	2,375
Budgeted fixed overhead	1,500	1,500	1,500
Budgeted total overhead	$3,550	$4,850	$3,875

EXHIBIT 23A.4

Factory Overhead Budget

Summary

C1 **Describe the importance and benefits of budgeting and the process of budget administration.** Planning is a management responsibility of critical importance to business success. Budgeting is the process management uses to formalize its plans. Budgeting promotes management analysis and focuses its attention on the future. Budgeting also provides a basis for evaluating performance, serves as a source of motivation, is a means of coordinating activities, and communicates management's plans and instructions to employees. Budgeting is a detailed activity that requires administration. At least three aspects are important: budget committee, budget reporting, and budget timing. A budget committee oversees the budget preparation. The budget period pertains to the time period for which the budget is prepared such as a year or month.

C2 **Describe a master budget and the process of preparing it.** A master budget is a formal overall plan for a company. It consists of plans for business operations and capital expenditures, plus the financial results of those activities. The budgeting process begins with a sales budget. Based on expected sales volume, companies can budget purchases, selling expenses, and administrative expenses. Next, the capital expenditures budget is prepared, followed by the cash budget and budgeted financial statements. Manufacturers also must budget production quantities, materials purchases, labor costs, and overhead.

A1 **Analyze expense planning using activity-based budgeting.** Activity-based budgeting requires management to identify activities performed by departments, plan necessary activity levels, identify resources required to perform these activities, and budget the resources.

P1 **Prepare each component of a master budget and link each to the budgeting process.** The term *master budget* refers to a collection of individual component budgets. Each component budget is designed to guide persons responsible for activities covered by that component. A master budget must reflect the components of a company and their interaction in pursuit of company goals.

P2   **Link both operating and capital expenditures budgets to budgeted financial statements.** The operating budgets, capital expenditures budget, and cash budget contain much of the information to prepare a budgeted income statement for the budget period and a budgeted statement of financial position at the end of the budget period. Budgeted financial statements show the expected financial consequences of the planned activities described in the budgets.

P3   **Prepare production and manufacturing budgets.** A manufacturer must prepare a *production budget* instead of a purchases budget. A *manufacturing budget* shows the budgeted production costs for direct materials, direct labor, and overhead.

Guidance Answers to Decision Maker and Decision Ethics

Budget Staffer   Your superior's actions appear unethical because she is using private information for personal gain. As a budget staffer, you are low in the company's hierarchical structure and probably unable to confront this superior directly. You should inform an individual with a position of authority within the organization about your concerns.

Entrepreneur   You must deal with two issues. First, because fashions and designs frequently change, you cannot heavily rely on previous budgets. As a result, you must carefully analyze the market to understand what designs are in vogue. This will help you plan the product mix and estimate demand. The second issue is the budgeting

period. An annual sales budget may be unreliable because tastes can quickly change. Your best bet might be to prepare monthly and quarterly sales budgets that you continuously monitor and revise.

Environmental Manager   You are unlikely to have data on this new position to use in preparing your budget. In this situation, you can use activity-based budgeting. This requires developing a list of activities to conduct, the resources required to perform these activities, and the expenses associated with these resources. You should challenge yourself to be absolutely certain that the listed activities are necessary and that the listed resources are required.

Guidance Answers to Quick Checks

1. Major benefits include promoting a focus on the future; providing a basis for evaluating performance; providing a source of motivation; coordinating the departments of a business; and communicating plans and instructions.

2. The budget committee's responsibility is to provide guidance to ensure that budget figures are realistic and coordinated.

3. Budget periods usually coincide with accounting periods and therefore cover a month, quarter, or a year. Budgets can also be prepared for longer time periods, such as five years.

4. Rolling budgets are budgets that are periodically revised in the ongoing process of continuous budgeting.

5. A master budget is a comprehensive or overall plan for the company that is generally expressed in monetary terms.

6. *b*

7. The master budget includes operating budgets, the capital expenditures budget, and financial budgets.

8. *c*; Computed as $(60\% \times 140) + 120 - 50 = 154$.

9. Merchandisers prepare merchandise purchases budgets; manufacturers prepare production and manufacturing budgets.

10. A just-in-time system keeps the level of inventory to a minimum and orders merchandise or materials to meet immediate sales demand. A safety stock system maintains an inventory that is large enough to meet sales demands plus an amount to satisfy unexpected sales demands and an amount to cover delayed shipments from suppliers.

11. *a*

12. (a) Operating budgets (such as sales, selling expense, and administrative budgets), (b) capital expenditures budget, (c) financial budgets: cash budget, budgeted income statement, and budgeted statement of financial position.

Key Terms   www.mheducation.asia/olc/wildkwokFAP

Activity-based budgeting (ABB) (p. 932)
Budget (p. 918)
Budgeted statement of financial position (p. 930)
Budgeted income statement (p. 930)
Budgeting (p. 918)

Capital expenditures budget (p. 928)
Cash budget (p. 928)
Continuous budgeting (p. 921)
General and administrative expense budget (p. 927)
Manufacturing budget (p. 938)
Master budget (p. 922)

Merchandise purchases budget (p. 925)
Production budget (p. 938)
Rolling budgets (p. 921)
Safety stock (p. 925)
Sales budget (p. 924)
Selling expense budget (p. 926)

Additional Quiz Questions are available at the book's Website.

1. A plan that reports the units or costs of merchandise to be purchased by a merchandising company during the budget period
   is called a
   a. Capital expenditures budget.
   b. Cash budget.
   c. Merchandise purchases budget.
   d. Selling expenses budget.
   e. Sales budget.

2. A hardware store has budgeted sales of $36,000 for its power
   tool department in July. Management wants to have $7,000 in
   power tool inventory at the end of July. Its beginning inventory
   of power tools is expected to be $6,000. What is the budgeted
   dollar amount of merchandise purchases?
   a. $36,000
   b. $43,000
   c. $42,000
   d. $35,000
   e. $37,000

3. A store has the following budgeted sales for the next five months.

May	$210,000
June	186,000
July	180,000
August	220,000
September	240,000

   Cash sales are 25% of total sales and all credit sales are expected
   to be collected in the month following the sale. The total amount
   of cash expected to be received from customers in September is

   a. $240,000
   b. $225,000
   c. $ 60,000
   d. $165,000
   e. $220,000

4. A plan that shows the expected cash inflows and cash outflows
   during the budget period, including receipts from loans needed
   to maintain a minimum cash balance and repayments of such
   loans, is called
   a. A rolling budget.
   b. An income statement.
   c. A statement of financial position.
   d. A cash budget.
   e. An operating budget.

5.^A The following sales are predicted for a company's next four
   months.

	September	October	November	December
Unit sales ..	480	560	600	480

   Each month's ending inventory of finished goods should be
   30% of the next month's sales. At September 1, the finished
   goods inventory is 140 units. The budgeted production of units
   for October is
   a. 572 units.
   b. 560 units.
   c. 548 units.
   d. 600 units.
   e. 180 units.

---

^A Superscript letter A denotes assignments based on Appendix 23A.
🔲 Icon denotes assignments that involve decision making.

1. 🔲 Identify at least three roles that budgeting plays in helping
   managers control and monitor a business.

2. What two common benchmarks can be used to evaluate actual
   performance? Which of the two is generally more useful?

3. 🔲 What is the benefit of continuous budgeting?

4. Identify three usual time horizons for short-term planning and
   budgets.

5. 🔲 Why should each department participate in preparing its
   own budget?

6. 🔲 How does budgeting help management coordinate and
   plan business activities?

7. 🔲 Why is the sales budget so important to the budgeting
   process?

8. What is a selling expense budget? What is a capital
   expenditures budget?

9. Budgeting promotes good decision making by requiring
   managers to conduct _____ and by focusing their attention on
   the _____.

10. **Nokia** prepares a cash budget. What is a cash budget? Why
    must operating budgets and the capital expenditures budget be
    prepared before the cash budget?

11.^A What is the difference between a production budget and a
    manufacturing budget?

12. 🔲 Would a manager of an **Apple** retail store participate
    more in budgeting than a manager at the corporate offices?
    Explain.

13. 🔲 Does the manager of a **Research In Motion** distribution
    center participate in long-term budgeting? Explain.

14. 🔲 Assume that **Palm**'s smartphone division is charged with
    preparing a master budget. Identify the participants—for
    example, the sales manager for the sales budget—and describe
    the information each person provides in preparing the master
    budget.

QUICK STUDY

QS 23-1
Budget motivation C1

The motivation of employees is one goal of budgeting. Identify three guidelines that organizations should follow if budgeting is to serve effectively as a source of motivation for employees.

QS 23-2
Budgeting process C1

Good management includes good budgeting. (1) Explain why the bottom-up approach to budgeting is considered a more successful management technique than a top-down approach. (2) Provide an example of implementation of the bottom-up approach to budgeting.

QS 23-3
Components of a master budget
C2

Which one of the following sets of items are all necessary components of the master budget?
1. Operating budgets, historical income statement, and budgeted statement of financial position.
2. Sales budget, operating budgets, and historical financial budgets.
3. Operating budgets, financial budgets, and capital expenditures budget.
4. Prior sales reports, capital expenditures budget, and financial budgets.

QS 23-4
Purchases budget P1

Rockgate Company's July sales budget calls for sales of $400,000. The store expects to begin July with $40,000 of inventory and to end the month with $50,000 of inventory. Gross margin is typically 30% of sales. Determine the budgeted cost of merchandise purchases for July.

QS 23-5
Computing budgeted accounts receivable
P2

Treehouse Company anticipates total sales for June and July of $420,000 and $398,000, respectively. Cash sales are normally 60% of total sales. Of the credit sales, 10% are collected in the same month as the sale, 70% are collected during the first month after the sale, and the remaining 20% are collected in the second month. Determine the amount of accounts receivable reported on the company's budgeted statement of financial position as at July 31.

QS 23-6
Cash budget
P1

Use the following information to prepare a cash budget for the month ended on March 31 for Sosa Company. The budget should show expected cash receipts and cash disbursements for the month of March and the balance expected on March 31.
a. Beginning cash balance on March 1, $82,000.
b. Cash receipts from sales, $300,000.
c. Budgeted cash disbursements for purchases, $120,000.
d. Budgeted cash disbursements for salaries, $80,000.
e. Other budgeted cash expenses, $55,000.
f. Cash repayment of bank loan, $30,000.

QS 23-7
Activity-based budgeting
A1

Activity-based budgeting is a budget system based on *expected activities*. (1) Describe activity-based budgeting, and explain its preparation of budgets. (2) How does activity-based budgeting differ from traditional budgeting?

QS 23-8[A]
Production budget
P3

Goldenlock Company manufactures watches and has a JIT policy that ending inventory must equal 20% of the next month's sales. It estimates that October's actual ending inventory will consist of 95,000 watches. November and December sales are estimated to be 350,000 and 400,000 watches, respectively. Compute the number of watches to be produced that would appear on the company's production budget for the month of November.

QS 23-9[A]
Factory overhead budget P3

Refer to information from QS 23-8[A]. Goldenlock Company assigns variable overhead at the rate of $1.75 per unit of production. Fixed overhead equals $5,000,000 per month. Prepare a factory overhead budget for November.

QS 23-10
Sales budget P1

Turks sells miniature digital cameras for $400 each. 900 units were sold in May, and it forecasts 5% growth in unit sales each month. Determine (a) the number of camera sales and (b) the dollar amount of camera sales for the month of June.

Refer to information from QS 23-10. Turks pays a sales manager a monthly salary of $4,000 and a commission of 10% of camera sales (in dollars). Prepare a selling expense budget for the month of June.

QS 23-11
Selling expense budget **P1**

Refer to information from QS 23-10. Assume 20% of Turks's sales are for cash. The remaining 80% are credit sales; these customers pay in the month following the sale. Compute the budgeted cash receipts for June.

QS 23-12
Cash budget **P1**

Following are selected accounts for a company. For each account, indicate whether it will appear on a budgeted income statement (BIS) or a budgeted statement of financial position. If an item will not appear on either budgeted financial statement, label it NA.

QS 23-13
Budgeted financial statements
P2

Sales	_____	Interest paid on bank loan	_____
Administrative salaries paid	_____	Cash dividends paid	_____
Accumulated depreciation	_____	Bank loan owed	_____
Depreciation expense	_____	Cost of goods sold	_____

The Candy Shoppe reports the following sales forecast: August, $110,000; September, $120,000. Cash sales are normally 25% of total sales and all credit sales are expected to be collected in the month following the date of sale. Prepare a schedule of cash receipts for September.

QS 23-14
Cash receipts **P1**

Zen Den reports the following sales forecast: September, $25,000; October, $36,000; and November, $30,000. All sales are on account. Collections of credit sales are received as follows: 15% in the month of sale, 60% in the first month after sale, 20% in the second month after sale, and 5% is uncollectible. Prepare a schedule of cash receipts for November.

QS 23-15
Cash receipts **P1**

T-Mart purchased $100,000 of merchandise in August and expects to purchase $120,000 in September. Merchandise purchases are paid as follows: 25% in the month of purchase and 75% in the following month. Compute cash disbursements for merchandise for September.

QS 23-16
Cash disbursements for
merchandise **P1**

Jam Co. forecasts merchandise purchases of $11,600 in January, $11,800 in February, and $15,400 in March; 40% of purchases are paid in the month of purchase and 60% are paid in the following month. At December 31 of the prior year, the balance of Accounts Payable (for December purchases) is $8,000. Prepare a schedule of cash disbursements for merchandise for each of the months of January, February, and March.

QS 23-17
Cash disbursements for
merchandise
P1

Splinter Company forecasts sales of 6,000 units for April. Beginning inventory is 1,000 units. The desired ending inventory is 30% higher than the beginning inventory. How many units should Splinter purchase in April?

QS 23-18
Computing purchases
P1

Li Company forecasts unit sales of 640,000 in April, 720,000 in May, 780,000 in June, and 620,000 in July. Beginning inventory on April 1 is 192,000 units, and the company wants to have 30% of next month's sales in inventory at the end of each month. Prepare a merchandise purchases budget for the months of April, May, and June.

QS 23-19
Computing purchases
P1

Kyoto, Inc. predicts the following sales in units for the coming three months:

QS 23-20[A]
Production budget
P3

	May	June	July
Sales in units	280	300	240

Each month's ending inventory of finished units should be 60% of the next month's sales. The April 30 finished goods inventory is 168 units. Compute Kyoto's budgeted production (in units) for May.

Zyton Corp. budgets production of 292 units in January and 264 units in February. Each finished unit requires five pounds of raw material Z, which costs $6 per pound. Each month's ending inventory of raw materials should be 30% of the following month's budgeted production. The January 1 raw materials inventory has 438 pounds of Z. Prepare a direct materials budget for January.

QS 23-21[A]
Direct materials budget
P3

QS 23-22[A]
Direct labor budget   **P3**

Tek Co. plans to produce 620 units in July. Each unit requires two hours of direct labor. The direct labor rate is $16 per hour. Prepare a direct labor budget for July.

QS 23-23
Sales budget   **P1**

Shay, Inc., is preparing its master budget for the quarter ending March 31. It sells a single product for $25 per unit. Budgeted sales for the next four months follow. Prepare a sales budget for the months of January, February, and March.

	January	February	March	April
Sales in units	1,200	1,000	1,600	1,400

QS 23-24
Cash receipts budget   **P1**

Refer to information in QS 23-23. In addition, sales are 40% cash and 60% on credit. All credit sales are collected in the month following the sale. The January 1 balance in accounts receivable is $10,000. Prepare a schedule of budgeted cash receipts for January, February, and March.

QS 23-25
Selling expense budget   **P1**

Refer to information in QS 23-23. In addition, sales commissions are 10% of sales and the company pays a sales manager a salary of $5,000 per month. Sales commissions and salaries are paid in the month incurred. Prepare a selling expense budget for January, February, and March.

QS 23-26
Budgeted loan activity
P1

Mink Company is preparing a cash budget for February. The company has $30,000 cash at the beginning of February and anticipates $75,000 in cash receipts and $96,250 in cash disbursements during February. What amount, if any, must the company borrow during February to maintain a $10,000 cash balance? The company has no loans outstanding on February 1.

QS 23-27
Operating budgets
P1

Royal Phillips Electronics of the Netherlands reports sales of EUR 23,200 million for a recent year. Assume that the company expects sales growth of 3% for the next year. Also assume that selling expenses are typically 20% of sales, while general and administrative expenses are 4% of sales.

Required

1. Compute budgeted sales for the next year.
2. Assume budgeted sales for next year is EUR 24,000 million, and then compute budgeted selling expenses and budgeted general and administrative expenses for the next year. Round amounts to one decimal.

■≣ connect·

EXERCISES

Exercise 23-1
Preparation of merchandise purchases budgets (for three periods)
P1

Formworks Company prepares monthly budgets. The current budget plans for a September ending inventory of 15,000 units. Company policy is to end each month with merchandise inventory equal to a specified percent of budgeted sales for the following month. Budgeted sales and merchandise purchases for the three most recent months follow. (1) Prepare the merchandise purchases budget for the months of July, August, and September. (2) Compute the ratio of ending inventory to the next month's sales for each budget prepared in part 1. (3) How many units are budgeted for sale in October?

	Sales (Units)	Purchases (Units)
July	120,000	138,000
August	210,000	204,000
September	180,000	159,000

Exercise 23-2
Preparation of cash budgets (for three periods)
P1

Kasik Co. budgeted the following cash receipts and cash disbursements for the first three months of next year.

	Cash Receipts	Cash Disbursements
January	$500,000	$450,000
February	300,000	250,000
March	400,000	500,000

According to a credit agreement with the company's bank, Kasik promises to have a minimum cash balance of $30,000 at each month-end. In return, the bank has agreed that the company can borrow up to $150,000 at an annual interest rate of 12%, paid on the last day of each month. The interest is computed based on the beginning balance of the loan for the month. The company has a cash balance of $30,000 and a loan balance of $60,000 at January 1. Prepare monthly cash budgets for each of the first three months of next year.

Use the following information to prepare the July cash budget for Sanchez Co. It should show expected cash receipts and cash disbursements for the month and the cash balance expected on July 31.

a. Beginning cash balance on July 1: $50,000.

b. Cash receipts from sales: 30% is collected in the month of sale, 50% in the next month, and 20% in the second month after sale (uncollectible accounts are negligible and can be ignored). Sales amounts are: May (actual), $1,720,000; June (actual), $1,200,000; and July (budgeted), $1,400,000.

c. Payments on merchandise purchases: 60% in the month of purchase and 40% in the month following purchase. Purchases amounts are: June (actual), $430,000; and July (budgeted), $600,000.

d. Budgeted cash disbursements for salaries in July: $211,000.

e. Budgeted depreciation expense for July: $12,000.

f. Other cash expenses budgeted for July: $150,000.

g. Accrued income taxes due in July: $80,000.

h. Bank loan interest due in July: $6,600.

Exercise 23-3
Preparation of a cash budget
P1

Use the information in Exercise 23-3 and the following additional information to prepare a budgeted income statement for the month of July and a budgeted statement of financial position for July 31.

a. Cost of goods sold is 44% of sales.

b. Inventory at the end of June is $80,000 and at the end of July is $64,000.

c. Salaries payable on June 30 are $50,000 and are expected to be $40,000 on July 31.

d. The equipment account balance is $1,600,000 on July 31. On June 30, the accumulated depreciation on equipment is $280,000.

e. The $6,600 cash payment of interest represents the 1% monthly expense on a bank loan of $660,000.

f. Income taxes payable on July 31 are $124,320, and the income tax rate applicable to the company is 30%.

g. The only other statement of financial position accounts are: Share Capital—Ordinary, with a balance of $600,000 on June 30; and Retained Earnings, with a balance of $1,072,000 on June 30.

Exercise 23-4
Preparing a budgeted income statement and statement of financial position
P2

Powerdyne Company's cost of goods sold is consistently 60% of sales. The company plans to carry ending merchandise inventory for each month equal to 40% of the next month's budgeted cost of good sold. All merchandise is purchased on credit, and 50% of the purchases made during a month is paid for in that month. Another 35% is paid for during the first month after purchase, and the remaining 15% is paid for during the second month after purchase. Expected unit sales are: August (actual), 150,000; September (actual), 350,000; October (estimated), 200,000; November (estimated), 300,000. Use this information to determine October's expected cash payments for purchases. (*Hint:* Use the layout of Exhibit 23.8, but revised for the facts given here.)

Exercise 23-5
Computing budgeted cash payments for purchases
P1

Sand Dollar Company purchases all merchandise on credit. It recently budgeted the following month-end accounts payable balances and merchandise inventory balances. Cash payments on accounts payable during each month are expected to be: May, $1,300,000; June, $1,450,000; July, $1,350,000; and August, $1,400,000. Use the available information to compute the budgeted amounts of (1) merchandise purchases for June, July, and August and (2) cost of goods sold for June, July, and August.

Exercise 23-6
Computing budgeted purchases and costs of goods sold
P1

	Accounts Payable	Merchandise Inventory
May 31	$120,000	$250,000
June 30	170,000	400,000
July 31	200,000	300,000
August 31	160,000	330,000

Exercise 23-7
Computing budgeted accounts payable and purchases—sales forecast in dollars
P1 P2

Check July purchases, $199,500; Sept. payments on accts. pay., $183,225

Sound Check, a merchandising company specializing in home computer speakers, budgets its monthly cost of goods sold to equal 70% of sales. Its inventory policy calls for ending inventory in each month to equal 25% of the next month's budgeted cost of goods sold. All purchases are on credit, and 20% of the purchases in a month is paid for in the same month. Another 50% is paid for during the first month after purchase, and the remaining 30% is paid for in the second month after purchase. The following sales budgets are set: July, $300,000; August, $240,000; September, $270,000; October, $240,000; and November, $210,000. Compute the following: (1) budgeted merchandise purchases for July, August, September, and October; (2) budgeted payments on accounts payable for September and October; and (3) budgeted ending balances of accounts payable for September and October. (*Hint:* For part 1, refer to Exhibits 23.7 and 23.8 for guidance, but note that budgeted sales are in dollars for this assignment.)

Exercise 23-8^A
Preparing production budgets (for two periods) **P3**

Check Second quarter production, 240,000 units

Nascar Company manufactures an innovative automobile transmission for electric cars. Management predicts that ending inventory for the first quarter will be 37,500 units. The following unit sales of the transmissions are expected during the rest of the year: second quarter, 225,000 units; third quarter, 262,500 units; and fourth quarter, 237,500 units. Company policy calls for the ending inventory of a quarter to equal 20% of the next quarter's budgeted sales. Prepare a production budget for both the second and third quarters that shows the number of transmissions to manufacture.

Exercise 23-9^A
Direct materials budget
P3

Refer to information from Exercise 23-8^A. Each transmission requires 0.60 pounds of a key raw material. Nascar Company aims to end each quarter with an ending inventory of direct materials equal to 50% of next quarter's budgeted materials requirements. Direct materials cost $175 per unit. Prepare a direct materials budget for the second quarter.

Exercise 23-10^A
Direct labor budget   **P3**

Refer to information from Exercise 23-8^A. Each transmission requires 4 direct labor hours, at a cost of $9 per hour. Prepare a direct labor budget for the second quarter.

Exercise 23-11
Budgeted cash disbursements
P1

Jake Company reports the following:

	July	August	September
Sales	$24,000	$32,000	$36,000
Purchases	14,400	19,200	21,600

Payments for purchases are made in the month after purchase. Selling expenses are 15% of sales, administrative expenses are 10% of sales, and both are paid in the month of sale. Rent expense of $2,400 is paid monthly. Depreciation expense is $1,300 per month. Prepare a schedule of budgeted cash disbursements for August and September.

Exercise 23-12
Budgeted cash receipts
P1

Emily Company has sales on account and for cash. Specifically, 60% of its sales are on account and 40% are for cash. Credit sales are collected in full in the month following the sale. The company forecasts sales of $525,000 for April, $535,000 for May, and $560,000 for June. The beginning balance of Accounts Receivable is $300,000 on April 1. Prepare a schedule of budgeted cash receipts for April, May, and June.

Exercise 23-13
Cash budget
P1

Kaizen Corp. requires a minimum $8,000 cash balance. If necessary, loans are taken to meet this requirement at a cost of 1% interest per month (paid monthly). Any excess cash is used to repay loans at month-end. The cash balance on July 1 is $8,400 and the company has no outstanding loans. Forecasted cash receipts (other than for loans received) and forecasted cash payments (other than for loan or interest payments) are:

	July	August	September
Cash receipts	$24,000	$32,000	$40,000
Cash disbursements	28,000	30,000	32,000

Prepare a cash budget for July, August, and September. Round interest payments to the nearest whole dollar.

Fabrice Corp. requires a minimum $6,000 cash balance. If necessary, loans are taken to meet this requirement at a cost of 1% interest per month (paid monthly). Any excess cash is used to repay loans at monthend. The cash balance on October 1 is $6,000 and the company has an outstanding loan of $2,000. Forecasted cash receipts (other than for loans received) and forecasted cash payments (other than for loan or interest payments) follow. Prepare a cash budget for October, November, and December. Round interest payments to the nearest whole dollar.

Exercise 23-14
Cash budget
P1

	October	November	December
Cash receipts	$22,000	$16,000	$20,000
Cash disbursements	24,000	15,000	16,000

Cambridge, Inc. is preparing its master budget for the quarter ended June 30. Budgeted sales and cash payments for merchandise for the next three months follow:

Exercise 23-15
Cash budget
P1

	April	May	June
Budgeted sales	$32,000	$40,000	$24,000
Budgeted cash payments for merchandise...................	20,200	16,800	17,200

Sales are 60% cash and 40% on credit. All credit sales are collected in the month following the sale. The March 30 statement of financial position includes balances of $12,000 in cash, $12,000 in accounts receivable, $11,000 in accounts payable, and a $2,000 balance in loans payable. A minimum cash balance of $12,000 is required. Loans are obtained at the end of any month when a cash shortage occurs. Interest is 1% per month based on the beginning of the month loan balance and is paid at each month-end. If an excess balance of cash exists, loans are repaid at the end of the month. Operating expenses are paid in the month incurred and consist of sales commissions (10% of sales), shipping (3% of sales), office salaries ($3,000 per month) and rent ($5,000 per month). Prepare a cash budget for each of the months of April, May, and June (round all dollar amounts to the nearest whole dollar).

Kool-Ray is preparing its master budget for the quarter ended September 30. Budgeted sales and cash payments for merchandise for the next three months follow:

Exercise 23-16
Cash budget
P1

	July	August	September
Budgeted sales	$64,000	$80,000	$48,000
Budgeted cash payments for merchandise...................	40,400	33,600	34,400

Sales are 20% cash and 80% on credit. All credit sales are collected in the month following the sale. The June 30 statement of financial position includes balances of $12,000 in cash; $45,000 in accounts receivable; $4,500 in accounts payable; and a $2,000 balance in loans payable. A minimum cash balance of $12,000 is required. Loans are obtained at the end of any month when a cash shortage occurs. Interest is 1% per month based on the beginning of the month loan balance and is paid at each month-end. If an excess balance of cash exists, loans are repaid at the end of the month. Operating expenses are paid in the month incurred and consist of sales commissions (10% of sales), office salaries ($4,000 per month), and rent ($6,500 per month). (1) Prepare a cash receipts budget for July, August, and September. (2) Prepare a cash budget for each of the months of July, August, and September. (Round all dollar amounts to the nearest whole dollar.)

Exercise 23-17
Budgeted statement of financial position
P2

The following information is available for Zhao Company:

a. The cash budget for March shows an ending bank loan of $10,000 and an ending cash balance of $48,000.

b. The sales budget for March indicates sales of $120,000. Accounts receivable are expected to be 70% of the current-month sales.

c. The merchandise purchases budget indicates that $89,000 in merchandise will be purchased on account in March. Purchases on account are paid 100% in the month following the purchase. Ending inventory for March is predicted to be 600 units at a cost of $35 each.

d. The budgeted income statement for March shows net profit of $48,000. Depreciation expense of $1,000 and $26,000 in income tax expense were used in computing net profit for March. Accrued taxes will be paid in April.

e. The statement of financial position for February shows equipment of $84,000 with accumulated depreciation of $30,000, ordinary shares of $25,000, and ending retained earnings of $8,000. There are no changes budgeted in the equipment or ordinary shares accounts.

Prepare a budgeted statement of financial position for March.

Exercise 23-18
Budgeted income statement
P2

Zulu, Inc., is preparing its master budget for the first quarter. The company sells a single product at a price of $25 per unit. Sales (in units) are forecasted at 40,000 for January, 60,000 for February, and 50,000 for March. Cost of goods sold is $14 per unit. Other expense information for the first quarter follows. Prepare a budgeted income statement for this first quarter.

Commissions	10% of sales
Rent	$20,000 per month
Advertising	15% of sales
Office salaries	$75,000 per month
Depreciation	$50,000 per month
Interest	15% annually on a $250,000 note payable
Tax rate	40%

Exercise 23-19[A]
Direct labor budget
P3

The production budget for Zink Company shows units to be produced as follows: July, 620; August, 680; September, 540. Each unit produced requires two hours of direct labor. The direct labor rate is currently $16 per hour but is predicted to be $16.75 per hour in September. Prepare a direct labor budget for the months July, August, and September.

Exercise 23-20[A]
Production budget
P3

Rad Co. provides the following sales forecast for the next four months:

	April	May	June	July
Sales (units)	500	580	530	600

The company wants to end each month with ending finished goods inventory equal to 20% of next month's sales. Finished goods inventory on April 1 is 174 units. Assume July's budgeted production is 540 units. Prepare a production budget for the months of April, May, and June.

Exercise 23-21[A]
Direct materials budget
P3

Refer to the information in Exercise 23-20[A]. In addition, assume each finished unit requires five pounds of raw materials and the company wants to end each month with raw materials inventory equal to 30% of next month's production needs. Beginning raw materials inventory for April was 663 pounds.

Prepare a direct materials budget for April, May, and June.

Match the definitions 1 through 9 with the term or phrase a through i.

A. Master budget

B. General and administrative expense budget

C. Budget

D. Safety stock

E. Budgeted income statement

F. Budgeted statement of financial position

G. Sales budget

H. Cash budget

I. Merchandise purchases budget

_____ **1.** A plan that shows the units or costs of merchandise to be purchased by a merchandising company during the budget period.

_____ **2.** An accounting report that presents predicted amounts of the company's assets, liabilities, and equity balances at the end of the budget period.

_____ **3.** A plan showing the units of goods to be sold and the sales to be derived; the usual starting point in the budgeting process.

_____ **4.** An accounting report that presents predicted amounts of the company's revenues and expenses for the budgeting period.

_____ **5.** A quantity of inventory or materials over the minimum to reduce the risk of running short.

_____ **6.** A comprehensive business plan that includes specific plans for expected sales, the units of product to be produced, the merchandise or materials to be purchased, the expenses to be incurred, the long-term assets to be purchased, and the amounts of cash to be borrowed or loans to be repaid, as well as a budgeted income statement and statement of financial position.

_____ **7.** A formal statement of a company's future plans, usually expressed in monetary terms.

_____ **8.** A plan that shows predicted operating expenses not included in the selling expenses budget.

_____ **9.** A plan that shows the expected cash inflows and cash outflows during the budget period, including receipts from any loans needed to maintain a minimum cash balance and repayments of such loans.

Exercise 23-22
Master budget definitions
C2

Participatory budgeting can sometimes lead to negative consequences. Identify three potential negative outcomes that can arise from participatory budgeting.

Exercise 23-23
Budget consequences C1

Kirk Co. CPA is preparing activity-based budgets for 2011. The partners expect the firm to generate billable hours for the year as follows:

Data entry	1,100 hours
Auditing	2,400 hours
Tax	2,150 hours
Consulting	375 hours

The company pays $8 per hour to data-entry clerks, $40 per hour to audit personnel, $50 per hour to tax personnel, and $50 per hour to consulting personnel. Prepare a schedule of budgeted labor costs for 2011 using activity-based budgeting.

Exercise 23-24
Activity-based budgeting
A1

connect

Pinsetter's Supply is a merchandiser of three different products. The company's February 28 inventories are footwear, 15,500 units; sports equipment, 70,000 units; and apparel, 40,000 units. Management believes that excessive inventories have accumulated for all three products. As a result, a new policy dictates that ending inventory in any month should equal 40% of the expected unit sales for the following month. Expected sales in units for March, April, May, and June follow.

	Budgeted Sales in Units			
	March	April	May	June
Footwear	10,000	20,000	30,000	33,000
Sports equipment	66,000	85,000	90,000	80,000
Apparel	36,000	30,000	30,000	18,000

PROBLEM SET A

Problem 23-1A
Preparation and analysis of merchandise purchases budgets

C2 P1

www.mheducation.asia/olc/wildkwokFAP

Required

1. Prepare a merchandise purchases budget (in units) for each product for each of the months of March, April, and May.

Analysis Component

2. The purchases budgets in part 1 should reflect fewer purchases of all three products in March compared to those in April and May. What factor caused fewer purchases to be planned? Suggest business conditions that would cause this factor to both occur and impact the company in this way.

Problem 23-2A
Preparation of cash budgets (for three periods)

C2   P2

www.mheducation.asia/olc/wildkwokFAP

During the last week of August, Apache Arts Company's owner approaches the bank for an $80,000 loan to be made on September 2 and repaid on November 30 with annual interest of 12%, for an interest cost of $2,400. The owner plans to increase the store's inventory by $60,000 during September and needs the loan to pay for inventory acquisitions. The bank's loan officer needs more information about Apache Arts' ability to repay the loan and asks the owner to forecast the store's November 30 cash position. On September 1, Apache Arts is expected to have a $3,000 cash balance, $135,000 of accounts receivable, and $100,000 of accounts payable. Its budgeted sales, merchandise purchases, and various cash disbursements for the next three months follow.

Budgeted Figures*	September	October	November
Sales	$220,000	$300,000	$380,000
Merchandise purchases	210,000	180,000	220,000
Cash disbursements			
Payroll	16,000	17,000	18,000
Rent	6,000	6,000	6,000
Other cash expenses	64,000	8,000	7,000
Repayment of bank loan			80,000
Interest on the bank loan			2,400

* Operations began in August; August sales were $180,000 and purchases were $100,000.

The budgeted September merchandise purchases include the inventory increase. All sales are on account. The company predicts that 25% of credit sales is collected in the month of the sale, 45% in the month following the sale, 20% in the second month, 9% in the third, and the remainder is uncollectible. Applying these percents to the August credit sales, for example, shows that $81,000 of the $180,000 will be collected in September, $36,000 in October, and $16,200 in November. All merchandise is purchased on credit; 80% of the balance is paid in the month following a purchase, and the remaining 20% is paid in the second month. For example, of the $100,000 August purchases, $80,000 will be paid in September and $20,000 in October.

Required

Prepare a cash budget for September, October, and November for Apache Arts Company. Show supporting calculations as needed.

Problem 23-3A
Preparation and analysis of cash budgets with supporting inventory and purchases budgets

C2   P2

Abacus Company sells its product for $125 per unit. Its actual and projected sales follow.

	Units	Dollars
April (actual)	8,000	$1,000,000
May (actual)	4,000	500,000
June (budgeted)	12,000	1,500,000
July (budgeted)...........	6,000	750,000
August (budgeted)	7,600	950,000

All sales are on credit. Recent experience shows that 20% of credit sales is collected in the month of the sale, 30% in the month after the sale, 48% in the second month after the sale, and 2% proves to be uncollectible. The product's purchase price is $100 per unit. All purchases are payable within 12 days. Thus, 60% of purchases made in a month is paid in that month and the other 40% is paid in the next month. The company has a policy to maintain an ending monthly inventory of 25% of the next month's unit sales plus a safety stock of 100 units. The April 30 and May 31 actual inventory levels are consistent with this policy. Selling and administrative expenses for the year are $1,200,000 and are paid evenly throughout the year in cash. The company's minimum cash balance at month-end is $60,000. This minimum is maintained, if necessary, by borrowing cash from the bank. If the balance exceeds $60,000, the company repays as much of the loan as it can without going below the minimum. This type of loan carries an annual 9% interest rate. On May 31, the loan balance is $32,000, and the company's cash balance is $60,000.

Required

1. Prepare a table that shows the computation of cash collections of its credit sales (accounts receivable) in each of the months of June and July.

2. Prepare a table that shows the computation of budgeted ending inventories (in units) for April, May, June, and July.

3. Prepare the merchandise purchases budget for May, June, and July. Report calculations in units and then show the dollar amount of purchases for each month.

4. Prepare a table showing the computation of cash payments on product purchases for June and July.

5. Prepare a cash budget for June and July, including any loan activity and interest expense. Compute the loan balance at the end of each month.

Analysis Component

6. Refer to your answer to part 5. Abacus's cash budget indicates the company will need to borrow more than $40,000 in June and will need to borrow $60,000 in July. Suggest some reasons that knowing this information in May would be helpful to management.

Check (1) Cash collections: June, $930,000; July, $840,000

(3) Budgeted purchases: May, $600,000; June, $1,050,000

(5) Budgeted ending loan balance: June, $72,240; July, $136,782

Lilliput, a one-product mail-order firm, buys its product for $60 per unit and sells it for $130 per unit. The sales staff receives a 10% commission on the sale of each unit. Its December income statement follows.

Problem 23-4A
Preparation and analysis of budgeted income statements

C2 P2

LILLIPUT COMPANY	
Income Statement	
For Month Ended December 31, 2011	
Sales	$1,300,000
Cost of goods sold	600,000
Gross profit	700,000
Expenses	
Sales commissions (10%)	(130,000)
Advertising	(200,000)
Store rent	(24,000)
Administrative salaries	(40,000)
Depreciation	(50,000)
Other expenses	(12,000)
Total expenses	(456,000)
Net profit	$ 244,000

Management expects December's results to be repeated in January, February, and March of 2012 without any changes in strategy. Management, however, has an alternative plan. It believes that unit sales will increase at a rate of 10% *each* month for the next three months (beginning with January) if the item's selling price is reduced to $115 per unit and advertising expenses are increased by 25% and remain at that level for all three months. The cost of its product will remain at $60 per unit, the sales staff will continue to earn a 10% commission, and the remaining expenses will stay the same.

Required

1. Prepare budgeted income statements for each of the months of January, February, and March that show the expected results from implementing the proposed changes. Use a three-column format, with one column for each month.

Check (1) Budgeted net profit: January, $102,500; February, $150,350; March, $202,985

Analysis Component

2. Use the budgeted income statements from part 1 to recommend whether management should implement the proposed changes. Explain.

Problem 23-5A
Preparation of a complete
master budget

C2 P1 P2

Near the end of 2011, the management of Simid Sports Co., a merchandising company, prepared the following estimated statement of financial position for December 31, 2011.

SIMID SPORTS COMPANY
Estimated Statement of Financial Position
December 31, 2011

Assets		
Cash		$ 18,000
Accounts receivable		262,500
Inventory		75,000
Total current assets		355,500
Equipment	$270,000	
Less accumulated depreciation	33,750	236,250
Total assets		$591,750

Liabilities and Equity		
Accounts payable	$180,000	
Bank loan payable	7,500	
Taxes payable (due 3/15/2012)	45,000	
Total liabilities		$232,500
Share capital—ordinary	236,250	
Retained earnings	123,000	
Total shareholders' equity		359,250
Total liabilities and equity		$591,750

To prepare a master budget for January, February, and March of 2012, management gathers the following information.

a. Simid Sports' single product is purchased for $30 per unit and resold for $55 per unit. The expected inventory level of 2,500 units on December 31, 2011, is more than management's desired level for 2012, which is 20% of the next month's expected sales (in units). Expected sales are: January, 3,500 units; February, 4,500 units; March, 5,500 units; and April, 5,000 units.

b. Cash sales and credit sales represent 25% and 75%, respectively, of total sales. Of the credit sales, 60% is collected in the first month after the month of sale and 40% in the second month after the month of sale. For the December 31, 2011, accounts receivable balance, $62,500 is collected in January and the remaining $200,000 is collected in February.

c. Merchandise purchases are paid for as follows: 20% in the first month after the month of purchase and 80% in the second month after the month of purchase. For the December 31, 2011, accounts payable balance, $40,000 is paid in January and the remaining $140,000 is paid in February.

d. Sales commissions equal to 20% of sales are paid each month. Sales salaries (excluding commissions) are $30,000 per year.

e. General and administrative salaries are $72,000 per year. Maintenance expense equals $1,000 per month and is paid in cash.

f. Equipment reported in the December 31, 2011, statement of financial position was purchased in January 2011. It is being depreciated over eight years under the straight-line method with no residual value. The following amounts for new equipment purchases are planned in the coming quarter: January, $18,000; February, $48,000; and March, $14,400. This equipment will be depreciated under the straight-line method over eight years with no residual value. A full month's depreciation is taken for the month in which equipment is purchased.

g. The company plans to acquire land at the end of March at a cost of $75,000, which will be paid with cash on the last day of the month.

h. Simid Sports has a working arrangement with its bank to obtain additional loans as needed. The interest rate is 12% per year, and interest is paid at each month-end based on the beginning balance. Partial or full payments on these loans can be made on the last day of the month. The company has agreed to maintain a minimum ending cash balance of $12,500 in each month.

i. The income tax rate for the company is 40%. Income taxes on the first quarter's income will not be paid until April 15.

Required

Prepare a master budget for each of the first three months of 2012; include the following component budgets (show supporting calculations as needed, and round amounts to the nearest dollar):

1. Monthly sales budgets (showing both budgeted unit sales and dollar sales).
2. Monthly merchandise purchases budgets.
3. Monthly selling expense budgets.
4. Monthly general and administrative expense budgets.
5. Monthly capital expenditures budgets.
6. Monthly cash budgets.
7. Budgeted income statement for the entire first quarter (not for each month).
8. Budgeted statement of financial position as at March 31, 2012.

Check   (2) Budgeted purchases: January, $57,000; February, $141,000
(3) Budgeted selling expenses: January, $41,000; February, $52,000
(6) Ending cash bal.: January, $15,050; February, $105,150
(8) Budgeted total assets at March 31, $784,325

Diamond Slope Company produces snow skis. Each ski requires 2 pounds of carbon fiber. The company's management predicts that 7,000 skis and 10,000 pounds of carbon fiber will be in inventory on June 30 of the current year and that 120,000 skis will be sold during the next (third) quarter. Management wants to end the third quarter with 4,000 skis and 5,000 pounds of carbon fiber in inventory. Carbon fiber can be purchased for $12 per pound.

Problem 23-6A[A]
Preparing production and direct materials budgets

C2 P3

Required

1. Prepare the third-quarter production budget for skis.
2. Prepare the third-quarter direct materials (carbon fiber) budget; include the dollar cost of purchases.

Check   (1) Units manuf., 117,000;
(2) Cost of carbon fiber purchases, $2,748,000

H20 Company is a merchandiser of three different products. The company's March 31 inventories are water skis, 40,000 units; tow ropes, 90,000 units; and life jackets, 250,000 units. Management believes that excessive inventories have accumulated for all three products. As a result, a new policy dictates that ending inventory in any month should equal 10% of the expected unit sales for the following month. Expected sales in units for April, May, June, and July follow.

PROBLEM SET B

Problem 23-1B
Preparation and analysis of merchandise purchases budgets

C2 P1

Budgeted Sales in Units			
	April	May	June	July
Water skis	70,000	90,000	130,000	140,000
Tow ropes	100,000	90,000	110,000	100,000
Life jackets	300,000	260,000	310,000	260,000

Required

1. Prepare a merchandise purchases budget (in units) for each product for each of the months of April, May, and June.

Check   (1) April budgeted purchases: Water skis, 39,000; Tow ropes, 19,000; Life jackets, 76,000

Analysis Component

2. The purchases budgets in part 1 should reflect fewer purchases of all three products in April compared to those in May and June. What factor caused fewer purchases to be planned? Suggest business conditions that would cause this factor to both occur and affect the company as it has.

During the last week of March, Siro Stereo's owner approaches the bank for a $125,000 loan to be made on April 1 and repaid on June 30 with annual interest of 10%, for an interest cost of $3,125. The owner plans to increase the store's inventory by $100,000 in April and needs the loan to pay for inventory acquisitions. The bank's loan officer needs more information about Siro Stereo's ability to repay the loan and asks the owner to forecast the store's June 30 cash position. On April 1, Siro Stereo is expected to have a $12,000 cash balance, $121,500 of accounts receivable, and $90,000 of accounts

Problem 23-2B
Preparation of cash budgets (for three periods)

C2 P2

payable. Its budgeted sales, merchandise purchases, and various cash disbursements for the next three months follow.

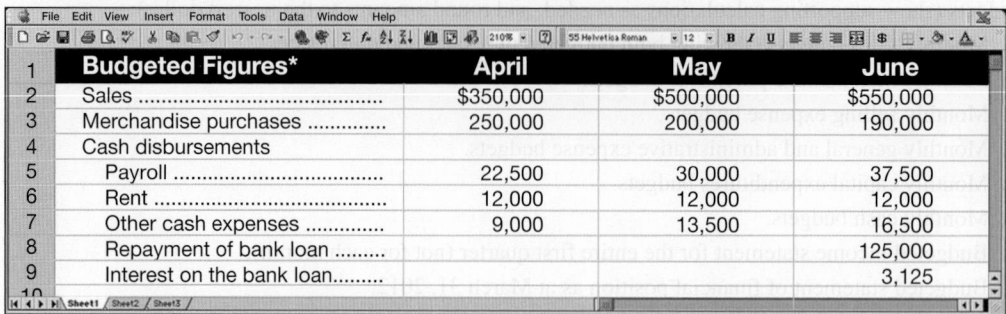

Budgeted Figures*	April	May	June
1			
2 Sales	$350,000	$500,000	$550,000
3 Merchandise purchases	250,000	200,000	190,000
4 Cash disbursements			
5 Payroll	22,500	30,000	37,500
6 Rent	12,000	12,000	12,000
7 Other cash expenses	9,000	13,500	16,500
8 Repayment of bank loan			125,000
9 Interest on the bank loan.........			3,125
10			

*Operations began in March; March sales were $135,000 and purchases were $90,000.

The budgeted April merchandise purchases include the inventory increase. All sales are on account. The company predicts that 10% of credit sales is collected in the month of the sale, 60% in the month following the sale, 25% in the second month, 3% in the third, and the remainder is uncollectible. Applying these percents to the March credit sales, for example, shows that $81,000 of the $135,000 will be collected in April, $33,750 in May, and $4,050 in June. All merchandise is purchased on credit; 80% of the balance is paid in the month following a purchase and the remaining 20% is paid in the second month. For example, of the $90,000 March purchases, $72,000 will be paid in April and $18,000 in May.

Check Budgeted cash balance: April, $137,500; May, $157,750; June, $200,175

Required

Prepare a cash budget for April, May, and June for Siro Stereo. Show supporting calculations as needed.

Problem 23-3B
Preparation and analysis of cash budgets with supporting inventory and purchases budgets

C2 P2

LaRocca Company sells its product for $20 per unit. Its actual and projected sales follow.

	Units	Dollars
January (actual)	18,000	$360,000
February (actual)	27,000	540,000
March (budgeted)	15,000	300,000
April (budgeted)	27,000	540,000
May (budgeted)	33,000	660,000

All sales are on credit. Recent experience shows that 40% of credit sales is collected in the month of the sale, 30% in the month after the sale, 25% in the second month after the sale, and 5% proves to be uncollectible. The product's purchase price is $12 per unit. All purchases are payable within 21 days. Thus, 30% of purchases made in a month is paid in that month and the other 70% is paid in the next month. The company has a policy to maintain an ending monthly inventory of 30% of the next month's unit sales plus a safety stock of 300 units. The January 31 and February 28 actual inventory levels are consistent with this policy. Selling and administrative expenses for the year are $1,440,000 and are paid evenly throughout the year in cash. The company's minimum cash balance for month-end is $45,000. This minimum is maintained, if necessary, by borrowing cash from the bank. If the balance exceeds $45,000, the company repays as much of the loan as it can without going below the minimum. This type of loan carries an annual 12% interest rate. At February 28, the loan balance is $12,000, and the company's cash balance is $45,000.

Required

Check (1) Cash collections: March, $372,000; April, $441,000

1. Prepare a table that shows the computation of cash collections of its credit sales (accounts receivable) in each of the months of March and April.

2. Prepare a table showing the computations of budgeted ending inventories (units) for January, February, March, and April.

(3) Budgeted purchases: February, $280,800; March, $223,200

3. Prepare the merchandise purchases budget for February, March, and April. Report calculations in units and then show the dollar amount of purchases for each month.

4. Prepare a table showing the computation of cash payments on product purchases for March and April.

(5) Ending cash balance: March, $45,000, April, $82,204

5. Prepare a cash budget for March and April, including any loan activity and interest expense. Compute the loan balance at the end of each month.

Analysis Component

6. Refer to your answer to part 5. LaRocca's cash budget indicates whether the company must borrow additional funds at the end of March. Suggest some reasons that knowing the loan needs in advance would be helpful to management.

Computa-Cations buys its product for $20 and sells it for $50 per unit. The sales staff receives a 10% commission on the sale of each unit. Its June income statement follows.

Problem 23-4B
Preparation and analysis of budgeted income statements

C2   P2

COMPUTA-CATIONS COMPANY
Income Statement
For Month Ended June 30, 2011

Sales	$1,000,000
Cost of goods sold	400,000
Gross profit	600,000
Expenses	
Sales commissions (10%)	(100,000)
Advertising	(100,000)
Store rent	(10,000)
Administrative salaries	(20,000)
Depreciation	(12,000)
Other expenses	(24,000)
Total expenses	(266,000)
Net profit	$ 334,000

Management expects June's results to be repeated in July, August, and September without any changes in strategy. Management, however, has another plan. It believes that unit sales will increase at a rate of 10% *each* month for the next three months (beginning with July) if the item's selling price is reduced to $45 per unit and advertising expenses are increased by 20% and remain at that level for all three months. The cost of its product will remain at $20 per unit, the sales staff will continue to earn a 10% commission, and the remaining expenses will stay the same.

Required

1. Prepare budgeted income statements for each of the months of July, August, and September that show the expected results from implementing the proposed changes. Use a three-column format, with one column for each month.

Check   Budgeted net profit:
July, $265,000; August, $310,100;
September, $359,710

Analysis Component

2. Use the budgeted income statements from part 1 to recommend whether management should implement the proposed plan. Explain.

Near the end of 2011, the management of Oasis Corp., a merchandising company, prepared the following estimated statement of financial position for December 31, 2011.

Problem 23-5B
Preparation of a complete master budget

C2   P1   P2

OASIS CORPORATION
Estimated Statement of Financial Position
December 31, 2011

Assets		
Cash		$ 160,000
Accounts receivable		400,000
Inventory		180,000
Total current assets		740,000
Equipment	$1,200,000	
Less accumulated depreciation	120,000	1,080,000
Total assets		$1,820,000

[continued on next page]

[continued from previous page]

Liabilities and Equity		
Accounts payable	$ 300,000	
Bank loan payable	20,000	
Taxes payable (due 3/15/2012)	200,000	
Total liabilities		$ 520,000
Share capital—ordinary	1,500,000	
Retained earnings	(200,000)	
Total shareholders' equity		1,300,000
Total liabilities and equity		$1,820,000

To prepare a master budget for January, February, and March of 2012, management gathers the following information.

a. Oasis Corp.'s single product is purchased for $10 per unit and resold for $24 per unit. The expected inventory level of 18,000 units on December 31, 2011, is more than management's desired level for 2012, which is 40% of the next month's expected sales (in units). Expected sales are: January, 30,000 units; February, 24,000 units; March, 40,000 units; and April, 50,000 units.

b. Cash sales and credit sales represent 40% and 60%, respectively, of total sales. Of the credit sales, 70% is collected in the first month after the month of sale and 30% in the second month after the month of sale. For the $400,000 accounts receivable balance at December 31, 2011, $280,000 is collected in January 2012 and the remaining $120,000 is collected in February 2012.

c. Merchandise purchases are paid for as follows: 80% in the first month after the month of purchase and 20% in the second month after the month of purchase. For the $300,000 accounts payable balance at December 31, 2011, $240,000 is paid in January 2012 and the remaining $60,000 is paid in February 2012.

d. Sales commissions equal to 10% of sales are paid each month. Sales salaries (excluding commissions) are $288,000 per year.

e. General and administrative salaries are $336,000 per year. Maintenance expense equals $6,000 per month and is paid in cash.

f. Equipment reported in the December 31, 2011, statement of financial position was purchased in January 2011. It is being depreciated over 10 years under the straight-line method with no residual value. The following amounts for new equipment purchases are planned in the coming quarter: January, $240,000; February, $120,000; and March, $96,000. This equipment will be depreciated using the straight-line method over 10 years with no residual value. A full month's depreciation is taken for the month in which equipment is purchased.

g. The company plans to acquire land at the end of March at a cost of $232,000, which will be paid with cash on the last day of the month.

h. Oasis Corp. has a working arrangement with its bank to obtain additional loans as needed. The interest rate is 12% per year, and interest is paid at each month-end based on the beginning balance. Partial or full payments on these loans can be made on the last day of the month. Oasis has agreed to maintain a minimum ending cash balance of $160,000 in each month.

i. The income tax rate for the company is 30%. Income taxes on the first quarter's income will not be paid until April 15.

Required

Prepare a master budget for each of the first three months of 2012; include the following component budgets (show supporting calculations as needed, and round amounts to the nearest dollar):

1. Monthly sales budgets (showing both budgeted unit sales and dollar sales).

2. Monthly merchandise purchases budgets.

3. Monthly selling expense budgets.

4. Monthly general and administrative expense budgets.

5. Monthly capital expenditures budgets.

6. Monthly cash budgets.

Check   (2) Budgeted purchases: January, $216,000; February, $304,000;

(3) Budgeted selling expenses: January, $96,000; February, $81,600

(6) Ending cash bal.: January, $160,000; February, $281,578

7. Budgeted income statement for the entire first quarter (not for each month).

8. Budgeted statement of financial position as at March 31, 2012.

(8) Budgeted total assets at March 31, $2,768,880

RBI Company produces baseball bats. Each bat requires 4 pounds of aluminum alloy. Management predicts that 10,000 bats and 28,000 pounds of aluminum alloy will be in inventory on March 31 of the current year and that 100,000 bats will be sold during this year's second quarter. Management wants to end the second quarter with 3,000 finished bats and 2,000 pounds of aluminum alloy in inventory. Aluminum alloy can be purchased for $3 per pound.

Problem 23-6B[A]

Preparing production and direct materials budgets

C2 P3

Required

1. Prepare the second-quarter production budget for bats.

2. Prepare the second-quarter direct materials (aluminum alloy) budget; include the dollar cost of purchases.

Check (1) Units manuf., 93,000;
(2) Cost of aluminum purchases, $1,038,000

(This serial problem began in Chapter 1 and continues through most of the book. If previous chapter segments were not completed, the serial problem can begin at this point.)

SERIAL PROBLEM

Business Solutions

P2

SP 23 Santana Rey expects second quarter 2012 sales of her new line of computer furniture to be the same as the first quarter's sales (reported below) without any changes in strategy. Monthly sales averaged 40 desk units (sales price of $1,250) and 20 chairs (sales price of $500).

BUSINESS SOLUTIONS
Segment Income Statement*
For Quarter Ended March 31, 2012

Sales[†]	$180,000
Cost of goods sold[‡]	115,000
Gross profit	65,000
Expenses	
Sales commissions (10%)	(18,000)
Advertising expenses	(9,000)
Other fixed expenses	(18,000)
Total expenses	(45,000)
Net profit	$ 20,000

* Reflects revenue and expense activity only related to the computer furniture segment.

[†] Revenue: (120 desks × $1,250) + (60 chairs × $500) = $150,000 + $30,000 = $180,000

[‡] Cost of goods sold: (120 desks × $750) + (60 chairs × $250) + $10,000 = $115,000

Santana Rey believes that sales will increase each month for the next three months (April, 48 desks, 32 chairs; May, 52 desks, 35 chairs; June, 56 desks, 38 chairs) *if* selling prices are reduced to $1,150 for desks and $450 for chairs, and advertising expenses are increased by 10% and remain at that level for all three months. The products' variable cost will remain at $750 for desks and $250 for chairs. The sales staff will continue to earn a 10% commission, the fixed manufacturing costs per month will remain at $10,000 and other fixed expenses will remain at $6,000 per month.

Required

1. Prepare budgeted income statements for each of the months of April, May, and June that show the expected results from implementing the proposed changes. Use a three-column format, with one column for each month.

2. Use the budgeted income statements from part 1 to recommend whether Santana Rey should implement the proposed changes. Explain.

Check (1) Budgeted income (loss):
April, $(660); May, $945

Beyond the Numbers

REPORTING IN ACTION

P2

BTN 23-1 Financial statements often serve as a starting point in formulating budgets. Access **Research In Motion**'s 2010 annual report from its Website **www.rim.com**, and review its financial statements to determine its cash paid for acquisitions of property, plant and equipment in the current year and the budgeted cash needed for such acquisitions in the next year.

Required

1. Which financial statement reports the amount of cash paid for acquisitions of property, plant, and equipment? Explain where on the statement this information is reported.

2. Indicate the amount of cash (a) paid for acquisitions of property, plant, and equipment in the year ended February 27, 2010, and (b) to be paid (budgeted for) next year under the assumption that annual acquisitions of property, plant and equipment equal 60% of the prior year's net profit.

Fast Forward

3. Access Research In Motion's financial statements for a year ending after February 27, 2010, from its Website. Compare your answer for part 2 with actual cash paid for acquisitions of property, plant and equipment for that financial year. Compute the error, if any, in your estimate. Speculate as to why cash paid for acquisitions of property, plant and equipment was higher or lower than your estimate.

COMPARATIVE ANALYSIS

P2

BTN 23-2 One source of cash savings for a company is improved management of inventory. To illustrate, assume that **Research In Motion** and **Apple** both have $200,000 per month in sales of one model of handheld devices in Canada, and both forecast this level of sales per month for the next 24 months. Also assume that both Research In Motion and Apple have a 20% contribution margin and equal fixed costs, and that cost of goods sold is the only variable cost. Assume that the main difference between Research In Motion and Apple is the distribution system. Research In Motion uses a just-in-time system and requires ending inventory of only 10% of next month's sales in inventory at each month-end. However, Apple is building an improved distribution system and currently requires 40% of next month's sales in inventory at each month-end.

Required

1. Compute the amount by which Apple can reduce its inventory level if it can match Research In Motion's system of maintaining an inventory equal to 10% of next month's sales. (*Hint:* Focus on the facts given and only on the Canada area.)

2. Explain how the analysis in part 1 that shows ending inventory levels for both the 40% and 10% required inventory policies can help justify a just-in-time inventory system. You can assume a 15% interest cost for resources that are tied up in ending inventory.

ETHICS CHALLENGE

C1

BTN 23-3 Both the budget process and budgets themselves can impact management actions, both positively and negatively. For instance, a common practice among not-for-profit organizations and government agencies is for management to spend any amounts remaining in a budget at the end of the budget period, a practice often called "use it or lose it." The view is that if a department manager does not spend the budgeted amount, top management will reduce next year's budget by the amount not spent. To avoid losing budget dollars, department managers often spend all budgeted amounts regardless of the value added to products or services. All of us pay for the costs associated with this budget system.

Required

Write a one-half page report to a local not-for-profit organization or government agency offering a solution to the "use it or lose it" budgeting problem.

COMMUNICATING IN PRACTICE

C2

BTN 23-4 The sales budget is usually the first and most crucial of the component budgets in a master budget because all other budgets usually rely on it for planning purposes.

Required

Assume that your company's sales staff provides information on expected sales and selling prices for items making up the sales budget. Prepare a one-page memorandum to your supervisor outlining concerns with the sales staff's input in the sales budget when its compensation is at least partly tied to these budgets. More generally, explain the importance of assessing any potential bias in information provided to the budget process.

BTN 23-5   Access information on e-budgets through The Manage Mentor: http://www.themanagementor.com/kuniverse/kmailers_universe/finance_kmailers/cfa/budgeting2.htm Read the information provided.

Required

1. Assume the role of a senior manager in a large, multidivision company. What are the benefits of using e-budgets?
2. As a senior manager, what concerns do you have with the concept and application of e-budgets?

BTN 23-6   Your team is to prepare a budget report outlining the costs of attending college (full-time) for the next two semesters (30 hours) or three quarters (45 hours). This budget's focus is solely on attending college; do not include personal items in the team's budget. Your budget must include tuition, books, supplies, club fees, food, housing, and all costs associated with travel to and from college. This budgeting exercise is similar to the initial phase in activity-based budgeting. Include a list of any assumptions you use in completing the budget. Be prepared to present your budget in class.

BTN 23-7   In the opening story, Esther of Cabela's says that a budget helps answer questions like "How can we increase the number of audits by 20% while keeping the total budget unchanged?"

Required

Explain how a budget can help answer Esther's question for her business.

BTN 23-8   Most companies begin their budgeting exercise with a forecast of sales. Sales, in turn, depend on a variety of factors, both internal and external to the company.

Required

Visit a local convenience store, for example, a 7-Eleven store. For a particular store (not the company as a whole) what are the factors likely to influence sales? Justify each factor.

BTN 23-9   View Adidas' target vs actual numbers at the following link: http://adidas-group.corporate-publications.com/2010/gb/en/additional-information/targets-vs-results.html.

Required

1. Link the targets to the various kinds of budgets such as sales budgets.
2. How does an investor in Adidas benefit from the targets, actual results, and outlook presentation?

ANSWERS TO MULTIPLE CHOICE QUIZ

1. c
2. e; Budgeted purchases = $36,000 + $7,000 − $6,000 = $37,000
3. b; Cash collected = 25% of September sales + 75% of August sales = (0.25 × $240,000) + (0.75 × $220,000) = $225,000
4. d
5. a; 560 units + (0.30 × 600 units) − (0.30 × 560 units) = 572 units

24

Flexible Budgets and Standard Costs

A Look Back

Chapter 23 explained the master budget and its component budgets as well as their usefulness for planning and monitoring company activities.

A Look at This Chapter

This chapter describes flexible budgets, variance analysis, and standard costs. It explains how each is used for purposes of better controlling and monitoring of business activities.

A Look Ahead

Chapter 25 focuses on capital budgeting decisions. It also explains and illustrates several procedures used in evaluating short-term managerial decisions.

Learning Objectives

CAP

CONCEPTUAL

C1 Define *standard costs* and explain how standard cost information is useful for management by exception. (p. 967)

C2 Describe variances and what they reveal about performance. (p. 969)

ANALYTICAL

A1 Analyze changes in sales from expected amounts. (p. 977)

PROCEDURAL

P1 Prepare a flexible budget and interpret a flexible budget performance report. (p. 964)

P2 Compute materials and labor variances. (p. 970)

P3 Compute overhead variances. (p. 974)

P4 *Appendix 24A*—Prepare journal entries for standard costs and account for price and quantity variances. (p. 984)

"Managing a dance studio allows me to share my passion for dancing."—**DERRICK LYE**

A Passion for Dance

Dreaming of dancing professionally? Or you just want to have a rock 'n' rolling good time? Perhaps you have two left feet and need someone to turn those awkward rheumatic steps into suave rhythmic moves? Meet at Mosaic Dance now!

The brainchild of Derrick Lye and Wee Tze Yi, **Mosaic Dance (www.mosaicdance.com.sg)** is a premium membership-based dance studio offering myriad get-your-body-moving classes ranging from sultry salsa and exotic rumba to Pilates and Stretch and Tone. "Mosaic Dance aims to promote dancing as a form of active and social lifestyle," says Derrick. Members pay a monthly membership fee for unlimited dance and fitness classes.

It takes two to tango, that's for sure, but for Derrick and Tze Yi, they didn't just waltz into Mosaic Dance without a few initial smart moves. "We started off with a marketing plan and a budget before raising funds," says Derrick. Looking for a dance studio alone took four months. In the meantime, they approached top dance instructors and other dance schools to offer classes at their dance studio. "Most of our marketing was done through social media networks due to its relevance and low cost of implementation," says Derrick.

Today, the duo's success rests partly on budgetary control. "Budgeting not Only encourages us to take a pragmatic approach to realize our company's marketing plan," asserts Derrick, "but it is also an effective tool for evaluating the performances of our marketing activities at meeting our sales pipeline and revenue target." Through budget reports that compare actual results to planned activities, for example, it was found that holding an open house performs better than conducting a road show as a promotional tool. Budgeting can also identify revenue gaps and thereby prompt additional marketing activities to address the discrepancies.

With only two persons running the show, the pair find it a challenge to plan and execute marketing activities while staying on top of day-to-day operations. But it's all worth it. "Managing a dance studio allows me to share my passion for dancing, fitness, and life with like-minded individuals," declares Derrick. "I feel pride and joy when members tell me that they love the concept and recommend it to their friends."

Budgeting helps organize and formalize management's planning activities. This chapter extends the study of budgeting to look more closely at the use of budgets to evaluate performance. Evaluations are important for controlling and monitoring business activities. This chapter also describes and illustrates the use of standard costs and variance analyses. These managerial tools are useful for both evaluating and controlling organizations and for the planning of future activities.

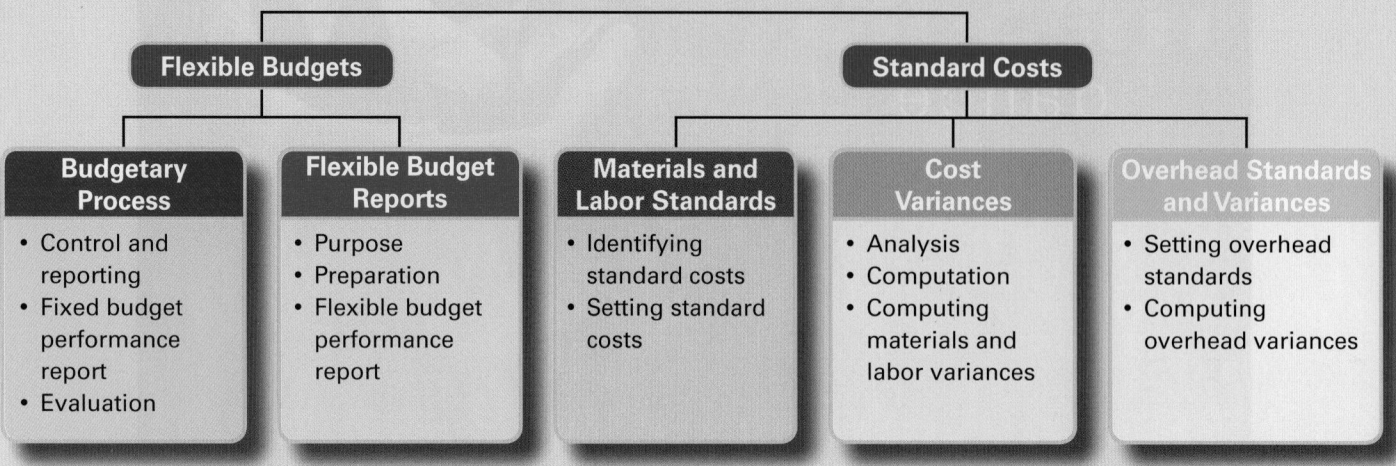

Flexible Budgets		Standard Costs		
Budgetary Process	**Flexible Budget Reports**	**Materials and Labor Standards**	**Cost Variances**	**Overhead Standards and Variances**
• Control and reporting • Fixed budget performance report • Evaluation	• Purpose • Preparation • Flexible budget performance report	• Identifying standard costs • Setting standard costs	• Analysis • Computation • Computing materials and labor variances	• Setting overhead standards • Computing overhead variances

Section 1—Flexible Budgets

This section introduces fixed budgets and fixed budget performance reports. It then introduces flexible budgets and flexible budget performance reports and illustrates their advantages.

BUDGETARY PROCESS

A master budget reflects management's planned objectives for a future period. The preparation of a master budget is based on a predicted level of activity such as sales volume for the budget period. This section discusses the effects on the usefulness of budget reports when the actual level of activity differs from the predicted level.

Budgetary Control and Reporting

Budgetary control refers to management's use of budgets to monitor and control a company's operations. This includes using budgets to see that planned objectives are met. **Budget reports** contain relevant information that compares actual results to planned activities. This comparison is motivated by a need to both monitor performance and control activities. Budget reports are sometimes viewed as progress reports, or *report cards,* on management's performance in achieving planned objectives. These reports can be prepared at any time and for any period. Three common periods for a budget report are a month, quarter, and year.

Point: Budget reports are often used to determine bonuses of managers.

The budgetary control process involves at least four steps: (1) develop the budget from planned objectives, (2) compare actual results to budgeted amounts and analyze any differences, (3) take corrective and strategic actions, and (4) establish new planned objectives and prepare a new budget. Exhibit 24.1 shows this continual process of budgetary control. Budget reports and

EXHIBIT 24.1

Process of Budgetary Control

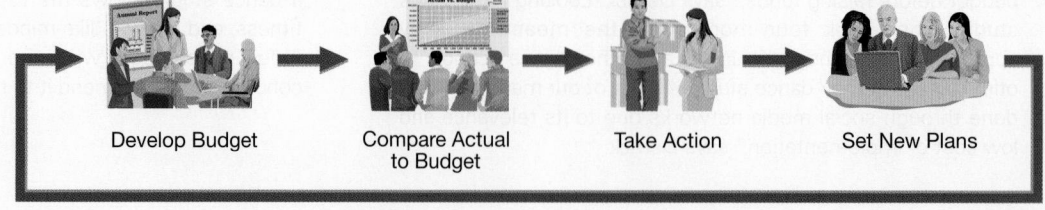

Develop Budget → Compare Actual to Budget → Take Action → Set New Plans

related documents are effective tools for managers to obtain the greatest benefits from this budgetary process.

Fixed Budget Performance Report

In a fixed budgetary control system, the master budget is based on a single prediction for sales volume or other activity level. The budgeted amount for each cost essentially assumes that a specific (or *fixed*) amount of sales will occur. A **fixed budget,** also called a *static budget,* is based on a single predicted amount of sales or other measure of activity.

One benefit of a budget is its usefulness in comparing actual results with planned activities. Information useful for analysis is often presented for comparison in a performance report. As shown in Exhibit 24.2, a **fixed budget performance report** for Optel compares actual results for January 2011 with the results expected under its fixed budget that predicted 10,000 (composite) units of sales. Optel manufactures inexpensive eyeglasses, frames, contact lens, and related supplies. For this report, its production volume equals sales volume (its inventory level did not change).

EXHIBIT 24.2

Fixed Budget Performance Report

OPTEL Fixed Budget Performance Report For Month Ended January 31, 2011	Fixed Budget	Actual Results	Variances*
Sales (in units)	10,000	12,000	
Sales (in dollars).........................	$100,000	$125,000	$25,000 F
Cost of goods sold			
Direct materials	10,000	13,000	3,000 U
Direct labor	15,000	20,000	5,000 U
Overhead			
Factory supplies	2,000	2,100	100 U
Utilities.............................	3,000	4,000	1,000 U
Depreciation—machinery..............	8,000	8,000	0
Supervisory salaries	11,000	11,000	0
Selling expenses			
Sales commissions	9,000	10,800	1,800 U
Shipping expenses	4,000	4,300	300 U
General and administrative expenses			
Office supplies	5,000	5,200	200 U
Insurance expenses	1,000	1,200	200 U
Depreciation—office equipment...........	7,000	7,000	0
Administrative salaries..................	13,000	13,000	0
Total expenses........................	88,000	99,600	11,600 U
Income from operations	$ 12,000	$ 25,400	$13,400 F

* F = Favorable variance; U = Unfavorable variance.

This type of performance report designates differences between budgeted and actual results as variances. We see the letters *F* and *U* located beside the numbers in the third number column of this report. Their meanings are as follows:

F = **Favorable variance**   When compared to budget, the actual cost or revenue contributes to a *higher* income. That is, actual revenue is higher than budgeted revenue, or actual cost is lower than budgeted cost.

U = **Unfavorable variance**   When compared to budget, the actual cost or revenue contributes to a *lower* income; actual revenue is lower than budgeted revenue, or actual cost is higher than budgeted cost.

This convention is common in practice and is used throughout this chapter.

Example: How is it that the favorable sales variance in Exhibit 24.2 is linked with so many unfavorable cost and expense variances? *Answer:* Costs have increased with the increase in sales.

Budget Reports for Evaluation

A primary use of budget reports is as a tool for management to monitor and control operations. Evaluation by Optel management is likely to focus on a variety of questions that might include these:

- Why is actual income from operations $13,400 higher than budgeted?
- Are amounts paid for each expense item too high?
- Is manufacturing using too much direct material?
- Is manufacturing using too much direct labor?

The performance report in Exhibit 24.2 provides little help in answering these questions because actual sales volume is 2,000 units higher than budgeted. A manager does not know if this higher level of sales activity is the cause of variations in total dollar sales and expenses or if other factors have influenced these amounts. This inability of fixed budget reports to adjust for changes in activity levels is a major limitation of a fixed budget performance report. That is, it fails to show whether actual costs are out of line due to a change in actual sales volume or some other factor.

Decision Insight

Green Budget Budget reporting and evaluation are used at the **Environmental Protection Agency (EPA)**. It regularly prepares performance plans and budget requests that describe performance goals, measure outcomes, and analyze variances. ∎

FLEXIBLE BUDGET REPORTS

Purpose of Flexible Budgets

To help address limitations with the fixed budget performance report, particularly from the effects of changes in sales volume, management can use a flexible budget. A **flexible budget,** also called a *variable budget,* is a report based on predicted amounts of revenues and expenses corresponding to the actual level of output. Flexible budgets are useful both before and after the period's activities are complete.

A flexible budget prepared before the period is often based on several levels of activity. Budgets for those different levels can provide a "what-if" look at operations. The different levels often include both a best case and worst case scenario. This allows management to make adjustments to avoid or lessen the effects of the worst case scenario.

A flexible budget prepared after the period helps management evaluate past performance. It is especially useful for such an evaluation because it reflects budgeted revenues and costs based on the actual level of activity. Thus, comparisons of actual results with budgeted performance are more likely to identify the causes of any differences. This can help managers focus attention on real problem areas and implement corrective actions. This is in contrast to a fixed budget, whose primary purpose is to assist managers in planning future activities and whose numbers are based on a single predicted amount of budgeted sales or production.

Point: A flexible budget yields an "apples to apples" comparison because budgeted activity levels are the same as the actual.

Preparation of Flexible Budgets

P1 Prepare a flexible budget and interpret a flexible budget performance report.

A flexible budget is designed to reveal the effects of volume of activity on revenues and costs. To prepare a flexible budget, management relies on the distinctions between fixed and variable costs. Recall that the cost per unit of activity remains constant for variable costs so that the total amount of a variable cost changes in direct proportion to a change in activity level. The total amount of fixed cost remains unchanged regardless of changes in the level of activity within a relevant (normal) operating range. (Assume that costs can be reasonably classified as variable or fixed within a relevant range.)

When we create the numbers constituting a flexible budget, we express each variable cost as either a constant amount per unit of sales or as a percent of a sales dollar. In the case of a fixed cost, we express its budgeted amount as the total amount expected to occur at any sales volume within the relevant range.

Exhibit 24.3 shows a set of flexible budgets for Optel for January 2011. Seven of its expenses are classified as variable costs. Its remaining five expenses are fixed costs. These classifications result from management's investigation of each expense. Variable and fixed expense categories are *not* the same for every company, and we must avoid drawing conclusions from specific cases. For example, depending on the nature of a company's operations, office supplies expense can be either fixed or variable with respect to sales.

Point: The usefulness of a flexible budget depends on valid classification of variable and fixed costs. Some costs are mixed and must be analyzed to determine their variable and fixed portions.

EXHIBIT 24.3

Flexible Budgets

	Flexible Budget		Flexible Budget for Unit Sales of 10,000	Flexible Budget for Unit Sales of 12,000	Flexible Budget for Unit Sales of 14,000
	Variable Amount per Unit	Total Fixed Cost			

OPTEL
Flexible Budgets
For Month Ended January 31, 2011

	Variable Amount per Unit	Total Fixed Cost	for Unit Sales of 10,000	for Unit Sales of 12,000	for Unit Sales of 14,000
Sales	$10.00		$100,000	$120,000	$140,000
Variable costs					
Direct materials	1.00		10,000	12,000	14,000
Direct labor	1.50		15,000	18,000	21,000
Factory supplies	0.20		2,000	2,400	2,800
Utilities	0.30		3,000	3,600	4,200
Sales commissions	0.90		9,000	10,800	12,600
Shipping expenses	0.40		4,000	4,800	5,600
Office supplies	0.50		5,000	6,000	7,000
Total variable costs	4.80		48,000	57,600	67,200
Contribution margin	$ 5.20		$ 52,000	$ 62,400	$ 72,800
Fixed costs					
Depreciation—machinery		$ 8,000	8,000	8,000	8,000
Supervisory salaries		11,000	11,000	11,000	11,000
Insurance expense		1,000	1,000	1,000	1,000
Depreciation—office equipment		7,000	7,000	7,000	7,000
Administrative salaries		13,000	13,000	13,000	13,000
Total fixed costs		$40,000	40,000	40,000	40,000
Income from operations			$ 12,000	$ 22,400	$ 32,800

The layout for the flexible budgets in Exhibit 24.3 follows a *contribution margin format*—beginning with sales followed by variable costs and then fixed costs. Both the expected individual and total variable costs are reported and then subtracted from sales. The difference between sales and variable costs equals contribution margin. The expected amounts of fixed costs are listed next, followed by the expected income from operations before taxes.

Example: Using Exhibit 24.3, what is the budgeted income from operations for unit sales of (a) 11,000 and (b) 13,000? *Answers:* $17,200 for unit sales of 11,000; $27,600 for unit sales of 13,000.

The first and second number columns of Exhibit 24.3 show the flexible budget amounts for variable costs per unit and each fixed cost for any volume of sales in the relevant range. The third, fourth, and fifth columns show the flexible budget amounts computed for three different sales volumes. For instance, the third column's flexible budget is based on 10,000 units. These numbers are the same as those in the fixed budget of Exhibit 24.2 because the expected volumes are the same for these two budgets.

Recall that Optel's actual sales volume for January is 12,000 units. This sales volume is 2,000 units more than the 10,000 units originally predicted in the master budget. When differences between actual and predicted volume arise, the usefulness of a flexible budget is apparent. For instance, compare the flexible budget for 10,000 units in the third column (which is the same as the fixed budget in Exhibit 24.2) with the flexible budget for 12,000 units in the fourth

Point: Flexible budgeting allows a budget to be prepared at the *actual* output level. Performance reports are then prepared comparing the flexible budget to actual revenues and costs.

column. The higher levels for both sales and variable costs reflect nothing more than the increase in sales activity. Any budget analysis comparing actual with planned results that ignores this information is less useful to management.

To illustrate, when we evaluate Optel's performance, we need to prepare a flexible budget showing actual and budgeted values at 12,000 units. As part of a complete profitability analysis, managers could compare the actual income of $25,400 (from Exhibit 24.2) with the $22,400 income expected at the actual sales volume of 12,000 units (from Exhibit 24.3). This results in a total favorable income variance of $3,000 to be explained and interpreted. This variance is markedly lower from the $13,400 favorable variance identified in Exhibit 24.2 using a fixed budget, but still suggests good performance. After receiving the flexible budget based on January's actual volume, management must determine what caused this $3,000 difference. The next section describes a flexible budget performance report that provides guidance in this analysis.

| **Decision Maker** | Answer — p. 986 |

Entrepreneur The heads of both the strategic consulting and tax consulting divisions of your financial services firm complain to you about the unfavorable variances on their performance reports. "We worked on more consulting assignments than planned. It's not surprising our costs are higher than expected. To top it off, this report characterizes our work as *poor!*" How do you respond? ∎

Flexible Budget Performance Report

A **flexible budget performance report** lists differences between actual performance and budgeted performance based on actual sales volume or other activity level. This report helps direct management's attention to those costs or revenues that differ substantially from budgeted amounts. Exhibit 24.4 shows Optel's flexible budget performance report for January. We prepare this report after the actual volume is known to be 12,000 units. This report shows a $5,000 favorable variance in total dollar sales. Because actual and budgeted volumes are both 12,000 units, the $5,000 sales variance must have resulted from a higher than expected selling price.

EXHIBIT 24.4

Flexible Budget
Performance Report

OPTEL — Flexible Budget Performance Report — For Month Ended January 31, 2011	Flexible Budget	Actual Results	Variances*
Sales (12,000 units)	$120,000	$125,000	$5,000 F
Variable costs			
Direct materials	12,000	13,000	1,000 U
Direct labor	18,000	20,000	2,000 U
Factory supplies	2,400	2,100	300 F
Utilities	3,600	4,000	400 U
Sales commissions	10,800	10,800	0
Shipping expenses	4,800	4,300	500 F
Office supplies	6,000	5,200	800 F
Total variable costs	57,600	59,400	1,800 U
Contribution margin	62,400	65,600	3,200 F
Fixed costs			
Depreciation—machinery	8,000	8,000	0
Supervisory salaries	11,000	11,000	0
Insurance expense	1,000	1,200	200 U
Depreciation—office equipment	7,000	7,000	0
Administrative salaries	13,000	13,000	0
Total fixed costs	40,000	40,200	200 U
Income from operations	$ 22,400	$ 25,400	$3,000 F

* F = Favorable variance; U = Unfavorable variance.

Further analysis of the facts surrounding this $5,000 sales variance reveals a favorable sales variance per unit of nearly $0.42 as shown here:

Actual average price per unit (rounded to cents)	$125,000/12,000 = $10.42
Budgeted price per unit	$120,000/12,000 = 10.00
Favorable sales variance per unit	$5,000/12,000 = $ 0.42

The other variances in Exhibit 24.4 also direct management's attention to areas where corrective actions can help control Optel's operations. Each expense variance is analyzed as the sales variance was. We can think of each expense as the joint result of using a given number of units of input and paying a specific price per unit of input. Optel's expense variances total $2,000 unfavorable, suggesting poor control of some costs, particularly direct materials and direct labor.

Each variance in Exhibit 24.4 is due in part to a difference between *actual price* per unit of input and *budgeted price* per unit of input. This is a **price variance.** Each variance also can be due in part to a difference between *actual quantity* of input used and *budgeted quantity* of input. This is a **quantity variance.** We explain more about this breakdown, known as **variance analysis,** later in the standard costs section.

Quick Check

Answers — p. 987

1. A flexible budget (*a*) shows fixed costs as constant amounts of cost per unit of activity, (*b*) shows variable costs as constant amounts of cost per unit of activity, or (*c*) is prepared based on one expected amount of budgeted sales or production.
2. What is the initial step in preparing a flexible budget?
3. What is the main difference between a fixed and a flexible budget?
4. What is the contribution margin?

Section 2—Standard Costs

Standard costs are preset costs for delivering a product or service under normal conditions. These costs are established by personnel, engineering, and accounting studies using past experiences and data. Management uses these costs to assess the reasonableness of actual costs incurred for producing the product or service. When actual costs vary from standard costs, management follows up to identify potential problems and take corrective actions. **Management by exception** means that managers focus attention on the most significant differences between actual costs and standard costs and give less attention to areas where performance is reasonably close to standard. Management by exception is especially useful when directed at controllable items, enabling top management to affect the actions of lower-level managers responsible for the company's revenues and costs.

Standard costs are often used in preparing budgets because they are the anticipated costs incurred under normal conditions. Terms such as *standard materials cost, standard labor cost,* and *standard overhead cost* are often used to refer to amounts budgeted for direct materials, direct labor, and overhead.

While many managers use standard costs to investigate manufacturing costs, standard costs can also help control *nonmanufacturing* costs. Companies providing services instead of products can also benefit from the use of standard costs. For example, while quality medical service is paramount, efficiency in providing that service is also important to medical professionals. The use of budgeting and standard costing is touted as an effective means to control and monitor medical costs, especially overhead.

C1 Define *standard costs* and explain how standard cost information is useful for management by exception.

Point: Since standard costs are often budgeted costs, they can be used to prepare both fixed budgets and flexible budgets.

Decision Ethics Answer — p. 986

Internal Auditor You discover a manager who always spends exactly what is budgeted. About 30% of her budget is spent just before the period-end. She admits to spending what is budgeted, whether or not it is needed. She offers three reasons: (1) she doesn't want her budget cut, (2) "management by exception" focuses on budget deviations; and (3) she believes the money is budgeted to be spent. What action do you take? ∎

MATERIALS AND LABOR STANDARDS

This section explains how to set materials and labor standards and how to prepare a standard cost card.

Identifying Standard Costs

Point: Business practice often uses the word *budget* when speaking of total amounts and *standard* when discussing per unit amounts.

Managerial accountants, engineers, personnel administrators, and other managers combine their efforts to set standard costs. To identify standards for direct labor costs, we can conduct time and motion studies for each labor operation in the process of providing a product or service. From these studies, management can learn the best way to perform the operation and then set the standard labor time required for the operation under normal conditions. Similarly, standards for materials are set by studying the quantity, grade, and cost of each material used. Standards for overhead costs are explained later in the chapter.

Example: What factors might be considered when deciding whether to revise standard costs? *Answer:* Changes in the processes and/or resources needed to carry out the processes.

Regardless of the care used in setting standard costs and in revising them as conditions change, actual costs frequently differ from standard costs, often as a result of one or more factors. For instance, the actual quantity of material used can differ from the standard, or the price paid per unit of material can differ from the standard. Quantity and price differences from standard amounts can also occur for labor. That is, the actual labor time and actual labor rate can vary from what was expected. The same analysis applies to overhead costs.

Decision Insight

Cruis'n Standards The **Toyota Camry** consists of hundreds of parts for which engineers set standards. Various types of labor are also involved in its production, including machining, assembly, painting, and welding, and standards are set for each. Actual results are periodically compared with standards to assess performance. ∎

Setting Standard Costs

To illustrate the setting of a standard cost, we consider a professional league baseball bat manufactured by ProBat. Its engineers have determined that manufacturing one bat requires 0.90 kg. of high-grade wood. They also expect some loss of material as part of the process because of inefficiencies and waste. This results in adding an *allowance* of 0.10 kg., making the standard requirement 1.0 kg. of wood for each bat.

Point: Companies promoting continuous improvement strive to achieve ideal standards by eliminating inefficiencies and waste.

The 0.90 kg. portion is called an *ideal standard;* it is the quantity of material required if the process is 100% efficient without any loss or waste. Reality suggests that some loss of material usually occurs with any process. The standard of 1.0 kg. is known as the *practical standard*, the quantity of material required under normal application of the process.

High-grade wood can be purchased at a standard price of $25 per kg. The purchasing department sets this price as the expected price for the budget period. To determine this price, the purchasing department considers factors such as the quality of materials, future economic conditions, supply factors (shortages and excesses), and any available discounts. The engineers also decide that two hours of labor time (after including allowances) are required to manufacture a bat. The wage rate is $20 per hour (better than average skilled labor is required). ProBat assigns all overhead at the rate of $10 per labor hour. The standard costs of direct materials, direct labor, and overhead for one bat are shown in Exhibit 24.5 in what is called a *standard cost card*. These cost amounts are then used to prepare manufacturing budgets for a budgeted level of production.

STANDARD COST CARD		▪ ◻ ✕
Production factor	**Cost factor**	**Total**
Direct materials (wood)	1 kg. @ $25 per kg.	$25
Direct labor	2 hours @ $20 per hour	40
Overhead	2 labor hours @ $10 per hour	20
	Total	**$85**

REMARKS:
Based on standard costs of direct materials, direct labor, and overhead for a single ProBat

SUMMARY:	
Materials	$25
Labor	40
Overhead	20
Total cost	$85

EXHIBIT 24.5

Standard Cost Card

COST VARIANCES

A **cost variance,** also simply called a *variance,* is the difference between actual and standard costs. A cost variance can be favorable or unfavorable. A variance from standard cost is considered favorable if actual cost is less than standard cost. It is considered unfavorable if actual cost is more than standard cost.[1] This section discusses variance analysis.

 C2 Describe variances and what they reveal about performance.

Cost Variance Analysis

Variances are usually identified in performance reports. When a variance occurs, management wants to determine the factors causing it. This often involves analysis, evaluation, and explanation. The results of these efforts should enable management to assign responsibility for the variance and then to take actions to correct the situation.

To illustrate, ProBat's standard materials cost for producing 500 bats is $12,500. Assume that its actual materials cost for those 500 bats is $13,000. The $500 unfavorable variance raises questions that call for answers that, in turn, can lead to changes to correct the situation and eliminate this variance in the next period. A performance report often identifies the existence of a problem, but we must follow up with further investigation to see what can be done to improve future performance.

Exhibit 24.6 shows the flow of events in the effective management of variance analysis. It shows four steps: (1) preparing a standard cost performance report, (2) computing and analyzing variances, (3) identifying questions and their explanations, and (4) taking corrective and strategic actions. These variance analysis steps are interrelated and are frequently applied in good organizations.

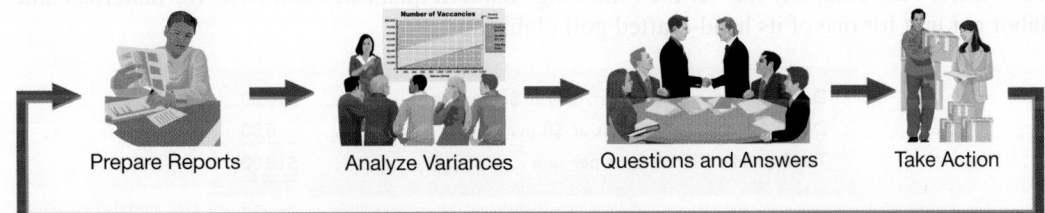

Prepare Reports   Analyze Variances   Questions and Answers   Take Action

EXHIBIT 24.6

Variance Analysis

Cost Variance Computation

Management needs information about the factors causing a cost variance, but first it must properly compute the variance. In its most simple form, a cost variance (CV) is computed as the difference between actual cost (AC) and standard cost (SC) as shown in Exhibit 24.7.

---

[1] Short-term favorable variances can sometimes lead to long-term unfavorable variances. For instance, if management spends less than the budgeted amount on maintenance or insurance, the performance report would show a favorable variance. Cutting these expenses can lead to major losses in the long run if machinery wears out prematurely or insurance coverage proves inadequate.

EXHIBIT 24.7

Cost Variance Formulas

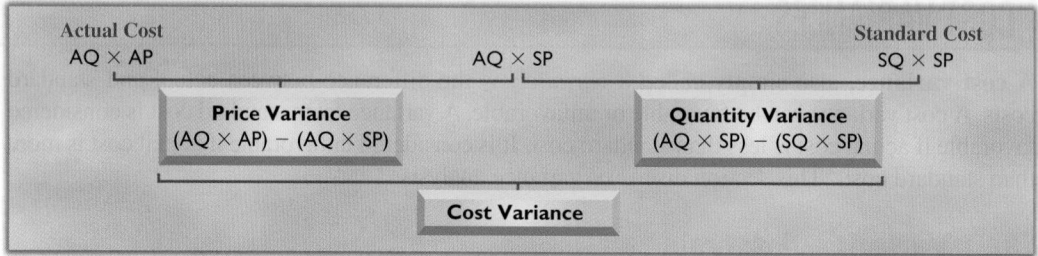

> **Cost Variance** (CV) = **Actual Cost** (AC) − **Standard Cost** (SC)
>
> where:
>
> **Actual Cost** (AC) = **Actual Quantity** (AQ) × **Actual Price** (AP)
>
> **Standard Cost** (SC) = **Standard Quantity** (SQ) × **Standard Price** (SP)

A cost variance is further defined by its components. Actual quantity (AQ) is the input (material or labor) used to manufacture the quantity of output. Standard quantity (SQ) is the expected input for the quantity of output. Actual price (AP) is the amount paid to acquire the input (material or labor), and standard price (SP) is the expected price.

Point: Price and quantity variances for direct labor are nearly always referred to as *rate* and *efficiency variances*, respectively.

Two main factors cause a cost variance: (1) the difference between actual price and standard price results in a *price* (or rate) *variance* and (2) the difference between actual quantity and standard quantity results in a *quantity* (or usage or efficiency) *variance*. To assess the impacts of these two factors in a cost variance, we use the formulas in Exhibit 24.8.

EXHIBIT 24.8

Price Variance and Quantity
Variance Formulas

Actual Cost		Standard Cost
AQ × AP	AQ × SP	SQ × SP

Price Variance	**Quantity Variance**
(AQ × AP) − (AQ × SP)	(AQ × SP) − (SQ × SP)

Cost Variance

In computing a price variance, the quantity (actual) is held constant. In computing a quantity variance, the price (standard) is held constant. The cost variance, or total variance, is the sum of the price and quantity variances. These formulas identify the sources of the cost variance. Managers sometimes find it useful to apply an alternative (but equivalent) computation for the price and quantity variances as shown in Exhibit 24.9.

EXHIBIT 24.9

Alternative Price Variance and
Quantity Variance Formulas

> **Price Variance** (PV) = [**Actual Price** (AP) − **Standard Price** (SP)] × **Actual Quantity** (AQ)
>
> **Quantity Variance** (QV) = [**Actual Quantity** (AQ) − **Standard Quantity** (SQ)] × **Standard Price** (SP)

The results from applying the formulas in Exhibits 24.8 and 24.9 are identical.

Computing Materials and Labor Variances

P2 Compute materials and labor variances.

We illustrate the computation of the materials and labor cost variances using data from G-Max, a company that makes specialty golf equipment and accessories for individual customers. This company has set the following standard quantities and costs for materials and labor per unit for one of its hand-crafted golf clubheads:

Direct materials (0.5 lb. per unit at $20 per lb.)	$10.00
Direct labor (1 hr. per unit at $8 per hr.)	8.00
Total standard direct cost per unit	$18.00

Materials Cost Variances   During May 2011, G-Max budgeted to produce 4,000 clubheads (units). It actually produced only 3,500 units. It used 1,800 pounds of direct materials (titanium) costing $21.00 per pound, meaning its total materials cost was $37,800. This information allows us to compute both actual and standard direct materials costs for G-Max's 3,500 units and its direct materials cost variance as follows:

Actual cost	1,800 lbs. @ $21.00 per lb.	= $37,800
Standard cost	1,750 lbs. @ $20.00 per lb.	= 35,000
Direct materials cost variance (unfavorable)		= $ 2,800

To better isolate the causes of this $2,800 unfavorable total direct materials cost variance, the materials price and quantity variances for these G-Max clubheads are computed and shown in Exhibit 24.10.

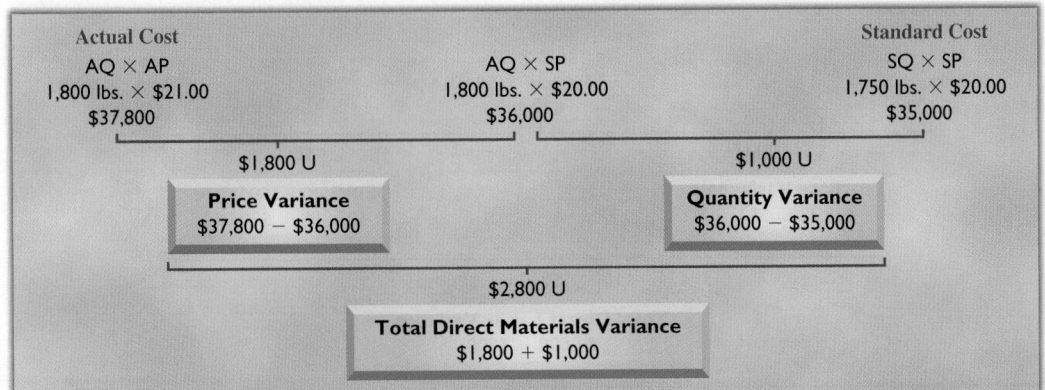

EXHIBIT 24.10

Materials Price and
Quantity Variances*

*AQ is actual quantity; AP is actual price; SP is standard price; SQ is standard quantity allowed for actual output.

The $1,800 unfavorable price variance results from paying $1 more per unit than the standard price, computed as 1,800 lbs. × $1. The $1,000 unfavorable quantity variance is due to using 50 lbs. more materials than the standard quantity, computed as 50 lbs. × $20. The total direct materials variance is $2,800 and it is unfavorable. This information allows management to ask the responsible individuals for explanations and corrective actions.

The purchasing department is usually responsible for the price paid for materials. Responsibility for explaining the price variance in this case rests with the purchasing manager if a price higher than standard caused the variance. The production department is usually responsible for the amount of material used and in this case is responsible for explaining why the process used more than the standard amount of materials.

Variance analysis presents challenges. For instance, the production department could have used more than the standard amount of material because its quality did not meet specifications and led to excessive waste. In this case, the purchasing manager is responsible for explaining why inferior materials were acquired. However, the production manager is responsible for explaining what happened if analysis shows that waste was due to inefficiencies, not poor quality material.

Sometimes reducing the number of suppliers used can result in decreasing material costs, which then results in a favorable price variance. For example, **Tops**, a chain of supermarkets in Thailand, moved from a system of having dozens of suppliers to a few "preferred" suppliers in early 2000. Major investments for a supermarket chain include the purchase of refrigerated trucks, standard crates, and the establishment of information systems. Transport and quality control costs could be decreased when the number of suppliers is reduced. Savings in transport costs resulting from a limited number of suppliers largely offset the rising costs for improving the transport equipment (refrigerated trucks). The share of quality control costs in total procurement costs could also be reduced. The resulting cost variances can be analyzed only in light of the strategy that Tops was trying to implement.

Labor Cost Variances   Labor cost for a specific product or service depends on the number of hours worked (quantity) and the wage rate paid to employees (price). When actual amounts for a task differ from standard, the labor cost variance can be divided into a rate (price) variance and an efficiency (quantity) variance.

To illustrate, G-Max's direct labor standard for 3,500 units of its hand-crafted clubheads is one hour per unit, or 3,500 hours at $8 per hour. Since only 3,400 hours at $8.30 per hour were actually used to complete the units, the actual and standard labor costs are

Actual cost	3,400 hrs. @ $8.30 per hr.	= $28,220
Standard cost	3,500 hrs. @ $8.00 per hr.	= 28,000
Direct labor cost variance (unfavorable)		= $ 220

Example: Identify at least two factors that might have caused the unfavorable quantity variance and the unfavorable price variance in Exhibit 24.10. *Answer:* Poor quality materials or untrained workers for the former; poor price negotiation or higher-quality materials for the latter.

This analysis shows that actual cost is merely $220 over the standard and suggests no immediate concern. Computing both the labor rate and efficiency variances reveals a different picture, however, as shown in Exhibit 24.11.

EXHIBIT 24.11

Labor Rate and
Efficiency Variances*

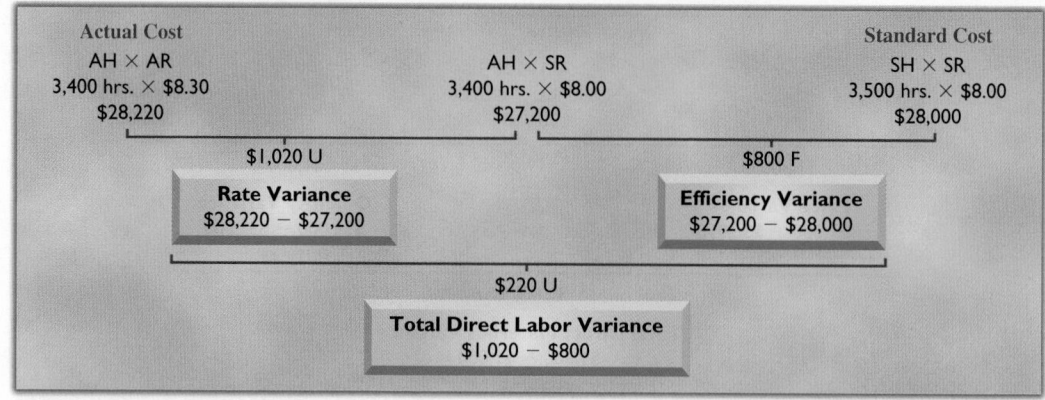

* AH is actual direct labor hours: AR is actual wage rate; SH is standard direct labor hours allowed for actual output; SR is standard wage rate.

Example: Compute the rate variance and the efficiency variance for Exhibit 24.11 if 3,700 actual hours are used at an actual price of $7.50 per hour. *Answer:* $1,850 favorable labor rate variance and $1,600 unfavorable labor efficiency variance.

The analysis in Exhibit 24.11 shows that an $800 favorable efficiency variance results from using 100 fewer direct labor hours than standard for the units produced, but this favorable variance is more than offset by a wage rate that is $0.30 per hour higher than standard. The personnel administrator or the production manager needs to explain why the wage rate is higher than expected. The production manager should also explain how the labor hours were reduced. If this experience can be repeated and transferred to other departments, more savings are possible.

One possible explanation of these labor rate and efficiency variances is the use of workers with different skill levels. If this is the reason, senior management must discuss the implications with the production manager who has the responsibility to assign workers to tasks with the appropriate skill level. In this case, an investigation might show that higher-skilled workers were used to produce 3,500 units of hand-crafted clubheads. As a result, fewer labor hours might be required for the work, but the wage rate paid these workers is higher than standard because of their greater skills. The effect of this strategy is a higher than standard total cost, which would require actions to remedy the situation or adjust the standard.

Decision Maker   Answer — p. 986

Human Resource Manager   You receive the manufacturing variance report for June and discover a large unfavorable labor efficiency (quantity) variance. What factors do you investigate to identify its possible causes? ■

Quick Check   Answers — p. 987

5. A standard cost (a) changes in direct proportion to changes in the level of activity, (b) is an amount incurred at the actual level of production for the period, or (c) is an amount incurred under normal conditions to provide a product or service.

6. What is a cost variance?

7. The following information is available for York Company.

Actual direct labor hours per unit	2.5 hours
Standard direct labor hours per unit	2.0 hours
Actual production (units)	2,500 units
Budgeted production (units)	3,000 units
Actual rate per hour	$3.10
Standard rate per hour	$3.00

The labor efficiency variance is (a) $3,750 U, (b) $3,750 F, or (c) $3,875 U.

8. Refer to Quick Check 7; the labor rate variance is (a) $625 F or (b) $625 U.

9. If a materials quantity variance is favorable and a materials price variance is unfavorable, can the total materials cost variance be favorable?

OVERHEAD STANDARDS AND VARIANCES

When standard costs are used, a predetermined overhead rate is used to assign standard overhead costs to products or services produced. This predetermined rate is often based on some overhead allocation base (such as standard labor cost, standard labor hours, or standard machine hours).

Setting Overhead Standards

Standard overhead costs are the amounts expected to occur at a certain activity level. Unlike direct materials and direct labor, overhead includes fixed costs and variable costs. This results in the average overhead cost per unit changing as the predicted volume changes. Since standard costs are also budgeted costs, they must be established before the reporting period begins. Standard overhead costs are therefore average per unit costs based on the predicted activity level.

To establish the standard overhead cost rate, management uses the same cost structure it used to construct a flexible budget at the end of a period. This cost structure identifies the different overhead cost components and classifies them as variable or fixed. To get the standard overhead rate, management selects a level of activity (volume) and predicts total overhead cost. It then divides this total by the allocation base to get the standard rate. Standard direct labor hours expected to be used to produce the predicted volume is a common allocation base and is used in this section.

To illustrate, Exhibit 24.12 shows the overhead cost structure used to develop G-Max's flexible overhead budgets for May 2011. The predetermined standard overhead rate for May is set before the month begins. The first two number columns list the per unit amounts of

Point: With increased automation, machine hours are frequently used in applying overhead instead of labor hours.

	Flexible Budget		Flexible Budget at 70% Capacity	Flexible Budget at 80% Capacity	Flexible Budget at 90% Capacity	Flexible Budget at 100% Capacity
	Variable Amount per Unit	Total Fixed Cost				
Production (in units)	1 unit		3,500	4,000	4,500	5,000
Factory overhead						
Variable costs						
Indirect labor	$0.40/unit		$1,400	$1,600	$1,800	$2,000
Indirect materials	0.30/unit		1,050	1,200	1,350	1,500
Power and lights	0.20/unit		700	800	900	1,000
Maintenance	0.10/unit		350	400	450	500
Total variable overhead costs	$1.00/unit		3,500	4,000	4,500	5,000
Fixed costs (per month)						
Building rent		$1,000	1,000	1,000	1,000	1,000
Depreciation—machinery		1,200	1,200	1,200	1,200	1,200
Supervisory salaries		1,800	1,800	1,800	1,800	1,800
Total fixed overhead costs		$4,000	4,000	4,000	4,000	4,000
Total factory overhead			$7,500	$8,000	$8,500	$9,000
Standard direct labor hours 1 hr./unit . .			3,500 hrs.	4,000 hrs.	4,500 hrs.	5,000 hrs.
Predetermined overhead rate per standard direct labor hour			$ 2.14	$ 2.00	$ 1.89	$ 1.80

G-MAX
Flexible Overhead Budgets
For Month Ended May 31, 2011

EXHIBIT 24.12

Flexible Overhead Budgets

variable costs and the monthly amounts of fixed costs. The four right-most columns show the costs expected to occur at four different levels of production activity. The predetermined overhead rate per labor hour is smaller as volume of activity increases because total fixed costs remain constant.

G-Max managers predicted an 80% activity level for May, or a production volume of 4,000 clubheads. At this volume, they budget $8,000 as the May total overhead. This choice implies a $2 per unit (labor hour) average overhead cost ($8,000/4,000 units). Since G-Max has a standard of one direct labor hour per unit, the predetermined standard overhead rate for May is $2 per standard direct labor hour. The variable overhead rate remains constant at $1 per direct labor hour regardless of the budgeted production level. The fixed overhead rate changes according to the budgeted production volume. For instance, for the predicted level of 4,000 units of production, the fixed rate is $1 per hour ($4,000 fixed costs/4,000 units). For a production level of 5,000 units, however, the fixed rate is $0.80 per hour ($4,000 fixed costs/5,000 units).

Point: Variable costs per unit remain constant, but fixed costs per unit decline with increases in volume. This means the average total overhead cost per unit declines with increases in volume.

When choosing the predicted activity level, management considers many factors. The level can be set as high as 100% of capacity, but this is rare. Factors causing the activity level to be less than full capacity include difficulties in scheduling work, equipment under repair or maintenance, and insufficient product demand. Good long-run management practices often call for some plant capacity in excess of current operating needs to allow for special opportunities and demand changes.

Decision Insight

Measuring Up In the spirit of continuous improvement, competitors compare their processes and performance standards against benchmarks established by industry leaders. According to a survey of 25 top management tools reported in "Management Tools and Trends 2013" by **Bain and Company**, **Benchmarking** ranks fourth globally and thirteenth in Asia Pacific region. ■

Total Overhead Cost Variance

P3 Compute overhead variances.

EXHIBIT 24.13

Overhead Cost Variance

When standard costs are used, the cost accounting system applies overhead to the good units produced using the predetermined standard overhead rate. At period-end, the difference between the total overhead cost applied to products and the total overhead cost actually incurred is called an **overhead cost variance** (total overhead variance), which is defined in Exhibit 24.13.

> **Overhead cost variance (OCV) = Actual overhead incurred (AOI) − Standard overhead applied (SOA)**

The standard overhead applied is based on the predetermined overhead rate and the standard number of hours that should have been used, based on the actual production. To illustrate, G-Max produced 3,500 units during the month, which should have used 3,500 direct labor hours. From Exhibit 24.12, G-Max's predetermined overhead rate at the predicted capacity level of 4,000 units was $2.00 per direct labor hour, so the standard overhead applied is $7,000 (computed as 3,500 × $2.00). Additional data from cost reports show that the actual overhead cost incurred in the month is $7,650. G-Max's total overhead variance is thus $650, computed as $7,650 − $7,000. This variance is unfavorable, as G-Max's actual overhead was higher than it should have been based on budgeted amounts.

Controllable and Volume Variances To help identify factors causing the overhead cost variance, managers analyze this variance separately for controllable and volume variances, as illustrated in Exhibit 24.14. The results provide information useful for taking strategic actions to improve company performance.

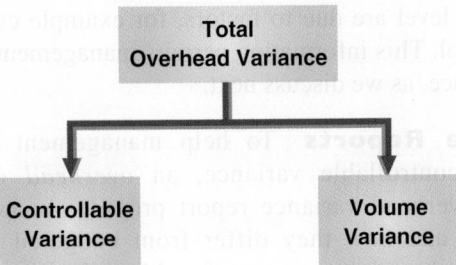

EXHIBIT 24.14

Framework for Understanding Total Overhead Variance

The **controllable variance** is the difference between actual overhead costs incurred and the budgeted overhead costs based on a flexible budget. The controllable variance is so named because it refers to activities usually under the control of management. A **volume variance** occurs when there is a difference between the actual volume of production and the standard volume of production. The budgeted fixed overhead amount is the same regardless of the volume of production (within the relevant range). This budgeted amount is computed based on the standard direct labor hours that the budgeted production volume allows. The applied total overhead is based, however, on the standard direct labor hours allowed for the actual volume of production, using the flexible budget. When a company operates at a capacity different from what it expected, the volume variance will differ from zero.

Returning to the G-Max data, the flexible budget in Exhibit 24.12 shows budgeted factory overhead of $7,500 at the production volume of 3,500 units during the month. The controllable variance is then computed as:

Actual total overhead (given)	$7,650
Applied total overhead (from flexible budget)	7,500
Controllable variance (unfavorable)	$ 150

We then compute the volume variance. It is important to note that the volume variance is based solely on *fixed* overhead. G-Max's budgeted fixed overhead at the predicted capacity level for the month was $4,000. Recall from Exhibit 24.12 that G-Max's predetermined fixed overhead at the predicted capacity level of 4,000 units was $1 per hour. Thus, G-Max's applied fixed overhead was $3,500, computed as 3,500 units $\times$ $1.00 per unit. G-Max's volume variance is then computed as:

Budgeted fixed overhead (at predicted capacity)	$4,000
Applied fixed overhead (3,500 $\times$ $1.00)	3,500
Volume variance (unfavorable)	$ 500

Analyzing Controllable and Volume Variances   How should the top management of G-Max interpret the unfavorable controllable and volume variances? An unfavorable volume variance implies that the company did not reach its predicted operating level. In this case, 80% of manufacturing capacity was budgeted but only 70% was used. Management needs to know why the actual level of production differs from the expected level. The main purpose of the volume variance is to identify what portion of the total overhead variance is caused by failing to meet the expected production level. Often the reasons for failing to meet

"Well, according to the books, you've got too much overhead."

EXHIBIT 24.15

Overhead Variance Report

this expected production level are due to factors, for example customer demand, that are beyond employees' control. This information permits management to focus on explanations for the controllable variance, as we discuss next.

Overhead Variance Reports To help management isolate the reasons for the $150 unfavorable controllable variance, an *overhead variance report* can be prepared. A complete overhead variance report provides managers information about specific overhead costs and how they differ from budgeted amounts. Exhibit 24.15 shows G-Max's overhead variance report for May. It reveals that (1) fixed costs and maintenance costs were incurred as expected, (2) costs for indirect labor and power and lights were higher than expected, and (3) indirect materials cost was less than expected.

G-MAX **Overhead Variance Report** **For Month Ended May 31, 2011**			
Volume Variance			
Expected production level	80% of capacity		
Production level achieved	70% of capacity		
Volume variance	$500 (unfavorable)		
	Flexible	**Actual**	
Controllable Variance	**Budget**	**Results**	**Variances***
Variable overhead costs			
Indirect labor	$1,400	$1,525	$125 U
Indirect materials	1,050	1,025	25 F
Power and lights	700	750	50 U
Maintenance	350	350	0
Total variable overhead costs	3,500	3,650	150 U
Fixed overhead costs			
Building rent	1,000	1,000	0
Depreciation—machinery	1,200	1,200	0
Supervisory salaries	1,800	1,800	0
Total fixed overhead costs	4,000	4,000	0
Total overhead costs	$7,500	$7,650	$150 U

* F = Favorable variance; U = Unfavorable variance.

The total controllable variance amount is also readily available from Exhibit 24.15. The overhead variance report shows the total volume variance as $500 unfavorable (shown at the top) and the $150 unfavorable controllable variance (reported at the bottom right). The sum of the controllable variance and the volume variance equals the total overhead variance of $650 unfavorable.

Appendix 24A describes an expanded analysis of overhead variances.

Quick Check   Answers — p. 987

10. Under what conditions is an overhead volume variance considered favorable?

11. To use management by exception, a company (*a*) need not study fixed overhead variances, (*b*) should compute variances from flexible budget amounts to allow management to focus its attention on significant differences between actual and budgeted results, or (*c*) should analyze only variances for direct materials and direct labor.

Decision Analysis

This chapter explained the computation and analysis of cost variances. A similar variance analysis can be applied to sales. To illustrate, consider the following sales data from G-Max for two of its golf products, Excel golf balls and Big Bert® drivers.

> **A1** Analyze changes in sales from expected amounts.

	Budgeted	Actual
Sales of Excel golf balls (units)...........	1,000 units	1,100 units
Sales price per Excel golf ball............	$10	$10.50
Sales of Big Bert® drivers (units)........	150 units	140 units
Sales price per Big Bert® driver..........	$200	$190

Using this information, we compute both the *sales price variance* and the *sales volume variance* as shown in Exhibit 24.16. The total sales price variance is $850 unfavorable, and the total sales volume variance is $1,000 unfavorable. Neither total variance implies anything positive about these two products. However, further analysis of these total sales variances reveals that both the sales price and sales volume variances for Excel golf balls are favorable, meaning that both the unfavorable total sales price variance and the unfavorable total sales volume variance are due to the Big Bert driver.

EXHIBIT 24.16

Computing Sales Variances*

Excel Golf Balls	Actual Results AS × AP	Flexible Budget AS × BP	Fixed Budget BS × BP
Sales dollars (balls)	(1,100 × $10.50) **$11,550**	(1,100 × $10) **$11,000**	(1,000 × $10) **$10,000**
	$550 F	$1,000 F	
	Sales Price Variance	Sales Volume Variance	
Big Bert® Drivers			
Sales dollars (drivers)	(140 × $190) **$26,600**	(140 × $200) **$28,000**	(150 × $200) **$30,000**
	$1,400 U	$2,000 U	
	Sales Price Variance	Sales Volume Variance	
Total	**$850 U**	**$1,000 U**	

* AS = actual sales units; AP = actual sales price; BP = budgeted sales price; BS = budgeted sales units (fixed budget).

Managers use sales variances for planning and control purposes. The sales variance information is used to plan future actions to avoid unfavorable variances. G-Max sold 90 total combined units (both balls and drivers) more than planned, but these 90 units were not sold in the proportion budgeted. G-Max sold fewer than the budgeted quantity of the higher-priced driver, which contributed to the unfavorable total sales variances. Managers use such detail to question what caused the company to sell more golf balls and fewer drivers. Managers also use this information to evaluate and even reward their salespeople. Extra compensation is paid to salespeople who contribute to a higher profit margin. Finally, with multiple products, the sales volume variance can be separated into a *sales mix variance* and a *sales quantity variance*. The sales mix variance is the difference between the actual and budgeted sales mix of the products. The sales quantity variance is the difference between the total actual and total budgeted quantity of units sold.

 **Decision** Maker   Answer — p. 986

Sales Manager   The current performance report reveals a large favorable sales volume variance but an unfavorable sales price variance. You did not expect to see a large increase in sales volume. What steps do you take to analyze this situation? ∎

DEMONSTRATION PROBLEM

Pacific Company provides the following information about its budgeted and actual results for June 2011. Although the expected June volume was 25,000 units produced and sold, the company actually produced and sold 27,000 units as detailed here:

	Budget (25,000 units)	Actual (27,000 units)
Selling price	$5.00 per unit	$5.23 per unit
Variable costs (per unit)		
Direct materials	1.24 per unit	1.12 per unit
Direct labor	1.50 per unit	1.40 per unit
Factory supplies*	0.25 per unit	0.37 per unit
Utilities*	0.50 per unit	0.60 per unit
Selling costs	0.40 per unit	0.34 per unit
Fixed costs (per month)		
Depreciation—machinery*	$3,750	$3,710
Depreciation—building*	2,500	2,500
General liability insurance	1,200	1,250
Property taxes on office equipment	500	485
Other administrative expense	750	900

* Indicates factory overhead item; $0.75 per unit or $3 per direct labor hour for variable overhead, and $0.25 per unit or $1 per direct labor hour for fixed overhead.

Standard costs based on expected output of 25,000 units

	Per Unit of Output	Quantity to Be Used	Total Cost
Direct materials, 4 oz. @ $0.31/oz.	$1.24/unit	100,000 oz.	$31,000
Direct labor, 0.25 hrs. @ $6.00/hr.	1.50/unit	6,250 hrs.	37,500
Overhead	1.00/unit		25,000

Actual costs incurred to produce 27,000 units

	Per Unit of Output	Quantity Used	Total Cost
Direct materials, 4 oz. @ $0.28/oz.	$1.12/unit	108,000 oz.	$30,240
Direct labor, 0.20 hrs. @ $7.00/hr.	1.40/unit	5,400 hrs.	37,800
Overhead	1.20/unit		32,400

Standard costs based on expected output of 27,000 units

	Per Unit of Output	Quantity to Be Used	Total Cost
Direct materials, 4 oz. @ $0.31/oz.	$1.24/unit	108,000 oz.	$33,480
Direct labor, 0.25 hrs. @ $6.00/hr.	1.50/unit	6,750 hrs.	40,500
Overhead			26,500

Required

1. Prepare June flexible budgets showing expected sales, costs, and net profit assuming 20,000, 25,000, and 30,000 units of output produced and sold.
2. Prepare a flexible budget performance report that compares actual results with the amounts budgeted if the actual volume had been expected.
3. Apply variance analysis for direct materials and direct labor.
4. Compute the total overhead variance, and the controllable and volume variances.
5. Compute spending and efficiency variances for overhead. (Refer to Appendix 24A.)
6. Prepare journal entries to record standard costs, and price and quantity variances, for direct materials, direct labor, and factory overhead. (Refer to Appendix 24A.)

PLANNING THE SOLUTION

- Prepare a table showing the expected results at the three specified levels of output. Compute the variable costs by multiplying the per unit variable costs by the expected volumes. Include fixed costs at the given amounts. Combine the amounts in the table to show total variable costs, contribution margin, total fixed costs, and income from operations.
- Prepare a table showing the actual results and the amounts that should be incurred at 27,000 units. Show any differences in the third column and label them with an *F* for favorable if they increase income or a *U* for unfavorable if they decrease income.
- Using the chapter's format, compute these total variances and the individual variances requested:
  - Total materials variance (including the direct materials quantity variance and the direct materials price variance).
  - Total direct labor variance (including the direct labor efficiency variance and rate variance).
  - Total overhead variance (including both controllable and volume overhead variances and their component variances).

SOLUTION TO DEMONSTRATION PROBLEM

1.

PACIFIC COMPANY
Flexible Budgets
For Month Ended June 30, 2011

	Flexible Budget — Variable Amount per Unit	Flexible Budget — Total Fixed Cost	Flexible Budget for Unit Sales of 20,000	Flexible Budget for Unit Sales of 25,000	Flexible Budget for Unit Sales of 30,000
Sales	$5.00		$100,000	$125,000	$150,000
Variable costs					
Direct materials	1.24		24,800	31,000	37,200
Direct labor	1.50		30,000	37,500	45,000
Factory supplies	0.25		5,000	6,250	7,500
Utilities	0.50		10,000	12,500	15,000
Selling costs	0.40		8,000	10,000	12,000
Total variable costs	3.89		77,800	97,250	116,700
Contribution margin	$1.11		22,200	27,750	33,300
Fixed costs					
Depreciation—machinery		$3,750	3,750	3,750	3,750
Depreciation—building		2,500	2,500	2,500	2,500
General liability insurance		1,200	1,200	1,200	1,200
Property taxes on office equipment		500	500	500	500
Other administrative expense		750	750	750	750
Total fixed costs.		$8,700	8,700	8,700	8,700
Income from operations			$ 13,500	$ 19,050	$ 24,600

2.

PACIFIC COMPANY
Flexible Budget Performance Report
For Month Ended June 30, 2011

	Flexible Budget	Actual Results	Variance*
Sales (27,000 units)	$135,000	$141,210	$6,210 F
Variable costs			
Direct materials	33,480	30,240	3,240 F
Direct labor	40,500	37,800	2,700 F
Factory supplies	6,750	9,990	3,240 U
Utilities	13,500	16,200	2,700 U
Selling costs	10,800	9,180	1,620 F
Total variable costs	105,030	103,410	1,620 F
Contribution margin	29,970	37,800	7,830 F
Fixed costs			
Depreciation—machinery	3,750	3,710	40 F
Depreciation—building	2,500	2,500	0
General liability insurance	1,200	1,250	50 U
Property taxes on office equipment	500	485	15 F
Other administrative expense	750	900	150 U
Total fixed costs	8,700	8,845	145 U
Income from operations	$ 21,270	$ 28,955	$7,685 F

* F = Favorable variance; U = Unfavorable variance.

3. Variance analysis of materials and labor costs.

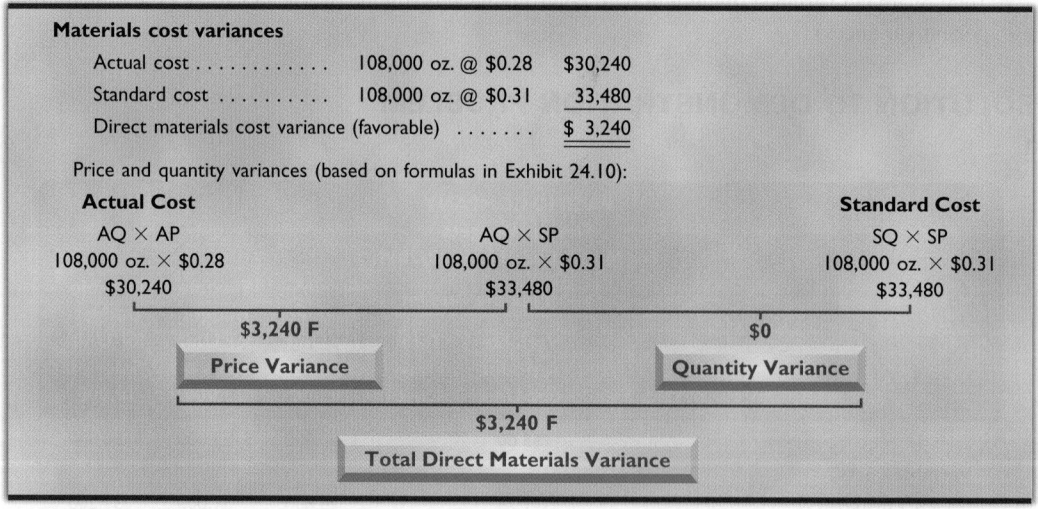

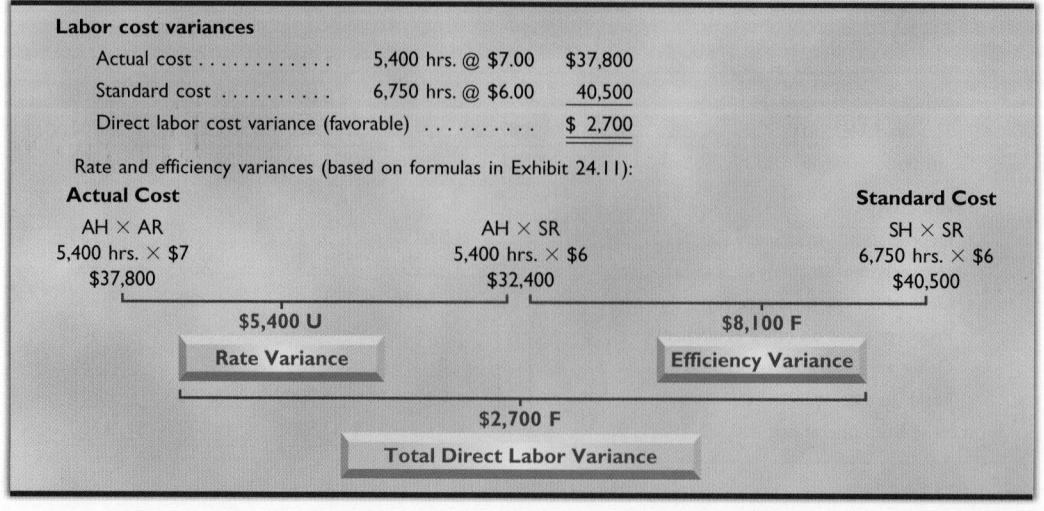

4. Total, controllable, and volume variances for overhead.

Overhead cost variances

Total overhead cost incurred	27,000 units @ $1.20	$32,400
Total overhead applied	27,000 units @ $1.00	27,000
Overhead cost variance (unfavorable)		$ 5,400

Controllable variance

Actual overhead (given)	$32,400
Applied overhead (from flexible budget for 27,000 units)	26,500
Controllable variance (unfavorable)	$ 5,900

Volume variance

Budgeted fixed overhead (at predicted capacity)	$ 6,250
Applied fixed overhead (6,750 × $1.00)	6,750
Volume variance (favorable)...........................	$ 500

5. Variable and fixed overhead spending and efficiency variances.

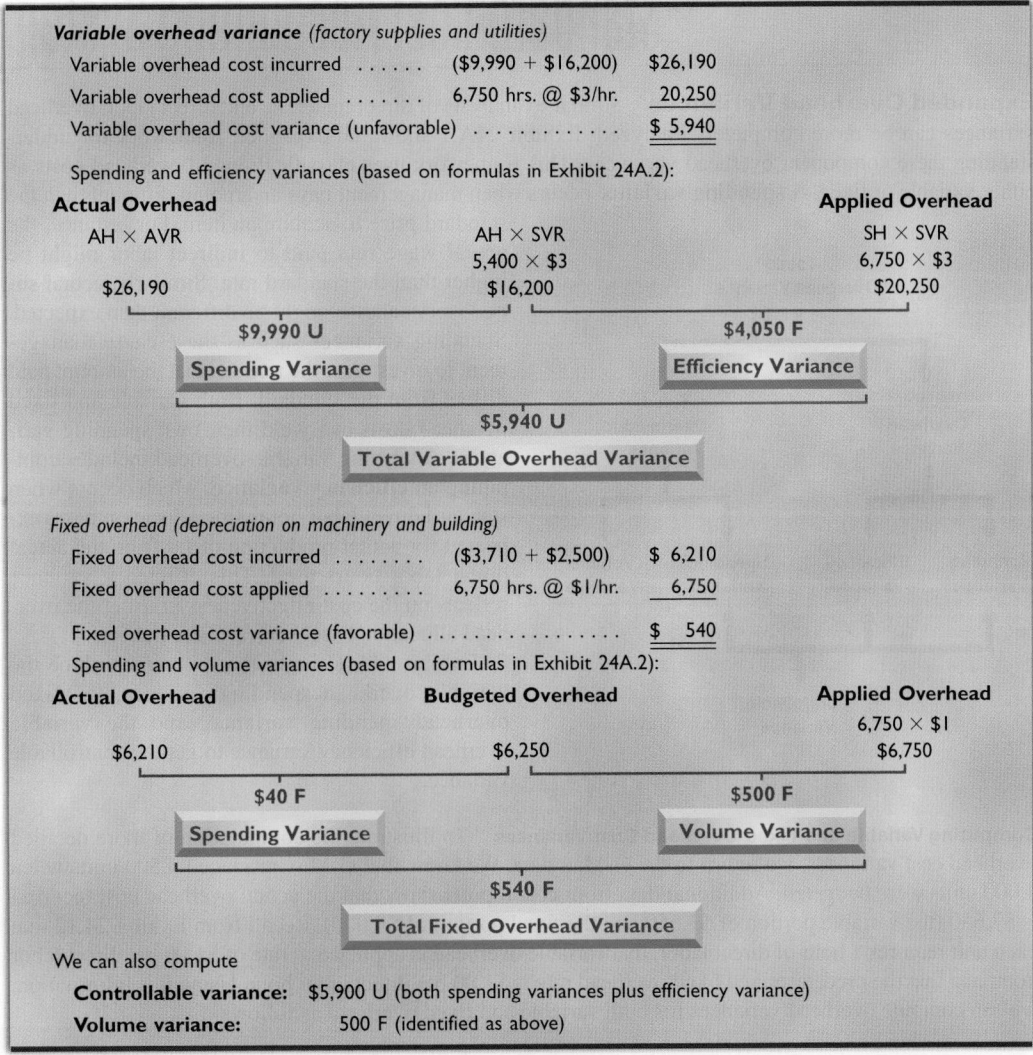

Variable overhead variance (factory supplies and utilities)

Variable overhead cost incurred	($9,990 + $16,200)	$26,190
Variable overhead cost applied	6,750 hrs. @ $3/hr.	20,250
Variable overhead cost variance (unfavorable)		$ 5,940

Spending and efficiency variances (based on formulas in Exhibit 24A.2):

Actual Overhead		**Applied Overhead**
AH × AVR	AH × SVR	SH × SVR
	5,400 × $3	6,750 × $3
$26,190	$16,200	$20,250

$9,990 U — **Spending Variance**

$4,050 F — **Efficiency Variance**

$5,940 U — **Total Variable Overhead Variance**

Fixed overhead (depreciation on machinery and building)

Fixed overhead cost incurred	($3,710 + $2,500)	$ 6,210
Fixed overhead cost applied	6,750 hrs. @ $1/hr.	6,750
Fixed overhead cost variance (favorable)		$ 540

Spending and volume variances (based on formulas in Exhibit 24A.2):

Actual Overhead	**Budgeted Overhead**	**Applied Overhead**
		6,750 × $1
$6,210	$6,250	$6,750

$40 F — **Spending Variance**

$500 F — **Volume Variance**

$540 F — **Total Fixed Overhead Variance**

We can also compute

Controllable variance:	$5,900 U (both spending variances plus efficiency variance)
Volume variance:	500 F (identified as above)

6.

Goods in Process Inventory	33,480	
Direct Materials Price Variance		3,240
Raw Materials Inventory		30,240
Goods in Process Inventory	40,500	
Direct Labor Rate Variance	5,400	
Direct Labor Efficiency Variance		8,100
Factory Payroll		37,800
Goods in Process Inventory*	27,000	
Variable Overhead Spending Variance	9,990	
Variable Overhead Efficiency Variance		4,050
Fixed Overhead Spending Variance		40
Fixed Overhead Volume Variance		500
Factory Overhead†		32,400

* \$20,250 + \$6,750   † \$26,190 + \$6,210

24A Expanded Overhead Variances and Standard Cost Accounting System

Expanded Overhead Variances   Similar to analysis of direct materials and direct labor, overhead variances can be more completely analyzed. Exhibit 24A.1 shows an expanded framework for understanding these component overhead variances. This framework uses classifications of overhead costs as either variable or fixed. A **spending variance** occurs when management pays an amount different than the standard price to acquire an item. For instance, the actual wage rate paid to indirect labor might be higher than the standard rate. Similarly, actual supervisory salaries might be different than expected. Spending variances such as these cause management to investigate the reasons that the amount paid differs from the standard. Both variable and fixed overhead costs can yield their own spending variances. Analyzing variable overhead includes computing an **efficiency variance,** which occurs when standard direct labor hours (the allocation base) expected for actual production differ from the actual direct labor hours used. This efficiency variance reflects on the cost-effectiveness in using the overhead allocation base (such as direct labor).

EXHIBIT 24A.1

Expanded Framework for Total Overhead Variance

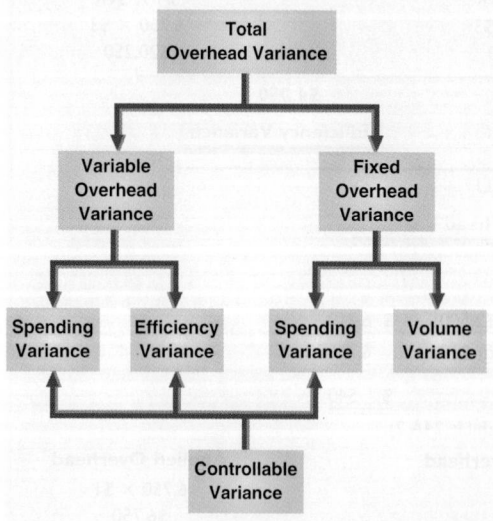

Exhibit 24A.1 shows that we can combine the variable overhead spending variance, the fixed overhead spending variance, and the variable overhead efficiency variance to get the controllable variance.

Computing Variable and Fixed Overhead Cost Variances   To illustrate the computation of more detailed overhead cost variances, we return to the G-Max data. We know that G-Max produced 3,500 units when 4,000 units were budgeted. Additional data from cost reports show that the actual overhead cost incurred is \$7,650 (the variable portion of \$3,650 and the fixed portion of \$4,000). Recall from Exhibit 24.12 that each unit requires 1 hour of direct labor, that variable overhead is applied at a rate of \$1.00 per direct labor hour, and that the predetermined fixed overhead rate is \$1.00 per direct labor hour. Using this information, we can compute overhead variances for both variable and fixed overhead as follows:

Actual variable overhead (given)	$3,650
Applied variable overhead (3,500 × $1.00)	3,500
Variable overhead variance (unfavorable)	$ 150

Actual fixed overhead (given)	$4,000
Applied fixed overhead (3,500 × $1.00)	3,500
Fixed overhead variance (unfavorable)	$ 500

Management should seek to determine the causes of these unfavorable variances and take corrective action. To help better isolate the causes of these variances, more detailed overhead variances can be used, as shown in the next section.

Expanded Overhead Variance Formulas   Exhibit 24A.2 shows formulas to use in computing detailed overhead variances that can better identify reasons for variable and fixed overhead variances.

EXHIBIT 24A.2

Variable and Fixed Overhead Variances

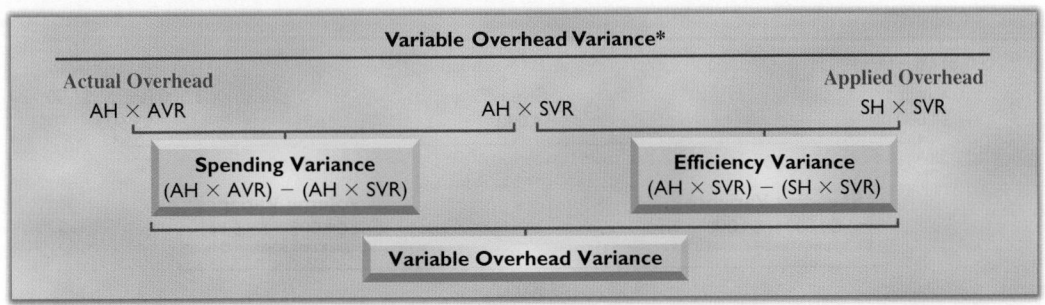

* AH = actual direct labor hours; AVR = actual variable overhead rate; SH = standard direct labor hours; SVR = standard variable overhead rate.

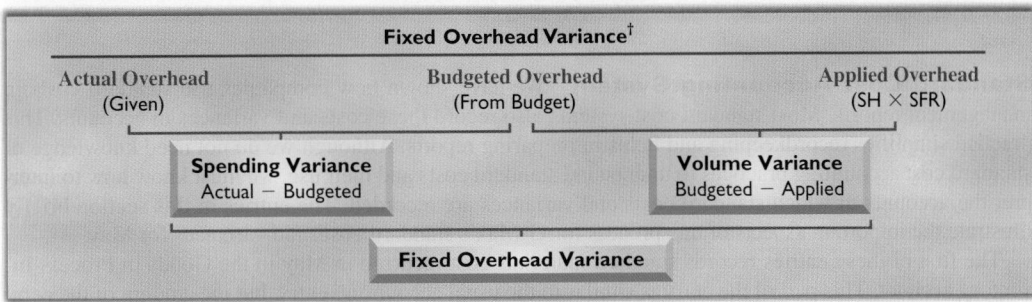

†SH = standard direct labor hours; SFR = standard fixed overhead rate.

Variable Overhead Cost Variances   Using these formulas, Exhibit 24A.3 offers insight into the causes of G-Max's $150 unfavorable variable overhead cost variance. Recall that G-Max applies overhead based on direct labor hours as the allocation base. We know that it used 3,400 direct labor hours to produce 3,500 units. This compares favorably to the standard requirement of 3,500 direct labor hours at one labor hour per unit. At a standard variable overhead rate of $1.00 per direct labor hour, this should have resulted in variable overhead costs of $3,400 (middle column of Exhibit 24A.3).

EXHIBIT 24A.3

Computing Variable Overhead Cost Variances

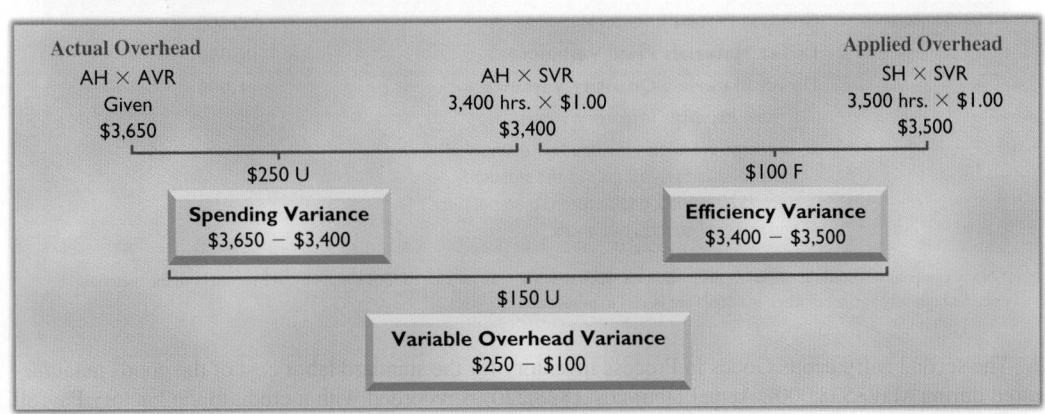

G-Max's cost records, however, report actual variable overhead of $3,650, or $250 higher than expected. This means G-Max has an unfavorable variable overhead spending variance of $250 ($3,650 − $3,400). On the other hand, G-Max used 100 fewer labor hours than expected to make 3,500 units, and its actual variable overhead is lower than its applied variable overhead. Thus, G-Max has a favorable variable overhead efficiency variance of $100 ($3,400 − $3,500).

Fixed Overhead Cost Variances   Exhibit 24A.4 provides insight into the causes of G-Max's $500 unfavorable fixed overhead variance. G-Max reports that it incurred $4,000 in actual fixed overhead; this amount equals the budgeted fixed overhead for May at the expected production level of 4,000 units (see Exhibit 24.12). Thus, the fixed overhead spending variance is zero, suggesting good control of fixed overhead costs. G-Max's budgeted fixed overhead application rate is $1 per hour ($4,000/4,000 direct labor hours), but the actual production level is only 3,500 units. Using this information, we can compute the fixed overhead volume variance shown in Exhibit 24A.4. The applied fixed overhead is computed by multiplying 3,500 standard hours allowed for the actual production by the $1 fixed overhead allocation rate. The volume variance of $500 occurs because 500 fewer units are produced than budgeted; namely, 80% of the manufacturing capacity is budgeted but only 70% is used.

EXHIBIT 24A.4

Computing Fixed Overhead
Cost Variances

Actual Overhead	Budgeted Overhead	Applied Overhead
Given	Given	3,500 hrs. × $1.00
$4,000	$4,000	$3,500

$0

Spending Variance
$4,000 − $4,000

$500 U

Volume Variance
$4,000 − $3,500

$500 U

Fixed Overhead Variance
$0 − $500

P4 Prepare journal entries for standard costs and account for price and quantity variances.

Standard Cost Accounting System   We have shown how companies use standard costs in management reports. Most standard cost systems also record these costs and variances in accounts. This practice simplifies recordkeeping and helps in preparing reports. Although we do not need knowledge of standard cost accounting practices to understand standard costs and their use, we must know how to interpret the accounts in which standard costs and variances are recorded. The entries in this section briefly illustrate the important aspects of this process for G-Max's standard costs and variances for May.

The first of these entries records standard materials cost incurred in May in the Goods in Process Inventory account. This part of the entry is similar to the usual accounting entry, but the amount of the debit equals the standard cost ($35,000) instead of the actual cost ($37,800). This entry credits Raw Materials Inventory for actual cost. The difference between standard and actual direct materials costs is recorded with debits to two separate materials variance accounts (recall Exhibit 24.10). Both the materials price and quantity variances are recorded as debits because they reflect additional costs higher than the standard cost (if actual costs were less than the standard, they are recorded as credits). This treatment (debit) reflects their unfavorable effect because they represent higher costs and lower income.

Assets = Liabilities + Equity
+35,000   −1,000
−37,800   −1,800

May 31			
	Goods in Process Inventory	35,000	
	Direct Materials Price Variance*	**1,800**	
	Direct Materials Quantity Variance	**1,000**	
	Raw Materials Inventory		37,800
	To charge production for standard quantity of materials used (1,750 lbs.) at the standard price ($20 per lb.), and to record material price and material quantity variances.		

* Many companies record the materials price variance when materials are purchased. For simplicity, we record both the materials price and quantity variances when materials are issued to production.

The second entry debits Goods in Process Inventory for the standard labor cost of the goods manufactured during May ($28,000). Actual labor cost ($28,220) is recorded with a credit to the Factory Payroll account. The difference between standard and actual labor costs is explained by two variances (see Exhibit 24.11). The direct labor rate variance is unfavorable and is debited to that account. The direct labor efficiency variance is favorable and that account is credited. The direct labor efficiency variance is favorable because it represents a lower cost and a higher net profit.

May 31	Goods in Process Inventory	28,000	
	Direct Labor Rate Variance	**1,020**	
	Direct Labor Efficiency Variance		**800**
	Factory Payroll		28,220
	To charge production with 3,500 standard hours of direct labor at the standard $8 per hour rate, and to record the labor rate and efficiency variances.		

Assets = Liabilities + Equity
+28,000   +28,220
                 − 1,020
                 +   800

The entry to assign standard predetermined overhead to the cost of goods manufactured must debit the $7,000 predetermined amount to the Goods in Process Inventory account. Actual overhead costs of $7,650 were debited to Factory Overhead during the period (entries not shown here). Thus, when Factory Overhead is applied to Goods in Process Inventory, the actual amount is credited to the Factory Overhead account. To account for the difference between actual and standard overhead costs, the entry includes a $250 debit to the Variable Overhead Spending Variance, a $100 credit to the Variable Overhead Efficiency Variance, and a $500 debit to the Volume Variance (recall Exhibits 24A.3 and 24A.4). An alternative (simpler) approach is to record the difference with a $150 debit to the Controllable Variance account and a $500 debit to the Volume Variance account (recall from Exhibit 24A.1 that controllable variance is the sum of both variable overhead variances and the fixed overhead spending variance).

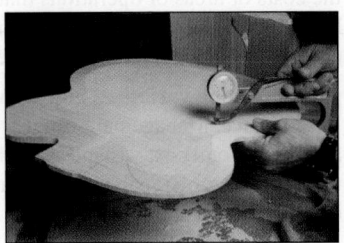

May 31	Goods in Process Inventory	7,000	
	Volume Variance	**500**	
	Variable Overhead Spending Variance..............	**250**	
	Variable Overhead Efficiency Variance		**100**
	Factory Overhead		7,650
	To apply overhead at the standard rate of $2 per standard direct labor hour (3,500 hours), and to record overhead variances.		

Assets = Liabilities + Equity
+7,000   +7,650
                − 250
                − 500
                + 100

The balances of these different variance accounts accumulate until the end of the accounting period. As a result, the unfavorable variances of some months can offset the favorable variances of other months.

These ending variance account balances, which reflect results of the period's various transactions and events, are closed at period-end. If the amounts are *immaterial,* they are added to or subtracted from the balance of the Cost of Goods Sold account. This process is similar to that shown in the job order costing chapter for eliminating an underapplied or overapplied balance in the Factory Overhead account. (*Note:* These variance balances, which represent differences between actual and standard costs, must be added to or subtracted from the materials, labor, and overhead costs recorded. In this way, the recorded costs equal the actual costs incurred in the period; a company must use actual costs in external financial statements prepared in accordance with generally accepted accounting principles.)

Point: If variances are material they can be allocated between Goods in Process Inventory, Finished Goods Inventory, and Cost of Goods Sold. This closing process is explained in advanced courses.

Quick Check
Answers — p. 987

12. A company uses a standard cost accounting system. Prepare the journal entry to record these direct materials variances:

Direct materials cost actually incurred.................	$73,200
Direct materials quantity variance (favorable)............	3,800
Direct materials price variance (unfavorable)............	1,300

13. If standard costs are recorded in the manufacturing accounts, how are recorded variances treated at the end of an accounting period?

Summary

C1 **Define *standard costs* and explain how standard cost information is useful for management by exception.** Standard costs are the normal costs that should be incurred to produce a product or perform a service. They should be based on a careful examination of the processes used to produce a product or perform a service as well as the quantities and prices that should be incurred in carrying out those processes. On a performance report, standard costs (which are flexible budget amounts) are compared to actual costs, and the differences are presented as variances. Standard cost accounting provides management information about costs that differ from budgeted (expected) amounts. Performance reports disclose the costs or areas of operations that have significant variances from budgeted amounts. This allows managers to focus attention on the exceptions and less attention on areas proceeding normally.

C2 **Describe variances and what they reveal about performance.** Management can use variances to monitor and control activities. Total cost variances can be broken into price and quantity variances to direct management's attention to those responsible for quantities used and prices paid.

A1 **Analyze changes in sales from expected amounts.** Actual sales can differ from budgeted sales, and managers can investigate this difference by computing both the sales price and sales volume variances. The *sales price variance* refers to that portion of total variance resulting from a difference between actual and budgeted selling prices. The *sales volume variance* refers to that portion of total variance resulting from a difference between actual and budgeted sales quantities.

P1 **Prepare a flexible budget and interpret a flexible budget performance report.** A flexible budget expresses variable costs in per unit terms so that it can be used to develop budgeted amounts for any volume level within the relevant range. Thus, managers compute budgeted amounts for evaluation after a period for the volume that actually occurred. To prepare a flexible budget, we express each variable cost as a constant amount per unit of sales (or as a percent of sales dollars). In contrast, the budgeted amount

of each fixed cost is expressed as a total amount expected to occur at any sales volume within the relevant range. The flexible budget is then determined using these computations and amounts for fixed and variable costs at the expected sales volume.

P2 **Compute materials and labor variances.** Materials and labor variances are due to differences between the actual costs incurred and the budgeted costs. The price (or rate) variance is computed by comparing the actual cost with the flexible budget amount that should have been incurred to acquire the actual quantity of resources. The quantity (or efficiency) variance is computed by comparing the flexible budget amount that should have been incurred to acquire the actual quantity of resources with the flexible budget amount that should have been incurred to acquire the standard quantity of resources.

P3 **Compute overhead variances.** Overhead variances are due to differences between the actual overhead costs incurred and the overhead applied to production. An overhead spending variance arises when the actual amount incurred differs from the budgeted amount of overhead. An overhead efficiency (or volume) variance arises when the flexible overhead budget amount differs from the overhead applied to production. It is important to realize that overhead is assigned using an overhead allocation base, meaning that an efficiency variance (in the case of variable overhead) is a result of the overhead application base being used more or less efficiently than planned.

P4ᴬ **Prepare journal entries for standard costs and account for price and quantity variances.** When a company records standard costs in its accounts, the standard costs of materials, labor, and overhead are debited to the Goods in Process Inventory account. Based on an analysis of the material, labor, and overhead costs, each quantity variance, price variance, volume variance, and controllable variance is recorded in a separate account. At period-end, if the variances are material, they are allocated among the balances of the Goods in Process Inventory, Finished Goods Inventory, and Cost of Goods Sold accounts. If they are not material, they are simply debited or credited to the Cost of Goods Sold account.

Guidance Answers to Decision Maker and Decision Ethics

Entrepreneur From the complaints, this performance report appears to compare actual results with a fixed budget. This comparison is useful in determining whether the amount of work actually performed was more or less than planned, but it is not useful in determining whether the divisions were more or less efficient than planned. If the two consulting divisions worked on more assignments than expected, some costs will certainly increase. Therefore, you should prepare a flexible budget using the actual number of consulting assignments and then compare actual performance to the flexible budget.

Internal Auditor Although the manager's actions might not be unethical, this action is undesirable. The internal auditor should report this behavior, possibly recommending that for the purchase of such discretionary items, the manager must provide budgetary requests using an activity-based budgeting process. The internal auditor would then be given full authority to verify this budget request.

Human Resource Manager As HR manager, you should investigate the causes for any labor-related variances although you may not be responsible for them. An unfavorable labor efficiency variance occurs because more labor hours than standard were used during the period. There are at least three possible reasons for this: (1) materials quality could be poor, resulting in more labor consumption due to rework; (2) unplanned interruptions (strike, breakdowns, accidents) could have occurred during the period; and (3) the production manager could have used a different labor mix to expedite orders. This new labor mix could have consisted of a larger proportion of untrained labor, which resulted in more labor hours.

Sales Manager The unfavorable sales price variance suggests that actual prices were lower than budgeted prices. As the sales manager, you want to know the reasons for a lower than expected price. Perhaps your salespeople lowered the price of certain products by offering quantity discounts. You then might want to know what prompted them to offer the quantity discounts (perhaps competitors were offering discounts). You want to break the sales volume variance into both the sales mix and sales quantity variances. You could find that although the sales quantity variance is favorable, the sales mix variance is not. Then you need to investigate why the actual sales mix differs from the budgeted sales mix.

Guidance Answers to Quick Checks

1. *b*

2. The first step is classifying each cost as variable or fixed.

3. A fixed budget is prepared using an expected volume of sales or production. A flexible budget is prepared using the actual volume of activity.

4. The contribution margin equals sales less variable costs.

5. *c*

6. It is the difference between actual cost and standard cost.

7. *a*; Total actual hours: 2,500 × 2.5 = 6,250

   Total standard hours: 2,500 × 2.0 = 5,000

   Efficiency variance = (6,250 − 5,000) × $3.00

   = $3,750 U

8. *b*; Rate variance = ($3.10 − $3.00) × 6,250 = $625 U

9. Yes, this will occur when the materials quantity variance is more than the materials price variance.

10. The overhead volume variance is favorable when the actual operating level is higher than the expected level.

11. *b*

12.

Goods in Process Inventory	75,700	
Direct Materials Price Variance	1,300	
Direct Materials Quantity Variance		3,800
Raw Materials Inventory		73,200

13. If the variances are material, they should be prorated among the Goods in Process Inventory, Finished Goods Inventory, and Cost of Goods Sold accounts. If they are not material, they can be closed to Cost of Goods Sold.

Key Terms   www.mheducation.asia/olc/wildkwokFAP

Benchmarking (p. 974)

Budget report (p. 962)

Budgetary control (p. 962)

Controllable variance (p. 975)

Cost variance (p. 969)

Efficiency variance (p. 982)

Favorable variance (p. 963)

Fixed budget (p. 963)

Fixed budget performance report (p. 966)

Flexible budget (p. 964)

Flexible budget performance report (p. 963)

Management by exception (p. 967)

Overhead cost variance (p. 974)

Price variance (p. 967)

Quantity variance (p. 967)

Spending variance (p. 982)

Standard costs (p. 967)

Unfavorable variance (p. 963)

Variance analysis (p. 967)

Volume variance (p. 975)

Multiple Choice Quiz   Answers on p. 1005   www.mheducation.asia/olc/wildkwokFAP

Additional Quiz Questions are available at the book's Website.

1. A company predicts its production and sales will be 24,000 units. At that level of activity, its fixed costs are budgeted at $300,000, and its variable costs are budgeted at $246,000. If its activity level declines to 20,000 units, what will be its fixed costs and its variable costs?

   a. Fixed, $300,000; variable, $246,000

   b. Fixed, $250,000; variable, $205,000

   c. Fixed, $300,000; variable, $205,000

   d. Fixed, $250,000; variable, $246,000

   e. Fixed, $300,000; variable, $300,000

2. Using the following information about a single product company, compute its total actual cost of direct materials used.

   • Direct materials standard cost: 5 lbs. × $2 per lb. = $10.

   • Total direct materials cost variance: $15,000 unfavorable.

   • Actual direct materials used: 300,000 lbs.

   • Actual units produced: 60,000 units.

   a. $585,000

   b. $600,000

   c. $300,000

   d. $315,000

   e. $615,000

3. A company uses four hours of direct labor to produce a product unit. The standard direct labor cost is $20 per hour. This period the company produced 20,000 units and used 84,160 hours of direct labor at a total cost of $1,599,040. What is its labor rate variance for the period?

   a. $83,200 F

   b. $84,160 U

   c. $84,160 F

   d. $83,200 U

   e. $ 960 F

4. A company's standard for a unit of its single product is $6 per unit in variable overhead (4 hours × $1.50 per hour). Actual data for the period show variable overhead costs of $150,000 and production of 24,000 units. Its total variable overhead cost variance is

     a. $ 6,000 F.
     b. $ 6,000 U.
     c. $114,000 U.
     d. $114,000 F.
     e. $ 0.

5. A company's standard for a unit of its single product is $4 per unit in fixed overhead ($24,000 total/6,000 units budgeted). Actual data for the period show total actual fixed overhead of $24,100 and production of 4,800 units. Its volume variance is

     a. $4,800 U.
     b. $4,800 F.
     c. $ 100 U.
     d. $ 100 F.
     e. $4,900 U.

A   *Superscript letter A denotes assignments based on Appendix 24A.*

   Icon denotes assignments that involve decision making.

Discussion Questions

1. What limits the usefulness to managers of fixed budget performance reports?

2. Identify the main purpose of a flexible budget for managers.

3. Prepare a flexible budget performance report title (in proper form) for Spalding Company for the calendar year 2011. Why is a proper title important for this or any report?

4. What type of analysis does a flexible budget performance report help management perform?

5. In what sense can a variable cost be considered constant?

6. What department is usually responsible for a direct labor rate variance? What department is usually responsible for a direct labor efficiency variance? Explain.

7. What is a price variance? What is a quantity variance?

8. What is the purpose of using standard costs?

9. **Nokia** monitors its fixed overhead. In an analysis of fixed overhead cost variances, what is the volume variance?

10. What is the predetermined standard overhead rate? How is it computed?

11. In general, variance analysis is said to provide information about _____ and _____ variances.

12. **Research In Motion** monitors its overhead. In an analysis of overhead cost variances, what is the controllable variance and what causes it?

13. What are the relations among standard costs, flexible budgets, variance analysis, and management by exception?

14. How can the manager of handheld devices at an **Apple** retail store use flexible budgets to enhance performance?

15. Is it possible for a retail store such as **Apple** to use variances in analyzing its operating performance? Explain.

16. Assume that **Palm** is budgeted to operate at 80% of capacity but actually operates at 75% of capacity. What effect will the 5% deviation have on its controllable variance? Its volume variance?

![connect]

QUICK STUDY

QS 24-1

Flexible budget performance report

P1

Santana Company sold 100,000 units of its product in May. For the level of production achieved in May, the budgeted amounts were: sales, $850,000; variable costs, $675,000; and fixed costs, $150,000. The following actual financial results are available for May. Prepare a flexible budget performance report for May.

Sales (100,000 units)	$837,500
Variable costs.	656,250
Fixed costs	150,000

QS 24-2

Management by exception

C1

Managers use *management by exception* for control purposes. (1) Describe the concept of management by exception. (2) Explain how standard costs help managers apply this concept to monitor and control costs.

QS 24-3

Standard cost card   **C1**

BatPro makes metal baseball bats. Each bat requires 1 kg. of aluminum at $20 per kg. and 0.50 direct labor hours at $16 per hour. Overhead is assigned at the rate of $40 per labor hour. What amounts would appear on a standard cost card for BatPro?

QS 24-4

Cost variances   **C2**

Refer to information in QS 24-3. Assume the actual cost to manufacture one metal bat was $54. Compute the cost variance and classify it as favorable or unfavorable.

Jacomo Company's output for the current period was assigned a $300,000 standard direct materials cost. The direct materials variances included a $44,000 favorable price variance and a $6,000 favorable quantity variance. What is the actual total direct materials cost for the current period?

QS 24-5
Materials cost variances   **P2**

Reflection Company's output for the current period results in a $40,000 unfavorable direct labor rate variance and a $20,000 unfavorable direct labor efficiency variance. Production for the current period was assigned an $800,000 standard direct labor cost. What is the actual total direct labor cost for the current period?

QS 24-6
Labor cost variances   **P2**

For the current period, Kawaga Company's manufacturing operations yield a $4,000 favorable price variance on its direct materials usage. The actual price per pound of material is $77; the standard price is $77.50. How many pounds of material are used in the current period?

QS 24-7
Materials cost variances   **P2**

Hewitt Company's output for the current period yields a $30,000 favorable overhead volume variance and a $50,400 unfavorable overhead controllable variance. Standard overhead charged to production for the period is $225,000. What is the actual total overhead cost incurred for the period?

QS 24-8
Overhead cost variances   **P3**

Refer to the information in QS 24-8. Hewitt records standard costs in its accounts. Prepare the journal entry to charge overhead costs to the Goods in Process Inventory account and to record any variances.

QS 24-9[A]
Preparing overhead entries   **P4**

Masters Company applies overhead using machine hours and reports the following information. Compute the total variable overhead cost variance.

QS 24-10[A]
Overhead cost variances
P3

Actual machine hours used	4,950 hours
Standard machine hours	5,000 hours
Actual variable overhead rate per hour	$4.10
Standard variable overhead rate per hour	$4.00

Refer to the information from QS 24-10. Compute the variable overhead spending variance and the variable overhead efficiency variance.

QS 24-11[A]
Overhead spending and efficiency variances   **P3**

VanWay, Inc. specializes in selling used SUVs. During the first six months of 2011, the dealership sold 100 trucks at an average price of $10,000 each. The budget for the first six months of 2011 was to sell 90 trucks at an average price of $10,500 each. Compute the dealership's sales price variance and sales volume variance for the first six months of 2011.

QS 24-12
Computing sales price and volume variances   **A1**

Based on predicted production of 12,000 units, a company anticipates $150,000 of fixed costs and $123,000 of variable costs. If the company actually produces 10,000 units, what are the flexible budget amounts of fixed and variable costs?

QS 24-13
Flexible budget   **P1**

Beck Company expects to produce 10,000 units for the year ending December 31. A flexible budget for 10,000 units of production reflects sales of $200,000; variable costs of $40,000; and fixed costs of $75,000. If the company instead produces and sells 13,000 units for the year, calculate the expected level of income from operations.

QS 24-14
Flexible budget
P1

Refer to information in QS 24-14. Assume that actual sales are $265,000, actual variable costs for the year are $59,000, and actual fixed costs for the year are $73,400. Prepare a flexible budget performance report for the year.

QS 24-15
Flexible budget performance report   **P1**

TenPro reports the following on one of its products. Compute the direct materials price and quantity variances.

QS 24-16
Materials variances
P2

Direct materials standard (4 lbs. @ $2/lb.)	$8 per finished unit
Actual direct materials used	150,000 lbs.
Actual finished units produced	30,000 units
Actual cost of direct materials used	$267,500

QS 24-17
Direct labor variances
P2

The following information describes a company's usage of direct labor in a recent period. Compute the direct labor rate and efficiency variances for the period.

Actual direct labor hours used	45,000
Actual direct labor rate per hour	$15
Standard direct labor rate per hour	$14
Standard direct labor hours for units produced	47,000

QS 24-18
Controllable overhead variance
P3

Funk Co. expects to produce 48,000 units for the year. The company's flexible budget for 48,000 units of production shows variable overhead costs of $72,000 and fixed overhead costs of $64,000. For the year, the company incurred actual overhead costs of $122,800 while producing 40,000 units. Compute the controllable overhead variance.

QS 24-19
Controllable overhead variance
P3

Aigne Corp. reports the following for November. Compute the controllable overhead variance for November.

Actual total factory overhead incurred	$28,175
Standard factory overhead:	
Variable overhead	$3.10 per unit produced
Fixed overhead	
($12,000/6,000 predicted units to be produced)	$2 per unit
Predicted units produced	6,000 units
Actual units produced	4,800 units

QS 24-20
Volume variance   **P3**

Refer to information in QS 24-19. Compute the volume variance for November.

QS 24-21
Sales variances   **A1**

In a recent year, **BMW** sold 216,944 of its 1 Series cars. Assume the company expected to sell 225,944 of these cars during the year. Also assume the budgeted sales price for each car was $30,000, and the actual sales price for each car was $30,200. Compute the sales price variance and the sales volume variance.

EXERCISES

Exercise 24-1
Preparation of flexible budgets
P1

Mesa Company's fixed budget for the first quarter of calendar year 2011 reveals the following. Prepare flexible budgets following the format of Exhibit 24.3 that show variable costs per unit, fixed costs, and three different flexible budgets for sales volumes of 7,500, 10,000, and 12,500 units.

Sales (10,000 units)		$3,000,000
Cost of goods sold		
Direct materials	$320,000	
Direct labor	680,000	
Production supplies	264,000	
Plant manager salary	60,000	1,324,000
Gross profit		1,676,000
Selling expenses		
Sales commissions	120,000	
Packaging	210,000	
Advertising	100,000	430,000
Administrative expenses		
Administrative salaries	80,000	
Depreciation—office equip.	30,000	
Insurance	18,000	
Office rent	24,000	152,000
Income from operations		$1,094,000

Check   Income (at 7,500 units), $742,500

KMAR Company manufactures and sells mountain bikes. It normally operates eight hours a day, six days a week. Using this information, classify each of the following costs as fixed or variable. If additional information would affect your decision, describe the information.

a. Incoming shipping expenses
b. Office supplies
c. Depreciation on tools
d. Taxes on property

e. Bike tires
f. Gas used for heating
g. Bike frames
h. Direct labor

i. Screws for assembly
j. Repair expense for tools
k. Management salaries

Exercise 24-2
Classification of costs as fixed or variable

P1

Cimarron Company's fixed budget performance report for July follows. The $630,000 budgeted expenses include $588,000 variable expenses and $42,000 fixed expenses. Actual expenses include $54,000 fixed expenses. Prepare a flexible budget performance report that shows any variances between budgeted results and actual results. List fixed and variable expenses separately.

Exercise 24-3
Preparation of a flexible budget performance report

P1

	Fixed Budget	Actual Results	Variances
Sales (in units)	8,400	10,800	
Sales (in dollars)	$840,000	$1,080,000	$240,000 F
Total expenses	630,000	756,000	126,000 U
Income from operations	$210,000	$ 324,000	$114,000 F

Check Income variance, $42,000 F

Daytec Company's fixed budget performance report for June follows. The $440,000 budgeted expenses include $300,000 variable expenses and $140,000 fixed expenses. Actual expenses include $130,000 fixed expenses. Prepare a flexible budget performance report showing any variances between budgeted and actual results. List fixed and variable expenses separately.

Exercise 24-4
Preparation of a flexible budget performance report

P1

	Fixed Budget	Actual Results	Variances
Sales (in units)	6,000	4,800	
Sales (in dollars)	$480,000	$422,400	$57,600 U
Total expenses	440,000	394,000	46,000 F
Income from operations	$ 40,000	$ 28,400	$11,600 U

Check Income variance, $24,400 F

After evaluating Zero Company's manufacturing process, management decides to establish standards of 1.5 hours of direct labor per unit of product and $11 per hour for the labor rate. During October, the company uses 3,780 hours of direct labor at a $45,360 total cost to produce 2,700 units of product. In November, the company uses 4,480 hours of direct labor at a $47,040 total cost to produce 2,800 units of product. (1) Compute the rate variance, the efficiency variance, and the total direct labor cost variance for each of these two months. (2) Interpret the October direct labor variances.

Exercise 24-5
Computation and interpretation of labor variances P2

Check (1) October rate variance, $3,780 U

Sonic Company set the following standard costs for one unit of its product for 2011.

Exercise 24-6[A]
Computation of total variable and fixed overhead variances

P3

Direct material (20 lbs. @ $2.50 per lb.)	$ 50.00
Direct labor (15 hrs. @ $8.00 per hr.)	120.00
Factory variable overhead (15 hrs. @ $2.50 per hr.)	37.50
Factory fixed overhead (15 hrs. @ $0.50 per hr.)	7.50
Standard cost	$215.00

The $3.00 ($2.50 + $0.50) total overhead rate per direct labor hour is based on an expected operating level equal to 75% of the factory's capacity of 50,000 units per month. The following monthly flexible budget information is also available.

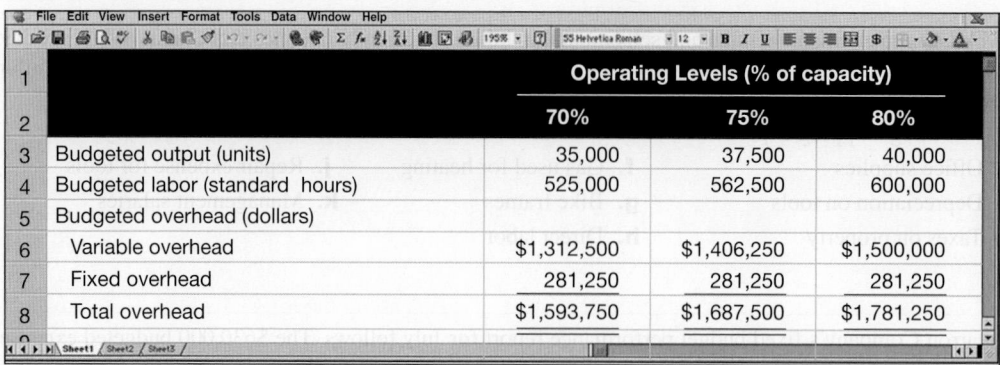

	Operating Levels (% of capacity)		
	70%	75%	80%
3 Budgeted output (units)	35,000	37,500	40,000
4 Budgeted labor (standard hours)	525,000	562,500	600,000
5 Budgeted overhead (dollars)			
6 Variable overhead	$1,312,500	$1,406,250	$1,500,000
7 Fixed overhead	281,250	281,250	281,250
8 Total overhead	$1,593,750	$1,687,500	$1,781,250

During the current month, the company operated at 70% of capacity, employees worked 500,000 hours, and the following actual overhead costs were incurred.

Variable overhead costs	$1,267,500
Fixed overhead costs	285,000
Total overhead costs	$1,552,500

Check (2) Variable overhead cost variance, $45,000 F

(1) Show how the company computed its predetermined overhead application rate per hour for total overhead, variable overhead, and fixed overhead. (2) Compute the variable and fixed overhead variances.

Exercise 24-7^A

Computation and interpretation of overhead spending, efficiency, and volume variances **P3**

Check (1) Variable overhead: Spending, $17,500 U; Efficiency, $62,500 F

Refer to the information from Exercise 24-6. Compute and interpret the following.

1. Variable overhead spending and efficiency variances.
2. Fixed overhead spending and volume variances.
3. Controllable variance.

Exercise 24-8

Computation and interpretation of materials variances **P2**

Check Price variance, $8,800 F

BTS Company made 6,000 bookshelves using 88,000 board feet of wood costing $607,200. The company's direct materials standards for one bookshelf are 16 board feet of wood at $7 per board foot. (1) Compute the direct materials variances incurred in manufacturing these bookshelves. (2) Interpret the direct materials variances.

Exercise 24-9^A

Materials variances recorded and closed

P4

Check (2) Cr. to Cost of Goods Sold, $64,800

Refer to Exercise 24-8. BTS Company records standard costs in its accounts and its material variances in separate accounts when it assigns materials costs to the Goods in Process Inventory account. (1) Show the journal entry that both charges the direct materials costs to the Goods in Process Inventory account and records the materials variances in their proper accounts. (2) Assume that BTS's material variances are the only variances accumulated in the accounting period and that they are immaterial. Prepare the adjusting journal entry to close the variance accounts at period-end. (3) Identify the variance that should be investigated according to the management by exception concept. Explain.

Exercise 24-10

Computation of total overhead rate and total overhead variance

P3

Check (1) Variable overhead rate, $7.00 per hour

Earth Company expects to operate at 80% of its productive capacity of 25,000 units per month. At this planned level, the company expects to use 40,000 standard hours of direct labor. Overhead is allocated to products using a predetermined standard rate based on direct labor hours. At the 80% capacity level, the total budgeted cost includes $40,000 fixed overhead cost and $280,000 variable overhead cost. In the current month, the company incurred $340,000 actual overhead and 39,000 actual labor hours while producing 19,500 units. (1) Compute its overhead application rate for total overhead. (2) Compute its total overhead variance.

Exercise 24-11

Computation of volume and controllable overhead variances

P3

Check (2) $27,000 U

Refer to the information from Exercise 24-10. Compute the (1) overhead volume variance and (2) overhead controllable variance.

Comp Wiz sells computers. During May 2011, it sold 500 computers at a $900 average price each. The May 2011 fixed budget included sales of 550 computers at an average price of $850 each. (1) Compute the sales price variance and the sales volume variance for May 2011. (2) Interpret the findings.

Match the terms a–e with their correct definition 1–5.

a. Standard cost

b. Practical standard

c. Standard cost card

d. Ideal standard

e. Management by exception

1. Record that accumulates standard cost information.

2. Quantity of input required if a production process is 100% efficient.

3. Managing by focusing on large differences from standard costs.

4. Quantity of input required under normal conditions.

5. Preset cost for delivering a product or service under normal conditions.

Presented below are terms preceded by letters a through j and a list of definitions 1 through 10. Enter the letter of the term with the definition, using the space preceding the definition.

a. Cost variance

b. Volume variance

c. Price variance

d. Quantity variance

e. Standard costs

f. Controllable variance

g. Fixed budget

h. Flexible budget

i. Variance analysis

j. Management by exception

_____ **1.** The difference between the total budgeted overhead cost and the overhead cost that was allocated to products using the predetermined fixed overhead rate.

_____ **2.** A planning budget based on a single predicted amount of sales or production volume; unsuitable for evaluations if the actual volume differs from the predicted volume.

_____ **3.** Preset costs for delivering a product, component, or service under normal conditions.

_____ **4.** A process of examining the differences between actual and budgeted sales or costs and describing them in terms of the amounts that resulted from price and quantity differences.

_____ **5.** The difference between actual and budgeted sales or cost caused by the difference between the actual price per unit and the budgeted price per unit.

_____ **6.** A budget prepared based on predicted amounts of revenues and expenses corresponding to the actual level of output.

_____ **7.** The difference between actual and budgeted cost caused by the difference between the actual quantity and the budgeted quantity.

_____ **8.** The combination of both overhead spending variances (variable and fixed) and the variable overhead efficiency variance.

_____ **9.** A management process to focus on significant variances and give less attention to areas where performance is close to the standard.

_____ **10.** The difference between actual cost and standard cost, made up of a price variance and a quantity variance.

Dee-Daw Co. provides the following results of April's operations: F indicates favorable and U indicates unfavorable. Applying the management by exception approach, which of the variances are of greatest concern? Why?

Direct materials price variance	$ 400 F
Direct materials quantity variance	2,000 U
Direct labor rate variance	100 U
Direct labor efficiency variance	1,200 F
Controllable overhead variance	400 U
Fixed overhead volume variance	600 F

Exercise 24-16
Direct materials and direct labor variances

P2

The following information describes production activities of Truzor Manufacturing for the year:

Actual raw materials used	16,000 lbs. at $4.05 per lb.
Actual factory payroll	5,545 hours for a total of $72,085
Actual units produced	30,000

Budgeted standards for each unit produced are 0.50 pounds of raw material at $4.15 per pound and 10 minutes of direct labor at $12.50 per hour. (1) Compute the direct materials price and quantity variances. Round to the nearest whole dollar. (2) Compute the direct labor rate and efficiency variances. Indicate whether each variance is favorable or unfavorable.

PROBLEM SET A

Problem 24-1A
Computation of materials, labor, and overhead variances

P2 P3

www.mheducation.asia/olc/wildkwokFAP

Tuna Company set the following standard unit costs for its single product.

Direct materials (25 lbs. @ $4 per lb.)	$100.00
Direct labor (6 hrs. @ $8 per hr.)	48.00
Factory overhead—variable (6 hrs. @ $5 per hr.)	30.00
Factory overhead—fixed (6 hrs. @ $7 per hr.)	42.00
Total standard cost	$220.00

The predetermined overhead rate is based on a planned operating volume of 80% of the productive capacity of 60,000 units per quarter. The following flexible budget information is available.

	Operating Levels		
	70%	80%	90%
Production in units	42,000	48,000	54,000
Standard direct labor hours	252,000	288,000	324,000
Budgeted overhead			
Fixed factory overhead	$2,016,000	$2,016,000	$2,016,000
Variable factory overhead	$1,260,000	$1,440,000	$1,620,000

During the current quarter, the company operated at 70% of capacity and produced 42,000 units of product; actual direct labor totaled 250,000 hours. Units produced were assigned the following standard costs:

Direct materials (1,050,000 lbs. @ $4 per lb.)	$4,200,000
Direct labor (252,000 hrs. @ $8 per hr.)	2,016,000
Factory overhead (252,000 hrs. @ $12 per hr.)	3,024,000
Total standard cost	$9,240,000

Actual costs incurred during the current quarter follow:

Direct materials (1,000,000 lbs. @ $4.25)	$4,250,000
Direct labor (250,000 hrs. @ $7.75)	1,937,500
Fixed factory overhead costs	1,960,000
Variable factory overhead costs	1,200,000
Total actual costs	$9,347,500

Required

Check (1) Materials variances: Price, $250,000 U; Quantity, $200,000 F.

(2) Labor variances: Rate, $62,500 F; Efficiency, $16,000 F

1. Compute the direct materials cost variance, including its price and quantity variances.
2. Compute the direct labor variance, including its rate and efficiency variances.
3. Compute the overhead controllable and volume variances.

Problem 24-2A[A]
Expanded overhead variances

P3

Refer to information in Problem 24-1A.

Required

Compute these variances: (a) variable overhead spending and efficiency, (b) fixed overhead spending and volume, and (c) total overhead controllable.

Pebco Company's 2011 master budget included the following fixed budget report. It is based on an expected production and sales volume of 20,000 units.

Problem 24-3A
Preparation and analysis of a flexible budget **P1**

PEBCO COMPANY
Fixed Budget Report
For Year Ended December 31, 2011

Sales		$3,000,000
Cost of goods sold		
Direct materials	$1,200,000	
Direct labor	260,000	
Machinery repairs (variable cost)	57,000	
Depreciation—plant equipment	250,000	
Utilities ($50,000 is variable)	200,000	
Plant management salaries	140,000	2,107,000
Gross profit		893,000
Selling expenses		
Packaging	80,000	
Shipping	116,000	
Sales salary (fixed annual amount)	160,000	356,000
General and administrative expenses		
Advertising expense	81,000	
Salaries	241,000	
Entertainment expense	90,000	412,000
Income from operations		$ 125,000

Required

1. Classify all items listed in the fixed budget as variable or fixed. Also determine their amounts per unit or their amounts for the year, as appropriate.

2. Prepare flexible budgets (see Exhibit 24.3) for the company at sales volumes of 18,000 and 24,000 units.

3. The company's business conditions are improving. One possible result is a sales volume of approximately 28,000 units. The company president is confident that this volume is within the relevant range of existing capacity. How much would operating income increase over the 2011 budgeted amount of $125,000 if this level is reached without increasing capacity?

4. An unfavorable change in business is remotely possible; in this case, production and sales volume for 2011 could fall to 14,000 units. How much income (or loss) from operations would occur if sales volume falls to this level?

Check (2) Budgeted income at 24,000 units, $372,400

(4) Potential operating loss, $(246,100)

Refer to the information in Problem 24-3A. Pebco Company's actual income statement for 2011 follows.

Problem 24-4A
Preparation and analysis of a flexible budget performance report

P1 P2 A1

www.mheducation.asia/olc/wildkwokFAP

PEBCO COMPANY
Statement of Income from Operations
For Year Ended December 31, 2011

Sales (24,000 units)		$3,648,000
Cost of goods sold		
Direct materials	$1,400,000	
Direct labor	360,000	
Machinery repairs (variable cost)	60,000	
Depreciation—plant equipment	250,000	
Utilities (fixed cost is $154,000)	218,000	
Plant management salaries	155,000	2,443,000
Gross profit		1,205,000
Selling expenses		
Packaging	90,000	
Shipping	124,000	
Sales salary (annual)	162,000	376,000
General and administrative expenses		
Advertising expense	104,000	
Salaries	232,000	
Entertainment expense	100,000	436,000
Income from operations		$ 393,000

Required

1. Prepare a flexible budget performance report for 2011.

Analysis Component

2. Analyze and interpret both the (a) sales variance and (b) direct materials variance.

Problem 24-5A
Flexible budget preparation; computation of materials, labor, and overhead variances; and overhead variance report

P1 P2 P3 C2

Kwikeze Company set the following standard costs for one unit of its product.

Direct materials (4.5 lbs. @ $6 per lb.)	$27.00
Direct labor (1.5 hrs. @ $12 per hr.)	18.00
Overhead (1.5 hrs. @ $16 per hr.)	24.00
Total standard cost.	$69.00

The predetermined overhead rate ($16 per direct labor hour) is based on an expected volume of 75% of the factory's capacity of 20,000 units per month. Following are the company's budgeted overhead costs per month at the 75% level.

Overhead Budget (75% Capacity)

Variable overhead costs		
Indirect materials	$22,500	
Indirect labor	90,000	
Power	22,500	
Repairs and maintenance	45,000	
Total variable overhead costs		$180,000
Fixed overhead costs		
Depreciation—building	24,000	
Depreciation—machinery	72,000	
Taxes and insurance.	18,000	
Supervision	66,000	
Total fixed overhead costs.		180,000
Total overhead costs		$360,000

The company incurred the following actual costs when it operated at 75% of capacity in October.

Direct materials (69,000 lbs. @ $6.10 per lb.)		$ 420,900
Direct labor (22,800 hrs. @ $12.30 per hr.)		280,440
Overhead costs		
Indirect materials	$21,600	
Indirect labor	82,260	
Power	23,100	
Repairs and maintenance	46,800	
Depreciation—building	24,000	
Depreciation—machinery	75,000	
Taxes and insurance	16,500	
Supervision	66,000	355,260
Total costs		$1,056,600

Required

1. Examine the monthly overhead budget to (a) determine the costs per unit for each variable overhead item and its total per unit costs, and (b) identify the total fixed costs per month.

2. Prepare flexible overhead budgets (as in Exhibit 24.12) for October showing the amounts of each variable and fixed cost at the 65%, 75%, and 85% capacity levels.

3. Compute the direct materials cost variance, including its price and quantity variances.

4. Compute the direct labor cost variance, including its rate and efficiency variances.
5. Prepare a detailed overhead variance report (as in Exhibit 24.15) that shows the variances for individual items of overhead.

(4) Labor variances: Rate, $6,840 U; Efficiency, $3,600 U

Kudos Company has set the following standard costs per unit for the product it manufactures.

Problem 24-6A^A

Materials, labor, and overhead variances; and overhead variance report

C2 P2 P3

Direct materials (10 lbs. @ $3 per lb.)...........	$30.00
Direct labor (4 hrs. @ $6 per hr.).............	24.00
Overhead (4 hrs. @ $2.50 per hr.)	10.00
Total standard cost	$64.00

The predetermined overhead rate is based on a planned operating volume of 80% of the productive capacity of 10,000 units per month. The following flexible budget information is available.

	Operating Levels		
	70%	80%	90%
Production in units	7,000	8,000	9,000
Standard direct labor hours	28,000	32,000	36,000
Budgeted overhead			
Variable overhead costs			
Indirect materials................	$ 8,750	$10,000	$11,250
Indirect labor	14,000	16,000	18,000
Power......................	3,500	4,000	4,500
Maintenance..................	1,750	2,000	2,250
Total variable costs	28,000	32,000	36,000
Fixed overhead costs			
Rent of factory building	12,000	12,000	12,000
Depreciation—machinery	20,000	20,000	20,000
Supervisory salaries	16,000	16,000	16,000
Total fixed costs	48,000	48,000	48,000
Total overhead costs	$76,000	$80,000	$84,000

During May, the company operated at 90% of capacity and produced 9,000 units, incurring the following actual costs.

Direct materials (92,000 lbs. @ $2.95 per lb.).........		$271,400
Direct labor (37,600 hrs. @ $6.05 per hr.)		227,480
Overhead costs		
Indirect materials	$10,000	
Indirect labor	16,000	
Power	4,500	
Maintenance	3,000	
Rent of factory building	12,000	
Depreciation—machinery	19,200	
Supervisory salaries	17,000	81,700
Total costs		$580,580

Required

1. Compute the direct materials variance, including its price and quantity variances.
2. Compute the direct labor variance, including its rate and efficiency variances.

Check (1) Materials variances: Price, $4,600 F; Quantity, $6,000 U
(2) Labor variances: Rate, $1,880 U; Efficiency, $9,600 U

3. Compute these variances: (a) variable overhead spending and efficiency, (b) fixed overhead spending and volume, and (c) total overhead controllable.

4. Prepare a detailed overhead variance report (as in Exhibit 24.15) that shows the variances for individual items of overhead.

Problem 24-7A^A
Materials, labor, and overhead variances recorded and analyzed

C1 P4

Loretto Company's standard cost accounting system recorded this information from its December operations.

Standard direct materials cost	$130,000
Direct materials quantity variance (unfavorable)	5,000
Direct materials price variance (favorable)	1,500
Actual direct labor cost	65,000
Direct labor efficiency variance (favorable)	7,000
Direct labor rate variance (unfavorable)	500
Actual overhead cost	250,000
Volume variance (unfavorable)	12,000
Controllable variance (unfavorable)	8,000

Required

Check (1) Dr. Goods in Process Inventory (for overhead), $230,000

1. Prepare December 31 journal entries to record the company's costs and variances for the month. (Do not prepare the journal entry to close the variances.)

Analysis Component

2. Identify the areas that would attract the attention of a manager who uses management by exception. Explain what action(s) the manager should consider.

PROBLEM SET B

Problem 24-1B
Computation of materials, labor, and overhead variances

P2   P3

Sabates Company set the following standard unit costs for its single product.

Direct materials (5 lbs. @ $10 per lb.)	$ 50.00
Direct labor (3 hrs. @ $15 per hr.)	45.00
Factory overhead—variable (3 hrs. @ $5 per hr.)	15.00
Factory overhead—fixed (3 hrs. @ $3 per hr.)	9.00
Total standard cost	$119.00

The predetermined overhead rate is based on a planned operating volume of 90% of the productive capacity of 100,000 units per quarter. The following flexible budget information is available.

	Operating Levels		
	80%	90%	100%
Production in units	32,000	36,000	40,000
Standard direct labor hours	96,000	108,000	120,000
Budgeted overhead			
Fixed factory overhead	$324,000	$324,000	$324,000
Variable factory overhead	480,000	540,000	600,000

During the current quarter, the company operated at 80% of capacity and produced 32,000 units of product; direct labor hours worked were 100,000. Units produced were assigned the following standard costs:

Direct materials (160,000 lbs. @ $10 per lb.)	$1,600,000
Direct labor (96,000 hrs. @ $15 per hr.)	1,440,000
Factory overhead (96,000 hrs. @ $8 per hr.)	768,000
Total standard cost	$3,808,000

Actual costs incurred during the current quarter follow:

Direct materials (155,000 lbs. @ $10.20)...........	$1,581,000
Direct labor (100,000 hrs. @ $14)................	1,400,000
Fixed factory overhead costs	370,000
Variable factory overhead costs	480,000
Total actual costs............................	$3,831,000

Required

1. Compute the direct materials cost variance, including its price and quantity variances.
2. Compute the direct labor variance, including its rate and efficiency variances.
3. Compute the total overhead controllable and volume variances.

Refer to information in Problem 24-1B.

Required

Compute these variances: (a) variable overhead spending and efficiency, (b) fixed overhead spending and volume, and (c) total overhead controllable.

Check (1) Materials variances:
Price, $31,000 U; Quantity, $50,000 F
(2) Labor variances: Rate,
$100,000 F; Efficiency, $60,000 U

Problem 24-2B^A
Expanded overhead variances
P3

Razorback Company's 2011 master budget included the following fixed budget report. It is based on an expected production and sales volume of 10,000 units.

Problem 24-3B
Preparation and analysis of a
flexible budget P1 A1

RAZORBACK COMPANY
Fixed Budget Report
For Year Ended December 31, 2011

Sales		$250,000
Cost of goods sold		
Direct materials	$100,000	
Direct labor	20,000	
Machinery repairs (variable cost)	3,000	
Depreciation—machinery	11,920	
Utilities (80% is variable cost)	8,000	
Plant manager salaries	6,000	148,920
Gross profit		101,080
Selling expenses		
Packaging	9,000	
Shipping	30,000	
Sales salary (fixed annual amount)	18,000	57,000
General and administrative expenses		
Advertising	4,000	
Salaries	9,360	
Entertainment expense	10,000	23,360
Income from operations		$ 20,720

Required

1. Classify all items listed in the fixed budget as variable or fixed. Also determine their amounts per unit or their amounts for the year, as appropriate.
2. Prepare flexible budgets (see Exhibit 24.3) for the company at sales volumes of 8,000 and 12,000 units.
3. The company's business conditions are improving. One possible result is a sales volume of approximately 14,400 units. The company president is confident that this volume is within the relevant range of existing capacity. How much would operating income increase over the 2011 budgeted amount of $20,720 if this level is reached without increasing capacity?
4. An unfavorable change in business is remotely possible; in this case, production and sales volume for 2011 could fall to 5,000 units. How much income (or loss) from operations would occur if sales volume falls to this level?

Check (2) Budgeted income at
12,000 units, $37,040

(4) Potential operating loss,
$(20,080)

Problem 24-4B
Preparation and analysis
of a flexible budget
performance report
P1 A1

Refer to the information in Problem 24-3B. Razorback Company's actual income statement for 2011 follows.

RAZORBACK COMPANY Statement of Income from Operations For Year Ended December 31, 2011		
Sales (12,000 units)		$288,000
Cost of goods sold		
Direct materials	$95,000	
Direct labor	16,000	
Machinery repairs (variable cost)	3,300	
Depreciation—machinery	11,920	
Utilities (variable cost, $7,160)	8,520	
Plant manager salaries	6,720	141,460
Gross profit		146,540
Selling expenses		
Packaging	10,800	
Shipping	37,200	
Sales salary (annual)	19,200	67,200
General and administrative expenses		
Advertising expense	4,200	
Salaries	9,360	
Entertainment expense	10,000	23,560
Income from operations		$ 55,780

Required

1. Prepare a flexible budget performance report for 2011.

Analysis Component

2. Analyze and interpret both the (a) sales variance and (b) direct materials variance.

Problem 24-5B
Flexible budget preparation;
computation of materials, labor,
and overhead variances; and
overhead variance report
P1 P2 P3 C2

Sunburst Company set the following standard costs for one unit of its product.

Direct materials (48 kgs. @ $4 per kg.)	$192.00
Direct labor (12 hrs. @ $9 per hr.)	108.00
Overhead (12 hrs. @ $4.50 per hr.)	54.00
Total standard cost	$354.00

The predetermined overhead rate ($4.50 per direct labor hour) is based on an expected volume of 50% of the factory's capacity of 10,000 units per month. Following are the company's budgeted overhead costs per month at the 50% level.

Overhead Budget (50% Capacity)		
Variable overhead costs		
Indirect materials	$40,000	
Indirect labor	80,000	
Power	20,000	
Repairs and maintenance	30,000	
Total variable overhead costs		$170,000
Fixed overhead costs		
Depreciation—building	20,000	
Depreciation—machinery	30,000	
Taxes and insurance	10,000	
Supervision	40,000	
Total fixed overhead costs		100,000
Total overhead costs		$270,000

The company incurred the following actual costs when it operated at 40% of capacity in December.

Direct materials (196,000 kgs. @ $4.00)		$ 784,000
Direct labor (46,000 hrs. @ $9.15)		420,900
Overhead costs		
Indirect materials	$30,000	
Indirect labor	66,000	
Power	15,600	
Repairs and maintenance	21,000	
Depreciation—building	20,000	
Depreciation—machinery	30,000	
Taxes and insurance	9,600	
Supervision	39,600	231,800
Total costs		$1,436,700

Required

1. Examine the monthly overhead budget to (a) determine the costs per unit for each variable overhead item and its total per unit costs, and (b) identify the total fixed costs per month.
2. Prepare flexible overhead budgets (as in Exhibit 24.12) for December showing the amounts of each variable and fixed cost at the 40%, 50%, and 60% capacity levels.
3. Compute the direct materials cost variance, including its price and quantity variances.
4. Compute the direct labor cost variance, including its rate and efficiency variances.
5. Prepare a detailed overhead variance report (as in Exhibit 24.15) that shows the variances for individual items of overhead.

Check (2) Budgeted total overhead at 6,000 units, $304,000

(3) Materials variances: Price, $0 U; Quantity, $16,000 U

(4) Labor variances: Rate, $6,900 U; Efficiency, $18,000 F

Carlsbad Company has set the following standard costs per unit for the product it manufactures.

Problem 24-6B[A]
Materials, labor, and overhead variances; and overhead variance report

C2 P2 P3

Direct materials (40 oz. @ $0.75 per oz.)		$ 30.00
Direct labor (2 hr. @ $20 per hr.)		40.00
Overhead (2 hr. @ $53.50 per hr.)		107.00
Total standard cost		$177.00

The predetermined overhead rate is based on a planned operating volume of 60% of the productive capacity of 3,000 units per month. The following flexible budget information is available.

	Operating Levels		
	50%	**60%**	**70%**
Production in units	1,500	1,800	2,100
Standard direct labor hours	3,000	3,600	4,200
Budgeted overhead			
Variable overhead costs			
Indirect materials	$ 18,000	$21,600	$25,200
Indirect labor	10,500	12,600	14,700
Power	7,500	9,000	10,500
Maintenance	4,500	5,400	6,300
Total variable costs	40,500	48,600	56,700
Fixed overhead costs			
Rent of factory building	48,000	48,000	48,000
Depreciation—machinery	44,000	44,000	44,000
Taxes and insurance.............	20,000	20,000	20,000
Supervisory salaries	32,000	32,000	32,000
Total fixed costs	144,000	144,000	144,000
Total overhead costs	$184,500	$192,600	$200,700

During March, the company operated at 70% of capacity and produced 2,100 units, incurring the following actual costs.

Direct materials (88,000 oz. @ $0.70 per oz.)...........		$ 61,600
Direct labor (4,000 hrs. @ $19.50 per hr.)		78,000
Overhead costs		
Indirect materials.............................	$23,600	
Indirect labor................................	14,800	
Power..	10,000	
Maintenance..................................	3,200	
Rent of factory building	48,000	
Depreciation—machinery	44,000	
Taxes and insurance...........................	24,000	
Supervisory salaries...........................	31,600	199,200
Total costs		$338,800

Required

Check (1) Materials variances:
Price, $4,400 F; Quantity, $3,000 U
     (2) Labor variances: Rate,
$2,000 F; Efficiency, $4,000 F

1. Compute the direct materials cost variance, including its price and quantity variances.
2. Compute the direct labor variance, including its rate and efficiency variances.
3. Compute these variances: (a) variable overhead spending and efficiency, (b) fixed overhead spending and volume, and (c) total overhead controllable.
4. Prepare a detailed overhead variance report (as in Exhibit 24.15) that shows the variances for individual items of overhead.

Problem 24-7B[A]
Materials, labor, and overhead
variances recorded and analyzed

C1   P4

Kincaid Company's standard cost accounting system recorded this information from its June operations.

Standard direct materials cost	$220,500
Direct materials quantity variance (favorable)	20,250
Direct materials price variance (favorable)	14,500
Actual direct labor cost	335,000
Direct labor efficiency variance (favorable)	26,700
Direct labor rate variance (unfavorable)	3,500
Actual overhead cost	359,000
Volume variance (unfavorable)	1,650
Controllable variance (unfavorable).................	32,500

Required

Check (1) Dr. Goods in Process
Inventory (for overhead), $324,850

1. Prepare journal entries dated June 30 to record the company's costs and variances for the month. (Do not prepare the journal entry to close the variances.)

Analysis Component

2. Identify the areas that would attract the attention of a manager who uses management by exception. Describe what action(s) the manager should consider.

SERIAL PROBLEM
Business Solutions

P1

(This serial problem began in Chapter 1 and continues through most of the book. If previous chapter segments were not completed, the serial problem can begin at this point.)

SP 24 Business Solutions' second quarter 2012 fixed budget performance report for its computer furniture operations follows. The $156,000 budgeted expenses include $108,000 in variable expenses for desks and $18,000 in variable expenses for chairs, as well as $30,000 fixed expenses. The actual expenses include $31,000 fixed expenses. Prepare a flexible budget performance report that shows any variances between budgeted results and actual results. List fixed and variable expenses separately.

	Fixed Budget	Actual Results	Variances
Desk sales (in units).............	144	150	
Chair sales (in units)	72	80	
Desk sales (in dollars)	$180,000	$186,000	$6,000 F
Chair sales (in dollars)...........	$ 36,000	$ 41,200	$5,200 F
Total expenses..................	$156,000	$163,880	$7,880 U
Income from operations	$ 60,000	$ 63,320	$3,320 F

Check   Variances: Fixed expenses, $1,000 U

Beyond the Numbers

BTN 24-1   Analysis of flexible budgets and standard costs emphasizes the importance of a similar unit of measure for meaningful comparisons and evaluations. When **Research In Motion** compiles its financial reports in compliance with GAAP, it applies the same unit of measurement, U.S. dollars, for most measures of business operations. One issue for Research In Motion is how best to adjust account values for its subsidiaries that compile financial reports in currencies other than the U.S. dollar.

REPORTING IN ACTION

C1

Required

1. Access Research In Motion's 2010 annual report from its Website www.rim.com. Read Note 1 and identify the financial statement where it reports the annual adjustment (remeasurement) for foreign currency translation.

2. Translating financial statements requires the use of a currency exchange rate. For each of the following three financial statement items, explain the exchange rate the company would apply to translate into U.S. dollars.

   a. Cash

   b. Sales revenue

   c. Property, plant and equipment

BTN 24-2   The usefulness of budgets, variances, and related analyses often depends on the accuracy of management's estimates of future sales activity.

COMPARATIVE ANALYSIS

A1

Required

1. Identify and record the prior three years' sales (in dollars) for **Research In Motion**, **Apple**, and **Palm**. For Research In Motion, use its 2010 annual report from its Website www.rim.com. For Apple and Palm, use their financial statements in Appendix A.

2. Using the data in part 1, predict all three companies' sales activity for the next two to three years. (If possible, compare your predictions to actual sales figures for these years.)

BTN 24-3   Setting materials, labor, and overhead standards is challenging. If standards are set too low, companies might purchase inferior products and employees might not work to their full potential. If standards are set too high, companies could be unable to offer a quality product at a profitable rate and employees could be overworked. The ethical challenge is to set a high but reasonable standard. Assume that as a manager, you are asked to set the standard materials price and quantity for the new 1,000 CKB Mega-Max chip, a technically advanced product. To properly set the price and quantity standards, you assemble a team of specialists to provide input.

ETHICS CHALLENGE

C1

Required

Identify four types of specialists that you would assemble to provide information to help set the materials price and quantity standards. Briefly explain why you chose each individual.

COMMUNICATING IN PRACTICE

P4   C2

BTN 24-4 The reason we use the words *favorable* and *unfavorable* when evaluating variances is made clear when we look at the closing of accounts. To see this, consider that (1) all variance accounts are closed at the end of each period (temporary accounts), (2) a favorable variance is always a credit balance, and (3) an unfavorable variance is always a debit balance. Write a one-half page memorandum to your instructor with three parts that answer the three following requirements. (Assume that variance accounts are closed to Cost of Goods Sold.)

Required

1. Does Cost of Goods Sold increase or decrease when closing a favorable variance? Does gross margin increase or decrease when a favorable variance is closed to Cost of Goods Sold? Explain.
2. Does Cost of Goods Sold increase or decrease when closing an unfavorable variance? Does gross margin increase or decrease when an unfavorable variance is closed to Cost of Goods Sold? Explain.
3. Explain the meaning of a favorable variance and an unfavorable variance.

TAKING IT TO THE NET

C1

BTN 24-5 Access iSixSigma's Website (iSixSigma.com) to search for and read information about *benchmarking* to complete the following requirements.

Required

1. Write a one-paragraph explanation (in layperson's terms) of benchmarking.
2. How does standard costing relate to benchmarking?

TEAMWORK IN ACTION

C2

BTN 24-6 Many service industries link labor rate and time (quantity) standards with their processes. One example is the standard time to board an aircraft. The reason time plays such an important role in the service industry is that it is viewed as a competitive advantage: best service in the shortest amount of time. Although the labor rate component is difficult to observe, the time component of a service delivery standard is often readily apparent—for example, "Lunch will be served in less than five minutes, or it is free."

Required

Break into teams and select two service industries for your analysis. Identify and describe all the time elements each industry uses to create a competitive advantage.

ENTREPRENEURIAL DECISION

C1   C2

BTN 24-7   Mosaic Dance is a two-person show. Yet Derrick Lye and Wee Tze Yi find budgeting important enough to merit allocation of their scarce time.

Required

1. Highlight the benefits that Derrick and Tze Yi see in budgeting.
2. "Budgeting can also identify revenue gaps and thereby prompt additional marketing activities to address the discrepancies." What do you think this comment means?

HITTING THE ROAD

C1

BTN 24-8 Try to set up an interview with the finance department head of your university. Interview him or her to understand how the university adjusts its budgets for deviations in student enrollments from what was planned. Document the findings.

BTN 24-9   View the target vs. actual numbers for Adidas at the following link: <u>http:adidas-group.</u> <u>corporate-publications.com/2010/gb/en/additional-information/targets-vs-results.html</u>.

Required

Identify the possible causes for the variance in operating margin. The target was 6.5% and the actual was 7.5%.

ANSWERS TO MULTIPLE CHOICE QUIZ

1. c; Fixed costs remain at $300,000; Variable costs = ($246,000/24,000 units) × 20,000 units = $205,000.

2. e; Budgeted direct materials + Unfavorable variance = Actual cost of direct materials used; or, 60,000 units × $10 per unit = $600,000 + $15,000 U = $615,000.

3. c; (AH × AR) − (AH × SR) = $1,599,040 − (84,160 hours × $20 per hour) = $84,160 F.

4. b; Actual variable overhead − Variable overhead applied to production = Variable overhead cost variance; or $150,000 − (96,000 hours × $1.50 per hour) = $6,000 U.

5. a; Budgeted fixed overhead − Fixed overhead applied to production = Volume variance; or $24,000 − (4,800 units × $4 per unit) = $4,800 U.

25

Capital Budgeting and Managerial Decisions

A Look Back

Chapter 24 discussed flexible budgets, variance analysis, and standard costs. It explained how management uses each to control and monitor business activities.

A Look at This Chapter

This chapter focuses on evaluating capital budgeting decisions. It also explains several tools and procedures used in making and evaluating short-term managerial decisions.

Learning Objectives

CAP

CONCEPTUAL

C1 Describe the importance of relevant costs for short-term decisions. (p. 1019)

ANALYTICAL

A1 Evaluate short-term managerial decisions using relevant costs. (p. 1020)

A2 Analyze a capital investment project using break-even time. (p. 1027)

PROCEDURAL

P1 Compute payback period and describe its use. (p. 1009)

P2 Compute accounting rate of return and explain its use. (p. 1011)

P3 Compute net present value and describe its use. (p. 1013)

P4 Compute internal rate of return and explain its use. (p. 1015)

"We require our people to understand our clients."—**NGUYEN TRUNG THANG**

Meet the Professionals

He has a realm of global work skills to impart, and he knows where they are needed the most—his home country of Vietnam.

With an impressive work record that culminated as regional Retail Development Manager in a multinational company, it was only a matter of time before the go-getting Nguyen Trung Thang struck out on his own. This was in the 2000s. Business management was a relatively foreign concept in Vietnamese enterprises, as was professionalism, which Thang values highly. In this "awkward" business environment, "I came up with the idea of applying my international experience in Vietnamese enterprises to enhance their value and success," he says.

Today, **Masso Group (www.massogroup.com),** which he founded to professionalize the business management of Vietnamese companies, is branded as a professional consulting and service group, specializing in integrated brand communication and management coaching. Within a decade, it has expanded its divisions from marketing consultancy and communications to brand building and acquisitions. The Group's success rests no less on its maxim that people come first. Stresses Thang, "We require our people to understand our clients at a level where they, the clients, can share all their difficulties and expectations."

Despite a challenging business climate—the majority of Vietnamese enterprises are small- and medium-sized enterprises, lacking in professionalism and business management knowledge, which poses challenges to consultancy services to begin with—astute managerial and investment decisions have helped the Group maneuver its way to success. On a day-to-day basis, the Group expertly tackles accounting issues pertaining to maintaining a viable level of resources, among other things. Capital budgeting, the process of analyzing alternative long-term investments and deciding which assets to acquire or sell, "is regularly planned, tracked, and reviewed from time to time" at Masso Group. Clearly this vigilance paid off when it acquired Emerald Digital Marketing, a digital-based communication outfit, thereby honing the Group's competitive edge even further.

"Young companies with committed entrepreneurship are our target," says Thang of future merger and acquisition activity while reiterating the foremost objective of delivering innovative solutions to clients. That and "adding more value from cooperation is what differentiates Masso Group from its competitors," he asserts. With that spirit, Masso Group may change not just the business environment in Vietnam but also people's lives.

Making business decisions involves choosing between alternative courses of action. Many factors affect business decisions, yet analysis typically focuses on finding the alternative that offers the highest return on investment or the greatest reduction in costs. Some decisions are based on little more than an intuitive understanding of the situation because available information is too limited to allow a more systematic analysis. In other cases, intangible factors such as convenience, prestige, and environmental considerations are more important than strictly quantitative factors. In all situations, managers can reach a sounder decision if they identify the consequences of alternative choices in financial terms. This chapter explains several methods of analysis that can help managers make those business decisions.

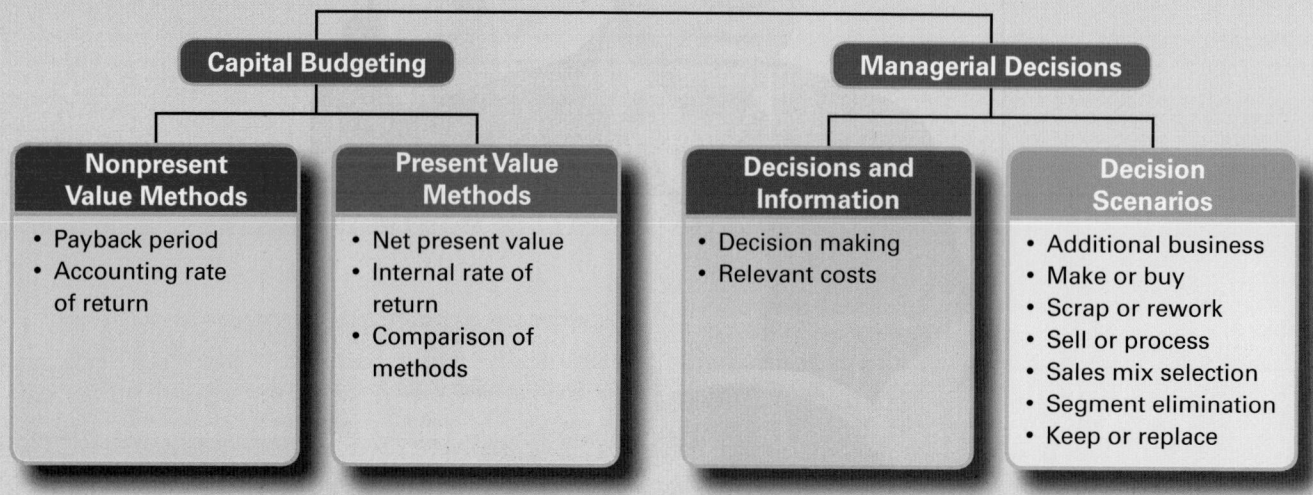

Capital Budgeting

Nonpresent Value Methods
- Payback period
- Accounting rate of return

Present Value Methods
- Net present value
- Internal rate of return
- Comparison of methods

Managerial Decisions

Decisions and Information
- Decision making
- Relevant costs

Decision Scenarios
- Additional business
- Make or buy
- Scrap or rework
- Sell or process
- Sales mix selection
- Segment elimination
- Keep or replace

Section 1—Capital Budgeting

The capital expenditures budget is management's plan for acquiring and selling property, plant and equipment. **Capital budgeting** is the process of analyzing alternative long-term investments and deciding which assets to acquire or sell. These decisions can involve developing a new product or process, buying a new machine or a new building, or acquiring an entire company. An objective for these decisions is to earn a satisfactory return on investment.

Capital budgeting decisions require careful analysis because they are usually the most difficult and risky decisions that managers make. These decisions are difficult because they require predicting events that will not occur until well into the future. Many of these predictions are tentative and potentially unreliable. Specifically, a capital budgeting decision is risky because (1) the outcome is uncertain, (2) large amounts of money are usually involved, (3) the investment involves a long-term commitment, and (4) the decision could be difficult or impossible to reverse, no matter how poor it turns out to be. Risk is especially high for investments in technology due to innovations and uncertainty.

Managers use several methods to evaluate capital budgeting decisions. Nearly all of these methods involve predicting cash inflows and cash outflows of proposed investments, assessing the risk of and returns on those flows, and then choosing the investments to make. Management often restates future cash flows in terms of their present value. This approach applies the time value of money: A dollar today is worth more than a dollar tomorrow. Similarly, a dollar tomorrow is worth less than a dollar today. The process of restating future cash flows in terms of their present value is called *discounting*. The time value of money is important when evaluating capital investments, but managers sometimes apply evaluation methods that ignore present value. This section describes four methods for comparing alternative investments.

Point: The nature of capital spending has changed with the business environment. Budgets for information technology have increased from about 25% of corporate capital spending 20 years ago to an estimated 35% today.

METHODS NOT USING TIME VALUE OF MONEY

All investments, whether they involve the purchase of a machine or another long-term asset, are expected to produce net cash flows. *Net cash flow* is cash inflows minus cash outflows. Sometimes managers perform simple analyses of the financial feasibility of an investment's net cash flow without using the time value of money. This section explains two of the most common methods in this category: (1) payback period and (2) accounting rate of return.

Payback Period

An investment's **payback period (PBP)** is the expected time period to recover the initial investment amount. Managers prefer investing in assets with shorter payback periods to reduce the risk of an unprofitable investment over the long run. Acquiring assets with short payback periods reduces a company's risk from potentially inaccurate long-term predictions of future cash flows.

| P1 | Compute payback period and describe its use. |

Computing Payback Period with Even Cash Flows   To illustrate use of the payback period for an investment with even cash flows, we look at data from FasTrac, a manufacturer of exercise equipment and supplies. (*Even cash flows* are cash flows that are the same each and every year; *uneven cash flows* are cash flows that are not all equal in amount.) FasTrac is considering several different capital investments, one of which is to purchase a machine to use in manufacturing a new product. This machine costs $16,000 and is expected to have an eight-year life with no residual value. Management predicts this machine will produce 1,000 units of product each year and that the new product will be sold for $30 per unit. Exhibit 25.1 shows the expected annual net cash flows for this asset over its life as well as the expected annual revenues and expenses (including depreciation and income taxes) from investing in the machine.

EXHIBIT 25.1

Cash Flow Analysis

FASTRAC Cash Flow Analysis—Machinery Investment January 15, 2011	Expected Accrual Figures	Expected Net Cash Flows
Annual sales of new product	$30,000	$30,000
Deduct annual expenses		
Cost of materials, labor, and overhead (except depreciation)	(15,500)	(15,500)
Depreciation—Machinery	(2,000)	
Additional selling and administrative expenses	(9,500)	(9,500)
Annual pretax accrual income	3,000	
Income taxes (30%)	900	900
Annual net profit	$ 2,100	
Annual net cash flow		$ 4,100

The amount of net cash flow from the machinery is computed by subtracting expected cash outflows from expected cash inflows. The cash flows column of Exhibit 25.1 excludes all noncash revenues and expenses. Depreciation is FasTrac's only noncash item. Alternatively, managers can adjust the projected net profit for revenue and expense items that do not affect cash flows. For FasTrac, this means taking the $2,100 net profit and adding back the $2,000 depreciation.

Point: Annual net cash flow in Exhibit 25.1 equals net profit plus depreciation (a noncash expense).

The formula for computing the payback period of an investment that yields even net cash flows is in Exhibit 25.2.

EXHIBIT 25.2

Payback Period Formula with Even Cash Flows

$$\text{Payback period} = \frac{\text{Cost of investment}}{\text{Annual net cash flow}}$$

The payback period reflects the amount of time for the investment to generate enough net cash flow to return (or pay back) the cash initially invested to purchase it. FasTrac's payback period for this machine is just under four years:

$$\text{Payback period} = \frac{\$16,000}{\$4,100} = 3.9 \text{ years}$$

The initial investment is fully recovered in 3.9 years, or just before reaching the halfway point of this machine's useful life of eight years.

Decision Insight

Payback Phones   Profits of telecoms have declined as too much capital investment chased too little revenue. Telecom success depends on new technology, and communications gear is evolving at a dizzying rate. Consequently, managers of telecoms often demand short payback periods and large expected net cash flows to compensate for the investment risk. ■

Computing Payback Period with Uneven Cash Flows   Computing the payback period in the prior section assumed even net cash flows. What happens if the net cash flows are uneven? In this case, the payback period is computed using the *cumulative total of net cash flows*. The word *cumulative* refers to the addition of each period's net cash flows as we progress through time. To illustrate, consider data for another investment that FasTrac is considering. This machine is predicted to generate uneven net cash flows over the next eight years. The relevant data and payback period computation are shown in Exhibit 25.3.

EXHIBIT 25.3

Payback Period Calculation with Uneven Cash Flows

Period*	Expected Net Cash Flows	Cumulative Net Cash Flows
Year 0	$(16,000)	$(16,000)
Year 1	3,000	(13,000)
Year 2	4,000	(9,000)
Year 3	4,000	(5,000)
Year 4	4,000	(1,000)
Year 5	5,000	4,000
Year 6	3,000	7,000
Year 7	2,000	9,000
Year 8	2,000	11,000
		Payback period = 4.2 years

* All cash inflows and outflows occur uniformly during the year.

Year 0 refers to the period of initial investment in which the $16,000 cash outflow occurs at the end of year 0 to acquire the machinery. By the end of year 1, the cumulative net cash flow is reduced to $(13,000), computed as the $(16,000) initial cash outflow plus year 1's $3,000 cash inflow. This process continues throughout the asset's life. The cumulative net cash flow amount changes from negative to positive in year 5. Specifically, at the end of year 4, the cumulative net cash flow is $(1,000). As soon as FasTrac receives net cash inflow of $1,000 during the fifth year, it has fully recovered the investment. If we assume that cash flows are received uniformly *within* each year, receipt of the $1,000 occurs about one-fifth of the way through the year. This is computed as $1,000 divided by year 5's total net cash flow of $5,000, or 0.20. This yields a payback period of 4.2 years, computed as 4 years plus 0.20 of year 5.

Using the Payback Period   Companies desire a short payback period to increase return and reduce risk. The more quickly a company receives cash, the sooner it is available for other uses and the less time it is at risk of loss. A shorter payback period also improves the company's ability to respond to unanticipated changes and lowers its risk of having to keep an unprofitable investment.

Payback period should never be the only consideration in evaluating investments. This is so because it ignores at least two important factors. First, it fails to reflect differences in the timing of net cash flows within the payback period. In Exhibit 25.3, FasTrac's net cash flows in the first five years were $3,000, $4,000, $4,000, $4,000, and $5,000. If another investment had predicted cash flows of $9,000, $3,000, $2,000, $1,800, and $1,000 in these five years, its payback period would also be 4.2 years, but this second alternative could be more desirable because it provides cash more quickly. The second important factor is that the payback period ignores *all* cash flows after the point where its costs are fully recovered. For example, one investment might pay back its cost in 3 years but stop producing cash after 4 years. A second investment might require 5 years to pay back its cost yet continue to produce net cash flows for another 15 years. A focus on only the payback period would mistakenly lead management to choose the first investment over the second.

"So what if I underestimated costs and overestimated revenues? It all averages out in the end."

Quick Check

Answers — pp. 1033–1034

1. Capital budgeting is (a) concerned with analyzing alternative sources of capital, including debt and equity, (b) an important activity for companies when considering what assets to acquire or sell, or (c) best done by intuitive assessments of the value of assets and their usefulness.

2. Why are capital budgeting decisions often difficult?

3. A company is considering purchasing equipment costing $75,000. Future annual net cash flows from this equipment are $30,000, $25,000, $15,000, $10,000, and $5,000. The payback period is (a) 4 years, (b) 3.5 years, or (c) 3 years.

4. If depreciation is an expense, why is it added back to an investment's net profit to compute the net cash flow from that investment?

5. If two investments have the same payback period, are they equally desirable? Explain.

Accounting Rate of Return

The **accounting rate of return,** also called *return on average investment,* is computed by dividing a project's after-tax net profit by the average amount invested in it. To illustrate, we return to FasTrac's $16,000 machinery investment described in Exhibit 25.1. We first compute (1) the after-tax net profit and (2) the average amount invested. The $2,100 after-tax net profit is already available from Exhibit 25.1. To compute the average amount invested, we assume that net cash flows are received evenly throughout each year. Thus, the average investment for each year is computed as the average of its beginning and ending carrying amounts. If FasTrac's $16,000 machine is depreciated $2,000 each year, the average amount invested in the machine for each year is computed as shown in Exhibit 25.4. The average for any year is the average of the beginning and ending carrying amounts.

P2 Compute accounting rate of return and explain its use.

	Beginning Carrying Amount	Annual Depreciation	Ending Carrying Amount	Average Carrying Amount
Year 1	$16,000	$2,000	$14,000	$15,000
Year 2	14,000	2,000	12,000	13,000
Year 3	12,000	2,000	10,000	11,000
Year 4	10,000	2,000	8,000	9,000
Year 5	8,000	2,000	6,000	7,000
Year 6	6,000	2,000	4,000	5,000
Year 7	4,000	2,000	2,000	3,000
Year 8	2,000	2,000	0	1,000
All years				**$ 8,000**

EXHIBIT 25.4

Computing Average Amount Invested (Carrying Amount)

Next we need the average carrying amount for the asset's entire life. This amount is computed by taking the average of the individual yearly averages. This average equals $8,000, computed as $64,000 (the sum of the individual years' averages) divided by eight years (see last column of Exhibit 25.4).

Point: General formula for *annual average investment* is the sum of individual years' average carrying amounts divided by the number of years of the planned investment.

If a company uses straight-line depreciation, we can find the average amount invested by using the formula in Exhibit 25.5. Because FasTrac uses straight-line depreciation, its average amount invested for the eight years equals the sum of the carrying amount at the beginning of the asset's investment period and the carrying amount at the end of its investment period, divided by 2, as shown in Exhibit 25.5.

EXHIBIT 25.5

Computing Average Amount Invested under Straight-Line Depreciation

$$\text{Annual average investment} = \frac{\text{Beginning carrying amount} + \text{Ending carrying amount}}{2}$$

(straight-line case only)

$$= \frac{\$16,000 + \$0}{2} = \$8,000$$

If an investment has a residual value, the average amount invested when using straight-line depreciation is computed as (Beginning carrying amount + residual value)/2.

Once we determine the after-tax net profit and the average amount invested, the accounting rate of return on the investment can be computed from the annual after-tax net profit divided by the average amount invested, as shown in Exhibit 25.6.

EXHIBIT 25.6

Accounting Rate of Return Formula

$$\text{Accounting rate of return} = \frac{\text{Annual after-tax net profit}}{\text{Annual average investment}}$$

This yields an accounting rate of return of 26.25% ($2,100/$8,000). FasTrac management must decide whether a 26.25% accounting rate of return is satisfactory. To make this decision, we must factor in the investment's risk. For instance, we cannot say an investment with a 26.25% return is preferred over one with a lower return unless we recognize any differences in risk. Thus, an investment's return is satisfactory or unsatisfactory only when it is related to returns from other investments with similar lives and risk.

When accounting rate of return is used to choose among capital investments, the one with the least risk, the shortest payback period, and the highest return for the longest time period is often identified as the best. However, use of accounting rate of return to evaluate investment opportunities is limited because it bases the amount invested on carrying amounts (not predicted market values) in future periods. Accounting rate of return is also limited when an asset's net profits are expected to vary from year to year. This requires computing the rate using *average* annual net profits, yet this accounting rate of return fails to distinguish between two investments with the same average annual net profit but different amounts of income in early years versus later years or different levels of income variability.

Quick Check

Answers — p. 1034

6. The following data relate to a company's decision on whether to purchase a machine:

Cost	$180,000
Residual value	15,000
Annual after-tax net profit	40,000

The machine's accounting rate of return, assuming the even receipt of its net cash flows during the year and use of straight-line depreciation, is (a) 22%, (b) 41%, or (c) 21%.

7. Is a 15% accounting rate of return for a machine a good rate?

METHODS USING TIME VALUE OF MONEY

Point: Use the Excel feature "Function/Financial/NPV" to find the present value of future cash flows, i.e., cash flows starting from time 1 to the end of a project. Add this present value to the cash flow (usually an outflow) in time 0 to get the NPV.

This section describes two methods that help managers with capital budgeting decisions and that use the time value of money: (1) net present value and (2) internal rate of return. *(To apply these methods, you need a basic understanding of the concept of present value. An expanded explanation of present value concepts is in Appendix B near the end of the book. You can use the present value tables at the end of Appendix B to solve many of this chapter's assignments that use the time value of money.)*

Net Present Value

Net present value analysis applies the time value of money to future cash inflows and cash outflows so management can evaluate a project's benefits and costs at one point in time. Specifically, **net present value (NPV)** is computed by discounting the future net cash flows from the investment at the project's required rate of return and then subtracting the initial amount invested. A company's required return, often called its hurdle rate, is typically its **cost of capital,** which is the rate the company must pay to its long-term creditors and shareholders. Cost of capital is the weighted average of *cost of debt* and *cost of equity*. Cost of capital depends on the cost of debt, cost of equity, and the mix of debt and equity. Since interest expense (the main element in cost of debt) is allowed as a tax deduction in most countries, cost of debt after tax, and consequently the cost of capital, are also affected by the tax rate.

To illustrate, let's return to FasTrac's proposed machinery purchase described in Exhibit 25.1. Does this machine provide a satisfactory return while recovering the amount invested? Recall that the machine requires a $16,000 investment and is expected to provide $4,100 annual net cash inflows for the next eight years. If we assume that net cash flows from this machine are received at each year-end and that FasTrac requires a 12% annual return, net present value can be computed as in Exhibit 25.7.

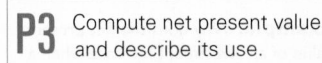

P3 Compute net present value and describe its use.

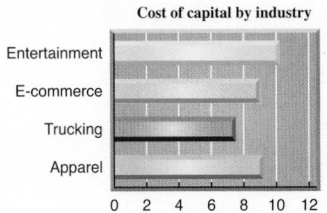

Cost of capital by industry

Net Cash Flows*	Present Value of 1 dollar at 12%†	Present Value of Net Cash Flows
Year 1 .... $ 4,100	0.8929	$ 3,661
Year 2 4,100	0.7972	3,269
Year 3 4,100	0.7118	2,918
Year 4 4,100	0.6355	2,606
Year 5 4,100	0.5674	2,326
Year 6 4,100	0.5066	2,077
Year 7 4,100	0.4523	1,854
Year 8 4,100	0.4039	1,656
Totals $32,800		20,367
Amount invested		(16,000)
Net present value		$ 4,367

EXHIBIT 25.7

Net Present Value Calculation with Equal Cash Flows

* Cash flows occur at the end of each year.

† Present value of 1 factors are taken from Table B.1 in Appendix B.

The first number column of Exhibit 25.7 shows the annual net cash flows. Present value of 1 factors, also called *discount factors,* are shown in the second column. Taken from Table B.1 in Appendix B, they assume that net cash flows are received at each year-end. *(To simplify present value computations and for assignment material at the end of this chapter, we assume that net cash flows are received at each year-end.)* Annual net cash flows from the first column of Exhibit 25.7 are multiplied by the discount factors in the second column to give present values shown in the third column. The last three lines of this exhibit show the final NPV computations. The asset's $16,000 initial cost is deducted from the $20,367 total present value of all future net cash flows to give this asset's NPV of $4,367. The machine is thus expected to (1) recover its cost, (2) provide a 12% compounded return, and (3) generate $4,367 above cost. We summarize this analysis by saying the present value of this machine's future net cash flows to FasTrac exceeds the $16,000 investment by $4,367.

Point: The assumption of end-of-year cash flows simplifies computations and is common in practice.

Point: The amount invested includes all costs that must be incurred to get the asset in its proper location and ready for use.

Example: What is the net present value in Exhibit 25.7 if a 10% return is applied? *Answer:* $5,873

Net Present Value Decision Rule The decision rule in applying NPV is as follows: When an asset's expected cash flows are discounted at the required rate and yield a *positive* net present value, the asset should be acquired. This decision rule is reflected in the graphic below. When comparing several investment opportunities of about the same cost and same risk, we prefer the one with the highest positive net present value.

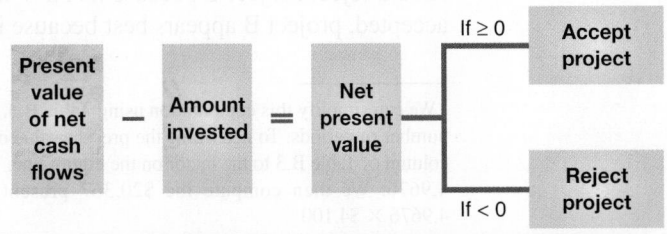

Simplifying Computations   The computations in Exhibit 25.7 use separate present value of 1 factors for each of the eight years. Each year's net cash flow is multiplied by its present value of 1 factor to determine its present value. The individual present values for each of the eight net cash flows are added to give the asset's total present value. This computation can be simplified in two ways if annual net cash flows are *equal in amount*. One way is to add the eight annual present value of 1 factors for a total of 4.9676 and multiply this amount by the annual $4,100 net cash flow to get the $20,367 total present value of net cash flows.[1] A second simplification is to use a calculator with compound interest functions or a spreadsheet program. We show how to use Excel functions to compute net present value in this chapter's Appendix. Whatever procedure you use, it is important to understand the concepts behind these computations.

■ **Decision Ethics** ──────────────────────────────   Answer — p. 1033

Systems Manager   Top management adopts a policy requiring purchases in excess of $5,000 to be submitted with cash flow projections to the cost analyst for capital budget approval. As systems manager, you want to upgrade your computers at a $25,000 cost. You consider submitting several orders all under $5,000 to avoid the approval process. You believe the computers will increase profits and wish to avoid a delay. What do you do? ■

Uneven Cash Flows   Net present value analysis can also be applied when net cash flows are uneven (unequal). To illustrate, assume that FasTrac can choose only one capital investment from among projects A, B, and C. Each project requires the same $12,000 initial investment. Future net cash flows for each project are shown in the first three number columns of Exhibit 25.8.

EXHIBIT 25.8

Net Present Value Calculation with Uneven Cash Flows

	Net Cash Flows			Present Value of 1 at 10%	Present Value of Net Cash Flows		
	A	**B**	**C**		**A**	**B**	**C**
Year 1	$ 5,000	$ 8,000	$ 1,000	0.9091	$ 4,546	$ 7,273	$ 909
Year 2	5,000	5,000	5,000	0.8264	4,132	4,132	4,132
Year 3	5,000	2,000	9,000	0.7513	3,757	1,503	6,762
Totals	$15,000	$15,000	$15,000		12,435	12,908	11,803
Amount invested					(12,000)	(12,000)	(12,000)
Net present value					$ 435	$ 908	$ (197)

The three projects in Exhibit 25.8 have the same expected total net cash flows of $15,000. Project A is expected to produce equal amounts of $5,000 each year. Project B is expected to produce a larger amount in the first year. Project C is expected to produce a larger amount in the third year. The fourth column of Exhibit 25.8 shows the present value of 1 factors from Table B.1 assuming 10% required return.

Computations in the right-most columns show that Project A has a $435 positive NPV. Project B has the largest NPV of $908 because it brings in cash more quickly. Project C has a $(197) *negative* NPV because its larger cash inflows are delayed. If FasTrac requires a 10% return, it should reject Project C because its NPV implies a return *under* 10%. If only one project can be accepted, project B appears best because it yields the highest NPV.

---

[1] We can simplify this computation using Table B.3, which gives the present value of 1 to be received periodically for a number of periods. To determine the present value of these eight annual receipts discounted at 12%, go down the 12% column of Table B.3 to the factor on the eighth line. This cumulative discount factor, also known as an *annuity* factor, is 4.9676. We then compute the $20,367 present value for these eight annual $4,100 receipts, computed as 4.9676 × $4,100.

Residual Value and Accelerated Depreciation FasTrac predicted the $16,000 machine to have zero residual value at the end of its useful life (recall Exhibit 25.1). In many cases, assets are expected to have residual values. If so, this amount is an additional net cash inflow received at the end of the final year of the asset's life. All other computations remain the same.

Depreciation computations also affect net present value analysis. FasTrac computes depreciation using the straight-line method. Accelerated depreciation is also commonly used, especially for income tax reports. Accelerated depreciation produces larger depreciation deductions in the early years of an asset's life and smaller deductions in later years. This pattern results in smaller income tax payments in early years and larger payments in later years. Accelerated depreciation does not change the basics of a present value analysis, but it can change the result. Using accelerated depreciation for tax reporting affects the NPV of an asset's cash flows because it produces larger net cash inflows in the early years of the asset's life and smaller ones in later years. Being able to use accelerated depreciation for tax reporting always makes an investment more desirable because early cash flows are more valuable than later ones.

Use of Net Present Value In deciding whether to proceed with a capital investment project, we approve the proposal if the NPV is positive but reject it if the NPV is negative. When considering several projects of similar investment amounts and risk levels, we can compare the different projects' NPVs and rank them on the basis of their NPVs. However, if the amount invested differs substantially across projects, the NPV is of limited value for comparison purposes. One means to compare projects, especially when a company cannot fund all positive net present value projects, is to use the **profitability index,** which is computed as:

$$\text{Profitability index} = \frac{\text{Net present value of cash flows}}{\text{Investment}}$$

A higher profitability index suggests a more desirable project. To illustrate, suppose that Project X requires a $1 million investment and provides a $100,000 NPV. Project Y requires an investment of only $100,000 and returns a $75,000 NPV. Ranking on the basis of NPV puts Project X ahead of Y, yet X's profitability index is only 0.10 ($100,000/$1,000,000) whereas Y's profitability index is 0.75. We must also remember that when reviewing projects with different risks, we computed the NPV of individual projects using different discount rates. The higher the risk, the higher the discount rate.

Inflation Large price-level increases should be considered in NPV analyses. Hurdle rates already include investor's inflation forecasts. Net cash flows can be adjusted for inflation by using *future value* computations. For example, if the expected net cash inflow in year 1 is $4,100 and 5% inflation is expected, then the expected net cash inflow in year 2 is $4,305, computed as $4,100 × 1.05 (1.05 is the future value of $1 (Table B.2) for 1 period with a 5% rate).

Internal Rate of Return

Another means to evaluate capital investments is to use the **internal rate of return (IRR),** which equals the rate that yields an NPV of zero for an investment. This means that if we compute the total present value of a project's net cash flows using the IRR as the discount rate and then subtract the initial investment from this total present value, we get a zero NPV.

To illustrate, we use the data for FasTrac's Project A from Exhibit 25.8 to compute its IRR. Exhibit 25.9 shows the two-step process in computing IRR.

EXHIBIT 25.9

Computing Internal Rate of Return
(with even cash flows)

Step 1: Compute the present value factor for the investment project.

$$\text{Present value factor} = \frac{\text{Amount invested}}{\text{Net cash flows}} = \frac{\$12,000}{\$5,000} = 2.4000$$

Step 2: Identify the discount rate (IRR) yielding the present value factor

Search Table B.3 for a present value factor of 2.4000 in the three-year row (equaling the 3-year project duration). The 12% discount rate yields a present value factor of 2.4018. This implies that the IRR is approximately 12%.*

* Since the present value factor of 2.4000 is not exactly equal to the 12% factor of 2.4018, we can more precisely estimate the IRR as follows:

Discount rate	Present Value Factor from Table B.3
12%	2.4018
15%	2.2832
	0.1186 = difference

Then, IRR = $12\% + \left[(15\% - 12\%) \times \dfrac{2.4018 - 2.4000}{0.1186} \right] = \underline{\underline{12.05\%}}$

When cash flows are equal, as with Project A, we compute the present value factor (as shown in Exhibit 25.9) by dividing the initial investment by its annual net cash flows. We then use an annuity table to determine the discount rate equal to this present value factor. For FasTrac's Project A, we look across the three-period row of Table B.3 and find that the discount rate corresponding to the present value factor of 2.4000 roughly equals the 2.4018 value for the 12% rate. This row is reproduced here:

Present Value of an Annuity of 1 for Three Periods

	Discount Rate				
Periods	1%	5%	10%	12%	15%
3	2.9410	2.7232	2.4869	2.4018	2.2832

The 12% rate is the Project's IRR. A more precise IRR estimate can be computed following the procedure shown in the note to Exhibit 25.9. Spreadsheet software and calculators can also compute this IRR. We show how to use an Excel function to compute IRR in this chapter's appendix.

Uneven Cash Flows If net cash flows are uneven, we must use trial and error to compute the IRR. We do this by selecting any reasonable discount rate and computing the NPV. If the amount is positive (negative), we recompute the NPV using a higher (lower) discount rate. We continue these steps until we reach a point where two consecutive computations result in NPVs having different signs (positive and negative). Because the NPV is zero using IRR, we know that the IRR lies between these two discount rates. We can then estimate its value. Spreadsheet programs and calculators can do these computations for us.

 **Decision Insight**

Fun-IRR Many theme parks use both financial and nonfinancial criteria to evaluate their investments in new rides and activities. The use of IRR is a major part of this evaluation. This requires good estimates of future cash inflows and outflows. It also requires risk assessments of the uncertainty of the future cash flows. ∎

Use of Internal Rate of Return   When we use the IRR to evaluate a project, we compare it to a predetermined **hurdle rate,** which is a minimum acceptable rate of return and is applied as follows.

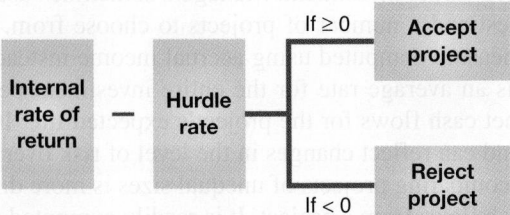

Top management selects the hurdle rate to use in evaluating capital investments. Financial formulas aid in this selection, but the choice of a minimum rate is subjective and left to management. For projects financed from borrowed funds, the hurdle rate must exceed the interest rate paid on these funds. The return on an investment must cover its interest and provide an additional profit to reward the company for its risk. For instance, if money is borrowed at 10%, an average risk investment often requires an after-tax return of 15% (or 5% above the borrowing rate). Remember that lower-risk investments require a lower rate of return compared with higher-risk investments.

 If the project is internally financed, the hurdle rate is often based on actual returns from comparable projects. If the IRR is higher than the hurdle rate, the project is accepted. Multiple projects are often ranked by the extent to which their IRR exceeds the hurdle rate. The hurdle rate for individual projects is often different, depending on the risk involved. IRR is not subject to the limitations of NPV when comparing projects with different amounts invested because the IRR is expressed as a percent rather than as an absolute dollar value in NPV.

Example: How can management evaluate the risk of an investment? *Answer:* It must assess the uncertainty of future cash flows.

Point: A survey reports that 41% of top managers would reject a project with an internal rate of return *above* the cost of capital, *if* the project would cause the firm to miss its earnings forecast. The roles of benchmarks and manager compensation plans must be considered in capital budgeting decisions.

 **Decision Maker**   Answer — p. 1033

Entrepreneur   You are developing a new product and you use a 12% discount rate to compute its NPV. Your banker, from whom you hope to obtain a loan, expresses concern that your discount rate is too low. How do you respond? ■

Comparison of Capital Budgeting Methods

We explained four methods that managers use to evaluate capital investment projects. How do these methods compare with each other? Exhibit 25.10 addresses that question. Neither the

EXHIBIT 25.10

Comparing Capital Budgeting Methods

	Payback Period	**Accounting Rate of Return**	**Net Present Value**	**Internal Rate of Return**
Measurement basis	● Cash flows	● Accrual income	● Cash flows ● Profitability	● Cash flows ● Profitability
Measurement unit	● Years	● Percent	● Dollars	● Percent
Strengths	● Easy to understand	● Easy to understand	● Reflects time value of money	● Reflects time value of money
	● Allows comparison of projects	● Allows comparison of projects	● Reflects varying risks over project's life	● Allows comparisons of dissimilar projects
Limitations	● Ignores time value of money	● Ignores time value of money	● Difficult to compare dissimilar projects	● Ignores varying risks over life of project
	● Ignores cash flows after payback period	● Ignores annual rates over life of project		
Acceptance or rejection criterion	● Accept if the payback period is less than a certain period decided by the management; otherwise reject	● Accept if the accounting rate of return is more than a percentage fixed by the management; otherwise reject	● Accept if NPV is zero or positive; otherwise reject	● Accept if IRR is higher than or equal to a hurdle rate fixed by the management; otherwise reject

payback period nor the accounting rate of return considers the time value of money. On the other hand, both the net present value and the internal rate of return do.

The payback period is probably the simplest method. It gives managers an estimate of how soon they will recover their initial investment. Managers sometimes use this method when they have limited cash to invest and a number of projects to choose from. The accounting rate of return yields a percent measure computed using accrual income instead of cash flows. The accounting rate of return is an average rate for the entire investment period. Net present value considers all estimated net cash flows for the project's expected life. It can be applied to even and uneven cash flows and can reflect changes in the level of risk over a project's life. Since it yields a dollar measure, comparing projects of unequal sizes is more difficult. The internal rate of return considers all cash flows from a project. It is readily computed when the cash flows are even but requires some trial and error estimation when cash flows are uneven. Because the IRR is a percent measure, it is readily used to compare projects with different investment amounts. However, IRR does not reflect changes in risk over a project's life.

Decision Insight

And the Winner Is . . . How do we choose among the methods for evaluating capital investments? Management surveys consistently show the internal rate of return (IRR) as the most popular method followed by the payback period and net present value (NPV). Few companies use the accounting rate of return (ARR), but nearly all use more than one method. ∎

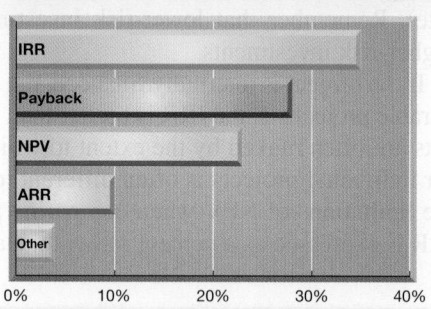

Company Usage of Capital Budgeting Methods

Quick Check

Answers — p. 1034

8. A company can invest in only one of two projects, A or B. Each project requires a $20,000 investment and is expected to generate end-of-period, annual cash flows as follows:

	Year 1	Year 2	Year 3	Total
Project A	$12,000	$8,500	$4,000	$24,500
Project B	4,500	8,500	13,000	26,000

Assuming a discount rate of 10%, which project has the higher net present value?

9. Two investment alternatives are expected to generate annual cash flows with the same net present value (assuming the same discount rate applied to each). Using this information, can you conclude that the two alternatives are equally desirable?

10. When two investment alternatives have the same total expected cash flows but differ in the timing of those flows, which method of evaluating those investments is superior, (a) accounting rate of return or (b) net present value?

Section 2—Managerial Decisions

This section focuses on methods that use accounting information to make several important managerial decisions. Most of these involve short-term decisions. This differs from methods used for longer-term managerial decisions that are described in the first section of this chapter and in several other chapters of this book.

DECISIONS AND INFORMATION

This section explains how managers make decisions and the information relevant to those decisions.

Decision Making

Managerial decision making involves five steps: (1) define the decision task, (2) identify alternative courses of action, (3) collect relevant information and evaluate each alternative, (4) select the preferred course of action, and (5) analyze and assess decisions made. These five steps are illustrated in Exhibit 25.11.

| Define Task and Goal | Identify Alternative Actions | Collect Relevant Information | Select Course of Action | Analyze and Assess Decision |

EXHIBIT 25.11

Managerial Decision Making

Both managerial and financial accounting information play an important role in most management decisions. The accounting system is expected to provide primarily *financial* information such as performance reports and budget analyses for decision making. *Nonfinancial* information is also relevant, however; it includes information on environmental effects, political sensitivities, and social responsibility.

The Principle of Relevant Costs

Most financial measures of revenues and costs from accounting systems are based on historical costs. Although historical costs are important and useful for many tasks such as product pricing and the control and monitoring of business activities, we sometimes find that an analysis of *relevant costs,* or *avoidable costs,* is especially useful. Three types of costs are pertinent to our discussion of relevant costs: sunk costs, out-of-pocket costs, and opportunity costs.

A *sunk cost* arises from a past decision and cannot be avoided or changed; it is irrelevant to future decisions. An example is the cost of computer equipment previously purchased by a company. Most of a company's allocated costs, including fixed overhead items such as depreciation and administrative expenses, are sunk costs.

An *out-of-pocket cost* requires a future outlay of cash and is relevant for current and future decision making. These costs are usually the direct result of management's decisions. For instance, future purchases of computer equipment involve out-of-pocket costs.

An *opportunity cost* is the potential benefit lost by taking a specific action when two or more alternative choices are available. An example is a student giving up wages from a job to attend summer school. Companies continually must choose from alternative courses of action. For instance, a company making standardized products might be approached by a customer to supply a special (nonstandard) product. A decision to accept or reject the special order must consider not only the profit to be made from the special order but also the profit given up by devoting time and resources to this order instead of pursuing an alternative project. The profit given up is an opportunity cost. Consideration of opportunity costs is important. The implications extend to internal resource allocation decisions. For instance, a computer manufacturer must decide between internally manufacturing a chip versus buying it externally. In another case, management of a multidivisional company must decide whether to continue operating or close a particular division.

Besides relevant costs, management must also consider the relevant benefits associated with a decision. **Relevant benefits** refer to the additional or *incremental* revenue generated by selecting a particular course of action over another. For instance, a student must decide the relevant benefits of taking one course over another. In sum, both relevant costs and relevant benefits are crucial to managerial decision making.

 C1 Describe the importance of relevant costs for short-term decisions.

Example: Depreciation and amortization are allocations of the original cost of plant and intangible assets. Are they out-of-pocket costs? *Answer:* No; they are sunk costs.

Point: Opportunity costs are not entered in accounting records. This does not reduce their relevance for managerial decisions.

DECISION MAKING USING RELEVANT COSTS

A1 Evaluate short-term managerial decisions using relevant costs.

Managers experience many different scenarios that require analyzing alternative actions and making a decision. We describe several different types of decision scenarios based on the principle of relevant costs in this section. These are (*a*) additional business, (*b*) make or buy, (*c*) scrap or rework, (*d*) sell or process, (*e*) sales mix selection, (*f*) segment elimination, and (*g*) keep or replace equipment. We set these tasks in the context of FasTrac, an exercise supplies and equipment manufacturer introduced earlier. *We treat each of these decision tasks as separate from each other.*

Additional Business

FasTrac is operating at its normal level of 80% of full capacity. At this level, it produces and sells approximately 100,000 units of product annually. Its per unit and annual total costs are shown in Exhibit 25.12.

EXHIBIT 25.12

Selected Operating Income Data

	Per Unit	Annual Total
Sales (100,000 units)	$10.00	$1,000,000
Direct materials	(3.50)	(350,000)
Direct labor	(2.20)	(220,000)
Overhead	(1.10)	(110,000)
Selling expenses	(1.40)	(140,000)
Administrative expenses	(0.80)	(80,000)
Total costs and expenses.	(9.00)	(900,000)
Operating income	$ 1.00	$ 100,000

A current buyer of FasTrac's products wants to purchase additional units of its product and export them to another country. This buyer offers to buy 10,000 units of the product at $8.50 per unit, or $1.50 less than the current price. The offer price is low, but FasTrac is considering the proposal because this sale would be several times larger than any single previous sale and it would use idle capacity. Also, the units will be exported, so this new business will not affect current sales.

To determine whether to accept or reject this order, management needs to know whether accepting the offer will increase net profit. The analysis in Exhibit 25.13 shows that if management relies on per unit historical costs, it would reject the sale because it yields a loss. However, historical costs are *not* relevant to this decision. Instead, the relevant costs are the additional costs, called **incremental costs.** These costs, also called *differential costs,* are the additional costs incurred if a company pursues a certain course of action. FasTrac's incremental costs are those related to the added volume that this new order would bring.

EXHIBIT 25.13

Analysis of Additional Business Using Historical Costs

	Per Unit	Total
Sales (10,000 additional units)	$ 8.50	$ 85,000
Direct materials	(3.50)	(35,000)
Direct labor	(2.20)	(22,000)
Overhead	(1.10)	(11,000)
Selling expenses	(1.40)	(14,000)
Administrative expenses	(0.80)	(8,000)
Total costs and expenses.	(9.00)	(90,000)
Operating loss	$(0.50)	$(5,000)

To make its decision, FasTrac must analyze the costs of this new business in a different manner. The following information regarding the order is available:

- Manufacturing 10,000 additional units requires direct materials of $3.50 per unit and direct labor of $2.20 per unit (same as for all other units).
- Manufacturing 10,000 additional units adds $5,000 of incremental overhead costs for power, packaging, and indirect labor (all variable costs).
- Incremental commissions and selling expenses from this sale of 10,000 additional units would be $2,000 (all variable costs).
- Incremental administrative expenses of $1,000 for clerical efforts are needed (all fixed costs) with the sale of 10,000 additional units.

We use this information, as shown in Exhibit 25.14, to assess how accepting this new business will affect FasTrac's income.

EXHIBIT 25.14

Analysis of Additional Business Using Relevant Costs

	Current Business	Additional Business	Combined
Sales	$1,000,000	$ 85,000	$1,085,000
Direct materials	(350,000)	(35,000)	(385,000)
Direct labor	(220,000)	(22,000)	(242,000)
Overhead	(110,000)	(5,000)	(115,000)
Selling expenses	(140,000)	(2,000)	(142,000)
Administrative expense	(80,000)	(1,000)	(81,000)
Total costs and expenses	(900,000)	(65,000)	(965,000)
Operating income	$ 100,000	$ 20,000	$ 120,000

The analysis of relevant costs in Exhibit 25.14 suggests that the additional business be accepted. It would provide $85,000 of added revenue while incurring only $65,000 of added costs. This would yield $20,000 of additional pretax income, or a pretax profit margin of 23.5%. More generally, FasTrac would increase its income with any price that exceeded $6.50 per unit ($65,000 incremental cost/10,000 additional units).

An analysis of the incremental costs pertaining to the additional volume is always relevant for this type of decision. We must proceed cautiously, however, when the additional volume approaches or exceeds the factory's existing available capacity. If the additional volume requires the company to expand its capacity by obtaining more equipment, more space, or more personnel, the incremental costs could quickly exceed the incremental revenue. Another cautionary note is the effect on existing sales. All new units of the extra business will be sold outside FasTrac's normal domestic sales channels. If accepting additional business would cause existing sales to decline, this information must be included in our analysis. The contribution margin lost from a decline in sales is an opportunity cost. If future cash flows over several time periods are affected, their net present value also must be computed and used in this analysis.

The key point is that *management must not blindly use historical costs, especially allocated overhead costs.* Instead, the accounting system needs to provide information about the incremental costs to be incurred if the additional business is accepted.

Example: Exhibit 25.14 uses quantitative information. Suggest some qualitative factors to be considered when deciding whether to accept this project. *Answer:* (1) Impact on relationships with other customers and (2) Improved relationship with customer buying additional units.

Decision Maker   Answer — p. 1033

Partner You are a partner in a small accounting firm that specializes in keeping the books and preparing taxes for clients. A local restaurant is interested in obtaining these services from your firm. Identify factors that are relevant in deciding whether to accept the engagement. ■

Make or Buy

The managerial decision to make or buy a component for one of its current products is commonplace and depends on incremental costs. To illustrate, FasTrac has excess productive capacity it can use to manufacture Part 417, a component of the main product it sells. The part is currently purchased and delivered to the plant at a cost of $1.20 per unit. FasTrac estimates that making Part 417 would cost $0.45 for direct materials, $0.50 for direct labor, and an undetermined amount for overhead. The task is to determine how much overhead to add to these costs so we can decide whether to make or buy Part 417. If FasTrac's normal predetermined overhead application rate is 100% of direct labor cost, we might be tempted to conclude that overhead cost is $0.50 per unit, computed as 100% of the $0.50 direct labor cost. We would then mistakenly conclude that total cost is $1.45 ($0.45 of materials + $0.50 of labor + $0.50 of overhead). A wrong decision in this case would be to conclude that the company is better off buying the part at $1.20 each than making it for $1.45 each.

Instead, as we explained earlier, only incremental overhead costs are relevant in this situation. Thus, we must compute an *incremental overhead rate*. Incremental overhead costs might include, for example, additional power for operating machines, extra supplies, added cleanup costs, materials handling, and quality control. We can prepare a per unit analysis in this case as shown in Exhibit 25.15.

EXHIBIT 25.15

Make or Buy Analysis

	Make	Buy
Direct materials	$0.45	—
Direct labor	0.50	—
Overhead costs	[?]	—
Purchase price	—	$1.20
Total incremental costs	$0.95 + [?]	$1.20

We can see that if incremental overhead costs are less than $0.25 per unit, the total cost of making the component is less than the purchase price of $1.20 and FasTrac should make the part. FasTrac's decision rule in this case is that any amount of overhead less than $0.25 per unit yields a total cost for Part 417 that is less than the $1.20 purchase price. FasTrac must consider several nonfinancial factors in the make or buy decision, including product quality, timeliness of delivery (especially in a just-in-time setting), reactions of customers and suppliers, and other intangibles such as employee morale and workload. It must also consider whether making the part requires incremental fixed costs to expand plant capacity. When these added factors are considered, small cost differences may not matter.

Point: Managers must consider nonfinancial factors when making decisions.

Decision Insight

Make or Buy Services   Companies apply make or buy decisions to their services. Many now outsource their payroll activities to a payroll service provider. It is argued that the prices paid for such services are close to what it costs them to do it, and without the headaches. ■

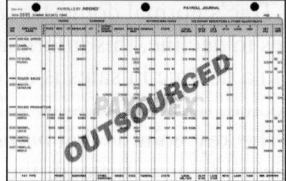

Scrap or Rework

Managers often must make a decision on whether to scrap or rework products in process. Remember that costs already incurred in manufacturing the units of a product that do not meet quality standards are sunk costs that have been incurred and cannot be changed. Sunk costs are irrelevant in any decision on whether to sell the substandard units as scrap or to rework them to meet quality standards.

To illustrate, assume that FasTrac has 10,000 defective units of a product that have already cost $1 per unit to manufacture. These units can be sold as is (as scrap) for $0.40 each, or they can be reworked for $0.80 per unit and then sold for their full price of $1.50 each. Should FasTrac sell the units as scrap or rework them?

To make this decision, management must recognize that the already incurred manufacturing costs of $1 per unit are sunk (unavoidable). These costs are *entirely irrelevant* to the decision. In addition, we must be certain that all costs of reworking defects, including interfering with normal operations, are accounted for in our analysis. For instance, reworking the defects means that FasTrac is unable to manufacture 10,000 *new* units with an incremental cost of $1 per unit and a selling price of $1.50 per unit, meaning it incurs an opportunity cost equal to the lost $5,000 net return from making and selling 10,000 new units. This opportunity cost is the difference between the $15,000 revenue (10,000 units × $1.50) from selling these new units and their $10,000 manufacturing costs (10,000 units × $1). Our analysis is reflected in Exhibit 25.16.

	Scrap	Rework
Sale of scrapped/reworked units	$ 4,000	$15,000
Less costs to rework defects		(8,000)
Less opportunity cost of not making new units		**(5,000)**
Incremental net profit................................	$4,000	$ 2,000

EXHIBIT 25.16

Scrap or Rework Analysis

The analysis yields a $2,000 difference in favor of scrapping the defects, yielding a total incremental net profit of $4,000. If we had failed to include the opportunity costs of $5,000, the rework option would have shown an income of $7,000 instead of $2,000, mistakenly making the reworking appear more favorable than scrapping.

Quick Check

Answers — p. 1034

11. A company receives a special order for 200 units that requires stamping the buyer's name on each unit, yielding an additional fixed cost of $400 to its normal costs. Without the order, the company is operating at 75% of capacity and produces 7,500 units of product at the following costs:

Direct materials	$37,500
Direct labor	60,000
Overhead (30% variable)	20,000
Selling expenses (60% variable)	25,000

The special order will not affect normal unit sales and will not increase fixed overhead and selling expenses. Variable selling expenses on the special order are reduced to one-half the normal amount. The price per unit necessary to earn $1,000 on this order is (*a*) $14.80, (*b*) $15.80, (*c*) $19.80, (*d*) $20.80, or (*e*) $21.80.

12. What are the incremental costs of accepting additional business?

Sell or Process

The managerial decision to sell partially completed products as is or to process them further for sale depends significantly on relevant costs. To illustrate, suppose that FasTrac has 40,000 units of partially finished Product Q. It has already spent $0.75 per unit to manufacture these 40,000 units at a $30,000 total cost. FasTrac can sell the 40,000 units to another manufacturer as raw material for $50,000. Alternatively, it can process them further and produce finished products X, Y, and Z at an incremental cost of $2 per unit. The added processing yields the products and revenues shown in Exhibit 25.17. FasTrac must decide whether the added revenues from selling finished products X, Y, and Z exceed the costs of finishing them.

Product	Price	Units	Revenues
Product X	$4.00	10,000	$ 40,000
Product Y..........	6.00	22,000	132,000
Product Z	8.00	6,000	48,000
Spoilage	—	2,000	0
Totals		40,000	$220,000

EXHIBIT 25.17

Revenues from
Processing Further

Exhibit 25.18 shows the two-step analysis for this decision. First, FasTrac computes its incremental revenue from further processing Q into products X, Y, and Z. This amount is the difference between the $220,000 revenue from the further processed products and the $50,000 FasTrac will give up by not selling Q as is (a $50,000 opportunity cost). Second, FasTrac computes its incremental costs from further processing Q into X, Y, and Z. This amount is $80,000 (40,000 units × $2 incremental cost). The analysis shows that FasTrac can earn incremental net profit of $90,000 from a decision to further process Q. (Notice that the earlier incurred $30,000 manufacturing cost for the 40,000 units of Product Q does not appear in Exhibit 25.18 because it is a sunk cost and as such is irrelevant to the decision.)

EXHIBIT 25.18

Sell or Process Analysis

Revenue if processed................	$220,000
Revenue if sold as is................	(50,000)
Incremental revenue	170,000
Cost to process...................	(80,000)
Incremental net profit	$90,000

Quick Check   Answers — p. 1034

13. A company has already incurred a $1,000 cost in partially producing its four products. Their selling prices when partially and fully processed follow with additional costs necessary to finish these partially processed units:

Product	Unfinished Selling Price	Finished Selling Price	Further Processing Costs
Alpha.............	$300	$600	$150
Beta.............	450	900	300
Gamma	275	425	125
Delta.............	150	210	75

Which product(s) should *not* be processed further, (a) Alpha, (b) Beta, (c) Gamma, or (d) Delta?

14. Under what conditions is a sunk cost relevant to decision making?

Sales Mix Selection

When a company sells a mix of products, some are likely to be more profitable than others. Management is often wise to concentrate sales efforts on more profitable products. If production facilities or other factors are limited, an increase in the production and sale of one product usually requires reducing the production and sale of others. In this case, management must identify the most profitable combination, or *sales mix* of products. To identify the best sales mix, management must know the contribution margin of each product, the facilities required to produce each product, any constraints on these facilities, and its markets.

To illustrate, assume that FasTrac makes and sells two products, A and B. The same machines are used to produce both products. A and B have the following selling prices and variable costs per unit:

	Product A	Product B
Selling price per unit................	$5.00	$7.50
Variable costs per unit	3.50	5.50
Contribution margin per unit.........	$1.50	$2.00

The variable costs are included in the analysis because they are the incremental costs of producing these products within the existing capacity of 100,000 machine hours per month. We consider three separate cases.

Demand Is Unlimited and Products Use Same Inputs   Assume that (1) each product requires 1 machine hour per unit for production and (2) the markets for these products are unlimited. Under these conditions, FasTrac should produce as much of Product B as it can because of its larger contribution margin of $2 per unit. At full capacity, FasTrac would produce $200,000 of total contribution margin per month, computed as $2 per unit times 100,000 machine hours.

Demand Is Unlimited and Products Use Different Inputs   Assume that (1) Product A requires 1 machine hour per unit, (2) Product B requires 2 machine hours per unit, and (3) the markets for these products are unlimited. Under these conditions, FasTrac should produce as much of Product A as it can because it has a contribution margin of $1.50 per machine hour compared with only $1 per machine hour for Product B. Exhibit 25.19 shows the relevant analysis.

	Product A	Product B
Selling price per unit	$5.00	$7.50
Variable costs per unit	3.50	5.50
Contribution margin per unit	$1.50	$2.00
Machine hours per unit..........................	1.0	2.0
Contribution margin per machine hour	**$1.50**	**$1.00**

EXHIBIT 25.19

Sales Mix Analysis

At its full capacity of 100,000 machine hours, FasTrac would produce 100,000 units of Product A, yielding $150,000 of total contribution margin per month. In contrast, if it uses all 100,000 hours to produce Product B, only 50,000 units would be produced yielding a contribution margin of $100,000. These results suggest that when a company faces excess demand and limited capacity, only the most profitable product per input should be manufactured.

Demand Is Limited   The need for a mix of different products arises when market demand is not sufficient to allow a company to sell all that it produces. For instance, assume that (1) Product A requires 1 machine hour per unit, (2) Product B requires 2 machine hours per unit, and (3) the market for Product A is limited to 80,000 units. Under these conditions, FasTrac should produce no more than 80,000 units of Product A. This would leave another 20,000 machine hours of capacity for making Product B. FasTrac should use this spare capacity to produce 10,000 units of Product B. This sales mix would maximize FasTrac's total contribution margin per month at an amount of $140,000.

Example: If Product B's variable costs per unit increase to $6, Product A's variable costs per unit decrease to $3, and the same machine hours per unit are used, which product should FasTrac produce? *Answer:* Product A. Its contribution margin of $2 per machine hour is higher than B's $.75 per machine hour.

■ Decision Insight

Companies such as **Gap, Abercrombie & Fitch**, and **American Eagle** must continuously monitor and manage the sales mix of their product lists. Selling their products in hundreds of countries and territories further complicates their decision process. The contribution margin of each product is crucial to their product mix strategies. ■

Segment Elimination

When a segment such as a department or division is performing poorly, management must consider eliminating it. Segment information on either net profit (loss) or its contribution to overhead is not sufficient for this decision. Instead, we must look at the segment's avoid-

Point: FasTrac might consider buying another machine to reduce the constraint on production. A strategy designed to reduce the impact of constraints or bottlenecks, on production, is called the *theory of constraints.*

able expenses and unavoidable expenses. **Avoidable expenses,** also called *escapable expenses,* are amounts the company would not incur if it eliminated the segment. **Unavoidable expenses,** also called *inescapable expenses,* are amounts that would continue even if the segment is eliminated.

To illustrate, FasTrac considers eliminating its treadmill division because its $48,300 total expenses are higher than its $47,800 sales. Classification of this division's operating expenses into avoidable or unavoidable expenses is shown in Exhibit 25.20.

EXHIBIT 25.20

Classification of Segment Operating Expenses for Analysis

	Total	Avoidable Expenses	Unavoidable Expenses
Cost of goods sold	$ 30,000	$ 30,000	—
Direct expenses			
Salaries expense	7,900	7,900	—
Depreciation expense—Equipment	200	—	$ 200
Indirect expenses			
Rent and utilities expense	3,150	—	3,150
Advertising expense	400	400	—
Insurance expense	400	300	100
Service department costs			
Share of office department expenses	3,060	2,200	860
Share of purchasing expenses	3,190	1,000	2,190
Total	$48,300	$41,800	$6,500

Example: How can insurance be classified as either avoidable or unavoidable? *Answer:* Depends on whether the assets insured can be removed and the premiums canceled.

FasTrac's analysis shows that it can avoid $41,800 expenses if it eliminates the treadmill division. Because this division's sales are $47,800, eliminating it will cause FasTrac to lose $6,000 of income. *Our decision rule is that a segment is a candidate for elimination if its revenues are less than its avoidable expenses.* Avoidable expenses can be viewed as the costs to generate this segment's revenues.

When considering elimination of a segment, we must assess its impact on other segments. A segment could be unprofitable on its own, but it might still contribute to other segments' revenues and profits. It is possible then to continue a segment even when its revenues are less than its avoidable expenses. Similarly, a profitable segment might be discontinued if its space, assets, or staff can be more profitably used by expanding existing segments or by creating new ones. Our decision to keep or eliminate a segment requires a more complex analysis than simply looking at a segment's performance report. Such reports provide useful information, but they do not provide all the information necessary for this decision.

Example: Give an example of a segment that a company might profitably use to attract customers even though it might incur a loss. *Answer:* Warranty and post-sales services.

Keep or Replace Equipment

Businesses periodically must decide whether to keep using equipment or replace it. Advances in technology typically mean newer equipment can operate more efficiently and at lower cost than older equipment. In making the decision to keep or replace equipment, managers must decide whether the reduction in *variable* manufacturing costs with the new equipment over its useful life is greater than the net purchase price of the equipment. In this setting, the net purchase price of the equipment is its total cost minus any trade-in allowance or cash receipt for the old equipment.

For example, FasTrac has a piece of manufacturing equipment with a carrying amount (cost minus accumulated depreciation) of $20,000 and a remaining useful life of four years. At the end of four years the equipment will have a residual value of zero. The market value of the equipment is currently $25,000.

FasTrac can purchase a new machine for $100,000 and receive $25,000 in return for trading in its old machine. The new machine will reduce FasTrac's variable manufacturing costs by

$18,000 per year over the four-year life of the new machine. FasTrac's incremental analysis is shown in Exhibit 25.21.

EXHIBIT 25.21

Keep or Replace Analysis

	Increase or (Decrease) in Net Profit
Cost to buy new machine	$(100,000)
Cash received to trade in old machine	25,000
Reduction in variable manufacturing costs*	72,000
Total increase (decrease) in net profit	$ (3,000)

*18,000 × 4 years

The analysis in Exhibit 25.21 shows that FasTrac should not replace the old equipment with this newer version as it will decrease income by $3,000. Note, the carrying amount of the old equipment ($20,000) is not relevant to this analysis. Carrying amount is a sunk cost, and it cannot be changed regardless of whether FasTrac keeps or replaces this equipment.

Qualitative Decision Factors

Managers must consider qualitative factors in making managerial decisions. Consider a decision on whether to buy a component from an outside supplier or continue to make it. Several qualitative decision factors must be considered. For example, the quality, delivery, and reputation of the proposed supplier are important. The effects from deciding not to make the component can include potential layoffs and impaired worker morale. Consider another situation in which a company is considering a one-time sale to a new customer at a special low price. Qualitative factors to consider in this situation include the effects of a low price on the company's image and the threat that regular customers might demand a similar price. The company must also  consider whether this customer is really a one-time customer. If not, can it continue to offer this low price in the long run? Clearly, management cannot rely solely on financial data to make such decisions.

Quick Check   Answers — p. 1034

15. What is the difference between avoidable and unavoidable expenses?
16. A segment is a candidate for elimination if (a) its revenues are less than its avoidable expenses, (b) it has a net loss, (c) its unavoidable expenses are higher than its revenues.

Break-Even Time      **Decision Analysis**

The first section of this chapter explained several methods to evaluate capital investments. Break-even time of an investment project is a variation of the payback period method that overcomes the limitation of not using the time value of money. **Break-even time (BET)** is a time-based measure used to evaluate a capital investment's acceptability. Its computation yields a measure of expected time, reflecting the

 A2 Analyze a capital investment project using break-even time.

time period until the *present value* of the net cash flows from an investment equals the initial cost of the investment. In basic terms, break-even time is computed by restating future cash flows in terms of present values and then determining the payback period using these present values.

To illustrate, we return to the FasTrac case described in Exhibit 25.1 involving a $16,000 investment in machinery. The annual net cash flows from this investment are projected at $4,100 for eight years. Exhibit 25.22 shows the computation of break-even time for this investment decision.

EXHIBIT 25.22

Break-Even Time Analysis*

Year	Cash Flows	Present Value of 1 at 10%	Present Value of Cash Flows	Cumulative Present Value of Cash Flows
0	$(16,000)	1.0000	$(16,000)	$(16,000)
1	4,100	0.9091	3,727	(12,273)
2	4,100	0.8264	3,388	(8,885)
3	4,100	0.7513	3,080	(5,805)
4	4,100	0.6830	2,800	(3,005)
5	4,100	0.6209	2,546	(459)
6	4,100	0.5645	2,314	1,855
7	4,100	0.5132	2,104	3,959
8	4,100	0.4665	1,913	5,872

* The time of analysis is the start of year 1 (same as end of year 0). All cash flows occur at the end of each year.

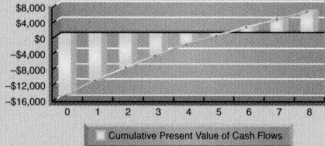
Cumulative Present Value of Cash Flows

The right-most column of this exhibit shows that break-even time is between 5 and 6 years, or about 5.2 years—also see margin graph (where the line crosses the zero point). This is the time the project takes to break even after considering the time value of money (recall that the payback period computed without considering the time value of money was 3.9 years). We interpret this as cash flows earned after 5.2 years contribute to a positive net present value that, in this case, eventually amounts to $5,872.

Break-even time is a useful measure for managers because it identifies the point in time when they can expect the cash flows to begin to yield net positive returns. Managers expect a positive net present value from an investment if break-even time is less than the investment's estimated life. The method allows managers to compare and rank alternative investments, giving the project with the shortest break-even time the highest rank.

◻ Decision Maker   Answer — p. 1033

Investment Manager   Management asks you, the investment manager, to evaluate three alternative investments. Investment recovery time is crucial because cash is scarce. The time value of money is also important. Which capital budgeting method(s) do you use to assess the investments? ◼

DEMONSTRATION PROBLEM

Determine the appropriate action in each of the following managerial decision situations.

1. Packer Company is operating at 80% of its manufacturing capacity of 100,000 product units per year. A chain store has offered to buy an additional 10,000 units at $22 each and sell them to customers so as not to compete with Packer Company. The following data are available.

Costs at 80% Capacity	Per Unit	Total
Direct materials	$ 8.00	$ 640,000
Direct labor	7.00	560,000
Overhead (fixed and variable)	12.50	1,000,000
Totals	$27.50	$2,200,000

In producing 10,000 additional units, fixed overhead costs would remain at their current level but incremental variable overhead costs of $3 per unit would be incurred. Should the company accept or reject this order?

2. Green Company uses Part JR3 in manufacturing its products. It has always purchased this part from a supplier for $40 each. It recently upgraded its own manufacturing capabilities and has enough excess capacity (including trained workers) to begin manufacturing Part JR3 instead of buying it. The company prepares the following cost projections of making the part, assuming that overhead is allocated to the part at the normal predetermined rate of 200% of direct labor cost.

Direct materials	$11
Direct labor	15
Overhead (fixed and variable) (200% of direct labor)	30
Total	$56

The required volume of output to produce the part will not require any incremental fixed overhead. Incremental variable overhead cost will be $17 per unit. Should the company make or buy this part?

3. Gold Company's manufacturing process causes a relatively large number of defective parts to be produced. The defective parts can be (a) sold for scrap, (b) melted to recover the recycled metal for reuse, or (c) reworked to be good units. Reworking defective parts reduces the output of other good units because no excess capacity exists. Each unit reworked means that one new unit cannot be produced. The following information reflects 500 defective parts currently available.

Proceeds of selling as scrap	$2,500
Additional cost of melting down defective parts	400
Cost of purchases avoided by using recycled metal from defects	4,800
Cost to rework 500 defective parts	
Direct materials	0
Direct labor	1,500
Incremental overhead	1,750
Cost to produce 500 new parts	
Direct materials	6,000
Direct labor	5,000
Incremental overhead	3,200
Selling price per good unit	40

Should the company melt the parts, sell them as scrap, or rework them?

4. White Company can invest in one of two projects, TD1 or TD2. Each project requires an initial investment of $100,000 and produces the year-end cash inflows shown in the following table. Use net present values to determine which project, if any, should be chosen. Assume that the company requires a 10% return from its investments.

	Net Cash Flows	
	TD1	TD2
Year 1	$ 20,000	$ 40,000
Year 2	30,000	40,000
Year 3	70,000	40,000
Totals	$120,000	$120,000

PLANNING THE SOLUTION

- Determine whether Packer Company should accept the additional business by finding the incremental costs of materials, labor, and overhead that will be incurred if the order is accepted. Omit fixed costs that the order will not increase. If the incremental revenue exceeds the incremental cost, accept the order.

- Determine whether Green Company should make or buy the component by finding the incremental cost of making each unit. If the incremental cost exceeds the purchase price, the component should be purchased. If the incremental cost is less than the purchase price, make the component.

- Determine whether Gold Company should sell the defective parts, melt them down and recycle the metal, or rework them. To compare the three choices, examine all costs incurred and benefits received from the alternatives in working with the 500 defective units versus the production of 500 new units. For the scrapping alternative, include the costs of producing 500 new units and subtract the $2,500 proceeds from selling the old ones. For the melting alternative, include the costs of melting the defective units, add the net cost of new materials in excess over those obtained from recycling, and add the direct labor and overhead costs. For the reworking alternative, add the costs of direct labor and incremental overhead. Select the alternative that has the lowest cost. The cost assigned to the 500 defective units is sunk and not relevant in choosing among the three alternatives.

- Compute White Company's net present value of each investment using a 10% discount rate.

SOLUTION TO DEMONSTRATION PROBLEM

1. This decision involves accepting additional business. Since current unit costs are $27.50, it appears initially as if the offer to sell for $22 should be rejected, but the $27.50 cost includes fixed costs. When the analysis includes only *incremental* costs, the per unit cost is as shown in the following table. The offer should be accepted because it will produce $4 of additional profit per unit (computed as $22 price less $18 incremental cost), which yields a total profit of $40,000 for the 10,000 additional units.

Direct materials	$ 8.00
Direct labor	7.00
Variable overhead (given)	3.00
Total incremental cost	$18.00

2. For this make or buy decision, the analysis must not include the $13 nonincremental overhead per unit ($30 − $17). When only the $17 incremental overhead is included, the relevant unit cost of manufacturing the part is shown in the following table. It would be better to continue buying the part for $40 instead of making it for $43.

Direct materials	$11.00
Direct labor	15.00
Variable overhead............	17.00
Total incremental cost	$43.00

3. The goal of this scrap or rework decision is to identify the alternative that produces the greatest net benefit to the company. To compare the alternatives, we determine the net cost of obtaining 500 marketable units as follows:

Incremental Cost to Produce 500 Marketable Units	Sell as Is	Melt and Recycle	Rework Units
Direct materials			
New materials	$ 6,000	$6,000	
Recycled metal materials		(4,800)	
Net materials cost		1,200	
Melting costs		400	
Total direct materials cost.	6,000	1,600	
Direct labor	5,000	5,000	$1,500
Incremental overhead.	3,200	3,200	1,750
Cost to produce 500 marketable units	14,200	9,800	3,250
Less proceeds of selling defects as scrap	(2,500)		
Opportunity costs*			5,800
Net cost	$11,700	$9,800	$9,050

* The $5,800 opportunity cost is the lost contribution margin from not being able to produce and sell 500 units because of reworking, computed as ($40 − [$14,200/500 units]) × 500 units.

The incremental cost of 500 marketable parts is smallest if the defects are reworked.

4. TD1:

	Net Cash Flows	Present Value of 1 at 10%	Present Value of Net Cash Flows
Year 1	$ 20,000	0.9091	$ 18,182
Year 2	30,000	0.8264	24,792
Year 3	70,000	0.7513	52,591
Totals	$120,000		95,565
Amount invested			(100,000)
Net present value			$ (4,435)

TD2:

	Net Cash Flows	Present Value of 1 at 10%	Present Value of Net Cash Flows
Year 1	$ 40,000	0.9091	$ 36,364
Year 2	40,000	0.8264	33,056
Year 3	40,000	0.7513	30,052
Totals	$120,000		99,472
Amount invested			(100,000)
Net present value			$ (528)

White Company should not invest in either project. Both are expected to yield a negative net present value, and it should invest only in positive net present value projects.

25A

Using Excel to Compute Net Present Value and Internal Rate of Return

Computing present values and internal rates of return for projects with uneven cash flows is tedious and error prone. These calculations can be performed simply and accurately by using functions built into Excel. Many calculators and other types of spreadsheet software can perform them too. To illustrate, consider FasTrac, a company that is considering investing in a new machine with the expected cash flows shown in the following spreadsheet. Cash outflows are entered as negative numbers, and cash inflows are entered as positive numbers. Assume FasTrac requires a 12% annual return, entered as 0.12 in cell C1.

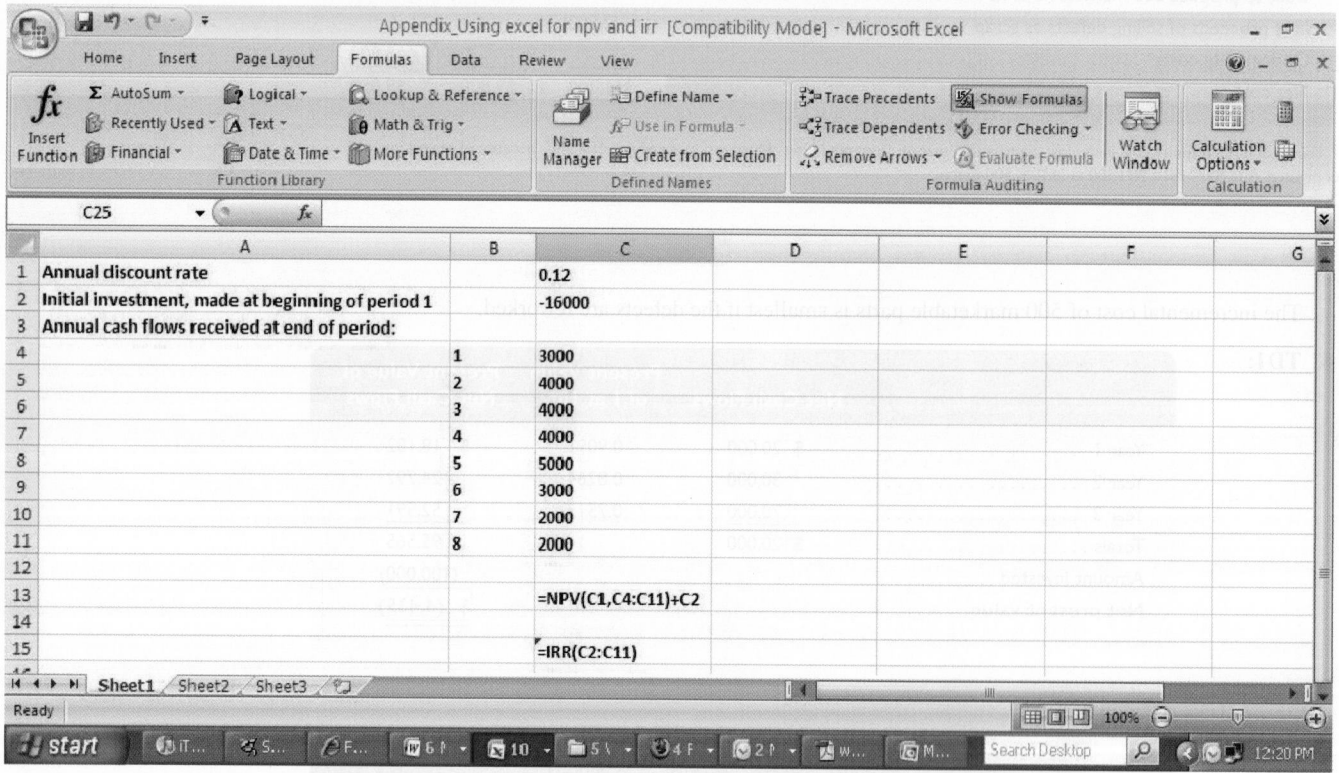

To compute the net present value of this project, the following is entered into cell C13:

$$=NPV(C1,C4:C11)+C2.$$

This instructs Excel to use its NPV function to compute the present value of the cash flows in cells C4 through C11, using the discount rate in cell C1, and then add the amount of the (negative) initial investment. For this stream of cash flows and a discount rate of 12%, the net present value is $1,326.03.

To compute the internal rate of return for this project, the following is entered into cell C15:

$$=IRR(C2:C11).$$

This instructs Excel to use its IRR function to compute the internal rate of return of the cash flows in cells C2 through C11. By default, Excel starts with a guess of 10%, and then uses trial and error to find the IRR. The IRR equals 14% for this project.

Summary

C1 **Describe the importance of relevant costs for short-term decisions.** A company must rely on relevant costs pertaining to alternative courses of action rather than historical costs. Out-of-pocket expenses and opportunity costs are relevant because these are avoidable; sunk costs are irrelevant because they result from past decisions and are therefore unavoidable. Managers must also consider the relevant benefits associated with alternative decisions.

A1 **Evaluate short-term managerial decisions using relevant costs.** Relevant costs are useful in making decisions such as to accept additional business, make or buy, and sell as is or process further. For example, the relevant factors in deciding whether to produce and sell additional units of product are incremental costs and incremental revenues from the additional volume.

A2 **Analyze a capital investment project using break-even time.** Break-even time (BET) is a method for evaluating capital investments by restating future cash flows in terms of their present values (discounting the cash flows) and then calculating the payback period using these present values of cash flows.

P1 **Compute payback period and describe its use.** One way to compare potential investments is to compute and compare their payback periods. The payback period is an estimate of the expected time before the cumulative net cash inflow from the investment equals its initial cost. A payback period analysis fails to reflect risk of the cash flows, differences in the timing of cash flows within the payback period, and cash flows that occur after the payback period.

P2 **Compute accounting rate of return and explain its use.** A project's accounting rate of return is computed by dividing the expected annual after-tax net profit by the average amount of investment in the project. When the net cash flows are received evenly throughout each period and straight-line depreciation is used, the average investment is computed as the average of the investment's initial carrying amount and its residual value.

P3 **Compute net present value and describe its use.** An investment's net present value is determined by predicting the future cash flows it is expected to generate, discounting them at a rate that represents an acceptable return, and then by subtracting the investment's initial cost from the sum of the present values. This technique can deal with any pattern of expected cash flows and applies a superior concept of return on investment.

P4 **Compute internal rate of return and explain its use.** The internal rate of return (IRR) is the discount rate that results in a zero net present value. When the cash flows are equal, we can compute the present value factor corresponding to the IRR by dividing the initial investment by the annual cash flows. We then use the annuity tables to determine the discount rate corresponding to this present value factor.

Guidance Answers to Decision Maker and Decision Ethics

Systems Manager Your dilemma is whether to abide by rules designed to prevent abuse or to bend them to acquire an investment that you believe will benefit the firm. You should not pursue the latter action because breaking up the order into small components is dishonest and there are consequences of being caught at a later stage. Develop a proposal for the entire package and then do all you can to expedite its processing, particularly by pointing out its benefits. When faced with controls that are not working, there is rarely a reason to overcome its shortcomings by dishonesty. A direct assault on those limitations is more sensible and ethical.

Entrepreneur The banker is probably concerned because new products are risky and should therefore be evaluated using a higher rate of return. You should conduct a thorough technical analysis and obtain detailed market data and information about any similar products available in the market. These factors might provide sufficient information to support the use of a lower return. You must convince yourself that the risk level is consistent with the discount rate used.

You should also be confident that your company has the capacity and the resources to handle the new product.

Partner You should identify the differences between existing clients and this potential client. A key difference is that the restaurant business has additional inventory components (groceries, vegetables, meats, etc.) and is likely to have a higher proportion of depreciable assets. These differences imply that the partner must spend more hours auditing the records and understanding the business, regulations, and standards that pertain to the restaurant business. Such differences suggest that the partner must use a different "formula" for quoting a price to this potential client vis-à-vis current clients.

Investment Manager You should probably focus on either the payback period or break-even time because both the time value of money and recovery time are important. Break-even time method is superior because it accounts for the time value of money, which is an important consideration in this decision.

Guidance Answers to Quick Checks

1. *b*

2. A capital budgeting decision is difficult because (1) the outcome is uncertain, (2) large amounts of money are usually involved, (3) a long-term commitment is required, and (4) the decision could be difficult or impossible to reverse.

3. *b*

4. Depreciation expense is subtracted from revenues in computing net profit but does not use cash and should be added back to net profit to compute net cash flows.

5. Not necessarily. One investment can continue to generate cash flows beyond the payback period for a longer time period than the other. The timing of their cash flows within the payback period also can differ.

6. *b*; Annual average investment = ($180,000 + $15,000)/2
$$= \$97,500$$
Accounting rate of return = $40,000/$97,500 = 41%

7. For this determination, we need to compare it to the returns expected from alternative investments with similar risk.

8. Project A has the higher net present value as follows:

		Project A		Project B	
Year	Present Value of 1 at 10%	Net Cash Flows	Present Value of Net Cash Flows	Net Cash Flows	Present Value of Net Cash Flows
1	0.9091	$12,000	$10,909	$ 4,500	$ 4,091
2	0.8264	8,500	7,024	8,500	7,024
3	0.7513	4,000	3,005	13,000	9,767
Totals		$24,500	$20,938	$26,000	$20,882
Amount invested			(20,000)		(20,000)
Net present value			**$ 938**		**$ 882**

9. No, the information is too limited to draw that conclusion. For example, one investment could be riskier than the other, or one could require a substantially larger initial investment.

10. *b*

11. *e*; Variable costs per unit for this order of 200 units follow:

Direct materials ($37,500/7,500)	$ 5.00
Direct labor ($60,000/7,500)	8.00
Variable overhead [(0.30 × $20,000)/7,500]	0.80
Variable selling expenses [(0.60 × $25,000 × 0.5)/7,500]	1.00
Total variable costs per unit	$14.80

Cost to produce special order: (200 × $14.80) + $400
$$= \$3,360.$$
Price per unit to earn $1,000: ($3,360 + $1,000)/200 = 21.80.

12. They are the additional (new) costs of accepting new business.

13. *d*;

	Incremental benefits		Incremental costs
Alpha	$300 ($600 − $300)	>	$150 (given)
Beta	$450 ($900 − $450)	>	$300 (given)
Gamma	$150 ($425 − $275)	>	$125 (given)
Delta	$ 60 ($210 − $150)	<	$ 75 (given)

14. A sunk cost is *never* relevant because it results from a past decision and is already incurred.

15. Avoidable expenses are ones a company will not incur by eliminating a segment; unavoidable expenses will continue even after a segment is eliminated.

16. *a*

Key Terms   www.mheducation.asia/olc/wildkwokFAP

Accounting rate of return (p. 1011)
Avoidable expense (p. 1026)
Break-even time (BET) (p. 1027)
Capital budgeting (p. 1008)
Cost of capital (p. 1013)

Hurdle rate (p. 1017)
Incremental cost (p. 1020)
Internal rate of return (IRR) (p. 1015)
Net present value (NPV) (p. 1013)
Payback period (PBP) (p. 1009)

Profitability index (p. 1015)
Relevant benefits (p. 1019)
Unavoidable expense (p. 1026)

Multiple Choice Quiz   Answers on p. 1050   www.mheducation.asia/olc/wildkwokFAP

Additional Quiz Questions are available at the book's Website.

1. A company inadvertently produced 3,000 defective MP3 players. The players cost $12 each to produce. A recycler offers to purchase the defective players as they are for $8 each. The production manager reports that the defects can be corrected for $10 each, enabling them to be sold at their regular market price of $19 each. The company should:
  a. Correct the defect and sell them at the regular price.
  b. Sell the players to the recycler for $8 each.
  c. Sell 2,000 to the recycler and repair the rest.
  d. Sell 1,000 to the recycler and repair the rest.
  e. Throw the players away.

2. A company's productive capacity is limited to 480,000 machine hours. Product X requires 10 machine hours to produce; and Product Y requires 2 machine hours to produce. Product X

sells for $32 per unit and has variable costs of $12 per unit; Product Y sells for $24 per unit and has variable costs of $10 per unit. Assuming that the company can sell as many of either product as it produces, it should:
  a. Produce X and Y in the ratio of 57% and 43%.
  b. Produce X and Y in the ratio of 83% X and 17% Y.
  c. Produce equal amounts of Product X and Product Y.
  d. Produce only Product X.
  e. Produce only Product Y.

3. A company receives a special one-time order for 3,000 units of its product at $15 per unit. The company has excess capacity and it currently produces and sells the units at $20 each to its regular customers. Production costs are $13.50 per unit, which includes $9 of variable costs. To produce the special order, the company must incur additional fixed costs of $5,000. Should the company accept the special order?

   a. Yes, because incremental revenue exceeds incremental costs.
   b. No, because incremental costs exceed incremental revenue.
   c. No, because the units are being sold for $5 less than the regular price.
   d. Yes, because incremental costs exceed incremental revenue.
   e. No, because incremental cost exceeds $15 per unit when total costs are considered.

4. A company is considering the purchase of equipment for $270,000. Projected annual cash inflow from this equipment is $61,200 per year. The payback period is:
   a. 0.2 years
   b. 5.0 years

   c. 4.4 years
   d. 2.3 years
   e. 3.9 years

5. A company buys a machine for $180,000 that has an expected life of nine years and no residual value. The company expects an annual net profit (after taxes of 30%) of $8,550. What is the accounting rate of return?
   a. 4.75%
   b. 42.75%
   c. 2.85%
   d. 9.50%
   e. 6.65%

Icon denotes assignments that involve decision making.

Discussion Questions

1. What is capital budgeting?
2. Identify four reasons that capital budgeting decisions by managers are risky.
3. Capital budgeting decisions require careful analysis because they are generally the _____ _____ and _____ decisions that management faces.
4. Identify two disadvantages of using the payback period for comparing investments.
5. Why is an investment more attractive to management if it has a shorter payback period?
6. What is the average amount invested in a machine during its predicted five-year life if it costs $200,000 and has a $20,000 residual value? Assume that net profit is received evenly throughout each year and straight-line depreciation is used.
7. If the present value of the expected net cash flows from a machine, discounted at 10%, exceeds the amount to be invested, what can you say about the investment's expected rate of return? What can you say about the expected rate of return if the present value of the net cash flows, discounted at 10%, is less than the investment amount?
8. Why is the present value of $100 that you expect to receive one year from today worth less than $100 received today? What is the present value of $100 that you expect to receive one year from today, discounted at 12%?

9. Why should managers set the required rate of return higher than the rate at which money can be borrowed when making a typical capital budgeting decision?
10. Why does the use of the accelerated depreciation method (instead of straight line) for income tax reporting increase an investment's value?
11. **Palm** has many types of costs. What is an out-of-pocket cost? What is an opportunity cost? Are opportunity costs recorded in the accounting records?
12. **Nokia** must confront sunk costs. Why are sunk costs irrelevant in deciding whether to sell a product in its present condition or to make it into a new product through additional processing?
13. Identify the incremental costs incurred by **Apple** for shipping one additional iPod from a warehouse to a retail store along with the store's normal order of 75 iPods.
14. **Apple** is considering expanding a store. Identify three methods management can use to evaluate whether to expand.
15. Assume that **Research In Motion** manufactures and sells 500,000 units of a product at $30 per unit in domestic markets. It costs $20 per unit to manufacture ($13 variable cost per unit, $7 fixed cost per unit). Can you describe a situation under which the company is willing to sell an additional 25,000 units of the product in an international market at $15 per unit?

---

connect

Ting Company is considering two alternative investments. The payback period is 3.5 years for investment A and 5 years for investment B. (1) If management relies on the payback period, which investment is preferred? (2) Why might Ting's analysis of these two alternatives lead to the selection of B over A?

QUICK STUDY

QS 25-1
Analyzing payback periods **P1**

QS 25-2
Payback period   P1

Fabiano Brothers Co. is considering an investment that requires immediate payment of $550,000 and provides expected cash inflows of $100,000 annually for eight years. What is the investment's payback period?

QS 25-3
Computation of
net present value   P3

If Kelsey K. Company invests $250,000 today, it can expect to receive $50,000 at the end of each year for the next seven years, plus an extra $32,000 at the end of the seventh year. What is the net present value of this investment assuming a required 8% return on investments?

QS 25-4
Computation of
accounting rate of return   P2

Cardinal Company is considering an investment expected to generate an average net profit after taxes of $1,300 for three years. The investment costs $30,000 and has an estimated $4,000 residual value. Compute the accounting rate of return for this investment; assume the company uses straight-line depreciation. Hint: Use the formula in Exhibit 25.5 when computing the average annual investment.

QS 25-5
Internal rate of return   P4

A company is considering investing in a new machine that requires a cash payment of $15,982 today. The machine will generate annual cash flows of $7,000 for the next three years. What is the internal rate of return if the company buys this machine?

QS 25-6
Relevant costs
C1

Label each of the following statements as either true ("T") or false ("F").
1. An opportunity cost is the potential benefit that is lost by taking a specific action when two or more alternative choices are available.
2. A sunk cost will change with a future course of action.
3. An out-of-pocket cost requires a current and/or future outlay of cash.
4. Relevant costs are also known as unavoidable costs.
5. Incremental costs are also known as differential costs.

QS 25-7
Analysis of incremental costs
A1

Mo-Kan Company incurs a $6 per unit cost for Product A, which it currently manufactures and sells for $9 per unit. Instead of manufacturing and selling this product, the company can purchase Product B for $5 per unit and sell it for $8 per unit. If it does so, unit sales would remain unchanged and $5 of the $6 per unit costs assigned to Product A would be eliminated. Should the company continue to manufacture Product A or purchase Product B for resale?

QS 25-8
Selection of sales mix
A1

Memory Lane Company can sell all units of computer memory X and Y that it can produce, but it has limited production capacity. It can produce four units of X per hour *or* three units of Y per hour, and it has 8,000 production hours available. Contribution margin is $10 for product X and $8 for product Y. What is the most profitable sales mix for this company?

QS 25-9
Decision to accept additional
business
A1

Kirk Company sells bikes for $600 each. The company currently sells 7,500 bikes per year and could make as many as 10,000 bikes per year. The bikes cost $450 each to make; $300 in variable costs per bike and $150 of fixed costs per bike. Kirk received an offer from a potential customer who wants to buy 1,500 bikes for $500 each. Incremental fixed costs to make this order are $100,000. No other costs will change if this order is accepted. Compute Kirk's additional income (ignore taxes) if it accepts this order.

QS 25-10
Scrap or rework
A1

Z-Tech mistakenly produced 10,000 defective cell phones. The phones cost $60 each to produce. A salvage company will buy the defective phones as they are for $30 each. It would cost Z-Tech $80 per phone to rework the phones. If the phones are reworked, Z-Tech could sell them for $125 each. Compute the incremental net profit from reworking the phones.

QS 25-11
Sell or process decision
A1

Bartel Company produces a product that can either be sold as is or processed further. Bartel has already spent $10,000 to produce 250 units that can be sold now for $13,500 to another manufacturer. Alternatively, Bartel can process the units further at an incremental cost of $36 per unit. If Bartel processes further, the units can be sold for $100 each. Compute the incremental income if Bartel processes further.

A guitar manufacturer is considering eliminating its electric guitar division because its $76,000 expenses are higher than its $72,000 sales. The company reports the following expenses for this division. Should the division be eliminated?

QS 25-12
Segment elimination
A1

	Avoidable Expenses	Unavoidable Expenses
Cost of goods sold	$55,000	
Direct expenses	6,250	$2,250
Indirect expenses	470	3,600
Service department costs	7,000	1,430

Tak Company has a machine with a carrying amount of $50,000 and a remaining five-year useful life. A new machine is available at a cost of $75,000, and Tak can also receive $40,000 for trading in its old machine. The new machine will reduce variable manufacturing costs by $12,000 per year over its five-year useful life. Should the machine be replaced?

QS 25-13
Keep or replace decision
A1

Soles, a shoe manufacturer, is evaluating the costs and benefits of new equipment that would custom fit each pair of athletic shoes. The customer would have his or her foot scanned by digital computer equipment; this information would be used to cut the raw materials to provide the customer a perfect fit. The new equipment costs $100,000 and is expected to generate an additional $35,000 in cash flows for five years. A bank will make a $100,000 loan to the company at a 10% interest rate for this equipment's purchase. Use the following table to determine the break-even time for this equipment. (Round the present value of cash flows to the nearest dollar.)

QS 25-14
Computation of break-even time
A2

Year	Cash Flows*	Present Value of 1 at 10%	Present Value of Cash Flows	Cumulative Present Value of Cash Flows
0	$(100,000)	1.0000		
1	35,000	0.9091		
2	35,000	0.8264		
3	35,000	0.7513		
4	35,000	0.6830		
5	35,000	0.6209		

* All cash flows occur at year-end.

Jester Company is considering two alternative projects. Project 1 requires an initial investment of $500,000 and has a net present value of cash flows of $1,200,000. Project 2 requires an initial investment of $3,500,000 and has a net present value of cash flows of $1,900,000. Compute the profitability index for each project. Based on the profitability index, which project should the company prefer? Explain.

QS 25-15
Profitability index
P3

Siemens AG invests EUR 80 million to build a manufacturing plant to build wind turbines. The company predicts net cash flows of EUR 16 million per year for the next 8 years. Assume the company requires an 8% rate of return from its investments. (1) What is the payback period of this investment? (2) What is the net present value of this investment?

QS 25-16
Capital budgeting methods
P1 P3

---

connect

Compute the payback period for each of these two separate investments (round the payback period to two decimals):

a. A new operating system for an existing machine is expected to cost $260,000 and have a useful life of five years. The system yields an incremental after-tax income of $75,000 each year after deducting its straight-line depreciation. The predicted residual value of the system is $10,000.

b. A machine costs $190,000, has a $10,000 residual value, is expected to last nine years, and will generate an after-tax income of $30,000 per year after straight-line depreciation.

EXERCISES

Exercise 25-1
Payback period computation;
even cash flows

P1

Exercise 25-2

Payback period computation; uneven cash flows

P1

Check 3.167 years

Wenro Company is considering the purchase of an asset for $90,000. It is expected to produce the following net cash flows. The cash flows occur evenly throughout each year. Compute the payback period for this investment.

	Year 1	Year 2	Year 3	Year 4	Year 5	Total
Net cash flows	$30,000	$20,000	$30,000	$60,000	$19,000	$159,000

Exercise 25-3

Payback period computation; declining-balance depreciation

P1

Check 2.265 years

A machine can be purchased for $300,000 and used for 5 years, yielding the following net profits. In project-ing net profits, double-declining balance depreciation is applied, using a 5-year life and a $50,000 residual value. Compute the machine's payback period (ignore taxes). (Round the payback period to two decimals.)

	Year 1	Year 2	Year 3	Year 4	Year 5
Net profits	$20,000	$50,000	$100,000	$75,000	$200,000

Exercise 25-4

Accounting rate of return   P2

A machine costs $500,000 and is expected to yield an after-tax net profit of $15,000 each year. Management predicts this machine has a 10-year service life and a $100,000 residual value, and it uses straight-line depreciation. Compute this machine's accounting rate of return.

Exercise 25-5

Payback period and accounting rate of return on investment

P1 P2

Check (1) 5.39 years (2) 20.42%

K2B Co. is considering the purchase of equipment that would allow the company to add a new product to its line. The equipment is expected to cost $240,000 with a 12-year life and no residual value. It will be depreciated on a straight-line basis. The company expects to sell 96,000 units of the equipment's product each year. The expected annual income related to this equipment follows. Compute the (1) payback period and (2) accounting rate of return for this equipment.

Sales	$150,000
Costs	
Materials, labor, and overhead (except depreciation).........	(80,000)
Depreciation on new equipment	(20,000)
Selling and administrative expenses	(15,000)
Total costs and expenses..............................	(115,000)
Pretax income	35,000
Income taxes (30%).................................	10,500
Net profit...	$ 24,500

Exercise 25-6

Computing net present value   P3

After evaluating the risk of the investment described in Exercise 25-5, K2B Co. concludes that it must earn at least a 8% return on this investment. Compute the net present value of this investment. (Round the net present value to the nearest dollar.)

Exercise 25-7

Computation and interpretation of net present value and internal rate of return

P3 P4

Check (1) C2 net present value, $2,152

Kase Company can invest in each of three cheese-making projects: C1, C2, and C3. Each project requires an initial investment of $190,000 and would yield the following annual cash flows.

	C1	C2	C3
Year 1.........	$ 10,000	$ 80,000	$150,000
Year 2	90,000	80,000	50,000
Year 3	140,000	80,000	40,000
Totals	$240,000	$240,000	$240,000

(1) Assuming that the company requires a 12% return from its investments, use net present value to determine which projects, if any, should be acquired. (2) Using the answer from part 1, explain whether the internal rate of return is higher or lower than 12% for project C2. (3) Compute the internal rate of return for project C2.

Exercise 25-8

NPV and profitability index   P3

Following is information on two alternative investments being considered by Jin Company. The company requires a 10% return from its investments.

	Project A	Project B
Initial investment	$(175,000)	$(145,000)
Expected net cash flows in year:		
1	40,000	32,000
2	56,000	50,000
3	80,295	66,000
4	90,400	72,000
5	55,000	29,000

For each alternative project compute the (a) net present value, and (b) profitability index. If the company can only select one project, which should it choose? Explain.

Refer to the information in Exercise 25-8. Create an Excel spreadsheet to compute the internal rate of return for each of the projects. Round the percentage return to two decimals.

Exercise 25-9^A
Using Excel to compute IRR   **P4**

Fill in each of the blanks below with the correct term.

1. Relevant costs are also known as _____.
2. An _____ requires a future outlay of cash and is relevant for current and future decision making.
3. An _____ is the potential benefit lost by taking a specific action when two or more alternative choices are available.
4. A _____ arises from a past decision and cannot be avoided or changed; it is irrelevant to future decisions.
5. _____ refer to the incremental revenue generated from taking one particular action over another.

Exercise 25-10
Relevant costs

C1

A company must decide between scrapping or reworking units that do not pass inspection. The company has 15,000 defective units that cost $6 per unit to manufacture. The units can be sold as is for $2.50 each, or they can be reworked for $4.50 each and then sold for the full price of $9 each. If the units are sold as is, the company will have to build 15,000 replacement units at a cost of $6 each, and sell them at the full price of $9 each. (1) What is the incremental income from selling the units as scrap? (2) What is the incremental income from reworking and selling the units? (3) Should the company sell the units as scrap or rework them?

Exercise 25-11
Scrap or rework

A1

Xu Company is considering replacing one of its manufacturing machines. The machine has a carrying amount of $45,000 and a remaining useful life of 4 years, at which time its residual value will be zero. It has a current market value of $55,000. Variable manufacturing costs are $34,000 per year for this machine. Information on two alternative replacement machines follows. Should Xu keep or replace its manufacturing machine? If the machine should be replaced, which alternative new machine should Xu purchase?

Exercise 25-12
Keep or replace

A1

	Alternative A	Alternative B
Cost	$115,000	$125,000
Variable manufacturing costs per year.........	22,000	12,000

Feist Co. expects to sell 200,000 units of its product in the next period with the following results.

Exercise 25-13
Decision to accept additional business or not

A1

Sales (200,000 units)	$3,000,000
Costs and expenses	
Direct materials	(400,000)
Direct labor	(800,000)
Overhead	(200,000)
Selling expenses	(300,000)
Administrative expenses	(514,000)
Total costs and expenses..........	(2,214,000)
Net profit......................	$ 786,000

The company has an opportunity to sell 20,000 additional units at $12 per unit. The additional sales would not affect its current expected sales. Direct materials and labor costs per unit would be the same for the additional units as they are for the regular units. However, the additional volume would create the following incremental costs: (1) total overhead would increase by 15% and (2) administrative expenses would increase by $86,000. Prepare an analysis to determine whether the company should accept or reject the offer to sell additional units at the reduced price of $12 per unit.

Check Income increase, $4,000

Exercise 25-14
Make or buy decision

A1

Check $10,000 increased costs to buy

Santos Company currently manufactures one of its crucial parts at a cost of $3.40 per unit. This cost is based on a normal production rate of 50,000 units per year. Variable costs are $1.50 per unit, fixed costs related to making this part are $50,000 per year, and allocated fixed costs are $45,000 per year. Allocated fixed costs are unavoidable whether the company makes or buys the part. Santos is considering buying the part from a supplier for a quoted price of $2.70 per unit guaranteed for a three-year period. Should the company continue to manufacture the part, or should it buy the part from the outside supplier? Support your answer with analyses.

Exercise 25-15
Sell or process decision

A1

Cantrell Company has already manufactured 20,000 units of Product A at a cost of $20 per unit. The 20,000 units can be sold at this stage for $500,000. Alternatively, the units can be further processed at a $300,000 total additional cost and be converted into 4,000 units of Product B and 8,000 units of Product C. Per unit selling price for Product B is $75 and for Product C is $50. Prepare an analysis that shows whether the 20,000 units of Product A should be processed further or not.

Exercise 25-16
Analysis of income effects from eliminating departments

A1

Suresh Co. expects its five departments to yield the following income for next year.

	File Edit View Insert Format Tools Data Window Help				
		Dept. M	**Dept. N**	**Dept. O**	**Dept. P**	**Dept. T**
1						
2	Sales	$31,500	$17,500	$28,000	$21,000	$ 14,000
3	Expenses					
4	Avoidable	4,900	18,200	11,200	7,000	18,900
5	Unavoidable	25,900	6,300	2,100	14,700	4,900
6	Total expenses	30,800	24,500	13,300	21,700	23,800
7	Net profit (loss)	$ 700	$ (7,000)	$14,700	$ (700)	$ (9,800)

Check Total profit (loss)
(2) $(10,500), (3) $3,500

Recompute and prepare the departmental income statements (including a combined total column) for the company under each of the following separate scenarios: Management (1) does not eliminate any department, (2) eliminates departments with expected net losses, and (3) eliminates departments with sales dollars that are less than avoidable expenses. Explain your answers to parts 2 and 3.

Exercise 25-17
Sales mix determination and analysis

A1

Bethel Company owns a machine that can produce two specialized products. Production time for Product TLX is two units per hour and for Product MTV is five units per hour. The machine's capacity is 2,200 hours per year. Both products are sold to a single customer who has agreed to buy all of the company's output up to a maximum of 3,750 units of Product TLX and 2,000 units of Product MTV. Selling prices and variable costs per unit to produce the products follow. Determine (1) the company's most profitable sales mix and (2) the contribution margin that results from that sales mix.

	Product TLX	Product MTV
Selling price per unit	$12.50	$7.50
Variable costs per unit	3.75	4.50

Check (2) $37,688

Exercise 25-18
Comparison of payback and BET

P1 A2

This chapter explained two methods to evaluate investments using recovery time, the payback period and break-even time (BET). Refer to QS 25-14 and (1) compute the recovery time for both the payback period and break-even time, (2) discuss the advantage(s) of break-even time over the payback period, and (3) list two conditions under which payback period and break-even time are similar.

≡connect

Elite Company is planning to add a new product to its line. To manufacture this product, the company needs to buy a new machine at a $300,000 cost with an expected four-year life and a $20,000 residual value. All sales are for cash, and all costs are out of pocket except for depreciation on the new machine. Additional information includes the following.

Expected annual sales of new product	$1,150,000
Expected annual costs of new product	
Direct materials	300,000
Direct labor	420,000
Overhead excluding straight-line depreciation on new machine	210,000
Selling and administrative expenses	100,000
Income taxes	30%

PROBLEM SET A

Problem 25-1A
Computation of payback period, accounting rate of return, and net present value
P1 P2 P3

Required

1. Compute straight-line depreciation for each year of this new machine's life. (Round depreciation amounts to the nearest dollar.)
2. Determine expected net profit and net cash flow for each year of this machine's life. (Round answers to the nearest dollar.)
3. Compute this machine's payback period, assuming that cash flows occur evenly throughout each year. (Round the payback period to two decimals.)
4. Compute this machine's accounting rate of return, assuming that income is earned evenly throughout each year. (Round the percentage return to two decimals.)
5. Compute the net present value for this machine using a discount rate of 7% and assuming that cash flows occur at each year-end. (*Hint:* Residual value is a cash inflow at the end of the asset's life. Round the net present value to the nearest dollar.)

Check (4) 21.88%

(5) $70,915

Pleasant Company has an opportunity to invest in one of two new projects. Project Y requires a $700,000 investment for new machinery with a four-year life and no residual value. Project Z requires a $700,000 investment for new machinery with a three-year life and no residual value. The two projects yield the following predicted annual results. The company uses straight-line depreciation, and cash flows occur evenly throughout each year.

Problem 25-2A
Analysis and computation of payback period, accounting rate of return, and net present value
P1 P2 P3

	Project Y	Project Z
Sales	$700,000	$560,000
Expenses		
Direct materials	(98,000)	(70,000)
Direct labor..........................	(140,000)	(84,000)
Overhead including depreciation	(252,000)	(252,000)
Selling and administrative expenses	(50,000)	(50,000)
Total expenses	(540,000)	(456,000)
Pretax income	160,000	104,000
Income taxes (30%)	48,000	31,200
Net profit	$112,000	$ 72,800

Required

1. Compute each project's annual expected net cash flows. (Round the net cash flows to the nearest dollar.)
2. Determine each project's payback period. (Round the payback period to two decimals.)
3. Compute each project's accounting rate of return. (Round the percentage return to one decimal.)
4. Determine each project's net present value using 8% as the discount rate. For part 4 only, assume that cash flows occur at each year-end. (Round the net present value to the nearest dollar.)

Check For Project Y: (2) 2.44 years, (3) 32%, (4) $250,573

Analysis Component

5. Identify the project you would recommend to management and explain your choice.

Problem 25-3A
Computation of cash flows and net present values with alternative depreciation methods

P3

Angiletta Corporation is considering a new project requiring a $30,000 investment in test equipment with no residual value. The project would produce $12,000 of pretax income before depreciation at the end of each of the next six years. The company's income tax rate is 40%. In compiling its tax return and computing its income tax payments, the company can choose between the two alternative depreciation schedules shown in the table.

	Straight-Line Depreciation	MACRS Depreciation*
Year 1	$ 3,000	$ 6,000
Year 2	6,000	9,600
Year 3	6,000	5,760
Year 4	6,000	3,456
Year 5	6,000	3,456
Year 6	3,000	1,728
Totals	$30,000	$30,000

* The modified accelerated cost recovery system (MACRS) for depreciation is discussed in Chapter 10.

Required

1. Prepare a five-column table that reports amounts (assuming use of straight-line depreciation) for each of the following for each of the six years: (a) pretax income before depreciation, (b) straight-line depreciation expense, (c) taxable income, (d) income taxes, and (e) net cash flow. Net cash flow equals the amount of income before depreciation minus the income taxes. (Round answers to the nearest dollar.)

2. Prepare a five-column table that reports amounts (assuming use of MACRS depreciation) for each of the following for each of the six years: (a) pretax income before depreciation, (b) MACRS depreciation expense, (c) taxable income, (d) income taxes, and (e) net cash flow. Net cash flow equals the income amount before depreciation minus the income taxes. (Round answers to the nearest dollar.)

Check   Net present value:
(3) $10,041, (4) $10,635

3. Compute the net present value of the investment if straight-line depreciation is used. Use 10% as the discount rate. (Round the net present value to the nearest dollar.)

4. Compute the net present value of the investment if MACRS depreciation is used. Use 10% as the discount rate. (Round the net present value to the nearest dollar.)

Analysis Component

5. Explain why the MACRS depreciation method increases this project's net present value.

Problem 25-4A
Analysis of income effects of additional business

A1

www.mheducation.asia/olc/wildkwokFAP

Cayman Products manufactures and sells to wholesalers approximately 300,000 packages per year of underwater markers at $4 per package. Annual costs for the production and sale of this quantity are shown in the table.

Direct materials	$384,000
Direct labor	96,000
Overhead	288,000
Selling expenses	120,000
Administrative expenses	80,000
Total costs and expenses.	$968,000

A new wholesaler has offered to buy 50,000 packages for $3.44 each. These markers would be marketed under the wholesaler's name and would not affect Cayman Products' sales through its normal channels. A study of the costs of this additional business reveals the following:

● Direct materials costs are 100% variable.

● Per unit direct labor costs for the additional units would be 50% higher than normal because their production would require overtime pay at one-and-one-half times the usual labor rate.

● 25% of the normal annual overhead costs are fixed at any production level from 250,000 to 400,000 units. The remaining 75% of the annual overhead cost is variable with volume.

• Accepting the new business would involve no additional selling expenses.

• Accepting the new business would increase administrative expenses by a $4,000 fixed amount.

Required

Prepare a three-column comparative income statement that shows the following:

1. Annual operating income without the special order (column 1).

2. Annual operating income received from the new business only (column 2).

3. Combined annual operating income from normal business and the new business (column 3).

Check Operating income:
(1) $232,000, (2) $44,000

Ortiz Company is able to produce two products, G and B, with the same machine in its factory. The following information is available.

Problem 25-5A

Analysis of sales mix strategies

A1

	Product G	Product B
Selling price per unit	$120	$160
Variable costs per unit.	40	90
Contribution margin per unit	$ 80	$ 70
Machine hours to produce 1 unit	0.8 hours	2.0 hours
Maximum unit sales per month.	400 units	350 units

The company presently operates the machine for a single eight-hour shift for 22 working days each month. Management is thinking about operating the machine for two shifts, which will increase its productivity by another eight hours per day for 22 days per month. This change would require $6,500 additional fixed costs per month.

Required

1. Determine the contribution margin per machine hour that each product generates.

2. How many units of Product G and Product B should the company produce if it continues to operate with only one shift? How much total contribution margin does this mix produce each month?

3. If the company adds another shift, how many units of Product G and Product B should it produce? How much total contribution margin would this mix produce each month? Should the company add the new shift? Explain.

4. Suppose that the company determines that it can increase Product G's maximum sales to 440 units per month by spending $2,000 per month in marketing efforts. Should the company pursue this strategy and the double shift? Explain.

Check Units of Product G: (2) 220,
(3) 400, (4) 440

Home Decor Company's management is trying to decide whether to eliminate Department 200, which has produced losses or low profits for several years. The company's 2011 departmental income statement shows the following.

Problem 25-6A

Analysis of possible elimination of a department

A1

HOME DECOR COMPANY Departmental Income Statements For Year Ended December 31, 2011			
	Dept. 100	Dept. 200	Combined
Sales	$872,000	$580,000	$1,452,000
Cost of goods sold	(524,000)	(414,000)	(938,000)
Gross profit	348,000	166,000	514,000
Operating expenses			
Direct expenses			
Advertising.	(34,000)	(24,000)	(58,000)
Store supplies used	(8,000)	(7,600)	(15,600)
Depreciation—Store equipment.	(10,000)	(6,600)	(16,600)
Total direct expenses	(52,000)	(38,200)	(90,200)

[continued on next page]

[continued from previous page]

Allocated expenses			
Sales salaries	(130,000)	(78,000)	(208,000)
Rent expense	(18,880)	(9,440)	(28,320)
Bad debts expense	(19,800)	(16,200)	(36,000)
Office salary	(37,440)	(24,960)	(62,400)
Insurance expense	(4,000)	(2,200)	(6,200)
Miscellaneous office expenses	(4,800)	(3,200)	(8,000)
Total allocated expenses	(214,920)	(134,000)	(348,920)
Total expenses	(266,920)	(172,200)	(439,120)
Net profit (loss)	$ 81,080	$ (6,200)	$ 74,880

In analyzing whether to eliminate Department 200, management considers the following:

a. The company has one office worker who earns $1,200 per week, or $62,400 per year, and four sales-clerks who each earn $1,000 per week, or $52,000 per year.

b. The full salaries of two salesclerks are charged to Department 100. The full salary of one salesclerk is charged to Department 200. The salary of the fourth clerk, who works half-time in both departments, is divided evenly between the two departments.

c. Eliminating Department 200 would avoid the sales salaries and the office salary currently allocated to it. However, management prefers another plan. Two salesclerks have indicated that they will be quit-ting soon. Management believes that their work can be done by the other two clerks if the one office worker works in sales half-time. Eliminating Department 200 will allow this shift of duties. If this change is implemented, half the office worker's salary would be reported as sales salaries and half would be reported as office salary.

d. The store building is rented under a long-term lease that cannot be changed. Therefore, Department 100 will use the space and equipment currently used by Department 200.

e. Closing Department 200 will eliminate its expenses for advertising, bad debts, and store supplies; 70% of the insurance expense allocated to it to cover its merchandise inventory; and 25% of the mis-cellaneous office expenses presently allocated to it.

Required

Check (1) Total expenses:
(a) $1,377,120, (b) $568,140

(2) Forecasted net profit without Department 200, $63,020

1. Prepare a three-column report that lists items and amounts for (a) the company's total expenses (including cost of goods sold)—in column 1, (b) the expenses that would be eliminated by closing Department 200—in column 2, and (c) the expenses that will continue—in column 3.

2. Prepare a forecasted annual income statement for the company reflecting the elimination of Depart-ment 200 assuming that it will not affect Department 100's sales and gross profit. The statement should reflect the reassignment of the office worker to one-half time as a salesclerk.

Analysis Component

3. Reconcile the company's combined net profit with the forecasted net profit assuming that Department 200 is eliminated (list both items and amounts). Analyze the reconciliation and explain why you think the department should or should not be eliminated.

PROBLEM SET B

Problem 25-1B
Computation of payback period, accounting rate of return, and net present value

P1 P2 P3

Concorde Company is planning to add a new product to its line. To manufacture this product, the company needs to buy a new machine at a $100,000 cost with an expected five-year life and a $25,000 residual value. All sales are for cash and all costs are out of pocket, except for depreciation on the new machine. Additional information includes the following.

Expected annual sales of new product	$350,000
Expected annual costs of new product	
Direct materials	150,000
Direct labor	50,000
Overhead excluding straight-line depreciation on new machine	100,000
Selling and administrative expenses	23,000
Income taxes	20%

Required

1. Compute straight-line depreciation for each year of this new machine's life. (Round depreciation amounts to the nearest dollar.)
2. Determine expected net profit and net cash flow for each year of this machine's life. (Round answers to the nearest dollar.)
3. Compute this machine's payback period, assuming that cash flows occur evenly throughout each year. (Round the payback period to two decimals.)
4. Compute this machine's accounting rate of return, assuming that income is earned evenly throughout each year. (Round the percentage return to two decimals.)
5. Compute the net present value for this machine using a discount rate of 12% and assuming that cash flows occur at each year-end. (*Hint:* Residual value is a cash inflow at the end of the asset's life.)

Check (4) 15.36%

(5) $2,862

Micelli Company has an opportunity to invest in one of two projects. Project A requires a $480,000 investment for new machinery with a three-year life and no residual value. Project B also requires a $480,000 investment for new machinery with a four-year life and no residual value. The two projects yield the following predicted annual results. The company uses straight-line depreciation, and cash flows occur evenly throughout each year.

Problem 25-2B
Analysis and computation of payback period, accounting rate of return, and net present value

P1 P2 P3

	Project A	Project B
Sales	$750,000	$800,000
Expenses		
Direct materials	(125,000)	(250,000)
Direct labor	(130,000)	(80,000)
Overhead including depreciation	(330,000)	(276,000)
Selling and administrative expenses	(120,000)	(120,000)
Total expenses	(705,000)	(726,000)
Pretax income	45,000	74,000
Income taxes (30%)	13,500	22,200
Net profit	$ 31,500	$ 51,800

Required

1. Compute each project's annual expected net cash flows. (Round net cash flows to the nearest dollar.)
2. Determine each project's payback period. (Round the payback period to two decimals.)
3. Compute each project's accounting rate of return. (Round the percentage return to one decimal.)
4. Determine each project's net present value using 10% as the discount rate. For part 4 only, assume that cash flows occur at each year-end. (Round net present values to the nearest dollar.)

Check For Project A: (2) 2.5 years, (3) 13.1%, (4) $(3,759)

Analysis Component

5. Identify the project you would recommend to management and explain your choice.

Cologne Corporation is considering a new project requiring a $25,000 investment in an asset having no residual value. The project would produce $15,000 of pretax income before depreciation at the end of each of the next six years. The company's income tax rate is 30%. In compiling its tax return and computing its income tax payments, the company can choose between two alternative depreciation schedules as shown in the table.

Problem 25-3B
Computation of cash flows and net present values with alternative depreciation methods

P3

	Straight-Line Depreciation	MACRS Depreciation*
Year 1	$ 2,500	$ 5,000
Year 2	5,000	8,000
Year 3	5,000	4,800
Year 4	5,000	2,880
Year 5	5,000	2,880
Year 6	2,500	1,440
Totals	$25,000	$25,000

* The modified accelerated cost recovery system (MACRS) for depreciation is discussed in Chapter 10.

Required

1. Prepare a five-column table that reports amounts (assuming use of straight-line depreciation) for each of the following items for each of the six years: (a) pretax income before depreciation, (b) straight-line depreciation expense, (c) taxable income, (d) income taxes, and (e) net cash flow. Net cash flow equals the amount of income before depreciation minus the income taxes. (Round answers to the nearest dollar.)

2. Prepare a five-column table that reports amounts (assuming use of MACRS depreciation) for each of the following items for each of the six years: (a) income before depreciation, (b) MACRS depreciation expense, (c) taxable income, (d) income taxes, and (e) net cash flow. Net cash flow equals the amount of income before depreciation minus the income taxes. (Round answers to the nearest dollar.)

Check Net present value:
(3) $19,437, (4) $19,914

3. Compute the net present value of the investment if straight-line depreciation is used. Use 15% as the discount rate. (Round the net present value to the nearest dollar.)

4. Compute the net present value of the investment if MACRS depreciation is used. Use 15% as the discount rate. (Round the net present value to the nearest dollar.)

Analysis Component

5. Explain why the MACRS depreciation method increases the net present value of this project.

Problem 25-4B
Analysis of income effects of additional business
A1

Windtrax Company manufactures and sells to local wholesalers approximately 200,000 units per month at a sales price of $1 per unit. Monthly costs for the production and sale of this quantity follow.

Direct materials	$ 30,000
Direct labor	12,000
Overhead	50,000
Selling expenses	7,500
Administrative expenses	31,500
Total costs and expenses.	$131,000

A new out-of-state distributor has offered to buy 20,000 units next month for $0.80 each. These units would be marketed in other states and would not affect Windtrax's sales through its normal channels. A study of the costs of this new business reveals the following:

- Direct materials costs are 100% variable.

- Per unit direct labor costs for the additional units would be 100% higher than normal because their production would require double overtime pay to meet the distributor's deadline.

- Eighty percent of the normal annual overhead costs are fixed at any production level from 120,000 to 300,000 units. The remaining 20% is variable with volume.

- Accepting the new business would involve no additional selling expenses.

- Accepting the new business would increase administrative expenses by a $750 fixed amount.

Required

Prepare a three-column comparative income statement that shows the following:

Check Operating income:
(1) $69,000, (2) $8,850

1. Monthly operating income without the special order (column 1).

2. Monthly operating income received from the new business only (column 2).

3. Combined monthly operating income from normal business and the new business (column 3).

Problem 25-5B
Analysis of sales mix strategies
A1

Digits Company is able to produce two products, 22 and 44, with the same machine in its factory. The following information is available.

	Product 22	Product 44
Selling price per unit	$175	$200
Variable costs per unit.	100	150
Contribution margin per unit	$ 75	$ 50
Machine hours to produce 1 unit	0.8 hours	0.5 hours
Maximum unit sales per month.	525 units	450 units

The company presently operates the machine for a single eight-hour shift for 23 working days each month. Management is thinking about operating the machine for two shifts, which will increase its productivity by another eight hours per day for 23 days per month. This change would require $5,000 additional fixed costs per month.

Required

1. Determine the contribution margin per machine hour that each product generates.

2. How many units of Product 22 and Product 44 should the company produce if it continues to operate with only one shift? How much total contribution margin does this mix produce each month?

3. If the company adds another shift, how many units of Product 22 and Product 44 should it produce? How much total contribution margin would this mix produce each month? Should the company add the new shift? Explain.

4. Suppose that the company determines that it can increase Product 44's maximum sales to 500 units per month by spending $500 per month in marketing efforts. Should the company pursue this strategy and the double shift? Explain.

Check Units of Product 44: (2) 368, (3) 450, (4) 500

Turftime Company's management is trying to decide whether to eliminate Department Z, which has produced low profits or losses for several years. The company's 2011 departmental income statement shows the following.

Problem 25-6B
Analysis of possible elimination of a department

A1

TURFTIME COMPANY
Departmental Income Statements
For Year Ended December 31, 2011

	Dept. A	Dept. Z	Combined
Sales	$350,000	$87,500	$437,500
Cost of goods sold	230,650	62,550	293,200
Gross profit	119,350	24,950	144,300
Operating expenses			
Direct expenses			
Advertising	(13,500)	(1,500)	(15,000)
Store supplies used	(2,800)	(700)	(3,500)
Depreciation—Store equipment	(7,000)	(3,500)	(10,500)
Total direct expenses	(23,300)	(5,700)	(29,000)
Allocated expenses			
Sales salaries	(35,100)	(11,700)	(46,800)
Rent expense	(11,040)	(2,760)	(13,800)
Bad debts expense	(10,500)	(2,000)	(12,500)
Office salary	(10,400)	(2,600)	(13,000)
Insurance expense	(2,100)	(700)	(2,800)
Miscellaneous office expenses	(850)	(1,250)	(2,100)
Total allocated expenses	(69,990)	(21,010)	(91,000)
Total expenses	(93,290)	(26,710)	(120,000)
Net profit (loss)	$ 26,060	$(1,760)	$ 24,300

In analyzing whether to eliminate Department Z, management considers the following items:

a. The company has one office worker who earns $250 per week or $13,000 per year and four salesclerks who each earn $225 per week or $11,700 per year.

b. The full salaries of three salesclerks are charged to Department A. The full salary of one salesclerk is charged to Department Z.

c. Eliminating Department Z would avoid the sales salaries and the office salary currently allocated to it. However, management prefers another plan. Two salesclerks have indicated that they will be quitting soon. Management believes that their work can be done by the two remaining clerks if the one office worker works in sales half-time. Eliminating Department Z will allow this shift of duties. If this change is implemented, half the office worker's salary would be reported as sales salaries and half would be reported as office salary.

    d. The store building is rented under a long-term lease that cannot be changed. Therefore, Department A will use the space and equipment currently used by Department Z.

    e. Closing Department Z will eliminate its expenses for advertising, bad debts, and store supplies; 65% of the insurance expense allocated to it to cover its merchandise inventory; and 30% of the miscellaneous office expenses presently allocated to it.

Required

1. Prepare a three-column report that lists items and amounts for (a) the company's total expenses (including cost of goods sold)—in column 1, (b) the expenses that would be eliminated by closing Department Z—in column 2, and (c) the expenses that will continue—in column 3.

2. Prepare a forecasted annual income statement for the company reflecting the elimination of Department Z assuming that it will not affect Department A's sales and gross profit. The statement should reflect the reassignment of the office worker to one-half time as a salesclerk.

Analysis Component

3. Reconcile the company's combined net profit with the forecasted net profit assuming that Department Z is eliminated (list both items and amounts). Analyze the reconciliation and explain why you think the department should or should not be eliminated.

SERIAL PROBLEM
Business Solutions

P1 P2

(This serial problem began in Chapter 1 and continues through most of the book. If previous chapter segments were not completed, the serial problem can begin at this point.)

SP 25   Santana Rey is considering the purchase of equipment for Business Solutions that would allow the company to add a new product to its computer furniture line. The equipment is expected to cost $300,000 and to have a six-year life and no residual value. It will be depreciated on a straight-line basis. Business Solutions expects to sell 100 units of the equipment's product each year. The expected annual income related to this equipment follows.

Sales	$375,000
Costs	
Materials, labor, and overhead (except depreciation).	(200,000)
Depreciation on new equipment	(50,000)
Selling and administrative expenses	(37,500)
Total costs and expenses	(287,500)
Pretax income	87,500
Income taxes (30%).	26,250
Net profit.	$ 61,250

Required

Compute the (1) payback period and (2) accounting rate of return for this equipment. (Record answers as percents, rounded to one decimal.)

Beyond the Numbers

REPORTING IN ACTION

P3

BTN 25-1   Assume **Research In Motion** invested $834 million to expand its manufacturing capacity. Assume that these assets have a seven-year life, and that Research In Motion requires a 12% internal rate of return on these assets.

Required

1. What is the amount of annual cash flows that Research In Motion must earn from these projects to have a 12% internal rate of return? (*Hint:* Identify the seven-period, 12% factor from the present value of an annuity table, and then divide $834 million by this factor to get the annual cash flows necessary.)

Fast Forward

2. Access RIM's financial statements for financial years ended after February 27, 2010, from its Website (www.rim.com).

 a. Determine the amount that RIM invested in capital assets for the most recent year. (*Hint:* Refer to the statement of cash flows.)

 b. Assume a seven-year life and a 12% internal rate of return. What is the amount of cash flows that RIM must earn on these new projects?

BTN 25-2   **Research In Motion**, **Apple**, and **Palm** sell several different products; most are profitable but some are not. Teams of employees in each company make advertising, investment, and product mix decisions. A certain portion of advertising for both companies is on a local basis to a target audience.

COMPARATIVE ANALYSIS

A1

Required

1. Find one major advertisement of a product or group of products for each company in your local newspaper. Contact the newspaper and ask the approximate cost of this ad space (for example, cost of one page or one-half page of advertising).

2. Estimate how many products this advertisement must sell to justify its cost. Begin by taking the product's sales price advertised for each company and assume a 20% contribution margin.

3. Prepare a one-half page memorandum explaining the importance of effective advertising when making a product mix decision. Be prepared to present your ideas in class.

BTN 25-3   A consultant commented that "too often the numbers look good but feel bad." This comment often stems from estimation error common to capital budgeting proposals that relate to future cash flows. Three reasons for this error often exist. First, reliably predicting cash flows several years into the future is very difficult. Second, the present value of cash flows many years into the future (say, beyond 10 years) is often very small. Third, it is difficult for personal biases and expectations not to unduly influence present value computations.

ETHICS CHALLENGE

P3

Required

1. Compute the present value of $100 to be received in 10 years assuming a 12% discount rate.

2. Why is understanding the three reasons mentioned for estimation errors important when evaluating investment projects? Link this response to your answer for part 1.

BTN 25-4   Payback period, accounting rate of return, net present value, and internal rate of return are common methods to evaluate capital investment opportunities. Assume that your manager asks you to identify the type of measurement basis and unit that each method offers and to list the advantages and disadvantages of each. Present your response in memorandum format of less than one page.

COMMUNICATING IN PRACTICE

P1 P2 P3 P4

BTN 25-5   Many companies must determine whether to internally produce their component parts or to outsource them. Further, some companies now outsource key components or business processes to international providers. Access the Website **BizBrim.com** and review the available information on outsourcing—especially as it relates to both the advantages and the negative effects of outsourcing.

TAKING IT TO THE NET

A1

Required

1. What does Bizbrim identify as the major advantages and the major disadvantages of outsourcing?

2. Does it seem that Bizbrim is generally in favor of or opposed to outsourcing? Explain.

BTN 25-6   Break into teams and identify four reasons that an international airline such as **Southwest**, **Delta**, or **American** would invest in a project when its direct analysis using both payback period and net present value indicate it to be a poor investment. (*Hint:* Think about qualitative factors.) Provide an example of an investment project supporting your answer.

TEAMWORK IN ACTION

P1 P3

ENTREPRENEURIAL DECISION

P1 P2 P3 P4

BTN 25-7   Masso Group is growing through acquisitions. "Young companies with committed entrepreneurship are our target," says its CEO Nguyen Trung Thang, of its future merger and acquisition activity.

Required

1. What are the management accounting tools that Masso can use in its acquisition activities?
2. What are the challenges in applying these tools to young companies in the context of Vietnam?

HITTING THE ROAD

P3

BTN 25-8   Visit a local taxi company. Interview a key manager to understand the management tools they apply in making decisions about buying new taxis. Document your findings.

GLOBAL DECISION

C1

BTN 25-9   Refer to page 11 of Adidas' 2010 Annual Report: http://adidas-group.corporate-publications.com/2010/gb/files/pdf/en/ADS_GB_2010_En.pdf. CEO Herbert Hainer responds to the interviewer by saying: "... I consider marketing an investment and not a cost." He then goes on to justify the marketing spending done by Adidas.

Required

1. If spending on marketing is an investment, how should Adidas analyze it before spending?
2. How should the spending be tracked post-spending?

ANSWERS TO MULTIPLE CHOICE QUIZ

1. a; Reworking provides incremental revenue of $11 per unit ($19 − $8); and, it costs $10 to rework them. The company is better off by $1 per unit when it reworks these products and sells them at the regular price.

2. e; Product X has a $2 contribution margin per machine hour [($32 − $12)/ 10 MH]; Product Y has a $7 contribution margin per machine hour [($24 − $10)/2 MH]. It should produce as much of Product Y as possible.

3. a; Total revenue from the special order = 3,000 units × $15 per unit = $45,000; and, Total costs for the special order = (3,000 units × $9 per unit) + $5,000 = $32,000. Net profit from the special order = $45,000 − $32,000 = $13,000. Thus, yes, it should accept the order.

4. c; Payback = $270,000/$61,200 per year = 4.4 years.

5. d; Accounting rate of return = $8,550/[($180,000 + $0)/2] = 9.5%.

Financial Statement Information

This appendix includes financial information for (1) Nestlé, (2) Adidas, and (3) Samsung. This information is taken from their annual reports. An **annual report** is a summary of a company's financial results for the year along with its current financial condition and future plans. This report is directed to external users of financial information, but it also affects the actions and decisions of internal users.

A company often uses an annual report to showcase itself and its products. Many annual reports include photos, diagrams, and illustrations related to the company. The primary objective of annual reports, however, is the *financial section,* which communicates much information about a company, with most data drawn from the accounting information system. The layout of an annual report's financial section is fairly established and typically includes the following:

- Letter to Shareholders
- Financial History and Highlights
- Management Discussion and Analysis
- Management's Report on Financial Statements and on Internal Controls
- Report of Independent Accountants (Auditor's Report) and on Internal Controls
- Financial Statements
- Notes to Financial Statements
- List of Directors and Officers

The appendix is organized as follows:

- Nestlé **A-2** through **A-41**
- Adidas **A-42** through **A-50**
- Samsung **A-51** through **A-59**

Many assignments at the end of each chapter refer to information in this appendix. We encourage readers to spend time with these assignments; they are especially useful in showing the relevance and diversity of financial accounting and reporting.

Nestlé Financial Report

Consolidated income statement
for the year ended 31 December 2013

In millions of CHF

	Notes	2013	2012 [a]
Sales	3	**92 158**	**89 721**
Other revenue		215	210
Cost of goods sold		(48 111)	(47 500)
Distribution expenses		(8 156)	(8 017)
Marketing and administration expenses		(19 711)	(19 041)
Research and development costs		(1 503)	(1 413)
Other trading income	4	120	141
Other trading expenses	4	(965)	(637)
Trading operating profit	3	**14 047**	**13 464**
Other operating income	4	616	146
Other operating expenses	4	(1 595)	(222)
Operating profit		**13 068**	**13 388**
Financial income	5	219	120
Financial expense	5	(850)	(825)
Profit before taxes, associates and joint ventures		**12 437**	**12 683**
Taxes	15	(3 256)	(3 259)
Share of results of associates and joint ventures	16	1 264	1 253
Profit for the year		**10 445**	**10 677**
of which attributable to non-controlling interests		430	449
of which attributable to shareholders of the parent (Net profit)		10 015	10 228
As percentages of sales			
Trading operating profit		15.2%	15.0%
Profit for the year attributable to shareholders of the parent (Net profit)		10.9%	11.4%
Earnings per share (in CHF)			
Basic earnings per share	17	3.14	3.21
Diluted earnings per share	17	3.13	3.20

(a) 2012 comparatives have been restated following the implementation of IFRS 11 and IAS 19 revised (see Note 22).

NESTLÉ

Consolidated statement of comprehensive income for the year ended 31 December 2013

In millions of CHF

	Notes	2013	2012 (a)
Profit for the year recognised in the income statement		**10 445**	**10 677**
Currency retranslations			
– Recognised in translation reserve		(3 160)	(1 053)
– Reclassified from translation reserve to income statement		214	–
Fair value adjustments on available-for-sale financial instruments			
– Recognised in fair value reserve		9	310
– Reclassified from fair value reserve to income statement		(532)	15
Fair value adjustments on cash flow hedges			
– Recognised in hedging reserve		161	(116)
– Reclassified from hedging reserve		85	266
Taxes	15	290	(31)
Share of other comprehensive income of associates and joint ventures	16	40	578
Items that are or may be reclassified subsequently to the income statement		(2 893)	(31)
Remeasurement of defined benefit plans	11	1 632	(1 534)
Taxes	15	(848)	386
Share of other comprehensive income of associates and joint ventures	16	47	(76)
Items that will never be reclassified to the income statement		831	(1 224)
Other comprehensive income for the year	19	**(2 062)**	**(1 255)**
Total comprehensive income for the year		**8 383**	**9 422**
of which attributable to non-controlling interests		371	393
of which attributable to shareholders of the parent		8 012	9 029

(a) 2012 comparatives have been restated following the implementation of IFRS 11 and IAS 19 revised (see Note 22).

NESTLÉ

Consolidated balance sheet
as at 31 December 2013

before appropriations

In millions of CHF

	Notes	2013	2012 (a)(b)
Assets			
Current assets			
Cash and cash equivalents	14/18	6 415	5 713
Short-term investments	14	638	3 583
Inventories	6	8 382	8 939
Trade and other receivables	7/14	12 206	13 048
Prepayments and accrued income		762	821
Derivative assets	14	230	576
Current income tax assets		1 151	972
Assets held for sale	2	282	368
Total current assets		**30 066**	**34 020**
Non-current assets			
Property, plant and equipment	8	26 895	26 576
Goodwill	9	31 039	32 688
Intangible assets	10	12 673	13 018
Investments in associates and joint ventures	16	12 315	11 586
Financial assets	14	4 550	4 979
Employee benefits assets	11	537	84
Current income tax assets		124	27
Deferred tax assets	15	2 243	2 899
Total non-current assets		**90 376**	**91 857**
Total assets		**120 442**	**125 877**

(a) 2012 comparatives have been restated following the implementation of IFRS 11 and IAS 19 revised (see Note 22).
(b) 2012 comparatives have been adjusted following the final valuation of the Wyeth Nutrition acquisition (see Note 22).

Consolidated balance sheet as at 31 December 2013

In millions of CHF

	Notes	2013	2012 (a)(b)
Liabilities and equity			
Current liabilities			
Financial debt	14	11 380	18 408
Trade and other payables	14	16 072	14 627
Accruals and deferred income		3 185	3 078
Provisions	13	523	452
Derivative liabilities	14	381	423
Current income tax liabilities		1 276	1 608
Liabilities directly associated with assets held for sale	2	100	1
Total current liabilities		**32 917**	**38 597**
Non-current liabilities			
Financial debt	14	10 363	9 008
Employee benefits liabilities	11	6 279	8 360
Provisions	13	2 714	2 827
Deferred tax liabilities	15	2 643	2 240
Other payables	14	1 387	2 181
Total non-current liabilities		**23 386**	**24 616**
Total liabilities		**56 303**	**63 213**
Equity	19		
Share capital		322	322
Treasury shares		(2 196)	(2 078)
Translation reserve		(20 811)	(17 924)
Retained earnings and other reserves		85 260	80 687
Total equity attributable to shareholders of the parent		**62 575**	**61 007**
Non-controlling interests		1 564	1 657
Total equity		**64 139**	**62 664**
Total liabilities and equity		**120 442**	**125 877**

(a) 2012 comparatives have been restated following the implementation of IFRS 11 and IAS 19 revised (see Note 22).
(b) 2012 comparatives have been adjusted following the final valuation of the Wyeth Nutrition acquisition (see Note 22).

Consolidated cash flow statement
for the year ended 31 December 2013

In millions of CHF

	Notes	2013	2012 (a)
Operating activities			
Operating profit	18	13 068	13 388
Non-cash items of income and expense	18	4 352	3 217
Cash flow before changes in operating assets and liabilities		**17 420**	**16 605**
Decrease/(increase) in working capital	18	1 360	2 015
Variation of other operating assets and liabilities	18	(574)	(95)
Cash generated from operations		**18 206**	**18 525**
Net cash flows from treasury activities	18	(351)	(324)
Taxes paid		(3 520)	(3 118)
Dividends and interest from associates and joint ventures	16	657	585
Operating cash flow		**14 992**	**15 668**
Investing activities			
Capital expenditure	8	(4 928)	(5 273)
Expenditure on intangible assets	10	(402)	(325)
Sale of property, plant and equipment		86	130
Acquisition of businesses	2	(321)	(10 916)
Disposal of businesses	2	421	142
Investments (net of divestments) in associates and joint ventures	16	(28)	(79)
Outflows from non-current treasury investments		(244)	(192)
Inflows from non-current treasury investments		2 644	1 561
Inflows/(outflows) from short-term treasury investments		400	677
Inflows from other investing activities (b)		1 187	89
Outflows from other investing activities		(421)	(305)
Cash flow from investing activities		**(1 606)**	**(14 491)**
Financing activities			
Dividend paid to shareholders of the parent	19	(6 552)	(6 213)
Dividends paid to non-controlling interests		(328)	(204)
Acquisition (net of disposal) of non-controlling interests		(337)	(165)
Purchase of treasury shares		(481)	(532)
Sale of treasury shares		60	1 199
Inflows from bonds and other non-current financial debt		3 814	5 226
Outflows from bonds and other non-current financial debt		(2 271)	(1 650)
Inflows/(outflows) from current financial debt		(6 063)	2 325
Cash flow from financing activities		**(12 158)**	**(14)**
Currency retranslations		(526)	(219)
Increase/(decrease) in cash and cash equivalents		**702**	**944**
Cash and cash equivalents at beginning of year		5 713	4 769
Cash and cash equivalents at end of year		**6 415**	**5 713**

(a) 2012 comparatives have been restated following the implementation of IFRS 11 and IAS 19 revised (see Note 22).
(b) Mainly relates to the disposal of Givaudan shares.

NESTLÉ

Consolidated statement of changes in equity
for the year ended 31 December 2013

In millions of CHF

	Share capital	Treasury shares	Translation reserve	Retained earnings and other reserves	Total equity attributable to shareholders of the parent	Non-controlling interests	Total equity
Equity as at 31 December 2011 as originally published	330	(6 722)	(16 927)	80 116	56 797	1 477	58 274
First application of IAS 19 revised	—	—	—	68	68	—	68
Equity restated as at 1 January 2012	330	(6 722)	(16 927)	80 184	56 865	1 477	58 342
Profit for the year [a]	—	—	—	10 228	**10 228**	449	**10 677**
Other comprehensive income for the year [a]	—	—	(997)	(202)	**(1 199)**	(56)	**(1 255)**
Total comprehensive income for the year [a]	—	—	(997)	10 026	**9 029**	393	**9 422**
Dividend paid to shareholders of the parent	—	—	—	(6 213)	**(6 213)**	—	**(6 213)**
Dividends paid to non-controlling interests	—	—	—	—	**—**	(204)	**(204)**
Movement of treasury shares [b]	—	501	—	599	**1 100**	—	**1 100**
Equity compensation plans	—	212	—	(39)	**173**	—	**173**
Changes in non-controlling interests	—	—	—	(94)	**(94)**	(9)	**(103)**
Reduction in share capital	(8)	3 931	—	(3 923)	**—**	—	**—**
Total transactions with owners	(8)	4 644	—	(9 670)	**(5 034)**	(213)	**(5 247)**
Other movements [c]	—	—	—	147	**147**	—	**147**
Equity restated as at 31 December 2012 [a]	322	(2 078)	(17 924)	80 687	61 007	1 657	62 664
Profit for the year	—	—	—	10 015	**10 015**	430	**10 445**
Other comprehensive income for the year	—	—	(2 887)	884	**(2 003)**	(59)	**(2 062)**
Total comprehensive income for the year	—	—	(2 887)	10 899	**8 012**	371	**8 383**
Dividend paid to shareholders of the parent	—	—	—	(6 552)	**(6 552)**	—	**(6 552)**
Dividends paid to non-controlling interests	—	—	—	—	**—**	(328)	**(328)**
Movement of treasury shares	—	(612)	—	190	**(422)**	—	**(422)**
Equity compensation plans	—	214	—	(39)	**175**	—	**175**
Other transactions settled with treasury shares [d]	—	280	—	—	**280**	—	**280**
Changes in non-controlling interests	—	—	—	(297)	**(297)**	(136)	**(433)**
Total transactions with owners	—	(118)	—	(6 698)	**(6 816)**	(464)	**(7 280)**
Other movements [c]	—	—	—	372	**372**	—	**372**
Equity as at 31 December 2013	322	(2 196)	(20 811)	85 260	62 575	1 564	64 139

(a) 2012 comparatives have been restated following the implementation of IFRS 11 and IAS 19 revised (see Note 22).
(b) Movements reported under retained earnings and other reserves mainly relate to written put options on own shares.
(c) Relates mainly to the adjustment for hyperinflation in Venezuela, considered as a hyperinflationary economy.
(d) The other transactions relate to the acquisition of a business (see Note 2).

Notes

1. Accounting policies

Accounting convention and accounting standards

The Consolidated Financial Statements comply with International Financial Reporting Standards (IFRS) issued by the International Accounting Standards Board (IASB), with the interpretations issued by the IFRS Interpretations Committee (IFRIC) and with Swiss law.

They have been prepared on an accrual basis and under the historical cost convention, unless stated otherwise. All significant consolidated companies, joint arrangements and associates have a 31 December accounting year-end.

The Consolidated Financial Statements 2013 were approved for issue by the Board of Directors on 12 February 2014 and are subject to approval by the Annual General Meeting on 10 April 2014.

Key accounting judgements, estimates and assumptions

The preparation of the Consolidated Financial Statements requires Group Management to exercise judgement and to make estimates and assumptions that affect the application of policies, reported amounts of revenues, expenses, assets and liabilities and disclosures. These estimates and associated assumptions are based on historical experience and various other factors that are believed to be reasonable under the circumstances. Actual results may differ from these estimates.

The estimates and underlying assumptions are reviewed on an ongoing basis. Revisions to accounting estimates are recognised in the period in which the estimate is revised if the revision affects only that period, or in the period of the revision and future periods if the revision affects both current and future periods. Those areas affect mainly provisions (see Note 13), goodwill impairment tests (see Note 9), employee benefits (see Note 11), allowance for doubtful receivables (see Note 7) and taxes (see Note 15).

Scope of consolidation

The Consolidated Financial Statements comprise those of Nestlé S.A. and of its affiliated companies, including joint arrangements and associates (the Group). The list of the principal companies is provided in the section "Companies of the Nestlé Group."

Consolidated companies

Companies, in which the Group has the power to exercise control, are fully consolidated. This applies irrespective of the percentage of interest in the share capital. The Group controls a company when it is exposed to, or has rights to, variable returns from its involvement with the company and has the ability to affect those returns through its power over the company. Non-controlling interests are shown as a component of equity on the balance sheet and the share of the profit attributable to non-controlling interests is shown as a component of profit for the year in the income statement.

Newly acquired companies are consolidated from the effective date of control, using the acquisition method.

Joint arrangements

Joint arrangements are contractual arrangements over which the Group exercises joint control with partners.

Joint ventures

Joint arrangements whereby the parties have rights to the net assets of the arrangement are joint ventures and are accounted for using the equity method.

Joint operations

The joint arrangements where the parties control the rights to the assets and obligations for the liabilities are joint operations and the individual assets, liabilities, income and expenses are consolidated in proportion to the Group's contractually specified share (usually 50%).

Associates

Companies where the Group has the power to exercise a significant influence but does not exercise control are accounted for using the equity method. The net assets and results are adjusted to comply with the Group's accounting policies. The carrying amount of goodwill arising from the acquisition of associates is included in the carrying amount of investments in associates.

Foreign currencies

The functional currency of the Group's entities is the currency of their primary economic environment.

In individual companies, transactions in foreign currencies are recorded at the rate of exchange at the date of the

1. Accounting policies

transaction. Monetary assets and liabilities in foreign currencies are translated at year-end rates. Any resulting exchange differences are taken to the income statement, except when deferred in other comprehensive income as qualifying cash flow hedges.

On consolidation, assets and liabilities of Group entities reported in their functional currencies are translated into Swiss Francs, the Group's presentation currency, at year-end exchange rates. Income and expense are translated into Swiss Francs at the annual weighted average rates of exchange or at the rate on the date of the transaction for significant items.

Differences arising from the retranslation of opening net assets of Group entities, together with differences arising from the restatement of the net results for the year of Group entities, are recognised in other comprehensive income.

The balance sheet and net results of Group entities operating in hyperinflationary economies are restated for the changes in the general purchasing power of the local currency, using official indices at the balance sheet date, before translation into Swiss Francs.

When there is a change of control in a foreign entity, exchange differences that were recorded in equity are recognised in the income statement as part of the gain or loss on disposal.

Segment reporting

Operating segments reflect the Group's management structure and the way financial information is regularly reviewed by the Group's chief operating decision maker (CODM), which is defined as the Executive Board.

The CODM considers the business from both a geographic and product perspective, through three geographic Zones and several Globally Managed Businesses (GMB). Zones and GMB that meet the quantitative threshold of 10% of sales, trading operating profit or assets, are presented on a stand-alone basis as reportable segments. Other business activities and operating segments, including GMB that do not meet the threshold, like Nestlé Professional, Nespresso and Nestlé Health Science are combined and presented in Other. Therefore, the Group's reportable operating segments are:
- Zone Europe;
- Zone Americas;
- Zone Asia, Oceania and Africa;
- Nestlé Waters;
- Nestlé Nutrition;
- Other.

As some operating segments represent geographic zones, information by product is also disclosed. The seven product groups that are disclosed represent the highest categories of products that are followed internally.

Finally, the Group provides information attributed to the country of domicile of the Group's parent company (Nestlé S.A. – Switzerland) and to the ten most important countries in terms of sales.

Segment results represent the contribution of the different segments to central overheads, research and development costs and the trading operating profit of the Group. Specific corporate expenses as well as specific research and development costs are allocated to the corresponding segments.

Segment assets and liabilities are aligned with internal reported information to the CODM. Segment assets comprise property, plant and equipment, intangible assets, goodwill, trade and other receivables, assets held for sale, inventories, prepayments and accrued income as well as specific financial assets associated to the reportable segments. Segment liabilities comprise trade and other payables, liabilities directly associated with assets held for sale, some other payables as well as accruals and deferred income. Eliminations represent inter-company balances between the different segments.

Segment assets by operating segment represent the situation at the end of the year. Assets and liabilities by product represent the annual average, as this provides a better indication of the level of invested capital for management purposes.

Capital additions represent the total cost incurred to acquire property, plant and equipment, intangible assets and goodwill, including those arising from business combinations. Capital expenditure represents the investment in property, plant and equipment only.

Depreciation of segment assets includes depreciation of property, plant and equipment and amortisation of intangible assets. Impairment of assets includes impairment related to property, plant and equipment, intangible assets and goodwill.

Unallocated items represent non-specific items whose allocation to a segment would be arbitrary. They mainly comprise:
- corporate expenses and related assets/liabilities;
- research and development costs and related assets/liabilities; and
- some goodwill and intangible assets.

Non-current assets by geography include property, plant and equipment, intangible assets and goodwill that are attributable to the ten most important countries and the country of domicile of Nestlé S.A.

1. Accounting policies

Valuation methods, presentation and definitions
Revenue
Sales represent amounts received and receivable from third parties for goods supplied to the customers and for services rendered. Revenue from the sales of goods is recognised in the income statement at the moment when the significant risks and rewards of ownership of the goods have been transferred to the buyer, which is mainly upon shipment. It is measured at the list price applicable to a given distribution channel after deduction of returns, sales taxes, pricing allowances, other trade discounts and couponing and price promotions to consumers. Payments made to the customers for commercial services received are expensed.

Other revenue is primarily license fees from third parties which have been earned during the period.

Expenses
Cost of goods sold is determined on the basis of the cost of production or of purchase, adjusted for the variation of inventories. All other expenses, including those in respect of advertising and promotions, are recognised when the Group receives the risks and rewards of ownership of the goods or when it receives the services.

Other trading income/(expenses)
These comprise restructuring costs, impairment of all assets except goodwill, litigations and onerous contracts, result on disposal of property, plant and equipment, and specific other income and expenses that fall within the control of operating segments.

Restructuring costs are restricted to dismissal indemnities and employee benefits paid to terminated employees upon the reorganisation of a business. Dismissal indemnities paid for normal attrition such as poor performance, professional misconduct, etc. are part of the expenses by functions.

Other operating income/(expenses)
These comprise impairment of goodwill, results on disposals of businesses, acquisition-related costs and other income and expenses that fall beyond the control of operating segments and relate to events such as natural disasters and expropriation of assets.

Net financial income/(expense)
Net financial income/(expense) includes net financing cost and net interest income/(expense) on defined benefit plans.

Net financing cost includes the interest expense on borrowings from third parties as well as the interest income earned on funds invested outside the Group. This heading also includes other financing related income and expense, such as exchange differences on loans and borrowings, results on foreign currency and interest rate hedging instruments that are recognised in the income statement. Certain borrowing costs are capitalised as explained under the section on Property, plant and equipment. Others are expensed.

Taxes
The Group is subject to taxes in different countries all over the world. Taxes and fiscal risks recognised in the Consolidated Financial Statements reflect Group Management's best estimate of the outcome based on the facts known at the balance sheet date in each individual country. These facts may include but are not limited to change in tax laws and interpretation thereof in the various jurisdictions where the Group operates. They may have an impact on the income tax as well as the resulting assets and liabilities. Any differences between tax estimates and final tax assessments are charged to the income statement in the period in which they are incurred, unless anticipated.

Taxes include current taxes on profit as well as actual or potential withholding taxes on current and expected transfers of income from Group companies and tax adjustments relating to prior years. Income tax is recognised in the income statement, except to the extent that it relates to items directly taken to equity or other comprehensive income, in which case it is recognised against equity or other comprehensive income.

Deferred taxation is the tax attributable to the temporary differences that arise when taxation authorities recognise and measure assets and liabilities with rules that differ from the principles of the Consolidated Financial Statements. It also arises on temporary differences stemming from tax losses carried forward.

Deferred taxes are calculated under the liability method at the rates of tax expected to prevail when the temporary differences reverse subject to such rates being substantially enacted at the balance sheet date. Any changes of the tax rates are recognised in the income statement unless related to items directly recognised against equity or other comprehensive income. Deferred tax liabilities are recognised on all taxable temporary differences excluding non-deductible goodwill. Deferred tax assets are recognised on all deductible temporary differences provided that it is probable that future taxable income will be available.

Financial instruments
Classes of financial instruments
The Group aggregates its financial instruments into classes based on their nature and characteristics. The details of financial instruments by class are disclosed in the notes.

1. Accounting policies

Financial assets

Financial assets are initially recognised at fair value plus directly attributable transaction costs. However when a financial asset at fair value to income statement is recognised, the transaction costs are expensed immediately. Subsequent remeasurement of financial assets is determined by their categorisation that is revisited at each reporting date.

Derivatives embedded in other contracts are separated and treated as stand-alone derivatives when their risks and characteristics are not closely related to those of their host contracts and the respective host contracts are not carried at fair value.

In case of regular way purchase or sale (purchase or sale under a contract whose terms require delivery within the time frame established by regulation or convention in the market place), the settlement date is used for both initial recognition and subsequent derecognition.

At each balance sheet date, the Group assesses whether its financial assets are to be impaired. Impairment losses are recognised in the income statement where there is objective evidence of impairment, such as where the issuer is in bankruptcy, default or other significant financial difficulty. In addition, for an investment in an equity security, a significant or prolonged decline in its fair value below its cost is objective evidence of impairment. Impairment losses are reversed when the reversal can be objectively related to an event occurring after the recognition of the impairment loss. For debt instruments measured at amortised cost or fair value, the reversal is recognised in the income statement. For equity instruments classified as available for sale, the reversal is recognised in other comprehensive income. Impairment losses on financial assets carried at cost because their fair value cannot be reliably measured are never reversed.

Financial assets are derecognised (in full or partly) when substantially all the Group's rights to cash flows from the respective assets have expired or have been transferred and the Group has neither exposure to substantially all the risks inherent in those assets nor entitlement to rewards from them.

The Group classifies its financial assets into the following categories: loans and receivables, financial assets designated at fair value through income statement, held-for-trading and available-for-sale assets.

Loans and receivables

Loans and receivables are non-derivative financial assets with fixed or determinable payments that are not quoted in an active market. This category includes the following classes of financial assets: loans; trade and other receivables and cash at bank and in hand.

Subsequent to initial measurement, loans and receivables are carried at amortised cost using the effective interest rate method less appropriate allowances for doubtful receivables.

Allowances for doubtful receivables represent the Group's estimates of losses that could arise from the failure or inability of customers to make payments when due. These estimates are based on the ageing of customers' balances, specific credit circumstances and the Group's historical bad receivables experience.

Loans and receivables are further classified as current and non-current depending whether these will be realised within twelve months after the balance sheet date or beyond.

Designated at fair value through income statement

Certain investments are designated at fair value through income statement because this reduces an accounting mismatch which would otherwise arise due the remeasurement of certain liabilities using current market prices as inputs.

Held-for-trading assets

Held-for-trading assets are derivative financial instruments.

Subsequent to initial measurement, held-for-trading assets are carried at fair value and all their gains and losses, realised and unrealised, are recognised in the income statement.

Available-for-sale assets

Available-for-sale assets are those non-derivative financial assets that are either designated as such upon initial recognition or are not classified in any of the other financial assets categories. This category includes the following classes of financial assets: bonds, equities, commercial paper, time deposits and other investments. They are included in non-current financial assets unless an investment matures or management intends to dispose of it within 12 months of the end of the reporting period. In that case it would be accounted for as short-term investments, or cash and cash equivalents, as appropriate.

Subsequent to initial measurement, available-for-sale assets are stated at fair value with all unrealised gains or losses recognised against other comprehensive income until their disposal when such gains or losses are recognised in the income statement.

Interest earned on available-for-sale assets is calculated using the effective interest rate method and is recognised in the income statement.

1. Accounting policies

Financial liabilities at amortised cost

Financial liabilities are initially recognised at the fair value of consideration received less directly attributable transaction costs.

Subsequent to initial measurement, financial liabilities are recognised at amortised cost unless they are part of a fair value hedge relationship (refer to fair value hedges). The difference between the initial carrying amount of the financial liabilities and their redemption value is recognised in the income statement over the contractual terms using the effective interest rate method. This category includes the following classes of financial liabilities: trade and other payables; commercial paper; bonds and other financial liabilities.

Financial liabilities at amortised cost are further classified as current and non-current depending whether these will fall due within 12 months after the balance sheet date or beyond.

Financial liabilities are derecognised (in full or partly) when either the Group is discharged from its obligation, they expire, are cancelled or replaced by a new liability with substantially modified terms.

Derivative financial instruments

A derivative is a financial instrument that changes its values in response to changes in the underlying variable, requires no or little net initial investment and is settled at a future date. Derivatives are mainly used to manage exposures to foreign exchange, interest rate and commodity price risk.

Derivatives are initially recognised at fair value. They are subsequently remeasured at fair value on a regular basis and at each reporting date as a minimum. The fair values of exchange-traded derivatives are based on market prices, while the fair value of the over-the-counter derivatives are determined using accepted mathematical models based on market data.

Derivatives are carried as assets when their fair value is positive and as liabilities when their fair value is negative.

The Group's derivatives mainly consist of currency forwards, futures, options and swaps; commodity futures and options; interest rate forwards, futures, options and swaps.

Hedge accounting

The Group designates and documents certain derivatives as hedging instruments against changes in fair values of recognised assets and liabilities (fair value hedges), highly probable forecast transactions (cash flow hedges) and hedges of net investments in foreign operations (net investment hedges). The effectiveness of such hedges is assessed at inception and verified at regular intervals and at least on a quarterly basis, using prospective and retrospective testing.

Fair value hedges

The Group uses fair value hedges to mitigate foreign currency and interest rate risks of its recognised assets and liabilities.

The changes in fair values of hedging instruments are recognised in the income statement. Hedged items are also adjusted for the risk being hedged, with any gain or loss being recognised in the income statement.

Cash flow hedges

The Group uses cash flow hedges to mitigate a particular risk associated with a recognised asset or liability or highly probable forecast transactions, such as anticipated future export sales, purchases of equipment and raw materials, as well as the variability of expected interest payments and receipts.

The effective part of the changes in fair value of hedging instruments is recognised in other comprehensive income, while any ineffective part is recognised immediately in the income statement. When the hedged item results in the recognition of a non-financial asset or liability, including acquired businesses, the gains or losses previously recognised in other comprehensive income are included in the measurement of the cost of the asset or of the liability. Otherwise the gains or losses previously recognised in other comprehensive income are removed and recognised in the income statement at the same time as the hedged transaction.

Net investment hedges

The Group uses net investment hedges to mitigate translation exposure on its net investments in affiliated companies.

The changes in fair values of hedging instruments are taken directly to other comprehensive income together with gains or losses on the foreign currency translation of the hedged investments. All of these fair value gains or losses are deferred in equity until the investments are sold or otherwise disposed of.

Undesignated derivatives

Undesignated derivatives are comprised of two categories. The first includes derivatives acquired in the frame of risk management policies for which hedge accounting is not applied. The second category relates to derivatives that are acquired with the aim of delivering performance over agreed benchmarks.

1. Accounting policies

Subsequent to initial measurement, undesignated derivatives are carried at fair value and all their gains and losses, realised and unrealised, are recognised in the income statement.

Fair value
The Group determines the fair value of its financial instruments on the basis of the following hierarchy:

i) The fair value of financial instruments quoted in active markets is based on their quoted closing price at the balance sheet date. Examples include commodity derivative assets and liabilities and other financial assets such as investments in equity and debt securities.

ii) The fair value of financial instruments that are not traded in an active market is determined by using valuation techniques using observable market data. Such valuation techniques include discounted cash flows, standard valuation models based on market parameters for interest rates, yield curves or foreign exchange rates, dealer quotes for similar instruments and use of comparable arm's length transactions. For example, the fair value of forward exchange contracts, currency swaps and interest rate swaps is determined by discounting estimated future cash flows using a risk-free interest rate.

iii) The fair value of financial instruments that are measured on the basis of entity specific valuations using inputs that are not based on observable market data (unobservable inputs). When the fair value of unquoted instruments cannot be measured with sufficient reliability, the Group carries such instruments at cost less impairment, if applicable.

Cash and cash equivalents
Cash and cash equivalents include cash at bank and in hand and other short-term highly liquid investments with maturities of three months or less from the initial recognition.

Short-term investments
Short-term investments are those which have maturities of more than three months at initial recognition and which are expected to be realised within 12 months after the reporting date.

Inventories
Raw materials and purchased finished goods are valued at purchase cost. Work in progress and manufactured finished goods are valued at production cost. Production cost includes direct production costs and an appropriate proportion of production overheads and factory depreciation. The cost of inventories includes the gains/losses on qualified cash flow hedges for the purchase of raw materials and finished goods.

Raw material inventories and purchased finished goods are accounted for using the FIFO (first in, first out) method. The weighted average cost method is used for other inventories.

An allowance is established when the net realisable value of any inventory item is lower than the value calculated above.

Prepayments and accrued income
Prepayments and accrued income comprise payments made in advance relating to the following year, and income relating to the current year, which will not be invoiced until after the balance sheet date.

Property, plant and equipment
Property, plant and equipment are shown on the balance sheet at their historical cost. Subsequent costs are included in the asset's carrying amount only when it is probable that future economic benefits associated with the item will be realised. The carrying amount of a replaced part is derecognised. All other repairs and maintenance are charged to the income statement.

Depreciation is provided on components that have homogenous useful lives by using the straight-line method so as to depreciate the initial cost down to the residual value over the estimated useful lives. The residual values are 30% on head offices and nil for all other asset types. The useful lives are as follows:

Buildings	20–40 years
Machinery and equipment	10–25 years
Tools, furniture, information technology and sundry equipment	3–10 years
Vehicles	3–8 years
Land is not depreciated.	

Useful lives, components and residual amounts are reviewed annually. Such a review takes into consideration the nature of the assets, their intended use including but not limited to the closure of facilities and the evolution of the technology and competitive pressures that may lead to technical obsolescence.

Depreciation of property, plant and equipment is allocated to the appropriate headings of expenses by function in the income statement.

Borrowing costs incurred during the course of construction are capitalised if the assets under construction are significant and if their construction requires a substantial period to complete (typically more than one year). The capitalisation rate is determined on the basis of the short-term borrowing rate for the period of construction. Premiums capitalised for leasehold land or buildings are amortised over the length of the lease. Government grants are recognised in accordance with the deferral method, whereby the grant is set up as

1. Accounting policies

deferred income which is released to the income statement over the useful life of the related assets. Grants that are not related to assets are credited to the income statement when they are received.

Leased assets

Leasing agreements which transfer to the Group substantially all the rewards and risks of ownership of an asset are treated as finance leases. All other leases are classified as operating leases.

Assets acquired under finance leases are capitalised and depreciated in accordance with the Group's policy on property, plant and equipment unless the lease term is shorter. Land and building leases are recognised separately provided an allocation of the lease payments between these categories is reliable. Finance leases are capitalised at the lower of the fair value of the leased property and the present value of the minimum lease payments. The associated obligations are included under financial debt.

Rentals under operating leases are charged to the income statement on a straight-line basis over the period of the lease.

The costs of the agreements that do not take the legal form of a lease but convey the right to use an asset are separated into lease payments and other payments if the entity has the control of the use or of the access to the asset or takes essentially all the output of the asset. Then the entity determines whether the lease component of the agreement is a finance or an operating lease.

Business combinations and related goodwill

Business combinations are accounted for using the acquisition method. Identifiable assets acquired and liabilities and contingent liabilities assumed in a business combination are measured initially at their fair values at the acquisition date. The consideration transferred is measured at fair value and includes the fair value of any contingent consideration. Subsequent changes in contingent consideration, when not classified as equity, are recognised in the income statement. The acquisition-related costs are charged to the income statement in the period in which they are incurred. Where not all of the equity of a subsidiary is acquired the non-controlling interests are recognised at the non-controlling interest's share of the acquiree's net identifiable assets. Upon obtaining control in a business combination achieved in stages, the Group remeasures its previously held equity interest at fair value and recognises a gain or a loss to the income statement.

Goodwill is recorded when the sum of the fair value of consideration transferred plus the fair value of any existing

Nestlé ownership interest in the acquiree and the amount of any non-controlling interest exceeds the fair value of the acquiree's net assets. If the fair value of the acquiree's net assets exceeds this amount a gain is recognised immediately in the income statement.

Acquisitions and disposals of non-controlling interests

The Group treats transactions with non-controlling interests that do not result in loss of control as transactions with equity holders in their capacity as equity holders. For purchases of shares from non-controlling interests, the difference between any consideration paid and the relevant share acquired of the carrying amount of net assets of the subsidiary is recorded in equity. The same principle is applied to disposals of shares to non-controlling interests.

Intangible assets

This heading includes intangible assets that are internally generated or acquired either separately or in a business combination when they are identifiable and can be reliably measured. Intangible assets are considered to be identifiable if they arise from contractual or other rights, or if they are separable (i.e. they can be disposed of either individually or together with other assets). Intangible assets comprise indefinite life intangible assets and finite life intangible assets. Internally generated intangible assets are capitalised, provided they generate future economic benefits and their costs are clearly identifiable.

Indefinite life intangible assets are those for which there is no foreseeable limit to their useful economic life as they arise from contractual or other legal rights that can be renewed without significant cost and are the subject of continuous marketing support. They are not amortised but tested for impairment annually or more frequently if an impairment indicator is triggered. They mainly comprise certain brands, trademarks and intellectual property rights. The assessment of the classification of intangible assets as indefinite is reviewed annually.

Finite life intangible assets are those for which there is an expectation of obsolescence that limits their useful economic life or where the useful life is limited by contractual or other terms. They are amortised over the shorter of their contractual or useful economic lives. They comprise mainly management information systems, patents and rights to carry on an activity (e.g. exclusive rights to sell products or to perform a supply activity). Finite life intangible assets are amortised on a straight-line basis assuming a zero residual value: management information systems over a period ranging from 3 to 5 years; and other finite life intangible assets over 5 to 20 years. Useful lives and residual values are reviewed annually. Amortisation of intangible assets

NESTLÉ

1. Accounting policies

is allocated to the appropriate headings of expenses by function in the income statement.

Research and development

Internal research costs are charged to the income statement in the year in which they are incurred. Development costs are only recognised as assets on the balance sheet if all the recognition criteria set by IAS 38 – Intangible Assets are met before the products are launched on the market. Development costs are therefore charged to the income statement in the year in which they are incurred due to uncertainties inherent in the development of new products because the expected future economic benefits cannot be reliably determined. As long as the products have not reached the market place, there is no reliable evidence that positive future cash flows would be obtained.

Payments made to third parties in order to in-license or acquire intellectual property rights, compounds and products are capitalised as they are separately identifiable and are expected to generate future benefits.

Other development costs (essentially management information system software) are capitalised provided that there is an identifiable asset that will be useful in generating future benefits in terms of savings, economies of scale, etc.

Impairment of goodwill and indefinite life intangible assets

Goodwill and indefinite life intangible assets are tested for impairment at least annually and upon the occurrence of an indication of impairment.

The impairment tests are performed annually at the same time each year and at the cash generating unit (CGU) level. The Group defines its CGU for goodwill impairment testing based on the way that it monitors and derives economic benefits from the acquired goodwill. For indefinite life intangible assets, the Group defines its CGU as the smallest identifiable group of assets that generates cash inflows that are largely independent of the cash inflows from other assets or groups of assets. The impairment tests are performed by comparing the carrying value of the assets of these CGU with their recoverable amount, based on their future projected cash flows discounted at an appropriate pre-tax rate of return. Usually, the cash flows correspond to estimates made by Group Management in financial plans and business strategies covering a period of five years. They are then projected to 50 years using a steady or declining growth rate given that the Group businesses are of a long-term nature. The Group assesses the uncertainty of these estimates by making sensitivity analyses. The discount rate reflects the current assessment of the time value of money and the risks specific to the CGU (essentially country risk). The business risk is

included in the determination of the cash flows. Both the cash flows and the discount rates exclude inflation.

An impairment loss in respect of goodwill is never subsequently reversed.

Impairment of property, plant and equipment and finite life intangible assets

Consideration is given at each balance sheet date to determine whether there is any indication of impairment of the carrying amounts of the Group's property, plant and equipment and finite life intangible assets. Indication could be unfavourable development of a business under competitive pressures or severe economic slowdown in a given market as well as reorganisation of the operations to leverage their scale. If any indication exists, an asset's recoverable amount is estimated. An impairment loss is recognised whenever the carrying amount of an asset exceeds its recoverable amount. The recoverable amount is the greater of the fair value less cost to sell and value in use. In assessing value in use, the estimated future cash flows are discounted to their present value, based on the time value of money and the risks specific to the country where the assets are located. The risks specific to the asset are included in the determination of the cash flows.

Assets that suffered an impairment are tested for possible reversal of the impairment at each reporting date if indications exist that impairment losses recognised in prior periods no longer exist or have decreased.

Assets held for sale and discontinued operations

Non-current assets held for sale (and disposal groups) are presented separately in the current section of the balance sheet. Immediately before the initial classification of the assets (and disposal groups) as held for sale, the carrying amounts of the assets (or all the assets and liabilities in the disposal groups) are measured in accordance with their applicable accounting policy. Non-current assets held for sale (and disposal groups) are subsequently measured at the lower of their carrying amount and fair value less cost to sell. Non-current assets held for sale (and disposal groups) are no longer depreciated.

Upon occurrence of discontinued operations, the income statement of the discontinued operations is presented separately in the consolidated income statement. Comparative information is restated accordingly. Balance sheet and cash flow information related to discontinued operations are disclosed separately in the notes.

1. Accounting policies

Provisions

Provisions comprise liabilities of uncertain timing or amount that arise from restructuring plans, environmental, litigation and other risks. Provisions are recognised when there exists a legal or constructive obligation stemming from a past event and when the future cash outflows can be reliably estimated. Obligations arising from restructuring plans are recognised when detailed formal plans have been established and when there is a valid expectation that such plans will be carried out by either starting to implement them or announcing their main features. Obligations under litigations reflect Group Management's best estimate of the outcome based on the facts known at the balance sheet date.

Contingent assets and liabilities

Contingent assets and liabilities are possible rights and obligations that arise from past events and whose existence will be confirmed only by the occurrence or non-occurrence of one or more uncertain future events not fully within the control of the Group. They are disclosed in the notes.

Post-employment benefits

The liabilities of the Group arising from defined benefit obligations, and the related current service cost, are determined using the projected unit credit method. Actuarial advice is provided both by external consultants and by actuaries employed by the Group. The actuarial assumptions used to calculate the defined benefit obligations vary according to the economic conditions of the country in which the plan is located. Such plans are either externally funded (in the form of independently administered funds) or unfunded.

The deficit or excess of the fair value of plan assets over the present value of the defined benefit obligation is recognised as a liability or an asset on the balance sheet. An excess of assets is recognised only to the extent that it represents a future economic benefit which is available in the form of refunds from the plan or reductions in future contributions to the plan. When these criteria are not met, it is not recognised but is disclosed in the notes. Impacts of minimum funding requirements in relation to past service are considered when determining pension obligations.

Pension cost charged to the income statement consists of service cost (current and past service cost, gains and losses arising from settlement), net interest expense or income and administration costs (other than costs of managing plan assets). Past service cost is recognised at the earlier of the following dates:
- when the plan amendment or curtailment occurs; and
- when the related restructuring costs or termination benefits are recognised.

Remeasurements of the defined benefit plans are reported in other comprehensive income. They correspond to the actual return on plan assets, excluding interest income, changes in actuarial assumptions and differences between actuarial assumptions and what has actually occurred.

Some benefits are also provided by defined contribution plans. Contributions to such plans are charged to the income statement as incurred.

Equity compensation plans

The Group has equity-settled and cash-settled share-based payment transactions.

Equity-settled share-based payment transactions are recognised in the income statement with a corresponding increase in equity over the vesting period. They are fair valued at grant date and measured using generally accepted pricing models. The cost of equity-settled share-based payment transactions is adjusted annually by the expectations of vesting, for the forfeitures of the participants' rights that no longer satisfy the plan conditions, as well as for early vesting.

Liabilities arising from cash-settled share-based payment transactions are recognised in the income statement over the vesting period. They are fair valued at each reporting date and measured using generally accepted pricing models. The cost of cash-settled share-based payment transactions is adjusted for the forfeitures of the participants' rights that no longer satisfy the plan conditions, as well as for early vesting.

Accruals and deferred income

Accruals and deferred income comprise expenses relating to the current year, which will not be invoiced until after the balance sheet date, and income received in advance relating to the following year.

Dividend

In accordance with Swiss law and the Company's Articles of Association, dividend is treated as an appropriation of profit in the year in which it is ratified at the Annual General Meeting and subsequently paid.

Events occurring after the balance sheet date

The values of assets and liabilities at the balance sheet date are adjusted if there is evidence that subsequent adjusting events warrant a modification of these values. These adjustments are made up to the date of approval of the Consolidated Financial Statements by the Board of Directors. Other non-adjusting events are disclosed in the notes.

NESTLÉ

NESTLÉ

3. Analyses by segment

3.1 Operating segments
Revenue and results

In millions of CHF

2013

	Sales [a]	Trading operating profit	Net other trading income/(expenses) *	of which impairment of assets other than goodwill	of which restructuring costs	Impairment of goodwill
Zone Europe	15 568	2 331	(115)	(33)	(54)	(2)
Zone Americas	28 375	5 151	(416)	(31)	(91)	—
Zone Asia, Oceania and Africa	18 859	3 558	(37)	(7)	(13)	—
Nestlé Waters	7 231	680	(23)	(11)	3	(5)
Nestlé Nutrition	9 826	1 961	(78)	(11)	(34)	(84)
Other [b]	12 299	2 175	(67)	(43)	(18)	(23)
Unallocated items [c]	—	(1 809)	(109)	(7)	(67)	—
Total	**92 158**	**14 047**	**(845)**	**(143)**	**(274)**	**(114)**

* included in Trading operating profit

In millions of CHF

2012

	Sales [a]	Trading operating profit	Net other trading income/(expenses) *	of which impairment of assets other than goodwill	of which restructuring costs	Impairment of goodwill
Zone Europe	15 388	2 363	(90)	(40)	(40)	—
Zone Americas	28 613	5 346	(247)	(13)	15	—
Zone Asia, Oceania and Africa	18 875	3 579	(10)	9	(19)	—
Nestlé Waters	7 174	640	(40)	(20)	(15)	(1)
Nestlé Nutrition	7 858	1 509	(32)	(3)	(6)	(12)
Other [b]	11 813	2 064	(60)	(5)	(23)	(1)
Unallocated items [c]	—	(2 037)	(17)	(2)	—	—
Total	**89 721**	**13 464**	**(496)**	**(74)**	**(88)**	**(14)**

* included in Trading operating profit

(a) Inter-segment sales are not significant.
(b) Mainly Nespresso, Nestlé Professional and Nestlé Health Science.
(c) Refer to the Segment reporting section of Note 1 – Accounting policies for the definition of unallocated items.

Refer to Note 3.3 for the reconciliation from trading operating profit to profit before taxes, associates and joint ventures.

3. Analyses by segment

Assets and other information

In millions of CHF

2013

	Segment assets	of which goodwill and intangible assets	Capital additions	of which capital expenditure	Depreciation and amortisation of segment assets
Zone Europe	11 779	2 229	980	964	(517)
Zone Americas	21 252	9 058	1 134	1 019	(769)
Zone Asia, Oceania and Africa	14 169	4 284	1 279	1 280	(520)
Nestlé Waters	6 033	1 575	405	377	(442)
Nestlé Nutrition	22 517	14 089	562	430	(337)
Other (a)	9 564	3 709	1 091	642	(437)
Unallocated items (b)	11 060	8 768	293	216	(143)
Inter-segment eliminations	(2 021)	—	—	—	—
Total segments	**94 353**	**43 712**	**5 744**	**4 928**	**(3 165)**
Non-segment assets	26 089				
Total	**120 442**				

In millions of CHF

2012

	Segment assets	of which goodwill and intangible assets	Capital additions	of which capital expenditure	Depreciation and amortisation of segment assets
Zone Europe	11 804	2 251	1 038	1 019	(533)
Zone Americas	22 485	9 555	1 149	1 073	(899)
Zone Asia, Oceania and Africa	14 329	4 454	1 699	1 564	(553)
Nestlé Waters	6 369	1 654	424	407	(491)
Nestlé Nutrition	24 279	15 515	10 902	426	(176)
Other (a)	9 081	3 460	596	550	(295)
Unallocated items (b)	11 208	8 817	236	234	(102)
Inter-segment eliminations	(1 937)	—	—	—	—
Total segments	**97 618**	**45 706**	**16 044**	**5 273**	**(3 049)**
Non-segment assets	28 259				
Total	**125 877**				

(a) Mainly Nespresso, Nestlé Professional and Nestlé Health Science.
(b) Refer to the Segment reporting section of Note 1 – Accounting policies for the definition of unallocated items.

3. Analyses by segment

3.2 Products
Revenue and results

In millions of CHF

2013

	Sales	Trading operating profit	Net other trading income/(expenses) *	of which impairment of assets other than goodwill	of which restructuring costs	Impairment of goodwill
Powdered and Liquid Beverages	20 495	4 649	(95)	(21)	(27)	—
Water	6 773	678	(21)	(9)	3	(5)
Milk products and Ice cream	17 357	2 632	(177)	(14)	(44)	—
Nutrition and HealthCare	11 840	2 228	(120)	(44)	(38)	(107)
Prepared dishes and cooking aids	14 171	1 876	(120)	(28)	(61)	—
Confectionery	10 283	1 630	(86)	(19)	(23)	—
PetCare	11 239	2 163	(117)	(1)	(17)	—
Unallocated items (a)	—	(1 809)	(109)	(7)	(67)	(2)
Total	**92 158**	**14 047**	**(845)**	**(143)**	**(274)**	**(114)**

* included in Trading operating profit

In millions of CHF

2012

	Sales	Trading operating profit	Net other trading income/(expenses) *	of which impairment of assets other than goodwill	of which restructuring costs	Impairment of goodwill
Powdered and Liquid Beverages	20 248	4 445	(92)	(8)	(31)	—
Water (b)	6 747	636	(39)	(20)	(15)	(1)
Milk products and Ice cream	17 344	2 704	(145)	(11)	(14)	—
Nutrition and HealthCare	9 737	1 778	(44)	(3)	(9)	(11)
Prepared dishes and cooking aids	14 394	2 029	(63)	(13)	(15)	(1)
Confectionery	10 441	1 765	(93)	(15)	(16)	—
PetCare	10 810	2 144	(3)	(2)	12	—
Unallocated items (a)	—	(2 037)	(17)	(2)	—	(1)
Total	**89 721**	**13 464**	**(496)**	**(74)**	**(88)**	**(14)**

* included in Trading operating profit

(a) Refer to the Segment reporting section of Note 1 – Accounting policies for the definition of unallocated items.
(b) Beverages other than Water sold by Nestlé Waters (mainly RTD Teas and Juices) have been reclassified to Powdered and Liquid Beverages.

Refer to Note 3.3 for the reconciliation from trading operating profit to profit before taxes, associates and joint ventures.

3. Analyses by segment

Assets and liabilities

In millions of CHF

2013

	Assets	of which goodwill and intangible assets	Liabilities
Powdered and Liquid Beverages	11 044	477	4 607
Water	6 209	1 621	1 747
Milk products and Ice cream	14 805	5 220	3 773
Nutrition and HealthCare	28 699	18 648	3 838
Prepared dishes and cooking aids	13 289	6 373	2 761
Confectionery	8 190	2 071	2 611
PetCare	14 064	9 185	1 819
Unallocated items (a) and intra-group eliminations	1 081	2 146	(2 821)
Total	**97 381**	**45 741**	**18 335**

In millions of CHF

2012

	Assets	of which goodwill and intangible assets	Liabilities
Powdered and Liquid Beverages	10 844	413	4 270
Water (b)	6 442	1 682	1 742
Milk products and Ice cream	14 995	5 336	3 607
Nutrition and HealthCare	19 469	11 475	3 212
Prepared dishes and cooking aids	13 479	6 451	2 753
Confectionery	8 343	2 104	2 374
PetCare	13 996	9 252	1 638
Unallocated items (a) and intra-group eliminations	1 004	2 151	(2 806)
Total	**88 572**	**38 864**	**16 790**

(a) Refer to the Segment reporting section of Note 1 – Accounting policies for the definition of unallocated items.
(b) Beverages other than Water sold by Nestlé Waters (mainly RTD Teas and Juices) have been reclassified to Powdered and Liquid Beverages.

3. Analyses by segment

3.3 Reconciliation from trading operating profit to profit before taxes, associates and joint ventures

In millions of CHF

	2013	2012
Trading operating profit	14 047	13 464
Impairment of goodwill	(114)	(14)
Net other operating income/(expenses) excluding impairment of goodwill	(865)	(62)
Operating profit	**13 068**	**13 388**
Net financial income/(expense)	(631)	(705)
Profit before taxes, associates and joint ventures	**12 437**	**12 683**

3.4 Customers

There is no single customer amounting to 10% or more of Group's revenues.

3.5 Geography (top ten countries and Switzerland)

In millions of CHF

	2013		2012	
	Sales	Non-current assets [a]	Sales	Non-current assets [a]
USA	23 334	15 161	23 265	16 309
Greater China Region	6 618	5 414	5 118	5 109
France	5 578	1 683	5 538	1 652
Brazil	5 116	1 057	5 054	1 164
Germany	3 321	1 598	3 206	1 429
Mexico	3 179	697	3 169	673
United Kingdom	2 824	1 111	2 730	976
Philippines	2 410	877	2 060	981
Italy	2 098	849	2 169	875
Canada	2 064	552	2 141	615
Switzerland [b]	1 512	2 846	1 504	2 605
Rest of the world and unallocated items	34 104	38 762	33 767	39 894
Total	**92 158**	**70 607**	**89 721**	**72 282**

(a) Relate to property, plant and equipment, intangible assets and goodwill.
(b) Country of domicile of Nestlé S.A.

The analysis of sales by geographic area is stated by customer location.

4. Net other trading and operating income/(expenses)

4.1 Net other trading income/(expenses)

In millions of CHF

	Notes	2013	2012
Profit on disposal of property, plant and equipment		24	53
Miscellaneous trading income		96	88
Other trading income		**120**	**141**
Loss on disposal of property, plant and equipment		(9)	(20)
Restructuring costs		(274)	(88)
Impairment of assets other than goodwill	8/10	(143)	(74)
Litigations and onerous contracts [a]		(380)	(369)
Miscellaneous trading expenses		(159)	(86)
Other trading expenses		**(965)**	**(637)**
Total net other trading income/(expenses)		**(845)**	**(496)**

(a) Mainly relates to numerous separate legal cases (for example labour, civil and tax litigations), liabilities linked to product withdrawals as well as several separate onerous contracts.

4.2 Net other operating income/(expenses)

In millions of CHF

	Notes	2013	2012
Profit on disposal of businesses		33	105
Miscellaneous operating income [a]		583	41
Other operating income		**616**	**146**
Loss on disposal of businesses	2	(1 221)	(3)
Impairment of goodwill	9	(114)	(14)
Miscellaneous operating expenses		(260)	(205)
Other operating expenses		**(1 595)**	**(222)**
Total net other operating income/(expenses)		**(979)**	**(76)**

(a) Mainly relates to the disposal of Givaudan shares, which were categorised as available for sale.

NESTLÉ

5. Net financial income/(expense)

In millions of CHF

	Notes	2013	2012
Interest income		199	108
Interest expense		(580)	(552)
Net financing cost		**(381)**	**(444)**
Interest income on defined benefit plans	11	20	12
Interest expense on defined benefit plans	11	(268)	(249)
Net interest income/(expense) on defined benefit plans		**(248)**	**(237)**
Other		(2)	(24)
Net financial income/(expense)		**(631)**	**(705)**

6. Inventories

In millions of CHF

	2013	2012
Raw materials, work in progress and sundry supplies	3 499	3 815
Finished goods	5 138	5 302
Allowance for write-down to net realisable value	(255)	(178)
	8 382	**8 939**

Inventories amounting to CHF 252 million (2012: CHF 238 million) are pledged as security for financial liabilities.

7. Trade and other receivables

7.1 By type

In millions of CHF

	2013	2012
Trade receivables	9 367	9 539
Other receivables	2 839	3 509
	12 206	**13 048**

The five major customers represent 11% (2012: 10%) of trade and other receivables, none of them individually exceeding 6% (2012: 5%).

7. Trade and other receivables

7.2 Past due and impaired receivables

In millions of CHF

	2013	2012
Not past due	10 175	10 633
Past due 1–30 days	1 054	1 329
Past due 31–60 days	284	429
Past due 61–90 days	116	166
Past due 91–120 days	103	93
Past due more than 120 days	851	772
Allowance for doubtful receivables	(377)	(374)
	12 206	**13 048**

7.3 Allowance for doubtful receivables

In millions of CHF

	2013	2012
At 1 January	374	365
Currency retranslations	(13)	(3)
Allowance made during the year	95	87
Amounts used and reversal of unused amounts	(74)	(75)
Modification of the scope of consolidation	(5)	—
At 31 December	**377**	**374**

Based on the historic trend and expected performance of the customers, the Group believes that the above allowance for doubtful receivables sufficiently covers the risk of default.

8. Property, plant and equipment

In millions of CHF

	Land and buildings	Machinery and equipment	Tools, furniture and other equipment	Vehicles	Total
Gross value					
At 1 January 2012	13 812	25 895	7 645	955	**48 307**
Currency retranslations	(147)	(642)	(30)	(28)	**(847)**
Capital expenditure (a)	1 395	2 803	947	128	**5 273**
Disposals	(168)	(543)	(609)	(94)	**(1 414)**
Reclassified as held for sale	(17)	(14)	(1)	—	**(32)**
Modification of the scope of consolidation (b)	585	467	(20)	(4)	**1 028**
At 31 December 2012	**15 460**	**27 966**	**7 932**	**957**	52 315
Currency retranslations	(655)	(1 398)	(222)	(27)	(2 302)
Capital expenditure (a)	1 330	2 453	1 066	79	4 928
Disposals	(82)	(339)	(774)	(104)	(1 299)
Reclassified as held for sale	(40)	(139)	(26)	(3)	(208)
Modification of the scope of consolidation	(25)	(110)	(159)	(22)	(316)
At 31 December 2013	**15 988**	**28 433**	**7 817**	**880**	53 118
Accumulated depreciation and impairments					
At 1 January 2012	(4 982)	(14 140)	(5 225)	(500)	**(24 847)**
Currency retranslations	65	259	63	10	**397**
Depreciation	(381)	(1 399)	(773)	(102)	**(2 655)**
Impairments	4	(57)	(21)	—	**(74)**
Disposals	120	486	551	78	**1 235**
Reclassified as held for sale	12	11	1	—	**24**
Modification of the scope of consolidation (b)	26	105	44	6	**181**
At 31 December 2012	**(5 136)**	**(14 735)**	**(5 360)**	**(508)**	(25 739)
Currency retranslations	187	602	190	17	996
Depreciation	(428)	(1 360)	(970)	(106)	(2 864)
Impairments	(15)	(74)	(20)	—	(109)
Disposals	57	269	739	83	1 148
Reclassified as held for sale	19	96	17	1	133
Modification of the scope of consolidation	16	104	81	11	212
At 31 December 2013	**(5 300)**	**(15 098)**	**(5 323)**	**(502)**	(26 223)
Net at 31 December 2012	**10 324**	**13 231**	**2 572**	**449**	26 576
Net at 31 December 2013	**10 688**	**13 335**	**2 494**	**378**	26 895

(a) Including borrowing costs.
(b) 2012 comparatives have been adjusted following the final valuation of the Wyeth Nutrition acquisition (see Note 2).

At 31 December 2013, property, plant and equipment include CHF 1510 million of assets under construction (2012: CHF 1322 million). Net property, plant and equipment held under finance leases amount to CHF 201 million (2012: CHF 154 million). Net property, plant and equipment of CHF 397 million are pledged as security for financial liabilities (2012: CHF 293 million). Fire risks, reasonably estimated, are insured in accordance with domestic requirements.

8. Property, plant and equipment

Impairment

Impairment of property, plant and equipment arises mainly from the plans to optimise industrial manufacturing capacities by closing or selling inefficient production facilities.

Commitments for expenditure

At 31 December 2013, the Group was committed to expenditure amounting to CHF 724 million (2012: CHF 517 million).

9. Goodwill

In millions of CHF

	Notes	2013	2012
Gross value			
At 1 January		34 387	30 554
Currency retranslations		(1 182)	(590)
Goodwill from acquisitions (a)	2	254	4 686
Disposals		(558)	(263)
Reclassified as held for sale	2	(271)	—
At 31 December		**32 630**	**34 387**
Accumulated impairments			
At 1 January		(1 699)	(1 941)
Currency retranslations		25	(7)
Impairments		(114)	(14)
Disposals		20	263
Reclassified as held for sale	2	177	—
At 31 December		**(1 591)**	**(1 699)**
Net at 31 December		31 039	32 688

(a) 2012 comparatives have been adjusted following the final valuation of the Wyeth Nutrition acquisition (see Note 2).

9.1 Impairment charge during the year

The 2013 impairment charge mainly relates to the Performance Nutrition business (CHF 84 million – see Note 2.3).

9.2 Annual impairment tests

Goodwill impairment reviews have been conducted for more than 200 goodwill items allocated to some 50 Cash Generating Units (CGU).

Detailed results of the impairment tests are presented below for the four largest goodwill items, representing more than 50% of the net book value at 31 December 2013. For the purpose of the tests, they have been allocated to the following CGU: Wyeth Nutrition (WN), PetCare by geographical zone, Infant Nutrition excluding WN (IN), Frozen Pizza and Ice Cream USA. For each of the CGU, the recoverable amount is higher than its carrying amount. The recoverable amount has been determined based upon a value-in-use calculation. Deflated cash flow projections covering the next 50 years, discounted at a deflated pre-tax weighted average rate, were used in this calculation. The cash flows for the first five years were based upon financial plans approved by Group Management; years six to ten were based upon Group Management's best expectations, which are consistent with the Group's

9. Goodwill

approved strategy for this period. WN cash flows were based on expectations for the first two years of activity and thereafter on the latest available business plan. Cash flows were assumed to be flat for years eleven to 50, although Group Management expects continuing growth for WN, PetCare and IN. A 1% increase per year has been assumed for years eleven to 50 for Frozen Pizza and Ice Cream USA. Cash flows have been adjusted to reflect the specific business risks.

9.2.1 Wyeth Nutrition

Goodwill related to the 2012 acquisition of Wyeth Nutrition has been allocated for impairment testing purposes to the CGU Wyeth Nutrition. As of 31 December 2013, the carrying amount of goodwill, denominated in various currencies, is CHF 4250 million (2012: CHF 4586 million). Intangible assets with indefinite useful life related to this CGU amount to CHF 4509 million (2012: CHF 4509 million).

Assumptions

A deflated pre-tax weighted average discount rate of 5.7% was used in this calculation.
The main assumptions were the following:
- sales: annual growth between 9.8 and 13.4% over the first ten-year period and flat thereafter;
- trading operating profit margin [a] evolution: improving over the ten-year period, in a range of 30 to 60 basis points per year.

Sensitivity analyses

The key sensitivity for the impairment test is the growth in sales and trading operating profit margin [a]. Assuming no sales growth and no improvement in trading operating profit margin [a] after year four would not result in the carrying amount exceeding the recoverable amount. An increase of 100 basis points in the discount rate assumption would not change the conclusions of the impairment test.

9.2.2 PetCare

The goodwill related to the acquisition of Ralston Purina in 2001 is allocated for impairment testing purposes to three distinct CGU corresponding to the three operating segments that are covering geographically the PetCare business: Zone Europe, Zone Americas and Zone Asia, Oceania and Africa.

As at 31 December, the carrying amounts of goodwill and intangible assets with indefinite useful life included in these CGU, denominated in various currencies, represent an equivalent of:

In millions of CHF

		2013			2012	
	Total	of which Zone Europe	of which Zone Americas	Total	of which Zone Europe	of which Zone Americas
Goodwill	8 665	1 773	6 833	8 781	1 753	6 957
Intangible assets with indefinite useful life	187	—	155	192	—	154
	8 852	1 773	6 988	8 973	1 753	7 111

(a) Before net other trading income/(expenses).

9. Goodwill

Assumptions

The main assumptions for the two most important CGU, PetCare Zone Europe and PetCare Zone Americas, were the following:

	Zone Europe	Zone Americas
Deflated pre-tax weighted average discount rate	6.4%	7.0%
Annual sales growth over the first ten-year period	between 3.0 and 6.9%	between 4.0 and 4.5%
Trading operating profit margin [a] evolution over the first ten-year period	steady improvement in a range of 10–60 basis points per year	generally flat

Assumptions used in the calculations are consistent with the expected long-term average growth rate of the PetCare businesses in the Zones concerned. The margin evolution is consistent with sales growth and portfolio optimisation.

Sensitivity analyses

The key sensitivity for the impairment tests is the growth in sales and trading operating profit margin [a]. For Zone Americas and Zone Europe, assuming no sales growth and no improvement in trading operating profit margin [a] over the entire period would not result in the carrying amount exceeding the recoverable amount. An increase of 100 basis points in the discount rate assumption would not change the conclusions of the impairment tests.

9.2.3 Infant Nutrition excluding Wyeth Nutrition

Goodwill related to the 2007 acquisition of Gerber has been allocated for impairment testing purposes to the CGU of the Infant Nutrition businesses excluding WN on a worldwide basis. As at 31 December 2013, the carrying amount of goodwill, denominated in various currencies, is CHF 3384 million (2012: CHF 3516 million). Intangible assets with indefinite useful life related to this CGU amount to CHF 1184 million (2012: CHF 1217 million).

Assumptions

A deflated pre-tax weighted average discount rate of 7.7% was used in this calculation.
The main assumptions, based on past experiences and current initiatives, were the following:
- sales: annual growth between 2.9 and 4.8% for North America over the first ten-year period and between 5.4 and 8.1% for the rest of the world over the first six-year period and flat thereafter;
- trading operating profit margin [a] evolution: improving over the ten-year period, in a range of 20 to 30 basis points per year.

Sensitivity analyses

The key sensitivity for the impairment test is the growth in sales and trading operating profit margin [a]. Assuming no sales growth and no improvement in trading operating profit margin [a] over the entire period would not result in the carrying amount exceeding the recoverable amount. An increase of 100 basis points in the discount rate assumption would not change the conclusions of the impairment test.

(a) Before net other trading income/(expenses).

9. Goodwill

9.2.4 Frozen Pizza and Ice Cream USA

Goodwill related to the Group's Ice cream businesses in the USA (Nestlé Ice Cream Company and Dreyer's) and related to the 2010 acquisition of the Kraft Food's frozen pizza business in the USA has been allocated to the CGU Frozen Pizza and Ice Cream USA. As at 31 December 2013, the carrying amount of goodwill, denominated in USD, is CHF 4045 million (2012: CHF 4159 million). Intangible assets with indefinite useful life related to this CGU amount to CHF 1593 million (2012: CHF 1638 million).

Assumptions

A deflated pre-tax weighted average discount rate of 7.1% was used in this calculation.
The main assumptions, based on past experiences and current initiatives, were the following:
- sales: annual growth between 1.2 and 3.2% over the first ten-year period;
- trading operating profit margin [a] evolution: steadily improving over the first four-year period, in a range of 80 to 210 basis points per year and then from a range of 0 to 50 basis points per year from year five to ten.

Sensitivity analyses

The key sensitivity for the impairment test is the growth in sales and trading operating profit margin [a]. Decreasing by 20 basis points the projected annual sales growth over the first ten year period, with cash flows remaining flat after year ten would not result in the carrying amount exceeding the recoverable amount. Limiting the improvement of the trading operating profit margin [a] by only 60 basis points per year over the first ten year period, with cash flows remaining flat after year ten would not result in the carrying amount exceeding the recoverable amount. An increase of 100 basis points in the discount rate assumption would not change the conclusions of the impairment test.

(a) Before net other trading income/(expenses).

10. Intangible assets

In millions of CHF

	Brands and intellectual property rights	Operating rights and others	Management information systems	Total	of which internally generated
Gross value					
At 1 January 2012	7 354	1 008	3 777	**12 139**	3 490
of which indefinite useful life	7 159	—	—	**7 159**	—
Currency retranslations	(122)	(24)	(62)	**(208)**	(56)
Expenditure	53	146	126	**325**	106
Disposals	(37)	(38)	(6)	**(81)**	—
Modification of the scope of consolidation (a)	4 461	(2)	(2)	**4 457**	(2)
At 31 December 2012	**11 709**	**1 090**	**3 833**	**16 632**	**3 538**
of which indefinite useful life	11 583	23	—	**11 606**	—
Currency retranslations	(119)	(26)	(124)	**(269)**	(118)
Expenditure	71	116	215	**402**	183
Disposals	(1)	(52)	(11)	**(64)**	—
Reclassified as held for sale	(23)	—	(14)	**(37)**	(13)
Modification of the scope of consolidation	(209)	(45)	(60)	**(314)**	—
At 31 December 2013	**11 428**	**1 083**	**3 839**	**16 350**	**3 590**
of which indefinite useful life (b)	11 305	35	—	**11 340**	—
Accumulated amortisation and impairments					
At 1 January 2012	(74)	(245)	(3 035)	**(3 354)**	(2 811)
Currency retranslations	1	5	47	**53**	43
Amortisation	(9)	(93)	(292)	**(394)**	(272)
Disposals	37	37	5	**79**	—
Modification of the scope of consolidation (a)	—	—	2	**2**	2
At 31 December 2012	**(45)**	**(296)**	**(3 273)**	**(3 614)**	**(3 038)**
Currency retranslations	1	3	116	**120**	111
Amortisation	(10)	(76)	(215)	**(301)**	(197)
Impairments	(31)	—	(3)	**(34)**	—
Disposals	1	48	8	**57**	—
Reclassified as held for sale	—	—	12	**12**	12
Modification of the scope of consolidation	7	49	27	**83**	—
At 31 December 2013	**(77)**	**(272)**	**(3 328)**	**(3 677)**	**(3 112)**
Net at 31 December 2012	**11 664**	**794**	**560**	**13 018**	**500**
Net at 31 December 2013	**11 351**	**811**	**511**	**12 673**	**478**

(a) 2012 comparatives have been adjusted following the final valuation of the Wyeth Nutrition acquisition (see Note 2).
(b) Annual impairment tests are performed in connection with goodwill impairment tests (refer to Note 9). Depending on the items tested, the CGU is equivalent to the CGU for goodwill impairment test or is at a lower level.

Internally generated intangible assets consist mainly of management information systems.

Commitments for expenditure
At 31 December 2013, the Group was committed to expenditure amounting to CHF 9 million (2012: CHF 2 million).

12. Equity compensation plans

The fair value of equity-settled RSU is determined on the basis of the market price of Nestlé S.A. shares at grant date, discounted at a risk-free interest rate and adjusted for the dividends that participants are not entitled to receive during the restricted period of three years. The weighted average fair value of the equity-settled RSU granted in 2013 is CHF 58.58 (2012: CHF 49.65).

For cash-settled outstanding RSU, the liability is re-measured at each reporting date based on subsequent changes in the market price of Nestlé S.A. shares. The average fair value of the cash-settled RSU outstanding at 31 December 2013 is CHF 63.36 (2012: CHF 57.72).

13. Provisions and contingencies

13.1 Provisions

In millions of CHF

	Restructuring	Environmental	Litigation	Other	Total
At 1 January 2012	630	26	2 525	473	3 654
Currency retranslations	4	(1)	(56)	(19)	(72)
Provisions made during the year (a)	92	1	384	141	618
Amounts used	(189)	(6)	(199)	(115)	(509)
Unused amounts reversed	(59)	(2)	(321)	(42)	(424)
Modification of the scope of consolidation (b)	1	—	—	11	12
At 31 December 2012	**479**	**18**	**2 333**	**449**	3 279
of which expected to be settled within 12 months					452
Currency retranslations	—	(1)	(78)	(16)	(95)
Provisions made during the year (a)	244	1	455	162	862
Amounts used	(167)	(2)	(205)	(85)	(459)
Unused amounts reversed	(35)	(1)	(258)	(63)	(357)
Modification of the scope of consolidation	—	—	(1)	8	7
At 31 December 2013	**521**	**15**	**2 246**	**455**	3 237
of which expected to be settled within 12 months					523

(a) Including discounting of provisions.
(b) 2012 comparatives have been adjusted following the final valuation of the Wyeth Nutrition acquisition (see Note 2).

Restructuring
Restructuring provisions arise from a number of projects across the Group. These include plans to optimise production, sales and administration structures, mainly in Europe. Restructuring provisions are expected to result in future cash outflows when implementing the plans (usually over the following two to three years).

Litigation
Litigation provisions have been set up to cover tax, legal and administrative proceedings that arise in the ordinary course of the business. These provisions cover numerous separate cases whose detailed disclosure could be detrimental to the Group interests. The Group does not believe that any of these litigation proceedings will have a material adverse impact on its financial position. The timing of outflows is uncertain as it depends upon the outcome of the proceedings. In that instance, these provisions are not discounted because their present value would not represent meaningful information. Group Management does not believe it is possible to make assumptions on the evolution of the cases beyond the balance sheet date.

13. Provisions and contingencies

Other

Other provisions are mainly constituted by onerous contracts and various damage claims having occurred during the year but not covered by insurance companies. Onerous contracts result from unfavourable leases, breach of contracts or supply agreements above market prices in which the unavoidable costs of meeting the obligations under the contracts exceed the economic benefits expected to be received or for which no benefits are expected to be received.

13.2 Contingencies

The Group is exposed to contingent liabilities amounting to a maximum potential payment of CHF 1669 million (2012: CHF 1823 million) representing potential litigations of CHF 1658 million (2012: CHF 1814 million) and other items of CHF 11 million (2012: CHF 9 million). Potential litigations relate mainly to labour, civil and tax litigations in Latin America.

Contingent assets for litigation claims in favour of the Group amount to a maximum potential recoverable amount of CHF 51 million (2012: CHF 189 million).

16. Associates and joint ventures

Reconciliation of the carrying amount

In billions of CHF

	2013	2012
Share held by the Group in the equity of L'Oréal	8.2	7.5
Goodwill and other adjustments	1.3	1.3
Carrying amount	**9.5**	**8.8**

16.2 Other associates
The Group holds a number of other associates that are individually not material for the Group.

16.3 Joint ventures
The Group holds 50% of a number of joint ventures operating in the food and beverages and in pharmaceutical activities. These joint ventures are individually not material for the Group, the main ones being Galderma and Cereal Partners Worldwide.

17. Earnings per share

	2013	2012
Basic earnings per share (in CHF)	3.14	3.21
Net profit (in millions of CHF)	10 015	10 228
Weighted average number of shares outstanding (in millions of units)	3 191	3 186
Diluted earnings per share (in CHF)	3.13	3.20
Net profit, net of effects of dilutive potential ordinary shares (in millions of CHF)	10 015	10 228
Weighted average number of shares outstanding, net of effects of dilutive potential ordinary shares (in millions of units)	3 200	3 195
Reconciliation of weighted average number of shares outstanding (in millions of units)		
Weighted average number of shares outstanding used to calculate basic earnings per share	3 191	3 186
Adjustment for share-based payment schemes, where dilutive	9	9
Weighted average number of shares outstanding used to calculate diluted earnings per share	3 200	3 195

18. Cash flow statement

18.1 Operating profit

In millions of CHF

	2013	2012
Profit for the year	10 445	10 677
Share of results of associates and joint ventures	(1 264)	(1 253)
Taxes	3 256	3 259
Financial income	(219)	(120)
Financial expense	850	825
	13 068	**13 388**

18.2 Non-cash items of income and expense

In millions of CHF

	2013	2012
Depreciation of property, plant and equipment	2 864	2 655
Impairment of property, plant and equipment	109	74
Impairment of goodwill	114	14
Amortisation of intangible assets	301	394
Impairment of intangible assets	34	—
Net result on disposal of businesses	1 188	(102)
Net result on disposal of assets	67	49
Non-cash items in financial assets and liabilities	(577)	(44)
Equity compensation plans	154	156
Other	98	21
	4 352	**3 217**

18.3 Decrease/(increase) in working capital

In millions of CHF

	2013	2012
Inventories	(157)	287
Trade and other receivables	(257)	(26)
Prepayments and accrued income	(48)	14
Trade and other payables	1 585	1 655
Accruals and deferred income	237	85
	1 360	**2 015**

18.4 Variation of other operating assets and liabilities

In millions of CHF

	2013	2012
Variation of employee benefits assets and liabilities	(887)	(174)
Variation of provisions	84	(50)
Other	229	129
	(574)	**(95)**

NESTLÉ

18. Cash flow statement

18.5 Net cash flows from treasury activities

In millions of CHF

	2013	2012
Interest paid	(505)	(559)
Interest and dividends received	105	115
Net cash flows from derivatives used to hedge foreign operations	29	133
Net cash flows from trading derivatives	20	(13)
	(351)	**(324)**

18.6 Reconciliation of free cash flow and net financial debt

In millions of CHF

	2013	2012
Operating cash flow	14 992	15 668
Capital expenditure	(4 928)	(5 273)
Expenditure on intangible assets	(402)	(325)
Sale of property, plant and equipment	86	130
Investments (net of divestments) in associates and joint ventures	(28)	(79)
Inflows from other investing activities	1 187	89
Outflows from other investing activities	(421)	(305)
Free cash flow	**10 486**	**9 905**
Acquisition of businesses	(321)	(10 916)
Financial liabilities and short-term investments acquired in business combinations	(1)	(8)
Disposal of businesses	421	142
Financial liabilities and short-term investments transferred on disposal of businesses	11	—
Acquisition (net of disposal) of non-controlling interests	(337)	(165)
Dividend paid to shareholders of the parent	(6 552)	(6 213)
Purchase of treasury shares	(481)	(532)
Sale of treasury shares	60	1 199
Reclassification of financial investments from non-current financial assets to net financial debt	366	2 841
Outflows from non-current treasury investments	(244)	(192)
Dividends paid to non-controlling interests	(328)	(204)
Cash inflows from hedging derivatives on net debt	41	250
Currency retranslations and exchange differences	399	47
Other movements	(90)	54
(Increase)/decrease of net financial debt	**3 430**	**(3 792)**
Net financial debt at beginning of year	(18 120)	(14 328)
Net financial debt at end of year	**(14 690)**	**(18 120)**

18. Cash flow statement

18.7 Cash and cash equivalents at end of year

In millions of CHF

	2013	2012
Cash at bank and in hand	4 524	3 499
Time deposits [a]	1 829	1 800
Commercial paper [a]	62	414
	6 415	**5 713**

(a) With maturity of three months or less as from the initial recognition.

19. Equity

19.1 Share capital issued

The ordinary share capital of Nestlé S.A. authorised, issued and fully paid is composed of 3 224 800 000 registered shares with a nominal value of CHF 0.10 each. Each share confers the right to one vote. No shareholder may be registered with the right to vote for shares which it holds, directly or indirectly, in excess of 5% of the share capital. Shareholders have the right to receive dividends.

19.2 Conditional share capital

The conditional capital of Nestlé S.A. amounts to CHF 10 million as in the preceding year. It confers the right to increase the ordinary share capital, through the exercise of conversion or option rights in connection with debentures and other financial market instruments, by a maximum of CHF 10 million by the issue of a maximum of 100 000 000 registered shares with a nominal value of CHF 0.10 each. Thus the Board of Directors has at its disposal a flexible instrument enabling it, if necessary, to finance the activities of the Company through convertible debentures.

19.3 Treasury shares

Number of shares in millions of units

	Notes	2013	2012
Purpose of holding			
Trading		18.2	18.0
Long-Term Incentive Plans	12	17.0	18.2
		35.2	**36.2**

At 31 December 2013, the treasury shares held by the Group represent 1.1% of the share capital (2012: 1.1%). Their market value amounts to CHF 2300 million (2012: CHF 2160 million).

19. Equity

19.4 Number of shares outstanding

Number of shares in millions of units

	Shares issued	Treasury shares	Outstanding shares
At 1 January 2012	3 300.0	(128.0)	3 172.0
Purchase of treasury shares	—	(9.1)	(9.1)
Sale of treasury shares	—	20.2	20.2
Treasury shares delivered in respect of options exercised	—	1.5	1.5
Treasury shares delivered in respect of equity compensation plans	—	4.0	4.0
Treasury shares cancelled	(75.2)	75.2	—
At 31 December 2012	**3 224.8**	**(36.2)**	**3 188.6**
Purchase of treasury shares	—	(7.7)	(7.7)
Treasury shares delivered in respect of options exercised	—	1.3	1.3
Treasury shares delivered in respect of equity compensation plans	—	3.3	3.3
Treasury shares delivered in respect of the acquisition of a business	—	4.1	4.1
At 31 December 2013	**3 224.8**	**(35.2)**	**3 189.6**

19.5 Translation reserve

The translation reserve comprises the cumulative gains and losses arising from translating the financial statements of foreign operations that use functional currencies other than Swiss francs. It also includes the changes in the fair value of hedging instruments used for net investments in foreign operations.

19.6 Retained earnings and other reserves

Retained earnings represent the cumulative profits, share premium, as well as remeasurement of defined benefit plans attributable to shareholders of the parent. Other reserves comprise the fair value reserve and the hedging reserve attributable to shareholders of the parent.

The fair value reserve includes the gains and losses on remeasuring available-for-sale financial instruments. At 31 December 2013, the reserve is CHF 50 million positive (2012: CHF 573 million positive).

The hedging reserve consists of the effective portion of the gains and losses on hedging instruments related to hedged transactions that have not yet occurred. At 31 December 2013, the reserve is CHF 42 million negative (2012: CHF 283 million negative).

19.7 Non-controlling interests

The non-controlling interests comprise the portion of equity of subsidiaries that are not owned, directly or indirectly, by Nestlé S.A. These non-controlling interests are individually not material for the Group.

19. Equity

19.8 Other comprehensive income

In millions of CHF

	Translation reserve	Retained earnings and other reserves	Total attributable to shareholders of the parent	Non-controlling interests	Total
2013					
Currency retranslations	(2 887)	—	(2 887)	(59)	(2 946)
Fair value adjustments on available-for-sale financial instruments	—	(523)	(523)	—	(523)
Fair value adjustments on cash flow hedges	—	246	246	—	246
Remeasurement of defined benefit plans	—	1 632	1 632	—	1 632
Taxes	—	(558)	(558)	—	(558)
Share of other comprehensive income of associates and joint ventures	—	87	87	—	87
Other comprehensive income for the year	**(2 887)**	**884**	**(2 003)**	**(59)**	**(2 062)**
2012					
Currency retranslations	(997)	—	(997)	(56)	(1 053)
Fair value adjustments on available-for-sale financial instruments	—	325	325	—	325
Fair value adjustments on cash flow hedges	—	150	150	—	150
Remeasurement of defined benefit plans	—	(1 534)	(1 534)	—	(1 534)
Taxes	—	355	355	—	355
Share of other comprehensive income of associates and joint ventures	—	502	502	—	502
Other comprehensive income for the year	**(997)**	**(202)**	**(1 199)**	**(56)**	**(1 255)**

19.9 Dividend

The dividend related to 2012 was paid on 18 April 2013 in accordance with the decision taken at the Annual General Meeting on 11 April 2013. Shareholders approved the proposed dividend of CHF 2.05 per share, resulting in a total dividend of CHF 6552 million.

Dividend payable is not accounted for until it has been ratified at the Annual General Meeting. At the meeting on 10 April 2014, a dividend of CHF 2.15 per share will be proposed, resulting in a total dividend of CHF 6927 million. For further details, refer to the Financial Statements of Nestlé S.A.

The Financial Statements for the year ended 31 December 2013 do not reflect this proposed distribution, which will be treated as an appropriation of profit in the year ending 31 December 2014.

NESTLÉ

Report of the Statutory Auditor on the Consolidated Financial Statements
to the General Meeting of Nestlé S.A.

As statutory auditor, we have audited the consolidated financial statements (income statement, statement of comprehensive income, balance sheet, cash flow statement, statement of changes in equity and notes on pages 74 to 148) of the Nestlé Group for the year ended 31 December 2013.

Board of Directors' responsibility
The Board of Directors is responsible for the preparation and fair presentation of the consolidated financial statements in accordance with International Financial Reporting Standards (IFRS) and the requirements of Swiss law. This responsibility includes designing, implementing and maintaining an internal control system relevant to the preparation and fair presentation of consolidated financial statements that are free from material misstatement, whether due to fraud or error. The Board of Directors is further responsible for selecting and applying appropriate accounting policies and making accounting estimates that are reasonable in the circumstances.

Auditor's responsibility
Our responsibility is to express an opinion on these consolidated financial statements based on our audit. We conducted our audit in accordance with Swiss law and Swiss Auditing Standards as well as International Standards on Auditing. Those standards require that we plan and perform the audit to obtain reasonable assurance whether the consolidated financial statements are free from material misstatement.

An audit involves performing procedures to obtain audit evidence about the amounts and disclosures in the consolidated financial statements. The procedures selected depend on the auditor's judgment, including the assessment of the risks of material misstatement of the consolidated financial statements, whether due to fraud or error. In making those risk assessments, the auditor considers the internal control system relevant to the entity's preparation and fair presentation of the consolidated financial statements in order to design audit procedures that are appropriate in the circumstances, but not for the purpose of expressing an opinion on the effectiveness of the entity's internal control system. An audit also includes evaluating the appropriateness of the accounting policies used and the reasonableness of accounting estimates made, as well as evaluating the overall presentation of the consolidated financial statements. We believe that the audit evidence we have obtained is sufficient and appropriate to provide a basis for our audit opinion.

Opinion
In our opinion, the consolidated financial statements for the year ended 31 December 2013 give a true and fair view of the financial position, the results of operations and the cash flows in accordance with International Financial Reporting Standards (IFRS) and comply with Swiss law.

Report of the Statutory auditor on the Consolidated Financial Statements

Report on other legal requirements

We confirm that we meet the legal requirements on licensing according to the Auditor Oversight Act (AOA) and independence (article 728 CO and article 11 AOA) and that there are no circumstances incompatible with our independence.

In accordance with article 728a paragraph 1 item 3 CO and Swiss Auditing Standard 890, we confirm that an internal control system exists, which has been designed for the preparation of consolidated financial statements according to the instructions of the Board of Directors.

We recommend that the consolidated financial statements submitted to you be approved.

KPMG

KPMG SA

Scott Cormack
Licensed Audit Expert
Auditor in charge

Fabien Lussu
Licensed Audit Expert

Geneva, 12 February 2014

Adidas Financial Report

Responsibility Statement

To the best of our knowledge, and in accordance with the applicable reporting principles, the consolidated financial statements give a true and fair view of the assets, liabilities, financial position and profit or loss of the Group, and the Group Management Report, which has been combined with the Management Report of adidas AG, includes a fair review of the development and performance of the business and the position of the Group, together with a description of the material opportunities and risks associated with the expected development of the Group.

Herzogenaurach, February 14, 2014

HERBERT HAINER
CEO

ROLAND AUSCHEL
Global Sales

GLENN BENNETT
Global Operations

ROBIN J. STALKER
CFO

ERICH STAMMINGER
Global Brands

ADIDAS

Auditor's Report

We have audited the consolidated financial statements prepared by adidas AG, Herzogenaurach, comprising the statement of financial position, income statement, statement of comprehensive income, statement of changes in equity, statement of cash flows and the notes, together with the management report of the Company and the Group for the business year from January 1 to December 31, 2013. The preparation of the consolidated financial statements and the Group management report in accordance with IFRS, as adopted by the EU, and the additional requirements of German commercial law pursuant to § 315a (1) HGB (Handelsgesetzbuch – "German Commercial Code") is the responsibility of the Company's Executive Board. Our responsibility is to express an opinion on the consolidated financial statements and on the Group management report based on our audit.

We conducted our audit of the consolidated financial statements in accordance with § 317 HGB and German generally accepted standards for the audit of financial statements promulgated by the Institut der Wirtschaftsprüfer (Institute of Public Auditors in Germany) (IDW). Those standards require that we plan and perform the audit such that misstatements materially affecting the presentation of the net assets, financial position and profit or loss in the consolidated financial statements in accordance with the applicable financial reporting framework and in the Group management report are detected with reasonable assurance. Knowledge of the business activities and the economic and legal environment of the Group and expectations as to possible misstatements are taken into account in the determination of audit procedures. The effectiveness of the accounting-related internal control system and the evidence supporting the disclosures in the consolidated financial statements and the Group management report are examined primarily on a test basis within the framework of the audit. The audit includes assessing the annual financial statements of the entities included in consolidation, the determination of entities to be included in consolidation, the accounting and consolidation principles used and significant estimates made by management, as well as evaluating the overall presentation of the consolidated financial statements and Group management report. We believe that our audit provides a reasonable basis for our opinion.

Our audit has not led to any reservations.

In our opinion, based on the findings of our audit, the consolidated financial statements comply with IFRS, as adopted by the EU, and the additional requirements of German commercial law pursuant to § 315a (1) HGB and give a true and fair view of the net assets, financial position and profit or loss of the Group in accordance with these requirements. The Group management report is consistent with the consolidated financial statements and as a whole provides a suitable view of the Group's position and suitably presents the opportunities and risks of future development.

Munich, February 14, 2014

KPMG AG
Wirtschaftsprüfungsgesellschaft

(Original German version signed by:)

Braun   Wolper
Wirtschaftsprüfer   Wirtschaftsprüfer
(German Public Auditor)   (German Public Auditor)

Consolidated Statement of Financial Position

.. ∕ **adidas AG Consolidated Statement of Financial Position (IFRS)** (€ in millions)

	Note	Dec. 31, 2013	Dec. 31, 2012	Change in %
ASSETS				
Cash and cash equivalents	4	1,587	1,670	(5.0)
Short-term financial assets	5	41	265	(84.4)
Accounts receivable	6	1,809	1,688	7.2
Other current financial assets	7	183	192	(5.1)
Inventories	8	2,634	2,486	5.9
Income tax receivables	33	86	76	12.7
Other current assets	9	506	489	3.7
Assets classified as held for sale	10	11	11	1.2
Total current assets		**6,857**	**6,877**	**(0.3)**
Property, plant and equipment	11	1,238	1,095	13.1
Goodwill	12	1,204	1,281	(6.1)
Trademarks	13	1,419	1,484	(4.4)
Other intangible assets	13	164	167	(2.3)
Long-term financial assets	14	120	112	7.9
Other non-current financial assets	15	30	21	40.6
Deferred tax assets	33	486	528	(8.0)
Other non-current assets	16	81	86	(4.8)
Total non-current assets		**4,742**	**4,774**	**(0.7)**
Total assets		**11,599**	**11,651**	**(0.4)**
LIABILITIES AND EQUITY				
Short-term borrowings	17	681	280	143.3
Accounts payable		1,825	1,790	1.9
Other current financial liabilities	18	113	83	37.4
Income taxes	33	240	275	(12.6)
Other current provisions	19	450	563	(20.1)
Current accrued liabilities	20	1,147	1,084	5.9
Other current liabilities	21	276	299	(8.0)
Total current liabilities		**4,732**	**4,374**	**8.2**
Long-term borrowings	17	653	1,207	(45.9)
Other non-current financial liabilities	22	22	17	28.3
Pensions and similar obligations	23	255	251	1.4
Deferred tax liabilities	33	338	368	(8.2)
Other non-current provisions	19	25	69	(63.4)
Non-current accrued liabilities	20	64	40	59.3
Other non-current liabilities	24	29	34	(11.6)
Total non-current liabilities		**1,386**	**1,986**	**(30.2)**
Share capital		209	209	—
Reserves		321	641	(49.8)
Retained earnings		4,959	4,454	11.3
Shareholders' equity	25	**5,489**	**5,304**	**3.5**
Non-controlling interests	26	(8)	(13)	37.9
Total equity		**5,481**	**5,291**	**3.6**
Total liabilities and equity		**11,599**	**11,651**	**(0.4)**

Rounding differences may arise in percentages and totals.
The accompanying notes are an integral part of these consolidated financial statements.

ADIDAS

Consolidated Income Statement

.. / **adidas AG Consolidated Income Statement (IFRS)** (€ in millions)

	Note	Year ending Dec. 31, 2013	Year ending Dec. 31, 2012	Change
Net sales	35	14,492	14,883	(2.6%)
Cost of sales		7,352	7,780	(5.5%)
Gross profit		**7,140**	**7,103**	**0.5%**
(% of net sales)		49.3%	47.7%	1.5pp
Royalty and commission income		104	105	(1.2%)
Other operating income	29	143	127	12.8%
Other operating expenses	11, 13, 30	6,133	6,150	(0.3%)
(% of net sales)		42.3%	41.3%	1.0pp
Goodwill impairment losses	12	52	265	(80.2%)
Operating profit		**1,202**	**920**	**30.6%**
(% of net sales)		8.3%	6.2%	2.1pp
Financial income	32	26	36	(28.2%)
Financial expenses	32	94	105	(11.2%)
Income before taxes		**1,134**	**851**	**33.3%**
(% of net sales)		7.8%	5.7%	2.1pp
Income taxes	33	344	327	5.3%
(% of income before taxes)		30.4%	38.4%	(8.0pp)
Net income		**790**	**524**	**50.7%**
(% of net sales)		5.4%	3.5%	1.9pp
Net income attributable to shareholders		**787**	**526**	**49.3%**
(% of net sales)		5.4%	3.5%	1.9pp
Net income attributable to non-controlling interests		**3**	**(2)**	**—**
Basic earnings per share (in €)	34	3.76	2.52	49.3%
Diluted earnings per share (in €)	34	3.76	2.52	49.3%

Rounding differences may arise in percentages and totals.
The accompanying notes are an integral part of these consolidated financial statements.

ADIDAS

Consolidated Statement of Comprehensive Income

.. ⁄ **adidas AG Consolidated Statement of Comprehensive Income (IFRS)** (€ in millions)

	Note	Year ending Dec. 31, 2013	Year ending Dec. 31, 2012
Net income after taxes		**790**	**524**
Items of other comprehensive income that will not be reclassified subsequently to profit or loss			
Remeasurements of defined benefit plans (IAS 19), net of tax [1]	23	5	(26)
Subtotal of items of other comprehensive income that will not be reclassified subsequently to profit or loss		**5**	**(26)**
Items of other comprehensive income that will be reclassified subsequently to profit or loss when specific conditions are met			
Net loss on cash flow hedges, net of tax	28	(13)	(134)
Currency translation differences		(309)	(43)
Subtotal of items of other comprehensive income that will be reclassified subsequently to profit or loss when specific conditons are met		**(322)**	**(177)**
Other comprehensive income		**(317)**	**(203)**
Total comprehensive income		**473**	**321**
Attributable to shareholders of adidas AG		467	321
Attributable to non-controlling interests		6	(0)

1) Includes actuarial gains or losses relating to defined benefit obligations, return on plan assets (excluding interest income) and the asset ceiling effect.
Rounding differences may arise in percentages and totals.
The accompanying notes are an integral part of these consolidated financial statements.

ADIDAS

Consolidated Statement of Changes in Equity

.. / **adidas AG Consolidated Statement of Changes in Equity (IFRS)** (€ in millions)

	Note	Share capital	Capital reserve
Balance at December 31, 2011		209	722
Net income recognised directly in equity			
Net income			
Total comprehensive income			
Dividend payment	25		
Acquisition of shares from non-controlling interest shareholders			
Convertible bond			55
Reclassifications of non-controlling interests in accordance with IAS 32	26		
Balance at December 31, 2012		209	777
Net income recognised directly in equity			
Net income			
Total comprehensive income			
Dividend payment	25		
Balance at December 31, 2013		209	777

1) Reserves for remeasurements of defined benefit plans (IAS 19), share option plans and acquisition of shares from non-controlling interest shareholders.
Rounding differences may arise in percentages and totals.
The accompanying notes are an integral part of these consolidated financial statements.

	Cumulative currency translation differences	Hedging reserves	Other reserves [1]	Retained earnings	Total share-holders' equity	Non-controlling interests	Total equity
	(6)	113	(38)	4,137	5,137	(9)	5,128
	(45)	(134)	(26)		(205)	2	(203)
				526	526	(2)	524
	(45)	(134)	(26)	526	321	(0)	321
				(209)	(209)	(3)	(212)
			(0)		(0)	(1)	(1)
					55		55
				0	0		0
	(51)	(21)	(64)	4,454	5,304	(13)	5,291
	(312)	(13)	5		(320)	3	(317)
				787	787	3	790
	(312)	(13)	5	787	467	6	473
				(282)	(282)	(1)	(283)
	(363)	(34)	(59)	4,959	5,489	(8)	5,481

Consolidated Statement of Cash Flows

.. ╱ adidas AG Consolidated Statement of Cash Flows (IFRS) (€ in millions)

	Note	Year ending Dec. 31, 2013	Year ending Dec. 31, 2012
Operating activities:			
Income before taxes		1,134	851
Adjustments for:			
Depreciation, amortisation and impairment losses	11, 12, 13, 30, 32	346	536
Reversals of impairment losses	29	(2)	(2)
Unrealised foreign exchange losses/(gains), net		10	(26)
Interest income	32	(25)	(35)
Interest expense	32	73	97
Losses on sale of property, plant and equipment, net		7	12
Other non-cash income	29, 30	(1)	(3)
Operating profit before working capital changes		**1,542**	**1,430**
Increase in receivables and other assets		(309)	(135)
(Increase)/decrease in inventories		(301)	23
Increase in accounts payable and other liabilities		164	94
Cash generated from operations before interest and taxes		**1,096**	**1,412**
Interest paid		(68)	(90)
Income taxes paid		(394)	(380)
Net cash generated from operating activities		**634**	**942**
Investing activities:			
Purchase of trademarks and other intangible assets		(52)	(58)
Proceeds from sale of trademarks and other intangible assets		1	1
Purchase of property, plant and equipment		(427)	(376)
Proceeds from sale of property, plant and equipment		4	19
Acquisition of subsidiaries and other business units net of cash acquired	3	—	(57)
Proceeds from disposal of subsidiaries net of cash		—	14
Proceeds from sale of short-term financial assets		226	195
(Purchase of)/proceeds from investments and other long-term assets		(20)	10
Interest received		25	35
Net cash used in investing activities		**(243)**	**(217)**
Financing activities:			
Repayments of long-term borrowings		—	(3)
Proceeds from issue of a convertible bond	17	—	496
Repayments of finance lease obligations		(2)	—
Dividend paid to shareholders of adidas AG	25	(282)	(209)
Dividend paid to non-controlling interest shareholders		(1)	(3)
Acquisition of non-controlling interests		—	(8)
Proceeds from short-term borrowings		67	—
Repayments of short-term borrowings		(221)	(231)
Net cash (used in)/generated from financing activities		**(439)**	**42**
Effect of exchange rates on cash		**(35)**	**(3)**
(Decrease)/increase of cash and cash equivalents		(83)	764
Cash and cash equivalents at beginning of the year	4	1,670	906
Cash and cash equivalents at the end of period	4	**1,587**	**1,670**

Rounding differences may arise in percentages and totals.
The accompanying notes are an integral part of these consolidated financial statements.

Samsung Financial Report

FINANCIAL STATEMENTS

Report of Independent Auditors

To the Board of Directors and
Shareholders of
Samsung Electronics Co., Ltd.

We have audited the accompanying consolidated financial statements of Samsung Electronics Co., Ltd. and its subsidiaries (collectively referred to as the "Company"), which comprise the consolidated statements of financial position as of December 31, 2012, December 31, 2011, and January 1, 2011, the related consolidated statements of income, comprehensive income, changes in equity and cash flow for the years ended December 31, 2012 and 2011, and the related notes. These financial statements are the responsibility of the Company's management. Our responsibility is to express an opinion on these consolidated financial statements based on our audit. We did not audit the financial statements of certain subsidiaries, whose financial statements represents 7.2% and 7.6% of the consolidated total assets as of December 31, 2012 and 2011, respectively, and 22.1% and 20.4% of the consolidated total sales for the year then ended, respectively. Those financial statements were audited by other auditors whose reports thereon have been furnished to us, and our opinion expressed herein, insofar as it relates to the amounts included for those subsidiaries, is based solely on the reports of the other auditors.

SAMSUNG

We conducted our audits in accordance with auditing standards generally accepted in the Republic of Korea. Those standards require that we plan and perform the audit to obtain reasonable assurance about whether the financial statements are free of material misstatement. An audit includes examining, on a test basis, evidence supporting the amounts and disclosures in the financial statements. An audit also includes assessing the accounting principles used and significant estimates made by management, as well as evaluating the overall financial statement presentation. We believe that our audits and the reports of the other auditors provide a reasonable basis for our opinion.

In our opinion, based on our audits, the consolidated financial statements referred to above present fairly, in all material respects, the financial position of Samsung Electronics Co., Ltd. and its subsidiaries as of December 31, 2012, December 31, 2011, and January 1, 2011, and their financial performance and cash flows for the years ended December 31, 2012 and 2011, in accordance with International Financial Reporting Standards as adopted by the Republic of Korea.

Samil PricewaterhouseCoopers
Seoul, Korea
February 1, 2013

This report is effective as of February 1, 2013, the audit report date. Certain subsequent events or circumstances, which may occur between the audit report date and the time of reading this report, could have a material impact on the accompanying financial statements and notes thereto. Accordingly, the readers of the audit report should understand that there is a possibility that the above audit report may have to be revised to reflect the impact of such subsequent events or circumstances, if any.

CONSOLIDATED STATEMENTS OF FINANCIAL POSITION

Samsung Electronics Co., Ltd. and its subsidiaries

(In millions of Korean won, in thousands of U.S dollars (Note 2.28))

	Notes	December 31 2012 KRW	December 31 2011 KRW	January 1 2011 KRW	December 31 2012 USD	December 31 2011 USD	January 1 2011 USD
Assets							
Current Assets							
Cash and cash equivalents	4, 6, 7	18,791,460	14,691,761	9,791,419	17,544,076	13,716,517	9,141,461
Short-term financial instruments	5, 6, 7	17,397,937	11,529,905	11,529,392	16,243,056	10,764,546	10,764,067
Available-for-sale financial assets	6, 9	1,258,874	655,969	1,159,152	1,175,309	612,426	1,082,207
Trade and other receivables	6, 7, 10	26,674,596	24,153,028	21,308,834	24,903,927	22,549,741	19,894,346
Advances		1,674,428	1,436,288	1,302,428	1,563,279	1,340,947	1,215,972
Prepaid expenses		2,262,234	2,329,463	2,200,739	2,112,066	2,174,832	2,054,653
Inventories	11	17,747,413	15,716,715	13,364,524	16,569,333	14,673,434	12,477,382
Other current assets	6	1,462,075	988,934	746,101	1,365,023	923,288	696,575
Total current assets		**87,269,017**	**71,502,063**	**61,402,589**	**81,476,069**	**66,755,731**	**57,326,663**
Non-current assets							
Available-for-sale financial assets	6, 9	5,229,175	3,223,598	3,040,206	4,882,060	3,009,614	2,838,396
Associates and joint ventures	12	8,785,489	9,204,169	8,335,290	8,202,305	8,593,193	7,781,990
Property, plant and equipment	13	68,484,743	62,043,951	52,964,594	63,938,701	57,925,451	49,448,785
Intangible assets	14	3,729,705	3,355,236	2,779,439	3,482,126	3,132,514	2,594,939
Deposits	6	814,693	791,863	655,662	760,613	739,299	612,139
Long-term prepaid expenses		3,515,479	3,454,205	3,544,572	3,282,120	3,224,914	3,309,282
Deferred income tax assets	29	2,516,080	1,783,086	1,144,068	2,349,062	1,664,724	1,068,124
Other non-current assets	6	727,189	442,092	442,383	678,919	412,746	413,018
Total assets		**181,071,570**	**155,800,263**	**134,308,803**	**169,051,975**	**145,458,186**	**125,393,336**

The accompanying notes are an integral part of these financial statements.

(In millions of Korean won, in thousands of U.S dollars (Note 2.28))

	Notes	December 31 2012 KRW	December 31 2011 KRW	January 1 2011 KRW	December 31 2012 USD	December 31 2011 USD	January 1 2011 USD
Liabilities and Equity							
Current liabilities							
Trade and other payables	6	16,889,350	18,509,490	16,049,800	15,768,229	17,280,823	14,984,409
Short-term borrowings	6,15	8,443,752	9,653,722	8,429,721	7,883,253	9,012,904	7,870,153
Advance received		1,517,672	1,450,733	883,585	1,416,928	1,354,433	824,932
Withholdings		966,374	1,715,070	1,052,555	902,226	1,601,223	982,686
Accrued expenses	6	9,495,156	7,823,728	7,102,427	8,864,864	7,304,386	6,630,965
Income tax payable		3,222,934	1,262,798	2,051,452	3,008,994	1,178,973	1,915,276
Current portion of long-term borrowings and debentures	6, 15, 16	999,010	30,292	1,123,934	932,695	28,281	1,049,327
Provisions	18	5,054,853	3,514,536	2,917,919	4,719,310	3,281,240	2,724,226
Other current liabilities	6	343,951	358,645	333,328	321,120	334,839	311,202
Total current liabilities		**46,933,052**	**44,319,014**	**39,944,721**	**43,817,619**	**41,377,102**	**37,293,176**
Non-current liabilities							
Non-current liabilities							
Long-term trade and other payables	6	1,165,881	1,024,804	1,072,661	1,088,489	956,777	1,001,457
Debentures	6, 16	1,829,374	1,280,124	587,338	1,707,940	1,195,149	548,350
Long-term borrowings	6, 15	3,623,028	3,682,472	634,381	3,382,530	3,438,028	592,271
Retirement benefit liabilities	17	1,729,939	1,119,188	823,486	1,615,105	1,044,896	768,823
Deferred income tax liabilities	29	3,429,467	2,333,442	1,618,523	3,201,818	2,178,547	1,511,085
Provisions	18	408,529	363,223	295,357	381,411	339,112	275,751
Other non-current liabilities	6	472,094	364,366	154,700	440,757	340,180	144,431
Total liabilities		**59,591,364**	**54,486,633**	**45,131,167**	**55,635,669**	**50,869,791**	**42,135,344**
Equity attributable to owners of the parent							
Preferred stock	20	119,467	119,467	119,467	111,537	111,537	111,537
Common stock	20	778,047	778,047	778,047	726,400	726,400	726,400
Share premium	20	4,403,893	4,403,893	4,403,893	4,111,561	4,111,561	4,111,561
Retained earnings	21	119,985,689	97,622,872	85,071,444	112,020,996	91,142,630	79,424,371
Other components of equity	23	(8,193,044)	(5,833,896)	(4,931,290)	(7,649,185)	(5,446,639)	(4,603,949)
Non-controlling interests		**4,386,154**	**4,223,247**	**3,736,075**	**4,094,997**	**3,942,906**	**3,488,072**
Total equity		**121,480,206**	**101,313,630**	**89,177,636**	**113,416,306**	**94,588,395**	**83,257,992**
Total liabilities and equity		**181,071,570**	**155,800,263**	**134,308,803**	**169,051,975**	**145,458,186**	**125,393,336**

The accompanying notes are an integral part of these financial statements.

SAMSUNG

CONSOLIDATED STATEMENTS OF INCOME

Samsung Electronics Co., Ltd. and its subsidiaries

(In millions of Korean won, in thousands of U.S dollars (Note 2.28))

	Notes	For the year ended December 31,			
		2012	2011	2012	2011
		KRW	KRW	USD	USD
Revenue		201,103,613	165,001,771	187,754,283	154,048,895
Cost of sales	25	126,651,931	112,145,120	118,244,730	104,700,887
Gross profit		74,451,682	52,856,651	69,509,553	49,348,008
Selling, general and administrative expenses	25, 26	45,402,344	37,212,360	42,388,520	34,742,191
Operating profit		29,049,338	15,644,291	27,121,033	14,605,817
Other non-operating income	27	1,552,989	2,251,019	1,449,901	2,101,596
Other non-operating expense	27	1,576,025	1,612,690	1,471,408	1,505,639
Share of profit or loss of associates and joint ventures	12	986,611	1,399,194	921,119	1,306,315
Finance income	28	7,836,554	7,403,525	7,316,361	6,912,076
Finance expense	28	7,934,450	7,893,421	7,407,758	7,369,453
Profit before income tax		29,915,017	17,191,918	27,929,248	16,050,712
Income tax expense	29	6,069,732	3,432,875	5,666,822	3,204,999
Profit for the year		23,845,285	13,759,043	22,262,426	12,845,713
Profit attributable to owners of the parent		23,185,375	13,382,645	21,646,322	12,494,300
Profit attributable to non-controlling interests		659,910	376,398	616,104	351,413
Earnings per share for profit attributable to the owners of the parent	30				
- Basic (in Korean won and US dollars)		154,020	89,229	143.80	83.31
- Diluted (in Korean won and US dollars)		153,950	89,146	143.73	83.23

The accompanying notes are an integral part of these financial statements.

CONSOLIDATED STATEMENTS OF COMPREHENSIVE INCOME

Samsung Electronics Co., Ltd. and its subsidiaries

(In millions of Korean won, in thousands of U.S dollars (Note 2.28))

	Notes	For the year ended December 31,			
		2012	2011	2012	2011
		KRW	KRW	USD	USD
Profit for the year		23,845,285	13,759,043	22,262,426	12,845,713
Items not to be reclassified subsequently to profit or loss :					
Remeasurement effect of employee benefit, net of tax		(504,120)	(385,214)	(470,656)	(359,643)
Items to be reclassified subsequently to profit or loss :	17, 23				
Changes in value of available-for-sale financial assets, net of tax	23	962,184	(572,028)	898,314	(534,057)
Share of associates and joint ventures, net of tax	23	(350,491)	(113,898)	(327,225)	(106,337)
Foreign currency translation, net of tax	23	(1,824,653)	183,655	(1,703,532)	171,463
Consolidated comprehensive income		22,128,205	12,871,558	20,659,327	12,017,139
Consolidated comprehensive income attributable to :					
Owners of the parent		21,499,343	12,439,116	20,072,209	11,613,403
Non-controlling interests		628,862	432,442	587,118	403,736

The accompanying notes are an integral part of these financial statements.

CONSOLIDATED STATEMENTS OF CHANGES IN EQUITY

Samsung Electronics Co., Ltd. and its subsidiaries

(In millions of Korean won)

2011 KRW	Notes	Preferred stock	Common stock	Share premium	Retained earnings	Other reserves	Equity attributable to owners of the parent	Non-controlling interests	Total
Balance at January 1, 2011		119,467	778,047	4,403,893	85,014,550	(4,726,398)	85,589,559	3,759,532	89,349,091
Cumulative effect of change in accounting policy	2	-	-	-	56,894	(204,892)	(147,998)	(23,457)	(171,455)
Revised balance at January 1, 2011		119,467	778,047	4,403,893	85,071,444	(4,931,290)	85,441,561	3,736,075	89,177,636
Profit for the year		-	-	-	13,382,645	-	13,382,645	376,398	13,759,043
Available-for-sale financial assets, net of tax,	9, 23	-	-	-	-	(567,186)	(567,186)	(4,842)	(572,028)
Share of associates and joint ventures, net of tax	12	-	-	-	-	(113,898)	(113,898)	-	(113,898)
Foreign currency translation, net of tax		-	-	-	-	123,434	123,434	60,221	183,655
Remeasurement effect of employee benefit, net of tax	17	-	-	-	-	(385,879)	(385,879)	665	(385,214)
Total comprehensive income		-	-	-	13,382,645	(943,529)	12,439,116	432,442	12,871,558
Dividends	22	-	-	-	(824,478)	-	(824,478)	(156,388)	(980,866)
Capital transaction under common control		-	-	-	-	(108,840)	(108,840)	78,155	(30,685)
Effect of business combination		-	-	-	-	-	-	131,564	131,564
Disposal of treasury stock	23	-	-	-	-	288,773	288,773	-	288,773
Stock option activities	24	-	-	-	-	(73,008)	(73,008)	-	(73,008)
Others		-	-	-	(6,739)	(66,002)	(72,741)	1,399	(71,342)
Total transactions with owners		-	-	-	(831,217)	40,923	(790,294)	54,730	(735,564)
Balance at December 31, 2011		119,467	778,047	4,403,893	97,622,872	(5,833,896)	97,090,383	4,223,247	101,313,630

The accompanying notes are an integral part of these consolidated financial statements.

(In thousands of U.S dollars (Note 2.28))

2011 USD	Notes	Preferred stock	Common stock	Share premium	Retained earnings	Other reserves	Equity attributable to owners of the parent	Non-controlling interests	Total
Balance at January 1, 2011		111,537	726,400	4,111,561	79,371,254	(4,412,658)	79,908,094	3,509,972	83,418,066
Cumulative effect of change in accounting policy	2	-	-	-	53,117	(191,291)	(138,174)	(21,900)	(160,074)
Revised balance at January 1, 2011		111,537	726,400	4,111,561	79,424,371	(4,603,949)	79,769,920	3,488,072	83,257,992
Profit for the year		-	-	-	12,494,300	-	12,494,300	351,413	12,845,713
Available-for-sale financial assets, net of tax,	9, 23	-	-	-	-	(529,536)	(529,536)	(4,521)	(534,057)
Share of associates and joint ventures, net of tax	12	-	-	-	-	(106,337)	(106,337)	-	(106,337)
Foreign currency translation, net of tax		-	-	-	-	115,240	115,240	56,224	171,464
Remeasurement effect of employee benefit, net of tax	17	-	-	-	-	(360,264)	(360,264)	621	(359,643)
Total comprehensive income		-	-	-	12,494,300	(880,897)	11,613,403	403,737	12,017,140
Dividends	22	-	-	-	(769,749)	-	(769,749)	(146,007)	(915,756)
Capital transaction under common control		-	-	-	-	(101,615)	(101,615)	72,967	(28,648)
Effect of business combination		-	-	-	-	-	-	122,831	122,831
Disposal of treasury stock	23	-	-	-	-	269,604	269,604	-	269,604
Stock option activities	24	-	-	-	-	(68,162)	(68,162)	-	(68,162)
Others		-	-	-	(6,292)	(61,620)	(67,912)	1,306	(66,606)
Total transactions with owners		-	-	-	(776,041)	38,207	(737,834)	51,097	(686,737)
Balance at December 31, 2011		111,537	726,400	4,111,561	91,142,630	(5,446,639)	90,645,489	3,942,906	94,588,395

The accompanying notes are an integral part of these consolidated financial statements.

(In millions of Korean won)

2012 KRW	Notes	Preferred stock	Common stock	Share premium	Retained earnings	Other reserves	Equity attributable to owners of the parent	Non-controlling interests	Total
Balance at January 1, 2012		119,467	778,047	4,403,893	97,622,872	(5,833,896)	97,090,383	4,223,247	101,313,630
Profit for the year		-	-	-	23,185,375	-	23,185,375	659,910	23,845,285
Available-for-sale financial assets, net of tax	9, 23	-	-	-	-	960,688	960,688	1,496	962,184
Share of associates and joint ventures, net of tax	12	-	-	-	-	(350,491)	(350,491)	-	(350,491)
Foreign currency translation, net of tax		-	-	-	-	(1,789,877)	(1,789,877)	(34,776)	(1,824,653)
Remeasurement effect of employee benefit, net of tax	17	-	-	-	-	(506,351)	(506,351)	2,231	(504,120)
Total comprehensive income		-	-	-	23,185,375	(1,686,031)	21,499,344	628,861	22,128,205
Dividends	22	-	-	-	(827,501)	-	(827,501)	(373,632)	(1,201,133)
Capital transaction under common control		-	-	-	-	(1,089,835)	(1,089,835)	(104,395)	(1,194,230)
Effect of business combination		-	-	-	-	-	-	12,844	12,844
Disposal of treasury stock	23	-	-	-	-	455,377	455,377	-	455,377
Stock option activities	24	-	-	-	-	(33,071)	(33,071)	-	(33,071)
Others		-	-	-	4,943	(5,588)	(645)	(771)	(1,416)
Total transactions with owners		-	-	-	(822,558)	(673,117)	(1,495,675)	(465,954)	(1,961,629)
Balance at December 31, 2012		119,467	778,047	4,403,893	119,985,689	(8,193,044)	117,094,052	4,386,154	121,480,206

The accompanying notes are an integral part of these consolidated financial statements.

(In thousands of U.S dollars (Note 2.28))

2012 USD	Notes	Preferred stock	Common stock	Share premium	Retained earnings	Other reserves	Equity attributable to owners of the parent	Non-controlling interests	Total
Balance at January 1, 2012		111,537	726,400	4,111,561	91,142,630	(5,446,639)	90,645,489	3,942,906	94,588,395
Profit for the year		-	-	-	21,646,322	-	21,646,322	616,104	22,262,426
Available-for-sale financial assets, net of tax	9, 23	-	-	-	-	896,917	896,917	1,397	898,314
Share of associates and joint ventures, net of tax	12	-	-	-	-	(327,225)	(327,225)	-	(327,225)
Foreign currency translation, net of tax		-	-	-	-	(1,671,064)	(1,671,064)	(32,468)	(1,703,532)
Remeasurement effect of employee benefit, net of tax	17	-	-	-	-	(472,739)	(472,739)	2,083	(470,656)
Total comprehensive income		-	-	-	21,646,322	(1,574,111)	20,072,211	587,116	20,659,327
Dividends	22	-	-	-	(772,571)	-	(772,571)	(348,830)	(1,121,401)
Capital transaction under common control		-	-	-	-	(1,017,491)	(1,017,491)	(97,466)	(1,114,957)
Effect of business combination		-	-	-	-	-	-	11,991	11,991
Disposal of treasury stock	23	-	-	-	-	425,149	425,149	-	425,149
Stock option activities	24	-	-	-	-	(30,876)	(30,876)	-	(30,876)
Others		-	-	-	4,615	(5,217)	(602)	(720)	(1,322)
Total transactions with owners		-	-	-	(767,956)	(628,435)	(1,396,391)	(435,025)	(1,831,416)
Balance at December 31, 2012		111,537	726,400	4,111,561	112,020,996	(7,649,185)	109,321,309	4,094,997	113,416,306

The accompanying notes are an integral part of these consolidated financial statements.

SAMSUNG

CONSOLIDATE STATEMENTS OF CASH FLOWS

Samsung Electronics Co., Ltd. and its subsidiaries

(In millions of Korean won, in thousands of U.S dollars (Note 2.28))

	Notes	For the year ended December 31,			
		2012	2011	2012	2011
		KRW	KRW	USD	USD
Cash flows from operating activities					
Profit for the year		23,845,285	13,759,043	22,262,426	12,845,713
Adjustments	31	22,759,559	16,450,629	21,248,771	15,358,630
Changes in operating assets and liabilities	31	(5,777,949)	4,057,345	(5,394,406)	(3,788,017)
Cash flows from operating activities		40,826,895	26,152,327	38,116,791	24,416,326
Interest received		789,397	755,859	736,997	705,685
Interest paid		(576,379)	(641,462)	(538,119)	(598,882)
Dividend received		1,112,940	628,585	1,039,063	586,859
Income tax paid		(4,180,044)	3,977,408	(3,902,572)	(3,713,385)
Net cash generated from operating activities		**37,972,809**	**22,917,901**	**35,452,160**	**21,396,603**
Cash flows from investing activities					
Net decrease (increase) in short-term financial instruments		(5,965,611)	75,666	(5,569,612)	70,643
Net decrease (increase) in short-term available-for-sale financial assets		(589,072)	518,479	(549,969)	484,062
Proceeds from disposal of long-term available-for-sale financial assets		106,208	415,096	99,158	387,542
Acquisition of long-term available-for-sale financial assets		(870,249)	(419,678)	(812,482)	(391,820)
Proceeds from disposal of associates and joint ventures		41,091	306,804	38,363	286,438
Acquisition of associates and joint ventures		(279,022)	(403,538)	(260,500)	(376,751)
Disposal of property and equipment		644,062	379,878	601,309	354,662
Purchases of property and equipment		(22,965,271)	(21,965,678)	(21,440,828)	(20,507,588)
Disposal of intangible assets		61,497	9,703	57,415	9,059
Purchases of intangible assets		(650,884)	(663,678)	(607,678)	(619,623)
Proceeds from deposits		313,043	461,454	292,263	430,823
Payment for deposits		(347,746)	(594,067)	(324,662)	(554,633)
Cash outflows from business combination		(464,279)	(522,740)	(433,460)	(488,040)
Cash inflows from disposal of business		-	925,454	-	864,022
Others		(355,321)	364,281	(331,735)	340,100
Net cash used in investing activities		**(31,321,554)**	**(21,112,564)**	**(29,242,418)**	**(19,711,104)**
Cash flows from financing activities					
Net (repayment) proceeds from shortterm borrowings		(800,579)	977,315	(747,436)	912,440
Disposal of treasury stock		88,473	160,827	82,600	150,151
Proceeds from long-term borrowings and debentures		1,862,256	3,925,406	1,738,639	3,664,836
Repayment of long-term borrowings and debentures		(522,899)	(1,145,167)	(488,189)	(1,069,150)
Payment of dividends		(1,265,137)	(874,608)	(1,181,157)	(816,551)
Net increase (decrease) in Non-controlling interests		(1,200,134)	363,417	(1,120,469)	339,293
Others		(26,488)	(297,461)	(24,729)	(277,715)
Net cash provided by (used in) financing activities		**(1,864,508)**	**3,109,729**	**(1,740,741)**	**2,903,304**
Effect of exchange rate changes on cash and cash equivalents		(687,048)	(14,724)	(641,442)	(13,747)
Net increase (decrease) in cash and cash equivalents		**4,099,699**	**4,900,342**	**3,827,559**	**4,575,056**
Cash and cash equivalents					
Beginning of the year		14,691,761	9,791,419	13,716,517	9,141,461
End of the year		**18,791,460**	**14,691,761**	**17,544,076**	**13,716,517**

The accompanying notes are an integral part of these consolidated financial statements.

Appendix

B

Time Value of Money

Learning Objectives

CAP

CONCEPTUAL

C1 Describe the earning of interest and the concepts of present and future values. (p. B-2)

PROCEDURAL

P1 Apply present value concepts to a single amount by using interest tables. (p. B-4)

P2 Apply future value concepts to a single amount by using interest tables. (p. B-5)

P3 Apply present value concepts to an annuity by using interest tables. (p. B-6)

P4 Apply future value concepts to an annuity by using interest tables. (p. B-7)

The concepts of present and future values are important to modern business, including the preparation and analysis of financial statements. The purpose of this appendix is to explain, illustrate, and compute present and future values. This appendix applies these concepts with reference to both business and everyday activities.

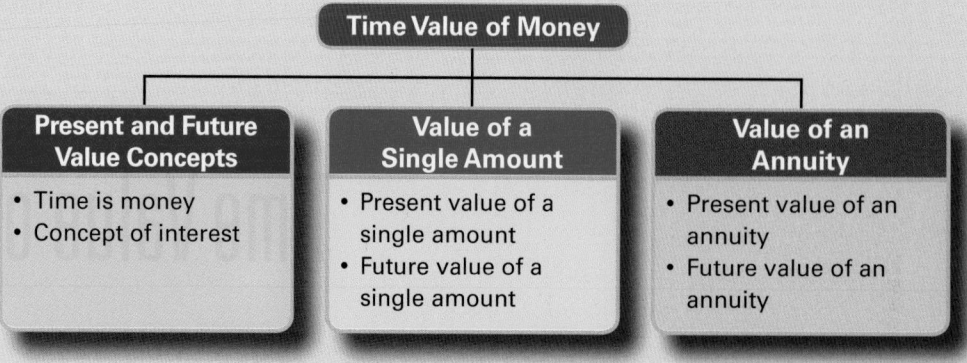

PRESENT AND FUTURE VALUE CONCEPTS

C1 Describe the earning of interest and the concepts of present and future values.

The old saying "Time is money" reflects the notion that as time passes, the values of our assets and liabilities change. This change is due to *interest,* which is a borrower's payment to the owner of an asset for its use. The most common example of interest is a savings account asset. As we keep a balance of cash in the account, it earns interest that the financial institution pays us. An example of a liability is a car loan. As we carry the balance of the loan, we accumulate interest costs on it. We must ultimately repay this loan with interest.

Present and future value computations enable us to measure or estimate the interest component of holding assets or liabilities over time. The present value computation is important when we want to know the value of future-day assets *today.* The future value computation is important when we want to know the value of present-day assets *at a future date.* The first section focuses on the present value of a single amount. The second section focuses on the future value of a single amount. Then both the present and future values of a series of amounts (called an *annuity*) are defined and explained.

Decision Insight

Keep That Job   Lottery winners often never work again. Kenny Dukes, a recent Georgia lottery winner, doesn't have that option. He is serving parole for burglary charges, and Georgia requires its parolees to be employed (or in school). For his lottery winnings, Dukes had to choose between $31 million in 30 annual payments or $16 million in one lump sum ($10.6 million after-tax); he chose the latter. ■

PRESENT VALUE OF A SINGLE AMOUNT

We graphically express the present value, called p, of a single future amount, called f, that is received or paid at a future date in Exhibit B.1.

EXHIBIT B.1

Present Value of a Single
Amount Diagram

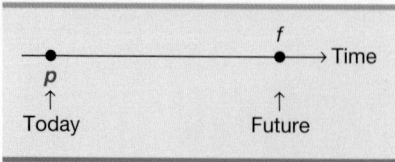

The formula to compute the present value of a single amount is shown in Exhibit B.2, where p = present value; f = future value; i = rate of interest per period; and n = number of periods. (Interest is also called the *discount,* and an interest rate is also called the *discount rate.*)

EXHIBIT B.2

Present Value of a Single
Amount Formula

$$p = \frac{f}{(1 + i)^n}$$

To illustrate present value concepts, assume that we need $220 one period from today. We want to know how much we must invest now, for one period, at an interest rate of 10% to provide for this $220. For this illustration, the p, or present value, is the unknown amount—the specifics are shown graphically as follows:

$$f = \$220$$
$$(i = 0.10)$$
$$p = ?$$

Conceptually, we know p must be less than $220. This is obvious from the answer to this question: Would we rather have $220 today or $220 at some future date? If we had $220 today, we could invest it and see it grow to something more than $220 in the future. Therefore, we would prefer the $220 today. This means that if we were promised $220 in the future, we would take less than $220 today. But how much less? To answer that question, we compute an estimate of the present value of the $220 to be received one period from now using the formula in Exhibit B.2 as follows:

$$p = \frac{f}{(1 + i)^n} = \frac{\$220}{(1 + 0.10)^1} = \$200$$

We interpret this result to say that given an interest rate of 10%, we are indifferent between $200 today or $220 at the end of one period.

We can also use this formula to compute the present value for *any number of periods.* To illustrate, consider a payment of $242 at the end of two periods at 10% interest. The present value of this $242 to be received two periods from now is computed as follows:

$$p = \frac{f}{(1 + i)^n} = \frac{\$242}{(1 + 0.10)^2} = \$200$$

Together, these results tell us we are indifferent between $200 today, or $220 one period from today, or $242 two periods from today given a 10% interest rate per period.

The number of periods (n) in the present value formula does not have to be expressed in years. Any period of time such as a day, a month, a quarter, or a year can be used. Whatever period is used, the interest rate (i) must be compounded for the same period. This means that if a situation expresses n in months and i equals 12% per year, then i is transformed into interest earned per month (or 1%). In this case, interest is said to be *compounded monthly.*

A present value table helps us with present value computations. It gives us present values (factors) for a variety of both interest rates (i) and periods (n). Each present value in a present value table assumes that the future value (f) equals 1. When the future value (f) is different from 1, we simply multiply the present value (p) from the table by that future value to give us the estimate. The formula used to construct a table of present values for a single future amount of 1 is shown in Exhibit B.3.

I will pay your allowance at the end of the month. Do you want to wait or receive its present value today?

EXHIBIT B.3

Present Value of 1 Formula

$$p = \frac{1}{(1 + i)^n}$$

This formula is identical to that in Exhibit B.2 except that f equals 1. Table B.1 at the end of this appendix is such a present value table. It is often called a **present value of 1 table**. A present value table involves three factors: p, i, and n. Knowing two of these three factors allows us to compute the third. (A fourth is f, but as already explained, we need only multiply the 1 used in the formula by f.) To illustrate the use of a present value table, consider three cases.

Case 1   (solve for p when knowing i and n). To show how we use a present value table, let's look again at how we estimate the present value of $220 (the f value) at the end of one period ($n = 1$) where the interest rate (i) is 10%. To solve this case, we go to the present value table (Table B.1) and look in the row for 1 period and in the column for 10% interest. Here we find a present value (p) of 0.9091 based on a future value of 1. This means, for instance, that $1 to be received one period from today at 10% interest is worth $0.9091 today. Since the future value in this case is not $1 but $220, we multiply the 0.9091 by $220 to get an answer of $200.

Case 2   (solve for n when knowing p and i). To illustrate, assume a $100,000 future value ($f$) that is worth $13,000 today ($p$) using an interest rate of 12% (i) but where n is unknown. In particular, we want to know how many periods (n) there are between the present value and the future value. To put this in context, it would fit a situation in which we want to retire with $100,000 but currently have only $13,000 that is earning a 12% return and we will be unable to save any additional money. How long will it be before we can retire? To answer this, we go to Table B.1 and look in the 12% interest column. Here we find a column of present values (p) based on a future value of 1. To use the present value table for this solution, we must divide $13,000 ($p$) by $100,000 ($f$), which equals 0.1300. This is necessary because *a present value table defines* f *equal to 1, and* p *as a fraction of 1*. We look for a value nearest to 0.1300 (p), which we find in the row for 18 periods (n). This means that the present value of $100,000 at the end of 18 periods at 12% interest is $13,000; alternatively stated, we must work 18 more years.

Case 3   (solve for i when knowing p and n). In this case, we have, say, a $120,000 future value ($f$) worth $60,000 today ($p$) when there are nine periods (n) between the present and future values, but the interest rate is unknown. As an example, suppose we want to retire with $120,000, but we have only $60,000 and we will be unable to save any additional money, yet we hope to retire in nine years. What interest rate must we earn to retire with $120,000 in nine years? To answer this, we go to the present value table (Table B.1) and look in the row for nine periods. To use the present value table, we must divide $60,000 ($p$) by $120,000 ($f$), which equals 0.5000. Recall that this step is necessary because a present value table defines f equal to 1 and p as a fraction of 1. We look for a value in the row for nine periods that is nearest to 0.5000 (p), which we find in the column for 8% interest (i). This means that the present value of $120,000 at the end of nine periods at 8% interest is $60,000 or, in our example, we must earn 8% annual interest to retire in nine years.

Quick Check   Answer — p. B-8

1. A company is considering an investment expected to yield $70,000 after six years. If this company demands an 8% return, how much is it willing to pay for this investment?

FUTURE VALUE OF A SINGLE AMOUNT

We must modify the formula for the present value of a single amount to obtain the formula for the future value of a single amount. In particular, we multiply both sides of the equation in Exhibit B.2 by $(1 + i)^n$ to get the result shown in Exhibit B.4.

EXHIBIT B.4

Future Value of a Single
Amount Formula

$$f = p \times (1 + i)^n$$

The future value (f) is defined in terms of p, i, and n. We can use this formula to determine that $200 ($p$) invested for 1 ($n$) period at an interest rate of 10% (i) yields a future value of $220 as follows:

$$f = p \times (1 + i)^n$$
$$= \$200 \times (1 + 0.10)^1$$
$$= \$220$$

This formula can also be used to compute the future value of an amount for *any number of periods* into the future. To illustrate, assume that $200 is invested for three periods at 10%. The future value of this $200 is $266.20, computed as follows:

P2 Apply future value concepts to a single amount by using interest tables.

$$f = p \times (1 + i)^n$$
$$= \$200 \times (1 + 0.10)^3$$
$$= \$266.20$$

A future value table makes it easier for us to compute future values (f) for many different combinations of interest rates (i) and time periods (n). Each future value in a future value table assumes the present value (p) is 1. As with a present value table, if the future amount is something other than 1, we simply multiply our answer by that amount. The formula used to construct a table of future values (factors) for a single amount of 1 is in Exhibit B.5.

$$f = (1 + i)^n$$

EXHIBIT B.5

Future Value of 1 Formula

Table B.2 at the end of this appendix shows a table of future values for a current amount of 1. This type of table is called a **future value of 1 table**.

There are some important relations between Tables B.1 and B.2. In Table B.2, for the row where $n = 0$, the future value is 1 for each interest rate. This is so because no interest is earned when time does not pass. We also see that Tables B.1 and B.2 report the same information but in a different manner. In particular, one table is simply the *inverse* of the other. To illustrate this inverse relation, let's say we invest $100 for a period of five years at 12% per year. How much do we expect to have after five years? We can answer this question using Table B.2 by finding the future value (f) of 1, for five periods from now, compounded at 12%. From that table we find $f = 1.7623$. If we start with $100, the amount it accumulates to after five years is $176.23 ($100 $\times$ 1.7623). We can alternatively use Table B.1. Here we find that the present value (p) of 1, discounted five periods at 12%, is 0.5674. Recall the inverse relation between present value and future value. This means that $p = 1/f$ (or equivalently, $f = 1/p$). We can compute the future value of $100 invested for five periods at 12% as follows: $f = \$100 \times (1/0.5674) = \$176.24$ (which equals the $176.23 just computed, except for a 1 cent rounding difference).

A future value table involves three factors: f, i, and n. Knowing two of these three factors allows us to compute the third. To illustrate, consider these three possible cases.

Case 1   (solve for f when knowing i and n). Our preceding example fits this case. We found that $100 invested for five periods at 12% interest accumulates to $176.24.

Case 2   (solve for n when knowing f and i). In this case, we have, say, $2,000 ($p$) and we want to know how many periods (n) it will take to accumulate to $3,000 ($f$) at 7% ($i$) interest. To answer this, we go to the future value table (Table B.2) and look in the 7% interest column. Here we find a column of future values (f) based on a present value of 1. To use a future value table, we must divide $3,000 ($f$) by $2,000 ($p$), which equals 1.500. This is necessary because *a future value table defines* p *equal to 1, and* f *as a multiple of 1.* We look for a value nearest to 1.50 (f), which we find in the row for six periods (n). This means that $2,000 invested for six periods at 7% interest accumulates to $3,000.

Case 3   (solve for i when knowing f and n). In this case, we have, say, $2,001 ($p$), and in nine years ($n$) we want to have $4,000 ($f$). What rate of interest must we earn to accomplish this? To answer that, we go to Table B.2 and search in the row for nine periods. To use a future value table, we must divide $4,000 ($f$) by $2,001 ($p$), which equals 1.9990. Recall that this is necessary because a future value table defines *p* equal to 1 and *f* as a multiple of 1. We look for a value nearest to 1.9990 (*f*), which we find in the column for 8% interest (*i*). This means that $2,001 invested for nine periods at 8% interest accumulates to $4,000.

Quick Check   Answer – p. B-8

2. Assume that you win a $150,000 cash sweepstakes. You decide to deposit this cash in an account earning 8% annual interest, and you plan to quit your job when the account equals $555,000. How many years will it be before you can quit working?

PRESENT VALUE OF AN ANNUITY

An *annuity* is a series of equal payments occurring at equal intervals. One example is a series of three annual payments of $100 each. An *ordinary annuity* is defined as equal end-of-period payments at equal intervals. An ordinary annuity of $100 for three periods and its present value (*p*) are illustrated in Exhibit B.6.

EXHIBIT B.6

Present Value of an Ordinary Annuity Diagram

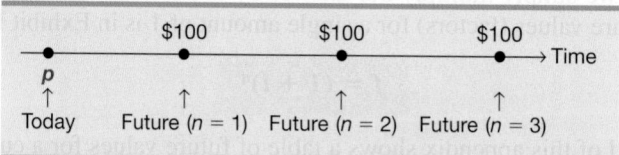

P3   Apply present value concepts to an annuity by using interest tables.

One way to compute the present value of an ordinary annuity is to find the present value of each payment using our present value formula from Exhibit B.3. We then add each of the three present values. To illustrate, let's look at three $100 payments at the end of each of the next three periods with an interest rate of 15%. Our present value computations are

$$p = \frac{\$100}{(1 + 0.15)^1} + \frac{\$100}{(1 + 0.15)^2} + \frac{\$100}{(1 + 0.15)^3} = \$228.32$$

This computation is identical to computing the present value of each payment (from Table B.1) and taking their sum or, alternatively, adding the values from Table B.1 for each of the three payments and multiplying their sum by the $100 annuity payment.

A more direct way is to use a present value of annuity table. Table B.3 at the end of this appendix is one such table. This table is called a **present value of an annuity of 1 table**. If we look at Table B.3 where *n* = 3 and *i* = 15%, we see the present value is 2.2832. This means that the present value of an annuity of 1 for three periods, with a 15% interest rate, equals 2.2832.

A present value of an annuity formula is used to construct Table B.3. It can also be constructed by adding the amounts in a present value of 1 table. To illustrate, we use Tables B.1 and B.3 to confirm this relation for the prior example:

From Table B.1		From Table B.3	
i = 15%, *n* = 1	0.8696		
i = 15%, *n* = 2	0.7561		
i = 15%, *n* = 3	0.6575		
Total	2.2832	*i* = 15%, *n* = 3	2.2832

We can also use business calculators or spreadsheet programs to find the present value of an annuity.

Decision Insight

Better Lucky Than Good   "I don't have good luck—I'm blessed," proclaimed Andrew "Jack" Whittaker, 55, a sewage treatment contractor, after winning the largest ever undivided jackpot in a U.S. lottery. Whittaker had to choose between $315 million in 30 annual installments or $170 million in one lump sum ($112 million after-tax). ■

Quick Check   Answer — p. B-8

3. A company is considering an investment paying $10,000 every six months for three years. The first payment would be received in six months. If this company requires an 8% annual return, what is the maximum amount it is willing to pay for this investment?

FUTURE VALUE OF AN ANNUITY

The future value of an *ordinary annuity* is the accumulated value of each annuity payment with interest as of the date of the final payment. To illustrate, let's consider the earlier annuity of three annual payments of $100. Exhibit B.7 shows the point in time for the future value (f). The first payment is made two periods prior to the point when future value is determined, and the final payment occurs on the future value date.

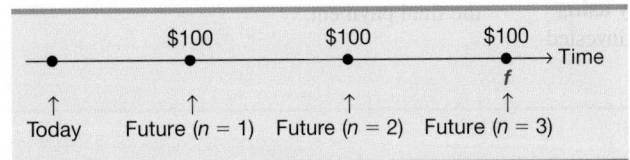

EXHIBIT B.7

Future Value of an Ordinary Annuity Diagram

One way to compute the future value of an annuity is to use the formula to find the future value of *each* payment and add them. If we assume an interest rate of 15%, our calculation is

$$f = \$100 \times (1 + 0.15)^2 + \$100 \times (1 + 0.15)^1 + \$100 \times (1 + 0.15)^0 = \$347.25$$

This is identical to using Table B.2 and summing the future values of each payment, or adding the future values of the three payments of 1 and multiplying the sum by $100.

A more direct way is to use a table showing future values of annuities. Such a table is called a **future value of an annuity of 1 table**. Table B.4 at the end of this appendix is one such table. Note that in Table B.4 when $n = 1$, the future values equal 1 ($f = 1$) for all rates of interest. This is so because such an annuity consists of only one payment and the future value is determined on the date of that payment—no time passes between the payment and its future value. The future value of an annuity formula is used to construct Table B.4. We can also construct it by adding the amounts from a future value of 1 table. To illustrate, we use Tables B.2 and B.4 to confirm this relation for the prior example:

P4   Apply future value concepts to an annuity by using interest tables.

From Table B.2		From Table B.4	
$i = 15\%, n = 0$	1.0000		
$i = 15\%, n = 1$	1.1500		
$i = 15\%, n = 2$	1.3225		
Total	3.4725	$i = 15\%, n = 3$	3.4725

Note that the future value in Table B.2 is 1.0000 when $n = 0$, but the future value in Table B.4 is 1.0000 when $n = 1$. Is this a contradiction? No. When $n = 0$ in Table B.2, the future value is determined on the date when a single payment occurs. This means that no interest is earned because no time has passed, and the future value equals the payment. Table B.4 describes annuities with equal payments occurring at the end of each period. When $n = 1$, the annuity has one payment, and its future value equals 1 on the date of its final and only payment. Again, no time passes between the payment and its future value date.

Quick Check

Answer — p. B-8

4. A company invests $45,000 per year for five years at 12% annual interest. Compute the value of this annuity investment at the end of five years.

Summary

C1 **Describe the earning of interest and the concepts of present and future values.** Interest is payment by a borrower to the owner of an asset for its use. Present and future value computations are a way for us to estimate the interest component of holding assets or liabilities over a period of time.

P1 **Apply present value concepts to a single amount by using interest tables.** The present value of a single amount received at a future date is the amount that can be invested now at the specified interest rate to yield that future value.

P2 **Apply future value concepts to a single amount by using interest tables.** The future value of a single amount invested at a specified rate of interest is the amount that would accumulate by the future date.

P3 **Apply present value concepts to an annuity by using interest tables.** The present value of an annuity is the amount that can be invested now at the specified interest rate to yield that series of equal periodic payments.

P4 **Apply future value concepts to an annuity by using interest tables.** The future value of an annuity invested at a specific rate of interest is the amount that would accumulate by the date of the final payment.

Guidance Answers to Quick Checks

1. $70,000 \times 0.6302 = \$44,114$ (use Table B.1, $i = 8\%$, $n = 6$).

2. $\$555,000/\$150,000 = 3.7000$; Table B.2 shows this value is not achieved until after 17 years at 8% interest.

3. $\$10,000 \times 5.2421 = \$52,421$ (use Table B.3, $i = 4\%$, $n = 6$).

4. $\$45,000 \times 6.3528 = \$285,876$ (use Table B.4, $i = 12\%$, $n = 5$).

---

connect

QUICK STUDY

QS B-1
Identifying interest rates in tables
C1

Assume that you must make future value estimates using the *future value of 1 table* (Table B.2). Which interest rate column do you use when working with the following rates?

1. 8% compounded quarterly
2. 12% compounded annually
3. 6% compounded semiannually
4. 12% compounded monthly

QS B-2
Interest rate on an investment   **P1**

Ken Francis is offered the possibility of investing $2,745 today and in return to receive $10,000 after 15 years. What is the annual rate of interest for this investment? (Use Table B.1.)

QS B-3
Number of periods of an investment   **P1**

Megan Brink is offered the possibility of investing $6,651 today at 6% interest per year in a desire to accumulate $10,000. How many years must Brink wait to accumulate $10,000? (Use Table B.1.)

QS B-4
Present value of an amount   **P1**

Flaherty is considering an investment that, if paid for immediately, is expected to return $140,000 five years from now. If Flaherty demands a 9% return, how much is she willing to pay for this investment?

QS B-5
Future value of an amount   **P2**

CII, Inc., invests $630,000 in a project expected to earn a 12% annual rate of return. The earnings will be reinvested in the project each year until the entire investment is liquidated 10 years later. What will the cash proceeds be when the project is liquidated?

Beene Distributing is considering a project that will return $150,000 annually at the end of each year for six years. If Beene demands an annual return of 7% and pays for the project immediately, how much is it willing to pay for the project?

QS B-6
Present value
of an annuity   P3

Claire Fitch is planning to begin an individual retirement program in which she will invest $1,500 at the end of each year. Fitch plans to retire after making 30 annual investments in the program earning a return of 10%. What is the value of the program on the date of the last payment?

QS B-7
Future value
of an annuity   P4

connect

EXERCISES

Bill Thompson expects to invest $10,000 at 12% and, at the end of a certain period, receive $96,463. How many years will it be before Thompson receives the payment? (Use Table B.2.)

Exercise B-1
Number of periods
of an investment   P2

Ed Summers expects to invest $10,000 for 25 years, after which he wants to receive $108,347. What rate of interest must Summers earn? (Use Table B.2.)

Exercise B-2
Interest rate on
an investment   P2

Jones expects an immediate investment of $57,466 to return $10,000 annually for eight years, with the first payment to be received one year from now. What rate of interest must Jones earn? (Use Table B.3.)

Exercise B-3
Interest rate on
an investment   P3

Keith Riggins expects an investment of $82,014 to return $10,000 annually for several years. If Riggins earns a return of 10%, how many annual payments will he receive? (Use Table B.3.)

Exercise B-4
Number of periods
of an investment   P3

Algoe expects to invest $1,000 annually for 40 years to yield an accumulated value of $154,762 on the date of the last investment. For this to occur, what rate of interest must Algoe earn? (Use Table B.4.)

Exercise B-5
Interest rate on
an investment   P4

Kate Beckwith expects to invest $10,000 annually that will earn 8%. How many annual investments must Beckwith make to accumulate $303,243 on the date of the last investment? (Use Table B.4.)

Exercise B-6
Number of periods
of an investment   P4

Sam Weber finances a new automobile by paying $6,500 cash and agreeing to make 40 monthly payments of $500 each, the first payment to be made one month after the purchase. The loan bears interest at an annual rate of 12%. What is the cost of the automobile?

Exercise B-7
Present value
of an annuity   P3

Spiller Corp. plans to issue 10%, 15-year, $500,000 par value bonds payable that pay interest semiannually on June 30 and December 31. The bonds are dated December 31, 2011, and are issued on that date. If the market rate of interest for the bonds is 8% on the date of issue, what will be the total cash proceeds from the bond issue?

Exercise B-8
Present value of bonds
P1 P3

McAdams Company expects to earn 10% per year on an investment that will pay $606,773 six years from now. Use Table B.1 to compute the present value of this investment. (Round the amount to the nearest dollar.)

Exercise B-9
Present value
of an amount   P1

Compute the amount that can be borrowed under each of the following circumstances:
1. A promise to repay $90,000 seven years from now at an interest rate of 6%.
2. An agreement made on February 1, 2011, to make three separate payments of $20,000 on February 1 of 2012, 2013, and 2014. The annual interest rate is 10%.

Exercise B-10
Present value of
an amount and
of an annuity   P1 P3

On January 1, 2011, a company agrees to pay $20,000 in three years. If the annual interest rate is 10%, determine how much cash the company can borrow with this agreement.

Exercise B-11
Present value
of an amount   P1

Exercise B-12
Present value
of an amount P1

Find the amount of money that can be borrowed today with each of the following separate debt agreements *a* through *f*. (Round amounts to the nearest dollar.)

Case	Single Future Payment	Number of Periods	Interest Rate
a.	$40,000	3	4%
b.	75,000	7	8
c.	52,000	9	10
d.	18,000	2	4
e.	63,000	8	6
f.	89,000	5	2

Exercise B-13
Present values of annuities
P3

C&H Ski Club recently borrowed money and agrees to pay it back with a series of six annual payments of $5,000 each. C&H subsequently borrows more money and agrees to pay it back with a series of four annual payments of $7,500 each. The annual interest rate for both loans is 6%.

1. Use Table B.1 to find the present value of these two separate annuities. (Round amounts to the nearest dollar.)
2. Use Table B.3 to find the present value of these two separate annuities. (Round amounts to the nearest dollar.)

Exercise B-14
Present value with semiannual compounding
C1 P3

Otto Co. borrows money on April 30, 2011, by promising to make four payments of $13,000 each on November 1, 2011; May 1, 2012; November 1, 2012; and May 1, 2013.

1. How much money is Otto able to borrow if the interest rate is 8%, compounded semiannually?
2. How much money is Otto able to borrow if the interest rate is 12%, compounded semiannually?
3. How much money is Otto able to borrow if the interest rate is 16%, compounded semiannually?

Exercise B-15
Future value
of an amount P2

Mark Welsch deposits $7,200 in an account that earns interest at an annual rate of 8%, compounded quarterly. The $7,200 plus earned interest must remain in the account 10 years before it can be withdrawn. How much money will be in the account at the end of 10 years?

Exercise B-16
Future value
of an annuity P4

Kelly Malone plans to have $50 withheld from her monthly paycheck and deposited in a savings account that earns 12% annually, compounded monthly. If Malone continues with her plan for two and one-half years, how much will be accumulated in the account on the date of the last deposit?

Exercise B-17
Future value of
an amount plus
an annuity P2 P4

Starr Company decides to establish a fund that it will use 10 years from now to replace an aging production facility. The company will make a $100,000 initial contribution to the fund and plans to make quarterly contributions of $50,000 beginning in three months. The fund earns 12%, compounded quarterly. What will be the value of the fund 10 years from now?

Exercise B-18
Future value of
an amount P2

Catten, Inc., invests $163,170 today earning 7% per year for nine years. Use Table B.2 to compute the future value of the investment nine years from now. (Round the amount to the nearest dollar.)

Exercise B-19
Using present and future
value tables
C1 P1 P2 P3 P4

For each of the following situations, identify (1) the case as either (*a*) a present or a future value and (*b*) a single amount or an annuity, (2) the table you would use in your computations (but do not solve the problem), and (3) the interest rate and time periods you would use.

a. You need to accumulate $10,000 for a trip you wish to take in four years. You are able to earn 8% compounded semiannually on your savings. You plan to make only one deposit and let the money accumulate for four years. How would you determine the amount of the one-time deposit?

b. Assume the same facts as in part (*a*) except that you will make semiannual deposits to your savings account.

c. You want to retire after working 40 years with savings in excess of $1,000,000. You expect to save $4,000 a year for 40 years and earn an annual rate of interest of 8%. Will you be able to retire with more than $1,000,000 in 40 years? Explain.

d. A sweepstakes agency names you a grand prize winner. You can take $225,000 immediately or elect to receive annual installments of $30,000 for 20 years. You can earn 10% annually on any investments you make. Which prize do you choose to receive?

TABLE B.1

Present Value of 1

$$p = 1/(1 + i)^n$$

Periods	1%	2%	3%	4%	5%	6%	7%	8%	9%	10%	12%	15%
1	0.9901	0.9804	0.9709	0.9615	0.9524	0.9434	0.9346	0.9259	0.9174	0.9091	0.8929	0.8696
2	0.9803	0.9612	0.9426	0.9246	0.9070	0.8900	0.8734	0.8573	0.8417	0.8264	0.7972	0.7561
3	0.9706	0.9423	0.9151	0.8890	0.8638	0.8396	0.8163	0.7938	0.7722	0.7513	0.7118	0.6575
4	0.9610	0.9238	0.8885	0.8548	0.8227	0.7921	0.7629	0.7350	0.7084	0.6830	0.6355	0.5718
5	0.9515	0.9057	0.8626	0.8219	0.7835	0.7473	0.7130	0.6806	0.6499	0.6209	0.5674	0.4972
6	0.9420	0.8880	0.8375	0.7903	0.7462	0.7050	0.6663	0.6302	0.5963	0.5645	0.5066	0.4323
7	0.9327	0.8706	0.8131	0.7599	0.7107	0.6651	0.6227	0.5835	0.5470	0.5132	0.4523	0.3759
8	0.9235	0.8535	0.7894	0.7307	0.6768	0.6274	0.5820	0.5403	0.5019	0.4665	0.4039	0.3269
9	0.9143	0.8368	0.7664	0.7026	0.6446	0.5919	0.5439	0.5002	0.4604	0.4241	0.3606	0.2843
10	0.9053	0.8203	0.7441	0.6756	0.6139	0.5584	0.5083	0.4632	0.4224	0.3855	0.3220	0.2472
11	0.8963	0.8043	0.7224	0.6496	0.5847	0.5268	0.4751	0.4289	0.3875	0.3505	0.2875	0.2149
12	0.8874	0.7885	0.7014	0.6246	0.5568	0.4970	0.4440	0.3971	0.3555	0.3186	0.2567	0.1869
13	0.8787	0.7730	0.6810	0.6006	0.5303	0.4688	0.4150	0.3677	0.3262	0.2897	0.2292	0.1625
14	0.8700	0.7579	0.6611	0.5775	0.5051	0.4423	0.3878	0.3405	0.2992	0.2633	0.2046	0.1413
15	0.8613	0.7430	0.6419	0.5553	0.4810	0.4173	0.3624	0.3152	0.2745	0.2394	0.1827	0.1229
16	0.8528	0.7284	0.6232	0.5339	0.4581	0.3936	0.3387	0.2919	0.2519	0.2176	0.1631	0.1069
17	0.8444	0.7142	0.6050	0.5134	0.4363	0.3714	0.3166	0.2703	0.2311	0.1978	0.1456	0.0929
18	0.8360	0.7002	0.5874	0.4936	0.4155	0.3503	0.2959	0.2502	0.2120	0.1799	0.1300	0.0808
19	0.8277	0.6864	0.5703	0.4746	0.3957	0.3305	0.2765	0.2317	0.1945	0.1635	0.1161	0.0703
20	0.8195	0.6730	0.5537	0.4564	0.3769	0.3118	0.2584	0.2145	0.1784	0.1486	0.1037	0.0611
25	0.7798	0.6095	0.4776	0.3751	0.2953	0.2330	0.1842	0.1460	0.1160	0.0923	0.0588	0.0304
30	0.7419	0.5521	0.4120	0.3083	0.2314	0.1741	0.1314	0.0994	0.0754	0.0573	0.0334	0.0151
35	0.7059	0.5000	0.3554	0.2534	0.1813	0.1301	0.0937	0.0676	0.0490	0.0356	0.0189	0.0075
40	0.6717	0.4529	0.3066	0.2083	0.1420	0.0972	0.0668	0.0460	0.0318	0.0221	0.0107	0.0037

TABLE B.2

Future Value of 1

$$f = (1 + i)^n$$

Periods	1%	2%	3%	4%	5%	6%	7%	8%	9%	10%	12%	15%
0	1.0000	1.0000	1.0000	1.0000	1.0000	1.0000	1.0000	1.0000	1.0000	1.0000	1.0000	1.0000
1	1.0100	1.0200	1.0300	1.0400	1.0500	1.0600	1.0700	1.0800	1.0900	1.1000	1.1200	1.1500
2	1.0201	1.0404	1.0609	1.0816	1.1025	1.1236	1.1449	1.1664	1.1881	1.2100	1.2544	1.3225
3	1.0303	1.0612	1.0927	1.1249	1.1576	1.1910	1.2250	1.2597	1.2950	1.3310	1.4049	1.5209
4	1.0406	1.0824	1.1255	1.1699	1.2155	1.2625	1.3108	1.3605	1.4116	1.4641	1.5735	1.7490
5	1.0510	1.1041	1.1593	1.2167	1.2763	1.3382	1.4026	1.4693	1.5386	1.6105	1.7623	2.0114
6	1.0615	1.1262	1.1941	1.2653	1.3401	1.4185	1.5007	1.5869	1.6771	1.7716	1.9738	2.3131
7	1.0721	1.1487	1.2299	1.3159	1.4071	1.5036	1.6058	1.7138	1.8280	1.9487	2.2107	2.6600
8	1.0829	1.1717	1.2668	1.3686	1.4775	1.5938	1.7182	1.8509	1.9926	2.1436	2.4760	3.0590
9	1.0937	1.1951	1.3048	1.4233	1.5513	1.6895	1.8385	1.9990	2.1719	2.3579	2.7731	3.5179
10	1.1046	1.2190	1.3439	1.4802	1.6289	1.7908	1.9672	2.1589	2.3674	2.5937	3.1058	4.0456
11	1.1157	1.2434	1.3842	1.5395	1.7103	1.8983	2.1049	2.3316	2.5804	2.8531	3.4785	4.6524
12	1.1268	1.2682	1.4258	1.6010	1.7959	2.0122	2.2522	2.5182	2.8127	3.1384	3.8960	5.3503
13	1.1381	1.2936	1.4685	1.6651	1.8856	2.1329	2.4098	2.7196	3.0658	3.4523	4.3635	6.1528
14	1.1495	1.3195	1.5126	1.7317	1.9799	2.2609	2.5785	2.9372	3.3417	3.7975	4.8871	7.0757
15	1.1610	1.3459	1.5580	1.8009	2.0789	2.3966	2.7590	3.1722	3.6425	4.1772	5.4736	8.1371
16	1.1726	1.3728	1.6047	1.8730	2.1829	2.5404	2.9522	3.4259	3.9703	4.5950	6.1304	9.3576
17	1.1843	1.4002	1.6528	1.9479	2.2920	2.6928	3.1588	3.7000	4.3276	5.0545	6.8660	10.7613
18	1.1961	1.4282	1.7024	2.0258	2.4066	2.8543	3.3799	3.9960	4.7171	5.5599	7.6900	12.3755
19	1.2081	1.4568	1.7535	2.1068	2.5270	3.0256	3.6165	4.3157	5.1417	6.1159	8.6128	14.2318
20	1.2202	1.4859	1.8061	2.1911	2.6533	3.2071	3.8697	4.6610	5.6044	6.7275	9.6463	16.3665
25	1.2824	1.6406	2.0938	2.6658	3.3864	4.2919	5.4274	6.8485	8.6231	10.8347	17.0001	32.9190
30	1.3478	1.8114	2.4273	3.2434	4.3219	5.7435	7.6123	10.0627	13.2677	17.4494	29.9599	66.2118
35	1.4166	1.9999	2.8139	3.9461	5.5160	7.6861	10.6766	14.7853	20.4140	28.1024	52.7996	133.1755
40	1.4889	2.2080	3.2620	4.8010	7.0400	10.2857	14.9745	21.7245	31.4094	45.2593	93.0510	267.8635

TABLE B.3

Present Value of an Annuity of 1

$$p = \left[1 - \frac{1}{(1 + i)^n}\right]/i$$

Periods						Rate						
	1%	2%	3%	4%	5%	6%	7%	8%	9%	10%	12%	15%
1	0.9901	0.9804	0.9709	0.9615	0.9524	0.9434	0.9346	0.9259	0.9174	0.9091	0.8929	0.8696
2	1.9704	1.9416	1.9135	1.8861	1.8594	1.8334	1.8080	1.7833	1.7591	1.7355	1.6901	1.6257
3	2.9410	2.8839	2.8286	2.7751	2.7232	2.6730	2.6243	2.5771	2.5313	2.4869	2.4018	2.2832
4	3.9020	3.8077	3.7171	3.6299	3.5460	3.4651	3.3872	3.3121	3.2397	3.1699	3.0373	2.8550
5	4.8534	4.7135	4.5797	4.4518	4.3295	4.2124	4.1002	3.9927	3.8897	3.7908	3.6048	3.3522
6	5.7955	5.6014	5.4172	5.2421	5.0757	4.9173	4.7665	4.6229	4.4859	4.3553	4.1114	3.7845
7	6.7282	6.4720	6.2303	6.0021	5.7864	5.5824	5.3893	5.2064	5.0330	4.8684	4.5638	4.1604
8	7.6517	7.3255	7.0197	6.7327	6.4632	6.2098	5.9713	5.7466	5.5348	5.3349	4.9676	4.4873
9	8.5660	8.1622	7.7861	7.4353	7.1078	6.8017	6.5152	6.2469	5.9952	5.7590	5.3282	4.7716
10	9.4713	8.9826	8.5302	8.1109	7.7217	7.3601	7.0236	6.7101	6.4177	6.1446	5.6502	5.0188
11	10.3676	9.7868	9.2526	8.7605	8.3064	7.8869	7.4987	7.1390	6.8052	6.4951	5.9377	5.2337
12	11.2551	10.5753	9.9540	9.3851	8.8633	8.3838	7.9427	7.5361	7.1607	6.8137	6.1944	5.4206
13	12.1337	11.3484	10.6350	9.9856	9.3936	8.8527	8.3577	7.9038	7.4869	7.1034	6.4235	5.5831
14	13.0037	12.1062	11.2961	10.5631	9.8986	9.2950	8.7455	8.2442	7.7862	7.3667	6.6282	5.7245
15	13.8651	12.8493	11.9379	11.1184	10.3797	9.7122	9.1079	8.5595	8.0607	7.6061	6.8109	5.8474
16	14.7179	13.5777	12.5611	11.6523	10.8378	10.1059	9.4466	8.8514	8.3126	7.8237	6.9740	5.9542
17	15.5623	14.2919	13.1661	12.1657	11.2741	10.4773	9.7632	9.1216	8.5436	8.0216	7.1196	6.0472
18	16.3983	14.9920	13.7535	12.6593	11.6896	10.8276	10.0591	9.3719	8.7556	8.2014	7.2497	6.1280
19	17.2260	15.6785	14.3238	13.1339	12.0853	11.1581	10.3356	9.6036	8.9501	8.3649	7.3658	6.1982
20	18.0456	16.3514	14.8775	13.5903	12.4622	11.4699	10.5940	9.8181	9.1285	8.5136	7.4694	6.2593
25	22.0232	19.5235	17.4131	15.6221	14.0939	12.7834	11.6536	10.6748	9.8226	9.0770	7.8431	6.4641
30	25.8077	22.3965	19.6004	17.2920	15.3725	13.7648	12.4090	11.2578	10.2737	9.4269	8.0552	6.5660
35	29.4086	24.9986	21.4872	18.6646	16.3742	14.4982	12.9477	11.6546	10.5668	9.6442	8.1755	6.6166
40	32.8347	27.3555	23.1148	19.7928	17.1591	15.0463	13.3317	11.9246	10.7574	9.7791	8.2438	6.6418

TABLE B.4

Future Value of an Annuity of 1

$$f = [(1 + i)^n - 1]/i$$

Periods						Rate						
	1%	2%	3%	4%	5%	6%	7%	8%	9%	10%	12%	15%
1	1.0000	1.0000	1.0000	1.0000	1.0000	1.0000	1.0000	1.0000	1.0000	1.0000	1.0000	1.0000
2	2.0100	2.0200	2.0300	2.0400	2.0500	2.0600	2.0700	2.0800	2.0900	2.1000	2.1200	2.1500
3	3.0301	3.0604	3.0909	3.1216	3.1525	3.1836	3.2149	3.2464	3.2781	3.3100	3.3744	3.4725
4	4.0604	4.1216	4.1836	4.2465	4.3101	4.3746	4.4399	4.5061	4.5731	4.6410	4.7793	4.9934
5	5.1010	5.2040	5.3091	5.4163	5.5256	5.6371	5.7507	5.8666	5.9847	6.1051	6.3528	6.7424
6	6.1520	6.3081	6.4684	6.6330	6.8019	6.9753	7.1533	7.3359	7.5233	7.7156	8.1152	8.7537
7	7.2135	7.4343	7.6625	7.8983	8.1420	8.3938	8.6540	8.9228	9.2004	9.4872	10.0890	11.0668
8	8.2857	8.5830	8.8923	9.2142	9.5491	9.8975	10.2598	10.6366	11.0285	11.4359	12.2997	13.7268
9	9.3685	9.7546	10.1591	10.5828	11.0266	11.4913	11.9780	12.4876	13.0210	13.5795	14.7757	16.7858
10	10.4622	10.9497	11.4639	12.0061	12.5779	13.1808	13.8164	14.4866	15.1929	15.9374	17.5487	20.3037
11	11.5668	12.1687	12.8078	13.4864	14.2068	14.9716	15.7836	16.6455	17.5603	18.5312	20.6546	24.3493
12	12.6825	13.4121	14.1920	15.0258	15.9171	16.8699	17.8885	18.9771	20.1407	21.3843	24.1331	29.0017
13	13.8093	14.6803	15.6178	16.6268	17.7130	18.8821	20.1406	21.4953	22.9534	24.5227	28.0291	34.3519
14	14.9474	15.9739	17.0863	18.2919	19.5986	21.0151	22.5505	24.2149	26.0192	27.9750	32.3926	40.5047
15	16.0969	17.2934	18.5989	20.0236	21.5786	23.2760	25.1290	27.1521	29.3609	31.7725	37.2797	47.5804
16	17.2579	18.6393	20.1569	21.8245	23.6575	25.6725	27.8881	30.3243	33.0034	35.9497	42.7533	55.7175
17	18.4304	20.0121	21.7616	23.6975	25.8404	28.2129	30.8402	33.7502	36.9737	40.5447	48.8837	65.0751
18	19.6147	21.4123	23.4144	25.6454	28.1324	30.9057	33.9990	37.4502	41.3013	45.5992	55.7497	75.8364
19	20.8109	22.8406	25.1169	27.6712	30.5390	33.7600	37.3790	41.4463	46.0185	51.1591	63.4397	88.2118
20	22.0190	24.2974	26.8704	29.7781	33.0660	36.7856	40.9955	45.7620	51.1601	57.2750	72.0524	102.4436
25	28.2432	32.0303	36.4593	41.6459	47.7271	54.8645	63.2490	73.1059	84.7009	98.3471	133.3339	212.7930
30	34.7849	40.5681	47.5754	56.0849	66.4388	79.0582	94.4608	113.2832	136.3075	164.4940	241.3327	434.7451
35	41.6603	49.9945	60.4621	73.6522	90.3203	111.4348	138.2369	172.3168	215.7108	271.0244	431.6635	881.1702
40	48.8864	60.4020	75.4013	95.0255	120.7998	154.7620	199.6351	259.0565	337.8824	442.5926	767.0914	1,779.0903

Glossary

Absorption costing Costing method that assigns both variable and fixed costs to products. *(p. 887)*

Accelerated depreciation method Method that produces larger depreciation charges in the early years of an asset's life and smaller charges in its later years. *(p. 400)*

Account Record within an accounting system in which increases and decreases are entered and stored in a specific asset, liability, equity, revenue, or expense. *(p. 51)*

Account balance Difference between total debits and total credits (including the beginning balance) for an account. *(p. 55)*

Accounting Information and measurement system that identifies, records, and communicates relevant information about a company's business activities. *(p. 4)*

Accounting cycle Recurring steps performed each accounting period, starting with analyzing transactions and continuing through the post-closing trial balance (or reversing entries). *(p. 146)*

Accounting equation Equality involving a company's assets, liabilities, and equity; Assets = Liabilities + Equity; also called *balance sheet equation*. *(p. 13)*

Accounting information system People, records, and methods that collect and process data from transactions and events, organize them in useful forms, and communicate results to decision makers. *(p. 272)*

Accounting period Length of time covered by financial statements; also called *reporting period*. *(p. 94)*

Accounting rate of return Rate used to evaluate the acceptability of an investment; equals the after-tax periodic income from a project divided by the average investment in the asset; also called *rate of return on average investment*. *(p. 1011)*

Accounts payable ledger Subsidiary ledger listing individual creditor (supplier) accounts. *(p. 277)*

Accounts receivable Amounts due from customers for credit sales; backed by the customer's general credit standing. *(p. 360)*

Accounts receivable ledger Subsidiary ledger listing individual customer accounts. *(p. 277)*

Accounts receivable turnover Measure of both the quality and liquidity of accounts receivable; indicates how often receivables are received and collected during the period; computed by dividing net sales by average accounts receivable. *(p. 374)*

Accrual basis accounting Accounting system that recognizes revenues when earned and expenses when incurred; the basis for GAAP. *(p. 95)*

Accrued expenses Costs incurred in a period that are both unpaid and unrecorded; adjusting entries for recording accrued expenses involve increasing expenses and increasing liabilities. *(p. 101)*

Accrued revenues Revenues earned in a period that are both unrecorded and not yet received in cash (or other assets); adjusting entries for recording accrued revenues involve increasing assets and increasing revenues. *(p. 103)*

Acid-test ratio Ratio used to assess a company's ability to settle its current debts with its most liquid assets; defined as quick assets (cash, short-term investments, and current receivables) divided by current liabilities. *(p. 194)*

Activity-based budgeting (ABB) Budget system based on expected activities. *(p. 932)*

Activity-based costing (ABC) Cost allocation method that focuses on activities performed; traces costs to activities and then assigns them to cost objects. *(p. 833)*

Activity cost driver Variable that causes an activity's cost to go up or down; a causal factor. *(p. 833)*

Activity cost pool Temporary account that accumulates costs a company incurs to support an activity. *(p. 833)*

Adjusted trial balance List of accounts and balances prepared after period-end adjustments are recorded and posted. *(p. 106)*

Adjusting entry Journal entry at the end of an accounting period to bring an asset or liability account to its proper amount and update the related expense or revenue account. *(p. 96)*

Aging of accounts receivable Process of classifying accounts receivable by how long they are past due for purposes of estimating uncollectible accounts. *(p. 368)*

Allowance for Doubtful Accounts Contra asset account with a balance approximating uncollectible accounts receivable; also called *Allowance for Uncollectible Accounts*. *(p. 365)*

Allowance method Procedure that (a) estimates and matches bad debts expense with its sales for the period and/or (b) reports accounts receivable at estimated realizable value. *(p. 365)*

Amortization Process of allocating the cost of an intangible asset to expense over its estimated useful life. *(p. 410)*

Amortized cost The amount at which a financial asset or financial liability is measured at initial recognition minus principal repayments, plus or minus the cumulative amortisation using the effective interest method of any difference between that initial amount and the maturity amount, and minus any reduction (directly or through the use of an allowance account) for impairment or uncollectibility. *(p. 576)*

Annual financial statements Financial statements covering a one-year period; often based on a calendar year, but any consecutive 12-month (or 52-week) period is acceptable. *(p. 94)*

Annual report Summary of a company's financial results for the year with its current financial condition and future plans; directed to external users of financial information. *(p. A-1)*

Annuity Series of equal payments at equal intervals. *(p. 549)*

Assets Resources a business owns or controls that are expected to provide current and future benefits to the business. *(p. 13)*

Asset carrying amount The net amount at which an asset is recognised after deducting any accumulated depreciation or amortization and accumulated impairment losses. *(p. 399)*

Audit Analysis and report of an organization's accounting system, its records, and its reports using various tests. *(p. 12)*

Authorized shares Total amount of shares that a corporation's charter authorizes it to issue. *(p. 494)*

Available-for-sale (AFS) securities Investments in debt and equity securities that are not classified as trading securities or held-to-maturity securities. *(p. 574)*

Average cost (See *weighted average cost*.)

Avoidable expense Expense (or cost) that is relevant for decision making; expense that is not incurred if a department, product, or service is eliminated. *(p. 1026)*

Bad debts Accounts of customers who do not pay what they have promised to pay; an expense of selling on credit; also called *uncollectible accounts*. *(p. 364)*

Balance column account Account with debit and credit columns for recording entries and another column for showing the balance of the account after each entry. *(p. 58)*

Statement of financial position Financial statement that lists types and dollar amounts of assets, liabilities, and equity at a specific date. *(p. 19)*

Balance sheet equation (See *accounting equation*.)

Balanced scorecard A system of performance measurement that collects information on several key performance indicators within each of four perspectives: customer, internal processes, innovation and learning, and financial. *(p. 846)*

Bank reconciliation Report that explains the difference between the book (company) balance of cash and the cash balance reported on the bank statement. *(p. 331)*

Bank statement Bank report on the depositor's beginning and ending cash balances, and a listing of its changes, for a period. *(p. 330)*

Basic earnings per share Net income less any preferred dividends and then divided by weighted-average common shares outstanding. *(p. 511)*

Batch processing Accumulating source documents for a period of time and then processing them all at once such as once a day, week, or month. *(p. 286)*

Bearer bonds Bonds made payable to whoever holds them (the *bearer*); also called *unregistered bonds*. *(p. 551)*

Benchmarking Practice of comparing and analyzing company financial performance or position with other companies or standards. *(p. 974)*

Bond Written promise to pay the bond's par (or face) value and interest at a stated contract rate; often issued in denominations of $1,000. *(p. 538)*

Bond certificate Document containing bond specifics such as issuer's name, bond par value, contract interest rate, and maturity date. *(p. 540)*

Bond indenture Contract between the bond issuer and the bondholders; identifies the parties' rights and obligations. *(p. 540)*

Bonus issue A corporation's distribution of additional shares to its shareholders without the receipt of any payment in return. *(p. 499)*

Book value per ordinary share Recorded amount of equity applicable to ordinary shares divided by the number of ordinary shares outstanding. *(p. 513)*

Bookkeeping (See *recordkeeping*.)

Break-even point Output level at which sales equals fixed plus variable costs; where income equals zero. *(p. 886)*

Break-even time (BET) Time-based measurement used to evaluate the acceptability of an investment; equals the time expected to pass before the present value of the net cash flows from an investment equals its initial cost. *(p. 1027)*

Budget Formal statement of future plans, usually expressed in monetary terms. *(p. 918)*

Budget report Report comparing actual results to planned objectives; sometimes used as a progress report. *(p. 962)*

Budgetary control Management use of budgets to monitor and control company operations. *(p. 962)*

Budgeted statement of financial position Accounting report that presents predicted amounts of the company's assets, liabilities, and equity balances as of the end of the budget period. *(p. 930)*

Budgeted income statement Accounting report that presents predicted amounts of the company's revenues and expenses for the budget period. *(p. 930)*

Budgeting Process of planning future business actions and expressing them as formal plans. *(p. 918)*

Business entity assumption Principle that requires a business to be accounted for separately from its owner(s) and from any other entity. *(p. 10)*

C corporation Corporation that does not qualify for nor elect to be treated as a proprietorship or partnership for income tax purposes and therefore is subject to income taxes; also called *C corp*. *(p. 466)*

Call price Amount that must be paid to call and retire a callable preferred stock or a callable bond. *(p. 503)*

Callable bonds Bonds that give the issuer the option to retire them at a stated amount prior to maturity. *(p. 551)*

Callable preference shares Preference shares that the issuing corporation, at its option, may retire by paying the call price plus any dividends in arrears. *(p. 503)*

Canceled checks Checks that the bank has paid and deducted from the depositor's account. *(p. 331)*

Capital budgeting Process of analyzing alternative investments and deciding which assets to acquire or sell. *(p. 1008)*

Capital expenditures Additional costs of plant assets that provide material benefits extending beyond the current period; also called *balance sheet expenditures*. *(p. 404)*

Capital expenditures budget Plan that lists dollar amounts to be both received from disposal of plant assets and spent to purchase plant assets. *(p. 928)*

Capitalize Record the cost as part of a permanent account and allocate it over later periods.

Carrying amount Asset's acquisition costs less its accumulated depreciation (or depletion, or amortization); also called *book value*. *(p. 100)*

Carrying amount (book value) of bonds Net amount at which bonds are reported on the balance sheet; equals the par value of the bonds less any unamortized discount or plus any unamortized premium; also called *carrying amount or book value. (pp. 100 & 542)*

Cash Includes currency, coins, and amounts on deposit in bank checking or savings accounts. *(p. 321)*

Cash basis accounting Accounting system that recognizes revenues when cash is received and records expenses when cash is paid. *(p. 95)*

Cash budget Plan that shows expected cash inflows and outflows during the budget period, including receipts from loans needed to maintain a minimum cash balance and repayments of such loans. *(p. 928)*

Cash disbursements journal Special journal normally used to record all payments of cash; also called *cash payments journal. (p. 284)*

Cash discount Reduction in the price of merchandise granted by a seller to a buyer when payment is made within the discount period. *(p. 183)*

Cash equivalents Short-term, investment assets that are readily convertible to a known cash amount or sufficiently close to their maturity date (usually within 90 days) so that market value is not sensitive to interest rate changes. *(p. 321)*

Cash flow on total assets Ratio of operating cash flows to average total assets; not sensitive to income recognition and measurement; partly reflects earnings quality. *(p. 629)*

Cash Over and Short Income statement account used to record cash overages and cash shortages arising from errors in cash receipts or payments. *(p. 323)*

Cash receipts journal Special journal normally used to record all receipts of cash. *(p. 281)*

Change in an accounting estimate Change in an accounting estimate that results from new information, subsequent developments, or improved judgment that impacts current and future periods. *(pp. 403 & 509)*

Chart of accounts List of accounts used by a company; includes an identification number for each account. *(p. 54)*

Check Document signed by a depositor instructing the bank to pay a specified amount to a designated recipient. *(p. 328)*

Check register Another name for a cash disbursements journal when the journal has a column for check numbers. *(pp. 284 & 340)*

Classified statement of financial position Balance sheet that presents assets and liabilities in relevant subgroups, including current and noncurrent classifications. *(p. 147)*

Clock card Source document used to record the number of hours an employee works and to determine the total labor cost for each pay period. *(p. 752)*

Closing entries Entries recorded at the end of each accounting period to transfer end-of-period balances in revenue, gain, expense, loss, and withdrawal (dividend for a corporation) accounts to the capital account (to retained earnings for a corporation). *(p. 143)*

Closing process Necessary end-of-period steps to prepare the accounts for recording the transactions of the next period. *(p. 142)*

Columnar journal Journal with more than one column. *(p. 278)*

Committee of Sponsoring Organizations (COSO) Committee devoted to improving the quality of financial reporting through effective internal controls, consisting of five interrelated components, along with other mechanisms (www.COSO.org). *(p. 317)*

Common-size financial statement Statement that expresses each amount as a percent of a base amount. In the balance sheet, total assets is usually the base and is expressed as 100%. In the income statement, net sales is usually the base. *(p. 667)*

Comparative financial statement Statement with data for two or more successive periods placed in side-by-side columns, often with changes shown in dollar amounts and percents. *(p. 662)*

Compatibility principle Information system principle that prescribes an accounting system to conform with a company's activities, personnel, and structure. *(p. 273)*

Complex capital structure Capital structure that includes outstanding rights or options to purchase common stock, or securities that are convertible into common stock. *(p. 511)*

Components of accounting systems Five basic components of accounting systems are source documents, input devices, information processors, information storage, and output devices. *(p. 273)*

Composite unit Generic unit consisting of a specific number of units of each product; unit comprised in proportion to the expected sales mix of its products. *(p. 894)*

Compound journal entry Journal entry that affects at least three accounts. *(p. 61)*

Comprehensive income Net change in equity for a period, excluding owner investments and distributions. *(p. 579)*

Computer hardware Physical equipment in a computerized accounting information system.

Computer network Linkage giving different users and different computers access to common databases and programs. *(p. 286)*

Computer software Programs that direct operations of computer hardware.

Conceptual framework for financing reporting A written framework to guide the development, preparation, and interpretation of financial accounting information. *(p. 11)*

Consignee Receiver of goods owned by another who holds them for purposes of selling them for the owner. *(p. 226)*

Consignor Owner of goods who ships them to another party who will sell them for the owner. *(p. 226)*

Consolidated financial statements Financial statements that show all (combined) activities under the parent's control, including those of any subsidiaries. *(p. 578)*

Contingent liability Obligation to make a future payment if, and only if, an uncertain future event occurs. *(p. 444)*

Continuous budgeting Practice of preparing budgets for a selected number of future periods and revising those budgets as each period is completed. *(p. 921)*

Continuous improvement Concept requiring every manager and employee continually to look to improve operations. *(p. 717)*

Contra account Account linked with another account and having an opposite normal balance; reported as a subtraction from the other account's balance. *(p. 99)*

Contract rate Interest rate specified in a bond indenture (or note); multiplied by the par value to determine the interest paid each period; also called *coupon rate, stated rate,* or *nominal rate. (p. 541)*

Contributed capital in excess of par value Difference between the par value of stock and its issue price when issued at a price above par.

Contribution margin Sales revenue less total variable costs.

Contribution margin income statement Income statement that separates variable and fixed costs; highlights the contribution margin, which is sales less variable expenses.

Contribution margin per unit Amount that the sale of one unit contributes toward recovering fixed costs and earning profit; defined as sales price per unit minus variable expense per unit. *(p. 886)*

Contribution margin ratio Product's contribution margin divided by its sale price. *(p. 886)*

Control Process of monitoring planning decisions and evaluating the organization's activities and employees. *(p. 703)*

Control principle Information system principle that prescribes an accounting system to aid managers in controlling and monitoring business activities. *(p. 272)*

Controllable costs Costs that a manager has the power to control or at least strongly influence. *(pp. 707 & 847)*

Controllable variance Combination of both overhead spending variances (variable and fixed) and the variable overhead efficiency variance. *(p. 975)*

Controlling account General ledger account, the balance of which (after posting) equals the sum of the balances in its related subsidiary ledger. *(p. 277)*

Conversion costs Expenditures incurred in converting raw materials to finished goods; includes direct labor costs and overhead costs. *(p. 713)*

Conversion costs per equivalent unit The combined costs of direct labor and factory overhead per equivalent unit. *(p. 799)*

Convertible bonds Bonds that bondholders can exchange for a set number of the issuer's shares. *(p. 551)*

Convertible preference shares Preference shares with an option to exchange it for ordinary shares at a specified rate. *(p. 503)*

Copyright Right giving the owner the exclusive privilege to publish and sell musical, literary, or artistic work during the creator's life plus 70 years. *(p. 411)*

Corporation Business that is a separate legal entity under state or federal laws with owners called *shareholders* or *stockholders*. *(pp. 10 & 492)*

Cost All normal and reasonable expenditures necessary to get an asset in place and ready for its intended use. *(p. 395)*

Cost accounting system Accounting system for manufacturing activities based on the perpetual inventory system. *(p. 746)*

Cost-based transfer pricing A form of pricing transfers between divisions of the same company based on costs to the transferring division; typically used when the transferring division has excess capacity. *(p. 849)*

Cost-benefit principle Information system principle that prescribes the benefits from an activity in an accounting system to outweigh the costs of that activity. *(p. 273)*

Cost center Department that incurs costs but generates no revenues; common example is the accounting or legal department. *(p. 837)*

Cost object Product, process, department, or customer to which costs are assigned. *(p. 707)*

Cost of capital Rate the company must pay to its long-term creditors and shareholders; also called *hurdle rate*. *(p. 1013)*

Cost of goods available for sale Consists of beginning inventory plus net purchases of a period.

Cost of goods manufactured Total manufacturing costs (direct materials, direct labor, and factory overhead) for the period plus beginning goods in process less ending goods in process; also called *net cost of goods manufactured* and *cost of goods completed*. *(p. 797)*

Cost of goods sold Cost of inventory sold to customers during a period; also called *cost of sales*. *(p. 180)*

Cost principle Accounting principle that prescribes financial statement information to be based on actual costs incurred in business transactions. *(p. 9)*

Cost variance Difference between the actual incurred cost and the standard cost. *(p. 969)*

Cost-volume-profit (CVP) analysis Planning method that includes predicting the volume of activity, the costs incurred, sales earned, and profits received. *(p. 880)*

Cost-volume-profit (CVP) chart Graphic representation of cost-volume-profit relations. *(p. 888)*

Coupon bonds Bonds with interest coupons attached to their certificates; bondholders detach coupons when they mature and present them to a bank or broker for collection. *(p. 551)*

Credit Recorded on the right side; an entry that decreases asset and expense accounts, and increases liability, revenue, and most equity accounts; abbreviated Cr. *(p. 55)*

Credit memorandum Notification that the sender has credited the recipient's account in the sender's records. *(p. 189)*

Credit period Time period that can pass before a customer's payment is due. *(p. 183)*

Credit terms Description of the amounts and timing of payments that a buyer (debtor) agrees to make in the future. *(p. 183)*

Creditors Individuals or organizations entitled to receive payments. *(p. 52)*

Cumulative preference shares Preference shares on which undeclared dividends accumulate until paid; ordinary shareholders cannot receive dividends until cumulative dividends are paid. *(p. 501)*

Current assets Cash and other assets expected to be sold, collected, or used within one year or the company's operating cycle, whichever is longer. *(p. 148)*

Current liabilities Obligations due to be paid or settled within one year or the company's operating cycle, whichever is longer. *(p. 149 & 437)*

Current portion of long-term debt Portion of long-term debt due within one year or the operating cycle, whichever is longer; reported under current liabilities. *(p. 442)*

Current ratio Ratio used to evaluate a company's ability to pay its short-term obligations, calculated by dividing current assets by current liabilities. *(p. 150)*

Curvilinear cost Cost that changes with volume but not at a constant rate. *(p. 882)*

Customer orientation Company position that its managers and employees be in tune with the changing wants and needs of consumers. *(p. 717)*

Cycle efficiency (CE) A measure of production efficiency, which is defined as value-added (process) time divided by total cycle time. *(p. 719)*

Cycle time (CT) A measure of the time to produce a product or service, which is the sum of process time, inspection time, move time, and wait time; also called *throughput time*. (*p. 719*)

Date of declaration Date the directors vote to pay a dividend. (*p. 498*)

Date of payment Date the corporation makes the dividend payment. (*p. 498*)

Date of record Date directors specify for identifying stockholders to receive dividends. (*p. 498*)

Days' sales in inventory Estimate of number of days needed to convert inventory into receivables or cash; equals ending inventory divided by cost of goods sold and then multiplied by 365; also called days' *stock on hand*. (*p. 238*)

Days' sales uncollected Measure of the liquidity of receivables computed by dividing the current balance of receivables by the annual credit (or net) sales and then multiplying by 365; also called *days' sales in receivables*. (*p. 335*)

Debit Recorded on the left side; an entry that increases asset and expense accounts, and decreases liability, revenue, and most equity accounts; abbreviated Dr. (*p. 55*)

Debit memorandum Notification that the sender has debited the recipient's account in the sender's records. (*p. 184*)

Debt ratio Ratio of total liabilities to total assets; used to reflect risk associated with a company's debts. (*p. 69*)

Debt-to-equity ratio Defined as total liabilities divided by total equity; shows the proportion of a company financed by non-owners (creditors) in comparison with that financed by owners. (*p. 552*)

Debtors Individuals or organizations that owe money. (*p. 51*)

Declining-balance method Method that determines depreciation charge for the period by multiplying a depreciation rate (often twice the straight-line rate) by the asset's beginning-period book value. (*p. 400*)

Degree of operating leverage (DOL) Ratio of contribution margin divided by pretax income; used to assess the effect on income of changes in sales. (*p. 896*)

Departmental accounting system Accounting system that provides information useful in evaluating the profitability or cost effectiveness of a department. (*p. 836*)

Departmental contribution to overhead Amount by which a department's revenues exceed its direct expenses. (*p. 843*)

Depletion Process of allocating the cost of natural resources to periods when they are consumed and sold. (*p. 409*)

Deposit ticket Lists items such as currency, coins, and checks deposited and their corresponding dollar amounts. (*p. 328*)

Deposits in transit Deposits recorded by the company but not yet recorded by its bank. (*p. 331*)

Depreciable cost Cost of an item of property, plant and equipment less its salvage value.

Depreciation Expense created by allocating the cost of plant and equipment to periods in which they are used; represents the expense of using the asset. (*pp. 99 & 397*)

Diluted earnings per share Earnings per share calculation that requires dilutive securities be added to the denominator of the basic EPS calculation. (*p. 511*)

Dilutive securities Securities having the potential to increase common shares outstanding; examples are options, rights, convertible bonds, and convertible preferred stock. (*p. 511*)

Direct costs Costs incurred for the benefit of one specific cost object. (*p. 707*)

Direct expenses Expenses traced to a specific department (object) that are incurred for the sole benefit of that department. (*p. 837*)

Direct labor Efforts of employees who physically convert materials to finished product. (*p. 712*)

Direct labor costs Wages and salaries for direct labor that are separately and readily traced through the production process to finished goods. (*p. 712*)

Direct material Raw material that physically becomes part of the product and is clearly identified with specific products or batches of product. (*p. 712*)

Direct material costs Expenditures for direct material that are separately and readily traced through the production process to finished goods. (*p. 712*)

Direct method Presentation of net cash from operating activities for the statement of cash flows that lists major operating cash receipts less major operating cash payments. (*p. 616*)

Direct write-off method Method that records the loss from an uncollectible account receivable at the time it is determined to be uncollectible; no attempt is made to estimate bad debts. (*p. 364*)

Discount on bonds payable Difference between a bond's par value and its lower issue price or carrying value; occurs when the contract rate is less than the market rate. (*p. 542*)

Discount on note payable Difference between the face value of a note payable and the (lesser) amount borrowed; reflects the added interest to be paid on the note over its life.

Discount period Time period in which a cash discount is available and the buyer can make a reduced payment. (*p. 183*)

Discount rate Expected rate of return on investments; also called *cost of capital, hurdle rate,* or *required rate of return*. (*p. B-3*)

Discounts lost Expenses resulting from not taking advantage of cash discounts on purchases. (*p. 341*)

Dividend in arrears Unpaid dividend on cumulative preference shares; must be paid before any regular dividends on preference shares and before any dividends on ordinary shares. (*p. 501*)

Dividends Corporation's distributions of assets to its owners.

Dividend yield Ratio of the annual amount of cash dividends distributed to ordinary shareholders relative to the ordinary share's market value (price). (*p. 512*)

Double-declining-balance (DDB) depreciation Depreciation equals beginning book value multiplied by 2 times the straight-line rate.

Double taxation Corporate income is taxed and then its later distribution through dividends is normally taxed again for shareholders. (*p. 493*)

Double-entry accounting Accounting system in which each transaction affects at least two accounts and has at least one debit and one credit. (*p. 55*)

Earnings (See *net income*.)

Earnings per share (EPS) Amount of income earned by each share of a company's outstanding common stock; also called *net income per share*. (*p. 511*)

Effective interest method Allocates interest expense over the bond life to yield a constant rate of interest; interest expense for a period is found by multiplying the balance of the liability at the beginning of the period by the bond market rate at issuance; also called *interest method*. *(p. 542)*

Efficiency Company's productivity in using its assets; usually measured relative to how much revenue a certain level of assets generates. *(p. 661)*

Efficiency variance Difference between the actual quantity of an input and the standard quantity of that input. *(p. 982)*

Electronic funds transfer (EFT) Use of electronic communication to transfer cash from one party to another. *(p. 329)*

Enterprise resource planning (ERP) software Programs that manage a company's vital operations, which range from order taking to production to accounting. *(p. 287)*

Entity Organization that, for accounting purposes, is separate from other organizations and individuals.

EOM Abbreviation for *end of month;* used to describe credit terms for credit transactions. *(p. 183)*

Equity Owner's claim on the assets of a business; equals the residual interest in an entity's assets after deducting liabilities; also called *net assets*. *(p. 13)*

Equity method Accounting method used for long-term investments when the investor has "significant influence" over the investee. *(p. 576)*

Equity ratio Portion of total assets provided by equity, computed as total equity divided by total assets. *(p. 676)*

Equity with control Long-term investment when the investor is able to exert controlling influence over the investee; investors owning 50% or more of voting stock are presumed to exert controlling influence. *(p. 577)*

Equity with significant influence Long-term investment when the investor is able to exert significant influence over the investee; investors owning 20 percent or more (but less than 50 percent) of voting stock are presumed to exert significant influence. *(p. 576)*

Equivalent units of production (EUP) Number of units that would be completed if all effort during a period had been applied to units that were started and finished. *(p. 791)*

Estimated liability Obligation of an uncertain amount that can be reasonably estimated. *(p. 443)*

Estimated line of cost behavior Line drawn on a graph to visually fit the relation between cost and sales. *(p. 883)*

Ethics Codes of conduct by which actions are judged as right or wrong, fair or unfair, honest or dishonest. *(pp. 7 & 706)*

Events Happenings that both affect an organization's financial position and can be reliably measured. *(p. 14)*

Expanded accounting equation Assets = Liabilities + Equity; Equity equals [Owner capital − Owner withdrawals + Revenues − Expenses] for a noncorporation; Equity equals [Contributed capital + Retained earnings + Revenues − Expenses] for a corporation where dividends are subtracted from retained earnings. *(p. 14)*

Expense recognition (or **matching) principle** (See *matching principle*.) *(pp. 10 & 96)*

Expenses Outflows or using up of assets as part of operations of a business to generate sales. *(p. 14)*

External transactions Exchanges of economic value between one entity and another entity. *(p. 14)*

External users Persons using accounting information who are not directly involved in running the organization. *(p. 5)*

Factory overhead Factory activities supporting the production process that are not direct material or direct labor; also called *overhead and manufacturing overhead*. *(p. 712)*

Factory overhead costs Expenditures for factory overhead that cannot be separately or readily traced to finished goods; also called *overhead costs*. *(p. 712)*

Favorable variance Difference in actual revenues or expenses from the budgeted amount that contributes to a higher income. *(p. 963)*

FIFO method (See *first-in, first-out*.) *(pp. 231 & 803)*

Financial accounting Area of accounting aimed mainly at serving external users. *(p. 5)*

Financial Accounting Standards Board (FASB) Independent group of full-time members responsible for setting accounting rules. *(p. 9)*

Financial leverage Earning a higher return on equity by paying dividends on preferred stock or interest on debt at a rate lower than the return earned with the assets from issuing preferred stock or debt; also called *trading on the equity*. *(p. 503)*

Financial reporting Process of communicating information relevant to investors, creditors, and others in making investment, credit, and business decisions. *(p. 661)*

Financial statement analysis Application of analytical tools to general-purpose financial statements and related data for making business decisions. *(p. 660)*

Financial statements Includes the balance sheet, income statement, statement of owner's (or stockholders') equity, and statement of cash flows.

Financing activities Transactions with owners and creditors that include obtaining cash from issuing debt, repaying amounts borrowed, and obtaining cash from or distributing cash to owners. *(p. 612)*

Finished goods inventory Account that controls the finished goods files, which acts as a subsidiary ledger (of the Inventory account) in which the costs of finished goods that are ready for sale are recorded. *(pp. 711 & 749)*

First-in, first-out (FIFO) Method to assign cost to inventory that assumes items are sold in the order acquired; earliest items purchased are the first sold. *(p. 231)*

Financial year Consecutive 12-month (or 52-week) period chosen as the organization's annual accounting period. *(p. 95)*

Fixed budget Planning budget based on a single predicted amount of volume; unsuitable for evaluations if the actual volume differs from predicted volume. *(p. 963)*

Fixed budget performance report Report that compares actual revenues and costs with fixed budgeted amounts and identifies the differences as favorable or unfavorable variances. *(p. 963)*

Fixed cost Cost that does not change with changes in the volume of activity. *(p. 706)*

Flexibility principle Information system principle that prescribes an accounting system be able to adapt to changes in the company, its operations, and needs of decision makers. *(p. 273)*

Flexible budget Budget prepared (using actual volume) once a period is complete that helps managers evaluate past performance; uses fixed and variable costs in determining total costs. *(p. 964)*

Flexible budget performance report Report that compares actual revenues and costs with their variable budgeted amounts based on actual sales volume (or other level of activity) and identifies the differences as variances. *(p. 966)*

FOB Abbreviation for *free on board;* the point when ownership of goods passes to the buyer; *FOB shipping point* (or *factory*) means the buyer pays shipping costs and accepts ownership of goods when the seller transfers goods to carrier; *FOB destination* means the seller pays shipping costs and buyer accepts ownership of goods at the buyer's place of business. *(p. 185)*

Foreign exchange rate Price of one currency stated in terms of another currency. *(p. 584)*

Franchises Privileges granted by a company or government to sell a product or service under specified conditions. *(p. 411)*

Full disclosure principle Principle that prescribes financial statements (including notes) to report all relevant information about an entity's operations and financial condition. *(p. 10)*

FVTOCI A financial instrument where changes in fair value is reported through the other comprehensive income section of the statement of comprehensive income. For a financial instrument not held for trading, an entity can make an irrevocable election at initial recognition to designate it as such. *(p. 587)*

FVTPL A financial instrument where changes in fair value is reported through the profit and loss account. A financial instrument held for trading or upon initial recognition designated by the entity as such. *(p. 587)*

FVTPL securities Debt or equity securities measured at fair value, with changes in fair value reported in the profit and loss account *(p. 573)*

GAAP (See *generally accepted accounting principles*.)

General accounting system Accounting system for manufacturing activities based on the *periodic* inventory system. *(p. 746)*

General and administrative expense budget Plan that shows predicted operating expenses not included in the selling expenses budget. *(p. 927)*

General journal All-purpose journal for recording the debits and credits of transactions and events. *(pp. 57 & 276)*

General ledger (See *ledger*.) *(p. 51)*

General partner Partner who assumes unlimited liability for the debts of the partnership; responsible for partnership management. *(p. 465)*

General partnership Partnership in which all partners have mutual agency and unlimited liability for partnership debts. *(p. 465)*

Generally accepted accounting principles (GAAP) Rules that specify acceptable accounting practices. *(p. 8)*

Generally accepted auditing standards (GAAS) Rules that specify auditing practices.

General-purpose financial statements Statements published periodically for use by a variety of interested parties; includes the income statement, balance sheet, statement of owner's equity (or statement of retained earnings for a corporation), statement of cash flows, and notes to these statements. *(p. 661)*

Going-concern assumption Principle that prescribes financial statements to reflect the assumption that the business will continue operating. *(p. 10)*

Goods and services tax (GST) A consumption tax charged at the point of purchase for certain goods and services; the tax amount is usually calculated by applying a percentage rate to the taxable price of a sale. *(p. 438)*

Goods in process inventory Account in which costs are accumulated for products that are in the process of being produced but are not yet complete; also called *work in process inventory*. *(pp. 711 & 748)*

Goodwill Amount by which a company's (or a segment's) value exceeds the value of its individual assets less its liabilities. *(p. 412)*

Gross margin (See *gross profit*.)

Gross margin ratio Gross margin (net sales minus cost of goods sold) divided by net sales; also called *gross profit ratio*. *(p. 194)*

Gross method Method of recording purchases at the full invoice price without deducting any cash discounts. *(p. 341)*

Gross pay Total compensation earned by an employee. *(p. 442)*

Gross profit Net sales minus cost of goods sold; also called *gross margin*. *(p. 180)*

Gross profit method Procedure to estimate inventory when the past gross profit rate is used to estimate cost of goods sold, which is then subtracted from the cost of goods available for sale. *(p. 248)*

Held-for-trading-securities Securities that are acquired principally for the purpose of selling or repurchasing them in the near term. *(p. 573)*

Held-to-maturity (HTM) debt Debt securities that a company has the intent and ability to hold until they mature. *(p. 575)*

High-low method Procedure that yields an estimated line of cost behavior by graphically connecting costs associated with the highest and lowest sales volume. *(p. 884)*

Horizontal analysis Comparison of a company's financial condition and performance across time. *(p. 662)*

Hurdle rate Minimum acceptable rate of return (set by management) for an investment. *(pp. 845 & 1017)*

Impairment Amount by which the carrying amount of an asset exceeds its recoverable amount. *(p. 406)*

Imprest system Method to account for petty cash; maintains a constant balance in the fund, which equals cash plus petty cash receipts.

Inadequacy Condition in which the capacity of plant assets is too small to meet the company's production demands. *(p. 397)*

Income (See *net income*.)

Income Summary Temporary account used only in the closing process to which the balances of revenue and expense accounts (including any gains or losses) are transferred; its balance is transferred to the capital account (or retained earnings for a corporation). *(p. 143)*

Incremental cost Additional cost incurred only if a company pursues a specific course of action. *(p. 1020)*

Indefinite life Asset life that is not limited by legal, regulatory, contractual, competitive, economic, or other factors. *(p. 410)*

Indirect costs Costs incurred for the benefit of more than one cost object. *(p. 707)*

Indirect expenses Expenses incurred for the joint benefit of more than one department (or cost object). *(p. 837)*

Indirect labor Efforts of production employees who do not work specifically on converting direct materials into finished products and who are not clearly identified with specific units or batches of product. *(p. 712)*

Indirect labor costs Labor costs that cannot be physically traced to production of a product or service; included as part of overhead. *(p. 712)*

Indirect material Material used to support the production process but not clearly identified with products or batches of product. *(p. 710)*

Indirect method Presentation that reports net income and then adjusts it by adding and subtracting items to yield net cash from operating activities on the statement of cash flows. *(p. 616)*

Information processor Component of an accounting system that interprets, transforms, and summarizes information for use in analysis and reporting. *(p. 274)*

Information storage Component of an accounting system that keeps data in a form accessible to information processors. *(p. 274)*

Input device Means of capturing information from source documents that enables its transfer to information processors. *(p. 274)*

Installment note Liability requiring a series of periodic payments to the lender. *(p. 548)*

Intangible assets Long-term assets (resources) used to produce or sell products or services; usually lack physical form and have uncertain benefits. *(pp. 147 & 410)*

Interest Charge for using money (or other assets) loaned from one entity to another. *(p. 370)*

Interim statements Financial statements covering periods of less than one year; usually based on one-, three-, or six-month periods. *(pp. 94 & 247)*

Internal controls or **Internal control system** All policies and procedures used to protect assets, ensure reliable accounting, promote efficient operations, and urge adherence to company policies. *(pp. 272, 316, & 706)*

Internal rate of return (IRR) Rate used to evaluate the acceptability of an investment; equals the rate that yields a net present value of zero for an investment. *(p. 1015)*

Internal transactions Activities within an organization that can affect the accounting equation. *(p. 14)*

Internal users Persons using accounting information who are directly involved in managing the organization. *(p. 6)*

International Accounting Standards Board (IASB) Group that identifies preferred accounting practices and encourages global acceptance; issues International Financial Reporting Standards (IFRS). *(p. 9)*

International Financial Reporting Standards (IFRS) International Financial Reporting Standards (IFRS) are required or allowed by over 100 countries; IFRS is set by the International Accounting Standards Board (IASB), which aims to develop a single set of global standards, to promote those standards, and to converge national and international standards globally. *(p. 9)*

Inventory Goods a company owns and expects to sell in its normal operations. *(p. 181)*

Inventory turnover Number of times a company's average inventory is sold during a period; computed by dividing cost of goods sold by average inventory; also called *merchandise turnover*. *(p. 238)*

Investing activities Transactions that involve purchasing and selling of long-term assets; includes making and collecting notes receivable and investments in other than cash equivalents. *(p. 611)*

Investment center Center of which a manager is responsible for revenues, costs, and asset investments. *(p. 837)*

Investment center residual income The actual net income an investment center earns above a target return on average invested assets. *(p. 845)*

Investment center return on total assets Center net income divided by average total assets for the center. *(p. 845)*

Investment turnover The efficiency with which a company generates sales from its available assets; computed as sales divided by average invested assets. *(p. 850)*

Invoice Itemized record of goods prepared by the vendor that lists the customer's name, items sold, sales prices, and terms of sale. *(p. 339)*

Invoice approval Document containing a checklist of steps necessary for approving the recording and payment of an invoice; also called *check authorization*. *(p. 339)*

Job Production of a customized product or service. *(p. 742)*

Job cost sheet Separate record maintained for each job. *(p. 748)*

Job lot Production of more than one unit of a customized product or service. *(p. 747)*

Job order cost accounting system Cost accounting system to determine the cost of producing each job or job lot. *(pp. 748 & 787)*

Job order production Production of special-order products; also called *customized production*. *(p. 746)*

Joint cost Cost incurred to produce or purchase two or more products at the same time. *(p. 855)*

Journal Record in which transactions are entered before they are posted to ledger accounts; also called *book of original entry*. *(p. 56)*

Journalizing Process of recording transactions in a journal. *(p. 56)*

Just-in-time (JIT) manufacturing Process of acquiring or producing inventory only when needed. *(p. 718)*

Known liabilities Obligations of a company with little uncertainty; set by agreements, contracts, or laws; also called *definitely determinable liabilities*. *(p. 438)*

Land improvements Assets that increase the benefits of land, have a limited useful life, and are depreciated. *(p. 396)*

Lean business model Practice of eliminating waste while meeting customer needs and yielding positive company returns. *(p. 717)*

Least-squares regression Statistical method for deriving an estimated line of cost behavior that is more precise than the high-low method and the scatter diagram. *(p. 885)*

Ledger Record containing all accounts (with amounts) for a business; also called *general ledger*. *(p. 51)*

Liabilities Creditors' claims on an organization's assets; involves a probable future payment of assets, products, or services that a company is obligated to make due to past transactions or events. *(p. 13)*

Licenses (See *franchises.*) *(p. 411)*

Limited liability company Organization form that combines select features of a corporation and a limited partnership; provides limited liability to its members (owners), is free of business tax, and allows members to actively participate in management. *(p. 466)*

Limited liability partnership Partnership in which a partner is not personally liable for malpractice or negligence unless that partner is responsible for providing the service that resulted in the claim. *(p. 465)*

Limited life (See *useful life.*)

Limited partners Partners who have no personal liability for partnership debts beyond the amounts they invested in the partnership. *(p. 465)*

Limited partnership Partnership that has two classes of partners, limited partners and general partners. *(p. 465)*

Liquid assets Resources such as cash that are easily converted into other assets or used to pay for goods, services, or liabilities. *(p. 321)*

Liquidation Process of going out of business; involves selling assets, paying liabilities, and distributing remainder to owners.

Liquidity Availability of resources to meet short-term cash requirements. *(pp. 321 & 661)*

List price Catalog (full) price of an item before any trade discount is deducted. *(p. 182)*

Long-term investments Long-term assets not used in operating activities such as notes receivable and investments in shares and bonds. *(p. 572)*

Long-term liabilities Obligations not due to be paid within one year or the operating cycle, whichever is longer. *(p. 437)*

Lower of cost and net realizable value (NRV) Required method to report inventory at market replacement cost when that market cost is lower than recorded cost. *(p. 234)*

Maker of the note Entity who signs a note and promises to pay it at maturity. *(p. 370)*

Management by exception Management process to focus on significant variances and give less attention to areas where performance is close to the standard. *(p. 967)*

Managerial accounting Area of accounting aimed mainly at serving the decision-making needs of internal users; also called *management accounting.* *(pp. 6 & 702)*

Manufacturer Company that uses labor and operating assets to convert raw materials to finished goods.

Manufacturing budget Plan that shows the predicted costs for direct materials, direct labor, and overhead to be incurred in manufacturing units in the production budget. *(p. 938)*

Manufacturing statement Report that summarizes the types and amounts of costs incurred in a company's production process for a period; also called *cost of goods manufacturing statement.* *(p. 715)*

Margin of safety Excess of expected sales over the level of break-even sales. *(p. 892)*

Market-based transfer price The market price of a good or service being transferred between divisions within a company; typically used when the transferring division does not have excess capacity. *(p. 855)*

Market prospects Expectations (both good and bad) about a company's future performance as assessed by users and other interested parties. *(p. 661)*

Market rate Interest rate that borrowers are willing to pay and lenders are willing to accept for a specific lending agreement given the borrowers' risk level. *(p. 541)*

Market value per share Price at which stock is bought or sold. *(p. 495)*

Master budget Comprehensive business plan that includes specific plans for expected sales, product units to be produced, merchandise (or materials) to be purchased, expenses to be incurred, plant assets to be purchased, and amounts of cash to be borrowed or loans to be repaid, as well as a budgeted income statement and balance sheet. *(p. 922)*

Matching (or expense recognition) principle Prescribes expenses to be reported in the same period as the revenues that were earned as a result of the expenses. *(p. 10)*

Materials consumption report Document that summarizes the materials a department uses during a reporting period; replaces materials requisitions. *(p. 788)*

Materials ledger card Perpetual record updated each time units are purchased or issued for production use. *(p. 750)*

Materials requisition Source document production managers use to request materials for production; used to assign materials costs to specific jobs or overhead. *(p. 751)*

Maturity date of a note Date when a note's principal and interest are due. *(p. 371)*

Measurement principle Accounting information is based on cost with potential subsequent adjustments to fair value; see also *cost principle.* *(p. 9)*

Merchandise (See *merchandise inventory.*) *(p. 180)*

Merchandise inventory Goods that a company owns and expects to sell to customers; also called *merchandise* or *inventory.* *(p. 181)*

Merchandise purchases budget Plan that shows the units or costs of merchandise to be purchased by a merchandising company during the budget period. *(p. 925)*

Merchandiser Entity that earns net income by buying and selling merchandise. *(p. 180)*

Mixed cost Cost that behaves like a combination of fixed and variable costs. *(p. 881)*

Monetary unit assumption Principle that assumes transactions and events can be expressed in money units. *(p. 10)*

Mortgage Legal loan agreement that protects a lender by giving the lender the right to be paid from the cash proceeds from the sale of a borrower's assets identified in the mortgage. *(p. 550)*

Multinational Company that operates in several countries. *(p. 584)*

Mutual agency Legal relationship among partners whereby each partner is an agent of the partnership and is able to bind the partnership to contracts within the scope of the partnership's business. *(p. 464)*

Natural business year Twelve-month period that ends when a company's sales activities are at their lowest point. *(p. 95)*

Natural resources Assets physically consumed when used; examples are timber, mineral deposits, and oil and gas fields; also called *wasting assets.* *(p. 409)*

Negotiated transfer price A price, determined by negotiation between division managers, to record transfers between divisions; typically lies between the variable cost and the market price of the item transferred. *(p. 855)*

Net assets (See *equity.*)

Net profit Amount earned after subtracting all expenses necessary for and matched with sales for a period; also called *income, profit,* or *earnings. (p. 14)*

Net loss Excess of expenses over revenues for a period. *(p. 14)*

Net method Method of recording purchases at the full invoice price less any cash discounts. *(p. 341)*

Net pay Gross pay less all deductions; also called *take-home pay. (p. 442)*

Net present value (NPV) Dollar estimate of an asset's value that is used to evaluate the acceptability of an investment; computed by discounting future cash flows from the investment at a satisfactory rate and then subtracting the initial cost of the investment. *(p. 1013)*

Net realizable value Estimated selling price in the ordinary course of business less the estimated costs of completion and the estimated costs necessary to make the sale. *(p. 226)*

Noncumulative preference shares Preference shares on which the right to receive dividends is lost for any period when dividends are not declared. *(p. 501)*

Noncurrent assets Assets not used up within one year or the operating cycle, whichever is longer. *(p. 149)*

Noncurrent liabilities Obligations not due within one year or the operating cycle, whichever is longer. *(p. 437)*

Noninterest-bearing note Note with no stated (contract) rate of interest; interest is implicitly included in the note's face value.

Nonparticipating preference shares Preference shares on which dividends are limited to a maximum amount each year. *(p. 502)*

Nonsufficient funds (NSF) check Maker's bank account has insufficient money to pay the check; also called *hot check.*

Non-value-added time The portion of cycle time that is not directed at producing a product or service; equals the sum of inspection time, move time, and wait time. *(p. 719)*

No-par value shares Share class that has not been assigned a par (or stated) value by the corporate charter. *(p. 495)*

Not controllable costs Costs that a manager does not have the power to control or strongly influence. *(p. 707)*

Note (See *promissory note.*)

Note payable Liability expressed by a written promise to pay a definite sum of money on demand or on a specific future date(s).

Note receivable Asset consisting of a written promise to receive a definite sum of money on demand or on a specific future date(s).

Obsolescence Condition in which, because of new inventions and improvements, a plant asset can no longer be used to produce goods or services with a competitive advantage. *(p. 397)*

Online processing Approach to inputting data from source documents as soon as the information is available. *(p. 286)*

Operating activities Activities that involve the production or purchase of merchandise and the sale of goods or services to customers, including expenditures related to administering the business. *(p. 611)*

Operating cycle Normal time between paying cash for merchandise or employee services and receiving cash from customers. *(p. 147)*

Operating leverage Extent, or relative size, of fixed costs in the total cost structure. *(p. 896)*

Operating segment Component of an entity (a) that engages in business activities from which it may earn revenues and incur expenses, (b) whose operating results are regularly reviewed by the entity's chief operating decision maker to make decisions about resources to be allocated to the segment and assess its performance, and (c) for which discrete financial information is available. *(p. 288)*

Opportunity cost Potential benefit lost by choosing a specific action from two or more alternatives. *(p. 708)*

Ordinary shares Corporation's basic ownership shares, also generally called *capital stock. (pp. 10 & 494)*

Organization expenses (costs) Costs such as legal fees and promoter fees to bring an entity into existence. *(p. 493)*

Other comprehensive income Equals net income less comprehensive income; includes unrealized gains and losses on available-for-sale securities, foreign currency adjustments, and pension adjustments. *(p. 579)*

Out-of-pocket cost Cost incurred or avoided as a result of management's decisions. *(p. 708)*

Output devices Means by which information is taken out of the accounting system and made available for use. *(p. 275)*

Outsourcing Manager decision to buy a product or service from another part of a *make-or-buy* decision; also called *make or buy.*

Outstanding checks Checks written and recorded by the depositor but not yet paid by the bank at the bank statement date. *(p. 331)*

Outstanding shares Corporation's shares held by its shareholders.

Overapplied overhead Amount by which the overhead applied to production in a period using the predetermined overhead rate exceeds the actual overhead incurred in a period. *(p. 757)*

Overhead cost variance Difference between the total overhead cost applied to products and the total overhead cost actually in-curred. *(p. 974)*

Owner, Capital Account showing the owner's claim on company assets; equals owner investments plus net income (or less net losses) minus owner withdrawals since the company's inception; also referred to as *equity. (p. 14)*

Owner investment Assets put into the business by the owner. *(p. 14)*

Owner's equity (See *equity.*)

Owner withdrawals Account used to record asset distributions to the owner. (See also *withdrawals.*) *(p. 14)*

Par value Value assigned to a share by the corporate charter when the shares are authorized. *(p. 495)*

Par value of a bond Amount the bond issuer agrees to pay at maturity and the amount on which cash interest payments are based; also called *face amount* or *face value* of a bond. *(p. 538)*

Par value share Class of share assigned a par value by the corporate charter. *(p. 495)*

Parent Company that owns a controlling interest in a corporation (requires more than 50% of voting stock). *(p. 578)*

Participating preference shares Preference shares that share with ordinary shareholders any dividends paid in excess of the percent stated on preference shares. *(p. 502)*

Partner return on equity Partner net income divided by average partner equity for the period. *(p. 476)*

Partnership Unincorporated association of two or more persons to pursue a business for profit as co-owners. *(pp. 10 & 464)*

Partnership contract Agreement among partners that sets terms under which the affairs of the partnership are conducted; also called *articles of partnership*. *(p. 464)*

Partnership liquidation Dissolution of a partnership by (1) selling noncash assets and allocating any gain or loss according to partners' income-and-loss ratio, (2) paying liabilities, and (3) distributing any remaining cash according to partners' capital balances. *(p. 473)*

Patent Exclusive right granted to its owner to produce and sell an item or to use a process for 20 years. *(p. 411)*

Payback period (PBP) Time-based measurement used to evaluate the acceptability of an investment; equals the time expected to pass before an investment's net cash flows equal its initial cost. *(p. 1009)*

Payee of the note Entity to whom a note is made payable. *(p. 370)*

Period costs Expenditures identified more with a time period than with finished products costs; includes selling and general administrative expenses. *(p. 708)*

Periodic inventory system Method that records the cost of inventory purchased but does not continuously track the quantity available or sold to customers; records are updated at the end of each period to reflect the physical count and costs of goods available. *(p. 182)*

Permanent accounts Accounts that reflect activities related to one or more future periods; balance sheet accounts whose balances are not closed; also called *real accounts*. *(p. 142)*

Perpetual inventory system Method that maintains continuous records of the cost of inventory available and the cost of goods sold. *(p. 182)*

Petty cash Small amount of cash in a fund to pay minor expenses; accounted for using an imprest system. *(p. 326)*

Planning Process of setting goals and preparing to achieve them. *(p. 702)*

Pledged assets to secured liabilities Ratio of the book value of a company's pledged assets to the book value of its secured liabilities.

Post-closing trial balance List of permanent accounts and their balances from the ledger after all closing entries are journalized and posted. *(p. 146)*

Posting Process of transferring journal entry information to the ledger; computerized systems automate this process. *(p. 56)*

Posting reference (PR) column A column in journals in which individual ledger account numbers are entered when entries are posted to those ledger accounts. *(p. 58)*

Predetermined overhead rate Rate established prior to the beginning of a period that relates estimated overhead to another variable, such as estimated direct labor, and is used to assign overhead cost to production. *(p. 754)*

Preemptive right Shareholders' right to maintain their proportionate interest in a corporation with any additional shares issued. *(p. 494)*

Preference shares Shares with a priority status over ordinary shareholders in one or more ways, such as paying dividends or distributing assets. *(p. 501)*

Premium on bonds Difference between a bond's par value and its higher carrying value; occurs when the contract rate is higher than the market rate; also called *bond premium*. *(p. 544)*

Premium on shares Difference between the par value of a share and its issue price when issued at a price below par value. *(p. 496)*

Prepaid expenses Items paid for in advance of receiving their benefits; classified as assets. *(p. 97)*

Price-earnings (PE) ratio Ratio of a company's current market value per share to its earnings per share; also called *price-to-earnings*. *(p. 511)*

Price variance Difference between actual and budgeted revenue or cost caused by the difference between the actual price per unit and the budgeted price per unit. *(p. 967)*

Prime costs Expenditures directly identified with the production of finished goods; include direct materials costs and direct labor costs. *(p. 713)*

Principal of a note Amount that the signer of a note agrees to pay back when it matures, not including interest. *(p. 370)*

Principles of internal control Principles prescribing management to establish responsibility, maintain records, insure assets, separate record-keeping from custody of assets, divide responsibility for related transactions, apply technological controls, and perform reviews. *(p. 317)*

Pro forma financial statements Statements that show the effects of proposed transactions and events as if they had occurred. *(p. 142)*

Process cost accounting system System of assigning direct materials, direct labor, and overhead to specific processes; total costs associated with each process are then divided by the number of units passing through that process to determine the cost per equivalent unit. *(p. 787)*

Process cost summary Report of costs charged to a department, its equivalent units of production achieved, and the costs assigned to its output. *(p. 796)*

Process operations Processing of products in a continuous (sequential) flow of steps; also called *process manufacturing* or *process production*. *(p. 784)*

Product costs Costs that are capitalized as inventory because they produce benefits expected to have future value; include direct materials, direct labor, and overhead. *(p. 708)*

Production budget Plan that shows the units to be produced each period. *(p. 938)*

Profit (See *net income*.)

Profit center Business unit that incurs costs and generates revenues. *(p. 837)*

Profit margin Ratio of a company's net income to its net sales; the percent of income in each dollar of revenue; also called *net profit margin*. *(pp. 108 & 850)*

Profitability Company's ability to generate an adequate return on invested capital. *(p. 661)*

Profitability index A measure of the relation between the expected benefits of a project and its investment, computed as the present value of expected future cash flows from the investment divided by the cost of the investment; a higher value indicates a more desirable investment, and a value below 1 indicates an unacceptable project. *(p. 1015)*

Promissory note (or **note**) Written promise to pay a specified amount either on demand or at a definite future date; is a *note receivable* for the lender but a *note payable* for the lendee. *(p. 370)*

Property, plant and equipment Tangible long-lived assets used to produce or sell products and services; also called *plant assets* or *fixed assets*. *(pp. 99 & 394)*

Property, plant and equipment age Estimate of the age of a company's property, plant and equipment, computed by dividing accumulated depreciation by depreciation expense. *(p. 413)*

Proprietorship (See *sole proprietorship.*) *(p. 10)*

Proxy Legal document giving a stockholder's agent the power to exercise the stockholder's voting rights. *(p. 493)*

Purchase discount Term used by a purchaser to describe a cash discount granted to the purchaser for paying within the discount period. *(p. 183)*

Purchase order Document used by the purchasing department to place an order with a seller (vendor). *(p. 338)*

Purchase requisition Document listing merchandise needed by a department and requesting it be purchased. *(p. 338)*

Purchases journal Journal normally used to record all purchases on credit. *(p. 283)*

Quantity variance Difference between actual and budgeted revenue or cost caused by the difference between the actual number of units and the budgeted number of units. *(p. 967)*

Ratio analysis Determination of key relations between financial statement items as reflected in numerical measures. *(p. 662)*

Raw materials inventory Goods a company acquires to use in making products. *(p. 710)*

Realizable value Expected proceeds from converting an asset into cash. *(p. 365)*

Receiving report Form used to report that ordered goods are received and to describe their quantity and condition. *(p. 339)*

Recordkeeping Part of accounting that involves recording transactions and events, either manually or electronically; also called *bookkeeping. (p. 4)*

Registered bonds Bonds owned by investors whose names and addresses are recorded by the issuer; interest payments are made to the registered owners. *(p. 551)*

Relevance principle Information system principle prescribing that its reports be useful, understandable, timely, and pertinent for decision making. *(p. 272)*

Relevant benefits Additional or incremental revenue generated by selecting a particular course of action over another. *(p. 1019)*

Relevant range of operations Company's normal operating range; excludes extremely high and low volumes not likely to occur. *(p. 889)*

Report form balance sheet Balance sheet that lists accounts vertically in the order of assets, liabilities, and equity.

Reportable segment Operating segment or aggregations of operating segments that meet specified criteria and quantitative thresholds. *(p. 288)*

Residual value Estimate of amount to be recovered at the end of an asset's useful life; also called *salvage value* or *scrap value. (p. 397)*

Responsibility accounting budget Report of expected costs and expenses under a manager's control. *(p. 848)*

Responsibility accounting performance report Responsibility report that compares actual costs and expenses for a department with budgeted amounts. *(p. 848)*

Responsibility accounting system System that provides information that management can use to evaluate the performance of a department's manager. *(p. 836)*

Reserves Can be any part of shareholders' equity, except for share capital. Most reserves result from accounting standards to reflect certain measurement changes in equity rather than the income statement, for example, asset revaluation surplus or reserve, foreign currency translation reserve, and other statutory reserves. *(p. 510)*

Retail inventory method Method to estimate ending inventory based on the ratio of the amount of goods for sale at cost to the amount of goods for sale at retail. *(p. 247)*

Retailer Intermediary that buys products from manufacturers or wholesalers and sells them to consumers. *(p. 180)*

Return Monies received from an investment; often in percent form. *(p. 26)*

Return on assets (See *return on total assets*) *(p. 22)*

Return on equity Ratio of net income to average equity for the period.

Return on total assets Ratio reflecting operating efficiency; defined as net income divided by average total assets for the period; also called *return on assets* or *return on investment. (p. 579)*

Revenue center Center of which a manager is responsible for achieving or exceeding budgeted revenues. *(p. 837)*

Revenue expenditures Expenditures reported on the current income statement as an expense because they do not provide benefits in future periods. *(p. 404)*

Revenue recognition principle The principle prescribing that revenue is recognized when earned. *(p. 9)*

Revenues Gross increase in equity from a company's business activities that earn income; also called *sales. (p. 14)*

Reversing entries Optional entries recorded at the beginning of a period that prepare the accounts for the usual journal entries as if adjusting entries had not occurred in the prior period. *(p. 154)*

Risk Uncertainty about an expected return. *(p. 26)*

Rolling budget New set of budgets a firm adds for the next period (with revisions) to replace the ones that have lapsed. *(p. 921)*

S corporation Corporation that meets special tax qualifications so as to be treated like a partnership for income tax purposes. *(p. 466)*

Safety stock Quantity of inventory or materials over the minimum needed to satisfy budgeted demand. *(p. 925)*

Sales (See *revenues.*)

Sales budget Plan showing the units of goods to be sold or services to be provided; the starting point in the budgeting process for most departments. *(p. 924)*

Sales discount Term used by a seller to describe a cash discount granted to buyers who pay within the discount period. *(p. 183)*

Sales journal Journal normally used to record sales of goods on credit. *(p. 278)*

Sales mix Ratio of sales volumes for the various products sold by a company. *(p. 893)*

Scatter diagram Graph used to display data about past cost behavior and sales as points on a diagram. *(p. 883)*

Schedule of accounts payable List of the balances of all accounts in the accounts payable ledger and their totals. *(p. 284)*

Schedule of accounts receivable List of the balances of all accounts in the accounts receivable ledger and their totals. *(p. 279)*

Secured bonds Bonds that have specific assets of the issuer pledged as collateral. *(p. 551)*

Securities and Exchange Commission (SEC) Federal agency Congress has charged to set reporting rules for organizations that sell ownership shares to the public. *(p. 9)*

Segment return on assets ratio Segment operating income divided by segment average (identifiable) assets for the period. *(p. 288)*

Selling expense budget Plan that lists the types and amounts of selling expenses expected in the budget period. *(p. 926)*

Serial bonds Bonds consisting of separate amounts that mature at different dates. *(p. 551)*

Service company Organization that provides services instead of tangible products.

Shareholders Owners of a corporation; also called *stockholders.* *(p. 10)*

Shareholders' equity A corporation's equity; also called *shareholders' equity* or *corporate capital.* *(p. 495)*

Share capital General term referring to a corporation's shares used in obtaining capital (owner financing). *(p. 494)*

Share dividend Corporation's distribution of its own shares to its shareholders without the receipt of any payment. *(p. 499)*

Share premium Amount received from issuance of shares that is in excess of the share's par value. *(p. 496)*

Share split Occurs when a corporation calls in its shares and replaces each share with more than one new share; decreases both the market value per share and any par or stated value per share. *(p. 500)*

Share subscription Investor's contractual commitment to purchase unissued shares at future dates and prices.

Shares Equity of a corporation divided into ownership units; also called *stock.* *(p. 10)*

Short-term investments Debt and equity securities that management expects to convert to cash within the next 3 to 12 months (or the operating cycle if longer); also called *temporary investments* or *marketable securities.* *(p. 572)*

Short-term note payable Current obligation in the form of a written promissory note. *(p. 439)*

Shrinkage Inventory losses that occur as a result of theft or deterioration. *(p. 190)*

Signature card Includes the signatures of each person authorized to sign checks on the bank account. *(p. 328)*

Simple capital structure Capital structure that consists of only common stock and nonconvertible preferred stock; consists of no dilutive securities. *(p. 511)*

Sinking fund bonds Bonds that require the issuer to make deposits to a separate account; bondholders are repaid at maturity from that account. *(p. 551)*

Sole proprietorship Business owned by one person that is not organized as a corporation; also called *proprietorship.* *(p. 10)*

Solvency Company's long-run financial viability and its ability to cover long-term obligations. *(p. 661)*

Source documents Source of information for accounting entries that can be in either paper or electronic form; also called *business papers.* *(p. 50)*

Special journal Any journal used for recording and posting transactions of a similar type. *(p. 276)*

Specific identification Method to assign cost to inventory when the purchase cost of each item in inventory is identified and used to compute cost of inventory. *(p. 229)*

Spending variance Difference between the actual price of an item and its standard price. *(p. 982)*

Spreadsheet Computer program that organizes data by means of formulas and format; also called *electronic work sheet.*

Standard costs Costs that should be incurred under normal conditions to produce a product or component or to perform a service. *(p. 967)*

Stated value share No-par share assigned a stated value per share; this amount is recorded in the share account when the share is issued. *(p. 495)*

Statement of cash flows A financial statement that lists cash inflows (receipts) and cash outflows (payments) during a period; arranged by operating, investing, and financing. *(pp. 19 & 610)*

Statement of changes in equity Report of changes in equity over a period; adjusted for increases (owner investment and net income) and for decreases (withdrawals and net loss). *(p. 19)*

Statement of partners' equity Financial statement that shows total capital balances at the beginning of the period, any additional investment by partners, the income or loss of the period, the partners' withdrawals, and the partners' ending capital balances; also called *statement of partners' capital.* *(p. 469)*

Statement of profit or loss and other comprehensive income The financial statement that shows all nonowner changes in equity and other comprehensive income. *(p. 507)*

Step-wise cost Cost that remains fixed over limited ranges of volumes but changes by a lump sum when volume changes occur outside these limited ranges. *(p. 882)*

Stock (See *shares.*)

Stockholders (See *shareholders.*)

Straight-line depreciation Method that allocates an equal portion of the depreciable cost of plant asset (cost minus salvage) to each accounting period in its useful life. *(pp. 99 & 398)*

Subsidiary Entity controlled by another entity (parent) in which the parent owns more than 50% of the subsidiary's voting shares. *(p. 578)*

Subsidiary ledger List of individual subaccounts and amounts with a common characteristic; linked to a controlling account in the general ledger. *(p. 276)*

Sunk cost Cost already incurred and cannot be avoided or changed. *(p. 707)*

Supplementary records Information outside the usual accounting records; also called *supplemental records.* *(p. 186)*

Supply chain Linkages of services or goods extending from suppliers, to the company itself, and on to customers.

T-account Tool used to show the effects of transactions and events on individual accounts. *(p. 55)*

Target cost Maximum allowable cost for a product or service; defined as expected selling price less the desired profit. *(p. 747)*

Temporary accounts Accounts used to record revenues, expenses, and withdrawals (dividends for a corporation); they are closed at the end of each period; also called *nominal accounts*. *(p. 142)*

Term bonds Bonds scheduled for payment (maturity) at a single specified date. *(p. 551)*

Throughput time (See *cycle time*.)

Time period assumption Assumption that an organization's activities can be divided into specific time periods such as months, quarters, or years. *(pp. 10 & 94)*

Time ticket Source document used to report the time an employee spent working on a job or on overhead activities and then to determine the amount of direct labor to charge to the job or the amount of indirect labor to charge to overhead. *(p. 752)*

Times interest earned Ratio of income before interest expense (and any income taxes) divided by interest expense; reflects risk of covering interest commitments when income varies. *(p. 447)*

Total asset turnover Measure of a company's ability to use its assets to generate sales; computed by dividing net sales by average total assets. *(p. 412)*

Total cost The sum of fixed and variable costs. *(p. 881)*

Total quality management (TQM) Concept calling for all managers and employees at all stages of operations to strive toward higher standards and reduce number of defects. *(p. 717)*

Trade discount Reduction from a list or catalog price that can vary for wholesalers, retailers, and consumers. *(p. 182)*

Trademark or **trade (brand) name** Symbol, name, phrase, or jingle identified with a company, product, or service. *(p. 412)*

Trading on the equity (See *financial leverage*.)

Transfer price The price used to record transfers of goods or services between divisions in the same company. *(p. 854)*

Transaction Exchange of economic consideration affecting an entity's financial position that can be reliably measured.

Treasury shares Corporation's own shares that it reacquired and still holds. *(p. 504)*

Trial balance List of accounts and their balances at a point in time; total debit balances equal total credit balances. *(p. 65)*

Unadjusted trial balance List of accounts and balances prepared before accounting adjustments are recorded and posted. *(p. 106)*

Unavoidable expense Expense (or cost) that is not relevant for business decisions; an expense that would continue even if a department, product, or service is eliminated. *(p. 1026)*

Unclassified statement of financial position statement of financial position that broadly groups assets, liabilities, and equity accounts. *(p. 147)*

Uncontrollable costs Costs that a manager does not have the power to determine or strongly influence. *(p. 847)*

Underapplied overhead Amount by which overhead incurred in a period exceeds the overhead applied to that period's production using the predetermined overhead rate. *(p. 757)*

Unearned revenue Liability created when customers pay in advance for products or services; earned when the products or services are later delivered. *(pp. 52 & 100)*

Unfavorable variance Difference in revenues or costs, when the actual amount is compared to the budgeted amount, that contributes to a lower income. *(p. 963)*

Unit contribution margin Amount a product's unit selling price exceeds its total unit variable cost.

Units-of-production depreciation Method that charges a varying amount to depreciation expense for each period of an asset's useful life depending on its usage. *(p. 400)*

Unlimited liability Legal relationship among general partners that makes each of them responsible for partnership debts if the other partners are unable to pay their shares. *(p. 465)*

Unsecured bonds Bonds backed only by the issuer's credit standing; almost always riskier than secured bonds; also called *debentures*. *(p. 551)*

Useful life Length of time an asset will be productively used in the operations of a business; also called *service life* or *limited life*. *(p. 397)*

Value-added time The portion of cycle time that is directed at producing a product or service; equals process time. *(p. 719)*

Value chain Sequential activities that add value to an entity's products or services; includes design, production, marketing, distribution, and service. *(p. 718)*

Variable cost Cost that changes in proportion to changes in the activity output volume. *(p. 706)*

Variable costing income statement An income statement which reports variable costs and fixed costs separately; also called a *contribution margin income statement*. *(p. 887)*

Variance analysis Process of examining differences between actual and budgeted revenues or costs and describing them in terms of price and quantity differences. *(p. 967)*

Vendee Buyer of goods or services. *(p. 339)*

Vendor Seller of goods or services. *(p. 338)*

Vertical analysis Evaluation of each financial statement item or group of items in terms of a specific base amount. *(p. 662)*

Volume variance Difference between two dollar amounts of fixed overhead cost; one amount is the total budgeted overhead cost, and the other is the overhead cost allocated to products using the predetermined fixed overhead rate. *(p. 975)*

Voucher Internal file used to store documents and information to control cash disbursements and to ensure that a transaction is properly authorized and recorded. *(p. 325)*

Voucher register Journal (referred to as *book of original entry*) in which all vouchers are recorded after they have been approved. *(p. 340)*

Voucher system Procedures and approvals designed to control cash disbursements and acceptance of obligations. *(p. 324)*

Warranty Agreement that obligates the seller to correct or replace a product or service when it fails to perform properly within a specified period. *(p. 443)*

Weighted average cost Method to assign inventory cost to sales; the cost of available-for-sale units is divided by the number of units available to determine per unit cost prior to each sale that is then multiplied by the units sold to yield the cost of that sale. *(p. 231)*

Weighted-average contribution margin Contribution margin for a multiproduct company; computed based on each products' percentage of the company's sales mix. *(p. 894)*

Weighted-average method (See *weighted average cost.*)

Wholesaler Intermediary that buys products from manufacturers or other wholesalers and sells them to retailers or other wholesalers. *(p. 180)*

Withdrawals Payment of cash or other assets from a proprietorship or partnership to its owner or owners. *(p. 14)*

Work sheet Spreadsheet used to draft an unadjusted trial balance, adjusting entries, adjusted trial balance, and financial statements. *(p. 138)*

Working capital Current assets minus current liabilities at a point in time. *(p. 671)*

Working papers Analyses and other informal reports prepared by accountants and managers when organizing information for formal reports and financial statements. *(p. 138)*

Credits

Index

Note: Page numbers followed by *n* indicate information found in footnotes; **boldface** entries indicate defined terms.